Y

ODES

N

tomic Bomb

merica

Ground

ON

Earth

t Safari

Secrets

Ungodly

Richard Rhodes

THE MAKING OF THE ATOMIC BOMB

SIMON AND SCHUSTER NEW YORK

Taken as a story of human achievement, and human blindness, the discoveries in the sciences are among the great epics.

Robert Oppenheimer

In an enterprise such as the building of the atomic bomb the difference between ideas, hopes, suggestions and theoretical calculations, and solid numbers based on measurement, is paramount. All the committees, the politicking and the plans would have come to naught if a few unpredictable nuclear cross sections had been different from what they are by a factor of two.

Emilio Segrè

Contents

PART ONE

PROFOUND AND NECESSARY TRUTH

It is a profound and necessary truth that the deep things in science are not found because they are useful; they are found because it was possible to find them.

Robert Oppenheimer

It is still an unending source of surprise for me to see how a few scribbles on a blackboard or on a sheet of paper could change the course of human affairs.

Stanislaw Ulam

1

Moonshine

In London, where Southampton Row passes Russell Square, across from the British Museum in Bloomsbury, Leo Szilard waited irritably one gray Depression morning for the stoplight to change. A trace of rain had fallen during the night; Tuesday, September 12, 1933, dawned cool, humid and dull. Drizzling rain would begin again in early afternoon. When Szilard told the story later he never mentioned his destination that morning. He may have had none; he often walked to think. In any case another destination intervened. The stoplight changed to green. Szilard stepped off the curb. As he crossed the street time cracked open before him and he saw a way to the future, death into the world and all our woe, the shape of things to come.

Leo Szilard, the Hungarian theoretical physicist, born of Jewish heritage in Budapest on February 11, 1898, was thirty-five years old in 1933. At five feet, six inches he was not tall even for the day. Nor was he yet the "short fat man," round-faced and potbellied, "his eyes shining with intelligence and wit" and "as generous with his ideas as a Maori chief with his wives," that the French biologist Jacques Monod met in a later year. Midway between trim youth and portly middle age, Szilard had thick, curly, dark hair and an animated face with full lips, flat cheekbones and dark brown eyes. In photographs he still chose to look soulful. He had reason.

His deepest ambition, more profound even than his commitment to science, was somehow to save the world.

The Shape of Things to Come was H. G. Wells' new novel, just published, reviewed with avuncular warmth in *The Times* on September 1. "Mr. Wells' newest 'dream of the future' is its own brilliant justification," *The Times* praised, obscurely. The visionary English novelist was one among Szilard's network of influential acquaintances, a network he assembled by plating his articulate intelligence with the purest brass.

In 1928, in Berlin, where he was a *Privatdozent* at the University of Berlin and a confidant and partner in practical invention of Albert Einstein, Szilard had read Wells' tract *The Open Conspiracy*. The Open Conspiracy was to be a public collusion of science-minded industrialists and financiers to establish a world republic. Thus to save the world. Szilard appropriated Wells' term and used it off and on for the rest of his life. More to the point, he traveled to London in 1929 to meet Wells and bid for the Central European rights to his books. Given Szilard's ambition he would certainly have discussed much more than publishing rights. But the meeting prompted no immediate further connection. He had not yet encountered the most appealing orphan among Wells' Dickensian crowd of tales.

Szilard's past prepared him for his revelation on Southampton Row. He was the son of a civil engineer. His mother was loving and he was well provided for. "I knew languages because we had governesses at home, first in order to learn German and second in order to learn French." He was "sort of a mascot" to classmates at his *Gymnasium*, the University of Budapest's famous Minta. "When I was young," he told an audience once, "I had two great interests in life; one was physics and the other politics." He remembers informing his awed classmates, at the beginning of the Great War, when he was sixteen, how the fortunes of nations should go, based on his precocious weighing of the belligerents' relative political strength:

> I said to them at the time that I did of course not know who would win the war, but I did know how the war ought to end. It ought to end by the defeat of the central powers, that is the Austro-Hungarian monarchy and Germany, and also end by the defeat of Russia. I said I couldn't quite see how this could happen, since they were fighting on opposite sides, but I said that this was really what ought to happen. In retrospect I find it difficult to understand how at the age of sixteen and without any direct knowledge of countries other than Hungary, I was able to make this statement.

He seems to have assembled his essential identity by sixteen. He believed his clarity of judgment peaked then, never to increase further; it "perhaps even declined."

His sixteenth year was the first year of a war that would shatter the political and legal agreements of an age. That coincidence—or catalyst—by itself could turn a young man messianic. To the end of his life he made dull men uncomfortable and vain men mad.

He graduated from the Minta in 1916, taking the Eötvös Prize, the Hungarian national prize in mathematics, and considered his further education. He was interested in physics but "there was no career in physics in Hungary." If he studied physics he could become at best a high school teacher. He thought of studying chemistry, which might be useful later when he picked up physics, but that wasn't likely either to be a living. He settled on electrical engineering. Economic justifications may not tell all. A friend of his studying in Berlin noticed as late as 1922 that Szilard, despite his Eötvös Prize, "felt that his skill in mathematical operations could not compete with that of his colleagues." On the other hand, he was not alone among Hungarians of future prominence in physics in avoiding the backwater science taught in Hungarian universities at the time.

He began engineering studies in Budapest at the King Joseph Institute of Technology, then was drafted into the Austro-Hungarian Army. Because he had a *Gymnasium* education he was sent directly to officers' school to train for the cavalry. A leave of absence almost certainly saved his life. He asked for leave ostensibly to give his parents moral support while his brother had a serious operation. In fact, he was ill. He thought he had pneumonia. He wanted to be treated in Budapest, near his parents, rather than in a frontier Army hospital. He waited standing at attention for his commanding officer to appear to hear his request while his fever burned at 102 degrees. The captain was reluctant; Szilard characteristically insisted on his leave and got it, found friends to support him to the train, arrived in Vienna with a lower temperature but a bad cough and reached Budapest and a decent hospital. His illness was diagnosed as Spanish influenza, one of the first cases on the Austro-Hungarian side. The war was winding down. Using "family connections" he arranged some weeks later to be mustered out. "Not long afterward, I heard that my own regiment," sent to the front, "had been under severe attack and that all of my comrades had disappeared."

In the summer of 1919, when Lenin's Hungarian protégé Bela Kun and his Communist and Social Democratic followers established a short-lived Soviet republic in Hungary in the disordered aftermath of Austro-Hungarian defeat, Szilard decided it was time to study abroad. He was twenty-one years old. Just as he arranged for a passport, at the beginning of August, the Kun regime collapsed; he managed another passport from the right-wing regime of Admiral Nicholas Horthy that succeeded it and left Hungary around Christmastime.

Still reluctantly committed to engineering, Szilard enrolled in the Technische Hochschule, the technology institute, in Berlin. But what had seemed necessary in Hungary seemed merely practical in Germany. The physics faculty of the University of Berlin included Nobel laureates Albert Einstein, Max Planck and Max von Laue, theoreticians of the first rank. Fritz Haber, whose method for fixing nitrogen from the air to make nitrates for gunpowder saved Germany from early defeat in the Great War, was only one among many chemists and physicists of distinction at the several government- and industry-sponsored Kaiser Wilhelm Institutes in the elegant Berlin suburb of Dahlem. The difference in scientific opportunity between Budapest and Berlin left Szilard physically unable to listen to engineering lectures. "In the end, as always, the subconscious proved stronger than the conscious and made it impossible for me to make any progress in my studies of engineering. Finally the ego gave in, and I left the Technische Hochschule to complete my studies at the University, some time around the middle of '21."

Physics students at that time wandered Europe in search of exceptional masters much as their forebears in scholarship and craft had done since medieval days. Universities in Germany were institutions of the state; a professor was a salaried civil servant who also collected fees directly from his students for the courses he chose to give (a *Privatdozent,* by contrast, was a visiting scholar with teaching privileges who received no salary but might collect fees). If someone whose specialty you wished to learn taught at Munich, you went to Munich; if at Göttingen, you went to Göttingen. Science grew out of the craft tradition in any case; in the first third of the twentieth century it retained—and to some extent still retains—an informal system of mastery and apprenticeship over which was laid the more recent system of the European graduate school. This informal collegiality partly explains the feeling among scientists of Szilard's generation of membership in an exclusive group, almost a guild, of international scope and values.

Szilard's good friend and fellow Hungarian, the theoretical physicist Eugene Wigner, who was studying chemical engineering at the Technische Hochschule at the time of Szilard's conversion, watched him take the University of Berlin by storm. "As soon as it became clear to Szilard that physics was his real interest, he introduced himself, with characteristic directness, to Albert Einstein." Einstein was a man who lived apart—preferring originality to repetition, he taught few courses—but Wigner remembers that Szilard convinced him to give them a seminar on statistical mechanics. Max Planck was a gaunt, bald elder statesman whose study of radiation emitted by a uniformly heated surface (such as the interior of a kiln) had led him to discover a universal constant of nature. He followed the canny tradition among leading scientists of accepting only the most promising students for tutelage; Szilard won his attention. Max von Laue, the handsome director of the university's Institute for Theoretical Physics, who founded the science of X-ray crystallography and created a popular sensation by thus making the atomic lattices of crystals visible for the first time, accepted Szilard into his brilliant course in relativity theory and eventually sponsored his Ph.D. dissertation.

The postwar German infection of despair, cynicism and rage at defeat ran a course close to febrile hallucination in Berlin. The university, centrally located between Dorotheenstrasse and Unter den Linden due east of the Brandenburg Gate, was well positioned to observe the bizarre effects. Szilard missed the November 1918 revolution that began among mutinous sailors at Kiel, quickly spread to Berlin and led to the retreat of the Kaiser to Holland, to armistice and eventually to the founding, after bloody riots, of the insecure Weimar Republic. By the time he arrived in Berlin at the end of 1919 more than eight months of martial law had been lifted, leaving a city at first starving and bleak but soon restored to intoxicating life.

"There was snow on the ground," an Englishman recalls of his first look at postwar Berlin in the middle of the night, "and the blend of snow, neon and huge hulking buildings was unearthly. You felt you had arrived somewhere totally strange." To a German involved in the Berlin theater of the 1920s "the air was always bright, as if it were peppered, like New York late in autumn: you needed little sleep and never seemed tired. Nowhere else did you fail in such good form, nowhere else could you be knocked on the chin time and again without being counted out." The German aristocracy retreated from view, and intellectuals, film stars and journalists took its place; the major annual social event in the city where an imperial palace stood empty was the Press Ball, sponsored by the Berlin Press Club, which drew as many as six thousand guests.

Ludwig Mies van der Rohe designed his first glass-walled skyscraper in postwar Berlin. Yehudi Menuhin made his precocious debut, with Einstein in the audience to applaud him. George Grosz sorted among his years of savage observation on Berlin's wide boulevards and published *Ecce Homo.* Vladimir Nabokov was there, observing "an elderly, rosy-faced beggar woman with legs cut off at the pelvis . . . set down like a bust at the foot of a wall and . . . selling paradoxical shoelaces." Fyodor Vinberg, one of the Czar's departed officers, was there, publishing a shoddy newspaper, promoting *The Protocols of the Elders of Zion,* which he had personally introduced into Germany from Russia—a new German edition of that pseudo-Machiavellian, patently fraudulent fantasy of world conquest sold more than 100,000 copies—and openly advocating the violent destruction of the Jews. Hitler was not there until the end, because he was barred from northern Germany after his release from prison in 1924, but he sent rumpelstiltskin Joseph Goebbels to stand in for him; Goebbels learned to break heads and spin propaganda in an open, lusty, jazz-drunk city he slandered in his diary as "a dark and mysterious enigma."

In the summer of 1922 the rate of exchange in Germany sank to 400 marks to the dollar. It fell to 7,000 to the dollar at the beginning of January 1923, the truly terrible year. One hundred sixty thousand in July. One million in August. And 4.2 *trillion* marks to the dollar on November 23, 1923, when adjustment finally began. Banks advertised for bookkeepers good with zeros and paid out cash withdrawals by weight. Antique stores filled to the ceiling with the pawned treasures of the bankrupt middle class. A theater seat sold for an egg. Only those with hard currency—mostly foreigners—thrived at a time when it was possible to cross Germany by first-class railroad carriage for pennies, but they also earned the enmity of starving Germans. "No, one did not feel guilty," the visiting Englishman crows, "one felt it was perfectly normal, a gift from the gods."

The German physicist Walter Elsasser, who later emigrated to the United States, worked in Berlin in 1923 during an interlude in his student years; his father had agreed to pay his personal expenses. He was no foreigner, but with foreign help he was able to live like one:

> In order to make me independent of [inflation], my father had appealed to his friend, Kaufmann, the banker from Basle, who had established for me an account in American dollars at a large bank. . . . Once a week I took half a day off to go downtown by subway and withdrew my allowance in marks; and it was more each time, of course. Returning to my rented room, I at once bought enough food staples to last the week, for within three days, all the prices would have risen appreciably, by fifteen percent, say, so that my allowance would have run short and would not have permitted such pleasures as an excursion to Potsdam or to the lake country on Sundays. . . . I was too young, much too callous, and too inexperienced to understand what this galloping inflation must have meant—actual starvation and misery—to people who had to live on pensions or other fixed incomes, or even to wage earners, especially those with children, whose pay lagged behind the rate of inflation.

So must Szilard have lived, except that no one recalls ever seeing him cook for himself; he preferred the offerings of delicatessens and cafés. He would have understood what inflation meant and some of the reasons for its extremity. But though Szilard was preternaturally observant—"During a long life among scientists," writes Wigner, "I have met no one with more imagination and originality, with more independence of thought and opinion"—his recollections and his papers preserve almost nothing of these Berlin days. Germany's premier city at the height of its postwar social, political and intellectual upheaval earns exactly one sentence from Szilard: "Berlin at that time lived in the heyday of physics." That was how much physics, giving extraordinary birth during the 1920s to its modern synthesis, meant to him.

Four years of study usually preceded a German student's thesis work. Then, with a professor's approval, the student solved a problem of his own conception or one his professor supplied. "In order to be acceptable," says Szilard, it "had to be a piece of really original work." If the thesis found favor, the student took an oral examination one afternoon and if he passed he was duly awarded a doctorate.

Szilard had already given a year of his life to the Army and two years to engineering. He wasted no time advancing through physics. In the summer of 1921 he went to Max von Laue and asked for a thesis topic. Von Laue apparently decided to challenge Szilard—the challenge may have been friendly or it may have been an attempt to put him in his place—and gave him an obscure problem in relativity theory. "I couldn't make any headway with it. As a matter of fact, I was not even convinced that this was a problem that could be solved." Szilard worked on it for six months, until the Christmas season, "and I thought Christmastime is not a time to work, it is a time to loaf, so I thought I would just think whatever comes to my mind."

What he thought, in three weeks, was how to solve a baffling inconsistency in thermodynamics, the branch of physics that concerns relationships between heat and other forms of energy. There are two thermodynamic theories, both highly successful at predicting heat phenomena. One, the phenomenological, is more abstract and generalized (and therefore more useful); the other, the statistical, is based on an atomic model and corresponds more closely to physical reality. In particular, the statistical theory depicts thermal equilibrium as a state of random motion of atoms. Einstein, for example, had demonstrated in important papers in 1905 that Brownian motion—the continuous, random motion of particles such as pollen suspended in a liquid—was such a state. But the more useful phenomenological theory treated thermal equilibrium as if it were static, a state of no change. That was the inconsistency.

Szilard went for long walks—Berlin would have been cold and gray, the grayness sometimes relieved by days of brilliant sunshine—"and I saw something in the middle of the walk; when I came home I wrote it down; next morning I woke up with a new idea and I went for another walk; this crystallized in my mind and in the evening I wrote it down." It was, he thought, the most creative period of his life. "Within three weeks I had produced a manuscript of something which was really quite original. But I didn't dare to take it to von Laue, because it was not what he had asked me to do."

He took it instead to Einstein after a seminar, buttonholed him and said he would like to tell him about something he had been doing.

"Well, what have you been doing?" Szilard remembers Einstein saying.

Szilard reported his "quite original" idea.

"That's impossible," Einstein said. "This is something that cannot be done."

"Well, yes, but I did it."

"How did you do it?"

Szilard began explaining. "Five or ten minutes" later, he says, Einstein understood. After only a year of university physics, Szilard had worked out a rigorous mathematical proof that the random motion of thermal equilibrium could be fitted within the framework of the phenomenological theory in its original, classical form, without reference to a limiting atomic model—"and [Einstein] liked this very much."

Thus emboldened, Szilard took his paper—its title would be "On the extension of phenomenological thermodynamics to fluctuation phenomena"—to von Laue, who received it quizzically and took it home. "And next morning, early in the morning, the telephone rang. It was von Laue. He said, 'Your manuscript has been accepted as your thesis for the Ph.D. degree.' "

Six months later Szilard wrote another paper in thermodynamics, "On the decrease of entropy in a thermodynamic system by the intervention of intelligent beings," that eventually would be recognized as one of the important foundation documents of modern information theory. By then he had his advanced degree; he was Dr. Leo Szilard now. He experimented with X-ray effects in crystals, von Laue's field, at the Kaiser Wilhelm Institute for Chemistry in Dahlem until 1925; that year the University of Berlin accepted his entropy paper as his *Habilitationsschrift,* his inaugural dissertation, and he was thereupon appointed a *Privatdozent,* a position he held until he left for England in 1933.

One of Szilard's sidelines, then and later, was invention. Between 1924 and 1934 he applied to the German patent office individually or jointly with his partner Albert Einstein for twenty-nine patents. Most of the joint applications dealt with home refrigeration. "A sad newspaper story. . .

caught the attention of Einstein and Szilard one morning," writes one of Szilard's later American protégés: "It was reported in a Berlin newspaper that an entire family, including a number of young children, had been found asphyxiated in their apartment as a result of their inhalation of the noxious fumes of the [chemical] that was used as the refrigerant in their primitive refrigerator and that had escaped in the night through a leaky pump valve." Whereupon the two physicists devised a method of pumping metallicized refrigerant by electromagnetism, a method that required no moving parts (and therefore no valve seals that might leak) except the refrigerant itself. A.E.G., the German General Electric, signed Szilard on as a paid consultant and actually built one of the Einstein-Szilard refrigerators, but the magnetic pump was so noisy compared to even the noisy conventional compressors of the day that it never left the engineering lab.

Another, oddly similar invention, also patented, might have won Szilard world acclaim if he had taken it beyond the patent stage. Independently of the American experimental physicist Ernest O. Lawrence and at least three months earlier, Szilard worked out the basic principle and general design of what came to be called, as Lawrence's invention, the cyclotron, a device for accelerating nuclear particles in a circular magnetic field, a sort of nuclear pump. Szilard applied for a patent on his device on January 5, 1929; Lawrence first thought of the cyclotron on about April 1, 1929, producing a small working model a year later—for which he won the 1939 Nobel Prize in Physics.

Szilard's originality stopped at no waterline. Somewhere along the way from sixteen-year-old prophet of the fate of nations to thirty-one-year-old open conspirer negotiating publishing rights with H. G. Wells, he conceived an Open Conspiracy of his own. He dated his social invention from "the mid-twenties in Germany." If so, then he went to see Wells in 1929 as much from enthusiasm for the Englishman's perspicacity as for his vision. C. P. Snow, the British physicist and novelist, writes of Leo Szilard that he "had a temperament uncommon anywhere, maybe a little less uncommon among major scientists. He had a powerful ego and invulnerable egocentricity: but he projected the force of that personality outward, with beneficent intention toward his fellow creatures. In that sense, he had a family resemblance to Einstein on a reduced scale." Beneficent intention in this instance is a document proposing a new organization: *Der Bund*—the order, the confederacy, or, more simply, the band.

The Bund, Szilard writes, would be "a closely knit group of people whose inner bond is pervaded by a religious and scientific spirit":

> If we possessed a magical spell with which to recognize the "best" individuals of the rising generation at an early age . . . then we would be able to train

> them to independent thinking, and through education in close association we could create a spiritual leadership class with inner cohesion which would renew itself on its own.

Members of this class would not be awarded wealth or personal glory. To the contrary, they would be required to take on exceptional responsibilities, "burdens" that might "demonstrate their devotion." It seemed to Szilard that such a group stood a good chance of influencing public affairs even if it had no formal structure or constitutional position. But there was also the possibility that it might "take over a more direct influence on public affairs as part of the political system, next to government and parliament, or in the place of government and parliament."

"The Order," Szilard wrote at a different time, "was not supposed to be something like a political party . . . but rather it was supposed to represent the state." He saw representative democracy working itself out somehow within the cells of thirty to forty people that would form the mature political structure of the Bund. "Because of the method of selection [and education] . . . there would be a good chance that decisions at the top level would be reached by fair majorities."

Szilard pursued one version or another of his Bund throughout his life. It appears as late as 1961, by then suitably disguised, in his popular story "The Voice of the Dolphins": a tankful of dolphins at a "Vienna Institute" begin to impart their compelling wisdom to the world through their keepers and interpreters, who are U.S. and Russian scientists; the narrator slyly implies that the keepers may be the real source of wisdom, exploiting mankind's fascination with superhuman saviors to save it.

A wild burst of optimism—or opportunism—energized Szilard in 1930 to organize a group of acquaintances, most of them young physicists, to begin the work of banding together. He was convinced in the mid-1920s that "the parliamentary form of democracy would not have a very long life in Germany" but he "thought that it might survive one or two generations." Within five years he understood otherwise. "I reached the conclusion something would go wrong in Germany . . . in 1930." Hjalmar Schacht, the president of the German Reichsbank, meeting in Paris that year with a committee of economists called to decide how much Germany could pay in war reparations, announced that Germany could pay none at all unless its former colonies, stripped from it after the war, were returned. "This was such a striking statement to make that it caught my attention, and I concluded that if Hjalmar Schacht believed he could get away with this, things must be rather bad. I was so impressed by this that I wrote a letter to my bank and transferred every single penny I had out of Germany into Switzerland."

A far more organized Bund was advancing to power in Germany with another and more primitive program to save the world. That program, set out arrogantly in an autobiographical book—*Mein Kampf*—would achieve a lengthy and bloody trial. Yet Szilard in the years ahead would lead a drive to assemble a Bund of sorts; submerged from view, working to more urgent and more immediate ends than utopia, that "closely knit group of people" would finally influence world events more enormously even than Nazism.

Sometime during the 1920s, a new field of research caught Szilard's attention: nuclear physics, the study of the nucleus of the atom, where most of its mass—and therefore its energy—is concentrated. He was familiar with the long record of outstanding work in the general field of radioactivity of the German chemist Otto Hahn and the Austrian physicist Lise Meitner, who made a productive team at the Kaiser Wilhelm Institute for Chemistry. No doubt he was also alert as always to the peculiar tension in the air that signaled the possibility of new developments.

The nuclei of some light atoms could be shattered by bombarding them with atomic particles; that much the great British experimental physicist Ernest Rutherford had already demonstrated. Rutherford used one nucleus to bombard another, but since both nuclei were strongly positively charged, the bombarded nucleus repelled most attacks. Physicists were therefore looking for ways to accelerate particles to greater velocities, to force them past the nucleus' electrical barrier. Szilard's design of a cyclotron-like particle accelerator that could serve such a purpose indicates that he was thinking about nuclear physics as early as 1928.

Until 1932 he did no more than think. He had other work and nuclear physics was not yet sufficiently interesting to him. It became compelling in 1932. A discovery in physics opened the field to new possibilities while discoveries Szilard made in literature and utopianism opened his mind to new approaches to world salvation.

On February 27, 1932, in a letter to the British journal *Nature,* physicist James Chadwick of the Cavendish Laboratory at Cambridge University, Ernest Rutherford's laboratory, announced the possible existence of a neutron. (He confirmed the neutron's existence in a longer paper in the *Proceedings of the Royal Society* four months later, but Szilard would no more have doubted it at the time of Chadwick's first cautious announcement than did Chadwick himself; like many scientific discoveries, it was obvious once it was demonstrated, and Szilard could repeat the demonstration in Berlin if he chose.) The neutron, a particle with nearly the same mass as the positively charged proton that until 1932 was the sole certain component of the atomic nucleus, had no electric charge, which meant it could pass through the surrounding electrical barrier and enter into the nucleus. The neutron would open the atomic nucleus to examination. It might even be a way to force the nucleus to give up some of its enormous energy.

Just then, in 1932, Szilard found or took up for the first time that appealing orphan among H. G. Wells' books that he had failed to discover before: *The World Set Free.* Despite its title, it was not a tract like *The Open Conspiracy.* It was a prophetic novel, published in 1914, before the beginning of the Great War. Thirty years later Szilard could still summarize *The World Set Free* in accurate detail. Wells describes, he says:

> . . . the liberation of atomic energy on a large scale for industrial purposes, the development of atomic bombs, and a world war which was apparently fought by an alliance of England, France, and perhaps including America, against Germany and Austria, the powers located in the central part of Europe. He places this war in the year 1956, and in this war the major cities of the world are all destroyed by atomic bombs.

More personal discoveries emerged from Wells' visionary novel—ideas that anticipated or echoed Szilard's utopian plans, responses that may have guided him in the years ahead. Wells writes that his scientist hero, for example, was "oppressed, he was indeed scared, by his sense of the immense consequences of his discovery. He had a vague idea that night that he ought not to publish his results, that they were premature, that some secret association of wise men should take care of his work and hand it on from generation to generation until the world was riper for its practical application."

Yet *The World Set Free* influenced Szilard less than its subject matter might suggest. "This book made a very great impression on me, but I didn't regard it as anything but fiction. It didn't start me thinking of whether or not such things could in fact happen. I had not been working in nuclear physics up to that time."

By his own account, a different and quieter dialogue changed the direction of Szilard's work. The friend who had introduced him to H. G. Wells returned in 1932 to the Continent:

> I met him again in Berlin and there ensued a memorable conversation. Otto Mandl said that now he really thought he knew what it would take to save mankind from a series of ever-recurring wars that could destroy it. He said that Man has a heroic streak in himself. Man is not satisfied with a happy idyllic life: he has the need to fight and to encounter danger. And he concluded that what mankind must do to save itself is to launch an enterprise aimed at leaving the earth. On this task he thought the energies of mankind

> could be concentrated and the need for heroism could be satisfied. I remember very well my own reaction. I told him that this was somewhat new to me, and that I really didn't know whether I would agree with him. The only thing I could say was this: that if I came to the conclusion that this was what mankind needed, if I wanted to contribute something to save mankind, then I would probably go into nuclear physics, because only through the liberation of atomic energy could we obtain the means which would enable man not only to leave the earth but to leave the solar system.

Such must have been Szilard's conclusion; that year he moved to the Harnack House of the Kaiser Wilhelm Institutes—a residence for visiting scientists sponsored by German industry, a faculty club of sorts—and approached Lise Meitner about the possibility of doing experimental work with her in nuclear physics. Thus to save mankind.

He always lived out of suitcases, in rented rooms. At the Harnack House he kept the keys to his two suitcases at hand and the suitcases packed. "All I had to do was turn the key and leave when things got too bad." Things got bad enough to delay a decision about working with Meitner. An older Hungarian friend, Szilard remembers—Michael Polanyi, a chemist at the Kaiser Wilhelm Institutes with a family to consider—viewed the German political scene optimistically, like many others in Germany at the time. "They all thought that civilized Germans would not stand for anything really rough happening." Szilard held no such sanguine view, noting that the Germans themselves were paralyzed with cynicism, one of the uglier effects on morals of losing a major war.

Adolf Hitler was appointed Chancellor of Germany on January 30, 1933. On the night of February 27 a Nazi gang directed by the head of the Berlin SA, Hitler's private army, set fire to the imposing chambers of the Reichstag. The building was totally destroyed. Hitler blamed the arson on the Communists and bullied a stunned Reichstag into awarding him emergency powers. Szilard found Polanyi still unconvinced after the fire. "He looked at me and said, 'Do you really mean to say that you think that [Minister] of the Interior [Hermann Göring] had anything to do with this?' and I said, 'Yes, this is precisely what I mean.' He just looked at me with incredulous eyes." In late March, Jewish judges and lawyers in Prussia and Bavaria were dismissed from practice. On the weekend of April 1, Julius Streicher directed a national boycott of Jewish businesses and Jews were beaten in the streets. "I took a train from Berlin to Vienna on a certain date, close to the first of April, 1933," Szilard writes. "The train was empty. The same train the next day was overcrowded, was stopped at the frontier, the people had to get out, and everybody was interrogated by the Nazis.

This just goes to show that if you want to succeed in this world you don't have to be much cleverer than other people, you just have to be one day earlier."

The Law for the Restoration of the Career Civil Service was promulgated throughout Germany on April 7 and thousands of Jewish scholars and scientists lost their positions in German universities. From England, where he landed in early May, Szilard went furiously to work to help them emigrate and to find jobs for them in England, the United States, Palestine, India, China and points between. If he couldn't yet save all the world, he could at least save some part of it.

He came up for air in September. By then he was living at the Imperial Hotel in Russell Square, having transferred £1,595 from Zurich to his bank in London. More than half the money, £854, he held in trust for his brother Béla; the rest would see him through the year. Szilard's funds came from his patent licenses, refrigeration consulting and *Privatdozent* fees. He was busy finding jobs for others and couldn't be bothered to seek one himself. He had few expenses in any case; a week's lodging and three meals a day at a good London hotel cost about £5.5; he was a bachelor most of his life and his needs were simple.

"I was no longer thinking about this conversation [with Otto Mandl about space travel], or about H. G. Wells' book either, until I found myself in London about the time of the British Association [meeting]." Szilard's syntax slips here: the crucial word is *until.* He had been too distracted by events and by rescue work to think creatively about nuclear physics. He had even been considering going into biology, a radical change of field but one that a number of able physicists have managed, in prewar days and since. Such a change is highly significant psychologically and Szilard was to make it in 1946. But in September 1933, a meeting of the British Association for the Advancement of Science, an annual assembly, intervened.

If on Friday, September 1, lounging in the lobby of the Imperial Hotel, Szilard read *The Times'* review of *The Shape of Things to Come,* then he noticed the anonymous critic's opinion that Wells had "attempted something of the sort on earlier occasions—that rather haphazard work, 'The World Set Free,' comes particularly to mind—but never with anything like the same continuous abundance and solidity of detail, or indeed, the power to persuade as to the terrifying probability of some of the more immediate and disastrous developments." And may have thought again of the atomic bombs of Wells' earlier work, of Wells' Open Conspiracy and his own, of Nazi Germany and its able physicists, of ruined cities and general war.

Without question Szilard read *The Times* of September 12, with its provocative sequence of headlines:

THE BRITISH ASSOCIATION

BREAKING DOWN
THE ATOM

TRANSFORMATION OF
ELEMENTS

Ernest Rutherford, *The Times* reported, had recited a history of "the discoveries of the last quarter of a century in atomic transmutation," including:

THE NEUTRON
NOVEL TRANSFORMATIONS

All of which made Szilard restive. The leading scientists in Great Britain were meeting and he wasn't there. He was safe, he had money in the bank, but he was only another anonymous Jewish refugee down and out in London, lingering over morning coffee in a hotel lobby, unemployed and unknown.

Then, midway along the second column of *The Times'* summary of Rutherford's speech, he found:

> HOPE OF TRANSFORMING ANY ATOM
>
> What, Lord Rutherford asked in conclusion, were the prospects 20 or 30 years ahead?
>
> High voltages of the order of millions of volts would probably be unnecessary as a means of accelerating the bombarding particles. Transformations might be effected with 30,000 or 70,000 volts. . . . He believed that we should be able to transform all the elements ultimately.
>
> We might in these processes obtain very much more energy than the proton supplied, but on the average we could not expect to obtain energy in this way. It was a very poor and inefficient way of producing energy, and anyone who looked for a source of power in the transformation of the atoms was talking moonshine.

Did Szilard know what "moonshine" meant—"foolish or visionary talk"? Did he have to ask the doorman as he threw down the newspaper and stormed out into the street? "Lord Rutherford was reported to have said that whoever talks about the liberation of atomic energy on an industrial scale is talking moonshine. Pronouncements of experts to the effect that something cannot be done have always irritated me."

"This sort of set me pondering as I was walking in the streets of London, and I remember that I stopped for a red light at the intersection of Southampton Row. . . . I was pondering whether Lord Rutherford might not prove to be wrong."

"It occurred to me that neutrons, in contrast to alpha particles, do not ionize [i.e., interact electrically with] the substance through which they pass.

"Consequently, neutrons need not stop until they hit a nucleus with which they may react."

Szilard was not the first to realize that the neutron might slip past the positive electrical barrier of the nucleus; that realization had come to other physicists as well. But he was the first to imagine a mechanism whereby more energy might be released in the neutron's bombardment of the nucleus than the neutron itself supplied.

There was an analogous process in chemistry. Polanyi had studied it. A comparatively small number of active particles—oxygen atoms, for example—admitted into a chemically unstable system, worked like leaven to elicit a chemical reaction at temperatures much lower than the temperature that the reaction normally required. Chain reaction, the process was called. One center of chemical reaction produces thousands of product molecules. One center occasionally has an especially favorable encounter with a reactant and instead of forming only one new center, it forms two or more, each of which is capable in turn of propagating a reaction chain.

Chemical chain reactions are self-limiting. Were they not, they would run away in geometric progression: 1, 2, 4, 8, 16, 32, 64, 128, 256, 512, 1024, 2048, 4096, 8192, 16384, 32768, 65536, 131072, 262144, 524288, 1048576, 2097152, 4194304, 8388608, 16777216, 33554432, 67108868, 134217736 . . .

"As the light changed to green and I crossed the street," Szilard recalls, "it . . . suddenly occurred to me that if we could find an element which is split by neutrons and which would emit *two* neutrons when it absorbs *one* neutron, such an element, if assembled in sufficiently large mass, could sustain a nuclear chain reaction.

"I didn't see at the moment just how one would go about finding such an element, or what experiments would be needed, but the idea never left me. In certain circumstances it might be possible to set up a nuclear chain reaction, liberate energy on an industrial scale, and construct atomic bombs."

Leo Szilard stepped up onto the sidewalk. Behind him the light changed to red.

2

Atoms and Void

Atomic energy requires an atom. No such beast was born legitimately into physics until the beginning of the twentieth century. The atom as an idea—as an invisible layer of eternal, elemental substance below the world of appearances where things combine, teem, dissolve and rot—is ancient. Leucippus, a Greek philosopher of the fifth century B.C. whose name survives on the strength of an allusion in Aristotle, proposed the concept; Democritus, a wealthy Thracian of the same era and wider repute, developed it. " 'For by convention color exists,' " the Greek physician Galen quotes from one of Democritus' seventy-two lost books, " 'by convention bitter, by convention sweet, but in reality atoms and void.' " From the seventeenth century onward, physicists postulated atomic models of the world whenever developments in physical theory seemed to require them. But whether or not atoms really existed was a matter for continuing debate.

Gradually the debate shifted to the question of what kind of atom was necessary and possible. Isaac Newton imagined something like a miniature billiard ball to serve the purposes of his mechanical universe of masses in motion: "It seems probable to me," he wrote in 1704, "that God in the beginning formed matter in solid, massy, hard, impenetrable, movable particles, of such sizes and figures, and with such other properties, and in such proportion to space, as most conduced to the end to which he formed them." The Scottish physicist James Clerk Maxwell, who organized the founding of the Cavendish Laboratory, published a seminal *Treatise on Electricity and Magnetism* in 1873 that modified Newton's purely mechanical universe of particles colliding in a void by introducing into it the idea of an electromagnetic field. The field permeated the void; electric and magnetic energy propagated through it at the speed of light; light itself, Clerk Maxwell demonstrated, is a form of electromagnetic radiation. But despite his modifications, Clerk Maxwell was as devoted as Newton to a hard, mechanical atom:

> Though in the course of ages catastrophes have occurred and may yet occur in the heavens, though ancient systems may be dissolved and new systems evolved out of their ruins, the [atoms] out of which [the sun and the planets] are built—the foundation stones of the material universe—remain unbroken and unworn. They continue this day as they were created—perfect in number and measure and weight.

Max Planck thought otherwise. He doubted that atoms existed at all, as did many of his colleagues—the particulate theory of matter was an English invention more than a Continental, and its faintly Britannic odor made it repulsive to the xenophobic German nose—but if atoms did exist he was sure they could not be mechanical. "It is of paramount importance," he confessed in his *Scientific Autobiography,* "that the outside world is something independent from man, something absolute, and the quest for laws which apply to this absolute appeared to me as the most sublime scientific pursuit in life." Of all the laws of physics, Planck believed that the thermodynamic laws applied most basically to the independent "outside world" that his need for an absolute required. He saw early that purely mechanical atoms violated the second law of thermodynamics. His choice was clear.

The second law specifies that heat will not pass spontaneously from a colder to a hotter body without some change in the system. Or, as Planck himself generalized it in his Ph.D. dissertation at the University of Munich in 1879, that "the process of heat conduction cannot be completely reversed by any means." Besides forbidding the construction of perpetual-motion machines, the second law defines what Planck's predecessor Rudolf Clausius named *entropy:* because energy dissipates as heat whenever work is done—heat that cannot be collected back into useful, organized form—the universe must slowly run down to randomness. This vision of increasing disorder means that the universe is one-way and not reversible; the second law is the expression in physical form of what we call time. But the equations of mechanical physics—of what is now called classical physics—

theoretically allowed the universe to run equally well forward or backward. "Thus," an important German chemist complained, "in a purely mechanical world, the tree could become a shoot and a seed again, the butterfly turn back into a caterpillar, and the old man into a child. No explanation is given by the mechanistic doctrine for the fact that this does not happen. . . . The actual irreversibility of natural phenomena thus proves the existence of phenomena that cannot be described by mechanical equations; and with this the verdict on scientific materialism is settled." Planck, writing a few years earlier, was characteristically more succinct: "The consistent implementation of the second law . . . is incompatible with the assumption of finite atoms."

A major part of the problem was that atoms were not then directly accessible to experiment. They were a useful concept in chemistry, where they were invoked to explain why certain substances—elements—combine to make other substances but cannot themselves be chemically broken down. Atoms seemed to be the reason gases behaved as they did, expanding to fill whatever container they were let into and pushing equally on all the container's walls. They were invoked again to explain the surprising discovery that every element, heated in a laboratory flame or vaporized in an electric arc, colors the resulting light and that such light, spread out into its rainbow spectrum by a prism or a diffraction grating, invariably is divided into bands by characteristic bright lines. But as late as 1894, when Robert Cecil, the third Marquis of Salisbury, chancellor of Oxford and former Prime Minister of England, catalogued the unfinished business of science in his presidential address to the British Association, whether atoms were real or only convenient and what structure they hid were still undecided issues:

> What the atom of each element is, whether it is a movement, or a thing, or a vortex, or a point having inertia, whether there is any limit to its divisibility, and, if so, how that limit is imposed, whether the long list of elements is final, or whether any of them have any common origin, all these questions remain surrounded by a darkness as profound as ever.

Physics worked that way, sorting among alternatives: all science works that way. The chemist Michael Polanyi, Leo Szilard's friend, looked into the workings of science in his later years at the University of Manchester and at Oxford. He discovered a traditional organization far different from what most nonscientists suppose. A "republic of science," he called it, a community of independent men and women freely cooperating, "a highly simplified example of a free society." Not all philosophers of science, which is what Polanyi became, have agreed. Even Polanyi sometimes called science an "orthodoxy." But his republican model of science is powerful in the same way successful scientific models are powerful: it explains relationships that have not been clear.

Polanyi asked straightforward questions. How were scientists chosen? What oath of allegiance did they swear? Who guided their research—chose the problems to be studied, approved the experiments, judged the value of the results? In the last analysis, who decided what was scientifically "true"? Armed with these questions, Polanyi then stepped back and looked at science from outside.

Behind the great structure that in only three centuries had begun to reshape the entire human world lay a basic commitment to a naturalistic view of life. Other views of life dominated at other times and places—the magical, the mythological. Children learned the naturalistic outlook when they learned to speak, when they learned to read, when they went to school. "Millions are spent annually on the cultivation and dissemination of science by the public authorities," Polanyi wrote once when he felt impatient with those who refused to understand his point, "who will not give a penny for the advancement of astrology or sorcery. In other words, our civilization is deeply committed to certain beliefs about the nature of things; beliefs which are different, for example, from those to which the early Egyptian or the Aztec civilizations were committed."

Most young people learned no more than the orthodoxy of science. They acquired "the established doctrine, the dead letter." Some, at university, went on to study the beginnings of method. They practiced experimental proof in routine research. They discovered science's "uncertainties and its eternally provisional nature." That began to bring it to life.

Which was not yet to become a scientist. To become a scientist, Polanyi thought, required "a full initiation." Such an initiation came from "close personal association with the intimate views and practice of a distinguished master." The practice of science was not itself a science; it was an art, to be passed from master to apprentice as the art of painting is passed or as the skills and traditions of the law or of medicine are passed. You could not learn the law from books and classes alone. You could not learn medicine. No more could you learn science, because nothing in science ever quite fits; no experiment is ever final proof; everything is simplified and approximate.

The American theoretical physicist Richard Feynman once spoke about his science with similar candor to a lecture hall crowded with undergraduates at the California Institute of Technology. "What do we mean by 'understanding' something?" Feynman asked innocently. His amused sense of human limitation informs his answer:

> We can imagine that this complicated array of moving things which constitutes "the world" is something like a great chess game being played by the gods, and we are observers of the game. We do not know what the rules of the game are; all we are allowed to do is to *watch* the playing. Of course, if we watch long enough, we may eventually catch on to a few of the rules. *The rules of the game* are what we mean by *fundamental physics.* Even if we know every rule, however . . . what we really can explain in terms of those rules is very limited, because almost all situations are so enormously complicated that we cannot follow the plays of the game using the rules, much less tell what is going to happen next. We must, therefore, limit ourselves to the more basic question of the rules of the game. If we know the rules, we consider that we "understand" the world.

Learning the feel of proof; learning judgment; learning which hunches to play; learning which stunning calculations to rework, which experimental results *not* to trust: these skills admitted you to the spectators' benches at the chess game of the gods, and acquiring them required sitting first at the feet of a master.

Polanyi found one other necessary requirement for full initiation into science: belief. If science has become the orthodoxy of the West, individuals are nevertheless still free to take it or leave it, in whole or in part; believers in astrology, Marxism and virgin birth abound. But "no one can become a scientist unless he presumes that the scientific doctrine and method are fundamentally sound and that their ultimate premises can be unquestioningly accepted."

Becoming a scientist is necessarily an act of profound commitment to the scientific system and the scientific world view. "Any account of science which does not explicitly describe it as something we believe in is essentially incomplete and a false pretense. It amounts to a claim that science is essentially different from and superior to all human beliefs that are not scientific statements—and this is untrue." Belief is the oath of allegiance that scientists swear.

That was how scientists were chosen and admitted to the order. They constituted a republic of educated believers taught through a chain of masters and apprentices to judge carefully the slippery edges of their work.

Who then guided that work? The question was really two questions: who decided which problems to study, which experiments to perform? And who judged the value of the results?

Polanyi proposed an analogy. Imagine, he said, a group of workers faced with the problem of assembling a very large, very complex jigsaw puzzle. How could they organize themselves to do the job most efficiently?

Each worker could take some of the pieces from the pile and try to fit them together. That would be an efficient method if assembling a puzzle was like shelling peas. But it wasn't. The pieces weren't isolated. They fitted together into a whole. And the chance of any one worker's collection of pieces fitting together was small. Even if the group made enough copies of the pieces to give every worker the entire puzzle to attack, no one would accomplish as much alone as the group might if it could contrive a way to work together.

The best way to do the job, Polanyi argued, was to allow each worker to keep track of what every other worker was doing. "Let them work on putting the puzzle together in the sight of the others, so that every time a piece of it is fitted in by one [worker], all the others will immediately watch out for the next step that becomes possible in consequence." That way, even though each worker acts on his own initiative, he acts to further the entire group's achievement. The group works independently together; the puzzle is assembled in the most efficient way.

Polanyi thought science reached into the unknown along a series of what he called "growing points," each point the place where the most productive discoveries were being made. Alerted by their network of scientific publications and professional friendships—by the complete openness of their communication, an absolute and vital freedom of speech—scientists rushed to work at just those points where their particular talents would bring them the maximum emotional and intellectual return on their investment of effort and thought.

It was clear, then, who among scientists judged the value of scientific results: every member of the group, as in a Quaker meeting. "The authority of scientific opinion remains *essentially mutual;* it is established *between* scientists, not *above* them." There were leading scientists, scientists who worked with unusual fertility at the growing points of their fields; but science had no ultimate leaders. Consensus ruled.

Not that every scientist was competent to judge every contribution. The network solved that problem too. Suppose Scientist M announces a new result. He knows his highly specialized subject better than anyone in the world; who is competent to judge him? But next to Scientist M are Scientists L and N. Their subjects overlap M's, so they understand his work well enough to assess its quality and reliability and to understand where it fits into science. Next to L and N are other scientists, K and O and J and P, who know L and N well enough to decide whether to trust their judgment about M. On out to Scientists A and Z, whose subjects are almost completely removed from M's.

"This network is the seat of scientific opinion," Polanyi emphasized; "of an opinion which is not held by any single human brain, but which, split

into thousands of different fragments, is held by a multitude of individuals, each of whom endorses the other's opinion at second hand, by relying on the consensual chains which link him to all the others through a sequence of overlapping neighborhoods." Science, Polanyi was hinting, worked like a giant brain of individual intelligences linked together. That was the source of its cumulative and seemingly inexorable power. But the price of that power, as both Polanyi and Feynman are careful to emphasize, is voluntary limitation. Science succeeds in the difficult task of sustaining a political network among men and women of differing backgrounds and differing values, and in the even more difficult task of discovering the rules of the chess game of the gods, by severely limiting its range of competence. "Physics," as Eugene Wigner once reminded a group of his fellows, "does not even try to give us complete information about the events around us—it gives information about the *correlations* between those events."

Which still left the question of what standards scientists consulted when they passed judgment on the contributions of their peers. Good science, original work, always went beyond the body of received opinion, always represented a dissent from orthodoxy. How, then, could the orthodox fairly assess it?

Polanyi suspected that science's system of masters and apprentices protected it from rigidity. The apprentice learned high standards of judgment from his master. At the same time he learned to trust his *own* judgment: he learned the possibility and the necessity of dissent. Books and lectures might teach rules; masters taught controlled rebellion, if only by the example of their own original—and in that sense rebellious—work.

Apprentices learned three broad criteria of scientific judgment. The first criterion was plausibility. That would eliminate crackpots and frauds. It might also (and sometimes did) eliminate ideas so original that the orthodox could not recognize them, but to work at all, science had to take that risk. The second criterion was scientific value, a composite consisting of equal parts accuracy, importance to the entire system of whatever branch of science the idea belonged to, and intrinsic interest. The third criterion was originality. Patent examiners assess an invention for originality according to the degree of surprise the invention produces in specialists familiar with the art. Scientists judged new theories and new discoveries similarly. Plausibility and scientific value measured an idea's quality by the standards of orthodoxy; originality measured the quality of its dissent.

Polanyi's model of an open republic of science where each scientist judges the work of his peers against mutually agreed upon and mutually supported standards explains why the atom found such precarious lodging in nineteenth-century physics. It was plausible; it had considerable scientific value, especially in systematic importance; but no one had yet made any surprising discoveries about it. None, at least, sufficient to convince the network of only about one thousand men and women throughout the world in 1895 who called themselves physicists and the larger, associated network of chemists.

The atom's time was at hand. The great surprises in basic science in the nineteenth century came in chemistry. The great surprises in basic science in the first half of the twentieth century would come in physics.

In 1895, when young Ernest Rutherford roared up out of the Antipodes to study physics at the Cavendish with a view to making his name, the New Zealand he left behind was still a rough frontier. British nonconformist craftsmen and farmers and a few adventurous gentry had settled the rugged volcanic archipelago in the 1840s, pushing aside the Polynesian Maori who had found it first five centuries before; the Maori gave up serious resistance after decades of bloody skirmish only in 1871, the year Rutherford was born. He attended recently established schools, drove the cows home for milking, rode horseback into the bush to shoot wild pigeons from the berry-laden branches of virgin miro trees, helped at his father's flax mill at Brightwater where wild flax cut from aboriginal swamps was retted, scutched and hackled for linen thread and tow. He lost two younger brothers to drowning; the family searched the Pacific shore near the farm for months.

It was a hard and healthy childhood. Rutherford capped it by winning scholarships, first to modest Nelson College in nearby Nelson, South Island, then to the University of New Zealand, where he earned an M.A. with double firsts in mathematics and physical science at twenty-two. He was sturdy, enthusiastic and smart, qualities he would need to carry him from rural New Zealand to the leadership of British science. Another, more subtle quality, a braiding of country-boy acuity with a profound frontier innocence, was crucial to his unmatched lifetime record of physical discovery. As his protégé James Chadwick said, Rutherford's ultimate distinction was "his genius to be astonished." He preserved that quality against every assault of success and despite a well-hidden but sometimes sickening insecurity, the stiff scar of his colonial birth.

His genius found its first occasion at the University of New Zealand, where Rutherford in 1893 stayed on to earn a B.Sc. Heinrich Hertz's 1887 discovery of "electric waves"—radio, we call the phenomenon now—had impressed Rutherford wonderfully, as it did young people everywhere in the world. To study the waves he set up a Hertzian oscillator—electrically charged metal knobs spaced to make sparks jump between metal plates—in a dank basement cloakroom. He was looking for a problem for his first independent work of research.

He located it in a general agreement among scientists, pointedly including Hertz himself, that high-frequency alternating current, the sort of current a Hertzian oscillator produced when the spark radiation surged rapidly back and forth between the metal plates, would not magnetize iron. Rutherford suspected otherwise and ingeniously proved he was right. The work earned him an 1851 Exhibition scholarship to Cambridge. He was spading up potatoes in the family garden when the cable came. His mother called the news down the row; he laughed and jettisoned his spade, shouting triumph for son and mother both: "That's the last potato I'll dig!" (Thirty-six years later, when he was created Baron Rutherford of Nelson, he sent his mother a cable in her turn: "Now Lord Rutherford, more your honour than mine.")

"Magnetization of iron by high-frequency discharges" was skilled observation and brave dissent. With deeper originality, Rutherford noticed a subtle converse reaction while magnetizing iron needles with high-frequency current: needles already saturated with magnetism became partly *demagnetized* when a high-frequency current passed by. His genius to be astonished was at work. He quickly realized that he could use radio waves, picked up by a suitable antenna and fed into a coil of wire, to induce a high-frequency current into a packet of magnetized needles. Then the needles would be partly demagnetized and if he set a compass beside them it would swing to show the change.

By the time he arrived on borrowed funds at Cambridge in September 1895 to take up work at the Cavendish under its renowned director, J. J. Thomson, Rutherford had elaborated his observation into a device for detecting radio waves at a distance—in effect, the first crude radio receiver. Guglielmo Marconi was still laboring to perfect his version of a receiver at his father's estate in Italy; for a few months the young New Zealander held the world record in detecting radio transmissions at a distance.

Rutherford's experiments delighted the distinguished British scientists who learned of them from J. J. Thomson. They quickly adopted Rutherford, even seating him one evening at the Fellows' high table at King's in the place of honor next to the provost, which made him feel, he said, "like an ass in a lion's skin" and which shaded certain snobs on the Cavendish staff green with envy. Thomson generously arranged for a nervous but exultant Rutherford to read his third scientific paper, "A magnetic detector of electrical waves and some of its applications," at the June 18, 1896, meeting of the Royal Society of London, the foremost scientific organization in the world. Marconi only caught up with him in September.

Rutherford was poor. He was engaged to Mary Newton, the daughter of his University of New Zealand landlady, but the couple had postponed marriage until his fortunes improved. Working to improve them, he wrote his fiancée in the midst of his midwinter research: "The reason I am so keen on the subject [of radio detection] is because of its practical importance. . . . If my next week's experiments come out as well as I anticipate, I see a chance of making cash rapidly in the future."

There is mystery here, mystery that carries forward all the way to "moonshine." Rutherford was known in later years as a hard man with a research budget, unwilling to accept grants from industry or private donors, unwilling even to ask, convinced that string and sealing wax would carry the day. He was actively hostile to the commercialization of scientific research, telling his Russian protégé Peter Kapitza, for example, when Kapitza was offered consulting work in industry, "You cannot serve God and Mammon at the same time." The mystery bears on what C. P. Snow, who knew him, calls the "one curious exception" to Rutherford's "infallible" intuition, adding that "no scientist has made fewer mistakes." The exception was Rutherford's refusal to admit the possibility of usable energy from the atom, the very refusal that irritated Leo Szilard in 1933. "I believe that he was fearful that his beloved nuclear domain was about to be invaded by infidels who wished to blow it to pieces by exploiting it commercially," another protégé, Mark Oliphant, speculates. Yet Rutherford himself was eager to exploit radio commercially in January 1896. Whence the dramatic and lifelong change?

The record is ambiguous but suggestive. The English scientific tradition was historically genteel. It generally disdained research patents and any other legal and commercial restraints that threatened the open dissemination of scientific results. In practice that guard of scientific liberty could molder into clubbish distaste for "vulgar commercialism." Ernest Marsden, a Rutherford-trained physicist and an insightful biographer, heard that "in his early days at Cambridge there were some few who said that Rutherford was not a cultured man." One component of that canard may have been contempt for his eagerness to make a profit from radio.

It seems that J. J. Thomson intervened. A grand new work had abruptly offered itself. On November 8, 1895, one month after Rutherford arrived at Cambridge, the German physicist Wilhelm Röntgen discovered X rays radiating from the fluorescing glass wall of a cathode-ray tube. Röntgen reported his discovery in December and stunned the world. The strange radiation was a new growing point for science and Thomson began studying it almost immediately. At the same time he also continued his experiments with cathode rays, experiments that would culminate in 1897 in his identification of what he called the "negative corpuscle"—the electron, the first atomic particle to be identified. He must have needed help. He would also have understood the extraordinary opportunity for original research that radiation offered a young man of Rutherford's skill at experiment.

To settle the issue Thomson wrote the grand old man of British science, Lord Kelvin, then seventy-two, asking his opinion of the commercial possibilities of radio—"before tempting Rutherford to turn to the new subject," Marsden says. Kelvin after all, vulgar commercialism or not, had developed the transoceanic telegraph cable. "The reply of the great man was that [radio] might justify a captial expenditure of a £100,000 Company on its promotion, but no more."

By April 24 Rutherford has seen the light. He writes Mary Newton: "I hope to make both ends meet somehow, but I must expect to dub out my first year. . . . My scientific work at present is progressing slowly. I am working with the Professor this term on Röntgen Rays. I am a little full up of my old subject and am glad of a change. I expect it will be a good thing for me to work with the Professor for a time. I have done one research to show I can work by myself." The tone is chastened and not nearly convinced, as if a ghostly, parental J. J. Thomson were speaking through Rutherford to his fiancée. He has not yet appeared before the Royal Society, where he was hardly "a little full up" of his subject. But the turnabout is accomplished. Hereafter Rutherford's healthy ambition will go to scientific honors, not commercial success.

It seems probable that J. J. Thomson sat eager young Ernest Rutherford down in the darkly paneled rooms of the Gothic Revival Cavendish Laboratory that Clerk Maxwell had founded, at the university where Newton wrote his great *Principia,* and kindly told him he could not serve God and Mammon at the same time. It seems probable that the news that the distinguished director of the Cavendish had written the Olympian Lord Kelvin about the commercial ambitions of a brash New Zealander chagrined Rutherford to the bone and that he went away from the encounter feeling grotesquely like a parvenu. He would never make the same mistake again, even if it meant strapping his laboratories for funds, even if it meant driving away the best of his protégés, as eventually it did. Even if it meant that energy from his cherished atom could be nothing more than moonshine. But if Rutherford gave up commercial wealth for holy science, he won the atom in exchange. He found its constituent parts and named them. With string and sealing wax he made the atom real.

The sealing wax was blood red and it was the Bank of England's most visible contribution to science. British experimenters used Bank of England sealing wax to make glass tubes airtight. Rutherford's earliest work on the atom, like J. J. Thomson's work with cathode rays, grew out of nineteenth-century examination of the fascinating effects produced by evacuating the air from a glass tube that had metal plates sealed into its ends and then connecting the metal plates to a battery or an induction coil. Thus charged with electricity, the emptiness inside the sealed tube glowed. The glow emerged from the negative plate—the cathode—and disappeared into the positive plate—the anode. If you made the anode into a cylinder and sealed the cylinder into the middle of the tube you could project a beam of glow—of cathode rays—through the cylinder and on into the end of the tube opposite the cathode. If the beam was energetic enough to hit the glass it would make the glass fluoresce. The cathode-ray tube, suitably modified, its all-glass end flattened and covered with phosphors to increase the fluorescence, is the television tube of today.

In the spring of 1897 Thomson demonstrated that the beam of glowing matter in a cathode-ray tube was not made up of light waves, as (he wrote drily) "the almost unanimous opinion of German physicists" held. Rather, cathode rays were negatively charged particles boiling off the negative cathode and attracted to the positive anode. These particles could be deflected by an electric field and bent into curved paths by a magnetic field. They were much lighter than hydrogen atoms and were identical "whatever the gas through which the discharge passes" if gas was introduced into the tube. Since they were lighter than the lightest known kind of matter and identical regardless of the kind of matter they were born from, it followed that they must be some basic constituent *part* of matter, and if they were a part, then there must be a whole. The real, physical electron implied a real, physical atom: the particulate theory of matter was therefore justified for the first time convincingly by physical experiment. They sang J. J.'s success at the annual Cavendish dinner:

The corpuscle won the day
And in freedom went away
And became a cathode ray.

Armed with the electron, and knowing from other experiments that what was left when electrons were stripped away from an atom was a much more massive remainder that was positively charged, Thomson went on in the next decade to develop a model of the atom that came to be called the "plum pudding" model. The Thomson atom, "a number of negatively-electrified corpuscles enclosed in a sphere of uniform positive electrification" like raisins in a pudding, was a hybrid: particulate electrons and diffuse remainder. It served the useful purpose of demonstrating mathematically that electrons could be arranged in stable configurations within an atom and that the mathematically stable arrangements could account for the similarities and regularities among chemical elements that the periodic table of the elements displays. It was becoming clear that electrons were responsible for chemical affinities between elements, that chemistry was ultimately electrical.

Thomson just missed discovering X rays in 1894. He was not so unlucky in legend as the Oxford physicist Frederick Smith, who found that photographic plates kept near a cathode-ray tube were liable to be fogged and merely told his assistant to move them to another place. Thomson noticed that glass tubing held "at a distance of some feet from the discharge-tube" fluoresced just as the wall of the tube itself did when bombarded with cathode rays, but he was too intent on studying the rays themselves to pursue the cause. Röntgen isolated the effect by covering his cathode-ray tube with black paper. When a nearby screen of fluorescent material still glowed he realized that whatever was causing the screen to glow was passing through the paper and the intervening air. If he held his hand between the covered tube and the screen, his hand slightly reduced the glow on the screen but in dark shadow he could *see its bones.*

Röntgen's discovery intrigued other researchers besides J. J. Thomson and Ernest Rutherford. The Frenchman Henri Becquerel was a third-generation physicist who, like his father and grandfather before him, occupied the chair of physics at the Musée d'Histoire Naturelle in Paris; like them also he was an expert on phosphorescence and fluorescence—in his case, particularly of uranium. He heard a report of Röntgen's work at the weekly meeting of the Académie des Sciences on January 20, 1896. He learned that the X rays emerged from the fluorescing glass, which immediately suggested to him that he should test various fluorescing materials to see if they also emitted X rays. He worked for ten days without success, read an article on X rays on January 30 that encouraged him to keep working and decided to try a uranium salt, uranyl potassium sulfate.

His first experiment succeeded—he found that the uranium salt emitted radiation—but misled him. He had sealed a photographic plate in black paper, sprinkled a layer of the uranium salt onto the paper and "exposed the whole thing to the sun for several hours." When he developed the photographic plate "I saw the silhouette of the phosphorescent substance in black on the negative." He mistakenly thought sunlight activated the effect, much as cathode rays released Röntgen's X rays from the glass.

The story of Becquerel's subsequent serendipity is famous. When he tried to repeat his experiment on February 26 and again on February 27 Paris was gray. He put the covered photographic plate away in a dark drawer, uranium salt in place. On March 1 he decided to go ahead and develop the plate, "expecting to find the images very feeble. On the contrary, the silhouettes appeared with great intensity. I thought at once that the action might be able to go on in the dark." Energetic, penetrating radiation from inert matter unstimulated by rays or light: now Rutherford had his subject, as Marie and Pierre Curie, looking for the pure element that radiated, had their backbreaking work.

Between 1898, when Rutherford first turned his attention to the phenomenon Henri Becquerel found and which Marie Curie named *radioactivity,* and 1911, when he made the most important discovery of his life, the young New Zealand physicist systematically dissected the atom.

He studied the radiations emitted by uranium and thorium and named two of them: "There are present at least two distinct types of radiation—one that is very readily absorbed, which will be termed for convenience the α [alpha] radiation, and the other of a more penetrative character, which will be termed the β [beta] radiation." (A Frenchman, P. V. Villard, later discovered the third distinct type, a form of high-energy X rays that was named gamma radiation in keeping with Rutherford's scheme.) The work was done at the Cavendish, but by the time he published it, in 1899, when he was twenty-seven, Rutherford had moved to Montreal to become professor of physics at McGill University. A Canadian tobacco merchant had given money there to build a physics laboratory and to endow a number of professorships, including Rutherford's. "The McGill University has a good name," Rutherford wrote his mother. "£500 is not so bad [a salary] and as the physical laboratory is the best of its kind in the world, I cannot complain."

In 1900 Rutherford reported the discovery of a radioactive gas emanating from the radioactive element thorium. Marie and Pierre Curie soon discovered that radium (which they had purified from uranium ores in 1898) also gave off a radioactive gas. Rutherford needed a good chemist to help him establish whether the thorium "emanation" was thorium or something else; fortunately he was able to shanghai a young Oxford man at McGill, Frederick Soddy, of talent sufficient eventually to earn a Nobel Prize. "At the beginning of the winter [of 1900]," Soddy remembers, "Ernest Rutherford, the Junior Professor of Physics, called on me in the laboratory and told me about the discoveries he had made. He had just returned with his bride from New Zealand . . . but before leaving Canada for his trip he had discovered what he called the thorium emanation. . . . I was, of course, intensely interested and suggested that the chemical character of the [substance] ought to be examined."

The gas proved to have no chemical character whatsoever. That, says Soddy, "conveyed the tremendous and inevitable conclusion that the element thorium was slowly and spontaneously transmuting itself into [chemically inert] argon gas!" Soddy and Rutherford had observed the spontaneous disintegration of the radioactive elements, one of the major discoveries of twentieth-century physics. They set about tracing the way uranium, radium and thorium changed their elemental nature by radiating away part of their substance as alpha and beta particles. They discovered that each different radioactive product possessed a characteristic "half-life," the time required for its radiation to reduce to half its previously measured intensity. The half-life measured the transmutation of half the atoms in an element into atoms of another element or of a physically variant form of the same element—an "isotope," as Soddy later named it. Half-life became a way to detect the presence of amounts of transmuted substances—"decay products"—too small to detect chemically. The half-life of uranium proved to be 4.5 billion years, of radium 1,620 years, of one decay product of thorium 22 minutes, of another decay product of thorium 27 days. Some decay products appeared and transmuted themselves in minute fractions of a second—in the twinkle of an eye. It was work of immense importance to physics, opening up field after new field to excited view, and "for more than two years," as Soddy remembered afterward, "life, scientific life, became hectic to a degree rare in the lifetime of an individual, rare perhaps in the lifetime of an institution."

Along the way Rutherford explored the radiation emanating from the radioactive elements in the course of their transmutation. He demonstrated that beta radiation consisted of high-energy electrons "similar in all respects to cathode rays." He suspected, and later in England conclusively proved, that alpha particles were positively charged helium atoms ejected during radioactive decay. Helium is found captured in the crystalline spaces of uranium and thorium ores; now he knew why.

An important 1903 paper written with Soddy, "Radioactive change," offered the first informed calculations of the amount of energy released by radioactive decay:

> It may therefore be stated that the total energy of radiation during the disintegration of one gram of radium cannot be less than 10^8 [i.e., 100,000,000] gram-calories, and may be between 10^9 and 10^{10} gram-calories. . . . The union of hydrogen and oxygen liberates approximately 4×10^3 [i.e., 4,000] gram-calories per gram of water produced, and this reaction sets free more energy for a given weight than any other chemical change known. The energy of radioactive change must therefore be at least twenty-thousand times, and may be a million times, as great as the energy of any molecular change.

That was the formal scientific statement; informally Rutherford inclined to whimsical eschatology. A Cambridge associate writing an article on radioactivity that year, 1903, considered quoting Rutherford's "playful suggestion that, could a proper detonator be found, it was just conceivable that a wave of atomic disintegration might be started through matter, which would indeed make this old world vanish in smoke." Rutherford liked to quip that "some fool in a laboratory might blow up the universe unawares." If atomic energy would never be useful, it might still be dangerous.

Soddy, who returned to England that year, examined the theme more seriously. Lecturing on radium to the Corps of Royal Engineers in 1904, he speculated presciently on the uses to which atomic energy might be put:

> It is probable that all heavy matter possesses—latent and bound up with the structure of the atom—a similar quantity of energy to that possessed by radium. If it could be tapped and controlled what an agent it would be in shaping the world's destiny! The man who put his hand on the lever by which a parsimonious nature regulates so jealously the output of this store of energy would possess a weapon by which he could destroy the earth if he chose.

Soddy did not think the possibility likely: "The fact that we exist is a proof that [massive energetic release] did not occur; that it has not occurred is the best possible assurance that it never will. We may trust Nature to guard her secret."

H. G. Wells thought Nature less trustworthy when he read similar statements in Soddy's 1909 book *Interpretation of Radium.* "My idea is taken from Soddy," he wrote of *The World Set Free.* "One of the good old scientific romances," he called his novel; it was important enough to him that he interrupted a series of social novels to write it. Rutherford's and Soddy's discussions of radioactive change therefore inspired the science-fiction novel that eventually started Leo Szilard thinking about chain reactions and atomic bombs.

In the summer of 1903 the Rutherfords visited the Curies in Paris. Mme. Curie happened to be receiving her doctorate in science on the day of their arrival; mutual friends arranged a celebration. "After a very lively evening," Rutherford recalled, "we retired about 11 o'clock in the garden, where Professor Curie brought out a tube coated in part with zinc sulphide and containing a large quantity of radium in solution. The luminosity was brilliant in the darkness and it was a splendid finale to an unforgettable day." The zinc-sulfide coating fluoresced white, making the radium's ejection of energetic particles on its progess down the periodic table from uranium to lead visible in the darkness of the Paris evening. The light was bright enough to show Rutherford Pierre Curie's hands, "in a very inflamed and painful state due to exposure to radium rays." Hands swollen with radiation burns was another object lesson in what the energy of matter could do.

A twenty-six-year-old German chemist from Frankfurt, Otto Hahn, came to Montreal in 1905 to work with Rutherford. Hahn had already discovered a new "element," radiothorium, later understood to be one of thorium's twelve isotopes. He studied thorium radiation with Rutherford; together they determined that the alpha particles ejected from thorium had the same mass as the alpha particles ejected from radium and those from another radioactive element, actinium. The various particles were probably therefore identical—one conclusion along the way to Rutherford's proof in 1908 that the alpha particle was inevitably a charged helium atom. Hahn went back to Germany in 1906 to begin a distinguished career as a discoverer of isotopes and elements; Leo Szilard encountered him working with physicist Lise Meitner at the Kaiser Wilhelm Institute for Physical Chemistry in the 1920s in Berlin.

Rutherford's research at McGill unraveling the complex transmutations of the radioactive elements earned him, in 1908, a Nobel Prize—not in physics but in chemistry. He had wanted that prize, writing his wife when she returned to New Zealand to visit her family in late 1904, "I may have a chance if I keep going," and again early in 1905, "They are all following on my trail, and if I am to have a chance for a Nobel Prize in the next few years I must keep my work moving." The award for chemistry rather than for physics at least amused him. "It remained to the end a good joke against him," says his son-in-law, "which he thoroughly appreciated, that he was thereby branded for all time as a chemist and no true physicist."

An eyewitness to the ceremonies said Rutherford looked ridiculously young—he was thirty-seven—and made the speech of the evening. He announced his recent confirmation, only briefly reported the month before, that the alpha particle was in fact helium. The confirming experiment was typically elegant. Rutherford had a glassblower make him a tube with extremely thin walls. He evacuated the tube and filled it with radon gas, a fertile source of alpha particles. The tube was gastight, but its thin walls allowed alpha particles to escape. Rutherford surrounded the radon tube with another glass tube, pumped out the air between the two tubes and sealed off the space. "After some days," he told his Stockholm audience triumphantly, "a bright spectrum of helium was observed in the outer vessel." Rutherford's experiments still stun with their simplicity. "In this Rutherford was an artist," says a former student. "All his experiments had style."

In the spring of 1907 Rutherford had left Montreal with his family—

by then including a six-year-old daughter, his only child—and moved back to England. He had accepted appointment as professor of physics at Manchester, in the city where John Dalton had first revived the atomic theory almost exactly a century earlier. Rutherford bought a house and went immediately to work. He inherited an experienced German physicist named Hans Geiger who had been his predecessor's assistant. Years later Geiger fondly recalled the Manchester days, Rutherford settled in among his gear:

> I see his quiet research room at the top of the physics building, under the roof, where his radium was kept and in which so much well-known work on the emanation was carried out. But I also see the gloomy cellar in which he had fitted up his delicate apparatus for the study of the alpha rays. Rutherford loved this room. One went down two steps and then heard from the darkness Rutherford's voice reminding one that a hot-pipe crossed the room at head-level, and to step over two water-pipes. Then finally, in the feeble light one saw the great man himself seated at his apparatus.

The Rutherford house was cheerier; another Manchester protégé liked to recall that "supper in the white-painted dining room on Saturdays and Sundays preceded pow-wows till all hours in the study on the first floor; tea on Sundays in the drawing room often followed a spin on the Cheshire roads in the motor." There was no liquor in the house because Mary Rutherford did not approve of drinking. Smoking she reluctantly allowed because her husband smoked heavily, pipe and cigarettes both.

Now in early middle age he was famously loud, a "tribal chief," as a student said, fond of banter and slang. He would march around the lab singing "Onward Christian Soldiers" off key. He took up room in the world now; you knew he was coming. He was ruddy-faced with twinkling blue eyes and he was beginning to develop a substantial belly. The diffidence was well hidden: his handshake was brief, limp and boneless; "he gave the impression," says another former student, "that he was shy of physical contact." He could still be mortified by condescension, blushing bright red and turning aside dumbstruck. With his students he was quieter, gentler, solid gold. "He was a man," pronounces one in high praise, "who never did dirty tricks."

Chaim Weizmann, the Russian-Jewish biochemist who was later elected the first president of Israel, was working at Manchester on fermentation products in those days. He and Rutherford became good friends. "Youthful, energetic, boisterous," Weizmann recalled, "he suggested anything but the scientist. He talked readily and vigorously on every subject under the sun, often without knowing anything about it. Going down to the refectory for lunch I would hear the loud, friendly voice rolling up the corridor." Rutherford had no political knowledge at all, Weizmann thought, but excused him on the grounds that his important scientific work took all his time. "He was a kindly person, but he did not suffer fools gladly."

In September 1907, his first term at Manchester, Rutherford made up a list of possible subjects for research. Number seven on the list was "Scattering of alpha rays." Working over the years to establish the alpha particle's identity, he had come to appreciate its great value as an atomic probe; because it was massive compared to the high-energy but nearly weightless beta electron, it interacted vigorously with matter. The measure of that interaction could reveal the atom's structure. "I was brought up to look at the atom as a nice hard fellow, red or grey in colour, according to taste," Rutherford told a dinner audience once. By 1907 it was clear to him that the atom was not a hard fellow at all but was substantially empty space. The German physicist Philipp Lenard had demonstrated as much in 1903 by bombarding elements with cathode rays. Lenard dramatized his findings with a vivid metaphor: the space occupied by a cubic meter of solid platinum, he said, was as empty as the space of stars beyond the earth.

But if there was empty space in atoms—void within void—there was something else as well. In 1906, at McGill, Rutherford had studied the magnetic deflection of alpha particles by projecting them through a narrow defining slit and passing the resulting thin beam through a magnetic field. At one point he covered half the defining slit with a sheet of mica only about three thousandths of a centimeter thick, thin enough to allow alpha particles to go through. He was recording the results of the experiment on photographic paper; he found that the edges of the part of the beam covered with the mica were blurred. The blurring meant that as the alpha particles passed through, the atoms of mica were deflecting—scattering—many of them from a straight line by as much as two degrees of angle. Since an intense magnetic field scattered the uncovered alpha particles only a little more, something unusual was happening. For a particle as comparatively massive as the alpha, moving at such high velocity, two degrees was an enormous deflection. Rutherford calculated that it would require an electrical field of about 100 million volts per centimeter of mica to scatter an alpha particle so far. "Such results bring out clearly," he wrote, "the fact that the atoms of matter must be the seat of very intense electrical forces." It was just this scattering that he marked down on his list to study.

To do so he needed not only to count but also to *see* individual alpha particles. At Manchester he accepted the challenge of perfecting the necessary instruments. He worked with Hans Geiger to develop an electrical device that clicked off the arrival of each individual alpha particle into a counting chamber. Geiger would later elaborate the invention into the familiar Geiger counter of modern radiation studies.

There was a way to make individual alpha particles visible using zinc sulfide, the compound that coated the tube of radium solution Pierre Curie had carried into the night garden in Paris in 1903. A small glass plate coated with zinc sulfide and bombarded with alpha particles briefly fluoresced at the point where each particle struck, a phenomenon known as "scintillation" from the Greek word for spark. Under a microscope the faint scintillations in the zinc sulfide could be individually distinguished and counted. The method was tedious in the extreme. It required sitting for at least thirty minutes in a dark room to adapt the eyes, then taking counting turns of only a minute at a time—the change signaled by a timer that rang a bell—because focusing the eyes consistently on a small, dim screen was impossible for much longer than that. Even through the microscope the scintillations hovered at the edge of visibility; a counter who expected an experiment to produce a certain number of scintillations sometimes unintentionally saw imaginary flashes. So the question was whether the count was generally accurate. Rutherford and Geiger compared the observation counts with matched counts by the electric method. When the observation method proved reliable they put the electric counter away. It could count, but it couldn't see, and Rutherford was interested first of all in locating an alpha particle's position in space.

Geiger went to work on alpha scattering, aided by Ernest Marsden, then an eighteen-year-old Manchester undergraduate. They observed alpha particles coming out of a firing tube and passing through foils of such metals as aluminum, silver, gold and platinum. The results were generally consistent with expectation: alpha particles might very well accumulate as much as two degrees of total deflection bouncing around among atoms of the plum-pudding sort. But the experiment was troubled with stray particles. Geiger and Marsden thought molecules in the walls of the firing tube might be scattering them. They tried eliminating the strays by narrowing and defining the end of the firing tube with a series of graduated metal washers. That proved no help.

Rutherford wandered into the room. The three men talked over the problem. Something about it alerted Rutherford's intuition for promising side effects. Almost as an afterthought he turned to Marsden and said, "See if you can get some effect of alpha particles directly reflected from a metal surface." Marsden knew that a negative result was expected—alpha particles shot *through* thin foils, they did not bounce *back* from them—but that missing a positive result would be an unforgivable sin. He took great care to prepare a strong alpha source. He aimed the pencil-narrow beam of alphas at a forty-five degree angle onto a sheet of gold foil. He positioned his scintillation screen on the same side of the foil, beside the alpha beam, so that a particle bouncing back would strike the screen and register as a scintillation. Between firing tube and screen he interposed a thick lead plate so that no direct alpha particles could interfere.

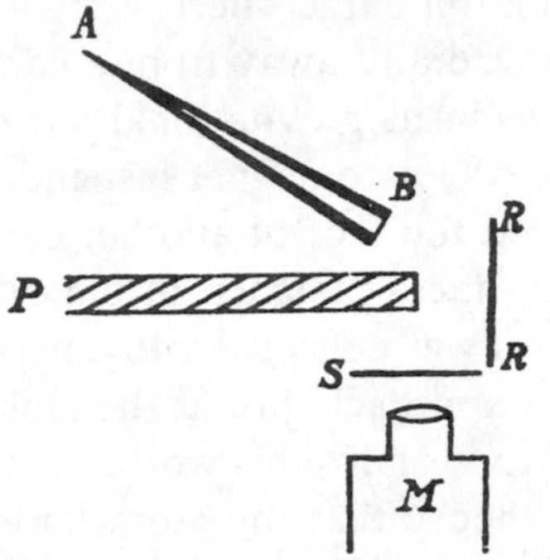

Arrangement of Ernest Marsden's experiment: A-B, alpha particle source. R-R, gold foil. P, lead plate. S, zinc sulfide scintillation screen. M, microscope.

Immediately, and to his surprise, he found what he was looking for. "I remember well reporting the result to Rutherford," he wrote, ". . .when I met him on the steps leading to his private room, and the joy with which I told him."

A few weeks later, at Rutherford's direction, Geiger and Marsden formulated the experiment for publication. "If the high velocity and mass of the α-particle be taken into account," they concluded, "it seems surprising that some of the α-particles, as the experiment shows, can be turned within a layer of 6×10^{-5} [i.e., .00006] cm. of gold through an angle of 90°, and even more. To produce a similar effect by magnetic field, the enormous field of 10^9 absolute units would be required." Rutherford in the meantime went off to ponder what the scattering meant.

He pondered, in the midst of other work, for more than a year. He had a first quick intuition of what the experiment portended and then lost it. Even after he announced his spectacular conclusion he was reluctant to promote it. One reason for his reluctance might be that the discovery contradicted the atomic models J. J. Thomson and Lord Kelvin had postulated earlier. There were physical objections to his interpretation of Marsden's discovery that would require working out as well.

Rutherford had been genuinely astonished by Marsden's results. "It was quite the most incredible event that has ever happened to me in my life," he said later. "It was almost as incredible as if you fired a 15-inch shell at a piece of tissue paper and it came back and hit you. On consideration I realised that this scattering backwards must be the result of a single collision, and when I made calculations I saw that it was impossible to get anything of that order of magnitude unless you took a system in which the greatest part of the mass of the atom was concentrated in a minute nucleus."

"Collision" is misleading. What Rutherford had visualized, making calculations and drawing diagrammatic atoms on large sheets of good paper, was exactly the sort of curving path toward and away from a compact, massive central body that a comet follows in its gravitational *pas de deux* with the sun. He had a model made, a heavy electromagnet suspended as a pendulum on thirty feet of wire that grazed the face of another electromagnet set on a table. With the two grazing faces matched in polarity and therefore repelling each other, the pendulum was deflected into a parabolic path according to its velocity and angle of approach, just as the alpha particles were deflected. He needed as always to visualize his work.

When further experiment confirmed his theory that the atom had a small, massive nucleus, he was finally ready to go public. He chose as his forum an old Manchester organization, the Manchester Literary and Philosophical Society—"largely the general public," says James Chadwick, who attended the historic occasion as a student on March 7, 1911, ". . . people interested in literary and philosophical ideas, largely business people."

The first item on the agenda was a Manchester fruit importer's report that he had found a rare snake in a consignment of Jamaica bananas. He exhibited the snake. Then it was Rutherford's turn. Only an abstract of the announcement survives, but Chadwick remembers how it felt to hear it: it was "a most shattering performance to us, young boys that we were. . . . We realized this was obviously the truth, this was it."

Rutherford had found the nucleus of his atom. He did not yet have an arrangement for its electrons. At the Manchester meeting he spoke of "a central electric charge concentrated at a point and surrounded by a uniform spherical distribution of opposite electricity equal in amount." That was sufficiently idealized for calculation, but it neglected the significant physical fact that the "opposite electricity" must be embodied in electrons. Somehow they would have to be arranged around the nucleus.

Another mystery. A Japanese theoretical physicist, Hantaro Nagaoka, had postulated in 1903 a "Saturnian" model of the atom with flat rings of electrons revolving like Saturn's rings around a "positively charged particle." Nagaoka adapted the mathematics for his model from James Clerk Maxwell's first triumphant paper, published in 1859, "On the stability of motion of Saturn's rings." All Rutherford's biographers agree that Rutherford was unaware of Nagaoka's paper until March 11, 1911—after the Manchester meeting—when he heard about it by postcard from a physicist friend: "Campbell tells me that Nagaoka once tried to deduce a big positive centre in his atom in order to account for optical effects." He thereupon looked up the paper in the *Philosophical Magazine* and added a discussion of it to the last page of the full-length paper, "The scattering of α and β particles by matter and the structure of the atom," that he sent to the same magazine in April. He described Nagaoka's atom in that paper as being "supposed to consist of a central attracting mass surrounded by rings of rotating electrons."

But it seems that Nagaoka had recently visited him, because the Japanese physicist wrote from Tokyo on February 22, 1911, thanking him "for the great kindness you showed me in Manchester."* Yet the two physicists seem not to have discussed atomic models, or Nagaoka would probably have continued the discussion in his letter and Rutherford, a totally honest man, would certainly have acknowledged it in his paper.

One reason Rutherford was unaware of Nagaoka's Saturnian model of the atom is that it had been criticized and abandoned soon after Nagaoka introduced it because it suffered from a severe defect, the same theoretical defect that marred the atom Rutherford was now proposing. The rings of Saturn are stable because the force operating between the particles of debris that make them up—gravity—is attractive. The force operating between the electrons of Nagaoka's Saturnian electron rings, however—negative electric charge—was repulsive. It followed mathematically that whenever two or more electrons equally spaced on an orbit rotated around the nucleus, they would drift into modes of oscillation—instabilities—that would quickly tear the atom apart.

What was true for Nagaoka's Saturnian atom was also true, theoretically, for the atom Rutherford had found by experiment. It the atom operated by the mechanical laws of classical physics, the Newtonian laws that govern relationships within planetary systems, then Rutherford's model should not work. But his was not a merely theoretical construct. It was the result of real physical experiment. And work it clearly did. It was as stable as the ages and it bounced back alpha particles like cannon shells.

Someone would have to resolve the contradiction between classical physics and Rutherford's experimentally tested atom. It would need to be someone with qualities different from Rutherford's: not an experimentalist but a theoretician, yet a theoretician rooted deeply in the real. He would need at least as much courage as Rutherford had and equal self-confidence. He would need to be willing to step through the mechanical looking glass

*Nagaoka indicates indirectly that the visit took place sometime prior to July 1910—after Marsden's 1909 discovery and before Rutherford's announcement to Geiger at Christmastime 1910 that he had worked out an explanation.

into a strange, nonmechanical world where what happened on the atomic scale could not be modeled with planets or pendulums.

As if he had been called to the cause, such a person abruptly appeared in Manchester. Writing to an American friend on March 18, 1912, Rutherford announced the arrival: "Bohr, a Dane, has pulled out of Cambridge and turned up here to get some experience in radioactive work." "Bohr" was Niels Henrick David Bohr, the Danish theoretical physicist. He was then twenty-seven years old.

3

Tvi

"There came into the room a slight-looking boy," Ernest Rutherford's McGill colleague and biographer A. S. Eve recalls of Manchester days, "whom Rutherford at once took into his study. Mrs. Rutherford explained to me that the visitor was a young Dane, and that her husband thought very highly indeed of his work. No wonder, it was Niels Bohr!" The memory is odd. Bohr was an exceptional athlete. The Danes cheered his university soccer exploits. He skied, bicycled and sailed; he chopped wood; he was unbeatable at Ping-Pong; he routinely took stairs two at a time. He was also physically imposing: tall for his generation, with "an enormous domed head," says C. P. Snow, a long, heavy jaw and big hands. He was thinner as a young man than later and his shock of unruly, combed-back hair might have seemed boyish to a man of Eve's age, twelve years older than Rutherford. But Niels Bohr was hardly "slight-looking."

Something other than Bohr's physical appearance triggered Eve's dissonant memory: probably his presence, which could be hesitant. He was "much more muscular and athletic than his cautious manner suggested," Snow confirms. "It didn't help that he spoke with a soft voice, not much above a whisper."All his life Bohr talked so quietly—and yet indefatigably—that people strained to hear him. Snow knew him as "a talker as hard to get to the point as Henry James in his later years," but his speech differed dramatically between public and private and between initial exploration of a subject and eventual mastery. Publicly, according to Oskar Klein, a student of Bohr's and then a colleague, "he took the greatest care to get the most accurately shaded formulation of the matter." Albert Einstein admired Bohr for "uttering his opinions like one perpetually groping and never like one who [believed himself to be] in the possession of definite truth." If Bohr groped through the exploratory phases of his deliberations, with mastery "his assurance grew and his speech became vigorous and full of vivid images," Lise Meitner's physicist nephew Otto Frisch noted. And privately, among close friends, says Klein, "he would express himself with drastic imagery and strong expressions of admiration as well as criticism."

Bohr's manner was as binary as his speech. Einstein first met Bohr in Berlin in the spring of 1920. "Not often in life," he wrote to Bohr afterward, "has a human being caused me such joy by his mere presence as you did," and he reported to their mutual friend Paul Ehrenfest, an Austrian physicist at Leiden, "I am as much in love with him as you are." Despite his enthusiasm Einstein did not fail to observe closely his new Danish friend; his verdict in Bohr's thirty-fifth year is similar to Eve's in his twenty-eighth: "He is like an extremely sensitive child who moves around the world in a sort of trance." At first meeting—until Bohr began to speak—the theoretician Abraham Pais thought the long, heavy face "gloomy" in the extreme and puzzled at that momentary impression when everyone knew "its intense animation and its warm and sunny smile."

Bohr's contributions to twentieth-century physics would rank second only to Einstein's. He would become a scientist-statesman of unmatched foresight. To a greater extent than is usually the case with scientists, his sense of personal identity—his hard-won selfhood and the emotional values he grounded there—was crucial to his work. For a time, when he was a young man, that identity was painfully divided.

Bohr's father, Christian Bohr, was professor of physiology at the University of Copenhagen. In Christian Bohr's case the Bohr jaw extended below a thick mustache and the face was rounded, the forehead not so high. He may have been athletic; he was certainly a sports enthusiast, who encouraged and helped finance the Akademisk Boldklub for which his sons would one day play champion soccer (Niels' younger brother Harald at the 1908 Olympics). He was progressive in politics; he worked for the emancipation of women; he was skeptical of religion but nominally conforming, a solid bourgeois intellectual.

Christian Bohr published his first scientific paper at twenty-two, took a medical degree and then a Ph.D. in physiology, studied under the distinguished physiologist Carl Ludwig at Leipzig. Respiration was his special subject and he brought to that research the practice, still novel in the early 1880s, of careful physical and chemical experiment. Outside the laboratory, a friend of his explains, he was a "keen worshipper" of Goethe; larger issues of philosophy intrigued him.

One of the great arguments of the day was vitalism versus mechanism, a disguised form of the old and continuing debate between those, including the religious, who believe that the world has purpose and those who believe it operates automatically and by chance or in recurring unprogressive cycles. The German chemist who scoffed in 1895 at the "purely mechanical world" of "scientific materialism" that would allow a butterfly to turn back into a caterpillar was disputing the same issue, an issue as old as Aristotle.

In Christian Bohr's field of expertise it emerged in the question whether organisms and their subsystems—their eyes, their lungs—were assembled to preexisting purpose or according to the blind and unbreathing laws of chemistry and of evolution. The extreme proponent of the mechanistic position in biology then was a German named Ernst Heinrich Haeckel, who insisted that organic and inorganic matter were one and the same. Life arose by spontaneous generation, Haeckel argued; psychology was properly a branch of physiology; the soul was not immortal nor the will free. Despite his commitment to scientific experiment Christian Bohr chose to side against Haeckel, possibly because of his worship of Goethe. He had then the difficult work of reconciling his practice with his views.

Partly for that reason, partly to enjoy the company of friends, he began stopping at a café for discussions with the philosopher Harald Høffding after the regular Friday sessions of the Royal Danish Academy of Sciences and Letters, of which they were both members. The congenial physicist C. Christensen, who spent his childhood as a shepherd, soon added a third point of view. The men moved from café meetings to regular rotation among their homes. The philologist Vilhelm Thomsen joined them to make a formidable foursome: a physicist, a biologist, a philologist, a philosopher. Niels and Harald Bohr sat at their feet all through childhood.

As earnest of his commitment to female emancipation Christian Bohr taught review classes to prepare women for university study. One of his students was a Jewish banker's daughter, Ellen Adler. Her family was cultured, wealthy, prominent in Danish life; her father was elected at various times to both the lower and upper houses of the Folketing, the Danish parliament. Christian Bohr courted her; they were married in 1881. She had a "lovable personality" and great unselfishness, a friend of her sons would say. Apparently she submerged her Judaism after her marriage. Nor did she matriculate at the university as she must originally have planned.

Christian and Ellen Bohr began married life in the Adler family townhouse that faced, across a wide street of ancient cobbles, Christianborg Palace, the seat of the Folketing. Niels Bohr was born in that favorable place on October 7, 1885, second child and first son. When his father accepted an appointment at the university in 1886 the Bohr family moved to a house beside the Surgical Academy, where the physiology laboratories were located. There Niels and his brother Harald, nineteen months younger, grew up.

As far back as Niels Bohr could remember, he liked to dream of great interrelationships. His father was fond of speaking in paradoxes; Niels may have discovered his dreaming in that paternal habit of mind. At the same time the boy was profoundly literal-minded, a trait often undervalued that became his anchoring virtue as a physicist. Walking with him when he was about three years old, his father began pointing out the balanced structure of a tree—the trunk, the limbs, the branches, the twigs—assembling the tree for his son from its parts. The literal child saw the wholeness of the organism and dissented: if it wasn't like that, he said, it wouldn't be a tree. Bohr told that story all his life, the last time only days before he died, seventy-eight years old, in 1962. "I was from first youth able to say something about philosophical questions," he summarized proudly then. And because of that ability, he said, "I was considered something of a different character."

Harald Bohr was bright, witty, exuberant and assumed at first to be the smarter of the two brothers. "At a very early stage, however," says Niels Bohr's later collaborator and biographer Stefan Rozental, "Christian Bohr took the opposite view; he realized Niels' great abilities and special gifts and the extent of his imagination." The father phrased his realization in what would have been a cruel comparison if the brothers had been less devoted. Niels, he pronounced, was "the special one in the family."

Assigned in the fifth grade to draw a house, Niels produced a remarkably mature drawing but counted the fence pickets first. He liked carpentry and metalworking; he was household handyman from an early age. "Even as a child [he] was considered the thinker of the family," says a younger colleague, "and his father listened closely to his views on fundamental problems." He almost certainly had trouble learning to write and always had trouble writing. His mother served loyally as his amanuensis: he dictated his schoolwork to her and she copied it down.

He and Harald bonded in childhood close as twins. "There runs like a leitmotif above all else," Rozental notices, "the inseparability that characterized the relationship between the two brothers." They spoke and thought *"à deux,"* recalls one of their friends. "In my whole youth," Bohr reminisced, "my brother played a very large part. . . . I had very much to do with my brother. He was in all respects more clever than I." Harald in his turn told whoever asked that he was merely an ordinary person and his brother pure gold, and seems to have meant it.

Speech is a clumsiness and writing an impoverishment. Not language but the surface of the body is the child's first map of the world, undifferentiated between subject and object, coextensive with the world it maps until awakening consciousness divides it off. Niels Bohr liked to show how a stick used as a probe—a blind man's cane, for example—became an extension of the arm. Feeling seemed to move to the end of the stick, he said. The observation was one he often repeated—it struck his physicist protégés as wondrous—like the story of the boy and the tree, because it was charged with emotional meaning for him.

He seems to have been a child of deep connection. That is a preverbal gift. His father, with his own Goethesque yearnings for purpose and wholeness—for natural unity, for the oceanic consolations of religion without the antique formalisms—especially sensed it. His overvalued expectation burdened the boy.

Religious conflict broke early. Niels "believed literally what he learnt from the lessons on religion at school," says Oskar Klein. "For a long time this made the sensitive boy unhappy on account of his parents' lack of faith." Bohr at twenty-seven, in a Christmastime letter to his fiancée from Cambridge, remembered the unhappiness as paternal betrayal: "I see a little boy in the snow-covered street on his way to church. It was the only day his father went to church. Why? So the little boy would not feel different from other little boys. He never said a word to the little boy about belief or doubt, and the little boy believed with all of his heart."

The difficulty with writing was a more ominous sign. The family patched the problem over by supplying him with his mother's services as a secretary. He did not compose mentally while alone and then call in his helper. He composed on the spot, laboriously. That was the whispering that reminded C. P. Snow of the later Henry James. As an adult Bohr drafted and redrafted even private letters. His reworking of scientific papers in draft and then repeatedly in proof became legendary. Once after continued appeals to Zurich for the incomparable critical aid of the Austrian theoretical physicist Wolfgang Pauli, who knew Bohr well, Pauli responded warily, "If the last proof is sent away, then I will come." Bohr collaborated first with his mother and with Harald, then with his wife, then with a lifelong series of younger physicists. They cherished the opportunity of working with Bohr, but the experience could be disturbing. He wanted not only their attention but also their intellectual and emotional commitment: he wanted to convince his collaborators that he was right. Until he succeeded he doubted his conclusions himself, or at least doubted the language of their formulation.

Behind the difficulty with writing lay another, more pervasive difficulty. It took the form of anxiety that without the extraordinary support of his mother and his brother would have been crippling. For a time, it was.

It may have emerged first as religious doubt, which appeared, according to Klein, when Niels was "a young man." Bohr doubted as he had believed, "with unusual resolution." By the time he matriculated at the University of Copenhagen in the autumn of 1903, when he was eighteen, the doubt had become pervasive, intoxicating him with terrifying infinities.

Bohr had a favorite novel. Its author, Poul Martin Møller, introduced *En Dansk Students Eventyr (The Adventures of a Danish Student)* as a reading before the University of Copenhagen student union in 1824. It was published posthumously. It was short, witty and deceptively lighthearted. In an important lecture in 1960, "The Unity of Human Knowledge," Bohr described Møller's book as "an unfinished novel still read with delight by the older as well as the younger generation in [Denmark]." It gives, he said, "a remarkably vivid and suggestive account of the interplay between the various aspects of our position [as human beings]." After the Great War the Danish government helped Bohr establish an institute in Copenhagen. The most promising young physicists in the world pilgrimaged to study there. "Every one of those who came into closer contact with Bohr at the Institute," writes his collaborator Léon Rosenfeld, "as soon as he showed himself sufficiently proficient in the Danish language, was acquainted with the little book: it was part of his initiation."

What magic was contained in the little book? It was the first Danish novel with a contemporary setting: student life, and especially the extended conversations of two student cousins, one a "licentiate"—a degree candidate—the other a "philistine." The philistine is a familiar type, says Bohr, "very soberly efficient in practical affairs"; the licentiate, more exotic, "is addicted to remote philosophical meditations detrimental to his social activities." Bohr quotes one of the licentiate's "philosophical meditations":

> [I start] to think about my own thoughts of the situation in which I find myself. I even think that I think of it, and divide myself into an infinite retrogressive sequence of "I's" who consider each other. I do not know at which "I" to stop as the actual, and in the moment I stop at one, there is indeed again an "I" which stops at it. I become confused and feel a dizziness as if I were looking down into a bottomless abyss.

"Bohr kept coming back to the different meanings of the word 'I,'" Robert Oppenheimer remembered, "the 'I' that acts, the 'I' that thinks, the 'I' that studies itself."

Other conditions that trouble the licentiate in Møller's novel might be taken from a clinical description of the conditions that troubled the young Niels Bohr. This disability, for example:

> Certainly I have seen thoughts put on paper before; but since I have come distinctly to perceive the contradiction implied in such an action, I feel completely incapable of forming a single written sentence. . . . I torture myself to solve the unaccountable puzzle, how one can think, talk, or write. You see, my friend, a movement presupposes a direction. The mind cannot proceed without moving along a certain line; but before following this line, it must already have thought it. Therefore one has already thought every thought before one thinks it. Thus every thought, which seems the work of a minute, presupposes an eternity. This could almost drive me to madness.

Or this complaint, on the fragmentation of the self and its multiplying duplicity, which Bohr in later years was wont to quote:

> Thus on many occasions man divides himself into two persons, one of whom tries to fool the other, while a third one, who is in fact the same as the other two, is filled with wonder at this confusion. In short, thinking becomes dramatic and quietly acts the most complicated plots with itself and for itself; and the spectator again and again becomes actor.

"Bohr would point to those scenes," Rosenfeld notes, "in which the licentiate describes how he loses the count of his many egos, or [discourses] on the impossibility of formulating a thought, and from these fanciful antinomies he would lead his interlocutor . . . to the heart of the problem of unambiguous communication of experience, whose earnestness he thus dramatically emphasized." Rosenfeld worshiped Bohr; he failed to see, or chose not to report, that for Bohr the struggles of the licentiate were more than "fanciful antinomies."

Ratiocination—that is the technical term for what the licentiate does, the term for what the young Bohr did as well—is a defense mechanism against anxiety. Thought spirals, panicky and compulsive. Doubt doubles and redoubles, paralyzing action, emptying out the world. The mechanism is infinitely regressive because once the victim knows the trick, he can doubt anything, even doubt itself. Philosophically the phenomenon could be interesting, but as a practical matter ratiocination is a way of stalling. If work is never finished, its quality cannot be judged. The trouble is that stalling postpones the confrontation and adds that guilt to the burden.

Anxiety increases; the mechanism accelerates its spiraling flights; the self feels as if it will fragment; the multiplying "I" dramatizes the feeling of impending breakup. At that point madness reveals its horrors; the image that recurred in Bohr's conversation and writing throughout his life was the licentiate's "bottomless abyss." We are "suspended in language," Bohr liked to say, evoking that abyss; and one of his favorite quotations was two lines from Schiller:

Nur die Fülle führt zur Klarheit,
Und im Abgrund wohnt die Wahrheit.

Only wholeness leads to clarity,
And truth lies in the abyss.

But it was not in Møller that Bohr found solid footing. He needed more than a novel, however apposite, for that. He needed what we all need for sanity: he needed love and work.

"I took a great interest in philosophy in the years after my [high school] examination," Bohr said in his last interview. "I came especially in close connection with Høffding." Harald Høffding was Bohr's father's old friend, the other charter member of the Friday-night discussion group. Bohr had known him from childhood. Born in 1843, he was twelve years older than Christian Bohr, a profound, sensitive and kindly man. He was a skillful interpreter of the work of Søren Kierkegaard and of William James and a respected philosopher in his own right: an anti-Hegelian, a pragmatist interested in questions of perceptive discontinuity. Bohr became a Høffding student. It seems certain he also turned personally to Høffding for help. He made a good choice. Høffding had struggled through a crisis of his own as a young man, a crisis that brought him, he wrote later, near "despair."

Høffding was twelve years old when Søren Kierkegaard died of a lung infection in chill November 1855, old enough to have heard of the near-riot at the grave a somber walk outside the city walls, old enough for the strange, awkward, fiercely eloquent poet of multiple pseudonyms to have been a living figure. With that familiarity as a point of origin Høffding later turned to Kierkegaard's writings for solace from despair. He found it especially in *Stages on Life's Way,* a black-humorous dramatization of a dialectic of spiritual stages, each independent, disconnected, bridgeable only by an irrational leap of faith. Høffding championed the prolific and difficult Dane in gratitude; his second major book, published in 1892, would help establish Kierkegaard as an important philosopher rather than merely a literary stylist given to outbursts of raving, as Danish critics had first chosen to regard him.

Kierkegaard had much to offer Bohr, especially as Høffding interpreted him. Kierkegaard examined the same states of mind as had Poul Martin Møller. Møller taught Kierkegaard moral philosophy at the university and seems to have been a guide. After Møller's death Kierkegaard dedicated *The Concept of Dread* to him and referred to him in a draft of the dedication as "my youth's enthusiasm, my beginning's *confidant,* mighty trumpet of my awakening, my departed friend." From Møller to Kierkegaard to Høffding to Bohr: the line of descent was direct.

Kierkegaard notoriously suffered from a proliferation of identities and doubts. The doubling of consciousness is a central theme in Kierkegaard's work, as it was in Møller's before him. It would even seem to be a hazard of long standing among the Danes. The Danish word for despair, *Fortvivlelse,* carries lodged at its heart the morpheme *tvi,* which means "two" and signifies the doubling of consciousness. *Tvivl* in Danish means "doubt"; *Tvivlesyg* means "skepticism"; *Tvetydighed,* "ambiguity." The self watching itself is indeed a commonplace of puritanism, closely akin to the Christian conscience.

But unlike Møller, who jollies the licentiate's *Tvivl* away, Kierkegaard struggled to find a track through the maze of mirrors. Høffding, in his *History of Modern Philosophy,* which Bohr would have read as an undergraduate, summarizes the track he understood Kierkegaard to have found: "His leading idea was that the different possible conceptions of life are so sharply opposed to one another that we must make a choice between them, hence his catchword *either-or;* moreover, it must be a choice which each particular person must make for himself, hence his second catchword, *the individual."* And, following: "Only in the world of possibilities is there continuity; in the world of reality decision always comes through a breach of continuity." Continuity in the sense that it afflicted Bohr was the proliferating stream of doubts and "I's" that plagued him; a breach of that continuity—decisiveness, function—was the termination he hoped to find.

He turned first to mathematics. He learned in a university lecture about Riemannian geometry, a type of non-Euclidean geometry developed by the German mathematician Georg Riemann to represent the functions of complex variables. Riemann showed how such multivalued functions (a number, its square root, its logarithm and so on) could be represented and related on a stack of coincident geometric planes that came to be called Riemann surfaces. "At that time," Bohr said in his last interview, "I really thought to write something about philosophy, and that was about this analogy with multivalued functions. I felt that the various problems in psychology—which were called the big philosophical problems, of the free will and such things—that one could really reduce them when one considered how one really went about them, and that was done on the analogy to multivalued functions." By then he thought the problem might be one of language, of the ambiguity—the multiple values, as it were—between different meanings of the word "I." Separate each different meaning on a different plane and you could keep track of what you were talking about. The confusion of identities would resolve itself graphically before one's eyes.

The scheme was too schematic for Bohr. Mathematics was probably too much like ratiocination, leaving him isolated within his anxiety. He thought of writing a book about his mathematical analogies but leapt instead to work that was far more concrete. But notice that the mathematical analogy begins to embed the problem of doubt within the framework of language, identifying doubt as a specialized form of verbal ambiguity, and notice that it seeks to clarify ambiguities by isolating their several variant meanings on separate, disconnected planes.

The solid work Bohr took up, in February 1905, when he was nineteen years old, was a problem in experimental physics. Each year the Royal Danish Academy of Sciences and Letters announced problems for study against a two-year deadline, after which the academy awarded gold and silver medals for successful papers. In 1905 the physics problem was to determine the surface tension of a number of liquids by measuring the waves produced in those liquids when they were allowed to run out through a hole (the braided cascade of a garden hose demonstrates such waves). The method had been proposed by the British Nobelist John William Strutt, Lord Rayleigh, but no one had yet tried it out. Bohr and one other contestant accepted the challenge.

Bohr went to work in the physiology laboratory where he had watched and then assisted his father for years, learning the craft of experiment. To produce stable jets he decided to use drawn-out glass tubes. Because the method required large quantities of liquid he limited his experiment to water. The tubes had to be flattened on the sides to make an oval cross section; that gave the jet of water the shape it needed to evolve braidlike waves. All the work of heating, softening and drawing out the tubes Bohr did himself; he found it hypnotic. Rosenfeld says Bohr "took such delight in this operation that, completely forgetting its original purpose, he spent hours passing tube after tube through the flame."

Each separate experimental determination of the surface-tension value took hours. It had to be done at night, when the lab was unoccupied, because the jets were easily disturbed by vibration. Slow work, but Bohr also dawdled. The academy had allowed two years. Toward the end of that time Christian Bohr realized his son was procrastinating to the point where he might not finish his paper before the deadline. "The experiments had no end," Bohr told Rosenfeld some years later on a bicycle ride in the country; "I always noticed new details that I thought I had first to understand. At last my father sent me out here, away from the laboratory, and I had to write up the paper."

"Out here" was Naerumgaard, the Adler country estate north of Copenhagen. There, away from the temptations of the laboratory, Niels wrote and Harald transcribed an essay of 114 pages. Niels submitted it to the academy on the day of deadline, but even then it was incomplete; three days later he turned in an eleven-page addendum that had been accidentally left off.

The essay, Bohr's first scientific paper, determined the surface tension only of water but also uniquely extended Rayleigh's theory. It won a gold medal from the academy. It was an outstanding achievement for someone so young and it set Bohr's course for physics. Unlike mathematicized philosophy, physics was anchored solidly in the real world.

In 1909 the Royal Society of London accepted the surface-tension paper in modified form for its *Philosophical Transactions.* Bohr, who was still only a student working toward his master's degree when the essay appeared, had to explain to the secretary of the society, who had addressed him by his presumed academic title, that he was "not a professor."

Retreating to the country had helped him once. It might help again. Naerumgaard ceased to be available when the Adler family donated it for use as a school. When the time came to study for his master's degree examinations, between March and May 1909, Bohr traveled to Vissenbjerg, on the island of Funen, the next island west from Copenhagen's Zealand, to stay at the parsonage of the parents of Christian Bohr's laboratory assistant. Niels procrastinated on Funen by reading *Stages on Life's Way.* The day he finished it he enthusiastically mailed the book to Harald. "This is the only thing I have to send," he wrote his younger brother; "nevertheless, I don't think I could easily find anything better. . . . It is something of the finest I have ever read." At the end of June, back in Copenhagen, again on deadline day, Bohr turned in his master's thesis, copied out in his mother's hand.

Harald had sprinted ahead of him by then, having won his M.Sc. in April and gone off to the Georgia-Augusta University in Göttingen, Germany, the center of European mathematics, to study for his Ph.D. He received that degree in Göttingen in June 1910. Niels wrote his younger brother tongue-in-cheek that his "envy would soon be growing over the rooftops," but in fact he was happy with his progress on his own doctoral dissertation despite having spent "four months speculating about a silly question about some silly electrons and [succeeding] only in writing circa fourteen more or less divergent rough drafts." Christensen had posed Bohr a problem in the electron theory of metals for his master's thesis; the subject interested Bohr enough to continue pursuing it as his doctoral work.

He was specializing in theoretical studies now; to try to do experimental work too, he explained, was "unpractical."

He returned to the parsonage at Vissenbjerg in the autumn of 1910. His work slowed. He may have recalled the licentiate's dissertation problems, for he again turned to Kierkegaard. "He made a powerful impression on me when I wrote my dissertation in a parsonage in Funen, and I read his works night and day," Bohr told his friend and former student J. Rud Nielsen in 1933. "His honesty and his willingness to think the problems through to their very limit is what is great. And his language is wonderful, often sublime. There is of course much in Kierkegaard that I cannot accept. I ascribe that to the times in which he lived. But I admire his intensity and perseverance, his analysis to the utmost limit, and the fact that through these qualities he turned misfortune and suffering into something good."

He finished his Ph.D. thesis, "Studies in the electron theory of metals," by the end of January 1911. On February 3, suddenly, at fifty-six, his father died. He dedicated his thesis "in deepest gratitude to the memory of my father." He loved his father; if there had been a burden of expectation he was free of that burden now.

As was customary, he publicly defended his thesis in Copenhagen on May 13. "Dr. Bohr, a pale and modest young man," the Copenhagen newspaper *Dagbladet* reported under a crude drawing of the candidate standing in white tie and tails at a heavy lectern, "did not take much part in the proceedings, whose short duration is a record." The small hall was crowded to overflowing. Christiansen, one of the two examiners, said simply that hardly anyone in Denmark was well enough informed on the subject to judge the candidate's work.

Before he died Christian Bohr had helped arrange a fellowship from the Carlsberg Foundation for his son for study abroad. Niels spent the summer sailing and hiking with Margrethe Nørland, the sister of a friend, a beautiful young student whom he had met in 1910 and to whom, shortly before his departure, he became engaged. Then he went off in late September to Cambridge. He had arranged to study at the Cavendish under J. J. Thomson.

29 Sept. 1911
Eltisley Avenue 10,
Newnham, Cambridge

Oh Harald!

Things are going so well for me. I have just been talking to J. J. Thomson and have explained to him, as well as I could, my ideas about radiation, magnetism, etc. If you only knew what it meant to me to talk to such a man. He was extremely nice to me, and we talked

> about so much; and I do believe that he thought there was some sense in what I said. He is now going to read [my dissertation] and he invited me to have dinner with him Sunday at Trinity College; then he will talk with me about it. You can imagine that I am happy. . . . I now have my own little flat. It is at the edge of town and is very nice in all respects. I have two rooms and eat all alone in my own room. It is very nice here; now, as I am sitting and writing to you, it blazes and rumbles in my own little fireplace.

Niels Bohr was delighted with Cambridge. His father's Anglophilia had prepared him to like English settings; the university offered the tradition of Newton and Clerk Maxwell and the great Cavendish Laboratory with its awesome record of physical discovery. Bohr found that his schoolboy English needed work and set out reading *David Copperfield* with an authoritative new dictionary at hand, looking up every uncertain word. He discovered that the laboratory was crowded and undersupplied. On the other hand, it was amusing to have to go about in cap and gown (once he was admitted to Trinity as a research student) "under threat of high fines," to see the Trinity high table "where they eat so much and so first-rate that it is quite unbelievable and incomprehensible that they can stand it," to walk "for an hour before dinner across the most beautiful meadows along the river, with the hedges flecked with red berries and with isolated windblown willow trees—imagine all this under the most magnificent autumn sky with scurrying clouds and blustering wind." He joined a soccer club; called on physiologists who had been students of his father; attended physics lectures; worked on an experiment Thomson had assigned him; allowed the English ladies, "absolute geniuses at drawing you out," to do their duty by him at dinner parties.

But Thomson never got around to reading his dissertation. The first meeting had not, in fact, gone so well. The new student from Denmark had done more than explain his ideas; he had shown Thomson the errors he found in Thomson's electron-theory work. "I wonder," Bohr wrote Margrethe soon after, "what he will say to my disagreement with his ideas." And a little later: "I'm longing to hear what Thomson will say. He's a great man. I hope he will not get angry with my silly talk."

Thomson may or may not have been angry. He was not much interested in electrons anymore. He had turned his attention to positive rays—the experiment he assigned Bohr concerned such rays and Bohr found it distinctly unpromising—and in any case had very little patience with theoretical discussions. "It takes half a year to get to know an Englishman," Bohr said in his last interview. ". . . It was the custom in England that they would be polite and so on, but they wouldn't be interested to see anybody. . . . I went Sundays to the dinner in Trinity College. . . . I was sitting there, and nobody spoke to me ever in many Sundays. But then they understood that I was not more eager to speak to them than they were to speak to me. And then we were friends, you see, and then the whole thing was different." The insight is generalized; Thomson's indifference was perhaps its first specific instance.

Then Rutherford turned up at Cambridge.

He "came down from Manchester to speak at the annual Cavendish Dinner," says Bohr. "Although on this occasion I did not come into personal contact with [him], I received a deep impression of the charm and power of his personality by which he had been able to achieve almost the incredible wherever he worked. The dinner"—in December—"took place in a most humorous atmosphere and gave the opportunity for several of Rutherford's colleagues to recall some of the many anecdotes which already then were attached to his name." Rutherford spoke warmly of the recent work of the physicist C. T. R. Wilson, the inventor of the cloud chamber (which made the paths of charged particles visible as lines of water droplets hovering in supersaturated fog) and a friend from Cambridge student days. Wilson had "just then," says Bohr, photographed alpha particles in his cloud chamber scattering from interactions with nuclei, "the phenomenon which only a few months before had led [Rutherford] to his epoch-making discovery of the atomic nucleus."

Bohr had matters on his mind that he would soon relate to the problem of the nucleus and its theoretically unstable electrons, but it was Rutherford's enthusiastic informality that most impressed him at the annual dinner. Remembering this period of his life long afterward, he would single out for special praise among Rutherford's qualities "the patience to listen to every young man when he felt he had any idea, however modest, on his mind." In contrast, presumably, to J. J. Thomson, whatever Thomson's other virtues.

Soon after the dinner Bohr went up to Manchester to visit "one of my recently deceased father's colleagues who was also a close friend of Rutherford," whom Bohr wanted to meet. The close friend brought them together. Rutherford looked over the young Dane and liked what he saw despite his prejudice against theoreticians. Someone asked him later about the discrepancy. "Bohr's different," Rutherford roared, disguising affection with bluster. "He's a football player!" Bohr was different in another regard as well; he was easily the most talented of all Rutherford's many students—and Rutherford trained no fewer than eleven Nobel Prize winners during his life, an unsurpassed record.

Bohr held up his decision between Cambridge and Manchester until he could go over everything with Harald, who visited him in Cambridge in January 1912 for the purpose. Then Bohr eagerly wrote Rutherford for permission to study at Manchester, as they had discussed in December. Rutherford had advised him then not to give up on Cambridge too quickly—Manchester is always here, he told him, it won't run away—and so Bohr proposed to arrive for spring term, which began in late March. Rutherford gladly agreed. Bohr felt he was being wasted at Cambridge. He wanted substantial work.

His first six weeks in Manchester he spent following "an introductory course on the experimental methods of radioactive research," with Geiger and Marsden among the instructors. He continued pursuing his independent studies in electron theory. He began a lifelong friendship with a young Hungarian aristocrat, George de Hevesy, a radiochemist with a long, sensitive face dominated by a towering nose. De Hevesy's father was a court councillor, his mother a baroness; as a child he had hunted partridge in the private game park of the Austro-Hungarian emperor Franz Josef next to his grandfather's estate. Now he was working to meet a challenge Rutherford had thrown at him one day to separate radioactive decay products from their parent substances. Out of that work he developed over the next several decades the science of using radioactive tracers in medical and biological research, one more useful offspring of Rutherford's casual but fecund paternity.

Bohr learned about radiochemistry from de Hevesy. He began to see connections with his electron-theory work. His sudden burst of intuitions then was spectacular. He realized in the space of a few weeks that radioactive properties originated in the atomic nucleus but chemical properties depended primarily on the number and distribution of electrons. He realized—the idea was wild but happened to be true—that since the electrons determined the chemistry and the total positive charge of the nucleus determined the number of electrons, an element's position on the periodic table of the elements was exactly the nuclear charge (or "atomic number"): hydrogen first with a nuclear charge of 1, then helium with a nuclear charge of 2 and so on up to uranium at 92.

De Hevesy remarked to him that the number of known radioelements already far outnumbered the available spaces on the periodic table and Bohr made more intuitive connections. Soddy had pointed out that the radioelements were generally not new elements, only variant physical forms of the natural elements (he would soon give them their modern name, isotopes). Bohr realized that the radioelements must have the same atomic number as the natural elements with which they were chemically identical. That enabled him to rough out what came to be called the radioactive dis-

1 H 1.0080																	2 He 4.0026
3 Li 6.941	4 Be 9.0122											5 B 10.81	6 C 12.011	7 N 14.0067	8 O 15.9994	9 F 18.9984	10 Ne 20.179
11 Na 22.9898	12 Mg 24.305											13 Al 26.9815	14 Si 28.086	15 P 30.9738	16 S 32.06	17 Cl 35.453	18 Ar 39.948
19 K 39.102	20 Ca 40.08	21 Sc 44.956	22 Ti 47.90	23 V 50.941	24 Cr 51.996	25 Mn 54.9380	26 Fe 55.847	27 Co 58.9332	28 Ni 58.71	29 Cu 63.54	30 Zn 65.37	31 Ga 69.72	32 Ge 72.59	33 As 74.9216	34 Se 78.96	35 Br 79.909	36 Kr 83.80
37 Rb 85.467	38 Sr 87.62	39 Y 88.906	40 Zr 91.22	41 Nb 92.906	42 Mo 95.94	43 Tc (99)	44 Ru 101.07	45 Rh 102.906	46 Pd 106.4	47 Ag 107.870	48 Cd 112.40	49 In 114.82	50 Sn 118.69	51 Sb 121.75	52 Te 127.60	53 I 126.9045	54 Xe 131.30
55 Cs 132.906	56 Ba 137.34	57 La 138.906	72 Hf 178.49	73 Ta 180.948	74 W 183.85	75 Re 186.2	76 Os 190.2	77 Ir 192.2	78 Pt 195.09	79 Au 196.967	80 Hg 200.59	81 Tl 204.37	82 Pb 207.2	83 Bi 208.981	84 Po (210)	85 At (210)	86 Rn (222)
87 Fr (223)	88 Ra (226)	89 Ac (227)															

Lanthanide Series

58 Ce 140.12	59 Pr 140.908	60 Nd 144.24	61 Pm (147)	62 Sm 150.4	63 Eu 151.96	64 Gd 157.25	65 Tb 158.925	66 Dy 162.50	67 Ho 164.930	68 Er 167.26	69 Tm 168.934	70 Yb 173.04	71 Lu 174.97

Actinide Series

90 Th (232)	91 Pa (231)	92 U (238)	93 Np (237)	94 Pu (242)

Periodic table of the elements. The lanthanide series ("rare earths"), beginning with lanthanum (57), and the actinide series, which begins with actinium (89) and includes thorium (90) and uranium (92), are chemically similar. Other families of elements read vertically down the table—at the far right, for example, the noble gases: helium, neon, argon, krypton, xenon, radon.

placement law: that when an element transmutes itself through radioactive decay it shifts its position on the periodic table two places to the left if it emits an alpha particle (a helium nucleus, atomic number 2), one place to the right if it emits a beta ray (an energetic electron, which leaves behind in the nucleus an extra positive charge).

All these first rough insights would be the work of other men's years to anchor soundly in theory and experiment. Bohr ran them in to Rutherford. To his surprise, he found the discoverer of the nucleus cautious about his own discovery. "Rutherford . . . thought that the meagre evidence [so far obtained] about the nuclear atom was not certain enough to draw such consequences," Bohr recalled. "And I said to him that I was sure that it would be the final proof of his atom." If not convinced, Rutherford was at least impressed; when de Hevesy asked him a question about radiation one day Rutherford responded cheerfully, "Ask Bohr!"

Rutherford was well prepared for surprises, then, when Bohr came to see him again in mid-June. Bohr told Harald what he was on to in a letter on June 19, after the meeting:

> It could be that I've perhaps found out a little bit about the structure of atoms. You must not tell anyone anything about it, otherwise I certainly could not write you this soon. If I'm right, it would not be an indication of the nature of a possibility . . . but perhaps a little piece of reality. . . . You understand that I may yet be wrong, for it hasn't been worked out fully yet (but I don't think so); nor do I believe that Rutherford thinks it's completely wild; he is the right kind of man and would never say that he was convinced of something that was not entirely worked out. You can imagine how anxious I am to finish quickly.

Bohr had caught a first glimpse of how to stabilize the electrons that orbited with such theoretical instability around Rutherford's nucleus. Rutherford sent him off to his rooms to work it out. Time was running short; he planned to marry Margrethe Nørland in Copenhagen on August 1. He wrote Harald on July 17 that he was "getting along fairly well; I believe I have found out a few things; but it is certainly taking more time to work them out than I was foolish enough to believe at first. I hope to have a little paper ready to show to Rutherford before I leave, so I'm busy, so busy; but the unbelieveable heat here in Manchester doesn't exactly help my diligence. How I look forward to talking to you!" By the following Wednesday, July 22, he had seen Rutherford, won further encouragement, and was making plans to meet Harald on the way home.

Bohr married, a serene marriage with a strong, intelligent and beautiful woman that lasted a lifetime. He taught at the University of Copenhagen through the autumn term. The new model of the atom he was struggling to develop continued to tax him. On November 4 he wrote Rutherford that he expected "to be able to finish the paper in a few weeks." A few weeks passed; with nothing finished he arranged to be relieved of his university teaching and retreated to the country with Margrethe. The old system worked; he produced "a very long paper on all these things." Then an important new idea came to him and he broke up his original long paper and began rewriting it into three parts. "On the constitution of atoms and molecules," so proudly and bravely titled—Part I mailed to Rutherford on March 6, 1913, Parts II and III finished and published before the end of the year—would change the course of twentieth-century physics. Bohr won the 1922 Nobel Prize in Physics for the work.

As far back as Bohr's doctoral dissertation he had decided that some of the phenomena he was examining could not be explained by the mechanical laws of Newtonian physics. "One must assume that there are forces in nature of a kind completely different from the usual mechanical sort," he wrote then. He knew where to look for these different forces: he looked to the work of Max Planck and Albert Einstein.

Planck was the German theoretician whom Leo Szilard would meet at the University of Berlin in 1921; born in 1858, Planck had taught at Berlin since 1889. In 1900 he had proposed a revolutionary idea to explain a persistent problem in mechanical physics, the so-called ultraviolet catastrophe. According to classical theory there should be an infinite amount of light (energy, radiation) inside a heated cavity such as a kiln. That was because classical theory, with its continuity of process, predicted that the particles in the heated walls of the cavity which vibrated to produce the light would vibrate to an infinite range of frequencies.

Obviously such was not the case. But what kept the energy in the cavity from running off infinitely into the far ultraviolet? Planck began his effort to find out in 1897 and pursued it for three hard years. Success came with a last-minute insight announced at a meeting of the Berlin Physical Society on October 19, 1900. Friends checked Planck's new formula that very night against experimentally derived values. They reported its accuracy to him the next morning. "Later measurements, too," Planck wrote proudly in 1947, at the end of his long life, "confirmed my radiation formula again and again—the finer the methods of measurement used, the more accurate the formula was found to be."

Planck solved the radiation problem by proposing that the vibrating particles can only radiate at certain energies. The permitted energies would be determined by a new number—"a universal constant," he says, "which I called *h*. Since it had the dimension of action (energy × time), I gave it the name, *elementary quantum of action.*" (*Quantum* is the neuter form of the Latin word *quantus,* meaning "how great.") Only those limited and finite energies could appear which were whole-number multiples of $h\nu$: of the frequency ν times Planck's *h*. Planck calculated *h* to be a very small number, close to the modern value of 6.63×10^{-27} erg-seconds. Universal *h* soon acquired its modern name: *Planck's constant.*

Planck, a thoroughgoing conservative, had no taste for pursuing the radical consequences of his radiation formula. Someone else did: Albert Einstein. In a paper in 1905 that eventually won for him the Nobel Prize,

Einstein connected Planck's idea of limited, discontinuous energy levels to the problem of the photoelectric effect. Light shone on certain metals knocks electrons free; the effect is applied today in the solar panels that power spacecraft. But the energy of the electrons knocked free of the metal does not depend, as common sense would suggest, on the brightness of the light. It depends instead on the *color* of the light—on its frequency.

Einstein saw a quantum condition in this odd fact. He proposed the heretical possibility that light, which years of careful scientific experiment had demonstrated to travel in waves, actually traveled in small individual packets—particles—which he called "energy quanta." Such photons (as they are called today), he wrote, have a distinctive energy $h\nu$ and they transfer most of that energy to the electrons they strike on the surface of the metal. A brighter light thus releases more electrons but not more energetic electrons; the energy of the electrons released depends on $h\nu$ and so on the frequency of the light. Thus Einstein advanced Planck's quantum idea from the status of a convenient tool for calculation to that of a possible physical fact.

With these advances in understanding Bohr was able to confront the problem of the mechanical instability of Rutherford's model of the atom. In July, at the time of the "little paper ready to show to Rutherford," he already had his central idea. It was this: that since classical mechanics predicted that an atom like Rutherford's, with a small, massive central nucleus surrounded by orbiting electrons, would be unstable, while in fact atoms are among the most stable of systems, classical mechanics was inadequate to describe such systems and would have to give way to a quantum approach. Planck had introduced quantum principles to save the laws of thermodynamics; Einstein had extended the quantum idea to light; Bohr now proposed to lodge quantum principles within the atom itself.

Through the autumn and early winter, back in Denmark, Bohr pursued the consequences of his idea. The difficulty with Rutherford's atom was that nothing about its design justified its stability. If it happened to be an atom with several electrons, it would fly apart. Even if it were a hydrogen atom with only one (mechanically stable) electron, classical theory predicted that the electron would radiate light as it changed direction in its orbit around the nucleus and therefore, the system losing energy, would spiral into the nucleus and crash. The Rutherford atom, from the point of view of Newtonian mechanics—as a miniature solar system—ought to be impossibly large or impossibly small.

Bohr therefore proposed that there must be what he called "stationary states" in the atom: orbits the electrons could occupy without instability, without radiating light, without spiraling in and crashing. He worked the numbers of this model and found they agreed very well with all sorts of experimental values. Then at least he had a plausible model, one that explained in particular some of the phenomena of chemistry. But it was apparently arbitrary; it was not more obviously a real picture of the atom than other useful models such as J. J. Thomson's plum pudding.

Help came then from an unlikely quarter. A professor of mathematics at King's College, London, J. W. Nicholson, whom Bohr had met and thought a fool, published a series of papers proposing a quantized Saturnian model of the atom to explain the unusual spectrum of the corona of the sun. The papers were published in June in an astronomy journal; Bohr didn't see them until December. He was quickly able to identify the inadequacies of Nicholson's model, but not before he felt the challenge of other researchers breathing down his neck—and not without noticing Nicholson's excursion into the jungle of spectral lines.

Oriented toward chemistry, communicating back and forth with George de Hevesy, Bohr had not thought of looking at spectroscopy for evidence to support his model of the atom. "The spectra was a very difficult problem," he said in his last interview. ". . . One thought that this is marvelous, but it is not possible to make progress there. Just as if you have the wing of a butterfly, then certainly it is very regular with the colors and so on, but nobody thought that one could get the basis of biology from the coloring of the wing of a butterfly."

Taking Nicholson's hint, Bohr now turned to the wings of the spectral butterfly.

Spectroscopy was a well-developed field in 1912. The eighteenth-century Scottish physicist Thomas Melvill had first productively explored it. He mixed chemical salts with alcohol, lit the mixtures and studied the resulting light through a prism. Each different chemical produced characteristic patches of color. That suggested the possibility of using spectra for chemical analysis, to identify unknown substances. The prism spectroscope, invented in 1859, advanced the science. It used a narrow slit set in front of a prism to limit the patches of light to similarly narrow lines; these could be directed onto a ruled scale (and later onto strips of photographic film) to measure their spacing and calculate their wavelengths. Such characteristic patterns of lines came to be called line spectra. Every element had its own unique line spectrum. Helium was discovered in the chromosphere of the sun in 1868 as a series of unusual spectral lines twenty-three years before it was discovered mixed into uranium ore on earth. The line spectra had their uses.

But no one understood what produced the lines. At best, mathematicians and spectroscopists who liked to play with wavelength numbers were able to find beautiful harmonic regularities among sets of spectral lines. Johann Balmer, a nineteenth-century Swiss mathematical physicist, identified in 1885 one of the most basic harmonies, a formula for calculating the wavelengths of the spectral lines of hydrogen. These, collectively called the Balmer series, look like this:

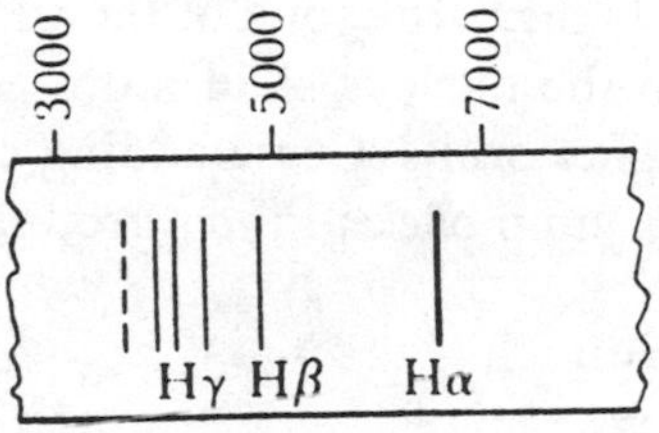

Balmer series

It is not necessary to understand mathematics to appreciate the simplicity of the formula Balmer derived that predicts a line's location on the spectral band to an accuracy of within one part in a thousand, a formula that has only one arbitrary number:

$$\lambda = 3645.6\left(\frac{n^2}{n^2 - 4}\right)$$

(the Greek letter λ, lambda, stands for the wavelength of the line; *n* takes the values 3, 4, 5 and so on for the various lines). Using his formula, Balmer was able to predict the wavelengths of lines to be expected for parts of the hydrogen spectrum not yet studied. They were found where he said they would be.

A Swedish spectroscopist, Johannes Rydberg, went Balmer one better and published in 1890 a general formula valid for a great many different line spectra. The Balmer formula then became a special case of the more general Rydberg equation, which was built around a number called the Rydberg constant. That number, subsequently derived by experiment and one of the most accurately known of all universal constants, takes the precise modern value of 109,677 cm^{-1}.

Bohr would have known these formulae and numbers from undergraduate physics, especially since Christensen was an admirer of Rydberg and had thoroughly studied his work. But spectroscopy was far from Bohr's field and he presumably had forgotten them. He sought out his old friend and classmate, Hans Hansen, a physicist and student of spectroscopy just returned from Göttingen. Hansen reviewed the regularity of line spectra with him. Bohr looked up the numbers. "As soon as I saw Balmer's formula," he said afterward, "the whole thing was immediately clear to me."

What was immediately clear was the relationship between his orbiting electrons and the lines of spectral light. Bohr proposed that an electron bound to a nucleus normally occupies a stable, basic orbit called a ground state. Add energy to the atom—heat it, for example—and the electron responds by jumping to a higher orbit, one of the more energetic stationary states farther away from the nucleus. Add more energy and the electron continues jumping to higher orbits. Cease adding energy—leave the atom alone—and the electrons jump back to their ground states, like this:

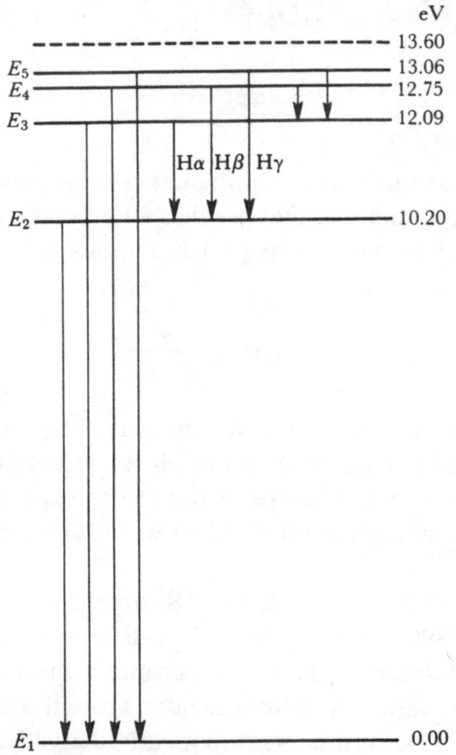

With each jump, each electron emits a photon of characteristic energy. The jumps, and so the photon energies, are limited by Planck's constant. Subtract the value of a lower-energy stationary state W_2 from the value of a higher energy stationary state W_1 and you get exactly the energy of the light as $h\nu$. So here was the physical mechanism of Planck's cavity radiation.

From this elegant simplification, $W_1 - W_2 = h\nu$, Bohr was able to derive the Balmer series. The lines of the Balmer series turn out to be exactly the energies of the photons that the hydrogen electron emits when it jumps down from orbit to orbit to its ground state.

Then, sensationally, with the simple formula

$$R = \frac{2\pi^2 me^4}{h^3}$$

(where *m* is the mass of the electron, *e* the electron charge and *h* Planck's constant—all fundamental numbers, not arbitrary numbers Bohr made up) Bohr produced Rydberg's constant, calculating it within 7 percent of its experimentally measured value! "There is nothing in the world which impresses a physicist more," an American physicist comments, "than a numerical agreement between experiment and theory, and I do not think that there can ever have been a numerical agreement more impressive than this one, as I can testify who remember its advent."

"On the constitution of atoms and molecules" was seminally important to physics. Besides proposing a useful model of the atom, it demonstrated that events that take place on the atomic scale are quantized: that just as matter exists as atoms and particles in a state of essential graininess, so also does process. Process is discontinuous and the "granule" of process—of electron motions within the atom, for example—is Planck's constant. The older mechanistic physics was therefore imprecise; though a good approximation that worked for large-scale events, it failed to account for atomic subtleties.

Bohr was happy to force this confrontation between the old physics and the new. He felt that it would be fruitful for physics. Because original work is inherently rebellious, his paper was not only an examination of the physical world but also a political document. It proposed, in a sense, to begin a reform movement in physics: to limit claims and clear up epistemological fallacies. Mechanistic physics had become authoritarian. It had outreached itself to claim universal application, to claim that the universe and everything in it is rigidly governed by mechanistic cause and effect. That was Haeckelism carried to a cold extreme. It stifled Niels Bohr as biological Haeckelism had stifled Christian Bohr and as a similar authoritarianism in philosophy and in bourgeois Christianity had stifled Søren Kierkegaard.

When Rutherford saw Bohr's Part I paper, for example, he immediately found a problem. "There appears to me one grave difficulty in your hypothesis," he wrote Bohr on March 20, "which I have no doubt you fully realise, namely, how does an electron decide what frequency it is going to vibrate at when it passes from one stationary state to the other? It seems to me that you would have to assume that the electron knows beforehand where it is going to stop." Einstein showed in 1917 that the physical answer to Rutherford's question is statistical—any frequency is possible, and the ones that turn up happen to have the best odds. But Bohr answered the question in a later lecture in more philosophical and even anthropomorphic terms: "Every change in the state of an atom should be regarded as an individual process, incapable of more detailed description, by which the atom goes over from one so-called stationary state to another. . . . We are here so far removed from a causal description that an atom in a stationary state may in general even be said to possess a free choice between various possible transitions." The "catchwords" here, as Harald Høffding might say, are *individual* and *free choice.* Bohr means the changes of state within individual atoms are not predictable; the catchwords color that physical limitation with personal emotion.

In fact the 1913 paper was deeply important emotionally to Bohr. It is a remarkable example of how science works and of the sense of personal authentication that scientific discovery can bestow. Bohr's emotional preoccupations sensitized him to see previously unperceived regularities in the natural world. The parallels between his early psychological concerns and his interpretation of atomic processes are uncanny, so much so that without the great predictive ability of the paper its assumptions would seem totally arbitrary.

Whether or not the will is free, for example, was a question that Bohr took seriously. To identify a kind of freedom of choice within the atom itself was a triumph for his carefully assembled structure of beliefs. The separate, distinct electron orbits that Bohr called stationary states recall Kierkegaard's stages. They also recall Bohr's attempt to redefine the problem of free will by invoking separate, distinct Riemann surfaces. And as Kierkegaard's stages are discontinuous, negotiable only by leaps of faith, so do Bohr's electrons leap discontinuously from orbit to orbit. Bohr insisted as one of the two "principal assumptions" of his paper that the electron's whereabouts between orbits cannot be calculated or even visualized. Before and after are completely discontinuous. In that sense, each stationary state of the electron is complete and unique, and in that wholeness is stability. By contrast, the continuous process predicted by classical mechanics, which Bohr apparently associated with the licentiate's endless ratiocination, tears the atom apart or spirals it into radiative collapse.

Bohr may have found his way through his youthful emotional crisis in part by calling up his childhood gift of literal-mindedness. He famously insisted on anchoring physics in fact and refused to carry argument beyond physical evidence. He was never a system-builder. "Bohr characteristically avoids such a word as 'principle,' " says Rosenfeld; "he prefers to speak of 'point of view' or, better still, 'argument,' i.e. line of reasoning; likewise, he rarely mentions the 'laws of nature,' but rather refers to 'regularities of the phenomena.' " Bohr was not displaying false humility with his choice of terms; he was reminding himself and his colleagues that physics is not a grand philosophical system of authoritarian command but simply a way, in his favorite phrase, of "asking questions of Nature." He apologized similarly for his tentative, rambling habit of speech: "I try not to speak more clearly than I think."

"He points out," Rosenfeld adds, "that the idealized concepts we use in science must ultimately derive from common experiences of daily life which cannot themselves be further analysed; therefore, whenever any two such idealizations turn out to be incompatible, this can only mean that some mutual limitation is imposed upon their validity." Bohr had found a solution to the spiraling flights of doubt by stepping out of what Kierkegaard called "the fairyland of the imagination" and back into the real world. In the real world material objects endure; their atoms cannot, then, ordinarily be unstable. In the real world cause and effect sometimes seem to limit our freedom, but at other times we know we choose. In the real world it is meaningless to doubt existence; the doubt itself demonstrates the existence of the doubter. Much of the difficulty was language, that slippery medium in which Bohr saw us inextricably suspended. "It is wrong," he told his colleagues repeatedly, "to think that the task of physics is to find out how nature *is*"—which is the territory classical physics had claimed for itself. "Physics concerns what we can *say* about nature."

Later Bohr would develop far more elaborately the idea of mutual limitations as a guide to greater understanding. It would supply a deep philosophical basis for his statecraft as well as for his physics. In 1913 he first demonstrated its resolving power. "It was clear," he remembered at the end of his life, "and that was *the* point about the Rutherford atom, that we had something from which we could not proceed at all in any other way than by radical change. And that was the reason then that [I] took it up so seriously."

4

The Long Grave Already Dug

Otto Hahn cherished the day the Kaiser came to visit. The official dedication of the first two Kaiser Wilhelm Institutes, one for chemistry, one for physical chemistry, on October 23, 1912—Bohr in Copenhagen was approaching his quantized atom—was a wet day in the suburb of Dahlem southwest of Berlin. The Kaiser, Wilhelm II, Victoria's eldest grandson, wore a raincloak to protect his uniform, the dark collar of his greatcoat turned out over the lighter shawl of the cloak. The officials who walked the requisite paces behind him, his scholarly friend Adolf von Harnack and the distinguished chemist Emil Fischer foremost among them, made do with dark coats and top hats; those farther back in the procession who carried umbrellas kept them furled. Schoolboys, caps in hand, lined the curbs of the shining street like soldiers on parade. They stood at childish attention, awe dazing their dreamy faces, as this corpulent middle-aged man with upturned dark mustaches who believed he ruled them by divine right passed in review. They were thirteen, perhaps fourteen years old. They would be soldiers soon enough.

Officials in the Ministry of Culture had encouraged His Imperial Majesty to support German science. He responded by donating land for a research center on what had been a royal farm. Industry and government then lavishly endowed a science foundation, the Kaiser Wilhelm

Society, to operate the proposed institutes, of which there would be seven by 1914.

The society began its official life early in 1911 with von Harnack, a theologian who was the son of a chemist, as its first president. The imperial architect, Ernst von Ihne, went briskly to work. The Kaiser came to Dahlem to dedicate the first two finished buildings, and the Institute for Chemistry especially must have pleased him. It was set back on a broad lawn at the corner of Thielallee and Faradayweg: three stories of cut stone filigreed with six-paned windows, a steep, gabled slate roof and at the roofline high above the entrance a classical pediment supported by four Doric columns. A wing angled off paralleling the cross street. Fitted between the main building and the wing like a hinge, a round tower rose up dramatically four stories high. Von Ihne had surmounted the tower with a dome. Apparently the dome was meant to flatter the Kaiser's taste. A sense of humor was not one of Wilhelm II's strong points and no doubt it did. The dome took the form of a giant *Pickelhaube,* the comic-opera spiked helmet that the Kaiser and his soldiers wore.

Leaving Ernest Rutherford in Montreal in 1906 Hahn had moved to Berlin to work with Emil Fischer at the university. Fischer was an organic chemist who knew little about radioactivity, but he understood that the field was opening to importance and that Hahn was a first-rate man. He made room for Hahn in a wood shop in the basement of his laboratories and arranged Hahn's appointment as a *Privatdozent,* which stirred less forward-looking chemists on the faculty to wonder aloud at the deplorable decline in standards. A chemist who claimed to identify new elements with a gold-foil electroscope must be at least an embarrassment, if not in fact a fraud.

Hahn found the university's physicists more congenial than its chemists and regularly attended the physics colloquia. At one colloquium at the beginning of the autumn term in 1907 he met an Austrian woman, Lise Meitner, who had just arrived from Vienna. Meitner was twenty-nine, one year older than Hahn. She had earned her Ph.D. at the University of Vienna and had already published two papers on alpha and beta radiation. Max Planck's lectures in theoretical physics had drawn her to Berlin for postgraduate study.

Hahn was a gymnast, a skier and a mountain climber, boyishly good-looking, fond of beer and cigars, with a Rhineland drawl and a warm, self-deprecating sense of humor. He admired attractive women, went out of his way to cultivate them and stayed friends with a number of them throughout his happily married life. Meitner was petite, dark and pretty, if also morbidly shy. Hahn befriended her. When she found she had free time she decided to experiment. She needed a collaborator. So did Hahn. A physicist and a radiochemist, they would make a productive team.

They required a laboratory. Fischer agreed that Meitner could share the wood shop on condition that she never show her face in the laboratory upstairs where the students, all male, worked. For two years she observed the condition strictly; then, with the liberalization of the university, Fischer relented, allowed women into his classes and Meitner above the basement. Vienna had been only a little more enlightened. Meitner's father, an attorney—the Meitners were assimilated Austrian Jews, baptized all around—had insisted that she acquire a teacher's diploma in French before beginning to study physics so that she would always be able to support herself. Only then could she prepare for university work. With the diploma out of the way Meitner crammed eight years of *Gymnasium* preparation into two. She was the second woman ever to earn a Ph.D at Vienna. Her father subsidized her research in Berlin until at least 1912, when Max Planck, by now a warm supporter, appointed her to an assistantship. "The German Madame Curie," Einstein would call her, characteristically lumping the Germanic peoples together and forgetting her Austrian birth.

"There was no question," says Hahn, "of any closer relationship between us outside the laboratory. Lise Meitner had had a strict, lady-like upbringing and was very reserved, even shy." They never ate lunch together, never went for a walk, met only in colloquia and in the wood shop. "And yet we were really close friends." She whistled Brahms and Schumann to him to pass the long hours taking timed readings of radioactivity to establish identifying half-lives, and when Rutherford came through Berlin in 1908 on his way back from the Nobel Prize ceremonies she selflessly accompanied Mary Rutherford shopping while the two men indulged themselves in long talks.

The close friends moved together to the new institute in 1912 and worked to prepare an exhibit for the Kaiser. In his first venture into radiochemistry, in London before he went to Montreal, Hahn had spied out what he took to be a new element, radiothorium, that was one hundred thousand times as radioactive as its modest namesake. At McGill he found a third substance intermediate between the other two; he named it "mesothorium" and it was later identified as an isotope of radium. Mesothorium compounds glow in the dark at a different level of faint illumination from radiothorium compounds. Hahn thought the difference might amuse his sovereign. On a velvet cushion in a little box he mounted an unshielded sample of mesothorium equivalent in radiation intensity to 300 milligrams of radium. He presented his potent offering to the Kaiser and asked him to compare it to "an emanating sample of radiothorium that produced in the dark very nice luminous moving shapes on [a] screen." No one warned His Majesty of the radiation hazard because no safety standards for radiation exposure had yet been set. "If I did the same thing today," Hahn said fifty years later, "I should find myself in prison."

The mesothorium caused no obvious harm. The Kaiser passed on to the second institute, half a block up Faradayweg northwest beyond the angled wing. Two senior chemists managed the Chemistry Institute where Hahn and Meitner worked, but the Institute for Physical Chemistry and Electrochemistry, to give it its full name, was established specifically for the man who was its first director, a difficult, inventive German-Jewish chemist from Breslau named Fritz Haber. It was a reward of sorts. A German industrial foundation paid for it and endowed it because in 1909 Haber had succeeded in developing a practical method of extracting nitrogen from the air to make ammonia. The ammonia would serve for artificial fertilizer, replacing Germany's and the world's principal natural source, sodium nitrate dug from the bone-dry northern desert of Chile, an expensive and insecure supply. More strategically, the Haber process would be invaluable in time of war to produce nitrates for explosives; Germany had no nitrates of its own.

Kaiser Wilhelm enlarged at the dedication on the dangers of firedamp, the explosive mixture of methane and other gases that accumulates in mines. He urged his chemists to find some early means of detection. That was a task, he said, "worthy of the sweat of noble brows." Haber, noble brow—he shaved his bullet head, wore round horn-rimmed glasses and a toothbrush mustache, dressed well, wined and dined in elegance but suffered bitter marital discord—set out to invent a firedamp whistle that would sound a different pitch when dangerous gases were present. With a fine modern laboratory uncontaminated by old radioactivity Hahn and Meitner went to work at radiochemistry and the new field of nuclear physics. The Kaiser returned from Dahlem to his palace in Berlin, happy to have lent his name to yet another organ of burgeoning German power.

In the summer of 1913 Niels Bohr sailed with his young wife to England. He followed the second and third parts of his epochal paper, which he had sent ahead by mail to Rutherford; he wanted to discuss them before releasing them for publication. In Manchester he met his friend George de Hevesy again and some of the other research men. One he met, probably for the first time, was Henry Gwyn Jeffreys Moseley, called Harry, an Eton boy and an Oxford man who had worked for Rutherford as a demonstrator, teaching undergraduates, since 1910. Harry Moseley at twenty-six was poised for great accomplishment. He needed only the catalyst of Bohr's visit to set him off.

Moseley was a loner, "so reserved," says A. S. Russell, "that I could neither like him nor not like him," but with the unfortunate habit of allowing no loose statement of fact to pass unchallenged. When he stopped work long enough to take tea at the laboratory he even managed to inhibit Ernest Rutherford. Rutherford's other "boys" called him "Papa." Moseley respected the boisterous laureate but certainly never honored him with any such intimacy; he rather thought Rutherford played the stage colonial.

Harry came from a distinguished line of scientists. His great-grandfather had operated a lunatic asylum with healing enthusiasm but without benefit of medical license, but his grandfather was chaplain and professor of natural philosophy and astronomy at King's College and his father had sailed as a biologist on the three-year voyage of H.M.S. *Challenger* that produced a fifty-volume pioneering study of the world ocean. Henry Moseley—Harry had his father's first name—won the friendly praise of Charles Darwin for his one-volume popular account, *Notes by a Naturalist on the 'Challenger';* Harry in his turn would work with Darwin's physicist grandson Charles G. Darwin at Manchester.

If he was reserved to the point of stuffiness he was also indefatigable at experiment. He would go all out for fifteen hours, well into the night, until he was exhausted, eat a spartan meal of cheese sometime before dawn, find a few hours for sleep and breakfast at noon on fruit salad. He was trim, carefully dressed and conservative, fond of his sisters and his widowed mother, to whom he regularly wrote chatty and warmly devoted letters. Hay fever threw off his final honors examinations at Oxford; he despised teaching the Manchester undergraduates—many were foreigners, "Hindoos, Burmese, Jap, Egyptian and other vile forms of Indian," and he recoiled from their "scented dirtiness." But finally, in the autumn of 1912, Harry found his great subject.

"Some Germans have recently got wonderful results by passing X rays through crystals and then photographing them," he wrote his mother on October 10. The Germans, at Munich, were directed by Max von Laue. Von Laue had found that the orderly, repetitive atomic structure of a crystal produces monochromatic interference patterns from X rays just as the mirroring, slightly separated inner and outer surfaces of a soap bubble produce interference patterns of color from white light. X-ray crystallography was the discovery that would win von Laue the Nobel Prize. Moseley and C. G. Darwin set out with a will to explore the new field. They acquired the necessary equipment and worked through the winter. By May 1913 they had advanced to using crystals as spectroscopes and were finishing up a first solid piece of work. X rays are energetic light of extremely short wavelength. The atomic lattices of crystals spread out their spectra much as a prism does visible light. "We find," Moseley wrote his mother on May 18, "that an X ray bulb with a platinum target gives out a sharp line spectrum of five wavelengths. . . . Tomorrow we search for the spectra of other elements. There is here a whole new branch of spectroscopy, which is sure to tell one much about the nature of the atom."

Then Bohr arrived and the question they discussed was Bohr's old insight that the order of the elements in the periodic table ought to follow the atomic number rather than, as chemists thought, the atomic weight. (The atomic number of uranium, for example, is 92; the atomic weight of the commonest isotope of uranium is 238; a rarer isotope of uranium has an atomic weight of 235 and the same atomic number.) Harry could look for regular shifts in the wavelengths of X-ray line spectra and prove Bohr's contention. Atomic number would make a place in the periodic table for all the variant physical forms that had been discovered and that would soon be named isotopes; atomic number, emphasizing the charge on the nucleus as the determiner of the number of electrons and hence of the chemistry, would strongly confirm Rutherford's nuclear model of the atom; the X-ray spectral lines would further document Bohr's quantized electron orbits. The work would be Moseley's alone; Darwin by then had withdrawn to pursue other interests.

Bohr and the patient Margrethe went on to Cambridge to vacation and polish Bohr's paper. Rutherford left near the end of July with Mary on an expedition to the idyllic mountains of the Tyrol. Moseley stayed in "unbearably hot and stuffy" Manchester, blowing glass. "Even now near midnight," he wrote his mother two days after Rutherford's departure, "I discard coat and waistcoat and work with windows and door open to try to get some air. I will come to you as soon as I can get my apparatus to work before ever I start measurements." On August 13 he was still at it. He wrote his married sister Margery to explain what he was after:

> I want in this way to find the wave-lengths of the X ray spectra of as many elements as possible, as I believe they will prove much more important and fundamental than the ordinary light spectra. The method of finding the wavelengths is to reflect the X rays which come from a target of the element investigated [when such a target is bombarded with cathode rays]. . . . I have then merely to find at which angles the rays are reflected, and that gives the wavelengths. I aim at an accuracy of at least one in a thousand.

The Bohrs returned to Copenhagen, the Rutherfords from the Tyrol, and now it was September and time for the annual meeting of the British

Association, this year in Birmingham. Bohr had not planned to attend, especially after lingering overlong in Cambridge, but Rutherford thought he should: his quantized atom with its stunning spectral predictions would be the talk of the conference. Bohr relented and rushed over. Birmingham's hotels were booked tight. He slept the first night on a billiard table. Then the resourceful de Hevesy found him a berth in a girls' college. "And that was very, very practical and wonderful," Bohr remembered afterward, adding quickly that "the girls were away."

Sir Oliver Lodge, president of the British Association, mentioned Bohr's work in his opening address. Rutherford touted it in meetings. James Jeans, the Cambridge mathematical physicist, allowed wittily that "the only justification at present put forward for these assumptions is the very weighty one of success." A Cavendish physicist, Francis W. Aston, announced that he had succeeded in separating two different weights of neon by tediously diffusing a large sample over and over again several thousand times through pipe clay—"a definite proof," de Hevesy noted, "that elements of different atomic weight can have the same chemical properties." Marie Curie came across from France, "shy," says A. S. Eve, "retiring, self-possessed and noble." She fended off the bulldog British press by praising Rutherford: "great developments," she predicted, were "likely to transpire" from his work. He was "the one man living who promises to confer some inestimable boon on mankind."

Harald Bohr reported to his brother that autumn that the younger men at Göttingen "do not dare to believe that [your paper] can be objectively right; they find the assumptions too 'bold' and 'fantastic.' " Against the continuing skepticism of many European physicists Bohr heard from de Hevesy that Einstein himself, encountered at a conference in Vienna, had been deeply impressed. De Hevesy passed along a similar tale to Rutherford:

> Speaking with Einstein on different topics we came to speak on Bohr's theory, he told me that he had once similar ideas but he did not dare to publish them. "Should Bohr's theory be right, it is of the greatest importance." When I told him about the [recent discovery of spectral lines where Bohr's theory had predicted they should appear] the big eyes of Einstein looked still bigger and he told me "Then it is one of the greatest discoveries."
>
> I felt very happy hearing Einstein saying so.

So did Bohr.

Moseley labored on. He had trouble at first making sharp photographs of his X-ray spectra, but once he got the hang of it the results were outstanding. The important spectral lines shifted with absolute regularity as he went up the periodic table, one step at a time. He devised a little staircase of strips of film by matching up the lines. He wrote to Bohr on November 16: "During the last fortnight or so I have been getting results which will interest you. . . . So far I have dealt with the K [spectral line] series from Calcium to Zinc. . . . The results are exceedingly simple and largely what you would expect. . . . K = N − 1, very exactly, N being the atomic number." He had calcium at 20, scandium at 21, titanium at 22, vanadium at 23, chromium at 24 and so on up to zinc at 30. He concludes that his results "lend great weight to the general principles which you use, and I am delighted that this is so, as your theory is having a splendid effect on Physics." Harry Moseley's crisp work gave experimental confirmation of the Bohr-Rutherford atom that was far more solidly acceptable than Marsden's and Geiger's alpha-scattering experiments. "Because you see," Bohr said in his last interview, "actually the Rutherford work was not taken seriously. We cannot understand today, but it was not taken seriously at all. . . . The great change came from Moseley."

Otto Hahn was called upon once more to demonstrate his radioactive preparations. In the early spring of 1914 the Bayer Dye Works at Leverkusen, near Cologne in the Rhineland, gave a reception to celebrate the opening of a large lecture hall. Germany's chemical industry led the world and Bayer was the largest chemical company in Germany, with more than ten thousand employees. It manufactured some two thousand different dyestuffs, large tonnages of inorganic chemicals, a range of pharmaceuticals. The firm's managing director, Carl Duisberg, a chemist who preferred industrial management along American lines, had invited the *Oberpräsident* of the Rhineland to attend the reception; he then invited Hahn to add a glow to the proceedings.

Hahn lectured to the dignitaries on radioactivity. Near the beginning of the lecture he wrote Duisberg's name on a sealed photographic plate with a small glass tube filled with strong mesothorium. Technicians developed the plate while he spoke; at the end Hahn projected the radiographic signature onto a screen to appreciative applause.

The high point of the celebration at the vast 900-acre chemical complex came in the evening. "In the evening there was a banquet," Hahn remembered with nostalgia; "everything was exquisite. On each of the little tables there was a beautiful orchid, brought from Holland by air." Orchids delivered by swift biplane might be adequate symbols of German prosperity and power in 1914, but the managing director wanted to demonstrate German technological superiority as well, and found exotic statement: "At many of the tables," says Hahn, evoking an unrecognizably futuristic past, "the wine was cooled by means of liquid air in thermos vessels."

When war broke out Niels and Harald Bohr were hiking in the Austrian Alps, covering as much as twenty-two miles a day. "It is impossible to describe how amazing and wonderful it is," Niels had written to Margrethe along the way, "when the fog on the mountains suddenly comes driving down from all the peaks, initially as quite small clouds, finally to fill the whole valley." The brothers had planned to return home August 6; the war suddenly came driving down like the mountain fog and they rushed across Germany before the frontiers closed. In October Bohr would sail with his wife from neutral Denmark to teach for two years at Manchester. Rutherford, his boys off to war work, needed help.

Harry Moseley was in Australia with his mother at the beginning of August, attending the 1914 British Association meeting, in his spare time searching out the duck-billed platypus and picturesque silver mines. The patriotism of the Australians, who immediately began mobilizing, triggered his own Etonian spirit of loyalty to King and country. He sailed for England as soon as he could book passage. By late October he had gingered up a reluctant recruiting officer to arrange his commission as a lieutenant in the Royal Engineers ahead of the waiting list.

Chaim Weizmann, the tall, sturdy, Russian-born Jewish biochemist who was Ernest Rutherford's good friend at Manchester, was a passionate Zionist at a time when many, including many influential British Jews, believed Zionism to be at least visionary and naïve if not wrongheaded, fanatic, even a menace. But if Weizmann was a Zionist he was also deeply admiring of British democracy, and one of his first acts after the beginning of the war was to cut himself off from the international Zionist organization because it proposed to remain neutral. Its European leaders hated Czarist Russia, England's ally, and so did Weizmann, but unlike them he did not believe that Germany in cultural and technological superiority would win the war. He believed that the Western democracies would emerge victorious and that Jewish destiny lay with them.

He, his wife and his young son had been en route to a holiday in Switzerland at the outbreak of the war. They worked their way back to Paris, where he visited the elderly Baron Edmond de Rothschild, financial mainstay of the pioneering Jewish agricultural settlements in Palestine. To Weizmann's astonishment Rothschild shared his optimism about the eventual outcome of the war and its possibilities for Jewry. Though Weizmann had no official position in the Zionist movement, Rothschild urged him to seek out and talk to British leaders.

That matched his own inclinations. His hope of British influence had deep roots. He was the third child among fifteen of a timber merchant who assembled rafts of logs and floated them down the Vistula to Danzig for milling and export. The Weizmanns lived in that impoverished western region of Russia cordoned off for the Jews known as the Pale of Settlement. When Chaim was only eleven he had written a letter that prefigured his work in the war. "The eleven-year-old boy," reports his biographer Isaiah Berlin, "says that the kings and nations of the world are plainly set upon the ruin of the Jewish nation; the Jews must not let themselves be destroyed; England alone may help them to return and rise again in their ancient land of Palestine."

Young Weizmann's conviction drove him inexorably west. At eighteen he floated on one of his father's rafts to West Prussia, worked his way to Berlin and studied at the Technische Hochschule. In 1899 he took his Ph.D. at the University of Fribourg in Switzerland, then sold a patent to Bayer that considerably improved his finances. He moved to England in 1904, a move he thought "a deliberate and desperate step. . . . I was in danger of degenerating into a *Luftmensch* [literally, an "air-man"], one of those well-meaning, undisciplined and frustrated 'eternal students.' " Chemical research would save him from that fate; he settled in Manchester under the sponsorship of William Henry Perkin, Jr., the head of the chemistry department there, whose father had established the British coal-tar dye industry by isolating aniline blue, the purple dye after which the Mauve Decade was named.

Returning to Manchester from France in late August 1914, Weizmann found a circular on his desk from the British War Office "inviting every scientist in possession of any discovery of military value to report it." He possessed such a discovery and forthwith offered it to the War Office "without remuneration." The War Office chose not to reply. Weizmann went on with his research. At the same time he began the approach to British leaders that he and Rothschild had discussed that would elaborate into some two thousand interviews before the end of the war.

Weizmann's discovery was a bacillus and a process. The bacillus was *Clostridium acetobutylicum Weizmann,* informally called B-Y ("bacillus-Weizmann"), an anerobic organism that decomposes starch. He was trying to develop a process for making synthetic rubber when he found it, on an ear of corn. He thought he could make synthetic rubber from isoamyl alcohol, which is a minor byproduct of alcoholic fermentation. He went looking for a bacillus—millions of species and subspecies live in the soil and on plants—that converted starch to isoamyl alcohol more efficiently than known strains. "In the course of this investigation I found a bacterium which produced considerable amounts of a liquid smelling very much like isoamyl alcohol. But when I distilled it, it turned out to be a mixture of acetone and butyl alcohol in very pure form. Professor Perkins advised me to pour the stuff down the sink, but I retorted that no pure chemical is useless or ought to be thrown away."

That creature of serendipity was B-Y. Mixed with a mash of cooked corn it fermented the mash into a solution of water and three solvents—one part ethyl alcohol, three parts acetone, six parts butyl alcohol (butanol). The three solvents could then be separated by straightforward distillation. Weizmann tried developing a process for making synthetic rubber from butanol and succeeded. In the meantime, in the years just prior to the beginning of the war, the price of natural rubber fell and the clamor for synthetic rubber stilled.

Pursuing his efforts toward a Jewish homeland, Weizmann acquired in Manchester a loyal and influential friend, C. P. Scott, the tall, elderly, liberal editor of the *Manchester Guardian.* Among his many connections, Scott was David Lloyd George's most intimate political adviser. Weizmann found himself having breakfast one Friday morning in January 1915 with the vigorous little Welshman who was then Chancellor of the Exchequer and who would become Prime Minister in the middle of the war. Lloyd George had been raised on the Bible. He respected the idea of a Jewish return to Palestine, especially when Weizmann eloquently compared rocky, mountainous, diminutive Palestine with rocky, mountainous, diminutive Wales. Besides Lloyd George, Weizmann was surprised to find interest in Zionism among such men as Arthur Balfour, the former Prime Minister who would serve as Foreign Secretary in Lloyd George's cabinet, and Jan Christiaan Smuts, the highly respected Boer who joined the British War Cabinet in 1917 after serving behind the scenes previously. "Really messianic times are upon us," Weizmann wrote his wife during this period of early hope.

Weizmann had cultured B-Y primarily for its butanol. He happened one day to tell the chief research chemist of the Scottish branch of the Nobel explosives company about his fermentation research. The man was impressed. "You know," he said to Weizmann, "you may have the key to a very important situation in your hands." A major industrial explosion prevented Nobel from developing the process, but the company let the British government know.

"So it came about," writes Weizmann, "that one day in March [1915], I returned from a visit to Paris to find waiting for me a summons to the British Admiralty." The Admiralty, of which Winston Churchill, at forty-one exactly Weizmann's age, was First Lord, faced a severe shortage of acetone. That acrid solvent was a crucial ingredient in the manufacture of cordite, a propellant used in heavy artillery, including naval guns, that takes its name from the cordlike form in which it is usually extruded. The explosive material that hurled the heavy shells of the British Navy's big guns from ship to ship and ship to shore across miles of intervening water was a mixture of 64 parts nitrocellulose and 30.2 parts nitroglycerin stabilized with 5 parts petroleum jelly and softened—gelatinized—with 0.8 percent acetone. Cordite could not be manufactured without acetone, and without cordite the guns would need to be extensively rebuilt to accommodate hotter propellants that would otherwise quickly erode their barrels.

Weizmann agreed to see what he could do. Shortly he was brought into the presence of the First Lord. As Weizmann remembered the experience of meeting the "brisk, fascinating, charming and energetic" Winston Churchill:

> Almost his first words were: "Well, Dr. Weizmann, we need thirty thousand tons of acetone. Can you make it?" I was so terrified by this lordly request that I almost turned tail. I answered: "So far I have succeeded in making a few hundred cubic centimeters of acetone at a time by the fermentation process. I do my work in a laboratory. I am not a technician, I am only a research chemist. But, if I were somehow able to produce a ton of acetone, I would be able to multiply that by any factor you chose." . . . I was given carte blanche by Mr. Churchill and the department, and I took upon myself a task which was to tax all my energies for the next two years.

That was part one of Weizmann's acetone experience. Part two came in early June. The British War Cabinet had been shuffled in May because of the enlarging disaster of the Dardanelles campaign at Gallipoli; Herbert Asquith, the Prime Minister, had required Churchill's resignation as First Lord of the Admiralty and replaced him with Arthur Balfour; Lloyd George had moved from Chancellor of the Exchequer to Minister of Munitions. Lloyd George thus immediately inherited the acetone problem in the wider context of Army as well as Navy needs. Scott of the *Manchester Guardian* alerted him to Weizmann's work and the two men met on June 7. Weizmann told him what he had told Churchill previously. Lloyd George was impressed and gave him larger carte blanche to scale up his fermentation process.

In six months of experiments at the Nicholson gin factory in Bow, Weizmann achieved half-ton scale. The process proved efficient. It fermented 37 tons of solvents—about 11 tons of acetone—from 100 tons of grain. Weizmann began training industrial chemists while the government took over six English, Scottish and Irish distilleries to accommodate them. A shortage of American corn—German submarines strangled British shipping in the First War as in the Second—threatened to shut down the operations. "Horse-chestnuts were plentiful," notes Lloyd George in his *War Memoirs,* "and a national collection of them was organised for the purpose of using their starch content as a substitute for maize." Eventually acetone production was shifted to Canada and the United States and back to corn.

"When our difficulties were solved through Dr. Weizmann's genius," continues Lloyd George, "I said to him: 'You have rendered great service to the State, and I should like to ask the Prime Minister to recommend you to His Majesty for some honour.' He said, 'There is nothing I want for myself.' 'But is there nothing we can do as a recognition of your valuable assistance to the country?' I asked. He replied: 'Yes, I would like you to do something for my people.' . . . That was the fount and origin of the famous declaration about the National Home for Jews in Palestine."

The "famous declaration" came to be called the Balfour Declaration, a commitment by the British government in the form of a letter from Arthur Balfour to Baron Edmond de Rothschild to "view with favour the establishment in Palestine of a national home for the Jewish people" and to "use their best endeavours to facilitate the achievement of this object." That document originated far more complexly than in simple payment for Weizmann's biochemical services. Other spokesmen and statesmen were at work as well and Weizmann's two thousand interviews need to be counted in. Smuts identified the relationship long after the war when he said that Weizmann's "outstanding war work as a scientist had made him known and famous in high Allied circles, and his voice carried so much the greater weight in pleading for the Jewish National Home."

But despite these necessary qualifications, Lloyd George's version of the story deserves better than the condescension historians usually accord it. A letter of one hundred eighteen words signed by the Foreign Secretary committing His Majesty's government to a Jewish homeland in Palestine at some indefinite future time, "it being clearly understood that nothing shall be done which may prejudice the civil and religious rights of existing non-Jewish communities in Palestine," can hardly be counted an unseemly reward for saving the guns of the British Army and Navy from premature senility. Chaim Weizmann's experience was an early and instructive example of the power of science in time of war. Government took note. So did science.

A heavy German artillery bombardment preceded the second battle of Ypres that began on April 22, 1915. Ypres was (or had been: it hardly existed anymore) a modest market town in southeastern Belgium about eight miles north of the French border and less than thirty miles inland from the

French port of Dunkirk. Around Ypres spread shell-cratered, soggy downland dominated by unpromising low hills—the highest of them, Hill 60 on the military maps, volcanically contested, only 180 feet elevation. A line of Allied and, parallel northeastward, of German trenches curved through the area, emplaced since the previous November.

Before then, the German attacking and the British defending, the two armies had run a race to the sea. The Germans had hoped to win the race to turn the flank of the Allies. Not yet fully mobilized for war, they even threw in Ersatz Corps of ill-trained high school and university students to bolster their numbers and took 135,000 casualties in what the German people came to call the *Kindermord,* the murder of the children. But at the price of 50,000 lives the British held the narrow flank. The war that was supposed to be surgically brief—a quick march through Belgium, France's capitulation, home by Christmas—turned to a stagnant war of opposing trenches, in the Ypres salient as everywhere along the battle line from the Channel to the Alps.

The April 22 bombardment, the beginning of a concerted German attempt at breakthrough, had driven the Canadians and French Africans holding the line at Ypres deep into their trenches. At sunset it lifted. German troops moved back from the front line along perpendicular communication trenches, leaving behind only newly trained *Pioniere*—combat engineers. A German rocket signal went up. The *Pioniere* set to work opening valves. A greenish-yellow cloud hissed from nozzles and drifted on the wind across no-man's-land. It blanketed the ground, flowed into craters, over the rotting bodies of the dead, through wide brambles of barbed wire, drifted then across the sandbagged Allied parapets and down the trench walls past the firesteps, filled the trenches, found dugouts and deep shelters: and men who breathed it screamed in pain and choked. It was chlorine gas, caustic and asphyxiating. It smelled as chlorine smells and burned as chlorine burns.

Masses of Africans and Canadians stumbled back in retreat. Other masses, surprised and utterly uncomprehending, staggered out of their trenches into no-man's-land. Men clawed at their throats, stuffed their mouths with shirttails or scarves, tore the dirt with their bare hands and buried their faces in the earth. They writhed in agony, ten thousand of them, serious casualties; and five thousand others died. Entire divisions abandoned the line.

Germany achieved perfect surprise. All the belligerents had agreed under the *Hague Declaration of 1899 Concerning Asphyxiating Gases* "to abstain from the use of projectiles the sole object of which is the diffusion of asphyxiating or deleterious gases." None seemed to think tear gas covered by this declaration, though tear gases are more toxic than chlorine in sufficient concentration. The French used tear gas in the form of rifle grenades as early as August 1914; the Germans used it in artillery shells fired against the Russians at Bolimow at the end of January 1915 and on the Western Front first against the British at Nieuport in March. But the chlorine attack at Ypres was the first major and deliberate poison-gas attack of the war.

As later with other weapons of unfamiliar effect, the chlorine terrorized and bewildered. Men threw down their rifles and decamped. Medical officers at aid stations were suddenly overwhelmed with casualties the cause of whose injuries was unknown. Chemists among the men who survived the attack recognized chlorine quickly enough, however, and knew how easy it was to neutralize; within a week the women of London had sewn 300,000 pads of muslin-wrapped cotton for soaking in hyposulfite—the first crude gas masks.

Even though the German High Command allowed the use of gas at Ypres, it apparently doubted its tactical value. It had massed no reserve troops behind the lines to follow up. Allied divisions quickly closed the gap. Nothing came of the attack except agony.

Otto Hahn, a lieutenant in the infantry reserve, helped install the gas cylinders, 5,730 of them containing 168 tons of chlorine, originally at a different place in the line. Shovel crews dug them into the forward walls of the trenches at firestep level and sandbagged them thickly to protect them from shellfire. To work them you connected lead pipe to their valves, ran the pipe over the parapet into no-man's-land, waited for a rocket to signal a start and opened the valves for a predetermined time. Chlorine boils at -28.5° F unpressurized; it boiled out eagerly when released. But the prevailing winds had been wrong where Hahn's team of *Pioniere* first installed the chlorine cylinders. By the time the High Command decided to remove them to Ypres along a four-mile front where the wind blew more favorably, Hahn had been sent off to investigate gas-attack conditions in the Champagne.

In January he was ordered to German-occupied Brussels to see Fritz Haber. Haber had just been promoted from reserve sergeant major to captain, an unprecedented leap in rank in the aristocratic Germany Army. He needed the rank, he told Hahn, to accomplish his new work. "Haber informed me that his job was to set up a special unit for gas-warfare." It seems that Hahn was shocked. Haber offered reasons. They were reasons that would be heard again in time of war:

> He explained to me that the Western fronts, which were all bogged down, could be got moving again only by means of new weapons. One of the weap-

> ons contemplated was poison gas. . . . When I objected that this was a mode of warfare violating the Hague Convention he said that the French had already started it—though not to much effect—by using rifle-ammunition filled with gas. Besides, it was a way of saving countless lives, if it meant that the war could be brought to an end sooner.

Hahn followed Haber to work on gas warfare. So did the physicist James Franck, head of the physics department at Haber's institute, who, like Haber and Hahn, would later win the Nobel Prize. So did a crowd of industrial chemists employed by I.G. Farben, a cartel of eight chemical companies assembled in wartime by the energetic Carl Duisberg of Bayer. The plant at Leverkusen with the new lecture hall turned up hundreds of known toxic substances, many of them dye precursors and intermediates, and sent them off to the Kaiser Wilhelm Institute for Physical Chemistry and Electrochemistry for study. Berlin acquired depots for gas storage and a school where Hahn instructed in gas defense.

He also directed gas attacks. In Galicia on the Eastern Front in mid-June 1915, "the wind was favourable and we discharged a very poisonous gas, a mixture of chlorine and phosgene, against the [Russian] enemy lines. . . . Not a single shot was fired. . . . The attack was a complete success."

Because of its massive chemical industry, which supplied the world before the war, Germany was far ahead of the Allies in the production of chemicals for gas warfare. Early in the war the British had even been reduced to buying German dyestuffs (not for gas, for dyeing) through neutral countries; when the Germans discovered the subterfuge they proposed, with what compounding of cynicism and labored Teutonic humor the record does not reveal, to trade dyestuffs for scarce rubber and cotton. But France and Britain went immediately to work. By the end of the war at least 200,000 tons of chemical warfare agents had been manufactured and used, half by Germany, half by the several Allies together.

Abrogating the Hague Convention opened an array of new ecological niches, so to speak, in weaponry. Types of gas and means of delivery then proceeded to diversify like Darwin's finches. Germany introduced phosgene next after chlorine, mixing it with chlorine for cloud-gas attacks like Hahn's because of its slow rate of evaporation. The French retaliated in early 1916 with phosgene artillery shells. Phosgene then became a staple of the war, dispensed from cylinders, artillery shells, trench mortars, canisters fired from mortarlike "projectors" and bombs. It smelled like new-mown hay but it was by far the most toxic gas used, ten times as toxic as chlorine, fatal in ten minutes at a concentration of half a milligram per liter of air. At higher concentrations one or two breaths killed in a matter of hours. Phosgene—carbonyl chloride—hydrolyzed to hydrochloric acid in contact with water; that was its action in the water-saturated air deep in the delicate bubbled tissue of the human lung. It caused more than 80 percent of the war's gas fatalities.

Chlorpicrin—the British called it vomiting gas, the Germans called it *Klop*—a vicious compound of picric acid and bleaching powder, came along next. German engineers used it against Russian soldiers in August 1916. Its special virtue was its chemical inertness. It did not react with the several neutralizing chemicals packed in gas-mask canisters; only the modest layer of activated charcoal in the canisters removed it from the air by adsorption. So a high concentration could saturate the charcoal and get through. It worked like tear gas but induced nausea, vomiting and diarrhea as well. Men raised their masks to vomit; if the *Klop* had been mixed with phosgene, as it frequently was, they might then be lethally exposed. Chlorpicrin's other advantage was that it was simple and cheap to make.

The most horrible gas of the war, the gas that started a previously complacent United States developing a chemical-warfare capacity of its own, was dichlorethyl sulfide, known for its horseradish- or mustard-like smell as mustard gas. The Germans first used it on the night of July 17, 1917, in an artillery bombardment against the British at Ypres. The attack came as a complete surprise and caused thousands of casualties. Defense in the form of effective masks and efficient gas discipline had caught up with offense by the summer of 1917; Germany introduced mustard gas to break the deadlock, just as it had introduced chlorine before. Shells marked with yellow crosses rained down on the men at Ypres. At first they experienced not much more than sneezing and many put away their masks. Then they began vomiting. Their skin reddened and began to blister. Their eyelids inflamed and swelled shut. They had to be led away blinded to aid stations, more than fourteen thousand of them over the next three weeks.

Though the gas smelled like mustard in dense concentrations, in low concentrations, still extremely toxic, it was hardly noticeable. It persisted for days and even weeks in the field. A gas mask alone was no longer sufficient protection. Mustard dissolved rubber and leather; it soaked through multiple layers of cloth. One man might bring enough back to a dugout on the sole of his boot to blind temporarily an entire nest of his mates. Its odor could also be disguised with other gases. The Germans sometimes chose to disguise mustard with xylyl bromide, a tear gas that smells like lilac, and so it came to pass in the wartime spring that men ran in terror from a breeze scented with blossoming lilac shrubs.

These are not nearly all the gases and poisons developed in the boisterous, vicious laboratory of the Great War. There were sneezing gases and arsenic powders and a dozen tear gases and every combination. The French loaded artillery shells with cyanide—to no point except hatred, as it turned out, because the resulting vapors were lighter than air and immediately lofted away. By 1918 a typical artillery barrage locomoting east or west over the front lines counted nearly as many gas shells as high-explosive. Germany, always logical at war to the point of inhumanity, blamed the French and courted a succession of increasingly desperate breakthroughs. The chemists, like bargain hunters, imagined they were spending a pittance of tens of thousands of lives to save a purseful more. Britain reacted with moral outrage but capitulated in the name of parity.

It was more than Fritz Haber's wife could bear. Clara Immerwahr had been Haber's childhood sweetheart. She was the first woman to win a doctorate in chemistry from the University of Breslau. After she married Haber and bore him a son, a neglected housewife with a child to raise, she withdrew progressively from science and into depression. Her husband's work with poison gas triggered even more desperate melancholy. "She began to regard poison gas not only as a perversion of science but also as a sign of barbarism," a Haber biographer explains. "It brought back the tortures men said they had forgotten long ago. It degraded and corrupted the discipline [i.e., chemistry] which had opened new vistas of life." She asked, argued, finally adamantly demanded that her husband abandon gas work. Haber told her what he had told Hahn, adding for good measure, patriot that he was, that a scientist belongs to the world in times of peace but to his country in times of war. Then he stormed out to supervise a gas attack on the Eastern Front. Dr. Clara Immerwahr Haber committed suicide the same night.

The Allied campaign at Gallipoli began on April 25, 1915. The rough, southward-descending Gallipoli Peninsula looked westward toward the Aegean; eastward, across the narrow strait known as the Dardanelles—to the ancients and to Lord Byron, the Hellespont—it faced Turkish Asia. Capture the peninsula; control the Dardanelles, then the Sea of Marmara above, then the narrow Bosporus Strait that divides Europe from Asia, then Constantinople, and you might control the Black Sea, into which the Danube drains—a vast flanking movement against the Central Powers. Such were the ambitions of the War Cabinet, chivvied by Winston Churchill, for the Dardanelles campaign. The Turks, whose land it was, backed by the Germans, opposed the operation with machine guns and howitzers.

One Australian, one New Zealand, one French colonial and two British divisions landed at Gallipoli to establish narrow beachheads. The water of one beachhead bay churned as white at first as a rapid, the Turks pouring down ten thousand rounds a minute from the steep cliffs above; then it bloomed thick and red with blood. Geography, error and six Turkish divisions under a skillful German commander forestalled any effective advance. By early May, when a British Gurkha and a French division arrived to replace the Allied depletions, both sides had chiseled trenches in the stony ground.

The standoff persisted into summer. Sir Ian Hamilton, the Allied commander, Corfu-born, literary, with a Boer-stiffened right arm and the best of intentions, appealed for reinforcements. The War Cabinet had reorganized itself and expelled Churchill; it assented with reluctance to Hamilton's appeal and shipped out five divisions more.

Harry Moseley shipped out among them. He was a signaling officer now, 38th Brigade, 13th Infantry Division, one of Lord Kitchener's New Army batches made up of dedicated but inexperienced civilian volunteers. At Gibraltar on June 20 he signaled his mother "Our destination no longer in doubt." At Alexandria on June 27 he made his will, leaving everything, which was £2,200, to the Royal Society strictly "to be applied to the furtherance of experimental research in Pathology Physics Physiology Chemistry or other branches of science but not in pure mathematics astronomy or any branch of science which aims merely at describing cataloguing or systematizing."

Alexandria was "full of heat flies native troops and Australians" and after a week they sailed on to Cape Helles on the southern extremity of the Gallipoli Peninsula, a relatively secure bay behind the trench lines. There they could ease into combat in the form of artillery shells lobbed over the Dardanelles to Europe, as it were, from Turkish batteries in Asia. If men were bathing in the bay a lookout on the heights blew a trumpet blast to announce a round coming in. Centipedes and sand, Harry dispensing chlorodyne to his men to cure them of the grim amebic dysentery everyone caught from the beaches, Harry in silk pajamas sharing out the glorious Tiptree blackberry jam his mother sent. "The one real interest in life is the flies," he wrote her. "No mosquitoes, but flies by day and flies by night, flies in the water, flies in the food."

Toward the end of July the divisions crossed to Lemnos to stage for the reinforcing invasion. That was to divide the peninsula, gain the heights and outflank the Turkish lines toward Helles. Hamilton secreted twenty thousand men by the dark of the moon into the crowded trenches at a beach called Anzac halfway up the peninsula and the Turks were none the wiser. The remainder, some seventeen thousand New Army men, came ashore on the night of August 6, 1915, at Sulva Bay north of Anzac, to very little opposition.

When the Turks learned of the invasion they moved new divisions down the peninsula by forced march. The objective of the 38th Brigade, what was left of it toward the end, after days and nights of continuous marching and fighting, was an 850-foot hill, Chanuk Bair, inland a mile and a half from Anzac. To the west of Chanuk Bair and lower down was another hill with a patch of cultivated ground: the Farm. Moseley's column, commanded by Brigadier A. H. Baldwin, struggling up an imprisoning defile a yard wide and six hundred feet deep, found its way blocked by a descending train of mules loaded with ammunition. That was scabby passage and the brigadier in a fury of frustration led off north toward the Farm "over ghastly country in the pitch dark," says the brigade machine gunner, the men "falling headlong down holes and climbing up steep and slippery inclines." But they reached the Farm.

Baldwin's force then held the far left flank of the line of five thousand British, Australians and New Zealanders precariously dug into the slopes below the heights of Chanuk Bair, which the Turks still commanded from trenches.

The Turkish reinforcements arrived at night and crowded into the Chanuk trenches, thirty thousand strong. They launched their assault at dawn on August 10 with the sun breaking blindingly at their backs. John Masefield, the British poet, was there and lived to report: "They came on in a monstrous mass, packed shoulder to shoulder, in some places eight deep, in others three or four deep." On the left flank "the Turks got fairly in among our men with a weight which bore all before it, and what followed was a long succession of British rallies to a tussle body to body, with knives and stones and teeth, a fight of wild beasts in the ruined cornfields of The Farm." Harry Moseley, in the front line, lost that fight.

When he heard of Moseley's death, the American physicist Robert A. Millikan wrote in public eulogy that his loss alone made the war "one of the most hideous and most irreparable crimes in history."

Six miles below Dover down the chalk southeastern coast of England the old resort and harbor town of Folkestone fills a small valley which opens steeply to the strait. Hills shelter the town to the north; the chalk cliff west sustains a broad municipal promenade of lawns and flower beds. The harbor, where Allied soldiers embarked in great numbers for France, offers the refuge of a deep-water pier a third of a mile long with berths for eight steamers. The town remembers William Harvey, the seventeenth-century physician who discovered the circulation of the blood, as its most distinguished native son.

At Folkestone on a sunny, warm Friday afternoon, May 25, 1917, housewives came out in crowds to shop for the Whitsun weekend. A few miles away at Shorncliffe camp, Canadian troops mustered on the parade ground. There was bustle and enthusiasm in town and camp alike. It was payday.

Without warning the shops and streets exploded. A line of waiting housewives crumpled outside a greengrocer's. A wine merchant returned to the front of his shop to find his only customer decapitated. Blast felled passersby in a narrow passage between two old buildings. Horses slumped dead between the shafts of carriages. Finely shattered glass suddenly iced a section of street, a conservatory shed its windows, a crater obliterated a tennis court. Fires bloomed from damaged stores.

Only after the first explosions did the people of Folkestone notice the sound of engines beating the air. They hardly understood what they heard. They screamed "Zepps! Zepps!" for until then Zeppelin dirigibles had been the only mechanism of air attack they knew. "I saw two aeroplanes," a clergyman remembered who ran outside amid the clamor, "not Zeppelins, emerging from the disc of the sun almost overhead. Then four more, or five, in a line and others, all light bright silver insects hovering against the blue of the sky. . . . There was about a score in all, and we were charmed with the beauty of the sight." Charmed because aircraft of any kind were new to the British sky and these were white and large. The results were less charming: 95 killed, 195 injured. The parade ground at Shorncliffe camp was damaged but no one was hurt.

Folkestone was the little Guernica of the Great War. German Gotha bombers—oversized biplanes—had attacked England for the first time, bringing with them the burgeoning concept of strategic bombing. The England Squadron had been headed for London but had met a solid wall of clouds inland from Gravesend. Twenty-one aircraft turned south then and searched for alternative targets. Folkestone and its nearby army camp answered the need.

A Zeppelin bombed Antwerp early in the war as the Germans pushed through Belgium. Churchill sent Navy fighters to bomb Zeppelin hangars at Düsseldorf. Gothas bombed Salonika and a British squadron bombed the fortress town of Maidos in the Dardanelles during the campaign for Gallipoli. But the Gothas that attacked Folkestone in 1917 began the first effective and sustained campaign of strategic civilian bombardment. It fitted Prussian military strategist Karl von Clausewitz's doctrine of total war in much the same way that submarine attack did, carrying fear and horror directly to the enemy to weaken his will to resist. "You must not suppose that we set out to kill women and children," a captured Zeppelin commander told the British authorities, another rationalization that would echo. "We have higher military aims. You would not find one officer in the German Army or Navy who would go to war to kill women and children. Such things happen accidentally in war."

At first the Kaiser, thinking of royal relatives and historic buildings, kept London off the bombing list. His naval staff pressed him to relent, which he did by stages, first allowing the docks to be bombed from naval airships, then reluctantly enlarging permission westward across the city. But the hydrogen-filled airships of Count Ferdinand von Zeppelin were vulnerable to incendiary bullets; when British pilots learned to fire them the stage was set for the bombers.

They came on in irregular numbers, dependent in those later years of the war not only on the vagaries of weather but also on the vagaries, enforced by the British blockade, of substandard engine parts and inferior fuel. A squadron flew against London by daylight on June 13, nineteen days after Folkestone, dropped almost 10,000 pounds of bombs and caused the most numerous civilian bombing casualties of the war, 432 injured and 162 killed, including sixteen horribly mangled children in the basement of a nursery school. London was nearly defenseless and at first the military saw no reason to change that naked condition; the War Minister, the Earl of Derby, told the House of Lords that the bombing was without military significance because not a single soldier had been killed.

So the Gothas continued their attacks. They crossed the Channel from bases in Belgium three times in July, twice in August, and averaged two raids a month through the autumn and winter and spring for a total of twenty-seven in all, first by day and then increasingly, as the British improved their home defenses, by night. They dropped almost a quarter of a million pounds of bombs, killing 835 people, injuring 1,972 more.

Lloyd George, by then Prime Minister, appealed to the brilliant, reliable Smuts to develop an air program, including a system of home defense. Early-warning mechanisms were devised: oversized binaural gramophone horns connected by stethoscope to keen blind listeners; sound-focusing cavities carved into sea cliffs that could pick up the *wong-wong* of Gotha engines twenty miles out to sea. Barrage balloons raised aprons of steel cable that girdled London's airspace; enormous white arrows mounted on the ground on pivots guided the radioless defenders in their Sopwith Camels and Pups toward the invading German bombers. The completed defense system around London was primitive but effective and it needed only technological improvement to ready it for the next war.

At the same time the Germans explored strategic offense. They extended the range of their Gothas with extra fuel tanks. When daylight bombing became too risky they learned to fly and bomb at night, navigating by the stars. They produced a behemoth new four-engine bomber, the Giant, a biplane with a wingspan of 138 feet, unmatched until the advent of the American B-29 Superfortress more than two decades later. Its effective range approached 300 miles. A Giant dropped the largest bomb of the war on London on February 16, 1918, a 2,000-pounder that was thirteen feet long; it exploded on the grounds of the Royal Hospital in Chelsea. As they came to understand strategic bombing, the Germans turned from high explosives to incendiaries, reasoning presciently that fires might cause more damage by spreading and coalescing than any amount of explosives alone. By 1918 they had developed a ten-pound incendiary bomb of almost pure magnesium, the Elektron, that burned at between 2000° and 3000° and that water could not dowse. Only hope of a negotiated peace restrained Germany from attempting major incendiary raids on London in the final months of the war.

The Germans bombed to establish "a basis for peace" by destroying "the morale of the English people" and paralyzing their "will to fight." They succeeded in making the British mad enough to think strategic bombing through. "The day may not be far off," Smuts wrote in his report to Lloyd George, "when aerial operations with their devastation of enemy lands and destruction of industrial and populous centres on a vast scale may become the principal operations of the war, to which the older forms of military and naval operations may become secondary and subordinate."

The United States Army was slow to respond to gas warfare because it assumed that masks would adequately protect U.S. troops. The civilian Department of the Interior, which had experience dealing with poison gases in mines, therefore took the lead in chemical warfare studies. The Army quickly changed its mind when the Germans introduced mustard gas in July 1917. Research contracts for poison-gas development went out to Cornell, Johns Hopkins, Harvard, MIT, Princeton, Yale and other universities. With what a British observer could now call "the great importance attached in America to this branch of warfare," Army Ordnance began construction in November 1917 of a vast war-gas arsenal at Edgewood, Maryland, on waste and marshy land.

The plant, which cost $35.5 million—a complex of 15 miles of roads, 36 miles of railroad track, waterworks and power plants and 550 buildings for the manufacture of chlorine, phosgene, chlorpicrin, sulfur chloride and mustard gas—was completed in less than a year. Ten thousand military and civilian workers staffed it. By the end of the war it was capable of filling 1.1 million 75-mm gas shells a month as well as several million other sizes and types of shells, grenades, mortar bombs and projector drums.

"Had the war lasted longer," the British observer notes, "there can be no doubt that this centre of production would have represented one of the most important contributions by America to the world war."

Gas in any case was far less efficient at maiming and killing men than were artillery and machine-gun fire. Of a total of some 21 million battle casualties gas caused perhaps 5 percent, about 1 million. It killed at least 30,000 men, but at least 9 million died overall. Gas may have evoked special horror because it was unfamiliar and chemical rather than familiar and mechanical in its effects.

The machine gun forced the opposing armies into trenches; artillery carried the violence over the parapets once they were there. So the general staffs learned to calculate that they would lose 500,000 men in a six-month offensive or 300,000 men in six months of "ordinary" trench warfare. The British alone fired off more than 170 million artillery rounds, more than 5 million tons, in the course of the war. The shells, if they were not loaded with shrapnel in the first place, were designed to fragment when they exploded on impact; they produced by far the most horrible mutilations and dismemberings of the war, faces torn away, genitals torn away, a flying debris of arms and legs and heads, human flesh so pulped into the earth that the filling of sandbags with that earth was a repulsive punishment. Men cried out against the monstrousness on all sides.

The machine gun was less mutilating but far more efficient, the basic slaughtering tool of the war. "Concentrated essence of infantry," a military theorist daintily labeled it. Against the criminally stubborn conviction of the professional officer corps that courage, *élan* and naked steel must carry the day the machine gun was the ultimate argument. "I go forward," a British soldier writes of his experience in an attacking line of troops, ". . . up and down across ground like a huge ruined honeycomb, and my wave melts away, and the second wave comes up, and also melts away, and then the third wave merges into the ruins of the first and second, and after a while the fourth blunders into the remnants of the others." He was describing the Battle of the Somme, on July 1, 1916, when at least 21,000 men died in the first hour, possibly in the first few minutes, and 60,000 the first day.

Americans invented the machine gun: Hiram Stevens Maxim, a Yankee from Maine; Colonel Isaac Lewis, a West Pointer, director of the U.S. Army coast artillery school; William J. Browning, a gunmaker and businessman; and their predecessor Richard Jordan Gatling, who correctly located the machine gun among automated systems. "It bears the same relation to other firearms," Gatling noted, "that McCormack's Reaper does to the sickle, or the sewing machine to the common needle." The military historian John Keegan writes:

> For the most important thing about a machine-gun is that it is a *machine,* and one of quite an advanced type, similar in some respects to a high-precision lathe, in others to an automatic press. Like a lathe, it requires to be set up, so that it will operate within desired and predetermined limits; this was done on the Maxim gun . . . by adjusting the angle of the barrel relative to its fixed firing platform, and tightening or loosening its traversing screw. Then, like an automatic press, it would, when actuated by a simple trigger, begin and continue to perform its functions with a minimum of human attention, supplying its own power and only requiring a steady supply of raw material and a little routine maintenance to operate efficiently throughout a working shift.

The machine gun mechanized war. Artillery and gas mechanized war. They were the hardware of the war, the tools. But they were only proximately the mechanism of the slaughter. The ultimate mechanism was a method of organization—anachronistically speaking, a software package. "The basic lever," the writer Gil Elliot comments, "was the *conscription law,* which made vast numbers of men available for military service. The civil machinery which ensured the carrying out of this law, and the *military organization* which turned numbers of men into battalions and divisions, were each founded on a bureaucracy. The *production* of resources, in particular guns and ammunition, was a matter for civil organization. The *movement* of men and resources to the front, and the trench system of defence, were military concerns." Each interlocking system was logical in itself and each system could be rationalized by those who worked it and moved through it. Thus, Elliot demonstrates, "It is reasonable to obey the law, it is good to organize well, it is ingenious to devise guns of high technical capacity, it is sensible to shelter human beings against massive firepower by putting them in protective trenches."

What was the purpose of this complex organization? Officially it was supposed to save civilization, protect the rights of small democracies, demonstrate the superiority of Teutonic culture, beat the dirty Hun, beat the arrogant British, what have you. But the men caught in the middle came to glimpse a darker truth. "The War had become undisguisedly mechanical and inhuman," Siegfried Sassoon allows a fictional infantry officer to see. "What in earlier days had been drafts of volunteers were now droves of victims." Men on every front independently discovered their victimization. Awareness intensified as the war dragged on. In Russia it exploded in revolution. In Germany it motivated desertions and surrenders. Among the

French it led to mutinies in the front lines. Among the British it fostered malingering.

Whatever its ostensible purpose, the end result of the complex organization that was the efficient software of the Great War was the manufacture of corpses. This essentially industrial operation was fantasized by the generals as a "strategy of attrition." The British tried to kill Germans, the Germans tried to kill British and French and so on, a "strategy" so familiar by now that it almost sounds normal. It was not normal in Europe before 1914 and no one in authority expected it to evolve, despite the pioneering lessons of the American Civil War. Once the trenches were in place, the long grave already dug (John Masefield's bitterly ironic phrase), then the war stalemated and death-making overwhelmed any rational response. "The war machine," concludes Elliot, "rooted in law, organization, production, movement, science, technical ingenuity, with its product of six thousand deaths a day over a period of 1,500 days, was the permanent and realistic factor, impervious to fantasy, only slightly altered by human variation."

No human institution, Elliot stresses, was sufficiently strong to resist the death machine. A new mechanism, the tank, ended the stalemate. An old mechanism, the blockade, choked off the German supply of food and matériel. The increasing rebelliousness of the foot soldiers threatened the security of the bureaucrats. Or the death machine worked too well, as against France, and began to run out of raw material. The Yanks came over with their sleeves rolled up, an untrenched continent behind them where the trees were not hung with entrails. The war putrified to a close.

But the death machine had only sampled a vast new source of raw material: the civilians behind the lines. It had not yet evolved equipment efficient to process them, only big guns and clumsy biplane bombers. It had not yet evolved the necessary rationale that old people and women and children are combatants equally with armed and uniformed young men. That is why, despite its sickening squalor and brutality, the Great War looks so innocent to modern eyes.

5

Men from Mars

The first subway on the European continent was dug not in Paris or Berlin but in Budapest. Two miles long, completed in 1896, it connected the thriving Hungarian capital with its northwestern suburbs. During the same year the rebuilding of the grand palace of Franz Josef I, in one of his Dual-Monarchial manifestations King of Hungary, enlarged that structure to 860 rooms. Across the wide Danube rose a grandiose parliament, its dimensions measured in acres, six stories of Victorian mansard-roofed masonry bristling with Neo-Gothic pinnacles set around an elongated Renaissance dome braced by flying buttresses. The palace in hilly, quiet Buda confronted the parliament eastward in flat, bustling Pest. "Horse-drawn droshkies," Hungarian physicist Theodor von Kármán remembers of that time, carried "silk-gowned women and their Hussar counts in red uniforms and furred hats through the ancient war-scarred hills of Buda." But "such sights hid deeper social currents," von Kármán adds.

From the hills of Buda you could look far beyond Pest onto the great Hungarian plain, the Carpathian Basin enclosed 250 miles to the east by the bow of the Carpathian Mountains that the Magyars had crossed to found Hungary a thousand years before. Pest expanded within rings of boulevards on the Viennese model, its offices busy with banking, brokering, lucrative trade in grain, fruit, wine, beef, leather, timber and industrial production only lately established in a country where more than 96 percent of the population had lived in settlements of fewer than 20,000 persons as recently as fifty years before. Budapest, combining Buda, Óbuda and Pest, had grown faster than any other city on the Continent in those fifty years, rising from seventeenth to eighth in rank—almost a million souls. Now coffeehouses, "the fountain of illicit trading, adultery, puns, gossip and poetry," a Hungarian journalist thought, "the meeting places for the intellectuals and those opposed to oppression," enlivened the boulevards; parks and squares sponsored a cavalry of equestrian bronzes; and peasants visiting for the first time the Queen City of the Danube gawked suspiciously at blocks of mansions as fine as any in Europe.

Economic take-off, the late introduction of a nation rich in agricultural resources to the organizing mechanisms of capitalism and industrialization, was responsible for Hungary's boom. The operators of those mechanisms, by virtue of their superior ambition and energy but also by default, were Jews, who represented about 5 percent of the Hungarian population in 1910. The stubbornly rural and militaristic Magyar nobility had managed to keep 33 percent of the Hungarian people illiterate as late as 1918 and wanted nothing of vulgar commerce except its fruits. As a result, by 1904 Jewish families owned 37.5 percent of Hungary's arable land; by 1910, although Jews comprised only 0.1 percent of agricultural laborers and 7.3 percent of industrial workers, they counted 50.6 percent of Hungary's lawyers, 53 percent of its commercial businessmen, 59.9 percent of its doctors and 80 percent of its financiers. The only other significant middle class in Hungary was a vast bureaucracy of impoverished Hungarian gentry that came to vie with the Jewish bourgeoisie for political power. Caught between predominantly Jewish socialists and radicals on one side and the entrenched bureaucracy on the other, both sides hostile, the Jewish commercial elite allied itself for survival with the old nobility and the monarchy; one measure of that conservative alliance was the dramatic increase in the early twentieth century of ennobled Jews.

George de Hevesy's prosperous maternal grandfather, S. V. Schossberger, became in 1863 the first unconverted Jew ennobled since the Middle Ages, and in 1895 de Hevesy's entire family was ennobled. Max Neumann, the banker father of the brilliant mathematician John von Neumann, was elevated in 1913. Von Kármán's father's case was exceptional. Mór Kármán, the founder of the celebrated Minta school, was an educator rather than a wealthy businessman. In the last decades of the nineteenth century he reorganized the haphazard Hungarian school system along German lines, to its great improvement—and not incidentally wrested control of education from the religious institutions that dominated it and passed that control to the state. That won him a position at court and the duty of planning the education of a young archduke, the Emperor's cousin. As a result, writes von Kármán:

> One day in August 1907, Franz Joseph called him to the Palace, and said he wished to reward him for his fine job. He offered to make my father an Excellency.
>
> My father bowed slightly and said: "Imperial Majesty, I am very flattered. But I would prefer something which I could hand down to my children."
>
> The Emperor nodded his agreement and ordained that my father be given a place in the hereditary nobility. To receive a predicate of nobility, my father had to be landed. Fortunately he owned a small vineyard near Budapest, so the Emperor bestowed upon him the predicate "von Szolloskislak" (small grape). I have shortened it to von, for even to me, a Hungarian, the full title is almost unpronounceable.

Jewish family ennoblements in the hundred years prior to 1900 totaled 126; in the short decade and a half between 1900 and the outbreak of the Great War the insecure conservative alliance bartered 220 more. Some thousands of men in these 346 families were ultimately involved. They were thus brought into political connection, their power of independent action siphoned away.

Out of the prospering but vulnerable Hungarian Jewish middle class came no fewer than seven of the twentieth century's most exceptional scientists: in order of birth, Theodor von Kármán, George de Hevesy, Michael Polanyi, Leo Szilard, Eugene Wigner, John von Neumann and Edward Teller. All seven left Hungary as young men; all seven proved unusually versatile as well as talented and made major contributions to science and technology; two among them, de Hevesy and Wigner, eventually won Nobel Prizes.

The mystery of such a concentration of ability from so remote and provincial a place has fascinated the community of science. Recalling that "galaxy of brilliant Hungarian expatriates," Otto Frisch remembers that his friend Fritz Houtermans, a theoretical physicist, proposed the popular theory that "these people were really visitors from Mars; for them, he said, it was difficult to speak without an accent that would give them away and therefore they chose to pretend to be Hungarians whose inability to speak any language without accent is well known; except Hungarian, and [these] brilliant men all lived elsewhere." That was amusing to colleagues and flattering to the Hungarians, who liked the patina of mystery that romanticized their pasts. The truth is harsher: the Hungarians came to live elsewhere because lack of scientific opportunity and increasing and finally violent anti-Semitism drove them away. They took the lessons they learned in Hungary with them into the world.

They all began with talent, variously displayed and remembered. Von Kármán at six stunned his parents' party guests by quickly multiplying six-figure numbers in his head. Von Neumann at six joked with his father in classical Greek and had a truly photographic memory: he could recite entire chapters of books he had read. Edward Teller, like Einstein before him, was exceptionally late in learning—or choosing—to talk. His grandfather warned his parents that he might be retarded, but when Teller finally spoke, at three, he spoke in complete sentences.

Von Neumann too wondered about the mystery of his and his compatriots' origins. His friend and biographer, the Polish mathematician Stanislaw Ulam, remembers their discussions of the primitive rural foothills on both sides of the Carpathians, encompassing parts of Hungary, Czechoslovakia and Poland, populated thickly with impoverished Orthodox villages. "Johnny used to say that all the famous Jewish scientists, artists and writers who emigrated from Hungary around the time of the first World War came, either directly or indirectly, from those little Carpathian communities, moving up to Budapest as their material conditions improved." Progress, to people of such successful transition, could be a metaphysical faith. "As a boy," writes Teller, "I enjoyed science fiction. I read Jules Verne. His words carried me into an exciting world. The possibilities of man's improvement seemed unlimited. The achievements of science were fantastic, and they were good."

Leo Szilard, long before he encountered the novels of H. G. Wells, found another visionary student of the human past and future to admire. Szilard thought in maturity that his "addiction to the truth" and his "predilection for 'Saving the World' " were traceable first of all to the stories his mother told him. But apart from those, he said, "the most serious influence on my life came from a book which I read when I was ten years old. It was a Hungarian classic, taught in the schools, *The Tragedy of Man.*"

A long dramatic poem in which Adam, Eve and Lucifer are central characters, *The Tragedy of Man* was written by an idealistic but disillusioned young Hungarian nobleman named Imre Madach in the years after the failed Hungarian Revolution of 1848. A modern critic calls the work "the most dangerously pessimistic poem of the 19th century." It runs Adam through history with Lucifer as his guide, rather as the spirits of Christmas lead Ebenezer Scrooge, enrolling Adam successively with such real historical personages as Pharaoh, Miltiades, the knight Tancred, Kepler. Its pessimism resides in its dramatic strategy. Lucifer demonstrates to Adam the pointlessness of man's faith in progress by staging not imaginary experiences, as in *Faust* or *Peer Gynt,* but real historical events. Pharaoh frees his slaves and they revile him for leaving them without a dominating god; Miltiades returns from Marathon and is attacked by a murderous crowd of citizens his enemies have bribed; Kepler sells horoscopes to bejewel his faithless wife. Adam sensibly concludes that man will never achieve his ultimate ideals but ought to struggle toward them anyway, a conclusion that Szilard continued to endorse as late as 1945. "In [Madach's] book," he said then, "the devil shows Adam the history of mankind, [ending] with the sun dying down. Only a few Eskimos are left and they worry chiefly because there are too many Eskimos and too few seals [the last scene before Adam returns to the beginning again]. The thought is that there remains a rather narrow margin of hope after you have made your prophecy and it is pessimistic."

Szilard's qualified faith in progress and his liberal political values ultimately set him apart from his Hungarian peers. He believed that group was shaped by the special environment of Budapest at the turn of the century, "a society where economic security was taken for granted," as a historian paraphrases him, and "a high value was placed on intellectual achievement." The Minta that Szilard and Teller later attended deeply gratified von Kármán when he went there in the peaceful 1890s. "My father [who founded the school]," he writes, "was a great believer in teaching everything—Latin, math, and history—by showing its connection with everyday living." To begin Latin the students wandered the city copying down inscriptions from statues and museums; to begin mathematics they looked up figures for Hungary's wheat production and made tables and drew graphs. "At no time did we memorize rules from a book. Instead we sought to develop them ourselves." What better basic training for a scientist?

Eugene Wigner, small and trim, whose father managed a tannery and who would become one of the leading theoretical physicists of the twentieth century, entered the Lutheran *Gimnásium* in 1913; John von Neumann followed the next year. "We had two years of physics courses, the last two years," Wigner remembers. "And it was very interesting. Our teachers were just enormously good, but the mathematics teacher was fantastic. He gave private classes to Johnny von Neumann. He gave him private classes because he realized that this would be a great mathematician."

Von Neumann found a friend in Wigner. They walked and talked mathematics. Wigner's mathematical talent was exceptional, but he felt less than first-rate beside the prodigious banker's son. Von Neumann's brilliance impressed colleagues throughout his life. Teller recalls a truncated syllogism someone proposed to the effect that (a) Johnny can prove anything and (b) anything Johnny proves is correct. At Princeton, where in 1933 von Neumann at twenty-nine became the youngest member of the newly established Institute for Advanced Study, the saying gained currency that the Hungarian mathematician was indeed a demigod but that he had made a thorough, detailed study of human beings and could imitate them perfectly. The story hints at a certain manipulative coldness behind the mask of bonhomie von Neumann learned to wear, and even Wigner thought his friendships lacked intimacy. To Wigner he was nevertheless the only authentic genius of the lot.

These earlier memories of *Gimnásium* days contrast sharply with the turmoil that Teller experienced. Part of the difference was personal. Teller was bored in first-year math at the Minta and quickly managed to insult his mathematics teacher, who was also the principal of the school, by improving on a proof. The principal took the classroom display unkindly. "So you are a genius, Teller? Well, I don't like geniuses." But whatever Teller's personal difficulties, he was also confronted directly, as a schoolboy of only eleven years, with revolution and counterrevolution, with riots and violent bloodletting, with personal fear. What had been usually only implicit for the Martians who preceded him was made explicit before his eyes. "I think this was the first time I was deeply impressed by my father," he told his biographers. "He said anti-Semitism was coming. To me, the idea of anti-Semitism was new, and the fact that my father was so serious about it impressed me."

Von Kármán studied mechanical engineering at the University of Budapest before moving on to Göttingen in 1906; de Hevesy tried Budapest in 1903 before going to the Technische Hochschule in Berlin in 1904 and on to work with Fritz Haber and then with Ernest Rutherford; Szilard had studied at the Technology Institute in Budapest and served in the Army before the post-Armistice turmoil made him decide to leave. In contrast, Wigner, von Neumann and particularly Teller experienced the breakdown of Hungarian society as adolescents—Teller at the impressionable beginning of puberty—and at first hand.

"The Revolution arrived as a hurricane," an eyewitness to the Hungarian Revolution of October 1918 recalls. "No one prepared it and no one arranged it; it broke out by its own irresistible momentum." But there were antecedents: a general strike of half a million workers in Budapest and other Hungarian industrial centers in January 1918; another general strike of similar magnitude in June. In the autumn of that year masses of soldiers, students and workers gathered in Budapest. This first brief revolution began with anti-military and nationalistic claims. By the time the Hungarian National Council had been formed under Count Mihály Károli ("We can't even manage a revolution without a count," they joked in Budapest), in late October, there was expectation of real democratic reform: the council issued a manifesto calling for Hungarian independence, an end to the war, freedom of the press, a secret ballot and even female suffrage.

The Austro-Hungarian Dual Monarchy collapsed in November. Austrian novelist Robert Musil explained that collapse as well as anybody in a dry epitaph: *Es ist passiert* ("It sort of happened"). Hungary won a new government on October 31 and ecstatic crowds filled the streets of Budapest waving chrysanthemums, which had become the symbol of the revolution, and cheering the truckloads of soldiers and workers that pushed through.

The victory was not easy after all. The revolution hardly extended beyond Budapest. The new government was unable to negotiate anything better than a national dismembering. The founding of the Republic of Hungary, proclaimed on November 16, 1918, was shadowed by another founding on November 20: of the Hungarian Communist Party, by soldiers returning from Russian camps where they had been radicalized as prisoners of war. On March 21, 1919, four months after it began, the Republic of Hungary bloodlessly metamorphosed into the Hungarian Soviet Republic, its head a former prisoner of war, disciple of Lenin, journalist, Jew born in the Carpathians of Transylvania: Béla Kun. Arthur Koestler, a boy of fourteen then in Budapest, heard for the first time "the rousing tunes of the *Marseillaise* and of the *Internationale* which, during the hundred days of the Commune, drowned the music-loving town on the Danube in a fiery, melodious flood."

It was a little more than a hundred days: 133. They were days of confusion, hope, fear, comic ineptitude and some violence. Toward the end of the war von Kármán had returned to Budapest from aeronautics work with the Austro-Hungarian Air Force, where he had participated in the development of an early prototype of the helicopter. De Hevesy had also returned. Von Kármán helped reorganize and modernize the university in the brief days of the Republic and even served as undersecretary for universities during the Kun regime. He remembered its naïveté more than its violence: "So far as I can recall, there was no terrorism in Budapest during the one hundred days of the Bolsheviks, although I did hear of some sadistic excesses." Lacking a qualified physicist, the university hired de Hevesy as a lecturer on experimental physics during the winter of 1918–19. Undersecretary von Kármán appointed him to a newly established professorship of physical chemistry in March, but de Hevesy found Commune working conditions unsatisfactory and went off in May to Denmark to visit Bohr. The two old friends agreed he would join Bohr's new institute in Copenhagen as soon as it was built.

Arthur Koestler remembers that food was scarce, especially if you tried to buy it with the regime's ration cards and nearly worthless paper money, but for some reason the same paper would purchase an abundance of Commune-sponsored vanilla ice cream, which his family therefore consumed for breakfast, lunch and dinner. He mentions this curiosity, he remarks, "because it was typical of the happy-go-lucky, dilettantish, and even surrealistic ways in which the Commune was run." It was, Koestler thought, "all rather endearing—at least when compared to the lunacy and savagery which was to descend upon Europe in years to come."

The Hungarian Soviet Republic affected von Neumann and Teller far more severely. They were not admirers like young Koestler nor yet members of the intellectual elite like de Hevesy and von Kármán. They were children of businessmen—Max Teller was a prosperous attorney. Max von Neumann took his family and fled to Vienna. "We left Hungary," his son testified many years later, "very soon after the Communists seized power. . . . We left essentially as soon as it was feasible, which was about 30 or 40 days later, and we returned about 2 months after the Communists had been put down." In Vienna the elder von Neumann joined the group of Hungarian financiers working with the conservative nobility to overthrow the Commune.

Lacking protective wealth, the Tellers stuck it out grimly in Budapest, living with their fears. They made forays into the country to barter with the peasants for food. Teller heard of corpses hung from lampposts, though as with von Kármán's "sadistic excesses" he witnessed none himself. Faced with an overcrowded city, the Commune had socialized all housing. The day came for the Koestlers as for the Tellers when soldiers charged with requisitioning bourgeois excesses of floor space and furniture knocked on their doors. The Koestlers, who occupied two threadbare rooms in a boarding house, were allowed to keep what they had, Arthur discovering in the meantime that working people were interesting and different. The Tellers acquired two soldiers who slept on couches in Max Teller's two office rooms, connected to the Teller apartment. The soldiers were courteous; they sometimes shared their food; they urinated on the rubber plant; but because they searched for hoarded money (which was safely stashed in the cover linings of Max Teller's law books) or simply because the Tellers felt generally insecure, their alien presence terrified.

Yet it was not finally Hungarian communism that frightened Edward Teller's parents most. The leaders of the Commune and many among its officials were Jewish—necessarily, since the only intelligentsia Hungary had evolved up to that time was Jewish. Max Teller warned his son that anti-Semitism was coming. Teller's mother expressed her fears more vividly. "I shiver at what my people are doing," she told her son's governess in the heyday of the Commune. "When this is over there will be a terrible revenge."

In the summer of 1919, as the Commune faltered, eleven-year-old Edward and his older sister Emmi were packed off to safety at their maternal grandparents' home in Rumania. They returned in the autumn; by then Admiral Nicholas Horthy had ridden into Budapest on a white horse behind a new national army to install a violent fascist regime, the first in Europe. The Red Terror had come and gone, resulting in some five hundred deaths by execution. The White Terror of the Horthy regime was of another order of magnitude: at least 5,000 deaths and many of those sadistic; secret torture chambers; a selective but unrelenting anti-Semitism that drove tens of thousands of Jews into exile. A contemporary observer, a socialist equally biased against either extreme, wrote that he had "no desire whatever to palliate the brutalities and atrocities of the proletarian dictatorship; its harshness is not to be denied, even if its terrorists operated more with insults and threats than with actual deeds. But the tremendous difference between the Red and the White Terror is beyond all question." A friend of the new regime, Max von Neumann brought his family home.

In 1920 the Horthy regime introduced a *numerus clausus* law restricting university admission which required "that the comparative numbers of the entrants correspond as nearly as possible to the relative population of the various races or nationalities." The law, which would limit Jewish admissions to 5 percent, a drastic reduction, was deliberately anti-Semitic. Though he was admitted to the University of Budapest and might have stayed, von Neumann chose instead to leave Hungary at seventeen, in 1921, for Berlin, where he came under the influence of Fritz Haber and studied first for a chemical engineering degree, awarded at the Technical Institute of Zürich in 1925. A year later he picked up a Ph.D. *summa cum laude* in mathematics at Budapest; in 1927 he became a *Privatdozent* at the University of Berlin; in 1929, at twenty-five, he was invited to lecture at Princeton. He was professor of mathematics at Princeton by 1931 and accepted lifetime appointment to the Institute for Advanced Study in 1933.

Von Neumann experienced no personal violence in Hungary, only upheaval and whatever anxiety his parents communicated. He nevertheless felt himself scarred. His discussion with Stanislaw Ulam went on more ominously from identifying Carpathian villages as the ultimate places of origin of Hungary's talented expatriates. "It will be left to historians of science," Ulam writes, "to discover and explain the conditions which catalyzed the emergence of so many brilliant individuals from that area. . . . Johnny used to say that it was a coincidence of some cultural factors which he could not make precise: an external pressure on the whole society of this part of Central Europe, a feeling of extreme insecurity in the individuals, and the necessity to produce the unusual or else face extinction."

Teller was too young to leave Hungary during the worst of the Horthy years. This was the adolescent period, as *Time* magazine paraphrased Teller later, when Max Teller "dinned into his son two grim lessons: 1) he would have to emigrate to some more favorable country when he grew up and 2) as a member of a disliked minority he would have to excel the average just to stay even." Teller added a lesson of his own. "I loved science," he told an interviewer once. "But also it offered a possibility for escaping this doomed society." Von Kármán embeds in his autobiography a similarly striking statement about the place of science in his emotional life. When the Hungarian Soviet Republic collapsed he retreated to the home of a wealthy friend, then found his way back to Germany. "I was glad to get out of Hungary," he writes of his state of mind then. "I felt I had had enough of politicians and government upheavals. . . . Suddenly I was enveloped in the feeling that only science is lasting."

That science can be a refuge from the world is a conviction common among men and women who turn to it. Abraham Pais remarks that Einstein "once commented that he had sold himself body and soul to science, being in flight from the 'I' and the 'we' to the 'it.' " But science as a means of escaping from the familiar world of birth and childhood and language when that world mounts an overwhelming threat—science as a way out, a portable culture, an international fellowship and the only abiding certitude—must become a more desperate and therefore a more total dependency. Chaim Weizmann gives some measure of that totality in the harsher world of the Russian Pale when he writes that "the acquisition of knowledge was not for us so much a normal process of education as the storing up of weapons in an arsenal by means of which we hoped later to be able to hold our own in a hostile world." He remembers painfully that "every division of one's life was a watershed."

Teller's experience in Hungary before he left it in 1926, at seventeen, for the Technical Institute at Karlsruhe was far less rigorous than Weizmann's in the Pale. But external circumstance is no sure measure of internal wounding, and there are not many horrors as efficient for the generation of deep anger and terrible lifelong insecurity as the inability of a father to protect his child.

"In the last few years," Niels Bohr wrote the German theoretical physicist Arnold Sommerfeld at Munich in April 1922, "I have often felt myself scientifically very lonesome, under the impression that my effort to develop the principles of the quantum theory systematically to the best of my ability has been received with very little understanding." Through the war years Bohr had struggled to follow, wherever it might lead, the "radical change" he had introduced into physics. It led to frustration. However stunning Bohr's prewar results had been, too many older European scientists still thought his inconsistent hypotheses *ad hoc* and the idea of a quantized atom repugnant. The war itself stalled advance.

Yet he persisted, groping his way forward in the darkness. "Only a rare and uncanny intuition," writes the Italian physicist Emilio Segrè, "saved Bohr from getting lost in the maze." He guided himself delicately by what he called the correspondence principle. As Robert Oppenheimer once explained it, "Bohr remembered that physics was physics and that Newton described a great part of it and Maxwell a great part of it." So Bohr assumed that his quantum rules must approximate, "in situations where the actions involved were large compared to the quantum, to the classical rules of Newton and of Maxwell." That correspondence between the reliable old and the unfamiliar new gave him an outer limit, a wall to feel his way along.

Bohr built his Institute for Theoretical Physics with support from the University of Copenhagen and from Danish private industry, occupying it on January 18, 1921, after more than a year of delay—he struggled with the architect's plans as painfully as he struggled with his scientific papers. The city of Copenhagen ceded land for the institute on the edge of the Faelledpark, broad with soccer fields, where a carnival annually marks the Danish celebration of Constitution Day. The building itself was modest gray stucco with a red tile roof, no larger than many private homes, with four floors inside that looked like only three outside because the lowest floor was built partly below grade and the top floor, which served the Bohrs at first as an apartment, extended into the space under the peaked roof (later, as Bohr's family increased to five sons, he built a house next door and the apartment served as living quarters for visiting students and colleagues). The institute included a lecture hall, a library, laboratories, offices and a popular Ping-Pong table where Bohr often played. "His reactions were very fast and accurate," says Otto Frisch, "and he had tremendous will power and stamina. In a way those qualities characterized his scientific work as well."

In 1922, the year his Nobel Prize made him a Danish national hero, Bohr accomplished a second great theoretical triumph: an explanation of the atomic structure that underlies the regularities of the periodic table of the elements. It linked chemistry irrevocably to physics and is now standard in every basic chemistry text. Around the nucleus, Bohr proposed, atoms are built up of successive orbital shells of electrons—imagine a set of nested spheres—each shell capable of accommodating up to a certain number of electrons and no more. Elements that are similar chemically are similar because they have identical numbers of electrons in their outermost shells, available there for chemical combination. Barium, for example, an alkaline earth, the fifty-sixth element in the periodic table, atomic weight 137.34, has electron shells filled successively by 2, 8, 18, 18, 8 and 2 electrons. Radium, another alkaline earth, the eighty-eighth element, atomic weight 226, has electron shells filled successively by 2, 8, 18, 32, 18, 8 and 2 electrons. Because the outer shell of each element has two valence electrons, barium and radium are chemically similar despite their considerable difference in atomic weight and number. "That [the] insecure and contradictory foundation [of Bohr's quantum hypotheses]," Einstein would say, "was sufficient to enable a man of Bohr's unique instinct and perceptiveness to discover the major laws of spectral lines and of the electron shells of the atom as well as their significance for chemistry appeared to me like a miracle. . . . This is the highest form of musicality in the sphere of thought."

Confirming the miracle, Bohr predicted in the autumn of 1922 that element 72 when discovered would not be a rare earth, as chemists expected and as elements 57 through 71 are, but would rather be a valence 4 metal like zirconium. George de Hevesy, now settled in at Bohr's institute, and a newly arrived young Dutchman, Dirk Coster, went to work using X-ray spectroscopy to look for the element in zircon-bearing minerals. They had not finished their checking when Bohr went off with Margrethe in early December to claim his Nobel Prize. They called him in Stockholm the night before his Nobel lecture, only just in time: they had definitely identified element 72 and it was chemically almost identical to zirconium. They named the new element hafnium after Hafnia, the old Roman name for Copenhagen. Bohr announced its discovery with pride at the conclusion of his lecture the next day.

Despite his success with it, quantum theory needed a more solid foundation than Bohr's intuition. Arnold Sommerfeld in Munich was an early contributor to that work; after the war the brightest young men, searching out the growing point of physics, signed on to help. Bohr remembered the period as "a unique cooperation of a whole generation of theoretical physicists from many countries," an "unforgettable experience." He was lonesome no more.

Sommerfeld brought with him to Göttingen in the early summer of 1922 his most promising student, a twenty-year-old Bavarian named Werner Heisenberg, to hear Bohr as visiting lecturer there. "I shall never forget the first lecture," Heisenberg wrote fifty years later, the memory still textured with fine detail. "The hall was filled to capacity. The great Danish physicist . . . stood on the platform, his head slightly inclined, and a friendly but somewhat embarrassed smile on his lips. Summer light flooded in through the wide-open windows. Bohr spoke fairly softly, with a slight Danish accent. . . . Each one of his carefully formulated sentences revealed a long chain of underlying thoughts, of philosophical reflections, hinted at but never fully expressed. I found this approach highly exciting."

Heisenberg nevertheless raised pointed objection to one of Bohr's statements. Bohr had learned to be alert for bright students who were not afraid to argue. "At the end of the discussion he came over to me and asked me to join him that afternoon on a walk over the Hain Mountain," Heisenberg remembers. "My real scientific career only began that afternoon." It is the memory of a conversion. Bohr proposed that Heisenberg find his way to Copenhagen eventually so that they could work together. "Suddenly, the future looked full of hope." At dinner the next evening Bohr was startled to be challenged by two young men in the uniforms of the Göttingen police. One of them clapped him on the shoulder: "You are arrested on the charge of kidnapping small children!" They were students, genial frauds. The small child they guarded was Heisenberg, boyish with freckles and a stiff brush of red hair.

Heisenberg was athletic, vigorous, eager—"radiant," a close friend says. "He looked even greener in those days than he really was, for, being a member of the Youth Movement . . . he often wore, even after reaching man's estate, an open shirt and walking shorts." In the Youth Movement young Germans on hiking tours built campfires, sang folk songs, talked of knighthood and the Holy Grail and of service to the Fatherland. Many were idealists, but authoritarianism and anti-Semitism already bloomed poisonously among them. When Heisenberg finally got to Copenhagen at Eastertime in 1924 Bohr took him off on a hike through north Zealand and asked him about it all. " 'But now and then our papers also tell us about more ominous, anti-Semitic, trends in Germany, obviously fostered by demagogues,' " Heisenberg remembers Bohr questioning. " 'Have you come across any of that yourself?' " That was the work of some of the old officers embittered by the war, Heisenberg said, "but we don't take these groups very seriously."

Now, as part of the "unique cooperation" Bohr would speak of, they went freshly to work on quantum theory. Heisenberg seems to have begun with a distaste for visualizing unmeasurable events. As an undergraduate, for example, he had been shocked to read in Plato's *Timaeus* that atoms had geometric forms: "It saddened me to find a philosopher of Plato's critical acumen succumbing to such fancies." The orbits of Bohr's electrons were similarly fanciful, Heisenberg thought, and Max Born and Wolfgang

Pauli, his colleagues at Göttingen, concurred. No one could see inside an atom. What was known and measurable was the light that came out of the atomic interior, the frequencies and amplitudes associated with spectral lines. Heisenberg decided to reject models entirely and look for regularities among the numbers alone.

He returned to Göttingen as a *Privatdozent* working under Born. Toward the end of May 1925 his hay fever flared; he asked Born for two weeks' leave of absence and made his way to Heligoland, a stormy sliver of island twenty-eight miles off the German coast in the North Sea, where very little pollen blew. He walked; he swam long distances in the cold sea; "a few days were enough to jettison all the mathematical ballast that invariably encumbers the beginning of such attempts, and to arrive at a simple formulation of my problem." A few days more and he glimpsed the system he needed. It required a strange algebra that he cobbled together as he went along where numbers multiplied in one direction often produced different products from the same numbers multiplied in the opposite direction. He worried that his system might violate the basic physical law of the conservation of energy and he worked until three o'clock in the morning checking his figures, nervously making mistakes. By then he saw that he had "mathematical consistency and coherence." And so often with deep physical discovery, the experience was elating but also psychologically disturbing:

> At first, I was deeply alarmed. I had the feeling that, through the surface of atomic phenomena, I was looking at a strangely beautiful interior, and felt almost giddy at the thought that I now had to probe this wealth of mathematical structures nature had so generously spread out before me. I was far too excited to sleep, and so, as a new day dawned, I made for the southern tip of the island, where I had been longing to climb a rock jutting out into the sea. I now did so without too much trouble, and waited for the sun to rise.

Back in Göttingen Max Born recognized Heisenberg's strange mathematics as matrix algebra, a mathematical system for representing and manipulating arrays of numbers on matrices—grids—that had been devised in the 1850s and that Born's teacher David Hilbert had extended in 1904. In three months of intensive work Born, Heisenberg and their colleague Pascual Jordan then developed what Heisenberg calls "a coherent mathematical framework, one that promised to embrace all the multifarious aspects of atomic physics." Quantum mechanics, the new system was called. It fit the experimental evidence to a high degree of accuracy. Pauli managed with heroic effort to apply it to the hydrogen atom and derive in a consistent way the same results—the Balmer formula, Rydberg's constant—that Bohr had derived from inconsistent assumptions in 1913. Bohr was delighted. At Copenhagen, at Göttingen, at Munich, at Cambridge, the work of development went on.

The bow of the Carpathians as they curve around northwestward begins to define the northern border of Czechoslovakia. Long before it can complete that service the bow bends down toward the Austrian Alps, but a border region of mountainous uplift, the Sudetes, continues across Czechoslovakia. Some sixty miles beyond Prague it turns southwest to form a low range between Czechoslovakia and Germany that is called, in German, the Erzgebirge: the Ore Mountains. The Erzgebirge began to be mined for iron in medieval days. In 1516 a rich silver lode was discovered in Joachimsthal (St. Joachim's dale), in the territory of the Count von Schlick, who immediately appropriated the mine. In 1519 coins were first struck from its silver at his command. *Joachimsthaler,* the name for the new coins, shortened to *thaler,* became "dollar" in English before 1600. Thereby the U.S. dollar descends from the silver of Joachimsthal.

The Joachimsthal mines, ancient and cavernous, shored with smoky timbers, offered up other unusual ores, including a black, pitchy, heavy, nodular mineral descriptively named pitchblende. A German apothecary and self-taught chemist, Martin Heinrich Klaproth, who became the first professor of chemistry at the University of Berlin when it opened its doors in 1810, succeeded in 1789 in extracting a grayish metallic material from a sample of Joachimsthal pitchblende. He sought an appropriate name. Eight years previously Sir William Herschel, the German-born English astronomer, had discovered a new planet and named it Uranus after the earliest supreme god of Greek mythology, son and husband of Gaea, father of Titans and Cyclopes, whose son Chronus with Gaea's help castrated him and from whose wounded blood, falling then on Earth, the three vengeful Furies sprang. To honor Herschel's discovery Klaproth named his new metal *uranium.* It was found to serve, in the form of sodium and ammonium diuranates, as an excellent coloring agent of ceramic glazes, giving a good yellow at 0.006 percent and with higher percentages successively orange, brown, green and black. Uranium mining for ceramics, once begun, continued modestly at Joachimsthal into the modern era. It was from Joachimsthal pitchblende residues that Marie and Pierre Curie laboriously separated the first samples of the new elements they named radium and polonium. The radioactivity of the Erzgebirge ores thus lent glamour to the region's several spas, including Carlsbad and Marienbad, which could now announce that their waters were not only naturally heated but dispersed tonic radioactivity as well.

In the summer of 1921 a wealthy seventeen-year-old American student, a recent graduate of the Ethical Culture School of New York, made his way to Joachimsthal on an amateur prospecting trip. Young Robert Oppenheimer had begun collecting minerals when his grandfather, who lived in Hanau, Germany, had given him a modest starter collection on a visit there when Robert was a small boy, before the Great War. He dated his interest in science from that time. "This was certainly at first a collector's interest," he told an interviewer late in life, "but it began to be also a bit of a scientist's interest, not in historical problems of how rocks and minerals came to be, but really a fascination with crystals, their structure, birefringence, what you saw in polarized light, and all the canonical business." The grandfather was "an unsuccessful businessman, born himself in a hovel, really, in an almost medieval German village, with a taste for scholarship." Oppenheimer's father had left Hanau for America at seventeen, in 1898, worked his way to ownership of a textile-importing company and prospered importing lining fabrics for men's suits at a time when ready-made suits were replacing hand tailoring in the United States. The Oppenheimers—Julius; his beautiful and delicate wife Ella, artistically trained, from Baltimore; Robert, born April 22, 1904; and Frank, Robert's sidekick brother, eight years younger—could afford to summer in Europe and frequently did so.

Julius and Ella Oppenheimer were people of dignity and some caution, nonpracticing Jews. They lived in a spacious apartment on Riverside Drive near 88th Street overlooking the Hudson River and kept a summer house at Bay Shore on Long Island. They dressed with tailored care, practiced cultivation, sheltered themselves and their children from real and imagined harm. Ella Oppenheimer's congenitally unformed right hand, hidden always in a prosthetic glove, was not discussed, not even by the boys out of earshot among their friends. She was loving but formal: in her presence only her husband presumed to raise his voice. Julius Oppenheimer, according to one of Robert's friends a great talker and social arguer, according to another was "desperately amiable, anxious to be agreeable," but also essentially kind. He belonged to Columbia University educator Felix Adler's Society for Ethical Culture, of which Robert's school was an extension, which declared that "man must assume responsibility for the direction of his life and destiny": man, as opposed to God. Robert Oppenheimer remembered himself as "an unctuous, repulsively good little boy." His childhood, he said, "did not prepare me for the fact that the world is full of cruel and bitter things. It gave me no normal, healthy way to be a bastard." He was a frail child, frequently ill. For that reason, or because she had lost a middle son shortly after birth, his mother did not encourage him to run in the streets. He stayed home, collected minerals and at ten years of age wrote poems but still played with blocks.

He was already working up to science. A professional microscope was a childhood toy. He did laboratory experiments in the third grade, began keeping scientific notebooks in the fourth, began studying physics in the fifth, though for many years chemistry would interest him more. The curator of crystals at the American Museum of Natural History took him as a pupil. He lectured to the surprised and then delighted members of the New York Mineralogical Club when he was twelve—from the quality of his correspondence the membership had assumed he was an adult.

When he was fourteen, to get him out of doors and perhaps to help him find friends, his parents sent him to camp. He walked the trails of Camp Koenig looking for rocks and discoursing with the only friend he found on George Eliot, emboldened by Eliot's conviction that cause and effect ruled human affairs. He was shy, awkward, unbearably precious and condescending and he did not fight back. He wrote his parents that he was glad to be at camp because he was learning the facts of life. The Oppenheimers came running. When the camp director cracked down on dirty jokes, the other boys, the ones who called Robert "Cutie," traced the censorship to him and hauled him off to the camp icehouse, stripped him bare, beat him up—"tortured him," his friend says—painted his genitals and buttocks green and locked him away naked for the night. Responsibly he held out to the end of camp but never went back. "Still a little boy," another childhood friend, a girl he liked more than she knew, remembers him at fifteen; ". . . very frail, very pink-cheeked, very shy, and very brilliant of course. Very quickly everybody admitted that he was different from all the others and very superior. As far as studies were concerned he was good in everything. . . . Aside from that he was physically—you can't say clumsy exactly—he was rather undeveloped, not in the way he behaved but the way he went about, the way he walked, the way he sat. There was something strangely childish about him."

He graduated as Ethical Culture's valedictorian in February 1921. In April he underwent surgery for appendicitis. Recovered from that, he traveled with his family to Europe and off on his side trip to Joachimsthal. Somewhere along the way he "came down with a heavy, almost fatal case of trench dysentery." He was supposed to enter Harvard in September, but "I was sick abed—in Europe, actually, at the time." Severe colitis following the bout of dysentery laid him low for months. He spent the winter in the family apartment in New York.

To round off Robert's convalescence and toughen him up, his father arranged for a favorite English teacher at Ethical Culture, a warm, supportive Harvard graduate named Herbert Smith, to take him out West for the summer. Robert was then eighteen, his face still boyish but steadied by arresting blue-gray eyes. He was six feet tall, on an extremely narrow frame; he never in his life weighed more than 125 pounds and at times of illness or stress could waste to 115. Smith guided his charge to a dude ranch, Los Piños, in the Sangre de Cristo Mountains northeast of Santa Fe, and Robert chowed down, chopped wood, learned to ride horses and live in rain and weather.

A highlight of the summer was a pack trip. It started in Frijoles, a village within sheer, pueblo-carved Cañon de los Frijoles across the Rio Grande from the Sangre de Cristos, and ascended the canyons and mesas of the Pajarito Plateau up to the Valle Grande of the vast Jemez Caldera above 10,000 feet. The Jemez Caldera is a bowl-shaped volcanic crater twelve miles across with a grassy basin inside 3,500 feet below the rim, the basin divided by mountainous extrusions of lava into several high valleys. It is a million years old and one of the largest calderas in the world, visible even from the moon. Northward four miles from the Cañon de los Frijoles a parallel canyon took its Spanish name from the cottonwoods that shaded its washes: Los Alamos. Young Robert Oppenheimer first approached it in the summer of 1922.

Like Eastern semi-invalids in frontier days, Oppenheimer's encounter with wilderness, freeing him from overcivilized restraints, was decisive, a healing of faith. From an ill and perhaps hypochondriac boy he weathered across a vigorous summer to a physically confident young man. He arrived at Harvard tanned and fit, his body at least in shape.

At Harvard he imagined himself a Goth coming into Rome. "He intellectually looted the place," a classmate says. He routinely took six courses for credit—the requirement was five—and audited four more. Nor were they easy courses. He was majoring in chemistry, but a typical year might include four semesters of chemistry, two of French literature, two of mathematics, one of philosophy and three of physics, these only the courses credited. He read on his own as well, studied languages, found occasional weekends for sailing the 27-foot sloop his father had given him or for all-night hikes with friends, wrote short stories and poetry when the spirit moved him but generally shied from extracurricular activities and groups. Nor did he date; he was still unformed enough to brave no more than worshiping older women from afar. He judged later that "although I liked to work, I spread myself very thin and got by with murder." The murder he got by with resulted in a transcript solid with A's sprinkled with B's; he graduated *summa cum laude* in three years.

There is something frantic in all this grinding, however disguised in traditional Harvard languor. Oppenheimer had not yet found himself—is that more difficult for Americans than for Europeans like Szilard or Teller, who seem all of a piece from their earliest days?—and would not manage to do so at Harvard. Harvard, he would say, was "the most exciting time I've ever had in my life. I really had a chance to learn. I loved it. I almost came alive." Behind the intellectual excitement there was pain.

He was always an intensely, even a cleverly, private man, but late in life he revealed himself to a group of sensitive friends, a revelation that certainly reaches back all the way to his undergraduate years. "Up to now," he told that group in 1963, "and even more in the days of my almost infinitely prolonged adolescence, I hardly took an action, hardly did anything or failed to do anything, whether it was a paper in physics, or a lecture, or how I read a book, how I talked to a friend, how I loved, that did not arouse in me a very great sense of revulsion and of wrong." His friends at Harvard saw little of this side—an American university is after all a safehouse—but he hinted of it in his letters to Herbert Smith:

> Generously, you ask what I do. Aside from the activities exposed in last week's disgusting note, I labor, and write innumerable theses, notes, poems, stories, and junk; I go to the math lib[rary] and read and to the Phil lib and divide my time between Meinherr [Bertrand] Russell and the contemplation of a most beautiful and lovely lady who is writing a thesis on Spinoza—charmingly ironic, at that, don't you think? I make stenches in three different labs, listen to Allard gossip about Racine, serve tea and talk learnedly to a few lost souls, go off for the weekend to distill the low grade energy into laughter and exhaustion, read Greek, commit faux pas, search my desk for letters, and wish I were dead. Voila.

Part of that exaggerated death wish is Oppenheimer making himself interesting to his counselor, but part of it is pure misery—considering its probable weight, rather splendidly and courageously worn.

Both of Oppenheimer's closest college friends, Francis Fergusson and Paul Horgan, agree that he was prone to baroque exaggeration, to making more of things than things could sustain on their own. Since that tendency would eventually ruin his life, it deserves to be examined. Oppenheimer was no longer a frightened boy, but he was still an insecure and uncertain young man. He sorted among information, knowledge, eras, systems, languages, arcane and apposite skills in the spirit of trying them on for size. Exaggeration made it clear that he knew you knew how awkwardly they fit (and self-destructively at the same time supplied the awkwardness). That was perhaps its social function. Deeper was worse. Deeper was self-loathing, "a very great sense of revulsion and of wrong." Nothing was yet his, nothing was original, and what he had appropriated through learning he thought stolen and himself a thief: a Goth looting Rome. He loved the loot but despised the looter. He was as clear as Harry Moseley was clear in his last will about the difference between collectors and creators. At the same time, intellectual controls were the only controls he seems to have found at that point in his life, and he could hardly abandon them.

He tried writing, poems and short stories. His college letters are those of a literary man more than of a scientist. He would keep his literary skills and they would serve him well, but he acquired them first of all for the access he thought they might open to self-knowledge. At the same time, he hoped writing would somehow humanize him. He read *The Waste Land,* newly published, identified with its *Weltschmerz* and began to seek the stern consolations of Hindu philosophy. He worked through the rigors of Bertrand Russell's and Alfred North Whitehead's three-volume *Principia Mathematica* with Whitehead himself, newly arrived—only one other student braved the seminar—and prided himself throughout his life on that achievement. Crucially, he began to find the physics that underlay the chemistry, as he had found crystals emerging in clarity from the historical complexity of rocks: "It came over me that what I liked in chemistry was very close to physics; it's obvious that if you were reading physical chemistry and you began to run into thermodynamical and statistical mechanical ideas you'd want to find out about them. . . . It's a very odd picture; I never had an elementary course in physics."

He worked in the laboratory of Percy Bridgman, many years later a Nobel laureate, "a man," says Oppenheimer, "to whom one wanted to be an apprentice." He learned much of physics, but haphazardly. He graduated a chemist and was foolhardy enough to imagine that Ernest Rutherford would welcome him at Cambridge, where the Manchester physicist had moved in 1919 to take over direction of the Cavendish from the aging J. J. Thomson. "But Rutherford wouldn't have me," Oppenheimer told a historian later. "He didn't think much of Bridgman and my credentials were peculiar and not impressive, and certainly not impressive to a man with Rutherford's common sense. . . . I don't even know why I left Harvard, but I somehow felt that [Cambridge] was more near the center." Nor would Bridgman's letter of recommendation, though well meant, have helped with Rutherford. Oppenheimer had a "perfectly prodigious power of assimilation," the Harvard physicist wrote, and "his problems have in many cases shown a high degree of originality in treatment and much mathematical power." But "his weakness is on the experimental side. His type of mind is analytical, rather than physical, and he is not at home in the manipulations of the laboratory." Bridgman said honestly that he thought

Oppenheimer "a bit of a gamble." On the other hand, "if he does make good at all, I believe that he will be a very unusual success." After another healing summer in New Mexico with Paul Horgan and old friends from the summer of 1921, Oppenheimer went off to Cambridge to attack the center where he could.

J. J. Thomson still worked at the Cavendish. He let Oppenheimer in. "I am having a pretty bad time," Oppenheimer wrote to Francis Fergusson at Oxford on November 1. "The lab work is a terrible bore, and I am so bad at it that it is impossible to feel that I am learning anything. . . . The lectures are vile." Yet he thought "the academic standard here would de-people Harvard overnight." He worked in one corner of a large basement room at the Cavendish (the Garage, it was called); Thomson worked in another. He labored painfully to make thin films of beryllium for an experiment he seems never to have finished—James Chadwick, who had moved down from Manchester and was now Rutherford's assistant director of research, later put them to use. "The business of the laboratory was really quite a sham," Oppenheimer recalled, "but it got me into the laboratory where I heard talk and found out a good deal of what people were interested in."

Postwar work on quantum theory was just then getting under way. It excited Oppenheimer enormously. He wanted to be a part of it. He was afraid he might be too late. All his learning had come easily before. At Cambridge he hit the wall.

It was as much an emotional wall as an intellectual, probably more. "The melancholy of the little boy who will not play because he has been snubbed," he described it three years later, after he broke through. The British gave him the same silent treatment they had given Niels Bohr, but he lacked Bohr's hard-earned self-confidence. Herbert Smith sensed the approaching disaster. "How is Robert doing?" he wrote Fergusson. "Is frigid England hellish socially and climatically, as you found it? Or does he enjoy its exoticism? I've a notion, by the way, that your ability to show him about should be exercised with great tact, rather than in royal profusion. Your [two] years' start and social adaptivity are likely to make him despair. And instead of flying at your throat . . . I'm afraid he'd merely cease to think his own life worth living." Oppenheimer wrote Smith in December that he had not been busy "making a career for myself. . . . Really I have been engaged in the far more difficult business of making myself for a career." It was worse than that. He was in fact, as he later said, "on the point of bumping myself off. This was chronic." He saw Fergusson at Christmastime in Paris and reported despair at his lab work and frustration with sexual ventures. Then, contradicting Smith's prediction, he flew at Fergusson's throat and tried to strangle him. Fergusson easily set him aside. Back at Cambridge Oppenheimer tried a letter of explanation. He wrote that he was sending Fergusson a "noisy" poem. "I have left out, and that is probably where the fun came in, just as I did in Paris, the awful fact of excellence; but as you know, it is that fact now, combined with my inability to solder two copper wires together, which is probably succeeding in getting me crazy."

The awful fact of excellence did not continue to elude him. As he approached a point of psychological crisis he also drove hard to extend himself, understanding deeply that his mind must pull him through. He was "doing a tremendous amount of work," a friend said, "thinking, reading, discussing things, but obviously with a sense of great inner anxiety and alarm." A crucial change that year was his first meeting with Bohr. "When Rutherford introduced me to Bohr he asked me what I was working on. I told him and he said, 'How is it going?' I said, 'I'm in difficulties.' He said, 'Are the difficulties mathematical or physical?' I said, 'I don't know.' He said, 'That's bad.' " But something about Bohr—his avuncular warmth at least, what C. P. Snow calls his simple and genuine kindness, his uninsipid "sweetness"—helped release Oppenheimer to commitment: "At that point I forgot about beryllium and films and decided to try to learn the trade of being a theoretical physicist."

Whether the decision precipitated the crisis or began to relieve it is not clear from the record. Oppenheimer visited a Cambridge psychiatrist. Someone wrote his parents about his problems and they hurried over as they had hurried to Camp Koenig years before. They pushed their son to see a new psychiatrist. He found one in London on Harley Street. After a few sessions the man diagnosed dementia praecox, the older term for what is now called schizophrenia, a condition characterized by early adult onset, faulty thought processes, bizarre actions, a tendency to live in an inner world, incapacity to maintain normal interpersonal relationships and an extremely poor prognosis. Given the vagueness of the symptomatology and Oppenheimer's intellectual dazzle and profound distress, the psychiatrist's mistake is easy enough to understand. Fergusson met Oppenheimer in Harley Street one day and asked him how it had gone. "He said . . . that the guy was too stupid to follow him and that he knew more about his troubles than the [doctor] did, which was probably true."

Resolution began before the consultations on Harley Street, in the spring, on a ten-day visit to Corsica with two American friends. What happened to bring Oppenheimer through is a mystery, but a mystery important enough to him that he deliberately emphasized it—tantalizingly and incompletely—to one of the more sensitive of his profilers, Nuel Pharr Davis. Corsica, Oppenheimer wrote his brother Frank soon after his visit, was "a great place, with every virtue from wine to glaciers, and from langouste to brigantines." To Davis, late in life, he emphasized that although the United States Government had assembled hundreds of pages of information about him across the years, so that some people said his entire life was recorded there, the record in fact contained almost nothing of real importance. To prove his point, he said, he would mention Corsica. "The [Cambridge] psychiatrist was a prelude to what began for me in Corsica. You ask whether I will tell you the full story or whether you must dig it out. But it is known to few and they won't tell. You can't dig it out. What you need to know is that it was not a mere love affair, not a love affair at all, but love." It was, he said, "a great thing in my life, a great and lasting part of it."

Whether a love affair or love, Oppenheimer found his vocation in Cambridge that year: that was the certain healing. Science saved him from emotional disaster as science was saving Teller from social disaster. He moved to Göttingen, the old medieval town in Lower Saxony in central Germany with the university established by George II of England, in the autumn of 1926, late Weimar years. Max Born headed the university physics department, newly installed in institute buildings on Bunsenstrasse funded by the Rockefeller Foundation. Eugene Wigner traveled to Göttingen to work with Born, as had Werner Heisenberg and Wolfgang Pauli and, less happily, the Italian Enrico Fermi, all future Nobel laureates. James Franck, having moved over from Haber's institute at the KWI, a Nobelist as of 1925, supervised laboratory classes. The mathematicians Richard Courant, Herman Weyl and John von Neumann collaborated. Edward Teller would show up later on an assistantship.

The town was pleasant, for visiting Americans at least. They could drink *frisches Bier* at the fifteenth-century Schwartzen Bären, the Black Bears, and sit to crisp, delicate *wiener Schnitzel* at the Junkernschänke, the Junkers' Hall, under a steel engraving of former patron Otto von Bismarck. The Junkernschänke, four hundred years old, occupied three stories of stained glass and flowered half-timber at the corner of Barefoot and Jew streets, which makes it likely that Oppenheimer dined there: he would have appreciated the juxtaposition. When a student took his doctorate at Göttingen he was required by his classmates to kiss the Goose Girl, a pretty, lifesize bronze maiden within a bronze floral arbor that decorates the fountain on the square in front of the medieval town hall. To reach the lips of the *Gänseliesel* required wading or leaping the fountain pool, the real point of the exercise, a baptism into professional distinction Oppenheimer must have welcomed.

The townspeople still suffered from the disaster of the war and the inflation. Oppenheimer and other American students lodged at the walled mansion of a Göttingen physician who had lost everything and was forced to take in boarders. "Although this society [at the university] was extremely rich and warm and helpful to me," Oppenheimer says, "it was parked there in a very miserable German mood . . . bitter, sullen, and, I would say, discontent and angry and with all those ingredients which were later to produce a major disaster. And this I felt very much." At Göttingen he first measured the depth of German ruin. Teller generalized it later from his own experience of lost wars and their aftermaths: "Not only do wars create incredible suffering, but they engender deep hatreds that can last for generations."

Two of Oppenheimer's papers, "On the quantum theory of vibration-rotation bands" and "On the quantum theory of the problem of the two bodies," had already been accepted for publication in the *Proceedings of the Cambridge Philosophical Society* when he arrived at Göttingen, which helped to pave the way. As he came to his vocation the papers multiplied. His work was no longer apprenticeship but solid achievement. His special contribution, appropriate to the sweep of his mind, was to extend quantum theory beyond its narrow initial ground. His dissertation, "On the quantum theory of continuous spectra," was published in German in the prestigious *Zeitschrift für Physik.* Born marked it "with distinction"—high praise indeed. Oppenheimer and Born jointly worked out the quantum theory of molecules, an important and enduring contribution. Counting the dissertation, Oppenheimer published sixteen papers between 1926 and 1929. They established for him an international reputation as a theoretical physicist.

He came home a far more confident man. Harvard offered him a job; so did the young, vigorous California Institute of Technology at Pasadena. The University of California at Berkeley especially interested him because it was, as he said later, "a desert," meaning it taught no theoretical physics yet at all. He decided to take Berkeley and Caltech both, arranging to lecture on the Bay Area campus in the autumn and winter and shift to Pasadena in the spring. But first he went back to Europe on a National Research Council fellowship to tighten up his mathematics with Paul Ehrenfest at Leiden and then with Pauli, now at Zurich, a mind more analytical and critical even than Oppenheimer's, a taste in physics more refined. After Ehrenfest Oppenheimer had wanted to work in Copenhagen with Bohr. Ehrenfest thought not: Bohr's "largeness and vagueness," in Oppenheimer's words, were not the proper astringent. "I did see a copy of the letter [Ehrenfest] wrote Pauli. It was clear that he was sending me there to be fixed up."

Before he left the United States for Leiden Oppenheimer visited the Sangre de Cristos with Frank. The two brothers found a cabin and a piece of land they liked—"house and six acres and stream," in Robert's terse description—up high on a mountain meadow. The house was rough-hewn timber chinked with caulk; it lacked even a privy. While Robert was in Europe his father arranged a long-term lease and set aside three hundred dollars for what Oppenheimer calls "restoration." A summer in the mountains was restoration for the celebrated young theoretician as well.

At the end of that summer of 1927 the Fascist government of Benito Mussolini convened an International Physical Congress at Como on the southwestern end of fjord-like Lake Como in the lake district of northern Italy. The congress commemorated the centennial of the death in 1827 of Alessandro Volta, the Como-born Italian physicist who invented the electric battery and after whom the standard unit of electrical potential, the volt, is named. Everyone went to Como except Einstein, who refused to lend his prestige to Fascism. Everyone went because quantum theory was beleaguered and Niels Bohr was scheduled to speak in its defense.

At issue was an old problem that had emerged in a new and more challenging form. Einstein's 1905 work on the photoelectric effect had demonstrated that light sometimes behaves as if it consists not of waves but of particles. Turning the tables, early in 1926 an articulate, cultured Viennese theoretical physicist named Erwin Schrödinger published a wave theory of matter demonstrating that matter at the atomic level behaves as if it consists of waves. Schrödinger's theory was elegant, accessible and completely consistent. Its equations produced the quantized energy levels of the Bohr atom, but as harmonics of vibrating matter "waves" rather than as jumping electrons. Schrödinger soon thereafter proved that his "wave mechanics" was mathematically equivalent to quantum mechanics. "In other words," says Heisenberg, ". . . the two were but different mathematical formulations of the same structure." That pleased the quantum mechanicists because it strengthened their case and because Schrödinger's more straightforward mathematics simplified calculation.

But Schrödinger, whose sympathies lay with the older classical physics, made more far-reaching claims for his wave mechanics. In effect, he claimed that it represented the reality of the interior of the atom, that not particles but standing matter waves resided there, that the atom was thereby recovered for the classical physics of continuous process and absolute determinism. In Bohr's atom electrons navigated stationary states in quantum jumps that resulted in the emission of photons of light. Schrödinger offered, instead, multiple waves of matter that produced light by the process known as constructive interference, the waves adding their peaks of amplitude together. "This hypothesis," says Heisenberg dryly, "seemed to be too good to be true." For one thing, Planck's quantized radiation formula of 1900, by now exhaustively proven experimentally, opposed it. But many traditional physicists, who had never liked quantum theory, greeted Schrödinger's work, in Heisenberg's words, "with a sense of liberation." Late in the summer, hoping to talk over the problem, Heisenberg turned up at a seminar in Munich where Schrödinger was speaking. He raised his objections. "Wilhelm Wien, [a Nobel laureate] who held the chair of experimental physics at the University of Munich, answered rather sharply that one must really put an end to quantum jumps and the whole atomic mysticism, and the difficulties I had mentioned would certainly soon be solved by Schrödinger."

Bohr invited Schrödinger to Copenhagen. The debate began at the railroad station and continued morning and night, says Heisenberg:

> For though Bohr was an unusually considerate and obliging person, he was able in such a discussion, which concerned epistemological problems which he considered to be of vital importance, to insist fanatically and with almost terrifying relentlessness on complete clarity in all arguments. He would not give up, even after hours of struggling, [until] Schrödinger had admitted that [his] interpretation was insufficient, and could not even explain Planck's law. Every attempt from Schrödinger's side to get round this bitter result was slowly refuted point by point in infinitely laborious discussions.

Schrödinger came down with a cold and took to his bed. Unfortunately he was staying at the Bohrs'. "While Mrs. Bohr nursed him and brought in tea and cake, Niels Bohr kept sitting on the edge of the bed talking at [him]: 'But you must surely admit that . . .' " Schrödinger approached desperation. "If one has to go on with these damned quantum jumps," he exploded, "then I'm sorry that I ever started to work on atomic theory." Bohr, always glad for conflicts that sharpened understanding, calmed his exhausted guest with praise: "But the rest of us are so grateful that you did, for you have thus brought atomic physics a decisive step forward." Schrödinger returned home discouraged but unconvinced.

Bohr and Heisenberg then went to work on the problem of reconciling the dualisms of atomic theory. Bohr hoped to formulate an approach that would allow matter and light to exist both as particle and as wave; Heisenberg argued consistently for abandoning models entirely and sticking to mathematics. In late February 1927, says Heisenberg, both of them "utterly exhausted and rather tense," Bohr went off to Norway to ski. The young Bavarian tried, using quantum-mechanical equations, to calculate something so seemingly simple as the trajectory of an electron in a cloud chamber and realized it was hopeless. Facing that corner, he turned around. "I began to wonder whether we might not have been asking the wrong sort of question all along."

Working late one evening in his room under the eaves of Bohr's institute Heisenberg remembered a paradox Einstein had thrown at him in a conversation about the value of theory in scientific work. "It is the theory which decides what we can observe," Einstein had said. The memory made Heisenberg restless; he went downstairs and let himself out—it was after midnight—and walked past the great beech trees behind the institute into the open soccer fields of the Faelledpark. It was early March and it would have been cold, but Heisenberg was a vigorous walker who did his best thinking outdoors. "On this walk under the stars, the obvious idea occurred to me that one should postulate that nature allowed only experimental situations to occur which could be described within the framework of the [mathematical] formalism of quantum mechanics." The bald statement sounds wondrously arbitrary; its test would be its consistent mathematical formulation and, ultimately, its predictive power for experiment. But it led Heisenberg immediately to a stunning conclusion: that on the extremely small scale of the atom, there must be inherent limits to how precisely events could be known. If you identified the position of a particle—by allowing it to impact on a zinc-sulfide screen, for example, as Rutherford did—you changed its velocity and so lost that information. If you measured its velocity—by scattering gamma rays from it, perhaps—your energetic gamma-ray photons battered it into a different path and you could not then locate precisely where it was. One measurement always made the other measurement uncertain.

Heisenberg climbed back to his room and began formulating his idea mathematically: the product of the uncertainties in the measured values of the position and momentum cannot be smaller than Planck's constant. So h appeared again at the heart of physics to define the basic, unresolvable granularity of the universe. What Heisenberg conceived that night came to be called the uncertainty principle, and it meant the end of strict determinism in physics: because if atomic events are inherently blurred, if it is impossible to assemble complete information about the location of individual particles in time and space, then predictions of their future behavior can only be statistical. The dream or bad joke of the Marquis de Laplace, the eighteenth-century French mathematician and astronomer, that if he knew at one moment the precise location in time and space of every particle in the universe he could predict the future forever, was thus answered late at night in a Copenhagen park: nature blurs that divine prerogative away.

Bohr ought to have liked Heisenberg's democratization of the atomic interior. Instead it bothered him: he had returned from his ski trip with a grander conception of his own, one that reached back for its force to his earliest understanding of doubleness and ambiguity, to Poul Martin Møller and Søren Kierkegaard. He was particularly unhappy that his Bavarian protégé had not founded his uncertainty principle on the dualism between particles and waves. He trained on him the "terrifying relentlessness" he had previously directed at Schrödinger. Oskar Klein, Bohr's amanuensis of the period, fortunately mediated. But Heisenberg was only twenty-six, however brilliant. He gave ground. The uncertainty principle, he agreed, was just a special case of the more general conception Bohr had devised. With that concession Bohr allowed the paper Heisenberg had written to go to the printer. And set to work composing his Como address.

At Como in pleasant September Bohr began with a polite reference to Volta, "the great genius whom we are here assembled to commemorate," then plunged in. He proposed to try to develop "a certain general point of view" which might help "to harmonize the apparently conflicting views taken by different scientists." The problem, Bohr said, was that quantum conditions ruled on the atomic scale but our instruments for measuring those conditions—our senses, ultimately—worked in classical ways. That inadequacy imposed necessary limitations on what we could know. An experiment that demonstrates that light travels in photons is valid within the limits of its terms. An experiment that demonstrates that light travels in waves is equally valid within its limits. The same is true of particles and waves of matter. The reason both could be accepted as valid is that "particles" and "waves" are words, are abstractions. What we know is not particles and waves but the equipment of our experiments and how that equipment changes in experimental use. The equipment is large, the interiors of atoms small, and between the two must be interposed a necessary and limiting translation.

The solution, Bohr went on, is to accept the different and mutually exclusive results as *equally valid* and stand them side by side to build up a composite picture of the atomic domain. *Nur die Fülle führt zur Klarheit:* only wholeness leads to clarity. Bohr was never interested in an arrogant reductionism. He called instead—the word appears repeatedly in his Como lecture—for "renunciation," renunciation of the godlike determinism of classical physics where the intimate scale of the atomic interior was concerned. The name he chose for this "general point of view" was *complementarity,* a word that derives from the Latin *complementum,* "that which fills up or completes." Light as particle and light as wave, matter as particle and matter as wave, were mutually exclusive abstractions that complemented each other. They could not be merged or resolved; they had to stand side by side in their seeming paradox and contradiction; but accepting that uncomfortably non-Aristotelian condition meant physics could know more than it otherwise knew. And furthermore, as Heisenberg's recently published uncertainty principle demonstrated within its limited context, the universe appeared to be arranged that way as far down as human senses would ever be able to see.

Emilio Segrè, who heard Bohr lecture at Como in 1927 as a young engineering student, explains complementarity simply and clearly in a history of modern physics he wrote in retirement: "Two magnitudes are complementary when the measurement of one of them prevents the accurate simultaneous measurement of the other. Similarly, two concepts are complementary when one imposes limitations on the other."

Carefully Bohr then examined the conflicts of classical and quantum physics one at a time and showed how complementarity clarified them. In conclusion he briefly pointed to complementarity's connection to philosophy. The situation in physics, he said, "bears a deep-going analogy to the general difficulty in the formation of human ideas, inherent in the distinction between subject and object." That reached back all the way to the licentiate's dilemma in *Adventures of a Danish Student,* and resolved it: the I who thinks and the I who acts are different, mutually exclusive, but complementary abstractions of the self.

In the years to come Bohr would extend the compass of his "certain general point of view" far into the world. It would serve him as a guide not only in questions of physics but in the largest questions of statesmanship as well. But it never commanded the central place in physics he hoped it would. At Como a substantial minority of the older physicists were predictably unpersuaded. Nor was Einstein converted when he heard. In 1926 he had written to Max Born concerning the statistical nature of quantum theory that "quantum mechanics demands serious attention. But an inner voice tells me that this is not the true Jacob. The theory accomplishes a lot, but it does not bring us closer to the secrets of the Old One. In any case, I am convinced that He does not play dice." Another physics conference, the annual Solvay Conference sponsored by a wealthy Belgian industrial chemist named Ernest Solvay, was held in Brussels a month after Como. Einstein attended, as did Bohr, Max Planck, Marie Curie, Hendrick Lorentz, Max Born, Paul Ehrenfest, Erwin Schrödinger, Wolfgang Pauli, Werner Heisenberg and a crowd of others. "We all stayed at the same hotel," Heisenberg remembers, "and the keenest arguments took place, not in the conference hall but during the hotel meals. Bohr and Einstein were in the thick of it all."

Einstein refused to accept the idea that determinism on the atomic level was forbidden, that the fine structure of the universe was unknowable, that statistics rule. " 'God does not throw dice' was a phrase we often heard from his lips in these discussions," writes Heisenberg. "And so he refused point-blank to accept the uncertainty principle, and tried to think up cases in which the principle would not hold." Einstein would produce a challenging thought experiment at breakfast, the debate would go on all day, "and, as a rule, by suppertime we would have reached a point where Niels Bohr could prove to Einstein that even his latest experiment failed to shake the uncertainty principle. Einstein would look a bit worried, but by next morning he was ready with a new imaginary experiment more complicated than the last." This went on for days, until Ehrenfest chided Einstein—they were the oldest of friends—that he was ashamed of him, that Einstein was arguing against quantum theory just as irrationally as his opponents had argued against relativity theory. Einstein remained adamant (he remained adamant to the end of his life where quantum theory was concerned).

Bohr, for his part, supple pragmatist and democrat that he was, never an absolutist, heard once too often about Einstein's personal insight into the gambling habits of the Deity. He scolded his distinguished colleague finally in Einstein's own terms. God does not throw dice? "Nor is it our business to prescribe to God how He should run the world."

6
Machines

After the war, under Ernest Rutherford's direction, the Cavendish thrived. Robert Oppenheimer suffered there largely because he was not an experimentalist; for experimental physicists, Cambridge was exactly the center that Oppenheimer had thought it to be. C. P. Snow trained there a little later, in the early 1930s, and in his first novel, *The Search*, published in 1934, celebrated the experience in the narrative of a fictional young scientist:

> I shall not easily forget those Wednesday meetings in the Cavendish. For me they were the essence of all the *personal* excitement in science; they were romantic, if you like, and not on the plane of the highest experience I was soon to know [of scientific discovery]; but week after week I went away through the raw nights, with east winds howling from the fens down the old streets, full of a glow that I had seen and heard and been close to the leaders of the greatest movement in the world.

More crowded than ever, the laboratory was showing signs of wear and tear. Mark Oliphant remembers standing in the hallway outside Rutherford's office for the first time and noticing "uncarpeted floor boards, dingy varnished pine doors and stained plastered walls, indifferently lit by a skylight with dirty glass." Oliphant also records Rutherford's appearance at that time, the late 1920s, when the Cavendish director was in his mid-fifties: "I was received genially by a large, rather florid man, with thinning fair hair and a large moustache, who reminded me forcibly of the keeper of the general store and post office in a little village in the hills behind Adelaide where I had spent part of my childhood. Rutherford made me feel welcome and at ease at once. He spluttered a little as he talked, from time to time holding a match to a pipe which produced smoke and ash like a volcano."

With simple experimental apparatus Rutherford continued to produce astonishing discoveries. The most important of them besides the discovery of the nucleus had come to fruition in 1919, shortly before he left Manchester for Cambridge—he sent off the paper in April. Afterward, at the Cavendish, he and James Chadwick followed through. The 1919 Manchester paper actually summarized a series of investigations Rutherford carried out in his rare moments of spare time during the four years of war, when he kept the Manchester lab going almost singlehandedly while doing research for the Admiralty on submarine detection. It appeared in four parts. The first three parts cleared the way for the fourth, "An anomalous effect in nitrogen," which was revolutionary.

Ernest Marsden, whose examination of alpha scattering had led Rutherford to discover the atomic nucleus, had found a similarly fruitful oddity in the course of routine experimental studies at Manchester in 1915. Marsden was using alpha particles—helium nuclei, atomic weight 4—emanating from a small glass tube of radon gas to bombard hydrogen atoms. He did that by fixing the radon tube inside a sealed brass box fitted at one end with a zinc-sulfide scintillation screen, evacuating the box of air and then filling it with hydrogen gas. The alpha particles emanating from the radon bounced off the hydrogen atoms (atomic weight approximately 1) like marbles, transferring energy to the H atoms and setting some of them in motion toward the scintillation screen; Marsden then measured their range by interposing pieces of absorbing metal foils behind the screen until the scintillations stopped. Predictably, the less massive H atoms recoiled farther as a result of their collisions with the heavier alpha particles than did the alphas—about four times as far, says Rutherford—just as smaller and larger marbles colliding in a marbles game do.

That was straightforward enough. But then Marsden noticed, Rutherford relates, while the box was evacuated, that the glass radon tube itself "gave rise to a number of scintillations like those from hydrogen." He tried a tube made of quartz, then a nickel disk coated with a radium compound, and found similarly bright, H-like scintillations. "Marsden concluded that there was strong evidence that hydrogen arose from the radioactive matter itself." This conjecture would have been stunning, if true—so far radioactive atoms had been found to eject only helium nuclei, beta electrons and gamma rays in the course of their decay—but it was not the only possible deduction. Nor was it one that Rutherford, who after all had discovered two of the three basic radiations and had never found hydrogen among them, was likely to accept out of hand. Marsden had returned to New Zealand in 1915 to teach; Rutherford pursued the strange anomaly. He had a good idea what he was after. "I occasionally find an odd half day to try a few of my own experiments," he wrote Bohr on December 9, 1917, "and have got I think results that will ultimately prove of great importance. I wish you were here to talk matters over with. I am detecting and counting the lighter atoms set in motion by [alpha] particles. . . . I am also trying to break up the atom by this method."

His equipment was similar to Marsden's, a small brass box fitted with stopcocks to admit and evacuate gases from its interior, with a scintillation screen mounted on one end. For an alpha source he used a beveled brass disk coated with a radium compound:

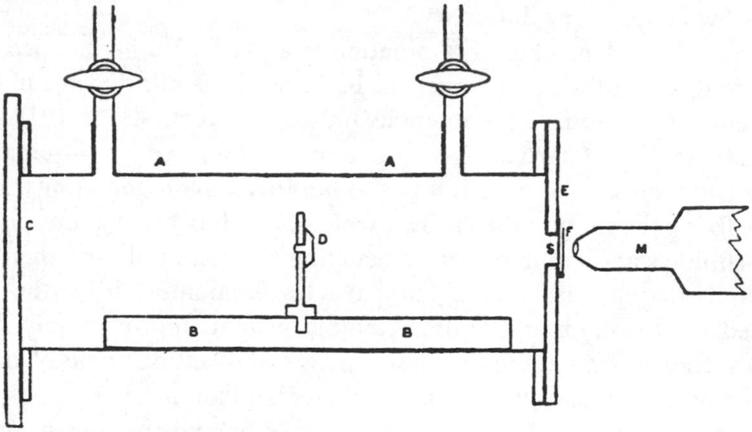

Arrangement of Ernest Rutherford's experiment: D, alpha source. S, zinc sulfide scintillation screen. M, microscope.

The likeliest explanation for Marsden's anomalous H atoms was contamination; hydrogen is light and chemically active and a minor component of the ubiquitous air. So Rutherford's problem was basically one of rigorous exclusion. He needed to narrow down the possible sources of hydrogen atoms in his box until he could conclusively prove their point of origin. He started by showing that they did not come from the radioactive materials alone. He established that they had the same mass and expected range as the H atoms that recoiled from alpha bombardment of hydrogen gas in Marsden's experiment. He admitted dry oxygen into the evacuated brass box, then carbon dioxide, and found in both cases that the H atoms coming off the radioactive source were slowed down by colliding with the atoms of those gases—fewer scintillations showed up on the screen.

Then he tried dry air. The result surprised him. Instead of decreasing the number of scintillations, as oxygen and carbon dioxide had done, dry air increased them—*doubled* them in fact.

These newfound scintillations "appeared to the eye to be about equal in brightness to H scintillations," Rutherford notes cautiously near the beginning of the revolutionary Part IV of his paper. He went after them. If they were H atoms, they still might be contaminants. He eliminated that possibility first. He showed that they could not be due merely to the hydrogen in water vapor (H_2O): drying the air even more thoroughly made little difference in their number. Dust might harbor H atoms like dangerous germs: he filtered the air he let into the box through long plugs of absorbent cotton but found little change.

Since the increase in H atoms occurred in air but not in oxygen or carbon dioxide, Rutherford deduced then that it "must be due either to nitrogen or to one of the other gases present in atmospheric air." And since air is 78 percent nitrogen, that gas appeared to be the likeliest candidate. He tested it simply, by comparing scintillations from air to scintillations from pure nitrogen. The test confirmed his hunch: "With pure nitrogen, the number of long-range scintillations under similar conditions was greater than in air." Finally, Rutherford established that the H atoms came in fact from the nitrogen and not from the radioactive source alone. And then he made his stunning announcement, couching it as always in the measured understatement of British science: "From the results so far obtained it is difficult to avoid the conclusion that the long-range atoms arising from collision of [alpha] particles with nitrogen are not nitrogen atoms but probably atoms of hydrogen. . . . If this be the case, we must conclude that the nitrogen atom is disintegrated." Newspapers soon published the discovery in plainer words: Sir Ernest Rutherford, headlines blared in 1919, had *split the atom.*

It was less a split than a transmutation, the first artificial transmutation ever achieved. When an alpha particle, atomic weight 4, collided with a nitrogen atom, atomic weight 14, knocking out a hydrogen nucleus (which Rutherford would shortly propose calling a *proton*), the net result was a new atom of oxygen in the form of the oxygen isotope O17: 4 plus 14 minus 1. There would hardly be enough O17 to breathe; only about one alpha particle in 300,000 crashed through the electrical barrier around the nitrogen nucleus to do its alchemical work.

But the discovery offered a new way to study the nucleus. Physicists had been confined so far to bouncing radiation off its exterior or measuring the radiation that naturally came out of the nucleus during radioactive decay. Now they had a technique for probing its insides as well. Rutherford and Chadwick soon went after other light atoms to see if they also could be disintegrated, and as it turned out, many of them—boron, fluorine, sodium, aluminum, phosphorus—could. But farther along the periodic table a barricade loomed. The naturally radioactive sources Rutherford used emitted relatively slow-moving alpha particles that lacked the power to penetrate past the increasingly formidable electrical barriers of heavier nuclei. Chadwick and others at the Cavendish began to talk of finding ways to accelerate particles to higher velocities. Rutherford, who scorned complex equipment, resisted. Particle acceleration was in any case difficult to do. For a time the newborn science of nuclear physics stalled.

Besides Rutherford's crowd of "boys," several individual researchers worked at the Cavendish, legatees of J. J. Thomson. One who pursued a different but related interest was a slim, handsome, athletic, wealthy experimentalist named Francis William Aston, the son of a Birmingham gunmaker's daughter and a Harborne metal merchant. As a child Aston made picric-acid bombs from soda-bottle cartridges and designed and launched huge tissue-paper fire balloons; as an adult, a lifelong bachelor, heir after 1908 to his father's wealth, he skied, built and raced motorcycles, played the cello and took elegant trips around the world, stopping off in Honolulu in 1909, at thirty-two, to learn surfing, which he thereafter declared to be the finest of all sports. Aston was one of Rutherford's regular Sunday partners at golf on the Gogs in Cambridge. It was he who had announced, at the 1913 meeting of the British Association, the separation of neon into two isotopes by laborious diffusion through pipe clay.

Aston trained originally as a chemist; Röntgen's discovery of X rays turned him to physics. J. J. Thomson brought him into the Cavendish in 1910, and it was because Thomson seemed to have separated neon into two components inside a positive-ray discharge tube that Aston took up the laborious work of attempting to confirm the difference by gaseous diffusion. Thomson found that he could separate beams of different kinds of atoms by subjecting his discharge tube to parallel magnetic and electrostatic fields. The beams he produced inside his tubes were not cathode rays; he was working now with "rays" repelled from the opposite plate, the positively charged anode. Such rays were streams of atomic nuclei stripped of their electrons: ionized. They could be generated from gas introduced into the tube. Or solid materials could be coated onto the anode plate itself, in which case ionized atoms of the material would boil off when the tube was evacuated and the anode was charged.

Mixed nuclei projected in a radiant beam through a magnetic field would bend into separated component beams according to their velocity, which gave a measure of their mass. An electrostatic field bent the component beams differently depending on their electrical charge, which gave a measure of their atomic number. "In this way," writes George de Hevesy, "a great variety of different atoms and atomic groupings were proved to be present in the discharge tube."

Aston thought hard about J. J.'s discharge tube while he worked during the war at the Royal Aircraft Establishment at Farnborough, southwest of London, developing tougher dopes and fabrics for aircraft coverings. He wanted to prove unequivocally that neon was isotopic—J. J. was still unconvinced—and saw the possibility of sorting the isotopes of other elements as well. He thought the positive-ray tube was the answer, but though it was good for general surveying, it was hopelessly imprecise.

By the time Aston returned to Cambridge in 1918 he had worked the problem out theoretically; he then began building the precision instrument he had envisioned. It charged a gas or a coating until the material ionized into its component electrons and nuclei and projected the nuclei through two slits that produced a knife-edge beam like the slit-narrowed beam of light in a spectrograph. It then subjected the beam to a strong electrostatic field; that sorted the different nuclei into separated beams. The separated beams proceeded onward through a magnetic field; that further sorted nuclei according to their mass, producing separated beams of isotopes. Finally the sorted beams struck the plateholder of a camera and marked their precise locations on a calibrated strip of film. How much the magnetic field bent the separated beams—where they blackened the strip of film—determined the mass of their component nuclei to a high degree of accuracy.

Aston called his invention a mass-spectrograph because it sorted elements and isotopes of elements by mass much as an optical spectrograph sorts light by its frequency. The mass-spectrograph was immediately and sensationally a success. "In letters to me in January and February, 1920," says Bohr, "Rutherford expressed his joy in Aston's work," which "gave such a convincing confirmation of Rutherford's atomic model." Of 281 naturally occurring isotopes, over the next two decades Aston identified 212. He discovered that the weights of the atoms of all the elements he measured, with the notable exception of hydrogen, were very nearly whole numbers, which was a powerful argument in favor of the theory that the elements were assembled in nature simply from protons and electrons—from hydrogen atoms, that is. Natural elements had not weighed up in whole numbers for the chemists because they were often mixtures of isotopes of different whole-number weights. Aston proved, for example, as he noted in a later lecture, "that neon consisted, beyond doubt, of isotopes 20 and 22, and that its atomic weight 20.2 was the result of these being present in the ratio of about 9 to 1." That satisfied even J. J. Thomson.

But why was hydrogen an exception? If the elements were built up from hydrogen atoms, why did the hydrogen atom itself, the elemental building block, weigh 1.008 alone? Why did it then shrink to 4 when it was packed in quartet as helium? Why not 4.032? And why was helium not exactly 4 but 4.002, or oxygen not exactly 16 but 15.994? What was the meaning of these extremely small, and varying, differences from whole numbers?

Atoms do not fall apart, Aston reasoned. Something very powerful holds them together. That glue is now called binding energy. To acquire it, hydrogen atoms packed together in a nucleus sacrifice some of their mass. This mass defect is what Aston found when he compared the hydrogen atom to the atoms of other elements following his whole-number rule. In addition, he said, nuclei may be more or less loosely packed. The density of their packing requires more or less binding energy, and that in turn requires more or less mass: hence the small variations. The difference between the measured mass and the whole number he expressed as a fraction, the packing fraction: roughly, the divergence of an element from its whole number divided by its whole number. "High packing fractions," Aston proposed, "indicate looseness of packing, and therefore low stability: low packing fractions the reverse." He plotted the packing fractions on a graph and demonstrated that the elements in the broad middle of the periodic table—nickel, iron, tin, for example—had the lowest packing fractions and were therefore the most stable, while elements at the extremes of the periodic table—hydrogen at the light end, for example, uranium at the heavy—had high packing fractions and were therefore the most unstable. Locked within all the elements, he said, but most unstably so in the case of those with high packing fractions, was mass converted to energy. Comparing helium to hydrogen, nearly 1 percent of the hydrogen mass was missing (4 divided by 4.032 = .992 = 99.2%). "If we were able to transmute [hydrogen] into [helium] nearly 1 percent of the mass would be annihilated. On the relativity equivalence of mass and energy now experimentally proved [Aston refers here to Einstein's famous equation $E = mc^2$], the quantity of energy liberated would be prodigious. Thus to change the hydrogen in a glass of water into helium would release enough energy to drive the 'Queen Mary' across the Atlantic and back at full speed."

Aston goes on in this lecture, delivered in 1936, to speculate about the social consequences of that energy release. Armed with the necessary knowledge, he says, "the nuclear chemists, I am convinced, will be able to synthesise elements just as ordinary chemists synthesise compounds, and it may be taken as certain that in some reactions sub-atomic energy will be liberated." And, continuing:

There are those about us who say that such research should be stopped by law, alleging that man's destructive powers are already large enough. So, no doubt, the more elderly and ape-like of our prehistoric ancestors objected to the innovation of cooked food and pointed out the grave dangers attending the use of the newly discovered agency, fire. Personally I think there is no doubt that sub-atomic energy is available all around us, and that one day man will release and control its almost infinite power. We cannot prevent him from doing so and can only hope that he will not use it exclusively in blowing up his next door neighbor.

The mass-spectrograph Francis Aston invented in 1919 could not release the binding energy of the atom. But with it he identified that binding energy and located the groups of elements which in their comparative instability might be most likely to release it if suitably addressed. He was awarded the Nobel Prize in Chemistry in 1922 for his work. After accepting the award alongside Niels Bohr—"Stockholm has been the city of our dreams ever since," his sister, who regularly traveled with him, reminisces—he returned to the Cavendish to build larger and more accurate mass-spectrographs, operating them habitually at night because he "particularly detested," his sister says, "various human noises," including even conversations muffled through the walls of his rooms. "He was very fond of animals, especially cats and kittens, and would go to any amount of trouble to make their acquaintance, but he didn't like dogs of the barking kind." Although Aston respected Ernest Rutherford enormously, the Cavendish director's great boom must ever have been a trial.

The United States led the way in particle acceleration. The American mechanical tradition that advanced the factory and diversified the armory now extended into the laboratory as well. A congressman in 1914 had questioned a witness at an appropriations hearing, "What is a physicist? I was asked on the floor of the House what in the name of common sense a physicist is, and I could not answer." But the war made evident what a physicist was, made evident the value of science to the development of technology, including especially military technology, and government support and the support of private foundations were immediately forthcoming. Twice as many Americans became physicists in the dozen years between 1920 and 1932 as had in the previous sixty. They were better trained than their older counterparts, at least fifty of them in Europe on National Research Council or International Education Board or the new Guggenheim fellowships. By 1932 the United States counted about 2,500 physicists, three times as many as in 1919. The *Physical Review,* the journal that has been to American physicists what the *Zeitschrift für Physik* is to German, was considered a backwater publication, if not a joke, in Europe before the

1920s. It thickened to more than twice its previous size in that decade, increased in 1929 to biweekly publication, and began to find readers in Cambridge, Copenhagen, Göttingen and Berlin eager to scan it the moment it arrived.

Psychometricians have closely questioned American scientists of this first modern generation, curious to know what kind of men they were—there were few women among them—and from what backgrounds they emerged. Small liberal arts colleges in the Middle West and on the Pacific coast, one study found, were most productive of scientists then (by contrast, New England in the same period excelled at the manufacture of lawyers). Half the experimental physicists studied and fully 84 percent of the theoreticians were the sons of professional men, typically engineers, physicians and teachers, although a minority of experimentalists were farmers' sons. None of the fathers of the sixty-four scientists, including twenty-two physicists, in the largest of these studies was an unskilled laborer, and few of the fathers of physicists were businessmen. The physicists were almost all either first-born sons or eldest sons. Theoretical physicists averaged the highest verbal IQ's among all scientists studied, clustering around 170, almost 20 percent higher than the experimentalists. Theoreticians also averaged the highest spatial IQ's, experimentalists ranking second.

The sixty-four-man study which included twenty-two physicists among its "most eminent scientists in the U.S." produced this composite portrait of the American scientist in his prime:

> He is likely to have been a sickly child or to have lost a parent at an early age. He has a very high I.Q. and in boyhood began to do a great deal of reading. He tended to feel lonely and "different" and to be shy and aloof from his classmates. He had only a moderate interest in girls and did not begin dating them until college. He married late . . . has two children and finds security in family life; his marriage is more stable than the average. Not until his junior or senior year in college did he decide on his vocation as a scientist. What decided him (almost invariably) was a college project in which he had occasion to do some independent research—to find out things for himself. Once he discovered the pleasures of this kind of work, he never turned back. He is completely satisfied with his chosen vocation. . . . He works hard and devotedly in his laboratory, often seven days a week. He says his work is his life, and he has few recreations. . . . The movies bore him. He avoids social affairs and political activity, and religion plays no part in his life or thinking. Better than any other interest or activity, scientific research seems to meet the inner need of his nature.

Clearly this is close to Robert Oppenheimer. The group studied, like the American physics community then, was predominantly Protestant in origin with a disproportionate minority of Jews and no Catholics.

A psychological examination of scientists at Berkeley, using Rorschach and Thematic Apperception Tests as well as interviews, included six physicists and twelve chemists in a total group of forty. It found that scientists think about problems in much the same way artists do. Scientists and artists proved less similar in personality than in cognition, but both groups were similarly different from businessmen. Dramatically and significantly, almost half the scientists in this study reported themselves to have been fatherless as children, "their fathers dying early, or working away from home, or remaining so aloof and nonsupportive that their sons scarcely knew them." Those scientists who grew up with living fathers described them as "rigid, stern, aloof, and emotionally reserved." (A group of artists previously studied was similarly fatherless; a group of businessmen was not.)

Often fatherless and "shy, lonely," writes the psychometrician Lewis M. Terman, "slow in social development, indifferent to close personal relationships, group activities or politics," these highly intelligent young men found their way into science through a more personal discovery than the regularly reported pleasure of independent research. Guiding that research was usually a fatherly science teacher. Of the qualities that distinguished this mentor in the minds of his students, not teaching ability but "masterfulness, warmth and professional dignity" ranked first. One study of two hundred of these mentors concludes: "It would appear that the success of such teachers rests mainly upon their capacity to assume a father role to their students." The fatherless young man finds a masterful surrogate father of warmth and dignity, identifies with him and proceeds to emulate him. In a later stage of this process the independent scientist works toward becoming a mentor of historic stature himself.

The man who would found big-machine physics in America arrived at Berkeley one year before Oppenheimer, in 1928. Ernest Orlando Lawrence was three years older than the young theoretician and in many ways his opposite, an extreme of the composite American type. Both he and Oppenheimer were tall and both had blue eyes and high expectations. But Ernest Lawrence was an experimentalist, from prairie, small-town South Dakota; of Norwegian stock, the son of a superintendent of schools and teachers' college president; domestically educated through the Ph.D. at the Universities of South Dakota, Minnesota and Chicago and at Yale; with "almost an aversion to mathematical thought" according to one of his protégés, the later Nobel laureate Luis W. Alvarez; a boyish extrovert whose strongest expletives were "Sugar!" and "Oh fudge!" who learned to stand at ease among the empire builders of patrician California's Bohemian Grove; a master salesman who paid his way through college peddling aluminum kitchenware farm to farm; with a gift for inventing ingenious machines. Lawrence arrived at Berkeley from Yale in a Reo Flying Cloud with his parents and his younger brother in tow and put up at the faculty club. Fired compulsively with ambition—for physics, for himself—he worked from early morning until late at night.

As far back as his first year of graduate school, 1922, Lawrence had begun to think about how to generate high energies. His flamboyant, fatherly mentor encouraged him. William Francis Gray Swann, an Englishman who had found his way to Minnesota via the Department of Terrestrial Magnetism of the District of Columbia's private Carnegie Institution, took Lawrence along with him first to Chicago and then to Yale as he moved up the academic ladder himself. After Lawrence earned his Ph.D. and a promising reputation Swann convinced Yale to jump him over the traditional four years of instructorship to a starting position as assistant professor of physics. Swann's leaving Yale in 1926 was one reason Lawrence had decided to move West, that and Berkeley's offer of an associate professorship, a good laboratory, as many graduate-student assistants as he could handle and $3,300 a year, an offer Yale chose not to match.

At Berkeley, Lawrence said later, "it seemed opportune to review my plans for research, to see whether I might not profitably go into nuclear research, for the pioneer work of Rutherford and his school had clearly indicated that the next great frontier for the experimental physicist was surely the atomic nucleus." But as Luis Alvarez explains, "the tedious nature of Rutherford's technique . . . repelled most prospective nuclear physicists. Simple calculations showed that one microampere of electrically accelerated light nuclei would be more valuable than the world's total supply of radium—if the nuclear particles had energies in the neighborhood of a million electron volts."

Alpha particles or, better, protons could be accelerated by generating them in a discharge tube and then repelling or attracting them electrically. But no one knew how to confine in one place for any useful length of time, without electrical breakdown from sparking or overheating, the million volts that seemed to be necessary to penetrate the electrical barrier of the heavier nuclei. The problem was essentially mechanical and experimental; not surprisingly, it attracted the young generation of American experimental physicists who had grown up in small towns and on farms experimenting with radio. By 1925 Lawrence's boyhood friend and Minnesota classmate Merle Tuve, another protégé of W. F. G. Swann now installed at the Carnegie Institution and working with three other physicists, had managed brief but impressive accelerations with a high-voltage transformer submerged in oil; others, including Robert J. Van de Graaff at MIT and Charles C. Lauritsen at Caltech, were also developing machines.

Lawrence pursued more promising studies but kept the high-energy problem in mind. The essential vision came to him in the spring of 1929, four months before Oppenheimer arrived. "In his early bachelor days at Berkeley," writes Alvarez, "Lawrence spent many of his evenings in the library, reading widely. . . . Although he passed his French and German requirements for the doctor's degree by the slimmest of margins, and consequently had almost no facility with either language, he faithfully leafed through the back issues of the foreign periodicals, night after night." Such was the extent of Lawrence's compulsion. It paid. He was skimming the German *Arkiv für Elektrotechnik,* an electrical-engineering journal physicists seldom read, and happened upon a report by a Norwegian engineer named Rolf Wideröe, *Über ein neues Prinzip zur Herstellung hoher Spannungen:* "On a new principle for the production of higher voltages." The title arrested him. He studied the accompanying photographs and diagrams. They explained enough to set Lawrence off and he did not bother to struggle through the text.

Wideröe, elaborating on a principle established by a Swedish physicist in 1924, had found an ingenious way to avoid the high-voltage problem. He mounted two metal cylinders in line, attached them to a voltage source and evacuated them of air. The voltage source supplied 25,000 volts of high-frequency alternating current, current that changed rapidly from positive to negative potential. That meant it could be used both to push and to pull positive ions. Charge the first cylinder negatively to 25,000 volts, inject positive ions into one end, and the ions would be accelerated to 25,000 volts as they left the first cylinder for the second. Alternate the charge then—make the first cylinder positive and the second cylinder negative—and the ions would be pushed and pulled to further acceleration. Add more cylinders, each one longer than the last to allow for the increasing speed of the ions, and theoretically you could accelerate them further still, until such a time as they scattered too far outward from the center and crashed into the cylinder walls. Wideröe's important innovation was the use of a relatively small voltage to produce increasing acceleration. "This new idea," says Lawrence, "immediately impressed me as the real answer which I had been looking for to the technical problem of accelerating positive ions, and without looking at the article further I then and there made estimates of the general features of a linear accelerator for protons in the energy range above one million [volts]."

Lawrence's calculations momentarily discouraged him. The accelerator tube would be "some meters in length," too long, he thought, for the laboratory. (Linear accelerators today range in length up to two miles.) "And accordingly, I asked myself the question, instead of using a large number of cylindrical electrodes in line, might it not be possible to use two electrodes over and over again by sending the positive ions back and forth through the electrodes by some sort of appropriate magnetic field arrangement." The arrangement he conceived was a spiral. "It struck him almost immediately," Alvarez later wrote, "that one might 'wind up' a linear accelerator into a spiral accelerator by putting it in a magnetic field," because the magnetic lines of force in such a field guide the ions. Given a well-timed push, they would swing around in a spiral, the spiral becoming larger as the particles accelerated and were thus harder to confine. Then, making a simple calculation for the magnetic-field effects, Lawrence uncovered an unsuspected advantage to a spiral accelerator: in a magnetic field slow particles complete their smaller circuits in exactly the same time faster particles complete their larger circuits, which meant they could all be accelerated together, efficiently, with each alternating push.

Exuberantly Lawrence ran off to tell the world. An astronomer who was still awake at the faculty club was drafted to check his mathematics. He shocked one of his graduate students the next day by bombarding him with the mathematics of spiral accelerations but mustering no interest whatever in his thesis experiment. "Oh, that," Lawrence told the questioning student. "Well, you know as much on that now as I do. Just go ahead on your own." A faculty wife crossing the campus the next evening heard a startling "I'm going to be famous!" as the young experimentalist burst past her on the walk.

Lawrence then traveled East to a meeting of the American Physical Society and discovered that not many of his colleagues agreed. To less inspired mechanicians the scattering problem looked insurmountable. Merle Tuve was skeptical. Jesse Beams, a Yale colleague and a close friend, thought it was a great idea if it worked. Despite Lawrence's reputation as a go-getter—perhaps because no one encouraged him, perhaps because the idea was solid and sure in his head but the machine on the laboratory bench might not be—he kept putting off building his spiral particle accelerator. He was not the first man of ambition to find himself stalling on the summit ridge of a famous future.

Oppenheimer arrived in a battered gray Chrysler in the late summer of 1929 from another holiday at the Sangre de Cristos ranch with Frank—the ranch was named Perro Caliente now, "hot dog," Oppenheimer's cheer when he had learned the property could be leased. He put up at the faculty club and the two opposite numbers, he and Lawrence, became close friends. Oppenheimer saw "unbelievable vitality and love of life" in Lawrence. "Work all day, run off for tennis, and work half the night. His interest was so primarily active [and] instrumental and mine just the opposite." They rode horses together, Lawrence in jodhpurs and using an

English saddle in the American West—to distance himself, Oppenheimer thought, from the farm. When Lawrence could get away they went off on long recreational drives in the Reo to Yosemite and Death Valley.

A distinguished experimentalist from the University of Hamburg, Otto Stern, a Breslau Ph.D., forty-one that year and on his way to a Nobel Prize (though Lawrence would beat him), gave Lawrence the necessary boost. Sometime after the Christmas holidays the two men dined out in San Francisco, a pleasant ferry ride across the unbridged bay. Lawrence rehearsed again his practiced story of particles spinning to boundless energies in a confining magnetic field, but instead of coughing politely and changing the subject, as so many other colleagues had done, Stern produced a Germanic duplicate of Lawrence's original enthusiasm and barked at him to leave the restaurant immediately and go to work. Lawrence waited in decency until morning, cornered one of his graduate students and committed him to the project as soon as he had finished studying for his Ph.D. exam.

The machine that resulted looked, in top and side views, like this:

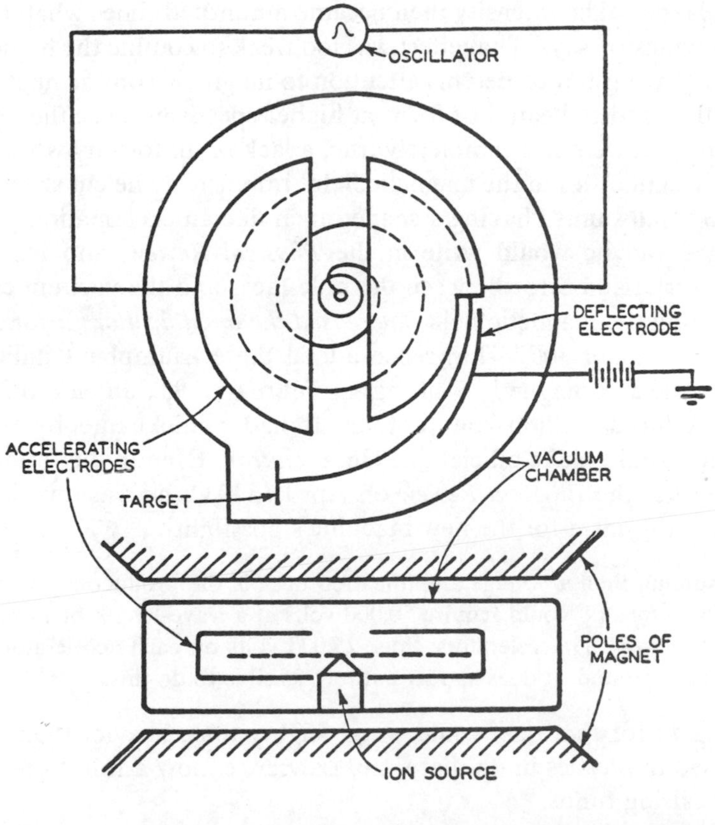

The two cylinders of the Wideröe accelerator have become two brass electrodes shaped like the cut halves of a cylindrical flask. These are contained completely within a vacuum tank and the vacuum tank is mounted between the round, flat poles of a large electromagnet.

In the space between the two electrodes (which came to be called *dees* because of their shape), at the center point, a hot filament and an outlet for hydrogen gas work together to produce protons which stream off into the magnetic field. The two dees, alternately charged, push and pull the protons as they come around. When they have been accelerated through about a hundred spirals the particles exit in a beam which can then be directed onto a target. With a 4.5-inch chamber and with less than 1,000 volts on the dees, on January 2, 1931, Lawrence and his student M. Stanley Livingston produced 80,000-volt protons.

The scattering problem solved itself at low accelerations when Livingston thought to remove the fine grid of wires installed in the gap between the dees that kept the accelerating electric field out of the drift space inside. The electric fields between the dee edges suddenly began functioning as lenses, focusing the spiraling particles by deflecting them back toward the middle plane. "The intensity then became a hundred times what it was before," Livingston says. That effect was too weak to confine the higher-speed particles. Livingston turned his attention to magnetic confinement. He suspected the particle beam lost focus at higher speeds because the pole faces of the magnet were not completely true, a lack of uniformity which in turn caused irregularities in the magnetic field. Impulsively he cut sheets of iron foil into small shims "having a shape much like an exclamation point," as Lawrence and he would write in the *Physical Review,* and inserted the shims by trial and error between the pole faces and the vacuum chamber. Thus tuning the magnetic field *"increased the amplification factor . . . from about 75 to about 300"*—Lawrence added these triumphant italics. With both electric and magnetic focusing, in February 1932 an eleven-inch machine produced million-volt protons. It had a nickname by then that Lawrence would make official in 1936: *cyclotron.* Even in the formal scientific report to the *Physical Review* on April 1, 1932, he was unable to contain his enthusiasm for the new machine's possibilities:

> Assuming then a voltage amplification of 500, the production of 25,000,000 volt-protons [!] would require 50,000 volts at a wave-length of 14 meters applied across the accelerators; thus, 25,000 volts on each accelerator with respect to ground. It does appear entirely feasible to do this.

The magnet for that one would weigh eighty tons, heavier than any machine used in physics up to that time. Lawrence, now a full professor, was already raising funds.

* * *

In his graduate-student days in Europe Robert Oppenheimer told a friend that he dreamed of founding a great school of theoretical physics in the United States—at Berkeley, as it happened, the second desert after New Mexico that he chose to colonize. Ernest Lawrence seems to have dreamed of founding a great laboratory. Both men coveted success and, each in his own way, the rewards of success, but they were differently driven.

Oppenheimer's youthful preciosity matured in Europe and the early Berkeley years into refinement that was usually admirable if still sometimes exquisite. Oppenheimer crafted that persona for himself at least in part from a distaste for vulgarity that probably originated in rebellion against his entrepreneurial father and that was not without elements of anti-Semitic self-hatred. Along the way he convinced himself that ambition and worldly success were vulgar, a conviction bolstered nicely by trust fund earnings to the extent of ten thousand dollars a year. Thereby he confounded his own strivings. The American experimental physicist I. I. Rabi would later question why "men of Oppenheimer's gifts do not discover everything worth discovering." His answer addresses one possible source of limitation:

> It seems to me that in some respects Oppenheimer was overeducated in those fields which lie outside the scientific tradition, such as his interest in religion, in the Hindu religion in particular, which resulted in a feeling for the mystery of the universe that surrounded him almost like a fog. He saw physics clearly, looking toward what had already been done, but at the border he tended to feel that there was much more of the mysterious and novel than there actually was. . . . Some may call it a lack of faith, but in my opinion it was more a turning away from the hard, crude methods of theoretical physics into a mystical realm of broad intuition.

But Oppenheimer's revulsion from what he considered vulgar, from just those "hard, crude methods" to which Rabi refers, must have been another and more directly punishing confusion. His elegant physics, so far as an outsider can tell—his scientific papers are nearly impenetrable to the nonmathematician and deliberately so—is a physics of bank shots. It works the sides and the corners and uses the full court but prefers not to drive relentlessly for the goal. Wolfgang Pauli and the hard, distant Cambridge theoretician Paul A. M. Dirac, Eugene Wigner's brother-in-law, both mathematicians of formidable originality, were his models. Oppenheimer first described the so-called tunnel effect whereby an uncertainly located particle sails through the electrical barrier around the nucleus on a light breeze of probability, existing—in particle terms—then ceasing to exist, then instantly existing again on the other side. But George Gamow, the antic

Russian, lecturing in Cambridge, devised the tunnel-effect equations that the experimenters used. Hans Bethe in the late 1930s first defined the mechanisms of carbon-cycle thermonuclear burning that fire the stars, work which won for him the Nobel Prize; Oppenheimer looked into the subtleties of the invisible cosmic margins, modeled the imploding collapse of dying suns and described theoretical stellar objects that would not be discovered for thirty and forty years—neutron stars, black holes—because the instruments required to detect them, radio telescopes and X-ray satellites, had not been invented yet. (Alvarez believes if Oppenheimer had lived long enough to see these developments he would have won a Nobel Prize for his work.) That was originality not so much ahead of its time as outside the frame.

Some of this psychological and creative convolution winds through a capsule essay on the virtues of discipline that Oppenheimer composed within a letter to his brother Frank in March 1932, when he was not quite twenty-eight years old. It is worth copying out at length; it hints of the long, self-punishing penance he expected to serve to cleanse any stain of crudity from his soul:

> You put a hard question on the virtue of discipline. What you say is true: I do value it—and I think that you do too—more than for its earthly fruit, proficiency. I think that one can give only a metaphysical ground for this evaluation; but the variety of metaphysics which gave an answer to your question has been very great, the metaphysics themselves very disparate: the bhagavad gita, Ecclesiastes, the Stoa, the beginning of the Laws, Hugo of St Victor, St Thomas, John of the Cross, Spinoza. This very great disparity suggests that the fact that discipline is good for the soul is more fundamental than any of the grounds given for its goodness. I believe that through discipline, though not through discipline alone, we can achieve serenity, and a certain small but precious measure of freedom from the accidents of incarnation, and charity, and that detachment which preserves the world which it renounces. I believe that through discipline we can learn to preserve what is essential to our happiness in more and more adverse circumstances, and to abandon with simplicity what would else have seemed to us indispensable; that we come a little to see the world without the gross distortion of personal desire, and in seeing it so, accept more easily our earthly privation and its earthly horror— But because I believe that the reward of discipline is greater than its immediate objective, I would not have you think that discipline without objective is possible: in its nature discipline involves the subjection of the soul to some perhaps minor end; and that end must be real, if the discipline is not to be factitious. Therefore I think that all things which evoke discipline: study, and our duties to men and to the commonwealth, war, and personal hardship, and even the need for subsistence, ought to be greeted by us with profound grati-

tude, for only through them can we attain to the least detachment; and only so can we know peace.

Lawrence, orders of magnitude less articulate than Oppenheimer, was also fiercely driven; the question is what drove him. A paragraph from a letter to his brother John, written at about the same time as Oppenheimer's essay, is revealing: "Interested to hear you have had a period of depression. I have them often—sometimes nothing seems to be OK—but I have gotten used to them now. I expect the blues and I endure them. Of course the best palliative is work, but sometimes it is hard to work under the circumstances." That work is only a "palliative," not a cure, hints at how blue the blues could be. Lawrence was a hidden sufferer, in some measure manic-depressive; he kept moving not to fall in.

To all these emotional troublings—Oppenheimer's and Lawrence's, as Bohr's and others' before and since—science offered an anchor: in discovery is the preservation of the world. The psychologist who studied scientists at Berkeley with Rorschach and TAT found that "uncommon sensitivity to experiences—usually sensory experiences" is the beginning of creative discovery in science. "Heightened sensitivity is accompanied in thinking by overalertness to relatively unimportant or tangential aspects of problems. It makes [scientists] look for and postulate significance in things which customarily would not be singled out. It encourages highly individualized and even autistic ways of thinking." Consider Rutherford playing his thoroughly unlikely hunch about alpha backscattering, Heisenberg remembering an obscure remark of Einstein's and concluding that nature only performed in consonance with his mathematics, Lawrence flipping compulsively through obscure foreign journals:

> Were this thinking not in the framework of scientific work, it would be considered paranoid. In scientific work, creative thinking demands seeing things not seen previously, or in ways not previously imagined; and this necessitates jumping off from "normal" positions, and taking risks by departing from reality. The difference between the thinking of the paranoid patient and the scientist comes from the latter's ability and willingness to test out his fantasies or grandiose conceptualizations through the systems of checks and balances science has established—and to give up those schemes that are shown not to be valid on the basis of these scientific checks. It is specifically because science provides such a framework of rules and regulations to control and set bounds to paranoid thinking that a scientist can feel comfortable about taking the paranoid leaps. Without this structuring, the threat of such unrealistic, illogical, and even bizarre thinking to overall thought and personality organization in general would be too great to permit the scientist the freedom of such fantasying.

At the leading edges of science, at the threshold of the truly new, the threat has often nearly overwhelmed. Thus Rutherford's shock at rebounding alpha particles, "quite the most incredible event that has ever happened to me in my life." Thus Heisenberg's "deep alarm" when he came upon his quantum mechanics, his hallucination of looking through "the surface of atomic phenomena" into "a strangely beautiful interior" that left him giddy. Thus also, in November 1915, Einstein's extreme reaction when he realized that the general theory of relativity he was painfully developing in the isolation of his study explained anomalies in the orbit of Mercury that had been a mystery to astronomers for more than fifty years. The theoretical physicist Abraham Pais, his biographer, concludes: "This discovery was, I believe, by far the strongest emotional experience in Einstein's scientific life, perhaps in all his life. Nature had spoken to him. He had to be right. 'For a few days, I was beside myself with joyous excitement.' Later, he told [a friend] that his discovery had given him palpitations of the heart. What he told [another friend] is even more profoundly significant: when he saw that his calculations agreed with the unexplained astronomical observations, he had the feeling that something actually snapped in him."

The compensation for such emotional risk can be enormous. For the scientist, at exactly the moment of discovery—that most unstable existential moment—the external world, nature itself, deeply confirms his innermost fantastic convictions. Anchored abruptly in the world, Leviathan gasping on his hook, he is saved from extreme mental disorder by the most profound affirmation of the real.

Bohr especially understood this mechanism and had the courage to turn it around and use it as an instrument of assay. Otto Frisch remembers a discussion someone attempted to deflect by telling Bohr it made him giddy, to which Bohr responded: "But if anybody says he can think about quantum problems without getting giddy, that only shows that he has not understood the first thing about them." Much later, Oppenheimer once told an audience, Bohr was listening to Pauli talking about a new theory on which he had recently been attacked. "And Bohr asked, at the end, 'Is this really crazy enough? The quantum mechanics was really crazy.' And Pauli said, 'I hope so, but maybe not quite.' " Bohr's understanding of how crazy discovery must be clarifies why Oppenheimer sometimes found himself unable to push alone into the raw original. To do so requires a sturdiness at the core of identity—even a brutality—that men as different as Niels Bohr and Ernest Lawrence had earned or been granted that he was unlucky enough to lack. It seems he was cut out for other work: for now, building that school of theoretical physics he had dreamed of.

* * *

On June 3, 1920, Ernest Rutherford delivered the Bakerian Lecture before the Royal Society of London. It was the second time he had been invited to fill the distinguished lectureship. He used the occasion to sum up present understanding of the "nuclear constitution" and to discuss his successful transmutation of the nitrogen atom reported the previous year, the usual backward glance of such formal public events. But unusually and presciently, he also chose to speculate about the possibility of a third major constituent of atoms besides electrons and protons. He spoke of "the possible existence of an atom of mass 1 which has zero nucleus charge." Such an atomic structure, he thought, seemed by no means impossible. It would not be a new elementary particle, he supposed, but a combination of existing particles, an electron and a proton intimately united, forming a single neutral particle.

"Such an atom," Rutherford went on with his usual perspicacity, "would have very novel properties. Its external [electrical] field would be practically zero, except very close to the nucleus, and in consequence it should be able to move freely through matter. Its presence would probably be difficult to detect by the spectroscope, and it may be impossible to contain it in a sealed vessel." Those might be its peculiarities. This would be its exceptional use: "On the other hand, it should enter readily the structure of atoms, and may either unite with the nucleus or be disintegrated by its intense field." A neutral particle, if such existed— a *neutron*—might be the most effective of all tools to probe the atomic nucleus.

Rutherford's assistant James Chadwick attended this lecture and found cause for disagreement. Chadwick was then twenty-nine years old. He had trained at Manchester and followed Rutherford down to Cambridge. He had accomplished much already—as a young man, two of his colleagues write, his output "was hardly inferior to that of Moseley"—but he had sat out the Great War in a German internment camp, to the detriment of his health and to his everlasting boredom, and he was eager to move the new work of nuclear physics along. A neutral particle would be a wonder, but Chadwick thought Rutherford had deduced it from flimsy evidence.

That winter he discovered his mistake. Rutherford invited him to participate in the work of extending the nitrogen transmutation results to heavier elements. Chadwick had improved scintillation counting by developing a microscope that gathered more light and by tightening up procedures. He also knew chemistry and might help eliminate hydrogen as a possible contaminant, a challenge to the nitrogen results that still bothered Rutherford. "But also, I think," said Chadwick many years later in a memorial lecture, "he wanted company to support the tedium of counting in the dark—and to lend an ear to his robust rendering of 'Onward, Christian Soldiers.' "

"Before the experiments," Chadwick once told an interviewer, "before we began to observe in these experiments, we had to accustom ourselves to the dark, to get our eyes adjusted, and we had a big box in the room in which we took refuge while Crowe, Rutherford's personal assistant and technician, prepared the apparatus. That is to say, he brought the radioactive source down from the radium room, put it in the apparatus, evacuated it, or filled it with whatever, put the various sources in and made the arrangements that we'd agreed upon. And we sat in this dark room, dark box, for perhaps half an hour or so, and naturally, talked." Among other things, they talked about Rutherford's Bakerian Lecture. "And it was then that I realized that these observations which I suspected were quite wrong, and which proved to be wrong later on, had nothing whatever to do with his suggestion of the neutron, not really. He just hung the suggestion on to it. Because it had been in his mind for some considerable time."

Most physicists had been content with the seemingly complete symmetry of two particles, the electron and the proton, one negative, one positive. Outside the atom—among the stripped, ionized matter beaming through a discharge tube, for example—two elementary atomic constituents might be enough. But Rutherford was concerned with how each element was assembled. "He had asked himself," Chadwick continues, "and kept on asking himself, how the atoms were built up, how on earth were you going to get—the general idea being at that time that protons and electrons were the constituents of an atomic nucleus . . . how on earth were you going to build up a big nucleus with a large positive charge? And the answer was a neutral particle."

From the lightest elements in the periodic table beyond hydrogen to the heaviest, atomic number—the nucleus' electrical charge and a count of its protons—differed from atomic weight. Helium's atomic number was 2 but its atomic weight was 4; nitrogen's atomic number was 7 but its atomic weight was 14; and the disparity increased farther along: silver, 47 but 107; barium, 56 but 137; radium, 88 but 226; uranium, 92 but 235 or 238. Theory at the time proposed that the difference was made up by additional protons in the nucleus closely associated with nuclear electrons that neutralized them. But the nucleus had a definite maximum size, well established by experiment, and as elements increased in atomic number and atomic weight there appeared to be less and less room in their nuclei for all the extra electrons. The problem worsened with the development in the 1920s of quantum theory, which made it clear that confining particles as light as electrons so closely would require enormous energies, energies that ought to show up when the nucleus was disturbed but never did. The only evidence for the presence of electrons in the nucleus was its occasional ejection of beta particles, energetic electrons. That was something to go on, but given the other difficulties with packing electrons into the nucleus it was not enough.

"And so," Chadwick concludes, "it was these conversations that convinced me that the neutron must exist. The only question was how the devil could one get evidence for it. . . . It was shortly after that I began to make experiments on the side when I could. [The Cavendish] was very busy, and left me little time, and occasionally Rutherford's interest would revive, but only occasionally." Chadwick would search for the neutron with Rutherford's blessing, but the frustrating work of experiment was usually his alone.

His temperament matched the challenge of discovering a particle that might leave little trace of itself in its passage through matter; he was a shy, quiet, conscientious, reliable man, something of a neutron himself. Rutherford even felt it necessary to scold him for giving the boys at the Cavendish too much attention, though Chadwick took their care and nurturing to be his primary responsibility. "It was Chadwick," remembers Mark Oliphant, "who saw that research students got the equipment they needed, within the very limited resources of the stores and funds at his disposal." If he seemed "dour and unsmiling" at first, with time "the kindly, helpful and generous person beneath became apparent." He tended, says Otto Frisch, "to conceal his kindness behind a gruff façade."

The façade was protective. James Chadwick was tall, wiry, dark, with a high forehead, thin lips and a raven's-beak nose. "He had," say his joint biographers, colleagues both, "a deep voice and a dry sense of humour with a characteristic chuckle." He was born in the village of Bollington, south of Manchester in Cheshire, in 1891. When he was still a small boy his father left their country home to start a laundry in Manchester; Chadwick's grandmother seems to have raised him. He sat for two scholarships to the University of Manchester at sixteen, an early age even in the English educational system, won them both, kept one and went off to the university.

He meant to read mathematics. The entrance interviews were held publicly in a large, crowded hall. Chadwick got into the wrong line. He had already begun to answer the lecturer's questions when he realized he was being questioned for a physics course. Since he was too timid to explain, he decided that the physics lecturer impressed him and he would read for physics. The first year he was sorry, his biographers report: "the physics classes were large and noisy." The second year he heard Rutherford lecture on his early New Zealand experiments and was converted. In his third year Rutherford gave him a research project. His timidity again confounded him, this time almost fatally for his career: he discovered a snag in the procedure Rutherford had recommended to him but could not bring himself to point it out. Rutherford thought he missed it. Man and boy found their way past that misunderstanding and Chadwick graduated from Manchester in 1911 with first-class honors.

He stayed on for his master's degree, working with A. S. Russell and following the research in those productive years of Geiger, Marsden, de Hevesy, Moseley, Darwin and Bohr. In 1913, taking his M.Sc., he won an important research scholarship that required him to change laboratories to broaden his training. By then Geiger had returned to Berlin; Chadwick followed. Which was a pleasure while it lasted—Geiger made a point of introducing Chadwick around, so that he became acquainted with Einstein, Hahn and Meitner, among others in Berlin—but the war intervened.

A reserve officer, Geiger was called up early. He fortified Chadwick with a personal check for two hundred marks before he left. Some of the young Englishman's German friends advised him to leave the country quickly, but others convinced him to wait to avoid the danger of encountering troop trains along the way. On August 2 Chadwick tried to buy a ticket home by way of Holland at the Cook's Tours office in Berlin. Cook's suggested going through Switzerland instead. That struck Chadwick's friends as risky. He again accepted their advice and settled in to wait.

Then it was too late. He was arrested along with a German friend for allegedly making subversive remarks—merely speaking English would have done the job in those first weeks of hysterical nationalism—and languished in a Berlin jail for ten days before Geiger's laboratory arranged his release. Once out he returned to the laboratory until chaos retreated behind order again and the Kaiser's government found time to direct that all Englishmen in Germany be interned for the duration of the war.

The place of internment was a race track at Ruhleben—the name means "quiet life"—near Spandau. Chadwick shared with five other men a box stall designed for two horses and must have thought of Gulliver. In the winter he had to stamp his feet till late morning before they thawed. He and other interns formed a scientific society and even managed to conduct experiments. Chadwick's cold, hungry, quiet life at Ruhleben continued for four interminable years. This was the time, he said later, making the best of it, when he really began to grow up. He returned to Manchester after the Armistice with his digestion ruined and £11 in his pocket. He was at least alive, unlike poor Harry Moseley. Rutherford took him in.

Some of the experiments Chadwick conducted at the Cavendish in the 1920s to look for the neutron, he says, "were so desperate, so far-fetched as to belong to the days of alchemy." He and Rutherford both thought of the neutron, as Rutherford had imagined it in his Bakerian Lecture, as a close union of proton and electron. They therefore conjured up various ways to torture hydrogen—blasting it with electrical discharges, searching out the effects on it of passing cosmic rays—in the hope that the H atom that had been stable since the early days of the universe would somehow agree to collapse into neutrality at their hands.

The neutral particle resisted their blandishments and the nucleus resisted attack. The laboratory, Chadwick remembers, "passed through a relatively quiet spell. Much interesting and important work was done, but it was work of consolidation rather than of discovery; in spite of many attempts the paths to new fields could not be found." It began to seem, he adds, that "the problem of the new structure of the nucleus might indeed have to be left to the next generation, as Rutherford had once said and as many physicists continued to believe." Rutherford "was a little disappointed, because it was so very difficult to find out anything really important." Quantum theory bloomed while nuclear studies stalled. Rutherford had felt optimistic enough in 1923 to shout at the annual meeting of the British Association, "We are living in the heroic age of physics!" By 1927, in a paper on atomic structure, he was a little less confident. "We are not yet able to do more than guess at the structure even of the lighter and presumably least complex atoms," he writes. He proposed a structure nonetheless, with electrons in the nucleus orbiting around nuclear protons, an atom within an atom.

They had other work. In hindsight, it was necessary preparation. The scintillation method of detecting radiation had reached its limit of effectiveness: it was unreliable if the counting rate was greater than 150 per minute or less than about 3 per minute, and both ranges now came into view in nuclear studies. A disagreement between the Cavendish and the Vienna Radium Institute convinced even Rutherford of the necessity of change. Vienna had reproduced the Cavendish's light-element disintegration experiments and published completely different results. Worse, the Vienna physicists attributed the discrepancy to inferior Cavendish equipment. Chadwick laboriously reran the experiments with a specially made microscope with zinc sulfide coated directly onto the lens of the microscope's objective, which greatly brightened the field. The results confirmed the Cavendish's earlier count. Chadwick then went to Vienna. "He found," write his biographers, "that the scintillation counting was done by three young women—it was thought that not only did women have better eyes than men but they were less likely to be distracted by thinking while counting!" Chadwick observed the young women at work and realized that because they understood what was expected of the experiments they produced the expected results, unconsciously counting nonexistent scintillations. To test the technicians he gave them, without explanation, an unfamiliar experiment; this time their counts matched his own. Vienna apologized.

Hans Geiger, among others, turned back to the electrical counter he had devised with Rutherford in 1908 and improved it. The result, the Geiger counter, was essentially an electrically charged wire strung inside a gas-filled tube with a thinly covered window that allowed charged particles to enter. Once inside the tube the charged particles ionized gas atoms; the electrons thus stripped from the gas atoms were drawn to the positively charged wire; that changed the current level in the wire; the change, in the form of an electrical pulse, could then be run through an amplifier and converted to a sound—typically a click—or shown as a jump in the sweep of a light beam on the television-like screen of an oscilloscope. The electrical counter could operate continuously and could count above and below the limits possible to fallible physicists peering at scintillation screens. But the early counters had a significant disadvantage: they were highly sensitive to gamma radiation, much more so than zinc sulfide, and the radium compounds the Cavendish used as alpha sources gave off plentiful gamma rays. Polonium, the radioactive element that Marie Curie had discovered in 1898 and named after her native Poland, could be an excellent alternative. It was a good alpha source and with a gamma-ray background 100,000 times less intense than radium it was much less likely to overload an electrical counter. Unfortunately, polonium was difficult to acquire. A ton of uranium ore contained only about 0.1 gram, too little for commercial separation. It was available practically only as a byproduct of the radioactive decay of radium, and radium too was scarce.

There was time in those years to recover from the bleakness of the war and get on with living. In 1925 Chadwick married Aileen Stewart-Brown, daughter of a family long established in business in Liverpool. He had been living at Gonville and Caius College; now he made plans for permanent residence. A year later, in the midst of house-building, when Rutherford asked him and another Cavendish man to take on part of the work of revising Rutherford's old textbook on radioactivity, he fitted in the duty at night, working bundled in an overcoat at a writing table moved close to the fireplace of a drafty temporary rental. When the fire burned low he even pulled on gloves.

At the end of the decade the Rutherfords suffered a personal tragedy. Their daughter Eileen, twenty-nine years old and the mother of three children—she was married to a theoretician, R. H. Fowler, who kept up that end of physics at the Cavendish—gave birth to a fourth; one week later, on

December 23, she was felled by a lethal blood clot. "The loss of his only child," writes A. S. Eve, "whom he loved and admired, aged Rutherford for a time; he looked older and stooped more. He continued his life and work with a manful purpose, and one of the delights of his life was his group of four grandchildren. His face always lit up when he spoke of them."

Rutherford was elevated to baron in the New Year's Honours List of 1931, the year he would turn sixty. A kiwi crested his armorial bearings; they were supported on the dexter side by a figure representing Hermes Trismegistus, the Egyptian god of wisdom who was supposed to have written alchemical books, and on the sinister side by a Maori holding a club; and the two crossed curves that quartered his escutcheon traced the matched growth and decay of activity that gives each radioactive element and isotope its characteristic half-life.

Around 1928 a German physicist, Walther Bothe, "a real physicist's physicist" to Emilio Segrè, and Bothe's student Herbert Becker began studying the gamma radiation excited by alpha bombardment of light elements. They surveyed the light elements from lithium to oxygen as well as magnesium, aluminum and silver. Since they were concentrating on gamma radiation excited from a target they wanted a minimum gamma background and used a polonium radiation source. "I don't know how [Bothe] got his sources," Chadwick puzzles, "but he did." Lise Meitner had generously sent polonium to Chadwick from the Kaiser Wilhelm Institutes, but it was too little to allow Chadwick to do the work Bothe was doing.

The Germans found gamma excitation with boron, magnesium and aluminum, as they had more or less expected, because alpha particles disintegrate those elements, but they also and unexpectedly found it with lithium and beryllium, which alphas in this reaction did not disintegrate. "Indeed," writes Norman Feather, one of Chadwick's colleagues at the Cavendish, "with beryllium, the intensity of the . . . radiation was nearly ten times as great as with any other element investigated." That was strange enough; equally strange was the oddity that beryllium emitted this intense radiation under alpha bombardment without emitting protons. Bothe and Becker reported their results briefly in August 1930, then more fully in December. The radiation they had excited from beryllium had more energy than the bombarding alpha particles. The principle of the conservation of energy required a source for the excess; they proposed that it came from nuclear disintegration despite the absence of protons.

Chadwick set one of his research students, an Australian named H. C. Webster, to work studying these unusual results. A French team began the same study a little later with better resources: Irène Curie, Mme. Curie's somber and talented daughter, then thirty-three, and her husband Frédéric Joliot, two years younger, a handsome, outgoing man trained originally as an engineer whose charm reminded Segrè of the French singer Maurice Chevalier.

Marie Curie's Radium Institute at the east end of the Rue Pierre Curie in the Latin Quarter, built just before the war with funds from the French government and the Pasteur Foundation, had the advantage in any studies that required polonium. Radon gas decays over time to three only mildly radioactive isotopes: lead 210, bismuth 210 and polonium 210, which thus become available for chemical separation. Medical doctors throughout the world then used radon sealed into glass ampules—"seeds"—for cancer treatment. When the radon decayed, which it did in a matter of days, the seeds no longer served. Many physicians sent them on to Paris as a tribute to the woman who discovered radium. They accumulated to the world's largest source of polonium.

The Joliot-Curies had worked independently for the two years since their marriage in 1927; in 1929 they decided to work in collaboration. They first developed new chemical techniques for separating polonium, and by 1931 had purified a volume of the element almost ten times more intense than any other existing source. With their powerful new source they turned their attention to the mystery of beryllium.

Chadwick's student H. C. Webster had progressed in the meantime, by the late spring of 1931, beyond recapitulation to discovery: he found, says Chadwick, "that the radiation from beryllium which was emitted in the same direction as the . . . alpha-particles was more penetrating than the radiation emitted in a backward direction." Gamma radiation, an energetic form of light, should be emitted equally in every direction from a point source such as a nucleus, just as visible light radiates equally from a lightbulb filament. A particle, on the other hand, would usually be bumped forward by an incoming alpha. "And that, of course," Chadwick adds, "was a point which excited me very much indeed, because I thought, 'Here's the neutron.' "

With twin daughters now, Chadwick had become a family man of regular habits. Among the most sacred of these was his annual June family vacation. The possibility of finding his long-sought neutron was not sufficient cause to change his plans. It might have been, but he thought he needed a cloud chamber for the next step in the search, and the one immediately available to him at the Cavendish was not in working order. He found a cloud chamber in other hands; its owner agreed to help Webster use it when he had finished using it himself. Still assuming that the neutron

1

1. English novelist H. G. Wells. His 1914 novel, *The World Set Free,* predicted atomic bombs, atomic war and world government.

2

2. As a young man, Hungarian physicist Leo Szilard dreamed of saving the world. "If we could find an element which is split by neutrons . . . "

3. Pierre and Marie Curie in their Paris laboratory, c. 1900. The elements they first isolated from pitchblende residues, polonium and radium, radiated far more energy than any chemical process could account for.

3

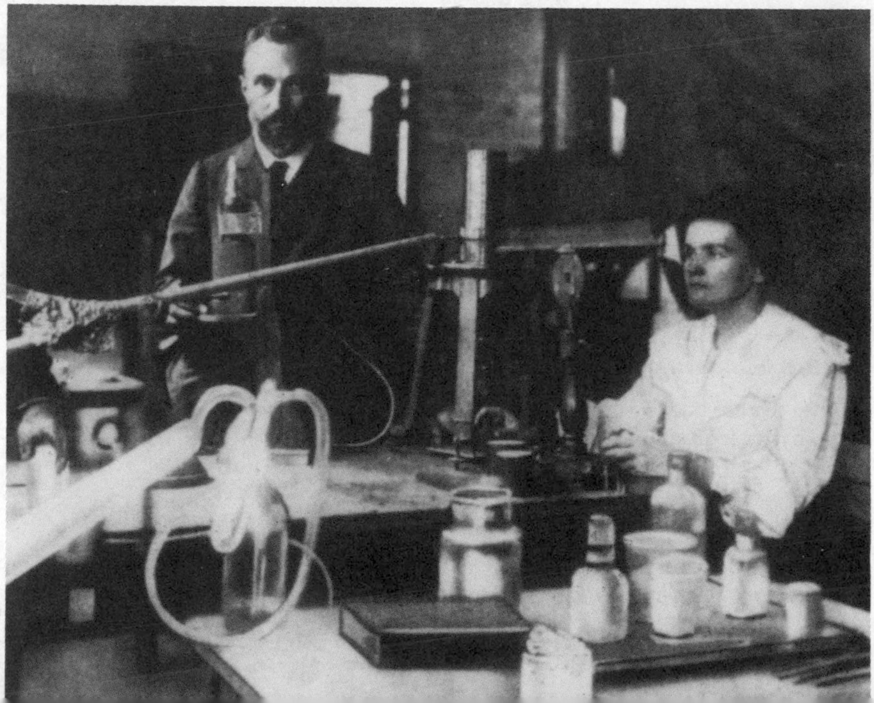

4

4. New Zealander Ernest Rutherford discovered the atomic nucleus. James Jeans called him "the Newton of atomic physics." C. 1902.

5

5. The Cavendish Laboratory in Cambridge, England, the world center of early-20th-century experimental physics.

6

6. Otto Hahn and Lise Meitner, chemist and physicist, made a productive team in Berlin.

7

7. Niels Bohr on the threshold of greatness, summer 1911, with his fiancée, Margrethe.

8

8. October 1912: The Kaiser led the way to dedicate the new institute built on farmland he donated in the Berlin suburb of Dahlem.
9. The Kaiser Wilhelm Institute for Chemistry, another measure of burgeoning German power.

9

10

10. Chemist Fritz Haber (*left*) and theoretician Albert Einstein, c. 1914. Haber guided German development of poison gases in the Great War; Einstein spoke out for pacifism and pursued the general theory of relativity. He had already formulated the fateful mass-energy equivalence, $E = mc^2$.

12

11

11. Cambridge physicist Harry Moseley, killed at Gallipoli, 1915. A eulogist said his death alone made the war a "hideous" and "irreparable" crime.

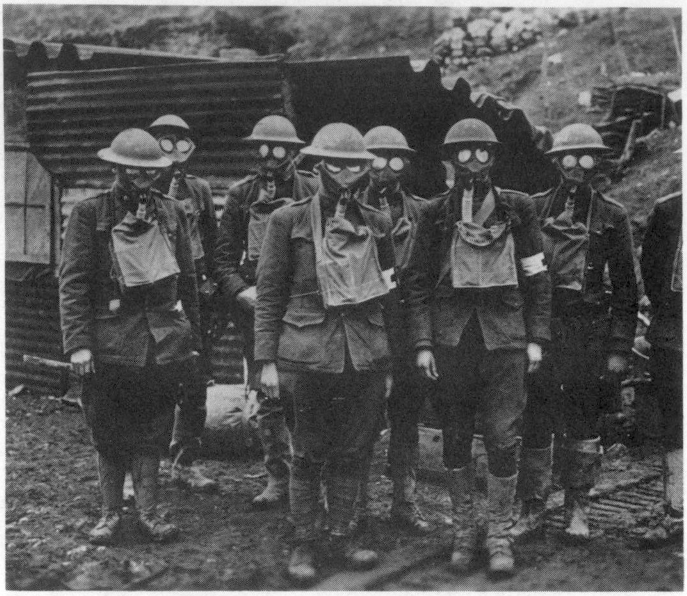

12. American soldiers preparing for gas drill, c. 1917. "It was a way of saving countless lives," Otto Hahn remembers Fritz Haber arguing of poison gas, ". . . if it meant that the war could be brought to an end sooner."

13

13. Niels Bohr's new Institute for Theoretical Physics in Copenhagen, completed in 1921. The best young physicists in the world pilgrimaged here to work and to learn.

14

14. Niels Bohr in the 1920s.

15

15. At Como, Italy, in 1927, Enrico Fermi, Werner Heisenberg and Wolfgang Pauli (*l. to r.*) heard Bohr define complementarity.

16

17

16. Fermi and his group in Rome prepared through the early 1930s for major work and found it bombarding the elements with neutrons to induce artificial radioactivities previously unknown. Uranium was a complex puzzle. *L. to r.,* Emilio Segrè, Enrico Persico and Enrico Fermi at Ostia, 1927. 17. The Physics Institute on the Via Panisperna.

18. Cambridge physicist Francis Aston's mass-spectrograph sorted out isotopes by mass. Their whole-number weights led to an understanding of binding energy, the glue that holds atoms together. "Personally I think there is no doubt that sub-atomic energy is available all around us," Aston lectured, "and that one day man will release and control its almost infinite power."

18

19

19. The first anti-Jewish law Adolf Hitler promulgated, in April 1933, stripped "non-Aryan" academics of their posts. More than 100 physicists fled Germany.

20

20. With Europe in turmoil, Bohr's annual Copenhagen conferences became job forums. In the front row (*l. to r.*): Oskar Klein, Bohr, Heisenberg, Pauli, George Gamow, Lev Landau, Hendrik Kramers.

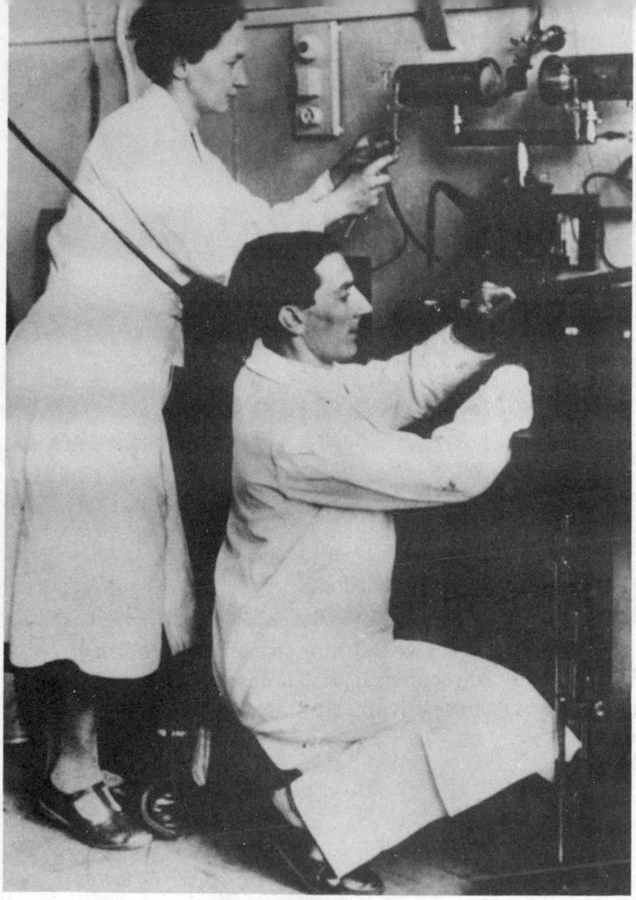

21

22

22. Identifying the third basic constituent of matter fell to Rutherford protégé James Chadwick. The discovery of the neutron in 1932 opened the atomic nucleus to detailed examination. Chadwick's colleagues hailed him as "the personification of the ideal experimentalist."

21. Frédéric and Irène Joliot-Curie at the Radium Institute in Paris discovered artificial radioactivity but missed the neutron. C. 1935.

23. At Berkeley in the 1930s theoretician Robert Oppenheimer (*left*) and experimentalist Ernest O. Lawrence built a great American school of physics.

23

24

24. Lawrence's Nobel Prize–winning cyclotron battered secrets from the nucleus and proved a potent source of neutrons. Here Lawrence examines the vacuum chamber of the 37-inch machine, completed in 1937.

25

25. Two distinguished Cavendish directors: J. J. Thomson (*left*) and Ernest Rutherford in the 1930s.

26

27

26. Mathematician John von Neumann departed Europe early for a lifetime appointment at the Institute for Advanced Study. 27. Leo Szilard, photographed by Gertrud Weiss at Oxford in 1936. The chain-reaction patent was already a British military secret.

28

29

28. After England, the physicists who escaped Nazi Germany emigrated in increasing numbers to the United States. Future Nobel laureate Hans Bethe won appointment at Cornell. 29. His Stuttgart professor's daughter Rose Ewald followed in 1936. "Rose was then twenty, and I fell in love with her."

30

30. The war against the Jews spread to Italy and threatened Laura Fermi. The 1938 Nobel Prize offered the couple escape with financial security; with their children Giulio and Nella they went on from Stockholm to New York. "We have founded the American branch of the Fermi family," Fermi mocked.

31

31. Lise Meitner at 59 in 1937. At Christmastime 1938 in Stockholm she heard from Otto Hahn of his stunning discovery with Fritz Strassmann that slow neutrons bombarding uranium made barium—the first evidence that the uranium atom split.

32

32. Otto Frisch, c. 1938. With Meitner, his aunt, he prized out the revolutionary meaning of the Hahn-Strassmann uranium discovery.

33

33. Otto Hahn at sixty in 1939. His "barium fantasy" would change the world.

34. One of Hahn's radiochemistry worktables at the Kaiser Wilhelm Institute for Chemistry.

34

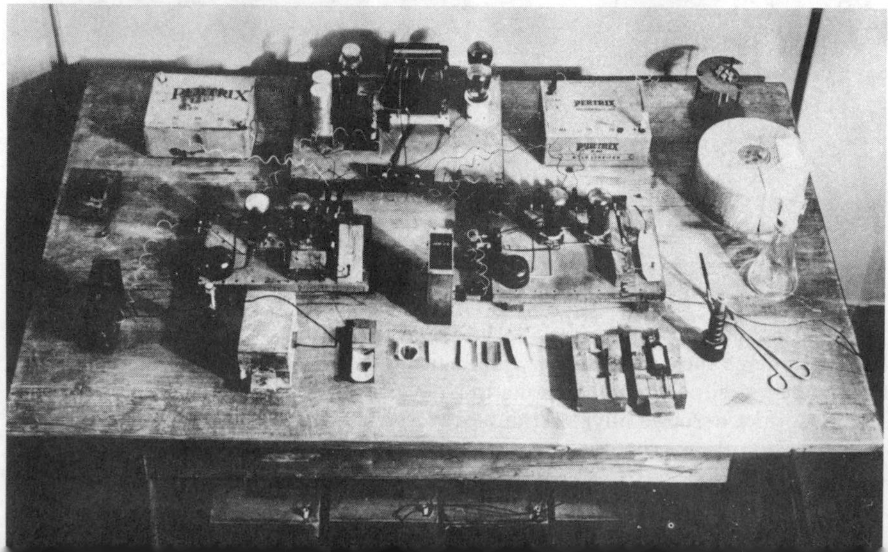

35

36

35. The medieval fortress at Kungälv, Sweden, that looked down upon Frisch and Meitner as they worked.

36. Herbert Anderson at Columbia first demonstrated nuclear fission in the United States in January 1939.

37

37. At Munich in September 1938, British Prime Minister Neville Chamberlain agreed to Nazi demands to partition Czechoslovakia. "Peace with honour," he told the London crowds. "Complete surrender," Winston Churchill charged.

38

38. The APO target room at the Carnegie Institution's Department of Terrestrial Magnetism, Washington, D.C., after the demonstration of fission there on the night of January 28, 1939. *L. to r.*, Robert Meyer, Merle Tuve, Fermi, Richard Roberts, Léon Rosenfeld, Erik Bohr, Niels Bohr, Gregory Breit, John Fleming.

39

39. Albert Einstein's 1939 letter to President Franklin Roosevelt reporting the possibility of German atomic bomb research led FDR to appoint a Uranium Committee headed by ineffectual Bureau of Standards director Lyman J. Briggs (*left*).

was an electron-proton doublet with enough residual electrical charge to ionize a gas at least weakly, Chadwick wanted Webster to aim the beryllium radiation into the cloud chamber and see if he could photograph its ionizing tracks. He left his student to the work and went off on holiday.

"Of course," Chadwick said in retrospect of the neutron he was hunting for, "they should not have seen anything" in the cloud chamber, nor did they. "They wrote and told me what had happened, that they hadn't found anything, which disappointed me very much." When Webster moved on to the University of Bristol, Chadwick decided to take over the beryllium research himself.

First he had to shift his laboratory to a different part of the Cavendish building, and that delayed him; then he had to prepare a strong polonium source. In the matter of polonium he was lucky. Norman Feather had spent the 1929–30 academic year in Baltimore, in the physics department at Johns Hopkins, and there befriended an English physician who was in charge of the radium supply at Baltimore's Kelly Hospital. The physician had stored away several hundred used radon seeds; "together," Feather remembers, "they contained almost as much polonium as was available to Curie and Joliot in Paris." The hospital donated them to the Cavendish and Feather brought them home. Chadwick accomplished the dangerous chemical separation that autumn.

Irène Joliot-Curie reported her first results to the French Academy of Sciences on December 28, 1931. The beryllium radiation, she found, was even more penetrating than Bothe and Becker had reported. She standardized her measurements and put the energy of the radiation at three times the energy of the bombarding alpha particle.

The Joliot-Curies decided next to see if the beryllium radiation would knock protons out of matter as alpha particles did. "They fitted their ionization chamber with a thin window," explains Feather, "and placed various materials close to the window in the path of the radiation. They found nothing, except with materials such as paraffin wax and cellophane which already contained hydrogen in chemical combination. When thin layers of these substances were close to the window, the current in the ionization chamber was greater than usual. By a series of experimental tests, both simple and elegant, they produced convincing evidence that this excess ionization was due to protons ejected from the hydrogenous material." The Joliot-Curies understood then that what they were seeing were elastic collisions—like the collisions of billiard balls or marbles—between the beryllium radiation and the nuclei of H atoms.

But they were still committed to their previous conviction that the penetrating radiation from beryllium was gamma radiation. They had not thought about the possibility of a neutral particle. They had not read Rutherford's Bakerian Lecture because such lectures were invariably, in their experience, only recapitulations of previously reported work. Rutherford and Chadwick alone had thought seriously about the neutron.

On January 18, 1932, the Joliot-Curies reported to the Academy of Sciences their discovery that paraffin wax emitted high-velocity protons when bombarded by beryllium radiation. But that was not the title and the argument of the paper they wrote. They titled their paper "The emission of protons of high velocity from hydrogenous materials irradiated with very penetrating gamma rays." Which was as unlikely as if a marble should deflect a wrecking ball. Gamma rays could deflect electrons, a phenomenon known as the Compton effect after its discoverer, the American experimental physicist Arthur Holly Compton, but a proton is 1,836 times heavier than an electron and not easily moved.

At the Cavendish in early February Chadwick found the *Comptes Rendus*, the French physics journal, in his morning mail, discovered the Joliot-Curie paper and read it with widening eyes:

> Not many minutes afterward Feather came to my room to tell me about this report, as astonished as I was. A little later that morning I told Rutherford. It was a custom of long standing that I should visit him about 11 a.m. to tell him any news of interest and to discuss the work in progress in the laboratory. As I told him about the Curie-Joliot observation and their views on it, I saw his growing amazement; and finally he burst out "I don't believe it." Such an impatient remark was utterly out of character, and in all my long association with him I recall no similar occasion. I mention it to emphasize the electrifying effect of the Curie-Joliot report. Of course, Rutherford agreed that one must believe the observations; the explanation was quite another matter.

No further duty interposed itself between Chadwick and his destiny. He went fervently to work, starting on February 7, 1932, a Sunday: "It so happened that I was just ready to begin experiment [when he read of the Joliot-Curie discovery]. . . . I started with an open mind, though naturally my thoughts were on the neutron. I was reasonably sure that the Curie-Joliot observations could not be ascribed to a kind of Compton effect, for I had looked for this more than once. I was convinced that there was something quite new as well as strange."

His simple apparatus consisted of a radiation source and an ionization chamber, the chamber connected to a vacuum-tube amplifier and thence to an oscilloscope. The radiation source, an evacuated metal tube strapped to a rough-sawn block of pine, contained a one-centimeter silver disk coated with polonium mounted close behind a two-centimeter disk of pure beryllium, a silver-gray metal that is three times as light as aluminum. Alpha particles from the polonium striking beryllium nuclei knocked out the penetrating beryllium radiation, which, Chadwick found immediately, would pass essentially unimpeded through as much as two centimeters of lead.

The half-inch opening into the small ionization chamber that faced this radiation source was covered with aluminum foil. Within the shallow chamber, in an atmosphere of air at normal pressure, a small charged plate collected electrons ionized by incoming radiation and moved their pulses along to the amplifier and oscilloscope. "For the purpose at hand," explains Norman Feather, "such an arrangement was ideal. If the amplifier were carefully designed, it was possible to ensure that the magnitude of the oscillograph deflection was directly proportional to the amount of ionization produced in the chamber. . . . The energy of the recoil atom producing the ionization could thus be calculated directly from the size of the deflection on the oscillograph record."

Chadwick mounted a sheet of paraffin two millimeters thick in front of the aluminum-foil window into the ionization chamber; immediately, he wrote in his final report on the experiment, "the number of deflections recorded by the oscillograph increased markedly." That showed that particles ejected from the paraffin were entering the chamber. Then he began interposing sheets of aluminum foil between the wax and the chamber window until no more kicks appeared on the oscilloscope; by scaling the absorptions of aluminum compared to air he calculated the range of the particles as just over 40 centimeters in air; that range meant "it was obvious that the particles were protons."

Thus repeating the Joliot-Curie work prepared the way. Now Chadwick broke new ground. He removed the paraffin sheet. He wanted to study what happens to other elements bombarded directly by the beryllium radiation. Elements in the form of solids he mounted in front of the chamber window: "In this way lithium, beryllium, boron, carbon and nitrogen, as paracyanogen, were tested." Elements in the form of gases he simply pumped into the chamber to replace the ambient air: "Hydrogen, helium, nitrogen, oxygen, and argon were examined in this way." In every case the kicks increased on the oscilloscope; the powerful beryllium radiation knocked protons out of all the elements Chadwick tested. It knocked about the same number out of each element. And, most important for his conclusion, the energies of the recoiling protons were significantly greater than they could possibly be if the beryllium radiation consisted of gamma rays. "In general," Chadwick wrote, "the experimental results show that if the recoil atoms are to be explained by collision with a [gamma-ray photon], we must assume a larger and larger energy for the [photon] as the mass of the struck atom increases." Then, quietly, in what in fact is a devastating criticism of the Joliot-Curie thesis, invoking the basic physical rule that no more energy or momentum can come out of an event than went into it: "It is evident that we must either relinquish the application of the conservation of energy and momentum in these collisions or adopt another hypothesis about the nature of the radiation." When they read that sentence the Joliot-Curies were deeply and properly chagrined.

The hypothesis Chadwick proposed adopting should come as no surprise: "If we suppose that the radiation is not a [gamma] radiation, but consists of particles of mass very nearly equal to that of the proton, all the difficulties connected with the collisions disappear, both with regard to their frequency and to the energy transfer to different masses. In order to explain the great penetrating power of the radiation we must further assume that the particle has no net charge. . . . We may suppose it [to be] the 'neutron' discussed by Rutherford in his Bakerian Lecture of 1920."

Chadwick then worked the numbers to show that his hypothesis was the correct one to explain the facts.

"It was a strenuous time," he said afterward. From beginning to end the work took ten days and he kept up his Cavendish responsibilities besides. He averaged perhaps three hours of sleep a night, labored over the weekend of February 13–14 as well, finished probably on the seventeenth, a Wednesday, the day he sent off a first brief report to *Nature* to establish priority of discovery. He titled that report, published as a letter to the editor, "Possible existence of a neutron." "But there was no doubt whatever in my mind or I should not have written the letter."

"To [Chadwick's] great credit," writes Segrè in tribute, "when the neutron was not present [in earlier experiments] he did not detect it, and when it ultimately was there he perceived it immediately, clearly and convincingly. These are the marks of a great experimental physicist."

A young Russian, Peter Kapitza, had come up to Cambridge in 1921 to work at the Cavendish. He was solid, dedicated, charming and technically inventive and he soon made himself the apple of Rutherford's eye, the only one among all the boys, even including Chadwick, who could convince the frugal director to allow large sums of money to be spent for apparatus. In 1936 Rutherford would attack Chadwick angrily for encouraging the construction of a cyclotron at the Cavendish; but already in 1932 Kapitza had a separate laboratory in an elegant new brick building in the Cavendish courtyard for his expensive experiments with powerful magnetic fields. As Kapitza had settled in at Cambridge he had noticed what he considered to be an excessive and unproductive deference of British physics students to their seniors. He therefore founded a club, the Kapitza Club, devoted to open and unhierarchical discussion. Membership was limited and coveted. Members met in college rooms and Kapitza frequently opened discussions with deliberate howlers so that even the youngest would speak up to correct him, loosening the grip of tradition on their necks.

That Wednesday Kapitza wined and dined the exhausted Chadwick into what Mark Oliphant calls "a very mellow mood," then brought him along to a Kapitza Club meeting. "The intense excitement of all in the Cavendish, including Rutherford," Oliphant remembers, "was already remarkable, for we had heard rumors of Chadwick's results." Oliphant says Chadwick spoke lucidly and with conviction, not failing to mention the contributions of Bothe, Becker, Webster and the Joliot-Curies, "a lesson to us all." C. P. Snow, who was also present, remembers the performance as "one of the shortest accounts ever made about a major discovery." When tall and birdlike Chadwick finished speaking he looked over the assembly and announced abruptly, "Now I want to be chloroformed and put to bed for a fortnight."

He deserved his rest. He had discovered a new elementary particle, the third basic constituent of matter. It was this neutral mass that compounded the weight of the elements without adding electrical charge. Two protons and 2 neutrons made a helium nucleus; 7 protons and 7 neutrons a nitrogen; 47 protons and 60 neutrons a silver; 56 protons and 81 neutrons a barium; 92 protons and 146 (or 143) neutrons a uranium.

And because the neutron was as massive as a proton but carried no electrical charge, it was hardly affected by the shell of electrons around a nucleus; nor did the electrical barrier of the nucleus itself block its way. It would therefore serve as a new nuclear probe of surpassing power of penetration. "A beam of thermal neutrons," writes the American theoretical physicist Philip Morrison, "moving at about the speed of sound, which corresponds to a kinetic energy of only about a fortieth of an electron volt, produces nuclear reactions in many materials much more easily than a beam of protons of millions of volts energy, traveling thousands of times faster." Ernest Lawrence's cyclotron, spiraling protons to million-volt energies for the first time the same month that Chadwick made his fateful discovery, fortunately proved to be adaptable to the production of neutrons. More than any other development, Chadwick's neutron made practical the detailed examination of the nucleus. Hans Bethe once remarked that he considered everything before 1932 "the prehistory of nuclear physics, and from 1932 on the history of nuclear physics." The difference, he said, was the discovery of the neutron.

Word of the discovery reached Copenhagen in the midst of preparations for an amateur theatrical, a parody of Goethe's *Faust*, to celebrate the tenth anniversary of the opening of Bohr's Institute for Theoretical Physics. Thc postdoctoral dramatists gave the new particle the last word. They had cast Wolfgang Pauli, a corpulent man with a smooth, round face and protuberant, heavy-lidded eyes who resembled the actor Peter Lorre, as Mephistopheles, Bohr as The Lord. Eclectically they cast Chadwick in absentia as Wagner and an anonymous illustrator drew him into the script, "*the personification of the ideal experimentalist*" according to the stage directions, balancing a vastly magnified neutron on his finger:

In Copenhagen, as before in Cambridge, Chadwick reports his discovery briefly and succinctly:

> *The* Neutron *has come to be.*
> *Loaded with Mass is he.*
> *Of Charge, forever free.*
> *Pauli, do you agree?*

Pauli steps forward to dispense his Mephistophelean blessing:

That which experiment has found—
Though theory has no part in—
Is always reckoned more than sound
To put your mind and heart in. . . .

And a chorus of clowning, friendly physicists, Bohr's brilliant young crew, dances out to sing a finale and bring the curtain down:

Now a reality,
Once but a vision.
What classicality,
Grace and precision!
Hailed with cordiality,
Honored in song,
Eternal Neutrality
Pulls us along!

It was the last peaceful time many of them would know for years to come.

7

Exodus

"Antisemitism is strong here and political reaction is violent," Albert Einstein wrote Paul Ehrenfest from Berlin in December 1919. The letter coincides with Einstein's discovery by the popular press, the beginning of his years of international celebrity. "A new figure in world history," the *Berliner Illustrirte Zeitung* described him under a cover photograph on December 14, ". . .whose investigations signify a complete revision of our concepts of nature, and are on a par with the insights of a Copernicus, a Kepler, a Newton." Immediately the anti-Semites and fascists set to work on him.

Einstein was already, at forty-three, respected in the first rank of theoretical physicists. He had been nominated for the Nobel Prize in all but two years since 1910, the secondings increasing in number after 1917; Max Planck, who was not given to exaggeration, wrote the Nobel Committee in 1919 that Einstein "made the first step beyond Newton." The award might have come sooner than in 1922 (belatedly for 1921: the 1922 prize was Bohr's) had relativity been less paradoxical a revelation.

Physically Einstein was not yet the amused, grandfatherly notabl his later American years. His mustache was still dark and his thick hair had only begun to gray. C. P. Snow would observe "a massi very heavily muscled." The Swabian-born physicist's friends t loud laugh boyish; his enemies thought it rude. "A powerfu

Snow suspected, suspecting also that Einstein took his sensuality to be "one of the chains of personality that ought to be slipped off." Nor had he yet learned, in the psychoanalyst Erik Erikson's words, "to look into cameras as if he were meeting the eyes of the future beholders of his image." In the past year Einstein had endured a stomach ulcer, jaundice and a painful divorce; he had lost and partly regained fifty-six pounds; his mother was dying of cancer: fatigue stained his expressive face. Leopold Infeld, a young Polish physicist who knocked at his door in postwar Berlin seeking a letter of recommendation, found him "dressed in a morning coat and striped trousers with one important button missing." Infeld knew Einstein's face from magazines and newsreels. "But no picture could reproduce the shining glow of his eyes." They were large and dark brown, and the diffident young visitor was one of many—Leo Szilard was another—who found comfort in those cold days in their honest warmth.

The immediate occasion for world notice was an eclipse of the sun. Einstein had presented a paper to the Prussian Academy of Sciences in Berlin on November 25, 1915, "The field equations of gravitation," in which, he reported happily, "finally the general theory of relativity is closed as a logical structure." The paper stands as his first finished statement of the general theory. It was susceptible of proof. It explained mysterious anomalies in the orbit of Mercury—that confirmed prediction was the one which left Einstein feeling something had snapped in him. The general theory also predicted that starlight would be deflected, when it passed a massive body like the sun, through an angle equal to twice the value Newtonian theory predicts. The Great War delayed measurement of the Einstein value. A total eclipse of the sun (which would block the sun's glare and make the stars beyond it visible) due on May 29, 1919, offered the first postwar occasion. The British, not the Germans, followed through. Cambridge astronomer Arthur Stanley Eddington led an expedition to Principe Island, off the West African coast; the Greenwich Observatory sent another expedition to Sobral, inland from the coast of northern Brazil. A joint meeting of the Royal Society and the Royal Astronomical Society at Burlington House in London on November 6, under a portrait of Newton, confirmed the stunning results: the Einstein value, not the Newton value, held good. "One of the greatest achievements in the history of human thought," J. J. Thomson told the assembled worthies. "It is not the discovery of an outlying island but of a whole continent of new scientific ideas."

That was news. *The Times* headlined it REVOLUTION IN SCIENCE and the word spread. From that day forward Einstein was a marked man.

It rankled German chauvinists, including rightist students and some physicists, that the eyes of the world should turn to a Jew who had declared himself a pacifist during the bloodiest of nationalistic wars and who spoke out for internationalism now. When Einstein prepared to offer a series of popular lectures in the University of Berlin's largest hall—everyone was lecturing on relativity that winter—students complained of the expense for coal and electricity. The student body president challenged Einstein to hire his own hall. He ignored the insult and spoke in the university hall as scheduled, but at least one of his lectures, in February, was disrupted.

He was challenged more seriously the following August by an organization assembled under obscure leadership and extravagant but clandestine financing that called itself the Committee of German Scientists for the Preservation of Pure Scholarship. The 1905 Nobel laureate Philipp Lenard, seeing relativity hailed and Einstein come to fame, retreated into a vindictive anti-Semitism and lent his respectability to the Committee, which attacked relativity theory as a Jewish corruption and Einstein as a tasteless self-promoter. The organization held a well-attended public meeting in Berlin's Philharmonic Hall on August 20. Einstein went to listen—one speaker, as Leopold Infeld recalled, "said that uproar about the theory of relativity was hostile to the German spirit"—and stayed to scorn the crackpot talk with laughter and satiric applause.

The criticism nevertheless stung. Einstein mistakenly thought the majority of his German colleagues subscribed to it. Rashly he struck off an uncharacteristically defensive statement. It appeared in the *Berliner Tageblatt* three days after the Philharmonic Hall meeting. "My Answer to the Antirelativity Theory Company Ltd." shocked his friends, but it presciently identified the deeper issues of the Committee attack. "I have good reason to believe that motives other than a desire to search for truth are at the bottom of their enterprise," Einstein wrote. And parenthetically, leaving his implications unstated in elision: "(Were I a German national, with or without swastika, instead of a Jew of liberal, international disposition, then . . .)." A month later his sense of humor had returned; he asked Max Born not to be too hard on him: "Everyone has to sacrifice at the altar of stupidity from time to time . . . and this I have done with my article." But before then he had seriously considered leaving Germany.

It would not be the first time. Einstein had renounced German citizenship and departed the country once before, at the extraordinary age of sixteen. That earlier rejection, which he reversed two decades later, prepared him for the final one, after the Weimar interlude, when Adolf Hitler came to power.

Germany had been united in empire for only eight years when Einstein was born in Ulm on March 14, 1879. He grew up in Munich. He was slow to speak, but he was not, as legend has it, slow in his studies; he consistently earned the highest or next-highest marks in mathematics and Latin in school and *Gymnasium*. At four or five the "miracle" of a compass his father showed him excited him so much, he remembered, that he "trembled and grew cold." It seemed to him then that "there had to be something behind objects that lay deeply hidden." He would look for the something which objects hid, though his particular genius was to discover that there was nothing behind them to hide; that objects, as matter and as energy, were all; that even space and time were not the invisible matrices of the material world but its attributes. "If you will not take the answer too seriously," he told a clamorous crowd of reporters in New York in 1921 who asked him for a short explanation of relativity, "and consider it only as a kind of joke, then I can explain it as follows. It was formerly believed that if all material things disappeared out of the universe, time and space would be left. According to the relativity theory, however, time and space disappear together with the things."

The quiet child became a rebellious adolescent. He was working his own way through Kant and Darwin and mathematics while the *Gymnasium* pounded him with rote. He veered off into religion—Judaism—and came back bitterly disillusioned: "Through the reading of popular scientific books I soon reached the conviction that much of the stories in the Bible could not be true. . . . The consequence was a positively fanatic free-thinking coupled with the impression that youth is intentionally being deceived by the state through lies; it was a crushing impression. Suspicion against every kind of authority grew out of this experience, a sceptical attitude towards the convictions which were alive in any specific social environment."

His father stumbled in business, not for the first time. The family moved across the Alps to Milan to start again, but Albert stayed behind in a boardinghouse to complete his *Gymnasium* work. He was probably expelled from the *Gymnasium* before he could quit. He acquired a doctor's certificate claiming nervous disorders. It was not only the autocracy of his German school that he despised. "Politically," he wrote later, "I hated Germany from my youth." He had thought of renouncing his citizenship while his family was still in Munich, as a rebellious adolescent of fifteen. That began a long family debate. He won it after he moved from Milan to Zurich to try again to finish his schooling; his father wrote the German authorities on his behalf. Einstein renounced his German citizenship officially on January 28, 1896. The Swiss took him aboard in 1901. He liked their doughty democracy and was prepared to serve in their militia but was found medically unfit (because of flat feet and varicose veins); but one reason he quit Germany was to avoid the duty of Prussian conscription, *Kadavergehorsamkeit*, the obedience of the corpse.

The boy and the young man rebelled to protect the child within—the "victorious child," Erik Erikson has it in Einstein's case, the child with its uninhibited creativity preserved into adulthood. Einstein grazes the point in a letter to James Franck:

> I sometimes ask myself how it came about that I was the one to develop the theory of relativity. The reason, I think, is that a normal adult never stops to think about problems of space and time. These are things which he has thought of as a child. But my intellectual development was retarded, as a result of which I began to wonder about space and time only when I had already grown up.

"Relativity" was a misnomer. Einstein worked his way to a new physics by demanding consistency and greater objectivity of the old. If the speed of light is a constant, then something else must serve as the elastic between two systems at motion in relation to one another—even if that something else is time. If a body gives off an amount *E* of energy its mass minutely diminishes. But if energy has mass, then mass must have energy: the two must be equivalent: $E = mc^2$, $E/c^2 = m$. (I.e., an amount of energy *E* in joules is equal to an amount of mass *m* in kilograms multiplied by the square of the speed of light, an enormous number, 3×10^8 meters per second times 3×10^8 m/s $= 9 \times 10^{16}$ or 90,000,000,000,000,000 joules per kilogram. Dividing *E* by c^2 demonstrates how large an amount of energy is contained within even a small mass.)

Einstein came to that beautiful, harrowing equivalency in 1907, in a long paper published in the *Jahrbuch der Radioaktivität und Elektronik*. "It is possible," he wrote there, "that radioactive processes may become known in which a considerably larger percentage of the mass of the initial atom is converted into radiations of various kinds than is the case for radium." Like Soddy and Rutherford earlier in England, he saw the lesson of radium that there was vast energy stored in matter, though he was not at all sure that it could be released, even experimentally. "The line of thought is amusing and fascinating," he confided to a friend at the time, "but I wonder if the dear Lord laughs about it and has led me around by the nose." He had his Ph.D. then from the University of Zurich and Max Planck had begun to correspond with him, but he had not yet left the patent office where he worked as a technical expert from 1902 to 1909, the years of his first great burst of papers including those on Brownian motion, the photoelectric effect and special relativity.

He habilitated as a *Privatdozent* at the University of Bern in 1908 but held on to the patent-office job for another year for security. Finally in October 1909, *after* receiving his first honorary doctorate, he moved up to associate professor at the University of Zurich. A full professorship enticed him to isolated Prague—he was married now, with a wife and two sons to support—but happily the Polytechnic in Zurich drew him back a year later with a matching offer. The academic hesitations measure how radically new was his work. It was 1913 before Max Planck, Fritz Haber and a muster of German notables, recognizing the waste, offered him a triple appointment in Berlin: a research position under the aegis of the Prussian Academy of Sciences, a research professorship at the university and the directorship of the planned Kaiser Wilhelm Institute for Physics. After the Germans left, Einstein quipped to his assistant, Otto Stern, that they were "like men looking for a rare postage stamp."

He arrived in Berlin in April 1914. In the war years, separated from his first wife and living alone, he completed the general theory. To Max Born that "great work of art" was "the greatest feat of human thinking about nature, the most amazing combination of philosophical penetration, physical intuition, and mathematical skill" even though "its connections with experience were slender." Einstein's crowning achievement ameliorated for him the universal madness of the war:

> I begin to feel comfortable amid the present insane tumult, in conscious detachment from all things which preoccupy the crazy community. Why should one not be able to live contentedly as a member of the service personnel in the lunatic asylum? After all, one respects the lunatics as the people for whom the building in which one lives exists. Up to a point, you can make your own choice of institution—though the distinction between them is smaller than you think in your younger years.

Einstein raised funds for the Zionist cause of a Hebrew university in Palestine on a first trip to the United States, with Chaim Weizmann, in April and May 1921. He had seen the crowds of Eastern Jews stumbling into Berlin in the wake of war and revolution, watched the German incitement against them and decided to take their part. His guide to Zionist thinking was the eloquent spokesman and organizer Kurt Blumenfeld, who also served in that capacity to the young Hannah Arendt. It was Blumenfeld who convinced him to accompany Weizmann to America—his relations with the forceful, singleminded Weizmann, Einstein told Abraham Pais once, "were, as Freud would say, ambivalent." He lectured on relativity at Columbia, the City College of New York and Princeton, met Fiorello La Guardia and President Warren G. Harding, conceived "a new theory of eternity" sitting through formal speeches at the annual dinner of the National Academy of Sciences and spoke to crowds of enthusiastic American Jews.

Back home he wrote that he "first discovered the Jewish people" in America. "I have seen any number of Jews, but the Jewish people I have never met either in Berlin or elsewhere in Germany. This Jewish people which I found in America came from Russia, Poland, and Eastern Europe generally. These men and women still retain a healthy national feeling; it has not yet been destroyed by the process of atomization and dispersion." The statement implicitly criticizes the Jews of Germany, whose "undignified assimilationist cravings and strivings," Einstein wrote elsewhere, had "always . . . annoyed" him. Blumenfeld propounded a radical, post-assimilatory Zionism and had taught him well. A decade later Hannah Arendt would write that "in a society on the whole hostile to Jews . . . it is possible to assimilate only by assimilating to anti-Semitism also." Einstein specialized in driving assumptions to their logical conclusions: clearly he had arrived at a similar understanding of the "Jewish question."

He was now not only the most famous scientist in the world but also a known spokesman for Jewish causes. In Berlin on June 24, 1922, right-wing extremists gunned down Walther Rathenau, the Weimar Republic's first Foreign Minister, a physical chemist and industrialist friend of Einstein and a highly visible Jew. It appeared that Einstein might be next. "I am supposed to belong to that group of persons whom the people are planning to assassinate," he wrote Max Planck. "I have been informed independently by serious persons that it would be dangerous for me in the near future to stay in Berlin or, for that matter, to appear anywhere in public in Germany." He lived privately until October, then left with his second wife, Elsa, on a long trip to the Far East and Japan, receiving notice of his Nobel Prize en route. He spent twelve days in Palestine on the way back and stopped over in Spain. By the time he returned to Berlin, German preoccupation with politics had temporarily retreated behind preoccupation with the Dadaistic mark, then soaring toward 54,000 to the dollar. Einstein went on with his work, including the Einstein-Szilard refrigerator pump and his first efforts toward a unified field theory, but began frequently to travel abroad.

The anti-Semitism Einstein found strong in Berlin in December 1919 was rampant in Munich. Pale, thin, thirty-year-old Adolf Hitler sat down that month at the single battered table in the cramped office of the German Workers Party, formerly a taproom, to draft his party's platform. A grotesque wood carving served as inspiration. It would follow its master into history; a touring Australian academic encountered it again in 1936:

> I was being shown round a famous collection of [Nazi] Party relics in Munich. The curator was a mild old man, a student of the old German academic class.

After showing me everything, he led, almost with bated breath, to his *pièce de résistance.* He produced a small sculptured wooden gibbet from which was suspended a brutally realistic figure of a dangling Jew. This piece of humourless sadism, he said, decorated the table at which Hitler founded the Party, seventeen years ago.

His pale blue eyes shining, Hitler read out the twenty-five points of his party's program the following February in the Festsaal of Munich's Hofbräuhaus before nearly two thousand people, the largest crowd the little German Workers Party had yet attracted. "These points of ours," he had shouted in triumph the day he finished drafting them, "are going to rival Luther's placard on the doors of Wittenberg!" All or part of six of them applied specifically to Jews: that Jews were not countrymen "of German blood" and therefore could not be citizens; that only citizens could hold public office or publish German-language newspapers; that no more non-Germans might immigrate into the country and that all non-Germans admitted since the beginning of the Great War should be expelled. The twenty-five points were never officially declared the program of the Nationalsozialistiche Deutsche Arbeiterpartei, the Nazi Party, which the German Workers Party evolved to, but their power was felt nevertheless.

The Beer Hall Putsch on November 8, 1923, delivered Hitler to a comfortable, sunlit cell in Landsberg prison, where he dictated his personal and political testament to his bashful acolyte Rudolf Hess. *Mein Kampf* has much to say about the Jews. Across the nearly seven hundred pages of its two volumes it refers to Jewry more frequently than to any other subject except Marxism—and Hitler considered Marxism a Jewish invention and a Jewish "weapon."

Jews, the future Chancellor of Germany declares in *Mein Kampf*, are "no lovers of water." He "often grew sick to my stomach from [their] smell." Their dress is "unclean," their appearance "generally unheroic." "A foreign people," they have "definite racial characteristics"; they are "inferior being[s]," "vampires" with "poison fangs," "yellow fist[s]" and "repulsive traits." "The personification of the devil as the symbol of all evil assumes the living shape of the Jew."

The attributes of the Jew are legion, Hitler goes on. The Jew is "a garbage separator, splashing his filth in the face of humanity." Or he is a "scribbler . . . who poison[s] men's souls like germ-carriers of the worst sort." Or "the cold-hearted, shameless, and calculating director of this revolting vice traffic in the scum of the big city." "Was there any form of filth or profligacy," Hitler asks rhetorically, ". . . without at least one Jew involved in it? If you cut even cautiously into such an abscess, you found, like a maggot in a rotting body, often dazzled by the sudden light—a kike!"

The Jew is "no German." Jews are a "race of dialectical liars"; a "people which lives only for this earth"; "the great masters of the lie"; "traitors, profiteers, usurers, and swindlers"; a "world hydra"; "a horde of rats." "Alone in this world they would stifle in filth and offal."

"Without any true culture," the Jew is "a *parasite* in the body of other peoples," "a sponger who like a noxious bacillus keeps spreading as soon as a favorable medium invites him." "He lacks idealism in any form." He is an "eternal blood-sucker" of "diabolical purposes," "restrained by no moral scruples," who "poisons the blood of others, but preserves his own." He "systematically ruins women and girls": "With satanic joy on his face, the black-haired Jewish youth lurks in wait for the unsuspecting girl whom he defiles with his blood, thus stealing her from her people." He is "master over bastards and bastards alone" and "it was and is Jews who bring the Negroes into the Rhineland, always with the same secret thought and clear aim of ruining the hated white race by the necessarily resulting bastardization." Syphilis is a "Jewish disease," a "Jewification of our spiritual life and mammonization of our mating instinct [that] will sooner or later destroy our entire offspring." The Jew "makes a mockery of natural feelings, overthrows all concepts of beauty and sublimity, of the noble and the good, and instead drags men down into the sphere of his own base nature." "An apparition in a black caftan and black hair locks," responsible for "spiritual pestilence worse than the Black Death of olden times," the Jew is a "coward," a "plunderer," a "menace," a "foreign element," a "viper," a "tyrant," a "ferment of decomposition."

The sun shines in the wide windows of Hitler's cell at Landsberg. Boyish in lederhosen, he remembers that he was blinded by mustard gas below Ypres. He wrote a poem during the war, a poem out of a dream, before he took shrapnel in the thigh on the Somme, before Ypres:

I often go on bitter nights
To Wotan's oak in the quiet glade
With dark powers to weave a union—
The runic letters the moon makes with its magic spell
And all who are full of impudence during the day
Are made small by the magic formula!

. . . . .

Hitler's testament is almost finished. He dictates, his blanched face tumefying:

> If at the beginning of the War and during the War twelve or fifteen thousand of these Hebrew corrupters of the people had been held under poison gas, as happened to hundreds of thousands of our very best German workers in the field, the sacrifice of millions at the front would not have been in vain.

* * *

The dispersion of the Jewish people from Palestine—the Diaspora—began in the sixth century B.C. when Babylon conquered the southern Palestinian kingdom of Judah, destroyed Solomon's temple and carried a large body of Jews into captivity. By the beginning of the Christian era, under Roman hegemony, Jews had established communities in Egypt, in Greece, around the Mediterranean and on the shores of the Black Sea and there were Jewish slaves with the Roman legions on the Rhine. Conditions worsened again for the Jews when the Empire was Christianized in the fourth century A.D. with the conversion of the Emperor Constantine; Christianity and Judaism competed, in a Darwinian sense, for the same Holy Land and the same holy books. Under systematic persecution only a small remnant of the Jewish people remained in Judea. The fantasy of Jews as a brotherhood of evil was invented during this era when Christianity fought its missionary way to dominance.

In the disorder of the Dark Ages the Jews lost even their vestigial Roman citizenship. Those who sought protection won it from rulers like Charlemagne's son Louis the Pious who knew their worth as merchants and craftsmen, but the price of protection was that they became the ruler's property. Their rights were thus no longer inherent but chartered. Against that threatening insecurity Jews could count their gain of judicial autonomy: within their communities they were allowed to administer their own laws. In parts of Spain they had the power even of life and death.

The medieval Church, challenged by the spread of learning and the militancy of Islam to shore up its defenses against heresy, exercised its increasing power over the Jews balefully. The Lateran Councils of 1179 and 1215 made the baleful conflict visible by denying Jews authority over Christians, denying them Christian servants, relegating moneylending to Jews by forbidding it to Christians, forbidding Christians lodging in Jewish quarters and thus officially sanctioning the establishment of ghettos and, most onerously, requiring every Jew to wear a distinguishing badge—frequently, on local authority, the yellow Magen David that the Nazis later restored. Every Jew who ventured from the ghetto distinctively marked was a painted bird, exposed to attack.

The fantasy of Jews as a brotherhood of evil swelled in medieval times to a full-blown demonology. The Jewish Messiah became the Antichrist. The Jews became sorcerers of Satan who poisoned wells, tortured the consecrated Host and murdered Christian children to collect their blood for diabolic rites. When the Black Death struck in the fourteenth century, a supposedly demonic people who poisoned wells were obvious suspects: they needed only to have infiltrated some more vicious poison into the water supply. A quarter of Europe died of plague, and in that time of horror tens of thousands of Jews were burned, drowned, hanged or buried alive in retaliation. Massacre became endemic; 350 Jewish communities were decimated in German lands alone.

The English were the first to expel the Jews entirely. The Jews of England belonged to the Crown, which had systematically extracted their wealth through a special Exchequer to the Jews. By 1290 it had bled them dry. Edward I thereupon confiscated what little they had left and threw them out. They crossed to France, but expulsion from that country followed in 1392; from Spain, at the demand of the Inquisition, in 1492; from Portugal in 1497. Since Germany was a region of multiple sovereignties, German Jews could not be generally expelled. They had been fleeing eastward from bitter German persecution in any case since the twelfth century.

The Jews expelled from Western Europe fled to Poland, a large and thinly populated kingdom where elected monarchs welcomed them with generous charters. The medieval German of these emigrant Ashkenazim evolved to Yiddish; they founded villages and towns; they dispersed up and down the long eastern Polish frontier and lived in relative peace for two hundred years.

Twenty-five thousand at the end of the fifteenth century had increased at least tenfold by the middle of the seventeenth. Then, in violent wars with Russia and Sweden, Poland began to break up. Cossacks and their peasant allies murdered great numbers of Jews and sacked hundreds of their communities. The Ukraine was split in two; Poland lost the northern half to Russia. War and disorder continued into the eighteenth century with Prussia, Austria and Turkey variously joining battle. When Russia invaded Poland in 1768, Prussia proposed a three-way partition with Austria to forestall a complete takeover. That led to Poland's partial dismemberment in 1772. In 1795, after another Russian invasion, the country was completely partitioned and ceased to exist. (Much truncated, it was revived by the Congress of Vienna in 1814 as Congress Poland, joined to Russia by the linkage of Polish kingship for the Czar.) Its Jewish population had increased by then to more than one million souls. Prussia acquired about 150,000 but promptly expelled them eastward. Austria acquired about 250,000. Russia, which soon controlled more than three-fourths of what had been the Polish commonwealth, then also controlled the fates of most of the Eastern Jews. But while Poland had welcomed them, Russia despised them. Its economy was too primitive to need their commercial skills and it abhorred their religion. To Catherine the Great her one million new subjects were first and foremost "the enemies of Christ."

The enemies of Christ became Russia's "Jewish problem." In Russia's benighted intolerance it framed only two solutions: assimilation (by conversion to Christianity) or expulsion. For the interim it practiced quarantine. A decree of 1791 limited Jewish residence to the formerly Polish territories and the unpopulated steppes above the Black Sea, a region that extended north across 286,000 square miles of central Europe to the Baltic: the Pale of Settlement ("pale" in its old sense of "enclosed by a boundary"). The Ashkenazim numbered one-ninth of the Pale's total population, and might have prospered there, but they were burdened with further restrictions. They were heavily taxed, they could not live in the villages as they had done for generations, they could not keep the village inns or sell liquor to the peasants. Their traditional local governments, the *kehillot*, were stripped of legal authority but required to collect Jewish taxes. More horribly, under Nicholas I after 1825 the *kehillot* were charged to conscript twelve-year-old Jewish children for a lifetime of forced service in the Russian Army—six years of brutal "education" followed by twenty-five years in the ranks—a fate that befell between 40,000 and 50,000 Jewish sons before the requirement was relaxed in 1856. The memory of that cruelty would endure: Edward Teller's grandmother responded to his childhood misbehavior, he reminisced once with a friend, by warning him to be a good boy or the Russians would get him.

While Eastern Jews toiled to survive in Mother Russia, emancipation was proceeding in the West. Small Jewish communities had reestablished themselves, made up partly of nominal converts to Christianity who had escaped Spain and Portugal for Holland and England and America, partly of Eastern returnees. The Austrian emperor Joseph II issued an Edict of Tolerance in 1782.

The edicts of emperors were less important to the political future of the Jewish people than the temper of the Enlightenment with its religious skepticism and its faith in the self-evident rights of man. The time had come in the evolution of European forms of government when no single group or class any longer had the power to dominate all others as the nobility had previously done. The nation-state evolved in part to remove this impasse by investing power in the state itself. Such a mechanism made no distinction between Jew and Christian. American Jews thus became American citizens automatically with the Revolution and the Bill of Rights.

The French, remembering ghettos and expulsions, found the emancipation of the Jews of France more difficult. "The Jews should be denied everything as a nation," the Count of Clermont-Tonnerre argued in the French National Assembly, "but granted everything as individuals. . . . It is intolerable that [they] should become a separate political formation or class in the country. Every one of them must individually become a citizen." When a Jewish community contracted its loyalty to a monarch in exchange for his protection it only did what other medieval classes and orders had done. But the nation-state was secular and it considered the autonomous Jewish theocracies lodged within its borders in secular terms. In secular terms a separate political body, theocratic or not, to which citizens gave their first loyalty was potentially a rival and inherently subversive. Much monstrosity would devolve from that reification. In the meantime Liberty, Equality and Fraternity prevailed and the Jews of France became *citoyens* on a September Tuesday in 1791.

Emancipations as they progressed within less revolutionary states included Holland-Belgium, 1795; Sweden, 1848; Denmark and Greece, 1849; England by a gradual unmuddling completely in 1866; Austria, 1867; Spain by the withdrawal of its 1492 order of expulsion in 1868; the new German Empire, 1871. Though they were influential out of all proportion to their numbers, the emancipated Jews of Western Europe, many of whom moved directly to assimilate, were only a minute fraction of the Diaspora. The preponderance of the Jewish people, increased by 1850 to 2.5 million, by 1900 to 5 million, struggled in increasing misery in the Pale.

At his coronation in 1856, amid remissions and amnesties, Czar Alexander II abolished the special conscription of Jewish children. Other alleviations followed, all designed to encourage Jewish assimilation. "Useful" Jews—wealthy merchants, university graduates, craftsmen and medical assistants—were allowed residence in the interior of Russia, beyond the Pale. The universities were restored to autonomy and Jews allowed to attend. Within the Pale Jews received limited civil rights and became eligible for local councils. But the Czar who freed 30 million peasants from serfdom was dismayed to discover that reform after so many centuries of repression might lead not to expressions of gratitude but to revolutionary agitation and revolt, as it did in Congress Poland in 1863, and the liberalization of Russian life stalled.

Revolutionaries—a splinter group that called itself "The People's Will"—murdered Alexander on March 13, 1881, by lobbing a hail of small bombs into his open carriage in broad daylight on a main street of St. Petersburg as he drove home from reviewing the Imperial Guards. One member of The People's Will, not a bomber, was Jewish; that was pretext enough, in the confused aftermath of regicide, to blame the assassination on the Jews. A wave of pogroms—the curious Russian word refers to a violent riot by one group against another—began that continued until 1884. "Jewish disorders," the dogmatic new Czar, Alexander III, called these murderous raids of drunken mobs on Jewish quarters everywhere in the Pale. They erupted with the active participation or tacit consent of the authorities. More than two hundred Jewish communities were attacked. The first wave of pogroms—there would be more in later decades—left

20,000 Jews homeless and 100,000 ruined. Women were raped, families murdered. The government blamed the violence on anarchists and moved to expel even the "useful" Jews back into the ghettos of the Pale.

With the pogroms came the 1882 May Laws, revising or repealing previous reforms and imposing catastrophic new restrictions. Between 1881 and 1900 more than 1 million Jews emigrated from Russia and central Europe to the United States and another 1.5 million between 1900 and 1920. A much smaller number of emigrants, like Chaim Weizmann, chose Western Europe and England. Most found less opportunity there than their American counterparts and more virulent anti-Semitism.

One of the important sources of German anti-Semitism in the years after the Great War was the strange forgery known as *The Protocols of the Elders of Zion*. Adolf Hitler took the *Protocols* as a text, to the extent that National Socialism had a text, for world domination. "I have read *The Protocols of the Elders of Zion*," Hitler told one of his loyalists; "it simply appalled me. The stealthiness of the enemy, and his ubiquity! I saw at once that we must copy it—in our own way, of course." Heinrich Himmler confirmed that connection: "We owe the art of government to the Jews." To the *Protocols*, he meant, which "the Führer learned by heart."

The *Protocols* were Russian work. They link the Jewish experience in Russia with the Jewish experience in Germany, where so few Jews actually lived—only about 500,000 in 1933, less than 1 percent of the German population. If Russia's hostility to the Jews was rooted in part in religious conflict, German anti-Semitism, by contrast, needed a secular myth. A half-educated apostate autodidact like Hitler especially needed some structure on which to hang his anti-Semitic pathology. German anti-Semitism had plentiful German antecedents—Richard Wagner's foamings were high on Hitler's list—but the *Protocols* happened to arrive at the right time and place to earn a prominent position well forward. In the 1920s and 1930s millions of copies of various translations and editions were sold throughout the world.

The book is cast in the form of lectures and begins in midsentence, its scene unset, as if torn from the evil hands of its perpetrators. To supply the missing background, editors usually bound in explanatory material. A popular preliminary was a chapter from the novel *Biarritz*, the work of a minor German postal official, entitled "In the Jewish Cemetery in Prague." Editors offered this lurid fiction, like the fiction of the *Protocols* themselves, as fact. The historian Norman Cohn summarizes its setting:

> At eleven o'clock the gates of the cemetery creak softly and the rustling of long coats is heard, as they touch against the stones and shrubbery. A vague white figure passes like a shadow through the cemetery until it reaches a cer-

> tain tombstone; here it kneels down, touches the tombstone three times with its forehead and whispers a prayer. Another figure approaches; it is that of an old man, bent and limping; he coughs and sighs as he moves. The figure takes its place next to its predecessor and it too kneels down and whispers a prayer. . . . Thirteen times this procedure is repeated. When the thirteenth and last figure has taken its place a clock strikes midnight. From the grave there comes a sharp, metallic sound. A blue flame appears and lights up the thirteen kneeling figures. A hollow voice [the thirteenth figure] says, "I greet you, heads of the twelve tribes of Israel." It is the Devil speaking; and the figures dutifully reply, "We greet you, son of the accursed."

The *Protocols* follow. They are twenty-four in all—some eighty pages in book form. "What I am about to set forth, then," explains the speaker at the beginning of the first Protocol, "is our system from the two points of view, that of ourselves and that of the *goyim*." Much about the system set forth is incoherent, but the *Protocols* elaborate three main themes: a bitter attack on liberalism, the political methods of the Jewish world conspiracy and an outline of the world government the Elders expect soon to install.

The attack on liberalism would be comical if the *Protocols* had not found such vicious use. Liberalism "produced Constitutional States . . . and a constitution, as you well know, is nothing else but a school of discords, misunderstandings, quarrels, disagreements, fruitless party agitations, party whims. . . . We replaced the ruler by a caricature of a government—by a president, taken from the mob, from the midst of our puppet creatures, our slaves." A touching loyalty to the Russian *ancien régime* surfaces from time to time and must have given European readers pause:

> The principal guarantee of stability of rule is to confirm the aureole of power, and this aureole is attained only by such a majestic inflexibility of might as shall carry on its face the emblems of inviolability from mystical causes—from the choice of God. Such was, until recent times, the Russian autocracy, the one and only serious foe we had in the world, without counting the Papacy.

In brief, the Elders have stage-managed the invention and dissemination of modern ideas—of the modern world. Everything more recent than the Russian imperial system of czar, landed nobility and serfs is part and parcel of their diabolical work. Which helps explain how so obscure a study as physics came in Germany in the 1920s to be counted part of the Jewish conspiracy.

The Elders work to establish a world autocracy ruled by a leader who is a "patriarchial paternal" guardian. Liberalism will be rooted out, the masses led away from politics, censorship strict, freedom of the press abolished. A third of the population will be recruited for amateur spying ("It will then be no disgrace to be a spy and informer, but a merit") and a vast secret police will keep order. All these were Nazi strategies, and certainly Hitler's debt to the *Protocols* is evident in *Mein Kampf* and explicitly acknowledged.

Russia's contribution to German anti-Semitism was plagiarized from a work of political satire, *Dialogues from Hell Between Montesquieu and Machiavelli*, written by a French lawyer, Maurice Joly, and first published in Brussels in 1864. Montesquieu speaks for liberalism, Machiavelli for despotism. The concoction of the *Protocols* was probably the work of the head of the czarist secret police outside Russia, a Paris-based agent named Pyotr Ivanovich Rachkovsky. Borrowing and paraphrasing Machiavelli's speeches without even bothering to change their order and attributing them to a secret Jewish council, Rachkovsky was attempting to discredit Russian liberalism by showing it to be a Jewish plot. A St. Petersburg newspaper serialized the earliest version of the *Protocols* in 1903. It was one of three books belonging to the Czarina Alexandra Feodorovna—the other two were the Bible and *War and Peace*—found among her possessions at Ekaterinburg after the murder of the imperial family by Communist revolutionaries on July 17, 1918.

That coincidence returned the *Protocols* west. Fyodor Vinberg, who arranged the German translation and publication of the *Protocols* in Berlin in 1920, was a colonel in the Imperial Guard. The Czarina had been an honorary colonel of his regiment and he had worshiped her. He escaped to Germany at the end of the Great War convinced that her murderers had been Jews. Thereafter revenge on the Jews was the central fixation of his life. He was a friend to Hitler's advisers, particularly the Nazi Party "philosopher," Russian-born Alfred Rosenberg, who published a study of the *Protocols* in 1923.

The fiction of a Jewish world conspiracy had practical value for the Nazi Party. As it had done for earlier anti-Semitic parties, writes Hannah Arendt, who was on the scene as a student in Berlin in the 1920s, it "gave them the advantage of a domestic program, and conditions were such that one had to enter the arena of social struggle in order to win political power. They could pretend to fight the Jews exactly as the workers were fighting the bourgeoisie. Their advantage was that by attacking the Jews, who were believed to be the secret power behind governments, they could openly attack the state itself."

The fiction also served for propaganda, to reassure the German people: if the Jews could dominate the world, then so could the Aryans. Arendt continues: "Thus the Protocols presented world conquest as a practical possibility, implied that the whole affair was only a question of inspired or shrewd know-how, and that nobody stood in the way of a German victory over the entire world but a patently small people, the Jews, who ruled it without possessing instruments of violence—an easy opponent, therefore, once their secret was discovered and their method emulated on a larger scale."

But the scurrilities of *Mein Kampf*, which on the evidence of their incoherence are not calculated manipulations but violent emotional outbursts, demonstrate that Hitler pathologically feared and hated the Jews. In black megalomania he masked an intelligent, industrious and much-persecuted people with the distorted features of his own terror. And that would make all the difference.

A German journalist had the temerity in 1931 to ask Adolf Hitler where he would find the brains to run the country if he took it over. Hitler snapped that *he* would be the brains but went on contemptuously to enlist the help of the German class that still resisted voting the Nazis into power:

> Do you think perhaps that, in the event of a successful revolution along the lines of my party, we would not inherit the brains in droves? Do you believe that the German middle class, this flower of the intelligentsia, would refuse to serve us and place their minds at our disposal? The German middle class would take its stand on the famed ground of the accomplished fact; we will do what we like with the middle class.

But what about the Jews, the journalist persisted—those talented people, war heroes among them, Einstein among them? "Everything they have created has been stolen from us," Hitler charged. "Everything that they know will be used against us. They should just go and foment their unrest among other peoples. We do not need them."

At noon on January 30, 1933, Adolf Hitler, forty-three years old, gleefully accepted appointment as Chancellor of Germany. With the Reichstag fire and the subsequent suspension of constitutional liberties, with the Enabling Act of March 23 by which the Reichstag voluntarily gave over its powers to the Hitler cabinet, the Nazis began to consolidate their control. They moved immediately to legalize anti-Semitism and abolish the civil rights of German Jews. Meeting at his country retreat in Berchtesgaden with Joseph Goebbels, now his propaganda minister, Hitler decided on a boycott of Jewish businesses as an opening sally. The national boycott began on Saturday, April 1. Already during the previous week Jewish judges and lawyers had been dismissed from practice in Prussia and Bavaria. Now newspapers conveniently published business addresses and teams of Nazi storm troopers stationed themselves at storefronts to direct the mobs. Jews caught in the streets were beaten while the police looked on. The boycott was a nationwide German pogrom and it lasted through a violent weekend.

A month earlier, the evening after the Reichstag fire, Wolfgang Pauli had dropped in on a Göttingen group that included Edward Teller. The group had discussed Germany's political situation and Pauli had declared emphatically that the idea of a German dictatorship was *Quatsch*, Pauli's favorite dismissal: rubbish, mush, nonsense. "I have seen dictatorship in Russia," he told them. "In Germany it just couldn't happen." In Hamburg Otto Frisch had mustered similar optimism, as indeed had many Germans. "I didn't take Hitler at all seriously at first," Frisch told an interviewer later. "I had the feeling, 'Well, chancellors come and chancellors go, and he will be no worse than the rest of them.' Then things began to change." The Third Reich promulgated its first anti-Jewish ordinance on April 7. The Law for the Restoration of the Professional Civil Service, the harbinger of some four hundred anti-Semitic laws and decrees the Nazis would issue, changed Teller's life, Pauli's, Frisch's, the lives of their colleagues decisively, forever. It announced bluntly that "civil servants of non-Aryan descent must retire." A decree defining "non-Aryan" followed on April 11: anyone "descended from non-Aryan, especially Jewish, parents or grandparents." Universities were state institutions. Members of their faculties were therefore civil servants. The new law abruptly stripped a quarter of the physicists of Germany, including eleven who had earned or would earn Nobel Prizes, of their positions and their livelihood. It immediately affected some 1,600 scholars in all. Nor were academics dismissed by the Reich likely to find other work. To survive they would have to emigrate.

Some had already left, among them Einstein and the older Hungarians. Einstein read the signs correctly because he was Einstein and because he had borne the brunt of the attack since immediately after the war; the Hungarians had become connoisseurs by now of advancing fascism.

Theodor von Kármán departed first, from Aachen. He had pioneered aeronautical physics; the California Institute of Technology, then vigorously assembling its future reputation, wanted to include that specialty in its curriculum. Aviation philanthropist Daniel Guggenheim was prevailed upon to contribute. The Guggenheim Aeronautical Laboratory, with a ten-foot wind tunnel, began operation under von Kármán's direction in 1930.

Caltech also courted Einstein. So did Oxford and Columbia, but he was attracted to the cosmological work of the dean of Caltech graduate studies, a Massachusetts-born physicist of Quaker background named Richard Chace Tolman. Ongoing observations at Mount Wilson Observatory, above Pasadena, might confirm the last of the three original predictions of the general theory of relativity, the gravitational red-shifting of the light of high-density stars. Tolman sent a delegation to Berlin; Einstein agreed to visit Pasadena in 1931 as a research associate.

He did, twice, returning to Berlin between, dining in Southern California with Charlie Chaplin, viewing a rough cut of Sergei Eisenstein's death-obsessed film *Que Viva Mexico!* with its sponsor Upton Sinclair. As his second visit approached, in December, Einstein was ready to reassess his future: "I decided today," he wrote in his diary, "that I shall essentially give up my Berlin position and shall be a bird of passage for the rest of my life."

The bird of passage was not to nest in Pasadena. Abraham Flexner, the American educator, sought out Einstein at Caltech. Flexner was in the process of founding a new institution, not yet located or named, chartered in 1930 with a $5 million endowment. The two men strolled for most of an hour up and down the halls of the club where Einstein was staying. They met again at Oxford in May and once more at the Einsteins' summer house at Caputh, outside Berlin, in June. "We sat then on the veranda and talked until evening," Flexner recalled, "when Einstein invited me to stay to supper. After supper we talked until almost eleven. By that time it was perfectly clear that Einstein and his wife were prepared to come to America." They walked together to the bus stop. "*Ich bin Feuer und Flamme dafür,*" Einstein told his guest as he put him on the bus: "I am fire and flame for it." The Institute for Advanced Study would be established in Princeton, New Jersey. Einstein was its first great acquisition. He had suggested a salary of $3,000 a year. His wife and Flexner negotiated a more respectable $15,000. It was what Caltech had been prepared to pay. But at Caltech, as in Zurich before, Einstein would have been expected to teach. At the Institute for Advanced Study his only responsibility was thought.

The Einsteins left Caputh in December 1932, scheduled to divide the coming year between Princeton and Berlin. Einstein knew better. "Turn around," he told his wife as they stepped off the porch of their house. "You will never see it again." She thought his pessimism foolish.

In mid-March the Nazi SA searched the empty house for hidden weapons. By then Einstein had spoken out publicly against Hitler and was returning to Europe to prepare to move. He settled temporarily at a resort town on the Belgian coast, Le Coq sur Mer, with his wife, his two stepdaughters, his secretary, his assistant and two Belgian guards: assassination threatened again. In Berlin his son-in-law arranged to have his furniture packed. The French obligingly transported his personal papers to Paris by diplomatic pouch. At the end of March 1933 the most original physicist of the twentieth century once again renounced his German citizenship.

Princeton University acquired John von Neumann and Eugene Wigner in 1930, in Wigner's puckish recollection, as a package deal. The university sought advice on improving its science from Paul Ehrenfest, who "recommended to them not to invite a single person but at least two . . . who already knew each other, who wouldn't feel suddenly put on an island where they have no intimate contact with anybody. Johnny's name was of course well known by that time the world over, so they decided to invite Johnny von Neumann. They looked: who wrote articles with John von Neumann? They found: Mr. Wigner. So they sent a telegram to me also." In fact, Wigner had already earned a high reputation in a recondite area of physics known as group theory, about which he published a book in 1931. He accepted the invitation to Princeton to look it over and perhaps to look America over as well. "There was no question in the mind of any person that the days of foreigners [in Germany], particularly with Jewish ancestry, were numbered. . . . It was so obvious that you didn't have to be perceptive. . . . It was like, 'Well, it will be colder in December.' Yes, it will be. We know it well."

Leo Szilard in Berlin debated his future in a musing letter to Eugene Wigner written on October 8, 1932. He was apparently still trying to organize his Bund: the knowledge had got into his blood that he had work to accomplish at the moment more noble than science, he wrote—bad luck, it couldn't be distilled out again. He understood he wasn't allowed to complain if such work commanded no office space in the world. He was considering a professorship in experimental physics in India since it would be essentially only a teaching post and he could therefore turn his creative energies elsewhere. Only the gods knew what might be available in Europe or on the American coast between Washington and Boston, places he might prefer, so he perforce might go to India. In any case, until he found a position he would at least be free to do science without feeling guilty.

Szilard promised to write Wigner again when he had an "actual program." He did not yet know that his actual program would be organizing the desperate rescue. He parked his bags at the Harnack House in Dahlem and sat down with Lise Meitner to talk about doing nuclear physics at the Kaiser Wilhelm Institute. She had Hahn, and Hahn was superb, but he was a chemist. She could use a jack-of-all-trades like Szilard. But the collaboration was not to be. Events moved too quickly. Szilard took his train from Berlin, the train that proved him, if not more clever than most people, at least a day earlier. That was "close to the first of April, 1933."

If Pauli, safe behind the lines in Zurich, had misread events before, he was clear enough once the new law was announced. Walter Elsasser, among the first to leave, chose neutral Switzerland, entrained for Zurich and homed on the physics building at the Polytechnic. "On entering the main door of this building one faces a broad and straight staircase leading directly to the second floor. Before I could take my first step on it, there appeared at the top of the stairs the moon-face of Wolfgang Pauli, who shouted down: 'Elsasser,' he said, 'you are the first to come up these stairs; I can see how in the months to come there will be many, many more to climb up here.' " The idea of a German dictatorship was no longer *Quatsch.*

Longstanding anti-Semitic discrimination in academic appointments weighted the civil service law dismissals in favor of the natural sciences, fields of study that had evolved more recently than the older disciplines of the liberal arts, that German scholarship had looked down upon as "materialistic" and that had therefore proved less impenetrable to Jews. Medicine incurred 423 dismissals, physics 106, mathematics 60—in the physical and biological sciences other than medicine, an immediate total of 406 scientists. The University of Berlin and the University of Frankfurt each lost a third of its faculty.

The promising young theoretical physicist Hans Bethe, then at Tübingen, first heard of his dismissal from one of his students, who wrote him to say he read of it in the papers and wondered what he should do. Bethe thought the question impertinent—it was he who had been dismissed, not the student—and asked for a copy of the news story. Hans Geiger was professor of experimental physics at Tübingen at the time, having moved there from Berlin. When Bethe joined the faculty as a theoretician in November 1932, "Geiger explained his experiments to me, and in other ways made a lot of me, so all seemed to be well on the personal level." Sensibly, then, Bethe wrote the vacationing Geiger for advice. "He wrote back a completely cold letter saying that with the changed situation it would be necessary to dispense with my further services—period. There was no kind word, no regret—nothing." A few days later the official notice arrived.

Bethe at twenty-seven was sturdy, indefatigable, a skier and mountain climber, exceptionally self-confident in physics if still socially diffident. His eyes were blue, his features Germanic; his thick, dark-brown hair, cut short, stood up on his head like a brush. His custom of plowing through difficulties eventually won Bethe comparison with a battleship, except that this particularly equable vessel usually boomed with laughter. He had already published important work.

Born in Strasbourg on July 2, 1906, Bethe moved during childhood to Kiel and then to Frankfurt as his father, a university physiologist, achieved increasing academic success. He did not think of himself as a Jew: "I was not Jewish. My mother was Jewish, and until Hitler came that made no difference whatever." His father's background was Protestant and Prussian; his mother was the daughter of a Strasbourg professor of medicine. He counted two Jewish grandparents, more than enough to trigger the Tübingen dismissal.

Bethe began university studies at Frankfurt in 1924. Two years later, recognizing his gift for theoretical work, his adviser sent him to Arnold Sommerfeld in Munich. Sommerfeld had trained nearly a third of the full professors of theoretical physics in the German-speaking world; his protégés included Max von Laue, Wolfgang Pauli and Werner Heisenberg. The American chemist Linus Pauling came to work with Sommerfeld while Bethe was there, as did the German Rudolf Peierls and Americans Edward U. Condon and I. I. Rabi. Edward Teller arrived from Karlsruhe in 1928, but before the relationship between the two young men could develop into friendship Teller was incapacitated in a streetcar accident, his right foot severed just above the ankle. By the time the amputation healed, Sommerfeld had gone off on a sixtieth-birthday trip around the world, leaving Bethe, who had just passed his doctoral examinations, to look for a job on his own; missing Sommerfeld, Teller chose to move on to Leipzig to study with Heisenberg. Bethe went to the Cavendish on a Rockefeller Fellowship, then to Rome, before accepting appointment at Tübingen.

Since Geiger refused to help challenge his Tübingen dismissal, Bethe appealed to Munich. "Sommerfeld immediately replied, 'You are most welcome here. I will have your fellowship again for you. Just come back.' " After a time in Munich Bethe was invited to Manchester, then to Copenhagen to work with Bohr. In the summer of 1934 Cornell University offered him an assistant professorship. One of his former students, now on the Ithaca physics faculty, had recommended him for the post. He accepted and shipped for America, arriving in early February 1935.

Teller took his Ph.D. under Heisenberg at Leipzig in 1930, stayed on there for another year as a research associate, then shifted to Göttingen to work in its Institute for Physical Chemistry. "His early papers," Eugene Wigner writes, "were entirely in the spirit of the times: the expanding world of the applications of quantum mechanics." Teller probed the more developed part of physics—chemical and molecular physics—with vigorous originality, producing some thirty papers between 1930 and 1936, most of them written with collaborators because he was sloppy at calculation and impatient with the detailed effort of following through.

"It was a foregone conclusion that I had to leave," Teller remembers. "After all, not only was I a Jew, I was not even a German citizen. I wanted to be a scientist. The possibility to remain a scientist in Germany and to have any chance of continuing to work had vanished with the coming of Hitler. I had to leave, as many others did, as soon as I could." The director of his institute, Arnold Eucken, "an old German nationalist," confirmed Teller's conclusion as they left on the same southbound train for spring vacation in March 1933. "I really want you here," Teller remembers Eucken equivocating, "but with this new situation, there is no point in your staying. I would like to help you, but you have no future in Germany." The problem then was where to go. Back in Göttingen after a tense confrontation with his parents in Budapest—they wanted him to stay in Hungary—Teller sat down to apply for a Rockefeller Fellowship to Copenhagen to work with Bohr.

In Hamburg Otto Frisch decided he would have to take Hitler seriously after all. Frisch, a personable young experimentalist with a gift for ingenious invention, worked for Otto Stern, the tubby Galician who apprenticed under Einstein and who had barked at Ernest Lawrence four years previously to get busy on his notion of a cyclotron. Stern was "quite shocked," Frisch writes, "to find that I was of Jewish origin, just as was he himself and another two of his four collaborators. He would have to leave and the three of us as well," although "the University of Hamburg—with the traditions of a Free Hansa city—was very reluctant to put the racial laws into effect, and I wasn't sacked until several months after the other universities had toed the line."

Before the Nazis promulgated the civil service law Frisch had applied for, and won, a Rockefeller Fellowship to work with Enrico Fermi in Rome. The program was designed to free promising young scientists from their immediate duties for a year of research abroad, after which they were expected to return to duty again. At a time of crisis the foundation unfortunately chose to enforce its rules narrowly. Frisch was soon "very disappointed and at first rather disgusted when [the foundation] told me that, the situation having changed because of the Hitler laws, they had to withdraw [their] offer of a grant because I no longer had a job to come back to."

In the meantime Bohr turned up in Hamburg. He was traveling throughout Germany to determine who needed help. "To me it was a great experience," Frisch writes, "to be suddenly confronted with Niels Bohr—an almost legendary name for me—and to see him smile at me like a kindly father; he took me by my waistcoat button and said: 'I hope you will come and work with us sometime; we like people who can carry out "thought experiments"!' " (Frisch had recently verified the prediction of quantum theory that an atom recoils when it emits a photon, a movement previously considered too slight to measure.) "That night I wrote home to my mother . . . and told her not to worry: the Good Lord himself had taken me by my waistcoat button and smiled at me. That was exactly how I felt."

Stern, secure personally in independent wealth and international reputation, set out to find places for his people. "Stern said he would go traveling," continues Frisch, "and see if he could sell his Jewish collaborators—I mean find places for them. And he said he would try to sell me to Madame Curie. So I said, 'Well, do what you can. I'll be very grateful for anything you can do. Just sell me to whoever wants to have me.' And when he came back [from visiting laboratories abroad] he said that Madame Curie had not bought me, but Blackett had." Patrick Maynard Stuart Blackett, London-born, tall, a Navy man, with a lean, vigorous face, was one of Rutherford's protégés and a future laureate. He had just departed the Cavendish for a workingmen's college in London, Birkbeck, after a furious argument over the extent of the Cavendish teaching load. "If physics laboratories have to be run dictatorially," Blackett had sworn, emerging white-faced from Rutherford's office, "I would rather be my own dictator." Birkbeck was a night school; experimenters could work at peace all day, except when Blackett's automatic cloud chamber, triggered by a passing cosmic ray, went off like a cannon in their midst. It was temporary duty. Frisch took it. When the appointment ran out the following year he crossed the North Sea to Copenhagen to work with the Good Lord.

He had the comfort of knowing that for the immediate future his aunt was safe. Lise Meitner was forbidden as of the following September to lecture at the University of Berlin, but because her citizenship was Austrian rather than German she was allowed to continue her work at the KWI. She had a subterfuge to confess, however. When Hahn, who had been lecturing on radiochemistry that spring at Cornell, returned hurriedly to salvage what he could from the wreckage of the Institutes' staff, Meitner sought him out. Her nephew explains:

> Lise Meitner had always kept quiet about her Jewish connection. She had never felt that she was in any way related to Jewish tradition. Although she was, racially speaking, a complete Jew, she had been baptized in her infancy and had never considered herself as anything but a Protestant who happened to have Jewish ancestors. And when all this [anti-Semitic] trouble began she felt, perhaps partly to let sleeping dogs lie and partly not to embarrass her friends, that she would keep quiet about it. It was rather an embarrassment when Hitler forced it all out into the open, so to say, and she had to go and tell Hahn, "You know, I am really Jewish and I am apt to be an embarrassment to you."

At Göttingen the Nobel laureate James Franck, a physical chemist, had a talk with Niels Bohr. Though Franck was Jewish, he was exempt from the civil service law because he had fought at the front in the Great War. He was no less outraged. The problem was deciding what to do. He listened to many people, but he told a friend long afterward that it was Bohr who persuaded him: Bohr insisted that individuals really were responsible for the political actions of their societies. Franck was director of Göttingen's Second Physical Institute. He resigned in protest on April 17 and made sure the newspapers knew.

Max Born shared Franck's convictions and admired his courage but disliked public confrontation. Placed on indefinite "leave of absence" as of April 25, but hearing from the university curator that arrangements might eventually be made to reinstate him, Born responded brusquely that he wanted no special treatment. "We decided to leave Germany at once," he writes. The Borns had already rented an apartment in an Alpine valley town for the summer; they slipped the possession date forward and went early. "Thus we left for the South Tyrol at the beginning of May." He passed the news to Einstein via Leiden. "Ehrenfest sent me your letter," Einstein responded on May 30 from Oxford, which was courting him. "I am glad that you have resigned your positions (you and Franck). Thank God there is no risk involved for either of you. But my heart aches at the thought of the young ones."

The young ones—the scientists and scholars just beginning to establish themselves, as yet unpublished, without international reputation—needed more than informal arrangements. They needed organized support.

Leo Szilard's early train delivered him to Vienna, where he put up at the Regina Hotel. The news of the Law for the Restoration of the Professional Civil Service reached him there, probably in the lobby, and he read the first list of dismissals. That outrage sent him into the street to walk. He encountered an old friend from Berlin, Jacob Marshack, an econometrician. Szilard insisted they had to do something to help. Together they went to see Gottfried Kuhnwald—"the old, hunchbacked Jewish adviser of the Christian Social party," a Szilard admirer explains. "Kuhnwald was a mysterious and shrewd man, very Austrian, with sideburns like Franz Josef. He agreed at once that there would be a great expulsion. He said that when it happened, the French would pray for the victims, the British would organize their rescue, and the Americans would pay for it."

Kuhnwald sent the conspirators to a German economist then visiting Vienna. He advised them in turn that Sir William Beveridge, the director of the London School of Economics, was also visiting Vienna at that time, working on the history of prices, and was registered at the Regina. Szilard bearded the Englishman in his room and found he had not yet thought further than the modest charity of appointing one dismissed economist to the school. That response was at least three orders of magnitude too timid for Szilard's taste and he prepared to assault Sir William with the truth.

Kuhnwald, Beveridge and Szilard met for tea and Szilard read out the list of academic dismissals. Beveridge then agreed, Szilard's admirer writes, "that as soon as he got back to England and got through the most important things on his agenda, he would try to form a committee to find places for the academic victims of Nazism; and he suggested that Szilard should come to London and occasionally prod him. If he prodded him long enough and frequently enough, he would probably be able to do something."

The busy economist required very little prodding. Szilard followed him to London and on a weekend at Cambridge in May Beveridge convinced Ernest Rutherford to head an Academic Assistance Council. The council announced itself on May 22, proposing "to provide a clearing house and centre of information" and to "seek to raise a fund." Among the distinguished academics who signed the announcement besides Beveridge and Rutherford were J. S. Haldane, Gilbert Murray, A. E. Housman, J. J. Thomson, G. M. Trevelyan and John Maynard Keynes.

At about the same time a similar response was building in the United States. John Dewey helped assemble a Faculty Fellowship Fund at Columbia University. There were other immediate private initiatives such as the hiring of Hans Bethe at Cornell. The major U.S. effort, the Emergency Committee in Aid of Displaced German Scholars, was organized under the auspices of the Institute for International Education.

Szilard beat the bushes that summer. He did not feel he could properly represent the Academic Assistance Council (though he ran its office for the month of August as an upaid volunteer), so he traveled and worked to coordinate existing groups and start new ones. A "long and satisfactory interview" early in May with Chaim Weizmann elicited support from English Jewry. Einstein had thought of creating a "university for exiles"; Szilard, working through Léon Rosenfeld, convinced him to devote his prestige to the common effort instead. In Switzerland he nudged the International Students' Service and the Intellectual Cooperation Section of the League of Nations; in Holland he nudged a nervous and disorganized Ehrenfest, who had a small fund available to support visiting theoretical physicists. The university rectors in Belgium were "sympathetic," Szilard reported back to Beveridge, but "war reminiscences make it difficult to establish in Belgium any organization for the helping of German scientists."

The Bohrs coordinated their own exhausting efforts with Szilard's. Bohr convened his usual summer conference in Copenhagen, but this time, writes Otto Frisch, "he proposed to use [it] as a sort of labour exchange." Frisch found it "a confusing affair, with so many people and so little time to sort them out."

It was Bohr with whom Edward Teller had hoped to work when he applied in Göttingen for a Rockefeller Fellowship. The foundation denied him an award on the same grounds it had removed Otto Frisch's: because he had no place of employment to return to. James Franck and Max Born interceded on Teller's behalf with the English, and shortly there arrived not one but two offers of temporary appointments. Teller accepted an assistantship in physics at University College, London. From there, at the beginning of 1934, with the Rockefeller to secure him, he shifted to Copenhagen.

Szilard had help from an American, a Columbia University man, a physicist named Benjamin Liebowitz who had invented a new kind of shirt collar and established himself in the business of shirt manufacturing. At forty-two, Liebowitz was seven years older than Szilard. The two men had met when Szilard had visited the United States briefly in early 1932 and had renewed their acquaintance afterward in Berlin. Like Szilard, Liebowitz had taken up unpaid relief work. The two threw in together, the New Yorker supplying Szilard with a useful American connection. Liebowitz characterized the German situation vividly in a letter back to New York in early May:

> It is impossible to describe the utter despair of all classes of Jews in Germany. The thoroughness with which they are being hounded out and stopped short in their careers is appalling. Unless help comes from the outside, there is no outlook for thousands, perhaps hundreds of thousands, except starvation or [suicide]. It is a gigantic "cold pogrom" and it is not only against Jews; Communists of course are included, but are not singled out racially; Social Democrats and Liberals generally are now or are coming under the ban, especially if they protest in the least against the Nazi movement. . . .
>
> Dr. Leo Szilard . . . proved to be the best prognosticator—he was able to foresee events better than anybody else I know. Weeks before the storm broke he began to formulate plans to provide some means of helping the scientists and scholars of Germany.

Szilard was becoming nervous about his own lack of anchorage. He had not, he wrote another friend in August, "dismissed the idea of going to India, neither has this idea grown stronger." He was not opposed to America, but he would very much prefer to live in England. Although he was "rather tired," he felt "very happy in England." His happiness darkened to gloom as soon as he looked ahead: "It is quite probable that Germany will rearm and I do not believe that this will be stopped by intervention of other powers within the next years. Therefore it is likely to have in a few years two heavily armed antagonistic groups in Europe, and the consequence will be that we shall get war automatically, probably against the wish of either of the parties."

That prepared him for that cool, humid, dull day in September when he would step off the Southampton Row curb and begin to shape the things to come.

Einstein crossed the Channel to England for the last time on September 9 and came under the flamboyant protection of a Naval Air Service commander, barrister and M.P. named Oliver Stillingfleet Locker-Lampson, who had the peculiar distinction of having been invited, while serving under the Grand Duke Nicholas of Russia, to murder Rasputin, an invitation which uncharacteristic discretion led him to decline. Locker-Lampson sent the distinguished physicist off the next morning to a vacation house isolated on moorlands on the east coast of England. Einstein had left Belgium at his wife's insistence: she feared for his life. While she organized their emigration he settled in at Roughton Heath, walking the moors "talking to the goats," he said. There he learned of the suicide of Paul Ehrenfest, one of his oldest and closest friends, on September 25; Ehrenfest had tried to kill his youngest son and blinded him and then killed himself.

The largest public event of the rescue was a mass meeting in Royal Albert Hall, the great circular auditorium in London below Kensington Gardens. Einstein was the featured speaker and therefore all the hall's ten thousand seats were filled and the aisles crowded. Ernest Rutherford came down from Cambridge to chair the event. Afterward Einstein packed his bags and left for America, joining his wife on the *Westernland* when it stopped at Southampton on its way from Antwerp to New York, on October 7.

The mass meeting had been meant to raise money. It raised very little. Cambridge physicist P. B. Moon remembers Rutherford's frustration:

> He did a very great deal for the refugees from Hitler's Germany, finding places for some of them in his laboratory and scraping together what money he could to keep them and their families going until they could find established posts. He told me that one of them had come to him and said he had discovered something or other. "I stopped him short and said 'plenty of people know that,' but you know, Moon, these chaps are living on the smell of an oil rag. They've *got* to push themselves forward."

With the possible exception of French prayer, in fact, Gottfried Kuhnwald's shrewd prediction held true for the first two years of the rescue effort: the British alone nearly equaled the rest of the world in temporary appointments, and American contributions, largely from foundations like the Rockefeller, matched the rest dollar for dollar. Then, as the Depression began to ease and the English academic system pinched, emigration increased to the United States. Under official Emergency Committee auspices thirty scientists and scholars arrived in 1933, thirty-two in 1934, only fifteen in 1935; but forty-three came in 1938, ninety-seven in 1939, fifty-nine in 1940, fifty in 1941. Nor were many of these physicists: with their international network of friendships and acquaintances the physicists were better able than most to provide for each other. About one hundred refugee physicists emigrated to the United States between 1933 and 1941.

Princeton, Einstein reported to his friend Elizabeth, the Queen of Belgium, "is a wonderful little spot, a quaint and ceremonious village of puny demigods on stilts. Yet, by ignoring certain social conventions, I have been able to create for myself an atmosphere conducive to study and free from distraction." Wigner noticed that von Neumann "fell in love with America on the first day. He thought: these are sane people who don't talk in these traditional terms which are meaningless. To a certain extent the materialism of the United States, which was greater than that of Europe, appealed to him." When Stanislaw Ulam arrived in Princeton in 1935 he found von Neumann comfortably ensconced in a "large and impressive house. A black servant let me in." The von Neumanns gave two or three parties a week. "These were not completely carefree," Ulam notes; "the shadow of coming world events pervaded the social atmosphere." Ulam's own enthusiasm for America, formulated a few years later when he was a Junior Fellow at Harvard, was tempered with a criticism of the extreme weather: "I used to tell my friends that the United States was like the little child in a fairy tale, at whose birth all the good fairies came bearing gifts, and only one failed to come. It was the one bringing the climate."

Leopold Infeld, riding the train through New Jersey from New York to Princeton, "was astonished at so many wooden houses; in Europe they are looked down upon as cheap substitutes which do not, like brick, resist the attack of passing time." Inevitably on that passage he noticed "old junked cars, piles of scrap iron." At Princeton the campus was deserted. He found a hotel and asked where all the students had gone. Perhaps to see Notre Dame, the clerk said. "Was I crazy?" Infeld asked himself. "Notre Dame is in Paris. Here is Princeton with empty streets. What does it all mean?" He soon found out. "Suddenly the whole atmosphere changed. It happened in a discontinuous way, in a split second. Cars began to run, crowds of people streamed through the streets, noisy students shouted and sang." Infeld arrived on a Saturday; in those days Princeton played Notre Dame at football.

His first night in the New World, Hans Bethe walked all over New York.

A chemist, Kurt Mendelssohn, vividly recalled the morning after his escape: "When I woke up the sun was shining in my face. I had slept deeply, soundly and long—for the first time in many weeks. [The previous night] I had arrived in London and gone to bed without fear that at 3 a.m. a car with a couple of S.A. men would draw up and take me away."

Before it is science and career, before it is livelihood, before even it is family or love, freedom is sound sleep and safety to notice the play of morning sun.

8

Stirring and Digging

The seventh Solvay Conference, held in Brussels in late October 1933, was George Gamow's ticket of escape from a Soviet Union rapidly becoming inhospitable to theoretical physicists who persisted in modern views. The previous summer the tall, blond, powerfully built Odessan and his wife Rho, also a physicist, had tried to escape by paddling a faltboat—a collapsible rubber kayak—170 miles south from the Crimea to Turkey across the Black Sea without benefit of a weather report. They took a pocket compass, carefully hoarded hard-boiled eggs, cooking chocolate, two bottles of brandy and a bag of fresh strawberries, set out in the morning ostensibly on a recreational excursion and paddled hard all day and into the night. The only document they carried was Gamow's Danish motorcycle-driver's license, souvenir of the 1930 winter he spent in Copenhagen after working with Rutherford at the Cavendish. Gamow planned to show the Turks the document, announce himself in Danish to be a Dane, head for the nearest Danish consulate and put himself long-distance in Bohr's capable hands. But the Black Sea is named for its storms. The wind thwarted the Gamows' escape, drenching them in heavy seas, exhausting them through a long, cold night and finally blowing them back to shore.

Back in Leningrad the following year Gamow received notice from his government that he was officially delegated to the Solvay Conference. "I could not believe my eyes," he writes in his autobiography. It was an easy way out of the country—except that Rho had not been included. Gamow determined to acquire a second passport or defiantly stay home. Through the Bolshevik economist Nikolai Bukharin, whom he knew, he arranged an interview with Party Chairman Vyacheslav Molotov at the Kremlin. Molotov wondered that the theoretician could not live for two weeks without his wife. Gamow feigned camaraderie:

> "You see," I said, "to make my request persuasive I should tell you that my wife, being a physicist, acts as my scientific secretary, taking care of papers, notes, and so on. So I cannot attend a large congress like that without her help. But this is not true. The point is that she has never been abroad, and after Brussels I want to take her to Paris to see the Louvre, the *Folies Bergère*, and so forth, and to do some shopping."

That Molotov understood. "I don't think this will be difficult to arrange," he told Gamow.

When the time arrived to collect the passports Gamow found that Molotov had changed his mind, preferring not to set an awkward precedent. Gamow stubbornly refused to cooperate. The passport office called him three times to pick up his passport and three times he insisted he would wait until there were two. The fourth time "the voice on the telephone informed me that both passports were ready. And indeed they were!" (After the conference the young defectors sailed to America. Gamow taught at the University of Michigan's summer school in pleasant Ann Arbor and from there moved to accept a professorship at George Washington University in Washington, D.C.)

The Solvay Conference, devoted for the first time to nuclear physics, drew men and women from the highest ranks of two generations: Marie Curie, Rutherford, Bohr, Lise Meitner among the older physicists; Heisenberg, Pauli, Enrico Fermi, Chadwick (eight men in all from Cambridge and no one from devastated Göttingen), Gamow, Irène and Frédéric Joliot-Curie, Patrick Blackett, Rudolf Peierls among the younger. Ernest Lawrence, his cyclotron humming, was the token American that year.

They debated the structure of the proton. Other topics they discussed may have seemed more far-reaching at the time. None would prove to be. On August 2, 1932, working with a carefully prepared cloud chamber, an American experimentalist at Caltech named Carl Anderson had discovered a new particle in a shower of cosmic rays. The particle was an electron with a positive instead of a negative charge, a "positron," the first indication that the universe consists not only of matter but of antimatter as well. (Its discovery earned Anderson the 1936 Nobel Prize.) Physicists everywhere immediately looked through their files of cloud-chamber photographs and identified positron tracks they had misidentified before (the Joliot-Curies, who had missed the neutron, saw that they had also missed the positron). The new particle raised the possibility that the positively charged proton might in fact be compound, might be not a unitary particle but a neutron in association with a positron. (It was not; there proved not to be room in the nucleus for electrons positive or negative.)

After they had identified the positrons they had missed before, the Joliot-Curies had started up their cloud chamber again and looked for the new particle in other experimental arrangements. They found that if they bombarded medium-weight elements with alpha particles from polonium, the targets ejected protons. Then they noticed that lighter elements, including in particular aluminum and boron, sometimes ejected a neutron and then a positron instead of a proton. That seemed evidence for a compound proton. They presented their evidence with enthusiasm as a report to the Solvay Conference.

Lise Meitner attacked the Joliot-Curies' report. She had performed similar experiments at the KWI and she was highly respected for the cautious precision of her work. In her experiments, she emphasized, she had been "unable to uncover a *single* neutron." Sentiment favored Meitner. "In the end, the great majority of the physicists present did not believe in the accuracy of our experiments," Joliot says. "After the meeting we were feeling rather depressed." Fortunately the theoreticians intervened. "But at that moment Professor Niels Bohr took us aside . . . and told us he thought our results were very important. A little later Pauli gave us similar encouragement." The Joliot-Curies returned to Paris determined to settle the issue once and for all.

Husband and wife were then thirty-three and thirty-six years old, with a small daughter at home. They sailed and swam together in summer, skied together in winter, worked together efficiently in the laboratory in the Latin Quarter on the Rue Pierre Curie. Irène had succeeded her mother as director of the Radium Institute in 1932: the long-widowed pioneer was mortally ill with leukemia induced by too many years of exposure to radiation.

It seemed likely that the appearance of neutrons and positrons rather than protons might depend on the energy of the alpha particles attacking the target. The Joliot-Curies could test that possibility by moving their polonium source away from the target, slowing the alphas by forcing them to batter their way through longer ranges of air. Joliot went to work. Without question he was seeing neutrons. When he shifted the polonium away from the aluminum-foil target "the emission of neutrons [ceased] altogether when a minimum velocity [was] reached." But something else happened then to surprise him. After neutron emission ceased, positron emission continued—not stopping abruptly but decreasing "only over a period of time, like the radiation . . . from a naturally radioactive element." What was going on? Joliot had been observing the particles with a cloud chamber, catching their ionizing tracks in its supersaturated fog. Now he switched to a Geiger counter and called in Irène. As he explained to a colleague the next day: "I irradiate this target with alpha rays from my source; you can hear the Geiger counter crackling. I remove the source: the crackling ought to stop, but in fact it continues." The strange activity declined to half its initial intensity in about three minutes. They would hardly yet have dared to think of that period as a half-life. It might merely mark the erratic performance of the Geiger counter.

A young German physicist who specialized in Geiger counters, Wolfgang Gentner, was working at the institute that year. Joliot asked him to check the lab instruments. The couple went off to a social evening they could find no excuse to avoid. "The following morning," writes the colleague to whom Joliot spoke that day, "the Joliots found on their desk a little hand-written note from Gentner, telling them that the Geiger counters were in perfect working order."

They were nearly certain then that they had discovered how to make matter radioactive by artificial means.

They calculated the probable reaction. An aluminum nucleus of 13 protons and 14 neutrons, capturing an alpha particle of 2 protons and 2 neutrons and immediately re-emitting 1 neutron must be converting itself into an unstable isotope of phosphorus with 15 protons and 15 neutrons (13 + 2 protons = 15; 14 + 2 - 1 neutrons = 15). The phosphorus then probably decayed to silicon (14 protons, 16 neutrons). The 3-minute period was the half-life of that decay.

They could not chemically trace the infinitesimal accumulation of silicon. Joliot explained why in 1935, when he and his wife accepted the Nobel Prize in Chemistry for their discovery: "The yield of these transmutations is very small, and the weights of elements formed . . . are less than 10^{-15} [grams], representing at most a few million atoms"—too few to find by chemical reaction alone. But they could trace the radioactivity of the phosphorus with a Geiger counter. If it did indeed signal the artificial transmutation of some of the aluminum to phosphorus, they should be able to separate the two different elements chemically. The radioactivity would go with the new phosphorus and leave the untransmuted aluminum behind. But they needed a definitive separation that could be carried out within three minutes, before the faint induced radioactivity faded below their Geiger counter's threshold.

The request perplexed a chemist in a nearby laboratory—"never having envisaged chemistry from that point of view," says Joliot—but he contrived the necessary procedure. The Joliot-Curies irradiated a piece of aluminum foil, dropped it into a container of hydrochloric acid and covered the container. The acid dissolved the foil, producing, by reaction, gaseous hydrogen, which should carry the phosphorus with it out of solution. They drew off the gas into an inverted test tube. The dissolved aluminum fell silent then but the gas made the Geiger counter chatter: whatever was radioactive had been carried along. A different chemical test proved that the radioactive substance was phosphorus. Joliot bounded like a boy.

The discovery might serve as an offering to Irène's ailing mother, who had prepared the daughter and sponsored the son-in-law:

> Marie Curie saw our research work and I will never forget the expression of intense joy which came over her when Irène and I showed her the first artificially radioactive element in a little glass tube. I can still see her taking in her fingers (which were already burnt with radium) this little tube containing the radioactive compound—as yet one in which the activity was very weak. To verify what we had told her she held it near a Geiger-Müller counter and she could hear the rate meter giving off a great many "clicks." This was doubtless the last great satisfaction of her life.

The Joliot-Curies reported their work—"one of the most important discoveries of the century," Emilio Segrè says in his history of modern physics—in the *Comptes Rendus* on January 15, 1934, and in a letter to *Nature* dated four days later. "These experiments give the first chemical proof of artificial transmutation," they concluded proudly. Rutherford wrote them within a fortnight: "I congratulate you both on a fine piece of work which I am sure will ultimately prove of much importance." He had tried a number of such experiments himself, he said, "but without any success"—high praise from the master of experiment.

They had demonstrated that it was possible not only to chip pieces off the nucleus, as Rutherford had done, but also to force it artificially to release some of its energy in radioactive decay. Joliot foresaw the potential consequences of that attack in his half of the joint Nobel Prize address. Given the progress of science, he said, "we are entitled to think that scientists, building up or shattering elements at will, will be able to bring about transmutations of an explosive type. . . . If such transmutations do succeed in spreading in matter, the enormous liberation of useful energy can be imagined." But he saw the possibility of cataclysm "if the contagion spreads to all the elements of our planet":

> Astronomers sometimes observe that a star of medium magnitude increases suddenly in size; a star invisible to the naked eye may become very brilliant and visible without any telescope—the appearance of a Nova. This sudden flaring up of the star is perhaps due to transmutations of an explosive character like those which our wandering imagination is perceiving now—a process that the investigators will no doubt attempt to realize while taking, we hope, the necessary precautions.

Leo Szilard received no invitation to the Solvay Conference. By October 1933 he had not accomplished any nuclear physics of note except within the well-equipped laboratory of his brain. In August he had written a friend that he was "spending much money at present for travelling about and earn of course nothing and cannot possibly go on with this for very long." The idea of a nuclear chain reaction "became a sort of obsession" with him. When he heard of the Joliot-Curies' discovery, in January, his obsession bloomed: "I suddenly saw that the tools were on hand to explore the possibility of such a chain reaction."

He moved to a less expensive hotel, the Strand Palace, near Trafalgar Square, and settled in to think. He had "a little money saved up" after all, "enough perhaps to live for a year in the style in which I was accustomed to live, and therefore I was in no particular hurry to look for a job"—the excitement of new ideas thus relieving his August urgency. The bath was down the hall. "I remember that I went into my bath . . . around nine o'clock in the morning. There is no place as good to think as a bathtub. I would just soak there and think, and around twelve o'clock the maid would knock and say, 'Are you all right, sir?' Then I usually got out and made a few notes, dictated a few memoranda."

One of the "memoranda" took the form of a patent application, filed March 12, 1934, relating to atomic energy. It was the first of several, that year and the next, all finally merged into one complete specification, "Improvements in or Relating to the Transmutation of Chemical Elements." (The same day Szilard applied for a patent, never issued, proposing the storage of books on microfilm.) Szilard had already realized—in September, in the context of inducing a chain reaction—that neutrons would be more efficient than alpha particles at bombarding nuclei. He applied that insight now to propose an alternative method for creating artificial radioactivity:

> In accordance with the present invention radio-active bodies are generated by bombarding suitable elements with neutrons. . . . Such uncharged nuclei penetrate even substances containing the heavier elements without ionization losses and cause the formation of radio-active substances.

That was a first step. It was also a cheeky piece of bravado. Szilard had only theoretical grounds for believing that neutrons might induce radioactivity artificially. He had not done the necessary experiments. Only the Joliot-Curies had carried out such experiments so far, and they used alpha particles. Szilard was pursuing more than artificial radioactivity. He was pursuing chain reactions, power generation, atomic bombs. He had not yet found patentable form for these excursions. He wondered which element or elements might emit two or more neutrons for each neutron captured. He decided at some point, he said later, "that the reasonable thing to do would be to investigate systematically all the elements. There were ninety-two of them. But of course this is a rather boring task, so I thought that I would get some money, have some apparatus built, and then hire somebody who would just sit down and go through one element after the other."

The task would hardly be boring. The truth is that Szilard lacked the resources for such work—access to a laboratory, a dedicated crew, sufficient financial support. "None of the physicists had any enthusiasm for this idea of a chain reaction," he would remember. Rutherford threw him out. Blackett told him, "Look, you will have no luck with such fantastic ideas in England. Yes, perhaps in Russia. If a Russian physicist went to the government and [said], 'We must make a chain reaction,' they would give him all the money and facilities which he would need. But you won't get it in England." Soaking in his bath against the London chill, Szilard turned back to mapping the future. The opportunity to explore the elements systematically for surprises by bombarding them with neutrons passed him by.

It fell instead to Enrico Fermi and his team of young colleagues in Rome. Fermi was prepared. He had all on hand that Szilard did not. He saw as soon as Szilard that the neutron would serve better than the alpha particle for nuclear bombardment. The point was not obvious. One used alphas to generate neutrons (as the Joliot-Curies had done along the way to chasing down their positrons). Since not all the alphas found targets, the neutral particles were correspondingly that much more scarce. As Otto Frisch would write: "I remember that my reaction and probably that of many others was that Fermi's was really a silly experiment because neutrons were much fewer than alpha particles. What that simple argument overlooked of course was that they are very much more effective."

Fermi was prepared because he had been organizing his laboratory for a major expedition into nuclear physics for more than four years. If Italy had been one of the hot centers of physical research he might have been too preoccupied to plan ahead so carefully. But Italian physics was a ruin as sere as Pompeii when he came to it. He had no choice but to push aside the debris and start fresh.

Both Fermi's biographers—his wife Laura and his protégé and fellow Nobel laureate Emilio Segrè—assign the beginning of his commitment to physics to the period of psychological trauma following the death of his older brother Giulio when Fermi was fourteen years old, in the winter of 1915. Only a year apart in age, the two boys had been inseparable; Giulio's death during minor surgery for a throat abscess left Enrico suddenly bereft.

That same winter young Enrico browsed on market day among the stalls of Rome's Campo dei Fiori, where a statue commemorates the philosopher Giordano Bruno, Copernicus' defender, who was burned at the stake there in 1600 by the Inquisition. Fermi found two used volumes in Latin, *Elementorum physicae mathematicae,* the work of a Jesuit physicist, published in 1840. The desolate boy used his allowance to buy the physics textbooks and carried them home. They excited him enough that he read them straight through. When he was finished he told his older sister Maria he had not even noticed they were written in Latin. "Fermi must have studied the treatise very thoroughly," Segrè would decide, looking through the old volumes many years later, "because it contains marginal notes, corrections of errors, and several scraps of paper with notes in Fermi's handwriting."

From that point forward Fermi's development as a physicist proceeded, with a single significant exception, rapidly and smoothly. A friend of his father, an engineer named Adolfo Amidei, guided his adolescent mathematical and physical studies, lending him texts in algebra, trigonometry, analytical geometry, calculus and theoretical mechanics between 1914 and 1917. When Enrico graduated from the *liceo* early, skipping his third year, Amidei asked him if he preferred mathematics or physics as a career and made a point of writing down, with emphasis, the young man's exact reply: "I studied mathematics with passion because I considered it necessary for the study of physics, *to which I want to dedicate myself exclusively.* . . . I've read all the best-known books of physics."

Amidei then advised Fermi to enroll not at the University of Rome but at the University of Pisa, because he could compete in Pisa to be admitted as a fellow to an affiliated Scuola Normale Superiore of international reputation that would pay his room and board. Among other reasons for the advice, Amidei told Segrè, he wanted to remove Fermi from his family home, where "a very depressing atmosphere prevailed . . . after Giulio's death."

When the Scuola Normale examiner saw Fermi's competition essay on the assigned theme "Characteristics of sound" he was stunned. It set forth, reports Segrè, "the partial differential equation of a vibrating rod, which Fermi solved by Fourier analysis, finding the eigenvalues and the eigenfrequencies . . . which would have been creditable for a doctoral examination." Calling in the seventeen-year-old *liceo* graduate, the examiner told him he was extraordinary and predicted he would become an important scientist. By 1920 Fermi could write a friend that he had reached the point of teaching his Pisa teachers: "In the physics department I am slowly becoming the most influential authority. In fact, one of these days I shall hold (in the presence of several magnates) a lecture on quantum theory, of which I'm always a great propagandist." He worked out his first theory of permanent value to physics while he was still a student in Pisa, a predictive deduction in general relativity.

The exception to his rapid progress came in the winter of 1923, when Fermi won a postdoctoral fellowship to travel to Göttingen to study under Max Born. Wolfgang Pauli was there then, and Werner Heisenberg and the brilliant young theoretician Pascual Jordan, but somehow Fermi's exceptional ability went unnoticed and he found himself ignored. Since he was, in Segrè's phrase, "shy, proud, and accustomed to solitude," he may have brought the ostracism on himself. Or the Germans may have been prejudiced against him by Italy's poor reputation in physics. Or, more dynamically, Fermi's visceral aversion to philosophy may have left him tongue-tied: he "could not penetrate Heisenberg's early papers on quantum mechanics, not because of any mathematical difficulties, but because the physical concepts were alien to him and seemed somewhat nebulous" and he wrote papers in Göttingen "he could just as well have written in Rome." Segrè has concluded that "Fermi remembered Göttingen as a sort of failure. He was there for a few months. He sat aside at his table and did his work. He didn't profit. They didn't recognize him." The following year Paul Ehrenfest sent along praise through the intermediary of a former student who looked up Fermi in Rome. A three-month fellowship then took the young Italian to Leiden for the traditional Ehrenfest tightening. After that Fermi could be sure of his worth.

He was always averse to philosophical physics; a rigorous simplicity, an insistence on concreteness, became the hallmark of his style. Segrè thought him inclined "toward concrete questions verifiable by direct experiment." Wigner noticed that Fermi "disliked complicated theories and avoided them as much as possible." Bethe remarked Fermi's "enlightening simplicity." Less generously, the sharp-tongued Pauli called him a "quantum engineer"; Victor Weisskopf, though an admirer, saw some truth in Pauli's canard, a difference in style from more philosophical originals like Bohr. "Not a philosopher," Robert Oppenheimer once sketched him.

"Passion for clarity. He was simply unable to let things be foggy. Since they always are, this kept him pretty active." An American physicist who worked with the middle-aged Fermi thought him "cold and clear. . . . Maybe a little ruthless in the way he would go directly to the facts in deciding any question, tending to disdain or ignore the vague laws of human nature."

Fermi's passion for clarity was also a passion to quantify. He seems to have attempted to quantify everything within reach, as if he was only comfortable when phenomena and relationships could be classified or numbered. "Fermi's thumb was his always ready yardstick," Laura Fermi writes. "By placing it near his left eye and closing his right, he would measure the distance of a range of mountains, the height of a tree, even the speed at which a bird was flying." His love of classification "was inborn," Laura Fermi concludes, "and I have heard him 'arrange people' according to their height, looks, wealth, or even sex appeal."

Fermi was born in Rome on September 29, 1901, into a family that had successfully made the transition during the nineteenth century from peasant agriculture in the Po Valley to career civil service with the Italian national railroad. His father was a *capo divisione* in the railroad's administration, a civil rank that corresponded to the military rank of brigadier general. In accord with a common Italian practice of the day, the infant Enrico was sent to live in the country with a wet nurse. So was his brother Giulio, but because Enrico's health was delicate he did not return to his mother and father until he was two and a half years old. Confronted then with a roomful of strangers purporting to be his family, and "perhaps," writes Laura Fermi, "missing the rough effusiveness of his nurse," he began to cry:

> His mother talked to him in a firm voice and asked him to stop at once; in this home naughty boys were not tolerated. Immediately the child complied, dried his tears, and fussed no longer. Then, as in later childhood, he assumed the attitude that there is no point in fighting authority. If *they* wanted him to behave that way, all right, he would; it was easier to go along with *them* than against.

In 1926, when he was twenty-five years old, Fermi was chosen under the Italian system of *concorsos*, national competitions, to become professor of theoretical physics at the University of Rome. An influential patron had seen to the creation of the new post, a Sicilian named Orso Mario Corbino, a short, dark, volatile man, forty-six when Fermi sought him out in 1921, the director of the university physics institute, an exceptional physicist and a Senator of the Kingdom. Since the old guard of Italian physicists resented Fermi's rapid promotion, he especially welcomed the protection of Corbino's patronage. Corbino found support for his efforts to improve Italian physics from the Fascist government of the bulletheaded former journalist Benito Mussolini, although the senator was not himself a party member.

In the later 1920s Corbino and his young professor agreed that the time was ripe for the small group they were assembling in Rome to colonize new territory on the frontier of physics. They chose as their territory the atomic nucleus, then finding description in quantum mechanics but not yet experimentally disassembled. Fermi's tall, erudite Pisa classmate Franco Rasetti signed on as Corbino's first assistant early in 1927. Rasetti and Fermi together recruited Segrè, who had been studying engineering, by taking him along to the Como conference and explaining the achievements of the assembled luminaries to him—by then, Segrè saw, Pauli and Heisenberg recognized Fermi's talents and included him among their friends. The son of the prosperous owner of a paper mill, Segrè contributed elegance to the group as well as brains.

Corbino added Edoardo Amaldi, the son of a mathematics professor at the University of Padua, by frankly raiding the engineering school. The group quickly nicknamed Fermi "the Pope" for his quantum infallibility; Corbino, like Rutherford at the Cavendish, called them all his "boys." Rasetti departed to Caltech, Segrè to Amsterdam, for seasoning. Fermi sent them out again in the early 1930s, after the decision to go into nuclear physics: Segrè to work with Otto Stern in Hamburg, Amaldi to Leipzig to the laboratory of the physical chemist Peter Debye, Rasetti to Lise Meitner at the KWI. By 1933, with a departmental budget above $2,000 a year, ten times the budget of most Italian physics departments, with a well-made cloud chamber and a nearby radium source and KWI training in the vagaries of Geiger counters, the group was ready to begin.

In the meantime, two months after the Solvay Conference, Fermi completed the major theoretical work of his life, a fundamental paper on beta decay. Beta decay, the creation and expulsion by the nucleus of high-energy electrons in the course of radioactive change, had needed a detailed, quantitative theory, and Fermi supplied it entire. He introduced a new type of force, the "weak interaction," completing the four basic forces known in nature: gravity and electromagnetism, which operate at long range, and the strong force and Fermi's weak force, which operate within nuclear dimensions. He introduced a new fundamental constant, now called the Fermi constant, determining it from existing experimental data. "A fantastic paper," Victor Weisskopf later praised it, ". . . a monument to Fermi's intuition." In London the editor of *Nature* rejected it on the grounds that it was too remote from physical reality, which Fermi found irritating but amusing; he published it instead in the little-known weekly journal of the Italian Research Council, *Ricerca Scientifica*, where Amaldi's wife Ginestra worked, and later in the *Zeitschrift für Physik*. With only minor adjustments Fermi's theory of beta decay continues to be definitive.

The *Comptes Rendus* reporting the Joliot-Curies' discovery of artificial radioactivity reached Rome shortly after Fermi returned from skiing in the Alps, in January 1934. "We had not yet found any [nuclear physics] problems to work on," Amaldi reminisces. ". . . Then came out the paper of Joliot, and Fermi immediately started to look for the radioactivity." Like Szilard, Fermi saw the advantages of using neutrons. I. I. Rabi catalogues those advantages in a lecture:

> Since the neutron carries no charge, there is no strong electrical repulsion to prevent its entry into nuclei. In fact, the forces of attraction which hold nuclei together may pull the neutron into the nucleus. When a neutron enters a nucleus, the effects are about as catastrophic as if the moon struck the earth. The nucleus is violently shaken up by the blow, especially if the collision results in the capture of the neutron. A large increase in energy occurs and must be dissipated, and this may happen in a variety of ways, all of them interesting.

When Fermi began his neutron-bombardment experiments he was thirty-three years old, short, muscular, dark, with thick black hair, a narrow nose and surprising gray-blue eyes. His voice was deep and he grinned easily. Marriage to the petitely beautiful Laura Capon, the daughter of a Jewish officer in the Italian Navy, had encouraged him in methodical habits: he worked for several hours privately at home, arrived at the physics institute at nine, worked until twelve-thirty, lunched at home, returned to the institute at four and continued work until eight in the evening, returning home then for dinner. With marriage he had also gained weight.

He and his team of young colleagues occupied the south section of the second floor of the institute, sharing the space with Corbino and with the chief physicist of Rome's Sanità Pubblica—its health department—a generous soul named G. C. Trabacchi who lent Corbino's boys some of the instruments and supplies they needed for their experiments (in return they cherished him, nicknaming him "Divine Providence"). Antonino Lo Sordo, a frustrated old-guard physicist, fended off the encroaching horde from an office at the north end of the floor. Corbino and his family lived above, the residence overlooking a private garden in back with a goldfish pond at its focus. The first floor served students; the basement held electrical generators and a lead-lined safe for the Sanità's gram of radium, worth 670,000 lire—about $34,000—in that year of its most historic use. Glass pipes passed through a wall of the special safe to carry radon, formed in the decay of radium, to a compact extraction plant, a modest refinery of glass-pipe towers that purified and dried the radioactive gas. The residential upper story of the institute, contracted above the longer lower floors to make room at one end for the dome of a small rotunda, was roofed with tile. "The location of the building in a small park on a hill near the central part of Rome was convenient and beautiful at the same time," Segrè recalls. "The garden, landscaped with palm trees and bamboo thickets, with its prevailing silence (except at dusk, when gatherings of sparrows populated the greenery), made the institute a most peaceful and attractive center of study." A gravel path that shone white in the golden Roman sun led down to the Via Panisperna.

As usual, Fermi hewed the neutron experiments by hand. In February and early March he personally assembled crude Geiger counters from aluminum cylinders acquired by cutting the bottoms off tubes of medicinal tablets. Wired, filled with gas, their ends sealed and leads attached, the counters were slightly smaller than rolls of breath mints and a hundred times less efficient than modern commercial units, but with Fermi to operate them they served. While he built Geiger counters he asked Rasetti to prepare a neutron source in the form of polonium evaporated onto beryllium. Since polonium emits relatively low-energy alpha particles, the resulting source emitted relatively few neutrons per second, and Fermi and Rasetti irradiated several samples without success.

At that point Rasetti, showing a surprising lack of eagerness for historic experiment, went off to Morocco for Easter vacation. Fermi cast about for some way to acquire a stronger neutron source. The rationale for using polonium in the first place, in Paris and Cambridge and Berlin as well as in Rome, had been that a stronger alpha emitter like radon also emitted strong beta and gamma radiation, which disturbed the instruments and interfered with measurements. Fermi realized suddenly that since he was trying to observe a *delayed* effect, he was measuring only *after* he removed the neutron source in any case—and therefore any beta and gamma radiation wouldn't matter and he could use radon. Trabacchi had the radon to spare and willingly dispensed it; with a half-life of only 3.82 days it was perishable in any case and his glowing gram of radium continually exhaled a fresh draft.

To the basement of the physics institute on the Via Panisperna, in his gray lab coat, in mid-March, Fermi thus carried a snippet of glass tubing no larger than the first joint of his little finger. It was flame-sealed at one end and partly filled with powdered beryllium. He set the sealed end of this capsule into a container of liquid air. The radon, directed from the outlet of the extraction plant into the capsule, condensed on its walls in the −200°C cold. Fermi then had to attempt quickly to heat and draw closed the other end of the capsule, without cracking the glass, before the radon evaporated and escaped. When he succeeded, he finished preparing the neutron source by dropping it into a two-foot length of glass tubing of larger diameter and sealing it into the far end so that it could be handled at a distance safe from dangerous exposure to its gamma rays. For all the tedious preparation its useful life was brief.

In the beginning Fermi worked alone. He intended eventually to irradiate most of the elements in the periodic table and he started methodically with the lightest. His source, he calculated, supplied him with more than 100,000 neutrons per second. "Small cylindrical containers filled with the substances tested," he would explain in his first report, "were subjected to the action of the radiation from this source during intervals of time varying from several minutes to several hours." Fermi first irradiated water—testing hydrogen and oxygen at the same time—then lithium, beryllium, boron and carbon without inducing them to radioactivity. Laura Fermi says he wavered then, discouraged by the lack of results, but Fermi seldom talked shop at home and doubt seems unlikely: he knew from the Joliot-Curie work that aluminum, a little farther along, reacted with alphas, and neutrons should prove even more effective.

In any case he succeeded on his next attempt, with fluorine: "Calcium fluoride, irradiated for a few minutes and rapidly brought into the vicinity of the counter, causes in the first few moments an increase of pulses; the effect decreases rapidly, reaching the half-value in about 10 seconds."

Soon he found a radioactivity in aluminum with a half-life of twelve minutes, different from the Joliot-Curies' discovery. Putting aluminum first to link his work with theirs, he reported his findings in a letter to the *Ricerca Scientifica* on March 25, 1934.

A Roman numeral *I* distinguishes that first report on "Radioactivity induced by neutron bombardment." The search was on. To move it along Fermi recruited Amaldi and Segrè and cabled Rasetti in Morocco to rush home. Segrè writes:

> We organized our activities this way: Fermi would do a good part of the experiments and calculations. Amaldi would take care of what we would now call the electronics, and I would secure the substances to be irradiated, the sources, etc. Now, of course, this division of labor was by no means rigid, and we all participated in all phases of the work, but we had a certain division of responsibility along these lines, and we proceeded at great speed. We needed all the help we could get, and we even enlisted the help of a younger brother of one of the students (probably 12 years old), persuading him that it was most interesting and important that he should prepare some neat paper cylinders in which we could irradiate our stuff.

The next letter that went to the *Ricerca Scientifica* (and in summary form to *Nature*) reported artificially induced radioactivity in iron, silicon, phosphorus, chlorine, vanadium, copper, arsenic, silver, tellurium, iodine, chromium, barium, sodium, magnesium, titanium, zinc, selenium, antimony, bromine and lanthanum. By then they had established a routine: they irradiated substances at one end of the second floor and tested them under the Geiger counters at the other end, down a long hall. That shielded the counters from stray radiation from the neutron source. But it also meant, whenever the half-life of an induced radioactivity was short, that someone had to run down the hall. "Amaldi and Fermi prided themselves on being the fastest runners," Laura Fermi notes, "and theirs was the task of speeding short-lived substances from one end of the corridor to the other. They always raced, and Enrico claims that he could run faster than Edoardo. But he is not a good loser." A dignified Spaniard showed up one day to confer with "His Excellency Fermi." Rome's young professor of theoretical physics, a dirty lab coat flying out behind him, nearly knocked the visitor down.

They came, finally, to uranium. They had roughly classified the effects they were seeing. Light elements generally transmuted to lighter elements by ejecting either a proton or an alpha particle. But the electrical barrier around the nucleus works against exits as well as entrances, and that barrier increases in strength with increasing atomic number. So heavy elements got heavier, not lighter: they captured the bombarding neutron, threw off its binding energy by emitting gamma radiation, and thus, with the addition of the neutron's mass, but with no added or subtracted charge, became a heavier isotope of themselves. Which then decayed by the delayed emission of a negative beta ray to an element with one more unit of atomic number. Uranium did the same; after a delay it emitted a beta electron. That should mean, Fermi realized, that bombarding uranium with neutrons was producing first a heavier isotope, uranium 239, and then a new, man-made transuranic element, atomic number 93, something never seen on earth before.

It was necessary to purify their uranium sample (uranium nitrate in solution, a light yellow liquid) of the obscuring beta activity its natural decay products gave off. (Uranium decays naturally through a series of fourteen complex steps down the periodic table to thorium, protactinium, radium, radon, polonium and bismuth to lead.) Trabacchi in his generosity had by then even lent the group a young chemist, Oscar D'Agostino, fresh from training in radiochemistry on the Rue Pierre Curie; D'Agostino accomplished the laborious purification in early May. They were using stronger sources now, up to 800 millicuries of radon, about a million neutrons per second. Irradiating the uranium nitrate gave "a very intense effect with several periods [of half-lives]: one period of about 1 minute, another of 13 minutes besides longer periods not yet exactly determined"—thus their May 10 report.

These several induced radioactivities were all beta emitters. They made whatever atom was emitting them heavier by one atomic number. It seemed to follow, then, that they were transmutations up the periodic table into the uncharted new region of man-made elements. To confirm that stunning possibility Fermi needed to demonstrate with chemical separations that the neutron bombardment was not unaccountably creating elements *lighter* than uranium. The one-minute half-life was too short to work with, so he concentrated on the thirteen-minute substance. D'Agostino diluted the irradiated uranium nitrate with 50 percent nitric acid, dissolved into the acid a small amount of manganese salt and set the solution to boil. By adding sodium chlorate to the boiling solution he precipitated crystals of manganese dioxide. When he filtered the crystals from the solution the radioactivity went with the manganese, much as the radioactivity the Joliot-Curies had induced in aluminum went off with the hydrogen gas. If the radioactivity could be precipitated out of the uranium solution along with a manganese carrier, then it must not be uranium anymore.

By adding other carriers and precipitating other compounds D'Agostino proved that the thirteen-minute substance was neither protactinium (91), thorium (90), actinium (89), radium (88), bismuth (83) nor lead (82). Its behavior excluded elements 87 (then known as ekacesium), and 86 (radon). Element 85 was unknown. Perhaps because the half-lives were different, Fermi made no attempt to check polonium (84). But he felt he had been sufficiently thorough. "This negative evidence about the identity of the 13 min-activity from a large number of heavy elements," he reported cautiously in *Nature* in June, "suggests the possibility that the atomic number of the element may be greater than 92."

Corbino injudiciously announced "a new element" at the annual convocation, the King of Italy in attendance, that closed the academic year, which set the press baying and gave Fermi a few sleepless nights. Having so splendidly accomplished Szilard's "rather boring task," the weary physicist was happy to depart after that with his wife and their small daughter Nella for a summer lecture tour sponsored by the Italian government through Argentina, Uruguay and Brazil.

Leo Szilard had emerged from his bath that spring of 1934 to pursue his favorite causes, not yet joined, of releasing the energy of the nucleus and of saving the world. In a late-April memorandum condemning the recent Japanese occupation of Manchuria he seemed to look ahead to a far future: "The discoveries of scientists," he wrote, "have given weapons to mankind which may destroy our present civilization if we do not succeed in avoiding further wars." He probably meant military aircraft; the horrors of strategic bombing and even its potential for deterrence through a balance of terror were much bruited at mid-decade. But almost certainly he was also thinking of atomic bombs.

Several weeks earlier, looking for a patron, he had sent Sir Hugo Hirst, the founder of the British General Electric Company, a copy of the first chapter of *The World Set Free*. "Of course," he wrote Sir Hugo with a touch of bitterness, still brooding on Rutherford's prediction, "all this is moonshine, but I have reason to believe that in so far as the industrial applications of the present discoveries in physics are concerned, the forecast of the writers may prove to be more accurate than the forecast of the scientists. The physicists have conclusive arguments as to why we cannot create at present new sources of energy for industrial purposes; I am not so sure whether they do not miss the point."

That Szilard saw beyond "energy for industrial purposes" to the possibility of weapons of war is evident in his next patent amendments, dated June 28 and July 4, 1934. Previously he had described "the transmutation of chemical elements"; now he added "the liberation of nuclear energy for power production and other purposes through nuclear transmutation." He proposed for the first time "a chain reaction in which particles which carry no positive charge and the mass of which is approximately equal to the proton mass or a multiple thereof [i.e., neutrons] form the links of the chain." He described the essential features of what came to be known as a "critical mass"—the volume of a chain-reacting substance necessary to make the chain reaction self-sustaining. He saw that the critical mass could be reduced by surrounding a sphere of chain-reacting substance with "some cheap heavy material, for instance lead," that would reflect neutrons back into the sphere, the basic concept for what came to be known (by analogy with the mud tamped into drill holes to confine conventional explosives) as "tamper." And he understood what would happen if he assembled a critical mass, spelling out the results simply on the fourth page of his application:

> If the thickness is larger than the critical value . . . I can produce an explosion.

As if to mark in some distant inhuman ledger the end of one age and the beginning of another, Marie Sklodowska Curie, born in Warsaw, Poland, on November 7, 1867, died that day of Szilard's filing, July 4, 1934, in

Savoy. Einstein's was the best eulogy: "Marie Curie is," he said, "of all celebrated beings, the only one whom fame has not corrupted."

There is nothing in the documentary record to indicate that Szilard was yet thinking of uranium. His June amendment describes a possible chain reaction using light, silvery beryllium, element number 4 on the periodic table.

To study that metal Szilard needed access to a laboratory and a source of radiation. The beryllium nucleus was so lightly bound he suspected he could knock neutrons out of it not only with alpha particles or neutrons but even with gamma rays or high-energy X rays. Radium emitted gamma rays and radium was available conveniently at the nearest large hospital. So Szilard, an unusually practical visionary, dropped in to see the director of the physics department at the medical college of St. Bartholomew's Hospital. Couldn't he use St. Bart's radium, "which was not much in use in summertime," for experiments? Something of value to medicine might emerge. The director thought he could if he teamed up with someone on the staff. "There was a very nice young Englishman, Mr. [T. A.] Chalmers, who was game, and so we teamed up and for the next two months we did experiments."

Their first experiment demonstrated a brilliantly simple method for separating isotopes of iodine by bombarding an iodine compound with neutrons. They then used this Szilard-Chalmers effect (as it came to be called), which was extremely sensitive, as a tool for measuring the production of neutrons in their second experiment: knocking neutrons out of beryllium using the gamma radiation from radium. "These experiments," Szilard reminisces wryly, "established me as a nuclear physicist, not in the eyes of Cambridge, but in the eyes of Oxford. [Szilard had in fact applied to Rutherford that spring to work at the Cavendish and Rutherford had turned him down.] I had never done work in nuclear physics before, but Oxford considered me an expert. . . . Cambridge . . . would never had made that mistake. For them I was just an upstart who might make all sorts of observations, but these observations could not be regarded as discoveries until they had been repeated at Cambridge and confirmed."

If Szilard's summer work helped establish his Oxford reputation, it was also a personal disappointment: beryllium proved an unsatisfactory candidate for chain reaction. The problem, not settled until 1935, lay with the established mass of helium. The one stable isotope of beryllium consists of two helium nuclei lightly bound by a neutron. Its apparently high mass, which was calculated from Francis Aston's measurements of the mass of helium, seemed to indicate that it should be unstable. But the mass spectrograph was a skittish instrument even in the hands of its inventor, and as

Bethe, Rutherford and others were about to demonstrate, Aston's measurements were inaccurate: he had set the mass of helium too high. One casualty of that error was beryllium's candidacy for chain reaction, for nuclear power and atomic bombs.

Emilio Segrè and Edoardo Amaldi pilgrimaged to Cambridge early in July, short on English but carrying with them a comprehensive report on the Rome neutron-bombardment investigations. They met Chadwick, Kapitza and the other regulars at the Cavendish; observed the retired J. J. Thomson making his rounds; noted Aston, says Amaldi innocently, "going on improving the accuracy of his measurements of atomic masses"; and had a memorable meeting with Rutherford, whose "strong personality dominated the whole laboratory."

The two young physicists had come to compare experiments with two of Rutherford's boys. An unanswered question hung over the neutron work, a question that called existing nuclear theory into doubt. The *Nature* paper they brought with them discussed the difficulty frankly. It concerned what is called "radiative capture," the typical reaction of the heavy elements to neutron bombardment: a nucleus captures a neutron, emits a photon of gamma radiation to stabilize itself energetically and thus becomes an isotope one mass unit heavier.

Theory at the time treated the nucleus as if it was one large particle. As such, it had a definite diameter, which was modest enough that a speeding neutron could go in one side and exit out the other in about 10^{-21} seconds, a billion times less than a trillionth of a second. Any capture process would have to work within that brief interval of time. Otherwise the neutron would be gone. Capturing a neutron means stopping it within a nucleus. To do that the nucleus has to absorb the neutron's energy of motion. The nucleus in turn has to get rid of the excess energy. Which it does: by emitting a gamma photon.

But the gamma-emission times Fermi's group had measured were different from what theory said they ought to be. The nuclei the Rome group had studied took at least 10^{-16} seconds to get around to gamma emission—one hundred thousand times too long. And that was unaccountable.

Definite proof of radiative capture would sharpen the challenge to theory. That required proving beyond doubt, by experiment, that a heavier isotope really forms when a heavy nucleus captures a neutron. The Cavendish team Segrè and Amaldi came to visit in the summer of 1934 accomplished the first part of the proof, using sodium, while the Italians were on hand. They then returned to Rome and enlisted D'Agostino's help to perform the confirming chemistry. In the heat of Roman August they looked for additional clear-cut examples and won a double prize: "We also found a second case of 'proven' radiative capture," Amaldi writes, "which was based on the discovery of a new radioisotope of [aluminum] with a lifetime of almost 3 minutes."

Fermi planned to stop off in London for an international physics conference on his way home from South America. His young colleagues sent him word of their aluminum discovery. He reported to the conference on the neutron work. (Szilard also attended, happy to hear praise for his summer experiments and well launched toward a paying fellowship at Oxford.) Fermi said his group had studied sixty elements so far and had induced radioactivity in forty of them. Discussing the radiative-capture problem he cited the Cavendish results "and those of Amaldi and Segrè on aluminium," which were both, he said, "to be considered particularly important." Segrè describes the tempestuous aftermath:

> Shortly afterwards I caught a cold and could not go to the laboratory for several days. Amaldi tried to repeat our experiments and found a different [half-life] for irradiated aluminum which showed that our so-called (n,γ) reaction [i.e., neutron in, gamma photon out] did not occur. This was hurriedly relayed to Fermi who resented having communicated a result which now looked to be in error. He strongly criticized us and did not conceal his displeasure. The whole business was becoming very troublesome because we could not find any fault with the various experiments which gave inconsistent results.

The chastened junior members had their work cut out for them. A new recruit joined them, a tall, broad-shouldered, handsome tennis champion from Pisa named Bruno Pontecorvo, as they set about polishing their first rough work. Neutron bombardment activated some elements more intensely than others. They had previously categorized that activation only generally as strong, medium or weak. Now they proposed to establish a quantitative scale of activibility. They needed some standard intensity against which to measure the intensity of other activations. They chose the convenient 2.3-minute half-life period that neutron bombardment induced in silver.

Amaldi and Pontecorvo got the assignment. They immediately found, to their surprise, that their silver cylinders activated differently in different parts of the laboratory. "In particular," writes Amaldi, "there were certain wooden tables near a spectroscope in a dark room which had miraculous properties, since silver irradiated on those tables gained much more activity than when it was irradiated on a marble table in the same room."

That was a mystery worth exploring. On October 18 they started a systematic investigation, a series of measurements made inside and outside a lead housing. By October 22 they were prepared to measure what might happen when only a lead wedge separated the neutron source from its target. But the experimenters had to give student examinations that morning and Fermi decided to go ahead on his own. He described the historic moment late in life to a colleague curious about the process of discovery in physics:

> I will tell you how I came to make the discovery which I suppose is the most important one I have made. We were working very hard on the neutron-induced radioactivity and the results we were obtaining made no sense. One day, as I came into the laboratory, it occurred to me that I should examine the effect of placing a piece of lead before the incident neutrons. Instead of my usual custom, I took great pains to have the piece of lead precisely machined. I was clearly dissatisfied with something: I tried every excuse to postpone putting the piece of lead in its place. When finally, with some reluctance, I was going to put it in its place, I said to myself: "No, I do not want this piece of lead here; what I want is a piece of paraffin." It was just like that with no advance warning, no conscious prior reasoning. I immediately took some odd piece of paraffin and placed it where the piece of lead was to have been.

The extraordinary result of substituting paraffin wax for a heavy element like lead was a dramatic increase in the intensity of the activation. "About noon," Segrè remembers, "everybody was summoned to watch the miraculous effects of the filtration by paraffin. At first I thought a counter had gone wrong, because such strong activities had not appeared before, but it was immediately demonstrated that the strong activation resulted from the filtering by the paraffin of the radiation that produced the radioactivity." Laura Fermi says "the halls of the physics building resounded with loud exclamations: 'Fantastic! Incredible! Black magic!' "

Not even his most important discovery kept Fermi from going home for lunch. He was alone; his wife and daughter would not return from a visit to the country until the following morning. He pondered in solitude and may have considered the difference between wood and marble tables as well as between paraffin and lead. When he returned in midafternoon he proposed an answer: the neutrons were colliding with the hydrogen nuclei in the paraffin and the wood. That slowed them down. Everyone had assumed that faster neutrons were better for nuclear bombardment because faster protons and alpha particles always had been better. But the analogy ignored the neutron's distinctive neutrality. A charged particle needed energy to push through the nucleus' electrical barrier. A neutron did not. Slowing down a neutron gave it more time in the vicinity of the nucleus, and that gave it more time to be captured.

The simple way to test Fermi's theory was to try some other material besides paraffin that contained hydrogen (other light nuclei would also work to slow neutrons down, but hydrogen would work best: its nuclei are protons, about the same size and mass as neutrons, and they therefore bounce hardest and soak up the most energy per collision). Down to the first floor and out the back door they marched with their silver cylinder and their neutron source extended in its long glass tube, to the pond in Corbino's garden where Rasetti had experimented with raising salamanders, where they had all caught the fad one summer of sailing candle-powered toy boats, where the dark, curving leaves and leathery gray drupes of an almond tree shaded the lively goldfish.

The hydrogen in water (and in goldfish) worked as well as paraffin. Back in the lab they quickly tested whatever they could lay hands on to irradiate: silicon, zinc, phosphorus, which did not seem to be affected by the slow neutrons; copper, iodine, aluminum, which did. They tried radon without beryllium to make sure the paraffin was affecting neutrons and not gamma rays. They replaced the paraffin with an oxygen compound and found much less increase in induced radioactivity.

They went home to dinner but met afterward at Amaldi's, whose wife had a typewriter, to prepare a first report. "Fermi dictated while I wrote," Segrè remembers. "He stood by me; Rasetti, Amaldi, and Pontecorvo paced the room excitedly, all making comments at the same time." Laura Fermi recreates the scene: "They shouted their suggestions so loudly, they argued so heatedly about what to say and how to say it, they paced the floor in such audible agitation, they left the Amaldis' house in such a state, that the Amaldis' maid timidly inquired whether the guests had all been drunk."

Ginestra Amaldi delivered the typed paper, "Influence of hydrogenous substances on the radioactivity produced by neutrons—I," to the director of the *Ricerca Scientifica* the next morning. Tucked away in its historic paragraphs was a quiet justification for the confusion over aluminum: "The case of aluminum is noteworthy. In water it acquires an activity showing a period slightly shorter than 3 minutes. . . . This activity under normal conditions is so weak that it almost disappears compared to other activities generated in the same element."

Amaldi and Segrè had not been wrong about aluminum. They had simply irradiated different samples of the element on different tables. The hydrogen in the wooden table had slowed down some of the neutrons and enhanced the almost-three-minute activity. As Hans Bethe once noted wittily, the efficiency of slow neutrons "might never have been discovered if Italy were not rich in marble. . . . A marble table gave different results from a wooden table. If it had been done [in America], it all would have been done on a wooden table and people would never have found out."

The discovery of slow-neutron radioactivity meant that Fermi's group had to work its way through the elements again looking for different and enhanced half-lives—which is to say, different isotopes and decay products.

While that work proceeded a paper appeared in the *Physical Review* criticizing the group's earlier study of uranium. The paper's primary author was Aristide von Grosse, who had been one of Otto Hahn's assistants at the KWI and who had purified the first substantial sample of protactinium, the element Hahn and Meitner had discovered in 1917. Von Grosse argued that when Fermi irradiated uranium he had created protactinium, atomic number 91, not a new transuranic element. The Rome group took the paper as a challenge to further experiment. At the same time Hahn and Meitner decided proprietarily to repeat Fermi's previous uranium work. "It was a logical decision," Hahn explains in his scientific autobiography; "having been the discoverers of protactinium, we knew its chemical characteristics." The increasing number of different half-lives that investigators in Berlin and Paris found when they irradiated uranium were puzzling; Hahn correctly felt that he was better qualified than anyone else in the world to accomplish the subtle radiochemistry necessary to sort everything out.

In January and February 1935, in the midst of other projects, Amaldi set to work looking for alpha-emitting reactions in uranium in addition to the beta reactions the group had originally found. If uranium emitted alpha particles when it captured neutrons it would be transmuting down the periodic table rather than up, which might indeed produce protactinium along the way. Amaldi chose to use an ionization chamber connected to a linear amplifier to capture and measure the radiation. "I began to irradiate some foil[s] of uranium," he writes, ". . . and put them immediately after irradiation in front of the thin-window ionization chamber." Nothing happened. Conceivably the half-lives were too brief for the run down the hall from the irradiation area to the ionization chamber. Amaldi decided to try irradiating his samples directly in front of the chamber. That required screening out unwanted radiation. The gamma rays from his neutron source, which would have disturbed the ionization chamber, he blocked by setting a piece of lead between the source and the chamber: the desirable neutrons would find the lead no obstacle.

He also wanted to filter out uranium's natural alpha background. To do that he took advantage of the basic law of radioactivity that shorter half-lives mean more energetic radiation. The half-life of natural uranium is about 4.5 billion years; its alphas are proportionately mild, mild enough to be blocked by a layer of aluminum foil. On the other hand, if there really were half-lives in his experiment so short that he had to irradiate directly in front of the ionization chamber to catch them, their alphas should be energetic enough to breeze easily through the aluminum and the chamber window and enter the chamber for counting. So Amaldi wrapped his uranium samples with aluminum foil. It did not occur to him that his shielding might also screen out other reaction products. In 1935, alpha, beta and gamma radiation were the only reaction products anyone knew. "The experiments," Amaldi concludes, "gave negative results." He found no artificially induced alphas from uranium.

The Italians thought it even more probable then that by irradiating uranium they were creating new, man-made elements. Hahn and Meitner reported they thought so too. Fermi's group rounded up its work in the *Proceedings of the Royal Society* in a paper Rutherford approvingly passed along to that journal on February 15:

> Through these experiments our hypothesis that the 13-minute and 100-minute induced activities of uranium are due to transuranic elements seems to receive further support. The simplest interpretation consistent with the known facts is to assume that the 15-second, 13-minute and 100-minute activities are chain products [i.e., one decays into the next], probably with atomic number 92, 93 and 94 respectively and atomic weight 239.

But the truth was, uranium was a confusion, and no one yet knew.

What else besides beryllium? Leo Szilard asked himself in London. Beryllium looked suspicious. What other elements might chain-react? He answered with an amended patent specification on April 9, 1935: "Other examples for elements from which neutrons can liberate multiple neutrons are uranium and bromine." He was guessing, and without research funds he saw no way to experiment. The physicists he talked to remained profoundly skeptical of his ideas. "So I thought, there is after all something called 'chain reaction' in chemistry. It doesn't resemble a nuclear chain reaction, but still it's a chain reaction. So I thought I would talk to a chemist." The chemist he thought he would talk to was someone even more skillful than Leo Szilard at raising funds: Chaim Weizmann, who now lived and worked in London. Weizmann received Szilard and "understood what I told him." He asked Szilard how much money he needed. Szilard said £2,000—about $10,000. Though he was certainly hard-pressed for funding himself, Weizmann said he would see what he could do. Szilard recalls:

> I didn't hear from him for several weeks, but then I ran into Michael Polanyi, who by that time had arrived in Manchester and was head of the chemistry

> department there. Polanyi told me that Weizmann had come to talk to him about my ideas for the possibility of a chain reaction, and he wanted Polanyi's advice on whether he should get me this money. Polanyi thought that this experiment should be done.

A decade passed before Szilard and Weizmann met again, a gulf of history. Weizmann had not neglected Szilard's request, he explained then in apology in late 1945; he had only not succeeded in raising the funds.

Since the beginning of his rescue work in England Szilard had been in occasional contact with the physicist Frederick Alexander Lindemann, who was professor of experimental philosophy at Oxford and director of the Clarendon Laboratory there. It was Lindemann, wealthy and well-connected, who was arranging a fellowship for Szilard, part of his continuing campaign to arm the decrepit Oxford science laboratory against its splendid Cambridge rival. Lindemann had made effective use in that campaign of the Nazi expulsion of the Jewish academics but had given as good as he got: immediately upon hearing of the civil service law he had gone to Imperial Chemical Industries and convinced its directors to establish a grant program, arguing that such an investment would be not charity but money well spent. ICI had already begun paying out its first grant on May 1, 1933, while Beveridge and Szilard were still laying plans. It was an ICI grant that Szilard missed winning the following August, perhaps because he had not yet accomplished his summer of impressive experiment at St. Bart's, but Lindemann was paying attention now.

The tall, handsome Englishman, forty-nine years old in 1935, had been born in Germany, at Baden-Baden, because his mother chose not to allow advanced pregnancy to interfere with a visit to that fashionable spa. To provide their son with an outstanding education his English parents had sent him to the *Gymnasium* in Darmstadt. As a student before the Great War at the Darmstadt Technische Hochschule, where he was a protégé of the physical chemist Walther Nernst (the 1920 chemistry Nobelist), he had enjoyed such exceptional family connections that he found himself at times playing tennis with the Kaiser or the Czar. Inevitably the war made suspect such golden afternoons. Lindemann was chagrined and angered in 1915 to find that the British Army, noting his German birth certificate and German-sounding name, was unwilling to extend him a commission.

The Army's decision injured him deeply and may have changed his life. He had served as a co-secretary to the 1911 Solvay Conference, standing up proudly with Nernst, Rutherford, Planck, Einstein, Mme. Curie, but even before that youthful apotheosis Nernst had predicted difficulty: "If your father were not such a rich man," the blunt German had said, "you would become a great physicist." When the Army questioned Lindemann's patriotism, writes a refugee colleague, "he became withdrawn to avoid exposing himself to slights and insults. Secretiveness about his personal life developed into a mania and he discouraged personal approaches by a stand-offishness which was easily mistaken for arrogance." Lindemann retreated from original work and became a talented administrator, "the Prof," an "unbending Victorian gentleman," always impeccable in bowler hat, summer gray suit, winter dark suit, rolled-up umbrella and long, dark coat. If he could not win a uniform he would adopt one of his own.

He worked for his country during the war at the Royal Aircraft Factory at Farnborough, designing what are now called avionics and doing aeronautical research. Tailspins were recognized maneuvers in air fighting by 1916, a good way to shake off an attacker. Lindemann was the first to study them scientifically. To do so he took flying lessons—only changing from civilian clothes to flying clothes on the runway beside the plane—then coolly flew spin after spin, memorizing his instrument readings as he plummeted and writing them down after he had recovered level flight.

After the war Lindemann accepted appointment to an Oxford still donnishly disdainful of science. He escaped from that further condescension, says his colleague, into "gracious living," enjoying weekends with the nobility that were seldom vouchsafed to less well-born Oxford dons. By then a Rolls-Royce was part of his regalia. In June 1921, on a weekend at the country estate of the Duke and Duchess of Westminster, Lindemann met Winston Churchill, twelve years his senior. "The two men, so different in background and character, took to each other immediately and their acquaintance soon turned into a close friendship." Churchill recalled that he "saw a great deal of Frederick Lindemann" during the 1930s. "Lindemann was already an old friend of mine. . . . We came much closer from 1932 onwards, and he frequently motored over from Oxford to stay with me at Chartwell. Here we had many talks into the small hours of the morning about the dangers which seemed to be gathering upon us. Lindemann . . . became my chief adviser on the scientific aspects of modern war."

To this illustrious personage, a vegetarian who daily consumed copious quantities of olive oil and Port Salut, Szilard turned in the early summer of 1935 to discuss "the question whether or not the liberation of nuclear energy . . . can be achieved in the immediate future." If "double neutrons" could be produced, Szilard wrote Lindemann on June 3, "then it is certainly less bold to expect this achievement in the immediate future than to believe the opposite." That meant trouble, Szilard thought, if Germany achieved a chain reaction first, and he argued for "an attempt, whatever small chance of success it may have . . . to control this development as long as possible." Secrecy was the way to achieve such control: first, by winning agreement from the scientists involved to restrict publication, and second, by taking out patents.

Michael Polanyi had cautioned Szilard late in 1934 that "there is an opposition to you on account of taking patents." The British scientific tradition that opposed patents assumed that those who filed them did so for mercenary purposes; Szilard explained his patents to Lindemann to clear his name:

> Early in March last year it seemed advisable to envisage the possibility that . . . the release of large amounts of energy . . . might be imminent. Realising to what extent this hinges on the "double neutron," I have applied for a patent along these lines. . . . Obviously it would be misplaced to consider patents in this field private property and pursue them with a view to commercial exploitation for private purposes. When the time is ripe some suitable body will have to be created to ensure their proper use.

For the time being, Szilard proposed to work at Oxford on finding his "double neutrons," possibly raising £1,000 on the side "from private persons" so that he could hire a helper or two. To bait Lindemann's Clarendon ambitions, he argued in conclusion that "this type of work could greatly accelerate the building up of nuclear physics at Oxford." As indeed, had it gone forward, it might have done.

When he learned, possibly from Lindemann, that he could keep his patents secret only by assigning them to some appropriate agency of the British government, Szilard offered them first to the War Office. Director of Artillery J. Coombes turned them down on October 8, noting that "there appears to be no reason to keep the specification secret so far as the War Department is concerned." If Lindemann heard of the rejection he must have remembered his own rejection by the Army in 1915. The following February 1936, he intervened on Szilard's behalf with the Admiralty, Churchill's old bailiwick, writing the head of the Department of Scientific Research and Development cannily:

> I daresay you remember my ringing you up about a man working here who had a patent which he thought ought to be kept secret. I enclose a letter from him on the subject as you suggested. I am naturally somewhat less optimistic about the prospects than the inventor, but he is a very good physicist and even if the chances were a hundred to one against it seems to me it might be worth keeping the thing secret as it is not going to cost the Government anything.

The patent, Szilard explained in the letter Lindemann enclosed, "contains information which could be used in the construction of explosive bodies . . . very many thousand times more powerful than ordinary bombs." He was concerned about "the disasters which could be caused by their use on the part of certain Powers which might attack this country." Wisely and withal inexpensively the Admiralty accepted the patent into its safekeeping.

Eight months in Copenhagen had suited Edward Teller. He met George Gamow on the Odessan's last visit there, after the Solvay Conference of the previous autumn; the two of them roared across Denmark and back during Easter vacation on Gamow's motorcycle, working over a problem in quantum mechanics. The Rockefeller Foundation did not approve of marriage during a fellowship period, but James Franck had interceded on his behalf and Teller had married his childhood sweetheart, Mici Harkanyi, in Budapest on February 26. He had also written an important paper. He returned to London with Mici in the summer of 1934 with his reputation enhanced and again took up his lectureship at University College. Assuming they would settle in England, the Tellers signed a nine-year lease just before Christmas on a pleasant three-room flat.

Two offers arrived in January, one of which changed Teller's mind. The first was from Princeton: a lectureship. The second was from Gamow: a full professorship at George Washington University. GWU wanted to strengthen its physics department; Gamow wanted company and liked Teller's verve.

Teller was twenty-six years old and a newlywed. He was less than sure about living in the United States, but a full professorship was not something he could sensibly refuse. His wife found someone to sublet the flat. The U.S. State Department refused nonquota immigration visas because Teller had only taught for one year—the Copenhagen time counted merely as a fellowship—and was required to have taught for two. He had not, however, tried for visas on the Hungarian immigration quota because he assumed the quota was full. In fact there was room. The Tellers followed the Gamows across the Atlantic in August 1935.

Niels Bohr celebrated his fiftieth birthday on October 7. "Bohr in those days seemed at the height of his powers, bodily and mentally," Otto Frisch observes. "When he thundered up the steep staircase [of the institute], two steps at a time, there were few of us younger ones that could keep pace with him. The peace of the library was often broken by a brisk game of ping-pong, and I don't remember ever beating Bohr at that game." To honor Denmark's leading physicist, George de Hevesy organized a fund-raising campaign; the Danish people contributed 100,000 kroner to buy Bohr 0.6

gram of radium for his birthday. De Hevesy divided the radium, in liquid solution, into six equal parts, mixed each with beryllium powder and allowed them to dry, making six potent neutron sources. He had them mounted on the ends of long rods and stored them in a dry well in the basement of the institute that had been dug originally to supply vibration-free housing for a spectrograph.

The institute's annual Christmas party continued to be held in the well room, Stefan Rozental recalls: "The lid of the well served as a table, a Christmas tree stood in the middle, and all the personnel were gathered, from the chief down to the youngest apprentice in the workshop, and served a modest meal of sausages and beer. During the party Niels Bohr used to make a speech in which he gave a sort of survey of the past year." Safely below the sausages, stuck in a gallon flask of carbon disulphide, the neutron sources silently transmuted sulfur to radioactive phosphorus for de Hevesy's biological radioisotope studies.

Bohr had won national distinction for his work and the enduring gratitude of refugees for his aid; he had also faced personal pain. In 1932 the Danish Academy offered him lifetime free occupancy of the Danish House of Honor, a palatial estate in Pompeiian style built originally for the founder of Carlsberg Breweries and subsequently reserved for Denmark's most distinguished citizen (Knud Rasmussen, the polar explorer, was its previous occupant). By then the institute buildings included a modest director's house, but the Bohrs shared it with five handsome sons. They moved to the mansion beside the brewery, the best address in Denmark after the King's.

Two years later an accident took the Bohrs' eldest son, Christian, nineteen years old. Father, son and two friends were sailing on the Öresund, the sea passage between Denmark and Sweden, when a squall blew up. Christian "was drowned by falling over[board] in a very rough sea from a sloop," Robert Oppenheimer reports, "and Bohr circled as long as there was light, looking for him." But the Öresund is cold. For a time Bohr retreated into grief. Exhausting as it was, the refugee turmoil helped him.

Everyone at the institute followed Fermi's neutron work with fascination. Frisch, the only physicist on hand who knew Italian, was drafted to translate the successive papers aloud as soon as each issue of the *Ricerca Scientifica* arrived. The Copenhagen group was puzzled that slow neutrons affected some elements more intensely than others; on the one-particle model of the nucleus even a slow neutron should almost always shoot completely through a nucleus without capture.

From Cornell Hans Bethe published a paper calculating the slim odds of neutron capture. They conflicted squarely with observation. Frisch remembers the colloquium in Copenhagen in 1935 when someone reported on Bethe's paper:

On that occasion Bohr kept interrupting, and I was beginning to wonder, with some irritation, why he didn't let the speaker finish. Then, in the middle of a sentence, Bohr suddenly stopped and sat down, his face completely dead. We looked at him for several seconds, getting anxious. Had he been taken unwell? But then he suddenly got up and said with an apologetic smile, "Now I understand it."

What Bohr understood about the nucleus he embodied in a landmark lecture to the Danish Academy on January 27, 1936, subsequently published in *Nature*. "Neutron capture and nuclear constitution" exploited the phenomenon of neutron capture to propose a new model of the nucleus; once again, as he had with Rutherford's planetary model of the atom, Bohr stood on the solid ground of experiment to argue for radical theoretical change.

He visualized a nucleus made up of neutrons and protons closely packed together—a model now familiar—rather than a single particle. (Nuclear particles collectively are known as nucleons.) A neutron entering such a crowded nucleus would not pass through; it would collide with the nearest nucleons, surrender its kinetic energy (as a cue ball does at break in billiards) and be captured by the strong force that holds the nucleus together. The energy added by the neutron would agitate the nearby nucleons; they would collide in turn with other nucleons beyond; the net effect would be a more generally agitated, "hotter" nucleus but one where no single component could quickly acquire enough energy to push through the electrical barrier and escape. If the nucleus then radiated its excess energy by ejecting a gamma photon, "cooling off," none of its nucleons could accrue enough energy to escape. The result, already confirmed by Fermi's experiments, would be the creation of a heavier isotope of the original element being bombarded.

More violent assaults on the nucleus, Bohr thought, would still disperse their energies throughout the compound nucleus created by their capture. Subsequent reconcentration of the energy might allow the nucleus to eject several charged or uncharged particles. Bohr did not think his compound model of the nucleus boded well for harnessing nuclear energy:

> For still more violent impacts, with particles of energies of about a thousand million volts, we must even be prepared for the collision to lead to an explosion of the whole nucleus. Not only are such energies, of course, at present far beyond the reach of experiments, but it does not need to be stressed that such effects would scarcely bring us any nearer to the solution of the much discussed problem of releasing the nuclear energy for practical purposes. Indeed, the more our knowledge of nuclear reactions advances the remoter this goal seems to become.

Thus by the mid-1930s the three most original living physicists had each spoken to the question of harnessing nuclear energy. Rutherford had dismissed it as moonshine; Einstein had compared it to shooting in the dark at scarce birds; Bohr thought it remote in direct proportion to understanding. If they seem less perceptive in their skepticism than Szilard, they also had a better grasp of the odds. The essential future is always unforeseen. They were experienced enough not to long for it.

In his lecture Bohr preferred to state only general principles, but to trace "the consequences of the general argument here developed" he had a specific mathematical model in mind. He published a discussion of that model the following year, in 1937. It reached all the way back to his doctoral dissertation on the surface tension of fluids to demonstrate the usefulness of treating the atomic nucleus as if it were a liquid drop.*

The tendency of molecules to stick together gives liquids a "skin" of surface tension. A falling raindrop thus rounds itself into a small perfect sphere. But any force acting on a liquid drop deforms it (think of the wobbles of a water-filled balloon thrown into the air and caught). Surface tension and deforming forces work against each other in complex ways; the molecules of the liquid bump and collide; the drop wobbles and distorts. Eventually the added energy dissipates as heat, and the drop steadies again.

The nucleus, Bohr proposed, was similar. The force that stuck the nucleons together was the nuclear strong force. Counteracting that strong force was the common electrical repulsion of the positively charged nuclear protons. The delicate balance between the two fundamental forces made the nucleus liquidlike. Energy added from the outside by particle bombardment deformed it; it wobbled like a liquid drop, oscillating complexly just as the braided streams of water Bohr had studied for his dissertation had oscillated. Which meant he could use Rayleigh's classical formulae for the surface tension of liquids to understand the complex nuclear energy levels and exchanges that Fermi's work had revealed. "This 1937 paper had to close with many issues not cleared up," writes the American theoretical physicist John Archibald Wheeler, who helped Bohr clear up more of them later. The liquid-drop model proved useful, however, and Frisch in Copenhagen and Meitner in Berlin, among others, took it to heart.

One fine October Thursday in 1937 Ernest Rutherford, a vigorous sixty-six, went out into the garden of his house on the green Cambridge Backs to

*George Gamow had proposed such a model in Copenhagen in 1928. Bohr credited it to Gamow at the October 1933 Solvay conference, as did Heisenberg. Bohr and his student Fritz Kalkar subsequently developed the model and physicists customarily attribute it to him.

trim a tree. He took a bad fall. He was "seedy" later in the day, Mary Rutherford said—nausea and indigestion—and she arranged for a masseur. Rutherford vomited that night. In the morning he called his family doctor. He suffered from a slight umbilical hernia, which he confined with a truss; his doctor found a possible strangulation, consulted with a specialist and directed the Rutherfords to the Evelyn Nursing Home for emergency surgery. Rutherford told his wife along the way that his business and financial affairs were all in order. She said his illness wasn't serious and asked him not to worry.

Surgery that evening confirmed a partial strangulation, released the imprisoned portion of the small intestine and restored its circulation. Saturday Rutherford seemed to be recovering but he began vomiting again on Sunday and there were signs of infection, deadly in those days before antibiotics. Monday he was worse; his doctors consulted the surgeon, a Melbourne man, who advised against a second operation given the patient's age and symptoms. Rutherford was made comfortable with intravenous saline, six pints by Tuesday, and a stomach tube. Tuesday morning, October 19, he was slightly improved, but though his wife judged him "a wonderful patient [who] bears his discomforts splendidly" and believed she discovered "just a thread of hope," he began that afternoon to weaken. A bequest he decided late in the day suggests he found gratitude in those last hours reviewing his life. "I want to leave a hundred pounds to Nelson College," he told Mary Rutherford. "You can see to it." And again loudly a little later: "Remember, a hundred to Nelson College." He died that evening. "Heart and circulation failed" because of massive infection, his doctor wrote, "and the end came peacefully."

An international gathering of physicists in Bologna that week celebrated the 200th anniversary of the birth of Luigi Galvani; Cambridge cabled the news of Rutherford's death on the morning of October 20. Bohr was on hand and accepted the grim duty of announcement. "When the meeting scheduled for that morning assembled," writes Mark Oliphant, "Bohr went to the front, and with faltering voice and tears in his eyes informed the gathering of what had happened." They were shocked at the abruptness of the loss. Bohr had visited Rutherford at Cambridge a few weeks earlier; the Cavendish men had seen their leader in fine fettle only days ago.

Bohr "spoke from the heart," says Oliphant, recalling "the debt which science owed so great a man whom he was privileged to call both his master and his friend." For Oliphant it was "one of the most moving experiences of my life." Remembering Rutherford in a letter to Oppenheimer on December 20 Bohr balanced loss with hope, complementarily: "Life is poorer without him; but still every thought about him will be a lasting encouragement." And in 1958, in a memorial lecture, Bohr said simply that "to me he had almost been as a second father."

The sub-dean of Westminster immediately approved interment of Rutherford's ashes in the nave of Westminster Abbey, just west of Newton's tomb and in line with Kelvin's. Eulogizing Rutherford at a conference in Calcutta the following January, James Jeans identified his place in the history of science:

> Voltaire said once that Newton was more fortunate than any other scientist could ever be, since it could fall to only one man to discover the laws which governed the universe. Had he lived in a later age, he might have said something similar of Rutherford and the realm of the infinitely small; for Rutherford was the Newton of atomic physics.

Ernest Rutherford unknowingly wrote his own more characteristic epitaph in a letter to A. S. Eve from his country cottage on the first day of that last October. He reported of his garden what he had also done for physics, vigorous and generous work: "I have made a still further clearance of the blackberry patch and the view is now quite attractive."

In September 1934, in the wake of Fermi's June *Nature* article "Possible production of elements of atomic number higher than 92," a curious paper appeared in a publication seldom read by physicists, the *Zeitschrift für Angewandte Chemie*—the *Journal of Applied Chemistry*. Its author was a respected German chemist, Ida Noddack, co-discoverer with her husband (in 1925) of the hard, platinum-white metallic element rhenium, atomic number 75. The paper was titled simply "On element 93" and it severely criticized Fermi's work. His "method of proof" was "not valid," Noddack wrote bluntly. He had demonstrated that "his new beta emitter" was not protactinium and then distinguished it from several other elements descending down the periodic table to lead, but it was "not clear why he chose to stop at lead." The old view that the radioactive elements form a continuous series beginning at uranium and ending at lead, wrote Noddack, was exactly what the Joliot-Curies' discovery of artificial radioactivity had disproved. "Fermi therefore ought to have compared his new radioelement with all known elements."

The fact was, Noddack went on, any number of elements could be precipitated out of uranium nitrate with manganese. Instead of assuming the production of a new transuranic element, "one could assume equally well that when neutrons are used to produce nuclear disintegrations, some distinctly new nuclear reactions take place which have not been observed previously." In the past, elements have transmuted only into their near neighbors. But "when heavy nuclei are bombarded by neutrons, it is conceivable that the nucleus breaks up into several large fragments, which would of course be isotopes of known elements but would not be neighbors." They would be, rather, much lighter elements farther down the periodic table than lead.

Segrè remembers reading the Noddack paper. He knows, because he asked them, that Hahn in Berlin and Joliot in Paris read it. It made very little sense to anyone. "I think whatever chemists read it," Frisch reminisces, "probably thought that this was quite pointless, carping criticism, and the physicists possibly even more so if they read it, because they would say, 'What's the use of criticizing unless you give some reason why that criticism would be valid?' Nobody had ever found a nuclear disintegration creating far-removed elements." Which was a point Noddack had carefully addressed, but was clearly one reason for the paper's neglect. The summary report for *Nature* on artificial radioactivity that Amaldi and Segrè had delivered to Rutherford in midsummer 1934 makes the assumption explicit: "It is reasonable to assume that the atomic number of the active element should be close to the atomic number . . . of the bombarded element."

But Fermi seldom left anything to assumption, however reasonable. He would certainly not have left to assumption this issue, about which he was already acutely sensitive because of Corbino's ill-timed speech (Noddack rubbed salt into that wound by referring to "the reports found in the newspapers"). He sat down and performed the necessary calculations. He later told at least Teller, Segrè and his American protégé Leona Woods that he had done so. Teller is quite sure he knows what those calculations were:

> Fermi refused to believe [Noddack]. . . . He knew how to calculate whether or not uranium could break in two. . . . He performed the calculation Mrs. Noddack suggested, and found that the probability was extraordinarily low. He concluded that Mrs. Noddack's suggestion could not possibly be correct. So he forgot about it. His theory was right . . . but . . . it was based on the . . . wrong experimental information.

Here Teller indicts Aston's measurement of the mass of helium (the same that had misled Szilard to beryllium), which "introduced a systematic error into calculating the mass and energy of nuclei."

Segrè finds Teller's version of the story possible but not persuasive. The helium mass number problem would not necessarily have ruled out breaking up the uranium nucleus. "You know, occasionally Fermi would tell you things, then you asked him, 'But really, how? Show me.' And then he would say, 'Oh, well, I know this on *c.i.f.*' He spoke Italian. '*C.i.f.*' meant '*con intuito formidable*,' 'with formidable intuition.' So how he did it, I don't know. On the other hand, Fermi made a lot of calculations which he kept to himself."

Leona Woods' version sheds light on Teller's:

> Why was Dr. Noddack's suggestion ignored? The reason is that she was ahead of her time. Bohr's liquid-drop model of the nucleus had not yet been formulated, and so there was at hand no accepted way to calculate whether breaking up into several large fragments was energetically allowed.

If Noddack's physics was *avant garde*, her chemistry was sound. By 1938 her article was gathering dust on back shelves, but Bohr had promulgated the liquid-drop model of the nucleus and the confused chemistry of uranium increasingly preoccupied Lise Meitner and Otto Hahn.

9

An Extensive Burst

"I believe all young people think about how they would like their lives to develop," Lise Meitner wrote in old age, looking back; "when I did so I always arrived at the conclusion that life need not be easy provided only that it was not empty. And this wish I have been granted." Sixty years old in 1938, the Austrian physicist had earned wide respect by hard and careful work. When Wolfgang Pauli had wished to propose an elusive, almost massless neutral particle to explain the energy that seemed to disappear in beta decay—it came to be called the neutrino—he had made his proposal in a letter to Lise Meitner and Hans Geiger. James Chadwick was "quite convinced that she would have discovered the neutron if it had been firmly in her mind, if she had had the advantage of, say, living in the Cavendish for years, as I had done." "Slight in figure and shy by nature," as her nephew Otto Frisch describes her, she was nevertheless formidable.

During the Great War she had volunteered as an X-ray technician with the Austrian Army; "there," says Frisch, "she had to cope with streams of injured Polish soldiers, not understanding their language, and with her medical bosses who interfered with her work, not understanding X-rays." She arranged her leaves from duty to coincide with Otto Hahn's and hurried to the Kaiser Wilhelm Institute for Chemistry in Dahlem to work with him; that was when they identified the element next down from uranium that they named protactinium. After the war she did physics separately until 1934, when, challenged by Fermi's work, she "persuaded Otto Hahn to renew our direct collaboration" to explore the consequences of bombarding uranium with neutrons. Meitner headed the physics department at the institute then, of which Hahn had become the director. She had attained by middle age, Hahn remarks fondly, "not only the dignity of a German professor, but also one of his proverbial attributes, absentmindedness." At a scientific gathering "a male colleague greeted her by saying, 'We met on an earlier occasion.' Not remembering that earlier occasion, she replied in all seriousness, 'You probably mistake me for Professor Hahn.' " Hahn supposed she was thinking of the many papers they had published together.

If she hid her shyness behind formidable reserve, among friends, Frisch says, "she could be lively and cheerful, and an excellent storyteller." Her nephew thought her "totally lacking in vanity." She wore her thick dark hair, now graying, pulled back and coiled in a bun and her youthful beauty had muted to bright but darkly circled eyes, a thin mouth, a prominent nose. She ate lightly but drank quantities of strong coffee. Music moved her; she followed it as other people follow trends and fashions in art (a family cultivation—her sister, Frisch's mother, was a concert pianist). She made a duet at the piano on visits with her musical nephew, "though hardly anybody else knew that she could play." She lived in an apartment at the KWI and when there was time she took long walks, ten miles or more a day: "It keeps me young and alert." Her most holy commitment, Frisch thought, "the vision she never lost" that filled her life, was "of physics as a battle for final truth."

The truth she battled for through the later 1930s was hidden somewhere in the complexities of uranium. She and Hahn, and beginning in 1935 a young German chemist named Fritz Strassmann, worked to sort out all the substances into which the heaviest of natural elements transmuted under neutron bombardment. By early 1938 they had identified no fewer than ten different half-life activities, many more than Fermi had demonstrated in his first pioneering survey. They assumed the substances must be either isotopes of uranium or transuranics. "For Hahn," says Frisch, "it was like the old days when new elements fell like apples when you shook the tree; [but] Lise Meitner found [the energetic reactions necessary to produce such new elements] unexpected and increasingly hard to explain."

Meanwhile Irène Curie had begun looking into uranium with a visiting Yugoslav, Pavel Savitch. They described a 3.5-hour activity the Germans had not reported and suggested it might be thorium, element 90, with which Curie had years of experience. If true, the Curie-Savitch suggestion would mean that a slow neutron somehow acquired the energy to knock an energetic alpha particle out of the uranium nucleus. The KWI trio scoffed, looked for the 3.5-hour activity, failed to find it and wrote the Radium Institute suggesting a public retraction. The French team identified the activity again and discovered they could separate it from their uranium by carrier chemistry using lanthanum (element 57, a rare earth). They proposed therefore that it must be either actinium, element 89, chemically similar to lanthanum but even harder than thorium to explain, or else a new and mysterious element.

Either way, their findings called the KWI work into doubt. Hahn met Joliot in May at a chemistry congress in Rome and told the Frenchman cordially but frankly that he was skeptical of Curie's discovery and intended to repeat her experiment and expose her error. By then, as Joliot undoubtedly knew, his wife had already raised the stakes, had tried to separate the "actinium" from its lanthanum carrier and had found it would not separate. No one imagined the substance could actually be lanthanum: how could a slow neutron transmute uranium into a much lighter rare earth thirty-four places down the periodic table? "It seems," Curie and Savitch reported that May in the *Comptes Rendus*, "that this substance cannot be anything except a transuranic element, possessing very different properties from those of other known transuranics, a hypothesis which raises great difficulties for its interpretation."

In the course of this exotic debate Meitner's status changed. Adolf Hitler bullied the young chancellor of Austria to a meeting at the German dictator's Berchtesgaden retreat in Bavaria in mid-February. "Who knows," Hitler threatened him, "perhaps I shall be suddenly overnight in Vienna: like a spring storm." On March 14 he was, triumphantly parading; the day before, with the raw new German Wehrmacht occupying its capital, Austria had proclaimed itself a province of the Third Reich and its most notorious native son had wept for joy. The *Anschluss*—the annexation—made Meitner a German citizen to whom all the ugly anti-Semitic laws applied that the Nazi state had been accumulating since 1933. "The years of the Hitler regime . . . were naturally very depressing," she wrote near the end of her life. "But work was a good friend, and I have often thought and said how wonderful it is that by work one may be granted a long respite of forgetfulness from oppressive political conditions." After the spring storm of the *Anschluss* her grant was abruptly withdrawn.

Max von Laue sought her out then. He had heard that Heinrich Himmler, head of the Nazi SS and chief of German police, had issued an order forbidding the emigration of any more academics. Meitner feared she might be expelled from the KWI and left unemployed and exposed. She made contact with Dutch colleagues including Dirk Coster, the physicist who had worked in Copenhagen with George de Hevesy in 1922 to discover hafnium. The Dutchmen persuaded their government to admit Meitner to Holland without a visa on a passport that was nothing more now than a sad souvenir.

Coster traveled to Berlin on Friday, July 16, arriving in the evening, and went straight to Dahlem to the KWI. The editor of *Naturwissenschaften*, Paul Rosbaud, an old friend, showed up as well, and together with Hahn the men spent the night helping Meitner pack. "I gave her a beautiful diamond ring," Hahn remembers, "that I had inherited from my mother and which I had never worn myself but always treasured; I wanted her to be provided for in an emergency."

Meitner left with Coster by train on Saturday morning. Nine years later she remembered the grim passage as if she had traveled alone:

> I took a train for Holland on the pretext that I wanted to spend a week's vacation. At the Dutch border, I got the scare of my life when a Nazi military patrol of five men going through the coaches picked up my Austrian passport, which had expired long ago. I got so frightened, my heart almost stopped beating. I knew that the Nazis had just declared open season on Jews, that the hunt was on. For ten minutes I sat there and waited, ten minutes that seemed like so many hours. Then one of the Nazi officials returned and handed me back the passport without a word. Two minutes later I descended on Dutch territory, where I was met by some of my Holland colleagues.

She was safe then. She moved on to Copenhagen for the emotional renewal of rest at the Carlsberg House of Honor with the Bohrs. Bohr had found a place for her in Sweden at the Physical Institute of the Academy of Sciences on the outskirts of Stockholm, a thriving laboratory directed by Karl Manne Georg Siegbahn, the 1924 Physics Nobel laureate for work in X-ray spectroscopy. The Nobel Foundation provided a grant. She traveled to that far northern exile, to a country where she had neither the language nor many friends, as if to prison.

Leo Szilard was looking for a patron. Frederick Lindemann had arranged an ICI fellowship for him at Oxford beginning in 1935, and for a while Szilard worked there, but the possibility of war in Europe made him restless. From Oxford in late March 1936 he had written Gertrud Weiss in Vienna that she should consider emigrating to America; he appears to have applied his reasoning to his own case as well. Szilard had met Weiss in his Berlin years and subsequently advised and quietly courted her. Now she had graduated from medical school. At his invitation she came to Oxford to see him. They walked in the country; she photographed him standing at roadside before a weathered log barrier, rounding at thirty-eight but not yet rotund, with a budding young tree filigreed behind him. "He told me he would be surprised if one could work in Vienna in two years. He said Hitler would be there. And he was"—the *Anschluss*—"almost to the day."

Szilard had written in his letter that England was "a *very* likeable country, but it would certainly be a lot smarter if you went to America. . . . In America you would be a free human being and very soon would not even be a 'stranger.' " (Weiss went, and stayed to become a distinguished expert in public health and, late in their wandering years, Szilard's wife.) During the same period Szilard wrote Michael Polanyi he would "stay in England until one year before the war, at which time I would shift my residence to New York City." The letter provoked comment, Szilard enjoyed recalling; it was "very funny, because how can anyone say what he will do one year *before* the war?" As it turned out, his prognostication was off by only four months: he arrived in the United States on January 2, 1938.

Before then Szilard had located a possible patron there, a Jewish financier of Virginia background named Lewis Lichtenstein Strauss, his first and middle names honoring his East Prussian maternal grandfather, his last name softened in Southern fashion to *straws*. Forty-two years old in 1938, Lewis Strauss was a full partner at the New York investment-banking house of Kuhn, Loeb, a self-made millionaire, an adaptable, clever but thin-skinned and pompous man.

Strauss had dreamed as a boy of becoming a physicist. The recession of 1913–14 had staggered his family's Richmond business—wholesale shoes—and his father had called on him at seventeen to drum a four-state territory. He did well; by 1917 he had saved twenty thousand dollars and was once again preparing to pursue a physics career. This time the Great War intervened. A childhood accident had left Strauss with marginal vision in one eye. His mother doted on him. She allowed his younger brother to volunteer for military service but looked for some less dangerous contribution for her favorite son. It turned up when Woodrow Wilson appointed the celebrated mining engineer and Belgian relief administrator Herbert Hoover as Food Administrator to manage U.S. supplies during the war. The wealthy Hoover was serving in Washington without pay and assembling a prosperous, unpaid young staff, Rhodes scholars preferred. Rosa Lichtenstein Strauss sent her boy.

He was twenty-one, knew how to ingratiate himself, knew also how to work. Improbable as it appears against a field of Rhodes scholars, within a month Hoover appointed the high-school-graduate wholesale shoe drummer as his private secretary. After the Armistice young Strauss shifted with Hoover to Paris, hastily picked up French at tutoring sessions over lunch and helped organize the allocation of 27 million tons of food and supplies to twenty-three countries. On the side he assisted the Jewish Joint Distribution Committee in its work of relieving the suffering of the hundreds of thousands of Jewish refugees streaming from Eastern Europe in the wake of war.

Strauss believed God had planned his life, which contributed greatly to his self-confidence. God let him take up employment when he was twenty-three, in 1919, at Kuhn, Loeb, a distinguished house with a number of major railroads among its clients. Four years later he married Alice Hanauer, daughter of one of the partners. His salary and participation reached $75,000 a year in 1926; the following year it escalated to $120,000. In 1929 he became a partner himself and settled into prosperous gentility.

The 1930s brought him pain and grief. After resisting Chaim Weizmann's attempts to convert him to Zionism at a Jewish conference in London in 1933—"My boy, you are difficult," Weizmann told him; "we will have to grind you down"—he returned to the United States to discover his mother terminally ill with cancer. She died early in 1935; the disease took his father as well in the hot summer of 1937. Strauss looked for a suitable memorial. "I became aware," he reports in his memoirs, "of the inadequate supply of radium for the treatment of cancer in American hospitals." He established the Lewis and Rosa Strauss Memorial Fund and turned up a young refugee physicist from Berlin, Arno Brasch. Brasch had designed a capacitor-driven discharge tube for producing bursts of high-energy X rays, a "surge generator." When Leo Szilard was working at St. Bart's with Chalmers in the summer of 1934 he had arranged for Brasch and his colleagues in Berlin to break up beryllium with hard X rays; the experiment had been a success and Brasch and four other contributors had signed the report to *Nature* along with Chalmers and Szilard. If X rays could break up beryllium they might at least induce radioactivity in other elements. "An isotope of cobalt thus produced," writes Strauss, "would be radioactive and would emit gamma rays similar to the radiation produced by radium. . . . Radioactive cobalt could be made . . . at a cost of a few dollars a gram. Radium was then priced at about fifty thousand dollars a gram. . . . I foresaw the possibility of producing the isotope in quantity and of giving it to hospitals as a memorial to my parents."

Enter Leo Szilard, still in England:

August 30, 1937

Dear Mr. Strauss:

I understand that you are interested in the development of a surge generator with the view of using it for producing artificially radioactive elements. . . .

> At present . . . I am not in the position of [offering manufacturing rights under this patent]. It is possible, however, that at a later date . . . I shall obtain full liberty of action concerning this patent. If this happens I shall let you have a non-exclusive license, royalty free, *but* limited to the production of radioactive elements by means of high voltage generated by a surge generator.
>
> Yours very truly,
> Leo Szilard

Brasch and Szilard owned the patent in question jointly. Szilard's letter offers to give his interest away free of charge nonexclusively to Strauss, a politic salutation to a rich man. But not even Leo Szilard could live on air, and as Strauss makes clear in his memoirs, the two young physicists eventually "asked me to finance them in the construction of a 'surge generator.' " On the other hand, Szilard as usual seems to have sought no personal financial gain from the project beyond, perhaps, basic support. In the time he could spare from observing the developing disaster in Europe he was apparently trying to promote the building of equipment with which he might explore further the possibility of a chain reaction.

He crossed the Atlantic in late September to reconnoiter. A friend remembers discussing the feasibility of an atomic bomb with Szilard during this period. "In the same conversation he spoke of his ideas for preserving peaches in tins in such a way that they would retain the texture and taste of the fresh fruit." When the surge-generator negotiations bogged down in debates among the lawyers, the resourceful Szilard distracted Strauss with the idea of using radiation to preserve and protect the natural products of farm and field. The tobacco worm might be exterminated, for example. But would irradiation harm the tobacco? Among Szilard's surviving papers is lodged a fading letter from Dr. M. Lenz of the Montefiore Hospital for Chronic Diseases that reports the decisive experiment:

> On April 14, 1938, at 2:30 p.m., your six cigars were irradiated with 100 kv., a filter focus distance of 20 cm. with ten minutes in front and ten minutes over the back of each cigar. This gave them 1000 r. in front and 1500 r. in back of each cigar.
>
> I hope that your friend finds the taste unchanged.

Szilard also bought pork from a meat market on Amsterdam Avenue, saving the receipt, and arranged its irradiation to see if X rays might kill the parasitic worm of trichinosis. He even dispatched his brother Béla to Chicago to discuss the matter with Swift & Company, which reported it had in fact made similar experiments of its own.

The surge-generator project developed through the year, incidentally giving Strauss the opportunity to meet Ernest Lawrence, who dropped by to pitch the new sixty-inch cyclotron he was building—the pole pieces were sixty inches across, but the magnet would weigh nearly two hundred tons. Lawrence and his brother John, a physician, had arrested their mother's cancer with accelerator radiation and intended to use the big cyclotron to further that research. Strauss remained loyal to the surge generator.

Segrè encountered Strauss's Hungarian wizard in New York that summer. The elegant Italian was professor of physics at Palermo by then, married to a German woman who had fled Breslau to escape the Nazis, with a young son:

> I left Palermo with a return ticket, and I arrived in New York. I met Szilard. "Oh, what are you doing here?" He was a good friend of mine. I knew him quite well. "What are you doing here? What's going on?"
>
> I said, "I'm going to Berkeley to look at the short-lived isotopes of element 43," which was my plan. "I'll work there the summer, and then I'll go back to Palermo."
>
> He said, "You are not going back to Palermo. By this fall, God knows what will happen! You can't go back."
>
> I said, "Well, I have a return ticket. Let's hope for the best."
>
> But I had gotten a passport for my wife and my son before leaving, because I smelled that the situation was dangerous. So I took the train in New York, Grand Central, and I bought the newspaper in Chicago. I still remember it. I will remember it as long as I live. I opened the newspaper, and I found out that Mussolini had started the antisemitic campaign and had fired everybody. So there I was. So I had the ticket and went to Berkeley. I started to work on my short-lived isotopes of technetium, but at the same time I tried to get some job. Then I got my wife here.

The pall of racism had dropped over Italy.

The physicists at the institute on Via Panisperna had been alert to the darkening Italian prospect since at least the mid-1930s. Segrè remembers asking Fermi in the spring of 1935 why the group's mood seemed less happy. Fermi suggested he look for an answer on the big table in the center of the institute reading room. Segrè did and found a world atlas there. He picked it up; it fell open automatically to a map of Ethiopia, which Italy in a show of Fascist bravado was about to invade. By the time the invasion began all but Amaldi were examining their options.

Fermi went off to the University of Michigan's summer school in Ann Arbor, renewing an affiliation he had begun with Laura in the summer of

1930. He liked America. "He was attracted," Segrè notes with an ear for Fermi's priorities, "by the well-equipped laboratories, the eagerness he sensed in the new generation of American physicists, and the cordial reception he enjoyed in academic circles. Mechanical proficiency and practical gadgets in America counterbalanced to an extent the beauty of Italy. American political life and political ideals were immeasurably superior to fascism." Fermi swam in Michigan's cool lakes and learned to enjoy American cooking. But the pressure of events in Italy was not yet sufficiently extreme, and Laura, Roman to her fine bones, was more than reluctant to leave the city of plane trees and classical ruins where she was born. Nor was anti-Semitism yet an issue in Italy—Mussolini had even declared he did not propose to make it one.

There was less to hold the other men. Rasetti summered at Columbia University that year, 1935, and decided to stay on. Segrè had shifted to Palermo but began looking toward Berkeley. Pontecorvo moved to Paris. D'Agostino went to work for the Italian National Research Council. Amaldi and Fermi pushed on alone, Amaldi remembers, Fermi even jettisoning his daily routine for the distraction of experiment:

> We worked with incredible stubbornness. We would begin at eight in the morning and take measurements [they were examining the unaccountably differing absorption of neutrons by different elements], almost without a break, until six or seven in the evening, and often later. The measurements . . . were repeated every three or four minutes, according to need, and for hours and hours for as many successive days as were necessary to reach a conclusion on a particular point. Having solved one problem, we immediately attacked another. . . . "Physics as soma" was our description of the work we performed while the general situation in Italy grew more and more bleak, first as a result of the Ethiopian campaign and then as Italy took part in the Spanish Civil War.

Fermi taught a summer course in thermodynamics at Columbia University in 1936 as the civil war began in Spain that would last three years, claim a million lives and set Mussolini decisively at Hitler's side. The following January Corbino died unexpectedly of pneumonia at sixty-one and the hostile occupant at the north end of the institute's second floor, Antonino Lo Sordo, a good Fascist, was appointed to succeed him. "That was a sign that Fermi's fortunes were declining in Italy," Segrè notes. "America," he concludes of those depressing years, "looked like the land of the future, separated by an ocean from the misfortunes, follies, and crimes of Europe."

If the *Anschluss* was a test of Hitler's strength, it was also a test of

Mussolini's willingness to acquiesce to complicity in crime. He had posed as Austria's protector; on the night of the March 1938 invasion Hitler waited near hysteria at the Chancellery in Berlin for a response from Rome to a letter he had sent justifying his action. The call came at 10:25 P.M. and the Führer snatched up the phone. "I have just come back from the Palazzo Venezia," his representative reported. "The Duce accepted the whole thing in a very friendly manner. He sends you his regards. . . . Mussolini said that Austria would be immaterial to him." Hitler replied: "Then please tell Mussolini I will never forget him for this! Never, never, never, no matter what happens! . . . As soon as the Austrian affair has been settled I shall be ready to go with him through thick and thin—through anything!" The Führer visited Rome in triumph in May, parading into districts the Duce had ordered hastily face-lifted to conceal their decay. Fermi's circle repeated the verse passed around the city by word of mouth by which an indignant Roman poet greeted the Nazi dictator:

Rome of travertine splendor
Patched with cardboard and plaster
Welcomes the little housepainter
As her next lord and master.

Italy would only be saved, Fermi told Segrè bitterly, if Mussolini went crazy and crawled on all fours.

The summer of 1938, July 14, brought the anti-Semitic *Manifesto della Razza* of which Segrè read in the Chicago newspaper on his way from New York to Berkeley. Italians are Aryans, the manifesto claimed. But "Jews do not belong to the Italian race." In Germany the vicious distinction had been commonplace; in Italy it was shocking. Italian Jews, only one in a thousand, were largely assimilated. The Fermis' two children—Giulio, a son, had been born in 1936—might be exempted since they were Catholic, born of a nominally Catholic father. But Laura was a Jew. She was spending the summer with the children in the Dolomites, the South Tyrol district named for the magnesian limestone that rings broad basin meadows with the flat, sharp formations Italians call "shovels." Enrico came up preoccupied in August to the meadow of San Martino di Castrozza to break the news. When Mussolini pushed through the first anti-Semitic laws early in September the Fermis decided to emigrate as soon as they could arrange their affairs. Fermi wrote four American universities and to avoid suspicion mailed each letter from a different Tyrolese town. Five schools shot back invitations. In confidence he accepted a professorship at Columbia and went off to Copenhagen to Bohr's annual gathering of the brethren.

The previous month the International Congress of Anthropological and Ethnological Sciences had invited Bohr to address it at a special session in Helsingør, Shakespeare's Elsinore, on the coast of Zealand north of Copenhagen. In the Renaissance castle there Denmark's most prominent citizen used the occasion to challenge Nazi racism publicly before the world. It was a brave statement by a brave man. Bohr understood that the major Western democracies were not likely to rally to the defense of his small, unprotected nation when Hitler eventually turned to look its way. George Placzek, a Bohemian theoretician working in Copenhagen whose tongue was almost as sharp as Pauli's, had already encapsulated that cruel truth. "Why should Hitler occupy Denmark?" Placzek quipped to Frisch one day. "He can just telephone, can't he?"

Against the brutal romanticism of German Blood and Earth, Bohr set the subtle corrective of complementarity. He spoke of "the dangers, well known to humanists, of judging from our own standpoint cultures developed within other societies." Complementarity, he proposed, offered a way to cope with the confusion. Subject and object interact to obscure each other in cultural comparisons as in physics and psychology; "we may truly say that different human cultures are complementary to each other. Indeed, each such culture represents a harmonious balance of traditional conventions by means of which latent possibilities of human life can unfold themselves in a way which reveals to us new aspects of its unlimited richness and variety."

The German delegates walked out. Bohr went on to say that the common aim of all science was "the gradual removal of prejudices," a complementary restorative to the usual pious characterization of science as a quest for incontrovertible truth. To a greater extent than any other scientist of the twentieth century Bohr perceived the institution of science to which he dedicated his life to be a profoundly political force in the world. The purpose of science, he believed, was to set men free. Totalitarianism, in Hannah Arendt's powerful image, drove toward "destroying all space between men and pressing men against each other." It was entirely in character that Bohr, at a time of increasing danger, publicly opposed that drive with the individualistic and enriching discretions of complementarity.

It was also entirely in character, when Fermi came to Copenhagen, that Bohr should lead him aside, take hold of his waistcoat button and whisper the message that his name had been mentioned for the Nobel Prize, a secret traditionally never foretold. Did Fermi wish his name withdrawn temporarily, given the political situation in Italy and the monetary restrictions, or would he like the selection process to go forward? Which was the same as telling Fermi he could have the Prize that year, 1938, if he wanted it and was welcome to use it to escape a homeland that threatened now despite the distinction he brought it to tear his wife from citizenship.

Leo Szilard's Cambridge collaborator Maurice Goldhaber emigrated to the United States in the late summer of 1938 and took up residence as an assistant professor of physics at the University of Illinois. Szilard appeared at Goldhaber's new apartment in Champaign in September to finish work they had begun together in England and stayed to follow the Munich crisis, for which purpose his host went out and bought a radio. Szilard understood, as Winston Churchill also understood and told his consituents at the end of August, that "the whole state of Europe and of the world is moving steadily towards a climax which cannot long be delayed." Before deciding between residency in England or the United States, Szilard said later, "I just thought I would wait and see."

The Sudetes, the border region of mountainous uplift that continues across Czechoslovakia from the Carpathians to the Erzgebirge, sustained at that time a German-speaking urban and industrialized population of some 2.3 million, about one-third of the population of western Czechoslovakia, formerly Bohemia. Nazi agitation began early in the Sudetenland; by 1935 a surrogate Nazi organization had become the largest political party in the Czechoslovakian republic. Hitler wanted Czechoslovakia next after Austria to facilitate his dream of German expansion, *Lebensraum*, and to deny airfields and support to the Soviet Union in the war he was well along in planning. The Sudetenland was his key. Czechoslovakia had built fortifications against German invasion across the Sudetes; after 1933 it imposed restrictions on the Sudeten Germans in an effort to protect that flank from subversion. Hitler opened his Czechoslovakian campaign even before the *Anschluss*, asserting the Reich's duty to protect the Sudeten Germans. Through the summer of 1938 German pressure on Czechoslovakia increased while the Western democracies maneuvered to avoid confrontation.

By the time Szilard began listening to Maurice Goldhaber's new radio the Czech government had established full martial law in the Sudetenland but also offered autonomy to the region in excess of what the Sudeten German Party had demanded. These developments prompted the British Prime Minister, Neville Chamberlain, to propose a meeting with Hitler. Hitler was delighted. He invited the Prime Minister to Berchtesgaden. The last outcome he wanted was a Czechoslovakian settlement. He signaled the Sudeten Nazis to increase their demands. Chamberlain heard the extremist proclamation on the radio on September 16 as he rode out by train from Munich: a call for immediate annexation to the German Reich. Back in

London on September 17 he recommended the annexation. Hitler, he said, "was in a fighting mood."

"The British and French cabinets at this time," writes Churchill, "presented a front of two overripe melons crushed together; whereas what was needed was a gleam of steel. On one thing they were all agreed: there should be no consultation with the Czechs. These should be confronted with the decision of their guardians. The Babes in the Wood had no worse treatment." The two governments, citing "conditions essential to security," decided that Czechoslovakia should cede to Germany all areas of the country where the population was more than 50 percent German. France had treaty obligations to Czechoslovakia but chose not to honor them. Facing such isolation, the small republic capitulated on September 21.

The Anglo-French proposals invoked self-determination for the German-speaking areas they defined. Hitler had agreed to such self-determination when he saw Chamberlain on September 16. Now the Prime Minister met with the Chancellor again, this time at Bad Godesberg on the Rhine outside Bonn, near Remagen. Hitler escalated his demands. "He told me," Chamberlain reported immediately afterward to the House of Commons, "that he never for one moment supposed that I should be able to come back and say that the principle [of self-determination] was accepted." Hitler wanted Czech acquiescence without self-determination by September 28 or he would invade. Chamberlain did not believe, however, he informed the Commons, that Hitler was deliberately deceiving him. The Nazi leader also told the Prime Minister "that this was the last of his territorial ambitions in Europe and that he had no wish to include in the Reich people of other races than Germans."

The Czechs mobilized a million and a half men. The French partly mobilized their army. The British fleet went active. At the same time a secret struggle may have been taking place between Hitler and the German general staff, which resisted any further plunge toward war. The result should have been stalemate, but Chamberlain moved again to concession. "Appeasement" was at that time a popular and not a pejorative word.

"How horrible, fantastic, incredible it is," the Prime Minister admonished the British people by radio on September 27, the night before Hitler's deadline, "that we should be digging trenches and trying on gas-masks here because of a quarrel in a faraway country between people of whom we know nothing!" He volunteered "to pay even a third visit to Germany." He was, he said, "a man of peace to the depths of my soul." He made the offer of a visit to Hitler at the same time directly by letter, and the Führer took him up on it the following afternoon. Chamberlain, French Premier Edouard Daladier, Mussolini and Hitler met at Munich on the evening of

September 29. By 2 A.M. the following morning the four leaders had agreed to Czech evacuation of the Sudetenland without self-determination within ten days beginning October 1. At Chamberlain's suggestion he and Hitler then met privately and agreed further to "regard the Agreement signed last night . . . as symbolic of the desire of our two peoples never to go to war with one another again." Before he left Munich, closeted with Mussolini, the Führer discussed Italian participation in the eventual invasion of the British Isles.

Chamberlain flew home. He read the joint declaration to the crowd gathered at the airport in welcome. Back in London he waved the declaration from an upper window of the Prime Minister's residence. "This is the second time there has come back from Germany to Downing Street peace with honour," he told the multitude below. "I believe it is peace in our time."

A group of refugee scientists was gathered outside the Clarendon Laboratory at Oxford the next morning discussing the Munich agreement when Frederick Lindemann drove up. Churchill had described the Czechoslovakian partition as amounting to "the complete surrender of the Western Democracies to the Nazi threat of force." Lindemann, Churchill's intimate adviser, was equally disgusted. One of the refugees asked him if he thought Chamberlain had something up his sleeve. "No," the Prof snapped, "something down his pants."

A cable came along to Lindemann then:

> HAVE ON ACCOUNT OF INTERNATIONAL SITUATION WITH GREAT REGRET POSTPONED MY SAILING FOR AN INDEFINITE PERIOD STOP WOULD BE VERY GRATEFUL IF YOU COULD CONSIDER ABSENCE AS LEAVE WITHOUT PAY STOP WRITING STOP PLEASE COMMUNICATE MY SINCERELY FELT GOOD WISHES TO ALL IN THESE DAYS OF GRAVE DECISIONS
>
> SZILARD

Szilard and Goldhaber found time during the crisis to write up a series of experiments with indium that they had started in England in 1937 and that Goldhaber and an Australian student, R. D. Hill, had completed before leaving for the United States. Szilard had thought indium might be a candidate for chain reaction but the results indicated that the radioactivity in indium of which Szilard had been suspicious was caused by a new type of reaction process, inelastic neutron scattering without neutron capture or loss. Szilard was discouraged. "As my knowledge of nuclear physics increased," he said later, "my faith in the possibility of a chain reaction gradually decreased." If other kinds of radiation also induced radioactivity in indium without producing neutrons, then he would have no more candidates for neutron multiplication and he would have to give up his belief in the process he still nicknamed "moonshine." That final experiment would be worked by friends at the University of Rochester in upstate New York, where he would travel in early December.

Otto Hahn opened the September 1938 issue of the *Comptes Rendus* to a shock. Part two of the Curie-Savitch study of the elusive 3.5-hour activity of uranium appeared there; amid much conjecture its most challenging conclusion was: "Taken altogether, the properties of $R_{3.5h}$ are those of lanthanum, from which it is not possible to separate it except by fractionation."*

Curie and Savitch believed that their $R_{3.5h}$ activity could be at least partly separated from lanthanum. It apparently did not occur to them that what was crystallizing out of solution might be another activity with a similar half-life, leaving a 3.5-hour lanthanum activity behind. They still could not believe—nor could anyone else—that uranium bombardment might produce an element thirty-five steps away down the periodic table. A Canadian radiochemist then visiting Dahlem records their German critic's response: "You can readily imagine Hahn's astonishment. . . . His reaction was that it just could not be, and that Curie and Savitch were very muddled up."

Despite his threat to Joliot in May, Hahn had not yet repeated the Curie-Savitch work. Now he passed the *Comptes Rendus* along to Fritz Strassmann. Strassmann studied the French paper and speculated that the muddle might have a physical cause—two similar radioactivities mixed together in the same solution. He told Hahn. Hahn laughed; the conclusion seemed improbable. On second thought, it was worth examining. As the Czechoslovakian crisis broke across Europe the two men bombarded uranium in peaceful Dahlem. They used a lanthanum carrier to precipitate rare-earth elements such as actinium (if any), a barium carrier to precipitate alkaline-earth elements such as radium (if any). (Carrier chemicals made it possible to separate from the parent solution the few thousand atoms of daughter substances produced by neutron bombardment. A chemically similar daughter substance, traceable by its unique half-life, would

*Fractionation—fractional crystallization—was a technique of chemical analysis pioneered by Marie Curie in the course of purifying polonium and radium. Most substances are more soluble at a high temperature than a low. Make a strong boiling solution of a substance—for rock candy, for example, sugar in water—cool the solution, and at some point the substance will emerge out of solution to form pure crystals. Fractional crystallization further involves separating out of the same solution several different, chemically similar substances by taking advantage of their tendency to crystallize at different temperatures according to differences in their atomic weights, lighter elements crystallizing first.

lodge in the spaces of the carrier's crystals as those regular solids formed from solution by chemical precipitation and would thus be carried away. Which carrier accomplished the carrying gave a clue to the part of the periodic table to which the unknown daughter substance belonged. Then it became a matter of further separating the daughter substance from the carrier by fractional crystallization, following it as before by tracing its characteristic radioactivity.)

After a hard week's work Hahn and Strassmann succeeded in identifying no fewer than sixteen different activities. Their barium separations gave them their most startling results: three previously unknown isotopes which they believed to be radium. They reported their findings in November in *Naturwissenschaften.* The creation of radium, element 88, from uranium, they pointed out, "must be due to the emission of two successive alpha particles."

If the physicists had found it hard to swallow that slow-neutron bombardment might produce thorium (90) or actinium (89), they found it even harder to swallow that it might produce radium. Lise Meitner wrote in warning from Stockholm suggesting pointedly that the two chemists check and recheck their results. Bohr invited Hahn to Copenhagen to lecture on the strange findings and tried to concoct a sufficiently crazy explanation:

> Bohr was skeptical and asked me if it was not highly improbable. . . . I had to reply that there was no other explanation, for our artificial radium could be separated only with weighable quantities of barium as carrier-substance. So apart from the radium only barium was present, and it was out of the question that it was anything but radium. Bohr suggested that these new radium isotopes of ours might perhaps in the end turn out to be strange transuranic elements.

Of the sixteen activities they had identified in neutron-bombarded uranium Hahn and Strassmann therefore now turned their full attention to the three controversial activities carried out of solution by barium.

Laura Fermi woke to the telephone early on the morning of November 10. A call would be placed from Stockholm, the operator advised her. Professor Fermi could expect it that evening at six.

Instantly awake to his wife's message, Fermi estimated the probability at 90 percent that the call would announce his Nobel Prize. As always he had planned conservatively, not counting on the award. The Fermis had prepared to leave for the United States from Italy shortly after the first of the year. Ostensibly Fermi was to lecture at Columbia for seven months and then return. For stays of longer than six months the United States required immigrant rather than tourist visas, and because Fermi was an academic he and his family could be granted such visas outside the Italian quota list. The ruse of a lecture series was devised to evade a drastic penalty: citizens leaving Italy permanently could take only the equivalent of fifty dollars with them out of the country. But the plan required circumspection. The Fermis could not sell their household goods or entirely empty their savings account without risking discovery. So the money from the Nobel Prize would be a godsend.

In the meantime they invested surreptitiously in what Fermi called "the refugee's trousseau." Laura's new coat was beaver and they distracted themselves on the day of the Stockholm call shopping for expensive watches. Diamonds, which had to be registered, they chose not to risk.

Near six o'clock the phone rang. It was Ginestra Amaldi wondering if they had heard. Everyone had gathered at the Amaldis to wait for the call, she reported. The Fermis turned on the six o'clock news. Laura long remembered the news:

> Hard, emphatic, pitiless, the commentator's voice read the second set of racial laws. The laws issued that day limited the activities and the civil status of the Jews. Their children were excluded from public schools. Jewish teachers were dismissed. Jewish lawyers, physicians, and other professionals could practice for Jewish clients only. Many Jewish firms were dissolved. "Aryan" servants were not allowed to work for Jews or to live in their homes. Jews were to be deprived of full citizenship rights, and their passports would be withdrawn.

The passports of Jews had already been marked. Fermi had contrived to keep his wife's passport clear.

They probably heard the news from Germany as well: of a vast pogrom the previous night—*Kristallnacht*, the night of glass. A seventeen-year-old Polish Jewish student had attempted to assassinate Ernst vom Rath, third secretary in the Germany Embassy in Paris, on November 7, in reprisal for Polish mistreatment of the student's parents. Vom Rath died on November 9 and the assassination served as an excuse for general anti-Semitic riot. Mobs torched synagogues, destroyed businesses and stores, dragged Jewish families from their homes and beat them in the streets. At least one hundred people died. A volume of plate glass was shattered that night across the Third Reich equal to half the annual production of its original Belgian sources. The SS arrested some thirty thousand Jewish men—"especially rich ones," its order had specified—and packed them into the concentration camps at Buchenwald, Dachau and Sachsenhausen, from which they could be ransomed only at the price of immediate pauperized emigration.

Fermi took the Stockholm call. The Nobel Prize, undivided, would be awarded for "your discovery of new radioactive substances belonging to the entire race of elements and for the discovery you made in the course of this work of the selective power of slow neutrons." In security the Fermis could leave the madness behind.

Lise Meitner had written Otto Hahn of her worries a few days before the Fermis arrived. "Most of the time I feel like a wind-up doll running on automatic," she told her old friend, "smiling along happily and empty of real life. From that you can judge for yourself how productive my efforts are at work. And still in the end I'm thankful for it because it forces me to keep my thoughts together, which isn't always easy." She was sorry Hahn's rheumatism had returned and was afraid he wasn't taking care of himself; she asked after Planck and von Laue by their private Hahn-Meitner nicknames, Max Sr. and Max Jr.; she greeted Hahn's wife, Edith, and wondered what Christmas plans he had for his son. His uranium work was "really very interesting." She hoped he would write again soon.

She was living in a small hotel room—there was hardly space to unpack—and having trouble sleeping. People told her she was too thin. Worse, conditions at the Physical Institute were not what she had expected them to be. A Swedish friend, Eva von Bahr-Bergius, a physicist she knew from Berlin who had been a lecturer at the University of Uppsala, had helped with arrangements and was gradually breaking the bad news. Manne Siegbahn had not wanted to take Meitner on. He had no money for her, he had complained; he could give her a place to work but no more. Von Bahr-Bergius had pursued the Nobel Foundation grant. But it provided nothing for equipment or assistance. Meitner blamed herself: "Of course it's my fault; I should have prepared much better and much earlier for my leaving, should at least have had drawings made of the most important apparatus [she would need]."

She was a strong woman, but she was miserable and alone. Hahn responded with sympathy. At midmonth she thanked him for that "dear letter," then changed moods and charged him with indifference: "Concerning myself I sometimes suspect you don't understand my way of thinking. . . . Right now I really don't know if anyone cares about my affairs at all or if they will ever be taken care of."

Hahn was pursuing Meitner's affairs as well as his own. With her moody letter at hand he stormed down to the revenue office, which was responsible for inventorying her furniture and other property before allowing its release, and laid on what he called "a little seizure of my 'ecstasy,' " after which "the matter went somewhat better." That news he wrote to Meitner on Monday evening, December 19, from the KWI. Only then did he report why he had not yet left the laboratory:

> As much as I can through all of this I am working, and Strassmann is working untiringly, on the uranium activities. . . . It's almost 11 at night; Strassmann will return at 11:30 so that I can see about going home. The fact is, there's something so strange about the "radium isotopes" that for the time being we are mentioning it only to you. The half-lives of the three isotopes are quite precisely determined; they can be separated from *all* elements except barium; all the processes are in tune. Just one is not—unless there are extremely unusual coincidences: the fractionation doesn't work. Our radium isotopes act like *barium*.

Hahn and Strassmann worked in three rooms on the ground floor of the Kaiser Wilhelm Institute for Chemistry, the building with the *Pickelhaube* dome: Hahn's large personal chemistry laboratory north off the main lobby, a measurement room across the hall at the near end of the wing that extended northwest along Faradayweg and an irradiation room at the far end of the wing. They separated the three functions of irradiation, measurement and chemistry to avoid contaminating one with radiation from another. All the rooms were fitted with worktables of unfinished raw pine roughed out by a careful carpenter who took the trouble to add a graceful taper to the legs. On the table in the irradiation room rested cylinders of beeswax-colored paraffin like angelfood cakes drilled for the neutron sources, which were gram-strength radium salts mixed with beryllium powder. Handmade Geiger counters, fixed in hinged, hollowed-out bricks of lead shielding on the table in the measurement room, connected through thin coiling wires back to breadboard amplifiers worked by silvered vacuum tubes like inverted bud vases. The amplifiers actuated gleaming brass clockwork counters with numbers showing black through angled miniature windows on their spines. Kraftboard-covered 90-volt Pertrix dry batteries that powered the system packed a shelf below the table. Hahn's laboratory table held the brackets, beakers, flasks, funnels and filters of radiochemistry. The two men moved in their work from room to room on a regular schedule determined by the duration of the half-lives they were studying. There would have been a pungency of nitrates in the air, mingled with the aroma of Hahn's inevitable cigar.

In his fifty-ninth year Hahn stooped slightly but looked younger than his age. His hairline had receded and his eyebrows had grown bushy; he had trimmed back to the edge of his upper lip the waxed Prussian mustache of his youth; his brown eyes still sparkled with warmth. By now he was unquestionably the ablest radiochemist in the world. He needed all his forty years' experience to decode uranium.

He and Strassmann had begun their renewed examination of the three "radium" isotopes early in December by attempting a purer separation from uranium. Strassmann suggested using barium chloride as a carrier rather than the customary barium sulfate because the chloride, Hahn explains, "forms beautiful little crystals" of exceptional purity. They wanted to be sure their separations would be free of contamination from other bombardment products with similar half-lives, the difficulty that had muddled Curie and Savitch. The procedure for the 86-minute activity they were studying, which they called "Ra-III," required them to irradiate about fifteen grams of purified uranium for twelve hours, wait several hours for their more intense 14-minute "Ra-II" to retreat from the foreground by decaying, then add barium chloride as a carrier and accomplish the separation. The Ra-III came out of the uranium solution with the barium, but it refused then to remain behind during fractionation when the barium crystallized away. Instead it crystallized with the barium.

"The attempts to separate our artificial 'radium isotopes' from barium in this way were unsuccessful," Hahn would explain in his Nobel Prize lecture; "no enrichment of the 'radium' was obtained. It was natural to ascribe this lack of success to the exceptionally low intensity of our preparations. It was always a question of merely a few thousands of atoms, which could only be detected as individual particles by the Geiger-Müller counter. Such a small number of atoms could be carried away by the great excess of inactive barium without any increase or decrease being perceptible." To check that possibility they retrieved from storage a known radium isotope they often worked with, the isotope they called "mesothorium." They diluted it to match the pale radioactivity of their few thousand atoms of Ra-III, then ran it through barium precipitation and fractionation. It separated away cleanly from the barium. Their technique was not at fault.

On Saturday, December 17, the day after Hahn stormed the revenue office on behalf of Meitner's furniture, he and Strassmann carried out a further heroic check. They mixed Ra-III with dilute mesothorium and precipitated and fractionated the two substances *together*. Then the chemical evidence was certain, whatever it might mean in physical terms: the mesothorium remained in solution when the barium carrier crystallized out but Ra-III went off with the barium, distributing itself uniformly and indivisibly throughout the small pure crystals. Hahn wrote an enthusiastic note in his pocket appointment book to mark the day: "Exciting fractionation of radium/barium/mesothorium."

It seemed their "radium" isotopes must be barium, element 56, slightly more than half as heavy as uranium and with just over half its charge. Hahn and Strassmann could hardly believe it. They conceived an even more convincing experiment. If their "radium" was really radium, then by beta decay it ought to transform itself one step up the periodic table to actinium (89). If, on the other hand, it was barium (56), then by beta decay it ought to transform itself one step up to lanthanum (57). And lanthanum could be separated from actinium by fractionation. They were carrying out this definitive project late Monday night, December 19, when Hahn sent Meitner the news.

"Perhaps you can suggest some fantastic explanation," he wrote. "We understand that it really *can't* break up into barium. . . . So try to think of some other possibility. Barium isotopes with much higher atomic weights than 137? If you can think of anything that might be publishable, then the three of us would be together in this work after all. We don't believe this is foolishness or that contaminations are playing tricks on us."

He closed by wishing his friend a "somewhat bearable" Christmas. Fritz Strassmann added "very warm greetings and best wishes." Hahn posted the letter to Stockholm late at night on his way home.

The two men took time from their readings to attend the annual KWI Christmas party the next day, though Hahn had little joy of it with Meitner gone. They continued the actinium-lanthanum experiment even as they worked up the radium-barium findings. After the party the institute would close for Christmas; they kept a typist busy until the end but were unable to finish their report. Hahn had called Paul Rosbaud at *Naturwissenschaften*, told him the news and asked him to make space in the next issue. Rosbaud was willing to pull a less urgent paper from the journal but cautioned that the manuscript must be delivered no later than Friday, December 23. Hahn arranged for a laboratory assistant to serve as typist on Thursday. In the meantime he and Strassmann would carry on alone.

Meitner received Hahn's Monday-night letter in Stockholm on Wednesday, December 21. It was startling; if the results held she saw it meant the uranium nucleus must fracture and she immediately wrote him back:

> Your radium results are very amazing. A process that works with slow neutrons and leads to barium! . . . To me for the time being the hypothesis of such an extensive burst seems very difficult to accept, but we have experienced so many surprises in nuclear physics that one cannot say without hesitation about anything: "It's impossible."

She was traveling on Friday to the village of Kungälv in the west of Sweden for a week's vacation, she told Hahn; "if you write me in the meantime please address your letter there." She sent him and his family "warmest greetings . . . and much love and the very best for the New Year."

That day Hahn and Strassmann had finished the actinium-lanthanum experiment—and confirmed lanthanum for barium decay. In the late evening, after they turned off their counters, Hahn wrote his exiled colleague again. The paper was not yet finished; a phrase from the letter would be reworked to more cautious language for the final draft: "Our radium proofs convince us that as chemists we must come to the conclusion that the three carefully-studied isotopes are not radium, but, from the standpoint of the chemist, barium."

Hahn had hoped Meitner might quickly find some physical explanation for his unprecedented chemistry. That would strengthen his conclusion and also put Meitner's name on the paper, the best possible Christmas gift. With the lanthanum confirmation at hand he could no longer delay. As it was he had withheld the news from physicists on his own staff and at the new physics institute nearby. Someone else—Curie and Savitch, for example—might very well have made the same discovery. And whatever the explanation, the discovery was clearly of major importance, a reaction unlike any other yet found. "We cannot hush up the results," Hahn wrote Meitner, "even though they may be absurd in physical terms. You can see that you will be performing a good deed if you find an alternative [explanation]. When we finish tomorrow or the day after I will send you a copy of the manuscript. . . . The whole thing is not very well suited for *Naturwissenschaften*. But they will publish it quickly."

Hahn mailed the letter to Stockholm. He did not yet know about Meitner's Kungälv vacation.

Leo Szilard's work at the University of Rochester confirmed that no neutrons came out when indium was irradiated. On December 21, as Hahn and Meitner exchanged their excited letters, Szilard advised the British Admiralty by letter:

> Further experiments . . . have definitely cleared up the anomalies which I have observed in 1936. . . . In view of this new work it does not now seem necessary to maintain [my] patent . . . nor would the waiving of the secrecy of this patent serve any useful purpose. I beg therefore to suggest that the patent be withdrawn altogether.

Szilard's faith in the possibility of a chain reaction, as he said later, had "just about reached the vanishing point."

Hahn and Strassmann had originally titled their paper "On the radium isotopes produced by the neutron bombardment of uranium and their behavior." With their new data they realized "radium" would no longer do. They considered changing "radium" to "barium" throughout the paper. But most of it had been written before the lanthanum experiment firmed their convictions. They would have had to rewrite from beginning to end, "especially," says Hahn in retrospect, "since in view of this result its major portion was not especially interesting any more." Christmas and the journal deadline were upon them and they had no time. They decided to jury-rig what was on hand. The results would be no less effective for being inelegant. They substituted the noncommittal phrase "alkaline-earth metals" for "radium isotopes" in the title—both barium and radium are alkaline-earth metals, as are beryllium, magnesium, calcium and strontium. They went through the draft putting equivocal quotation marks around their many references to radium and actinium. Then they attached seven cautious paragraphs at the end.

"Now we still have to discuss some newer experiments," this final section began, "which we publish rather hesitantly due to their peculiar results." They then summarized their series of experiments:

> We wanted to identify beyond any doubt the chemical properties of the parent members of the radioactive series which were separated with the barium and which have been designated as "radium isotopes." We have carried out fractional crystallizations and fractional precipitations, a method which is well-known for concentrating (or diluting) radium in barium salt solutions. . . .
>
> When we made appropriate tests with radioactive barium samples which were free of any later decay products, *the results were always negative. The activity was distributed evenly among all the barium fractions.* . . . We come to the conclusion that our "radium isotopes" have the properties of barium. As chemists we should actually state that the new products are not radium, but rather barium itself. Other elements besides radium or barium are out of the question.

They discussed actinium then, distinguished their work from that of Curie and Savitch and pointed out that all so-called transuranics would have to be reexamined. Not quite prepared to usurp the prerogative of the physicists, they closed on a tentative note:

> As chemists we really ought to revise the decay scheme given above and insert the symbols Ba, La, Ce [cerium], in place of Ra, Ac, Th [thorium]. However as "nuclear chemists," working very close to the field of physics, we cannot bring ourselves yet to take such a drastic step which goes against all previous laws of nuclear physics. There could perhaps be a series of unusual coincidences which has given us false indications.

Promising further experiments, they prepared to release their news to the world. Hahn mailed the paper and then felt the whole thing to be so improbable "that I wished I could get the document back out of the mail box"; or Paul Rosbaud came around to the KWI the same evening to pick it up. Both stories survive Hahn's later recollection. Since Rosbaud knew the paper's importance and dated its receipt December 22, 1938, he probably picked it up. But Hahn also visited the mailbox that night, to send a carbon copy of the seminal paper to Lise Meitner in Stockholm. His misgivings at publishing without her—or some dawning glimmer of the fateful consequences that might follow his discovery—may have accounted for his remembered apprehension.

The Swedish village of Kungälv—the name means King's River—is located some ten miles above the dominant western harbor city of Göteborg and six miles inland from the Kattegat coast. The river, now called North River, descends from Lake Vänern, the largest freshwater lake in Western Europe; at Kungälv it has cut a sheer granite southward-facing bluff, the precipice of Fontin, 335 feet high. The modern village is built along a single cobblestone lane on the narrow talus between the bluff and the river, its back to the wall.

As Norwegian Kongahalla the village was founded at a less constricted place downstream around A.D. 800. But an island hill rises from the river at Kungälv and is thus guarded by a natural moat, a defensive geography which the precipice of Fontin reinforces. In 1308, to mark the border there between Norway and Sweden, the Norwegians began to build on that island hill a monumental granite fortress, Bohus' Fäste (i.e., King Bohus' Fort), sod-ridged block walls mazing inward and upward to a cylindrical tower of thick stone with a conical roof that dominates the entire coastal valley. An accident of placement of three of the deep windows that penetrate the tower—two open above, one centered below—transforms it into a face staring with hollow eyes toward the Fontin bluff. To soften the grimness of that face the people of the valley named the tower *Fars Hatt*, Father's Hat, as if it evoked a workman in a cap. Through four hundred years of occupation Bohus' Fäste was besieged fourteen times while the settlements in the valley were put to the torch and the graveyard filled on the island below its hard walls.

The village was ordered moved upriver onto the island in 1612. The Danes ruled Norway from the fifteenth century to the early nineteenth century; they ceded the Kungälv region, Bohuslän, to Sweden by the Treaty of Roskilde in 1658. Fire in 1676 burned the island village and its burghers shifted for safety to the narrow shore. They laid out their lane and strip of houses extending west and east from a cobblestone marketplace where the talus widened to make room. Despite its fortress Kungälv is peaceful, especially in winter with the river frozen and a depth of clean snow on the ground. Its snug wooden houses, painted pastel, enclose rooms cozy with ships' chests and china cabinets and lace curtains, warmed by corner fireplaces faced with decorative tile, aromatic with coffee and baking. Eva von Bahr-Bergius and her husband Niklas built a house there in 1927, larger than most Kungälv houses but constructed in the same style. In 1938 Lise Meitner was alone in Stockholm. Otto Frisch was alone in Copenhagen, his mother, Meitner's sister, beyond reach in Vienna, his father incarcerated at Dachau, a victim of *Kristallnacht*. The Bergiuses therefore considerately invited aunt and nephew to Kungälv for Christmas dinner.

Meitner left Stockholm Friday morning, two days before Christmas. Frisch took the train ferry across from Denmark. His aunt arrived before him and registered at a quiet inn on Västra gatan, West Street, where they both would stay, a pale green building much like its modest neighbors but with a café on the ground floor. It faced a shadowed strip of garden north across the lane; above the stunted garden trees the dark bluff loomed. The other way, behind the inn, the flat, snow-covered flood plain of the river extended into open woods. The Bergiuses' house was a short walk eastward past the marketplace and the white church. Tired from travel, Frisch and Meitner met only briefly in the evening when Frisch came in.

In Copenhagen that winter he had been studying the magnetic behavior of neutrons. To further his work he needed a strong, uniform magnetic field, and on his way to Kungälv he had sketched out a large magnet he meant to design and build. He came downstairs on the morning before Christmas prepared to interest his aunt in his plans. She was already at breakfast and had no intention of discussing magnets: she had brought Hahn's December 19 letter downstairs with her and insisted Frisch read it. He did. "Barium," he told her, "I don't believe it. There's some mistake." He tried to change the subject to his magnet; she changed it back to barium. "Finally," says Meitner, ". . . we both became absorbed in my problem." They decided to go for a walk to see what they could puzzle out.

Frisch had brought cross-country skis and wanted to use them. He was concerned that his aunt would be unable to keep up. She could walk as fast as he could ski on level ground, she told him. She could and did. He fetched his skis and they went out, probably eastward to the Kungälv marketplace, which gave onto the flood plain of the river, then across the frozen river and into the open woods beyond.

"But it's impossible," Frisch remembers them saying in their collective effort to understand. "You couldn't chip a hundred particles off a nucleus in one blow. You couldn't even cut it across. If you tried to estimate the nuclear forces, all the bonds you'd have to cut all at once—it's fantastic. It's quite impossible that a nucleus could do that." Thirty years afterward Frisch summarized their thinking in more formal terms:

> But how could barium be formed from uranium? No larger fragments than protons or helium nuclei (alpha particles) had ever been chipped away from nuclei, and the thought that a large number of them should be chipped off at once could be dismissed; not enough energy was available to do that. Nor was it possible that the uranium nucleus could have been cleaved right across. Indeed a nucleus was not like a brittle solid that could be cleaved or broken; Bohr had stressed that a nucleus was much more like a liquid drop.

The liquid-drop model made a division of the nucleus seem possible. They sat down on a log. Meitner found a scrap of paper and a pencil in her purse. She drew circles. "Couldn't it be this sort of thing?"

Frisch: "Now, she always rather suffered from an inability to visualize things in three dimensions, whereas I had that ability quite well. I had, in fact, apparently come around to the same idea, and I drew a shape like a circle squashed in at two opposite points."

"Well, yes," Meitner said, "that is what I mean." She had meant to draw what Frisch had drawn, a liquid drop elongated like a dumbbell, but had drawn it end-on, indicating with a smaller dashed circle inside a larger solid circle the dumbbell's waist.

Frisch: "I remember that I immediately at that instant thought of the fact that electric charge diminishes surface tension." The liquid drop is held together by surface tension, the nucleus by the analogous strong force. But the electrical repulsion of the protons in the nucleus works against the strong force, and the heavier the element, the more intense the repulsion. Frisch continues:

> And so I promptly started to work out by how much the surface tension of a nucleus would be reduced. I don't know where we got all our numbers from, but I think I must have had a certain feeling for the binding energies and could make an estimate of the surface tension. Of course we knew the charge and the size reasonably well. And so, as an order of magnitude, the result was that at a charge [i.e., an atomic number] of approximately 100 the surface tension of the nucleus disappears; and therefore uranium at 92 must be pretty close to that instability.

They had discovered the reason no elements beyond uranium exist naturally in the world: the two forces working against each other in the nucleus eventually cancel each other out.

They pictured the uranium nucleus as a liquid drop gone wobbly with the looseness of its confinement and imagined it hit by even a barely energetic slow neutron. The neutron would add its energy to the whole. The nucleus would oscillate. In one of its many random modes of oscillation it might elongate. Since the strong force operates only over extremely short distances, the electric force repelling the two bulbs of an elongated drop would gain advantage. The two bulbs would push farther apart. A waist would form between them. The strong force would begin to regain the advantage within each of the two bulbs. It would work like surface tension to pull them into spheres. The electric repulsion would work at the same time to push the two separating spheres even farther apart.

Eventually the waist would give way. Two smaller nuclei would appear where one large nucleus had been before—barium and krypton, for example:

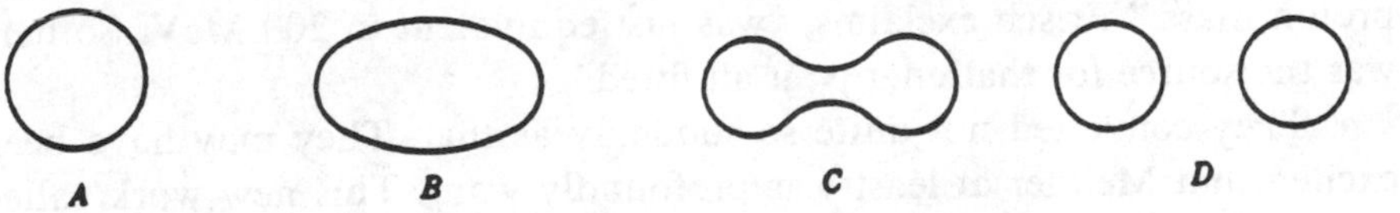

"Then," Frisch recalls, "Lise Meitner was saying that if you really do form two such fragments they would be pushed apart with great energy." They would be pushed apart by the mutual repulsion of their gathered protons at one-thirtieth the speed of light. Meitner or Frisch calculated that energy to be about 200 MeV: 200 million electron volts. An electron volt is the energy necessary to accelerate an electron through a potential difference of one volt. Two hundred million electron volts is not a large amount of energy, but it is an extremely large amount of energy from one atom. The most energetic chemical reactions release about 5 eV per atom. Ernest Lawrence was that year building a cyclotron with a nearly 200-ton magnet with which he hoped to accelerate particles by as much as 25 MeV. Frisch would calculate later that the energy from each bursting uranium nucleus would be sufficient to make a visible grain of sand visibly jump. In each mere gram of uranium there are about 2.5×10^{21} atoms, an absurdly large number, 25 followed by twenty zeros: 2,500,000,000,000,000,000,000.

They asked themselves what the source of all that energy could be. That was the crux of the problem and the reason no one had credited the possibility before. Neutron captures that had been observed before had involved much smaller energy releases.

When she was thirty-one, in 1909, Meitner had met Albert Einstein for the first time at a scientific conference in Salzburg. He "gave a lecture on the development of our views regarding the nature of radiation. At that time I certainly did not yet realize the full implications of his theory of relativity." She listened eagerly. In the course of the lecture Einstein used the theory of relativity to derive his equation $E = mc^2$, with which Meitner was then unfamiliar. Einstein showed thereby how to calculate the conversion of mass into energy. "These two facts," she reminisced in 1964, "were so overwhelmingly new and surprising that, to this day, I remember the lecture very well."

She remembered it in 1938, on the day before Christmas. She also "had the packing fractions in her head," says Frisch—she had memorized Francis Aston's numbers for the mass defects of nuclei. If the large uranium nucleus split into two smaller nuclei, the smaller nuclei would weigh less in total than their common parent. How much less? That was a calculation she could easily work: about one-fifth the mass of a proton less. Process one-fifth of the mass of a proton through $E = mc^2$. "One fifth of a proton mass," Frisch exclaims, "was just equivalent to 200 MeV. So here was the source for that energy; it all fitted!"

They converted not quite so suddenly as that. They may have been excited, but Meitner at least was profoundly wary. This new work called her previous four years' work with Hahn and Strassmann into doubt; if she was right about the one she was wrong about the other, just when she had escaped from Germany into the indifferent world of exile and needed most to confirm her reputation. "Lise Meitner sort of kept saying, 'We couldn't have seen it. This was so totally unexpected. Hahn is a good chemist and I trusted his chemistry to correspond to the elements he said they corresponded to. Who could have thought that it would be something so much lighter?' "

Christmas dinner at the Bergiuses' came and went. Frisch skied and Meitner walked. Nineteen thirty-eight was ticking to its end. With a week to pass in a small village they would certainly have visited the fortress and looked down from its ramparts onto the snow-covered valley, onto centuries of violent graves. Though they understood its energetics now, the discovery was still only physics to them; they did not yet imagine a chain reaction.

Hahn's letter of December 21, confirming lanthanum, was still not forwarded from Stockholm, nor was the carbon copy of the *Naturwissenschaften* paper. Hahn was eager to win Meitner's support and wrote Kungälv directly on the Wednesday after Christmas to woo her. Careful not to seem to usurp her place, he called the discovery his "barium fantasy" and questioned everything except the presence of barium and the absence of actinium, taking the humble chemist's part. "Naturally, I would be very interested to hear your frank opinion. Perhaps you could compute and publish something." He had continued to hold off telling other physicists, though he itched for physical confirmation of his chemistry. It was as though a maker of hand axes had discovered fire by striking flints while the sorcerers pondered how to harness lightning. He might hardly believe his luck and urgently seek their authentication even though he knew what burned his hand was real.

The letter reached Kungälv on Thursday; by return mail that day Meitner responded that the radium-barium finding was "very exciting. Otto R[obert] and I have already puzzled over it." But she let slip no answer to the puzzle and she asked about the lanthanum result.

Friday she sent Hahn a postcard: "Today the manuscript arrived." An important page was missing but it was all "very amazing." Nothing more; Hahn must have bitten his lip.

In Dahlem Rosbaud passed along the galley proofs. Hahn was more certain now of his findings. The manuscript had set the barium results "against all previous laws of nuclear physics." He moderated the phrase in proof to "against all previous experience."

But even with the carbon copy, the missing page and the December 21 letter finally at hand in Kungälv, Meitner hesitated to leap. On January 1, after conveying New Year's greetings to Hahn, she wrote: "We have read your work very thoroughly and consider it *perhaps* possible energetically after all that such a heavy nucleus bursts." She veered off to worry about their misbegotten transuranics, "not a good reference for my new start." Frisch added a New Year's wish of his own and a more genial reservation: "If your new findings are really true, it would certainly be of the greatest interest and I am very curious about further results."

Meitner returned to Stockholm later that day and Frisch to Copenhagen. He was "keen to submit our speculations—it wasn't really more at that time—to Bohr." The note of hesitancy in their letter to Hahn suggests they sought the authority of Bohr's blessing. Frisch saw him on January 3: "I had hardly begun to tell him, when he struck his forehead with his hand and exclaimed, 'Oh what idiots we have all been! Oh but this is wonderful! This is just as it must be!' " Their conversation lasted only a few minutes, Frisch wrote his aunt that day, "since Bohr immediately and in every respect was in agreement with us. . . . [He] still wants to consider this quantitatively this evening and to talk with me again about it tomorrow."

In Stockholm that day Meitner had received Hahn's revised proofs. Independently they quieted her doubt. She wrote Hahn emphatically: "I am fairly *certain* now that you really have a splitting towards barium and I consider it a wonderful result for which I congratulate you and Strassmann very warmly. . . . You now have a wide, beautiful field of work ahead of you. And believe me, even though I stand here very empty-handed at the moment, I am still happy about the marvelousness of these findings."

Now those findings needed interpretation. Aunt and nephew outlined a theoretical paper by long-distance telephone. Frisch drafted it Friday, January 6, and that evening took the trolley to the House of Honor to discuss it with Bohr, who was leaving for the United States the next morning for a term of work at the Institute for Advanced Study. There was time the next morning to type only part of the draft; Frisch delivered two pages to Bohr at the train station from which he and his nineteen-year-old son Erik were departing for Göteborg harbor. On the assumption that Frisch would immediately send the paper along to *Nature* Bohr promised not to mention it to their American colleagues until he heard from Frisch that it had been received and was in press. Among the notes he brought to that final discussion Frisch mentioned an experiment to confirm by physical means the Dahlem chemistry.

Hahn's and Strassmann's article had been published in Berlin on January 6. When it arrived in Copenhagen the next day Frisch thought to go over the whole business with George Placzek. Placzek was characteristically skeptical and characteristically witty about it. Uranium already suffered from alpha decay, Frisch remembers him scoffing; to think that it could be made to burst as well "was like dissecting a man killed by a falling brick and finding that he would have died of cancer." Placzek suggested that Frisch use a cloud chamber to look for energetic fragments that would prove the nucleus had split. The institute's radium-based neutron sources would fog a cloud-chamber photograph with gamma radiation, Frisch realized. But a simple ionization chamber would do. "One would expect fast-moving nuclei, of atomic number about 40-50 and atomic weight 100-150, and up to 100 MeV energy to emerge from a layer of uranium bombarded with neutrons," he explained his experiment in a subsequent report. "In spite of their high energy, these nuclei should have a range, in air, of a few millimetres only, on account of their high effective charge . . . which implies very dense ionization." In the course of their short passage his highly charged nuclear fragments would strip about 3 million electrons from the nuclei of air gases. They should be easy to find.

His chamber consisted of "two metal plates separated by a glass ring about 1 cm. high." The charged plates, which would collect the air ions, connected to a simple amplifier, which connected to an oscilloscope. To the bottom plate he attached a piece of uranium-coated foil. He set up the experiment in the basement of the institute and retrieved three of the neutron sources from the covered well. He placed the sources close to the foil and looked for the expected nuclei to emerge. Since they were highly energetic and strongly ionizing they would create quick, sharp, vertical pulses of the sweeping green beam of the oscilloscope.

Frisch started measurements on the afternoon of Friday, January 13, and "pulses at about the predicted amplitude and frequency (one or two per minute) were seen within a few hours." He ran checks with either the neutron sources or the uranium lining removed. He wrapped the sources with paraffin to slow the neutrons and "enhanced the effect by a factor of two." He continued measurements "until six in the morning to verify that the apparatus was working consistently." As had Werner Heisenberg before him, he lived upstairs at the institute; exhausted, he climbed the stairs to bed. He remembers thinking that 13 had proved once again to be his lucky number.

Even luckier than that: "At seven in the morning I was knocked out of bed by the postman who brought a telegram to say that my father had been released from concentration camp." His parents would move to Stockholm and share an apartment with his aunt, whose possessions, thanks to Hahn, were eventually shipped.

In "a state of slight confusion" Frisch spent the next day repeating the experiment for anyone who cared to see. One who came down in the morning to the basement laboratory was a black-haired, blue-eyed American biologist of Irish heritage named William A. Arnold who was studying on a Rockefeller Fellowship with George de Hevesy. Arnold was thirty-four, Frisch's age, on leave from the Hopkins Marine Station at Pacific Grove, California. He had made his way to Europe from San Francisco the previous September by freighter with his wife and young daughter. He could have gone to Berkeley to pick up radioisotope technique, but would have missed living in Copenhagen, learning from de Hevesy—would have missed contributing a coinage to the gamble that is history. Frisch showed the American the experiment and pointed out the pulses on the oscilloscope. "From the size of the spikes," Arnold recalls, "it was clear that they must represent 100-200 MeV, very much larger than the spikes from [uranium's natural background of] alpha particles."

> Later that day Frisch looked me up and said, "You work in a microbiology lab. What do you call the process in which one bacterium divides into two?" And I answered, "binary fission." He wanted to know if you could call it "fission" alone, and I said you could.

Frisch the sketch artist, good at visualizing as his aunt was not, had metamorphosed his liquid drop into a dividing living cell. Thereby the name for a multiplication of life became the name for a violent process of destruction. "I wrote home to my mother," says Frisch, "that I felt like someone who has caught an elephant by the tail."

Aunt and nephew conferred by telephone further over the weekend to prepare not one but two papers for *Nature*: a joint explanation of the reaction and Frisch's report of the confirming evidence of his experiment. Both reports—"Disintegration of uranium by neutrons: a new type of nuclear reaction" and "Physical evidence for the division of heavy nuclei under neutron bombardment"—used the new term "fission." Frisch finished the two papers on Monday evening, January 16, and posted them airmail to London the next morning. Since he and Bohr had already discussed the theoretical paper and since the experiment only confirmed the Hahn-Strassmann discovery, he did not hurry to let Bohr know.

Bohr sailed on the Swedish-American liner *Drottningholm* with his son Erik and the Belgian theoretician Léon Rosenfeld. "As we were boarding the ship," Rosenfeld recalls, "Bohr told me he had just been handed a note by Frisch, containing his and Lise Meitner's conclusions; we should 'try to understand it.' " That meant a working voyage; a blackboard was duly installed in Bohr's stateroom. The North Atlantic was stormy in that season; it made him "rather miserable, all the time on the verge of seasickness" but hardly stopped the work. The first question he wanted to answer was why, if the nucleus oscillated more or less randomly when it was bombarded, it seemed to prefer splitting into two parts rather than some other number. He was satisfied when he saw that the heaviest nuclei, because of their instability, require no more energy to split than they do to emit a single particle. It was a question of probabilities and two fragments were greatly more probable than a crowd.

The Fermis had arrived in New York on January 2, Laura feeling distinctly alien, Enrico announcing with his usual mock solemnity, "We have founded the American branch of the Fermi family." They put up temporarily at the King's Crown Hotel, opposite Columbia University, where Szilard was also living. George Pegram, the tall, soft-spoken Virginian who was chairman of the physics department and dean of graduate studies at Columbia, had met the Fermis as they debarked the *Franconia*; now in turn they waited at dockside to meet Bohr. The American theoretician John Archibald Wheeler, then twenty-nine years old, who had worked with Bohr in Copenhagen in the mid-1930s and would be working with him again at Princeton, joined them on the crowded West 57th Street pier. He had taught his regular Monday morning class, then caught a midday train.

As the *Drottningholm* berthed, at 1 P.M. on January 16, Laura Fermi saw Bohr on an upper deck leaning on the railing searching the crowd. She

ht, was "an ivory tower; people did not have any
e facts of life and so forth and they looked down
other job and found one at the University of Wis-
m the second day on I felt at home there. Some-
the track and we ran around the track and we were
nly about the most difficult problems but about the
wn to earth almost." He met a young American
hey were quickly married. She became ill:

from her that she had cancer and that there was no hope
e was in a hospital in Madison and then she went to see
ent with her but I didn't want to stay with her parents, of
as, after all, a stranger to her parents. I went for a little
igan, Ann Arbor, and then I came back and saw her in her
And then she told me essentially that she knows that she is
said, "Should I tell you where our suitcases are?" So she
ked to me. I tried to conceal it from her because I felt that it
f a reasonably young person does not realize that she is
e, we are all doomed.

eton in 1938, the university by then having more sen-
rth (a sophisticated and highly respected theoretician,
Nobel Prize in Physics in 1963 for his work on the
leus).
rrival Szilard traveled down from New York to visit his
a long-overdue surprise:

of Hahn's discovery. Hahn found that uranium breaks into
it absorbs a neutron. . . . When I heard this I immediately saw
ments, being heavier than corresponds to their charge, must
and if enough neutrons are emitted . . . then it should be, of
e to sustain a chain reaction. All the things which H. G. Wells
eared suddenly real to me.

side in the Princeton infirmary the two Hungarians de-
.
time Bohr had sent his letter for *Nature* to Frisch in Co-
him to forward it on "if, as I hope, Hahn's article has al-
lished and your and your aunt's note has already been
asked for the "latest news" on that front and wondered
ments are proceeding." In a postscript he added that he had
ahn-Strassmann paper in *Naturwissenschaften*.

thought him w
since our visit t
last few months
ation in Europe,
carrying a heavy
one to the other c
about Europe. He

He had busin
Wheeler took Léon
Frisch, Bohr had n
Frisch-Meitner inte
glected to tell Rose
Meitner had already
pretation priority. He
him. "In those days,"
evening journal club"-
cuss the latest studies t
"It was the custom to g
thing hot, as I had lea
heard the news of the sp
crossed the Atlantic—at
the chill Monday evening
the American physicists,"
than the fission phenomen
in all directions."

Bohr arrived in Prince
senfeld casually mentioned
frightened," Bohr wrote his
would wait until Hahn's not
more than a point of honor, t
to trigger the Bohr conscience.
ugees who could use so specta
in exile. Bohr had at hand the
aboard the *Drottningholm*; for t
into a letter to *Nature* that wo
Meitner and Frisch. Three days
was for Niels Bohr great haste.

"Can you guess where I foun
Wigner. "In . . . the [Princeton] i
and was in the infirmary for six we
mediately got along; in 1936 "the

Princeton then, he thoug
normal thinking about t
upon me." He sought an
consin at Madison. "Fr
body suggested we go to
friends. We talked not c
daily events. We got d
woman in Wisconsin; t

I tried to conceal it
for her surviving. S
her parents and I w
course, because I w
while away to Mich
bed at her parents'
close to death. She
knew when she ta
would be better i
doomed. Of cours

He returned to Prin
sibly assessed his w
Wigner shared the
structure of the nuc
After Bohr's a
sick friend and wo

Wigner told m
two parts when
that these frag
emit neutrons,
course, possib
predicted app

At Wigner's bed
bated what to d
In the mea
penhagen, askin
ready been pu
submitted." He
"how the exper
just seen the H

Ideas infect like viruses. The point of origin of the fission infection was Dahlem. From there it spread to Stockholm, to Kungälv, to Copenhagen. It crossed the Atlantic with Bohr and Rosenfeld. I. I. Rabi and the young California-born theoretician Willis Eugene Lamb, Jr., two Columbia men working at Princeton that week, both heard the news, Lamb perhaps from Wheeler, Rabi from Bohr himself. They returned to New York—"probably Friday night," Lamb thinks. Rabi says he told Fermi. In 1954 Fermi credited Lamb: "I remember one afternoon Willis Lamb came back very excited and said that Bohr had leaked out great news." Lamb recalls "spreading it around" but does not recall specifically telling Fermi. Possibly both men talked to the Italian laureate within a space of hours; it was information he of all physicists would most need to hear, since the Nobel lecture he had delivered only a month earlier, not yet printed, was now partly obsolete and an embarrassment. (Fermi confined revision to a footnote: "The discovery by Hahn and Strassmann . . . makes it necessary to re-examine all the problems of the transuranic elements, as many of them might be found to be products of a splitting of uranium." The many other radioactivities he and his group identified and his slow-neutron discovery still secured his Nobel Prize.)

Szilard also hoped to talk to Fermi: "I thought that if neutrons are in fact emitted in fission, this fact should be kept secret from the Germans. So I was very eager to contact Joliot and to contact Fermi, the two men who were most likely to think of this possibility." He had borrowed Wigner's apartment and had not yet left Princeton. "I got up one morning and wanted to go out. It was raining cats and dogs. I said, 'My God, I am going to catch cold!' Because at that time, the first years I was in America, each time I got wet I invariably caught a bad cold." He had to go out anyway. "I got wet and came home with a high fever, so I was not able to contact Fermi."

Fever or not, by January 25—Wednesday—Szilard had returned to New York, had seen the Hahn-Strassmann paper and was writing Lewis Strauss, whose patronage might now be more important than ever:

> I feel I ought to let you know of a very sensational new development in nuclear physics. In a paper . . . Hahn reports that he finds when bombarding uranium with neutrons the uranium breaking up. . . . This is entirely unexpected and exciting news for the average physicist. The Department of Physics at Princeton, where I spent the last few days, was like a stirred-up ant heap.
>
> Apart from the purely scientific interest there may be another aspect of this discovery, which so far does not seem to have caught the attention of those to whom I spoke. First of all it is obvious that the energy released in this new reaction must be very much higher than all previously known cases. . . .

> This in itself might make it possible to produce power by means of nuclear energy, but I do not think that this possibility is very exciting, for . . . the cost of investment would probably be too high to make the process worthwhile. . . .
>
> I see . . . possibilities in another direction. These might lead to large-scale production of energy and radioactive elements, unfortunately also perhaps to atomic bombs. This new discovery revives all the hopes and fears in this respect which I had in 1934 and 1935, and which I have as good as abandoned in the course of the last two years. At present I am running a high temperature and am therefore confined to my four walls, but perhaps I can tell you more about these new developments some other time.

The same day Fermi stepped into the office of John R. Dunning, a Columbia experimentalist whose specialty was neutrons, to propose an experiment. Dunning, his graduate student Herbert Anderson and others at Columbia had built a small cyclotron in the basement of Pupin Hall, the modern thirteen-story physics tower that faces downtown Manhattan from behind the library on the upper campus. A cyclotron was a potent source of neutrons; the two men talked about using it to perform an experiment similar to Frisch's experiment of January 13-14, of which they were as yet unaware. They discussed arrangements over lunch at the Columbia faculty club and afterward back at Pupin.

While Fermi was away from his desk Bohr arrived to tell him what he already knew. Finding an empty office, Bohr took the elevator to the basement, to the cyclotron area, where he turned up Herbert Anderson:

> He came right over and grabbed me by the shoulder. Bohr doesn't lecture you, he whispers in your ear. "Young man," he said, "let me explain to you about something new and exciting in physics." Then he told me about the splitting of the uranium nucleus and how naturally this fits in with the idea of the liquid drop. I was quite enchanted. Here was the great man himself, impressive in his bulk, sharing his excitement with me as if it were of the utmost importance for me to know what he had to say.

Bohr was en route to a conference in Washington on theoretical physics that would begin the next afternoon; he left to catch his train without seeing Fermi. As soon as Bohr was gone Anderson hunted up the Italian, who had returned to his office by now. "Before I had a chance to say anything," Anderson remembers, "he smiled in a friendly fashion and said, 'I think I know what you want to tell me. Let *me* explain it to you. . . .' I have to say that Fermi's explanation was even more dramatic than Bohr's."

Fermi helped Anderson and Dunning begin organizing the experiment he had discussed with Dunning earlier in the day. Anderson happened not long before to have built an ionization chamber and linear amplifier. "All we had to do was prepare a layer of uranium on one electrode and insert it into the chamber. That same afternoon we set up everything at the cyclotron. But the cyclotron was not working very well that day. Then I remembered some radon and beryllium which had been used as a source of neutrons in earlier experiments. It was a lucky thought." It came too late in the day; Fermi was also attending the Washington conference and had to leave. Anderson and Dunning closed up shop.

The Washington Conferences on Theoretical Physics, of which the 1939 meeting would be the fifth, were a George Gamow invention. He had stipulated their creation as a condition of his employment at George Washington University in 1934. He took Bohr's annual gathering in Copenhagen for a model; since there was no comparable assembly in the United States at the time, the Washington Conferences met with immediate success. At the instigation of Merle Tuve, Ernest Lawrence's boyhood friend and the driving force at the Department of Terrestrial Magnetism of the Carnegie Institution of Washington, the Carnegie Institution co-sponsored the conferences with GWU, though expenses were modest, for travel only, no more in total than five or six hundred dollars a year. People attended because they were interested. Edward Teller recalls the meetings as "in general small and exciting, thoroughly absorbing, and also a little tiring. Somehow, most of the running of the conferences Gamow left to me." The two men simply chose a topic and made up a list of invitees. Graduate students crowded in to listen. This year's topic was low-temperature physics.

Bohr sought out Gamow as soon as he arrived in Washington that evening. Gamow in turn called Teller: "Bohr has just come in. He has gone crazy. He says a neutron can split uranium." Teller thought of Fermi's experiments in Rome and the mess of radioactivities they produced and "suddenly understood the obvious." In Washington Fermi learned to his further disappointment from Bohr that Frisch was supposed to have done an experiment similar to the one left unfinished at Columbia. "Fermi . . . had no idea before that Frisch had made the experiment," Bohr wrote Margrethe a few days later. "I had no right to prevent others from experimentation, but I emphasized that Frisch had also spoken of an experiment in his notes. I said that it was all my fault that they all heard about Frisch and Meitner's explanation, and I earnestly asked them to wait [to make a public announcement] until I received a copy of Frisch's note to *Nature,* which I hoped would be waiting for me at Princeton [i.e., after the conference]." Fermi, understandably, seems to have argued against further delay.

Herbert Anderson returned to the basement of Pupin Hall that evening. He retrieved his neutron source. He calculated how many alpha particles the uranium oxide coated on a metal plate inside his ionization chamber would eject spontaneously in its normal process of radioactive decay: three thousand per minute. He calculated the probability of ten of those alphas appearing simultaneously to produce a spurious high-energy kick of the scanning beam of his oscilloscope: "practically never," he concluded in his laboratory notebook.

He set the neutron source beside the ionization chamber a little after 9 P.M. and began observing the effect on the oscilloscope. "Most kicks are due to .4 cm range α part[icles] [of approximately] .65 M[e]V," he noted. Then he saw what he was looking for: "Now large kicks which occur infrequently about 1 every 2 minutes." He counted them against the clock. In 60 minutes he had counted 33 large kicks. He removed the neutron source. "In 20 min" without a neutron source, he wrote, "0 counts." It was the first intentional observation of fission west of Copenhagen.

Dunning showed up later that evening, Anderson remembers, and "was very excited by the result I'd gotten." Anderson thought Dunning would telegraph Fermi immediately, but he seems not to have done so. Frisch, as he told Bohr later, had cabled no news of his confirming Copenhagen experiment because it seemed to him "just additional evidence of a discovery already made" and "cabling to you would have appeared unmodest to me." Dunning, despite his excitement at seeing the new phenomenon for himself, may have felt the same way.

Bohr woke to his dilemma. The conference would begin at two. As recently as three days previously he had written Frisch again, chiding him for not sending a copy of his and Meitner's *Nature* note. But he was less concerned now with that delay than he was with protecting the priority of Frisch's experiment, if any. Reluctantly he acceded to public announcement, stressing, he wrote Frisch afterward, "that no public account . . . could legitimately appear without mentioning your and your aunt's original interpretation of the Hahn results."

Fifty-one participants sat for a photograph in the course of the Fifth Washington Conference, and even a partial list of their names confirms the event's prestige. Otto Stern attended; Fermi; Bohr; Harold Urey of Columbia, who won the 1934 Nobel Prize in Chemistry for isolating a heavy form of hydrogen, deuterium, that carried a neutron in its nucleus; Gregory Breit, a waspish but inspired theoretician; Rabi; George Uhlenbeck, then at Columbia, who had been Paul Ehrenfest's assistant; Gamow; Teller; Hans Bethe down from Cornell; Léon Rosenfeld; Merle Tuve. Conspicuously absent was the Western crowd, probably because the two sponsoring institutions chose not to budget such long-distance travel.

Gamow opened the meeting by introducing Bohr. His news galvanized the room. A young physicist watching from the back saw an immediate application. Richard B. Roberts, Princeton-trained, worked with Tuve at the Department of Terrestrial Magnetism, the experimental section of the Carnegie Institution, located in a parklike setting in the Chevy Chase area of the capital. Roberts—thin, vigorous, with a strong jaw and wavy dark hair—still remembered the occasion vividly in 1979 in a draft autobiography:

> The Theo. Phys. Conference for 1939 was on the topic of low temperatures and I was not eager to attend. However, I went down to sit in the back row of the meeting.... Bohr and Fermi arrived and Bohr proceeded to reveal his news concerning the Hahn and Strassmann experiments.... He also told of Meitner's interpretation that the uranium had split. As usual he mumbled and rambled so there was little in his talk beyond the bare facts. Fermi then took over and gave his usual elegant presentation including all the implications.

Roberts noted in a letter to his father the Monday after the conference ended that "Fermi also . . . described an obvious experiment to test the theory"—Frisch's experiment, Fermi's, Dunning's and Anderson's experiment. "The remarkable thing is that this reaction results in 200 million volts of energy liberated and brings back the possibility of atomic power."

Bohr was calling the fission fragments "splitters." For the time being everyone borrowed that comical usage. Lawrence R. Hafstad, a longtime associate of Tuve, was sitting beside Roberts. When Fermi finished, the two men looked at each other, got up, left the meeting and lit out for the DTM. If "splitters" issued forth from uranium they intended to be among the first to see them.

In New York that day Szilard dragged himself to the nearest Western Union office and cabled the British Admiralty:

> KINDLY DISREGARD MY RECENT LETTER STOP WRITING

The secret patent had revived.

Naturwissenschaften reached Paris about January 16. One of Frédéric Joliot's associates recalls that "in a rather moving meeting [Joliot] made a report on this result to Madame Joliot and myself after having locked himself in for a few days and not talked to anybody." The Joliot-Curies were once again appalled to find they had barely missed a major discovery. In the next few days Joliot independently deduced the large energy release and considered the possibility of a chain reaction, as Szilard had thought he might. He tried to track down the neutrons from fission first, found that approach difficult, then set up an experiment somewhat like Frisch's. He detected fission fragments on January 26.

* * *

The newest building on the DTM grounds was the Atomic Physics Observatory, the working contents of which had just been brought on line two weeks before: a new 5 MV pressure Van de Graaff generator that Tuve, Roberts and their colleagues had built for $51,000 to extend their studies in the structure of the nucleus. The Van de Graaff was named for the Alabama-born physicist who invented it, but Tuve was the first—in 1932—to put it to practical use in experiment. It was essentially a monumental static-electricity generator, an insulated motor-driven pulley belt that picked up ions from discharge needles in its metal base, carried them up through an insulated support cylinder into a smooth metal storage sphere and deposited them on the sphere. As ions accumulated the sphere's voltage increased. The voltage could then be discharged as a spark—Van de Graaffs discharging lightning-bolt sparks have been staples of mad-scientist movies—or drawn off to power an accelerator tube. The new machine was built inside a pear-shaped pressure tank, as large as the tank of a water tower, that helped reduce accidental sparking.

When Tuve had first proposed the Van de Graaff to the zoning board of the prosperous Chevy Chase neighborhood the board had turned him down. Smashing atoms smacked of industrial process and the neighborhood had its property values to consider. Tuve noted the popularity of the Naval Observatory, across Connecticut Avenue a few miles west, and rechristened his project the Atomic Physics Observatory, which it was. As the APO it won approval.

Roberts and Hafstad chose to work with the APO. They had intended to use the old 1 MV Van de Graaff in the building next door to make neutrons for their splitter experiment, but that machine's ion-source filament was burned out. Although the APO's vacuum accelerator tube leaked, finding the leak looked to be less tedious than replacing the filament. In fact it needed two days. Hafstad went off Friday night on a ski weekend and another young Tuve protégé, R. C. Meyer, took his place.

Roberts' laboratory notebook entries summarize Saturday's work:

> *Sat 4:30 PM*
>
> *Set up ionization chamber to try to detect*
>
> $U_{92}^{238} + n \rightarrow U_{92}^{239} \rightarrow Ba_{56}^{?} + Kr_{36}^{?}$
>
> *Neutrons from Li + D* [accelerated deuterium nuclei bombarding lithium]
>
> . . .
>
> *With uranium lined I.C. observed*
> α's [approximately] *1-2 mm and occasional 35 mm kicks* (*Ba + Kr?*)

The APO's target room was a small circular basement accessible down a steel ladder, a chilly kiva that smelled pleasantly of oil. As soon as Roberts saw the "tremendous pulses corresponding to very large energy release" he and Meyer ran every test they could think of. "We promptly tried the effect of paraffin (for slow neutrons) and the cadmium to remove the slow neutrons. We also tried all the other heavy elements available [to determine if they would split] and saw the same [i.e., fission] with thorium." Having made that original discovery (Frisch had made it independently in Copenhagen before them) they stopped to eat. "I told Tuve after supper and he immediately called Bohr and Fermi and they came out Saturday night."

Not only Bohr and Fermi came, in heavy, dark, pin-striped three-piece suits, Fermi swarthy with a day's growth of beard, but also Tuve; Rosenfeld; Teller; Erik Bohr, handsome in a heavy overcoat over a decorative Danish sweater; Gregory Breit, owlish in spectacles; and John A. Fleming, the conservative director of the DTM, who had the presence of mind to bring along a photographer. All except Teller posed in the target room with Meyer and Roberts for a historic photograph. The box of the ionization chamber in the foreground is stacked with disks of paraffin; Bohr holds the stub of an after-dinner cigar; Fermi's grin reveals the gap between his front teeth left by a baby tooth he shed late; Roberts looks into the camera weary but satisfied. Fermi had been amazed at the ionization pulses on the oscilloscope and had insisted they check for equipment malfunctions: he had never seen such pulses in Rome (they were captured by the aluminum foil Amaldi had wrapped around his uranium to block its alpha background). Bohr was still fretting. "I had to stand and look at the first [*sic*] experiment," he wrote Margrethe, "without knowing certainly if Frisch had done the same experiment and sent a note to *Nature*." Back at Princeton on Sunday he learned from other family letters that Frisch had. "There followed," Roberts concludes, "several days of excitement, press releases and phone calls."

Science reporter Thomas Henry had attended the conference; his story appeared in the *Washington Evening Star* on Saturday afternoon. The Associated Press picked it up. Shortened, it earned a place on an inside page of the Sunday *New York Times*. Dunning may have seen it there; he finally wired Fermi news that morning of the Columbia experiment. As Herbert Anderson remembers it, "Fermi . . . rushed back to Columbia and straightaway called me into his office. My notebook lists the experiments he felt we should do right away. The date was January 29, 1939." They had already agreed, says Anderson, that "I would teach him Americana, and he would teach me physics." Both lessons began in earnest.

The *San Francisco Chronicle* picked up the wire-service story. Luis W. Alvarez, Ernest Lawrence's tall, ice-blond protégé, a future Nobelist whose father was a prominent Mayo Clinic physician, read it at Berkeley sitting in a barber chair in Stevens Union having his hair cut. "So [I told] the barber to stop cutting my hair and I got right out of that barber chair and ran as fast as I could to the Radiation Lab . . . where my student Phil Abelson . . . had been [trying to identify] what transuranium elements were produced when neutrons hit uranium; he was so close to discovering fission that it was almost pitiful." Abelson still remembers the painful moment: "About 9:30 a.m. I heard the sound of running footsteps outside, and immediately afterward Alvarez burst into the laboratory. . . . When [he] told me the news, I almost went numb as I realized that I had come close but had missed a great discovery. . . . For nearly 24 hours I remained numb, not functioning very well. The next morning I was back to normal with a plan to proceed." By the end of the day Abelson found iodine as a decay product of tellurium from uranium irradiation, another way the nucleus could split (i.e., tellurium 52 + zirconium 40 = U 92).

Alvarez wired Gamow for details, learned of the Frisch experiment, then tracked down Oppenheimer:

> I remember telling Robert Oppenheimer that we were going to look for [ionization pulses from fission] and he said, "That's impossible" and gave a lot of theoretical reasons why fission couldn't really happen. When I invited him over to look at the oscilloscope later, when we saw the big pulses, I would say that in less than fifteen minutes Robert had decided that this was indeed a real effect and . . . he had decided that some neutrons would probably boil off in the reaction, and that you could make bombs and generate power, all inside of a few minutes. . . . It was amazing to see how rapidly his mind worked, and he came to the right conclusions.

The following Saturday Oppenheimer discussed the discovery in a letter to a friend at Caltech, outlining all the experiments Alvarez and others had accomplished during the week and speculating on applications:

> The U business is unbelievable. We first saw it in the papers, wired for more dope, and have had a lot of reports since. . . In how many ways does the U come apart? At random, as one might guess, or only in certain ways? And most of all, are there many neutrons that come off during the splitting, or from the excited pieces? If there are, then a 10 cm cube of U deuteride (one would need the D [deuterium, heavy hydrogen] to slow them without capture) should be quite something. What do you think? It is I think exciting, not in the rare way of positrons and mesotrons, but in a good honest practical way.

The next day, in a letter to George Uhlenbeck at Columbia, "quite something" became "might very well blow itself to hell." One of Oppenheimer's students, the American theoretical physicist Philip Morrison, recalls that "when fission was discovered, within perhaps a week there was on the blackboard in Robert Oppenheimer's office a drawing—a very bad, an execrable drawing—of a bomb."

Enrico Fermi made similar estimates. George Uhlenbeck, who shared an office with him in Pupin Hall, was there one day to overhear him. Fermi was standing at his panoramic office window high in the physics tower looking down the gray winter length of Manhattan Island, its streets alive as always with vendors and taxis and crowds. He cupped his hands as if he were holding a ball. "A little bomb like that," he said simply, for once not lightly mocking, "and it would all disappear."

PART TWO

A PECULIAR SOVEREIGNTY

The Manhattan District bore no relation to the industrial or social life of our country; it was a separate state, with its own airplanes and its own factories and its thousands of secrets. It had a peculiar sovereignty, one that could bring about the end, peacefully or violently, of all other sovereignties.

Herbert S. Marks

We must be curious to learn how such a set of objects—hundreds of power plants, thousands of bombs, tens of thousands of people massed in national establishments—can be traced back to a few people sitting at laboratory benches discussing the peculiar behavior of one type of atom.

Spencer R. Weart

10
Neutrons

At the end of January 1939, still ill with a feverish cold that had laid him low for more than a week but determined to prevent information on the possibility of a chain reaction in uranium from reaching physicists in Nazi Germany, Leo Szilard raised himself from his bed in the King's Crown Hotel on West 116th Street in Manhattan and went out into the New York winter to take counsel of his friend Isador Isaac Rabi. Rabi, no taller than Szilard but always a trimmer and cooler man, who would be the 1944 Nobel laureate in physics, was born in Galicia in 1898 and emigrated to the United States with his family as a small child. Yiddish had been his first language; he grew up on New York's Lower East Side, where his father worked in a sweatshop making women's blouses until he accumulated enough savings to open a grocery store. Because his family was Orthodox and fundamentalist in its Judaism, Rabi had not known that the earth revolved around the sun until he read it in a library book. A frightening vision of the vast yellow face of the rising moon seen as a child down a New York street had begun his turn toward science, as had his childhood reading of the cosmological first verses of the Book of Genesis. He was a man of abrupt and honest bluntness who did not easily tolerate fools. One reason for his impatience was certainly that it guarded from harm his deeply emotional commitment to science: he thought physics "infinite," he told a biographer in late middle age, and he was disappointed that young physicists of that later day, intent on technique, seemed to miss what he had found, "the mystery of it: how very different it is from what you can see, and how profound nature is."

Szilard learned from Rabi that Enrico Fermi had discussed the possibility of a chain reaction in his public presentation at the Fifth Washington Conference on Theoretical Physics that had met the week before. Szilard adjourned to Fermi's office but did not find him there. He went back to Rabi and asked him to talk to Fermi "and say that these things ought to be kept secret." Rabi agreed and Szilard returned to his sickbed.

He was recovering; a day or two later he again sought Rabi out:

> I said to him: "Did you talk to Fermi?" Rabi said, "Yes, I did." I said, "What did Fermi say?" Rabi said, "Fermi said 'Nuts!' " So I said, "Why did he say 'Nuts!'?" and Rabi said, "Well, I don't know, but he is in and we can ask him." So we went over to Fermi's office, and Rabi said to Fermi, "Look, Fermi, I told you what Szilard thought and you said 'Nuts!' and Szilard wants to know why you said 'Nuts!' " So Fermi said, "Well . . . there is the remote possibility that neutrons may be emitted in the fission of uranium and then of course perhaps a chain reaction can be made." Rabi said, "What do you mean by 'remote possibility'?" and Fermi said, "Well, ten per cent." Rabi said, "Ten per cent is not a remote possibility if it means that we may die of it. If I have pneumonia and the doctor tells me that there is a remote possibility that I might die, and it's ten percent, I get excited about it."

But despite Fermi's facility with American slang and Rabi's with probabilities Fermi and Szilard were unable to agree. For the time being they left the discussion there.

Fermi was not misleading Szilard. It was easy to estimate the explosive force of a quantity of uranium, as Fermi would do standing at his office window overlooking Manhattan, if fission proceeded automatically from mere assembly of the material; even journalists had managed that simple calculation. But such obviously was not the case for uranium in its natural form, or the substance would long ago have ceased to exist on earth. However energetically interesting a reaction, fission by itself was merely a laboratory curiosity. Only if it released secondary neutrons, and those in sufficient quantity to initiate and sustain a chain reaction, would it serve for anything more. "Nothing known then," writes Herbert Anderson, Fermi's young partner in experiment, "guaranteed the emission of neutrons. Neutron emission had to be observed experimentally and measured quantitatively." No such work had yet been done. It was, in fact, the new work Fermi had proposed to Anderson immediately upon returning from Washington. Which meant to Fermi that talk of developing fission into a weapon of war was absurdly premature.

Many years later Szilard succinctly summed up the difference between his position and Fermi's. "From the very beginning the line was drawn," he said. ". . . Fermi thought that the conservative thing was to play down the possibility that [a chain reaction] may happen, and I thought the conservative thing was to assume that it would happen and take all the necessary precautions."

Once he was well again Szilard had catching up to do. He cabled Oxford to ship him the cylinder of beryllium he had left behind at the Clarendon when he came to the United States, preliminary to mounting a neutron-emission experiment of his own. At Lewis Strauss's request he spent a day with the financier discussing the possible consequences of fission, which included, Strauss notes wistfully in his memoirs, making "the performance of our surge generator in Pasadena insignificant. The device had just been completed." The surge generator in which he had invested some tens of thousands of dollars had been cut down to size. The Strausses were scheduled to leave that evening by overnight train for a Palm Beach vacation; Szilard rode along as far as Washington to continue the discussion. He was massaging his patron: he needed to rent radium to combine with his beryllium to make a neutron source and hoped Strauss might be persuaded to support the expense.

Arriving late at Union Station in Washington, Szilard called the Edward Tellers. They were still recovering from the work of hosting the Washington Conference. Mici Teller protested the surprise visit, her husband remembers: "No! We are both much too tired. He must go to a hotel." They met Szilard anyway, whereupon to Teller's surprise Mici invited their countryman to stay with them:

> We drove to our home, and I showed Szilard to his room. He felt the bed suspiciously, then turned to me suddenly and said: "Is there a hotel nearby?" There was, and he continued: "Good! I have just remembered sleeping in this bed before. It is much too hard."
>
> But before he left, he sat on the edge of the hard bed and talked excitedly: "You heard Bohr on fission?"
>
> "Yes," I replied.
>
> Szilard continued: "You know what that means!"

What it meant to Szilard, Teller remembers, was that "Hitler's success could depend on it."

The next day Szilard discussed his plan for voluntary secrecy with Teller, then entrained for Princeton to pursue the same subject with Eugene Wigner, who was still drydocked in the infirmary with jaundice. Szilard was thus present in Princeton when yet another momentous insight struck Niels Bohr.

Bohr and Léon Rosenfeld were staying at the Nassau Club, the Princeton faculty center. On Sunday, February 5, George Placzek joined them at breakfast in the club dining room. The Bohemian theoretician had arrived in Princeton from Copenhagen the night before, another refugee from Nazi persecution. Talk turned to fission. "It is a relief that we are now rid of those transuranians," Rosenfeld remembers Bohr saying, referring to the confusing radioactivities Hahn, Meitner and Strassmann had found in the late 1930s that Bohr assumed could now be attributed to existing lighter elements—barium, lanthanum and the many other fission products researchers were beginning to identify.

Placzek was skeptical. "The situation is more confused than ever," he told Bohr. He began then to specify the sources of confusion. He was directly challenging the relevance of Bohr's liquid-drop model of the nucleus. The Danish laureate paid attention.

Physicists use a convenient measurement they call a "cross section" to indicate the probability that a particular nuclear reaction will or will not happen. The theoretical physicist Rudolf Peierls once explained the measurement with this analogy:

> For example, if I throw a ball at a glass window one square foot in area, there may be one chance in ten that the window will break, and nine chances in ten that the ball will just bounce. In the physicists' language, this particular window, for a ball thrown in this particular way, has a "disintegration cross-section" of 1/10 square foot and an "elastic cross-section" of 9/10 square foot.

Cross sections can be measured for many different nuclear reactions, and they are expressed not in square feet but in minute fractions of square centimeters, customarily 10^{-24}, because the diminutive nucleus is the target window of Peierls' analogy. The cross section that concerned Placzek in his discussion with Bohr was the capture cross section: the probability that a nucleus will capture an approaching neutron. In terms of Peierls' analogy, the capture cross section measures the chance that the window might be open when the ball arrives and might therefore admit the ball into the living room.

Nuclei capture neutrons of certain energies more frequently than they capture neutrons of other energies. They are naturally tuned, so to speak, to certain specific energy levels—as if Peierls' window opened more easily to balls thrown at only certain speeds. This phenomenon is known as resonance. The confusion Placzek delighted in reporting concerned a resonance in the capture cross sections of uranium and thorium.

Placzek pointed out that uranium and thorium both exhibit a capture resonance for neutrons with medium-range energies of about 25 electron volts. That meant, first of all, that although fission was one behavior uranium could exhibit under neutron bombardment, capture and subsequent transmutation continued to be another. Bohr was not ever to be rid of those inconvenient "transuranians." Some of them were real.

If a neutron penetrated a uranium nucleus, for example, the result might be fission. But if the neutron happened to be traveling at the appropriate energy when it penetrated—somewhere around 25 eV—the nucleus would probably capture it without fissioning. Beta decay would follow, increasing the nuclear charge by one unit; the result should be a new, as-yet-unnamed transuranic element of atomic number 93. That was one of Placzek's points. It would prove in time to be crucial.

The other source of confusion was more straightforward. It was also more immediately relevant to the question of how to harness nuclear energy. It concerned differences between uranium and thorium.

Thorium, element 90, a soft, heavy, lustrous, silver-white metal, was first isolated by the celebrated Swedish chemist Jöns Jakob Berzelius in 1828. Berzelius named the new element after Thor, the Norse god of thunder. Its oxide found commercial use beginning in the late nineteenth century as the primary component of the fragile woven mantles of gas lanterns: heat incandesces it a brilliant white. Because it is mildly radioactive, and radioactivity was once considered tonic, thorium was also for some years incorporated into a popular German toothpaste, Doramad. Auer, the company that made German gas mantles, also made the toothpaste. Hahn, Meitner and Strassmann, the Joliot-Curies and others had regularly studied thorium alongside uranium. Its behavior was often similar. Otto Frisch had first demonstrated that it fissioned. He bombarded it next after uranium in the course of his January experiment in Copenhagen, the experiment he had discussed with Bohr after he returned from Kungälv and Bohr had worked so hard in the United States to protect.

Frisch was then also the first to notice that the fission characteristics of thorium differed from those of uranium. Thorium did not respond to the magic of paraffin; it was unaffected by slow neutrons. Richard B. Roberts and his colleagues at the Department of Terrestrial Magnetism of the Carnegie Institution of Washington had just independently confirmed and extended Frisch's findings. With their 5 million volt Van de Graaff they could generate neutrons of several different, known energies. Continuing their experiments after their Saturday-night show for the Washington Conference group, they had compared uranium and thorium fission responses at varying energies as Frisch with his single neutron source could not. They found to their surprise (Frisch's paper had not yet appeared in *Nature*) that while both uranium and thorium fissioned under bombardment by fast neutrons, only uranium fissioned under bombardment by slow neutrons. Some energy between 0.5 MeV and 2.5 MeV marked a lower threshold for fast-neutron fission for both elements. (Bohr and John Wheeler, beginning work at Princeton on fission theory, had estimated the threshold energy to be about 1 MeV.) The slow neutrons that also fissioned uranium were effective at far lower energies. "From these comparisons," the DTM group concluded in a February paper, "it appears that the uranium fissions are produced by different processes for fast and slow neutrons."

Why, Placzek now prodded Bohr, should both uranium and thorium have similar capture resonances and similar fast-neutron thresholds but different responses to slow neutrons? If the liquid-drop model had any validity at all, the difference made no sense.

Bohr abruptly saw why and was struck dumb. Not to lose what he had only barely grasped, oblivious to courtesy, he pushed back his chair and strode from the room and from the club. Rosenfeld hurried to follow. "Taking a hasty leave of Placzek, I joined Bohr, who was walking silently, lost in deep meditation, which I was careful not to disturb." The two men tramped speechless through the snow across the Princeton campus to Fine Hall, the Neo-Gothic brick building where the Institute for Advanced Study was then lodged. They went in to Bohr's office, borrowed from Albert Einstein. It was spacious, with leaded windows, a fireplace, a large blackboard, an Oriental rug to warm the floor. No peripatetic like Bohr, Einstein had judged it too large and moved into a small secretarial annex nearby.

"As soon as we entered the office," Rosenfeld remembers, "[Bohr] rushed to the blackboard, telling me: 'Now listen: I have it all.' And he started—again without uttering a word—drawing graphs on the blackboard."

The first graph Bohr drew looked like this:

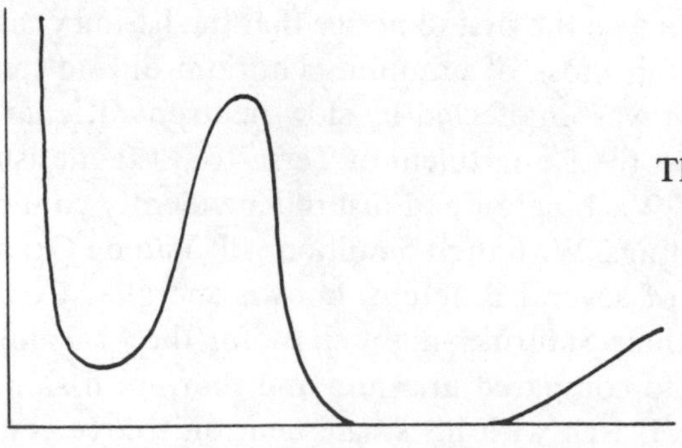

The horizontal axis plotted neutron energy left to right—low to high, slow to fast. The vertical axis charted cross sections—the probability of a particular nuclear reaction—and served a double purpose. The lazy S that filled most of the frame represented thorium's cross section for capture at different neutron energies, the steep central peak demonstrating the 25 eV resonance in the middle range. The tail that waved from the horizontal axis on the right side represented a different thorium cross section: its cross section for fission beginning at that high 1 MeV threshold. What Bohr had drawn was thus a visualization of thorium's changing response to bombardment by neutrons of increasing energy.

Bohr moved to the next section of blackboard and drew a second graph. He labeled it with the mass number of the isotope most plentiful in natural uranium. "He wrote the mass number 238 with very large figures," Rosenfeld says; "he broke several pieces of chalk in the process." Bohr's urgency marked the point of his insight. The second graph looked exactly like the first:

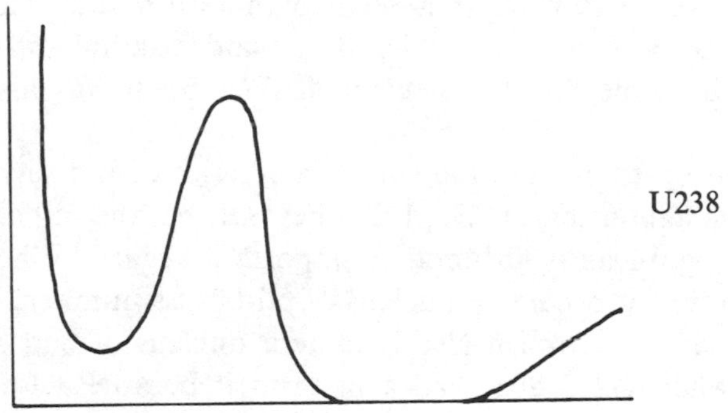

But a third graph was coming.

Francis Aston had found only U238 when he first passed uranium through his mass spectrograph at the Cavendish. In 1935, using a more powerful instrument, physicist Arthur Jeffrey Dempster of the University of Chicago detected a second, lighter isotope. "It was found," Dempster announced in a lecture, "that a few seconds' exposure was sufficient for the main component at 238 reported by Dr. Aston, but on long exposures a faint companion of mass number 235 was also present." Three years later a gifted Harvard postdoctoral fellow named Alfred Otto Carl Nier, the son of working-class German emigrants to Minnesota, measured the ratio of U235 to U238 in natural uranium as 1:139, which meant that U235 was present to the extent of about 0.7 percent. By contrast, thorium in its natural form is essentially all one isotope, Th232. And that natural difference in the composition of the two elements was the clue that set Bohr off. He drew his third graph. It depicted one cross section, not two:

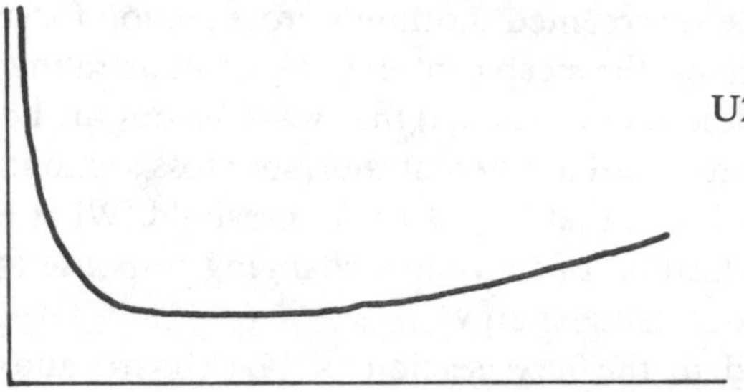

Having made a hard copy of his abrupt vision, Bohr was finally ready to explain himself.

Both thorium and U238 could be expected on theoretical grounds to behave similarly, he pointed out to Rosenfeld: to fission only with fast neutrons above 1 MeV. And it seemed that they did. That left U235. It followed as a matter of logic, Bohr said triumphantly, that U235 must be responsible for slow-neutron fission. Such was his essential insight.

He went on to explore the subtle energetics of the several reactions. Thorium was lighter than U235, U238 heavier, but the middle isotope differed more significantly in another important regard. When Th232 absorbed a neutron it became a nucleus of odd mass number, Th233. When U238 absorbed a neutron it also became a nucleus of odd mass number, U239. But when U235 absorbed a neutron it became a nucleus of even mass number, U236. And the vicissitudes of nuclear rearrangement are such, as Fermi would explain one day in a lecture, that "changing from an odd number of neutrons to an even number of neutrons released one or two MeV." Which meant that U235 had an inherent energetic advantage over its two competitors: it accrued energy toward fission simply by virtue of its change of mass; they did not.

Lise Meitner and Otto Frisch had realized in Kungälv that a certain amount of energy was necessary to agitate the nucleus to fission, but they had not considered in detail the energetics of that input. They were distracted by the enormous 200 MeV output. In fact, the uranium nucleus required an input of about 6 MeV to fission. That much energy was necessary to roil the nucleus to the point where it elongated and broke apart. The absorption of any neutron, regardless of its velocity, made available a binding energy of about 5.3 MeV. But that left U238 about 1 MeV short, which is why it needed fast neutrons of at least that threshold energy before it could fission.

U235 also earned 5.3 MeV when it absorbed a neutron. But it won Fermi's "one or two MeV" in addition simply by adjusting from an odd to an even mass. That put its total above 6 MeV. So *any neutron at all* would fission U235—slow, fast or in between. Which was what Bohr's third graph demonstrated: the probably continuous fission cross section of U235. From slow neutrons on the left only a fraction of an electron volt above zero energy, to fast neutrons on the right above 1 MeV that would also fission U238, any neutron an atom of U235 encountered would agitate it to fission. Natural uranium masked U235's continuous fissibility; the more abundant U238 captured most of the neutrons. Only by slowing the neutrons with paraffin below the U238 capture resonance at 25 eV had experimenters like Hahn, Strassmann and Frisch been able to coax the highly fissionable U235 out of hiding. In a burst of insight Bohr had answered Placzek's objections and replenished his liquid drop.

In January Bohr had produced a 700-word paper in three days to protect his European colleagues' priorities. Now, in his eagerness to spread the news of U235's special role in fission, he produced an 1,800-word paper in two days, mailing it to the *Physical Review* on February 7. "Resonance in uranium and thorium disintegrations and the phenomenon of nuclear fission" was nevertheless written with care, more care than it received in the reading. Everyone understood its basic hypothesis—that U235, not U238, is responsible for slow-neutron fission in uranium—though not everyone concurred without the confirmation of experiment. But probably because, as Fermi recalled, isotopes at that time "were considered almost magically inseparable," everyone overlooked its further implications. Szilard explained to Lewis Strauss that month that "slow neutrons seem to split a uranium isotope which is present in an abundance of about 1% in uranium." Richard Roberts at the DTM, in a 1940 draft report of considerable significance, asserted that "Bohr . . . ascribed the [slow] neutron reaction to U235 and the fast neutron reaction to U238." Roberts' misstatement was probably no more than a rough first approximation that he would have corrected in a polished report. Szilard's and Roberts' comments illustrate, however, that the slow-neutron fission of U235 preoccupied the physicists at first to the exclusion of a more ominous potentiality.

Bohr acknowledged it indirectly in his paper for the *Physical Review.* The slow-neutron fission of U235 occupied the foreground of his discussion because it explained the puzzling difference between uranium and thorium. But Bohr also considered U235's behavior under fast-neutron bombardment. "For fast neutrons," he wrote near the end of the paper, ". . .because of the scarcity of the isotope concerned, the fission yields will be much smaller than those obtained from neutron impacts on the abundant isotope." The statement implies but does not ask a pregnant question: what would the yields be for fast neutrons if U235 could be separated from U238?

The latest incarnation of Orso Corbino's garden fish pond in Rome was a tank of water three feet wide and three feet deep that Fermi and Anderson set up that winter in the basement of Pupin Hall. They planned to insert a radon-beryllium neutron source into the center of a five-inch spherical bulb and suspend the bulb in the middle of the tank. Neutrons from the beryllium would then diffuse through the surrounding water, which would slow them down. The neutrons would induce a characteristic 44-second half-life in strips of rhodium foil, Fermi's favorite neutron detector, set at various distances away from the bulb. Once he established a baseline of neutron activity using the Rn + Be source alone, Fermi intended to pack uranium oxide into the bulb around the source and make a second series of measurements. If more neutrons turned up in the water tank with uranium than without, he could deduce that uranium produced secondary neutrons when it fissioned and could roughly estimate their number. One neutron out for each neutron in was not enough to sustain a chain reaction, since inevitably some would be captured and others drift away: it needed something more than one secondary for each primary, preferably at least two.

Upstairs on the seventh floor Szilard discovered a different experiment in progress. Walter Zinn, a tall, blond Canadian postdoctoral research associate who taught at City College, was bombarding uranium with 2.5 MeV neutrons from a small accelerator. He had reasoned in terms of neutron energy rather than quantity; he was trying to demonstrate secondary neutron production by looking for neutrons faster than the 2.5 MeV's he supplied. So far he had managed only inconclusive results.

"Szilard watched my experiment with great interest," Zinn recalls, "and then suggested that perhaps it would be more successful if lower energy neutrons were available. I said, 'That's fine, but where do you get them?' Leo said, 'Just leave it to me, I'll get them.' "

Szilard meant to help Zinn, but he also coveted Zinn's ionization chamber. "All we needed to do," he said later, "was to get a gram of radium, get a block of beryllium, expose a piece of uranium to the neutrons which come from the beryllium, and then see by means of the ionization chamber which Zinn had built whether fast neutrons were emitted in the process. Such an experiment need not take more than an hour or two to perform, once the equipment has been built and if you have the neutron source. But of course we had no radium."

The problem was still money. The Radium Chemical Company of New York and Chicago, a subsidiary of the Union Minière du Haut-Katanga of Belgium, the dominant source of world radium supplies, was willing to rent a gram of radium for a minimum of three months for $125 a month. Szilard wrote Lewis Strauss at his Virginia farm on February 13 "to see whether you could sanction the expenditures" and presciently briefed the financier on the meaning of the latest developments. The letter's crucial paragraph addresses Bohr's new hypothesis that U235 is responsible for slow-neutron fission in natural uranium:

> If this isotope could be used for maintaining chain reactions, it would have to be separated from the bulk of uranium. This, no doubt, would be done if necessary, but it might take five to ten years before it can be done on a technical scale. Should small scale experiments show that the thorium and the bulk of uranium would not work, but the rare isotope of uranium would, we would have the task immediately to attack the question of concentrating the rare isotope of uranium.*

Strauss's surge-generator losses had inoculated him against further investment in the nuclear enterprise. He wanted to know, Szilard says, "just how sure I was that this would work." Since Szilard could offer no guarantees, Strauss offered no support. Szilard turned then to Benjamin Liebowitz. "He was not poor but he was not exactly wealthy. . . . I told him what this was all about, and he said, 'How much money do you need?' I said, 'Well, I'd like to borrow $2,000.' He took out his checkbook, he wrote out a check, I cashed the check, I rented the . . . radium, and in the meantime the beryllium block arrived from England."

The cylinder of beryllium, which Walter Zinn thought "a strange and unique object" and took for proof of Szilard's magic ways, arrived on February 18. The same day Szilard heard from Teller about significant work in

*The distinction between U235 and U238 had already fired a debate. "Fermi and a number of others," says John Dunning, "had considerable doubts about U-235 or even disagreed—they thought it was U-238 [that was responsible for slow-neutron fission]." The disagreement incensed Bohr, who told Léon Rosenfeld he was "outraged" that Fermi should question the logic of his argument that thorium and U238 stood on one side and U235 on the other. "It was both the strength and the weakness of Fermi," writes Rosenfeld, "to be so intent on following his own lines of thought that he was impervious to any outside influence. . . . He fancied there could be a different interpretation of the evidence discussed by Bohr, and that only experiment could decide." Dunning, on the other hand, "immediately accepted Bohr's argument." The important outcome was that Dunning began to think of isotope separation, while Fermi continued to pursue the possibility of a chain reaction in natural uranium. With unusual and uncharacteristically Fermian conservatism, so did Szilard.

Washington at the DTM. Richard Roberts and R. C. Meyer were preparing a letter to the *Physical Review* reporting the discovery of delayed neutrons from fission. These were not the instantaneous secondary neutrons the Columbia researchers were seeking, but they did confirm that the fission fragments had neutrons to spare and would give them up spontaneously.

The general excitement Teller found at the busy DTM laboratories impressed him more:

> As soon as I began taking interest in uranium, sharp discussion started on the practical significance. Tuve, Hafstad, and Roberts are entirely aware of what is involved. They also know of Fermi's experiments. Of course, I didn't say anything. The above-mentioned letter [to the *Physical Review*] cannot cause any harm. . . .
>
> I do not know their detailed plans, but I believe that urgent action [to maintain secrecy] is required. Very many people have discovered already what is involved. Those in Washington would like to persuade the Carnegie Institution that it should provide more money for U-research in view of the practical significance of the matter. . . . But right now this has no reality unless the [Carnegie] leadership becomes more interested than it has been so far. . . .
>
> I repeat that there is a chain-reaction mood in Washington. I only had to say "uranium" and then could listen for two hours to their thoughts.

The president of the Carnegie Institution was a New England Yankee, the grandson of two sea captains, an electrical engineer, inventor and former dean of the school of engineering at the Massachusetts Institute of Technology named Vannevar Bush. If Bush was initially less willing to invest in chain-reaction experiments than Teller would have liked him to be, he kept good company; neither Ernest Lawrence at Berkeley nor Otto Hahn in Dahlem nor Lise Meitner, visiting Copenhagen that February to work with Otto Frisch, chose to pursue moonshine. Only Columbia and Paris mounted early experiments, though the DTM would soon follow the Columbia lead.

Frédéric Joliot and two colleagues, a cultivated Austrian named Hans von Halban and a huge, keen Russian named Lew Kowarski, began an experiment similar to Fermi's the last week in February to identify secondary neutrons from fission. They also used a tank of water with a central neutron source but dissolved their uranium in the water rather than packing it around the source. More important to their priority of research, they had immediate access to the Radium Institute's ample radium supply.

Because Fermi's neutron source relied on radon rather than radium it induced an ambiguity into his experiment that Szilard caught and called to his attention: radon ejected much faster neutrons from beryllium than did radium; at least part of any increase in neutrons Fermi found in his tank might therefore result not from fission but from another, competing reaction in beryllium. Fermi thought the ambiguity trivial, but agreed, as Zinn had before, to repeat the experiment using a radium-beryllium source. Szilard generously offered his. But the radium to energize it was not yet in hand; Szilard was still negotiating its rental because his lack of official affiliation made the Radium Chemical Company nervous.

He got his radium, two grams sealed in a small brass capsule, early in March, after he arranged admission to the Columbia laboratories for three months as a guest researcher. He and Zinn immediately set up their experiment. They made an ingenious nest, like Chinese boxes, of its various components: a large cake of paraffin wax, the beryllium cylinder set at the bottom of a blind hole in the paraffin, the radium capsule fitted into the beryllium cylinder; resting on the beryllium, inside the paraffin, a box lined with neutron-absorbing cadmium filled with uranium oxide; pushed into that box, but shielded from the radium's gamma radiation by a lead plug, the ionization tube itself, which connected to an oscilloscope. With this arrangement, says Szilard, they could measure the flux of neutrons from the uranium with and without the cadmium shield:

> Everything was ready and all we had to do was to turn a switch, lean back, and watch the screen of a television tube. If flashes of light appeared on the screen, that would mean that neutrons were emitted in the fission process of uranium and this in turn would mean that the large-scale liberation of atomic energy was just around the corner. We turned the switch and saw the flashes. We watched them for a little while and then we switched everything off and went home.

They had made a rough estimate of neutron production: "We find the number of neutrons emitted per fission to be about two." With radium available merely by picking up the phone, the French team a week earlier had found "more than one neutron . . . produced for each neutron absorbed." Fermi and Anderson estimated "a yield of about two neutrons per each neutron captured." Szilard immediately alerted Wigner and Teller. Teller remembers the moment well:

> I was at my piano, attempting with the collaboration of a friend and his violin to make Mozart sound like Mozart, when the telephone rang. It was Szilard, calling from New York. He spoke to me in Hungarian, and he said only one thing: "I have found the neutrons."

Szilard also wired Lewis Strauss:

> PERFORMED TODAY PROPOSED EXPERIMENT WITH BERYLLIUM BLOCK WITH STRIKING RESULT. VERY LARGE NEUTRON EMISSION FOUND. ESTIMATE CHANCES FOR REACTION NOW ABOVE 50%.

Szilard had known what the neutrons would mean since the day he crossed the street in Bloomsbury: the shape of things to come. "That night," he recalled later, "there was very little doubt in my mind that the world was headed for grief."

Though he was still recovering from jaundice, Eugene Wigner responded vigorously to Szilard's disturbing news while a storm of betrayal broke over Central Europe. Hitler ordered the President and the Foreign Minister of Czechoslovakia to Berlin on March 14 and threatened to bomb Prague to rubble unless they surrendered their country. With the Nazi leader's encouragement the Slovaks formally seceded from the republic that day. Ruthenia, Czechoslovakia's narrow eastern extension along the Carpathians, also claimed independence as Carpatho-Ukraine, an exercise in grave-robbing abruptly terminated the following morning when the fascist Hungary of Admiral Horthy invaded the new nation with German endorsement. Hitler flew in triumph to Prague. On March 16 he decreed what was left of Czechoslovakia—Bohemia and Moravia—to be a German protectorate. The country that France and Great Britain had abandoned at Munich was partitioned without resistance.

Wigner caught the train to New York. On the morning of March 16 he met with Szilard, Fermi and George Pegram in Pegram's office. Since at least the end of January Szilard had been promoting a new version of his Bund—he called it the Association for Scientific Collaboration—to monitor research, collect and disburse funds and maintain secrecy, a civilian organization that might guide the development of atomic energy. He had discussed it with Lewis Strauss on the train to Washington, with Teller after the night of the hard bed, with Wigner in Princeton the weekend Bohr drew his graphs. As far as Wigner was concerned, the time for such amateurism was over. He "strongly appealed to us," says Szilard, "immediately to inform the United States government of these discoveries." It was "such a serious business that we could not assume responsibility for handling it."

At sixty-three George Braxton Pegram was a generation older than the two Hungarians and the Italian who debated in his office that morning. A South Carolinian who had earned his Ph.D. from Columbia in 1903 working with thorium, he had studied under Max Planck at the University of Berlin and corresponded with Ernest Rutherford when Rutherford was still progressing in fruitful exile at McGill. Pegram was tall and athletic, a champion at tennis well into his sixties, a canoeist when young who enjoyed paddling and sailing an eighteen-foot sponson around Manhattan Island. His interest in radioactivity may have been aroused by his father, a chemistry professor; "probably the most important problem before the physicist today," the senior Pegram told the North Carolina Academy of Sciences in 1911, "is that of making the enormous energy [within the atom] available for the world's work." The next year, as an associate professor of physics at Columbia, Pegram had written Albert Einstein encouraging him to come to New York to lecture on relativity theory. Pegram had brought Rabi and Fermi to Columbia, building the university's international reputation for nuclear research. He was gray now, with thinning hair, wire-rimmed glasses, protuberant ears, a strong, square, wide-chinned jaw. Radioactivity intrigued him still, but a university dean's well-worn conservatism counseled him to caution.

He knew someone in Washington, he told Wigner: Charles Edison, Undersecretary of the Navy. Wigner insisted Pegram immediately call the man. Pegram was willing to do so, but first the group should discuss logistics. Who would carry the news? Fermi was traveling to Washington that afternoon to lecture in the evening to a group of physicists; he could meet with the Navy the next day. His Nobel Prize should give him exceptional credibility. Pegram called Washington. Edison was unavailable; his office directed Pegram to Admiral Stanford C. Hooper, technical assistant to the Chief of Naval Operations. Hooper agreed to hear Fermi out. Pegram's call was the first direct contact between the physicists of nuclear fission and the United States government.

The next topic on the morning's agenda was secrecy. Fermi and Szilard had both written reports on their secondary-neutron experiments and were ready to send them to the *Physical Review.* With Pegram's concurrence they decided to go ahead and mail the reports to the *Review,* to establish priority, but to ask the editor to delay publishing them until the secrecy issue could be resolved. Both papers went off that day.

Pegram prepared a letter of introduction for Fermi to carry along to his appointment. It stated a hesitant case dense with hypotheticals:

> Experiments in the physics laboratory at Columbia University reveal that conditions may be found under which the chemical element uranium may be able to liberate its large excess of atomic energy, and that this might mean the possibility that uranium might be used as an explosive that would liberate a million times as much energy per pound as any known explosive. My own feeling is that the probabilities are against this, but my colleagues and I think that the bare possibility should not be disregarded.

Thus lightly armed, Fermi departed to engage the Navy.

The debate was hardly ended, nor Wigner's long day done. He returned to Princeton with Szilard in tow for an important meeting with Niels Bohr. It had been planned in advance; John Wheeler and Léon Rosenfeld would attend and Teller was making a special trip up from Washington. If Bohr could be convinced to swing his prestige behind secrecy, the campaign to isolate German nuclear physics research might work.

They met in the evening in Wigner's office. "Szilard outlined the Columbia data," Wheeler reports, "and the preliminary indications from it that at least two secondary neutrons emerge from each neutron-induced fission. Did this not mean that a nuclear explosive was certainly possible?" Not necessarily, Bohr countered. "We tried to convince him," Teller writes, "that we should go ahead with fission research but we should not publish the results. We should keep the results secret, lest the Nazis learn of them and produce nuclear explosions first. Bohr insisted that we would never succeed in producing nuclear energy and he also insisted that secrecy must never be introduced into physics."

Bohr's skepticism, says Wheeler, concerned "the enormous difficulty of separating the necessary quantities of U235." Fermi noted in a later lecture that "it was not very clear [in 1939] that the job of separating large amounts of uranium 235 was one that could be taken seriously." At the Princeton meeting, Teller remembers, Bohr insisted that "it can never be done unless you turn the United States into one huge factory."

More crucial for Bohr was the issue of secrecy. He had worked for decades to shape physics into an international community, a model within its limited franchise of what a peaceful, politically united world might be. Openness was its fragile, essential charter, an operational necessity, as freedom of speech is an operational necessity to a democracy. Complete openness enforced absolute honesty: the scientist reported *all* his results, favorable and unfavorable, where all could read them, making possible the ongoing correction of error. Secrecy would revoke that charter and subordinate science as a political system—Polanyi's "republic"—to the anarchic competition of the nation-states. No one was more anguished than Bohr by the menace of Nazi Germany; Laura Fermi remembers of this period, "two months after his landing in the United States," that "he spoke about the doom of Europe in increasingly apocalyptic terms, and his face was that of a man haunted by one idea." If U235 could be separated easily from U238, that misfortune might be cause for temporary compromise with principle in the interest of survival. Bohr thought the technology looked not even remotely accessible. The meeting dragged on inconclusively past midnight.

The next afternoon Fermi turned up at the Navy Department on

Constitution Avenue for his appointment with Admiral Hooper. He had probably planned a conservative presentation. The contempt of the desk officer who went in to announce him to the admiral encouraged that approach. "There's a wop outside," Fermi overheard the man say. So much for the authority of the Nobel Prize.

In what Lewis Strauss, by now a Navy volunteer, calls "a ramshackle old board room" Hooper assembled an audience of naval officers, officers from the Army's Bureau of Ordnance and two civilian scientists attached to the Naval Research Laboratory. One of the civilians, a bluff physicist named Ross Gunn, had watched Richard Roberts demonstrate fission in the target room of the 5 MV Van de Graaff at the DTM not long after Fermi passed through at the time of the Fifth Washington Conference. Gunn worked on submarine propulsion; he was eager to learn more about an energy source that burned no oxygen.

Fermi led his auditors through an hour of neutron physics. If the notes of one of the participants, a naval officer, are comprehensive, Fermi emphasized his water-tank measurements rather than Szilard's more direct ionization-chamber work. New experiments in preparation might confirm a chain reaction, Fermi explained. The problem then would be to assemble a sufficiently large mass of uranium to capture and use the secondary neutrons before they escaped through the surface of the material.

The officer taking notes interrupted. What might be the size of this mass? Would it fit into the breech of a gun?

Rather than look at physics down a gun barrel Fermi withdrew to the ...undane. It might turn out to be the size of a small star, he said, smil...
...nowing better.
...s diffusing through a tank of water: it was all too vague. Ex...
...s Gunn, the meeting came to nothing. "Enrico himself . . .
...ce of his predictions," says Laura Fermi. The Navy re...
... in maintaining contact; representatives would un...
...bia premises. Fermi smelled the condescension

...ilard traveled down to Washington from
... the weekend. They got together, re...
... these things"—the *Physical Review*
... and I thought that they should
...er a long discussion, Fermi
...cracy; if the majority was
...sh of the majority." Within a
...roup learned of the Joliot/von
...*Nature* on March 18. "From that

moment on," Szilard notes, "Fermi was adamant that withholding publication made no sense."

The following month, on April 22, Joliot, von Halban and Kowarski published a second paper in *Nature* concerning secondary neutrons. This one, "Number of neutrons liberated in the nuclear fission of uranium," rang bells. Calculating on the basis of the experiment previously reported, the French team found 3.5 secondary neutrons per fission. "The interest of the phenomenon discussed here as a means of producing a chain of nuclear reactions," the three men wrote, "was already mentioned in our previous letter." Now they concluded that if a sufficient amount of uranium were immersed in a suitable moderator, "the fission chain will perpetuate itself and break up only after reaching the walls limiting the medium. Our experimental results show that this condition will most probably be satisfied." That is, uranium would most probably chain-react.

Joliot's was an authoritative voice. G. P. Thomson, J.J.'s son, who was professor of physics at Imperial College, London, heard it. "I began to consider carrying out certain experiments with uranium," he told a correspondent later. "What I had in mind was something rather more than a piece of pure research, for at the back of my thoughts there lay the possibility of a weapon." He applied forthwith to the British Air Ministry for a ton of uranium oxide, "ashamed of putting forward a proposal apparently so absurd."

More ominously, two initiatives originated simultaneously in Germany as a result of the French report. A physicist at Göttingen alerted the Reich Ministry of Education. That led to a secret conference in Berlin on April 29, which led in turn to a research program, a ban on uranium exports and provision for supplies of radium from the Czechoslovakian mines at Joachimsthal. (Otto Hahn was invited to the conference but arranged to be elsewhere.) The same week a young physicist working at Hamburg, Paul Harteck, wrote a letter jointly with his assistant to the German War Offic

> We take the liberty of calling to your attention the newest development i clear physics, which, in our opinion, will probably make it possible to pr an explosive many orders of magnitude more powerful than the conve ones. . . . That country which first makes use of it has an unsurpass vantage over the others.

The Harteck letter reached Kurt Diebner, a competent nucle stuck unhappily in the Wehrmacht's ordnance department s explosives. Diebner carried it to Hans Geiger. Geiger recor suing the research. The War Office agreed.

A public debate in Washington on April 29 paralleled the secret conference in Berlin. The *New York Times* account accurately summarizes the divisions in the U.S. physics community at the time:

> Tempers and temperatures increased visibly today among members of the American Physical Society as they closed their Spring meeting with arguments over the probability of some scientist blowing up a sizable portion of the earth with a tiny bit of uranium, the element which produces radium.
>
> Dr. Niels Bohr of Copenhagen, a colleague of Dr. Albert Einstein at the Institute for Advanced Study, Princeton, N.J., declared that bombardment of a small amount of the pure Isotope U235 of uranium with slow neutron particles of atoms would start a "chain reaction" or atomic explosion sufficiently great to blow up a laboratory and the surrounding country for many miles.
>
> Many physicists declared, however, that it would be difficult, if not impossible, to separate Isotope 235 from the more abundant Isotope 238. The Isotope 235 is only 1 per cent of the uranium element.
>
> Dr. L. Onsager of Yale University described, however, a new apparatus in which, according to his calculations, the isotopes of elements can be separated in gaseous form in tubes which are cooled on one side and heated to high temperatures on the other.
>
> Other physicists argued that such a process would be almost prohibitively expensive and that the yield of Isotope 235 would be infinitesimally small. Nevertheless, they pointed out that, if Dr. Onsager's process of separation should work, the creation of a nuclear explosion which would wreck as large an area as New York City would be comparatively easy. A single neutron particle, striking the nucleus of a uranium atom, they declared, would be sufficient to set off a chain reaction of millions of other atoms.

The *Times* story assumes the truth of Bohr's argument in favor of U235, although even Bohr was apparently still emphasizing only a slow-neutron reaction. Fermi and others were not yet convinced of U235's role. The two uranium isotopes might not easily be separated in quantity, but it had occurred to John Dunning earlier in the month that they could be separated in microscopic amounts in Alfred Nier's mass spectrograph. Dunning had immediately written Nier a long, impassioned letter asking him, in effect, to resolve the dispute between Fermi and Bohr and push chain-reaction research dramatically forward. Nier, Dunning and Fermi all attended the American Physical Society meeting. In person Dunning urged Nier to try for a separation much as he had urged him in the key paragraph of his letter:

> There is one line of attack that deserves strong effort, and that is where we need your cooperation. . . . It is of the utmost importance to get some uranium

> isotopes separated in enough quantities for a real test. If you could separate effectively even tiny amounts of the two main isotopes [a third isotope, U234, is present in natural uranium to the trace extent of one part in 17,000], there is a good chance that [Eugene T.] Booth and I could demonstrate, by bombarding them with the cyclotron, which isotope is responsible. There is no other way to settle this business. If we could all cooperate and you aid us by separating some samples, then we could, by combining forces, settle the whole matter.

The important point for Dunning, the reason for his passion, was that if U235 was responsible for slow-neutron fission, then its fission cross section must be 139 times as large as the slow-neutron fission cross section of natural uranium, since it was present in the natural substance to the extent of only one part in 140. "By separating the 235 isotope," Herbert Anderson emphasizes in a memoir, "it would be much easier to obtain the chain reaction. More than this, with the separated isotope the prospect for a bomb with unprecedented explosive power would be very great."

Fermi urged Nier in similar terms; Nier recalls that he "went back and figured out how we might soup up our apparatus some in order to increase the output. . . . I did work on the problem, but at first it seemed like such a farfetched thing that I didn't work on it as hard as I might have. It was just one of a number of things I was trying to do."

Fermi in any case was more interested in pursuing a chain reaction in natural uranium than in attempting to separate isotopes. "He was not discouraged by the small cross-section for fission in the natural [element]," comments Anderson. " 'Stay with me,' he advised, 'we'll work with natural uranium. You'll see. We'll be the first to make the chain reaction.' I stuck with Fermi."

By mid-April Szilard had managed to borrow about five hundred pounds of black, grimy uranium oxide free of charge from the Eldorado Radium Corporation, an organization owned by the Russian-born Pregel brothers, Boris and Alexander. Boris had studied at the Radium Institute in Paris; Eldorado speculated in rare minerals and owned important uranium deposits at Great Bear Lake in the Northwest Territories of Canada.

Like Fermi's and Anderson's previous experiment, the new project involved measuring neutron production in a tank of liquid. For a more accurate reading the experimenters needed a longer exposure time than their customary rhodium foils activated to 44-second half-life would allow. They planned instead simply to fill the tank with a 10 percent solution of manganese, an ironlike metal that gives amethyst its purple color and that activates upon neutron bombardment to an isotope with a nearly 3-hour half-life. "The [radio]activity induced in manganese," they explained afterward in their report, "is proportional to the number of [slow] neutrons present." So the hydrogen in the water would serve to slow both the primary neutrons from the central neutron source and any secondary neutrons from fission, and the manganese in the water would serve to measure them—a nice economy of design.

Atoms on the surface of a mass of uranium are exposed to neutrons more efficiently than atoms deeper inside. Fermi and Szilard therefore decided not to bulk their five hundred pounds of uranium oxide into one large container but to distribute it throughout the tank by packing it into fifty-two cans as tall and narrow as lengths of pipe—two inches in diameter and two feet long.

Packing cans and mixing manganese solutions, which had to be changed and the manganese concentrated after each experimental run, was work. So was staying up half the night taking readings of manganese radioactivity. Fermi accepted the challenge with gusto. "He liked to work harder than anyone else," Anderson notes, "but everyone worked very hard." Except Szilard. "Szilard thought he ought to spend his time thinking." Fermi was insulted. "Szilard made a mortal sin," Segrè remembers, echoing Fermi. "He said, 'Oh, I don't want to work and dirty my hands like a painter's assistant.' " When Szilard announced that he had hired a stand-in, a young man whom Anderson remembers as "very competent," Fermi acceded to the arrangement without comment. But he never again pursued an experiment jointly with Szilard.

The arrangement as finally consummated looked like this:

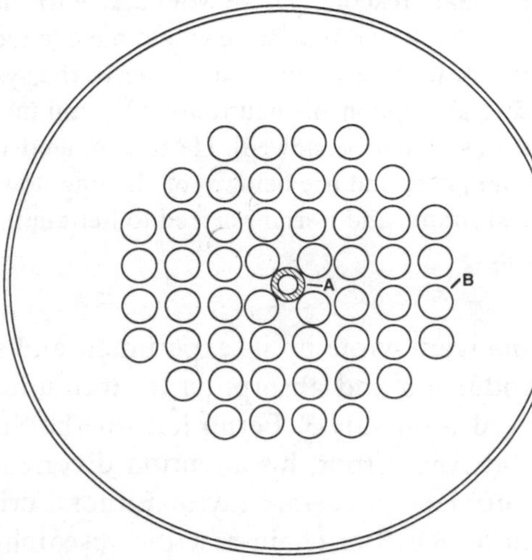

Szilard's Ra + Be source stands in the center of the tank, which holds 143 gallons of manganese solution; the fifty-two cans of UO_2 gather around.

It worked. The three physicists found neutron activity "about ten percent higher with uranium oxide than without it. This result shows that in our arrangement more neutrons are emitted by uranium than are absorbed by uranium." But the experiment raised puzzling questions. Resonance absorption, for example, was clearly a problem, capturing neutrons that might otherwise serve the chain reaction. The report estimates "an average emission [of secondary neutrons] of about 1.2 neutrons per thermal neutron" but notes that "this number should be increased, to perhaps 1.5," because some of the neutrons had obviously been captured without fissioning—demonstrating the big capture resonance around 25 eV that Bohr had attributed on his graphs to U238.

Another problem was the use of water as a moderator. As Fermi's team had discovered in Rome in 1934, hydrogen was more efficient than any other element at slowing down neutrons, and slow neutrons avoided the parasitic capture resonance of U238. But hydrogen itself also absorbed some slow neutrons, reducing further the number available for fission. And it was already clear that every possible secondary neutron would have to be husbanded carefully if a chain reaction was to be initiated in natural uranium. George Placzek came down from Cornell, where he had found a new home, for a visit, looked over the arrangement and insightfully foreclosed its future. As Szilard tells it:

> We were inclined to conclude that . . . the water-uranium system would sustain a chain reaction. . . . Placzek said that our conclusion was wrong because in order to make a chain reaction go, we would have to eliminate the absorption of [neutrons by the] water; that is, we would have to reduce the amount of water in the system, and if we reduced the water in the system, we would increase the parasitic absorption of [neutrons by] uranium [because with less water fewer neutrons would be slowed]. He recommended that we abandon the water-uranium system and use helium for slowing down the neutrons. To Fermi this sounded funny, and Fermi referred to helium thereafter invariably as Placzek's helium.

In June the Columbia team wrote up its experiment and sent the resulting paper, "Neutron production and absorption in uranium," to the *Physical Review,* which received it on July 3. Fermi left for the Summer School of Theoretical Physics at Ann Arbor, his attention diverted, says Anderson, "by an interesting problem in cosmic rays." Either Fermi did not share Szilard's sense of the urgency of chain-reaction research or he was withdrawing for a time from the Navy's indifference and Placzek's persuasive criticism of his uranium-water system; probably both. Anderson settled down to study resonance absorption in uranium, a project that would evolve into his doctoral dissertation.

Szilard remained in the steamy city: "I was left alone in New York. I still had no position at Columbia; my three months [of laboratory privileges] were up, but there were no experiments going on anyway and all I had to do was to think."

Szilard thought first about an alternative to water. The next common material up the periodic table that might work—that had a capture cross section considerably smaller than hydrogen's, that was cheap, that would be thermally and chemically stable—was carbon. The mineral form of carbon, chemically identical to diamond but the product of a different structure of crystallization, is graphite, a black, greasy, opaque, lustrous material that is the essential component of pencil lead. Although carbon slows neutrons much less rapidly than hydrogen, even that difference might be put to advantage by careful design.

Lewis Strauss was leaving for Europe the week of July 2. Hoping that the financier might coax support for uranium research from Belgium's Union Minière, Szilard sent Strauss a last-minute letter arguing that a chain reaction in uranium "is an immediate possibility" but chose not to mention his new uranium-graphite conception. Apparently he wanted to discuss it first with Fermi; the same day, July 3, he wrote the Italian laureate at length. "It seems to me now," he reported, "that there is a good chance that carbon might be an excellent element to use in place of hydrogen, and there is a strong temptation to gamble on this chance." He wanted to try "a large-scale experiment with a carbon-uranium-oxide mixture" as soon as they could acquire enough material. In the meantime he thought he would set up a small experiment to measure more accurately carbon's capture cross section, only the upper limit of which was then known. If carbon should prove unsuitable their "next best guess might be heavy water," rich in deuterium, though they would need "a few tons" of that scarce and expensive liquid. (Deuterium, H2, has a much smaller cross section for neutron capture than ordinary hydrogen.)

Across the one hundred sixty-third anniversary of the Declaration of Independence Szilard's ideas evolved rapidly. On July 5 he visited the National Carbon Company of New York to look into purchasing graphite blocks of high purity (because impurities such as boron with large capture cross sections would soak up too many neutrons). He wrote Fermi his finding the same day: "It seems that it will be possible to get sufficiently pure carbon at a reasonable price." He also mentioned arranging the uranium and carbon in layers.

Fermi sat down in Ann Arbor at the end of the week to respond to Szilard's first report. Independently he had arrived at a similar plan:

> Thank you for your letter. I was also considering the possibility of using carbon for slowing down the neutrons. . . . According to my estimates a possible recipe might be about 39,000 kg of carbon mixed with 600 kg of uranium. If it were really so the amounts of materials would certainly not be too large.
>
> Since however the amount of uranium that can be used, especially in a homogeneous mixture, is exceedingly small . . . *perhaps the use of thick layers of carbon separated by layers of uranium might allow use of a somewhat larger percentage of uranium.*

The idea of layering or in some other way separating the uranium from the graphite originated in calculations Fermi made in June for the manganese water-tank experiment. Fermi's calculations led both men to consider partitioning the oxide from the graphite in the new design they were independently evolving. Partitioning would give the fast secondary neutrons room to slow down, bouncing around in the moderator, before they encountered any U238 nuclei. Szilard's next letter, on July 8, mentions that "the carbon and the uranium oxide would not be mixed but built up in layers, or in any case used in some canned form." Both the July 5 and July 8 letters apparently crossed with Fermi's letter in the mail.

By the time he heard from Fermi, Szilard had seen still farther and realized that small spheres of uranium arranged within blocks of graphite would be "even more favorable from the point of view of a chain reaction than the system of plane uranium layers which was initially considered." The arrangement Szilard had in mind he called a "lattice." (A geodesic dome would represent such a lattice arrangement schematically if it were a complete sphere and if all its interior volume were filled like its surface with evenly spaced points.) His calculations indicated somewhat larger volumes of material than had Fermi's: "perhaps 50 tons of carbon and 5 tons of uranium." The entire experiment, he thought, would cost about $35,000.

If a chain reaction would work in graphite and uranium, Szilard assumed, then a bomb was probable. And if he had managed these conclusions, he further assumed, then so had his counterparts in Nazi Germany. He sought out Pegram in those early July days and tried to convince him of the urgent need for a large-scale experiment to settle the question. The dean resisted the assault: "He took the position that even though the matter appeared to be rather urgent, this being summer and Fermi being away there was really nothing that usefully could be done until the fall."

For several weeks Szilard had been trying on his own to raise funds from the U.S. military. In late May he had asked Wigner to contact the Army's Aberdeen Proving Ground, its weapons-development facility in Maryland. While he was thinking through the possibilities of a uranium-graphite system he had talked to Ross Gunn about Navy support. Now Fermi's letter of July 9 and a July 10 letter from Gunn arrived to discourage him. Fermi wrote of layering the carbon and uranium but calculated in terms of a homogeneous system—of graphite and uranium oxide crushed and mixed together. Szilard concluded he was being mocked: "I knew very well that Fermi . . . computed the homogeneous mixture only because it was the easiest to compute. This showed me that Fermi did not take this really seriously." Gunn in turn reported that "it seems almost impossible . . . to carry through any sort of an agreement [with the Navy] that would be really helpful to you. I regret this situation but see no escape."

Despite his Olympian ego not even Leo Szilard felt capable of saving the world entirely alone. He called on his Hungarian compatriots now for moral support. Edward Teller had moved to Manhattan for the summer to teach physics at Columbia; Eugene Wigner came up from Princeton to conspire with them. In later years Szilard would recount several different versions of how their conversation went, but a letter he wrote on August 15, 1939, offers reliable contemporary testimony: "Dr. Wigner is taking the stand that it is our duty to enlist the cooperation of the [Roosevelt] Administration. A few weeks ago he came to New York in order to discuss this point with Dr. Teller and me." Szilard had shown Wigner his uranium-graphite calculations. "He was impressed and he was concerned." Both Teller and Wigner, Szilard wrote in a background memorandum in 1941, "shared the opinion that no time must be lost in following up this line of development and in the discussion that followed, the opinion crystallized that an attempt ought to be made to enlist the support of the Government rather than that of private industry. Dr. Wigner, in particular, urged very strongly that the Government of the United States be advised."

But the discussion slipped away from that project into "worry about what would happen if the Germans got hold of large quantities of the uranium which the Belgians were mining in the Congo." Perhaps Szilard emphasized the futility of the government contacts that he and Fermi had already made. "So we began to think, through what channels could we approach the Belgian government and warn them against selling any uranium to Germany?"

It occurred to Szilard then that his old friend Albert Einstein knew the Queen of Belgium. Einstein had met Queen Elizabeth in 1929 on a trip to Antwerp to visit his uncle; thereafter the physicist and the sovereign maintained a regular correspondence, Einstein addressing her in plainspoken letters simply as "Queen."

The Hungarians were aware that Einstein was summering on Long Island. Szilard proposed visiting Einstein and asking him to alert Elizabeth of Belgium. Since Szilard owned no car and had never learned to drive he enlisted Wigner to deliver him. They called Einstein's office at the Institute for Advanced Study and learned he was staying at a summer house on Old Grove Pond on Nassau Point, the spit of land that divides Little from Great Peconic Bay on the northeastern arm of the island.

They called Einstein to arrange a day. At this time Szilard also furthered Wigner's proposal to contact the United States government by seeking advice from a knowledgeable emigré economist, Gustav Stolper, a Berliner resettled in New York who had once been a member of the Reichstag. Stolper offered to try to identify an influential messenger.

Wigner picked up Szilard on the morning of Sunday, July 16, and drove out Long Island to Peconic. They reached the area in early afternoon but had no luck soliciting directions to the house until Szilard thought to ask for it in Einstein's name. "We were on the point of giving up and going back to New York"—two world-class Hungarians lost among country lanes in summer heat—"when I saw a boy aged maybe seven or eight standing on the curb. I leaned out of the window and I said, 'Say, do you by any chance know where Professor Einstein lives?' The boy knew that and he offered to take us there."

C. P. Snow had visited Einstein at the same summer retreat two years before, also losing his way, and makes the scene familiar:

> He came into the sitting room a minute or two after we arrived. There was no furniture apart from some garden chairs and a small table. The window looked out on to the water, but the shutters were half closed to keep out the heat. The humidity was very high.
>
> At close quarters, Einstein's head was as I had imagined it: magnificent, with a humanizing touch of the comic. Great furrowed forehead; aureole of white hair; enormous bulging chocolate eyes. I can't guess what I should have expected from such a face if I hadn't known. A shrewd Swiss once said it had the brightness of a good artisan's countenance, that he looked like a reliable old-fashioned watchmaker in a small town who perhaps collected butterflies on a Sunday.
>
> What did surprise me was his physique. He had come in from sailing and was wearing nothing but a pair of shorts. It was a massive body, very heavily muscled: he was running to fat round the midriff and in the upper arms, rather like a footballer in middle-age, but he was still an unusually strong man. He was cordial, simple, utterly unshy. The large eyes looked at me, as though he was thinking: what had I come for, what did I want to talk about?

> . . . The hours went on. I have a hazy memory that several people drifted in and out of the room, but I do not remember who they were. Stifling heat. There appeared to be no set time for meals. He was already, I think, eating very little, but he was still smoking his pipe. Trays of open sandwiches—various kinds of wurst, cheese, cucumber—came in every now and then. It was all casual and Central European. We drank nothing but soda water.

Similarly settled, Szilard told Einstein about the Columbia secondary-neutron experiments and his calculations toward a chain reaction in uranium and graphite. Long afterward he would recall his surprise that Einstein had not yet heard of the possibility of a chain reaction. When he mentioned it Einstein interjected, *"Daran habe ich gar nicht gedacht!"*—"I never thought of that!" He was nevertheless, says Szilard, "very quick to see the implications and perfectly willing to do anything that needed to be done. He was willing to assume responsibility for sounding the alarm even though it was quite possible that the alarm might prove to be a false alarm. The one thing most scientists are really afraid of is to make fools of themselves. Einstein was free from such a fear and this above all is what made his position unique on this occasion."

Einstein hesitated to write Queen Elizabeth but was willing to contact an acquaintance who was a member of the Belgian cabinet. Wigner spoke up to insist again that the United States government should be alerted, pointing out, Szilard goes on, "that we should not approach a foreign government without giving the State Department an opportunity to object." Wigner suggested that they send the Belgian letter with a cover letter through State. All three men thought that made sense.

Einstein dictated a letter to the Belgian ambassador, a more formal contact appropriate to their State Department plan, and Wigner took it down in longhand in German. At the same time Szilard drafted a cover letter. Einstein's was the first of several such compositions—they served in succession as drafts—and the origin of most of the statements that ultimately found their way into the letter he actually sent.

Wigner carried the first Einstein draft back to Princeton, translated it into English and on Monday gave it to his secretary to type. When it was ready he mailed it to Szilard. Then he left Princeton to drive to California on vacation.

A message from Gustav Stolper awaited Szilard at the King's Crown. "He reported to me," Szilard wrote Einstein on July 19, "that he had discussed our problems with Dr. Alexander Sachs, a vice-president of the Lehman Corporation, biologist and national economist, and that Dr. Sachs wanted to talk to me about this matter." Eagerly Szilard arranged an appointment.

Alexander Sachs, born in Russia, was then forty-six years old. He had come to the United States when he was eleven, graduated from Columbia in biology at nineteen, worked as a clerk on Wall Street, returned to Columbia to study philosophy and then went on to Harvard with several prestigious fellowships to pursue philosophy, jurisprudence and sociology. He contributed economics text to Franklin Roosevelt's campaign speeches in 1932; beginning in 1933 he worked for three years for the National Recovery Administration, joining the Lehman Corporation in 1936. He had thick curls and a receding chin and looked and sounded like the comedian Ed Wynn. His associates at the NRA used to point him out to visiting firemen under that *nom de guerre* as ultimate proof, if the NRA itself was not sufficient, of Roosevelt's gift for radical innovation. Sachs communicated in dense, florid prose (he had been thinking that spring of writing a book entitled *The Inter-War Retreat from Reason as Exemplified in the Mis-history of the Recent Past and in the Contemporaneous Conduct of International Political and Economic Affairs by the United States and Great Britain*) but could coruscate in committee.

Sachs heard Szilard out. Then, as Szilard wrote Einstein, he "took the position, and completely convinced me, that these were matters which first and foremost concerned the White House and that the best thing to do, also from the practical point of view, was to inform Roosevelt. He said that if we gave him a statement he would make sure it reached Roosevelt in person." Among those who valued Sachs' opinions and called him from time to time for talks, it seems, was the President of the United States.

Szilard was stunned. The very boldness of the proposal won his heart after all the months when he had confronted caution and skepticism: "Although I have seen Dr. Sachs once," he told Einstein, "and really was not able to form any judgment about him, I nevertheless think that it could not do any harm to try this way and I also think that in this regard he is in a position to fulfill his promise."

Szilard met Sachs shortly after returning from Peconic—between Sunday and Wednesday. Unable at midweek to reach Wigner en route to California, he tracked down Teller, who thought Sachs' proposal preferable to the plan they had previously worked out. Drawing on the first Einstein draft, Szilard now prepared a draft letter to Roosevelt. He wrote it in German because Einstein's English was insecure, added a cover letter and mailed it to Long Island. "Perhaps you will be able to tell me over the telephone whether you would like to return the draft with your marginal comments by mail," he proposed in the cover letter, "or whether I should come out to discuss the whole thing once more with you." If he visited Peconic again, Szilard wrote, he would ask Teller to drive him, "not only because I believe his advice is valuable but also because I think you might enjoy getting to know him. He is particularly nice."

Einstein preferred to review a letter to the President in person. Teller therefore delivered Szilard to Peconic, probably on Sunday, July 30, in his sturdy 1935 Plymouth. "I entered history as Szilard's chauffeur," Teller aphorizes the experience. They found the Princeton laureate in old clothes and slippers. Elsa Einstein served tea. Szilard and Einstein composed a third text together, which Teller wrote down. "Yes, yes," Teller remembers Einstein commenting, "this would be the first time that man releases nuclear energy in a direct form rather than indirectly." Directly from fission, he meant, rather than indirectly from the sun, where a different nuclear reaction produces the copious radiation that reaches the earth as sunlight.

Einstein apparently questioned if Sachs was the best man to carry the news to Roosevelt. On August 2 Szilard wrote Einstein hoping "at long last" for a decision "upon whom we should try to get as middle man." He had seen Sachs in the interim; the economist, who certainly coveted the assignment of representing Albert Einstein to the President, had generously listed the financier Bernard Baruch or Karl T. Compton, the president of MIT, as possible alternates. On the other hand, he had strongly endorsed Charles Lindbergh, though he must have known that Roosevelt despised the famous aviator for his outspoken pro-German isolationism. Szilard wrote that he and Sachs had discussed "a somewhat longer and more extensive version" of the letter Einstein had written with Szilard at their second Peconic meeting; he now enclosed both the longer and shorter versions and asked Einstein to return his favorite along with a letter of introduction to Lindbergh.

Einstein opted for the longer version, which incorporated the shorter statement that had originated with him but carried additional paragraphs contributed by Szilard in consultation with Sachs. He signed both letters and returned them to Szilard in less than a week with a note hoping "that you will finally overcome your inner resistance; it's always questionable to try to do something too cleverly." That is, be bold and get moving. "We will try to follow your advice," Szilard rejoined on August 9, "and as far as possible overcome our inner resistances which, admittedly, exist. Incidentally, we are surely not trying to be too clever and will be quite satisfied if only we don't look too stupid."

Szilard transmitted the letter in its final form to Sachs on August 15 along with a memorandum of his own that elaborated on the letter's discussion of the possibilities and dangers of fission. He had not given up contacting Lindbergh—he drafted a letter to the aviator the following day—but he seems to have decided to try Sachs in the meantime, probably in the interest of moving the project on; he pointedly asked Sachs either to deliver the letter to Roosevelt or to return it.

One of the discussions Szilard had added to the longer draft that Einstein chose concerned who should serve as liaison between "the Administration and the group of physicists working on chain reactions in America." In his letter of transmittal to Sachs, Szilard now tacitly offered himself for that service. "If a man, having courage and imagination, could be found," he wrote, "and if such a man were put—in accordance with Dr. Einstein's suggestion—in the position to act with some measure of authority in this matter, this would certainly be an important step forward. In order that you may be able to see of what assistance such a man could be in our work, allow me please to give you a short account of the past history of the case." The short account that followed, an abbreviated and implicit *curriculum vitae,* essentially outlined Szilard's own role since Bohr's announcement of the discovery of fission seven crowded months earlier.

Szilard's offer was as innocent of American bureaucratic politics as it was bold. It was surely also the apotheosis of his drive to save the world. By this time the Hungarians at least believed they saw major humanitarian benefit inherent in what Eugene Wigner would describe in retrospect as "a horrible military weapon," explaining:

> Although none of us spoke much about it to the authorities [during this early period]—they considered us dreamers enough as it was—we did hope for another effect of the development of atomic weapons in addition to the warding off of imminent disaster. We realized that, should atomic weapons be developed, no two nations would be able to live in peace with each other unless their military forces were controlled by a common higher authority. We expected that these controls, if they were effective enough to abolish atomic warfare, would be effective enough to abolish also all other forms of war. This hope was almost as strong a spur to our endeavors as was our fear of becoming the victims of the enemy's atomic bombings.

From the horrible weapon which they were about to urge the United States to develop, Szilard, Teller and Wigner—"the Hungarian conspiracy," Merle Tuve was amused to call them—hoped for more than deterrence against German aggression. They also hoped for world government and world peace, conditions they imagined bombs made of uranium might enforce.

Alexander Sachs intended to read aloud to the President when he met with him. He believed busy people saw so much paper they tended to dismiss the printed word. "Our social system is such," he told a Senate committee in 1945, "that any public figure [is] punch-drunk with printer's ink. . . . This was a matter that the Commander in Chief and the head of the Nation must know. I could only do it if I could see him for a long stretch and read the material so it came in by way of the ear and not as a soft mascara on the eye." He needed a full hour of Franklin Delano Roosevelt's time.

History intervened to crowd the President's calendar. Having won the Rhineland, Austria and Czechoslovakia simply by taking them, having signed the Pact of Steel with Italy on May 22 and a ten-year treaty of non-aggression and neutrality with the USSR on August 23, Adolf Hitler ordered the invasion of Poland beginning at 4:45 A.M. on September 1, 1939, and precipitated the Second World War. The German invasion fielded fifty-six divisions against thirty Polish divisions strung thinly across the long Polish frontier; Hitler had ten times the aircraft, including plentiful squadrons of Stuka dive-bombers, and nine divisions of Panzer tanks against Polish horse cavalry armed with swords and spears. The assault was "a perfect specimen of the modern Blitzkrieg," writes Winston Churchill: "the close interaction on the battlefield of army and air force; the violent bombardment of all communications and of any town that seems an attractive target; the arming of an active Fifth Column; the free use of spies and parachutists; and above all, the irresistible forward thrusts of great masses of armour."

The mathematician Stanislaw Ulam had just returned from visiting Poland, bringing with him on a student visa his sixteen-year-old brother, Adam:

> Adam and I were staying in a hotel on Columbus Circle. It was a very hot, humid, New York night. I could not sleep very well. It must have been around one or two in the morning when the telephone rang. Dazed and perspiring, very uncomfortable, I picked up the receiver and the somber, throaty voice of my friend the topologist Witold Hurewicz began to recite the horrible tale of the start of war: "Warsaw has been bombed, the war has begun," he said. This is how I learned about the beginning of World War II. He kept describing what he had heard on the radio. I turned on my own. Adam was asleep; I did not wake him. There would be time to tell him the news in the morning. Our father and sister were in Poland, so were many other relatives. At that moment, I suddenly felt as if a curtain had fallen on my past life, cutting it off from my future. There has been a different color and meaning to everything ever since.

One of Roosevelt's first acts was to appeal to the belligerents to refrain from bombing civilian populations. Revulsion against the bombing of cities had grown in the United States since at least the Japanese bombing of

Shanghai in 1937. When Spanish Fascists bombed Barcelona in March 1938, Secretary of State Cordell Hull had condemned the atrocity publicly: "No theory of war can justify such conduct," he told reporters. ". . . I feel that I am speaking for the whole American people." In June the Senate passed a resolution condemning the "inhuman bombing of civilian populations." As war approached, revulsion began to give way to impulses of revenge; in the summer of 1939 Herbert Hoover could urge an international ban on the bombing of cities and still argue that "one of the impelling reasons for the unceasing building of bombing planes is to prepare reprisals." Bombing was bad because it was enemy bombing. *Scientific American* saw through to a darker truth: "Although . . . aerial bombing remains an unknown, indeterminate quantity, the world may be sure that the unwholesome atrocities which are happening today are but curtain raisers on insane dramas to come."

So although Roosevelt had asked Congress for increased funds for long-range bombers nine months before, in appealing to the belligerents on September 1, 1939, he could still articulate the moral indignation of millions of Americans:

> The ruthless bombing from the air of civilians in unfortified centers of population during the course of the hostilities which have raged in various quarters of the earth during the past few years, which has resulted in the maiming and in the death of thousands of defenseless men, women and children, has sickened the hearts of every civilized man and woman, and has profoundly shocked the conscience of humanity.
>
> If resort is had to this form of inhuman barbarism during the period of the tragic conflagration with which the world is now confronted, hundreds of thousands of innocent human beings who have no responsibility for, and who are not even remotely participating in, the hostilities which have now broken out, will lose their lives. I am therefore addressing this urgent appeal to every Government which may be engaged in hostilities publicly to affirm its determination that its armed forces shall in no event, and under no circumstances, undertake the bombardment from the air of civilian populations or of unfortified cities, upon the understanding that these same rules of warfare will be scrupulously observed by all of their opponents. I request an immediate reply.

Great Britain agreed to the President's terms the same day. Germany, busy bombing Warsaw, concurred on September 18.

The invasion of Poland brought Britain and France into the war on September 3. Abruptly Roosevelt's schedule filled to overflowing. In early September in particular he was working overtime with a reluctant Congress to revise the Neutrality Act to terms more favorable to Britain; Sachs was unable even to discuss arranging an interview until after the first week in September.

By September Kurt Diebner's new War Office department had consolidated German fission research under its authority. Diebner enlisted a young Leipzig theoretician named Erich Bagge and together the two physicists planned a secret conference to consider the feasibility of a weapons project. They had the authority to enlist the services of any German citizen they wished and they used it, sending out papers that left Hans Geiger, Walther Bothe, Otto Hahn and a number of other exceptional older men nervously uncertain if they were being invited to Berlin for consultation or ordered to active military service.

At the conference in Berlin on September 16 the physicists learned that German intelligence had discovered the beginnings of uranium research abroad—meaning, presumably, in the United States and Britain. They discussed the long, thorough theoretical paper by Niels Bohr and John Wheeler, "The mechanism of nuclear fission," that had been published in the September *Physical Review* and especially its conclusion, which Bohr and Wheeler had elaborated from Bohr's Sunday-morning graph work, that U235 was probably the isotope of uranium responsible for slow-neutron fission. Hahn like Bohr argued that isotope separation was difficult to the point of impossibility. Bagge proposed calling in Werner Heisenberg, his superior at Leipzig, to adjudicate.

Heisenberg therefore attended a second Berlin conference on September 26 and discussed two possible ways to harness the energy from fission: by slowing secondary neutrons with a moderator to make a "uranium burner" and by separating U235 to make an explosive. Paul Harteck, the Hamburg physicist who had written the War Office the previous April, traveled to the second conference armed with a paper he had just finished on the importance of layering uranium and moderator to avoid the U238 capture resonance—the same insight that had come independently to Fermi and Szilard in early July. Harteck's study, however, considered using heavy water as moderator, even though Harteck had worked with Rutherford at the Cavendish and knew from personal experience how expensive heavy-water production could be—water in which deuterium replaced hydrogen had to be tediously distilled from tons of ordinary H_2O.

Diebner and Bagge had outlined for the second conference a "Preparatory Working Plan for Initiating Experiments on the Exploitation of Nuclear Fission." Heisenberg would head up theoretical investigation. Bagge would measure deuterium's cross section for collision to establish how effectively heavy water might slow secondary neutrons. Harteck would look into isotope separation. Others would experiment to determine other significant nuclear constants. The War Office would take over the Kaiser Wilhelm Institute of Physics, finished in 1937 and beautifully equipped. Adequate funds would be forthcoming.

The German atomic bomb project was well begun.

It may have been no less complicated by humanitarian ambiguities than the project the Hungarians in the United States proposed. One young but highly respected German physicist involved in the work from near the beginning was Carl Friedrich von Weizsäcker, the son of the German Undersecretary of State. In a 1978 memoir von Weizsäcker remembers discussing the possibility of a bomb with Otto Hahn in the spring of 1939. Hahn opposed secrecy then partly on the grounds of scientific ethics but also partly because he "felt that if it were to be made, it would be worst for the entire world, even for Germany, if Hitler were to be the only one to have it." Like Szilard, Teller and Wigner, von Weizsäcker remembers realizing in discussions with a friend "that this discovery could not fail to radically change the political structure of the world":

> To a person finding himself at the beginning of an era, its simple fundamental structures may become visible like a distant landscape in the flash of a single stroke of lightning. But the path toward them in the dark is long and confusing. At that time [i.e., 1939] we were faced with a very simple logic. Wars waged with atom bombs as regularly recurring events, that is to say, nuclear wars as institutions, do not seem reconcilable with the survival of the participating nations. But the atom bomb exists. It exists in the minds of some men. According to the historically known logic of armaments and power systems, it will soon make its physical appearance. If that is so, then the participating nations and ultimately mankind itself can only survive if war as an institution is abolished.

Both sides might work from fear of the other. But some on both sides would be working also paradoxically believing they were preparing a new force that would ultimately bring peace to the world.

As September extended its violence Szilard grew impatient. He had heard nothing from Alexander Sachs. Pursuing Sachs' previous suggestions and his own leads, he arranged for Eugene Wigner to give him a letter of introduction to MIT president Karl T. Compton; recontacted a businessman of possible influence whom he had once interested in the Einstein-Szilard refrigerator pump; read a newspaper account of a Lindbergh speech and reported to Einstein that the aviator "is in fact not our man." Finally, the last week in September, he and Wigner visited Sachs and found to their dismay that the economist still held Einstein's letter. "He says he has spoken repeatedly with Roosevelt's secretary," Szilard reported to Einstein on October 3, "and has the impression that Roosevelt is so overburdened that it would be wiser to see him at a later date. He intends to go to Washington this week." The two Hungarians were ready to start over: "There is a distinct possibility that Sachs will be of no use to us. If this is the case, we must put the matter in someone else's hands. Wigner and I have decided to accord Sachs ten days' grace. Then I will write you again to let you know how matters stand."

But Alexander Sachs did indeed travel to Washington, not that week but the next, and on Wednesday, October 11, presented himself, probably in the late afternoon, at the White House. Roosevelt's aide, General Edwin M. Watson, "Pa" to Roosevelt and his intimates, sitting with his own executive secretary and military aide, reviewed Sachs' agenda. When he was convinced that the information was worth the President's time, Watson let Sachs into the Oval Office.

"Alex," Roosevelt hailed him, "what are you up to?"

Sachs liked to warm up the President with jokes. His sense of humor tended to learned parables. Now he told Roosevelt the story of the young American inventor who wrote a letter to Napoleon. The inventor proposed to build the emperor a fleet of ships that carried no sail but could attack England in any weather. He had it in his power to deliver Napoleon's armies to England in a few hours without fear of wind or storm, he wrote, and he was prepared to submit his plans. Napoleon scoffed: ships without sails? "Bah! Away with your visionists!"

The young inventor, Sachs concluded, was Robert Fulton. Roosevelt laughed easily; probably he laughed at that.

Sachs cautioned the President to listen carefully: what he had now to impart was at least the equivalent of the steamboat inventor's proposal to Napoleon. Not yet ready to listen, Roosevelt scribbled a message and summoned an aide. Shortly the aide returned with a treasure, a carefully wrapped bottle of Napoleon brandy that the Roosevelts had preserved in the family for years. The President poured two glasses, passed one to his visitor, toasted him and settled back.

Sachs had made a file for Roosevelt's reading of Einstein's letter and Szilard's memorandum. But neither document had suited his sense of how to present the information to a busy President. "I am an economist, not a scientist," he would tell friends, "but I had a prior relationship with the President, and Szilard and Einstein agreed I was the right person to make the relevant elaborate scientific material intelligible to Mr. Roosevelt. No scientist could sell it to him." Sachs had therefore prepared his own version of the fission story, a composite and paraphrase of the contents of the Einstein and Szilard presentations. Though he left those statements with Roosevelt, he read neither one of them aloud. He read not Einstein's subsequently famous letter but his own eight-hundred-word summation, the first authoritative report to a head of state of the possibility of using nuclear energy to make a weapon of war. It emphasized power production first, radioactive materials for medical use second and "bombs of hitherto unenvisaged potency and scope" third. It recommended making arrangements with Belgium for uranium supplies and expanding and accelerating experiment but imagined that American industry or private foundations would be willing to foot the bill. To that end it proposed that Roosevelt "designate an individual and a committee to serve as a liaison" between the scientists and the Administration.

Sachs had intentionally listed the peaceful potentials of fission first and second among its prospects. To emphasize the "ambivalence" of the discovery, he said later, the "two poles of good and evil" it embodied, he turned near the end of the discussion to Francis Aston's 1936 lecture, "Forty Years of Atomic Theory"—it had been published in 1938 as part of a collection, *Background to Modern Science,* which Sachs had brought along to the White House—where the English spectroscopist had ridiculed "the more elderly and apelike of our prehistoric ancestors" who "objected to the innovation of cooked food and pointed out the grave dangers attending the use of the newly discovered agency, fire." Sachs read the entire last paragraph of the lecture to Roosevelt, emphasizing the final sentences:

> Personally I think there is no doubt that sub-atomic energy is available all around us, and that one day man will release and control its almost infinite power. We cannot prevent him from doing so and can only hope that he will not use it exclusively in blowing up his next door neighbor.

"Alex," said Roosevelt, quickly understanding, "what you are after is to see that the Nazis don't blow us up."

"Precisely," Sachs said.

Roosevelt called in Watson. "This requires action," he told his aide.

Meeting afterward with Sachs, Watson went by the book. He proposed a committee consisting initially of the director of the Bureau of Standards, an Army representative and a Navy representative. The Bureau of Standards, established by Act of Congress in 1901, is the nation's physics laboratory, charged with applying science and technology in the national interest and for public benefit. Its director in 1939 was Dr. Lyman J. Briggs, a Johns Hopkins Ph.D. and a government scientist for forty-three years who had been nominated by Herbert Hoover and appointed by FDR. The military representatives were Lieutenant Colonel Keith F. Adamson and Commander Gilbert C. Hoover, both ordnance experts.

"Don't let Alex go without seeing me again," Roosevelt had directed Watson. Sachs met the same evening with Briggs, briefed him and proposed he and his committee of two get together with the physicists working on fission. Briggs agreed. Sachs saw the President again and declared himself satisfied. That was good enough for Roosevelt.

Briggs set a first meeting of the Advisory Committee on Uranium for October 21 in Washington, a Saturday. Sachs proposed to invite the emigrés; to counterbalance them Briggs invited Tuve, who found a schedule conflict and deputized Richard Roberts as his stand-in. Fermi, still nursing his Navy grievance, refused to attend but was willing to allow Teller to speak in his behalf. On the appointed day the Hungarian conspiracy breakfasted with Sachs at the Carleton Hotel, the out-of-towners having arrived the night before. From the hotel they proceeded to the Department of Commerce. The meeting then counted nine participants: Briggs, a Briggs assistant, Sachs, Szilard, Wigner, Teller, Roberts, Adamson for the Army and Hoover for the Navy.

Szilard began by emphasizing the possibility of a chain reaction in a uranium-graphite system. Whether such a system would work, he said, depended on the capture cross section of carbon and that was not yet sufficiently known. If the value was large, they would know that a large-scale experiment would fail. If the value was extremely small, a large-scale experiment would look highly promising. An intermediate value would necessitate a large-scale experiment to decide. He estimated the destructive potential of a uranium bomb to be as much as twenty thousand tons of high-explosive equivalent. Such a bomb, he had written in the memorandum Sachs carried to Roosevelt, would depend on fast neutrons and might be "too heavy to be transported by airplane," which meant he was still thinking of exploding natural uranium, not of separating U235.

Adamson, openly contemptuous, butted in. "In Aberdeen," Teller remembers him sneering, "we have a goat tethered to a stick with a ten-foot rope, and we have promised a big prize to anyone who can kill the goat with a death ray. Nobody has claimed the prize yet." As for twenty thousand tons of high explosive, the Army officer said, he'd been standing outside an ordance depot once when it blew up and it hadn't even knocked him down.

Restraining himself, Wigner spoke after Szilard, supporting his compatriot's argument.

Roberts raised serious objection. He was convinced that Szilard's optimism for a chain reaction was premature and his notion of a fast-neutron weapon made of natural uranium misguided. Roberts had co-authored a review of the subject just one month before. It agreed with Szilard that "there are not yet sufficient data to say definitely whether or not a uranium powerhouse is a possibility." But it also assessed—because the DTM had begun assessing—the question of the fast-neutron fission of natural uranium and found, because of resonance capture and extensive scattering of fast neutrons, that it was "very unlikely that the fast neutrons can producc a sufficient number of fissions to maintain a [chain] reaction."

The DTM physicist also pointed out that other lines of research might be more promising than a slow-neutron chain reaction in natural uranium. He meant isotope separation. At the University of Virginia Jesse Beams, formerly Ernest Lawrence's colleague at Yale, was applying to the task the high-speed centrifuges he was developing there. Roberts thought answers to these questions might require several years of work and that research should be left in the meantime to the universities.

Briggs spoke up to defend his committee. He argued vigorously that any assessment of the possibilities of fission at a time when Europe was at war had to include more than physics; it had to include the potential impact of the development on national defense.

Szilard was "astonished," as he told Pegram the next day, at Sachs' "active and enthusiastic" participation in the meeting. Sachs seconded Briggs and the Hungarians. "The issue was too important to wait," he recalled his argument, "and the important thing was to be helpful because if there was something to it there was danger of our being blown up. We had to take time by the forelock, and we had to be ahead."

Then it was Teller's turn. For himself, he announced in his deep, heavily accented voice, he strongly supported Szilard. But he had also been given the task of serving as messenger for Fermi and Tuve, who had discussed these issues in New York and had come to some agreement about them. "I said that this needed a little support. In particular we needed to acquire a good substance to slow down the neutrons, therefore we needed pure graphite, and this is expensive." Jesse Beams' centrifuge work also required support, Teller added.

"How much money do you need?" Commander Hoover wanted to know.

Szilard had not planned to ask for money. "The diversion of Government funds for such purposes as ours appears to be hardly possible," he explained to Pegram the next day, "and I have therefore myself avoided to make any such recommendation." But Teller answered Hoover promptly, probably speaking for Fermi: "For the first year of this research we need six thousand dollars, mostly in order to buy the graphite." ("My friends blamed me because the great enterprise of nuclear energy was to start with such a pittance," Teller reminisces; "they haven't forgiven me yet." Szilard, who would write Briggs on October 26 that the graphite alone for a large-scale experiment would cost at least $33,000, must have been appalled.)

Adamson had anticipated just such a raid on the public treasury. "At this point," says Szilard, "the representative of the Army started a rather longish tirade":

> He told us that it was naive to believe that we could make a significant contribution to defense by creating a new weapon. He said that if a new weapon is created, it usually takes two wars before one can know whether the weapon is any good or not. Then he explained rather laboriously that it is in the end not weapons which win the wars, but the morale of the troops. He went on in this vein for a long time until suddenly Wigner, the most polite of us, interrupted him. [Wigner] said in his high-pitched voice that it was very interesting for him to hear this. He always thought that weapons were very important and that this is what costs money, and this is why the Army needs such a large appropriation. But he was very interested to hear that he was wrong: it's not weapons but the morale which wins the wars. And if this is correct, perhaps one should take a second look at the budget of the Army, and maybe the budget could be cut.

"All right, all right," Adamson snapped, "you'll get your money."

The Uranium Committee produced a report for the President on November 1. It narrowly emphasized exploring a controlled chain reaction "as a continuous source of power in submarines." In addition, it noted, "If the reaction turns out to be explosive in character, it would provide a possible source of bombs with a destructiveness vastly greater than anything now known." The committee recommended "adequate support for a thorough investigation." Initially the government might undertake to supply four tons of pure graphite (this would allow Fermi and Szilard to measure the capture cross section of carbon) and, if justified later, fifty tons of uranium oxide.

Briggs heard from Pa Watson on November 17. The President had read the report, Watson wrote, and wanted to keep it on file. On file is where it remained, mute and inactive, well into 1940.

Even with Szilard and Fermi stalled, fission studies continued at many other American laboratories. Prodded by a late-October letter from Fermi, for example, Alfred Nier at the University of Minnesota finally began preparing to separate enough U235 from U238, using his mass spectroscope, to determine experimentally which isotope is responsible for slow-neutron fission. But to American physicists and administrators in and out of government a bomb of uranium seemed a remote possibility at best. However intense their sympathies, the war was still a European war.

11
Cross Sections

In the days before the war, Otto Frisch remembers, in Hamburg with Otto Stern, he used to run experiments by day and think intensely about physics well into the night. "I regularly came home," Frisch told an interviewer once, "had dinner at seven, had a quarter of an hour's nap after dinner, and then I sat down happily with a sheet of paper and a reading lamp and worked until about one o'clock at night—until I began to have hallucinations. . . . I began to see queer animals against the background of my room, and then I thought, 'Oh, well, better go to bed.' " The young Austrian's hypnagogic visions were "unpleasant feelings" but otherwise "it was an ideal life. I'd never had such a pleasant life, ever—this concentrated five hours work every night."

Through the spring of 1939, in contrast, after his early experiments with fission, Frisch found himself "in a state of complete doldrums. I had a feeling war was coming. What was the use of doing any research? I simply couldn't brace myself. I was in a pretty bad state, feeling, 'Nothing I start now is going to be any good.' " As his aunt, Lise Meitner, worried about her isolation in Stockholm, Frisch worried about his vulnerability in Copenhagen; when British colleagues visited he uncharacteristically campaigned among them:

> I first spoke to Blackett and then Oliphant when they passed through Copenhagen and said that I had a fear that Denmark would soon be overrun by

Hitler, and if so, would there be a chance for me to go to England in time, because I'd rather work for England than do nothing or be compelled in some way or other to work for Hitler or be sent to a concentration camp.

Mark Oliphant directed the physics department at the University of Birmingham. Rather than initiate some complicated sponsorship he simply invited Frisch to visit him that summer to talk over the problem. "So I packed two small suitcases and traveled by ship and train, just like any tourist." The war overtook him safe in the English Midlands but with nothing more of his possessions on hand than the contents of his two small suitcases. His friends in Copenhagen had to store his belongings and arrange the repossession of the piano he was buying.

Oliphant found him work as an auxiliary lecturer. In that relative security he began to think about physics again. Fission still intrigued him. He lacked the neutron source he would need for direct attack. But he had followed Bohr's theoretical work: the distinction between the fissile characteristics of U235 and U238 in February; the major Bohr-Wheeler paper in September just as the German invasion of Poland brought war, "a great feeling of tense sobriety." He wondered if Bohr was right that U235 was the isotope responsible for slow-neutron fission. He conceived a way to find out: by preparing "a sample of uranium in which the proportions of the two isotopes were changed." That meant at least partly separating the isotopes, as Fermi and Dunning had encouraged Nier to do for the same reason. Frisch read up on methods. The simplest, he decided, was gaseous thermal diffusion, a technique developed by the German physical chemist Klaus Clusius. For equipment it required little more than a long tube standing on end with a heated rod inside running down its center. Fill the tube with some gaseous form of the material to be separated, cool the tube wall by flushing it with water, and "material enriched in the lighter isotope would accumulate near the top . . . while the heavier isotope would tend to go to the bottom."

Frisch set out to assemble his Clusius tube. Progress was slow. He planned to make the tube of glass, but the laboratory glassblower's first priority was Oliphant's secret war work, work about which Frisch, technically an enemy alien, was not supposed to know. Two physicists on Oliphant's staff, James Randall and H. A. H. Boot, were in fact developing the cavity magnetron, an electron tube capable of generating intense microwave radiation for ground and airborne radar—in C. P. Snow's assessment "the most valuable English scientific innovation in the Hitler war."

Meanwhile the British Chemical Society asked Frisch to write a review of advances in experimental nuclear physics for its annual report. "I managed to write that article in my bed-sitter where in daytime, with the gas fire going all day, the temperature rose to 42° Fahrenheit . . . while at night the water froze in the tumbler at my bedside." He wore his winter coat, set his typewriter on his lap and pulled his chair close to the fire. "The radiation from the gas fire stimulated the blood supply to my brain, and the article was completed on time."

Frisch's review article mentioned the possibility of a chain reaction only to discount it. He based that conclusion on Bohr's argument that the U238 in natural uranium would scatter fast neutrons, slowing them to capture-resonance energies; the few that escaped capture would not suffice, he thought, to initiate a slow-neutron chain reaction in the scarce U235. Slow neutrons in any case could never produce more than a modest explosion, Frisch pointed out; they took too long slowing down and finding a nucleus. As he explained later:

> That process would take times of the order of a sizeable part of a millisecond [i.e., a thousandth of a second], and for the whole chain reaction to develop would take several milliseconds; once the material got hot enough to vaporize, it would begin to expand and the reaction would be stopped before it got much further. So the thing might blow up like a pile of gunpowder, but no worse, and that wasn't worth the trouble.

Not long from Nazi Germany, Frisch found his argument against a violently explosive chain reaction reassuring. It was backed by the work of no less a theoretician than Niels Bohr. With satisfaction he published it.

It had seen the light of day before, most notably in an August 5, 1939, letter from Member of Parliament Winston Churchill to the British Secretary of State for Air. Concerned that Hitler might bluff Neville Chamberlain with threats of a new secret weapon, Churchill had collected a briefing from Frederick Lindemann and written to caution the cabinet not to fear "new explosives of devastating power" for at least "several years." The best authorities, the distinguished M.P. emphasized with a nod to Niels Bohr, held that "only a minor constituent of uranium is effective in these processes." That constituent would need to be laboriously extracted for any large-scale effects. "The chain process can take place only if the uranium is concentrated in a large mass," Churchill continued, slightly muddling the point. "As soon as the energy develops, it will explode with a mild detonation before any really violent effects can be produced. It might be as good as our present-day explosives, but it is unlikely to produce anything very much more dangerous." He concluded optimistically: "Dark hints will be dropped and terrifying whispers will be assiduously circulated, but it is to be hoped that nobody will be taken in by them."

40

40. The leaders of wartime American science, 1940. *L. to r,* Ernest Lawrence, Arthur Compton, Vannevar Bush, James Bryant Conant, Karl Compton, Alfred Loomis.

41. War came to Europe with the German invasion of Poland on September 1, 1939. Here Polish citizens in Warsaw study Nazi proclamations. Roosevelt appealed to the belligerents to refrain from bombing civilians.

41

42

42. Genia and Rudolf Peierls. While American efforts stalled, Peierls and Otto Frisch in England in 1940 worked out the essential theory of a fast-fission uranium bomb fueled with U235 and convinced his British colleagues that it was feasible.

43

44

44. Economist Alexander Sachs had carried the Einstein letter of warning to Roosevelt; he pushed the conservative Briggs committee without success for another year.

43. Eugene T. Booth (*left*) and John Dunning (*right*) decided in 1940 to experiment with gaseous barrier diffusion to separate U235 from U238. The British took the same route.

46. Alfred O. C. Nier separated a sample of U235 with his mass-spectrograph; Columbia used it to confirm the rare isotope's responsibility for slow-neutron fission.

45

45. Nobel laureate theoretician Eugene P. Wigner, the third member of the "Hungarian conspiracy" with Szilard and Edward Teller. Szilard called him "the conscience of the project" from beginning to end.

46

47

48

47. Australian Mark Oliphant visited the United States in 1941 and helped goad the American atomic-bomb program to commitment.

48. Glenn Seaborg, the codiscoverer of plutonium, with his bride-to-be, Helen Griggs, Los Angeles, 1942.

49

49. Strategic bombing soon bridged the barrier of the English Channel. Here: Coventry Cathedral, destroyed by German bombs.

50

50. The Japanese surprise attack on Pearl Harbor, December 7, 1941, finally precipitated the entry of the United States into the war against not only Japan but Germany and Italy as well. Immediately U.S. atomic bomb development accelerated.

51

51. Franklin Roosevelt saw the long-term potential and instinctively reserved nuclear-weapons policy to himself.

52

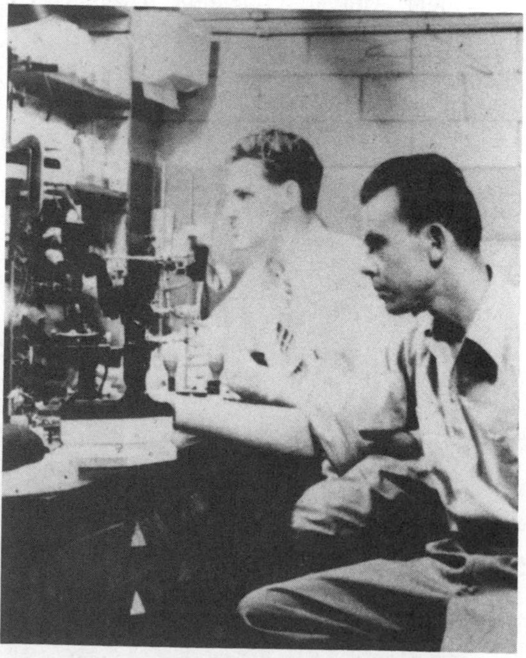

52. Louis B. Werner and Burris Cunningham in Chicago the day they isolated the first pure sample of plutonium, August 20, 1942.

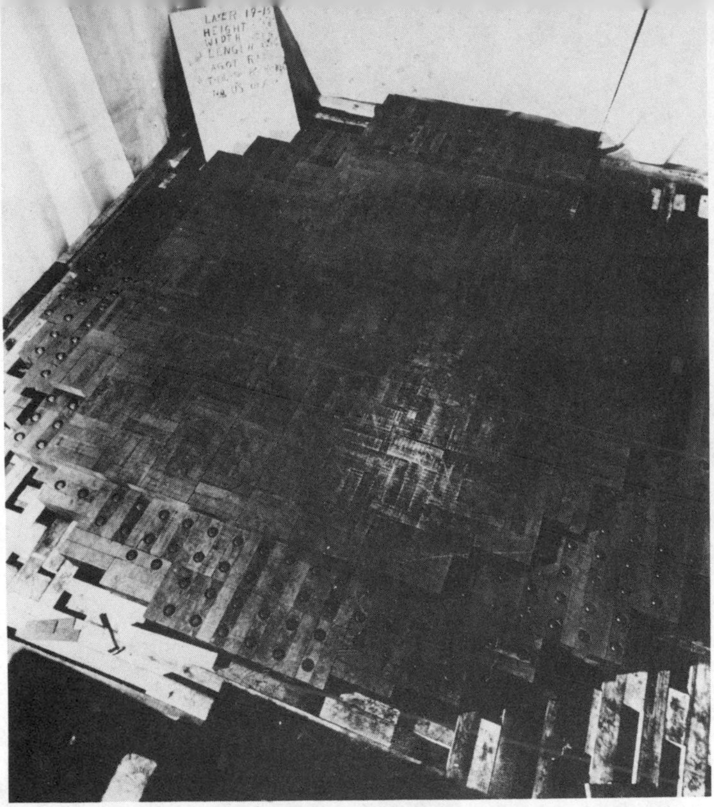

53

53. Chicago Pile Number One, the first man-made nuclear reactor, under construction at the University of Chicago, November 1942. Lower layer holds uranium oxide pseudospheres, unfinished dead layer overlying. Note hammer in foreground for scale.

54

54. Oak Ridge Alpha I calutron racetrack for electromagnetic separation of U235. Silver-wound magnets protrude like ribs spaced by semicircular mass-spectrometer tanks. Spare tanks in left foreground.

55

55. K-25 gaseous-diffusion plant, Oak Ridge, Tennessee. Built to monumental scale, the structure is half a mile long with 42.6 acres under roof.

56. William S. "Deke" Parsons and Philip Abelson. Parsons directed ordnance development at Los Alamos; Abelson pioneered liquid thermal diffusion for uranium enrichment.

56

57

57. Abelson's liquid thermal diffusion rack. Steam circulated through an inner pipe, cooling water through an outer, causing U235 to diffuse inward and circulate upward. The resulting enriched material fed Ernest Lawrence's hungry calutrons.

58

59

58. U.S. plutonium-production complex on the Columbia River at Hanford, Washington. Twelve-hundred-ton graphite reactors drilled with 2,004 channels held uranium slugs; neutrons from fission transmuted 250 parts per million of U238 to plutonium. D pile in foreground between water tanks. 59. Pile face showing slug channels.

60

61

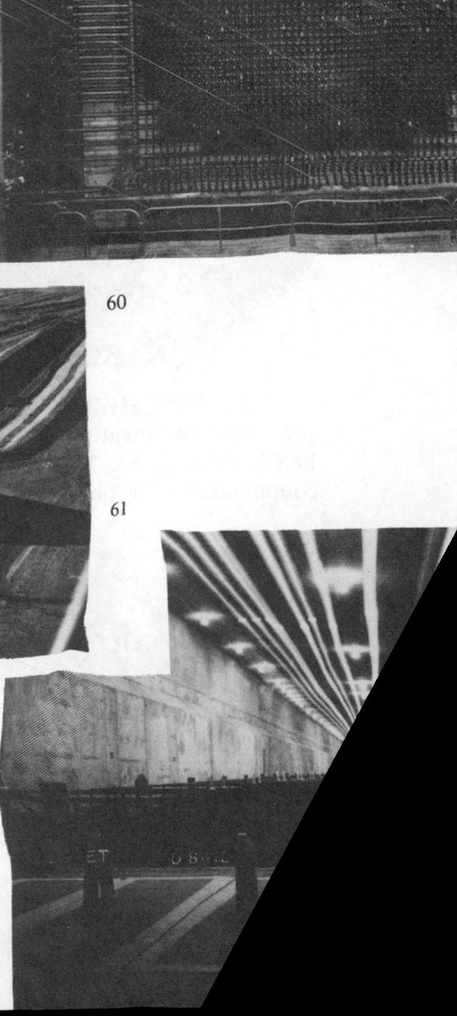

…ary" plutonium sepa-
…anford. Dissolved ir-
…rogressed by remote
… separation stages
…of this 800-foot con-
…1. Interior showing

62

63

62. The Norsk Hydro hydrogen electrolysis plant at Vemork, Norway, produced heavy water for German uranium research until disabled by Allied bombing. 63. The ferry *Hydro* on Lake Tinnsjö, Norway, sunk by commandos while carrying the last Norsk Hydro heavy water to Germany.

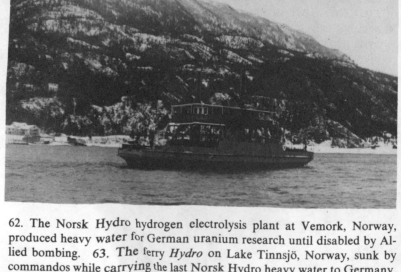

64. A secret laboratory was established in 1943 north of Santa Fe, New Mexico, on the forested Los Alamos mesa 7,200 feet. Here scientists a engineers assembled to de and build the first at bombs. The Army Co Engineers constructed f family apartments f

58

59

58. U.S. plutonium-production complex on the Columbia River at Hanford, Washington. Twelve-hundred-ton graphite reactors drilled with 2,004 channels held uranium slugs; neutrons from fission transmuted 250 parts per million of U238 to plutonium. D pile in foreground between water tanks. 59. Pile face showing slug channels.

60

61

60. "Queen Mary" plutonium separation plant, Hanford. Dissolved irradiated slugs progressed by remote control through separation stages down the length of this 800-foot concrete building. 61. Interior showing processing cells.

62

63

62. The Norsk Hydro hydrogen electrolysis plant at Vemork, Norway, produced heavy water for German uranium research until disabled by Allied bombing. 63. The ferry *Hydro* on Lake Tinnsjö, Norway, sunk by commandos while carrying the last Norsk Hydro heavy water to Germany.

64

64. A secret laboratory was established in 1943 north of Santa Fe, New Mexico, on the forested Los Alamos mesa at 7,200 feet. Here scientists and engineers assembled to design and build the first atomic bombs. The Army Corps of Engineers constructed fourplex family apartments for housing.

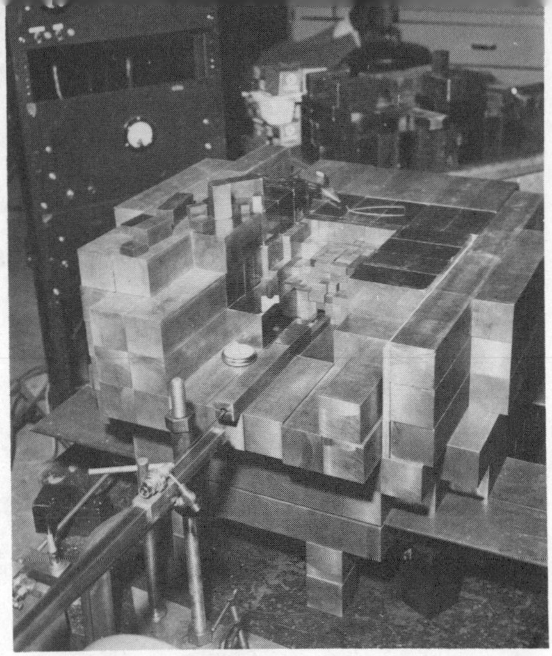

65

65. Experiments at Los Alamos determined the critical masses of U235 and Pu239. Adding U235 cubes to a subcritical assembly within blocks of beryllium tamper measurably increased neutron flux. 66. The Los Alamos Tech Area.

66

67

67. The guillotine mechanism for studying supercritical assemblies (the Dragon experiment). 68. The first RaLa test. Note Army tanks for observers, lower left.

68

69

69. Niels Bohr learned of the U.S. program in 1943. The bomb, he foresaw, would end major war and challenge the nation-states to move toward an open world.

70

70. Polish mathematician Stanislaw Ulam calculated hydrodynamics at Los Alamos; in 1951 he conceived the essential breakthrough arrangement for a workable H-bomb.

71. Hungarian theorist Edward Teller (*left*) helped make the plutonium bomb work; Navy physicist Norris Bradbury directed its test assembly at Trinity. Teller guided H-bomb theoretical studies at Los Alamos.

71

72

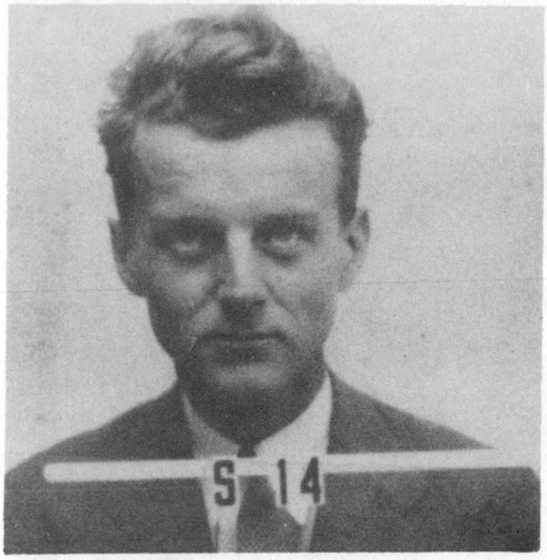

73

72. Seth Neddermeyer. His idea of using explosives to squeeze a nuclear core to criticality saved the plutonium bomb when impurities threatened its design. 73. Kitty Oppenheimer at Los Alamos with Peter.

74. The Los Alamos staff worked a six-day week; Sundays there was time for recreation. Shown here on a Sunday hike, *l. to r.*, standing, Emilio Segrè, Enrico Fermi, Hans Bethe, H. H. Staub, Victor Weisskopf; seated, Erika Staub, Elfriede Segrè.

74

75

75. The Normandy invasion in May 1944 led ultimately to Allied victory in Europe 12 months later. Supreme Commander Dwight D. Eisenhower visited the front lines.

76

76. Ferocious Japanese resistance claimed increasing U.S. casualties in the Pacific—30,000 of the 60,000 Americans committed on Iwo Jima, where 20,000 Japanese died.

77

77. At Los Alamos, Ukrainian chemist George Kistiakowsky (here riding Crisis) manufactured and tested the explosive lenses for the Fat Man bomb.

78

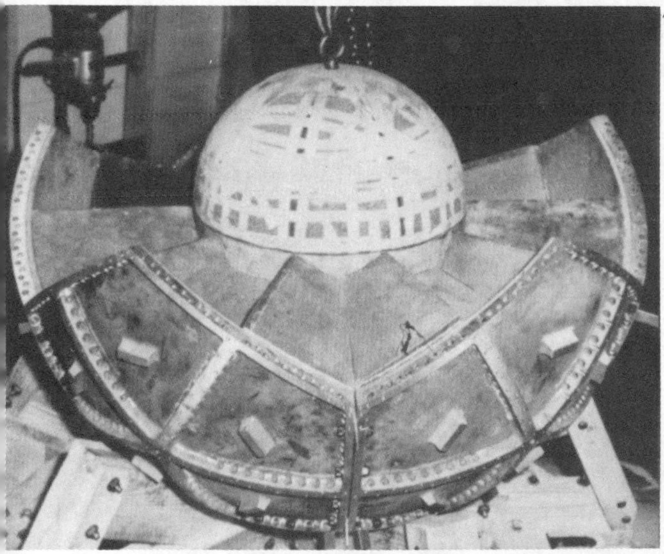

78. Early model Fat Man implosion bomb, upper segments removed to show interior. Overall diameter is about 5 feet.

79

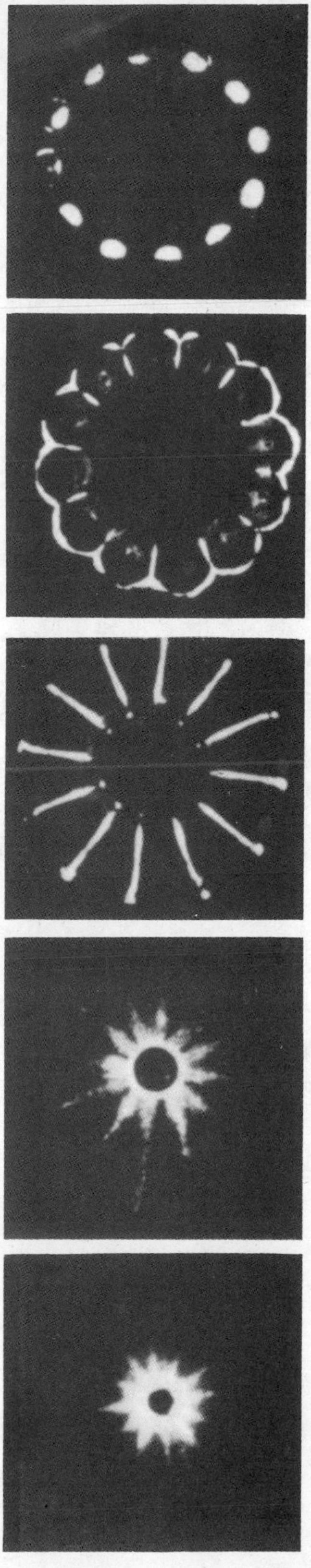

79. X-ray motion picture frames of implosion experiment. Note compression of core in final frames.

81

80. Shot tower at Trinity Site in the desert north of Alamogordo, N.M., where Los Alamos prepared in the spring of 1945 to test the plutonium bomb. 81. Base Camp.

80

82

83

82. The bomb explosive assembly arrived by truck from Los Alamos on Friday, July 13, 1945. Here the assembly is hoisted from the truck bed at the base of the 100-foot shot tower. 83. Firing and instrumentation bunkers.

84

84. Theoretician Philip Morrison (*left*), here with Ernest Lawrence, escorted the plutonium core to Trinity.

85

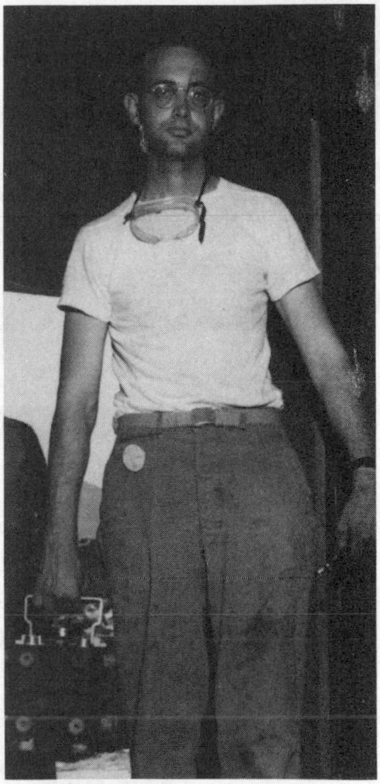

85. Sgt. Herbert Lehr delivered the core in its shock-mounted case to the McDonald Ranch assembly room at Trinity about 6 P.M., July 12, 1945. Assembly proceeded the following morning.

86

87

86. After inserting the initiator into the core and mounting the assembly in a cylindrical plug of tamper, the crew delivered it to the tower for insertion into the bomb. 87. The completely assembled Trinity bomb in its tower, with Norris Bradbury attending, July 15, 1945.

88–93. The first man-made nuclear explosion: Trinity, 0529:45 hours et seq., July 16, 1945. The sequence runs down this page and up the next. Note change of scale as the fireball expands. "This power of nature which we had first understood it to be," said I. I. Rabi, "—well, there it was."

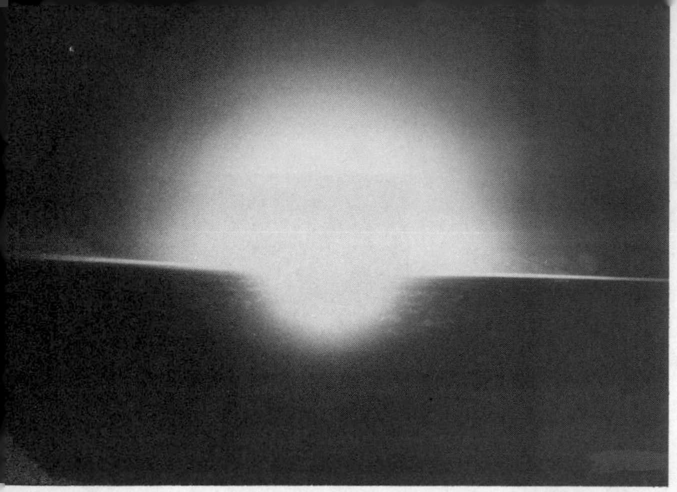

88

89

90

93

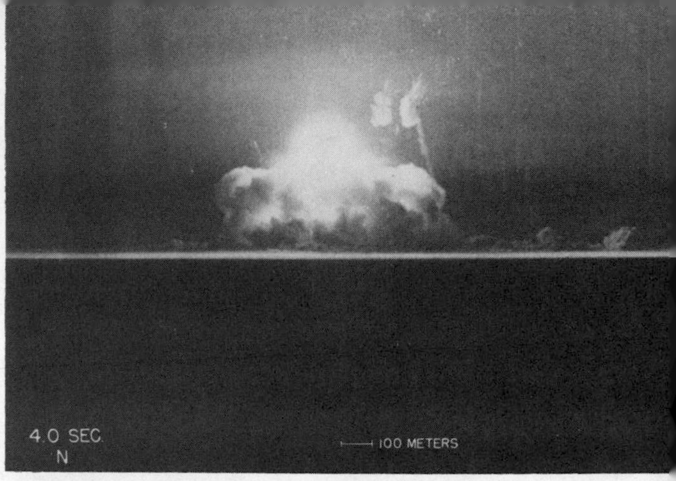

92

91

94

94. Twenty-four hours later Trinity, seen from the air, revealed a radioactive crater of green, glassy, fused desert sand. (Smaller crater to the south marks the 100-ton explosive test.)

95. Los Alamos director Robert Oppenheimer (*left*) subsequently visited the site with Manhattan Project commanding general Leslie R. Groves and found only the reinforcing rods of the tower footings left unvaporized.

96. In a final postwar celebration the British mission at Los Alamos pantomimed the war years. A stepladder stood in for the Trinity shot tower. Note Otto Frisch (third from left) in skirt playing housemaid.

95

96

Frisch found a friend that year in a fellow emigré at Birmingham, the theoretician Rudolf Peierls. A well-off Berliner, a slender man with a boyish face, a notable overbite and a mind of mathematical austerity, Peierls was born in 1907 and had arrived in England in 1933 on a Rockefeller Fellowship to Cambridge. With the Nazi purge of the German universities he chose to remain in England. He would be naturalized as a British citizen in February 1940, but until then he was technically an enemy alien. When Oliphant consulted with him from time to time on the mathematics of resonant cavities—important for microwave radar—both men were careful to pretend that the question was purely academic.

Peierls had already contributed significantly to the debate on the possible explosive effects of fission. The previous May one of Frédéric Joliot's associates in Paris, Francis Perrin, had published a first approximate formula for calculating the critical mass of uranium—the amount of uranium necessary to sustain a chain reaction. A lump smaller than a critical mass would be inert; a lump of critical size would explode spontaneously upon assembly.

The possibility of a critical mass is anchored in the fact that the surface area of a sphere increases more slowly with increasing radius than does the volume (as nearly r^2 to r^3). At some particular volume, depending on the density of the material and on its cross sections for scattering, capture and fission, more neutrons should find nuclei to fission than find surface to escape from; that volume is then the critical mass. Estimating the several cross sections of natural uranium, Francis Perrin put its critical mass at forty-four tons. A tamper around the uranium of iron or lead to bounce back neutrons might reduce the requirement, Perrin calculated, to only thirteen tons.

Peierls saw immediately that he could sharpen Perrin's formula. He did so in a theoretical paper he worked out in May and early June 1939 that the Cambridge Philosophical Society published in its *Proceedings* in October. Because a critical-mass formula based on slow-neutron fission would be mathematically complicated, requiring that the characteristics of the moderator be taken into account, Peierls proposed to consider "a simplified case": fission by unmoderated fast neutrons. Plugging in the fission cross section of natural uranium, which was essentially the fission cross section of U238, gave a critical mass, notes Peierls, "of the order of tons." As a weapon, an object of that size was too unwieldy to take seriously. "There was of course no chance of getting such a thing into any aeroplane, and the paper appeared to have no practical significance." Peierls was aware of the British and American concern for secrecy, but in this case he saw no reason not to publish.

The USSR opportunistically invaded Finland at the end of November. In the rest of Europe the strange standoff prevailed that isolationist Idaho senator William Borah would label the "phony war." The Peierlses moved to a larger house; early in the new year they generously invited Frisch to live with them. Genia Peierls, who was Russian, took the bachelor Austrian in hand. She "ran her house," writes Frisch, "with cheerful intelligence, a ringing Manchester voice and a Russian's sovereign disregard of the definite article. She taught me to shave every day and to dry dishes as fast as she washed them, a skill that has come in useful many times since." Life at the Peierlses was entertaining, but Frisch walked home through ominous blackouts so dark that he sometimes stumbled over roadside benches and could distinguish fellow pedestrians only by the glow of the luminous cards they had taken to wearing in their hatbands. Thus reminded of the continuing threat of German bombing, he found himself questioning his confident Chemical Society review: "Is that really true what I have written?"

Sometime in February 1940 he looked again. There had always been four possible mechanisms for an explosive chain reaction in uranium:

(1) slow-neutron fission of U238;
(2) fast-neutron fission of U238;
(3) slow-neutron fission of U235; and
(4) fast-neutron fission of U235.

Bohr's logical distinction between U238 and thorium on the one hand and U235 on the other ruled out (1): U238 was not fissioned by slow neutrons. (2) was inefficient because of scattering and the parasitic effects of the capture resonance of U238. (3) was possibly applicable to power production but too slow for a practical weapon. But what about (4)? Apparently no one in Britain, France or the United States had asked the question quite that way before.

If Frisch now glimpsed an opening into those depths he did so because he had looked carefully at isotope separation and had decided it could be accomplished even with so fugitive an isotope as U235. He was therefore prepared to consider the behavior of the pure substance unalloyed with U238, as Bohr, Fermi and even Szilard had not yet been. "I wondered—assuming that my Clusius separation tube worked well—if one could use a number of such tubes to produce enough uranium-235 to make a truly explosive chain reaction possible, not dependent on slow neutrons. How much of the isotope would be needed?"

He shared the problem with Peierls. Peierls had his critical-mass formula. In this case it required the cross section for fast-neutron fission of U235, a number no one knew because no one had yet separated a sufficient amount of the rare isotope to determine its cross section by experiment, the only way the number could be reliably known. Nevertheless, says Peierls, "we had read the paper of Bohr and Wheeler and had understood it, and it seemed to convince us that in those circumstances for neutrons in U235 the cross-section would be dominated by fission." Peierls could state simply what followed: "If a neutron hit the [U235] nucleus something was bound to happen."

What followed thus made the cross section intuitively obvious: it would be more or less the same as the familiar cross section that expressed the odds of hitting the uranium nucleus with a neutron at all—the geometric cross section, 10^{-23} square centimeters, an entire order of magnitude larger than the fission cross sections previously estimated for natural uranium that were small multiples of 10^{-24}.

"Just sort of playfully," Frisch writes, he plugged 10^{-23} cm^2 into Peierls' formula. "To my amazement" the answer "was very much smaller than I had expected; it was not a matter of tons, but something like a pound or two." A volume less than a golf ball for a substance so heavy as uranium.

But would that pound or two explode or fizzle? Peierls easily produced an estimate. The chain reaction would have to proceed faster than the vaporizing and swelling of the heating metal ball. Peierls calculated the time between neutron generations, between $1 \times 2 \times 4 \times 8 \times 16 \times 32 \times 64 \ldots$, to be about four millionths of a second, much faster than the several thousandths of a second Frisch had estimated for slow-neutron fission.

Then how destructive was the consequent explosion? Some eighty generations of neutrons—as many as could be expected to multiply before the swelling explosion separated the atoms of U235 enough to stop the chain reaction—still millionths of a second in total, gave temperatures as hot as the interior of the sun, pressures greater than the center of the earth where iron flows as a liquid. "I worked out the results of what such a nuclear explosion would be," says Peierls. "Both Frisch and I were staggered by them."

And finally, practically: Could even a few pounds of U235 be separated from U238? Frisch writes:

> I had worked out the possible efficiency of my separation system with the help of Clusius's formula, and we came to the conclusion that with something like a hundred thousand similar separation tubes one might produce a pound of reasonably pure uranium-235 in a modest time, measured in weeks. At that point we stared at each other and realized that an atomic bomb might after all be possible.

"The cost of such a plant," Frisch adds for perspective, "would be insignificant compared with the cost of the war."

"Look, shouldn't somebody know about that?" Frisch then asked Peierls. They hastened their calculations to Mark Oliphant. "They convinced me," Oliphant testifies. He told them to write it all down.

They did, succinctly, in two parts, one part three typewritten pages, the other even briefer. Talking about it made them nervous, Peierls recalls (by then it was March and the exceptional cold had given way to warmer weather):

> I remember we were writing our memorandum . . . together in my room in the Physics Lab on the ground floor; it was a fine day and the window was open . . . and while we were discussing the wording a face suddenly appeared in the open window. And we were a little worried! It turned out that just underneath the window (which was facing south) people were growing some tomato plants, and somebody had been there bending down inspecting what these plants were doing.

The first of the two parts they titled "On the construction of a 'super-bomb'; based on a nuclear chain reaction in uranium." It was intended, they wrote, "to point out and discuss a possibility which seems to have been overlooked in . . . earlier discussions." They proceeded to cover the same ground they had previously covered together in private, noting that "the energy liberated by a 5 kg bomb would be equivalent to that of several thousand tons of dynamite." They described a simple mechanism for arming the weapon: making the uranium sphere in two parts "which are brought together first when the explosion is wanted. Once assembled, the bomb would explode within a second or less." Springs, they thought, might pull the two small hemispheres together. Assembly would have to be rapid or the chain reaction would begin prematurely, destroying the bomb but not much else. A byproduct of the explosion—about 20 percent of its energy, they thought—would be radiation, the equivalent of "a hundred tons of radium" that would be "fatal to living beings even a long time after the explosion." Effective protection from the weapon would be "hardly possible."

The second report, "Memorandum on the properties of a radioactive 'super-bomb,' " a less technical document, was apparently intended as an alternative presentation for nonscientists. This study explored beyond the technical questions of design and production to the strategic issues of possession and use; it managed at the same time both seemly innocence and extraordinary prescience:

> 1. As a weapon, the super-bomb would be practically irresistible. There is no material or structure that could be expected to resist the force of the explosion. . . .

> 2. Owing to the spreading of radioactive substances with the wind, the bomb could probably not be used without killing large numbers of civilians, and this may make it unsuitable as a weapon for use by this country. . . .
>
> 3. . . . It is quite conceivable that Germany is, in fact, developing this weapon. . . .
>
> 4. If one works on the assumption that Germany is, or will be, in the possession of this weapon, it must be realised that no shelters are available that would be effective and could be used on a large scale. The most effective reply would be a counter-threat with a similar weapon.

Thus in the first months of 1940 it was already clear to two intelligent observers that nuclear weapons would be weapons of mass destruction against which the only apparent defense would be the deterrent effect of mutual possession.

Frisch and Peierls finished their two reports and took them to Oliphant. He quizzed the men thoroughly, added a cover letter to their memoranda ("I have considered these suggestions in some detail and have had considerable discussion with the authors, with the result that I am convinced that the whole thing must be taken rather seriously, if only to make sure that the other side are not occupied in the production of such a bomb at the present time") and sent letter and documents off to Henry Thomas Tizard, an Oxford man, a chemist by training, the driving force behind British radar development, the civilian chairman of the Committee on the Scientific Survey of Air Defense—better known as the Tizard Committee—which was the most important British committee at the time concerned with the application of science to war.

"I have often been asked," Otto Frisch wrote many years afterward of the moment when he understood that a bomb might be possible after all, before he and Peierls carried the news to Mark Oliphant, "why I didn't abandon the project there and then, saying nothing to anybody. Why start on a project which, if it was successful, would end with the production of a weapon of unparalleled violence, a weapon of mass destruction such as the world had never seen? The answer was very simple. We were at war, and the idea was reasonably obvious; very probably some German scientists had had the same idea and were working on it."

Whatever scientists of one warring nation could conceive, the scientists of another warring nation might also conceive—and keep secret. That early in 1939 and early 1940, the nuclear arms race began. Responsible men who properly and understandably feared a dangerous enemy saw their own ideas reflected back to them malevolently distorted. Ideas that appeared defensive in friendly hands seen the other way around appeared aggressive. But they were the same ideas.

* * *

Werner Heisenberg sent his considered conclusions to the German War Office on December 6, 1939, while Fermi and Szilard waited for the $6,000 the Briggs Uranium Committee had allocated to them for graphite studies and Frisch prepared his pessimistic Chemical Society review. Heisenberg thought fission could lead to energy production even with ordinary uranium if a suitable moderator could be found. Water would not do, but "heavy water [or] very pure graphite would, on the other hand, suffice on present evidence." The surest method for building a reactor, Heisenberg wrote, "will be to enrich the uranium-235 isotope. The greater the degree of enrichment, the smaller the reactor can be made." Enrichment—increasing the proportion of U235 to U238—was also "the only method of producing explosives several orders of magnitude more powerful than the strongest explosives yet known." (The phrase indicates Heisenberg understood the possibility of fast-neutron fission even before Frisch and Peierls did.)

During the same period Paul Harteck in Hamburg was building a Clusius separation tube; in December he tested it by successfully separating isotopes of the heavy gas xenon. He traveled to Munich at Christmastime to discuss design improvements with Clusius, who was professor of physical chemistry at the university there. Auer, the thorium specialists, purveyors of gas mantles and radioactive toothpaste, delivered the first ton of pure uranium oxide processed from Joachimsthal ores to the War Office in January 1940. German uranium research was thriving.

Acquiring a suitable moderator looked more difficult. The German scientists favored heavy water, but Germany had no extraction plant of its own. Harteck calculated at the beginning of the year that a coal-fired installation would require 100,000 tons of coal for each ton of heavy water produced, an impossibility in wartime. The only source of heavy water in quantity in the world was an electrochemical plant built into a sheer 1,500-foot granite bluff beside a powerful waterfall at Vemork, near Rjukan, ninety miles west of Oslo in southern Norway. Norsk Hydro-Elektrisk Kvaelstofaktieselskab produced the rare liquid as a byproduct of hydrogen electrolysis for synthetic ammonia production.

I.G. Farben, the German chemical cartel assembled by Bayer's Carl Duisberg in the 1920s, owned stock in Norsk Hydro; learning of the War Office's need it approached the Norwegians with an offer to buy all the heavy water on hand, about fifty gallons worth some $120,000, and to order more at the rate of at least thirty gallons a month. Norsk Hydro was then producing less than three gallons a month, enough in the prewar years to glut the small physics-laboratory market. It wanted to know why Germany needed so vast a quantity. I.G. Farben chose not to say. In February the

Norwegian firm refused either to sell its existing stock or to increase production.

Heavy water also impressed the French team, a fact Joliot pased on to the French Minister of Armament, Raoul Dautry. When Dautry heard about the German bid for Norsk Hydro's supply he decided to win the water for France. A French bank, the Banque de Paris et des Pays Bas, controlled a majority interest in the Norwegian company and a former bank officer, Jacques Allier, was now a lieutenant in Dautry's ministry. Dautry briefed the balding, bespectacled Allier with Joliot on hand on February 20: the minister wanted the lieutenant to lead a team of French secret-service agents to Norway to acquire the heavy water.

Allier slipped into Oslo under an assumed name and met with the general manager of Norsk Hydro at the beginning of March. The French officer was prepared to pay up to 1.5 million kroner for the water and even to leave half for the Germans, but once the Norwegian heard what military purpose the substance might serve he volunteered his entire stock and refused payment. The water, divided among twenty-six cans, left Vemork by car soon afterward on a dark midnight. From Oslo Allier's team flew it to Edinburgh in two loads—German fighters forced down for inspection a decoy plane Allier had pretended to board at the time of the first loading—and then transported it by rail and Channel ferry to Paris, where Joliot prepared through the winter and spring of the phony war to use it in both homogeneous and heterogeneous uranium-oxide experiments.

Nuclear research in the Soviet Union during this period was limited to skillful laboratory work. Two associates of Soviet physicist Igor Kurchatov reported to the *Physical Review* in June 1940 that they had observed rare spontaneous fissioning in uranium. "The complete lack of any American response to the publication of the discovery," writes the American physicist Herbert F. York, "was one of the factors which convinced the Russians that there must be a big secret project under way in the United States." It was not yet big, but by then it had begun to be secret.

Japanese studies toward an atomic bomb began first within the military. The director of the Aviation Technology Research Institute of the Imperial Japanese Army, Takeo Yasuda, a lieutenant general and an alert electrical engineer, conscientiously followed the international scientific literature that related to his field; in the course of his reading in 1938 and 1939 he noticed and tracked the discovery of nuclear fission. In April 1940, foreseeing fission's possible consequences, he ordered an aide who was scientifically trained, Lieutenant Colonel Tatsusaburō Suzuki, to prepare a full report. Suzuki went to work with a will.

* * *

Niels Bohr had returned from Princeton to Copenhagen at the beginning of May 1939, preoccupied with the gathering European apocalypse. His friends had urged him to send for his family and remain in the United States. He had not been tempted. Refugees still escaping from Germany and now fleeing Central Europe as well needed him; his institute needed him; Denmark needed him. Hitler proposed on May 31 to compromise the neutrality of the Scandinavian countries with nonagression pacts. The pragmatic Danes alone accepted, fully aware the pact was worthless and even demeaning but unwilling to invite invasion for a paper victory. By autumn, when the John Wheelers offered to shelter one of Bohr's sons in Princeton for the duration of the conflict, Bohr reserved the offer against future need. "We are aware that a catastrophe might come any day," he wrote in the midst of Poland's agony.

Catastrophe for Denmark waited until April 1940 and came then with brutal efficiency. Bohr was lecturing in Norway. The British had announced their intention to mine Norwegian coastal waters against shipment of Norwegian iron ore to Nazi Germany. On the final evening of his lecture tour, April 8, Bohr dined with the King of Norway, Haakon VII, and found King and government lost in gloom at the prospect of a German attack. After dinner he boarded the night train for Copenhagen. A train ferry carried the cars across the Öresund at night to Helsingør while the passengers slept. Danish police pounding on compartment doors woke them to the news: the Germans had invaded not only Norway but Denmark as well. Two thousand German troops hidden in coal freighters moored near Langelinie, the Copenhagen pier of Hans Christian Andersen's Little Mermaid, had stormed ashore in the early morning, so unexpected a sight that night-shift workers bicycling home thought a motion picture was being filmed. A major German force had marched north through Schleswig-Holstein onto the Danish peninsula as well, crossing the border before dawn. German aircraft marked with black crosses dominated the air. German warships commanded the Kattegat and Skagerrak passages that open Denmark and southern Norway to the North Sea.

The Norwegians fought back, determined that their King, court and parliament must escape to exile. The Danes, in their flat country where Panzers might roll, did not. Rifle fire crackled in the streets of Copenhagen in the early morning, but King Christian X ordered an immediate cease-fire, which took effect at 6:25 A.M. By the time Bohr's train arrived in the capital city what Churchill would call "this ruthless *coup*" was complete, the streets littered with green surrender leaflets, the King preparing to receive the German chief of staff. Danish resistance would be dedicated and effective, but it would take less suicidal forms than open battle with the Wehrmacht.

The American Embassy quickly passed word that it could guarantee the Bohrs safe passage to the United States. Bohr again chose duty. His immediate concern was to burn the files of the refugee committee that had helped hundreds of emigrés to escape to exile. "It was characteristic of Niels Bohr," his collaborator, Stefan Rozental, writes, "that one of the first things he did was to contact the Chancellor of the University and other Danish authorities in order to protect those of the staff at the Institute whom the Germans might be expected to persecute." Those were Poles first of all, but Bohr also sought out government leaders to argue for concerted Danish resistance to any German attempt to install anti-Semitic laws in Denmark.

He even found time on the day of the occupation to worry about the large gold Nobel Prize medals that Max von Laue and James Franck had given him for safekeeping. Exporting gold from Germany was a serious criminal offense and their names were engraved on the medals. George de Hevesy devised an effective solution—literally: he dissolved the medals separately in acid. As solutions of black liquid in unmarked jars they sat out the war innocently on a laboratory shelf. Afterward the Nobel Foundation recast them and returned them to their owners.

Norsk Hydro was a prime German objective and there was heavy fighting around Rjukan, which held out until May 3, the last town in southern Norway to surrender. Then a management under duress reported to Paul Harteck that its heavy-water facility, the Vemork High Concentration Plant, could be expanded to increase production of the ideal neutron moderator to as much as 1.5 tons per year.

"What I should like," Henry Tizard wrote Mark Oliphant after he had studied the Frisch-Peierls memoranda, "would be to have quite a small committee to sit soon to advise what ought to be done, who should do it, and where it should be done, and I suggest that you, Thomson, and say Blackett, would form a sufficient nucleus for such a committee." Thomson was G. P. Thomson, J.J.'s son, the Imperial College physicist who had ordered up a ton of uranium oxide the previous year to study and felt ashamed at the absurdity. He had concluded after neutron-bombardment experiments that a chain reaction in natural uranium was unlikely and a war project therefore impractical. Tizard, who had been skeptical to begin with and had taken Thomson's conclusions as support for his skepticism, appointed Thomson chairman of the small committee; James Chadwick, now at Liverpool, his assistant P. B. Moon and Rutherford protégé John

Douglas Cockcroft were added to the list. Blackett was busy with other war work, although he would join the committee later. The group met informally for the first time on April 10 in the Royal Society's quarters at Burlington House.

It probably met as much to hear a visitor, the ubiquitous Jacques Allier of the Banque de Paris and the French Ministry of Armament, as to discuss the Frisch-Peierls work. Allier warned the British physicists about the German interest in heavy-water production and bid for collaboration on nuclear research between Britain and France. Only then, Thomson notes in the minutes he kept, did they consider "the possibility of separating isotopes . . . and it was agreed that the prospects were sufficiently good to justify small-scale experiments on uranium hexafluoride [a gaseous uranium compound]." They proposed rather ungenerously to remind Frisch to avoid "any possible leakage of news in view of the interest shown by the Germans." They were willing to inform him that his memorandum was being considered but not to supply details. (Peierls' name seems not yet to have made an impression on Thomson, and Tizard apparently retained the second Frisch-Peierls memorandum in his files.) "We entered the project with more scepticism than belief," the committee would report later, "though we felt it was a matter which had to be investigated." Thomson's minutes make that skepticism evident. Tizard for his part wrote Lindemann's brother Charles, a science adviser to the British Embassy in Paris, that he considered the French "unnecessarily excited" about the perils of German nuclear research. "I still . . . think that [the] probability of anything of real military significance is very low," he estimated in a note written the same week to the British War Cabinet staff.

It might have been as unpromising a start as the first meeting of the Briggs Uranium Committee had been, but the men on the Thomson committee were active, competent physicists, not military ordnance specialists, and whatever their initial skepticism they understood where the numbers Frisch and Peierls had used came from and what they might mean. At a second meeting on April 24 Thomson recorded laconically that "Dr. Frisch produced some notes to show that the uranium bomb was feasible." Many years later Oliphant recalled a more expansive response: "The Committee generally was electrified by the possibility." Chadwick's good opinion helped. He had just begun exploring fast-neutron fission himself with his new Liverpool cyclotron, the first in England, when he saw the Frisch-Peierls memorandum. At the April 24 meeting he awarded the emigrés' work chagrined confirmation: he "was embarrassed," says Oliphant, "confessing that he had reached similar conclusions, but did not feel justified in reporting them until more was known about the neutron cross sections from experiments. Peierls and Frisch had used calculated values. However, this confirmatory evidence led the Committee to pay great attention to the development of techniques for . . . separation."

Chadwick agreed to undertake the necessary studies. For several more weeks, until their protests through Oliphant registered with Thomson, Frisch and Peierls would be walled off from their own secrets. But work toward a bomb of chain-reacting uranium was now fairly begun, and this time it had found the right—fast—track.

Szilard chafed. The months after the first Uranium Committee meeting became "the most curious period of my life." No one called. "We heard nothing from Washington at all. . . . I had assumed that once we had demonstrated that in the fission of uranium neutrons are emitted, there would be no difficulty in getting people interested; but I was wrong." The Uranium Committee's November 1 report had in fact been languishing in Roosevelt's files; Watson finally decided on his own in early February 1940 to bring it up again. He asked Lyman Briggs if he had anything to add. Briggs reported the transfer, finally, of the $6,000 for Fermi's work on neutron absorption in graphite. That was "a crucial undertaking," Briggs said; he imagined it would determine "whether or not the undertaking has a practical application." He proposed to wait for results.

Something other than Briggs' penurious methodology triggered a new burst of activity from Szilard. He had spent the winter preparing a thorough theoretical study, "Divergent chain reactions in systems composed of uranium and carbon"—divergent in this case meaning chain reactions that continue to multiply once begun (the document's first footnote, numbered zero, cited "H. G. Wells, The World Set Free [1913]"). Early in the new year Joliot's group reported a uranium-water experiment that "seemed to come so close to being chain-reacting," says Szilard, "that if we improved the system somewhat by replacing water with graphite, in my opinion we should have gotten over the hump." He arranged lunch with Fermi to discuss the French paper. "I asked him, 'Did you read Joliot's paper?' He said he did. I asked him, 'What did you think of it?' and Fermi said, 'Not much.' " Szilard was furious. "At which point I saw no reason to continue the conversation and went home."

He traveled again to Princeton to see Einstein. They worked up another letter and sent it under Einstein's signature to Sachs. It emphasized the secret German uranium research at the Kaiser Wilhelm Institutes, about which they had learned from the physical chemist Peter Debye, the 1936 Nobel laureate in chemistry and director of the physics institute at Dahlem, who had been expelled recently to the United States, ostensibly on leave of absence, when he refused to give up Dutch citizenship and join the Nazi Reich. Sachs sent the Einstein letter on to Pa Watson for FDR. But Watson thought it sensible to check first with the Uranium Committee. Adamson responded, echoing Briggs: everything depended on the graphite measurements at Columbia. Watson proposed to wait for the official report. Sachs may have rebutted; Roosevelt wrote the gadfly economist on April 5 emphasizing that the Briggs committee was "the most practical method of continuing this research" but also calling for another committee meeting that Sachs might attend. Briggs dutifully scheduled it for Saturday afternoon, April 27.

In the meantime another development intervened. Alfred Nier at the University of Minnesota had gone to work, after Fermi wrote urging him again to do so, to prepare to separate measurable samples of U235 and U238. John Dunning sent him uranium hexafluoride, a highly corrosive compound that is a white solid at room temperature but volatilizes to a gas when heated to 140°F. "I worked with this for a couple of months in late 1939," Nier remembers. Unfortunately the gas was too volatile; it dispersed through Nier's three-foot glass spectrometer tube despite the best efforts of his vacuum pump to clear it and contaminated the collector plates:

> Finally I said, "This won't do." A new instrument was built in about 10 days in February, 1940. Our glass blower bent the horseshoe-shaped mass spectrometer tube for me; I made the metal parts myself. As a source of uranium, I used the less volatile uranium tetrachloride and tetrabromide left over from [his earlier] Harvard experiments. The first separation of U-235 and U-238 was actually accomplished on February 28 and 29, 1940. It was a leap year, and on Friday afternoon, February 29, I pasted the little samples [collected on nickel foil] on the margin of a handwritten letter and delivered them to the Minneapolis Post Office at about six o'clock. The letter was sent by airmail special delivery and arrived at Columbia University on Saturday. I was aroused early Sunday morning by a long-distance telephone call from John Dunning [who had worked through the night bombarding the samples with neutrons from the Columbia cyclotron]. The Columbia test of the samples clearly showed that U-235 was responsible for the slow neutron fission of uranium.

The demonstration vindicated Bohr's hypothesis, but it also led Briggs to even greater suspicion of the value of natural uranium; it was "very doubtful," he reported to Watson on April 9 "whether a chain reaction can be established without separating 235 from the rest of the uranium." Nier, Dunning and their collaborators Eugene T. Booth and Aristide von Grosse had written much the same thing in the *Physical Review* on March 15:

"These experiments emphasize the importance of uranium isotope separation on a larger scale for the investigation of chain reaction possibilities in uranium." But isotope separation was Dunning's approach to the problem in the first place and his enthusiasm as well; the slow-neutron finding hardly ruled out the Fermi-Szilard system. More misleading may have been the measurements Nier and the Columbia team published on April 15 using larger (but still microscopic) samples: "Furthermore, the number of fissions/microgram of U^{238} observed under these neutron intensity conditions, is sufficient to account for practically all the fast neutron fission observed in unseparated U." The statement was correct within the limits of measurement for such small samples, but its wording seems to deprecate U235 fast-neutron fission. In fact, Nier had not collected enough U235 to allow Columbia to measure that possibility. All anyone knew by then was that the U235 cross section for fast-neutron fission was less than the isotope's cross section for slow-neutron fission. But that cross section, as the first Nier/Columbia paper reported, was a whopping 400 to 500 $\times 10^{-24}$ cm^2.

Predictably, then, when the Uranium Committee met on April 27, with Sachs, Pegram, Fermi, Szilard and Wigner in attendance, it listened to the renewed debate, squared its shoulders at Sachs' exhortation to plunge ahead—and never wavered in its adamant conviction that a large-scale uranium-graphite experiment should await the outcome of Fermi's graphite measurements.

Now that the $6,000 had been paid, Columbia was able to buy the graphite Szilard had tracked down for Fermi's use. "Cartons of carefully-wrapped graphite bricks began to arrive at the Pupin Laboratory," Herbert Anderson remembers, four tons in all. "Fermi returned to the chain reaction problem with enthusiasm. This was the kind of physics he liked best. Together we stacked the graphite bricks in a neat pile. We cut narrow slots in some of the bricks for the rhodium foil detectors we wanted to insert, and soon we were ready to make measurements."

"So the physicists on the seventh floor of Pupin Laboratories started looking like coal miners," adds Fermi, "and the wives to whom these physicists came back tired at night were wondering what was happening."

The arrangement was designed to determine how far neutrons from a radon-beryllium source set in paraffin on the floor under the graphite column would diffuse up the column through the graphite after first slowing down in scattering collisions: the farther the neutrons traveled, the smaller was carbon's absorption cross section and therefore the better moderator it would be. The Pupin seventh floor became a racetrack like the second floor of the institute in Rome. Anderson describes the scene:

> A precise schedule was followed for each measurement. With the rhodium in place in the graphite, the source was inserted in its position inside the pile and removed after a one-minute exposure. To get the rhodium foil under the Geiger counter in the allotted 20 seconds [because its induced half-life is only 44 seconds] took coordination and some fast legwork. The division of labor was typical. I removed the source on signal; Fermi, stopwatch in hand, grabbed the rhodium and raced down the hall at top speed. He had just enough time to place the foil carefully into position, close the lead shield and, at the prescribed moment, start the count. Then with obvious satisfaction at seeing everything go right, he would watch the flashing lights on the scaler, tapping his fingers on the bench in time with the clicking of the register. Such a display of the phenomenon of radioactivity never failed to delight him.

The absorption cross section, as Fermi and Anderson subsequently calculated it, proved usefully small: 3×10^{-27} cm^2. And could be made smaller still, they thought, with purer graphite. The measurement strongly supported Fermi's and Szilard's plan to attempt to induce a slow-neutron chain reaction in natural uranium.

But while such a plan might demonstrate a potential future source of power, the American scientists and administrators who were advising Briggs could not yet identify any military use. In April the British Thomson committee asked A. V. Hill, a scientific adviser to the British Embassy in Washington, to find out what the Americans were doing about fission. According to the official history of the British atomic energy program, Hill talked to unidentified "scientists of the Carnegie Institution," whose opinions he reported pungently:

> It is not inconceivable that practical engineering applications and war use may emerge in the end. But I am assured by American colleagues that there is no sign of them at present and that it would be a sheer waste of time for people busy with urgent matters in England to turn to uranium as a war investigation. If anything likely to be of war value emerges they will certainly give us a hint of it in good time. A large number of American physicists are working on or interested in the subject; they have excellent facilities and equipment: they are extremely well disposed towards us: and they feel that it is much better that they should be pressing on with this than that our people should be wasting their time on what is scientifically very interesting, but for present practical needs probably a wild goose chase.

The opinion from the Carnegie may have been hardheaded, but it was based on more than prejudice. Roberts, Hafstad and fellow DTM physicist Norman P. Heydenburg had improved their measurements of cross sections for fast-neutron fission, scattering and capture in natural uranium.

Using their numbers, Edward Teller in one of the many calculations he made during this period arrived at a critical mass in excess of thirty tons, the same order of magnitude as Perrin and Peierls had calculated before him. With only slightly more pessimistic assumptions Roberts concluded that "the cross-section for capture [in natural uranium] is sufficiently large that it now seems impossible for a fast-neutron chain reaction to occur, even in an infinitely large block of pure uranium." By the spring of 1940 experiments at Columbia and the DTM had thus ruled out both slow- and significant fast-neutron fission in U238 and ruled in slow-neutron fission in U235. The asymmetry might have been a clue. No one picked it up.

Since at least the time of Einstein's first letter to FDR, Edward Teller had debated within himself the morality of weapons work. His life had twice been cruelly uprooted by totalitarianism. He understood Germany's frightening technological advantages at the outset of the war. "I came to the United States in 1935," he notes. ". . . The handwriting was on the wall. At that time, I believed that Hitler would conquer the world unless a miracle happened." But pure science still pacified him. "To deflect my attention from physics, my full-time job which I liked, to work on weapons, was not an easy matter. And for quite a time I did not make up my mind."

The accidental juxtaposition of two events led him to decision. "In the spring of 1940 it was announced that President Roosevelt would speak to a Pan American Scientific Congress in Washington, and as one of the professors of George Washington University I was invited. I did not intend to go." The other event of that crucial day, May 10, 1940, reversed his intention: the phony war abruptly ended. With seventy-seven divisions and 3,500 aircraft Germany without declaration or warning invaded Belgium, the Netherlands and Luxembourg to make way for the invasion of France. Teller thought Roosevelt might speak to that outrage. In his voluntary prewar isolation he had never bothered, Teller says, to visit the Capitol or listen to one of FDR's radio talks or otherwise involve himself in the political life of his adopted country, but he wanted now to see the President of the United States in person.

Alone among the scientists at the congress Teller knew about the Einstein letter. It was a direct link, he was an emotional man and the encounter with Roosevelt was eerily personal: "We had never met, but I had an irrational feeling he was talking to me." The President mentioned the German invasion, its challenge to "the continuance of the type of civilization" the people of the Americas valued, the distances of the modern world shortened by modern technology to timetables that removed the "mystic immunity" Americans once felt from European war. "Then he started to talk about the role of the scientist," Teller recalls, "who has been accused of inventing deadly weapons. He concluded: 'If the scientists in the free countries will not make weapons to defend the freedom of their countries, then freedom will be lost.' " Teller believed Roosevelt was not proposing what scientists *may* do "but something that was our duty and that we *must* do—to work out the military problems, because without the work of the scientists the war and the world would be lost."

Teller's memory of Roosevelt's speech differs from its text. The President said that most people abhor "conquest and war and bloodshed." He said that the search for truth was a great adventure but that "in other parts of the world, teachers and scholars are not permitted" that search—an observation of which Teller had personal knowledge. And then, cannily, Roosevelt offered absolution in advance for war work:

> You who are scientists may have been told that you are in part responsible for the debacle of today . . . but I assure you that it is not the scientists of the world who are responsible. . . . What has come about has been caused solely by those who would use, and are using, the progress that you have made along lines of peace in an entirely different cause.

"My mind was made up," Teller reports, "and it has not changed since."

Vannevar Bush made a similar choice that spring. The sharp-eyed Yankee engineer, who looked like a beardless Uncle Sam, had left his MIT vice presidency for the Carnegie Institution in the first place to position himself closer to the sources of government authority as war approached. Karl Compton had offered to move up to chairman of the MIT corporation and give him the presidency to keep him, but Bush had larger plans.

As a young man, with a doctorate in engineering behind him jointly from MIT and Harvard earned in one intense year, Bush in 1917 had gone patriotically to work for a research corporation developing a magnetic submarine detector. The device was effective, and one hundred sets got built; but because of bureaucratic confusion they were never put to use against German submarines. "That experience," Bush writes in a memoir, "forced into my mind pretty solidly the complete lack of proper liaison between the military and the civilian in the development of weapons in time of war, and what that lack meant."

In Washington after the invasion of Poland the Carnegie president gathered with a group of fellow science administrators—Frank Jewett, president of Bell Telephone Laboratories and the National Academy of Sciences; James Bryant Conant, the young president of Harvard, a distinguished chemist; Richard Tolman of Caltech, the theoretician who had wooed Einstein; Karl Compton—to worry about the approaching conflict:

> It was during the period of the "phony" war. We were agreed that the war was bound to break out into an intense struggle, that America was sure to get into it in one way or another sooner or later, that it would be a highly technical struggle, that we were by no means prepared in this regard, and finally and most importantly, that the military system as it existed . . . would never fully produce the new instrumentalities which we would certainly need.

They devised a national organization to do the job. Bush had learned his way around Washington and took the lead. The organization Bush wanted needed independent authority. He thought it should report directly to the President rather than through military channels and should have its own source of funds. He drafted a proposal. Then he arranged an introduction to Harry Hopkins.

A small-town Iowa boy, idealistic and energetic, Harry Lloyd Hopkins had fallen into New York social work after four years at Grinnell and won appointment at the beginning of the Depression administering emergency state relief. When the governor of New York was elected President, Hopkins moved with Roosevelt to Washington to help out with the New Deal. He ran the vast Works Progress Administration, then took over as Secretary of Commerce. His performance moved him closer and closer to the President, who picked up talent wherever he could find it; as war approached, Roosevelt invited Hopkins to dinner at the White House one evening and moved the man in for the duration as his closest adviser and aide. Hopkins was tall, a chain smoker and emaciated to the point of cachexia, his ghastly health the result of cancer surgery that took most of his stomach and left him unable to absorb much protein and therefore slowly starving to death. He kept an office in the White House basement but usually worked out of a cluttered bedroom suite—the Lincoln Bedroom—down the hall from FDR's.

When Bush met Hopkins, though the presidential aide was a liberal Democrat and the Carnegie president an admirer of Herbert Hoover and a self-styled Tory, "something meshed," writes Bush, "and we found we spoke the same language." Hopkins had a scheme for an Inventors Council. Bush countered with his more comprehensive National Defense Research Council. "Each of us was trying to sell something to the other." Bush won. Hopkins liked his plan.

In early June Bush made the rounds of Washington touching bases: the Army, the Navy, Congress, the National Academy of Sciences. On June

12 "Harry and I then went in to see the President. It was the first time I had met Franklin D. Roosevelt. . . . I had the plan for N.D.R.C. in four short paragraphs in the middle of a sheet of paper. The whole audience lasted less than ten minutes (Harry had no doubt been there before me). I came out with my 'OK-FDR' and all the wheels began to turn."

The National Defense Research Council immediately absorbed the Uranium Committee. That had been part of its purpose. Briggs was a cautious and frugal man, but his committee had also lacked the authority of a source of funds independent of the military. The white-haired director of the National Bureau of Standards would continue to be responsible for fission work. He would report now to James Bryant Conant, Harvard's wiry president, boyish in appearance but in practice cool and reserved, whom Bush had enlisted as soon as FDR authorized the new council.

The NDRC gave research in nuclear fission an articulate lobby within the executive branch. But though Bush and Conant felt challenged by German science—"the threat of a possible atomic bomb," writes Bush, "was in all our minds"—both men, concerned about scarce scientific resources, were initially more interested in proving the impossibility of such a weapon than in rushing to build one: the Germans could not do what could not be done. When Briggs wrapped up his pre-NDRC committee work in a report to Bush on July 1 he asked for \$140,000, \$40,000 of it for research on cross sections and other fundamental physical constants, \$100,000 for the Fermi-Szilard large-scale uranium-graphite experiment (the military had decided to grant \$100,000 on its own through the Naval Research Laboratory to isotope-separation studies). Bush allotted Briggs only the \$40,000. Once again Fermi and Szilard were left to bide their time.

Winston Churchill had accepted George VI's invitation to form a government upon Neville Chamberlain's resignation the day Germany invaded the Lowlands; he shouldered the prime ministership calmly but felt the somber weight of office. C. P. Snow recalls a more paradoxical mood:

> I remember—I shall not forget it while I live—the beautiful, cloudless, desperate summer of 1940. . . . Oddly enough, most of us were very happy in those days. There was a kind of collective euphoria over the whole country. I don't know what we were thinking about. We were very busy. We had a purpose. We were living in constant excitement, usually, if we examined the true position, of an unpromising kind. In one's realistic moments, it was difficult to see what chance we had. But I doubt if most of us had many realistic moments, or thought much at all. We were all working like mad. We were sustained by a surge of national emotion, of which Churchill was both symbol and essence, evocator and voice.

Not only native-born Englishmen felt that surge. So did the emigré scientists whom Britain had sheltered. Franz Simon, an outstanding chemist whom Frederick Lindemann had extracted from Germany in 1933 for the Clarendon, wrote his old friend Max Born on the eve of the Battle of France that he longed to "use my whole force in the struggle for this country." Though he may not yet have realized it, Simon's opportunity had already arrived. Early in the year, when Frisch and Peierls were first beginning to discuss the ideas that would lead to their important memoranda, Peierls had consulted Simon about methods of isotope separation. Frisch had chosen to work with gaseous thermal diffusion—his Clusius tube—because it seemed to him the simplest method, but Simon had begun then to think about other systems. Half a dozen approaches had been tried in the past. You couldn't spit on the floor without separating isotopes, Simon joked; the problem was to collect them. He wanted to find a method adaptable to mass production, because with a 1:139 isotope ratio, uranium separation would have to proceed on a vast scale, as Frisch's calculation of 100,000 Clusius tubes demonstrated. Frisch dramatized the difficulty with a simile: "It was like getting a doctor who had after great labour made a minute quantity of a new drug and then saying to him: 'Now we want enough to pave the streets.' "

The surge of national emotion sustained Mark Oliphant as well, and in that mood he found even less patience than usual for obstructive rules. When P. B. Moon questioned the assumption that gaseous thermal diffusion was the method of choice for isotope separation, he won no encouragement from the Thomson committee, but back in Birmingham Oliphant simply told him to go ahead and talk it over with Peierls. "Within a week or two," writes Moon, "Peierls identified ordinary diffusion as a logically superior process and wrote directly to Thomson on the matter." Peierls proposed that the Thomson committee consult with Simon, the best man around. The committee hesitated, even though Simon was a naturalized citizen. Oliphant then authorized Peierls out of hand to visit Simon at Oxford.

Simon in the meantime had been working to convert a skeptical Lindemann. At Simon's suggestion Peierls had written to Lindemann on June 2. Together at Oxford later in June they approached Lindemann in person. "I do not know him sufficiently well to translate his grunts correctly," Peierls reported of the meeting. But he felt sure he had "convinced him that the whole thing ought to be taken seriously."

Like Peierls, Simon had settled on "ordinary" gaseous diffusion (as opposed to gaseous *thermal* diffusion) as the best method of isotope separation after winnowing through the alternatives. Gases diffuse through porous materials at rates that are determined by their molecular weight, lighter gases diffusing faster than heavier gases. Francis Aston had applied this principle in 1913 when he separated two isotopes of neon by diffusing a mixed sample several thousand times over and over through pipe clay—that is, unglazed bisque of the sort used to make clay pipes. Thick materials like pipe clay worked too slowly to be effective at factory scale; Simon sought a more efficient mechanism and concluded that a metal foil punctured with millions of microscopic holes would work faster. Divide a cylinder down its length with such a foil barrier, pump a gas of mixed isotopes into one side of the divided cylinder, and gas would diffuse through the barrier as it flowed from one end of the cylinder to the other. Compared to the gas left behind, the gas that diffused through the barrier would be selectively enriched in lighter isotopes. In the case of uranium hexafluoride the enrichment factor would be slight, 1.0043 under ideal conditions. But with enough repetitions of the process any degree of enrichment was possible, up to nearly 100 percent.

The immediate problem, Simon saw, was barrier material. The smaller the holes, the higher the pressures a separation system could sustain, and the higher the pressure, the smaller the equipment could be. Whatever the material, it would have to resist corrosion by uranium hexafluoride—"hex," they were beginning to call it, not necessarily in tribute to its evil contrarities—or the gas would clog its microscopic pores.

One morning that June, inspired, Simon took a hammer to a wire strainer he found in his kitchen. He carried the results to the Clarendon and called together two of his assistants—a Hungarian, Nicholas Kurti, and a big Rhodes scholar from Idaho, H. S. Arms. "Arms, Kurti," Simon announced, holding up the strainer, "I think we can now separate the isotopes." He had hammered the wires flat in demonstration, reducing the spaces between to pinholes.

"The first thing we used," Kurti recalls, "was 'Dutch cloth,' as I think it is called—a very fine copper gauze which has many hundreds of holes to the inch." The assistants hammered the holes even finer by hand. They tested the copper barrier not with hex but with a mixture of water vapor and carbon dioxide, "in other words something much like ordinary sodawater"—the first in an urgent series of experiments carried out through the summer and fall to study materials, pore size, pressures and other basic parameters preliminary to any equipment design.

In late June G. P. Thomson gave his committee a new name to disguise its activities: MAUD. The initials appear to form an acronym but do not. They arrived as a mysterious word in a cable from Lise Meitner to an English friend: MET NIELS AND MARGRETHE RECENTLY BOTH WELL BUT UNHAPPY ABOUT EVENTS PLEASE INFORM COCKCROFT AND MAUD RAY KENT.

Meitner's friend passed the message to Cockcroft, who decided, he wrote Chadwick, that MAUD RAY KENT was "an anagram for 'radium taken.' This agrees with other information that the Germans are getting hold of all the radium they can." Thomson borrowed the first word of Cockcroft's mysterious anagram for a suitably misleading name. The committee members did not learn until 1943 that Maud Ray was the governess who had taught Bohr's sons English; she lived in Kent.

The war crossed the Channel first in the air. As a result of the German bombing of Warsaw in the autumn of 1939, an act Germany represented as tactical because the Polish city was heavily fortified, the British Air Ministry had repudiated its pledge to refrain from strategic bombing. But neither belligerent was eager to exchange bombing raids, and although nightly blackouts added inconvenience and apprehension to the wartime burden of the people of both nations, the implicit truce held until mid-May 1940. Then within a week two events triggered British action. German raiders targeted for French airfields at Dijon lost their way and bombed the southern German city of Freiburg instead, killing fifty-seven people; the German Ministry of Propaganda brazenly denounced the bombing as British or French and threatened fivefold retaliation. Blacker and more violent non sequitur destroyed the city center of Rotterdam. Dutch forces were holding out stubbornly as late as May 14 in the northern section of that old Netherlands port. The German commanding general ordered a "short but devastating air raid" that he hoped might decide the battle. Negotiations with the Dutch advanced, the air raid was canceled, but the abort message arrived too late to stop half the hundred Heinkel 111's ordered into action from dropping 94 tons of bombs. The bombs started massive fires in stores of fats and margarine. The first official Dutch statement, issued from the embassy in Washington, placed casualties in the devastated city at 30,000, and the Western democracies responded with outrage. Actual deaths totaled about 1,000; some 78,000 people went homeless.

The British retaliated on May 15 by dispatching ninety-nine bombers to attack railway centers and supply depots in the Ruhr. Busy with the Battle of France, Hitler did not immediately strike back, but he issued a directive that prepared the way. He ordered the Luftwaffe "to undertake a full-scale offensive against the British homeland as soon as sufficient forces are available."

The initial German air attack, the Battle of Britain, began in mid-August: a month of ferocious daylight contests between the Luftwaffe and British Fighter Command for air supremacy in advance of Operation Sea Lion, Germany's planned cross-Channel invasion. It was not yet an attack on cities. British airfields and aircraft factories were primary targets. Hitler had reserved for himself the decision to bomb London, just as the Kaiser had done before him. Cities would soon go on the targeting list, however; the Luftwaffe was scheduled to raid Liverpool at night on August 28. Accident again intervened: German bombers aiming for oil storage tanks along the Thames overflew their targets on August 24 and bombed central London instead.

Churchill immediately retaliated, hurling four bombing raids in one week at Berlin. They accomplished little physical damage but incited Hitler to hysterical revenge:

> And if the British air force drops two or three or four thousand kilograms of bombs, then we will drop in a single night 150,000, 180,000, 230,000, 300,000, 400,000, a million kilograms. If they announce that they will attack our cities on a large scale, then we shall wipe their cities out!

The Luftwaffe was losing the Battle of Britain in any case, taking unacceptable losses—some 1,700 German aircraft compared to about 900 British. Night bombing would alleviate the losses, curtaining the bombers in dark asylum. But night bombing was notably less accurate than daylight bombing in those days before effective radar and required correspondingly larger targets. Cities and their civilian populations thus fell victim partly by default, because the technology necessary for more accurate targeting was not yet at hand. In any case terror was a weapon that Hitler especially prized, the destruction of what he called the enemy's "will-to-resist," and early in September he told his Sea Lion planners that "a systematic and long-drawn-out bombardment of London might produce an attitude in the enemy which will make Sea Lion unnecessary." He ordered the bombardment. Since it rained from the skies for months, it was hardly *Blitzkrieg,* lightning war, but the citizens exposed beneath it were not in the mood for fine distinctions, and they soon named it the Blitz.

Gresham's Law operated with air raid shelters as it operates with good and bad money: the basements of better department stores like Dickens and Jones, where clerks carried around refreshments—chocolates and ice cream—filled up first. Because the bombing followed regularly, night after night, Londoners had time to get used to it, but adjustment could go either way, the confident beginner slowly unraveling, the frightened beginner moving beyond fear.

More Londoners by far lived out the dangerous raids in their homes than in shelters: 27 percent fled to corrugated-iron Anderson shelters in back gardens, 9 percent to street shelters, only 4 percent into the Tube. By mid-November 13,700 tons of high explosives had fallen and 12,600 tons of incendiary canisters, an average of 201 tons per night; for the entire Blitz, September to May, the total tonnage reached 18,800—18.8 kilotons by modern measure, spread across nine months. London civilian deaths in 1940 and 1941 totaled 20,083, civilian deaths elsewhere in Britain 23,602, for a total death by Blitz in the second and third year of the war (about which the United States was still officially neutral) of 43,685. After that the bombing went the other way. Only twenty-seven Londoners lost their lives to bombs in 1942.

At Oxford in December 1940, Franz Simon, now officially working for the MAUD Committee, produced a report nearly as crucial to the future of uranium-bomb development as the original Frisch-Peierls memoranda had been. It was titled "Estimate of the size of an actual separation plant." Its aim, Simon wrote, was "to provide data for the size and costs of a plant which separates 1 kg per day of ^{235}U from the natural product." He estimated such a plant would cost about £5,000,000 and outlined its necessities in careful detail.

Simon had never trusted the mails. He trusted them even less at the height of the Blitz. He duplicated some forty copies of his report, accumulated enough rationed gasoline for a round trip and shortly before Christmas drove from Oxford into bomb-threatened London to deliver the fruit of half a year's hard work, his whole force in the struggle for his country, to G. P. Thomson.

The Germans may have been collecting radium, as Cockcroft thought MAUD RAY KENT signaled. They were certainly laying in industrial stocks of uranium. In June 1940, about the time Simon was hammering out his kitchen strainer, Auer ordered sixty tons of refined uranium oxide from the Union Minière in occupied Belgium. Paul Harteck in Hamburg tried that month to measure neutron multiplication in an ingenious arrangement of uranium oxide and dry ice—frozen carbon dioxide, a source of carbon free from any impurity other than oxygen—but was unable to convince Heisenberg to lend him enough uranium to guarantee unambiguous results. Heisenberg had larger plans. He had allied himself with von Weizsäcker at the KWI. In July they began designing a wooden laboratory building to be constructed on the grounds of the Kaiser Wilhelm Institute for Biology and Virus Research, next to the physics institute. To discourage the curious they named the building the Virus House. They intended to build a subcritical uranium burner there.

Germany had access to the world's only heavy-water factory and to thousands of tons of uranium ore in Belgium and the Belgian Congo. It had chemical plants second to none and competent physicists, chemists and engineers. It lacked only a cyclotron for measuring nuclear constants. The Fall of France—Paris was occupied June 14, an armistice signed June 22—filled that need. Kurt Diebner, the War Office's resident nuclear physics expert, rushed to Paris. Perrin, von Halban and Kowarski, he found, had escaped to England and taken Allier's twenty-six cans of heavy water with them, but Joliot had chosen to remain in France. (The French laureate would become president of the Directing Committee of the National Front, the largest Resistance organization of the war.)

German officers interrogated Joliot at length when he returned to his laboratory after the occupation began. Their interpreter, sent along from Heidelberg, turned out to be Wolfgang Gentner, the former Radium Institute student who had confirmed that Joliot's Geiger counter was working properly when Joliot discovered artificial radioactivity in 1933. Gentner arranged a secret meeting one evening at a student café and warned Joliot that the cyclotron he was building might be seized and shipped to Germany. Rather than allow that outrage Joliot negotiated a compromise: the cyclotron would stay but German physicists could use it for purely scientific experiments; Joliot would be allowed in turn to continue as laboratory director.

The Virus House was finished in October. Besides a laboratory the structure contained a special brick-lined pit, six feet deep, a variant of Fermi's water tank for neutron-multiplication studies. By December Heisenberg and von Weizsäcker had prepared the first of several such experiments. With water in the pit to serve as both reflector and radiation shield they lowered down a large aluminum canister packed with alternating layers of uranium oxide and paraffin. A radium-beryllium source in the center of the canister supplied neutrons, but the German physicists were able to measure no neutron multiplication at all. The experiment confirmed what Fermi and Szilard had already demonstrated: that ordinary hydrogen, whether in the form of water or paraffin, would not work with natural uranium to sustain a chain reaction.

That understanding left the German project with two possible moderator materials: graphite and heavy water. In January a misleading measurement reduced that number to one. At Heidelberg Walther Bothe, an exceptional experimentalist who would eventually share a Nobel Prize with Max Born, measured the absorption cross section of carbon using a 3.6-foot sphere of high-quality graphite submerged in a tank of water. He found a cross section of 6.4×10^{-27} cm^2, more than twice Fermi's value, and concluded that graphite, like ordinary water, would absorb too many neutrons to sustain a chain reaction in natural uranium. Von Halban and Kowarski, now at Cambridge and in contact with the MAUD Committee, similarly overestimated the carbon cross section—the graphite in both experiments was probably contaminated with neutron-absorbing impurities such as boron—but their work was eventually checked against Fermi's. Bothe could make no such check. The previous fall Szilard had assaulted Fermi with another secrecy appeal:

> When [Fermi] finished his [carbon absorption] measurement the question of secrecy again came up. I went to his office and said that now that we had this value perhaps the value ought not to be made public. And this time Fermi really lost his temper; he really thought this was absurd. There was nothing much more I could say, but next time when I dropped in his office he told me that Pegram had come to see him, and Pegram thought that this value should not be published. From that point the secrecy was on.

It was on just in time to prevent German researchers from pursuing a cheap, effective moderator. Bothe's measurement ended German experiments on graphite. Nothing in the record indicates the overestimate was deliberate, but it is worth noting that Walther Bothe, a protégé of Max Planck, had been hounded from the directorship of the physics institute of the University of Heidelberg in 1933 because he was anti-Nazi. "These galling fights so affected my health," he wrote later in a brief unpublished memoir, "that I had to spend a long period in a Badenweiler sanitorium." When Bothe was well again Planck appointed him to the Kaiser Wilhelm Society's Heidelberg physics institute, but "the Nazis continued to harass me, even to the accusation of scientific fraud."

At nearly the same time—early 1941—Harteck learned at Hamburg what Otto Frisch had recently learned at Liverpool. Frisch had moved to the industrial port city in the northwest of England to work with Chadwick and Chadwick's cyclotron. He built a Clusius tube there with a student assistant Chadwick assigned him—they moved in such energetic coordination through the laboratory that they won the nickname "Frisch and Chips"—and discovered, says Frisch, that "uranium hexafluoride is one of the gases for which the Clusius method does not work." The discovery set the British program back not at all, since Simon was already hard at work on gaseous barrier diffusion. But the German researchers had placed such faith in thermal diffusion that they had not bothered to develop alternatives. They quickly began doing so and identified several promising methods; oddly enough, barrier diffusion was not among them. Restudying the separation problem made it even clearer that U235 and U238 could only be separated by brute-force methods and at great expense.

When Harteck reported to the War Office in March 1941, following a conference with his colleagues, he stressed their consensus that isotope separation would be feasible "only for special applications in which cheapness is but a secondary consideration." Only for a bomb, he meant—so he told the historian David Irving after the war. The German physicists gave "special applications" second place on their list; they recommended urgent work first of all on the production of heavy water. Like Fermi and Szilard, they opted initially for a slow-neutron chain reaction in natural uranium. Make that reaction work and "special applications" might follow. Knowing no more than they knew, they hardly had a choice.

Lieutenant Colonel Suzuki reported back to Lieutenant General Yasuda in October 1940. He confined his report to a basic issue: the availability to Japan of uranium deposits. He looked beyond Japan to Korea and Burma and concluded that his country had access to sufficient uranium. A bomb was therefore possible.

Yasuda turned then to the director of Japan's Physical and Chemical Research Institute, who passed the problem on to his country's leading physicist, Yoshio Nishina. Nishina, born late in the Meiji era and fifty years old in 1940, known for theoretical work on the Compton Effect, had studied with Niels Bohr in Copenhagen, where he was remembered as a cosmopolitan and exceptional man. He had built a small cyclotron at his Tokyo laboratory, the Riken, and with help from an assistant who had trained at Berkeley was building in 1940 a 60-inch successor with a 250-ton magnet, the plans for which had been donated by Ernest Lawrence. More than one hundred young Japanese scientists, the cream of the crop, worked under Nishina at the Riken; to them he was *Oyabun,* "the old man," and he ran his laboratory Western-style with warmth and informality.

The Riken began measuring cross sections in December. In April 1941 the official order came through: the Imperial Army Air Force authorized research toward the development of an atomic bomb.

Leo Szilard was known by now throughout the American physics community as the leading apostle of secrecy in fission matters. To his mailbox, late in May 1940, came a puzzled note from a Princeton physicist, Louis A. Turner. Turner had written a Letter to the Editor of the *Physical Review,* a copy of which he enclosed. It was entitled "Atomic energy from U^{238}" and he wondered if it should be withheld from publication. "It seems as if it was wild enough speculation so that it could do no possible harm," Turner told Szilard, "but that is for someone else to say."

Turner had published a masterly twenty-nine-page review article on nuclear fission in the January *Reviews of Modern Physics* citing nearly one hundred papers that had appeared since Hahn and Strassmann reported their discovery twelve months earlier; the number of papers indicates the impact of the discovery on physics and the rush of physicists to explore it. Turner had also noted the recent Nier/Columbia report confirming the attribution of slow-neutron fission to U235. (He could hardly have missed it; the *New York Times* and other newspapers publicized the story widely. He wrote Szilard irritably or ingenuously that he found it "a little difficult to figure out the guiding principle [of keeping fission research secret] in view of the recent ample publicity given to the separation of isotopes.") His reading for the review article and the new Columbia measurements had stimulated him to further thought; the result was his *Physical Review* letter.

Since U235 is responsible for slow-neutron fission, the letter pointed out, and ordinary uranium contains only one part in 140 of that isotope, "it is natural to conclude that only 1/140 of any quantity of U can be considered as a possible source of atomic energy if slow neutrons are to be used." But the truth may be otherwise, Turner went on. The fission energy of most of the U238, if it could not be used directly, might yet find indirect release.

Turner was referring to the possibility that bombarding uranium with neutrons converted some of the uranium to transuranic elements, the transuranics that Bohr had hoped might have been banished by the discovery of fission. When an atom of U238 captured a neutron it became the isotope U239. That substance itself might fission, Turner suggested. But whether or not U239 did so, it was energetically unstable and would probably decay by beta emission to new elements heavier than uranium. And one or more of those new elements might be fissionable by slow neutrons—which would thereby indirectly put U238 to work.

The next element up the periodic table from uranium would be element 93. Turner selected as the likeliest candidate for fission not ${}_{93}X^{239}$, however, but the element next along, the element that 93 would probably decay to, ${}_{94}X^{239}$, which he called "eka-osmium."* And ${}_{94}\text{EkaOs}^{239}$, Turner proposed, changing from an odd to an even number of neutrons when it absorbed a neutron preparatory to fissioning (239 nucleons − 94 protons = 145 neutrons + 1 = 146) just as U235 changed to U236, ought to be even more fissionable than the lighter uranium isotope: "In ${}_{94}\text{EkaOs}^{240}$ . . . the excess energy would be even larger than in ${}_{92}U^{236}$ and a large cross section for fission would be expected."

* Although Bohr had speculated many years earlier that the transuranic elements, if any, would probably be chemically similar to uranium, researchers still commonly assumed that the transuranics would be chemically similar to the series of metals in the periodic table that begins with rhenium and osmium and includes platinum and gold. "Eka" is an old prefix meaning "beyond."

While Turner was thinking these theories through, two Berkeley men, Edwin M. McMillan and Philip M. Abelson, were moving independently toward demonstrating them. McMillan, a slim, freckled, California-born experimentalist, had been one of the men most responsible in the 1930s for improving Ernest Lawrence's cyclotrons to the point where they worked steadily and produced reliable results. Soon after the news of the discovery of fission reached Berkeley in late January 1939 he had devised an elegantly simple experiment to explore the phenomenon. "When a nucleus of uranium absorbs a neutron and fission takes place," McMillan told an audience later, "the two resulting fragments fly apart with great violence, sufficient to propel them through the air, or other matter, for some distance. This distance, called the 'range,' is a quantity of some interest, and I undertook to measure it." He did so first with thin sheets of aluminum foil "like the pages of a book" stacked on a layer of uranium oxide backed with filter paper. He bombarded the uranium with slow neutrons. Some of the fission fragments recoiled up into the stack of foils; each fragment embedded itself in a single sheet of foil at the end of its range, which depended on its mass; McMillan could then simply check successive sheets of foil in an ionization chamber, look for the characteristic half-lives of various fission products and read out the range (the uranium nucleus splits in many different ways, producing many different lighter-element nuclei).

But aluminum itself is activated by neutron bombardment, which made half-life measurements difficult. So McMillan replaced the foils with a stack of cigarette papers previously treated with acid to remove any trace of minerals that might develop radioactivity under bombardment. "Nothing very interesting about the fission fragments came out of this," he comments. The uranium coating on the filter paper under the stack of cigarette papers, on the other hand, "showed something very interesting." It showed two half-life activities different from those of the fission products that had recoiled away. And since whatever had remained in the uranium layer had not recoiled, the two different activities were probably not fission products. They were probably radioactivities induced in the uranium by captured neutrons. McMillan suspected that one of the two activities, the one with a half-life of 23 minutes, was one that Hahn, Meitner and Strassmann had identified in the 1930s as U239, "a uranium isotope produced by resonance neutron capture." The other activity left behind in the uranium layer had a longer half-life, about 2 days. In his report on his foil and cigarette-paper experiments McMillan chose not to speculate on what that second activity might be, but privately, he remembers, he thought "the two-day period could . . . be the product of the beta-decay of U-239, and therefore an isotope of [transuranic] element 93; in fact, this was the most reasonable explanation."

To check that explanation McMillan needed some hint of the substance's chemical identity. He expected that element 93 would behave chemically like the metal rhenium, element 75, next to osmium on the periodic table—would be "eka-rhenium" in the old terminology. He bombarded a larger uranium sample and enlisted the aid of Emilio Segrè, who was now working as a research associate at Berkeley. "Segrè was very familiar with the chemistry of [rhenium], since he and his co-workers [studying rhenium] had discovered [a similar element], now called technetium, in 1937." Segrè began a chemical analysis of the irradiated uranium; in the meantime McMillan sharpened his half-life measurement to 2.3 days. Segrè, says McMillan, "showed that the 2.3-day material had none of the properties of rhenium, and indeed acted like a rare earth instead." The rare earths, elements 57 (lanthanum) to 71 (lutetium), form a chemically closely related and odd series between barium and hafnium. Because of their middle-table atomic weights near barium, they often turn up as fission products. When Segrè found the 2.3-day activity acting not like rhenium, as expected, but like a rare earth, McMillan assumed that was what it was: "Since rare earths are prominent among the fission products, this discovery seemed at the time to end the story." Segrè even published a paper on his work titled "An unsuccessful search for transuranic elements."

McMillan might have left it there, but the fact that the 2.3-day substance did not recoil away from the uranium layer nagged at him. "As time went on and the fission process became better understood, I found it increasingly difficult to believe that one fission product should behave in a way so different from the rest, and early in 1940 I returned to the problem." The 60-inch cyclotron, with a massive rectangular-framed magnet spacious enough to shelter Lawrence's entire crew between its poles for a photograph—twenty-seven men, two rows seated on the lower jaw of the beast, Lawrence prominent at center, and a third row standing inside its maw—was up and running by then; McMillan used it to study the 2.3-day activity in more detail. He studied the activity chemically as well and managed the significant observation that it did not always fractionally crystallize out of solution as a rare earth would.

"By now it was the spring of 1940," McMillan continues, "and Dr. Philip Abelson came to Berkeley for a short vacation." Abelson was the young experimentalist for whose benefit Luis Alvarez had vacated his Berkeley barber chair half-shorn to pass along the news of the discovery of fission. He had finished his Berkeley Ph.D. and signed on with Merle Tuve at the DTM. Like McMillan, he had become suspicious of the conclusion that the 2.3-day activity was merely another rare-earth fission product. He found time in April 1940 to begin sorting out its chemistry—although he was a physicist by graduate training, he had earned his B.S. in chemistry at

Washington State. But he needed a bigger sample of bombarded uranium than he could produce with DTM equipment. "When he arrived for his vacation," says McMillan, "and our mutual interest became known to one another, we decided to work together." McMillan made up a new batch of irradiated uranium. Abelson pursued its chemistry.

"Within a day," Abelson recalls, "I established that the 2.3-day activity had chemical properties different from those of any known element. . . . [It] behaved much like uranium." Apparently the transuranics were not metals like rhenium and osmium but were part of a new series of rare-earth-like elements similar to uranium. For a rigorous proof that they had found a transuranic the two men isolated a pure uranium sample with strong 23-minute U239 activity and demonstrated with half-life measurements that the 2.3-day activity increased in intensity as the 23-minute activity declined. If the 2.3-day activity was different chemically from any other element and was created in the decay of U239, then it must be element 93. McMillan and Abelson wrote up their results. McMillan had already thought of a name for the new element—neptunium, for the next planet out beyond Uranus—but they chose not to offer the name in their report. They mailed the report, "Radioactive element 93," to the *Physical Review* on May 27, 1940, the same day Louis Turner sent Szilard his transuranic theories: anticipation and discovery can cut that close in science.

Presumably Szilard did not yet know of the Berkeley work (published June 15) when he answered Turner's letter on May 30, since he makes no mention of it, but he recognized the logic of Turner's argument, told him "it might eventually turn out to be a very important contribution"—and proposed he keep it secret. Szilard saw beyond what Turner had seen. He saw that a fissile element bred in uranium could be chemically separated away: that the relatively easy and relatively inexpensive process of chemical separation could replace the horrendously difficult and expensive process of physical separation of isotopes as a way to a bomb. But unstable element 93, neptunium, was not yet that fissile element and Szilard did not yet realize how small a quantity of pure fissile material was needed to make a critical mass. (Turner was first with his observation, but he was not alone. The idea occurred independently to von Weizsäcker one day in July, before the June *Physical Review* reached him in Germany with the McMillan-Abelson news, while he was riding the Berlin subway, though he assumed element 93 would do the job; he offered the idea to the War Office in a five-page report. A British team at the Cavendish worked it out and presented it to the MAUD Committee early in 1941. But the Germans thought only heavy water could make a uranium burner go in which the new elements might breed, and the British had become optimistic about isotope separation. Neither group therefore pursued the Turner approach.)

After Abelson returned to Washington, McMillan pressed on. Unstable neptunium decayed by beta emission with a 2.3-day half-life; he suspected it decayed to element 94. By analogy with uranium, which emits alpha particles naturally, element 94 should also be a natural alpha emitter. McMillan therefore looked for alphas with ranges different from the uranium alphas coming off his mixed uranium-neptunium samples. By autumn he had identified them. He tried some chemical separations, "finding that the alpha-activity did not belong to an isotope of protactinium, uranium or neptunium." He was that close.

But American science, spurred on by British appeals, was finally gearing up for war. Churchill had sent over Henry Tizard in the late summer of 1940 with a delegation of experts and a black-enameled metal steamer trunk, the original black box, full of military secrets. The prize specimen among them was the cavity magnetron developed in Mark Oliphant's laboratory at Birmingham. John Cockcroft, a future Nobel laureate with a vital mission, traveled along to explain the high-powered microwave generator. The Americans had never seen anything like it before. Cockcroft got together one weekend in October with Ernest Lawrence and multimillionaire physicist-financier Alfred Loomis, the last of the gentlemen scientists, at Loomis' private laboratory in the elegant suburban New York colony of Tuxedo Park. That meeting laid the groundwork for a major new NDRC laboratory at MIT. To keep its work secret it was named the Radiation Laboratory, as if serious scientists might actually be pursuing applications so dubious as those bruited by visionaries from nuclear physics. Loomis wanted Lawrence to direct the new laboratory. Lawrence preferred to stay at Berkeley laying plans and raising funds for a new 184-inch cyclotron but was willing to encourage his best people to move to Cambridge. He convinced McMillan: "I left Berkeley in November 1940 to take part in the development of radar for national defense." Lawrence's and McMillan's priorities are a measure of the priorities of American science in late 1940. Peacetime cyclotrons and radar for air defense came first before superbombs. With a different perspective on the matter, James Chadwick at Liverpool was so uncharacteristically incensed by the publication of the McMillan-Abelson paper reporting element 93 that he asked for, and got, an official protest through the British Embassy. An attaché was duly dispatched to Berkeley to scold Ernest Lawrence, the 1939 Nobel laureate in physics, for giving away secrets to the Germans in perilous times.

Laura and Enrico Fermi and their two children had moved from a Manhattan apartment in the summer of 1939 across the George Washington Bridge and beyond the Palisades to the pleasant suburb of Leonia, New

Jersey. Harold Urey, a short, intense, enthusiastic man, was a resident along with other Columbia families and had convinced the Fermis to buy a house there, praising Leonia's "excellent public schools," Laura writes, and extolling "the advantages of living in a middle-class town where one's children may have all that other children have." Among much good advice Urey cautioned the Italian couple to wage eternal war on crabgrass. Fermi was a product of Roman apartments; he quickly identified *Digitaria sanguinalis* neutrally as "an unlicensed annual" and chose to ignore it. Laura prepared to do battle but was unable to distinguish crabgrass from sod. Urey dropped by one day to give her counsel and identified the problem. "D'you know what's wrong with your lawn, Laura?" the chemistry laureate asked her compassionately. "It's *all* crab grass." Life was pleasant in Leonia; Fermi practiced fitting in. Segrè remembers that his friend "purposely studied contemporary Americana and read the comic strips. . . . Among adult immigrants, I have never seen a comparably earnest effort toward Americanization."

Segrè traveled to Indiana toward the end of 1940 to interview at Purdue, perfunctory interviewing because he meant to stay at Berkeley—"the machine was so good, I could do these things that nowhere else could I do." He continued eastward to visit the Fermis in Leonia. Independently of Turner, Segrè recalls, both he and Fermi had been thinking about element 94. On December 15, he writes, "we had a long walk along the Hudson, in freezing weather, during which we spoke of the possibility that the isotope of mass 239 of element 94 . . . might be a slow neutron fissioner. If this proved to be true, [it] could substitute for ^{235}U as a nuclear explosive. Furthermore, a nuclear reactor fueled with ordinary uranium would produce [the new element]. This gave an entirely new perspective on the making of nuclear explosives, eliminating the need to separate uranium isotopes, at that time a truly scary problem."

Lawrence happened to be visiting New York. "Fermi, Lawrence, Pegram and I met in Dean Pegram's office at Columbia University and developed plans for a cyclotron irradiation that could produce a sufficient amount of [element 94]." After Christmas Segrè returned to Berkeley.

A young chemist there, Glenn T. Seaborg, had already begun working toward identifying and isolating element 94. Born in Michigan of Swedish-American parents, Seaborg had grown up in Los Angeles and taken his Ph.D. at Berkeley in chemistry in 1937, when he was twenty-five. He was exceptionally tall, thin, guarded in the Swedish way but gifted and comfortable at work. The published record of Otto Hahn's 1933 Cornell lectures, *Applied Radiochemistry,* had been his guidebook in graduate school: radiochemistry was his passion. He had been practicing it at Berkeley in

January 1939 when the news of fission arrived; like Philip Abelson, he was excited by the discovery and chagrined to have missed it and had walked the streets for hours the night he heard.

As early as the end of August he had bombarded a sample of uranium to produce neptunium and had assigned one of his second-year graduate students, Arthur C. Wahl, to study its chemistry. His other collaborator in the search for 94 was Joseph W. Kennedy, like Seaborg a Berkeley chemistry instructor. By late November the group had progressed through four more bombardments, unraveling enough of neptunium's chemistry to devise techniques for isolating highly purified samples. Seaborg then wrote McMillan at MIT, a letter he summarizes in a careful history he wrote later that he cast as a contemporary diary: "I suggested that since he has now left Berkeley . . . and is therefore not in a position to continue this work [of studying neptunium and looking for element 94], that we would be very glad to carry on in his absence as his collaborators." McMillan acceded in mid-December; by the time Segrè returned to Berkeley Seaborg had separated out significant fractions of material from his bombarded samples, including uranium, fission products, purified neptunium and a rare-earth fraction that might contain 94.

Two searches were thus to proceed simultaneously. Seaborg's team would follow one especially intense alpha emitter it had identified in the hope of demonstrating that it was an isotope of 94, chemically different from all other known elements. At the same time, Segrè and Seaborg would produce neptunium 239 in quantity, look for its decay product (which ought to be 94^{239}) and attempt to measure that substance's fissibility.

Segrè and Seaborg bombarded ten grams of a solid uranium compound, uranyl nitrate hexahydrate (UNH), for six hours in the 60-inch cyclotron on January 9. They bombarded five more grams for an hour the next morning. By afternoon they knew from ionization-chamber measurements that they could make 94 by cyclotron bombardment; one kilogram of UNH, they calculated, suitably irradiated, should produce about 0.6 microgram (one millionth of a gram) from neptunium after allowing time for beta decay.

Seaborg's team identified an alpha-emitting daughter of Np238 on January 20. Definitive proof that it was 94 required chemical separation, and that delicate, tedious work proceeded during February. The crucial breakthrough came at the beginning of a week when everyone routinely labored past midnight to pursue the difficult fractionations to their end. On Sunday afternoon, February 23, Wahl discovered he could precipitate the alpha emitter from acid solution using thorium as a carrier. But he was not then able to separate the alpha emitter from the thorium. He talked to a

Berkeley chemistry professor who suggested using a more powerful oxidizing agent.

That evening Seaborg and Segrè began bombarding 1.2 kilograms of UNH in the 60-inch cyclotron to transmute some of its uranium into neptunium. They packed the UNH into glass tubes, set the tubes in holes drilled into a 10-inch block of paraffin and set the paraffin in a wooden box. Then they arranged the wooden box behind the beryllium target of the big cyclotron, which battered copious quantities of neutrons from the beryllium with powerful 16 MeV deuterons—favorite cyclotron projectiles, deuterium nuclei from heavy water. With the UNH in place in the cyclotron Seaborg climbed the stairs to the third floor of Gilman Hall where Wahl brewed fractionations under the roof in a cramped room relieved by a small balcony. Wahl tried the new oxidation chemistry that evening with Seaborg at his side. It worked; the thorium precipitated from solution and the alpha emitter stayed behind, enough of it to read out about 300 kicks per minute on the linear amplifier. That, writes Seaborg, was the "key step in its discovery," but they still needed a precipitate of the alpha emitter and they pushed on through the night. Seaborg remembers noticing the new day—lightning over San Francisco to the west across the Bay—when he stepped out onto the balcony to clear his lungs of fumes. Working again past midnight on Tuesday, Wahl filtered out a precipitate cleared of thorium. "With this final separation from Th," Seaborg records with emphasis, "it has been demonstrated that our alpha activity can be separated from all known elements and thus it is now clear that our *alpha activity is due to the new element with the atomic number 94.*"

The bombardment of Segrè's and Seaborg's kilogram sample, interrupted from time to time by other experiments that commanded the cyclotron, continued for a week. The UNH was rendered more intensely radioactive; the radioactivity would increase dangerously as they concentrated the Np239 they had made. They began working with goggles and lead shielding, dissolving the uranium first in two liters of ether and then proceeding through a series of laborious precipitations.

Their fifth and sixth reprecipitations they finished on Thursday, March 6. From 1.2 kilograms of UNH they had now separated less than a millionth of a gram of pure Np239 mixed with sufficient carrier to stain a miniature platinum dish that measured two-thirds of an inch across and half an inch deep. When they had dried this speck of matter God had not welcomed at the Creation they simply snipped off the sides of the platinum dish, covered the sample with a protective layer of Duco Cement, glued the dish to a piece of cardboard labeled Sample A and set it aside until it decayed completely to 94^{239}.

On Friday, March 28 (of the week when Field Marshal Erwin Rommel, commander of the Afrika Korps, opened a major offensive in North Africa; when the British meat ration was reduced to six ounces per person per week; when British torpedo bombers successfully attacked the Italian fleet as it returned from the Aegean, a performance that greatly interested the Japanese), Seaborg recorded:

> This morning Kennedy, Segrè and I made our first test for the fissionability of 94^{239} using Sample A. . . .
>
> Kennedy has constructed during the past few weeks a portable ionization chamber and linear amplifier suitable for detecting fission pulses. . . . Sample A (estimated to contain 0.25 micrograms of 94^{239}) was placed near the screened window of the ionization chamber embedded in paraffin near the beryllium target of the 37-inch cyclotron. The neutrons produced by the irradiation of the beryllium target with 8 MeV deuterons give a fission rate of 1 count per minute per microampere. When the ionization chamber is surrounded by a cadmium shield, the fission rate drops to essentially zero. . . .
>
> *This gives strong indications that 94^{239} undergoes fission with slow neutrons.*

Not until 1942 would they officially propose a name for the new element that fissioned like U235 but could be chemically separated from uranium. But Seaborg already knew what he would call it. Consistent with Martin Klaproth's inspiration in 1789 to link his discovery of a new element with the recent discovery of the planet Uranus and with McMillan's suggestion to extend the scheme to Neptune, Seaborg would name element 94 for Pluto, the ninth planet outward from the sun, discovered in 1930 and named for the Greek god of the underworld, a god of the earth's fertility but also the god of the dead: *plutonium.*

Frisch and Peierls had calculated a small U235 critical mass on the basis of sensible theory. Through the winter Merle Tuve's group at the DTM had continued to refine its cross-section measurements; in March Tuve was able to send to England a measured U235 fast-fission cross section that the British used to confirm a critical mass somewhat larger than the Frisch-Peierls estimate: about eighteen pounds untamped, nine or ten pounds surrounded by a suitably massive and reflective tamper. "This first test of theory," Peierls wrote triumphantly that month, "has given a completely positive answer and there is no doubt that the whole scheme is feasible (provided the technical problems of isotope separation are satisfactorily solved) and that the critical size for a U sphere is manageable."

Chadwick had also made further cross-section measurements. He was already a sober man; when he saw the new numbers a more intense sobriety seized him. He described the change in 1969 in an interview:

> I remember the spring of 1941 to this day. I realized then that a nuclear bomb was not only possible—it was inevitable. Sooner or later these ideas could not be peculiar to us. Everybody would think about them before long, and some country would put them into action. And I had nobody to talk to. You see, the chief people in the laboratory were Frisch and [Polish experimental physicist Joseph] Rotblat. However high my opinion of them was, they were not citizens of this country, and the others were quite young boys. And there was nobody to talk to about it. I had many sleepless nights. But I did realize how very very serious it could be. And I had then to start taking sleeping pills. It was the only remedy. I've never stopped since then. It's 28 years, and I don't think I've missed a single night in all those 28 years.

12

A Communication from Britain

James Bryant Conant traveled to London in the winter of 1941 to open a liaison office between the British government and the National Defense Research Council. Conant was the first American scientist of administrative rank to visit the beleaguered nation following the ad hoc exchanges of the Tizard Mission and he came to count the trip "the most extraordinary experience of my life." "I was hailed as a messenger of hope," he writes in his autobiography. "I saw a stouthearted population under bombardment. I saw an unflinching government with its back against the wall. Almost every hour I saw or heard something that made me proud to be a member of the human race."

The Harvard president, who would be forty-seven late in March, was welcomed not only because of his university affiliation or his distinction as a member of the NDRC. He had been an outspoken opponent of American isolationism during the long months of the phony war and was therefore welcomed especially as a sign—with only the Prime Minister dissenting. Churchill was less than delighted at the prospect of lunching with the president of Harvard. "What shall I talk to him about?" he was heard to ask. "He thought you would be an old man with a white beard, exuding learning and academic formality," Brendon Bracken, Churchill's aide, told Conant afterward. But braced by the American's belligerently pro-British views and put at ease by the tweed suit he chose to wear, the Prime Minister eventually warmed over lunch in the bomb-shelter basement at 10 Downing Street, proffering a Churchillian monologue during which he repeated one of his choicer recent coinages: "Give us the tools, and we will finish the job."

In 1920, at twenty-seven, when Conant was courting the woman he would marry—she was the only child of the Nobel laureate Harvard chemist T. W. Richards, a pioneer in measuring atomic weights—he had shared hopes for a grand future with her that coming from a less able man might have sounded absurd. "I said that I had three ambitions. The first was to become the leading organic chemist in the United States; after that I would like to be president of Harvard; and after that, a Cabinet member, perhaps Secretary of the Interior." Those may not seem conjoint ambitions, but Conant managed a version of each in turn. He was born of a Massachusetts family that had resided in the state since 1623. After Roxbury Latin and Harvard College he had taken a double Ph.D. under his future father-in-law in organic and physical chemistry. He emerged from the Great War with the rank of major for his work in poison-gas research at Edgewood. In his autobiography, written late in life, he justified his participation:

> I did not see in 1917, and do not see in 1968, why tearing a man's guts out by a high-explosive shell is to be preferred to maiming him by attacking his lungs or skin. All war is immoral. Logically, the 100 percent pacifist has the only impregnable position. Once that is abandoned, as it is when a nation becomes a belligerent, one can talk sensibly only in terms of the violation of agreements about the way war is conducted, or the consequences of a certain tactic or weapon.

Like Vannevar Bush, Conant was a patriot who believed in the application of advanced technology to war.

"Conant achieved an international reputation in both natural products chemistry and in physical-organic chemistry," writes the Ukrainian-born Harvard chemist George B. Kistiakowsky. Natural products include chlorophyll and hemoglobin and Conant contributed to the unraveling of both those vital molecules. His studies also helped generalize the concept of acids and bases, a concept now considered fundamental. If not the leading American organic chemist of his day, he ranked among the leaders. When Caltech tried to lure him away with a large research budget Harvard topped the offer and refused to let him go.

Number two on Conant's youthful list, the presidency of his alma mater, he won in 1933. He told the members of the Harvard Corporation who approached him that he didn't want the job, which was apparently a prerequisite, but would serve if elected. He was forty at the time of his election. He created the modern Harvard of eminent scholarship and publish-or-perish, up-or-out.

Conant's third ambition achieved approximate fulfillment after the war in high, though less than cabinet-rank, appointment; his long span of voluntary government service began with the NDRC.

In England in the late winter of 1941 he met with the leaders of the British government, had an audience with the King, picked up an honorary degree at Cambridge and walked the Backs afterward to see the crocuses in bloom, made room for the NDRC mission among hostile U.S. military and naval attachés, lunched with Churchill again. His mission in Britain was diplomatic rather than technical. He discussed gas warfare and explosives manufacture but was unable to share in the intense exchange of information on radar because he knew very little about electronics. But although he was familiar with the work on uranium and it fell within his official NDRC responsibilities, secrecy and his "strong belief in the 'need to know' principle" kept Conant from learning what the British had learned about the possibility of a bomb.

He met a "French scientist" at Oxford, probably Hans von Halban, who complained of inaction on uranium–heavy water research. "Since his complaints were clearly 'out of channels,' I quickly terminated the conversation and forgot the incident." That reaction was understandable: Conant could hardly know what security arrangements the British might have made with the Free French. But he also shied from Lindemann. They were lunching alone at a London club. "He introduced the subject of the study of the fission of uranium atoms. I reacted by repeating the doubts I had expressed and heard expressed at NDRC meetings." Lindemann brushed them aside and pounced:

> "You have left out of consideration," said [Lindemann], "the possibility of the construction of a bomb of enormous power." "How would that be possible?" I asked. "By first separating uranium 235," he said, "and then arranging for the two portions of the element to be brought together suddenly so that the resulting mass would spontaneously undergo a self-sustaining reaction."

Remarkably, the chairman of the chemistry and explosives division of the NDRC adds that, as late as March 1941, "this was the first I had heard about even the remote possibility of a bomb." Nor did he pursue the matter. "I assumed, quite correctly, that if and when Bush wished to be in touch with the atomic energy work in England, he would do so through channels involving Briggs." No wonder the Hungarian conspirers continued to tear their hair.

Then for the first time a ranking American physicist joined the debate whose voice could not be ignored. Even before Seaborg and Segrè confirmed the fissibility of plutonium, Ernest Lawrence had measured the prevailing American skepticism and conservatism against the increasing enthusiasm of his British friends and responded with characteristic fervor. Ralph H. Fowler, Ernest Rutherford's widower son-in-law, had visited Berkeley during the 1930s and attended picnics and weekend parties with the inventor of the cyclotron. Fowler was British scientific liaison officer in Washington now and from that close vantage he urged Lawrence to get involved. So did Mark Oliphant, whom Lawrence had met and liked on a visit to the Cavendish after the 1933 Solvay Conference.

Lawrence had encouraged the search for plutonium partly because he saw little hope for isotope separation by any of the methods so far discussed—by centrifuge, thermal diffusion or barrier diffusion. But around the beginning of the year he began thinking about separating isotopes electromagnetically, by the process that had already worked on a microscopic scale for Alfred Nier. It occurred to Lawrence that he could modify his superseded 37-inch cyclotron into a big mass spectrometer. The fact that Nier thought electromagnetic separation on an industrial scale impossible only spurred the Berkeley laureate on. Lawrence lived from machine to machine, as it were; conceiving a machine to do the job of liberating U235 from its confinement within U238 (while Fermi's uranium-graphite reactor manufactured Berkeley-born plutonium) gave him something solid to fight for, a tangible program to push.

It assembled itself by stages. He was not yet ready emotionally to set aside his peacetime plans. Warren Weaver, the director of the division of natural sciences at the Rockefeller Foundation, visited Berkeley in February to see how construction was progressing on the 4,900-ton, 184-inch cyclotron for which the foundation had awarded a $1,150,000 grant less than twelve months earlier. Lawrence took time to complain about the Uranium Committee's sloth—Weaver worked with another division of the NDRC—but then drove up behind the university to the cyclotron site on the hillside and first irritated and then enthralled the Rockefeller administrator with visions of a superior and much larger machine.

Lawrence rehearsed his complaint again in March when Conant, back from London, traveled out to deliver an address. "Light a fire under the Briggs committee," the energetic Californian badgered the president of Harvard. "What if German scientists succeed in making a nuclear bomb before we even investigate possibilities?" That prepared Lawrence for a full assault. He launched it on March 17 when he met with Karl Compton and Alfred Loomis at MIT.

Loomis had turned to physics after a lucrative career in the law and investment banking. Compton was a physicist of distinction who had taught for fifteen years at Princeton, where he took his Ph.D., before becoming president of MIT in 1930. Both men understood the politics of organizations. Yet they were sufficiently seized with Lawrence's fervor that Compton telephoned Vannevar Bush almost as soon as Lawrence left the room and dictated a follow-up letter the same day. Briggs was "by nature slow, conservative, methodical and accustomed to operate at peacetime government bureau tempo," Compton wrote, conveying Lawrence's blunt complaints, and had been "following a policy consistent with these qualities and still further inhibited by the requirement of secrecy." The British were ahead even though America had "the most in number and the best in quality of the nuclear physicists of the world." The Germans were "very active." Briggs had invited only a very few U.S. nuclear physicists into the work. There were other possibilities in fission research besides the pursuit of a slow-neutron chain reaction for power, possibilities "capable, if successful, of far more important military usage."

Though they felt free thus to lecture Bush, both Loomis and Compton stood in awe of Lawrence—Loomis had recently contributed $30,000 to a private fund simply to make it easier for Lawrence to travel around the country—and thought Bush could do no better than to turn him loose: "I hasten to say that the idea of Ernest himself taking an active part in any reorganization was in no sense suggested by him or even in his mind, but I do believe that it would be an ideal solution."

Bush's ego was commensurate with his responsibilities, as Loomis and Compton ought to have known. It might have been politic to welcome Lawrence's campaign, especially since Loomis was a first cousin and close friend of Henry L. Stimson, the respected and influential Secretary of War; but Bush decided instead to take it as a challenge to his authority, the first the physics community had mounted since he invented the NDRC, welcoming a fight he knew he could win. He met Lawrence in New York two days after the MIT meeting and let fly:

> I told him flatly that I was running the show, that we had established a procedure for handling it, that he could either conform to that as a member of the NDRC and put in his kicks through the internal mechanism, or he could be utterly on the outside and act as an individual in any way that he saw fit. He got into line and I arranged for him to have with Briggs a series of excellent conferences. However, I made it very clear to Lawrence that I proposed to

> make available to Briggs the best advice and consultation possible, but that in the last analysis I proposed to back up Briggs and his committee in their decision unless there was some decidedly strong case for entering into it personally. I think this matter was thoroughly straightened out, therefore, but it left its trail behind.

By threatening to push Ernest Lawrence out into the cold with the emigrés Bush managed temporarily to confine the uranium problem. Confinement lasted less than a month.

In 1940 Lawrence had recruited a Harvard experimentalist named Kenneth Bainbridge, by trade a nuclear physicist—Bainbridge built the Harvard cyclotron—to work on radar at MIT. When Conant went to London to open the new NDRC office there, Bainbridge and others had followed, to work with the British each in his own field of competence. But since Bainbridge knew nuclear physics as well as radar and had even looked into isotope separation, the British allowed him also to attend a full-dress meeting of the MAUD Committee. To Bainbridge's surprise, the committee had "a very good idea of the critical mass and [bomb] assembly [mechanism], and urged the exchange of personnel. . . . Their estimate was that a minimum of three years would be required to solve all the problems involved in producing an atomic weapon." Bainbridge immediately contacted Briggs and suggested he send someone over to represent the United States in uranium matters.

Beneath Bush's organizational bristle lay genuine perplexity. "I am no atomic scientist," he writes candidly; "most of this was over my head." As he saw the situation that April, "it would be possible to spend a very large amount of money indeed, and yet there is certainly no clear-cut path to defense results of great importance lying open before us at the present time." But he felt the increasing pressure—Lawrence's prodding, Bainbridge's confirmation of British progress—and reached out now for help.

"It was Bush's strategy," writes the American experimental physicist Arthur Compton, Karl's younger brother, "as co-ordinator of the nation's war research, to use the National Academy [of Sciences] as the court of final appeal for important scientific problems." On a Tuesday in mid-April, after meeting with Briggs, Bush wrote Frank B. Jewett, the senior Bell Telephone engineer who was president of the National Academy. Briggs had heard from Bainbridge and alerted Bush; Bush and Briggs, "disturbed," had conferred. "The British are apparently doing fully as much as we are, if not more, and yet it seems as though, if the problem were of really great importance, we ought to be carrying most of the burden in this country." Bush wanted "an energetic but dispassionate review of the entire situation by a highly competent group of physicists." The men chosen ought to have "sufficient knowledge to understand and sufficient detachment to cold bloodedly evaluate."

At a regular Washington meeting of the National Academy the following Friday Jewett, Bush and Briggs recruited their review group. They put Lawrence on the committee and the recently retired director of the research laboratory at General Electric, a physical chemist named William D. Coolidge. Then they sought out Arthur Compton, a Nobel laureate and professor of physics at the University of Chicago, and proposed he head the review. Compton humbly questioned his "fitness for the task" and jumped at the chance.

Arthur Holly Compton was the son of a Presbyterian minister and professor of philosophy at the College of Wooster in Wooster, Ohio. Compton's Mennonite mother was dedicated to missionary causes and had been the 1939 American Mother of the Year. He followed his older brother Karl into science and surpassed him in achievement but preserved the family piety as well. "Arthur Compton and God were daily companions," notes Leona Woods, Enrico Fermi's young protégé at the University of Chicago. She judged Compton nevertheless "a fine scientist and a fine man. . . . He was remarkably handsome all his life and athletically spare and strong." Fermi had concluded, writes Woods, that "tallness and handsomeness usually were inversely proportional to intelligence," but "he excepted Arthur Compton . . . whose intelligence he respected enormously."

Compton's physics was first-rate, as Fermi's respect implies. He graduated from the College of Wooster and took his Ph.D. at Princeton. In 1919, the first year of the program, he was appointed a National Research Council fellow and used the appointment to study under Rutherford at the Cavendish. The difficult work he began there—examining the scattering and absorption of gamma rays—led directly to the discovery of what came to be called the Compton effect, for which he won the Nobel Prize.

In 1920, Compton writes, he accepted a professorship at Washington University in St. Louis, "a small kind of place," to get out of the mainstream of physics so that he could concentrate on his scattering studies, which he was then extending from gamma rays to X rays. He scattered X rays with a graphite block and caught them and measured their wavelengths Moseley-style with a calcite-crystal X-ray spectrograph. He found that the X rays scattered by the graphite came out with wavelengths longer than their wavelengths going in: as if a shout bounced off a distant wall came back bizarrely deepened to a lower pitch. If X rays—light—were only a motion of waves, then their wavelengths would not have changed; Compton had in fact demonstrated in 1923 what Einstein had postulated in

1905 in his theory of the photoelectric effect: that light was wave but also simultaneously particle, photon. An X-ray photon had collided elastically with an electron, as billiard balls collide, had bounced off and thereby given up some of its energy. The calcite crystal revealed the energy loss as a longer wavelength of X-ray light. Arnold Sommerfeld hailed the Compton effect—elastic scattering of a photon by an electron—as "probably the most important discovery which could have been made in the current state of physics" because it proved that photons exist, which hardly anyone in 1923 yet believed, and demonstrated clearly the dual nature of light as both particle and wave.

The subtle experimenter lost his subtlety when he shifted from doing science to proselytizing for God. Rigor slipped to Chautauqua logic and he perpetrated such howlers as the notion that Heisenberg's uncertainty principle somehow extends beyond the dimensions of the atom into the human world and confirms free will. Bohr heard Compton's Free Will lecture when he visited the United States in the early 1930s and scoffed. "Bohr spoke highly of Compton as a physicist and a man," a friend of the Danish laureate remembers, "but he felt that Compton's philosopohy was too primitive: 'Compton would like to say that for God there is no uncertainty principle. That is nonsense. In physics we do not talk about God but about what we can know. If we are to speak of God we must do so in an entirely different manner.' "

In 1941 war work had already been kind to Arthur Compton's brother, moving Karl to national prominence within the science community and winning an important secret laboratory for MIT. Arthur wanted as much or more. There was the problem of pacifism, his mother's Mennonite creed and a course much discussed at that time in American vestries, a churchly counterpart to isolationism:

> In 1940, my forty-eighth year, I began to feel strongly my responsibility as a citizen for taking my proper part in the war that was then about to engulf my country, as it had already engulfed so much of the world. I talked, among others, with my minister in Chicago. He wondered why I was not supporting his appeal to the young people of our church to take a stand as pacifists. I replied in this manner: "As long as I am convinced, as I am, that there are values worth more to me than my own life, I cannot in sincerity argue that it is wrong to run the risk of death or to inflict death if necessary in the defense of those values."

Arthur Compton was ready, then, "a short time later," when Bush and the National Academy asked him to serve.

The review committee met immediately with some of Briggs' associates in Washington. A week later, May 5, 1941, it met again in Cambridge to hear from other Uranium Committee members and from Bainbridge. "There followed," writes Compton, "two weeks spent in discussing the military possibilities of uranium with others who were actively interested." Compton worked quickly to complete a seven-page report and delivered it to Jewett on May 17.

The report began with the statement that the committee was concerned with "the matter of possible military aspects of atomic fission" and listed three of those possibilities: "production of violently radioactive materials . . . carried by airplanes to be scattered as bombs over enemy territory," "a power source on submarines and other ships" and "violently explosive bombs." Radioactive dust would need a year's preparation after "the first successful production of a chain reaction," which meant "not earlier than 1943." A power source would need at least three years after a chain reaction. Bombs required concentrating U235 or possibly making plutonium in a chain reaction, so "atomic bombs can hardly be anticipated before 1945."

And that was that: no mention of fast-neutron fission, or critical mass, or bomb assembly mechanisms. The bulk of the report discussed "progress toward securing a chain reaction" and considered uranium-graphite, uranium-beryllium and uranium–heavy water systems. The committee proposed giving Fermi all the money he needed for his intermediate experiment and beyond. It also, more originally, discovered and emphasized the decisive long-range challenge of the new field:

> It would seem to us unlikely that the use of nuclear fission can become of military importance within less than two years. . . . If, however, the chain reaction can be produced and controlled, it may rapidly become a determining factor in warfare. Looking, therefore, to a struggle which may continue for a decade or more, it is important that we gain the lead in this development. That nation which first produces and controls the process will have an advantage which will grow as its applications multiply.

Bush was in the process of reorganizing government science when he received the NAS report. The NDRC, empowered equally with the military laboratories and the National Advisory Committee for Aeronautics, had served for research but lacked the authority to pursue engineering development. Bush proposed a new umbrella agency with wide authority over all government science in the service of war, the Office of Scientific Research and Development. Its director—Bush—would report personally to Roosevelt. Bush prepared to move up to the OSRD by calling in Conant to take over the NDRC. "And only after it was clear that I should shortly have a new position," writes Conant, "did Bush begin to take me into his confidence as he pondered on what to do with the Briggs Committee." Against the background of his British experience Conant told Bush his reaction to Compton's report was "almost completely negative."

Jewett had delivered the report to Bush with a cover letter calling it "authoritative and impressive," but privately he cautioned Bush that he had "a lurking fear" that the report "might be over-enthusiastic in parts and not so well balanced." Jewett also passed it to several senior colleagues for comment, including the 1923 Nobel laureate in physics, Robert A. Millikan of Caltech, and sent their comments along to Bush in early June. Bush responded with exasperation compounded with astonishing confusion about the developments in Britain:

> This uranium business is a headache! I have looked over Millikan's comments, and it is quite clear that he wrote them without realizing the present situation. The British have apparently definitely established the possibility of a chain reaction with 238 [*sic*], which entirely changes the complexion of the whole affair. Millikan bases his comments on the conviction that only 235 holds promise. This is natural, since he has not been brought in touch with recent developments which the British have told us about in great confidence.

He agreed that the work "ought to be handled in a somewhat more vigorous form," but he was still profoundly skeptical of its promise:

> Even if the physicists get all that they expect, I believe that there is a very long period of engineering work of the most difficult nature before anything practical can come out of the matter, unless there is an explosive involved, which I very much doubt.

The OSRD director was not yet convinced despite new word of plutonium's remarkable fissibility. Segrè and Seaborg had continued working through the spring of 1941 to determine the man-made element's various cross sections. On Sunday, May 18, having finally prepared a sample thin enough for accurate measurement, they calculated plutonium's cross section for slow-neutron fission at 1.7 times that of U235. When Lawrence heard the news on Monday, says Seaborg, he swung into action:

> We told Lawrence about our definitive demonstration yesterday of the slow neutron fissionability of 94^{239} and he was quite excited. He immediately phoned the University of Chicago to give the news to Arthur H. Compton. . . . Compton made an immediate attempt to phone (unsuccessfully) and then sent a telegram to Vannevar Bush. . . . In his telegram Compton indicated that the demonstration . . . greatly increases the importance of the fission problem since the available material [i.e., U238 transmuted to plutonium] is thus in-

creased by over 100 times. . . . He said that Alfred Loomis and Ernest Lawrence accordingly have requested him to urge anew the vital importance of pushing the [uranium-graphite] work at Columbia.

* * *

Whenever the U.S. program bogged down in bureaucratic doubt Hitler and his war machine rescued it. That summer's massive escalation, code-named Operation Barbarossa, was the opening of the Eastern Front at dawn on the morning of Sunday, June 22, a surge eastward with 164 divisions, including Finnish and Rumanian components, toward *Blitzkrieg* invasion of the USSR. The Führer's ambitious intention, declared with emphasis in a secret directive six months earlier, was "*to crush Soviet Russia in a quick campaign* even before the conclusion of the war against England." Hitler meant to push all the way to the Urals before winter and commandeer the Soviet Union's industrial and agricultural base; by July Panzers had crossed the Dnieper and were threatening Kiev.

The effect on Conant of his London experiences and the widening war was paradoxically to increase his skepticism of the program he had just accepted assignment to administer:

> What worried me about Compton's first report, I told Bush, was the assumption that achieving a chain reaction was so important that a large expenditure of both money and manpower was justified. To me, the defense of the free world was in such a dangerous state that only efforts which were likely to yield results within a matter of months or, at most, a year or two were worthy of serious consideration. In that summer of 1941, with recollections of what I had seen and heard in England fresh in my mind, I was impatient with the arguments of some of the physicists associated with the Uranium Committee whom I met from time to time. They talked in excited tones about the discovery of a new world in which power from a uranium reactor would revolutionize our industrialized society. These fancies left me cold. I suggested that until Nazi Germany was defeated all our energies should be concentrated on one immediate objective.

Having experienced the London Blitz, Conant had developed a siege mentality; Bush, as Conant points out, "was faced with a momentous decision as to priorities." Both men wanted a hard, practical assessment. They decided Compton's report needed an injection of common sense in the form of engineering expertise. Compton discreetly retired from the line; W. D. Coolidge, the General Electric scientist, temporarily took his place. Conant added an engineer from Bell Laboratories and another from Westinghouse and early in July the enlarged committee reviewed the first review.

Briggs was a convincing witness. By then he had received the April 9 minutes of a MAUD technical subcommittee meeting where Peierls reported that cross-section measurements confirmed the feasibility of a fast-neutron bomb. Briggs had also just learned from Lawrence that plutonium had a cross section for fast fission some ten times that of U238. Lawrence even submitted a separate report on element 94 that emphasized for the first time in U.S. official deliberations the importance of fast fission over slow. But Briggs was still preoccupied with a slow-neutron chain reaction for power production and so was the second NAS report. "In the summer of 1941," John Dunning's associate Eugene Booth remembers, "Briggs visited us in the basement of Pupin at Columbia to see our experiment for the separation of U235 by [gaseous] diffusion of uranium hexafluoride. He was interested, blessed us, but sent us no money."

The American program was in danger for its life that summer, Compton thought: "The government's responsible representatives were . . . very close to dropping fission studies from the war program." He believed the program was saved because of Lawrence's proposal to use plutonium to make a bomb. The fissibility of 94 may have convinced Compton. It was not decisive for the government's responsible representatives. They were hard men and needed hard facts. Those began to arrive. "More significant than the arguments of Compton and Lawrence," writes Conant, "was the news that a group of physicists in England had concluded that the construction of a bomb made out of uranium 235 was entirely feasible."

The British had been trying all winter and spring to pass the word. In July they tried again. G. P. Thomson had assembled a draft final report for the MAUD Committee to consider on June 23, the day after Barbarossa exploded across the Balkans and eastern Poland. Charles C. Lauritsen of Caltech, a respected senior physicist, was beginning work for the NDRC developing rockets and happened to be in London conferring with the British at the time of the MAUD draft. The committee invited him to attend its July 2 meeting at Burlington House. Lauritsen listened carefully, took notes and afterward talked individually with eight of the twenty-four physicists now attached to the work. When he returned to the United States the following week he immediately reported the MAUD findings to Bush. "In essence," says Conant, "he summarized the 'draft report.' " The physicists Lauritsen had interviewed had all pushed for a U.S.-built gaseous-diffusion plant.

The British government would not officially transmit the final MAUD Report to the United States government until early October, but the committee approved it on July 15 (and thereupon promptly disbanded) and by then Bush had been passed a copy of the Thomson draft, which embodied the essential findings. The MAUD Report differed from the two National

Academy studies as a blueprint differs from an architect's sketch. It announced at the outset:

> We have now reached the conclusion that it will be possible to make an effective uranium bomb which, containing some 25 lb of active material, would be equivalent as regards destructive effect to 1,800 tons of T.N.T. and would also release large quantities of radioactive substances. . . . A plant to produce 2¼ lb (1 kg) per day [of U235] (or 3 bombs per month) is estimated to cost approximately £5,000,000. . . . In spite of this very large expenditure we consider that the destructive effect, both material and moral, is so great that every effort should be made to produce bombs of this kind. . . . The material for the first bomb could be ready by the end of 1943. . . . Even if the war should end before the bombs are ready the effort would not be wasted, except in the unlikely event of complete disarmament, since no nation would care to risk being caught without a weapon of such destructive capabilities.

Of conclusions and recommendations the report offered, crisply, three:

> (i) The committee considers that the scheme for a uranium bomb is practicable and likely to lead to decisive results in the war.
> (ii) It recommends that this work continue on the highest priority and on the increasing scale necessary to obtain the weapon in the shortest possible time.
> (iii) That the present collaboration with America should be continued and extended especially in the region of experimental work.

"With the news from Great Britain unofficially in hand," Conant concludes in a secret history of the project he drafted in 1943, ". . . it became clear to the Director of OSRD and the Chairman of NDRC that a major push along the lines outlined was in order."

They still did not immediately organize that push. Nor was Conant, to his postwar recollection, yet convinced that a uranium bomb would work as described. British research and considered judgment had at least proposed a clear-cut program of *military* development. Bush took it to Vice President Henry Wallace, his White House sounding board, who was the only scientist in the cabinet, a plant geneticist who had developed several varieties of hybrid corn. "During July," writes Conant, "Bush had a discussion with Vice President Wallace about the question of spending a large amount of government money on the uranium program." After which Bush apparently decided to wait for official transmittal of the final MAUD Report.

"If each necessary step requires ten months of deliberation," Leo Szilard had complained to Alexander Sachs in 1940, "then obviously it will not be possible to carry out this development efficiently." The American program was moving faster now than that, but not by much.

While Lawrence and Compton championed plutonium that summer, a big, rawboned, war-battered Austrian hiding out within the German physics establishment tried to keep the fissile new element out of sight. He was an old friend of Otto Frisch:

> Fritz Houtermans and I had met in Berlin, but in London [before the war] I saw a lot more of that impressive eagle of a man, half Jewish as well as a Communist who had narrowly escaped the Gestapo. His father had been a Dutchman, but he was very proud of his mother's Jewish origin and liable to counter anti-semitic remarks by retorting "When your ancestors were still living in the trees mine were already forging cheques!" He was full of brilliant ideas.

Houtermans had taken a Ph.D. in experimental physics at Göttingen but was strong in theory. One of his brilliant ideas, developed in the late 1920s at the University of Berlin with a visiting British astronomer, Robert Atkinson, concerned the production of energy in stars. Atkinson was familiar with recent estimates by his older colleague Arthur Eddington that the sun and other stars burn at temperatures of 10 million and more degrees and have life spans of billions of years—a prodigious and unexplained expenditure of energy. On a walking tour near Göttingen in the summer of 1927 the two men had wondered if nuclear transformations of the sort Rutherford was producing at the Cavendish might account for the enduring stellar fires. They quickly worked out a basic theory, as Hans Bethe later described it, "that at the high temperatures in the interior of a star, the nuclei in the star could penetrate into other nuclei and cause nuclear reactions, releasing energy." The energy would be released when hot (and therefore fast-moving) hydrogen nuclei collided with enough force to overcome their respective electrical barriers and fused together, making helium nuclei and giving up binding energy in the process. With George Gamow, Houtermans and Atkinson later named these events *thermonuclear* reactions because they proceeded at such high temperatures.

In 1933 Houtermans emigrated to the Soviet Union, "but fell victim," writes Frisch, "to one of Stalin's purges and spent a couple of years in prison; his wife with two small children managed to escape and get to the U.S.A. When Hitler made his temporary pact with Stalin in 1939 it included an exchange of prisoners, and Houtermans was handed back to the Gestapo." Max von Laue, whom Frisch celebrates as "one of the few German scientists with the prestige and courage to stand up against the Nazis," managed to free Houtermans and arranged for him to work with a wealthy German inventor, Baron Manfred von Ardenne, who had studied physics and who maintained a private laboratory in Lichterfelde, outside Berlin. Von Ardenne was pursuing uranium research independently of Heisenberg and the War Office; to raise funds for the work he had approached the German Post Office, which commanded a large and largely unused budget for research. The Minister of Posts, imagining himself handing Hitler the decisive secret weapon of the war, had funded the building of a million-volt Van de Graaff and two cyclotrons, all under construction in 1941. Until they came on line Houtermans turned his attention to theory.

By August he had independently worked out all the basic ideas necessary to a bomb. He discussed them in a thirty-nine-page report, "On the question of unleashing chain reactions," that considered fast-neutron chain reactions, critical mass, U235, isotope separation and element 94. Houtermans emphasized making 94. "Every neutron which, instead of fissioning uranium-235, is captured by uranium-238," he wrote, "creates in this way a new nucleus, fissionable by thermal neutrons." He discussed his ideas privately with von Weizsäcker and Heisenberg, but he saw to it that the Post Office kept his report in its safe secure from War Office eyes. He had learned to cooperate for survival in the Soviet Union, where the NKVD—the KGB of its day—had knocked out all his teeth and kept him in solitary confinement for months. But in Germany as in the USSR he withheld as much information as he dared. His private endorsement of 94, to be transmuted by chain reaction from natural uranium, probably contributed to the neglect of isotope separation in Germany. After the summer of 1941 the German bomb program depended entirely on uranium and Vemork heavy water.

The British, at least, knew where they were going. Tizard was skeptical of the MAUD Report and doubted that a bomb could be produced before the end of the war. Lindemann—he was Lord Cherwell now, a baron, courtesy of his friend the P.M.—did not. Cherwell had followed the MAUD work carefully. He respected Thomson; Simon was an old friend; Peierls had read his grunts correctly after all. He trusted their judgment and set to work to reduce the lengthy report to a memorandum for Churchill. Churchill liked his documents held to half a page. So important was this one that Cherwell allowed it to run on for two and a half pages. He thought research should continue for six months and then face further review. He thought an isotope-separation plant should be erected not in the United States but in England—despite manpower shortages and the risk of German bombing—or "at worst" in Canada. In that conclusion he differed from the

MAUD Committee. "The reasons in favor [of an English location]," he wrote, "are the better chance of maintaining secrecy . . . but above all the fact that whoever possesses such a plant should be able to dictate terms to the rest of the world. However much I may trust my neighbor and depend on him, I am very much averse to putting myself completely at his mercy. I would, therefore, not press the Americans to undertake this work." His summation narrowed the odds but decisively raised the stakes:

> People who are working on these problems consider the odds are ten to one on success within two years. I would not bet more than two to one against or even money. But I am quite clear that we must go forward. It would be unforgivable if we let the Germans defeat us in war or reverse the verdict after they had been defeated.

Churchill received Cherwell's recommendation on August 27. Three days later he minuted his military advisers, alluding ironically to the effects of the Blitz: "Although personally I am quite content with the existing explosives, I feel we must not stand in the path of improvement, and I therefore think that action should be taken in the sense proposed by Lord Cherwell."

The British chiefs of staff concurred on September 3.

Mark Oliphant helped goad the American program over the top. "If Congress knew the true history of the atomic energy project," Leo Szilard said modestly after the war, "I have no doubt but that it would create a special medal to be given to meddling foreigners for distinguished services, and Dr. Oliphant would be the first to receive one." Conant in his 1943 secret history thought the "most important" reason the program changed direction in the autumn of 1941 was that "the all-out advocates of a head-on attack on the uranium problem had become more vocal and determined" and mentioned Oliphant's influence first of all.

Oliphant flew to the United States in late August—he considered the Pan-American Clipper through Lisbon too slow and usually traveled by unheated bomber—to work with his NDRC counterparts on radar. But he was also charged with inquiring why the United States was ignoring the MAUD Committee's findings. "The minutes and reports . . . had been sent to Lyman Briggs . . . and we were puzzled to receive virtually no comment. . . . I called on Briggs in Washington, only to find that this inarticulate and unimpressive man had put the reports in his safe and had not shown them to members of his Committee." Oliphant was "amazed and distressed."

's story should be given serious consideration." Infor
been available in the United States—at least the MAU
ing Peierls' April 9 statement—but Briggs had locke
ing. Oliphant returned to Birmingham wondering
pression at all.

e was already moving. He called Arthur Compton in C
left Berkeley. "Certain developments made him beli
ible to make an atomic bomb," Compton paraphrases
'Such a bomb, if developed in time, might determine t
war. The activity of the Germans in this field made it seem
of great urgency for us to press its development." It was no
d had argued two years earlier. Lawrence was scheduled to
on September 25. Conant would be in town to receive an
Compton proposed to invite both men together to his
ould then press the NDRC chairman directly.

ion for political commitment at the Pan American Sci-
Edward Teller had continued teaching at George
ty but sought work in fission research. In March 1941,
ne of their sponsors, the Tellers swore allegiance to
l became American citizens. Hans Bethe, who was
or the spring term on temporary leave from Cornell,
month. At the end of the term Bethe recommended
eller to replace him. To work more closely with
l to adjudicate their disputes, which he did with
ed and moved to Manhattan, to an apartment on

riment Fermi found time to theorize. He and
niversity Club one pleasant day in September.
Pupin—"out of the blue," Teller says—Fermi
bomb might serve to heat a mass of deuterium
uclear fusion. Such a mechanism, a bomb fus-
ld be three orders of magnitude as energetic
aper in terms of equivalent explosive force.
away. Teller found it a surpassing challenge

ground. When he understood something
n without waiting for experimental confir-
ic bomb. He moved on to consider the
He made extensive calculations. They
hat deuterium could not be ignited by
Sunday, we went on a walk. The Ferm

He met then with the Uranium Commi
committee member, a talented experi
Compton at the University of Chicago. Ol
lison recalls, "... and said '*bomb*' in nc
must concentrate every effort on the b
work on power plants or anything bu
twenty-five million dollars, he said, a
the manpower, so it was up to us."
the committee in the dark. "I thou
submarines."

In desperation Oliphant reac
knew in the United States. He
Washington to meet at a conve
September he did.

Lawrence drove Oliph
the site of the 184-inch c
overheard. Oliphant rehe
not yet seen. Lawrence
netic separation of U23
nium. "How much I s
laboratory," Olipha
sure that in your ha
plete consideratio
and arranged for
ten summary of

In Washin
terest. Bush m
minutes. Ne
port. "Gos
characteri

Olip
ate mor
and n

F
visit
sec
st

that O
had indee
utes, includ
for safekeep
made any im

Lawrenc
after Oliphan
would be poss
conversation. "
outcome of the
to him a matter
more than Szilar
speak in Chicago
honorary degree.
home. Lawrence c

Following his decisi
entific Conference,
Washington Univers
with Merle Tuve as
the United States an
teaching at Columbia
took the oath the same
that Columbia invite T
Fermi and Szilard—an
sensitivity—Teller accep
Morningside Drive.

In the midst of exp
Teller had lunch at the U
Afterward, walking back t
wondered aloud if an atomi
sufficiently to begin thermon
ing hydrogen to helium, sho
as a fission bomb and far ch
For Fermi the idea was a thro
and took it to heart.

Teller liked to break new
theoretically he usually moved
mation. He understood the ato
possibility of a hydrogen bomb
were disappointing. "I decided
atomic bombs," he recalls. "Next

and the Tellers. And I explained to Enrico why a hydrogen bomb could never be made. And he believed me." For a while, Teller even believed himself.

Enrico Fermi and Edward Teller were not, however, the first to conceive of using a nuclear chain reaction to initiate a thermonuclear reaction in hydrogen. That distinction apparently belongs to Japanese physicist Tokutaro Hagiwara of the faculty of science of the University of Kyoto. Hagiwara had followed world fission research and had conducted studies of his own. In May 1941 he lectured on "Super-explosive U235," reviewing existing knowledge. He was aware that an explosive chain reaction depended on U235 and understood the necessity of isotope separation: "Because of the potential application of this explosive chain reaction a practical method of achieving this must be found. Immediately, it is very important that a means of manufacturing U-235 on a large scale from natural uranium be found." He then discussed the linkage he saw between nuclear fission and thermonuclear fusion: "If by any chance U-235 could be manufactured in a large quantity and of proper concentration, U-235 has a great possibility of becoming useful as the initiating matter for a quantity of hydrogen. We have great expectations for this."

But before the Japanese or the Americans could build a hydrogen bomb they would have to build an atomic bomb. And in neither country was major support yet secure.

"It was a cool September evening," Arthur Compton remembers. "My wife greeted Conant and Lawrence as they came into our home and gave each of us a cup of coffee as we gathered around the fireplace. Then she busied herself upstairs so the three of us might talk freely."

Lawrence spoke with passion. He was "very vigorous in his expression of dissatisfaction with the U.S. program," writes Conant. "Dr. Oliphant had seen him during the summer and by recounting the British hopes had further fired Lawrence's zeal for more action in this whole field." Conant knew all about the British hopes, knew talk was cheap and chose to play the devil's advocate, easily gulling Compton, who thought his arguments turned the tide:

> Conant was reluctant. As a result of the reports so far received he had concluded that the time had come to drop the support of nuclear research as a subject for wartime study. . . . We could not afford to spend either our scientific or our industrial effort on an atomic program of highly questionable military value when every ounce of our strength was needed for the nation's defense.
>
> I rallied to Lawrence's support. . . .
>
> Conant began to be convinced.

"I could not resist the temptation," says the Harvard president, "to cut behind [Lawrence's] rhetoric by asking if he was prepared to shelve his own research programs." Compton cranks Conant's challenge to high melodrama:

> "If this task is as important as you men say," [Conant] remarked, "we must get going. I have argued with Vannevar Bush that the uranium project be put in wraps for the war period. Now you put before me plans for making a definite, highly effective weapon. If such a weapon is going to be made, we must do it first. We can't afford not to. But I'm here to tell you, nothing significant will happen on such a job as this unless we get into it with everything we've got."
>
> He turned to Lawrence. "Ernest, you say you are convinced of the importance of these fission bombs. Are you ready to devote the next several years of your life to getting them made?"
>
> . . . The question brought Lawrence up with a start. I can still recall the expression in his eyes as he sat there with his mouth half open. Here was a serious personal decision. . . . He hesitated only a moment: "If you tell me this is my job, I'll do it."

Back in Washington Conant briefed Bush on what he calls "the results of the involuntary conference in Chicago to which [I] had been exposed." The two administrators decided to order up a third National Academy report, enlarging Compton's committee this time to include W. K. Lewis, a chemical engineer with an outstanding reputation for estimating the potential success at industrial scale of laboratory processes, and Conant's Harvard colleague George B. Kistiakowsky, the resident NDRC explosives expert.

Tall, big-boned, boisterous, with a flat Slavic face and abiding self-confidence, Kistiakowsky had volunteered at eighteen for the White Russian Army and fought in the Russian Revolution. "I grew up in a family in which the question of civil rights, human freedom, was an important one," he told an interviewer late in life. "My father was a professor of sociology and wrote articles and books on the subject and got into trouble with the Czar's regime, very substantial trouble. Mother was also politically oriented. I think both of them went through a short period of being Marxists and then rejected it. That's why I really joined the anti-Bolshevik armies in '18. It was certainly not because I loved Czarism. Of course, I got completely disgusted with the White Army long before it was all over." Kistiakowsky escaped to Germany and took his doctorate at the University of Berlin in 1925. He might have stayed, but his professor advised him to look elsewhere. "He told me that if I wanted to go into an academic career I should emigrate; I would never get a job in Germany—'Here you will always be a Russian.' " Princeton accepted the Ukrainian chemist on a fellowship and soon hired him for its faculty. Then Harvard discovered and courted him. In 1930 he moved, becoming professor of chemistry in 1938.

Conant had been among those who lured Kistiakowsky from Princeton to Harvard. He valued highly his friend and fellow chemist's opinion. "When I retailed to him the idea that a bomb could be made by the rapid assembly of two masses of fissionable material, his first remark was that of a doubting Thomas. 'It would seem to be a difficult undertaking on a battlefield,' he remarked." But it was Kistiakowsky's judgment that finally convinced Conant, as British hopes and physicists' entreaties had not:

> A few weeks later when we met, his doubts were gone. "It can be made to work," he said. "I am one hundred percent sold."
>
> My doubts about Briggs' project evaporated as soon as I heard George Kistiakowsky's considered verdict. I had known George for many years. . . . I had asked him to be head of the NDRC division on explosives. . . . I had complete faith in his judgment. If he was sold on Arthur Compton's program, who was I to have reservations?

Oliphant convinced Lawrence, Lawrence convinced Compton, Kistiakowsky convinced Conant. Conant says Compton's and Lawrence's attitudes "counted heavily with Bush." But "more significant" was the MAUD Report, which G. P. Thomson, now British scientific liaison officer in Ottawa, officially transmitted to Conant on October 3. On October 9, without waiting for the third National Academy of Sciences review, Bush carried the report directly to the President.

Franklin Roosevelt, Henry Wallace and the director of the OSRD met that Thursday at the White House. In a memorandum Bush wrote to Conant the same day he makes it clear that the MAUD Report was the basis for the discussion: "I told the conference of the British conclusions." He told the President and the Vice President that the explosive core of an atomic bomb might weigh twenty-five pounds, that it might explode with a force equivalent to some eighteen hundred tons of TNT, that a vast industrial plant costing many times as much as a major oil refinery would be necessary to separate the U235, that the raw material might come from Canada and the Belgian Congo, that the British estimated the first bombs might be ready by the end of 1943. Bush tried to explain that an atomic bomb plant would produce no more than two or three bombs a month but doubted if the President took in that "relatively low yield." He emphasized that he was basing his statements "primarily on calculation with some laboratory investigation, but not on a proved case" and therefore could not guarantee success.

Bush was presenting, essentially, British calculations and British conclusions. Such a presentation made it appear that Britain was further advanced in the field than America. The discussion therefore shifted to the question of how the United States was attached or might attach itself to the British program. "I told of complete interchange with Britain on technical matters, and this was endorsed." Bush explained that the "technical people" in Britain had also formulated policy—had proposed that the government develop the atomic bomb as a weapon of war—and had passed their formulations along directly to the War Cabinet. In the United States, Bush said, an NDRC section and an advisory committee considered technical matters and only he and Conant considered policy.

Policy was the President's prerogative. As soon as Bush exposed it to view Roosevelt seized it. Bush took that decision to be the most important outcome of the meeting and put it emphatically first in his memorandum to Conant. Roosevelt wanted policy consideration restricted to a small group (it came to be called the Top Policy Group). He named its members: Vice President Wallace, Secretary of War Henry L. Stimson, Army Chief of Staff George C. Marshall, Bush and Conant. Every man owed his authority to the President. Roosevelt had instinctively reserved nuclear weapons policy to himself.

Thus at the outset of the U.S. atomic energy program scientists were summarily denied a voice in deciding the political and military uses of the weapons they were proposing to build. Bush accepted the usurpation happily. To him it was simply a matter of who would run the show. It left him on top and inside and he put it to use immediately to shoulder the physics community into line. Within hours, as he wrote Frank Jewett in November, he had "emphasized to Arthur Compton and his people the fact that they are asked to report upon the techniques, and that consideration of general policy has not been turned over to them as a subject."

Significantly, Bush associated the reservation of policy with relief from criticism: "Much of the difficulty in the past has been due to the fact that Ernest Lawrence in particular had strong ideas in regard to policy, and talked about them generally. . . . I cannot . . . bring him into the discussions, as I am not authorized by the President to do so." He applied just this test—silence on policy—to measure Lawrence's and Compton's loyalty: "I think [Lawrence] now understands this, and I am sure that Arthur Compton does, and I think our difficulties in this regard are over."

A scientist could choose to help or not to help build nuclear weapons. That was his only choice. The surrender of any further authority in the matter was the price of admission to what would grow to be a separate, secret state with separate sovereignty linked to the public state through the person and by the sole authority of the President.

Patriotism contributed to many decisions, but a deeper motive among the physicists, by the measure of their statements, was fear—fear of German triumph, fear of a thousand-year Reich made invulnerable with atomic bombs. And deeper even than fear was fatalism. The bomb was latent in nature as a genome is latent in flesh. Any nation might learn to command its expression. The race was therefore not merely against Germany. As Roosevelt apparently sensed, the race was against time.

There are indications in Bush's memorandum that Roosevelt was concerned less with a German challenge than with the long-term consequences of acquiring so decisive a new class of destructive instruments. "We discussed at some length after-war control," Bush wrote Conant, "together with sources of raw material" (sources of raw material were then believed to be few and far between; whoever commanded them might well, it seemed, monopolize the bomb). Roosevelt was thinking beyond developing bombs for the war that the United States had not yet entered. He was thinking about a military development that would change the political organization of the world.

Bush, who was a successful administrator partly because he knew the limits of his charter, then suggested that a "broader program"—industrial production—ought to be handled when the time came by some larger organization than the OSRD. Roosevelt agreed. Summarizing his assignment, Bush told the President he understood he was to expedite in every possible way the necessary research but was "not [to] proceed with any definite steps on this expanded plan until further instructions from him. . . . He indicated that this was correct." The money, the President told him, "would have to come from a special source available for such an unusual purpose and . . . he could arrange this."

The United States was not yet committed to building an atomic bomb. But it was committed to exploring thoroughly whether or not an atomic bomb could be built. One man, Franklin Roosevelt, decided that commitment—secretly, without consulting Congress or courts. It seemed to be a military decision and he was Commander in Chief.

Bush and Conant proceeded to order up from Arthur Compton a third NAS review. Compton asked Samuel Allison for the name of someone who could help him calculate the critical mass of U235. Allison had been corresponding with Enrico Fermi on the subject of carbon absorption cross sections and recommended him highly. Compton "called on Fermi in his office at Columbia University. Stepping to the blackboard he worked out for me, simply and directly, the equation from which could be calculated the critical size of a chain-reacting sphere. He had at his fingertips the most recent experimental values of the constants. He discussed for me the reliability of the data. . . . Even the most conservative estimate showed that the amount of fissionable metal needed to effect a nuclear explosion could hardly be greater than a hundred pounds."*

Compton moved on to Harold Urey's office to look into isotope separation. Urey was the recognized world leader in the field as a result of his Nobel Prize–winning work with hydrogen isotopes; he had directed isotope separation studies for the Uranium Committee and the Naval Research Laboratory since the beginning. He personally investigated chemical separation of U235 (which turned out to be impossible given the chemical compounds of the day) and separation by centrifuge. Estimating that a centrifuge plant that would produce one kilogram of U235 per day would require 40,000 to 50,000 yard-long centrifuges and would cost about $100 million, he had recently contracted with Westinghouse in the name of the Uranium Committtee for a prototype unit.

Urey was initially skeptical of gaseous barrier diffusion. He and John Dunning were not compatible, perhaps because they were both enthusiasts, and only when centrifuge development was well under way, in late 1940, did Urey turn his attention to the process that Dunning and Eugene Booth were working hard at their own expense to develop. They had chosen gaseous diffusion at dinner one evening in 1940 on their way home from a trip to Schenectady by systematically ruling out other methods as unsuitable for large-scale production, much as Peierls and Simon had done. They were interested in nuclear power, Booth remembers, not bomb-making. "Our reasons for pursuing the isotope separation path toward power production were simple and general. If a chain reaction became possible with normal uranium, a smaller and probably cheaper power plant could be made with enriched uranium."

Dunning and Urey produced a joint appraisal of the gaseous-diffusion process in November 1940. Dunning's barrier material at the time was fritted glass—partially fused and therefore porous silica, the material from which porcelain is made—which uranium hexafluoride was likely to cor-

*Compton's memory errs toward more optimism than Fermi's calculations warranted. After Compton's visit Gregory Breit, Briggs' theoretician on the Uranium Committee, asked Fermi to work his formulae on paper. Fermi was busy with his uranium-graphite experiment and produced, on October 6, a sketchy set of notes. He guessed at the cross sections and came up with 130,000 grams—287 pounds. "One cannot," he added, "in my opinion, exclude the possibility that [the critical mass] may be as low as 20,000 grams [44 pounds] or as high as one or more tons."

rode. They estimated that a gaseous-diffusion plant would involve some five thousand separate barrier tanks—"stages"—but made no attempt to determine cost and power requirements.

By the autumn of 1941, without official support, Dunning and Booth had nevertheless made significant progress. They had switched to brass barriers from which the zinc had been etched (brass is an alloy of copper and zinc; etching away the zinc made the material porous). In November, the month after Compton's visit, they would successfully enrich a measurable quantity of uranium with their equipment.

Compton traveled next to Princeton to see Eugene Wigner, who had been working closely with Fermi. Wigner clarified for Compton the difference between fast- and slow-neutron fission. He endorsed the uranium-graphite system Fermi was developing as a method for producing 94. "He urged me," writes Compton, "almost in tears, to help get the atomic program rolling. His lively fear that the Nazis would make the bomb first was the more impressive because from his life in Europe he knew them so well."

Back in Chicago Compton talked to Glenn Seaborg, who had come east from Berkeley at Compton's request. Seaborg was confident he could devise a large-scale, remote-controlled technology for separating 94 chemically from uranium.

Armed with this new round of information Compton called a meeting of his committee for October 21 in Schenectady. He prepared for the meeting by writing a draft report. A letter came from Lawrence saying he wanted to bring along Robert Oppenheimer: "I have a great deal of confidence in Oppie, and I'm anxious to have the benefit of his judgment in our deliberation." Conant had scolded Lawrence at Compton's fireside when he learned that Lawrence had asked Oppenheimer, still an outsider, for help with theory, but now Lawrence's request was granted.

A dispute between Lawrence and Oppenheimer about what Lawrence called the theoretician's "leftwandering activities" almost excluded him from the atomic bomb project. Oppenheimer, married now to the former Katherine Puening, known as Kitty, with a six-month-old son, had begun to wish for assignment. "Many of the men I had known went off to work on radar and other aspects of military research," he testified later. "I was not without envy of them." He learned the price of admission when he invited Lawrence to an organizational meeting at his elegant new home on Eagle Hill for a professional union, the American Association of Scientific Workers, of which Arthur Compton, among others, was a senior member. Lawrence wanted no part in any "causes and concerns," as he called political activities, and barred his staff as well: "I don't think it's a good idea," he told them. "I don't want you to join it. I know nothing wrong with it, but we're planning big things in connection with the war effort, and it wouldn't be right. I want no occasion for somebody in Washington to find fault with us." Oppenheimer was not so easily put off; he debated Lawrence's point, arguing that humanity was everyone's responsibility and that the more fortunate should help "underdogs." The Nazis came first, Lawrence countered. He told Oppenheimer about Conant's scolding. Oppenheimer reserved judgment. The October 21 meeting, where he could measure the scientific leaders of the uranium program against his own formidable gifts, changed his mind. "It was not until my first connection with the rudimentary atomic-energy enterprise," he testifies, "that I began to see any way in which I could be of direct use." When he saw his way to war work he quickly sacrificed his underdogs, writing Lawrence on November 12:

> I . . . assure you that there will be no further difficulties at any time with the A.A.S.W. . . . I doubt very much whether anyone will want to start at this time an organization which could in any way embarrass, divide or interfere with the work we have in hand. I have not yet spoken to everyone involved, but all those to whom I have spoken agree with us: so you can forget it.

Lawrence opened the Schenectady meeting by reading Oliphant's summary of the MAUD Report. Compton followed with a review based on his October travels. Oppenheimer weighed in during the discussion of U235's critical mass with an estimate of 100 kilograms, 220 pounds, close to Fermi's estimate of 130,000 grams. "Kistiakowsky," writes Compton, "explained the great economic advantage of being able to deliver a heavy blow with a bomb carried by a single plane."

But Compton was distressed to discover he could not move the engineers on the review committee—the practical souls Bush had insisted be added to bring the NAS reviews down to earth—to estimate either how much time it would take to build a bomb or how much the enterprise would cost:

> With one accord they refused. . . . There weren't enough data. The fact was that they had before them all the relevant information that existed, and some kind of answer was needed, however rough it might be, for otherwise our recommendation could not be acted upon. After some discussion, I suggested a total time of between three and five years, and a total cost . . . of some hundreds of millions of dollars. None of the committee members objected.

So the American numbers came out of a scientist's hat, as the British numbers had. Atomic energy was still too new for engineering.

If Compton was distressed by the refusal of commitment, Lawrence was appalled. Within twenty-four hours he mailed the committee chairman a bracing challenge edged with threat:

> In our meeting yesterday, there was a tendency to emphasize the uncertainties, and accordingly the possibility that uranium will not be a factor in the war. This to my mind, was very dangerous. . . .
>
> It will not be a calamity if, when we get the answers to the uranium problem, they turn out negative from the military point of view, but if the answers are fantastically positive and we fail to get them first, the results for our country may well be tragic disaster. I feel strongly, therefore, that anyone who hesitates on a vigorous, all-out effort on uranium assumes a grave responsibility.

But Compton had already been threatened by an expert, Vannevar Bush, and knew his duty well, though he did not yet know that Bush was already committed to expedition and expansion. He had difficulty estimating "the destructiveness of the bomb." The calculation "involved problems of gas pressure, specific heats at hitherto unknown temperatures, the transmission of radiations and particles through the material, and forces of inertia." He asked Gregory Breit for help. Breit was even more obsessed with secrecy than Briggs. "No help was forthcoming," says Compton, gritting his teeth. He turned then to Oppenheimer. "I had known 'Oppie' for some fourteen years and had found him most competent in seeing the essentials of an intricate problem and in interpreting what he saw. So I was glad to get a letter from him with helpful suggestions." Through the end of October Compton worked on.

At Leipzig in September Werner Heisenberg received the first forty gallons of heavy water from Norsk Hydro and immediately prepared another chain-reaction experiment like the unsuccessful effort at the Virus House in Dahlem the year before: a thirty-inch aluminum sphere filled with alternating layers of heavy water and uranium oxide, more than three hundred pounds of it, arranged around a central neutron source, the sphere itself then immersed in water in a laboratory tank. This time Heisenberg found some increase in neutrons, enough to extrapolate eventual success. The German laureate knew now from the work of von Weizsäcker and Houtermans that a sustained chain reaction in natural uranium would breed element 94. "It was from September 1941," he remarks in consequence, "that we saw an open road ahead of us, leading to the atomic bomb."

He decided to talk to Bohr. To what end he thought Bohr might help him he never unambiguously explained. His wife Elisabeth believes "he was lonely in Germany. Niels Bohr had become a father figure to him.... He thought that he could talk about anything with Bohr.... The advice of an older friend, more experienced in human and political affairs, had always been important to him." He "saw himself confronted with the spectre of the atomic bomb," Elisabeth Heisenberg explains, "and he wanted to signal to Bohr that Germany neither would nor could build a bomb.... Secretly he even hoped that his message could prevent the use of an atomic bomb on Germany one day. He was constantly tortured by this idea.... This vague hope was probably the strongest motivation for his trip."

Heisenberg and von Weizsäcker attended a scientific meeting in Copenhagen at the end of October, a meeting Bohr routinely boycotted as he boycotted all joint Danish and German activities, to emphasize his refusal to collaborate. He was willing to see Heisenberg, however, and received him, according to the German physicist's wife, "with great warmth and hospitality."

Heisenberg saved his crucial conversation for a long evening walk with Bohr through the brewery district around the Carlsberg House of Honor. "Being aware that Bohr was under the surveillance of the German political authorities," he recalled after the war, "and that his assertions about me would probably be reported to Germany, I tried to conduct this talk in such a way as to preclude putting my life into immediate danger." Heisenberg remembers asking Bohr if it was right for physicists to work on "the uranium problem" in wartime when there was a possibility that such work could lead to "grave consequences in the technique of war." Bohr, who had returned from the United States convinced that a bomb was practically impossible, "understood the meaning of the question immediately, as I realized from his slightly frightened reaction." Heisenberg apparently thought Bohr was privy to American secrets and was reacting guiltily to implicit exposure. But Bohr's next response suggests that he had been, rather, stunned at Heisenberg's revelation: he asked Heisenberg if a bomb really was possible. Heisenberg says he answered that a "terrific technical effort" would be necessary, which he hoped could not be realized in the present war. "Bohr was shocked by my reply, obviously assuming that I had intended to convey to him that Germany had made great progress in the direction of manufacturing atomic weapons. Although I tried subsequently to correct this false impression I probably did not succeed.... I was very unhappy about the result of this conversation."

Thus Heisenberg's version of the evening walk. Bohr's is less detailed. His son Aage, a Nobel laureate in his turn and his father's successor as director of the Copenhagen institute, summarizes it in a memoir:

> The impression that in Germany great military importance was given to [atomic energy research] was strengthened by the visit to Copenhagen in the autumn of 1941 of Werner Heisenberg and C. F. von Weizsäcker. . . . In a private conversation with my father Heisenberg brought up the question of the military applications of atomic energy. My father was very reticent and expressed his scepticism because of the great technical difficulties that had to be overcome, but he had the impression that Heisenberg thought that the new possibilities could decide the outcome of the war if the war dragged on. . . . [Heisenberg's] account [of the meeting] has no basis in actual events.

Robert Oppenheimer, who also had the story direct from Bohr, condenses the meeting to the comment: "Heisenberg and von Weizsäcker came over from Germany, and so did others. Bohr had the impression that they came less to tell what they knew than to see if Bohr knew anything that they did not; I believe that it was a standoff."

The two accounts are not incompatible, but both leave out a crucial fact: that Heisenberg passed to Bohr a drawing of the experimental heavy-water reactor he was working to build. If he did so clandestinely he certainly risked his life. If he did so cynically and with Nazi approval to misdirect Allied intelligence he was certainly no longer attached to Bohr as a father figure, as Elisabeth Heisenberg writes. Whatever his intent, it had the wrong effect on Bohr. Elisabeth Heisenberg thinks "Bohr essentially heard only one single sentence: The Germans knew that atomic bombs could be built. He was deeply shaken by this, and his consternation was so great that he lost track of all else." But Aage Bohr's and Oppenheimer's accounts imply a further response from Bohr: indignation, even incredulity, that Heisenberg would think Bohr might be willing in any way, for any reason, to cooperate with Nazi Germany. Heisenberg, in turn, was aghast that Bohr would fail to see and credit his reservations, would not understand, as his wife writes, that his "bond to his country and its people was not tantamount to a bond to the regime." To the contrary, she adds, "Bohr told Heisenberg that he understood completely that one had to use all of one's abilities and energies for one's country in time of war." Not surprisingly, since it implied Bohr thought the worst of him—that he was willing to work for the Nazis—"Heisenberg was deeply shocked by Bohr's reply."

The meeting, and especially the drawing Heisenberg passed, gave Bohr more to worry about, but he continued to doubt that any nation could afford sufficient industrial capacity, especially in wartime, to pursue isotope separation. He must have been pained at what he took to be the treachery of a brilliant and formerly devoted protégé. Heisenberg for his part found himself, says his wife, in "a state of confusion and despair." Even at risk he had not convinced Bohr of his sincerity nor in any way begun a dialogue to avert possible catastrophe. In the absence of such dialogue he had only managed potentially to alarm Germany's most powerful enemy further with news of progress in approaching the chain reaction. That news must necessarily accelerate Allied efforts to build a bomb. As Rudolf Peierls writes of this period in Heisenberg's life, "he had agreed to sup with the devil, and perhaps he found that there was not a long enough spoon."

Arthur Compton sent draft copies of the third National Academy of Sciences report to Vannevar Bush and Frank Jewett before the weekend of November 1. The new report was brief—six double-spaced typewritten pages (with forty-nine pages of technical appendices and figures)—and finally and emphatically to the point: "The special objective of the present report is to consider *the possibilities of an explosive fission reaction with U235.*" Progress toward separating uranium isotopes, Compton wrote, made renewed consideration urgent (a rationale somewhat less than candid: British progress had spurred the change).

This time the report knew what it was about: "*A fission bomb of superlative destructive power will result from bringing quickly together a sufficient mass of element U235.* This seems to be as sure as any untried prediction based upon theory and experiment can be." On the second page an estimate of critical mass elicited for the first time among the three NAS reports a mention of fast fission: "*The mass of U235 required to produce explosive fission under appropriate conditions can hardly be less than 2 kg nor greater than 100 kg.* These wide limits reflect chiefly the experimental uncertainty in the capture cross-section of U235 for fast neutrons."

The NAS estimate of destructiveness was low compared to the MAUD Report estimate, some 30 tons of TNT equivalent per kilogram of U235 (for 25 pounds, 300 tons compared to MAUD's 1,800 tons), but the American report attempted to compensate for its doubts about the efficacy of an intense energy release from a small amount of matter by emphasizing that the destructive effects on life of a bomb's radioactivity "may be as important as those of the explosion itself."

The centrifuge and gaseous diffusion programs were noted to be "approaching the stage of practical test." Fission bombs might be available "in significant quantity within three or four years." Like its predecessors the report stressed not the German challenge but the long-term prospect: "The possibility must be seriously considered that within a few years the use of bombs such as described here, or something similar using uranium fission, may determine military superiority. Adequate care for our national defense seems to demand urgent development of this program."

In detailed appendices Compton calculated the critical mass of a bomb heavily constrained in tamper at no more than 3.4 kilograms; Kistiakowsky debated whether a fission explosion would be as destructive in terms of energy produced as the explosion of an equivalently energetic mass of TNT and confirmed the feasibility of firing together two pieces of uranium at a speed of several thousand feet per second; and a senior physicist on Compton's committee reported favorably on the isotope-separation systems then under consideration and recommended "the principle of *parallel development,*" meaning pursuing them all at once, an expensive way to save time in case one or more failed.

Notably missing from the third report was any mention of the uranium-graphite work going on at Columbia or of plutonium. Compton remembers that a U235 bomb looked "more straightforward and more certain of accomplishment" than a plutonium bomb, but the omission also measures the extent to which Briggs' judgment of priorities, and Briggs himself, had been set aside. Bush writing Jewett before he met with Compton had already mentioned "leaving Briggs in charge of a section devoted as it is at the present time to physical measurements"—small potatoes indeed—and constituting "a new group under a full-time head to handle development." He was considering Ernest Lawrence but still thought Lawrence talked too much: "The matter . . . would have to be handled under the strictest sort of secrecy. This is the reason that I hesitate at the name of Ernest Lawrence."

If the third and last NAS report only rationalized a previous presidential decision, it at least served to check the British findings independently and to commit the American physics community to the cause. The United States had finally set its wheels to the bomb track. Its inertia was proportional to the juggernaut of its scientific, engineering and industrial might. Acceleration overcoming inertia, it now began to roll.

No document Franklin Delano Roosevelt signed authenticates the fateful decision to expedite research toward an atomic bomb that Vannevar Bush reported in his October 9 memorandum to James Bryant Conant: the archives divulge no smoking gun. The closest the records come to a piece of paper that changed the world is a banality. Bush personally delivered the third National Academy of Sciences report to the President on November 27, 1941. Roosevelt returned it to him two months later with a note on White House stationery written in black ink with a broad-nibbed pen, a note that would communicate only a commonplace of the housekeeping of state secrets except for the authority of its first vernacular expression and the initials it bears:

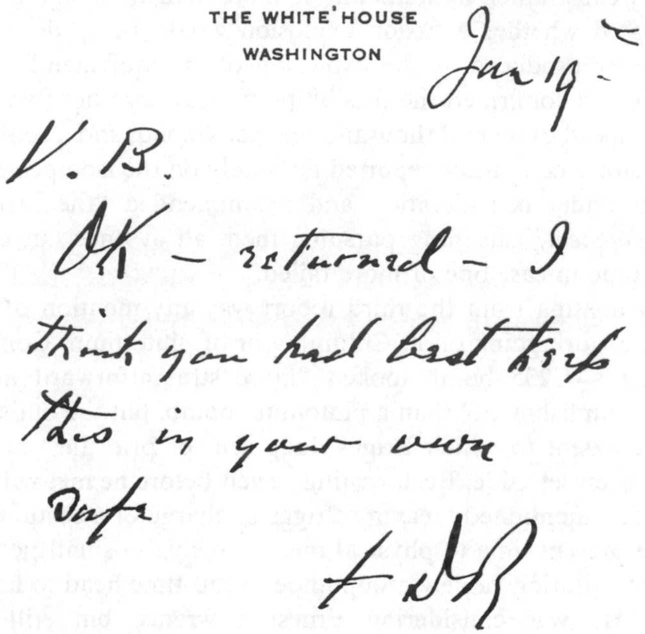
THE WHITE HOUSE
WASHINGTON

Jan 19 —
V.B.
OK — returned — I think you had best keep this in your own safe
FDR

Text reads: "Jan 19— V.B. OK —returned— I think you had best keep this in your own safe FDR"

Still orphaned was plutonium, which Lawrence and Compton believed so promising. Compton found his chance to speak for it in early December when Bush and Conant called the members of the Uranium Committee to Washington to announce the reorganization of their work. Harold Urey would develop gaseous diffusion at Columbia, Bush and Conant had decided. Lawrence would pursue electromagnetic separation at Berkeley. A young chemical engineer, Eger V. Murphree, the director of research for Standard Oil of New Jersey, would supervise centrifuge development and look into broader questions of engineering. Compton in Chicago would be responsible for theoretical studies and the actual design of the bomb. "The meeting adjourned," writes Compton, "with the understanding that we would meet again in two weeks to compare progress and shape our plans more firmly."

Bush, Conant and Compton went to lunch at the Cosmos Club on Lafayette Square. There the Chicago physicist spoke up for plutonium. He argued that the advantage of chemical extraction rather than isotope separation made element 94 "a worthy competitor." Bush was wary. Conant pointed out that the new element's chemistry was still largely unknown. Compton recalls their exchange:

> "Seaborg tells me that within six months from the time [plutonium] is formed [by chain reaction] he can have it available for use in the bomb," was my comment.
>
> "Glenn Seaborg is a very competent young chemist, but he isn't that good," said Conant.

How good a chemist Glenn Seaborg might be remained to be seen. Compton, Conant remembers, went on to argue that "the construction of a self-sustaining chain reaction [in natural uranium—Fermi's and Szilard's project] would be a magnificent achievement" even if plutonium flunked as bomb material; "it would prove that the measurements and theoretical calculations were correct":

> I never knew whether it was this near-certainty of demonstrating a slow-neutron reaction which settled the matter in Van's mind, or whether he was impressed with Compton's faith in the production of a plutonium bomb, against my lack of faith as a chemist. At all events, within a matter of weeks he agreed to Arthur Compton's setting up at Chicago a highly secret project.

Bush had called the Washington meeting on a weekend to accommodate busy men. They had assembled on Saturday, December 6, 1941. Almost immediately they found themselves busier yet.

At 7 A.M. Hawaiian time on Sunday, December 7, 1941, near Kahuku Point at the northernmost reach of the island of Oahu, two U.S. Army privates in the process of shutting down the Opana mobile radar station, an aircraft reconnaissance unit which they had manned since 4 A.M., noticed an unusual disturbance on their oscilloscope screen. They checked and confirmed no malfunction and decided the large merged blur of light "must be a flight of some sort." Their plotting board indicated a bearing out of the northeast at a distance of 132 miles. More than fifty planes appeared to be involved. One of the men called the information center at Fort Shafter, at the other end of the island, where radar and visual reconnaissance reports were combined on a tabletop map. The lieutenant who took the phone heard the radar operator call the sightings "the biggest . . . he had ever seen." The operator did not, however, report his estimate of their number.

Both the Army and the Navy had been warned of imminent danger of

Japanese attack. The Japanese had convinced themselves that dominance over East Asia was vital to their survival. The American reaction to militant Japanese expansion into Manchuria and China—as many as 200,000 men, women and children were brutally slaughtered by the Japanese Army in Shanghai in 1937—had been to embargo war materials and freeze Japanese assets in the United States. Aviation fuel, steel and scrap iron went on the embargo list in September 1940 when the Japanese moved into French Indochina with the timid approval of Vichy France. After that the Japanese estimated they could survive no more than eighteen months without access to Asian oil and iron ore. For some time they had prepared for war while continuing to negotiate. Now negotiations had collapsed.

Lieutenant General Walter C. Short, commander of the Army's Hawaiian Department, received a coded message on November 27 signed in the name of the Chief of Staff—George Marshall—that read in part:

> Negotiations with Japan appear to be terminated to all practical purposes with only the barest possibility that the Japanese Government might come back and offer to continue. Japanese future action unpredictable but hostile action possible at any moment. If hostilities cannot, repeat cannot be avoided the United States desires that Japan commit the first overt act. . . . Measures should be carried out so as not, repeat not, to alarm civil population or disclose intent.

Short had at option three levels of alert, escalating from "a defense against sabotage, espionage and subversive activities without any threat from the outside" to full defense against "an all-out attack." He thought it obvious that the War Department message "was written basically for General MacArthur in the Philippines" and chose the limited sabotage defense, Alert No. 1.

Admiral Husband E. Kimmel, Commander in Chief of the U.S. Pacific Fleet, which was based at Pearl Harbor west of Honolulu on the southern coast of Oahu, received a similar but even more pointed message from the Navy Department a few hours later:

> This dispatch is to be considered a war warning. Negotiations with Japan looking toward stabilization of conditions in the Pacific have ceased and an aggressive move by Japan is expected within the next few days. The number and equipment of Japanese troops and the organization of naval task forces indicates an amphibious expedition against either the Philippines, Thai or Kra Peninsula or possibly Borneo. Execute an appropriate defensive deployment preparatory to carrying out the tasks assigned.

Kimmel noted the references to other theaters of potential conflict. When he and Short exchanged messages he noted the "more cautious phrasing" of the Army warning. "Appropriate defensive deployment" meant, he thought, full security measures for ships at sea. A surprise submarine attack seemed possible and he ordered the depth-bombing of any submarines discovered in the waters around Oahu.

The Army lieutenant who took the Opana radar call therefore had no expectation of danger. He looked for a routine explanation of the unusual report and found it. The Army paid radio station KGMB in Honolulu to play Hawaiian music throughout the night whenever it ferried aircraft to the Islands, giving its navigators a signal to seek. The lieutenant had heard such music on the radio that morning on his way to the information center. He decided that the radar must be picking up a flight of B-17's. The heading plotted at Opanu was the usual direction of approach from California. "Well, don't worry about it," the lieutenant told the radar men.

Pearl Harbor is a shallow, compound basin sheltered inland through a narrow outer channel from the sea. A bulge of land, Pearl City, and a midbasin island, Ford Island, canalize the main anchorage of the harbor into a loop of narrow inlets. In 1941 drydocks, oil storage tanks and a submarine base occupied the harbor's irregular eastern shore. Seven battleships rode at anchor immediately southeast of Ford Island that Sunday morning: *Nevada* anchored alone; *Arizona* inboard of the repair ship *Vestal; Tennessee* inboard of *West Virginia; Maryland* inboard of *Oklahoma; California* alone. An eighth battleship, *Pennsylvania*, wedged naked in drydock nearby.

Lieutenant Commander Mitsuo Fuchida of the Japanese Imperial Navy, thirty-nine years old, who wore a red shirt to disguise from his men any blood he might shed and a white *hachimaki* tied around his flight helmet brushed with the calligraphic characters for "Certain Victory," called out *"Tora! Tora! Tora!"* at 0753 hours as his pilot banked around Barber's Point southwest of Pearl: *"Tiger!"* three times invoked to announce to the listening Japanese Navy that his first wave of 183 planes had achieved complete surprise. The 43 fighters, 49 high-level bombers, 51 dive-bombers and 40 torpedo planes he commanded had flown from six carriers holding station 200 miles to the north, carriers formidably escorted by battleships, heavy cruisers, destroyers and submarines that had left Hitokappu Bay on the northern Japanese island of Etorofu on November 25 and sailed blacked out in radio silence across the stormy but empty northern Pacific for almost two weeks to achieve this stunning rendezvous.

The torpedo bombers divided into groups of twos and threes and dived. The aircrews had prepared themselves to ram the battleships if necessary, but nothing restrained their attack. At 0758 the Ford Island command center radioed its frantic message to the world: AIR RAID PEARL HARBOR. THIS IS NOT DRILL. Admiral Kimmel saw the attack begin from a neighbor's lawn—"in utter disbelief and completely stunned," the neighbor remembers, "as white as the uniform he wore." Torpedoes struck a light cruiser and a target ship, a minelayer, another light cruiser, then the battleships: *Arizona* lifted out of the water; *West Virginia* washed by a huge waterspout; *Oklahoma* hit by three torpedoes one after another and immediately listing steeply to port; the bottom blown out of *Arizona;* three torpedoes into *California;* two more into *West Virginia*; a fourth into *Oklahoma* that bounced the big ship and rolled it over bottom up; *Arizona* taking a bomb that detonated its forward explosive stores, ripped the ship apart, killed at least a thousand men and blew high into the air a grisly rain of bodies, hands, legs and heads; a torpedo tearing out *Nevada*'s port bow. Thick black smoke rolled up to foul the blue Hawaiian morning and in the water, burning, screaming men attempted to swim through a dense scum of burning oil. Japanese fighters and bombers destroyed aircraft on the ground and strafed soldiers and marines pouring out of barracks at Hickam Field and Ewa Field and Wheeler. An hour later a second wave of 167 more attack aircraft deployed to further destruction. The two raids accounted for eight battleships, three light cruisers, three destroyers and four other ships sunk, capsized or damaged and 292 aircraft damaged or wrecked, including 117 bombers. And 2,403 Americans, military and civilian, killed, 1,178 wounded, in unprovoked assaults that lasted only minutes. The following afternoon, Franklin Roosevelt, addressing Congress in joint session, requested and won a declaration of war against not only Japan but Germany and Italy as well.

The man who conceived and planned the surprise attack on Pearl Harbor, Admiral Isoroku Yamamoto, Commander in Chief of the Japanese Combined Fleet, had few illusions about the ultimate success of a war against the United States. He had studied at Harvard and served as a naval attaché in Washington and knew America's strength. But if war had to come he meant "to give a fatal blow to the enemy fleet" when it was least expected, at the outset. By that act he hoped he could win his country six months to a year during which it might establish its Greater East Asia Co-Prosperity Sphere and dig in.

The torpedoes had been a challenge. Pearl Harbor was only forty feet deep. Torpedoes dropped from planes routinely sank seventy feet or more before bobbing up to attack depth. The Japanese had to reduce that plunge signficantly or bury their weapons in the Pearl mud.

They found in repeated experiments that they could sometimes manage a shallower drop by flying only forty feet above the water and holding down their air speed—the maneuver demanded skilled flying—but further improvement required torpedo redesign, largely by trial and error. As late as mid-October Fuchida's flyers were still managing no better than sixty-foot plunges, still far too deep.

A new stabilizer fin, originally designed for aerial stability, saved the mission. Tested during September, it consistently held the torpedo to less than forty feet and steadied it as well. But the pilots still needed aiming practice. Only thirty of the modified weapons could be promised by October 15, another fifty by the end of the month and the last hundred on November 30, after the task force was scheduled to sail.

The manufacturer did better. Realizing the weapons were vital to a secret program of unprecedented importance, manager Yukiro Fukuda bent company rules, drove his lathe and assembly crews overtime and delivered the last of the 180 specially modified torpedoes by November 17. Mitsubishi Munitions contributed decisively to the success of the first massive surprise blow of the Pacific War by the patriotic effort of its torpedo factory on Kyushu, the southernmost Japanese island, three miles up the Urakami River from the bay in the old port city of Nagasaki.

13

The New World

Enrico Fermi's team at Columbia University had been hard at work through 1941 while the government deliberated. Fermi, Leo Szilard, Herbert Anderson and the young physicists who had joined them may never have known how close they came to orphanhood. The isolation of plutonium at Berkeley added a potential military application to their reasons for pursuing a slow-neutron chain reaction in uranium and graphite, but given the necessary resources Fermi at least would certainly have pursued the chain reaction anyway as a physical experiment of fundamental and historic worth. He had missed discovering fission by the thickness of a sheet of aluminum foil; he would not willingly leave to someone else the demonstration of atomic energy's first sustained release. Thanks largely to Arthur Compton his work found continued support, which may help explain why he admired the pious Woosterite's intelligence so extravagantly.

Szilard had finally gone on the Columbia payroll on November 1, 1940, when the $40,000 National Defense Research Committee contract came through for physical-constant measurements. To help Fermi without the friction the two men generated when they worked side by side, Szilard undertook to apply his special talent for enlightened cajolery to the problem of procuring supplies of purified uranium and graphite. The record is thick with his correspondence with American graphite manufacturers dismayed to discover that what they thought were the purest of materials were in fact hopelessly contaminated, usually with traces of boron. The cross section for neutron absorption of that light, ubiquitous, silicon-like element, number 5 on the periodic table, was tremendous and poisonous. "Szilard at that time took extremely decisive and strong steps to try to organize the early phases of production of pure materials," says Fermi. ". . . He did a marvelous job which later on was taken over by a more powerful organization than was Szilard himself. Although to match Szilard it takes a few able-bodied customers."

In August and September the Columbia team prepared to assemble the largest uranium-graphite lattice yet devised. A slow-neutron chain reaction in natural uranium, like its fast-neutron counterpart U235, requires a critical mass: a volume of uranium and moderator sufficient to sustain neutron multiplication despite the inevitable loss of neutrons from its outer surface. No one yet knew the specifications of that critical volume, but it was obviously vast—on the order of some hundreds of tons. One way to create a self-sustaining chain reaction might be simply to continue stacking uranium and graphite together. But so crude an experiment, if it worked at all, would teach the experimenter very little about controlling the resulting reaction and might culminate in a disastrous and lethal runaway. Fermi proposed to approach the problem by the more circumspect route of a series of subcritical experiments designed to determine the necessary quantities and arrangements and to establish methods of control.

As always, he built directly on previous experience. He and Anderson had calculated the absorption cross section of carbon by measuring the diffusion of neutrons from a neutron source up a column of graphite. The new experiments would enlarge that column to take advantage of the increased stocks of graphite available and to make room for regularly spaced inclusions of uranium oxide: simplicity itself, but in physical form a thick, black, grimy, slippery mass of some thirty tons of extruded bars of graphite confining eight tons of oxide. Fermi named the structure a "pile." "Much of the standard nomenclature in nuclear science was developed at this time," Segrè writes. ". . . I thought for a while that this term was used to refer to a source of nuclear energy in analogy with Volta's use of the Italian term *pila* to denote his own great invention of a source of electrical energy [i.e., the Voltaic battery]. I was disillusioned by Fermi himself, who told me that he simply used the common English word *pile* as synonymous with *heap*." The Italian laureate was continuing to master the plainsong of American speech.

The exponential pile Fermi proposed to build (so called because an exponent entered into the calculation of its relationship to a full-scale reactor) would be too big for any of the laboratories in Pupin. He sought larger quarters:

> We went to Dean Pegram, who was then the man who could carry out magic around the university, and we explained to him that we needed a big room. And when we say big we meant a really big room. Perhaps he made a crack about a church not being the most suited place for a physics laboratory . . . but I think a church would have been just precisely what we wanted. Well, he scouted around the campus and we went with him to dark corridors and under various heating pipes and so on to visit possible sites for this experiment and eventually a big room, not a church, but something that might have been compared in size with a church was discovered in Schermerhorn [Hall].

There, Fermi goes on, they began to build "this structure that at that time looked again in order of magnitude larger than anything that we had seen before. . . . It was a structure of graphite bricks and spread through these graphite bricks in some sort of pattern were big cans, cubic cans, containing uranium oxide." The cans, 8 by 8 by 8 inches, 288 of them in all, were made of tinned iron sheet; each could hold about 60 pounds of uranium oxide. Each cubic "cell" of the uranium-graphite lattice—a can and its surrounding graphite—was 16 inches on a side. Spheres of uranium in an arrangement of spherical cells would have been more efficient. In these beginning experiments, with materials of doubtful purity, Fermi was pursuing order-of-magnitude estimates, a first rough mapping of new territory. "This structure was chosen because of its constructional simplicity," the experimenters wrote afterward, "since it could be assembled without cutting our graphite bricks of 4″ by 4″ by 12″. Although we did not expect that the structure would approach too closely the optimum proportions, we thought it desirable to obtain some preliminary information as soon as possible." Promising results might also win further NDRC support.

"We were faced with a lot of hard and dirty work," Herbert Anderson recalls. "The black uranium oxide powder had to be . . . heated to drive off undesired moisture and then packed hot in the containers and soldered shut. To get the required density, the filling was done on a shaking table. Our little group, which by that time included Bernard Feld, George Weil, and Walter Zinn, looked at the heavy task before us with little enthusiasm. It would be exhausting work." Then Pegram to the rescue in Fermi's telling:

> We were reasonably strong, but I mean we were, after all, thinkers. So Dean Pegram again looked around and said that seems to be a job a little bit beyond your feeble strength, but there is a football squad at Columbia that contains a

dozen or so of very husky boys who take jobs by the hour just to carry them through college. Why don't you hire them?

And it was a marvelous idea; it was really a pleasure for once to direct the work of these husky boys, canning uranium—just shoving it in—handling packs of 50 or 100 pounds with the same ease as another person would have handled three or four pounds.

"Fermi tried to do his share of the work," Anderson adds; "he donned a lab coat and pitched in to do his stint with the football men, but it was clear that he was out of his class. The rest of us found a lot to keep us busy with measurements and calibrations that suddenly seemed to require exceptional care and precision."

For this first exponential experiment and the many similar experiments to come, Fermi defined a single fundamental magnitude for assessing the chain reaction, "the reproduction factor *k*." *k* was the average number of secondary neutrons produced by one original neutron in a lattice of infinite size—in other words, if the original neutron had all the room in the world in which to drift on its way to encountering a uranium nucleus. One neutron in the zero generation would produce *k* neutrons in the first generation, k^2 neutrons in the second generation, k^3 in the third generation and so on. If *k* was greater than 1.0, the series would diverge, the chain reaction would go, "in which case the production of neutrons is infinite." If *k* was less than 1.0, the series would eventually converge to zero: the chain reaction would die out. *k* would depend on the quantity and quality of materials used in the pile and the efficiency of their arrangement.

The cubical lattice that the Columbia football squad stacked in Schermerhorn Hall in September 1941 extrapolated to a disappointing first *k* of 0.87. "Now that is by 0.13 less than one," Fermi comments—13 percent less than the minimum necessary to make a chain reaction go—"and it was bad. However, at the moment we had a firm point to start from, and we had essentially to see whether we could squeeze the extra 0.13 or preferably a little bit more." The cans were made of iron, and iron absorbs neutrons. "So, out go the cans." Cubes of uranium were less efficient than spheres; next time the Columbia group would press the oxide into small rounded lumps. The materials were impure. "So, now, what do these impurities do?—clearly they can do only harm. Maybe they make harm to the tune of 13 percent." Szilard would continue his quest for materials of higher purity. "There was some considerable gain to be made . . . there."

"Well," concludes Fermi, "this brings us to Pearl Harbor."

Arthur Compton had less than two weeks to throw together a program between his discussion with Vannevar Bush and James Bryant Conant at the

Cosmos Club luncheon on December 6 and the first meeting on December 18 of the new leaders of what was now to be called the S-1 program. (S-1 for Section One of the Office of Scientific Research and Development: Conant would administer S-1, but the National Defense Research Committee was no longer directly involved; the bomb program had advanced from research into development.) On December 18, Conant notes in the secret history of the project he wrote in 1943, "the atmosphere was charged with excitement—the country had been at war nine days, an expansion of the S-1 program was now an accomplished matter. Enthusiasm and optimism reigned." Compton offered his program to Bush, Conant and Briggs the next day and followed up on December 20 with a memorandum. The projects that had come under his authority were scattered across the country at Columbia, Princeton, Chicago and Berkeley. For the time being he proposed leaving them there.

With the arrival of war, not to breathe a word of the mysteries they were exploring, the project leaders had adopted an informal code: plutonium was "copper," U235 "magnesium," uranium generically in the nonsensical British coinage "tube alloy." "On the basis of the present data," Compton wrote, optimism reigning, "it appears that explosive units of copper need be only half the size of those using magnesium, and that premature explosions can be ruled out." Because of the difficulty of engineering a remotely controlled chemical plant to extract plutonium, however, he thought that "the production of useful quantities of copper will take longer than the production of magnesium." For a timetable he offered:

> Knowledge of conditions for chain reaction by June 1, 1942.
> Production of chain reaction by October 1, 1942.
> Pilot plant for using reaction for copper production, October 1, 1943.
> Copper in usable quantities by December 31, 1944.

His schedule was designed to show that plutonium might be produced in time to influence the outcome of the war, the standard which Conant was insisting upon after Pearl Harbor even more vehemently than before. But the uranium-graphite work had not yet won even Compton's full confidence. If graphite proved impractical and "copper production" had to wait for heavy water (of which Harold Urey was urging the extraction at an existing plant in Canada), Compton's schedule would slip by "from 6 months to 18 months." And that might be too late to make a difference.

For the next six months, Compton estimated, the pile studies at Columbia, Princeton and Chicago would cost $590,000 for materials and $618,000 for salaries and support. "This figure seemed big to me," he remembers modestly, "accustomed as I was to work on research that needed not more than a few thousand dollars per year."

He had met with Pegram and Fermi to prepare this part of his proposal and concluded that when metallic uranium became available the project should be concentrated at Columbia. Over Christmas and through the first weeks of January it fell to Herbert Anderson, the native son, to find a building in the New York City area large enough to house a full-scale chain-reacting pile. Not to be outdone in the matter of informal codes, the Columbia team had named that culmination "the egg-boiling experiment." Anderson stumped the wintry boroughs and turned up seven likely locations for boiling uranium eggs. He proposed them to Szilard on January 21; they included a Polo Grounds structure, an aircraft hangar on Long Island that belonged to Curtiss-Wright and the hangar Goodyear used to house its blimps.

But as Compton reviewed the work of the several groups that had come under his authority, bringing their leaders together in Chicago three times during January, their disagreements and duplications made it obvious that all the developmental work on the chain reaction and on plutonium chemistry should be combined at one location. Pegram offered Columbia. They considered Princeton and Berkeley and industrial laboratories in Cleveland and Pittsburgh. Compton offered Chicago. No one wanted to move.

The third meeting of the new year, on Saturday, January 24, Compton conducted from his sickbed in one of the sparsely furnished spare bedrooms on the third floor of his large University Avenue house: he had the flu. Risking infection, Szilard attended, Ernest Lawrence, Luis Alvarez—Lawrence and Alvarez sitting together on the next bed—and several other men. "Each was arguing the merits of his own location," Compton writes, "and every case was good. I presented the case for Chicago." He had already won the support of his university's administration. "We will turn the university inside out if necessary to help win this war," its vice president had sworn. That was Compton's first argument: he knew the management and had its support. Second, more scientists were available to staff the operation in the Midwest than on the coasts, where faculties and graduate schools had been "completely drained" for other war work. Third, Chicago was conveniently and centrally located for travel to other sites.

Which convinced no one. Szilard had forty tons of graphite on hand at Columbia and a going concern. The arguments continued. Compton, who was notoriously indecisive, suffered their brunt as long as he could bear it. "Finally, wearied to the point of exhaustion but needing to make a firm decision, I told them that Chicago would be [the project's] location."

Lawrence scoffed. "You'll never get a chain reaction going here," he baited his fellow laureate. "The whole tempo of the University of Chicago is too slow."

"We'll have the chain reaction going here by the end of the year," Compton predicted.

"I'll bet you a thousand dollars you won't."

"I'll take you on that," Compton says he answered, "and these men here are the witnesses."

"I'll cut the stakes to a five-cent cigar," Lawrence hedged.

"Agreed," said Compton, who never smoked a cigar in his life.

After the crowd left, Compton shuffled wearily to his study and called Fermi. "He agreed at once to make the move to Chicago," Compton writes. Fermi may have agreed, but he found the decision burdensome. He was preparing further experiment. His group was exactly the right size. He owned a pleasant house in a pleasant suburb. He and Laura had buried a cache of Nobel Prize money in a lead pipe under the concrete floor of their basement coal bin against the possibility that as enemy aliens their assets would be frozen. Laura Fermi "had come to consider Leonia as our permanent home," she writes, "and loathed the idea of moving again." She says her husband "was unhappy to move. *They* (I did not know who they were) had decided to concentrate all *that* work (I did not know what it was) in Chicago and to enlarge it greatly, Enrico grumbled. It was the work he had started at Columbia with a small group of physicists. There is much to be said for a small group. It can work quite efficiently." But the country was at war. Fermi traveled back and forth by train until the end of April, then camped in Chicago. Laura dug up their buried treasure and followed at the end of June.

To Szilard, the day after the sickbed meeting—he had returned promptly to New York—Compton sent a respectful telegram: THANK YOU FOR COMING TO PRESENT ABLY COLUMBIA'S SITUATION. NOW WE NEED YOUR HELP IN ORGANIZING THE METALLURGICAL LABORATORY OF O.S.R.D. IN CHICAGO. CAN YOU ARRIVE HERE WEDNESDAY MORNING WITH FERMI AND WIGNER . . . TO DISCUSS DETAILS OF MOVING AND ORGANIZATION. Unlike the Radiation Laboratory at MIT, the new Metallurgical Laboratory hardly disguised its purpose in its name. Who would imagine its goal was the transmutation of the elements to make baseball-sized explosive spheres of unearthly metal?

Before Fermi and his team moved to Illinois they built one more exponential pile, this one loaded with cylindrical lumps of pressed uranium oxide three inches long and three inches in diameter that weighed four pounds each, some two thousand in all, set in blind holes drilled directly into graphite. A new recruit, a handsome, dark-haired young experimentalist named John Marshall, located a suitable press for the work in a junkyard in Jersey City and set it up on the seventh floor of Pupin; Walter Zinn designed stainless steel dies; the powdered oxide bound together under pressure as medicinal tablets pressed from powder—aspirin, for example—do.

Fermi was concerned to free the pile as completely as possible of moisture to reduce neutron absorption. He had canned the oxide before; now he decided to can the entire nine-foot graphite cube. "There are no ready-made cans of the needed size," Laura Fermi says dryly, "so Enrico ordered one." That, writes Albert Wattenberg, who joined the group in January, "required soldering together many strips of sheet metal. We were very fortunate in getting a sheet metal worker who made excellent solder joints. It was, however, quite a challenge to deal with him, since he could neither read nor speak English. We communicated with pictures, and somehow he did the job." Laura Fermi picks up the story: "To insure proper assembly, they marked each section with a little figure of a man: if the can were put together as it should be, all men would stand on their feet, otherwise on their heads." The Columbia men preheated the oxide lumps to 480°F before loading. They heated the contents of the room-sized can to the boiling point of water and pumped down a partial vacuum. Their heroic efforts reduced the pile's moisture to 0.03 percent. With the same relatively impure uranium and graphite they had used before but with these improved conditions and arrangements they measured *k* at the end of April at an encouraging 0.918.

In Chicago in the meantime Samuel Allison had built a smaller seven-foot exponential pile and measured *k* for his arrangement of 0.94. The University of Chicago had long ago sacrificed football to scholarship; Compton took over the warren of disused rooms under the west stands of Stagg Field, which was conveniently located immediately north of the main campus, and made space available there to Allison. Below solid masonry façades set with Gothic windows and crenellated towers the stands concealed ball courts as well as locker areas. The unheated room Allison had used for his experiment, sixty feet long, thirty feet wide, twenty-six feet high and sunk half below street level, was a doubles squash court.

December 6, 1941, the day of the bomb program expansion, marked another tidal event: Soviet forces under General Georgi Zhukov counterattacked across a two-hundred-mile front against the German Army congealed in snow and −35°F cold only thirty miles outside Moscow. "Like the supreme military genius who had trod this road a century before him," Churchill writes, evoking Napoleon Bonaparte, "Hitler now discovered what Russian winter meant." Zhukov's hundred divisions came as a bitter surprise—"well-fed, warmly clad and fresh Siberians," a German general describes them, "fully equipped for winter fighting" as the Wehrmacht troops were not—and armies that had advanced half a thousand miles to push within sight of the Kremlin stumbled back toward Germany nearly in rout. For the first time since Hitler began his conquests *Blitzkrieg* had failed. "The winter had fallen," Churchill writes. "The long war was certain." Hitler relieved his Army commander in chief of duty and appropriated that office to himself. By the end of March his casualties in the East, counting not the sick but only the wounded, numbered nearly 1.2 million men.

It was clear in Berlin that the German economy had reached the limits of its expansion. Tradeoffs must follow. The Minister of Munitions installed a rule similar to the rule upon which Conant was insisting in the United States, and the director of Reich military research promulgated it to the physicists studying uranium: "The work . . . is making demands which can be justified in the current recruiting and raw materials crisis only if there is a certainty of getting some benefit from it in the near future." After considering the question the War Office decided to reduce the priority of uranium research by assigning most of it to the Ministry of Education under Bernhard Rust, the scientifically illiterate SS *Obergruppenführer* and former provincial schoolteacher who had refused to sanction Lise Meitner's emigration following the *Anschluss.* The academic physicists were happy to be out from under the Army but chagrined to be consigned to a backwater ministry run by a party hack. Rust delegated authority to the Reich Research Council. That organization was part of the Reich Bureau of Standards. The KWI physicists considered its physics section head, Abraham Esau, incompetent. In effect, the German uranium program had slipped in status to the level of the old U.S. Uranium Committee and now had its Briggs.

The Research Council decided to appeal directly to the highest levels of the Reich for support. It organized an elaborate presentation and invited such dignitaries as Hermann Göring, Martin Bormann, Heinrich Himmler, Navy commander in chief Admiral Erich Raeder, Field Marshal Wilhelm Keitel and Albert Speer, Hitler's admired patrician architect who was Minister of Armaments and War Production. Heisenberg, Hahn, Bothe, Geiger, Clusius and Harteck were scheduled to speak at the February 26 meeting, Rust presiding, and an "Experimental Luncheon" would be served offering entrées prepared from frozen foods basted with synthetic shortening and bread made with soy flour.

Unfortunately for the council's ambitious plans, the secretary assigned to send out invitations enclosed the wrong lecture program. A secret scientific conference under the auspices of Army Ordnance had been scheduled at the Kaiser Wilhelm Society's Harnack House for the same day. Its program listed twenty-five highly technical scientific papers. That was the program the leaders of the Reich mistakenly received. Himmler regretted: he would be away from Berlin that day. Keitel was "too busy at the moment." Raeder would send a representative. None of the leaders chose to attend.

What Heisenberg had to say might have surprised them. He emphasized atomic energy for power but also discussed military uses. "Pure uranium-235 is thus seen to be an explosive of quite unimaginable force," he told his staff-level auditors. "The Americans seem to be pursuing this line of research with particular urgency." Inside a uranium reactor "a new element is created [i.e., plutonium] . . . which is in all probability as explosive as pure uranium-235, with the same colossal force." At the same time at Harnack House, where Leo Szilard once lodged, bags packed, Army Ordnance was learning that "it would suffice to bring together two lumps of this explosive, weighing a total of ten to a hundred kilograms, for it to detonate."

Basic knowledge of one direct route to an atomic bomb—via plutonium—was at hand. What was lacking was money and materials. The February 26 meeting won over at least the Minister of Education. "The first time large funds were available in Germany," Heisenberg recalled at the end of the war, "was in the spring of 1942, after that meeting with Rust, when we convinced him that we had absolutely definite proof that it could be done." Heisenberg's "large" is relative to the modest funds that had been available before, however. Not Bernhard Rust but Albert Speer needed to be convinced of the military promise of atomic energy to swell the scale of funding anywhere near the billions of reichsmarks that production of even ten kilograms of U235 or plutonium would require.

Speer did not recall the February 26 invitation after the war. Atomic energy first came to his attention, he writes in his memoirs, at one of his regular private luncheons with General Friedrich Fromm, the commander of the Home Army. "In the course of one of these meetings, at the end of April 1942, [Fromm] remarked that our only chance of winning the war lay in developing a weapon with totally new effects. He said he had contacts with a group of scientists who were on the track of a weapon which could annihilate whole cities. . . . Fromm proposed that we pay a joint visit to these men." Speer also heard that spring from the president of the Kaiser Wilhelm Society, who complained of lack of support for uranium research. "On May 6, 1942, I discussed this situation with Hitler and proposed that Göring be placed at the head of the Reich Research Council—thus emphasizing its importance."

That shift to the obese Reichsmarshal who commanded the Luftwaffe and whom Hitler had designated to be his successor carried only symbolic promotion. More crucial was a June 4 conference at Harnack House that Speer, Fromm, automobile and tank designer Ferdinand Porsche and other military and industrial leaders attended. In February Heisenberg had devoted most of his lecture to nuclear power. This time he emphasized military prospects. The secretary of the Kaiser Wilhelm Society was surprised: "The word 'bomb' which was used at this conference was news not only to me but for many others present, as I could see from their reaction." It was not news to Speer. When Heisenberg took questions from the floor, one of Speer's deputies asked how large a bomb capable of destroying a city would have to be. Heisenberg cupped his hands as Fermi had done sighting down Manhattan Island from Pupin Hall. "As large as a pineapple," he said.

After the briefings Speer questioned Heisenberg directly. How could nuclear physics be applied to the manufacture of atomic bombs? The German laureate seems to have shied from committing himself. "His answer was by no means encouraging," Speer remembers. "He declared, to be sure, that the scientific solution had already been found. . . . But the technical prerequisites for production would take years to develop, two years at the earliest, even provided that the program was given maximum support." They were crippled by an absence of cyclotrons, Heisenberg said. Speer offered to build cyclotrons "as large as or larger than those in the United States." Heisenberg demurred that German physicists lacked experience building large cyclotrons and would have to start small. Speer "urged the scientists to inform me of the measures, the sums of money and the materials they would need to further nuclear research." A few weeks later they did, but their requests looked picayune to a Reichsminister accustomed to dealing in billions of marks. They requested "an appropriation of several hundred thousand marks and some small amounts of steel, nickel, and other priority metals. . . . Rather put out by these modest requests in a matter of such crucial importance, I suggested that they take one or two million marks and correspondingly larger quantities of materials. But apparently more could not be utilized for the present, and in any case I had been given the impression that the atom bomb could no longer have any bearing on the course of the war."

Speer saw Hitler regularly and duly reported the findings of the June conferences:

> Hitler had sometimes spoken to me about the possibility of an atom bomb, but the idea quite obviously strained his intellectual capacity. He was also

> unable to grasp the revolutionary nature of nuclear physics. In the twenty-two hundred recorded points of my conferences with Hitler, nuclear fission comes up only once, and then is mentioned with extreme brevity. Hitler did sometimes comment on its prospects, but what I told him of my conferences with the physicists confirmed his view that there was not much profit in the matter. Actually, Professor Heisenberg had not given any final answer to my question whether a successful nuclear fission could be kept under control with absolute certainty or might continue as a chain reaction. Hitler was plainly not delighted with the possibility that the earth under his rule might be transformed into a glowing star. Occasionally, however, he joked that the scientists in their unworldly urge to lay bare all the secrets under heaven might some day set the globe on fire. But undoubtedly a good deal of time would pass before that came about, Hitler said; he would certainly not live to see it.

Following that, according to Speer, "on the suggestion of the nuclear physicists we scuttled the project to develop an atom bomb . . . after I had again queried them about deadlines and been told that we could not count on anything for three or four years." Work on what Speer calls "an energy-producing uranium motor for propelling machinery"—the heavy-water pile—would continue. "In the upshot," Heisenberg wrote in *Nature* in 1947, summarizing the war years, German physicists "were spared the decision as to whether or not they should aim at producing atomic bombs. The circumstances shaping policy in the critical year of 1942 guided their work automatically toward the problem of the utilization of nuclear energy in prime movers." But the Allies had not yet been informed.

"We may be engaged in a race toward realization," Vannevar Bush wrote Franklin Roosevelt on March 9, 1942; "but, if so, I have no indication of the status of the enemy program, and have taken no definite steps toward finding out." Why Bush was not more curious remains a mystery. Conant, Lawrence and Compton, not to mention the emigrés, fretted continually about the possibility of a German bomb. It was their primary reason for urging an American bomb. It was not Bush's or Roosevelt's—to them the bomb offered offensive advantage first of all—but the two leaders were alert to the German danger and surprisingly indifferent to assessing it.

The report that accompanied Bush's letter stated that five to ten pounds of "active material" would be "fairly certain" to explode with a force equivalent to 2,000 tons of TNT, up from 600 tons in the third National Academy of Sciences report of the previous November 6. It recommended building a centrifuge plant at a cost of $20 million that could produce enough U235 for one bomb a month and estimated that such a plant could be completed by December 1943. A gaseous diffusion plant, its cost unspecified, might deliver by the end of 1944. An electromagnetic separation plant—Ernest Lawrence's project—won the most attention in the report: it might "offer a short-cut," wrote Bush, and deliver "fully practicable quantities of material by the summer of 1943, with a time saving of perhaps six months or even more." In summary, "present opinion indicates that successful use is possible, and that this would be very important and might be determining in the war effort. It is also true that if the enemy arrived at results first it would be an exceedingly serious matter. The best estimate indicates completion in 1944, if every effort is made to expedite."

Roosevelt responded two days later: "I think the whole thing should be pushed not only in regard to development, but also with due regard to time. This is very much of the essence." Time, not money, was becoming the limiting factor in atomic bomb development.

A meeting on May 23 brought all the program leaders together with Conant to decide which of several methods of making a bomb should be moved on to the pilot-plant and industrial engineering stages. The centrifuge, gaseous barrier diffusion, electromagnetic and graphite or heavy-water plutonium-pile approaches all looked equally promising. Given wartime scarcities and budget priorities, which should be advanced? Conant used an arms-race argument to identify the point of decision:

> While all five methods now appear to be about equally promising, clearly the time of production of a dozen bombs by the five routes will certainly not be the same but might vary by six months or a year because of unforeseen delays. Therefore, if one discards one or two or three of the methods now, one may be betting on the slower horse unconsciously. To my mind the decision as to how "all out" the effort should be might well turn on the military appraisal of what would occur if either side had a dozen or two bombs before the other.

To that point Conant reviewed the evidence for a German bomb program, including new indications of espionage activity: information from the British that the Germans had a ton of heavy water; Peter Debye's report when he arrived in the United States eighteen months earlier that his colleagues at the KWI were hard at work; and "the recently intercepted instruction to their agents in this country [that] shows they are interested in what we are doing." Conant thought this last evidence the best. "If they are hard at work, they cannot be far behind since they started in 1939 with the same initial facts as the British and ourselves. There are still plenty of competent scientists left in Germany. They may be ahead of us by as much as a year, but hardly more."

If time, not money, was the crucial issue—in Conant's words, "if the possession of the new weapon in sufficient quantities would be a determining factor in the war"—then "three months' delay might be fatal." It followed that all five methods should be pushed at once, even though "to embark on this Napoleonic approach to the problem would require the commitment of perhaps $500,000,000 and quite a mess of machinery."

Glenn Seaborg arrived in Chicago aboard the streamliner City of San Francisco at 9:30 A.M. Sunday, April 19, 1942, his thirtieth birthday. As he left the station he noticed first that Chicago was cold compared to Berkeley—forty degrees that spring morning. Then headlines at a newsstand caught him up on the developing Pacific war: the Japanese reported American aircraft had bombed Tokyo and three other Honshu cities, a surprise attack that neither Southwest Pacific commander General Douglas MacArthur nor Washington acknowledged (it was Jimmy Doolittle's morale raid of sixteen B-25 bombers launched one-way across Japan to landing fields in China from the U.S. aircraft carrier *Hornet*). "This day . . . marks a transition point in my life," Seaborg writes in his carefully documented diary-style memoir, "for tomorrow I will take on the added responsibility of the 94 chemistry group at the Metallurgical Laboratory on the University of Chicago campus, the central component of the Metallurgical Project."

Transmuting U238 to plutonium in a chain-reacting pile was one thing, extracting the plutonium from the uranium quite another. The massive production piles that Compton's people were already beginning to plan would create the new element at a maximum concentration in the uranium of about 250 parts per million—a volume, uniformly dispersed through each two tons of mingled uranium and highly radioactive fission products, equal to the volume of one U.S. dime. Seaborg's work was somehow to pull that dime's worth out.

He had made a good beginning at Berkeley, exploring plutonium's unusual chemistry. Oxidizing agents are chemicals that strip electrons from the outer shells of atoms. Reducing agents conversely add electrons to the outer shells of atoms. Plutonium, it seemed, precipitated differently when it was treated with oxidizing agents than when it was treated with reducing agents. In a +4 oxidation state, the Berkeley team had found, the man-made element could be precipitated out of solution using a rare-earth compound such as lanthanum fluoride as a carrier. Oxidize the same plutonium to a +6 oxidation state and the precipitation no longer worked; the carrier crystallized but the plutonium remained behind in solution. That gave Seaborg a basic approach to extraction:

> We conceived the principle of the oxidation-reduction cycle. . . . This principle applied to any process involving the use of a substance which carried plutonium in one of its oxidation states but not in another. . . . For example, a carrier could be used to carry plutonium in one oxidation state and thus to separate it from uranium and the fission products. Then the carrier and the plutonium [now solid crystals] could be dissolved, the oxidation state of the plutonium changed, and the carrier reprecipitated, leaving the plutonium in solution. The oxidation state of the plutonium could again be changed and the cycles repeated. With this type of procedure, only a contaminating element having a chemistry nearly identical with the plutonium itself would fail to separate if a large number of oxidation-reduction cycles were employed.

A two-day chemistry conference began on Wednesday, April 23, with Eugene Wigner, Harold Urey, Princeton theoretician John A. Wheeler and a number of chemists already assigned to the Met Lab on hand. The scientists discussed seven possible ways to extract plutonium from irradiated uranium. They favored four that seemed particularly adaptable to remote control, not including precipitation. Seaborg, the new man, disagreed: "I, however, expressed confidence in the use of precipitation." They would nevertheless investigate all seven methods proposed. That would require the full-time work of forty men. One of Seaborg's jobs for months to come was recruiting. It worried him: "Sometimes I feel a little apprehensive about inviting . . . people to give up their secure university positions and come to work at the Met Lab. They must gamble on the future of their careers, and how long they will be diverted from them nobody knows." But if no one knew how long the work would last, most of them came to believe it transcendently important: "There is a statement of rather common currency around here and Berkeley that goes something like this: 'No matter what you do with the rest of your life, nothing will be as important to the future of the World as your work on this Project right now.' "

So far Seaborg had studied plutonium by following the characteristic radioactivity of minute amounts vastly diluted in carrier, the same tracer chemistry that Hahn, Fermi and the Joliot-Curies had used. Chemical reactions often proceed differently at different dilutions, however. To prove that an extraction process would work at industrial scale, Seaborg knew he would have to demonstrate it at industrial-scale concentrations. In peacetime he might have waited until a pile large enough to transmute at least gram quantities of plutonium was built and operating. That normal procedure was a luxury the bomb program could not afford.

Seaborg looked instead for a way to make more plutonium without a pile and a way to work with concentrated solutions of the little he might make. The resources of the OSRD came to his aid in the first instance, his own imagination and ingenuity in the second. He commandeered the 45-inch cyclotron at Washington University in St. Louis, where Compton had once hidden out, and arranged to have 300-pound batches of uranium nitrate hexahydrate bombarded heroically with neutrons for weeks and months at a time. So long and intense a bombardment would give him microgram quantities of plutonium—several hundred millionths of a gram, amounts hardly visible to the naked eye. He then somehow had to devise techniques for mixing, measuring and analyzing them.

Visiting New York earlier that month to deliver a lecture, Seaborg had sought out a quaint soul named Anton Alexander Benedetti-Pichler, a professor at Queens College in Flushing who had pioneered ultramicrochemistry, a technology for manipulating extremely small quantities of chemicals. Benedetti-Pichler had briefed Seaborg thoroughly and promised to send a list of essential equipment. Seaborg hired one of Benedetti-Pichler's former students and together the two men planned an ultramicrochemistry laboratory. "We looked for a good spot that would be vibration-free for the microbalances and settled on Room 405 (a former darkroom) in Jones Laboratory which has a concrete bench." The former darkroom, hardly six feet by nine, was scaled to the work.

Another specialist in ultramicrochemistry, Paul Kirk, taught at Berkeley. Seaborg hired a recent Ph.D. whom Kirk had trained, Burris Cunningham, and a graduate student, Louis B. Werner. "I always thought I was tall," the chemistry laureate comments, but Werner at six feet seven topped him by four inches, "a tight fit" in the small laboratory.

With the special tools of ultramicrochemistry the young chemists could work on undiluted quantities of chemicals as slight as tenths of a microgram (a dime weighs about 2.5 grams— 2,500,000 micrograms). They would manage their manipulations on the mechanical stage of a binocular stereoscopic microscope adjusted to 30-power magnification. Fine glass capillary straws substituted for test tubes and beakers; pipettes filled automatically by capillary attraction; small hypodermic syringes mounted on micromanipulators injected and removed reagents from centrifuge microcones; miniature centrifuges separated precipitated solids from liquids. The first balance the chemists used consisted of a single quartz fiber fixed at one end like a fishing pole stuck into a riverbank inside a glass housing that protected it from the least breath of air. To weigh their Lilliputian quantities of material they hung a weighing pan, made of a snippet of platinum foil that was itself almost too small to see, to the free end of the quartz fiber and measured how much the fiber bent, a deflection which was calibrated against standard weights. A more rugged balance developed at Berkeley had double pans suspended from opposite ends of a quartz-fiber beam strung with microscopic struts. "It was said," notes Seaborg, "that 'invisible material was being weighed with an invisible balance.' "

In addition to his new Met Lab responsibilities Seaborg still coordinated basic scientific studies of uranium and plutonium at Berkeley. At the beginning of June he traveled to California to meet with "the fellows on the third floor of Gilman Hall" and to marry Ernest Lawrence's secretary. On June 6, returning to Chicago through Los Angeles, where Seaborg's parents lived, bride and groom prepared for a quick Nevada wedding. They got off the train in Caliente, Nevada, stored their bags with the telegraph operator at the station and asked directions to the city hall. "But to our vexation we learned there is no city hall here and in order to get our marriage license we would have to go to the county seat, a town called Pioche, some 25 miles to the north." Providentially the deputy sheriff who served as Caliente's travel adviser and all-around troubleshooter turned out to be a June graduate of the Berkeley chemistry department. He arranged for the professor and his bride, Helen Griggs, to ride to Pioche in a mail truck. "Our witnesses were a janitor whom we recruited and [a] friendly clerk. We returned to Caliente on the mail truck's 4:30 run and checked into the local hotel here for our overnight stay."

Arriving in Chicago on June 9 Seaborg delivered his wife to the apartment he had rented before he left for California and proceeded immediately to his office. His mail informed him that Edward Teller was joining the Chicago project to work in the theoretical group under Eugene Wigner.

Two days later Robert Oppenheimer turned up in Chicago and dropped by to see Seaborg; they were old friends but "it was more than just a social call." Gregory Breit, the Wisconsin-based theoretician on the Uranium Committee who had been responsible for fast-neutron studies, had resigned from the bomb project in protest over what he felt were serious violations of security. "I do not believe that secrecy conditions are satisfactory in Dr. Compton's project," he had written Briggs on May 18. His litany of examples approached paranoia. "Within the Chicago project there are several individuals strongly opposed to secrecy. One of the men, for example, coaxed my secretary there to give him some official reports out of my safe while I was away on a trip. . . . The same individual talks quite freely within the group. . . . I have heard him advocate the principle that all parts of the work are so closely interrelated that it is desirable to discuss them as a whole." The dangerous individual Breit chose not to name was Enrico Fermi, pushing to make the chain reaction go. Compton had appointed Oppenheimer to replace Breit and Oppenheimer was visiting Seaborg for a briefing on the fast-neutron studies Seaborg was coordinating at

Berkeley. Studying fast-neutron reactions, Seaborg notes, was "a prerequisite to the design of an atomic bomb." Oppenheimer had found a place for himself on the ground floor.

The Washington University cyclotron crew moved the first 300 pounds of uranium nitrate hexahydrate into position around the machine's beryllium target on June 17. The UNH was scheduled for a month's bombardment, 50,000 microampere-hours. Though the chain reaction had not yet been proved and no one had yet seen plutonium, the various Met Lab councils of which Seaborg was a member had already begun debating the design and location of the big 250,000-kilowatt production piles that would create pounds of the strange metal if all went well. Fermi thought plutonium production needed an area a mile wide and two miles long for safety. Compton proposed building piles of increasing power to work up to full-scale production and was considering alternative sites in the Lake Michigan Dunes area and in the Tennessee Valley.

A question that would eventually encompass many other issues, some of them profound, was how to cool the big piles. Early in the organization of the Met Lab Compton had appointed an engineering council to consider such questions; besides an engineer and an industrial chemist the council included Samuel Allison, Fermi, Seaborg, Szilard and John A. Wheeler among its membership. By late June its discussions had progressed to the point of tentative commitment. Helium was one prospective coolant, to be circulated at high pressure inside a sealed steel shell; its zero cross section for neutron absorption was only one of its several advantages. Water was another coolant possibility, the heat-exchange medium most familiar to engineers but corrosive to uranium. An exotic third was bismuth, a metal with a low 520°F melting point that serves as a watchful solid in fuses and automatic fire alarms. Melted to a liquid it would transfer heat far more efficiently than helium or water. Szilard championed a liquid-bismuth cooling system in part because the metal could be circulated through the pile with a scaled-up version of the magnetic pump he and Albert Einstein had invented for refrigerators, a mechanism that had no moving parts to leak or fail.

The engineering council ruled out liquid cooling, Seaborg writes, "because of potential chemical action, danger of leaks and difficulty in transferring heat from oxide. . . . There was general agreement to use helium." Eugene Wigner had not been invited onto the council despite his interest in its problems and his thorough knowledge of chemical engineering. Wigner strongly favored water cooling, says Szilard, because "a water cooled system could be built in a much shorter time." Seaborg corroborates Wigner's continuing desperate concern about a German bomb:

> Compton repeated a conversation that ensued between him and Wigner on a possible schedule of the Germans. Like us, they have had three years since the discovery of fission to prepare a bomb. Assuming they know about [plutonium], they could run a heavy water pile for two months at 100,000 kw and produce six kilograms of it; thus it would be possible for them to have six bombs by the end of this year [1942]. On the other hand, we don't plan to have bombs in production until the first part of 1944.

Compton encouraged Wigner's group to design a water-cooled pile but ordered up detailed engineering studies only of a system using helium.

The basic issue behind the technical dispute was control, which Szilard at least understood they were systematically signing away to the U.S. government. A meeting on June 27 intensified the conflict. Bush's latest status report to Roosevelt on June 17 had proposed dividing the work of development and ultimate production between the OSRD and the U.S. Army Corps of Engineers, bringing in the Army to build and run the factories as Bush had planned to do all along. Roosevelt initialed Bush's cover letter "OK. FDR." and returned it immediately. The same day the Chief of Engineers ordered Colonel James C. Marshall of the Syracuse Engineer District, a 1918 West Point graduate with experience building air bases, to report to Washington for duty. Marshall selected the Boston construction engineering corporation of Stone & Webster as principal contractor for the bomb project. To report the reorganization Compton called the June 27 meeting of his group leaders and planning board. Allison, Fermi, Seaborg, Szilard, Teller, Wigner and Zinn attended, among others.

"Compton opened the meeting with a pep talk," Seaborg remembers, "asking us to go ahead with all vigor possible. He said our aim the past half-year has been to investigate the possibilities of producing an atomic bomb—now we have the responsibility to proceed from the military point of view on the assumption it can be done and we can assume we have a project for the entire duration of the war." Compton was stealthily working his way to the new arrangements. He emphasized the program's secrecy. "Only about six men in the U.S. Army are permitted to know what is going on," Seaborg paraphrases him; those privileged few included Secretary of War Henry L. Stimson—heady company for men who had only recently been graduate students or obscure academics—and "two construction experts," generals whom Compton then named. He described the responsibilities of the "construction experts" and finally broke the news: "It is hoped to have a contractor assume responsibility for the production plant." A contractor already had.

Compton's announcement had the effect he seems to have feared, Seaborg goes on: "A number of the people present expressed great concern about working for an industrial contractor because of their fear that this would not be a compatible environment in which to work." They would not have to work *for* such a contractor, though they would obviously have to work *with* one, but to make the reorganization palatable Compton hinted at worse that might be yet to come: "There was considerable talk about our being absorbed into the Army [i.e., commissioned as officers] and what the advantages and disadvantages might be. There were vigorous objections from most of the people present."

The problem would fester all summer and burst through again in the fall. Szilard would define it precisely in a memorandum: "Stated in abstract form, the trouble at Chicago arises out of the fact that the work is organized along somewhat authoritative [*sic*: authoritarian] rather than democratic lines." The visionary Hungarian physicist did not believe science could function by fiat. "In 1939," he had already written Vannevar Bush passionately in late May, before the cooling-system and contractor debates, "the Government of the United States was given a unique opportunity by Providence; this opportunity was lost. Nobody can tell now whether we shall be ready before German bombs wipe out American cities. Such scanty information as we have about work in Germany is not reassuring and all one can say with certainty is that we could move at least twice as fast if our difficulties were eliminated."

Three hundred pounds of irradiated UNH—yellowish crystals like rock salt—arrived from St. Louis by truck on July 27, a Monday:

> The UNH was surrounded by a layer of lead bricks. [Truman] Kohman and [Elwin H.] Covey were detailed to unload the shipment and carry it up to our lab on the fourth floor for extraction of the 94^{239}. The UNH crystals came packaged in small boxes of various sizes, made to fit into the various niches around the cyclotron target. Some of the boxes were made of masonite, but most of them were of quarter inch plywood. Unfortunately, some of the seams and edges had cracked open, allowing crystals of hot [i.e., radioactive] UNH to creep out. We could not get hold of any instrument to measure the radioactivity. I told Kohman and Covey their best protection would be to wear rubber gloves and a lab coat. . . . Although they struggled for half the day to get all the boxes and lead bricks upstairs into the storage area, I think they were conscientious and kept their radiation exposure to a minimum.

While Seaborg's high-spirited crew of young chemists began attempting to extract plutonium 239 from the bulky St. Louis UNH, wrestling with carboys of ether and heavy three-liter separatory funnels held at arm's length from behind lead shields, Cunningham and Werner in narrow Room 405 started toward isolating plutonium as a pure compound. They first measured out a 15-milliliter solution of UNH irradiated earlier that summer in the 60-inch Berkeley cyclotron. They assumed their solution then contained about one microgram of plutonium 239. (*Pu*239, that is: Seaborg had chosen the abbreviation Pu rather than Pl partly to avoid confusion with platinum, Pt, but also "facetiously," he says, "to create attention"—P.U. the old slang for putrid, something that raises a stink.) Working with their ultramicrochemical equipment—slow, tedious operations via micromanipulator gearing down large motions to microscopically small—on August 15, a Saturday, they mixed the rare earths cerium and lanthanum into their solution as carriers, partially evaporated it and precipitated the carriers and the Pu as fluorides. They dissolved the precipitated crystals in a few drops of sulfuric acid and evaporated the resulting solution to a volume of about one milliliter, a thousandth of a liter, some twenty drops. They checked the larger volume of solution left behind and found essentially no alpha activity, evidence that the alpha-active Pu had crystallized out with the rare earths. That was a day's work and they stored the precipitate solution carefully for Monday and went home.

On Monday, August 17, Cunningham and Werner began by oxidizing their small volume of precipitate to change the oxidation state of its Pu. They repeated the oxidation and reduction cycles on the solution several times. At the end of the day their quartz centrifuge microcone contained a minute drop of liquid that radiated some 57,000 alpha particles per minute. They set it in a steam bath to concentrate it.

On Tuesday the two men transferred the concentrated solution to a shallow platinum dish to prepare to concentrate it further. It began creeping over the sides. Rather than lose it they moved it quickly to the only larger dish at hand, which was contaminated with lanthanum. Their misjudgment of volume condemned them to another day of repurifying. Upstairs in the attic and on the roof Seaborg's bulk UNH crew stirred large-volume extractions of ether and water. It was hot and heavy work.

Room 405 had a purified concentrate again to process Wednesday morning. It was still contaminated with a potassium compound and with silver. Cunningham and Werner diluted it and precipitated out the silver as a chloride. They added five micrograms of lanthanum and precipitated out the Pu along with the lanthanum carrier. They dissolved the precipitate, oxidized it once more to change over the Pu and precipitated out the lanthanum. That left pure plutonium in solution, one more morning's work to bring down.

Of Thursday, August 20, 1942, Seaborg writes:

> Perhaps today was the most exciting and thrilling day I have experienced since coming to the Met Lab. Our microchemists isolated pure element 94 for

> the first time! This morning Cunningham and Werner set about fuming . . . yesterday's 94 solution containing about one microgram of 94^{239}, added hydrofluoric acid whereupon the reduced 94 precipitated as the fluoride . . . free of carrier material. . . .
>
> This precipitate of 94, which was viewed under the microscope and which was also visible to the naked eye, did not differ visibly from the rare-earth fluorides. . . .
>
> It is the first time that element 94 . . . has been beheld by the eye of man.

By afternoon "a holiday spirit prevailed in our group." After several hours' exposure to air "the precipitated [plutonium] had taken on a pinkish hue." Someone photographed Cunningham and Werner at their crowded bench in the narrow, tile-walled room—trim, strong-jawed young men looking weary. The crew upstairs that muscled carboys and lead bricks shuffled in like clumsy shepherds to peer through the microscope at the miracle of the tiny pinkish speck.

In the summer of 1942 Robert Oppenheimer gathered together at Berkeley a small group of theoretical physicists he was amused to call the "luminaries." Their job was to throw light on the actual design of an atomic bomb.

Hans Bethe, now thirty-six and a highly respected professor of physics at Cornell, had resisted joining the bomb project because he doubted the weapon's feasibility. "I considered . . . an atomic bomb so remote," Bethe told a biographer after the war, "that I completely refused to have anything to do with it. . . . Separating isotopes of such a heavy element [as uranium] was clearly a very difficult thing to do, and I thought we would never succeed in any practical way." But Bethe may well have headed the list of luminaries Oppenheimer wanted to attract. By 1942 the Cornell physicist had established himself as a theoretician of the first rank. His most outstanding contribution, for which he would receive the 1967 Nobel Prize in Physics, was to elucidate the production of energy in stars, identifying a cycle of thermonuclear reactions involving hydrogen, nitrogen and oxygen that is catalyzed by carbon and culminates in the creation of helium. Among other important work during the 1930s Bethe had been principal author of three lengthy review articles on nuclear physics, the first comprehensive survey of the field. Bound together, the three authoritative studies came to be called "Bethe's Bible."

He had wanted to help oppose Nazism. "After the fall of France," he says, "I was desperate to do something—to make some contribution to the war effort." First he developed a basic theory of armor penetration. On the recommendation of Theodor von Kármán, whom he consulted at Caltech, he and Edward Teller in 1940 extended and clarified shock-wave theory. In

1942 he joined the Radiation Laboratory at MIT to work on radar. That was where Oppenheimer found him.

Oppenheimer cleared his plan with Lee A. DuBridge, the director of the Rad Lab, then set a senior American theoretician, John H. Van Vleck, professor of physics at Harvard, to snare Bethe for the Berkeley summer study. "The essential point," he counseled Van Vleck, "is to enlist Bethe's interest, to impress on him the magnitude of the job we have to do . . . and to try to convince him, too, that our present plans . . . are the appropriate machinery." Oppenheimer felt the weight of the work. "Every time I think about our problem a new headache appears," he told the Harvard professor. "We shall certainly have our hands full." Van Vleck arranged to meet Bethe conspiratorially in Harvard Yard and succeeded in convincing him he was needed. The prearranged signal to Oppenheimer was a Western Union Kiddygram, an inexpensive standardized telegram with a message like "Brush your teeth."

Oppenheimer also invited Edward Teller. In 1939 Bethe had married Rose Ewald, the attractive and intelligent daughter of his Stuttgart physics professor Paul Ewald; Edward and Mici Teller, "our best friends in this country," had attended the New Rochelle wedding. Setting out for Berkeley in early July 1942, the Bethes stopped over in Chicago to pick up the Tellers. Teller showed Bethe Fermi's latest exponential pile. "He had a setup under one of the stands in Stagg Field," Bethe remembers—"in a squash court—with tremendous stacks of graphite." A chain reaction that made plutonium would bypass the problem of isotope separation. "I then," says Bethe, "became convinced that the atomic-bomb project was real, and that it would probably work."

The other luminaries enlisted for the summer study were Van Vleck, the Swiss-born Stanford theoretician Felix Bloch, Oppenheimer's former student and close collaborator Robert Serber, a young Indiana theoretician named Emil Konopinski and two postdoctoral assistants. Konopinski and Teller had arrived at the Met Lab at about the same time earlier that year. "We were newcomers in the bustling laboratory," Teller writes in a memoir, "and for a few days we were given no specific jobs." Teller proposed that he and Konopinski review his calculations that seemed to prove the impossibility of using an atomic bomb to ignite a thermonuclear reaction in deuterium:

> Konopinski agreed, and we tackled the job of writing a report to show, once and for all, that it could not be done. . . . But the more we worked on our report, the more obvious it became that the roadblocks which I had erected for Fermi's idea were not so high after all. We hurdled them one by one, and concluded that heavy hydrogen actually could be ignited by an atomic bomb

to produce an explosion of tremendous magnitude. By the time we were on our way to California . . . we even thought we knew precisely how to do it.

That was not news Edward Teller was likely to hide under a bushel, whatever Oppenheimer's official agenda. Bethe was ushered into the glare as the streamliner clicked west: "We had a compartment on the train to California, so we could talk freely. . . . Teller told me that the fission bomb was all well and good and, essentially, was now a sure thing. In reality, the work had hardly begun. Teller likes to jump to conclusions. He said that what we really should think about was the possibility of igniting deuterium by a fission weapon—the hydrogen bomb."

At Berkeley the luminaries began meeting in Oppenheimer's office, "in the northwest corner of the fourth floor of old LeConte [Hall]," an older colleague remembers. "Like all those rooms, it had French doors opening out onto a balcony, to which there was easy access from the roof. Accordingly a very strong wire netting was fastened securely over his balcony." Only Oppenheimer had a key. "If a fire had ever started . . . in Oppenheimer's absence, it would have been tragic." But the fires that summer were still only theoretical.

The theoreticians let Teller's bomb distract them. It was new, important and spectacular and they were men with a compulsion to know. "The theory of the fission bomb was well taken care of by Serber and two of his young people," Bethe explains. They "seemed to have it well under control so we felt we didn't need to do much." The essentials of fast-neutron fission were firm—it needed experiment more than theory. The senior men turned their collective brilliance to fusion. They had not yet bothered to name generic bombs of uranium and plutonium. But from the pre-anthropic darkness where ideas abide in nonexistence until minds imagine them into the light, the new bomb emerged already chased with the technocratic euphemism of art deco slang: the Super, they named it.

Rose Bethe, who was then twenty-four, understood instantly. "My wife knew vaguely what we were talking about," says Bethe, "and on a walk in the mountains in Yosemite National Park she asked me to consider carefully whether I really wanted to continue to work on this. Finally, I decided to do it." The Super "was a terrible thing." But the fission bomb had to come first in any case and "the Germans were presumably doing it."

Teller had examined two thermonuclear reactions that fuse deuterium nuclei to heavier forms and simultaneously release binding energy. Both required that the deuterium nuclei be hot enough when they collided—energetic enough, violently enough in motion—to overcome the nuclear electrical barrier that usually repels them. The minimum necessary energy was thought at the time to come to about 35,000 electron volts, which corresponds to a temperature of about 400 million degrees. Given that temperature—and on earth only an atomic bomb might give it—both thermonuclear reactions should occur with equal probability. In the first, two deuterium nuclei collide and fuse to helium 3 with the ejection of a neutron and the release of 3.2 million electron volts of energy. In the second the same sort of collision produces tritium—hydrogen 3, an isotope of hydrogen with a nucleus of one proton and two neutrons that does not occur naturally on earth—with the ejection of a proton and the release of 4.0 MeV of energy.

The D + D reactions' release of 3.6 MeV was slightly less by mass than fission's net of 170 MeV. But fusion was essentially a thermal reaction, not inherently different in its kindling from an ordinary fire; it required no critical mass and was therefore potentially unlimited. Once ignited, its extent depended primarily on the volume of fuel—deuterium—its designers supplied. And deuterium, Harold Urey's discovery, the essential component of heavy water, was much easier and less expensive to separate from hydrogen than U235 was from U238 and much simpler to acquire than plutonium. Each kilogram of heavy hydrogen equaled about 85,000 tons TNT equivalent. Theoretically, 12 kilograms of liquid heavy hydrogen—26 pounds—ignited by one atomic bomb would explode with a force equivalent to 1 million tons of TNT. So far as Oppenheimer and his group knew at the beginning of the summer, an equivalent fission explosion would require some 500 atomic bombs.

That reckoning alone would have been enough to justify devoting the summer to imagining the Super a little way out of the darkness. Teller found something else as well, or thought he did, and with his usual pellmell facility he scattered it before them. There are many other thermonuclear reactions besides the D + D reactions. Bethe had examined a number of them methodically when looking for those that energized massive stars. Now Teller offered several which a fission bomb or a Super might inadvertently trigger. He proposed to the assembled luminaries the possibility that their bombs might ignite the earth's oceans or its atmosphere and burn up the world, the very result Hitler occasionally joked about with Albert Speer.

"I didn't believe it from the first minute," Bethe scoffs. "Oppie took it sufficiently seriously that he went to see Compton. I don't think I would have done it if I had been Oppie, but then Oppie was a more enthusiastic character than I was. I would have waited until we knew more." Oppenheimer had other urgent business with Compton in any case: the Super itself. Not to risk their loss, the bomb-project leaders were no longer allowed to fly. Oppenheimer tracked Compton by telephone at the beginning of a

July weekend to a country store in northern Michigan where he had stopped to pick up the keys to his lakeside summer cottage, got directions and caught the next train east. In the meantime Bethe applied himself to Teller's calculations.

The Cornell physicist's instant skepticism gives perspective to Compton's melodramatic recollection of his meeting with Oppenheimer:

> I'll never forget that morning. I drove Oppenheimer from the railroad station down to the beach looking out over the peaceful lake. There I listened to his story. . . .
>
> Was there really any chance that an atomic bomb would trigger the explosion of the nitrogen in the atmosphere or the hydrogen in the ocean? This would be the ultimate catastrophe. Better to accept the slavery of the Nazis than to run a chance of drawing the final curtain on mankind!
>
> We agreed there could be only one answer. Oppenheimer's team must go ahead with their calculations.

Bethe already had. "I very soon found some unjustified assumptions in Teller's calculations which made such a result extremely unlikely, to say the least. Teller was very soon persuaded by my arguments." The arguments—Bethe's and others'—against a runaway explosion appear most authoritatively in a technical history of the bomb design program prepared under Oppenheimer's supervision immediately after the war:

> It was assumed that only the most energetic of several possible [thermonuclear] reactions would occur, and that the reaction cross sections were at the maximum values theoretically possible. Calculation led to the result that no matter how high the temperature, energy loss would exceed energy production by a reasonable factor. At an assumed temperature of three million electron volts [compare the 35,000 eV known for D + D] the reaction failed to be self-propagating by a factor of 60. This temperature exceeded the calculated initial temperature of the deuterium reaction by a factor of 100, and that of the fission bomb by a larger factor. . . . The impossibility of igniting the atmosphere was thus assured by science and common sense.

Oppenheimer returned to that good news and they proceeded with the Super. Teller recaptures the mood: "My theories were strongly criticized by others in the group, but together with new difficulties, new solutions emerged. The discussions became fascinating and intense. Facts were questioned and the questions were answered by still more facts. . . . A spirit of spontaneity, adventure, and surprise prevailed during those weeks in Berkeley, and each member of the group helped move the discussion toward a positive conclusion."

There was serious trouble with Teller's D + D Super. The reactions would proceed too slowly to reach ignition before the fission trigger blew the assembly apart. Konopinski came to the rescue: "Konopinski suggested that, in addition to deuterium, we should investigate the reactions of the heaviest form of hydrogen, tritium." This, Teller explains, was at that time "only . . . a conversational guess." One tritium reaction of obvious interest was the fusion of a deuterium nucleus with a tritium nucleus, D + T, which results in the formation of a helium nucleus with the ejection of a neutron and the release of 17.6 MeV of energy. The D + T reaction kindled at a mere 5,000 eV, which corresponds to a temperature of 40 million degrees. But since tritium does not exist on earth it would have to be created. Neutrons bombarding an isotope of lithium, Li6, would transmute some of that light metal to tritium much as neutrons made plutonium from U235, but the only obvious source of such necessarily copious quantities of neutrons was Fermi's unproven pile. The luminaries did, however, consider the possibility of making tritium within the Super itself by packing the bomb with a dry form of lithium, lithium deuteride. But lithium in its natural form, like uranium in its natural form, contained too little of the desired isotope; to be effective, the Li6 would have to be separated. But lithium—element number 3 on the periodic table—would be much easier to separate than uranium . . . So the arguments progressed across the pleasant Berkeley summer. "We were forever inventing new tricks," Bethe says, "finding ways to calculate, and rejecting most of the tricks on the basis of the calculations. Now I could see at first-hand the tremendous intellectual power of Oppenheimer who was the unquestioned leader of our group. . . . The intellectual experience was unforgettable."

At the end of the summer, merging the Serber subgroup's work with their own, the luminaries concluded that the development of an atomic bomb would require a major scientific and technical effort. Glenn Seaborg heard Oppenheimer's deduction from that outcome at a meeting of the Met Lab technical council in Chicago on September 29. "Fast neutron work has no home," Seaborg paraphrases the Berkeley theoretician "[and] may need one." "Oppenheimer has plans in mind for fast neutron work," Compton told the council. Oppenheimer was scouting a site where the bomb might be designed and assembled. He thought such an operation might find a home in Cincinnati or with the plutonium production piles in Tennessee.

James Bryant Conant heard the results of the Berkeley summer study at a meeting of the S-1 Executive Committee in late August 1942 and jotted down a page of notes under the heading "Status of the Bomb." The fission bomb, he wrote, would explode according to the luminaries with "150 times energy of previous calculation" but, bad news, would require a critical mass "6 times the previous [estimated] size[:] 30 kg U235." Twelve kilograms of U235 were enough to explode, Conant noted, but inefficiently with "only 2% of energy." News of the Super then startled the NDRC chairman to a slip of the pencil:

> To denotate [*sic*: detonate] 5–10 kg of heavy hydrogen liquid would require 30 kg U235
>
> If you use 2 or 3 Tons of liquid deuterium and 30 kg U235 this would be equivalent 10^8 [i.e., 100,000,000] tons of TNT.
>
> Estimate devastation area of 1000 sq. km [or] 360 sq miles. Radioactivity lethal over same area for a few days.

Conant then drew a bold line with a steady hand and initialed the file note "JBC." As an afterthought or at a later time he added: "S-1 Executive Committee thinks the above probable. Heavy water is being pushed as hard as it can. [First] 100 kg of D will be available by fall of 1943 before 60 kg of U235 will be ready!"

A formal status report went off immediately from the Executive Committee to Bush. It predicted enough fissionable material for a test in eighteen months—by March 1944. It estimated that a 30-kilogram bomb of U235 "should have a destructive effect equivalent to the explosion of over 100,000 tons of TNT," much more than the mere 2,000 tons estimated earlier. And it dramatically announced the Super:

> If this [U235] unit is used to detonate a surrounding mass of 400 kg of liquid deuterium, the destructiveness should be equivalent to that of more than 10,000,000 tons of TNT. This should devastate an area of more than 100 square miles.

The committee—Briggs, Compton, Lawrence, Urey, Eger Murphree and Conant—concluded by judging the bomb project important beyond all previous estimates: "We have become convinced that success in this program before the enemy can succeed is necessary for victory. We also believe that success of this program will win the war if it has not previously been terminated."

On August 29 Bush bumped the status report up to the Secretary of War, noting that "the physicists of the Executive Committee are unanimous in believing that this large added factor [i.e., the Super] can be obtained. . . . The ultimate potential possibilities are now considered to be very much greater than at the time of the [last] report."

The hydrogen bomb was thus under development in the United States onward from July 1942.

The problem that Leo Szilard would call "the trouble at Chicago"—the problem of authority and responsibility for pile-cooling design and much more—erupted in a brief rebellion at the Met Lab in September. Stone & Webster, the construction engineers the Army had hired, had spent the summer studying plutonium production. "Classical engineers," Leona Woods calls them, "who knew bridges and structures, canals, highways, and the like, but who had a very weak grasp or none at all of what was needed in the new nuclear industry." The firm sent one of its best engineers to brief Met Lab leaders on production plans. "The scientists sat deadly still with curled lips. The briefer was ignorant; he enraged and frightened everyone."

An exasperated Compton protégé, Volney Wilson, an idealistic young physicist responsible for pile instrumentation, called a confrontation meeting soon afterward on a hot autumn evening. (As a student Wilson had analyzed the motions of swimming fish and invented the competition swimming style known as the Dolphin; with it he had won in Olympics tryouts in 1938 but then suffered disqualification because the style was new and thus unauthorized, a purblindness on the part of the Olympics judges which may have conditioned Wilson's attitude toward authority.) In his memoirs Compton mixes up the autumn meeting with the similar disagreement in June; Woods, who worked for Wilson, remembers it better:

> We (some 60 or 70 scientists) assembled quietly in the commons room at Eckhart Hall, open windows bringing hot, humid air in with an infinitesimal breeze. No one spoke—it was a Quaker meeting. Finally Compton entered carrying a Bible. . . .
>
> Compton thought that the issue of Wilson's meeting was whether the plutonium production should be undertaken by large-scale industry or should be carried out by the scientists of the Metallurgical Project, keeping control in their hands. Instead, it seemed to me that the primary issue was to get rid of Stone & Webster.

Compton vouchsafed a parable. Without introduction he opened his Bible to Judges 7: 5–7 and read to Leo Szilard and Enrico Fermi, to Eugene Wigner, to John Wheeler and threescore serious scientists the story of how the Lord helped Gideon sort among His people to find a few good men to fight the Midianites when there were too many volunteers at hand to demonstrate clearly that the victory would be entirely the work of the Lord. "When Compton finished reading," Woods remembers, "he sat down." Not surprisingly, "there was more Quaker-meeting silence." Or astonishment. Then Volney Wilson stood to direct "well-considered fire and brimstone . . . at the incompetence of Stone & Webster." Many others in the group spoke as well, all opposing the Boston engineers. "After a while, silence fell and finally everyone got up and disbanded." Compton had reduced the discussion to a demand that the Met Lab capitulate to his authority. Fortunately the assembly of scientists ignored him. The Army would soon move the responsibility for plutonium production into more experienced hands than Stone & Webster's. When the change was proposed Compton eagerly endorsed it.

Szilard responded to the struggles at the Met Lab with anger that by now, after four years of frustration, had begun to harden into stoicism. Late in September he drafted a long memorandum to his colleagues that addressed specific Met Lab problems but also considered the deeper issue of the responsibility of scientists for their work. In draft and more moderately in finished form his examination by turns compliments and savages Compton's leadership: "In talking to Compton I frequently have the feeling that I am overplaying a delicate instrument." Beyond personality Szilard pointed to a destructive abdication by those whom Compton led: "I have often thought . . . that things would have been different if Compton's authority had actually originated with our group, rather than with the OSRD." He elaborates in the finished memorandum:

> The situation might be different if Compton considered himself as our representative in Washington and asked in our name for whatever was necessary to make our project successful. He could then refuse to make a decision on any of the issues which affect our work until he had an opportunity fully to discuss the matter with us.
>
> Viewed in this light, it ought to be clear to us that we, and we alone, are to be blamed for the frustration of our work.

An authoritarian organization had moved in—had been allowed to move in—to take over work that had been democratically begun. "There is a sprinkling of democratic spots here and there, but they do not form a coherent network which could be functional." Szilard was convinced that authoritarian organization was no way to do science. So were Wigner and the more detached Fermi. "If we brought the bomb to them all ready-made on a silver platter," Szilard remembers hearing Fermi say, "there would still be a fifty-fifty chance that they would mess it up." But beyond debating the virtues of contractors and cooling systems only Szilard continued to rebel:

> We may take the stand that the responsibility for the success of this work has been delegated by the President to Dr. Bush. It has been delegated by Dr.

> Bush to Dr. Conant. Dr. Conant delegates this responsibility (accompanied by only part of the necessary authority) to Compton. Compton delegates to each of us some particular task and we can lead a very pleasant life while we do our duty. We live in a pleasant part of a pleasant city, in the pleasant company of each other, and have in Dr. Compton the most pleasant "boss" we could wish to have. There is every reason why we should be happy and since there is a war on, we are even willing to work overtime.
>
> Alternatively, we may take the stand that those who have originated the work on this terrible weapon and those who have materially contributed to its development have, before God and the World, the duty to see to it that it should be ready to be used at the proper time and in the proper way.
>
> I believe that each of us has now to decide where he feels that his responsibility lies.

The Army had been involved in the bomb project since June, but the Corps of Engineers' Colonel Marshall had been unable to drive the project ahead of other national military priorities. Divided between the OSRD and the Army it began to look as if it might lose its way. Bush thought he saw a solution in an authoritative new Military Policy Committee that would retain the project under partly civilian control but delegate direction to a dynamic Army officer and back him up. "From my own point of view," he wrote at the end of August 1942, "faced as I am with the unanimous opinion of a group of men that I consider to be among the greatest scientists in the world, joined by highly competent engineers, I am prepared to recommend that nothing should stand in the way of putting this whole affair through to conclusion . . . even if it does cause moderate interference with other war efforts."

Bush had discussed his problems with the general in charge of the Army Services of Supply, Brehon Somervell. Independently Somervell worked out a solution of his own: assigning entire responsibility to the Corps of Engineers, which was under his command. The program would need a stronger leader. He had a man in mind. In mid-September he sought him out.

"On the day I learned that I was to direct the project which ultimately produced the atomic bomb," Albany-born Leslie Richard Groves wrote later, "I was probably the angriest officer in the United States Army." The West Point graduate, forty-six years old in 1942, goes on to explain why:

> It was on September 17, 1942, at 10:30 a.m., that I got the news. I had agreed, by noon that day, to telephone my acceptance of a proposed assignment to duty overseas. I was then a colonel in the Army Engineers, with most of the headaches of directing ten billion dollars' worth of military construction in

> the country behind me—for good, I hoped. I wanted to get out of Washington, and quickly.
>
> Brehon B. Somervell . . . my top superior, met me in a corridor of the new House of Representatives Office Building when I had finished testifying about a construction project before the Military Affairs Committee.
>
> "About that duty overseas," General Somervell said, "you can tell them no."
>
> "Why?" I inquired.
>
> "The Secretary of War has selected you for a very important assignment."
>
> "Where?"
>
> "Washington."
>
> "I don't want to stay in Washington."
>
> "If you do the job right," General Somervell said carefully, "it will win the war."
>
> Men like to recall, in later years, what they said at some important or possibly historic moment in their lives. . . . I remember only too well what I said to General Somervell that day.
>
> I said, "Oh."

As deputy chief of construction for the entire U.S. Army, Groves knew enough about the bomb project to recognize its dubious claim to decisive effect and be thoroughly disappointed. He had just finished building the Pentagon, the most visible work of his career. He had seen the S-1 budget; it amounted in total to less than he had been spending in a week. He wanted assignment commanding troops. But he was career Army and understood he hardly had a choice. He crossed the Potomac to the Pentagon office of Somervell's chief of staff, Brigadier General Wilhelm D. Styer, for a briefing. Styer implied the job was well along and ought to be easy. The two officers worked up an order for Somervell to sign authorizing Groves "to take complete charge of the entire . . . project." Groves discovered he would be promoted to brigadier—for authority and in compensation—in a matter of days. He proposed to delay official appointment until the promotion came through. "I thought that there might be some problems in dealing with the many academic scientists involved in the project," he remembers of his initial innocence, "and I felt that my position would be stronger if they thought of me from the first as a general instead of as a promoted colonel." Styer agreed.

Groves was one inch short of six feet tall, jowly, with curly chestnut hair, blue eyes, a sparse mustache and sufficient girth to balloon over his webbing belt above and below its brass military buckle. Leona Woods thought he might weigh as much as 300 pounds; he was probably nearer

250 then, though he continued to expand. He had graduated from the University of Washington in 1914, studied engineering intensely for two years at MIT and gone on to West Point, where he graduated fourth in his class in 1918. Years at the Army Engineer School, the Command and General Staff College and the Army War College in the 1920s and 1930s completed his extensive education. He had seen duty in Hawaii, Europe and Central America. His father was a lawyer who left the law for the ministry and served in a country parish and an urban, working-class church before Grover Cleveland's Secretary of War convinced him to enlist as an Army chaplain on the Western frontier. "Entering West Point fulfilled my greatest ambition," Groves testifies. "I had been brought up in the Army, and in the main had lived on Army posts all my life. I was deeply impressed with the character and outstanding devotion to duty of the officers I knew." The dynamic engineer was married, with a thirteen-year-old daughter and a plebe son at West Point.

"A tremendous lone wolf," one of his subordinates describes Groves. Another, whose immediate superior Groves was about to become, distills their years together into grudgingly admiring vitriol. Lieutenant Colonel Kenneth D. Nichols—balding, bespectacled, thirty-four in 1942, West Point, Ph.D. in hydraulic engineering at Iowa State—remembers Groves as

> the biggest sonovabitch I've ever met in my life, but also one of the most capable individuals. He had an ego second to none, he had tireless energy—he was a big man, a heavy man but he never seemed to tire. He had absolute confidence in his decisions and he was absolutely ruthless in how he approached a problem to get it done. But that was the beauty of working for him—that you never had to worry about the decisions being made or what it meant. In fact I've often thought that if I were to have to do my part all over again, I would select Groves as boss. I hated his guts and so did everybody else but we had our form of understanding.

Nichols' previous boss, Colonel Marshall, had worked out of an office in Manhattan (where in August he had disguised the project to build an atomic bomb behind the name Manhattan Engineer District). But decisions of priority and supply were made in wartime in hurly-burly Washington offices, not in Manhattan, and to fight those battles the colonel had chosen the capable Nichols. Groves therefore sought out Nichols next after Styer. And found the project in even worse condition than he had feared: "I was not happy with the information I received; in fact, I was horrified."

He took Nichols with him to the Carnegie Institution on P Street to confront Vannevar Bush. Somervell had overlooked clearing Groves' appointment with Bush and the OSRD director was infuriated. He evaded

Groves' questions brusquely, which puzzled Groves. Controlling his anger until Groves and Nichols left, Bush then paid Styer a visit, which he describes in a contemporary memorandum:

> I told him (1) that I still felt, as I had told him and General Somervell previously, that the best move was to get the military commission first, and then the man to carry out their policies second; (2) that having seen General Groves briefly, I doubted whether he had sufficient tact for such a job.
>
> Styer disagreed on (1) and I simply said I wanted to be sure he understood my recommendation. On (2) he agreed the man is blunt, etc., but thought his other qualities would overbalance. . . . I fear we are in the soup.

Bush changed his mind within days. Groves immediately tackled his worst problems and solved them.

One of the first issues the heavyweight colonel had raised with Nichols was ore supply: was there sufficient uranium on hand? Nichols told him about a recent and fortuitous discovery: some 1,250 tons of extraordinarily rich pitchblende—it was 65 percent uranium oxide—that the Union Minière had shipped to the United States in 1940 from its Shinkolobwe mine in the Belgian Congo to remove it beyond German reach. Frédéric Joliot and Henry Tizard had independently warned the Belgians of the German danger in 1939. The ore was stored in the open in two thousand steel drums at Port Richmond on Staten Island. The Belgians had been trying for six months to alert the U.S. government to its presence. On Friday, September 18, Groves sent Nichols to New York to buy it.

On Saturday Groves drafted a letter in the name of Donald Nelson, the civilian head of the War Production Board, assigning a first-priority AAA rating to the Manhattan Engineer District. Groves personally carried the letter to Nelson. "His reaction was completely negative; however, he quickly reversed himself when I said that I would have to recommend to the President that the project should be abandoned because the War Production Board was unwilling to co-operate with his wishes." Groves was bluffing but it was not the bluster that swayed Nelson; he had probably heard by then from Bush and Henry Stimson. He signed the letter. "We had no major priority difficulties," notes Groves, "for nearly a year."

The same day Groves approved a directive that had been languishing on his predecessor's desk throughout the summer for the acquisition of 52,000 acres of land along the Clinch River in eastern Tennessee. Site X, the Met Lab called it. District Engineer Marshall had thought to wait to buy the land at least until the chain reaction was proved.

On September 23, the following Wednesday, Groves' promotion to brigadier came through. He hardly had time to pin on his stars before attending a command performance in the office of the Secretary of War called to assemble Bush's outmaneuvered Military Policy Committee with Stimson, Army Chief of Staff George Marshall, Bush, Conant, Somervell, Styer and an admiral on hand. Groves described how he intended to operate. Stimson proposed a nine-man committee to supervise. Groves held out for a more workable three and won his point. Discussion continued. Abruptly Groves asked to be excused: he needed to catch a train to Tennessee, he explained, to inspect Site X. The startled Secretary of War agreed and Leslie Richard Groves, the new broom that would sweep the Manhattan Engineer District clean, departed for Union Station. "You made me look like a million dollars," Somervell praised Groves when he got back to Washington. "I'd told them that if you were put in charge, things would really start moving." They did.

Enrico Fermi began planning a full-scale chain-reacting pile in May 1942 when one of the exponential piles his team built in the west stands of Stagg Field indicated its *k* at infinity would muster 0.995. The Met Lab was searching out higher-quality graphite and sponsoring production of pure uranium metal, denser than oxide; those and other improvements should push *k* above 1.0. "I remember I talked about the experiment on the Indiana dunes," Fermi told his wife after the war, "and it was the first time I saw the dunes. . . . I liked the dunes: it was a clear day, with no fog to dim colors. . . . We came out of the water, and we walked along the beach."

As they began preparations that summer Leona Woods remembers swimming "in frigid Lake Michigan every afternoon at five o'clock, off the huge breakwater rocks at the 55th street promontory"—she, Herbert Anderson, Fermi. She was still a graduate student, twenty-two and shy. "One evening, Enrico gave a party, inviting Edward and [Mici] Teller, Helen and Robert Mulliken (my research professor), and Herb Anderson, John Marshall, and me." They played Murder, the parlor game then in fashion. "The second the lights went out on this particular evening, I shrank into a corner and listened with astonishment to these brilliant, accomplished, famous sophisticated people shrieking and poking and kissing each other in the dark like little kids." All nice people are shy, Fermi consoled her when he knew her better; he had always been dominated by shyness. She records his sly self-mockery: "As he frequently said, he was amazed when he thought how modest he was."

Woods was finishing her thesis work during the summer but sometimes helped Anderson scour Chicago for lumber. CP-1—Chicago Pile Number One—Fermi planned to build in the form of a sphere, the most efficient shape to maximize *k*. Since the pile's layers of graphite bricks would enlarge concentrically up to its equator, they would need external support, and wood framing was light and easy to shape and assemble. "I was the buyer for a lot of lumber," Anderson says. "I remember the Sterling Lumber Company, how amazed they were by the orders I gave them, all with double X priority. But they delivered the lumber with no questions asked. There was almost no constraint on money and priority to get what we wanted."

Horseback riding one Saturday afternoon in the Cook County Forest Preserve twenty miles southwest of Chicago, Arthur and Betty Compton found an isolated, scenic site for the pile building, a terminal moraine forested with hawthorne and scrub oak known as the Argonne Forest. The Army's Nichols negotiated with the county to use the land; Stone & Webster began planning construction.

The Fermis rented a house from a businessman moving to Washington for war work; since they were enemy aliens and not allowed to own a shortwave radio the man had to have his big all-band Capehart temporarily disabled of its long-distance frequencies, though it continued to supply dance music to the party room on the third floor. Fermi was angry to find his mail being opened and complained indignantly until the practice was stopped (or managed more surreptitiously). The Comptons gave a series of parties to welcome newcomers to the Met Lab. "At each of these parties," Laura Fermi writes, "the English film *Next of Kin* was shown. It depicted in dark tones the consequences of negligence and carelessness. A briefcase laid down on the floor in a public place is stolen by a spy. English military plans become known to the enemy. Bombardments, destruction of civilian homes, and an unnecessarily high toll of lives on the fighting front are the result. . . . Willingly we accepted the hint and confined our social activities to the group of 'metallurgists.'" Compton, who describes himself as "one of those who must talk over important problems with his wife," arranged uniquely to have Betty Compton cleared. None of the other wives was supposed to know about her husband's work. Laura Fermi found out, like many others, only at the end of the war.

In mid-August Fermi's group could report a probable k for a graphite–uranium oxide pile of "close to 1.04." They were working on control-rod design and testing the vacuum properties of both metal sheet and balloon cloth. The cloth was Anderson's idea, a possible alternative to canning the pile to exclude neutron-absorbing air. It proved serviceable and Anderson followed up: "For the balloon cloth enclosure I went to the Goodyear Rubber Company in Akron, Ohio. The company had a good deal of experience in building blimps and rubber rafts but a square balloon 25′ on a side seemed a bit odd to them." They made it anyway, "with no questions asked." It should be good for a 1 percent improvement in k.

Between September 15 and November 15 Anderson, Walter Zinn and their crews also built sixteen successive exponential piles in the Stagg Field west stands to measure the purity of the various shipments of graphite, uranium oxide and metal they had begun to receive in quantity. Not all the uranium was acceptable. But Mallinckrodt Chemical Works in St. Louis, specialists at handling the ether necessary for oxide extraction, began producing highly purified brown oxide at the rate of thirty tons a month, and the National Carbon Company and a smaller supplier, by using purified petroleum coke for raw material and doubling furnace time, significantly improved graphite supplies (graphite is molded as coke, then baked in a high-temperature electric-arc oven for long hours until it crystallizes and its impurities vaporize away). By September regular deliveries began to arrive in covered trucks. Physicists doubled as laborers to unload the bricks and cans and pass them into the west stands for finishing.

Walter Zinn took charge of preparing the materials for the pile. The graphite came in from various manufacturers as rough 4¼ by 4¼-inch bars in 17- to 50-inch lengths. So that the bars would fit closely together they had to be smoothed and cut to standard 16½-inch lengths. About a fourth of them also had to be drilled for the lumps of uranium they would hold. A few required slots machined through to make channels for control rods. The uranium oxide needed to be compressed into what the physicists called "pseudospheres"—stubby cylinders with round-shouldered ends—for which purpose the press from the Jersey City junkyard had been shipped to Chicago the previous winter.

For crew Zinn had half a dozen young physicists, a thoroughly able carpenter and some thirty high school dropouts earning pocket money until their draft notices came through. They were Back of the Yards boys from the tough neighborhood beyond the Chicago stockyards and Zinn improved the fluency of his swearing keeping them in line.

Machining the graphite was like sharpening thousands of giant pencils. Zinn used power woodworking tools. A jointer first made two sides of each graphite brick perpendicular and smooth; a planer finished the other two surfaces; a swing saw cut the bricks to length. That processing produced 14 tons of bricks a day; each brick weighed 19 pounds.

To drill the blind, round-bottomed 3¼-inch holes for the uranium pseudospheres, two to a brick, Zinn adapted a heavy lathe. He mounted a 3¼-inch spade bit in the headstock of the lathe, where the material to be turned would normally be mounted, and forced the graphite up against the tool with the lathe carriage. Dull bits caused problems. Zinn tried tough carballoy bits first, but they were tedious to resharpen. He began making bits from old steel files, sharpening them by hand whenever they dulled. One sharpening was good for 60 holes, about an hour's work. Before they were through they would shape and finish 45,000 graphite bricks and drill 19,000 holes.

General Groves made his first appearance at the Met Lab on October 5 and delivered his first pronouncement. The technical council was debating cooling systems again. "The War Department considers the project important," Seaborg paraphrases Groves' formula, which they would all learn by heart. "There is no objection to a wrong decision with quick results. If there is a choice between two methods, one of which is good and the other looks promising, then build both." Get the cooling-system decision into Compton's hands by Saturday night, Groves demanded. It was Monday. They had been debating for months.

Groves moved on to Berkeley more impressed with their work than his Met Lab auditors realized. "I left Chicago feeling that the plutonium process seemed to offer us the greatest chances for success in producing bomb material," he recalls. "Every other process . . . depended upon the physical separation of materials having almost infinitesimal differences in their physical properties." Transmutation by chain reaction was entirely new, but the rest of the plutonium process, chemical separation, "while extremely difficult and completely unprecedented, did not seem to be impossible."

At the beginning of the month, to Compton's great relief, the brigadier had convinced E. I. du Pont de Nemours, the Delaware chemical and explosives manufacturers, to take over building and running the plutonium production piles under subcontract to Stone & Webster. He meant to involve the industrial chemists more extensively than that—meant for them to take over the plutonium project in its entirety. Du Pont resisted the increasing encroachment. "Its reasons were sound," writes Groves: "the evident physical operating hazards, the company's inexperience in the field of nuclear physics, the many doubts about the feasibility of the process, the paucity of proven theory, and the complete lack of essential technical design data." Du Pont also suspected, once it had sent an eight-man review team to Chicago at the beginning of November, that the plutonium project was the least promising of the several then under development and might even fail, tarnishing the company's reputation. Nor was it happy at the prospect of identifying itself with a secret weapon of mass destruction; it still remembered the general condemnation it had received for selling munitions to Britain and France before the United States entered the First World War. Groves told the Du Pont executive committee that the Germans were probably hard at work and the only defense against a Nazi atomic bomb would be an American bomb. And added what he took to be a clinching argument: "If we were successful in time, we would shorten the war and thus save tens of thousands of American casualties." The second week in November Du Pont admitted the possibility of regular production by 1945 and accepted the assignment (limiting itself to a profit of one dollar to avoid arms-merchant stigma), but made its skepticism and reluctance clear.

By then Stone & Webster's construction workers had gone on strike. The pile building scheduled for completion by October 20 would be indefinitely delayed. Fermi lived with the problem only long enough to recalculate the risks of pile control. In early November he cornered Compton in his office and proposed an alternative site: the doubles squash court where his team had built its series of exponential piles. A *k* greater than 1.0 presented an entirely different order of risk from a *k* of less than 1.0, however; Compton had, in Seaborg's words, a "dreadful decision" to make. "We did not see how a true nuclear explosion, such as that of an atomic bomb, could possibly occur," Compton writes with more calm than he probably felt at the time. "But the amount of potentially radioactive material present in the pile would be enormous and anything that would cause excessive ionizing radiation in such a location would be intolerable." He asked for Fermi's analysis of the probability of control.

No doubt Fermi discussed the various hand and automatic control rods he planned for the pile. But even slow-neutron fission generations had been calculated to multiply in thousandths of a second, which might flash the pile to dangerous levels of heat and radiation before any merely mechanical control system could move into position. The "most significant fact assuring us that the chain reaction could be controlled," says Compton, was one of the Richard Roberts team's earliest discoveries at the Carnegie Institution's Department of Terrestrial Magnetism following Bohr's announcement of the discovery of fission in 1939—in Compton's words, that "a certain small fraction of the neutrons associated with the fission process are not emitted at once but come off a few seconds after fission occurs." With a pile operating at *k* only marginally above 1.0, such delayed neutrons would slow the response sufficiently to allow time for adjustment.

For once Compton made a quick decision: with control seemingly assured, he allowed Fermi to build CP-1 in the west stands. He chose not to inform the president of the University of Chicago, Robert Maynard Hutchins, reasoning that he should not ask a lawyer to judge a matter of nuclear physics. "The only answer he could have given would have been—no. And this answer would have been wrong. So I assumed the responsibility myself." The word *meltdown* had not yet entered the reactor engineer's vocabulary—Fermi was only then inventing that specialty—but that is what

Compton was risking, a small Chernobyl in the midst of a crowded city. Except that Fermi, as he knew, was a formidably competent engineer.

In mid-November Fermi reorganized his team into two twelve-hour shifts, a day crew under Walter Zinn (who continued to supervise materials production as well), a night crew under Herbert Anderson. Construction began on Monday morning, November 16, 1942. From the balcony of the doubles squash court in the west stands of Stagg Field Fermi directed the hanging of the cubical dark-gray Goodyear balloon as his men hauled it into place with block and tackle. It dominated the room: bottom panel smoothed on the floor, top and three sides secured to the ceiling and the walls, the fourth side facing the balcony furled up out of the way like an awning. Someone drew a circle on the floor panel to locate the first layer of graphite and without ceremony the crew began positioning the dark, slippery bricks. The first layer was "dead" graphite that carried no load of uranium: solid crystalline carbon to diffuse and slow the neutrons that fission would generate. Up the pile as it stacked, the crews would alternate one layer of dead graphite with two layers of bricks each drilled and loaded with two five-pound uranium pseudospheres. That created a cubic cell of neutron-diffusing graphite around every lump of uranium.

To build the wooden framing, Herbert Anderson recalls, "Gus Knuth, the millwright, would be called in. We would show him . . . what we wanted, he would take a few measurements, and soon the timbers would be in place. There were no detailed plans or blueprints for the frame or the pile." Since they had batches of graphite, oxide and metal of varying purity, they improvised the placement of materials as they went along. Fermi, says Anderson, "spent a good deal of time calculating the most effective location for the various grades of [material] on hand."

They were soon averaging not quite two layers a shift, handing the bricks along from their delivery skids, sliding them to the workers on the pile, singing together to pass the time. The bricks in the dead graphite layers alternated direction, three running east and west and the next three north and south. That gave support to the oxide layers, which all ran together from front to back except at the outer edges, where dead graphite formed an outer shell. The physicist bricklayers had to be careful to line up the slots for the ten control-rod channels that passed at widely distributed points completely through the pile. "A simple design for a control rod was developed," says Anderson, "which could be made on the spot: cadmium sheet nailed to a flat wood strip. . . . The [thirteen-foot] strips had to be inserted and removed by hand. Except when the reactivity of the pile was being measured, they were kept inside the pile and locked using a simple hasp and padlock, the only keys to which were kept by Zinn and myself." Cadmium, which has a gargantuan absorption cross section for slow neutrons, held the pile quiescent.

As it grew they assembled wooden scaffolding to stand on and ran loads of bricks up to the working face on a portable materials elevator. Before the arrival of the elevator, during the period when they were building large exponential piles, they had simply leaned over from the precarious 2 by 12-inch scaffolding and reached the bricks up from the men on the floor below. Groves walked in on them one day and dressed them down for risking their necks. The elevator appeared unbidden soon after.

When they achieved the fifteenth layer Zinn and Anderson began measuring neutron intensity at the end of each shift at a fixed point near the center of the pile with the control rods removed. They used a boron trifluoride counter Leona Woods had devised that worked much like a Geiger counter, clicking off the neutron count. Standard indium foils bombarded to radioactivity by pile neutrons gave daily checks on the boron counter's calibration. Fermi had complained to Segrè in October that he was doing physics by telephone; now he moved a little closer to the work. "Each day we would report on the progress of the construction to Fermi," Anderson notes, "usually in his office in Eckhart Hall. Then we would present our sketch of the layers that we had assembled and reach some agreement on what would be added during the following shifts." Fermi took the raw boron-counter and indium measurements and calculated a countdown. As the pile approached its slow-neutron critical mass the neutrons generated within it by spontaneous fission multiplied through more and more generations before they were absorbed. At $k = 0.99$, for example, each neutron would multiply through an average one hundred generations before its chain of generations died out. Fermi divided the square of the radius of the pile by a measure of the intensity of radioactivity the pile induced in indium and got a number that would decrease to zero as the pile approached criticality. At layer 15 the countdown stood at 390; at layer 19 it dropped to 320. It was 270 at layer 25 and down to 149 at layer 36.

As winter locked down, the unheated west stands turned bitterly cold. Graphite dust blackened walls, floors, hallways, lab coats, faces, hands. A black haze dispersed light in the floodlit air. White teeth shone. Every surface was slippery, hands and feet routine casualties of dropped blocks. The men building the pile, lifting tons of materials every shift, stayed warm enough, but the unlucky security guards stationed at doors and entrances froze. Zinn scavenged rakish makeshift to thaw them out:

> We tried charcoal fires in empty oil drums—too much smoke. Then we secured a number of ornamental, imitation log, gas-fired fireplaces. These were

hooked up to the gas mains, but they gobbled up the oxygen and replaced it with fumes which burned the eyes. . . . The University of Chicago came to the rescue. Years before, big league football had been banned from the campus; we found in an old locker a supply of raccoon fur coats. Thus, for a time we had the best dressed collegiate-style guards in the business.

Fermi had originally designed his first full-scale pile as a 76-layer sphere. Some 250 tons of better graphite from National Carbon now promised to reduce neutron absorption below previous estimates; more than 6 tons of high-purity uranium metal in the form of 2¼-inch cylinders began arriving from Iowa State College at Ames, where one of the Met Lab's chemistry group leaders, Frank Spedding, had converted a laboratory to backyard mass production. "Spedding's eggs," dropped in place of oxide pseudospheres into drilled graphite blocks that were then stacked in spherical configuration close to the center of the CP-1 lattice, significantly increased the value of *k*. Adjusting for the improvements, Fermi saw that they would not need to seal the Goodyear balloon and evacuate the air from the pile and could eliminate some 20 layers: his countdown should converge to zero, $k = 1.0$, between layers 56 and 57. Instead of a sphere the pile would take the form of a doorknob as big as a two-car garage, a flattened rotational ellipsoid 25 feet wide at the equator and 20 feet high from pole to pole:

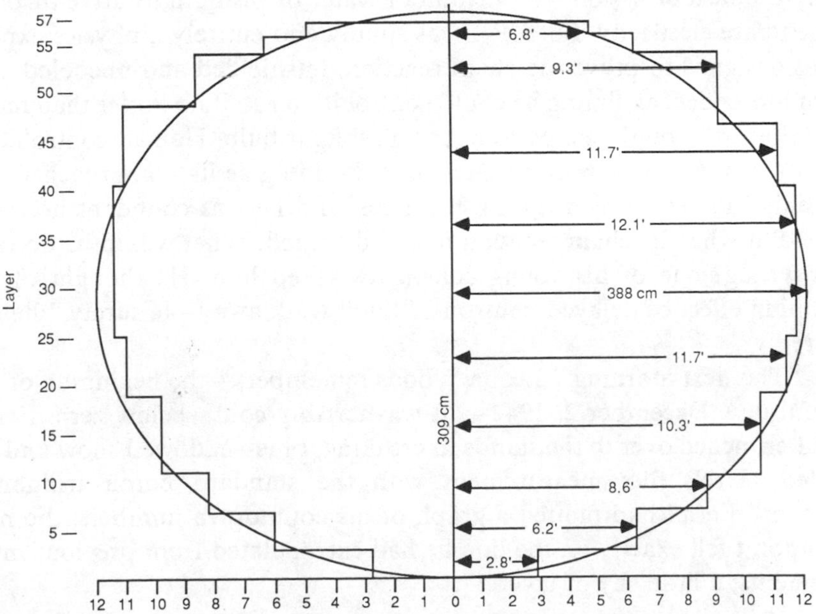

Anderson's crew assembled this final configuration on the night of December 1:

> That night the construction proceeded as usual, with all cadmium covered wood in place. When the 57th layer was completed, I called a halt to the work, in accordance with the agreement we had reached in the meeting with Fermi that afternoon. All the cadmium rods but one were removed and the neutron count taken following the standard procedure which had been followed on the previous days. It was clear from the count that once the only remaining cadmium rod was removed, the pile would go critical. I resisted great temptation to pull the final cadmium strip and be the first to make a pile chain react. However, Fermi had foreseen this temptation and extracted a promise from me to make the measurement, record the result, insert all cadmium rods, and lock them all in place.

Which Anderson dutifully did, and closed up the squash court and went home to bed.

The pile as it waited in the dark cold of Chicago winter to be released to the breeding of neutrons and plutonium contained 771,000 pounds of graphite, 80,590 pounds of uranium oxide and 12,400 pounds of uranium metal. It cost about $1 million to produce and build. Its only visible moving parts were its various control rods. If Fermi had planned it for power production he would have shielded it behind concrete or steel and pumped away the heat of fission with helium or water or bismuth to drive turbines to generate electricity. But CP-1 was simply and entirely a physics experiment designed to prove the chain reaction, unshielded and uncooled, and Fermi intended, assuming he could control it, to run it no hotter than half a watt, hardly enough energy to light a flashlight bulb. He had controlled it day by day for the seventeen days of its building as its *k* approached 1.0, matching its responses with his estimates, and he was confident he could control it when its chain reaction finally diverged. What would he do if he was wrong? one of his young colleagues asked him. He thought of the damping effect of delayed neutrons. "I will walk away—leisurely," he answered.

"The next morning," Leona Woods remembers—the beginning of the fateful day, December 2, 1942—"it was terribly cold—below zero. Fermi and I crunched over to the stands in creaking, blue-shadowed snow and repeated Herb's flux measurement with the standard boron trifluoride counter." Fermi had plotted a graph of his countdown numbers; the new data point fell exactly on the line he had extrapolated from previous measurements, a little shy of layer 57:

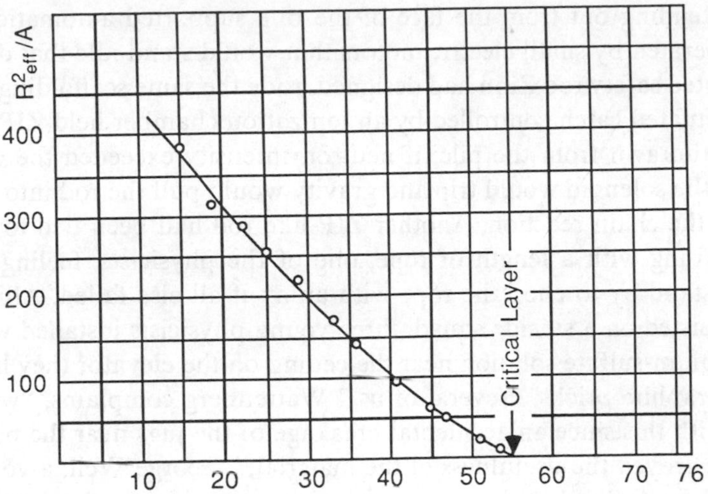

Fermi discussed a schedule for the day with Zinn and Volney Wilson, Woods continues; "then a sleepy Herb Anderson showed up. . . . Herb, Fermi and I went over to the apartment I shared with my sister (it was close to the stands) for something to eat. I made pancakes, mixing the batter so fast that there were bubbles of dry flour in it. When fried, these were somewhat crunchy between the teeth, and Herb thought I had put nuts in the batter."

Outside was raw wind. On the second day of gasoline rationing Chicagoans jammed streetcars and elevated trains, leaving almost half their usual traffic of automobiles at home. The State Department had announced that morning that two million Jews had perished in Europe and five million more were in danger. The Germans were preparing counterattack in North Africa; American marines and Japanese soldiers struggled in the hell of Guadalcanal.

> Back we mushed through the cold, creaking snow. . . . Fifty-seventh Street was strangely empty. Inside the hall of the west stands, it was as cold as outside. We put on the usual gray (now black with graphite) laboratory coats and entered the doubles squash court containing the looming pile enclosed in the dirty, grayish-black balloon cloth and then went up on the spectators' balcony. The balcony was originally meant for people to watch squash players, but now it was filled with control equipment and read-out circuits glowing and winking and radiating some gratefully received heat.

The instrumentation included redundant boron trifluoride counters for lower neutron intensities and ionization chambers for higher. A wooden pier extending out from the face of the pile supported automatic control rods operated by small electric motors that would stand idle that day. ZIP, a weighted safety rod Zinn had designed, rode the same scaffolding. A solenoid-actuated catch controlled by an ionization chamber held ZIP in position withdrawn from the pile; if neutron intensity exceeded the chamber setting the solenoid would trip and gravity would pull the rod into position to stop the chain reaction. Another ZIP-like rod had been tied to the balcony railing with a length of rope; one of the physicists, feeling foolish, would stand by to chop the rope with an ax if all else failed. Allison had even insisted on a suicide squad, three young physicists installed with jugs of cadmium-sulfate solution near the ceiling on the elevator they had used to lift graphite bricks; "several of us," Wattenberg complains, "were very upset with this since an accidental breakage of the jugs near the pile could have destroyed the usefulness of the material." George Weil, a young veteran of the Columbia days, took up position on the floor of the squash court to operate one of the cadmium control rods by hand at Fermi's order. Fermi had scalers that counted off boron trifluoride readings with loud clicks and a cylindrical pen recorder that performed a similar function silently, graphing pile intensities in ink on a roll of slowly rotating graph paper. For calculations he relied on his own trusted six-inch slide rule, the pocket calculator of its day.

Around midmorning Fermi began the crucial experiment. First he ordered all but the last cadmium rod removed and checked to see if the neutron intensity matched the measurement Anderson had made the night before. With that first comparison Volney Wilson's team working on the balcony took time to adjust its monitors. Fermi had calculated in advance the intensity he expected the pile to reach at each step of the way as George Weil withdrew the last thirteen-foot cadmium rod by measured increments.

When Wilson's team was ready, writes Wattenberg, "Fermi instructed Weil to move the cadmium rod to a position which was about half-way out. [The adjustment brought the pile to] well below critical condition. The intensity rose, the scalers increased their rates of clicking for a short while, and then the rate became steady, as it was supposed to." Fermi busied himself at his slide rule, calculating the rate of increase, and noted the numbers on the back. He called to Weil to move the rod out another six inches. "Again the neutron intensity increased and leveled off. The pile was still subcritical. Fermi had again been busy with his little slide rule and seemed very pleased with the results of his calculations. Every time the intensity leveled off, it was at the values he had anticipated for the position of the control rod."

The slow, careful checking continued through the morning. A crowd began to gather on the balcony. Szilard arrived, Wigner, Allison, Spedding whose metal eggs had flattened the pile. Twenty-five or thirty people accumulated on the balcony watching, most of them the young physicists who had done the work. No one photographed the scene but most of the spectators probably wore suits and ties in the genteel tradition of prewar physics and since it was cold in the squash court, near zero, they would have kept warm in coats and hats, scarves and gloves. The room was dingy with graphite dust. Fermi was calm. The pile rising before them, faced with raw 4 by 6-inch pine timbers up to its equator, domed bare graphite above, looked like an ominous black beehive in a bright box. Neutrons were its bees, dancing and hot.

Fermi called for another six-inch withdrawal. Weil reached up to comply. The neutron intensity leveled off at a rate outside the range of some of the instruments. Time passed, says Wattenberg, the watchers abiding in the cold, while Wilson's team again adjusted the electronics:

> After the instrumentation was reset, Fermi told Weil to remove the rod another six inches. The pile was still subcritical. The intensity was increasing slowly—when suddenly there was a very loud crash! The safety rod, ZIP, had been automatically released. Its relay had been activated by an ionization chamber because the intensity had exceeded the arbitrary level at which it had been set. It was 11:30 a.m., and Fermi said, "I'm hungry. Let's go to lunch." The other rods were put into the pile and locked.

At two in the afternoon they prepared to continue the experiment. Compton joined them. He brought along Crawford Greenewalt, the tall, handsome engineer who was the leader of the Du Pont contingent in Chicago. Forty-two people now occupied the squash court, most of them crowded onto the balcony.

Fermi ordered all but one of the cadmium rods again unlocked and removed. He asked Weil to set the last rod at one of the earlier morning settings and compared pile intensity to the earlier reading. When the measurements checked he directed Weil to remove the rod to the last setting before lunch, about seven feet out.

The closer k approached 1.0, the slower the rate of change of pile intensity. Fermi made another calculation. The pile was nearly critical. He asked that ZIP be slid in. That adjustment brought the neutron count down. "This time," he told Weil, "take the control rod out twelve inches." Weil withdrew the cadmium rod. Fermi nodded and ZIP was winched out as well. "This is going to do it," Fermi told Compton. The director of the plutonium project had found a place for himself at Fermi's side. "Now it will become self-sustaining. The trace [on the recorder] will climb and continue to climb; it will not level off."

Herbert Anderson was an eyewitness:

> At first you could hear the sound of the neutron counter, clickety-clack, clickety-clack. Then the clicks came more and more rapidly, and after a while they began to merge into a roar; the counter couldn't follow anymore. That was the moment to switch to the chart recorder. But when the switch was made, everyone watched in the sudden silence the mounting deflection of the recorder's pen. It was an awesome silence. Everyone realized the significance of that switch; we were in the high intensity regime and the counters were unable to cope with the situation anymore. Again and again, the scale of the recorder had to be changed to accommodate the neutron intensity which was increasing more and more rapidly. Suddenly Fermi raised his hand. "The pile has gone critical," he announced. No one present had any doubt about it.

Fermi allowed himself a grin. He would tell the technical council the next day that the pile achieved a *k* of 1.0006. Its neutron intensity was then doubling every two minutes. Left uncontrolled for an hour and a half, that rate of increase would have carried it to a million kilowatts. Long before so extreme a runaway it would have killed anyone left in the room and melted down.

"Then everyone began to wonder why he didn't shut the pile off," Anderson continues. "But Fermi was completely calm. He waited another minute, then another, and then when it seemed that the anxiety was too much to bear, he ordered 'ZIP in!' " It was 3:53 P.M. Fermi had run the pile for 4.5 minutes at one-half watt and brought to fruition all the years of discovery and experiment. Men had controlled the release of energy from the atomic nucleus.

The chain reaction was moonshine no more.

Eugene Wigner reports how they felt:

> Nothing very spectacular had happened. Nothing had moved and the pile itself had given no sound. Nevertheless, when the rods were pushed back in and the clicking died down, we suddenly experienced a let-down feeling, for all of us understood the language of the counter. Even though we had anticipated the success of the experiment, its accomplishment had a deep impact on us. For some time we had known that we were about to unlock a giant; still, we could not escape an eerie feeling when we knew we had actually done it. We felt as, I presume, everyone feels who has done something that he knows will have very far-reaching consequences which he cannot foresee.

Months earlier, realizing that the importation of Italian wine had been cut off by the war, Wigner had searched the liquor stores of Chicago for a celebratory *fiasca* of Chianti. He produced it now in a brown paper bag and

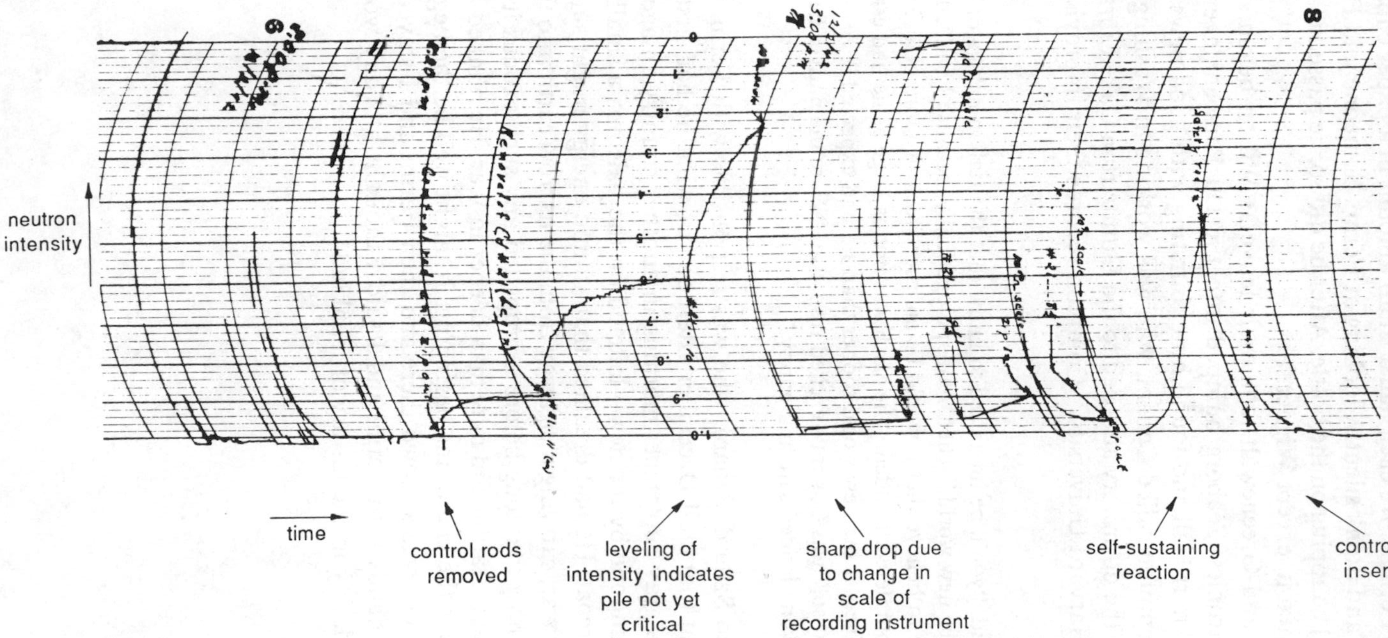

Neutron intensity in the pile as recorded by the chart recorder

presented it to Fermi. "We each had a small amount in a paper cup," Wattenberg says, "and drank silently, looking at Fermi. Someone told Fermi to sign the [straw] wrapping on the bottle. After he did so, he passed it around, and we all signed it, except Wigner."

Compton and Greenewalt took their leave as Wilson began shutting down the electronics. Seaborg bumped into the Du Pont engineer in the corridor of Eckhart Hall and found him "bursting with good news." Back in his office Compton called Conant, who was working in Washington "in my quarters in the dormitory attached to the Dumbarton Oaks Library and Collection of Harvard University." Compton records their improvised dialogue:

> "Jim," I said, "you'll be interested to know that the Italian navigator has just landed in the new world." Then, half apologetically, because I had led the S-1 Committee to believe that it would be another week or more before the pile could be completed, I added, "the earth was not as large as he had estimated, and he arrived at the new world sooner than he had expected."
>
> "Is that so," was Conant's excited response. "Were the natives friendly?"
>
> "Everyone landed safe and happy."

Except Leo Szilard. Szilard, who was responsible with Fermi for the accomplishment that chill December afternoon of what he had first imagined alone on a gray September morning in another country an age ago—the old world undone by the new—loitered on the balcony, a small round man in an overcoat. He had dreamed that atomic energy might substitute exploration for war, carrying men away from the narrow earth into the cosmos. He knew now that long before it propelled any such exodus it would increase war's devastation and mire man deeper in fear. He blinked behind his glasses. It was the end of the beginning. It might well be the beginning of the end. "There was a crowd there and then Fermi and I stayed there alone. I shook hands with Fermi and I said I thought this day would go down as a black day in the history of mankind."

14 Physics and Desert Country

Robert Oppenheimer was thirty-eight years old in 1942. He had done by then what Hans Bethe calls "massive scientific work." He was known and respected as a theoretician throughout the world of physics. Up to the time of the Berkeley summer study, however, few of his peers seem to have thought him capable of decisive leadership. Though he had matured deeply across the decade of the 1930s, his persistent mannerisms, especially his caustic tongue, may have screened his maturity from his colleagues' eyes. Yet the 1930s shaped Oppenheimer for the work that was now to challenge him.

His distinctive appearance sharpens the memory of an admiring new friend of that decade, a Berkeley professor and translator of French literature named Haakon Chevalier:

> [Oppenheimer] was tall, nervous and intent, and he moved with an odd gait, a kind of jog, with a great deal of swinging of his limbs, his head always a little to one side, one shoulder higher than the other. But it was the head that was the most striking: the halo of wispy black curly hair, the fine, sharp nose, and especially the eyes, surprisingly blue, having a strange depth and intensity, and yet expressive of a candor that was altogether disarming. He looked like a young Einstein, and at the same time like an overgrown choir boy.

Chevalier's portrait identifies Oppenheimer's youthfulness and sensitivity but misses the self-destructiveness: the chain-smoking, the persistent cough persistently ignored, the ravaged teeth, the usually empty stomach assaulted by highly praised martinis and highly spiced food. Oppenheimer's emaciation suggests he had an aversion to incorporating the world. His body embarrassed him and he seldom allowed himself to appear, as at the beach, undressed. At school he wore gray suits, blue shirts and well-polished black shoes. At home (a small spare apartment at first; later, after his marriage, the elegant house in the Berkeley hills he bought with a check the day he first toured it) he preferred jeans and blue chambray work shirts, the jeans hung on his narrow hips with a wide Western silver-buckled belt. It was not a common look in the 1930s—he had picked it up in New Mexico—and it was another detail that made him seem different.

Women thought him handsome and dashing. Before a party he might send gardenias not only to his own date but to his friends' dates as well. "He was great at a party," a female acquaintance of his later adulthood comments, "and women simply loved him." His unfailing attentiveness probably elicited that admiration: "He was always," writes Chevalier, "without seeming effort, aware of, and responsive to, everyone in the room, and was constantly anticipating unspoken wishes."

Men he could antagonize or amuse. Edward Teller first met Oppenheimer in 1937. The meeting, Teller says, was "painful but characteristic. On the evening I was to talk at a Berkeley colloquium, he took me out to a Mexican restaurant for dinner. I didn't have the practice in speaking that I've had since, and I was already a little nervous. The plates were so hot, and the spices were so hot—as you might suspect if you knew Oppenheimer—and his personality was so overpowering, that I lost my voice." Emilio Segrè notes that Oppenheimer "sometimes appeared amateurish and snobbish." Out of curiosity in 1940, while visiting Berkeley to deliver a lecture, Enrico Fermi attended a seminar one of Oppenheimer's protégés led in the master's style. "Emilio," Fermi joked afterward with Segrè, "I am getting rusty and old. I cannot follow the highbrow theory developed by Oppenheimer's pupils anymore. I went to their seminar and was depressed by my inability to understand them. Only the last sentence cheered me up; it was: 'and this is Fermi's theory of beta decay.' " Although Segrè found Oppenheimer "the fastest thinker I've ever met," with "an iron memory . . . brilliance and solid merits," he also saw "grave defects" including "occasional arrogance . . . [that] stung scientific colleagues where they were most sensitive." "Robert could make people feel they were fools," Bethe says simply. "He made me, but I didn't mind. Lawrence did. The two disagreed while they were both still at Berkeley. I think Robert would give Lawrence a feeling that he didn't know physics, and since that is what cyclotrons are for, Lawrence didn't like it." Oppenheimer recognized the habit without diagnosing it in a letter to his younger brother Frank: "But it is not easy—at least it is not easy for me—to be quite free of the desire to browbeat somebody or something." He called the behavior "beastliness." It did not win him friends.

Oppenheimer's mother died after a long battle with leukemia in late 1931; that was when he announced himself to Herbert Smith, his former Ethical Culture teacher, to be "the loneliest man in the world." His father died suddenly of a heart attack in 1937. The two deaths frame the beginning years of the unworldly physicist's discovery of the suffering in the world. Later he testified to the surprise of that discovery:

> My friends, both in Pasadena and in Berkeley, were mostly faculty people, scientists, classicists, and artists. I studied and read Sanskrit with Arthur Ryder. I read very widely, mostly classics, novels, plays, and poetry; and I read something of other parts of science. I was not interested in and did not read about economics or politics. I was almost wholly divorced from the contemporary scene in this country. I never read a newspaper or a current magazine like *Time* or *Harper's;* I had no radio, no telephone; I learned of the stock market crash in the fall of 1929 only long after the event; the first time I ever voted was in the Presidential election of 1936. To many of my friends, my indifference to contemporary affairs seemed bizarre, and they often chided me with being too much of a highbrow. I was interested in man and his experience; I was deeply interested in my science; but I had no understanding of the relations of man to his society. . .
>
> Beginning in late 1936, my interests began to change.

Oppenheimer reports three reasons for the change. "I had had a continuing, smouldering fury about the treatment of the Jews in Germany," he mentions first. "I had relatives there, and was later to help in extricating them and bringing them to this country." They arrived only a few days after his father's death and he and Frank volunteered responsibility for them.

Second, says Oppenheimer, "I saw what the Depression was doing to my students." Philip Morrison, one of the wittiest of the young theoreticians, polio-crippled and poor, remembers in compensation the "very grave, very profound involvement in physics, the love of the whole thing, which we all had in those days." Oppenheimer could take his admiring students to dinner; he was unable to find them jobs. "And through them," he testifies, "I began to understand how deeply political and economic events could affect men's lives. I began to feel the need to participate more fully in the life of the community."

He had no framework yet. A woman would help him with that, her involvement the third reason he gives for his entry into the world: Jean Tatlock, the lithe, chiaroscuro daughter of an anti-Semite Berkeley medievalist. "In the autumn [of 1936], I began to court her, and we grew close to each other. We were at least twice close enough to marriage to think of ourselves as engaged." Tatlock was bright, passionate and compassionate, frequently depressed; their relationship was an ocean of storms. But so were Tatlock's other commitments. "She told me about her Communist Party memberships; they were on again, off again affairs, and never seemed to provide for her what she was seeking." The couple began to move together among what he calls "leftwing friends. . . . I liked the new sense of companionship, and at the time felt that I was coming to be part of the life of my time and country." He was taken with the causes of the Loyalists in the Spanish Civil War and the migrant workers in California, to both of which he contributed time and money. He read Engels and Feuerbach and all of Marx, finding their dialectics less rigorous than his taste: "I never accepted Communist dogma or theory; in fact, it never made sense to me."

He met his wife, Kitty, in the summer of 1939 in Pasadena. She was petite and dark, with a broad, high forehead, brown eyes, prominent cheekbones and a wide, expressive mouth. On the rebound she had married a young British physician, "Dr. [Stewart] Harrison, who was a friend and associate of the [Richard] Tolmans, [Charles C.] Lauritsens, and others of the California Institute of Technology faculty [Harrison was doing cancer research]. I learned of her earlier marriage to Joe Dallet, and of his death fighting in Spain. He had been a Communist Party official, and for a year or two during their brief marriage my wife was a Communist Party member. When I met her I found in her a deep loyalty to her former husband, a complete disengagement from any political activity, and a certain disappointment and contempt that the Communist Party was not in fact what she had once thought it was." The involvement was apparently immediate and intense.

Probably with his wife's encouragement, but certainly with his own growing good sense, Oppenheimer began to jettison political commitments that had come to seem parochial. "I went to a big Spanish relief party the night before Pearl Harbor," he testifies in example, "and the next day, as we heard the news of the outbreak of war, I decided that I had had about enough of the Spanish cause, and that there were other and more pressing crises in the world." He was willing similarly to abandon the American Association of Scientific Workers at Lawrence's insistence in order to help, as he supposed, to beat the Nazis to the atomic bomb.

By then, says Bethe, though Oppenheimer had been a poor teacher when he began, pitching quantum theory well above his students' untrained range, he had "created the greatest school of theoretical physics that the United States has ever known." Bethe's explanation for that evolution reveals the seedbed of Oppenheimer's later administrative leadership:

> Probably the most important ingredient he brought to his teaching was his exquisite taste. He always knew what were the important problems, as shown by his choice of subjects. He truly lived with those problems, struggling for a solution, and he communicated his concern to his group. . . . He was interested in everything, and in one afternoon [he and his students] might discuss quantum electrodynamics, cosmic rays, electron pair production and nuclear physics.

During the same period Oppenheimer's clumsiness with experiment evolved to appreciation and he consciously mastered experimental work—hands off. "He began to observe, not manipulate," a former student notes. "He learned to see the apparatus and to get a feeling of its experimental limitations. He grasped the underlying physics and had the best memory I know of. He could always see how far any particular experiment would go. When you couldn't carry it any farther, you could count on him to understand and to be thinking about the next thing you might want to try."

It remained for Oppenheimer to learn to control his "beastliness" and submerge his mannerisms. But he was always a quick study. Significantly, he was least convoluted, most direct, least mannered, most natural living simply at his unadorned ranch in the Pecos Valley high in the Sangre de Cristo Mountains of northern New Mexico.

Oppenheimer first met General Leslie R. Groves when Groves came to Berkeley from Chicago on his initial inspection tour early in October 1942. They attended a luncheon given by the president of the university; afterward they talked. Oppenheimer had already discussed the need for a fast-neutron laboratory at the Met Lab technical council meeting on September 29. He envisioned more responsibilities for that laboratory than basic fission studies, as he testified after the war:

> I became convinced, as did others, that a major change was called for in the work on the bomb itself. We needed a central laboratory devoted wholly to this purpose, where people could talk freely with each other, where theoretical ideas and experimental findings could affect each other, where the waste and

> frustration and error of the many compartmentalized experimental studies could be eliminated, where we could begin to come to grips with chemical, metallurgical, engineering, and ordnance problems that had so far received no consideration.

Memory compresses the laboratory's evolution here, however; Oppenheimer is not likely to have discussed eliminating Groves' cherished compartmentalization at their first meeting. To the contrary, he goes on to say, the two men first considered making the laboratory "a military establishment in which key personnel would be commissioned as officers," and he carried the idea far enough before he left Berkeley to visit a nearby military post to begin the process of commissioning.

Groves remembers that his "original impression gained from our first conversation in Berkeley" was that a central laboratory was a good idea; he felt strongly that "the work [of bomb design] should be started at once in order that one part of our operation, at any rate, could progress at what I hoped would be a comfortable pace." His immediate concern was leadership; he believed that the right man at the helm could sail even the most ungovernable boat. Ernest Lawrence would have been Groves' first choice, but the general doubted if anyone else could make electromagnetic isotope separation work. Compton had his hands full in Chicago. Harold Urey was a chemist. "Outside the project there may have been other suitable people, but they were all fully occupied on essential work, and none of those suggested appeared to be the equal of Oppenheimer." Groves had already sized up his man.

"It was not obvious that Oppenheimer would be [the new laboratory's] director," Bethe notes. "He had, after all, no experience in directing a large group of people. The laboratory would be devoted primarily to experiment and to engineering, and Oppenheimer was a theorist." Worse—in the eyes of the project leaders, Nobel laureates all—he had no Nobel Prize to distinguish him. There was also what Groves calls the "snag" of Oppenheimer's left-wing background, which "included much that was not to our liking by any means." Groves had not yet wrested control of Manhattan Project security from Army counterintelligence, and that organization adamantly refused to clear someone whose former fiancée, wife, brother and sister-in-law had all been members of the Communist Party once and perhaps, gone underground, still were.

The general wanted Oppenheimer anyway. "He's a genius," Groves told an interviewer off the record immediately after the war. "A real genius. While Lawrence is very bright he's not a genius, just a good hard worker. Why, Oppenheimer knows about everything. He can talk to you about anything you bring up. Well, not exactly. I guess there are a few things he doesn't know about. He doesn't know anything about sports."

Groves proposed Oppenheimer's name to the Military Policy Committee. It balked. "After much discussion I asked each member to give me the name of a man who would be a better choice. In a few weeks it became apparent that we were not going to find a better man; so Oppenheimer was asked to undertake the task." The physicist demurred later that he was chosen "by default. The truth is that the obvious people were already taken and that the Project had a bad name." Rabi would come to think that "it was a real stroke of genius on the part of General Groves, who was not generally considered to be a genius, to have appointed him," but at the time it seemed "a most improbable appointment. I was astonished." Groves on his way from Chicago to New York asked Oppenheimer on October 15, 1942, to ride on the train with him as far as Detroit to discuss the appointment. The two men met with Vannevar Bush in Washington on October 19. That long meeting was apparently decisive. Security questions would have to wait.

The next problem was where to locate the new laboratory. Already at his first meeting with Oppenheimer in Berkeley, Groves had stressed the need for isolation; however much or little the scientists who gathered at the new center would be allowed to talk to each other, the general intended to divide them away from the populace. "For this reason," Oppenheimer wrote his Illinois colleague John H. Manley in mid-October, "some rather far reaching geographical change in plans seems to be in the cards." (In the same letter Oppenheimer proposed "start[ing] now on a policy of absolutely unscrupulous recruiting of anyone we can lay hands on." He wanted the best he could get, and soon asked Groves for the likes of Bethe, Segrè, Serber and Teller.)

Site Y, as the hypothetical laboratory was initially called, needed good transportation, an adequate supply of water, a local labor force and a moderate climate for year-round construction and for experiment conducted outdoors. In his memoirs Groves lists safety as the primary reason he insisted on isolation— "so that nearby communities would not be adversely affected by any unforeseen results from our activities" —but the high steel fence topped with triple strands of barbed wire that eventually surrounded the laboratory was clearly not designed to confine explosions. Groves was in the midst of selecting sites for Manhattan Project production centers; the difference between his criteria for those locations and his criteria for Site Y was that at the bomb-design laboratory "we were faced with the necessity of importing a group of highly talented specialists, some of whom would be prima donnas, and of keeping them satisfied with their working and living conditions." If that in fact was Groves' intention, it was one of the few wartime goals he failed to achieve.

The general assigned the task of identifying a suitable location for the laboratory to Major John H. Dudley of the Manhattan Engineer District. Groves gave Dudley criteria more specific than satisfying prima donnas: room for 265 people, location at least two hundred miles from any international boundary but west of the Mississippi, some existing facilities, a natural bowl with the hills nearby that shaped the bowl so that fences might be strung on top and guarded. Traveling by air, rail, auto, jeep and horse through most of the American Southwest, Dudley found the perfect place: Oak City, Utah, "a delightful little oasis in south central Utah." But to claim it the Army would have had to evict several dozen families and remove a large area of farmland from production. Dudley thereupon recommended his second choice: Jemez Springs, New Mexico, a deep canyon about forty miles northwest of Santa Fe on the western slope of the Jemez Mountains— "a lovely spot," Oppenheimer thought in early November before he toured it, "and in every way satisfactory."

When the newly appointed director arrived on November 16 to inspect the Jemez Springs location with Dudley and Edwin McMillan, who was helping start the laboratory, he changed his mind. The canyon felt confining; Oppenheimer knew the region's grand scenic vistas and decided he wanted a laboratory with a view. McMillan also remembers expressing "considerable reservations about this site":

> We were arguing [with Dudley] when General Groves showed up. This had been planned. He would come in sometime in the afternoon and receive our report. As soon as Groves saw the site he didn't like it; he said, "This will never do." . . . At that point Oppenheimer spoke up and said "if you go on up the canyon you come out on top of the mesa and there's a boys' school there which might be a usable site."

Oppenheimer proposed the boys' school site, grouses Dudley, "as though it was a brand new idea." Dudley had already scouted the mesa twice, rejecting it because it failed to meet Groves' criteria. But a mesa is an inverted bowl, its perimeter similarly fencible. And the first requirement was to make the longhairs happy. "As I . . . knew the roads (or trails)," Dudley says sardonically, ". . . we drove directly there."

"The school was called Los Alamos," the daughter of its founder writes, "after the deep canyon which bordered the mesa to the south and which was groved with cottonwood trees along the sandy trickle of its stream." Ashley Pond, the founder, had been a sickly boarding-school boy sent West for his health, like Oppenheimer, who returned to New Mexico in later adulthood when his father died and left him with independent means. He opened the Los Alamos Ranch School on the 7,200-foot mesa in 1917. It was organized to invigorate pale scions, as Pond had been invigorated: boys slept on unheated porches of a chinked-log dormitory and wore shorts in winter snow; each was assigned a horse to ride and groom. It was, Emilio Segrè writes, "beautiful and savage country" : the dark Jemez Mountains to the west that formed the higher rim of the Jemez Caldera, the slumped cone of the old volcano of which Los Alamos was eroded tuffaceous spill; precipitously down from the mesa eastward the valley of the Rio Grande, "hot and barren" except for the green meander of the river, writes Laura Fermi, with "sand, cacti, a few piñon trees hardly rising above the ground, and space, immense, transparent, with no fog or moisture"; farther east the wall of the Rocky Mountains as that range extends south into New Mexico to form the Sangre de Cristo, reversing hue from green to red progressively at sunset. "I remember arriving [at Los Alamos]," McMillan continues of that first inspection, "and it was late in the afternoon. There was a slight snow falling. . . . It was cold and there were the boys and their masters out on the playing fields in shorts. I remarked that they really believed in hardening up the youth. As soon as Groves saw it, he said, in effect, 'This is the place.' "

"My two great loves are physics and desert country," Robert Oppenheimer had written a friend once; "it's a pity they can't be combined." Now they would be.

Leo Szilard, urban man, habitué of hotel lobbies, took a different view of the location when he heard about it. "Nobody could think straight in a place like that," he told his Met Lab colleagues. "Everybody who goes there will go crazy." The Corps of Engineers' appraisal prepared on November 21 describes a large forested site thirty-five miles by road northwest of Santa Fe with no gas or oil lines, one one-wire Forest Service telephone, average annual precipitation of 18.53 inches and an annual range of temperatures from −12° to 92°F. The land and improvements, including the boys' school with its sixty horses, two tractors, two trucks, fifty saddles, eight hundred cords of firewood, twenty-five tons of coal and sixteen hundred books, was worth $440,000. The school was willing to sell. The Manhattan Project acquired its scenic laboratory site.

Groves convinced the University of California to serve as contractor to operate the secret installation. Construction—of cheap, barracks-like buildings not intended to outlast the war, with coal-burning stoves and no sidewalks on which to escape the mire of spring and autumn mud—began almost immediately. "What we were trying to do," writes John Manley, the

University of Illinois physicist working with Oppenheimer then, "was build a new laboratory in the wilds of New Mexico with no initial equipment except the library of Horatio Alger books or whatever it was that those boys in the Ranch School read, and the pack equipment that they used going horseback riding, none of which helped us very much in getting neutron-producing accelerators." Robert R. Wilson, a young Berkeley Ph.D. teaching at Princeton, went up to Harvard for Oppenheimer and negotiated with Percy Bridgman for the Harvard cyclotron; Wisconsin would contribute two Van de Graaffs; from other laboratories, including Berkeley and the University of Illinois, Manley scavenged other gear. In the meantime Oppenheimer crisscrossed the country recruiting:

> The prospect of coming to Los Alamos aroused great misgivings. It was to be a military post; men were asked to sign up more or less for the duration; restrictions on travel and on the freedom of families to move about would be severe. . . . The notion of disappearing into the New Mexico desert for an indeterminate period and under quasi-military auspices disturbed a good many scientists, and the families of many more. But there was another side to it. Almost everyone realized that this was a great undertaking. Almost everyone knew that if it were completed successfully and rapidly enough, it might determine the outcome of the war. Almost everyone knew that it was an unparalleled opportunity to bring to bear the basic knowledge and art of science for the benefit of his country. Almost everyone knew that this job, if it were achieved, would be a part of history. This sense of excitement, of devotion and of patriotism in the end prevailed. Most of those with whom I talked came to Los Alamos.

One of the most tough-minded, I. I. Rabi, did not. His reasons are revealing. He continued developing radar at the Radiation Laboratory at MIT. "Oppenheimer wanted me to be the associate director," he told an interviewer many years later. "I thought it over and turned him down. I said, 'I'm very serious about this war. We could lose it with insufficient radar.' " The Columbia physicist thought radar more immediately important to the defense of his country than the distant prospect of an atomic bomb. Nor did he choose to work full time, he told Oppenheimer, to make "the culmination of three centuries of physics" a weapon of mass destruction. Oppenheimer responded that he would take "a different stand" if he thought the atomic bomb would serve as such a culmination. "To me it is primarily the development in time of war of a military weapon of some consequence." Either Oppenheimer had not yet thought his way through to a more millenarian view of the new weapon's implications or he chose to avoid discussing those implications with Rabi. He asked Rabi only to participate in an inaugural physics conference at Los Alamos in April 1943 and to help convince others, particularly Hans Bethe, to sign on. Eventually Rabi would come and go as a visiting consultant, one of the very few exceptions to Groves' compartmentalization and isolation rules.

Oppenheimer talked to the Bethes in Cambridge in snowy New England December; they questioned him at length about the life they would be asked to lead. Extracts from his letter of response sketch the invention of an instant community: "Laboratory . . . town . . . utilities, schools, hospitals . . . a sort of city manager . . . city engineer . . . teachers . . . M.P. camp . . . a laundry . . . two eating places . . . a recreation officer . . . libraries, pack trips, movies . . . bachelor apartments . . . a so-called Post Exchange . . . a vet . . . barbers and such like . . . a cantina where we can have beer and cokes and light lunches." The Bethes' best guarantee of satisfaction, Oppenheimer concluded, "is in the great effort and generosity that . . . Groves [has] brought to setting up this odd community and in [Groves'] evident desire to make a real success of it. In general [he is] not interested in saving money, but . . . in saving critical materials, in cutting down personnel, and in doing nothing which would attract Congressional attention to our hi-jinks." He chose not to mention the security arrangements, in the development of which he was participating: the perimeter fence, the pass controls, the virtual elimination of telephones ("Oppenheimer's idea was one telephone for himself," says Dudley, "one for the post commander, and any volume business would go out over a teletype."). By March Teller found Bethe taking "a very optimistic view, and there was no need whatever to persuade him to come."

Teller felt underemployed in Chicago and was eager to move to the new laboratory. John Manley asked him to write a prospectus to help with recruiting, which Teller sent to Oppenheimer in early January. During the Berkeley summer study the two men had begun what another participant judged a "mental love affair." Teller "liked and respected Oppie enormously. He kept wanting to talk about him with others who knew him, kept bringing up his name in conversation." Bethe noticed then and later that despite their many outward differences Teller and Oppenheimer were "fundamentally . . . very similar. Teller had an extremely quick understanding of things, so did Oppenheimer. . . . They were also somewhat alike in that their actual production, their scientific publications, did not measure up in any way to their capacity. I think Teller's mental capacity is very high, and so was Oppenheimer's but, on the other hand, their papers, while they included some very good ones, never reached really the top standards. Neither of them ever came up to the Nobel Prize level. I think you just cannot get to that level unless you are somewhat introverted." (Luis Alvarez, the 1968 physics Nobel laureate, disagrees, at least where Oppenheimer is concerned. He believes Oppenheimer would have won a Nobel Prize for his astrophysical work if he had lived long enough to see his predictions concerning exotic stellar objects—neutron stars, black holes—confirmed, as they have been, by discovery.) Both Oppenheimer and Teller wrote poetry; Oppenheimer pursued literature as Teller pursued music; and for a time in 1942 and 1943 the Hungarian apparently admired the older and socially more sophisticated New Yorker and hoped to count him for an ally.

As Oppenheimer traveled the country recruiting he discovered to his surprise that few of his colleagues were attracted to the notion of joining the Army. It fell to Rabi and his Rad Lab colleague Robert F. Bacher, during the weeks before Rabi decided to stay in Cambridge, to lead the revolt. The necessity of "scientific autonomy" was one crucial reason they cited for resisting militarization, Oppenheimer wrote Conant at the beginning of February 1943, and they insisted as a corollary that although "the execution of the security and secrecy measures should be in the hands of the military . . . the decision as to what measures should be applied must be in the hands of the Laboratory." On that point Oppenheimer concurred, "because I believe it is the only way to assure the cooperation and the unimpaired morale of the scientists." The stakes were higher than simply losing Rabi and Bacher, Oppenheimer told Conant: "I believe that the solidarity of physicists is such that if these conditions are not met, we shall not only fail to have the men from M.I.T with us, but that many men who have already planned to join the new Laboratory will reconsider their commitments or come with such misgivings as to reduce their usefulness." A rebellion, he concluded, would mean "a real delay in our work."

Groves had wanted the scientists commissioned as a security measure and because their work might be hazardous. He was hardly interested in the politics of the question, but delay was unthinkable. He compromised. Conant wrote a letter, co-signed by Groves, that Oppenheimer could use in recruiting; it allowed the new laboratory civilian administration and civilian staff until the time of hazardous large-scale trials. Then anyone who wanted to stay would have to accept a commission (a provision Groves chose later not to pursue). The Army would administer the community it was building around the laboratory. Laboratory security would be Oppenheimer's responsibility, and he would report to Groves.

Robert Oppenheimer thus acquired for Los Alamos what Leo Szilard had not been able to organize in Chicago: scientific freedom of speech. The price the new community paid, a social but more profoundly a political price, was a guarded barbed-wire fence around the town and a second guarded barbed-wire fence around the laboratory itself, emphasizing that the scientists and their families were walled off where knowledge of their work was concerned not only from the world but even from each other. "Several of the European-born were unhappy," Laura Fermi notes, "because living inside a fenced area reminded them of concentration camps."

The heavy-water installation at Vemork in southern Norway became a target of British sabotage operations in the winter of 1942–43. The British had been planning to send in two glider-loads of demolition experts, thirty-four trained volunteers; when Groves requested Allied action soon after his appointment to administer the Manhattan Project they moved ahead to comply. An advance party of four Norwegian commandos parachuted into the Rjukan area on October 18 to prepare the way, but bad planning and bad weather brought disaster to the gliders on the night of November 19 when they crossed the North Sea from Scotland; both crashed in Norway, one into a mountainside, and the fourteen men who survived the separate disasters were captured by German occupation forces and executed the same day.

R. V. Jones, an Oxford protégé of Cherwell who was now director of intelligence for the British Air Staff, then had "one of the most painful decisions that I had to make" —whether to send another demolition party after the first. "I reasoned that we had already decided, before the tragedy of the first raid and therefore free from sentiment, that the heavy water plant must be destroyed; casualties must be expected in war, and so if we were right in asking for the first raid we were probably right in asking that it be repeated."

This time six men, Norwegians native to the region and trained as Special Forces, parachuted onto a frozen lake thirty miles northwest of Vemork on February 16, 1943, the night of a full moon. "Here lay the Hardanger Vidda," one of them, Knut Haukelid, writes of the high plateau that surrounded the lake, "the largest, loneliest and wildest mountain area in northern Europe." The men wore white jumpsuits over British Army uniforms and parachuted with skis, supplies, a shortwave radio and eighteen sets of plastic explosives, one for each of the eighteen stainless-steel electrolysis cells of the High Concentration Plant—which happened to have been designed by a refugee physical chemist, Lief Tronstad, who was now responsible to the Norwegian High Command in London for intelligence and sabotage. Haukelid, a powerfully built mountaineer, says they weathered "one of the worst storms I have ever experienced in the mountains" to rendezvous some days later with the four Norwegians of the original advance party, who had been forced to hide out on the barren Hardanger

Vidda and were malnourished and weak. The new arrivals fattened up their compatriots while one of them skied on to Rjukan to gather the latest information about the plant. He returned to report minefields laid around the obvious approaches, guards on the suspension bridge that crossed the sheer gorge above the shelf on which the hydrochemical facility was built but only fifteen German soldiers on duty despite the forewarning of the failed glider attack. The factory itself was fitted with searchlights and guarded with machine guns.

The commandos set out mid-evening on Saturday, February 27, leaving one man behind to guard the radios. They carried cyanide capsules and agreed that if anyone was wounded he would take his own life rather than allow himself to be captured and risk betraying his comrades. They had camped high on the mountain across the gorge from the plant, which was located to take advantage of the fall of water from the lake that fed it, Tinnsjö. "Halfway down we sighted our objective for the first time, below us on the other side. The great seven-storey factory building bulked large on the landscape. . . . [The wind] was blowing fairly hard, but nevertheless the hum of the machinery came up to us through the ravine. We understood how the Germans could allow themselves to keep so small a guard there. The colossus lay like a mediaeval castle, built in the most inaccessible place, protected by precipices and rivers."

They crashed down through soft snow all the way to the bottom of the gorge, crossed the frozen river, climbed up toward the plant on the other side. Above at the elevation of the shelf was a seldom-used railroad siding leading into the compound that they hoped the Germans had chosen not to mine. "It was a dark night and there was no moon," Haukelid remembers. The searchlights were kept turned off and the high wind "drowned all the noise we made. Half an hour before midnight we came to a snow-covered building five hundred yards from Vemork, where we ate a little chocolate and waited for the change of sentries." They divided into two groups, a demolition party and a covering party. "We were well armed: five tommy-guns among nine men, and everyone had a pistol, a knife and hand grenades."

In an hour, time for the sentries to settle, they attacked. Haukelid in the covering party led the way. With bolt cutters they snipped "the thin little iron chain which barred the way to one of the most important military objectives in Europe." The covering party dispersed to its prearranged positions—Haukelid and one other man took up posts twenty yards from the Wehrmacht barracks, a flimsy wooden building they saw they could easily shoot through—and the demolition party moved ahead. The doors on the ground floor of the plant were locked, but Tronstad in London had identified for the commandos a cable intake that they could crawl along that led directly to the heavy-water facility. Two men looked for some other entrance while two disappeared into the cable intake.

After what seemed to Haukelid an interminable delay he heard an explosion, "but an astonishingly small, insignificant one. Was this what we had come over a thousand miles to do?" The guards were slow to check; only one German soldier appeared and seemed not to realize what had happened; he tried the doors to the plant, found them locked, looked to see if snow falling from the mountain above had detonated a land mine and returned to his quarters. The Norwegians moved out fast. They had descended to the river before the sirens began to sound.

The operation was successful. No one was injured on either side. All eighteen cells had been blown open, spilling nearly half a ton of heavy water into the drains. Not only would the plant require weeks to repair; because it was a cascade, pumping water of increasing deuterium concentration from one cell to the next, it would need almost a year of operation after repair simply to reach equilibrium again on its own and begin producing. General Nikolaus von Falkenhorst, the commander in chief of the occupying German Army in Norway, called the Vemork attack "the best coup I have ever seen." Whatever German physicists might be doing with heavy water, they would do it more slowly now.

In Japan both the Army Air Force and the Imperial Navy had moved separately since 1941 to promote atomic bomb research. The Riken, Yoshio Nishina's prestigious Tokyo laboratory, primarily served the Army, exploring the theoretical possibilities of U235 separation by way of the gaseous barrier diffusion, gaseous thermal diffusion, electromagnetic and centrifuge processes. In the spring of 1942 the Navy committed itself to developing nuclear power for propulsion:

> The study of nuclear physics is a national project. Research in this field is continuing on a broad scale in the United States, which has recently obtained the services of a number of Jewish scientists, and considerable progress has been made. The objective is the creation of tremendous amounts of energy through nuclear fission. Should this research prove successful, it would provide a stupendous and dependable source of power which could be used to activate ships and other large pieces of machinery. Although it is not expected that nuclear energy will be realized in the near future, the possibility of it must not be ignored. The Imperial Navy, accordingly, hereby affirms its determination to foster and assist studies in this field.

Soon after that nonviolent affirmation, however, the Naval Technological Research Institute appointed a secret committee of leading Japanese scientists—corresponding to the U.S. National Academy of Sciences committee—to meet monthly to follow research progress until it could report decisively for or against a Japanese atomic bomb. The committee included Nishina, who was forthwith elected chairman. An elderly appointee was Hantarō Nagaoka, whose Saturnian atomic model had nearly anticipated Ernest Rutherford's planetary model in the early years of the century.

The Navy committee met first on July 8 with the Navy's chief technical officers at an officers' club at Shiba Park in Tokyo. It noted that the United States was probably working on a bomb and agreed that whether and how soon Japan could produce such a weapon was as yet uncertain. To the task of answering those questions the Navy appropriated 2,000 yen, about $4,700, somewhat less than the Uranium Committee had summoned from the U.S. Treasury at Edward Teller's request at the beginning of the American program in 1939.

Nishina hardly participated in the Navy committee meetings. The fact that he was already working for the Army probably constrained him; the two services, both of which were responsible directly to the Emperor without detour through the civilian government, operated far more independently than their American counterparts and were increasingly bitter rivals. Nishina was coming to conclusions of his own, however, and at the end of 1942, when the Navy committee began to report discouragement, he met privately with a young cosmic-ray physicist in his laboratory, Tadashi Takeuchi, told his young colleague he meant to carry forward isotope separation studies and asked him to help. Takeuchi agreed.

Between December 1942 and March 1943 the Navy committee organized a ten-session physics colloquium to work through to a decision. By then it was understood that a bomb would necessitate locating, mining and processing hundreds of tons of uranium ore and that U235 separation would require a tenth of the annual Japanese electrical capacity and half the nation's copper output. The colloquium concluded that while an atomic bomb was certainly possible, Japan might need ten years to build one. The scientists believed that neither Germany nor the United States had sufficient spare industrial capacity to produce atomic bombs in time to be of use in the war.

After the final March 6 meeting the Navy representative at the colloquium reported discouragement: "The best minds of Japan, studying the subject from the point of view of their respective fields of endeavor as well as from that of national defense, came to a conclusion that can only be regarded as correct. The more they considered and discussed the problem, the more pessimistic became the atmosphere of the meeting." As a result the Navy dissolved the committee and asked its members to devote themselves to more immediately valuable research, particularly radar.

Nishina continued isotope studies for the Army, deciding on March 19 to focus on thermal diffusion as the only practical separation technology at a time of increasing national shortages. He spoke to his staff of processing several hundred tons of uranium after first building laboratory-scale diffusion apparatus. He envisioned a major program run in parallel, as the Manhattan Project was beginning to be, with weapon design and development proceeding simultaneously with U235 production.

Meanwhile a different branch of the Navy, the Fleet Administration Center, sponsored a new project in atomic bomb development at the University of Kyoto, where Tokutaro Hagiwara had made his startling early prediction of the possibility of a thermonuclear explosive. The university won support in 1943 to the extent of 600,000 yen—nearly $1.5 million—much of which it budgeted to build a cyclotron.

Robert Oppenheimer moved to Santa Fe with a small team of aides on March 15, 1943, brisk early spring. Scientists and their families arrived by automobile and train during the next four weeks. Not much was ready on the mesa, which they began to call the Hill. Groves wanted no breaches of security in the lobbies of Santa Fe hotels; the Army commandeered guest ranches in the area for quarters suitably remote and bought up Santa Fe's feeble stock of used cars and jitneys to serve as transportation through ruts and mud up and down the terrifying unbarricaded dirt switchback of the mesa access road. After flat tires and mirings, hours could be short on the Hill. Box lunches assembled in Santa Fe gave cold comfort when the delivery truck made it through.

The hardships only mattered because they slowed the work. Oppenheimer had sold it as work that would end the war to end all wars and his people believed him. The unit of measurement for wasted hours was therefore human lives. Construction crews unwilling to vary the specifications of a laboratory door or hang an unauthorized shelf initially bore the brunt of the scientists' impatience. John Manley remembers inspecting the chemistry and physics building. It needed a basement at one end for an accelerator and a solid foundation at the other end for the two Van de Graaffs—which end for which was unimportant. Rather than adjust the construction plans for terrain the contractor had drilled the basement from solid rock and used the rock debris as fill for the foundation. "This was my introduction to the Army Engineers."

Fuller Lodge, a Ranch School hall elegantly assembled of monumental hand-hewn logs, was kept to serve as a dining room and guest house. The pond south of the lodge—predictably named Ashley Pond after the Ranch School's founder—offered winter ice-skating and summer canoeing and the easeful harmonic wakes of swimming ducks. The engineers preserved the stone icehouse beside the pond that the school had used to store winter cuttings of ice and the row of tree-shaded faculty residences northeast of the lodge. Across the dirt main road that divided the mesa south of the pond the Tech Area went up in a style the Army called modified mobilization: plain one-story buildings like elongated barracks with clapboard sides and shingled roofs. T Building would house Oppenheimer and his staff and the Theoretical Physics Division; behind T, connected by a covered walkway, would be the much longer chemistry and physics building with its Van de Graaffs; behind that the laboratory shops. Farther south near the rim of the mesa above Los Alamos canyon contractors would hammer up a cryogenics laboratory and the building that would shelter Harvard's cyclotron. West and north of the Tech Area the first two-story, four-unit family apartments, painted drab green, urbanized last year's pastures and fields; more apartments, and dormitories for the unmarried, would follow.

At the beginning of April Oppenheimer assembled the scientific staff—"about thirty persons" at that point of the hundred scientists initially hired, says Emilio Segrè, who was one among them—for a series of introductory lectures. Robert Serber, thin and shy, delivered the lectures with authority despite the distraction of a lisp; they summed up the conclusions of the Berkeley summer study and incorporated the experimental fast-fission work of the past year. Edward U. Condon, the crew-cut, Alamogordo-born theoretician from Westinghouse whom Oppenheimer had chosen for associate director, revised his notes of Serber's lectures into the new laboratory's first report, a document called the *Los Alamos Primer* that was subsequently handed to all new Tech Area arrivals cleared for Secret Limited access. In twenty-four mimeographed pages the *Primer* defined the laboratory's program to build the first atomic bombs.

Serber's lectures startled the chemists and experimental physicists whom compartmentalization had kept in the dark; the scientists' euphoria at finally learning in detail what they had only previously guessed or heard hinted measures the extent to which secrecy had contorted their emotional commitment to the work. Now, following the lead of their mentors—their average age was twenty-five; Oppenheimer, Bethe, Teller, McMillan, Bacher, Segrè and Condon were older men—they could apply themselves at last with devotion. In that heady new freedom they seldom noticed the barbed wire. Similarly confined but kept uninformed because Oppenheimer and Groves decided it so, the wives served harder time.

"The object of the project," Condon summarizes what Serber told the scientists, "is to produce a *practical military weapon* in the form of a bomb in which the energy is released by a fast neutron chain reaction in one or more of the materials known to show nuclear fission." Serber said one kilogram of U235 was approximately equal to 20,000 tons of TNT and noted that nature had almost located that conversion beyond human meddling: "Since only the last few generations [of the chain reaction] will release enough energy to produce much expansion [of the critical mass], it is just possible for the reaction to occur to an interesting extent before it is stopped by the spreading of the active material." If fission had proceeded more energetically the bombs would have slept forever in the dark beds of their ores.

Serber discussed fission cross sections, the energy spectrum of secondary neutrons, the average number of secondary neutrons per fission (measured by then to be about 2.2), the neutron capture process in U238 that led to plutonium and why ordinary uranium is safe (it would have to be enriched to at least 7 percent U235, the young theoretician pointed out, "to make an explosive reaction possible"). He was already calling the bomb "the gadget," its nickname thereafter on the Hill, a bravado metonymy that Oppenheimer probably coined. The calculations Serber reported indicated a critical mass for metallic U235 tamped with a thick shell of ordinary uranium of 15 kilograms: 33 pounds. For plutonium similarly tamped the critical mass might be 5 kilograms: 11 pounds. The heart of their atomic bomb would then be a cantaloupe of U235 or an orange of Pu239 surrounded by a watermelon of ordinary uranium tamper, the combined diameter of the two nested spheres about 18 inches. Shaped of such heavy metal the tamper would weigh about a ton. The critical masses would eventually have to be determined by actual test, Serber said.

He went on to speak of damage. Out to a radius of a thousand yards around the point of explosion the area would be drenched with neutrons, enough to produce "severe pathological effects." That would render the area uninhabitable for a time. It was clear by now—it had not been clear before—that a nuclear explosion would be no less damaging than an equivalent chemical explosion. "Since the one factor that determines the damage is the energy release, our aim is simply to get as much energy from the explosion as we can. And since the materials we use are very precious, we are constrained to do this with as high an efficiency as is possible."

Efficiency appeared to be a serious problem. "The reaction will not go to completion in an actual gadget." Untamped, a bomb core even as large as twice the critical mass would completely fission less than 1 percent of its nuclear material before it expanded enough to stop the chain reaction from proceeding. An equally disadvantageous secondary effect also tended to stop the reaction: "as the pressure builds up it begins to blow off material at the outer edge of the [core]." Tamper always increased efficiency; it reflected neutrons back into the core and its inertia—not its tensile strength, which was inconsequential at the pressures a chain reaction would generate—slowed the core's expansion and helped keep the core surface from blowing away. But even with a good tamper they would need more than one critical mass per bomb for reasonable efficiency.

Detonation was equally a problem. To detonate their bombs they would have to rearrange the core material so that its effective neutron number, which corresponded to Fermi's *k,* changed from less than 1 to more than 1. But however they rearranged the material—firing one subcritical piece into another subcritical piece inside the barrel of a cannon seemed to be the simplest option—they would have no slow, smooth transition as Fermi had with CP-1. If they fired one piece into another at the high velocity of 3,000 feet per second it would take the pieces about a thousandth of a second to assemble themselves. But since more than one critical mass was necessary for an efficient explosion the pieces would be supercritical before they had completely mated. If a stray neutron then started a chain reaction, the resulting inefficient explosion would proceed from beginning to end in a few millionths of a second. "An explosion started by a premature neutron will be all finished before there is time for the pieces to move an appreciable distance." Which meant that the neutron background—spontaneous-fission neutrons from the tamper, neutrons knocked from light-element impurities, neutrons from cosmic rays—would have to be kept as low as possible and the rearrangement of the core material managed as fast as possible. On the other hand, they did not have to worry that a fizzle would drop an intact bomb into enemy hands; even a fizzle would release energy equivalent to at least sixty tons of TNT.

Predetonation would reduce the bomb's efficiency, Serber repeated; so also might postdetonation. "When the pieces reach their best position we want to be very sure that a neutron starts the reaction before the pieces have a chance to separate and break." So there might be a third basic component to their atomic bomb besides nuclear core and confining tamper: an initiator—a Ra + Be source or, better, a Po + Be source, with the radium or polonium attached perhaps to one piece of the core and the beryllium to the other, to smash together and spray neutrons when the parts mated to start the chain reaction.

Firing the pieces of core together, the Berkeley theoretician continued, "is the part of the job about which we know least at present." The summer-study group had examined several ingenious designs. The most favorable fired a cylindrical male plug of core and tamper into a mated female sphere of tamper and core, illustrated here in cross section from the *Los Alamos Primer:*

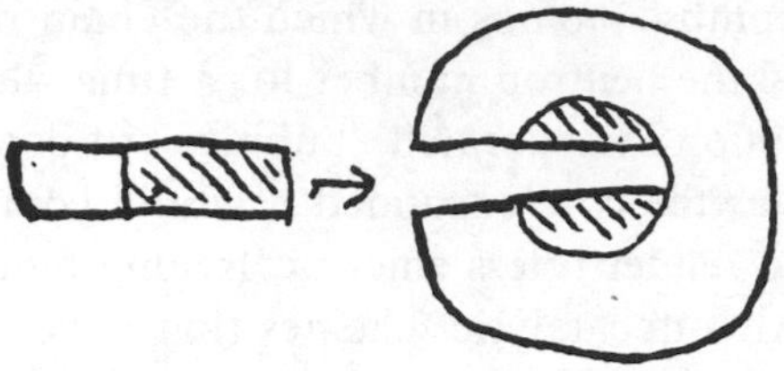

The target sphere could be simply welded to the muzzle of a cannon; then the cylinder, which might weigh about a hundred pounds, could be fired up the barrel like a shell:

> The highest muzzle velocity available in U.S. Army guns is one whose bore is 4.7 inches and whose barrel is 21 feet long. This gives a 50 lb. projectile a muzzle velocity of 3150 ft/sec. The gun weighs 5 tons. It appears that the ratio of projectile mass to gun mass is about constant for different guns so a 100 lb. projectile would require a gun weighing about 10 tons.

For a mechanism eight times lighter or with double the effective muzzle velocity they could weld two guns together at their muzzles and fire two projectiles into each other. Synchronization would be a problem with such a design and efficiency might require four critical masses instead of two, a demand which would significantly delay delivering a usable bomb.

Serber also described more speculative arrangements: sliced ellipsoidal core-tamper assemblies like halves of hard-boiled eggs that slid together; wedge-shaped quarters of core/tamper like sections of a quartered apple mounted on a ring. That was an odd and striking design, sketched in the mimeographed *Primer* as probably on a blackboard before, and it did not go unnoticed. "If explosive material were distributed around the ring and fired the pieces would be blown inward to form a sphere":

Autocatalytic bombs—bombs in which the chain reaction itself, as it proceeded, increased the neutron number for a time—looked less promising. The cleverest notion incorporated "bubbles" of boron-coated paraffin into the U235 core; as the core expanded it would compress the neutron-absorbing boron and render it less efficient, freeing more neutrons for fission chains. But: "All autocatalytic schemes that have been thought of so far require large amounts of active material, are low in efficiency unless very large amounts are used, and are dangerous to handle. Some bright ideas are needed."

Their immediate work of experiment, Serber concluded, would be measuring the neutron properties of various materials and mastering the ordnance problem—the problem, that is, of assembling a critical mass and firing the bomb. They would also have to devise a way to measure a critical mass for fast fission with subcritical amounts of U235 and Pu239. They had a deadline: workable bombs ready when enough uranium and plutonium was ready. That probably gave them two years.

The Japanese physics colloquium in Tokyo had decided in March 1943 that an atomic bomb was possible but not practically attainable by any of the belligerents in time to be of use in the present war. Robert Serber's lectures at Los Alamos in early April asserted to the contrary that for the United States an atomic bomb was both possible and probably attainable within two years. The Japanese assessment was essentially technological. Like Bohr's assessment in 1939, it overestimated the difficulty of isotope separation and underestimated U.S. industrial capacity. It also, as the Japanese government had before Pearl Harbor, underestimated American dedication. Collective dedication was a pattern of Japanese culture more than of American. But Americans could summon it when challenged, and couple it with resources of talent and capital unmatched anywhere else in the world.

The Europeans at Los Alamos complained of the barbed wire. With the exception, apparently, only of Edward Condon, who found security so oppressive he quit the project within weeks of his arrival and went back to Westinghouse, the Americans accepted the fences around their work and their lives as a necessity of war. The war was a manifestation of nationalism, not of science, and such did their duty on the Hill appear at first to be. There was "relatively little nuclear physics" at Los Alamos, Bethe says, mostly cross-section calculations. They thought they were assembled to engineer a *"practical military weapon."* That was first of all a national goal. Science—a fragile, nascent political system of limited but increasing franchise—would have to wait until the war was won. Or so it seemed. But a few among the men and women gathered at Los Alamos—certainly Robert

Oppenheimer—sniffed a paradox. They proposed in fact to win the war with an application of their science. They dreamed further that by that same application they might forestall the next war, might even end war as a means of settling differences between nations. Which must in the long run have decisive consequences, one way or the other, for nationalism.

By the time Robert Serber finished his orientation lectures at Los Alamos in mid-April most of the scientific and technical staff was on hand, many lodged temporarily in the surviving buildings of the Ranch School. Now began a second phase of the conference, to plan the laboratory's work. "If there were any ground-breaking ceremonies at Los Alamos like champagne or cutting ribbons," John Manley comments, "I was unaware of them. Most of us who were there felt that the conference in April, 1943, was really the ground-breaking ceremony." Rabi, Fermi and Samuel Allison arrived from Cambridge and Chicago to serve as senior consultants. Groves appointed a review committee—W. K. Lewis again, an engineer named E. L. Rose who was thoroughly experienced in ordnance design, Van Vleck, Tolman and one other expert—to follow planning and advise. Groves despite his formidable competence as an organizer and administrator was intellectually insecure around so many distinguished scientists, as who would not be?

They laid their plans, often during hikes into the uninhabited wild surroundings of the mesa. They had to rely heavily on theoretical anticipations of the effects they wanted to study; that was their basic constraint. Any experimental device that demonstrated a fast-neutron chain reaction to completion would use up at least one critical mass: there could be no controlled, laboratory-scale bomb tests, no squash-court demonstrations. They decided they had to analyze the explosion theoretically and work out ways to calculate the stages of its development. They needed to understand how neutrons would diffuse through the core and the tamper. They needed a theory of the explosion's hydrodynamics—the complex dynamic motions of its fluids, which the core and tamper would almost instantly become as their metals heated from solid to liquid to gas.

They needed detailed experiments to observe bomb-related nuclear phenomena and they needed integral experiments to duplicate as much as possible the full-scale operation of the bomb. They had to develop an initiator to start the chain reaction. They had to devise technology for reducing uranium and plutonium to metal, for casting and shaping that metal, possibly for alloying it to improve its properties. Particularly with plutonium, they had to discover and measure those properties in the first place and do so quickly when more than microgram quantities began to arrive.

As a sideline, because they agreed that work on the Super should continue at second priority, they wanted to construct and operate a plant for liquefying deuterium at −429°F—the cryogenics plant to be built near the south rim of the mesa.

Ordnance work was crucial. From the April discussions came immediate breakthroughs. An Oppenheimer recruit from the National Bureau of Standards who had been a protégé at Caltech, a tall, thin, thirty-six-year-old experimental physicist named Seth Neddermeyer, imagined an entirely different strategy of assembly. Neddermeyer could not quite remember after the war the complex integrations by which he came to it. An ordnance expert had been lecturing. The expert had quibbled at the physicists' use of the word "explosion" to describe firing the bomb parts together. The proper word, the expert said, was "implosion." During Serber's lectures Neddermeyer had already been thinking about what must happen when a heavy cylinder of metal is fired into a blind hole in an even heavier metal sphere. Spheres and shock waves made him think about spherically symmetrical shock waves, whatever those might be. "I remember thinking of trying to push in a shell of material against a plastic flow," Neddermeyer told an interviewer later, "and I calculated the minimum pressures that would have to be applied. Then I happened to recall a crazy thing somebody had published about firing bullets against each other. It may have had a photograph of two bullets liquefied on impact. That is what I was thinking when the ballistics man mentioned implosion."

Two bullets fired against each other recall the double-gun model of the *Los Alamos Primer.* There were other clues to Neddermeyer's new strategy placed evocatively in the *Primer* as well. That document notes that when the surface of the bomb core blows off, it "expands into the tamper material, starting a shock wave which compresses the tamper material sixteenfold." The *Primer* emphasizes more than once that the expansion of the core would be the greatest obstacle to an efficient explosion. It may have occurred to Neddermeyer that if a tamper merely by its inertia—by its tendency to stay where it is when the swelling core begins to push out against it—could resist the core's expansion and thereby increase the efficiency of the explosion, a tamper that somehow *pushed back* against the core might do even better. The compressing of the boron bubbles in the autocatalytic bomb may also have been suggestive. Finally, the *Primer* offered the interesting model of four apple-quarter wedges of core/tamper fired together by an encompassing explosive ring. "At this point," says Neddermeyer, "I raised my hand."

He proposed packing a spherical layer of high explosives around a spherical assembly of tamper and a hollow but thick-walled spherical core.

Detonated at many points simultaneously, the HE would blow inward. The shock wave from that explosion would squeeze the tamper from all sides, which in turn would squeeze the core. Squeezing the core would change its geometry from hollow shell to solid ball. What had been subcritical because of its geometry would be squeezed critical far faster and more efficiently than any mere gun could fire. "The gun will compress in one dimension," Manley remembers Neddermeyer telling them. "Two dimensions would be better. Three dimensions would be better still."

A three-dimensional squeeze inward was *implosion.* Neddermeyer had just defined a possible new way to fire an atomic bomb. The idea had been suggested previously, but no one had carried it beyond conversation. "At a meeting on ordnance problems late in April," records the Los Alamos technical history, "Neddermeyer presented the first serious theoretical analysis of the implosion. His arguments showed that the compression of a . . . sphere by detonation of a surrounding high-explosive layer was feasible, and that it would be superior to the gun method both in its high velocity and shorter path of assembly."

The response at the time was not encouraging. "Neddermeyer faced stiff opposition from Oppenheimer and, I think, Fermi and Bethe," Manley says. How do you make a shock wave spherically symmetrical? How do you keep tamper and core from squirting out in every direction as water does when squeezed between cupped hands? "Nobody . . . really took [implosion] very seriously," Manley adds. But Oppenheimer had been wrong before—even about the possibility of fission when Luis Alvarez dropped by to report it in 1939, wrong for the fifteen minutes it took him to think past the stubbornness with which he rejected any possibility he had not himself foreseen. Apparently he was learning to steer by that grudging incredulity as Bohr steered by the madness of a truly original idea. "This will have to be looked into," he told Neddermeyer in private conference after the dismissive public debate. He took his revenge for the trouble Neddermeyer was causing him by appointing that thoroughgoing loner to the newly invented post of group leader in the Ordnance Division for implosion experimentation.

The other fresh insight remembered from the April conference corrected an error that everyone wondered afterward how anyone could have overlooked. The error is perhaps a measure of how unfamiliar the physicists were with ordnance. E. L. Rose, the research engineer on Groves' review committee, woke up one day to realize that the Army cannon the physicists were basing their estimates on weighed five tons only because it had to be sturdy enough for repeated firing. A gun that wore an atomic bomb welded to its muzzle could be flimsier: it would be fired only once, after which it would vaporize and drift away. That specification cut its weight drastically and promised a practical, flyable bomb.

Fermi, superb experimentalist that he was, contributed valuably to the program of experimental studies, defining with clarity problems that needed to be examined. For him the war work was duty, however, and the eager conviction he found on the Hill puzzled him. "After he had sat in on one of his first conferences here," Oppenheimer recalls, "he turned to me and said, 'I believe your people actually *want* to make a bomb.' I remember his voice sounded surprised."

The leaders attended a party one night that April at Oppenheimer's house, the log-and-stucco former residence of the Ranch School headmaster. Edward Condon, whose father had been a builder of railroads in the West, who had worked as a newspaper reporter in tough Oakland, found occasion at Oppenheimer's party to satirize Los Alamos' Panglossian mood. He was an exceptional theoretician; he and Oppenheimer had boarded together at Göttingen; Condon thought they were fast friends. He would soon clash bitterly with Groves over compartmentalization and find that his friend the director had higher priorities than backing him up. Now, sitting in a corner at the director's house, Condon pulled from a bookshelf a copy of Shakespeare's *The Tempest* and skimmed it for speeches meant for Prospero's enchanted island that might play contrapuntally against Oppenheimer's high and dry and secret mesa where no one had a street address, where mail was censored, where drivers' licenses went nameless, where children would be born and families live and a few people die behind a post-office box in devotion to the cause of harnessing an obscure force of nature to build a bomb that might end a brutal war. There are many speeches in *The Tempest* that would have fit the occasion but one certainly that Condon would not have missed reading aloud to the assembled, Miranda's speech that Aldous Huxley borrowed for an ironic title:

O, wonder!
How many goodly creatures are there here!
How beauteous mankind is! O brave new world
That has such people in't!

The British had chosen not to bomb Vemork because Lief Tronstad, the physical chemist attached to Norwegian intelligence in London, had warned that hitting the hydrochemical facility's liquid-ammonia storage tanks would almost certainly kill large numbers of Norwegian workers. But the British had in any case long since abandoned precision bombing.

Winston Churchill had declared himself strongly in favor of strategic air attack early in the war, speaking even of extermination. In July 1940, in the desperate time after the debacle of Dunkirk and at the beginning of the Battle of Britain, Churchill had written his Minister of Aircraft Production to that effect: "But when I look round to see how we can win the war I see that there is only one sure path . . . and that is absolutely devastating, exterminating attack by very heavy bombers from this country upon the Nazi homeland. We must be able to overwhelm them by this means, without which I do not see a way through."

The slide from precision bombing attacks on industry to general attacks on cities followed less from political decisions than from inadequate technology. Bomber Command had attempted long-distance daylight precision bombing early in the war but had been unable to defend its aircraft against German fighters and flak so far from home. It therefore switched to night bombing, which reduced losses but severely impaired accuracy. If it was logical to bomb factories and other strategic targets to reduce the enemy's ability to wage war, it began to seem equally logical to bomb the blocks of workers' housing that surrounded those targets; the workers, after all, made the factories run. Sir Arthur Harris, who became chief of Bomber Command in early 1942, notes in his war memoirs of this transitional period in the summer of 1941 that "the targets chosen were in congested industrial areas and were carefully picked so that bombs which overshot or undershot the actual railway centers under attack [in this instance] should fall on these areas, thereby affecting morale. This programme amounted to a halfway stage between area and precision bombing." "Morale" is here and elsewhere in the literature of air power a euphemism for the bombing of civilians. Another sign of halfway status at this stage was permission to dump bombs before exiting Germany if crews had missed their targets.

Churchill says he authorized a study of bombing accuracy at Frederick Lindemann's suggestion which discovered in the summer of 1941 "that although Bomber Command believed they had found the target, two-thirds of crews actually failed to strike within five miles of it. . . . Unless we could improve on this there did not seem much use in continued night bombing." In November the government ordered its bomber arm to reduce operations over Germany.

To reduce strategic bombing operations was to admit failure in both theory and practice, and it was to do so at a time when the USSR was fully engaged with the German armies on the Eastern Front and Joseph Stalin was demanding the Allies open a second front in the West. Neither Britain nor the United States was nearly prepared yet to invade Europe on the ground, but both nations might offer such aid as air attack could bring.

Soviet Union was a political justification for continuing some kind of strategic bombing campaign, though it hardly placated Stalin. Headlines proclaiming almost daily bombing raids also helped keep the home front happy when the ground war stalled.

Yet Allied politics and domestic propaganda could not have been the primary reasons for the drift from precision to area bombing, because U.S. air forces beginning to arrive in Britain in 1942 planned and carried out precision daylight bombing, though not often effectively, until much later in the war. Rather, Bomber Command switched programs in order to justify its continued existence as a service with a mission separate from Army and Navy tactical support, cutting theory to fit the facts. It found an ally in the newly ennobled Lindemann, Lord Cherwell, who calculated in March 1942 that bombing might destroy the housing of a third of the German population within a year if sufficiently pursued against industrial urban areas. Patrick Blackett and Henry Tizard thought Cherwell's estimate far too optimistic and dissented vigorously, but Cherwell had the Prime Minister's ear.

Sir Arthur Harris—"Butch," his staff came to call him, short for "the Butcher"—took over Bomber Command in February and promulgated a new approach to the air war: "It has been decided that the primary objective of your operations should now be focussed on the morale of the enemy civil population and in particular, of the industrial workers." Harris had witnessed the London Blitz; it convinced him, he writes, that "a bomber offensive of adequate weight and the right kind of bombs would, if continued for long enough, be something that no country in the world could endure." His argument was valid, of course, though what "the right kind of bombs" might be would require the work of the Manhattan Project to reveal. Hitler's terror bombing taught Britain not terror but forceful imitation. Harris certainly despised the Germans for starting and perpetuating two world wars. But he seems to have thought less about killing civilians than about solving the problem of making Bomber Command a measurably effective force. If night bombing and area bombing were the only tactics that paid a reasonable return in destruction at a reasonable price in lost aircraft and aircrew lives, then he would dedicate Bomber Command to perfecting those tactics and measure success not in factories rendered inoperative but in acres of cities flattened. Which is to say, area bombing was invented to give bombers targets they could hit.

An incendiary attack on the old Baltic port of Lübeck in March burned much of the town and produced four-figure casualties for the first time in the bombing campaign. On May 20, to demonstrate Bomber Command's effectiveness at a time of public debate, Harris mustered every aircraft he could find—hundreds of two-engine bombers of light payload and even training planes—to launch a thousand-bomber raid on Cologne. For that successful assault he organized what came to be called a bomber "stream," the aircraft flying in massed continuous formations to overwhelm defenses rather than in small and vulnerable packets as before, and destroyed some eight square miles of the ancient city on the Rhine with 1,400 tons of bombs, two-thirds of them incendiary. Finally, in August, encouraged by Cherwell, Bomber Command deployed a Pathfinder force: skilled advance crews that marked targets with colored flares so that less experienced pilots following in the lethal stream could more easily find their aiming points.

No fleet of bombers could yet accurately deliver enough high explosives to raze a city. The Lübeck bombing had been planned to test the theory that area bombing worked best by starting fires. If the bombloads were incendiary, then the massed aircraft might combine their destructiveness, wind and weather cooperating, rather than disperse it on isolated targets. The theory worked at Lübeck and again at Cologne and because it worked it won adoption. At the end of 1942 the British Chiefs of Staff called for "the progressive destruction and dislocation of the enemy's war industrial and economic system, and the undermining of his morale to a point where his capacity for armed resistance is fatally weakened." Churchill and Roosevelt affirmed the British plan for an aerial war of attrition in a directive issued at the conclusion of the Casablanca Conference in late January 1943.

On May 27, 1943, as work began at Los Alamos following the April conferences, Bomber Command ordered Hamburg attacked. Its *Most Secret Operation Order No. 173* stated its new policy of mass destruction explicitly:

> INFORMATION
>
> The importance of HAMBURG, the second largest city in Germany with a population of one and a half millions, is well known . . . . The total destruction of this city would achieve immeasurable results in reducing the industrial capacity of the enemy's war machine. This, together with the effect on German morale, which would be felt throughout the country, would play a very important part in shortening and in winning the war.
>
> 2. The "Battle of Hamburg" cannot be won in a single night. It is estimated that at least 10,000 tons of bombs will have to be dropped to complete the process of elimination . . . . This city should be subjected to sustained attack . . . .
>
> 3. . . . It is hoped that the night attacks will be preceded and/or followed by heavy daylight attacks by the United States VIIIth Bomber Command.
>
> INTENTION
>
> 4. To destroy HAMBURG.

The operation was code-named Gomorrah. Notice the significant claim that it would help shorten and win the war.

Operation Gomorrah began on the night of July 24, 1943, a hot summer Saturday in Hamburg under clear skies. Pathfinder bombers used radar to aid marking, and the initial Hamburg aiming point was chosen not for its strategic significance but for its distinctive radar reflection: a triangle of land at the junction of the Alster and North Elbe rivers, near the oldest part of the city and far from any war industry. Bomber Command had learned to adjust targeting for creep-back, the tendency of bombardiers to release their bombs as quickly as possible upon approaching the flak-infested aiming point that led to a gradual backup of impacts. From the ground the bombs seemed to unroll in the direction of the bomber stream's approach; survivors named the phenomenon "carpet bombing." Targeters incorporated creep-back into their calculations by setting the aiming point several miles forward of the intended target area. The creep-back districts behind the Hamburg aiming point to a distance of four miles were entirely residential.

To give the bombers further advantage Churchill had authorized the first use of the secret radar-jamming device known as Window: bales of 10.5-inch strips of aluminum foil to be pushed out of the bombers en route to the target to disperse on the wind and cloud German defensive radar. Window worked so well that of the 791 planes of the initial raid only twelve were lost.

Hamburg sustained heavy damage that first night but not damage even on the scale of Cologne; 1,300 tons of high explosives and almost 1,000 tons of incendiaries killed about 1,500 people and left many thousands homeless. More important for what would follow, the first raid seriously disrupted communications and overwhelmed firefighting forces.

Daylight precision bombing by American B-17's followed on July 25 and 26, attacks meant for a submarine yard and an aircraft engine factory. Smoke from the British bombing and from German defensive generators obscured the targets and they were only lightly damaged.

Harris ordered a maximum bombing effort against Hamburg again for the night of July 27. Targeters fixed the same aiming point but aligned the bomber stream to approach from the northeast rather than the north to set its creep-back over districts dense with workers' apartment buildings. Since the mix of 787 bombers for this second raid would include more Halifaxes and Stirlings, and they could carry less weight of weapons and fuel than the longer-distance Lancasters, the mix of bombs was also changed, high explosives reduced and incendiaries increased to more than 1,200 tons. More experienced pilots also came aboard, higher-ranking officers signing on to observe the effects of Window. These accidents of arrangement contributed their share to the night's catastrophe.

At 6 P.M. in Hamburg on July 27 the temperature was 86 degrees and the humidity 30 percent. Fires still burned in stores of coal and coke in the western sector of the city. Since the fires would render a blackout ineffective most of Hamburg's firefighting equipment had been moved to the area to douse them. "It was completely quiet," recalls a German woman who lived in a district targeted for creep-back, miles to the northeast. ". . . It was an enchantingly beautiful summer night."

Pathfinders started dropping yellow markers and bombs at fifty-five minutes past midnight on July 28. Five minutes later the main bomber stream arrived. Marking was good and creep-back was slow. Later arrivals began to notice a difference between this raid and others they had flown: "Most of the raids we did looked like gigantic firework displays over the target area," a flight sergeant remarks, "but this was 'the daddy of them all.' " A flight lieutenant distinguishes the difference:

> The burning of Hamburg that night was remarkable in that I saw not many fires but one. Set in the darkness was a turbulent dome of bright red fire, lighted and ignited like the glowing heart of a vast brazier. I saw no flames, no outlines of buildings, only brighter fires which flared like yellow torches against a background of bright red ash. Above the city was a misty red haze. I looked down, fascinated but aghast, satisfied yet horrified. I had never seen a fire like that before and was never to see its like again.

The summer heat and low humidity, the mix of high-explosive and incendiary bombs that made kindling and then ignited it and the absence of firefighting equipment in the bombed districts conspired to assemble a new horror. An hour after the bombing began the horror had a name, recorded first in the main log of the Hamburg Fire Department: *Feuersturm*: firestorm. A Hamburg factory worker remembers its beginning, some twenty minutes into the one-hour bombing raid:

> Then a storm started, a shrill howling in the street. It grew into a hurricane so that we had to abandon all hope of fighting the [factory] fire. It was as though we were doing no more than throwing a drop of water on to a hot stone.The whole yard, the canal, in fact as far as we could see, was just a whole, great, massive sea of fire.

Small fires had coalesced into larger fires and, greedy for oxygen, had sucked air from around the coalescing inferno and fanned further fires there. That created the wind, a thermal column above the city like an invisible chimney above a hearth; the wind heated the fury at the center of the firestorm to more than 1,400 degrees, heat sufficient to melt the windows of a streetcar, wind sufficient to uproot trees. A fifteen-year-old Hamburg girl recalls:

> Mother wrapped me in wet sheets, kissed me, and said, "Run!" I hesitated at the door. In front of me I could see only fire—everything red, like the door to a furnace. An intense heat struck me. A burning beam fell in front of my feet. I shied back but, then, when I was ready to jump over it, it was whirled away by a ghostly hand. I ran out to the street. The sheets around me acted as sails and I had the feeling that I was being carried away by the storm. I reached . . . a five-storey building in front of which we had arranged to meet again. . . . Someone came out, grabbed me by the arm, and pulled me into the doorway.

The fire filled the air with burning embers and melted the streets, a nineteen-year-old milliner reports:

> We came to the door which was burning just like a ring in a circus through which a lion has to jump. . . . The rain of large sparks, blowing down the street, were each as large as a five-mark piece. I struggled to run against the wind in the middle of the street but could only reach a house on the corner . . . .
>
> We got to the Löschplatz [park] all right but I couldn't go on across the Eiffestrasse because the asphalt had melted. There were people on the roadway, some already dead, some still lying alive but stuck in the asphalt. They must have rushed on to the roadway without thinking. Their feet had got stuck and then they had put out their hands to try to get out again. They were on their hands and knees screaming.

The firestorm completely burned out some eight square miles of the city, an area about half as large as Manhattan. The bodies of the dead cooked in pools of their own melted fat in sealed shelters like kilns or shriveled to small blackened bundles that littered the streets. Or worse, as the woman who was once the fifteen-year-old girl horribly recreates:

> Four-storey-high blocks of flats [the next day] were like glowing mounds of stone right down to the basement. Everything seemed to have melted and pressed the bodies away in front of it. Women and children were so charred as to be unrecognizable; those that had died through lack of oxygen were half-charred and recognizable. Their brains had tumbled from their burst temples and their insides from the soft parts under the ribs. How terribly these people must have died. The smallest children lay like fried eels on the pavement.

Bomber Command killed at least 45,000 Germans that night, the majority of them old people, women and children.

The bombing of Hamburg was hardly unique. It was one atrocity in a war of increasing atrocities. Between 1941 and 1943 the German Army on the Eastern Front captured and enclosed in prisoner-of-war camps without food or shelter some two million Soviet soldiers; at least one million of them died of exposure and starvation. During the same period the Final Solution to the Jewish Question—the vast Nazi program to exterminate the European Jews—began in deadly earnest after the Wannsee Conference of coordinating agencies met in suburban Berlin on January 20, 1942. Whatever moral issues such atrocities raise, they resulted from the progressive escalation of the war by all its belligerents in pursuit of victory. (Even the Final Solution: because the Nazis believed the Jews constituted a separate nation lodged subversively in their midst—nationality being defined in the Nazi canon primarily in terms of race—and as such the nation with which the Third Reich was preeminently at war. It was Hitler's particular perversity to define victory over the Jews as extermination; the Allies in their defensive war against Germany and Japan wanted only total surrender, in return for which the mass killing of combatants and civilians would stop.)

One way the belligerents could escalate was to improve their death technologies. Better bombers and better bomber defenses such as Window were hardware improvements; so were the showers at the death camps efficiently pumped with the deadly fumigant Zyklon B. The bomber-stream system and allowance for creep-back were software improvements; so were the schedules Adolf Eichmann devised that kept the trains running efficiently to the camps.

The other way the belligerents could escalate was to enlarge the range of permissible victims their death technologies might destroy. Civilians had the misfortune to be the only victims left available. Better hardware and software began to make them also accessible in increasing numbers. No great philosophical effort was required to discover acceptable rationales. War begot psychic numbing in combatants and civilians alike; psychic numbing prepared the way for increasing escalation.

Extend war by attrition to include civilians behind the lines and war becomes total. With improving technology so could death-making be. The bombing of Hamburg marked a significant step in the evolution of death technology itself, massed bombers deliberately churning conflagration. It was still too much a matter of luck, an elusive combination of weather and organization and hardware. It was still also expensive in crews and matériel. It was not yet perfect, as no technology can ever be, and therefore seemed to want perfecting.

The British and the Americans would be enraged to learn of Japanese brutality and Nazi torture, of the Bataan Death March and the fathomless horror of the death camps. By a reflex so mindlessly unimaginative it may be merely mammalian, the bombing of distant cities, out of sight and sound and smell, was generally approved, although neither the United States nor Great Britain admitted publicly that it deliberately bombed civilians. In Churchill's phrase, the enemy was to be "de-housed." The Jap and the Nazi in any case had started the war. "We must face the fact that modern warfare as conducted in the Nazi manner is a dirty business," Franklin Roosevelt told his countrymen. "We don't like it—we didn't want to get in it—but we are in it and we're going to fight it with everything we've got."

The Los Alamos review committee headed by W.K. Lewis of MIT reported its findings on May 10, 1943. It approved the laboratory's nuclear physics research program. It recommended that theoretical investigation of the thermonuclear bomb continue at second priority, subordinate to fission bomb work. It proposed a major change in the chemistry program: final purification of plutonium on the Hill, because Los Alamos would be ultimately responsible for the performance of the plutonium bomb and because the scarce new element would be used and reused for experiments during the months before a sufficient quantity accumulated to load a bomb and would have to be frequently repurified. The Lewis committee also concurred in a recommendation Robert Oppenheimer had made in March that ordnance development and engineering should begin immediately at Los Alamos rather than wait until nuclear physics studies were complete. General Groves accepted the committee's findings; they dictated an immediate doubling of Hill personnel. Thereafter until the end of the war the Los Alamos working population would double every nine months. The dust of construction never settled; housing would always be short, water scarce, electricity intermittent. Groves spent not a penny more than necessary on comforts for civilians.

The bottom pole piece of the Harvard cyclotron had been laid on April 14; by the first week in June Robert Wilson's cyclotron group saw signs of a beam. The Wisconsin long-tank Van de Graaff came on line at 4 million volts on May 15 and the 2 MV short-tank Van de Graaff on June 10. In July the first physics experiment completed at Los Alamos counted the number of secondary neutrons Pu239 emitted when it fissioned. "In this experiment," says the Los Alamos technical history, "the neutron number was measured from an almost invisible speck of plutonium and found to be somewhat greater even than for U^{235}." The experiment thus established what had not yet been confirmed despite the expensive rush of building: that plutonium emitted sufficient secondary neutrons to chain-react.

The speck of plutonium was Glenn Seaborg's 200-milligram sample of Met Lab oxide, which he had sent to Los Alamos at the beginning of the month. Seaborg had worked himself sick at the Met Lab that spring—an upper respiratory infection compounded with exhaustion and a persistent fever—and came to New Mexico with his wife during July to vacation. ("I guess I deliberately chose to be near the plutonium," he muses. "I wonder why?") Too much peace and quiet at a guest ranch threatened to exhaust him further and on July 21 he and his wife moved to the adobe-style La Fonda del Sol Hotel in Santa Fe. Compartmentalization put Los Alamos off limits. The Seaborgs were ready to return to Chicago on Friday, July 30, and Seaborg proposed to carry the Pu sample, most of the world's supply, back with him on the train. Robert Wilson and another physicist made the transfer before dawn in the restaurant where the Seaborgs were having breakfast in Santa Fe, Wilson arriving in a pickup armed Western-style with his personal Winchester .32 deer-hunting rifle to guard a highly valuable but barely visible treasure. "Then I just put it in my pocket and then into my suitcase," Seaborg remembers. He proceeded to Chicago unarmed.

To direct the expanded Ordnance Division Groves asked the Military Policy Committee in Washington to recommend a good man, preferably a military officer. Vannevar Bush knew a *naval* officer—would Groves mind? "Of course not," the general humphed. Bush proposed Captain William S. "Deke" Parsons, a 1922 Annapolis graduate then responsible under Bush for field-testing the proximity fuse.*

Parsons had also worked on early radar development and served as gunnery officer on a destroyer and experimental officer at the Naval Proving Ground in Dahlgren, Virginia. He was forty-three, cool, vigorous, trim, nearly bald, spit-and-polish but innovative; "all his life," one of the men who worked for him at Los Alamos testifies in praise, "he fought the silly regulations and the conservatism of the Navy." Groves liked him; "within a few minutes [of meeting him]," the general says, "I was sure he was the man for the job." Oppenheimer interviewed the man for the job in Washington and agreed. Parsons was married to Martha Cluverius, a Vassar graduate and the daughter of an admiral; with two blond daughters and a cocker spaniel the couple arrived at Los Alamos in an open red convertible in June.

Parsons' first order of business was the plutonium gun. Because it needed a muzzle velocity of at least 3,000 feet per second it would have to

*The proximity fuse was a miniature radar unit shaped to replace the ballistic nose of anti-aircraft shells. It sensed its proximity to a target—an enemy plane—and exploded the shell it rode at a preset range, often turning a miss into a kill. Its development was another of Bush's responsibilities and it was one of science's most important contributions to the war. Merle Tuve, Richard Roberts and most of the physics team at the Department of Terrestrial Magnetism of the Carnegie Institution had turned from fission research in August 1940 to develop it.

be 17 feet long. It should weigh no more than a ton, a fifth of the usual weight of a gun that size, which meant it would have to be machined from strong high-alloy steel. It would not require rifling but needed three independently operated primers to make sure it fired. Parsons arranged for the Navy's gun-design section to engineer it.

Norman F. Ramsey, a tall young Columbia physicist, the son of a general, served under Parsons as group leader for delivery: for devising a way to deliver the bombs to their targets and drop them. In June he contacted the U.S. Air Force to identify a combat aircraft that could carry a 17-foot bomb. "As a result of this survey," Ramsey writes, "it was apparent that the B-29 was the only United States aircraft in which such a bomb could be conveniently carried internally, and even this plane would require considerable modification so that the bomb could extend into both front and rear bomb bays. . . . Except for the British Lancaster, all other aircraft would require such a bomb to be carried externally." The Air Force was not about to allow a historic new weapon of war to be introduced to the world in a British aircraft, but the B-29 Superfortress was a new design still plagued with serious problems. The first service-test model had not yet flown when Ramsey began his aircraft survey in June; a flight-test model had crashed into a Seattle packing house in February and killed the plane's entire test crew and nineteen packing-house workers.

Ramsey did not have to wait for access to a B-29 to begin collecting data on the long bomb's ballistics, however. He mocked up a scale model and arranged to see it dropped:

> On August 13, 1943, the first drop tests of a prototype atomic bomb were made at the Dahlgren Naval Proving Ground [by a Navy TBF aircraft] to determine stability in flight. These tests were on a 14/23 scale model of a bomb shape which was then thought probably suitable for a gun assembly. Essentially, the model consisted of a long length of 14-inch pipe welded into the middle of a split standard 500-pound bomb. It was officially known at Dahlgren as the "Sewer Pipe Bomb." . . . The first test . . . was an ominous and spectacular failure. The bomb fell in a flat spin such as had rarely been seen before. However, an increase in fin area and a forward movement of the center of gravity provided stability in subsequent tests.

In the meantime Seth Neddermeyer, whose implosion experimentation group Parsons inherited, had visited a U.S. Bureau of Mines laboratory at Bruceton, Pennsylvania, to experiment with high explosives. Edwin McMillan, who was interested in implosion, went with the Caltech physicist:

> At that point it was just Seth and myself with a few helpers. The first cylindrical implosions were done at Bruceton. You take a piece of iron pipe, wrap the explosives around it, and ignite it at several points so that you get a converging wave and squash the cylinder in. That was the birth of the experimental work on implosion, long before experimental work on the gun method.

Back at Los Alamos Neddermeyer set up a small research station on South Mesa, the next mesa south of the Hill across Los Alamos canyon. He fired his first tests in an arroyo on Independence Day, 1943, using iron pipe set in cans packed with TNT. Experimenting with cylinders rather than spheres simplified calculation. Because he wanted to recover the results he packed only limited amounts of explosive. "Those tests of course could not be very sophisticated," says McMillan. ". . . They did show that you could take metal pipes and close them right in so that they became like solid bars, indicating that this was a practical method." They also showed that the squeeze was far from uniform: the pipes emerged from the arroyo dust twisted and deformed.

When Parsons, a thoroughly pragmatic engineer, had time to look over Neddermeyer's work he was openly contemptuous. He doubted if implosion could ever be made reliable enough for field use. Neddermeyer presented his initial results at one of the weekly colloquia Oppenheimer had instituted at Hans Bethe's suggestion to keep everyone with a white badge—everyone cleared for secrets—informed of Tech Area progress. Richard P. Feynman, a brilliant, outspoken New York–born graduate-student theoretician from Princeton, summarized the opinion of the assembly in a phrase: "It stinks." In the name of lightheartedness Parsons was crueler. "With everyone grinding away in such dead earnest here," he told the group, "we need a touch of relief. I question Dr. Neddermeyer's seriousness. To my mind he is gradually working up to what I shall refer to as the Beer-Can Experiment. As soon as he gets his explosives properly organized, we will see this done. The point to watch for is whether he can blow in a beer can without splattering the beer." Implosion was even harder to do than that.

John von Neumann, the Hungarian mathematician who had come to the United States in 1930 and joined the Institute for Advanced Study, had been examining for the NDRC the complex hydrodynamics of shock waves formed by shaped charges, technology which was being applied to the American tank-killing infantry weapon known as the bazooka. Like Rabi, von Neumann had agreed to serve as an occasional Oppenheimer consultant. He visited Los Alamos at the end of the summer and looked into implosion theory, another warren of hydrodynamic complexity. Neddermeyer had devised "a simple theory that worked up to a certain level of violence in the shockwave." Von Neumann, he says, "is generally credited with originating the science of large compressions. But I knew it before and had done it in a naive way. Von Neumann's was more sophisticated."

"Johnny was quite interested in high explosives," Edward Teller remembers. Teller and von Neumann renewed their youthful acquaintance during the mathematician's visit to the Hill. "In my discussions with him some crude calculations were made," Teller continues. "The calculation is indeed simple as long as you assume that the material to be accelerated is incompressible, which is the usual assumption about solid matter. . . . In materials driven by high explosives, pressures of more than 100,000 atmospheres occur." Von Neumann knew that, Teller says, as he did not. On the other hand:

> If a shell moves in one-third of the way toward the center you obtain under the assumption of an incompressible material a pressure in excess of eight million atmospheres. This is more than the pressure in the center of the earth and it was known to me (but not to Johnny), that at these pressures, iron is not incompressible. In fact I had rough figures for the relevant compressibilities. The result of all this was that in the implosion significant compressions will occur, a point which had not been previously discussed.

It had been clear from the beginning that implosion, by squeezing a hollow shell of plutonium to a solid ball, could effectively "assemble" it as a critical mass much faster than the fastest gun could fire. What von Neumann and Teller now realized, and communicated to Oppenheimer in October 1943, was that implosion at more violent compressions than Neddermeyer had yet attempted should squeeze plutonium to such unearthly densities that a solid subcritical mass could serve as a bomb core, avoiding the complex problem of compressing hollow shells. Nor would predetonation threaten from light-element impurities. Develop implosion, in other words, and they could deliver a more reliable bomb more quickly.

It was possible at that point to estimate roughly the size and shape of a bomb that worked by fast implosion. The big gun bomb would be just under 2 feet in diameter and 17 feet long. An implosion bomb—a thick shell of high explosives surrounding a thick shell of tamper surrounding a plutonium core surrounding an initiator—would be just under 5 feet in diameter and a little over 9 feet long: a man-sized egg with tail fins.

Norman Ramsey started planning full-scale drop tests that autumn as the aspens brightened to yellow at Los Alamos. He offered to practice with a Lancaster. The Air Force insisted he practice with a B-29 even though the

97

97. Beginning in 1944, U.S. Air Force B-29's systematically firebombed Japanese cities. *L. to r.,* Generals Lauris Norstad, Curtis LeMay and Thomas Power.

98

98. At the Potsdam Conference in July 1945 President Harry Truman welcomed the bomb as a substitute for Soviet entry into the Pacific war. *L. to r.,* Soviet Premier Joseph Stalin, Truman, British Prime Minister Winston Churchill.

99. Henry L. Stimson, Secretary of War, directed bomb development. 100. Jimmy Byrnes, Secretary of State, advised Truman to use the bomb to force the unconditional surrender of the Japanese.

99

100

101

101. The Hiroshima bomb, Little Boy, was a cannon with a U235 bullet and three U235 target rings fitted to its muzzle. Tinian, August 1945.

102

102. Hiroshima pre-strike briefing on Tinian. *L. to r.,* first row, unknown; second row, Norman Ramsey, Paul Tibbets; third row, Thomas Ferrell, Adm. Parnell, Deke Parsons, Luis Alvarez; fourth row, left of Parsons, Charles Sweeney, right of Parsons, Thomas Ferebee, right of Alvarez, Theodore Van Kirk; Harold Agnew.

103. Crew of the *Enola Gay* before Hiroshima mission: *l. to r.*, standing, John Porter (ground maintenance officer), Theodore Van Kirk (navigator), Thomas Ferebee (bombardier), Paul Tibbets (pilot), Robert Lewis (copilot), Jacob Beser (radar countermeasures officer); kneeling, Joseph Stiborik (radar operator), Robert Caron (tail gunner), Richard Nelson (radio operator), Robert Shumard (assistant engineer), Wyatt Duzenbury (flight engineer). Not shown: Deke Parsons (weaponeer), Morris Jeppson (electronics test officer).

104

104. The mushroom cloud over Hiroshima, August 6, 1945, photographed from the strike mission B-29. 105. The *Enola Gay* landing at Tinian after the Hiroshima strike.

105

106

106. A panorama of Hiroshima damage. Some roads have been cleared. Buildings left standing were earthquake-reinforced. Little Boy exploded with a yield equivalent to 12,500 tons of TNT (12.5 KT). Modern atomic artillery shells deliver equal yield; one Minuteman III missile is armed with the equivalent of 84 Hiroshimas.

107

107. Miyuki Bridge, Hiroshima, 1.4 miles from the hypocenter, 11 A.M., August 6, 1945.

108

108. The Hiroshima fireball instantly raised surface temperatures within a mile of the hypocenter well above 1,000° F.

109

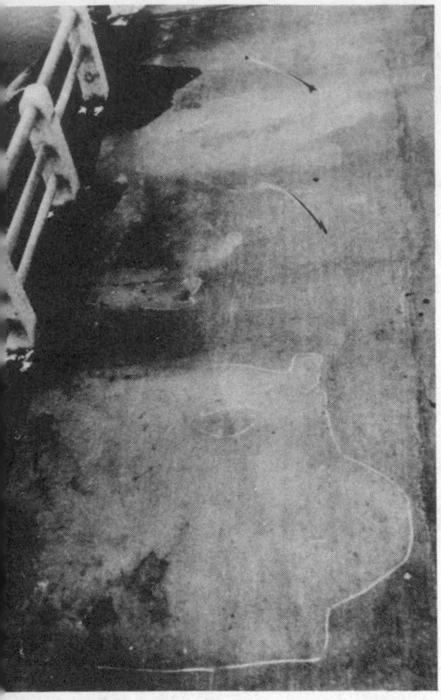

109. A man pulling a cart shadowed in unburned asphalt, Hiroshima.

110

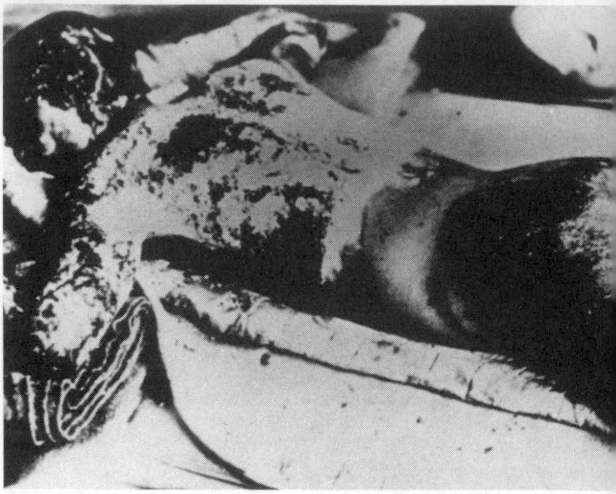

110. Thermal burns on a soldier exposed within half a mile of the Hiroshima hypocenter. His sash protected his waist.

111

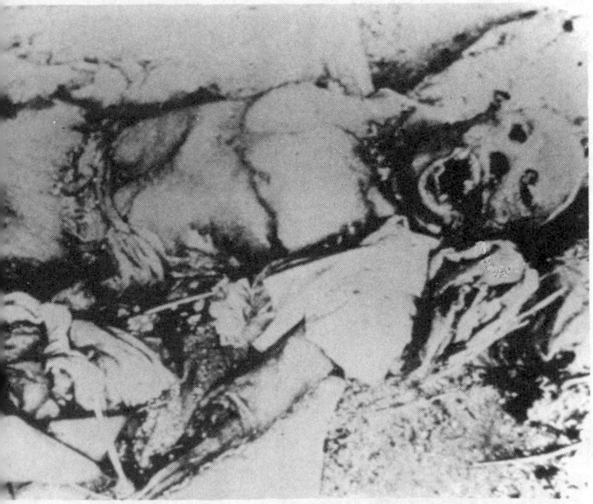

111. Unidentified corpse, Hiroshima. Deaths to the end of 1945 totaled 140,000.

112

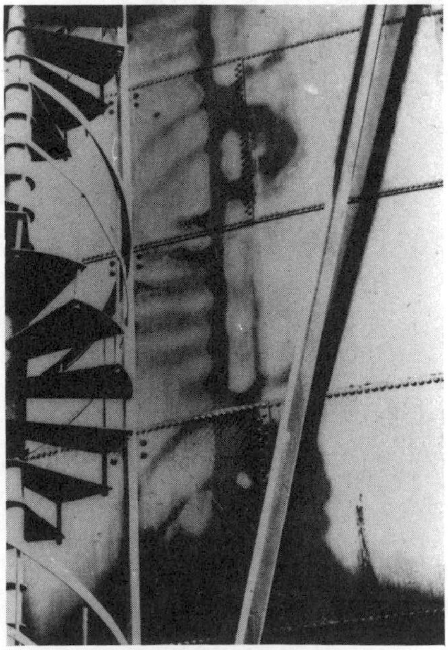

112. Staircase on a gas storage tank shadowed in uncharred paint, Hiroshima.

113. Fat Man was ready on Tinian on August 8, 1945, and flew the following day. Note graffiti on tail assembly.

113

114

114. The plutonium bomb exploded over Nagasaki near the largest Christian church in Japan at 1102 hours, August 9, 1945, with a yield estimated at 22 kilotons.

115

115. Fat Man snapped trees at Nagasaki; the less powerful Hiroshima bomb only knocked them down. 116. Collecting the dead for cremation.

116

117

117. A student exposed half a mile from the Nagasaki hypocenter.

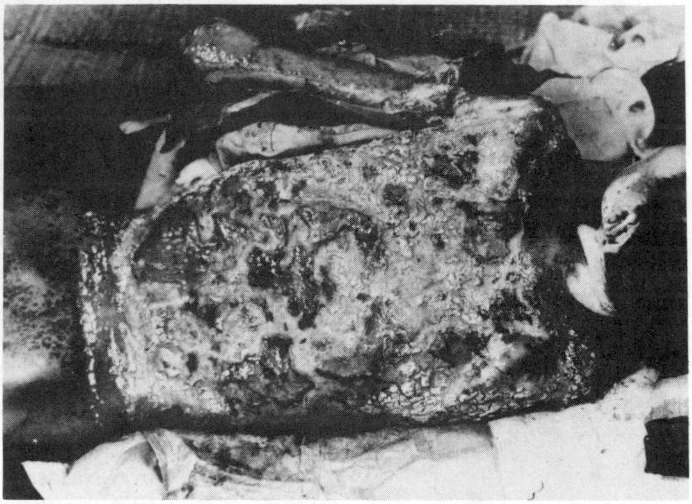

118

118. Flash burns, Nagasaki.

119. Near the Nagasaki hypocenter, noon, August 10, 1945.

119

120

121

120. Dr. Michihiko Hachiya, director of the Hiroshima Communications Hospital. His diary chronicled the disaster.

121. Emperor Hirohito decided after Nagasaki, over his ministers' objections, to end the war and cited "a new and most cruel bomb" in his August 15 surrender proclamation.

122. Los Alamos received the Army-Navy E for excellence for its work.

122

123

123. Mike I, the first true thermonuclear bomb, tested at Eniwetok in the Marshall Islands on November 1, 1952. Yield: 10.4 megatons (i.e., millions of tons of TNT equivalent). Pipes carried off radiation to diagnostic equipment; their arrangement confirms the linear Teller-Ulam configuration. Note man seated in foreground for scale. 124. Mike vaporized the island of Elugelab and left a crater half a mile deep and two miles wide. 125. The Mark 17 H-bomb, the first deliverable thermonuclear weapon. Yield: megaton-range. Weight: 21 tons.

124

125

126. The Mike shot. Its fireball expanded to a diameter of 3 miles.

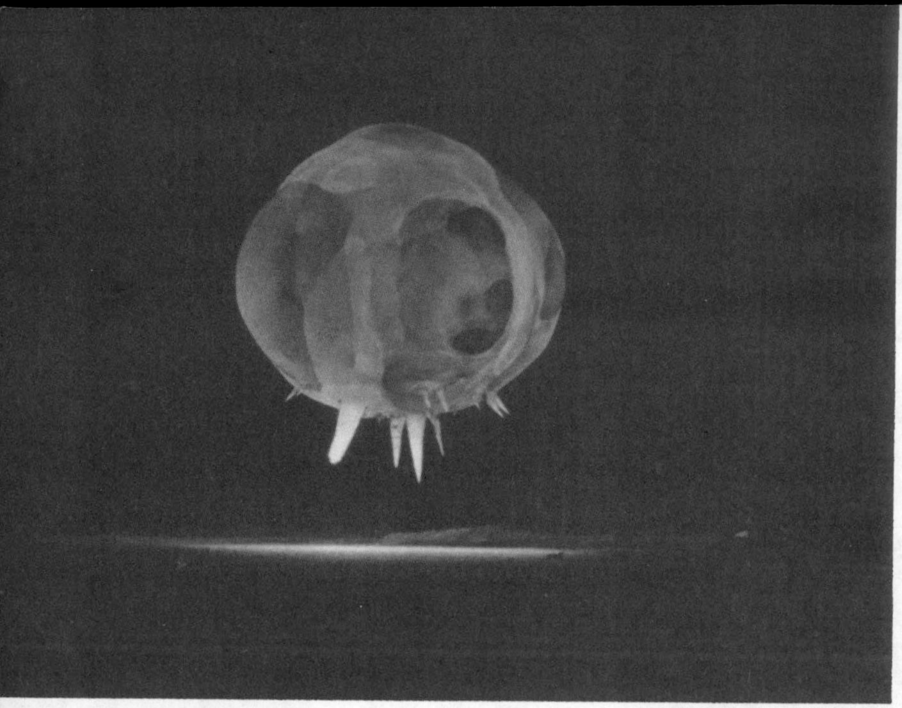

127

127. Early fireball of a postwar atomic bomb test. "I could see a great bare eyeball," Michihiko Hachiya dreamed after Hiroshima, "bigger than life, hovering over my head, staring point-blank at me."

128. Margrethe and Niels Bohr at their summer cottage in Tisvilde. "We are in a completely new situation that cannot be resolved by war."

128

new polished-aluminum intercontinental bombers were just beginning production and still scarce. "In order that the aircraft modifications could begin," Ramsey writes in his third-person report on this work, "Parsons and Ramsey selected two external shapes and weights as representative of the current plans at Site Y. . . . For security reasons, these were called by the Air Force representatives the 'Thin Man' and the 'Fat Man,' respectively; the Air Force officers tried to make their phone conversations sound as though they were modifying a plane to carry Roosevelt (the Thin Man) and Churchill (the Fat Man). . . . Modification of the first B-29 officially began November 29, 1943."

A captain of the Danish Army who was also a member of the Danish underground visited Niels Bohr at the House of Honor in Copenhagen early in 1943. After tea the two men retired to Bohr's greenhouse where hidden microphones might not overhear their conversation. The British had instructed the underground that they would soon be sending Bohr a set of keys. Blind holes had been drilled in the bows of two of the keys, identical microdots implanted and the holes sealed. A captioned diagram located the holes. "Professor Bohr should gently file the keys at the point indicated until the hole appears," the document explained. "The message can then be syringed or floated out onto a micro-slide." The captain offered to extract the microdot and have it enlarged. Bohr was no secret agent; he accepted the offer gratefully.

When the message arrived it proved to be a letter from James Chadwick. "The letter contained an invitation to my father to go to England, where he would find a very warm welcome," Aage Bohr remembers. ". . . Chadwick told my father that he would be able to work freely on scientific matters. But it was also mentioned that there were special problems in which his co-operation would be of considerable help." Bohr understood that Chadwick might be hinting about work on nuclear fission. The Danish physicist was still skeptical of its application. He would not stay in Denmark, he wrote Chadwick in return, "if I felt that I could be of real help . . . but I do not think that this is probable. Above all I have to the best of my judgment convinced myself that, in spite of all future prospects, any immediate use of the latest marvelous discoveries of atomic physics is impracticable." If an atomic bomb were a serious possibility Bohr would leave. Otherwise he had compelling reasons to stay "to help resist the threat against the freedom of our institutions and to assist in the protection of the exiled scientists who have sought refuge here."

The threat against Danish institutions that Bohr was helping to resist was peculiar to the German occupation of Denmark. Germany relied heavily on Danish agriculture, which supplied meat and butter rations to 3.6 million Germans in 1942 alone. It was a labor-intensive agriculture of small farms and it could only continue with the cooperation of the farmers and, more broadly, of the entire Danish population. Not to arouse resistance the Nazis had allowed Denmark to keep its constitutional monarchy and continue to govern itself. The Danes in turn had extracted an extraordinary price for agreeing to cooperate under foreign occupation: the security of Danish Jews. To the Danes the eight thousand Jews in Denmark, 95 percent of them in Copenhagen, were Danish citizens first of all; their security was therefore a test of German good faith. "Danish statesmen and heads of government," reports a historian, "one after the other, had made the security of the Jews a *conditio sine qua non* for the maintenance of a constitutional Danish government."

But resistance, especially strikes and sabotage, gradually increased as the Danish people felt the occupation's burden and as the tides of war began to turn against the Axis powers. The German surrender at Stalingrad on February 2, 1943, may have appeared to many Danes to be a turning point. Mussolini's resignation and arrest the following summer on July 25 and the impending surrender of Italy certainly did. On August 28 the Nazi plenipotentiary for Denmark, Dr. Karl Rudolf Werner Best, presented the Danish government with an ultimatum at Hitler's orders demanding that it declare a state of national emergency, forbid strikes and meetings and introduce a curfew, a ban on arms, press censorship at German hands and the death penalty for harboring arms and for sabotage. With the King's permission the government refused. On August 29 the Nazis reoccupied Copenhagen, disarmed the Danish Army, blockaded the royal palace and confined the King.

One reason for the takeover was Nazi determination to eliminate the Danish Jews, whose exemption from the Final Solution infuriated Hitler. The Nazis had arrested several Jewish notables on August 29 (they had planned to arrest Bohr but had decided the deed would be less obvious during a general roundup). In early September Bohr learned from the Swedish ambassador in Copenhagen that his emigré colleagues, including his collaborator Stefan Rozental, were slated for arrest. He contacted the underground, which helped the emigrés escape across the Öresund to Sweden. Rozental endured nine stormy hours crowded with other refugees in a rowboat borrowed from a city park before his exhausted party made Swedish landfall.

Bohr's turn came soon after. The Swedish ambassador took tea at the House of Honor on September 28 and hinted that Bohr would be arrested within a few days. *Even professors* were leaving Denmark, Margrethe Bohr remembers the diplomat emphasizing. The next morning word came through her brother-in-law that an anti-Nazi German woman working at Gestapo offices in Copenhagen had seen orders authorized in Berlin for the arrest and deportation of Niels and Harald Bohr.

"We had to get away the same day," Margrethe Bohr said afterward. "And the boys would have to follow later. But many were helping. Friends arranged for a boat, and we were told we could take one small bag." In the late afternoon of September 29 the Bohrs walked through Copenhagen to a seaside suburban garden and hid in a gardener's shed. They waited for night. At a prearranged time they left the shed and crossed to the beach. A motorboat ran them out to a fishing boat. Threading minefields and German patrols they crossed the Öresund by moonlight and landed at Linhamm, near Malmö.

Bohr had learned at the last minute that the Nazis planned to round up all the Danish Jews the next evening and deport them to Germany. Leaving his wife in southern Sweden to await the crossing of their sons he rushed to Stockholm to appeal to the Swedish government for aid. He discovered that the Swedes had offered to intern the Danish Jews but the Germans had denied that any roundup was planned.

In fact it proceeded on schedule while Bohr worked his way through the Swedish bureaucracy, but fell far short of success. The Danes, warned in advance, had spontaneously hidden their Jewish fellow citizens away. Only some 284 elderly rest-home residents had been seized. The more than seven thousand Jews remaining in Denmark were temporarily safe. But few of them planned at first to leave the country; it was far from certain that Sweden would accept them and there seemed nowhere else to go.

Meeting with the Swedish Undersecretary for Foreign Affairs on September 30 Bohr had urged that Sweden make public its protest note to the German Foreign Office. He saw that publicity would alert the potential victims, signal Swedish sympathy and bring pressure to bear on the Nazis to desist. The Undersecretary told him Sweden planned no further intervention beyond the confidential note. Bohr appealed to the Foreign Minister on October 2, failed to win publication of the note and determined to dispense with intermediaries. Rozental says the Danish laureate "went to see Princess Ingeborg (the sister of the Danish king Christian X) and while there expressed the desire to be received by the King of Sweden." Bohr also contacted the Danish ambassador and influential Swedish academic colleagues. Rozental describes the crucial meeting with the King:

> The audience . . . took place that afternoon. . . . King Gustaf said that the Swedish Government had tried a similar approach to the Germans once be-

> fore, when the occupying power had started deporting Jews from Norway. The . . . approach, however, had been rejected. . . . Bohr objected that in the meantime the situation had changed decisively by reason of the Allied victories, and he suggested that the offer by the Swedish government to assume responsibility for the Danish Jews should be made public. The King promised to talk to the Foreign Minister at once, but he emphasized the great difficulties of putting the plan into operation.

The difficulties were overcome. Swedish radio broadcast the Swedish protest that evening, October 2, and reported the country ready to offer asylum. The broadcast signaled a route of escape; in the next two months 7,220 Jews crossed to safety in Sweden with the active help of the Swedish coast guard. One refugee's report of what first alerted him in hiding to the idea of escape is typical: "At the pastor's house I heard on the Swedish radio that the Bohr brothers had fled to Sweden by boat and that the Danish Jews were being cordially received." With personal intervention on behalf of the principle of openness, which exposes crime as well as error to public view, Niels Bohr played a decisive part in the rescue of the Danish Jews.

Stockholm was alive with German agents and there was fear that Bohr would be assassinated. "The stay in Stockholm lasted only a short time," remembers Aage Bohr. ". . . A telegram was received from Lord Cherwell . . . with an invitation to come to England. My father immediately accepted and requested that I should be permitted to accompany him." Aage was twenty-one at the time and a promising young physicist. "It was not possible for the rest of the family to follow; my mother and brothers stayed in Sweden."

Bohr went first. The British flew their diplomatic pouch back and forth from Stockholm in an unarmed two-engine Mosquito bomber, a light, fast aircraft that could fly high enough to avoid the German anti-aircraft batteries on the west coast of Norway—flak usually topped out at 20,000 feet. The Mosquito's bomb bay was fitted for a single passenger. On October 6 Bohr donned a flight suit and strapped on a parachute. The pilot supplied him with a flight helmet with built-in earphones for communication with the cockpit and showed him the location of his oxygen hookup. Bohr also took delivery of a stick of flares. In case of attack the pilot would dump the bomb bay and Bohr would parachute into the cold North Sea; the flares would aid his rescue if he survived.

"The Royal Air Force was not used to such great heads as Bohr's," says Robert Oppenheimer wryly. Aage Bohr describes the near-disaster:

> The Mosquito flew at a great height and it was necessary to use oxygen masks; the pilot gave word on the inter-com when the supply of oxygen should be

> turned on, but as the helmet with the earphones did not fit my father's head, he did not hear the order and soon fainted because of lack of oxygen. The pilot realized that something was wrong when he received no answer to his inquiries, and as soon as they had passed over Norway he came down and flew low over the North Sea. When the plane landed in Scotland, my father was conscious again.

The vigorous fifty-eight-year-old was none the worse for wear. "Once in England and recovered," Oppenheimer continues the story, "he learned from Chadwick what had been going on." Aage arrived a week later and father and son toured Britain observing the developing activities there of the Tube Alloys project, which included a section of a pilot-scale gaseous-diffusion plant. But the center of gravity had long since shifted to the United States. The British were preparing to recover a share of the initiative by sending a mission to Los Alamos to help design the bombs; they wanted Bohr on their team to increase its influence and prestige. By then the Danish theoretician had taken what Oppenheimer calls a "good first look." At how nuclear weapons would change the world, Oppenheimer means. He emphasizes Bohr's developing understanding then with a potent simile: "It came to him as a revelation, very much as when he learned of Rutherford's discovery of the nucleus [thirty] years before."

So Niels Bohr prepared in the early winter of 1943 to travel to America once again with an important and original revelation in hand, this one in the realm not of physics but of the political organization of the world.

He was willing to be impressed by a mighty progress of industry. "The work on atomic energy in the USA and in England proved to have advanced much further than my father had expected," Aage Bohr understates. Robert Oppenheimer pitches his summary closer to the shock of surprise a refugee released from the suspended animation that had been occupied Denmark would have felt: "To Bohr the enterprises in the United States seemed completely fantastic."

They were.

15

Different Animals

The 59,000 acres of Appalachian semiwilderness along the Clinch River in eastern Tennessee that Brigadier General Leslie R. Groves acquired for the Manhattan Engineer District as one of his first official acts, in September 1942, extended from the Cumberland foothills in a series of parallel, southwestern-running ridge valleys. Groves liked the geology, which offered isolation for his several enterprises, but the new reservation was nearly as primitive as Los Alamos would be. The Clinch, a meandering tributary of the Tennessee, defined the reservation's southeastern and southwestern boundaries. Eastward twenty miles was Knoxville, a city of nearly 112,000, farther east the wall of Great Smoky Mountains National Park. Five unpaved county roads traversed the ninety-two square miles of depleted valleys and scrub-oak ridges, an area seventeen miles long and seven miles wide that supported only about a thousand families in rural poverty. In the ridge-barricaded valleys of this impoverished hill country, far from prying eyes, the United States Army intended to construct the futuristic factories that would separate U235 from U238 in quantity sufficient to make an atomic bomb.

To do so it had first to improve communications and build a town. Into the gummy red eastern-Tennessee clay in the winter of 1942 and the spring of 1943 its contractors cut fifty-five miles of rail roadbed and three hundred miles of paved roads and streets. They improved the important county roads to four-lane highways. Stone & Webster, the hard-pressed Boston engineering corporation, laid out a town plan so unimaginative that the MED rejected it and passed the assignment to the ambitious young architectural firm of Skidmore, Owings and Merrill, which produced a well-sited arrangement of housing using innovative new materials that saved enough money to allow for such amenities in the best residences as fireplaces and porches. The new town, planned initially for thirteen thousand workers, took its name from its location lining a long section of the northwesternmost valley: Oak Ridge. The entire reservation, fenced with barbed wire and controlled through seven guarded gates, was named, after a nearby Tennessee community, the Clinton Engineer Works. Its workers would come to call it Dogpatch in homage to the hillbilly comic strip "Li'l Abner." The new gates closed off public access on April 1.

Groves planned to build electromagnetic isotope separation plants and a gaseous-diffusion plant at Clinton; plutonium production, he realized during his first months on the project, would proceed at such a scale and generate so vast a quantity of potentially dangerous radioactivity that it would require a separate reservation of its own. Of the three processes, Ernest Lawrence's electromagnetic method was farthest along.

Electromagnetic isotope separation enlarged and elaborated Francis Aston's 1918 Cavendish invention, the mass spectrograph. As a 1945 report prepared by Lawrence's staff explains, the method "depends on the fact that an electrically charged atom traveling through a magnetic field moves in a circle whose radius is determined by its mass"—which was also a basic principle of Lawrence's cyclotron. The lighter the atom, the tighter the circle it made. Form ions of a vaporous uranium compound and start them moving at one side of a vacuum tank permeated by a strong magnetic field and the moving ions as they curved around would separate into two beams. Lighter U235 atoms would follow a narrower arc than heavier U238 atoms; across a four-foot semicircle the separation might be about three-tenths of an inch. Set a collecting pocket at the point where the U235 ion beam separately arrived and you could catch the ions. "When the ions strike the bottom of the collecting pocket . . . they give up their charge and are deposited as flakes of metal." Schematically, with slotted electrodes to accelerate the ions, the arrangement would look like the illustration on page 488.

Late in 1941 Lawrence had installed such a 180-degree mass spectrometer in place of the dees in the Berkeley 37-inch cyclotron. By running it continuously for a month his crews produced a partially separated 100-microgram sample of U235. That was several hundred million times less than the 100 kilograms Robert Oppenheimer had originally estimated would be

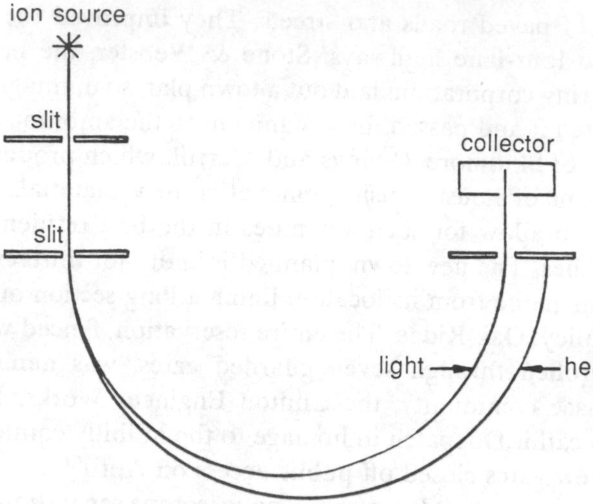

Magnetic field perpendicular to plane of drawing

necessary to make a bomb. The demonstration proved the basic principle of electromagnetic separation even as it dramatized the method's monumental prodigality: Lawrence was proposing to separate uranium atom by individual atom.

Enlarging the equipment, increasing the accelerating voltage, multiplying the number of sources and collectors set side by side between the poles of the same magnet were obvious ways to improve output and efficiency. Lawrence had committed his time to winning the war; now he committed his beautiful new 184-inch cyclotron. Instead of cyclotron dees he had D-shaped mass-spectrometer tanks installed between the pole faces of its 4,500-ton magnet. Making the new instrument work, through the spring and summer of 1942, solved the most difficult design problems. It acquired a name along the way: *calutron*, another *tron* from the *U*niversity of *Cal*ifornia.

To separate 100 grams—about 4 ounces—of U235 per day, Lawrence estimated in the autumn of 1942, would require some 2,000 4-foot calutron tanks set among thousands of tons of magnets. If a bomb needed 30 kilograms—66 pounds—of U235 for reasonable efficiency, as the Berkeley summer study group had just worked out, 2,000 such calutrons could enrich material enough for one bomb core every 300 days. That assumed the system worked reliably, which so far its laboratory predecessors had hardly done. Yet in 1942 electromagnetic separation still looked so much more promising to James Bryant Conant than either the plutonium approach or gaseous barrier diffusion that he had offered up for debate the possibility of pursuing it exclusively. Lawrence was self-confident but not foolhardy; he insisted that the two dark horses should continue to run the race alongside the favorite.

Groves was less impressed. So was the first Lewis committee that had visited Chicago and Berkeley when Fermi was building CP-1 in the winter of 1942. The Lewis committee judged gaseous diffusion the best approach because it was most like existing technology—diffusion was a phenomenon familiar to petroleum engineers and a gaseous-diffusion plant would be essentially an enormous interconnected assemblage of pipes and pumps. Electromagnetic separation by contrast was a batch process untested at such monumental scale; Berkeley planned a system of 4-foot tanks set vertically between the pole faces of large square electromagnets, two tanks to a gap and a total of 96 tanks per unit. To reduce the amount of iron needed for the magnet cores the arrangement would be not rectangular but oval, like a racetrack:

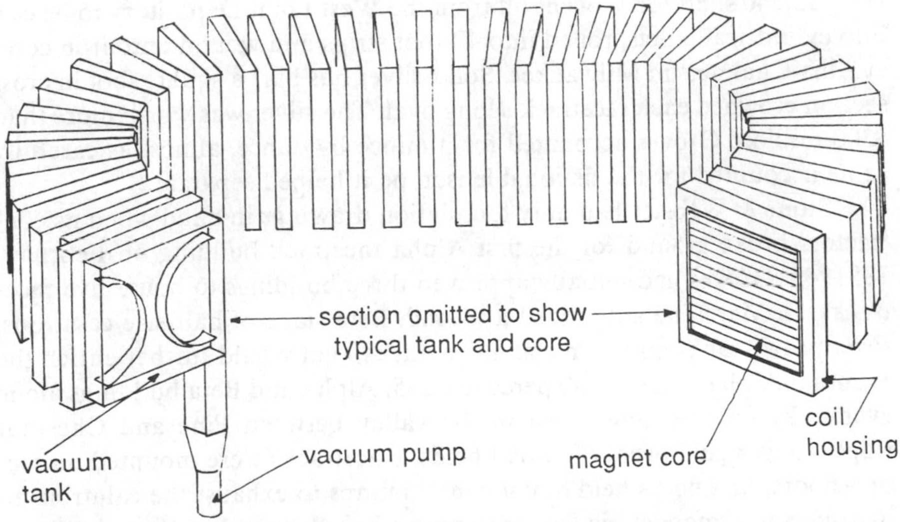

And *racetrack* it was called, though its official designation was Alpha. Berkeley could promise only 5 grams of enriched uranium per day per racetrack, but Groves thought 2,000 tanks well beyond Stone & Webster's capability and cut the number back to 500, reasoning, as Lawrence recalled later, "that the art and science of the process would go forward and that by the time the plant was built substantially higher production rates would be assured." Five grams per day per racetrack with only five racetracks would mean 1,200 days per 30-kilogram bomb even if the Alpha calutrons produced nearly pure U235, which they did not—their best production was around 15 percent. Groves counted on improvements and forged ahead.

He had to begin building before he knew precisely what to build. He worked from the general to the particular, from outline to detail. Fully six months before he decided how many calutrons to authorize, his predecessors, Colonel James Marshall and Lieutenant Colonel Kenneth Nichols, had moved to solve one serious problem of supply. The United States was critically short of copper, the best common metal for winding the coils of electromagnets. For recoverable use the Treasury offered to make silver bullion available in copper's stead. The Manhattan District put the offer to the test, Nichols negotiating the loan with Treasury Undersecretary Daniel Bell. "At one point in the negotiations," writes Groves, "Nichols . . . said that they would need between five and ten thousand tons of silver. This led to the icy reply: 'Colonel, in the Treasury we do not speak of tons of silver; our unit is the Troy ounce.' " Eventually 395 million troy ounces of silver—13,540 short tons—went off from the West Point Depository to be cast into cylindrical billets, rolled into 40-foot strips and wound onto iron cores at Allis-Chalmers in Milwaukee. Solid-silver bus bars a square foot in cross section crowned each racetrack's long oval. The silver was worth more than $300 million. Groves accounted for it ounce by ounce, almost as carefully as he accounted for the fissionable isotope it helped separate.

Stone & Webster had only foundation drawings in hand when its contractors broke ground for the first Alpha racetrack building on February 18, 1943. Groves had initially approved three buildings to house five racetracks. In March he authorized a second, Beta stage of half-size calutrons, seventy-two tanks on two rectangular tracks, that would further enrich the eventual Alpha output to 90 percent U235. Alpha and Beta buildings alone eventually covered more area in the valley between Pine and Chestnut ridges than would twenty football fields. Racetracks were mounted on second floors; first floors held monumental pumps to exhaust the calutrons to high vacuum, more cubic feet of vacuum than the combined total volume pumped down everywhere else on earth at that time. Eventually the Y-12 complex counted 268 permanent buildings large and small—the calutron structures of steel and brick and tile, chemistry laboratories, a distilled water plant, sewage treatment plants, pump houses, a shop, a service station, warehouses, cafeterias, gatehouses, change houses and locker rooms, a paymaster's office, a foundry, a generator building, eight electric substations, nineteen water-cooling towers—for an output measured in the best of times in grams per day. An inspection trip in May 1943 awed even Ernest Lawrence.

By August, twenty thousand construction workers swarmed over the area. An experimental Alpha unit saw successful operation. Lawrence was urging Groves then to double the Alpha plant. With ten Alpha racetracks instead of five he estimated he could separate half a kilogram of U235 per day at 85 percent enrichment. An Army engineer's less exuberant summary, written six days after Lawrence's, predicted 900 grams per month with existing Alpha and Beta stages beginning in November 1943, for a total of 22 kilograms of bomb-grade U235 in the first year of operation. Faced with new estimates from Los Alamos that summer that an efficient uranium gun would probably require 40 kilograms—88 pounds—of the rarer uranium isotope, Groves bought Lawrence's proposal. The doubling would add four new 96-tank tracks of advanced design designated Alpha II and a proportionate number of Beta tracks, at a cost of $150 million more than the $100 million already authorized. If everything worked at Y-12, Groves justified his proposal to the Military Policy Committee, he would then have a 40-kilogram bomb core around the beginning of 1945.

The Army had contracted with Tennessee Eastman, a manufacturing subsidiary of Eastman Kodak, to operate the electromagnetic separation plant. By late October 1943, when Stone & Webster finished installing the first Alpha racetrack, the company had assembled a work force of 4,800 men and women. They were trained to run and maintain the calutrons—without knowing why—twenty-four hours a day, seven days a week.

The big square racetrack magnets wrapped with silver windings were encased in boxes of welded steel. Oil that circulated through the boxes was supposed to insulate the windings and carry heat away. The first magnets tested at the end of October leaked electricity. If moisture in the circulating oil was shorting out the coils, the normal heat of operation would correct the problem by evaporating the water. Tennessee Eastman pushed on. Vacuum leaks in the calutron tanks were numerous and hard to find—one supervisor remembers spending most of a month looking for one leak. Inexperienced operators had trouble striking and maintaining a steady ion beam. Groves recalls that the powerful magnets unexpectedly "moved the intervening tanks, which weighed some fourteen tons each, out of position by as much as three inches. . . . The problem was solved by securely welding the tanks into place, using heavy steel tie straps. Once that was done, the tanks stayed where they belonged."

The magnets dried out but continued to short. Something was seriously wrong. Early in December Tennessee Eastman shut the entire 96-tank racetrack down. The company's engineers would have to break open one of the windings and examine it. That was major trauma; the unit must then be returned to Allis-Chalmers and rebuilt.

The inspectors found disaster: two major troubles. "The first lay in the design," writes Groves, "which placed the heavy current-carrying silver bands too close together. The other lay in the excessive amount of rust and other dirt particles in the circulating oil. These bridged the too narrow gap between the silver bands and resulted in shorting." Groves arrived seething from Washington on December 15 to view the remains. The design's inadequacy forced the general to order all forty-eight magnets hauled back to Milwaukee to be cleaned and rebuilt. The second Alpha track would not come on line until mid-January 1944. They would lose at least a month of production.

Tennessee Eastman's 4,800 employees reported for work in the shambles of gloomy halls. Rather than lose them from boredom the company scheduled classes, conferences, lectures, motion pictures, games. Serious men in double-breasted suits scouted the state for chess and checker sets. At the end of 1943 Y-12 was dead in the water with hardly a gram of U235 to show for all its enormous expense.

Gaseous-diffusion research had progressed at Columbia University since John Dunning and Eugene Booth had first demonstrated measurable U235 separation in November 1941. By the spring of 1942 Harold Urey could note in a progress report that "three methods for the separation of the uranium isotopes have now reached the engineering stage. They are the English and the American diffusion methods, and the centrifuge method." With the authorization of the full-scale plant Dunning's staff, which had grown to include about ninety people, increased in early 1943 to 225. Franz Simon's diffusion method would have operated at low gas pressures and in incremental ten-unit stages but required extremely large pumps; Columbia designed a high-pressure system with more conventional pumps, a continuous, interconnected cascade of some four thousand stages. In a postwar memoir Groves reviews the design, which was both reliably simple and expensively tedious:

> The method was completely novel. It was based on the theory that if uranium gas was pumped against a porous barrier, the lighter molecules of the gas, containing U-235, would pass through more rapidly than the heavier U-238 molecules. The heart of the process was, therefore, the barrier, a porous thin metal sheet or membrane with millions of submicroscopic openings per square inch. These sheets were formed into tubes which were enclosed in an airtight vessel, the diffuser. As the gas, uranium hexafluoride, was pumped through a long series, or cascade, of these tubes it tended to separate, the enriched gas moving up the cascade while the depleted moved down. However, there is so little difference in mass between the hexafluoride of U-238 and U-235 that it was impossible to gain much separation in a single diffusion step. That was why there had to be several thousand successive stages.

In schematic cross section the stages looked like this:

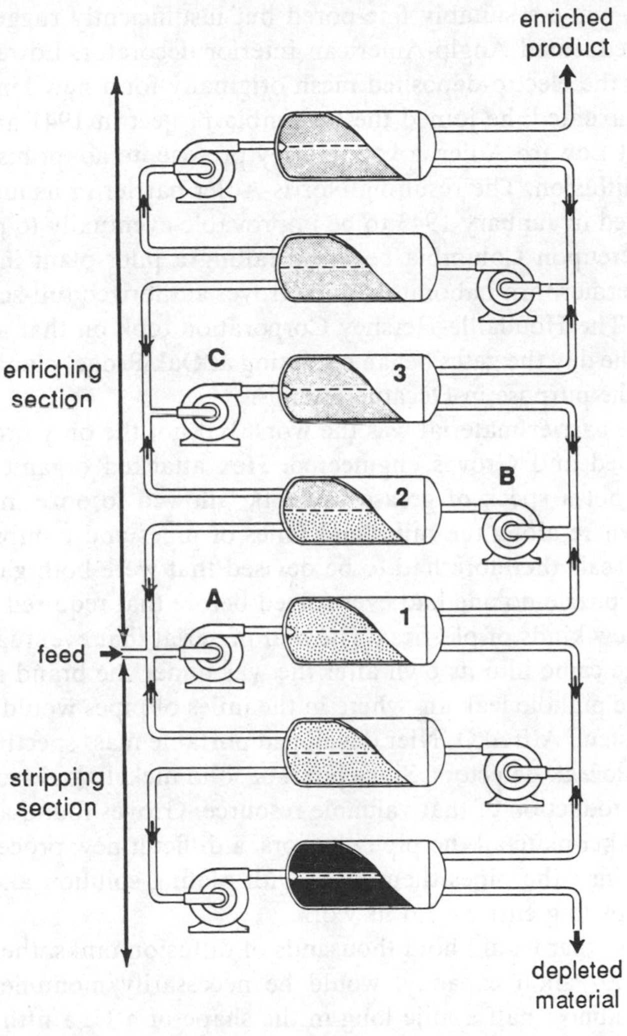

"Further development of barriers is needed," Urey had concluded in his progress report, "but we now feel confident that the problem can be solved." It had not been solved when Groves committed the Manhattan Project to a $100 million gaseous-diffusion plant, however; no practical barrier was yet in hand. The American process required finer-pored material than the British; the material also had to be rugged enough to withstand the higher pressure of the heavy, corrosive gas.

Columbia had been experimenting with copper barriers but abandoned them late in 1942 in favor of nickel, the only common metal that resisted hexafluoride corrosion. Compressed nickel powder made a suitably rugged but insufficiently fine-pored barrier material; electro-deposited nickel mesh made a suitably fine-pored but insufficiently rugged alternative. A self-educated Anglo-American interior decorator, Edward Norris, had devised the electro-deposited mesh originally for a new kind of paint sprayer he invented; he joined the Columbia project in 1941 and worked with chemist Edward Adler, a young Urey protégé, to adapt his invention to gaseous diffusion. The resulting Norris-Adler barrier in its nickel incarnation seemed in January 1943 to be improvable eventually to production quality, whereupon Columbia began installing a pilot plant in the basement of Schermerhorn Laboratory and Groves authorized full-scale barrier production. The Houdaille-Hershey Corporation took on that assignment on April 1, the day the gates began operating at Oak Ridge, planning a new factory for the purpose in Decatur, Illinois.

Suitable barrier material was the worst but not the only problem Columbia studied and Groves engineered. Hex attacked organic materials ferociously: not a speck of grease could be allowed to ooze into the gas stream anywhere along the miles and miles of pipes and pumps and barriers. Pump seals therefore had to be devised that were both gastight and greaseless, a puzzle no one had ever solved before that required the development of new kinds of plastics. (The seal material that eventually served at Oak Ridge came into its own after the war under the brand name Teflon.) A single pinhole leak anywhere in the miles of pipes would confound the entire system; Alfred O. Nier developed portable mass spectrometers to serve as subtle leak detectors. Since pipes of solid nickel would exhaust the entire U.S. production of that valuable resource, Groves found a company willing to nickel-plate all the pipe interiors, a difficult new process accomplished by filling the pipes themselves with plating solution and rotating them as the plating current did its work.

The plant that would hold thousands of diffusion tanks, the largest of them of 1,000 gallon capacity, would be necessarily monumental: four stories high, almost half a mile long in the shape of a U, a fifth of a mile wide, 42.6 acres under roof, some 2 million square feet, more than twice the total ground area of Y-12's Alpha and Beta buildings. K-25, as the gaseous-diffusion complex was designated, needed more than a narrow ridge valley. The building and operating contractors, Kellex and Union Carbide, found a relatively flat site along the Clinch River at the southwestern end of the reservation; the first surveying, for the coal-fired power plant needed to run the factory, began on May 31, 1943.

Rather than designing and setting thousands of different columns for footings the construction contractors leveled and compacted the entire K-

25 foundation area, plowing, drying and moving in the process nearly 100,-000 cubic yards of red clay. That took months; the first concrete—200,000 cubic yards—was not poured until October 21. By then the continuing failure to develop an adequate barrier material had led Groves to decide to lop off the unfinished plant's upper stages and limit its enrichment potential to less than 50 percent U235—it would have been capable of taking natural uranium all the way to pure U235 with its full complement of diffusers—and to use this enriched material to feed the Beta calutrons at Y-12.

Kellex succeeded in devising a promising new barrier material in the autumn of 1943 that combined the best features of the Norris-Adler barrier and the compressed nickel-powder barrier. The problem then was what to do about the Houdaille-Hershey plant under construction in Decatur, which was designed to produce Norris-Adler. Should it be stripped and reequipped to manufacture the new barrier at the price of some delay in starting up K-25? Or should the several barrier-development teams make a final concerted effort to improve Norris-Adler to production quality? Over these significant questions Groves and Harold Urey violently clashed.

Kellex wanted to strip the Houdaille-Hershey plant and convert it, preferring delay to the risk of failure. Urey thought abandoning the Norris-Adler barrier would mean forgoing the production of U235 by gaseous diffusion in time to shorten the war. In which case he saw no reason to continue building K-25; its high priority, he argued, would even hinder the war effort by displacing more immediately useful production.

Groves decided to submit the dispute to an unusual review committee: the experts who had worked on gaseous diffusion in England. With the renewal of interchange between the British and American atomic bomb programs that autumn the British had arranged to send a delegation to work in America. Led by Wallace Akers of ICI, the group included Franz Simon and Rudolf Peierls. It met with both sides—Kellex and Columbia—on December 22 and then settled in to review American progress.

The participants reconvened early in January 1944. The new barrier, the British concluded, would probably be superior eventually to the Norris-Adler, but they thought the months of research on the Norris-Adler must count decisively in its favor if time was of the essence. The new barrier had been manufactured so far only by hand in small batches. Yet K-25 would require acres of it to fill the planned 2,892 stages of the diffusion plant's cascade.

Then Kellex set a trap: it proposed to produce the new barrier by hand by piecework—thousands of workers each duplicating the simple laboratory process Kellex had initially devised—and claimed that by doing so it could match or beat the Norris-Adler production schedule. When the British had recovered from their surprise at the novelty of the proposal they signaled their preference for the new barrier by agreeing that if production was possible it ought to be pursued. That agreement sprang the trap; with the British implicitly committed, the American engineers revealed that they could only manufacture the new barrier by stripping the Houdaille-Hershey plant and forgoing Norris-Adler production entirely.

Groves in any case had already decided, the day before the January meeting, to switch over to the new barrier; the British review then simply ratified his decision. By changing barriers rather than abandoning gaseous diffusion he confirmed what many Manhattan Project scientists had not yet realized: that the commitment of the United States to nuclear weapons development had enlarged from the seemingly urgent but narrow goal of beating the Germans to the bomb. Building a gaseous-diffusion plant that would interfere with conventional war production, would eventually cost half a billion dollars but would almost certainly not contribute significantly to shortening the war meant that nuclear weapons were thenceforth to be counted a permanent addition to the U.S. arsenal. Urey saw the point and withdrew; "from that time forward," write his colleague biographers, "his energies were directed to the control of atomic energy, not its applications."

Twelve days after Enrico Fermi proved the chain reaction in Chicago on December 2, 1942, Groves had assembled a list of criteria for a plutonium production area and definitely and finally ruled out Tennessee. "The Clinton site . . . was not far from Knoxville," he comments, "and while I felt that the possibility of serious danger was small, we could not be absolutely sure; no one knew what might happen, if anything, when a chain reaction was attempted in a large reactor. If because of some unknown and unanticipated factor a reactor were to explode and throw great quantities of highly radioactive materials into the atmosphere when the wind was blowing toward Knoxville, the loss of life and the damage to health in the area might be catastrophic." Such an accident might "wipe out all semblance of security in the project," Groves could imagine, and it might render the electromagnetic and gaseous-diffusion plants "inoperable." Better to site plutonium production somewhere far away.

The production piles needed plentiful electricity and water for blowing and cooling the helium that was planned to cool them. For safety they needed space. Those criteria suggested the great river systems of the Far West, particularly the Columbia River basin. Groves sent out an officer who would administer the plutonium reservation along with the civilian engineer who would supervise construction for Du Pont. Besides picking the site he wanted the two men to get used to working together. They did, agreeing on a promising location in south-central Washington State, and arrived back in Groves' office on New Year's Eve to report. The general received a real estate appraisal on January 21, 1943. By then he had already personally walked the ground.

Eastward of the Cascade Range, twenty air miles east of the city of Yakima, the blue, cold, fast-running Columbia River bends east, then northeast, abruptly ninety degrees southeast and finally due south through a flat, arid scrubland on its last excursion toward the continental interior before it makes its great bend below Pasco to course directly westward two hundred fifty miles to the sea. Even that far inland the river is wide and deep and veined in season with salmon, but the sandy plain surrounding wins little of the river's water and the barrier of the Cascades denies it more than six inches a year of rain.

The site Groves' representatives discovered, and Groves acquired at the end of January at a cost of about $5.1 million, was contained within the eastward excursion of the Columbia: some 500,000 acres, about 780 square miles, devoted primarily to sheep grazing but varied with a few irrigated orchards and vineyards and a farm or two thriving in wartime on irrigated crops of peppermint. Temperatures ranged from a maximum of 114° in the long, dry summers to rare −27° winter lows. Roads were sparse on the roughly circular thirty-mile tract. A Union Pacific railroad line crossed one corner; a double electric power line of 230 kilovolts traversed the northwest sector on its way from Grand Coulee Dam to Bonneville Dam. Gable Mountain, an isolated basalt outcropping that rose five hundred feet above the sedimentary plain a few miles southwest of the ninety-degree river bend, divided the riverside land at the bend from the interior. Midway down the tract where a ferry crossed the Columbia, a half-abandoned riverside village, population about 100, supplied a base of buildings and gave the Hanford Engineer Works its name.

Groves could hardly build Hanford until he knew more about the plant that would go there. It was clear that he would need enormous quantities of concrete to shield the production piles and chemical processing buildings; his Hanford engineer searched out accessible beds of gravel and aggregate to quarry. An accident might release radioactivity into the air; that called for thorough meteorological work. The river water needed study; so did the river's valuable salmon, to see how they would take to mild doses of transient radioactivity from pile discharge flow. Roads had to be paved, power sources tapped, hutments and barracks built for tens of thousands of construction workers.

What had come up once again for discussion early in 1943 was how the plutonium production piles—the Du Pont engineers were beginning to call them *reactors*—should be cooled. Crawford Greenewalt, in charge of plutonium production for Du Pont, continued to plan for helium cooling because the noble gas had no absorption cross section at all for neutrons. But it would need to be pumped through the piles under high pressure; that would require large, powerful compressors Greenewalt was not at all sure he had time to build. Enormous steel tanks would be needed to contain the gas; they would have to allow access to the pile but still remain airtight, a formidable challenge to engineer or even simply to weld.

Eugene Wigner came to the project's rescue. Fermi had found *k* for CP-1 higher than he expected. The Stagg Field pile had been assembled largely from uranium oxide. Its graphite had varied in quality, improving along the way. A production pile of pure uranium metal and high-quality graphite would find *k* higher yet—high enough, Wigner calculated, to make water cooling practical.

Wigner's team designed a 28- by 36-foot graphite cylinder lying on its side and penetrated through its entire length horizontally by more than a thousand aluminum tubes. Two hundred tons of uranium slugs the size of rolls of quarters would fill these tubes. Chain-reacting within 1,200 tons of graphite, the uranium would generate 250,000 kilowatts of heat; cooling water pumped through the aluminum tubes around the uranium slugs at the rate of 75,000 gallons per minute would dissipate that heat. The slugs would not go naked into the torrent; Wigner intended that they also should be separately sheathed in aluminum—canned. When they had burned long enough—100 days—to transmute about 1 atom in every 4,000 into plutonium the irradiated slugs could be pushed out the back of the pile simply by loading fresh slugs in at the front. The hot slugs would fall into a deep pool of pure water that would safely confine their intense but short-lived fission-product radioactivity. After 60 days they could be fished out and carted off for chemical separation.

The Wigner design was elegantly simple. Greenewalt saw engineering problems—in particular the question whether corrosion of the aluminum tubes would block the flow of cooling water—and studied helium and water side by side until the middle of February. Corrosion studies were promising. "With water of high purity," writes Arthur Compton, "the evidence indicated that no serious difficulties from this source should arise." Greenewalt opted then for water cooling. Wigner, whom Leo Szilard calls "the conscience of the Project from its early beginnings to its very end," who worried constantly about German progress, wondered angrily why it had taken Du Pont three months to see the value of a system he and his group had judged superior in the summer of 1942.

With that basic decision construction could begin at Hanford. Three production piles would go up at six-mile intervals along the Columbia River, two upstream and one downstream of its ninety-degree bend. Ten miles south, screened behind Gable Mountain, Du Pont would build four chemical-separation plants paired at two sites. The former town of Hanford would become a central construction camp serving all five construction areas.

The work proceeded slowly, dogged by recruiting problems. The nation at war had moved beyond full employment to severe labor shortages and men and women willing to camp out on godforsaken scrubland far from any major city were hard to find. Frequent sandstorms plagued the area, writes Leona Woods, now Leona Marshall after marrying fellow physicist John Marshall of Fermi's staff. "Local storms were caused by tearing up the desert floor for roads, and construction sites were suffocating. Wind-blown sand covered faces, hair, and hands and got into eyes and teeth. . . . After each storm, the number of people quitting might be as much as twice the average. When the storms were at their worst, buses and other traffic came to a stop until the roads were visible through the grey-black clouds of dust." Stoics who stayed on called the dust "termination powder."

"The most essential thing to bring with you is a padlock," a project recruiting pamphlet ominously announced. "The next important things are towels, coat hangers and a thermos bottle. Don't bring cameras or guns." Hanford, says Marshall, "was a tough town. There was nothing to do after work except fight, with the result that occasionally bodies were found in garbage cans the next morning." Du Pont built saloons with windows hinged for easy tear-gas lobbing. Eventually some 5,000 construction workers struggled in the desert dust and Du Pont built more than two hundred barracks to house them. Meat rationing stopped at the edge of the reservation; there were no meatless Tuesdays in the vast Hanford mess halls, a significant enticement for recruiting. The gray coyotes of the region fed sleek in turn on rabbits killed by cars and trucks driving the new reservation roads.

By August 1943 work had begun on the water-treatment plants for the three piles, capacity sufficient to supply a city of one million people. Du Pont released pile-design drawings in Wilmington, Delaware, on October 4 and the company's engineers staked out the first pile, 100-B, beside the Columbia on October 10. After excavating, reports an official history, "work gangs began to lay the first of 390 tons of structural steel, 17,400 cubic yards of concrete, 50,000 concrete blocks, and 71,000 concrete bricks that went into the pile buildings. Starting with the foundations for the pile and the deep water basins behind it where the irradiated slugs would be collected after discharge, the work crews were well above ground by the end of the year." The forty-foot windowless concrete monolith they were building was hollow, however: installation of B pile would not begin until February 1944.

"There was a large change of scale from the Chicago to the Hanford piles," Laura Fermi remarks. "As Fermi would have put it, they were different animals." So also were Ernest Lawrence's behemoth mass spectrometers and John Dunning's gaseous-diffusion factory with its 5 million barrier tubes. The mighty scale of the works at Clinton and Hanford is a measure of the desperation of the United States to protect itself from the most serious potential threat to its sovereignty it had yet confronted—even though that threat, of a German atomic bomb, proved to be an image in a darkened mirror. It is also a measure of the sheer recalcitrance of heavy-metal isotopes. Niels Bohr had insisted in 1939 that U235 could be separated from U238 only by turning the country into a gigantic factory. "Years later," writes Edward Teller, "when Bohr came to Los Alamos, I was prepared to say, 'You see . . .' But before I could open my mouth, he said, 'You see, I told you it couldn't be done without turning the whole country into a factory. You have done just that.' "

The monumental scale reveals another desperation as well: how ambitiously the nation was moving to claim the prize. And to deny it to others, even to the British until Winston Churchill turned Franklin Roosevelt's head at the conference in Quebec in August 1943, where Operation Overlord, the 1944 invasion of Europe across the beaches of Normandy, was planned. Before then, in June, Groves had demonstrated this last desperation at its most overweening: he proposed to the Military Policy Committee that the United States attempt to acquire total control of all the world's known supplies of uranium ore. When the Union Minière refused to reopen its flooded Shinkolobwe Mine in the Belgian Congo, Groves had to turn to the British, who owned a significant minority interest in the Belgian firm, for help; after Quebec the partnership evolved into an agreement between the two nations known as the Combined Development Trust to search out world supplies. That uranium is common in the crust of the earth to the extent of millions of tons Groves may not have known. In 1943, when the element in useful concentrations was thought to be rare, the general, acting on behalf of the nation to which he gave unquestioning devotion, exercised himself to hoard for his country's exclusive use every last pound. He might as well have tried to hoard the sea.

Work toward an atomic bomb had begun in the USSR in 1939. A thirty-six-year-old nuclear physicist, Igor Kurchatov, the head of a major laboratory since his late twenties, alerted his government then to the possible military significance of nuclear fission. Kurchatov suspected that fission research might be under way already in Nazi Germany. Soviet physicists realized in 1940 that the United States must also be pursuing a program when the names of prominent physicists, chemists, metallurgists and mathematicians disappeared from international journals: secrecy itself gave the secret away.

The German invasion of the USSR in June 1941 temporarily ended what had hardly been begun. "The advance of the enemy turned everyone's thoughts and energies to one single job," writes Academician Igor Golovin, a colleague of Kurchatov and his biographer: "to halt the invasion. Laboratories were deserted. Equipment, instruments and books were packed up, and valuable records shipped east for safety." The invasion rearranged research priorities. Radar now took first place, naval mine detection second, atomic bombs a poor third. Kurchatov moved to Kazan, four hundred miles east of Moscow beyond Gorky, to study defenses against naval mines.

In Kazan at the end of 1941 he heard from George Flerov, one of the two young physicists in his Moscow laboratory who had discovered the spontaneous fission of uranium in 1940 and reported their discovery in a cable to the *Physical Review.** Flerov had attended an international meeting of scientists in Moscow in October and heard Peter Kapitza, Ernest Rutherford's protégé, when asked what scientists could do to help the war effort, respond in part:

> In recent years a new possibility—nuclear energy—has been discovered. Theoretical calculations show that, if a contemporary bomb can for example destroy a whole city block, an atomic bomb, even of small dimensions, if it can be realized, can easily annihilate a great capital city having a few million inhabitants.

Thus recalled to their earlier work, Flerov challenged Kurchatov as he had already in a similar letter challenged the State Defense Committee that "no time must be lost in making a uranium bomb." The first requirement was fast-neutron research, he wrote. The MAUD Report had only just made that necessity clear to the United States.

Kurchatov disagreed. Research toward a uranium weapon seemed too far removed from the immediate necessities of war. But the Soviet government in the meantime had assembled an advisory committee that included Kapitza and the senior Academician Abram Joffe, Kurchatov's mentor. The

* Spontaneous fission, a relatively rare nuclear event, differs from fission caused by neutron bombardment; it occurs without outside stimulus as a natural consequence of the instability of heavy nuclei.

committee endorsed atomic bomb research and recommended Kurchatov to head it. Somewhat reluctantly he accepted.

"So it was that from early 1943 on," writes his colleague A. P. Alexandrov, "work on this difficult problem was resumed in Moscow under the leadership of Igor Kurchatov. Nuclear scientists were recalled from the front, from industry, from the research institutes which had been evacuated to the rear. Auxiliary work began in many places." Auxiliary work included building a cyclotron. Kurchatov moved his institute out of the Soviet capital to an abandoned farm near the Moscow River in the summer of 1943. An artillery range nearby offered an area for explosives testing; "Laboratory No. 2" would be the Soviet Union's Los Alamos. By January 1944 Kurchatov had assembled a staff of only about twenty scientists and thirty support personnel. "Even so," writes Herbert York, "they did experiments and made theoretical calculations concerning the reactions involved in both nuclear weapons and nuclear reactors, they began work designed to lead to the production of suitably pure uranium and graphite, and they studied various possible means for the separation of uranium isotopes." But the Soviet Bear was not yet fully aroused.

"The kind of man that any employer would have fired as a troublemaker." Thus Leslie Groves described Leo Szilard in an off-the-record postwar interview, as if the general had arrived first at fission development and Szilard had only been a hireling. Groves seems to have attributed Szilard's brashness to the fact that he was a Jew. Upon Groves' appointment to the Manhattan Project he almost immediately judged Szilard a menace. They proceeded to fight out their profound disagreements hand to hand.

The heart of the matter was compartmentalization. Alice Kimball Smith, the historian of the atomic scientists whose husband Cyril was associate division leader in charge of metallurgy at Los Alamos, defines the background of the conflict:

> If the Project could have been run on ideas alone, says Wigner, no one but Szilard would have been needed. Szilard's more staid scientific colleagues sometimes had trouble adjusting to his mercurial passage from one solution to another; his army associates were horrified, and to make matters worse, Szilard freely indulged in what he once identified as his favorite hobby—baiting brass hats. General Groves, in particular, had been outraged by Szilard's unabashed view that army compartmentalization rules, which forbade discussion of lines of research that did not immediately impinge on each other, should be ignored in the interests of completing the bomb.

The issue for Szilard was openness within the project to facilitate its work. "There is no way of telling beforehand," he wrote in a 1944 discussion of the problem, "what man is likely to discover and invent a new method which will make the old methods obsolete." The issue for Groves, to the contrary, was security.

At first Szilard bent the rules and Groves threatened him. In late October 1942, while Fermi moved toward building CP-1, Szilard apparently badgered the Du Pont engineers who arrived in Chicago to take over pile design. Arthur Compton saw this activity as obstructive but not necessarily subversive; on October 26 he wired Groves that he had given Szilard two days TO REMOVE BASE OF OPERATIONS TO NEW YORK. ACTION BASED ON EFFICIENT OPERATION OF ORGANIZATION NOT ON RELIABILITY. ANTICIPATE PROBABLE RESIGNATION. Compton did not know his man. Szilard would not resign, for the simple reason that he believed he was needed to help beat Germany to the bomb. Compton proposed surveillance: SUGGEST ARMY FOLLOW HIS MOTIONS BUT NO DRASTIC ACTION NOW. Two days later Compton hurriedly wired Groves to desist: SZILARD SITUATION STABILIZED WITH HIM REMAINING CHICAGO OUT OF CONTACT WITH ENGINEERS. SUGGEST YOU NOT ACT WITHOUT FURTHER CONSULTATION CONANT AND MYSELF.

Groves had prepared drastic action indeed. On the stationery of the Office of the Chief of Engineers, over a signature block reserved for the Secretary of War, he had drafted a letter to the U.S. Attorney General calling Leo Szilard an "enemy alien" and proposing that he "be interned for the duration of the war." Compton's telegram forestalled an ugly arrest and the letter was never signed or sent.

But the incident raised the issue of Szilard's loyalty and prejudiced Groves implacably against him. Szilard responded forthrightly; he assembled a large collection of documents from the 1939–40 period demonstrating his part in carrying the news of fission to Franklin Roosevelt and, pointedly, his efforts to enforce voluntary secrecy among physicists in the United States, Britain and France. Compton, waffling, sent the documents to Groves in mid-November with an implicit endorsement of Szilard's stand. The first Groves-Szilard confrontation thus ended in stalemate. Szilard saw how much raw power Groves commanded. Groves learned how deep were Szilard's roots in the evolution of atomic energy research and perhaps also that men he considered vital to the project—Fermi, Teller, Wigner—were Szilard colleagues of long standing and would have to be taken into account.

As political dissidents have done in the Soviet Union, Szilard embarked next on a careful campaign to negotiate changes by insisting meticulously on the enforcement of his legal rights. His opening sally came December 4, two days after Fermi proved the chain reaction. In a quiet memorandum to Arthur Compton he noted that the official responsible for handling NDRC patents had requested patent applications "for inventions relating to the chain reaction." That raised the question, Szilard wrote, of how to deal with inventions "made and disclosed before we had the benefit of the financial support of the government." He and Fermi would be glad to file a joint application, but only if they could be sure they retained their rights to their earlier separate inventions. The memorandum continues in this straightforward style until its final paragraph, which throws down the gauntlet:

> My present request clearly represents a change of [my] attitude with respect to patents on the uranium work, and I would appreciate an opportunity to explain to you and also to the government agency which may be involved, my reasons for it.

Previously Szilard had believed he would have equal voice in fission development. Since he had now been compartmentalized, his freedom of speech restrained, his loyalty challenged, he was prepared to actuate the only leverage at hand, his legal right to his inventions.

Compton sent Szilard's request to Lyman Briggs, whose responsibilities within the OSRD included patent matters; Briggs thought the Army ought to handle it. Szilard waited until the end of December, heard nothing and advanced further into the field. In a second memorandum he told Compton he wanted to apply for a patent on "the basic inventions which underlie our work on the chain reaction on unseparated uranium . . . which were made before government support for this research was forthcoming." The patent could be registered in his name alone or jointly with Fermi; he would be willing "to assign this patent at this time to the government for such financial compensation as may be deemed fair and equitable." The memorandum mentions no amount; according to Army security files Szilard asked for $750,000. But the issue was not compensation; the issue was representation:

> I wish to take this opportunity to mention that the question of patents was discussed by those who were concerned in 1939 and 1940. At that time it was proposed by the scientists that a government corporation should be formed which would look after the development of this field and . . . be the recipient of the patents. It was assumed that the scientists would have adequate representation within this government owned corporation. . . .
>
> In the absence of such a government owned corporation in which the scientists can exert their influence on the use of funds, I do not now propose to

> assign to the government, without equitable compensation, patents covering the basic inventions.

Burdened by Manhattan Project security, with Du Pont taking over plutonium production and the Army moving hundreds of thousands of cubic yards of earth in unprecedented construction, Leo Szilard was advancing singlehandedly to attempt to extricate the process of decision from governmental restraints and to return it to the hands of the atomic scientists.

Compton understood the extent of the challenge. He sent Szilard's two memoranda directly to Conant, whose office received them on January 11, 1943. "Szilard's case is perhaps unique," Compton wrote the NDRC chairman, "in that for a number of years the development of this project has continuously occupied his primary attention. . . . There is no doubt that he is among the few to whom the United States Government can look for establishing basic claims for invention. The matter is thus one of real importance to our Government."

Before Washington could respond Szilard had to fight off a harassing attack from the flank. It strengthened his resolve. He discovered that a French patent filed originally by Frédéric Joliot's group had been published in Australia and he and Fermi had missed the deadline for filing challenges. Some of their claims overlapped the French work. "This is, I am afraid, an irreparable loss," he told Compton. He had now started writing down his own inventions, he said, and hoped to file a number of patents in the near future. Until he had done so he wanted to be removed from the payroll of the University of Chicago to avoid legal complications. In the meantime he would toil on once again as a free volunteer: "It would not be my intention to interrupt or slow down the work which I am doing in the laboratory at present."

Conant bumped Compton's letter up to Bush, who answered it personally and to the point with Yankee canniness. Inventions scientists made after joining the project belonged to the project, Bush told Compton; unless Szilard had disclosed his previous inventions to the University of Chicago at the time of his employment he had only a very short leg to stand on, if any at all. Genially the OSRD director outlined the proper legal procedure for secret patent filings and then kicked at the leg Szilard had left: "It is my understanding that none of this procedure has been gone through with in the case of Dr. Szilard." Bush either did not understand or chose to misunderstand Szilard's idea of an autonomous organization of scientists to guide nuclear energy development: "I gather that Dr. Szilard is particularly anxious that the proceeds arising from his early activity in invention in this field, if such eventuate, should in some way become available for the furtherance of scientific research." He thought that was admirable, but he also thought it had nothing to do with the government. Nor did he intend that it should.

By the time Bush's letter reached Compton the Met Lab director had gone another round with Szilard. Szilard asked for a raise based upon the value to the project of his inventions. Compton took the position that Szilard had signed over all his rights to his inventions to the government for as long as he was in the government's employ. Szilard would not sign a renewal contract under those terms. Trying to keep him aboard, Compton proposed raising his salary from $550 to $1,000 a month on the basis that the higher level was "comparable with the other original sponsors of this project, Messrs. Fermi and Wigner." That might have been acceptable to Szilard, since it tacitly acknowledged the special worth of the three physicists' participation, including presumably their early inventions, but Compton had to clear it with Conant. Until the arrangement was cleared and a new contract signed Szilard would remain off the payroll.

Compton reported Bush's response to Szilard in late March. There matters stood until early May, when Szilard with restrained exasperation proposed to proceed with filing patent applications. He asked that Groves designate someone to act as his legal adviser. The Army general supplied a Navy captain, Robert A. Lavender, who was attached to the OSRD in Washington, and Szilard met frequently with Lavender in the spring and early summer to discuss his claims.

Somewhere along the way Groves put Szilard under surveillance. The brigadier still harbored the incredible notion that Leo Szilard might be a German agent. The surveillance was already months old in mid-June when the MED's security office suggested discontinuing it. Groves rejected the suggestion out of hand: "The investigation of Szilard should be continued despite the barrenness of the results. One letter or phone call once in three months would be sufficient for the passing of vital information and until we know for certain that he is 100% reliable we cannot entirely disregard this person." He apparently equated disagreement with disloyalty and scaled the ratio of the two conditions directly: anyone who caused him as much pain as Leo Szilard must be a spy. It followed that he ought to be watched.

The surveillance of an innocent but eccentric man makes gumshoe comedy. Szilard traveled to Washington on June 20, 1943, and in preparation for the visit an Army counterintelligence agent reviewed his file:

> The surveillance reports indicate that Subject is of Jewish extraction, has a fondness for delicacies and frequently makes purchases in delicatessen stores, usually eats his breakfast in drug stores and other meals in restaurants, walks

> a great deal when he cannot secure a taxi, usually is shaved in a barber shop, speaks occasionally in a foreign tongue, and associates mostly with people of Jewish extraction. He is inclined to be rather absent minded and eccentric, and will start out a door, turn around and come back, go out on the street without his coat or hat and frequently looks up and down the street as if he were watching for someone or did not know for sure where he wanted to go.

Armed with these profundities a Washington agent observed the Subject arriving at the Wardman Park Hotel at 2030 hours—8:30 P.M.—on June 20 and composed a contemporary portrait:

> Age, 35 or 40 yrs; height, 5′6″; weight, 165 lbs; medium build; florid complexion; bushy brown hair combed straight back and inclined to be curly, slight limp in right leg causing droop in right shoulder and receding forehead. He was wearing brown suit, brown shoes, white shirt, red tie and no hat.

Szilard worked the next morning at the Carnegie Institution with Captain Lavender. Wigner arrived at the Wardman Park for an overnight stay ("Mr. Wigner is approximately 40 years of age, medium build, bald head, Jewish features and was conservatively dressed") and the two Hungarians, both of them presumably with justice on their minds, went off for a tour of the Supreme Court (the cabbie "said that they did not talk in a foreign tongue and there was nothing in their conversation to attract his attention. . . . He said they more or less gave him the impression that they were 'on a lark' "). In the evening they sat "on a bench by the [hotel] tennis courts where both pulled off their coats, rolled up their sleeves and talked in a foreign language for some time."

Wigner checked out early in the morning; Szilard took a cab to the Navy Building at 17th and Constitution Avenue, "entered the reception room . . . and told one of the ladies that he wished to see Commander Lewis Strauss about personal business. He stated that he had an appointment. . . . He also told the lady that he was a friend of Commander Strauss' and was interested in getting into a branch of the Navy." The Naval Research Laboratory had continued work on nuclear power for submarine propulsion independently of the Manhattan Project and that institution may have been the one Szilard had in mind. Or he may have been practicing misdirection. Strauss took him to lunch at the Metropolitan Club and apparently discouraged him from transferring; back at his hotel he wired Gertrud Weiss that he expected to arrive at the King's Crown at 8:30 P.M. and left that afternoon for New York.

Since he worked for Vannevar Bush, Lavender was hardly a disinterested consultant; when he met again with Szilard on July 14 he informed the physicist that his documents "failed to disclose an operable pile," meaning that in his opinion Szilard could not claim a patentable invention. (Ten years after the end of the war Szilard and Fermi won a joint patent for their invention of the nuclear reactor.) Szilard realized then, if not before, that he needed private counsel and asked that an attorney who could act in his behalf be cleared.

The battle was almost decided. Szilard retreated to New York. He negotiated now not only with Lavender but with Army Lieutenant Colonel John Landsdale, Jr., Groves' chief of security. In an October 9 letter to Szilard, Groves summed up the blunt exchange over which the three men bargained: "You were assured [by Lavender and Landsdale] that as soon as you were able to convey full rights [to any inventions made prior to government employment], negotiations would be entered into with a view to acquisition by the Government of any rights you may have and your reemployment on Government contracts. . . . I repeat this assurance." That is, Szilard could trade his patent rights, if any, for the privilege of working to beat the Germans to the bomb.

Groves and Szilard arranged a temporary truce—the general may have imagined it was a surrender—at a meeting in Chicago on December 3. The Army agreed to pay Szilard $15,416.60 to reimburse him for the twenty months when he worked unpaid and out-of-pocket at Columbia and for lawyers' fees.

The general had attempted several times to force Szilard to sign a document promising "not to give any information of any kind relating to the project to any unauthorized person." Szilard had consistently agreed verbally to that restriction and just as consistently refused as a matter of honor to sign. He meant to continue protesting and on January 14, 1944, he began again with a three-page letter to Vannevar Bush. He knew fifteen people, he told Bush, "who at one time or another felt so strongly about [compartmentalization] that they intended to reach the President." The central issue as always was freedom of scientific speech: "Decisions are often clearly recognized as mistakes at the time when they are made by those who are competent to judge, but . . . there is no mechanism by which their collective views would find expression or become a matter of record."

In this letter for the first time Szilard emphasized a purpose to his urgency beyond beating the Germans to the bomb: that the bomb might be used and become grimly known.

> If peace is organized before it has penetrated the public's mind that the potentialities of atomic bombs are a reality, it will be impossible to have a peace that is based on reality. . . . Making some allowances for the further development of the atomic bomb in the next few years . . . this weapon will be so pow-

> erful that there can be no peace if it is simultaneously in the possession of any two powers unless these two powers are bound by an indissoluble political union. . . . It will hardly be possible to get political action along that line unless high efficiency atomic bombs have actually been used in this war and the fact of their destructive power has deeply penetrated the mind of the public.

Which was the explanation Szilard now gave for challenging the Army and Du Pont: "This for me personally is perhaps the main reason for being distressed by what I see happening around me."

Bush insisted in return that all was well. "I feel that the record when this effort is over," he wrote Szilard, "will show clearly that there has never at any time been any bar to the proper expression of opinion by scientists and professional men within their appropriate sphere of activity in this whole project." But he was willing to meet with Szilard if that was what the physicist wanted. In February, preparing for that meeting, Szilard drafted forty-two pages of notes. Much in those notes is specific and local; here and there basic issues are joined.

Since invention is unpredictable, Szilard writes, "the only thing we can do in order to play safe is to encourage sufficiently large groups of scientists to think along those lines and to give them all the basic facts which they need to be encouraged to such activity. This was not done in the past [in the Manhattan Project] and it is not being done at present." He tracked the consequences of the government's policies of restriction:

> The attitude taken toward foreign born scientists in the early stages of this work had far reaching consequences affecting the attitude of the American born scientists. Once the general principle that authority and responsibility should be given to those who had the best knowledge and judgment is abandoned by discriminating against the foreign born scientists, it is not possible to uphold this principle with respect to American born scientists either. If authority is not given to the best men in the field there does not seem to be any compelling reason to give it to the second-best men and one may give it to the third- or fourth- or fifth-best men, whichever of them appears to be the most agreeable on purely subjective grounds.

Wigner's early discouragement was an "incalculable loss," Szilard thought; the fact that Fermi was excluded from centrifuge development work at Columbia "visibly affected" him "and he has from that time on shown a very marked attitude of being always ready to be of service rather than considering it his duty to take the initiative."

Finally, Szilard judged the Met Lab moribund, its services rejected and its spirit broken, and pronounced its epitaph:

> The scientists are annoyed, feel unhappy and incapable of living up to their responsibility which this unexpected turn in the development of physics has thrown into their lap. As a consequence of this, the morale has suffered to the point where it almost amounts to a loss of faith. The scientists shrug their shoulders and go through the motions of performing their duty. They no longer consider the overall success of this work as their responsibility. In the Chicago project the morale of the scientists could almost be plotted in a graph by counting the number of lights burning after dinner in the offices in Eckhart Hall. At present the lights are out.

But Leo Szilard at least was not yet done with protest.

Enrico Fermi took the initiative at least once during the war. Perhaps influenced by the enthusiasm he found at Los Alamos for weapons-making, he proposed at the time of the April 1943 conference—privately to Robert Oppenheimer, it appears—that radioactive fission products bred in a chain-reacting pile might be used to poison the German food supply.

The possibility of using radioactive material bred in a nuclear reactor as a weapon of war had been mentioned by Arthur Compton's National Academy of Sciences committee in 1941. German development of such a weapon began worrying the scientists at the Met Lab late in 1942, on the assumption that Germany might be a year or more ahead of the United States in pile development. If CP-1 went critical in December 1942, they argued, the Germans might have had time by then to run a pile long enough to create fiercely radioactive isotopes that could be mixed with dust or liquid to make radioactive (but not fissionable) bombs. Germany might then logically attempt preemptively to attack the Met Lab, if not American cities. German development of radioactive warfare, another vision in a dark mirror, seemed to the leaders of the Manhattan Project to require countering by examination into parallel U.S. development; the S-1 Committee gave such assignment to a subcommittee consisting of James Bryant Conant as chairman and Arthur Compton and Harold Urey as members. That subcommittee went to work sometime before May 1943, probably before February.

Fermi would have known of the Met Lab discussions. His proposal to Oppenheimer at the April conference was different from those essentially defensive concerns, however, and clearly offensive in intent. He may well have been motivated in part by his scientific conservatism: may have asked himself what recourse was open to the United States if a fast-fission bomb proved impossible—it could not be demonstrated by experiment for at least two years—and have found the answer in the formidable neutron flux of CP-1 and its intended successors. Oppenheimer swore Fermi to intimate secrecy within the larger secrecy of the Manhattan Project; when the Italian laureate returned to Chicago he went quietly to work.

In May Oppenheimer traveled to Washington. Among other duties he reported Fermi's ideas to Groves and learned of the Conant subcommittee. Back at Los Alamos on May 25 he wrote Fermi a warm letter reporting what he had found. He attributed the subcommittee assignment to a request from the Army Chief of Staff, George Marshall, although it seems far likelier that the study originated within the Manhattan Project. "I therefore, with Groves' knowledge and approval, discussed with [Conant] the application [i.e., poisoning German food supplies] which seemed to us so promising."

Oppenheimer had also discussed Fermi's idea with Edward Teller. The isotope the men identified that "appears to offer the highest promise" was strontium, probably strontium 90, which the human body takes up in place of calcium and deposits dangerously and irretrievably in bone. Teller thought that separating the strontium from other pile products "is not a very major problem." Oppenheimer wanted to delay the work until "the latest safe date," he told Fermi further, so that they would have "a much better chance of keeping your plan quiet." He did not even want to include Compton in any immediate discussion. Summarizing, he wrote in part:

> I should recommend delay if that is possible. (In this connection I think that we should not attempt a plan unless we can poison food sufficient to kill a half a million men, since there is no doubt that the actual number affected will, because of non-uniform distribution, be much smaller than this.)

There is no better evidence anywhere in the record of the increasing bloody-mindedness of the Second World War than that Robert Oppenheimer, a man who professed at various times in his life to be dedicated to *Ahimsa* ("the Sanscrit word that means doing no harm or hurt," he explains) could write with enthusiasm of preparations for the mass poisoning of as many as five hundred thousand human beings.

Mid-1943 was in any case a season of great apprehension among the atomic scientists, who saw Nazi Germany beginning to lose the war and sensed that country's desperation. The Manhattan Project expected to produce atomic bombs by early 1945; if Germany had begun fission research in 1939 at similar scale it should have bombs nearly in hand. Hans Bethe and Edward Teller wrote Oppenheimer in a memorandum on August 21:

> Recent reports both through the newspapers and through secret service, have given indications that the Germans may be in possession of a powerful new weapon which is expected to be ready between November and January. There

> seems to be a considerable probability that this new weapon is tubealloy [i.e., uranium]. It is not necessary to describe the probable consequences which would result if this proves to be the case.
>
> It is possible that the Germans will have, by the end of this year, enough material accumulated to make a large number of gadgets which they will release at the same time on England, Russia and this country. In this case there would be little hope for any counter-action. However, it is also possible that they will have a production, let us say, of two gadgets a month. This would place particularly Britain in an extremely serious position but there would be hope for counter-action from our side before the war is lost, provided our own tubealloy program is drastically accelerated in the next few weeks.

The memorandum goes on to criticize the handling of production "entirely by large companies" —the Hungarian threnody Szilard and Wigner also sounded—and to propose a crash program directed by Urey and Fermi to build heavy-water piles. Nothing seems to have come of the Bethe-Teller proposal—Hitler's secret weapons proved to be the V-1 and V-2 rockets then in development at Peenemünde, the first of which crossed the English coast on June 13, 1944—but it captures the mid-war mood.

Less worrisome was radioactive dusting. Conant's subcommittee considered the possibilities and concluded that they were "rather remote." Conant emphasized that he thought it *"extremely* unlikely that a radioactive weapon will be used against the U.S. and unlikely the weapon will be used at all." Groves eventually proposed to George Marshall that a handful of officers be trained in the use of Geiger counters and sent to England to observe. Preparing for the Normandy invasion, Marshall approved.

It was easier for Americans guarded by the wide moat of the Atlantic than for the British to dismiss the possibility of radioactive attack. Sir John Anderson, Chancellor of the Exchequer, a scientist and the member of Churchill's cabinet responsible for the Tube Alloys program, discussed the question with Conant at lunch at the Cosmos Club in Washington in August 1943. He was concerned particularly about German heavy-water production because British scientists believed they had found a way to separate light from heavy water at five times the efficiency of existing processes and feared their German counterparts might have made the same discovery. Heavy water would certainly work to moderate a chain-reacting pile. And such a machine might be used to breed radioactive isotopes for dusting London.

The British therefore kept closer watch on the High Concentration Plant at Vemork in Norway. It had not been damaged beyond repair. To the contrary, intelligence sources reported that summer, it had begun production again in April; German scientists had shipped heavy water from laboratory stocks in Germany to refill the various cells and speed restoration of the cascade.

When Niels Bohr escaped from Stockholm to Scotland on October 6, 1943, he carried with him Werner Heisenberg's drawing of an experimental heavy-water reactor. Bohr met more than once in London that autumn with Sir John Anderson; Anderson matched up Bohr's information with the Conant subcommittee's radioactive-warfare study and the Norwegian underground's news of Vemork's renewed production and concluded that the plant once again urgently required attack. The Nazis had significantly increased security at Vemork, which ruled out another commando raid. After British and American representatives discussed the problem in Washington George Marshall authorized precision bombing.

American Eighth Air Force B-17's climbed northeast from British bases before dawn on the morning of November 16. To minimize Norwegian casualties the aircraft were scheduled to drop their bombs during the Norsk Hydro lunch period, between 11:30 A.M. and noon. No German fighters came up from the defensive airfields of western Norway to delay them and they elected to circle over the North Sea to kill time before penetrating the Scandinavian peninsula. That alerted German flak, which took a limited toll as the bombers crossed the coast. One hundred forty got through to Vemork and released more than seven hundred 500-pound bombs. None hit the aiming point but four destroyed the power station and two damaged the electrolysis unit that supplied hydrogen to the High Concentration Plant, effectively shutting it down.

Abraham Esau of the Reich Research Council decided then to rebuild in Germany. To expedite construction the council planned to dismantle the Vemork plant and remove it to the Reich. The Norwegian underground reported that decision to London. Anderson was less concerned with the plant itself—Germany had only limited hydroelectricity to divert to its operation—than with the heavy water preserved in its cascade. British intelligence asked the Norwegians to keep watch.

Word came by way of clandestine shortwave radio from the Rjukan area on February 9, 1944, that the heavy water would be transported under guard to Germany within a week or two—not enough warning to prepare and drop in a squad of saboteurs. Knut Haukelid, who had spent the past year living on the land and organizing future military operations, was the only trained commando in the area except for the radio operator. He would have to destroy the heavy water alone with whatever amateur help he could assemble.

Haukelid slipped into Rjukan at night and met secretly with the new chief engineer at Vemork, Alf Larsen. Larsen agreed to help and they discussed possible operations. The heavy water, of enrichments varying from 97.6 down to 1.1 percent, would be transferred to some thirty-nine drums labeled potash-lye. "A one-man attack on Vemork," writes Haukelid, "I considered out of the question. . . . The only practical possibility, therefore, was to try to carry out an attack on the transport in one way or another." He and Larsen, joined later by the Vemork transport engineer, considered the various stages of the journey. The drums of water would go by train from Rjukan to the head of Lake Tinnsjö. From there the cars would be run onto a rail ferry to travel the length of the lake, proceeding beyond Tinnsjö again by train to the port where they would be loaded aboard a ship bound for Germany. Blowing up the trains would be difficult and bloody, since they would be crowded with Norwegian passengers; Haukelid finally decided to attempt to sink the ferry, which also carried passengers, into the 1,300-foot lake. The transport engineer agreed to arrange to dispatch the heavy water on a Sunday morning, when the ferry was usually least crowded.

Sabotaging the boat would almost certainly mean the deaths of some of the shipment's German guards, which would call down heavy reprisals in the Tinnsjö area against the Norwegian population. Haukelid radioed London for permission, emphasizing that his engineer compatriots had questioned if the results were worth the reprisals:

> The fact that the Germans were using heavy water for atomic experiments, and that an atomic explosion might possibly be brought about, was a thing we now talked of openly. At Rjukan they doubted very much whether the Germans had come in sight of a solution. They also doubted whether an explosion of the kind could be brought about at all.

The British begged to differ:

> The answer came from London the same day:
>
> "Matter has been considered. It is thought very important that the heavy water shall be destroyed. Hope it can be done without too disastrous results. Send our best wishes for success in the work. Greetings."

So Knut Haukelid laid his plans. He put on workman's clothes, packed his Sten gun into a violin case, identified which ferry would make the run on Sunday, February 20, 1944, the appointed day, and rode it with one eye on his watch. The *Hydro* was flat and bargelike with twin smokestacks jutting up side by side through its boxy superstructure. It reached the deepest part of the lake about thirty minutes after sailing and took twenty minutes then to cross to shallower waters. "We had therefore a margin of twenty minutes in which the explosion must take place." For even such generous leeway Haukelid needed something better than a time fuse: he needed electric detonators and a clock. He visited a Rjukan hardware-store owner at night for the detonators but was suspiciously turned away. One of his local compatriots had better luck. A handyman retired from Norsk Hydro donated one alarm clock to the cause; Alf Larsen supplied a backup. Haukelid modified them so that their hammers struck not bells but contact plates, closing a battery-powered electrical circuit that could fire the detonators.

Months earlier the British had dropped supplies to the Norwegian commando that included sticks of plastic explosive. Haukelid strung the stubby sticks together to make a circumferential loop to cut a hole in the bottom of the ferry. "As the Tinnsjö is narrow, the ferry must sink in less than five minutes, or else it would be possible to beach her. I . . . spent many hours sitting and calculating how large the hole must be for the ferry to sink quickly enough." To test his timing mechanism he hooked up a few spare detonators at his cabin on the mountain above Rjukan after a long night's work, set the alarm for evening and lay down to sleep. The detonators went off on schedule; he bolted bewildered from bed, grabbed the nearest gun and reflexively covered the door. "The timing apparatus seemed to be working properly."

On Saturday Haukelid and a local compatriot, Rolf Sörlie, slipped into Rjukan. It was crowded with German soldiers and SS police. An hour before midnight "Rolf and I went over to the bridge which crossed the river Maan and had a look at our target." The freight cars "had been run up under some lamps, and were guarded. . . . The train was to go at eight next morning, and the ferry was due to leave . . . at ten."

From the bridge the two men slipped to a back street where they met their driver in a car Haukelid had arranged with its owner to steal in the name of the King and return on Sunday morning. The owner had modified the car to run on methane and they were a long hour starting it. They picked up Larsen, who was prepared to escape Norway to avoid arrest after the work was done. He brought a suitcase of valuables and had come directly from a dinner party where he had heard a visiting concert violinist mention plans to leave on the morning ferry and had tried unsuccessfully to convince the musician to stay in the area one more day to sample its excellent skiing. Another Rjukan man also joined them. They drove to the lake well past the middle of the night:

> Armed with Sten guns, pistols and hand-grenades, we crept . . . down toward the ferry. The bitterly cold night set everything creaking and crackling; the ice on the road snapped sharply as we went over it. When we came out on the

> bridge by the ferry station, there was as much noise as if a whole company was on the march.
>
> Rolf and the other Rjukan man were told to cover me while I went on board to reconnoitre. All was quiet there. Was it possible that the Germans had omitted to place a guard at the weakest point in the whole route to the transport?
>
> Hearing voices in the crew's quarters, forward, I stole to the companion[way] and listened. There must be a party going on down there, and a game of poker. The other two followed me on to the deck of the ferry. We went down to the third-class accommodation and found a hatchway leading to the bilges. But before we had got the hatch open we heard steps, and took cover behind the nearest table or chair. The ferry watchman was standing in the doorway.

Haukelid thought fast. "The situation was awkward, but not dangerous." He told the watchman they were escaping the Gestapo and needed a place to hide:

> The watchman immediately showed us the hatchway in the deck, and told us that they had several times had illicit things with them on their trips.
>
> The Rjukan man now proved invaluable. He talked and talked with the watchman, while Rolf and I flung our sacks down under the deck and began to work.
>
> It was an anxious job, and it took time.

Haukelid and Sörlie found themselves standing on the bottom plates of the boat in a foot of cold water. They had to tape the two alarm-clock timers to one of the steel stringers that braced the ferry's hull, attach four electric detonators to the timers, attach high-speed fuses to the loop of plastic explosive, lay the charge of explosive on the bottom plates and then, most dangerously, hook up batteries to detonators and detonators to fuses.

"The charge was placed in the water and concealed. It consisted of nineteen pounds of high explosive laid in the form of a sausage. We laid it forward, so that the rudder and propeller would rise above the surface when water began to come in [to prevent navigating the boat to shallower water]. . . . When the charge exploded, it would blow about eleven square feet out of the ship's side." The sausage was some twelve feet around.

Sörlie went up on deck. Haukelid set his alarms to go off at 10:45 A.M. "Making the last connection was a dangerous job; for an alarm clock is an uncertain instrument, and contact between the hammer and the alarm was avoided by not more than a third of an inch. Thus there was one third of an inch between us and disaster." Everything worked and he finished at 4 A.M.

The Rjukan man had convinced the watchman by then that the escapees he had sheltered needed to return to Rjukan to collect their possessions. Haukelid considered warning their benefactor but decided that might endanger the mission and only thanked him and shook his hand.

Ten minutes from the ferry station Haukelid and Larsen left the car to ski to Kongsberg, forty miles away around the lake, where they would catch a train for the first leg of their escape to Sweden. Sörlie carried a report for London to the clandestine radio. The driver returned the stolen car and he and the Rjukan man strolled home. At Haukelid's suggestion the Norsk Hydro transport engineer had arranged a foolproof alibi: over the weekend doctors at the local hospital operated on him for appendicitis, no questions asked.

With fifty-three people aboard including the concert violinist the *Hydro* sailed on time. Forty-five minutes into the crossing Haukelid's charge of plastic explosive blew the hull. The captain felt the explosion rather than heard it, and though Tinnsjö is landlocked he thought they might have been torpedoed. The bow swamped first as Haukelid had intended; while the passengers and crew struggled to release the lifeboats, the freight cars with their thirty-nine drums of heavy water—162 gallons mixed with 800 gallons of dross—broke loose, rolled overboard and sank like stones. Of passengers and crew twenty-six drowned. The concert violinist slipped high and dry into a lifeboat; when his violin case floated by, someone was kind enough to fish it out for him.

Kurt Diebner of German Army Ordnance counted the full effect on German fission research of the Vemork bombing and the sinking of the *Hydro* in a postwar interview:

> When one considers that right up to the end of the war, in 1945, there was virtually no increase in our heavy-water stocks in Germany . . . it will be seen that it was the elimination of German heavy-water production in Norway that was the main factor in our failure to achieve a self-sustaining atomic reactor before the war ended.

The race to the bomb, such as it was, ended for Germany on a mountain lake in Norway on a cold Sunday morning in February 1944.

Despite Pearl Harbor and the subsequent Japanese sweep across a million square miles of Southeast Asia and the western Pacific, the Pacific theater commanded less attention in the United States in the earlier years of the war than did the European. Partly that neglect was a result of the deliberate national policy that gave priority to Europe. "Europe was Washington's darling," Pacific Fleet Admiral William F. Halsey would write in a memoir, "the South Pacific was only a stepchild." But Americans also found it difficult at first to take seriously an Asian island people who were small in stature and radically different in culture. Reporting from the Solomon Islands east of New Guinea late in 1942, *Time-Life* correspondent John Hersey found the typical U.S. marine "very uneasy about what he feels is Washington's ignorance of the Pacific. Sure, he argues, Hitler has to be beaten, but that doesn't mean we have to go on thinking of the Japs as funny little ring-tailed monkeys." The U.S. Ambassador to Japan at the time of the Pearl Harbor attack, Boston-born Joseph C. Grew, confronted a similar skepticism when he returned from Japanese internment and battled it by traveling the nation lecturing:

> The other day a friend, an intelligent American, said to me: "Of course there must be ups and downs in this war; we can't expect victories every day, but it's merely a question of time before Hitler will go down to defeat before the steadily growing power of the combined air and naval and military forces of the [Allies]—and then, we'll mop up the Japs." Mark well those words, please. "And then we'll mop up the Japs."

Grew thought such bravado ill-advised. "The Japanese have known what we thought of them," he told his audiences— "that they were little fellows physically, that they were imitative, that they were not really very important in the world of men and nations." To the contrary, said Grew, they were "united," "frugal," "fanatical" and "totalitarian" :

> At this very moment, the Japanese feel themselves, man for man, superior to you and to me and to any of our peoples. They admire our technology, they may have a lurking dread of our ultimate superiority of resources, but all too many of them have contempt for us as human beings. . . . The Japanese leaders *do* think that they can and will win. They are counting on our underestimates, on our apparent disunity before—and even during—war, on our unwillingness to sacrifice, to endure, and to fight.

So far Grew's lecture might have been merely exhortation. But he went on to emphasize a phenomenon that Americans fighting in the Pacific were just then beginning to encounter. " 'Victory or death' is no mere slogan for these soldiers," Grew noted. "It is plain, matter-of-fact description of the military policy that controls their forces, from the highest generals to the newest recruits. The man who allows himself to be captured has disgraced himself and his country."

Which was exactly what Marine Major General Alexander A. Vandegrift was finding at the time, late 1942, in the Solomons at Guadalcanal.

"General," he wrote the Marine Commandant in Washington, "I have never heard or read of this kind of fighting. These people refuse to surrender. The wounded will wait until men come up to examine them . . . and blow themselves and the other fellow to death with a hand grenade."

It was frightening. It required a corresponding escalation of violence to combat. John Hersey felt the need to explain:

> A legend has grown up that this young man [i.e., the U.S. marine] is a killer; he takes no prisoners, and gives no quarter. This is partly true, but the reason is not brutality, not just vindictive remembrance of Pearl Harbor. He kills because in the jungle he must, or be killed. This enemy stalks him, and he stalks the enemy as if each were a hunter tracking a bear cat. Quite frequently you hear marines say: "I wish we were fighting against Germans. They are human beings, like us. Fighting against them must be like an athletic performance—matching your skill against someone you know is good. Germans are misled, but at least they react like men. But the Japs are like animals. Against them you have to learn a whole new set of physical reactions. You have to get used to their animal stubbornness and tenacity. They take to the jungle as if they had been bred there, and like some beasts you never see them until they are dead."

As an explanation for unfamiliar behavior, bestiality had the advantage that it made killing a formidable enemy easier emotionally. But it also, by dehumanizing him, made him seem yet more alien and dangerous. So did the other common attribution that evolved during the war to explain Japanese behavior: that the Japanese were fanatics, believers, as Grew had preached, "in the incorruptible certainty of their national cause." The historian William Manchester, a marine at Guadalcanal, argues more objectively from a longer perspective postwar:

> At the time it was impolitic to pay the slightest tribute to the enemy, and Nip determination, their refusal to say die, was commonly attributed to "fanaticism." In retrospect it is indistinguishable from heroism. To call it anything less cheapens the victory, for American valor was necessary to defeat it.

Whether bestiality, fanaticism, or heroism, the refusal of Japanese soldiers to surrender required new tactics and strong stomachs to defeat. In his best-selling 1943 book *Guadalcanal Diary* war correspondent Richard Tregaskis reported those tactics from the first land battles of the Pacific war at Guadalcanal:

> The general summarized the fighting. . . . The toughest job, he said, had been to clean out scores of dugout caves filled with Japs. Each cave, he said, had

> been a fortress in itself, filled with Japs who were determined to resist until they were all killed. The only effective way to finish off these caves, he said, had been to take a charge of dynamite and thrust it down the narrow cave entrance. After that had been done, and the cave blasted, you could go in with a submachine gun and finish off the remaining Japs. . . .
>
> "You've never seen such caves and dungeons," said the general. "There would be thirty or forty Japs in them. And they absolutely refused to come out, except in one or two isolated cases."

The statistics of the Solomons campaign told the same story: of 250 Japanese manning the garrison on Guadalcanal when the marines first landed only three allowed themselves to be taken prisoner; more than 30,000 Japanese shipped in to fight died before the island was secure, compared to 4,123 Americans. Similar patterns obtained elsewhere. The proportion of captured to dead Japanese in the North Burma campaign was 142 to 17,166, about 1:120 when a truism among Western nations is that the loss of one-fourth to one-third of an army—4:1—usually bodes surrender. Paralleling Japanese resistance, Allied losses grew.

As the slow, bloody push up the Pacific toward the Japanese home islands gained momentum through 1943, the question the behavior of Japanese soldiers raised was whether such standards applied not only to the military but to the civilians of Japan as well. Grew had sought to answer that question in his lectures the year before:

> I know Japan; I lived there for ten years. I know the Japanese intimately. The Japanese will not crack. They will not crack morally or psychologically or economically, even when eventual defeat stares them in the face. They will pull in their belts another notch, reduce their rations from a bowl to a half bowl of rice, and fight to the bitter end. Only by utter physical destruction or utter exhaustion of their men and materials can they be defeated. That is the difference between the Germans and the Japanese. That is what we are up against in fighting Japan.

In the meantime the United States manufactured flamethrowers to burn Japanese soldiers from their caves. A seasoned journalist who had traveled in Japan before the war, Henry C. Wolfe, called in *Harper's* for the firebombing of Japan's "inflammable," "matchbox" cities. "It seems brutal to be talking about burning homes," Wolfe explained. "But we are engaged in a life-and-death struggle for national survival, and we are therefore justified in taking any action that will save the lives of American soldiers and sailors. We must strike hard with everything we have at the spot where it will do the most damage to the enemy."

The month Wolfe's call to aerial battle appeared in *Harper's* —January 1943—Franklin Roosevelt met with Winston Churchill at Casablanca. In the course of the meeting the two leaders discussed what terms of surrender they would eventually insist upon; the word "unconditional" was discussed but not included in the official joint statement to be read at the final press conference. Then, on January 24, to Churchill's surprise, Roosevelt inserted the word ad lib: "Peace can come to the world," the President read out to the assembled journalists and newsreel cameras, "only by the total elimination of German and Japanese war power. . . . The elimination of German, Japanese and Italian war power means the unconditional surrender of Germany, Italy, and Japan." Roosevelt later told Harry Hopkins that the surprising and fateful insertion was a consequence of the confusion attending his effort to convince French General Henri Girard to sit down with Free French leader Charles de Gaulle:

> We had so much trouble getting those two French generals together that I thought to myself that this was as difficult as arranging the meeting of Grant and Lee—and then suddenly the Press Conference was on, and Winston and I had had no time to prepare for it, and the thought popped into my mind that they had called Grant "Old Unconditional Surrender," and the next thing I knew I had said it.

Churchill immediately concurred— "Any divergence between us, even by omission, would on such an occasion and at such a time have been damaging or even dangerous to our war effort" —and unconditional surrender became official Allied policy.

16

Revelations

"How would you like to work in America?" James Chadwick asked Otto Frisch in Liverpool one day in November 1943.

"I would like that very much," Frisch remembers responding.

"But then you would have to become a British citizen."

"I would like that even more."

Within a week the British had cleared the Austrian emigré for citizenship. Following instructions "to pack all my necessary belongings into one suitcase and to come to London by the night train" Frisch made the rounds of government offices with other emigré scientists in one crowded day—swearing allegiance to the King, picking up a passport, collecting a visa stamp at the American Embassy—and hurried back to Liverpool, where the delegation would board the converted luxury liner *Andes* the next morning. Headed by Wallace Akers of ICI, the British group included the men General Groves would ask to review barrier development as well as men going to Los Alamos: Frisch, Rudolf Peierls, William G. Penney, George Placzek, P. B. Moon, James L. Tuck, Egon Bretscher and Klaus Fuchs among others. Chadwick would join them, as would the hydrodynamicist Geoffrey Taylor.

Akers maneuvered around the transport shortage by loading them for the Liverpool pier in black mortuary limousines; a hearse for the luggage completed the cortège. On the *Andes* Frisch had an entire eight-berth cabin to himself. Unconvoyed they zigzagged west. America was luxury; traveling up from Newport News Frisch's train stopped in Richmond, Virginia:

> I wandered out into the streets. There I was greeted by a completely incredible spectacle: fruit stalls with pyramids of oranges, illuminated by bright acetylene flares! After England's blackout, and not having seen an orange for a couple of years, that sight was enough to send me into hysterical laughter.

Groves in Washington lectured them on security. A succession of trains delivered them into a fantastic landscape—Frisch and another man in December, the larger group early in 1944—and there in the bright sunlight of a pine-shouldered mesa was Robert Oppenheimer smoking a pipe and shading his close-cropped military haircut with a pork-pie hat: "Welcome to Los Alamos, and who the devil are you?"

They were Churchill's flying wedge. The bomb had been theirs to begin with as much as anybody's, but more immediate urgencies had demanded their attention and now they were couriers sent along to help build it and then to bring it home. America was giving the bomb away to another sovereign state, proliferating. Churchill had negotiated the renewed collaboration at Quebec in August:

> It is agreed between us
>
> First, that we will never use this agency against each other.
>
> Secondly, that we will not use it against third parties without each other's consent.
>
> Thirdly, that we will not either of us communicate any information about Tube Alloys to third parties except by mutual consent.

Niels Bohr and his son Aage followed next as consultant to the Tube Alloys directorate and junior scientific officer, respectively; the British were paying their salaries. Groves' security men met father and son at dockside, assigned them cover names—Nicholas and James Baker—and spirited them off to a hotel, there to discover NIELS BOHR stenciled bold and black on the Danish laureate's luggage. At Los Alamos, warmly welcomed, Nicholas and James Baker became Uncle Nick and Jim.

The first order of business was Heisenberg's drawing of a heavy-water reactor, which Bohr had previously revealed to Groves. Oppenheimer convened a conference of experts on the last day of 1943 to see if they could find any new reason to believe a pile might serve as a weapon. "It was clearly a drawing of a reactor," Bethe recalled after the war, "but when we saw it our conclusion was that these Germans were totally crazy—did they want to throw a reactor down on London?" That was not Heisenberg's purpose, but Bohr wanted to be sure. Bethe and Teller prepared the consequent report, "Explosion of an inhomogeneous uranium–heavy water pile." It found that such an explosion "will liberate energies which are probably smaller, and certainly not much larger, than those obtainable by the explosion of an equal mass of TNT."

If Heisenberg's drawing told the physicists anything it ought to have told them that the Germans were far behind; it depicted sheets of uranium rather than lumps, an inefficient arrangement Heisenberg had clung to for a time even when his colleagues had argued the advantages of a three-dimensional lattice. Samuel Goudsmit, a Dutch physicist in America who would soon lead a front-line Manhattan Project intelligence mission into Germany, remembers a more convoluted conclusion: "At that time we thought this meant simply that they had succeeded in keeping their real aims secret, even from a scientist as wise as Bohr."

Oppenheimer appreciated the salutary effect of Bohr's presence. "Bohr at Los Alamos was marvelous," he told an audience of scientists after the war. "He took a very lively technical interest. . . . But his real function, I think for almost all of us, was not the technical one." Here two texts of the postwar lecture diverge; both versions illuminate Oppenheimer's state of mind in 1944 as he remembered it. In unedited transcript he said Bohr "made the enterprise which looked so macabre seem hopeful" ; edited, that sentence became: "He made the enterprise seem hopeful, when many were not free of misgiving."

How Bohr did so Oppenheimer and even Bohr had work to explain. Oppenheimer outlines an explanation in his lecture:

> Bohr spoke with contempt of Hitler, who with a few hundred tanks and planes had tried to enslave Europe for a millennium. He said nothing like that would ever happen again; and his own high hope that the outcome would be good, and that in this the role of objectivity, the cooperation which he had experienced among scientists would play a helpful part; all this, all of us wanted very much to believe.

"He said nothing like that would ever happen again" is a key; Austrian emigré theoretician Victor Weisskopf supplies another:

> In Los Alamos we were working on something which is perhaps the most questionable, the most problematic thing a scientist can be faced with. At that time physics, our beloved science, was pushed into the most cruel part of reality and we had to live it through. We were, most of us at least, young and somewhat inexperienced in human affairs, I would say. But suddenly in the midst of it, Bohr appeared in Los Alamos.

> It was the first time we became aware of the sense in all these terrible things, because Bohr right away participated not only in the work, but in our discussions. Every great and deep difficulty bears in itself its own solution. . . . This we learned from him.

"They didn't need my help in making the atom bomb," Bohr later told a friend. He was there to another purpose. He had left his wife and children and work and traveled in loneliness to America for the same reason he had hurried to Stockholm in a dark time to see the King: to bear witness, to clarify, to win change, finally to rescue. His revelation—which was equivalent, as Oppenheimer said, to his revelation when he learned of Rutherford's discovery of the nucleus—was a vision of the complementarity of the bomb. In London and at Los Alamos Bohr was working out its revolutionary consequences. He meant now to communicate his revelation to the heads of state who might act on it: to Franklin Roosevelt and Winston Churchill first of all.

In December, before he first went out to Los Alamos, at a small reception at the Danish Embassy in Washington where he and Aage lived when they visited that city, Bohr had renewed his acquaintance with Supreme Court Associate Justice Felix Frankfurter. The justice was short, crackling, bright, Vienna-born, an agnostic Zionist Jew, an ardent patriot, a close friend of Franklin Roosevelt and one of the President's longtime advisers. Bohr had met him in England in 1933 in connection with the rescue of the emigré academics; when Bohr visited Washington in 1939, the year Frankfurter was elevated to the Court, the two men developed what Frankfurter calls a "warm friendly relation." The December tea offered no opportunity to talk privately, but on his way out Frankfurter proposed to invite Bohr to lunch in chambers at the Supreme Court. He already understood that something was up.

The justice was three years older than the physicist, born in 1882, the same year as Roosevelt. He had emigrated to the United States with his family in 1894, grown up on New York's Lower East Side, graduated at nineteen from the City College of New York and made a brilliant showing at Harvard Law. He worked for Henry Stimson when Stimson was U.S. Attorney for the Southern District of New York, before the Great War, and in Washington when Stimson served as Secretary of War the first time, under William Howard Taft. Harvard invited Frankfurter to a professorship at its law school in 1914. He held that post until Roosevelt appointed him to the Supreme Court, but he was intensely active politically across those academic years, a one-man recruiting agency for the New Deal, a loyal friend who supported Roosevelt's ill-advised 1937 scheme to pack the Court to overwhelm its conservative resistance to his innovative legislation.

After Bohr returned to Washington from Los Alamos, in mid-February, the two men kept their appointment for lunch. Both left wartime memoranda describing the meeting. "We talked about the recent events in Denmark," Frankfurter writes, "the probable course of the war, the state of England . . . our certainty of German defeat and what lay ahead. Professor Bohr never remotely hinted the purpose of his visit to this country."

Fortunately Frankfurter had heard about the project he called X. He says he heard from "some distinguished American scientists," but he certainly heard from a distraught young Met Lab scientist who had penetrated all the way to Frankfurter and Eleanor Roosevelt in 1943 with complaints about Du Pont. "I had thus become aware of X—aware, that is, that there was such a thing as X and of its significance." Since Frankfurter knew Bohr's field he assumed X was the reason for Bohr's visit:

> And so . . . I made a very oblique reference to X so that if I was right in my assumption that Professor Bohr was sharing in it, he would know that I knew something about it. . . . He likewise replied in an innocent remote way, but it soon became clear to both of us that two such persons, who had been so long and so deeply preoccupied with the menace of Hitlerism and who were so deeply engaged in the common cause, could talk about the implications of X without either of us making any disclosure to the other.

Eminent jurist and eminent physicist thus easily dispatched that modest obstacle.

"Professor Bohr then expressed to me," Frankfurter goes on, "his conviction that X might be one of the greatest boons to mankind or might become the greatest disaster . . . and he made it clear to me that there was not a soul in this country with whom he could or did talk about these things except Lord Halifax [the British ambassador] and Sir Ronald Campbell [a British representative on the Anglo-American Combined Policy Committee]." Bohr picks up the narrative in third-person voice: "On hearing this F said that, knowing President Roosevelt, he was confident that the President would be very responsive to such ideas as B outlined."

Bohr had found his go-between. "B met F again one of the last days of March," Bohr records in his wartime memorandum, "and learned that in the meantime F had had occasion to speak with the President and that the President shared the hope that the project might bring about a turning point in history." Frankfurter describes his meeting with Roosevelt:

> On this particular occasion I was with the President for about an hour and a half and practically all of it was consumed by this subject. He told me the whole thing "worried him to death" (I remember the phrase vividly), and he

> was very eager for all of the help he could have in dealing with the problem. He said he would like to see Professor Bohr and asked me whether I would arrange it. When I suggested to him that the solution of this problem might be more important than all the schemes for a world organization, he agreed and authorized me to tell Professor Bohr that he, Bohr, might tell our friends in London that the President was most eager to explore the proper safeguards in relation to X.

Much controversy surrounds this meeting, because Roosevelt later implicitly repudiated it. Why, if the President was worried to death about the postwar implications of the bomb, did he entrust a mission to the British to so informal an arrangement? He had not even met Niels Bohr. An answer to this question would answer a more substantive question: whether Roosevelt was in fact interested in exploring ideas of international control or whether he was already committed to perpetuating an Anglo-American monopoly (the Quebec Agreement implied commitment, and he had recently discussed cornering the world uranium and thorium markets with Groves and Bush).

Why did Roosevelt entrust so important a mission to Bohr? In fact, the commission worked the other way around: Bohr had come to the United States representing the British, representing at least Sir John Anderson, who had encouraged his visit as much to promote discussing the issues Bohr had raised as to bolster the British Los Alamos mission. If the commission was informal it was no more so than any number of other back-channel arrangements between the British and the Americans. Roosevelt simply responded to what he took to be a British approach. He seems to have assumed—correctly—that British statesmen around Churchill were using Bohr to communicate to the President ideas about wartime and postwar arrangements to which Churchill was not yet committed. He responded candidly with loyalty to his British counterpart, Bohr adds: "F also informed B that as soon as the question had been brought up, the President had said it was a matter for Prime Minister Churchill and himself to find the best ways of handling the project to the benefit of all mankind, and that he should heartily welcome any suggestion to this purpose from the Prime Minister." The President would be happy to discuss new ideas for postwar relations, but the British would first have to convince the P.M. ; Roosevelt would not deal behind Churchill's back. Frankfurter implies this understanding: "I wrote out such a formula for Bohr to take to London—a communication to Sir John Anderson, who was apparently Bohr's connecting link with the British government."

Complicating Bohr's discussions, in March and later, was the question of what to do about the USSR. Bohr considered the question in the following perspective. Tell the Soviet Union soon, before the first bombs were nearly built, that a bomb project was under way, and the confidence might lead to negotiations on postwar arms control. Let the Soviet Union discover the information on its own, build the bombs and drop them, oppose the Soviets at the end of the war with an Anglo-American nuclear monopoly, and the likeliest outcome was a nuclear arms race.

Bohr's revelation of the complementarity of the bomb was far more fundamental than this contemporary political question. But the contemporary political question was an aspect of the larger issue and partly obscured it from view. The bomb was opportunity and threat and would always be opportunity and threat—that was the peculiar, paradoxical hopefulness. But political conditions would necessarily differ before and after it was deployed.

At the end of March 1944, Bohr seemingly had a mandate from the President of the United States to talk to the Prime Minister of Great Britain. The British in whom Bohr had been confiding were properly impressed. "Halifax considered this development to be so important," writes Aage Bohr, "that he thought my father should go to London immediately." Father and son crossed the Atlantic again, this time by military aircraft, in early April.

Anderson had been working to soften Churchill up. The tall, dark Chancellor of the Exchequer, whom Oppenheimer describes as a "conservative, dour, remarkably sweet man," sent the Prime Minister a long memorandum on March 21. He suggested opening Tube Alloys to wider discussion within the British government. Echoing Bohr, he saw the possibility of international proliferation of nuclear weapons after the war. He thought the only alternative to a vicious arms race was international agreement. He proposed "communicating to the Russians in the near future the bare fact that we expected, by a given date, to have this devastating weapon; and . . . inviting them to collaborate with us in preparing a scheme for international control."

Churchill circled "collaborate" and wrote in the margin: "on no account."

When Bohr arrived Anderson wrote the Prime Minister again, going over the same arguments but adding that he now believed Roosevelt was attending the subject and would welcome discussion. He even supplied a draft message Churchill might send to initiate an exchange. The response was equally waspish: "I do not think any such telegram is necessary nor do I wish to widen the circle who are informed."

Churchill was in no mood to see Bohr; the Danish laureate cooled his heels for weeks. While he waited he heard from the Soviets. Peter Kapitza had written Bohr shortly after the Bohrs escaped from Denmark—the letter found its way from Stockholm to the Soviet Embassy in London— "to let you know that you will be welcome to the Soviet Union where everything will be done to give you and your family a shelter and where we now have all the necessary conditions for carrying on scientific work." After alerting the Tube Alloys security officer Bohr went to the embassy in Kensington Gardens to collect the letter; on his return he reported his conversation with the embassy's counsellor. Amid much talk about the greatness of Russian science and how few friends Russia had counted before the war was the heart of the matter:

> The Counsellor then said that he knew that B had recently been to America, and B said that he had received from the journey many encouraging expressions of the wish for international cultural co-operation and that he hoped soon to come to Russia also. The Counsellor next asked what information B had received about the work of American scientists during the war, and B answered that the American scientists, just like the Russian and the British, had surely made very large contributions to the war effort which would no doubt be of great importance for an appreciation of science everywhere after the war. B thereafter told a little about the situation in Denmark during the occupation.

Quickly changing the subject. But for Bohr the blunt question and Kapitza's invitation to come to Moscow were enough to indicate that the Soviets had at least an inkling of the bomb project and might be working on their own. Which meant there was very little time left to convince them that a secret arms race had not already begun. He carried that urgency with him when he was called with Cherwell, finally, on May 16, to 10 Downing Street.

"We came to London full of hopes and expectations," Aage Bohr remembers. "It was, of course, a rather novel situation that a scientist should thus try to intervene in world politics, but it was hoped that Churchill, who possessed such imagination and who had often shown such great vision, would be inspired by the new prospects." Niels Bohr cherished that hope. His British friends had not prepared him.

"One of the blackest comedies of the war," C. P. Snow characterizes the disastrous confrontation. The definitive account is from R. V. Jones, Cherwell's protégé, who had helped make arrangements and who was surprised to find Bohr wandering a few hours later in Old Queen Street outside the Tube Alloys office:

> When I asked him how the meeting had gone he said: "It was terrible. He scolded us like two schoolboys!" From what he told me at that time and af-

> terwards, it appeared that the meeting misfired from the start. Churchill was in a bad mood, and he berated Cherwell for not having arranged the interview in a more regular manner. He then said he knew why Cherwell had done it—it was to reproach him about the Quebec Agreement. This, of course, was quite untrue, but it meant that Bohr's "set piece" talk was thrown right out of gear. Bohr, who used to say that accuracy and clarity were complementary (and so a short statement could never be precise), was not easy to hear, and all that Churchill seemed to gather was that he was worried about the likely state of the post-war world and that he wanted to tell the Russians about the progress towards the bomb. As regards the post-war world Churchill told him: "I cannot see what you are talking about. After all this new bomb is just going to be bigger than our present bombs. It involves no difference in the principles of war. And as for any post-war problems there are none that cannot be amicably settled between me and my friend, President Roosevelt."

Bohr got only the bare thirty minutes of his scheduled appointment, most of which Churchill had monopolized. "As he was leaving," Aage Bohr concludes, "my father asked for permission to write Churchill, whereupon the latter answered, 'It will be an honour for me to receive a letter from you,' adding, 'but not about politics!' "

"We did not speak the same language," Bohr said afterward. His son found him "somewhat downcast." He was angrier than that; in his seventy-second year, still stinging, he told an old friend: "It was terrible that no one over there" —England and America both— "had worked on the solution of the problems that would arise when it became possible to release nuclear energy; they were completely unprepared." And further, "It was perfectly absurd to believe that the Russians cannot do what others can. . . . There never was any secret about nuclear energy."

Churchill's obduracy was compound but straightforward. He was up to his neck in preparations for the Normandy invasion; he sniffed conspirators encroaching back-channel and instinctively swatted them down; he resented the awe his colleagues accorded this certified great man ("I did not like the man when you showed him to me, with his hair all over his head, at Downing Street," he gnawed at Cherwell afterward); he could not listen carefully enough, or was too certain of his own opinions, to be convinced that the bomb would change the rules. A year later the seventy-year-old Prime Minister had budged no further. "In all the circumstances," he wrote Anthony Eden in 1945, "our policy should be to keep the matter so far as we can control it in American and British hands and leave the French and Russians to do what they can. You can be quite sure that any power that gets hold of the secret will try to make the article and this touches the existence of human society. This matter is out of all relation to anything else that exists in the world, and I could not think of participating in any disclosure to third or fourth parties at the present time."

"He had always had a naive faith in 'secrets,' " concludes C. P. Snow. "He had been told by the best authorities that this 'secret' wasn't keepable and that the Soviets would soon have the bomb themselves. Perhaps, with one of his surges of romantic optimism, he deluded himself into not believing it. He was only too conscious that British power, and his own, was now just a vestige. So long as the Americans and British had the bomb in sole possession, he could feel that that power hadn't altogether slipped away. It is a sad story."

Bohr wrote Churchill on May 22; the letter was circumspect but political after all and conveyed what he had not been allowed to convey at the meeting: "that the President is deeply concerned in his own mind with the stupendous consequences of the project, in which he sees grave dangers, but also unique opportunities." Bohr did not spell out these opportunities. He even seemed to step back from offering advice: "The responsibility for handling the situation rests, of course, with the statesmen alone. The scientists who are brought into confidence can only offer the statesmen all such information about technical matters as may be of importance for their decisions." Those technical matters, however, Bohr made sure to note, included the probability of proliferation and of bigger bombs—he had learned of the Super at Los Alamos.

Apparently Churchill did not trouble himself to respond.

Bohr stayed on in London for several more weeks. He was thus on hand for D-Day, Tuesday, June 6, 1944. "The greatest amphibious assault ever attempted," Dwight D. Eisenhower, the Supreme Allied Commander, called that invasion of Europe across the English Channel with an initial force of 156,000 British, Canadian and American soldiers supported by 1,200 warships, 1,500 tanks and 12,000 aircraft. By the time Bohr and his son left England at the end of the week to return to the United States the Allies had secured the invasion beaches and begun advancing inland with a force bolstered now to 326,000 men. "The way home," Eisenhower instructed his armies, "is via Berlin."

For Bohr the way home was via Washington. He reported his dismal experience with Churchill to Felix Frankfurter on June 18. Frankfurter immediately carried the news to Roosevelt, who was amused to hear another tale of Churchillian pugnacity:

> About a week later F told B that this information had been heartily welcomed by the President who had said that he regarded the steps taken as a favourable development. During the talk the President had expressed the wish to see B,

> and as a preliminary step F advised B to give an account of his views in a brief memorandum.

The Bohrs turned to the task as Washington steamed, the last days of June and the first days of July dawning in the high eighties and sweltering above 100° by afternoon. Aage Bohr recalls the document's preparation:

> It was worked out in the tropical heat of Washington and, like all my father's work, underwent many stages before it was ready for delivery. In the morning, my father would usually bring up new ideas for alterations that he had thought out during the night. There was no secretary to whom we could entrust such documents, and therefore I typed them; meanwhile my father darned socks and sewed buttons on for us, a job which he carried out with his usual thoroughness and manual skill.

Sewing on buttons, darning socks, suffering in the heat that seemed equatorial to a Dane of the cold North Sea, Bohr worked and reworked his memorandum to maximum generality of expression, a political analysis as reserved as any scientific paper. It says all that he had seen up to that time, which was almost everything essential.

Late in life Bohr explained the starting point of his revelation in a single phrase. "*We are in a completely new situation that cannot be resolved by war,*" he confided to a friend. He had already grasped that fundamental point when he arrived at Los Alamos in 1943 and told Oppenheimer that nothing like Hitler's attempt to enslave Europe would ever happen again. "First of all," Oppenheimer confirms, "[Bohr] was clear that if it worked, this development was going to bring an enormous change in the situation of the world, in the whole situation of war and the tolerability of war."

The weapon devised as an instrument of major war would end major war. It was hardly a weapon at all, the memorandum Bohr was writing in sweltering Washington emphasized; it was "a far deeper interference with the natural course of events than anything ever before attempted" and it would "completely change all future conditions of warfare." When nuclear weapons spread to other countries, as they certainly would, no one would be able any longer to *win.* A spasm of mutual destruction would be possible. But not war.

That was new ground, ground the nations had never walked before. It was new as Rutherford's nucleus had been new and unexplored. Bohr had searched the forbidding territory of the atom when he was young and discovered multiple structures of paradox; now he searched it again by the dark light of the energy it released and discovered profound political change.

Nations existed in a condition of international anarchy. No hierarchical authority defined their relations with one another. They negotiated voluntarily as self-interest moved them and took what they could get. War had been their final negotiation, brutally resolving their worst disputes.

Now an ultimate power had appeared. If Churchill failed to recognize it he did so because it was not a battle cry or a treaty or a committee of men. It was more like a god descending to the stage in a gilded car. It was a mechanism that nations could build and multiply that harnessed unlimited energy, a mechanism that many nations *would* build in self-defense as soon as they learned of its existence and acquired the technical means. It would seem to confer security upon its builders, but because there would be no sure protection against so powerful and portable a mechanism, in the course of time each additional unit added to the stockpiles would *decrease* security by adding to the general threat until insecurity finally revealed itself to be total at every hand.

By the necessity, commonly understood, to avoid triggering a nuclear holocaust, the *deus ex machina* would have accomplished then what men and nations had been unable to accomplish by negotiation or by conquest: the abolition of major war. Total security would be indistinguishable from total insecurity. A menacing standoff would be maintained suspiciously, precariously, at the brink of annihilation. Before the bomb, international relations had swung between war and peace. After the bomb, major war among nuclear powers would be self-defeating. No one could win. World war thus revealed itself to be historical, not universal, a manifestation of destructive technologies of limited scale. Its time would soon be past. The pendulum now would swing wider: between peace and national suicide; between peace and total death.

Bohr saw that far ahead—all the way to the present, when menacing standoff has been achieved and maintained for decades without formal agreement but at the price of smaller client wars and holocaustal nightmare and a good share of the wealth of nations—and stepped back. He wondered if such apocalyptic precariousness was necessary. He wondered if the war-weary statesmen of the day, taught the consequences of his revelation, could be induced to forestall those consequences, to adjourn the game when the stalemate revealed itself rather than illogically to play out the menacing later moves. It was clear at least that the new weapons would be appallingly dangerous. If the statesmen could be brought to understand that the danger of such weapons would be common and mutual, might they not negotiate commonly and mutually to ban them? If the end would be a warless world either way, but one way with the holocaustal machinery in place and the other way with its threat only considered and understood, what did they have to lose? Negotiating peace rather than allowing the *deus ex machina* inhumanly to impose standoff might show the common threat to contain within itself, complementarily, common promise. Much good might follow. *"It appeared to me,"* Bohr wrote in 1950 of his lonely wartime initiative, *"that the very necessity of a concerted effort to forestall such ominous threats to civilization would offer quite unique opportunities to bridge international divergencies."* That, in a single sentence, was the revelation of the complementarity of the bomb.

"Much thought has naturally been given to the question of [arms] control," Bohr flattered Franklin Roosevelt in his 1944 document, knowing that hardly any thought had yet been given, "but the further the exploration of the scientific problems concerned is proceeding" —to thermonuclear weapons, Bohr means— "the clearer it becomes that no kind of customary measures will suffice for this purpose and that especially the terrifying prospect of a future competition between nations about a weapon of such formidable character can only be avoided through a universal agreement in true confidence."

Bohr was no fool. Obviously no nation could be expected to trust another nation's bare word about something so vital to survival. Each would want to see for itself that the other was not secretly building bombs. That meant the world would have to open up. He knew very well how suspicious the Soviet Union would be of such an idea; he hoped, however, that the dangers of a nuclear arms race might appear serious enough to make evident the compensating advantages:

> The prevention of a competition prepared in secrecy will therefore demand such concessions regarding exchange of information and openness about industrial efforts including military preparations as would hardly be conceivable unless at the same time all partners were assured of a compensating guarantee of common security against dangers of unprecedented acuteness.

Nor was the urge to suspicious secrecy unique to the Soviets; the Americans and the British were even then risking an arms race by keeping their work on the atomic bomb secret from their Soviet allies. Oppenheimer elaborates:

> [Bohr] was clear that one could not have an effective control of . . . atomic energy . . . without a very open world; and he made this quite absolute. He thought that one would have to have privacy, for he needed privacy, as we all do; we have to make mistakes and be charged with them only from time to time. One would have to have respect for individual quiet, and for the quiet process of government and management; but in principle everything that

might be a threat to the security of the world would have to be open to the world.

Openness would accomplish more than forestalling an arms race. As it did in science, it would reveal error and expose abuse. Men performed in secrecy, behind closed doors and guarded borders and silenced printing presses, what they were ashamed or afraid to reveal to the world. Bohr talked to George Marshall after the war, when the Chief of Staff had advanced to Secretary of State. "What it would mean," he told him, "if the whole picture of social conditions in every country were open for judgment and comparison, need hardly be enlarged upon." The great and deep difficulty that contained within itself its own solution was not, finally, the bomb. It was the inequality of men and nations. The bomb in its ultimate manifestation, nuclear holocaust, would eliminate that inequality by destroying rich and poor, democratic and totalitarian alike in one final apocalypse. It followed complementarily that the opening up of the world necessary to prevent (or reverse) an arms race would also progressively expose and alleviate inequality, but in the direction of life, not death:

> Within any community it is only possible for the citizens to strive together for common welfare on the basis of public knowledge of the general conditions of the country. Likewise, real co-operation between nations on problems of common concern presupposes free access to all information of importance for their relations. Any argument for upholding barriers of information and intercourse, based on concern for national ideals or interests, must be weighed against the beneficial effects of common enlightenment and the relieved tension resulting from such openness.

That statement, from an open letter Bohr wrote to the United Nations in 1950, is preceded by another, a vision of a world evolved to the relative harmony of the nations of Scandinavia that once confronted each other and the rest of Europe as aggressively and menacingly as the Soviet Union and the United States had come by 1950 to do. Notice that Bohr does not propose a world government of centralized authority but a consortium: "An open world where each nation can assert itself solely by the extent to which it can contribute to the common culture and is able to help others with experience and resources must be the goal to put above everything else." And most generally and profoundly: "The very fact that knowledge is itself the basis for civilization points directly to openness as the way to overcome the present crisis."

Such an effort would begin with the United States, Bohr suggested to Roosevelt in the summer of 1944, because the United States had achieved clear advantage: "The present situation would seem to offer a most favourable opportunity for an early initiative from the side which by good fortune has achieved a lead in the efforts of mastering mighty forces of nature hitherto beyond human reach." Concessions would demonstrate goodwill; "indeed, it would appear that only when the question is taken up . . . of what concessions the various powers are prepared to make as their contribution to an adequate control arrangement, [will it] be possible for any one of the partners to assure themselves of the sincerity of the intentions of the others."

The untitled memorandum Bohr prepared for Franklin Roosevelt in Washington in 1944 went to Felix Frankfurter for review on July 5 along with a cover letter apologizing for its inadequacies. Bohr worried through the hot night and composed another apology the next day: "I have had serious anxieties," he confided, "that [the memorandum] may not correspond to your expectations and perhaps not at all be suited for the purpose." Frankfurter had the good sense to recognize the document's merit—it is still the only comprehensive and realistic charter for a postnuclear world—and about a week later told Bohr he had handed it to the President. Bohr and his son left Washington soon after, on a Friday in mid-July, to work at Los Alamos, understanding that Roosevelt would arrange a meeting in good time.

That time came in August as the President prepared to meet the Prime Minister in Quebec. Bohr returned to the U.S. capital; "on August 26th at 5 p.m.," he writes, "B was received by the President in the White House in a completely private manner." Roosevelt "was very cordial and in excellent spirits," says Aage Bohr, as well he might have been after the rapid advances of the Allied armies across Europe. He had read Bohr's memorandum; he "most kindly gave B an opportunity to explain his views and spoke in a very frank and encouraging manner about the hopes he himself entertained." FDR liked to charm; he charmed Bohr with stories, Aage Bohr recounts:

> Roosevelt agreed that an approach to the Soviet Union of the kind suggested must be tried, and said that he had the best hopes that such a step would achieve a favourable result. In his opinion Stalin was enough of a realist to understand the revolutionary importance of this scientific and technical advance and the consequences it implied. Roosevelt described in this connection the impression he had received of Stalin at the meeting in Teheran, and also related humorous anecdotes of his discussion and debates with Churchill and Stalin. He mentioned that he had heard how the negotiations with Churchill in London had gone, but added that the latter had often reacted in this way at the first instance. However, Roosevelt said, he and Churchill always managed

to reach agreement, and he thought that Churchill would eventually come around to sharing his point of view in this matter. He would discuss the problems with Churchill at their forthcoming meeting and hoped to see my father soon afterwards.

The interview lasted an hour and a half. To Robert Oppenheimer in 1948 Bohr reported a more specific commitment from the President: he "left with Professor Bohr the impression," Oppenheimer writes, "that, after discussion with the Prime Minister, he might well ask [Bohr] to undertake an exploratory mission to the Soviet Union."

"It is hardly necessary to mention the encouragement and gratitude my father felt after his talk with Roosevelt," Aage Bohr goes on; "these were days filled with the greatest optimism and expectation." Bohr saw Frankfurter in Boston and told him about the meeting. Frankfurter suggested Bohr restate his case in a thank-you note, which Bohr managed to compress into one long page by September 7. Frankfurter passed it to Roosevelt's aide. Bohr settled in eagerly to wait.

The two heads of state saved their Tube Alloy discussions for the end of the conference, late September, when they retreated to Roosevelt's estate in the Hudson Valley at Hyde Park. "This was another piece of black comedy," writes C. P. Snow. " . . .Roosevelt surrendered without struggle to Churchill's view of Bohr." The result was a secret aide-mémoire, obviously of Churchill's composition, that misrepresented Bohr's proposals, repudiated them and recorded for the first time the Anglo-American position on the new weapon's first use:

> The suggestion that the world should be informed regarding tube alloys, with a view to an international agreement regarding its control and use, is not accepted. The matter should continue to be regarded as of the utmost secrecy; but when a "bomb" is finally available, it might perhaps, after mature consideration, be used against the Japanese, who should be warned that this bombardment will be repeated until they surrender.
>
> 2. Full collaboration between the United States and the British Government in developing tube alloys for military and commercial purposes should continue after the defeat of Japan unless and until terminated by joint agreement.
>
> 3. Enquiries should be made regarding the activities of Professor Bohr and steps taken to ensure that he is responsible for no leakage of information particularly to the Russians.

The next day, September 20, Churchill wrote Cherwell in high dudgeon:

> The President and I are much worried about Professor Bohr. How did he come into this business? He is a great advocate of publicity. He made an un-

> authorized disclosure to Chief Justice [*sic*] Frankfurter who startled the President by telling him he knew all the details. He says he is in close correspondence with a Russian professor, an old friend of his in Russia to whom he has written about the matter and may be writing still. The Russian professor has urged him to go to Russia in order to discuss matters. What is all this about? It seems to me Bohr ought to be confined or at any rate made to see that he is very near the edge of mortal crimes. I had not visualized any of this before. . . . I do not like it at all.

Anderson, Halifax and Cherwell all defended Bohr to Churchill after the Hyde Park outburst, as did Bush and Conant to FDR. The Danish laureate was not confined. But neither was he invited to meet again with the President of the United States. There would be no exploratory mission to the USSR.

How much the world lost that September is immeasurable. The complementarity of the bomb, its mingled promise and threat, would not be canceled by the decisions of heads of state; their frail authority extends not nearly so far. Nuclear fission and thermonuclear fusion are not acts of Parliament; they are levers embedded deeply in the physical world, discovered because it was possible to discover them, beyond the power of men to patent or to hoard.

Edward Teller had arrived at Los Alamos in the April of its founding in 1943 prepared to participate fully in its work. He was then thirty-five years old, dark, with bushy, mobile black eyebrows and a heavy, uneven step; "youthful," Stanislaw Ulam remembers, "always intense, visibly ambitious, and harboring a smouldering passion for achievement in physics. He was a warm person and clearly desired friendship with other physicists." Teller's son Paul, his first child, had been born in February. The Tellers had shipped to the primitive New Mexico mesa two machines they considered vital to their peace of mind, a Steinway concert grand piano Mici Teller had bought for her husband for two hundred dollars at a Chicago hotel sale and a new Bendix automatic washer. They were assigned an apartment; the Steinway nearly filled the living room.

Teller had striven on behalf of nuclear energy since Bohr's first public announcement of the discovery of fission in Washington in 1939. He had helped Robert Oppenheimer organize Los Alamos and recruit its staff. He expected to contribute to the planning of the new laboratory's program and he did. "It was essential that the whole laboratory agree on one or a very few major lines of development," writes Hans Bethe, "and that all else be considered of low priority. Teller took an active part in the decision on what were to be the major lines. . . . A distribution of work among the members of the Theoretical Division was agreed upon in a meeting of all scientists of the division and Teller again had a major voice."

But Teller had received no concomitant administrative appointment that April, and the omission aggrieved him. He was qualified to lead the Theoretical Division; Oppenheimer appointed Hans Bethe instead. He was qualified to lead a division devoted to work toward a thermonuclear fusion weapon, a Super, but no such division was established. The laboratory had decided at its opening conference, and the Lewis committee had affirmed in May, that thermonuclear research should be restricted largely to theoretical studies and held to distant second priority behind fission: an atomic bomb, since it would trigger any thermonuclear arrangement, necessarily came first; there was a war on and manpower was limited.

"That I was named to head the [Theoretical] division," Bethe comments, "was a severe blow to Teller, who had worked on the bomb project almost from the day of its inception and considered himself, quite rightly, as having seniority over everyone then at Los Alamos, including Oppenheimer." Bethe believed he was chosen because his "more plodding but steadier approach to life and science would serve the project better at that stage of its development, where decisions had to be adhered to and detailed calculations had to be carried through, and where, therefore, a good deal of administrative work was inevitable." Teller saw his old friend's steadier approach differently: "Bethe was given the job to organize the effort and, in my opinion, in which I may well have been wrong, he overorganized it. It was much too much of a military organization, a line organization." On the other hand, Teller has repeatedly praised Oppenheimer's direction of Los Alamos, direction which included Bethe's appointment and ratified Bethe's decisions:

> Throughout the war years, Oppie knew in detail what was going on in every part of the Laboratory. He was incredibly quick and perceptive in analyzing human as well as technical problems. Of the more than ten thousand people who eventually came to work at Los Alamos, Oppie knew several hundred intimately, by which I mean that he knew what their relationships with one another were and what made them tick. He knew how to organize, cajole, humor, soothe feelings—how to lead powerfully without seeming to do so. He was an exemplar of dedication, a hero who never lost his humanness. Disappointing him somehow carried with it a sense of wrongdoing. Los Alamos' amazing success grew out of the brilliance, enthusiasm and charisma with which Oppenheimer led it.

"I believe maybe [Teller] resented my being placed on top of him," Bethe concludes. "He resented even more that there would be an end to free and general discussion. . . . He resented even more that he was removed [by lack of administrative contact] from Oppenheimer."

The theoretical complexity of the Super challenged Teller as the fission bomb had not; it also offered a line of work along which he might lead. "When Los Alamos was established in the spring of 1943," he writes and the technical history of the laboratory confirms, "the exploration of the Super was among its objectives." He accepted the postponement of that exploration through the summer of 1943, helping Bethe with the more immediate problem of developing means to calculate the critical mass and nuclear efficiency of various bomb designs. During the summer, experimental studies at Purdue found that the fusion reaction cross section for deuterium was much larger than expected; Teller cited that result to the Purdue Los Alamos Governing Board in September to propose renewing the Super investigation. Then John von Neumann arrived on the Hill to endorse and extend Seth Neddermeyer's implosion work and for a few months Teller was caught up in reconnoitering that new territory.

Emilio Segrè won a new workshop that 1943 autumn. At Berkeley he had measured the rate of spontaneous fission—naturally occurring fission without neutron bombardment—in uranium and plutonium. The measurements were difficult because the rates were low for the small samples Segrè had to use, but they were crucial. They determined how cleansed of light-element impurities the bomb cores would have to be—there was no point in purifying past the spontaneous background—and they determined how fast the gun assemblies would have to fire to avoid predetonation. Segrè moved off the Los Alamos mesa to protect his new and more capacious measuring instruments from the radiation other experiments generated there:

> At this time I acquired a special small laboratory for measuring spontaneous fission, the like of which I have never seen before or since. It was a log cabin that had been occupied by a ranger and it was located in a secluded valley a few miles from Los Alamos. It could be reached only by a jeep trail that passed through fields of purple and yellow asters and a canyon whose walls were marked with Indian carvings. On this trail we once found a large rattlesnake. The cabin-laboratory, in a grove shaded by huge broadleaf trees, occupied one of the most picturesque settings one could dream of.

In December at this Pajarito Canyon field station Segrè made a significant discovery. The spontaneous fission rate for natural uranium was much the same at the field station as at Berkeley, but at the field station the rate was seemingly higher for U235. Segrè deduced that cosmic-ray neutrons, which were usually too slow to fission U238 but effective to fission

U235, caused the difference. Cosmic rays batter neutrons from the upper reaches of the atmosphere and the field station was 7,300 feet nearer that region than was sea-level Berkeley. Shield out such stray neutrons and the U235 bomb core could be purified less rigorously than they had assumed. Predetonation would be less likely: the gun that assembled the U235 to critical mass would need less muzzle velocity and could be significantly shorter and lighter. Thus was Little Boy engendered, Thin Man's modest brother, a gun assembly six feet long instead of seventeen that would weigh less than 10,000 pounds, an easy load for a B-29: in a log cabin in a grove beyond fields of bright asters, up a trail visited by rattlesnakes.

Gun research was already advanced. "The first task of the gun group," Edwin McMillan remembers, "was to set up a test stand where experiments could be done. You have to have a gun emplacement, and a gun, and a sand butt, which is nothing but a huge box full of sand that you fire projectiles into so that you can find the pieces afterwards, and because there might be somebody else out there." The site they chose was Anchor Ranch, a former working ranch three miles southwest of the mesa that the Army had bought as part of the reservation; they fired the first shot on September 17, 1943.

Until the following March the group used a three-inch Navy anti-aircraft gun fitted with unrifled barrels. With it they tested propellants—eventually choosing cordite—and studied scale-model projectiles and targets. Knowing that the uranium bullet would complete a critical assembly they decided that it should not impact upon the target core but pass freely through; within microseconds of its arrival at spherical configuration it would in any case have vaporized.

From the beginning the plutonium gun with its nearly unattainable muzzle velocity of 3,000 feet per second had been a gamble. When von Neumann that autumn celebrated the advantages of implosion the Governing Board gave the novel approach its strong endorsement. Through the fall and early winter of 1943 Neddermeyer's experiments made only slow progress, however. He added few men to his group. He continued to work methodically with metal cylinders wrapped with solid slabs of high explosive. By spacing several detonators symmetrically around the wrap he could start implosion simultaneously at different points on the HE surface. From each point of detonation a detonation wave shaped like an expanding bubble would travel inward toward the metal cylinder; by varying the spacing of the detonators and the thickness of the HE Neddermeyer hoped to find a configuration that smoothed the convex, multiple shock waves to one uniform cylindrical squeeze. He was working to the same end with small metal balls, scale models of an eventual bomb core. But "the first successful HE flash photographs of imploding cylinders," notes the Los Alamos technical history, "showed that there were . . . very serious asymmetries in the form of jets which traveled ahead of the main mass. A number of interpretations of these jets were proposed, including the possibility that they were optical illusions." They were all too real. "Absolutely awful results," says Bethe. Oppenheimer decided Neddermeyer needed help. Groves agreed. Conant knew just the man.

"Everything in books [about the Manhattan Project] looks so simple, so easy, and everybody was friends with everybody," George Kistiakowsky told an audience wryly long after the war. He remembered a different Los Alamos. The tall, outspoken Ukrainian-born Harvard chemist had begun studying explosives for the National Defense Research Committee in 1940; "by 1943 I thought I knew something about them." What he knew about them was original and unorthodox: "that they could be made into precision instruments, a view which was very different from that of military ordnance." He had already won von Neumann to his view, which had prepared the Hungarian mathematician in turn to endorse the precision instrument of implosion. Conant similarly trusted Kistiakowsky's judgment. In 1941 Conant had abandoned his skepticism toward the atomic bomb because of Kistiakowsky; now the explosives expert found the Harvard president seeking his help to advance Neddermeyer's work:

> I began going to Los Alamos as a consultant in the Fall of 1943, and then pressure was put on me by Oppenheimer and General Groves and particularly Conant, which really mattered, to go there on full time. I didn't want to, partly because I didn't think the bomb would be ready in time and I was interested in helping win the war. I also had what looked like an awfully interesting overseas assignment all fixed up for myself. Well, instead, unwillingly, I went to Los Alamos. That gave me a wonderful opportunity to act as a reluctant bride throughout the life of the project, which helped at times.

Kistiakowsky arrived in late January 1944 and took up residence in a small stone cabin that had been the Ranch School's pump house, an accommodation he negotiated in preference to the men's dormitory—he was forty-four years old and divorced. He quickly discovered, as he suspected, that everything was not easy and everybody was not friends:

> After a few weeks . . . I found that my position was untenable because I was essentially in the middle trying to make sense of the efforts of two men who were at each other's throats. One was Captain [Deke] Parsons who tried to run his division the way it is done in military establishments—very conservative. The other was, of course, Seth Neddermeyer, who was the exact opposite of

Parsons, working away in a little corner. The two never agreed about anything and they certainly didn't want me interfering.

While Kistiakowsky struggled with that dilemma the theoreticians began to glimpse how a successful implosion mechanism might be designed.

The previous spring the Polish mathematician Stanislaw Ulam, then thirty-four years old and a member of the faculty at the University of Wisconsin, had found himself unhappy merely teaching in the midst of war: "It seemed a waste of my time; I felt I could do more for the war effort." He had noticed that letters from his old friend John von Neumann often bore Washington rather than Princeton postmarks and deduced that von Neumann was involved in war work; now he wrote asking for advice. Von Neumann proposed they meet between trains in Chicago to talk and turned up impressively chaperoned by two bodyguards. Eventually Hans Bethe sent along an official invitation. In the winter of 1943 Ulam and his wife Françoise, who was then two months pregnant, rode the Sante Fe Chief to New Mexico as so many others had done before them. "The sun shone brilliantly, the air was crisp and heady, and it was warm even though there was a lot of snow on the ground—a lovely contrast to the rigors of winter in Madison."

The day of his arrival Ulam met Edward Teller for the first time—he was assigned to Teller's group—who "talked to me on that first day about a problem in mathematical physics that was part of the necessary theoretical work in preparation for developing the idea of a 'super' bomb." Teller's preemption of Ulam's first days at Los Alamos for Super calculations was symptomatic of the discord that had been widening between him and Hans Bethe, who needed every available theoretical physicist and mathematician to concentrate on the difficult problem of implosion. Teller had contributed enthusiastically and crucially to the most interesting part of the work. "However," Bethe complains, "he declined to take charge of the group which would perform the detailed calculations on the implosion. Since the theoretical division was very shorthanded, it was necessary to bring in new scientists to do the work that Teller declined to do." That was one reason the British team had been invited to Los Alamos.

Teller recalls no specific refusal. "[Bethe] wanted me to work on calculational details at which I am not particularly good," he counters, "while I wanted to continue not only on the hydrogen bomb, but on other novel subjects."

The Los Alamos Governing Board reevaluated the Super once again in February 1944, learning that despite deuterium's more favorable cross section it would still be difficult to ignite. A Super would almost certainly require tritium. The small tritium samples studied so far had been transmuted in a cyclotron by bombarding lithium with neutrons. Large-scale tritium production, like large-scale plutonium production, would require production reactors, but the piles at Hanford were unfinished and previously committed. "Both because of the theoretical problems still to be solved and because of the posssibility that the Super would have to be made with tritium," reports the Los Alamos technical history, "it appeared that the development would require much longer than originally anticipated." Work could continue—the Super was too portentous a weapon to ignore—but only to the extent that it "did not interfere with the main program."

Von Neumann soon drafted Ulam to help work out the hydrodynamics of implosion. The problem was to calculate the interactions of the several shock waves as they evolved through time, which meant trying to reduce the continuous motion of a number of moving, interacting surfaces to some workable mathematical model. "The hydrodynamical problem was simply stated," Ulam comments, "but very difficult to calculate—not only in detail, but even in order of magnitude."

He remembers in particular a long discussion early in 1944 when he questioned "all the ingenious shortcuts and theoretical simplifications which von Neumann and other . . . physicists suggested." He had argued instead for "simpleminded brute force—that is, more realistic, massive numerical work." Such work could not be done reliably by hand with desktop calculating machines. Fortunately the laboratory had already ordered IBM punchcard sorters to facilitate calculating the critical mass of odd-shaped bomb cores. The IBM equipment arrived early in April 1944 and the Theoretical Division immediately put it to good use running brute-force implosion numbers. Hydrodynamic problems, detailed and repetitious, were particularly adaptable to machine computation; the challenge apparently set von Neumann thinking about how such machines might be improved.

Then a member of the newly arrived British mission made a proposal that paid his mission's way. James L. Tuck was a tall, rumpled Cherwell protégé from Oxford who had worked in England developing shaped charges for armor-piercing shells. A shaped charge is a charge of high explosive arranged in such a way—usually hollowed out like an empty ice cream cone with the open end pointed forward—that its normally divergent, bubble-shaped shock wave converges into a high-speed jet. Such a ferocious jet can punch its way through the thick armor of a tank to spray death inside.

It had just become clear from theoretical work that the several diverging shock waves produced by multiple detonators in Neddermeyer's experiments reinforced each other where they collided and produced points of high pressure; such pressure nodes in turn caused the jets and irregularities that spoiled the implosion. Rather than continue trying to smooth out a colliding collection of divergent shock waves, Tuck sensibly proposed that the laboratory consider designing an arrangement of explosives that would produce a converging wave to begin with, fitting the shock wave to the shape it needed to squeeze. Such explosive arrangements were called lenses by analogy with optical lenses that similarly focus light.

No one wanted to tackle anything so complex so late in the war. Geoffrey Taylor, the British hydrodynamicist, arrived in May to offer further insight into the problem. He had developed an understanding of what came to be called Raleigh-Taylor instabilities, instabilities formed at the boundaries between materials. Accelerate heavy material against light material, he demonstrated mathematically, and the boundary between the two will be stable. But accelerate light material against heavy material and the boundary between the two will be unstable and turbulent, causing the two materials to mix in ways extremely difficult to predict. High explosive was light compared to tamper. All of the tamper materials under consideration except uranium were significantly lighter than plutonium. Raleigh-Taylor instabilities would constrain subsequent design. They would also make it difficult to predict bomb yield.

As the IBM results clarified shock-wave behavior the physicists began seriously to doubt if a uniform wrap of HE could ever be made to produce a symmetrical explosion. Complex though explosive lenses might be, they were apparently the only way to make implosion work. Von Neumann turned to their formulation. "You have to assume that you can control the velocity of the detonation wave in a chemical explosive very accurately," Kistiakowsky explains, "so if you start the wave at certain points by means of detonators you can predict exactly where it will be at a given time. Then you can design the charge." It was soon clear that the velocity of the converging shock waves from the several explosive lenses that would surround the bomb core could vary by no more than 5 percent. That was the demanding limit within which von Neumann designed and Kistiakowsky, Neddermeyer and their staffs began to work.

In the spring of 1944 the two difficult personal conflicts—between Teller and Bethe and between Kistiakowsky and Neddermeyer—forced Oppenheimer to intervene. First, Bethe writes, Teller withdrew from fission development:

> With the pressure of work and lack of staff, the Theoretical Division could ill afford to dispense with the services of any of its members, let alone one of

> such brilliance and high standing as Teller. Only after two failures to accomplish the expected and necessary work, and only on Teller's own request, was he, together with his group, relieved of further responsibility for work on the wartime development of the atomic bomb.

A letter from Oppenheimer to Groves on May 1, 1944, seeking to replace Teller with Rudolf Peierls, corroborates Bethe's account: "These calculations," it says in part, "were originally under the supervision of Teller who is, in my opinion and Bethe's, quite unsuited for this responsibility. Bethe feels that he needs a man under him to handle the implosion program." It was, Oppenheimer notes, a question of the "greatest urgency."

Ulam remembers that Teller threatened to leave. Oppenheimer stepped in then to save him for the project. He encouraged Teller to give himself over to the Super—encouragement, Teller wrote in 1955, perhaps disingenuously, that he needed to move him on from the immediate task at hand:

> Oppenheimer . . . continued to urge me with detailed and helpful advice to keep exploring what lay beyond the immediate aims of the laboratory. This was not easy advice to give, nor was it easy to take. It is easier to participate in the work of the scientific community, particularly when a goal of the highest interest and urgency has been clearly defined. Every one of us considered the present war and the completion of the A-bomb as the problems to which we wanted to contribute most. Nevertheless, Oppenheimer . . . and many of the most prominent men in the laboratory continued to say that the job at Los Alamos would not be complete if we should remain in doubt whether or not a thermonuclear bomb was feasible.

To that end Oppenheimer in May discussed tritium production with Groves and Du Pont's Crawford Greenewalt. The chemical company had built a pilot-scale air-cooled pile at Oak Ridge that produced neutrons to spare; Greenewalt agreed to put some of them to use bombarding lithium.

Teller departed the Theoretical Division. Rudolf Peierls took his place. Oppenheimer arranged then to meet with Teller weekly for an hour of freewheeling talk. That was a remarkable concession when the laboratory was working overtime six days a week to build a bomb before the end of the war. Oppenheimer may well have thought Teller's imaginative originality worth it. He also understood his extreme sensitivity to slight. Later that summer, when Cherwell visited Los Alamos, Oppenheimer gave a party and inadvertently failed to invite Peierls, who was deputy head of the British mission under James Chadwick. Oppenheimer sought out Peierls the next day and apologized, adding: "But there is an element of relief in this situation: it might have happened with Edward Teller."

George Kistiakowsky adjusted himself to Seth Neddermeyer until he felt that not only he but also the project was suffering; then he reviewed his alternatives and, on June 3, wrote Oppenheimer a memorandum. He and Neddermeyer had established a certain *modus vivendi,* he wrote, but it was not what he had been asked to do, which was to administer implosion work while Neddermeyer did the science, and it was "not based on mutual confidence and a friendly give-and-take."

He proposed three possible solutions. He could resign, the solution he thought best and fairest to Neddermeyer. Or Neddermeyer could resign, but that would disturb his staff and slow the work; it would also be unfair to a good physicist. Or Neddermeyer could "take over more vigorous scientific and technical direction of the project but dissociate himself completely from all administrative and personnel matters."

Oppenheimer had come to value Kistiakowsky too highly to choose any of these alternatives. He proposed a fourth. Kistiakowsky worked out the details and the men met painfully to present it to Neddermeyer on a Thursday evening in mid-June: Kistiakowsky would assume full responsibility for implosion work as an associate division leader under Parsons. Neddermeyer and Luis Alvarez, recently arrived from Chicago, would become senior technical advisers. Neddermeyer left the meeting early, as well he might. "I am asking you to accept the assignment," Oppenheimer wrote him the same evening. ". . . In behalf of the success of the whole project, as well as the peace of mind and effectiveness of the workers in the H. E. program, I am making this request of you. I hope you will be able to accept it." With enduring bitterness Neddermeyer did.

The air-cooled, pilot-scale reactor at Oak Ridge had gone critical at five o'clock in the morning on November 4, 1943; the loading crews, realizing during the night that they were nearing criticality sooner than expected, had enjoyed rousting Arthur Compton and Enrico Fermi out of bed at the Oak Ridge guest house to witness the event. The pile, which was designated X-10, was a graphite cube twenty-four feet on a side drilled with 1,248 channels that could be loaded with canned uranium-metal slugs and through which large fans blew cooling air. The channels extended for loading through the seven feet of high-density concrete that composed the pile face; at the back they opened onto a subterranean pool like the pools planned for Hanford into which irradiated slugs could be pushed to shield them until they lost their more intense short-term radioactivity. Chemists then processed the slugs in a remote-controlled pilot-scale separations plant using the chemical separation processes Glenn Seaborg and his colleagues had developed at ultramicrochemical scale in Chicago.

A few days before Compton moved to Oak Ridge to supervise the X-10 operation, at the end of November, workers discharged the first five tons of irradiated uranium from the pile. Chemical separations began the following month. By the summer of 1944 batches of plutonium nitrate containing gram quantities of plutonium had begun arriving at Los Alamos. The man-made element was quickly used and reused in extensive experiments to study its unfamiliar chemistry and metallurgy—more than two thousand separate experiments by the end of the summer.

Not chemistry or metallurgy but physics nearly condemned the plutonium bomb to failure that summer. More than a year previously Glenn Seaborg had warned that the isotope Pu240 might form along with desirable Pu239 when uranium was irradiated to make plutonium. Pu240, an even-numbered isotope, was likely to exhibit a much higher rate of spontaneous fission than Pu239. The plutonium samples Emilio Segrè had studied at his isolated log-cabin laboratory fissioned spontaneously at acceptable rates. They had been transmuted from uranium in one of the Berkeley cyclotrons. U238 needed one neutron to transmute to Pu239; for Pu240 it required two, and far more neutrons bombarded the uranium slugs cooking in the X-10 pile than a cyclotron could generate. When Segrè measured the spontaneous fission rate of the X-10 plutonium he found it much higher than the Berkeley rate. The rate for Hanford plutonium, which would be exposed to an even heavier neutron flux, was likely to be higher still. That meant they would not need to cleanse the plutonium so thoroughly of light-element impurities. But it also signaled catastrophe. They could not use a gun to assemble a critical mass of such stuff: approaching each other even at 3,000 feet per second, the plutonium bullet and target would melt down and fizzle before the two parts had time to join.

Oppenheimer alerted Conant on July 11. The two men met with Compton, Groves, Nichols and Fermi in Chicago six days later and the next day Oppenheimer wrote Groves to confirm their conclusions. Pu240 was apparently long-lived, and since the two isotopes were elementally identical it could not be removed chemically. They had not considered separating Pu239 from Pu240 electromagnetically. Such an effort with isotopes that differed by only one mass unit and were highly toxic would dwarf the vast calutron operation at Oak Ridge and could not possibly be accomplished in time to influence the outcome of the war. "It appears reasonable," Oppenheimer ended, "to discontinue the intensive effort to achieve higher purity for plutonium and to concentrate attention on methods of assembly which do not require a low neutron background for their success. At the present time the method to which an over-riding priority must be assigned is the method of implosion."

That necessity was painful, as the Los Alamos technical history makes clear: "The implosion was the only real hope, and from current evidence not a very good one." Oppenheimer agonized over the problem to the point that he considered resigning his directorship. Robert Bacher, the sturdy leader of the Experimental Physics Division, took long walks with him in those days to share his pain and eventually dissuaded him. There was no one else who could do the job, Bacher argued; without Oppenheimer there would be no bomb in time to shorten the war and save lives.

Action changed Oppenheimer's mood. "The Laboratory had at this time strong reserves of techniques, of trained manpower, and of morale," says the technical history. "It was decided to attack the problems of the implosion with every means available, 'to throw the book at it.' " Going over the prospects with Bacher and Kistiakowsky, Oppenheimer decided to carve two new divisions out of Parsons' Ordnance Division: G (for Gadget) under Bacher to master the physics of implosion and X (for eXplosives) under Kistiakowsky to perfect explosive lenses. The Navy captain howled, Kistiakowsky remembers:

> [Oppenheimer] called a big meeting of all the group heads, and there he sprang on Parsons the fact that I had plans for completely re-designing the explosives establishment. Parsons was furious—he felt that I had by-passed him and that was outrageous. I can understand perfectly how he felt but I was a civilian, so was Oppie, and I didn't have to go through him. . . . From then on Parsons and I were not on good terms. He was extremely suspicious of me.

Parsons had his hands full in any case designing the uranium gun, Little Boy, and arranging its eventual use. Oppenheimer prevailed: they would throw the book at implosion. In the months ahead the laboratory, which had swollen to 1,207 full-time employees by the previous May 1, would once again double and redouble in size.

Philip Abelson, the young Berkeley physicist to whom Luis Alvarez had run from his barber chair in January 1939 to announce the news of fission, had moved to the Naval Research Laboratory in 1941 to work on uranium enrichment for the Navy and had made valuable progress independently of the Manhattan Project in the intervening years. The Navy was interested in nuclear power as a motive force for submarines, to extend their range and to allow them to travel farther submerged. But a pile of the sort Fermi would build would be unwieldy; "it had become pretty obvious," Abelson recalls, "that a reactor fueled with natural uranium would be big as a barn." Increase the ratio of U235 to U238 in the reactor fuel—enrich the uranium—and the reactor could be correspondingly smaller; with enough enrichment, small enough to fit inside the hull of a submarine in the space previously reserved for diesel engines, batteries and fuel.

Enrichment and separation are different goals, but the same technologies achieve them. Abelson began work by looking up the record of those technologies. Gaseous barrier diffusion was under study then at Columbia, electromagnetic separation at Berkeley, centrifuge separation at the University of Virginia. Abelson decided to try a process that had been pioneered in Germany before the war: liquid thermal diffusion (using glass tubes, Otto Frisch had experimented unsuccessfully with a similar process, gaseous thermal diffusion, at Birmingham). Thermal diffusion relied on the tendency of lighter isotopes to diffuse toward a hotter region while heavier isotopes diffused toward a colder region. The mechanism for driving such diffusion could be simple: a hot pipe inside a cold pipe with liquid uranium hexafluoride flowing between the two pipe walls. Depending on the difference in temperature and the spacing between the two pipes more or less diffusion would occur. At the same time the heating and cooling of the hex would start a convection current flowing up the hot pipe wall and down the cold. That would bring the U235-enriched fluid to the top of the column where it could be tapped off. To increase the enrichment a number of columns could be connected in series to make a cascade like the cascade of barrier tanks planned for K-25.

Abelson's first technical contribution, in 1941, was inventing a relatively cheap way to make uranium hexafluoride. He processed the first hundred kilograms of hex produced in the United States. For the nominal sum of one dollar the Army contracted to borrow his patented process for Oak Ridge. He never saw the dollar.

The experimental thermal-diffusion columns Abelson built at the Naval Research Laboratory in 1941 and 1942 were 36 feet tall, each consisting of three pipes arranged one inside the other. The hot inner pipe, 1¼ inches in diameter, carried high-pressure steam at about 400° F. Surrounding that nickel pipe a copper pipe contained the liquid hex. The critical spacing between the two pipes where the hex flowed measured only about one-tenth of an inch. Surrounding both pipes a 4-inch pipe of galvanized iron carried water at about 130°, just above hex's melting point, to cool the hex.

Pumps that circulated the water were the only moving parts. "The apparatus was run continuously with no shut down or break down what so ever," Abelson reported to the Navy early in 1943. "Indeed, so constant were the various temperatures and operating characteristics that practically no attention was required to insure successful operation. Many days passed in which operating personnel did not touch any control device." To stop the flow of the hex out of a column Abelson simply dipped the bend of a U-shaped metal drain tube into a bucket of dry ice and alcohol, which froze the hex and plugged the tube. A flame to warm the tube started the flow again.

Abelson's January 4, 1943, report, submitted jointly with his NRL colleague Ross Gunn, indicated that uranium could be enriched within a single thermal-diffusion column from its natural U235 content of 0.7 percent up to 1 percent or better. With several thousand columns connected in series Abelson thought he could produce 90 percent pure U235 at the rate of 1 kilogram per day at a total construction cost of no more than $26 million. Ninety percent purity was entirely sufficient to make a bomb. (That estimate proved optimistic, however, and equilibrium time for such a cascade appeared to be as long as 600 days.)

Another choice, more in keeping with the Navy's interest in submarine propulsion, emphasized quantity enrichment rather than quality. Abelson proposed building a plant of 300 48-foot columns operating in parallel to make large amounts of slightly enriched uranium immediately. Chicago could use such slightly enriched uranium to advance its pile work, Abelson thought. He did not yet know that CP-1 had gone critical just one month before his report. "Information concerning the many experiments performed by [the Chicago] workers in the last six months has been denied to us," he complained. "It is vitally necessary that there be an exchange of technical information if proper plans are to be made for future plants." The NRL had been the first research center Groves visited when he took charge of the Manhattan Project in September 1942. Months before then, Franklin Roosevelt had specifically instructed Vannevar Bush to exclude the Navy from atomic bomb development. Groves followed the NRL's research and Bush encouraged its funding through the Military Policy Committee. But by 1943 the official flow of information on nuclear energy research ran from the Navy to the Army one-way only.

Unofficially, however, several of Groves' compartments leaked. In November 1943 the Navy authorized Abelson to build his 300-column plant. He had searched for a sufficient source of steam—thermal diffusion used volcanic magnitudes of steam, one reason the Manhattan Project had chosen not to pursue it—and located the Naval Boiler and Turbine Laboratory at the Philadelphia Navy Yard. "They were testing good-sized boilers that would go into ships," Abelson says. "They had the capability of making quantities of steam at a thousand pounds per square inch and they had Navy people standing twenty-four-hour watches to deliver the steam." The boiler laboratory's waste steam would supply his 300-column plant, but before scaling up that far he planned to test his design by building and operating only the first 100 columns. Construction began in January 1944, with completion scheduled for July. By now Abelson knew more about the

Manhattan Project. He knew that the barriers which Houdaille-Hershey had been stripped and reequipped to manufacture were not yet passing inspection and that K-25, the gaseous-diffusion plant, was therefore woefully behind schedule. He knew Los Alamos had been founded with Robert Oppenheimer as its director. He knew Berkeley was struggling to make its calutrons work. He saw that his thermal-diffusion process might come to the bomb project's rescue and he was generous enough and worried enough about the war to offer it despite the Army's several previous rebuffs.

He chose not to work through the limited official channels that the Army and the OSRD had devised to constrict the flow of information. "I wanted to let Oppenheimer know what we were doing. Someone in the Bureau of Ships knew one of the people in the [Navy] Bureau of Ordnance who was going out to Los Alamos. I remember that I met the man at the old Warner Theater here in Washington, up in the balcony—real cloak and dagger stuff." Abelson briefed the BuOrd officer about the plant he was building. He said that he expected to be producing 5 grams a day of material enriched to 5 percent U235 by July. This vital information the BuOrd man carried to Los Alamos and passed along to Edward Teller. Teller in turn briefed Oppenheimer. Oppenheimer apparently conspired then with Deke Parsons, the Hill's ranking Navy man, to concoct a cover story: that Parsons had learned of the Abelson work on a visit to the Philadelphia Navy Yard. With the Navy thus protected, Oppenheimer on April 28 alerted Groves.

Oppenheimer had seen Abelson's January 1943 report only a few months previously, a year after it was written. He was not impressed. Like his colleagues Oppenheimer had considered only those processes that enriched natural uranium all the way up to bomb grade, a requirement thermal diffusion could not efficiently meet. Now he realized that Abelson's process offered a valuable alternative, the alternative Abelson had proposed in his report to help Chicago advance its pile work: slight enrichment of larger quantities. Feeding even slightly enriched material into the Oak Ridge calutrons would greatly increase their efficiency. A thermal-diffusion plant could therefore substitute at least temporarily for the stalled lower stages of the K-25 plant and supplement the output of the Alpha calutrons. Abelson's 100-column plant with the columns operating in parallel, Oppenheimer calculated, should produce about 12 kilograms a day of uranium of 1 percent enrichment.

"Dr. Oppenheimer . . . suddenly told me that we had [made] a terrible scientific blunder," Groves testified after the war. "I think he was right. It is one of the things that I regret the most in the whole course of the operation.

We had failed to consider [thermal diffusion] as a portion of the process as a whole." From the beginning the leaders of the Manhattan Project had thought of the several enrichment and separation processes as competing horses in a race. That had blinded them to the possibility of harnessing the processes together. Groves had partly opened his eyes when barrier troubles delayed K-25; then he had decided to cancel the upper stages of the K-25 cascade and feed the lower-stage product to the Beta calutrons for final enrichment. So he was prepared to understand immediately Oppenheimer's similar point about the value of a thermal-diffusion plant: "I at once decided that the idea was well worth investigating."

Groves appointed a committee of men thoroughly experienced by now in Manhattan Project troubleshooting: W. K. Lewis, Eger Murphree and Richard Tolman. They visited the Philadelphia Navy Yard on June 1 and turned in their conclusions on June 3. They thought Oppenheimer's estimate of 12 kilograms a day of 1 percent U235 optimistic but emphasized the possibility—with 300 columns instead of 100—of producing 30 kilograms per day of 0.95 percent U235.

Groves thought bigger than that. He had a power plant with 238,000 kilowatts rated capacity coming on line within weeks in the K-25 area at Oak Ridge that K-25 would not be ready to draw on until the end of the year. It was designed to generate electricity to run the barrier diffusers but it made electricity by making steam. The steam could serve a thermal-diffusion plant that would enrich uranium for the Alpha and Beta calutrons until such a time as K-25 needed electricity. Then the permanent K-25 installation could be phased in gradually and the temporary thermal-diffusion plant phased out.

The proposal cleared the Military Policy Committee on June 12, 1944. On June 18 Groves contracted with the engineering firm of H. K. Ferguson to build a 2,100-column thermal-diffusion plant beside the power plant on the Clinch River in ninety days or less. That extraordinary deadline allowed no time for design. Ferguson would assemble the operation from twenty-one identical copies—"Chinese copies," Groves called them—of Philip Abelson's 100-column unit in the Philadelphia Navy Yard.

The general must have appreciated the fortuity of his decision when he learned the following month of the plutonium crisis at Los Alamos. But the thermal-diffusion plant was not immediately Oak Ridge's savior. Ferguson managed to build a capacious 500-foot barn of black metal siding and began operating the first rack of columns in sixty-nine days, by September 16, but steam leaked out almost as fast as it could be blown in and couplings needed extensive repair and even partial redesign. The gaseous-diffusion plant, K-25, was more than half completed but no barrier tubes shipped from Houdaille-Hershey yet met even minimum standards. The Alpha calutrons smeared uranium all over the insides of their vacuum tanks, catching no more than 4 percent of the U235; that valuable fraction, reprocessed and fed into the Beta calutrons, reached the Beta collectors in turn at only 5 percent efficiency. Five percent of 4 percent is two thousandths. A speck of U235 stuck to an operator's coveralls was well worth searching out with a Geiger counter and retrieving delicately with tweezers. No essence was ever expressed more expensively from the substance of the world with the possible exception of the human soul.

In the Pacific the island war advanced. As the Army under General Douglas MacArthur pushed up from Australia across New Guinea toward the Philippines, the Marines under Admiral Chester Nimitz island-hopped from Guadalcanal to Bougainville in the Solomons, north across the equator to Tarawa in the Gilberts, farther north to Kwajalein and Eniwetok in the Marshalls. That brought them, by the summer of 1944, within striking distance of the Japanese inner defense perimeter to the west. Its nearest bastions were the Marianas, a chain of volcanic islands at the right corner of a roughly equilateral triangle of which the Philippine main island of Luzon was the left corner and the Japanese main island of Honshu the apex. The United States wanted the Marianas as primary bases for further advance: Guam for the Navy; Saipan and Tinian for the new B-29 Superfortresses that the Army Air Force had begun deploying temporarily at great risk and expense in China's Szechwan province, ferrying aviation fuel and bombs over the Himalayas to support their mission, which was the high-altitude precision bombing of Japan. By contrast, only fifteen hundred miles of open water separated Saipan and Tinian from Tokyo and the islands could be supplied securely by sea.

Nimitz named the Marianas campaign Operation Forager; it began in mid-June with heavy bombing of the island airfields. Then 535 ships carrying 127,571 troops sailed from Eniwetok, the largest force of men and ships yet assembled for a Pacific naval operation. "We are through with flat atolls now," Holland Smith, the Marine commanding general, briefed his officers. "We learned to pulverize atolls, but now we are up against mountains and caves where Japs can dig in. A week from now there will be a lot of dead Marines."

Intelligence estimates put 15,000 to 17,000 Japanese troops on Saipan, 10,000 on smaller Tinian three miles to the south. The marines invaded Saipan first, on the morning of June 15, and won a long but shallow beachhead onto which, by afternoon, amphtracs had delivered 20,000 men. *Time* correspondent Robert Sherrod was among them dodging shells from

Japanese artillery inland; he had seen action before on the Aleutian island of Attu and on Tarawa and knew the Japanese as America had come to know them:

> Nowhere have I seen the nature of the Jap better illustrated than it was near the airstrip at dusk. I had been digging a foxhole for the night when one man shouted: "There is a Jap under those logs!" The command post security officer was dubious, but he handed concussion grenades to a man and told him to blast the Jap out. Then a sharp ping of the Jap bullet whistled out of the hole and from under the logs a skinny little fellow—not much over 5 ft. tall—jumped out waving a bayonet.
>
> An American tossed a grenade and it knocked the Jap down. He struggled up, pointed his bayonet into his stomach and tried to cut himself open in approved hara-kiri fashion. The disemboweling never came off. Someone shot the Jap with a carbine. But, like all Japs, he took a lot of killing. Even after four bullets had thudded into his body he rose to one knee. Then the American shot him through the head and the Jap was dead.

While the marines advanced into Saipan, fighting off the harrowing Japanese frontal assaults they learned to call banzai charges, 155-millimeter Long Toms brought ashore and set up in the southern sector of the island began softening up Tinian. That smaller island of thirty-eight square miles, ten miles long and shaped much like Manhattan, was far less rugged than Saipan. Its highest elevation, Mount Lasso, rose only 564 feet above sea level; its lowlands were planted in sugar cane; it had roads and a railway to recommend it to tank operations. To the disadvantage of amphibious assault the island was a raised platform protected on all sides by steep cliffs 500 to 600 feet high—The Rock, the marines would come to call it. It had two major beaches, one near Tinian Town on the southwest coast and the other, which the marines named Yellow, on the east coast at the island's waist. Navy frogmen explored both by night and found them heavily mined and defended.

Two other smaller beaches on the northwest coast hardly deserved the name; one was 60 yards long and the other 150 yards. The United States had made no division-strength landing across any beach less than twice the length of those two toeholds combined in the entire course of the war. The Japanese on Tinian accordingly defended them with nothing more than a few mines and two 25-man blockhouses. The marines coded them White 1 and White 2 and chose them for their assault.

The invasion of Tinian began on July 24, two weeks after Saipan had been secured. Because of the larger island's proximity the marines could deploy shore-to-shore rather than ship-to-shore, embarking in LST's and smaller craft directly from Saipan. A feint at Tinian Town beach decoyed the Japanese defenses and the invaders achieved complete tactical surprise, rushing ashore and pushing inland as fast as possible to escape the dangerously narrow landings. By the end of the day, when the advance halted to organize a solid defense against the Japanese troops rushing up the island from Tinian Town, most of the tanks had been brought ashore, four howitzer batteries were in place and a spare battalion was even at hand. The defenders had killed fifteen marines and wounded fewer than two hundred; the American perimeter extended inland more than two miles.

With the coming of darkness the Japanese began a mortar barrage. Near midnight their artillery arrived and they added it in. The marines answered with their howitzers. To watch for the expected Japanese counterattack they illuminated the area with flares. The attack started at 0300 hours, Japanese soldiers rushing the American lines head-on in the naked light of the flares. Against strong Marine defenses challenge quickly became slaughter.

The marines needed only four days to advance down the island. They encountered tanks and infantry and in the mild terrain easily destroyed them. They took Tinian Town on July 31, that night shattered a last banzai charge from the south and the next day, August 1, 1944, declared the island secure. More than 6,000 Japanese combatants died compared to 300 Americans. Another 1,500 marines were wounded. Soon the Seabees would arrive to begin bulldozing airfields.

Saipan before had been bloodier: 13,000 U.S. casualties, 3,000 marines killed, 30,000 Japanese defenders dead. But a more grotesque slaughter had engulfed the island's population of civilians. Believing as propaganda had prepared them that the Americans would visit upon them rape, torture, castration and murder, 22,000 Japanese civilians had made their way to two sea cliffs 80 and 1,000 feet high above jagged rocks and, despite appeals from Japanese-speaking American interpreters and even fellow islanders, had flung themselves, whole families at a time, to their deaths. The surf ran red with their blood; so many broken bodies floated in the water that Navy craft overrode them to rescue. Not all the dead had volunteered their sacrifice; many had been rallied, pushed or shot by Japanese soldiers.

The mass suicide on Saipan—a Jonestown of its day—instructed Americans further in the nature of the Jap. Not only soldiers but also civilians, ordinary men and women and children, chose death before surrender. On their home islands the Japanese were 100 million strong, and they would take a lot of killing.

"The view was stupendous, and the wind was bitter cold," Leona Marshall recalls of a day at Hanford, Washington, in September 1944 when she,

Enrico Fermi and Crawford Greenewalt climbed giddily to the top of a twelve-story tower to survey the secret reservation. They could see the Columbia River running deep and blue in both directions out of sight over the horizon; they could see the gray desert and the distant hazy mountains. By then construction was more than two-thirds completed and nearer at hand they overlooked a city of industrial buildings and barracks and three massive blockhouses, the three plutonium production reactors sited on the river's western shore. The number of construction workers had peaked at 42,400 the previous June. Marshall was working now at Hanford; Fermi and Greenewalt had traveled out to monitor the start-up of the B pile, the first one finished. The day the construction teams left it, September 13, Fermi had inserted the first aluminum-canned uranium slug to begin the loading, the Pope conferring his blessing as he had on the piles at Chicago and Oak Ridge.

Slug canning had almost come to a crisis. Two years of trial-and-error effort had not produced canning technology adequate to seal the uranium slugs, which quickly oxidized upon exposure to air or water, away from corrosion. Only in August had the crucial step been devised, by a young research chemist who had followed the problem from Du Pont in Wilmington to Chicago and then to Hanford: putting aside elaborate dips and baths he tried soaking the bare slugs in molten solder, lowering the aluminum cans into the solder with tongs and canning the slugs submerged. The melting point of the aluminum was not much higher than the melting point of the solder, but with careful temperature control the canning technique worked.

Greenewalt then pushed production around the clock. Slugs accumulated in the reactor building faster than the loading crews could use them and Marshall and Fermi observed them there on one of their inspections:

> Enrico and I went to the reactor building . . . to watch the loading.The slugs were brought to the floor in solid wooden blocks in which holes were drilled, each of a size to contain a slug, and the wooden blocks were stacked much as had been the slug-containing graphite bricks in CP-1. Idly I teased Fermi saying it looked like a chain-reacting pile. Fermi turned white, gasped, and reached for his slide rule. But after a couple of seconds he relaxed, realizing that under no circumstances could natural uranium and natural wood in any configuration cause a chain reaction.

Tuesday evening, September 26, 1944, the largest atomic pile yet assembled on earth was ready. It had reached dry criticality—the smaller loading at which it would have gone critical without cooling water if its operators had not restrained it with control rods—the previous Friday. Now the Columbia circulated through its 1,500 loaded aluminum tubes. "We arrived in the control room as the du Pont brass began to assemble," Marshall remembers. "The operators were all in place, well-rehearsed, with their start-up manuals on their desks." Some of the observers had celebrated with good whiskey; their exhalations braced the air. Marshall and Fermi strolled the room checking readings. The operators withdrew the control rods in stages just as Fermi had once directed for CP-1; once again he calculated the neutron flux on his six-inch slide rule. Gradually gauges showed the cooling water warmed, flowing in at 50°F and out at 140°. "And there it was, the first plutonium-production reactor operating smoothly and steadily and quietly. . . . Even in the control room one could hear the steady roaring sound of the high-pressure water rushing through the cooling tubes."

The pile went critical a few minutes past midnight; by 2 A.M. it was operating at a higher level of power than any previous chain reaction. For the space of an hour all was well. Then Marshall remembers the operating engineers whispering to each other, adjusting control rods, whispering more urgently. "Something was wrong. The pile reactivity was steadily decreasing with time; the control rods had to be withdrawn continuously from the pile to hold it at 100 megawatts. The time came when the rods were completely withdrawn. The reactor power began to drop, down and down."

Early Wednesday evening B pile died. Marshall and Fermi had slept by then and returned. They talked over the mystery with the engineers, who first suspected a leaking tube or boron in the river water somehow plating out on the cladding. Fermi chose to remain open-minded. The charts, which seemed to show a straight-line failure, might be hiding the shallow curve of an exponential decline in reactivity, which would mean a fission product undetected in previous piles was poisoning the reaction.

Early Thursday morning the pile came back to life. By 7 A.M. it was running well above critical again. But twelve hours later it began another decline.

Princeton theoretician John A. Wheeler had counseled Crawford Greenewalt on pile physics since Du Pont first joined the project. He was stationed at Hanford now and he followed the second failure of the pile closely. He had been "concerned for months," he writes, "about fission product poisons." B pile's heavy breathing convinced him such a poisoning had occurred. The mechanism would be compound: "A non-[neutron-]absorbing mother fission product of some hours' half-life decays to a daughter dangerous to neutrons. This poison itself decays with a half-life of some hours into a third nuclear species, non-absorbing and possibly even stable." So the pile would chain-react, making the mother product; the mother product would decay to the daughter; as the volume of daughter product increased, absorbing neutrons, the pile would decline; when sufficient daughter product was present, enough neutrons would be absorbed to starve the chain reaction and the pile would shut down. Then the daughter product would decay to a non-absorbing third element; as it decayed the pile would stir; eventually too little daughter product would remain to inhibit the chain reaction and the pile would go critical again.

Fermi had left for the night; Wheeler on watch calculated the likely half-lives based on the blooming and fading of the pile. By morning he thought he needed two radioactivities with half-lives totaling about fifteen hours:

> If this explanation made sense, then an inspection of the chart of nuclei showed that the mother had to be 6.68 hr [iodine]^{135} and the daughter 9.13 hr [xenon]^{135}. Within an hour Fermi arrived with detailed reactivity data which checked this assignment. Within three hours two additional conclusions were clear. (a) The cross section for absorption of thermal neutrons by Xe^{135} was roughly 150 times that of the most absorptive nucleus previously known, [cadmium]^{113}. (b) Almost every Xe^{135} nucleus formed in a high flux reactor would take a neutron out of circulation. Xenon had thrust itself in as an unexpected and unwanted extra control rod. To override this poison more reactivity was needed.

Greenewalt called Samuel Allison in Chicago on Friday afternoon. Allison passed the bad news to Walter Zinn at Argonne, the laboratory in the forest south of Chicago where CP-1 was meant to be housed and where several piles now operated. Zinn had just shut down CP-3, a shielded six-foot tank filled with 6.5 tons of heavy water in which 121 aluminum-clad uranium rods were suspended. Disbelieving, Zinn started the 300-kilowatt reactor up again and ran it at full power for twelve hours. It was primarily a research instrument and it had never been run so long at full power before. He found the xenon effect. Laborious calculations at Hanford over the next three days confirmed it.

Groves received the news acidly. He had ordered Compton to run CP-3 at full power full time to look for just such trouble. Ever the optimist, Compton apologized in the name of pure science: the mistake was regrettable but it had led to "a fundamentally new discovery regarding neutron properties of matter." He meant xenon's consuming appetite for neutrons. Groves would have preferred to blaze trails less flamboyantly.

If Du Pont had built the Hanford production reactors to Eugene Wigner's original specifications, which were elegantly economical, all three piles would have required complete rebuilding now. Fortunately Wheeler had fretted about fission-product poisoning. After the massive wooden shield blocks that formed the front and rear faces of the piles had been pressed, a year previously, he had advised the chemical company to increase the count of uranium channels for a margin of safety. Wigner's 1,500 channels were arranged cylindrically; the corners of the cubical graphite stacks could accommodate another 504. That necessitated drilling out the shield blocks, which delayed construction and added millions to the cost. Du Pont had accepted the delay and drilled the extra channels. They were in place now when they were needed, although not yet connected to the water supply.

D pile went critical with a full 2,004-tube loading on December 17, 1944; B pile followed on December 28. Plutonium production in quantity had finally begun. Groves was enthusiastic enough at year's end to report to George Marshall that he expected to have eighteen 5-kilogram plutonium bombs on hand in the second half of 1945. "Looks like a race," Conant noted for his history file on January 6, 1945, "to see whether a fat man or a thin man will be dropped first and whether the month will be July, August or September."

17
The Evils of This Time

The bombs James Bryant Conant speculated about early in 1945 were crude designs of uncertain yield. The previous October he had traveled out to Los Alamos to ascertain their prospects. To Vannevar Bush he reported that the gun method of detonation seemed "as nearly certain as any untried new procedure can be." The availability of a uranium gun bomb, which Los Alamos expected would explode with a force equivalent to about 10,000 tons of TNT, now depended only on the separation of sufficient U235. Implosion looked far more questionable; intensive work was just then getting under way following Oppenheimer's August reorganization of the laboratory. Conant estimated the yield of the first implosion design, whether lensed or not, "as an order of magnitude only" at about 1,000 tons TNT equivalent. That was so relatively modest a result that he invited Bush to consider the gun bomb strategic and the implosion bomb tactical.

For the past three years Bush and Conant had concentrated their efforts entirely on these first crude bombs. Now they were interested in improvements. During the summer of 1944, Conant says, on an earlier inspection trip to Los Alamos, he and Bush had found leisure and privacy to discuss "what the policy of the United States should be after the war was over." As a result they had sent Secretary of War Henry L. Stimson a joint memorandum on September 19 that independently raised some of the issues Niels Bohr had raised with Franklin Roosevelt in August, in particular that "the progress of this art and science is bound to be so rapid in the next five years in some countries that it would be extremely dangerous for this government to assume that by holding secret its present knowledge we should be secure." They did not see the bomb's complementarity, but did see that whatever control arrangement the United States and Great Britain devised—they favored a treaty—would somehow have to include the Soviet Union; if the Soviets were not informed, as Bush told Conant, the exclusion would lead "to a very undesirable relationship indeed on the subject with Russia."

Roosevelt had returned from Hyde Park troubled that Felix Frankfurter and Bohr had somehow breached Manhattan Project security, Bush and perhaps Conant had talked to Bohr and the two administrators had submitted to Stimson at his request a more detailed proposal incorporating Bohr's ideas. In doing so they had explicitly recommended that the United States sacrifice some portion of its national sovereignty in exchange for effective international control, understanding as they did so that they would have to answer vigorous opposition:

> In order to meet the unique situation created by the development of this new art we would propose that free interchange of all scientific information on this subject be established under the auspices of an international office deriving its power from whatever association of nations is developed at the close of the present war. We would propose further that as soon as practical the technical staff of this office be given free access in all countries not only to the scientific laboratories where such work is contained, but to the military establishments as well. We recognize that there will be great resistance to this measure, but believe the hazards to the future of the world are sufficiently great to warrant this attempt.

But how great in fact were the hazards? That was something else Conant traveled to Los Alamos in October to find out. If the argument for allowing the nation's military establishments to be inspected depended on the dangers of a thermonuclear explosive, it was speculative and therefore weak: the thermonuclear was still only an idea on paper that might not work. How much could fission weapons be improved? How much destructiveness of either kind might a bomber—or, as Bush and Conant briefed Stimson, "a robot plane or guided missile"—eventually visit upon the cities of the world?

What Conant learned first of all was that others had already begun to ask the same questions. The technological imperative, the urge to improvement even if the objects to be improved are weapons of mass destruction, was already operating at Los Alamos. Under intense pressure to produce a first crude weapon in time to affect the outcome of the war, people had found occasion nevertheless to think about building a better bomb. Conant reported to Bush:

> By various methods that seem quite possible of development within six months after the first bomb is perfected, it should be possible to increase the efficiency . . . in which case the same amount of material would yield something like 24,000 Tons TNT equivalent. Further developments along this same line hold a possibility of producing a single bomb with such amounts of materials and such efficiencies as to run this figure up to several hundred thousand Tons TNT equivalent, or even perhaps a million Tons TNT equivalent. . . . All these possibilities reside only in perfecting the efficiency of the use of elements "25"[U235] and "49"[Pu239]. You will thus see that a considerable "super" bomb is in the offing quite apart from the use of other nuclear reactions.

A million tons TNT equivalent was devastation indeed—the world war then raging would consume a total of about three million tons of explosives by its end—but Edward Teller, Conant found, had already dismissed such improvements as picayune:

> It seems that the possibility of inciting a thermonuclear reaction involving heavy hydrogen is somewhat less now than appeared at first sight two years ago. I heard an hour's talk on this subject by the leading theoretical man at L.A. The most hopeful procedure is to use tritium (the radioactive isotope of hydrogen made in a pile) as a sort of booster in the reaction, the fission bomb being used as the detonator and the reaction involving the atoms of liquid deuterium being the prime explosive. Such a gadget should produce an explosive equivalent to 100,000,000 Tons of TNT, which in turn should produce Class B damage over an area of 3,000 square miles!
>
> This last real super bomb is probably at least as distant now as was the fission bomb when you and I first heard of the enterprise.

The thermonuclear was something of a Rorschach test. If it could be made to work at all it was, like a fire, potentially unlimited; to build it larger you only piled on more heavy hydrogen. As Los Alamos paid less attention to Teller's Super his projection of its destructive potential grew more-grandiose.

Robert Oppenheimer also commited himself at that time to exploring the thermonuclear—after the war was won—in a letter to Richard Tolman on September 20, 1944. "I should like," he emphasized, ". . . to put in writing at an early date the recommendation that the subject of initiating violent thermonuclear reactions be pursued with vigor and diligence, and promptly." A way station on the road to a full-scale thermonuclear might be a boosted fission bomb with a small charge of heavy hydrogen confined possibly within the core of an implosion device:

> In this connection I should like to point out that [fission] gadgets of reasonable efficiency and suitable design can almost certainly induct significant thermonuclear reactions in deuterium even under conditions where these reactions are not self-sustaining. . . . It is not at all clear whether we shall actually make this development during the present project, but it is of great importance that such . . . gadgets form an experimentally possible transition from a simple gadget to the super and thus open the possibility of a not purely theoretical approach to the latter.

(In fact not deuterium but tritium proved to be the necessary ingredient of a boosted fission bomb, and such weapons were not developed until long after the end of the war.)

Alluding then to the larger consequences that Bohr had revealed, Oppenheimer emphasized once more the urgency he attached to the pursuit of an H-bomb: "In general, not only for the scientific but also for the political evaluation of the possibilities of our project, the critical, prompt, and effective exploration of the extent to which energy can be released by thermonuclear reactions is clearly of profound importance."

Working against the clock to build weapons that might end a long and bloody war strained life at Los Alamos but also heightened it. "I always pitied our Army doctors for their thankless job," comments Laura Fermi:

> They had prepared for the emergencies of the battlefields, and they were faced instead with a high-strung bunch of men, women, and children. High-strung because altitude affected us, because our men worked long hours under unrelenting pressure; high-strung because we were too many of a kind, too close to one another, too unavoidable even during relaxation hours, and we were all [as Groves had warned his officers not entirely tongue-in-cheek] crackpots; high-strung because we felt powerless under strange circumstances, irked by minor annoyances that we blamed on the Army and that drove us to unreasonable and pointless rebellion.

They made the best of it. Mici Teller waged pointed rebellion saving the backyard trees to preserve a playground for her son. "I told the soldier in his big plow to leave me please the trees here," one of her friends remembers her recounting, "so Paul could have shade but he said, 'I got orders to level off everything so we can plant it,' which made no sense as it was planted by wild nature and suits me better than dust. The soldier left, but was back next day and insisted he had more orders 'to finish this neck of the woods.' So I called all the ladies to the danger and we put chairs under the trees and sat on them. So what could he do? He shook his head and went away and has not come again." Contrariwise, to clear a ski area on the hill to the west of the mesa, George Kistiakowsky wrapped the trees with half-necklaces of plastic explosive and thus noisily but efficiently cut them down. "Then we scrounged equipment to build a rope tow and it became a nice little ski slope," he recalls.

The Fermis moved to Los Alamos in September 1944 and requested one of the less coveted fourplex apartments rather than the Ranch School faculty cottage that had been prepared for them, to make a point about social snobbery. The Peierls, Rudolf and energetic Genia—Otto Frisch's dish-drying coach in Birmingham—lived below. The mix of birthplaces and citizenships was typical of the Hill: Peierls a German Jew, his wife a Russian, both with British citizenship; Laura Fermi still nostalgic for Rome but she and her husband new American citizens as of July. "Oppie has whistled," Fermi would announce with a yawn when the morning siren sounded. "It is time to get up." The Italian laureate directed a new operation, F (for Fermi) Division, a catchall designed to take advantage of his versatility as both theoretician and experimentalist. One of the groups he caught was Teller's. "That young man has imagination," the forty-three-year-old Italian emigré told his wife drolly of the thirty-six-year-old Hungarian. "Should he take full advantage of his inventiveness, he will go a long way." Teller stayed up late at night working out ideas and playing the piano and hardly ever appeared in the Tech Area before late morning.

"Parties," remembers Fuze Development group leader Robert Brode's articulate wife Bernice, "both big and brassy and small and cheerful, were an integral part of mesa life. It was a poor Saturday night that some large affair was not scheduled, and there were usually several of them. . . . On [Saturday nights] we raised whoopie, on Sundays we took trips, the rest of the week we worked." Single men and women sponsored dorm parties fueled with tanks of punch made potent with mixed liquors and pure Tech Area grain alcohol and invited wall-to-wall crowds. The singles removed all the furniture from their dormitory common rooms to make areas for dancing and by unwritten rule kept their upstairs doors open through the night.

Square dancing evolved as a natural Saturday evening activity in that Southwestern setting. ("Everybody was wearing Western clothes—jeans, boots, parkas," Stanislaw Ulam's French wife Françoise remembers noticing with surprise when she and her husband arrived on the Hill. "There was a feeling of mountain resort, in addition to army camp.") The dances were first held in Deke Parsons' living room, then the theater, then Fuller Lodge, finally expanding to crowd the large mess hall. Eventually even the Fermis attended with their daughter Nella to learn the vigorous reels. Long after mother and daughter had been persuaded from the sidelines Fermi sat unbudging, mentally working out the steps. When he was ready he asked Bernice Brode, one of the leaders, to be his partner. "He offered to be head couple, which I thought most unwise for his first venture, but I couldn't do anything about it and the music began. He led me out on the exact beat, knew exactly each move to make and when. He never made a mistake, then or thereafter, but I wouldn't say he enjoyed himself. . . . He [danced] with his brains instead of his feet."

Theater sometimes supplied a Saturday alternative. At a performance of *Arsenic and Old Lace* Robert Oppenheimer surprised and delighted the audience by appearing powdered sepulchrally white with flour as the first of the crowd of corpses emerging from the cellar in the last act. Donald Flanders, tall and bearded, known as Moll, Computation group leader in the Theoretical Division, wrote a comic ballet, *Sacre du Mesa,* set to George Gershwin music. Despite his beard and his lack of ballet training Flanders danced the part of General Groves. Samuel Allison's son Keith appeared as Oppenheimer, dancing on a large table wearing suitably casual clothes and a pork-pie hat. "The main stage prop," Bernice Brode notes, "was a mechanical brain with flashing lights and noisy bangs and sputters, which did consistently wrong calculations, for example, 2 + 2 = 5. In the grand but hectic finale, the wrong calculations were revealed as the real sacred mystery of the mesa."

Kistiakowsky preferred less formally intellectual entertainment:

> I played a lot of poker with important people like Johnny Von Neumann, Stan Ulam, etc. . . . When I came to Los Alamos I discovered that these people didn't know how to play poker and offered to teach them. At the end of the evening they got annoyed occasionally when we added up the chips. I used to point out that if they had tried to learn violin playing, it would cost them even more per hour. Unfortunately, before the end of the war, these great theoretical minds caught on to poker and the evening's accounts became less attractive from my point of view.

And Robert Wilson, Cyclotron Program group leader, who served on the advisory Town Council, discovered even more elemental activities on the Hill despite security screening before employment and roving military police:

> Of the many problems that were presented to us during my term of office, the most memorable was when the M.P.'s who guarded the site chose to place one of our women's dorms off-limits. They recommended that we close the dorm and dismiss the occupants. A tearful group of young ladies appeared before us to argue to the contrary. Supporting them, a determined group of bachelors argued even more persuasively against closing the dorm. It seems that the girls

had been doing a flourishing business of requiting the basic needs of our young men, and at a price. All understandable to the army until disease reared its ugly head, hence their interference. By the time we got that matter straightened out—and we did decide to continue it—I was a considerably more learned physicist than I had intended to be a few years earlier when going into physics was not all that different from taking the cloth.

Married or single, the occupants of Post Office Box 1663 were young and healthy; they produced so many babies that Groves ordered either the reservation commander or the laboratory director—both versions of the story survive—to staunch the flood. Oppenheimer, if Oppenheimer it was, refused the duty. With justification: his wife Kitty bore him a second child, a daughter, Katherine, called Toni, on December 7, 1944. So many people wanted to see the boss's baby that the hospital identified the crib with a sign and lines formed to file past the nursery window.

Crowded together behind a fence, Hill families worried about epidemic disease. A pet dog that had bitten several children turned up rabid and pet owners debated angrily with parents about which category of dependent should be kept on a leash. More frightening was the sudden death of a young chemist, a group leader's wife, from an unidentified form of paralysis. Fearing an outbreak of poliomyelitis, doctors closed the schools, put Santa Fe off limits and ordered all children indoors.

No new cases appeared, the danger abated with the continuation of cold weather and work and play resumed. "I don't think I shall ever again live in a community where so many brains were," comments Edwin McMillan's wife Elsie, Ernest Lawrence's sister-in-law, "nor shall I ever live in a community so confined that visitors expected us to fight with each other. We didn't have telephones, we didn't have the bright lights, but I don't think I shall ever live in a community that had such deep roots of cooperation and friendship."

Some reserved Sundays for church and hobbies; others devoted the day to outings. The Oppenheimers maintained magnificent riding horses and rode regularly on Sunday morning but only once in three years found time for an overnight excursion. Kistiakowsky bought one of Oppenheimer's quarter horses and refreshed himself trailing in the mountains after his late Saturday poker nights; the Army stabled the private animals along with the remuda it kept for the mounted MP's who patrolled the mesa fences. Emilio Segrè found excellent fly-fishing. "The streams are full of big trouts," he announced happily to newcomers. "All you have to do is throw in a line and they bite you, even if you are shouting." Fermi took up angling, says Segrè, "but he went about it in a peculiar way. He had tackle different from what anyone else used for trout fishing, and he developed theories about the way fish should behave. When these were not substantiated by experiment, he showed an obstinacy that would have been ruinous in science." Fermi insisted on fishing for trout with worms, arguing that the condemned creatures should be offered an authentic final meal, not the dry flies of tradition. Segrè made a point of reviewing the subtleties of trout fishing with his old friend. "Oh, I see, Emilio," Fermi eventually countered, "it is a battle of wits."

Mountain climbing had long been a Hans Bethe hobby. He and Fermi, among others, sometimes scaled Lake Peak across the Rio Grande in the Sangre de Cristos, one of Bethe's admiring group leaders remembers, to "sit there in the sunshine" at 12,500 feet "discussing physics problems. This is how many discoveries were made." Leona Marshall, who moved with Fermi to Los Alamos, recalls less Olympian hours with "nothing to do but admire the view and gasp for breath."

Equally strenuous excursions went out to area landmarks. Genia Peierls and Bernice Brode determined to find the Stone Lions, prehistoric lifesized twin effigies of crouching mountain lions carved in tuff, reported beside a ruined pueblo on a distant mesa. They gathered up a carload of Navy ensigns and another of young bachelors from the British mission and drove within ten miles of their goal, then set out walking, Genia Peierls leading the way in tennis shoes without socks: "Best for stones, best for bunions." Lunch at two in the afternoon by a cool canyon stream encouraged the weary ensigns to drop anchor, but Mrs. Peierls had cowed the young British mission men from similar protest. "OK, we proceed to Stone Lions without U. S. Navy. All aboard." More hiking, crossing desert country from mesa to mesa, the Rio Grande below. The American woman was impressed with the Stone Lions; not so the Russian. "House cats only, my dear, not well made and maybe not even old." "On the way back," Bernice Brode recalls, "the young men . . . looked out over the wide expanse of the desert region and the ribbon of water shining in the setting sun. One of them, dark and slim, wearing tortoise shell rimmed glasses, spoke in his soft voice with a slight German accent. 'I have not seen New York, nor Chicago, but I have seen the Stone Lions.' He smiled pleasantly as we walked on. His name was Klaus Fuchs." Penny-in-the-slot Fuchs, Genia Peierls nicknamed him, because the quiet, hardworking emigré theoretician only spoke when spoken to.

On a hike through Frijoles Canyon with the Fermis, Niels Bohr stopped to admire a skunk, an animal unknown to Europeans, but it chose not to instruct the vigorous Dane in the pungency of its defenses. Bears sometimes appeared on the trails, prompting warnings in the daily bulletin: "Remember that these are not tame bears like those in Yellowstone Park."

A family cat turned up with a suppurating jaw; the Hill's Army veterinarian recognized the bone necrosis as a sign of radiation poisoning from Tech Area contamination and kept the animal alive to observe its unusual symptomatology, about which not much was yet known. Its tongue swelled and its hair fell out in patches; its heartsick owner eventually asked that the animal be destroyed.

A low-power radio station began broadcasting to Hill residents on Christmas Eve, 1943, drawing on several fine collections of classical records, including Oppenheimer's; the few New Mexicans beyond the Hill who could receive the station's signals were puzzled that announcers never introduced live performers by their last names. The "Otto" who occasionally played classical piano selections was Otto Frisch. A golf course opened in June 1944. Men and women fielded baseball, softball and basketball teams. The Army divided up the old Ranch School truck garden east of Fuller Lodge into victory-gardening plots but had no water to spare for irrigation.

Life was rougher for construction workers, machinists, soldiers and WAC's: minimal barracks, jerrybuilt dormitories, muddy trailer courts. Hillbilly construction families invited once in the interest of authenticity to the square dancing at the mess hall arrived drunk and nearly caused a riot; thereafter a man in uniform guarded the door. Hans Bethe recalls that one wild machinist late in the war, when the laboratory took what help it could find, slit a fellow worker's throat "from cover to cover." The Indians from San Ildefonso and other pueblos and ranches in the area lived better for their work on the Hill as cleaning women and maintenance men. The hand-coiled black pottery of Maria Martinez soon graced many Los Alamos apartments.

In winter a pall of coal smoke hung over the mesa. The men the Army assigned to service the apartment furnaces stoked them so hot that apartment walls sometimes sizzled. Los Alamos sat high and dry surrounded by pine forests, and fire worried everyone. The main machine shop in the Tech Area caught fire one night early in 1945; Eleanor Jette remembers watching her husband Eric, Metal Reduction group leader in the Chemistry and Metallurgy Division, standing with Oppenheimer and the Hill commanding officer on the fire escape of the administration building grimly overseeing the firefighters. "Jesus," she heard someone say, "let's be thankful it isn't D building. That place is as hot as seven million dollars. Every time it gets too hot for them to work, they slap on another coat of paint." Her husband worked in D building; she did not know he worked with plutonium but understood that "hot" meant radioactive. "Damn," he told her when she asked. "You mustn't be upset. We're so careful it's fantastic." A fire in the plutonium-handling areas would be a major disaster; after the machine-shop fire Groves ordered a fireproof plutonium works built with steel walls and a steel roof and filtering systems for both incoming and outgoing air.

Robert Oppenheimer oversaw all this activity with self-evident competence and an outward composure that almost everyone came to depend upon. "Oppenheimer was probably the best lab director I have ever seen," Teller repeats, "because of the great mobility of his mind, because of his successful effort to know about practically everything important invented in the laboratory, and also because of his unusual psychological insight into other people which, in the company of physicists, was very much the exception." "He knew and understood everything that went on in the laboratory," Bethe concurs, "whether it was chemistry or theoretical physics or machine shop. He could keep it all in his head and coordinate it. It was clear also at Los Alamos that he was intellectually superior to us." The Theoretical Division leader elaborates:

> He understood immediately when he heard anything, and fitted it into the general scheme of things and drew the right conclusions. There was just nobody else in that laboratory who came even close to him. In his knowledge. There was human warmth as well. Everybody certainly had the impression that Oppenheimer cared what each particular person was doing. In talking to someone he made it clear that that person's work was important for the success of the whole project. I don't remember any occasion at Los Alamos in which he was nasty to any person, whereas before and after the war he was often that way. At Los Alamos he didn't make anybody feel inferior, not anybody.

Yet Oppenheimer felt inferior himself, had always felt for the actions of his life, as he confessed many years afterward, "a very great sense of revulsion and of wrong." At Los Alamos for the first time he seems to have found alleviation of that loathing. He may have discovered there a process of self-analysis anchored in complementarity that served him more comprehensively later in his life: "In an attempt to break out and be a reasonable man, I had to realize that my own worries about what I did were valid and were important, but that they were not the whole story, that there must be a complementary way of looking at them, because other people did not see them as I did. And I needed what they saw, and needed them." Certainly he found the more traditional alleviation of losing himself in work.

Whatever his burden of morale and work in those years, Oppenheimer also carried his full share of private pain. He was kept under constant surveillance, his movements monitored and his rooms and telephones bugged; strangers observed his most intimate hours. His home life cannot have been happy. Kitty Oppenheimer responded to the stress of living at isolated Los Alamos by drinking heavily; eventually Martha Parsons, the admiral's daughter, took over the duties of social leadership on the Hill. Army security officers hounded the director of the central laboratory of the nation's most important secret war project mercilessly; at least one of them, Peer de Silva, was convinced Oppenheimer was a Soviet spy. They interrogated him frequently, fishing for the names of people he knew or believed to be members of the Communist Party, hoping to trip him up. He invented circumstances and volunteered the names of friends to protect his own, indiscretions that would return in time to haunt him.

During the first Los Alamos summer he heard from Jean Tatlock, the unhappy woman he had loved before he met his wife. Loyally, even though she had been and still might be a Communist and he knew himself to be spied upon, he went to her; an FBI document coldly summarizes a security man's peepshow version of that meeting:

> On June 14, 1943, Oppenheimer traveled via Key Railway from Berkeley to San Francisco on the evening of June 14, 1943, where he was met by Jean Tatlock who kissed him. They dined at the Xochimilcho Cafe, 787 Broadway, San Francisco, then proceeded at 10:50 P.M. to 1405 Montgomery Street and entered a top floor apartment. Subsequently, the lights were extinguished and Oppenheimer was not observed until 8:30 A.M. next day when he and Jean Tatlock left the building together.

In January 1944 Jean Tatlock committed suicide. "I wanted to live and to give and I got paralyzed somehow," her suicide note said. It was a paralysis of the spirit Oppenheimer seemingly had to resist in himself.

Planning began in March 1944 for a full-scale test of an implosion weapon. Sometime between March and October Oppenheimer proposed a code name for that test. The first man-made nuclear explosion would be a historic event and its designation therefore a name that history might remember. Oppenheimer coded the test and the test site Trinity. Groves wrote him in 1962 to find out why, speculating that he chose the name because it is common to rivers and peaks in the American West and would be inconspicuous.

"I did suggest it," Oppenheimer responded, "but not on [that] ground. . . . Why I chose the name is not clear, but I know what thoughts were in my mind. There is a poem of John Donne, written just before his death, which I know and love. From it a quotation:

> *As West and East*
> *In all flatt Maps—and I am one—are one,*
> *So death doth touch the Resurrection."*

The poem was Donne's "Hymne to God My God, in My Sicknesse," and among its subtleties it construes a complementarity that parallels the complementarity of the bomb that Bohr had recently revealed to Oppenheimer. ("Bohr was deeply in this," Bethe testifies, "and this was his real interest, and Bohr had long conversations with Oppenheimer which brought Oppenheimer into this at a very early stage. Oppenheimer was very much indoctrinated by Bohr's ideas of international control.") That dying leads to death but might also lead to resurrection—as the bomb for Bohr and Oppenheimer was a weapon of death that might also end war and redeem mankind—is one way the poem expresses the paradox.

"That still does not make a Trinity," Oppenheimer's letter to Groves goes on, "but in another, better known devotional poem Donne opens, 'Batter my heart, three person'd God;—.' Beyond this, I have no clues whatever." Nor must Groves have had; but the fourteenth of Donne's *Holy Sonnets* equally explores the theme of a destruction that might also redeem:

Batter my heart, three person'd God; for you
As yet but knocke, breathe, shine, and seeke to mend;
That I may rise, and stand, o'erthrow mee, and bend
Your force to breake, blowe, burn and make me new.
I, like an usurpt towne, to another due,
Labour to admit you, but Oh, to no end;
Reason, your viceroy in mee, mee should defend,
But is captiv'd, and proves weake or untrue.
Yet dearly I love you, and would be loved faine,
But am betroth'd unto your enemie:
Divorce me, untie, or breake that knot againe,
Take mee to you, imprison me, for I
Except you enthrall me, never shall be free,
Nor ever chaste, except you ravish me.

That is poetry perhaps martial enough, ardent enough and sufficiently fraught with paradox to supply a code name for the first secret test of a millennial force newly visited upon the world.

Oppenheimer did not doubt that he would be remembered to some degree, and reviled, as the man who led the work of bringing to mankind for the first time in its history the means of its own destruction. He cherished the complementary compensation of knowing that the hard riddle the bomb would pose had two answers, two outcomes, one of them transcendent. Such understanding justified the work at Los Alamos if anything did, and the work in turn healed the split between self and overweening conscience that hurt him. He had long recognized the possibility of such a convalescence and evoked it explicitly in the epistle on discipline he wrote his brother Frank in 1932 that concluded in Pauline measure: "Therefore I think that all things which evoke discipline: study, and our duties to men and to the commonwealth, war, and personal hardship, and even the need for subsistence, ought to be greeted by us with profound gratitude; for only through them can we attain to the least detachment; and only so can we know peace." At Los Alamos, if only for a time, he located that detachment in duties to men and to the commonwealth that Bohr was teaching him to believe might be worthy, not macabre. He was not the first man to find himself in war.

To develop implosion Los Alamos had to develop diagnostics, ways to see and to measure events that began and ended in considerably less time than the blink of an eye. The iron pipes Seth Neddermeyer imploded could be studied by aiming a high-speed flash camera down their bores, but how could the physicists of G Division observe the shaping of a detonation wave as it passed through solid blocks of high explosives, or the compression of the metal sphere which those explosives completely surrounded? They were competent research scientists who had been working within narrow technological constraints for a year and a half; diagnostics demanded imagination and they brought all their frustrated creativity to the task.

X-raying was a reliable approach; the Ordnance Division had already used X rays to study the behavior of small spherical arrangements of explosives. X rays reveal differences in density—dense bone casts a darker shadow than lighter flesh—and since the detonation wave of a developing implosion changed the density of the explosive material as it burned its way through, X rays could make that wave visible. But adapting X-ray diagnostics to implosion studies on an increasing scale meant protecting fragile X-ray equipment from the repeated blasts of as much as two hundred pounds of high explosives at a time. That challenge the physicists met by the unorthodox expedient of mounting their implosion tests between two closely spaced blockhouses with the X-ray unit in one building and the radiography equipment in the other, accessible to the test event through protected ports. Ultimately flash X-ray equipment—high-current X-ray tubes that pulsed as rapidly as every ten-millionth of a second—proved most useful for detonation-wave studies.

The behavior of a test unit's HE shell was easier to study with X rays and high-speed photography than was the compression of its denser metal core. For following the metal core as it squeezed to less than half its previous volume Los Alamos developed several different diagnostic methods and used them in complement.

One method set the test unit within a magnetic field and measured changes in field configuration as the metal sphere compressed. Since HE is essentially transparent to magnetism, this method allowed the physicists eventually to study full-scale assemblies. It gave reliable measure of shock waves reflected from the core and of the troublesome detonation-wave intersections that caused jets and spalling.

Carefully spaced prearranged wires contacted by the metal sphere as it imploded supplied information not only about the timing of the implosion but also about material velocities at various depths within the core. That provided direct, quantitative data which the Theoretical Division could use to check how well its hydrodynamic theory fit the facts. The Electric Method group began by measuring the high-explosive acceleration of flat metal plates. Early in 1945 it adapted its techniques to partial spheres and eventually to spheres surrounded by HE lens systems with only one lens removed to access the necessary wires.

Duplicated at another test site, the blockhouse arrangement that served to protect ordinary X-ray equipment also served to shield the most unusual diagnostic method the scientists devised: firing pulsed X rays from a betatron through scale-model implosion units into a cloud chamber and photographing the resulting ionization tracks with a stereoscopic camera.* The betatron method needed an ingenious timing circuit to trigger in quick but precise sequence the explosive charge, the betratron X-ray pulse, the expansion of the diaphragm of the cloud chamber that made the ionization tracks visible as droplets in the fog and the camera shutters that photographed them.

The fifth successful method G Division developed varied the betatron method by incorporating an intense source of gamma radiation within the core itself. The source, radioactive lanthanum extracted from among fission products of the Oak Ridge air-cooled pile, gave the method its name: RaLa. Not a cloud chamber but alignments of rugged ionization chambers served to register the changing patterns of radiation from the RaLa cores as they compressed. Since no one knew at first how extensively the radiolanthanum would contaminate the test site, Luis Alvarez, who coordinated the first experiment, borrowed two tanks from the Army's Dugway Proving Ground in Utah to use as temporary blockhouses. He recalls spectacular results:

> I was sitting in the tank when the first explosion went off. George Kistiakowsky was in one tank and I was in the other. We were looking through the periscopes and all that happened was that it blew a lot of dust in our eyes.

* A betatron accelerates electrons to high speeds in a magnetic field; such beta ray-like electrons can then be directed onto a target to produce intense beams of high-energy X rays.

And then—we hadn't thought about this possibility at all—the whole forest around us caught on fire. These pieces of white-hot metal went flying off into the wild blue yonder setting trees on fire. We were almost surrounded.

Implosion lens development had begun the previous winter, says Bethe, when John von Neumann "very quickly designed an arrangement which was obviously correct from the theoretical point of view—I had tried and failed." Now in the fall and winter of 1944–45 Kistiakowsky had to make the theoretical arrangement work.

An optical lens takes advantage of the fact that light travels at different velocities in different media. Light traveling through air slows when it encounters glass. If the glass curves convexly, as a magnifying glass is curved, the light that encounters the thicker center must follow a longer path than the light that encounters the thinner edges. The effect of these differing path lengths is to direct the light toward a focal point.

The implosion lens system von Neumann designed was made up of truncated pyramidal blocks about the size of car batteries. The assembled lenses formed a sphere with their smaller ends pointing inward. Each lens consisted of two different explosive materials fitted together—a thick, fast-burning outer layer and a shaped slow-burning solid inclusion that extended to the surface of the face of the block that pointed toward the bomb core:

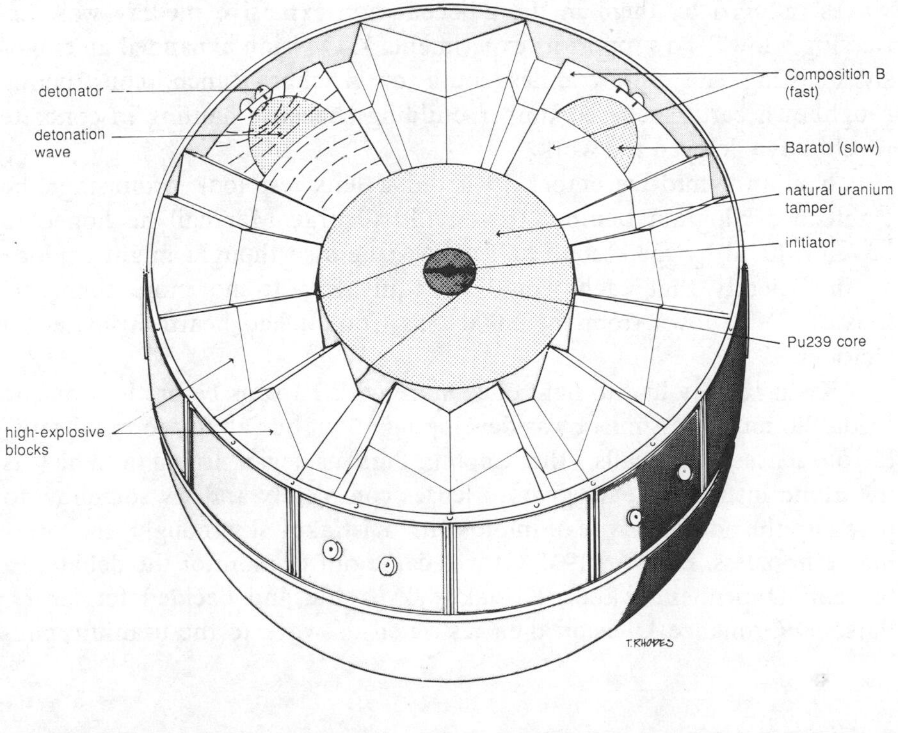

The fast-burning outer layer functioned for the detonation wave as air around an optical lens functions for light. The slower-burning shaped inclusion functioned as a magnifying glass, directing and reshaping the wave. A detonator would ignite the fast-burning explosive. That material would develop a spherical detonation wave. When the apex of the wave advanced into the apex of the inclusion, however, it would begin burning more slowly. The delay would give the rest of the wave time to catch up. As the detonation wave encountered and burned through the inclusion it thus reshaped itself from convex to concave, from a spherical wave expanding from a point to a spherical wave converging on a point, emerging fitted to the convex curve of the spherical tamper. Before the reshaped wave reached the tamper it passed through a second layer of solid blocks of fast-burning explosive to add to its force. The heavy natural-uranium tamper then served to smooth out any minor irregularities as the spherical shock wave compressed it passing through to the plutonium core.

Kistiakowsky would apologize after the war for a research program "too frequently reduced to guesswork and empirical shortcuts" because the field had been grossly neglected. "Prior to this war the subject of explosives attracted very little scientific interest," he wrote in an introduction to a technical history of X Division's work, "these materials being looked upon as blind destructive agents rather than precision instruments; the level of fundamental knowledge concerning detonation waves—and strong shock waves induced by them in the adjacent non-explosive media—was distressingly low." To support its experiments X Division expanded an explosives-casting site a few miles south of Anchor Ranch, constructing roughhewn earth-sheltered timber buildings because hauling in concrete would have delayed the work.

Not until mid-December 1944 did a lens test look promising; the eighteen 5-kilogram bombs Groves told George Marshall he hoped to have on hand by the second half of 1945 he also thought might explode so inefficiently that each would be equivalent to no more than 500 tons of TNT, down from the 1,000 tons Conant had heard estimated in October.

Kistiakowsky had to fight once more with Parsons before he won the field. "So much pessimism was developing about our ability to build satisfactory lenses," he recalls, "that Captain Parsons began urging (and he was not alone in this) that we give up lenses completely and try somehow to patch up the non-lens type of implosion." Kistiakowsky thought that alternative hopeless. Early in 1945 Groves came out to monitor the debate. In the end Oppenheimer took Kistiakowsky's side and decided for lenses. Parsons' Ordnance Division then restricted its work to the uranium gun,

Little Boy, and to engineering the weapons for the battlefield. X and G Divisions worried about implosion.

Finishing the high-explosive castings by machining them was the most dramatic innovation Kistiakowsky introduced. He wanted to shape the HE components entirely by machining from solid pre-cast blocks but lacked sufficient time to develop and build the elaborate remote-controlled machinery the innovative technology would have required. He settled instead for precision casting with machine finishing and used his limited supply of machinists primarily to turn out the necessary molds. Molds gave him "the greatest agony," he remembers; the HE components of the bomb totaled "something in the nature of a hundred or so pieces, which had to fit together to within a precision of a few thousandths of an inch on a total size of five feet and make a sphere. So we had to have very precise molds." Eventually mold procurement paced Fat Man's testing and delivery.

But even with the necessary molds on hand, casting HE was far from simple, another technology that had to be learned by trial and error. In February 1945 Kistiakowsky chose an explosive called Composition B to serve as the fast-burning component of Fat Man's lenses and a mixture he had commissioned from a Navy research laboratory, Baratol, for the slow-burning component. Composition B was poured as a hot slurry of wax, molten TNT and a non-melting crystalline powder, RDX, that was 40 percent more powerful than TNT alone. Baratol slurried barium nitrate and aluminum powder with TNT, stearoxyacetic acid and nitrocellulose:

> We learned gradually that these large castings, fifty pounds and more each, had to be cooled in just certain ways, otherwise you get air bubbles in the middle or separations of solids and liquids, all of which screwed up the implosion completely. So it was a slow process. The explosive was poured in and then people sat over that damned thing watching it as if it was an egg being hatched, changing the temperature of the water running through the various cooling tubes built into the mold.

The wilderness reverberated that winter to the sounds of explosions, gradually increasing in intensity as the chemists and physicists applied small lessons at larger scale. "We were consuming daily," says Kistiakowsky, "something like a ton of high performance explosives, made into dozens of experimental charges." The total number of castings, counting only those of quality sufficient to use, would come to more than 20,000. X Division managed more than 50,000 major machining operations on those castings in 1944 and 1945 without one explosive accident, vindication of Kistiakowsky's precision approach. A RaLa test on February 7, 1945, showed definite improvement in implosion symmetry. On March 5, after a strained round of conferences, Oppenheimer froze lens design. However scarce plutonium might be, no one doubted that Fat Man would have to be tested at full scale before a military weapon could be trusted to work.

A problem small in scale but difficult of solution was the initiator, the minuscule innermost component of the bombs. The chain reaction required a neutron or two to start it off. No one wanted to trust a billion dollars' worth of uranium or several hundred million dollars' worth of plutonium to spontaneous fission or a passing cosmic ray. Neutron sources had been familiar laboratory devices for more than a decade, ever since James Chadwick bombarded beryllium with alpha particles from polonium and broke the elusive neutral particle free in the first place. In his early lectures at Los Alamos Robert Serber had discussed using a radium-beryllium source in a gun bomb with the radium attached to one piece of core material and the beryllium to the other, arranged to smash together when the gun was fired and the two core components mated to complete a critical assembly. Radium released dangerous quantities of gamma radiation, however, and Edward Condon noted in the *Los Alamos Primer* that "some other source such as polonium . . . will probably prove more satisfactory." Polonium emitted copious quantities of alpha particles energetic enough to knock neutrons from beryllium but very little gamma radiation.

The challenge of initiator development was to design a source of sufficient neutron intensity that released those neutrons only at the precise moment they were needed to initiate the chain reaction. In the case of the uranium gun that requirement would be relatively easy to meet, since the alpha source and the beryllium could be separated with the bullet and the target core. But the implosion bomb offered no such convenient arrangement for separation and for mixing. Polonium and beryllium had to be intimately conjoined in Fat Man at the center of the plutonium core but inert as far as neutrons were concerned until the fraction of a microsecond when the imploding shock wave squeezed the plutonium to maximum density. Then the two materials needed instantaneously to mix.

Polonium, element 84 on the periodic table, was a strange metal. Marie and Pierre Curie had isolated it by hand from pitchblende residues (at backbreaking concentrations of a tenth of a milligram per ton of ore) in 1898 and named it in honor of Marie Curie's native Poland. Physically and chemically it resembled bismuth, the next element down the periodic table, except that it was a softer metal and emitted five thousand times as much alpha radiation as an equivalent mass of radium, which caused the ionized, excited air around a pure sample to glow with an unearthly blue light.

Po210, the isotope of polonium that interested Los Alamos, decayed to lead 206 with the emission of an alpha particle and a half-life of 138.4 days. The range of Po210's alphas was some 38 millimeters in air but only a few hundredths of a millimeter in solid metals; the alphas gave up their energies ionizing atoms along the way and finally came to a stop. That meant the polonium for an initiator could be safely confined within a sandwich of metal foils. Sandwiching the foils in turn might be concentric shells of light, silvery beryllium. The entire unit need be no larger than a hazelnut.

"I think I probably had the first idea [for an initiator design]," Bethe remembers, "and Fermi had a different idea, and I thought mine was better for once, and then I was the chairman of a committee of three to watch the development of the initiator." Segregating the Po210 from the beryllium was straightforward. Making sure the two elements mixed thoroughly at the right instant was not, and the primary difference between initiator designs—many were invented and tested during the winter of 1944–45—was their differing mixing mechanisms. A quantity of Po210 equivalent in alpha activity to 32 grams of radium, thoroughly mixed with beryllium, would produce some 95 million neutrons per second, but that would be no more than nine or ten neutrons in the brief ten-millionth of a second when they would be useful in an imploding Fat Man to start the chain reaction; therefore the mixing had to be certain and thorough. Initiator design has never been declassified, but irregularities machined into the beryllium outer surface that induced turbulence in the imploding shock wave probably did the job: the Fat Man initiator may have been dimpled like a golf ball.

To supply ten neutrons to initiate a chain reaction men labored for years. Bertrand Goldschmidt, a French chemist who had once been Marie Curie's personal assistant and who came to the United States after the invasion of France to work with Glenn Seaborg at the Met Lab, extracted the first half-curie of initiator polonium from old radon capsules at a New York cancer hospital (polonium is a daughter product of radium decay). Quantity production required using scarce neutrons from the Oak Ridge air-cooled pile to transmute bismuth one step up the periodic table to Po. Charles A. Thomas, research director for the Monsanto Chemical Company, a consultant on chemistry and metallurgy, took responsibility for purifying the Po, for which purpose he borrowed the indoor tennis court on his mother-in-law's large and securely isolated estate in Dayton, Ohio, and converted it to a laboratory.

Thomas shipped the Po on platinum foil in sealed containers, but another nasty characteristic of polonium caused shipping troubles: for reasons never satisfactorily explained by experiment, the metal migrates from place to place and can quickly contaminate large areas. "This isotope has been observed to migrate upstream against a current of air," notes a postwar British report on polonium, "and to translocate under conditions where it would appear to be doing so of its own accord." Chemists at Los Alamos learned to look for it embedded in the walls of shipping containers when Thomas' foils came up short.

Initiator studies proceeded in G Division at a test site established in Sandia Canyon, one mesa south of the Hill. The Initiator group drilled blind holes in large turbine ball bearings—screwballs, the experimenters called them—inserted test initiators and plugged the holes with bolts. After imploding the screwballs they recovered the remains and examined them to see how well the Po and Be had mixed. Mixing, unfortunately, could not be a conclusive measure of effectiveness. Bethe's committee selected the most promising design on May 1, 1945, but only a full-scale test culminating in a chain reaction could prove definitively that the design worked.

Progress toward a Japanese atomic bomb, never rapid, slowed to frustration and futility across the middle years of the Pacific war. After the Imperial Navy had bowed out of atomic energy research Yoshio Nishina had continued patriotically to pursue it even though he privately believed that Japan in challenging the United States had invited certain disaster. On July 2, 1943, Nishina had met with his Army liaison, a Major General Nobuuji, to report that he had "great expectations" for success. He noted that the Air Force had asked him to study uranium as a possible aircraft fuel, as an explosive and as a source of power, and he had recently received a request for assistance from another Army laboratory, which had contributed 2,000 yen to his expenses. Nobuuji promptly discouraged such consultations. "The main point," Nishina agreed, "is to complete the project as rapidly as possible." His calculations, he told Nobuuji, indicated that 10 kilograms of U235 of at least 50 percent purity should make a bomb, although cyclotron experiments would be necessary to determine "whether 10 kg. will be sufficient, or whether it will require 20 kg. or even 50 kg." He wanted help finishing his 60-inch cyclotron:

> The 250-ton, 1.5 meter accelerator is ready for operation except for certain components which are unavailable as they are being used in the construction of munitions. If this accelerator is completed we believe we can accomplish a great deal. At this moment the U.S. plans to construct an accelerator ten times as great but we are unsure as to whether they can accomplish this.

The previous March Nishina had discarded as impractical under wartime conditions in Japan all methods of isotope separation except gaseous thermal diffusion. Otto Frisch had tried gaseous thermal diffusion (differing from Philip Abelson's *liquid* thermal diffusion) at Birmingham early in 1941 and proved it inadequate for separating uranium isotopes, but Nishina had no knowledge of that secret work. The Riken team had designed a thermal column much like the laboratory-scale column Abelson had built at the Naval Research Laboratory in Washington: of concentric 17-foot pipes, the inner pipe heated to 750°F—electrically heated in the Riken configuration—and the outer pipe cooled with water.

Nishina did not meet again with Nobuuji until seven months later, in February 1944, when he reported difficulty producing uranium hexafluoride. His team had managed to develop a method for generating elemental fluorine but had not yet been able to combine the gas with uranium using an old and inefficient process that Abelson in the United States had discarded before he began his thermal-diffusion studies. Nishima also had a problem with his diffusion column that Abelson would have appreciated: it leaked. "To achieve an airtight system," Nishina told Nobuuji, "we used [sealing] wax and finally achieved our goal. Solder could not be used because of the corrosive properties of the fluorine." He was "in the middle of developing this [hexafluoride-generating] process but can see the end in sight." His 1.5-meter cyclotron was now in operation but only at low energy; his explanation for that compromise comments pointedly on the condition of the Japanese industrial economy by 1944:

> We have been unable to obtain any superior, high-frequency-generating vacuum tubes . . . for the cyclotron. . . . As a result of this constraint, the low operating voltages limit the population of neutrons we can produce. . . . In order to liberate many high-energy neutrons, a high-voltage vacuum tube is required. But, unfortunately, they are difficult to acquire.

By summer Nishina's group had manufactured some 170 grams of uranium hexafluoride—in the United States hex was now being produced by the ton—and in July attempted a first thermal separation. Gauges at the top and bottom of the column, intended to measure a difference in pressure—showing that separation was taking place—indicated no difference at all. "Well, don't worry," Nishina told his team. "Just keep on with it, just keep giving it more gas."

He reconvened with Nobuuji on November 17, 1944, to report that "since February of this year there has not been a great deal of progress." He was losing as much as half his hexafluoride to corrosion effects:

> We thought the materials we had used to make this apparatus for working with the [hexafluoride] were made of impure metals. Therefore we next used the most highly-refined metals available for the system. However, they were

> still eaten away. It was therefore necessary to reduce the pressure of the system . . . to compensate for this erosion.

The cyclotron was operating at higher but not yet full power; Nishina was using it, he told Nobuuji, "to assay the concentrated, separated material." Significantly missing from the November 17 conference report is any mention of measurable separation of U235 from U238. Nishina's staff had understood for more than a year that he did not believe his country could build an atomic bomb in time to affect the outcome of the war. Whether he continued research out of loyalty, or because he thought such knowledge would be valuable after the war, or to win support for his laboratory and deferment from military service for his young men, the bare record does not reveal. On the occasion of the November 17 conference he once again complained of the lack of sufficiently powerful vacuum tubes for his cyclotron and told Nobuuji, contrary to the evidence of experiment, that the Riken's efforts at isotope separation were "now at a midpoint in their practical solution." Nobuuji might have been more helpful if he had understood even the most basic facts of the work. An exchange between the two men late in the meeting indicates the military liaison was as innocent of nuclear physics as a stone:

> *Nobuuji:* If uranium is to be used as an explosive, 10 kg is required. Why not use 10 kg of a conventional explosive?
>
> *Nishina:* That's nonsense.

A B-29, specially modified, first dropped an atomic bomb—a dummy Thin Man—at Muroc Army Air Force Base in California on March 3, 1944. Restrained by sway-bracing, a bomb hung singly in the B-29's bomb bay from a single release, and the first series of tests ended ignominiously that season when a release cable loosened and dumped one onto closed bomb-bay doors at 24,000 feet. "The doors were then opened," a technical report notes, "and the bomb tore free, considerably damaging the doors." A second series of tests in June went better. Word that Fat Man would be heavier than previously estimated encouraged Norman Ramsey's Delivery group to replace the original bomb-release mechanism, which had been modified from a standard glider tow release, with a sturdier British Lancaster bomber design.

Lessons learned, the Air Force began modifying seventeen more B-29's at the Glenn L. Martin plant in Omaha, Nebraska, in August; that month the service prepared to train a special group to deliver the first atomic bombs. The 393rd Bombardment Squadron, then based at Fairmont, Nebraska, in training for Europe, would form the nucleus of the new organization. Late in August Henry H. ("Hap") Arnold, the commanding general of the U.S. Army Air Forces, approved the assignment of an Illinois-born lieutenant colonel, Paul W. Tibbets, twenty-nine years old, to be group commander.

Tibbets may well have been the best bomber pilot in the Air Force. He had led the first B-17 bombing mission from England into Europe, had carried Dwight Eisenhower to his Gibraltar command post before the invasion of North Africa and had led the first bomber strike of that invasion. More recently he had been test-piloting the B-29, which in 1944 was just beginning to come on line, working with the physics department of the University of New Mexico in Albuquerque to determine how well the new bomber could defend itself against fighter attack at high altitude. He was a man of medium height and stocky build with dark, wavy hair and a widow's peak, full-faced and square-jawed, a pipe smoker. His father was a candy wholesaler in Florida and a disciplinarian from whom Tibbets probably acquired his reserved perfectionism; he was closer to his mother, the former Enola Gay Haggard of Glidden, Iowa. He had chosen an Air Force career, he told a postwar interviewer, after his mother had supported him in that choice against his father's opposition:

> When I was in college, studying to be a doctor, I realized that I had always wanted to fly. In 1936, my desire to do something about it reached the point where a family showdown on the subject developed. During the discussion, a few tempers flared, but my mother never said a word. In the end, still undecided, I got her off to the side and asked her what she thought. Despite the things that had been said on the subject, and the fact that most of the people in the discussion had included the statement, "You'll kill yourself in an airplane," Mother said, quite calmly and with positive assurance, "You go ahead and fly. You will be all right."

So far he had been, and now he had won a new assignment. He flew to Second Air Force headquarters in Colorado Springs at the beginning of September 1944 to report to commanding Major General Uzal Ent. An aide installed him in the general's anteroom. An officer came out, introduced himself, took Tibbets aside and asked him if he had ever been arrested. Tibbets considered the situation and decided to answer honestly to this stranger that he had been, as a teenager in North Miami Beach, caught *in flagrante delicto* in the backseat of a car with a girl. Lieutenant Colonel John Lansdale, Jr., who was responsible to Groves for atomic bomb intelligence and security, knew about the arrest and had questioned Tibbets to test his honesty. Now he led him into Ent's office. Norman Ramsey and

Deke Parsons were waiting there. "I'm satisfied," Lansdale said. The physicist and the Navy officer briefed Tibbets on the Manhattan Project and the Muroc bombing tests. Lansdale cautioned him at length on security. After the three men left, Ent specified Tibbets' assignment. "You have to put together an outfit and deliver this weapon," the pilot remembers the Second Air Force commander saying. "We don't know anything about it yet. We don't know what it can do. . . . You've got to mate it to the airplane and determine the tactics, the training, and the ballistics—everything. These are all parts of your problem. This thing is going to be very big. I believe it has the potential and possibility of ending the war." The delivery program within the Air Force had been codenamed Silverplate, Ent told him. If Tibbets needed anything, he had only to use that magic word; Arnold had accorded it the highest priority in the service.

The Air Force chose Wendover Field, Utah, as home base for the new organization. Tibbets flew to Utah early in September, looked the base over and liked what he saw. It was sited between low mountain ranges on the desert salt flats in gritty and secure isolation 125 miles west of Salt Lake City near the Utah-Nevada border; the flat basin, the sink of an ancient and enormous freshwater lake of which the Great Salt Lake is a brackish remnant, offered miles of desolation for bombing practice. Pioneers bound for California had suffered the crossing once—their wagon ruts could still be viewed nearby. The 393rd moved to Wendover in September and with the addition of troop-carrier and other support components became the 509th Composite Group. In October it began receiving its new B-29's.

A Boeing product, the B-29 was a revolutionary aircraft, the first intercontinental bomber. It was conceived in the late 1930s by ambitious officers within what was then still the Army Air Corps as the vehicle of their vision of wars fought at great distance by strategic air power. As early as September 1939 they proposed its use from bases in the Philippines, Siberia or the Aleutians in the event of war against Japan. It was the world's first pressurized bomber and at 70,000 pounds the heaviest production bomber ever built, 135,000 pounds loaded, a weight that required an 8,000-foot runway to lumber airborne. In appearance it was a sleek, polished-aluminum tube 99 feet long intersected by huge 141-foot wings—two B-29's would fill a football field—with a classic sinusoidal tail nearly three stories tall. Four Wright 18-cylinder radial engines that each developed 2,200 horsepower propelled it at altitude at 350 miles per hour maximum speed—it cruised at 220—and it was designed to fly a 4,000-mile mission with up to 20,000 pounds of bombs, though 12,000 pounds was nearer its operational load. It could cruise above 30,000 feet, out of range of flak and of most enemy fighters. Turbosuperchargers boosted engine power; outsized 16.5-foot propellers turned more slowly than those of any other aircraft; wing flaps, the world's largest, adjusted a fifth of wing area to adapt the high-speed, long-range, low-drag wing for takeoff and landing.

On the ground the B-29 rested level on three point landing gear: retractable wheels at the nose and under each wing. The plane's eleven-man crew occupied two pressurized sections within the five joined sections of the fuselage; tandem bomb bays fore and aft of the wings separated the nose section from the waist and tail, and to pass back from the nose to the waist required crawling through a pressurized one-man tunnel. The standard B-29 crew counted pilot, copilot, bombardier, flight engineer, navigator and radio operator in the nose section, three gunners and a radar operator in the waist and another gunner in the tail. Because electrical wiring was less vulnerable to battle damage than pneumatic or hydraulic tubing, the aircraft systems with the exception of the hydraulic wheel brakes operated entirely on electric motors, more than 150 in all, with a gasoline-powered donkey engine in the rear fuselage supplying current on the ground. Analog computers ran a central gun-control system, but all the guns were stripped from 509th bombers except the 20-millimeter cannon in the tail.

If the B-29's engines were powerful they were also notoriously susceptible to fires. To improve their horsepower-to-weight ratio Wright had used magnesium for their crankcases and accessory housings. Engine cooling was inadequate and exhaust valves tended to overheat and stick; an engine would then sometimes swallow a valve and catch fire. If the fire reached the magnesium, a metal commonly used in incendiary bombs, the engine would usually burn through the main wing spar and peel off the wing. To prevent such disasters Boeing improved engine cooling but the basic design fault persisted; there was no time to develop a new power plant if the aircraft was to serve the war for which it was invented. (One Delivery group physicist remembers skimming along at Wendover for miles after takeoff, mowing sagebrush, to cool the engines before climbing to altitude.)

Once at altitude the flight crews of the 509th practiced bombing runs, bombardiers aiming from above 30,000 feet through their Norden bombsights at progressively smaller target circles limed on the ground. Crews that had flown in cloudy Europe wondered why they were training in visual bombing; an odd evasive maneuver instructed them at least in the explosive potential of the unknown weapon they would carry. Tibbets briefed no one on the atomic bomb but directed his crews to nose their aircraft over into a sharp 155-degree diving turn immediately after bomb release. Diving the huge bombers rapidly increased their airspeed; by perfecting the maneuver the crews could escape ten miles from the delayed explosion, "safe from destruction" by a bomb of 20,000 tons TNT equivalent, writes Groves, "by a factor of two." Before they practiced their diving turns they dropped bombs of concrete and bombs filled with HE. These crudely riveted Fat Man imitations, painted bright orange for visibility, they called Pumpkins. The 509th worked hard; the winter wind howled over the Wendover reservation, trapping tumbleweeds on the barbed-wire fences; crews careened into Salt Lake City on weekends to blow out. Tibbets opened their mail, bugged their telephones, had them followed and shipped off those who broke security to the secure but miserable Aleutians for the duration of the war. He held authority over 225 officers and 1,542 enlisted men. With his silverplated requisitions he commandeered from around the world the best pilots, bombardiers, navigators and flight engineers he could find.

One of them, Captain Robert Lewis of Brooklyn, New York, stocky and blond, twenty-six years old, an abrasive but gifted pilot whom Tibbets had personally trained, had spent part of the summer of 1944 at Grand Island, Nebraska, teaching a senior officer with hundreds of combat hours behind him to fly B-29's. Thus checked out, Major General Curtis LeMay rode a C-54 to India late in August to take over the 20th Bomber Command, based in India with forward airfields in China from which it was attempting with fewer than two hundred B-29's to bomb Japan. The bombers had to ferry their own fuel and ordnance from India to China over the Himalayas before each mission—seven supply flights for each bombing strike, up to twelve gallons burned for each one gallon delivered. "It didn't work," LeMay writes in his autobiography. "No one could have made it work. It was founded on an utterly absurd logistic basis. Nevertheless, our entire Nation howled like a pack of wolves for an attack on the Japanese homeland."

Curtis LeMay was a wild man, hard-driving and tough, a bomber pilot, a big-game hunter, a chewer of cigars, dark, fleshy, smart. "I'll tell you what war is about," he once said bluntly—but he said it after the war—"you've got to kill people, and when you've killed enough they stop fighting." Through most of the war he seems to have held to the preference for precision bombing over area bombing that had distinguished the U.S. Air Force from the British since Churchill's and Cherwell's intervention of 1942. Sometimes in Europe precision bombing had served, though never decisively. Over Japan, so far, it had failed. And failure was LeMay's *bête noire.*

His father had been a failure, an odd-job drifter, forever moving his family around. The LeMays lived all over Ohio, in Pennsylvania, out in the wilds in Montana, in California. Curtis Emerson LeMay, born in Columbus, Ohio, in 1906, was the first of seven children. The two memories of early childhood he chooses to offer in his autobiography are linked. Of first seeing an airplane and chasing it madly: "I wanted not only the substance of the mysterious object, not only that part I could have touched with my hands. I wished also in vague yet unforgettable fashion for the drive and speed and energy of the creature." And of compulsively running away from home: "truancy" that "bordered on mania," his mother told him. "I had to grow older," LeMay writes, "and be burdened with a lot of responsibilities, and begin to nourish ambition—I had to do these things before I could manage to control my temper and discipline my activities."

He delivered telegrams and packages and boxes of candy. He delivered newspapers, sold newspapers, wholesaled newspapers to delivery boys, supporting himself and sometimes his family: "When the grocer hesitates about putting that latest basket of groceries on the bill, then you'd better be ready to come up with cash in hand. Very early in life I was convinced bitterly of this necessity. . . . The larder was a vague mystery which Pop didn't bother to penetrate." LeMay resented the missing childhood but moved on. He paid his own way through Ohio State by working nights at a steel foundry. ROTC in college led to the Ohio National Guard because the Guard had higher priority on Army flying-school enrollments than the Army Reserve. He won his wings in 1929 and never looked back: mess officer, navigation officer, General Headquarters navigator, B-10's, B-17's. In England in 1943 and 1944 he worked night and day to improve precision bombing. He won quick promotion.

Arnold sent him to the Pacific because he needed someone who could get the job done:

> General Arnold, fully committed to the B-29 program all along, had crawled out on a dozen limbs about a thousand times, in order to achieve physical resources and sufficient funds to build those airplanes and get them into combat. . . . So he finds they're not doing too well. He has to keep juggling missions and plans and people until the B-29s *do* do well. General Arnold was absolutely determined to get results out of this weapons system.

The B-29 had to be used, that is, successfully used, or men who had staked their careers and their convictions would be shamed, resources squandered that might have aided elsewhere in the war, lives lost futilely and millions of dollars wasted. The justification recurs.

The first B-29 to arrive in the Marianas landed on Saipan on October 12, 1944. Brigadier General Haywood S. Hansell, Jr., assigned to lead the 21st Bomber Command, flew it. As Arnold's chief of staff Hansell had helped formulate the doctrine of precision bombing and believed strongly in its central premise—that wars could be won by selectively destroying the enemy's key industries of war. A stream of new bombers followed the new commander out to the Marianas; the first U.S. aircraft to fly over Tokyo since the Doolittle raid of 1942 was a B-29 on November 1 soaring high and light on a photoreconnaissance mission. A French journalist living in Tokyo at the time, Robert Guillain, remembers his sense of anticlimax:

> The city waited. Millions of lives were suspended in the silence of the radiant autumn afternoon. For a moment, antiaircraft fire shook the horizon with a noise of doors slamming in the sky. Then—nothing: the all-clear was sounded without sight of a plane. The radio announced that a single B-29 had flown over the capital without dropping any bombs.

That seemed a reprieve and for a time only reconnaissance missions disturbed the ill-defended city. "One day the visitor finally appeared, flying at 35,000 feet," Guillain continues; "he even left his signature chalked on the blue sky: a line of pure white like some living thing that seemed to nose an almost imperceptible silver fly ahead of it." Back in the Marianas Hansell was teaching his men to navigate together, to fly in formation; they had trained in the United States only as individual crews.

Hansell received his first target directive on November 11. The Joint Chiefs of Staff had approved it and it reflected their conviction that bombing and naval blockade alone could not bring the Pacific war to a timely end. In September the Combined Chiefs—British and American together—had established a planning date for the end of the war: eighteen months after the defeat of Germany. The U.S. Joint Chiefs judged an invasion of the Japanese home islands essential to achieve that goal. The target directive Hansell received therefore gave first priority to the precision bombing of the Japanese aircraft industry (to cripple Japanese air defenses before an American invasion), second priority to supporting Pacific operations (MacArthur was even then reoccupying the Philippines, returning as he had promised he would) and third priority to testing the efficacy of area incendiary attacks. These priorities, putting precision bombing first, suited Hansell's own.

His crews flew their first raid on Japan from Saipan on November 24. Their target was the Musashi aircraft engine factory north of Tokyo ten miles from the Imperial Palace. A hundred planes began the mission. Seventeen aborted; six were unable to release their bombs. Flak was heavy and the target buried in undercast. But totally unexpected at the high altitude at which the bombers flew was a 140-mile-per-hour wind. They were blown with it over the target and their ground speed was therefore nearly 450 mph, impossible for the bombardiers. As a result only twenty-four planes managed to bomb the factory area—the rest scattered their loads over the docks and warehouses around Tokyo Bay—and only sixteen bombs hit the target. "I did not anticipate the extremely high wind velocities above thirty thousand feet," Hansell said later, "and they came as a very disagreeable surprise." The Air Force had discovered the jet stream.

LeMay was then still working with his 20th Bomber Command out of India and China. Supporting the indifferent military campaigns of Chiang Kai-shek was an activity he abhorred but was sometimes forced to perform. For six months Claire Chennault, the leathery Texan who headed the U.S. air staff assigned to the Nationalist Chinese Army, had been promoting the bombing of Hankow, the riverside city on the Yangtze five hundred miles inland from Shanghai from which Japan supplied its Asian mainland armies. With a renewed Japanese drive in interior China in November Chennault pressed for a Hankow attack. LeMay resisted diverting his command from Japanese home-island targets; the Joint Chiefs had to compel his participation. B-24's and B-25's were also massing for the strike; Chennault particularly wanted LeMay to load his aircraft with incendiaries and bomb from 20,000 feet rather than from above 30,000 feet in order to sow a denser pattern. LeMay reserved one aircraft in five for high explosives. Seventy-seven B-29's took part in the raid on December 18 and burned the Hankow river district down; fires raged out of control for three days. The lesson was not lost on Washington, nor on LeMay.

At Los Alamos the same week Groves, Parsons, Conant, Oppenheimer, Kistiakowsky, Ramsey and several other leaders met in Oppenheimer's office to discuss preparing Pumpkins—they called them blockbusters—for Tibbets' 509th Composite Group. The first Fat Man design, the 1222, had already been changed because it had proved so difficult to assemble—assembly required inserting, threading nuts onto and tightening more than 1,500 bolts—and redesign meant the loss of about 80 percent of the tooling work done at the Pacific Aviation Company in Los Angeles through the autumn. The first unit of a new, simpler design, the 1291, would be ready in three days, on December 22. "Captain Parsons said that the blockbuster production for the 1291 gadget between 15 February and 15 March would require a minimum of 30 blockbusters," the minutes of the meeting report, "so that each B-29 could drop at least two. . . . An additional 20 blockbusters should be produced for H.E. testing. . . . Following that, 75 units should be produced for overseas shipment."

Groves wanted none of it. He wanted no dummy 1291's drop-tested outside the continental United States and he saw no reason to build 75

Pumpkins for overseas target practice for Tibbets' crews. It was the end of 1944 and he was feeling the pressure of accumulating Manhattan Project delays: "General Groves indicated that too much valuable time was being taken from other problems to devote time to the blockbuster program." Conant asked how long the blockbuster program would have to continue; Parsons answered combatively that it would have to continue as long as Tibbets' group operated so that 509th crews could maintain their bombing skills. He relented to reveal that "Colonel Tibbets' Group expected to reach peak combat training by 1 July."

Since Parsons had not succeeded in person in convincing Groves of the importance of bomb-assembly and bombing practice he wrote the general a forceful memorandum on the day after Christmas. There were major differences, he pointed out, between the "gun gadget" and the "implosion gadget," particularly in terms of final assembly:

> It is believed fair to compare the assembly of the gun gadget to the normal field assembly of a torpedo, as far as mechanical tests are involved. . . . The case of the implosion gadget is very different, and is believed comparable in complexity to rebuilding an airplane in the field. Even this does not fully express the difficulty, since much of the assembly involves bare blocks of high explosives and, in all probability, will end with the securing in position of at least thirty-two boosters and detonators, and then connecting these to firing circuits, including special coaxial cables and high voltage condenser circuit. . . . I believe that anyone familiar with advance base operations . . . would agree that this is the most complex and involved operation which has ever been attempted outside of a combined laboratory and ammunition depot.

Parsons' simple and compelling point: the assembly team as well as the bombardiers needed practice. Groves relented; Tibbets got his Pumpkins.

More conventional bombs were falling regularly now on Japan, if not yet to devastating effect. Robert Guillain, the French journalist, remembers the first night raid over Tokyo at the end of November:

> Suddenly there was an odd, rhythmic buzzing that filled the night with a deep, powerful pulsation and made my whole house vibrate: the marvelous sound of the B-29s passing invisibly through a nearby corner of sky, pursued by the barking of antiaircraft fire. . . . I went up on my terrace roof. . . . The B-29s caught in the sweeping searchlight beams went tranquilly on their way followed by the red flashes of ack-ack bursts which could not reach them at that altitude. A pink light spread across the horizon behind a near hill, growing bigger, bloodying the whole sky. Other red splotches lit up like nebulas else-

where on the horizon. It was soon to be a familiar sight. Feudal Tokyo was called Edo, and the people there had always been terrified by the frequent accidental fires they euphemistically called "flowers of Edo." That night, all Tokyo began to blossom.

While Parsons and Groves were debating Pumpkins, Lauris Norstad, who had succeeded Hansell in Washington as Hap Arnold's chief of staff when Hansell moved to the Marianas, passed along word to his predecessor that a trial fire raid on Nagoya, Japan's third-largest city, was an "urgent requirement." Hansell resisted. "With great difficulty," he wrote Norstad, he had "implanted the principle that our mission is the destruction of primary targets by sustained and determined attacks using precision bombing methods both visual and radar" and he was "beginning to get results." Ironically, he feared that area bombing would slacken his crews' hard-won skills. Norstad sympathized but insisted that Nagoya was only a test, "a special requirement resulting from thc necessity of future planning." Nearly one hundred of Hansell's B-29's flew incendiaries to Nagoya, at the southern end of the Nobi Plain two hundred miles southwest of Tokyo, on January 3, 1945, and started numerous small fires that resisted coalescing.

In three months of hard flying, taking regular losses, Hansell had managed to destroy none of his nine high-priority targets. His determination not to rise to the bait Washington was offering—Billy Mitchell, the Air Force's earliest strategic champion, had pointed out the vulnerability of Japanese cities to fire as long ago as 1924—doomed his command. Norstad flew out to Guam to relieve Hansell of duty on January 6. Curtis LeMay arrived from China the next day. "LeMay is an operator," Norstad told Hansell, "the rest of us are planners. That's all there is to it." As if to encourage the new commander to independence, Hap Arnold suffered a major heart attack on January 15 and withdrew for a time to Miami sunshine to heal.

LeMay officially took command on January 20. He had 345 B-29's in the Marianas and more arriving. He had 5,800 officers and 46,000 enlisted men. And he had all Hansell's problems to solve: the jet stream; the terrible Japanese weather, seven days of visual bombing a month with luck and not much weather prediction because the Soviets refused to cooperate from Siberia, whence the weather came; B-29 engines that overheated and burned out while straining up the long climb to altitude; indifferent bombing:

> General Arnold needed results. Larry Norstad had made that very plain. In effect he had said: "You go ahead and get results with the B-29. If you don't get results, you'll be fired. If you don't get results, also, there'll never be any Strategic Air Forces of the Pacific. . . . If you don't get results it will mean

eventually a mass amphibious invasion of Japan, to cost probably half a million more American lives."

LeMay set his crews to intensive training. They were beginning to get radar units and he saw to it that they were able at least to identify the transition from water to land. He ordered high-altitude precision strikes but experimented with firebombing as well; 159 tons on Kobe on February 3 burned out a thousand buildings. Not good enough: "another month of indifferent operations," LeMay calls February:

> When I summed it all up, I realized that we had not accomplished very much during those six or seven weeks. We were still going in too high, still running into those big jet stream winds upstairs. Weather was almost always bad.
>
> I sat up nights, fine-tooth-combing all the pictures we had of every target which we had attacked or scouted. I examined Intelligence reports as well.
>
> Did actually very much in the way of low-altitude flak exist up there in Japan? I just couldn't find it.
>
> There was food for thought in this.

There was food for thought as well in two compelling February horrors. One occurred halfway around the world, in Europe, where LeMay had flown so often before. The other began nearby. The hardbitten general from Ohio who despised failure and was failing in Japan could not have avoided learning in detail of both.

The European event was the bombing of Dresden, the capital of the German state of Saxony, on the Elbe River 110 miles south of Berlin, famous for its art and its graceful and delicate architecture. In February 1945 the Russian front advanced to less than eighty miles to the east; refugees streamed west from that deadly harrowing and into the Saxon city. Lacking significant war industry, Dresden had not been a bombing target before and was essentially undefended. It counted in its suburbs 26,000 Allied prisoners of war.

Winston Churchill instigated the Dresden raid. The Secretary of State for Air responded to a phone call from the Prime Minister sometime in January with tactical proposals; the P.M. countered as testily as he had countered in the matter of Niels Bohr:

> I did not ask you last night about plans for harrying the German retreat from Breslau. On the contrary, I asked whether Berlin, and no doubt other large cities in East Germany should not now be considered especially attractive targets. I am glad that this is "under consideration." Pray report to me tomorrow what is going to be done.

Dresden's number thus came up. On the cold night of February 13, 1,400 Bomber Command aircraft dropped high explosives and nearly 650,000 incendiaries on the city; six planes were lost. The firestorm that ensued was visible two hundred miles away. The next day, just after noon, 1,350 American heavy bombers flew over to attack the railroad marshaling yards with high explosives but found nine-tenths cover of cloud and smoke and bombed a far larger area, encountering no flak at all.

The American novelist Kurt Vonnegut, Jr., was a young prisoner of war in Dresden at the time of the attack. He described his experience to an interviewer long after the war:

> The first fancy city I'd ever seen. A city full of statues and zoos, like Paris. We were living in a slaughterhouse, in a nice new cement-block hog barn. They put bunks and straw mattresses in the barn, and we went to work every morning as contract labor in a malt syrup factory. The syrup was for pregnant women. The damned sirens would go off and we'd hear some other city getting it—*whump a whump a whumpa whump.* We never expected to get it. There were very few air-raid shelters in town and no war industries, just cigarette factories, hospitals, clarinet factories. Then a siren went off—it was February 13, 1945—and we went down two stories under the pavement into a big meat locker. It was cool there, with cadavers hanging all around. When we came up the city was gone.... The attack didn't sound like a hell of a lot either. *Whump.* They went over with high explosives first to loosen things up, and then scattered incendiaries.... They burnt the whole damn town down....
>
> Every day [afterward] we walked into the city and dug into basements and shelters to get the corpses out, as a sanitary measure. When we went into them, a typical shelter, an ordinary basement usually, looked like a streetcar full of people who'd simultaneously had heart failure. Just people sitting there in their chairs, all dead. A fire storm is an amazing thing. It doesn't occur in nature. It's fed by the tornadoes that occur in the midst of it and there isn't a damned thing to breathe. We brought the dead out. They were loaded onto wagons and taken to parks, large, open areas in the city which weren't filled with rubble. The Germans got funeral pyres going, burning the bodies to keep them from stinking and from spreading disease. One hundred thirty thousand corpses were hidden underground.

Nearer at hand Curtis LeMay could see the intensity and ferocity of Japanese resistance increasing as American forces fought their way toward the home islands. The latest hellhole was Iwo Jima—Sulfur Island—a mass of volcanic ash and rock only seven square miles in area with a dormant volcano at one end, Mount Suribachi, that had risen from the sea within historic times. Miasmic with sulfur fumes, a steam of rotten eggs, Iwo lacked fresh water but supported two airfields from which Japanese fighter-bombers departed to attack LeMay's B-29's shining on their hardstands on Guam, Saipan and Tinian. It was nine hundred miles closer to Tokyo than the Marianas and its radar outposts gave Honshu antiaircraft batteries and defensive fighter units ample warning when B-29's dispatched for strategic assault passed overhead.

The Japanese understood the island's strategic position and had prepared for months, often under bombardment from U.S. Navy and Air Force planes, to defend it. Fifteen thousand men turned Iwo Jima into a fortress of bunkers, ditches, trenches, 13,000 yards of tunnels, 5,000 pillboxes and fortified cave entrances, vast galleys and wards built into Suribachi, blockhouses with thick concrete walls. The emplacements were armed with the largest concentration of artillery the Japanese had assembled anywhere up to that day: coastal defense guns in concrete bunkers, fieldpieces of all calibers shielded in caves, rocket launchers, tanks buried in the sand up to their turrets, 675-pound spigot mortars, long-barreled anti-aircraft guns cranked down parallel to the ground. The Japanese commander, Lieutenant General Tadamichi Kuribayashi, taught his men a new strategy: "We would all like to die quickly and easily, but that would not inflict heavy casualties. We must fight from cover as long as we possibly can." His soldiers and marines, increased in strength now to more than 21,000, would no longer throw away their lives in banzai charges. They would resist to the death. "I am sorry to end my life here, fighting the United States of America," Kuribayashi wrote his wife. "But I want to defend this island as long as I can." He expected no rescue. "They meant to make the conquest of Iwo so costly," says William Manchester, who fought not this battle but the next one, Okinawa, "that the Americans would recoil from the thought of invading their homeland."

Washington secretly considered sanitizing the island with artillery shells loaded with poison gas lobbed in by ships standing well offshore; the proposal reached the White House but Roosevelt curtly vetoed it. It might have saved thousands of lives and hastened the surrender—arguments used to justify most of the mass slaughters of the Second World War, and neither the United States nor Japan had signed the Geneva Convention prohibiting such use—but Roosevelt presumably remembered the world outcry that had followed German introduction of poison gas in the First World War and decided to leave the sanitizing of Iwo Jima to the U.S. Marines.

They began landing on Saturday, February 19, at 9 A.M., after weeks of naval barrage and bombing. A less well-defended foe would have been pulverized by that battering; the Japanese dug in on Iwo Jima were only groggy from the long disturbance of their sleep. The Navy ferried the marines to shore in amphtracs, gave them over to the deep and treacherous black pumice of the beaches and ran out to reload. The Japanese commanded Suribachi, the high ground; they had zeroed in on every point of consequence on the flat island and now stood back to fire. On the beaches, says Manchester, men were more often killed by artillery than by bullets:

> The invaders were taking heavy mortar and artillery fire. Steel sleeted down on them like the lash of a desert storm. By dusk 2,420 of the 30,000 men on the beachhead were dead or wounded. The perimeter was only four thousand yards long, seven hundred yards deep in the north and a thousand yards in the south. It resembled Doré's illustrations of the *Inferno*. Essential cargo—ammo, rations, water—was piled up in sprawling chaos. And gore, flesh, and bones were lying all about. The deaths on Iwo were extraordinarily violent. There seemed to be no clean wounds; just fragments of corpses. It reminded one battalion medical officer of a Bellevue dissecting room. Often the only way to distinguish between Japanese and marine dead was by the legs; Marines wore canvas leggings and Nips khaki puttees. Otherwise identification was completely impossible. You tripped over strings of viscera fifteen feet long, over bodies which had been cut in half at the waist. Legs and arms, and heads bearing only necks, lay fifty feet from the closest torsos. As night fell the beach reeked with the stench of burning flesh.

After that first awful night, when the Japanese might have squandered themselves in counterattacks but chose instead to hold fast to their defensive redoubts, the leaders of the invasion understood that they would pay with American lives for every foot of the island they captured. Kuribayashi's final order to his men demanded of them the same sacrifice: "We shall infiltrate into the midst of the enemy and annihilate them," he exhorted. "We shall grasp bombs, charge the enemy tanks and destroy them. With every salvo we will, without fail, kill the enemy. Each man will make it his duty to kill ten of the enemy before dying!" Slow, cruel fighting continued for most of a month. In the end, late in March, when shell and fire had changed the very landscape, victory had cost 6,821 marines killed and 21,865 wounded of some 60,000 committed, a casualty ratio of 2 to 1, the highest in Marine Corps history. Of Japanese defenders, 20,000 died on Iwo Jima; only 1,083 allowed themselves to be captured.

That so many were dying to protect his B-29 crews when their results were inconsequential to the war catalyzed LeMay to radical departure. The deaths had to be justified, the debt of death repaid.

One more incendiary test, 172 planes over Tokyo on February 23, produced the best results of any bombing so far, a full square mile of the city burned out. But LeMay had long known that fire would burn down

Japan's wooden cities if properly set. Proper setting, not firebombing itself, was the problem he struggled to solve.

He studied strike photographs. He reviewed intelligence reports. "The Japanese just didn't seem to have those 20- and 40-millimeter [antiaircraft] guns," he remembers realizing. "That's the type of defense which must be used against bombers coming in to attack at a low or medium altitude. Up at twenty-five or thirty thousand feet they have to shoot at you with 80- or 90-millimeter stuff, or they're never going to knock you down. . . . But 88-millimeter guns, *if you come in low,* are impotent. You're moving too fast."

Low-altitude firebombing had other important advantages. Flying low saved fuel coming and going from the Marianas: the B-29's could carry more bombs. Flying low put less strain on the big Wright engines: fewer aircraft would have to abort or ditch. LeMay added in another variable and proposed to bomb at night; his intelligence sources indicated that Japanese fighters lacked airborne radar units. With little or no light flak or fighter cover Tokyo would be nearly defenseless. Why not, then, LeMay reasoned, take out B-29 guns and gunners and further increase the bomb load? He decided to leave the tail gunner as an observer and pull the rest.

He discussed his plan with only a few members of his staff. They worked out a target zone, a flat, densely crowded twelve square miles of workers' houses adjacent to the northeast corner of the Imperial Palace in central Tokyo. Even two decades after the war LeMay felt the need to justify the site as in some sense industrial: "All the people living around that Hattori factory where they make shell fuses. That's the way they disperse their industry: little kids helping out [at home], working all day, little bits of kids." The U.S. Strategic Bombing Survey notes frankly that 87.4 percent of the target zone was residential, and LeMay goes on to more candid admission later in his autobiography:

> No matter how you slice it, you're going to kill an awful lot of civilians. Thousands and thousands. But, if you don't destroy the Japanese industry, we're going to have to invade Japan. And how many Americans will be killed in an invasion of Japan? Five hundred thousand seems to be the lowest estimate. Some say a million.
>
> . . . We're at war with Japan. We were attacked by Japan. Do you want to kill Japanese, or would you rather have Americans killed?

A little later in the war a spokesman for the Fifth Air Force would point out that since the Japanese government was mobilizing civilians to resist invasion, "the entire population of Japan is a proper military target."

Onto the proper military target of working-class Tokyo LeMay decided to drop two kinds of incendiaries. His lead crews would carry M47's, 100-pound oil-gel bombs, 182 per aircraft, each of which was capable of starting a major fire. Behind those crews his major force would sow M69's, 6-pound gelled-gasoline bombs, 1,520 per aircraft. He eschewed magnesium bombs because those more rigid weapons smashed all the way through the tile roofs and light wooden floors of Japanese houses and buried themselves ineffectually in the earth. LeMay also remembers including a few high explosives in the mix to demoralize the firemen.

He delayed seeking approval of his plan until the day before the raid was scheduled to go, taking responsibility for it himself and determined to risk the gamble. Norstad approved on March 8 and alerted the Air Force public relations staff to the possibility of "an outstanding strike." Arnold was informed the same afternoon. LeMay's crews were stunned to hear they would fly their sorties unarmed at staggered levels between five and seven thousand feet. "You're going to deliver the biggest firecracker the Japanese have ever seen," LeMay told them. Some of them thought he was crazy and considered mutiny. Others cheered.

From Guam first, from Saipan next and then from Tinian 334 B-29's took off for Tokyo in the late afternoon of March 9. They were loaded with more than 2,000 tons of incendiaries.

They flew toward a city that an Associated Press correspondent who knew it well had described in 1943 in a best-selling book as "grim, drab and grubby." Freed from Japanese detention in Manila and then in Shanghai, Russell Brines had brought home a message about the people he had lived among before the war and whose language he spoke:

> "We will fight," the Japanese say, "until we eat stones!" The phrase is old; now revived and ground deeply into Japanese consciousness by propagandists skilled in marshaling their sheeplike people. . . . [It] means they will continue the war until every man—perhaps every woman and child—lies face downward on the battlefield. Thousands of Japanese, maybe hundreds of thousands, accept it literally. To ignore this suicide complex would be as dangerous as our pre-war oversight of Japanese determination and cunning which made Pearl Harbor possible. . . .
>
> American fighting men back from the front have been trying to tell America this is a war of extermination. They have seen it from foxholes and barren strips of bullet-strafed sand. I have seen it from behind enemy lines. Our picture coincides. This *is* a war of extermination. The Japanese militarists have made it that way.

The fighting men of the Navy and the Air Force had seen particular evidence of Japanese doggedness that autumn and winter in the appearance of kamikazes, planes loaded with high explosives and deliberately flown to ram ships. Between October and March young Japanese pilots, most of them barely qualified university students, sacrificed themselves in some nine hundred sorties. Navy fighters and antiaircraft guns shot most of the kamikazes down. About four hundred U.S. ships were hit and only about one hundred sunk or severely damaged in a fleet of thousands, but the attacks were alien and terrifying; they served to confirm for Americans the extent of Japanese desperation even as they further depleted Japan's waning air defenses.

LeMay's pathfinders arrived first over Tokyo a little after midnight on March 10. On the district of Shitamachi on the flatlands east of the Sumida River where 750,000 people lived crowded into wood-and-paper houses they marked a diagonal of fire and then crossed it to ignite a gigantic, glowing X. At 0100 the main force of B-29's came on and began methodically bombing the flatlands. The wind was blowing at 15 miles per hour. The bombers carried their 1,520 M69's in 500-pound clusters that broke apart a few hundred feet above the ground. Main-force intervalometers—the bomb-bay mechanisms that spaced the release of the clusters—had been set for 50-foot intervals. Each planeload then covered about a third of a square mile of houses. If only a fifth of the incendiaries started fires, that was one fire for every 30,000 square feet—one fire for every fifteen or twenty closely spaced houses. Robert Guillain remembers a deadlier density:

> The inhabitants stayed heroically put as the bombs dropped, faithfully obeying the order that each family defend its own house. But how could they fight the fires with that wind blowing and when a single house might be hit by ten or even more of the bombs . . . that were raining down by the thousands? As they fell, cylinders scattered a kind of flaming dew that skittered along the roofs, setting fire to everything it splashed and spreading a wash of dancing flames everywhere.

By 0200 the wind had increased to more than 20 miles per hour. Guillain climbed to his roof to observe:

> The fire, whipped by the wind, began to scythe its way through the density of that wooden city. . . . A huge borealis grew. . . . The bright light dispelled the night and B-29's were visible here and there in the sky. For the first time, they flew low or middling high in staggered levels. Their long, glinting wings, sharp as blades, could be seen through the oblique columns of smoke rising from the city, suddenly reflecting the fire from the furnace below, black silhouettes gliding through the fiery sky to reappear farther on, shining golden against the dark roof of heaven or glittering blue, like meteors, in the searchlight beams spraying the vault from horizon to horizon. . . . All the Japanese in the gar-

> dens near mine were out of doors or peering up out of their holes, uttering cries of admiration—this was typically Japanese—at this grandiose, almost theatrical spectacle.

Something worse than a firestorm was kindled in Tokyo that night. The U.S. Strategic Bombing Survey calls it a conflagration, begun when the high wind heeled over the pillar of hot and burning gases that the fires had volatilized and convection had carried up into the air:

> The chief characteristic of the conflagration . . . was the presence of a fire front, an extended wall of fire moving to leeward, preceded by a mass of preheated, turbid, burning vapors. The pillar was in a much more turbulent state than that of [a] fire storm, and being usually closer to the ground, it produced more flame and heat, and less smoke. The progress and destructive features of the conflagration were consequently much greater than those of [a] fire storm, for the fire continued to spread until it could reach no more material. . . . The 28-mile-per-hour wind, measured a mile from the fire, increased to an estimated 55 miles at the perimeter, and probably more within. An extended fire swept over 15 square miles in 6 hours. Pilots reported that the air was so violent that B-29s at 6,000 feet were turned completely over, and that the heat was so intense, even at that altitude, that the entire crew had to don oxygen masks. The area of the fire was nearly 100 percent burned; no structure or its contents escaped damage. The fire had spread largely in the direction of the natural wind.

A bombardier who flew through the black turbulence above the conflagration remembers it as "the most terrifying thing I've ever known."

In the shallower canals of Shitamachi, where people submerged themselves to escape the fire, the water boiled.

The Sumida River stopped the conflagration from sweeping more than 15.8 square miles of the city. The Strategic Bombing Survey estimates that "probably more persons lost their lives by fire at Tokyo in a 6-hour period than at any [equivalent period of] time in the history of man." The fire storm at Dresden may have killed more people but not in so short a space of time. More than 100,000 men, women and children died in Tokyo on the night of March 9–10, 1945; a million were injured, at least 41,000 seriously; a million in all lost their homes. Two thousand tons of incendiaries delivered that punishment—in the modern notation, two kilotons. But the wind, not the weight of bombs alone, created the conflagration, and therefore the efficiency of the slaughter was in some sense still in part an act of God.

Hap Arnold sent LeMay a triumphant telex: CONGRATULATIONS. THIS MISSION SHOWS YOUR CREWS HAVE GOT THE GUTS FOR ANYTHING. Certainly

LeMay did; having gambled and succeeded, he quickly pushed on. His B-29's firebombed Nagoya on March 11; firebombed Osaka by radar on March 13; firebombed Kobe on March 16—stocks of M69's were running low and M17A1 clusters of 4-pound magnesium thermite bombs, less effective, had to be substituted; firebombed Nagoya again on March 18. "Then," says LeMay, "we ran out of bombs. Literally." In ten days and 1,600 sorties the Twentieth Air Force burned out 32 square miles of the centers of Japan's four largest cities and killed at least 150,000 people and almost certainly tens of thousands more. "I consider that for the first time," LeMay wrote Norstad privately in April, "strategic air bombardment faces a situation in which its strength is proportionate to the magnitude of its task. I feel that the destruction of Japan's ability to wage war lies within the capability of this command." He had found a method, LeMay had begun to believe, whereby the Air Force might end the Pacific war without invasion.

At Oak Ridge guests removed their shoes before entering a house. Hiring was still increasing on the muddy Tennessee reservation and construction continuing, challenges to the meager ground cover that a Tennessee Eastman employee was moved to immortalize anonymously in verse:

In order not to check in late,
I've had to lose a lot of weight,
From swimming through a fair-sized flood
And wading through the goddam mud.

I've lost my rubbers and my shoes
Perpetually I have the blues
My spirits tumble with a thud
Because of all this goddam mud.

It's in my system so that when
I cut my finger now and then
Instead of bleeding just plain blood
Out pours a stream of goddam mud.

Mud measured progress: Ernest Lawrence's calutrons, built at such great expense, had begun enriching uranium. A minimum of 100 grams per day—3.5 ounces—of 10 percent U235 came through the Alpha racetracks beginning in late September 1944. But poor planning for chemical recovery of that feed from the Beta tanks wasted some 40 percent of it, as Mark Oliphant reported to James Chadwick from Oak Ridge early in November: "This loss or hold-up . . . has resulted in a very serious delay in the production of material for the first weapon. . . . The chemistry, viewed as a whole, I believe to present an appalling example of lack of coordination, of inefficiency, and bad management."

A copy of Oliphant's complaint went to Groves, who must have acted quickly; the troubleshooting Australian physicist could report to the general two weeks later that "the output from the beta tracks has shown an abrupt and very satisfying upward trend." In his letter to Chadwick, Oliphant had noted a Beta output of only 40 grams per day; now "an output of about 90 grams per day [has] been reached and there [is] reason for believing that this level would be maintained, or even increased, during the coming months." He concluded optimistically that "there is now a definite hope that continued effort on the part of the operating company and others will lead early in the New Year to a plant output of the order of that expected."

As of January 1945 on any given day about 85 percent of some 864 Alpha calutron tanks operated to produce 258 grams—9 ounces—of 10 percent enriched product; at the same time 36 Beta tanks converted the accumulated Alpha product to 204 grams—7.2 ounces—per day of 80 percent enriched U235, sufficient enrichment to make a bomb. James Bryant Conant calculated in his handwritten history notes on January 6 that a kilogram of U235 per day would mean one gun bomb every six weeks. It follows that the gun bomb required about 42 kilograms—92.6 pounds, about 2.8 critical masses—of U235. Without further improvement the calutrons alone could produce that much material in 6.8 months, and Conant noted after conferring with Groves that "it looks as if 40–45 kg . . . will be obtained by July 1." Ernest Lawrence's monumental effort had succeeded; every gram of U235 in the one Little Boy that should be ready by mid-1945 would pass at least once through his calutrons.

Conant also contrasted his assumptions of June 1944 with his assumptions at the beginning of the new year to draw up a problematic balance sheet: while he had previously "believed a few bombs might do the trick" of ending the war, at the beginning of 1945 he was "convinced many bombs will now be required (German experience)." The German experience was probably the determined German resistance that was prolonging the war in Europe, particularly the counteroffensive through the Ardennes known as the Battle of the Bulge that had begun in mid-December and still threatened Allied lines at the time of Conant's notes. It was partly Allied frustration with such continuing resistance that would lead in another month to the atrocity of the Dresden bombing.

Houdaille-Hershey was finally delivering satisfactory barrier tubes for the K-25 gaseous-diffusion plant. Union Carbide had scheduled barrier delivery to take advantage of K-25's organization as a cascade; as individual tanks, called converters, arrived, workers hooked them into the system and tested them for leaks in atmospheres of nitrogen and helium with the portable mass spectrometers that Alfred Nier had designed. When a stage was leakproof and otherwise ready it could be operated without further delay, and the first stage of the enormous K-25 cascade was charged with uranium hexafluoride on January 20, 1945. Enrichment by gaseous barrier diffusion in the most advanced automated industrial plant in the world had begun. It would proceed efficiently with only normal maintenance for decades.

The pipes in Philip Abelson's scaled-up thermal-diffusion plant, S-50, leaked so badly they had to be welded, which delayed production, but all twenty-one racks had begun enriching uranium by March. Juggling the different enrichment processes to produce maximum output in minimum time then became a complex mathematical and organizational challenge. Lieutenant Colonel Kenneth D. Nichols, Groves' talented and long-suffering assistant, worked out the scheduling. Based on Nichols' schedule Groves decided in mid-March not to build more Alpha calutrons, as Lawrence had proposed, but to construct instead a second gaseous-diffusion plant and a fourth Beta plant. Though he certainly expected his atomic bombs to end the war, Groves seems to have justified the new construction by the Joint Chiefs' conservative estimate that the Pacific war would end eighteen months after the European; his new plants could not be completed before February 15, 1946, he explained in his proposal, but "on the assumption that the war with Japan will not be over before July, 1946, it is planned to proceed with the additions to the two plants unless instructions to the contrary are received." Perhaps he was simply being prudent.

Early in 1945 Oak Ridge began shipping bomb-grade U235 to Los Alamos. Between shipments Groves took no chances with a substance far more valuable gram for gram than diamonds. Although the Army had condemned all the land and ejected the original inhabitants from the Clinton reservation area, at the dead end of a dusty reservation back road cattle grazed in a pasture beside a white farmhouse. A concrete silo towered over the road, which was sheltered by a steep bluff. From the air the scene resembled any number of small Tennessee holdings, but the silo was a machine-gun emplacement, the farm was manned by security guards, and built into the side of the bluff a concrete bunker shielded a bank-sized vault completely encircled with guarded walkways. In this pastoral fortress Groves stored his accumulating grams of U235. Armed couriers transported it as uranium tetrafluoride in special luggage by car to Knoxville, where they boarded the overnight express to Chicago. They passed on the luggage the next morning to their Chicago counterparts, who held reserved space on the Santa Fe Chief. Twenty-six hours later, in midafternoon, the Chicago couriers debarked at Lamy, the stranded desert way station that served Santa Fe. Los Alamos security men met the train and completed the transfer to the Hill, where chemists waited eagerly to reduce the rare cargo to metal.

Plutonium production at Hanford depended as much on chemical separation as it did on chain-reacting piles. The chemistry was Glenn Seaborg's, spectacularly scaled up a billionfold directly from his team's earlier ultramicrochemical work. The plutonium in the slugs irradiated in the Hanford piles emerged mixed to the extent of only about 250 parts per million with uranium and highly radioactive fission products. Carrier chemistry—the fractional crystallization of Marie Curie and Otto Hahn—was therefore required to help the scant plutonium along. The man-made metal is extremely poisonous if ingested but only mildly radioactive. To make it safe to handle it also needed to be purified to less than 1 part in 10 million of fission products. And because the pile slugs developed such a burden of radioactivity, all but the final chemical processing had to be carried out by remote control behind thick shielding.

Seaborg's team developed two separation processes to take advantage of the different chemistries of plutonium's several different valence states. One process used bismuth phosphate as a carrier; the other used lanthanum fluoride. Bismuth phosphate, scaled up directly from Met Lab experiments, served the primary purpose of uranium and fission-product decontamination. Lanthanum fluoride, applied at pilot scale at Oak Ridge, then concentrated the plutonium from the large volume of solution in which it was suspended.

Hanford was the largest plant Du Pont had ever constructed and operated; not least among its facilities were the chemical separation buildings. "Originally eight separation plants were considered necessary," writes Groves, "then six, then four. Finally, with the benefit of the operating experience and information obtained from the Clinton semi-works, we decided to build only three, of which two would operate and one would serve as a reserve." For safety the plants went up behind Gable Mountain ten miles southwest of the riverside piles. Each building was 800 feet long, 65 feet wide and 80 feet tall, poured-concrete structures so massive the workers called them Queen Marys; the British ocean liner of that name was only a fifth again as long. The Queen Marys were essentially large concrete boxes, says Groves, containment buildings "in which there were individual cells containing the various parts involved in the process equipment. To provide protection from the intense radioactivity, the cells were surrounded by concrete walls seven feet thick and were covered by six feet of concrete."

Each Queen Mary contained forty cells, and each cell's lid, which could be removed by an overhead crane that rolled the length of the building's long canyon, weighed 35 tons. Irradiated slugs ejected from a production pile would be stored in pools of water 16.5 feet deep to remain until the most intense and therefore short-lived of their fission-product radioactivities decayed away, the water glowing blue around them with Cerenkov radiation, a sort of charged-particle sonic boom. The slugs would then move in shielded casks on special railroad cars to one of the Queen Marys, where they would first be dissolved in hot nitric acid. A standard equipment group occupied two cells: a centrifuge, a catch tank, a precipitator and a solution tank, all made of specially fabricated corrosion-resistant stainless steel. The liquid solution that the slugs had become would move through these units by steam-jet syphoning, a low-maintenance substitute for pumps. There were three necessary steps to the separation process: solution, precipitation and centrifugal removal of the precipitate. These would repeat from equipment group to equipment group down the canyon of the separation building. The end products would be radioactive wastes, stored on site in underground tanks, and small quantities of highly purified plutonium nitrate.

Once the Queen Marys were contaminated with radioactivity no repair crews could enter them. Equipment operators had to be able to maintain them entirely by remote control. The operators trained at Du Pont in Delaware, at Oak Ridge and on mockups at Hanford, but the engineer in charge, Raymond Genereaux, sought more authoritative qualification. And found it: he required his operators, one hundred of whom arrived at Hanford in October 1944, to install the process equipment into the first completed separation building by remote control, pretending the canyon was already radioactive. They did, awkwardly at first but with increasing confidence as practice improved their remote-manipulation skills.

"When the Queen Marys began to function," Leona Marshall remembers, "dissolving the irradiated slugs in concentrated nitric acid, great plumes of brown fumes blossomed above the concrete canyons, climbed thousands of feet into the air, and drifted sideways as they cooled, blown by winds aloft." B-pile slugs traveled by rail into the 221-T separation plant beginning on December 26, 1944. "The yields in the first plant runs . . . ranged between 60 and 70 per cent," Seaborg notes proudly, and "reached 90 per cent early in February 1945." Lieutenant Colonel Franklin T. Matthias, Groves' representative at Hanford, personally carried the first small batch of plutonium nitrate by train from Portland to Los Angeles, where he turned it over to a Los Alamos security courier. Thereafter shipments—small subcritical batches in metal containers in wooden boxes—

traveled in convoy by Army ambulance via Boise, Salt Lake City, Grand Junction and Pueblo to Los Alamos.

Bertrand Goldschmidt, the French chemist who worked with Glenn Seaborg, puts the Manhattan Engineer District at the height of its wartime development in perspective with a startling comparison. It was, he writes in a memoir, "the astonishing American creation in three years, at a cost of two billion dollars, of a formidable array of factories and laboratories—as large as the entire automobile industry of the United States at that date."

One of the mysteries of the Second World War was the lack of an early and dedicated American intelligence effort to discover the extent of German progress toward atomic bomb development. If, as the record repeatedly emphasizes, the United States was seriously worried that Germany might reverse the course of the war with such a surprise secret weapon, why did its intelligence organizations, or the Manhattan Project, not mount a major effort of espionage?

Vannevar Bush had raised the question of espionage with Franklin Roosevelt at their crucial meeting on October 9, 1941, when Bush apprised the President of the MAUD Report, but the OSRD director got no satisfactory answer, probably because the United States was not yet a belligerent. Groves in his memoirs passes the buck to the existing intelligence agencies—Army G-2, the Office of Naval Intelligence and the Office of Strategic Services, the forerunner of the CIA—and attributes the inadequacy of their information to "the unfortunate relationships that had grown up among [them]." Why he failed to confront the issue himself until late 1943, when George Marshall asked him directly to do so, he chooses not to say. One reason was certainly security, a Groves obsession; in order to know what to look for, intelligence agents would have to be briefed on at least isotope-separation technologies and nuclear-fission research, which would mean that any agent captured or turned might well give American secrets away. When Groves finally did take responsibility for intelligence gathering he picked scientific personnel who had not worked within the Manhattan Project and authorized paramilitary operations to advance only into areas already occupied. That at least is how he intended his intelligence unit to operate; in practice it frequently claimed its prizes in the no-man's-land between fighting fronts, by hook or by crook.

The unit Groves authorized in late 1943 somehow acquired the name Alsos, Greek for "grove" and thus obscurely revealing; the brigadier thought to have it renamed, "but I decided that to change it . . . would only draw attention to it." To head the Alsos mission he chose Lieutenant Colonel Boris T. Pash, a former high school teacher turned Army G-2 security officer, FBI trained, who had made himself notorious in domestic intelligence circles for his flamboyant investigation of Communist activities among members of the staff of Ernest Lawrence's Berkeley laboratory. Pash, trim and Slavic, with rimless glasses and light, thin hair, spoke Russian fluently and was a great hunter of Communists. His background helps explain why: his Russian emigré father was the Metropolitan—senior bishop—of the Eastern Orthodox Church in North America. It was Pash who had interrogated Robert Oppenheimer about his Communist affiliations while a clandestine recording device in the next room preserved the physicist's damaging evasions on blank sound motion picture film; he concluded without hard evidence that Oppenheimer was a Communist Party member gone underground and possibly a spy. Whatever Groves thought of Pash's Red-baiting, he chose him to head Alsos because he delivered the goods: "his thorough competence and great drive had made a lasting impression on me."

Pash set up a base in London in 1944 as the Allied armies pushed through France after the Normandy invasion. He then crossed the Channel with a squad of Alsos enlisted men and wheeled toward Paris by jeep. "The ALSOS advance party joined the 102nd U.S. Cavalry Group on Highway 188 at Orsay," a contemporary military intelligence report notes. The American force stopped outside Paris—Charles de Gaulle had persuaded Franklin Roosevelt to allow the Free French to enter the city first—but Pash decided to improvise: "Colonel Pash and party then proceeded to cut across-country to Highway 20 and joined second elements of a French armored division. The ALSOS Mission then entered the City of Paris 0855 hrs., 25 August 1944. The party proceeded to within the city in the rear of the first five French vehicles to enter, being the first American unit to enter Paris." The five French vehicles were tanks. In his unarmored jeep Pash drew repeated sniper fire. He dodged among the back streets of Paris and by the end of the day had achieved his goal, the Radium Institute on the Rue Pierre Curie. There he settled in for the evening to drink celebratory champagne with Frédéric Joliot.

Joliot knew less about German uranium research than anyone had expected. Pash moved his base to liberated Paris and began following up promising leads. One of the most significant pointed to Strasbourg, the old city on the Rhine in Alsace-Lorraine, which Allied forces began occupying in mid-November. Pash found a German physics laboratory installed there in a building on the grounds of Strasbourg Hospital. His scientific counterpart on the Alsos team was Samuel A. Goudsmit, a Dutch theoretical physicist and Paul Ehrenfest protégé who had studied criminology and had previously worked at the MIT Radiation Laboratory. Goudsmit followed

Pash to Strasbourg, began laboriously examining documents and hit the jackpot. He recalls the experience in a postwar memoir:

> It is true that no precise information was given in these documents, but there was far more than enough to get a view of the whole German uranium project. We studied the papers by candlelight for two days and nights until our eyes began to hurt. . . . The conclusions were unmistakable. The evidence at hand proved definitely that Germany had no atom bomb and was not likely to have one in any reasonable form.

But paper evidence was not good enough for Groves; as far as he was concerned, he could close the books on the German program only when he had accounted for all the Union Minière uranium ore the Germans had confiscated when they invaded Belgium in 1940, some 1,200 tons in all, the only source of untraced bomb material available to them during the war with the mines at Joachimsthal under surveillance and the Belgian Congo cut off.

Pash had already liberated part of that supply, some 31 tons, from a French arsenal in Toulouse where it had been diverted and secretly stored. Moving into Germany with the Allied armies after they crossed the Rhine late in March he acquired a larger force of men, two armored cars mounted with .50-caliber machine guns and four machine-gun-mounted jeeps and began tracking the German atomic scientists themselves. "Washington wanted absolute proof," Pash remembers, "that no atomic activity of which it did not know was being carried on by the Nazis. It also wanted to be sure that no prominent German scientist would evade capture or fall into the hands of the Soviet Union." Alsos moved through Heidelberg and picked up Walther Bothe, whose laboratory contained Germany's only functioning cyclotron. Documents there pointed to Stadtilm, near Weimar, as the location of Kurt Diebner's laboratory. The small town proved to have become the central office of the German atomic research program as well, and although Werner Heisenberg and his group from the Kaiser Wilhelm Institutes had moved to southern Germany to escape Allied bombing and the advancing Russian and Allied armies, there was a small amount of uranium oxide at Stadtilm to reward Pash's search.

Pash missed the ore rescue. Groves' liaison man with the British had been watching a factory at Stassfurt, near Magdeburg in northern Germany, since late 1944, when documents captured in Brussels indicated it might house the balance of the Belgium ore. By early April 1945 the Red Army had advanced too close to that prize to leave it uninspected any longer; Groves arranged to assemble a mixed British and American strike force led by Lieutenant Colonel John Lansdale, Jr., the security officer who had cleared Paul Tibbets, to move in. The team met with the Twelfth Army Group's G-2 in Göttingen to seek approval for the Stassfurt mission; Lansdale describes the confrontation in a report:

> We outlined to him our proposal and advised him that if we found the material we were after we proposed to remove it and that it would be necessary that we act with the utmost secrecy and greatest dispatch inasmuch as a meeting between the Russian armies and Allied armies apparently would soon take place and the area in which the material appeared to be was a part of the proposed Russian zone of occupation. [The G-2] was very perturbed at our proposal and foresaw all kinds of difficulties with the Russians and political repercussions at home. Said he must see the Commanding General.

That was calm, no-nonsense Omar Bradley:

> He went alone in to see General Bradley, who at that time was in conference with [the] Ninth Army Commander within whose area Stassfurt then was. Both of them gave unqualified approval to our project, General Bradley being reported to have remarked "to hell with the Russians."

On April 17, led by an infantry-division intelligence officer familiar with the area, Lansdale and his team struck for Stassfurt:

> The plant was a mess both from our bombings and from looting by the French workmen. After going through mountains of paper we located the lager or inventory of papers which disclosed the presence of the material we sought at the plant. . . . This ore was fortunately stored above ground. It was in barrels in open sided sheds and had obviously been there a long time, many of the barrels being broken open. Approximately 1100 tons of ore were stored there. This was in various forms, mostly the concentrates from Belgium and about eight tons of uranium oxide.

Lansdale instructed his group to take inventory and went off to Ninth Army headquarters. That organization assigned him two truck companies. He moved on to the nearest railhead within the permanent American zone of occupation but found the commanding officer there too busy evacuating some ten thousand Allied prisoners of war to be able to offer more help than half a dozen men for guard duty. Lansdale improvised, located empty airport hangars nearby where the ore could be stored awaiting shipment out of Germany and arranged to have them cleared of booby traps. Then he returned to Stassfurt:

> Many of the barrels in which the material was packed were broken open and the majority of those not broken open were in such a weakened condition that

they could not stand transportation. [A British and an American officer] and I took a jeep and scouting around the country found in one small town a paper bag factory which had a large supply of very heavy bags. We later sent a truck and obtained 10,000 of these. We also discovered in a mill a quantity of wire and the necessary implements for closing the bags. By the evening of 19th April we had a large crew busily engaged in repacking the material and that night the movement of the material to [the railhead] started.

Boris Pash in the meantime continued to chase down the German atomic scientists. Alsos documents placed Werner Heisenberg, Otto Hahn, Carl von Weizsäcker, Max von Laue and the others in their organization in the Black Forest region of southwestern Germany in the resort town of Haigerloch. By late April the German front had broken and the French were moving ahead. Pash and his forces, which now included a battalion of combat engineers, got word in the middle of the night and raced around Stuttgart in their jeeps and trucks and armored cars to beat the French to Haigerloch. They drew German fire along the way and returned it. In the meantime Lansdale in London reassembled his British-American team and flew over to follow Pash in. The story is properly Pash's:

> Haigerloch is a small, picturesque town straddling the Eyach River. As we approached it, pillowcases, sheets, towels and other white articles attached to flagpoles, broomsticks and window shutters flew the message of surrender.
>
> . . . While our engineer friends were busy consolidating the first Alsos-directed seizure of an enemy town, [Pash's men] led teams in a rapid operation to locate Nazi research facilities. They soon found an ingenious set-up that gave almost complete protection from aerial observation and bombardment—a church atop a cliff.
>
> Hurrying to the scene, I saw a box-like concrete entrance to a cave in the side of an 80-foot cliff towering above the lower level of the town. The heavy steel door was padlocked. A paper stuck on the door indicated the manager's identity.
>
> . . . When the manager was brought to me, he tried to convince me that he was only an accountant. When he hesitated at my command to unlock the door, I said: "Beatson, shoot the lock off. If he gets in the way, shoot him."
>
> The manager opened the door.
>
> . . . In the main chamber was a concrete pit about ten feet in diameter. Within the pit hung a heavy metal shield covering the top of a thick metal cylinder. The latter contained a pot-shaped vessel, also of heavy metal, about four feet below the floor level. Atop the vessel was a metal frame. . . . [A] German prisoner . . . confirmed the fact that we had captured the Nazi uranium "machine" as the Germans called it—actually an atomic pile.

Pash left Goudsmit and his several colleagues behind at Haigerloch on April 23 and rushed to nearby Hechingen. There he found the German scientists, all except Otto Hahn, whom he picked up in Tailfingen two days later, and Werner Heisenberg, whom he located with his family at a lake cottage in Bavaria.

The pile at Haigerloch had served for the KWI's final round of neutron-multiplication studies. One and a half tons of carefully husbanded Norsk-Hydro heavy water moderated it; its fuel consisted of 664 cubes of metallic uranium attached to 78 chains that hung down into the water from the metal "shield" Pash describes. With this elegant arrangement and a central neutron source the KWI team in March had achieved nearly sevenfold neutron multiplication; Heisenberg had calculated at the time that a 50 percent increase in the size of the reactor would produce a sustained chain reaction.

"The fact that the German atom bomb was not an immediate threat," Boris Pash writes with justifiable pride, "was probably the most significant single piece of military intelligence developed throughout the war. Alone, that information was enough to justify Alsos." But Alsos managed more: it prevented the Soviet Union from capturing the leading German atomic scientists and acquiring a significant volume of high-quality uranium ore. The Belgian ore confiscated at Toulouse was already being processed through the Oak Ridge calutrons for Little Boy.

At Los Alamos in late 1944 Otto Frisch, always resourceful at invention, proposed a daring program of experiments. Enriched uranium had begun arriving on the Hill from Oak Ridge. By compounding the metal with hydrogen-rich plastic to make uranium hydride it had become possible to approach an assembly of critical mass responsive to fast as well as slow neutrons. Frisch was leader of the Critical Assemblies group in G Division. Making a critical assembly involved stacking several dozen 1½-inch bars of hydride one at a time and measuring the increased neutron activity as the cubical stack approached critical mass. Usually the small bars were stacked within a boxlike framework of larger machined bricks of beryllium tamper to reflect back neutrons and reduce the amount of uranium required. Dozens of these critical-assembly experiments had gone forward during 1944. "By successively lowering the hydrogen content of the material as more U^{235} became available," the Los Alamos technical history points out, "experience was gained with faster and faster reactions."

But it was impossible to assemble a complete critical mass by stacking bars; such an assembly would run away, kill its sponsors with radiation and melt down. Frisch nearly caused a runaway reaction one day by leaning too close to a naked assembly—he called it a Lady Godiva—that was just subcritical, allowing the hydrogen in his body to reflect back neutrons. "At that moment," he remembers, "out of the corner of my eye I saw that the little red [monitoring] lamps had stopped flickering. They appeared to be glowing continuously. The flicker had speeded up so much that it could no longer be perceived." Instantly Frisch swept his hand across the top of the assembly and knocked away some of the hydride bars. "The lamps slowed down again to a visible flicker." In two seconds he had received by the generous standards of the wartime era a full day's permissible dose of radiation.

Despite that frightening experience, Frisch wanted to work with full critical masses to determine by experiment what Los Alamos had so far been able to determine only theoretically: how much uranium Little Boy would need. Hence his daring proposal:

> The idea was that the compound of uranium-235, which by then had arrived on the site, enough to make an explosive device, should indeed be assembled to make one, but leaving a big hole so that the central portion was missing; that would allow enough neutrons to escape so that no chain reaction could develop. But the missing portion was to be made, ready to be dropped through the hole so that for a split second there was the condition for an atomic explosion, although only barely so.

Brilliant young Richard Feynman laughed when he heard Frisch's plan and named it: he said it would be like tickling the tail of a sleeping dragon. The Dragon experiment it became.

At a remote laboratory site in Omega Canyon that Fermi also used, Frisch's group built a ten-foot iron frame, the "guillotine," that supported upright aluminum guides. The experimenters surrounded the guides at table level with blocks of uranium hydride. To the top of the guillotine they raised a hydride core slug about two by six inches in size. It would fall under the influence of gravity, accelerating at 32 feet per second/per second. When it passed between the blocks it would momentarily form a critical mass. Mixed with hydride, the U235 would react much more slowly than pure metal would react later in Little Boy. But the Dragon would stir, and its dangerous stirring would give Frisch a measure of the fit between theory and experiment:

> It was as near as we could possibly go towards starting an atomic explosion without actually being blown up, and the results were most satisfactory. Everything happened exactly as it should. When the core was dropped through the hole we got a large burst of neutrons and a temperature rise of several degrees in that very short split second during which the chain reaction proceeded as a sort of stifled explosion. We worked under great pressure be-

cause the material had to be returned by a certain date to be made into metal. . . . During those hectic weeks I worked about seventeen hours a day and slept from dawn till mid-morning.

The official Los Alamos history measures the significance of Frisch's Dragon-tickling:

> These experiments gave direct evidence of an explosive chain reaction. They gave an energy production of up to twenty million watts, with a temperature rise in the hydride up to 2°C per millisecond. The strongest burst obtained produced 10^{15} neutrons. The dragon is of historical importance. It was the first controlled nuclear reaction which was supercritical with prompt neutrons alone.

By April 1945 Oak Ridge had produced enough U235 to allow a near-critical assembly of pure metal without hydride dilution. The little bars arrived at the Omega site packed in small, heavy boxes everyone took pains to set well apart; unpacked and unwrapped, the metal shone silver in Frisch's workbench light. Gradually it oxidized, to blue and then to rich plum. Frisch had walked in the snow at Kungälv puzzling out the meaning of Otto Hahn's letters to his aunt; in the basement at Bohr's institute in Copenhagen he had borrowed a name from biology for the process that made these small exotic bars deadly beyond measure; at Birmingham with Rudolf Peierls he had toyed with a formula and had first seen clearly that no more plum-colored metal than now lay scattered on his workbench would make a bomb that would change the world. At Los Alamos in Southwestern spring, dénouement: he would assemble as near a critical mass of U235 as anyone might ever assemble by hand and not be destroyed.

April 12, Thursday, was the day Frisch completed his critical assembly experiments with metallic U235. The previous day Robert Oppenheimer had written Groves the cheering news that Kistiakowsky had managed to produce implosive compressions so smoothly symmetrical that their numbers agreed with theoretical prediction. April 12 in America was Friday, April 13, in Japan, and on the night of that unlucky day B-29's bombing Tokyo bombed the Riken. The wooden building housing Yoshio Nishina's unsuccessful gaseous thermal diffusion experiment did not immediately burn; firemen and staff managed to extinguish the fires that threatened it. But after the other fires were out the building suddenly burst into flame. It burned to the ground and took the Japanese atomic bomb project with it. In Europe John Lansdale was preparing to rush to Stassfurt to confiscate what remained of the Belgian uranium ore; when Groves heard of the success of that adventure later in April he wrote a memorandum to George Marshall that closed the German book:

> In 1940 the German Army in Belgium confiscated and removed to Germany about 1200 tons of uranium ore. So long as this material remained hidden under the control of the enemy we could not be sure but that he might be preparing to use atomic weapons.
>
> Yesterday I was notified by cable that personnel of my office had located this material near Stassfurt, Germany and that it was now being removed to a safe place outside of Germany where it will be under the complete control of American and British authorities.
>
> The capture of this material, which was the bulk of uranium supplies available in Europe, would seem to remove definitely any possibility of the Germans making use of an atomic bomb in this war.

The day these events cluster around, April 12, saw another book closed: at midday, in Warm Springs, Georgia, while sitting for a portrait, Franklin Delano Roosevelt in the sixty-third year of his life was shattered by a massive cerebral hemorrhage. He lingered comatose through the afternoon and died at 3:35 P.M. He had served his nation as President for thirteen years.

When the news of Roosevelt's death reached Los Alamos, Oppenheimer came out from his office onto the steps of the administration building and spoke to the men and women who had spontaneously gathered there. They grieved as Americans everywhere grieved for the loss of a national leader. Some also worried about whether the Manhattan Project would continue. Oppenheimer scheduled a Sunday morning memorial service that everyone in and out of the Tech Area might attend.

"Sunday morning found the mesa deep in snow," Philip Morrison recalls of that day, April 15. "A night's fall had covered the rude textures of the town, silenced its business, and unified the view in a soft whiteness, over which the bright sun shone, casting deep blue shadows behind every wall. It was no costume for mourning, but it seemed recognition of something we needed, a gesture of consolation. Everybody came to the theater, where Oppie spoke very quietly for two or three minutes out of his heart and ours." It was Robert Oppenheimer at his best:

> When, three days ago, the world had word of the death of President Roosevelt, many wept who are unaccustomed to tears, many men and women, little enough accustomed to prayer, prayed to God. Many of us looked with deep trouble to the future; many of us felt less certain that our works would be to a good end; all of us were reminded of how precious a thing human greatness is.

> We have been living through years of great evil, and of great terror. Roosevelt has been our President, our Commander-in-Chief and, in an old and unperverted sense, our leader. All over the world men have looked to him for guidance, and have seen symbolized in him their hope that the evils of this time would not be repeated; that the terrible sacrifices which have been made, and those that are still to be made, would lead to a world more fit for human habitation. . . .
>
> In the Hindu scripture, in the Bhagavad-Gita, it says, "Man is a creature whose substance is faith. What his faith is, he is." The faith of Roosevelt is one that is shared by millions of men and women in every country of the world. For this reason it is possible to maintain the hope, for this reason it is right that we should dedicate ourselves to the hope, that his good works will not have ended with his death.

Vice President Harry S. Truman of Independence, Missouri, who knew only the bare fact of the Manhattan Project's existence, said later that when he heard from Eleanor Roosevelt that he must assume the Presidency in Franklin Roosevelt's place, "I kept thinking, 'The lightning has struck. The lightning has struck!' " Between the Thursday of Roosevelt's death and the Sunday of the memorial service on the Hill, Otto Frisch delivered to Robert Oppenheimer his report on the first experimental determination of the critical mass of pure U235. Little Boy needed more than one critical mass, but the fulfillment of that requirement was now only a matter of time. The lightning had struck at Los Alamos as well.

PART THREE

LIFE AND DEATH

What will people of the future think of us? Will they say, as Roger Williams said of some of the Massachusetts Indians, that we were wolves with the minds of men? Will they think that we resigned our humanity? They will have the right.

C. P. Snow

I see that as human beings we have two great ecstatic impulses in us. One is to participate in life, which ends in the giving of life. The other is to avoid death, which ends tragically in the giving of death. Life and death are in our gift, we can activate life and activate death.

Gil Elliot

18

Trinity

Within twenty-four hours of Franklin Roosevelt's death two men told Harry Truman about the atomic bomb. The first was Henry Lewis Stimson, the upright, white-haired, distinguished Secretary of War. He spoke to the newly sworn President following the brief cabinet meeting Truman called after taking the oath of office on the evening of the day Roosevelt died. "Stimson told me," Truman reports in his memoirs, "that he wanted me to know about an immense project that was under way—a project looking to the development of a new explosive of almost unbelievable destructive power. That was all he felt free to say at the time, and his statement left me puzzled. It was the first bit of information that had come to me about the atomic bomb, but he gave me no details."

Truman had known of the Manhattan Project's existence since his wartime Senate work as chairman of the Committee to Investigate the National Defense Program, when he had attempted to explore the expensive secret project's purpose and had been rebuffed by the Secretary of War himself. That a senator of watchdog responsibility and bulldog tenacity would call off an investigation into unaccounted millions of dollars in defense-plant construction on Stimson's word alone gives some measure of the quality of the Secretary's reputation.

Stimson was seventy-seven years old when Truman assumed the Presidency. He could remember stories his great-grandmother told him of her childhood talks with George Washington. He had attended Phillips Andover when the tuition at that distinguished New England preparatory school was sixty dollars a year and students cut their own firewood. He had graduated from Yale College and Harvard Law School, had served as Secretary of War under William Howard Taft, as Governor General of the Philippines under Calvin Coolidge, as Secretary of State under Herbert Hoover. Roosevelt had called him back to active service in 1940 and with able assistance especially from George Marshall and despite insomnia and migraines that frequently laid him low he had built and administered the most powerful military organization in the history of the world. He was a man of duty and of rectitude. "The chief lesson I have learned in a long life," he wrote at the end of his career, "is that the only way you can make a man trustworthy is to trust him; and the surest way to make him untrustworthy is to distrust him and show your distrust." Stimson sought to apply the lesson impartially to men and to nations. In the spring of 1945 he was greatly worried about the use and consequences of the atomic bomb.

The other man who spoke to Truman, on the following day, April 13, was James Francis Byrnes, known as Jimmy, sixty-six years old, a private citizen of South Carolina since the beginning of April but before then for three years what Franklin Roosevelt had styled "assistant President": Director of Economic Stabilization and then Director of War Mobilization, with offices in the White House. While FDR ran the war and foreign affairs, that is, Byrnes had run the country. "Jimmy Byrnes . . . came to see me," writes Truman of his second briefing on the atomic bomb, "and even he told me few details, though with great solemnity he said that we were perfecting an explosive great enough to destroy the whole world." Then or soon afterward, before Truman met with Stimson again, Byrnes added a significant twist to his tale: "that in his belief the bomb might well put us in a position to dictate our own terms at the end of the war."

At that first Friday meeting Truman asked Byrnes to transcribe his shorthand notes on the Yalta Conference, three months past, which Byrnes had attended as one of Roosevelt's advisers and about which Truman, merely the Vice President then, knew little. Yalta represented nearly all Byrnes' direct experience of foreign affairs. It was more than Truman had. Under the circumstances the new President found it sufficient and informed his colleague that he meant to make him Secretary of State. Byrnes did not object. He insisted that he be given a free hand, however, as Roosevelt had given him in domestic affairs, and Truman agreed.

"A small, wiry, neatly made man," a team of contemporary observers describes Jimmy Byrnes, "with an odd, sharply angular face from which his sharp eyes peer out with an expression of quizzical geniality." Dean Acheson, then an Assistant Secretary of State, thought Byrnes overconfident and insensitive, "a vigorous extrovert, accustomed to the lusty exchange of South Carolina politics." Truman assayed the South Carolinian most shrewdly a few months after their April discussion in a private diary he intermittently kept:

> Had a long talk with my able and conniving Secretary of State. My but he has a keen mind! And he is an honest man. But all country politicians are alike. They are sure all other politicians are circuitous in their dealings. When they are told the straight truth, unvarnished, it is never believed—an asset *sometimes.*

A politician's politician, Byrnes had managed in his thirty-two years of public life to serve with distinction in all three branches of the federal government. He was self-made from the ground up. His father died before he was born. His mother learned dressmaking to survive. Young Jimmy found work at fourteen, his last year of formal education, in a law office, but in lieu of classroom study one of the law partners kindly guided him through a comprehensive reading list. His mother in the meantime taught him shorthand and in 1900, at twenty-one, he earned appointment as a court reporter. He read for the law under the judge whose circuit he reported and passed the bar in 1904. He ran first, in 1908, for solicitor, the South Carolina equivalent of district attorney, and made himself known prosecuting murderers. More than forty-six stump debates won him election to Congress in 1910; in 1930, after fourteen years in the House and five years out of office, he was elected to the Senate. By then he was already actively promoting Franklin Roosevelt's approaching presidential bid. Byrnes served as one of the candidate's speechwriters during the 1932 campaign and afterward worked hard as Roosevelt's man in the Senate to push through the New Deal. His reward, in 1941, was a seat on the United States Supreme Court, which he resigned in 1942 to move to the White House to take over operating the complicated wartime emergency program of wage and price controls, the assistant Presidency of which Roosevelt spoke.

In 1944 everyone understood that Roosevelt's fourth term would be his last. The man he selected for Vice President would therefore almost certainly take the Democratic Party presidential nomination in 1948. Byrnes expected to be that man and Roosevelt encouraged him. But the assistant President was a conservative Democrat from the Deep South, and at the last minute Roosevelt compromised instead on the man from Missouri, Harry S. Truman. "I freely admit that I was disappointed," Byrnes writes with understatement approaching lockjaw, "and felt hurt by President Roosevelt's action." He made a point of visiting the European front with George Marshall in September 1944, in the midst of the presidential campaign; when he returned FDR had to appeal to him formally by letter—a document Byrnes could show around—to endorse the ticket with a speech.

Byrnes undoubtedly regarded Truman as a usurper: if not Truman but he had been Roosevelt's choice he would be President of the United States now. Truman knew Byrnes' attitude but needed the old pro badly to help him run the country and face the world. Hence the prize of State. The Secretary of State was the highest-ranking member of the cabinet and under the rules of succession then obtaining was the officer next in line for the Presidency as well when the Vice Presidency was vacant. Short of the Presidency itself, State was the most powerful office Truman had to give.

Vannevar Bush and James Bryant Conant had needed months to convince Henry Stimson to take up consideration of the bomb's challenge in the postwar era. He had not been ready in late October 1944 when Bush pressed him for action and he had not been ready in early December when Bush pressed him again. By then Bush knew what he thought the problem needed, however:

> We proposed that the Secretary of War suggest to the President the establishment of a committee or commission with the duty of preparing plans. These would include the drafting of legislation and the drafting of appropriate releases to be made public at the proper time. . . . We were all in agreement that the State Department should now be brought in.

Stimson allowed one of his trusted aides, Harvey H. Bundy, a Boston lawyer, father of William P. and McGeorge, at least to begin formulating a membership roster and list of duties for such a committee. But he did not yet know even in broad outline what basic policy to recommend.

Bohr's ideas, variously diluted, floated by that time in the Washington air. Bohr had sought to convince the American government that only early discussion with the Soviet Union of the mutual dangers of a nuclear arms race could forestall such an arms race once the bomb became known. (He would try again in April to see Roosevelt; Felix Frankfurter and Lord Halifax, the British ambassador, would be strolling in a Washington park discussing Bohr's best avenue of approach when the bells of the city's churches began tolling the news of the President's death.) Apparently no one within the executive branch was sufficiently convinced of the *inevitability* of Bohr's vision. Stimson was as wise as any man in government, but late in December he cautioned Roosevelt that the Russians should earn the right to hear the baleful news:

> I told him of my views as to the future of S-1 [Stimson's code for the bomb] in connection with Russia: that I knew they were spying on our work but had not yet gotten any real knowledge of it and that, while I was troubled about the possible effect of keeping from them even now that work, I believed that it was essential not to take them into our confidence until we were sure to get a real quid pro quo from our frankness. I said I had no illusions as to the possibility of keeping permanently such a secret but that I did not think it was yet time to share it with Russia. He said he thought he agreed with me.

In mid-February, after talking again to Bush, Stimson confided to his diary what he wanted in exchange for news of the bomb. Bohr's conviction that only an open world modeled in some sense on the republic of science could answer the challenge of the bomb had drifted, in Bush's mind, to a proposal for an international pool of scientific research. Of such an arrangement Stimson wrote that "it would be inadvisable to put it into full force yet, until we had gotten all we could in Russia in the way of liberalization in exchange for S-1." That is, the quid pro quo Stimson thought the United States should demand from the Soviet Union was the democratization of its government. What for Bohr was the inevitable outcome of a solution to the problem of the bomb—an open world where differences in social and political conditions would be visible to everyone and therefore under pressure to improve—Stimson imagined should be a precondition to any initial exchange.

Finally in mid-March Stimson talked to Roosevelt, their last meeting. That talk came to no useful end. In April, with a new President in the White House, he prepared to repeat the performance.

In the meantime the men who had advised Franklin Roosevelt were working to convince Harry Truman of the increasing perfidy of the Soviet Union. Averell Harriman, the shrewd multimillionaire Ambassador to Moscow, had rushed to Washington to brief the new President. Truman says Harriman told him the visit was based on "the fear that you did not understand, as I had seen Roosevelt understand, that Stalin is breaking his agreements." To soften that condescension Harriman added that he feared Truman "could not have had time to catch up with all the recent cables." The self-educated Missourian prided himself on how many pages of documents he could chew through per day—he was a champion reader—and undercut Harriman's condescension breezily by instructing the ambassador to "keep on sending me long messages."

Harriman told Truman they were faced with a "barbarian invasion of Europe." The Soviet Union, he said, meant to take over its neighbors and install the Soviet system of secret police and state control. "He added that he was not pessimistic," the President writes, "for he felt that it was possible for us to arrive at a workable basis with the Russians. He believed that this would require a reconsideration of our policy and the abandonment of any illusion that the Soviet government was likely soon to act in accordance with the principles to which the rest of the world held in international affairs."

Truman was concerned to convince Roosevelt's advisers that he meant to be decisive. "I ended the meeting by saying, 'I intend to be firm in my dealings with the Soviet government.' " Delegates were arriving in San Francisco that April, for example, to formulate a charter for a new United Nations to replace the old and defunct League. Harriman asked Truman if he would "go ahead with the world organization plans even if Russia dropped out." Truman remembers responding realistically that "without Russia there would not be a world organization." Three days later, having heard from Stalin in the meantime and met the arriving Soviet Foreign Minister, Vyacheslav Molotov, he retreated from realism to bluster. "He felt that our agreements with the Soviet Union had so far been a one-way street," an eyewitness recalls, "and that he could not continue; it was now or never. He intended to go on with the plans for San Francisco and if the Russians did not wish to join us they could go to Hell."

Stimson argued for patience. "In the big military matters," Truman reports him saying, "the Soviet government had kept its word and the military authorities of the United States had come to count on it. In fact . . . they had often done better than they had promised." Although George Marshall seconded Stimson's argument and Truman could not have had two more reliable witnesses, it was not counsel the new and untried President wanted to hear. Marshall added a crucial justification that Truman took to heart:

> He said from the military point of view the situation in Europe was secure but that we hoped for Soviet participation in the war against Japan at a time when it would be useful to us. The Russians had it within their power to delay their entry into the Far Eastern war until we had done all the dirty work. He was inclined to agree with Mr. Stimson that the possibility of a break with Russia was very serious.

Truman could hardly tell the Russians to go to hell if he needed them to finish the Pacific war. Marshall's justification for patience meant Stalin had the President over a barrel. It was not an arrangement Harry Truman intended to perpetuate.

He let Molotov know. They had sparred diplomatically at their first meeting; now the President attacked. The issue was the composition of the postwar government of Poland. Molotov discussed various formulas, all favoring Soviet dominance. Truman demanded the free elections that he understood had been agreed upon at Yalta: "I replied sharply that an agreement had been reached on Poland and that there was only one thing to do, and that was for Marshal Stalin to carry out that agreement in accordance with his word." Molotov tried again. Truman replied sharply again, repeating his previous demand. Molotov hedged once more. Truman proceeded to lay him low: "I expressed once more the desire of the United States for friendship with Russia, but I wanted it clearly understood that this could be only on a basis of the mutual observation of agreements and not on the basis of a one-way street." Those are hardly fighting words; Molotov's reaction suggests that the President spoke more pungently at the time:

> "I have never been talked to like that in my life," Molotov said.
>
> I told him, "Carry out your agreements and you won't get talked to like that."

If Truman felt better for the exchange, it disturbed Stimson. The new President had acted without knowledge of the bomb and its potentially fateful consequences. It was time and past time for a full briefing.

Truman agreed to meet with Stimson at noon on Wednesday, April 25. The President was scheduled to address the opening session of the United Nations conference in San Francisco by radio that evening. One more conditioning incident intervened; on Tuesday he received a communication from Joseph Stalin, "one of the most revealing and disquieting messages to reach me during my first days in the White House." Molotov had reported Truman's tough talk to the Soviet Premier. Stalin replied in kind. Poland bordered on the Soviet Union, he wrote, not on Great Britain or the United States. "The question [of] Poland had the same meaning for the security of the Soviet Union as the question [of] Belgium and Greece for the security of Great Britain"—but "the Soviet Union was not consulted when those governments were being established there" following the Allied liberation. The "blood of the Soviet people abundantly shed on the fields of Poland in the name of the liberation of Poland" demanded a Polish government friendly to Russia. And finally:

> I am ready to fulfill your request and do everything possible to reach a harmonious solution. But you demand too much of me. In other words, you demand that I renounce the interests of security of the Soviet Union, but I cannot turn against my country.

With this blunt challenge on his mind Truman received his Secretary of War.

Stimson had brought Groves along for technical backup but left him waiting in an outer office while he discussed issues of general policy. He began dramatically, reading from a memorandum:

> Within four months we shall in all probability have completed the most terrible weapon ever known in human history, one bomb of which could destroy a whole city.

We had shared the development with the British, Stimson continued, but we controlled the factories that made the explosive material "and no other nation could reach this position for some years." It was certain that we would not enjoy a monopoly forever, and "probably the only nation which could enter into production within the next few years is Russia." The world "in its present state of moral advancement compared with its technical development," the Secretary of War continued quaintly, "would be eventually at the mercy of such a weapon. In other words, modern civilization might be completely destroyed."

Stimson emphasized what John Anderson had emphasized to Churchill the year before: that founding a "world peace organization" while the bomb was still a secret "would seem to be unrealistic":

> No system of control heretofore considered would be adequate to control this menace. Both inside any particular country and between the nations of the world, the control of this weapon will undoubtedly be a matter of the greatest difficulty and would involve such thorough-going rights of inspection and internal controls as we have never heretofore contemplated.

That brought Stimson to the crucial point:

> Furthermore, in the light of our present position with reference to this weapon, the question of sharing it with other nations and, if so shared, upon what terms, becomes a primary question of our foreign relations.

Bohr had proposed to inform other nations of the common dangers of a nuclear arms race. At the hands of Stimson and his advisers that sensible proposal had drifted to the notion that the issue was sharing the weapon itself. As Commander in Chief, as a veteran of the First World War, as a man of common sense, Truman must have wondered what on earth his Secretary of War was talking about, especially when Stimson added that "a certain moral responsibility" followed from American leadership in nuclear technology which the nation could not shirk "without very serious responsibility for any disaster to civilization which it would further." Was the United States morally obligated to give away a devastating new weapon of war?

Now Stimson called in Groves. The general brought with him a report on the status of the Manhattan Project that he had presented to the Secretary of War two days earlier. Both Stimson and Groves insisted Truman read the document while they waited. The President was restive. He had a threatening note from Stalin to deal with. He had to prepare to open the United Nations conference even though Stimson had just informed him that allowing the conference to proceed in ignorance of the bomb was a sham. A scene of darkening comedy followed as the proud man who had challenged Averell Harriman to keep sending him long messages tried to avoid public instruction in the minutiae of a secret project he had fought doggedly as a senator to investigate. Groves misunderstood completely:

> Mr. Truman did not like to read long reports. This report was not long, considering the size of the project. It was about twenty-four pages and he would constantly interrupt his reading to say, "Why, I don't like to read papers." And Mr. Stimson and I would reply: "Well we can't tell you this in any more concise language. This is a big project." For example, we discussed our relations with the British in about four or five lines. It was that much condensed. We had to explain all the processes and we might just say what they were and that was about all.

After the reading of the lesson, Groves notes, "a great deal of emphasis was placed on foreign relations and particularly on the Russian situation"—Truman reverting to his immediate problems. He "made it very definite," Groves adds for the record, "that he was in entire agreement with the necessity for the project."

The final point in Stimson's memorandum was the proposal Bush and Conant had initiated to establish what Stimson called "a select committee . . . for recommending action to the Executive and legislative branches of our government." Truman approved.

In his memoirs the President describes his meeting with Stimson and Groves with tact and perhaps even a measure of private humor: "I listened with absorbed interest, for Stimson was a man of great wisdom and foresight. He went into considerable detail in describing the nature and the power of the projected weapon. . . . Byrnes had already told me that the weapon might be so powerful as to be capable of wiping out entire cities and killing people on an unprecedented scale." That was when Byrnes had crowed that the new bombs might allow the United States to dictate its own terms at the end of the war. "Stimson, on the other hand, seemed at least as much concerned with the role of the atomic bomb in the shaping of history as in its capacity to shorten this war. . . . I thanked him for his enlightening presentation of this awesome subject, and as I saw him to the door I felt how fortunate the country was to have so able and so wise a man in its service." High praise, but the President was not sufficiently impressed at the outset with Stimson and Harriman to invite either man to accompany him to the next conference of the Big Three. Both found it necessary, when the time came, to invite themselves. Jimmy Byrnes went at the President's invitation and sat at the President's right hand.

Discussion between Truman and his various advisers was one level of discourse in the spring of 1945 on the uses of the atomic bomb. Another was joined two days after Stimson and Groves briefed the President when a Target Committee under Groves' authority met for the first time in Lauris Norstad's conference room at the Pentagon. Brigadier General Thomas F. Farrell, who would represent the Manhattan Project as Groves' deputy to the Pacific Command, chaired the committee; besides Farrell it counted two other Air Force officers—a colonel and a major—and five scientists, including John von Neumann and British physicist William G. Penney. Groves opened the meeting with a variant of his usual speech to Manhattan Project working groups: how important their duty was, how secret it must be kept. He had already discussed targets with the Military Policy Committee and now informed his Target Committee that it should propose no more than four.

Farrell laid down the basics: B-29 range for such important missions no more than 1,500 miles; visual bombing essential so that these untried and valuable bombs could be aimed with certainty and their effects photographed; probable targets "urban or industrial Japanese areas" in July, August or September; each mission to be given one primary and two alternate targets with spotter planes sent ahead to confirm visibility.

Most of the first meeting was devoted to worrying about the Japanese weather. After lunch the committee brought in the Twentieth Air Force's top meteorologist, who told them that June was the worst weather month in Japan; "a little improvement is present in July; a little bit better weather is present in August; September weather is bad." January was the best month, but no one intended to wait that long. The meteorologist said he could forecast a good day for bombing operations only twenty-four hours ahead, but he could give two days' notice of bad weather. He suggested they station submarines near the target areas to radio back weather readings.

Later in the afternoon they began considering targets. Groves had extended Farrell's guidelines:

> I had set as the governing factor that the targets chosen should be places the bombing of which would most adversely affect the will of the Japanese people to continue the war. Beyond that, they should be military in nature, consisting either of important headquarters or troop concentrations, or centers of production of military equipment and supplies. To enable us to assess accurately the effects of the bomb, the targets should not have been previously damaged by air raids. It was also desirable that the first target be of such size that the damage would be confined within it, so that we could more definitely determine the power of the bomb.

But such pristine targets had already become scarce in Japan. If the first choice the Target Committee identified at its first meeting was hardly big enough to confine the potential damage, it was the best the enemy had left to offer:

> Hiroshima is the largest untouched target not on the 21st Bomber Command priority list. Consideration should be given to this city.

"Tokyo," the committee notes continue, "is a possibility but it is now practically all bombed and burned out and is practically rubble with only the palace grounds left standing. Consideration is only possible here."

The Target Committee did not yet fully understand the level of authority it commanded. With a few words to Groves it could exempt a Japanese city from Curtis LeMay's relentless firebombing, preserving it through spring mornings of cherry blossoms and summer nights of wild monsoons for a more historic fate. The committee thought it took second priority behind LeMay rather than first priority ahead, and in emphasizing these mistaken priorities the colonel who reviewed the Twentieth Air Force's bombing directive for the committee revealed what the United States' policy in Japan in all its deadly ambiguity had become:

> It should be remembered that in our selection of any target, the 20th Air Force is operating primarily to laying waste all the main Japanese cities, and that they do not propose to save some important primary target for us if it interferes with the operation of the war from their point of view. Their existing procedure has been to bomb the hell out of Tokyo, bomb the aircraft, manufacturing and assembly plants, engine plants and in general paralyze the aircraft industry so as to eliminate opposition to the 20th Air Force operations. The 20th Air Force is systematically bombing out the following cities with the prime purpose in mind of not leaving one stone lying on another:
>
> Tokyo, Yokohama, Nagoya, Osaka, Kyoto,
> Kobe, Yawata & Nagasaki.

If the Japanese were prepared to eat stones, the Americans were prepared to supply them.

The colonel also advised that the Twentieth Air Force planned to increase its delivery of conventional bombs steadily until it was dropping 100,000 tons a month by the end of 1945.

The group decided to study seventeen targets including Tokyo Bay, Yokohama, Nagoya, Osaka, Kobe, Hiroshima, Kokura, Fukuoka, Nagasaki and Sasebo. Targets already destroyed would be culled from the list. The weather people would review weather reports. Penney would consider "the size of the bomb burst, the amount of damage expected, and the ultimate distance at which people would be killed." Von Neumann would be responsible for computations. Adjourning its initial meeting the Target Committee planned to meet again in mid-May in Robert Oppenheimer's office at Los Alamos.

A third level of discourse on the uses of the bomb revealed itself as Henry Stimson assembled the committee that Bush and Conant had proposed to him and he had proposed in turn to the President. On May 1, the day German radio announced the suicide of Adolf Hitler in the ruins of Berlin, George L. Harrison, a special Stimson consultant and the president of the New York Life Insurance Company, prepared for the Secretary of War an entirely civilian committee roster consisting of Stimson as chairman, Bush, Conant, MIT president Karl Compton, Assistant Secretary of State William L. Clayton, Undersecretary of the Navy Ralph A. Bard and a special representative of the President whom the President might choose. Stimson modified the list to include Harrison as his alternate and carried it to Truman for approval on May 2. Truman agreed and Stimson apparently assumed his interest in the project, but the President significantly did not even bother to name his own man to the list. Stimson wrote in his diary that night:

> The President accepted the present members of the committee and said that they would be sufficient even without a personal representative of himself. I said I should prefer to have such a representative and suggested that he should be a man (a) with whom the President had close personal relations and (b) who was able to keep his mouth shut.

Truman had not yet announced his intention to appoint Byrnes Secretary of State because the holdover Secretary, Edward R. Stettinius, Jr., was heading the United States delegation to the United Nations in San Francisco and the President did not want to undercut his authority there. But word of the forthcoming appointment had diffused through Washington.

Acting on it, Harrison suggested that Stimson propose Byrnes. On May 3 Stimson did, "and late in the day the President called me up himself and said that he had heard of my suggestion and it was fine. He had already called up Byrnes down in South Carolina and Byrnes had accepted." Bundy and Harrison, Stimson told his diary, "were tickled to death." They thought their committee had acquired a second powerful sponsor. In fact they had just welcomed a cowbird into their nest.

Stimson sent out invitations the next day. He proposed calling his new group the Interim Committee to avoid appearing to usurp congressional prerogatives: "when secrecy is no longer required," he explained to the prospective members, "Congress might wish to appoint a permanent Post War Commission." He set the first informal meeting of the Interim Committee for May 9.

The membership would assemble in the wake of momentous change. The war in Europe had finally ground to an end. Supreme Allied Commander Dwight D. Eisenhower celebrated the victory on national radio the evening of Tuesday, May 8, 1945, V-E Day:

> I have the rare privilege of speaking for a victorious army of almost five million fighting men. They, and the women who have so ably assisted them, constitute the Allied Expeditionary Force that has liberated western Europe. They have destroyed or captured enemy armies totalling more than their own strength, and swept triumphantly forward over the hundreds of miles separating Cherbourg from Lübeck, Leipzig and Munich. . . .
>
> These startling successes have not been bought without sorrow and suffering. In this Theater alone 80,000 Americans and comparable numbers among their Allies, have had their lives cut short that the rest of us might live in the sunlight of freedom. . . .
>
> But, at last, *this* part of the job is done. No more will there flow from this Theater to the United States those doleful lists of death and loss that have brought so much sorrow to American homes. The sounds of battle have faded from the European scene.

Eisenhower had watched Colonel General Alfried Jodl sign the act of military surrender in a schoolroom in Rheims—the temporary war room of the Supreme Headquarters Allied Expeditionary Force—in the early morning hours of May 7. Eisenhower's aides had attempted then to draft a suitably eloquent message to the Combined Chiefs reporting the official surrender. "I tried one myself," Eisenhower's chief of staff Walter Bedell Smith remembers, "and like all my associates, groped for resounding phrases as fitting accolades to the Great Crusade and indicative of our dedication to the great task just accomplished." The Supreme Commander listened quietly for a time, thanked everyone for trying and dictated his own unadorned report:

> The mission of this Allied force was fulfilled at 0241, local time, May 7th, 1945.

Better to be brief, better than resounding phrases. Twenty million Soviet soldiers and civilians died of privation or in battle in the Second World War. Eight million British and Europeans died or were killed and another five million Germans. The Nazis murdered six million Jews in ghettos and concentration camps. Manmade death had ended thirty-nine million human lives prematurely; for the second time in half a century Europe had become a charnel house.

There remained the brutal conflict Japan had begun in the Pacific and refused despite her increasing destruction to end by unconditional surrender.

Officially Byrnes was retired to South Carolina. In fact he was visiting Washington surreptitiously, absorbing detailed evening briefings by State Department division chiefs at his apartment at the Shoreham Hotel. On the afternoon of V-E Day he spent two hours closeted alone with Stimson. Then Harrison, Bundy and Groves joined them. "We all discussed the function of the proposed Interim Committee," Stimson records. "During the meeting it became very evident what a tremendous help Byrnes would be as a member of the committee."

The next morning the Interim Committee met for the first time in Stimson's office. The gathering was preliminary, to fill in Byrnes, State's Clayton and the Navy's Bard on the basic facts, but Stimson made a point of introducing the former assistant President as Truman's personal representative. The membership was thus put on notice that Byrnes enjoyed special status and that his words carried extra weight.

The committee recognized that the scientists working on the atomic bomb might have useful advice to offer and created a Scientific Panel adjunct. Bush and Conant put their heads together and recommended Arthur Compton, Ernest Lawrence, Robert Oppenheimer and Enrico Fermi for appointment.

Between the first and second meetings of the Interim Committee its *Doppelgänger,* the Target Committee, met again for two days, May 10 and 11, at Los Alamos. Added to the full committee as advisers were Oppenheimer, Parsons, Tolman and Norman Ramsey and for part of the deliberations Hans Bethe and Robert Brode. Oppenheimer took control by devising and presenting a thorough agenda:

A. Height of Detonation
B. Report on Weather and Operations
C. Gadget Jettisoning and Landing
D. Status of Targets
E. Psychological Factors in Target Selection
F. Use Against Military Objectives
G. Radiological Effects
H. Coordinated Air Operations
I. Rehearsals
J. Operating Requirements for Safety of Airplanes
K. Coordination with 21st [Bomber Command] Program

Detonation height determined how large an area would be damaged by blast and depended crucially on yield. A bomb detonated too high would expend its energy blasting thin air; a bomb detonated too low would expend its energy excavating a crater. It was better to be low than high, the committee minutes explain: "The bomb can be detonated as much as 40% below the optimum with a reduction of 24% in area of damage whereas a detonation [only] 14% above the optimum will cause the same loss in area." The discussion demonstrates how uncertain Los Alamos still was of bomb yield. Bethe estimated a yield range for Little Boy of 5,000 to 15,000 tons TNT equivalent. Fat Man, the implosion bomb, was anybody's guess: 700, 2,000, 5,000 tons? "With the present information the fuse would be set at 2,000 tons equivalent but fusing for the other values should be available at the time of final delivery. . . . Trinity data will be used for this gadget."

The scientists reported and the committee agreed that in an emergency a B-29 in good condition could return to base with a bomb. "It should make a normal landing with the greatest possible care. . . . The chances of [a] crash initiating a high order [i.e., nuclear] explosion are . . . sufficiently small [as to be] a justifiable risk." Fat Man could even survive jettisoning into shallow water. Little Boy was less forgiving. Since the gun bomb contained more than two critical masses of U235, seawater leaking into its casing could moderate stray neutrons sufficiently to initiate a destructive slow-neutron chain reaction. The alternative, jettisoning Little Boy onto land, might loose the U235 bullet down the barrel into the target core and set off a nuclear explosion. For temperamental Little Boy, the minutes note, unluckily for the aircrew, "the best emergency procedure that has so far been proposed is . . . the removal of the gun powder from the gun and the execution of a crash landing."

Target selection had advanced. The committee had refined its qualifications to three: "important targets in a large urban area of more than three miles diameter" that were "capable of being damaged effectively by blast" and were "likely to be unattacked by next August." The Air Force had agreed to reserve five such targets for atomic bombing. These included:

> (1) *Kyoto*—This target is an urban industrial area with a population of 1,000,000. It is the former capital of Japan and many people and industries are now being moved there as other areas are being destroyed. From the psychological point of view there is the advantage that Kyoto is an intellectual center for Japan and the people there are more apt to appreciate the significance of such a weapon as the gadget. . . .
>
> (2) *Hiroshima*—This is an important army depot and port of embarkation in the middle of an urban industrial area. It is a good radar target and it is such a size that a large part of the city could be extensively damaged. There are adjacent hills which are likely to produce a focusing effect which would considerably increase the blast damage. Due to rivers it is not a good incendiary target.

The other three targets proposed were Yokohama, Kokura Arsenal and Niigata. An unsung enthusiast on the committee suggested a spectacular sixth target for consideration, but wiser heads prevailed: "The possibility of bombing the Emperor's palace was discussed. It was agreed that we should not recommend it but that any action for this bombing should come from authorities on military policy."

So the Target Committee sitting in Oppenheimer's office at Los Alamos under the modified Lincoln quotation that Oppenheimer had posted on the wall—THIS WORLD CANNOT ENDURE HALF SLAVE AND HALF FREE—remanded four targets to further study: Kyoto, Hiroshima, Yokohama and Kokura Arsenal.

The committee and its Los Alamos consultants were not unmindful of the radiation effects of the atomic bomb—its most significant difference in effect from conventional high explosives—but worried more about radiation danger to American aircrews than to the Japanese. "Dr. Oppenheimer presented a memo he had prepared on the radiological effect of the gadget. . . . The basic recommendations of this memo are (1) for radiological reasons no aircraft should be closer than 2½ miles to the point of detonation (for blast reasons the distance should be greater) and (2) aircraft must avoid the cloud of radio-active materials."

Since the expected yields of the bombs under discussion made them something less than city-busters, the Target Committee considered following Little Boy and Fat Man with conventional incendiary raids. Radioactive clouds that might endanger LeMay's follow-up crews worried the targeters, though they thought an incendiary raid delayed one day after an atomic bombing might be safe and "quite effective."

With a better sense for having visited Los Alamos of the weapons it was targeting, the Target Committee scheduled its next meeting for May 28 at the Pentagon.

Vannevar Bush thought the second Interim Committee meeting on May 14 produced "very frank discussions." The group, he decided, was "an excellent one." These judgments he passed along to Conant, who had been unable to attend. Stimson won approval of the Scientific Panel as constituted and discussed the possibility of assembling a similar group of industrialists. As his agenda noted, such a group would "advise of [the] likelihood of other nations repeating what our industry has done"—that is, whether other nations could build the vast, innovative industrial plant necessary to produce atomic bombs.

That May Monday morning the committee received copies of Bush's and Conant's September 30, 1944, memorandum to Stimson, the discussion framed on Bohr's ideas of the free exchange of scientific information and inspection not only of laboratories throughout the world but also of military installations. Bush promptly hedged his commitment to so open a world:

> I . . . said that while we made the memorandum very explicit, that it certainly did not indicate that we were irrevocably committed to any definite line of action but rather felt that we ought to express our ideas early in order that there might be discussion as [a] result of which we might indeed change our thoughts as we studied into the subject further, and I said also that we would undoubtedly write the memorandum a little differently today due to the lapse of time since last September.

At the end of the meeting Byrnes took his copy along and studied it with interest.

The Secretary of State–designate was learning fast. When the Interim Committee met again on Friday, May 18, with Groves sitting in, Byrnes brought up the Bush-Conant memorandum as soon as draft press releases announcing the dropping of the first atomic bomb on Japan had been reviewed. It was Bush's turn to be absent; Conant passed along the news:

> Mr. Byrnes spent considerable time discussing our memorandum of last fall, which he had read carefully and with which he was much impressed. It apparently stimulated his thinking (which was all that we had originally desired I imagine). He was particularly impressed with our statement that the Russians might catch up in three to four years. This premise was violently opposed by the General [i.e., Groves], who felt that twenty years was a much better figure. . . . The General is basing his long estimate on a very poor view of Russian ability, which I think is a highly unsafe assumption. . . .

> There was some discussion about the implications of a time interval as short as four years and various international problems were discussed, particularly the question of whether or not the President should tell the Russians of the existence of the weapon after the July test.

Bohr's proposal to enlist the Soviet Union in discussions before the atomic bomb became a reality here slips to the question of whether or not to tell the Soviets the bare facts after the first bomb had been tested but before the second was dropped on Japan. Byrnes thought the answer to that question might depend on how quickly the USSR could duplicate the American accomplishment. The Interim Committee's recording secretary, 2nd Lieutenant R. Gordon Arneson, remembered after the war of this confrontation that "Mr. Byrnes felt that this point was a very important one." The veteran of House and Senate cloakrooms was at least as concerned as Henry Stimson to extract a quid pro quo for any exchange of information, as Conant's next comment to Bush demonstrates:

> This question [i.e., whether or not to tell the Russians about the atomic bomb before using it on Japan] led to the review of the Quebec Agreement which was shown once more to Mr. Byrnes. He asked the General what we had got in exchange, and the General replied only the arrangements controlling the Belgium-Congo [*sic*]. . . . Mr. Byrnes made short work of this line of argument.

The Quebec Agreement of 1943 renewed the partnership of the United States and Great Britain in the nuclear enterprise; Groves was justifying it as an exchange for British help in securing the Union Minière's agreement to sell the two nations all its uranium ore. The British-American relation was built on deeper foundations than that, and Conant moved quickly to limit the damage of Groves' blunder:

> Some of us then pointed out the historic background and [that] our connection with England flowed from the original agreement as to the complete exchange of scientific information. . . . I can foresee a great deal of trouble on this front. It was interesting that Mr. Byrnes felt that Congress would be most curious about this phase of the matter.

If Byrnes had begun his service on the Interim Committee respecting the men who had carried the Manhattan Project forward, he must have conceived less respect for them now. Both Stimson and Bush, Conant told Byrnes, had talked to Churchill in Quebec. If, as it seemed, they could be conned by the British into giving away the secrets of the bomb—whatever

Byrnes imagined those might be—for the price of a few tons of uranium ore, how much was their judgment worth? Why give away something so stupendous as the bomb unless you got something equally stupendous in return? Byrnes believed international relations worked like domestic politics. The bomb was power, newly minted, and power was to politics as money was to banking, a medium of enriching exchange. Only naïfs and fools gave it away.

Enter Leo Szilard.

As the man who had thought longer and harder than anyone else about the consequences of the chain reaction, Szilard had chafed at his continuing exile from the high councils of government. Another politically active Met Lab scientist, Eugene Rabinowitch, a younger man, confirms "the feeling which was certainly shared . . . by others that we were surrounded by a kind of soundproof wall so that you could write to Washington or go to Washington and talk to somebody but you never got any reaction back." With the successful operation of the production reactors and separation plants at Hanford the work of the Met Lab had slowed; Compton's people, Szilard particularly, found time to think about the future. Szilard says he began to examine "the wisdom of testing bombs and using bombs." Rabinowitch remembers "many hours spent walking up and down the Midway [the wide World's Fair sward south of the University of Chicago main campus] with Leo Szilard and arguing about these questions and about what can be done. I remember sleepless nights."

There was no point in talking to Groves, Szilard reasoned in March 1945, nor to Bush or Conant for that matter. Secrecy barred discussion with middle-level authorities. "The only man with whom we were sure we would be entitled to communicate," Szilard recalls, "was the President." He prepared a memorandum for Franklin Roosevelt and traveled to Princeton to enlist once again the durable services of Albert Einstein.

Except for some minor theoretical calculations for the Navy, Einstein had been excluded from wartime nuclear development. Bush explained why to the director of the Institute for Advanced Study early in the war:

> I am not at all sure that if I place Einstein in entire contact with his subject he would not discuss it in a way that it should not be discussed. . . . I wish very much that I could place the whole thing before him . . . but this is utterly impossible in view of the attitude of people here in Washington who have studied into his whole history.

The great theoretician whose letter to Roosevelt helped alert the United States government to the possibility of an atomic bomb was thus spared by concern for security and by hostility to his earlier outspoken politics—his pacifism and probably also his Zionism—from contributing to that weapon's development. Szilard could not show Einstein his memorandum. He told his old friend simply that there was trouble ahead and asked for a letter of introduction to the President. Einstein complied.

From Chicago Szilard approached Roosevelt through his wife. Eleanor Roosevelt agreed to see him on May 8 to pursue the matter. Thus fortified, he wandered to Arthur Compton's office to confess his out-of-channel sins. Compton surprised him by cheering him on. "Elated by finding no resistance where I expected resistance," Szilard reports, "I went back to my office. I hadn't been in my office for five minutes when there was a knock on the door and Compton's assistant came in, telling me that he had just heard over the radio that President Roosevelt had died. . . .

"So for a number of days I was at a complete loss for what to do," Szilard goes on. He needed a new avenue of approach. Eventually it occurred to him that a project as large as the Met Lab probably employed someone from Kansas City, Missouri, Harry Truman's original political base. He found a young mathematician named Albert Cahn who had worked for Kansas City boss Tom Pendergast's political machine to earn money for graduate school. Cahn and Szilard traveled to Kansas City later that month, dazzled Pendergast's hoodlum elite with who knows what Szilardian tale "and three days later we had an appointment at the White House."

Truman's appointments secretary, Matthew Connelly, barred the door. After he read the Einstein letter and the memorandum he relaxed. "I see now," Szilard remembers him saying, "this is a serious matter. At first I was a little suspicious, because the appointment came through Kansas City." Truman had guessed the subject of Szilard's concern. At the President's direction Connelly sent the wandering Hungarian to Spartansburg, South Carolina, to talk to a private citizen named Jimmy Byrnes.

A University of Chicago dean, a scientist named Walter Bartky, had accompanied Szilard to Washington. For added authority Szilard enlisted Nobel laureate Harold Urey and the three men boarded the overnight train south. Compartmentalization was working: "We did not quite understand why we were sent by the President to see James Byrnes. . . . Was he to . . . be the man in charge of the uranium work after the war, or what? We did not know." Truman had alerted Byrnes that the delegation was on its way. The South Carolinian received it warily at his home. He read the letter from Einstein first—"I have much confidence in [Szilard's] judgment," the theoretician of relativity testified—then turned to the memorandum.

It was a prescient document. It argued that in preparing to test and then use atomic bombs the United States was "moving along a road leading to the destruction of the strong position [the nation] hitherto occupied in the world." Szilard was referring not to a moral advantage but to an industrial: as he wrote elsewhere that spring, U.S. military strength was "essentially due to the fact that the United States could outproduce every other country in heavy armaments." When other countries acquired nuclear weapons, as they would in "just a few years," that advantage would be lost: "Perhaps the greatest immediate danger which faces us is the probability that our 'demonstration' of atomic bombs will precipitate a race in the production of these devices between the United States and Russia."

Much of the rest of the memorandum asked the sort of questions the Interim Committee was also asking about international controls versus attempting to maintain an American monopoly. But Szilard echoed Bohr in pleading for what no one among the national leaders concerned with the problem seemed able to grasp, that "these decisions ought to be based not on the *present* evidence relating to atomic bombs, but rather on the situation which can be expected to confront us in this respect a few years from now." By present evidence the bombs were modest and the United States held them in monopoly; the difficulty was deciding what the future would bring. Szilard first offended Byrnes in his memorandum by concluding that "this situation can be evaluated only by men who have first-hand knowledge of the facts involved, that is, by the small group of scientists who are actively engaged in this work." Having thus informed Byrnes that he thought him unqualified, Szilard then proceeded to tell him how his inadequacies might be corrected:

> If there were in existence a small subcommittee of the Cabinet (having as its members the Secretary of War, either the Secretary of Commerce or the Secretary of the Interior, a representative of the State Department, and a representative of the President, acting as the secretary of the Committee), the scientists could then submit to such a committee their recommendations.

It was H. G. Wells' Open Conspiracy emerging again into the light; it amused Byrnes, a man who had climbed to the top across forty-five years of hard political service, not at all:

> Szilard complained that he and some of his associates did not know enough about the policy of the government with regard to the use of the bomb. He felt that scientists, including himself, should discuss the matter with the Cabinet, which I did not feel desirable. His general demeanor and his desire to participate in policy making made an unfavorable impression on me.

Byrnes proceeded to demonstrate the dangers of a lack of firsthand knowledge, Szilard remembers:

> When I spoke of my concern that Russia might become an atomic power, and might become an atomic power soon, if we demonstrated the power of the bomb and if we used it against Japan, his reply was, "General Groves tells me there is no uranium in Russia."

So Szilard explained to Byrnes what Groves, busy buying up the world supply of high-grade ore, apparently did not understand: that high-grade deposits are necessary for the extraction of so rare an element as radium but that low-grade ores, which undoubtedly existed in the Soviet Union, were entirely satisfactory where so abundant an element as uranium was concerned.

To Szilard's argument that using the atomic bomb, even testing the atomic bomb, would be unwise because it would disclose that the weapon existed, Byrnes took a turn at teaching the physicist a lesson in domestic politics:

> He said we had spent two billion dollars on developing the bomb, and Congress would want to know what we had got for the money spent. He said, "How would you get Congress to appropriate money for atomic energy research if you do not show results for the money which has been spent already?"

But Byrnes' most dangerous misunderstanding from Szilard's point of view was his reading of the Soviet Union:

> Byrnes thought that the war would be over in about six months. . . . He was concerned about Russia's postwar behavior. Russian troops had moved into Hungary and Rumania, and Byrnes thought it would be very difficult to persuade Russia to withdraw her troops from these countries, that Russia might be more manageable if impressed by American military might, and that a demonstration of the bomb might impress Russia. I shared Byrnes' concern about Russia's throwing around her weight in the postwar period, but I was completely flabbergasted by the assumption that rattling the bomb might make Russia more manageable.

Shadowed by one of Groves' ubiquitous security agents, the three discouraged men caught the next train back to Washington.

There on the same day the Target Committee was meeting, this time with Paul Tibbets as well as Tolman and Parsons on hand. Much of the discussion concerned Tibbets' training program for the 509th Composite Group. He had sent his best crews to Cuba for six weeks to give them radar experience and flying time over water. "On load and distance tests," the committee minutes report, "Col. Tibbets stated crews had taken off at 135,000 lbs. gross load, flown 4300 miles with 10,000 lb. bomb load, bombed from 32,000 ft. and returned to base with 900 gallons of fuel. This is in excess of the expected target run and further tests will reduce the loading to reach the S.O.P. [standard operating procedure] of 500 gallons of fuel on return." The 509th was in the process of staging out to Tinian. Pumpkin production was increasing; nineteen had been shipped to Wendover and some of them dropped.

LeMay was also keeping busy. "The 3 reserved targets for the first unit of this project were announced. With current and prospective rate of [Twentieth Air Force] H.E. bombing, it is expected to complete strategic bombing of Japan by 1 Jan 46 so availability of future targets will be a problem." If the Manhattan Project did not hurry, that is, there would be no cities left in Japan to bomb.

Kyoto, Hiroshima and Niigata were the three targets reserved. The committee completed its review by abandoning any pretension that its objectives there were military:

> The following conclusions were reached:
>
> (1) not to specify aiming points, this is to be left to later determination at base when weather conditions are known.
> (2) to neglect location of industrial areas as pin point target, since on these three targets such areas are small, spread on fringes of cities and quite dispersed.
> (3) to endeavor to place first gadget in center of selected city; that is, not to allow for later 1 or 2 gadgets for complete destruction.

And that was that; the Target Committee would schedule no more meetings but would remain on call.

Stimson abhorred bombing cities. As he wrote in his third-person memoir after the war, "for thirty years Stimson had been a champion of international law and morality. As soldier and Cabinet officer he had repeatedly argued that war itself must be restrained within the bounds of humanity. . . . Perhaps, as he later said, he was misled by the constant talk of 'precision bombing,' but he had believed that even air power could be limited in its use by the old concept of 'legitimate military targets.' " Firebombing was "a kind of total war he had always hated." He seems to have conceived the idea that even the atomic bomb could be somehow humanely applied, as he discussed with Truman on May 16:

> I am anxious to hold our Air Force, so far as possible, to the "precision" bombing which it has done so well in Europe. I am told that it is possible and adequate. The reputation of the United States for fair play and humanitarianism is the world's biggest asset for peace in the coming decades. I believe the same rule of sparing the civilian population should be applied, as far as possible, to the use of any new weapons.

But the Secretary of War had less control over the military forces he was delegated to administer than he would have liked, and nine days later, on May 25, 464 of LeMay's B-29's—nearly twice as many as flew the first low-level March 9 incendiary raid—once again successfully burned out nearly sixteen square miles of Tokyo, although the Strategic Bombing Survey asserts that only a few thousand Japanese were killed compared to the 86,000 it totals for the earlier conflagration. The newspapers made much of the late-May fire raid; Stimson was appalled.

On May 30 Groves crossed the river from his Virginia Avenue offices and hove into view. Stimson's frustration at the bombing of Japanese cities ignited a fateful exchange, as the general later told an interviewer:

> I was over in Mr. Stimson's office talking to him about some matter in connection with the bomb when he asked me if I had selected the targets yet. I replied that I had that report all ready and I expected to take it over to General Marshall the following morning for his approval. Mr. Stimson then said: "Well, your report is all finished, isn't it?" I said: "I haven't gone over it yet, Mr. Stimson. I want to be sure that I've got it just right." He said: "Well, I would like to see it" and I said: "Well, it's across the river and it would take a long time to get it." He said: "I have all day and I know how fast your office operates. Here's a phone on this desk. You pick it up and you call your office and have them bring that report over." Well, it took about fifteen or twenty minutes to get that report there and all the time I was stewing and fretting internally over the fact that I was shortcutting General Marshall. . . . But there was nothing I could do and when I protested slightly that I thought it was something that General Marshall should pass on first, Mr. Stimson said: "This is one time I'm going to be the final deciding authority. Nobody's going to tell me what to do on this. On this matter I am the kingpin and you might just as well get that report over here." Well in the meantime he asked me what cities I was planning to bomb, or what targets. I informed him and told him that Kyoto was the preferred target. It was the first one because it was of such size that we would have no question about the effects of the bomb. . . . He immediately said: "I don't want Kyoto bombed." And he went on to tell me about its long history as a cultural center of Japan, the former ancient capital, and a great many reasons why he did not want to see it bombed. When the report came over and I handed it to him, his mind was made up. There's no question

> about that. He read it over and he walked to the door separating his office from General Marshall's, opened it and said: "General Marshall, if you're not busy I wish you'd come in." And then the Secretary really double-crossed me because without any explanation he said to General Marshall: "Marshall, Groves has just brought me his report on the proposed targets." He said: "I don't like it. I don't like the use of Kyoto."

So Kyoto at least, the Rome of Japan, founded in 793, famous for silk and cloisonné, a center of the Buddhist and Shinto religions with hundreds of historic temples and shrines, would be spared, though Groves would continue to test his superior's resolve in the weeks to come. The Imperial Palace in Tokyo had been similarly spared even as Tokyo was laid waste around it. There were still limits to the destructiveness of war: the weapons were still modest enough to allow such fine discriminations.

The Interim Committee was to meet in full dress with its Scientific Panel on Thursday, May 31, and on Friday, June 1, with its industrial advisers. The Joint Chiefs of Staff prepared the ground for those meetings on May 25 when they issued a formal directive to the Pacific commanders and to Hap Arnold defining U.S. military policy toward Japan in the months to come:

> The Joint Chiefs of Staff direct the invasion of Kyushu (operation OLYMPIC) target date 1 November 1945, in order to:
>
> (1) Intensify the blockade and aerial bombardment of Japan.
> (2) Contain and destroy major enemy forces.
> (3) Support further advances for the purpose of establishing the conditions favorable to the decisive invasion of the industrial heart of Japan.

Truman had not yet signed on for the Japanese invasion. One of his advisers favored a naval blockade to starve the Japanese to surrender. The President would soon tell the Joint Chiefs that he would judge among his options "with the purpose of economizing to the maximum extent possible the loss of American lives." Marshall, with MacArthur concurring from the field, estimated that casualties—killed, wounded and missing—in the first thirty days following an invasion of the southernmost Japanese home island would not exceed 31,000. An invasion of the main island of Honshu across the plain of Tokyo would be proportionately more violent.

When Szilard returned to Washington from South Carolina he looked up Oppenheimer, just arrived in town for the Interim Committee meeting, to lobby him. So hard was the Los Alamos director working to complete the first atomic bombs that Groves had doubted two weeks earlier if he could break free for the May 31 meeting. Oppenheimer would not for the world have missed the chance to advise at so high a level. But his candid vision of the future of the weapon he was building was as unromantic as his understanding of its immediate necessity was, in Szilard's view, misinformed:

> I told Oppenheimer that I thought it would be a very serious mistake to use the bomb against the cities of Japan. Oppenheimer didn't share my view. He surprised me by starting the conversation by saying, "The atomic bomb is shit." "What do you mean by that?" I asked him. He said, "Well, this is a weapon which has no military significance. It will make a big bang—a very big bang—but it is not a weapon which is useful in war." He thought that it would be important, however, to inform the Russians that we had an atomic bomb and that we intended to use it against the cities of Japan, rather than taking them by surprise. This seemed reasonable to me. . . . However, while this was necessary it was certainly not sufficient. "Well," Oppenheimer said, "don't you think that if we tell the Russians what we intend to do and then use the bomb in Japan, the Russians will understand it?" And I remember that I said, "They'll understand it only too well."

Stimson's insomnia troubled him on the night of May 30 and he arrived at the Pentagon the next morning feeling miserable. His committee assembled at 10 A.M. Marshall, Groves, Harvey Bundy and another aide attended by invitation, but Stimson's attention was focused on the four scientists, three of them Nobel laureates. The elderly Secretary of War welcomed them warmly, congratulated them on their accomplishments and was concerned to convince them that he and Marshall understood that the product of their labor would be more than simply an enlarged specimen of ordnance. The handwritten notes he prepared emphasize the awe in which he held the bomb; he was not normally a histrionic man:

S.1

Its *size* and *character*
We don't think it *mere* new *weapon*
Revolutionary Discovery of Relation of man to universe
Great History Landmark like
    Gravitation
    Copernican Theory
But,
Bids fair [to be] *infinitely greater,* in *respect* to its *Effect*
    —on the ordinary affairs of man's life.
May *destroy* or *perfect* International *Civilization*
May [be] *Frankenstein or* means for World Peace

Oppenheimer was surprised and impressed. When Roosevelt died, he told an audience late in life, he had felt "a terrible bereavement . . . partly because we were not sure that anyone in Washington would be thinking of what needed to be done in the future." Now he saw that "Colonel Stimson was thinking hard and seriously about the implications for mankind of the thing we had created and the wall into the future that we had breached." And though Oppenheimer knew Stimson had never sat down to talk with Niels Bohr, the Secretary seemed to be speaking in terms derived at some near remove from Bohr's understanding of the complementarity of the bomb.

After Stimson's introduction Arthur Compton offered a technical review of the nuclear business, concluding that a competitor would need perhaps six years to catch up with the United States. Conant mentioned the thermonuclear and asked Oppenheimer what gestation period that much more violent mechanism would require; Oppenheimer estimated a minimum of three years. The Los Alamos director took the floor then to review the explosive forces involved. First-stage bombs, he said, meaning crude bombs like Fat Man and Little Boy, might explode with blasts equivalent to 2,000 to 20,000 tons of TNT. That was an upward revision of the estimate Bethe had supplied the Target Committee at Los Alamos in mid-May. Second-stage weapons, Oppenheimer went on—meaning presumably advanced fission weapons with improved implosion systems—might be equal to 50,000 to 100,000 tons of TNT. Thermonuclear weapons might range from 10 million to 100 million tons TNT equivalent.

These were numbers most of the men in the room had seen before and were inured to. Apparently Byrnes had not; they worried him gravely: "As I heard these scientists . . . predict the destructive power of the weapon, I was thoroughly frightened. I had sufficient imagination to visualize the danger to our country when some other country possessed such a weapon." For now the President's personal representative bided his time.

Entirely in energetic character, Ernest Lawrence spoke up for staying ahead of the rest of the world by knowing more and doing more than any other country. He made explicit a future course for the nation about which the previous record of all the meetings and deliberations is oddly silent, a course based on assumptions diametrically opposite to Oppenheimer's profound insight that the atomic bomb was shit:

> Dr. Lawrence *recommended* that a program of plant expansion be vigorously pursued and at the same time a sizable stock pile of bombs and material should be built up. . . . Only by vigorously pursuing the necessary plant expansion and fundamental research . . . could this nation stay out in front.

That was a prescription for an arms race as soon as the Soviet Union took up the challenge. Arthur Compton immediately signed on. So did his brother Karl. Oppenheimer contented himself with a footnote about materials allocation. Stimson eventually summarized the discussion:

1. *Keep our industrial plant intact.*
2. *Build up sizeable stock piles of material for military use and for industrial and technical use.*
3. *Open the door to industrial development.*

Oppenheimer demurred that the scientists should be released to return to their universities and get back to basic science; during the war, he said, they had been plucking the fruits of earlier research. Bush emphatically agreed.

The committee turned to the question of international control and Oppenheimer took the lead. His exact words do not survive, only their summary in the meeting notes kept by the young recording secretary, Gordon Arneson, but if that summary is accurate, then Oppenheimer's emphasis was different from Bohr's and misleading:

> *Dr. Oppenheimer* pointed out that the immediate concern had been to shorten the war. The research that had led to this development had only opened the door to future discoveries. Fundamental knowledge of this subject was so widespread throughout the world that early steps should be taken to make our developments known to the world. He thought it might be wise for the United States to offer to the world free interchange of information with particular emphasis on the development of peace-time uses. The basic goal of all endeavors in the field should be the enlargement of human welfare. If we were to offer to exchange information before the bomb was actually used, our moral position would be greatly strengthened.

Where was Bohr's understanding that the bomb was a source of terror but for that very reason also a source of hope, a means of welding together nations by their common dread of a menacing nuclear standoff? The problem was not exchanging information to improve America's moral standing; the problem was leaders sitting down and negotiating a way beyond the mutual danger the new weapons would otherwise install. The opening up would emerge *out of* those negotiations, necessarily, to guarantee safety; it could not in the real world of secrecy and suspicion realistically *precede* them. In 1963, lecturing on Bohr, Oppenheimer understood well enough the fundamental weakness of his proposal:

> Bush and Compton and Conant were clear that the only future they could envisage with hope was one in which the whole development would be interna-

> tionally controlled. Stimson understood this; he understood that it meant a very great change in human life; and he understood that the central problem at that moment lay in our relations with Russia. . . . But there were differences: Bohr was for action, for timely and responsible action. He realized that it had to be taken by those who had the power to commit and to act. He wanted to change the whole framework in which this problem would appear, early enough so that the problem would be altered by it. He believed in statesmen; he used the word over and over again; he was not very much for committees. The Interim Committee was a committee, and proved itself by appointing another committee, the scientific panel.

No one should presume to judge these men as they struggled with a future that even a mind as fundamental as Niels Bohr's could only barely imagine. But if Robert Oppenheimer ever had a chance to present Bohr's case to those who had the power to commit and to act he had it that morning. He did not speak the Dane's hard plain truths. He spoke instead as Aaron to Bohr's Moses. And Bohr, though he waited nearby in Washington, had not been invited to appear in the star chamber of that darkly paneled room.

Even Stimson thought Oppenheimer's proposals misguided. He asked immediately "what would be the position of democratic governments as against totalitarian regimes under such a program of international control coupled with scientific freedom"—as if opening up the world would leave either democratic or totalitarian nations unchanged, a confusion that Oppenheimer's confusion inspired. Which led to further confusion: "The Secretary said . . . it was his own feeling that the democratic countries had fared pretty well in this war. *Dr. Bush* endorsed this view vigorously." Bush then unwittingly outlined a domestic model of what Bohr's larger open world might be: "He said that our tremendous advantage stemmed in large measure from our system of team work and free interchange of information." And promptly lapsed back into Stimson's extended status quo: "He expressed some doubt, however, of our ability to remain ahead permanently if we were to turn over completely to the Russians the results of our research under free competition with no reciprocal exchange."

Odder and odder, and Byrnes sitting among them trying to imagine a weapon equivalent to 100 million tons of TNT, trying to imagine what it would mean to possess such a weapon and listening to these highly educated men, men almost entirely of the Eastern establishment, of Harvard and MIT and Princeton and Yale, blithely proposing, it seemed, to give away the knowledge of how to make such a weapon.

Stimson left to attend a White House ceremony and they went on to speak of Russia, which Byrnes knew as an advancing brutality currently devouring Poland, and Oppenheimer again took the lead:

> *Dr. Oppenheimer* pointed out that Russia had always been very friendly to science and suggested that we might open up this subject with them in a tentative fashion and in the most general terms without giving them any details of our productive effort. He thought we might say that a great national effort had been put into this project and express hope for cooperation with them in this field. He felt strongly that we should not prejudge the Russian attitude in this matter.

Oppenheimer found an ally then in George Marshall, who "discussed at some length the story of charges and counter-charges that have been typical of our relations with the Russians, pointing out that most of these allegations have proven unfounded." Marshall thought Russia's reputation for being uncooperative "stemmed from the necessity of maintaining security." He believed a way to begin was to forge "a combination among like-minded powers, thereby forcing Russia to fall in line by the very force of this coalition." Such bulldozing had worked in the gunpowder days now almost past but it would not work in the days of the bomb; that power would be big enough, as Oppenheimer's estimates clarified, to make one nation alone a match for the world.

The surprise of the morning was perhaps Marshall's idea for an opening to Moscow: "He raised the question whether it might be desirable to invite two prominent Russian scientists to witness the [Trinity] test." Groves must have winced; after the years of secrecy, after the thousands of numb man-hours of security work, that would be a renunciation worthy of Bohr himself.

Byrnes had heard enough. He had sat behind Franklin Roosevelt at Yalta making notes. In all but the formalities he outranked even Henry Stimson. He put his foot down and the seasoned committeemen moved smoothly into line:

> *Mr. Byrnes* expressed a fear that if information were given to the Russians, even in general terms, Stalin would ask to be brought into the partnership. He felt this to be particularly likely in view of our commitments and pledges of cooperation with the British. In this connection *Dr. Bush* pointed out that even the British did not have any of our blue prints on plants. *Mr. Byrnes* expressed the view, *which was generally agreed to by all present,* that the most desirable program would be to push ahead as fast as possible in production and research to make certain that we stay ahead and at the same time make every effort to better our political relations with Russia.

When Stimson returned, Compton summed up the sense of the crucial discussion the Secretary of War had missed—"the need for maintaining ourselves in a position of superiority while at the same time working toward adequate political agreements." Marshall left them for duty and the rest of the committee trooped off to lunch.

They sat at adjoining tables in a Pentagon dining room. They were a civilian committee; separate conversations converged on the same question, only briefly mentioned during the morning and not taken up: was there no way to let this cup pass from them? Must Little Boy be dropped on the Japanese in surprise? Could their stubborn enemy not be warned in advance or a demonstration arranged?

Stimson, at the focus of one conversation (Byrnes the center of the other), may have spoken then of his outrage at the mass murder of civilians and his complicity; Oppenheimer remembered such a statement at some time during the day and lunch was the only unstructured occasion:

> [Stimson emphasized] the appalling lack of conscience and compassion that the war had brought about . . . the complacency, the indifference, and the silence with which we greeted the mass bombings in Europe and, above all, Japan. He was not exultant about the bombings of Hamburg, of Dresden, of Tokyo. . . . Colonel Stimson felt that, as far as degradation went, we had had it; that it would take a new life and a new breath to heal the harm.

The only recorded response to Stimson's *mea culpa* is Oppenheimer's admiration for it, but there were a number of responses to the question of warning the Japanese or demonstrating the atomic bomb. Oppenheimer could not think of a suitably convincing demonstration:

> You ask yourself would the Japanese government as then constituted and with divisions between the peace party and the war party, would it have been influenced by an enormous nuclear firecracker detonated at a great height doing little damage and your answer is as good as mine. I don't know.

Since the Secretary of State–designate had power to commit and to act, the significant responses to the question are Byrnes'. In a 1947 memoir he recalled several:

> We feared that, if the Japanese were told that the bomb would be used on a given locality, they might bring our boys who were prisoners of war to that area. Also, the experts had warned us that the static test which was to take place in New Mexico, even if successful, would not be conclusive proof that a bomb would explode when dropped from an airplane. If we were to warn the

> Japanese of the new highly destructive weapon in the hope of impressing them and if the bomb then failed to explode, certainly we would have given aid and comfort to the Japanese militarists. Thereafter, the Japanese people probably would not be impressed by any statement we might make in the hope of inducing them to surrender.

In a later television interview he emphasized a more political concern: "The President would have had to take the responsibility of telling the world that we had this atomic bomb and how terrific it was . . . and if it didn't prove out what would have happened to the way the war went God only knows."

Someone among the assembled, Ernest Lawrence remembers, concluded that the "number of people that would be killed by the bomb would not be greater in general magnitude than the number already killed in fire raids," making those slaughters a baseline, as indeed before the awful potential of the new weapon they were.

These troubled men returned to Stimson's office and spent most of the afternoon considering the effect of the bombing on the Japanese and their will to fight. Someone unnamed chose to discredit the atomic bomb's destructiveness, asserting it "would not be much different from the effect caused by any Air Corps strike of present dimensions." Oppenheimer defended his creation's pyrotechnics, citing the electromagnetic and nuclear radiation it would expel:

> *Dr. Oppenheimer* stated that the visual effect of an atomic bombing would be tremendous. It would be accompanied by a brilliant luminescence which would rise to a height of 10,000 to 20,000 feet. The neutron effect of the explosion would be dangerous to life for a radius of at least two-thirds of a mile.

It was probably during this afternoon discussion that Oppenheimer reported an estimate prepared at Los Alamos of how many deaths an atomic bomb exploded over a city might cause. Arthur Compton remembers the number as 20,000, an estimate based on the assumption, he says, that the city's occupants would seek shelter when the air raid began and before the bomb went off. He recalls Stimson bringing up Kyoto then, "a city that must not be bombed." The Secretary still insisted passionately that "the objective was military damage . . . not civilian lives."

The contradiction in Stimson's caveat persisted into his summary of the afternoon's findings, which he offered before he left the meeting at three thirty:

> After much discussion concerning various types of targets and the effects to be produced, *the Secretary expressed the conclusion, on which there was general*

> *agreement, that we could not give the Japanese any warning; that we could not concentrate on a civilian area; but that we should seek to make a profound psychological impression on as many of the inhabitants as possible. At the suggestion of Dr. Conant the Secretary agreed that the most desirable target would be a vital war plant employing a large number of workers and closely surrounded by workers' houses.*

Which had been the general formula in Europe, but according to Curtis LeMay the Japanese worked at home, as families:

> We were going after military targets. No point in slaughtering civilians for the mere sake of slaughter. Of course there is a pretty thin veneer in Japan, but the veneer was there. It was their system of dispersal of industry. All you had to do was visit one of those targets after we'd roasted it, and see the ruins of a multitude of tiny houses, with a drill press sticking up through the wreckage of every home. The entire population got into the act and worked to make those airplanes or munitions of war . . . men, women, children. We knew we were going to kill a lot of women and kids when we burned [a] town. Had to be done.

Stimson had now left the meeting. Arthur Compton wanted to talk about problems at the Met Lab. Before that final discussion the spirit of Leo Szilard bustled through the room. Groves had just learned of another round of Szilardian conspiracy. The general was wrathful: "*General Groves* stated that the program has been plagued since its inception by the presence of certain scientists of doubtful discretion and uncertain loyalty." Szilard had traveled on to New York after talking to Oppenheimer and that very morning had looked up Boris Pregel, the Russian-born French metals speculator and bon vivant who had helped out in the early Columbia days and whose mine on Great Bear Lake supplied the Manhattan Project with uranium ore. On May 16 Szilard had sent Pregel a version of his Truman memorandum. (Groves knew all this from what he calls "secret intelligence sources.") Meeting with Pregel fresh from the May 28 meeting with Byrnes, Szilard had "expressed the opinion," says Groves, "that someone high in the Government [i.e., Byrnes] had been completely misinformed as to [Russian] sources of ore by the [U.S.] Army. He claimed that the misinformation was given intentionally." Two could play at sniffing conspiracy, and even in the midst of debate on the necessity of total death in total war, they did.

The next morning, June 1, the Interim Committee met with four industrialists. Walter S. Carpenter, the president of Du Pont, estimated that the Soviet Union would need "at least four or five years" to construct a plutonium production facility like Hanford. James White, president of Tennessee Eastman, "doubted whether Russia would be able to secure sufficient precision in its equipment to make [an electromagnetic separation plant] possible" at all. George Bucher, the president of Westinghouse, thought that if the Soviets acquired the services of German technicians and scientists they might build an electromagnetic operation in three years. A vice president of Union Carbide, James Rafferty, offered the longest odds: ten years to build a gaseous-diffusion plant from the ground up—but only three years if the Soviets ferreted out barrier technology by espionage.

Mentally Byrnes added processing time to plant construction: "I concluded that any other government would need from seven to ten years, at least, to produce a bomb." From a political point of view seven years was a millennium.

Stimson still quailed at destroying entire cities with atomic bombs. In the afternoon, absenting himself from the Interim Committee discussions, he distanced that horror by pursuing the precision-bombing question further with Hap Arnold, whom he says he "sternly questioned." "I told him of my promise from [War Department Undersecretary for Air Robert] Lovett that there would be only precision bombing in Japan. . . . I wanted to know what the facts were." Arnold told Stimson the one about dispersed Japanese industry. Area bombing was the only way to get at all those drill presses. "He told me, however, that they were trying to keep it down as far as possible." Stimson was willing a few days later to pass that tale along to Truman, with a brace of ambivalent motives thrown in for good measure:

> I told him how I was trying to hold the Air Force down to precision bombing but that with the Japanese method of scattering its manufacture it was rather difficult to prevent area bombing. I told him I was anxious about this feature of the war for two reasons: First, because I did not want to have the United States get the reputation for outdoing Hitler in atrocities; and second, I was a little fearful that before we could get ready, the Air Force might have Japan so thoroughly bombed out that the new weapon would not have a fair background to show its strength. He said he understood.

While Stimson was away Byrnes swiftly and decisively co-opted the committee. "Mr. Byrnes felt that it was important there be a final decision on the question of the use of the weapon," recording secretary Arneson recalled after the war. He described the decision-making process in the minutes he took on June 1:

> *Mr. Byrnes recommended,* and the Committee *agreed,* that the Secretary of War should be advised that, while recognizing that the final selection of the target was essentially a military decision, the present view of the Committee

was that the bomb should be used against Japan as soon as possible; that it be used on a war plant surrounded by workers' homes; and that it be used without prior warning.

It remained to carry the decision to the President for endorsement. Byrnes headed straight for the White House as soon as the Interim Committee adjourned:

> I told the President of the final decision of his Interim Committee. Mr. Truman told me he had been giving serious thought to the subject for many days, having been informed as to the investigation of the committee and the consideration of alternative plans, and that with reluctance he had to agree that he could think of no alternative and found himself in accord with what I told him the Committee was going to recommend.

Truman saw his Secretary of War five days later. The President, Stimson noted in his diary, "said that Byrnes had reported to him already about [the Interim Committee's decision] and that Byrnes seemed to be highly pleased with what had been done."

Harry Truman did not give the order to drop the atomic bomb on June 1. But he appears to have made the decision then, with a little help from Jimmy Byrnes.

After the Interim Committee meeting on May 31 Robert Oppenheimer had sought out Niels Bohr. "I was very deeply impressed with General Marshall's wisdom," he remembered in 1963, "and also that of Secretary Stimson; and I went over to the British mission and met Bohr and tried to comfort him; but he was too wise and too worldly to be comforted, and he left for England very soon after that, quite uncertain about what, if anything, would happen."

Before Bohr left, late in June, he attempted one last time to see a high official of the United States government—Stimson—Harvey Bundy sending in a message on June 18 to the Secretary: "Do you want to try and work in a meeting with Professor Bohr, the Dane, before you get away this week?"

At the side of the memorandum, in bold script, whether from exhaustion or impatience or because he understood that the matter had been taken out of his hands, Henry Stimson struck finally: "No."

No one doubted that Little Boy would work if any design would. Otto Frisch's Dragon experiments had proven the efficacy of the fast-neutron chain reaction in uranium. The gun mechanism was wasteful and inefficient but U235 was forgiving. It remained to test implosion. While doing so the physicists could also compare their theory of the progress of such an exotic release of energy with the huge blinding fact. Trinity would be the largest physics experiment ever attempted up to that time.

The hard work of finding a proving ground sufficiently barren and remote and organizing it fell to a compact, close-cropped Harvard experimental physicist named Kenneth T. Bainbridge. His task, the Los Alamos technical history notes, "was one of establishing under conditions of extreme secrecy and great pressure a complex scientific laboratory in a barren desert." Bainbridge was well qualified. From Cooperstown, New York, the son of a wholesale stationer, he had worked under Ernest Rutherford at the Cavendish and had designed and built the Harvard cyclotron that now served the Manhattan Project's purposes on the Hill. He had brought back word of the MAUD Committee report to Vannevar Bush in the summer of 1941 and had worked at MIT and in Great Britain on radar. Robert Bacher had recruited him for Los Alamos in the summer of 1943. Beginning in March 1944 he took charge of Trinity.

He needed a flat, desolate site with good weather, near enough to Los Alamos to make travel convenient but far enough away to obscure obvious connection. From map data he chose eight sites, including a desert training area in southern California, the Texas Gulf sandbar region now known as Padre Island and several barren dry valleys in southern New Mexico. Riding three-quarter-ton weapons carriers with Robert Oppenheimer and a team of Army officers in May 1944, Bainbridge led an exploration of the New Mexico sites through late snow; carrying along food and water and sleeping bags, he remembers, they "followed unmapped ranch trails past deserted areas of dry farming lands beaten by too many years of drought and high winds." For Oppenheimer it was a rare escape from the daily burdens of directing Los Alamos, one he was not able to repeat. Several explorations later Bainbridge chose a flat scrub region some sixty miles northwest of Alamogordo between the Rio Grande and the Sierra Oscura, known ominously from Spanish times as the Jornada del Muerto—the dry and therefore dangerous Dead Man's Trail, the Journey of Death. Two hundred ten miles south of Los Alamos, the Jornada formed the northwest sector of the Alamogordo Bombing Range; with the permission of Second Air Force Commander Uzal Ent, Bainbridge staked out an eighteen-by-twenty-four-mile claim.

The demands of the implosion crisis in the autumn of 1944 reduced Trinity's priority, says Bainbridge, "almost to zero . . . until the end of February 1945." With bomb physics well in hand by then Oppenheimer set the test shot's target date at July 4 and Bainbridge got busy. His staff of twenty-five increased across the next five months to more than 250. Herbert Anderson, P. B. Moon, Emilio Segrè and Robert Wilson carried major responsibilities; William G. Penney, Enrico Fermi and especially Victor Weisskopf served as consultants.

The Army leased the David McDonald ranch in the middle of the Jornada site and renovated it for a field laboratory and Military Police station. About 3,400 yards northwest of McDonald Ranch Bainbridge marked out Ground Zero. From that center, at compass points roughly north, west and south at 10,000-yard distances, Corps of Engineers contractors built earth-sheltered bunkers with concrete slab roofs supported by oak beams thicker than railroad ties. N-10000, 5.7 miles from Zero, would house recording instruments and searchlights; W-10000 would house searchlights and banks of high-speed cameras; S-10000 would serve as the control bunker for the test. Another five miles south beyond S-10000 a Base Camp of tents and barracks took shape.

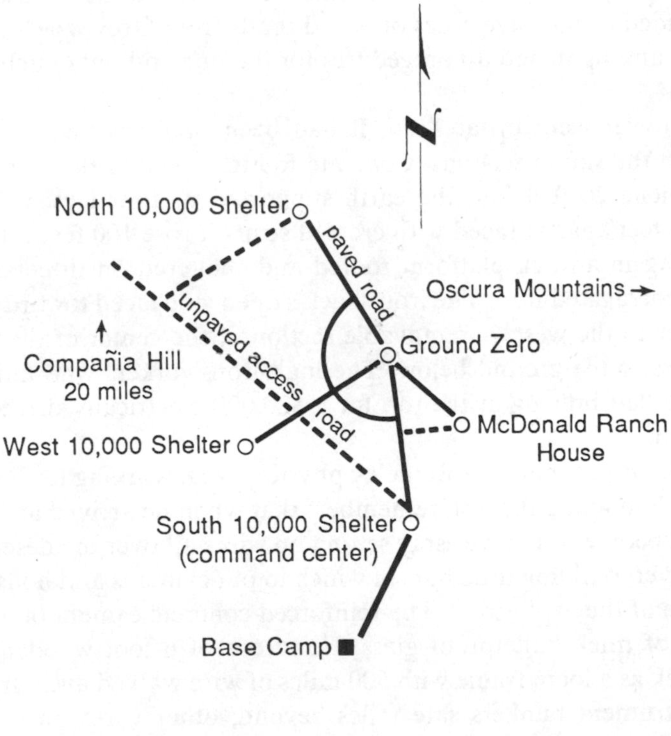

A hill named Compañia twenty miles northwest of Zero on the edge of the Jornada would serve as a VIP scenic overlook. The Oscuras to the east rose more than 4,000 feet above the high alkaline plain.

The Jornada was host to gray hard mesquite, to yucca sharp as the swords of samurai, to scorpions and centipedes men shook in the morning from their boots, to rattlesnakes and fire ants and tarantulas. The MP's hunted antelope with machine guns for fresh meat and for sport. Groves authorized only cold showers for his troops; their isolated duty would win them eventual award for the lowest VD rate in the entire U.S. Army. The well water, fouled with gypsum, made a sovereign purgative. It also stiffened the hair.

Contractors built two towers. One, 800 yards south of Zero, they bolted together 20 feet high in trestles of heavy beams like those that framed the bunkers. It supported a wide platform like an outdoor dance floor and one day in early May the builders returned from a mandated layoff to find it had vanished. Bainbridge had seen it stacked with 100 tons of high explosives in wooden boxes, had packed canisters of dissolved hot Hanford slugs at the center and before dawn on May 7 had blown the entire stack, the largest chemical explosion ever deliberately set off, merely to practice routines and try out instruments. The dirt roads had caused delays; he demanded twenty-five miles of paved roads from Groves as a result and got them, and tightened up procedures for the one and only nuclear test to come.

The tower went up at Zero. It had been prefabricated of steel and shipped to the site in sections. Concrete footings poured through the hard desert caliche 20 feet into the earth supported its four legs, which were spaced 35 feet apart; braced with crossed struts it rose 100 feet into the air, culminating in an oak platform roofed and sheltered on three sides with sheets of corrugated iron. The iron shack's open side faced toward the camera bunker to the west. A removable section at the center of the platform gave access to the ground below. The high-iron workers who finished the tower installed bracing at the top for a $20,000 electrically driven heavy-duty winch.

Frank Oppenheimer, a Berkeley physics Ph.D. working for his brother now troubleshooting the test, remembers that when he arrived at Trinity in late May "people were feverishly setting up wires all over the desert, building the tower, building little huts in which to put cameras and house people at the time of the explosion." The reinforced concrete camera bunkers had portholes of thick bulletproof glass. Hundreds of 6-foot wooden T-poles strung thick as a loom frame with 500 miles of wire walked away from Zero to the instrument bunkers safe miles beyond; other wires buried underground ran protected inside miles of premium garden hose.

Besides photographic studies three kinds of experiments concerned Bainbridge and his team. One set, by far the most extensive, would measure blast, optical and nuclear effects with seismographs, geophones, ionization chambers, spectrographs, films and a variety of gauges. A second would study the implosion in detail and check the operation of the new exploding-wire detonators Luis Alvarez had invented. Experiments planned by Herbert Anderson to reveal the explosive yield radiochemically made up the third category. Harvard physicist David Anderson (no relation) arranged to acquire two Army tanks for that work and to pressurize them and line them with lead; Herbert Anderson and Fermi meant to ride them close to the crater at Zero immediately after the shot, scoop up some of the radioactive debris with a tethered cup hitched to a rocket fired into the crater and retrieve the material for laboratory measurement. Its ratio of fission products to unfissioned plutonium would reveal the yield.

By May 31 enough plutonium had arrived at Los Alamos from Hanford to begin critical-mass experiments. Seth Neddermeyer's shell-configured core had been abandoned even though thin-walled shells give the highest compressions in implosion. Designing out their hydrodynamic instabilities required calculations too dificult to accomplish by hand. Berkeley theoretician Robert Christy designed a more conservative solid core, two mated hemispheres totaling less than one critical mass that implosion would squeeze to at least double their previous density, shortening the distance that fission neutrons would have to travel between nuclei and rendering the mass supercritical. Frisch's group confirmed the core configuration experimentally on June 24. For the high-density form of Pu the critical mass within a heavy tamper is eleven pounds; even with a nut-sized central hollow to encapsulate an initiator the Trinity core cannot have been larger than a small orange.

Delivery of full-sized molds for the implosion lens segments paced the test; they began arriving in quantity only in June, and on June 30 the committee responsible for deciding the test date moved it back to July 16 at the earliest. Kistiakowsky's group worked night and day at S-Site to make enough lenses. "Most troublesome were the air cavities in the interior of the large castings," he recalled after the war, "which we detected by x-ray inspection techniques but could not repair. More rejects than acceptable castings were usually our unfortunate lot."

Groves met with Oppenheimer and Parsons on June 27 to lay plans for shipping the first atomic bombs to the Pacific. They agreed to send the Little Boy U235 projectile by water and the several U235 target pieces later by air; the shipping program acquired the code name Bronx because of that New York borough's adjacency to Manhattan. The metallurgists at Los Alamos cast one target piece before the end of June and the U235 bullet on July 3. The next day, Independence Day, the Combined Policy Committee met in Washington and the British officially gave their approval, as the Quebec Agreement provided, for the use of atomic bombs on Japan.

Truman had agreed to meet with Stalin and Churchill in the Berlin suburb of Potsdam sometime during the summer; he told Stimson on June 6 that he had succeeded in postponing the conference until July 15 "on purpose," Stimson wrote in his diary, "to give us more time." Though Truman and Byrnes had not yet decided to tell Stalin about the atomic bomb, a successful test would change the Pacific equation; they might not need a Soviet invasion of Manchuria to challenge the Japanese and might therefore have to trade away less in Europe. To make sure the President had news of the test at Potsdam, Groves decided during the first week in July to fix the test date at July 16, subject to the vagaries of the weather. He had learned late in June of the possibility of dangerous radioactive fallout over populated areas of New Mexico—"What are you," he berated the Los Alamos physician who gave him the news, "some kind of Hearst propagandist?"—or he would not have waited even on the weather.

So the shot was set for sometime in mid-July, in the heat of the desert summer when the temperature on the Jornada often burned above 100° late in the day. Oppenheimer wired Arthur Compton and Ernest Lawrence: ANY TIME AFTER THE 15TH WOULD BE A GOOD TIME FOR OUR FISHING TRIP. BECAUSE WE ARE NOT CERTAIN OF THE WEATHER WE MAY BE DELAYED SEVERAL DAYS.

The senior men arranged a betting pool with a one-dollar entry fee, wagering on the explosive yield. Edward Teller optimistically picked 45,000 tons TNT equivalent. Hans Bethe picked 8,000 tons, Kistiakowsky 1,400. Oppenheimer chose a modest 300 tons. Norman Ramsey took a cynical zero. When I. I. Rabi arrived a few days before the test the only bet left was for 18,000 tons; whether or not he believed that might be the Trinity yield, he bought it.

As of July 9 Kistiakowsky did not yet have enough quality lens castings on hand to assemble a complete charge. Oppenheimer further compounded his troubles by insisting on firing a Chinese copy of the gadget a few days before the Trinity shot to test its high-explosive design at full scale with a nonfissionable core. Each unit would require ninety-six blocks of explosive. Kistiakowsky resorted to heroic measures:

> In some desperation, I got hold of a dental drill and, not wishing to ask others to do an untried job, spent most of one night, the week before the Trinity test, drilling holes in some faulty castings so as to reach the air cavities indicated on our x-ray inspection films. That done, I filled the cavities by pouring molten explosive slurry into them, and thus made the castings acceptable. Overnight, enough castings were added to our stores by my labors to make more than two spheres.

"You don't worry about it," he adds fatalistically. "I mean, if fifty pounds of explosives goes in your lap, you won't know it."

Navy Lieutenant Commander Norris E. Bradbury, a brisk, energetic Berkeley physics Ph.D., took charge of assembling the high explosives. On Wednesday, July 11, he met with Kistiakowsky to sort the charges according to their quality. "The castings were personally inspected by Kistiakowsky and Bradbury for chipped corners, cracks, and other imperfections," writes Bainbridge. ". . . Only first-quality castings which were not chipped or which could be easily repaired were used for the Trinity assembly. The remainder of the castings were diverted for the Creutz charge"—so named for Edward Creutz, the physicist who was running the Chinese copy test. The castings were waxy, mottled, brown with varnish. They weighed in total, for each device, about 5,000 pounds.

Everyone felt the pressure of the approaching test. It took its toll. "That last week in many ways dragged," Elsie McMillan remembers; "in many ways it flew on wings. It was hard to behave normally. It was hard not to think. It was hard not to let off steam. We also found it hard not to overindulge in all the natural activities of life." In a letter to Eleanor Roosevelt in 1950 Oppenheimer recalled an odd group delusion:

> Very shortly before the test of the first atomic bomb, people at Los Alamos were naturally in a state of some tension. I remember one morning when almost the whole project was out of doors staring at a bright object in the sky through glasses, binoculars and whatever else they could find; and nearby Kirtland Field reported to us that they had no interceptors which had enabled them to come within range of the object. Our director of personnel was an astronomer and a man of some human wisdom; and he finally came to my office and asked whether we would stop trying to shoot down Venus. I tell this story only to indicate that even a group of scientists is not proof against the errors of suggestion and hysteria.

By then the two small plutonium hemispheres had been cast, and plated against corrosion and to absorb alpha particles with nickel, which made the assembly, as metallurgist Cyril Smith would write, "beautiful to gaze upon." But "an unscheduled change began to be evident three or four days before the scheduled date." Plating solution trapped beneath the plating on the flat faces of the hemispheres began to blister the nickel, spoiling the fit. "For a time," says Smith, "postponement of the whole event was threatened." Completely filing off the blisters would expose the plutonium. The metallurgists salvaged the castings by grinding only partway through the blisters and smoothing the bumpy fit with sheets of gold foil. The core of the first atomic bomb would go to its glory dressed in improvised offerings of nickel and gold.

A tropical air mass moved north over Trinity on July 10, just as the test meteorologist, Caltech-trained Jack M. Hubbard, thirty-nine years old, had predicted. Hubbard had resisted the July 16 date, a Monday, since he first heard of it; he expected bad weather that weekend. The Gulf air suspended salt crystals that diffused a slight haze. On July 12, worrying about Potsdam, Groves confirmed the test for the morning of July 16. Bainbridge passed the word to Hubbard. "Right in the middle of a period of thunderstorms," the meteorologist stormed to his journal, "what son-of-a-bitch could have done this?" Groves had been awarded such scurrilous genealogy before.

The general's decision started Norris Bradbury and his crews of Special Engineering Detachment GI's—SED's, the science-trained recruits were called—assembling the Trinity and Creutz high-explosive charges at two separate canyon sites near Los Alamos mesa that Thursday. They debated filling the small air spaces between the castings with grease. Kistiakowsky decided against such filler, writes Bainbridge, "on the basis that the castings assembled were much better than any previously made and that the air spaces left by the spacer materials were insignificant." The charges, each of which had been X-rayed one last time and numbered, were papered into snugness instead with facial tissue and Scotch tape. The simplified and improved casing of the unit to be tested, which was designated model 1561, differed from the earlier 1222 casing of bolted pentagons; it featured an equatorial band of five segments machined from dural castings to which were bolted large upper and lower domed polar caps. When the explosives that lined the lower hemisphere had been papered into place Bradbury's SED's winched down the heavy tamper sphere of natural uranium, which filled the cavity like the pit in an avocado. The tamper was missing a cylindrical plug; the resulting hole would receive the core assembly. The explosive blocks that formed the upper shell followed next.

For transport to Trinity one set of castings was temporarily left out, replaced by a trapdoor plug through which the core assembly could be positioned in the tamper. The reserved castings—an inner of solid Composition B, an outer lensed—were boxed separately with one spare of each type. The men completed preparing the HE assembly for the slow drive down to Trinity by bagging it in waterproof Butvar plastic, boxing it in a braced shipping crate of knotty pine and lashing the resulting package securely to the bed of a five-ton Army truck. A tarpaulin then muffled its secrets in inconclusive drape.

The plutonium core left the Hill first, at three that Thursday afternoon, shock-mounted in a field carrying case studded with rubber bumpers with a strong wire bail. It rode with Philip Morrison in the backseat of an Army sedan like a distinguished visitor, a carload of armed guards clearing the way ahead and another of pit-assembly specialists bringing up the rear. Morrison also delivered a real and a simulated initiator. At about six o'clock a sunburned young sergeant in a white T-shirt and summer uniform pants carried the plutonium core in its field case into the room at McDonald Ranch where it would spend the night. Guards surrounded the ranchhouse to keep vigil.

For security and to encounter less road traffic the HE assembly would make the trip by night; Kistiakowsky deliberately scheduled that more conspicuous convoy to leave at one minute after midnight on Friday, July 13, to put reverse English on the day's unlucky reputation. He rode in the lead car with the security guards. He soon dozed off and was then startled awake by the scream of the car's siren as the convoy ran through Santa Fe; the Army wanted no late-night drunken drivers rolling out of sidestreets to collide with its truckload of handmade high explosives. Beyond Santa Fe the convoy slowed again to below thirty miles an hour; the haul to Trinity took eight hours and Kistiakowsky got some sleep.

On Friday morning at nine the pit-assembly team gathered in white lab coats at McDonald Ranch to begin the final phase of its work. Brigadier General Thomas Farrell was on hand as Groves' deputy, Robert Bacher as the team's senior adviser. Bainbridge looked in; so did Oppenheimer. The ranchhouse room where the core had spent the night had been thoroughly vacuumed in preparation and its windows sealed against dust with black electrical tape to convert it to a makeshift clean room. On a table there the assemblers spread crisp brown wrapping paper and laid out the pieces of their puzzle: two gold-faced, nickel-plated hemispheres of plutonium, a shiny beryllium initiator hot with polonium alphas and, to confine these crucial elements, the several pieces of plum-colored natural uranium that formed the cylindrical 80-pound plug of tamper. Before assembly began Bacher asked for a receipt from the Army for the material it would soon explode. Los Alamos was officially an extension of the University of California working for the Army under contract and Bacher wanted to document the university's release from responsibility for some millions of dollars' worth of plutonium that would soon be vaporized. Bainbridge thought the ceremony a waste of time but Farrell saw its point and agreed. To relieve the tension Farrell insisted on hefting the hemispheres first to confirm that he was getting good weight. Like polonium but much less intensely, plutonium is an alpha emitter; "when you hold a lump of it in your hand," says Leona Marshall, "it feels warm, like a live rabbit." That gave Farrell pause; he set the hemispheres down and signed the receipt.

The parts were few but the men worked carefully. They nested the initiator between the two plutonium hemispheres; they nested the nickel ball in turn in its hollowed plug of tamper. That required the morning and half the afternoon. Two men lugged the heavy boxed assembly on a barrow out to the car. It arrived in its lethal dignity at Zero at 3:18 P.M.

There Norris Bradbury's crew had been busy with the five-foot sphere of high explosives Kistiakowsky had delivered that morning. At 1 P.M. the truck driver had backed his load under the tower. The men had used a jib winch to lift off the wooden packing crate, had swung it aside and lowered around the sphere a massive set of steel tongs suspended from the main winch anchored one hundred feet up at the top of the tower. With the tongs securing the sphere its two tons were winched up off the truck bed; the driver pulled the truck away and the winch lowered the preassembled unit to a skid set on the asphalt-paved ground. "We were scared to death that we would drop it," Bradbury recalls, "because we didn't trust the hoist and it was the only bomb immediately available. It wasn't that we were afraid of setting it off, but we might damage it in some way." Before they opened the upper polar cap to expose the trapdoor plug they erected a white tent over the assembly area; thereafter a diffused glow of sunlight illuminated their work.

Inserting the plug courted disaster, team member Boyce McDaniel remembers:

> The [high-explosive] shell was incomplete, one of the lenses was missing. It was through this opening that the cylindrical plug containing the plutonium and initiator was to be inserted. . . . In order to maximize the density of the uranium in the total assembly, the clearance between the plug and the spherical shell had been reduced to a few thousandths of an inch. Back at Los Alamos, three sets of these plugs and [tamper spheres] had been made. However, in the haste of last minute production, the various units had not been made interchangeable, so not all of the plugs would fit into all [holes]. Great care had been exercised to make sure, however, that mating pieces had been shipped to [Trinity].
>
> Imagine our consternation when, as we started to assemble the plug in the hole, deep down in the center of the high explosive shell, it would not enter! Dismayed, we halted our efforts in order not to damage the pieces, and stopped to think about it. Could we have made a mistake. . . ?

Bacher saw the cause and calmed them: the plug had warmed and expanded in the hot ranchhouse but the tamper, set deep within the insulation of its shell of high explosives, was still cool from Los Alamos. The men left the two pieces of heavy metal in contact and took a break. When they checked the assembly again the temperatures had equalized. The plug slid smoothly into place.

Then it was the turn of the explosives crew. Oppenheimer watched over them, conspicuous in his pork-pie hat, wasted to 116 pounds by a recent bout of chicken pox and the stress of months of late nights and seven-day weeks. In the motion picture that documents this historic assembly he darts in and out of the frame like a foraging water bird, pecking at the open well of the bomb. Someone hands Bradbury a strip of Scotch tape and his arms disappear into the well to secure a block of explosive. He finished the work in late evening under lights. The detonators were not yet installed. That would be the next day's challenge after the unit had been hauled to the top of the tower.

The following morning, Saturday, around eight, Bradbury supervised raising the test device to its high platform. The openings into the casing where the detonators would be inserted had been covered and taped to keep out dust; as the bulky sphere rose into the air it revealed itself generously bandaged as if against multiple wounds. It stopped at fifteen feet long enough to allow a crew of GI's to stack depths of striped ticking-covered Army mattresses up nearly to its skid, a prayer in cotton batting against a damaging fall. Then it started up again, twisting slowly, seeming on its thin, braided steel cable to levitate, rising the full height of the tower and diminishing slightly with distance as it rose. Two sergeants received it into the tower shack through the open floor, replaced the floor panel and lowered the unit onto its skid, positioning it with its north and south polar caps at left and right rather than above and below as they had been positioned during assembly, the same posture in which its militant armored twin, Fat Man, would ride to war in the bomb bay of a B-29. The delicate work of inserting the detonators then began.

Disaster loomed again that day. The Creutz group at Los Alamos had fired the Chinese copy, measured the simultaneity of its implosion by the magnetic method and called Oppenheimer to report the dismaying news that the Trinity bomb was likely to fail. "So of course," says Kistiakowsky, "I immediately became the chief villain and everybody lectured me." Groves flew in to Albuquerque in his official plane with Bush and Conant at noon; they were appalled at the news and added their complaints to Kistiakowsky's full burden:

> Everybody at headquarters became terribly upset and focused on my presumed guilt. Oppenheimer, General Groves, Vannevar Bush—all had much to say about that incompetent wretch who forever after would be known to the world as the cause of the tragic failure of the Manhattan Project. Jim

> Conant, a close personal friend, had me on the carpet it seemed for hours, coldly quizzing me about the causes of the impending failure.
>
> Sometime later that day Bacher and I were walking in the desert and as I timidly questioned the results of the magnetic test Bob accused me of challenging no less than Maxwell's equations themselves! At another point Oppenheimer became so emotional that I offered him a month's salary against ten dollars that our implosion charge would work.

In the midst of this contretemps all of Little Boy but its U235 target pieces slipped away. With two Army officers in escort, a closed black truck and seven carloads of security guards left Los Alamos Saturday morning for Kirtland Air Force Base in Albuquerque. A manifest describes the truck's expensive cargo:

> a. 1 box, wt. about 300 lbs, containing projectile assembly of active material for the gun type bomb.
> b. 1 box, wt. about 300 lbs, containing special tools and scientific instruments.
> c. 1 box, wt. about 10,000 lbs, containing the inert parts for a complete gun type bomb.

Two DC-3's waiting at Kirtland flew the crates and their officer escorts to Hamilton Field, near San Francisco, from which another security convoy escorted them to Hunter's Point Naval Shipyard to await the sailing of the U.S.S. *Indianapolis,* the heavy cruiser that would deliver them to Tinian.

At Trinity gloom was everywhere. A physical chemist from Los Alamos, Joseph O. Hirschfelder, remembers Oppenheimer's discomfiture that Saturday evening at the hotel where the guests invited to view the test had begun to assemble: "We drove to the Hilton Hotel in Albuquerque, where Robert Oppenheimer was meeting with a large group of generals, Nobel laureates, and other VIP's. Robert was very nervous. He told [us] about some experimental results which Ed Creutz had obtained earlier in the day which indicated that the [Trinity] atom bomb would be a dud."

Oppenheimer searched for calm in the midst of this latest evidence of the physical world's relentlessness and found a breath of it in the *Bhagavad-Gita,* the seven-hundred-stanza devotional poem interpolated into the great Aryan epic *Mahabharata* at about the same time that Greece was declining from its golden age. He had discovered the *Gita* at Harvard; at Berkeley he had learned Sanskrit from the scholar Arthur Ryder to set himself closer to the original text and thereafter a worn pink copy occupied an honored place on the bookshelf closest to his desk. There are meanings enough for a lifetime in the *Gita,* dramatized as a dialogue between a warrior prince named Arjuna and Krishna, the principal avatar of Vishnu (and

Vishnu the third member of the Hindu godhead with Brahma and Shiva—a Trinity again). Vannevar Bush records the particular meaning Oppenheimer clutched that desperate Saturday in July:

> His was a profoundly complex character. . . . So my comment will be brief. I simply record a poem, which he translated from the Sanscrit, and which he recited to me two nights before [Trinity]:
>
> *In battle, in forest, at the precipice in the mountains,*
> *On the dark great sea, in the midst of javelins and arrows,*
> *In sleep, in confusion, in the depths of shame,*
> *The good deeds a man has done before defend him.*

Back at Base Camp Oppenheimer slept no more than four hours that night; Farrell heard him stirring restlessly on his bunk in the next room of the quarters they shared, racked with coughing. Chain-smoking as much as meditative poetry drove him through his days.

Sturdy Hans Bethe found a way back from the precipice, Kistiakowsky remembers:

> Sunday morning another phone call came with wonderful news. Hans Bethe spent the whole night of Saturday analyzing the electromagnetic theory of this experiment and discovered that the instrumental design was such that even a perfect implosion could not have produced oscilloscope records different from what was observed. So I became again acceptable to local high society.

When Groves called, Oppenheimer chatted happily about the Bethe results. The general interrupted: "What about the weather?" "The weather is whimsical," the whimsical physicist said. The Gulf air mass had stagnated over the test site. But change was coming. Jack Hubbard, the meteorologist, predicted light and variable winds the next day.

Stagnation exacerbated the July heat. Camera crews replacing battery packs damaged by a blown circuit burned their hands on metal camera housings. Frank Oppenheimer, thin enough not to suffer the heat unduly, hurried to construct a last-minute experiment less aloof than readings of light and radiation: he set out boxes filled with excelsior and posts nailed with corrugated iron strips to simulate the fragile Japanese houses where LeMay's ubiquitous drill presses lurked. Groves had forbidden the construction of full-scale housing for the test, more scientific tomfoolery, a waste of money and time. Norris Bradbury's instructions for bomb assembly as of Saturday listed *"Gadget complete"*; for "Sunday, 15 July, all day," he advised his crews to "look for rabbits' feet and four-leaved clovers.

Should we have the Chaplain down there?" Rabbits' feet would turn up, but even chaplains would have had trouble finding a stem of clover on the Jornada.

Oppenheimer, Groves, Bainbridge, Farrell, Tolman and an Army meteorologist met with Hubbard at McDonald Ranch at four that afternoon to consider the weather. Hubbard reminded them that he had never liked the July 16 date. He thought the shot could go as scheduled, he noted in his journal, "in less than optimum conditions, which would require sacrifices." Groves and Oppenheimer repaired to another room to confer. They decided to wait and see. They had scheduled a last weather conference for the next morning at 0200 hours; they would make up their minds then. The shot was set for 0400 and they let that time stand.

Sometime early that evening Oppenheimer climbed the tower to perform a final ritual inspection. There before him crouched his handiwork. Its bandages had been removed and it was hung now with insulated wires that looped from junction boxes to the detonator plugs that studded its dark bulk, an exterior ugly as Caliban's. His duty was almost done.

At dusk the tired laboratory director was calm. He stood with Cyril Smith beside the reservoir at McDonald Ranch where cattle had watered and spoke of families and home, even of philosophy, and Smith found himself soothed. A storm was blowing up. Oppenheimer looked beneath it to anchorage, to the darkening Oscuras. "Funny how the mountains always inspire our work," the metallurgist heard him say.

With the weather changing from stagnant to violent and with everyone short of sleep, moods swung at Base Camp. The occasion of Fermi's satire that evening made Bainbridge furious. It merely irritated Groves:

> I had become a bit annoyed with Fermi . . . when he suddenly offered to take wagers from his fellow scientists on whether or not the bomb would ignite the atmosphere, and if so, whether it would merely destroy New Mexico or destroy the world. He had also said that after all it wouldn't make any difference whether the bomb went off or not because it would still have been a well worth-while scientific experiment. For if it did fail to go off, we would have proved that an atomic explosion was not possible.

On the realistic grounds, the Italian laureate explained with his usual candor, that the best physicists in the world would have tried and failed.

Bainbridge was furious because Fermi's "thoughtless bravado" might scare the soldiers, who did not have the benefit of a knowledge of thermonuclear ignition temperatures and fireball cooling effects. But a new force was about to be loosed on the world; no one could be absolutely certain—

Fermi's point—of the outcome of its debut. Oppenheimer had assigned Edward Teller the deliciously Tellerian task of trying to think of any imaginable trick or turn by which the explosion might escape its apparent bounds. Teller at Los Alamos that evening raised the same question Fermi had, but questioned Robert Serber, no mere uninformed GI:

> Trying to find my way home in the darkness, I bumped into an acquaintance, Bob Serber. That day we had received a memo from our director . . . saying that we would have to be [at Trinity] well before dawn, and that we should be careful not to step on a rattlesnake. I asked Serber, "What will you do tomorrow about the rattlesnakes?" He said, "I'll take a bottle of whiskey." I then went into my usual speech, telling him how one could imagine that things might get out of control in this, that, or a third manner. But we had discussed these things repeatedly, and we could not see how, in actual fact, we could get into trouble. Then I asked him, "And what do you think about it?" There in the dark Bob thought for a moment, then said, "I'll take a second bottle of whiskey."

Rabi, the real mystic among them, spent the evening playing poker.

Bainbridge managed a little sleep. He headed the Arming Party charged with arming the bomb. He was due at Zero by 11 P.M. to prepare the shot. An MP sergeant woke him at ten; he picked up Kistiakowsky and Joseph McKibben, the tall, lanky Missouri-born physicist responsible for running the countdown, and assembled with Hubbard and his crew and two security men. "On the way in," Bainbridge remembers, "I stopped at S 10,000 and locked the main sequence timing switches. Pocketing the key I returned to the car and continued to Point Zero." A young Harvard physicist, Donald Hornig, was busy in the tower. He had designed the 500-pound X-unit of high-voltage capacitors that fired Fat Man's multiple detonators with microsecond simultaneity, a crucial Luis Alvarez invention, and now was disconnecting the unit Bainbridge's crews had used for practice runs and connecting the new unit reserved for the shot. In static test this Fat Man would be fired through cables from the S-10000 control bunker; the one to be shipped to Tinian, self-contained, would carry onboard batteries. Cables or batteries would charge the X-unit and on command it would discharge its capacitors to the detonators, vaporizing wires imbedded in the explosive blocks to start shock waves to set off the HE. "Soon after our arrival," says Bainbridge, "Hornig completed his work and returned to S 10,000. Hornig was the last man to leave the top of the tower."

Hubbard operated a portable weather station at the tower; to measure wind speed and direction the two sergeants who worked with him inflated and released helium balloons. At eleven o'clock he found the wind blowing across Zero toward N-10000. At midnight the Gulf air mass had thickened to 17,000 feet and arranged two inversions—cooler air above warmer—within its layered depths that might loop the radioactive Trinity column back down to the ground directly below.

To an observer traveling toward the desert from Los Alamos "the night was dark with black clouds, and not a star could be seen."

Thunderstorms began lashing the Jornada at about 0200 hours on July 16, drenching Base Camp and S-10000. "It was raining cats and dogs, lightning and thunder," Rabi remembers. "[We were] really scared [that] this object there in the tower might be set off accidentally. So you can imagine the strain on Oppenheimer." Winds gusted to thirty miles an hour. Hubbard hung on at Zero for last-minute readings—only misting drizzle had yet reached the tower area—and arrived eight minutes late for the 0200 weather conference at Base Camp, to find Oppenheimer waiting for him outside the weather center there. Hubbard told him they would have to scrub 0400 but should be able to shoot between 0500 and 0600. Oppenheimer looked relieved.

Inside they found an agitated Groves waiting with his advisers. "What the hell is wrong with the weather?" the general greeted his forecaster. Hubbard took the opportunity to repeat that he had never liked July 16. Groves demanded to know when the storm would pass. Hubbard explained its dynamics: a tropical air mass, night rain. Afternoon thunderstorms took their energy from the heating of the earth and collapsed at sunset; this one, contrariwise, would collapse at dawn. Groves growled that he wanted a specific time, not an explanation. I'm giving you both, Hubbard rejoined. He thought Groves was ready to cancel the shot, which seems unlikely given the pressure from Potsdam. He told Groves he could postpone if he wanted but the weather would relent at dawn.

Oppenheimer applied himself to soothe his bulky comrade. Hubbard was the best man around, he insisted, and they ought to trust his forecast. The others at the meeting—Tolman and two Army meteorologists, one more than before—agreed. Groves relented. "You'd better be right on this," he threatened Hubbard, "or I will hang you." He ordered the meteorologist to sign his forecast and set the shot for 0530. Then he went off to roust the governor of New Mexico out of bed to the telephone to warn him he might have to declare martial law.

Bainbridge at Zero was less concerned with local effects than with distant, even though he had personally locked open the circuits that communicated with the shelters. "Sporadic rain was a disturbing factor," he recalls. ". . . We had none of the lightning reported by those at the Base Camp about 16,000 yards away or at S 10,000, but it made interesting conversation as many of the wires from N, S, W 10,000 ended at the tower." About 0330 a gust of wind at Base Camp collapsed Vannevar Bush's tent; he found his way to the mess hall, where from 0345 the cooks began serving a breakfast of powdered eggs, coffee and French toast.

The gods sent Emilio Segrè happier amusement. He had distracted himself through the evening with André Gide's *The Counterfeiters* and slept through the worst of the Base Camp storm. "But my attention was attracted by an unbelievable noise whose nature escaped me completely. As the noise persisted, Sam Allison and I went out with a flashlight and, much to our surprise, found hundreds of frogs in the act of making love in a big hole that had filled with water."

Hubbard departed Base Camp at 0315 for S-10000. The rain had moved on. He telephoned Zero; one of his men there said the clouds were opening and a few stars shone. By 0400 the wind was shifting toward the southwest, away from the shelters. The meteorologist prepared his final forecast at S-10000. He called Bainbridge at 0440. "Hubbard gave me a complete weather report," the Trinity director recalls, "and a prediction that at 5:30 a.m. the weather at Point Zero would be possible but not ideal. We would have preferred no inversion layer at 17,000 feet but not at the expense of waiting over half a day. I called Oppenheimer and General Farrell to get their agreement that 5:30 a.m. would be T = 0." Hubbard, Bainbridge, Oppenheimer and Farrell each had veto over the shot. They all agreed. Trinity would fire at 0530 hours July 16, 1945—just before dawn.

Bainbridge had arranged to report each step of the final arming process to S-10000 in case anything went wrong. "I drove McKibben to W 900 so that he could throw the timing and sequence switches there while I checked off his list." Back at Zero Bainbridge called in the next step "and threw the special arming switch which was not on McKibben's lines. Until this switch was closed the bomb could not be detonated from S 10,000. The final task was to switch on a string of lights on the ground which were to serve as an 'aiming point' for a B-29 practice bombing run. The Air Force wanted to know what the blast effects would be like on a plane 30,000 feet up and some miles away. . . . After turning on the lights, I returned to my car and drove to S 10,000." Kistiakowsky, McKibben and the security guards rode with him. They were the last to leave the site. Behind them searchlight beams converged on the tower.

The Arming Party arrived at S-10000, the earth-sheltered concrete control bunker, at about 0508. Hubbard gave Bainbridge his signed forecast. "I unlocked the master switches," Bainbridge concludes, "and McKibben started the timing sequence at −20 minutes, 5:09:45 a.m." Oppenheimer would watch the shot from S-10000, as would Farrell, Donald

Hornig and Samuel Allison. With the beginning of the final countdown Groves left by jeep for Base Camp. For protection against common disaster he wanted to be physically separated from Farrell and Oppenheimer.

Busloads of visitors from Los Alamos and beyond had begun arriving at Compañia Hill, the viewing site twenty miles northwest of Zero, at 0200. Ernest Lawrence was there, Hans Bethe, Teller, Serber, Edwin McMillan, James Chadwick come to see what his neutron was capable of and a crowd of other men, including Trinity staff no longer needed down on the plain. "With the darkness and the waiting in the chill of the desert the tension became almost unendurable," one of them remembers. The shortwave radio requisitioned to advise them of the schedule refused to work until after Allison began broadcasting the countdown. Richard Feynman, a future Nobel laureate who had entered physics as an adolescent via radio tinkering, tinkered the radio to life. Men began moving into position. "We were told to lie down on the sand," Teller protests, "turn our faces away from the blast, and bury our heads in our arms. No one complied. We were determined to look the beast in the eye." The radio went dead again and they were left to watch for the warning rockets to be fired from S-10000. "I wouldn't turn away . . . but having made all those calculations, I thought the blast might be rather bigger than expected. So I put on some suntan lotion." Teller passed the lotion around and the strange prophylaxis disturbed one observer: "It was an eerie sight to see a number of our highest-ranking scientists seriously rubbing sunburn lotion on their faces and hands in the pitch-blackness of the night, twenty miles from the expected flash."

The countdown continued at S-10000. At 0525 a green Very rocket went up. That signaled a short wail of the siren at Base Camp. Shallow trenches had been bulldozed below the south rim of the Base Camp reservoir for protection and since these men watched ten miles closer to Zero than the crowd on Compañia Hill they planned to use them. Rabi lay down next to Kenneth Greisen, a Cornell physicist, facing south away from Zero. Greisen remembers that he was "personally nervous, for my group had prepared and installed the detonators, and if the shot turned out to be a dud, it might possibly be our fault." Groves found refuge between Bush and Conant, thinking "only of what I would do if, when the countdown got to zero, nothing happened." Victor Weisskopf remembers that "groups of observers had arranged small wooden sticks at a distance of 10 yds from our observation place in order to estimate the size of the explosion." The sticks were posted on the rim of the reservoir. "They were arranged so that their [height] corresponded to 1000 ft. at zero point." Philip Morrison relayed the countdown to the Base Camp observers by loudspeaker.

The two-minute-warning rocket fizzled. A long wail of the Base Camp siren signaled the time. The one-minute warning rocket fired at 0529. Morrison also meant to look the beast in the eye and lay down on the slope of the reservoir facing Zero. He wore sunglasses and held a stopwatch in one hand and a piece of welder's glass in the other. The welder's glass was stockroom issue: Lincoln Super-visibility Lens, Shade #10.

At S-10000 someone heard Oppenheimer say, "Lord, these affairs are hard on the heart." McKibben had been marking off the minutes and Allison broadcasting them. At 45 seconds McKibben turned on a more precise automatic timer. "The control post was rather crowded," Kistiakowsky notes, "and, having now nothing to do, I left as soon as the automatic timer was thrown in . . . and went to stand on the earth mound covering the concrete dugout. (My own guess was that the yield would be about 1 kt [i.e., 1,000 tons, 1 kiloton], and so five miles seemed very safe.)"

Teller prepared himself further at Compañia Hill: "I put on a pair of dark glasses. I pulled on a pair of heavy gloves. With both hands I pressed the welder's glass to my face, making sure no stray light could penetrate around it. I then looked straight at the aim point."

Donald Hornig at S-10000 monitored a switch that could cut the connection between his X-unit in the tower and the bomb, the last point of interruption if anything went wrong. At thirty seconds before T = 0 four red lights flashed on the console in front of him and a voltmeter needle flipped from left to right under its round glass cover to register the full charging of the X-unit. Farrell noticed that "Dr. Oppenheimer, on whom had rested a very heavy burden, grew tenser as the last seconds ticked off. He scarcely breathed. He held on to a post to steady himself. For the last few seconds, he stared directly ahead."

At ten seconds a gong sounded in the control bunker. The men lying in their shallow trenches at Base Camp might have been laid out for death. Conant told Groves he never imagined seconds could be so long. Morrison studied his stopwatch. "I watched the second-hand until T = −5 seconds," he wrote the day of the shot, "when I lowered my head onto the sand bank in such a way that a slight rise in the ground completely shielded me from Zero. I placed the welding glass over the right lens of my sun glasses, the left lens of which was covered by an opaque cardboard shield. I counted seconds and at zero began to raise my head just over the protecting rise." Ernest Lawrence on Compañia Hill had planned to watch the shot through the windshield of a car, allowing the glass to filter out damaging ultraviolet, "but at the last minute decided to get out . . . (evidence indeed I was excited!)." Robert Serber, his bottles of whiskey to succor him, stared twenty miles toward distant Zero with unprotected eyes. The last decisive inaction was Hornig's:

> Now the sequence of events was all controlled by the automatic timer except that I had the knife switch which could stop the test at any moment up until the actual firing . . . I don't think I have ever been keyed up as I was during those final seconds . . . I kept telling myself "the least flicker of that needle and you have to act." It kept on coming down to zero. I kept saying, "Your reaction time is about half a second and you can't relax for even a fraction of a second." . . . My eyes were glued on the dial and my hand was on the switch. I could hear the timer counting . . . three . . . two . . . one. The needle fell to zero. . . .

Time: 0529:45. The firing circuit closed; the X-unit discharged; the detonators at thirty-two detonation points simultaneously fired; they ignited the outer lens shells of Composition B; the detonation waves separately bulged, encountered inclusions of Baratol, slowed, curved, turned inside out, merged to a common inward-driving sphere; the spherical detonation wave crossed into the second shell of solid fast Composition B and accelerated; hit the wall of dense uranium tamper and became a shock wave and squeezed, liquefying, moving through; hit the nickel plating of the plutonium core and squeezed, the small sphere shrinking, collapsing into itself, becoming an eyeball; the shock wave reaching the tiny initiator at the center and swirling through its designed irregularities to mix its beryllium and polonium; polonium alphas kicking neutrons free from scant atoms of beryllium: one, two, seven, nine, hardly more neutrons drilling into the surrounding plutonium to start the chain reaction. Then fission multiplying its prodigious energy release through eighty generations in millionths of a second, tens of millions of degrees, millions of pounds of pressure. Before the radiation leaked away, conditions within the eyeball briefly resembled the state of the universe moments after its first primordial explosion.

Then expansion, radiation leaking away. The radiant energy loosed by the chain reaction is hot enough to take the form of soft X rays; these leave the physical bomb and its physical casing first, at the speed of light, far in front of any mere explosion. Cool air is opaque to X rays and absorbs them, heating; "the very hot air," Hans Bethe writes, "is therefore surrounded by a cooler envelope, and only this envelope"—hot enough at that—"is visible to observers at a distance." The central sphere of air, heated by the X rays it absorbs, reemits lower-energy X rays which are absorbed in turn at its boundaries and reemitted beyond. By this process of downhill leapfrogging, which is known as radiation transport, the hot sphere begins to cool itself. When it has cooled to half a million degrees—

in about one ten-thousandth of a second—a shock wave forms that moves out faster than radiation transport can keep up. "The shock therefore separates from the very hot, nearly isothermal [i.e., uniformly heated] sphere at the center," Bethe explains. Simple hydrodynamics describes the shock front: like a wave in water, like a sonic boom in air. It moves on, leaving behind the isothermal sphere confined within its shell of opacity, isolated from the outside world, growing only slowly by radiation transport on this millisecond scale of events.

What the world sees is the shock front and it *cools* into visibility, the first flash, milliseconds long, of a nuclear weapon's double flash of light, the flashes too closely spaced to distinguish with the eye. Further cooling renders the front transparent; the world if it still has eyes to see looks *through* the shock wave into the hotter interior of the fireball and "because higher temperatures are now revealed," Bethe continues, "the total radiation increases toward a second maximum": the second, longer flash. The isothermal sphere at the center of the expanding fireball continues opaque and invisible, but it also continues to give up its energy to the air beyond its boundaries by radiation transport. That is, as the shock wave cools, the air behind it heats. A cooling wave moves in reverse of the shock wave, eating into the isothermal sphere. Instead of one simple thing the fireball is thus several things at once: an isothermal sphere invisible to the world; a cooling wave moving inward toward that sphere, eating away its radiation; a shock front propagating into undisturbed air, air that has not yet heard the news. Between each of these parts lay further intervening regions of buffering air.

Eventually the cooling wave eats the isothermal sphere completely away and the entire fireball becomes transparent to its own radiation. Now it cools more slowly. Below about 9000°F it can cool no more. Then, concludes Bethe, "any further cooling can only be achieved by the rise of the fireball due to its buoyancy, and the turbulent mixing associated with this rise. This is a slow process, taking tens of seconds."

The high-speed cameras at W-10000 recorded the later stages of the fireball's development, Bainbridge reports, tracking its huge swelling from the eyeball it had been:

> The expansion of the ball of fire before striking the ground was almost symmetric . . . except for the extra brightness and retardation of a part of the sphere near the bottom, a number of blisters, and several spikes that shot radially ahead of the ball below the equator. Contact with the ground was made at 0.65 ms [i.e., thousandths of a second]. Thereafter the ball became rapidly smoother. . . . Shortly after the spikes struck the ground (about 2 ms) there appeared on the ground ahead of the shock wave a wide skirt of lumpy mat-

> ter. . . . At about 32 ms [when the fireball had expanded to 945 feet in diameter] there appeared immediately behind the shock wave a dark front of absorbing matter, which traveled slowly out until it became invisible at 0.85 s [the fireball now 2,500 feet across]. The shock wave itself became invisible [earlier] at about 0.10 s. . . .
>
> The ball of fire grew even more slowly to a [diameter] of about [2,000 feet], until the dust cloud growing out of the skirt almost enveloped it. The top of the ball started to rise again at 2 s. At 3.5 s a minimum horizontal diameter, or neck, appeared one-third of the way up the skirt, and the portion of the skirt above the neck formed a vortex ring. The neck narrowed, and the ring and fast-growing pile of matter above it rose as a new cloud of smoke, carrying a convection stem of dust behind it. . . . The stem appeared twisted like a left-handed screw.

But men saw what theoretical physics cannot notice and what cameras cannot record, saw pity and terror. Rabi at Base Camp felt menaced:

> We were lying there, very tense, in the early dawn, and there were just a few streaks of gold in the east; you could see your neighbor very dimly. Those ten seconds were the longest ten seconds that I ever experienced. Suddenly, there was an enormous flash of light, the brightest light I have ever seen or that I think anyone has ever seen. It blasted; it pounced; it bored its way right through you. It was a vision which was seen with more than the eye. It was seen to last forever. You would wish it would stop; altogether it lasted about two seconds. Finally it was over, diminishing, and we looked toward the place where the bomb had been; there was an enormous ball of fire which grew and grew and it rolled as it grew; it went up into the air, in yellow flashes and into scarlet and green. It looked menacing. It seemed to come toward one.
>
> A new thing had just been born; a new control; a new understanding of man, which man had acquired over nature.

To Teller at Compañia Hill the burst "was like opening the heavy curtains of a darkened room to a flood of sunlight." Had astronomers been watching they could have seen it reflected from the moon, literal moonshine.

Joseph McKibben made a comparison at S-10000: "We had a lot of flood lights on for taking movies of the control panel. When the bomb went off, the lights were drowned out by the big light coming in through the open door in the back."

It caught Ernest Lawrence at Compañia Hill in the act of stepping from his car: "Just as I put my foot on the ground I was enveloped with a warm brilliant yellow white light—from darkness to brilliant sunshine in an instant and as I remember I momentarily was stunned by the surprise."

To Hans Bethe at Compañia Hill "it looked like a giant magnesium flare which kept on for what seemed a whole minute but was actually one or two seconds."

Serber at Compañia Hill risked blindness but glimpsed an earlier stage of the fireball:

> At the instant of the explosion I was looking directly at it, with no eye protection of any kind. I saw first a yellow glow, which grew almost instantly to an overwhelming white flash, so intense that I was completely blinded. . . . By twenty or thirty seconds after the explosion I was regaining normal vision. . . . The grandeur and magnitude of the phenomenon were completely breathtaking.

Segrè at Base Camp imagined apocalypse:

> The most striking impression was that of an overwhelmingly bright light. . . . I was flabbergasted by the new spectacle. We saw the whole sky flash with unbelievable brightness in spite of the very dark glasses we wore. . . . I believe that for a moment I thought the explosion might set fire to the atmosphere and thus finish the earth, even though I knew that this was not possible.

Not light but heat disturbed Morrison at Base Camp:

> From ten miles away, we saw the unbelievably brilliant flash. That was not the most impressive thing. We knew it was going to be blinding. We wore welder's glasses. The thing that got me was not the flash but the blinding heat of a bright day on your face in the cold desert morning. It was like opening a hot oven with the sun coming out like a sunrise.

It unfolded in silence, a ballistics expert watching from Compañia Hill realized with awe:

> The flash of light was so bright at first as to seem to have no definite shape, but after perhaps half a second it looked bright yellow and hemispherical with the flat side down, like a half-risen sun but about twice as large. Almost immediately a turgid rising of this luminous mass began, great swirls of flame seeming to ascend within a rather rectangular outline which expanded rapidly in height. . . . Suddenly out of the center of it there seemed to rise a narrower column to a considerably greater height. Then as a climax, which was exceedingly impressive in spite of the fact that the blinding brightness had subsided, the top of the slenderer column seemed to mushroom out into a thick parasol of a rather bright but spectral blue. . . . All this seemed very fast . . .

> and was followed by a feeling of letdown that it was all over so soon. Then came the awe-inspiring realization that it was twenty miles away, that what had flared up and died so brilliantly and quickly was really a couple of miles high. The feeling of the remoteness of this thing which had seemed so near was emphasized by the long silence while we watched the grey smoke grow into a taller and taller twisting column, a silence broken after a minute or so that seemed much longer by a quite impressive bang, about like the crack of a five-inch anti-aircraft gun at a hundred yards.

"Most experiences in life can be comprehended by prior experiences," Norris Bradbury comments, "but the atom bomb did not fit into any preconceptions possessed by anybody."

As the fireball rose into the air, Joseph W. Kennedy reports, "the overcast of strato-cumulus clouds directly overhead [became] pink on the underside and well illuminated, as at a sunrise." Weisskopf noticed that "the path of the shock wave through the clouds was plainly visible as an expanding circle all over the sky where it was covered by clouds." "When the red glow faded out," writes Edwin McMillan, "a most remarkable effect made its appearance. The whole surface of the ball was covered with a purple luminescence, like that produced by the electrical excitation of the air, and caused undoubtedly by the radioactivity of the material in the ball."

Fermi had prepared an order-of-magnitude experiment to determine roughly the bomb's yield:

> About 40 seconds after the explosion the air blast reached me. I tried to estimate its strength by dropping from about six feet small pieces of paper before, during and after the passage of the blast wave. Since, at the time, there was no wind, I could observe very distinctly and actually measure the displacement of the pieces of paper that were in the process of falling while the blast was passing. The shift was about 2½ meters, which, at the time, I estimated to correspond to the blast that would be produced by ten thousand tons of T.N.T.

"From the distance of the source and from the displacement of the air due to the shock wave," Segrè explains, "he could calculate the energy of the explosion. This Fermi had done in advance having prepared himself a table of numbers, so that he could tell immediately the energy liberated from this crude but simple measurement." "He was so profoundly and totally absorbed in his bits of paper," adds Laura Fermi, "that he was not aware of the tremendous noise."

Frank Oppenheimer found his brother watching beside him outside the control bunker at S-10000:

And so there was this sense of this ominous cloud hanging over us. It was so brilliant purple, with all the radioactive glowing. And it just seemed to hang there forever. Of course it didn't. It must have been just a very short time until it went up. It was very terrifying.

And the thunder from the blast. It bounced on the rocks, and then it went—I don't know where else it bounced. But it never seemed to stop. Not like an ordinary echo with thunder. It just kept echoing back and forth in that Jornada del Muerto. It was a very scary time when it went off.

And I wish I would remember what my brother said, but I can't—but I think we just said, "It worked." I think that's what we said, both of us. "It worked."

Trinity director Bainbridge appropriately pronounced its benediction: "No one who saw it could forget it, a foul and awesome display."

At Base Camp Groves "personally thought of Blondin crossing Niagara Falls on his tightrope, only to me the tightrope had lasted for almost three years, and of my repeated, confident-appearing assurances that such a thing was possible and that we would do it." Sitting up in their trenches before the blast wave arrived, he and Conant and Bush ceremoniously shook hands.

The blast had knocked Kistiakowsky down at S-10000. He scrambled up to watch the fireball rise and darken and mushroom purple auras, then moved to claim his bet. "I slapped Oppenheimer on the back and said, 'Oppie, you owe me ten dollars.' " The distracted Los Alamos director searched his wallet. "It's empty," he told Kistiakowsky, "you'll have to wait." Bainbridge went around congratulating the S-10000 leaders on the success of the implosion method. "I finished by saying to Robert, 'Now we are all sons of bitches.' . . . [He] told my younger daughter later that it was the best thing anyone said after the test."

"Our first feeling was one of elation," Weisskopf remembers, "then we realized we were tired, and then we were worried." Rabi elaborates:

Naturally, we were very jubilant over the outcome of the experiment. While this tremendous ball of flame was there before us, and we watched it, and it rolled along, it became in time diffused with the clouds. . . . Then it was washed out with the wind. We turned to one another and offered congratulations, for the first few minutes. Then, there was a chill, which was not the morning cold; it was a chill that came to one when one thought, as for instance when I thought of my wooden house in Cambridge, and my laboratory in New York, and of the millions of people living around there, and this power of nature which we had first understood it to be—well, there it was.

Oppenheimer looked again into the *Gita* for a model sufficiently scaled:

> We waited until the blast had passed, walked out of the shelter and then it was extremely solemn. We knew the world would not be the same. A few people laughed, a few people cried. Most people were silent. I remembered the line from the Hindu scripture, the *Bhagavad-Gita:* Vishnu is trying to persuade the Prince that he should do his duty and to impress him he takes on his multi-armed form and says, "Now I am become Death, the destroyer of worlds." I suppose we all thought that, one way or another.

Other models also came to mind, Oppenheimer told an audience shortly after the war:

> When it went off, in the New Mexico dawn, that first atomic bomb, we thought of Alfred Nobel, and his hope, his vain hope, that dynamite would put an end to wars. We thought of the legend of Prometheus, of that deep sense of guilt in man's new powers, that reflects his recognition of evil, and his long knowledge of it. We knew that it was a new world, but even more we knew that novelty itself was a very old thing in human life, that all our ways are rooted in it.

The successful director of the Los Alamos bomb laboratory left with Farrell in a jeep. Rabi watched him arrive at Base Camp and saw a change:

> He was in the forward bunker. When he came back, there he was, you know, with his hat. You've seen pictures of Robert's hat. And he came to where we were in the headquarters, so to speak. And his walk was like "High Noon"—I think it's the best I could describe it—this kind of strut. He'd done it.

"When Farrell came up to me," Groves continues the story, "his first words were, 'The war is over.' My reply was, 'Yes, after we drop two bombs on Japan.' I congratulated Oppenheimer quietly with 'I am proud of you,' and he replied with a simple 'Thank you.' " The theoretical physicist who was also a poet, who found physics, as Bethe says, "the best way to do philosophy," had staked his claim on history. It was a larger claim, but more ambivalent, than any Nobel Prize.

The horses in the MP stable still whinnied in fright; the paddles of the dusty Aermotor windmill at Base Camp still spun away the energy of the blast; the frogs had ceased to make love in the puddles. Rabi broke out a bottle of whiskey and passed it around. Everyone took a swig. Oppenheimer went to work with Groves on a report for Stimson at Potsdam. "My faith in the human mind has been somewhat restored," Hubbard overheard him say. He estimated the blast at 21,000 tons—21 kilotons. Fermi knew from his paper experiment that it was at least 10 KT. Rabi had wagered 18. Later that morning Fermi and Herbert Anderson would don white surgical scrub suits and board the two lead-lined tanks to drive near Zero. Fermi's tank broke down after only a mile of approach and he had to walk back. Anderson clanked on. Through the periscope the young physicist studied the crater the bomb had made. The tower—the $20,000 winch, the shack, the wooden platform, the hundred feet of steel girders—was gone, vaporized down to the stubby twisted wreckage of its footings. What had been asphalt paving was now fused sand, green and translucent as jade. The cup strung to Anderson's rocket scooped up debris. His later radiochemical measurements confirmed 18.6 KT. That was nearly four times what Los Alamos had expected. Rabi won the pot.

Fermi experienced a delayed reaction, he told his wife: "For the first time in his life on coming back from Trinity he had felt it was not safe for him to drive. It had seemed to him as if the car were jumping from curve to curve, skipping the straight stretches in between. He had asked a friend to drive, despite his strong aversion to being driven." Stanislaw Ulam, who chose not to attend the shot, watched the buses returning: "You could tell at once they had had a strange experience. You could see it on their faces. I saw that something very grave and strong had happened to their whole outlook on the future."

A bomb exploded in a desert damages not much besides sand and cactus and the purity of the air. Stafford Warren, the physician responsible for radiological safety at Trinity, had to search to discover more lethal effects:

> Partially eviscerated dead wild jack rabbits were found more than 800 yards from zero, presumably killed by the blast. A farm house three miles away had doors torn loose and suffered other extensive damage. . . .
>
> The light intensity was sufficient at nine miles to have caused temporary blindness and this would be longer lasting at shorter distances. . . . The light together with the heat and ultraviolet radiation would probably cause severe damage to the unprotected eye at 5–6 miles; damage sufficient to put personnel out of action several days if not permanently.

The boxes of excelsior Frank Oppenheimer had set out, and the pine boards, also recorded the coming of the light: they were charred beyond 1,000 yards, slightly scorched up to 2,000 yards. At 1,520 yards—nine-tenths of a mile—exposed surfaces had heated almost instantly to 750°F.

William Penney, the British physicist who had studied blast effects for the Target Committee, held a seminar at Los Alamos five days after Trinity. "He applied his calculations," Philip Morrison remembers. "He predicted that this [weapon] would reduce a city of three or four hundred thousand people to nothing but a sink for disaster relief, bandages, and hospitals. He made it absolutely clear in numbers. It was reality."

Around the time of the Trinity shot, in the predawn dark at Hunter's Point in San Francisco Bay, a floodlit crane had loaded onto the deck of the *Indianapolis* the fifteen-foot crate that carried the Little Boy gun assembly. Two sailors carried aboard the Little Boy bullet in a lead bucket shouldered between them on a crowbar. They followed the two Los Alamos Army officers to the cabin of the ship's flag lieutenant, who had vacated it for the voyage. Eyebolts had been welded to its deck. The sailors strapped the lead bucket to the eyebolts. One of the officers padlocked it into place. They would take turns guarding it around the clock for the ten-day voyage to Tinian.

At 0836 Pacific War Time, four hours after the light flung from the Jornada del Muerto blanched the face of the moon, the *Indianapolis* sailed with its cargo under the Golden Gate and out to sea.

19

Tongues of Fire

At the end of March 1945, as Curtis LeMay's bombers shuttled back and forth burning cities, Colonel Elmer E. Kirkpatrick, a plainspoken Army engineer, arrived in the Marianas to locate a small corner where he could lodge Paul Tibbets' 509th Composite Group. Kirkpatrick met with LeMay and then with Pacific Fleet commander Chester Nimitz on Guam on the day he arrived, March 30, and found the commanding officers cooperative. LeMay personally flew Kirkpatrick to Tinian on April 3. The next day, he reported to Groves, he "covered most of the island [and] decided on our sites and the planning forces went to work on layouts." Though there was no shortage of B-29's, he found that cement and buildings were scarce; "housing and life here is a little rugged for everyone except [general] officers & the Navy. Tents or open barracks." Kirkpatrick flew back to Guam on April 5 "to dig up some materials some place" and "to get authority for the work I required," threaded his way through the Air Force and Navy chains of command with his letters of authority from Washington and by the end of the day had seen a telex sent to Saipan "directing them to give me enough material to get the essential things done." A Navy construction battalion—the SeaBees—would build the buildings and hardstands and dig the pits from which the bombs, too large for ground-level clearance, would be lifted up into the bomb bays of Tibbets' B-29's.

By early June, when Tibbets arrived to inspect the accommodations and confer with LeMay, Kirkpatrick could report that "progress has been very satisfactory and I have the feeling now that we can't miss." He sat in on an evening meeting between Tibbets and LeMay and heard evidence that the Twentieth Air Force commander did not yet appreciate the power of an atomic bomb:

> LeMay does not favor high altitude bombing. Work is not as accurate but, more important, visibility at such altitudes is extremely poor especially during the period June to November. Tibbets advised him that the weapon would destroy a plane using it at an altitude of less than 25,000 feet.

Kirkpatrick demonstrated his progress to Groves with an impressive list: five warehouses, an administration building, roads and parking areas and nine magazines completed; pits completed except for lifts; hardstands for parking the 509th aircraft completed except for asphalt paving; generator buildings and compressor shed completed; one air-conditioned building where the bombs would be assembled to be completed by July 1; two more assembly buildings to be completed by August 1 and August 15. Of the 509th's men more than 1,100 had already staged out by ship "and more [are] coming in every week."

The first of Tibbets' combat crews arrived June 10, flying themselves to Tinian in advanced, specially modified new B-29's. The early-model aircraft delivered to the group the previous autumn had become obsolete, Tibbets explained to readers of the *Saturday Evening Post* after the war:

> Tests showed us that the B-29's we had weren't good enough for atom bombing. They were heavy, older types. Top cylinders were overheating and causing valve failures in the long climb to 30,000 feet at 80 per cent of full power. . . .
>
> I asked for new, light-weight B-29's and fuel-injection systems to replace carburetors.

He got those improvements and more: quick-closing pneumatic bomb doors, fuel flow meters, reversible electric propellers.

The new aircraft had been modified to accommodate the special bombs they would carry and the added crew. The cylindrical tunnel that connected the pressurized forward and waist sections of the plane had to be partly cut away and reworked so that the larger bomb, Fat Man, would fit in the forward bomb bay. Guide rails were installed to prevent the tail assemblies from hanging up during fallout. An extra table, chair, oxygen outlet and interphone station for the weaponeers responsible for monitoring a bomb during flight went in forward of the radio operator's station in the forward section. "The performance of these special B-29's was exceptional," writes the engineer in charge of their procurement. "They were without doubt the finest B-29's in the theater." By the end of June, eleven of the new bombers shone on their hardstands in the Pacific sun.

To men used to the blizzards and dust of Wendover, Utah, the 509th's historian claims, Tinian "looked like the Garden of Paradise." The surrounding blue ocean and the palm groves may have occasioned that vision. Philip Morrison, who came out after Trinity to help assemble Fat Man, saw more reverberantly what the island had become, as he told a committee of U.S. Senators later in 1945:

> Tinian is a miracle. Here, 6,000 miles from San Francisco, the United States armed forces have built the largest airport in the world. A great coral ridge was half-leveled to fill a rough plain, and to build six runways, each an excellent 10-lane highway, each almost two miles long. Beside these runways stood in long rows the great silvery airplanes. They were there not by the dozen but by the hundred. From the air this island, smaller than Manhattan, looked like a giant aircraft carrier, its deck loaded with bombers. . . .
>
> And all these gigantic preparations had a grand and terrible outcome. At sunset some day the field would be loud with the roar of motors. Down the great runways would roll the huge planes, seeming to move slowly because of their size, but far outspeeding the occasional racing jeep. One after another each runway would launch its planes. Once every 15 seconds another B-29 would become air-borne. For an hour and a half this would continue with precision and order. The sun would go below the sea, and the last planes could still be seen in the distance, with running lights still on. Often a plane would fail to make the take-off, and go skimming horribly into the sea, or into the beach to burn like a huge torch. We came often to sit on the top of the coral ridge and watch the combat strike of the 313th wing in real awe. Most of the planes would return the next morning, standing in a long single line, like beads on a chain, from just overhead to the horizon. You could see 10 or 12 planes at a time, spaced a couple of miles apart. As fast as the near plane would land, another would appear on the edge of the sky. There were always the same number of planes in sight. The empty field would fill up, and in an hour or two all the planes would have landed.

A resemblance in shape between Tinian and Manhattan had inspired the SeaBees to name the island's roads for New York City streets. The 509th happened to be lodged immediately west of North Field at 125th Street and Eighth Avenue, near Riverside Drive, in Manhattan, the environs of Columbia University where Enrico Fermi and Leo Szilard had identified secondary neutrons from fission: the wheel had come full circle.

"The first half of July," Norman Ramsey writes of 509th activity, "was occupied with establishing and installing all of the technical facilities needed for assembly and test work at Tinian." In the meantime the group's flight crews practiced navigating to Iwo Jima and back and bombing with standard general-purpose bombs and then with Pumpkins such bypassed islands still nominally in Japanese hands as Rota and Truk.

Harry Truman and Jimmy Byrnes left suburban Potsdam in an open car to tour ravaged Berlin at about the same time on July 16, 1945, that Groves and Oppenheimer at Trinity were preparing their first report of the tower shot's success. The Potsdam Conference, appropriately coded TERMINAL, was supposed to have begun that afternoon, but Joseph Stalin was late arriving by armored train from Moscow. (He apparently suffered a mild heart attack the previous day.) The Berlin tour gave Truman an opportunity to view at close hand the damage Allied bombing and Red Army shelling had done.

Byrnes was officially Secretary of State now, invested in a sweltering ceremony in the White House Rose Garden on July 3 attended by a crowd of his former House, Senate and Supreme Court colleagues. After Byrnes swore the oath of office Truman had kidded him: "Jimmy, kiss the Bible." Byrnes complied, then gave as good as he got: passed the Bible to the President and bade him kiss it as well. Truman did so; understanding the byplay between the former Vice President and the man who had missed his turn, the crowd laughed. Four days later the two leaders boarded the cruiser *Augusta* for the Atlantic crossing to Antwerp and now they rode side by side into Berlin, conquerors in snap-brim hats and natty worsteds.

Though he had arrived before them in Potsdam, Henry Stimson did not accompany the President and his favorite adviser on their tour. The Secretary of War had consulted with Truman the day before Byrnes' swearing-in—proposing to give the Japanese "a warning of what is to come and definite opportunity to capitulate"—and as he was leaving had asked the President plaintively if he had not invited his Secretary of War to attend the forthcoming conference out of solicitude for his health. That was it, Truman had said quickly, and Stimson had replied that he could manage the trip and would like to go, that Truman ought to have advice "from the top civilians in our Department." The next day, the day of Byrnes' investiture, Truman accorded the elderly statesman permission. But Stimson had traveled separately on the military transport *Brazil* via Marseilles, was lodged separately in Potdam from the President and his Secretary of State and would not be included in their daily private discussions. One of Stimson's aides felt that "Secretary Byrnes was a little resentful of Mr. Stimson's presence there. . . . The Secretary of the Navy wasn't there so why should Mr. Stimson be there?" Byrnes in his 1947 account of his career, *Speaking Frankly,* narrates an entire chapter about Potsdam without once mentioning Stimson's name, relegating his rival to a brief separate discussion of the decision to use the atomic bomb on Japan and awarding him there the dubious honor of having chosen the targets. In fact, Stimson at Potsdam would be reduced to serving Truman and Byrnes as not much more than a messenger boy. But the messages he brought were fateful.

"We reviewed the Second Armored Division," Truman reports his Berlin tour in his impromptu diary, ". . . Gen. [J. H.] Collier, who seemed to know his stuff, put us in a reconnaissance car built with side seats and no top, just like a hoodlum wagon minus the top, or a fire truck with seats and no hose, and we drove slowly down a mile and a half of good soldiers and some millions of dollars worth of equipment—which had amply paid its way to Berlin." The destroyed city fired an uneasy burst of associations:

> Then we went on to Berlin and saw absolute ruin. Hitler's folly. He overreached himself by trying to take in too much territory. He had no morals and his people backed him up. Never did I see a more sorrowful sight, nor witness retribution to the nth degree. . . .
>
> I thought of Carthage, Baalbec, Jerusalem, Rome, Atlantis; Peking, Babylon, Nineveh; Scipio, Rameses II, Titus, Hermann, Sherman, Jenghis Khan, Alexander, Darius the Great. But Hitler only destroyed Stalingrad—and Berlin. I hope for some sort of peace—but I fear that machines are ahead of morals by some centuries and when morals catch up perhaps there'll be no reason for any of it.
>
> I hope not. But we are only termites on a planet and maybe when we bore too deeply into the planet there'll be a reckoning—who knows?

The "Proposed Program for Japan" that Stimson had offered to Truman on July 2 had reckoned up that country's situation—which included the possible entry of the Soviet Union, at present neutral, into the Pacific war—and judged it desperate:

> Japan has no allies.
>
> Her navy is nearly destroyed and she is vulnerable to a surface and underwater blockade which can deprive her of sufficient food and supplies for her population.
>
> She is terribly vulnerable to our concentrated air attack upon her crowded cities, industrial and food resources.
>
> She has against her not only the Anglo-American forces but the rising forces of China and the ominous threat of Russia.

> We have inexhaustible and untouched industrial resources to bring to bear against her diminishing potential.
>
> We have great moral superiority through being the victim of her first sneak attack.

On the other hand, Stimson had argued, because of the mountainous Japanese terrain and because "the Japanese are highly patriotic and certainly susceptible to calls for fanatical resistance to repel an invasion," America would probably "have to go through with an even more bitter finish fight than in Germany" if it attempted to invade. Was there, then, any alternative? Stimson thought there might be:

> I believe Japan *is* susceptible to reason in such a crisis to a much greater extent than is indicated by our current press and other current comment. Japan is not a nation composed wholly of mad fanatics of an entirely different mentality from ours. On the contrary, she has within the past century shown herself to possess extremely intelligent people, capable in an unprecedentedly short time of adopting not only the complicated technique of Occidental civilization but to a substantial extent their culture and their political and social ideas. Her advance in these respects . . . has been one of the most astounding feats of national progress in history. . . .
>
> It is therefore my conclusion that a carefully timed warning be given to Japan. . . .
>
> I personally think that if in [giving such a warning] we should add that we do not exclude a constitutional monarchy under her present dynasty, it would substantially add to the chances of acceptance.

Within the text of his proposal the Secretary of War several times characterized it as "the equivalent of an unconditional surrender," but others did not see it so. Before Byrnes left for Potsdam he had carried the document to ailing Cordell Hull, a fellow Southerner and Franklin Roosevelt's Secretary of State from 1933 to 1944, and Hull had immediately plucked out the concession to the "present dynasty"—the Emperor Hirohito, in whose mild myopic figure many Americans had personified Japanese militarism—and told Byrnes that "the statement seemed too much like appeasement of Japan."

It may have been, but by the time they arrived in Potsdam, Stimson, Truman and Byrnes had learned that it was also the minimum condition of surrender the Japanese were prepared to countenance, whatever their desperate situation. U.S. intelligence had intercepted and decoded messages passing between Tokyo and Moscow instructing Japanese ambassador Naotake Sato to attempt to interest the Soviets in mediating a Japanese surrender. "The foreign and domestic situation for the Empire is very serious," Foreign Minister Shigenori Togo had cabled Sato on July 11, "and even the termination of the war is now being considered privately. . . . We are also sounding out the extent to which we might employ the USSR in connection with the termination of the war. . . . [This is] a matter with which the Imperial Court is . . . greatly concerned." And pointedly on July 12:

> It is His Majesty's heart's desire to see the swift termination of the war. . . . However, as long as America and England insist on unconditional surrender our country has no alternative but to see it through in an all-out effort for the sake of survival and the honor of the homeland.

Unconditional surrender seemed to the Japanese leadership a demand to give up its essential and historic polity, a demand that under similar circumstances Americans also might hesitate to meet even at the price of their lives: hence Stimson's careful qualification of his proposed terms of surrender. But to the extent that the imperial institution was tainted with militarism, an offer to preserve it might also seem an offer to preserve the militaristic government that ran the country and that had started and pursued the war. Certainly many Americans might think so and might conclude in consequence that their wartime sacrifices were being callously betrayed.

Hull considered these difficulties while Byrnes sailed the Atlantic and sent along a cable of further advice on July 16. The Japanese might reject a challenge to surrender, the former Secretary of State argued, even if it allowed the Emperor to remain on the throne. In that case not only would the militarists among them be encouraged by what they would take to be a sign of weakening Allied will, but also "terrible political repercussions would follow in the U.S. . . . Would it be well *first* to await the climax of Allied bombing and Russia's entry into the war?"

The point of warning the Japanese was to encourage an early surrender in the hope of avoiding a bloody invasion; the trouble with waiting until the Soviet Union entered the war was that it left Truman where he had dangled uncomfortably for months: over Stalin's barrel, dependent on the USSR for military intervention in Manchuria to tie up the Japanese armies there. Hull's delaying tactic might improve the first prospect; but it might also secure the second.

Another message arrived in Potsdam that evening, however, that changed the terms of the equation, a message for Stimson from George Harrison in Washington announcing the success of the Trinity shot:

> Operated on this morning. Diagnosis not yet complete but results seem satisfactory and already exceed expectations. Local press release necessary as in-

terest extends great distance. Dr. Groves pleased. He returns tomorrow. I will keep you posted.

"Well," Stimson remarked to Harvey Bundy with relief, "I have been responsible for spending two billions of dollars on this atomic venture. Now that it is successful I shall not be sent to prison in Fort Leavenworth." Happily the Secretary of War carried the cable to Truman and Byrnes, just returned to Potsdam from Berlin.

In Stimson's welcome news Byrnes saw a more general reprieve. It informed his overnight response to Hull. "The following day" Hull says, "I received a message from Secretary Byrnes agreeing that the statement [warning the Japanese] should be delayed and that, when it was issued, it should not contain this commitment with regard to the Emperor." Byrnes had good reason to delay a warning now: to await the readying of the first combat atomic bombs. Those weapons would answer Hull's first objection; if the Japanese ignored a warning, then the United States could deliver a brutally retributive response. With such weapons in the U.S. arsenal unconditional surrender need not be compromised. And America no longer required the Soviet Union's aid in the Pacific; the problem now would be not dealing the Soviets in but stalling to keep them out. "Neither the President nor I," Byrnes affirms, "were anxious to have them enter the war after we had learned of this successful test."

Byrnes and others within the American delegation came to realize that preserving the Emperor might be sensible policy if Hirohito alone could persuade the far-flung Japanese armies, undefeated and with a year's supply of ammunition on hand, to lay down their arms. The new Secretary of State, who was drafting a suitable declaration, sought a formula that would not arouse the American people but might reassure the Japanese. The Joint Chiefs produced its first version: "Subject to suitable guarantees against further acts of aggression, the Japanese people will be free to choose their own form of government." The Japanese polity resided in the Imperial House, not in the people, but provision for popular government was as conditional an unconditional surrender as the enemy would be allowed.

George Harrison cabled Stimson on July 21 that "all your local military advisors engaged in preparation definitely favor your pet city": Groves still coveted Kyoto. Stimson quickly returned that he was "aware of no factors to change my decision. On the contrary new factors here tend to confirm it."

Harrison also asked Stimson to alert him by July 25 "if [there is] any change in plans" because "[the] patient [is] progressing rapidly." At the same time Groves requested permission from George Marshall to brief Douglas MacArthur, who had not yet been told about the new weapon, in view of "the imminence of the use of the atomic fission bomb in operations against Japan, 5 to 10 August." The 509th had begun flying Pumpkin missions over Japan the previous day for combat experience and to accustom the enemy to small, unescorted flights of B-29's at high altitude.

Groves' eyewitness narrative of the Trinity test had arrived that Saturday just before noon. Stimson sought out Truman and Byrnes and had the satisfaction of riveting them to their chairs by reading it aloud. Groves estimated "the energy generated to be in excess of the equivalent of 15,000 to 20,000 tons of TNT" and allowed his deputy, Thomas F. Farrell, to call the visual effects "unprecedented, magnificent, beautiful, stupendous and terrifying." Kenneth Bainbridge's "foul and awesome display" became at Farrell's hand "that beauty the great poets dream about but describe most poorly and inadequately," which Farrell presumably meant for a superlative. "As to the present war," Farrell opined, "there was a feeling that no matter what else might happen, we now had the means to insure its speedy conclusion and save thousands of American lives." Stimson saw that Truman was "tremendously pepped up" by the report. "[He] said it gave him an entirely new feeling of confidence."

The President met the next day to discuss Groves' results with Byrnes, Stimson and the Joint Chiefs, including Marshall and Hap Arnold. Arnold had long maintained that conventional strategic bombing by itself could compel the Japanese to surrender. In late June, when invasion was being decided, he had rushed LeMay to Washington to work the numbers. LeMay figured he could complete the destruction of the Japanese war machine by October 1. "In order to do this," writes Arnold, "he had to take care of some 30 to 60 large and small cities." Between May and August LeMay took care of fifty-eight. But Marshall disagreed with the Air Force assessment. The situation in the Pacific, he had told Truman in June, was "practically identical" to the situation in Europe after Normandy. "Airpower alone was not sufficient to put the Japanese out of the war. It was unable alone to put the Germans out." He explained his reasoning at Potsdam to an interviewer after the war:

> We regarded the matter of dropping the [atomic] bomb as exceedingly important. We had just gone through a bitter experience at Okinawa [the last major island campaign, when the Americans lost more than 12,500 men killed and missing and the Japanese more than 100,000 killed in eighty-two days of fighting]. This had been preceded by a number of similar experiences in other Pacific islands, north of Australia. The Japanese had demonstrated in each case they would not surrender and they would fight to the death. . . . It was

> expected that resistance in Japan, with their home ties, would be even more severe. We had had the one hundred thousand people killed in Tokyo in one night of [conventional] bombs, and it had had seemingly no effect whatsoever. It destroyed the Japanese cities, yes, but their morale was not affected as far as we could tell, not at all. So it seemed quite necessary, if we could, to shock them into action. . . . We had to end the war; we had to save American lives.

Before Groves' report arrived, Dwight Eisenhower, a hard and pragmatic commander, had angered Stimson with a significantly different assessment. "We'd had a nice evening together at headquarters in Germany," the Supreme Allied Commander remembers, "nice dinner, everything was fine. Then Stimson got this cable saying the bomb had been perfected and was ready to be dropped." The cable was the second Harrison had sent, the day after the Trinity test when Groves arrived back in Washington:

> Doctor has just returned most enthusiastic and confident that the little boy is as husky as his big brother. The light in his eyes discernible from here to Highhold and I could have heard his screams from here to my farm.

Highhold was Stimson's Long Island estate, 250 miles from Washington—the Trinity flash had been visible even farther from Zero than that. Harrison's farm was 50 miles outside the capital. Eisenhower found the allegorical code less than amusing and the subject baleful:

> The cable was in code, you know the way they do it. "The lamb is born" or some damn thing like that. So then he told me they were going to drop it on the Japanese. Well, I listened, and I didn't volunteer anything because, after all, my war was over in Europe and it wasn't up to me. But I was getting more and more depressed just thinking about it. Then he asked for my opinion, so I told him I was against it on two counts. First, the Japanese were ready to surrender and it wasn't necessary to hit them with that awful thing. Second, I hated to see our country be the first to use such a weapon. Well . . . the old gentleman got furious. And I can see how he would. After all, it had been his responsibility to push for all the huge expenditure to develop the bomb, which of course he had a right to do, and *was* right to do. Still, it was an awful problem.

Eisenhower also spoke to Truman, but the President concurred in Marshall's judgment, having already formed his own. "Believe Japs will fold up before Russia comes in," he confided to his diary almost as soon as he heard of the Trinity success. "I am sure they will when Manhattan appears over their homeland."

When to issue the Potsdam Declaration now became essentially a question of when the first atomic bombs would be ready to be dropped. Stimson queried Harrison, who responded on July 23:

> Operation may be possible any time from August 1 depending on state of preparation of patient and condition of atmosphere. From point of view of patient only, some chance August 1 to 3, good chance August 4 to 5 and barring unexpected relapse almost certain before August 10.

Stimson had also asked for a target list, "always excluding the particular place against which I have decided. My decision has been confirmed by highest authority." Harrison complied: "Hiroshima, Kokura, Niigata in order of choice here."

Which meant that Nagasaki had not yet, as of the last full week in July, been added to the list. Within days it would be. Official Air Force historians speculate that LeMay's staff proposed it. The requirement for visual bombing was probably the reason. Hiroshima was 440 miles southwest of Niigata. Nagasaki, over the mountains from Kokura on Kyushu, was a further 220 miles southwest of Hiroshima. If one city was socked in, another might be clear. Nagasaki was certainly also added because it was one of the few major cities left in Japan that had not yet been burned out.

A revealing third cable completed the day's communications from Harrison (the metallurgists at Los Alamos had finished the Pu core for Fat Man that day). It concerned possible future deliveries of atomic bombs and hinted at a forthcoming change in design, probably to the so-called "mixed" implosion bomb with a core of U235 and plutonium alloyed together. Such a core could draw on the resources of both Oak Ridge and Hanford:

> First one of tested type [i.e., Fat Man] should be ready at Pacific base about 6 August. Second one ready about 24 August. Additional ones ready at accelerating rate from possibly three in September to we hope seven or more in December. The increased rate above three per month entails changes in design which Groves believes thoroughly sound.

Stimson reported Harrison's several estimates to Truman on Tuesday morning, July 24. The President was pleased and said he would use them to time the release of the Potsdam Declaration. The Secretary took advantage of the moment to appeal to Truman to consider assuring the Japanese privately that they could keep their Emperor if they persisted in making that concession a condition of surrender. Deliberately noncommittal, the President said he had the point in mind and would take care of it.

Stimson left and Byrnes joined Truman for lunch. They discussed how to tell Stalin as little as possible about the atomic bomb. Truman wanted protective cover when Stalin learned that his wartime allies had developed an epochal new weapon behind his back but wanted to give as little as possible away. Byrnes also devised a more immediate reason for circumspection, he told the historian Herbert Feis in 1958:

> As a result of his experience with the Russians during the first week of the Conference he had come to the conclusion that it would be regrettable if the Soviet Union entered the [Pacific] war, and . . . he was afraid that if Stalin were made fully aware of the power of the new weapon, he might order the Soviet Army to plunge forward at once.

But in fact Stalin already knew about the Trinity test. His agents in the United States had reported it to him. It appears he was not immediately impressed. There is gallows humor in Truman's elaborately offhand approach to the Soviet Premier at the end of that day's plenary session at the Cecilienhof Palace, stripped and shabby, where pale German mosquitoes homing through unscreened windows dined on the sanguinary conquerors. Truman left behind his translator, rounded the baize-covered conference table and sidled up to his Soviet counterpart, both men dissimulating. "I casually mentioned to Stalin that we had a new weapon of unusual destructive force. The Russian Premier showed no special interest. All he said was that he was glad to hear it and hoped we would make 'good use of it against the Japanese.' " "That," concludes Robert Oppenheimer dryly, knowing how much at that moment the world lost, "was carrying casualness rather far."

If Stalin was not yet impressed with the potential of the bomb, Truman in his private diary was waxing apocalyptic, biblical visions mingling in his autodidact's mind with doubt that the atom could be decomposed and denial that the new weapon would be used to slaughter civilians:

> We have discovered the most terrible bomb in the history of the world. It may be the fire destruction prophesied in the Euphrates Valley Era, after Noah and his fabulous Ark.
>
> Anyway we "think" we have found a way to cause a disintegration of the atom. An experiment in the New Mexican desert was startling—to put it mildly. . . .
>
> This weapon is to be used against Japan between now and August 10th. I have told the Sec. of War, Mr. Stimson, to use it so that military objectives and soldiers and sailors are the target and not women and children. Even if the Japs are savages, ruthless, merciless and fanatic, we as the leader of the world for the common welfare cannot drop this terrible bomb on the old Capital or the new.

> He & I are in accord. The target will be a purely military one and we will issue a warning statement asking the Japs to surrender and save lives. I'm sure they will not do that, but we will have given them the chance. It is certainly a good thing for the world that Hitler's crowd or Stalin's did not discover this atomic bomb. It seems to be the most terrible thing ever discovered, but it can be made the most useful.

The Tuesday Truman mentioned the new weapon to Stalin the Combined Chiefs met with their Soviet counterparts; Red Army chief of staff General Alexei E. Antonov announced that Soviet troops were assembling on the Manchurian border and would be ready to attack in the second half of August. Stalin had said August 15 before. Byrnes was anxious that the Soviets might prove uncharacteristically punctual.

That afternoon in Washington Groves drafted the historic directive releasing the atomic bomb to use. It passed up through Harrison for transmission by radio EYES ONLY to Marshall "in order that your approval and the Secretary of War's approval might be obtained as soon as possible." (A small map of Japan cut from a large National Geographic Society map and a one-page description of the chosen targets, which now included Nagasaki, followed by courier.) Marshall and Stimson approved the directive at Potsdam and presumably showed it to Truman, though it does not record his formal authorization; it went out the next morning to the new commander of the Strategic Air Force in the Pacific:

> To General Carl Spaatz, CG, USASTAF:
>
> 1. The 509 Composite Group, 20th Air Force will deliver its first special bomb as soon as weather will permit visual bombing after about 3 August 1945 on one of the targets: Hiroshima, Kokura, Niigata and Nagasaki. . . .
>
> 2. Additional bombs will be delivered on the above targets as soon as made ready by the project staff. . . .
>
> 3. Dissemination of any and all information concerning the use of the weapon against Japan is reserved to the Secretary of War and the President of the United States. . . .
>
> 4. The foregoing directive is issued to you by direction and with the approval of the Secretary of War and of the Chief of Staff, USA.

As Groves drafted the directive the metallurgists at Los Alamos finished casting the rings of U235 that fitted together to form the gun bomb's target assembly, the last components needed to complete Little Boy.

Strategy and delivery intersected on July 26 and synchronized. The *Indianapolis* arrived at Tinian. Three Air Transport Command C-54 cargo planes departed Kirtland Air Force Base with the three separate pieces of the Little Boy target assembly; two more ATC C-54's departed with Fat Man's initiator and plutonium core. Meanwhile Truman's staff released the Potsdam Declaration to the press at 7 P.M. for dispatch from Occupied Germany at 9:20. It offered on behalf of the President of the United States, the President of Nationalist China and the Prime Minister of Great Britain to give Japan "an opportunity to end this war":

> Following are our terms. We will not deviate from them. There are no alternatives. We shall brook no delay.
>
> There must be eliminated for all time the authority and influence of those who have deceived and misled the people of Japan into embarking on world conquest. . . .
>
> Until such a new order is established . . . points in Japanese territory . . . shall be occupied.
>
> . . . Japanese sovereignty shall be limited to the islands of Honshu, Hokkaido, Kyushu, Shikoku and such minor islands as we determine.
>
> The Japanese military forces, after being completely disarmed, shall be permitted to return to their homes with the opportunity to lead peaceful and productive lives.
>
> We do not intend that the Japanese shall be enslaved as a race or destroyed as a nation, but stern justice shall be meted out to all war criminals. . . . Freedom of speech, of religion, and of thought, as well as respect for the fundamental human rights shall be established.
>
> Japan shall be permitted to maintain such industries as will sustain her economy. . . .
>
> The occupying forces of the Allies shall be withdrawn from Japan as soon as these objectives have been accomplished and there has been established in accordance with the freely expressed will of the Japanese people a peacefully inclined and responsible government.
>
> We call upon the government of Japan to proclaim now the unconditional surrender of all Japanese armed forces. . . . The alternative for Japan is prompt and utter destruction.

"We faced a terrible decision," Byrnes wrote in 1947. "We could not rely on Japan's inquiries to the Soviet Union about a negotiated peace as proof that Japan would surrender unconditionally without the use of the bomb. In fact, Stalin stated the last message to him had said that Japan would 'fight to the death rather than accept unconditional surrender.' Under the circumstances, agreement to negotiate could only arouse false hopes. Instead, we relied upon the Potsdam Declaration."

The text of that somber document went out by radio to the Japanese from San Francisco; Japanese monitors picked it up at 0700 hours Tokyo time July 27. The Japanese leaders debated its mysteries all day. A quick Foreign Office analysis noted for the ministers that the Soviet Union had preserved its neutrality by not sponsoring the declaration, that it specified what the Allies meant by unconditional surrender and that the term itself had been applied specifically only to the nation's armed forces. Foreign Minister Togo disliked the demand for occupation and the stripping away of Japan's foreign possessions; he recommended waiting for a Soviet response to Ambassador Sato's representations before responding.

The Prime Minister, Baron Kantaro Suzuki, came during the day to the same position. The military leaders disagreed. They recommended immediate rejection. Anything less, they argued, might impair morale.

The next day Japanese newspapers published a censored version of the Potsdam text, leaving out in particular the provision allowing disarmed military forces to return peacefully to their homes and the assurance that the Japanese would not be enslaved or destroyed. In the afternoon Suzuki held a press conference. "I believe the Joint Proclamation by the three countries," he told reporters, "is nothing but a rehash of the Cairo Declaration. As for the Government, it does not find any important value in it, and there is no other recourse but to ignore it entirely and resolutely fight for the successful conclusion of the war." In Japanese Suzuki said there was no other recourse but to *mokusatsu* the declaration, which could also mean "treat it with silent contempt." Historians have debated for years which meaning Suzuki had in mind, but there can hardly be any doubt about the rest of his statement: Japan intended to fight on.

"In the face of this rejection," Stimson explained in *Harper's* in 1947, "we could only proceed to demonstrate that the ultimatum had meant exactly what it said when it stated that if the Japanese continued the war, 'the full application of our military power, backed by our resolve, will mean the inevitable and complete destruction of the Japanese armed forces and just as inevitably the utter devastation of the Japanese homeland.' For such a purpose the atomic bomb was an eminently suitable weapon."

The night of Suzuki's press conference the five C-54's from Albuquerque arrived at Tinian, six thousand miles nearer Japan, while three B-29's departed Kirtland each carrying a Fat Man high-explosive preassembly.

The U.S. Senate in the meantime ratified the United Nations Charter.

The *Indianapolis* had sailed on to Guam after unloading the Little Boy gun and bullet at Tinian on July 26; from Guam it continued unescorted toward Leyte in the Philippines, where two weeks of training would ready the crew, 1,196 men, to join Task Force 95 at Okinawa preparing for the

November 1 Kyushu invasion. With the destruction of the Japanese surface fleet and air force, unescorted sailing had become commonplace on courses through rear areas, but the *Indianapolis,* an older vessel, lacked sonar gear for submarine detection and was top-heavy. Japanese submarine I-58 discovered the heavy cruiser in the Philippine Sea a little before midnight on Sunday, July 29, and mistook it for a battleship. Easily avoiding detection while submerging to periscope depth, I-58 fired a fanwise salvo of six torpedoes from 1,500 yards. Lieutenant Commander Mochitsura Hashimoto, I-58's commanding officer, remembers the result:

> I took a quick look through the periscope, but there was nothing else in sight. Bringing the boat on to a course parallel with the enemy, we waited anxiously. Every minute seemed an age. Then on the starboard side of the enemy by the forward turret, and then by the after turret there rose columns of water, to be followed immediately by flashes of bright red flame. Then another column of water rose from alongside Number 1 turret and seemed to envelop the whole ship—"A hit, a hit!" I shouted as each torpedo struck home, and the crew danced round with joy. . . . Soon came the sound of a heavy explosion, far greater than that of the actual hits. Three more heavy explosions followed in quick succession, then six more.

The torpedoes and following explosions of ammunition and aviation fuel ripped away the cruiser's bow and destroyed its power center. Without power the radio officer was unable to send a distress signal—he went through the motions anyway—or the bridge to communicate with the engine room. The engines pushed the ship forward unchecked, scooping up water through the holes in the hull and leaving behind the sailors thrown overboard who had been sleeping on deck in the tropical heat. The order to abandon ship, when it came, had to be passed by word of mouth.

With the ship listing to 45 degrees frightened and injured men struggled to follow disaster drill. Fires lit the darkness and smoke sickened. The ship's medical officer found some thirty seriously burned men in the port hangar where the aviation fuel had exploded; at best they got morphine for their screams and rough kapok lifejackets strapped on over their burns. They went overboard with the others into salt water scummed with nauseating fuel oil. It was possible to walk down the hull to the keel and jump into the water but the spinning number three screw with its lethal blades chopped to death the unwary.

Some 850 men escaped. The stern rose up a hundred feet straight into the air and the ship plunged. The survivors heard screams from within the disappearing hull. Then they were left to the night and the darkness in twelve-foot swells.

Most had kapok lifejackets. Few had found their way to life rafts. They floated instead in clusters, linked together, stronger men swimming the circumferences to catch sleepers before they drifted away; one group numbered between three and four hundred souls. They pushed the wounded to the center where the water was calmer and prayed the distress call had gone out.

The captain had found two empty life rafts and later that night encountered one more occupied. He ordered the rafts lashed together. They sheltered ten men and he thought them the only survivors. Through the night a current carried the swimmers southwest while wind blew the rafts northeast; by the light of morning rafts and swimmers had separated beyond discovery.

More than fifty injured swimmers died during the night. Their comrades freed them from their jackets in the morning and let them go. The wind abated and the sun glared from the oil slick, blinding them with painful photophobia. And then the sharks came. A seaman swimming for a floating crate of potatoes thrashed in the water and was gone. Elemental terror: the men pressed together in their groups, some clusters deciding to beat the water, some to hang immotile as flotsam. A shark snapped away both a sailor's legs and his unbalanced torso, suspended in its lifejacket, flipped upside down. One survivor remembered counting twenty-five deadly attacks; the ship's doctor in his larger group counted eighty-eight.

They won no rescue. They passed through Monday and Monday night and Tuesday and Tuesday night without water, sinking lower and lower in the sea as the kapok in their lifejackets waterlogged. Eventually the thirst-crazed drank seawater. "Those who drank became maniacal and thrashed violently," the doctor testifies, "until the victims became comatose and drowned." The living were blinded by the sun; their lifejackets abraded their ulcerating skin; they burned with fever; they hallucinated.

Wednesday and Wednesday night. The sharks circled and darted in to foray after flesh. Men in the grip of group delusions followed one swimmer to an island he thought he saw, another to the ghost of the ship, another down into the ocean depths where fountains of fresh water seemed to promise to slake their thirst; all were lost. Fights broke out and men slashed each other with knives. Saturated lifejackets with waterlogged knots dragged other victims to their deaths. "We became a mass of delirious, screaming men," says the doctor grimly.

Thursday morning, August 2, a Navy plane spotted the survivors. Because of negligence at Leyte the *Indianapolis* had not yet even been missed. A major rescue effort began, ships steaming to the area, PBY's and PBM's dropping food and water and survival gear. The rescuers found 318 naked and emaciated men. The fresh water they drank, one of them remembers, tasted "so sweet [it was] the sweetest thing in your life." Through the 84-hour ordeal more than 500 men had died, their bodies feeding sharks or lost to the depths of the sea.

After making good his escape, submarine commander Hashimoto reminisces, "at length, on the 30th, we celebrated our haul of the previous day with our favorite rice with beans, boiled eels, and corned beef (all of it tinned)."

The day of the I-58's feast of canned goods Carl Spaatz telexed Washington with news:

> HIROSHIMA ACCORDING TO PRISONER OF WAR REPORTS IS THE ONLY ONE OF FOUR TARGET CITIES . . . THAT DOES NOT HAVE ALLIED PRISONER OF WAR CAMPS.

It was too late to reconsider targets, prisoners of war or not. Washington telexed back the next day:

> TARGETS ASSIGNED . . . REMAIN UNCHANGED. HOWEVER IF YOU CONSIDER YOUR INFORMATION RELIABLE HIROSHIMA SHOULD BE GIVEN FIRST PRIORITY AMONG THEM.

The die was cast.

Once Trinity proved that the atomic bomb worked, men discovered reasons to use it. The most compelling reason Stimson stated in his *Harper's* apologia in 1947:

> My chief purpose was to end the war in victory with the least possible cost in the lives of the men in the armies which I had helped to raise. In the light of the alternatives which, on a fair estimate, were open to us I believe that no man, in our position and subject to our responsibilities, holding in his hands a weapon of such possibilities for accomplishing this purpose and saving those lives, could have failed to use it and afterwards looked his countrymen in the face.

The Scientific Panel of the Interim Committee—Lawrence, Compton, Fermi, Oppenheimer—had been asked to conjure a demonstration of sufficient credibility to end the war. Meeting at Los Alamos on the weekend of July 16–17, debating long into the night, it found in the negative. Even Fermi's ingenuity was not sufficient to the task of devising a demonstration persuasive enough to decide the outcome of a long and bitter conflict. Recognizing "our obligation to our nation to use the weapons to help save American lives in the Japanese war," the panel first surveyed the opinions of scientific colleagues and then stated its own:

> Those who advocate a purely technical demonstration would wish to outlaw the use of atomic weapons, and have feared that if we use the weapons now our position in future negotiations will be prejudiced. Others emphasize the opportunity of saving American lives by immediate military use, and believe that such use will improve the international prospects, in that they are more concerned with the prevention of war than with the elimination of this specific weapon. We find ourselves closer to these latter views; we can propose no technical demonstration likely to bring an end to the war; we see no acceptable alternative to direct military use.

The bomb was to prove to the Japanese that the Potsdam Declaration meant business. It was to shock them to surrender. It was to put the Russians on notice and serve, in Stimson's words, as a "badly needed equalizer." It was to let the world know what was coming: Leo Szilard had dallied with that rationale in 1944 before concluding in 1945 on moral grounds that the bomb should not be used and on political grounds that it should be kept secret. Teller revived a variant rationale in early July 1945, in replying to Szilard about a petition Szilard was then circulating among Manhattan Project scientists protesting the bomb's impending use:

> First of all let me say that I have no hope of clearing my conscience. The things we are working on are so terrible that no amount of protesting or fiddling with politics will save our souls. . . .
>
> But I am not really convinced of your objections. I do not feel that there is any chance to outlaw any one weapon. If we have a slim chance of survival, it lies in the possibility to get rid of wars. The more decisive the weapon is the more surely it will be used in any real conflicts and no agreements will help.
>
> Our only hope is in getting the facts of our results before the people. This might help to convince everybody that the next war would be fatal. For this purpose actual combat-use might even be the best thing.

The bomb was also to be used to pay for itself, to justify to Congress the investment of $2 billion, to keep Groves and Stimson out of Leavenworth prison.

"To avert a vast, indefinite butchery," Winston Churchill summarizes in his history of the Second World War, "to bring the war to an end, to give peace to the world, to lay healing hands upon its tortured peoples by a manifestation of overwhelming power at the cost of a few explosions, seemed, after all our toils and perils, a miracle of deliverance."

The few explosions did not seem a miracle of deliverance to the civilians of the enemy cities upon whom the bombs would be dropped. In their behalf—surely they have claim—something more might be said about reasons. The bombs were authorized not because the Japanese refused to surrender but because they refused to surrender unconditionally. The debacle of conditional peace following the First World War led to the demand for unconditional surrender in the Second, the earlier conflict casting its dark shadow down the years. "It was the insistence on unconditional surrender that was the root of all evil," writes the Oxford moralist G. E. M. Anscombe in a 1957 pamphlet opposing the awarding of an honorary degree to Harry Truman. "The connection between such a demand and the need to use the most ferocious methods of warfare will be obvious. And in itself the proposal of an unlimited objective in war is stupid and barbarous."

As before in the Great War for every belligerent, that was what the Second World War had become: stupid and barbarous. "For men to choose to kill the innocent as a means to their ends," Anscombe adds bluntly, "is always murder, and murder is one of the worst of human actions. . . . In the bombing of [Japanese] cities it was certainly decided to kill the innocent as a means to an end." In the decision of the Japanese militarists to arm the Japanese people with bamboo spears and set them against a major invasion force to fight to the death to preserve the homeland it was certainly decided to kill the innocent as a means to an end as well.

The barbarism was not confined to the combatants or the general staffs. It came to permeate civilian life in every country: in Germany and Japan, in Britain, in Russia, certainly in the United States. It was perhaps the ultimate reason Jimmy Byrnes, the politician's politician, and Harry Truman, the man of the people, felt free to use and compelled to use a new weapon of mass destruction on civilians in undefended cities. "It was the psychology of the American people," I. I. Rabi eventually decided. "I'm not justifying it on military grounds but on the existence of this mood of the military with the backing of the American people." The mood, suggests the historian Herbert Feis, encompassed "impatience to end the strain of war blended with a zest for victory. They longed to be done with smashing, burning, killing, dying—and were angry at the defiant, crazed, useless prolongation of the ordeal."

In 1945 *Life* magazine was the preeminent general-circulation magazine in the United States. It served millions of American families for news and entertainment much as television a decade later began to do. Children read it avidly and reported on its contents in school. In the last issue of *Life* before the United States used the atomic bomb a one-page picture story appeared, titled, in 48-point capitals, A JAP BURNS. Its brief text, for those who could tear their eyes away from the six postcard-sized black-and-white photographs showing a man being burned alive long enough to read the words, savored horror while complaining of ugly necessity:

> When the 7th Australian Division landed near Balikpapan on the island of Borneo last month they found a town strongly defended by Japanese. As usual, the enemy fought from caves, from pillboxes, from every available hiding place. And, as usual, there was only one way to advance against them: burn them out. Men of the 7th, who had fought the Japs before, quickly applied their flamethrowers, soon convinced some Japs that it was time to quit. Others, like the one shown here, refused. So they had to be burned out.
>
> Although men have fought one another with fire from time immemorial, the flamethrower is easily the most cruel, the most terrifying weapon ever developed. If it does not suffocate the enemy in his hiding place, its quickly licking tongues of flame sear his body to a black crisp. But so long as the Jap refuses to come out of his holes and keeps killing, this is the only way.

In a single tabloid page *Life* had assembled a brutal allegory of the later course of the Pacific war.

Little Boy was ready on July 31. It lacked only its four sections of cordite charge, a precaution prepared when the weapon was designed at Los Alamos but decided upon at Tinian, for safety on takeoff and in the event visual bombing proved impossible, in which case Tibbets had orders to bring the bomb back. Three of Tibbets' full complement of fifteen B-29's flew a last test that last day of July with a dummy Little Boy. They took off from Tinian, rendezvoused over Iwo Jima, returned to Tinian, dropped unit L6 into the sea and practiced their daredevil diving turn. "With the completion of this test," writes Norman Ramsey, "all tests preliminary to combat delivery of a Little Boy with active material were completed." That unit would be number L11, and the sturdy tungsten-steel target holder screwed to its muzzle, the best in stock, was the first one Los Alamos had received; it had served four times for firing tests at Anchor Ranch late in 1944 before being packed in cosmoline for the voyage out to Tinian.

Since everything was ready, Farrell telexed Groves to report that the mission could be flown on August 1; he would assume that the Spaatz directive of July 25 authorized such initiative unless Groves replied to the contrary. The commanding general of the Manhattan Project let his deputy's interpretation stand. Little Boy would have flown on August 1 if a typhoon had not approached Japan that day to intervene.

So the mission waited on the weather. On August 2, Thursday, the three B-29's that carried Fat Man preassemblies arrived from New Mexico.

The assembly team of Los Alamos scientists and military ordnance technicians went to work immediately to prepare one Fat Man for a drop test and a second with higher-quality HE castings for combat. The third preassembly would be held in reserve for the plutonium core scheduled to be shipped from Los Alamos in mid-August. "By August 3," recalls Paul Tibbets, "we were watching the weather and comparing it to the [long-range] forecast. The actual and forecast weather were almost identical, so we got busy."

Among other necessities, getting busy involved briefing the crews of the seven 509th B-29's that would fly the first mission for weather reporting, observation and bombing. Tibbets scheduled the briefing for 1500 hours on August 4. The crews arrived between 1400 and 1500 to find the briefing hut completely surrounded by MP's armed with carbines. Tibbets walked in promptly at 1500; he had just returned from checking out the aircraft he intended to use to deliver Little Boy, usually piloted by Robert Lewis: B-29 number 82, as yet unnamed. Deke Parsons joined him on the briefing platform. A radio operator, Sergeant Abe Spitzer, kept an illegal diary of his experiences at Tinian that describes the briefing.

The moment had arrived, Tibbets told the assembled crews. The weapon they were about to deliver had recently been tested successfully in the United States; now they were going to drop it on the enemy.

Two intelligence officers undraped the blackboards behind the 509th commander to reveal aerial photographs of the targets: Hiroshima, Kokura, Nagasaki. (Niigata was excluded, apparently because of weather.) Tibbets named them and assigned three crews—"finger crews"—to fly ahead the day of the drop to assess their cloud cover. Two more aircraft would accompany him to photograph and observe; the seventh would wait beside a loading pit on Iwo Jima as a spare in case Tibbets' plane malfunctioned.

The 509th commander introduced Parsons, who wasted no words. He told the crews the bomb they were going to drop was something new in the history of warfare, the most destructive weapon ever made: it would probably almost totally destroy an area three miles across.

They were stunned. "It is like some weird dream," Spitzer mused, "conceived by one with too vivid an imagination."

Parsons prepared to show a motion picture of the Trinity test. The projector refused to start. Then it started abruptly and began chewing up leader. Parsons told the projectionist to shut the machine off and improvised. He described the shot in the Jornada del Muerto: how far away the light had been seen, how far away the explosion had been heard, the effects of the blast wave, the formation of the mushroom cloud. He did not identify the source of the weapon's energy, but with details—a man knocked down at 10,000 yards, men 10 and 20 miles away temporarily blinded—he won their rapt attention.

Tibbets took over again. They were now the hottest crews in the Air Force, he warned them. He forbade them to write letters home or to discuss the mission even among themselves. He briefed them on the flight. It would probably go, he said, early on the morning of August 6. An air-sea rescue officer described rescue operations. Tibbets closed with a challenge, a final word Spitzer paraphrases in his diary:

> The colonel began by saying that whatever any of us, including himself, had done before was small potatoes compared to what we were going to do now. Then he said the usual things, but he said them well, as if he meant them, about how proud he was to have been associated with us, about how high our morale had been, and how difficult it was not knowing what we were doing, thinking maybe we were wasting our time and that the "gimmick" was just somebody's wild dream. He was personally honored and he was sure all of us were, to have been chosen to take part in this raid, which, he said—and all the other big-wigs nodded when he said it—would shorten the war by at least six months. And you got the feeling that he really thought this bomb would end the war, period.

The following morning, Sunday, Guam reported that weather over the target cities should improve the next day. "At 1400 on August 5," Norman Ramsey records, "General LeMay officially confirmed that the mission would take place on August 6."

That afternoon the loading crew winched Little Boy onto its sturdy transport dolly, draped it with a tarpaulin to protect it from prying eyes—there were still Japanese soldiers hiding out on the island, hunted at night by security forces like raccoons—and wheeled it to one of the 13 by 16-foot loading pits Kirkpatrick had prepared. A battery of photographers followed along to record the proceedings. The dolly was wheeled over the nine-foot pit on tracks; the hydraulic lift came up to relieve it of its bomb and detachable cradle; the crew wheeled the dolly away, removed the tracks, rotated the bomb 90 degrees and lowered it into the pit.

The world's first combat atomic bomb looked like "an elongated trash can with fins," one of Tibbets' crew members thought. With its tapered tail assembly that culminated in a boxed frame of stabilizing baffle plates it was 10½ feet long and 29 inches in diameter. It weighed 9,700 pounds, an armored cylinder jacketed in blackened dull steel with a flat, rounded nose. A triple fusing system armed it. The main fusing component was a radar unit adapted from a tail-warning mechanism developed to alert combat pilots

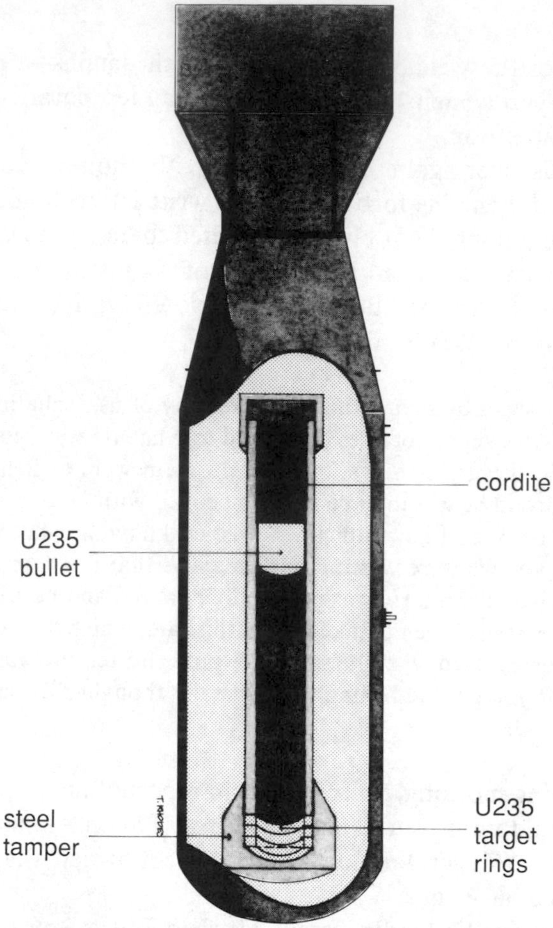

when enemy aircraft approached from behind. "This radar device," notes the Los Alamos technical history, "would close a relay [i.e., a switch] at a predetermined altitude above the target." For reliability Little Boy and Fat Man each carried four such radar units, called Archies. Rather than an approaching enemy aircraft, the bomb Archies would bounce their signals off the approaching enemy ground. An agreed reading by any two of the units would send a firing signal into the next stage of the fusing system, the technical history explains:

> This stage consisted of a bank of clock-operated switches, started by arming wires which were pulled out of the clocks when the bomb dropped from the plane's bomb bay. These clock switches were not closed until 15 seconds after the bomb was released. Their purpose was to prevent detonation in case the A[rchie] units were fired by signals reflected from the plane. A second arming

device was a [barometric] pressure switch, which did not close until subject to a pressure corresponding to 7000 feet altitude.

Once it passed through the clock and barometric arming devices the Little Boy firing signal went directly to the primers that lit the cordite charges to fire the gun. Externally the fusing system revealed itself in trailing whips of radar antennae, clock wires threaded into holes in the weapon's upper waist and holes in its tapered tail assembly that admitted external air to guarantee accurate barometry.

Loading the bomb was delicate: the fit was tight. A ground crew towed the B-29 to a position beside the loading pit, running onto a turntable the main landing gear on the wing nearer the pit. Towing the aircraft around on the turntable through 180 degrees positioned it over the pit. The hydraulic lift raised Little Boy to a point directly below the open bomb doors. A plumb bob hung from the single bomb shackle for a point of reference and jacks built into the bomb cradle allowed the crew to line up the bomb eye.

"The operation can be accomplished in 20 to 25 minutes," a Boeing engineer commented in an August report, "but is a rather ticklish procedure, as there is very little clearance with the catwalks and, once installed, nothing holds the bomb but the single shackle and adjustable sway braces bearing on it."

Though he flew it as his own, Robert Lewis had never named B-29 number 82. The day of the loading Tibbets consulted the officers in Lewis' crew—but not Lewis—and did so. The 509th commander chose not pinups or puns but his mother's given names, Enola Gay, because she had assured him he would not be killed flying when he fought out with his father his decision to become a pilot. "Through the years," Tibbets told an interviewer once, "whenever I got in a tight spot in a plane I always remembered her calm assurance. It helped. In getting ready for the big one I rarely thought of what might happen, but when I did, those words of Mom's put an end to it." He "wrote a note on a slip of paper," located a sign painter among the service personnel—the man had to be dragged away from a softball game—and told him to "paint that on the strike ship, nice and big." Foot-high, squared brushstrokes went on at a 30-degree angle beneath the pilot's window of the bullet-nosed plane, the middle name flush-right below the first.

Lewis, a sturdy, combative two-hundred-pounder, had known for a day or two that Tibbets would pilot the mission, a disappointment, but still considered the special B-29 his own. When he dropped by late in the afternoon to inspect it and found ENOLA GAY painted on its fuselage he was furious. "What the hell is *that* doing on *my* plane?" one of his crew mates remembers him yelling. He found out that Tibbets had authorized the christening and marched off to confront him. The 509th commander told him coolly, rank having its privileges, that he didn't think the junior officer would mind. Lewis minded, but he could do no more than stow away his resentment for the war stories he would tell.

"By dinnertime on the fifth," Tibbets narrates, "all [preparations were] completed. The atom bomb was ready, the planes were gassed and checked. Takeoff was set for [2:45] a.m. I tried to nap, but visitors kept me up. [Captain Theodore J.] Dutch [Van Kirk, the *Enola Gay*'s navigator,] swallowed two sleeping tablets, then sat up wide awake all night playing poker." The weapon waiting in the bomb bay took its toll on nerves.

"Final briefing was at 0000 of August 6," Ramsey notes—midnight. Tibbets emphasized the power of the bomb, reminded the men to wear the polarized goggles they had been issued, cautioned them to obey orders and follow their protocols. A weather officer predicted moderate winds with clouds over the targets clearing at dawn. Tibbets called forward a Protestant chaplain who delivered a prayer composed for the occasion on the back of an envelope; it asked the Almighty Father "to be with those who brave the heights of Thy heaven and who carry the battle to our enemies."

After the midnight briefing the crews ate an early breakfast of ham and eggs and Tibbets' favorite pineapple fritters. Trucks delivered them to their hardstands. At the *Enola Gay*'s hardstand, writes Ramsey, "amid brilliant floodlights, pictures were taken and retaken by still and motion picture photographers (as though for a Hollywood premiere)." A photograph shows ten of the twelve members of the strike plane's crew posed in flight coveralls under the forward fuselage by the nose wheel: boyish Van Kirk in overseas cap with his coveralls unzipped down his chest to expose a white T-shirt; Major Thomas Ferebee, the bombardier, a handsome Errol Flynn copy with an Errol Flynn mustache, resting a friendly hand on Van Kirk's shoulder; Tibbets standing at the center of it all easily smiling, belted and trim, his hands in his pockets; at Tibbets' left Robert Lewis, the only crew member wearing a weapon; small, wiry Lieutenant Jacob Beser beside Lewis awkwardly smiling, a Jewish technician from Baltimore added for the flight, responsible for electronic countermeasures to screen the Archie units from Japanese radar. In front of the officers kneel the slimmer, mostly younger enlisted men (though the entire flight crew was young, Tibbets now all of thirty years old): radar operator Sergeant Joseph Stiborik; tail gunner Staff Sergeant Robert Caron, Brooklyn-born, wearing a Dodgers baseball cap; radio operator Private Richard R. Nelson; assistant engineer Sergeant Robert H. Shumard; flight engineer Staff Sergeant

Wyatt Duzenbury, thirty-two, a former Michigan tree surgeon who thought the bomb looked like a tree trunk. An eleventh member of the crew, 2nd Lieutenant Morris Jeppson, an ordnance expert, would assist Deke Parsons in arming and monitoring Little Boy. Parsons, the twelfth man, resisted photographing but was flying the mission as weaponeer.

The three weather planes and the Iwo Jima standby had already left. Tibbets ordered Wyatt Duzenbury to start engines at 0227 hours. Pilot and copilot sat side by side just back of the point where the cylindrical fuselage began to curve inward to form the bullet-shaped nose; Ferebee, the bombardier, sat a step down ahead of them within the nose itself, an exposed position but a good view. Almost everything inside the aircraft was painted a dull lime green. "It was just another mission," Tibbets says, "if you didn't let imagination run away with your wits." As Dimples Eight Two, the *Enola Gay*'s unlikely designation that day, he reconstructs his dialogue with the Tinian control tower:

> I forgot the atom bomb and concentrated on the cockpit check.
>
> I called the tower. "Dimples Eight Two to North Tinian Tower. Taxi-out and take-off instructions."
>
> "Dimples Eight Two from North Tinian Tower. Take off to the east on Runway A for Able."
>
> At the end of the runway, another call to the tower and a quick response: "Dimples Eight Two cleared for take-off."
>
> Bob Lewis called off the time. Fifteen seconds to go. Ten seconds. Five seconds. Get ready.

At that moment the *Enola Gay* weighed 65 tons. It carried 7,000 gallons of fuel and a four-ton bomb. It was 15,000 pounds overweight. Confident the aircraft was maintained too well to falter, Tibbets decided to use as much of the two-mile runway as he needed to build RPM's and manifold pressure before roll-up.

He eased the brakes at 0245, the four fuel-injected Wright Cyclone engines pounding. "The B-29 has lots of torque in take-off," he notes. "It wants to swerve off the runway to the left. The average mass-production pilot offsets torque by braking his right wheels. It's a rough ride, you lose ten miles an hour and you delay the take-off." Nothing so crude for Tibbets. "Pilots of the 509th Group were taught to cancel torque by leading in with the left engines, advancing throttles ahead of the right engines. At eighty miles an hour, you get full rudder control, advance the right-hand engines to full power and, in a moment, you're airborne." Takeoff needed longer than a moment for the *Enola Gay*'s overloaded flight. As the runway disappeared beneath the big bomber Lewis fought the urge to pull back the yoke. At the last possible takeoff point he thought he did. Not he but Tibbets did and abruptly they were flying, an old dream of men, climbing above a black sea.

Ten minutes later they crossed the northern tip of Saipan on a course northwest by north at 4,700 feet. The air temperature was a balmy 72°. They were flying low not to burn fuel lifting fuel and for the comfort of the two weaponeers, Parsons and Jeppson, who had to enter the unpressurized, unheated bomb bay to finish assembling the bomb.

That work began at 0300. It was demanding in the cramped confines of the loaded bomb bay but not dangerous; there was only minimal risk of explosion. The green plugs that blocked the firing signal and prevented accidental detonation were plugged into the weapon; Parsons confirmed that fact first of all. Next he removed a rear plate; removed an armor plate beneath, exposing the cannon breech; inserted a wrench into the breech plug and rotated the wrench about sixteen times to unscrew the plug; removed it and placed it carefully on a rubber pad. He inserted the four sections of cordite one at a time, red ends to breech. He replaced the breech plug and tightened it home, connected the firing line, reinstalled the two metal plates and with Jeppson's help removed and secured the tools and the catwalk. Little Boy was complete but not yet armed. The charge loading took fifteen minutes. They spent another fifteen minutes checking monitoring circuitry at the panel installed at the weaponeer's position in the forward section. Then, except for monitoring, their work was done until time to arm the bomb.

Robert Lewis kept a journal of the flight. William L. Lawrence, the *New York Times* science editor attached to the Manhattan Project, had traveled out to Tinian expecting to go along. When he learned to his bitter disappointment that his participation had been deleted he asked Lewis to take notes. The copilot imagined himself writing a letter to his mother and father but appears to have sensed that the world would be looking over his shoulder and styled his entries with regulation Air Force bonhomie. "At forty-five minutes out of our base," he began self-consciously, "everyone is at work. Colonel Tibbets has been hard at work with the usual tasks that belong to the pilot of a B-29. Captain Van Kirk, navigator, and Sergeant Stiborik, radio operator, are in continuous conversation, as they are shooting bearings on the northern Marianas and making radar wind runs." No mention of Parsons or Jeppson, oddly enough, though Lewis could have seen the bomb hanging in its bay through the round port below the tunnel opening straight back from his copilot's seat.

The automatic pilot, personified as George, was flying the plane, which Tibbets stationed below 5,000 feet. The commander realized he was tired, Lewis records: "The colonel, better known as 'the Old Bull,' shows signs of a tough day. With all he's had to do to get this mission off, he is deserving of a few winks, so I'll have a bite to eat and look after 'George.' "

Rather than sleep Tibbets crawled through the thirty-foot tunnel to chat with the waist crew, wondering if they knew what they were carrying. "A chemist's nightmare," the tail gunner, Robert Caron, guessed, then "a physicist's nightmare." "Not exactly," Tibbets hedged. Tibbets was leaving by the time Caron put two and two together:

> [Tibbets] stayed . . . a little longer, and then started to crawl forward up the tunnel. I remembered something else, and just as the last of the Old Man was disappearing, I sort of tugged at his foot, which was still showing. He came sliding back in a hurry, thinking maybe something was wrong. "What's the matter?"
>
> I looked at him and said, "Colonel, are we splitting atoms today?"
>
> This time he gave me a really funny look, and said, "That's about it."

Caron's third try, which he styles "a lucky guess," apparently decided Tibbets to complete the crew's briefing; back in his seat he switched on the interphone, called "Attention!" and remembers saying something like "Well, boys, here's the last piece of the puzzle." They carried an atomic bomb, he told them, the first to be dropped from an airplane. They were not physicists; they understood at least that the weapon was different from any other ever used in war.

Lewis took control from George to weave his way through a mass of towering cumuli, clouds black in the darkness that swept aside to reveal a sky shot with stars. "At 4:30," he jotted, "we saw signs of a late moon in the east. I think everyone will feel relieved when we have left our bomb with the Japs and get half way home. Or, better still, all the way home." Ferebee in the nose was quiet; Lewis suspected he was thinking of home, "in the midwest part of old U.S.A." The bombardier was in fact from Mocksville, North Carolina, close enough to the Midwest for a native of New York. Dawn lightening a little past 0500 cheered them; "it looks at this time," Lewis wrote coming out of the clouds, "that we will have clear sailing for a long spell."

At 0552 they approached Iwo Jima and Tibbets began climbing to 9,300 feet to rendezvous with the observation and photography planes. The *Enola Gay* circled left over Iwo, found its two escorts and moved on, its course continuing northwest by north toward the archipelago of green islands the men called the Empire.

"After leaving Iwo we began to pick up some low stratus," Lewis resumes his narrative, "and before long we were flying on top of an undercast. At 07:10 the undercast began to break up a little bit. Outside of a high thin cirrus and the low stuff it's a very beautiful day. We are now about two hours from Bombs Away." They flew into history through a middle world, suspended between sky and sea, drinking coffee and eating ham sandwiches, engines droning, the smell of hot electronics in the air.

At 0730 Parsons visited the bomb bay for the last time to arm Little Boy, exchanging its green plugs for red and activating its internal batteries. Tibbets was about to begin the 45-minute climb to altitude. Jeppson worked his console. Parsons told Tibbets that Little Boy was "final." Lewis overheard:

> The bomb was now independent of the plane. It was a peculiar sensation. I had a feeling the bomb had a life of its own now that had nothing to do with us. I wished it were over and we were at this same position on the way back to Tinian.

"Well, folks, it won't be long now," the copilot added as Tibbets increased power to climb.

The weather plane at Hiroshima reported in at 0815 (0715 Hiroshima time). It found two-tenths cloud cover lower and middle and two-tenths at 15,000 feet. The other two target weather reports followed. "Our primary is the best target," Lewis wrote enthusiastically, "so, with everything going well so far, we will make a bomb run on Hiroshima." "It's Hiroshima," Tibbets announced to the crew.

They leveled at 31,000 feet at 0840. They had pressurized the aircraft and heated it against an outside temperature of −10° F. Ten minutes later they achieved landfall over Shikoku, the smaller home island east of Hiroshima, a city which looks southeastward from the coast of Honshu into the Inland Sea. "As we are approaching our target, Ferebee, Van Kirk and Stiborik are coming into their own, while the colonel and I are standing by and giving the boys what they need." Correcting course, Lewis means, aligning the plane. He got excited then or busy: "There will be a short intermission while we bomb our target." But bombing the target was the main event.

The crew pulled on heavy flak suits, cumbersome protection the pilots disdained. No Japanese fighters came up to meet them, nor were they bothered by flak.

The two escort planes dropped back to give the *Enola Gay* room. Tibbets reminded his men to wear their protective goggles.

They carried no maps. They had studied aerial photographs and knew the target city well. It was distinctive in any case, sited on a delta divided by the channels of seven distributaries. "Twelve miles from the target," Tibbets remembers, "Ferebee called, 'I see it!' He clutched in his bombsight and took control of the plane from me for a visual run. Dutch [Van Kirk] kept giving me radar course corrections. He was working with the radar operator. . . . I couldn't raise them on the interphone to tell them Ferebee had the plane." The bombardier flew the plane through his bombsight, the knurled knobs he adjusted instructing the automatic pilot to make minor corrections in course. They crossed the Inland Sea on a heading only five degrees south of due west. Van Kirk noticed eight large ships south of them in Hiroshima harbor. The *Enola Gay*'s ground speed then was 285 knots, about 328 miles per hour.

Above a fork in the Ōta River in central Hiroshima a T-shaped bridge spanned the river and connected to the island formed by the two distributaries. The Aioi Bridge, not a war plant surrounded by workers' houses, was Ferebee's chosen aiming point. Second Army headquarters was based nearby. Tibbets had called the bridge the most perfect AP he'd seen in the whole damn war:

> Ferebee had the drift well killed but the rate was off a little. He made two slight corrections. A loud "blip" on the radio notified the escort B-29's that the bomb would drop in two minutes. After that, Tom looked up from his bombsight and nodded to me; it was going to be okay.
>
> He motioned to the radio operator to give the final warning. A continuous tone signal went out, telling [the escorts]: "In fifteen seconds she goes."

The distant weather planes also heard the radio signal. So did the spare B-29 parked on Iwo Jima. It alerted Luis Alvarez in the observation plane to prepare to film the oscilloscopes he had installed there; the radio-linked parachute gauges he had designed to measure Little Boy's explosive yield hung in the bomb bay waiting to drop with the bomb and float down toward the city.

Hiroshima unrolled east to west in the cross hairs of Thomas Ferebee's Norden bombsight. The bomb-bay doors were open. Ferebee had flown sixty-three combat missions in Europe before returning to the United States to instruct and then to join the 509th. Before the war he had wanted to be a baseball player and had got as far as spring tryouts with a major-league team. He was twenty-four years old.

"The radio tone ended," Tibbets says tersely, "the bomb dropped, Ferebee unclutched his sight." The arming wires pulled out to start Little Boy's clocks. The first combat atomic bomb fell away from the plane, then nosed down. It was inscribed with autographs and messages, some of them obscene. "Greetings to the Emperor from the men of the *Indianapolis,*" one challenged.

Four tons lighter, the B-29 jumped. Tibbets dove away:

> I threw off the automatic pilot and hauled *Enola Gay* into the turn.
>
> I pulled antiglare goggles over my eyes. I couldn't see through them; I was blind. I threw them to the floor.
>
> A bright light filled the plane. The first shock wave hit us.
>
> We were eleven and a half miles slant range from the atomic explosion, but the whole airplane cracked and crinkled from the blast. I yelled "Flak!" thinking a heavy gun battery had found us.
>
> The tail gunner had seen the first wave coming, a visible shimmer in the atmosphere, but he didn't know what it was until it hit. When the second wave came, he called out a warning.
>
> We turned back to look at Hiroshima. The city was hidden by that awful cloud . . . boiling up, mushrooming, terrible and incredibly tall.
>
> No one spoke for a moment; then everyone was talking. I remember Lewis pounding my shoulder, saying, "Look at that! Look at that! Look at that!" Tom Ferebee wondered about whether radioactivity would make us all sterile. Lewis said he could taste atomic fission. He said it tasted like lead.

"Fellows," Tibbets announced on the interphone, "you have just dropped the first atomic bomb in history."

Van Kirk remembers the two shock waves—one direct, one reflected from the ground—vividly:

> [It was] very much as if you've ever sat on an ash can and had somebody hit it with a baseball bat. . . . The plane bounced, it jumped and there was a noise like a piece of sheet metal snapping. Those of us who had flown quite a bit over Europe thought that it was anti-aircraft fire that had exploded very close to the plane.

The apparent proximity of the explosion would be one of its trademarks, much as its heat had seemed intimate to Philip Morrison and his colleagues at Trinity.

Turning, diving, circling back to watch, the crew of the *Enola Gay* missed the early fireball; when they looked again Hiroshima smothered under a pall. Lewis in a postwar interview:

> I don't believe anyone ever expected to look at a sight quite like that. Where we had seen a clear city two minutes before, we could now no longer see the city. We could see smoke and fires creeping up the sides of the mountains.

Van Kirk:

> If you want to describe it as something you are familiar with, a pot of boiling black oil. . . . I thought: Thank God the war is over and I don't have to get shot at any more. I can go home.

It was a sentiment hundreds of thousands of American soldiers and sailors would soon express, and it was hard-earned.

Leaving the scene the tail gunner, Robert Caron, had a long view:

> I kept shooting pictures and trying to get the mess down over the city. All the while I was describing this on the intercom. . . . The mushroom itself was a spectacular sight, a bubbling mass of purple-gray smoke and you could see it had a red core in it and everything was burning inside. As we got farther away, we could see the base of the mushroom and below we could see what looked like a few-hundred-foot layer of debris and smoke and what have you.
>
> I was trying to describe the mushroom, this turbulent mass. I saw fires springing up in different places, like flames shooting up on a bed of coals. I was asked to count them. I said, "Count them?" Hell, I gave up when there were about fifteen, they were coming too fast to count. I can still see it—that mushroom and that turbulent mass—it looked like lava or molasses covering the whole city, and it seemed to flow outward up into the foothills where the little valleys would come into the plain, with fires starting up all over, so pretty soon it was hard to see anything because of the smoke.

Jacob Beser, the electronic countermeasures officer, an engineering student at Johns Hopkins before he enlisted, found an image from the seashore for the turmoil he saw:

> That city was burning for all she was worth. It looked like . . . well, did you ever go to the beach and stir up the sand in shallow water and see it all billow up? That's what it looked like to me.

Little Boy exploded at 8:16:02 Hiroshima time, 43 seconds after it left the *Enola Gay,* 1,900 feet above the courtyard of Shima Hospital, 550 feet southeast of Thomas Ferebee's aiming point, Aioi Bridge, with a yield equivalent to 12,500 tons of TNT.

"It was all impersonal," Paul Tibbets would come to say. It was not impersonal for Robert Lewis. "If I live a hundred years," he wrote in his journal, "I'll never quite get these few minutes out of my mind." Nor would the people of Hiroshima.

* * *

In my mind's eye, like a waking dream, I could still see the tongues of fire at work on the bodies of men.

Masuji Ibuse, *Black Rain*

The settlement on the delta islands of the Ōta River in southwestern Honshu was named Ashihara, "reed field," or Gokaura, "five villages," before the feudal lord Terumoto Mōri built a fortress there between 1589 and 1591 to secure an outlet for his family holdings on the Inland Sea. Mōri called his fortress Hiro-shima-jō, "broad-island castle," and gradually the town of merchants and artisans that grew up around it acquired its name. It was an 800-foot rectangle of massive stone walls protected within a wide rectangular moat, one corner graced by a high white pagoda-like tower with five progressively inset roofs. The Mōri family soon lost its holdings to the stronger Fukushima family, which lost them in turn to the Asano family in 1619. The Asanos had the good sense to have allied themselves closely with the Tokugawa Shogunate and ruled Hiroshima fief within that alliance for the next two and a half centuries. Across those centuries the town prospered. The Asanos saw to its progressive enlargement by filling in the estuarial shallows to connect its islands. Divided then into long, narrow districts by the Ōta's seven distributaries, Hiroshima assumed the form of an open, extended hand.

The restoration of the Meiji emperor in 1868 and the abolition of the feudal clan system transformed Hiroshima fief into Hiroshima Prefecture and the town, like the country, began vigorously to modernize. A physician was appointed its first mayor in 1889 when it officially became a city; the population that celebrated the change numbered 83,387. Five years of expensive landfill and construction culminated that year in the opening of Ujina harbor, a reclamation project that established Hiroshima as a major commercial port. Railroads came through at the turn of the century.

By then Hiroshima and its castle had found further service as an army base and the Imperial Army Fifth Division was quartered in barracks within and around the castle grounds. The Fifth Division was the first to be shipped to battle when Japan and China initiated hostilities in 1894; Ujina harbor served as a major point of embarkation and would continue in that role for the next fifty years. The Meiji emperor moved his headquarters to the castle in Hiroshima in September, the better to direct the war, and the Diet met in extraordinary session in a provisional Diet building there. Until the following April, when the limited mainland war ended with a Japanese victory that included the acquisition of Formosa and the southern part of Manchuria, Hiroshima was *de facto* the capital of Japan. Then the emperor returned to Tokyo and the city consolidated its gains.

It acquired further military and industrial investments in the first three decades of the twentieth century as Japan turned to increasing international adventure. By the Second World War, an American study noted in the autumn of 1945, "Hiroshima was a city of considerable military importance. It contained the 2nd Army headquarters, which commanded the defense of all of southern Japan. The city was a communication center, a storage point, and an assembly area for troops. To quote a Japanese report, 'Probably more than a thousand times since the beginning of the war did the Hiroshima citizens see off with cries of "Banzai" the troops leaving from the harbor.' " From Hiroshima in 1945 the Japanese Army general staff prepared to direct the defense of Kyushu against the impending American invasion.

Earlier in the war the city's population had approached 400,000, but the threat of strategic bombing, so ominously delayed, had led the authorities to order a series of evacuations; on August 6 the resident population numbered some 280,000 to 290,000 civilians plus about 43,000 soldiers. Given that proportion of civilian to military—more than six to one—Hiroshima was not, as Truman had promised in his Potsdam diary, a "purely military" target. It was not without responsibility, however, in serving the ends of war.

"The hour was early, the morning still, warm, and beautiful," a Hiroshima physician, Michihiko Hachiya, the director of the Hiroshima Communications Hospital, begins a diary of the events Little Boy entrained on August 6. "Shimmering leaves, reflecting sunlight from a cloudless sky, made a pleasant contrast with shadows in my garden." The temperature at eight o'clock was 80 degrees, the humidity 80 percent, the wind calm. The seven branches of the Ōta flowed past crowds of citizens walking and bicycling to work. The streetcars that clanged outside Fukuya department store two blocks north of Aioi Bridge were packed. Thousands of soldiers, bare to the waist, exercised at morning calesthenics on the east and west parade grounds that flanked Hiroshima Castle a long block west of the T-shaped bridge. More than eight thousand schoolgirls, ordered to duty the day before, worked outdoors in the central city helping to raze houses to clear firebreaks against the possibility of an incendiary attack. An air raid alert at 7:09—the 509th weather plane—had been called off at 7:31 when the B-29 left the area. Three more *B-sans* approaching just before 8:15 sent hardly anyone to cover, though many raised their eyes to the high silver instruments to watch.

"Just as I looked up at the sky," remembers a girl who was five years old at the time and safely at home in the suburbs, "there was a flash of white light and the green in the plants looked in that light like the color of dry leaves."

Closer was more brutal illumination. A young woman helping to clear firebreaks, a junior-college student at the time, recalls: "Shortly after the voice of our teacher, saying 'Oh, there's a B!' made us look up at the sky, we felt a tremendous flash of lightning. In an instant we were blinded and everything was just a frenzy of delirium."

Closer still, in the heart of the city, no one survived to report the coming of the light; the constrained witness of investigative groups must serve instead for testimony. A Yale Medical School pathologist working with a joint American-Japanese study commission a few months after the war, Averill A. Liebow, observes:

> Accompanying the flash of light was an instantaneous flash of heat. . . Its duration was probably less than one tenth of a second and its intensity was sufficient to cause nearby flammable objects . . . to burst into flame and to char poles as far as 4,000 yards away from the hypocenter [i.e., the point on the ground directly below the fireball]. . . . At 600–700 yards it was sufficient to chip and roughen granite. . . . The heat also produced bubbling of tile to about 1,300 yards. It has been found by experiment that to produce this effect a temperature of [3,000° F] acting for four seconds is necessary, but under these conditions the effect is deeper, which indicates that the temperature was higher and the duration less during the Hiroshima explosion.

"Because the heat in [the] flash comes in such a short time," adds a Manhattan Project study, "there is no time for any cooling to take place, and the temperature of a person's skin can be raised [120° F] . . . in the first millisecond at a distance of [2.3 miles]."

The most authoritative study of the Hiroshima bombing, begun in 1976 in consultation with thirty-four Japanese scientists and physicians, reviews the consequences of this infernal insolation, which at half a mile from the hypocenter was more than three thousand times as energetic as the sunlight that had shimmered on Dr. Hachiya's leaves:

> The temperature at the site of the explosion . . . reached [5,400° F] . . . and primary atomic bomb thermal injury . . . was found in those exposed within [2 miles] of the hypocenter. . . . Primary burns are injuries of a special nature and not ordinarily experienced in everyday life.

This Japanese study distinguishes five grades of primary thermal burns ranging from grade one, red burn, through grade three, white burn, to grade five, carbonized skin with charring. It finds that "severe thermal burns of over grade 5 occurred within [0.6 to 1 mile] of the hypocenter . . . and those of grades 1 to 4 [occurred as far as 2 to 2.5 miles] from the hypocenter. . . . Extremely intense thermal energy leads not only to carbonization but also to evaporation of the viscerae." People exposed within half a mile of the Little Boy fireball, that is, were seared to bundles of smoking black char in a fraction of a second as their internal organs boiled away. "Doctor," a patient commented to Michihiko Hachiya a few days later, "a human being who has been roasted becomes quite small, doesn't he?" The small black bundles now stuck to the streets and bridges and sidewalks of Hiroshima numbered in the thousands.

At the same instant birds ignited in midair. Mosquitoes and flies, squirrels, family pets crackled and were gone. The fireball flashed an enormous photograph of the city at the instant of its immolation fixed on the mineral, vegetable and animal surfaces of the city itself. A spiral ladder left its shadow in unburned paint on the surface of a steel storage tank. Leaves shielded reverse silhouettes on charred telephone poles. The black-brushed calligraphy burned out of a rice-paper name card posted on a school building door; the dark flowers burned out of a schoolgirl's light blouse. A human being left the memorial of his outline in unspalled granite on the steps of a bank. Another, pulling a handcart, protected a handcart- and human-shaped surface of asphalt from boiling. Farther away, in the suburbs, the flash induced dark, sunburn-like pigmentation sharply shadowed deep in human skin, streaking the shape of an exposed nose or ear or hand raised in gesture onto the faces and bodies of startled citizens: the mask of Hiroshima, Liebow and his colleagues came to call that pigmentation. They found it persisting unfaded five months after the event.

The world of the dead is a different place from the world of the living and it is hardly possible to visit there. That day in Hiroshima the two worlds nearly converged. "The inundation with death of the area closest to the hypocenter," writes the American psychiatrist Robert Jay Lifton, who interviewed survivors at length, "was such that if a man survived within a thousand meters (.6 miles) and was out of doors . . . more than nine tenths of the people around him were fatalities." Only the living, however inundated, can describe the dead; but where death claimed nine out of ten or, closer to the hypocenter, ten out of ten, a living voice describing necessarily distorts. Survivors are like us; but the dead are radically changed, without voice or civil rights or recourse. Along with their lives they have been deprived of participation in the human world. "There was a fearful silence which made one feel that all people and all trees and vegetation were dead," remembers Yōko Ōta, a Hiroshima writer who survived. The silence was the only sound the dead could make. In what follows among the living, remember them. They were nearer the center of the event; they died because they were members of a different polity and their killing did not therefore count officially as murder; their experience most accurately models the worst case of our common future. They numbered in the majority in Hiroshima that day.

Still only light, not yet blast: Hachiya:

> I asked Dr. Koyama what his findings had been in patients with eye injuries.
>
> "Those who watched the plane had their eye grounds burned," he replied. "The flash of light apparently went through the pupils and left them with a blind area in the central portion of their visual fields.
>
> "Most of the eye-ground burns are third degree, so cure is impossible."

And a German Jesuit priest reporting on one of his brothers in Christ:

> Father Kopp . . . was standing in front of the nunnery ready to go home. All of a sudden he became aware of the light, felt that wave of heat, and a large blister formed on his hand.

A white burn with the formation of a bleb is a grade-four burn.

Now light and blast together; they seemed simultaneous to those close in. A junior-college girl:

> Ah, that instant! I felt as though I had been struck on the back with something like a big hammer, and thrown into boiling oil. . . . I seem to have been blown a good way to the north, and I felt as though the directions were all changed around.

The first junior-college girl, the one whose teacher called everyone to look up:

> The vicinity was in pitch darkness; from the depths of the gloom, bright red flames rise crackling, and spread moment by moment. The faces of my friends who just before were working energetically are now burned and blistered, their clothes torn to rags; to what shall I liken their trembling appearance as they stagger about? Our teacher is holding her students close to her like a mother hen protecting her chicks, and like baby chicks paralyzed with terror, the students were thrusting their heads under her arms.

The light did not burn those who were protected inside buildings, but the blast found them out:

> That boy had been in a room at the edge of the river, looking out at the river when the explosion came, and in that instant as the house fell apart he was blown from the end room across the road on the river embankment and landed on the street below it. In that distance he passed through a couple of windows inside the house and his body was stuck full of all the glass it could hold. That is why he was completely covered with blood like that.

The blast wave, rocketing several hundred yards from the hypocenter at 2 miles per second and then slowing to the speed of sound, 1,100 feet per second, threw up a vast cloud of smoke and dust. "My body seemed all black," a Hiroshima physicist told Lifton, "everything seemed dark, dark all over. . . . Then I thought, 'The world is ending.' " Yōko Ōta, the writer, felt the same chill:

> I just could not understand why our surroundings had changed so greatly in one instant. . . . I thought it might have been something which had nothing to do with the war, the collapse of the earth which it was said would take place at the end of the world.

"Within the city," notes Hachiya, who was severely injured, "the sky looked as though it had been painted with light *sumi* [i.e., calligraphy ink], and the people had seen only a sharp, blinding flash of light; while outside the city, the sky was a beautiful, golden yellow and there had been a deafening roar of sound." Those who experienced the explosion within the city named it *pika,* flash, and those who experienced it farther away named it *pika-don,* flash-boom.

The houses fell as if they had been scythed. A fourth-grade boy:

> When I opened my eyes after being blown at least eight yards, it was as dark as though I had come up against a black-painted fence. After that, as if thin paper was being peeled off one piece at a time, it gradually began to grow brighter. The first thing that my eyes lighted upon then was the flat stretch of land with only dust clouds rising from it. Everything had crumbled away in that one moment, and changed into streets of rubble, street after street of ruins.

Hachiya and his wife ran from their house just before it collapsed and terror opened out into horror:

> The shortest path to the street lay through the house next door so through the house we went—running, stumbling, falling, and then running again until in headlong flight we tripped over something and fell sprawling into the street. Getting to my feet, I discovered that I had tripped over a man's head.
>
> "Excuse me! Excuse me, please!" I cried hysterically.

A grocer escaped into the street:

> The appearance of people was . . . well, they all had skin blackened by burns. . . . They had no hair because their hair was burned, and at a glance you couldn't tell whether you were looking at them from in front or in

back. . . . They held their arms [in front of them] . . . and their skin—not only on their hands, but on their faces and bodies too—hung down. . . . If there had been only one or two such people . . . perhaps I would not have had such a strong impression. But wherever I walked I met these people. . . . Many of them died along the road—I can still picture them in my mind—like walking ghosts. . . . They didn't look like people of this world. . . . They had a very special way of walking—very slowly. . . . I myself was one of them.

The peeled skin that hung from the faces and bodies of these severely injured survivors was skin that the thermal flash had instantly blistered and the blast wave had torn loose. A young woman:

I heard a girl's voice clearly from behind a tree. "Help me, please." Her back was completely burned and the skin peeled off and was hanging down from her hips. . . .

The rescue party . . . brought [my mother] home. Her face was larger than usual, her lips were badly swollen, and her eyes remained closed. The skin of both her hands was hanging loose as if it were rubber gloves. The upper part of her body was badly burned.

A junior-college girl:

On both sides of the road, bedding and pieces of cloth had been carried out and on these were lying people who had been burned to a reddish-black color and whose entire bodies were frightfully swollen. Making their way among them are three high school girls who looked as though they were from our school; their faces and everything were completely burned and they held their arms out in front of their chests like kangaroos with only their hands pointed downward; from their whole bodies something like thin paper is dangling—it is their peeled-off skin which hangs there, and trailing behind them the unburned remnants of their puttees, they stagger exactly like sleepwalkers.

A young sociologist:

Everything I saw made a deep impression—a park nearby covered with dead bodies waiting to be cremated . . . very badly injured people evacuated in my direction. . . . The most impressive thing I saw was some girls, very young girls, not only with their clothes torn off but with their skin peeled off as well. . . . My immediate thought was that this was like the hell I had always read about.

A five-year-old boy:

That day after we escaped and came to Hijiyama Bridge, there were lots of naked people who were so badly burned that the skin of their whole body was hanging from them like rags.

A fourth-grade girl:

> The people passing along the street are covered with blood and trailing the rags of their torn clothes after them. The skin of their arms is peeled off and dangling from their finger tips, and they go walking silently, hanging their arms before them.

A five-year-old girl:

> People came fleeing from the nearby streets. One after another they were almost unrecognizable. The skin was burned off some of them and was hanging from their hands and from their chins; their faces were red and so swollen that you could hardly tell where their eyes and mouths were. From the houses smoke black enough to scorch the heavens was covering the sky. It was a horrible sight.

A fifth-grade boy compiling a list:

> The flames which blaze up here and there from the collapsed houses as though to illuminate the darkness. The child making a suffering, groaning sound, his burned face swollen up balloon-like and jerking as he wanders among the fires. The old man, the skin of his face and body peeling off like a potato skin, mumbling prayers while he flees with faltering steps. Another man pressing with both hands the wound from which blood is steadily dripping, rushing around as though he has gone mad and calling the names of his wife and child—ah—my hair seems to stand on end just to remember. This is the way war really looks.

But skin peeled by a flash of light and a gust of air was only a novelty among the miseries of that day, something unusual the survivors could remember to remember. The common lot was random, indiscriminate and universal violence inflicting terrible pain, the physics of hydraulics and leverage and heat run riot. A junior-college girl:

> Screaming children who have lost sight of their mothers; voices of mothers searching for their little ones; people who can no longer bear the heat, cooling their bodies in cisterns; every one among the fleeing people is dyed red with blood.

The thermal flash and the blast started fires and very quickly the fires became a firestorm from which those who could ambulate ran away and those who sustained fractures or were pinned under houses could not; two months later Liebow's group found the incidence of fractures among Hiroshima survivors to be less than 4.5 percent. "It was not that injuries were few," the American physicians note; "rather, almost none who had lost the capacity to move escaped the flames." A five-year-old girl:

> The whole city . . . was burning. Black smoke was billowing up and we could hear the sound of big things exploding. . . . Those dreadful streets. The fires were burning. There was a strange smell all over. Blue-green balls of fire were drifting around. I had a terrible lonely feeling that everybody else in the world was dead and only we were still alive.

Another girl the same age:

> I really have to shudder when I think of that atom bomb which licked away the city of Hiroshima in one or two minutes on the 6th of August, 1945. . . .
>
> We were running for our lives. On the way we saw a soldier floating in the river with his stomach all swollen. In desperation he must have jumped into the river to escape from the sea of fire. A little farther on dead people were lined up in a long row. Al little farther on there was a woman lying with a big log fallen across her legs so that she couldn't get away.
>
> When Father saw that he shouted, "Please come and help!"
>
> But not a single person came to help. They were all too intent on saving themselves.
>
> Finally Father lost his patience, and shouting, "Are you people Japanese or not?" he took a rusty saw and cut off her leg and rescued her.
>
> A little farther on we saw a man who had been burned black as he was walking.

A first-grade girl whose mother was pinned under the wreckage of their house:

> I was determined not to escape without my mother. But the flames were steadily spreading and my clothes were already on fire and I couldn't stand it any longer. So screaming, "Mommy, Mommy!" I ran wildly into the middle of the flames. No matter how far I went it was a sea of fire all around and there was no way to escape. So beside myself I jumped into our [civil defense] water tank. The sparks were falling everywhere so I put a piece of tin over my head to keep out the fire. The water in the tank was hot like a bath. Beside me there were four or five other people who were all calling someone's name. While I was in the water tank everything became like a dream and sometime or other I became unconscious. . . . Five days after that [I learned that] Mother had finally died just as I had left her.

Similarly a woman who was thirteen at the time who was still haunted by guilt when Lifton interviewed her two decades later:

> I left my mother there and went off. . . . I was later told by a neighbor that my mother had been found dead, face down in a water tank . . . very close to the

> spot where I left her. . . . If I had been a little older or stronger I could have rescued her. . . . Even now I still hear my mother's voice calling me to help her.

"Beneath the wreckage of the houses along the way," recounts the Jesuit priest, "many have been trapped and they scream to be rescued from the oncoming flames."

"I was completely amazed," a third-grade boy remembers of the destruction:

> While I had been thinking it was only my house that had fallen down, I found that every house in the neighborhood was either completely or half-collapsed. The sky was like twilight. Pieces of paper and cloth were caught on the electric wires. . . . On that street crowds were fleeing toward the west. Among them were many people whose hair was burned, whose clothes were torn and who had burns and injuries. . . . Along the way the road was full to overflowing with victims, some with great wounds, some burned, and some who had lost the strength to move farther. . . . While we were going along the embankment, a muddy rain that was dark and chilly began to fall. Around the houses I noticed automobiles and footballs, and all sorts of household stuff that had been tossed out, but there was no one who stopped to pick up a thing.

But against the background of horror the eye of the survivor persisted in isolating the exceptional. A thirty-five-year-old man:

> A woman with her jaw missing and her tongue hanging out of her mouth was wandering around the area of Shinsho-machi in the heavy, black rain. She was heading toward the north crying for help.

A four-year-old boy:

> There were a lot of people who were burned to death and among them were some who were burned to a cinder while they were standing up.

A sixth-grade boy:

> Nearby, as if he were guarding these people, a policeman was standing, all covered with burns and stark naked except for some scraps of his trousers.

A seventeen-year-old girl:

> I walked past Hiroshima Station . . . and saw people with their bowels and brains coming out. . . . I saw an old lady carrying a suckling infant in her arms. . . . I saw many children . . . with dead mothers. . . . I just cannot put into words the horror I felt.

At Aioi Bridge:

> I was walking among dead people. . . . It was like hell. The sight of a living horse burning was very striking.

A schoolgirl saw "a man without feet, walking on his ankles." A woman remembers:

> A man with his eyes sticking out about two inches called me by name and I felt sick. . . . People's bodies were tremendously swollen—you can't imagine how big a human body can swell up.

A businessman whose son was killed:

> In front of the First Middle School there were . . . many young boys the same age as my son . . . and what moved me most to pity was that there was one dead child lying there and another who seemed to be crawling over him in order to run away, both of them burned to blackness.

A thirty-year-old woman:

> The corpse lying on its back on the road had been killed immediately. . . . Its hand was lifted to the sky and the fingers were burning with blue flames. The fingers were shortened to one-third and distorted. A dark liquid was running to the ground along the hand.

A third-grade girl:

> There was also a person who had a big splinter of wood stuck in his eye—I suppose maybe he couldn't see—and he was running around blindly.

A nineteen-year-old Ujina girl:

> I saw for the first time a pile of burned bodies in a water tank by the entrance to the broadcasting station. Then I was suddenly frightened by a terrible sight on the street 40 to 50 meters from Shukkeien Garden. There was a charred body of a woman standing frozen in a running posture with one leg lifted and her baby tightly clutched in her arms. Who on earth could she be?

A first-grade girl:

> A streetcar was all burned and just the skeleton of it was left, and inside it all the passengers were burned to a cinder. When I saw that I shuddered all over and started to tremble.

"The more you hear the sadder the stories get," writes a girl who was five years old at Hiroshima. "Since just in my family there is so much sadness from it," deduces a boy who was also five, "I wonder how much sadness other people must also be having."

Eyes watched as well from the other side. A history professor Lifton interviewed:

> I went to look for my family. Somehow I became a pitiless person, because if I had pity, I would not have been able to walk through the city, to walk over those dead bodies. The most impressive thing was the expression in people's eyes—bodies badly injured which had turned black—their eyes looking for someone to come and help them. They looked at me and knew that I was stronger than they. . . . I saw disappointment in their eyes. They looked at me with great expectation, staring right through me. It was very hard to be stared at by those eyes.

Massive pain and suffering and horror everywhere the survivors turned was their common lot. A fifth-grade boy:

> I and Mother crawled out from under the house. There we found a world such as I had never seen before, a world I'd never even heard of before. I saw human bodies in such a state that you couldn't tell whether they were humans or what. . . . There is already a pile of bodies in the road and people are writhing in death agonies.

A junior-college girl:

> At the base of the bridge, inside a big cistern that had been dug out there, was a mother weeping and holding above her head a naked baby that was burned bright red all over its body, and another mother was crying and sobbing as she gave her burned breast to her baby. In the cistern the students stood with only their heads above the water and their two hands, which they clasped as they imploringly cried and screamed, calling their parents. But every single person who passed was wounded, all of them, and there was no one to turn to for help.

A six-year-old boy:

> Near the bridge there were a whole lot of dead people. There were some who were burned black and died, and there were others with huge burns who died with their skins bursting, and some others who died all stuck full of broken glass. There were all kinds. Sometimes there were ones who came to us asking

for a drink of water. They were bleeding from their faces and from their mouths and they had glass sticking in their bodies. And the bridge itself was burning furiously. . . . The details and the scenes were just like Hell.

Two first-grade girls:

We came out to the Miyuki Bridge. Both sides of the street were piled with burned and injured people. And when we looked back it was a sea of bright red flame.

*

The fire was spreading furiously from one place to the next and the sky was dark with smoke. . . .

The [emergency aid station] was jammed with people who had terrible wounds, some whose whole body was one big burn. . . . The flames were spreading in all directions and finally the whole city was one sea of fire and sparks came flying over our heads.

A fifth-grade boy:

I had the feeling that all the human beings on the face of the earth had been killed off, and only the five of us [i.e., his family] were left behind in an uncanny world of the dead. . . . I saw several people plunging their heads into a half-broken water tank and drinking the water. . . . When I was close enough to see inside the tank I said "Oh!" out loud and instinctively drew back. What I had seen in the tank were the faces of monsters reflected from the water dyed red with blood. They had clung to the side of the tank and plunged their heads in to drink and there in that position they had died. From their burned and tattered middy blouses I could tell that they were high school girls, but there was not a hair left on their heads; the broken skin of their burned faces was stained bright red with blood. I could hardly believe that these were human faces.

A physician sharing his horror with Hachiya:

Between the [heavily damaged] Red Cross Hospital and the center of the city I saw nothing that wasn't burned to a crisp. Streetcars were standing at Kawaya-cho and Kamiya-cho and inside were dozens of bodies, blackened beyond recognition. I saw fire reservoirs filled to the brim with dead people who looked as though they had been boiled alive. In one reservoir I saw a man, horribly burned, crouching beside another man who was dead. He was drinking blood-stained water out of the reservoir. . . . In one reservoir there were so many dead people there wasn't enough room for them to fall over. They must have died sitting in the water.

A husband helping his wife escape the city:

> While taking my severely-wounded wife out to the riverbank by the side of the hill of Nakahiro-machi, I was horrified, indeed, at the sight of a stark naked man standing in the rain with his eyeball in his palm. He looked to be in great pain but there was nothing that I could do for him.

The naked man may have been the same victim one of Hachiya's later visitors remembered noticing, or he may have been another:

> There were so many burned [at a first-aid station] that the odor was like drying squid. They looked like boiled octopuses. . . . I saw a man whose eye had been torn out by an injury, and there he stood with his eye resting in the palm of his hand. What made my blood run cold was that it looked like the eye was staring at me.

The people ran to the rivers to escape the firestorm; in the testimony of the survivors there is an entire subliterature of the rivers. A third-grade boy:

> Men whose whole bodies were covered with blood, and women whose skin hung from them like a kimono, plunged shrieking into the river. All these become corpses and their bodies are carried by the current toward the sea.

A first-grade girl:

> We were still in the river by evening and it got cold. No matter where you looked there was nothing but burned people all around.

A sixth-grade girl:

> Bloated corpses were drifting in those seven formerly beautiful rivers; smashing cruelly into bits the childish pleasure of the little girl, the peculiar odor of burning human flesh rose everywhere in the Delta City, which had changed to a waste of scorched earth.

A young ship designer whose response to the bombing was to rush home immediately to Nagasaki:

> I had to cross the river to reach the station. As I came to the river and went down the bank to the water, I found that the stream was filled with dead bodies. I started to cross by crawling over the corpses, on my hands and knees. As I got about a third of the way across, a dead body began to sink under my weight and I went into the water, wetting my burned skin. It pained severely. I

> could go no further, as there was a break in the bridge of corpses, so I turned back to the shore.

A third-grade boy:

> I got terribly thirsty so I went to the river to drink. From upstream a great many black and burned corpses came floating down the river. I pushed them away and drank the water. At the margin of the river there were corpses lying all over the place.

A fifth-grade boy:

> The river became not a stream of flowing water but rather a stream of drifting dead bodies. No matter how much I might exaggerate the stories of the burned people who died shrieking and of how the city of Hiroshima was burned to the ground, the facts would still be clearly more terrible.

Terrible was what a Hachiya patient found beyond the river:

> There was a man, stone dead, sitting on his bicycle as it leaned against a bridge railing. . . . You could tell that many had gone down to the river to get a drink of water and had died where they lay. I saw a few live people still in the water, knocking against the dead as they floated down the river. There must have been hundreds and thousands who fled to the river to escape the fire and then drowned.
>
> The sight of the soldiers, though, was more dreadful than the dead people floating down the river. I came onto I don't know how many, burned from the hips up; and where the skin had peeled, their flesh was wet and mushy. . . .
>
> And they had no faces! Their eyes, noses and mouths had been burned away, and it looked like their ears had melted off. It was hard to tell front from back.

The suffering in the crowded private park of the Asano family was doubled when survivors faced death a second time, another Hachiya confidant saw:

> Hundreds of people sought refuge in the Asano Sentei Park. They had refuge from the approaching flames for a little while, but gradually, the fire forced them nearer and nearer the river, until at length everyone was crowded onto the steep bank overlooking the river. . . .
>
> Even though the river is more than one hundred meters wide along the border of the park, balls of fire were being carried through the air from the opposite shore and soon the pine trees in the park were afire. The poor people faced a fiery death if they stayed in the park and a watery grave if they

> jumped in the river. I could hear shouting and crying, and in a few minutes they began to fall like toppling dominoes into the river. Hundreds upon hundreds jumped or were pushed in the river at this deep, treacherous point and most were drowned.

"Along the streetcar line circling the western border of the park," adds Hachiya, "they found so many dead and wounded they could hardly walk."

The setting of the sun brought no relief. A fourteen-year-old boy:

> Night came and I could hear many voices crying and groaning with pain and begging for water. Someone cried, "Damn it! War tortures so many people who are innocent!" Another said, "I hurt! Give me water!" This person was so burned that we couldn't tell if it was a man or a woman.
>
> The sky was red with flames. It was burning as if scorching heaven.

A fifth-grade girl:

> Everybody in the shelter was crying out loud. Those voices. . . . They aren't cries, they are moans that penetrate to the marrow of your bones and make your hair stand on end. . . .
>
> I do not know how many times I called begging that they would cut off my burned arms and legs.

A six-year-old boy:

> If you think of Brother's body divided into left and right halves, he was burned on the right side, and on the inside of the left side. . . .
>
> That night Brother's body swelled up terribly badly. He looked just like a bronze Buddha. . . .
>
> [At Danbara High School field hospital] every classroom . . . was full of dreadfully burned people who were lying about or getting up restlessly. They were all painted with mercurochrome and white salve and they looked like red devils and they were waving their arms around like ghosts and groaning and shrieking. Soldiers were dressing their burns.

The next morning, remembers a boy who was five years old at the time, "Hiroshima was all a wasted land." The Jesuit, coming in from a suburb to aid his brothers, testifies to the extent of the destruction:

> The bright day now reveals the frightful picture which last night's darkness had partly concealed. Where the city stood, everything as far as the eye could reach is a waste of ashes and ruin. Only several skeletons of buildings completely burned out in the interior remain. The banks of the rivers are covered with dead and wounded, and the rising waters have here and there covered

> some of the corpses. On the broad street in the Hakushima district, naked, burned cadavers are particularly numerous. Among them are the wounded who are still alive. A few have crawled under the burned-out autos and trams. Frightfully injured forms beckon to us and then collapse.

Hachiya corroborates the priest's report:

> The streets were deserted except for the dead. Some looked as if they had been frozen by death while still in the full action of flight; others lay sprawled as though some giant had flung them to their death from a great height. . . .
>
> Nothing remained except a few buildings of reinforced concrete. . . . For acres and acres the city was like a desert except for scattered piles of brick and roof tile. I had to revise my meaning of the word destruction or choose some other word to describe what I saw. Devastation may be a better word, but really, I know of no word or words to describe the view.

The history professor Lifton interviewed is similarly at a loss:

> I climbed Hikiyama Hill and looked down. I saw that Hiroshima had disappeared. . . . I was shocked by the sight. . . . What I felt then and still feel now I just can't explain with words. Of course I saw many dreadful scenes after that—but that experience, looking down and finding nothing left of Hiroshima—was so shocking that I simply can't express what I felt. . . . Hiroshima didn't exist—that was mainly what I saw—Hiroshima just didn't exist.

Without familiar landmarks, the streets filled with rubble, many had difficulty finding their way. For Yōko Ōta the city's history itself had been demolished:

> I reached a bridge and saw that the Hiroshima Castle had been completely leveled to the ground, and my heart shook like a great wave. . . . The city of Hiroshima, entirely on flat land, was made three-dimensional by the existence of the white castle, and because of this it could retain a classical flavor. Hiroshima had a history of its own. And when I thought about these things, the grief of stepping over the corpses of history pressed upon my heart.

Of 76,000 buildings in Hiroshima 70,000 were damaged or destroyed, 48,000 totally. "It is no exaggeration to say," reports the Japanese study, "that the whole city was ruined instantaneously." Material losses alone equaled the annual incomes of more than 1.1 million people. "In Hiroshima many major facilities—prefectural office, city hall, fire departments, police stations, national railroad stations, post offices, telegram and telephone offices, broadcasting station, and schools—were totally demolished

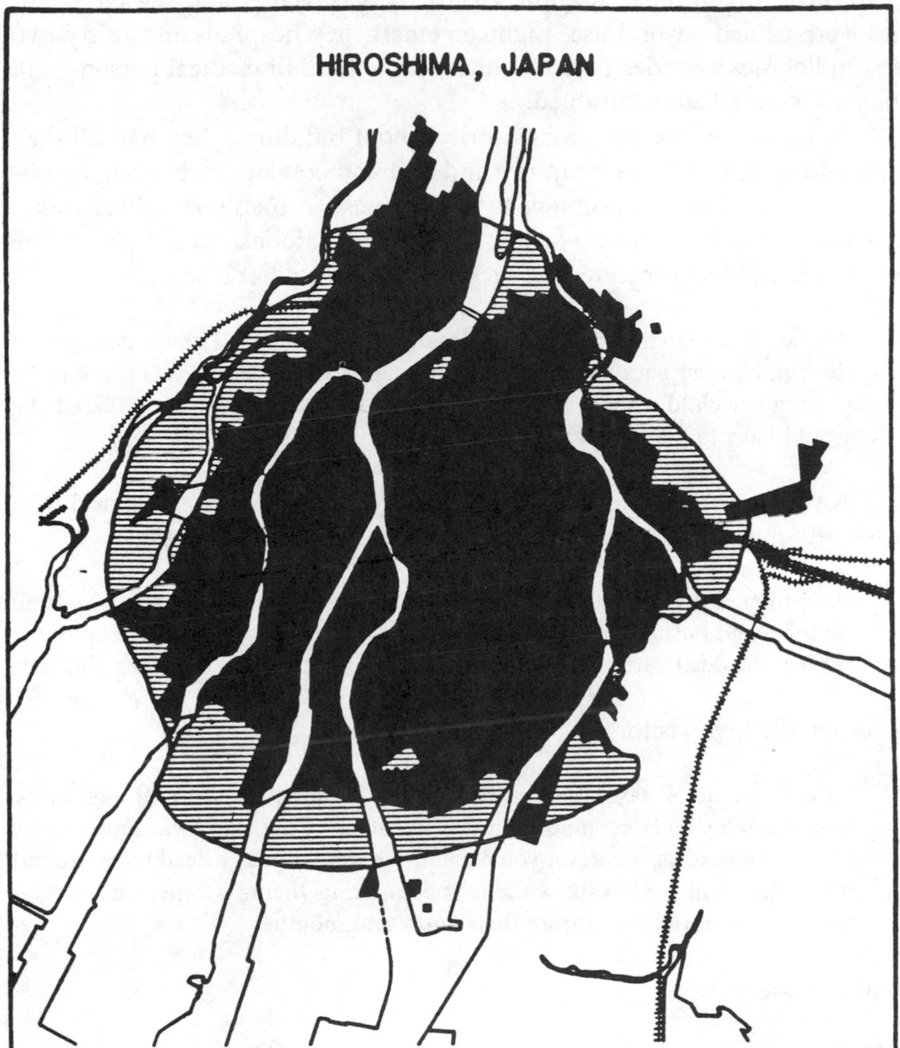
HIROSHIMA, JAPAN
LEGEND
STRUCTURAL (FIRE & BLAST)
STRUCTURAL (BLAST ONLY)
SCALE
MILE
1/2 1/4 0 1/2
U.S. STRATEGIC BOMBING SURVEY
PHYSICAL DAMAGE DIV.
FIGURE 32 B

or burned. Streetcars, roads, and electricity, gas, water, and sewage facilities were ruined beyond use. Eighteen emergency hospitals and thirty-two first-aid clinics were destroyed." Ninety percent of all medical personnel in the city were killed or disabled.

Not many of the survivors worried about buildings; they had all they could do to deal with their injuries and find and cremate their dead, an obligation of particular importance to the Japanese. A man remembers seeing a woman bloody in torn wartime *mompei* pantaloons, naked above the waist, her child strapped to her back, carrying a soldier's helmet:

> [She was] in search of a place to cremate her dead child. The burned face of the child on her back was infested with maggots. I guess she was thinking of putting her child's bones in a battle helmet she had picked up. I feared she would have to go far to find burnable material to cremate her child.

A young woman who had been in charge of a firebreak group and who was badly burned on one shoulder recalls the mass cremations:

> We gathered the dead bodies and made big mountains of the dead and put oil on them and burned them. And people who were unconscious woke up in the piles of the dead when they found themselves burning and came running out.

Another Hachiya visitor:

> After a couple of days, there were so many bodies stacked up no one knew who was who, and decomposition was so extensive the smell was unbearable. During those days, wherever you went, there were so many dead lying around it was impossible to walk without encountering them—swollen, discolored bodies with froth oozing from their noses and mouths.

A first-grade girl:

> On the morning of the 9th, what the soldiers on the clearance team lifted out of the ruins was the very much changed shape of Father. The Civil Defense post [where he worked] was at Yasuda near Kyobashi, in front of the tall chimney that was demolished last year. He must have died there at the foot of it; his head was already just a white skull. . . . Mother and my little sister and I, without thinking, clutched that dead body and wailed. After that Mother went with it to the crematory at Matsukawa where she found corpses piled up like a mountain.

Having moved his hospital sickbed to a second-floor room with blown-out windows that fire had sterilized, Hachiya himself could view and smell the ruins:

> Towards evening, a light southerly wind blowing across the city wafted to us an odor suggestive of burning sardines. . . . Towards Nigitsu was an especially large fire where the dead were being burned by the hundreds. . . . These glowing ruins and the blazing funeral pyres set me to wondering if Pompeii had not looked like this during its last days. But I think there were not so many dead in Pompeii as there were in Hiroshima.

Those who did not die seemed for a time to improve. But then, explains Lifton, they sickened:

> Survivors began to notice in themselves and others a strange form of illness. It consisted of nausea, vomiting, and loss of appetite; diarrhea with large amounts of blood in the stools; fever and weakness; purple spots on various parts of the body from bleeding into the skin . . . inflammation and ulceration of the mouth, throat and gums . . . bleeding from the mouth, gums, throat, rectum, and urinary tract . . . loss of hair from the scalp and other parts of the body . . . extremely low white blood cell counts when those were taken . . . and in many cases a progressive course until death.

Only gradually did the few surviving and overworked Japanese doctors realize that they were seeing radiation sickness; "atomic bomb illness," explains the authoritative Japanese study, "is the first and only example of heavy lethal and momentary doses of whole body irradiation" in the history of medicine. A few human beings had been accidentally overexposed to X rays and laboratory animals had been exposed and sacrificed for study but no large population had ever experienced so extensive and deadly an assault of ionizing radiation before.

The radiation brought further suffering, Hachiya reports in his diary:

> Following the *pika,* we thought that by giving treatment to those who were burned or injured recovery would follow. But now it was obvious that this was not true. People who appeared to be recovering developed other symptoms that caused them to die. So many patients died without our understanding the cause of death that we were all in despair. . . .
>
> Hundreds of patients died during the first few days; then the death rate declined. Now, it was increasing again. . . . As time passed, anorexia [i.e., loss of appetite] and diarrhea proved to be the most persistent symptoms in patients who failed to recover.

Direct gamma radiation from the bomb had damaged tissue throughout the bodies of the exposed. The destruction required cell division to manifest itself, but radiation temporarily suppresses cell division; hence the delayed onset of symptoms. The blood-forming tissues were damaged worst, particularly those that produce the white blood cells that fight infection. Large doses of radiation also stimulate the production of an anti-clotting factor. The outcome of these assaults was massive tissue death, massive hemorrhage and massive infection. "Hemorrhage was the cause of death in all our cases," writes Hachiya, but he also notes that the pathologist at his hospital "found changes in every organ of the body in the cases he . . . autopsied." Liebow reports "evidence of generalization of infection with masses of bacteria in . . . organs as remote from the surface [of the body] as the brain, bone marrow and eye." The operator of a crematorium in the Hiroshima suburbs, a connoisseur of mortality, told Lifton "the bodies were black in color . . . most of them had a peculiar smell, and everyone thought this was from the bomb. . . . The smell when they burned was caused by the fact that these bodies were decayed, many of them even before being cremated—some of them having their internal organs decay even while the person was living." Yōko Ōta raged:

> We were being killed against our will by something completely unknown to us. . . . It is the misery of being thrown into a world of new terror and fear, a world more unknown than that of people sick with cancer.

In the depths of his loss a boy who was a fourth-grader at Hiroshima found words for the unspeakable:

> Mother was completely bedridden. The hair of her head had almost all fallen out, her chest was festering, and from the two-inch hole in her back a lot of maggots were crawling in and out. The place was full of flies and mosquitoes and fleas, and an awfully bad smell hung over everything. Everywhere I looked there were many people like this who couldn't move. From the evening when we arrived Mother's condition got worse and we seemed to see her weakening before our eyes. Because all night long she was having trouble breathing, we did everything we could to relieve her. The next morning Grandmother and I fixed some gruel. As we took it to Mother, she breathed her last breath. When we thought she had stopped breathing altogether, she took one deep breath and did not breathe any more after that. This was nine o'clock in the morning of the 19th of August. At the site of the Japan Red Cross Hospital, the smell of the bodies being cremated is overpowering. Too much sorrow makes me like a stranger to myself, and yet despite my grief I cannot cry.

Not human beings alone died at Hiroshima. Something else was destroyed as well, the Japanese study explains—that shared life Hannah Arendt calls the common world:

> In the case of an atomic bombing . . . a community does not merely receive an impact; the community itself is destroyed. Within 2 kilometers of the atomic

> bomb's hypocenter all life and property were shattered, burned, and buried under ashes. The visible forms of the city where people once carried on their daily lives vanished without a trace. The destruction was sudden and thorough; there was virtually no chance to escape.... Citizens who had lost no family members in the holocaust were as rare as stars at sunrise....
>
> The atomic bomb had blasted and burned hospitals, schools, city offices, police stations, and every other kind of human organization.... Family, relatives, neighbors, and friends relied on a broad range of interdependent organizations for everything from birth, marriage, and funerals to firefighting, productive work, and daily living. These traditional communities were completely demolished in an instant.

Destroyed, that is, were not only men, women and thousands of children but also restaurants and inns, laundries, theater groups, sports clubs, sewing clubs, boys' clubs, girls' clubs, love affairs, trees and gardens, grass, gates, gravestones, temples and shrines, family heirlooms, radios, classmates, books, courts of law, clothes, pets, groceries and markets, telephones, personal letters, automobiles, bicycles, horses—120 war-horses—musical instruments, medicines and medical equipment, life savings, eyeglasses, city records, sidewalks, family scrapbooks, monuments, engagements, marriages, employees, clocks and watches, public transportation, street signs, parents, works of art. "The whole of society," concludes the Japanese study, "was laid waste to its very foundations." Lifton's history professor saw not even foundations left. "Such a weapon," he told the American psychiatrist, "has the power to make everything into nothing."

There remains the question of how many died. The U.S. Army Medical Corps officer who proposed the joint American-Japanese study to Douglas MacArthur thought as late as August 28 that "the total number of casualties reported at Hiroshima is approximately 160,000 of which 8,000 are dead." The Jesuit priest's contemporary reckoning approaches the appalling reality and illuminates further the destruction of the common world:

> How many people were a sacrifice to this bomb? Those who had lived through the catastrophe placed the number of dead at at least 100,000. Hiroshima had a population of 400,000. Official statistics place the number who had died at 70,000 up to September 1st, not counting the missing—and 130,000 wounded, among them 43,500 severely wounded. Estimates made by ourselves on the basis of groups known to us show that the number of 100,000 dead is not too high. Near us there are two barracks, in each of which forty Korean workers lived. On the day of the explosion they were laboring on the streets of Hiroshima. Four returned alive to one barracks and sixteen to the other. Six hun-

> dred students of the Protestant girls' school worked in a factory, from which only thirty or forty returned. Most of the peasant families in the neighborhood lost one or more of their members who had worked at factories in the city. Our next door neighbor, Tamura, lost two children and himself suffered a large wound since, as it happened, he had been in the city on that day. The family of our reader suffered two dead, father and son; thus a family of five members suffered at least two losses, counting only the dead and severely wounded. There died the mayor, the president of the central Japan district, the commander of the city, a Korean prince who had been stationed in Hiroshima in the capacity of an officer, and many other high-ranking officers. Of the professors of the University thirty-two were killed or severely wounded. Especially hard-hit were the soldiers. The Pioneer Regiment was almost entirely wiped out. The barracks were near the center of the explosion.

More recent estimates place the number of deaths up to the end of 1945 at 140,000. The dying continued; five-year deaths related to the bombing reached 200,000. The death rate for deaths up to the end of 1945 was 54 percent, an extraordinary density of killing; by contrast, the death rate for the March 9 firebombing of Tokyo, 100,000 deaths among 1 million casualties, was only 10 percent. Back at the U.S. Army Institute of Pathology in Washington in early 1946 Liebow used a British invention, the Standardized Casualty Rate, to compute that Little Boy produced casualties, including dead, 6,500 times more efficiently than an ordinary HE bomb. "Those scientists who invented the . . . atomic bomb," writes a young woman who was a fourth-grade student at Hiroshima—"what did they think would happen if they dropped it?"

Harry Truman learned of the atomic bombing of Hiroshima at lunch on board the *Augusta* en route home from Potsdam. "This is the greatest thing in history," he told a group of sailors dining at his table. "It's time for us to get home."

Groves called Oppenheimer from Washington on August 6 at two in the afternoon to pass along the news:

> Gen. G: I'm very proud of you and all of your people.
> Dr. O: It went all right?
> Gen. G: Apparently it went with a tremendous bang.
> Dr. O: When was this, was it after sundown?
> Gen. G: No, unfortunately, it had to be in the daytime on account of security of the plane and that was left in the hands of the Commanding General over there. . . .
> Dr. O: Right. Everybody is feeling reasonably good about it and I extend my heartiest congratulations. It's been a long road.

Gen. G: Yes, it has been a long road and I think one of the wisest things I ever did was when I selected the director of Los Alamos.

Dr. O: Well, I have my doubts, General Groves.

Gen. G: Well, you know I've never concurred with those doubts at any time.

If Oppenheimer, who knew nothing yet of the extent of the destruction, was only feeling "reasonably good" about his handiwork, Leo Szilard felt terrible when the story broke. The press release issued from the White House that day called the atomic bomb "the greatest achievement of organized science in history" and threatened the Japanese with "a rain of ruin from the air, the like of which has never been seen on this earth." In Chicago on Quadrangle Club stationery Szilard scribbled a hasty letter to Gertrud Weiss:

> I suppose you have seen today's newspapers. Using atomic bombs against Japan is one of the greatest blunders of history. Both from a practical point of view on a 10-year scale and from the point of view of our moral position. I went out of my way and very much so in order to prevent it but as today's papers show without success. It is very difficult to see what wise course of action is possible from here on.

Otto Hahn, interned with the German atomic scientists on a rural estate in England, was shattered:

> At first I refused to believe that this could be true, but in the end I had to face the fact that it was officially confirmed by the President of the United States. I was shocked and depressed beyond measure. The thought of the unspeakable misery of countless innocent women and children was something that I could scarcely bear.
>
> After I had been given some gin to quiet my nerves, my fellow-prisoners were also told the news. . . . By the end of a long evening of discussion, attempts at explanation, and self-reproaches I was so agitated that Max von Laue and the others became seriously concerned on my behalf. They ceased worrying only at two o'clock in the morning, when they saw that I was asleep.

But if some were disturbed by the news, others were elated, Otto Frisch found at Los Alamos:

> Then one day, some three weeks after [Trinity], there was a sudden noise in the laboratory, of running footsteps and yelling voices. Somebody opened my door and shouted, "Hiroshima has been destroyed!"; about a hundred thousand people were thought to have been killed. I still remember the feeling of

> unease, indeed nausea, when I saw how many of my friends were rushing to the telephone to book tables at the La Fonda Hotel in Santa Fe, in order to celebrate. Of course they were exalted by the success of their work, but it seemed rather ghoulish to celebrate the sudden death of a hundred thousand people, even if they were "enemies."

The American writer Paul Fussell, an Army veteran, emphasizes "the importance of experience, sheer vulgar experience, in influencing one's views about the first use of the bomb." The experience Fussell means is "that of having come to grips, face to face, with an enemy who designs your death":

> I was a 21-year-old second lieutenant leading a rifle platoon. Although still officially in one piece, in the German war I had been wounded in the leg and back severely enough to be adjudged, after the war, 40 percent disabled. But even if my leg buckled whenever I jumped out of the back of the truck, my condition was held to be satisfactory for whatever lay ahead. When the bombs dropped and news began to circulate that [the invasion of Japan] would not, after all, take place, that we would not be obliged to run up the beaches near Tokyo assault-firing while being mortared and shelled, for all the fake manliness of our facades we cried with relief and joy. We were going to live. We were going to grow up to adulthood after all.

In Japan the impasse persisted between civilian and military leaders. To the civilians the atomic bomb looked like a golden opportunity to surrender without shame, but the admirals and the generals still despised unconditional surrender and refused to concur. Foreign Minister Togo continued to pursue Soviet mediation as late as August 8. Ambassador Sato asked for a meeting with Molotov that day; Molotov set the meeting for eight in the evening, then moved it up to five o'clock. Despite earlier notice of the power of the new weapon, news of the devastation of a Japanese city by an American atomic bomb had surprised and shocked Stalin and prompted him to accelerate his war plans; Molotov announced that afternoon to the Japanese ambassador that the Soviet Union would consider itself at war with Japan as of the next day, August 9. Well-armed Soviet troops, 1.6 million strong, waited in readiness on the Manchurian border and attacked the ragged Japanese an hour after midnight.

In the meantime a progaganda effort that originated in the U.S. War Department was developing in the Marianas. Hap Arnold cabled Spaatz and Farrell on August 7 ordering a crash program to impress the facts of atomic warfare on the Japanese people. The impetus probably came from George Marshall, who was surprised and shocked that the Japanese had not immediately sued for peace. "What we did not take into account," he said long afterward, "... was that the destruction would be so complete that it would be an appreciable time before the actual facts of the case would get to Tokyo. The destruction of Hiroshima was so complete that there was no communication at least for a day, I think, and maybe longer."

The Navy and the Air Force both lent staff and facilities, including Radio Saipan and a printing press previously used to publish a Japanese-language newspaper distributed weekly over the Empire by B-29s. The working group that assembled on August 7 in the Marianas decided to attempt to distribute 6 million leaflets to forty-seven Japanese cities with populations exceeding 100,000. Writing the leaflet occupied the group through the night. A historical memorandum prepared for Groves in 1946 notes that the working group discovered in a midnight conference with Air Force commanders "a certain reluctance to fly single B-29's over the Empire, reluctance arising from the fact that enemy opposition to single flights was expected to be increased as the result of the total damage to Hiroshima by one airplane."

The proposed text of the leaflet was ready by morning and was flown from Saipan to Tinian at dawn for Farrell's approval. Groves' deputy edited it and ordered the revised text called to Radio Saipan by inter-island telephone for broadcast to the Japanese every fifteen minutes; radio transmission probably began the same day. The text described the atomic bomb as "the equivalent in explosive power to what 2,000 of our giant B-29's can carry on a single mission," suggested skeptics "make inquiry as to what happened to Hiroshima" and asked the Japanese people to "petition the Emperor to end the war." Otherwise, it threatened, "we shall resolutely employ this bomb and all our other superior weapons." Printing millions of copies of a leaflet took time, and distribution was delayed some hours further by a local shortage of T-3 leaflet bombs. Such was the general confusion that Nagasaki did not receive its quota of warning leaflets until August 10.

Assembly of Fat Man unit F31 was progressing at Tinian in the air-conditioned assembly building designed for that purpose. F31 was the second Fat Man with real high explosives that the Tinian team had assembled; the first, with lower-quality HE castings and a non-nuclear core, unit F33, had been ready since August 5 for a test drop but would not be dropped until August 8 because the key 509th crews were busy delivering Little Boy and being debriefed. The F31 Fat Man, Norman Ramsey writes,

> was originally scheduled for dropping on August 11 local time. . . . However, by August 7 it became apparent that the schedule could be advanced to August 10. When Parsons and Ramsey proposed this change to Tibbets, he expressed regret that the schedule could not be advanced two days instead of

> only one since good weather was forecast for August 9 and the five succeeding days were expected to be bad. It was finally agreed that [we] would try to be ready for August 9 provided all concerned understood that the advancement of the date by two full days introduced a large measure of uncertainty into the probability of meeting such a drastically revised schedule.

One member of the Fat Man assembly team, a young Navy ensign named Bernard J. O'Keefe, remembers the mood of urgency in the Marianas, where the war was still a daily threat:

> With the success of the Hiroshima weapon, the pressure to be ready with the much more complex implosion device became excruciating. We sliced off another day, scheduling it for August 10. Everyone felt that the sooner we could get off another mission, the more likely it was that the Japanese would feel that we had large quantities of the devices and would surrender sooner. We were certain that one day saved would mean that the war would be over one day sooner. Living on that island, with planes going out every night and people dying not only in B-29s shot down, but in naval engagements all over the Pacific, we knew the importance of one day; the *Indianapolis* sinking also had a strong effect on us.

Despite that urgency, O'Keefe adds, August 9 sat less well; "the scientific staff, dog-tired, met and warned Parsons that cutting two full days would prevent us from completing a number of important checkout procedures, but orders were orders."

The young Providence, Rhode Island, native had been a student at George Washington University in 1939 and had attended the conference there on January 25 at which Niels Bohr announced the discovery of fission. Now on Tinian more than six years later, on the night of August 7, it became O'Keefe's task to check out Fat Man for the last time before its working parts were encased beyond easy access in armor. In particular, he was required to connect the firing unit mounted on the front of the implosion sphere with the four radar units mounted in the tail by plugging in a cable inaccessibly threaded around the sphere inside its dural casing:

> When I returned at midnight, the others in my group left to get some sleep; I was alone in the assembly room with a single Army technician to make the final connection. . . .
>
> I did my final checkout and reached for the cable to plug it into the firing unit. It wouldn't fit!
>
> "I must be doing something wrong," I thought. "Go slowly; you're tired and not thinking straight."
>
> I looked again. To my horror, there was a female plug on the firing set

> and a female plug on the cable. I walked around the weapon and looked at the radars and the other end of the cable. Two male plugs. . . . I checked and double-checked. I had the technician check; he verified my findings. I felt a chill and started to sweat in the air-conditioned room.
>
> What had happened was obvious. In the rush to take advantage of good weather, someone had gotten careless and put the cable in backward.

Removing the cable and reversing it would mean partly disassembling the implosion sphere. It had taken most of a day to assemble it. They would miss the window of good weather and slip into the five days of bad weather that had worried Paul Tibbets. The second atomic bomb might be delayed as long as a week. The war would go on, O'Keefe thought. He decided to improvise. Although "nothing that could generate heat was ever allowed in an explosive assembly room," he determined to "unsolder the connectors from the two ends of the cable, reverse them, and resolder them":

> My mind was made up. I was going to change the plugs without talking to anyone, rules or no rules. I called in the technician. There were no electrical outlets in the assembly room. We went out to the electronics lab and found two long extension cords and a soldering iron. We . . . propped the door open so it wouldn't pinch the extension cords (another safety violation). I carefully removed the backs of the connectors and unsoldered the wires. I resoldered the plugs onto the other ends of the cable, keeping as much distance between the soldering iron and the detonators as I could as I walked around the weapon. . . . We must have checked the cable continuity five times before plugging the connectors into the radars and the firing set and tightening up the joints. I was finished.

So, the next day, was Fat Man, the two armored steel ellipsoids of its ballistic casing bolted together through bathtub fittings to lugs cast into the equatorial segments of the implosion sphere, its boxed tail sprouting radar antennae just as Little Boy's had done. By 2200 on August 8 it had been loaded into the forward bomb bay of a B-29 named *Bock's Car* after its usual commander, Frederick Bock, but piloted on this occasion by Major Charles W. Sweeney. Sweeney's primary target was Kokura Arsenal on the north coast of Kyushu; his secondary was the old Portuguese- and Dutch-influenced port city of Nagasaki, the San Francisco of Japan, home of that country's largest colony of Christians, where the Mitsubishi torpedoes used at Pearl Harbor had been made.

Bock's Car flew off Tinian at 0347 on August 9. The Fat Man weaponeer, Navy Commander Frederick L. Ashworth, remembers the flight to rendezvous:

> The night of our takeoff was one of tropical rain squalls, and flashes of lightning stabbed into the darkness with disconcerting regularity. The weather forecast told us of storms all the way from the Marianas to the Empire. Our rendezvous was to be off the southeast coast of Kyushu, some fifteen hundred miles away. There we were to join with our two companion observation B-29s that took off a few minutes behind us.

Fat Man was fully armed at takeoff except for its green plugs, which Ashworth changed to red only ten minutes into the mission so that Sweeney could cruise above the squalls at 17,000 feet, St. Elmo's fire glowing on the propellers of his plane. The pilot soon discovered he would enjoy no reserve of fuel; the fuel selector that would allow him to feed his engines from a 600-gallon tank of gasoline in his aft bomb bay refused to work. He circled over Yakoshima between 0800 and 0850 Japanese time waiting for his escorts, one of which never did catch up. The finger plane at Kokura reported three-tenths low clouds, no intermediate or high clouds and improving conditions, but when *Bock's Car* arrived there at 1044 heavy ground haze and smoke obscured the target. "Two additional runs were made," Ashworth notes in his flight log, "hoping that the target might be picked up after closer observation. However, at no time was the aiming point seen."

Jacob Beser controlled electronic countermeasures on the Fat Man mission as he had done on the Little Boy mission before. He remembers of Kokura that "the Japs started to get curious and began sending fighters up after us. We had some flak bursts and things were getting a little hairy, so Ashworth and Sweeney decided to make a run down to Nagasaki, as there was no sense dragging the bomb home or dropping it in the ocean."

Sweeney had enough fuel left for only one pass over the target before nursing his aircraft to an emergency landing on Okinawa. When he approached Nagasaki he found the city covered with cloud; with his fuel low he could either bomb by radar or jettison a bomb worth several hundred million dollars into the sea. It was Ashworth's call and rather than waste the bomb he authorized a radar approach. At the last minute a hole opened in the cloud cover long enough to give the bombardier a twenty-second visual run on a stadium several miles upriver from the original aiming point nearer the bay. Fat Man dropped from the B-29, fell through the hole and exploded 1,650 feet above the steep slopes of the city at 11:02 A.M., August 9, 1945, with a force later estimated at 22 kilotons. The steep hills confined the larger explosion; it caused less damage and less loss of life than Little Boy.

But 70,000 died in Nagasaki by the end of 1945 and 140,000 altogether

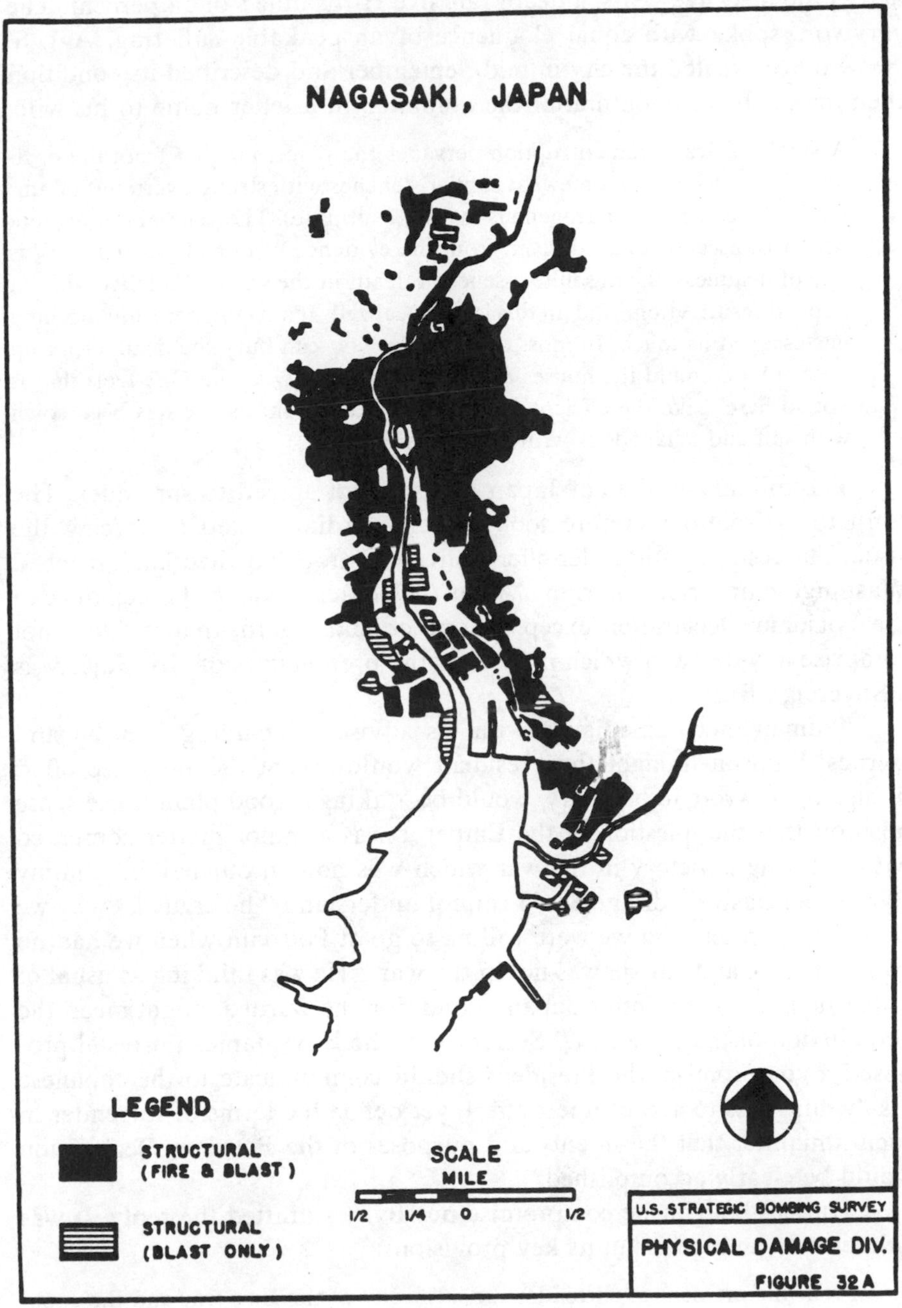
NAGASAKI, JAPAN
LEGEND
STRUCTURAL (FIRE & BLAST)
STRUCTURAL (BLAST ONLY)
SCALE
MILE
1/2 1/4 0 1/2
U.S. STRATEGIC BOMBING SURVEY
PHYSICAL DAMAGE DIV.
FIGURE 32 A

across the next five years, a death rate like Hiroshima's of 54 percent. The survivors spoke with equal eloquence of unspeakable suffering. A U.S. Navy officer visited the city in mid-September and described its condition then, more than a month after the bombing, in a letter home to his wife:

> A smell of death and corruption pervades the place, ranging from the ordinary carrion smell to somewhat subtler stenches with strong overtones of ammonia (decomposing nitrogenous matter, I suppose). The general impression, which transcends those derived from the evidence of our physical senses, is one of deadness, the absolute essence of death in the sense of finality without hope of resurrection. And all this is not localized. It's everywhere, and nothing has escaped its touch. In most ruined cities you can bury the dead, clean up the rubble, rebuild the houses and have a living city again. One feels that is not so here. Like the ancient Sodom and Gomorrah, its site has been sown with salt and ichabod* is written over its gates.

The military leaders of Japan had still not agreed to surrender. The Emperor Hirohito therefore took the extraordinary step of forcing the issue. The resulting surrender offer, delivered through Switzerland, reached Washington on Friday morning, August 10. It acknowledged acceptance of the Potsdam Declaration except in one crucial regard: that it "does not comprise any demand which prejudices the prerogatives of His Majesty as a Sovereign Ruler."

Truman met immediately with his advisers, including Stimson and Byrnes. Stimson thought the President would accept the Japanese offer; doing so, he wrote in his diary, would be "taking a good plain horse sense position that the question of the Emperor was a minor matter compared with delaying a victory in the war which was now in our hands." Jimmy Byrnes persuasively disagreed. "I cannot understand," he argued, "why we should go further than we were willing to go at Potsdam when we had no atomic bomb, and Russia was not in the war." He was thinking as usual of domestic politics; accepting Japan's condition, he warned, might mean the "crucifixion of the President." Secretary of the Navy James Forrestal proposed a compromise: the President should communicate to the Japanese his "willingness to accept [their offer], yet define the terms of surrender in such a manner that the intents and purposes of the Potsdam Declaration would be clearly accomplished."

Truman bought the compromise but Byrnes drafted the reply. It was deliberately ambiguous in its key provisions:

> From the moment of surrender the authority of the Emperor and the Japanese Government to rule the state shall be subject to the Supreme Commander of the Allied Powers. . . .

* "The glory is departed."

> The Emperor and the Japanese High Command will be required to sign the surrender terms. . . .
>
> The ultimate form of government shall, in accordance with the Potsdam Declaration, be established by the freely expressed will of the Japanese people.

Nor did Byrnes hurry the message along; he kept it in hand overnight and only released it for broadcast by radio and delivery through Switzerland the following morning.

Stimson, still trying to bring his Air Force under control, had argued at the Friday morning meeting that the United States should suspend bombing, including atomic bombing. Truman thought otherwise, but when he met with the cabinet that afternoon he had partly reconsidered. "We would keep up the war at its present intensity," Forrestal paraphrases the President, "until the Japanese agreed to these terms, with the limitation however that there will be no further dropping of the atomic bomb." Henry Wallace, the former Vice President who was now Secretary of Commerce, recorded in his diary the reason for the President's change of mind:

> Truman said he had given orders to stop the atomic bombing. He said the thought of wiping out another 100,000 people was too horrible. He didn't like the idea of killing, as he said, "all those kids."

The restriction came none too soon. Groves had reported to Marshall that morning that he had gained four days in manufacture and expected to ship a second Fat Man plutonium core and initiator from New Mexico to Tinian on August 12 or 13. "Provided there are no unforeseen difficulties in manufacture, in transportation to the theatre or after arrival in the theatre," he concluded cautiously, "the bomb should be ready for delivery on the first suitable weather after 17 or 18 August." Marshall told Groves the President wanted no further atomic bombing except by his express order and Groves decided to hold up shipment, a decision in which Marshall concurred.

The Japanese government learned of Byrnes' reply to its offer of conditional surrender not long after midnight on Sunday, August 12, but civilian and military leaders continued to struggle in deadlocked debate. Hirohito resisted efforts to persuade him to reverse his earlier commitment to surrender and called a council of the imperial family to collect pledges of support from the princes of the blood. The Japanese people were not yet told of the Byrnes reply but knew of the peace negotiations and waited in suspense. The young writer Yukio Mishima found the suspense surreal:

> It was our last chance. People were saying that Tokyo would be [atomic-bombed] next. Wearing white shirts and shorts, I walked about the streets. The people had reached the limits of desperation and were now going about their affairs with cheerful faces. From one moment to the next, nothing happened. Everywhere there was an air of cheerful excitement. It was just as though one was continuing to blow up an already bulging toy balloon, wondering: "Will it burst now? Will it burst now?"

Strategic Air Forces commander Carl Spaatz cabled Lauris Norstad on August 10 proposing "placing [the] third atomic bomb . . . on Tokyo," where he thought it would have a salutary "psychological effect on government officials." On the other hand, continuing area incendiary bombing disturbed him; "I have never favored the destruction of cities as such with all inhabitants being killed," he confided to his diary on August 11. He had sent off 114 B-29's on August 10; because of bad weather and misgivings he canceled a mission scheduled for August 11 and restricted operations thereafter to "attacks on military targets visually or under very favorable blind bombing conditions." American weather planes over Tokyo were no longer drawing anti-aircraft fire; Spaatz thought that fact "unusual."

The vice chief of the Japanese Navy's general staff, the man who had conceived and promoted the kamikaze attacks of the past year that had added to American bewilderment and embitterment at Japanese ways, crashed a meeting of government leaders on the evening of August 13 with tears in his eyes to offer "a plan for certain victory": "sacrifice 20,000,000 Japanese lives in a special [kamikaze] attack." Whether he meant the 20 million to attack the assembled might of the Allies with rocks or bamboo spears the record does not reveal.

A B-29 leaflet barrage forced the issue the next morning. Leaflet bombs showered what remained of Tokyo's streets with a translation of Byrnes' reply. The Lord Keeper of the Privy Seal knew such public revelation would harden the military against surrender. He carried the leaflet immediately to the Emperor and just before eleven that morning, August 14, Hirohito assembled his ministers and counselors in the imperial air raid shelter. He told them he found the Allied reply "evidence of the peaceful and friendly intentions of the enemy" and considered it "acceptable." He did not specifically mention the atomic bomb; even that terrific leviathan submerged in the general misery:

> I cannot endure the thought of letting my people suffer any longer. A continuation of the war would bring death to tens, perhaps even hundreds, of thousands of persons. The whole nation would be reduced to ashes. How then could I carry on the wishes of my imperial ancestors?

He asked his ministers to prepare an imperial rescript—a formal edict—that he might broadcast personally to the nation. The officials were not legally bound to do so—the Emperor's authority lay outside the legal structure of the government—but by older and deeper bonds than law they were bound, and they set to work.

In the meantime Washington had grown impatient. Groves was asked on August 13 about "the availability of your patients together with the time estimate that they could be moved and placed." Stimson recommended proceeding to ship the nuclear materials for the third bomb to Tinian. Marshall and Groves decided to wait another day or two. Truman ordered Arnold to resume area incendiary attacks. Arnold still hoped to prove that his Air Force could win the war; hc called for an all-out attack with every available B-29 and any other bombers in the Pacific theater and mustered more than a thousand aircraft. Twelve million pounds of high-explosive and incendiary bombs destroyed half of Kumagaya and a sixth of Isezaki, killing several thousand more Japanese, even as word of the Japanese surrender passed through Switzerland to Washington.

The first hint of surrender reached American bases in the Pacific by radio in the form of a news bulletin from the Japanese news agency Dōmei at 2:49 P.M. on August 14—1:49 A.M. in Washington:

> Flash! Flash! Tokyo, Aug. 14—It is learned an imperial message accepting the Potsdam Proclamation is forthcoming soon.

The bombers droned on even after that, but eventually that day the bombs stopped falling. Truman announced the Japanese acceptance in the afternoon. There were last-minute acts of military rcbellion in Tokyo—a high officer assassinated, an unsuccessful attempt to steal the phonograph recording of the imperial rescript, a brief takeover of a division of Imperial Guards, wild plans for a coup. But loyalty prevailed. The Emperor broadcast to a weeping nation on August 15; his 100 million subjects had never heard the high, antique Voice of the Crane before:

> Despite the best that has been done by everyone . . . the war situation has developed not necessarily to Japan's advantage, while the general trends of the world have all turned against her interest. Moreover, the enemy has begun to employ a new and most cruel bomb, the power of which to do damage is indeed incalculable, taking the toll of many innocent lives. . . . This is the reason why We have ordered the acceptance of the provisions of the Joint declaration of the Powers. . . .
>
> The hardships and sufferings to which Our nation is to be subjected hereafter will be certainly great. We are keenly aware of the inmost feelings of all

ye, Our subjects. However, it is according to the dictate of time and fate that We have resolved to pave the way for a grand peace for all generations to come by enduring the unendurable and suffering what is insufferable. . . .

Let the entire nation continue as one family from generation to generation.

"If it had gone on any longer," writes Yukio Mishima, "there would have been nothing to do but go mad."

"An atomic bomb," the Japanese study of Hiroshima and Nagasaki emphasizes, ". . . is a weapon of mass slaughter." A nuclear weapon is in fact a total-death machine, compact and efficient, as a simple graph prepared from Hiroshima statistics demonstrates:

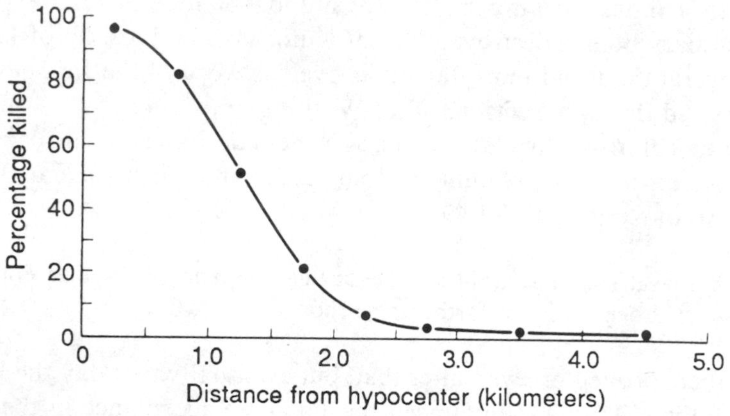

The percentage of people killed depends simply on distance from the hypocenter; the relation between death percentage and distance is inversely proportional and the killing, as Gil Elliot emphasizes, is no longer selective:

> By the time we reach the atom bomb, Hiroshima and Nagasaki, the ease of access to target and the instant nature of macro-impact mean that both the choice of city and the identity of the victim has become completely randomized, and human technology has reached the final platform of self-destructiveness. The great cities of the dead, in numbers, remain Verdun, Leningrad and Auschwitz. But at Hiroshima and Nagasaki the "city of the dead" is finally transformed from a metaphor into a literal reality. The city of the dead of the future is our city and its victims are—not French and German soldiers, nor Russian citizens, nor Jews—but all of us without reference to specific identity.

"The experience of these two cities," the Japanese study emphasizes, "was the opening chapter to the possible annihilation of mankind."

On August 24, having recently heard about the man holding an eyeball, Dr. Michihiko Hachiya suffered a nightmare. Like the myth of the Sphinx—destruction to those who cannot answer its riddle, whom ignorance or inattention or arrogance misleads—the dream of this Japanese doctor who was wounded in the world's first atomic bombing and who ministered to hundreds of victims must be counted one of the millennial visions of mankind:

> The night had been close with many mosquitoes. Consequently, I slept poorly and had a frightful dream.
>
> It seems I was in Tokyo after the great earthquake and around me were decomposing bodies heaped in piles, all of whom were looking right at me. I saw an eye sitting on the palm of a girl's hand. Suddenly it turned and leaped into the sky and then came flying back towards me, so that, looking up, I could see a great bare eyeball, bigger than life, hovering over my head, staring point blank at me. I was powerless to move.

"I awakened short of breath and with my heart pounding," Michihiko Hachiya remembers.

So do we all.

Epilogue

The atomic bombing of Hiroshima and Nagasaki horrified Leo Szilard. He felt a full measure of guilt for the development of such terrible weapons of war; the shape of things to come that he had first glimpsed as he crossed Southampton Row in Bloomsbury in 1933 had found ominous residence in the world partly at his invitation. In the petition to the President that he had circulated among the atomic scientists in July 1945—the petition Edward Teller in consultation with Robert Oppenheimer had decided not to sign, writing Szilard he felt "that I should do the wrong thing if I tried to say how to tie the little toe of the ghost to the bottle from which we just helped it to escape"—Szilard had argued that large moral responsibilities devolved upon the United States in consequence of its possession of the bomb:

> The development of atomic power will provide the nations with new means of destruction. The atomic bombs at our disposal represent only the first step in this direction, and there is almost no limit to the destructive power which will become available in the course of their future development. Thus a nation which sets the precedent of using these newly liberated forces of nature for purposes of destruction may have to bear the responsibility of opening the door to an era of devastation on an unimaginable scale.

The United States set that precedent in Japan; Szilard wrote Gertrud Weiss his despairing August 6 letter saying it was difficult to see what wise course of action was possible after that; but within days he was moving to protest and debate. Upon hearing of the Nagasaki bombing he immediately asked the chaplain of the University of Chicago to include a special prayer for the dead and a collection for the survivors of the two Japanese cities in any service commemorating the end of the war. He drafted a second petition to the President calling the atomic bombings "a flagrant violation of our own moral standards" and asking that they be stopped. The Japanese surrender mooted the issue and the petition was never sent.

Besides White House and War Department press releases the United States government immediately published a detailed report on the scientific aspects of atomic bomb development, in preparation during the preceding year by Princeton physicist Henry DeWolf Smyth. *Atomic Energy for Military Purposes* was another faded echo of Niels Bohr's appeal for openness. It appalled the British, enlightened the Soviets on which approaches to isotope separation not to pursue and—Groves' intention in releasing it— defined what might be public and what secret about the atomic bomb program, thereby forestalling information leaks.

With the atomic secret, such as it was, made public Szilard went to see the Chicago chancellor, Robert Maynard Hutchins, "and told him that something needed to be done to get thoughtful and influential people to think about what the bomb might mean to the world, and how the world and America could adjust to its existence. I proposed that the University of Chicago call a three-day meeting and assemble about twenty-five of the best men to discuss the subject." Hutchins liked the idea and began contacting twice that many participants, including Henry Wallace, Tennessee Valley Authority chairman David E. Lilienthal, the ubiquitous Charles Lindbergh and a number of academics and scientists. The meeting took shape for late September.

The day after the Nagasaki bombing Ernest Lawrence had flown to New Mexico, partly to escape newspaper reporters clamoring for interviews, partly to work with Oppenheimer on a report on postwar planning that the Interim Committee had solicited from its Scientific Panel. The inventor of the cyclotron, who approved of the use of the bombs to avoid invasion and force a Japanese surrender, found his Los Alamos colleague weary, guilty and depressed. Oppenheimer wondered if the dead at Hiroshima and Nagasaki were not luckier than the survivors, whose exposure to the bombs would have lifetime effects. His mood that weekend found expression during the next weeks in letters. "You will believe that this undertaking has not been without its misgivings," he wrote his former Ethical

Culture School teacher Herbert Smith, the confessor of his youth; "they are heavy on us today, when the future, which has so many elements of high promise, is yet only a stone's throw from despair." To Haakon Chevalier, his friend at Berkeley in Depression days, Oppenheimer repeated that "the circumstances are heavy with misgiving, and far, far more difficult than they should be, had we power to remake the world to be as we think it."

Lawrence could muster only limited patience for Oppenheimer's remorse. He thought the atomic bomb a "terrible swift sword" that would end the war and might succeed in "ending all wars." He also seems to have claimed it as his own. "In one newspaper interview out of many published the day after Hiroshima," notes Stanislaw Ulam mischievously, "E. O. Lawrence 'modestly admitted,' according to the interviewer, 'that he more than anyone else was responsible for the atomic bomb.' "

From secret participants in a top-secret project the two men and their colleagues had emerged as public heroes, the artificers of a military revolution. "With the discovery of fission," C. P. Snow comments, ". . . physicists became, almost overnight, the most important military resource a nation-state could call upon." The letter on postwar planning that the Berkeley and Los Alamos directors polished that last weekend of the war tried out their new authority; in it the members of the Interim Committee Scientific Panel—Lawrence, Oppenheimer, Compton, Fermi—set aside merely technical advice to propose a radical rethinking of national policy. In doing so they began to outline the nuclear dilemma as they understood it.

They were convinced, they wrote, "that weapons quantitatively and qualitatively far more effective than now available will result from further work on these problems." (Among such weapons they thought the "technical prospects of the realization of the super bomb" to be "quite favorable.") They could not, however, "devise or propose effective military countermeasures for atomic weapons" and it was their "firm opinion that no military countermeasures will be found." They were not only "unable to outline a program that would assure this nation for the next decades hegemony in the field of atomic weapons," but were "equally unable to insure that such hegemony, if achieved, could protect us from the most terrible destruction." What followed, they thought, was the necessity of *political* change:

> The development, in the years to come, of more effective atomic weapons, would appear to be a most natural element in any national policy of maintaining our military forces at great strength; nevertheless we have grave doubts that this further development can contribute essentially or permanently to the prevention of war. We believe that the safety of this nation—as opposed to its ability to inflict damage on an enemy power— cannot lie

> wholly or even primarily in its scientific or technical prowess. It can be based only on making future wars impossible. It is our unanimous and urgent recommendation to you that, despite the present incomplete exploitation of technical possibilities in this field, all steps be taken, all necessary international arrangements be made, to this one end.

Oppenheimer had discovered such convictions in his discussions with Bohr, but Lawrence had advised the Interim Committee only two months earlier to build up stockpiles. For a time at the end of the war the reality of the bomb seems to have moved the Berkeley laureate to at least limited internationalism. "There is no doubt in my mind," he wrote during this period, "that the best channel of information about what is going on in Russia would be developed by encouraging free interchange of science and scientists. In fact it is the only avenue I can think of that has a reasonable chance of working."

Oppenheimer carried the Scientific Panel's letter to Washington a few days after the surrender and found Henry Stimson out of town. He talked instead to Stimson's aide George L. Harrison and to Vannevar Bush. "I emphasized of course that all of us would earnestly do whatever was really in the national interest, no matter how desperate and disagreeable," he wrote Lawrence after he returned to New Mexico; "but that we felt reluctant to promise that much real good could come of continuing the atomic bomb work—just like poison gases after the last war." But no more than Leo Szilard before him was Oppenheimer successful at influencing policy from outside the political process, whatever his newfound authority as a consultant:

> I had the fairly clear impression from the talks [with Harrison and Bush] that things had gone badly at Potsdam, and that little or no progress had been made in interesting the Russians in collaboration or control. I don't know how seriously an effort was made: apparently neither Churchill nor Attlee nor Stalin was any help at all, but this is only my conjecture. While I was in Washington two things happened, both rather gloomy: the President issued an absolute Ukase, forbidding any disclosures on the atomic bomb—and the terms were broad—without his personal approval. The other was that Harrison took our letter to [Jimmy] Byrnes, who sent back word just as I was leaving that "in the present critical international situation there was no alternative to pushing the [Manhattan Project] program full steam ahead." . . .I do not come away from [i.e., I still feel] a profound grief, and a profound perplexity about the course we should be following.

The Conference on Atomic Energy Control at the University of Chicago convened on a Thursday and Friday in late September. David Lilienthal kept shorthand notes; their highlights reveal remarkable prescience among the participants, as does Szilard's memory of the event. Jacob Viner, an influential University of Chicago economist, told the conference that the atomic bomb was the cheapest way yet devised of killing human beings. With two giants, he argued—the Soviet Union and the United States—world government would be impossible. "Degree of peace we have had in the past two or three centuries," Lilienthal noted of Viner's comments, "has been due to uncertainty as to who was your natural enemy. . . . Now no ambiguity as to target, where there are only two giants. Already having psychological effects in this country." Viner thought "atomic bomb warfare more largely a war of nerves. . . . Psychological warfare begins when two countries have atomic bombs. . . Believes atomic bomb will be peacemaking in effect; deterrent effect—the cost when it is used against you." Only five weeks after the first use of nuclear weapons in war Viner had ferreted out the essential principle of deterrence, of the balance of terror in a nuclear-armed world.

Szilard presented his ideas to the group on Friday. He emphasized that the bombs would get bigger, bypassing secrecy by quoting a public statement of Mark Oliphant's to the effect that weapons "corresponding to one million and to ten million tons of TNT . . . are entirely possible." Of Szilard's talk Lilienthal noted:

> We are in an armament race.
>
> If Russia starts making atomic bombs in two or three years—perhaps five or six years—then we have an armed peace, and it will be a durable peace.
>
> But we will not have permanent peace at lesser cost than world government. But this cannot come without changed loyalty of people. If we can't have that, all we can have is a durable peace [i.e., deterrence]. Only purpose of a durable peace would be to create conditions 20–30 years from now [that] can bring about world peace. That requires shift of loyalties.
>
> If we are *sure* to get a Third World War, the later it comes the worse for us.
>
> Victor of next war will *make* a world government, even if that victor should be the United States, having lost 25 million people dead.

Szilard himself came to believe his predictions unimpressive. He thought Viner did better:

> The wisest remarks that were made at this meeting were made by Jake Viner, and what he said was this: "None of these things will happen. There will be no preventive war, and there will be no international agreement involving inspection. America will be in [sole] possession for a number of years, and the

> bomb will exert a certain subtle influence; it will be present at every diplomatic conference in the consciousness of the participants and will exert its effect. Then, sooner or later, Russia will also have the bomb, and then a new equilibrium will establish itself."

No longer shackled to Army secrecy, Leo Szilard would continue and increase his participation in the political life of his adopted country. But whether from guilt, or because nuclear physics no longer seemed to him a frontier, or because he had come to understand that the liberation of atomic energy was far more likely to enable man to destroy the earth than to leave it behind for the stars—the cause for which he had taken up studying the nucleus in the first place—he closed the loop he opened in 1932, went off in 1947 to Cold Spring Harbor Laboratory on Long Island to audit the phage course offered there and turned away from physics to biology.

H. G. Wells lived to know of Hiroshima and Nagasaki. Deeply pessimistic in his final years, he died at eighty on August 13, 1946.

Immediately after Trinity Edward Teller and Enrico Fermi had renewed theoretical work on the problem of thermonuclear ignition. "The end sought," explains the Los Alamos technical history, "was a bomb burning about a cubic meter of liquid deuterium. For such a bomb the energy release will be about ten million tons of TNT." But with the Japanese surrender hydrogen bomb studies at Los Alamos temporarily slowed and stopped. General Groves, Oppenheimer would testify later, "was unclear whether his mandate and therefore mine extended to fiddling with this next project. I so reported to the people in the laboratory, who were thinking about it." Teller, frustrated, suspected his colleagues had "[lost] their appetites for weapons work." Some had. Most simply wanted to go home. "We all felt," Hans Bethe remembers, "that, like the soldiers, we had done our duty and that we deserved to return to the type of work that we had chosen as our life's career, the pursuit of pure science and teaching. . . . Moreover, it was not obvious in [1945 and] 1946 that there was any need for a large effort on atomic weapons in peacetime."

Teller passionately disagreed. "He expressed himself as terribly pessimistic about relations with Russia," Bethe remembers of a conversation the two theoreticians had that winter. "He was terribly anti-communist, terribly anti-Russian. Now I knew that he had been anti-communist during the communist takeover in Hungary when he was about eleven, but now it came out in a much more forceful way. Teller said we had to continue research on nuclear weapons . . . it was really wrong of all of us to want to leave. The war was not over and Russia was just as dangerous an enemy as

Germany had been. I just couldn't go along with that. I thought it was more important to go home and get the universities restarted, to train young physicists again."

Bethe was returning to Cornell. Oppenheimer had offers from every direction; he turned down Harvard in late September, believing, he wrote James Bryant Conant, "that I would like to go back to California for the rest of my days." Fermi had accepted appointment to the faculty of the University of Chicago. Teller had been invited to work at Fermi's side. Leaving Los Alamos would mean leaving the Super to others, but staying at Los Alamos would mean becoming part of what Oppenheimer, free once more to indulge in casual cruelty, was calling the second team.

Norris Bradbury, the vigorous Berkeley-trained Navy physicist who had organized the assembly of the Trinity bomb, was replacing Oppenheimer as director. "In the months immediately following the war," Bradbury recalled in 1948, "the Laboratory struggled for existence and there is no better way to put it":

> Here was Los Alamos in September, 1945. The senior civilian scientists, weary of living under wartime conditions, under wartime security, on a wartime Army post, and under conditions of wartime urgency, thought longingly of their academic laboratories and classrooms. The more junior civilians thought of the academic degrees they did not have and the further education they ought to have. . . .
>
> There was even no agreement as to what sort of future should be planned for Los Alamos. There was one school of thought which held that Los Alamos should become a monument, a ghost laboratory, and that all work on the military use of atomic energy should cease. Another group looked with increasing pessimism on the deterioration of our international relations and contended that Los Alamos should become a factory for atomic weapons. The majority agreed that, for the present at least, the United States required a research laboratory devoted to the study of fundamental nuclear physics and chemistry and their possible application to military use.

Bradbury asked Teller to continue at Los Alamos as head of the Theoretical Division, the position Teller had believed he deserved when the laboratory was founded and that Oppenheimer had given to Bethe. Teller would sign on only if Bradbury promised major commitment in return. "I said we either should make a great effort to build a hydrogen bomb in the shortest possible time or develop new models of fission explosives and speed progress by at least a dozen [weapons] tests a year. Bradbury said he would like to see either program, but that neither was realistic. There no longer was governmental support for weapons work. No one was interested." Either the new director was misinformed or Teller misrepresents his position; Jimmy Byrnes had charged Oppenheimer only a few weeks earlier to maintain "full steam ahead." The immediate postwar problem at Los Alamos was not lack of support but lack of authority. The Army had run the Manhattan Project in wartime. Now the work needed congressional authorization and funding, and that was slow in coming because it depended on legislation dealing with atomic energy, a revolutionary new field. "To demand, as Teller did as a condition of his staying," writes Bethe, "that Los Alamos tackle the super-bomb on a large scale, or plan for twelve tests a year on fission bombs, was plainly unrealistic to say the least."

Teller went looking for Oppenheimer, "seeking his advice and support":

> I told him about my conversation with Bradbury, and then said: "This has been your laboratory, and its future depends on you. I will stay if you will tell me that you will use your influence to help me accomplish either of my goals, if you will help enlist support for work toward a hydrogen bomb or further development of the atomic bomb."
>
> Oppenheimer's reply was quick: "I neither can nor will do so."
>
> It was obvious and clear to me that Oppenheimer did not want to support further weapons work in any way. It was equally obvious that only a man of Oppenheimer's stature could arouse governmental interest in either program. I was not willing to work without backing, and told Oppenheimer that I would go to Chicago. He smiled: "You are doing the right thing."

Deke Parsons gave a party that night. Teller says Oppenheimer sought him out and asked him, "Now that you have decided to go to Chicago, don't you feel better?" Teller complained that he did not feel better; he felt that their work had been only a beginning. "We have done a wonderful job here," Oppenheimer countered, "and it will be many years before anyone can improve on our work in any way." The insensitivity of the remark rankled Teller as its ambiguity confused him. He would quote it frequently in the years after 1945, always to demonstrate its self-deception. It might have meant: the Soviets will not soon build a bomb. Or it might have meant: the Oppenheimer team had accomplished in fission development what a Teller team could not soon improve in thermonuclear development. Teller would read it both ways and like neither reading.

His immediate response was to take his problem to Fermi. Fermi apparently argued with him, consistent with the Interim Committee Scientific Panel letter of August 17, that the solution to the problem of nuclear weapons must be a political solution. Fermi thought Teller was overly optimistic as well about the early prospects for a successful thermonuclear. Not only was thermonuclear burning itself a hard problem; the atomic bomb would also have to be better understood and considerably improved before it could be made efficient enough to serve as a thermonuclear trigger. But the two men were good friends, and Fermi encouraged Teller to write him a letter expressing his dissent; he would be happy to pass it along to the Secretary of War for the Interim Committee file.

A year earlier, in the midst of war, James Bryant Conant had visited Los Alamos and talked to Teller about the Super. Teller had predicted then, as Conant reported to Vannevar Bush, that the Super was "probably at least as distant now as was the fission bomb when . . . I first heard of the enterprise." That estimate—between four and five years—was already optimistic compared to Fermi's. Now, in October 1945, Teller set it as an upper limit. He also first stated for the record many of the arguments for pursuing technological security that he would elaborate in the decades to come.

"When," he asked in the question-and-answer format he adopted, "could the first super bomb be tried out?" He answered with two numbers, the second an early example of what has come to be called threat inflation:

> It is my belief that five years is a conservative estimate of this time. This assumes that the development will be pursued with some vigor. The job, however, may be much easier than expected and may take no more than two years. In considering future dangers it is important not to disregard this eventuality.

How soon could another country produce such a superbomb? Faster than the United States, Teller apparently thought, despite his adopted nation's commanding technological and industrial lead: "The time needed . . . may not be much longer than the time needed by them to produce an atomic bomb."

What about moral objections? They were meaningless before the onrush of technology:

> There is among my scientific colleagues some hesitancy as to the advisability of this development on the grounds that it might make the international problems even more difficult than they are now. My opinion is that this is a fallacy. If the development is possible, it is out of our powers to prevent it.

Teller thought that civil defense measures such as the dispersal of cities might prove effective against atomic bombs but "very much less so against super bombs." He could not yet offer detailed plans for the peaceful use of thermonuclear explosives. "But I consider it a certainty that the super bomb will allow us to extend our power over natural phenomena far beyond anything we can at present imagine."

He filed his dissent as he prepared to depart Los Alamos. Teller was not one to fight for lost causes. He might have stayed, but the first team was leaving. His wife was expecting their second child. He packed his grand piano and moved to a professorship at the University of Chicago to do physics with Enrico Fermi. For a few years he would find security in family and teaching and research.

General Leslie R. Groves traveled to Los Alamos in mid-October to present a certificate of appreciation to the laboratory from the Secretary of War. "Under a brilliant New Mexico sky," Alice Kimball Smith remembers, "virtually the entire population of the mesa assembled for the outdoor ceremony" on October 16, Oppenheimer's last day as director. He still thought he would return to California and to teaching, but accepting the certificate he struck the theme that would occupy the next full decade of his life:

> It is our hope that in years to come we may look at this scroll, and all that it signifies, with pride.
>
> Today that pride must be tempered with a profound concern. If atomic bombs are to be added as new weapons to the arsenals of a warring world, or to the arsenals of nations preparing for war, then the time will come when mankind will curse the names of Los Alamos and Hiroshima.
>
> The peoples of the world must unite, or they will perish. This war, that has ravaged so much of the earth, has written these words. The atomic bomb has spelled them out for all men to understand. Other men have spoken them, in other times, of other wars, of other weapons. They have not prevailed. There are some, misled by a false sense of human history, who hold that they will not prevail today. It is not for us to believe that. By our works we are committed, committed to a world united, before the common peril, in law, and in humanity.

Besides the certificate the men and women of Los Alamos each received a memento that day: a sterling-silver pin the size of a dime stamped with a large letter *A* framing the small word BOMB. Before Oppenheimer rushed off to Washington to testify on atomic energy to House and Senate committees a newspaper reporter asked him if the atomic bomb had any significant limitations. "The limitations lie in the fact that you don't want to be on the receiving end of one," he quipped. Then he ventured prophecy: "If you ask: 'Can we make them more terrible?' the answer is yes. If you ask: 'Can we make a lot of them?' the answer is yes. If you ask: 'Can we make them terribly more terrible?' the answer is probably." *Time* featured the remarks in its International section at the end of the month with a photograph of Oppenheimer holding a pipe and looking persuasive. He was "the smartest of the lot," the newsmagazine quoted an unnamed colleague on his behalf. The public romance had begun.

I. I. Rabi returned to Columbia University, Eugene Wigner to Princeton, Luis Alvarez, Glenn Seaborg and Emilio Segrè to Berkeley, George Kistiakowsky to Harvard. Victor Weisskopf went to MIT. Stanislaw Ulam briefly and unhappily tried UCLA, then came back to Los Alamos. James Chadwick and most of the British Mission returned to Great Britain with pockets full of secrets. In September the British had given a formal farewell party for their friends on the Hill, the Brobdingnagian log cabin of Fuller Lodge jammed with men in black tie and even white tie and tails and women in long gowns not completely aired of mothballs. Genia Peierls had cooked buckets of thick soup; steak and kidney pie was served on paper plates; Winifred Moon supplied several hundred paper cartons of trifle, a dessert which she swore she would never look upon again without nausea. The Oppenheimers and the Peierlses sat at high table above the fray (the Chadwicks had not come out from Washington) and the convivial and sometimes bibulous James Tuck served as toastmaster. After dinner, Bernice Brode notes, the British staged an original pantomime based on *Babes in the Woods:*

> Good Uncle Winnie had sent his Babes to join forces with Good Uncle Franklin, to out-wit Bad Uncles Adolf and Benito. All that befell the children on their hazardous journey to the Unknown Desert was acted out by the entire Mission. . . . The end, the grand finale was a re-enacting of the [Trinity] test, with [a stepladder for] a high tower from which a pail of stuff was overturned making flashes and bangs and clatters for several minutes. This was not entirely comprehensible to many of the women, but made a tremendous hit with the men, particularly some of the details of the bangs. It was indeed a real smash hit.

Later they cleared the floor and danced, as they had danced so many Saturday nights in that strange wilderness retreat through the long years of war.

Niels Bohr, resettled in the Carlsberg House of Honor in Copenhagen, wrote Oppenheimer on November 9:

> I was very sorry that I should not see you again before my return to Denmark, but, due to difficulties in arranging passage for Margrethe and me, we could not, as we had intended to, return to U.S.A. before the secret of the project was lifted, and then it was thought advisable that I no longer postponed my return to Denmark.

> I need not say how often Aage and I think of all the kindness you and Kitty showed us in these last eventful years, where your understanding and sympathy have meant so much to me, and how closely I feel connected with you in the hope that the great accomplishment may contribute decisively to bringing about harmonious relationships between nations. . . .
>
> I trust that the whole matter is developing in a favorable way.

It was not, as Bohr knew; there was loud talk in the United States of an atomic "secret" that America would keep and protect. How little might be secret was revealed that autumn and early winter in a series of reports of Soviet stirrings in the field. The War Department learned in the middle of September, writes the historian Herbert Feis, "that the Soviet authorities were compelling the commanders of the Czechoslovak Army to give orders that all German plans, parts, models and formulas regarding the use of atomic energy, rocket weapons, and radar be turned over to them. Russian infantry and technical troops occupied Jachimov . . . and St. Joachimstal, the town and the factory—the only place in central Europe where at this time uranium was being produced." The old mine from the residues of which Martin Klaproth had first isolated the heavy gray metal he named uranium, the mine young Robert Oppenheimer had explored on a walking tour in 1921, had fallen into Soviet hands.

An attaché at the U.S. Embassy in Moscow warned on December 24 that "the U.S.S.R. is out to get the atomic bomb. This has been officially stated. The meager evidence available indicates that great efforts are being made and that super-priority will be given to the enterprise." At home was incomprehension, Herbert York remembers: "To most . . . of us, Russia was as mysterious and remote as the other side of the moon and not much more productive when it came to really new ideas or inventions. A common joke of the time said that the Russians could not surreptitiously introduce nuclear bombs in suitcases into the United States because they had not yet been able to perfect a suitcase." But if American leaders did not believe the Soviet Union could soon achieve an atomic bomb, what it would do otherwise and what were its motives had become a matter of intense debate within the U.S. government.

Tragically, that debate obscured the deeper issue then confronting the world for the first time in history. Robert Oppenheimer had testified before Congress; he had begun to work his way into the corridors of power; now, on a stormy Friday night at the beginning of November 1945, he stepped forward to examine the nuclear dilemma publicly. Freed from the constraints of the Los Alamos directorship he spoke to five hundred members of the Association of Los Alamos Scientists, a new political organization, crowded into the larger movie theater on the Hill. An unrevised transcript preserves his words much as his listeners heard them; thunder above the mesa orchestrated his bare reconnaissance. It framed anew the prospects Bohr had revealed and defined limitations and opportunities that have persisted into the present.

"I should like to talk tonight—if some of you have long memories perhaps you will regard it as justified—as a fellow scientist," Oppenheimer began with humor, "and at least as a fellow worrier about the fix we are in." Involved, he thought, were "issues which are quite simple and quite deep." One of those issues for him was *why* scientists had built the atomic bomb. He listed a number of motives: fear that Nazi Germany would build it first, hope that it would shorten the war, curiosity, "a sense of adventure," or so that the world might know "what can be done . . . and deal with it." But he thought the basic motivation was moral and political:

> When you come right down to it the reason that we did this job is because it was an organic necessity. If you are a scientist you cannot stop such a thing. If you are a scientist you believe that it is good to find out how the world works; that it is good to find out what the realities are; that it is good to turn over to mankind at large the greatest possible power to control the world and to deal with it according to its lights and its values. . . .
>
> It is not possible to be a scientist unless you believe that the knowledge of the world, and the power which this gives, is a thing which is of intrinsic value to humanity, and that you are using it to help in the spread of knowledge, and are willing to take the consequences.

The defining trust in the value of knowledge that Oppenheimer ascribes here to science echoes Bohr's succinct formulation of the value of openness: "The very fact that knowledge is itself the basis of civilization points directly to openness as the way to overcome the present crisis." Long before them Thomas Jefferson, secure in his understanding of the core principles of democracy, professed a similar conviction. "I know no safe depository of the ultimate powers of the society but the people themselves," he wrote late in life; "and if we think them not enlightened enough to exercise that control with a wholesome discretion, the remedy is not to take it from them, but to inform their discretion."

Oppenheimer went on to examine the political changes he believed the new weapons challenged mankind to explore:

> But I think the advent of the atomic bomb and the facts which will get around that they are not too hard to make, that they will be universal if people wish to make them universal, that they will not constitute a real drain on the economy

> of any strong nation, and that their power of destruction will grow and is already incomparably greater than that of any other weapon—I think these things create a new situation, so new that there is some danger, even some danger in believing, that what we have is a new argument for arrangements, for hopes, that existed before this development took place. By that I mean that much as I like to hear advocates of a world federation, or advocates of a United Nations organization, who have been talking of these things for years—much as I like to hear them say that here is a new argument, I think that they are in part missing the point, because the point is not that atomic weapons constitute a new argument. There have always been good arguments. The point is that atomic weapons constitute also a field, a new field, and a new opportunity for realizing preconditions. I think when people talk of the fact that this is not only a great peril, but a great hope, this is what they should mean . . .[:] the simple fact that in this field, because it is a threat, because it is a peril . . . there exists a possibility of realizing, of beginning to realize, those changes which are needed if there is to be any peace.
>
> Those are very far-reaching changes. They are changes in the relations between nations, not only in spirit, not only in law, but also in conception and feeling. I don't know which of these is prior; they must all work together, and only the gradual interaction of one or the other can make a reality. I don't agree with those who say the first step is to have a structure of international law. I don't agree with those who say the only thing is to have friendly feelings. All of these things will be involved. I think it is true to say that atomic weapons are a peril which affects everyone in the world, and in that sense a completely common problem, as common a problem as it was for the Allies to defeat the Nazis.

Solving that common problem, he continued, could serve as "a pilot plant for a new type of international collaboration":

> I speak of it as a pilot plant because it is quite clear that the control of atomic weapons cannot be in itself the unique end of such operation. The only unique end can be a world that is united, and a world in which war will not occur.

Half a century of circumscribed and often cynical negotiations for arms control has not altered Oppenheimer's essential point, which was Bohr's hopeful vision first of the complementarity of the bomb.

Next he discussed what Bohr would have called the necessity of renunciation. Oppenheimer offered an American analogy:

> The one point I want to hammer home is what an enormous change in spirit is involved. There are things which we hold very dear, and I think rightly hold

> very dear; I would say that the word democracy perhaps stood for some of them as well as any other word. There are many parts of the world in which there is no democracy. There are other things which we hold dear, and which we rightly should. And when I speak of a new spirit in international affairs I mean that even to these deepest of things which we cherish, and for which Americans have been willing to die—and certainly most of us would be willing to die—even in those deepest things, we realize that there is something more profound than that; namely, the common bond with other men everywhere. It is only if you do that that this makes sense; because if you approach the problem and say, "We know what is right and we would like to use the atomic bomb to persuade you to agree with us," then you are in a very weak position. . . .
>
> I want to express the utmost sympathy with the people who have to grapple with this problem and in the strongest terms to urge you not to underestimate its difficulty. I can think of an analogy. . . : in the days in the first half of the nineteenth century there were many people, mostly in the North, but some in the South, who thought that there was no evil on earth more degrading than human slavery, and nothing that they would more willingly devote their lives to than its eradication. Always when I was young I wondered why it was that when Lincoln was President he did not declare that the war against the South, when it broke out, was a war that slavery should be abolished, that this was the central point, the rallying point, of that war. Lincoln was severely criticized by many of the Abolitionists as you know, by many then called radicals, because he seemed to be waging a war which did not hit the thing that was most important. But Lincoln realized, and I have only in the last months come to appreciate the depth and wisdom of it, that beyond the issue of slavery was the issue of the community of the people of this country, and the issue of the Union. . . . In order to preserve the Union Lincoln had to subordinate the immediate problem of the eradication of slavery—and trust—and I think if he had had his way it would have gone so—to the conflict of these ideas in a united people to eradicate it.

For such understanding Oppenheimer celebrated Bohr, "who was here so much during the difficult days, who had many discussions with us, and who helped us reach the conclusion [that a universal renunciation of the use of force] was not only a desirable solution, but that it was the unique solution, that there were no other alternatives."

Little more in Oppenheimer's talk that stormy night carries weight down the years: practical matters of legislation, counsel to his fellow scientists to accept responsibility for the consequences of their work. In closing he delivered a final burst of realism about a timetable for change:

> I'm not sure that the greatest opportunities for progress do not lie somewhat further in the future than I had for a long time thought. . . .

> The plain fact is that in the actual world, and with the actual people in it, it has taken time, and it may take longer, to understand what this is all about. And I'm not sure, as I have said before, that in other lands it won't take longer than it does in this country.

These basic questions engaged men in 1945; they engage us still, as if the clock had stopped while only the machinery of armament with terrible and terribly more terrible weapons has kept on running.

Edward Teller returned to Los Alamos in April 1946 to chair a secret conference. Its purpose, according to a subsequent report, was "to review work that has been done on the Super for completeness and accuracy and to make suggestions concerning further work that would be needed in this field if actual construction and test of the Super were planned." John von Neumann, Stanislaw Ulam and Norris Bradbury attended the conference, as did Emil Konopinski, John Manley, Philip Morrison, Canadian theoretician J. Carson Mark and a crowd of other participants. One whose presence would vitally affect U.S. nuclear weapons policy later was Klaus Fuchs.

The Super conference examined only one design for a thermonuclear weapon, the design Teller and his group had developed during the war, the so-called classical Super, with an estimated explosive force of 10 million tons TNT equivalent—10 megatons. The ingredients for the classical Super would be an atomic bomb, a cubic meter of liquid deuterium and an indefinite amount of the rare second isotope of hydrogen, tritium, which because of its short 12.26-year half-life does not normally exist in nature but can be created in a nuclear reactor by bombarding lithium with neutrons. How these components would have been arranged in the classical Super is still secret: probably spherically, the fission trigger and hydrogen isotopes physically contiguous and contained within a heavy tamper.

"It is likely," the conference decided on the basis of the Teller group's calculations, "that a super-bomb can be constructed and will work. Definite proof of this can hardly ever be expected and a final decision can be made only by a test of the completely assembled super-bomb." The conference called for "a detailed calculation" to study mathematically the probable progress of the explosion (the hand calculations that Teller and his group had made to arrive at the classical Super were necessarily, given the complexity of the problem, rough and incomplete). The conference also found that Teller's design was "on the whole workable." Some participants had doubts; "should the doubts prove well-founded, simple modifications of the design will render the model feasible." In conclusion:

> The undertaking of the new and important Super Bomb project would necessarily involve a considerable fraction of the resources which are likely to be devoted to work on atomic developments in the next years. . . . We feel it appropriate to point out that further decision in a matter so filled with the most serious implications as is this one can properly be taken only as part of the highest national policy.

In June 1946, three months after the Super conference, the U.S. nuclear weapons stockpile consisted of only nine Fat Man bombs, of which no more than seven could be made operational for lack of initiators. The stockpile held only thirteen bombs a year later, two years after the end of the war. Plutonium production was the crucial bottleneck. The high neutron flux of the Hanford production piles had proven damaging. One had been unloaded in May to prevent further damage and the other damped back to 80 percent of its full capacity. Anything Los Alamos could do, therefore, to improve fission bomb design would significantly bolster the U.S. nuclear arsenal at a time of increasing conflict with the Soviet Union. Nevertheless, about half the Theoretical Division's time between 1946 and 1950 went to the Super. Atomic bombs by then were a matter more of engineering than of theoretical physics, to be sure, but the complexities of the thermonuclear problem also tantalized.

There ensued a curious period of optimism in Teller's life. His wife Mici bore him a second child, a daughter, in the summer of 1946 and he found more time for his family. He was caught up again in the grandeur and the deeply satisfying creativity of basic science. "The years after Los Alamos," writes Eugene Wigner, "and until the renewal of his preoccupation with national security, were perhaps Teller's most fruitful years scientifically." Teller taught, co-authored thirteen scientific papers, regularly visited Los Alamos to consult, wrote articles for the new *Bulletin of the Atomic Scientists.* In the *Bulletin* he called for an end to secrecy where "purely scientific data" are concerned. He praised as "ingenious, daring and basically sound" the Acheson-Lilienthal Report that became the basis of the Baruch Plan for international control of nuclear weapons that the United States offered to the United Nations in 1946. He recognized the absolutes of the absolute weapon in April 1946, the same month as the Super conference, in a surprising profession of faith: "Nothing that we can plan as a defense for the next generation is likely to be satisfactory; that is, nothing but world-union."

A year later he still saw no defense against atomic weapons. He described with compassionate horror the terrible devastation of Hiroshima: "One is struck by the picture of fires raging unopposed, wounds remaining unattended, sick men killing themselves with the exertions of helping their fellows." It was even possible to imagine, he wrote, "that the effects of an atomic war will endanger the survival of man." He thought in December 1947, in the wake of Soviet rejection of the Baruch Plan, that "agreement with the Russians still seems possible"; the Danes, he noted waggishly, were once similarly imperialistic and ambitious. "We must now work for world law and world government. . . . Even if Russia should not join immediately, a successful, powerful, and patient world government may secure their cooperation in the long run. . . . We [scientists] have two clear-cut duties: to work on atomic energy and to work for world government which alone can give us freedom and peace."

The extreme swings in Edward Teller's outlook remain somewhat mysterious. The British theoretician Freeman Dyson, then one of Teller's students, wrote his family from postwar Chicago that his teacher, whom he liked and admired, was nevertheless "a good example of the saying that no man is so dangerous as an idealist." The emotional timbre of Teller's Chicago-period writing differs notably from his later work. It is less choleric and more optimistic, of course, but a deeper difference is that it is informed by a much greater degree of trust in his fellow man and in the possibility that human institutions might serve to restrain the conflicts of nations. Even Russia became, for a time, "this fabulous monster," not the threatening presence Teller described to Bethe in 1945 and would invoke with increasing urgency in the years after 1949: "World government," he wrote in the *Bulletin* as late as July 1948, "is our only hope for survival. . . . I believe that we should cease to be infatuated with the menace of this fabulous monster, Russia. Our present necessary task of opposing Russia should not cause us to forget that in the long run we cannot win by working against something. We must work for something. We must work for World Government." The reasons for this difference of attitude must be partly personal and inaccessible, perhaps even to the man himself. But it would appear from subsequent events that a crucial reason for Teller's sense of security in the immediate postwar years was America's sole possession of the atomic bomb.

But hardly anyone was listening. The Cold War had begun in earnest. Oppenheimer had found his way into the high councils of government; now director of the Institute for Advanced Study at Princeton and chairman of the scientific General Advisory Committee of the newly established U.S. Atomic Energy Commission, he was internationally famous, a household name. A plaintive footnote in a 1948 Teller *Bulletin* review of the first year's work of the Atomic Energy Commission reveals the Hungarian physicist's isolation from power in those days: "Due to the limited experience of the author the account is necessarily incomplete."

In the early summer of 1949 Teller returned to Los Alamos on leave of absence from Chicago. He did not easily wrench himself away. Oppenheimer had sought him out and encouraged him; Bradbury had then sent a delegation that included Stanislaw Ulam to invite him back. He said later he went because he had decided that his writing, public speaking and political action were less than productive and that "the best contribution I could make would be to go back to Los Alamos to help develop weapons—something I knew about and that could yield concrete results." He was undoubtedly influenced by the Soviet coup in Czechoslovakia in the winter of 1948, by the blockade of Berlin that began the following summer and by the impending Communist victory over Nationalist forces in China. A more personal challenge was the fate of Hungary, which had briefly experienced democratic government once more as a republic under the protection of the Allied Control Commission. But the Red Army remained in occupation and by 1948 the Communist Party had maneuvered itself into power. A one-slate election on May 15, 1949, finished the job. Teller's father, mother, sister and nephew had survived the destruction of Hungarian Jewry and still lived in Budapest. Now they were cut off from him.

Teller was thus back at weapons work when Harry Truman announced, on September 23, 1949, the explosion of Joe I, the first Soviet atomic bomb. Like most Americans, Teller had not expected the Soviet success so soon. He called Oppenheimer on the day the Soviet test was announced in a state of arousal sufficient to cause Oppenheimer to advise him sharply, "Keep your shirt on." He testified later that his mind "did not immediately turn in the direction of working on the thermonuclear bomb," but in fact he discussed that prospect intensely at Los Alamos early in October with Ernest Lawrence and Luis Alvarez, who encouraged him. The American nuclear monopoly had ended. The fabulous monster had real claws. If the Soviet Union had tested an atomic bomb, could a Soviet hydrogen bomb be far behind? Teller decided that the only possible hope for continued national security was an all-out American effort to build the Super.

The first concrete act of the United States government in response to the Soviet Union's demonstrated mastery of explosive fission was to approve, in October 1949, a program to expand the production of uranium and plutonium. In the meantime a secret debate raged within the government: what should the United States do? Herbert York, at the time a Teller protégé, describes the debate's constituents:

> Especially considering the enormity of the issue—and most of those involved were fully aware of its enormity—the participants in the secret debate were

> very few: the members of the GAC [the AEC's General Advisory Committee], the members of the AEC and a few of their staff, the members of the [Senate and House Joint Committee on Atomic Energy] and a few of their staff, a very few top officials in the Defense Department, and a very small group of concerned scientists. . . . Altogether, there were less than one hundred people, most of whom thought of themselves—probably correctly—as being involved in making one of the most fateful decisions of all time.

Another crucial figure in the debate was Dean Acheson, now Secretary of State. Truman listened to Acheson, Secretary of Defense Louis Johnson and the Joint Chiefs of Staff more than he listened to the scientists. The Joint Chiefs told Truman, without much staff evaluation, that a Soviet H-bomb would be "intolerable." So, in as many words, did Acheson. None of the groups that participated in the debate studied the possibility that the result of the American initiative might be an arms race. The H-bomb appeared to its supporters to offer a return to nuclear superiority. On January 31, 1950, Truman announced in favor of proceeding to develop it.

Teller took the President's decision as a personal victory. Since at least the September afternoon of Oppenheimer's blunt advice to keep his shirt on he seems to have felt that his fellow physicist was personally attempting to impede him. Oppenheimer was chairman of the GAC, which had been asked in October to advise the AEC commissioners in the matter. Teller went to Washington to lobby past that committee. Among others he talked to Kenneth D. Nichols, now a general and with Groves' retirement the Army's resident nuclear weapons expert. One autumn Sunday morning on Nichols' front porch Teller argued so emotionally that Nichols finally challenged him: "Edward, why are you worrying about the situation so much?" "I'm not really worrying about the situation," Nichols remembers Teller responding; "I'm worrying about the people who should be worrying about it."

The GAC met on October 29 and 30 (Oppenheimer, Conant, Fermi, Rabi, Caltech president Lee DuBridge, metallurgist Cyril Smith, Bell Laboratories president Oliver E. Buckley, engineer Hartley Rowe, Glenn Seaborg absent). It recommended in response to the Soviet achievement that the AEC look further into increasing the production of fissionable materials. It called for "an intensification of efforts to make atomic weapons available for tactical purposes." It proposed building facilities to produce more neutrons for weapons research and development. And it strongly recommended pursuing an existing Los Alamos program to use small quantities of tritium in atomic bombs to "boost" those bombs to more efficient and more powerful explosions (an invention that was successfully tested in May 1951).

But the committee also recommended against pursuing "with high priority the development of the super bomb." It based its recommendation on essentially two arguments: that at ten megatons a Super would be a weapon of mass destruction only, with no other apparent military use; and that it would not obviously improve the security of the United States. It would not do so, in particular, because the design then under consideration—the design reviewed at the Super conference in 1946, Teller's design, the classical Super—looked as if it would require large amounts of tritium, and plutonium and tritium, both created in nuclear reactors, would compete for existing plant capacity. Tritium was as well eighty times as expensive to make, gram for gram, as plutonium. The U.S. nuclear stockpile in late 1949 consisted of about two hundred atomic bombs. Slowing production of bombs that worked for a new weapon that might not work made no sense to the scientists and engineers of the GAC. As Oppenheimer summarized in later testimony, "The [H-bomb] program we had in 1949 was a tortured thing that you could well argue did not make a great deal of technical sense. It was therefore possible to argue also that you did not want it even if you could have it."

The GAC members divided themselves into a majority and a minority to write explanatory annexes to their October 30 report. Conant drafted the majority annex, which Oppenheimer, DuBridge, Rowe, Smith and Buckley signed. It said that a Super "might become a weapon of genocide." It said such a bomb "should never be produced. . . . To the argument that the Russians may succeed in developing this weapon, we would reply that our undertaking it will not prove a deterrent to them. Should they use the weapon against us, reprisals by our large stock of atomic bombs would be comparably effective to the use of a super." Rabi drafted the minority annex, which he and Fermi signed. It argued that the H-bomb question might serve as a springboard for new arms-control efforts. It described the Super as "a weapon which in practical effect is almost one of genocide," then for good measure went even further in condemnation: "It is an evil thing considered in any light."

Teller had been the leading proponent of this enormously powerful weapon since before Pearl Harbor. His Manhattan Project colleagues on the GAC—Oppenheimer, Conant, Fermi, Rabi, Smith—had encouraged him and even worked alongside him. Nothing was said then of evil, of genocide. They who had won high position building weapons used in the mass destruction of two Japanese cities now condemned another, more ingenious weapon. They who were scientists and understood that kindling a sustained thermonuclear reaction on the earth was a historic experiment in fundamental physics proposed the indefinite postponement of that experiment, thus probably handing the triumph gratuitously to the Russians. A courier delivered a copy of the committee's report to Los Alamos in advance of a delegation of interested congressmen who had already seen it. With AEC chairman David Lilienthal's approval, John Manley, associate director of the laboratory and executive secretary of the GAC, showed it to division heads, including Teller. "Edward was of course just completely aghast," Manley recalls, "and his reaction was to offer me a bet that if we did not proceed immediately with a crash program on the Super, he would be a prisoner of war of the Russians in the United States."

Teller explained his reaction to a *Time-Life* interviewer in 1954, using an ironic variation of the argument he accepted from Oppenheimer in 1945 when he rejected Szilard's petition:

> The reasons they gave just made me mad. . . . The important thing in any science is to do the things that can be done. Scientists naturally have a right and a duty to have opinions. But their science gives them no special insight into public affairs. There is a time for scientists and movie stars and people who have flown the Atlantic to restrain their opinions lest they be taken more seriously than they should be.

It is sometimes difficult even for other scientists to remember that the atomic and hydrogen bombs were developed not only as weapons of terrible destruction. They were also, as Fermi once said, "superb physics."

At the time of the Truman announcement, J. Carson Mark headed the Theoretical Division at Los Alamos. "Truman's words," Mark comments, "didn't necessarily mean we did anything much different from what we had been doing because we really didn't know how to make a gadget that would work as a hydrogen bomb." In February 1950, when Washington learned that for seven crucial years, from 1942 to 1949, Klaus Fuchs had passed along secret information to the Soviet Union, Truman turned to a special committee of the National Security Council for advice. The committee recommended that the President clarify his somewhat vague January 31 directive to put energetic development of a hydrogen bomb clearly on record. It emphasized at the same time that there was no obvious way to speed up the weapons test schedule and no guarantee of success. Truman promulgated the committee's report as official policy.

The necessary next step toward a workable thermonuclear weapon was elaborate mathematical simulation. Without a mathematical model of the evolution of thermonuclear burning from a fission trigger event, Mark explains, "no conclusive evidence was possible short of a successful stab in the dark, since a [test] failure would not necessarily establish unfeasibility, but possibly only that the system chosen [Teller's classical Super, for example] was unsuitable." The Super problem, as the simulation came to be called, was the largest mathematical effort ever undertaken up to that time, "vastly larger," writes Stanislaw Ulam, "than any astronomical calculation done to that date on hand computers." It involved calculating the blooming of a thermonuclear explosion—its heating, its extremely complex hydrodynamics, its evolving physical reactions—in progressive increments of less than one ten-millionths of a second. The 1946 Super conference had called for such calculations, but until the further development of the electronic computer they simply could not be accomplished in any reasonable period of time. Teller said as much in a September 1947 report, discussing choosing between his classical Super and an alternative design: "I think that the decision whether considerable effort is to be put on the development of the TX-14 or the Super should be postponed for approximately two years; namely, until such time as these experiments, tests, and calculations have been carried out."

In late 1949, before the H-bomb decision, Los Alamos began detailed work preparing a machine calculation for the first primitive electronic computer, the ENIAC at the Aberdeen Proving Grounds in Maryland. After the H-bomb decision Ulam and the Theoretical Division's Cornelius J. Everett decided to go ahead by hand with a simplified version of the calculation. "We started to work each day for four to six hours with slide rule, pencil, and paper," Ulam remembers, "making frequent quantitative guesses. . . . Much of our work was done by guessing values of geometrical factors, imagining intersections of solids, estimating volumes, and estimating chances of points escaping. We did this repeatedly for hours, liberally sprinkling the guesses with constant slide-rule calculations. It was long and arduous work." They were calculating part 1 of a two-part problem, trying to see if a fission trigger heating a specified amount of deuterium and tritium would start a thermonuclear reaction. Teller's group had calculated a cruder version of part 1 between 1944 and 1946. By February 1950 Ulam saw that the amount of tritium Teller had estimated earlier was not nearly sufficient. "The result of the calculations," Ulam reported, "seems to be that the model considered is a fizzle." He increased the estimated tritium volume and began again. Even with more tritium Teller's classical Super looked distinctly unpromising. Late in April Ulam went off to Princeton to discuss his pessimistic results with von Neumann and Fermi. The three men talked with Oppenheimer as well; Ulam noticed that he "seemed rather glad to learn of the difficulties."

Ulam returned to Los Alamos and broke the news to Teller. "He was pale with fury yesterday literally," Ulam reported to von Neumann—"but I think is calmed down today." Teller at first refused to believe the calculations. He also questioned Ulam's motives for performing them; according to the official AEC history it was necessary for von Neumann to offer Teller "reassurances that the motives behind the changes [in tritium estimates] were constructive." Ironically, Ulam had favored building the Super from the beginning.

The Super problem went on the ENIAC on schedule in June. The evolving results confirmed Ulam's and Everett's findings. "In the course of the calculation," Ulam recalls, "in spite of an initial, hopeful-looking 'flare up,' the whole assembly started slowly to cool down. Every few days Johnny [von Neumann] would call in some results. 'Icicles are forming,' he would say dejectedly." At the same time Ulam and Fermi, who was visiting Los Alamos for the summer, began hand-calculating the next phase of the Super problem, which concerned the propagation of the initial thermonuclear reaction. That work, says Ulam, "turned out to be basic to the technology of thermonuclear explosions." It also predicted that Teller's Super would fizzle. The Super was simply a bad design, Hans Bethe explains, a dead end:

> That Ulam's calculations had to be done at all was proof that the H-bomb project was not ready for a "crash" program when Teller first advocated such a program in the Fall of 1949. Nobody will blame Teller because the calculations of 1946 were wrong, especially because adequate computing machines were not then available. But he was blamed at Los Alamos for leading the Laboratory, and indeed the whole country, into an adventurous program on the basis of calculations which he himself must have known to have been very incomplete. The technical skepticism of the GAC on the other hand had turned out to be far more justified than the GAC itself had dreamed in October 1949.

Between October 1950 and January 1951, Bethe goes on, Teller "was desperate. . . . He proposed a number of complicated schemes to save [the classical Super], none of which seemed to show much promise. It was evident that he did not know of any solution." He was nevertheless unwilling to retrench. He wanted most of the laboratory's time for at least another year and a half. He did not know how to make a thermonuclear, he told the GAC at an October meeting, but he was convinced it could be done. He insisted that the bottleneck was a lack of theoreticians at Los Alamos and a lack of imagination. If the Greenhouse tests of thermonuclear feasibility scheduled for the spring of 1951 at Eniwetok atoll in the Marshall Islands proved a hydrogen bomb impossible, he concluded, Los Alamos might be strong enough to continue; if the tests proved a bomb possible, the laboratory might not be strong enough to follow through. Teller's assessment won him few friends at Los Alamos.

Severe stress can be creative. So can long familiarity with a problem. By February 1951 Ulam was angry with Teller and Teller was angry with everyone. The result was a novel, entirely unexpected invention. Not even Teller had anticipated it. Bethe supplies a context for lay assessment: "The new concept was to me, who had been rather closely associated with the program, about as surprising as the discovery of fission had been to physicists in 1939." The concept has come to be called the Teller-Ulam configuration.

Afterward Teller would variously deny, acknowledge and claim credit for Ulam's contribution. Ulam would consistently acknowledge Teller's part but quietly insist upon his own. Others—Lothar Nordheim of the Theoretical Division, Herbert York—confirm, as Nordheim wrote in 1954 to the *New York Times,* that "a general principle was formulated by Dr. Stanislaw Ulam in collaboration with Teller, who shortly afterward gave it its technically practical form." Teller's most nearly generous acknowledgment appears in his 1955 essay "The Work of Many People": "Two signs of hope came within a few weeks: one sign was an imaginative suggestion by Ulam; the other sign was a fine calculation by [physicist Frederick] de Hoffmann." His unwillingness consistently to acknowledge Ulam's contribution, in contradiction of scientific ethics, suggests the importance he attached to historic rank in the matter. He came to dislike being called "the father of the H-bomb," but asserted his paternity in 1954 with a curiously explicit allegory of his on-again, off-again relationship with Los Alamos:

> It is true that I am the father in [the] biological sense that I performed a necessary function and let nature take its course. After that a child had to be born. It might be robust or it might be stillborn, but *something* had to be born. The process of conception was by no means a pleasure; it was filled with difficulty and anxiety for both parties. My act . . . aroused the emotions associated with such behavior.

Bethe sifts the evidence the other way, drolly tongue-in-cheek: "I used to say that Ulam was the father of the hydrogen bomb and Edward was the mother, because he carried the baby for quite a while."

The mechanism of the Teller-Ulam H-bomb was revealed in general terms in an official Los Alamos publication in 1983, on the occasion of the fortieth anniversary of the laboratory's founding:

> The first megaton-yield explosives (hydrogen bombs) were based on the application of x-rays produced by a primary nuclear device to compress and ignite a physically distinct secondary nuclear assembly. The process by which the time-varying radiation source is coupled to the secondary is referred to as radiation transport.

Stanislaw Ulam's basic contribution appears to have emerged from a closer look at the early development of the fission fireball, which initially radiates most of its energy as X rays. These, traveling at the speed of light, advance outward ahead of any shock wave. The classical Super and other previous designs presumably tried to pack the entire mass of thermonuclear material into the evolving fission explosion to heat it hydrodynamically—more spheres within spheres, a fatter and unworkable Fat Man. Those designs always promised to blow apart before thermonuclear burning could make much headway. Ulam suddenly realized, it seems, that if the thermonuclear materials were *physically separated* from the fission primary, the enormous flux of X rays coming off the primary might be applied somehow to start thermonuclear burning in the brief fraction of a second before the slower shock wave caught up and blew everything apart.

Ulam and Teller proceeded to develop Ulam's idea. The X rays from the primary might heat the thermonuclear secondary directly (as microwaves heat food in a microwave oven) but they could not squeeze it efficiently to the greater density that would promote fusion. Some other material would need to intervene. It turned out that ordinary plastic would serve. Dump so large a flux of X rays into a layer of dense plastic foam wrapped around a cylindrical stick of thermonuclear materials and the plastic would heat instantaneously to a plasma—a hot, ionized gas—expanding explosively at pressures thousands of times more intense than the pressures high explosives can generate. So a fission primary—a little Fat Man, no larger in today's efficient weapons than a soccer ball—might occupy one end of an evacuated cylindrical casing. Farther along the casing a layer of plastic might wrap a cylindrical arrangement of thermonuclear material. Fire the primary and the X-ray flux would radiate into the plastic at the speed of light, much faster than the expanding fission shock wave coming up behind. Configuring the plastic would be much simpler than configuring high-explosive lenses; the light-swift X rays would irradiate it simultaneously along its entire length and the resulting implosion would be beautifully symmetrical.

That, to the extent that continuing secrecy allows its reconstruction, is probably what Ulam first conceived and Teller made practical. Though it was the necessary breakthrough, it was not the end of invention. Even with

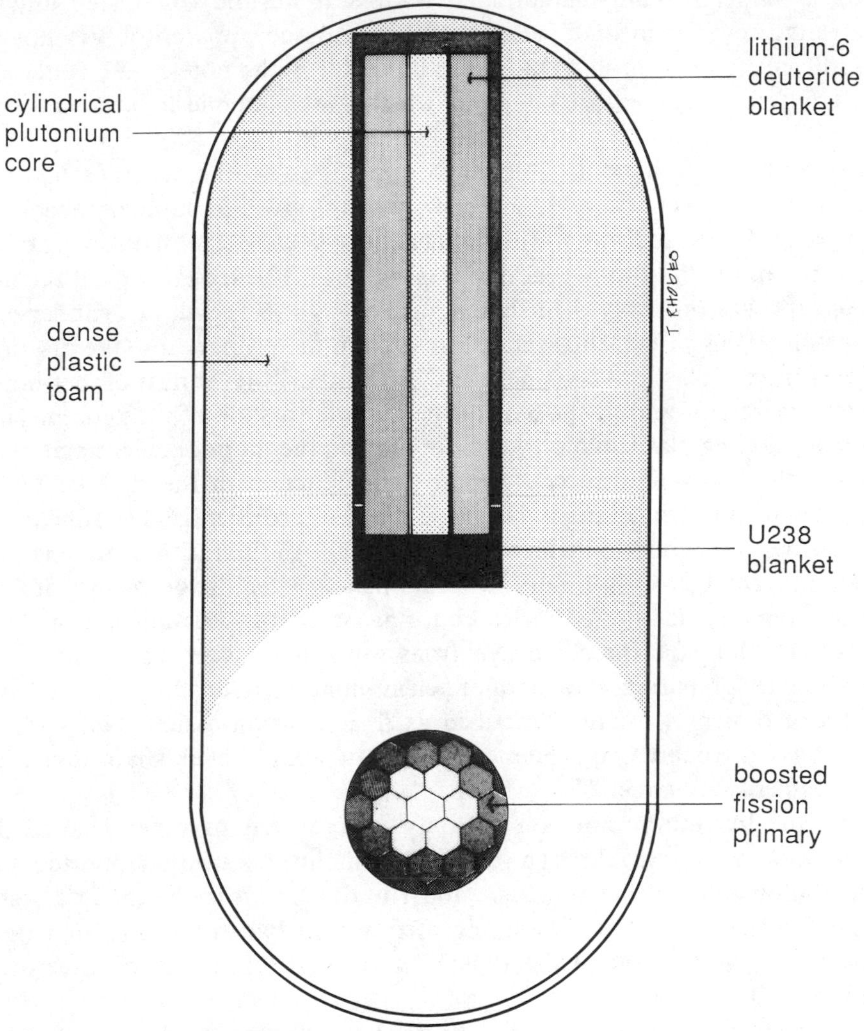

the greater heat and pressure of irradiated plastic implosion the design apparently would not evolve sufficient heat long enough to kindle a full-scale thermonuclear reaction. Such reactions depend on heating light atoms such as deuterium and tritium—increasing their velocity of motion—sufficiently to force them through the electrical barrier of the nucleus so that they can fuse to helium. The process requires heat and pressure but no critical mass. Once fusion has begun, the binding energy released in the reaction (for deuterium and tritium, 17.6 MeV) promotes further burning. A fusion weapon can therefore be made arbitrarily large, as a fire can be made arbitrarily large, by piling on more fuel. But first it must be well started, and the arrangement Ulam and Teller initially proposed apparently was not yet sufficient to do the job. "On March 9, 1951," Bethe notes, ". . . Teller and Ulam published a [classified] paper which contained one-half the new concept."

But "within a month," Bethe goes on, "the very important second half of the new concept occurred to Teller, and was given preliminary checks by [Frederick] de Hoffmann. This immediately became the main focus of attention of the thermonuclear design program." The second half of the new concept was probably a further nesting of cylinders within cylinders: an outside casing of U238 to scatter X rays from the primary into the plastic; a layer next of plastic; a layer next of U238 tamper; a layer next of thermonuclear materials; and at the axis of the cylinder a stick of plutonium. Now the imploding plastic would work not only on the thermonuclear materials. It would also start a second fission chain reaction in the stick of Pu by squeezing it to critical mass. That would add a further huge flux of heat and pressure to the thermonuclear materials and push the fusion reactions over the top. The U238 layer, in turn, would benefit from the dense flux of neutrons released in thermonuclear burning and would fission above the 1 MeV U238 fission threshold. Neutrons from that fission would then contribute to preparing the thermonuclear materials for further burning.* Such a design is usually described as fission-fusion-fission. Not without reason did Robert Oppenheimer call the two-part Teller-Ulam invention "technically . . . sweet."

The Institute for Advanced Study director, among others, hailed the invention as a breakthrough. "Dr. Oppenheimer warmly supported this new approach," Teller testifies, "and I understand that he made a statement to the effect that if anything of this kind had been suggested right away [i.e., at the time of the 1949 H-bomb debate] he would never have opposed it."

Work on a thermonuclear advanced rapidly at Los Alamos through 1951, but by then Teller's relationships had deteriorated to the point of no return. (Three years later, in a time of trial, Oppenheimer would note on a yellow pad a damning remark of Teller's that summarized the Hungarian physicist's turnabout from proponent of world government to aggressive weaponeer, a remark that echoes all the way back to his traumatic experience of revolution and counterrevolution in the Hungary of his youth: " 'Since I cannot work w[ith] the appeasers, I will work with the Fascists.' . . . Someone heard E. T. say this. Who?") In 1952, with Ernest Lawrence's

* In modern "dry" bombs, by making tritium from lithium^{6} deuteride.

support and Defense Department backing, Teller won a second weapons laboratory in the Livermore Valley, fifty miles inland from Berkeley. Los Alamos was left to build the first experimental thermonuclear device, banally coded Mike.

Teller chose not to attend the Mike shot at Eniwetok on November 1, 1952. He was busy starting up his new weapons laboratory and could hardly spare the time; he certainly also felt unwelcome. The Mike device was fueled with liquid tritium and deuterium; the liquids required a cryogenic refrigeration plant to maintain their low temperature. The complex assembly weighed some 65 tons and occupied an entire laboratory building on the small island of Elugelab. Shrouded in black tar paper, shimmering in the heat, the cubic building looked in the distance like a diabolic twin to the Kaaba of Mecca.

Teller contrived nevertheless to follow the progress of the test. He stationed himself at a seismograph in a basement room of the Berkeley geology building. Herbert York, acting director at Livermore, tuned a shortwave radio to the frequency of the Mike shot telemetry. When the shot was fired he called Teller in Berkeley. The two physicists had calculated the time a seismic wave from a successful shot would require to travel under the Pacific basin to northern California—about fifteen minutes, Teller remembers:

> I watched with little patience, the seismograph making at each minute a clearly visible vibration which served as a time signal. At last the time signal came that had to be followed by the shock from the explosion and there it seemed to be: the luminous point appeared to dance wildly and irregularly. Was it only that the pencil which I held as a marker trembled in my hand?

Mike was expected to explode with an energy of a few megatons. But its designers had engineered every component to maximize its yield. It yielded 10.4 million tons TNT equivalent, a thousand times more violent than Little Boy. "This thing is the plague of Thebes," Oppenheimer once complained of the H-bomb. Now the plague found incarnation.

The test was secret. No report would reach Los Alamos until security officers on Eniwetok had time to examine and encode it. Teller knew Mike had worked before its builders did. He dictated a telegram to York to send on to Los Alamos. The message was brief but barbed: "It's a boy."

"The fireball," writes Leona Marshall Libby, "expanded to 3 miles in diameter. Observers, all evacuated to 40 miles or more away, saw millions of gallons of [atoll] lagoon water, turned to steam, appear as a giant bubble.

When the steam had evaporated, they saw that the island of Elugelab, where the bomb [building] had been, had vanished, vaporized also. In its place, a crater ½ mile deep and 2 miles wide had been torn in the reef."

The Soviet Union exploded a device with a small hydrogen component in August 1953. Its yield was probably several hundred kilotons, about half the yield of the largest fission weapon the United States had tested up to that time. "This was not a true H-bomb," Hans Bethe comments, "as I know very well because I was chairman of the committee analyzing the Russian [fallout]."

At 65 tons Mike was too large and complex a mechanism to serve as a deliverable bomb. Its designers had fueled it with liquid deuterium and tritium for simplicity in measuring the thermonuclear reactions it would test. For a deliverable bomb the thermonuclear material of choice would be lithium deuteride, a stable powder, the lithium in the form of the isotope Li6, which constitutes 7.4 percent of natural lithium but can be separated from it relatively easily. Neutrons from the fission components of a lithium-fueled bomb would produce tritium almost instantly from Li6, which would then fuse with the deuteride to develop thermonuclear burning just as the wet and bulky liquid hydrogen isotopes had done in Mike. The dry design was tested during Operation Castle in the spring of 1954; "the very first test of the series," writes Herbert York, "the *Bravo* test, was of a device using LiD as its fuel and yielding 15 megatons. It was in a form readily adaptable for delivery by aircraft, and thus was the first large American hydrogen bomb." A true Soviet thermonuclear, dropped from an aircraft in test, followed on November 23, 1955.

When Niels Bohr arrived at Los Alamos in 1943, writes Robert Oppenheimer, "his first serious question was, 'Is it really big enough?' " The bomb, Bohr meant: big enough to end world war, big enough to challenge mankind to find its way beyond man-made death to a world more open and more humane. "I do not know whether it was," Oppenheimer adds; "it did finally get to be." By 1955, if not before, the bomb had worked an essential change upon the world. Oppenheimer had already found succinct metaphoric expression of that change in a commencement address he delivered early in 1946. "It did not take atomic weapons to make war terrible," he said then. ". . . It did not take atomic weapons to make man want peace, a peace that would last. But the atomic bomb was the turn of the screw. It has made the prospect of future war unendurable. It has led us up those last few steps to the mountain pass; and beyond there is a different country."

Gil Elliot's *Twentieth Century Book of the Dead* is a useful guide to that progress. Elliot is a Scottish writer of original mind who lives in London. It occurred to him to look into the question of how many human beings have died by man-made violence in this most bloody of centuries. He discovered that few historians or statisticians have bothered to count past the men in uniform. He worked out order-of-magnitude estimates and arrived at a total (including combatants) of about 100 million dead. He calls this uncelebrated multitude a nation of the dead:

> We know as much about the nation of the dead as we might have known about any living nation fifty years ago when the techniques of social measurement were still at an early stage. The population is around one hundred million. A proper census has not yet been possible but the latest estimate based on samples of the population suggests a figure of a hundred and ten million. That's about the size of it. A large modern nation. It's very much a twentieth-century nation, as cosmopolitan in its origins as the United States. The people have always been mixed, but the real growth began in 1914. Between then and the early 1920s the population reached twenty million, and steady growth over the next twenty years brought it to almost forty million by the outbreak of the Second World War. In the early 1940s the population more than doubled, with annual increases reaching peaks of 10/12 million. Since 1945 the growth-rate has declined below any previous levels since the late 1920s. This has been accompanied by a gigantic increase in the *capacity* for expansion.

Elliot went on from counting to examine how this silent nation assembled itself, the manner of its murder. He found the weapons to have been hardware and privation: big guns, small arms in combat, small arms in massacre, aerial bombs; ghettos, camps, sieges, occupations, dislocations, famines, blockades. Behind the weapons Elliot encountered a phenomenon more basic and more malign: the war machine evolving across the decades into a total-war machine and the total-war machine managing variously and intermittently to create areas of total death: Verdun, Leningrad, Auschwitz, Hiroshima.

The most compact, efficient, inexpensive, inexorable mechanisms of total death are nuclear weapons. Since 1945 they have therefore come to dominate the field. "The lesson we should learn from all this," I. I. Rabi remarks, "and the frightening thing which we did learn in the course of the war, was . . . how easy it is to kill people when you turn your mind to it. When you turn the resources of modern science to the problem of killing people, you realize how vulnerable they really are."

The change from a total-war machine capable of gouging out pockets of total death in a living landscape to a total-death machine capable of burning and blasting and poisoning and chilling the human world is Oppenheimer's turn of the screw. Elliot elaborates:

> The hundred million or so man-made deaths of the twentieth century . . . are more directly comparable with the scale of death from disease and plague which was the accepted norm before this century. Indeed, man-made death has largely replaced these as a source of untimely death. This is the kind of change that Hegel meant when he said that a quantitative change, if large enough, could bring about a qualitative change. The quality of this particular change becomes clear if we connect the present total of deaths with the scale of death inherent in the weapons now possessed by the large powers. Nuclear strategists talk in terms of hundreds of millions of deaths, of the destruction of whole nations and even of the entire human race.

Less efficient machines required two-thirds of a century to assemble a nation of the dead; the nuclear death machine could manage it in half an hour. The nuclear death machine has become capable of creating not merely cities of the dead or nations of the dead but a world of the dead. (Even before detailed studies appeared of the potentially widespread disaster known as nuclear winter, the World Health Organization had estimated—in 1982—that a major nuclear war would kill half the population of the earth: two billion people.) Therefore, Elliot deduces:

> The moral significance is inescapable. If morality refers to relations between individuals, or between the individual and society, then there can be no more fundamental moral issue than the continuing survival of individuals and societies. The scale of man-made death is the central moral as well as material fact of our time.

This identifies what we are talking about—the modern phenomenon of total death, that is, not capitalism versus communism or democracy versus the police state—but does not explain how we arrived at the brink of so absolute an abyss. Elliot supplies a clue to the answer in his discussion of the First World War. "The one thing that stands out overall," he observes, "is that at no time, before, during or after the war, was there a living organic structure in society [e.g., church, political party, custom, body of law] with sufficient strength to resist the new man-made and machine-made creation: [organized] death."

War is ancient. That it traditionally exposes to maximum danger a biologically surplus and relatively powerless subset of the population—young males—suggests that in some circumstances of traditional intersocial conflict it confers reproductive advantage. Nor were mass slaughters ever rare. The Old Testament regularly celebrates their carnage. The histories of empires bulk thick with them.

World war differed not only in scale but also in essential organization from such more limited earlier conflicts. Total death differs from the surround of mass slaughter in its time-dependent, assembly-line linearity. Both kinds of violence emerge from a distinctly modern process: the nation-state parasitizing applied science and industrial technology to protect itself and to further its ambitions.

Though it dominates the world, the nation-state owns no long history of legitimacy. It developed in the eighteenth and nineteenth centuries, its nationalism "a doctrine invented in Europe," writes the political scientist Elie Kedourie, that "pretends to supply a criterion for the determination of the unit of population proper to enjoy a government exclusively its own. . . . Briefly, the doctrine holds that humanity is naturally divided into nations, that nations are known by certain characteristics which can be ascertained, and that the only legitimate type of government is national self-government."

> Not the least triumph of this doctrine is that such propositions have become accepted and are thought to be self-evident, that the very word nation has been endowed by nationalism with a meaning and a resonance which until the end of the eighteenth century it was far from having. These ideas have become firmly naturalized in the political rhetoric of the West which has been taken over for the use of the whole world. But what now seems natural once was unfamiliar, needing argument, persuasion, evidences of many kinds; what seems simple and transparent is really obscure and contrived, the outcome of circumstances now forgotten and preoccupations now academic, the residue of metaphysical systems sometimes incompatible and even contradictory.

Nationalism differed radically from the hierarchical feudal organization that preceded it in the West. It offered every member of society who was included within its definition the security, invested with powerful emotion, of merger into a welcoming crowd. Not the king or the nobility but the people would be its essential polity: *L'état c'est moi et moi et moi.* That was the increase in political freedom its invention installed. But complementarily, notes the economist Barbara Ward, "its essential nature is [as well] to leave other people out. . . . It can even divorce from all community of brotherhood and goodwill fellowmen who simply happen to live on the other side of a river."

The power of the state, when nationalism succeeded in acquiring it—enlarging such power in the process—amplified that essential tension. Whole populations discovered political and emotional investment in their national causes. But outlanders became certainly more alien; the Other was confirmed in his Otherness; and between nation-states so radically divided—divided, as they believed, by nature itself—opened gulfs of threatening anarchy. Bridging them was difficult in the best of circumstances and no hierarchical authority survived to mediate as the Church had once done. In international affairs the worst case came to be counted the most reliable.

Then industrial technology and applied science enormously amplified the nation-state's power and when the smoke cleared the cities of the dead and gradually the nation of the dead revealed themselves to view. "Once men lose all grip on reality," observes Barbara Ward, "there seems to be no limit to the horrors of hatred and passion and rage they can dredge up from their psychological depths, horrors which normally we use all our social institutions to check. Unleashed nationalism on the contrary removes the checks."

Which suggests, reverting to Elliot's clue, that no living organic structure could be found sufficiently strong to resist the new death organization because the entire nation was implicated: the death organization was the nation-state itself. It followed that once mechanisms could be devised with which to attack civilian populations, civilian populations would be attacked. The enemy was the enemy nation, which was no more than the corporate body of all the enemy citizens, each of whom, in uniform or not, regardless of age or sex, was individually the enemy.

But the nation-state was not the only new political system invented in early modern times. Through the two centuries of the nation-state's evolution the republic of science had been evolving in parallel. Founded on openness, international in scope, science survived in the nation-state's midst by limiting its sovereignty to a part of the world which interested the larger system hardly at all: observable natural phenomena. Within that limited compass it proved spectacularly successful, lighting up the darkness, healing the sick, feeding the multitudes. And finally with the release of nuclear energy its success brought it into direct confrontation with the political system within which it operated. In 1945 science became the first living organic structure strong enough to challenge the nation-state itself.

The conflict between science and the nation-state that has continued and enlarged since 1945 is different from traditional forms of political conflict. Bohr visited the statesmen of his day to explain it but chose to be diplomatic rather than blunt. He explained that with the coming of nuclear weapons the world would arrive at an entirely new situation that could not be resolved by war. The situation might be resolved by statesmen sitting down together and negotiating for mutual security. If they did so, the inevitable outcome of such negotiations, given the understandable suspicion on every side, must be an open world. To Winston Churchill and apparently also to Franklin Roosevelt Bohr's scenario appeared dangerously naïve. In his role as spokesman for the republic of science Bohr certainly carried news of danger, but he was never naïve. He was warning the statesmen that science was about to hand them control over a force of nature that would destroy their political system. Considering the slaughter that political system had perpetrated upon the twentieth century, he was polite enough not to add, the mechanism of its dismantling had turned up none too soon.

The bomb that science found hidden in the world and made manifest would destroy the nation-state paradoxically by rendering it defenseless. Against such small and cheap and holocaustal weapons no defense could ever be certain. The thickest shields, from fighter aircraft to Star Wars, could be penetrated merely by multiplying weapons, decoys and delivery systems. The only security from the bomb would be political: negotiation toward an open world, which would increase security by decreasing national sovereignty and damping out the violence that attended it.

The consequence of refusing to negotiate would be a temporary monopoly followed by an arms race. That road to nowhere looked so much more familiar than Bohr's open world, which even Oppenheimer sometimes confused with World Government, that the nations preferred it and took it. The bomb might be a wall, but until the wall was tested escalation by escalation, new weapons system by new weapons system, who could prove that clever men—or threatening enemies—might not find a way under its fastness or around? Nuclear weapons might also be enterprise and profit and steady work. They might secure the citadel. They might permit the nation not to send its favored sons to war. More significantly, they would deter major war and freeze into permanence the political status quo. The nation-state could roll on into perpetuity with its sovereignty intact.

So it seemed along the way. So it still seems to many. But rather than a guarantor of sovereignty the arms race has proven a *reductio ad absurdum* of sovereignty. Though they bristle with holocaustal weapons, the superpowers confront each other today totally vulnerable, totally dependent for their continued survival on mutual and reasonable restraint, their sovereignties so thoroughly compromised that they can exercise their military ambitions only through third-world skirmishes that seldom find conclusive end. The bomb, the final word on the accumulation of power—that matter properly arranged is *all* power—has saturated national sovereignty and shorted it out.

Bohr would surely emphasize that the result of either course—negotiation or arms race—must be the foreclosure of the nation-state. Negotiation to an open world would replace the nation-state with some more tolerant and peaceful and international arrangement that recognized the reality of the bomb. Alternatively the death machine that we have installed in our midst will destroy the nation-state, ours and our rival's, along with most of the rest of the human world. The weapons with which the superpowers have armed themselves—collectively the equivalent of more than one million Hiroshimas—are linked together through their warning systems into a hair-trigger, feedback-looped contrivance, and no human contrivance has ever worked perfectly nor ever will. Each side is hostage to the other side's errors. The clock ticks. Accidents happen. Nuclear war would abolish the nation-state as certainly as negotiation but instead of a living, open world would replace it with a world of the dead, a world completely closed.

Science is sometimes blamed for the nuclear dilemma. Such blame confuses the messenger with the message. Otto Hahn and Fritz Strassmann did not invent nuclear fission; they discovered it. It was there all along waiting for us, the turn of the screw. If the bomb seems brutal and scientists criminal for assisting at its birth, consider: would anything less absolute have convinced institutions capable of perpetrating the First and Second World Wars, of destroying with hardware and callous privation 100 million human beings, to cease and desist? Nor was escalation inevitable. To the contrary, it resulted from a series of deliberate choices the superpowers made in pursuit of national interests.

But if the arms race is not a creation of science (however much men trained as scientists and applying the discoveries of science may have helped it along), what constitutes that republic's armament in its continuing conflict with the nation-state?

Oddly from the perspective of previous conflicts, science's highly effective armament is the basic scientific principle of openness. Science fights the exclusivity of the nation-state, an exclusivity that has revealed itself capable of preparing to convert the living world into a dead world of corpses, by sharing its discoveries freely—in Oppenheimer's words, by "turn[ing] over to mankind at large the greatest possible power to control the world and to deal with it according to its lights and its values." That deep trust in the promise of openness to remake the world must inspire even at the brink of the abyss. Science in conflict with the nation-state demonstrates how an open world could function without chartered violence. The effectiveness of such profound civility is obscured at present because it necessarily operates from within the nation-state itself. Turning around and looking back across the half-century since 1945 demonstrates its power: it forced an end to world war, in itself an enormous deliverance.

If the arms race now makes that deliverance seem a leap out of the frying pan into the fire, science's response has been to continue to confront the nation-state with the facts and probabilities it discovers in the course of its daily work. Nuclear winter, whatever its level of severity, is one of those probabilities. Damage to the ozone layer is another. The likelihood of widespread epidemics after a nuclear war and of mass starvation because of disruptions in food transport are two more. The nation-states may have understood that nuclear weapons spoil war. The continuing arms race unfortunately demonstrates they have not yet understood that the nationalist system of exclusion and international confrontation has now become suicidal. Each new contribution to understanding—more knowledge turned over to mankind—must further erode that stubborn and potentially genocidal ignorance. Additional knowledge will certainly continue to emerge. It is not likely to prove massive armaments a blessing.

Change is possible. Americans who want the Soviet Union to change first, as Henry Stimson did, should realize that they can only pursue that cause peacefully; the Soviet Union controls a deterrent fully as dangerous as the United States' deterrent. And patriots may need reminding that the national security state is not where holy democracy began. The American Revolution foresaw a future much like Bohr's open world, in part because the framers of that revolution and the founders of the republic of science drew from a common body of Enlightenment ideas. The national security state that the United States has evolved toward since 1945 is significantly a denial of the American democratic vision: suspicious of diversity, secret, martial, exclusive, monolithic, paranoid. "Nationalism conquered both the American thesis and the Russian antithesis of the universalist faith," writes Barbara Ward. "The two great federated experiments, based upon a revolutionary concept of the destiny of all mankind, have ended, in counterpoint, as the two most powerful nation-states in history." But other nations have moderated their belligerence and tempered their ambitions without losing their souls. Sweden was once the scourge of Europe. It gave way; the empty fortress at Kungälv testifies to that. Now it abides honorably and peacefully among the nations.

Change is possible because the choice is bare: change is the only alternative to total death. The conditions have already been established, irrevocably, for the destruction of the human world or its modification into some more collegial commonality. The necessity now is to begin to dismantle the death machine. The energies rich and intelligent peoples have squandered on the elaboration of death need to be turned to the elaboration of life.

Bohr's great vision of the complementarity of the bomb can bring hope to the prospect of change. The death machine's suicidal destructiveness is ample reason to work for its dismantling. But although that road is now necessarily longer, the promise still holds, as it has held from the beginning, that negotiating away from chartered violence will be identical to negotiating toward an open world. Democracy has nothing to fear from such a world.

Negotiation is in fact already ongoing, partly by necessity, partly by inadvertence. It began when the United States and Great Britain decided to build nuclear weapons secretly and spring them on the world in surprise, thereby precipitating an arms race with the Soviet Union that eventually came to stalemate. It continued when the United States resisted preemptive war in the brief years of its nuclear monopoly; when new delivery systems made defense impossible and thereby further undermined national sovereignty; when nations tolerated overflights and then satellite reconnaissance of their previously sacrosanct territories. It elaborates in custom and tradition every time confrontation leads to prudent stand-down or front- or back-channel resolution. It progresses as commoners in every country slowly come to understand that in a nuclear world their national leaders cannot, no matter how much tribute and control they exact, protect even their citizens' bare lives, the minimum demand the commons have made in exchange for the political authority that is ultimately theirs alone to award.

It can be useful to categorize nuclear weapons as a more virulent strain of plague, to consider man-made death as a phenomenon that parallels the older phenomenon of biological death that the people of all the nations, working in peaceful concert, have brought under a measure of control. Elliot draws this comparison productively:

> Our societies are dedicated to the preservation and care of life. . . . Public death was first recognized as a matter of civilized concern in the nineteenth century, when some health workers decided that untimely death was a question between men and society, not between men and God. Infant mortality and endemic disease became matters of social responsibility. Since then, and for that reason, millions of lives have been saved. They are not saved by accident or goodwill. Human life is daily deliberately protected from nature by accepted practices of hygiene and medical care, by the control of living conditions and the guidance of human relationships. Mortality statistics are constantly examined to see if the causes of death reveal any areas needing special attention. Because of the success of these practices, the area of public death has, in advanced societies, been taken over by man-made death—once an insignificant or "merged" part of the spectrum, now almost the whole.
>
> When politicians, in tones of grave wonder, characterize our age as one of vast effort in saving human life, and enormous vigor in destroying it, they seem to feel they are indicating some mysterious paradox of the human spirit.

> There is no paradox and no mystery. The difference is that one area of public death has been tackled and secured by the forces of reason; the other has not. The pioneers of public health did not change nature, or men, but adjusted the active relationship of men to certain aspects of nature so that the relationship became one of watchful and healthy respect. In doing so they had to contend with and struggle against the suspicious opposition of those who believed that to interfere with nature was sinful, and even that disease and plague were the result of something sinful in the nature of man himself.

The pioneers of public health who proposed to secure the biological death machine for the forces of reason must have felt, at the beginning, a despair at the magnitude of the task like the despair many thoughtful citizens today feel at the magnitude of the task of similarly securing the man-made death machine. They persisted and triumphed.

Bohr's open world has already been negotiated and installed against the biological death machine. No one any longer considers disease a political issue and only modern primitives consider it a judgment of God. When the World Health Organization worked through the 1960s and 1970s to eradicate smallpox from the earth—a program the Soviet Union initiated—both the Soviet Union and the United States shared the cost of the campaign with the third-world countries involved. The Soviets were not charged with expansionism nor the Americans with imperialism. WHO health workers of diverse national origin usually found welcome; once they demonstrated progress and overcame skepticism that containment and then eradication of so pervasive a disease was possible they won enthusiastic local support. "The eradication of smallpox will represent a major milestone in the history of medicine," the director of the campaign, the American physician Donald A. Henderson, wrote in its final phase. "It will have demonstrated what can be achieved when governments throughout the world join an international organization in a common purpose." It did: the most devastating and feared natural pestilence in human history is gone, a great victory for mankind.

Man-made death is evidently more intractable than biological death. Whether the unarmed republic of science, dedicated to human felicity rather than to the accumulation of power, can force nation-states armed to the teeth to change before they destroy themselves remains to be seen. That no world wars have engulfed us since 1945 is our interim guarantee that the opening up of the world is well begun, though at any time accident or miscalculation could close it forever. That nuclear weapons proliferate and the superpowers exhaust their economies attempting to outmaneuver each other to unattainable dominance demonstrates how irrationally tenacious is our hold on traditional forms of control.

In the spring of 1957 former AEC chairman Gordon Dean asked Robert Oppenheimer to comment on Henry Kissinger's forthcoming book *Nuclear Weapons and Foreign Policy.* Oppenheimer responded:

> Of course Kissinger is right in conceiving the problems of policy planning and strategy in terms of national power, in rough analogy to the national struggles of the 19th century; yet I have the impression that there are deep things abroad in the world, which in time are going to turn the flank of all struggles so conceived. This will not happen today, nor easily as long as Soviet power continues great and unaltered; but nevertheless I think in time the transnational communities in our culture will begin to play a prominent part in the political structure of the world, and even affect the exercise of power by the states.

The preeminent transnational community in our culture is science. With the release of nuclear energy in the first half of the twentieth century that model commonwealth decisively challenged the power of the nation-state. The confrontation is ongoing and inextricably embedded in mortal risk, but it offers at least a distant prospect of felicity.

The different country that still opens before us is Bohr's open world.

Kansas City, Missouri
1981–1986

Acknowledgments

These men and women who participated in the events of this book generously made time for interviews and correspondence: Philip Abelson, Luis W. Alvarez, David L. Anderson, William A. Arnold, Hans Bethe, Rose Bethe, Eugene T. Booth, Sakae Itoh, Shigetoshi Iwamatsu, George Kistiakowsky, Willis E. Lamb, Jr., Leon Love, Alfred O. C. Nier, I. I. Rabi, Stefan Rozental, Glenn Seaborg, Emilio Segrè, Edward Teller, Stanislaw Ulam, Eugene Wigner and Herbert York.

Michael Korda took the chance of sponsorship. David Halberstam, Geoffrey Ward and Edward O. Wilson vouched for me to the Ford Foundation. Arthur L. Singer, Jr., saved the day. The Cockefair Chair in Continuing Education at the University of Missouri–Kansas City and its director, Michael Mardikes, lent support. Louis Brown offered physics coaching and wise counsel far beyond the call of any duty and is not responsible for lapses in either regard. Egon Weiss went out of his way to arrange access to the Szilard Papers. The Linda Hall Library of Science and its former director, Larry X. Besant, and the UMKC Library and its former director, Kenneth LaBudde, never failed.

I visited or corresponded with a number of institutions; their staffs guided me with competence and courtesy: American Institute of Physics Niels Bohr Library; Argonne National Laboratory; Bibliothek und Archiv für Geschichte der Max-Planck-Gesellschaft, Dahlem; Columbia University; Department of Terrestrial Magnetism, Carnegie Institution of Washington; Hiroshima Peace Culture Foundation; J. Robert Oppenheimer Memorial Committee; Lawrence Berkeley Laboratory; Library of Congress; Los Alamos National Laboratory; National Archives; Niels Bohr Institute, Copenhagen; The Readers Digest of Japan; United States Air Force Museum, Wright-Patterson AFB; United States Military Academy Library; University of California—San Diego; University of Chicago Library.

Friends and colleagues helped with research, advice, encouragement, aid: Millicent Abell, Hans and Elisabeth Archenhold, John Aubrey, Dan Baca, Roy and Sandra Beatty, David Butler, Margaret Conyngham, Gil Elliot, Jon Else, Susie Evans, Peter Francis, Kimball Higgs, Jack Holl, Ulla Holm, Joan and Frank Hood, Jim and Reiko Ishikawa, Sigurd Johansson, Tadao Kaizuka, Edda and Rainer König, Barbro Lucas, Thomas Lyons, Karen McCarthy, Donald and Britta McNemar, Yasuo Miyazaki, Hiroyuki Nakagawa, Kimiko Nakai, Rolf Neuhaus, Issei Nishimori, Fredrik Nordenham, Patricia O'Connell, Gena Peyton, Edward Quattlebaum, P. Wayne Reagan, Edward Reese, Katherine Rhodes, Timothy Rhodes, Bill Jack Rodgers, Siegfried Ruschin, Robert G. Sachs, Silva Sandow, Sabine Schaffner, Ko Shioya, R. Jeffrey Smith, Robert Stewart, Lewis H. Strauss, Linda Talbot, Sharon Gibbs Thibodeau, Josiah Thompson, Kosta Tsipsis, Erma Valenti, Joan Warnow, Spencer Weart, Paul Williams, Edward Wolowiec, Mike Yoshida.

Luis Alvarez and Emilio Segrè were kind enough to read the galleys and offered invaluable suggestions.

Mary saw it through.

Notes

ABBREVIATIONS AND SOURCES:

OHI: Oral history interview.
AIP: Center for the History of Physics, American Institute of Physics, New York, N.Y.
AHQP: Archives for the History of Quantum Physics, available at the AIP and several other repositories.
Bush-Conant File: Vannevar Bush–James B. Conant files, Office of Scientific Research and Development, S-1 (Record Group 227), National Archives.
MED: Manhattan Engineer District Records (Record Group 77), National Archives.
JRO Papers: J. Robert Oppenheimer Papers, Library of Congress.
Strauss Papers: Lewis L. Strauss Papers, Herbert Hoover Library, West Branch, Iowa.
Szilard Papers: Leo Szilard Papers, University of California at San Diego.

Chapter 1: Moonshine

PAGE

13. September 12, 1933: I derive this date from Leo Szilard's statement at Szilard (1972), p. 529, that he read about Ernest Rutherford's speech to the British Association "one morning . . . in the newspapers" and "that day . . . was walking down Southampton Row." The British Association story appeared prominently on p. 7 of *The Times* on Sept. 12.
13. "short fat man . . . wives": Szilard (1972), p. xv.
14. "Mr. Wells . . . justification": *The Times,* p. 6.
14. He knew Wells personally: Shils (1964), p. 38.
14. Szilard read Wells' tract: Weart and Szilard (1978), p. 22n.
14. he traveled to London in 1929: ibid.
14. Szilard bid: Shils (1964), p. 38.
14. "I knew languages. . . .mascot": Weart and Szilard (1978), p. 4.
14. "When I was young . . . politics": Szilard (1972), p. xix.
14. "I said to them . . . this statement": Weart and Szilard (1978), pp. 4–5.

PAGE

14. his clarity of judgment: ibid., p. 5.
15. the Eötvös Prize: von Kármán and Edson (1967), p. 22.
15. "no career in physics": Weart and Szilard (1978), p. 5.
15. "felt that his skill . . . colleagues": Wigner (1964), p. 338.
15. saved his life: Weart and Szilard (1978), p. 8.
15. "family connections": ibid., p. 7.
15. "Not long afterward . . . disappeared": ibid., p. 8.
16. around Christmastime: ibid.
16. "In the end . . . '21": ibid., p. 9.
16. "As soon . . . Einstein": Wigner (1964), p. 338.
16. Wigner remembers: ibid.
17. Szilard won his attention: Segrè (1970), p. 106.
17. von Laue . . . accepted Szilard: Weart and Szilard (1978), Fig. 1, p. 10.
17. "There was snow . . . strange": de Jonge (1978), p. 125.
17. "the air . . . counted out": ibid., p. 130.
17. Press Ball: ibid., p. 132.

PAGE

17. Mies van der Rohe: Friedrich (1972), p. 163.
17. Yehudi Menuhin: ibid., p. 219.
17. George Grosz: Grosz (1923); Friedrich (1972), p. 152.
17. "an elderly . . . shoelaces": quoted in ibid., p. 90.
17. Fyodor Vinberg: ibid., pp. 95–96.
18. "a dark . . . enigma": quoted in ibid., p. 190.
18. "No, one . . . gods": de Jonge (1978), p. 99.
18. "In order . . . of inflation": Elsasser (1978), pp. 31–32.
18–19. "During a . . . and opinion": Wigner (1964), p. 337.
19. "Berlin . . . of physics": Weart and Szilard (1978), p. 8.
19. "In order . . . original work": ibid., p. 9.
19. "I couldn't . . . to my mind": ibid.
19. Einstein, for example: Cf. Einstein's own evaluation: "Because of the understanding of the essence of Brownian motion, suddenly all doubts vanished about the correctness of Boltzmann's [statistical] interpretation of the thermodynamic laws." Cited in Pais (1982), p. 100. Cf. also Szilard (1972), p. 31ff.
19–20. "and I saw . . . to do": Weart and Szilard (1978), p. 9.
20. "Well . . . very much": ibid., p. 9ff.
20. "and next . . . degree": ibid., p. 11.
20. Six months later: ibid.
20. accepted as *Habilitationsschrift:* Szilard (1972), p. 6.
20. Szilard patents: ibid., pp. 697–706.
20–21. "A sad . . . valve": Feld (1984), p. 676.
21. pumping refrigerant: Weart and Szilard (1978), p. 12.
21. January 5, 1929: Szilard (1972), p. 528.
21. April 1, 1929: Childs (1968), p. 138ff.
21. "the mid-twenties in Germany": Weart and Szilard (1978), p. 22.
21. "had a . . . scale": Snow (1981), p. 44.
21. *Der Bund:* Weart and Szilard (1978), p. 23ff.
21. "a closely . . . spirit": ibid., p. 23.
21–22. "If we . . . own": ibid., p. 24.
22. "take over . . . parliament": ibid., p. 25.
22. "The Order . . . state": ibid., p. 28n.
22. "The Voice of the Dolphins": Szilard (1961).

PAGE

22. banding together: Weart and Szilard (1978), p. 22.
22. "the parliamentary . . . generations": ibid.
22. "I reached . . . Switzerland": ibid., p. 13.
23. Chadwick *Nature* letter: Chadwick (1932a).
23. Chadwick *Proc. Roy. Soc.* paper: Chadwick (1932b).
24. Szilard found orphan: Weart and Szilard (1978), p. 16.
24. "the liberation . . . bombs": ibid.
24. "oppressed . . . application": Wells (1914), p. 46.
24. "This book . . . time": Weart and Szilard (1978), p. 16.
24–25. "I met . . . system": ibid.
25. Such must . . . nuclear physics: ibid., pp. 12–13.
25. "All I . . . too bad": ibid., p. 13.
25. Things got . . . Meitner: ibid.
25. "They all . . . happening": ibid.
25. "He looked . . . eyes": ibid., p. 14.
25–26. "I took . . . day earlier": ibid.
26. £1595: Bank receipt dated 6 September 1933 in Szilard Papers.
26. £854: Letter to "Béla" dated 31 August 1933 in Szilard Papers.
26. "I was . . . Association": Weart and Szilard (1978), p. 17.
26. "attempted . . . developments": *The Times,* p. 6.
27–28. "Lord Rutherford . . . irritated me": Szilard (1972), p. 529.
28. "This sort of . . . Row": Weart and Szilard (1978), p. 17.
28. "I was . . . be wrong": Szilard (1972), p. 530.
28. "It occurred . . . may react": ibid., p. 183.
28. Polanyi: Semenoff (1935), p. 5.
28. "As the light . . . the street": Szilard (1972), p. 530.
28. "it suddenly . . . atomic bombs": Weart and Szilard (1978), p. 17.

Chapter 2: Atoms and Void

29. "For by convention . . . void": quoted in *Scientific American* (1949), p. 49.
29–30. "It seems . . . formed them": in *Optics,* quoted in Guillemin (1968), p. 15.
30. "Though in . . . and weight": quoted in Pais (1982), p. 82.
30. "It is . . . pursuit in life": Planck (1949), p. 13.
30. "the process . . . by any means": ibid., p. 17.

PAGE

31. "Thus . . . is settled": W. Ostwald, at a meeting of the Deutsche Gesellschaft für Naturforscher und Ärzte in 1895, quoted in Pais (1982), p. 83.
31. "The consistent . . . finite atoms": in 1883, quoted in ibid., p. 82.
31. "What the atom . . . as ever": quoted in Chadwick (1954), p. 436.
31. "republic of science": Polanyi (1962).
31. "a highly . . . free society": ibid., p. 5.
32. "Millions are . . . committed": Polanyi (1974), p. 63.
32. "the established . . . letter": Polanyi (1946), p. 43.
32. "uncertainties . . . nature": ibid.
32. "a full initiation": ibid.
32. "close personal . . . master": ibid.

32–33. "what do we . . . the world": Feynman (1963), p. 2-1.

33. "no one . . . accepted": Polanyi (1946), p. 45.
33. "Any account . . . is untrue": Polanyi (1974), p. 51.
33. an analogy: Polanyi (1962), p. 6ff.
34. "Let them . . . consequence": ibid., p. 7.
34. "growing points": ibid., p. 15.
34. "The authority . . . *above* them": ibid., p. 14. His emphasis.

34–35. "*This network* . . . neighborhoods": ibid.

35. "Physics . . . those events": Wigner (1981), p. 8.
35. three broad criteria: cf. discussion in Polanyi (1962), p. 10ff.
36. one thousand . . . physicists: cf. Segrè (1980), p. 9.
36. "his genius . . . astonished": Chadwick (1954), p. 440. Details of Rutherford's childhood selected from Eve (1939), Feather (1940) and Crowther (1974).
36. sickening insecurity: the phrase is C. P. Snow's in Snow (1967), p. 11.
37. "That's the last potato": Eve (1939), p. 11.
37. "Now Lord . . . mine": ibid., p. 342.
37. "Magnetization of . . . discharges": 1894, in Rutherford (1962), pp. 25–57.
37. the world record: Marsden (1962), p. 3.
37. "like an . . . lion's skin": Eve (1939), p. 24.
37. "A magnetic detector . . . applications": Rutherford (1962), pp. 80–104.
37. Marconi . . . in September: cf. Eve (1939), p. 35.
38. "The reason . . . the future": ibid., p. 23.

PAGE

38. "You cannot serve . . . time": quoted in Kapitza (1980), p. 267.
38. "one curious . . . mistakes": Snow (1967), p. 7.
38. "I believe . . . commercially": Oliphant (1972), p. 140ff.
38. "in his . . . cultured man": Marsden (1962), p. 16.
39. "before tempting . . . more": ibid., p. 3.
39. "I hope . . . by myself": Eve (1939), p. 34.
39. Bank of England sealing wax: Blackett (1933), p. 72: "It is curious that the most universally successful vacuum cement available for many years should have been a material of common use for quite other purposes. At one time it might have been hard to find in an English laboratory an apparatus which did not use red Bank of England sealing-wax as a vacuum cement."
40. "the almost . . . passes": J. J. Thompson in Conn and Turner (1965), p. 53.
40. "the corpuscle . . . cathode ray": Crowther (1974), p. 123.
40. "a number . . . electrification": J. J. Thompson in Conn and Turner (1965), p. 97.
41. Thompson . . . discovering X rays: cf. ibid., p. 33.
41. Frederick Smith: cf. Andrade (1957), p. 444.
41. "at a . . . discharge-tube": J. J. Thompson in Conn and Turner (1965), p. 33.
41. Röntgen, Becquerel: these details from Segrè (1980), p. 19ff.
41. "exposed . . . on the negative": quoted in ibid., p. 28.
42. "expecting . . . in the dark": quoted in ibid., p. 29.
42. "There are . . . [beta] radiation": Rutherford (1962), p. 175.
42. P. V. Villard: Segrè (1980), p. 50.
42. "The McGill . . . cannot complain": Eve (1939), p. 57.
42. In 1900 . . . radioactive gas: "A radioactive substance emitted from thorium compounds." Rutherford (1962), pp. 220–231.
42. "At the beginning . . . be examined": Soddy (1953), p. 124ff.
43. "conveyed the . . . gas!": ibid., p. 126.
43. an "isotope": Soddy (1913), p. 400.
43. "for more than . . . an institution": Soddy (1953), p. 127.

PAGE

43. "similar . . . cathode rays": Rutherford (1962), p. 549.
43. "It may . . . molecular charge": ibid., p. 606ff.
44. "playful suggestion . . . in smoke": Eve (1939), p. 102.
44. "some fool . . . unawares": ibid.
44. "It is . . . secret": Soddy (1953), p. 95.
44. "My idea . . . romances": quoted in Dickson (1969), p. 228.
44–45. "After a very . . . radium rays": Eve (1939), p. 93.
45. "I may . . . keep going": ibid., p. 123.
45. "they are . . . moving": ibid., p. 127.
45. "it remained . . . true physicist": R. H. Fowler, quoted in ibid., p. 429.
45. An eyewitness: ibid., p. 183.
45. reported the month before: "The Nature of the α Particle," Nov. 3, 1908; Rutherford (1963), pp. 134–135.
45. "After some days . . . vessel": ibid., p. 145.
45. "In this . . . style": Russell (1950), p. 91.
46. "I see . . . his apparatus": quoted in Eve (1939), p. 239.
46. "supper in . . . the motor": Russell (1950), p. 88.
46. his handshake: Oliphant (1972), p. 22.
46. "he gave . . . physical contact": ibid.
46. He could still be mortified: cf. his response to the bishop in gaiters who presumed to compare the South Island to Stoke-on-Trent in Russell (1950), p. 96.
46. "He was . . . tricks": ibid., p. 89.
46–47. "Youthful . . . fools gladly": Weizmann (1949), p. 118.
47. "Scattering of . . . rays": Feather (1940), p. 117.
47. "I was . . . to taste": Eve (1939), p. 384.
47. Philipp Lenard: cf. Andrade (1957), p. 441.
47. 100 million volts: Rutherford's calculation in 1906 cited in Feather (1940), p. 131.
47. "Such results . . . electrical forces": ibid.
48. rang a bell: Blackett (1933), p. 77.
48. But the experiment was troubled: details from Marsden (1962), p. 8ff.
48. "See if . . . surface": ibid., p. 8.
49. "I remember . . . told him": ibid.
49. "If the . . . be required": H. Geiger and E. Marsden, "On a diffuse reflection of α-particles" in Conn and Turner (1965), p. 135ff.

PAGE

49. a first quick intuition: cf. Norman Feather in Rutherford (1963), p. 22.
49–50. "It was . . . minute nucleus": quoted in Conn and Turner (1965), p. 136ff.
50. sheets of good paper: cf. photographs of these historic notes in Rutherford (1963), following p. 240.
50. a model . . . pendulum: cf. Eve (1939), p. 197.
50. "largely . . . people": Chadwick OHI, AIP, p. 11.
50. a rare snake: ibid. Cf. also Chadwick (1954), p. 442n.
50. "a most . . . it": Chadwick OHI, AIP, p. 12.
50. "a central . . . in amount": Rutherford (1963), p. 212.
50. Nagaoka had postulated: cf. Conn and Turner (1965), p. 112ff, for partial text.
50. "Campbell tells . . . optical effects": quoted in Feather (1940), p. 136.
51. "supposed to . . . rotating electrons": Rutherford (1963), p. 254.
51. "for the . . . in Manchester": Nagaoka refers in his letter to "your paper on the calculation of alpha particles which was in progress when I visited Manchester." That paper, "The number of ***a*** particles emitted by uranium and thorium and by uranium minerals," was written with Hans Geiger, appeared in the *Philosophical Magazine* in Oct. 1910 and was sent July 1910. For the text of Nagaoka's letter cf. Eve (1939), p. 200.
51. the same theoretical defect: cf. discussion in Heilbron and Kuhn (1969), p. 241ff.
52. "Bohr . . . radioactive work": Eve (1939), p. 218.

Chapter 3: Tvi

53. *Tvi:* conversations with Josiah Thompson greatly enlightened this discussion.
53. "There came . . . Niels Bohr!": Eve (1939), p. 218.
53. "an enormous . . . head": Snow (1981), p. 19.
53. "much more . . . later years": ibid.
54. "he took . . . the matter": quoted in Rozental (1967), p. 78.
54. "uttering his . . . truth": quoted in Pais (1982), p. 417.
54. "his assurance . . . vivid images": Frisch (1979), p. 94.

PAGE

54. "he would . . . as criticism": quoted in Rozental (1967), p. 79.
54. "Not often . . . of trance": quoted in Pais (1982), pp. 416–417.
54. "gloomy . . . smile": quoted in Rozental (1967), p. 215.
55. "keen worshipper": Harald Høffding, quoted in ibid., p. 13.
55. "lovable personality": the surgeon Ole Chievitz, quoted in ibid., p. 15.
56. great interrelationships: Petersen (1963), p. 9: "Bohr has said that as far back as he could remember he liked to dream of great interrelationships."
56. speaking in paradoxes: according to Høffding in his *Memoirs*, quoted in Rozental (1967), p. 13.
56. "I was . . . different character": Bohr OHI, AIP, p. 1.
56. "At a . . . his imagination": Rozental (1967), p. 15.
56. "the special . . . the family": quoted in ibid.
56. "Even as . . . fundamental problems": Petersen (1963), p. 9.
56. trouble learning to write: cf. Segrè (1980), p. 119.
56. "There runs . . . two brothers": Rozental (1967), p. 23.
57. "*à deux*": Vilhelm Slomann, quoted in ibid., p. 25.
57. "In my . . . than I": Bohr OHI, AIP, p. 1.
57. Harald . . . told whoever asked: cf. for example Richard Courant in Rozental (1967), p. 301.
57. a stick used as a probe: e.g., Rozental (1967), p. 306.
57. "believed literally . . . of faith": quoted in ibid., p. 74.
57. "I see . . . his heart": quoted without citation in Moore (1966), p. 35. Moore was allowed access to some of Bohr's unpublished private correspondence.
57. Bohr drafted . . . private letters: cf. Rozental (1967), p. 30.
57. "If the . . . will come": quoted in Cline (1965), p. 214.
58. Bohr's anxiety: this discussion is based on Lewis S. Feuer's excellent analysis in Feuer (1982) but differs in emphasis and to some extent in conclusions. Holton (1973) is also an essential source.
58. "a young . . . unusual resolution": quoted in Rozental (1967), p. 74.

PAGE

58. "an unfinished . . . in [Denmark]": Bohr (1963), p. 13.
58. "a remarkably . . . position [as human beings]": ibid.
58. "Every one . . . his initiation": quoted in Rozental (1967), p. 121.
58. "very soberly . . . social activities": Bohr (1963), p. 13.
58. "[I start] . . . bottomless abyss": ibid.
59. "Bohr kept . . . studies itself": Oppenheimer (1963), II, pp. 25–26.
59. "Certainly I . . . to madness": quoted in Rosenfeld (1963), p. 48.
59. "Thus on . . . becomes actor": quoted in ibid., p. 49.
59. "Bohr would . . . emphasized": Rozental (1967), p. 121.
60. the image that recurred: cf. ibid., pp. 77, 327–328. Examples abound in the written record.
60. "suspended in language": quoted in Petersen (1963), p. 10.
60. *"Nur die . . . die Wahrheit":* quoted in Holton (1973), p. 148.
60. "I took . . . with Høffding": Bohr OHI, AIP, p. 1.
60. Harald Høffding: cf. biographical note at Bohr (1972), p. xx.
60. "despair": Holton (1973) notes this confession on p. 144.
61. Møller taught Kierkegaard: cf. Thompson (1973), p. 88.
61. "my youth's . . . departed friend": quoted in ibid.
61. The Danish word . . . "ambiguity": paraphrased from ibid., p. 155.
61. "His leading . . . *the individual*": quoted in Holton (1973), p. 146.
61. "Only in . . . of continuity": quoted in ibid., p. 147.
61. "At that . . . multivalued functions": Bohr OHI, AIP, p. 1.
62. the solid work: cf. Bohr (1972), p. 4.
62. "took such . . . the flame": Rosenfeld (1979), p. 325.
62–63. "the experiments . . . the paper": quoted in Rosenfeld (1963), p. 39.
63. "not a professor": Bohr (1972), p. 10.
63. "This is . . . ever read": ibid., p. 501.
63. "envy would . . . the rooftops": ibid., p. 95, adjusting the idiom.
63. "four months . . . rough drafts": ibid.
64. "unpractical": Bohr OHI, AIP, p. 2.
64. "He made . . . something good": quoted in Nielsen (1963), pp. 27–28.
64. "in deepest . . . my father": Bohr (1972), p. 295.

PAGE

64. "Dr. Bohr . . . a record": quoted in ibid., pp. 98–99.
64–65. "Oh Harald! . . . little fireplace": ibid., p. 519.
65. "under threat . . . stand it": ibid., p. 523.
65. "for an . . . blustering wind": quoted in Rozental (1967), p. 44, adjusting the idiom.
65. "absolute geniuses . . . you out": quoted in ibid., p. 40.
65. "I wonder . . . his ideas": quoted in Moore (1966), p. 32.
65. "I'm longing . . . silly talk": quoted in ibid., p. 33.
65–66. "It takes . . . was different": Bohr OHI, AIP, pp. 13–14.
66. "came down . . . his name": Bohr (1963), p. 31. My chronology of Bohr's visits to Manchester and his arrangements to work there generally follows the plausible conjectures of Heilbron and Kuhn (1969), p. 233, n. 57.
66. "just then . . . atomic nucleus": Bohr (1963), p. 31.
66. Bohr had matters on his mind: cf. his letter to C. W. Oseen on Dec. 1, 1911: "I am at the moment very enthusiastic about the quantum theory (I mean its experimental side), but I am still not sure this is not due to my ignorance." Quoted in Heilbron and Kuhn (1969), p. 230, with a following discussion.
66. "the patience . . . his mind": Bohr (1963), p. 32.
66. "one of . . . of Rutherford": ibid., p. 31.
66. "Bohr's different . . . football player!": quoted in Rozental (1967), p. 46.
66. eleven Nobel Prize winners: cf. Zuckerman (1977), p. 103.
67. Manchester is always here: cited by A. S. Russell in Birks (1962), p. 93ff.
67. "an introductory . . . research": Bohr (1963), p. 32.
67. Bohr learned about radiochemistry: cf. ibid., pp. 32–33.
68–69. "Rutherford . . . thought . . . his atom": Bohr OHI, AIP, p. 13.
69. "Ask Bohr!": quoted in Rozental (1967), p. 46.
69. "It could . . . quickly": Heilbron and Kuhn (1969), p. 238; Bohr (1972), p. 559; selecting the most idiomatic phrases from each translation.

PAGE

69. "getting along . . . to you!": Bohr (1972), p. 561, adjusting the idiom.
69. July 22: Bohr to Harald Bohr, ibid.
69. "to be . . . few weeks": quoted in Heilbron and Kuhn (1969), p. 256.
69. "a very . . . these things": quoted in ibid.
70. "One must . . . mechanical sort": quoted in ibid., p. 214. My discussion here generally follows this excellent monograph.
70. "Later measurements . . . to be": Planck (1949), p. 41.
70. "a universal . . . *of action*": ibid., p. 43.
72. "The spectra . . . a butterfly": quoted in Heilbron and Kuhn (1969), p. 257, n. 117.
74. "As soon . . . to me": quoted in ibid., p. 265.
75. "There is . . . its advent": Darrow (1952), p. 53.
75–76. "There appears . . . to stop": quoted in Bohr (1963), p. 41.
76. "Every change . . . possible transitions": quoted in Feuer (1982), p. 137.
76. "principal assumptions": cf. Shamos (1959), p. 338.
76–77. "Bohr characteristically . . . phenomena": Rosenfeld (1979), p. 318.
77. "asking questions of Nature": Rosenfeld (1963), p. 51.
77. "I try . . . I think": Oppenheimer (1963), I, p. 7.
77. "He points . . . their validity": Rosenfeld (1979), p. 318.
77. "the fairyland of the imagination": quoted in Thompson (1973), p. 176.
77. "It is . . . about nature": Petersen (1963), p. 12.
77. "It was . . . so seriously": Bohr OHI, AIP, p. 13.

Chapter 4: The Long Grave Already Dug

78. October 23, 1912: Hahn (1966), p. 70. Hahn (1970), p. 102, says Oct. 12. The official program confirms the later date.
78. a wet day, etc.: cf. photo "The dedication of the Kaiser Wilhelm Institute for Chemistry" in Hahn (1966), following p. 72.
78–79. the Kaiser Wilhelm Society: details from Haber (1971), pp. 49–50.
79. an embarrassment: cf. Hahn (1966), p. 50.
79. Hahn admired women: cf. Hahn (1970), passim.

PAGE

80. For details of Meitner's early life: cf. Frisch (1979), p. 3.
80. "There was . . . close friends": Hahn (1970), p. 88.
80–81. "an emanating . . . screen": Hahn (1966), p. 71.
81. "If I . . . in prison": Hahn (1970), p. 110.
81. "worthy of . . . noble brows": quoted in ibid., p. 102.
81. Moseley: this discussion relies on Heilbron (1974).
82. "so reserved . . . like him": quoted in ibid., p. 57.
82. "Hindoos, Burmese . . . 'scented dirtiness' ": Moseley to his mother, ibid., p. 176.
82. "Some Germans . . . photographing them": ibid., p. 193.
83. "We find . . . the atom": ibid., p. 205.
83. "unbearably hot . . . start measurements": ibid., p. 206.
83. "I want . . . a thousand": ibid., pp. 207–208.
84. a billiard table: Bohr OHI, AIP, p. 7.
84. "And that . . . were away": ibid.
84. "the only . . . of success": quoted in Rozental (1967), p. 58.
84. "a definite . . . chemical properties": quoted in Eve (1939), p. 224.
84. "shy . . . and noble": ibid., p. 223.
84. "great developments . . . on mankind": quoted in ibid., p. 224.
84. "do not . . . and 'fantastic' ": Bohr (1972), p. 567.
84. "Speaking with . . . saying so": quoted in Eve (1939), p. 226.
85. "During the . . . on Physics": Heilbron (1974), pp. 211–213.
85. "Because you . . . from Moseley": Bohr OHI, AIP, p. 4.
85. Bayer Dye Works: cf. Haber (1971), p. 128.
85–86. "In the . . . thermos vessels": Hahn (1970), p. 107.
86. "It is . . . whole valley": quoted in Rozental (1967), p. 64.
87. "The eleven- . . . of Palestine": quoted in Weisgal and Carmichael (1963), p. 20.
87. "a deliberate . . . 'eternal students' ": Weizmann (1949), p. 93.
87. "inviting every . . . remuneration": ibid., p. 171.
87–88. "In the . . . thrown away": ibid., p. 134.
88. January 1915: Stein (1961), p. 140.

PAGE

88. "Really messianic . . . upon us": quoted in ibid., p. 137n.
88. "You know . . . your hands": quoted in Weizmann (1949), p. 171.
88. "So it . . . British Admiralty": ibid., p. 172. Weizmann writes 1916, but this is clearly a slip of memory. Cf. Stein (1961), p. 118. Churchill was no longer First Lord in 1916.
89. "brisk, fascinating . . . two years": Weizmann (1949), p. 173.
90. "Horse-chestnuts . . . for maize": Lloyd George (1933), pp. 49–50.
90. "When our . . . in Palestine": ibid., p. 50. Vera Weizmann affirmed the authenticity of this conversation; cf. Stein (1961), p. 120n.
90. "view with . . . this object": cf. frontispiece facsimile, Stein (1961).
90. "outstanding war . . . National Home": quoted in ibid., p. 120n.
90. "it being . . . in Palestine": ibid., frontispiece facsimile.
91. a German rocket signal, etc.: these details at Lefebure (1923), pp. 36–37; Goran (1967), p. 68; and Hahn (1970), pp. 119–120.
91. "to abstain . . . deleterious gases": Carnegie Endowment for International Peace (1915), p. 1.
92. 300,000 pads: Pound (1964), p. 131.
92. Otto Hahn helped: cf. Hahn (1970), p. 118ff.
92. 5,730 of them: Prentiss (1937), p. 148.
92. "Haber informed . . . gas-warfare": Hahn (1970), p. 118.
93. James Franck: according to ibid., p. 119ff.
93. I. G. Farben: cf. Lefebure (1923), p. 86; Haber (1971), pp. 279–280.
93. mid-June 1915: as Hahn remembers it in Hahn (1970), p. 120. Prentiss (1937) says phosgene was first used by the Germans in a cloud-gas attack against the British at Nieltje on Dec. 19, 1915. Hahn may have meant 1916.
93. "the wind . . . success": Hahn (1970), p. 120.
93. buying German dyestuffs: cf. Haber (1971), p. 189.
93. phosgene: cf. Prentiss (1937), p. 154ff.
94. chlorpicrin: cf. ibid., p. 161ff.
94. mustard gas: cf. ibid., p. 177.
95. a typical artillery barrage: estimated from the figures given at Lefebure (1923), pp. 77–80.

PAGE

95. "She began . . . of life": Goran (1967), p. 71.
95. a scientist belongs: according to ibid.
96. "Our destination . . . in doubt": Heilbron (1974), p. 271.
96. "to be . . . or systematizing": ibid., p. 271ff.
96. "full of . . . and Australians": ibid., p. 272.
96. "The one . . . food": ibid., p. 274.
97. "over ghastly . . . slippery inclines": G. E. Chadwick, quoted in ibid., p. 122.
97. "They came . . . The Farm": Masefield (1916), p. 206.
97. "one of . . . in history": quoted in Kevles (1979), p. 113.
97. Folkestone: this section relies primarily on Fredette (1976).
98. "I saw . . . the sight": quoted in ibid., pp. 20–21.
98–99. "You must . . . in war": quoted in ibid., p. 30.
100. "a basis . . . to fight": ibid., p. 39.
100. "The day . . . and subordinate": quoted in ibid., p. 111.
100. research contracts: Prentiss (1937), p. 84.
100. "the great . . . of warfare": Lefebure (1923), p. 173.
100. a vast war-gas arsenal: cf. Prentiss (1937), p. 85, for these details and statistics.
101. "Had the . . . war": Lefebure (1923), p. 176.
101. 500,000 . . . 300,000: cf. Ellis (1976), p. 62.
101. 170 million rounds: ibid.
101. "Concentrated essence of infantry": J. F. C. Fuller, quoted in Keegan (1976), p. 228.
101. "I go . . . others": Edmund Blunden, quoted in Ellis (1975), pp. 137–138.
101. 21,000 men: cf. Keegan (1976), p. 255.
101–102. "It bears . . . common needle": quoted in Ellis (1975), p. 16.
102. "For the . . . working shift": Keegan (1976), pp. 229–230.
102. a software package: this discussion benefits from Elliot (1972), p. 20ff.
102. "The basic . . . trenches": ibid., p. 20.
102. "The War . . . of victims": Sassoon (1937), II, p. 143.
103. the long grave already dug: Masefield (1916), p. 104.
103. "The war . . . human variation": Elliot (1972), p. 23.
103. Elliot stresses: ibid., p. 25.

Chapter 5: Men from Mars

PAGE

104. "Horse-drawn . . . social currents": von Kármán (1967), p. 14.
105. "the fountain . . . to oppression": Paul Ignotus, quoted in Fermi (1971), pp. 38–39.
105. 33 percent . . . illiterate: Jászi (1924), p. 7.
105. 37.5 percent of . . . arable land: McCagg (1970), p. 186.
105. 1910 statistics: cf. Nagy-Talavera (1970), p. 41n.
105. S. V. Schossberger: cf. McCagg (1970), p. 132. My discussion of this phenomenon generally follows McCagg.
106. "one day . . . almost unpronounceable": von Kármán (1967), p. 17.
106. Jewish family ennoblements: cf. McCagg (1970), p. 63.
106. "galaxy of . . . lived elsewhere": Frisch (1979), pp. 173–174.
107. Von Kármán at six: von Kármán (1967), pp. 15–16.
107. Von Neumann at six: cf. Goldstine (1972), pp. 166–167.
107. Edward Teller . . . late . . . to talk: cf. Blumberg and Owens (1976), p. 6.
107. "Johnny used . . . improved": Ulam (1976), p. 111.
107. "As a . . . were good": Teller (1962), p. 81.
107. "addiction to . . . *of Man*": Weart and Szilard (1978), p. 4.
107. "the most . . . 19th century": E. F. Kunz, quoted in Madach (1956), p. 7.
108. "In [Madach's] . . . is pessimistic": *New York Post,* Nov. 24, 1945, quoted in Weart and Szilard (1978), p. 3n.
108. "a society . . . achievement": Smith (1960), p. 78.
108. "My father . . . them ourselves": von Kármán (1967), p. 21.
108. "We had . . . mathematician": interview with Eugene Wigner, Princeton, N.J., Jan. 21, 1983.
108. Teller recalls . . . syllogism: cf. Blumberg and Owens (1976), p. 137.
109. At Princeton: cf. Goldstine (1972), p. 176.
109. even Wigner thought: cf. Heims (1980), p. 43.
109. the only authentic genius: cf. Fermi (1971), pp. 53–54.
109. "So you . . . like geniuses": Blumberg and Owens (1976), pp. 15–16.

PAGE

109. "I think . . . impressed me": ibid., p. 23.
109. "The Revolution . . . irresistible momentum": Ferenc Göndör, quoted in Völgyes (1971), p. 31.
110. "*Es ist passiert*": quoted in ibid., p. 12.
110. "the rousing . . . melodious flood": Koestler (1952), p. 63.
110. "So far . . . sadistic excesses": von Kármán (1967), p. 93.
111. "because it . . . to come": Koestler (1952), p. 67.
111. "We left . . . put down": USAEC (1954), p. 654.
111. the group of Hungarian financiers: McCagg (1970), p. 16.
111. Teller heard of corpses: Blumberg and Owens (1976), p. 18.
111. The Tellers acquired two soldiers: cf. ibid.
111–112. "I shiver . . . terrible revenge": quoted in ibid., p. 19.
112. five hundred deaths: I use Koestler's figure ("under five hundred"), the larger of the two I have found. Koestler (1952), p. 67.
112. at least five thousand deaths: Heims (1980), p. 47, citing Rudolf L. Tökes, *Béla Kun and the Hungarian Soviet Republic* (Praeger, 1967), p. 214.
112. "no desire . . . all question": Jászi (1923), p. 160, the atrocities in detail ff.
112. "that the . . . nationalities": quoted in ibid., p. 186.
112–113. "It will . . . face extinction": Ulam (1976), p. 111.
113. "dinned into . . . stay even": *Time,* Nov. 19, 1957, p. 22.
113. "I loved . . . doomed society": Coughlan (1963), p. 89.
113. "I was . . . is lasting": von Kármán (1967), p. 95.
113. "once commented . . . the 'it' ": Pais (1982), p. 39.
113. "the acquisition . . . hostile world": Weizmann (1949), p. 18.
113. "every division . . . a watershed": ibid., p. 29.
113–114. "In the . . . little understanding": Born (1981), p. 39.
114. "Only a . . . the maze": Segrè (1980), p. 124.
114. "Bohr remembered . . . of Maxwell": Oppenheimer (1963), I, p. 21.
114. "His reactions . . . as well": Rozental (1967), p. 138.

PAGE

115. "That . . . of thought": quoted in Segrè (1980), p. 124.
115. "a unique . . . unforgettable experience": Bohr (1963), p. 54.
115–116. "I shall . . . highly exciting": Heisenberg (1971), pp. 37–38.
116. "At the . . . that afternoon": ibid., p. 38.
116. "Suddenly, the . . . of hope": ibid., p. 42.
116. "You are . . . small children!": Gamow (1966), p. 51.
116. "radiant . . . walking shorts": quoted in Jungk (1958), p. 26.
116. "But now . . . very seriously": Heisenberg (1971), p. 55.
116. "It saddened . . . such fancies": ibid., p. 8.
117. "a few . . . to rise": ibid., p. 61.
117. "a coherent . . . atomic physics": ibid., p. 62.
119. "This was . . . scholarship": the interviewer was Thomas Kuhn, in 1963, quoted in Smith and Weiner (1980), p. 3.
119. one of Robert's friends: Francis Fergusson, cited in ibid., p. 2.
119. "desperately amiable . . . be agreeable": Paul Horgan, quoted in ibid.
119. "an unctuous . . . a bastard": quoted in Royal (1969), pp. 15–16.
120. "tortured him": quoted in ibid., p. 23.
120. "Still a . . . about him": Jane Didisheim Kayser, quoted in Smith and Weiner (1980), p. 6.
120. "came down . . . the time": ibid., p. 7.
121. a Goth coming into Rome: Royal (1969), p. 27.
121. "He intellectually . . . the place": quoted in ibid. Michelmore (1969), p. 11, however, has Oppenheimer himself saying: "I . . . just raided the place intellectually."
121. a typical year: cf. Smith and Weiner (1980), p. 45.
121. "although I . . . with murder": ibid., p. 46.
122. "the most . . . came alive": Michelmore (1969), p. 11.
122. "Up to . . . of wrong": Seven Springs Farm transcript, p. 5, in JRO Papers, Box 66.
122. "Generously, you . . . dead. Voila": Smith and Weiner (1980), p. 54.
122. Both of Oppenheimer's . . . friends: they are quoted in this regard in ibid., p. 32.

PAGE

123. "It came . . . in physics": ibid., pp. 45–46.
123. "a man . . . an apprentice": ibid. , p. 69.
123. "But Rutherford . . . the center": ibid., p. 75.
123–124. "perfectly prodigious . . . success": quoted in ibid., p. 77.
124. "I am . . . Harvard overnight": ibid., p. 87.
124. "The business . . . interested in": ibid, p. 88ff.
124. "The melancholy . . . been snubbed": ibid., p. 128.
124. "How is . . . worth living": ibid., p. 86.
124. "making a . . . a career": ibid., p. 90.
124. "on the . . . was chronic": quoted in Royal (1969), p. 35.
125. "noisy . . . me crazy": Smith and Weiner (1980), p. 92.
125. "doing a . . . and alarm": John Edsall, quoted in ibid.
125. "When Rutherford . . . That's bad": ibid., p. 96.
125. "sweetness": Snow (1981), p. 60.
125. "At that . . . theoretical physicist": Smith and Weiner (1980), p. 96.
125. "He said . . . probably true": quoted in ibid., p. 94.
125–126. "a great . . . to brigantines": ibid., p. 95.
126. "The [Cambridge] . . . but love": quoted in Davis (1968), p. 22.
126. "a great . . . it": quoted in ibid., p. 21.
127. "Although this . . . very much": Smith and Weiner (1980), p. 103.
127. "Not only . . . for generations": Teller (1980), p. 137.
127. "a desert": second AHQP interview, p. 18.
127. "largeness and . . . fixed up": Smith and Weiner (1980), p. 121.
128. "house and . . . and stream": ibid., p. 126.
128. Everyone went . . . except Einstein: Segrè (1980) gives Einstein's reason at p. 168.
128. "In other . . . same structure": Heisenberg (1971), p. 71.
128–129. "This hypothesis . . . be true": ibid., p. 72.
129. "with . . . liberation": ibid., p. 71.
129. "Wilhelm Wien . . . by Schrödinger": Heisenberg in Rozental (1967), p. 103.
129. "For though . . . laborious discussions": ibid.
129. "While Mrs. . . . admit that": Heisenberg (1971), pp. 75–76.

PAGE

129. "If one . . . step forward": quoted in Rozental (1967), pp. 103–104.
129–130. "utterly . . .all along": Heisenberg (1971), p. 77.
130. "It is . . . can observe": quoted in ibid.
130. "On this . . . quantum mechanics": Heisenberg in Rozental (1967), p. 105.
130. Bohr ought to have liked: cf. Heisenberg's discussion in ibid., p. 106.
131. "the great . . . scientists": Bohr (1961), p. 52.
131. "renunciation": e.g., ibid., pp. 77, 80.
132. "Two magnitudes . . . the other": Segrè (1980), p. 167.
132. "bears a . . . and object": Bohr (1961), p. 91.
132. "quantum mechanics . . . play dice": quoted in Holton (1973), p. 120.
132. "We all . . . it all": Heisenberg (1971), p. 79.
133. " 'God does . . . the last": ibid., p. 80.
133. "Nor is . . . the world": quoted in ibid., p. 81.

Chapter 6: Machines

134. "I shall . . . world": Snow (1958), p. 88.
134. "uncarpeted floor . . . volcano": Oliphant (1972), p. 19.
135. "An anomalous effect in nitrogen": Rutherford (1963), p. 585ff.
135. "gave rise . . . itself": ibid., p. 547.
136. "I occasionally . . . this method": quoted in Bohr (1963), p. 50.
137. "appeared to . . . H scintillations": Rutherford (1963), p. 585.
137. "must be . . . in air": ibid., p. 587.
137. "From the . . . is disintegrated": ibid., p. 589.
137. one . . . in 300,000: Rutherford (1965), p. 24.
138. Francis William Aston: biographical details from de Hevesy (1947).
139. "In this . . . discharge tube": ibid., p. 637.
139. building the precision instrument: cf. Aston (1927, 1933).
139. "In letters . . . atomic model": Bohr (1963), p. 52.
139–140. "that neon . . . to 1": Aston (1938), p. 105.
140. "High packing . . . the reverse": Aston (1927), p. 958.
140. "If we . . . full speed": Aston (1938), p. 106.
140–141. "the nuclear . . . door neighbor": ibid., pp. 113–114.

PAGE

141. "Stockholm . . . ever since": quoted in de Hevesy (1947), p. 645.
141. "particularly detested . . . barking kind": quoted in ibid., p. 644.
141. "What is . . . not answer": quoted in Kevles (1977), p. 96. Numbers of American physicists given here and ff.
142. Psychometricians: e.g., Eiduson (1962), Goodrich et al. (1951), Roe (1952) and Terman (1955).
142. IQ scores: cf. Roe (1952), p. 24.
142. "He is . . . his nature": ibid. , p. 22.
143. A psychological examination: Eiduson (1962).
143. "their fathers . . . knew them": ibid., p. 65.
143. "rigid . . . reserved": ibid., p. 22.
143. "shy, lonely . . . or politics": Terman (1955), p. 29.
143. a fatherly science teacher: cf. Goodrich et al. (1951), p. 17.
143. "masterfulness . . . dignity": ibid.
143. "It would . . . their students": ibid.
143. Ernest Orlando Lawrence: biographical details from Alvarez (1970), Childs (1968) and Davis (1968).
143. "almost . . . mathematical thought": Alvarez (1970), p. 253.
144. "it seemed . . . atomic nucleus": Lawrence (1951), p. 430.
144. "the tedious . . . electron volts": Alvarez (1970), p. 260.
145. "In his . . . after night": ibid., p. 261.
145–146. "This new . . . arrangement": Lawrence (1951), p. 431.
146. "It struck . . . magnetic field": Alvarez (1970), p. 261.
146. "Oh, that . . . your own": quoted in Davis (1968), p. 19.
146. "I'm going . . . famous!": quoted in Childs (1968), p. 140.
146. a battered gray Chrysler: cf. Smith and Weiner (1980), p. 135.
146. "unbelievable vitality . . . the opposite": quoted in Childs (1968), p. 143.
148. "The intensity . . . was before": quoted in Davis (1968), p. 38.
148. "having a . . . *about 300*": Lawrence and Livingston (1932), p. 32.
148. "Assuming then . . . do this": ibid., p. 34.
149. Oppenheimer told a friend: cf. Davis (1968), p. 23.
149. "men of . . . broad intuition": Rabi (1969), p. 7.
149. the tunnel effect: cf. Bethe (1968), p. 393: "This work led him on to a treatment of the ionization of the hydrogen atom by electric fields, probably the first paper describing the penetration of a potential barrier."
150. dying suns: e.g. Oppenheimer and Snyder (1939).
150–151. "You put . . . know peace": Smith and Weiner (1980), pp. 155–156.
151. "Interested to . . . the circumstances": quoted in Childs (1968), p. 174.
151. "uncommon sensitivity . . . of thinking": Eiduson (1962), p. 105–106.
151. "Were this . . . such fantasying": ibid., p. 106.
152. "This discovery . . . in him": Pais (1982), p. 253.
152. "But if . . . about them": quoted in Rozental (1967), p. 139.
152. "And Bohr . . . not quite' ": Oppenheimer (1963), I, p. 3.
153. The Bakerian Lecture: "Nuclear constitution of atoms" in Rutherford (1965), p. 14ff.
153. "the possible . . . intense field": ibid., p. 34.
153. James Chadwick: biographical details in Massey and Feather (1976). Cf. also Chadwick's various recollections.
153. "was hardly . . . of Moseley": Massey and Feather (1976), p. 50.
153–154. "But also . . . Soldiers' ": Chadwick (1954), p. 443.
154. "Before the . . . neutral particle": Chadwick OHI, AIP, pp. 35–36.
155. "And so . . . only occasionally": ibid., p. 36.
155. "It was . . . disposal": Oliphant (1972), p. 67.
155. "dour and . . . became apparent": ibid., p. 68.
155. "to conceal . . . gruff façade": quoted in Wilson (1975), p. 57.
155. "He had . . . chuckle": Massey and Feather (1976), p. 66.
155. "the physics . . . noisy": ibid., p. 12.
156. he said later: paraphrased in ibid., p. 15.
156. "were so . . . of alchemy": Chadwick (1964), p. 159.
157. "passed through . . . be found": Chadwick (1954), p. 445.
157. "the problem . . . to believe": ibid., p. 444.
157. "was a . . . really important": James Chadwick OHI, AIP, p. 49.
157. "We are . . . physics!": Snow (1967), p. 3.
157. "We are . . . complex atoms": Rutherford (1965), p. 181.

PAGE

157. the scintillation method: this discussion follows Feather (1964), esp. p. 136ff.
157. "He found . . . while counting!": Massey and Feather (1976), p. 19.
159. "The loss . . . of them": Eve (1939), p. 341.
159. his armorial bearings: cf. illustration and description in ibid., p. 342.
159. "a real . . . physicist": Segrè (1980), p. 180.
159. "I don't . . . he did": James Chadwick OHI, AIP, p. 70.
159. "Indeed . . . element investigated": Feather (1964), p. 138.
160. "that the . . . backward direction": James Chadwick OHI, AIP, p. 161.
160. "And that . . . the neutron": James Chadwick OHI, AIP, p. 71.
161. "Of course . . . very much": ibid.
161. "together . . . in Paris": Feather (1964), p. 142.
161. "They fitted . . . hydrogenous material": ibid., p. 140.
162. "Not many . . . strange": Chadwick (1964), p. 161.
162. The radiation source: cf. photograph at Crowther (1974), p. 196.
163. "For the . . . oscillograph record": Feather (1964), p. 141.
163. "the number . . . protons": Chadwick (1932b), p. 695.
163. "In this . . . were tested": ibid.
163. "Hydrogen . . . this way": ibid., p. 696.

163–164. "In general . . . of 1920": ibid., p. 697.

164. "It was . . . time": James Chadwick OHI, AIP, p. 71.
164. "But there . . . the letter": ibid., p. 72.
164. "To [Chadwick's] . . . physicist": Segrè (1980), p. 184.
165. That Wednesday: the Kapitza Club traditionally met on Tuesday, but I take it that Chadwick finished the first intense phase of his work with the writing of his letter to *Nature* dated this day, Feb. 17, 1932. His remark about wanting to be chloroformed (see below) indicates he had not yet rested from his ten-day marathon.
165. "a very . . . us all": Oliphant (1972), p. 76.
165. "one of . . . a fortnight": Snow (1981), p. 35.
165. "A beam . . . times faster": Morrison (1951), p. 48.

PAGE

165. "the prehistory . . . nuclear physics": Bethe OHI, AIP, p. 3.
166. *"the personification . . . experimentalist":* Gamow (1966), p. 213. The complete *Faust* text is translated here by Barbara Gamow.
166. "The *Neutron* . . . you agree?: ibid., p. 213.
167. "That which . . . heart in": ibid., p. 214.
167. "Now a . . . along!": ibid.

Chapter 7: Exodus

168. "Antisemitism . . . is violent": Nathan and Norden (1960), p. 37
168. "A new . . . Newton": Pais (1982), Plate II.
168. Nobel Prize nominations: cf. ibid., p. 502ff.
168. "made . . . beyond Newton": quoted in ibid., p. 508.
168. "a massive . . . muscled": Snow (1967a), p. 52.

168–169. "A powerful . . . slipped off": ibid., p. 49.

169. "to look . . . his image": Erikson, "Psychoanalytic Reflections on Einstein's Centenary," p. 157, in Holton and Elkana (1982).
169. "dressed in . . . his eyes": Infeld (1941), p. 92.
169. "finally the . . . structure": quoted in Pais (1982), p. 239. The paper is A. Einstein, *PAW* (1915), p. 844.
169. "One of . . . scientific ideas": quoted in Clark (1971), p. 290.
170. popular lectures: cf. Feuer (1982), p. 82.
170. disrupted lecture: cf. Pais (1982), p. 315ff.
170. "said that . . . German spirit": quoted in Clark (1971), p. 318.
170. Einstein mistakenly thought: cf. Einstein to Arnold Sommerfeld, Sept. 6, 1920: "I attached too much importance to that attack on me, in that I believed that a great part of our physicists took part in it. So I really thought for two days that I would 'desert' as you call it. But soon there came reflection." Quoted in ibid., p. 323ff.
170. " 'My Answer . . . disposition, then": quoted in ibid., p. 319.
170. "Everyone . . . my article": quoted in Pais (1982), p. 316.
171. "miracle . . . deeply hidden": quoted in ibid., p. 37.

PAGE

171. "If you . . . the things": quoted in Clark (1971), p. 469.
171. "Through the . . . social environment": quoted in ibid., p. 36.
171. His father stumbled: for a careful reconstruction of this period in Einstein's life cf. ibid., p. 39ff.
171. "Politically . . . my youth": quoted in ibid., p. 315.
171. medically unfit: Pais (1982), p. 45n.
172. "victorious child": Holton and Elkana (1982), p. 151.
172. "I sometimes . . . grown up": quoted in Clark (1971), p. 27.
172. $E = mc^2$: the paper is A. Einstein, *Jahrb. Rad. Elektr.* 4, 411 (1907).
172. "It is . . . for radium": quoted in Pais (1982), p. 149.
172. "The line . . . the nose": revised from ibid., p. 148ff.
173. "like men . . . postage stamp": quoted in Holton and Elkana (1982), p. 326.
173. "great work . . . were slender": quoted in Clark (1971), p. 252.
173. "I begin . . . younger years": c. 1915, revised from Pais (1982), p. 243.
173. "were . . . ambivalent": quoted in ibid., p. 315.
173. "a new . . . eternity": quoted in Clark (1971), p. 473.
174. "first discovered . . . and dispersion": quoted in ibid., p. 475.
174. "undignified . . . annoyed": quoted in Pais (1982), p. 314.
174. "in a . . . anti-Semitism also": quoted in Young-Bruehl (1982), p. 92.
174. "I am . . . in Germany": quoted in Feuer (1982), p. xxvi.
174. 54,000 marks: deJonge (1978), p. 240.
174–175. "I was . . . years ago": Roberts (1938), p. 265.
175. "These points . . . Wittenberg!": quoted in Toland (1976), p. 96.
175. refers to Jewry more frequently: cf. Hitler (1971), index.
175–176. "no lovers . . . of decomposition": ibid., passim.
176. The sun shines in: cf. photograph of Hitler's cell in Toland (1976), between pp. 172–173.
176. lederhosen: cf. photograph of Hitler at Landsberg, ibid.
176. "I often . . . magic formula!": quoted in ibid., p. 64.
176. "If at . . . in vain": Hitler (1971), p. 679.
177. The Jewish people: sources for this discussion include Arendt (1973), Bauer (1982), Cohn (1967), Dawidowicz (1967, 1975), Laqueur (1965), Litvinoff (1976), Mendelsohn (1970), Mendes-Flohr and Reinharz (1980), Parkes (1964), Patai (1977), *The Protocols of the Meetings of the Learned Elders of Zion* (1934), Rosenberg (1970), Veblen (1919), Weizmann (1949).
177. The fantasy of Jews: cf. Cohn (1967), p. 254.
178. "the enemies of Christ": Parkes (1964) attributes this canard to Catherine II in 1762. The *Encyclopedia Judaica,* however, ascribes it to the Czarina Elizabeth Petrovna in 1742. Whether mother- or daughter-in-law made the statement, it clearly reflects imperial opinion of the Jews at the time of the Polish partition.
179. Edward Teller's grandmother: interview with Herbert York, La Jolla, Calif., June 27, 1983.
179. "The Jews . . . a citizen": Mendes-Flohr and Reinharz (1980), p. 104.
180. "Jewish disorders": quoted in Levin (1977), p. 18.
181. Jews to the U.S.: for annual numbers cf. Mendes-Flohr and Reinharz (1980), p. 374.
181. "I have . . . of course": reported by Herman Rauschning, quoted in Cohn (1967), p. 60.
181. "We owe . . . by heart": quoted in Arendt (1973), p. 360.
181–182. "At eleven . . . the accursed": Cohn (1967), p. 34.
182. "What I . . . the *goyim*": *Protocols* (1934), p. 142.
182. "produced . . . our slaves": ibid., p. 175ff.
182. "The principal . . . the Papacy": ibid., p. 193.
183. "It will . . . a merit": ibid., p. 205.
183. *Protocols* plagiarized: the best discussions of the bizarre history of the *Protocols* are Cohn (1967) and Laqueur (1965).
183. "gave them . . . state itself": Arendt (1973), p. 39.
184. "Thus the . . . larger scale": ibid., p. 360.
184. "Do you . . . need them": Richard Breitling was the journalist. Quoted in Beyerchen (1977), p. 10.
184. meeting with Goebbels: cf. Goebbels' diary entry quoted in Dawidowicz (1975), p. 68.

PAGE

185. "I have . . . couldn't happen": quoted in Blumberg and Owens (1976), p. 51.
185. "I didn't . . . to change": Otto Frisch OHI, AIP, p. 12.
185. "Civil . . . must retire": quoted in Dawidowicz (1975), p. 77.
185. "descended from . . . grandparents": quoted in ibid., p. 78.
185. a quarter of the physicists: Beyerchen (1977), p. 44.
185. Some 1,600 scholars: ibid.
186. "I decided . . . my life": quoted in Clark (1971), p. 539.
186. "We sat . . . to America": quoted in ibid., p. 543.
186. *"Ich bin . . . dafür":* quoted in ibid., p. 544.
186. fifteen thousand: according to Pais (1982), p. 450. Clark (1971), p. 544, has $16,000.
186. "Turn around . . . again": quoted in Pais (1982), p. 318.
187. "recommended . . . me also": Eugene Wigner OHI, AIP, p. 2.
187. "There was . . . it well": ibid., p. 6.
187. Leo Szilard to Eugene Wigner: Oct. 8, 1932, Egon Weiss personal papers, USMA Library, West Point, N.Y. Trans. Edda König.
187. "close . . . 1933": Weart and Szilard (1978), p. 14.
188. "On entering . . . up here": Elsasser (1978), p. 161.
188. numbers of dismissals: Beyerchen (1977), p. 44.
188. Bethe's dismissal: cf. Bernstein (1980), p. 34.
188. "Geiger . . . personal level": ibid., p. 33.
188. "He wrote . . . nothing": ibid., p. 35.
188. Bethe at 27: telephone interview with Rose Bethe, Jan. 18, 1984.
188–189. "I was . . . whatever": interview with Hans Bethe, Ithaca, N.Y., Sept. 12, 1982.
189. "Sommerfeld . . . come back": Bernstein (1980), p. 35.
189. "His early . . . mechanics": Wigner (1969), p. 2.
189–190. "It was . . . I could": interview with Edward Teller, Stanford, Calif., June 19, 1982.
190. "an old German nationalist": quoted in Blumberg and Owens (1976), p. 49.
190. "I really . . . in Germany": ibid.
190. "quite shocked . . . the line": Frisch (1979), p. 52.

PAGE

190. "very disappointed . . . back to": Otto Frisch OHI, AIP, p. 14.
190. "To me . . . I felt": Rozental (1967), p. 137.
191. "Stern . . . Blackett had": Frisch OHI, AIP, p. 14.
191. "If physics . . . dictator": quoted in "Patrick Maynard Stuart Blackett," *Biog. Mem. F.R.S.* 21, p. 22.
191. "Lise Meitner . . . to you": Frisch OHI, AIP, p. 12ff.
192. Bohr persuaded him: so Franck told Alice Kimball Smith: Smith, "The Politics of Control—The Role of the Chicago Scientists." Symposium on the 40th Anniversary of the First Chain Reaction, University of Chicago, Dec. 2, 1982. Franck's daughters have emphasized to the contrary that his decision to resign in protest was made "for himself and by himself and nobody else had any part in making it": Beyerchen (1977), p. 16; p. 215, n. 8.
192. Max Born's reinstatement: according to Beyerchen (1977), p. 21.
192. "We decided . . . of May": Born (1971), p. 113.
192. "Ehrenfest . . . young ones": ibid., p. 113ff.
192. "the old . . . for it": Shils (1964). Shils tells the Vienna story here at length and notes that he heard it not from Szilard but from "other persons." It was, he writes, "absolutely characteristic of Szilard to launch a campaign of aid and claim no credit later for himself."
193. "that as . . . do something": ibid., p. 38.
193. the major U.S. effort: cf. Duggan and Drury (1948) and Weiner (1969).
193. "a long . . . interview": Weart and Szilard (1978), p. 32.
193. "university of exiles": Born (1971), p. 114.
193. In Switzerland: Szilard reports these activities in a letter to Beveridge dated May 23, 1933. Leo Szilard Papers.
193. "sympathetic . . . German scientists": Szilard to Beveridge, ibid.
193. "he proposed . . . them out": Frisch (1979), p. 53.
194. Benjamin Liebowitz: for biographical data cf. "A memorial service for BENJAMIN LIEBOWITZ," Egon Weiss personal papers, West Point.

PAGE

194. "It is . . . Germany": Liebowitz to Ernest P. Boas, May 5, 1933. Szilard Papers.
194. "dismissed . . . stronger": Weart and Szilard (1978), p. 36.
194–195. "rather tired . . . the parties": ibid., p. 35.
195. Locker-Lampson: cf. Clark (1971), p. 566ff.
195. "talking . . . goats": quoted in ibid., p. 603.
195. "He did . . . forward": Moon (1974), p. 23.
195. British appointments: Bentwich (1953), p. 13, puts this number at 155.
195. American contributions: ibid., p. 19: "The total American financial contribution by 1935 equalled that of the rest of the world."
196. Emergency Committee arrivals: cf. Duggan and Drury (1948), p. 25.
196. one hundred physicists: Weiner (1969), p. 217.
196. "is a . . . distraction": Nathan and Norden (1960), p. 245.
196. "fell in . . . to him": Wigner OHI, AIP, p. 5.
196. "large and . . . atmosphere": Ulam (1976), p. 69ff.
196. "I used . . . the climate": ibid., p. 158.
196. "was astonished . . . and sang": Infeld (1941), p. 245.
197. Hans Bethe walked: Hans Bethe OHI, AIP.
197. "When I . . . me away": Mendelssohn (1973), p. 164.

Chapter 8: Stirring and Digging

198. Stirring and Digging: cf. Francis Bacon, *The Advancement of Learning:* "Surely to alchemy this right is due, that it may be compared to the husbandman whereof Aesop makes the fable: that, when he died, told his sons that he had left unto them gold buried underground in his vineyard; and they digged all over the ground, and gold they found none; but by reason of their stirring and digging the mould about the roots of their vines, they had a great vintage the year following: so assuredly the search and stir to make gold hath brought to light a great number of good and fruitful inventions and experiments." Quoted in Seaborg (1958), p. xxi.

PAGE

198. the Gamows' escape: cf. Gamow (1970), p. 108ff.
198–199. "I . . . my eyes": ibid., p. 120.
199. "You see . . . to arrange": ibid., p. 122.
199. "the voice . . . they were!": ibid., p. 123.
200. "unable . . . neutron": quoted in Weart (1979), p. 44.
200. "In the . . . encouragement": revised from ibid., p. 44, and Biquard (1962), p. 36.
200–201. "the emission . . . element": Joliot, quoted in Biquard (1962), p. 36.
201. "I irradiate . . . it continues": quoted in ibid., p. 32.
201. "The following . . . working order": ibid., p. 37.
201. "The yield . . . million atoms": Joliot (1935), p. 370.
202. "never . . . of view": quoted in Weart (1979), p. 46.
202. "Marie Curie . . . her life": quoted in Biquard (1962), p. 33.
202. "one of . . . the century": Segrè (1980), p. 197ff.
202. "These . . . transmutation": ibid., p. 198, where the letter to *Nature* is reproduced as Fig. 9.15.
202. "I congratulate . . . any success": quoted in Biquard (1962), p. 39.
202–203. "we are . . . necessary precautions": Joliot (1935), p. 373.
203. "spending much . . . very long": Weart and Szilard (1978), p. 36.
203. "became . . . chain reaction": ibid., p. 17.
203. "a little . . . a job": ibid.
203. "I remember . . . memoranda": ibid., p. 19ff.
203. a patent application: cf. Szilard (1972), p. 622ff.
203. March 12, 1934: LS completed the application on Saturday, March 10. He had to wait until Monday to file.
203. books on microfilm: cf. Szilard (1972), p. 722.
203. "In accordance . . . substances": ibid., p. 622. The balance of the application seems to concern a rough early conception of a thermonuclear fusion reactor of the Shiva type with a blanket for breeding heavy-element transmutations!
204. "that the . . . the other": Weart and Szilard (1978), p. 18.
204. "None of . . . England": ibid.

PAGE

204. Fermi was prepared: cf. Holton (1974), for evidence and a discussion.
204. "I remember . . . effective": Frisch (1976b), p. 46.
205. Both Fermi's biographers: L. Fermi (1954) and Segrè (1970).
205. "Fermi must . . . handwriting": Segrè (1970), p. 8.
205. "I studied . . . physics": quoted in ibid., p. 10.
205. "a very . . . death": quoted in ibid., p. 11.
206. "the partial . . . examination": ibid., p. 12.
206. "In the . . . propagandist": Fermi to Enrico Persico, Jan. 30, 1920, in ibid., p. 194. Segrè translates the extant Fermi-Persico correspondence in an appendix, p. 189ff.
206. "shy . . . solitude": ibid., p. 33.
206. "could not . . . nebulous": ibid., p. 23.
206. "he . . . in Rome": ibid., p. 33.
206. "Fermi remembered . . . recognize him": interview with Emilio Segrè, Lafayette, Calif., June 29, 1983.
206. "toward . . . experiment": Segrè (1970), p. 23.
206. "disliked . . . possible": quoted in ibid., p. 55.
206. "enlightening simplicity": ibid.
206. "quantum engineer": quoted by Weisskopf in Weiner (1972), p. 188.
206–207. "Not a . . . pretty active": quoted in Davis (1968), p. 266.
207. "cold . . . nature": quoted in ibid., p. 265.
207. "Fermi's thumb . . . flying": L. Fermi (1954), p. 7ff.
207. "was . . . sex appeal": ibid., p. 10.
207. "perhaps . . . than against": ibid., p. 15. LF's emphasis.
208. the time was ripe: sources for this discussion include Holton (1974) and Amaldi (1977) as well as L. Fermi (1954) and Segrè (1970).
208. "A fantastic . . . intuition": quoted in Holton (1974), p. 172.
209. too remote: according to Segrè (1970), p. 72.
209. Fermi found amusing: Segrè interview, June 29, 1983.
209. Fermi skiing: L. Fermi in Badash (1980), p. 89.
209. "We had . . . radioactivity": quoted in Holton (1974), p. 173, n. 81.
209. "Since the . . . interesting": Rabi (1970), p. 16.

PAGE

210. "The location . . . of study": Segrè (1970), p. 53.
210. crude Geiger counters: cf. Amaldi (1977), p. 301, Fig. 3, and Libby (1979), p. 41.
211. 100,000 neutrons: cf. Fermi paper (hereafter FP) 84*b,* Fermi (1962), p. 674.
211. "Small cylindrical . . . seconds": ibid.
211–212. "We organized . . . our stuff": Segrè (1955), p. 258ff.
212. The next letter: FP 85*b,* Fermi (1962), p. 676.
212. "Amaldi . . . good loser": L. Fermi (1954), p. 89.
213. 800 millicuries: cf. FP 99, Fermi (1962), p. 748.
213. "a very . . . determined": FP 86*b,* ibid., p. 678.
213. "This negative . . . than 92": FP 99, ibid., p. 750.
213. "a new element": cf. partial text of Corbino's address in Segrè (1970), p. 76.
214. "The discoveries . . . wars": Weart and Szilard (1978), p. 37.
214. "Of course . . . the point": ibid., p. 39.
214. "the liberation . . . the chain": Szilard (1972), p. 639.
214. critical mass: cf. ibid., p. 642.
214. "some cheap . . . an explosion": ibid.
215. "Marie Curie . . . not corrupted": quoted in Eve (1939), p. 388.
215. "which was . . . experiments": Weart and Szilard (1978), p. 20.
215. Szilard applied to Rutherford: cf. LS to Ernest Rutherford, June 7, 1934, Szilard Papers.
215. "These experiments . . . confirmed": Weart and Szilard (1978), p. 20.
215. the problem with helium: cf. Brown (n.d.), p. 53ff.
216. early in July: Amaldi (1977), p. 305.
216. "going on . . . laboratory": ibid.
216. an unanswered question: cf. Amaldi (1977), p. 310, and FP 98 (p. 744), FP 103 (p. 755) and p. 641 of Fermi (1962).
217. "We also . . . 3 minutes": Amaldi (1977), p. 310.
217. radiative-capture problem: cf. FP 103, Fermi (1962), p. 754ff.
217. "and those . . . important": ibid., p. 756.
217. "Shortly afterwards . . . results": ibid., p. 641.
217. "In particular . . . same room": Amaldi (1977), p. 311ff.

PAGE

218. "I will . . . have been": quoted in Segrè (1970), p. 80. The colleague was Subrahmanyan Chandrasekhar.
218. "About noon . . . radioactivity": ibid.
218. "the halls . . . magic!": L. Fermi (1954), p. 98.
219. water worked: cf. FP 105*b*, Fermi (1962), p. 761ff.
219. "Fermi dictated . . . time": Segrè (1970), p. 81.
219. "They shouted . . . drunk": L. Fermi (1954), p. 100.
219. "Influence of . . . neutrons—I": FP 105*b*, Fermi (1962).
219. "The case . . . same element": ibid., p. 761.
219–220. "might never . . . found out": Hans Bethe OHI, AIP, p. 30.
220. *Physical Review* paper: A. von Grosse, *Phys. Rev.* 46:241 (1934).
220. "It was . . . characteristics": Hahn (1966), p. 141.
220. "I began . . . chamber": Amaldi (1977), p. 317.
221. "The experiments . . . results": ibid.
221. "Through these . . . weight 239": FP 107, Fermi (1962), p. 791.
221. "Other examples . . . bromine": Szilard (1972), p. 646.
221. "So I . . . a chemist": Weart and Szilard (1978), p. 18.
221–222. "understood . . . done": ibid., p. 19.
222. Frederick Alexander Lindemann: cf. especially Mendelssohn (1973), p. 168ff.
222. "If your . . . physicist": quoted in ibid., p. 168.
223. "he became . . . for arrogance": ibid., p. 169.
223. "unbending . . . gentlemen": ibid., p. 168.
223. "gracious living . . . friendship": ibid., p. 171.
223. "saw a . . . modern war": Churchill (1948), p. 79ff.
223. "the question . . . as possible": Weart and Szilard (1978), p. 41.
224. "there is . . . taking patents": ibid., p. 40.
224. "Early in . . . proper use": ibid., p. 42.
224. "from private . . . at Oxford": ibid.
224. "there appears . . . concerned": quoted in ibid., p. 18, n. 28.
224. "I daresay . . . Government anything": quoted in Szilard (1972), p. 733.
224–225. "contains . . . this country": ibid., p. 734.

PAGE

225. "Bohr in . . . that game": Rozental (1967), p. 138.
226. "The lid . . . past year": ibid., p. 153.
226. "was drowned . . . for him": Oppenheimer (1963), II, p. 30.
227. "On that . . . understand it": Frisch (1979), p. 102.
227. "Neutron capture and nuclear constitution": Bohr (1936).
227. "For still . . . to become": ibid., p. 348.
228. "the consequences . . . developed": ibid.
228. "This 1937 . . . cleared up": Wheeler (1963b), p. 40.
228–229. Rutherford's death: cf. Eve (1939), p. 424ff, and Oliphant (1972), p. 153ff.
229. "seedy": quoted in Oliphant (1972), p. 154.
229. "a wonderful . . . of hope": quoted in ibid., p. 155.
229. "I want . . . Nelson College": quoted in Eve (1939), p. 425.
229. "When the . . . life": Oliphant (1972), p. 155.
229–230. "Life is . . . encouragement": Smith and Weiner (1980), p. 204.
230. "to me . . . father": Bohr (1958), p. 73.
230. "Voltaire . . . atomic physics": quoted in Eve (1939), p. 430ff.
230. "I have . . . attractive": ibid., p. 424.
230. "On element 93": *Zeitschrift für Angewandte Chemie* 47: 653. Cf. translation in Graetzer and Anderson (1971), p. 16ff.
231. Segrè remembers: cf. Emilio Segrè OHI, AIP, p. 24, and my Segrè interview.
231. "I think . . . elements": Otto Frisch OHI, AIP, p. 38.
231. "It is . . . element": FP 98, Fermi (1962), p. 734.
231. He later told Teller, Segrè, Woods: e.g., the three citations ff.
231. "Fermi refused . . . of nuclei": Teller (1979), p. 140.
231–232. "You know . . . to himself": Segrè interview, June 29, 1983.
232. "Why was . . . allowed": Libby (1979), p. 43.

Chapter 9: An Extensive Burst

233. "I believe . . . been granted": Meitner (1964), p. 2.
233. "quite convinced . . . had done": James Chadwick OHI, AIP, p. 76.
233. "Slight . . . by nature": Frisch (1968), p. 414.

PAGE

233. "there . . . X-rays": Frisch (1978), p. 427.
234. "persuaded . . . collaboration": Meitner (1962), p. 6.
234. "not only . . . Professor Hahn": Hahn (1966), p. 66.
234. "she could . . . story-teller": Frisch (1968), p. 414.
234. "totally . . . vanity": Frisch (1978), p. 426.
234. "though . . . could play": Frisch (1968), p. 414.
234. "It . . . alert": Axelsson (1946), p. 31.
234. "the vision . . . final truth": Frisch (1978), p. 426.
234. "For Hahn . . . to explain": ibid., p. 428.
235. Hahn met Joliot: Weart (1979), p. 57.
235. "It seems . . . its interpretation": quoted in Graetzer and Anderson (1971), p. 37.
235. "Who knows . . . storm": quoted in Churchill (1948), p. 262.
235. "The years . . . conditions": Meitner (1959), p. 12.
235. Meitner feared: cf. Frisch (1968), p. 410ff.
236. "I gave . . . an emergency": an important detail; after the war Meitner bitterly accused Hahn of railroading her out of Germany so that he would not have to share the discovery of fission with her—as if he foresaw it in July. Cf. Hahn (1970), p. 199.
236. "I took . . . Holland colleagues": Axelsson (1946), p. 31.
236. Physical Institute: such is LM's address in Meitner and Frisch (1939). In his postwar recollections Frisch consistently places her at the "newly-built" Nobel Institute.
236. she photographed him: cf. Szilard (1972), p. 18.
237. "He told . . . the day": quoted in Leigh Fenly, "The Agony of the Bomb, and Ecstasy of Life with Leo Szilard." *San Diego Union,* Nov. 19, 1978, p. D-8.
237. "a *very* . . . a 'stranger' ": LS to Gertrud Weiss, March 26, 1936. Trans. Edda König. Szilard Papers.
237. "stay in . . . the war?": Weart and Szilard (1978), p. 20ff.
237. Lewis L. Strauss: details of his life from Pfau (1984), which Dr. Pfau was kind enough to allow me to read in MS.

PAGE

238. "My boy . . . you down": quoted in ibid.
238. "I became . . . hospitals": Strauss (1962), p. 163.
238. the report to *Nature:* cf. Szilard (1972), pp. 140, 147ff.
238. "An isotope . . . my parents": Strauss (1962), p. 164.
238–239. "August 30 . . . Leo Szilard": Szilard Papers.
239. owned patent jointly: "Patents which have been taken out by Dr. Brasch and Dr. Szilard were to be brought into this foundation." File memorandum, Szilard Papers.
239. "asked me . . . 'surge generator' ": Strauss (1962), p. 164.
239. "In the . . . fresh fruit": Shils (1964), p. 39.
239. debates among lawyers: cf. file memorandum, Szilard Papers.
239. "On April . . . taste unchanged": M. Lenz to LS, April 15, 1938. Szilard Papers.
240. "I left . . . wife here": Emilio Segrè OHI, AIP, p. 31.
240. a map of Ethiopia: Segrè (1970), p. 87.
241. "He was . . . to fascism": ibid., p. 63.
241. "We worked . . . Civil War": quoted in ibid., p. 90.
241. "That was . . . Italy": ibid., p. 91.
241. "America . . . of Europe": ibid., p. 92.
242. "I have . . . through anything": quoted in Shirer (1960), p. 343.
242. "Rome of . . . and master": revised from Segrè (1970), p. 95.
242. Fermi told Segrè: ibid., p. 96.
242. "Jews . . . Italian race": quoted in L. Fermi (1954), p. 119.
243. "Why should . . . can't he?": quoted in Frisch (1979), p. 108.
243. "the dangers . . . other societies": Bohr (1958), p. 23.
243. "we may . . . and variety": ibid., p. 30.
243. the German delegates: according to Moore (1966), p. 218.
243. "the . . . prejudices": Bohr (1958), p. 31.
243. "destroying . . . each other": Arendt (1951), p. 478.
243. Bohr and Fermi's Nobel: cf. L. Fermi (1954), p. 120ff.
244. Goldhaber: cf. Szilard (1972), p. 141ff.
244. "the whole . . . be delayed": Churchill (1948), p. 292.

PAGE

244. "I just . . . and see": Weart and Szilard (1978), p. 21.
245. "was . . . mood": quoted in Churchill (1948), p. 301.
245. "The British . . . worse treatment": ibid., p. 301ff.
245. "conditions . . . security": quoted in ibid., p. 302.
245. "He told . . . was accepted": quoted in ibid., p. 306.
245. "that this . . . than Germans": quoted in ibid., p. 309.
245. "How horrible . . . my soul": quoted in ibid., p. 315.
246. "regard the . . . another again": quoted in ibid., p. 318.
246. invasion of British Isles: cf. ibid.
246. "This is . . . our time": quoted in ibid.
246. Lindemann drove up: this story and Lindemann's remark appear in Mendelssohn (1973), p. 172.
246. "the complete . . . of force": Churchill (1948), p. 303.
246. HAVE ON . . . DECISIONS: Weart and Szilard (1978), p. 48.
246. "As my . . . decreased": Szilard (1972), p. 185.
247. University of Rochester: Goldhaber, Hill and Szilard, *Phys. Rev.* 55:47, refers to these experiments "to be reported in the following paper." They are therefore not reported in *Phys. Rev.* 55:47 as Weart and Szilard (1978) assert (p. 53, n.1). Szilard in Weart and Szilard (1978), p. 53, says to the point: "I went up to Rochester and stayed there for two weeks and made some experiments on indium which finally cleared up the mystery." Since he wrote the Admiralty on Dec. 21, 1938 (cf. Weart and Szilard, p. 60), the Rochester work probably occurred in late November–early December.
247. "Taken . . . by fractionation": quoted in Graetzer and Anderson (1971), p. 38.
247. "You can . . . muddled up": quoted in ibid., p. 39ff.
247. Strassmann speculated: cf. Irving (1967), p. 21. Irving interviewed both Strassmann and Hahn.
248. "must be . . . alpha particles": quoted in Graetzer and Anderson (1971), p. 42.
248. Meitner wrote in warning: according to Frisch (1979), p. 115. Frisch says elsewhere that this letter has been lost. It is not included among the Hahn-Meitner correspondence in Hahn (1975). All translations from the Hahn-Meitner correspondence by Edda König.

PAGE

248. "Bohr was . . . elements": Hahn (1970), p. 150.
249. "Hard . . . be withdrawn": L. Fermi (1954), p. 123.
249. "especially rich ones": quoted in Dawidowicz (1975), p. 135.
250. "your discovery . . . slow neutrons": quoted in Segrè (1970), p. 98.
250. "Most of . . . very interesting": Hahn (1975), p. 75ff.
250. Meitner's living conditions: cf. ibid., pp. 91, 93, 103.
250. Eva von Bahr-Bergius: Johansson (n.d.), p. 1, and Hahn (1975), p. 103.
250. "Of course . . . important apparatus": Hahn (1975), p. 99.
250. "Concerning . . . care of": ibid., p. 76.
250. "a little . . . somewhat better": ibid., p. 77.
251. "As much . . . like *barium*": ibid., p. 77ff.
251. KWI layout: cf. floor plan, Max Planck Society Library and Archive, Berlin-Dahlem, and illustration accompanying "Die Kernspaltung," *Bild der Wissenschaft,* Dec. 1978, pp. 68–69.
251. KWI tables: the composite worktable preserved at the Deutsches Museum in Munich would appear to be the measurement-room table with a paraffin block, flasks and filters added to represent the other work areas.
252. "forms . . . crystals": Hahn (1966), p. 154ff.
252. "The attempts . . . being perceptible": Hahn (1946), p. 58.
252. "Exciting . . . mesothorium": quoted in Irving (1967), p. 23.
253. "Perhaps you . . . somewhat bearable": Hahn (1975), p. 78ff.
253. "very warm . . . wishes": ibid., p. 79.
253. Hahn had little joy: cf. ibid., p. 78: "How much I am looking forward to it—after such a long time without you—you can imagine."
253. *Naturwissenschaften:* cf. ibid.: "But before the institute closes we still want to write something . . . for Naturwiss." (Dec. 19, 1938); p. 81: "Since yesterday we have been putting together our Ra-Ba proofs. . . . On Friday the work is supposed to be turned

PAGE

in to Naturwiss. . . . The whole thing is not very well suited for [them] but they will publish it quickly" (Dec. 21, 1938). Cf. also Irving (1967), p. 27. Irving has it nearly right.

253. "Your radium . . . impossible": Hahn (1975), p. 79.
253. "if you . . . New Year": ibid., p. 79ff.
254. "Our radium . . . it quickly": ibid., p. 81.
254. "Further experiments . . . altogether": Weart and Szilard (1978), p. 80.
254. "just about . . . point": Szilard (1972), p. 185.
254. Hahn's and Strassmann's paper: all quotations from Hahn and Strassmann (1939a), trans. Hans G. Graetzer.
255. "especially . . . any more": Hahn (1966), p. 157.
256. "that I . . . box": Jungk (1958), p. 68. The Rosebaud pickup version is in Irving (1967), p. 27.
256. Kungälv: for much of this history cf. Claesson (1959).
257. Frisch and Meitner in Kungälv: sources for this episode, one of the most confused in the entire story, are Frisch (1967b, 1968, 1978, 1979); Frisch OHI, AIP; Rozental (1967); Clark (1980); Meitner (1962, 1964). A close reading of Hahn (1975) is extremely important for straightening out the accumulated errors of memory.
257. a quiet inn: the building, at No. 9, had become in 1982 a veterans' hall.
257. met in the evening: Frisch OHI, AIP, p. 33.
257. a large magnet: ibid.
257. insisted Frisch read it: Rozental (1967), p. 144: "But she wouldn't listen; I had to read that letter."
257. "Barium . . . mistake": Frisch OHI, AIP, p. 33.
257. "Finally . . . my problem": Meitner (1962), p. 7.
257–258. "But it's . . . that": Frisch OHI, AIP, p. 34.
258. "But how . . . drop": Rozental (1967), p. 144.
258. "Couldn't . . . of thing": Frisch OHI, AIP, p. 34.
258. "Now . . . opposite points": ibid.
258. "Well . . . I mean": ibid.
258. "I remember . . . instability": ibid.
259. "Then . . . energy": ibid.

PAGE

259–260. "gave a . . . well": Meitner (1964), p. 4.
260. "had . . . her head": Frisch OHI, AIP, p. 34.
260. "One fifth . . . fitted": Frisch (1979), p. 116.
260. "Lise . . . much lighter": Frisch OHI, AIP, p. 37.
260. Hahn's letter of Dec. 21: cf. LM to OH, Dec. 29, 1938: "Furthermore, how about the so-called actinium? Can they be separated from lanthanum or not?" Hahn (1975), p. 83. Hahn reported that result in his Dec. 21 letter; if Meitner had received it she would have known.
260. "barium fantasy . . . something": Hahn (1975), p. 82.
261. "very exciting . . . it": ibid., p. 83.
261. "Today . . . amazing": ibid.
261. "against . . . experience": quoted in Weart (1979), p. 59.
261. "We have . . . start": Hahn (1975), p. 84.
261. "If your . . . results": ibid.
261. "keen . . . Bohr": Rozental (1967), p. 145.
261. OF-NB meeting on Jan. 3: cf. OF to LM, Jan. 13, 1939: "Only today was I able to speak with Bohr about the bursting uranium." Stuewer (1985), p. 50.
261. "I had . . . be!": Rozental (1967), p. 145. Frisch misplaces this conversation to a later time.
261. "since Bohr . . . tomorrow": quoted in Stuewer (1985), p. 51.
261–262. "I am . . . findings": Hahn (1975), p. 85ff.
262. chronology of paper development and meeting with Bohr: Stuewer (1985), p. 51, quoting a contemporary letter from OF to LM.
262. Frisch mentioned experiment to Bohr: cf. Bohr's letter to his wife quoted at Moore (1966), p. 233: "I emphasized that Frisch had also spoken of an experiment in his notes." Note that according to OF this discussion occurred before he talked to Placzek. Placzek probably did not, therefore, as OF later remembered, suggest the experiment.
262. chronology of Placzek discussion: OF to LM, Jan. 8, 1939, quoted in Stuewer (1985), p. 53.
262. "was like . . . cancer": Stuewer (1979), p. 72.

PAGE

262. "One would . . . high": Frisch (1939), p. 276.
263. Jan. 13 until 6 A.M.: Frisch confirms date and time from his original laboratory notes in Stuewer (1979), p. 72.
263. "pulses at . . . two": Frisch (1939), p. 276.
263. "At seven . . . camp": Frisch OHI, AIP, p. 35.
263. "a state . . . confusion": ibid.
263. William A. Arnold: personal communication.
263. a dividing living cell: "Bohr had always urged that a nucleus behaved like a small droplet; a uranium nucleus . . . might divide itself into two smaller nuclei . . . much as a living cell becomes two smaller cells by fission." Frisch (1978), p. 428.
264. "I wrote . . . tail": Frisch OHI, AIP, p. 36.
264. two papers for *Nature:* Meitner and Frisch (1939); Frisch (1939).
264. papers posted: Stuewer (1985), p. 53.
264. "As we . . . seasickness": Rosenfeld (1979), p. 342.
264. "We . . . Fermi family": L. Fermi (1954), p. 139.
265. "During the . . . none": ibid., p. 154.
265. Rosenfeld thought paper sent: cf. Rosenfeld (1979), p. 343.
265. "In those . . . train": Stuewer (1979), p. 77.
265. "The effect . . . directions": Rosenfeld (1979), p. 343.
265. "I was . . . off": quoted in Moore (1966), p. 231.
265. Bohr letter to *Nature:* Bohr (1939a).
265. "Can you . . . weeks": Eugene Wigner OHI, AIP, p. 28.
265-266. "they said . . . doomed": interview with Eugene Wigner, Princeton N.J., Jan. 21, 1983.
266. "Wigner told . . . me": Weart and Szilard (1978), p. 53.
266. "if, as . . . proceeding": quoted in Stuewer (1985), p. 52.
267. Rabi from Bohr himself: as he remembers it. Telephone interview Feb. 27, 1984.
267. "probably . . . night": telephone interview with Willis E. Lamb, Jr., Feb. 24, 1984.
267. Rabi told Fermi: but remembers doing so as early as Jan. 17, 1939, which is difficult to reconcile with Fermi's proposal to Dunning of a confirming experiment on Jan. 25.
267. "I remember . . . news": Fermi (1962), p. 996.
267. "spreading . . . around": Lamb interview, Feb. 24, 1984.
267. "The discovery . . . uranium": quoted in Segrè (1970), p. 217.
267. "I thought . . . Fermi": Weart and Szilard (1978), p. 53.
267-268. "I feel . . . time": ibid., p. 62.
268. Fermi/Dunning/Anderson experiment: cf. Wilson (1975), p. 69ff, and Sachs (1984), p. 18ff.
268. "He came . . . say": Wilson (1975), p. 69ff.
268. "Before I . . . Bohr's": ibid., p. 71.
269. "All we . . . thought": ibid., p. 72.
269. "in general . . . me": quoted in Blumberg and Owens (1976), p. 70.
269. "Bohr has . . . obvious": Teller (1962), p. 8ff.
269. "Fermi . . . at Princeton": quoted in Moore (1966), p. 233.
269. Anderson returned to Pupin: cf. Anderson's account in Sachs (1984), p. 24ff, which includes photostats of Anderson's entries that night in his laboratory notebook, quoted here.
270. thought Dunning would telegraph: Evidence that Dunning had not wired Fermi as of Saturday night is Fermi's unusual response to the Roberts experiment at the DTM. Cf. Bolton (n.d.), p. 18. Frisch's explanation to Bohr is quoted in Stuewer (1985), p. 53.
270. Bohr chiding Frisch: quoted in Stuewer (1985), p. 53.
270. "that no . . . results": quoted in ibid., p. 55.
270. 51 participants: cf. group portrait, Carnegie Institution archives, Washington, D.C.
270. Gamow introduced Bohr: Roberts, et al. (1939). Roberts says Tuve wrote the introductory paragraph to this contemporary paper; the conference, it says, "began . . . with a discussion by Professor Bohr and Professor Fermi." Cf. also R. B. Roberts to E. T. Roberts, Jan. 30, 1939: "The annual theoretical physics conference started Thursday with an announcement by Bohr that Hahn in Germany had discovered a radioactive isotope of barium as a product

PAGE

of bombarding uranium with neutrons." DTM archives, Carnegie Institution.

271. "The Theo . . . implications": Roberts (1979), p. 29.
271. "Fermi . . . atomic power": RBR to ETR, Jan. 30, 1939.
271. KINDLY . . . WRITING: Weart and Szilard (1978), p. 60.
271. "in a . . . anybody": quoted in Weart (1979), p. 63.
271. Joliot's response: cf. ibid., p. 63ff.
272. APO: Dr. Louis Brown, DTM, personal communication.
272. "Sat 4:30 . . . Kr?)": R. B. Roberts laboratory notes (n.p.), DTM archives.
273. "tremendous . . . energy release": RBR to ETR, Jan. 30, 1939.
273. "We promptly . . . thorium": Roberts (1979), p. 29.
273. "I told . . . night": RBR to ETR, Jan. 30, 1939.
273. all except Teller: RBR's laboratory notes.
273. Fermi amazed: Bolton (n.d.), p. 18. Bolton talked to both Roberts and Meyer; both agreed on Fermi's response.
273. "I had . . . *Nature*": quoted in Moore (1966), p. 236.
273. "There . . . phone calls": Roberts (1979), p. 30.
273. "Fermi . . . 1939": Wilson (1975), p. 73.
273. "I would . . . physics": ibid., p. 72.

273–274. "So . . . almost pitiful": Luis Alvarez OHI, AIP.

274. "About 9:30 . . . proceed": Wilson (1975), p. 28ff.
274. "I remember . . . conclusions": Alvarez OHI, AIP.
274. "The U . . . way": Smith and Weiner (1980), p. 270ff, conjecture this letter to have been written on Jan. 28, 1939. The "papers" JRO refers to must be Henry's AP story, which reached Berkeley via the *Chronicle* on Sunday, Jan. 29 (on the evidence of Abelson's "About 9:30 a.m."). JRO dated the letter "Saturday"; probably therefore Feb. 4, 1939.
274. "might . . . to hell": Smith and Weiner (1980), p. 209.

274–275. "when fission . . . bomb": quoted in Weiner (1972), p. 90.

275. "A little . . . disappear": quoted in Kevles (1977), p. 324.

Chapter 10: Neutrons

PAGE

279. I. I. Rabi: cf. Bernstein (1975).
279. "infinite": ibid., p. 64.
280. "the mystery . . . nature is": ibid., p. 50.
280. Szilard learned: cf. Weart and Szilard (1978), p. 54.
280. "and say . . . about it": ibid.
280. "Nothing known . . . quantitatively": Wilson (1975), p. 76.
281. "From the . . . precautions": Weart and Szilard (1978), p. 54.
281. at Strauss' request: Strauss (1962), p. 172.
281. "the performance . . . been completed": ibid., p. 171.
281. "No! . . . on it": Teller (1962), p. 9ff.
282. "It is . . . than ever": Rosenfeld (1979), p. 343.
282. "For example . . . square foot": quoted in Clark (1980), p. 86.
284. "From these . . . slow neutrons": Roberts et al. (1939a), p. 417.
284. "Taking a . . . blackboard": Rosenfeld (1979), p. 343.
285. "He wrote . . . the process": ibid., p. 344.
285. "It was . . . also present": Dempster (1935), p. 765.
285. Nier measured the ratio: Nier (1939).
286. "changing from . . . two MeV": Fermi (1949), p. 166.
287. "Resonance in . . . nuclear fission": Bohr (1939b).
287. "were . . . inseparable": Fermi (1962), p. 999.
287. "slow neutrons . . . in uranium": Weart and Szilard (1978), p. 64.
287. "Bohr . . . to U238": Roberts et al. (1940), second page of introduction (unnumbered).

287–288. "For fast . . . abundant isotope": Bohr (1939b), p. 419.

288. a tank of water: cf. Fermi (1962), p. 5ff.
288. "Szilard watched . . . get them' ": Booth (1969), p. 11.

288–289. "All we . . . no radium": Weart and Szilard (1978), p. 55.

289. "to see . . . uranium": ibid., p. 64.
289. "just . . . from England": Weart and Szilard (1978), p. 55.
289. "a strange . . . object": Booth (1969), p. 11.

289*n*. "Fermi and . . . was U-238": Booth (1969), p. 20.

PAGE

289*n*. "outraged": quoted in Moore (1966), p. 248.
289*n*. "It was . . . Bohr's argument": Rosenfeld (1979), p. 345.
290. Roberts' and Meyer's *Phys. Rev.* letter: Roberts et al. (1939b).
290. "As soon . . . their thoughts": Weart and Szilard (1978), p. 66.
291. Szilard-Zinn experiment: cf. Szilard (1972), p. 158ff.
291. "Everything was . . . went home": Weart and Szilard (1978), p. 55.
291. "We find . . . about two": Szilard (1972), p. 158.
291. "more than . . . absorbed": Joliot et al. (1939a), p. 471.
291. "a yield . . . captured": Fermi (1962), p. 6.
291. "I was . . . the neutrons": Teller (1962), p. 10.
292. PERFORMED . . . 50%: Strauss (1962), p. 174.
292. "That night . . . for grief": Weart and Szilard (1978), p. 55.
292. "strongly appealed . . . discoveries": LS to A. H. Compton, Nov. 12, 1942, p. 3. MED 201.
292. "such a . . . handling it": Weart and Szilard (1978), p. 56.
292. G. B. Pegram: cf. Embrey (1970).
293. "probably the . . . world's work": quoted in ibid., p. 378.
293. "Experiments in . . . be disregarded": quoted in L. Fermi (1954), p. 162.
294. "Szilard . . . certainly possible?": Stuewer (1979), p. 282.
294. "We tried . . . into physics": Teller (1979), p. 143.
294. "the enormous . . . of U235": Stuewer (1979), p. 282.
294. "it was . . . taken seriously": Fermi (1962), p. 999.
294. "it can . . . huge factory": Blumberg and Owens (1976), p. 89.
294. "two months . . . one idea": L. Fermi (1954), p. 155.
295. "There's a wop": Hans Bethe interview, Sept. 12, 1982.
295. "a . . . board room": Strauss (1962), p. 236.
295. officer taking notes: these details in ibid., p. 238.
295. "Enrico . . . predictions": L. Fermi (1954), p. 165.
295. "to discuss . . . the majority": Weart and Szilard (1978), p. 56.
295. Joliot et al. paper: Joliot et al. (1939a).

PAGE

295–296. "From that . . . no sense": Weart and Szilard (1978), p. 57.
296. a second Joliot paper: Joliot et al. (1939b).
296. "The interest . . . satisfied": ibid.
296. "I began . . . absurd": quoted in Clark (1981), p. 58ff.
296. German initiatives: cf. especially Irving (1967), the basic reference to this subject.
296. "We take . . . others": quoted in ibid., p. 34.
297. "Tempers and . . . atoms": *New York Times,* April 30, 1939, p. 35.
297–298. "There is . . . whole matter": quoted in Groueff (1967), p. 191.
298. "By separating . . . very great": Wilson (1975), p. 75.
298. "went back . . . to do": Booth (1969), p. 27.
298. "He was . . . Fermi": Wilson (1975), p. 76.
299. "The [radio] . . . neutrons present": Fermi (1962), p. 12.
299. "He liked . . . time thinking": Wilson (1975), p. 78.
299. "Szilard made . . . assistant": Emilio Segrè interview, June 29, 1983.
299. "very competent": Wilson (1975), p. 78.
300. "about ten . . . by uranium": Fermi (1962), p. 12.
300. "an average . . . perhaps 1.5": ibid., p. 13.
300. "We were . . . Placzek's helium": Weart and Szilard (1978), p. 81.
300. the resulting paper: Fermi (1962), p. 11ff.
300. "by an . . . rays": ibid., p. 15.
301. "I was . . . to think": Weart and Szilard (1978), p. 81.
301. "is an . . . possibility": ibid., p. 88.
301–302. "It seems . . . reasonable price": Szilard (1972), p. 195.
302. "Thank you . . . *of uranium*": ibid., p. 197. Fermi's emphasis.
302. "the carbon . . . canned form": ibid., p. 196.
302. "even more . . . considered": ibid., p. 213.
302. "perhaps 50 . . . uranium": ibid., p. 196.
302. about $35,000: LS to "Bill Richards," July 9, 1939. Szilard Papers.
302. "He took . . . fall": Weart and Szilard (1978), p. 82.
303. "I knew . . . really seriously": ibid.
303. "it seems . . . no escape": ibid., p. 90.

PAGE

303. "Dr. Wigner . . . and me": ibid., p. 98.
303. "He was . . . concerned": ibid., p. 82.
303. "shared the . . . be advised": Szilard (1972), p. 214.
303. "worry about . . . to Germany?": Weart and Szilard (1978), p. 82.
304. Gustav Stolper: LS implies in ibid., p. 84, that he first contacted Stolper after his first visit to Long Island. His letter to Einstein of July 19, 1939 (p. 90), however, makes it clear that he talked to Stolper before his first visit but that Stolper did not connect him to Alexander Sachs until *after* that visit. In 1945 (Hellman [1945], p. 70) Sachs implied that he had been in touch with Einstein, Wigner and Szilard before this introduction. The contemporary record cited here indicates otherwise.
304. Sunday, July 16: the letter that resulted from the first meeting was transcribed by Wigner's secretary on Monday morning; July 16, 1939, is the only Sunday between LS's July 9 letter to Fermi and his post-meeting July 19 letter to AE.
304. "We were . . . us there": Weart and Szilard (1978), p. 83.
304–305. "He came . . . soda water": Snow (1967), p. 52ff.
305. "*Daran . . . gedacht!*": Nathan and Norden (1960), p. 291; Clark (1971), p. 669ff.
305. "very quick . . . to object": Weart and Szilard (1978), p. 83.
305. Einstein dictated a letter: cf. ibid. for an English paraphrase of this first Einstein draft. The letter to Roosevelt that eventually resulted is often erroneously attributed to LS. As will become apparent, that letter grew directly from this first draft.
305. "He reported . . . this matter": ibid., p. 90.
306. Alexander Sachs: cf. Hellman (1945). Sachs' book title appears on the cover page of Notes on imminence world war in perspective accrued errors and cultural crisis of the inter-war decades, March 10, 1939, MED 319.7.
306. "took the . . . in person": Weart and Szilard (1978), p. 91.
306. "Although I . . . his promise": ibid.
306. Teller midweek: cf. LS to AE, July 19, 1939, ibid., p. 90.
306–307. "Perhaps you . . . particularly nice": Weart and Szilard (1978), p. 91.

PAGE

307. July 30: I find no reference to this date except the garbled account in Blumberg and Owens (1976), p. 94, which gives it for the earlier LS-Wigner visit. It fell somewhere between July 20, 1939, when LS called AE to confirm his proposal by letter of July 19, and August 2, 1939, when LS again wrote AE. July 30 looks possible.
307. "I entered . . . chauffeur": NOVA (1980), p. 2.
307. a third text: cf. LS to AE, July 2, 1939: "I am enclosing the German text which we drafted together in Peconic." Weart and Szilard (1978), p. 92.
307. "Yes, yes . . . than indirectly": quoted in Teller (1979), p. 144.
307. "at long . . . middle man": Weart and Szilard (1978), p. 92.
307. "that you . . . too cleverly": AE to LS (n.d.). Szilard Papers. Trans. Edda König.
307. "We will . . . too stupid": Weart and Szilard (1978), p. 96. Translation revised.
307. Lindbergh letter: cf. ibid., p. 99.
308. "the Administration . . . in America": ibid., p. 95. This is the letter Sachs ultimately delivered to Roosevelt for AE. Szilard's accompanying memorandum is in Szilard (1972), p. 201ff.
308. "If a . . . the case": Weart and Szilard (1978), p. 97ff.
308. "a horrible . . . atomic bombings": Wigner (1945), p. 28.
308. "the Hungarian conspiracy": E. P. Wigner, memorandum to LS, April 16, 1941. Szilard Papers.
308–309. "Our social . . . the eye": U.S. Senate (1945), p. 7.
309. "a perfect . . . of armour": Churchill (1948), p. 447.
309. "Adam and . . . ever since": Ulam (1976), p. 116.
309. revulsion against bombings: this discussion follows Hopkins (1966).
310. "No theory . . . people": quoted in ibid., p. 454.
310. "inhuman . . . populations": quoted in ibid., p. 455.
310. "one of . . . reprisals": quoted in ibid., p. 457.
310. "Although . . . to come": ibid.
310. "The ruthless . . . immediate reply": Roosevelt (1939), p. 454.

PAGE

311. a secret conference: cf. Irving (1967), p. 40ff.
311. Bohr-Wheeler paper: Bohr and Wheeler (1939c).
311. "Preparatory . . . Fission": Irving (1967), p. 46n.
312. "felt that . . . is abolished": von Weizsäcker (1978), p. 199ff.
312. "is . . . our man": Weart and Szilard (1978), p. 100.
313. "He says . . . matters stand": ibid., p. 101.
313. late afternoon: on the evidence of the brandy and of Sachs' evening meeting with Briggs.
313. Watson meeting: according to AS to E. Wigner, Oct.17, 1939, MED 319.7. Hewlett and Anderson (1962) identify the two participants besides Watson as Adamson and Hoover, the ordnance specialists subsequently appointed to the Uranium Committee, citing a 1947 statement filed by Adamson. Sachs' contemporary letter is more authoritative.
313. "Alex . . . up to?": Moore (1966), p. 268. I have found no other source for this quotation or the Napoleon story but take it Moore interviewed Sachs.
313. Napoleon story: ibid. Moore places this story near the end of the meeting, but it was clearly designed to catch FDR's attention. Cf. also Hellman (1945), p. 71: "The October 11th White House interview was one of a considerable series, during which Sachs, according to friends, would ease the President into the discussion with a few learned jokes."
313. "Bah! . . . visionists!": A. C. Sutcliffe, *Robert Fulton* (Macmillan, 1915), p. 98.
313. "I am . . . to him": quoted in Hellman (1945), p. 70.
314. Sachs did not read the Einstein letter: there is considerable evidence in the record to this point; cf. especially Sachs' almost- explicit admission at U.S. Senate (1945), p. 10: "The Einstein letter of August 2, from which I quoted in part in my own letter, was left with the President, along with my own letter." Hewlett and Anderson (1962), p. 17, confirm the omission: "Sachs read aloud his covering letter, which emphasized the same ideas as the Einstein communication but was more pointed on the need for funds." The scientific authority behind the meeting was nevertheless AE's, as FDR wrote AE on Oct. 19, 1939: "I found this data of such import that I have convened a board . . . to thoroughly investigate the possibilities of your suggestion." Nathan and Norden (1960), p. 297. Some have questioned the effect of the Einstein/Szilard/Sachs contact. Its effect was to convince FDR to appoint the Advisory Committee on Uranium. The emigrés were hardly to blame for the inadequacies of that committee.
314. Sachs summation: Sachs (1945).
314. Sachs intentionally: U.S. Senate (1945), p. 7.
314. "ambivalence . . . and evil": ibid., p. 9.
314. "the more . . . door neighbor": Aston (1938), p. 113ff. Also quoted in ibid.
314. "Alex . . . requires action": U.S. Senate (1945), p. 9.
315. "Don't let . . . me again": ibid.
315. Tuve deputized Roberts: Roberts (1979), p. 37.
315. Sachs breakfast: AS to E. Wigner, Oct. 17, 1939. MED 319.7.
315. Szilard began: cf. his Oct. 26, 1939, memorandum to L. Briggs (Szilard [1972], p. 204ff), which embodies "the statements and recommendations made by me at the meeting of October 21st": LS to LB, Oct. 26, 1939. Weart and Szilard (1978), p.110ff.
315. "too heavy . . . airplane": Szilard (1972), p. 202.
315. "In Aberdeen . . . prize yet": quoted in Teller (1979), p. 144.
315. ordnance depot: cf. Blumberg and Owens (1976), p. 98.
315. Roberts raised objection: Sachs notes "a strong objection" (Sachs [1945] p. 7) from "scientists who were not as much concerned as these refugee scientists"—U.S. Senate (1945), p. 11. The only other American scientist at the meeting besides Briggs was Mohler. He may have concurred with Roberts, but Roberts had the necessary fast-neutron measurements.
316. "there are . . . possibility": Roberts (1939c), p. 613.
316. the DTM had begun assessing: Roberts writes: "After Florida [i.e., March 1939] I continued work . . . on neutron scattering but my main efforts went into measuring cross-section for

PAGE

fission for neutrons of various energies. These were essential in calculating whether a chain reaction would run." Roberts (1979), p. 37. Roberts "made rough measurements of the fission cross-section for neutrons in the energy range 500–2000 kv." Roberts (1940), p. 2.

316. "very unlikely . . . reaction": Roberts (1939c), p. 613.
316. Briggs spoke up: Sachs (1945), p. 11.
316. "astonished . . . enthusiastic": Weart and Szilard (1978), p. 110.
316. "The issue . . . ahead": U.S. Senate (1945), p. 11.
316. "I said . . . is expensive": Blumberg and Owens (1976), p. 98.
316. "How much . . . need": Eugene Wigner interview, Jan. 21, 1983.
316. "The diversion . . . such recommendation": Weart and Szilard (1978), p. 110.
316–317. "For the . . . me yet": Teller (1979), p. 145.
317. $33,000: Szilard (1972), p. 205.
317. "At this . . . be cut": Weart and Szilard (1978), p. 85.
317. "All right . . . your money": Hewlett and Anderson (1962), p. 20.
317. Uranium Committee report: excerpts at Sachs (1945), p. 7ff.
317. Fermi letter: EF to AOCN, Oct. 28, 1939. A.O.C. Nier, personal communication.
317. Nier finally began preparing: A.O.C. Nier, personal communication.

Chapter 11: Cross Sections

318. "I regularly . . . every night": Otto Frisch OHI, AIP, p. 12.
318. "in a . . . any good": ibid., p. 40.
318–319. "I first . . . concentration camp": ibid., p. 39ff.
319. "So I . . . tourist": Frisch (1979), p. 120.
319. "a great . . . sobriety": ibid., p. 121.
319. "a sample . . . changed": ibid., p. 123ff.
319. "material enriched . . . bottom": ibid., p. 124.
319. "the most . . . Hitler war": Snow (1981), p. 105.
319–320. "I managed . . . on time": Frisch (1979), p. 125.
320. "That process . . . the trouble": Frisch (1971), p. 22.
320. "new explosives . . . by them": Churchill (1948), p. 386ff.

PAGE

321. when Oliphant consulted Peierls: cf. Frisch (1971), p. 123.
321. Perrin's formula: Perrin (1939).
321. Peierls' formula: Peierls (1939).
321. "of the . . . practical significance": Clark (1981), p. 85.
322. "ran her . . . times since": Frisch (1979), p. 130.
322. "Is that . . . written?": Frisch OHI, AIP, p. 39.
322. "I wondered . . . be needed?": Frisch (1979), p. 126.
323. "we had . . . to happen": Frisch (1977), p. 23.
323. 10^{-23} cm^2: ibid.
323. "Just . . . playfully": ibid., p. 22
323. "To my . . . or two": Frisch (1979), p. 126.
323. four millionths/second: Gowing (1964), p. 391.
323. "I worked . . . by them": quoted in Clark (1981), p. 88.
323. "I had . . . be possible": Frisch (1979), p. 126.
323. "The cost . . . the war": Wilson (1975), p. 55.
324. "Look . . . about that?": Frisch OHI, AIP, p. 39.
324. "They . . . me": Oliphant (1982), p. 17.
324. "I remember . . . were doing": Frisch (1977), p. 25.
324. "On the . . . in uranium": the full text appears at Gowing (1964), p. 389ff.
324. "to point . . . discussions": ibid., p. 389.
324. "the energy . . . or less": ibid., p. 391.
324. "Memorandum . . . 'super-bomb' ": Ronald M. Clark found this document among the papers of Henry Tizard and published it in Clark (1965), p. 214ff.
325. "I have . . . present time": quoted in ibid., p. 218.
325. "I have . . . on it": Frisch (1979), p. 126.
326. "heavy water . . . yet known": Irving (1967), p. 49.
326. Norsk Hydro: cf. ibid., pp. 49ff, 56ff.
327. Allier and heavy water: cf. Weart (1979), p. 130ff.
327. "The complete . . . United States": York (1976), p. 30. For York on Soviet research cf. p. 29ff.
327. Japanese studies: cf. Pacific War Research Society (1972) (hereafter PWRS) and Shapley (1978).

PAGE

327. Takeo Yasuda: PWRS (1972), p. 18ff.
328. "We are . . . any day": quoted in Moore (1966), p. 267.
328. "this . . . *coup*": Churchill (1948), p. 600.
329. "It was . . . to persecute": Rozental (1967), p. 160ff.
329. Nobel Prize medals: cf. de Hevesy (1962), p. 27.
329. 1.5 tons heavy water: Irving (1967), p. 61.
329. "What I . . . a committee": quoted in Clark (1965), p. 218.
330. "the possibility . . . the Germans": quoted in Clark (1981), p. 92ff.
330. "We entered . . . be investigated": Gowing (1964), p. 394.
330. "unnecessarily excited": quoted in Clark (1981), p. 94.
330. "I still . . . very low": quoted in Clark (1965), p. 219.
330. "Dr. Frisch . . . was feasible": quoted in Clark (1981), p. 95.
330-331. "The Committee . . . separation": Oliphant (1982), p. 17.
331. "the most . . . was wrong": Weart and Szilard (1978), p. 115.
331. Watson decided: Hewlett and Anderson (1962), p. 21.
331. "a crucial . . . application": quoted in ibid.
331. "Divergent chain . . . and carbon": Szilard (1972), p. 216ff.
331. "seemed to . . . went home": Weart and Szilard (1978), p. 115.
332. "the most . . . this research": ibid., p. 122.
332. "I worked . . . of uranium": Booth et al. (1969), p. 28.
332. "very doubtful . . . uranium": quoted in Hewlett and Anderson (1962), p. 20.
333. "These experiments . . . in uranium": Nier et al. (1940a).
333. "Furthermore . . . unseparated U": Nier et al. (1940b).
333. 400 to 500 $\times 10^{-24}$ cm^2: Nier et al. (1940a).
333. "Cartons of . . . make measurements": Wilson (1975), p. 83ff. Anderson recalls 1.5 tons of graphite here; but Fermi (1962), FP 136, p. 34, the report of this experiment, confirms the larger figure.
333. "So physicists . . . happening": Fermi (1962), p. 1000.
334. "A precise . . . delight him": Wilson (1975), p. 84.

PAGE

334. 3×10^{-27} cm^2: Fermi (1962), p. 32.
334. "scientists . . . Institution": Gowing (1964), p. 43.
334. "It is . . . goose chase": quoted in Clark (1965), p. 220.
335. Teller calculation: Hewlett and Anderson (1962), p. 32.
335. "the cross-section . . . pure uranium": Roberts et al. (1940), Introduction, second page.
335. "I came . . . miracle happened": Teller (1977), p. 11.
335. "To deflect . . . my mind": Blumberg and Owens (1976), p. 100.
335. "In the . . . to go": Teller (1979), p. 145.
335. Teller had never bothered: cf. ibid.
335. "We had . . . to me": quoted in *Forbes,* Feb. 18, 1980, p. 62.
335. "the continuance . . . mystic immunity": Roosevelt (1941), p. 184.
335-336. "Then he . . . be lost": Teller (1979), p. 145ff.
336. "but something . . . be lost": Blumberg and Owens (1976), p. 101.
336. "conquest and . . . different cause": Roosevelt (1941), pp. 184–187.
336. "My mind . . . changed since": Blumberg and Owens (1976), p. 101.
336. "That experience . . . lack meant": Bush (1970), p. 74.
337. "It was . . . certainly need": ibid., p. 33.
337. "something meshed . . . language": ibid., p. 35.
337-338. "Each of . . . to turn": ibid., p. 36.
338. "the threat . . . our minds": ibid., p. 34.
338. Bush and Conant proving impossibility: this insightful assessment comes from Dupree (1972), p. 456.
338. "I remember . . . and voice": Snow (1967b), p. 149ff.
339. Franz Simon: cf. Arms (1966).
339. "use my . . . this country": ibid., p. 111.
339. Simon joked: ibid., p. 109.
339. "It was . . . the streets": quoted in Clark (1981), p. 108.
339. "Within a . . . the matter": Moon (1977), p. 544.
339. "I do . . . taken seriously": quoted in Gowing (1964), p. 47.
340. hammered kitchen strainer: Arms (1966), p. 109, says this occurred in "late spring." Fitted against other events June is a reasonable surmise.
340. "Arms . . . separate isotopes": ibid.

PAGE

340. "The first . . . soda-water": quoted in Clark (1981), p. 110.
340. MET . . . KENT: quoted in ibid., p. 95.
341. "an anagram . . . they can": quoted in ibid., p. 96.
341. strategic bombing: cf. Burns (1967); Kennett (1982); Saundby (1961).
341. "short . . . air raid": quoted in Kennett (1982), p. 112.
341. "to undertake . . . are available": quoted in ibid., p. 113.
341–342. Hitler reserved London: ibid., p. 118.
342. "And if . . . cities out!": quoted in ibid., p. 119.
342. "will-to-resist": quoted in ibid., p. 118.
342. "a systematic . . . Lion unnecessary": quoted in ibid., p. 120.
342. HE tonnage: Harrisson (1976), p. 128.
343. deaths: ibid., p. 265.
343. Simon report: reproduced, probably in rewritten form, under a different title as part of the MAUD Report and given in this form in Gowing (1964), p. 416ff. I quote from the MAUD version, p. 416.
343. Simon delivered report: Arms (1966), p. 111.
343. Auer ordered sixty tons: Irving (1967), p. 65.
344. Joliot: the cyclotron episode appears at Weart (1979), p. 156ff.
344. Bothe graphite measurements: Bothe (1944).
345. "When . . . was on": Weart and Szilard (1978), p. 116.
345. "These galling . . . scientific fraud": Bothe (1951), p. 1ff. Trans. Louis Brown.
345. "uranium . . . not work": Frisch (1979), p. 138.
346. "only for . . . consideration": Irving (1967), p. 80. Irving's report of Harteck's meaning is here and on p. 277; the heavy-water recommendation is also here.
346. Suzuki report/Nishina: PWRS (1972), p. 19ff; Shapley (1978), p. 153.
346. Turner letter to *Phys. Rev.*: Turner (1946).
346. "It seems . . . to say": Weart and Szilard (1978), p. 126ff.
346. Turner review article: Turner (1940).
347. "a little . . . of isotopes": Weart and Szilard (1978), p. 126.
347. "it is . . . be used": Turner (1946).
347. "In $_{94}$ EkaOs^{240} . . . be expected": Turner (1946).

PAGE

347*n*. Bohr had speculated: cf. Nobel Committee presentation speech preceding McMillan (1951), p. 310ff.
348. "When a . . . a book": McMillan (1951), p. 314.
348. "Nothing very . . . very interesting": ibid., p. 315.
348. "a uranium . . . neutron capture": McMillan (1939).
348. "the two-day . . . explanation": McMillan (1951), p. 316.
349. "Segrè . . . the story": ibid., p. 317.
349. "As time . . . vacation": ibid., p. 318.
350. "When he . . . work together": ibid., p. 319.
350. "Within a . . . like uranium": Wilson (1975), p. 33.
350. "Radioactive element 93": McMillan and Abelson (1940).
350. "it might . . . contribution": Weart and Szilard (1978), p.127.
350. idea occurred to von Weizsäcker: cf. Irving (1967), p. 68.
351. "finding that . . . neptunium": McMillan (1951), p. 321.
351. "I left . . . national defense": ibid., p. 322.
352. "excellent public . . . children have": L. Fermi (1954), p. 145.
352. "an . . . annual": ibid., p. 148.
352. " 'D'you know . . . crab grass": quoted in ibid., p. 147.
352. "purposely studied . . . Americanization": Segrè (1970), p. 104.
352. Segrè at Purdue: Segrè discusses this episode, including Lawrence's attitude, in Emilio Segrè OHI, AIP, p. 33.
352. "the machine . . . I do": ibid.
352. "we had . . . scary problem": Segrè (1981), p. 11.
352. "Fermi . . . 94]": ibid.
353. "I suggested . . . his collaborators": Seaborg (1976), p. 5.
353. Two searches: both of which may be followed day by day in ibid.
353. 0.6 microgram: ibid., p. 13.
354. "key step . . . discovery": Seaborg (1958), p. 4.
354. Seaborg remembers: cf. Bickel (1980), p. 188.
354. "With this . . . *94*": Seaborg (1976), p. 25.
355. "This morning . . . *neutrons*": ibid., p. 34.
355. larger critical mass: Gowing (1964), p. 68.

PAGE

355. "This first . . . is manageable": quoted in ibid., p. 67ff.
356. "I remember . . . 28 years": James Chadwick OHI, AIP, p. 105.

Chapter Twelve: A Communication from Britain

357. Conant: cf. Conant (1970), Kistiakowsky and Westheimer (1979).
357. "the most . . . race": Conant (1970), p. 252.
357. "What shall . . . formality": quoted in ibid., p. 253.
358. "I said . . . the Interior": ibid., p. 52.
358. "I did . . . or weapon": ibid., p. 49.
358. "Conant achieved . . . chemistry": Kistiakowsky and Westheimer (1979), p. 212.
359-360. "strong belief . . . involving Briggs": Conant (1970), p. 276ff.
360-361. "Light a . . . possibilities?": quoted in Childs (1968), p. 311.
361. Compton follow-up letter: K. Compton to V. Bush, March 17, 1941. OSRD S-1, Bush-Conant File, folder 19.
361. "by nature . . . solution": ibid.
361-362. "I told . . . trail behind": VB to F. Jewett, June 7, 1941. Bush-Conant File, f. 4.
362. "a very . . . atomic weapon": Wilson (1975), p. 205.
362. Bainbridge contacted Briggs: on the evidence of V. Bush to F. Jewett, April 15, 1941: "The immediate reason being a suggestion from Bainbridge that we send a member of our group to London on the uranium problem." Bush-Conant File, f. 19.
362. "I am . . . my head": Bush (1970), p. 60.
362. "it would . . . present time": VB to FJ, April 15, 1941.
362. "It was . . . scientific problems": Compton (1956), p. 45.
362-363. "disturbed . . . bloodedly evaluate": VB to FJ, April 15, 1941.
363. "fitness . . . task": Compton (1956), p. 46.
363. "Arthur Compton . . . and strong": Libby (1979), p. 91ff.
363. "tallness . . . enormously": ibid., p. 16.
363. "a small . . . place": Compton (1967), p. 31.
364. "probably the . . . of physics": quoted in Pais (1982), p. 414.
364. "Bohr spoke . . . different manner' ": Nielson (1963), p. 27.

PAGE

364. "In 1940 . . . time later": Compton (1967), p. 44.
365. "There followed . . . interested": Compton (1956), p. 46.
365. first NAS report (May 17, 1941): Bush-Conant File, f. 3.
365. "the matter . . . applications multiply": ibid.
365-366. "And only . . . negative": Conant (1970), p. 278.
366. "authoritative and impressive": discussed in FJ to VB, June 6, 1941. Bush-Conant File, f. 4.
366. "a lurking . . . well balanced": ibid.
366. "This uranium . . . doubt": VB to FJ, June 7, 1941. Bush-Conant File, f. 4.
366-367. "We told . . . at Columbia": Seaborg (1976), p. 42.
367. "*to crush* . . . against England": Hitler directive #21, "Operation Barbarossa," Dec. 18, 1940, quoted in Churchill (1949), p. 589.
367. "What worried . . . to priorities": Conant (1970), p. 278ff. Conant (1943), p. 5, confirms this recollection.
368. Briggs learned from Lawrence: a letter dated July 10, 1941, according to Conant (1943), p. 13.
368. "In the . . . no money": Eugene T. Booth, personal communication.
368. "The government's . . . war program": Compton (1956), p. 49.
368. "More significant . . . entirely feasible": Conant (1970), p. 280.
368. eight of twenty-four physicists: Conant (1943), p. 20.
368. "In essence . . . 'draft report' ": ibid.
368. MAUD Report: given in full in Gowing (1946), p. 394ff.
369. "With the . . . in order": Conant (1943), p. 21.
369. "During July . . . uranium program": Conant (1970), p. 279.
369-370. "If each . . . efficiently": Weart and Szilard (1978), p. 138.
370. "Fritz Houtermans . . . brilliant ideas": Frisch (1979), p. 71ff.
370. "that at . . . energy": Bethe (1967), p. 216.
370. "but fell . . . the Nazis": Frisch (1979), p. 72ff.
371. Houtermans report: cf. Irving (1967), p. 84.
371. "Every neutron . . . thermal neutrons": quoted in ibid., p. 85.
371-372. "at worst . . . been defeated": quoted in Clark (1981), p. 126.

PAGE

372. "Although personally . . . Lord Cherwell": Churchill (1950), p. 814.
372. "If Congress . . . receive one": Weart and Szilard (1978), p. 146.
372. "most important . . . and determined": Conant (1943), p. 19.
372. "The minutes . . . and distressed": Oliphant (1982), p. 17.
373. "came to . . . for submarines": quoted in Davis (1968), p. 112.
373. "I'll even . . . in Berkeley": quoted in Childs (1968), p. 315. Childs attributes this wire to Lawrence. Since he was in Berkeley and Oliphant in Washington, I take it to be Oliphant's.
373. "How much . . . complete consideration": quoted in ibid., p. 316ff.
373. Oliphant sees Conant and Bush: cf. Bickel (1980), p. 166. Bickel interviewed Oliphant at length.
373. "gossip . . . subjects": Conant (1943), p. 19.
373. "non-committal . . . of fission": quoted in Gowing (1964), p. 84n.
373–374. "that the . . . serious consideration": quoted in Conant (1943), p. 20.
374. "Certain developments . . . its development": Compton (1956), p. 6.
374. "out of the blue": interview with Edward Teller, Stanford, Calif., June 19, 1982.
374. "I decided . . . bombs": Blumberg and Owens (1976), p. 110.
374–375. "Next Sunday . . . believed me": NOVA (1980), p. 3.
375. Hagiwara lecture: quoted in "Concerning uranium, Tonizo Laboratory, April 43." Document copy and translation in the private collection of P. Wayne Reagan, Kansas City, Mo.
375. Chicago meeting: Conant lists Pegram as a fourth participant. Compton, who believed the meeting to be crucial to his future and who describes it in detail, does not.
375. "It was . . . talk freely": Compton (1956), p. 7.
375. "very vigorous . . . whole field": Conant (1943), p. 21.
375. "Conant was . . . be convinced": Compton (1956), p. 7ff.
376. "I could . . . research programs": Conant (1970), p. 280.
376. "If this . . . do it": Compton (1956), p. 8.
376. "the results . . . been exposed": Conant (1943), p. 22.

PAGE

376–377. "I grew . . . a Russian' ": interview with George Kistiakowsky, Cambridge, Mass., Jan. 15, 1982.
377. "When I . . . have reservations?": Conant (1970), p. 279.
377. "counted . . . significant": ibid., p. 280.
377. Bush memorandum: VB to J. B. Conant, Oct. 9, 1941. Bush-Conant File, f. 4. Quotations describing Bush's meeting with FDR come from this memo.
378. "emphasized to . . . are over": VB to F. Jewett, Nov. 4, 1941. Bush-Conant File, f. 4.
379. Bush to expedite research: cf. VB to FDR, March 9, 1942: "In accordance with your instructions [on October 9] I have since expedited this work in every way possible." Bush-Conant File, f. 13.
379–380. "called . . . hundred pounds": Compton (1956), p. 53ff.
380. Dunning and Booth choosing gaseous diffusion: Booth et al. (1975), p. 1ff.
380. "Our . . . enriched uranium": Eugene T. Booth, personal communication.
380. barrier materials: cf. Cohen et al. (1983), p. 636ff.
380*n*. "One cannot . . . more tons": FP 143, Fermi (1962), p. 99. Herbert Anderson's headnote here confirms the chronology of this incident.
381. "He urged . . . so well": Compton (1956), p. 55.
381. October 21 in Schenectady: Compton (1956), p. 56, says Cambridge, but Hewlett and Anderson (1962), p. 46, referring to the minutes of the meeting, locate it here.
381. "I have . . . deliberation": quoted in Childs (1968), p. 321.
381. Conant scolded Lawrence: ibid., p. 319.
381. "leftwandering activities": quoted in ibid.
381. "Many of . . . of them": USAEC (1954), p. 11.
381–382. "causes and . . . with us": quoted in Childs (1968), p. 319.
382. Oppenheimer debated Lawrence: cf. ibid.
382. "It was . . . direct use": USAEC (1954), p. 11.
382. "I . . . forget it": Smith and Weiner (1980), p. 220.
382. "Kistiakowsky . . . members objected": Compton (1956), p. 56ff.

PAGE

383. "In our . . . grave responsibility": quoted in Childs (1968), p. 321.
383. "the destructiveness . . . of inertia": Compton (1956), p. 57.
383. "No help . . . helpful suggestions": ibid., p. 58.
383. "It was . . . atomic bomb": quoted in Irving (1967), p. 93.
383–384. "he was . . . his trip": E. Heisenberg (1984), p. 77ff.
384. "with . . . hospitality": ibid., p. 78.
384. "Being aware . . . this conversation": quoted in Jungk (1958), p. 103ff.
385. "The impression . . . actual events": Rozental (1967), p. 193.
385. "Heisenberg and . . . a standoff": Oppenheimer (1963), III, p. 7.
385. Heisenberg reactor drawing: reported by Hans Bethe in Bernstein (1979), p. 77.
385. "Bohr . . . all else": E. Heisenberg (1984), p. 81.
385. "bond to . . . Bohr's reply": ibid., p. 80.
386. "a state . . . despair": ibid., p. 81.
386. "he had . . . enough spoon": Mott and Peierls (1977), p. 230.
386. third NAS report: Report to the President of the National Academy of Sciences by the Academy Committee on Uranium, Nov. 6, 1941. Bush-Conant File, f. 18.
386. "The special . . . *with U235*": ibid., p. 1.
386. "*a fission* . . . can be": ibid.
386. "*The mass* . . . fast neutrons": ibid., p. 2.
386. "may be . . . itself": ibid., p. 3.
386. "approaching . . . test": ibid., p. 4.
386. "in . . . four years": ibid.
386–387. "The possibility . . . this program": ibid., p. 6.
387. "more . . . of accomplishment": Compton (1956), p. 61.
387. "leaving Briggs . . . Ernest Lawrence": VB to FJ, Nov. 4, 1941. Bush-Conant File, f. 4.
388. "Jan 19 . . . FDR": Bush-Conant File, f. 13.
388. "The meeting . . . more firmly": Compton (1956), p. 70.
389. "a worthy . . . said Conant": ibid., p. 70ff.
389. "the construction . . . secret project": Conant (1970), p. 282.
389. December 7, 1941: I rely primarily on Prange (1982) for this summary reconstruction, but cf. also Murukami (1982), Coffey (1970) and Toland (1970).

PAGE

389. "must be . . . ever seen": quoted in Prange (1982), p. 500.
390. "Negotiations with . . . disclose intent": quoted in ibid., p. 402.
390. "a defense . . . Philippines": quoted in ibid., p. 403.
390. "This dispatch . . . tasks assigned": quoted in ibid., p. 406.
390. "more . . . phrasing": quoted in ibid., p. 409.
391. "Well . . . it": quoted in ibid., p. 501.
393. Nagasaki torpedoes: cf. ibid., p. 323.

Chapter 13: The New World

395. "Szilard at . . . customers": Fermi (1962), p. 1003.
395. thirty tons of graphite: ibid., p. 546.
395. "Much of . . . with *heap*": Segrè (1970), p. 116.
396. "We . . . oxide": Fermi (1962), p. 1002.
396. The cans: cf. FP 150, ibid., p. 128.
396. "This structure . . . as possible": ibid.
396. "We were . . . exhausting work": Wilson (1975), p. 86.
396–397. "We . . . four pounds": Fermi (1962), p. 1002.
397. "Fermi tried . . . and precision": Wilson (1975), p. 87.
397. *k:* cf. FP 149, Fermi (1962), p. 120.
397. "Now that . . . Pearl Harbor": ibid., p. 1002ff.
398. "the atmosphere . . . optimism reigned": Conant (1943), II, p. 2.
398. the next day: i.e., Dec. 19, 1941. Compton gives Dec. 20 but cf. Hewlett and Anderson (1962), p. 53.
398. "On the . . . 18 months": AHC to VB et al., Dec. 20, 1941, p. 2. Bush-Conant File, folder 5.
398–399. "This figure . . . per year": Compton (1956), p. 72.
399. Anderson scouting locations: cf. his letter to Szilard, Jan. 21, 1942, Szilard Papers.
399. "egg-boiling": ibid.
399. "Each was . . . for Chicago": Compton (1956), p. 80.
399. "We will . . . war": quoted in Compton, "Operation of the Metallurgical Project," memorandum, July 28, 1944. Bush-Conant File, f. 20a.
399–400. "Finally, wearied . . . to Chicago": Compton (1956), p. 81.
400. "had come . . . moving again": L. Fermi (1954), p. 174.

PAGE

400. "was unhappy . . . quite efficiently": ibid., p. 169.
400. THANK YOU . . . ORGANIZATION: AHC to LS, Jan. 25, 1942. Szilard Papers.
401. uranium press: Libby (1979), p. 70. Libby's chronology here is garbled, however.
401. "There are . . . ordered one": L. Fermi (1954), p. 186. LF believed the pile was canned to exclude the air, but cf. FP 151, Fermi (1962), p. 137: "Particular care was taken to eliminate as much as possible the moisture."
401. "required soldering . . . the job": Wattenberg (1982), p. 23.
401. "To insure . . . their heads": L. Fermi (1954), p. 186.
401–402. "Like the . . . winter meant": Churchill (1950), p. 536.
402. "well-fed . . . fighting": Guderian, quoted in Shirer (1960), p. 862.
402. "The winter . . . certain": Churchill (1950), p. 537.
402. "The work . . . near future": quoted in Irving (1967), p. 94.
402. "Experimental Luncheon": cf. Goudsmit (1947), p. 170.
403. "too busy . . . moment": quoted in ibid., p. 171.
403. "Pure uranium-235 . . . colossal force": quoted in Irving (1967), p. 99.
403. "it would . . . to detonate": quoted in ibid., p. 100.
403. "The first . . . be done": quoted in Groves (1962), p. 335. Note that this is testimony obtained surreptitiously by bugging while its subjects, who have claimed it was mistranslated and misinterpreted, were prisoners of war. To the extent that it is reliable it is far more candid than published statements, however.
403. "In the . . . its importance": Speer (1970), p. 225.
404. "The word . . . reaction": quoted in Irving (1967), p. 108.
404. "As . . . a pineapple": quoted in ibid., p. 109.
404. "His answer . . . the war": Speer (1970), p. 226.
404–405. "Hitler had . . . see it": ibid., p. 227.
405. "on the . . . propelling machinery": ibid.
405. "In the . . . prime movers": Heisenberg (1947), p. 214.
405. "We may . . . finding out": VB to FDR, March 9, 1942. Bush-Conant File, f. 13.

PAGE

405. March 9 report: "Report to the President, status of tubealloy development" (n.d.). Bush-Conant File, f. 13.
406. "I think . . . the essence": FDR to VB, March 11, 1942. Bush-Conant File, f. 13.
406. "While all . . . the other": JBC to VB, May 14, 1942. Bush-Conant File, f. 5.
406. Conant reviewed the evidence: cf. ibid.
407. "if the . . . of machinery": ibid.
407. Seaborg to Chicago: chronology and details of this section follow Seaborg (1977).
407. "This day . . . Project": ibid., p. 2.
407. 250 ppm: Seaborg (1958), p. 16.
408. "We conceived . . . were employed": ibid., p. 8.
408. "I . . . precipitation": Seaborg (1977), p. 9.
408. "Sometimes I . . . right now": ibid., p. 42.
409. "We looked . . . concrete bench": ibid., p. 56.
409. "I always . . . fit": ibid., p. 112.
410. "It was . . . balance": Seaborg (1958), p. 38.
410. "the fellows . . . Hall": Seaborg (1977), p. 66.
410. "But to . . . the north": ibid., p. 68.
410. "Our witnesses . . . stay": ibid., p. 70.
410. "it was . . . call": ibid., p. 75.
410. "I do . . . a whole": G. Breit to L. Briggs, May 18, 1942. Bush-Conant File, f. 5.
411. "a prerequisite . . . bomb": Seaborg (1977), p. 75.
411. "because . . . use helium": ibid., p. 91.
411. "a water . . . time": Weart and Szilard (1978), p. 157.
412. "Compton repeated . . . of 1944": Seaborg (1977), p. 86ff.
412–413. "Compton opened . . . people present": ibid., p. 93ff.
413. "Stated in . . . lines": Weart and Szilard (1978), p. 156.
413. "In 1939 . . . were eliminated": ibid., p. 152.
413. "The UNH . . . a minimum": Seaborg (1977), p. 148.
414. "facetiously . . . attention": interview with Glenn Seaborg, Berkeley, Calif., June 22, 1982.
414–415. "Perhaps today . . . of man": Seaborg (1977), p. 192ff.
415. "a holiday . . . hue": ibid., p. 193.

PAGE

415. "luminaries": Smith and Weiner (1980), p. 227.
415. "I considered . . . practical way": quoted in Bernstein (1980), p. 70.
415. "After the . . . effort": quoted in ibid., p. 61.
416. "The essential . . . hands full": Smith and Weiner (1980), p. 226.
416. Kiddygram: cf. ibid.
416. "our best . . . country": quoted in Bernstein (1980), p. 55.
416. early July: on July 9, 1942, Teller told Seaborg he was leaving for a month in Berkeley. Seaborg (1977), p. 111.
416. "He had . . . probably work": quoted in Bernstein (1980), p. 71.
416–417. "We were . . . do it": Teller (1962), p. 38.
417. "We had . . . hydrogen bomb": quoted in Bernstein (1980), p. 72ff.
417. "in the . . . been tragic": "Remarks by Raymond T. Birge," May 5, 1964, p. 5ff. JRO Papers, Box 248.
417. "The theory . . . do much": interview with Hans Bethe, Ithaca, N.Y., Sept. 12, 1982.
417. "My wife . . . doing it": quoted in Bernstein (1980), p. 73.
418. 35,000 eV/400 million degrees: Hawkins (1947), p. 14.
418. 85,000 tons: ibid., p. 15.
418. 500 atomic bombs: based on Bush's March estimate of 2 KT per "unit."
418. "I didn't . . . know more": Bethe interview, Sept. 12, 1982.
419. "I'll never . . . their calculations": Compton (1956), p. 127ff.
419. "I very . . . my arguments": Bethe interview, Sept. 12, 1982.
419. "It was . . . common sense": Hawkins (1947), p.15.
419. "My theories . . . conclusion": Teller (1962), p. 39.
420. "Konopinski . . . guess": ibid.
420. lithium deuteride: cf. Teller to Oppenheimer, Sept. 5, 1942, JRO Papers, Box 71: "In connection with these reactions it occurred to me that our Lithium Deuterite estimate which we made at Berkeley might be wrong . . . But even so I agree that Lithium Hydride will probably not be possible without some change in isotopic composition."
420. "We were . . . unforgettable": Bethe (1968), p. 398.
420. a major effort: cf. Hawkins (1947), p. 2.

PAGE

420. "Fast neutron . . . work": Seaborg (1977), pp. 269–271.
420. Cincinnati/Tennessee: ibid.
420. Conant notes: handwritten on yellow legal pad paper, headed "August 26, 1942. Status of the Bomb." Bush-Conant File, f. 14a.
421. Executive Committee report: "Status of Atomic Fission Project," (n.d.), Bush-Conant File, f. 12.
421. "the physicists . . . report": via Harvey Bundy. Cf. VB, "Memorandum for Mr. Bundy," July 29, 1942. OSRD S-1 Bush Report March 1942 #58.
422. "Classical engineers . . . everyone": Libby (1979), p. 90ff.
422. Wilson's meeting: Leona (Woods) Libby's is the more detailed recollection and squares with the timing of the Stone & Webster appointment in June, following which the engineering firm conducted preliminary studies during the summer. Compton apparently confuses the meeting Wilson called with the June meeting Seaborg describes when the decision to turn Pu production over to industry was first announced—also a rowdy meeting. Cf. Libby (1979), p. 90ff; Compton (1956), p. 108ff; Seaborg (1977), p. 93ff.
422. "We (some . . . & Webster": Libby (1979), p. 91.
422–423. "When Compton . . . and disbanded": ibid., p. 91ff.
423. Szilard memorandum: Weart and Szilard (1978), p. 153ff, and draft "Memorandum" dated Sept. 19, 1942, Szilard Papers.
423. "In talking . . . instrument": LS, draft "Memorandum," p. 5.
423. "I have . . . OSRD": ibid., p. 4.
423. "The situation . . . our work": Weart and Szilard (1978), p. 155.
423. "There is . . . be functional": ibid., p. 156.
423. "If we . . . it up": quoted in ibid., p. 147.
423–424. "We may . . . responsibility lies": ibid., p. 159ff.
424. "From my . . . war efforts": VB to Harvey Bundy, Aug. 29, 1942. OSRD S-1 Bush Report March 1942 #58, p. 4.
424–425. "On the . . . Oh": Groves (1948), p. 15.
425. "to take . . . project": "Memorandum

PAGE

for the Chief of Engineers," Sept. 17, 1942. MD I/I/f.25b.

425. "I thought . . . colonel": Groves (1962), p. 5.
426. Groves' father: cf. Groves (n.d.), "The Army As I Saw It."
426. "Entering West . . . I knew": ibid., p. 103.
426. "A . . . wolf": quoted in Davis (1968), p. 244.
426. "the biggest . . . of understanding": quoted in Goodchild (1980), p. 56ff.
426. "I was . . . horrified": Groves (1962), p. 19.
427. "I told . . . the soup": quoted in ibid., p. 20.
427. "His reaction . . . his wishes": ibid., p. 22.
427. "We had . . . a year": ibid., p. 23.
428. "You made . . . start moving": quoted in Groueff (1967), p. 15n. Groueff interviewed Groves at length.
428. $k = 0.995$: Hewlett and Anderson (1962), p. 70.
428. "I remember . . . beach": L. Fermi (1954), p. 191.
428. "in frigid . . . promontory": Libby (1979), p. 2.
428. "One evening . . . little kids": ibid., p. 4.
428. "As he . . . he was": ibid., p. 1.
429. "I was . . . we wanted": R. Sachs (1984), p. 33.
429. "At each . . . 'metallurgists' ": L. Fermi (1954), p. 176.
429. "one of . . . his wife": Compton (1956), p. 207.
429. "close to 1.04": Fermi (1962), p. 207.
429. "For the . . . questions asked": Wilson (1975), p. 91.
429. 1 percent improvement in *k:* Fermi (1962), p. 212.
430. Zinn preparations: cf. FP 181 ibid.; Wattenberg (1982); Wilson (1975), p. 108ff.
431. "The War . . . build both": Seaborg (177), p. 284ff.
431. "I left . . . be impossible": Groves (1962), p. 41.
431. "Its reasons . . . design data": ibid., p. 48.

431–432. "if we . . . casualties": ibid., p. 49.

432. "dreadful decision": Seaborg (1977), p. 343.
432. "We did . . . be intolerable": Compton (1956), p. 137.
432. "most significant . . . fission occurs": ibid., p. 136ff.

PAGE

432. delayed neutrons: Roberts et al. (1939b).
432. "The only . . . myself": Compton (1956), p. 138.
433. building CP-1: cf. Allardice and Trapnell (1955); Compton (1956), p. 132ff; FP 181, Fermi (1962); L. Fermi (1954), p. 176ff; Groueff (1967), p. 54ff; Libby (1979), p. 118ff and passim; R. Sachs (1984), pp. 32ff and 281ff; Seaborg (1977), p. 388ff; Segrè (1970), p. 120ff; Wigner (1967), p. 228ff; Wilson (1975), pp. 91ff and 108ff.
433. "Gus Knuth . . . on hand": Wilson (1975), p. 92.
433. number of layers: 57 layers/17 days/2 shifts = 1.7 per shift.

433–434. "A simple . . . and myself": Wilson (1975), p. 93.

434. "Each day . . . following shifts": Fermi (1962), p. 268.
434. pile countdown: these numbers charted in ibid., FP 181, p. 275.

434–435. "We tried . . . the business": quoted in Wilson (1975), p. 94.

436. "That night . . . in place": Fermi (1962), p. 269.
436. "I will . . . leisurely": ibid., p. 270.

436–437. "The next . . . the batter": Libby (1979), p. 120.

437. "Back we . . . received heat": ibid.
438. "several of . . . the material": Wattenberg (1982), p. 30.
438. "Fermi instructed . . . supposed to": ibid., p. 31.
438. "Again the . . . control rod": ibid.
439. "After the . . . and locked": ibid.
439. "This time . . . level off": quoted in ibid., p. 32.
440. "at first . . . about it": Wilson (1975), p. 95.
440. Fermi told tech council: cf. Seaborg (1977), p. 394. Seaborg gives $k = 1.006$, presumably a typographical error; cf. FP 181, Fermi (1962), p. 276.
440. "Then everyone . . . ZIP in!": Wilson (1975), p. 95.
440. "Nothing very . . . cannot foresee": Wigner (1967), p. 240.
442. "We each . . . except Wigner": Wattenberg (1982), p. 32.
442. "bursting . . . news": Seaborg (1977), p. 390.
442. "in my . . . University": Conant (1970), p. 290.

PAGE

442. "Jim . . . and happy": Compton (1956), p. 144.
442. "There was . . . of mankind": Weart and Szilard (1978), p. 146.

Chapter 14: Physics and Desert Country

443. "massive . . . work": Bethe (1968), p. 396.
443. "[Oppenheimer] . . . choir boy": Chevalier (1965), p. 11.
444. "He was . . . loved him": Dorothy McKibben, quoted in Else (1980), p. 9.
444. "He was . . . unspoken wishes": Chevalier (1965), p. 21.
444. "painful but . . . my voice": quoted in Davis (1968), p. 129.
444. "sometimes appeared . . . most sensitive": Segrè (1970), p. 134.
444–445. "Robert could . . . like it": quoted in Davis (1968), p. 103.
445. "But it . . . or something": Smith and Weiner (1980), p. 135.
445. "the loneliest . . . world": quoted in ibid., p. 145.
445. "My friends . . . to change": USAEC (1954), p. 8.
445. "I had . . . my students": ibid.
445. "very grave . . . those days": interview with Philip Morrison, Cambridge, Mass., Jan. 1982.
445–446. "And through . . . the community": USAEC (1954), p. 8.
446. "In the . . . and country": ibid.
446. "I never . . . to me": ibid., p. 10.
446. "Dr. [Stewart] . . . it was": ibid.
446. "I went . . . the world": ibid., p. 9.
447. "created the . . . nuclear physics": Bethe (1968), p. 396.
447. "He began . . . to try": quoted in Davis (1968), p. 79.
447. JRO meeting Groves: cf. LRG to JRO, Sept. 27, 1960. JRO Papers, Box 36.
447–448. "I became . . . no consideration": USAEC (1954), p. 12.
448. "a military . . . as officers": ibid.
448. "original . . . in Berkeley": LLG to JRO, Sept. 27, 1960.
448. "the work . . . pace": Groves (1962), p. 60.
448. "Outside the . . . Oppenheimer": ibid., p. 62.
448. "It was . . . a theorist": Bethe (1968), p. 399.
448. "snag . . . any means": Groves (1962), p. 63.

PAGE

448–449. "He's a . . . about sports": interview, March 8, 1946. Szilard Papers.
449. "After much . . . the task": Groves (1962), p. 62ff.
449. "by default . . . bad name": quoted in Davis (1968), p. 159.
449. "it was . . . astonished": Else (1980), p. 11.
449. October 15 and 19: cf. LLG to JRO, Sept. 27, 1960.
449. "For this . . . hands on": Smith and Weiner (1980), p. 231.
449. Bethe, Segrè et al.: Kunetka (1982), p. 48.
449–450. "so that . . . conditions": Groves (1962), p. 64.
450. Groves' criteria: cf. Badash (1980), p. 3ff.
450. "a delightful . . . Utah": ibid., p. 4.
450. "a lovely . . . satisfactory": Smith and Weiner (1980), p. 236.
450. "considerable . . . usable site": Badash (1980), p. 14ff.
450. "as though . . . directly there": ibid., p. 5.
450. "The school . . . its stream": Church (1960), p. 4.
451. "beautiful . . . country": Segrè (1970), p. 135.
451. "hot and . . . or moisture": L. Fermi (1954), p. 204.
451. "I remember . . . the place' ": Badash (1980), p. 15.
451. "My two . . . be combined": quoted in Royal (1969), p. 49; cf. also Brode (1960), first page of Introduction. I merge these two versions of JRO's statement; the sense is the same and the exact remark is variously attested.
451. "Nobody could . . . go crazy": quoted in Davis (1968), p. 163.
451. Corps of Engineers' appraisal: MED 319.1.
451–452. "What we . . . accelerators": Badash (1980), p. 30.
452. "The prospect . . . Los Alamos": USAEC (1954), p. 12ff.
452. "Oppenheimer . . . radar": Moyers (1984).
452. "the culmination . . . physics": quoted by JRO in Smith and Weiner (1980), p. 250.
452. "To me . . . consequence": ibid.
453. "Laboratory . . . our hi-jinks": ibid., p. 243ff.
453. "Oppenheimer's . . . a teletype": Badash (1980), p. 10.

PAGE

453. "a very . . . to come": ET to JRO, March 6, 1943. JRO Papers, Box 71.
453. Teller's prospectus: referred to in ET to JRO, Jan. 4, 1943 (misdated 1942). JRO Papers, Box 71.
453. "mental love . . . in conversation": quoted in Coughlan (1963), p. 90.
453. "fundamentally . . . somewhat introverted": quoted in Blumberg and Owens (1976), p. 77.
453–454. Alvarez disagrees: personal communication.
454. "scientific autonomy . . . our work": Smith and Weiner (1980), p. 247ff.
455. "Several of . . . camps": L. Fermi (1954), p. 201.
455. Vemork raid: cf. Haukelid (1954); Irving (1967); Jones (1967).
455. "one of . . . be repeated": Jones (1967), p. 1422.
455. "Here lay . . . Europe": Haukelid (1954), p. 71.
455. "one of . . . mountains": ibid., p. 73.
456. "Halfway down . . . and rivers": ibid., p. 92ff.
456. "It was . . . of sentries": ibid., p. 94.
456. "We were . . . grenades": ibid., p. 95.
456. "the thin . . . Europe": ibid.
457. "but an . . . to do?": ibid., p. 98.
457. "the best . . . seen": quoted in Irving (1967), p. 149.
457. Japan: cf. Pacific War Research Society (1972), p. 27ff, and Shapley (1978).
457. "The study . . . field": quoted in PWRS (1972), p. 26.
458. "The best . . . the meeting": ibid., p. 35.
459. "This was . . . Engineers": Badash (1980), p. 31.
460. "about thirty persons": Segrè (1970), p. 135.
460. *Los Alamos Primer:* Condon (1943). Designated LA-1.
460–461. "The object . . . nuclear fission": ibid., p. 1.
461. "Since only . . . active material": ibid., p. 2.
461. 7 percent U235: Condon says at least tenfold; 1/140th × 10 = 7%. Condon (1943), p. 5.
461. "to make . . . possible": ibid.
461. "the gadget": ibid., p. 7.
461. "severe . . . effects": ibid., p. 9.
461. "Since . . . is possible": ibid., p. 10.
461. "The reaction . . . gadget": ibid., p. 11.
461. "as the . . . [core]": ibid., p. 13.

PAGE

462. "An explosion . . . distance": ibid., p. 16.
462. "When the . . . break": ibid., p. 18.
462. "is . . . at present": ibid., p. 21.
463. illustration: Condon's drawing, ibid.
463. "The highest . . . 10 tons": ibid.
463. "If explosive . . . sphere": ibid., p. 22.
463. illustration: Condon's drawing, ibid.
464. "All autocatalytic . . . needed": ibid., p. 24.
464. "relatively . . . physics": Hans Bethe OHI, AIP, p. 59.
465. "If there . . . ceremony": Badash (1980), p. 31ff.
465. April conference plans: cf. Hawkins (1947), p. 16ff.
466. Neddermeyer's thoughts: as reported to Davis (1968), p. 170ff.
466. "I remember . . . implosion": quoted in ibid., p. 171.
466. "expands . . . sixteenfold": Condon (1943), p. 15.
466. "At this . . . hand": quoted in Davis (1968), p. 171.
467. "The gun . . . better still": quoted in ibid., p. 172.
467. "At a . . . of assembly": Hawkins (1947), p. 23.
467. "Neddermeyer . . . and Bethe": quoted in Davis (1968), p. 173.
467. "Nobody . . . seriously": Badash (1980). p. 34.
467. "This will . . . into": quoted in Davis (1968), p. 173.
468. "After he . . . surprised": quoted in ibid., p. 182.
468. Condon and *The Tempest:* cf. Smith and Weiner (1980), p. 252.
468. the bombing of Hamburg: cf. Kennett (1982), Middlebrook (1980), Overy (1980).
469. "But when . . . way through": quoted in Jones (1966), p. 80ff.
469. "the targets . . . bombing": quoted in Kennett (1982), p. 128.
469. "that although . . . night bombing": Churchill (1950), p. 279.
470. Headlines proclaiming raids: for a discussion of this point cf. Hopkins (1966), p. 461ff.
470. "It has . . . workers": quoted in Kennett (1982), p. 129.
470. "a bomber . . . endure": quoted in ibid., p. 130.
471. "INFORMATION . . . HAMBURG": quoted in Middlebrook (1980), p. 95.
472. Operation Gomorrah: I rely here on Middlebrook (1980).

PAGE

473. "It was . . . night": quoted in ibid., p. 253.
473. "Most of . . . them all": quoted in ibid., p. 244.
473. "The burning . . . like again": quoted in ibid.
473. "Then a . . . of fire": quoted in ibid., p. 259.
474. "Mother wrapped . . . the doorway": quoted in ibid., p. 264.
474. "We came . . . knees screaming": quoted in ibid., p. 266ff.
474. "Four-storey . . . the pavement": quoted in ibid., p. 276.
475. two million Soviet soldiers: Elliot (1972), p. 48. Elliot puts total Soviet military POWs at 5 million and POW deaths at 3 million; I use his number here of those enclosed in occupied Russia, of which he writes: "Total deprivation of entire enclosed populations . . . does not exist elsewhere in human history." The other 3 million were treated with more customary brutality.
475–476. mammalian reflex: cf. Kruuk (1972).
476. "We must . . . we've got": quoted in Hopkins (1966), p. 464.
476. Lewis committee findings: cf. Hawkins (1947), p. 24.
476. "In this . . . for U^{235}": ibid., p. 71.
477. "I guess . . . why?": interview with Glenn Seaborg, Berkeley, Calif., June 22, 1982.
477. "Then I . . . suitcase": ibid.
477. "Of course not": Groves (1962), p. 160.
477. "all his . . . the Navy": Joseph Hirschfelder, quoted in Badash (1980), p. 82.
477. "within a . . . the job": Groves (1962), p. 160.
477*n*. Tuve reassignment: cf. V. Bush to MT, Aug.14, 1941. Bush-Conant File, f. 4.
478. "As a . . . externally": Ramsey (1946), p. 6ff.
478. B-29: cf. Birdsall (1980). The first service-test model flew June 27, 1943 (ibid., p. 18).
478. "On August . . . subsequent tests": Ramsey (1946), p. 7.
479. "At that . . . gun method": Badash (1980), p. 17.
479. "Those tests . . . practical method": ibid.
479. "It stinks": quoted in Davis (1968), p. 216.

PAGE

479. "With everyone . . . the beer": quoted in ibid.
480. "a simple . . . sophisticated": quoted in ibid., p. 217.
480. "Johnny was . . . previously discussed": quoted in Blumberg and Owens (1976), p. 455.
480. JvN and ET to JRO: the official record says "autumn." I conjecture October because the governing board met Oct. 28, 1943. Hawkins (1947), p. 76.
481. "In order . . . 1943": Ramsey (1946), p. 8ff.
481. "Professor Bohr . . . micro-slide": Rozental (1967), p. 192 plate.
481. "The letter . . . help": ibid., p. 193ff.
481. "if I . . . refuge here": quoted in ibid., p. 194.
482. 3.6 million Germans: Yahil (1969), p. 118.
482. "Danish statesmen . . . government": ibid., p. 200ff.
482–483. Margrethe Bohr remembers: cf. Moore (1966), p. 302.
483. "We had . . . small bag": quoted in ibid., p. 303.
483. Bohr appeals to Swedish government: Flender (1963), p. 76. Flender interviewed Bohr at length; his account is garbled, however.
483. 284 people: Yahil (1969), p. 187.
483. Sept. 30, 1943: Yahil (1969), p. 328, puts this meeting "the day after [Bohr's] arrival in Stockholm," i.e., Oct. 1, 1943. But cf. Rozental (1967), p. 168: "on the same evening. . . ."
483. "went to . . . of Sweden": Rozental (1967), p. 169.
483. contacted the Danish ambassador: Yahil (1969), p. 330.
483–484. "The audience . . . operation": Rozental (1967), p. 169.
484. "At the . . . received": quoted in Yahil (1969), p. 219.
484. "The stay . . . in Sweden": Rozental (1967), p. 195.
484. "The Royal . . . as Bohr's": Oppenheimer (1963), III (Los Alamos version), p. 7.
484–485. "The Mosquito . . . conscious again": Rozental (1967), p. 196.
485. "Once in . . . going on": Oppenheimer (1963), III, p. 7.
485. "good first . . . years before": ibid., p. 8.
485. "The work . . . expected": Rozental (1967), p. 196.

PAGE

485. "To Bohr . . . fantastic": Oppenheimer (1963), III, p. 7.

Chapter 15: Different Animals

487. "depends on . . . its mass": Brobeck and Reynolds (1945), p. 4.
487. "When the . . . of metal": ibid., p. 5.
487. 100-microgram sample: ibid., p. 7.
489. "that . . . be assured": EOL to LRG, Aug. 3, 1943. Bush-Conant file, f. 19.
490. "At one . . . Troy ounce": Groves (1962), p. 107.
490. electromagnetic separation buildings: "Pertinent reference data, CEW." Dec. 1, 1944. MED 319.1, p. 3ff.
491. 20,000 workers: W. E. Kelley to E. H. Marsden, Aug. 9, 1943. MED misc., f. 4.
491. 40 kg U235: JRO to LRG, Sept. 25, 1943, p. 3 MED 337.
491. Army engineer's summary: W. E. Kelley to E. H. Marsden, Aug. 9, 1943. MED misc., f.4.
491. one supervisor remembers: interview with Leon Love, Oak Ridge, Tenn., 1975.
491. "moved the . . . they belonged": Groves (1962), p. 105ff.

491–492. "The first . . . shorting": ibid., p. 104ff.

492. Dunning's staff: Cohen (1983), p. 641.
492. "three methods . . . method": quoted in ibid., p. 637ff.
492. "The method . . . stages": Groves (1962), p. 111.
493. "Further . . . be solved": quoted in Cohen (1983), p. 637ff.
495. 2,892 stages: Cave Brown (1977), p. 311.
496. "from that . . . applications": Cohen (1983), p. 643.
496. "The Clinton . . . inoperable": Groves (1962), p. 69ff.
497. real estate appraisal: "Gross Appraisal, Gable Project." Jan. 21, 1943. MED 319.1.
497. Hanford description: ibid.
498. dimensions: Cave Brown (1977), p. 322.
498. 1:4000: Seaborg (1977), p. 548.
498. "With water . . . arise": Compton (1956), p. 170.
498. "the conscience . . . very end": Weart and Szilard (1978), p. 148.
499. "Local storms . . . dust": Libby (1979), p. 167.
499. "The most . . . guns": quoted in Groueff (1967), p. 141.

PAGE

499. "was a . . . morning": Libby (1979), p. 167.

499–500. "work gangs . . . the year": Hewlett and Anderson (1962), p. 216ff.

500. Forty-foot pile building: Hewlett and Anderson (1962), p. 217, give 120 feet; that measurement includes the detached exhaust stack, however. Cf. Libby (1979), p.167, and Hewlett and Anderson (1962), photo following p. 224.
500. "There was . . . animals": Badash (1980), p. 91.
500. "Years later . . . that": Teller (1962), p. 211.

500–501. Soviet research: cf. York (1976), p. 29ff; Alexandrov (1967); Golovin (1967); Szulc (1984).

501. "The advance . . . safety": Golovin (1967), p. 14.
501. "In recent . . . inhabitants": quoted in York (1976), p. 30.
501. "no time . . . bomb": ibid.
502. "So it . . . places": Alexandrov (1967), p. 12.
502. "Even so . . . isotopes": York (1976), p. 31.
502. Groves' anti-Semitism: cf. transcript of Groves interview of March 8, 1946, Szilard Papers: "Only a man with [Szilard's] brass would have pushed through to the President. Take Wigner or Fermi—they're not Jewish—they're quiet, shy, modest, just interested in learning . . . Of course, most of [Szilard's] ideas are bad, but he has so many. . . . And I'm not prejudiced. I don't like certain Jews and I don't like certain well-known characteristics of theirs but I'm not prejudiced."
502. "If the . . . bomb": Smith (1965), p. 27.
503. "There is . . . obsolete": Weart and Szilard (1978), p. 165.
503. TO REMOVE . . . NOW: AHC to LRG, Oct. 26, 1942. MED 201, Leo Szilard.
503. SZILARD . . . MYSELF: AHC to LRG, Oct. 28, 1942. MED 201, Leo Szilard.
503. "enemy alien . . . war": draft Sec. of War to Atty. Gen., Oct. 28, 1942. MED 201, Leo Szilard.
503. Compton to Groves mid-November: Nov. 13, 1942. MED 201, Leo Szilard.
504. "for inventions . . . it": LS to AHC, Dec. 4, 1942. Bush-Conant File, f. 13.
504. Compton to Briggs: cf. AHC to JBC, Jan. 7, 1943. Bush-Conant File, f. 13.

PAGE

504–505. "the basic . . . inventions": LS to AHC, Dec. 29, 1942. MED 072, Szilard patents.

504. $750,000: undated memorandum, "Leo Szilard," p. 3. MED 12, Intelligence and security.

505. "Szilard's case . . . Government": AHC to JBC, Jan. 7, 1943. Bush-Conant File, f. 13.

505. "This is . . . present": LS to AHC, Jan. 13, 1943. MED 072, Szilard patents.

505–506. "It is . . . research": VB to AHC, Jan. 29, 1943. Bush-Conant File, f. 13.

506. "comparable . . . Wigner": AHC to JBC, Feb. 3, 1943. MED 072. Compton notes at the head of this letter that it was never sent but was communicated orally.

506. "The investigation . . . person": LRG to Capt. Calvert, June 12, 1943. MED 201.

506–507. "The surveillance . . . to go": "Memorandum for the officer in charge," June 24, 1943. MED 201.

507. "Age, 35 . . . no hat": ibid.

507. "(Mr. Wigner . . . the Navy": ibid.

508. "failed to . . . pile": RAL to LRG (n.d.), "copy made for Maj. Peterson 8-2-43." MED 072.

508. "You were . . . assurance": LRG to LS, Oct. 9, 1943. MED 201.

508. Dec. 3 Chicago meeting: H. E. Metcalfe, "A memorandum of a conference held at the Chicago Area Office, U.S. Engineers, on 3 December 1943." MED 072.

508. "not to . . . person": LRG to LS, Oct. 8, 1943. MED 072.

508–509. "who at . . . around me": LS to VB, Jan. 14, 1944. Bush-Conant File, f. 13. Reprinted in Weart and Szilard (1978), p. 161ff.

509. "I feel . . . project": VB to LS, Jan. 18, 1944. Bush-Conant File, f. 13.

509. "the only . . . at present": Weart and Szilard (1978), p. 165.

509. "The attitude . . . initiative": ibid., p. 177.

510. "The scientists . . . are out": ibid., p. 178.

510. Fermi and poisoning food: cf. JRO to EF, May 25, 1943. JRO Papers, Box 33.

510. Met Lab worries: cf. A. H. Compton, J. B. Conant, H. Urey, "Radioactive material as a military weapon." MED 319.1, Literature. Appendix IV, p. 7.

PAGE

510. May 1943/before February: May is the month of JRO's letter to Fermi, which mentions the subcommittee; February is the date of a table of biological effects given in ibid., Appendix I, p. 4ff.

511. "I therefore . . . than this": JRO to EF, May 25, 1943. JRO Papers, Box 33.

511. "the Sanscrit . . . or hurt": quoted in Davis (1968), p. 330.

511–512. "Recent reports . . . large companies": HAB and ET to JRO, July 21, 1943. JRO Papers, Box 20.

512. Conant subcommittee report: MED 319.1.

512. Cosmos Club: Irving (1967), p. 166.

512–513. Vemork bombing and ferry sinking: cf. ibid., p. 174ff; Haukelid (1954), p. 149ff.

514. 97.6 to 1.1 percent: Irving (1967), p. 188.

514. "a one-man . . . another": Haukelid (1954), p. 156.

514. "The fact . . . at all": ibid., p. 160.

514. "The answer . . . Greetings": ibid., p. 161.

514–515. "We had . . . place": ibid., p. 163.

515. "As the . . . enough": ibid., p. 167ff.

515. "The timing . . . properly": ibid., p. 163.

515. "Rolf . . . at ten": ibid., p. 165.

515–516. "Armed with . . . took time": ibid., p. 166ff.

516. "The charge . . . side": ibid., p. 167.

516. "Making the . . . disaster": ibid., p. 168.

517. "When one . . . war ended": quoted in Irving (1967), p. 191.

517–518. "Europe was . . . stepchild": quoted in Costello (1981), p. 354.

518. "very uneasy . . . monkeys": Hersey (1942), p. 36.

518. "The other . . . the Japs": Grew (1942), p. 81.

518. "The Japanese . . . and nations": ibid., p. 79.

518. "united . . . totalitarian": ibid., p. 80.

518. "At this . . . to fight": ibid., p. 80ff.

518. " 'Victory or . . . his country": ibid., p. 82.

519. "General . . . hand grenade": quoted in Manchester (1980), p. 183.

519. "A legend . . . or dead": Hersey (1942), p. 36.

519. "in the . . . cause": Grew (1942), p. 80.

519. "At the . . . defeat it": Manchester (1980), p. 240.

PAGE

519-520. "The general . . . isolated cases": Tregaskis (1943), p. 79.
520. "I know . . . fighting Japan": Grew (1942), p. 82.
520. "It seems . . . the enemy": Wolfe (1943), p. 190.
521. unconditional surrender: cf. Churchill (1950), p. 695ff.
521. "We had . . . war effort": quoted in ibid., p. 687.

Chapter 16: Revelations

522. "How would . . . night train": Frisch (1979), p. 145ff.
522. hearse: Clark (1980), p. 154.
523. "I wandered . . . laughter": Frisch (1979), p. 148.
523. "Welcome . . . you?": quoted in ibid., p. 150.
523. Quebec Agreement: for complete text cf. Gowing (1964), p. 439ff.
523. Bohr's luggage: cf. Frisch (1979), p. 169.
523-524. "It was . . . London": quoted in Bernstein (1980), p. 77.
524. "Explosion . . . of pile": MED 337. Cf. also JRO to LRG, Jan. 1, 1944, same file.
524. "At that . . . Bohr": Goudsmit (1947), p. 177.
524. "Bohr at . . . one": Oppenheimer (1963), III (Los Alamos version), p. 10ff.
524. "made . . . hopeful": Oppenheimer (1963), III, p. 11.
524. "He made . . . misgiving": Oppenheimer (1963), III (Los Alamos version), p. 11.
524. "Bohr spoke . . . believe": ibid.
524-525. "In Los . . . from him": quoted in Moore (1966), p. 330.
525. "They . . . bomb": quoted in Nielson (1963), p. 29.
525. "warm . . . relation": FF memorandum headed "Private," April 18, 1945. JRO Papers, Box 34.
526. "We talked . . . Campbell": ibid.
526. "On hearing . . . B outlined": unsigned Bohr memorandum, May 6, 1945. JRO Papers, Box 34.
526. "B met . . . in history": ibid.
526-527. "On this . . . to X": FF memorandum, April 18, 1945.
527. "F also . . . Minister": NB memorandum, May 6, 1945.
527. "I wrote . . . government": FF memorandum, April 18, 1945.

PAGE

528. "Halifax . . . immediately": Rozental (1967), p. 203.
528. "conservative . . . man": Oppenheimer (1963), III (Los Alamos version), p. 8.
528. Anderson memorandum, March 21, 1944: cf. Clark (1980), p. 169—where a portion is quoted confusingly *after* a later memorandum—and Gowing (1964), p. 350ff.
528. "communicating . . . account": quoted in Clark (1980), p. 169.
528. "I do . . . informed": quoted in Gowing (1964), p. 352.
529. "to let . . . work": PK to NB, Oct. 23, 1943. JRO Papers, Box 34.
529. "The Counsellor . . . the occupation": "Conversation between B and Counsellor Zinchenko at the Soviet Embassy in London on April 20th, 1944, at 5 p.m." JRO Papers, Box 34.
529. "We came . . . new prospects": Rozental (1967), p. 203.
529. "One of . . . the war": Snow (1981), p. 112.
529. R. V. Jones: cf. Jones (1966), p. 88ff.
529-530. "When I . . . Roosevelt": ibid., p. 88.
530. "As he . . . politics!": Rozental (1967), p. 204.
530. "We . . . language": quoted in Gowing (1964), p. 355.
530. "downcast": Rozental (1967), p. 204.
530. "It was . . . nuclear energy": quoted in Nielson (1963), p. 29.
530. "I did . . . Street": quoted in Clark (1980), p. 177.
530-531. "In all . . . present time": quoted in Sherwin (1975), p. 108.
531. "He had . . . sad story": Snow (1981), p. 116.
531. "that the . . . their decisions": NB to WC, May 22, 1944. JRO Papers, Box 34.
531. "The way . . . Berlin": Chandler (1970), III, p. 1865.
531-532. "About a . . . memorandum": NB memorandum, May 6, 1945.
532. "It was . . . manual skill": Rozental (1967), p. 205ff.
532. Bohr FDR memorandum: July 3, 1944. JRO Papers, Box 21. Relevant portions of the text of this unpublished document are quoted in NB's "Open Letter to the United Nations" reprinted in Rozental (1967), p. 341.
532. "We are . . . *by war*": quoted in Nielson (1963), p. 29ff. My italics.

PAGE

532. "First of . . . of war": Oppenheimer (1963), III (Los Alamos version) p. 8.
532. "a far . . . warfare": NB memorandum, July 3, 1944.
534. *"It appeared . . . divergencies":* Rozental (1967), p. 341. My italics.
534. "Much thought . . . confidence": NB memorandum, July 3, 1944.
534. "The prevention . . . acuteness": ibid.
534–535. "[Bohr] . . . the world": Oppenheimer (1963), III (Los Alamos version) p. 9.
535. "What it . . . enlarged upon": quoted in ibid.
535. "Within any . . . openness": Rozental (1967), p. 350.
535. "An open . . . else": ibid.
535. "The very . . . crisis": ibid., p. 351.
536. "The present . . . the others": NB memorandum, July 3, 1944.
536. "I have . . . purpose": NB to FF, July 6, 1944. JRO Papers, Box 34.
536. "on August . . . manner": NB memorandum, May 6, 1945.
536. "was very . . . spirits": Rozental (1967), p. 205.
536. "most kindly . . . entertained": NB memorandum, May 6, 1945.
536–537. "Roosevelt . . . afterwards": Rozental (1967), p. 206ff.
537. "left with . . . Union": unsigned memorandum "Notes on Bohr" dated May 20, 1948, on the stationery of the office of the Director of the Institute for Advanced Study. JRO Papers, Box 21.
537. "It is . . . expectation": Rozental (1967), p. 207.
537. "This was . . . of Bohr": Snow (1981), p. 116.
537. "The suggestion . . . Russians": quoted in Gowing (1964), p. 447.
537–538. "The President . . . at all": quoted in Clark (1981), p. 177.
538. "youthful . . . physicists": Ulam (1976), p. 151.
538–539. "It was . . . major voice": Bethe (1982). Communicated in manuscript; Ms. p. 2.
539. thermonuclear research: cf. Hawkins (1947), p. 24.
539. "That I . . . inevitable": quoted in Bernstein (1980), p. 81.
539. "Bethe was . . . organization": quoted in Blumberg and Owens (1976), p. 129ff.
539. "Throughout the . . . led it": Teller (1983), p. 190ff.

PAGE

539–540. "I believe . . . Oppenheimer": quoted in Blumberg and Owens (1976), p. 129ff.
540. "When Los . . . objectives": Teller (1955), p. 269.
540. the laboratory history confirms: cf. Hawkins (1947), p. 96.
540. "At this . . . dream of": Segrè (1970), p. 137.
541. "The first . . . out there": Badash (1980), p. 17.
541. bullet passing through: cf. Hawkins (1947), p. 131.
541–542. "the first . . . illusions": ibid., p. 77.
542. "Absolutely . . . results": quoted in Bernstein (1980), p. 85.
542. "Everything in . . . everybody": Badash (1980), p. 49.
542. "by 1943 . . . ordnance": ibid.
542. GK won JvN to his view: interview with George Kistiakowsky, Cambridge, Mass., Jan. 15, 1982.
542. "I began . . . at times": Badash (1980), p. 49ff.
542–543. "After a . . . interfering": quoted a Goodchild (1980), p. 112ff.
543. "It seemed . . . effort": Ulam (1976), p. 141.
543. "The sun . . . Madison": ibid., p. 145.
543. "talked to . . . bomb": ibid., p. 148ff.
543. "However . . . to do": Bethe (1982), Ms. p. 2.
543. "[Bethe] . . . novel subjects": quoted in Blumberg and Owens (1976), p. 131.
544. "Both . . . main program": Hawkins (1947), p. 97.
544. "the hydrodynamical . . . magnitude": Ulam (1976), p. 154.
544. "all the . . . work": ibid., p. 154ff.
545. "You have . . . the charge": Kistiakowsky interview, Jan. 15, 1982.
545. 5 percent variation: Hawkins (1947), p. 91.
545–546. "With the . . . bomb": Bethe (1982), Ms. p. 3.
546. "These calculations . . . urgency": JRO to LRG, May 1, 1944. MED 201, Peierls, R.
546. "Oppenheimer . . . was feasible": Teller (1955), p. 269.
546. "But there . . . Teller": quoted in Smith and Weiner (1980), p. 273.
547. Kistiakowsky memorandum: GBK to JRO, June 3, 1944. JRO Papers, Box 43.
547. "I am . . . accept it": quoted in Kunetka (1979), p. 88.

PAGE

548. 2000+ experiments: 2,500; cf. Smith and Weiner (1980), p. 282.
548. "It appears . . . implosion": JRO to LRG, July 18, 1944. Bush-Conant File, f. 3.
549. "The implosion . . . one": Hawkins (1947), p. 82.
549. "The Laboratory . . . at it' ": ibid.
549. "[Oppenheimer] . . . of me": quoted in Goodchild (1980), p. 118.
549. 1,207 employees: "Personnel employed at 'Y' technical area, May 1, 1944." MED 201, Personnel.
549. "it had . . . a barn": interview with Philip Abelson, Washington, D.C., Sept. 17, 1982.
550. the dollar: ibid.
550. thermal diffusion experiments: cf. Abelson (1943).
550. "The apparatus . . . device": ibid., p. 5.
551. "Information . . . future plants": ibid., p. 20.
551. "They were . . . steam": Abelson interview, Sept. 17, 1982.
551–552. Abelson knew Manhattan Project: ibid.
552. "I wanted . . . dagger stuff": telephone interview with Philip Abelson, Oct.16, 1984.
552. BuOrd man: Hewlett and Anderson (1962), p. 168, cite a visit by Deke Parsons to the Navy Yard as the origin of this contact. Abelson remembers no such visit. The official AEC historians apparently found the Parsons version in JRO's memorandum to LRG. Groves was concerned after the war to discredit a Szilard recounting of this story similar to Abelson's version. Abelson remembers quite clearly that he initiated the contact; asked if he deliberately breached compartmentalization, he answers, "I sure as hell did!" Telephone interview, Oct. 16, 1984.
552–553. "Dr. Oppenheimer . . . a whole": USAEC (1954), p. 164ff.
553. "I at . . . investigating": Groves (1962), p. 120.
553. Lewis/Murphree/Tolman conclusions: cf. "Possible utilization of Navy pilot thermal diffusion plant," dated June 3, 1944. Bush-Conant File, f. 3.
553. "Chinese copies": Groves (1962), p. 120.
554. "We are . . . Marines": quoted in Costello (1981), p. 476.

PAGE

555. "Nowhere have . . . was dead": Sherrod (1944), p. 32.
555. Tinian: cf. esp. Hough (1947).
556. "The view . . . cold": Libby (1979), p. 177.
557. "Enrico and . . . reaction": ibid., p. 178ff.
557–558. "We arrived . . . cooling tubes": ibid., p. 179ff.
558. "Something was . . . and down": ibid., p. 180ff.
558. Fermi open-minded: cf. ibid., p. 181.
558. "concerned for . . . even stable": Wheeler (1962), p. 34.
559. "If this . . . was needed": ibid., p. 34ff.
559. "a fundamentally . . . matter": quoted in Hewlett and Anderson (1962), p. 307.
560. Groves' report to Marshall: cf. J. B. Conant handwritten "Notes on history of S-1" dated Jan. 6, 1945. Bush-Conant File, f. 19.
560. "Looks like . . . September": ibid.

Chapter 17: The Evils of This Time

561. Conant to Bush: "Report on visit to Los Alamos—October 18, 1944." Bush-Conant File, f. 3.
561. "what the . . . over": Conant (1970), p. 300.
562. Niels Bohr: NB's influence on VB and JBC can be traced by careful reading. The two administrators knew little or nothing of NB's ideas on Sept. 19, 1944, when they sent their own to HLS: when VB met with Cherwell and FDR on Sept. 22, VB was disturbed that FDR was discussing postwar arrangements without benefit of briefing and gathered, apparently from FDR, that NB wanted the British and the Americans to maintain peace via bilateral postwar monopoly. Between Sept. 22 and 30, however, at least VB must have talked to NB: the memorandum he and JBC sent HLS on that later date contains and endorses all NB's basic ideas. Since Bohr was in the doghouse with FDR at the time, VB and JBC were probably politic not to credit him as their source. Cf. VB/JBC to HLS, Sept. 19, 1944, MED 76, S-1 interim committee scientific panel; VB to JBC, "Memorandum of conference," Sept. 22, 1944, Bush-Conant File, f. 20a; VB to JBC, Sept. 23, 1944, ibid.; VB/JBC to HLS,

PAGE

Sept. 30, 1944, Bush-Conant File, f. 20a.

562. "the progress . . . be secure": VB/JBC to HLS, Sept. 19, 1944.

562. "to a . . . Russia": VB to JBC, Sept. 22, 1944.

562. "In order . . . attempt": VB/JBC to HLS, Sept. 30, 1944.

562. "a robot . . . missile": ibid.

563. "By various . . . enterprise": JBC to VB, Oct. 20, 1944. Bush-Conant File, f. 3.

563–564. "I should . . . importance": USAEC (1954), p. 954ff.

564. Los Alamos: This discussion draws especially on Badash (1980), Brode (1960), L. Fermi (1954), Jette (1977), Libby (1979), Lyon and Evans (1984) and Segrè (1970).

564. "I always . . . rebellion": L. Fermi (1954), p. 231ff.

564–565. "I told . . . come again": quoted in Brode (1960), I, 7.

565. "Then we . . . slope": Badash (1980), p. 61.

565. "Oppie . . . get up": quoted in L. Fermi (1954), p. 227.

565. "That young . . . long way": quoted in ibid., p. 219.

565. "Parties . . . we worked": Brode (1960), X, 5.

565. "Everybody . . . army camp": Else (1980), p. 9.

566. "He offered . . . feet": Brode (1960), VIII, 5.

566. "The main . . . mesa": ibid., X, 7.

566. "I played . . . of view": Badash (1980), p. 61.

566–567. "Of the . . . cloth": Wilson (1975), p. 160.

567. "I don't . . . friendship": Badash (1980), p. 43.

567. "The streams . . . shouting": quoted in Brode (1960), IX, 7.

567–568. "but he . . . science": Segrè (1970), p. 140.

568. "Oh, I . . . wits": quoted in Ulam (1976), p. 165.

568. "sit there . . . made": Badash (1980), p. 81.

568. "nothing . . . breath": Libby (1979), p. 204ff.

568. "Best for . . . Fuchs": Brode (1960), IX, 7.

568. "Remember . . . Park": quoted in Lyon and Evans (1984), p. 31.

569. "from . . . cover": Hans Bethe OHI, AIP, p. 159.

PAGE

569–570. "Jesus . . . fantastic": Jette (1977), p. 84.

570. "Oppenheimer . . . exception": interview with Edward Teller, Stanford, Calif., June 19, 1982.

570. "He knew . . . us": Else (1980), p. 10.

570. "He understood . . . anybody": interview with Hans Bethe, Ithaca, N.Y., Sept. 12, 1982.

570. "a very . . . them": "Seven Springs meeting, 5/63," p. 5. JRO Papers, Box 66.

571. volunteered names to protect his own: cf. Stern and Green (1969), p. 48ff.

571. "On June . . . together": D. M. Ladd to Director FBI, Dec. 17, 1953, p. 9. JRO FBI file, doc. 65.

571. "I wanted . . . somehow": quoted in Goodchild (1980), p. 128.

571. between March and October: between the beginning of planning and the first mention of Trinity I find in the record, JBC to VB, Oct. 18, 1944.

571. "I did . . . Resurrection": JRO to LRG, Oct. 20, 1962. JRO Papers, Box 36.

572. "Bohr was . . . control": Hans Bethe OHI, AIP, p. 62.

572. "That still . . . whatever": JRO to LRG, Oct. 20, 1962.

572. Oppenheimer did not doubt: cf. his famous remark to Truman that he had blood on his hands.

572. healed the split: cf. Dyson (1979), p. 81ff, esp. Kitty Oppenheimer's choice of George Herbert's "The Collar" as "a poem . . . that she found particularly appropriate to describe how Robert had appeared to himself." "The Collar" works complementarities similar to Donne's.

573. "Therefore I . . . peace": Smith and Weiner (1980), p. 156.

574–575. "I was . . . surrounded": interview with Luis Alvarez, Berkeley, Calif., June 22, 1982.

575. "very quickly . . . failed": Bethe interview, Sept. 12, 1982.

576. "too frequently . . . shortcuts": Kistiakowsky (1949a), I-1.

576. "Prior to . . . low": ibid., I-2.

576. "So much . . . implosion": Badash (1980), p. 54.

577. "the greatest . . . molds": interview with George Kistiakowsky, Cambridge, Mass., Jan. 15, 1982.

577. Composition B/Baratol: cf. Kistiakowsky (1949b).

PAGE

577. "We learned . . . mold": Kistiakowsky interview, Jan. 15, 1982.
577. "We were . . . charges": Kistiakowsky (1980), p. 19.
578. initiator: Dr. Louis Brown, DTM, Carnegie Institution of Washington, contributed valuably to this discussion.
578. "some other . . . satisfactory": Condon (1943), p. 19.
579. "I think . . . initiator": Bethe interview, Sept. 12, 1982.
579–580. "This isotope . . . accord": quoted in Trenn (1980), p. 98.
580. screwballs: cf. Groueff (1967), p. 327.
580. Nishina's private belief: cf. Pacific War Research Society (1972) (hereafter PWRS), p. 23.
580. first Nishina/Nobuuji meeting: "Uranium project research meeting," July 2, 1943. Copies of original documents and translations in the private collection of P. Wayne Reagan, Kansas City, Mo.
581. second Nishina/Nobuuji meeting: "Uranium project research meeting," Feb. 2, 1944. P. Wayne Reagan collection.
581. 170 grams: PWRS (1972), p. 48.
581. "Well, don't . . . gas": quoted in ibid., p. 49.
581. third Nishina/Nobuuji meeting: "Uranium project research meeting," Nov. 17, 1944. P Wayne Reagan collection.
582. Nishina's staff had understood: cf. PWRS (1972), p. 41.
582. "The doors . . . doors": Ramsey (1946), p. 126.
583. "When I . . . right": quoted in Marx (1967), p. 98.
584. "I'm satisfied": quoted in Tibbets (1973), p. 51.
584. "You have . . . war": ibid.
584. Air Force chose Wendover: Tibbets has remembered making the choice, but it was determined before his appointment; no doubt he confirmed it. Cf. Capt. Derry to LRG, Aug. 29, 1944. MED 5c, Preparation and movement of personnel and equipment to Tinian.
584. B-29: cf. Birdsall (1980).
584. Sept. 1939 proposal: ibid., p. 2.
585. one Delivery group physicist: David L. Anderson interview, Oberlin, Ohio, 1981.

PAGE

585–586. "safe . . . of two": Groves (1962), p. 286.
586. Tibbets: besides previous references cf. also Thomas and Witts (1977).
586. "It didn't . . . homeland": LeMay (1965), p. 322.
586. "I'll tell . . . fighting": quoted in Powers (1984), p. 60.
587. "I wanted . . . creature": LeMay (1965), p. 14.
587. "truancy . . . mania": ibid., p. 16.
587. "I had . . . activities": ibid., p. 17.
587. "When the . . . penetrate": ibid., p. 30.
587. "General Arnold . . . system": ibid., p. 338.
588. "The city . . . of it": Guillain (1981), p. 174.
588. Hansell target directive: cf. Birdsall (1980), p. 107.
589. "I did . . . surprise": quoted in ibid., p. 144.
589. blockbluster meeting: on Dec. 19, 1944. Cf. Capt. Derry to LRG, Jan. 9, 1945. MED 4, Trinity test.
590. Parsons memorandum: WSP to LRG, Dec. 26, 1944. MED 51, Memos from Parsons (misc).
590–591. "Suddenly there . . . blossom": Guillain (1981), p. 176.
591. "urgent . . . future planning": quoted in Birdsall (1980), p. 131, whose argument I follow here.
591. "LeMay is . . . it": quoted in ibid., p. 143.
591–592. "General Arnold . . . lives": LeMay (1965), p. 347.
592. "another month . . . this": ibid., p. 345.
592. Churchill instigated: cf. Irving (1963), p. 90ff.
592. "I did . . . done": quoted in ibid., p. 92.
593. "The first . . . underground": I was the interviewer. Rhodes et al. (1977), p. 213ff.
593. Iwo Jima: cf. esp. Wheeler (1980).
594. "We would . . . can": quoted in ibid., p. 28.
594. "I am . . . can": quoted in ibid., p. 29.
594. "They meant . . . homeland": Manchester (1980), p. 339.
594. poison gas: cf. Wheeler (1980), p. 13.
595. "The invaders . . . flesh": Manchester (1980), p. 340.
595. "We shall . . . dying!": quoted in Costello (1981), p. 546.
596. "The Japanese . . . fast": LeMay (1965), p. 346; his italics.

PAGE

596. Tokyo raid: cf. *United States Strategic Bombing Survey* (1976) (hereafter *USSBS*); Birdsall (1980); Guillain (1981); Kennett (1982); Overy (1980).
596. "All the . . . kids": LeMay (1965), p. 349.
596. 87.4 percent: *USSBS* #96, p. 105.
596. "No matter . . . killed": LeMay (1965), p. 352; his ellipses.
596. "the entire . . . target": quoted in Kennett (1982), p. 176.
597. "outstanding strike": quoted in Birdsall (1980), p. 180.
597. Arnold informed: LeMay remembers otherwise, but cf. ibid.
597. "You're going . . . seen": quoted in Costello (1981), p. 548.
597. "grim . . . grubby": Brines (1944), p. 292.
597. "We will . . . possible": ibid., p. 9.
597. "American fighting . . . way": ibid., p. 11.
598. "The inhabitants . . . everywhere": Guillain (1981), p. 184.
598–599. "The fire . . . spectacle": ibid., p. 182.
599. "The chief . . . wind": *USSBS* #96, p. 96ff.
599. "the most . . . known": quoted in Birdsall (1980), p. 195.
599. "probably more . . . man": *USSBS* #96, p. 95.
599. CONGRATULATIONS . . . ANYTHING: quoted in Birdsall (1980), p. 196.
600. "Then . . . Literally": LeMay (1965), p. 354.
600. 32 sq. mi.: *USSBS* #96, p. 39.
600. "I consider . . . command": quoted in Overy (1980), p. 100.
600. "In order . . . mud": quoted in Johnson and Jackson (1981), p. 19.
600. 100 gms., etc.: these numbers and dates from M. L. Oliphant to J. Chadwick, Nov. 2, 1944. MED 201, Chadwick, J.
600–601. "This loss . . . management": ibid.
601. "the output . . . expected": MLO to LRG, Nov. 13, 1944. MED 201, Oliphant, M. L.
601. Jan. 1945, data: Brobeck and Reynolds (1945).
601. Conant notes on Jan. 6: "Notes on history of S-1." Bush-Conant File, f. 19.
601. U235 critical mass: Conant cites 13 ± 2 kg in JBC to VB, Oct. 18, 1944; King (1979) cites 15 kg for U235 surrounded by a thick U tamper.

PAGE

602. "on the . . . received": quoted in Hewlett and Anderson (1962), p. 301.
602. Groves' U235 farm: toured on a visit to Oak Ridge in 1975, when the bluff-side bunker had been converted to an air-pollution sampling station.
603. 250 ppm: Seaborg (1958), p. 16.
603. "Originally eight . . . concrete": Groves (1962), p. 85.
604. "When the . . . aloft": Libby (1979), p. 174.
604. "The yields . . . 1945": Seaborg (1958), p. 50ff.
605. "the astonishing . . . date": Goldschmidt (1964), p. 35.
605. "the unfortunate . . . [them]": Groves (1962), p. 186.
605. "but I . . . it": ibid., p. 191.
606. "his thorough . . . me": ibid., p. 193.
606. "The ALSOS . . . Paris": Lt. Col. G. R. Eckman to Chief, Military Intelligence Service, Sept. 1, 1944. MED 371.2, Goudsmit mission.
607. "It is . . . form": Goudsmit (1947), p. 70ff.
607. "Washington wanted . . . Union": Pash (1969), p. 191.
608. "We outlined . . . oxide": JL, "Capture of material," draft report, July 10, 1946. MED 7, War Dept. special operations (tab E-F).
608–609. "Many of . . . started": ibid. Note that Groves (1962), p. 237, remembers these paper bags as fruit barrels and invents a two-week plant run in the midst of contending armies to manufacture them. Such is memory; JL's is the eyewitness account, confirmed by his contemporary report JL to LRG, May 5, 1945. MED 7 (tab A-C).
609. "Haigerloch is . . . pile": Pash (1969), p. 206ff.
609–610. Haigerloch pile: cf. Irving (1967), p. 244ff.
610. "The fact . . . Alsos": Pash (1969), p. 157ff.
610. "By successively . . . reactions": Hawkins (1947), p. 229.
610–611. "At that . . . flicker": Frisch (1979), p. 161.
611. "The idea . . . so": ibid., p. 159.
611. Feynman named it: cf. ibid.
611–612. "It was . . . mid-morning": ibid., p. 159ff.
612. "These experiments . . . alone": Hawkins (1947), p. 230.
613. "In 1940 . . . war": LRG to GCM, April 23, 1945. MED 7 (tab E-F).

PAGE

613. "Sunday morning . . . ours": quoted in Smith and Weiner (1980), p. 287.
613–614. "When, three . . . death": ibid., p. 288.
614. "I kept . . . struck!": quoted in Bishop (1974), p. 598.

Chapter 18: Trinity

617. "Stimson told . . . details": Truman (1955), p. 10.
618. "The chief . . . distrust": Stimson and Bundy (1948), p. 544.
618. "assistant President": quoted in Byrnes (1958), p. 155.
618. "Jimmy Byrnes . . . world": Truman (1955), p. 11.
618. "that in . . . war": ibid., p. 87.
618–619. "A small . . . geniality": Joseph Alsop and Robert Kitner, quoted in Mee (1975), p. 2.
619. "a vigorous . . . politics": quoted in ibid.
619. "Had a . . . *sometimes*": Ferrell (1980), p. 39.
619–620. "I freely . . . action": Byrnes (1958), p. 230.
620. "We proposed . . . in": "Memorandum of conference," Dec. 8, 1944. Bush-Conant File, f. 20a.
621. "I told . . . me": "Extract from notes made after a conference with the President, December 31, 1944." MED 24, Memos to file by LRG covering two meetings with the President.
621. "it would . . . S-1": quoted in Sherwin (1975), p. 136.
621. "the fear . . . messages": Truman (1955), p. 72.
621–622. "barbarian invasion . . . affairs": ibid., p. 71.
622. "I ended . . . government' ": ibid., p. 72.
622. "go ahead . . . organization": ibid.
622. "He felt . . . Hell": Charles Bohlen, quoted in Giovannitti and Freed (1965), p. 46. Note Truman's nearly identical language, sans cuss word and imperative, at Truman (1955), p. 77.
622. "In the . . . promised": Truman (1955), p. 77.
622. "He said . . . serious": ibid., p. 79.
623. "I replied . . . like that": ibid., p. 82.
623. "one of . . . House": ibid., p. 85.
623. April 24 message from Stalin: quoted in full in ibid., p. 85ff.
624. Stimson memorandum: "Memo discussed with the President," April 25, 1945. MED 60, S-1 White House.

PAGE

625. "Mr. Truman . . . all": quoted in Giovannitti and Freed (1965), p. 80.
625. "a great . . . project": "Report of meeting with the President," April 25, 1945. MED 24.
625–626. "I listened . . . service": Truman (1955), p. 87.
626. first Target Committee meeting: Groves (1962), p. 268, dates this occasion May 2, 1945, but cf. "Notes on initial meeting of target committee" dated April 27, 1945, from which all indicated quotations following are extracted. MED 5D, Selection of targets.
627. "I had . . . bomb": Groves (1962), p. 267.
628. May 1 Harrison memorandum: Bush-Conant File, f. 20A.
628. "The President . . . shut": quoted in Giovannitti and Freed (1965), p. 54.
629. "and late . . . accepted": ibid.
629. "were . . . death": quoted in Sherwin (1975), p. 170.
629. "when secrecy . . . Commission": HLS to VB, April 4, 1945. Bush-Conant File, f. 20b.
629. "I have . . . scene": Eisenhower (1970), IV, p. 2673ff.
629. "I tried . . . accomplished": quoted in ibid., p. 2696.
630. "The mission . . . 1945": ibid.
630. deaths: from Elliot (1972) except for Holocaust victims; that number from Dawidowicz (1975), p. 544.
630. "We all . . . committee": quoted in Giovannitti and Freed (1965), p. 56.
630. Stimson introducing Byrnes: cf. R. Gordon Arneson, "Memorandum for the files," May 24, 1946. Bush-Conant File, f. 6.
631. "A. Height . . . Program": J. A. Derry and N. F. Ramsey, "Summary of Target Committee meetings on 10 and 11 May 1945." MED 5D.
633. "very frank . . . one": VB to JBC, May 14, 1945. Bush-Conant File, f. 20B.
633. Stimson's agenda: copy (misdated May 12, 1945) with notes in HLS's hand in Bush-Conant File, f. 100.
633. "I . . . said . . . September": VB to JBC, May 14, 1945.
633–634. "Mr. Byrnes . . . test": JBC to VB, May 18, 1945. Bush-Conant File, f. 12.
634. "Mr. Byrnes . . . one": quoted in Giovannitti and Freed (1965), p. 62.

PAGE

634. "This question . . . argument": JBC to VB, May 18, 1945.
634. "Some of . . . matter": ibid.
634. Conant told Byrnes: cf. ibid.
635. "the feeling . . . back": quoted in Giovannitti and Freed (1965), p. 116ff.
635. "the wisdom . . . bombs": Weart and Szilard (1978), p. 182.
635. "many hours . . . nights": quoted in Giovannitti and Freed (1965), p. 115.
635. "The only . . . President": Weart and Szilard (1978), p. 181.
635. "I am . . . history": quoted in Clark (1970), p. 685.
636. "Elated by . . . House": Weart and Szilard (1978), p. 182.
636. "I see . . . City": ibid., p. 183.
636. "We did . . . know": ibid.
636. "I have . . . judgment": ibid., p. 205.
636. Szilard memorandum: although Document 101 in ibid., p. 196ff, is usually cited as the memorandum Byrnes read, his memory of the contents—discussed below—makes it clear that he read the enclosure given as part of Document 102, p. 205ff, which Weart and Szilard describe as an "enclosure to Einstein's letter."
637. "essentially due . . . armaments": ibid., p. 198.
637. "Szilard complained . . . me": Byrnes (1958), p. 284.
638. "When I . . . Russia": Weart and Szilard (1978), p. 183.
638. "He said . . . already?": ibid., p. 184.
638. "Byrnes thought . . . manageable": ibid.
638. May 28 Target Committee meeting: minutes at MED 5D.
639. "for thirty . . . hated": Stimson and Bundy (1948), p. 632.
640. "I am . . . weapons": diary, quoted in Steiner (1974), p. 473.
640. May 30: on the evidence of LRG to Lauris Norstad, May 30, 1945, reporting Stimson's decision "this AM." MED 5B.
640–641. "I was . . . Kyoto": quoted in Giovannitti and Freed (1965), p. 40ff.
641. "The Joint . . . Japan": quoted in Feis (1966), p. 7.
641. "with the . . . lives": quoted in ibid., p. 8.
641. 31,000 casualties: cf. ibid., p. 8ff.
642. Groves had doubted: cf. VB to JBC, May 14, 1945.
642. "I told . . . well": Weart and Szilard (1978), p. 185.

PAGE

642. May 31 Interim Committee meeting: cf. notes at Bush-Conant File, f. 100.
642. "S.1 . . . World Peace": handwritten notes "To the Four," May 31, 1945. Bush-Conant File, f. 100.
643. "a terrible . . . breached": Oppenheimer (1961), p. 11.
643. "As I . . . weapon": the deleted phrase is "and industrialists." Byrnes would not meet with the industrialists until the next day and presumably merges the two meetings in memory. The context is the May 31 meeting. Byrnes (1958), p. 283.
644–645. "Bush and . . . panel": Oppenheimer (1963), III (Los Alamos version), p. 15.
647. question mentioned during morning: according to E. O. Lawrence; cf. Sherwin (1975), p. 207.
647. "[Stimson emphasized] . . . harm": Oppenheimer (1961), p. 12.
647. "You ask . . . know": quoted in Giovannitti and Freed (1965), p. 104.
647–648. "We feared . . . surrender": Byrnes (1958), p. 261.
648. "The President . . . knows": quoted in Feis (1966), p. 47.
648. "number of . . . raids": quoted in Sherwin (1975), p. 207ff.
648. 20,000 deaths: Compton (1956), p. 237.
648. "a city . . . lives": ibid. AHC locates this discussion A.M. P.M. is likelier; much else in his memory of this meeting is misplaced.
649. "We were . . . done": LeMay (1965), p. 384.
649. "secret intelligence . . . intentionally": unsigned memorandum dated June 1, 1945, on War Dept. stationery; Top Secret classification authorized by LRG. MED 12.
649. June 1 Interim Committee meeting: minutes at MED 100.
650. "I concluded . . . bomb"; quoted in Feis (1966), p. 44.
650. "sternly questioned": Stimson and Bundy (1948), p. 632.
650. "I told . . . understood": Stimson's diary, quoted in Giovannitti and Freed (1965), p. 36.
650. "Mr. Byrnes . . . weapon": quoted in ibid., p. 107.
650–651. Byrnes to White House: ibid., p. 109.
651. "I told . . . recommend": quoted in ibid., p. 110.
651. "said that . . . done": quoted in ibid.

PAGE

651. "I was . . . happen": Oppenheimer (1963) III (Los Alamos version), p. 15.
651. "Do you . . . No": MED 19, Bohr, Dr. Niels.
651–652. Trinity: cf. esp. Badash (1980), Bainbridge (1945), Else (1980), Lamont (1965), Szasz (1984), and Wilson (1975).
652. "was one . . . desert": Hawkins (1947), p. 271.
652. "followed unmapped . . . winds": Wilson (1975), p. 210.
652. "almost to . . . 1945": Bainbridge (1945), p. 5.
654. "people were . . . explosion": Else (1980), p. 16.
655. Pu critical mass: cf. King (1979), p. 7.
655. "Most troublesome . . . lot": Kistiakowsky (1980), p. 20.
655. June 27 LRG/JRO/WSP meeting: JRO/WSP to LRG, June 29, 1945. MED 50. Preparations and movement of personnel to Tinian.
656. "on purpose . . . time": quoted in Sherwin (1975), p. 193.
656. "What are . . . propagandist?": quoted in Szasz (1984), p. 65.
656. ANY . . . DAYS: quoted in Groueff (1967), p. 340.
656. July 9: Bainbridge (1945), p. 39.
656. "In some . . . spheres": Kistiakowsky (1980), p. 20.
657. "You don't . . . it": interview with G. B. Kistiakowsky, Cambridge, Mass., Jan. 15, 1982.
657. "The castings . . . charge": Bainbridge (1945), p. 39.
657. "That last . . . life": Badash (1980), p. 46.
657. "Very shortly . . . hysteria": JRO to ER, May 19, 1950. JRO Papers, Box 62.
657. nickel: Bill Jack Rodgers, LANL, personal communication.
657. "beautiful to . . . threatened": Smith (1954), p. 88.
658. "Right in . . . this?": quoted in Szasz (1984), p. 72.
658. "on the . . . insignificant": Bainbridge (1945), p. 39.
659–660. "when you . . . rabbit": Libby (1979), p. 171.
660. "We were . . . way": quoted in Johnson (1970), p. 11.
660. "The [high- . . . mistake": Wilson (1975), p. 185ff.
661. "So of . . . me": Badash (1980), p. 59.

PAGE

661–662. "Everybody at . . . work": Kistiakowsky (1980), p. 21.
662. "a. 1 box . . . bomb": J. A. Derry to Adm. W. S. DeLany, July 17, 1945. MED 50.3, Shipment of special materials (bomb).
662. "We drove . . . dud": Badash (1980), p. 75ff.
663. "His was . . . him": Bush (1970), p. 148.
663. "Sunday morning . . . society": Badash (1980), p. 59.
663. "What about . . . whimsical": quoted in Lamont (1965), p. 184.
663–664. "*Gadget complete* . . . there?": Bainbridge (1945), p. 43.
664. "in less . . . sacrifices": quoted in Szasz (1984), p. 75.
664. JRO climbed tower: Lamont puts this visit at 1600, when JRO was in conference with Hubbard. Lamont (1965), p. 190.
664. "Funny how . . . work": quoted in ibid., p. 193.
664. "I had . . . possible": Groves (1962), p. 296ff.
664. "thoughtless bravado": Wilson (1975), p. 225.
665. "Trying to . . . whiskey": Teller (1979), p. 147.
665. "On the . . . Zero": Wilson (1975), p. 227.
665. "Soon after . . . tower": ibid.
666. "the night . . . seen": Lawrence (1946), p. 5.
666. "It was . . . Oppenheimer": Else (1980).
666. 0200 weather conference: details from Szasz (1984), p. 76ff., who finds them in Hubbard's contemporary journal.
666. "What the . . . weather": quoted in ibid., p. 76.
666. "or . . . you": quoted in ibid., p. 77.
666–667. "Sporadic rain . . . tower": Wilson (1975), p. 228.
667. "But my . . . water": Segrè (1970), p. 146.
667. "Hubbard gave . . . = 0": Wilson (1975), p. 228.
667. "I drove . . . S 10,000": ibid., p. 228ff.
667. "I unlocked . . . 5:09:45 a.m.": ibid., p. 229.
668. "With the . . . unendurable": Lawrence (1946), p. 6.
668. "We were . . . eye": Teller (1962), p. 17.
668. "I wouldn't . . . lotion": Teller (1979), p. 148.

PAGE

668. "It was . . . flash": Lawrence (1946), p. 7.
668. "personally nervous . . . fault": MED 319.1, Trinity test reports (misc.).
668. "only of . . . happened": Groves (1962), p. 296.
668. "groups of . . . point": MED 319.1.
669. "Lord, these . . . heart": quoted in Lamont (1965), p. 226.
669. "The control . . . safe)": GBK to Richard Hewlett (n.d.), JRO Papers, Box 43.
669. "I put . . . point": Teller (1979), p. 148.
669. "Dr. Oppenheimer . . . ahead": quoted in Groves (1962), p. 436.
669. "I watched . . . rise": MED 319.1.
669. "but at . . . excited!)": ibid.
670. "Now the . . . zero": quoted in Giovannitti and Freed (1965), p. 196.
670. "the very . . . distance": Bethe (1964), p. 13.
671. "The shock . . . center": ibid.
671. "because higher . . . maximum": ibid., p. 14ff.
671. "any further . . . seconds": ibid., p. 92ff.
671-672. "The expansion . . . screw": Bainbridge (1945), p. 60.
672. "We were . . . nature": Rabi (1970), p. 138.
672. "was like . . . sunlight": Teller (1962), p. 17.
672. "We had . . . back": quoted in *Los Alamos: beginning of an era 1943–1945* (n.d.) (hereafter *LABE*), p. 52.
672. "Just as . . . surprise": MED 319.1.
673. "it looked . . . seconds": quoted in *LABE,* p. 53.
673. "At the . . . breath-taking": MED 319.1.
673. "The most . . . possible": Segrè (1970), p. 147.
673. "From ten . . . sunrise": quoted in Terkel (1984), p. 512ff.
673-674. "The flash . . . yards": D. R. Inglis, MED 319.1.
674. "Most experiences . . . anybody": quoted in *LABE,* p. 53.
674. "the overcast . . . sunrise": MED 319.1.
674. "the path . . . clouds": ibid.
674. "When the . . . ball": ibid.
674. "About 40 . . . T.N.T.": ibid.
674. "From the . . . measurement": Segrè (1970), p. 147ff.

PAGE

674. "He was . . . noise": L. Fermi (1954), p. 239.
675. "And so . . . worked": Else (1980).
675. "No one . . . display": Wilson (1975), p. 230.
675. "personally thought . . . it": Groves (1962), p. 439.
675. "I slapped . . . dollars": Badash (1980), p. 60.
675. "It's empty . . . wait": quoted in Lamont (1965), p. 237.
675. "I finished . . . test": Wilson (1975), p. 230.
675. "Our first . . . worried": quoted in Szasz (1984), p. 91.
675. "Naturally, we . . . was": Rabi (1970), p. 138.
676. "We waited . . . another": quoted in Giovannitti and Freed (1965), p. 197.
676. "When it . . . it": Oppenheimer (1946), p. 265.
676. "He was . . . it": Else (1980).
676. "When Farrell . . . you": Groves (1962), p. 298.
676. "the best . . . philosophy": quoted in Davis (1968), p. 184.
676. "My faith . . . restored": quoted in Szasz (1984), p. 89.
677. 21 KT, 18 KT: cf. telephone notes of 7:55 A.M. LRG to Jean O'Leary, July 16, 1945. MED 319.1.
677. 18.6 KT: Bainbridge (1945), p. 67.
677. "For the . . . driven": L. Fermi (1954), p. 238.
677. "You could . . . future": quoted in Szasz (1984), p. 91.
677. "Partially eviscerated . . . permanently": SW to LRG, July 21, 1945. MED 4, Trinity test.
677. Frank Oppenheimer experiment: Bainbridge (1945), p. 48.
678. "He applied . . . reality": quoted in Terkel (1984), p. 513.
678. 0836 PWT: Ethridge (1982), p. 81.

Chapter 19: Tongues of Fire

679. Kirkpatrick reported to Groves: cf. handwritten reports dated March 31, April 11, and May 10, 1945, at MED 5C, Preparation and movement of personnel and equipment to Tinian.
680. "Tests showed . . . carburetors": Tibbets (1946), p. 133.
681. "The performance . . . theater": Ramsey (1946), p. 146.
681. eleven B-29's: Peer DeSilva to John Lansdale, Jr., June 28, 1945. MED 371.2.

PAGE

681. "looked . . . Paradise": quoted in Craven and Cate (1958), V, p. 707.
681. "Tinian is . . . landed": Morrison (1946), p. 177.
682. "The first . . . Tinian": Ramsey (1946), p. 147.
682. "Jimmy . . . Bible": quoted in Messer (1982), p. 6.
682. "a warning . . . capitulate": Stimson and Bundy (1948), p. 621.
682. "from the . . . Department": quoted in Giovannitti and Freed (1965), p. 180.
682–683. "Secretary Byrnes . . . there?": quoted in ibid.
683. "We reviewed . . . knows?": Ferrell (1980), p. 41.
683. "Proposed Program for Japan": cf. Stimson and Bundy (1948), p. 620ff.
684. "the statement . . . Japan": quoted in Giovannitti and Freed (1965), p. 185.
684–685. "The foreign . . . concerned": quoted in Feis (1966), p. 67.
685. "It is . . . homeland": quoted in ibid., p. 68.
685. "terrible political . . . war?": quoted in Giovannitti and Freed (1965), p. 203.
685–686. "Operated on . . . posted": MED 5E, Terminal cables.
686. "Well . . . Leavenworth": quoted in Bundy (1957), p. 57.
686. "The following . . . Emperor": quoted in Giovannitti and Freed (1965), p. 203.
686. "Neither the . . . test": quoted in ibid.
686. a year's supply of ammunition: production, that is, "which is estimated to equal 350 division months of defensive fighting from fixed positions." *Effects of Strategic Bombing* (n.d.), cover memorandum dated July 25, 1945, p. 5. MED 319.2, Misc.
686. "Subject to . . . government": quoted in Feis (1966), p. 81.
686. "all your . . . city": MED 5E.
686. "aware of . . . it": ibid.
686. "If any . . . rapidly": ibid.
687. "the imminence . . . August": ibid.
687. Groves' narrative: cf. Groves (1962), p. 433ff.
687. "tremendously pepped . . . confidence": quoted in Feis (1966), p. 85.
687. October 1: Arnold (1949), p. 564.
687. "In order . . . cities": ibid.
687. fifty-eight cities: Overy (1980), p. 100.
687. "practically identical . . . out": quoted in Wolk (1975), p. 60.

PAGE

687–688. "We regarded . . . lives": quoted in Mosley (1982), p. 337ff.
688. "We'd had . . . dropped": quoted in "Ike on Ike," *Newsweek*, Nov. 11, 1963, p. 108.
688. "Doctor has . . . farm": MED 5E.
688. "The cable . . . problem": "Ike on Ike."
688. "Believe Japs . . . homeland": Ferrell (1980), p. 42.
689. "Operation may . . . 10": MED 5E.
689. "always . . . authority": ibid.
689. "Hiroshima . . . here": ibid.
689. Official Air Force historians: i.e., Craven and Cate (1958), V; cf. p. 710.
689. "First one . . . sound": MED 5E.
690. "As a . . . once": Feis (1966), p. 101.
690. Stalin knew of Trinity: according to a secret U.S. intelligence agency history of the Soviet atomic bomb program reported in Szulc (1984), p. 3.
690. "I casually . . . Japanese": Truman (1955), p. 416.
690. "That . . . far": Oppenheimer (1963), III (Los Alamos version), p. 16.
690–691. "We have . . . useful": Ferrell (1980), p. 42.
691 the historic directive: WAR 37683, MED 5E.
691. "in order . . . possible": ibid.
692. C-54's: cf. J. A. Derry to Adm. W.S. DeLany, Aug. 17, 1945. MED 5C.
692. Potsdam Declaration: cf. Truman (1955), p. 390ff.
692. "We faced . . . Declaration": Byrnes (1947), p. 262.
693. Japanese response: this discussion follows Feis (1966), p. 107ff.
693. "I believe . . . war": quoted in ibid., p. 109ff.
693. "In the . . . weapon": Stimson and Bundy (1948), p. 625.
693. three B-29's: J. A. Derry to Adm. W. S. DeLany, Aug. 17, 1945.
693. *Indianapolis:* cf. esp. Ethridge (1982).
694. "I took . . . more": Hashimoto (1954), p. 224.
695. "Those who . . . drowned": quoted in Ethridge (1982), p. 89.
695. "We . . . men": quoted in ibid.
696. "so sweet . . . life": quoted in ibid., p. 92.
696. "at length . . . tinned)": Hashimoto (1954), p. 226.
696. HIROSHIMA . . . THEM: MED 5B.
696. "My chief . . . face": Stimson and Bundy (1948), p. 632.

PAGE

697. "our obligation . . . use": cf. report at MED 76.
697. "badly . . . equalizer": quoted in Giovannitti and Freed (1965), p. 237.
697. "First of . . . thing": ET to LS, July 2, 1945. MED 201, Leo Szilard.
697. "To avert . . . deliverance": Churchill (1953), p. 639.
698. "It was . . . end": Anscombe (1981), p. 64.
698. "It was . . . people": Moyers (1984).
698. "impatience to . . . ordeal": Feis (1966), p. 120.
698. A JAP BURNS: *Life,* Aug. 13, 1945, p. 34. This issue appeared on Aug. 6, postdated as is customary to extend newsstand life. Luis Alvarez suggested to me this exercise in examining the popular mood.
699. cordite charge: not, as some have written mistakenly, its bullet. Cf. "Check list for loading charge in plane. . . ." MED 5B.
699. precaution prepared at Los Alamos: cf. Hawkins (1947), p. 225.
699. orders to bring bomb back: Craven and Cate (1958), V, p. 716.
699. "With the . . . completed": Ramsey (1946), p. 149.
699. Farrell telexed Groves: Feis (1966), p. 114.
699. August 2: J. A. Derry to Adm. W. S. DeLany, Aug. 7, 1945.
700. one Fat Man for drop test: cf. Ramsey (1946), p. 150.
700. "By August . . . busy": Tibbets (1973), p. 55.
700. Spitzer diary: quoted in Thomas and Witts (1977).
701. "At 1400 . . . 6": Ramsey (1946), p. 151.
701. bomb-loading procedure: cf. Harold S. Gladwin, Jr., to Boeing Service Dept., Eng. Div., Aug. 20, 1945. MED 5B.
701. "an elongated . . . fins": Jacob Beser, quoted in Thomas and Witts (1977), p. 216.
702–703. "This radar . . . altitude": Hawkins (1947), p. 225ff.
703. "The operation . . . it": H. S. Gladwin, Jr., to Boeing Service Dept., Aug. 20, 1945.
703. "Through the . . . paper": quoted in Marx (1967), p. 98ff.
703. "paint that . . . big": quoted in Thomas and Witts (1977), p. 232.

PAGE

704. "What . . . plane?"; quoted in ibid., p. 233.
704. "By dinnertime . . . poker": Tibbets (1946), p. 135.
704. "Final . . . 6": Ramsey (1946), p. 151.
704. "to be . . . enemies": quoted in Thomas and Witts (1977), p. 237.
704. "amid . . . premiere)": Ramsey (1946), p. 151.
705. "It was . . . ready": Tibbets (1946), p. 135.
705. "The B-29 . . . airborne": ibid.
706. course, altitude, etc.: cf. navigator's charts printed as end papers to Marx (1967).
706. cordite loading: cf. "Check list for loading charge in plane. . . ." MED 5B. For times cf. Parson's log at Cave Brown and MacDonald (1977), p. 522ff.
706. "At forty- . . . runs": quoted in Lawrence (1946), p. 220.
707. "The colonel . . . 'George' ": quoted in variant forms in Marx (1967), p. 78, and Lawrence (1946), p. 220.
707. "A chemist's . . . guess": quoted in Marx (1967), p. 106, and Lawrence (1946), p. 220ff.
707. "Attention! . . . puzzle": quoted in Talk of the Town (1946), p. 16.
707. "At 4:30 . . . spell": quoted in Lawrence (1946), p. 220.
708. "After leaving . . . Away": quoted in ibid. and in Marx (1967), p. 135ff.
708. "The bomb . . . Tinian": quoted in Marx (1967), p. 136.
708. "Well . . . now": quoted in Lawrence (1946), p. 221.
708. "Our primary . . . Hiroshima": quoted in ibid.
708. "It's Hiroshima": quoted in Marx (1967), p. 143.
708. "As we . . . target": quoted ibid., p. 157.
709. "Twelve miles . . . plane": Tibbets (1946), p. 136.
709. perfect aiming point: Thomas and Witts (1977), p. 220.
709. "Ferebee had . . . goes": Tibbets (1946), p. 136.
709–710. "The radio . . . lead": ibid.
710. "Fellows . . . history": according to Jacob Beser, quoted in Marx (1967), p. 173.
710. "[It was] . . . plane": quoted in Giovannitti and Freed (1965), p. 250.
710. "I don't . . . mountains": quoted in ibid.

PAGE

711. "If you . . . home": quoted in ibid.
711. "I kept . . . smoke": quoted in Marx (1967), p. 171ff.
711. "That city . . . me": quoted in ibid., p. 174.
711. 8:16:02: cf. The Committee for the Compilation of Materials on Damage Caused by the Atomic Bombs in Hiroshima and Nagasaki (1981)—hereafter cited as Committee—p. 21. All statistics from this source unless otherwise indicated. The official time according to Hiroshima City is 8:15.
711. "It . . . impersonal": Tibbets (1973), p. 55.
711. "If I . . . mind": quoted in Marx (1967), p. 221.
711. Hiroshima: cf. in particular Cave Brown and MacDonald (1977); Committee (1981); Hachiya (1955); Liebow et al. (1949); Liebow (1965); Lifton (1967); NHK (1977); Osada (1982); *USSBS* (1976), X.
712. Hiroshima history: cf. Kosaki (1980).
712–713. "Hiroshima was . . . harbor": Cave Brown and MacDonald (1977), p. 554.
713. "The hour . . . garden": Hachiya (1955), p. 1.
713. "Just as . . . leaves": Osada (1982), p. 8.
713–714. "Shortly after . . . delirium": ibid., p. 305.
714. "Accompanying the . . . explosion": Liebow (1965), p. 68.
714. "Because the . . . miles]": Cave Brown and MacDonald (1977), p. 570.
714. "The temperature . . . life": Committee (1977), p. 119.
714. "severe thermal . . . viscerae": ibid.
715. "Doctor . . . he?": Hachiya (1955), p. 92.
715. "The inundation . . . fatalities": Lifton (1967), p. 21.
715. "There was . . . dead": quoted in ibid., p. 27.
716. "I asked . . . impossible": Hachiya (1955), p. 114.
716. "Father Kopp . . . hand": Cave Brown and MacDonald (1977), p. 542.
716. "Ah, that . . . around": Osada (1982), p. 352.
716. "The vicinity . . . arms": ibid., p. 305.
716. "That boy . . . that": ibid., p. 194.
717. "My body . . . ending' ": quoted in Lifton (1967), p. 22.

PAGE

717. "I just . . . world": quoted in ibid., p. 23.
717. "Within the . . . sound": Hachiya (1955), p. 164.
717. "When I . . . ruins": Osada (1982), p. 224.
717. "The shortest . . . hysterically": Hachiya (1955), p. 2.
717–718. "The appearance . . . them": quoted in Lifton (1967), p. 27.
718. "I heard . . . burned": NHK (1977), p. 12ff.
718. "On both . . . sleepwalkers": Osada (1982), p. 313.
718. "Everything I . . . about": quoted in Lifton (1967), p. 29.
718. "That day . . . rags": Osada (1982), p. 10.
719. "The people . . . them": ibid., p. 258.
719. "People came . . . sight": ibid., p. 97.
719. "The flames . . . looks": ibid., p. 234.
719. "Screaming children . . . blood": ibid., p. 305.
719–720. "It was . . . flames": Liebow et al. (1949), p. 856ff.
720. "The whole . . . alive": Osada (1982), p. 8ff.
720. "I really . . . walking": ibid., p. 65ff.
720. "I was . . . her": ibid., p. 122ff.
720–721. "I left . . . her": quoted in Lifton (1967), p. 40.
721. "Beneath the . . . flames": Cave Brown and MacDonald (1977), p. 544.
721. "I was . . . thing": Osada (1982), p. 137ff.
721. "A woman . . . help": NHK (1977), p. 49.
721. "There were . . . up": Osada (1982), p. 43.
721. "Nearby . . . trousers": ibid., p. 364.
721. "I walked . . . felt": quoted in Lifton (1967), p. 50.
722. "I was . . . striking": NHK (1977), p. 39.
722. "a man . . . ankles": quoted in Mary McGrory, "Hiroshima Horrors Relived," *Kansas City Times,* March 24, 1982. p. A13.
722. "A man . . . up": quoted in Lifton (1967), p. 42.
722. "In front . . . blackness": quoted in ibid., p. 49ff.
722. "The corpse . . . hand": NHK (1977), p. 96.
722. "There was . . . blindly": Osada (1982), p. 154.
722. "I saw . . . be?": NHK (1977), p. 52.

PAGE

722. "A streetcar . . . tremble": Osada (1982), p. 55.
723. "The more . . . get": ibid., p. 77.
723. "Since just . . . having": ibid., p. 83.
723. "I went . . . eyes": quoted in Lifton (1967), p. 36.
723. "I and . . . agonies": Osada (1982), p. 230.
723. "At the . . . help": ibid., p. 352ff.
723–724. "Near the . . . Hell": ibid., p. 79ff.
724. "We came . . . flame": ibid., p. 62.
724. "The fire . . . heads": ibid., p. 72.
724. "I had . . . faces": ibid., p. 237.
724. "Between the . . . water": Hachiya (1955), p. 19.
725. "While taking . . . him": NHK (1977), p. 48.
725. "There were . . . me": Hachiya (1955), p. 101.
725. "Men whose . . . sea": Osada (1982), p. 178.
725. "We . . . around": ibid., p. 94.
725. "Bloated corpses . . . earth": ibid., p. 334.
725–726. "I had . . . shore": quoted in Trumbull (1957), p. 76.
726. "I got . . . place": Osada (1982), p. 173.
726. "The river . . . terrible": ibid., p. 219.
726. "There was . . . back": Hachiya (1955), p. 15.
726–727. "Hundreds of . . . drowned": ibid., p. 77ff.
727. "Along the . . . walk": ibid., p. 184.
727. "Night came . . . heaven": NHK (1977), p. 44.
727. "Everybody in . . . legs": Osada (1982), p. 280.
727. "If you . . . burns": ibid., p. 99ff.
727. "Hiroshima . . . land": ibid., p. 54.
727–728. "The bright . . . collapse": Cave Brown and MacDonald (1977), p. 546.
728. "The streets . . . height": Hachiya (1955), p. 8.
728. "Nothing . . . view": ibid., p. 31.
728. "I climbed . . . exist": quoted in Lifton (1967), p. 29.
728. "I reached . . . heart": quoted in ibid., p. 86.
728. "It is . . . instantaneously": Committee (1977), p. 61.
728–730. "In Hiroshima . . . destroyed": ibid., p. 379.
730. "[She was] . . . child": NHK (1977), p. 70.
730. "We gathered . . . out": interview with Sakae Itoh, Hiroshima, Aug. 5, 1982.

PAGE

730. "After a . . . mouths": Hachiya (1955), p. 164.
730. "On the . . . mountain": Osada (1982), p. 72ff.
731. "Towards evening . . . Hiroshima": Hachiya (1955), p. 32.
731. "Survivors began . . . death": Lifton (1967), p. 57.
731. "atomic bomb . . . irradiation": Committee (1977), p. 115.
731. "Following the . . . recover": Hachiya (1955), p. 97.
731. gamma radiation: cf. Hempelmann et al. (1952), p. 286ff.
731–732. anti-clotting factor: cf. Liebow et al. (1949), p. 927.
732. "Hemorrhage was . . . cases": Hachiya (1955), p. 147ff.
732. "found . . . autopsied": ibid., p. 145.
732. "evidence of . . . eye": Liebow et al. (1949), p. 923.
732. "the bodies . . . living": quoted in Lifton (1967), p. 66.
732. "We were . . . cancer": quoted in ibid., p. 61.
732. "Mother was . . . cry": Osada (1982), p. 227.
732–733. "in the . . . instant": Committee (1977), p. 6.
733. "The whole . . . foundations": ibid., p. 336.
733. "Such a . . . nothing": quoted in Lifton (1967), p. 79.
733. "the total . . . dead": quoted in Liebow (1965), p. 82.
733–734. "How many . . . explosion": Cave Brown and MacDonald (1977), p. 549.
734. Standardized Casualty Rate: cf. Liebow (1965), p. 235.
734. "Those scientists . . . it?": Osada (1982), p. 264.
734. "This is . . . home": Truman (1955), p. 421.
734–735. "Gen G . . . time": Aug. 6, 1945, transcript, MED 201, Groves, L. R., telephone conversations.
735. "The greatest . . . earth": quoted in Truman (1955), p. 422.
735. "I suppose . . . on": LS to GW, Aug. 6, 1945. Egon Weiss, personal communication.
735. "At first . . . asleep": Hahn (1970), p. 170.
735–736. "Then one . . . enemies": Frisch (1979), p. 176.
736. "the importance . . . all": "From the Rubble of Okinawa: A Different

PAGE

View of Hiroshima." *Kansas City Star,* Aug. 30, 1981, p. I1.

736. propaganda effort: cf. J. F. Moynahan to L. R. Groves, May 23, 1946. MED 314.7, History.

736-737. "What we . . . longer": quoted in Mosley (1982), p. 340.

737. "a certain . . . airplane": J. F. Moynahan to L. R. Groves, May 23, 1946.

737. "the equivalent . . . weapons": ibid.

737. Nagasaki leaflets: ibid.

737-738. "was originally . . . schedule": Ramsey (1946), p. 153.

738. "With the . . . orders": O'Keefe (1983), p. 97.

738-739. "When I . . . backward": ibid., p. 98.

739. "nothing that . . . resolder them": ibid., p. 99.

739. "My mind . . . finished": ibid., p. 100ff.

739. 0347: Ramsey (1946), p. 154.

740. "The night . . . us": Cave Brown and MacDonald (1977), p. 557.

740. Ashworth changed plugs: cf. his log at Ramsey (1946), p. 154.

740. "Two . . . seen": quoted in ibid., p. 155.

740. "the Japs . . . ocean": quoted in Marx (1967), p. 202.

742. "A smell . . . gates": William C. Bryson, Capt., USN, Sept. 14, 1945. *Bul. Atom. Sci.* Dec. 82, p. 35.

742. surrender offer: this discussion relies in part on Bernstein (1977).

742. "does not . . . Ruler": quoted in Butow (1954), p. 244.

742. "taking a . . . hands": quoted in Bernstein (1977), p. 5.

742. "I cannot . . . war": quoted in ibid., p. 6.

742. "crucifixion . . . President": quoted in ibid., p. 5.

742. "willingness to . . . accomplished": quoted in ibid., p. 6ff.

742-743. "From the . . . people": quoted in Feis (1966), p. 134.

743. "We would . . . bomb": quoted in Bernstein (1977), p. 9.

743. "Truman said . . . kids": quoted in Herken (1980), p. 11.

743. "Provided there . . . August": LRG to Chief of Staff, Aug. 10, 1945. MED 5B.

744. "It was . . . now?": quoted in Scott-Stokes (1974), p. 109.

744. "placing . . . officials": quoted in Bernstein (1977), p. 13.

PAGE

744. "I have . . . unusual": quoted in ibid., p. 15ff.

744. "a plan . . . attack": quoted in Feis (1966), p. 205.

744. "evidence of . . . ancestors?": quoted in ibid., p. 208.

745. "the . . . placed": quoted in Bernstein (1977), p. 13.

745. "Flash! . . . soon": quoted in Feis (1966), p. 209n.

745-746. "Despite the . . . generation": quoted in ibid., p. 248.

746. "If it . . . mad": quoted in Scott-Stokes (1974), p. 109.

746. "An atomic . . . slaughter": Committee (1977), p. 335.

746. "By the . . . identity": Elliot (1972), p. 138ff.

746. "The experience . . . mankind": Committee (1977), p. 340.

747. "The night . . . pounding": Hachiya (1955), p. 114ff.

Epilogue

749. "that I . . . escape": ET to LS, July 2, 1945. Weart and Szilard (1978), p. 209.

749. "The development . . . scale": ibid., p. 211.

750. special prayer: cf. ibid., p. 230.

750. second petition: cf. ibid., p. 231.

750. "and told . . . subject": ibid., p. 223

750. Oppenheimer wondered: according to EOL's memory of the weekend as reported in Childs (1968), p. 366.

750-751. "You will . . . despair": Smith and Weiner (1980), p. 297.

751. "the circumstances . . . it": quoted in Else (1980).

751. "terrible swift . . . wars": quoted in Childs (1968), p. 365.

751. "In one . . . bomb": Ulam (1976), p. 170.

751. "With the . . . upon": Snow (1981), bound galleys, p. 89. I do not find this comment in the published book.

751. letter on postwar planning: Scientific Panel to the Secretary of War, Aug. 17, 1945. Smith and Weiner (1980), p. 293ff.

752. "There is . . . working": quoted in Childs (1968), p. 366.

752. "I emphasized . . . following": Smith and Weiner (1980), p. 301.

752-753. Lilienthal notes: cf. Lilienthal (1964), II, p. 637ff.

753-754. "The wisest . . . itself": Weart and Szilard (1978), p. 223.

PAGE

754. Szilard to biology: Wigner (1964) dates this conversion from 1949, the year of LS's first biology paper, but LS himself says 1946. Cf. ibid., p. 16.
754. "The end ... TNT": Hawkins (1947), p. 214.
754. "was unclear ... it": quoted in Clark (1980), p. 262.
754. "[lost] ... work": Teller (1962), p. 22.
754. "We all ... peacetime": Bethe (1982), p. 45.
754–755. "He expressed ... again": quoted in Blumberg and Owens (1976), p. 185.
755. "that I ... days": Smith and Weiner (1980), p. 308.
755. "In the ... it": Bradbury (1948), p. 10.
755. "Here was ... use": ibid., p. 7.
755–756. "I said ... interested": Teller (1962), p. 22ff.
756. "To demand ... least": Bethe (1982), p. 45.
756. "seeking his ... thing": Teller (1962), p. 23.
756. "Now that ... way": ibid.
757. Teller letter: ET to EF, Oct. 31, 1945. MED Harrison and Bundy File, f. 76.
758. "Under a ... ceremony": Smith and Weiner (1980), p. 210.
758. "It is ... humanity": quoted in Hawkins (1947), p. 294.
758–759. "The limitations ... lot": *Time,* Oct. 29, 1945, p. 30.
759. "Good Uncle ... hit": Brode (1960), XI, p. 8.
759–760. "I was ... way": NB to JRO, Nov. 9, 1945. JRO Papers.
760. "that the ... produced": Feis (1966), p. 173n.
760. "the U.S.S.R. ... enterprise": quoted in Clark (1980), p. 208.
760. "To most ... suitcase": York (1970), p. 107.
760. Oppenheimer ALAS speech: Smith and Weiner (1980), p. 315ff.
764. "to review ... were planned": Teller et al. (1950), p. 1.
764–765. "It is ... national policy": Teller et al. (1980), pp. 44–46.
765. numbers of weapons stockpiled: cf. Norris et al. (1985), p. 107; Rearden (1984), p. 439; Rosenberg (1982).
765. half the T Division's time: Mark (1974), p. 3.
765. "The years ... scientifically": Wigner in Mark and Fernbach (1969), p. 4.
765. "purely scientific data": Teller (1946a), p. 10.

PAGE

765. "ingenious ... sound": Teller (1946b), p. 13.
765. "Nothing ... world-union": Teller (1946c), p. 13.
765. He saw no defense: Teller (1947a), p. 85.
765–766. "One is ... of man": ibid.
766. "agreement with ... and peace": Teller (1947b), p. 356.
766. "a good ... idealist": Dyson (1979), p. 89.
766. "World government ... Government": Teller (1948b), p. 204.
766. "Due to ... incomplete": Teller (1948a), p. 5.
767. Oppenheimer sought him out: USAEC (1954), p. 714.
767. Bradbury sent delegation: Alfred P. Sloan Foundation H-bomb history symposium, videotape transcript (n.d.), Part I, p. 15.
767. "the best ... results": Coughlan (1963), p. 91.
767. Teller had not expected: according to S. Ulam, Sloan transcript I, p. 40.
767. "Keep your shirt on": quoted by Teller, USAEC (1954), p. 714.
767. "did not ... bomb": ibid.
767–768. "Especially ... all time": York (1976), p. 45ff.
768. "intolerable": quoted in Hewlett and Duncan (1969), p. 395.
768. So did Acheson: cf. Acheson (1969), p. 349: "The American people simply would not tolerate a policy of delaying nuclear research in so vital a matter."
768. "Edward ... about it": Sloan transcript II, pp. 30–31.
768. The GAC recommended: the report and annexes are reproduced in York (1976), p. 150ff.
769. two arguments: for an informed and thorough discussion cf. York (1976).
769. 200 bombs: estimated from Rosenberg (1982), p. 26.
769. "The [H-bomb] ... it": USAEC (1954), p. 251.
770. "Edward was ... United States": Sloan transcript II, p. 26.
770. "The reasons ... should be": Coughlan (1954), p. 65ff.
770. "Truman's words ... bomb": interview with J. Carson Mark et al., *Los Alamos Science* 4: 7 (Winter/Spring 1983), p. 36.
771. "no conclusive ... unsuitable": Mark (1974), p. 10.

PAGE

771. "vastly larger . . . computers": Ulam (1976), p. 213.
771. "I think . . . out": quoted in Mark (1974), p. 9.
771. "We started . . . work": Ulam (1976), p. 214.
771. By February 1950: Mark (1974), p. 8.
771. "the result . . . fizzle": quoted in Hewlett and Duncan (1969), p. 440.
771. more tritium: Mark (1974), p. 8.
771. "seemed rather . . . difficulties": Ulam (1976), p. 217.
772. "He was . . . today": quoted in Hewlett and Duncan (1969), p. 440.
772. Teller refused to believe: cf. Teller (1955), p. 272: "I felt at the time that these calculations, which seemed to be in conflict with earlier results obtained on machines, were hard to believe."
772. "reassurances . . . constructive": Hewlett and Duncan (1969), p. 440.
772. "In the . . . dejectedly": Ulam (1976), p. 212. Ulam places this work at Princeton, confusing it in memory with the later calculation carried out on the MANIAC there. The MANIAC was not built in the summer of 1950; when it was, it calculated the hydrodynamics of the successful Teller-Ulam design: icicles did not form.
772. "turned out . . . explosions": ibid., p. 219.
772. "That Ulam's . . . 1949": Bethe (1982), p. 47.
772. "was desperate . . . solution": ibid., p. 48.
772. the laboratory's time: ibid.
772. Teller told the GAC: cf. Hewlett and Duncan (1969), p. 530.
773. few friends: Bethe (1982), p. 48.
773. "The new . . . 1939": ibid., p. 49.
773. Lothar Nordheim: undated draft letter in Teller-Strauss correspondence file, Strauss Papers.
773. Herbert York: interview with Herbert York, La Jolla, Calif., June 27, 1983.
773. "Two signs . . . de Hoffmann": Teller (1955), p. 273.
773. "It is . . . behavior": Coughlan (1954).
773. "I used . . . while": Bernstein (1980), p. 95.
774. "The first . . . transport": *Los Alamos Science* 4:7 (Winter/Spring 1983), p. 112.
774. Ulam studying fission fireball: cf. Bethe (1982), p. 48: "Ulam . . . made his discovery while studying some aspects of fission weapons."

PAGE

774. Those designs blow apart: cf. Ulam (1966), p. 597: "For the wartime schemata for the 'Super,' the hydrodynamical disassembly proceeded faster than the buildup and maintenance of the reaction."
774. Teller-Ulam invention: Howard Morland, who pieced together odds and ends of information that had escaped the security system and reached the right conclusion, deserves a vote of thanks in any discussion of the mechanism of the H-bomb. His book—Morland (1981)—is invaluable. Further confirming the role of plastic foam in the thermonuclear is a description in Cahn (1984) of an inertially confined fusion reactor fuel pellet, which is effectively a miniature spherical H-bomb brought to fusion temperature (its designers hope) by laser pulse: "The essential parts consist of a glass microballoon coated internally with a layer of deuterium-tritium fuel and externally with a dense 'pusher' layer, the whole separated by plastic foam from an external dense metal pusher layer which itself is coated by an ablative plastic layer which creates the 'rocket' effect." In a conference room at the Lawrence Livermore Laboratory in 1984 I saw relegated to a dusty window ledge three display spheres labeled "plutonium," "lithium" and "foam." Cf. also Allred and Rosen (1976); Bell (1965); Bethe (1982); DeVolpi et al. (1981); Mark (1974); Teller (1980); Teller et al. (1950); Ulam (1966).
776. "On March . . . program": Bethe (1982), p. 48.
776. "technically . . . sweet": USAEC (1954), p. 251.
776. "Dr. Oppenheimer . . . it": ibid., p. 720.
776. "Since I . . . who?": JRO Papers, Box 205.
777. "I watched . . . hand?": Teller (1955), p. 274ff.
777. "This thing . . . Thebes": Davis (1968) reports the remark but oddly attributes it to Lewis Strauss' birthday party.
777. "It's a boy": York interview. This response is frequently misplaced to the

PAGE

earlier George shot on May 8, 1951, which tested thermonuclear feasibility, one of the Greenhouse tests. Teller's response on that earlier occasion—which he attended—was silently to hand Ernest Lawrence a five-dollar bill to pay off a bet that the shot would not succeed.

777–778. "The fireball . . . reef": Libby (1979), p. 303.

778. August 1953 Soviet shot yield: York (1976), p. 85.

778. "This was . . . [fallout]": Bethe (1982), p. 53.

778. "the very . . . bomb": York (1976), p. 85.

778. Nov. 23, 1955: ibid., p. 93.

778. "his first . . . be": Oppenheimer (1963), III (Los Alamos version), p. 8.

778. "It did . . . country": Oppenheimer (1946), p. 265.

PAGE

779. "We know . . . expansion": Elliot (1972), p. 187.

779. "The lesson . . . are": Rabi (1970), p. 70.

780. "The hundred . . . race": Elliot (1972), p. 5ff.

780. "The moral . . . time": ibid.

780. "The one . . . death": ibid., p. 24.

781. "a doctrine . . . contradictory": Kedourie (1960), p. 9.

781. "its essential . . . river": Ward (1966), p. 14.

782. "Once men . . . checks": ibid., p. 56.

785. "Nationalism . . . history": ibid., p. 99.

786–787. "Our societies . . . himself": Elliot (1972), p. 8.

787. "The eradication . . . purpose": Henderson (1976), p. 33.

788. "Of course . . . states": JRO to GD, May 16, 1957. JRO Papers, Box 43.

Bibliography

Abelson, Phillip. 1939. Cleavage of the uranium nucleus. *Phys. Rev.* 56:418.
———, et al. 1943. *Progress Report on Liquid Thermal Diffusion.* Naval Research Laboratory report No. 0-1977.
Acheson, Dean. 1969. *Present at the Creation.* W. W. Norton.
Alexandrov, A. P. 1967. The heroic deed. *Bul. Atom. Sci.* Dec.
Allardice, Corbin, and Edward R. Trapnell. 1955. *The First Pile.* U.S. Atomic Energy Commission.
Allison, Samuel K. 1965. Arthur Holly Compton. *Biog. Mem. Nat. Ac. Sci.* 38:81.
Allred, John, and Louis Rosen. 1976. First fusion neutrons from a thermonuclear weapon device. In Bogdan Maglich, ed., *Adventures in Experimental Physics.* World Science Education.
Alperovitz, Gar. 1985. *Atomic Diplomacy.* Penguin.
Alvarez, Luis W. 1970. Ernest Orlando Lawrence. *Biog. Mem. Nat. Ac. Sci.* 41:251.
Amaldi, E. 1977. Personal notes on neutron work in Rome in the 30s and post-war European collaboration in high-energy physics. In Charles Weiner, ed., *History of Twentieth Century Physics. Academic Press.*
Anderson, Herbert L., et al. 1939a. The fission of uranium. Phys. Rev. 55:511.
———. 1939b. Production of neutrons in uranium bombarded by neutrons. *Phys. Rev.* 55:797.
———. 1939c. Neutron production and absorption in uranium. *Phys. Rev.* 56:284.
Andrade, E. N. da C. 1956. The birth of the nuclear atom. *Scientific American.* Nov.
———. 1957. The birth of the nuclear atom. *Proc. Roy. Soc. A.* 244:437.
Anscombe, G.E. M. 1981. *The Collected Philosophical Papers.* v. III. University of Minnesota Press.
Arendt, Hannah. 1973. *The Origins of Totalitarianism.* Harcourt Brace Jovanovich.
Arms, Nancy. 1966. *A Prophet in Two Countries.* Pergamon Press.

Arnold, H. H. 1949. *Global Mission.* Harper & Bros.
Aston, Francis. 1920. Isotopes and atomic weights. *Nature* 105:617.
———. 1927. A new mass-spectrograph and the whole number rule. *Proc. Roy. Soc. A.* 115:487.
———. 1938. Forty years of atomic theory. In Joseph Needham and Walter Pagel, eds., *Background to Modern Science.* Macmillan.
Axelsson, George. 1946. Is the atom terror exaggerated? *Sat. Even. Post.* Jan. 5.
Bacher, R. F., and V. F. Weisskopf. 1966. The career of Hans Bethe. In R. E. Marshak, ed., *Perspectives in Modern Physics.* Interscience.
Bacon, Francis. 1627. *The New Atlantis.* Oxford University Press, 1969.
Badash, Lawrence, et al. 1980. *Reminiscences of Los Alamos.* D. Reidel.
Bainbridge, Kenneth T. 1945. *Trinity.* Los Alamos Scientific Laboratory, 1976.
Barber, Frederick A. 1932. *The Horror of It.* Brewer, Warren & Putnam.
Batchelor, John, and Ian Hogg. 1972. *Artillery.* Ballantine.
Bauer, Yehuda. 1982. *A History of the Holocaust.* Franklin Watts.
Bell, George I. 1965. Production of heavy nuclei in the Par and Barbel devices. *Phys. Rev.* 139: B1207.
Belote, James and William. 1970. *Typhoon of Steel.* Harper & Row.
Benedict, Ruth. 1946. *The Chrysanthemum and the Sword.* New American Library, 1974.
Bentwich, Norman. 1953. *The Rescue and Achievement of Refugee Scholars.* Martinus Nijhoff.
Bernstein, Barton J. 1977. The perils and politics of surrender: ending the war with Japan and avoiding the third atomic bomb. *Pacific Historical Review.* Feb.
Bernstein, Jeremy. 1975. Physicist. *New Yorker.* I: Oct. 13. II: Oct. 20.
———. 1980. *Hans Bethe: Prophet of Energy.* Basic Books.
Bethe, Hans. 1935. Masses of light atoms from transmutation data. *Phys. Rev.* 47:633.
———. 1953. What holds the nucleus together? *Scientific American.* Sept.
———. 1964. *Theory of the Fireball.* Los Alamos Scientific Laboratory.
———. 1965. The fireball in air. *J. Quant. Spectrosc. Radiative Transfer* (GB) 5:9.
———. 1967. Energy production in stars. Nobel Lecture.
———. 1968. J. Robert Oppenheimer. *Biog. Mem. F. R. S.* 14:391.
———. 1982. Comments on the history of the H-bomb. *Los Alamos Science.* Fall.
Beyerchen, Alan D. 1977. *Scientists Under Hitler.* Yale University Press.
Bickel, Lennard. 1980. *The Deadly Element.* Stein and Day.
Biquard, Pierre. 1962. *Frédéric Joliot-Curie.* Paul S. Eriksson.
Birdsall, Steve. 1980. *Saga of the Superfortress.* Doubleday.
Bishop, Jim. 1974. *FDR's Last Year.* William Morrow.
Blackett, P. M. S. 1933. The craft of experimental physics. In Harold Wright, ed., *University Studies.* Ivor Nelson & Watson.
Blumberg, Stanley A., and Gwinn Owens. 1976. *Energy and Conflict.* G. P. Putnam's Sons.
Bohr, Niels. 1909. Determination of the surface-tension of water by the method of jet vibration. *Phil. Trans. Roy. Soc.* 209:281.
———. 1936. Neutron capture and nuclear constitution. *Nature* 137:344.
———.1939a. Disintegration of heavy nuclei. *Nature* 143:330.
———. 1939b. Resonance in uranium and thorium disintegrations and the phenomenon of nuclear fission. *Phys. Rev.* 56:418.
———. 1958. *Atomic Physics and Human Knowledge.* John Wiley.
———. 1963. *Essays 1958–1963 on Atomic Physics and Human Knowledge.* Interscience.
———. 1972. *Collected Works,* v. I. North-Holland.
———. 1981. *Collected Works,* v. II. North-Holland.
———, and J. A. Wheeler. 1939. The mechanism of nuclear fission. *Phys. Rev.* 56:426.

Bolle, Kees. 1979. *The Bhagavadgītā.* University of California Press.
Bolton, Ellis. n.d. A few days in January 1939. Unpublished MS.
Booth, Eugene, et al. 1969. *The Beginnings of the Nuclear Age.* Newcomen Society.
Born, Max. 1971. *The Born-Einstein Letters.* Macmillan.
Bothe, W. 1944. Die Absorption thermischer Neutronen in Kohlenstoff. *Zeitschrift für Physik* 122:749.
———. 1951. Lebensbeschreibung. In Ruth Drossel, *Walther Bothe, Bemerkungen zu seinen kernphysikalischen Arbeiten auf Grund der Durchsicht seiner Laborbucher.* Max-Planck-Institut für Kernphysik, Heidelberg. Unpublished. 1975.
Bradbury, Norris E. 1949. Peace and the atomic bomb. *Pomona College Bulletin.* Feb.
Bretall, Robert, ed. 1946. *A Kierkegaard Anthology.* Modern Library.
Brines, Russell. 1944. *Until They Eat Stones.* J. B. Lippincott.
British Information Services. 1945. Statements relating to the atomic bomb. *Rev. Mod. Phys.* 17:472.
Brobeck, W. M., and W. B. Reynolds. 1945. *On the Future Development of the Electromagnetic System of Tubealloy Isotope Separation.* MED G-14-74.
Brode, Bernice. 1960. Tales of Los Alamos. *LASL Community News.* June 2 and Sept. 22.
Brode, Harold L. 1968. Review of nuclear weapons effects. *Ann Rev. Nucl. Sci.* 18:153.
Brown, Louis. n.d. *Beryllium-8.* Unpublished MS
Bundy, Harvey H. 1957. Remembered words. *Atlantic.* Mar.
Bundy, McGeorge. 1969. To cap the volcano. *Foreign Affairs.* Oct.
Burckhardt, Jacob. 1943. *Force and Freedom.* Pantheon.
Burns, E. L. M. 1966. *Megamurder.* Pantheon.
Bush, Vannevar. 1954. Lyman J. Briggs and atomic energy. *Scientific Monthly.* 78:275.
———. 1970. *Pieces of the Action.* William Morrow.
Butow, Robert J. C. 1954. *Japan's Decision to Surrender.* Stanford University Press.
Byrnes, James F. 1947. *Speaking Frankly.* Harper & Bros.
———. 1958. *All in One Lifetime.* Harper & Bros.
Cahn, Robert W. 1984. Making fuel for inertially confined fusion reactors. *Nature* 311:408.
Canetti, Elias. 1973. *Crowds and Power.* Continuum.
Carnegie Endowment for International Peace. 1915. *The Hague Declaration* (IV, 2) *of 1899 Concerning Asphyxiating Gases.*
Cary, Otis. 1979. Atomic bomb targeting—myths and realities. *Japan Quarterly* 26/4.
Casimir, Hendrick. 1983. *Haphazard Reality.* Harper & Row.
Cave Brown, Anthony, and Charles B. MacDonald. 1977. *The Secret History of the Atomic Bomb.* Delta.
Chadwick, James. 1932a. Possible existence of a neutron. *Nature* 129:312.
———. 1932b. The existence of a neutron. *Proc. Roy. Soc.* 136A:692.
———. 1935. The neutron and its properties. Nobel Lecture.
———. 1954. The Rutherford Memorial Lecture. *Proc. Roy. Soc.* 224:435.
———. 1964. Some personal notes on the search for the neutron. *Proceedings of the Tenth Annual Congress of the History of Science.* Hermann.
Chandler, Alfred D., Jr., ed. 1970. *The Papers of Dwight David Eisenhower.* Johns Hopkins Press.
Chevalier, Haakon. 1965. *The Story of a Friendship.* Braziller.
Childs, Herbert. 1968. *An American Genius.* E. P. Dutton.
Chivian, Eric, et al., ed. 1982. *Last Aid.* W. H. Freeman.
Church, Peggy Pond. 1960. *The House at Otowi Bridge.* University of New Mexico Press.
Churchill, Winston. 1948. *The Gathering Storm.* Houghton Mifflin.
———. 1949. *Their Finest Hour.* Houghton Mifflin.

———. 1950. *The Grand Alliance.* Houghton Mifflin.
———. 1950. *The Hinge of Fate.* Houghton Mifflin.
———. 1951. *Closing the Ring.* Houghton Mifflin.
———. 1953. *Triumph and Tragedy.* Houghton Mifflin.
Claesson, Claes. 1959. *Kungälvsbygden.* Bohusläns Grafiska Aktiebolag.
Clark, Ronald W. 1971. *Einstein.* Avon.
———. 1980. *The Greatest Power on Earth.* Harper & Row.
Cline, Barbara Levett. 1965. *The Questioners.* Crowell.
Cockburn, Stewart, and David Ellyard. 1981. *Oliphant.* Axiom Books.
Coffey, Thomas M. 1970. *Imperial Tragedy.* World.
Cohen, K. P., et al. 1983. Harold Clayton Urey. *Biog. Mem. F. R. S.* 29:623.
Cohn, Norman. 1967. *Warrant for Genocide.* Harper & Row.
Colinvaux, Paul. 1980. *The Fate of Nations.* Simon and Schuster.
Collier, Richard. 1979. *1940.* Hamish Hamilton.
The Committee for the Compilation of Materials on Damage Caused by the Atomic Bombs in Hiroshima and Nagasaki. 1977, 1981. *Hiroshima and Nagasaki.* Basic Books.
Compton, Arthur Holly.1935. *The Freedom of Man.* Greenwood Press, 1969.
———. 1956. *Atomic Quest.* Oxford University Press.
———. 1967. *The Cosmos of Arthur Holly Compton.* Knopf.
Conant, James Bryant. 1943. *A History of the Development of an Atomic Bomb.* Unpublished MS. OSRD S-1, Bush-Conant File, folder 5. National Archives.
———. 1970. *My Several Lives.* Harper & Row.
Condon, Edward U. 1943. *The Los Alamos Primer.* Los Alamos Scientific Laboratory.
———. 1973. Reminiscences of a life in and out of quantum mechanics. *Proceedings of the 7th International Symposium on Atomic, Molecular, Solid State Theory and Quantum Biology.* John Wiley & Sons.
Conn, G. K. T., and H. D. Turner. 1965. *The Evolution of the Nuclear Atom.* American Elsevier.
Costello, John. 1981. *The Pacific War.* Rawson, Wade.
Coughlan, Robert. 1954. Dr. Edward Teller's magnificent obsession. *Life.* Sept. 6.
———. 1963. The tangled drama and private hells of two famous scientists. *Life.* Dec. 13.
Craig, William. 1967. *The Fall of Japan.* Penguin.
Craven, Wesley Frank, and James Lea Cate, eds. 1948–58. *The Army Air Forces in World War II.* University of Chicago Press.
Crowther, J. G. 1974. *The Cavendish Laboratory 1874–1974.* Science History Publications.
Curie, Eve. 1937. *Madam Curie.* Doubleday, Doran.
Dainton, F. S. 1966. *Chain Reactions.* John Wiley & Sons.
Darrow, Karl K. 1952. The quantum theory. *Scientific American.* Mar.
Davis, Nuel Pharr. 1968. *Lawrence and Oppenheimer.* Simon and Schuster.
Dawidowicz, Lucy S. 1967. *The Golden Tradition.* Holt, Rinehart and Winston.
———. 1975. *The War Against the Jews 1933–1945.* Bantam.
de Hevesy, George. 1947. Francis William Aston. *Obituary Notices of F. R. S.* 16:635.
———. 1962. *Adventures in Radioisotope Research.* Pergamon.
de Jonge, Alex. 1978. *The Weimar Chronicle.* Paddington Press.
Demster, Arthur Jeffrey. 1935. New methods in mass spectroscopy. *Proc. Am. Phil. Soc.* 75:755.
DeVolpi, A., et al. 1981. *Born Secret.* Pergamon.
Dickson, Lovat. 1969. *H. G. Wells.* Atheneum.
Draper, Theodore. 1985. Pie in the sky. *NYRB.* Feb. 4.
Duggan, Stephen, and Betty Drury. 1948. *The Rescue of Science and Learning.* Macmillan.

Dupre, A. Hunter. 1972. The *great instauration* of 1940: the organization of scientific research for war. In Gerald Holton, ed., *The Twentieth Century Sciences,* W. W. Norton.

Dyson, Freeman. 1979. *Disturbing the Universe.* Harper & Row.

Eiduson, Bernice T. 1962. *Scientists: Their Psychological World.* Basic Books.

Einstein, Albert, and Leopold Infeld. 1966. *The Evolution of Physics.* Simon and Schuster.

Elliot, Gil. 1972. *Twentieth Century Book of the Dead.* Charles Scribner's Sons.

———. 1978. *Lucifer.* Wildwood House.

Ellis, John. 1975. *The Social History of the Machine Gun.* Pantheon.

———. 1976. *Eye-Deep in Hell.* Pantheon.

Elsasser, Walter M. 1978. *Memoirs of a Physicist in the Atomic Age.* Science History Publications.

Else, Jon. 1980. *The Day After Trinity.* KTEH-TV, San Jose CA.

Embry, Lee Anna. 1970. George Braxton Pegram. *Biog. Mem. Nat. Ac. Sci.* 41:357.

Ethridge, Kenneth E. 1982. The agony of the *Indianapolis. American Heritage.* Aug.–Sept.

Eve, A. S. 1939. *Rutherford.* Macmillan.

Everett, Susanne. 1980. *World War I.* Rand McNally.

Feather, Norman. 1940 *Lord Rutherford.* Priory Press.

———. 1964. The experimental discovery of the neutron. In *Proceedings of the Tenth Annual Congress of the History of Science.* Hermann.

———. 1974. Chadwick's neutron. *Contemp. Phys.* 6:565.

Feis, Herbert. 1966. *The Atomic Bomb and the End of World War II.* Princeton University Press.

Feld, Bernard. 1984. Leo Szilard, scientist for all seasons. *Social Research.* Autumn.

Fermi, Enrico. 1949. *Nuclear Physics.* University of Chicago Press.

———. 1962. *Collected Papers.* University of Chicago Press.

Fermi, Laura. 1954. *Atoms in the Family.* University of Chicago Press.

———. 1971. *Illustrious Immigrants.* University of Chicago Press.

Ferrell, Robert H., ed. 1980. Truman at Potsdam. *American Heritage.* June–July.

Feuer, Lewis S. 1963. *The Scientific Intellectual.* Basic Books.

———. 1982. *Einstein and the Generations of Science.* Transaction Books.

Feyerabend, Paul. 1975. *Against Method.* Verso.

Feynman, Richard P. 1985. *Surely You're Joking, Mr. Feynman.* W. W. Norton.

———, et al. 1963. *The Feynman Lectures on Physics,* v. I. Addison-Wesley.

Flender, Harold. 1963. *Rescue in Denmark.* Simon and Schuster.

Fredette, Raymond H. 1976. *The Sky on Fire.* Harcourt Brace Jovanovich.

Friedrich, Otto. 1972. *Before the Deluge.* Harper & Row.

Frisch, Otto. 1939. Physical evidence for the division of heavy nuclei under neutron bombardment. *Nature* 143:276.

———. 1954. Scientists and the hydrogen bomb. *Listener.* Apr. 1.

———. 1967a. The life of Niels Bohr. *Scientific American.* June.

———. 1967b. The discovery of fission. *Physics Today.* Nov.

———. 1968. Lise Meitner. *Biog. Mem. F. R. S.* 16:405.

———. 1971. Early steps toward the chain reaction. In I. J. R. Aitchison and J. E. Paton, eds., *Rudolf Peierls and Theoretical Physics.* Pergamon Press.

———. 1975. A walk in the snow. *New Scientist* 60:833.

———. 1978. Lise Meitner, nuclear pioneer. *New Scientist.* Nov. 9.

———. 1979. *What Little I Remember.* Cambridge University Press.

Gamow, George. 1966. *Thirty Years That Shook Physics.* Doubleday.

———. 1969. Origin of galaxies. In Hans Mark and Sidney Fernbach, eds., *Properties of Matter Under Unusual Conditions.* Interscience.

———. 1970. *My World Line.* Viking.

Giovannitti, Len, and Fred Freed. 1965. *The Decision to Drop the Bomb.* Coward-McCann.
Glasstone, Samuel. 1967. *Sourcebook on Atomic Energy.* D. Van Nostrand.
———, and Philip J. Dolan. 1977. *The Effects of Nuclear Weapons.* U. S. Department of Defense.
Goldschmidt, Bertrand. 1964. *Atomic Adventure.* Pergamon.
———. 1982. *The Atomic Complex.* American Nuclear Society.
Goldstine, Herman H. 1972. *The Computer from Pascal to von Neumann.* Princeton University Press.
Golovin, Igor. 1967. Father of the Soviet bomb. *Bul. Atom. Sci.* Dec.
Goodchild, Peter. 1980. *J. Robert Oppenheimer: Shatterer of Worlds.* Houghton Mifflin.
Goodrich, H. B., et al. 1951. The origins of U. S. scientists. *Scientific American.* July.
Goran, Morris. 1967. *The Story of Fritz Haber.* University of Oklahoma Press.
Goudsmit, Samuel A. 1947. *Alsos.* Henry Schuman.
Gowing, Margaret. 1964. *Britain and Atomic Energy 1939–1945.* Macmillan.
Graetzer, Hans G., and David L. Anderson. 1971. *The Discovery of Nuclear Fission.* Van Nostrand Reinhold.
Grew, Joseph C. 1942. Report from Tokyo. *Life.* Dec. 7.
———. 1952. *Turbulent Era.* Houghton Mifflin.
Grodzins, Morton, and Eugene Rabinowitch. 1963. *The Atomic Age.* Basic Books.
Grosz, George. 1923. *Ecce Homo.* Brussel & Brussel.
Groueff, Stephane. 1967. *Manhattan Project.* Little, Brown.
Groves, Leslie R. 1948. The atom general answers his critics. *Sat. Even. Post.* May 19.
———. 1962. *Now It Can Be Told.* Harper & Row.
———. n.d. *For My Grandchildren.* Unpublished MS, U.S. Military Academy Library.
Guillain, Robert. 1981. *I Saw Tokyo Burning.* Doubleday.
Guillemin, Victor. 1968. *The Story of Quantum Mechanics.* Charles Scribner's Sons.
Hachiya, Michihiko. 1955. *Hiroshima Diary.* University of North Carolina Press.
Hahn, Otto. 1936. *Applied Radiochemistry.* Cornell University Press.
———. 1946. From the natural transmutations of uranium to its artificial fission. Nobel Lecture.
———. 1958. The discovery of fission. *Scientific American.* Feb.
———. 1966. *A Scientific Autobiography.* Charles Scribner's Sons.
———. 1970. *My Life.* Herder and Herder.
———. 1975. *Erlebnisse und Erkenntnisse.* Econ Verlag.
———, and F. Strassmann. 1939. Concerning the existence of alkaline earth metals resulting from the neutron irradiation of uranium. *Naturwiss.* 27:11 (Trans., Hans G. Graetzer, *Am. Jour. Phys.* 32:10. 1964.)
Haldane, J. B. S. 1925. *Callinicus.* Dutton.
Harris, Benedict R., and Marvin A. Stevens. 1945. Experiences at Nagasaki, Japan. *Conn. St. Medical Journal* 12:913.
Harrisson, Tom. 1976. *Living Through the Blitz.* Collins.
Harrod, R. F. 1959. *The Prof.* Macmillan.
Harwell, Mark A. 1984. *Nuclear Winter.* Springer-Verlag.
Hashimoto, Mochitsura. 1954. *Sunk.* Henry Holt.
Haukelid, Knut. 1954. *Skis Against the Atom.* William Kimber.
Hawkins, David. 1947. *Manhattan District History, Project Y, The Los Alamos Project,* v. I. Los Alamos Scientific Laboratory.
Heibut, Anthony. 1983. *Exiled in Paradise.* Viking.
Heilbron, J. L. 1974. *H. G. J. Moseley.* University of California Press.
———, and Thomas S. Kuhn. 1969. The genesis of the Bohr atom. *Historical Studies in the Physical Sciences* 1:211.
Heims, Steve J. 1980. *John von Neumann and Norbert Weiner.* MIT Press.

Heisenberg, Elisabeth. 1984. *Inner Exile.* Birkhäuser.
Heisenberg, Werner. 1947. Research in Germany on the technical application of atomic energy. *Nature* 160:211.
———. 1968. The Third Reich and the atomic bomb. *Bul. Atom. Sci.* June.
———. 1971. *Physics and Beyond.* Harper.
Hellman, Geoffrey T. 1945. The contemporaneous memoranda of Dr. Sachs. *New Yorker.* Dec. 1.
Hempelmann, Louis H., et al. 1952. The acute radiation syndrome: a study of nine cases and a review of the problem. *Annals of Internal Medicine* 36/2:279.
Henderson, Donald A. 1976. The eradication of smallpox. *Scientific American.* Oct.
Herken, Gregg. 1980. *The Winning Weapon.* Knopf.
Hersey, John. 1942. The marines on Guadalcanal. *Life.* Nov. 9.
———. 1946. *Hiroshima.* Modern Library.
Hewlett, Richard G., and Oscar E. Anderson, Jr. 1962. *The New World, 1939/1946.* Pennsylvania State University Press.
———, and Francis Duncan. 1969. *Atomic Shield, 1947/1952.* Pennsylvania State University Press.
Hitler, Adolf. 1927. *Mein Kampf.* Houghton Mifflin, 1971.
Hogg, I. V., and L. F. Thurston. 1972. *British Atillery Weapons and Ammunition.* Ian Allan.
Holton, Gerald. 1973. *Thematic Origins of Scientific Thought.* Harvard University Press.
———. 1974. Striking gold in science: Fermi's group and the recapture of Italy's place in physics. *Minerva* 12:159.
———, and Yehuda Elkana, eds. 1982. *Albert Einstein: Historical and Cultural Perspectives.* Princeton University Press.
Hopkins, George E. 1966. Bombing and the American conscience during World War II. *The Historian* 28:451.
Hough, Frank O. 1947. *The Island War.* Lippincott.
Howorth, Muriel. 1958. *Pioneer Research on the Atom.* New World.
Hughes, H. Stuart. 1975. *The Sea Change.* Harper & Row.
Ibuse, Masuji. 1969. *Black Rain.* Kodansha International.
Infeld, Leopold. 1941. *Quest.* Chelsea, 1980.
Irving, David. 1963. *The Destruction of Dresden.* Holt, Rinehart and Winston.
———. 1967. *The Virus House.* William Kimber. (In U.S.: *The German Atomic Bomb,* Simon and Schuster, 1968.)
Iwamatsu, Shigetoshi. 1982. A perspective on the war crimes. *Bul. Atom. Sci.* Feb.
Jaki, Stanley L. 1966. *The Relevance of Physics.* University of Chicago Press.
Jammer, Max. 1966. *The Conceptual Development of Quantum Mechanics.* McGraw-Hill.
Jászi, Oscar. 1924. *Revolution and Counter-Revolution in Hungary.* P. S. King and Son.
Jette, Eleanor. 1977. *Inside Box 1663.* Los Alamos Historical Society.
Johansson, Sigurd. n.d. *Atomålderns vagga stod i. Kungälv.* Unpublished MS.
Johnson, Charles W., and Charles O. Jackson. 1981. *City Behind a Fence.* University of Tennessee Press.
Johnson, Ken. 1970. A quarter century of fun. *The Atom.* Los Alamos Scientific Laboratory. Sept.
Joliot, Frédéric. 1935. Chemical evidence of the transmutation of elements. Nobel Lecture.
———, H. von Halban, Jr., and L. Kowarski. 1939a. Liberation of neutrons in the nuclear explosion of uranium. *Nature* 143:470.
———. 1939b. Number of neutrons liberated in the nuclear explosion of uranium. *Nature* 143:680.
Joliot-Curie, Irène. 1935. Artificial production of radioactive elements. Nobel Lecture.

Jones, R. V. 1966. Winston Leonard Spencer Churchill. *Biog. Mem. F. R. S.* 12:35.
———. 1967. Thicker than heavy water. *Chemistry and Industry.* Aug. 26.
Jungk, Robert. 1958. *Brighter Than a Thousand Suns.* Harcourt, Brace.
Kapitza, Peter. 1968. *On Life and Science.* Macmillan.
———. 1980. *Experiment, Theory, Practice.* D. Reidel.
Kedourie, Elie. 1960. *Nationalism.* Hutchinson University Library.
Keegan, John. 1976. *The Face of Battle.* Viking.
Kennedy, J. W., et al. 1941. Properties of 94(239). *Phys. Rev.* 70:555 (1946).
Kennett, Lee. 1982. *A History of Strategic Bombing.* Charles Scribner's Sons.
Kevles, Daniel J. 1979. *The Physicists.* Vintage.
Kierkegaard, Søren. 1959. *Either/Or.* Doubleday.
King, John Kerry. 1970. *International Political Effects of the Spread of Nuclear Weapons.* USGPO.
Kistiakowsky, George B. 1949a. *Explosives and Detonation Waves. Part I, Introduction.* (LA-1043).
———. 1949b. *Explosives and Detonation Waves. Part IV, The Making of Explosive Charges.* (LA-1052)
———. 1949c. *Explosives and Detonation Waves. Part IV, The Making of Explosive Charges, cont.* (LA-1053)
———. 1980. Trinity—a reminiscence. *Bul. Atom. Sci.* June.
———, and F. H. Westheimer. 1979. James Bryant Conant. *Biog. Mem. F. R. S.* 25:209.
Koestler, Arthur. 1952. *Arrow in the Blue.* Macmillan.
Korda, Michael. 1979. *Charmed Lives.* Random House.
Kosakai, Yoshiteru. 1980. *Hiroshima Peace Reader.* Hiroshima Peace Culture Foundation.
Kruuk, Hans. 1972. The urge to kill. *New Scientist.* June 28.
Kuhn, Thomas S., et. al. 1962. Interview with Niels Bohr.
Kunetka, James W. 1979. *City of Fire.* University of New Mexico Press.
———. 1982. *Oppenheimer.* Prentice-Hall.
Lamont, Lansing. 1965. *Day of Trinity.* Atheneum.
Lang, Daniel. 1959. *From Hiroshima to the Moon.* Simon and Schuster.
Langer, Walter C. 1972. *The Mind of Adolf Hitler.* Basic Books.
Laqueur, Walter. 1965. *Russia and Germany.* Little, Brown.
Lash, Joseph P., ed. 1975. *From the Diaries of Felix Frankfurter.* W. W. Norton.
Lawrence, Ernest O. 1951. The evolution of the cyclotron. Nobel Lecture.
———, and M. Stanley Livingston. 1932. The production of high speed ions without the use of high voltages. *Phys. Rev.* 40:19.
Lawrence, William L. 1946. *Dawn Over Zero.* Knopf.
Lawson, Ted W. 1943. *Thirty Seconds Over Tokyo.* Random House.
Leachman, R. B. 1965. Nuclear fission. *Scientific American.* Aug.
Lefebure, Victor. 1923. *The Riddle of the Rhine.* Dutton.
LeMay, Curtis E., with McKinlay Kantor. 1965. *Mission with LeMay.* Doubleday.
Levin, Nora. 1977. *While Messiah Tarried.* Schocken.
Libby, Leona Marshall. 1979. *The Uranium People.* Crane Russak.
Liebow, Averill A. 1965. Encounter with disaster—a medical diary of Hiroshima, 1945. *Yale Journal of Biology and Medicine* 37:60.
———, et al. 1949. Pathology of atomic bomb casualties. *American Journal of Pathology* 5:853.
Lifton, Robert Jay. 1967. *Death in Life.* Random House.
Lilienthal, David E. 1964. *The Journals of David E. Lilienthal.* Harper & Row.
Litvinoff, Barnet. 1976. *Weizmann.* Hodder and Stoughton.
Lloyd George, David. 1933. *War Memoirs.* Little, Brown.

Los Alamos: beginning of an era 1943–1945. n.d. Los Alamos Scientific Laboratory.
Lyon, Fern, and Jacob Evans, eds. 1984. *Los Alamos: The First Forty Years.* Los Alamos Historical Society.
McCagg, William O., Jr. 1972. *Jewish Nobles and Geniuses in Modern Hungary.* East European Quarterly.
McMillan, Edwin. 1939. Radioactive recoils from uranium activated by neutrons. *Phys. Rev.* 55:510
———. 1951. The transuranium elements: early history. Nobel Lecture.
———, and Philip H. Abelson. 1940. Radioactive element 93. *Phys. Rev.* 57:1185.
Madach, Imre. 1956. *The Tragedy of Man.* Pannonia.
Manchester, William. 1980. *Goodbye Darkness.* Little, Brown.
Mark, Hans, and Sidney Fernbach, eds. 1969. *Properties of Matter Under Unusual Conditions.* Interscience.
Mark, J. Carson. 1974. *A Short Account of Los Alamos Theoretical Work on Thermonuclear Weapons, 1946–1950.* (LA-5647-MS)
Marsden, Ernest. 1962. Rutherford at Manchester. In J. B. Birks, ed., *Rutherford at Manchester.* Heywood & Co.
Marx, Joseph L. 1967. *Seven Hours to Zero.* G. P. Putnam's Sons.
Masefield, John. 1916. *Gallipoli.* Macmillan.
Massie, Harrie, and N. Feather. 1976. James Chadwick. *Biog. Mem. F. R. S.* 22:11.
Mee, Charles L., Jr., 1975. *Meeting at Potsdam.* M. Evans.
Meitner, Lise. 1959. Otto Hahn zum 80. Geburtstag. *Otto Hahn zum 8. März 1959.* Max-Planck-Gesellschaft.
———. 1962. Right and wrong roads to the discovery of nuclear energy. *IAEA Bulletin.* Dec. 2.
———. 1964. Looking back. *Bul. Atom. Sci.* Nov.
———, and O. R. Frisch. 1939. Disintegration of uranium by neutrons: a new type of nuclear reaction. *Nature* 143:239.
Mendelsohn, Ezra. 1970. *Class Struggle in the Pale.* Cambridge University Press.
Mendelssohn, Kurt. 1973. *The World of Walter Nernst.* University of Pittsburgh Press.
Mendes-Flohr, Paul R., and Jehuda Reinharz, eds. 1980. *The Jew in the Modern World.*
Messer, Robert L. 1982. *The End of the Alliance.* University of North Carolina Press.
Middlebrook, Martin. 1980. *The Battle of Hamburg.* Allen Lane.
Moon, P. B. 1974. *Ernest Rutherford and the Atom.* Priory Press.
———. 1977. George Paget Thompson. *Biog. Mem. F. R. S.* 23:529.
Moore, Ruth. 1966. *Niels Bohr.* Knopf.
Moorehead, Alan. 1956. *Gallipoli.* Harper & Bros.
Morison, Elting E. 1960. *Turmoil and Tradition.* Houghton Mifflin.
Morland, Howard. 1981. *The Secret that Exploded.* Random House.
Morrison, Philip. 1946. Beyond imagination. *New Republic.* Feb. 11.
———, and Emily Morrison. 1951. The neutron. *Scientific American.* Oct.
Morse, Philip M. 1976. Edward Uhler Condon. *Biog. Mem. Nat. Ac. Sci.* 48:125.
Morton, Louis. 1957. The decision to use the atomic bomb. *Foreign Affairs.* Jan.
Mosley, Leonard. 1982. *Marshall.* Hearst.
Moyers, Bill. 1984. Meet I. I. Rabi. *A Walk Through the 20th Century.* NET.
Murakami, Hyōe. 1982. *Japan: The Years of Trial.* Kodansha International.
Murrow, Edward R. 1967. *In Search of Light.* Knopf.
Nagy-Talavera, Nicholas M. 1970. *The Green Shirts and Others.* Hoover Institution.
Nathan, Otto, and Heinz Norden, eds. 1960. *Einstein on Peace.* Simon and Schuster.
NHK (Japanese Broadcasting Corporation), eds. 1977. *Unforgettable Fire.* Pantheon.
Nielson, J. Rud. 1963. Memories of Niels Bohr. *Physics Today.* Oct.
Nier, Alfred O. 1939. The isotopic constitution of uranium and the half-lifes of the uranium isotopes. *Phys. Rev.* 55:150.
———, et al. 1940a. Nuclear fission of separated uranium isotopes. *Phys. Rev.* 57:546.

———. 1940b. Further experiments on fission of separated uranium isotopes. *Phys. Rev.* 57:748.
———. 1940c. Neutron capture by uranium (238). *Phys. Rev.* 58:475.
Nincic, Miroslav. 1982. *The Arms Race.* Praeger.
Norris, Robert S., et al. 1985. History of the nuclear stockpile. *Bul. Atom. Sci.* Sept.
NOVA. 1980. *A is for Atom, B is for Bomb.* WGBH Transcripts.
O'Keefe, Bernard J. 1972. *Nuclear Hostages.* Houghton Mifflin.
Oliphant, Mark. 1972. *Rutherford.* Elsevier.
———. 1982. The beginning: Chadwick and the neutron. *Bul. Atom. Sci.* Dec.
———, and Penny. 1968. John Douglas Cockcroft. *Biog. Mem. F. R. S.* 14:139.
Oppenheimer, J. Robert. 1946. The atom bomb and college education. *The General Magazine and Historical Chronicle.* University of Pennsylvania General Alumni Society.
———. 1957. Talk to undergraduates. *Engineering and Science Monthly.* California Institute of Technology.
———. 1961. Secretary Stimson and the atomic bomb. *Andover Bulletin.* Spring.
———. 1963. Niels Bohr and his times. Three lectures, unpublished MSS. Oppenheimer Papers, Box 247.
———, and H. Snyder. 1939. On continued gravitational contraction. *Phys. Rev.* 56:455.
———, et al. 1946. *A Report on the International Control of Atomic Energy.* Department of State.
Osada, Arata, comp. 1982. *Children of the A-Bomb.* Midwest Publishers International.
Overy, R. J. 1980. *The Air War 1939–1945.* Europe Publications.
Pacific War Research Society. 1972. *The Day Man Lost.* Kodansha International.
Pais, Abraham. 1982. *'Subtle Is the Lord. . .'* Oxford University Press.
Parkes, James. 1964. *A History of the Jewish People.* Penguin.
Pash, Boris T. 1969. *The Alsos Mission.* Award Books.
Patai, Raphael. 1977. *The Jewish Mind.* Charles Scribner's Sons.
Paterson, Thomas G. 1972. Potsdam, the atomic bomb and the Cold War: a discussion with James F. Byrnes. *Pacific Historical Review.* May.
Peattie, Lisa. 1984. Normalizing the unthinkable. *Bul. Atom. Sci.* Mar.
Peierls, Rudolf. 1939. Critical conditions in neutron multiplication. *Proc. Camb. Phil. Soc.* 35:610.
———. 1959. The atomic nucleus. *Scientific American.* Jan.
———. 1981. Otto Robert Frisch. *Biog. Mem. F. R. S.* 27:283.
———. 1985. *Bird of Passage.* Princeton University Press.
———, and Nevill Mott. 1977. Werner Heisenberg. *Biog. Mem. F. R. S.* 23:213.
Perrin, Francis. 1939. Calcul relatif aux conditions éventuelles de transmutation en chaîne de l'uranium. *Comptes Rendus* 208:1394.
Peterson, Aage. 1963. The philosophy of Niels Bohr. *Bul. Atom. Sci.* Sept.
Pfau, Richard. 1984. *No Sacrifice Too Great.* University Press of Virginia.
Planck, Max. 1949. *Scientific Autobiography.* Philosophical Library.
Polanyi, Michael. 1946. *Science, Faith and Society.* University of Chicago Press.
———. 1962. *The Republic of Science.* Roosevelt University.
Pound, Reginald. 1964. *The Lost Generation of 1914.* Coward-McCann.
Powers, Thomas. 1984. Nuclear winter and nuclear strategy. *Atlantic.* Nov.
Prange, Gordon W. 1981. *At Dawn We Slept.* Penguin.
Prentiss, Augustin M. 1937. *Chemicals in War.* McGraw-Hill.
The Protocols of the Meetings of the Learned Elders of Zion. 1934. Trans. Victor E. Marsden, n.p.
Purcell, Edward M. 1964. Nuclear physics without the neutron: clues and contradictions. *Proceedings of the Tenth Annual Congress of the History of Science.* Hermann.
Rabi, I. I. 1945. The physicist returns from the war. *Atlantic.* Oct.

———. 1970. *Science: the Center of Culture.* World.
———, et al. 1969. *Oppenheimer.* Scribner's.
Ramsey, Norman, ed. 1946. *Nuclear Weapons Engineering and Delivery.* Los Alamos Technical Series, v. XXIII. Los Alamos Scientific Laboratory.
Rearden, Steven L. 1984. *History of the Office of the Secretary of Defense,* v. I. Office of the Secretary of Defense.
Rhodes, Richard, et al. 1977. Kurt Vonnegut, Jr. In George Plimpton, ed., *Writers at Work.* Viking, 1984.
Roberts, Richard Brooke. 1979. Autobiography. Unpublished MS.
——, et al. 1939a. Droplet fission of uranium and thorium nuclei. *Phys. Rev.* 55:416.
———. 1939b. Further observations on the splitting of uranium and thorium. *Phys. Rev.* 55:510.
———. 1940. Fission cross-sections for fast neutrons. Unpublished MS. Department of Terrestrial Magnetism Archives, Carnegie Institution of Washington.
———, and J. B. H. Kuper. 1939. Uranium and atomic power. *J. Appl. Phys.* 10:612.
Roberts, Stephen H. 1938. *The House that Hitler Built.* Harper & Bros.
Robison, George O. 1950. *The Oak Ridge Story.* Southern Publishers.
Roe, Anne. 1952. A psychologist examines 64 eminent scientists. *Scientific American.* Nov.
Roosevelt, Franklin D. 1939. *The Public Papers and Addresses, VIII.* Russell & Russell.
———. 1941. *The Public Papers and Addresses, IX.* Russell & Russell.
Rosenberg, Alfred. 1970. *Race and Race History.* Harper & Row.
Rosenberg, David Alan. 1982. U.S. nuclear stockpile, 1945 to 1950. *Bul. Atom. Sci.* May.
Rosenfeld, Léon. 1963. Niels Bohr's contribution to epistemology. *Phys. Today.* Oct.
———. 1979. *Selected Papers.* D. Reidel.
Royal, Denise. 1969. *The Story of J. Robert Oppenheimer.* St. Martin's Press.
Rozental, Stefan, ed. 1967. *Niels Bohr.* North-Holland.
Russell, A. S. 1962. Lord Rutherford: Manchester, 1907–19: a partial portrait. In J. B. Birks, ed., *Rutherford at Manchester.* Heywood & Co.
Rutherford, Ernest. 1962. *The Collected Papers,* v. I. Allen and Unwin.
———. 1963. *The Collected Papers,* v. II. Interscience.
———. 1965. *The Collected Papers,* v. III. Interscience.
Sachs, Alexander. 1945. Early history atomic project in relation to President Roosevelt, 1939–40. Unpublished MS. MED 319.7, National Archives.
Sachs, Robert G., ed. 1984. *The Nuclear Chain Reaction—Forty Years Later.* University of Chicago Press.
Sassoon, Siegfried. 1937. *The Memoirs of George Sherston.* Doubleday, Doran.
———. 1961. *Collected Poems 1908–1956.* Faber and Faber.
Saundby, Robert. 1961. *Air Bombardment.* Harper & Bros.
Schell, Jonathan. 1982. *The Fate of the Earth.* Knopf.
———. 1984. *The Abolition.* Knopf.
Schonland, Basil. 1968. *The Atomists.* Oxford University Press.
Scott-Stokes, Henry. 1974. *The Life and Death of Yukio Mishima.* Farrar, Straus & Giroux.
Seaborg. Glenn T. 1951. The transuranium elements: present status. Nobel Lecture.
———. 1958. *The Transuranium Elements.* Yale University Press.
———. 1976. *Early History of Heavy Isotope Production at Berkeley.* Lawrence Berkeley Laboratory.
———. 1977. *History of Met Lab Section C-I, April 1942 to April 1943.* Lawrence Berkeley Laboratory.

———. 1978. *History of Met Lab Section C-I, May 1943 to April 1944.* Lawrence Berkeley Laboratory.
———, et al. 1946a. Radioactive element 94 from deuterons on uranium. *Phys. Rev.* 69:366.
———. 1946b. Radioactive element 94 from deuterons on uranium. *Phys. Rev.* 69:367.
Segrè, Emilio. 1939. An unsuccessful search for transuranic elements. *Phys. Rev.* 55:1104.
———. 1955. Fermi and neutron physics. *Rev. Mod. Phys.* 28:262.
———. 1964. The consequences of the discovery of the neutron. *Proceedings of the Tenth Annual Congress of the History of Science.* Hermann.
———. 1970. *Enrico Fermi, Physicist.* University of Chicago Press.
———. 1980. *From X-Rays to Quarks.* W. H. Freeman.
———. 1981. Fifty years up and down a strenuous and scenic trail. *Ann. Rev. Nucl. Part. Sci.* 31:1.
Semenoff, N. 1935. *Chemical Kinetics and Chain Reactions.* Clarendon Press.
Shamos, Morris H. 1959. *Great Experiments in Physics.* Holt, Rinehart and Winston.
Shapley, Deborah. 1978. Nuclear weapons history: Japan's wartime bomb projects revealed. *Science* 199:152.
Sherrod, Robert. 1944. Beachhead in the Marianas. *Time.* July 3.
Sherwin, Martin J. 1975. *A World Destroyed.* Knopf.
Shils, Edward. 1964. Leo Szilard: a memoir. *Encounter.* Dec.
Shirer, William L. 1960. *The Rise and Fall of the Third Reich.* Simon and Schuster.
Smith, Alice Kimball. 1960. The elusive Dr. Szilard. *Harper's,* Aug.
———. 1965. *A Peril and a Hope.* MIT Press.
———, and Charles Weiner. 1980. *Robert Oppenheimer: Letters and Recollections.* Harvard University Press.
Smith, Cyril Stanley. 1954. Metallurgy at Los Alamos 1943–1945. *Met. Prog.* 65(5):81.
Smith, Lloyd P., et al. 1947. On the separation of isotopes in quantity by electromagnetic means. *Phys. Rev.* 72:989.
Smyth, Henry DeWolf. 1945. *Atomic Energy for Military Purposes.* USGPO.
Snow, C. P. 1958. *The Search.* Charles Scribner's Sons.
———. 1961. *Science and Government.* Harvard University Press.
———. 1967a. On Albert Einstein. *Commentary.* Mar.
———. 1967b. *Variety of Men.* Scribner's.
———. 1981. *The Physicists.* Little, Brown.
Soddy, Frederick. 1913. Inter-atomic charge. *Nature* 92:400.
———. 1953. *Atomic Transmutation.* New World.
Spector, Ronald H. 1985. *Eagle Against the Sun.* Free Press.
Speer, Albert. 1970. *Inside the Third Reich.* Macmillan.
Spence, R. 1970. Otto Hahn. *Biog. Mem. F. R. S.* 16:279.
Stein, Leonard. 1961. *The Balfour Declaration.* Simon and Schuster.
Stimson, Henry L., and McGeorge Bundy. 1948. *On Active Service in Peace and War.* Harper & Bros.
Strauss, Lewis L. 1962. *Men and Decisions.* Doubleday.
Stuewer, Roger H. 1979. *Nuclear Physics in Retrospect.* University of Minnesota Press.
———. 1985. Bringing the news of fission to America. *Phys. Today.* Oct.
Szasz, Ferenc Morton. 1984. *The Day the Sun Rose Twice.* University of New Mexico Press.
Szilard, Leo. 1945. We turned the switch. *Nation.* Dec. 22.
———. 1961. *The Voice of the Dolphins.* Simon and Schuster.
———. 1972. *The Collected Works: Scientific Papers.* MIT Press.
———, and Walter H. Zinn. 1939. Instantaneous emission of fast neutrons in the interaction of slow neutrons with uranium. *Phys. Rev.* 55:799.

Szulc, Tad. 1984. The untold story of how Russia "got the bomb." *Los Angeles Times,* IV:1. Aug. 26.
Talk of the Town. 1946. Usher. *New Yorker.* Jan. 5.
Teller, Edward. 1946a. Scientists in war and peace. *Bul. Atom. Sci.* Mar.
———. 1946b. The State Dep't report— "a ray of hope." *Bul. Atom. Sci.* Apr.
———. 1946c. Dispersal of cities and industries. *Bul. Atom. Sci.* Apr.
———. 1947a. How dangerous are atomic weapons? *Bul. Atom. Sci.* Feb.
———. 1947b. Atomic scientists have two responsibilities. *Bul. Atom. Sci.* Mar.
———. 1948a. The first year of the Atomic Energy Commission. *Bul. Atom. Sci.* Jan.
———. 1948b. Comments on the "draft of a world constitution." *Bul. Atom. Sci.* July.
———. 1955. The work of many people. *Science* 121:267.
———. 1962. *The Legacy of Hiroshima.* Doubleday.
———. 1977. *In Search of Solutions for Defense and for Energy.* Stanford University Press.
———. 1979. *Energy from Heaven and Earth.* W. H. Freeman.
———. 1980a. Hydrogen bomb. *Encyclopedia Americana,* v. XIV.
———. 1980b. *In Pursuit of Simplicity.* Pepperdine University Press.
———. 1983. Seven hours of reminiscences. *Los Alamos Science.* Winter/Spring.
———, et al. 1950. *Report of Conference on the Super* (LA-575, Deleted). Los Alamos Scientific Laboratory.
Terkel, Studs. 1984. *"The Good War."* Pantheon.
Terman, Lewis M. 1955. Are scientists different? *Scientific American.* Jan.
Thomas, Gordon, and Max Morgan Witts. 1977. *Enola Gay.* Stein and Day.
Thompson, Josiah. 1973. *Kierkegaard.* Knopf.
Tibbets, Paul W. 1946. How to drop an atom bomb. *Sat. Even. Post.* June 8.
———. 1973. Training the 509th for Hiroshima. *Air Force Magazine.* Aug.
Toland, John. 1970. *The Rising Sun.* Random House.
———. 1976. *Adolf Hitler.* Doubleday.
Tregaskis, Richard. 1943. *Guadalcanal Diary.* Random House.
Trenn, Thaddeus J. 1980. The phenomenon of aggregate recoil: the premature acceptance of an essentially incorrect theory. *Ann. Sci.* 37:81.
Truman, Harry S. 1955. *Year of Decision.* Doubleday.
Trumbull, Robert. 1957. *Nine Who Survived Hiroshima and Nagasaki.* E. P. Dutton.
Truslow, Edith C., and Ralph Carlisle Smith. 1946–47. *The Los Alamos Project,* v. II. Los Alamos Scientific Laboratory.
Turner, Louis A. 1940. Nuclear fission. *Rev. Mod. Phys.* 12:1.
———. 1946. Atomic energy from U238. *Phys. Rev.* 69:366.
Ulam. Stanislaw. 1966. Thermonuclear devices. In R. E. Marshak, ed., *Perspectives in Modern Physics.* Interscience.
———. 1976. *Adventures of a Mathematician.* Scribner's.
United States Atomic Energy Commission. 1954. *In the Matter of J. Robert Oppenheimer.* MIT Press, 1971.
United States Special Committee on Atomic Energy. 1945. *Hearings pursuant to S. Res. 179.* USGPO.
United States Strategic Bombing Survey, v. X. 1976. Garland.
Urey, Harold C., et al. 1932. A hydrogen isotope of mass 2 and its concentration. *Phys. Rev.* 40:1.
Veblen, Thorstein. 1919. The intellectual pre-eminence of Jews in modern Europe. *Political Science Quarterly.* Mar.
Völgyes, Ivan, ed. 1971. *Hungary in Revolution.* University of Nebraska Press.
von Kármán, Theodore. 1967. *The Wind and Beyond.* Little, Brown.
von Weizsäcker, Carl Friedrich. 1978. *The Politics of Peril.* Seabury Press.
Waite, Robert G. 1977. *The Psychopathic God: Adolf Hitler.* Basic Books.

Ward, Barbara. 1966. *Nationalism and Ideology.* Norton.

Wattenberg, Albert. 1982. December 2, 1942: the event and the people. *Bul. Atom. Sci.* Dec.

Weart, Spencer R. 1979. *Scientists in Power.* Harvard University Press.

———, and Gertrud Weiss Szilard, eds. 1978. *Leo Szilard: His Version of the Facts.* MIT Press.

Weinberg, Alvin M., and Eugene P. Wigner. 1958. *The Physical Theory of Neutron Chain Reactors.* University of Chicago Press.

Weiner, Charles. 1967. Interview with Otto Frisch, AIP.

———. 1967. Interview with Emilio Segrè, AIP.

———. 1969. Interview with James Chadwick, AIP.

———. 1969. A new site for the seminar: the refugees and American physics in the Thirties. In Donald Fleming and Bernard Bailyn, eds., *The Intellectual Migration.* Harvard University Press.

———, ed. 1972. *Exploring the History of Nuclear Physics.* AIP Conference Proceedings No. 7. American Institute of Physics.

———, and Jagdish Mehra. 1966. Interview with Hans Bethe, AIP.

———. 1966. Interview with Eugene Wigner, AIP.

Weisgal, Meyer W., and Joel Carmichael, eds. 1963. *Chaim Weizmann.* Atheneum.

Weizmann, Chaim. 1949. *Trial and Error.* Harper & Bros.

Wells, H. G. 1914. *The World Set Free.* E. P. Dutton.

———. 1931. *What Are We to Do with Our Lives?* Doubleday, Doran.

Wheeler, John A. 1962. Fission then and now. *IAEA Bulletin.* Dec. 2.

———. 1963a. No fugitive and cloistered virtue. *Phys. Today.* Jan.

———. 1963b. Niels Bohr and nuclear physics. *Phys. Today.* Oct.

Wheeler, Richard. 1980. *Iwo.* Lippincott & Crowell.

Wiesner, Jerome B. 1979. Vannevar Bush. *Biog. Mem. Nat. Ac. Sci.* 50:89.

Wigner, Eugene P. 1945. Are we making the transition wisely? *Sat Rev.* Nov. 17.

———. 1964. Leo Szilard. *Biog. Mem. Nat. Ac. Sci.* 40:337.

———. 1967. *Symmetries and Reflections.* Indiana University Press. Reprint OxBow Press, 1979.

———. 1969. An appreciation on the 60th birthday of Edward Teller. In Hans Mark and Sidney Fernbach, eds., *Properties of Matter Under Unusual Conditions.* Interscience.

Wilson, David. 1983. *Rutherford.* MIT Press.

Wilson, Jane, ed. 1975. *All in Our Time.* Bulletin of the Atomic Scientists.

Wolfe, Henry C. 1943. Japan's nightmare. *Harper's.* Jan.

Wolk, Herman S. 1975. The B-29, the A-Bomb, and the Japanese surrender. *Air Force Magazine.* Feb.

Yahil, Leni. 1969. *The Rescue of Danish Jewry.* Jewish Publication Society of America.

Yergin, Daniel. 1977. *Shattered Peace.* Houghton Mifflin.

York, Herbert. 1970. *Race to Oblivion.* Simon and Schuster.

———. 1976. *The Advisors.* W. H. Freeman.

Young-Bruehl, Elisabeth. 1982. *Hannah Arendt.* Yale University Press.

Zuckerman, Harriet. 1977. *Scientific Elite.* Free Press.

PHOTO CREDITS

1. Culver *2.* Egon Weiss *3.* E. Scott Barr Collection, AIP Niels Bohr Library *4.* Courtesy Otto Hahn and Lawrence Badash, AIP Niels Bohr Library *5.* Mary Evans Rhodes *6.* Bibliothek und Archiv für Geschichte der Max-Planck-Gesellschaft *7.* Niels Bohr Institute *8/9.* Bibliothek und Archiv für Geschichte der Max-Planck-Gesellschaft *10.* AIP Niels Bohr Library *11.* University of California Press *12.* Culver *13/14.* Niels Bohr Institute *15–17.* Emilio Segrè *18.* AIP Niels Bohr Library *19.* Picture People *20.* Niels Bohr Institute *21.* Société Française de Physique, Paris/ AIP Niels Bohr Library *22.* W. F. Meggers Collection, AIP Niels Bohr Library *23/24.* Lawrence Berkeley Laboratory *25.* Photo by D. Schoenberg, Bainbridge Collection, AIP Niels Bohr Library *26.* Françoise Ulam *27.* Egon Weiss *28/29.* Rose Bethe *30.* Wide World *31.* Bibliothek und Archiv für Geschichte der Max-Planck-Gesellschaft *32.* Segrè Collection, AIP Niels Bohr Library *33/34.* Bibliothek und Archiv für Geschichte der Max-Planck-Gesellschaft *35.* Mary Evans Rhodes *36.* Argonne National Laboratory *37.* Picture People *38.* Department of Terrestrial Magnetism, Carnegie Institution of Washington *39.* Wide World

40. Lawrence Berkeley Laboratory *41.* Picture People *42.* Rudolf Peierls *43.* Smithsonian Institution Science Service Collection, AIP Niels Bohr Library *44.* UPI/Bettmann Newsphotos *45.* UPI/Bettmann Newsphotos *46.* Alfred O. C. Nier *47.* Photo by P. Ehrenfest, Weisskopf Collection, AIP Niels Bohr Library *48.* Lawrence Berkeley Laboratory *49.* Picture People *50.* UPI/Bettmann Newsphotos *51.* Picture People *52.* Lawrence Berkeley Laboratory *53.* Argonne National Laboratory *54/55.* Martin Marietta *56.* Philip Abelson *57–61.* National Archives *62/63.* Norsk Hydro *64–67.* Los Alamos National Laboratory *68.* Luis W. Alvarez *69.* Niels Bohr Institute *70.* Françoise Ulam *71/72.* Los Alamos National Laboratory *73.* Oppenheimer Memorial Committee *74.* Emilio Segrè *75.* Picture People *76.* Picture People *77.* Mrs. George Kistiakowsky *78–83.* Los Alamos National Laboratory *84.* AIP Niels Bohr Library *85–96.* Los Alamos National Laboratory

97. USAF *98.* Picture People *99.* Henry L. Stimson Papers, Yale University Library *100.* Robert Muldrow Cooper Library, Clemson University *101.* National Archives *102.* Harold Agnew *103–105.* USAF *106.* Yoshito Matsushige *107.* Hiroshima Peace Memorial Museum *108/109.* Hiroshima Peace Culture Foundation *110/111.* Hiroshima Peace Memorial Museum *112.* Hiroshima Peace Culture Foundation *113.* National Archives *114/115.* Issei Nishimori *116.* Hiroshima Peace Memorial Museum *117.* Yosuke Yamabata *118.* Issei Nishimori *119.* Yosuke Yamabata *120.* Peter Wyden *121.* UPI/Bettmann Newsphotos *122–126.* Los Alamos National Laboratory *127.* Dr. Harold E. Edgerton, MIT, Cambridge, MA *128.* Niels Bohr Institute

Index

177 – Jewish persecution

Rhodes, Richard

The making of the atomic bomb

2/87

$22.45

DATE			
MAR 7 '87	MAY 02 1990		
MAR 21 '87	MAY 17 1990		
APR 19 '87	JUN 01 1990		
JUN 17 '87	JUN 27 1990		
AUG 22 '87	SEP 24 1992		
OCT 16 '87			
OCT 31 '87	OCT 7 1992		
NOV 14 '87			
APR 06 '88	MAY 22 [illegible]		
DEC 28 1988			
JAN 06 1989			
APR 14 1989			

1987

strategic victory. The allied plan of invasion was foiled. Allied losses were more than 10,000 killed, 5,000 captured (mostly wounded), and about 15,000 additional wounded. French casualties were nearly 10,000.

TURENNE'S RHINELAND CAMPAIGN, 1674–1675

Turenne was again given the mission of protecting Alsace. The Elector of Brandenburg and a number of other German princes had now entered the war against France. His principal opponents were imperial Generals **Enea Sylvio Caprara,** Prince **Alexandre-Hippolyte of Bournonville,** and Duke Charles Leopold of Lorraine, assembling armies north and south of Heidelberg.

1674, June 14. Turenne Crosses the Rhine. Deciding to strike before imperial forces could concentrate, he crossed at Philippsburg.

1674, June 16. Battle of Sinsheim. Caprara and Lorraine had moved with 9,000 men (7,000 being cavalry) to block Turenne's advance. Caprara thought his position behind the Elsenz River was inaccessible. Turenne thought otherwise. He crossed the river, drove the imperial outposts out of Sinsheim, then forced a way up rugged heights to a plateau where Caprara's main force was deployed. After a hard struggle, Turenne won a complete victory. The French lost 1,200 men killed, the imperialists 2,000 killed and 600 captured. Under orders from Paris, Turenne soon thereafter retired back across the Rhine.

1674, July–September. Summer Maneuvers. Reinforced to 16,000 men, Turenne again crossed at Philippsburg (July 3). The allies withdrew behind the Main after an engagement near **Heidelberg** (July 7). Under orders from Paris, Turenne devastated the region between the Main and the Neckar. Then he returned across the Rhine to block a threatened invasion along the Moselle. His army was reinforced to 20,000 men. The allied army, now under Bournonville, crossed and recrossed the Rhine near Speyer, then, while Turenne was occupied to the northwest, seized neutral Strasbourg (September 24). Turenne immediately moved to the vicinity, seeking an opportunity to attack his more numerous, but cautious, foes.

1674, October 4. Battle of Enzheim. Turenne, with 22,000 men and 30 guns, deliberately attacked Bournonville's 38,000, with 50 guns in defensive position covered by entrenchments. One English regiment was there under John Churchill, later Duke of Marlborough. Although his army had been marching for two days and two nights, Turenne held the initiative throughout most of the day, but was unable to drive the allies from their position. He withdrew from the inconclusive battle at the end of the day. The allies withdrew simultaneously. French casualties were about 3,500, those of the allies about 3,000.

1674, October–November. Watchful Waiting. Allied forces in Alsace were augmented to 57,000 by the arrival of the Great Elector. They made their winter quarters in all the towns from Belfort to Strasbourg; Turenne camped at Dettweiler. To mislead the enemy he displayed activity by placing the fortresses of middle Alsace in a state of defense, while he was quietly taking his whole field army (28,000 men) to Lorraine.

1674, November 29–December 29. Advance into Alsace. Turenne marched secretly southward behind the Vosges; in the last stages of the movement, he split his forces into many small bodies to further misguide enemy spies. After having marched over snow-covered mountains, the French reunited near Belfort and hastened into Alsace from the south. Bournonville tried unsuccessfully to stop them at **Mulhouse** (December 29). The scattered imperial forces could only retreat toward Strasbourg. Turenne's advance continued to Colmar, where the Great Elector stood with forces slightly greater than his.

1675, January 5. Battle of Turckheim. In a battle reminiscent of Enzheim, Turenne attacked vigorously, despite exhaustion of his troops. After perfunctory resistance and light casualties the allies retreated, leaving the field to the victorious Turenne. Thus was completed one of the most brilliant campaigns in military annals.

1675. General Operations. The French

recaptured some fortresses in the Meuse Valley and took Liége and Limburg. The expeditionary forces in Sicily continued to be successful, and Schomburg invaded Catalonia.

1675, June–July. Operations in Germany. The dejected Elector had withdrawn to Brandenburg and Montecuccoli resumed command of the imperial armies. In a war of maneuver east of the Rhine between Philippsburg and Strasbourg, Turenne prevented Montecuccoli from retaking Strasbourg.

1675, July 27. Death of Turenne. Forcing Montecuccoli's more numerous army to withdraw, Turenne was typically preparing to attack the imperial army in defensive position at Nieder-Sasbach, when he was killed by a cannonball (July 27). Thereupon the French were driven by Montecuccoli across the Rhine almost to the Vosges.

1675, August–October. Operations in Lorraine. French Marshal Créqui was defeated and captured by Charles of Lorraine at the **Battle of Conzer-Brucke** (August 11) on the Moselle. The allies then recaptured Trier (September 6) and prepared to invade France. Condé left Luxembourg in charge in Flanders and proceeded to take over the command of Turenne's and Créqui's armies. Condé forced Montecuccoli to retreat across the Rhine. These 2 men, the best generals of the era after Turenne, both retired from their commands at the end of the year.

1676, January–April. Operations in and around Sicily. After Admiral Marquis **Abraham Duquesne** repulsed De Ruyter's Hispano-Dutch naval attack on Messina (January), French Marshal **Louis Victor de R. Vivonne** defeated the Spanish army in Sicily in the **Battle of Messina** (March 25) and was named viceroy of Sicily. De Ruyter was defeated by Duquesne and mortally wounded in the **Naval Battle of Messina** (April 22).

1676, April–August. Operations in the North. Again Louis and Vauban conducted the campaign. They captured Condé-sur-l'Escaut (April 26), then maneuvered against William III near Valenciennes. William was repulsed from Maastricht by Schomburg (August). Rochefort still held the Meuse Valley.

1676. Operations in the Rhineland. Créqui, who had been exchanged, held Lorraine, but lost Philippsburg to the imperialists (September 17). The French now laid waste the land between the Meuse and Moselle to prevent it from supporting an invasion army. At the end of the year, Charles of Lorraine was engaged in a war of maneuver with Luxembourg on the upper Rhine.

1677. Operations in the North. Against the advice of his marshals, Louis approved Vauban's bold plan for an assault on besieged Valenciennes, which was completely successful (March 17). The French then besieged St.-Omer. William's relieving army was defeated by Duke **Philippe d'Orléans** at the **Battle of Mont Cassel** (April 11) and St.-Omer soon surrendered. During the summer William and Luxembourg carried on an indecisive campaign of maneuver, the French having the better of it.

1677. Operations in the Rhineland. Créqui drove Charles of Lorraine to the Rhine. Another imperial army, attempting to cross the Rhine at Philippsburg, was isolated on a river island. Lorraine sent a large relieving force, which was smashed by Créqui in the **Battle of Kochersberg,** near Strasbourg (October 17). The invested army was then forced to surrender. Créqui followed up his successes by capturing Freiburg (November 14).

1678. French Successes in the North. Louis captured Ghent and Ypres (March). With his armies generally victorious, but threatened with the intervention of England on the side of the coalition, and informed by Colbert that the war was financially disastrous, Louis decided to make peace. Over William's objections the States General entered into negotations.

1678, July 6. Battle of Rheinfelden. Créqui defeated the imperial armies.

1678, July 23. Battle of Gengenbach. Créqui was again victorious, and seized Kehl.

1678, August 10. Treaty of Nijmegen with Holland. Holland pledged its neutrality for the return of its territories.

1678, August 14. Battle of Saint Denis (near Mons). Presumably unaware that the treaty had been signed, William attacked Luxembourg and was defeated after a fierce struggle.

1678, September 17. Treaty of Nijmegen with Spain. France retained Franche-Comté, Valenciennes, Cambrai, Cambresis, Aire, St.-Omer, Ypres, Condé, Bouchain, Maubeuge, and other frontier fortresses. Spain received back Charleroi, Binche, Oudenarde, Ath, Courtrai, Limburg, Ghent, and others.

1679, February 6. Treaty of Nijmegen with the Emperor. France received Freiburg and gave up the right to garrison Philippsburg. Charles of Lorraine was permitted to regain his duchy, but refused to accept French conditions.

1679, June 29. Treaty of St. Germain with Brandenburg. The Elector surrendered nearly all of his conquests in Pomerania to Sweden (see p. 569).

LOUIS AT THE HEIGHT OF HIS POWER, 1679–1700

1680–1684. Chambers of Reunion. Louis, taking advantage of his superior position and the weakness of the Empire, set up courts of claims (chambers of reunion) to determine what dependencies had belonged to the towns and territories France had received in the peace treaties. Based on the decisions of his tribunals, he annexed many additional towns (such as Strasbourg). This policy of reunion involved an invasion of the Spanish Netherlands and the occupation of Luxembourg and Trier (1684). Lorraine was permanently annexed.

1684. Treaty of Regensburg. Louis, the Emperor, and the Empire concluded a 20-year truce; Louis retained everything he had claimed by reunion up to August 1, 1681.

1685, October 18. Repeal of the Edict of Nantes. This denial of Protestant freedom of worship led to the emigration of more than 50,000 families.

1688–1697. The War of the Grand Alliance (League of Augsburg; see p. 546).

GERMANY

1576–1612. Reign of Rudolph. Marked by continuing warfare against the Turks in Southeastern Europe and by Catholic-Protestant dissension.

1612–1619. Reign of Matthias. Growing tension between the Protestants and Catholics.

1618–1648. The Thirty Years' War. (See p. 533.)

1619–1637. Reign of Ferdinand II (of Styria). An ardent Catholic, his accession brought problems to his hereditary dominions and precipitated a serious Bohemian crisis.

1658–1705. Reign of Leopold I. He had been destined for the church and was very reluctant to become a temporal ruler. His prime interest was the promotion of the Catholic Church; the interests of the house of Hapsburg and Austria were secondary.

1658, August 16–1667. The Confederation of the Rhine. A defensive alliance of Catholic and Protestant princes to execute the Peace of Westphalia, to prevent foreign wars, and to defend the Rhineland.

1662–1664. War with the Turks. (See p. 581.)

1672–1679. The French Wars, or Dutch Wars. (See p. 563.)

1682–1699. War against the Turks for the Liberation of Hungary. (See p. 582.)

1688–1697. The War of the Grand Alliance. (See p. 546.)

SCANDINAVIA

Denmark and Norway

1588–1648. Reign of Christian IV.

1611–1613. War of Kalmar. Caused by rivalry with Sweden in the Baltic, and by Swedish efforts to gain control of Finnmark. Christian sent forces to the mouth of the Gota and to Kalmar, which fell to the Danes after a long siege, despite relief attempts of **Charles IX of Sweden.** Charles died on his way home after the summer campaign, during which 16-year-old Prince **Gustavus Adolphus** of Sweden distinguished himself (October, 1611). The following campaign was inconclusive; border provinces of both sides were harried. Mediation of James I of England resulted in the **Peace of Knarod** (January, 1613). Finnmark was given to Denmark and Norway.

1618–1648. The Thirty Years' War. (See p. 533.)

1648–1670. Reign of Frederick III. A monarchical coup d'état (1660) supported by the clergy and burghers transformed the king into a hereditary and absolute ruler.

1656–1660. Danish Participation in the First Northern War. (See below.)

1670–1699. Reign of Christian V.

1675–1679. The Dutch War. (See p. 563.) The Danes, allied to the Dutch, saw an opportunity to regain lost territory from Sweden, France's ally. Though the Danes were successful at sea, this was offset by Swedish land victories at **Lund** (1676) and elsewhere.

Sweden

THE RISE OF SWEDEN, 1600–1655

1604–1611. Reign of Charles IX. Charles led the intervention of Sweden in Russia during the Time of Troubles (see p. 576). His attempt to extend Swedish rule from Finnmark up to the Arctic led to war with Denmark.

1611–1613. War of Kalmar. (See above.)

1611–1632. Reign of Gustavus II (Adolphus). Height of Swedish power.

1613–1617. War with Russia. (See p. 577.)

1617–1629. Wars in Poland. This resulted from a dynastic dispute with **Sigismund of Poland** (see pp. 483 and 573).

1630–1648. Swedish Participation in the Thirty Years' War. (See p. 537.)

1644–1654. Reign of Christina. Decline of Swedish power.

1654–1660. Reign of Charles X Gustavus.

THE FIRST NORTHERN WAR, 1655–1660

To extend Sweden's possessions in the southern Baltic, Charles X declared war against Poland. He was encouraged by Russia's current invasion of Poland and the internal dissension and weakness of Poland. His war plan provided for a double offensive: from Pomerania against western Poland, and from Livonia against Lithuania. His pretext was the failure of **John Casimir,** King of Poland, to recognize his own special status of "Protector of Poland."

1655, Summer. Invasion of Poland. Count **Arfwid von Wittenberg,** with a force of 17,000, occupied western Poland. Charles arrived soon after with reinforcements, increasing the Swedish army to 32,000 men. He advanced into central Poland.

1655, September 8. Swedish Capture of Warsaw. Cracow fell soon afterward. John Casimir fled to Silesia. Meanwhile Lithuania, simultaneously invaded by the Russians and the Swedes, had been surrendered by Hetman **Janusz Radziwill** to Sweden.

1655, October–January. Intervention of Brandenburg. Frederick William, taking advantage of Poland's collapse, seized West Prussia, a Polish fief. Charles immediately invaded Brandenburg, besieged Berlin, and forced the Great Elector to sign the **Treaty of Königsberg,** whereby East Prussia became a fief of Poland and the Elector became vassal of Charles as "Protector of Poland."

1655–1656. Revival of Polish National Resistance. Swedish atrocities, desecration of churches, and plunder of public and private property inflamed the Poles against the Swedes. The gentry formed military detachments all over the country; the partisans harassed the Swedes. John Casimir returned to Poland and assumed the leadership of the struggle.

1656, Spring. Charles X Returns to Poland. At the news of John Casimir's return to Poland, Charles rushed back from Prussia with 10,000 men. After some minor successes he was repulsed from the fortress of Zamosc, and near **Sandomierz** was surrounded by superior Polish forces in a triangle formed by the Vistula and the San rivers. In an extraordinary feat of bravery and skill, but with heavy loss, Charles broke out of encirclement and retreated to Prussia harassed by the cavalry of Hetman **Czarniecki** and ambushed in the forests by merciless peasant partisans. He reached Prussia with only 4,000 men. His remaining forces were dispersed as garrisons in Polish cities and fortresses.

1656, June. John Casimir Retakes Warsaw. He captured its Swedish garrison under Wittenberg. By the end of the same month, however, Charles X, reinforced by the army (18,000) of his new vassal and ally, Frederick William of Brandenburg, invaded Poland.

1656, July. Battle of Warsaw. Casimir and General Stefan Czarniecki, with 50,000 men, were defeated in a 3-day battle in which Brandenburg General **Georg von Derfflinger** distinguished himself. Charles reoccupied Warsaw, but the Elector refused to send his army deeper into seething Poland.

1657, February–July. Transylvanian Intervention. Another Swedish ally, Prince **George Rakoczy** of Transylvania, crossed the Carpathians and invaded Poland with 30,000 men. By summer, however, he was surrounded by Polish forces and capitulated. He left Poland with only 400 horsemen, his army being destroyed during the retreat by the Tartars.

1657, Spring. Russia Enters the War. The Russians invaded Livonia and besieged Riga.

1657, Spring. Support for Poland. The Emperor made an alliance with John Casimir, sending 12,000 troops to help the Poles recapture Cracow. Denmark declared war on Sweden (June 1) and was soon joined by the Elector, who deserted the Swedish cause. The overextended Swedes withdrew from Poland to protect threatened possessions around the Baltic.

1657, July. Swedish Invasion of Mainland Denmark. Charles and 6,000 troops crossed the frontier of Holstein and expelled the Danes from Bremen.

1657, October 24. Battle of Frederiksodde. Swedish Count Karl Gustav Wrangel and 4,000 men stormed the city. Danish Marshal **Bilde** was killed and more than 3,000 of his men surrendered. The Swedes now commanded the mainland of Denmark.

1658, January. Invasion of Insular Denmark. Charles led a daring advance over the ice from Jutland to Fyn and then to Zealand. Denmark sued for peace.

1658, February 27. Treaty of Roeskilde. Denmark relinquished its possessions in the Swedish peninsula. Both countries agreed to make common cause to keep enemy fleets out of the Sound.

1658, June. Renewal of the Danish War. Danish delays in carrying out the peace terms and Dutch activity in Denmark made Charles fearful that more hostilities would be forthcoming, so he decided to crush Denmark completely.

1658, July. Repulse at Copenhagen. Charles ordered Wrangel to attack Copenhagen, Kronberg (Elsinore), and Christiania. A national patriotic movement enabled Copenhagen to withstand the Swedish assault, and Charles faced a bloody siege.

1658, September. Fall of Kronberg. International interest in the Baltic Straits now became important in frustrating Charles's design to control the Sound.

1658, October 29. Dutch-English Intervention. A fleet of 35 ships under Admiral **Opdam** joined the Danes and temporarily relieved Copenhagen.

1659, February 11. Dutch Intervention. Following renewal of the Swedish blockade, a Dutch fleet arrived to relieve Copenhagen, driving the Swedish fleet away.

1659, November. Battle of Nyborg. Michael de Ruyter transported 9,000 Danish troops from Jutland to Fyn. They defeated **Philip of Sulzbach** and 6,000 Swedish troops.

1660, February 13. Death of Charles X. Sweden, under a regency of nobles, immediately sought peace.

1660, May. Treaty of Oliva. Peace between Sweden and Poland. Both gave up respective monarchical-dynastic claims. Livonia was confirmed to Sweden. Brandenburg received full title to East Prussia.

1660, June. Treaty of Copenhagen. Denmark formally surrendered Skane, the southern portion of the Scandinavian peninsula. She and Sweden agreed to guarantee access of foreign vessels to the Sound.

1661. Treaty of Kardis. This confirmed the *status quo ante bellum* between Sweden, Poland, and Russia.

THE REIGN OF CHARLES XI, 1660–1697

1672–1679. The Dutch War. (See p. 563.) Sweden was allied with Louis XIV of France.

1675, June 28. Battle of Fehrbellin. An army of 12,000 Swedes invading Brandenburg were defeated by Field Marshal Derfflinger. The Brandenburgers then took the offensive and invaded Swedish Pomerania, taking Stettin, Stralsund, and **Griefswald.**

1676, May 25. Battle of Jasmund. The Swedish Navy was defeated by the Danes under Admiral **Niels Juel.**

1676–1679. Campaigns of Charles XI. The young king took the field to win impressive victories against Danes and Brandenburgers, and retain Sweden's pre-eminence in Northern Europe. He decisively defeated the Danes in the campaigns of 1677 and 1678. Danish Admiral Juel, however, again defeated the Swedes, under **Evert Horn,** near Copenhagen at **Kjöge Bight** (1677, June 30).

1679, June 29. Peace of St. Germain-en-Laye. The Elector returned to Sweden nearly all of the conquests he had made in Pomerania.

1697–1718. Reign of Charles XII. (**See p. 644.**)

THE NETHERLANDS

1609–1621. The Twelve Years' Truce. The desultory, indecisive fighting with Spain ended temporarily and the northern provinces consolidated their independence.

1621, August 9. Renewal of the War with Spain. As soon as the 12 years' truce expired, hostilities broke out. This became part of the Thirty Years' War (see p. 533). Maurice commanded the Dutch; Spinola again commanded the Spanish.

1624, August 28–1625, June 5. Spinola's Siege and Capture of Breda. Maurice was repulsed in attempts to relieve the siege.

1625, April 23. Death of Maurice. He was succeeded as stadholder by his brother **Frederick Henry.**

1626–1629. Dutch Successes. The Dutch captured Oldenzaal (1626), Gral (1627), 's Hertogenbosch, and Wesel (1629). These latter successes interrupted Spanish and imperial communications along the Rhine.

1631. Naval Battle of the Slaak. A Dutch fleet defeated a Spanish invasion fleet.

1632. Dutch Capture of Maastricht. Peace negotiations were undertaken, but without results.

1635. Dutch-French Alliance.

1637. Dutch Recapture of Breda.

1639, October 21. Battle of the Downs. Maarten Tromp engaged and dealt a blow to a fleet of Spanish warships and transports commanded by **António de Oquendo.** The Dutch now held complete mastery of the seas.

1643. Battle of Rocroi. (**See p. 543.**) Peace negotiations were begun anew.

1644–1645. Dutch Successes. Capture of Sas van Ghent gave Frederick Henry a foothold on the southern bank of the Scheldt (1644). Next year the Dutch captured Hulst.

1648. Treaty of Münster (**Part of the Peace of Westphalia**). This ended the long "Eighty Years'" war with Spain. The frontiers that had been established were recognized, as was the independence of the United Provinces.

1647–1650. William II as Stadholder. He disapproved of the Treaty of Münster because it left France and Spain at war. He entered into secret negotiations to re-enter the war in alliance with France, but he died suddenly of smallpox (November 6, 1650).

1650–1672. Holland Without a Stadholder. William's posthumous son William III was now head of the House of Orange. **Jan de Witt** was the strong man who became the Grand Pensionary (1653) and maintained Dutch prestige for the next 20 years.

1652, May–1654, April 5. First Anglo-Dutch War. (**See p. 555.**)

1657–1660. The First Northern War. Holland intervened on the side of Denmark to prevent the takeover of the entrance of the Baltic by Sweden (see p. 568).

1657–1661. War with Portugal. This was over the expulsion of the Dutch from Brazil (1654; see p. 607). The Dutch were unsuccessful.

1664. Undeclared Hostilities with England. England seized Dutch posts on the West African coast and the New Netherlands Colony, whose capital, New Amsterdam, was renamed New York.

1665–1667. Second Anglo-Dutch War. (**See p. 556.**)

1668, January 13. The Triple Alliance. (**See p. 563.**)

1672–1678. War with France and England. (**See p. 557.**)

1672, August 27. Overthrow and Murder of de Witt. A popular uprising established the young son of William II as stadholder.

1672–1702. William III as Stadholder. Aided by the Emperor, the Elector of Brandenburg, and the withdrawal of the British (1674), William held off the

French and emerged from the **Treaty of Nijmegen** (1678) without losses (see p. 566).

1678, March. Anglo-Dutch Defense Alliance.

1686. The League of Augsburg Formed by William. (See p. 558.)

1688, November 5. The Glorious Revolution. William, whose wife was Mary, daughter of James II, landed in Torbay, England, in response to an appeal from the opponents of James II (see p. 558). William and Mary became rulers of England.

1689–1697. War of the Grand Alliance (**League of Augsburg; see p. 546.**)

SWITZERLAND

The Swiss Confederation was a very loose kind of union with the cantons divided among themselves on religious questions. Fighting was the main occupation and Swiss mercenaries continued to be employed by foreign states, especially France. The principal events were:

1602. Savoyard Invasion. The invaders, supported by Spain, were repulsed from Geneva.

1618–1648. The Thirty Years' War. The Swiss Confederation was officially neutral. Acceptance of the principle of neutrality was significant. Swiss mercenaries were hired by both sides and much material was sold to the belligerents at a profit.

1620. Spanish Seizure of the Valtelline Passes. This was the most convenient link in communications to the Spanish Netherlands (and also to Hapsburg Austria) from the Spanish Hapsburg possessions around Milan, Italy. A Swiss effort to expel the Spanish was unsuccessful (1621).

1625. Swiss Seizure of the Valtelline. The Swiss were led by the French **Marquis de Coeuvres.**

1626. Treaty of Monzon. As a result of the mediation of Pope **Urban VIII,** France and Spain agreed on rights in the Valtelline. Spain retained control.

1637. Swiss Seizure of the Valtelline. A subsequent treaty with Spain (1639) left the passes open to the use of Spanish troops, but reinstated Grisons sovereignty.

1648. The Treaty of Westphalia. European recognition of the Swiss Confederation's independence of the German Empire.

1656, January 24. First Villmergen War. The Catholic cantons under **Christopher Pfyffer** defeated the Protestants from Bern and Zurich.

ITALY

Italy continued to be divided into numerous political entities, many under foreign rule. There was a general decline in prosperity. The papacy tried to be neutral in the conflicts between the Bourbons and the Hapsburgs. In Savoy the French and Spanish factions met in sporadic conflicts which brought about a decisive weakening of the ducal power. Naples continued under Spanish rule. Venice maintained independence and became an advocate of peace and neutrality despite her wars with the Turks. The *status quo* was restored in Italy by the **Peace of the Pyrenees** (1659) as Spain kept her traditional territories and France retained Pinerolo with its control over Savoy.

IBERIAN PENINSULA

Spain

1598–1621. Philip III. He devoted himself to the needs of the church rather than the country. Spain entered a period of decline and decadence.

1609, April 9. Twelve Years' Truce with the Netherlands. This followed 45 years of wasteful warfare (see p. 570).

1609–1614. Expulsion of the Moriscos. (**See p. 488.**)

1618–1648. The Thirty Years' War. (**See p. 533.**)

1621–1665. Reign of Philip IV. The military and economic decline of Spain accelerated.

1640. Independence of Portugal. (**See below.**)

1648. The Treaty of Münster. This ended the Thirty Years' War and the long war with the United Provinces; war with France continued (see p. 545).

1659, November 7. The Peace of the Pyrenees. (**See p. 562.**) This treaty marked the end of Spanish ascendancy in Europe and the beginning of French ascendancy. For the first time in 40 years, Spain was free from foreign war.

1665–1700. Reign of Charles II. (**See p. 563.**) A half-mad monarch, the last of the Spanish Hapsburgs.

1667–1668. War of Devolution. (**See p. 563.**)

1673–1678. The Dutch War, or War of the First Coalition Against Louis XIV. (**See p. 563.**) Disastrous to Spain.

Portugal

1640, November–December. Portuguese Independence. Revolt against Spanish rule. Spain was unsuccessful in attempts to regain control (1640–1668).

1640–1656. Reign of John IV. First king of the house of Braganza. He was recognized by France and Holland, but Spain continued sporadic hostilities.

1641, January. Surrender of Malacca to the Dutch. (**See p. 597.**)

1644, May 26. Battle of Montijo. A Portuguese force commanded by General **Mathias d'Albuquerque** and backed by England and France successfully invaded Spain. After this victory near Badajoz, Portugal was left in peace for several years.

1657–1661. War with Holland. The Dutch were unable to regain the foothold in Brazil from which they had been driven (1654).

1661–1663. Spanish Invasion. Philip IV of Spain attempted to reconquer his lost kingdom. Don Juan and some 20,000 men crossed the border from Estremadura while a smaller force entered Portugal from the north. The Portuguese, aided by an English auxiliary force under Schomberg, were successful in halting the Spanish. Between 1662 and 1663 Don Juan was able to overrun Alentejo Province.

1662. English Assistance. Charles II of England married the daughter of John IV, **Catherine,** and in return for the dowry provided men and arms for the war with Spain.

1663, June 8. Battle of Ameixal. Sancho de Vita Flor defeated Don Juan.

1663, June 17. Battle of Montes Claras. Antonio de Marialva routed the Spanish.

1664–1665. Portuguese Successes. Desultory warfare.

1665, June. Battle of Villa Viciosa. Marialva and Schomberg defeated Count **Caracina** in a bitter 8-hour hand-to-hand battle. This ended Spain's efforts to reconquer Portugal.

1668, February 13. Peace with Spain. Through the mediation of Charles II of England, Spain finally recognized Portugal's independence.

EASTERN EUROPE

POLAND

This was a century of almost continuous wars, offensive in the first half of the century and defensive in the second. These exhausting conflicts contributed to Poland's downfall in the 18th century.

At a time of infantry predominance in Western Europe, cavalry remained the principal arm in Poland, and the charges of Polish cavalry armed with lance and heavy sword broke many pike squares. Polish heavy cavalry wore armor (mail shirts), discarded in the West. At the same time, Polish horsemen were highly skilled in warfare against the elusive Tartars. Camps fortified by several rows of chained carts were widely used as field fortresses. The principal events were:

1587–1632. The Reign of Sigismund III (Vasa). (See p. 483.) His refusal to abandon his claim to the Swedish throne led to incessant Polish-Swedish wars.

First Polish-Swedish War for Livonia, 1600–1611

1600. Swedish Invasion of Estonia. Swedish forces under **Charles of Sunderland** (uncle of Sigismund; later Charles IX) invaded and occupied Estonia (except for Riga) and most of Livonia.

1601. Polish Counteroffensive. Successfully defending Riga, the Poles reconquered most of Livonia. In subsequent campaigns Hetman **Jan Karo Chodkiewicz** was victorious at **Dorpat, Revel,** and **Weissenstein.**

1604. Battle of Kircholm. Newly crowned Swedish King Charles IX landed in Estonia with a fresh army of 14,000 men and marched toward Riga. Chodkiewicz with 3,500 men, two-thirds horsemen, routed the Swedish Army with an impetuous charge. Charles narrowly escaped captivity. The Swedes lost 9,000 killed.

1604–1611. Intermittent Operations. A truce was agreed to after the death of Charles IX (1611).

1605–1609. Polish Intervention in Russia. (See p. 576.)

1609–1618. Polish-Russian War. (See p. 577.)

Polish-Turkish War, 1614–1621

This was provoked by Polish Cossack raids upon Turkish ports along the western and southern Black Sea coasts, and by Polish support of revolts in Moldavia and Walachia (present Rumania). In retaliation, devastating Turkish and Tartar raids overran the Polish Ukraine while Poland was primarily occupied in Russia (1614–1618).

1620, September 20. Battle of Jassy. Hetman **Stanislas Zolkiewski** with about 10,000 men decisively defeated a much larger Turkish and Tartar army. As a result the Ottoman Sultan, **Osman II,** led a large army north from Constantinople. Zolkiewski began to retreat.

1620, December. Battle of Cecora. Zolkiewski and his army of 9,000 men were annihilated in Moldavia.

1621, Fall. Battle of Chocim (Chotyn, or Hotin). A Polish army of 75,000 under Hetmen Chodkiewicz and **Stanislas Lubomirski** had the better of an inconclusive struggle on the Dniester River against Sultan Osman's Turkish Army of some 200,000. This was followed by a truce confirming the *status quo*. Nevertheless Cossack raids upon Turkey and Tartar raids upon Poland continued.

The Second Polish-Swedish War, 1617–1629

Gustavus Adolphus took advantage of Poland's simultaneous involvement in major wars with Turkey and Moscow by reconquering the eastern littoral of the Baltic Sea.

1617. Gustavus Victorious in Livonia. He captured several Baltic ports in Livonia, and compelled Hetman **Krzysztof Radziwill** to conclude an armistice until 1620.

1621. Gustavus Invades Estonia. His 12,000 Swedes were reinforced by 4,000 Estonians. He besieged and captured **Riga,** the political and commercial center of Livonia (September 15).

1622–1625. Armistice. Radziwill was again forced to conclude an armistice.

1625. Gustavus Occupies Livonia. After landing in Riga, he occupied all Livonia and Kurland against minor resistance.

1626. Swedish Invasion of Prussia. Gustavus landed at Pillau (vassal of Poland) with 15,000 men and quickly occupied all northern Prussia, threatening Poland's access to the Baltic. Only Gdansk (Danzig) rejected his demand of surrender. Gustavus left forces to blockade Danzig and returned to Sweden.

1626–1627. Polish Counteroffensive. Under Hetman **Alexander Koniecpolski** the Poles attempted to reopen the Vistula and relieve blockaded Danzig. Koniecpolski captured the fortified port of Puck (a fortress on the Vistula south of Tczew and west of Danzig), but could not cut the Swedish line of communication with Pillau. He intercepted and captured 4,000 Germans recruited in Germany for Gustavus.

1627, May. Gustavus Adolphus Returns from Sweden. He brought reinforcements, giving him 14,000 against Koniecpolski's 9,000. Koniecpolski was repulsed at the **Battle of Tczew** (Dirschau), where Gustavus was wounded. For the first time Swedish cavalry fought Polish cavalry on equal terms. Sigismund III organized a small fleet of privateers; these harassed the Swedish fleet, but Sweden retained control of the sea.

1628. Swedish Advance. With his army increased to 32,000 and recovered from his wounds, Gustavus forced Koniecpolski to retreat south. The Poles fought a war of harassment. By winter Gustavus withdrew to Prussia.

1629. Imperial Support from Germany. The Emperor sent Sigismund III a corps of 7,000 men to prevent Gustavus' proposed march from Prussia to Germany to enter the 30 Years' War. Koniecpolski immediately started an offensive, surprising Gustavus and a detachment of cavalry on the march.

1629. Battle of Sztum. The Swedes had the worst of an inconclusive cavalry action. Gustavus, wounded in the back, narrowly escaped capture. Because of the 2 wounds he received during this war, Gustavus could never wear armor again. The Swedish hold on the Baltic coast was unshaken.

1629. Truce of Altmark. Poland needed peace and Gustavus wanted to be free to enter the war in Germany. Poland lost Livonia north of the Dvina River. Sweden was permitted to use all Prussian ports—except for Königsberg, Danzig, and Puck—for 6 years. The lower Vistula ports (Marienburg, Sztum, and Glova) were temporarily left in the hands of the Elector of Brandenburg.

1632–1634. Russo-Polish War. (See p. 577.)

1632–1648. Reign of Ladislas IV.

1634–1653. "Bloodless War" with Sweden. Taking advantage of Swedish involvement in the Thirty Years' War (see p. 533), Ladislas assembled an army of 24,000 men on the lower Vistula and, while threatening Swedish ports in Prussia, began negotiations with Sweden with regard to the eastern littoral of the Baltic. This led to the **Treaty of Sztumsdorff,** which provided for a 26-year truce and restored all Prussia to Poland; most of Livonia south of the Dvina River was returned to Poland.

1648–1668. Reign of John II Casimir.

Cossack Uprising in the Ukraine, 1648–1654

The rebellious Cossacks were led by **Bogdan Chmielnicki.** There was great ferocity and cruelty on both sides; the Ukraine was devastated and depopulated. Chmielnicki recruited not only Cossacks but also masses of rebellious Ukrainian peasants. He formed an alliance with the Crimean khan and was assisted by a Tartar army.

1648. Cossack Victories. These were at the **Battles of Zolte Wody** and **Korsun.**

1649. Battle of Pilawce. A Polish force of 36,000 was defeated by the Cossacks.

1648–1649. Poland on the Defensive. The Poles held their strategic fortresses of Lwow (1648), Zamosc (1648), and Zbaraz (1649) against Cossack attacks.

1649. Treaty of Zborow. A temporary Polish-Cossack peace.

1651. Resumption of Hostilities. At the **Battle of Beresteczko,** 34,000 Poles under John Casimir decisively defeated 200,000 Cossacks and Tartars under Chmielnicki (July 1).

1651. Treaty of Biala Cerkew. The Cossacks made peace. Chmielnicki, however, continued the war with a few followers.

1654. Treaty of Pereiaslavl. The Cossacks placed the Ukraine under the protection of Czar **Alexis,** provoking a war between Poland and Moscow.

1654–1656. Polish-Russian War. (See p. 578.)

1655–1660. First Northern War. War with Sweden (see p. 568).

1657. Transylvanian Invasion. (See p. 581.)

1658. Treaty of Hadziak. Regent **Wyhowski** of the Ukraine, alarmed by the Russo-Polish alliance in the Northern War, reached an agreement with Poland which proclaimed equality of the Ukrainian, Polish, and Lithuanian peoples and creation of an autonomous Ukrainian duchy ruled by a Hetman confirmed by the Polish king, and sending senators and representatives to the Polish Diet. This provoked war with Moscow at a time when Poland was suffering the ordeal of repeated Swedish invasions.

1658–1666. Polish-Russian War. (See p. 579.)

1668. Abdication of John Casimir. A violent struggle for the throne ensued.

1669–1673. Reign of Michael Wisniowiecki. This was a period of turmoil and struggle between partisans and enemies of the incompetent monarch. A principal leader of the opponents was **John Sobieski.**

Polish-Turkish War, 1671–1677

The Ukraine had been divided along the Dnieper River between Russia and Poland after a long war (1667; see p. 579). The Cossack chieftain **Peter Doroshenko,** in Polish Poland, refused to accept Polish authority and acknowledged Turkish sovereignty (1668). As a result of Polish efforts to suppress the Cossack revolt, as they considered it, Turkey demanded cession of the Ukraine. Though unprepared for war, Poland refused.

1671, December 9. Declaration of War by Sultan Mohammed IV.

1672, Summer. Invasion of Poland. Grand Vizier **Ahmed** led a huge army of more than 200,000 into southeastern Poland. The Turks and their Tartar vassals and Cossack allies besieged and captured the strategic fortress of Kamieniec. Most of the garrison of 1,100 perished under the debris of the castle, which they blew up after a 12-day siege. The Turks then took Lublin against little resistance.

1672, October. Treaty of Buczacz. Michael, unable to organize his disintegrating kingdom, ceded to Turkey the province of Podolia. Doroshenko was granted independence in the western Ukraine. Poland also agreed to pay an annual tribute. The treaty was never ratified by the Polish Diet.

1672–1673. Sobieski Rallies Poland. In the face of the deadly Turkish menace, Grand Hetman John Sobieski, renowned for earlier victories over Tartars, formed an army of 40,000. He marched against the Turks.

1673, November 11. Second Battle of Chocim (Chotyn). Sobieski annihilated a Turkish army of 30,000 men. He then took the fortress of Chocim. Other Turkish forces withdrew from Poland without fighting. King Michael had died one day before the battle. On learning this, Sobieski suspended further offensive operations, and disposed his forces for the protection of the frontiers. He then hastened to Warsaw, where he was elected king (May 21, 1674).

1674–1696. Reign of John III Sobieski. Internal turmoil and intrigue continued.

1675. Turkish Invasion. Some 60,000 Turks and 100,000 Tartars invaded Podolia and the Ukraine. They recaptured Chocim and threatened Lwow.

1675. Battle of Lwow. Sobieski defeated the Turks. Gradually he drove the invaders back, winning several small battles and liberating all of Poland except Kamieniec. Internal difficulties hampered his efforts to raise a large army to invade Turkey.

1676, September. Turkish Invasion. An army of 200,000 under **Ibrahim Pasha** again invaded southeastern Poland.

1676, September–October. Battle of Zorawno. Sobieski with 16,000 men repulsed the Turks from his strongly fortified camp on the Dniester in an inconclusive 2-week battle.

1676, October 16. Treaty of Zorawno. The Turks agreed to the return of the western Ukraine to Poland. They retained Podolia, including Kamieniec and Chocim.

1676–1681. Continuing War in the Ukraine. Meanwhile, Moscow, also engaged in an unrelated war against Turkey (see p.

579), had frequently violated the truce agreement of Andrussovo and invaded the Polish Ukraine, devastating it and inciting the Cossacks to continue rebellion against Poland. The continuing Russo-Turkish war, largely waged in the eastern part of the Polish Ukraine, turned this rich land into a desert.

1683, March 31. Alliance with the Empire. Turkey, having waged inconclusive wars with Poland and Moscow, turned against Austria. John Sobieski believed that if Austria was defeated, the next Turkish blow would be directed against Cracow, the heart of Poland. He concluded a defensive-offensive alliance with the Empire and prepared for war.

1683, July–September. Siege of Vienna. (See **p. 582.**) The high point in Sobieski's career.

1683–1699. Desultory Warfare. The war against the Turks dragged on with varying results. Sobieski, unable to reach any agreement with the Russians and obtaining no assistance from jealous Emperor Leopold, bore the brunt of the war and was hard put to hold the Ukraine. Meanwhile Poland continued to be wracked by internal intrigue and violence.

1696, June 17. Death of Sobieski.

RUSSIA

The military power of Moscow developed in relative isolation from the West, and reflected the general backwardness of the country. At the beginning of the 17th century, Moscow's army, comprised of relatively ill-armed and poorly trained levies, was often defeated by considerably smaller Swedish and Polish forces. However, in the defense of fortresses the Russians showed tenacity, resourcefulness, and courage. In 1612, Polish and Swedish invaders of Muscovy were forced to retreat by masses of popular militia and not by the army.

By the middle of the century a new system of recruitment was introduced, based on compulsory service of peasants and city dwellers, and permanent infantry and cavalry regiments replaced the old levy. In addition to these semiregular troops, there were nearly 150,000 Cossacks eager for war. By the end of the century, Moscow in emergency was able to mobilize an armed force of over 300,000 men, mostly poorly trained.

Early in the 17th century, Moscow suffered its "Time of Troubles." A combination of violent internal upheavals and Polish and Swedish interventions ruined the country and led to territorial losses. By the middle of the century, however, the czardom had recovered its political and economic strength, and, owing to Poland's mounting difficulties, in the second half of the century Moscow conquered much of the northeastern Ukraine from Poland.

The "Time of Troubles," 1604–1613

This began with the appearance of a false **Dmitri,** a pretender who claimed to be the murdered son of **Ivan IV** and who was supported by the Poles and Cossacks. After the death of **Boris Godunov** (1605; see p. 492), the struggle for power among various boyar factions threw the country into a state of extreme confusion and brought Polish and Swedish intervention. The principal events were:

1605. Brief Reign of Theodore (or Fëdor, Son of Boris). He was murdered by hostile boyars. The false Dmitri briefly took the throne, but also was soon murdered by the boyars.

1605–1609. Polish Intervention. Several Polish magnates supported the claims of the false Dmitri. As chaos mounted in the Moscow czardom, Polish intervention was increasingly persistent.

1606–1610. Reign of Basil Shuisky. He was bitterly opposed internally and by the Poles.

1608. Battle of Balkhov. A Polish army, reinforced by 45,000 rebellious Cossacks, defeated Basil. Soon after, the Poles and

Cossacks defeated Basil again at the **Battle of the Chadyuka River,** bringing a second "false Dmitri" to power. This was followed by an uprising of the Cossacks and peasants in the east and south in support of the pretender. Basil requested Swedish aid at the price of the cession of Karelia to Sweden.

WAR WITH POLAND, 1609–1618

1609. Sigismund III of Poland Declares War. Claiming the disputed throne of Moscow for himself, he invaded Russia.

1609–1611. The Siege of Smolensk. Michael Shein, commander of Smolensk, stubbornly and skillfully defended the fortress against repeated assaults. The garrison of 12,000 was reinforced by 70,000 civilians.

1610, September. The Battle of Klushino. A Russian army of 30,000 men, including 8,000 Swedes, led by **Dmitri Shuisky** marching to relieve Smolensk, was surprised and annihilated by a small Polish corps of 4,000 (3,800 horsemen and 200 infantry with 2 small cannon) led by Hetman Stanislas Zolkiewski. The Russians left 15,000 killed on the battlefield. Shuisky fled to Moscow. Zolkiewski, reinforced to 23,000, moved on Moscow. Smolensk surrendered early the following year.

1610, October 8. Capture of Moscow. Polish troops entered Moscow and the Kremlin. The boyars deposed Czar Basil Shuisky.

1610–1611. Protracted Negotiations. The boyars were prepared to elect Ladislas (son of Sigismund) to the Moscow throne, but negotiations broke down when Sigismund insisted on having the throne for himself.

1611. Rising of Russia. Rebellion of the populace against the invaders broke out in Moscow. A Polish garrison was besieged in the Kremlin. The uprising spread in the northern and eastern part of the country under the leadership of Prince **Pazharsky.** The second "false Dmitri" died.

1612. Polish Withdrawal. The Polish army, unable to relieve the Polish garrison of the Kremlin, withdrew from Moscow. Desultory frontier fighting continued. The Poles in the Kremlin surrendered and were massacred.

The Swedish and Polish Wars, 1613–1667

1613–1645. Reign of Michael Romanov. This weak ruler founded Russia's greatest dynasty.

RUSSO-SWEDISH WAR, 1613–1617

1613. Novgorod Expedition. Moscow sent troops against Novgorod, occupied by the Swedes. Swedish troops intercepted and severely defeated the Russian corps.

1614. Invasion of Moscow. Gustavus Adolphus transferred military operations into Moscow territory. Pskov, the strongest Russian frontier fortress, resisted his assault successfully and, following a 7-month siege, Gustavus withdrew to Swedish territory. Since Moscow expected a Polish invasion and Gustavus was preparing an attack on Polish Livonia, both Moscow and Sweden were anxious to conclude peace.

1617. Treaty of Stolbovo. This terminated the Russo-Swedish War. Sweden restored Novgorod and several other towns to Moscow, and the Russians ceded to Sweden their last footholds on the Gulf of Finland. Thus Moscow lost its outlet to the Baltic.

1617. Renewed Polish Invasion. Ladislas marched to Moscow, claiming the Moscow throne as czar-elect. After the rejection of his claim by Michael, Hetman Chodkiewicz tried to capture Moscow by direct attack, but failed. Peace negotiations followed.

1618. Truce of Devlin. Poland was confirmed in possession of all border towns conquered in 1609–1611 (including Smolensk).

1618–1632. Military Reorganization. Michael hired foreign mercenaries in England, Holland, Denmark, and Sweden and formed of them several foreign regiments. Several Russian regiments were also trained by foreigners and according to foreign regulations. Guns, arms, and powder were purchased.

RUSSO-POLISH WAR, 1632–1634

1632, September. Russian Invasion of Poland. Boris Shein with 30,000 men advanced to besiege Smolensk, which had a garrison of only 3,000.

1632–1633. Siege of Smolensk. After a gallant defense of 11 months, the provisions of the garrison were nearly exhausted.

1633, September. Battle of Smolensk. Ladislas IV with an army of 40,000 men decisively defeated the Russians, then surrounded Shein's decimated army, which was in turn besieged for 6 months before it surrendered (February, 1634). Shein was permitted to withdraw his troops to Moscow, where he was unjustly accused of treason and executed.

1634. Treaty of Polianovo. This confirmed the Treaty of Deulin. Ladislas renounced his claims to the czardom and recognized Michael as czar.

1637. Capture of Azov. The Cossacks seized the fortified port of Azov from the Crimean Tartars and offered it to the Czar, but Michael, afraid of a conflict with Turkey, refused the offer. Azov therefore was returned to the Tartars.

1645–1676. Reign of Czar Alexis.

RUSSO-POLISH WAR, 1654–1656

Seeking revenge for past defeats at the hands of Poland, the Russians took advantage of Poland's deep involvement in the struggle with the Cossacks in the Ukraine (see p. 574). The Cossack leader, Bogdan Chmielnicki, offered to surrender the Ukraine to the Czar.

1654, July–October. Operations in Lithuania. Alexis personally led an army of over 100,000 into Lithuania. He captured Smolensk after a 3-month siege (July 2–September 26), then at the **Battle of Borisov** overwhelmed a small Polish corps. The Russians then occupied defenseless Lithuania as far as the Berezina River until winter stopped the operations.

1654. Operations in the Ukraine. Simultaneously, a smaller Russian force of 40,000 invaded the Ukraine and occupied Kiev. Between the two Russian armies, a Cossack force under Hetman **Zolotarenko** utterly devastated the area of the Pripet Marshes and massacred its population.

1655, January. Polish Counteroffensive in the Ukraine. In spite of bitter cold, Hetman **Stanislas Lanckoronski** defeated a much larger joint Russo-Cossack army at the **Battle of Okhmatov.** The Russians promptly retreated.

1655, May–October. Resumed Russian Offensives. In Lithuania the Russian advance was facilitated by simultaneous Swedish attacks on Poland from Livonia (see pp. 568 and 574). Alexis advanced to the Niemen River and proclaimed himself Grand Duke of Lithuania. His troops, however, were harassed by partisans. Simultaneously, Russo-Cossack forces reoccupied most of the Ukraine and even sent raids into central Poland. They were unable to take the fortified cities of Kamieniec and Lwow.

1655, November. Tartar Intervention. Poland's ally, Crimean Khan **Mahmet Girei,** invaded the Ukraine with 150,000 men. He defeated and captured Chmielnicki at **Zalozce,** and forced the Russians to withdraw precipitously toward the north.

1656, November 3. Treaty of Nimieza. After prolonged negotiations the war was terminated by the conclusion of a three-year truce and an anti-Swedish alliance between Russia and Poland.

RUSSO-SWEDISH WAR, 1656–1658

Alarmed by Sweden's expansion in the Baltic area, Alexis, rejecting Swedish offers of alliance against Poland, instead concluded alliances with Poland and Denmark against Sweden. This was part of the First Great Northern War (see p. 568).

1656. Russian Northern Offensive. Advancing toward the Gulf of Finland, the Russians captured the strong fortresses of Schlüsselburg and Nienshanz, near the Neva River's mouth.

1656, July–August. Battle of Riga. Alexis advanced from Polotsk down the Dvina River, captured Dinaburg (whose defenders were massacred), and then took the fortress of Kokenhuzen. Riga, whose small garrison was commanded by **Magnus De La Gardie,** was besieged. After the arrival of considerable reinforcements, De La Gardie made a sortie, defeating the much more numerous entrenched Russians, who lost 8,000 killed and 14,000 wounded and prisoners. Alexis retreated, pursued energetically.

1657. Swedish Counteroffensives. The Swedes devastated Karelia. At the same time Swedish troops advanced overland from Finland to Riga to strengthen its defense.

1658. Renewed Russian Offensive. A small Russian force captured Yamburg and besieged Narva, but soon was ejected from the Baltic and the Gulf of Finland by the Swedes, who recaptured all previously lost towns.

1658. Three-Year Truce. Alexis conceded defeat, and decided to make peace so he could renew the war with Poland. The Swedes kept all the towns along the Baltic coast and the Gulf of Finland.

RUSSO-POLISH WAR, 1658–1666

The Russo-Polish Truce of Nimieza expired. Moscow resumed hostilities.

1658–1659. Invasion of Lithuania. Prince **George Dolgoruki** surprised and captured Hetman **Wincenty Gosiewski** at Werki and occupied Wilno, which he devastated with fire and sword. Prince **Chowansky** captured Grodno, Nowogrodek (1659), and besieged the fortress of Lachowicze.

1658–1659. Invasion of the Ukraine. A Russian force of 150,000, under command of Prince **Trubetskoi,** was temporarily successful, but was severely beaten by the Ukrainian Hetman John Wyhowski in the **Battle of Konotop,** with the loss of 30,000 killed (1659).

1660. Operations in Lithuania. The Russians took the initiative, but were defeated by increased Polish forces, freed by the peace with Sweden. Hetmen Stefan Czarniecki and **Paul Sapieha** defeated Dolgoruki and Chowansky, and forced them to withdraw to Polotsk and Smolensk. The Poles not only liberated Lithuania but invaded the area of Vitebsk, Polotsk, and Velikie Luki.

1660. Operations in the Ukraine. Russian General **Sheremetiev** led 60,000 well-trained and equipped troops against Lwow; was defeated and captured at the **Battle of Lubar** (1660) by Hetmen Czarniecki and George Lubomirski, who had 20,000 Poles assisted by 20,000 Tartars. Another army of pro-Moscow Cossacks—numbering 40,000 and led by Chmielnicki—attempting to join Sheremetiev, was defeated by George Lubomirski at the **Battle of Slobodyszcze.** Chmielnicki pledged obedience to the Polish king.

1661–1667. Polish Initiative. There followed several years of sporadic frontier fighting.

1667. Treaty of Andrusovo. The Ukraine was partitioned between Poland and Moscow with the Dnieper River as the dividing line. Kiev, though located on the southern Polish bank, was ceded to Moscow for 2 years (it never returned to Poland). Smolensk was also ceded to Moscow.

Beginnings of the Turkish Wars, 1667–1700

1667–1678. Friction with Turkey. The acquisition of northeastern Ukraine brought Moscow into contact with Turkish possessions, and frontier friction soon began.

1676–1682. Reign of Theodore III (or Fëdor, Son of Alexis).

1678–1681. First Russo-Turkish War. Cossack Hetman Doroshenko was dissatisfied with the results of the Treaty of Zorawno (see p. 575), and asked Russian assistance against Poland and Turkey. At the same time, Sultan Mohammed IV claimed the Ukraine. He sent a large army under Vizier **Kara Mustafa** to drive out the Poles and Russians. The area of operations was mostly in the eastern part of the Polish Ukraine, which had been utterly devastated in the Polish war against Turkey (see p. 575). Russo-Cossack forces under the command of Prince **Romodanowsky** withdrew without offering serious opposition. The Turks captured and destroyed a number of Ukrainian fortresses and cities.

1681, January 8. Treaty of Radzin. Turkey renounced her claims to the Ukraine, but under condition that the population of the area between the rivers Bug and Dniester should be evacuated and this area should remain unpopulated. Podolia was returned to Poland. The Cossacks were to have special rights throughout the Ukraine.

1682–1689. Joint Reigns of Peter I and Ivan V.

1689–1725. Reign of Peter I, the Great. He initiated Russia's struggle for access to the sea, beginning with the Black Sea.

1695–1700. Russo-Turkish War for Azov. The first Russian offensive, under the personal command of Peter, reached Azov via the Volga and Don rivers, but was repulsed with heavy losses. Having no navy, the Russians were unable to blockade the water approaches to the fortress.

1695–1696. Peter Builds a Navy. Peter built a fleet near Voronezh and sent it to Azov down the Don River in the spring.

1696, July 28. Capture of Azov. The Russian army, increased to 75,000, advanced partly by land, partly by river. This time the fortress was captured by combined operations of ground and naval forces which repulsed the Turkish warships and blockaded approach to Azov from the sea.

COMMENT. *The possession of Azov, which was located on the Sea of Azov and was separated from the Black Sea by the Strait of Kerch, solidly blocked by Turkey, could not solve the problem of Russian access to the Black Sea. Its selection as the strategic objective of the war can be explained only by lack of means for an attack on the Crimea. The cost of Azov in heavy Russian losses was disproportionate to its relative importance to Russia.*

1698. Mutiny in Moscow. Peter, who had been traveling incognito in Western Europe (1697–1698), returned to suppress an army mutiny and to reform the Russian government and nation.

1700. Truce with Turkey. The war was terminated by a truce for 30 years.

HUNGARY

During most of the 17th century, Hungary was the main battleground in the continuing but sporadic struggle between the Hapsburg and Ottoman Empires. The Hapsburgs' involvement in the Thirty Years' War and in other conflicts of Central and Western Europe long prevented them from taking advantage of the gradual decline of Turkish power. During much of this period, Transylvania, nominally a fief of the Ottoman Empire, was virtually independent and played the two empires and Poland off against each other. Toward the end of the century, brief Turkish resurgence enabled them to reconquer Transylvania and to overrun practically all of Hapsburg Hungary, culminating in a siege of Vienna. Repulsed from Vienna, thanks to the intervention of Poland's John Sobieski, the Turkish decline accelerated. By the end of the century, practically all of Hungary was controlled by the Hapsburgs. The principal events were:

The Rise and Fall of Transylvania, 1593–1662

1593–1606. The Long War. (See p. 491.)

1599–1601. Struggle for Transylvania. The country was briefly dominated by **Michael the Brave,** Voivode of Wallachia and Rumania's national hero. Driven out of Transylvania by a Magyar revolt (1601), Michael regained power briefly by a victory at the **Battle of Goroslau,** won with the assistance of Hapsburg General **George Basta.** Soon afterward, however, Basta procured Michael's murder, and began a reign of terror which led to the rise of **Stephen Bocskay** and his successful alliance with the Turks (see p. 491).

1606, June 23. Treaty of Vienna. Stephen Bocskay was recognized as sovereign Prince of Transylvania by Emperor **Rudolf.** Rights of Transylvanian (and other) Protestants in Hapsburg Hungary were guaranteed.

1606, November 11. Treaty of Zsitva-Torok. End of the Long War. The territorial status of Hungary was unchanged, but the emperor was no longer required to pay tribute to the sultan. Transylvania was still nominally under Ottoman suzerainty.

1606, December 29. Death of Bocskay. He was probably poisoned; a scramble for power followed.

1608–1613. Reign of Gabriel Bathory of Transylvania (Son of Stephen; see p. 490.) Cruel and tyrannical, he was overthrown and murdered.

1613–1629. Reign of Bethlen Gabor of Transylvania. He was a wise prince and able soldier.

1618–1629. Transylvanian Participation in the Thirty Years' War. Bethlen briefly besieged Vienna (1619) and, though driven away from the Austrian capital (see p. 534), overran most of Hapsburg Hungary (1620). The Hapsburgs recognized him as Prince of Transylvania, and ceded much of Hapsburg Hungary to him in the **Treaty of Nikolsburg** (December 21, 1621). Subsequent campaigns were inconclusive.

1630–1648. Reign of George Rakoczy I of Transylvania. He increased the power, size, and independence of Transylvania.

1645. Renewed War with the Hapsburgs. George defeated the Hapsburgs and (by the **Treaty of Linz,** December 16, 1645) forced renewed grant of religious freedom to Protestants as well as Catholics in Hapsburg Hungary.

1648–1660. Reign of George Rakoczy II of Transylvania. In an undeclared frontier war between Turks and Austrians Rakoczy supported his nominal suzerain, the sultan of Turkey (1648–1652).

1657. Transylvanian Invasion of Poland. Hoping to take advantage of Poland's early defeats in the First Northern War (see p. 568), Rakoczy invaded southern Poland, hoping to seize the throne. This move, without his permission, enraged the Sultan, who still coveted the Ukraine. The Khan of the Crimean Tartars, a Turkish vassal, was ordered to eject Rakoczy from Poland. Rakoczy briefly occupied Warsaw, but, deserted by the Swedes, was forced to retreat. During the withdrawal his rear guard was overwhelmed by the Tartars at the **Battle of Trembowla,** near Tarnopol (July 31), and its commander, **Janos Kemeny,** was captured. Rakoczy reached Transylvania with only a fraction of his army.

1657–1662. War with Turkey. Mohammed Koprulu, Grand Vizier of Turkey, attempted to depose Rakoczy, but failed. Rakoczy at first defeated Koprulu's invading army at the **Battle of Lippa** (May, 1658), but was driven out of Transylvania to his estates in Hapsburg Hungary by the convergence of the Ottoman Army and that of their Crimean Tartar vassals. **Akos Barcsay** was proclaimed Prince of Transylvania by Koprulu (November, 1658). Rakoczy drove Barcsay out of the country (1659), but was in turn so hard-pressed by the Turks that he appealed for Hapsburg assistance in return for the cession of some border provinces.

1660. Battle of Fenes. Attempting to halt an invasion by **Ahmed Sidi,** Pasha of Buda, Rakoczy was defeated and mortally wounded. He died in Nagyvarad, where his forces were besieged by the Turks. After a 4-month siege, Nagyvarad finally fell to Turkish assault (August 27), while an Austrian army stood idly nearby.

1661. Janos Kemeny Elected Prince of Transylvania. He had recently returned from imprisonment in the Crimea. Despite some assistance from a small Austrian army under Raimondo Montecuccoli, Kemeny was unable to repel a Turkish invasion.

1662, January 22. Battle of Nagyszollos. Kemeny was defeated and killed by a Turkish army under **Mehmed Kucuk.** Turkish control was restored to Transylvania and **Mihaly Apafi** was proclaimed Prince by the Turks.

Renewal of the Hapsburg-Ottoman Struggle for Hungary, 1662–1683

1663–1664. Turkish Invasion of Hapsburg Hungary. The new Grand Vizier, **Fazil Ahmed Koprulu Pasha** (son of Koprulu), invaded Hapsburg Hungary with the intention of advancing on Vienna. The Turks were halted by the gallant defense of Neuhause, under **Adam Forgach.** When Neuhause finally surrendered (September, 1663), Ahmed decided to postpone the advance on Vienna until the following spring. But when he renewed the advance, the Austrians were better prepared, and he was again slowed by resistance of fortresses. Peace negotiations began in late summer at Vasvar.

1664, August 1. Battle of the Raab River (or of St. Gotthard Abbey). Ahmed, attempting to force the Austrians to accept the peace terms, crossed the river to attack Montecuccoli's army. Despite greatly superior numbers, the Turks were repulsed, and retreated to Buda; the Austrians did not pursue.

1664, August 11. Peace of Vasvar. A 20-year peace was agreed. Autonomous Transylvania remained under Turkish suzerainty. The Turks were also allowed to retain the frontier fortresses they had captured.

1664–1673. Unrest in Hapsburg Hungary. Partly because of bitterness at the unfavorable terms of the Treaty of Vasvar, partly because of religious persecution, Magyar conspiracies against the Hapsburgs in Hungary were widespread, even to the extent of seeking Turkish assistance. The Austrians subdued the unrest and minor uprisings with ease, and repression increased.

1678–1682. Revolt against Austria. Rebels under the leadership of Count **Imre Thokoly** gained control of most of northern and western Hungary. But popular support faded as Leopold made concessions to the Magyars; Thokoly turned to the Turks for aid. A Turkish army, dispatched by the Grand Vizier, Kara Mustafa, helped Thokoly to overrun northeastern Hungary. Thokoly was declared King of Hungary, as a vassal of the Sultan. Unable to gain concessions from Austria, the Turks prepared for an invasion the following year. Leopold hastily made peace with Thokoly, leaving him virtual master of all Hungary, save for Transylvania.

1683, March 31. Austro-Polish Alliance. Austria and Poland, both at war with Turkey, and aware of Kara Mustafa's forces gathering at Adrianople and Belgrade, became allies in mutual defense against invasion.

Vienna Campaign, 1683

1683, March–May. Turkish Advance. Sultan **Mohammed IV** personally led the Turkish Army from Adrianople toward Belgrade (March 31). Continuing north from Belgrade, under the actual leadership of Kara Mustafa, the Turks were joined by a Transylvanian force under Apafi, bringing their total strength to nearly 200,000 men. Meanwhile, a Hungarian army under Thokoly advanced against the Austrians in Slovakia, but was repulsed at Pressburg.

1683, June. Invasion of Austria. Leaving a force to besiege Gyor, the Turkish Army, now about 150,000 men, continued up the Danube into Austria. Leopold and his court fled to Passau. Duke Charles of Lorraine, with an Austrian army of about 30,000, retreated from Vienna to Linz. Count **Rudiger von Starhemberg,** governor of Vienna, was left with a garrison of about 15,000 men.

1683, July 14. Turks Reach Vienna. Immediate investment of the city began.

1683, July 17–September 12. Siege of Vienna. The Turks were handicapped by insufficient heavy artillery; only a few big guns had been brought up the river by barge. The defending guns were superior in both quality and quantity. The Turks were also hampered by the vigor of the defenders, who made frequent sorties. Meanwhile, Charles of Lorraine kept contact with the defenders via the river, and blocked Turkish raids up the Danube Valley. However, the energetic Turks opened several breaches in the walls and forced their way into portions of the city, where their advance was stopped by hastily erected fortifications (September 1). The defenders by this time had lost about half of their strength and were running short of ammunition and other supplies.

1683, August–September. Arrival of Sobieski. Faithful to his treaty, and also responding to an appeal from the pope, John Sobieski marched to the relief of Vienna with 30,000 men. His main body made the march of 220 miles from Warsaw in 15 days, an unusual speed in those times. The arrival of the Poles and their juncture with the Austrians and Germans west of Vienna completely surprised Kara Mustafa. The allied army advanced on the Turkish camp (September 11).

1683, September 12. Battle of Vienna. Sobieski assumed supreme command of the allied army of 76,000 (his Poles and 46,000 Austrians and Germans). The Poles were on the right wing, the Austrians under Charles of Lorraine on the left, and various German corps in the center. The allies advanced slowly because of difficult terrain; Sobieski planned to attack the next day. Noticing, however, that Turkish resistance was weak, at 5 P.M. he ordered a general attack. At the same time the Vienna garrison attacked the siege lines. For an hour an inconclusive infantry struggle raged between the river and the Turkish camp. Sobieski and his Polish cavalry charged toward Kara Mustafa's headquarters. Kara Mustafa and his army fled in panic; Turkish losses were extremely heavy. Sobieski suspended the pursuit because of fear of ambush in the dark, and the Turkish army escaped destruction. Sobieski sent the captured Imperial Banner of the Prophet to the pope.

1683, September–December. Sobieski's Pursuit. Leopold, jealous of Sobieski's victory, was cool to his savior, who nevertheless led a pursuit of the Turks and helped liberate Grau (October) and much of northwestern Hungary.

Hapsburg Conquest of Hungary, 1683–1688

1684, March 31. Treaty of Linz. At the instigation of Pope **Innocent XI,** a crusading **Holy League** against Turkey was created. Original members were the empire, Poland, and Venice. Moscow later joined (April, 1686).

1684–1685. Inconclusive Frontier Warfare. The Hapsburgs retained the upper hand.

1686, September 2. Capture of Buda. Charles of Lorraine took the Turkish capital of Hungary after a siege of nearly 2 months.

1687. Battle of Nagyharsany (Harkány). Charles decisively defeated the Turks near the site of the Battle of Mohacs (see p. 497), establishing Hapsburg control over all of southern Hungary and much of Transylvania. The Hungarians were forced to accept the Hapsburgs as hereditary monarchs.

1688, September 6. Capture of Belgrade. The stronghold was taken after a siege immortalized by the anonymous alliterative poem which begins: "An Austrian army awfully arrayed/Boldly by battery besieged Belgrade." Most of Serbia was taken by the Austrians.

Turkish Efforts to Reconquer Hungary, 1688–1699

1690. Turkish Invasion of Transylvania. Sultan **Suleiman II,** having nominated Thokoly as Prince of Transylvania after the death of Apafi, sent him into Transylvania. He defeated a combined Hapsburg-Transylvanian army at the **Battle of Zernyest** (August). **Louis of Baden** then marched from Belgrade with the main imperial army, overrunning much of Transylvania, Serbia, and parts of Macedonia.

1690, August–October. Turkish Reconquest of Serbia. The new Turkish Grand Vizier, **Mustafa Koprulu,** took advantage of Louis's expedition to conduct a lightning campaign, recapturing Nish, Smederevo, Vidin, and Belgrade. Thousands of Serbian refugees flocked into southern Hungary.

1691, August 19. Battle of Szalánkemen. Mustafa and Thokoly were decisively defeated by Louis of Baden. Mustafa and 20,000 Turks were killed. Transylvania was now firmly in Hapsburg hands.

1691–1696. Inconclusive Frontier Campaigns.

1697. Battle of Zenta. Prince **Eugene of Savoy** marched to oppose a major Turkish invasion of Hungary from Belgrade under the personal command of Sultan **Mustafa II.** The armies met near the Theiss River; Eugene attacked and practically annihilated the Turkish Army. This was the last serious Turkish threat to Hungary.

1699, January 26. Treaty of Karlowitz. Austria received all of Hungary and Transylvania except the Banat. Venice obtained the Peloponnesus and much of Dalmatia. Poland recovered Podolia. Turkey retained Belgrade. Austria was now the predominant power of Southeastern Europe, despite considerable internal Hungarian unrest and discontent with the Hapsburg monarchy which had been imposed upon her.

EURASIA AND THE MIDDLE EAST

THE OTTOMAN EMPIRE

The slow decline of the Ottoman Empire continued. Yet at midcentury the empire stretched over three continents; the frontier in Europe was only 80 miles from Vienna; it included all of North Africa except Morocco; the Black Sea and the Red Sea were Turkish lakes, and in the east it stretched to the shores of the Caspian and the Persian Gulf. The heart of the empire included the provinces of Rumelia, Anatolia, and the territories along the coasts of the Aegean and the Mediterranean. The Christian principalities of Moldavia, Wallachia, and Transylvania were autonomous; they were administered locally and were not garrisoned by Turkish forces, but their princes were appointed by the Porte and they had to provide corn and sheep for the Turkish army and pay tribute. The Khanate of the Crimea, an autonomous Moslem state, had similar status; the Tartar khans paid no tribute but had to participate in Turkish campaigns with some 20,000 to 30,000 horsemen, and were responsible for defending Ottoman territories against Cossack raids. The Barbary States (Tripoli, Tunis, and Algiers) were more or less independent, having their own military and administrative organization. They pursued their piracy without concern for Ottoman alliances or policies.

The military strength on which the Ottoman Empire depended was deteriorating. The regular army consisted of the Janissaries—originally slaves of the Sultan, but now a privileged social class, recruited from the Moslem population. Lax in their duties and unruly, their popular support precluded disbanding. The spahis and the feudal cavalry were declining both in numbers and in quality. As a result, the Porte was forced to place increasing reliance on Tartar horsemen from the Crimea, on untrained levies, and on undisciplined volunteers.

These factors all contributed to speeding the decline of Turkish power by the end of the century. The principal events were:

1595–1606. War with Austria. So-called Long War (see p. 491).

1602–1612. War with Persia. (See p. 586.)

1603–1606. Revolt of Kurds and Druses. Janbulad, Kurdish governor of Klis, and **Fakhr-ad-Din,** Prince of the Druses, joined in revolutionary alliance. Janbulad was defeated by Ottoman forces and fled to Fakhr-ad-Din in Lebanon. The Druse prince, maintaining himself in his mountainous territory, made a temporary truce with the Porte, and paid tribute.

1603–1617. Reign of Ahmed I (14 Years Old). A period of revolt, turmoil, and discord within the empire.

1606. Treaty of Zsitva-Torok. Peace with Austria, which the Ottomans were forced to recognize as an equal, nontributary power.

1610–1613. Renewed Druse Revolt. Fakhr-ad-Din had plotted with European Christian princes—including the pope and the leaders of the Empire, Spain, and Tuscany—to help them recover the Holy Land. He seized Baalbek and threatened Damascus. Overthrown by a combined Turkish land and sea invasion, he fled to Italy.

1614–1621. War with Poland. (See p. 573.)

1616–1618. War with Persia. (See p. 586.) The Turks lost Azerbaijan and Georgia.

1617–1621. Reign of Osman II.

1621–1622. Janissary Revolt. Osman attempted to reform the Janissaries, but they revolted and overthrew him and put his imbecile brother **Mustafa I** on the throne. Mustafa soon abdicated in favor of Ahmed I's fifth son, **Murad IV.**

1623–1640. Reign of Murad IV. Eleven years old at accession, the first 9 years of his reign were under the regency of his mother, **Kosem Sultan,** while the mutinous Janissaries virtually ruled the country.

1623–1638. War with Persia. (See p. 586).

1631–1635. Renewed Druse Revolt. Fakhr-ad-Din returned from Italy and began fomenting revolt (1618). During the Persian war he gained control of much of Syria, and defeated a Turkish army attempting to go into winter quarters in Syria between campaigns against Persia (1631). Again the Turks mounted a land and sea invasion (1633), and Fakhr-ad-Din's son was defeated and killed in a decisive battle north of Damascus. Fakhr-ad-Din took refuge in the mountains again, but was captured and beheaded in Constantinople (April 13, 1633).

1638–1640. Military Reforms of Murad. Last of the warrior sultans, he was strong enough to initiate long-needed reforms in the Janissary organization. The reforms ended with his death (1640).

1640–1648. Reign of Ibrahim I. Another son of Ahmed, his reign was dominated by strong-willed Kosem Sultan. Turkey's decline continued.

1645–1670. War with Venice over Crete. This resulted from capture of Ibrahim's wives by Maltese corsairs, based on Venetian ports in Crete. A Turkish expedition of 50,000 men aided by the Greek inhabitants, who hated the Venetians, captured Canea (August, 1645) and Retino (1646).

1648–1669. Siege of Candia. The Turks had great difficulty in protecting their supply lines to Crete against the more modern Venetian fleet, which was able to keep Candia supplied and reinforced. Venice also captured Clissa, in Dalmatia, and the islands of Lemnos and Tenedos, blockading the Dardanelles (1648).

1648. Revolt in Constantinople. This was partly stimulated by famine caused by the Venetian blockade. Ibrahim was overthrown and killed. His 7-year-old son **Mohammed IV** was placed on the throne, and Kosem Sultan continued to rule.

1649. First Naval Battle of the Dardanelles. A Turkish fleet, attempting to open the blockade, was defeated by the Venetians.

1651. Death of Kosem Sultan. She was strangled at the instigation of the mother of Mohammed IV, **Turhan Sultan,** who became regent.

1656. Mohammed Koprulu Becomes Grand Vizier. An Albanian pasha, Koprulu was appointed by Turhan Sultan. He halted the decline of the empire by his energy, firmness, and wisdom.

1656. Second Naval Battle of the Dardanelles. Another Venetian victory maintained the blockade. A Venetian fleet briefly threatened Constantinople. This led Koprulu to devote a massive effort to rebuilding the Turkish Navy (1656–1657).

1656–1661. Reorganization of the Ottoman Government. Koprulu succeeded in a major reform of the civil and military sides of the government. He ruthlessly suppressed a revolt and executed all who opposed him. At least 50,000 people were killed, mostly rebels.

1657. Revolt in Transylvania. **(See p. 581.)**

1657. Third Naval Battle of the Dardanelles. The Turks were victorious, then reconquered Tenedos and Lemnos. They then proceeded to take several other Venetian islands in the Aegean (1657–1658). Regaining control of the Aegean, the Turks sent substantial reinforcements to their hard-pressed army on Crete.

1661. Death of Koprulu. He was succeeded as grand vizier by his son, Fazil Ahmed Koprulu.

1662–1664. War with Austria. **(See p. 581.)** Despite Fazil Ahmed's defeat in the Battle of the Raab, he obtained favorable peace terms.

1664–1669. French Operations against the Barbary Pirates. **(See p. 563.)** Because of this involvement against Turkish vassals, the Venetians attempted to persuade France to enter an alliance against the Ottoman Empire. Louis XIV did send a fleet and a force of 7,000 men to Candia (1669).

1666–1669. Turkish Efforts Intensified on Crete. Ahmed went to Crete and assumed command of the siege of Candia.

1669, September 6. Fall of Candia. Seeing defeat inevitable, the French contingent withdrew, and Venetian General **Francesco Morosini** was forced to surrender. In the subsequent treaty, Venice lost all of Crete save for 3 small seaports. Venice also lost most of its Aegean islands and much of Dalmatia to Turkey.

1671–1677. War with Poland over the Ukraine. **(See p. 575.)**

1678–1681. Revolt of the Cossacks and War with Russia. **(See p. 579.)**

1678. Kara Mustafa Becomes Grand Vizier.

1682–1699. War with Austria and Poland and the "Holy League." **(See pp. 576–582.)** The Turkish defeat at Vienna precipitated a series of disasters which eventually caused Turkey to lose all of Hungary.

1687. Turmoil in Constantinople. Following news of the defeat at the **Battle of Nagyharsany** (see p. 583), there was panic in Constantinople; the Janissaries mutinied. **Mohammed IV** abdicated and was succeeded by his brother.

1687–1691. Reign of Suleiman II.

1685–1688. Venetian Offensives. Under Francesco Morosini the Venetians were successful in Dalmatia and southern Greece. He overran the Peloponnesus (1686); advanced through the Isthmus of Corinth; besieged and captured Athens (September, 1687). He later was forced to abandon Athens, but held most of the Peloponnesus.

1690. Mustafa Koprulu Becomes Grand Vizier. Temporarily he stopped the disasters and retook the lost fortress of Belgrade (see p. 583).

1691. Venetian Capture of Chios.

1693. Austrians Repulsed at Belgrade.

1695. Turkish Successes. Chios was recaptured from the Venetians. At the **Battle of Lippa,** Austrian Field Marshal **Friedrich von Veterani** was defeated and killed.

1697, September 11. Battle of Zenta. (See **p. 583.**) Climactic Austrian victory.

1699. Treaty of Karlowitz. (**See p. 583.**)

PERSIA

Under brilliant soldier, statesman, and administrator Shah Abbas, Safawid Persia briefly became the most powerful nation of Southern and Western Asia. His successors, however, soon lost what he had gained from the Turks and Uzbeks, and by the end of the century the Safawid Dynasty was on the verge of collapse. The principal events were:

1587–1629. Reign of Shah Abbas the Great. (See p. 505.)

1602–1612. War with Turkey. Abbas took advantage of Turkish internal troubles and wars in Europe. Marching rapidly from Isfahan (the new Persian capital), his efficient modern army easily defeated local Turkish forces and besieged Tabriz, which capitulated after a long siege (October 21, 1603).

1603–1604. Reconquest of South Caucasus Region. Abbas captured Erivan (after a 6-month siege), Shirvan, and Kars. In little over a year he had regained the territories surrendered to Turkey a decade earlier.

1605–1606. Consolidation and Preparation. While Abbas consolidated his control over the reconquered territories, the Turks, under young and vigorous Sultan Ahmed, prepared to get them back.

1606. Battle of Sis (or Urmia). Ahmed with an army of 100,000 met Abbas with 62,000 near Lake Urmia. The Turks followed their traditional battle plan against the Persians: a meeting engagement of cavalry, designed to draw the essentially cavalry Persian army within range of the guns of Turkish infantry and artillery. Abbas, however, sent a detachment to carry out a demonstration behind the Turks. This caused much of the Turkish army to face to the rear, thinking this the main Persian threat. Then, with his main force of disciplined cavalry, infantry, and artillery, Abbas made his main effort. The Turks were routed, losing more than 20,000 dead. Following this the Persians occupied all of Azerbaijan, Kurdistan, Baghdad, Mosul, and Diarbekh.

1612. Peace with Turkey. Turkey renounced all claim to the conquests of Sultans Murad and Mohammed III. In a face-saving gesture, Abbas agreed to give the Sultan 200 camel loads of silk annually.

1613–1615. Expedition against Georgia. Georgia acknowledged Abbas' suzerainty. This being an area considered in the Ottoman sphere of interest, and since Abbas had made no payment of silk, Turkey prepared for war.

1616–1618. War with Turkey. A powerful Turkish army laid siege to Erivan, but was repulsed. Forced by winter weather to withdraw, the Turks lost heavily from the cold and from Persian harassment (1616–1617). After a year's lull, the Turks again invaded, advancing rapidly on Tabriz. A portion of their army was ambushed by a Persian force and suffered severely, but the main Turkish army continued to advance, at a reduced rate. Peace negotiations opened; the terms of the treaty of 1612 were reaffirmed, save that the silk tribute from Abbas was reduced to 100 camel loads annually.

1622–1623. War with the Mogul Empire. Abbas led an army which captured Kandahar (see p. 587).

1623–1638. War with Turkey. Turkey again invaded the areas lost to Abbas, this time attempting to recapture Baghdad. After a 6-month siege, Abbas arrived with a relieving army (1625). Fierce fighting was inconclusive, until a mutiny forced the Turks to withdraw (1626). They suffered severe losses in their retreat. For several years there were no campaigns of importance, but incessant border warfare. Renewing active warfare, Sultan Murad IV sent an invasion army through Kurdistan (1630). Capturing Mosul en route, the Turks defeated a Persian army, then besieged and captured Hamadan. They continued on to Baghdad, but were repulsed and retreated to Mosul (1630). Internal unrest in Turkey and a series of mutinies in the Turkish Army provided a respite to the Persians (1631–1634). Murad led an invading army in person to capture Erivan and Tabriz (1635). Murad having returned to Constantinople, **Shah Safi** (see below) besieged Erivan and after a long winter siege captured the town (1636). Following another lull, Murad took the field again and, showing great personal energy and skill, assaulted and captured Baghdad (1638). Peace was now made; the Turks kept Baghdad and the Persians kept Erivan.

1629–1642. Reign of Shah Safi (Grandson of Abbas). He was a weak and cruel ruler. He lost Kandahar to the Uzbeks (1630; see p. 591).

1638. War with the Moguls. Shah Jahan's army reconquered Kandahar (see p. 588).

1642–1667. Reign of Shah Abbas II. He halted the decline of the Safawid Dynasty.

1649–1653. War with the Moguls. Abbas personally led the army which recaptured Kandahar (1649). His troops then repulsed Aurangzeb's repeated attempts to reconquer the city (see p. 588).

1659. Revolt in Georgia. Abbas repressed an uprising led by **Tahmurath** Khan.

1664. Cossack Raid into Mazandaran. Instigated by Czar Alexis of Moscow, the Cossacks raided deep into Persia, at the base of the Caspian Sea, but were driven out after causing considerable loss and damage. This was the first Russian aggression against Persia.

1667–1694. Reign of Shah Suleiman. Persia declined rapidly during this drunken reign. The Dutch seized the port of Kishm and the Uzbeks made numerous inroads into Khorasan.

SOUTH ASIA

NORTH INDIA

1605. Death of Akbar. Probably the result of poisoning by his son Salim, who ascended the throne with the title **Jahangir** (1605–1627).

1606. Revolt in the Punjab. Jahangir's example of filial insubordination was followed by his own son **Khusru,** who seized Lahore. Jahangir promptly marched to the Punjab and at **Jallundur** defeated and captured his errant son, whom he caused to be partially blinded and imprisoned.

1607–1612. Rebellion in Bengal. Smoldering Afghan opposition to the Moguls broke into open warfare in Bengal, but was suppressed by Jahangir.

1610–1629. War with Ahmadnagar. During most of his reign Jahangir was involved in a desultory war in the Deccan with Ahmadnagar. Its prime minister and general, an Abyssinian named **Malik Ambar,** realizing that his small forces could not meet those of Jahangir in a pitched battle, resorted successfully to guerrilla tactics.

1622–1623. War with Persia. The Persian Emperor, Shah Abbas, captured Kandahar (1622). Rebellion of Jahangir's second son, **Khurram,** prevented Mogul retaliation.

1623. Khurram's Rebellion. He was defeated at the **Battle of Balochpur,** and fled (1623).

1625. Revolt. This unsuccessful revolt was led by Jahangir's chief general, **Mahabat Khan.**

1627–1658. Reign of Shah Jahan. He was creator of the Taj Mahal, erected as a tomb to his lovely wife, **Mumtaz Mahal.**

1629–1636. Conquest in the Deccan. Shah Jahan renewed his predecessors' efforts to dominate the Deccan. After the death of Malik Ambar, he conquered and annexed Ahmadnagar (1633). Golconda and Bijapur were defeated and forced to acknowledge Mogul sovereignty (1635–1636).

1631–1632. War with the Portuguese. The Portuguese were meddling in Bengal and had also encouraged piracy against all merchant ships but their own. Shah Jahan sent an army which captured the Portuguese fort at Hooghly, in the Ganges-Brahmaputra delta; the defenders were all killed or brought to Agra as captive slaves (1632).

1637–1646. Unrest in the Deccan. The conquered territories were pacified by Shah Jahan's young second son, Aurangzeb.

1638. Recapture of Kandahar from the Persians and Uzbeks. (See p. 591.)

1649–1653. War with Persia over Kandahar. The Persians again seized Kandahar (1649). Three attempts by Aurangzeb to recapture the fortress failed (1650, 1652, 1653).

1653–1658. Revolt in the Deccan. Due to the Maratha Revolt (see below), Jahan sent Aurangzeb back to the Deccan. He reconquered Golconda and Bijapur (1658), but the Maratha leader Sivaji was still unconquered.

1657–1659. War of Succession. The illness of Shah Jahan was followed by an internecine struggle among his 4 sons. Aurangzeb, prevailing after the **Battles of Samugarh** (May, 1658) and **Khajwa** (January, 1659), imprisoned his father in Agra Fort (where he remained, within sight of the Taj Mahal, until his death in 1666).

1658–1707. Reign of Aurangzeb. He crowned himself emperor at Delhi (July, 1658). Soon afterward he conquered Assam (1661–1663) and annexed Chittagong (1666).

1664–1707. Persecution of Non-Moslems. Aurangzeb's revival of persecution and discrimination alienated the Hindu masses and encouraged revolts. The consequent unrest resulted in constant turmoil during most of his long reign.

1675–1681. Rajput Revolt. Aurangzeb's persecution of the Sikhs turned that peace-loving religious group into a community of fanatic warriors dedicated to the destruction of Moslem rule. His policies caused the same reaction among the formerly conciliated Rajputs. Under a popular Mewar leader named **Durgadas,** the Rajputs drove out most of the Mogul garrisons (1675–1679).

1681. Revolt of Akbar. Aurangzeb's son Akbar joined the Rajput rebels, but was defeated by his father and forced to flee to Persia.

1681–1707. Continuing Conflict in Rajputana. This resulted in the elimination from the imperial army of the Rajput cavalry, one of its most effective components. This loss was particularly serious at a time when the empire was becoming engaged in a major military effort in the south.

1681–1689. Renewed War in the Deccan. The continuous exploits and victories of Sivaji and the consequent rise of the Marathas (see below) now caused Aurangzeb to take the field personally with his Grand Army in the Deccan. He overran the Maratha country, captured and executed Sivaji's son **Sambhuji** (1689), and recaptured both Bijapur (1686) and Golconda (1687). The Marathas refused to acknowledge defeat and resorted to protracted guerrilla war, leaving the land unconquered and unconquerable (see p. 589).

1689–1707. The Decline of Aurangzeb. His large empire bankrupt and exhausted, many of his soldiers mutinous, his policy of expansion and conquest unconsolidated, it was only through tremendous personal vitality and will power that Aurangzeb succeeded in holding his realm together until his death.

SOUTH INDIA

1610–1629. Revival of Ahmadnagar. Though nominally the prime minister, the virtual ruler of Ahmadnagar for nearly 2 decades was the Abyssinian General Malik Ambar. He defeated the Moguls, then retained the independence of the nation in a protracted series of partisan wars (see p. 587).

1636. Mogul Reconquest of Ahmadnagar. After the death of Malik Ambar the Moguls reconquered the country.

1646–1680. Rise of the Marathas; Reign of Sivaji. The Marathas, a hardy, frugal Hindu people living generally in arid mountains of the west-central Deccan, east and southeast of modern Bombay, were essentially the descendants of the former Yavada Kingdom of Devagiri; their major employment had been as mercenary soldiers in other states. A growing feeling of religious and national consciousness was sparked into a flame by the rise of the young Yavada Prince **Sivaji.** At the age of 19 he rose against the Moslem principality of Bijapur and established an independent Maratha principality in the western Ghat Mountains.

1646–1664. Expansion of the Marathas. Slowly Sivaji increased his strength and power, initially at the expense of Bijapur, and then through incursions and conquests in the Mogul provinces to the north. He created a navy (1659) which enabled him to carry the war to Mogul lands bordering the Arabian Sea. It proved itself very effective as a bulwark against the Portuguese and English fleets and as a mercantile force trading between India and Arabia.

1664. Sack of Surat. Sivaji captured and sacked the principal Mogul port. Subsequently defeated by a Mogul army under the Rajput **Jai Singh,** he made peace, and was sent to Delhi as a nominal ambassador but virtual prisoner. After more than a year in Delhi, Sivaji made a dramatic escape and returned to the Deccan.

1670–1674. Renewed Maratha-Mogul War. Sivaji was successful and established himself as king of an independent Maratha kingdom.

1674–1680. Expansion of the Maratha Kingdom. A first-rate soldier and able adminstrator, Sivaji continued to gain power and prestige until his untimely death (1680). His military success was due to his use of inaccessible hill forts as bases of operations for guerrilla warfare, and to the exceptional efficiency of the regular army he created, compensating his lack of quantity by quality. Since this arid country could not support such an army, he found provender and the wealth he needed for his military budget by constantly raiding Moslem lands, or receiving "protection" tribute from those who wished to escape his depredations. The Marathas, good horsemen, rode light, devoid of luxuries, heavy baggage, equipment, and tents. In the actual conduct of operations Sivaji followed the traditions of Hindu chivalry in his treatment of defeated enemies and of noncombatants.

1683–1689. Renewed Maratha-Mogul War. **(See p. 588.)**

1689–1707. Resurgence of the Marathas. Slowly the Marathas, in desperate guerrilla warfare, wore down the strength of the Mogul Grand Army. They received an assist from nature when most of the Mogul army was wiped out in a flood of the Bhima River (1695). Aurangzeb returned personally to the field in his old age, but died in Ahmadnagar (1707). Following this, the Grand Army withdrew northward, leaving the Marathas again dominant in the Deccan.

THE EUROPEANS IN INDIA AND THE INDIAN OCEAN

1601–1603. Arrival of the Dutch. Appearance of Dutch ships on the Gujerat and Coromandel coasts ended Portuguese monopoly of Indian overseas trade.

1602. Portuguese Loss of Bahrein. Arab vassals of Persia recaptured the island.

1608. Arrival of the English. William Hawkins of the British East India Company arrived at Surat on the Gujerat coast and tried to gain a trading-concessions treaty with Jahangir.

1612–1630. English-Portuguese Conflict. Trading rights were obtained at Surat when **Thomas Best** defeated a much superior Portuguese fleet (1612). Portuguese hostilities persisted, but Portuguese warships were once again defeated by **Nicholas Dowton** (1614). In following years the Dutch and British East India Companies established trading posts scattered along the coast. The Indians welcomed the newcomers because they envisaged an opportunity to play off the 3 European nations against each other.

1616. England Begins Trade with Persia. The first merchant ship of the East India Company evaded Portuguese warships and arrived at the Persian port of Jask.

1618. English-Portuguese Conflict in the Persian Gulf. A small English squadron, operating from Surat for the purpose of keeping the Persian Gulf open to English trade, defeated a larger Portuguese fleet in two engagements off **Jask.** This gave the English superiority in the Arabian Sea.

1621. English Recognition by the Moguls. Jahangir granted the English additional trade rights, and established the East India Company as a naval auxiliary of the Mogul Empire.

1621–1622. English Capture of Ormuz. An English fleet, cooperating with a Persian land army, captured the major Portuguese base of Ormuz. After this disaster the

Portuguese moved their Persian Gulf base to Muscat.

1624–1630. English-Dutch Cooperation against the Portuguese. A major Portuguese effort to re-establish supremacy in the Indian Ocean caused the English and Dutch to cooperate. After some indecisive actions in the Arabian Sea and Persian Gulf (1624–1625), Portuguese power continued its slow decline. A Portuguese effort to retake Ormuz failed completely (1630).

1640. First Fortified English Post. Fort Saint George (the site of modern Madras) became the company's headquarters on the Coromandel coast.

1641–1663. Dutch Encroachment against the Portuguese. The Dutch attempted to eliminate Portuguese land bases in the Indian Ocean area, capturing Malacca (1641), Colombo (1656), Negapatam (1658), and Cochin (1663). Goa held out against several determined Dutch attacks.

1650. Portuguese Loss of Muscat. The base was captured by the Imam of Oman.

1651. English in Bengal. A post was established at Hooghly. They later decided to fortify in the face of Mogul threats (1681).

1666. Arrival of the French. The French entered the Indian trade later than their Dutch and English rivals, but they established a number of posts, the most important being Chandernagore (1670) on the Ganges delta near Hooghly, and Pondichery (1673) on the Coromandel coast near Fort Saint George.

1667. Establishment of Bombay. The British established a fort and trading post on the island of Bombay.

1686. War in Bengal. Desultory fighting erupted between the British at Hooghly and the Mogul governor of Bengal. This resulted in the building and fortification of Fort William lower down the river (the site of modern Calcutta).

EAST AND CENTRAL ASIA

INNER ASIA

At the outset of the 17th century, Inner Asia was inhabited by 3 major groups of largely nomadic peoples: the Turks, the Mongols and Tartars, and the Tibetans. The 2 most important of the Turkic peoples were the Uzbeks of southern and central Turkestan and the Kazakhs of northern Turkestan. The Uzbeks dominated the Turkoman nomads, who inhabited the desert region between the Caspian and Aral seas, and the Tajiks, who lived in the highlands north of the Hindu Kush Mountains. Most important of the many Mongol tribes were the Khalkas, who lived north of the Gobi Desert; the Kalmucks, who inhabited western Mongolia and the Altai region; and the Kirghiz, who lived in the valleys of the Tien Shan Mountains.

During this century began a process which would, in the following century, completely extinguish the traditional independence of these warlike peoples of Inner Asia. This was the steady expansion of Czarist Russia from the west and of Manchu (or Ch'ing) China from the east. That the Mongols and Turks, traditionally conquerors, should themselves now be conquered was not due to any decline in their warlike proclivities, but rather to the fact that the evolution of the art of war had progressed beyond the capacity of essentially nomadic peoples. Their economic resources would not permit the production or purchase of muskets and cannon, and their cavalry could not stand up to modern musketry and artillery.

For our purposes we shall deal with the principal events of Inner Asia in this century under three headings: the Uzbeks, the Mongols, and Russian expansion. Chinese expansion is dealt with under China.

The Uzbeks

1599. Independence of Bokhara. Bokhara, under the Ashtarkanids, threw off the rule of the decaying Shaibanid Dynasty. Bokhara now again became the principal seat of Uzbek power, but its emirs shared control of southern Turkestan with the khans of Khiva (successors of the Shaibanids).

1608–1646. Reign of Imam Kuli of Bokhara. Bokharan Uzbeks raided occasionally into Persian Khorasan and Afghanistan. Sporadic efforts to conquer the Kirghiz were invariably repulsed by the mountain Mongol tribes.

1630–1634. Conquest of Kandahar. Bokhara seized Kandahar from the Persians, but the Uzbeks were soon driven out by Mogul Shah Jahan (1638; see p. 587).

1688. Conquest of Khiva by the Persians. The Khan of Khiva retained autonomy as a vassal of the Persian Shah.

Mongolia

The innumerable wars between the great Mongol tribal groupings, among the tribes within the groupings, and with the neighboring Tibetans, Chinese, Tartars, Turks, and Russians were too many, and too confused, for simple and concise summarization. During most of this century the Mongols dominated Tibet. The principal events were:

1623–1633. Conquest of Inner Mongolia by the Manchus. (See p. 592.) The Ordos Mongols became virtually assimilated by the Chinese.

1636. Migration of the Western Kalmucks. They fought their way through Kirghiz and Kazakh territory to cross the Emba River. They subsequently settled in the Trans-Volga steppe, raiding Russian settlements on both sides of the river. Submitting to Russia (1646), they maintained autonomy under their own khan. They became an excellent source of light cavalry for the Russians, who later used them in their campaigns against the Krim Tartars and in Central Asia.

1672. Raid of the Torgut Mongols. Ayuka Khan of the Torgut Mongols raided through western Siberia, across the Urals and the Volga, as far as Kazan in Russia. He then made peace with the Russians and, supported by this, was able to maintain his lands in relative peace for the remainder of the century.

c. 1680–1688. Expansion of Galdan's Dzungar Empire. Under the leadership of **Galdan** (Kaldan) Khan (also known as Bushtu Khan), the Dzungars—a subdivision of the Kalmucks inhabiting the region around Lake Balkash—conquered most of Kashgar, Yarkand, and Khotan from the Kirghiz, and also expanded into Kazakh territory.

1688–1689. Galdan Attacks the Khalkas. The Khalka Mongols, hard-pressed by the Dzungars, appealed to the Manchus for aid. A Manchu army helped them.

1689. Congress of Dolonor. (See p. 594.)

1690–1695. Galdan Harasses the Khalkas and the Chinese.

1696. Battle of Chao-Modo (Urga). (See p. 594.)

1697. Death of Galdan. (See p. 594.)

Expansion of Russia into Central Asia

The initial movements of the Russians east of the Urals late in the 16th century had been made in the high latitudes, carefully avoiding the still-formidable Kalmucks who inhabited the region which now comprises central Siberia.

1604. Founding of Tomsk. Russian expansion extended eastward as far as the middle Yenisei River.

1618. Russians Reach the Upper Yenisei. They established the fort of Yaniseisk.

1628. Russians Reach the Middle Lena River.

1630. Founding of Kirensk.

1632. Founding of Yakutsk.

1639. Russians Reach the Sea of Okhotsk. This was their first foothold on the Pacific.

1641–1652. Conquest of the Buryat Mongols. This gave the Russians control of the region around Lake Baikal.

1643–1646. Penetration into the Amur Val-

ley. A Russian expedition from Yakutsk under **Vasily Poyarkov** made the first contact with Chinese civilization.

1644. Russians at the Mouth of the Kolyma River. This brought them to the Arctic Ocean.

1648. Founding of Okhotsk.

1651. Founding of Irkutsk and Khabarovsk.

1651–1653. Occupation of Amur Valley. Yerofey Khabarov established Russian forts in the Amur Valley and in the Daur land to the north.

1653–1685. Clashes with China. The Manchus, relatively uninterested in the Amur Valley, were aroused by Russian persecution of Chinese and Manchu settlers in the region. Occasional Manchu raids made the Russian position precarious.

1660. Manchus Eject the Russians from the Amur Valley. (**See p. 593.**)

1683–1685. War with the Manchus. The Russians were again ejected from the Amur Valley (see p. 593).

1689. Treaty of Nerchinsk. (**See p. 594.**)

CHINA, 1600–1700

1600–1615. Emergence of a Manchu State. Nurhachi erected a 3- or 4-walled fortress in his capital, Liaoyang, and welded the former Ming garrison system (*wei*) into a primitive military and administrative bureaucracy of 4 (later 8) "banners" (1600–1615). Manchu nobles formed an officer corps, usurping the traditional command functions of tribal chieftains. By 1644, the Manchu army included 278 Manchu, 120 Mongol, and 165 Chinese companies, each company (*niru*) consisting of approximately 300 men.

1618. Outbreak of War between Manchus and Mings. Nurhachi's army seized a Ming stronghold at Fushun, then defeated a Ming retaliatory force. The Ming recruited 20,000 Koreans, traditional allies of the Chinese dynasty, to help put down the Manchu revolt.

1621. Capture of Mukden (**Shenyang**). The Manchus drove the Ming from the Liao Basin and attacked Mukden. The city capitulated after Ming troops, dispatched from the garrison to meet Nurhachi's advance, were trapped when traitors within Mukden destroyed the single bridge spanning the fortress moat.

1623. Manchu Advance Halted. Nurhachi was defeated near the **Great Wall** by a Ming provincial governor, **Yuang Ch'ung-huan;** the Ming artillery, provided by European Jesuit missionaries, overpowering the Manchu longbows. The Manchus thereupon turned west and began to expand into Mongolia.

1624–1625. The Dutch Reach Taiwan. They established several posts on Taiwan.

1626. Death of Nurhachi. He was succeeded by his son, **Abahai** (or T'ai Tsung), who immediately augmented the banners.

1627, February. Manchu Invasion of Korea. They crossed the frozen Yalu and subdued the Ming ally prior to invading China.

1628. Manchus Again Repulsed. A renewed effort to invade China was again halted by Yuang with his Ming artillery.

1629–1634. Raids into Northern China. Repeated Manchu raids into northern China through the Jehol Pass were repulsed by the Ming. Manchu forces also raided Shansi Province (1632 and 1634). During this period, Abahai began developing his own highly effective artillery to permit his troops to face the Ming Army in open battle.

1633. Manchu Conquest of Inner Mongolia. This was facilitated by Mongol soldiers defecting to escape harsh conditions in the Mongolian Army. Subsequently, there was large-scale assimilation of Mongol troops into the Manchu banners.

1635–1644. Decline of the Ming. Widespread rebellions throughout China.

1636–1637. Conquest of Korea. Upon the failure of the Koreans to pay tribute and their reluctance to participate in campaigns against the Ming, Abahai led 100,000 Manchus into Korea and compelled a formal renunciation of the Chinese dynasty.

1636–1644. Consolidation of the Amur Basin. In 4 expeditions, Abahai secured control over the entire Amur region.

1636. Establishment of Ch'ing Dynasty. At Mukden, the Manchus proclaimed an imperial dynasty; Abahai took the title of **Ch'ung Teh.**

1643. Death of Abahai. His 5-year-old son, **Shun Chih,** assumed the imperial title. Actual power passed to Abahai's brother, the regent, Prince **Dorgon.**

1643–1661. Reign of Shun Chih. Ming resistance in the south persisted throughout Shun Chih's reign.

1643–1646. Russian Explorations in the Amur Region.

1644, May 26. Collapse of the Ming Dynasty. A rebel brigand, **Li Tzu-ch'eng,** seized Peking. **Wu San-kuei,** a Ming general (and later viceroy), enlisted Manchu aid to overthrow the rebel regime. In a great battle just south of the **Great Wall** the Manchus defeated Li and seized Peking.

1644–1645. Expansion to the Yangtze. Prince **Fu** of the Ming Dynasty set up a new government at Nanking, defying the invaders. Prince Dorgon defeated the Ming Army in a 7-day battle in and around **Yangchow.** A bloody and indiscriminate massacre of the defeated army and the inhabitants followed. Nanking soon fell, with little struggle, and Prince Fu fled into oblivion. Several Ming cousins, however, claimed the imperial throne and continued scattered resistance to the invaders.

1645–1647. Conquest of Fukien. Taking advantage of dissension among the Ming claimants, the Manchus swept through Fukien Province (1645–1646). They next seized Canton (1647). Strong resistance continued, however, in Shensi, Shansi, and Szechwan.

1648–1651. Campaigns of Kuei Wang. Prince **Kuei Wang,** last of the Mings, now became the rallying point for Chinese opposition to the invaders. An able soldier, he briefly controlled most of south China. Dorgon quickly consolidated control of the Yangtze Valley, however, then systematically overran most of south China. Kuei Wang fled to the mountainous southwest, where he briefly retained control of Kweichow and Yunnan.

1651–1659. Conquest of the Southwest. Despite desperate resistance and difficulties of terrain, the Manchus established control over most of the southwest, although they were unable to capture Kuei Wang before his death (1662).

1652–1662. War against the Pirates. A family of pirates, whose most renowned member was **Cheng Ch'eng-kung** (known to Europeans as **Koxinga**), conducted incessant warfare on behalf of the Ming against both Manchus and Europeans in China. Koxinga captured Amoy (1653) and Ch'ung-ming Island (1656) and unsuccessfully assaulted Nanking (1657). He attacked Taiwan with 900 vessels and besieged Fort Zelanda (at Anping), compelling the Dutch to capitulate (1661–1662). The Ch'ing Dynasty evacuated 6 coastal provinces and installed their inhabitants behind a guarded barrier some 10 miles from the sea (1661). Pirate power faded, however, after Koxinga's death (1662).

1659–1683. Manchu Consolidation. The conquerors strengthened the garrison at Peking, surrounding it with about 25 smaller posts, and established stout garrisons in 9 provincial capitals and at other strategic sites. "Tartar generals" (*chiang-chun*) and Manchu brigade generals commanded these fortifications on a rotational basis. Local police operations in 14 provinces were conducted by the Chinese Army of the Green Standard under Chinese officers.

1660. Clash with the Russians. Manchu troops forced the Russians to evacuate their posts in the Amur and lower Sungari River regions.

1662–1722. Reign of K'ang-hsi. The height of modern Chinese culture and glory.

1663–1664. Dutch Operations against the Pirates. With Manchu support, a Dutch fleet forced **Cheng Chin,** Koxinga's son, to retire from his Fukien coastal stronghold to Taiwan.

1674–1681. Revolt of the Three Viceroys. K'ang-hsi, wary of the growing power of the governors (or viceroys) of Yunnan, Fukien, and Kiangsi, decreed their removal (1673). Wu San-kuei of Yunnan (the former Ming general) resisted the imperial decree and held Szechuan, Kweichow, Hunan, and Kwangsi (1674–1679). He was joined in revolt by the other 2 governors. Ultimately the uprising was quelled.

1675. Revolt in Chahar. Suppressed by the Manchus.

1683. Taiwan Annexed. Cheng K'e-shuang, the son and successor of Cheng Chin, surrendered Taiwan to the Manchus.

1683–1685. Clash with the Russians. The Russians had re-established themselves securely in the Amur Valley (1670) while the Manchus were engaged in suppressing the revolt in southern China. A Manchu military commission studied the Russian penetration (1682) and concluded that about 2,000 troops would be required to counter the advance; 1,500 were dispatched to the Zeya River (1683). The following year the Russians were expelled from the lower Sungari area. A Manchu army then marched on the Russian stronghold at Albasin and forced the garrison to surrender (1685). When the Manchus withdrew, however, later that year, another Russian contingent reconstructed the fortifications. The Manchus began to prepare for a more extensive war.

1689, August. Treaty of Nerchinsk. Distracted by events in Russia and Europe (see p. 580), Peter the Great was anxious to resolve the Albasin dispute by pacific means. Chinese war preparations and the skillful diplomacy of Jean François Gerbillon, a Jesuit member of the Manchu delegation, caused the Russians, led by **Fyodor Golovin,** to compromise their original rigid demands and to abandon Albasin and the area north of the Amur River. The terms of the Treaty of Nerchinsk, supplemented by the primarily commercial **Treaty of Kiakhta** (1727), regulated Russian-Chinese relations for 175 years.

1688–1689. Dzungar Raids into Mongolia. (**See p. 591.**)

1689. Congress of Dolonor. The Mongols formally accepted Manchu suzerainty. Prolonged resistance of elements of the Khalka and Kalmuck tribes continued, but K'ang-hsi's operations in the Gobi finally prevailed (1721).

1696. War in the Ili Valley and Turkestan. After 5 years of desultory raiding by the Dzungars into central Mongolia, K'ang-hsi led 7 columns of 80,000 troops across Mongolia and, with the decisive use of the Manchu artillery, crushed Galdan at **Chao-Modo** (Urga). The Dzungar leader fled and committed suicide (1697). Mongol bands continued to wage sporadic war in the northwest.

JAPAN, 1600–1700

Within 2 years of the death of Hideyoshi (1598), the joint regency of his most powerful vassals had disintegrated into a struggle for supremacy between Ieyasu and the combined forces of Ishida, Uesugi, Mori, Ukita, Konishi, and Shimazu.

1600, October 21. Battle of Sekigahara (Barrier Field). Ieyasu's 70,000 troops decisively defeated a coalition force of 120,000, torn by internal dissension. About 40,000 confederates were reportedly killed. This victory, and Mori's subsequent surrender of Osaka Castle, enabled Ieyasu to consolidate control over Honshu.

1603. Ieyasu Proclaimed Shogun. The capital was established at Edo (Tokyo). His Tokugawa Shogunate was to rule Japan until the second half of the 19th century.

1606–1614. Tokugawa Exclusion Policy. Fear of the political objectives of missionary activities—and of possible intervention of Spain and Portugal in a violent Franciscan-Jesuit controversy—led to the wide-scale deportation of European priests. Persecution of Christians was intensified under **Iyemitsu** (1623–1651).

1609, June. Sinking of the Madre de Dios. Following a Japanese-Portuguese flare-up at Macao, Ieyasu ordered seizure of a Portuguese merchant ship, the *Madre de Dios,* moored in Nagasaki Harbor. A Japanese fleet, carrying over 1,200 troops, surrounded the vessel. After 3 days of combat, the Portuguese captain, **Pessoa,** blew up his ship, its crew, many of his assailants, and over 1 million crowns' worth of cargo.

1614, December–1615, June. Siege of Osaka Castle. Hideyoshi's son, **Hideyori,** had retired to Osaka Castle after the Battle of Sekigahara. During the first decade of the Tokugawa Shogunate, the castle became the center of potential resistance as some 90,000 alienated warriors (*ronin*) gathered at Osaka. A siege of the castle, conducted by Edo forces between December and January, was terminated by a truce. This respite enabled the besieging force to fill the outer moats and, in the following June, to successfully storm the stronghold.

1616, June 1. Death of Ieyasu. He was succeeded by his son, **Hidetada** (1616–1623).

1623–1651. Shogunate of Iyemitsu.

1624. Japanese Isolation Policy. Following the voluntary withdrawal of English traders (1623), the Spanish were forcibly driven from Japan. The shogun ordered the destruction of all large Japanese vessels in order to prevent the mass embarkation of any disaffected subjects.

1637–1638, April 12. Shimabara Revolt. Christianized peasants on the Shimabara peninsula and Amakusa Islands rose against the oppressive religious and agrarian practices of the Tokugawa regime. Between 20,000 and 37,000 insurgents gathered at the ancient fortress of Hara; for nearly 3 months they were besieged by 100,000 Edo troops supported by a Dutch man-of-war dispatched from Hirado. Exhaustion of supplies and ammunition compelled the insurgents to capitulate; most were massacred.

1637–1638. Exclusion Edict. Iyemitsu, suspecting that Portuguese traders had encouraged the insurgents, demanded their expulsion from Japan. Only 2 foreign settlements and trade outposts remained in Japan: the Dutch outpost at Hirado and the Chinese at Nagasaki.

1651–1680. Shogunate of Ietsune. Two attempted coups, the last until the 19th century, were readily suppressed at Edo (1651–1652).

1653–1700. Internal Peace in Japan.

KOREA

1606. Peace with Japan. Good relations were restored after the Tokugawa shoguns came to power (1600) and lasted without a break until the second half of the 19th century.

1624. Military Uprising. This was caused by renewed factional dispute in Korea. It swept the northern half of the peninsula before it was suppressed.

1627–1637. Wars with the Manchus. The Koreans, as vassals of the Ming, became involved in the wars with the rising Manchu power on the northern frontiers of Korea (see p. 592).

c. 1630. The Hermit Kingdom. A policy of national seclusion was introduced. Although the Yi Dynasty maintained its traditional tributary relationship with Manchu China, Korea, become known as the Hermit Kingdom, stagnated.

1650–1700. Internal Factional Strife.

SOUTHEAST ASIA

BURMA

1600. Destruction of Pegu. As a result of the incursions of Arakan, Ayuthia, and Toungoo (see p. 514), Burma was broken up into several small states.

1601–1605. Revival of Burma. The **Nyaungyan** Prince, descendant of the old royal family, held Ava. He embarked on a series of campaigns to re-establish authority in Upper Burma and the Shan States.

1602. Arrival of the Portuguese. Philip de Brito established a base at Syriam.

1605–1628. Reign of Anaukpetlun. Son of the Nyaungyan Prince, Anaukpetlun reconquered much of south Burma. He took Prome (1607) and Toungoo (1610).

1613. Conquest of Syriam. Anaukpetlun captured the Portuguese base; de Brito was impaled.

1613–1614. Repulse from Tenasserim. Anaukpetlun was driven out by Siamese and Portuguese forces.

1628. Murder of Anaukpetlun. A brief civil war followed.

1629–1648. Reign of Thalun. He transferred the capital from Pegu to Ava.

1648–1661. Reign of Pindale.

1658–1661. War with China. Prince **Yung Li,** last of the Mings, fled from Yunnan to Burma after defeat by the Manchus (1658). Pindale gave political asylum to the prince in Sagaing, and for 3 years was harassed by repeated raids of Ming supporters in Upper Burma.

1660–1662. War with Siam. (See p. 596.)

1661–1672. Reign of Pye (Brother and Murderer of Pindale). At the outset Pye was confronted by a Manchu army of 20,000 men and was forced to surrender the Ming prince (1662).

SIAM

1600, May. Repulse from Toungoo. King **Naresuen** returned to Siam, leaving Burma in a state of chaos (see p. 514).

1603–1618. Expedition to Cambodia. Prince **Srisup'anma,** accompanied by an army of 6,000 men, became King of Cambodia as a vassal of Siam.

1604–1605. Naresuen's Last Campaign.

Naresuen went north with a large army to meet the Nyaungyan Prince of Burma, who was attempting to reconquer the Shan States. Naresuen fell ill and died. His successors abandoned the effort, and the Shan States returned to Burmese domination.

1610–1628. Reign of Songt'am the Just. He suppressed an insurrection incited by Japanese traders (1610). He then turned to defeat a simultaneous invasion from Laos.

1612. Portuguese-Siamese Dispute. The Siamese governor of Pegu and Philip de Brito quarreled over their alliance against Toungoo and withdrew their support from each other. As a result de Brito and Syriam fell to Anaukpetlun (see p. 595) and Siam lost most of its Peguan possessions.

1614. Repulse of Burmese. Siamese forces, aided by Portuguese mercenaries, defended Tenasserim against Anaukpetlun's invasion (see p. 595).

1618. Truce between Burma and Siam.

1622. War with Cambodia. Srisup'anma died and his successor proclaimed Cambodia independent. Songt'am invaded Cambodia by land and by sea. The Siamese fleet returned to Siam without seeing any action, but the Siamese army suffered heavy losses in men, horses, and elephants, and withdrew.

1630–1656. Reign of Prasat T'ong. He was a usurper who soon established friendly relations with the Dutch, who were given special trading privileges.

1634–1636. Rebellion of the Patani. This state, in the lower Malay Peninsula, refused to recognize Prasat T'ong. Two Siamese expeditions to Patani were total failures, and Patani became virtually independent.

1657–1688. Reign of Narai.

1660–1662. Campaigns around Chiengmai. King Narai, taking advantage of Burma's preoccupation with the Ming raiders, marched upon Chiengmai. After one repulse (1660), another effort was made, capturing Chiengmai (1662, March).

1662. Repulse of Burmese. The Mons, who were rebelling against the Burmese and fleeing into Siam, called on King Narai to protect them from pursuing Burmese troops. Narai repulsed the pursuers, then undertook a series of punitive raids into Lower Burma (see p. 595).

1687, August. War against the British East India Company. This followed a series of disputes with the British and the Dutch. The French East India Company supported Narai, sending a force of some 600 men to help man coastal forts. The French soon were at odds with the Siamese.

1688–1703. Reign of P'ra P'etraja. He reached understandings with both the English and French. The reign was plagued by serious internal rebellions in the provinces.

LAOS

1624–1637. War of Succession. Finally ended when **Souligna-Vongsa** defeated 4 rivals.

1637–1694. Reign of Souligna-Vongsa.

1651–1652. War with Tran Ninn. Souligna, denied the hand of the daughter of the king of Tran Ninn (a small state between Annam and Laos), sent a military force to bring back the princess. After an initial repulse Xieng-Khouang, capital of Tran Ninn, was captured and the princess seized.

1694–1700. Turmoil in Laos. Three-way struggle for the throne.

VIETNAM

While the Le Dynasty was recognized as the only legitimate ruling force in Vietnam, rivalry and partition between the Trinh family (north) and the Nguyen family (south) led to seven campaigns. The Trinh had an army and fleet of 100,000 men, 500 elephants, 500 large junks, and cannons. The Nguyen had numerically inferior forces, but as early as 1615 had been producing heavy guns under Portuguese auspices. The shipments of modern weapons from Portugal and the Portuguese military advisers enabled the Nguyen to successfully resist the Trinh offensive. The Nguyen reinforced their natural defenses by constructing 2 huge walls across the main avenues of approach, north of Hué. The Truong-duc wall was 6 miles long, contained a camp for troops, and was an obstacle for passage up the Nhat-Le River. The Dong-hoi wall was 11 miles long and fortified with heavy cannons. In over 50 years of fighting, the Trinh never managed to break through both of these walls. The Nguyen also began constructing arsenals, cannon foundries, rifle ranges, and training grounds for infantry, cavalry, and elephants (1631). The battles generally took place south of Ha-Tinh and north of Hué, or in the wall region of Dong-hoi. The principal encounters were:

1633. Naval Battle of Nhat-Le. The Nguyen defeated the Trinh fleet.

1642–1643. Expeditions of Trinh-Trang. He and his Dutch allies were defeated on land and sea by the Nguyen.

1648. Battle of Truong-duc. The Trinh were repulsed with heavy losses at the wall.

1658–1660. Nguyen Offensives. There followed 2 years of inconclusive attacks and counterattacks.

1673. Peace. After the sixth and seventh campaigns, the Linh River was recognized as the boundary line between the 2 territories.

CAMBODIA

1603–1618. Reign of Srisup'anma. (**See p. 595.**) He was a puppet of Naresuen of Siam.

1618. Accession of Jai Jett'a (Son of Srisup'anma). He proclaimed Cambodia to be independent of Siam.

1622. Siamese Invasion. (**See p. 596.**) This was repulsed.

1679. War of Succession. Sri Jai Jett'a's accession to the throne was disputed by **Nak Norr.** With assistance of Narai of Siam, Sri Jai Jett'a defeated Nak Norr, who fled.

MALAYA AND INDONESIA

1600–1641. Three-Way War. Bickering between the Achenese, the Sultan of Johore, and the Portuguese.

1606–1607. Dutch Repulsed from Malacca. Despite this failure, the Dutch did succeed in ousting the Portuguese from the Spice Islands of east Indonesia and strangling their trade in the Straits by cutting off Malacca from the main sea routes.

1607. Portuguese Repulsed from Johore.

1607–1629. Rise and Expansion of Acheh. A new ruler, **Iskandar** Shah (1607–1636) controlled most of Sumatra and several mainland territories.

1613–1615. Achenese Sackings of Johore.

1616. Acheh and Johore Repulsed from Malacca.

1629. Naval Battle of Malacca. The Achenese were defeated by combined fleets of Portugal, Johore, and Patani. Decline of Acheh begins.

1637. Alliance of Johore with the Dutch.

1640–1641. Dutch Capture of Malacca. The Malaccan fortress **A Famosa** had walls 32 feet high, 24 feet thick. It was garrisoned by 260 Portuguese and 2,000 or 3,000 Asiatics. The Dutch, aided by Johore's fleet, blockaded the port (June, 1640). The siege began in August. A Famosa did not surrender until January, 1641, after an estimated 7,000 had died in battle or by sickness and famine. The Dutch, establishing a garrison at Malacca, enforced their trade monopoly of the Straits.

1666–1689. War between Johore and Jambi. Johore's power was reduced.

1681. Arrival of the Bugis. The Bugis came from Celebes as a result of their growing maritime strength and the benefits of an alliance with the Dutch. A warlike people, using chain armor, they gained a reputation as sea fighters—invincible on sea and on land. They were primarily river pirates, mercenaries, and homeless adventurers whose presence was disturbing to the Malays.

AFRICA

NORTH AFRICA

All 4 of the North African nations supported themselves largely by piracy and the slave trade. The Barbary pirates became the terror of European mariners; their galleys and sailing vessels ranged over much of the Mediterranean and the eastern Atlantic Ocean. The Moroccans and Algerians, and to a lesser extent the Tunisians, also sent raiding parties across the Sahara to capture slaves from the Negro nations to the south. During this period Tripoli was more directly controlled by Turkey than were Algeria and Tunis.

Morocco

1608–1628. Reign of Sultan Zidan. The decline of the Sa'ad Dynasty began.

1618. Abandonment of Timbuktu. Expense in man power and other resources in retaining control of the sub-Saharan colony did not bring any real financial return to Morocco. Zidan wisely withdrew his forces; Moroccan colonists remained, however (see below). Slave raiding continued.

c. 1645–1668. Civil War. The Hassani Berber tribes, living on the edge of the desert, rose against the Sa'adis.

1649. Hassani Capture of Fez. Mohammed XIV established the Hassani Dynasty, still ruling in Morocco. It was almost 2 decades before the conquest was completed by the Hassani capture of Marrakech (1668).

1662. Portugal Cedes Tangier to Britain.

1668–1672. Consolidation. This was done by **Rashid II.**

1672–1727. Reign of Sultan Mulay Ismail. Known as "the Bloodthirsty." The relatively stable history of Morocco during this and subsequent reigns was due to his creation of a special Negro bodyguard, the Bukharis, who were, in effect, a small and efficient standing army. Tied to the Sultan by religious oaths and his paternal care, they not only protected the royal person and palace but also were rotated on garrison duty at forts scattered throughout the empire.

1684. British Abandon Tangier to Morocco.

Algeria

Algeria, nominally ruled by the Ottomans, was in fact almost completely independent by the close of the century. The autonomous coastal towns and the central government at Algiers lived mainly on the proceeds of piratical plunder. During the latter part of the century, the ruling deys established a licensing system for all Algerian pirates whereby the dey was paid a percentage of all loot and ransom money. Toward the end of the century, more or less successful French punitive expeditions against the Barbary pirates forced the deys of Algiers to release their Christian slaves (1684–1688).

Tunis

During the early years of the century, the deys of Tunis were elected by Ottoman Janissaries, who at first were an army of occupation. The beys, originally administrative subordinates of the ruling deys, and responsible for administering the inland tribes, became increasingly powerful in Tunis toward midcentury.

1650. Ali Bey Ruler of Tunis. The deys were supplanted.

1655. Blake's Expedition against Porto Farina. English Admiral Blake bombarded the corsair base, destroying many of the pirate vessels and the coastal fortifications.

WEST AFRICA

In the interior savannah region, south of the Sahara and north of the tropical rain-forest belt, there was a more or less continuous struggle between Negro and Arab-Negro nomadic kingdoms and empires—some Moslem, some pagan. Along the narrow coastal ledge, the European colonial powers fought each other for bases and favored positions in the growing and profitable slave trade. In between were the jungle peoples, generally more fragmented and less land-hungry than their nomadic neighbors to the north and northeast, but less easily exploited by European slave traders than were the relatively docile tribes along the narrow coastal lowlands. The principal events were:

1591–1618. Moroccan Wars. The Moroccan conquerors of Timbuktu (see p. 517) spread their control gradually into the old Songhoi and Hausa empires, but with difficulty and at great cost.

1600–1700. Rise of the Ashanti Union. The Akan people, in various tribal groupings, having migrated from the west, settled in the jungle region west of the Volta and formed a loose confederation for defensive purposes. During the century they gradually expanded and increased their power in the Volta basin and farther west, coming in contact inland with the nomads and along the coast with the Europeans.

1618–1660. Turmoil in the Old Songhoi Empire. Official withdrawal of the Moroccans (see above) left control of Timbuctoo and the neighboring region in the hands of various pashas, mostly of Moroccan descent, who paid nominal allegiance to Morocco. Under pressure from the neighboring Negro and Negro-Arab peoples, and particularly the briefly resurgent Songhois, the Moorish colonials were confined to a decreasing area around Timbuctoo itself.

c. 1620–1654. Dutch-Portuguese Wars. The growing maritime power of the Netherlands began to take advantage of the earlier incorporation of Portugal into Spain (see p. 572) to raid and capture Portuguese bases on both sides of the Atlantic. Although the Dutch abandoned the initiative after the independence of Portugal (1640; see p. 572), the Portuguese continued the conflict for several more years until they had recovered a number of their lost bases.

1621. Dutch Seizure of the Portuguese Bases of Arguin and Goree.

1626. Establishment of St. Louis. This was the first French base at the mouth of the Senegal River.

1631. Establishment of Kormantine. This was the first English base on the African coast.

1637–1645. Portuguese-Dutch Conflicts. The Dutch seized Elmina from Portugal. In retaliation the Portuguese reconquered São Thome and Loanda from the Dutch (1640–1648), while the Dutch seized St. Helena (1645).

1660. Rise of the Bambara Kingdoms. The Negro nomadic states of Segu and Kaarta on the upper Niger began to expand into the vacuum left by the decay of the Mali, Songhoi, and Moroccan empires.

1662. British Base at the Mouth of the Gambia River.

1664–1665. Anglo-Dutch War. The British took Cape Coast Castle (10 miles from Elmina) from the Dutch (1664). Next year they took St. Helena from the Dutch, who captured Kormantine from the British (1665).

1670. Defeat of Mandingo and Timbuktu by the Bambaras. The remnants of the old Mali and Moroccan empires became tributary to Segu and Kaarta.

1677. French Capture Arguin and Goree from the Dutch. Goree became the main French base on the West African coast.

1697. French Begin Expansion up the Senegal River.

EAST AFRICA

While Bantu tribes, migrating from the north and west, broke up the old Monomotopa Empire and simultaneously disrupted the neighboring Portuguese coastal possessions, the Portuguese found themselves facing a more lasting threat from the north. During most of this century the Portuguese and the Omanis from Arabia struggled bitterly for control of the entire western coast of the Indian Ocean, its raw-materials resources, and the even more valuable African slave trade with Asia. The principal events were:

1590–1620. Turmoil in the Monomotopa Empire. The Sotho and Ngoni Bantu tribes completely broke up the empire and left it in chaos as they continued their great migration southward to and across the Limpopo River (see below).

1622–1650. Omani Conquest of the Northeastern Coast. Taking advantage of Portugal's decline under Spanish rule, the sultans of Oman evicted the Portuguese from their coastal bases north of Mozambique, gaining tenuous control of the entire littoral.

1626. First French Settlements on Madagascar.

1633. Expulsion of the Portuguese from Abyssinia. European penetration and influence were checked for nearly a century.

1643. The French Settle Réunion Island.

1650–1750. Coastal War of Portugal and Oman. Portugal, somewhat resurgent after independence from Spain, began to carry the war against the Arabs back northward along the coast. The Portuguese regained some of their bases, but reached the effective limit of their power when they were repulsed from Mombasa (1728–1730).

1686. French Annexation of Madagascar. Proclaimed by Louis XIV. They did not exercise any effective control over the vast island.

1699. French Embassy to Abyssinia. The French arrived at Gondar via Cairo and the Nile.

SOUTH AFRICA

South Africa, inhabited by the primitive Hottentots and Bushmen, was the scene of near-simultaneous migrations from the north and the south. Overland from the north came warlike Bantu Negro tribes. By sea, to the southern tip of the continent, came Dutch colonists. The migrating races, unaware of their approaching historic confrontation, did not come into any substantial contact during this century.

c. 1620. Arrival of the Bantus in South Africa. Fresh from the turmoil they had created in East Africa (see above), the Sotho and Ngoni tribes crossed the Limpopo River and spread slowly southward.

1652, April 6. Arrival of the Dutch. Colonists in 3 ships, under **Jan van Riebeeck,** arrived at the site of modern Capetown, and established the first European settlement in South Africa.

1652–1700. Dutch Expansion Inland. By the end of the century, Dutch settlers had established themselves more than 250 miles inland.

1658. Arrival of the First Slaves at the Cape.

1686. Dutch Coastal Expansion. They reached Mossel Bay. Intermittent conflict began with the Bushmen.

1688. Arrival of Huguenot Refugees at the Cape.

THE AMERICAS

During the early 17th century, the increasingly competitive commercial and colonial activities of European states in North and South America, and their challenge to the native Indians, led to frequent conflicts which, in some localities, were incessant. The very process of colonization and combat between the colonial powers on the American continents often was a reflex or phase of European strife. Thus, **Jean de Ribaut**'s attempt to establish a colony in Florida (1562) had been an element in Admiral Coligny's projected attack on Spain (see p. 477). At times, European forces enlisted Indian support in their campaigns (for example, the French counterattack on Spanish-held St. Augustine, August 22, 1567–June 2, 1568; see p. 521). Expeditions conducted ostensibly for pacific purposes of exploration, colonization, and commerce often employed military means or sought military ends. These had been initiated by Drake's circumnavigation (1577–1580), which constituted a sustained assault upon Spanish shipping (see p. 465), and by Sir Walter Raleigh's expedition of 1584, which served both to explore the mainland and to reconnoiter Spain's Caribbean defenses (see p. 518).

INDIAN WARFARE

The character and duration of warfare between Indians and Europeans varied according to region. At the time of the first European settlements in the Americas, there were some 16 million native inhabitants scattered from Hudson Bay to Cape Horn, comprising a vast array of tribes, cultures, and military attitudes, practices, and values. By far the most civilized, and possessing the most advanced military techniques, had been the Mexican tribes (particularly the Aztecs) and the Incas of Peru. As we have seen, these were smashed by the Spanish in the 16th century (see p. 520). In North America the Iroquois confederacy constituted a remarkably civilized form of politico-military organization. Similarly, Iroquois linear and assault tactics proved relatively sophisticated.

Lack of discipline and cohesiveness, far more than crudity of weapons, put the Indians at great disadvantage in opposing the Europeans, although a long series of successful raids and massacres testify to some degree of adroitness and, perhaps more significantly, colonial unpreparedness. Several tribes proved invaluable allies (for example, Mohawk intervention in the Dutch-Algonquin conflict of 1645) and some became tenacious enemies, as the French discovered after Champlain's folly in firing upon a band of Iroquois in 1609. However, from the first, Indian prospects were doomed; increasingly effective European weapons, the curious reluctance of the Indians to exploit tactical victories, and an inability to cope with the fundamental problem of supply proved fatal.

GENERAL COLONIAL MILITARY EXPERIENCE

The British home government, like the French, afforded its North American colonies scant military assistance, whether in money, supplies, or men. For example, New York was the only colony to house British troops regularly throughout the period of British suzerainty. Similarly, at no point did the French post large regular forces in Canada (estimates vary from between 2,000 and 5,000); a request for reinforcements during a Seneca uprising (1686) merely brought an admonition from Paris that peace was desirable. The Spanish military establishment, also operating with small numbers in the Americas, attempted to shield the sprawling empire; thus, with Spanish troops already stationed in Cuba, Mexico, and Peru, 2 companies totaling 280 men were dispatched to the stone fort at St. Augustine (1672) to hold Florida. However, as piracy and marauding intensified, the inadequacy of numbers in the face of such extensive geographic demands became apparent (see p. 521).

The initial reluctance of the colonial powers to provide aid is understandable when one considers (1) the potentially enormous economic drain (the colonies expended over £90,000 in King Philip's War, a considerable sum in the 17th century), (2) crucial commitments in Europe, (3) the distraction of domestic discord (for instance, the English Civil War and the French Fronde), and (4) the relative autonomy of the colonizing companies. This philosophy of colonial self-sufficiency was articulated explicitly in a later British declaration (1742), cautioning the colonies that they must bear the responsibility for their own defense.

Confronted with what Burke labeled "salutary neglect," the early settlers developed militia in accordance with familiar European models. In the British colonies, the tradition of the citizen-soldier was transplanted from England as early as 1638; in 1643, Massachusetts instituted a compulsory policy requiring 4 to 6 days of military training for all males (with the exception of doctors, ministers, educators, the Harvard student body, and other peripheral groups). The other British colonies, except Pennsylvania, followed suit, creating forces whose composition was usually one-third pikemen and two-thirds musketeers. As the pike proved itself inapplicable to combat in the wilderness, the pikemen became musketeers. The colonial militia was characterized by the absence of a staff hierarchy. Generally, the governor assumed military command (although in Massachusetts, the sergeant major general performed the function). Lack of intercolonial military coordination was one of the most critical problems facing the English colonies. The failure of effective cooperation was exposed in the Pequot War; an attempt to rectify it by the creation of a New England Confederation proved futile. Furthermore, there was the inherited English distrust of a standing and powerful military establishment as a threat to civil institutions. This fear was expressed as early as 1638 at the formation of the Ancient and Honorable Artillery Company.

The fascinating problem of the adaptability of European concepts of war to American conditions recurs throughout early colonial history. For example, although dense forest growth undermined the utility of cavalry, it remained the most prestigious branch of the New England militia. Between 1607 and 1689, the need to adapt and modify at times served as a catalyst to improvement of weapons. Thus the inadequacies of the matchlock were underscored in the North American setting and the flintlock was adopted extensively before it was in general use by European armies. By 1650, European armor, although effective against Indian projectiles, had been largely abandoned (first in New England, in the course of the Pequot War, and later in Virginia) and replaced by lighter and less cumbersome protective garb of cloth and leather.

By the time of the first major clashes between European forces in North America, much of the wilderness in the British New England, Middle Atlantic, and Southern colonies had been at least partially subdued, and physical conditions more closely approximated those of Europe. After the 1680's, and into the 18th century, only minor military improvements were made as a result of the colonial experience; the muzzle-loading, smoothbore musket and pistol reigned for nearly a century, colonial units clinging to European traditions.

BRITISH AMERICA

Virginia and Maryland

1607. The First Colony. A London Company expedition settled at Jamestown.

1622, March 22. Indian Massacre at Jamestown. This led to reprisals by the colonists.

1635–1644. Intermittent Warfare between Virginia and Maryland. William Claiborne, secretary of the Virginia colony, established a trade post on Kent Island, a parcel included in the Maryland tract granted to the first Lord Baltimore. His refusal to acknowledge the legitimacy of the second **Lord Baltimore**'s proprietary claim led to intermittent hostilities, supported in the Council of Virginia, and strained his relations with **Leonard Calvert,** brother of Lord Baltimore and the first governor of the colony. Clashes occurred at sea (1635). Claiborne's unsuccessful appeal to the crown was followed by his seizure of Kent Island (1644).

1644–1646. Religious War in Maryland. A Protestant trader, **Richard Ingle,** captured the predominantly Catholic settlement of St. Mary's. Governor Calvert fled to Virginia; enlisted the aid of Sir **William Berkeley,** governor of Virginia; and recaptured the settlement.

1649–1689. The Civil Wars and Glorious Revolution. Both colonies suffered considerable unrest during this period of strife and turmoil in the mother country.

1675–1676. Indian Depredations. Susquehannock warriors crossed the Potomac into Virginia, conducted a series of raids, and repulsed a joint Maryland and Virginia retaliatory force at Piscataway Creek. The raids were intensified, resulting in the abandonment of frontier homes. Critics of Berkeley attacked his refusal to dispatch a punitive force, alleging a personal interest in the preservation of the fur trade.

1676, May 10–December. Bacon's Rebellion. Nathaniel Bacon, a civilian, disgusted with Berkeley's inaction, led a force to the Roanoke River and destroyed a band of Susquehannocks. He was declared a traitor, arrested, and eventually pardoned by Berkeley. Bacon then marched on Jamestown with a force of 500 men and secured a commission. Again he was declared a traitor. Failing to consolidate military support, Berkeley fled. On September 18, the insurgents ousted Berkeley's troops from Jamestown and burned the settlement. One month later Bacon died of malaria. His sudden death fragmented his following; during November and December, rebel groups were captured or chose to surrender in response to a promise of amnesty. The subsequent execution of 23 insurgents elicited royal censure of Berkeley.

New England

1620. Colony Established at Plymouth.

1633. English and Dutch Claims in the Connecticut Valley. Following exploration of the Connecticut Valley by **Edward Winslow** of Plymouth, the Dutch claimed the region and sent a ship up the Connecticut River. A Dutch fort and trading post were erected at Fort Good Hope (Hartford).

1636, July 30–1637, July 28. Pequot War. The murder of a trader by the Pequots called forth retaliation by the colonists and, in turn, reprisals by the Indians. A Connecticut band destroyed the major Pequot base near Stonington (May 26). On July 28, near New Haven, a force composed of contingents from Plymouth, Massachusetts, and Connecticut annihilated the fleeing survivors of the May attack.

1638. The First American Military Unit. The Ancient and Honorable Artillery Company was created in Boston. Fears were expressed in some quarters regarding the possible ascendancy of military over political leadership.

1643, May 19. The New England Confederation. The Pequot War had revealed the inadequacy of military coordination between colonies. This realization, coupled with the threat of Dutch expansion, led to a union of Massachusetts, Plymouth, Connecticut, and New Haven (the United Colonies of New England). Military expenses were to be shared by the colonies in proportion to their male populations. Save for a brief period during King Philip's War (see below), the confederation accomplished little.

1675, June 20–1678, April 12. King Philip's War. Colonial expansion brought conflict with the Wampanoags under **Philip.** Following raids in southern New England, the New England Confederation declared war. At first Indian attacks were frequent and generally successful. However, a severe food shortage later drained Wampanoag strength (spring, 1676). Widespread surrender followed a successful campaign waged by a combined Connecticut Valley and Mohegan force (June, 1676). Philip was killed (August). Although major operations soon ceased, Indian raids in the north persisted until peace was concluded (April, 1678). During the 3-year conflict, over £90,000 was devoted to the war effort, 500 settlers were captured or killed, and between 10 and 20 towns were destroyed or abandoned and many others damaged.

1689. The "Glorious Revolution." Upon news of the flight of James II (see p. 558), the people of Boston revolted and imprisoned unpopular Governor Sir **Edmund Andros.**

The Carolinas

By 1653, settlers from Virginia had established the Albemarle Colony (North Carolina). English expansion in the south was stimulated by the English victory over Spanish forces on Jamaica in 1655 (see p. 607). Stirred by suspicions of a Spanish and Indian conspiracy, Charles Town colonists attacked and defeated the Kusso tribe (1671). The following years were marked by continued English expansion, occasional Indian strife, and intermittent conflict with the Spanish.

FRENCH AMERICA

1609–1627. French Penetration of the St. Lawrence. With the aid of Montaignais, Algonquins, and Hurons, the French drove the Iroquois from the valley. **Samuel de Champlain** led joint French-Algonquin and French-Huron expeditions in an attempt to push the Five Nations southward and to preserve contact between the allies (1609, 1616).

1613. English Raids. French settlements bordering the Bay of Fundy were destroyed.

1629, July 20. Capture of Quebec. The combined attacking force, under Sir **William Alexander** and Sir **David Kirke,** was unaware of a truce in the Anglo-French War (see p. 549).

1632, March 29. Peace Settlement. England returned Acadia and the St. Lawrence settlements to France.

1654–1670. New England Occupation of Acadia. A New England force under Major **Robert Sedgwick** departed from Boston for the purpose of attacking New Netherlands (the 1st Anglo-Dutch War; see p. 555). Instead, the colonists struck Acadia (July 1) in an attempt to destroy French competition in the fur trade. The English retained the province until 1670, when it was restored to France in accordance with the Treaty of Breda (see p. 557).

1642–1653. Iroquois War. The Dutch, seeking to attract the Algonquin and Huron fur trade, provided the Iroquois with arms to use against the French and their Indian allies. The Five Nations struck first against the Hurons, ultimately extending their raids as far as Montreal. After a brief truce (July 4, 1645), the Iroquois set fire to Fort Richelieu, drove the Hurons westward, and forced the Jesuits to abandon missions in Huron country. Attacks along the St. Lawrence continued until the Five Nations concluded a peace treaty with the French (November 5, 1653).

1661–1681. French Expansion in the Caribbean. They established themselves in the Lesser Antilles, a base for piracy against Spain.

1665–1666. Renewed Iroquois War. After allying themselves with the English, the Iroquois resumed hostilities against the French. The flare-up proved brief and the Five Nations were compelled to seek peace in 1666.

1668–1688. Conflict over Hudson Bay. An expedition, supported by an English syndicate and led by French explorer **Pierre-Esprit Radisson,** sailed to Hudson Bay (June, 1668). Later Radisson rejected his sponsors and pledged his allegiance to France; he then changed his mind and reaffirmed loyalty to the company (1680). A French force, led by Sieur **Pierre Le**

Moyne d'Iberville, captured the company posts at James Bay (1688). The English retained isolated posts at the mouths of the Hayes and Severn rivers.

1684, July. La Salle's Expedition to Texas. During the Franco-Spanish conflict of 1683–1684 (see p. 567), Sieur **Robert Cavelier de La Salle** sailed from France to the Gulf of Mexico to establish a colony at the mouth of the Mississippi, near the center of Spanish colonial power. He missed the Mississippi and landed at Matagorda Bay. The disobedience of **Beaujeu,** naval commander of the expedition, and a series of misfortunes led to insubordination and La Salle's assassination (1687). His colony was destroyed by the Indians (1689).

1684–1689. Renewed Iroquois War. The Indians were incited by **Thomas Dongan,** governor of New York. Raiding parties reached the Mississippi and swept across Lakes Erie and Ontario, disrupting the flow of the French lake trade. An unsuccessful attempt at retaliation provoked Indian reprisals in the St. Lawrence Valley; 200 French were killed and 90 captured.

1689, May 12–1697, September 20. King William's War. (War of the League of Augsburg; see p. 546.) In America the war encompassed conflict in Hudson Bay, in the St. Lawrence Valley and upper Hudson Valley, and in Acadia. The English were aided by the Iroquois, while the French were assisted by most of the other Indian tribes.

1690–1697. Frontenac's Indian Raids. Count **Louis de Buade of Pallau and Frontenac** led a series of combined French and Indian assaults along the entire northwestern frontier of the English colonies. The Abenaki, French allies, raided independently in New York and Massachusetts. Frontenac also conducted a western campaign against the Iroquois (1693–1696).

1690, May 1. Albany Conference. Representatives from Plymouth, Massachusetts, Connecticut, and New York elected to invade Canada with 2 land forces and to send a heterogeneous fleet of 34 vessels up the St. Lawrence (see below).

1690, May 11. Capture of Port Royal. New England (Massachusetts) troops under Sir **William Phips** seized the capital of French Acadia. This was the single effective Anglo-American operation.

1690–1691. Abortive Expeditions against the St. Lawrence. The planned colonial expedition against Quebec and St. Lawrence by the New England and New York colonies failed. The French retook Port Royal, but lost it in the Treaty of Ryswick (see p. 548).

1690–1694. Hudson Bay Operations. Iberville drove the English from their posts at the mouths of the Severn (1690) and the Hayes (1694). However, the English regained the James Bay area (1693).

NEW NETHERLANDS AND NEW YORK

1614. Dutch Establish Fort Nassau Near Albany.

1624. Additional Dutch Settlements. They founded their first settlements on Manhattan and at Fort Nassau on the Delaware (Gloucester, N.J.).

1638, March. New Sweden. In defiance of Dutch protest, a Swedish expedition reached the Delaware (abandoned by the Dutch in 1627) and established Fort Christina (Wilmington).

1641–1645. Algonquin War. The Algonquins, provoked by colonial expansion, raided Staten Island and Manhattan. Reprisals and counterreprisals resulted in damage to Dutch and nearby English settlements and plantations. The Dutch, aided by the Mohawks, imposed peace (August 9, 1645).

1647–1655. Dutch-Swedish Hostilities. John Bjornsson Printz, governor of New Sweden, constructed a chain of blockhouses on Tinicum Island (1634) and Fort New Krisholm (1647). In response, the Dutch built forts overlooking the approaches to New Sweden by the Delaware and Schuylkill rivers. The Swedes burned Fort Beversrede on the Schuylkill (May and November, 1648) and seized Fort Casimir (Newcastle, 1653). The Dutch, under Governor **Peter Stuyvesant,** held Beversrede and retook Casimir. They then captured the Swedish stronghold, Fort Christina (September, 1655). This ended Swedish attempts to colonize North America.

1650. Treaty of Hartford. Following encroachments of English settlers on Dutch settlements, a number of incidents led to this boundary settlement between the Dutch and the New England Confederation.

1652–1654. First Anglo-Dutch War. There was no formal declaration of war, but the English seized some Dutch frontier posts. Connecticut forces entered Westchester and Long Island, compelling Stuyvesant to acknowledge English dominion over English settlements on Long Island (1653).

1655–1664. Dutch-Indian Wars. There were 3 major episodes, the first extending from Manhattan to Esopus and Long Island (1655). The second was centered near Esopus (1663). The wars ended with the Indian surrender of the Esopus Valley after the third episode (1664).

1664–1667. Second Anglo-Dutch War. Even before formal outbreak of war in Europe, James, Duke of York, directed Colonel **Richard Nicolls** to capture New Netherlands. The arrival of 4 frigates in New Amsterdam Harbor in late August resulted in the surrender of New Amsterdam (September 7). The English took Fort George and replaced the Dutch in their alliance with the Iroquois.

1672, March–1674, October 31. Third Anglo-Dutch War. Dutch naval and land forces seized New York (August, 1673). Subsequently, Albany, New Jersey, and western Long Island yielded to the Dutch. However, the **Treaty of Westminster** (see p. 558) restored the settlements to England.

1689–1691. Leisler's Rebellion. Reports of the arrest of Sir Edmund Andros in Boston (see p. 604) encouraged anti-Catholic agitation in New York City and on Long Island (May, 1689). The militia captured Fort James and turned it over to **Jacob Leisler,** the rebel leader, who declared his allegiance to William and Mary. He refused to give up his authority and was seized by British troops (March 30, 1691). He was executed (May 26).

SPANISH AMERICA

North America

Spanish Jesuits extended their missionary activities on the Pacific coast. Settlements around the missions in the Mayo and Yaqui river valleys led to Indian attacks, which were met by punitive expeditions under Captain **Diego Martínez de Hurdiade** (c. 1625). In New Mexico, dissension among the Pueblos, fostered by Spanish slavery practices and attempts to convert the Indians, exploded in a Pueblo revolt (1680), in which 400 Spaniards were killed and over 2,000 others expelled. However, the Pueblos, terrorized by constant Apache attacks, acquiesced in resumption of control by Governor **Don Diego de Vargas** (1692–1696).

English expansion and raiding in the south—Florida and the Carolinas—led to Spanish reprisals against English settlements.

Central and South America

During this century Spain assumed a defensive posture to preserve the empire which she had acquired in the preceding century. Encroachments by France, England, and Holland (particularly in the West Indies) both contributed to, and were symptoms of, the decline of Spanish power. Conflict in the Caribbean region and farther south, as in North America, reflected the shifting alliances and antagonisms of Europe. Three prime characteristics marked the period: (1) Indian unrest, particularly among the Araucanians of southern Chile, the Piajos of Peru, and the Chiriguanes, between Las Charcas and Paraguay; (2) the Corsarios Lutheranos, or pirates (often encouraged if not directly subsidized by the European powers, particularly England); and (3) relatedly, an extensive contraband traffic. By the end of the century, Spain had attempted to compensate for her naval inadequacy by heavy fortification of the coastal and Caribbean communities. Typical of this defensive policy was the atrophy of highly vulnerable Santo Domingo and the development of Cartagena with its round fortress, walls of a 40-foot diameter, and an easily blocked channel. The principal events were:

1624–1629. War with the Dutch. The Dutch captured Bahia (1624), but were dispossessed in the following year by a Spanish naval force. However, soon after, as a preliminary to an invasion of Pernambuco, the Dutch recaptured Bahia (1627). Dutch buccaneers, under **Piet Heyn,** seized a Spanish silver shipment off the Cuban coast (1628). Subsequently, Heyn was made an admiral in the Dutch Navy. A Dutch force of 60 vessels captured Pernambuco and Recife (1629).

1629–1660. Punitive Expeditions against Other Colonies. The Spanish drove English settlers from the islands of Nevis and St. Christopher (1629). They returned upon the departure of the Spaniards. English Puritans were forced from the Providence Islands, off Central America (1641). In reprisal, a band organized by the Providence Company and the Earl of Warwick assaulted the Venezuelan coast and briefly seized Jamaica (1643). Some years later the Spanish ousted English and French colonists in the Lesser Antilles (1660).

1654. English Seizure of Jamaica. Cromwell ordered Admiral **William Penn** to capture Santo Domingo; the operation failed and Penn proceeded to take Jamaica.

1668–1671. Morgan's Panama Raids. Led by **Henry Morgan,** a force of 2,000 buccaneers plundered Porto Bello and Panama City. Morgan was knighted by Charles II.

1670. Treaty of Madrid. England promised to halt piracy in the Caribbean. Spain recognized English sovereignty over Jamaica.

1679. English Pirates Raid Panama.

PORTUGUESE AMERICA

1609–1642. Portuguese Slave Traders Repulsed from Paraguay. Spanish Jesuits armed mission Indians and successfully resisted the penetration of Paraguay by Portuguese slave traders.

1615. French Expelled from Brazil. The Portuguese seized the French colony on Maranhão Island and subsequently settled Belém, ruining French efforts to colonize South America.

c. 1620–1654. Dutch-Portuguese Wars. (**See p. 572.**) Insurrection of the Portuguese population in Brazil ended in the withdrawal of the Dutch (1654). Holland relinquished all claim to the region (1661).

1680. Conflict over the Rio de la Plata. Portugal established a fort, Colonia del Sacramento, across from Buenos Aires, asserting its claim to the northern and eastern bank of the Rio de la Plata. The Spanish seized the post. English intervention (in Europe) resulted in the return of the fort to Portugal (recognized formally in 1701).

XV

THE MILITARY SUPREMACY OF EUROPE: 1700–1750

MILITARY TRENDS

During this half-century Europe became pre-eminent in world affairs. Save for the meteorlike passage of Nadir Shah's Persian Empire, only three major non-European powers still existed—Manchu China, Mogul India, and Ottoman Turkey—all declining in strength and incapable of exerting great influence outside of their borders. Tiny Europe, on the other hand, contained five major powers with intercontinental interests, influence, or ambitions—Britain, France, Spain, Russia, and Austria—and two other powers with modest strength in Europe, but great influence elsewhere: Portugal and Holland. And there was in Europe one new power—Prussia—with wholly continental interests and contacts, but whose military prowess was beginning to have worldwide repercussions.

In military and nonmilitary affairs, Europe set the pace; others followed if they could. Europe led the world in part by default and in part because of a growing, and apparently irresistible, superiority in technology.

All of the important military leaders of the period were European—again with the significant exception of **Nadir Shah,** last of the great Asian conquerors. There was one general of great-captain rank: **Frederick the Great** of Prussia. And there were four other generals of truly outstanding ability: Prince **Eugene of Savoy** and of Austria, **John Churchill, Duke of Marlborough** of England, **Charles XII** of Sweden, and **Claude, Duke of Villars** of France. Hardly less competent were **Maurice de Saxe,** the German who fought for France; **James, Duke of Berwick,** the English expatriate who fought for France; **Louis, Duke of Vendôme,** also of France; and **Peter the Great** of Russia. Otherwise, even though this was a period of almost incessant—though extremely limited—warfare, leadership was for the most part unimaginative and pedantic.

Naval affairs were dominated by Britain to an extent almost unmatched in prior or subsequent history, although imaginative leadership was largely stultified in the Royal Navy (though for reasons quite different from the stultification on land). At least two British admirals, however, deserve recognition for achieving imaginative victories despite this stultification: **George, Lord Anson** and **Edward, Baron Hawke.**

EIGHTEENTH-CENTURY WARFARE

The example of Gustavus Adolphus was the military basis of 18th-century European warfare. A handful of his imitators had sufficient ability to apply his example with imagination and energy comparable to his. Most, however, were satisfied to adopt the external aspects of Gustavus' military organization with little or no understanding of the fact that his success was due to flexibility in the employment of novel weapons and organization in accordance with old principles. Here is a perfect example of what Toynbee has called "a cycle of invention, triumph, lethargy and [eventually] disaster."*

There were, however, social, political, and economic factors which affected the conduct of 18th-century warfare at least as much as this military cycle.

The economic aspects in themselves were perhaps least important. They reflected relatively little change from previous eras, although they were soon to be completely overturned by the effects of the Industrial Revolution. The economic limitations on war in the 18th century, as earlier, were primarily those of agricultural and industrial production. The vast majority of people were employed in agriculture, producing sufficient food for themselves, with but little left over for the much smaller percentage of the population engaged in handicraft industries, in services, or in the military forces. In time of war it was simply impossible to raise very large armies. The soldiers came mostly from the farms, thus simultaneously reducing the number of producers while increasing the demand for food for non-producers. In addition, the limited industrial capacities of nations prior to the introduction of mass-production techniques, could not provide sufficient weapons, equipment, and other munitions to equip large armies engaged in active and wasteful warfare.

The colonial expansion of Europe, with its increased trade and growing mercantilism, only served to accentuate these major economic limitations. The manpower demands of colonialism and mercantilism attracted farmers and handicrafters from their old tasks at a time when the expansion of the economy was placing ever-increasing demands upon agricultural and industrial production.

The social conditions existing in 18th-century Europe exerted an influence upon military systems very closely related to the economic considerations. The manpower demands of the economic expansion dictated the recruitment of armies from among the least productive elements of the populations. The officers were from the nobility, a generally unproductive stratum of the society, while the soldiers came from riffraff and the unemployed, who were also unproductive.

Social considerations, in turn, were closely related to the political factors which governed the conduct of wars. For all practical purposes governments were organizational structures used by monarchs in the administration of their domains. Wars were fought for personal or dynastic objectives. While the growing sense of nationalism and the widespread existence of patriotic sentiments cannot be dismissed, these were linked to monarchical loyalty, and otherwise were relatively unimportant in the rigidly stratified political and social organizations of society. Rigidity was indeed the dominant characteristic of the era, an economic, social, and cultural rigidity which reinforced and contributed to unimaginative military pedantry.

---

* Arnold J. Toynbee, *A Study of History,* Somervell Abridgment (Vols. 1–6), Oxford, N.Y., 1947, p. 336.

Take, for instance, discipline. Discipline and precision had been fundamental to the successes of Gustavus; therefore they were considered by his imitators to be goals in themselves. Furthermore, only through harsh, ironbound discipline and the most rigid physical and mental controls could the riffraff of the average European army be controlled and trained. The dregs of society could not be allowed to wander freely among the productive communities; either they would terrorize the civilians through the exercise of their newly learned military skills or, more likely, they would desert. Because of the relatively small segment of a nation's man power available for military service, because there was difficulty in recruiting new soldiers, and because it took time to train men in the precise military drills necessitated by existing weaponry, losses by desertion were as serious as battle losses.

When on campaign armies could not be allowed to forage off the country—not to spare the citizenry, but because the civilian economy could not stand ravaging and looting by hordes of soldiers, and the military economy could not stand the inevitable desertions. Therefore, a campaign could not be initiated until the commanders had assembled large stores of food and equipment in storage depots called magazines; armies could not be allowed to maneuver any great distance—usually four or five days' march at the most—from these magazines.

It was also important to avoid the risk of losing expensively trained soldiers in combat. Consequently, a commander was unwilling to fight a battle unless he calculated his chances of success to be near certainty. His opponent, who was capable of making a roughly comparable estimate of the situation, would naturally seek to avoid battle under such circumstances, and would do so by placing himself more than four or five days' distance from the enemy's nearest magazine. Under such circumstances battles were infrequent, and decisive actions resulted only from the energy of exceptionally good commanders or the foolhardiness of exceptionally stupid ones.

But once battles were joined, they were fought with ferocity and tenacity. Grim testimony to this are the casualty figures for such engagements as Blenheim, Malplaquet, and Fontenoy. But, given the nature of the warfare and the composition of the armies, such losses did not create serious strains on the national economies or societies of the opponents.

It must not be assumed, however, that the era (including the late 17th century) did not have its share of capable military commanders. We have previously noted Turenne, Cromwell, and Condé, and this chapter will consider comparable leaders. But none of these men had the genius—and perhaps also lacked opportunity—to overcome the rigid military system within which they operated and to which, therefore, they adapted themselves and their strategies. Not even Frederick the Great—one of the undoubted geniuses of warfare—was able completely to break the rigid shackles. Frederick's greatest military weakness—his failure to pursue after a decisive victory—probably reflected a fear that his army would melt away in desertion were he to unleash it in pursuit.

It would take the cataclysm of the French Revolution, combined with the impact of the growing Industrial Revolution, harnessed by the ruthless genius of Napoleon, to shatter completely the rigid system of 18th-century warfare.

WEAPONS DEVELOPMENTS

As might be expected in this era of conventionality and conservatism, significant developments or innovations in weapons were few. What technological progress there was lay primarily in the refinement of existing weapons.

The basic small-arms weapon was the flintlock musket—typified by Britain's "Brown Bess"—with its offset ring bayonet. The Prussians produced two refinements to improve its utility in combat. They introduced a double-ended iron ramrod (about 1718), much more reliable (and thus faster) than the relatively insubstantial wooden ramrod. The Prussians also developed the funnel-shaped touchhole, making it easier to prime the musket, particularly in the stress of battle. When these innovations were combined with the speedy and precise loading drill demanded by Frederick the Great, Prussian infantry soldiers could fire about twice as fast as those in other armies.

In artillery also there was little real change. The French improved on their earlier standardization efforts, and abolished all mobile pieces larger than 24-pounders. The few major developments were tactical, and again—significantly—Prussia led the way.

TACTICS OF LAND WARFARE

With warfare primarily governed by convention, there was relatively little new in tactics. As we have seen, most generals preferred to avoid battle, relying solely on ponderous maneuvering. Tactical formations were generally the same as those that had emerged in the previous century, except that they tended to be somewhat more elaborate and somewhat slower. Tactical perfection was considered to consist in the ability to form perfect lines, and to maintain these lines even during the heat of battle. The lines themselves, due to increased rates of fire, were often reduced to four ranks instead of six.

The principal exception to these generalities was to be found in the tactical developments of Frederick the Great, which were beginning to make themselves felt by the close of the War of the Austrian Succession at midcentury. Frederick was just as concerned as other 18th-century generals with discipline and drill, and with precision in tactical infantry maneuver. But with him these were means to an end, rather than conformance or acceptance of convention. In fact his Prussian armies had even more ruthless discipline, had a greater emphasis on drill, and were required to meet higher standards of precision than any other army in Europe. But Frederick added two significant elements: speed and battlefield maneuver. The result was an instrument of war probably unsurpassed in technical military perfection for its time by any army save possibly that of Alexander of Macedon.

Frederick carried one step farther the artillery tactical developments of Gustavus Adolphus. He created the concept of horse artillery (as opposed to conventional horse-*drawn* artillery) in which every cannoneer and ammunition handler was mounted, so that the light guns could keep up with the fast-moving, hard-riding Prussian cavalry. He also exploited the high trajectory of the howitzer by striking at enemy reserves concealed behind trees and hills, and in the process gave to artillerymen their first glimmering of the concept of indirect fire.

The only other significant tactical development of the period was improved organization and employment of light infantry. In Europe this was primarily an Austrian-Hungarian innovation and was to some extent a result of necessity in the War of the Austrian Succession, when Maria Theresa's generals had to adapt the Hungarian light-infantry soldier, accustomed to informal border skirmishing with the Turks, to operations against the Prussians and French. But there was also a trend toward comparable light-infantry development in the operations in the American colonies, a trend that would become increasingly important by the end of the century.

MILITARY ORGANIZATION

The armies of the early 18th century were generally small, were highly professional, to a large extent were still mercenary, and the troops had little enthusiastic passion for the dynastic cause for which they fought. In organization and structure there was little change from the new systems which had emerged at the close of the preceding century.

As we have seen, armies were largely composed of vagabonds and nobles. As a consequence there was probably a greater gulf between officers and men than at any other time in history. It is not much of an overstatement to suggest that soldiers fought in battle mainly because they feared their own officers more than they did the foe. This was because armies of this sort could be held together and kept from deserting only by iron, ruthless discipline.

NAVAL WARFARE

Tactics

Up to 1750, naval tactics were as blunt as a sledgehammer. Opposing fleets, each sailing in a single column (line ahead) on parallel courses, attempted to close with one another and engage ship against ship. Individual vessels fought broadside to broadside, sometimes actually side by side, pounding away until one or the other gave in. England dominated the seas, not through new concepts of conflict, but through the momentum gained by her great admirals of an earlier era, and by numerical superiority in numbers of fighting ships.

The French Navy was second, having clearly surpassed the Dutch. Ship for ship, French war vessels were better built than the British, but they were usually fewer in number—and in general English seamanship was the better. The basic distinction between English and French battle tactics was that the French, usually outnumbered, were forced to save their vessels. In fleet actions they followed the principle that "He who fights and runs away will live to fight another day." In consequence French admirals preferred to enter action on the leeward side of their adversaries, which would enable a quick breakoff of conflict if necessary, and their gunnery was directed at the spars and rigging of the enemy to slow him down. Contrariwise, the English sought the "weather gauge" (position to windward of the adversary), facilitating closing in; their fire was directed at the enemy's hull, seeking to sink or pulverize him.

Broadside fire power dominated the action; seamanship and shiphandling were part and parcel of the art of naval gunnery, for fire power was merely a statistic unless the ship herself was so maneuvered as to bring her almost rigid guns to bear on the target. One might have thought that under such conditions individualism in battle would be a *sine qua non* among the admirals and captains of the Royal Navy. Far from it; the "Fighting Instructions" of the Royal Navy had become frozen into law (1691), and the line (a rigid single file) was gospel. Woe betide the captain who broke from its frozen mediocrity. Since no other navy had a system any better, or even as good, only an exceptional naval commander was able to achieve any major success against a force even approximately the strength of his own. There were few decisive naval actions. Attempts to experiment or innovate were discouraged; frequently they led to court-martial and disgrace. In fact, it would seem that almost every important engagement of the Royal Navy during this period culminated in a court-martial.

The Ships

This was the golden age of the ship of the line with her multitiered broadside batteries. As her name signified, she was large enough and carried sufficient armament to slug it out in the line of battle. She averaged about 200 feet in length, with a maximum tonnage of 2,500. The biggest of these vessels carried a crew of about 1,000 men. By the end of this period warships had become assorted into six "rates." The first three of these classes were ships of the line: a 1st-rate carried 100 or more guns on three decks; a 2nd-rate had about 90 guns on three decks; the 3rd-rate—the workhorse of the battle fleet—carried from 64 to 74 guns on two decks. The 4th-rater was a compromise, a 50-gun vessel (two gun decks) called a frigate, but sometimes used in the line of battle. Like all compromises in naval construction, she was not powerful enough to play her part in the line, and she was usually too clumsy to act as a cruiser. The real cruisers were the smaller frigates—5th- and 6th-raters—carrying from 24 to 40 guns, all on one gun deck. These vessels, relatively lighter and faster than ships of the line, were built for commerce destruction, scouting, and screening. All the foregoing vessels were, in the true nautical term, ships—square-rigged three-masters.

Below these rates came the sloops of war (the term "sloop" had nothing to do with the rig), carrying from 16 to 24 guns, usually brigs (two masts, square-rigged) or brigantines (two masts, square-rigged on the fore only). And finally came cutters and other small craft, usually known by the name of their rig (sloop, schooner, or ketch).

Naval Ordnance

The main batteries of ships of the line and frigates had become fairly standardized by this time: 16-, 18-, and 24-pounder cannon. The multitiered vessels usually carried 16's on their upper decks, 24's on the lower. Lighter craft mounted 4-, 6-, and 9-pounders, and the big ships frequently carried some lighter guns in addition to their normal armament.

Naval Developments

Only two innovations appeared during the period, but they were important. The tiller, the great beam projecting inboard from the rudder by which the ship was steered, by 1700 had been rigged by cables to a steering wheel mounted on the quarter-deck, greatly facilitating the conning of the ship. And underwater sheathing of copper was being introduced, protecting the oaken bottoms to a great extent from the ravages of the dreaded teredo (marine worm attacking wood), and barnacles.

Morale

Living conditions on board ship in all navies of the period were abominable. It is hard to imagine, for instance, how 1,000 men could exist in a 2,500-ton vessel, carrying, in addition to ammunition, enough food and water for extended cruises of a year or more without entering port or reprovisioning. The nature of the food, and its condition after months at sea, can be imagined. The principal item of diet was weevil-infested, brick-hard biscuits, with a few sips of brackish water. The addition of some rum to the water—to make "grog"—helped. The physical effects of the diet were apparently severe. Sailors who survived battle usually aged quickly and died young. The English discovered that lime juice inhibited scurvy, and from their use of limes comes the word "Limey," meaning an Englishman.

To these cruel living conditions was added even more cruel discipline. Punishments were atrocious. The gulf between officers and men was at least as great as that in the ground forces, and commanders exercised almost unquestioned life-and-death authority over their men. This, of course, was probably the only way of assuring obedience from men who to a large extent had not volunteered, but who had been impressed into service against their wills.

As a social institution, the principal characteristics of the Royal Navy of this time have been aptly summed up by Winston Churchill: "Rum, buggery, and the lash!"

MAJOR WARS

THE GREAT NORTHERN WAR, 1700–1721

1698–1699. Alliance against Sweden. Peter I of Russia, **Augustus II** of Poland (also Elector of Saxony), and **Frederick IV** of Denmark entered into a secret alliance against Sweden, hoping to take advantage of the youth of **Charles XII** (aged 16) to end Sweden's dominance in the Baltic.

1700, April. Danish Invasion of Schleswig. Conquest from the Duke of Holstein-Gottorp, ally of Sweden.

1700, June. Polish-Saxon Invasion of Livonia. Augustus' Saxon troops besieged Riga.

1700, August. Russian Invasion of Ingria. Peter's army of 40,000 besieged Narva (October 4).

1700, August 4. Charles Invades Zealand. Against the advice of his admiral, the 18-year-old Swedish monarch boldly took his fleet and army across supposedly unnavigable waters, and immediately advanced on Copenhagen. The Danes sued for peace.

1700, August 18. Treaty of Travendal. Denmark returned Schleswig to the Duke of Holstein-Gottorp; agreed not to engage in further hostilities against Sweden.

1700, October 6. Charles Lands in Livonia. Arriving at Pernau with a few men, he had planned to relieve Riga. While awaiting reinforcements he decided instead to march to the relief of hard-pressed Narva.

1700, November 13–19. Advance on Narva. Charles with 8,000 men scattered Russian forces attempting to block the approaches (November 18). Revealing more perception than courage, Peter fled.

1700, November 20. Battle of Narva. In a 2-hour battle, during a snowstorm, Charles virtually annihilated the Russian army, nearly 5 times as numerous as his own. He lost 2,000 men. During the winter he prepared to march on Livonia.

1701, June 17. Battle of Riga. Charles defeated a Russian-Polish-Saxon army and relieved Riga, besieged for almost a year.

1701, July. Swedish Invasion of Poland. Considering Augustus and Poland to be more formidable foes than Peter and Russia (reasonable under the circumstances, but wrong in retrospect), Charles decided to deal with Poland first. He crossed the Dvina, defeated a Saxon-Russian army at the **Battle of Dunamunde** (July 9), occupied and annexed Courland, then moved into Lithuania.

1702, January–May. Advance on Warsaw. Charles occupied the undefended Polish capital (May 14). He then boldly marched westward, seeking battle with Augustus.

1702, January–December. Russian Invasion of Ingria. Peter defeated Swedish General **Schlippenbach** at the **Battle of Errestfer** (January 7). He defeated the Swedes again at the **Battle of Hummselsdorf** (July 18), and seized the Neva Valley (December).

1702, July 2. Battle of Kliszow. Charles routed a much larger Polish-Saxon army. He then marched on through hostile country to seize Cracow.

1702–1703. Consolidation of Poland. Charles systematically eliminated Augustus' control.

1703, April 13. Battle of Pultusk. Charles defeated another much larger Augustan army, then besieged and captured Thorn (May–December).

1703, May 16. Peter Founds St. Petersburg. Russian troops occupied and fortified the mouth of the Neva River, regaining an outlet on the Baltic.

1704. Charles Places Stanislas Leszczynski on Polish Throne. Civil war raged through Poland between the adherents of Augustus and Stanislas.

1704, July 4. Peter Recaptures Dorpat.

1704, August 9. Peter Recaptures Narva. All Swedish inhabitants were massacred.

1705–1706. Charles Pacifies Poland. Defeating the Saxons at the **Battles of Punitz** and **Wszowa** (1705), Charles then hastened to Lithuania to meet a Russian army under Scottish General **Ogilvie** which had occupied Courland (1705). The Russians avoided major battle, but Charles finally chased them out of Lithuania and as far as Pinsk, where he halted (July, 1706). Meanwhile, Augustus attempted to retake Poland, but was routed by a much smaller Swedish army under General **Karl G. Rehnskjold** at the **Battle of Franstadt** (February 3, 1706).

1706, August–September. Charles Invades Saxony. The Swedish Army seized Leipzig, practically without opposition. Augustus sued for peace.

1706, September 24. Treaty of Altranstadt. Augustus abdicated the Polish throne, recognized Stanislas as king, and broke his alliance with Russia. Peter sued for peace, but Charles, determined on revenge, refused to negotiate.

1706–1707. Quarrel with the Empire. Charles, poised menacingly in Saxony, demanded restitution for mistreatment of Silesian Protestants under the provisions of the Treaty of Osnabrück (see p. 545). Fearful that Sweden would join France in the War of the Spanish Succession (see p. 617), the allies persuaded the emperor to accede to Swedish demands (August, 1707). Charles at once marched from Saxony into Poland to prepare for an invasion of Russia. Peter concentrated an army at Grodno and Minsk.

1708, January 1. Invasion of Russia. Charles, waiting until the rivers were frozen, crossed the Vistula with an army of 45,000 men, the largest he ever commanded. He took Grodno, abandoned by Peter (January 26), and continued toward Moscow. He waited near Minsk during the spring thaw (March–June).

1708, June 29. Charles Crosses the Berezina at Borisov.

1708, July 4. Battle of Holowczyn. Assaulting a Russian army defending the line of the Bibitch River, Charles penetrated and scattered the defenders. He then advanced to the Dnieper at Mogilev (July 8).

1708, July–October. Scorched Earth. The Russians retreated slowly, destroying food and crops as they withdrew. They refused battle, though Charles forced one brief engagement at **Dobry** (September 9). The Swedes, short of food and fodder, began to suffer severely. Charles decided not to retreat, but to go into the Ukraine to join **Ivan Mazeppa,** the Cossack leader, who secretly agreed to rise against the Russians with 30,000 men. Charles ordered a small relief army under General **Adam Loewenhaupt** to march in from Livonia, with a tremendous wagon train of supplies, to join him in the Ukraine. This was Charles' worst military decision. He should have concentrated his forces and made adequate logistical arrangements before marching deeper into Russia.

1708, September–October. Repulse at St. Petersburg. Swedish General **Lybecker** was forced to retreat into Finland.

1708, October. Ousting of Mazeppa. Learning of Mazeppa's planned revolt, Peter sent a Russian army into the Ukraine to seize and burn his capital, Baturin. Mazeppa and a small force fled to join Charles at Horki in Severia (November 6).

1708, October 9–10. Battle of Lyesna. Loewenhaupt's army of 11,000 men was attacked and defeated by much larger Russian forces in a 2-day battle just east of the Dnieper. Loewenhaupt, forced to burn all of his supply train, reached Charles with 6,000 exhausted and hungry survivors (October 21).

1708–1709. Winter Struggle for Survival. The Swedes, harassed by the Russians, were forced to fight continuously. This, perhaps the coldest winter ever experienced in Europe, caused severe hardships and losses to the Swedes. Charles did wonders to hold his army together, but by spring he barely had about 20,000 men fit for action. He had only 34 artillery pieces and almost no powder for his guns.

1709, May–July. Siege of Poltava. Charles advanced on Voronezh, but stopped to capture the Russian fortification at Poltava (May 2). Peter immediately marched on Poltava with a relieving army of 80,000 men and more than 100 artillery pieces. The 2 armies maneuvered cautiously, preparing for battle. In preliminary skirmishing Charles was badly wounded in the foot and had to be carried in a litter (June 17).

1709, June 28. Battle of Poltava. Seriously short of ammunition, Charles needed a quick victory. His initial attacks went according to plan; the Swedish left and center were successful. Peter was on the verge of retreat, when he realized that there was little or no coordination among the 3 major elements of the overextended Swedish army. Rallying his army, the Czar awaited the climactic Swedish charge—7,000 strong—with 40,000 fresh troops. Overwhelming strength, more and better weapons, and adequate ammunition soon reversed the tide of battle. The Swedish infantry was practically annihilated, the cavalry scattered. Charles was lifted from his litter and placed on a horse. Accompanied by Mazeppa and about 1,500 horsemen—half Cossacks and half Swedes—he fled to Turkish Moldavia. The 12,000 Swedish cavalry survivors surrendered to the Russians at Perevolchna, on the Dnieper, 2 days after the battle. The Russians lost 1,345 killed and 3,290 wounded. The Swedes lost 9,234 killed and wounded and 18,794 prisoners.

1709, August–December. Russian Occupation of Poland. Peter marched westward to occupy Poland, placing back on the throne his ally Augustus II, who had renounced the Treaty of Altranstadt and returned to Poland when he heard the news of Poltava. By virtue of military occupation, however, Peter was the real ruler of Poland. Stanislas fled to Swedish Pomerania; his former adherents were ruthlessly persecuted.

1709–1710. The Allies Collect the Spoils. The Danes took Schleswig and the Swedish possessions of Bremen and Verden, which were in turn given to Hanover as an inducement to enter the war. A Danish army overran Skane, in southern Sweden. Another Danish force and a Polish-Saxon army invaded Swedish Pomerania, but were held at bay. Meanwhile the Russians occupied Carelia, Livonia, Estonia, and the remainder of Ingria.

1710, February. Battle of Helsingborg. Swedish General **Magnus Stenbock** defeated the Danes in southern Sweden and forced them to withdraw across the Sound. Stenbock then proceeded to Germany to protect Swedish possessions there.

1710, October. Turkey Enters the War as Ally of Sweden. Responding to the appeals of Charles XII, still a refugee at Bender in Moldavia, the sultan declared war on Russia and sent **Baltaji Mehmet,** the grand vizier, to the Russian frontier with an army nearly 200,000 strong.

1711, March–July. Moldavian Campaign. Overconfident after Poltava, Peter invaded Moldavia with about 60,000 men, to be outmaneuvered by the larger Turkish army and driven back against the Pruth River, where his starving army entrenched itself and was surrounded. Instead of investing the Russians, Baltaji opened negotiations. Had he persevered, Peter would have been forced to surrender, with historical consequences unimaginable.

1711, July 21. Treaty of the Pruth. Peter returned Azov to Turkey, dismantled Taganrog and other fortresses, and agreed to withdraw from Poland and to refrain from interfering in Polish internal affairs. (He never carried out the latter two provisions.) Charles, who had been granted free passage to Sweden, was bitterly disappointed at the easy escape of his rival. Refusing to leave Turkey for 3 years, he continued vain efforts to get Turkey to undertake major operations against Russia. He was finally imprisoned by his Turkish allies after a fierce hand-to-hand struggle (February 1, 1713).

1712–1713. Operations in Northern Germany. Stenbock defeated a Danish army at the **Battle of Gadebusch** (1712), but was soon afterward set upon by a much larger allied army and forced to capitulate at **Toningen** (1713). Meanwhile the Saxons and Russians were being repulsed from Stralsund (1713). Despite disasters, Sweden continued the war, and the Swedish Navy still dominated the Baltic.

1713. Peace of Adrianople. Peace between Russia and Turkey.

1713–1714. Russian Conquest of Finland.

1714. Naval Battle of Gangut (Hanko). Peter's newly created Russian fleet defeated the Swedes to gain control of the Gulf of Finland, facilitating the conquest of Finland. Swedish predominance in the Baltic was ended, although the Russians did not yet feel strong enough to offer a climactic challenge.

1714, November 11. Arrival of Charles at Stralsund. Finally despairing of Turkish action, Charles, fleeing from virtual house arrest in Turkey, made a daring journey across Europe with 1 servant.

1714–1715. Charles Revitalizes Sweden. Unwisely refusing to consider opportunities for peace negotiations, Charles would not compromise his determination to achieve complete victory. After repulsing a series of allied assaults on Stralsund, he returned to Sweden (December, 1715), now threatened by another invasion from Denmark and Norway. He raised an army of 20,000 and moved into Skane, causing his enemies to abandon their invasion plans (1716).

1717–1718. Norwegian Campaigns. Charles, taking the initiative, invaded Danish Norway. He hoped that the conquest of Norway would give him a stronger base for further operations, as well as territory which he could trade in eventual peace negotiations.

1718, December 11. Death of Charles. As his army was preparing to assault besieged Fredriksten, Charles, peering over the front-trench parapet, was shot through the head by a Danish bullet.

1719–1720. Russian Raids against Sweden. The Russian fleet now controlled the Baltic. Repeated landings on the Swedish coast near Stockholm were repulsed by the exhausted Swedes with the greatest difficulty; the Swedish Riksdag sued for peace.

1719–1721. Treaties of Stockholm. The *status quo* was restored between Sweden, Saxony, and Poland. Prussia kept Stettin and part of Pomerania, and also paid an indemnity. Denmark gave up her conquests, save for Schleswig, but received an indemnity from Sweden.

1721, August 30. Treaty of Nystad. Russia kept Livonia, Estonia, Ingria, part of Carelia, and many Baltic islands. She returned Finland (except for Vyborg) and paid an indemnity to Sweden. By this treaty Russia supplanted Sweden as the dominant power in the Baltic, and became a major European power.

WAR OF THE SPANISH SUCCESSION, 1701–1714

Charles II, last of the Spanish Hapsburg line, was childless. There were 2 major contenders for the throne of Spain: (1) **Louis XIV** of France, son of the elder daughter of Philip III of Spain and husband of the elder daughter of Philip IV; (2) **Leopold I,** Hapsburg emperor, son of the younger daughter of Philip III and husband of the younger daughter of Philip IV. Neither of the maritime powers—England and Holland—was willing to see Spain united with either France or Austria, and because of this Louis was claiming the Spanish throne for his second grandson, **Philip of Anjou,** while Leopold's claim was for his second son, the **Archduke Charles.**

1700, March 13. Charles's Will. Philip of Anjou was declared heir to the Spanish throne.

1700, November 1. Death of Charles. Philip of Anjou was proclaimed Philip V, and assumed the throne in Spain.

Operations in Western and Central Europe

1701, March. French Occupy Fortresses of Spanish Netherlands. England and Holland prepared for war. Since Leopold still claimed the Spanish Netherlands, Austria also prepared for war. Prince **Eugene** assembled an Austrian army in the Tyrol. A larger French army under Marshal **Nicolas de Catinat** occupied the defile of Rivoli (May).

1701, May 28. Eugene Arrives in Italy. Traveling little-used roads in a surprise and secret march, the Austrians by-passed Catinat and reached Vicenza. The French withdrew westward to avoid being cut off.

1701, May–August. Maneuvers in Lombardy. Despite the superior size of the

French Army, Eugene maneuvered Catinat back to the Oglio. Paris replaced Catinat by aging Marshal Duke **François de Villeroi** (August).

1701, September 1. Battle of Chiari. The French attacked Eugene's fortified position and were repulsed with heavy loss. They withdrew to Cremona and went into winter quarters. Eugene went into winter quarters farther east, blockading the French-Spanish garrison of Mantua.

1701, September 7. Establishment of the Grand Alliance. The enemies of France were England, Holland, Austria, Prussia, most of the other German states, and (later) Portugal. At this time French allies were Savoy, Mantua, Cologne, and (later) Bavaria. (Savoy soon changed sides.)

1702, February 1. Battle of Cremona. Eugene made a surprise raid, captured Villeroi, then withdrew after causing considerable damage. Paris sent Marshal Louis Josef, Duke of Vendôme to replace Villeroi.

1702, May 15. England Declares War. John Churchill, Earl of Marlborough was sent to Holland as captain general of combined English and Dutch forces.

1702, June–July. Marlborough Invades the Spanish Netherlands. With an army of 50,000 (12,000 being British), Marlborough attempted to force French Marshal **Louis, Duke of Boufflers** into battle. To his intense disgust, the Dutch governmental deputies who had veto power over his use of Dutch troops refused on 4 different occasions to permit him to fight.

1702, July. Austrian Threat to Alsace. Prince **Louis, Margrave of Baden,** led an imperial army across the Rhine at Spires. Marshal Catinat was sent to protect Strasbourg.

1702, July 29–September 12. Siege of Landau. Louis of Baden prepared to move into Alsace after capturing the town.

1702, August 15. Battle of Luzzara. Drawn battle between Eugene and Vendôme. No other important operations in Italy, as Eugene skillfully maintained himself despite greatly superior French and Spanish strength.

1702, September–October. Marlborough on the Meuse. The allies opened the lower Rhine and Meuse Rivers. Since there was no risk of battle, and since their security and trade routes were both involved, the Dutch agreed to Marlborough's efforts against the Meuse fortresses; he captured Venloo (September 15), Ruremonde (October 7), and Liége (October 15). As a result he was made Duke of Marlborough.

1702, September. Bavarian Declaration of War. Bavarian troops seized Ulm. Louis of Baden recrossed the Rhine to protect his country. Catinat sent a small army after him under the command of General **Claude L. H. de Villars.**

1702, October 14. Battle of Friedlingen. Villars defeated Louis of Baden. He was promoted to the rank of marshal.

1703. Opposing Plans. Marlborough planned to reopen communications with Austria via the Rhine, and then to penetrate and shatter the French cordon of forts in the Spanish Netherlands and to seize Antwerp. The French planned to send Villars to join the Elector of Bavaria on the Danube, and then march to capture Vienna.

1703, April–May. Villars Marches through the Black Forest. He first seized Kehl, to have a base east of the Rhine. He then plunged into the Black Forest. Arriving at Ulm, he left a small force to contain Louis of Baden, joined the elector (May 8), and urged an immediate advance on Vienna. But timid Maximilian insisted instead upon a junction with Vendôme in the Tyrol before attempting to take Vienna.

1703, May. Marlborough Takes Bonn. This opened the Rhine Valley, and Marlborough then turned to his second objective, Antwerp.

1703, June–August. Bavarian Tyrol Adventure. Maximilian occupied the Tyrol, while Villars remained in the Danube Valley to hold off Louis of Baden and an Austrian army under Count **Styrum.** Vendôme was slow in starting from Italy, and the Austrians in the Tyrol, supported by an aroused local population, drove the Bavarians out (August). Vendôme, who had been marching toward the Brenner, remained in Italy.

1703, June–October. Failure in the Netherlands. Marlborough was frustrated in the Netherlands by a combination of superior French forces under Villeroi (who had been exchanged) and by lack of Dutch cooperation.

1703, July–September. Villars in the Danube Valley. Louis of Baden and Styrum advanced separately into the Danube Valley, Villars skillfully concentrating against each in turn. He repulsed Louis's efforts against Augsburg at the **Battle of Munderkingen** (July 31), then, in collaboration with the elector, defeated Styrum decisively at the **Battle of Hochstadt,** losing only 1,000 men, while the Austrians lost 11,000 out of 20,000. Louis had taken advantage of this brief campaign to seize Augsburg (September 6), but hastily withdrew and went into winter quarters as Villars approached. Villars again urged Maximilian to join him in a dash to Vienna, which was simultaneously being menaced by Hungarian rebels from the east (see p. 642). But the fainthearted elector refused, and after a violent quarrel Villars gave up his command and returned to France. He was replaced by Marshal **Marsin.**

1703, August–November. Operations along the Middle Rhine. To assure better communications with the army in Bavaria, Marshal Count **Camille de Tallard** was given the mission of securing the middle Rhine. An army under the aging Vauban besieged and captured **Alt Breisach,** most important fortification on the right bank of the Rhine south of Kehl (September 6). Tallard cleared the allies from the Bavarian Palatinate by a victory at **Speyer,** and recaptured **Landau** (November 12).

1703, October 25. Savoy Changes Sides. Duke **Victor Amadeus,** distrustful of the French, allied himself with the emperor.

1703, November–December. Recall of Eugene from Italy. Leopold, alarmed by the situation in southern Germany, and with his southern flank now guarded by Savoy, recalled Eugene from Italy to protect Vienna.

1704. Opposing Plans. The French planned to send Tallard to reinforce Marsin and the elector for a powerful thrust at Vienna. Villeroi, meanwhile, was expected to contain Marlborough along the Netherlands frontiers. Marlborough, as captain general of Anglo-Dutch forces, decided to send the Archduke Charles and an expeditionary force for an invasion of Spain to Lisbon. Admiral Sir **George Rooke** was then to take the fleet, and additional troops, to attack Toulon and to support Huguenot rebels (the Camisards) in southern France. These operations, however, were primarily diversionary. The allied main effort was to be a concentration of forces under Eugene and Marlborough in the Danube Valley to save Vienna, to drive the French out of Germany, and to knock Bavaria out of the war. It is not clear whether this bold concept was Marlborough's or Eugene's; more likely it was the Austrian's, though either general was capable of it.

BLENHEIM CAMPAIGN, 1704

1704, April. French Reinforcements to Bavaria. The strength of Maximilian and Marsin, concentrated around Ulm, was brought to about 55,000 men. Tallard with 30,000 was at Strasbourg, preparing to march east. The Austrians had 30,000 around Vienna, Eugene had about 10,000 men south of Ulm, and Louis of Baden had about 30,000 at Stollhofen, on the Rhine north of Kehl.

1704, May–June. Marlborough's March to the Danube. Leaving about 60,000 men to protect Holland, Marlborough, without informing the Dutch of his intentions, marched toward the Rhine Valley (May 20) with 35,000 men, of whom less than one-third were British and the remainder German forces in British pay. At Mondelsheim he met Eugene and Louis of Baden for a planning conference (June 10–13). Marlborough and Baden continued toward the Danube, while Eugene returned to Stollhofen to prevent Tallard (now at Landau) and Villeroi (now at Strasbourg) from reinforcing Maximilian and Marsin. Distribution of forces was as follows (June 30): Allies: Marlborough and Baden advancing eastward toward Donauwörth, 70,000 men; Eugene at Stollhofen, 30,000. French and Bavarians: Maximilian and Marsin, near Ulm, 60,-000; Villeroi at Strasbourg, 60,000; Tallard, advancing east across the Rhine from Landau, 30,000.

1704, July 2. Battle of the Schellenberg. An audacious surprise attack by Marlborough on the fortified Schellenberg Hill overlooking Donauwörth. Despite heavy losses, Marlborough took the hill, and then Donauwörth, without a siege.

1704, July–August. Maneuvers in Southern Germany. Marsin and Maximilian moved to Augsburg to block Marlborough's approach to Munich. Since Maximilian and Marsin refused battle until they received reinforcements, Marlborough and Baden began to devastate western Bavaria. Meanwhile, Tallard had marched to Ulm (July 29), and soon thereafter joined Marsin and Maximilian south of the Danube. Eugene, misleading Villeroi into thinking he was staying near the Rhine, marched hastily eastward with about 20,000 men to join Marlborough. Villeroi, not knowing where Eugene had gone, decided to stay near Strasbourg to protect Alsace. With battle approaching, Marlborough sent Baden (for whom he had low regard) to besiege Ingolstadt, and prepared to march west to join Eugene.

1704, August 10. French and Bavarians Cross the Danube. Knowing Eugene had arrived near Donauwörth, and that Marlborough was still in western Bavaria, Tallard (real commander of Maximilian's Franco-Bavarian army) moved to attack Eugene, or at least force him and Marlborough to retreat northward to protect their lines of communication. Eugene sent a message urging Marlborough to join him.

1704, August 12. Marlborough and Eugene Join Forces. The combined allied force totaled about 56,000 men. The Franco-Bavarians, encamped behind a little stream near Blenheim, just north of the Danube, totaled about 60,000, almost equally divided between the armies of Tallard and of Marsin-Maximilian.

1704, August 12–13. The Allied Advance. Marlborough and Eugene decided to attack. Marlborough's larger army, on the left, was to make the main effort against Tallard, while Eugene was to contain Marsin and Maximilian with an aggressive holding attack. Following carefully prepared plans, the allied armies, deployed in battle order, marched from their camps near Donauwörth at 2 A.M. in 9 columns. Marlborough's 5 columns, going over easy ground, arrived on the heights east of the Nebel stream at 7 A.M., and began skirmishing with French outposts and exchanging long-range fire with the artillery of the surprised and hastily deploying Franco-Bavarians. Eugene's troops, having a longer and more difficult route, did not reach their appointed positions until nearly noon.

1704, August 13. Battle of Blenheim. Marlborough and Eugene attacked simultaneously across the Nebel at 12:30. Marlborough initially attacked the villages of Blenheim (beside the river) and Oberglau (about 2 miles inland) to pin down French reserves. The British lost heavily, but the purpose was accomplished; Tallard poured in his reserves. Learning that Eugene was advancing very slowly in heavy fighting on the right, in accordance with plan, Marlborough at 4:30 launched his cavalry squadrons in an attack which after about an hour of tough fighting broke through Tallard's center. Tallard's army was shattered and he was captured. Many of the fleeing troops drowned in the Danube. Before Marlborough could complete a right turn, in the dusk Marsin and Maximilian were able to extract most of their army from the jaws of Eugene's and Marlborough's double envelopment. Allied losses were 4,500 killed and 7,500 wounded. The French and Bavarians lost a total of 38,600 in killed, wounded, and prisoners.

COMMENT. *There is probably no finer example in history of allied coordination and cooperation than that of Eugene and Marlborough in this campaign and battle. The prestige of France and French armies was shattered; the Elector of Bavaria had to flee his country, which was annexed by Austria.*

1705. Stalemate in the Low Countries. Marlborough, back in the Netherlands, was opposed in a desultory campaign by Villeroi and the Elector of Bavaria. His offensive inclinations were again frustrated by the overcautious Dutch.

1705. Stalemate on the Rhine. Equally inconclusive were the maneuverings of Villars and Louis of Baden.

1705. Stalemate in Italy. After Vendôme had overrun much of Savoy, Eugene was sent to the aid of Victor Amadeus. No further results were achieved. The only major action was the drawn **Battle of Cassano** (August 16).

THE RAMILLIES CAMPAIGN, 1706

1706, April–May. Convergence on Namur. Villeroi, rightly believing that Marlbor-

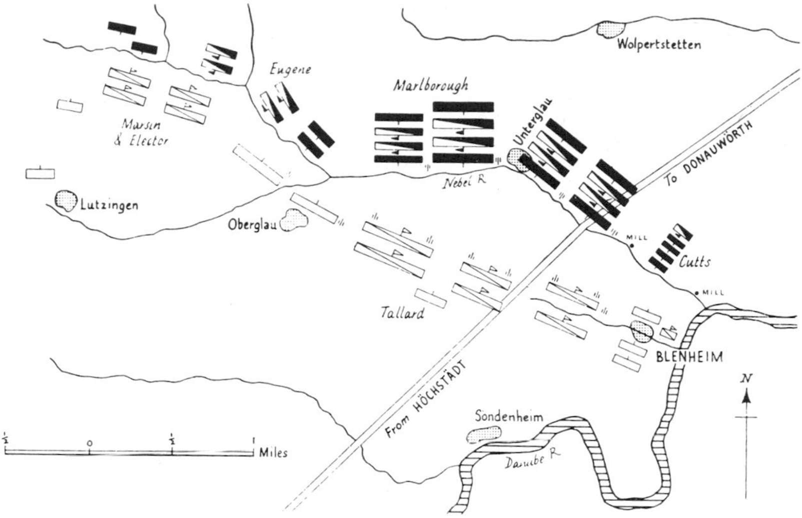

Battle of Blenheim

ough intended to seize Namur, moved with about 60,000 men to protect the city. He was intercepted at Ramillies by the allied army in about equal strength.

1706, May 23. Battle of Ramillies. The French drew themselves up on high ground in a defensive position, partially entrenched. Marlborough, in a typical maneuver, feinted against the French left, causing Villeroi to shift his reserves and to draw some units out of his right wing. Marlborough then launched his main attack against the weakened French right. The outnumbered French right defended itself gallantly, but was overwhelmed by the strength and power of the allied attack. The entire French line wavered, and Marlborough ordered a general attack, driving the French off the field in great disorder. He pursued vigorously, inflicting heavy losses. French casualties were about 8,000 killed and wounded and 7,000 prisoners. The allies lost 1,066 men killed and 3,633 wounded.

1706, June–October. Marlborough Consolidates the Spanish Netherlands. He captured the following important fortifications, among others: Antwerp (June 6), Dunkirk (July 6), Menin (August 22), Dendermonde (September 5), Ath (October 4). In these operations the allies took about 14,000 additional prisoners.

1706, August. Vendôme to Command in the North. Hurriedly called north from Italy (see below), he replaced the incompetent Villeroi. Louis XIV also made tentative peace overtures.

THE TURIN CAMPAIGN, 1706

1706, April 19. Vendôme Seizes the Initiative. With an army of over 100,000, opposed to about 30,000 Savoyards and less than 40,000 Austrians, he boldly divided his field forces into 2 main groups of about 40,000 each. With one he drove the Austrians, under Count **Reventlau,** from central Lombardy back to the Adige River. The remaining French besieged Turin, capital of Savoy.

1706, April 22. Arrival of Eugene. Eugene, who had been in Vienna, took command and halted the Austrian retreat. He remained on the Adige, maneuvering against Vendôme, for more than a month.

1706, July–August. Eugene's Advance on Turin. Having received reinforcements, which brought his strength about equal to that of the French on the Adige, Eugene responded to appeals from Victor Amadeus by adroitly marching south with 25,000 men, leaving 18,000 on the Adige in front of Vendôme. Swinging around Vendôme's right, he threatened the French line of communications, causing Vendôme to fall back. Vendôme was now called north to retrieve the disaster of

Ramillies (see above). He left the young **Duke of Orléans** in command, with Marshal Marsin as his second in command. Suddenly, to the amazement of the French, Eugene marched due west, abandoning his line of communications and living off the countryside, something almost unheard of in 18th-century warfare. He seized Parma (August 15), then turned northwestward. Orléans, confused by Eugene's maneuvers, rushed back to Turin, just as Eugene met Victor Amadeus on the upper Po (August 31). The combined allied army was then about 36,000, with another 6,000 Piedmontese east of Turin, and about 15,000 in the besieged city. Orléans had about 60,000 in the lines west of the Po at Turin, with another 20,000 facing the Piedmontese detachment. Another 20,000 or more French were scattered through northwest Italy in garrisons. The French lines of circumvallation around Turin were very strong. Eugene, in a favorable position on the French lines of communication, but with only half the strength of his strongly entrenched enemy, decided to attack.

1706, September 7. Battle of Turin. Selecting a relatively isolated portion of the French lines between the Dura and Stura rivers, tributaries of the Po, Eugene and the Piedmontese attacked vigorously, smashing through the defending lines before Orléans could send adequate reinforcements. As more French troops arrived, however, the allied attack was halted. Eugene reformed, then vigorously resumed his bold attack against the more numerous enemy just as the garrison made a sortie. The French could not cope with these converging attacks. Orléans was wounded, Marsin mortally wounded, and the French army collapsed and fled, abandoning all of its baggage, 100 pieces of artillery, and heavy equipment. French losses were 2,000 killed, 1,200 wounded, and 6,000 prisoners. The allies lost 950 killed and 2,300 wounded. The routed French fled to France, pursued by Austrian and Piedmontese detachments.

1706, September–December. Eugene Sweeps the French from Italy. By the end of the year Eugene had captured all of the remaining French garrisons in north Italy.

COMMENT. *This was probably the most brilliant campaign of the war.*

1707. Inconclusive Operations. Vendôme held the Flanders frontier, while Marlborough and the Dutch continued their debates. In the most daring operation of the year, Villars, on the Rhine, drove the Austrians from their lines at **Stollhofen** (May 22), then raided into south-central Germany as far as Bavaria, living off the countryside (June–September). In Italy Eugene and Victor Amadeus invaded southern France, but without result (see p. 626).

OUDENARDE CAMPAIGN, 1708

Deployment of Forces. The French Flanders army, about 100,000 strong, under the nominal command of the young **Duke of Burgundy,** but with Vendôme exercising actual operational command, was located around Mons. The **Duke of Berwick*** and **Maximilian** of Bavaria had another French army of about 50,000 at Strasbourg, while Villars had about 20,000 in the Vosges near Switzerland. On the allied side Marlborough had nearly 70,000 at Brussels, Eugene had 35,000 at Coblenz, and the **Duke of Hanover** had about 50,000 opposite Strasbourg.

1708, April. Allied Planning Conference. Marlborough and Eugene, at The Hague, agreed that Eugene's army would join Marlborough in the Netherlands when another allied army, gathering in central Germany, arrived on the Rhine to replace him. Eugene was under strict imperial orders not to leave the Rhine until these reinforcements arrived.

1708, May–June. Maneuvers in Flanders. Vendôme aggressively seized the initiative. He gave Marlborough no opportunity to attack, even when he approached allied positions near Louvain (late June).

1708, July 1–9. Vendôme Threatens Oudenarde. The French army suddenly moved westward to capture Ghent (July 4) and Bruges (July 5) in a *coup de main.* Vendôme then turned south to threaten the allied garrison of Oudenarde. Knowing

* Nephew of Marlborough, illegitimate son of James II and Arabella Churchill.

that Eugene's army had started westward from Coblenz, he was anxious for battle before the Austrians arrived. Marlborough, realizing he had been outmaneuvered, and with Dutch morale plummeting, also sought battle. He had been reinforced and his field strength was about 80,000, about equal to that of Burgundy and Vendôme, west of the Scheldt. Furthermore, although Eugene's army was still marching from the Rhine, Eugene himself arrived to join the allied army. He also urged battle.

1708, July 10. French Command Troubles. With battle obviously imminent, young Burgundy became nervous and insisted that Vendôme avoid battle. While the prince and the general argued, the French army stood aimlessly in scattered units north of Oudenarde, instead of moving to block the allied passage of the Scheldt.

1708, July 10–11. Marlborough's Advance. The allied army marched 28 miles in 22 hours. Marlborough turned the right wing of his army over to Eugene. They hastily prepared a plan roughly similar to Blenheim.

1708, July 11. Battle of Oudenarde. While the allies swarmed across the river in the morning and early afternoon, Burgundy ordered a retreat. However, Vendôme finally convinced the prince that he would be cut off from France if he did not stand and fight. Reluctantly Burgundy gave his permission for a defensive battle; Vendôme hastily deployed the army on the heights north of Oudenarde. Despite the royal orders, Vendôme ordered an attack just as Marlborough and Eugene were beginning their own attack (about 2 P.M.). There was little plan on either side, and the result was a long, confused, bloody struggle, in which the allies held a slight advantage due to the vigor, determination, and field generalship of their joint commanders; the French had perhaps been discouraged by the obvious vacillation in their command. By dusk Marlborough had achieved an envelopment of the French right and, as Eugene continued to press forward, the allies drove the French from the field in the gathering darkness. French losses were 4,000 killed, 2,000 wounded, 9,000 prisoners, and 3,000 missing (deserters). Allied losses were 2,000 killed and 5,000 wounded.

1708, July 12. Allied Repulse at Ghent. Vendôme, brilliantly rallying his defeated troops, repulsed the pursuing allies at Ghent. As a result, the French retained control of western Flanders, and regained a secure line of communications to France.

COMMENT. *It is interesting to speculate on the result if Vendôme had been initially free to fight this campaign as he wished.*

1708, July 15. Arrival of Eugene's Army. The allies now had a clear-cut superiority of force, totaling about 120,000 men. Vendôme, reinforced by Berwick, had 96,000. Marlborough's plan of invading France was vetoed by the Dutch. Surprising Vendôme, Marlborough moved suddenly south against Lille (August).

1708, August 14–December 11. Siege of Lille. The siege was conducted by Eugene with 40,000 men, while Marlborough covered with 70,000 in strong defensive positions. Boufflers gave up the city due to lack of food, but withdrew into the citadel with his garrison (October 22). At this point Vendôme marched northeastward to threaten Brussels, hoping this would force the allies to raise the siege, but Marlborough moved after him vigorously and Vendôme fell back (November 24). Boufflers was finally forced to surrender (December 11). Because of his skill and gallantry, Marlborough and Eugene let him dictate his own surrender terms.

1708, December–1709, January. French Withdrawal. Marlborough, refusing to go into winter quarters, decided to force the French out of western Flanders. He besieged and captured Ghent (January 2), and then took Bruges. The French withdrew to their own borders, and both sides went into winter quarters.

1708–1709. Fruitless Peace Negotiations. Louis again sought terms, but refused harsh allied conditions. The French people gave full support to Louis's decision to continue the war.

MALPLAQUET CAMPAIGN, 1709

1709, Spring. Deployments in Flanders. The French army, about 112,000 strong, under Villars, with Boufflers, his senior, voluntarily serving under his command, was entrenched generally north of the border. Villars was instructed from Paris to avoid general battle if possible. The allied army, about 110,000, under Marlborough and Eugene, occupied most of the Spanish Netherlands. Their objective was to try to get past, or through, the French fortified line, or to entice the French to leave that line for battle on conditions favorable to the allies.

1709, June–August. Inconclusive Maneuvering. The most important of many minor incidents was the siege and capture of Tournai by the allies (June 28–July 29). Gradually the allies were able to reach a position to threaten Mons, held by the French.

1709, September 4–October 26. Siege of Mons. Villars now received orders from Paris to fight to hold Mons. He immediately concentrated 90,000 men at Malplaquet, where he entrenched, knowing that this threat to the besieging forces would attract them to attack him. Marlborough and Eugene, leaving about 20,000 men to continue the siege, eagerly advanced with about 90,000 to accept Villars' challenge (September 9–10).

1709, September 11. Approach to Battle. The allies advanced with, as usual, Eugene on the right and Marlborough on the left. Eugene was to make a holding attack on the French left, while part of Marlborough's force was making a secondary holding attack on the French right; the remainder of Marlborough's command would make the main effort near the French center after French reserves had been committed. This simple tactical scheme had been effective at Blenheim and Ramillies, and something similar had won the day at Oudenarde. This, however, was the first time allied generals had been opposed by Villars, a commander of ability comparable to their own.

1709, September 11. Battle of Malplaquet. The vigor of the early allied flank attacks led Villars to weaken his center, mainly to oppose Eugene. In the bitter fighting on the French left and allied right, Eugene was twice wounded, but refused to leave the field; Villars was so badly wounded while leading a counterattack that he had to turn the command over to Boufflers. During the early afternoon Marlborough launched his typical hammer-blow cavalry-infantry attack against the French center, and broke through. Boufflers, following Villars' plan, promptly counterattacked with his last reserves, re-establishing the line. Marlborough and Eugene now committed their remaining reserves and renewed the vigor of their attacks, again penetrating the French center. Boufflers thereupon ordered a general withdrawal, which was carried out in good order. The allies, who had suffered fearful losses, were unable to pursue. French losses were about 4,500 killed and 8,000 wounded. The allies lost about 6,500 killed and more than 14,000 wounded. Both sides had fought superbly, and the leadership was excellent on both sides at all levels. The allied victory was primarily due to the absolute determination of Eugene and Marlborough, who persisted in attacks after most generals would have admitted defeat. The battle had no results other than to permit the allies to continue the siege of Mons, which they eventually captured (October 26). Both armies then went into winter quarters.

1709–1710. The "Ne Plus Ultra" Lines. During the winter the French built a strong line of fortifications along the frontier.

1710–1711. Inconclusive Maneuvering. Marlborough and Eugene captured a few more border fortresses, including Douai (1710, June 10) and Bethune (August 30). Nothing further of real significance occurred during that year. The following year Eugene was ordered to Frankfurt to protect that city during the coronation of new Emperor **Charles VI**—the former Archduke Charles. Because none of the allies would accept Charles both as Emperor and as King of Spain, the alliance began to fall apart. In Flanders, Villars and Marlborough treated each other with cautious respect.

1711, December 31. Recall of Marlborough. The new Tory cabinet relieved him of his command, ending his military career.

1712. Peace Negotiations. While negotiators met at Utrecht, Eugene assumed command in the Netherlands. He was no more successful than Marlborough in getting the Dutch to agree to aggressive action, particularly with negotiations under way. Eugene nevertheless crossed the Scheldt with 120,000 men (May) to try to force a battle on Villars, who was entrenched from Cambrai to Arras with 100,000 men. Unknown to Eugene, however, his English contingent, now under **James Butler, Duke of Ormonde,** had been ordered not to fight, and suddenly was withdrawn. The remainder of the allied army was forced to halt, while Eugene attempted to obtain reinforcements.

1712. Battle of Denain. Villars, by prompt and energetic action, overwhelmed a portion of Eugene's army in a bayonet attack. About 8,000 allied soldiers were killed or drowned in the Scheldt; the French lost 500. Eugene, who arrived too late to take part in the action, decided to withdraw across the river.

1712, August–October. Villars on the Offensive. The French now advanced, besieging and recapturing a number of the fortresses they had lost in previous years, including Douai, Quesnoy, and Bouchain. These successes materially aided the French negotiators at Utrecht.

1713, April 11. Treaty of Utrecht. Agreed to by all participants save the Emperor, who continued the war. France recognized the Protestant succession in England, and ceded Newfoundland and parts of Canada to England. Philip V was recognized as King of Spain, but France gave assurances that the crowns of France and Spain would remain permanently separated. Savoy received Sicily and some lands in northern Italy from Spain. Prussia was recognized as a monarchy. Portugal received a favorable correction of colonial boundaries in South America. The Empire was to receive the Spanish Netherlands (meanwhile administered by Holland) and all Spanish possessions in Italy, save those given to Savoy.

1713, May–November. Operations on the Rhine. Eugene, given only 60,000 men and poorly supported by Austria, was opposed by Villars with 130,000. Villars besieged and captured Speyer, Landau, and Freiburg.

1713–1714. Peace Negotiations. These were concluded by Eugene and Villars.

1714, March–September. Treaties of Rastatt and Baden. At Rastatt Austrian Emperor Charles VI made peace with France. As Holy Roman Emperor, he made peace at Baden. Generally the terms confirmed Utrecht. The Emperor still refused to recognize Bourbon rule in Spain.

Operations in Spain and the Mediterranean

1702, August–September. Allied Repulse at Cádiz. An Anglo-Dutch force of 50 ships and 15,000 men under Rooke (land force under the **Duke of Ormonde**) was repulsed in a fiasco of mismanagement.

1702, October 12. Naval Action at Vigo Bay. Rooke's allied force, returning from the failure at Cádiz, discovered in Vigo Bay the Spanish treasure fleet from the River Plate, protected by a Franco-Spanish squadron including 24 French ships of the line. In a combined action, the Duke of Ormonde's troops took the fortifications overlooking the bay while the fleet forced the boom and entered the harbor. Rooke destroyed or captured the entire treasure fleet and its convoy. The booty of £2 million was perhaps the largest ever taken in one action.

1703, May. Portugal Joins the Alliance. The Portuguese agreed to make bases available to the allies for operations against Spain by land and by sea (known as the **Methuen Treaty**).

1704, February. Charles at Lisbon. The Archduke Charles and 2,000 English and Dutch troops were landed at Lisbon by Rooke's English fleet.

1704, March–June. Rooke in the Mediterranean. Rooke passed through the Straits of Gibraltar, hoping to join the Duke of Savoy in an attack on Toulon, but Victor Amadeus did not cooperate. Arrival of the French Brest fleet, which outsailed the English to reach Toulon unscathed, gave the French numerical superiority in the Mediterranean, and Rooke returned through the Straits to join another Anglo-Dutch fleet under Admiral **Clowdisley Shovell** near Cádiz. The combined allied fleet then returned to the Mediterranean.

1704, July 23–24. Capture of Gibraltar. An English fleet under Vice-Admiral Viscount **George Byng of Torrington** bombarded Gibraltar, which was seized next day by 1,800 English marines, commanded by Prince **George of Hesse-Darmstadt.**

1704, August 13. Naval Battle of Malaga. The allied (English and Dutch) fleet under Rooke defeated the combined French fleet under the **Count of Toulouse.** This secured the British capture of Gibraltar.

1704, August–1705, March. Siege of Gibraltar. A Franco-Spanish force under Marshal Count **R. de Fromlay Tessé** besieged Gibraltar, which Prince George held successfully with only 900 marines. He was reinforced and resupplied (December), and after a supporting French naval force was destroyed (see below), Tessé raised the siege.

1705, March 10. Naval Battle of Marbella. An English naval squadron under Admiral Sir **John Leake** destroyed a French squadron under Admiral **de Pointis** near Gibraltar.

1705, June. Allied Landing in Catalonia. Admiral Shovell and **Charles Mordaunt,** Lord **Peterborough,** as joint commanders, landed in Catalonia, accompanied by Charles. They beseiged and captured Barcelona (October 3). Prince George, who had joined at Gibraltar, was killed during the final assault. The main fleet returned to the Atlantic, leaving a squadron under Leake to support the land force.

1705, November–1706, April. Siege of Barcelona. Philip and Tessé marched from Madrid to besiege Barcelona, supported by the French Toulon fleet. Leake, outmaneuvering the French, forced them to return to Toulon, and the French army abandoned the siege (April 30), to return westward to face an invasion of Spain from Portugal under English Lord **Henry Galway** (see below).

1706, May–September. Leake's Coastal Operations. The English fleet captured Cartagena (June 1), Alicante (August 24), and the Balearic islands of Mallorca and Iviza (September).

1706, June 26. Allied Capture of Madrid. Galway's invading force from Portugal seized the capital and proclaimed Charles king.

1706, October. French Recapture Madrid. The Duke of Berwick took command of French and Spanish forces in Spain. Accompanied by Philip, he forced the allies to abandon Madrid. Galway and the Portuguese returned directly to Portugal, but Charles and other allied contingents retreated to Valencia.

1707, April. Allied Advance toward Madrid. Galway, who had returned to the east coast by sea, led an army of 33,000 from Valencia toward Madrid. Berwick, with an equal force, marched to meet him.

1707, April 25. Battle of Almanza. Berwick decisively defeated Galway. French losses were slight; the allies lost 5,000 killed and wounded and 10,000 prisoners. Galway retreated to Valencia, closely pursued by Berwick. With only 16,000 men left, Galway continued his retreat to Catalonia (October). The French now had effective control over practically all of Spain. Both armies went into winter quarters near Barcelona.

1707, July–August. Allied Invasion of France; Blockade of Toulon. The allied fleet under Shovell blockaded Toulon by sea, while Eugene and Victor Amadeus led an imperial-Savoy army across the Maritime Alps. Marshal Tessé, however, who had just arrived from Spain with veterans of Almanza, repulsed the allied land force, thanks mainly to the Duke of Savoy's refusal to cooperate closely with Eugene (July 26). The French, expecting to lose Toulon, had sunk their 50 ships in the harbor, giving the allies uncontested control of the Mediterranean. The allied army returned to Italy, while the main allied fleet returned to the Atlantic.

1708, August. Allied Capture of Sardinia. Admiral Leake, his marines, and a contingent of Savoy troops captured the island.

1708, September. Capture of Minorca. The English force was commanded by General **James Stanhope.**

1708–1709. Stalemate in Catalonia. Berwick, recalled to the Netherlands after the French disasters at Ramillies and Turin, left the Duke of Orléans in command. Despite French superiority, there was little action. The allies in Catalonia were now commanded by Stanhope.

1710, May–December. Madrid Campaign. Stanhope's force, about 26,000 men, was opposed by about 35,000 under Philip in Catalonia. A Portuguese army of 33,000 was at Elvas. Advancing rapidly, and expecting to meet the Portuguese at Madrid, Stanhope won victories at **Almenar, Lérida,** and **Saragossa,** then marched on Madrid, accompanied by Charles. The Portuguese, however, had withdrawn when opposed by a much smaller Franco-Spanish force. The Spanish people made clear their preference of Philip over Charles. Vendôme arrived in Spain, collected the scattered French forces, and advanced on Saragossa with 27,000 men, cutting Stanhope's line of communications (October). As the French approached Madrid, Stanhope, who had only 16,000, retreated toward Valencia, closely pursued by Vendôme. The French caught up with the allied rear guard, under Stanhope's personal command, defeating and capturing him at the **Battle of Brihuega** (December 10). The remainder of the allied force, under General **Guido von Starhemberg,** retreating to Barcelona, was again defeated en route at the **Battle of Villaviciosa.**

1714, September 11. Fall of Barcelona. Finally captured by the French under Berwick; last major action of the war.

1715, February. Treaty of Madrid. Peace with Portugal, officially ending the war.

WAR OF THE QUADRUPLE ALLIANCE, 1718–1720

After the death of Louis XIV of France (1715), his grandson, Philip of Spain, uncle of **Louis XV,** hoped to gain the crown of France himself. These ambitions seem to have been fanned by the designs and intrigues of his powerful and unscrupulous prime minister, Cardinal **Giulio Alberoni.** At the same time other, and equally aggressive, ambitions were being entertained by Philip's second wife, **Elizabeth Farnese** of Parma, who wished her children to inherit the family's possessions in Italy, and perhaps all Italy. The maritime powers—England and Holland—were unalterably opposed to any union of France and Spain. The Emperor Charles VI, aside from his continuing enmity toward Philip as a result of the War of the Spanish Succession, had equally strong dynastic reasons to oppose any return of Spanish power to Italy. The Empire, however, was engaged in a major war against Turkey, hence Charles was unprepared to precipitate another war in Italy or Western Europe.

1717, January 4. The Triple Alliance. England, France, and Holland agreed to oppose the ambitions of Philip and of Spain both in France and in Italy.

1717, November. Spanish Occupation of Sardinia. Taking advantage of Austria's war with Turkey, Philip sent an army to seize Sardinia, formerly a Spanish possession, but granted to Austria by the Treaties of Utrecht and Rastatt (see p. 625).

1718, July. Spanish Occupation of Sicily. This former Spanish colony, awarded to Savoy by the Treaty of Utrecht, provided a second base for further political and military action in Italy. It was seized by an army of 30,000 under the **Marquis of Lede.**

1718, August 2. Formation of the Quadruple Alliance. Austria joined the Triple Alliance. France, Austria, and England (Holland, though in the alliance, was not at this time active against Spain) demanded Spanish withdrawal from Sicily. Spain refused. An English fleet immediately landed a force of 3,000 Austrian troops near Messina, where they blockaded the Spanish garrison (August).

1718, August 11. Naval Battle of Cape Passaro (off Syracuse). Byng's English fleet of 21 ships of the line completely overwhelmed a somewhat smaller, but much weaker, Spanish fleet under Admiral Castenada. The British sank or captured 16 Spanish ships of the line and 4 frigates; only 2 or 3 Spanish ships escaped.

1718, December. Declaration of War. Holland later joined her allies in the war (August, 1719).

1718–1719. Operations in Sicily. Austrian troops, supported by an English fleet, operated against Spanish forces based in Messina. The Austrians captured Messina (October, 1719).

1719, March. Spanish Expedition to Scotland. This force, which included 6,000 men and a large store of supplies of weapons for Scottish Jacobites, was scattered by a storm off Scotland (see p. 638).

1719, April. French Invasion of Spain. A

French army of 30,000, under Berwick, invaded the Basque provinces of Spain. Berwick ranged through northern Spain almost unopposed before disease and bad weather caused him to return to France (November).

1719, October. English Operations along the Galician Coast. Amphibious forces captured Vigo and Pontevedra.

1719, December. Dismissal of Alberoni. Philip finally recognized that the recent series of disasters to Spanish arms had largely been the result of the intrigues of his prime minister.

1720, February 17. Treaty of The Hague. Philip abandoned his Italian claims in return for Austrian agreement that his son Charles could succeed to the duchies of Parma, Piacenza, and Tuscany upon the impending extinction of the male Farnese line. Sicily was ceded to Austria; Savoy got Sardinia in return. Victor Amadeus of Savoy was recognized as King of Sardinia.

WAR OF THE POLISH SUCCESSION, 1733–1738*

During the Great Northern War (see p. 614), Stanislas Leszczynski was briefly installed as King of Poland by Charles XII, but the eventual defeat of Charles left Augustus II (protégé of Peter the Great of Russia) on the throne. As the death of Augustus II approached, there were 2 major claimants to the throne of Poland: Stanislas Leszczynski, now the father-in-law of Louis XV, and thus supported by France (and also by Spain and Sardinia); and **Augustus III of Saxony,** son of Augustus II, supported by Austria and Russia.

1733, February. Death of Augustus II.

1733, September. Arrival of Stanislas in Warsaw. The former king was popularly re-elected to his former throne.

1733, October. Russian Invasion. An army of 30,000 Russians, later joined by 10,000 Saxons, marched on Warsaw to support the claims of Augustus III. There was no effective Polish army, and Stanislas fled to Danzig.

1734, January–June. Siege of Danzig. Despite the arrival by sea of a French relief force of 2,200 men, the Russians and Saxons captured the town. Stanislas escaped to Prussia just before the capitulation.

1734, April–September. Operations in the Rhineland. The only important event of this inconclusive campaign was the French capture of Philippsburg, after overrunning Lorraine. Of greater historical interest is the fact that it was the last campaign of 2 great soldiers: Prince Eugene of Savoy, the magnificent Frenchman who had fought all his life for Austria, and the Duke of Berwick, the gifted Englishman who had fought all of his life for France. Berwick was killed during the siege of Philippsburg (June 12). Also significant was the first appearance of a Russian army in the Rhine Valley after the campaign had come to its languid close and peace negotiations had begun.

1734–1735. Operations in Italy. Following French and Spanish invasions of Lombardy, Naples, and Sicily, the Austrians won the **Battle of Parma** (June 29), the French the **Battle of Luzzara** (September 19), and the Austrians had slightly the better of the final engagements of the war at the **Battle of Bitonto** (May 25, 1735).

1734–1735. Civil War in Poland. Stanislas, more popular among the Poles than his rival Augustus, attempted to revive his fallen fortunes, but received little help from France, whose prime minister, Cardinal **André H. de Fleury,** was anxious to restore peace on terms favorable to France.

1738, November. Treaty of Vienna. Stanislas abdicated the throne of Poland; the coronation of Augustus (which had taken place at Cracow, September, 1734) was recognized, but Leszczynski was created Duke of Lorraine (and permitted to retain the title of King of Poland), while possession of Lorraine was to go to the French crown upon his death. **Charles Bourbon** (son of Philip of Spain) was recognized as King of the Two Sicilies, in return for which his 3 duchies were ceded to Austria.

* Since the Polish monarchy was elective and not hereditary, Polish historians designate this more accurately as the "War for the Polish Throne."

AUSTRO-RUSSIAN-TURKISH WAR, 1736–1739

This was an outgrowth of the War of the Polish Succession (see above). France urged Turkey to join her in the war against the Ottoman Empire's traditional enemies: Russia and Austria. Turkey postponed her participation in the European war until she had concluded an ongoing war against Persia. By this time the War of the Polish Succession was over, and so a new and different war resulted: Russia, learning of Turkish intentions, and anxious to gain revenge for the Treaty of the Pruth (see p. 616), declared war (late 1735).

1736. Operations in the Ukraine. Two Russian armies invaded the Turkish-Tartar regions north of the Black Sea. The army under Marshal Count **Peter Lacy** captured Azov after a fierce struggle, but lost so heavily in the campaign that Lacy abandoned the fortress and retreated into the Russian Ukraine. The army under Marshal Count **Burkhardt C. von Munnich** invaded the Crimea and captured the Tartar capital. Losses from disease, exhaustion, and starvation, however, resulted in a mutiny, and Munnich retreated, having lost 30,000 dead out of his army of 58,000.

1736–1737. Tartar Raids in the Ukraine. Retaliating for the invasion of their territory, an army of 100,000 Tartars devastated much of the Russian Ukraine.

1737, January. Austrian Declaration of War. Revealing a secret treaty with Russia, Austria sent invading armies under Marshal Count **Friedcrich H. von Seckendorf** into Bosnia, Wallachia, and southern Serbia, capturing Nish. A Turkish counteroffensive, however, threw the Austrians out of most of the regions they had conquered. The Austrians and Russians made no attempt to coordinate their operations.

1737. Renewed Russian Offensives. While one Russian army raided into the Ukraine and another reoccupied Azov without serious opposition, the main army under Munnich overran most of the Turkish Ukraine and captured Ochakov, at the mouth of the Bug River. Again the Russians were stricken with disease, and Munnich was fortunate in being able to withdraw without serious opposition from large Turkish forces waiting passively in Moldavia and Bessarabia.

1738. Operations in the Balkans. The Turks, retaining the initiative, by the end of the campaign had thrown an army across the Danube into the Banat, and were threatening Belgrade. There were no major battles, as Austrian Count **Lothar J. G. Konigsegg-Rothenfels** conducted a typical 18th-century campaign.

1738. Operations in the Ukraine. One Russian force conducted an inconclusive and meaningless raid into the Crimea, while Munnich threatened Moldavia. Repulsed at the **Battle of Bendery,** in an effort to cross the Dniester River, he was once more forced to retreat, leaving half of his army dead (from battle, disease, and starvation) while abandoning almost all of his artillery.

1739. Operations in the Balkans. An Austrian army commanded by General Count **Georg O. von Wallis** was forced to fight a greatly superior Turkish army advancing on Belgrade. Wallis, decisively defeated in the **Battle of Kroszka,** fell back into Belgrade, where he was besieged.

1739. Operations in Moldavia. Munnich's fourth offensive was finally successful. Advancing through Polish Podolia, he invaded Moldavia with an army of 68,000. He defeated 90,000 Turks in the **Battle of Khotin** (or Stavuchany, August 17); captured the fortress of Khotin; seized Jassy, capital of Moldavia; and prepared for an advance on Constantinople.

1739, September. Negotiations at Belgrade. The Austrians, dismayed by the successes of their Russian allies, immediately entered negotiations with the Turks at Belgrade.

1739, September 18. Treaty of Belgrade. Austria abandoned all of the gains of the Treaty of Passarowitz (see p. 642) save for the Banat, giving up northern Serbia, Belgrade, and portions of Bosnia and Wallachia. The victorious Turkish army now moved to strike the right flank of Munnich's armies in Moldavia, eastern Wallachia, and Bessarabia.

1739, October 3. Treaty of Nissa. Abandoned by Austria and threatened by the convergence of two larger Turkish armies, the Russians made peace. They surrendered all of their important conquests save for Azov, where they agreed to demolish the fortifications. They also agreed not to build a navy or merchant marine in the Black Sea. As a result of the war, however, the effective Russian frontier on the Ukrainian steppes was pushed about 50 miles closer to the Black Sea.

WAR OF THE AUSTRIAN SUCCESSION, 1740–1748

Background

1711. Death of Emperor Joseph I. He was succeeded as Emperor and as heir to the Hapsburg dominions by his half-brother, **Charles VI,** who had been one of the two major claimants to the Spanish succession (see pp. 617 and 642).

1713, April 19. The Pragmatic Sanction. Having no male children, Charles established the order of succession to be followed after his death, so as to avoid a disputed succession. The main provisions were (1) the lands of the Hapsburg Austrian Empire were to be held intact; (2) if he had no male heirs, the succession should go to his daughters—the eldest being **Maria Theresa**—and their heirs in accordance with the laws of primogeniture; (3) if this line should fail, the succession would go to the daughters of Joseph I and their heirs. This Pragmatic Sanction was accepted by Hungary (1723) and by the major European powers except Bavaria.

1725–1740. Claim of Charles Albert, Elector of Bavaria. As a descendant of the eldest daughter of Ferdinand I, he interpreted Ferdinand's will to assure him the succession in the event of a failure of Ferdinand's male descendants.

1740, October 20. Death of Charles VI. Maria Theresa inherited the Hapsburg Empire, in accordance with the Pragmatic Sanction. Her succession was disputed by the following claimants: Charles Albert of Bavaria, **Philip V** of Spain on grounds largely arising from his successful claim to the Spanish throne (see p. 625), and Augustus III of Saxony, husband of the eldest daughter of Joseph I.

1740, November. Involvement of Frederick II of Prussia. He recognized Maria Theresa's succession, offered his aid against the other claimants, but announced that in return he would occupy Silesia, pending settlement of an old Brandenburg claim for the province. Maria Theresa refused.

1740, December 16. Frederick Invades Silesia.

First Silesian War, 1740–1742

This war had nothing to do with the Austrian succession. It did, however, precipitate the wider conflict. Maria Theresa appealed to all guarantors of the Pragmatic Sanction to assist her against Frederick. There were no responses.

1741, January–February. Prussian and Austrian Actions. Frederick consolidated control over Silesia, save for a few towns held by Austrian garrisons. Investing Neisse and Glogau, Frederick put the remainder of his army in winter quarters. Meanwhile, Count **Adam A. Neipperg** was quietly collecting an Austrian army in Bohemia.

1741, March 9. Assault on Glogau. Prince **Leopold of Anhalt-Dessau** (son of the "Old Dessauer") led the efficient and successful assault.

1741, March–April. Austrian Invasion of Silesia. Unprepared for Neipperg's move while the passes from Bohemia were still covered with snow, Frederick hastily collected his scattered forces. Meanwhile Neipperg overran much of the province. By relieving the beleaguered garrison of Neisse, he cut Frederick off from Prussia.

1741, April 10. Battle of Mollwitz. At the outset of the battle superior Austrian cavalry drove the Prussian right-wing cavalry off the field. Frederick, commanding on that wing, was reluctantly persuaded by Marshal Count **Kurt C. von Schwerin** to flee with his men. Schwerin, however, stayed, and with the magnificent Prussian infantry smashed repeated attacks by the Austrian cavalry and infantry, then drove the Austrians off the field. This was the first and last time Frederick left a still-disputed battlefield.

1741, May–August. The War Spreads. Charles Albert of Bavaria, gambling to gain the Imperial crown and the Hapsburg lands, sent an army to invade Bohemia. France, allied to Bavaria, sent an army under Marshal **François M. de Broglie** into southern Germany to support the Bavarians. This force was described by the French both as "volunteers" and as "auxiliaries"; most of the officers wore Bavarian insignia. Saxony and Savoy both joined Bavaria in the war against Austria. England and Holland then immediately announced their support for Maria Theresa, and prepared for war. Sweden, influenced by France, supported Prussia and used this as an excuse to attack Russia (which supported the Pragmatic Sanction) in revenge for the Great Northern War (see p. 614).

1741, April–October. Maneuvering in Silesia. Frederick recovered much of the territory he had lost before Mollwitz, reopened his line of communications to Prussia, and cautiously maneuvered against Neippberg.

1741, July–September. Bavarian Invasion of Upper Austria. Charles Albert seized Passau (July) and was soon joined by a French army. They rejected Frederick's suggestion of a converging advance on Vienna.

1741, October 9. Truce of Klein Schnellendorf. This was a secret truce, following several weeks of secret Austrian-Prussian negotiations. In return for Frederick's agreement not to carry out further operations against the Austrians, he was to be allowed to capture Neisse after a mock siege, and was to be left in virtual control of Silesia. Neipperg immediately withdrew his army from Silesia to join the gathering Austrian forces preparing for campaigns in Bohemia and Bavaria.

1741, October. Franco-Bavarian Invasion of Bohemia. The allies marched on Prague, hoping to be joined by Frederick.

1741, November–December. Austrian Mobilization. An army under the Grand Duke **Francis of Lorraine** (Maria Theresa's consort) ineptly opposed the French-Bavarian invasion of Bohemia; additional forces gathered in Vienna. Maria Theresa, as Queen of Hungary, had made a successful appeal to the Hungarian nobles, who contributed substantial forces, mostly light troops. Additional forces were gathered from Austria and other Hapsburg dominions. The principal army, under Marshal Count **Ludwig A. von Khevenhüller,** prepared to invade Bavaria. Additional forces, under Marshal Prince **Charles of Lorraine** (younger brother of Francis) prepared to go to Bohemia.

1741, November 26. Fall of Prague. The French and Bavarians quickly consolidated control of western and central Bohemia. Charles Albert was crowned King of Bohemia (December 19).

1741, December. Renewal of War in Silesia. With her forces mobilized, Maria Theresa thought she could recover Silesia from Frederick, as well as defeat the Bavarians and French. She divulged the terms of the secret Truce of Klein Schnellendorf to embarrass Frederick with his allies. Frederick immediately sent Marshal Schwerin to Bohemia, and soon followed himself, intending to operate in conjunction with the Bavarians and French.

1741, December 27. Khevenhüller Invades Bavaria. Pushing aside weak Bavarian forces (their main army was in Bohemia), Khevenhüller invested Linz and marched on to capture Munich (January 24).

1742, January 24. Election of Charles Albert as Emperor. The same day he became Charles VII, the new Emperor's capital was being captured by the Austrians (see above).

1742, January–April. Operations in Bohemia. Planned cooperation of the Prussians, Bavarians, and French collapsed when the Bavarians had to rush back to protect what was left of their country from the Austrians. The French, under Broglie, were too weak to leave the vicinity of Prague. Leaving a force to observe the French, Charles of Lorraine, now commanding in Bohemia, moved against Frederick, who was overrunning Moravia and had even sent cavalry raiders to the outskirts of Vienna. But Charles's threats to his line of communications, combined with a Hungarian invasion of

Silesia, forced Frederick to return to Silesia. Charles followed closely.

1742, May 17. Battle of Chotusitz. In a hard-fought battle Frederick was victorious, thanks largely to the results of his intensive efforts to improve the combat capability of his cavalry.

1742, May 27. Battle of Sahay. Taking advantage of the absence of Charles, Broglie attacked and defeated the Austrian covering force in an engagement near Budweis.

1742, June 11. Treaty of Breslau. Practical Maria Theresa decided to make peace with Prussia, ceding Silesia to Frederick. She hoped that a later opportunity would permit her to recover the province. This ended the First Silesian War and (temporarily) Frederick's participation in the War of the Austrian Succession.

Operations in Bohemia and South Germany, 1742–1743

1742, June–September. Blockade of Prague. Charles, returning from Silesia, virtually besieged the French in Prague.

1742, August–September. French Invasion of Franconia. Marshal **Jean B. F. D. Maillebois** advanced from the Rhine toward Amberg. Charles raised the siege of Prague (September 14) and marched to meet the French, calling Khevenhüller to join him.

1742, October–December. Maneuvers in Bavaria and Bohemia. After an abortive demonstration toward Prague, Maillebois timidly fell back to the Danube west of Regensburg. As the Austrians again concentrated against Prague, Broglie was ordered to leave the forces there under the command of Marshal Duke **Charles L. A. F. Belle-Isle** and to take over Maillebois's army. Broglie did so, and quickly overran most of Bavaria. Charles and Khevenhüller fell back to the line between Linz and Passau, to cover the approaches to Vienna, leaving a force under Prince **Johann G. Lobkowitz** to cover Prague. Lobkowitz denuded the countryside, so that the French could obtain no provisions. Belle-Isle therefore withdrew from Bohemia (December 16–26), leaving a garrison in Prague under General **François de Chevert.** (Early the following year, after a gallant defense of the city, Chevert was allowed to evacuate with all honors of war and to rejoin the main French army.) Meanwhile, Charles VII and an imperial-Bavarian army under General **Seckendorf** joined Broglie in the Danube Valley in eastern Bavaria.

1743, April–May. Austrian Convergent Invasions of Bavaria. As Prince Charles advanced up the Danube, Khevenhüller marched into southern Bavaria from Salzburg, and Lobkowitz moved from Bohemia down the Naab. Broglie and Seckendorf could not agree on a defensive plan or strategy. After Khevenhüller defeated Seckendorf at the **Battle of Braunau** (May 9), the French and Bavarians withdrew westward from Bavaria.

1743, May–June. Advance of the Pragmatic Army. King **George II** of England, who was also the Elector of Hanover, had collected a multinational army on the lower Rhine. The principal elements were Hanoverian, English, and Dutch, with contingents from other German allies of Austria and guarantors of the Pragmatic Sanction. This army, about 40,000 strong, advanced slowly up the Rhine and into the Main and Neckar valleys. A French army of 30,000, under Marshal Duke **Adrien M. Noailles,** advanced from the middle Rhine to block the Pragmatic advance, and to protect the withdrawal of Broglie's command. The armies of George and Noailles approached each other in the Main Valley, between Hanau and Aschaffenburg. Noailles, far more skillful than George II, soon had the Pragmatic army virtually blockaded in the Main River defiles.

1743, June 27. Battle of Dettingen. In a battle typical both of English sturdiness and Hanoverian royal stubbornness, George extricated himself from the dangerous situation into which he had ineptly brought his army. At the outset a French cavalry charge came close to overwhelming the allied left wing. When his horse bolted and tried to gallop off the field, George dismounted and, sword in hand, led his English and Hanoverian infantry in counterattack. When the day was over, the allies held the field and Noailles was forced to retreat. This was the last time that an English monarch personally commanded and led his troops on the battlefield. England was still not officially at war with France.

1743, July–October. Operations along the

Rhine. Threats by both Prince Charles and King George to invade France were both frustrated by inept attempts to cross the Rhine. All armies went into winter quarters.

1743–1744. French Plans to Invade Britain. An army under Marshal **Maurice de Saxe** was assembled at Dunkirk to go to England with Prince **Charles Stuart** (pretender to the English throne). The movement was foiled by weather and the Royal Navy (see p. 637).

1744, April. French Declaration of War. France now officially entered the war. A French army of 90,000, under the personal supervision of Louis XV, prepared to invade the Spanish Netherlands. Saxe and Prince Charles Stuart were still at Dunkirk, but Saxe was soon shifted to take operational command of the main army under Louis. Another army, under Marshal **François Coigny,** collected on the middle Rhine opposite Prince Charles. Still another under Prince **Louis François de Bourbon-Conti** prepared to join the Spanish against the Austrians in northern Italy (see p. 636).

1744, June–August. Operations along the Rhine. Charles seized the initiative, crossed the Rhine near Philippsburg (July 1), and advanced on Weissenburg, cutting Coigny off from his base in Alsace. Louis XV, who had barely begun his invasion of the Austrian Netherlands, now left Saxe in Flanders and moved southeast with half of his army into Lorraine, while Coigny in a series of confused running fights fought his way through the Austrian Army at Weissenberg and re-established himself near Strasbourg. At this point, with Charles threatened by the convergence of the 2 French armies, Louis XV became ill and all French activity ceased.

Second Silesian War, 1744–1745

1744, August. Frederick Re-enters the War. Concerned by the completeness of the Austrian and allied victories of 1743, and realizing that Maria Theresa still hoped to regain Silesia, Frederick made an alliance with Louis XV.

1744, August–September. Prussian Invasion of Bohemia. Believing Charles to be in danger in northern Alsace, Frederick suddenly advanced with 80,000 men in 3 columns through Saxony, Lusatia, and Silesia into Bohemia, converging on Prague, which he quickly besieged and captured (September 2–6). He at once moved due south on Budweis, from whence he could threaten the Danube Valley and Vienna.

1744, September–November. Austrian Reaction. Inspired by Maria Theresa, new units were raised in Austria and Hungary, and regular garrisons hastily assembled to cover the approaches to Vienna. Marshal **Otto F. von Traun,** in combination with Saxon forces, held Frederick in check, while Prince Charles marched hastily east across the Rhine toward Bohemia. Frederick, finding himself opposed by the entire might of Austria and her allies, while his French allies sat on their hands, began a reluctant retreat into Silesia. Meanwhile, in the west, Louis recovered, secured the Rhine Valley, then returned to Flanders, where his army went into winter quarters.

1744, December 27. Death of Charles VII. He was succeeded as Elector of Bavaria by his son, **Maximilian Joseph,** who decided not to contend for the Imperial election.

1745, January 7. Battle of Amberg. The Austrians, in a surprise invasion of Bavaria, caught the Bavarian Army in winter quarters and in a few weeks overran most of the country (January–March).

1745, January 8. The Quadruple Alliance. At Warsaw, Austria, Saxony, England, and Holland united themselves formally against France, Bavaria, and Prussia.

1745, April 22. Treaty of Füssen. Peace between Austria and Bavaria. Maximilian renounced all pretensions to the Austrian crown and promised his vote to Francis Stephen, husband of Maria Theresa, in the coming Imperial elections. In return, Austria restored all of his possessions to the young elector. Frederick was now completely isolated from his only allies, the French, who seemed interested only in operations in Flanders.

FONTENOY CAMPAIGN, 1745

1745, May. French Advance in Flanders. Marshal Saxe (illegitimate son of Augustus II of Saxony) led a French army of about 70,000 in an advance on Tournai, which the French invested (May 10). The army was accompanied by Louis XV and the Dauphin. Opposed to Saxe was the Pragmatic army, about 50,000 strong, commanded by the young **William Augustus, Duke of Cumberland** (son of George II), who moved slowly to relieve Tournai.

1745, May 10. Battle of Fontenoy. Leaving part of his army to continue the siege, Saxe drew up about 52,000 in position at Fontenoy to block the allied advance. Dominating the French line of entrenchments were 3 hastily constructed redoubts. Saxe was so ill with the dropsy that he had himself carried to the field on a litter, but refused to relinquish command. The allies mounted an unimaginative frontal attack shortly after dawn, but were soon halted by the French defensive line. After some inconclusive skirmishing, Cumberland decided to attempt to smash his way through the center of the French position with a force of about 15,000 infantry, drawn up in 3 lines, the first 2 English (mainly consisting of the Guards Brigade), the third Hanoverian. While skirmishing continued along the line, Cumberland led these troops toward the center of the French line, between one of the redoubts and Fontenoy. As the ponderous mass, an almost square column, approached the French lines, Cumberland halted them to dress ranks and reorganize prior to a final assault. Lt. Col. Lord **Charles Hay,** commanding the Grenadier Guards, walked out between the lines; the French infantry and artillery fire slackened and came to a virtual halt. Facing the French Guards, Hay pulled out a flask, drank a toast, shouted a polite taunt, then saluted, led his troops in 3 hearty cheers, and dashed back to his own lines. (He almost certainly did not invite the French Guards to fire first, as apocryphal legend tells us.) As the amazed French were returning the salute and cheers, a tremendous volley was fired from the English line, which then resumed the advance, smashing through the shattered first French line. Louis XV, urged to flee, refused and stood fast as panicking soldiers ran past him. Saxe roused himself from his litter, mounted his horse, and established a second line which, in an exchange of smashing volleys, brought the English attack to a halt. Prominent among the French units in this new line was the Irish Brigade, refugees and supporters of the Stuarts. Saxe now brought up artillery, and soon a combined artillery-infantry-cavalry assault smashed the great English-Hanoverian square. The survivors withdrew in small groups, stubbornly returning the French fire and repulsing pursuing French cavalry. Cumberland withdrew his army in good order. Allied losses were reported as 7,500 killed and wounded, but the assaulting column alone must have lost that number; French losses were 7,200 killed and wounded.

1745, May–September. French Conquest of Flanders. Following up his victory, Saxe took Tournai, Ghent, Bruges, Oudenarde, Ostend, and Brussels.

HOHENFRIEDBERG CAMPAIGN, 1745

1745, April–May. Skirmishing in Silesia. Austrian and Hungarian irregular troops harassed the Prussian army. Frederick concentrated 60,000 men at Frankenstein, between Glatz and Neisse. At the same time Charles marched across the passes from Bohemia with an army of about 80,000. He concentrated at Landshut, in the mountains of western Silesia, threatening Breslau. Frederick at once marched north to Striegau.

1745, June 3. Austrian Advance to Hohenfriedberg. Charles, not realizing that Frederick had left southern Silesia, marched toward Breslau and camped near Hohenfriedberg. After dark Frederick marched quickly and secretly to Hohenfriedberg, and before dawn drew his army up in order of battle.

1745, June 4. Battle of Hohenfriedberg. At dawn the Prussians struck, completely overwhelming the Austrians and Saxons. By 8 A.M. the battle was over. The allies lost more than 9,000 killed and wounded, about 7,000 prisoners, and 66 guns. Frederick's total losses were barely 1,000 men.

1745, June–September. Pursuit into Bohemia. As the Austrian and Saxon refugees fled into Bohemia, Frederick pursued aggressively with about half of his army, leaving the remainder to deal with the Austrian and Hungarian irregulars in the south. In Bohemia, Charles was reinforced, and soon reorganized his shaken troops. He was reluctant to risk another battle with Frederick, however, and the Prussian king did not have enough strength to force the Austrians to fight. After 3 months of inconclusive maneuvers along the upper Elbe in northeastern Bohemia, Frederick, whose army had gradually shrunk to 18,000 men, began to withdraw to Silesia, followed by Charles, who had about 39,000 men. Frederick halted at Sohr (Soor).

1745, September 30. Battle of Sohr. Expecting an Austrian attack, Frederick formed his army for battle, only to find that Charles had outmaneuvered him, and in a surprise night march had seized the heights to the right rear of his army. The Prussian line of retreat was cut. Frederick immediately swung his army in a great right wheel, under heavy Austrian fire. In the middle of this maneuver the Prussian pivot suddenly advanced against the Austrian left wing. The result was an oblique formation which suddenly threw itself on the Austrians, who had no thought that Frederick would be foolhardy enough to attack. Overwhelming Prussian strength smashed the Austrian left. The dazed Austrians retreated to the northwest, leaving the passes to Silesia open. Frederick's losses were relatively light, while the Austrians lost 8,000 killed and wounded, and abandoned 22 guns to the Prussians. Frederick and his army then returned deliberately to Silesia.

1745, October–November. Allied Invasion of Prussia. Collecting reinforcements, Charles marched north into the territory of his Saxon allies, while another Austrian army from the west joined the main Saxon army under Marshal **Rutowski** in western Saxony. The two allied forces then slowly advanced toward Berlin. Frederick immediately marched from Silesia into Saxony toward Dresden, forcing Charles to halt and face eastward.

1745, November 24–25. Battles of Katholisch Hennersdorf and Görlitz. Before the Austrian general could concentrate his scattered marching columns, they were struck 2 sharp blows by Frederick on successive days. Charles retreated back into Bohemia.

1745, November–December. Operations on the Elbe. Meanwhile another Prussian army under elderly Leopold of Anhalt-Dessau (the "Old Dessauer") marched up the Elbe from Magdeburg to meet Rutowski and his allied army. Rutowski, though considerably superior in numbers, took up a defensive position between Meissen and Dresden.

1745, December 14. Battle of Kesselsdorf. Leopold, marching against the allied defensive position in battle order, surprised and overwhelmed Rutowski. The allies retreated in disorder, after suffering heavy losses.

1745, December 25. Treaty of Dresden. This unbroken series of Prussian victories, following so soon after Saxe's successes in Flanders and the withdrawal of the English army to deal with civil war at home (see p. 639), caused Maria Theresa to seek immediate peace. She again recognized Frederick's conquest of Silesia, while he recognized the election of her husband as Emperor. (This had taken place on September 13.)

Final Campaigns in the Netherlands, 1746–1748

1746. French Successes in the Austrian Netherlands. Saxe continued his deliberate operations against the major fortresses of the Austrian Netherlands, taking Antwerp, then clearing the region between Brussels and the Meuse. Charles of Lorraine, who had been sent to oppose the French, made only one major effort to interfere, and was defeated in the **Battle of Raucoux** (Rocourt), near Liége (October 11). The armies then went into winter quarters, on opposite sides of the Meuse.

1747. French Invasion of Holland. Saxe was now opposed by the Prince of Orange and by the Duke of Cumberland, who had returned from England after suppressing the insurrection of "the '45" (see p. 639). Saxe met and defeated the allied army at the **Battle of Lauffeld,** near Maastricht (July 2). He then sent a corps under General Count **Ulrich F. V. de Lowendahl** to besiege and capture Bergen-op-Zoom (September 18), while with his main body he virtually isolated Maastricht before the armies again went into winter quarters.

1748. Concluding Operations. While a large Russian army marched across Germany to join the allies in the Netherlands, Maastricht fell to Saxe's assault

(May 7). There were no further operations of importance while the diplomats concluded peace negotiations.

1748, October 18. Treaty of Aix-la-Chapelle. With a few exceptions, all conquests were restored on both sides. In Italy, Parma, Piacenza, and Guastella were ceded to Spanish Prince **Don Philip.** Also reaffirmed were Prussian conquest of Silesia, the Pragmatic Sanction in Austria, and the retention of both the electorate of Hanover and the English throne by the House of Hanover.

Operations in Italy, 1741–1748

1741–1743. Desultory Warfare. Spanish and Neapolitan armies, hoping to conquer the Austrian Duchy of Milan, were generally outmaneuvered by Austrian Marshal Traun. The Austrians were joined by Sardinia (Savoy, 1742), while at the same time the Neapolitans were forced to return home to protect their country against British amphibious threats.

1744. Intensification of the War. The tempo of the war speeded up as the French army in Dauphiné under the Prince of Conti attempted to join the main Spanish army on the lower Po River under General Count **John B. D. de Gages.** King **Charles Emmanuel I** of Sardinia, with considerable Austrian assistance, succeeded in holding up the French advance. The French besieged **Cuneo,** where they were joined by a Spanish force. Charles Emmanuel, attempting to relieve Cuneo, suffered a series of defeats at **Villefranche** and **Montalban** (April), **Peyre-Longue** (July 18), and in the major **Battle of Madonna del Olmo** near Cuneo (September 30). Conti, however, was repulsed in his efforts to take Cuneo, and retired into Dauphiné for winter quarters. The Austrians, now under Lobkowitz, had driven the main Spanish army southward out of northern Italy, but were halted and defeated by a combined Spanish-Neapolitan army in the inconclusive **Battle of Velletri** (August 11). Lobkowitz withdrew northward, but the Spanish were too weak to follow him closely. The year ended with the Austrians and Sardinians firmly in control of the Po Valley.

1745, March. Genoa Enters the War. She joined France, Spain, and Naples. De Gages and a French army under Maillebois joined forces south of Piacenza. Outmaneuvering Lobkowitz, the allies decisively defeated the Sardinians at the **Battle of Bassignano** (September 27), then quickly captured Alessandria and other Po fortresses.

1746, April–May. The Pendulum Swings. Reinforcements from Austria, released by the peace with Frederick, again permitted the Austrians, now under Marshal Count **Maximilian U. von Browne,** to regain the initiative.

1746, June 16. Battle of Piacenza. After a series of extremely confused maneuvers, in which Maillebois distinguished himself, the combined French and Spanish army, under Infante Don Philip, engaged the Austrians and Sardinians in an inconclusive battle. Interference from Don Philip prevented Maillebois from winning; as it was, the French and Spanish armies were separated and forced to retreat.

1746, August 12. Battle of Rottofreddo. Maillebois repulsed the pursuing Austrians, and made good his escape to Genoa.

1746, September. Austrian Conquest of Genoa. The arrival of Browne's army caused Maillebois to retreat along the Riviera to France; the Austrians took the city.

1746, December 5–11. Genoese Uprising. The Austrians were driven out. Communications were briefly restored with France, but the city was besieged by an Austrian army early the next year.

1747–1748. French Initiative. The French, now under Marshal Belle-Isle, advanced across the Maritime Alps and relieved besieged Genoa (July, 1747). The Austrians withdrew into Lombardy, followed by Belle-Isle. There were no further operations of importance. When the war ended, the Austrians still held most of the Duchy of Milan.

Operations at Sea

1739–1741. War of Jenkins's Ear. (See p. 661). This colonial war in the Caribbean was soon engulfed in the larger war.

1739, November. Vernon Captures Porto Bello. (See p. 661.)

1740. Vernon Repulsed at Cartagena. (See p. 661.)

1740, September–1744, July. Anson's Cruise.

A squadron under Commodore **George Anson** was dispatched to raid the Spanish Pacific coast possessions. Only his flagship, the **Centurion,** succeeded in getting around Cape Horn. In the 2 following years Anson ravaged the west coast of the Americas, then sailed west to intercept and capture the famed "Manila Galleon." He then continued westward, circumnavigating the globe.

1742–1744. Blockade of Toulon. Although France and England were not yet officially at war, the British maintained a loose blockade of Toulon, where a combined French and Spanish fleet lay idle. The principal mission of the English blockaders was to prevent the Spanish from reinforcing their land forces in Italy by seaborne convoys.

1744, February 11. Battle of Toulon. The Franco-Spanish fleet sailed south from Toulon under Admirals **de la Bruyère de Court** and **Don José Navarro.** The British fleet, under Admiral **Thomas Matthews,** approximately equal in strength to the French and Spanish, sailed to intercept. Matthews believed that de Court was trying to lure him away from the coast, so that a Spanish troop convoy could take reinforcements to Italy. He ordered an immediate attack without waiting to form his fleet in line ahead, since he feared that otherwise de Court would get away. His orders were not clearly understood; his principal subordinate, Admiral **Richard Lestock** probably deliberately went out of his way not to understand. The result was an inconclusive fight, in which the French and Spanish inflicted somewhat more damage than they received. Matthews was courtmartialed and dismissed from the Royal Navy for having failed to adhere to its rigid and formal "Fighting Instructions." Lestock, who should have been convicted of gross disobedience of orders was acquitted through political influence.

1744, March–April. French Threats in the Channel. A convoy of French troops at Dunkirk was ready to sail for England (see p. 633) and a French fleet of 20 ships of the line on at least 2 occasions sailed from Brest, and then from Cherbourg, to convoy the troops to invade England. Admiral Sir **John Norris,** age 84, stayed at sea in the Channel with 25 British ships, despite wintry gales, and the French did not attempt to fight their way through.

1745. Expedition to Louisburg. (See p. 661.)

1746, July 25. Battle of Negapatam. French Admiral **Mahé de la Bourdonnais** outmaneuvered Commodore **Edward Peyton** in an inconclusive action, in which the English suffered more damage than the French. Peyton sailed away, permitting the French to capture Madras.

1747, May 3. First Battle of Finisterre. Anson with 14 ships intercepted a French convoy escorted by a French squadron of 9 ships under Admiral **de la Jonquière.** In a bold, brilliant action, the English fleet captured every French warship and several of the convoy.

1747, October. Second Battle of Finisterre. Under similar circumstances, Admiral **Edward Hawke** with 15 ships encountered a French convoy heading for the West Indies, escorted by a squadron of 9 commanded by Admiral **de l'Etenduère.** The odds were less than they might seem, because 8 of the French ships were bigger, better, and faster than any of the British. Hawke, fighting a bold battle, largely ignoring the "Fighting Instructions," captured all but 2 of the French warships. The convoy escaped, heading for the West Indies. But Hawke sent a sloop to warn the British West Indies fleet to be on the lookout; most of the convoy was captured in the Leeward Islands.

1748, October. Battle of Havana. Admiral **Charles Knowles** defeated a Spanish fleet under Admiral **Reggio** in a close-fought but relatively inconclusive engagement.

WESTERN EUROPE

GREAT BRITAIN

In this half-century modern Great Britain emerged as a political entity, and as the predominant world power. Also during this period the last important English dynastic struggle came to a close, and with it the end of serious threats to the internal security of Great Britain. The principal events were:

1699, February. Disbanding Act. Parliament, to limit involvement of William III in European wars, reduced the standing army to a total of 7,000 men.

1701, June 12. Act of Settlement. Succession to the crown (after **Anne,** second daughter of James II) was established by Parliament to **Sophia,** Princess of Hanover (granddaughter of James I) and her issue. All future sovereigns were to be Protestant (thus barring James II and his male, Catholic, issue) and (in rebuke to William) were not to leave the country without Parliament's permission, were not to involve England in war for defense of their foreign possessions, and were not to grant office to foreigners. The act asserted the right of ministers to be responsible for the actions of the sovereign.

1701, September 16. Death of James II in France. He was succeeded as the Stuart Pretender to the English throne by **James Edward,** known to English history as the "Old Pretender." He was recognized as King of England by Louis XIV.

1701–1713. War of the Spanish Succession. (**See p. 617.**)

1702, March 8. Death of William III. Since Mary, his wife, was dead (December 28, 1694), he was succeeded by Mary's younger sister, Anne.

1702–1714. Reign of Anne. Last Stuart sovereign of England.

1707, May 1. Union of England with Scotland. This established the United Kingdom of Great Britain.

1707, October 21. Shovell's Disaster. Six ships of his squadron returning from Toulon (see p. 626) crashed on a Scilly Islands reef. Shovell went down with his flagship and 2 other ships of the line.

1708, March. Landing of James Edward in Scotland. He was disappointed both in the lack of a spontaneous rising in his favor and by the failure of a French expeditionary force to follow him, although part of the French fleet did reach the Firth of Forth before being scattered by a storm. He returned to France.

1710, August. Fall of the Whig Ministry. Tory enemies of Marlborough came to power.

1711, December. Dismissal of Marlborough. The new Tory Parliament acted for political reasons as well as on not completely disproved charges of financial peculation on the part of the Duke while captain general on the Continent. He was replaced by the Duke of Ormonde as commander of British land forces in Europe, but for all practical purposes the new Parliament withdrew the nation from the war (see pp. 624–625).

1713, April 11. Treaty of Utrecht. (**See p. 625.**) Louis XIV renounced the Pretender (who left France) and recognized the Protestant succession in England. He also dismantled (temporarily) Dunkirk's fortifications, and ceded to England French American possessions of Hudson Bay, Acadia, Newfoundland, and St. Kitts. Spain ceded Gibraltar, and also gave Britain limited slave-trading rights in the Spanish-American colonies.

1714, August 1. Death of Anne. She was succeeded by **George,** Elector of Hanover, eldest son of Sophia.

1715, September–1716, February. "The Fifteen." Jacobite rebellion in Scotland, led by **John Erskine, Earl of Mar,** who raised an army of 4,000 Scotsmen.

1715, November 13. Battles of Preston and Sheriffmuir. While Mar fought an inconclusive battle at Sheriffmuir with loyal troops under **Archibald Campbell, Duke of Argyll,** other regular troops recaptured **the town of Preston from a Jacobite garrison under James Radcliffe, Earl of Derwentwater.**

1715, December. Arrival of James Edward. The Pretender landed at Peterhead and started south, but the advance of Argyll caused him to retreat to Montrose and then, as his dispirited Highlanders dispersed, he sailed again for France (February 5, 1716).

1718–1720. War of the Quadruple Alliance. (**See p. 627.**)

1719. Spanish Expedition to Scotland. A Spanish fleet sailed to Scotland with the objective of replacing the Stuarts on the throne, but the expedition was scattered by a storm. (See p. 627.)

1727–1760. Reign of George II.

1727–1729. War with Spain. (See p. 640.)

1739–1748. War with Spain (War of Jenkins's Ear). For all practical purposes this colonial and naval war became a part of the War of the Austrian Succession (see p. 661).

1740–1748. War of the Austrian Succession. (See p. 630.)

"The Forty-five," 1745–1746

Jacobite rebellion in Scotland, inspired against the advice of his followers by young Prince **Charles Edward Stuart** ("Bonnie Prince Charlie" or "the Young Pretender"), son of James Edward.

1745, July 13. Charles Sails from Nantes. He arrived, practically alone, in the Hebrides (August 3).

1745, August–September. Rising of the Clans. With a Highland army of about 2,000, Charles marched on Edinburgh. Tactical command was exercised by able Lord **George Murray.**

1745, September 17. Capture of Edinburgh. Charles occupied the city, and Holyrood Palace, but the English garrison, under General **Joshua Guest** held Edinburgh Castle.

1745, September 20. Battle of Prestonpans. Charles and Murray decisively defeated a British army of about 3,000 under General Sir **John Cope.**

1745, November–December. Invasion of England. Charles and Murray, with about 5,000 men, hoped both for a rising of English Stuart sympathizers, and for direct aid from France. Charles was disappointed on both counts. He did, however, capture Carlisle and Manchester, and reached Derby (December 4). Many of his Highlanders had meanwhile deserted, and 2 strong English armies were advancing against him. Charles retreated north (December 6), closely followed by the Duke of Cumberland, who had returned from France (see p. 635).

1745, December–1746, February. Siege of Stirling. Cumberland having stopped at the border due to bad weather, Charles vainly tried to capture Stirling.

1745, December 18. Battle of Penrith. Jacobite rear-guard victory over an English detachment, while Charles' main army invested Stirling.

1746, January 17. Battle of Falkirk. English General **Henry Hawley,** who had recaptured Edinburgh, advanced to try to raise the siege of Stirling, but was defeated by Charles and Murray.

1746, February–March. Inconclusive Operations in Northern Scotland.

1746, April 8. Cumberland Advances from Aberdeen. With 9,000 regulars Cumberland advanced on Inverness, where Charles had about 5,000 men (practically all Highlanders).

1746, April 16. Battle of Culloden. Charles and Murray, attempting to surprise Cumberland, made a night march, but found the English ready for them at dawn. Under heavy artillery fire, the tired Highlanders nonetheless attacked, but were repulsed by the steady English infantry, then cut down and routed by cavalry charges. Charles fled. The Highlanders lost about 1,000 killed and about 1,000 captured. Most of the prisoners were killed out of hand, or later summarily executed, earning for Cumberland the sobriquet of "Butcher."

1746, April–September. Charles a Fugitive. Although his cause had been smashed forever at Culloden, Charles stayed in Scotland, spurned by most of his formerly ardent supporters, who were now terrorized by Cumberland's ruthless executions of most of the leaders who had taken part in the rebellion. Charles finally returned to France (September 20).

FRANCE

1701–1714. War of the Spanish Succession. (See p. 617.)

1715, September 1. Death of Louis XIV.

1715–1774. Reign of Louis XV (5 Years Old; Great-Grandson of Louis XIV). The early years of the reign (1715–1723) were under the regency of Duke **Philippe of Orléans,** nephew of Louis XIV, who reversed his uncle's policies and entered alliances with England and Holland.

1718–1720. War of the Quadruple Alliance. (See p. 627.)

1727–1729. War with Spain. (See p. 640.)

1733–1738. War of the Polish Succession. (**See p. 628.**) France gained Lorraine.

1740–1748. War of the Austrian Succession. (**See p. 630.**)

THE IBERIAN PENINSULA

Spain

1700, November 1. Death of Charles II. Without issue, the king's death precipitated the War of the Spanish Succession.

1700–1724. First Reign of Philip V.

1701–1715. War of the Spanish Succession. (**See p. 617.**)

1718–1720. War of the Quadruple Alliance. (**See p. 627.**)

1724. Abdication of Philip. The king abdicated in favor of his son, **Louis I,** apparently to pursue his efforts to gain the French crown.

1724–1746. Second Reign of Philip V. He returned to the Spanish throne when Louis died.

1727–1729. War with England and France. An almost bloodless war resulted from refusal of England and France to permit Charles (son of Philip) to go to Italy to take over the duchies to which he had received succession rights in the Treaty of The Hague (see p. 628). Spanish troops besieged Gibraltar; minor naval engagements took place in the West Indies. Due to the mediation of Cardinal Fleury of France, however, overt hostilities ended almost immediately (May, 1727) and peace negotiations soon began (March, 1728).

1729, November. Treaty of Seville. France and England again agreed to succession of Prince Charles to the Italian duchies, as in the Treaty of The Hague. Spain recognized British possession of Gibraltar.

1731. Charles Inherits the Farnese Duchies (Parma, Piacenza, and Tuscany).

1733–1738. War of the Polish Succession. (**See p. 628.**) Philip took advantage of Austrian occupation in Central Europe and the Balkans to expand his family's dominions, and his own interests, in Italy.

1733. Spanish Conquest of Sicily and Naples. Charles was crowned King of the Two Sicilies. By treaty with Austria, he relinquished his 3 duchies in order to obtain recognition of his new crown (1735). Philip and Charles agreed that the crowns of Spain and the Two Sicilies would never be united.

1738, November 13. Treaty of Vienna. (**See p. 628.**) The Austrian-Spanish agreements on Italy and Sicily were ratified.

1739–1741. The War of Jenkins's Ear. (**See p. 661.**)

1740–1748. War of the Austrian Succession. (**See p. 630.**)

1746–1759. Reign of Ferdinand VI (Third Son of Philip). He brought needed and welcome peace to a country which had been at war during 40 of the 46 years of his father's reign.

Portugal

Save for unsuccessful participation in the War of the Spanish Succession, this was a period of relative peace and great prosperity for Portugal. The prosperity came from a combination of expanding trade with Britain as a result of the Methuen Treaty (see p. 625) and the discovery of great natural wealth in Brazil.

THE NETHERLANDS

In the War of the Spanish Succession the Dutch Republic declined from great-power status. The war exhausted the country physically and financially. The principal events were:

1702, November 1. Death of William III. The States General refused to accede to William's will; for nearly 45 years there was no Stadholder (1702–1747).

1702–1713. War of the Spanish Succession. (**See p. 617.**)

1743–1748. War of the Austrian Succession. The Dutch played a minor role militarily in the early part of the conflict.

1747. French Invasion of the Netherlands. (**See p. 635.**) In desperation, in the face of Saxe's advance, the Dutch people rose in a bloodless revolution against the States General and installed **William IV** of Orange, a distant cousin of William III, as stadholder. Simultaneously the war was drawing to a close with the **Treaty of Aix-la-Chapelle,** which practically ignored Holland (see p. 636).

ITALY

As in previous centuries, Italy was again a battleground of the neighboring great powers. The decline of Venice and Genoa continued, while Savoy—which became the Kingdom of Sardinia—began to emerge as the strongest and most aggressive of the many Italian principalities. The principal events were:

1675–1730. Reign of Victor Amadeus II of Savoy and Sardinia. The beginning of the steady rise of the House of Savoy that would lead, more than a century later, to the unification of Italy.

1701–1713. War of the Spanish Succession. (**See p. 617.**)

1707. Austrian Occupation of Naples. Spannish occupying garrisons were defeated and ejected.

1713. Treaty of Utrecht. (**See p. 625.**) Savoy received formerly Spanish Sicily; Victor Amadeus was recognized as King of Sicily. Austria received Naples and most other Spanish possessions in Italy.

1718. Treaty of Passarowitz. (**See p. 642.**) Venice lost the Morea to Turkey, but gained bases in Albania and Dalmatia.

1718–1720. War of the Quadruple Alliance. (**See p. 627.**) Savoy remained virtually neutral although, despite Spanish seizure of Sicily, Victor Amadeus concluded an alliance with Spain.

1720. Treaty of The Hague. (**See p. 628.**) Savoy surrendered Sicily to Austria in return for Sardinia; Victor Amadeus changed his title to King of Sardinia.

1730–1773. Reign of Charles Emmanuel of Savoy and Sardinia.

1730–1768. Endemic Revolt in Corsica. Local Corsican chieftains became virtually independent of Genoa, which finally requested and received French assistance in reconquering the island, which Genoa then sold to France (1768).

1733–1738. War of the Polish Succession. (**See p. 628.**) Austria ceded Naples and Sicily to the Spanish Bourbons (1735; see p. 640).

1742–1748. War of the Austrian Succession. (**See p. 630.**)

SWITZERLAND

Switzerland played little part in international events of this period. Swiss mercenaries were still an important source of foreign exchange for the country, and fought on both sides in the War of the Spanish Succession. But no longer did the Swiss troops have an influence on the outcome of battles disproportionate to their numbers. Internally, the country was still rent by Protestant-Catholic conflict, which gradually declined by the middle of the century.

GERMANY

Central Europe was still a mass of small, unimportant, and relatively ineffectual principalities. To a greater extent than previously, however, a coalescence of German interests and rudimentary nationalism had begun. This was to a considerable extent inspired by a common hatred of France and the French, arising largely from the repeated invasions of Germany by the armies of Louis XIV and Louis XV.

Austria (or the Empire)

The House of Hapsburg became increasingly identified with the still-expanding Austrian Empire, which it controlled directly from its capital at Vienna. At the same time the Hapsburgs' nominal responsibilities as emperors of the almost meaningless Holy Roman (or German) Empire became less important. Expansion continued in the Balkans at the expense of the Ottoman Empire. Although the military and political fortunes of the Hapsburgs were mixed elsewhere in Europe, Austrian power and influence reached their zenith during the reign of Maria Theresa. The principal events were:

1658–1705. Reign of Leopold I.

1701–1714. War of the Spanish Succession. (See p. 617.)

1703–1711. Revolt in Hungary. Hungarian nationalists, resentful of Austrian control over their country, revolted under the leadership of **Francis II Rakoczy.** The rebels gained control over most of the country, and on several occasions directly threatened Vienna. The Austrians slowly gained the upper hand, however, particularly after Rakoczy was defeated at the **Battle of Trencin** (1708). Guerrilla war continued.

1705–1711. Reign of Joseph I (Son of Leopold).

1711–1740. Reign of Charles VI (Brother of Joseph). He had been the Hapsburg claimant to the throne of Spain in the War of the Spanish Succession (see p. 617). His accession to the imperial and Austrian crowns caused virtual withdrawal of England and Holland from the alliance that had been supporting his claims to the Spanish throne (see p. 000).

1711, May. Peace of Szatinar. The Hungarians accepted Charles VI's assurances that Austria would respect Hungary's national rights and liberties. Rakoczy, still coveting the Hungarian throne, fled to Turkey.

1716–1718. War with Turkey. Austria joined Venice, already at war with Turkey (since 1714; see p. 647). With Turkish support, Rakoczy returned to Hungary to lead an insurrection, but failed completely.

1716, August 5. Battle of Peterwardein. Prince Eugene with 60,000 men met and (after a fierce fight) routed a Turkish army of nearly 150,000. The Turks lost 6,000 killed, an unknown number of wounded, and all of their 164 guns. The Austrians lost 3,000 killed and 2,000 wounded.

1716, August–October. Siege and Capture of Temesvár (Timisoara). Eugene captured the last Turkish stronghold in Hungary after a 5-week siege.

1717, July–August. Siege of Belgrade. Eugene, with about 20,000 men, besieged Belgrade, the strongest Turkish fortification in the Balkans, garrisoned by 30,000 troops. While he was preparing for an assault, a Turkish relieving army of 200,000 approached under Grand Vizier **Khahil Pasha.**

1717, August 16. Battle of Belgrade. While a detachment repulsed an attempted sortie by the garrison, Eugene typically and boldly attacked the main Turkish host. Although wounded (for the 13th and last time), Eugene remained on the field, and his army smashed the Turks, whose casualties were estimated at over 20,000. Austrian losses were 2,000. Belgrade soon surrendered (August 21).

1717–1718. Austrian Successes in the Balkans. Eugene and other Austrian commanders occupied much of Serbia, Wallachia, and the Banat. Eugene was actually contemplating an advance on Constantinople when Turkey sued for peace. Despite Venetian desire to continue the war (which had earlier gone badly for Venice in the Morea), Charles was also anxious for peace in order to respond to Spanish aggression and threats in Sardinia and Italy (see p. 627).

1718, July 21. Treaty of Passarowitz. Austria gained Temesvar (thus completely liberating Hungary), part of Wallachia, and Belgrade. Venice gave up the Morea, but was given new coastal strongholds in Albania and Dalmatia.

1718–1720. War of the Quadruple Alliance. (See p. 627.)

1733–1738. War of the Polish Succession. (See p. 628.)

1737–1739. War with Turkey. (See p. 629.) Most of the gains of Passarowitz were lost.

1740–1780. Reign of Maria Theresa. Hapsburg Queen of Bohemia and of Hungary, and Archduchess of Austria. Her husband later became Emperor (see below), and thus for all practical purposes she was Empress Regnant as well.

1740–1748. War of the Austrian Succession. (**See p. 630.**)

1742–1745. Reign of Charles VII as Emperor. Charles Albert of Bavaria, principal rival of Maria Theresa, reigned briefly after his election. Had he not died during the war, he almost certainly would have been deposed.

1745–1765. Reign of Francis I as Emperor. Francis of Lorraine, husband of Maria Theresa, founded the House of Lorraine-Hapsburg, the line which followed Maria Theresa.

Prussia

By the end of the 17th century, the Electorate of Brandenburg had become the most powerful state of northern Germany, thanks to 2 strong Hohenzollern rulers: **Frederick William** ("the Great Elector") and his son, **Frederick I,** who crowned himself King of Prussia early in the 18th century. Frederick's son, **Frederick William,** the third strong ruler of the line, increased the strength and influence of Prussia. Frederick William contemptuously considered his eldest son a weakling, but as **Frederick II** ("the Great") that son was destined to make Prussia a great power, establishing the base upon which modern Germany is founded. By the middle of the century, Frederick had taught himself to be one of the greatest soldiers of history in 2 small, successful wars. His greatest achievements, and their consolidation, took place in the latter half of the century. The principal events up to 1750 were:

1688–1713. Reign of Frederick I. He started his reign as Elector of Brandenburg.

1701, January 18. Establishment of the Kingdom of Prussia. Frederick proclaimed himself king.

1701–1713. War of the Spanish Succession. (**See p. 617.**) Prussian contingents particularly distinguished themselves in Marlborough's great victories: Blenheim, Ramillies, Oudenarde, and Malplaquet. Prussia's status as a kingdom was recognized by the Treaty of Utrecht, signed shortly after Frederick's death (see p. 625).

1713–1740. Reign of Frederick William. He built up the strength of the Prussian Army to 80,000 men, largest per capita in Europe, thanks largely to his parsimony. His men were recruited (or shanghaied) from the dregs of society; his officers were rather reluctantly conscripted from the nobility. By iron discipline and brutal tyranny the monarch (assisted by his able training genius, Prince **Louis of Anhalt-Dessau**—the "Old Dessauer") transformed this unlikely material into the best army in Europe.

1713, January 24. Birth of Karl Frederick. The fourth of 14 children, destined to become Frederick the Great.

1730. Frederick Sentenced to Death. Frederick William decreed that his "weakling" son should be strangled for some minor disciplinary infractions. He was dissuaded only by threats of mutiny among his courtiers, and by the representations of foreign ambassadors.

1740–1786. Reign of Frederick II. His personality, accomplishments, and genius defy ready or simple analysis. He was a sensitive, cultured intellectual, and at the same time a ruthless, coldhearted disciplinarian. A man of great personal honor, as a monarch he was a sly, treacherous, and untrustworthy foe and ally. He was in many respects a typical 18th-century monarch and a typical 18th-century soldier. He accepted the military system as he found it (unlike Gustavus and Napoleon). But he recognized its tactical weaknesses: slowness, ponderousness, lack of imagination, slow rates of fire. So he became a conservative innovator. He injected mobility, speed, and rapidity of fire, thus roughly doubling his infantry effectiveness. He used cavalry vigorously, like Marlborough and Eugene, but he acted much more quickly than either of them did, particularly in the approach to battle and in the early stages. He was always inferior in strength to his enemies; he always attacked first. He created horse artillery to give increased fire power to his fast-moving cavalry. He emphasized the howitzer for two reasons: its greater lightness made it more mobile; its higher trajectory enabled it to get at enemy reserves concealed behind hills. He learned that by speed and agility he could concentrate superior power at a critical point before his more ponderous foes could react effectively. He achieved his mobility and speed by re-emphasizing the drill and disciplinary methods inherited from his father.

1740–1748. War of the Austrian Succession. (**See p. 630.**) Precipitated by Frederick, in the **First Silesian War.** After gaining Silesia, Frederick made peace, then reentered the conflict in the **Second Silesian War** to prevent Austria from recovering sufficient strength to oust him from Silesia. Both foes and allies had reason to respect both the military prowess and slippery political double-dealing of the young king.

SCANDINAVIA

Sweden

The undisciplined and rash military genius of **Charles XII** of Sweden was the direct cause of his nation's rapid decline from great-power status. Treacherously attacked by his neighbors in the Great Northern War, Charles defeated all of them decisively in a series of campaigns that are among the most brilliant in military annals. These great victories did not satisfy his thirst for vengeance, or his ambitions for military honor and conquest. By rejecting his foes' peace overtures, Charles assured his own eventual defeat at the hands of emerging Russia. After his death Sweden made peace—with honor but with great loss of territory and prestige. One subsequent attempt to gain vengeance against Russia led to further losses and decline of influence. The principal events were:

1697–1718. Reign of Charles XII.

1700–1721. The Great Northern War. (**See p. 614.**)

1718–1720. Reign of Ulrica Eleonora (**Sister of Charles**).

1720–1751. Reign of Frederick I (**Husband of Ulrica**).

1741–1743. War with Russia. (**See p. 646.**)

Norway and Denmark

Save for participation in the Great Northern War (1700–1721; see p. 614), this half-century was relatively uneventful militarily in Denmark.

EASTERN EUROPE

POLAND

This was a period of rapid political, military, economic, and moral decline in Poland. Impoverished and exhausted by the wars and uprisings of the 17th century, her population diminished by one-third, Poland found herself surrounded by 3 powerful and wealthy enemies: Austria, Russia, and Prussia. Her central government was weak and ineffective; there were deep distrust and suspicion between the foreign king (Augustus II) and the Poles; there was dissension among the leading magnates, the economy was backward, and the treasury was empty. The imposition by Russia of a second Saxon king (Augustus III) merely made Poland weaker and more divided. The principal events were:

1697–1733. Reign of Augustus II. One of the least attractive figures of world history.

1700–1721. Great Northern War. **(See p. 614.)** Poland was ruined economically and demoralized politically by this war, during which the nation was a battleground for Saxony, Sweden, and Russia.

1715–1717. Revolt against Augustus II. This rising of the gentry was provoked by huge and arbitrary Saxon requisitions of food and fodder, and by the murder of two Polish officials. Hostilities were terminated by a Russian-supported agreement which was approved without discussion by the "mute" Diet (1717).

1718–1719. Anti-Russian Unrest. Augustus, whose relations with Peter of Russia had deteriorated, concluded an anti-Russian alliance with Austria and England, the so-called **Treaty of Vienna** (1719), providing for enforced evacuation of the Russian troops.

1720. Russian Withdrawal from Poland. Under this pressure the czar withdrew his troops from Poland, but simultaneously concluded in Potsdam the first secret Russo-Prussian alliance.

1721. Treaty of Nystad. **(See p. 617.)** Without Polish participation, the treaty provided for cession of the eastern coast of the Baltic, including Polish Livonia, to Russia.

1727. Russian Occupation of Polish Courland.

1733–1738. War of the Polish Succession. **(See p. 628.)**

1734–1763. Reign of Augustus III. Continued decline of Poland under an inept and uninterested foreign king.

RUSSIA

During the first quarter of the 18th century, Russia under Peter the Great rose to be one of the great military and political powers of Europe. Following this came a decline during the reigns of Peter's mediocre successors. The principal events were:

1689–1725. Reign of Peter I. This cruel, ruthless ruler reformed the archaic and Asiatic government, economy, and society of Russia, primarily to assure an adequate civilian base for military conquest. He reformed and modernized the army, and learned the art of war from his arch-enemy, Charles XII of Sweden. He conquered the eastern coast of the Baltic and relegated Sweden to the position of a second-rate power. He ruined Poland, his other main rival. He built a navy, but failed to gain unrestricted access to the Black Sea. When he died, he left Russia exhausted, her population diminished by 20 per cent, but equipped with a regular army of 212,000 veterans hardened in continuous campaigns and reinforced by 110,000 Cossacks, and a strong navy. There was no immediate successor who could use this powerful instrument for further conquests and expansion of the Russian Empire until the reign of Catherine II in the second half of the 18th century.

1700–1721. Great Northern War. **(See p. 614.)**

1722–1723. War with Persia. **(See p. 649.)**

1725–1741. Successors of Peter I the Great. There was a series of short reigns of weak rulers, preventing Russia from conducting a consistent and effective foreign policy. They also neglected the Russian military forces. In only one policy was there Russian consistency: keeping Poland weak.

1725–1736. Guerrilla Rebellion in the Caucasus. Native partisans engaged in constant guerrilla warfare against Russia in the lands recently conquered from Persia. Soon one-quarter of the Russian Army was engaged in the Caucasus-Caspian region (1730).

1736. Restoration of Land to Persia. Russia restored to Persia the Caspian littoral, with the towns of Derbent and Baku, be-

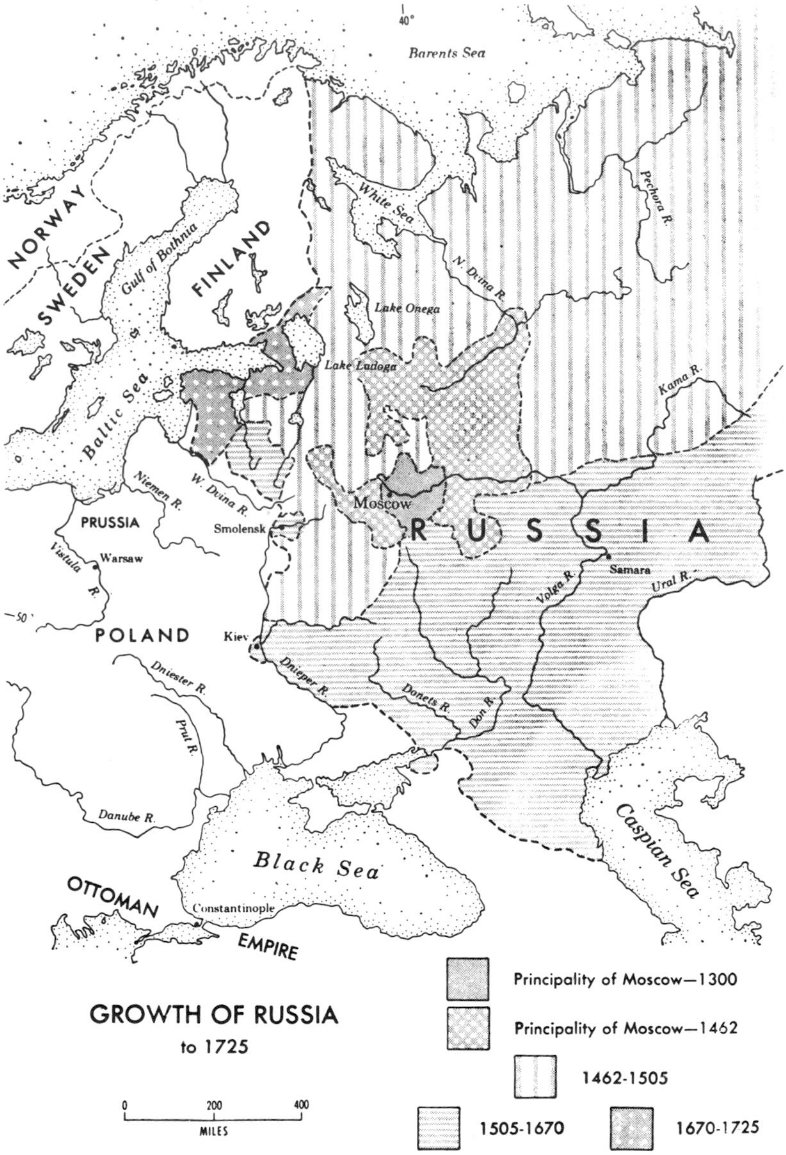

cause their defense against native partisans became too heavy a drain on the Russian Army.

1736–1739. War with Turkey. (See p. 630.)

1741–1762. Reign of Elizabeth I. One of Russia's strong rulers.

1741–1743. Russo-Swedish War. Under the influence of France, Sweden saw in the War of the Austrian Succession an opportunity to gain revenge on Russia, which had declared its support of Maria Theresa and the Pragmatic Sanction (see p. 000). The timing was bad for Sweden, whose army was only 15,000 men, because after the conclusion of peace with Turkey (1739) the entire Russian Army could be used against Sweden.

1741. The Battle of Wilmanstrand. The Swedes, 6,000 strong, were defeated with great loss by 10,000 Russians. Swedish losses were 3,300 killed and wounded and 1,300 prisoners; Russian losses were 2,400 killed and wounded.

1742. Russian Invasion of Finland. The

Russians cut the road of retreat of the main Swedish Army at Helsinki. The Swedes (17,000) surrendered, virtually ending the war.

1743, August 7. Peace with Sweden. Russia obtained some new territory in Finland, where the frontier was fixed on the Kymmene River.

EURASIA AND THE MIDDLE EAST

THE OTTOMAN EMPIRE

The decline of the Ottoman Empire continued, but at a slower pace than in the previous century. In part this was due to the fact that England and France, separately and without coordination, were becoming aware of the possible threat to their Mediterranean interests, and to the European balance of power, if either Russia or Austria were to gain control of the Straits and of the eastern Mediterranean. Thus French and English diplomacy—while not pro-Turkish, and rarely deliberately coordinated—was directed toward maintaining the *status quo* in the Balkans and Anatolia. Another reason for the deceleration of Ottoman decline was the jealousy of Austria and Russia, each afraid that the other might displace Turkey in control of the Balkans and of the Straits. Perhaps the most important reason for Turkey's continuing, even though weakened, power was the inherent toughness and fighting qualities of the Turkish soldier, displayed on battlefield after battlefield against Austrians, Russians, Venetians, and Persians. The principal events were:

1703. Janissary Revolt. Sultan Mustafa II was forced to abdicate.

1703–1730. Reign of Ahmed II (Brother of Mustafa II).

1710–1711. War with Russia. (See p. 616.) Ended by favorable **Treaty of the Pruth.**

War with Venice and Austria, 1714–1718

1714. Revolt in Montenegro. Quelled by the Turks, who believed it had been instigated by Venice.

1714. Turkey Declares War on Venice.

1715. Turkish Offensives. Energetic and skillful Grand Vizier **Damad Ali** conquered the Peloponnesus (Morea) in a 100-day campaign of successful sieges without any pitched battles. All Venetian fortresses were taken, their 8,000 defenders captured. The Ottoman fleet, reinforced by ships from Egypt and the Barbary States, drove the Venetians out of the Aegean Islands. The remaining Venetian fortresses on Crete were taken.

1716, January–December. Venetian Gains. The Venetians repulsed a Turkish attack on Corfu and received naval reinforcements from Spain, Portugal, and some other Italian states.

1716, January. Austria Joins Venice. The grand vizier marched north from Belgrade toward Peterwardein (June–July).

1716, August 5. Battle of Peterwardein. (See p. 642.)

1717. Belgrade Campaign. (See p. 642.)

1718, July 21. Treaty of Passarowitz. (See p. 642.) Unfavorable to Turkey.

1722–1727. Expansion in Persia. Both Turkey and Russia took advantage of Persian weakness and involvement with an Afghan invasion to seize and divide between them large portions of northwestern Persia (see p. 649). Division of the spoils was agreed on by the **Treaty of Constantinople** (1724).

1730–1736. War with Persia. (See p. 649.)

1730, September–October. Revolt in Constantinople. News of the disastrous Turkish defeat at Hamadan (see p. 649) led to a popular rising. The grand vizier was killed; the sultan abdicated. The city continued to be plagued by unrest and riots for 2 years.

1730–1754. Reign of Mahmud I.

1733, 1736. Peace of Baghdad. (See p. 650.) Ended the inconclusive war with Nadir Shah of Persia; Turkey lost some of the land seized earlier.

1736–1739. War with Austria and Russia. (See p. 629.) Ended by the favorable **Treaty of Belgrade.**

1743–1747. War with Persia. (See p. 650.) Turkey's last major war with Persia. Turkey was forced to give up all the lands seized 20 years earlier.

PERSIA

In this short half-century Persia virtually collapsed, conquered by Afghan invaders and her provinces divided at the conference table between Russia and Turkey. Then briefly and astonishingly Persia revived for one of her most glorious military episodes, before another disastrous collapse. The period was dominated by **Nadir Kuli Beg,** later **Nadir Shah,** one of the greatest soldiers in Persian history and the last great Asian conqueror. He drove out, then conquered, the Afghan invaders, repeatedly defeated the Turks, overawed the Russians, conquered Mogul India, and conquered the Uzbek khanates of the Oxus region. His empire collapsed at his death. The principal events were:

1694–1722. Reign of Shah Husain. His strong emphasis on Shi'i doctrine aroused resentment among Sunnite subjects and neighbors, reopening the wounds of ancient Moslem religious differences.

1709. Afghan Revolt at Kandahar. Under the leadership of **Mir Vais,** leader of the Ghilzai Afghans, a separate Afghan state established its independence. Repeated Persian efforts to reconquer Kandahar were repulsed (1709–1711). The struggle was embittered by the religious dispute.

1711. Siege of Kandahar. A Persian army under **Khusru Khan** defeated Mir Vais and besieged Kandahar. Mir Vais was ready to surrender, but Persian insistence upon unconditional surrender stimulated the defenders to greater efforts. When the besiegers began to suffer from food shortages, Mir Vais sortied and defeated them. Khusru was killed; only 1,000 of the 25,000 Persians escaped. Subsequent Persian reconquest efforts were repulsed.

1715. Death of Mir Vais. He was succeeded by his brother **Abdulla,** and then by his son **Mahmud** (1717).

1717. Afghan Revolt at Herat. Under the leadership of **Asadullah Khan,** the Abdali Afghans revolted. They joined with the Uzbeks to plunder Khorasan.

1719. Battle of Herat. A Persian army of 30,000 under **Safi Kuli Khan** attempted to reconquer Herat. Asadullah met them with 15,000. In a hard-fought battle, Asadullah was saved by confusion in the Persian army, which resulted in the defeat and capture of Safi.

1720. Afghan Raid into Persia. Mahmud Khan (son of Mir Vais) invaded Persia and captured Kerman. The Afghans were routed when capable Persian general **Lutf Ali Khan** surprised their camp and pursued them back to Kandahar. Lutf was preparing for a full-scale invasion when he was dismissed due to the jealousy of the grand vizier, his brother-in-law.

1721. Frontier Raids. The Abdalis raided unchecked in Khorasan, while the Lesgians of Daghestan sacked Shamaka, capital of Shirvan. Mahmud prepared for a major invasion of Persia.

1722, January. Mahmud's Invasion. Advancing with about 20,000 men, he again captured Kerman, but was repulsed from its citadel. Moving on to Yezd, he was again repulsed. He continued on to the walls of the capital, Isfahan. He rejected a handsome ransom to return to Afghanistan; with about 10,000 men he encamped at Gulnabad, 11 miles east of Isfahan, and waited for a higher offer.

1722, March. Battle of Gulnabad. A Persian army of about 30,000 now advanced against Mahmud. The Afghans attacked, defeated the Persians, and, after capturing some outlying fortifications, invested Isfahan.

1722, March–October. Siege of Isfahan. Mahmud repelled, or bribed off, a few halfhearted efforts to relieve the city. The Shah's son **Tahmasp** fought his way out with 600 men, but in the city garrison and people began to starve. The shah surrendered, abdicating in favor of Mahmud.

1722–1725. Reign of Mahmud. The Afghan conqueror controlled only part of the country. His accession was challenged by Tahmasp, who raised resistance in Mazandaran.

1722–1727. Russian and Turkish Aggression. Peter of Russia, nominally supporting Tahmasp, seized Derbent (1722), and then Resht and Baku (1723). In return for promised Russian support, Tahmasp agreed to cede Shirvan, Daghestan, Gilan, Mazandaran, and Astrabad to the Russians. Turkey, anxious to regain the provinces lost to Shah Abbas, and fearful of Russian penetration, also moved into northwest Persia, seizing Tiflis, capital of Georgia (1723). By the **Treaty of Constantinople** (1724), Russia and Turkey agreed to divide northern and western Persia. The Turks then occupied Tabriz, Hamadan, and Kermanshah (1724–1725).

1724–1725. Chaos in Isfahan. Mahmud became insane and was eventually put to death by his followers.

1725–1730. Reign of Ashraf Shah (Cousin of Mahmud). Order was re-established in central and southern Persia.

1726–1727. Turkish Invasion. Ashraf repulsed the invaders at the **Battle of Isfahan** (1726). He then made peace, allowing the Turks to retain the extensive border provinces they had seized in return for Ottoman recognition of his accession (1727).

1726–1729. Rise of Tahmasp. Supported by **Nadir Kuli Beg,** an obscure Khorasan chieftain, Tahmasp conquered Meshed and Herat (1728). Marching on Isfahan, he and Nadir defeated Ashraf at the **Battle of the Mehmandost,** near Dourghan, and again at the **Battle of Murchakhar,** near Isfahan, and then seized the capital (1729). Ashraf fell back on Shiraz, pursued by Nadir, who decisively defeated the Afghans at the **Battle of Zarghan** (1730). In trying to return to Kandahar, Ashraf was murdered.

1730–1732. Reign of Tahmasp. The shah was a figurehead; the real ruler of Persia was brilliant soldier Nadir Kuli Beg, who was made viceroy of most of northern and eastern Persia by the grateful Shah.

1730. Conquest of Meshed. Nadir marched on Meshed, where an independent Afghan chieftain, **Malik Mahmud,** had established himself (1722) and now refused to submit to the new shah. Nadir defeated Malik outside the city, which he then captured through treachery. Malik was captured and later killed.

1730–1736. War with Turkey. The Turks refusing to give up the Persian territories they had seized, Nadir decided to fight to recover the lost provinces. He marched on Hamadan.

1730. Battle of Hamadan. Nadir decisively defeated the Turks. He quickly occupied Iraq and Azerbaijan, and laid siege to Erivan.

1731–1732. Campaign against the Abdalis. With Nadir now occupied in the west, there were outbreaks in Khorasan, largely inspired and exploited by the Abdali Afghans of Herat. Nadir raised the siege of Erivan, marched 1,400 miles east, defeated the Abdalis, invested and captured Herat (1732).

1731. Second Battle of Hamadan. Tahmasp, hoping to complete the reconquest of the eastern provinces from Turkey during the absence of Nadir, took the field himself and invested Erivan. He withdrew when a Turkish relief army appeared. The Turks pursued and decisively defeated him. Tahmasp, now having lost all the territories conquered by Nadir the previous year, made peace to forestall a Turkish invasion, recognizing the Turkish conquests.

1732. Tahmasp Deposed. Nadir, returning from the east, deposed Tahmasp, installed his 8-month-old son **Abbas** on the throne, repudiated the treaty with the Turks, and renewed the war.

1732. Treaty of Resht. The Russians gave up their claims to Gilan, Mazandaran, and Astrabad (see p. 645).

1732–1736. Reign of Abbas III. Nadir, as regent, was the real ruler in this reign, the last of the Safawids.

1733. Nadir's Invasion of Mesopotamia. Nadir defeated the Turkish governor, **Ahmed Pasha,** near **Baghdad.** He invested the city with a portion of his army, then turned to meet a powerful Turkish relief army under **Topal Osman.** At the **Battle of Karkuk,** near Samarra, the Turks decisively defeated Nadir's smaller Persian army. The garrison of Baghdad then sortied to overwhelm the small Persian detachment Nadir had left in the trenches around the city. Despite these twin disasters, Nadir rallied his troops and held off Topal while awaiting reinforcements. When these arrived he again took the offensive, defeated Topal at the **Battle of Leilan,** near Karkuk, then marched again on Baghdad. News of a revolt in Fars led him to make a favorable peace with Ahmed Pasha (**Treaty of Baghdad**) and he then returned to suppress the revolt in Fars.

1734–1735. Operations in Transcaucasia. Turkish Sultan Mahmud refused to recognize the Treaty of Baghdad. A Turkish army of 80,000 under **Abdulla Koprulu** assembled near Kars. On the approach of Nadir the Turks went into an entrenched camp. Nadir threatened Tiflis, Erivan, and Ganja, but was unable to entice the Turks into battle.

1735. Treaty with Russia. Nadir, knowing Russia was planning war against Turkey in Europe, sent troops against Baku and Derbent, threatening to join Turkey in war against Russia. The Russians quickly negotiated an alliance with Nadir, returning Baku and Derbent to Persia.

1735. Battle of Baghavand. Nadir invaded Turkey. When he sent off a number of detachments from his main army in the plain of Baghavand, near Kars, Koprulu decided to risk battle. By so doing, he fell into a trap set by Nadir, who counterattacked and won a complete victory. Nadir then quickly captured Tiflis, Erivan, and Ganja.

1736. Peace with Turkey. Sultan Mahmud, anxious to make peace so that he could deal with Russia and Austria, recognized the terms of the Treaty of Baghdad; Persia recovered part of the lost provinces. Nadir agreed not to join Russia in the new war.

1736. Death of Abbas. Nadir was elected shah by the Persian chieftains. A devout Sunnite, he accepted only on condition that the Shi'i heresy be abandoned. The condition was nominally accepted, but had little practical effect.

1736–1747. Reign of Nadir Shah. He devoted himself to restoring the old frontiers of Persia.

1737–1738. Invasion of Afghanistan. Nadir Shah took Kandahar after a 9-month siege (1738). During the siege Nadir sent smaller forces to occupy and pacify the former Persian provinces of Balkh and Baluchistan. When Kandahar surrendered, he treated the Afghans leniently, and many joined his army.

1738–1739. Invasion of India. The Mogul Emperor, **Mohammed Shah** having given assistance to the Afghans, Nadir invaded India. He captured Ghazni and Kabul (September, 1738), then turned toward the Punjab. With 50,000 men he bypassed a Mogul army holding the Khyber Pass, instead went over the nearby Tsatsobi Pass (where Alexander had crossed), and then turned to attack the Moguls in the rear at the successful **Battle of the Khyber Pass.** He then advanced rapidly into India, seizing Peshawar and Lahore, and crossing the Indus to Attock.

1739, February. Battle of Karnal. Mohammed marched from Delhi to meet the Persians with an army of 80,000 men. Nadir, enticing the Moguls to battle from their entrenched camp, defeated them, then besieged the camp. Mohammed surrendered. Nadir, treating him well, occupied Delhi.

1739, March. Massacre of Delhi. Nadir ruthlessly suppressed a rising of the population. Then, leaving Mohammed on the throne, but taking an indemnity of more than $100 million in precious metals and jewels and annexing all of India west and north of the Indus, he returned to Persia.

1740. Conquest of Bokhara and Khiva. Defeating the Uzbeks at the **Battles of Charjui** and **Khiva,** Nadir annexed the region south of the Aral Sea.

1741. Failure in Daghestan. Nadir attempted to subdue a rising of the Lesgians, but was frustrated when the people took to the mountains in guerrilla war.

1742–1747. Growing Unrest. Nadir's cruelty, his poor administration, and his efforts to force unpopular religious beliefs on his people caused bitterness and hatred to spread through the country.

1743–1747. War with Turkey. Ostensibly for religious reasons, but mainly to exploit the growing unrest in Persia, Turkey again invaded Persia. Nadir, outmaneuvering the more numerous invaders, blocked their advance east of Kars.

1745. Battle of Kars. Nadir once more decisively defeated the Turks, and occupied most of Armenia.

1747. Peace with Turkey. The boundaries were re-established as they had been at the time of Turkish Sultan Murad (1640).

1747. Death of Nadir. He was assassinated by his own bodyguard.

1747–1750. Anarchy in Persia. The empire fell apart in civil war. A new Afghan state was created by **Ahmad Khan Durani,** one of Nadir's leading generals. Georgia declared its independence.

SOUTH ASIA

AFGHANISTAN

During this century, modern Afghanistan emerged from the ruins of the Persian and Mogul empires. For most of the period the history of Afghanistan was inextricably bound up with that of Persia. But upon the death of Nadir Shah, Ahmad Khan Durani, a young Afghan of the Abdali tribe who had joined Nadir

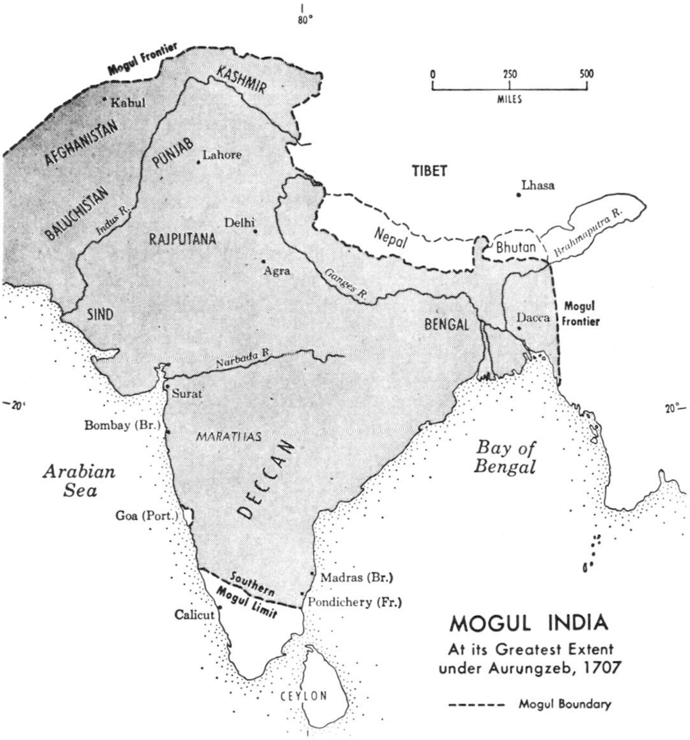

Shah after the Persian conquest of Kandahar (1738) and had become a Persian general, seized control of most of the region now known as Afghanistan. Known as Ahmad Shah Durani (or Abdali), he quickly began to expand his small kingdom at the expense of both Persia and India. Having been with Nadir during the invasion of India, he was well aware of the weakness of the Mogul Empire. He had no sooner seized control of Afghanistan than he made the first of his 10 major invasions of India. This first invasion (1747) was unsuccessful, but in later years he became the strongest ruler in northern India, and annexed much of the remains of the Mogul Empire (see pp. 651 and 653).

INDIA

During this half-century the Mogul Empire declined rapidly. The decline was hastened by Nadir Shah's successful invasion, and by the steady advance of Maratha power from the Deccan into northern India. As the period ended there were 4 major powers competing for a dominant place in India to supplant the nearly extinct Mogul Empire. These were the Maratha Confederacy, the Afghan empire of Ahmad Shah, the French, and the English. The principal events were:

c. 1700. Rise of the Sikhs. A militant Hindu sect, they became powerful in Rajputana and the Punjab.

1700–1707. Maratha Struggle for Existence. The Marathas, with difficulty, maintained their independence against the last powerful efforts of aged Mogul Emperor Aurangzeb (see p. 588).

1700. Consolidation of East India Company Bases in Bengal. Sir **Charles Eyre** became governor.

1701. Expansion of French East India Company. A new base was established at Calicut. French bases were already established at Surat, Pondichery, Masulipatam, Chandernagore, Balasore, and Kasimbazar.

1707. Death of Aurangzeb.

1707–1712. Reign of Bahadur Shah (Son of Aurangzeb). He assumed the throne in the absence of his elder brother, **Muazim,** governor of Kabul. He made peace with the Marathas and Rajputs, and repressed the rising ambitions of the Sikhs.

1708. Battle of Agra. Bahadur defeated and killed his brother Muazim, who was returning to claim the throne.

1708–1748. Reign of Sahu, the Maratha. Son of Sivaji, he had been imprisoned by Aurangzeb. He was released by Bahadur and set on the Maratha throne. His allegiance to the Moguls soon became less than nominal.

1710. Campaign against the Sikhs. Bahadur, concerned by the rise of Sikh power, defeated them in an inconclusive campaign.

1712–1719. Mogul Interregnum. After the death of Bahadur the situation in the empire became anarchic; in a series of bloody struggles for the throne, some 5 puppets reigned in Delhi, but the real power was in the hands of the nobles and court officials.

1712. Appointment of the First Maratha Peshwa. Sahu appointed able **Balaji Visvanath Bhat** as his prime minister, with title of Peshwa. From this time until his death (1720) Balaji was the virtual ruler of what had become a confederacy of the Maratha kingdoms of Baroda, Gwalior, Indore, Nagpur, and the Peshwa's dominions. The position of Peshwa became hereditary, and his successors continued to be the real leaders of the Maratha Confederacy.

1712–1720. Spread of Maratha Power. The Marathas gained strength and spread northward into Hindustan, taking advantage of anarchy in the Mogul Empire.

1713. Nizam ul-Mulk Viceroy of the Deccan. During the struggle in Delhi, **Asaf Jah** (also known as Chin Kilich Khan), a Turkoman who had been one of Aurangzeb's best generals, quietly had himself appointed as subahdar, or viceroy, of the Mogul dominions in the Deccan, with the title of **Nizam ul-Mulk.** Not troubling the autonomous Marathas, he re-established firm Mogul control over the central and eastern Deccan.

1719–1748. Reign of Mohammed Shah as Mogul Emperor. He was supported by Nizam ul-Mulk and the Marathas in gaining the throne. The Nizam became the wazir, or prime minister, but remained subahdar of the Deccan (1720).

1720–1740. Rule of Peshwa Baji Rao Bhat over Marathas. The Maratha Confederacy continued its expansion northward and eastward at the expense of the Mogul Empire.

1721. French Base Established at Mahé.

1724–1748. Reign of Nizam ul-Mulk over Hyderabad. With the Mogul Empire obviously approaching collapse, Nizam ul-Mulk left Delhi (1722) and established the independent Kingdom of Hyderabad in his Deccan viceroyalty. He appointed

Dost Ali as nawab, or governor, of the Carnatic.

1737. **Battle of Delhi.** Baji Rao and the Marathas defeated Mohammed Shah's imperial army outside of Delhi. The emperor made peace, ceding Malwa to the Marathas. In the following years they also seized Gujerat, Orissa, and Bundelkhand.

1739. **Nadir Shah's Invasion. (See p. 650.)** This accelerated the decline of the Mogul Empire.

1739. **Baji Rao Takes Bassein from the Portuguese.**

1740. **Bengal Independent of the Mogul Empire.**

1740–1761. **Rule of Peshwa Balaji Baji Rao Bhat over Marathas.**

1741. **Marquis Joseph Dupleix Appointed French Governor General.** He had been governor of Chandernagore; he moved to Pondichery.

1743. **Death of Dost Ali.** The Nizam appointed **Anwar-ud-din** the new Nawab of the Carnatic, refusing the claim of **Chanda Sahib,** Dost Ali's son-in-law.

First Carnatic War, 1744–1748

This was part of the War of the Austrian Succession (see p. 630). Word of hostilities in Europe having reached India, Dupleix sought neutrality between the French and British East India Companies.

1745. **Arrival of a British Fleet.** Commodore **Curtis Barnett** swept French shipping off the nearby seas. Dupleix sent an urgent plea for help to Count **Mahé de la Bourdonnais,** an able French admiral, commanding at Mauritius.

1746, **June. Arrival of la Bourdonnais.** A fleet of 8 ships of the line, carrying 1,200 French troops, arrived at Pondichery.

1746, **July 25. Naval Battle of Negapatam. (See p. 637.)** Commodore **Edward Peyton** (who had succeeded to command after Barnett's death) was outmaneuvered and driven away by la Bourdonnais. Peyton sailed to Hooghly.

1746, **September 2–10. Seizure of Madras.** Dupleix invested the main British base, while la Bourdonnais blockaded it by sea. Madras surrendered after brief resistance.

1746, **September 21. Battle of Madras.** Nawab Anwar-ud-din, who had allied himself with the British, arrived near Madras with a large army. The French sortied from the captured city and easily defeated the Nawab's army.

1746, **November 3. Battle of St. Thomé.** A French detachment of 230 Europeans and 730 sepoys (native troops) attacked and routed a force of 10,000 of the Nawab's troops near Madras.

1746, **November–1748, April. Siege of Fort St. George.** The French tried unsuccessfully for 18 months to take the British base near Madras. Dupleix finally had to raise the siege due to the arrival of a new British fleet, under Admiral **Edward Boscawen,** with reinforcements.

1747. **Ahmad Shah's First Invasion of India.** The Afghans were halted at the inconclusive **Battle of Sirkind** by a mixed Mogul-Rajput force, and forced to retreat to Afghanistan.

1748, **August–October. Siege of Pondichery.** Boscawen unsuccessfully tried to take Pondichery, ably defended by Dupleix. Onset of the monsoon forced the British fleet to withdraw.

1748. **Treaty of Aix-la-Chapelle. (See p. 636.)** News of the treaty reached India at the end of the year. Madras was returned to Britain, in return for Louisbourg in Nova Scotia.

1749. **Ahmad Shah's Second Invasion of India.** This was a combined raid and reconnaissance in force, but led him to believe that he could conquer the Punjab and Kashmir.

Second Carnatic War, 1749–1754

Despite formal peace between France and Britain, hostilities between the 2 East India companies continued, through their involvement in Indian conflicts. Following the death of Nizam ul-Mulk (1748), Chanda Sahib began to conspire for the nawabship of the Carnatic, and was supported by Dupleix. At the same time, **Muzaffar Jang,** grandson of Nizam ul-Mulk, had received the blessing of the new and ineffectual Mogul emperor to succeed as the Nizam of Hyderabad, instead of his father **Nasir Jang,** who had automatically succeeded to the throne as Nizam. Dupleix also supported Muzaffar Jang. The British East India Company, under the able leadership of **Thomas Saunders,** supported the incumbents: Nasir Jang, the new Nizam; and Anwar-ud-din, the Nawab of the Carnatic.

1749. Battle of Ambur. The combined forces of Chanda, Muzaffar, and the French under the Marquis **Charles de Bussy** defeated and killed Anwar-ud-din. Chanda was proclaimed Nawab of the Carnatic, with Dupleix the actual ruler. However, **Mohammed Ali,** claiming to be the successor to Anwar-ud-din, retained control of Trichinopoly, where he was recognized and supported by the British.

1749–1750. Nasir Jang in the Carnatic. With English support, Nasir Jang invaded the Carnatic in a partially successful effort to re-establish Hyderabad control.

1750, December. Assassination of Nasir Jang. Following the death of his father (for which he was probably responsible), Muzaffar Jang seized power as the new nizam. He was proclaimed Subahdar of the Deccan by Dupleix. In return he appointed Dupleix governor of all former Mogul lands in the eastern Deccan from the Krishna River to Cape Comorin. Dupleix put his small but efficient army, commanded by de Bussy, at the disposal of the new Nizam. (For operations after 1750, see p. 700.)

EAST AND CENTRAL ASIA

CHINA

The Manchu Dynasty of China reached its height of power, prestige, and influence during this period. During the latter years of his reign, the great Emperor K'ang-hsi consolidated the Manchu conquest of China and Mongolia, and continued the expansion of the empire into Tibet. His grandson, Ch'ien-lung, continued the expansion of China into neighboring areas, and by midcentury had become the most powerful monarch of China since Kublai Khan. The principal events were:

1662–1722. Reign of K'ang-hsi. (**See also p. 593.**)

1700. Chinese Troops to Tibetan Frontier. Chinese troops occupied parts of the border region between Tibet and China because of K'ang-hsi's concern about the growing influence in Tibet of the Eleuth (or Dzungar) Mongols (part of the Oirat Mongols).

1705. Chinese Intervention in Tibet. Chinese troops installed a new Dalai Lama, against the opposition of most Tibetans.

1716–1718. Dzungar Intervention in Tibet. A Dzungar force of 6,000 men, under Galdan's nephew, **Chewanlaputan** (Tsewang Araptan), invaded Tibet to join in the continuing dispute over the succession to the Dalai Lama. They seized Lhasa and imprisoned the incumbent Dalai Lama. A Manchu force, coming to his assistance, was ambushed and destroyed (1718).

1720. Manchu Conquest of Tibet. K'ang-hsi sent 2 armies into Tibet, 1 from Kansu and 1 from Szechwan. They smashed the Dzungars and drove out the survivors. Meanwhile another Chinese army advanced into Dzungaria to capture Urumchi and Turfan. This was the first war in which Mongol forces made extensive use of musketry; they were not very effective, however, against the larger, better-armed, better-equipped Chinese troops. A new and more popular Dalai Lama was installed by K'ang-hsi, and a Manchu garrison was left in Lhasa.

1721. Revolt in Formosa. Rebels, led by **Chu I-kuei,** were quickly overwhelmed by Chinese troops.

1723–1735. Reign of Yung-cheng (Son of K'ang-hsi). China was peaceful, but there was considerable conflict along the western frontiers with Central Asian tribes.

1727. Treaty of Kiakhta. A treaty with Russia, delineating frontiers and regulating trade and other relations.

1727–1728. Civil War in Tibet. A Chinese army of 15,000 restored order. The Dalai Lama was exiled for 7 years. The Chinese garrison was increased.

1729–1735. Campaigns against the Dzungars. Continuing Dzungar opposition to Chinese policy in Tibet and frontier depredations in western China resulted in a series of Chinese punitive expeditions. At first, largely due to poor management, the Chinese were not very successful. After reorganization (1732), the Dzungars were soundly defeated.

1736–1795. Reign of Ch'ien Lung (or Kâo Tsung). Height of Manchu power and prestige.

1747–1749. Tibetan Frontier Campaigns. Renewed unrest along the Tibetan frontier was suppressed in hard, inconclusive partisan warfare.

INNER ASIA

The Russian and Chinese empires continued their expansions into Inner Asia. Apparently oblivious of what was happening to them, the Mongol and Turkic tribes continued their interminable bitter quarrels with each other, in the process weakening themselves and their neighbors so that they could not offer any truly sustained opposition to the colonial encroachment from east and west. The principal events were:

1714–1717. Russian Expedition against Khiva. Peter the Great sent the expedition, expecting that Khiva would accept a protectorate. Instead, the Khivans ambushed and annihilated the Russian expedition.

1720. Chinese Expedition in Dzungaria. (**See p. 654.**)

1722. Peace of Astrakhan. A meeting between Peter of Russia and the aged Torgut Khan **Ayuka** confirmed the submission of the Torguts to Russia.

1727. Treaty of Kiakhta. Russia and China (see above).

1729–1735. Chinese Campaigns in Dzungaria. (See above.)

1730–1731. Kazakh Acceptance of Russian Suzerainty. Russia thereby gained control of tribes inhabiting areas claimed by Khiva and Bokhara.

1738. Conquest of Balkh by Persia. (**See p. 650.**)

1740. Conquest of Khiva and Bokhara by Persia. (**See p. 650.**)

1741. Discovery of Bering Strait. This was by **Vitus Bering,** a Danish navigator in Russian service.

1747. Khiva Regains Independence. This was the result of the collapse of Nadir Shah's empire (see p. 650).

JAPAN

Under the Tokugawa Shogunate Japan continued to exclude herself from practically all contact with the outside world, while internal peace reigned within the kingdom.

SOUTHEAST ASIA

BURMA

This was a period of weakness and decline in Burma. The country was ravaged by raids from weak and small neighbors (Manipur and Arakan), as well as by unrest and revolt at home. There was no leadership capable of dealing with these problems. The principal events were:

1714–1749. Manipuri Raids. Under Raja **Gharib Newaz** of Manipur, repeated cavalry raids into Upper Burma devastated the country. The Manipuris swept to the very gates of Ava (most notably, 1738), plundering and pillaging at will.

1740–1752. Mon Revolt. The Mons, or Talaings, of Lower Burma, seeing the weakness and ineptitude of the kings of Ava, revolted to set up an independent kingdom. They seized Toungoo, original home of the ruling family, and raided frequently into Upper Burma as far as the walls of Ava. Finally, under the leadership of King **Binnya Dala,** they began a systematic conquest of Upper Burma, ending in the capture of Ava and overthrow of the Toungoo Dynasty (1752; see p. 702).

SIAM

Stability marked this period in Siam. There was one major foreign war, there was one major civil war, and there were the usual sort of border bickerings which were practically continuous in Southeast Asia. In relative terms, however, it was a quiet period. The principal events were:

1717. Invasion of Cambodia. (See p. 657.) Although one of two Siamese armies was destroyed, the expedition was eventually successful.

1733–1758. Reign of King Boromokot. This began with a violent struggle between Boromokot, younger brother of previous King **T'ai Sra,** and the son of the dead king. Eventually successful, Boromokot ruthlessly revenged himself by killing all of his principal enemies, then ruled wisely and well.

LAOS

Laos was rocked by violence and civil war at the outset of the century. This soon led to the division of the kingdom into the two hostile kingdoms of Luang Prabang and Vientiane. Although a condition of war was endemic in the country, there were no outstanding events.

VIETNAM

This was a period of internal truce in Vietnam between the Trinh and Nguyen families. The Nguyens took advantage of this internal peace to extend the power and territory of Vietnam to the south and west at the expense of Cambodia and Laos. The major military activity centered around Vietnamese ambitions in Cambodia, resulting in 3 major wars: 1714–1717, 1739, and 1749 (see below).

CAMBODIA

During the first part of this period Cambodia was the victim of expansionist aims of Vietnam and of Siam. In the process Vietnam annexed a considerable part of Cambodia. Later, as a measure of strength and stability was restored, Cambodia attempted to regain her lost provinces, but was unsuccessful, and in the subsequent prolonged fighting was forced to cede more territory to Vietnam. The principal events were:

1714–1716. Civil War and Vietnamese Intervention. In a struggle for succession, King **Prea Srey Thomea** was driven from his throne by his uncle, **Keo Fa,** who had the support of a Vietnamese army and a small Laotian force. Prea Srey Thomea fled to Siam to request help from King **T'ai Sra** (1709–1733).

1717. Siamese Invasion. Two large Siamese expeditionary forces entered Cambodia. The southern force was disastrously defeated at the **Battle of Bantea Meas,** mostly because of a panic apparently caused by the destruction of the supporting Siamese naval force in a storm at sea. The northern expedition, however, defeated the Cambodians and their Vietnamese allies in a series of engagements and reached Udong, Keo Fa's capital. Keo Fa thereupon offered his allegiance to Siam. This was accepted, and Prea Srey Thomea's cause was abandoned. Meanwhile, however, the Vietnamese had annexed several small border provinces of Cambodia in the Mekong River region.

1739–1749. War with Vietnam. A Cambodian army attempted to regain the coastal region of Ha-tien, which had been taken by Vietnam during the previous war. The Cambodians were repulsed. In retaliation, Vietnamese forces again invaded Cambodia. Further parcels of Cambodian territory were annexed in the Mekong River area.

MALAYA

A period of confused warfare in the Strait of Malacca area, involving the principality of Siak (in Sumatra) and the Malay states of Johore, Kedah, Perak, and Selangor. The Dutch avoided involvement. Taking advantage of internal troubles in Johore, and of warfare between Siak and Johore, the martial Buginese pirates (see p. 597), who had established a pirate maritime state in the Riau Archipelago, soon established their ascendancy over Johore, Kedah, Perak, and Selangor. The principal Bugi leader was **Daing Parani,** who was ably supported by 4 equally daring and ruthless brothers. By the end of the period, however, the Buginese were facing the possibility of trouble with the Dutch, who found the growing Buginese power and maritime interests a threat to their own position in Indonesia and in the Malacca Strait.

INDONESIA

During this period the Dutch established virtually complete control over Java, and also expanded their holdings elsewhere in the islands of the archipelago. The principal events were:

1704–1705. First Javanese War of Succession. Finding their trade, and their position in Batavia, threatened by a dispute within the royal family of Mataram (which still held most of eastern and central Java), the Dutch intervened, deposed an unfriendly monarch, and placed a puppet on the throne. They also extended the area of their dominion in western Java and annexed the eastern half of Madura.

1706–1707. Dutch War with Surapati. This Balinese soldier of fortune had carved out a kingdom for himself in the northeastern portion of Java, near Surabaya, at the expense of Mataram. He had played an important role in the intrigues which had led to the First Javanese War of Succession. His overthrow and death gave virtual control of northeast Java to the Dutch.

1712–1719. Continued Turmoil in Northeast Java. Followers and successors of Surapati tried to eject the Dutch, but were finally wiped out.

1719–1723. Second Javanese War of Succession. Another struggle for the succession to the throne of Mataram caused chaos on Java and again led to Dutch intervention and subsequent territorial expansion.

1740–1743. Chinese War. This was a rebellion, started by Dutch persecution of Chinese merchant residents of Batavia and other Javanese cities, the initial incident being a panicky massacre of Chinese in Batavia. The Chinese survivors fled to the country and, linking up with Javanese dissidents, stirred up a major rebellion. The Dutch finally suppressed this, and annexed the entire north coast of Java and the remainder of Madura.

1743–1744. Rebellion in Madura. Madurans, who had fought beside the Dutch in the Chinese War, expected thereby to gain their independence. When this was not forthcoming, they revolted, but were suppressed after hard fighting.

1749–1757. Third Javanese War of Succession. A conflict was stirred up when Baron **Gustaaf van Imhoff,** Dutch governor general, became unnecessarily involved in an internal dynastic feud in the remnant of Mataram. This was the most bitter of all the Java wars, and was complicated for the Dutch by a simultaneous revolt in western Java. The Dutch were defeated by **Mangku Bumi,** the opposing Mataram ruler, at the **Battle of the Bogowonto River** (1751) and the Dutch commander, **De Clercq,** was killed. Determined fighting and internal discord among the Javanese finally brought Dutch victory.

AFRICA

NORTH AFRICA

During this period Tripolitania for all practical purposes became independent of Turkey. Tripolitania, Morocco, and Algeria (and Tunisia to a lesser extent) maintained themselves by piracy and by shipborne and overland slave trade. The heyday of Barbary piracy was beginning to pass, however, due to active and aggressive opposition of the European Mediterranean powers.

Morocco

Morocco was by far the most powerful and most extensive of the North African states at the beginning of the century. Under the strong and able rule of Sultan **Mulay Ismail** ("The Bloodthirsty"), Moroccan influence and territorial claims extended in all directions across the Sahara Desert, reaching as far as the Sudan (1672–1727). After Mulay Ismail's death, however, the country was thrown into turmoil by struggles among the oligarchical military caste which he had created. Moroccan power and influence practically disappeared beyond the Atlas Mountains.

Algeria

This was a period of Algerian decline. Central rule was weak, and European naval activity reduced the activity and profits of the corsairs. Oran was captured from Spain (1708), which was then busily engaged in wars north of the Mediterranean, but was recaptured by Spanish forces a few years later (1732). Algeria was still nominally a Turkish possession.

Tunisia

Tunisia was the first of the Barbary States to turn from piracy to normal maritime trade relations. This trend was begun by **Hussein ben Ali,** the leading soldier of Tunisia, who made himself bey, overthrew the last of the deys, and virtually ended Turkish rule (1705). He entered into trade treaties with the main European Mediterranean powers, but this led to opposition, and his nephew, **Ali Pasha,** rebelled, seized power, and beheaded Hussein. During the subsequent reign of Ali Pasha (1710–1756) relatively peaceful relations with Europe were retained, but with less cordiality than during the brief reign of Hussein.

Tripolitania

Tripolitania became virtually independent from Turkey (1714) under the leadership of **Ahmed Pasha Karamanli.** Nominal tribute to Constantinople continued, paid out of receipts from piracy.

EGYPT

Under the Mamelukes, Egypt, like the three North African lands farther west, became virtually independent of Turkey, though continuing nominal allegiance. It was a half-century of intrigue and conflict between the 2 major Mameluke factions, the Kasimites and the Fikarites. By the middle of the century one of the greatest of Egypt's Mameluke rulers, **Ali Bey,** was fighting his way to a position of preeminence in Egypt (1750).

WEST AFRICA

The slave trade had begun to ruin, and to fatally weaken, the coastal regions of West Africa. The inland peoples, of whom the Ashantis had now become the most important, were less affected by this trade, but they too were suffering from it, and contributed to its evils by selling the captives taken in their interminable wars either to the European slave merchants on the coast or to the Arab slave traders from across the Sahara. (The Arab brought the Islamic religion with them, and it generally spread along all of the territories bounding the Sahara on the southwest.) The rise of the Ashantis was due in large part to the able leadership and fighting ability of 2 chiefs, **Osei Tutu** (1697–1731) and **Opuku Ware** (1731–1742). Osei Tutu was defeated and killed by the neighboring Akim people, but his death was soon avenged by Opuku Ware, who conquered the Akim and other highland people.

SOUTH AFRICA

The converging advances of the Boers from the southwest and the Bantus from the north and east continued. By midcentury these 2 dynamic and aggressive peoples were beginning to meet in an arc extending from Orange River Valley in the north and west to the coast more than 550 miles northeast of Capetown. Although the Boers had been engaged in continuing minor military pacifications against Hottentots and bushmen in the interior, there had been no major clash with the Bantus before midcentury.

EAST AFRICA

The Sultanate of Oman consolidated its control of the East African coast above Cape Delgado, repulsing the last weak efforts of the Portuguese to re-establish themselves on this coast. The Omani slave trade into the Red Sea, Persian Gulf, and coast of India was almost as profitable as that on the east coast.

ABYSSINIA

At the outset of the century the Negus, or Emperor, **Jesus** (a member of a dynasty claiming unbroken descent from Solomon) had established a strong, centralized rule from his capital, Gondar. He was assassinated, however (1708), and in the following decades the country reverted to anarchic feudalism.

THE AMERICAS

NORTH AMERICA

Queen Anne's War, 1702–1713

This was the American version of the War of the Spanish Succession (see p. 617).

1702, December. Sack of St. Augustine. Hostilities were begun in a destructive raid by a combined force of Carolinians and Indians.

1703–1704. Operations along the Southern Frontier. Carolinian-Indian attacks destroyed Spanish missions in the Apalachee region; however, Choctaw resistance prevented raids on French communities in the Gulf area.

1703–1707. Operations in the Northeast. Abenaki and French bands conducted raids from Maine to the Connecticut Valley. Five hundred New Englanders were dispatched to Acadia in an attempt to disrupt Abenaki supply lines and to capture fisheries (1704). English-colonial forces twice vainly attempted to take the main French base at Port Royal, Nova Scotia (1704, 1707). Farther north, a French and Indian attack destroyed the Newfoundland settlement of Bonavista (August 18–29, 1704); later, the French consolidated control of the area by seizing St. John's (1708).

1710, October 16. Capture of Port Royal. A British force of 4,000, with naval support, seized Port Royal which was renamed Annapolis Royal.

1711. Failure in the St. Lawrence. In planned land and naval attacks, **Francis Nicholson** was to lead a mixed group of colonists and Iroquois against Montreal; simultaneously, an English force, including 7 crack Marlborough regiments, was to strike Quebec by sea. However, the loss of 10 ships on the St. Lawrence rendered the joint campaign stillborn.

1713. Treaty of Utrecht. An uneasy peace in North America was established.

1711–1712. Tuscarora War. A Tuscarora uprising in the Carolinas was suppressed after the slaughter of 200 settlers. Tuscarora survivors moved to New York State and became the sixth nation of the Iroquois Confederacy.

1715–1728. Yamassee War. The Yamassees and lower Creeks drove South Carolina settlers from the territory west of Savannah. A concerted Carolinian and Cherokee effort pushed the Yamassee confederation into Florida (1716). The colonists erected fortifications on the Altamaha, Savannah, and Santee rivers to protect the Carolina communities from French and Spanish aggression (1716–1721). The inefficiency of the proprietary regime in prosecuting the Yamassee War (and generally in providing defenses against Indian raids and piracy) led the Board of Trade to substitute royal for proprietary government (Act of Parliament, 1729).

1720–1738. Fortification of the Great Lakes. The French erected Fort Niagara (1720) as a headquarters for the Iroquois campaigns and in order to gain control of the lower Great Lakes. In response, the British built Fort Oswego on Lake Ontario (1725). New England settlers fortified the frontier in anticipation of Abenaki raids.

1733–1739. English Expansion in Georgia. James Oglethorpe, one of 20 trustees of the territory extending from the Savannah to the Altamaha rivers, supervised construction of a series of forts on St. Simon's, St. Andrew's, Cumberland, and Amelia islands. Oglethorpe was also instrumental in establishing peaceful relations with the Creeks and lesser tribes.

1739–1743. War of Jenkins's Ear. Prolonged Anglo-Spanish discord concerning the boundaries of Florida, the commercial provisions of the Treaty of Utrecht and the **Assiento** (a contract providing for an English monopoly of the slave trade with the Spanish colonies), and Spanish abuse of British seamen caused England to declare war (October 19). The immediate cause of war was the claim of a British merchant ship captain, named Jenkins, that his ear had been cut off by Spanish officials. British forces under Admiral **Edward Vernon** seized Porto Bello (1739) and Chagres (1740). An assault on Cartagena was repulsed (1740). Under Oglethorpe, Carolina, Georgia, and Virginia contingents—protected on the west by the Creeks, Cherokees, and Chickasaws—captured 2 forts on the San Juan River (January, 1740) and unsuccessfully assaulted St. Augustine (May–July). The following year, an English attack on Cuba failed. In the **Battle of Bloody Swamp** (1742), a Spanish attack on St. Simon's Island was repulsed. Oglethorpe's troops again attempted to seize St. Augustine, but were compelled to withdraw from Florida (1743).

King George's War, 1740–1748

This was the American version of the War of the Austrian Succession (see p. 630).

1744. French Attack on Annapolis. The French were repulsed from Annapolis Royal (formerly Port Royal), Nova Scotia.

1745, April–June. Siege of Louisbourg. A New England expedition under **William Pepperell,** supported by British vessels, engaged in the most notable American operation of the war, a siege of the heavily fortified stronghold at Louisbourg. The fort surrendered (June 16). This marked one of the first uses of field artillery in North America.

1746. French Expedition against Nova Scotia and Cape Breton Island. The assault force was demolished in a storm off the coast of Nova Scotia.

1746–1748. Operations on the Northern Frontier. A New England campaign to penetrate into Canada provoked French and Indian raids on Maine settlements. **William Johnson,** New York commissioner for Indian affairs, and **Conrad Weiser,** who pressed Iroquois land claims at the expense of the Delawares, secured the support of the Six Nations.

1748. Treaty of Aix-la-Chapelle. An uneasy peace settled over northern North America. To the disgust of the colonists, Louisbourg was restored to the French in return for Madras.

LATIN AMERICA

Spanish America

1702–1713. War of the Spanish Succession. (See pp. 617 and 660.) In its American phase, the conflict was restricted primarily to the North American continent and to naval operations in the Caribbean and among the Antilles.

1718–1720. French and Spanish War on the Gulf Coast. This was a part of the War of the Quadruple Alliance (see p. 627). Clashes occurred in Florida and Texas.

1720–1722. Spanish Occupation of Texas. This was intended to prevent French expansion from Louisiana.

1721–1725. Rebellion in Paraguay. José de Antiquera, governor of Asunción, disturbed by the increasing dominance of Buenos Aires traders, rebelled. He refused to accept a new governor sent from Lima, ousted the Jesuits, and defeated a force from Buenos Aires (1724). Although Antiquera was captured (1726), the insurrection persisted for 9 more years until an expedition under Governor **Zabala** of Buenos Aires crushed the rebels.

1723. Araucanian Revolt. The restless and warlike Araucanian Indians (see p. 520) attempted unsuccessfully to oust the Spaniards from southern Chile.

1726. Establishment of Montevideo. This was to prevent Portuguese expansion in the Banda Oriental (Uruguay), a region disputed between Spain and Portugal because of differing interpretations of the Treaty of Tordesillas (see p. 518).

1736–1737. Oruro Revolt. Harsh labor conditions in the mines of central Peru caused the Oruros to revolt. Led by **Juan Santos,** they seriously damaged the city of Oruro before the uprising was quelled.

1739–1748. War of Jenkins's Ear and War of the Austrian Succession. (See pp. 661 and 630.) Although combat extended over a wide area, the emphasis remained on North America. Nevertheless, British forces operated in the Caribbean: Porto Bello and Chagres were captured while attacks on Cuba and Cartagena failed (see pp. 636 and 661). In addition, there was British raiding along the coast of Venezuela.

1749. Insurrection in Venezuela. Uprisings among the Venezuelan Creoles were suppressed by force.

Portuguese America

1701–1713. War of the Spanish Succession. The French made repeated raids and attacks along the Brazilian coast. Colonia was captured and held temporarily (1702), and Rio de Janeiro was captured, sacked, and held for ransom by able French Admiral **René Duguay-Trouin** (1711).

1708–1709. War of the Emboabas. The Portuguese government suppressed and brought under control the adventurous, expansionist, and semi-independent **Paulistas** (Portuguese inhabitants of São Paulo).

1710–1711. War of the Mascates. A small-scale conflict between the inhabitants of Olinda and Recife, in Pernambuco, over the primacy of the 2 towns.

1735–1737. Spanish-Portuguese War. This was a part of the War of the Polish Succession (see p. 628). Spain seized Colonia (1735), but was persuaded by Britain to return the port to Portugal (1737). Colonia, the main Portuguese foothold on the River Plate (since 1680), continued to be a source of friction between Portugal and Spain in their dispute over the Banda Oriental (Uruguay).

XVI

THE DOMINANCE OF MANEUVER ON LAND AND SEA: 1750–1800

MILITARY TRENDS

Maneuver—the tactical manipulation of fire and movement on the battlefield—was the predominant military characteristic of this period on both land and sea. This was due in part to improvements in weaponry, but mainly evolved through the genius of four of history's greatest captains.

On land, the period opened with **Frederick II** of Prussia—**Frederick the Great**—in the full flower of his military capacity. **George Washington*** emerged in mid-period, and before the half-century closed **Napoleon Bonaparte**'s star was shining over the horizon of war. On the sea, **Horatio Nelson,** exploring down the path previously opened by France's **Pierre André Suffren** and England's **John Jervis** and **George Brydges Rodney,** shattered the old order of naval tactics.

The trend toward maneuver progressed through the three major wars of the period: the Seven Years' War, 1756–1763; the American Revolution, 1775–1783; and the French Revolutionary Wars, 1791–1800. These embraced not only Europe and the North American continent but also much of the rest of the world. As a result of these wars and their subsidiary operations, the French colonial empires in both North America and India were destroyed, a worldwide British Empire was firmly established, and the United States of America came into being. Paradoxically, the close of the period saw France the predominant military land power in Europe.

Sea power's importance became firmly established, although it is doubtful whether many people realized it at the time. Certainly **William Pitt** the elder, George Washington, and Horatio Nelson did. Frederick the Great, whose operations were confined to the land, had no reason to understand sea power. Bonaparte never did adequately appreciate it, a blind spot in his genius which would be most costly to him.

* Military and other historians have tended to underrate Washington's generalship. Those who disagree with the authors' firm conviction that he merits comparison with Frederick, Napoleon, and Nelson are referred to their *Compact History of the Revolutionary War,* New York, 1963, Appendix V, "The Historians and the Generalship of George Washington."

WEAPONS AND TACTICS ON LAND

The continued employment of the flintlock musket and its increased rate of fire (see p. 611) caused a still further thinning of Gustavus' 6-man line into one which was at first 4 men deep, then 3, and finally 2. This created a radical new problem in control. The already rigid discipline of early 18th-century warfare became even more stringent. It was maintained in all European armies. Frederick the Great went further. The individual Prussian soldier, through incessant, brutal, rigid drill discipline, including the cadenced step, became an automaton. Prussian units could change direction or front simultaneously or by small groups in succession; could shift into battle formation from marching column or vice versa, even over broken and irregular terrain. In addition, fire by platoon replaced the more formalized volley fire by larger formations.

The net result was a mobile infantry which could be so shifted and massed at will on the battlefield as to produce the maximum effect of fire and shock action

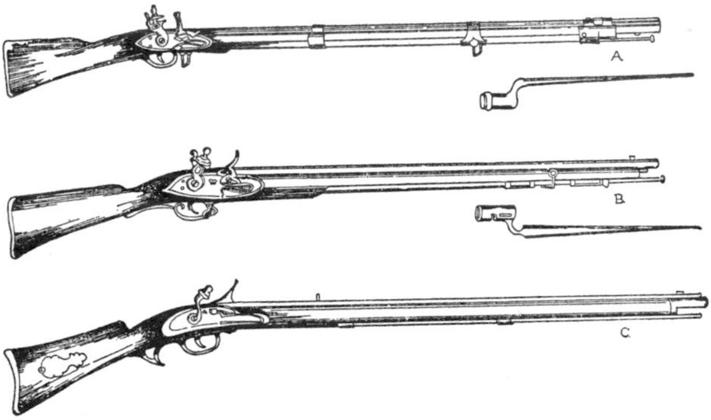

Eighteenth-century flintlocks: (a) French regulation musket; (b) British "Brown Bess" musket; (c) American frontier rifle

at a chosen spot. This rendered possible Frederick's oblique attack, with Leuthen (see p. 671) as prime example.

Another weapon affecting infantry tactics was the rifle, which came slowly into military use toward the end of the period. Originally a sporting weapon, this heavy, cumbersome hand arm, whose grooved barrel imparted a twist to its bullet, achieved amazing accuracy and range as compared to the smoothbore musket. It had crept oversea to North America from its original habitat, the Rhineland, where the huntsman—the jäger or "yager"—had used it for nearly 200 years. It skipped New England, but German craftsmen in Pennsylvania began turning out a somewhat lighter and longer-barreled rifle for the woodsman. The rifle had a slower rate of fire than the musket, since to load it each bullet (wrapped in a greased patch) had to be hammered down into the grooved barrel with a mallet. It was an individual arm, used by individualists along the western fringes of the thirteen colonies. It carried no bayonet. As a result of experience in the American Revolution, the rifle and the rifleman had become an element in European warfare as the period closed. The German and Austrian jäger battalions were armed with the rifle.

Out of the French and Indian War also came further mobility. Skirmishers—light troops covering the front of the field of battle—had always been present in one way or another. Previous to 1756, in Europe these units were usually "expendables," irregulars. But as a result of Braddock's defeat (see p. 706), experiments were made in the British Army leading to the establishment in each foot regiment (or battalion) of a "light" company, usually detached from its battalion for covering the advance, or for some other special mission. By the time of the American Revolution it was British practice to separate the light companies from their regiments for action, organizing them into provisional units. In addition, the grenadier companies—also one to each regiment—were separated and gathered into special units in combat. These grenadier companies were composed of the largest men in the regiment—a selection dating from the time of the 3-or-more-pound hand grenade (discarded by this time) best hurled by powerful men. The fault of this British system was that the grenadier (not to be confused with the Grenadier Guards Regiment) and light companies became an elite, thus inducing a feeling of inferiority in the remainder of each regiment—the "line" companies. However, the use of regular troops for skirmishing also led to the establishment of "light" and "rifle" regiments in the British service. At the beginning of the French Revolutionary Wars (1792), the untrained French conscripts hurriedly gathered wholesale by the *levée en masse* were literally herded into battle. Perforce, "line" tactics were abandoned and the French infantry, with bayonets fixed, advanced to the assault in deep, dense formations—somewhat erroneously called "columns"—covered by a cloud of skirmishers. This forced compromise would remain, even though the later well-disciplined armies of Bonaparte would include regiments of *chasseurs à pied* and *voltigeurs* (light infantry), while the elite were organized into grenadier regiments.

The role of the cavalry was clarified in Western Europe. During the previous century it had become common practice to intermingle masses of cavalry and infantry in the battle line. Save in Sweden and France, where the saber and shock action were often employed, the horsemen, armed with light muskets and pistols, employed fire action while advancing, and when and if they charged it was only at a slow trot. During the early part of the 18th century, shock action was more generally employed, but infantry and cavalry were still intermingled. This hybrid cavalry-infantry formation was last used in 1759 at Minden (see p. 673), where British infantry broke the French cavalry.

Frederick, however, long before Minden, had restored his cavalry to its original functions: shock action on the battlefield and reconnaissance off the battlefield. He prohibited the firearm as a cavalry weapon (excepting always dragoons, who were taught to fight on foot as well as on horseback). Frederick's cavalry, who went into action first in a 3-rank and later a 2-rank formation, charged boot-to-boot at full gallop. They were never interspersed among their own infantry; their principal weapon was the saber.

Field artillery, despite the efficient Frederick's improvements through the Seven Years' War, was still a cumbersome arm, its matériel of many differing calibers and most of it too heavy for efficient mobile use. But in 1765 a Frenchman, **Jean Baptiste de Gribeauval,** began to revolutionize the arm, which a quarter-century later would really come into its own under Napoleon's direction. Gribeauval standardized the French field artillery into 4-, 8- and 12-pounder guns and 6-inch howitzers, smoothbores cast of iron or bronze. The pieces were lightened, carriages strengthened; horses were harnessed in pairs instead of in tandem; drivers—heretofore usually hired civilians (despite the example of Gustavus) unreliable on the battlefield—became soldiers; caissons and limbers were provided; tangent scales and elevating screws increased ease and accuracy of laying. For nearly a century to come, Gribeauval's 12-pounder gun—much later called the "Napoleon" in honor of Napoleon III—would dominate battlefields the world over.

Toward the end of the period, two inventions—one British, the other American—radically affected future warfare. In 1784, Lieutenant **Henry Shrapnel,** R.A., invented the artillery shell which would bear his name—in essence a canister filled with lead bullets surrounded by a bursting charge. Exploding in air, shrapnel spread its hail over an extended area, lethal to troops in the open. In 1798, **Eli Whitney,** New England inventor of the cotton gin, turned his hand to making small arms. By invention of a jig and the distribution of his labor force, he manufactured muskets whose various parts were interchangeable; here was the initial mass pro-

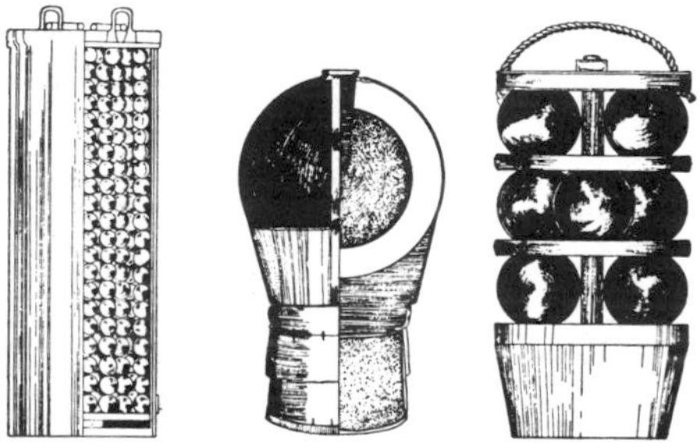

Types of artillery ammunition: (a) caseshot, or canister; (b) shell; (c) grapeshot

duction of weapons. An earlier approach had been made in Britain in 1702–1704 by the Tower of London armories in producing the Brown Bess (or Tower) musket. Two other refinements were the semaphore telegraph of **Claude Chappe** and the military observation balloon, both developed by the French during the Wars of the French Revolution.

Logistically, it was Frederick who during the period evolved the basic principles of modern military supply. Breaking away from slavish dependence on depots, 3 days' rations were carried in the Prussian soldier's knapsack, 8 days' bread supply in the regimental trains and a month's supply in the army trains. A fairly well-organized transport system linked Frederick's armies to such depots as he did organize. His troops, too, were prepared to live off the country when necessary.

TACTICS AND WEAPONS AT SEA

Brilliant English naval iconoclasts smashed the "Permanent Fighting Instructions" of the Royal Navy, which up to this period had frozen initiative by limiting battle formations to a rigid line ahead (see p. 532). Until a new school of British naval officers dared to try it and succeeded, it was unthinkable that vessels should leave the line of battle and sail in, bow-on, toward enemy ships (which could rake them with entire broadsides), break through the opposing line, and, falling upon separated parts of the hostile formation, destroy them in succession by concentration of superior fire power. But by 1800 this method—the Nelsonian touch—had been added to naval warfare. And this was why, as the period ended, Britannia indeed "ruled the waves."

Naval gunnery of the period was still of two schools (see p. 612). The British so aimed their guns as to hull the enemy; smash in her oaken sides and sink or disable her. The French aimed for the enemy's top hamper, to immobilize her by shooting away masts and rigging. To increase fire power, the British introduced the carronade, a short, squatty piece hurling a 32-pound or larger ball; its smashing power at close range was far superior to that of the long 12-, 16-, and 24-pounder guns comprising the normal armament of ships of the line and frigates. The carronade was cheaper to manufacture than the long gun and, being lighter, easier to handle aboard ship. It had much to do with British victories during the period, but it had one major drawback which would not become critical until the War of 1812: the carronade-armed ship had to be much faster and handier than an opponent armed with long guns, or she would be demolished before her carronades came in range.

British technical ingenuity during the period brought forth several innovations in naval gunnery, contributing to superior fire power. These included a flintlock device, flashing a spark into the touchhole, instead of the loose powder priming and the linstock—the slow match previously used; also improvements in powder bags, and the wetting of the wads between powder and ball to prevent premature firings. Metal springs were added to the rope breechings which held the gun in recoil, and inclined planes of wood were placed under the carriage wheels further to ease recoil. Block-and-tackle purchases enabled the traversing of individual guns to right or left—a tremendous advance, this, in naval gunnery, since one no longer had to steer the entire vessel at a right angle to the target when firing. Another invention was the firing of red-hot cannon shot at wooden ships, a procedure first introduced by the British at Gibraltar in 1782. This incendiary weapon, fired with relative accuracy, was a vast improvement over the employment of drifting fire ships and fire rafts, necessarily chancy and haphazard in results. The crowning development was in tactical control: an improved flag signal code, whereby for the first time in naval history a commander could maintain control and issue orders right up until battle was joined. These improvements appeared gradually during the period; by its end all had proved their efficacy.

The period closed with a massive mutiny in England of the enlisted personnel of the Royal Navy (1797). This, as it turned out, was a blessing in disguise, for public attention was drawn to the injustices and horrors suffered by the sailors and caused immediate remedial action (see p. 613).

MAJOR EUROPEAN WARS*

SEVEN YEARS' WAR, 1756–1763

Land Operations in Europe

The Holy Roman Empire (Austria), France, Russia, Sweden, and Saxony, alarmed by Prussia's growing power and territorial expansion under Frederick, joined in a coalition to cripple or destroy Prussia (May–June, 1756). England, already involved in colonial and maritime war with France in the French and Indian War in North America (see p. 705) and in India (see p. 699), supported Prussia. The 7 principal land campaigns of this war—also known as the Third Silesian War—were fought in Europe east of the Rhine, but naval operations spread over the Atlantic and Indian Oceans and the Mediterranean and Caribbean Seas.

* The French and Indian War (an extension of the Seven Years' War) and the American Revolution (which had European and worldwide repercussions) are covered below, pp. 705–708.

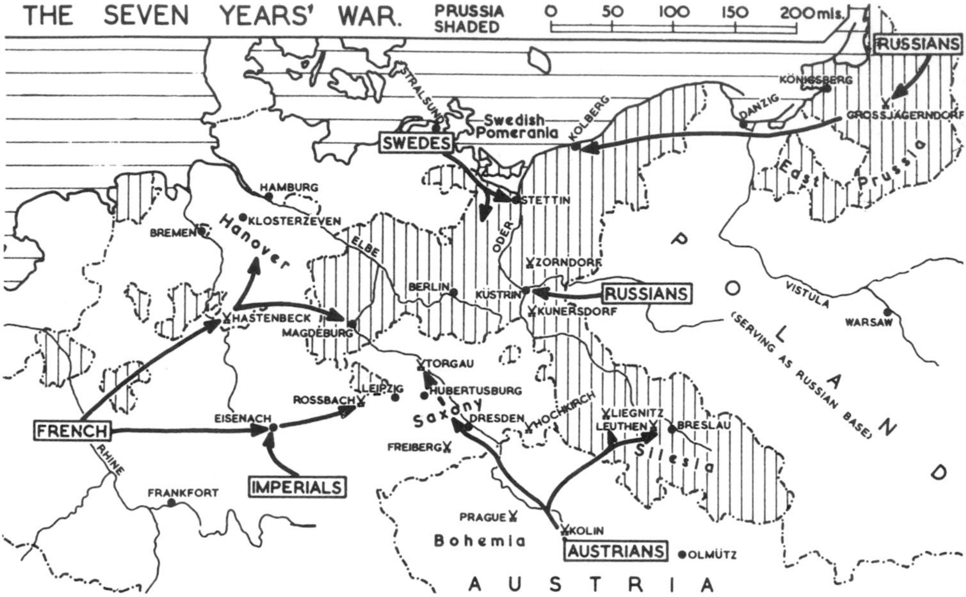

1756, August 29. Frederick Strikes First. Learning the intentions of his enemies, Frederick crossed the Saxon frontier with 70,000 men, the remaining 80,000 men of his army guarding the northern and eastern frontiers. He occupied Dresden (September 10), Saxon forces, only 14,000 strong, falling back to the fortified camp of Pirna, on the Elbe, where they were blockaded.

1756, October 1. Battle of Lobositz (Lovocize). Frederick, learning that an Austrian army of 50,000 men under Marshal **Maximilian U. von Browne** was approaching to relieve the Saxons, marched south with equal strength and defeated the Austrians in the rugged Erzgebirge. Casualties on each side were approximately 3,000. The Saxons at Pirna surrendered. Saxony fell into Frederick's possession, and the Saxon troops were incorporated into his army.

1757, April. Invasion of Bohemia. The coalition had 132,000 Austrian troops in northern Bohemia; none of the other allies were ready. Frederick now had nearly 175,000 men under arms. Almost half of these were scattered along the Bohemian frontier in three groups: the left under Marshal **Kurt C. von Schwerin** and **August Wilhelm, Duke of Brunswick-Bevern,** and the center and right under Frederick's personal command. An additional force of about 40,000 Prussians and 10,000 English under **William Augustus, Duke of Cumberland** stood in Hanover to guard against any French move; another 50,000 guarded the frontiers of Swedish Pomerania and Russia. Frederick sent his left wing south across the mountains east of the Elbe, while with the bulk of his army (about 65,000 men) he pressed from Pirna on Prague, where the Austrians had concentrated about 70,000 troops under Prince Charles of Lorraine.

1757, May 6. Battle of Prague (Praha). The Austrians were defeated in a short, savage battle by Frederick. His initial attack against the Austrian right having been repulsed, he sent his cavalry to envelop the enemy right flank. A gap appeared in the Austrian formation as they tried to meet this envelopment. Penetrating the gap (in the "Prague Maneuver"), Frederick broke the Austrian army in two, and threw it back into the city, which he invested. Losses on both sides were heavy: 14,275 Austrians killed, wounded, and captured; 13,200 Prussian casualties included Marshal von Schwerin, who was killed while leading the first infantry assault.

1757, May–June. Approach of Austrian Relief Army. Marshal **Leopold J. von Daun**

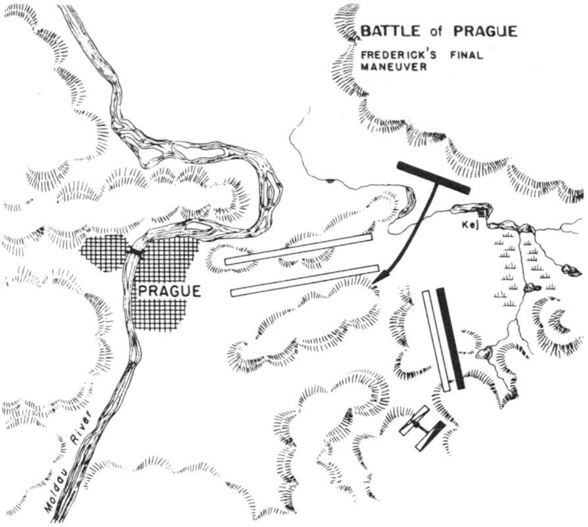

with 60,000 fresh troops moved leisurely to the relief of beleaguered Prague.

1757, June 18. Battle of Kolin. Frederick gathered all the forces he could spare from the siege—34,000 men—and attacked Daun's entrenched camp. The Prussians were repulsed, losing 12,090 men, while the Austrians had 8,000 casualties. Frederick was forced to raise the siege of Prague and to evacuate Bohemia.

1757, July. Allied Invasions of Prussia and Hanover. A French army of 100,000 men, under Marshal **Louis d'Estrées,** invaded Hanover. Simultaneously another 24,000 French under **Charles, Duke of Soubise** and 60,000 Austrians under Prince **Joseph of Saxe-Hildburghausen** were moving northeast from Franconia to join d'Estrées. The main Austrian army, 110,000 strong, under Prince Charles of Lorraine and Marshal Daun, was in Bohemia, advancing toward Prussia. Also a Russian army of 100,000 under Marshal **Stepan Apraksin** was invading East Prussia, and 16,000 Swedes had landed in Pomerania.

1757, July 26. Battle of Hastenbeck. The Duke of Cumberland with 54,000 men was defeated and driven from Hanover by d'Estrées.

1757, July 30. Battle of Gross-Jägersdorf. Prussian General **Hans von Lehwald,** with 30,000 men, was defeated by Apraksin's Russians. The road to Berlin was open. Poor Russian supply arrangements kept them from exploiting promptly.

ROSSBACH-LEUTHEN CAMPAIGN, 1757

1757, September–October. The Allies Converge on Berlin. Frederick, leaving a small force in Silesia under the Duke of Brunswick-Bevern, moved west by forced marches with only 23,000 men to meet the most pressing threat: the juncture, in Prussian Saxony, of the main French army under the **Duke of Richelieu** (who had replaced d'Estrées) and Hildburghausen's and Soubise's Austro-French army. But Richelieu's army did not move, and Soubise and Hildburghausen—who had taken Magdeburg—declined to give battle and retreated to Eisenach. Frederick then dashed back to Silesia to stop Charles' and Daun's attempted Austrian invasion from Bohemia, and to block the lethargic Russian advance on Berlin. He learned that Austrian raiders had entered and plundered Berlin (October 16).

1757, October 18–November 4. Maneuvers in Saxony. While a small force was detached to rescue his capital, Frederick again marched westward, having learned that Soubise and Hildburghausen were again advancing. By the end of the month Frederick was west of the Saale River, again endeavoring to entice his enemies into battle, in the vicinity of the village of Rossbach.

1757, November 5. Battle of Rossbach. Hildburghausen and Soubise had 64,000 men on commanding ground, facing east.

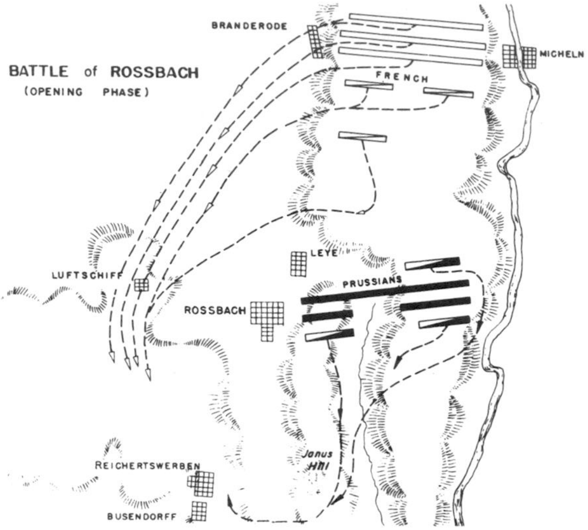

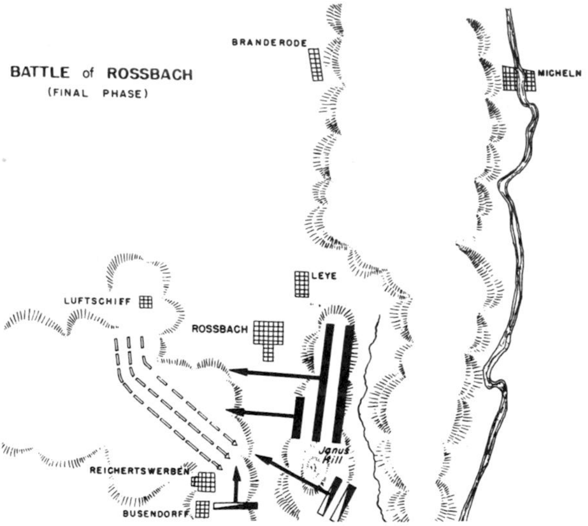

The allies decided to envelop Frederick's left flank. The king diagnosed his enemy's intentions. As 3 parallel allied columns marched southward, 41,000 strong, Frederick pretended to withdraw his 21,000 men to the east from Rossbach. His cavalry, 38 squadrons under General **Friederick Wilhelm von Seydlitz,** swung wide to the east, while the infantry, much more mobile than those of the allies, shortly changed direction to the south, screened by hills from the sight of the allies. As a result, when the allied army completed its circling around the original Prussian flank and headed north to deploy, it was met head on by heavy Prussian artillery fire, supported by 7 battalions of infantry. At the same time the Prussian cavalry charged into the allied right flank, throwing the columns into confusion. The Prussian main effort then attacked the enemy mass, in echelon (overlapping succession) from the left. In less than an hour and a half the allied army was completely routed, with loss of about 8,000 men. The fugitives were joined by the 20,000-odd allied troops that had not been engaged. Frederick's casualties totaled 500, including Seydlitz, who was badly wounded.

1757, November 6–December 5. Return to Silesia. Frederick immediately hurried back to Silesia, where the Austrians were advancing toward Breslau (Wroclaw). En route he learned that Charles of Lorraine and Marshal Daun had defeated and captured August Wilhelm of Brunswick-Bevern at **Breslau** (November 22), and had driven Brunswick-Bevern's troops west of the Oder. With 13,000 men Frederick covered 170 miles in 12 days, to unite with Brunswick-Bevern's survivors near Liegnitz (Legnica). The king, who now had about 36,000 men, at once took the offensive, marching east.

1757, December 6. Battle of Leuthen. Prince Charles' Austrian army, nearly 80,000 strong, lay in a 5-mile-long line of battle, facing west in undulating country a few miles from Breslau. Cavalry protected both flanks. The Austrian reserves lay behind the partially entrenched left wing, in anticipation that Frederick would attempt his favorite enveloping maneuver on favorable terrain. The right flank lay on a marsh. Frederick moved toward the Austrian right, in 4 columns, the inner 2 columns made up of infantry, the outer ones composed of cavalry. Under cover of a range of low hills, he changed direction obliquely to the right, leaving his left-hand column of cavalry in his rear, to begin a demonstration against the Austrian right. Still out of sight of the Austrians, the infantry was thus marching past the enemy front in 2 columns, the remainder of the cavalry having taken the lead.

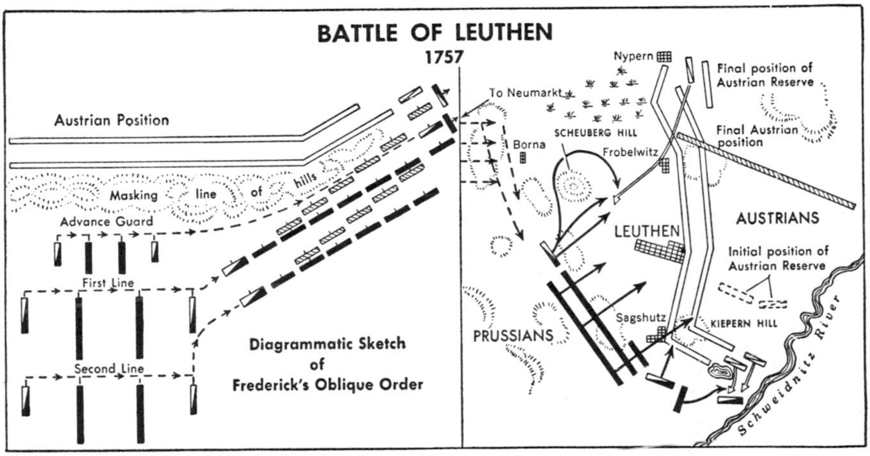

Charles, meanwhile, had moved his reserves to bolster his apparently threatened right wing. When Frederick's marching columns, still concealed behind the hills, began to overlap the Austrian left, the king faced his infantry to the left and attacked in 2 lines echeloned from the right, the pressure increasing as each successive battalion moved in. At the same time, massed Prussian artillery fire shot at the apex of the Austrian left flank, ranged in a vee. The Prussian cavalry on the right flank, under General **Hans J. von Ziethen,** charged into the broken Austrian left and threw it back on the center. Charles attempted to form a new line against this attack, at the same time throwing his right-wing cavalry against the Prussian left flank. But the Austrian horse was caught and scattered by the rear half of Frederick's cavalry, who then charged in on the Austrian right flank. Thus caught off balance, the Austrians never rallied, despite efforts by Charles and Daun. Nightfall alone enabled the escape of the vanquished across the Schwiednitz River to Breslau. Charles's army had been ruined; more than 20,000 were captured, 6,750 killed or wounded, additional thousands scattered to the four winds. Frederick captured 116 guns and 51 colors. Only about half of the original Austrian strength returned to Bohemia and winter quarters. Prussian losses in this desperate fight were 6,150 killed and wounded. Breslau surrendered five days later, ending the campaign.

COMMENT. *"Masterpiece of maneuver and resolution," said Napoleon. Leuthen is generally considered to be the chef-d'oeuvre of the man who was perhaps the ablest tactician of military history.*

1758, January. Renewed Russian Invasion. The Russians, now under the command of General Count **Wilhelm Fermor,** attempted to occupy east Prussia, but were soon immobilized by muddy roads.

1758, May–July. Operations in Moravia. Frederick, certain that he had nothing to fear from the Russians or the Swedes until midsummer, again opened operations by moving into Moravia against the Austrians. An attempt to invest Olmütz (Olomouc) was unsuccessful. Frederick now learned that the Russians, marching into Prussia from the east, were approaching the Oder River. Raising the siege (July 1), by skillful maneuver Frederick deceived the Austrians and marched against the Russians. Meanwhile in the west, Duke **Ferdinand of Brunswick** drove the French back over the Rhine, defeating them at **Crefeld** (June 23).

1758, August 20. Across the Oder River. Frederick arrived at the Oder, across the river from Kustrin (Kostrzyn), which Fermor with 45,000 men was besieging. Feinting a concentration and crossing at that point, Frederick instead moved northward in a rapid, brilliantly conceived night march, crossed the river, and put himself on Fermor's line of communications in a wide, right turning movement. Fermor, raising the siege, turned and moved to a defensive position at the hamlet of Zorndorf, on high ground. The Russians were arrayed in 3 irregular masses, beyond mutual supporting distances, facing north.

1758, August 25. Battle of Zorndorf. Frederick, who had 36,000 men, attacked again in his oblique formation, passing completely around the Russian front to fall on their right (east) flank. Fermor, forming a new front, repulsed the Prussian attack until Seydlitz with his cavalry crossed marshy ground on the Russian right to charge into their masses, smashing the square. Frederick, shifting his attack to the new Russian right (southwest) flank, was checked until Seydlitz, having reformed his cavalry, again rode into the Russian infantry. An inconclusive butchery followed, ending at nightfall. Almost half of the Russian army had fallen, while Frederick had lost some 14,000. Next day Fermor retreated to Königsberg (Kaliningrad); the Prussians were too exhausted to pursue. The Russian threat was ended for the time being.

1758, September–October. Meeting the Austrians in Saxony. Frederick, learning that Daun was threatening his brother, Prince **Henry of Prussia,** not far from Dresden, hurried back with part of his army by forced marches, making 22 miles a day. On his arrival the Austrians withdrew (September 12). After a short rest, Frederick with 37,000 men took the offensive again. Overconfident, he was surprised by Daun, who surrounded the Prussian army with 90,000 men during the night and attacked at dawn.

1758, October 14. Battle of Hochkirch. Frederick's army fought hard against overwhelming force. An escape route was opened and held by General **Hans J. von Ziethen**'s cavalry. Through it the Prussian army retreated, leaving behind 101 guns and some 9,500 men killed, wounded, and prisoners. Daun's army, with losses of about 8,000, was so shaken that no pursuit was made.

1758, October–November. Frederick Regains the Initiative. Daun now laid siege to Dresden, but on learning that Frederick had been reinforced and was moving to attack him, withdrew to the fortified camp at Pirna. The close of the campaign found Frederick in firm possession of Saxony and Silesia, while both the Russians and the small Swedish invading force had evacuated Prussia.

COMMENT. *This had been a costly campaign. Frederick could still keep 150,000 men in the field, but the combat value of the Prussian Army was deteriorating. In 3 years of campaigning he had lost 100,000 of his superbly trained and disciplined troops.*

MINDEN CAMPAIGN, 1759

1759, April. Prussian Failure in West-Central Germany. Duke Ferdinand of Brunswick, reinforced by British troops, advanced with 30,000 men from the line Münster-Paderborn-Cassel, held during the winter, to drive out the French, based on Frankfurt and Wesel. Rebuffed at **Bergen** (near Frankfurt) by sheer weight of numbers, he was forced to retire again, and the French, seizing the bridges across the Weser at Minden, occupied a position too strong for direct attack.

1759, August 1. Battle of Minden. Marquis **Louis de Contades,** commanding both his own troops and those of Duke **Victor de Broglie,** had 60,000 men near Minden. Ferdinand, who now had 45,000, feinted against the French right with a fraction of his command. Contades moved out in force to overwhelm it. As he did, Ferdinand launched a counterassault, in 8 columns. Bad weather delayed the movement, and the French, reforming, were overwhelming the Prussians when the British infantry brigade attacked the French cavalry, who were drawn up in the center of the line of battle and protected by artillery. The British were met by a cavalry charge; with an amazing discipline and gallantry (of 4,434 men, 1,330 became casualties) they not only drove off the French horse by fire but then advanced with the bayonet against French infantry and pierced the center of Contades' line of battle. Ferdinand, realizing that victory was in his hand, at once ordered the British cavalry, 5 regiments strong, to charge and complete the rout. Lieutenant General **George, Lord Sackville** thrice refused to move. As a result the French, though disorganized and beaten, and having lost 10,000 prisoners and 115 guns, retired from the field unhindered. Ferdinand, following them almost to the Rhine, checked his advance only when he had to send reinforcements to assist King Frederick (see below).

COMMENT. *Sackville, tried by court-martial for his disobedience, was cashiered from the British Army. However, 12 years later he returned as a favorite of King George III, to become Lord* **Germain** *and contribute mightily to the ineptness of the British military effort in the American Revolution (see p. 713).*

1759, July–August. Russian and Austrian Invasion. The Russians (now under Count **Peter S. Soltikov**) defeated the Prussian covering forces along the Oder line at **Kay** (July 23) and moved on Frankfurt, linking with 35,000 men of Daun's Austrian army under Lieutenant General **Gideon E. von Laudon.** Frederick, gathering all available forces, moved to meet the combination.

1759, August 12. Battle of Kunersdorf. The Austro-Russian armies, 90,000 strong, lay entrenched in the sand hills 4 miles east of Frankfurt. Frederick, with 50,000 men, crossed the Oder and attempted a double envelopment. But his columns lost their way in the woods and their attacks were delivered piecemeal. Thrown back at all points, Frederick insisted upon continuing the vain attacks. He lost more than 20,000 men, 178 guns, and 28 colors in 6 hours —the greatest calamity ever to befall him. Completely discouraged, he contemplated abdication. Fortunately for the Prussians, their enemies (who had lost 15,700 men) were too sluggish to reap advantage from their victory.

1759, August–November. Frederick Retrieves the Initiative. Frederick, receiving reinforcements from Ferdinand, recovered his determination and reorganized his army in the field. The Russians, having exhausted all the food and forage in the vicinity, later retired to their own frontier, and Frederick turned his attention to Daun, who had occupied Dresden (September 4).

1759, November 21. Battle of Maxen. Frederick sent a detachment of 12,000 men under General **Frederick von Finck** to envelop Daun's army. But the Austrians concentrated 42,000 to overwhelm the detachment; the survivors surrendered. Both sides now spent the winter in relative quiet. This had been Frederick's worst year.

1760. Renewed Allied Convergence on Prussia. The allies planned to move concentrically upon Frederick; Austria's Daun with 100,000 men in Saxony, and Laudon with 50,000 more in Silesia, would work in unison with Russia's Soltikov (50,000 strong) in East Prussia. If Frederick turned on one, the others would converge on Berlin. Frederick with 40,000 faced Daun on the Elbe; Prince Henry with 34,000 was in Silesia, and 15,000 additional Prussians were covering additional Russian and Swedish forces ravaging Pomerania. In the west, Duke Ferdinand's Prussian-British army of 70,000 faced 125,000 French troops in Hanover.

1760, June–October. Ferdinand Maneuvers in the West. Ferdinand, following the instructions and example of his king, played a successful game of march, maneuver, and quick battle against the French armies of the Duke de Broglie and **Claude, Count of St. Germain.** In this campaign the British contingent, commanded by Lieutenant General Sir **John M. Granby** (successor to the incompetent Sackville), played a conspicuous part. Highlight of the British effort was the storming of Warburg (July 31) by Granby's cavalry, who took 1,500 prisoners and 10 guns. Ferdinand outfoxed the French, driving them back to the Rhine, but there he was repulsed at **Kloster-Kamp** (October 16) and withdrew to Lippstadt and Warburg for the winter.

1760, June–August. Frederick Maneuvers in the East. While Prince Henry engaged the Russians in operations sterile for both sides, and Laudon destroyed a Prussian detachment at **Landeshut** (June 23), Frederick with his main army began shuttling between Laudon—who was besieging Glatz (Klodzko)—and Daun. When Daun marched to help Laudon, Frederick turned back to besiege Dresden (July 12). Daun came hurrying to its relief and almost surrounded Frederick, who slipped away in the nick of time (July 29). That same day Glatz fell to Laudon. Frederick, summoning Prince Henry's army to join him, now plunged into Silesia with 30,000 troops in a remarkable series of forced marches.

1760, August 15. Battle of Liegnitz. With the 60,000 men of Laudon and Daun closing in on him and 30,000 Russians under Czernichev not far behind, Frederick in a brilliant night attack (August 15) cut his way to safety, leaving 10,000 Austrian casualties on the field and capturing 82 guns. Tricking Czernichev by a false message which led him to believe the Austrians had been totally defeated, Frederick resumed his maneuvering against Daun, while the Russians hurriedly retreated, no more to appear in this campaign.

1760, October 9. Capture of Berlin. Learning that Austrian and Russian raiders had again seized and partly burned his capital, Frederick turned to its relief. On his approach the allies hurriedly evacuated the city (October 12) and the main Austrian army, 64,000 strong, began concentrating near Torgau. Frederick, gathering 45,000 men, moved against the Austrian entrenched camp.

1760, November 3. Battle of Torgau. The Austrians, under Daun, lay in a formidable position on high ground west of the Elbe. Frederick, advancing from the south, planned to move half of his army entirely around the Austrian right, through dense woods, and attack their rear. Ziethen, with the other half, was to make a simultaneous frontal attack. Through a combination of errors and bad

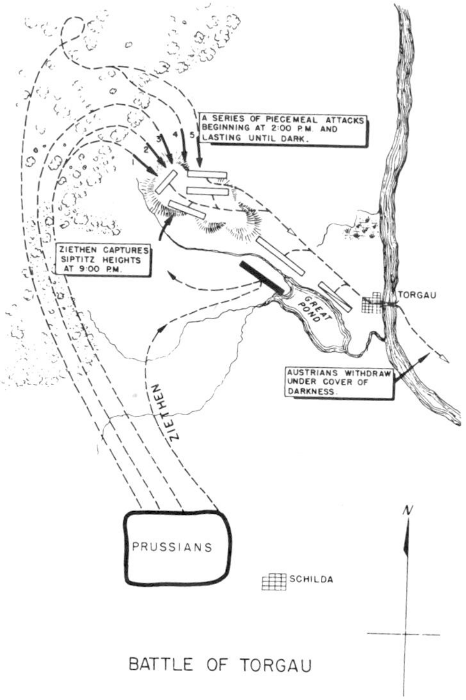

BATTLE OF TORGAU

weather, Frederick's wing became disorganized. Surprise was lost and the Austrians regrouped their forces to meet the threat. Meanwhile Ziethen allowed himself to be diverted by a small force in his front and opened a premature attack. Frederick, hearing the cannonade, assumed Ziethen was assaulting the main Austrian position and threw his own forces in piecemeal. For 2½ hours all his attacks were repulsed. By that time all Frederick's reserves had been committed. It seemed to be another Kunersdorf. But as dusk was falling Ziethen finally reached his appointed position and attacked. Frederick renewed his assaults in darkness.

Austrian resistance collapsed; Daun withdrew from the position and across the river. Frederick had squandered 13,000 men, while Austrian losses were more than 4,000 killed and wounded and 7,000 more made prisoner. Both sides having fought themselves to exhaustion, the campaign ended for the year.

1761. Operations in the West. Duke Ferdinand had some success against the French as the campaign opened, but by October they had pushed him eastward to Brunswick.

1761. Frederick at Bay in the East. He could scrape together barely 100,000 troops, and was facing thrice that number of Austrians and Russians in Silesia. Despite brilliant maneuvering, he was finally cut off from Prussia by the junction of the armies of Laudon and Russian General **Alexander Buturlin,** near Liegnitz. Frederick retired (August 20) to the entrenched camp of Bunzewitz, 20 miles east of Glatz, in the vicinity of Jauernick (Javornik). Situated in the Eulen Gebirge hills on what is now the northern frontier of Czechoslovakia, the Bunzewitz camp was a natural fortress, improved by elaborate field fortifications extemporized in 10 days and nights of frantic effort—time granted by the vacillation of the allied commanders. Laudon wanted to attack, Buturlin refused. Then (September 9) the Russians withdrew permanently, and the Austrians soon fell back into winter quarters. Frederick, the pressure relieved, did the same.

1761, December. Frederick on the Brink of Defeat. Although Prince Henry in Saxony had held his own against Daun, Ferdinand's army in the west was dwindling; **George III** of England, succeeding **George II** in 1760, had begun withdrawing part of the British contingent, and now threatened to cut off all subsidies. Frederick could only muster 60,000 troops. He was at the end of his rope.

1762, January 5. Death of Elizabeth of Russia. Her successor, **Peter III,** an admirer of Frederick, immediately began peace negotiations.

1762, May 15. The Treaty of St. Petersburg. This ended the war between Russia and Prussia, and saved Frederick from almost certain defeat. Peter loaned a Russian army corps to Frederick.

1762, May 22. Treaty of Hamburg. This brought peace between Prussia and Sweden. Frederick could now concentrate against the Austrians while Ferdinand held off the French.

1762, June 24. Battle of Wilhelmstal. Duke Ferdinand's Prusso-British army defeated the French in Westphalia, Granby's British brigades delivering the vital assault.

1762, July 9. Collapse of the Russian Alliance. Peter was deposed. His wife, **Catherine II** of Russia, broke off the alliance with Prussia, but did not renew the war.

1762, July 21. Battle of Burkersdorf. In Silesia, Frederick defeated Daun. The exhausted armies maneuvered inconclusively, but Frederick steadily strengthened his hold on the province.

1762, October 29. Battle of Freiberg. In Saxony, Prince Henry, assisted by Seydlitz, defeated Austrian Marshal **Serbelloni.**

1762, October–November. Ferdinand Drives the French across the Rhine.

1762, November. Armistice. All concerned were exhausted by the years of protracted conflict. France was already making peace with England.

1763, February 16. Treaty of Hubertusburg. Austria agreed to the return of the *status quo* in Europe. Frederick retained Silesia.

Naval Operations, 1755–1763

PRE-WAR CONFLICT, 1755–1756

1755. Franco-British Rivalry in North America. This led to the French and Indian War (see p. 705); it also brought about naval warfare nearly a year before formal declaration of hostilities. Shortly after Britain sent General **Edward Braddock** to the American colonies, the French sent a naval squadron and transports with reinforcements and supplies for Canada. A British fleet under Admiral **Edward Boscawen** was sent to intercept the French squadron before it reached the St. Lawrence River.

1755, June 8. Action of the Strait of Belle Isle. Boscawen found the French squadron, but was able to capture only 2 transports; the remainder of the French ships escaped and reached Quebec. The English now began to seize all French ships wherever found. British Admiral Sir **Ed-**

ward Hawke, cruising off the coast of France, captured a large number of ships in a convoy from the French colonies in America. In retaliation, **Louis XV**'s government seemingly prepared for an invasion of the British Isles, but still without declaring war. Britain, alarmed by this threat, paid little attention to a French joint army-navy expeditionary force preparing at Toulon.

1756, April 9. British Squadron to the Mediterranean. Belatedly concerned about the Toulon preparations, the British Admiralty sent Admiral **John Byng** (son of Viscount George Byng of Torrington; see p. 625) with 10 ships of the line to the Mediterranean. He was to protect the British possessions of Gibraltar and Minorca.

1756, April 12. French Expedition to Minorca. Admiral Count **Augustin de la Gallissonnière,** with 12 ships of the line, convoying 150 transports carrying 15,000 troops under Marshal Duke **Louis de Richelieu,** sailed from Toulon for Minorca. One week later (while Byng was still out on the Atlantic Ocean) the French landed and invested Port Mahon, the island's capital, while the fleet blockaded the port. The British garrison of 3,000 men was in peril when Byng finally appeared off the island (May 19).

1756, May 20. Battle of Minorca. Byng, who now had 13 ships, tried to bring his column (in line ahead) into action against the French, ship for ship. But he came in on an angle. One of his center vessels, disabled by French fire, held up the rest. Meanwhile the 5 leading British warships were badly hammered by the entire French squadron. Instead of letting his ships sail on individually to join the van of his squadron, Byng now attempted to carry on in his original formation, which gave the French squadron time to sail away. Byng gathered up his damaged vessels, making no attempt to land the army battalion he had on board, which he felt was insignificant in comparison to the French army. He returned to Gibraltar. A victim of restrictive Admiralty instructions, and later of Whig-Tory politics, he was tried by court-martial, convicted of failure to do his utmost, and was shot. Minorca surrendered (May 28).

WARTIME OPERATIONS, 1756–1763

1756, May 17. War Formally Declared. The British reinforced squadrons in the Mediterranean and western Atlantic. Britain had 130 ships of the line; France had 63; Spain had 46. The British were superior in equipment and personnel.

1757. Aggressive British Naval Policy. The reins of government were in the hands of the elder **William Pitt** (later Earl of Chatham), who knew sea power's value.

1757–1758. Planning in North America. Admiral Boscawen and General **Jeffrey Amherst** prepared a joint expedition against France's fortress of Louisbourg on Cape Breton Island which would end successfully (see p. 706).

1758, April 29. Battle of the Bay of Bengal. Admiral Sir **George Pocock,** with 7 ships of the line, engaged French Commodore Count **Anne Antoine d'Aché**'s 8 ships in an inconclusive action off Fort St. David. The Frenchman was carrying reinforcements to Pondichery while the British fleet was vainly attempting to relieve the besieged port.

1758, August 3. Battle of Negapatam. In a renewed battle between Pocock and d'Aché near the site of the previous battle, the French squadron was so cut up that d'Aché withdrew, to the detriment of French land forces in India (see p. 700).

1758, September. British Repulsed at St. Cas Bay. This concluded a series of fruitless minor British expeditions against the French coast.

1759. Operations in North America. British army-navy cooperation resulted in the capture of Quebec and the conquest of Canada (see p. 707).

1759–1760. Operations in the West Indies. A British joint task force, repulsed at **Martinique** (January), took **Guadeloupe** in a long campaign (February–April). Another force took **Dominica (1760).**

1759, August 18. Battle of Lagos. Meanwhile a French plan to invade England and Scotland was in the making, its initial success dependent upon the junction at Brest of 2 French squadrons. Commodore **de la Clue** left Toulon for Brest with 12 ships of the line (August 15) and reached the Straits of Gibraltar on the 17th, unaware that Boscawen, now commanding in the Mediterranean, had taken his squadron into Gibraltar to refit. A patrolling English frigate sighted the French and gave the alarm. Boscawen, with 14 ships of the line, gave chase. De la Clue headed for the open sea, but 5 of his ships broke away and fled to Cádiz. The remainder got away momentarily, thanks to the gallantry of the rear ship, whose captain fought 5 English ships for 5 hours. But de le Clue's case was hopeless, so he ran the remainder of his squadron ashore on the Portuguese coast, near Lagos. Boscawen, with the usual British disdain for neutrality, captured them.

1759, September 10. Naval Battle of Pondichery. D'Aché reappeared off the Coromandel coast with 11 ships to fight a third tactically inconclusive battle with Pocock. The French ships were so badly damaged that d'Aché departed, never to return. With him went the last hope for French forces in India (see p. 701).

1759, November. Operations off the Coast of Brittany. The French squadron in Brest, 21 ships of the line and several frigates, was under Admiral **Hubert de Conflans.** Off the port stood British Admiral Edward Hawke with 25 sail of the line, plus 4 50-gun ships and 9 frigates. A tremendous gale drove Hawke off station and into Torbay for shelter, whereupon Conflans put to sea. Off Quiberon Bay on the Breton coast, he fell in with some British ships on blockade duty, and at the same time Hawke, who had hurried out when the storm subsided, caught up with him. Conflans, outnumbered by at least 2 ships of the line and the 4 50-gun ships, fled for Quiberon Bay, hoping that his opponent would not dare to follow him through the treacherous banks and reefs of the entrance. But Hawke did just that.

1759, November 20. Battle of Quiberon Bay. Engaging his enemy in the crowded bay, on a lee shore, in heavy weather, Hawke destroyed or captured 7 French ships and the remainder were so scattered that they were unable to reassemble. Hawke lost 2 ships, wrecked on a reef; his losses in action were negligible. This battle ended France's naval power for the remainder of the war.

1760–1763. England Supreme at Sea. Although French privateers had taken heavy toll—10 per cent—of British merchant vessels, French commerce, with the French Navy swept from the sea, was completely destroyed.

1761. Spanish Intervention. Charles III of Spain chose this unpropitious time to ally himself with France, and broke off diplomatic relations with England. France gave Minorca to Spain, which soon declared war (January 4).

1762, January 4. British West Indies Offensive. Admiral **George B. Rodney** proceeded against Martinique, the last French stronghold in the West Indies. Its surrender (February 12) was followed by seizure of Grenada, St. Lucia, and St. Vincent. While Rodney was securing the West Indies, Pocock, back from the East Indies, promptly sailed from England for Havana with 19 ships of the line and transports bearing 10,000 army troops (March).

1762, June 20–August 10. Operations against Havana. Pocock and Rodney, joining forces, sailed to Havana (June). Morro Castle was taken (July 30) after a 40-day siege by troops under **George Keppel, Earl of Albemarle.** The Spaniards then surrendered the port, with 12 ships of the line and more than $15 million in money and merchandise. It was a body blow to Spain's economy and prestige, since all Spanish-American commerce funneled through Havana.

1762, October 5. Capture of Manila. Another British joint expedition, mounted in India and commanded by Admiral Sir **Samuel Cornish** and Lieutenant General Sir **William Draper,** sailed into Manila Bay and captured the city. A ransom of $4 million was levied (in lieu of the normal practice of looting). The Acapulco galleon with $3 million on board also fell into the expedition's hands. As an additional jolt, out in the Atlantic an English squadron bagged a treasure ship from Lima carrying $4 million in silver to Spain. King Charles at once joined France in negotiations for peace; his brief excursion into war had cost Spain much.

1763, February 10. Treaty of Paris. France renounced to England all claims to Canada, Nova Scotia, and the St. Lawrence River islands, the Ohio Valley, and all territory east of the Mississippi except the city of New Orleans. Spain traded Florida (all Spanish possessions east of the Mississippi) to England for the return of Havana. She also returned Minorca to England. Spain had already been compensated for her alliance in the secret **Treaty of San Ildefonso*** (November 3, 1762) by receiving from France New Orleans and all Louisiana west of the Mississippi. In the West Indies, Guadeloupe and Martinique were returned to France. Of the "neutral" islands of the Lesser Antilles all but St. Lucia went to England. In India, the British East India Company had become the supreme power in Bengal. Pondichery was returned to France, but its fortifications were razed, and limits were set on French military strength on the Coromandel coast; French stations in Bengal were to be strictly commercial.

Commentary

On land, the Seven Years' War decided nothing politically. Militarily, it proved that loose-knit, bumbling coalitions, regardless of superiority of numbers, are at a disadvantage when waging war against a determined, disciplined, single-purposed nation under capable military leadership. Frederick the Great, through indomitable courage, tactical genius, and brilliant strategic use of interior lines, preserved the integrity of Prussia against amazing odds. He placed his country in the ranks of the great powers, laying the foundation for a united Germany. His campaigns in the Seven Years' War proved him to be a master tactician, one of the great captains of history. At sea, the Royal Navy firmly established the British Empire and destroyed the colonial pretensions of France and severely shook those of Spain—now Britain's only overseas rival. Sea power had come into its own.

WARS OF THE FRENCH REVOLUTION, 1792–1800

War of the First Coalition, 1792–1798

BACKGROUND

1791, August 2. Declaration of Pillnitz, Saxony. The growing strength and violence of the French Revolutionary movement, and the parlous situation of **Louis XVI,** led King **Frederick William II** of Prussia and the Emperor **Leopold II** of Austria to declare themselves ready to join with all the other European powers to restore the monarchy to power in France. Russia and Sweden agreed to raise contingents (subsidized by Spain). England declined to join. The French Legislative Assembly, alarmed by this threat, hastily organized armies to protect the eastern frontiers.

1792, February 7. Austro-Prussian Alliance. Partly in response to pleas of French monarchical émigrés, and partly to take military and political advantage of the chaos in France, Austria and Prussia formed an alliance and began to move troops toward the frontiers. The Kingdom of Sardinia (or Piedmont) joined the alliance soon afterward.

LAND OPERATIONS, 1792–1793

1792, April 20. The French Assembly Declares War against Austria. Fighting began at once along the Flanders frontier. The French Army, though disorganized by the republican movement, still retained some of its previous discipline, as well as a few of its professional officers. Patriotic enthusiasm brought flocks of volunteers to the colors. The result was an uneasy mixture of professionals and amateurs (National Guard and volunteers), easily brushed aside by the Austrians in the opening skirmishes near Lille, which the Austrians besieged. Disgusted with the conduct of his troops, Marshal Compte **de Rochambeau** resigned command of the Army of the North, and was succeeded by the Marquis **de Lafayette,** who had been in command of the Army of the Center.

1792, July 11. Assembly of an Allied Army. Karl Wilhelm, Duke of Brunswick had 80,000 men (42,000 Prussians, 30,000 Austrians, and small contingents of Hessians and French émigrés) gathering at Coblenz.

1792, August 10. Storming of the Tuileries.

* One of three Treaties of San Ildefonso in this century; see pp. 689 and 726.

A Paris mob stormed the royal palace, massacring the Swiss Guards. Louis took refuge with the Assembly and was deprived of his few remaining powers. Lafayette, who had briefly thought of marching on Paris to restore order, was relieved of his command, and fled across the frontier to surrender to the Austrians (August 20).

1792, August 19. Allied Invasion of France. Capturing the fortresses of Longwy and Verdun, Brunswick's army moved very slowly through the Argonne Forest, heading toward Paris, weakly opposed by the small French Army of the Center, commanded by General **François C. Kellermann.**

1792, August–September. French Preparations for Defense. General **Charles C. Dumouriez** was appointed by the Assembly to replace Lafayette in command of the Army of the North. With part of this army he hastened to join Kellermann in an attempt to halt the advance of Brunswick's army.

1792, September 20. Battle of Valmy. Dumouriez and Kellermann were able to bring together 36,000 troops of questionable quality to oppose 34,000 veteran regulars of Brunswick. (The remainder of the allies were spread out along the line of communications.) Fortunately for the French, the main bodies never became engaged, the Prussian infantry being thrown back by accurate fire from 54 French guns —manned by regulars of the old army. Brunswick, who had never been enthusiastic about the invasion, was so discouraged by this cannonade that he withdrew to Germany.

1792. Other Operations. In the south, French forces invaded Piedmont, overrunning Savoy and capturing Nice. From Alsace, General **Adam Philippe Custine** led a French offensive which captured Mainz and got into Germany as far as Frankfurt. Dumouriez returned north and pushed into Flanders. Meanwhile (September 21) the newly elected National Convention installed itself as the government of France and abolished the monarchy.

1792, November 6. Battle of Jemappes. On Dumouriez's approach the Austrians raised the siege of Lille and went into winter quarters at Jemappes, just across the border in Belgium (the Austrian Netherlands). The French army of 40,000 men and 100 guns followed and defeated the Austrians, who numbered only 13,000. This victory stimulated the French republicans; Brussels was captured (November 16) and a French squadron pushed up the Scheldt to besiege Antwerp, arousing fear in England.

1792, December. Allied Successes. Brunswick, with 43,000 men, drove Custine back to the Rhine. Frankfurt was retaken (December 2). Custine retired to Mainz and winter quarters.

1793, January 21. Execution of Louis XVI. The beheading of the French king sparked England to oust the French ambassador, whereupon France, already at war with Austria, Prussia, and Piedmont, declared war on England, Holland, and Spain. National conscription was decreed, Belgium annexed to France, and Dumouriez ordered to invade Holland. But the allies were already on the offensive. **Friedrich Josias, Prince of Saxe-Coburg** with 40,000 Austrians crossed the Meuse to recover Belgium; Brunswick's 60,000 Prussians besieged Custine in Mainz. Other allied troops took positions along the Rhine and in Luxembourg.

1793, March 18. Battle of Neerwinden. Dumouriez with 45,000 men attacked Saxe-Coburg, attempting to turn his left. The French, advancing in 8 columns, were repulsed in disorder.

1793, April–July. French Defeats and Demoralization. The Austrians recaptured Brussels. Dumouriez, falsely accused of treason, turned against France and fled to the allies; with him went the **Duke of Chartres** (Prince **Louis Philippe**). General **Picot Dampierre** assumed command and tried to stem the advance of Coburg's allied army, but was killed in action near besieged **Condé** (May 8). Custine was now placed in command of the demoralized French Army of the North. A defeat near besieged **Valenciennes** (May 21–23) resulted in the beheading of Custine by order of the Committee of Public Safety, establishing a pattern which would thereafter menace all French republican commanders. Condé was captured by Coburg (July 10) and Valenciennes fell soon afterward (July 29). The Army of the North retreated to Arras under its new commander, **Jean Nicolas Houchard.**

1793, July–August. The Reign of Terror. France was now assailed from within and without, while the Reign of Terror was beginning in Paris under **Maximilien F. de Robespierre** and the Committee of Public Safety.

1793, August. France Approaches Collapse. The Allies recaptured Mainz. In the Vendée a monarchist counterrevolution was in full swing. Lyon and Marseilles declared for the monarchy. Prince **Frederick Augustus, Duke of York,** with a British-Hanoverian army, was investing Dunkirk, while the **Prince of Orange**'s Netherlands forces linked York to the Austrians farther east. A British-Spanish fleet closed in on Toulon, which declared for the monarchy (August 21).

1793, August 23. The Levée en Masse. The Committee of Public Safety decreed conscription of the entire male population of France. Fourteen armies were hastily put into the field in the next few weeks. Symbolic of the revitalization of France was the recovery of Marseille by the Republicans on the day of the decree (August 23).

1793, September 8. Battle of Hondschoote. With 42,000 men Houchard assailed the Duke of York's 13,000 disciplined English and Hanoverian troops just east of Dunkirk. The uncoordinated but desperate charges of the French recruits forced York back by sheer weight of numbers; he extricated himself, although losing his siege artillery.

1793, September 13. Battle of Menin. Houchard routed the Prince of Orange, but he failed in efforts to maneuver the Austrians out of eastern France. He was removed and guillotined, General **Jean Baptiste Jourdan** taking his place.

1793, September. Lazare Nicolas Carnot. The war minister of the Committee of Public Safety joined the army, and ordered Jourdan to relieve Maubeuge, besieged by 30,000 Austrians under Saxe-Coburg.

1793, October 15–16. Battle of Wattignies. The French, 50,000 strong, were at first repulsed by the better-disciplined allies. Next day, however, Jourdan enveloped and drove back Saxe-Coburg's left. The Austrians abandoned the siege of Maubeuge and retired eastward.

COMMENT. *These 3 battles (Hondschoote, Menin, Wattignies) are remarkable because, beginning with Hondschoote, not only did they demonstrate an amazing will to win on the part of the new French levies, but in addition, at Wattignies, the new army for the first time used maneuver on the battlefield. A peculiar mixture of patriotism and terror was transforming armed mobs into soldiers. What had happened was mainly due to the incessant efforts of one man: Lazare Carnot, a stern, uncompromising soldier of the old regime, who amalgamated the raw conscripts with the remnants of the old professional army, and brought discipline to enthusiastic hordes of Frenchmen filled with the valor of ignorance. Carnot built the prototype of the instrument that Bonaparte would use later on. In his 2-year tenure of office, Carnot's efforts in organizing the national defense caused him to become known as the "Organizer of Victory."*

1793, October–December. French Revival. Elsewhere the Vendée uprising was finally suppressed, and Lyon was retaken (October 20) by Kellermann. Toulon, besieged by the Republicans, fell (December 19; see p. 681). Along the Rhine and in Alsace an indeterminate campaign ended when General **Louis Lazare Hoche,** after being checked by Brunswick at **Kaiserslautern** (November 28–30), defeated the Prussians at **Fröschwiller** (December 22), then turned on Austrian General **Dagobert Wurmser** in Alsace and defeated him at **Geisberg** (December 26). By the year's end the invaders were back across the Rhine; Alsace and the Palatinate had been cleared and Mainz recaptured. Fighting along the Spanish and Italian frontiers was sporadic and inconclusive.

WAR AT SEA, 1792–1793

1792. Sad State of the French Navy. Its professional officer corps had been purged; its enlisted force, disrupted by a succession of mutinies, was a mob. Merchant marine officers, recruited for the emergency, had no knowledge of naval tactics. Administratively, ships, navy yards, and stores had been completely neglected. Less than half of the 76 ships of the line could be manned.

1792. State of the Allied Navies. Spain had only 56 serviceable capital ships; its personnel were of less than mediocre ability. Holland's 49 ships were good, but light. Portugal had 6 capital ships, Naples 4. The English Navy consisted of 115 ships of the line, in good shape, commanded by professionals, but many were undermanned. The 2 principal British operational forces were the Channel Fleet under Admiral Lord **Richard Howe** and the Mediterranean Fleet under Admiral Sir **Samuel Hood.**

1792. No Naval Operations of Significance.

1793, August–September. Inconclusive Maneuvering. The French fleet, under Admiral **Morad de Galles,** tentatively put to sea off the Atlantic coast of France. He avoided battle with Howe. De Galles was a capable sailor, but was unable to control his unruly crews. By the end of the summer he had given up his command; the fleet remained in port.

1793, August 27–December 19. Siege of Toulon. Hood, with 21 ships of the line, entered the port, which at once declared for the monarchy. The British seized the great naval arsenal together with about 70 vessels, 30 of them ships of the line, nearly half of the French Navy. A Spanish squadron under Admiral **Juan de Langara** accompanied the British. Republican land forces invested the fortress (September 7), but little was done until 2 inept commanders were replaced by General **Jacques E. Dugommier,** who adopted a plan prepared by young Colonel **Napoleon Bonaparte,** commanding an artillery brigade. The forts commanding the anchorage were soon carried by the French troops (December 16). The allied naval forces hastily left (December 19). The British destroyed or carried away part of the French fleet, but 15 ships of the line were left untouched, through Spanish neglect. The Spanish Navy took no further part in the war as an ally of Britain. Colonel Bonaparte was promoted to brigadier general.

OPERATIONS ON LAND, 1794–1795

1794. Opposing Plans in the North. The allied "plan of annihilation" was proposed by Baron **Karl Mack von Leiberich,** Austrian chief of staff. It was matched by Carnot's plan to clear the invaders from French territory.

1794, May 11. Courtrai. The French forces of General **Charles Pichegru**'s Army of the North defeated the Allied English and Austrian army of Field Marshal Clerfayt.

1794, May 18. Battle of Tourcoing. Pichegru's army (temporarily commanded by General **Joseph Souham**) defeated Saxe-Coburg's badly managed Austro-British-Hanoverian concentration.

1794, May 23. Battle of Tournai. A fiercely fought drawn battle, between forces almost equal in strength (about 50,000 each). Both sides retreated, with losses of about 3,000 each.

1794, June 17. Battle of Hooglede. A fierce French counterattack retrieved victory from defeat. The allies began to withdraw northward.

1794, June. Formation of the Army of the Sambre and Meuse. Jourdan's Army of the Moselle had moved north and invested Charleroi (June 12). He was now placed in command of the combined armies, totaling 75,000–80,000 men.

1794, June 26. Battle of Fleurus. Coburg, with 52,000 men, moved to relieve Charleroi. Unaware the town had fallen (June 25), 5 allied columns struck the 73,000 French grouped in a 20-mile circumference around the town. At first successful all along the line, the allied right was halted by French counterattacks, General **Jean B. Kléber** driving the Prince of Orange from the field. Jourdan led a counterblow in the center. Despite the success of his left against the overextended French right, Saxe-Coburg called off the attack. Next day he retreated. Jourdan pursued at once.

1794, July–August. French Victories in Belgium and on the Rhine. They entered Brussels (July 10), Antwerp was occupied (July 27), and the British contingent sailed home. Belgium was abandoned forever by the Austrians. Jourdan followed Coburg across the Roer and cleared the left bank of the Rhine in desultory operations against the Prussians.

1794, September–December. French Victories Elsewhere. General **Jean Victor Moreau,** who had distinguished himself under Jourdan's command in Belgium, was given command of a newly formed Army of the Rhine and Moselle; in late summer he advanced into the Rhineland and pressed forward despite a setback near **Kaiserslautern;** by October he had forced the allies to cross the upper Rhine and had laid siege to Mainz. An army under Pichegru invaded Holland. In the Alps and along the Mediterranean coast the French had also had minor successes, driving the allies completely out of Savoy, and pressing eastward as far as Savona on the Mediterranean coast. In the southwest French armies had penetrated both flanks of the Pyrenees.

1795, January–March. French Occupation of the Netherlands. Pichegru's cavalry in midwinter rode over the frozen Texel to capture the Dutch fleet. Holland now became the Batavian Republic, a satellite and active military ally of republican France.

1795, April 5–June 22. Treaties of Basel. Prussia, financially exhausted, made peace with France. Saxony, Hanover, and Hesse-Cassel followed suit. So did Spain, ceding Santo Domingo to France.

1795, June 27. Landing on Quiberon. French émigrés, landed from British warships, attempted to invade Brittany. They were disastrously defeated by the waiting French Army of the West under Hoche (July 16–20). A small force of accompanying British troops was safely re-embarked (July 20–21).

1795, August 22. The Directory. Republican France rocked internally when a new government—a 5-man group—was established by the Constitution of 1795. After a monarchist outbreak in Paris was put down by General Bonaparte (October 5), the Convention was dissolved. Military operations in the field continued, Carnot remaining in control.

1795. Operations along the Rhine. Jourdan's Army of the Sambre and Meuse, about 100,000 strong, was west of Coblenz. Pichegru's Army of the Rhine and Moselle, about 90,000 men, was in Alsace and blockading Mainz in the Palatinate. Another force captured Luxembourg after a siege of 8 months (June 26). Opposite Jourdan were about 100,000 allies under Austrian Marshal Count **Charles von Clerfayt;** Wurmser had 85,000 east of the upper Rhine. Jourdan attempted an invasion of Germany (September 3–6) which Wurmser ignored. Jourdan, advancing toward Frankfurt, was outmaneuvered near **Höchst** by Clerfayt (early October). Clerfayt then defeated Pichegru's forces blockading **Mainz** (October 29) and invaded the Palatinate. Then, unaccountably, he consented to a general armistice (December 21). Jourdan's defeat was attributable to the treachery of Pichegru, who, involved in the royalist plot, had defected to the Austrians, after betraying the invasion plans.

1795. Operations in Italy. The French Army of Italy, under the over-all command of General **Barthélemy Schérer,** had progressed slightly eastward and northeastward along the Mediterranean coast. The principal action in this area was at **Loano** (November 23–25), where General **André Masséna** dislodged allied forces from their positions in the mountains.

1795–1796. Operations in the Vendée. Revolt blazed briefly again. A British expedition with 2,500 troops approached the Ile d'Yeu off the Poitou coast. Before it could disembark, French troops crushed the uprising and the British withdrew (November 15). By next spring pacification of the Vendée had been brutally completed by Hoche.

WAR AT SEA, 1794–1795

1794, May 29–June 1. Battle of the First of June. In an extraordinary effort to avert famine in France, 130 merchant ships laden with purchased foodstuffs sailed from the United States (April). To protect its safe arrival at Brest, Admiral **Louis T. Villaret de Joyeuse** put to sea with his fleet. Howe intercepted the French fleet in the Atlantic, 400-odd miles off Ushant. When the fight started the opponents had each 26 ships of the line, but before it ended 4 additional French vessels joined Villaret. The 4-day running fight ended when Howe flung his entire fleet into the midst of the French. In an epic melee, 6 French ships were taken and a seventh vessel sunk. The French fleet broke off combat, returning to Brest, to find the food convoy had arrived safely. Tactically a British victory, the French admiral had nevertheless accomplished his mission by drawing the British from the convoy's path. No other actions of major importance occurred in the Atlantic for the rest of the year.

1794. Operations in the West Indies. Admiral Sir **John Jervis** completed the occupation of Martinique, St. Lucia, and Guadeloupe (April). These islands were later recovered by the French governor, **Victor Hugues.** In the flux of naval maneuvering, however, the British Navy retained the upper hand, destroying a great part of the French merchant marine.

1794, August 10. Capture of Corsica. Accomplished by a British joint operation.

1795. Operations in the Atlantic. Only 2 minor actions took place, both in connection with the ill-fated landings in Quiberon Bay (see p. 682). Admiral **William Cornwallis** with 5 blockading ships escaped Villaret's 12 in the Bay of Biscay (June 8–12). Villaret was prevented from attacking the convoy of troop transports only by luck and the boldness of Admiral **John Warren,** the convoy commander. Shortly after this (June 23), Admiral Lord **Alexander Hood of Bridport** (younger brother of Samuel Hood) with 12 ships engaged Villaret off Ile de Groix, capturing 3 French vessels. For most of the year, both sides engaged in commerce destruction, the British Channel Fleet being held in port, while the French fleet at Brest was in too poor condition to put to sea.

1795. Operations in the Mediterranean. Admiral Lord **William Hotham** twice clashed inconclusively with Admiral **Pierre Martin**'s refurbished Toulon fleet. Tactically, the British were favored; strategically, the honors went to France. In November, efficient Sir John Jervis succeeded indolent Hotham.

OPERATIONS ON LAND, 1796–1798

War was waged in two major theaters—Germany and Italy—under the overall direction of the efficient Carnot, who was now in effect both minister of war and chief of staff. The character of the conflict changed from a defense of national territory to a war of conquest by France. The motivation was partly missionary zeal in spreading the gospel of "Liberty, Equality, Fraternity" throughout Europe, but there was also a definite economic-logistic impulse: France could no longer feed the vast citizen armies she had raised for defense. Carnot's plan was a pincers movement against Austria: the Armies of the Sambre and Meuse and of the Rhine and Moselle, driving through Germany, would unite at Vienna with the Army of Italy.

Germany; the Northern Front

East of the Rhine a vast war of maneuver took place in the triangle Dusseldorf-Basel-Ratisbon, with the youthful **Archduke Charles** of Austria, utilizing interior lines, pitted against Jourdan and Jean Victor Moreau. Charles had complete liberty of action; the French generals, independent one of the other, were hampered by the orders of the Directory. Jourdan's mission was to attract Charles to the north so as to permit Moreau to invade Bavaria. Jourdan would then join Moreau in an advance into Austria.

1796, June–July. Jourdan's Invasion. With 72,000 men, he crossed the Rhine at Düsseldorf (June 10), penetrated to Wetzlar. Charles repulsed the French advance at **Wetzlar** (June 16). His mission accomplished, Jourdan fell back across the Rhine (July).

1796, June–August. Moreau's Invasion. With 78,000 troops, he crossed at Strasbourg (June 23–27). Charles, leaving General **Alexander H. Wartensleben** with 36,000 men to observe Jourdan, marched with 20,000 against Moreau. According to plan, Jourdan recrossed the Rhine and drove Wartensleben back. After the indecisive **Battle of Malsch** (July 9), Charles fought an inconclusive battle at **Neresheim** (August 11), and was pushed across the Danube by Moreau, between Ulm and Donauwörth (August 12).

1796, August 24. Battles of Amberg and Friedberg. Charles, reinforced, recrossed the Danube, left 30,000 men under General **Latour** to watch Moreau, and hurried north with 27,000 to find Jourdan still pressing Wartensleben near Amberg. Charles struck the French right flank while Wartensleben attacked frontally. Jourdan, decisively defeated, retired. That same day, Moreau attacked and defeated Latour at **Friedberg.** Jourdan, learning this, regrouped near Würzburg on the Main. Charles pressed after him.

1796, September 3. Battle of Würzburg. Charles enveloped both French flanks in a brilliant maneuver, the Austrian cavalry distinguishing themselves. Jourdan managed to disengage and fell back to the Rhine in a series of running fights. An armistice was concluded here, and Charles turned his attention to Moreau in Bavaria, who, learning of Jourdan's defeat, broke off his pursuit of Latour and retired. Reaching the Rhine at Hunningen, he crossed to safety (October 26).

1797, April 18. New French Offensive. Hoche, who had superseded Jourdan, as commander of the Army of the Sambre and Meuse, moved up the right bank of the Rhine to assist Moreau's Army of the Rhine and Moselle in a planned crossing at Kehl. Charles had been sent to meet Bonaparte's threat in Italy (see below). Latour commanded the Austrians opposite Moreau; under him General **Werneck** held the lower Rhine. Crossing the Rhine between Düsseldorf and Coblenz, Hoche struck Werneck near Neuwied, and defeated him in the **Battle of the Lahn** (April 18). Moreau crossed the river two days later. The Austrians were driven back to Rastatt. Operations ended with the **Peace of Leoben** (see p. 688).

Italy; the Southern Front

1796, March 27. Bonaparte Commands the Army of Italy. This army, some 45,000 ill-fed, poorly clothed men, lay along the Riviera from Nice almost to Genoa. British sea power blockaded the coast ports, while beyond the hills to the north on the edge of the Lombardy Plain lay 2 allied armies: Baron **Colli** (Piedmontese) with 25,000 men and **Jean Pierre Beaulieu** (Austrian) with 35,000. Their widely separated dispositions invited attack. Bonaparte concentrated for an offensive just as Beaulieu extended his own left to the sea at Voltri.

1796, April 12. Battle of Montenotte. Striking north between his opponents, Bonaparte drove in Beaulieu's right flank, widening the gap between the allied armies.

1796, April 14–15. Battle of Dego. Pressing his advantage, Bonaparte drove the Austrians out of the town, but a counterattack regained it. Bonaparte in person gathered reserves who threw the Austrians out again. Beaulieu retreated northeast to Acqui. Instead of pursuing, Bonaparte turned west, on Colli's army, which had begun retirement.

1796, April 21. Battle of Mondovi. Colli, attempting a stand, held back one French assault, but was finally driven out. Bonaparte's rapid pursuit ended when Colli sued for an armistice (April 23), which put Piedmont out of the war (April 28).

1796, April 23–May 6. Advance to the Po. Bonaparte shifted to the northeast. On the north bank of the river, Beaulieu had spread his army out in cordon defense, covering all possible crossing places along a 60-mile front.

1796, May 7–8. Crossing at Piacenza. Bonaparte, having demonstrated on a wide front along the river line, suddenly surprised Beaulieu by a swift crossing, jeopardizing the Austrian left and its line of communications with Mantua. Beaulieu retreated east in haste, abandoning Pavia and Milan.

1796, May 10. Battle of Lodi. The Austrian rear guard bitterly contested a bridge over the Adda. Putting himself at the head of a massed column of infantry, Bonaparte led a bayonet charge across the bridge which decided the day, and won from his soldiers his soubriquet of "Little Corporal." While Beaulieu continued his retreat toward the Tyrol, Bonaparte entered Milan in triumph (May 15). The Austrian garrison of Milan surrendered the citadel six weeks later (June 29). Piedmont made peace with France (May 21); King Victor Amadeus II surrendered Savoy and Nice to France, and granted the French army the right to garrison fortresses in Piedmont.

COMMENT. *In 17 days Bonaparte had defeated 2 enemies in detail and had conquered Lombardy. After a few days of rest*

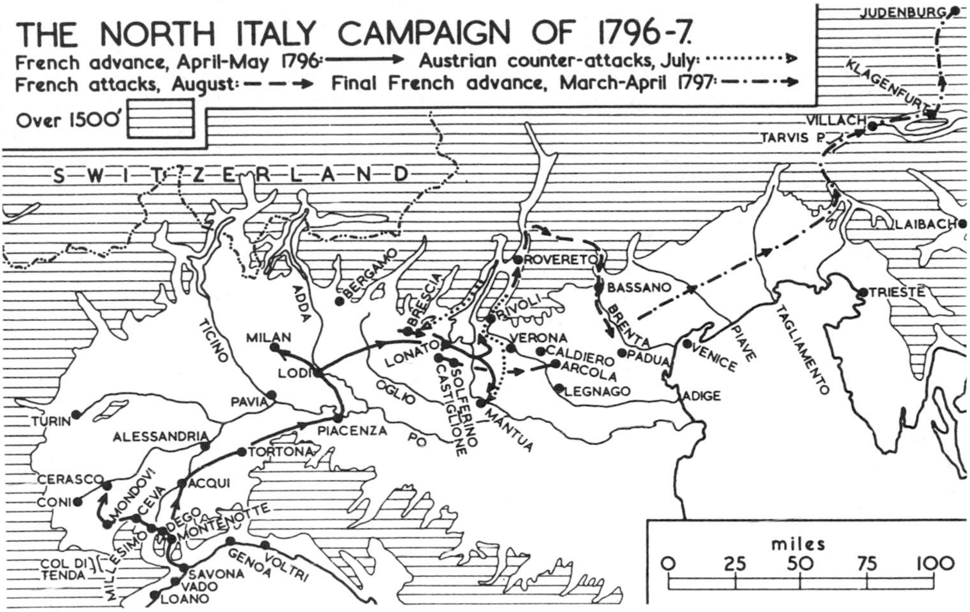

and reorganization, he proceeded after the Austrians.

1796, May 30. Passage of the Mincio. Beaulieu had reorganized his own forces, holding with 19,000 men the line of the Mincio River from Lake Garda south to Mantua, where he had an additional 11,000. Bonaparte, who had arrived at the Mincio (May 29) with 28,000, concentrated his forces and thrust through this cordon defense at Borghetto. Beaulieu, barely saving himself from destruction, hurriedly retreated across the Adige and into the Tyrol. Except for Mantua, with a garrison of 13,000 men, all north Italy was in Bonaparte's hands. He invested Mantua (June 4); most of the French army was deployed along the Adige to cover the siege operations.

1796, July–August. Arrival of Wurmser. He hurried south from the Tyrol with a new Austrian army. Sending General **Quasdanovich** with 18,000 men down the west side of Lake Garda, toward Brescia, to cut the French communications, the elderly Wurmser himself with 24,000 came down the east side, through the Adige Valley, to relieve Mantua; another detachment of 5,000 came down the Brenta Valley. Abandoning the siege of Mantua and recalling his troops from the Adige, Bonaparte, who had 47,000 men in all, concentrated southwest of Lake Garda against Quasdanovich, leaving Wurmser to move south unopposed to join the 13,000-man garrison of Mantua. Quasdanovich had split his force in 3 columns; he cut the Milan-Mantua road (July 31). Advancing southeast, he expected to unite with Wurmser, who by this time had come around the south end of the lake, hoping to complete a double envelopment of the French.

1796, August 3. Battle of Lonato. While General **Pierre F. C. Augereau**'s division delayed Wurmser, Bonaparte threw the remainder of his army against Quasdanovich north of Lonato, defeating the 3 columns in detail. One of Quasdanovich's columns surrendered; the shattered remainder retreated north to the head of the lake.

1796, August 5. Battle of Castiglione. Bonaparte's entire army now turned upon Wurmser. Attacked on both flanks and struck in the rear by a turning movement around his left, the Austrian retreated with difficulty across the Mincio and began a general retirement to the Tyrol, having lost 16,000 casualties.

COMMENT. *Again Bonaparte, throwing himself between 2 enemy forces, had con-*

centrated on each in turn and defeated them in detail.

1796, August 24. Resumption of the Siege of Mantua. The Austrian garrison, reinforced by fugitives from Wurmser's army, was now 17,000 men.

1796, September. French Advance on Trent. Bonaparte moved north with 34,000 men, leaving 8,000 to invest Mantua. At the same time, Wurmser, who had regrouped, also decided to resume the offensive, but again he divided his forces. General **Paul Davidovich** with 20,000 would defend the Tyrol, while Wurmser himself with 26,000 would march down the Brenta Valley on Mantua. Bonaparte, unaware of the Austrian plan, defeated Davidovich at **Caliano** on the upper Adige and drove him back through Trent (September 2–5). Learning of Wurmser's movement down the Brenta, Bonaparte followed, overhauling the Austrians at Bassano after a series of forced marches.

1796, September 8. Battle of Bassano. Augereau and Masséna each attacked an Austrian flank; 1 entire Austrian division was cut off and surrendered, only a few units escaping to the east. Wurmser, however, reached Mantua with the remainder of his army and fought his way into the city, swelling its garrison to 28,000 (September 13). He attempted to expand the defended area by a sortie, but was driven back into the city by blockading French troops under Masséna and General **Charles Kilmaine** (September 15).

1796, November 1. Third Austrian Attempt to Relieve Mantua. Baron **Josef Alvintzy** sent Davidovich with 16,000 men down the Adige, while he moved on Vicenza with 27,000, east of the Brenta. Alvintzy expected to join Davidovich at Verona, then move south of Mantua. Bonaparte, with 30,000 men (not counting the 9,000 containing Wurmser's 28,000 in Mantua), interposed. Leaving General **Pierre A. Dubois** with 8,000 to delay Davidovich, he hurried east with 18,000 to meet Alvintzy; 4,000 were in reserve at Verona.

1796, November 12. Battle of Caldiero. Attacking Alvintzy's advance guard, the French were checked by a rapid Austrian build-up and finally withdrew to Verona, having lost 2,000 men. Alvintzy, however, hesitated to advance.

1796, November 15–17. Battle of Arcola. Bonaparte, swinging south around Alvintzy, crossed the Adige, then turned north, moving through a marshy area, to cut the Austrian communications. Despite Napoleon's personal attempt—flag in hand—to storm a bridge over the Alpone at Arcola, continuous French attacks across the causeway were repulsed. But on the third day, Augereau crossed by a trestle bridge below the village, Masséna made another assault on the main bridge, and at the same time a detachment of French cavalry rode to the rear of the Austrian position, blowing bugles. Fearing that they were encircled, Alvintzy's troops broke and retreated. That same day Davidovich drove Dubois back toward Verona, but Bonaparte, shifting from pursuit of Alvintzy, turned on Davidovich and chased him back into Trent (November 19).

1797, January. Fourth Attempt to Relieve Mantua. Once more Alvintzy divided his forces. With 30,000 men, he marched south down the Adige Valley, sending 15,000 more toward Verona and Mantua from the east. Bonaparte ordered the concentration of the bulk of his forces on the plateau of Rivoli, between the Adige and Lake Garda. He was there with 10,000 men under General **Barthélemy C. Joubert,** while Masséna with 6,000 more was hurrying up from Verona, and Generals **Antoine Rey** and **Claude P. Victor,** with 6,000 additional, were also approaching. Augereau with 9,000 at Verona was holding the line of the Adige against the threat from the east. General **Jean M. P. Serurier** with 8,000 continued the investment of Wurmser's 28,000 in Mantua.

1797, January 14. Battle of Rivoli. Alvintzy began a complicated attack in 6 columns; 3 of these were to attack Bonaparte's position on the Rivoli plateau frontally, while 1 each would envelop the French flanks; the sixth column would advance down the east bank of the river to cross over at Rivoli behind Bonaparte's main body. Joubert's division, despite a stout defense and the inspiration of Bonaparte's personal presence, was pressed back by the main Austrian assault, and the eastern Austrian flanking column had reached the plateau to threaten the French right flank when Masséna arrived. The penetration on the French right flank was smothered; the right of the Austrian cen-

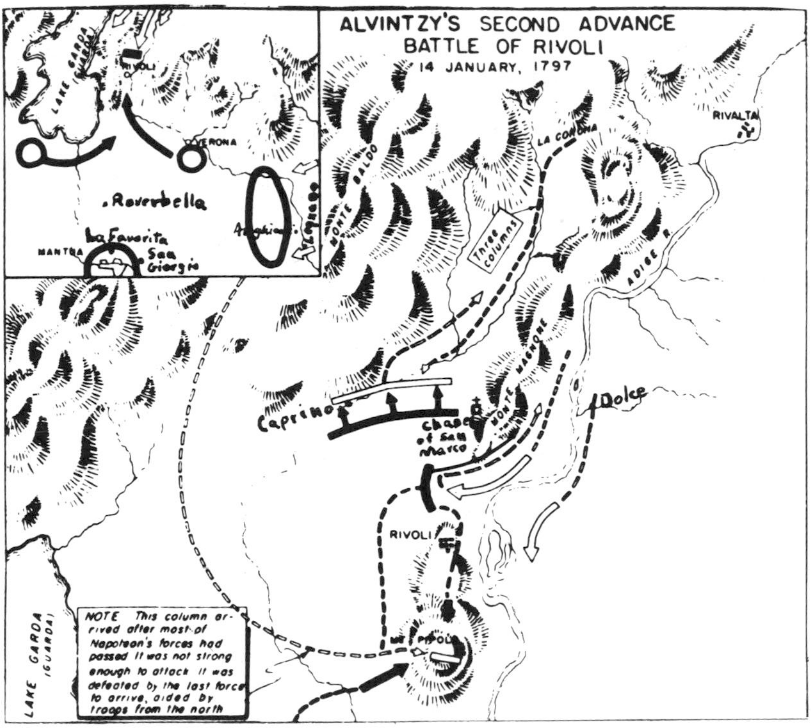

ter was assailed, and the western Austrian flanking column surrounded. By late afternoon, Alvintzy had been driven from the field. Bonaparte pursued immediately, sending Rey's division through the mountains to strike the flank and rear of the retreating Austrians. Spearhead of this pursuit was a regiment of infantry under Colonel **Joachim Murat** which had been ferried across Lake Garda, marching across Monte Baldo just in time to smash Alvintzy's efforts to reorganize.

1797, January 14–February 2. Operations around Mantua. Meanwhile 2 Austrian columns advanced toward Verona and Mantua from the east. One of these, 9,000 strong, under General **Provera,** slipped around Augereau and moved west across the Adige. Reaching the outskirts of Mantua (January 16), Provera attacked the French besiegers, while Wurmser simultaneously attempted a sortie. While Serurier drove Wurmser back into Mantua, Bonaparte hurried up from Rivoli with Masséna and, joining Augereau, surrounded Provera's column and forced him to surrender. Wurmser's garrison of 16,000 in Mantua capitulated (February 2). In this campaign the French captured 39,000 prisoners, nearly 1,600 guns, and 24 colors. During the siege 18,000 Austrians had died, mostly from disease.

1797, March. Arrival of Archduke Charles. He replaced Alvintzy. In the Tyrol he had 14,000 regulars and 10,000 Tyrolese volunteer riflemen, with 27,000 more under his immediate command along the Tagliamento.

1797, March 10. Invasion of Austria. Having been reinforced from France, again Bonaparte interposed himself between two enemy forces. With 41,000 men he moved against Charles on the Tagliamento, leaving Joubert with 12,000 to operate in the Tyrol. Charles retired behind the Isonzo (March 18), but had to fall back again to avoid envelopment after Masséna smashed a detachment at **Malborghetto** (March 23). Bonaparte, in pursuit, crossed the snowy passes of the Julian and Carnic Alps in 3 columns. These united at Klagenfurt and advanced to Leoben, 95 miles from Vienna (April 6). At the same time Joubert, having driven in the Austrian forces opposing him in the Tyrol, had reached Lienz on the way to join Bonaparte in front of Vienna. The emperor sent emissaries to discuss peace with the Republican general.

1797, April 18. Preliminary Peace of Leoben. Bonaparte, knowing well that behind him lay a conquered country whose seething inhabitants were threatening his communications, boldly dictated truce terms without any reference to the Directory. They were accepted; Bonaparte then returned to Paris.

1797, October 17. Treaty of Campo Formio. The terms laid down by Bonaparte at Leoben were formally accepted and the face of Europe changed. Belgium became a part of France, and a northern Italian (Cisalpine) Republic was recognized by Austria, which in return for its losses was given the Republic of Venice. From Basel to Aldernach the left bank of the Rhine was French.

COMMENTARY. *The French victory in this War of the First Coalition was due to a number of complex factors. The most important of these were (1) the sweeping social and political changes brought about by the French Revolution, which were epitomized by the* levée en masse *of free citizens whose patriotic obligation brought them together in a people's army to defend the state; (2) revolutionary fervor which inspired the rank and file of the French army to prodigies of valor and energy which could not be matched by the better-trained, better-disciplined, stolid professionals of 18th-century Europe; (3) the first flowering of the Industrial Revolution, permitting the mobilized state to raise and support a larger proportion of its population than heretofore had been possible in purely agrarian economies; (4) the organizing genius of Carnot in taking advantage of these revolutionary changes; (5) the strategic and tactical genius of young Bonaparte, who applied classical principles of war with skill, ingenuity, and audacity that entirely baffled the 18th-century pedestrian soldiers, and whose brilliant campaign culminated in the dictation of peace terms in the heart of Austria.*

1798, January. Continuing War with Britain. Bonaparte was placed in command of an Army of England assembling at Dunkirk for proposed invasion. Convinced that this was a very doubtful project in the light of British command of the sea, Bonaparte suggested to the Directory (February) an expedition to Egypt, which he recognized as being a crossroads of the world. With Egypt under French control, he visualized an outlet to the Orient and a base from which the British could be driven from India.

1798, February. French Occupation of Rome. The pope was captured; a Roman Republic was proclaimed. (For subsequent operations in Italy in 1798, see p. 690.)

1798, April. Occupation of Switzerland. A new Helvetian Republic was established.

EGYPTIAN CAMPAIGN, 1798–1800

1798, April 12. Establishment of the Army of the Orient. The French Directory appointed Bonaparte to command. The politicians were glad to have this dynamic, popular leader out of the country. Immediately he began to assemble his new army at Toulon; meanwhile, the concentration at Dunkirk continued as a feint to keep the British fleet out of the Mediterranean.

1798, May 19–July 1. Voyage to Egypt. Bonaparte sailed from Toulon with 40,000 men, escorted by Admiral **François P. Brueys** with 13 ships of the line. Capturing Malta en route (June 12), the expedition landed near Alexandria.

1798, July 2. Storming of Alexandria. The French advanced on Cairo.

1798, July 21. Battle of the Pyramids. Marching up the left bank of the Nile, Bonaparte was harassed by the Egyptian forces, whose main component consisted of the Mamelukes—courageous horsemen unaccustomed to organized modern warfare. The Egyptians, 60,000 strong, concentrated under **Murad** and **Ibrahim** near Embabeh, with their left flank resting on the Pyramids at Gizeh. The French army attacked to turn the Egyptian left, its divisions formed in squares in checkerboard fashion. A wild charge of the Mameluke horsemen was repulsed, their entrenched camp stormed, and the Egyptians dispersed with great loss.

1798, July–August. Occupation of Egypt. Cairo was seized (July 22). French forces moved in pursuit of Ibrahim, who had retreated toward Syria.

1798, August–December. Allied Reaction. Nelson's annihilation of the French fleet (see p. 690) disrupted Bonaparte's entire plan. The French army in Egypt was completely isolated from the homeland and surrounded by an actively hostile population. A Turkish army under **Achmed Pasha** (the "Butcher") gathered in Syria; another assembled at Rhodes to invade Egypt under escort of an English squadron.

1799, January 31. Bonaparte Takes the Offensive. He marched into Syria with 8,000 men. El Arish (February 14–15) and Jaffa (March 3–7) were taken in turn, and Acre invested (March 17). British Navy Captain Sir **Sidney Smith** took command of the garrison.

1799, April 17. Battle of Mount Tabor. Achmed's army attempted to relieve Acre. Kléber's division, in hollow squares, was surrounded, but Bonaparte enveloped the Turkish force with the remainder of his troops. Under a combined attack the Turks were defeated and driven across the Jordan.

1799, May 20–June 14. Retreat from Acre. After Acre resisted several assaults, and plague broke out in his army, Napoleon retired. After a grueling retreat, continually harassed, the French reached Cairo (June 14). He had lost 2,200 dead, nearly half from disease.

1799, July 25. Battle of Aboukir. Under English escort, the Turkish force from Rhodes, 18,000 strong, landed at Aboukir and entrenched (July 15). Bonaparte at once concentrated all available forces—6,000 men—and moved to the Delta. The Turks lay in 2 concentric positions. The outer position was rapidly brushed away by French attack. An assault on the inner ring was repulsed, but a second assault, led by General **Jean Lannes,** was successful. Murat's cavalry at the same time broke through, and the Turks were annihilated. The citadel of Aboukir surrendered (August 2). Napoleon's losses were 900 killed and wounded.

1799, August 23–October 9. Return to France. Bonaparte, satisfied that he had stabilized the Egyptian situation, realizing that further conquest and glory were unlikely without possibility of reinforcements from France, and alarmed by developments in Europe, turned over the command to Kléber. He returned to France in a fast frigate, eluding British naval forces on the way.

WAR AT SEA, 1796–1800

1796–1798. The War of Commerce Destruction. This was continuous. Frigates of both sides preyed on the commerce of the other, with honors rather evenly divided.

1796. Inconclusive Operations. The British rather ineffectively blockaded the main French naval bases of Brest and Toulon, and at the same time observed both Dutch and Spanish activities. French Admiral **Richery** broke out of Toulon (September 14) with a small squadron, cruised to Newfoundland where he harassed the Canadian fishing industry, captured a number of merchantmen, and returned safely. A more imposing joint force left to invade Ireland from Brest (December 15); 43 warships and transports, under Admiral de Galles, carried some 13,000 troops under Hoche's command. Ill-fitted and badly managed, the flotilla was scattered by bad weather. A portion arrived at Bantry Bay (December 21), but foul weather prevented landing and the project was abandoned. Five ships were lost in storms, 6 more captured by the British; the remainder finally got back. The only significant British naval activity in the Mediterranean was Captain **Horatio Nelson**'s singlehanded harassment and commerce destruction along the Franco-Italian coast, which hampered the sea communications of the French Army of Italy.

1796, August 19. Treaty of San Ildefonso. Spain joined France in the war against Britain. The British position in the Mediterranean was gravely threatened, and it was decided to withdraw. Corsica and Elba were evacuated, and the Mediterranean fleet, now under Jervis, moved to Gibraltar (December 1) and transferred its activities to the Atlantic coasts of Spain and Portugal.

1797, February 14. Battle of Cape St. Vincent. Spanish Admiral **José de Córdova,** with 27 ships of the line, sailed from the Mediterranean past Gibraltar en route to Brest and a planned junction with the French fleet, and a proposed invasion of England. Jervis with the former British Mediterranean fleet, 15 ships of the line, cruising off the Portuguese coast to prevent such a move, met the Spanish off

Cape St. Vincent. Cordova's ships—in 2 groups of 9 and 18, respectively—were good, but their officers and crews relatively untrained. Jervis sailed between them in line, then turned on the larger group, which might have escaped had not Nelson, commanding H.M.S. *Captain,* broken away from the British line without orders and after a wide sweep placed his vessel in the path of the Spanish flotilla. He engaged the 7 leading ships until the rest of Jervis' squadron swarmed among them. In the resulting melee 4 Spanish ships were captured—2 by Nelson, who boarded them in quick succession. The shattered Spanish fleet escaped next day to Cádiz. Jervis' victory marked the end of the Spanish threat to England. It was also significant in definitely confirming the tactical superiority of the melee over the more formal line of battle, at least when initiated by a more aggressive force with superior seamanship.

1797, April–August. "The Breeze at Spithead." The Royal Navy in home ports was rocked by mutinies at Spithead (April 16), the Nore (May 12), and other home ports—revolts of the enlisted men against existing brutality, poor food, and poor pay. The mutineers asserted willingness to return to duty if the French fleet put to sea. Suppressed after several weeks of uproar, the mutinies nevertheless resulted in great improvement in the British seaman's status.

1797, October 11. Battle of Camperdown. British Admiral **Adam Duncan,** with 16 capital ships, attacked Admiral **Jan Willem de Winter**'s Dutch fleet of 15 as it emerged from the Texel. Duncan charged the Dutch line in 2 columns, broke it into 3 groups, and in the resulting melee captured 9 vessels, including the flagship. The Dutch put up bitter opposition; the British suffered severe damage and the prizes were so badly battered as to be completely unusable.

1798, May–June. British Return to the Mediterranean. News of Bonaparte's troop movement to Egypt in June caused the Admiralty to send a small British fleet to the Mediterranean under young Admiral Nelson. The French expedition evaded his search; but shortly after its landing in Egypt (see p. 688), Nelson discovered the French fleet of 13 ships of the line anchored in the Bay of Aboukir.

1798, August 1. Battle of the Nile. French Admiral Brueys was entirely unprepared; part of his crews were ashore. Nelson attacked in the late afternoon, a portion of his 13 ships carefully sailing between the French line and the shallow coastal waters, the remainder closing from the outer side, bringing the French between 2 fires. In the dusk and through the night the British fleet cruised slowly down the French line, concentrating on ship after ship in succession. By dawn only 3 French vessels remained; one was run aground and burned by her crew and the other 2 escaped. Brueys was among the killed in this catastrophic defeat.

1798, August 22. Invasion of Ireland. General **Jean J. A. Humbert** landed with 1,200 troops at Killala Bay. The invaders were surrounded and forced to surrender by Lord **Charles Cornwallis** (September 8). A reinforcing squadron under Admiral **J. B. F. Bompard** was overtaken and destroyed by Sir **John Warren** (October 12).

1798–1800. Operations on Malta. A Maltese uprising broke out against the French occupation force (September, 1798). Nelson sent ships and men to assist the Maltese guerrillas against French General Vaubois, who was driven into Valetta and besieged. Starvation finally forced the French to surrender (September 5, 1800).

1798–1800. British Domination of the Seas.

War of the Second Coalition, 1798–1800

1798, December 24. Russo-British Alliance. While Napoleon's Egyptian campaign was continuing, Emperor **Paul I** of Russia organized the Second Coalition, England being his principal partner. Austria, Portugal, Naples, the Vatican, and the Ottoman Empire joined (these latter 3 already being at war with France). Preliminary operations had been going on in Italy: French General Joubert overran Piedmont in November and early December, while a Neapolitan army, commanded by Austrian General **Karl Mack von Leiberich,** had attacked the Roman Republic and captured Rome (November 29), only to be driven out by French General **Jean**

Etienne Championnet (December 15). The over-all allied plan contemplated that an Anglo-Russian army under the **Duke of York** would drive the French from the Netherlands, an Austrian army under the Archduke Charles was to oust them from Germany and Switzerland, and a Russio-Austrian army under 70-year-old Marshal **Alexander Suvarov** would expel them from Italy. Available allied forces totaled about 300,000 men, not counting Mack's 60,000 unreliable Neapolitans. French strength was about 200,000, in 5 separate armies: Jourdan with 46,000 was on the upper Rhine; Masséna had 30,000 in Switzerland; Scherer with 80,000 was in northern Italy; Championnet had about 30,000 mixed French and Italian troops invading Naples in southern Italy; approximately 24,000 (including the satellite Batavian army) were in Holland under General **Guillaume Brune.** Already France was incorporating vassal legions in her armies: Dutch, Piedmontese, Italian, and Swiss. (In Egypt, Bonaparte had recruited Mameluke, Maltese, and Coptic groups.) Despite the Allied preponderance of force, Carnot ordered an early advance on all fronts.

ITALY—THE SOUTHERN FRONT

1799, January 11. Capitulation at Capua. Mack fled to the French lines to save his life from his mutinous Neapolitan troops. Championnet then stormed Naples (January 24). Establishment of the satellite Parthenopean Republic followed.

1799, March. Action along the Adige. Farther north, Scherer with 53,000 men moved against General **Paul Kray**'s 52,000 Austrians, hoping to win a victory before Suvarov's Russian army and Austrian reinforcements could join Kray. Late in March, French probes around Verona were repulsed. Both armies now moved to attack each other south of Verona.

1799, April 5. Battle of Magnano. Scherer's attack, at first successful, was checked. Kray threw his reserves at the French right flank and broke it in. Scherer retired in considerable disorder. Flamboyant, eccentric Suvarov arrived soon after. Assuming command of the allied army, he advanced westward with 90,000 men, driving the French before him. Leaving Kray with 20,000 men to besiege Mantua and Peschiera, he caught up with the French midway between Brescia and Milan.

1799, April 27. Battle of Cassano. Moreau, who had replaced Scherer, had about 30,000 men to oppose nearly 65,000 allies. After desperate resistance, he was driven off the field. Suvarov entered Milan in triumph (April 28), then seized Turin. Largely because of differences with the Austrian government, Suvarov gave up his pursuit of the French, and allied forces were scattered around northern Italy besieging French garrisons. Meanwhile General **Jacques E. J. A. Macdonald,** who now commanded the French army in southern Italy, was hastening north with 35,000 men. Moreau, based on Genoa, attempted with some success to distract Suvarov's attention from this reinforcement. Suddenly, in mid-June, the Russian general, who had about 40,000 men scattered around Alessandria, found himself between the 2 French armies.

1799, June 17–19. Battle of the Trebbia. Concentrating 25,000 men unexpectedly against Macdonald, Suvarov defeated him in a hard-fought engagement. French losses were some 10,000, allied casualties 7,000. Macdonald, closely pursued through hostile country by energetic Suvarov, finally joined Moreau near Genoa, losing another 5,000 men en route. Suvarov now pressed into the Apennines to drive the Army of Italy back to the Riviera. Moreau was relieved of his command by the Directory and replaced by Joubert (August 5).

1799, August 15. Battle of Novi. Joubert with 35,000 men attacked Suvarov with 50,000. But Joubert was killed, and his army decisively defeated with the loss of 11,000 men. Suvarov, who had lost 8,000, promptly pursued and drove the French across the Apennines. The pursuit was halted, however, when he discovered that the French Army of the Alps, some 30,000 strong, under Championnet, had entered Italy via the Mt. Cenis Pass. Suvarov turned northward, but before he could deal with Championnet, he was ordered to march to Switzerland with 20,000 Russians, leaving operations in Italy to Marshal **Michael Melas,** with about 60,000 Austrians.

1799, November 4. Battle of Genoa. Melas defeated Championnet, driving the French back across the Alps.

COMMENT. *By year's end practically all of Bonaparte's gains of 1796–1797 had been erased; the credit goes almost entirely to doughty old Suvarov.*

GERMANY AND THE NETHERLANDS

1799, March. Jourdan's Invasion of Germany. The Army of Mayence, 40,000 strong, crossed the Rhine at Kehl and commenced operations against the Archduke Charles, who had about 80,000. Checked at **Ostrach** (March 21), Jourdan boldly determined to attack the archduke at Stockach, with his main effort against the Austrian right. Charles, unaware of Jourdan's intentions, at the same time was leading half of his army forward on a reconnaissance in force.

1799, March 25. Battle of Stockach. Jourdan's initial assault gained some ground, and at first he thought he had won a victory. But Charles held on grimly and sent for the remainder of his army, giving him 60,000 men on the field to Jourdan's 35,000. The Austrian counterattack smashed through the center of Jourdan's loosely linked divisions. Austrian losses were 6,000 against the French 3,600, but Jourdan's offensive had been wrecked. He withdrew his shaken army at nightfall and made good his retreat to the Rhine. There he resigned his post. His army was put under Masséna (see below). There was little further action in Germany for the remainder of the year, the attention of both sides being focused instead on operations south of the upper Rhine in Switzerland, and west of the lower Rhine in the Netherlands.

1799, August. Operations in the Netherlands. A British force, 27,000 strong, under the **Duke of York,** landed on the tip of Holland's peninsula, south of the Texel. The Dutch Republican fleet in the Texel surrendered to a British squadron without fighting (August 30). Reinforced by 2 Russian divisions, the Duke of York took the offensive.

1799, September 16. First Battle of Bergen. The combined Russo-British army, 35,000 strong, was met by Brune with 22,000 Franco-Batavian troops. The Russians and English could not coordinate their operations, and were defeated. Allied losses were 4,000; the French had 3,000 casualties. Two weeks later the allied forces advanced again.

1799, October 2. Second Battle of Bergen. This time the allies drove the republican forces from the field, each side losing about 2,000 men. Pressing his advantage, York continued south.

1799, October 6. Battle of Castricum. The allies were checked in a spirited action along the sand dunes of the North Sea coast, losing 3,500 men to the republicans' 2,500. Lack of Russo-British liaison again contributed to York's defeat. Realizing that he did not have sufficient force to drive the French from Holland, and since his principal mission—destruction of the Dutch fleet—had been accomplished, he withdrew northward.

1799, October 18. The Convention of Alkmaar. This ended hostilities in the Netherlands. The allied army withdrew from Dutch territory; 8,000 French and Dutch prisoners held in England were returned, but the Dutch fleet remained in British hands.

SWITZERLAND AND THE ALPS

1799, March. Operations in Switzerland. Masséna had nearly 30,000 men in central Switzerland. In accordance with Carnot's over-all plan, he was to advance through the mountainous Vorarlberg and Grisons regions, covering the right flank of Jourdan's army. Surprising the Austrians by his early advance through the snowy passes, Masséna quickly crossed the upper Rhine near Mayenfeld, and captured most of the 7,000-man force around Chur in the Grisons. The Austrian garrison of Feldkirch, on Masséna's left flank, however, repulsed 2 efforts to capture the town (March 7 and 23). Masséna now held up his advance to await developments north of the Rhine. Meanwhile he sent a column of 10,000 men under General **Claude Lecourbe,** from the vicinity of the Splugen Pass, raiding down the valley of the upper Inn into the Tyrol. Here Lecourbe was joined by a small French column which had marched north from the Army of Italy, the combined force creating consternation in the western Tyrol.

1799, April. Increasing Austrian Pressure. The defeats of the French armies in Germany and Italy exposed Masséna's northern and southern flanks. Austrian Generals **Heinrich J. J. Bellegarde** and **Friedrich von Hotze** brought overwhelming numbers to bear on Lecourbe's force in the Inn Valley. This was driven back to the upper Rhine.

1799, May. Formation of the Army of the Danube. Masséna took over Jourdan's defeated army as well as his own. He was responsible for defense of the Rhine south of Mainz, as well as of Switzerland. With his main body of 45,000 he withdrew slowly toward Zurich, followed by the Archduke Charles and Hotze, with about 80,000 men. Masséna repulsed an Austrian attack on his entrenchments at **Zurich** (June 4), but the pressure of superior numbers and the doubtful loyalty of the Swiss caused him to withdraw farther westward (June 7). Things remained quiet in Switzerland for the next 2 months, since Charles did not feel his strength permitted further advance.

1799, August. Masséna Resumes the Initiative. He defeated Charles's left wing in the rugged mountains of the upper Rhine and Rhone valleys. He then advanced against **Zurich,** but was repulsed (August 14). Two days later he repulsed an Austrian attack against his left flank at **Dottingen.**

1799, August–September. New Allied Plans. Charles was to march north through western Germany to join the Russo-British force of the Duke of York in driving the French from the Netherlands. Suvarov with his Russians would march north from Italy to Switzerland to drive Masséna back into France. The departure of Charles left less than 40,000 allies in Switzerland under General **Aleksander M. Korsakov,** with Suvarov still advancing from Italy. While Lecourbe with 12,000 men held the St. Gotthard Pass, Masséna with 40,000 struck in central Switzerland.

1799, September 25. Third Battle of Zurich. Masséna swept Korsakov's 20,000 from the field, inflicting 8,000 casualties and loss of 100 guns. Suvarov, arriving at the foot of the St. Gotthard, found himself unexpectedly blocked. He fought his way through the pass, at great cost, only to learn of Korsakov's disaster. He managed to struggle back across the central Alpine spine to Ilanz, on the upper Rhine. Flighty, unstable Czar Paul relieved him of command, a sad ending for the last and most glorious campaign of a great soldier. Meanwhile the disaster at Zurich, combined with the Russo-British defeat in the Netherlands, forced Charles to abandon his proposed march toward the Low Countries.

COMMENT. *The campaign of 1799 had been disappointing to both sides. The French had been driven from Italy, though they managed to hold their own elsewhere, despite several costly defeats. The allies, on the other hand, had failed miserably to take advantage of their opportunities, which would not come again for many years. Russia in disgust withdrew from the coalition.*

EUROPE

GREAT BRITAIN

1756–1763. The Seven Years' War. (See p. 667.)

1760–1820. Reign of George III.

1775–1783. War of the American Revolution. (See p. 708.)

1792–1800. Wars of the French Revolution. (See p. 678.)

1795–1797. United Irishmen Revolt. These nationalists, inspired by **Wolf Tone, Napper Tandy,** and others, rose in armed rebellion to secure separation from England. They expected French help, but what little materialized was abortive and weak (see pp. 689 and 690). The uprising was savagely repressed (1796–1797) by British General **Gerard Lake.**

1797, April–August. The Naval Mutinies. (See p. 690.)

1798, June 12. Battle of Vinegar Hill. The Irish revolt flared again when an armed mob without competent military direction stormed and burned Enniscorthy, County Wexford, after which they encamped on Vinegar Hill, overlooking the town. Surrounded by Lake's troops, the rebels surrendered after a short struggle. Again violence and brutality marked the suppression of the revolt.

FRANCE

1715–1774. Reign of Louis XV.
1756–1763. The Seven Years' War. (See p. 667.)
1774–1792. Reign of Louis XVI.
1778–1783. French Intervention in the American Revolution. (See p. 716).
1789, July 14. The Storming of the Bastille. Traditional date for the beginning of the French Revolution.
1792–1800. Wars of the French Revolution. (See p. 678.)

IBERIAN PENINSULA

Spain

1759–1788. Reign of Charles III.
1761–1763. Spanish Participation in Seven Years' War. (See p. 677). Plans were made to invade Portugal, England's ally.
1761–1762. Spain Invades Portugal. Bragança and Almeida were seized. The Portuguese Army, reorganized under command of **William of Lippe** and reinforced by a British contingent under General **John Burgoyne,** repelled the invasion.
1779–1783. American Revolution. **(See p. 716.)**
1793–1795. War with France. (See p. 679.)
1796–1799. War with England. (See p. 689.)

Portugal

1761–1763. War with Spain. (See above.)

THE NETHERLANDS

1780–1784. Dutch-English War. This was an extension of the American Revolution (see p. 718). Holland lost several possessions in both the West and East Indies.
1785–1787. Civil War. Emergence of the Patriot party (pro-French) brought internal conflict between Stadholder **William V** and the States General. William called in Prussian troops (1787) to restore his authority.
1793–1795. War with France. (See p. 679.) Holland was conquered and became the Batavian Republic.

SCANDINAVIA

Sweden

1751–1771. Reign of Adolphus Frederick.
1771–1792. Reign of Gustavus III. A brilliant, although controversial, ruler and soldier. He was also one of Sweden's greatest authors.
1772, August 19. Royal Coup d'État. Since the reign of Ulrica Eleonora (1718), Sweden had been a constitutional monarchy, with most power shared by the Riksdag and the Royal Council. Gustavus seized power in a series of well-planned military moves. The remainder of his reign was plagued by continuous internal unrest. The *coup d'état* also aroused fears in Denmark and Russia; they contemplated war, but were deterred by Gustavus' readiness for war.
1788–1790. War with Russia and Denmark (see p. 696). Denmark played little part.
1792, March 29. Assassination of Gustavus. This was the culmination of an aristocratic conspiracy.
1792–1809. Reign of Gustavus IV.

Denmark and Norway

This was a period of relatively minor military interest or activity in Denmark. Danish participation as Russia's ally in the war against Sweden (see above, and p. 696) was nominal.

GERMANY

Austria and Hungary

The Hapsburgs continued to wear 2 imperial crowns: that of the Holy Roman Empire (or Germany) and that of their hereditary Danubian lands, now commonly known as the Austrian Empire. Austria continued to be involved as a primary participant in all of the major wars of Western and Central Europe, and was also still engaged in frequent wars in the Balkans, mostly against Turkey. The principal events were:

1740–1780. Reign of Maria Theresa.

1756–1763. The Seven Years' War. (See p. 667.)

1765–1790. Reign of Joseph II (as Holy Roman Emperor). He was coregent with his mother over Hapsburg lands, but with little influence until her death.

1772. First Partition of Poland. (See below.)

1785. Revolt in Transylvania. The Rumanian peasants rose and massacred many Magyar nobles. The rising was crushed ruthlessly.

WAR WITH TURKEY, 1787–1791

1787. Austrian Alliance with Russia.

1788. Austrian Failures. Joseph, personally leading his armies, was completely unsuccessful in efforts in Transylvania and Serbia.

1789. Capture of Belgrade. After repulsing a Turkish invasion of Bosnia, the Austrians captured Belgrade.

1790. Peace Negotiations. Threats of Prussian intervention, the weakening of Russian cooperation because of her war with Sweden, revolt in the Austrian Netherlands (see below), and widespread unrest throughout the empire led Joseph and his successor, **Leopold,** to seek peace and to negotiate an armistice with Turkey (July–September).

1791, August 4. Treaty of Sistova. Austria returned Belgrade to Turkey in return for a strip of northern Bosnia.

1789–1790. Brabant Revolt. Imperial infringement of established civil rights in the Austrian Netherlands (see below) resulted in armed insurrection, led by **Henry van der Noot.** The rebellion was suppressed, but its objectives were achieved; Joseph restored the former constitution and privileges.

1790–1792. Reign of Leopold II.

1792–1800. Wars of the French Revolution. (See p. 678.) These were disastrous to Austria.

1792–1835. Reign of Francis II.

1793. The Second Partition of Poland. (See p. 696.)

1795. The Third Partition of Poland. (See p. 696.)

Prussia

By virtue of his victories in the War of the Austrian Succession, Frederick the Great made his nation a major power and a rival to Austria in Germany and the Empire.

1756–1763. The Seven Years' War. (See p. 667.) Frederick and Prussia emerged with enhanced power and prestige.

1772. First Partition of Poland. (See below.)

1777–1779. War of the Bavarian Succession. Death of Elector **Maximilian III** caused a crisis when Austria and Prussia selected different candidates for succession. Frederick mobilized and marched into Bohemia (July, 1778). An Austrian army marched to oppose him, and for more than a year the 2 armies faced each other without battle. The bloodless conflict (also known as the "Potato War" because of the soldiers' diet) was ended by the **Treaty of Teschen** (May 13, 1779).

1786–1797. Reign of Frederick William II.

1790. Preparations to Intervene in the Austro-Turkish War. Frederick was satisfied when Austria made peace with Turkey (see above).

1792–1800. Wars of the French Revolution. (See p. 678.)

1793. Second Partition of Poland. (See p. 696.)

1795. Third Partition of Poland. (See p. 696.)

1797–1840. Reign of Frederick William III.

POLAND

1768–1776. Civil War and Russian Invasion. A group of Polish noblemen ("Confederation of the Bar") organized an armed movement to defend the country against Russian religious and political aggression. Despite the efforts of French General Dumouriez, sent by France to command the dissidents, the movement failed, largely because of Russian armed intervention in support of the pro-Russian government.

1772. First Partition of Poland. Engineered

by Frederick the Great to prevent Austria, jealous of Russian successes against Turkey, from going to war. Guerrilla war continued throughout Poland.

1792. Russian Invasion of Poland. This was caused by constitutional changes that would have stabilized the weak Polish monarchy. Prussia at once also invaded to prevent Russian conquest.

1793. Second Partition of Poland. Russia and Prussia made a bargain at Poland's expense.

1794. National Uprising. The Polish nation rose in revolt against Russian and Prussian domination. **Thaddeus Kosciusko,** whose democratic principles had brought him to America to take part in the American Revolution, led a popular uprising.

1794, April 3. Battle of Raclawice. Kosciusko, with 4,000 troops and some 2,000 peasants armed only with scythes and pikes, defeated a force of 5,000 Russian troops. The Russian garrison of Warsaw (Warszawa) was driven out (April 17) after several days of street fighting.

1794, April–August. Russian and Prussian Invasions. The allied forces converged on the unfortunate country and after several desperate encounters Kosciusko's forces were invested in Warsaw by Frederick William of Prussia with 25,000 men and 179 guns, and Russian General **Fersen** with 65,000 men and 74 guns. Another Russian force of 11,000 occupied the right bank of the Vistula (Wisla) across from the capital.

1794, August 26–September 6. Defense of Warsaw. The Poles, 35,000 strong, with 200 guns, resisted 2 successive assaults and the siege was lifted. There was, however, no cohesion between the Polish forces in the field.

1794, October 10. Battle of Maciejowice. Kosciusko, with only 7,000 men, was crushed by Fersen's 16,000 Russians when 1 of his divisions failed to support him. Kosciusko, seriously wounded, was made prisoner. The entire uprising now collapsed.

1795. Third Partition of Poland. The ancient Polish nation disappeared; Russia had a permanent hold in Central Europe.

RUSSIA

1741–1762. Reign of Elizabeth (**Youngest Daughter of Peter the Great**).

1756–1763. Seven Years' War. (**See p. 667.**)

1762. Revolution. Peter III was deposed by his nobles and generals after a 6-month reign.

1762–1796. Reign of Catherine II (**the Great**). She was the German-born wife of Peter III.

1766–1772. Russian Intervention in Poland. (**See p. 695.**)

1768–1774. First War of Catherine the Great against Turkey. (**See p. 697.**)

1773–1774. Peasant and Cossack Revolt. Russian efforts against Turkey were hampered by **Emelyan I. Pugachev**'s revolt in southeast Russia. This was put down only with difficulty by Suvarov.

1783. Annexation of the Crimea. England and Austria persuaded Turkey not to go to war.

1787–1792. Second War of Catherine the Great against Turkey. (**See p. 698.**)

War with Sweden, 1788–1790

1788. Swedish Invasion. Gustavus III invaded Russian Finland to offset possible future moves against his country by either Russia or Prussia. Bold assaults on land and sea brought success to the Swedes at first, causing consternation in Catherine's court, already occupied by the Turkish war. Gustavus' efforts on land ended with a Swedish repulse before the fortress of **Svataipol,** and a sudden Danish attack on Sweden further hampered him.

1789, August 24. First Naval Battle of Svensksund. The Swedish fleet, under Count **Karl A. Ehrensvard,** was decisively defeated by the Russian Admiral **Krose,** with loss of 33 ships. However, within a year, the Swedish Navy had been completely restored by the intensive efforts of Gustavus.

1790, July 2–9. Second Battle of Svensksund. The Swedish fleet, under the **Duke of Sudermania,** attacking in single file in a narrow channel, successfully ran the gantlet of the Russian fleet until the explosion of a powder ship threw the line into confusion, and the Swedes withdrew to the protection of the guns of Sveaborg (then a Swedish fortress). On the 9th, the reorganized Swedish fleet again put to sea to meet the Russians, who advanced in a crescent formation. The excellent Swedish gunnery chopped gaps in the Russian line and the Swedes, who had in all 195 ships to the Russians' 151, defeated their enemy piecemeal in the greatest sea fight in Scandinavian history. Russian losses were 53 ships sunk or captured. The stupidity and poor leadership of **Charles H. N. O. Nassau-Siegen,** an international adventurer in the Russian service, contributed to the disaster. British **William Sidney Smith** served brilliantly with the Swedes.

1790, August 15. Treaty of Wereloe. Peace with Sweden followed, restoring the *status quo ante.*

1792–1800. Wars of the French Revolution. (See p. 678.)

1793. Second Partition of Poland. (See p. 696.)

1795. Third Partition of Poland. (See p. 696.)

EURASIA AND THE MIDDLE EAST

TURKEY

First War against Catherine of Russia, 1768–1774

1768, October. Turkey Declares War. Poland pleaded for assistance against Russian intervention (see p. 695), but Turkey merely protested until Russian troops pursued Poles into Turkish territory and destroyed the Turkish town of Balta. The Crimean Tartars at once invaded the Ukraine.

1769. Russian Invasion of the Caucasus. The Turks were defeated in the Kabardia and in Georgia.

1769. Russian Invasion of the Balkans. Russian Count **Peter Rumiantsev** defeated the main Turkish army on the banks of the **Dniester.** He then seized Jassy and overran Moldavia and Wallachia, including the occupation of Bucharest.

1769–1773. Revolt in Egypt. Ali Bey, governor of Egypt, revolted and declared Egypt independent. He received Russian support.

1770. Russians Incite and Support Rebellion in Greece. Admiral **Aleksei G. Orlov**'s Russian Baltic fleet sailed to the Mediterranean and captured Navarino (April) and several other small places in the Morea. The Turks, however, assembled a large army, mostly Albanian, ruthlessly suppressed the revolt, and drove the Russians away (June).

1770, July 6. Naval Battle of Chesme (Çeşme). Orlov defeated the Turkish fleet near the island of Chios, off the coast of Anatolia. Scottish Admiral **Samuel Greig,** serving under Orlov, was largely responsible for the victory.

1770, August. Battle of Karkal. A Turkish and Tartar army, attempting to drive the Russians from Moldavia, were badly defeated by Rumiantsev. The Turks were forced to retreat behind the Danube. The Russians then systematically captured the Turkish fortresses along the Danube and Pruth Rivers.

1771. Egyptian Invasion of Syria. The Egyptians, under **Abu'l Dhahab,** captured Damascus. Abu'l then negotiated secretly with the Turks, evacuated Syria, and marched back to attack Egypt for Turkey.

1771. Invasion of the Crimea. A Russian army under Prince **Vasily Dolgoruky** stormed the Isthmus of Perekop and conquered the Crimea.

1772–1773. Truce. Peace negotiations were fruitless. The Turks took advantage of the lull to reorganize and revitalize their army.

1772–1773. Confused War in Egypt and Syria. As Abu'l returned to Egypt to reconquer it for Turkey, Ali marched to Syria to reconquer it. Abu'l consolidated Egypt, and Ali consolidated Palestine.

1773, April 19–21. Battle of Salihia. After initial success, Ali was defeated and captured. Egypt returned to Turkish control. Abu'l was governor.

1773. Operations on the Danube. Count Peter Rumiantsev, commanding Russian forces on the Danube, advanced south toward the main Turkish army under the Grand Vizier **Muhsinzade.** The Turks fell back on Shumla (Shumen or Kolarovgrad). Other Russian forces besieged the Turkish fortresses of Varna and Silistria.

1773. Peace Negotiations. The grand vizier began to negotiate for peace with Rumiantsev. The Russians, too, were eager for peace because of a vast Cossack and peasant revolt in southeast Russia (see p. 696).

1774, June. Battle of Kozludzha. Suvarov, subordinate to Rumiantsev, defeated a large portion of the Turkish army near Shumla.

1774, July 16. Treaty of Kuchuk Kainarji. Russia returned Wallachia, Moldavia, and Bessarabia, but was given the right to protect Christians in the Ottoman Empire, and to intervene in Wallachia and Moldavia in case of Turkish misrule. The Crimea was declared independent, but the sultan remained the religious leader of the Tartars as the Moslem caliph. Russia gained Kabardia in the Caucasus, unlimited sovereignty over the port of Azov, part of the Kuban near Azov, the Kerch peninsula in the Crimea, and the land between the Bug and Dnieper rivers and at the mouth of the Dnieper. Russian merchant vessels were to be allowed passage of the Dardanelles. Russia thus gained 2 outlets to the Black Sea, which was no longer a Turkish lake. Russian troops were withdrawn north of the Danube. Suvarov was sent to deal with the Cossacks.

1783. Russian Annexation of the Crimea. (See p. 696.)

1786. Revolt in Egypt. Suppressed by an Ottoman army.

Second War with Catherine of Russia, 1787–1792

1787. Russia Precipitates War. This resulted from encroachments in Georgia and demands that Turkey recognize a Russian protectorate over Georgia. Turkey was also intriguing with the Crimean Tartars to rise against Russia. Austria joined Russia on the basis of a secret alliance. Prince **Peter** of Montenegro rebelled against Turkey (1788).

1788. Turkish Repulse at Kinburn. Suvarov defeated a Turkish attempt to reconquer the Crimea.

1788. Russian Invasion of Moldavia. Rumiantsev captured the cities of Chocim and Jassy, then advanced to the seacoast. After **John Paul Jones**'s naval victories (see below), Prince **Grigori Potemkin** took Ochakov, at the mouth of the Danube, opposite Kinburn. He seems to have ordered the massacre of all Turkish inhabitants of the captured cities, men, women, and children.

1788, June 17 and 27. Naval Battles of the Liman (Lagoons near the Mouth of the Dnieper). John Paul Jones, commanding the Russian Black Sea fleet, defeated **Hasan el Ghasi**'s Turkish flotilla in 2 sharp actions. Nassau-Siegen, who was vying with Jones for command, botched the opening of the first battle, but Jones's leadership retrieved the situation, and the Turkish ships drew off. The second battle brought disaster to the Turks, who lost 15 ships, 3,000 men killed, and more than 1,600 taken prisoner. Russian losses were 1 frigate, 18 men killed, and 67 wounded.

1788. Operations in Serbia and Transylvania. The Turks repulsed the Austrian armies under Joseph II.

1789. Operations in Moldavia and Wallachia. The Russians invaded Moldavia from the north, the Austrians from the west. The Austrians and 2 of the Russian armies (under Prince Potemkin and Count Rumiantsev) were generally unsuccessful against a revitalized Turkish army. But a Russo-Austrian army under Suvarov and Saxe-Coburg smashed the Turks at **Focsani** (August 1) and **Rimnik** (September 22). Suvarov's victorious advance then forced the Turks to withdraw to the Danube.

1789. Operations in Serbia. The Austrians, now commanded by General Gideon E. von Laudon, repulsed a Turkish invasion of Bosnia, then besieged and captured Belgrade by assault.

1790, July 27. Truce with Austria. (See p. 695.)

1790. Revolt in Greece. This seriously interfered with Turkish operations for the remainder of the war.

1790, December. Storming of Ismail. After a prolonged siege, Suvarov captured this fortress at the mouth of the Danube.

1791. Treaty of Sistova. (See p. 695.) Peace with Austria.

1791. Peace Negotiations. Russia was anxious for peace because of Prussian activity in Poland.

1792, January 9. Treaty of Jassy. Russia returned Moldavia and Bessarabia to Turkey. She retained all conquered territory east of the Dniester River, including the port of Ochakov.

1798–1800. War with France; Bonaparte's Invasion of Egypt. (See p. 688.)

PERSIA, 1747–1800

1747–1750. Struggle for the Throne. After the death of **Nadir Shah,** a protracted 3-cornered fight for control of the empire ensued between **Mohammed Husain,** who held the Caspian provinces; **Karim Khan,** strong in the south; and **Azad** in Azerbaijan. Karim Khan was successful and established unquestioned control over Persia.

1750–1779. Reign of Karim Khan. A period of relative peace and prosperity.

1779–1794. Civil War. This was a revolt of **Agha Mohammed,** an able eunuch general, against the successors of Karim Khan.

1794–1797. Reign of Agha Mohammed. A cruel and brutal ruler.

1795–1796. Invasion of Georgia. This nation had fallen away from Persian rule after the death of Nadir Shah. Defeating the Georgian King **Heraclius,** Agha Mohammed brutally reimposed Persian sovereignty over Georgia.

1797. Assassination of Agha Mohammed.

1798. Invasion of Afghanistan. The new Shah, **Fath Ali,** was incited by the British. This began a long-drawn-out series of wars weakening both Asian kingdoms.

SOUTH ASIA

AFGHANISTAN

Ahmad Shah, assuming control of the Afghan provinces of Persia after the death of **Nadir Shah** of Persia (see p. 651), established the Durani Dynasty. His military operations extended over much of Central Asia, including 9 invasions of India. The high point of his Indian incursions was a great victory over a numerically superior Maratha army at the **Battle of Panipat** (see p. 701). On his death the Afghan Empire extended over eastern Persia and all the region south of the Oxus, including Baluchistan, Kashmir, the Punjab, and Sind. His son, **Timur Shah** (1773–1793), weak and ineffectual, permitted loss of Sind and other Indian territory and the slow disintegration of Afghan sovereignty over the entire empire. Timur's son, **Zaman Murza** (1793–1799) in 1799 ceded Lahore to Sikh **Ranjit Singh** (see p. 784). Meanwhile, a protracted war with Persia had begun (1798; see above).

INDIA

When the period opened, 4 European nations were milking India for their own purposes. Waning Dutch exploitation was soon eliminated (1759), and Portugal's influence was frozen in her possessions of Goa, Diu, and Daman. Only England and France continued their battle for supremacy amid the wreckage of the Mogul Empire, while the Marathas were simultaneously rising to power. Both European nations took advantage of native rivalries in an unabashed and almost continual warfare with but one objective—the exploitation of India's riches for the benefit of European investors. Both masked their national rivalry through agencies—for France the **Compagnie des Indes,** for England the **British East India Company** ("John Company"). This latter remarkable organization had the delegated power of a sovereign state, including the making of both war and peace "with any non-Christian nation." It had its own army, composed of European adventurers and native troops, under English commanders. Further English military influence was furnished (1754) by an English regular regiment, the 39th Foot (later the Dorsetshire Regiment), at Madras. This became the backbone of English military operations in India. Many of its officers and men later transferred to the company's service. At midcentury France and her native allies controlled a great part of southern India; **Joseph François Dupleix** (see p. 653) was governor general of all French establishments in India; his subordinate, General **Charles J. P. Bussy-Castelnau,** was operating in Hyderabad in the Deccan.

1751, September–October. Capture and Siege of Arcot. Chanda Sahib, France's puppet Nawab of the Carnatic, was besieging a small English garrison at Trichinopoly (Tiruchirappalli). Young **Robert Clive,** former East India Company clerk turned soldier, with 500 men and 3 guns moved suddenly from Madras and captured Arcot, Chanda Sahib's capital, as a diversion to relieve the siege (September 12). The nawab's son, **Raja** Sahib, with 10,000 men, at once returned to invest Arcot. After a siege of 50 days, in which Clive's troops were reduced to 120 Europeans and 200 sepoys, the Indians assaulted, driving ahead a herd of elephants, their heads armed with iron plates, to batter down the gates. But the elephants stampeded when they came under musket fire. Another assault across the moat was repelled, and then the assailants withdrew after an hour's fight, having lost 400 casualties. Clive's losses were only 5 or 6 men. This exploit greatly enhanced England's prestige, to the disadvantage of the French, whose campaign now broke down. Dupleix, a most capable administrator, whose greatest trouble had been lack of understanding by and support from the home government, was summarily relieved in 1754.

COMMENT. *This was the beginning of Clive's career, which would lead to England's domination of India and his own fame as one of Britain's foremost captains and colonizers.*

1756, June 20. Capture of Calcutta. Suraja Dowla, Nawab of Bengal, after a 4-day siege, seized the town, founded by the British and now the focal point of their activities. Europeans unable to escape were forced into a small subterranean dungeon —the **Black Hole**—in which it has been alleged 123 out of 146 perished overnight. Historians today are still not certain of the numbers actually involved.

1757, January 2. Recapture of Calcutta. This was by a joint expedition from Madras under Clive and Admiral **Charles Watson.**

1757, March 23. Capture of Chandernagore. This French post was seized by Clive after a spirited fight. This permitted Clive to march inland against Suraja without fear for his line of communications with Calcutta.

1757, June 23. Battle of Plassey. Clive, pursuing Suraja, found him entrenched on the far side of the Bhagirathi River near the village of Plassey. The Indian army was 50,000 strong, with 53 guns. Clive had 1,100 Europeans, 2,100 native troops, and 10 guns. He crossed the river and massed his force in a mango grove. The Nawab's army moved to surround it in a large semicircle, its guns—under French command—massed on the right flank. A sudden rainstorm wet the Nawab's powder. As the firing ceased, a cavalry charge swept up to the British position, but Clive's gunners had covered their ammunition from the rain and repulsed the charge, inflicting great loss. Clive, counting rightly on the disaffection of part of the Indian army, advanced to cannonade the Nawab's entrenchments at short range. An Indian infantry sortie was repulsed and Clive now assaulted the position, in which only the French gunners, under M. **St. Frais,** continued fighting to the last. Plassey decided the fate of Bengal. Suraja was assassinated a few days later and was succeeded by Clive's ally, **Mir Jafar.**

1758. Arrival of French Reinforcements. An expeditionary force under Baron **Thomas Lally** arrived at Pondicherry, capital of French interests. He immediately marched to besiege and capture British **Fort St. David,** south of Pondicherry (March–June 2).

1758, December–1759, February. Siege of Madras. Lally failed in efforts to take the city. He was hampered by lack of naval support, while the British garrison was supplied by sea (see p. 676).

1759, January 25. Battle of Masulipatam. A British relieving force, arriving by sea, under **Francis Forde** defeated Lally, forcing him to raise the siege of Madras.

1759. Operations against the Dutch. A Dutch naval expedition was repulsed by the British at the mouth of the Hooghly River, and Forde captured the Dutch port of **Chinsura.**

1760, January 22. Battle of Wandiwash. Lally was defeated by General Sir **Eyre Coote** and forced to retire to Pondicherry. There he was besieged.

1760, August–1761, January 15. Fall of Pondicherry. Lally capitulated to Clive's troops (Clive had returned ill to England) there being no hope for reinforcements from France (see p. 677).

1761, January 14. Battle of Panipat. The Afghan armies of **Ahmad Shah Durani** had been ravaging northern and central India (since 1747). Ahmad reached and captured Delhi (1757). The **Maratha** revolt which had demolished the Mogul Dynasty had swept north into the Punjab (1753), but Ahmad, again invading, slowly drove the Mahrathas back, routing them completely at Panipat. Ahmad's later withdrawal, caused by a Sikh insurrection, left India in complete chaos, facilitating British consolidation of their position in Bengal.

1763. Treaty of Paris. Pondicherry was restored to France (see p. 677), but the Compagnie des Indes was soon dissolved (1769).

1763–1765. Operations in Bengal. Sporadic conflicts between the British East India Company's troops and the native rulers continued. A mutiny in the company's Bengal Army, near Patna (1763), inspired by the Nawab of Bengal, was summarily quelled at **Buxar** (October 23, 1764), and 24 of the ringleaders blown from gun muzzles by Major **Hector Munro** to avenge the massacre at Patna.

1766–1769. First Mysore War. Haidar Ali, ruler of Mysore, fought British troops to a standstill, then signed a treaty of defensive alliance with the East India Company.

1771. Mysore-Maratha War. Inconclusive.

1774. Rohilla War. Governor General **Warren Hastings** loaned a brigade of East India Company troops to **Shuju-ud-Dowla,** Wazir of Oudh and a British ally, to help conquer the territory of the Rohillas, a fierce Afghan tribe in the Ganges-Jumna river region west of Oudh (April). He offset the threat of growing Maratha strength, but his employment of Company troops in a native war was contrary to British and Company policy.

1779–1782. First Maratha War. Inconclusive despite British success in Gujarat and the capture of the fortress of Gwalior (1780).

Second Mysore War, 1780–1783

1780. Haidar Ali Declares War. He was smarting from failure of the British to support him in his own war with the Marathas. After British troops moved against French holdings in 1778 (see p. 716), he joined France. The British had taken Pondicherry and Mahé from the French. But Haidar Ali, in the Carnatic, attacked and cut to pieces a small British force at **Perambakam** (September 10), and swept up to the gates of Madras.

1781, June 1. Battle of Porto Novo. Coote, with 8,000 men sent by sea from Bengal, attacked and defeated Ali's 60,000, saving the Madras Presidency.

1781, August–September. British Victories. Haidar was defeated at **Pollilur** (August 27) and at **Sholingarh** a month later.

1782, August 30. Capture of Trincomalee. French Admiral **Pierre de Suffren** captured the port from the British and was thus able to send help to Haidar Ali. He retained tenuous control of the Indian Ocean until the signing of peace between England and France in 1783 (see p. 724).

1783. Withdrawal of French Aid Ends the War. Haidar Ali having died, his son **Tippoo Sahib** made peace.

1789–1792. Third Mysore War. Tippoo attacked Travancore. **Lord Cornwallis,** who had succeeded Hastings as governor general of India, invaded Mysore; stormed the fortress of Bangalore, its capital; and drove Tippoo into Seringapatam, where he was besieged. Tippoo made peace (March 16, 1792) by ceding half his dominions to the British.

1795–1796. British Expedition to Ceylon. The Dutch were easily defeated. The independent King of Kandy soon recognized British sovereignty, and Ceylon became a crown colony (1798).

1799. Fourth Mysore War. Governor General **Richard Wellesley** (then Lord Mornington), as directed by Pitt, moved actively to suppress the last vestiges of French influence in India, lest Bonaparte invade it. French troops in the employ of the Maratha Confederacy were disbanded on Wellesley's demand. Tippoo, however, was carrying on secret correspondence with the French government; on his refusal to cooperate with the British, Wellesley sent 2 armies into Mysore. General **George Harris** drove Tippoo once again into Seringapatam and then took the place by storm. Tippoo was killed while fighting bravely in the breached wall. Wellesley's younger brother, General **Arthur Wellesley** (later Duke of Wellington) distinguished himself in the campaign and was appointed governor of Seringapatam.

SOUTHEAST ASIA

BURMA

1740–1752. Mon Revolt. The inhabitants of Lower Burma rose up against the Burmese Toungoo Dynasty, drove them out, and overran much of Upper Burma, capturing Ava (1752). The Toungoo Dynasty was completely destroyed. The Mons (or Talaings) re-established their former capital at Pegu (see p. 656).

1752–1757. Rise of Alaungpaya. This obscure lord of the Shwebo district united the demoralized Burmans. He began to repel the Mons from Upper Burma, and reconquered most of Lower Burma (1754–1755). The Mons were able to hold only the regions around Syriam and Pegu. In these operations Alaungpaya proved himself probably the ablest military leader of Burmese history. His successes, thanks also to strong lieutenants, established a strong dynasty.

1753. British Post at Negrais. This small fortified trading post was unrecognized by the Mons, but Alaungpaya recognized it.

1755, 1758. Alaungpaya's Operations in Manipur. This was a punitive response to Manipuri raids (1715–1749). When the local inhabitants rose up against the garrisons he left there, Alaungpaya returned to devastate Manipur (1758).

1755–1756. Siege of Syriam. It was captured after a long struggle, and despite French assistance to the Mons. Alaungpaya also captured 2 French warships in the narrow river channel near the town. He killed the officers but spared the crews, incorporating them into his own army.

1756–1757. Siege of Pegu. After driving the remaining Mon army into the city, Alaungpaya finally wore down the defenders and captured the town by assault. This, and the ensuing massacre, ended Mon national existence in Burma, though there was an abortive uprising (1758) while Alaungpaya was absent on his punitive expedition to Manipur.

1759. Capture of Negrais. Alaungpaya massacred most of the small English and Mon garrison.

1760. Invasion of Siam. Alaungpaya advanced to besiege Ayuthia, the capital. While directing the fire of his siege batteries, he was seriously wounded by a gun explosion. Because of either this or an epidemic of malaria, the siege was raised and the army retreated to Burma, suffering some losses from Siamese harassment. The king died en route.

1764. Invasion of Manipur. Hsinbyushin (1763–1776), the second son of Alaungpaya, carried off much of the population into slavery.

1764–1767. Invasion of Siam. This culminated in the capture of Ayuthia. The operation was very well conducted, and the victory was due mainly to the able Burmese General **Maha Nawraha,** who died just before the surrender of Ayuthia.

1765–1769. Chinese Invasion. The Chinese, aggravated by Burmese frontier forays, invaded Burma in great force. They seized most of eastern Burma from Bhamo south to Lashio and west almost to the Irrawaddy at Singaung. The Burmese, however, refused to accept defeat. Holding on to a number of strategically located fortified stockades in the jungles, avoiding open battle against the larger Chinese armies, and aggressively and incessantly raiding the Chinese lines of communication, they soon had the Chinese armies cut up into several segments and isolated in north-central Burma. As a result of heavy casualties, of their inability to come to grips with the elusive Burmese in the jungles, and of losses from disease and starvation, the Chinese asked for terms. Burmese General **Maha Thihathura,** realizing that, if the war continued, China had inexhaustible supplies of man power, granted terms to the Chinese, who withdrew.

COMMENT. *This was one of the most glorious episodes of Burmese military history.*

1768–1776. Defeat in Siam. Exhausted by the struggle with the Chinese, and unable to follow an effective and consistent policy in Siam, the Burmese were being expelled from Siam by **P'ya Taksin** (see below).

1770. Invasion of Manipur. Maha Thihathura and other Burmese leaders, to divert the king's mind from foolhardy operations against the Siamese or Chinese, and fearful of execution if they tried to reason with him, diverted their armies into operations against a minor foe.

1775–1776. War with Siam. (**See below.**)

1782–1819. Reign of Bodawpaya (Youngest Son of Alaungpaya). He gained the throne after a violent struggle with several other rivals.

1784–1785. Conquest of Arakan.

1785–1792. Renewed War with Siam. A Burmese invasion (1785–1786) was generally unsuccessful, probably largely due to the utterly incompetent leadership of the king. Burma did, however, annex the regions of Tavoy and Tenasserim after sporadic border warfare.

SIAM

1760. Alaungpaya's Invasion. (**See p. 702.**)

1764. Burmese Invasion of Southern Siam. General P'ya Taksin finally halted the invasion at **P'etchaburi,** but only after most of the Malay Peninsula provinces of Siam had been overrun.

1764–1767. Burmese Invasion of Central Siam. This resulted in the capture and destruction of Ayuthia (see p. 702). P'ya Taksin, however, had been able to fight his way through the Burmese besieging lines with a few troops, and escaped southward to raise a new army.

1767–1768. Burmese Ejected from Central Siam. P'ya Taksin assumed the throne. The country, however, was in turmoil, with two other claimants to royal power; at the same time the Burmese were planning to invade the country again, and trouble with Vietnam was brewing in Cambodia, an area which had long been under Siamese suzerainty.

1769. Repulse at Chiengmai. P'ya Taksin failed in an effort to win the region back from Burma. He was, however, able to defeat his 2 major rivals and to secure his rule over the nation.

1770–1773. Operations in Cambodia. The fortunes of war fluctuated widely. The Siamese defeated a Vietnamese-supported puppet ruler and regained full control of Cambodia.

1775–1776. Renewed War with Burma. P'ya Taksin reconquered Chiengmai (1775). He then repulsed an attempted Burmese invasion (1776).

1778. Invasion of Laos. The Siamese seized Vientiane, which recognized Siamese suzerainty.

1780–1782. Intervention in Vietnam. This ended with the death of P'ya Taksin (see below).

1782. Death of P'ya Taksin. He had become insane, and was killed in an uprising. General **Chakri** took the throne as King **Rama I** (1782–1809). He founded the modern city of Bangkok as his capital.

1785–1792. Sporadic Warfare with Burma. (**See above.**)

VIETNAM

1755–1760. Expansion in Cambodia. The Khmer, their Siamese allies occupied with a struggle against Burma, were helpless against the Vietnamese aggressors.

1769–1773. War with Siam over Cambodia. After initial success, the Vietnamese were driven out.

1773–1801. Civil War. Long and complicated, it resulted in the elimination of the Trinh family and a briefly emergent Tay Son family, with **Nguyen Anh** eventually victorious and assuming the imperial title of **Gia Long** at the capital of Hué (1802).

During this struggle, Nguyen Anh received considerable assistance from Siam, with the result that Siamese control over Cambodia was strengthened and Siamese influence became a political issue in Vietnam.

CAMBODIA

Cambodia, as we have seen, was essentially simply a football to the conflicting ambitions of Siam and Vietnam.

LAOS

Laos, divided into the 2 principalities of Luang Prabang and Vientiane, was a pawn in the great struggle between Burma and Siam. Dominated at first by Burma as a result of the victories of Alaungpaya and his successors, toward the end of the century the 2 principalities of Laos were generally under Siamese control, though some southeastern regions were under strong Vietnamese influence.

MALAYA AND INDONESIA

There were no significant military activities in Malaya or Indonesia during this period. The Dutch-English trade rivalry continued, with the Dutch consolidating their hold on most of Indonesia, save for strong British influence in Borneo; at the same time, the English established a foothold in Malaya at Penang (1771) to initiate a challenge to the powerful Dutch position in the peninsula.

The conquest of the Netherlands by France in 1795, during the War of the First Coalition (see p. 682), gave Britain an opportunity to break the Dutch trade monopoly in this area. At the "request" of the Dutch government in exile, England took Cape Colony (the important Dutch base at the top of Africa, controlling the southwest approach to the Indian Ocean), Ceylon (the main intermediate base), all the Dutch posts in India and on the west coast of Sumatra, the Spice Islands, and Malacca. A solemn promise was made to return these to the rightful Dutch government when peace was made.

EAST AND CENTRAL ASIA

CHINA

1736–1796. Reign of Ch'ien Lung (or Kao Tsung). Under this able and energetic emperor, the Manchu Empire reached its greatest geographical extent and the zenith of its power. In particular, imperial Chinese control of Central Asia was tightened.

1751. Invasion of Tibet. Tibet, nominally under Chinese control since 1662, had revolted (1750). Ch'ien Lung sent an invasion force which quickly captured Lhasa and forced the Dalai Lama to submit to even stricter Chinese control.

1755–1757. Mongol Revolt in the Ili Valley. This was promptly suppressed by General **Chao Hui,** who seized this opportunity to strengthen over-all Chinese control over western Mongolia.

1758–1759. Conquest of Kashgaria. Chao Hui now turned southwestward to establish Chinese control once more over the Tarim Basin and the surrounding regions. Sinkiang was now organized as a Chinese province.

1774–1797. Minor Rebellions. These plagued the latter years of the reign of Emperor Ch'ien Lung. All were quickly suppressed, but they presaged a general weakening of powei of the Ch'ing Dynasty. These revolts were in Shantung (1774), Kansu (1781 and 1784), Formosa (1786–1787), and Hunan and Kweichow (1795–1797).

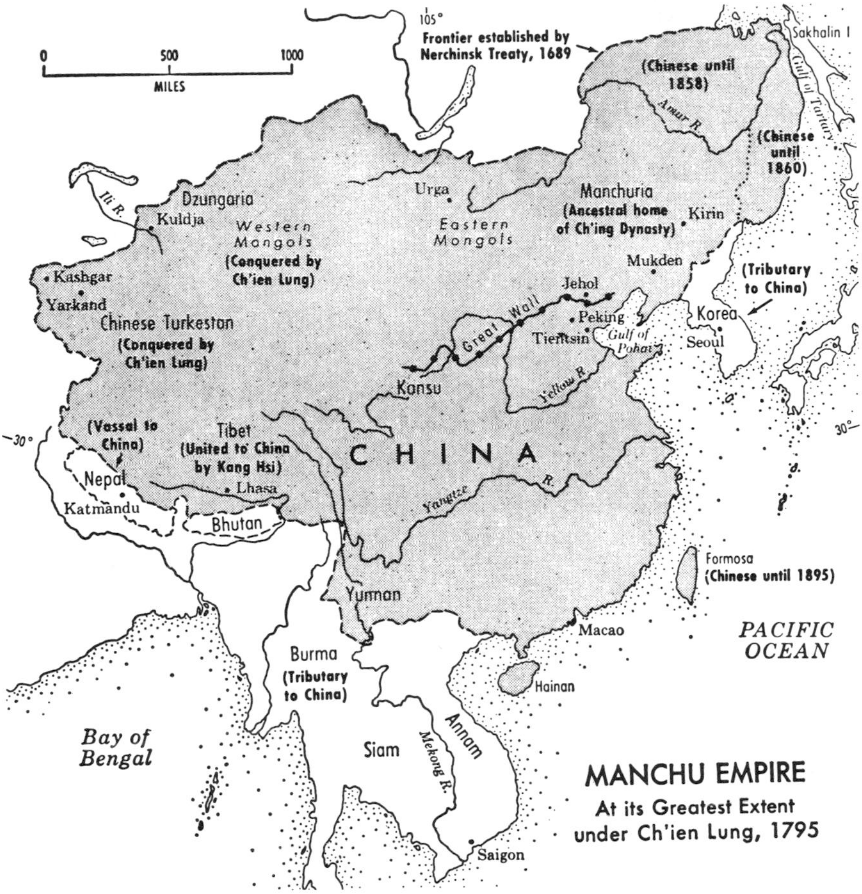

MANCHU EMPIRE
At its Greatest Extent
under Ch'ien Lung, 1795

KOREA AND JAPAN

This was a period of relative peace and prosperity in both of these isolated East Asiatic kingdoms. No military operations of any significance took place.

NORTH AMERICA

FRENCH AND INDIAN WAR, 1754–1763

1754, February–July. Fort Necessity Campaign. Alarmed by increasing French influx from Canada into the Ohio Valley, Lieutenant Governor **Robert Dinwiddie** of Virginia sent Lieutenant Colonel **George Washington** with a detachment of Virginia militia to construct a fort at the confluence of the Allegheny and Monongahela rivers (present Pittsburgh). Finding the French had already erected Fort Duquesne on this site, Washington built Fort Necessity at Great Meadows (near modern Uniontown, Pa.). Here he was attacked by the French. After vigorous resistance, he was forced to capitulate to superior numbers (July 3). He was allowed to march out with the honors of war.

1755, April 14. Arrival of Major General Edward Braddock in Virginia. The new commander in chief in America brought 2 British regiments. A conference with several provincial governors resulted in a plan to attack the French with 4 separate expeditions. Braddock himself, with 1,400 regulars and 450 colonials, moved to attack Fort Duquesne and to establish British control of the Ohio basin.

1755, June. Arrival of French Reinforcements. A French fleet slipped into the St. Lawrence past the blockade of Admiral **Edward Boscawen.**

1755, June. Bay of Fundy Expedition. From Boston, a provincial force accompanied by a few English regulars, under Colonels **Robert Monckton** and **John Winslow,** sailed into the Bay of Fundy, capturing Forts St. John and Beausejour (June 19). All the Fundy area was soon in British hands (June 30). The French Acadians were cruelly exiled (October).

1755, July 9. Battle of the Monongahela. As his force approached Fort Duquesne, Braddock was surprised and routed by 900 French and Indians. He was killed with more than half of his force. Washington, who accompanied the expedition as a volunteer, helped to lead the remnants back to Virginia. The rigid linear formations of European warfare had succumbed to the elusive individualism of wilderness combat.

1755, August–September. Crown Point Expeditions. A force of 3,500 provincials and 300 Indians advanced from Albany toward Crown Point under **William Johnson,** a civilian with wide influence among the Indian tribes, commissioned a brigadier general. A mixed force of 2,000 French regulars, Canadians, and Indians under Baron **Ludwig A. Dieskau** simultaneously moved up the Richelieu River to defend Crown Point. The 2 forces met at the head of Lake George.

1755, September 8. Battle of Lake George. Dieskau was defeated and captured, but Johnson, plagued by militia discontent, contented himself with building Fort William Henry; he left a small garrison there and the remainder of his force dispersed to their homes. The French entrenched themselves at Ticonderoga.

1755, August–September. Expedition against Fort Niagara. Governor **William Shirley** of Massachusetts, who had replaced Braddock in command, marched with 1,500 men up the Mohawk Valley to Oswego. There Shirley decided the task was too great against French reinforcements, and returned to Albany.

1755–1756. Establishment of the Royal Americans. Spurred by Braddock's defeat, the British War Office took steps to meet the tactical situation imposed by wilderness warfare. A 4-battalion regiment of light infantry was authorized (1755). At Governors Island, N.Y., the Royal Americans (now the King's Royal Rifle Corps)—actually composed of equal parts of German-American settlers and Germans recruited abroad—began light-infantry training (1756). Many of the officers were soldiers of fortune.

1756. Seven Years' War Begins in Europe. **(See p. 667.)**

1756, May 11. Arrival of Marquis Louis Joseph de Montcalm. The new commander of all French forces in Canada brought reinforcements.

1756, July 23. Arrival of General John Campbell (Earl of Loudoun). He was appointed to the command in North America.

1756, August. Montcalm Takes the Offensive. He crossed Lake Ontario and captured Oswego, destroying the settlement. Returning to Montreal, he took station finally at Ticonderoga with a force of 5,000 regulars and militia. Loudoun, who had 10,000 men between Albany and Lake George, made no offensive move.

1756–1757. Winter Quarters. The regulars on both sides withdrew, leaving garrisons at Forts Ticonderoga and William Henry, respectively. The provincial militiamen went home.

1757, June–September. Expedition against Louisbourg. Loudoun arrived at Halifax to meet a British squadron which would take part in the expedition (June 30) only to learn that Louisbourg had been strongly reinforced and a French fleet was in the harbor. The British blockading squadron, under Admiral **Francis Holborne,** was scattered by a storm and the expedition abandoned (September 24). Loudoun's 12,000 troops returned to New York.

1757, August 9. Massacre at Fort William Henry. Montcalm, taking advantage of the absence of the British troops, had meanwhile moved from Ticonderoga with 4,000 troops and 1,000 Indians to besiege and capture Fort William Henry. The garrison, under Colonel **Monro,** marching out with the honors of war, was treacherously attacked by Montcalm's Indians and many were killed. Content with destroying the fort, Montcalm withdrew, and both sides went into winter quarters.

1757–1758. British Plans. The British government, now headed by **William Pitt,** decided to make a major effort to eliminate France from North America. General **James Abercrombie** arrived to replace ineffective Loudoun (December 30). General **Jeffrey Amherst** soon followed (February 19) with troops to take Louisbourg. Abercrombie was directed also to attack Forts Ticonderoga and Duquesne.

1758, May 30–July 27. Louisbourg Expedition. Amherst with young Brigadier General **James Wolfe** took 9,000 British regulars and 500 colonials from Halifax to Louisbourg, escorted by Admiral Boscawen's squadron. Twelve French sail of the line were shut up in the harbor, while the troops invested the fortress (June 2). It surrendered (July 27) after considerable fighting. Wolfe particularly distinguished himself.

1758, July 8. Battle of Fort Ticonderoga. Abercrombie, with 12,000 men, 6,000 being British regulars, moved from Lake George (late June) to attack Fort Ticonderoga. Montcalm, with but 3,000, defended a ridge in front of the fort. Abercrombie's frontal attack was repulsed with the loss of some 1,600 men killed or wounded. He withdrew. He was later relieved and replaced by Amherst (September 18).

1758, July–November. Fort Duquesne Expedition. Brigadier General **John Forbes,** retracing Braddock's steps, cut a road through the Blue Ridge and after some hard fighting advanced upon Fort Duquesne, which the French blew up and abandoned (November 24). Backbone of Forbes's force was a battalion of the Royal Americans, under Major **Henri Bouquet,** Swiss soldier of fortune in British service. The former French post now became Fort Pitt. Forbes's operations were methodical and efficient, Bouquet's new system of light-infantry tactics in extended order and rapid deployment proved its worth, and Colonel George Washington, who commanded a Virginia regiment, assisted in planning the campaign.

1758, August 27. Capture of Fort Frontenac. This fortress (modern Kingston) at the entrance to the St. Lawrence, on Lake Ontario, was captured by a provincial force under Colonel **John Bradstreet** which marched up the Mohawk.

1758–1759. French Situation. The year ended with the French hard-pressed on both flanks of their North American colony, but clinging firmly to Ticonderoga in the center.

1759. Pitt's Plan. He ordered a 3-pronged campaign to drive the French out of Canada: (1) capture of Fort Niagara to cut western Canada off from the St. Lawrence, (2) an offensive through the Champlain Valley to the St. Lawrence, and (3) an amphibious assault against Quebec.

1759, June–July. Fort Niagara Operations. Brigadier General **John Prideaux** with 2,000 British regulars marched up the Mohawk Valley, reoccupied Oswego and, moving by water on Lake Ontario, captured Fort Niagara (July 25). Prideaux was killed during the siege.

1759, June–July. Ticonderoga Campaign. Amherst, commanding 11,000 regulars and provincials, captured Ticonderoga (July 26) and Crown Point (July 31), where he spent the winter.

1759, June–September. Quebec Campaign. Wolfe, young military perfectionist, with some 9,000 men, escorted by Admiral **Charles Saunders'** squadron, departed from Louisbourg to disembark on Orléans Island, just below Quebec (June 26). Montcalm, with some 14,000 troops and some Indians, defended an almost impregnable fortress, standing high above the St. Lawrence River. For 2 months all Wolfe's efforts to gain a foothold were foiled. Admiral Saunders, fearing that his ships might be caught in winter ice, threatened to leave. Then a footpath winding up the precipitous cliffs just north of the city was discovered. Wolfe sent his 1 battalion of provincial rangers (light infantry), under Colonel **William Howe,** followed by 4 regular battalions, up this path during the night of September 12. They gained the plateau above, and the main body followed. By dawn Wolfe's command—4,800 strong—was in line of battle in front of the city.

1759, September 13. Battle of the Plains of Abraham. Montcalm attacked at once. He had about 4,500 men, but lacked artillery—**Pierre François de Vaudreuil,** the French governor, would not release guns to him. Excellent British musketry threw the French back into the city. Both commanders were mortally wounded. Wolfe died during the battle, Montcalm that night. Quebec capitulated (September 18), and the backbone of French resistance in Canada had been broken. Leaving a garrison in the city, the expedition sailed away.

1760, April. French Attack on Quebec. General **François G. de Lévis** led an expedition from Montreal. He invested Quebec, but the siege was broken by the timely arrival of a British naval squadron.

1760, September. Advance on Montreal. Three columns converged: Amherst, moving down the St. Lawrence from Oswego, Colonel **William Haviland** from Crown Point down the Richelieu, and Brigadier General **James Murray,** with the Quebec command, up the St. Lawrence.

1760, September 8. Surrender of Canada. Governor Vaudreuil capitulated, ending French dominion of Canada.

1762, January–February. British Conquest of Martinique. The island was captured by Admiral George Rodney.

COMMENT. *The effects of the French and Indian War upon British infantry tactics and techniques were enormous. The colonists' successful combination of discipline and loose-knit Indian fighting impressed the English soldiers. The Royal American Regiment under its 2 Swiss-born battalion commanders, Henri Bouquet and* **Frederick Haldimand,** *showed its efficiency during all the campaigns after 1756; Colonel* **Robert Rogers** *of Connecticut, whose battalion of Rangers became a component of the British Army in America, and Howe at Quebec further proved the worth of disciplined light infantry.*

1763, February 10. Treaty of Paris. **(See p. 677.)**

PRE-REVOLUTION, 1763–1774

1763, May 23–November 28. Pontiac's Rebellion. Unhappy over the substitution of British control for French along the northwestern frontier, and fearful of a growing influx of settlers, the Indian tribes became restless, then went on the warpath. **Pontiac,** chief of the Ottawa, after a surprise attack upon Detroit failed, destroyed nearly every other British fort west of the Niagara except Fort Pitt.

1763, August 4–6. Battle of Bushy Run. Colonel Bouquet, moving to Fort Pitt from Carlisle, Pa., with a relief expedition composed of his Royal Americans, the Black Watch (42nd Foot), and other light companies, 500 men, was surprised as Braddock had been in 1755. He formed a circle about his train, where the troops lay all night. Next morning Bouquet enticed the Indians to attack, then cleverly fell on their flank and routed them. Fort Pitt was relieved (August 10). Pontiac, abandoning the siegē of Detroit, later submitted to British authority.

1769–1807. Yankee-Pennamite Wars. Connecticut's claim to transcontinental dominion "from sea to sea" led to bitter strife between Connecticut and Pennsylvania settlers in the Wyoming Valley of the Susquehanna River. Drafting of Connecticut settlers for the Revolutionary War so depleted manpower that the settlement fell easy prey in 1778 to a bloody massacre by New York Tories (see p. 716). Sporadic bickering continued until 1807. (See p. 725.)

1770–1774. Growing Violence and Unrest. Colonial resentment of royal rule led to repressive measures by British troops in the so-called **"Battle of Golden Hill"** in New York and the **"Boston Massacre"** (January, March, 1770). The "Boston Tea Party" (December 16, 1773), caused Parliament to put Boston under military rule. To unify colonial reaction and protest against this and other "intolerable" acts, the 1st Continental Congress met at Philadelphia (September 5–October 26, 1774).

1771. Uprising in Western North Carolina. A group of frontier settlers, calling themselves "Regulators," defied royal rule. Governor **William Tryon** sent a force of militia which suppressed the rebellion at **Alamance Creek** (May 16).

1774. Lord Dunmore's War. Governor **John Murray, Earl of Dunmore,** of Virginia, sent a force of militia under General **Andrew Lewis** to suppress a Shawnee uprising on the Virginia-Kentucky frontier. A contingent from the Watauga Association, from the area where Virginia, North Carolina, and Tennessee now meet, took part in this campaign. The Indians made peace after Lewis won a decisive victory at **Point Pleasant** (mouth of Great Kanahwa; October 10).

WAR OF THE AMERICAN REVOLUTION, 1775–1783

The War on Land, 1775–1776

1775, April 19. Lexington and Concord. Long-standing and ever-increasing differences between the thirteen colonies and the motherland flamed into open rebellion when General **Thomas Gage,** governor of Massachusetts, sent 700 men from the British garrison in Boston (April 18) to capture arms and ammunition gathered by the colonists at Concord. Forewarned by the "midnight ride" of **Paul Revere, William Dawes,** and Dr. **Samuel Prescott,** "minute companies" of militia began gathering. The British advance guard under Major **John Pitcairn** met Captain **John Parker**'s company of 70 men assembled on Lexington Common. The "shot heard 'round the world"* (no one knows who fired it) brought British volleys. The Americans scattered, leaving 8 men dead and 10 wounded. Proceeding to Concord, the British found most of the supplies removed, but they destroyed what remained. Harassed all the way back to Boston by swarms of militiamen, British losses were 73 killed, 174 wounded and 26 missing; in all, 93 Americans were killed, wounded, or missing.

1775–1776. Siege of Boston. The Massachusetts Provincial Congress authorized the raising of 13,600 militia, Major General **Artemas Ward** to command. Calls for assistance were answered by Rhode Island, Connecticut, and New Hampshire. Boston and its British garrison were besieged by some 15,000 colonists.

1775, May 10. Capture of Ticonderoga. Colonel **Benedict Arnold** was authorized to attack the fort on Lake Champlain. Colonel **Ethan Allen** of Vermont with his Green Mountain Boys, refusing to accept Arnold's command, captured the post by surprise (May 10). Arnold accompanied the expedition. Crown Point was soon captured (May 12).

1775, June 12. Seizure of the *Margaretta*. At Machias Bay, Me., a party of lumbermen led by **Jeremiah O'Brien** captured the British armed cutter *Margaretta,* the first naval action of the war.

1775, June 15. Washington Commands an Army. The 2nd Continental Congress at Philadelphia (since May 10), accepting the colonial forces besieging Boston as a Continental Army, authorized the raising of 6 companies of riflemen and commissioned Colonel George Washington of Virginia as a general, to command the whole. He started north on June 23.

1775, June 17. Battle of Bunker Hill. Gage had been reinforced (May 25) by British troops from overseas; with them came Generals **John Burgoyne, William Howe,** and **Henry Clinton.** The garrison of 7,000 was sufficient to hold the city but too few to attack the besiegers. The Massachusetts Committee of Safety ordered Ward (June 15) to fortify Bunker (Bunker's) Hill on Charlestown Heights overlooking Boston Harbor. Next night 1,200 men under Colonel **William Prescott** occupied not Bunker Hill but Breed's Hill, a lower and more vulnerable eminence, and threw up an earthen fort. Gage responded at dawn by a naval bombardment and an amphibious attack. Howe, crossing the bay with a picked force of 2,200 men, was twice repelled. A third assault, with fixed bayonets, was successful when the defenders' ammunition gave out. The affair, badly mismanaged by the Americans, was distinguished by gallantry on both sides. The British lost practically half of their strength; of less than 1,500 colonials actually engaged, 140 were killed, 271 wounded, and 30 captured.

COMMENT. *Tactically a British victory, the result left the local situation unchanged. But psychologically the effect on the colonies was tremendous; Americans had met British regulars in battle and had been defeated only when their ammunition was exhausted. The significance of the earthworks was largely overlooked.*

1775, July 3. Birth of the Continental Army. Washington, on Cambridge Common, assumed command of all Continental forces and began the stupendous job of transforming an armed rabble into an army while maintaining the siege of Boston throughout the remainder of the year.

NORTHERN CAMPAIGN; EXPEDITIONS AGAINST CANADA

1775, August–November. Operations against Montreal. General **Philip Schuyler,** with 1,000 men, invaded Canada from Ticonderoga, laying siege to St. Johns on the Richelieu River (September 6); falling ill, he was replaced (September 13) by General **Richard Montgomery.** St. Johns's 600 defenders capitulated (November 2).

* Poetically, Emerson attributes this to Concord.

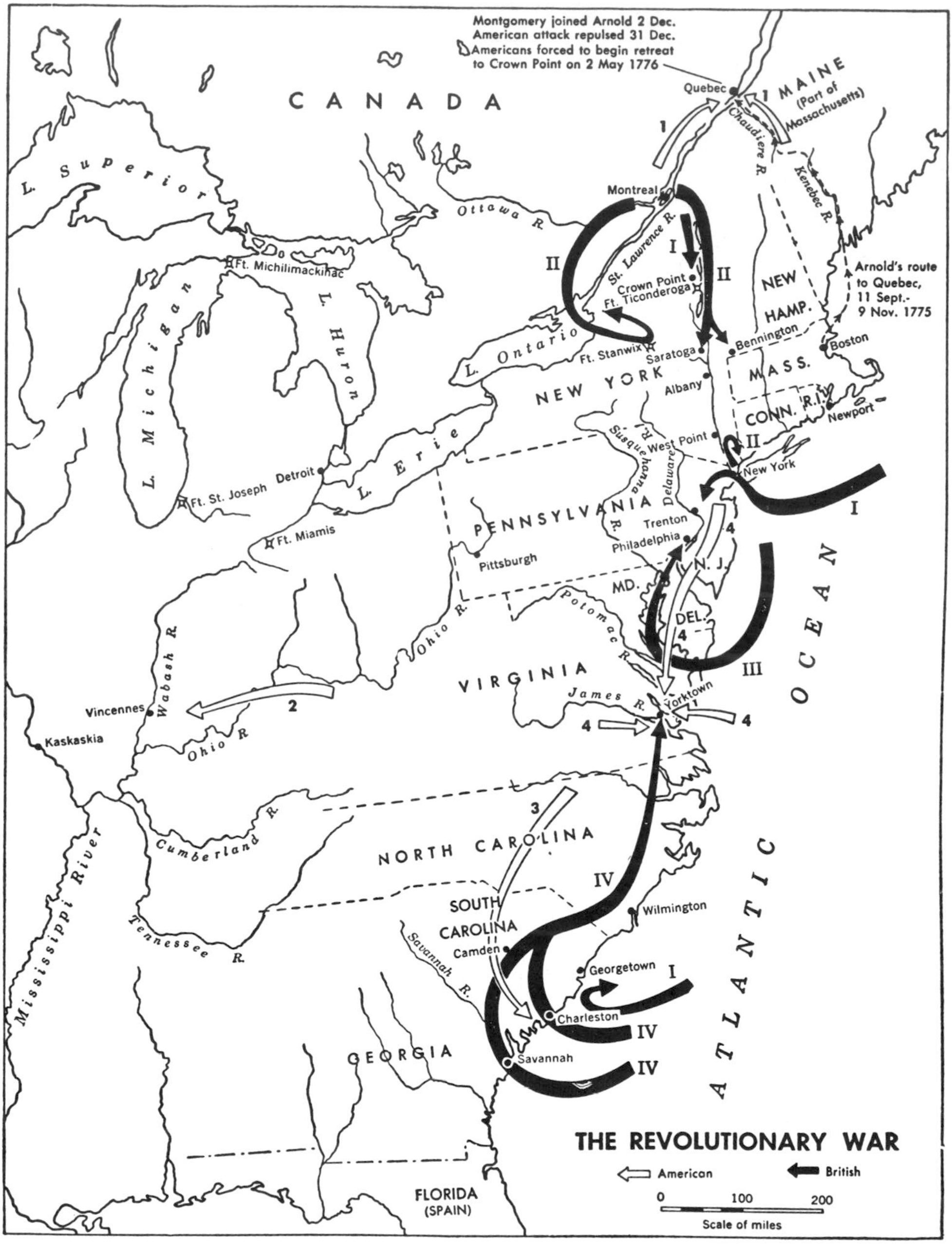

American Offensives

(1) 1775—Invasion of Canada by Montgomery and Arnold

(2) 1779—Clark in the West

(3) 1781—Greene in the South

(4) 1781—Yorktown Campaign

British Offensives

(I) 1776—Three-pronged offensive: Lake Champlain, New York, Charleston

(II) 1777—Converging drives on Albany by Burgoyne, St. Leger, Clinton

(III) 1777—Howe's offensive to Philadelphia

(IV) 1780–1781—Invasion of South by Clinton and Cornwallis

Meanwhile a harebrained attempt by Ethan Allen to capture Montreal was repulsed and Allen captured. Montgomery pushed on to Montreal, occupying it (November 13) and capturing a British river flotilla. Sir **Guy Carleton,** British governor general of Canada, withdrew to Quebec.

1775, September–December. Arnold's Expedition to Quebec. With Washington's approval, Arnold and 1,100 volunteers left Cambridge (September 12). After an amazing autumn march through the freezing Maine wilderness, the expedition arrived on the St. Lawrence, opposite Quebec (November 8). Only 600 men completed the trek. Crossing the river (November 13), Arnold was joined by Montgomery from Montreal with 300 men (December 3). Montgomery took command.

1775, December 31. Assault on Quebec. Attacking under cover of a driving snowstorm, the Americans were disastrously repulsed by Carleton's 1,800-man garrison. Montgomery was killed, Arnold wounded; nearly 100 Americans were killed or wounded and 300 more captured.

1776, January–May. Retreat to Montreal. The survivors, still under Arnold's command, maintained a tenuous hold outside the city for the next 5 months, but retired to Montreal upon the arrival from England (May 6) of General Burgoyne with British and German reinforcements for Carleton. General **John Sullivan,** now commanding the Americans, received additional troops from General Washington and attempted a counterstroke to stabilize conditions on the upper St. Lawrence.

1776, June 8. Trois Rivières. American General **William Thompson,** with 2,000 men, discovered that instead of a supposed garrison of 600, Burgoyne's 8,000 were concentrating there. The Americans were completely dispersed.

1776, June–July. Retreat from Canada. Sullivan, abandoning Montreal, hastily retired first to Crown Point and then to Ticonderoga. Both sides now occupied themselves with extemporizing naval forces to dispute possession of Lake Champlain as Carleton prepared to march into New York.

1776, October 11. Battle of Valcour Island. The makeshift flotilla built and manned by American soldiers through Benedict Arnold's efforts was attacked by Carleton's flotilla—also makeshift, but manned by sailors drafted from the transports which had carried Burgoyne's troops, and more heavily armed. Most of the American vessels were destroyed or crippled. Arnold slipped away in the night with the remainder, but at Split Rock (October 13) Carleton's ships caught up and destroyed them. The American flotilla had, however, served its purpose, delaying Carleton's advance for so long that after occupying Crown Point briefly he postponed further advance and withdrew into Canada.

CENTRAL CAMPAIGN; NEW YORK AND THE JERSEYS

1776, March 17. Evacuation of Boston. Threatened by the growing strength of Washington's army (20,000 Continentals, 6,000 militia, and heavy ordnance dragged from Ticonderoga), Howe, now commanding at Boston, evacuated the city, sailing to Halifax. Washington shortly began transferring his forces to New York as the most likely place for the next British move.

1776. French and Spanish Assistance. Louis XVI of France authorized the supplying of munitions to the Americans; **Charles III** of Spain followed suit.

1776, April. British Plans. The British government decided to take the offensive and crush the revolution. General Howe was to sail to New York from Halifax with considerable reinforcement from England under escort of a fleet commanded by his brother, Admiral **Richard Howe.**

1776, July 4. Declaration of Independence.

1776, July–August. Concentrations Near New York. After arriving off New York Harbor (July 2), Howe landed his 32,000 men on Staten Island. These included 9,000 Hessian mercenaries. Washington, instructed by the Congress to hold New York, attempted to guard against attack by land or water or both. Earthworks were thrown up across Brooklyn Heights and batteries manned on lower Manhattan and Governors Island. Half of Washington's army of 13,000, under General

Israel Putnam, was deployed across the Flatbush area of Long Island; the remainder held on Manhattan.

1776, August 27. Battle of Long Island. Howe, landing 20,000 men on Long Island (August 22–25), skillfully turned Putnam's left flank. The Americans were thrown back into Brooklyn Heights with losses of 200 killed and nearly 1,000 captured. British casualties were 400. While Howe slowly approached the Brooklyn Heights line, Washington evacuated Long Island in a brilliant operation (August 29–30).

1776, September 6–7. The "American Turtle." Sergeant **Ezra Lee** in **David Bushnell**'s 1-man submarine attacked the British fleet off Staten Island. Though unsuccessful, he created much alarm. This was the first use of the submarine in war.

1776, September 12. The Americans Abandon New York.

1776, September 12. Washington Decides to Abandon New York.

1776, September 15. Action at Kip's Bay. American troops fled as British troops assaulted across the East River from Brooklyn.

1776, September 16. Battle of Harlem Heights. Washington halted Howe's slow pursuit. But the British advance up the East River endangered Washington's communications and he fell back again.

1776, October 28. Battle of White Plains. After obstinate resistance the British regulars drove the Americans off the field.

1776, November 16–20. Forts Washington and Lee. Fort Washington on northern Manhattan, overlooking the Hudson, fell with the capture of 2,800 Americans. Fort Lee on the west bank was evacuated (November 20), with the loss of much badly needed materiel.

1776, November–December. Retreat through New Jersey. Washington with the bulk of his remaining troops retreated southward. General **Charles Lee,** left behind to cover the retreat, allowed himself and many of his 4,000 men to be captured near Morristown. Washington and the remaining 3,000 men of the Continental Army crossed the Delaware River into Pennsylvania. Congress, fleeing from Philadelphia to Baltimore (December 12), in desperation turned over dictatorial powers to Washington. Confident of a speedy conclusion, Howe went into winter quarters, the bulk of his army at New York with garrisons scattered in several sections of southern New Jersey.

1776, December 26. Battle of Trenton. Washington, whose little army was disintegrating as enlistments expired, took a desperate chance. Crossing the Delaware 9 miles north of Trenton with 2,400 men on Christmas night, during a snowstorm, at dawn he fell on the Hessian garrison at Trenton. His victory was complete. Of 1,400 Hessians, nearly 1,000 were captured and a great amount of booty—small arms, cannon, and other munitions—taken. Thirty Hessians, including their commander, Colonel **Johann Rall,** were killed. American losses were 2 men frozen to death and 5 more wounded. In immediate reaction, 8,000 British troops under Lord Cornwallis moved to box Washington's army between the Delaware River and the Atlantic Ocean.

1777, January 2. Confrontation at Trenton. Cornwallis faced the American position with 5,000 men, while behind him at Princeton, 12 miles away, were 2,500 more under orders to join. Cornwallis ordered an assault for the next day. Washington now had 1,600 regulars and 3,600 unreliable militia. Leaving his campfires burning, he slipped away to the eastward in the night over a disused road, behind Cornwallis.

1777, January 3. Battle of Princeton. Washington met and defeated British reinforcements advancing from Princeton, captured a large quantity of military stores in that town, and hastened away to Morristown before fuming Cornwallis could return from Trenton.

COMMENT. *Washington's outstanding personal leadership had in 10 short days fanned the dying embers of the Revolution into lively flame. Frederick the Great characterized these operations as one of the most brilliant campaigns in military history. With Washington now flanking their communications, all British garrisons in central and western New Jersey were evacuated.*

SOUTHERN CAMPAIGN; THE CAROLINAS

1775, December. Uprising in Virginia. After a minor engagement at **Great Bridge,** near Norfolk, Governor Dunmore fled to take refuge on a British warship.

1776, February 27. Battle of Moores Creek Bridge. A force of 1,100 North Carolina patriots defeated about 1,800 Tories marching toward Wilmington, where they had hoped to establish a British coastal base.

1776, June 4. Charleston Expedition. General Sir **Henry Clinton** with troops from Boston and reinforcements from England arrived off Charleston, S.C., after abandoning his plan to land at Wilmington as a result of the Battle of Moores Creek Bridge (see above). General Charles Lee had earlier been sent by Congress to organize the defense of the most important American port south of Philadelphia.

1776, June 28. Battle of Sullivan's Island. The palmetto-log fortification on this island was the key to the harbor defenses. Admiral Sir **Peter Parker**'s squadron, which had convoyed the British expedition, attacked the fort. But American artillery under Colonel **William Moultrie** did amazing damage to the British ships; the squadron withdrew and shortly afterward Clinton re-embarked his troops and left to join Howe at New York. (Rechristened Fort Moultrie, the island post so well defended was destined to further fame in the Civil War.) There would be no further operations by the regular British forces in the Carolinas for 2 years to come.

War at Sea, 1776–1777

1776, February 17. Bahamas Cruise. Commodore **Esek Hopkins** with a squadron of 6 small extemporized warships sailed from Philadelphia for the Bahamas. He attacked New Providence, sending a landing party ashore and capturing a quantity of cannon and powder (March 3–4). Hopkins returned to Providence, R.I., where the squadron remained for the rest of the year.

1776, March 23. Congress Authorizes Privateering. This became a profitable business throughout the war.

1776–1777. The New Navy Is Blockaded. Thirteen frigates authorized by Congress were building. However, the overwhelming strength of the Royal Navy dominated the entire eastern seaboard.

War on Land, 1777–1779

NORTHERN CAMPAIGN, 1777

1777. British Plans. They intended to seize the Hudson River Valley, thus splitting the colonies. Burgoyne was to move south from Canada via Lake Champlain, while Howe was to move north from New York, joining Burgoyne at Albany. A third column under Colonel **Barry St. Leger,** moving up the St. Lawrence to Lake Ontario, would land at Oswego and, in conjunction with Iroquois Indians and Tories under Sir **John Johnson,** sweep down the Mohawk Valley to unite with the others at Albany. While perhaps an attractive plan on the map, success was entirely dependent upon close coordination and timing, which would be most difficult to achieve under the circumstances of the time in the trackless forests of North America. Furthermore, the entire affair—originally conceived by Burgoyne—was bungled by Lord **George Germain** (see p. 673), who as secretary of state for the colonies in Lord **North**'s cabinet was in control of operations in America. There was no coordination. Burgoyne had been ordered to meet Howe, but Howe's operations were left to his own discretion. The results were disastrous to England.

1777, April 25. Danbury Raid. A British force under General William Tryon, Governor of New York, destroyed an American supply depot at Danbury, but was severely harassed by local militia gathered and led by General Benedict Arnold.

1777, July 5. Capture of Ticonderoga. Burgoyne, with 7,200 regulars—including 4,000 British and 3,200 Hessian-Brunswicker mercenaries—as well as a small number of Tories and Indians, reached Fort Ticonderoga July 1, emplacing his artillery on a dominating height. American General **Arthur St. Clair** evacuated the post the night of July 5–6, the 2,500 poorly armed and equipped Americans retreating into Vermont over a bridge spanning Lake Champlain; the sick and the baggage went by boat to Skenesboro (now Whitehall). Burgoyne pursued immediately, his main body up the lake, his advance corps over the road.

1777, July 7. Battle of Hubbardton. The American rear guard was overtaken and defeated; the baggage and supplies at Skenesboro captured. However, **Seth Warner**'s delaying action saved St. Clair's army. He fled to Rutland, thence south to join General Schuyler at Fort Edward.

1777, July–August. Burgoyne's Pursuit. He sent his heavy equipage from Ticonderoga via Lake George, but the Americans had completely devastated the rough roads southward, so that it took him 3 weeks to reach Fort Edward. By that time Schuyler had retreated to Stillwater. The American forces had been strengthened to some 3,000 Continentals and 1,600 militia, and Washington had also sent Generals Benedict Arnold and **Benjamin Lincoln** to assist Schuyler as well as Colonel **Daniel Morgan**'s rifle regiment.

1777, August 3. Burgoyne Learns of Howe's Nonparticipation. Howe was bound south, hunting Washington. Burgoyne decided to strike on for Albany anyway, hoping to meet St. Leger there.

1777, July 25–August 25. St. Leger on the Mohawk. Arriving at Oswego, St. Leger, with 875 British, Tory, and Hessian troops and 1,000 Iroquois under **Joseph Brant,** invested Fort Stanwix (also called Fort Schuyler) on the present site of Rome, N.Y., garrisoned by 750 Continentals and militia. General **Nicholas Herkimer** of the county militia hurried to the rescue with 800 men.

1777, August 6. Battle of Oriskany. Herkimer was ambushed by Brant with Indians and Tories 6 miles from the fort. The Americans successfully fought off the attack, but Herkimer was mortally wounded; having lost nearly half its strength, the relief column retreated. While the action was on, a sortie from the fort ravaged St. Leger's camp. The siege was resumed. At Stillwater, Schuyler, with Burgoyne only 24 miles away, detached 1,000 volunteers under Arnold to relieve the fort.

1777, August 16. Battle of Bennington. Burgoyne, short of supplies, meanwhile had sent 700 Brunswickers under Colonel **Friedrich Baum** to capture military stores at Bennington, and to scour the countryside for horses. Colonel **John Stark,** with 2,000 New Hampshire, Vermont, and Massachusetts militiamen, surrounded Baum and destroyed his force. Reinforcements for Baum, 650 Brunswickers under Colonel **Heinrich von Breymann,** arriving later that day, were defeated by Stark and Seth Warner's 400 Green Mountain Boys, who had made a forced march from Manchester. Breymann escaped with less than two-thirds of his force. British casualties were 207 dead and 700 captured; the Americans lost 30 killed and 40 wounded. Much-needed small arms, cannon, and wagons were captured.

1777, August 23. Relief of Fort Stanwix. St. Leger's Indians were put in panic through a ruse, and he abandoned the siege before Arnold's arrival, leaving behind him tents, cannon, and stores as he retreated precipitately to Oswego.

1777, September 13. Burgoyne Crosses the Hudson Near Saratoga. Having reached the point of no return, he crossed to attack the American forces entrenched on Bemis Heights, with General **Horatio Gates** now in command. Burgoyne also sent an urgent call for help to General Clinton in New York, commanding in Howe's absence.

1777, September 19. Battle of Freeman's Farm. Burgoyne's attack on the American left was repulsed with 600 casualties; American losses were 300. Arnold, who distinguished himself, requested reinforcements to counterattack, but these were refused by Gates.

1777, October 3. Clinton's Gesture. Down in New York, Clinton, with 7,000 remaining British and Germans, took 4,000 men up the Hudson, capturing Forts Clinton and Montgomery in the highlands (October 6). Satisfied that he had created a diversion helpful to Burgoyne, Clinton then returned to New York after his ships had burned Esopus (Kingston, New York).

1777, October 7. Battle of Bemis Heights. Burgoyne, who had entrenched in the hope that Clinton would come to his help, made one last desperate attempt to turn the American left. Arnold, who had been deprived of command by Gates, nevertheless led an American counterattack which drove the British back against the river with loss of 600 men to the Americans' 150. Morgan's riflemen played a leading part in the victory. Withdrawing toward Saratoga, Burgoyne was soon surrounded by a force thrice his remaining strength of 5,700.

1777, October 17. Burgoyne's Surrender.

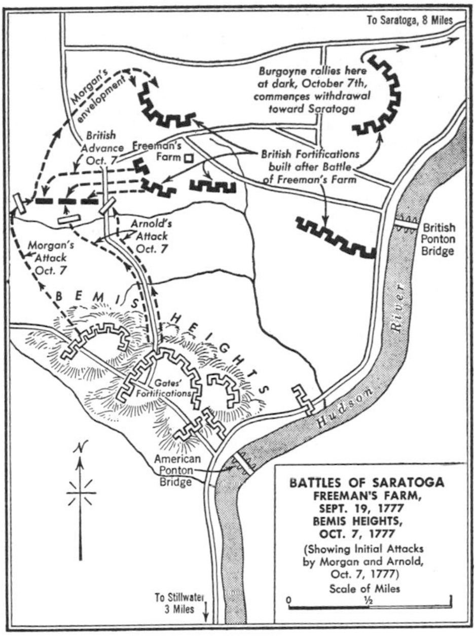

By the terms of the "Convention of Saratoga," the disarmed British army was to be marched to Boston and shipped to England on parole. These terms were later shamefully repudiated by the American Congress; the British and German soldiers were not permitted to return home.

COMMENT. *The Saratoga victory was the turning point in the Revolution. To the American people it more than balanced the reverses of the central campaign related below. British forces were redistributed. Ticonderoga and Crown Point were evacuated; Clinton abandoned the Hudson highlands. The British held only New York City, part of Rhode Island, and Philadelphia. Overseas, France recognized the independence of the United States, a forerunner of her active participation in the war.*

CENTRAL CAMPAIGN, 1777–1778

1777. Maneuvers in New Jersey. Spring and early summer were taken up by fruitless maneuvers as Howe attempted to coax Washington into battle.

1777, July 23. Howe Sails from New York. He took some 18,000 men in transports. Washington, puzzled and anxious about Burgoyne's expedition in the north, detached Arnold and Morgan with reinforcements to Schuyler, but held his army north of the Delaware until he received word that Howe's expedition had sailed up Chesapeake Bay and was landing (August 25) at the Head of Elk (Elkton). Washington, with 10,500 men, then barred the way to Philadelphia on the east bank of Brandywine Creek. Howe advanced, brushing aside light American resistance at **Cooch's Bridge** (south of Wilmington; September 2).

1777, September 11. Battle of the Brandywine. Howe skillfully turned the American right, forcing Washington back toward Philadelphia with losses of 1,000 men; the British lost 576.

1777, September 21. Action at Paoli. A surprise British night attack routed the brigade of General **Anthony Wayne.** Philadelphia was evacuated, the Congress fleeing to Lancaster and then to York. Again it left dictatorial powers to Washington.

1777, September 26. Howe Occupies Philadelphia. With the assistance of his brother's fleet he cleared the Delaware River as a supply route despite the desperate and gallant American defense of **Forts Mifflin** and **Mercer** (October 22–November 20).

1777, September 25–December 23. Conway Cabal. Colonel **Thomas Conway,** Irish soldier of fortune who left the French service to join the Americans, attempted to stir congressional dissatisfaction with the direction of the war into the elevation of Gates over Washington. Unsuccessful, Conway resigned (December 23).

1777, October 4. Battle of Germantown. Washington, reinforced to a strength of 13,000, attempted a complicated movement against Howe's main encampment at Germantown, but through the blunders of his officers was defeated, incurring 700 casualties and losing 400 prisoners.

1777–1778. Ordeal at Valley Forge. The American army spent an agonizing winter, while the British enjoyed the comforts of Philadelphia.

1778, January–June. The Impact of Baron Augustus H. F. von Steuben. This German volunteer instilled discipline and tactical skill in the remnants of the starving little Continental Army at Valley Forge.

1778, February 6. Franco-American Alliance. Two treaties were signed: one of amity and commerce, the other an alliance effective if and when war broke out between France and England.

1778, June 17. Outbreak of War between France and England.

1778, June 18. British Evacuation of Philadelphia. Sir Henry Clinton, succeeding to command from Howe, removed his 13,000 troops over land toward New York, intending to institute a more vigorous campaign. Washington's army, recruited to equal strength and hardened by von Steuben's training, followed by a more northern road, seeking a chance to give battle under favorable circumstances.

1778, June 28. Battle of Monmouth. On Washington's orders General Charles Lee,* heading the American advance guard, moved toward Clinton's rear guard, but at a critical moment fell back, throwing the army into confusion. Clinton turned to give battle. Washington's personal leadership rallied his army, repulsing repeated British attacks. An all-day fight in intense heat finished with both armies bivouacking on the field, but during the night Clinton hurriedly withdrew. Reported losses were about 350 on each side; they were undoubtedly much greater. The Continental troops had proved themselves equal to the British regulars. Clinton reached New York safely, where he was blockaded by Washington, who took position at White Plains July 30. Lee was cashiered for his shameful conduct.

NORTHERN, CENTRAL, AND WESTERN CAMPAIGNS, 1778–1779

1778–1781. Operations in the North. There were no major operations in the northern or central theaters, though there was hard fighting, both in organized warfare and in guerrilla actions. Tory and Indian atrocities rocked northern Pennsylvania and New York: the **Wyoming Valley** (July 3, 1778) and **Cherry Valley** (November 11, 1778) **Massacres** were monuments to the bloodthirsty **Johnson** family, the **Butlers**—**John** and **Walter**—and Chief **Joseph** (**Thayendanegea**) **Brant**'s Indians. An expedition into northwestern New York, under Generals Sullivan and James Clinton, reduced the Tory-Indian threat (August–September, 1779). Simultaneously Col. **Daniel Brodhead** led an expedition from Fort Pitt to ravage Indian villages in the Allegheny Valley (August 11–September 14). A Franco-American expedition against **Newport** (August, 1778) failed because of bad weather and faulty cooperation between General Sullivan's American land forces and Admiral **Jean Baptiste d'Estaing**'s French fleet. In the lower Hudson Valley the British capture of **Stony Point** (May 31, 1779) was quickly followed by Wayne's brilliant and successful bayonet assault (July 15–16), which recaptured the post and ended a threat to West Point, key American fortress on the Hudson. A similar American attack by Major **Henry "Lighthorse Harry" Lee** on **Paulus Hook** on the New Jersey shore of New York harbor, was also successful (August 19).

1778–1779. Operations of George Rogers Clarke in the West. With a handful of militia, he waged a campaign tactically minor but strategically most important. His final capture of Vincennes, Ind. (February 25, 1779), secured to the United States in the later peace treaty the entire region from the Alleghenies to the Mississippi, a territory larger than the thirteen original colonies.

1779, June 21. Spain Declares War against England. King **Charles III**, however, and his wily Prime Minister, Count **José de Floridablanca**, refused to recognize American independence.

* He had been exchanged as a prisoner of war.

SOUTHERN CAMPAIGNS, 1778–1779

For nearly 2 years, the southern colonies had writhed in a continuous guerrilla warfare between Tories and patriots, but no major operations took place until Clinton, after the evacuation of Philadelphia, was ordered to the Carolinas.

1778, December 29. Capture of Savannah. Lieutenant Colonel **Archibald Campbell**, with 3,500 men of Clinton's command, crushed 1,000 American militia under General **Robert Howe** and occupied the city.

1779, January–June. War Flames in the South. Tory hopes rose as British General **Augustine Prevost** moved up from Florida, while Campbell seized Augusta, Ga. (January 29). In South Carolina, Moultrie at **Port Royal** repulsed an attack by Prevost (February 3), and **Andrew Pickens'** militia defeated a Tory brigade at **Kettle Creek** (February 14). An American attempt to recapture Augusta failed at **Briar Creek** (March 3). General Lincoln, sent by Washington to command the Southern Department, arrived in the area with a force of Continentals. Prevost failed in an effort to take Charleston. He withdrew and, despite Lincoln's unsuccessful attack at **Stono Ferry** (June 19), safely regained Savannah. In isolated actions, North Carolina and Virginia militia raided Chickamauga Indian villages in Tennessee, while British Admiral Sir **George Collier** sacked and burned Portsmouth and neighboring towns on the Virginia coast (May).

1779, September 3–October 28. Siege of Savannah. D'Estaing's fleet with 4,000 French troops, returning from the West Indies (see below), arrived off the port, capturing 2 British warships and 2 supply ships. Disembarking his French troops (September 12), d'Estaing invested the place. Lincoln with 600 Continentals and 750 militia joined him (September 16–23). Prevost, commanding the British garrison, had some 3,500 men and his defenses were strong. Discouraged by slow progress of the siege, and anxious lest his fleet meet disaster in seasonal storms, the French admiral after a futile bombardment insisted on an assault (October 8). At dawn next day, 5 allied columns advanced. Warned by a deserter, the British were waiting for them and the assaults were thrown back after hand-to-hand fighting in the most severe conflict of the war since Bunker Hill. Allied losses were more than 800 killed and wounded, among them Polish Count **Casimir Pulaski.** British losses amounted to 150. Refusing to continue the siege, d'Estaing embarked his troops and sailed away. Lincoln returned to Charleston.

COMMENT. *A serious blow had been struck against the cause of independence; Tory spirits soared, while the disheartened patriots' confidence in the French dropped sharply.*

1779, December 26. Clinton Sails South. After withdrawing British troops from Newport, Rhode Island (October 11), and placing German General **Wilhelm von Knyphausen** in command at New York, Clinton sailed with 8,000 men to attack Charleston. All available British pressure would now be put on the South.

Operations at Sea, 1778–1779

1778, April–May. Exploits of John Paul Jones. In U.S.S. *Ranger,* after terrorizing British shipping in the Irish Sea, he landed at Whitehaven in England, spiked the guns of the local fort, then, crossing Solway Firth to St. Mary's Island, seized the residence of the **Earl of Selkirk** (April 23). This was the first purely foreign invasion of England since the Norman Conquest. Jones then cruised over to northern Ireland and, after a 1-hour fight with H.M.S. *Drake* off Carrickfergus, captured her (April 24) and took her into Brest. Jones's activities threw the British into a ferment.

1778, July 11–22. Arrival of the French Fleet. Admiral Count d'Estaing arrived from France off Sandy Hook, blockading New York for a short time. He then sailed for Narragansett Bay, lying offshore and making contact with American General Sullivan for planned operations against Newport (see p. 716).

1778, July 27. Battle of Ushant. British Admiral **Augustus Keppel,** with 30 ships of the line, met and clashed briefly and inconclusively off the coast of Brittany with French Admiral Count **d'Orvilliers'** squadron of equal strength.

1778, August. Maneuvers of Howe and d'Estaing. Howe's fleet, based at New York, tried to come to grips with d'Estaing's fleet off Newport, but a storm dispersed both squadrons before they could come into general contact with each other (August 11). D'Estaing then withdrew from Newport to repair storm damage at Boston; as a consequence, Sullivan, without naval support, had to abandon the Newport operation.

1778, November 4. Departure of d'Estaing. He left Boston, cruising to the West Indies, where local French forces had seized Dominica (September 8), and British Admiral **Samuel Barrington** took St. Lucia (November 13).

1779. Operations in the West Indies. D'Estaing captured St. Vincent (June 16) and Grenada (July 4) while British Admiral **John Byron** was hunting for him.

1779, June 21–1783, February 6. Siege of Gibraltar. The successful defense of the fortress by General **George Augustus Eliott** with the assistance of the Royal Navy was one of the great combined arms exploits of the British armed forces.

1779, July 6. Battle of Grenada. Off Georgetown Byron's squadron was roughly handled by d'Estaing's superior French force and 4 British ships were dismasted. D'Estaing sailed to Savannah (see p. 717).

1779, July 25–August 14. Penobscot Expedition. An amphibious force under Continental Navy Commodore Dudley Saltonstall and Massachusetts militia Brigadier General Solomon Lovell tried ineptly to seize the British timber base on Penobscot Bay, Maine. A British squadron destroyed the flotilla; the land force dispersed in the Maine wilderness.

1779, September 23, *U.S.S. Bonhomme Richard* vs. *H.M.S. Serapis*. John Paul Jones in a converted 42-gun Indiaman, off Flamborough Head, defeated the British frigate *Serapis,* 44, in one of history's most remarkable single-ship actions. Jones's flaming ship was sinking, but he refused British Captain **Richard Pearson**'s hail to surrender with, "I have not yet begun to fight!" Pearson, his mainmast shot away, his gun deck swept by a powder explosion touched off by an American grenade, at last surrendered. Jones moved his crew to the *Serapis* and brought his prize into Texel, Netherlands(October 3).

SPANISH OPERATIONS IN THE SOUTH AND WEST 1779–1781

1779, August–September. Expedition up the Lower Mississippi. Don **Bernardo de Galvez,** Spanish governor of Louisiana, recognized the threat to New Orleans of Britain's West Florida posts on the Mississippi above the city. After Spain declared war, with a few troops he quickly took **Manchac** (September 7), **Baton Rouge** (September 20), and **Natchez** (September 30).

1780, February–March. Mobile Campaign. Galvez landed troops from New Orleans and captured Mobile, capital of British West Florida (March 14). Major General **John Campbell,** coming from Pensacola with reinforcements, turned back.

1780–1781. Raid into Michigan. Galvez sent Captain **Eugenio Pourré** up the Mississippi from St. Louis. He surprised and captured the British garrison of **Fort St. Joseph,** on Lake Michigan (1781, January), and returned to St. Louis.

1781, February–May. Pensacola Campaign. With troops from Havana and Mobile and his naval squadron from New Orleans, Galvez besieged **Fort St. George** near Pensacola (March 10). After a Spanish hit blew up the fort's powder magazine, General Campbell surrendered (May 9).

WAR ON LAND, 1779–1783

SOUTHERN CAMPAIGN, 1780–1781

American Disasters, 1780

1780, February 28. Russia's Armed Neutrality. Britain's blockade of French and Spanish supply to the United States suffered when **Catherine II** declared her navy would protect her trade against all belligerents. Denmark (July 9) and Sweden (August 1) accepted her invitation to join; within 2 years the Netherlands, Prussia, Portugal, Austria, and the Kingdom of the Two Sicilies (Naples) joined.

1780, July 10. French Army at Newport. Lieutenant General Count **Jean Baptiste de Rochambeau** with 5,000 men, convoyed by 7 ships of the line under Admiral **De Ternay,** landed at Newport. British ships blockaded the harbor, preventing proposed Franco-American operations against New York.

1780, September 23. Treason of Benedict Arnold. His plans to deliver his command, West Point, guardian of the Hudson Valley, to Clinton were captured with British Major **John André.** Arnold escaped and received a British brigadier general's commission and substantial cash. Thereafter he fought for England. André was hanged as a spy.

1780, December 20. England Declares War on the Netherlands. This was because of clandestine Dutch trade with the American states.

1780–1781. American Mutinies. Continental currency depreciation and supply deficiencies led to six quickly suppressed mutinies, at West Point (January 1, 1780), at Morristown (May 25, 1780), Ft. Stanwix (June 1780), Morristown (January 1, 1781), Pompton (January 20, 1781), and again Morristown (May 1781).

1780–1781. Blockade of New York. Washington maintained a cordon about the British in New York.

1780, February 11–May 12, Siege of Charleston. Clinton's expedition disembarked near Charleston, bringing the British forces in the area to 14,000. Despite Lincoln's energetic efforts, Clinton slowly completed the investment (April 11) and began siege operations. Admiral **Marriot Arbuthnot's** squadron in the harbor added to the heavy bombardment from the land. Lincoln finally surrendered with 5,400 men, plus cannon, small arms, and ammunition, in the worst American disaster of the war (May 12). Leaving Cornwallis with 8,000 men in South Carolina, Clinton returned to New York.

1780, May–August. Pacification and Reaction. Cornwallis's severe measures, particularly the brutality of Sir **Banastre Tarleton's** Tory cavalry, caused strong guerrilla opposition, led by **Francis Marion, Thomas Sumter,** and **Andrew Pickens.** Tarleton's massacre of a small American force at **Waxhaw Creek** (May 29) aroused the countryside. Washington sent Brigadier General **Johann de Kalb** and 900 Continentals to South Carolina. Congress put Horatio Gates in command of the Southern Department, independent of Washington.

1780, August 16. Battle of Camden. Gates with some 3,000 men, mostly militia, met Cornwallis with 2,400 British and Tory regulars at dawn. The militia broke; Tarleton's cavalry charged from the rear. The Continentals, struggling gallantly, were overwhelmed. Gates fled 160 miles to Hillsboro, N.C., followed by the remnants of his army. Nearly 900, including De Kalb, were killed and 1,000 captured. Two days later Tarleton smashed Sumter's guerrilla force at **Fishing Creek.**

The Turn of the Tide, 1780–1781

1780, October 6. Congress Returns Control to Washington. He at once appointed **Nathanael Greene,** his "right arm," to command in the south.

1780, October 7. Battle of King's Mountain. British Colonel **Patrick Ferguson**'s corps of Tory riflemen, 1,100 strong, was demolished by 1,400 sharpshooting Carolinian "mountain men" and Virginians—all militia—led by Colonels **Isaac Shelby** and **Richard Campbell.** Ferguson was killed.

COMMENT. *The fight was remarkable in that all participants on both sides were Americans, save Ferguson himself. This disaster, combined with widespread disorders in South Carolina, led Cornwallis to abandon a proposed invasion of North Carolina. He retreated to winter quarters at Winnsborough, N.C., and took stern measures against rebellious colonists.*

1780, December 2. Greene Assumes Command. His army at Charlotte had 1,482 men, 949 of them Continentals, all ill-clothed and badly equipped. By mid-December this force had grown to some 3,000—1,400 of whom were Continentals—thanks to reinforcements sent by Washington. Meanwhile, Cornwallis had also been reinforced to a strength of 4,000 well-equipped, well-trained regulars.

1780, December 20. Greene Takes the Offensive. He deliberately (and mistakenly) divided his forces, sending Brigadier General **Daniel Morgan** with 1,000 men on a wide western sweep. Greene moved with the remainder to a camp at Cheraw Hill, S.C., nearer to Charleston than Cornwallis. The American forces were now separated by 140 miles. Cornwallis, instead of concentrating against one of the American forces, unwisely split his own command. He sent Tarleton with 1,100 men against Morgan, while General **Alexander Leslie** with a comparable force was to contain the Americans at Cheraw Hill. Cornwallis with the main body followed Tarleton.

1781, January 17. Battle of Cowpens. Tarleton, catching up with Morgan, was decisively defeated in a brilliant double envelopment. The British lost 110 killed and 830 captured of their 1,100 strength; Morgan lost 12 killed and 61 wounded.

COMMENT. *This American "Cannae" was one of the most brilliant tactical operations ever fought on American soil.*

1781, January–February. Retreat to the Dan. Greene and Morgan, reuniting, hastily retreated into southern Virginia, closely pursued by Cornwallis. The British general, destroying his baggage in order to increase his mobility, pursued to the unfordable Dan River, then retired to Hillsboro again. Greene turned and followed him, his army having been reinforced to a total of about 4,400 men, of whom more than two-thirds were untrained militia or newly raised Continentals. Crippling arthritis prevented Morgan from remaining in the field.

1781, March 15. Battle of Guilford Courthouse. Cornwallis, with 1,900 effectives, attacked Greene, who had chosen his ground carefully. The outnumbered British with great gallantry gained the upper hand and drove the militia from the field; Greene broke off the action in order to avoid disaster and retreated in good order with the remainder of his army. Cornwallis' victory was costly: 93 killed and 439 wounded, against 78 Americans killed and 183 wounded. The British general marched eastward to Wilmington, N.C., then, deciding he could no longer hold Georgia and the Carolinas, proceeded with 1,500 men into Virginia (see below).

Greene's Later Operations, 1781

Left behind in the Carolinas were several isolated British garrisons, against whom Greene now proceeded, his operations aided and supported by the guerrilla activities of Marion, Sumter, and Pickens.

1781, April 19. Battle of Hobkirk's Hill (near Camden). Greene was repulsed by a British force under Colonel **Francis Rawdon.** As Greene prepared to renew his advance, the British withdrew toward Charleston.

1781, May 22–June 19. Siege of Fort Ninety-six. Greene was again unsuccessful when a relieving force rescued the garrison and then withdrew to Charleston. Most of Carolina was now liberated from the British.

1781, September 8. Battle of Eutaw Springs. Approaching Charleston, Greene with 2,400 men attacked Lieutenant Colonel **Alexander Stewart** with some 2,000. The Americans were at first successful, but the British rallied and repulsed the Americans. Greene withdrew. Next day, Stewart, whose losses had been very heavy, fell back on Charleston, which, with Savannah, was 1 of only 2 remaining British footholds south of Virginia.

COMMENT. *Greene's strategical task had been competently accomplished, despite his failure to win a single tactical victory.*

YORKTOWN CAMPAIGN, 1781

Preliminaries in Virginia

1780, December 30–1781, March 26. Arnold's Operations in Virginia. The American traitor, with a force of 1,600 men, arrived at Hampton Roads to carry out Clinton's instructions to destroy military stores, to prevent reinforcements from reaching Greene, and to rally Tories. He seized and devastated Richmond (January 5). He then returned to Portsmouth, maneuvering inconclusively against von Steuben.

1781, March–May. Phipps's Operations in Virginia. British Major General **William Phipps** was sent with reinforcements to command in Virginia over Arnold. After some further destruction of supplies and goods, Phipps and Arnold marched southwest to meet Cornwallis, arriving from North Carolina (see p. 719). Phipps died at Petersburg (May 10).

1781, April 29. Lafayette Reaches Richmond. He had been sent from New York by Washington with reinforcements to take command in Virginia. His total force, including new troops being trained by Steuben, was 3,550 men, of whom 1,200 were veteran Continentals. Washington sent Wayne with his brigade of 1,000 Continentals from Pennsylvania to join Lafayette (June 10). Von Steuben was also sent to Virginia, where he gave a poor performanec as a field commander but again demonstrated his superb training talents.

1781, May 20. Arrival of Cornwallis at Petersburg. He took command of British forces in Virginia. Counting the garrison of Portsmouth, these totaled 8,000.

1781, May–July. Maneuvers around Virginia. Cornwallis attempted to bring the Americans to battle, but Lafayette, keeping out of reach, led the British in a chase around eastern Virginia. Cornwallis, ordered by Clinton to send part of his force back to New York, reluctantly returned to Portsmouth, closely followed by Lafayette. In a well-planned ambush near **Jamestown Ford** (July 6) on the banks of the James River, Cornwallis caught Wayne's brigade by surprise, but the Americans, despite heavy losses, repulsed the British attack, counterattacked, then retreated in good order. Cornwallis continued on to Portsmouth.

1781, August 4. Cornwallis Moves to Yorktown. New orders from Clinton (July 20) permitted Cornwallis to keep all of his troops, and directed him to occupy the tip of the Virginia Peninsula. He moved by water to Yorktown with more than 7,000 troops, planning to keep a link by sea with Clinton in New York. Lafayette, who now had 4,500, cautiously moved to nearby West Point, Virginia, closely observing the British. He sent a report to Washington.

Washington's Plans and Movements, May–September, 1781

1781, May 21. Washington and Rochambeau Confer near New York. They reached the joint conclusion that British strength now lay in 2 points: New York and Chesapeake Bay. In the West Indies at this time was Admiral **François J. P. de Grasse,** with a powerful French fleet (see p. 723). Were de Grasse to cut the sea communications between these 2 British centers, joint land and sea operations against either would be favored. A French frigate was sent to de Grasse with the word from Washington that sea power was essential to success. At the same time Rochambeau's army moved from Newport to join Washington's outside New York.

1781, August 13. De Grasse Sails North. His fleet headed for Chesapeake Bay, carrying an additional 3,000 French troops. He had earlier sent word to Washington that the fleet would be available until mid-October. Washington received the message (August 14) just after getting Lafayette's report of Cornwallis' move to Yorktown. Washington at once recognized that if de Grasse could keep command of the sea, Cornwallis' army could be destroyed. Rochambeau agreed.

1781, August 21. Washington Marches South. Leaving **William Heath** with 2,000 men to contain Clinton's 17,000 in New York, Washington led the allied armies south by forced marches. They reached Philadelphia before Clinton, deceived by a pretended attack, realized what was happening.

1781, August 30. De Grasse Arrives off Yorktown. He disembarked his troops, who reinforced Lafayette. A British fleet under Admiral **Thomas Graves** rushed from New York, appearing off the entrance of the Bay.

1781, September 5–9. Battle of the Capes. (**See p. 723.**) More French ships arrived from Newport, strengthening victorious de Grasse and bringing siege artillery for the allies. Graves sailed away for New York, leaving command of the sea to the French and sealing Cornwallis' fate.

1781, September 14–26. Arrival of Washington's and Rochambeau's Troops. Most were transported by French ships from Head of Elk, Baltimore, and Annapolis, and put ashore at Williamsburg.

Operations against Yorktown

1781, September 28. Investment of Yorktown. Washington had some 9,500 Americans and 7,800 splendidly equipped French regulars (Rochambeau had put himself without reservation under Washington's orders) with a variety of artillery—including the Gribeauval field guns of the French, here to receive their baptism of fire. Cornwallis had 8,000 men in all.

1781, September–October. Siege of Yorktown. Hoping to receive aid soon from Clinton, Cornwallis withdrew to his inner fortifications (September 30), thus enabling the allies to bring their siege artillery within range of his entire position. Bombardment soon began (October 9). Two key redoubts were stormed by Franco-American detachments (October 14) and new batteries established. A British counterattack was sharply repulsed (October 16). Cornwallis' situation was now impossible. A desperate scheme to evacuate part of his troops across the York River was thwarted by storm.

1781, October 17. Cornwallis Opens Negotiations for Capitulation. Washington allowed 2 days for written proposals, but insisted on complete surrender.

1781, October 19. Surrender of Cornwallis. Yorktown's garrison marched out and laid down all their arms. To all intents and purposes the war was over.

1781, October 24. Clinton's Belated Arrival. Graves convoyed him and 7,000 reinforcements to Chesapeake Bay. But, deterred by the presence of de Grasse's fleet and realizing that he was too late, Clinton put back to New York. De Grasse, fearful of hurricanes, declined to participate in Washington's suggestion of an attack on Charleston or the British base at Wilmington, and sailed for the West Indies.

COMMENT. *Sea power, and Washington's brilliant strategic grasp of its importance, combined with superb allied tactics, had won the decisive battle of the war.*

FINAL LAND OPERATIONS, 1781–1783

1781, November. Washington Marches Back to the Investment of New York. He established his headquarters at Newburgh.

1781–1782. French Activities. Rochambeau's army spent the winter in Virginia, returned to Rhode Island (fall, 1782),

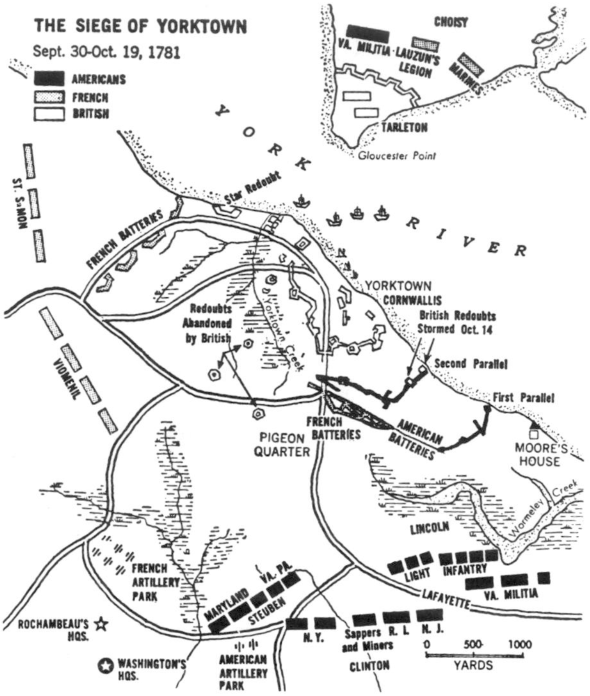

and embarked from Boston for France (December 24, 1782).

1781–1782. Greene Secures the South. He moved to invest British-held Charleston, while sending detachments to secure Georgia in a few minor engagements.

1782. Britain Sues for Peace. Lord North's ministry collapsed (March 20) and peace negotiations were opened (April 12). Sir Guy Carleton succeeded Clinton in the United States (May 9). All British troops were concentrated in New York. (Wilmington had been evacuated in January; Savannah was cleared July 11 and Charleston December 14.)

1782, August. Canadian and Indian Raid into Kentucky. An irregular force of about 240 men under American turncoat **Simon Girty** raided across the Ohio to attack **Bryan's Station** (August 15). Repulsed, they ambushed a pursuing American force at **Blue Licks** (August 19). Colonel **Daniel Boone,** who had warned his companions of a possible ambush, distinguished himself. The victorious raiders withdrew.

1782, November 30. The Treaty of Paris. This treaty recognized the independence of the United States, and concluded the war between the United States and Great Britain; it was to become effective upon conclusion of Britain's war with France and Spain, now being pursued in the West Indies, off the Indian coast, and in the Mediterranean.

1783, April 15. Congress Ratifies the Treaty. Hostilities elsewhere having ended, the war was now officially concluded. Disbandment of the Continental Army (June) set a pattern for hasty demobilization which would be followed in the United States thereafter.

1783, November 25. British Evacuation of New York. The last English troops embarked; Washington with Governor George Clinton entered the city. The British transports stood out to sea (December 4). That same day Washington took leave of his officers at Fraunces' Tavern.

War at Sea, 1780–1783

RODNEY'S OPERATIONS, 1780

1780, January 16. The "Moonlight Battle." British Admiral **George B. Rodney,** with 22 ships of the line and a large convoy of transports under orders to assist Gibraltar (under siege by the Spaniards on land since July 1779), fell in with Admiral **Langara**'s squadron of 11 Spanish ships off Cape St. Vincent. The Spaniards were defeated in a night action, 1 ship being sunk and 6 captured. After reinforcing Gibraltar, Rodney made for the West Indies, where he was to take command.

1780, March–August. Operations in the West Indies. French Admiral **Lucurbain de Guichen** met Rodney in equal strength in 3 indecisive actions (April). The Frenchman was then reinforced by a Spanish squadron, but through disease and indecision the allied effort aborted. De Guichen sailed for France (August).

1780, September. Rodney Sails North. Leaving half his fleet, he sailed with the remainder for New York, foiling Washington's plan for a joint Franco-American land and sea assault on the city. Returning to the West Indies (December), Rodney seized the Dutch islands of St. Eustatius and St. Martin (February), crippling the contraband trade on which the United States depended. He then sailed for England, leaving Admiral **Samuel Hood** in command.

THE PERIOD OF FRENCH PREDOMINANCE

1781, March 16. First Battle of the Virginia Capes. When Washington sent Lafayette to Virginia to catch Arnold, French Commodore **Sochet Destouches** at Newport sailed for Chesapeake Bay with 8 ships of the line and a detachment of French troops to join Lafayette. British Admiral Arbuthnot, off New York, gave chase with 8 ships. Destouches had the better of the resultant engagement; 3 British ships were crippled. But Destouches returned to Newport, leaving command of the sea to the British. (Sometimes called Battle of the Chesapeake Capes.)

1781, March 22. De Grasse Leaves Brest. He had 26 ships of the line and a large convoy of troop transports. He headed for the West Indies and, possibly, the United States. Off the Azores, Admiral **Pierre André de Suffren,** with 5 ships, parted company, bound for the East Indies. De Grasse arrived off Martinique (April 28).

1781, April–August. Fencing in the West Indies. De Grasse had somewhat the better of inconclusive operations against Hood. He received Washington's message (see p. 721) off Haiti.

1781, August. The Fleets Move North. Promptly gathering all available French troops (3,500) on Haiti, de Grasse sailed by a roundabout route, arriving at Lynnhaven with 28 ships of the line (August 30). Hood, following de Grasse, had actually reached Chesapeake Bay 2 days before the main French fleet, but finding it empty went on to New York to join Admiral **Thomas Graves,** who as senior officer took command of the combined force, 19 ships of the line. Graves returned to the Chesapeake to find de Grasse already there.

1781, September 5–9. Second Battle of the Capes. De Grasse with 24 ships promptly put to sea to meet Graves. The 8 leading French ships rounded Cape Henry well ahead of the remainder, but Graves failed to seize the opportunity to crush them. Some British ships were roughly handled in an inconclusive action, and one was abandoned. Due to hidebound adherence to outmoded tactics, Graves never closed in. After 5 days of fruitless maneuvering, he returned to New York, leaving command of the sea to the French admiral. At this time the French Newport squadron—8 ships of the line—now under Commodore **de Barras,** arrived at the Capes, convoying transports carrying Rochambeau's siege artillery. (Sometimes called Battle of the Virginia Capes.)

1782, February 5. French-Spanish Conquest of Minorca. An allied force under General **Duke Louis de Crillon** had occupied all of Minorca except Port Mahon (July–August, 1781). Port Mahon fell after a six-months' siege.

AMERICAN OPERATIONS, 1780–1781

1780, June 1. *USS Trumbull vs HMP Watt.* The *Trumbull,* 28, fought a bloody, drawn battle with the 34-gun British privateer.

1781. American Privateering at Its Peak. During this year there was a total of 449 American privateers in action.

1781, May 29. Cruise of the *Alliance.* Sole American regular naval action this year was that of Captain **John Barry** in the *Alliance* frigate, which cruised to France and back, fighting and taking, on the return journey, the British sloops of war *Atlanta* and *Trepassy*. Barry also captured 2 British privateers.

SUFFREN'S OPERATIONS, 1781–1782

1781, April 16. Battle of Porto Praya. Suffren, who was bound for the Cape of Good Hope to preserve that Dutch colony from England, found British Commodore **George Johnstone** with 5 ships and 35 transports at anchor in Porto Praya in the Cape Verde Islands. Johnstone was also on his way to the Cape. Suffren, disregarding neutrality, attacked and so injured Johnstone's flotilla that the British expedition was called off. Suffren made for India (see p. 701).

1782, February–September. Operations off India. The first of 5 violent actions to be fought against British Admiral Sir **Edward Hughes** took place south of **Madras** (February 17). In this, as in the 4 subsequent actions (April 12, near **Trincomalee;** July 6, off **Cuddalore;** September 3, again near **Trincomalee;** and April 20, 1783 again near **Cuddalore**) Suffren had the best of the encounter, although no ships were lost or captured by either side. Suffren received less than full support from several of his subordinates; nonetheless he attacked with such vigor that the British were invariably forced on the defensive and in each instance broke off the action. As a result Suffren was able to give considerable support to French land forces, thus offsetting the great British superiority in India. The most amazing aspect of Suffren's operations in the Indian Ocean was that he was able to maintain his squadron without the help of a port in which he could refit, and that he at least temporarily checked the rise of British supremacy in India by actually seizing the strategically important anchorage of Trincomalee (August 30, 1782). In these operations, the French admiral proved himself to be the greatest naval man of his nation and one of the outstanding sailors of history.

BRITAIN REGAINS MASTERY OF THE SEAS, 1781–1782

1781, August 5. Battle of Dogger Bank. Sir Hyde Parker with 7 ships of the line, escorting a merchant convoy from the Baltic, encountered Admiral **Johann A. Zoutman**'s Dutch squadron, also 7 ships, convoying a merchant fleet to the Baltic. Parker had the best of the engagement; the Dutch ships returned to port.

1781, December 12. Second Battle of Ushant. Following months of maneuvering by Franco-Spanish fleets against English forces along the Atlantic coast of Europe, British Admiral **Richard Kempenfelt** defeated de Guichen's squadron escorting merchantmen and supply vessels to the West Indies, capturing 20 transports.

1782, April 12. Battle of the Saints. After 2 clashes with Rodney and Hood (January), de Grasse met their combined squadrons between Dominica and Guadaloupe. The British fleet, 34 ships of the line, and the French, 29 ships, each maneuvered in line ahead until Rodney unorthodoxically burst through the middle of the French line. In a short time de Grasse's fleet was broken into 3 detachments and utterly defeated. Seven ships were captured, including the French flagship; 2 more fell to Hood a week later as the scattered French vessels were pursued. But this restoration of British sea command was too late to affect the outcome of the Revolution.

1782, September 13–14. Franco-Spanish Attack on Gibraltar. For 3 years, the fortress garrison of 7,000 men under Sir **George Augustus Eliott** had maintained a grim defense against Spanish blockade and bombardment by land and sea. Twice British squadrons had sent in reinforcements and supplies (see pp. 722 and 723). Following the capture of Port Mahon and Minorca (see p. 723), the Duke of Crillon launched an attack on Gibraltar. Ten floating batteries, with overhead and side armor of green wood some 6 feet thick, moved close to the walls of the fortress and opened heavy fire. British projectiles failed to pierce the armor until **Eliott's** gunners began, for the first time in history, to use red-hot shot. The balls, heated on grates and handled by tongs, were rammed home against wet wads protecting the powder charges, then fired at once. The device was most successful. In all, 8,300 rounds were fired. Before noon next day all 10 of the armored batteries had either been blown up or burned to the water's edge. The siege continued, but the garrison, close to starvation, was reinforced and supplied for the third time by a fleet under Lord Howe (October).

1783, January 20. Treaty of Versailles. Peace between England and the Franco-Spanish Alliance. England proclaimed cessation of hostilities (February 4).

UNITED STATES, 1783–1800

Disbanding of the Continental Army following the Revolution left the United States practically without Federal forces as Indian unrest again swept the frontier. An uneasy truce halted bloody Yankee-Pennamite fighting in the Wyoming Valley (see p. 708), finally leading to settlement of the dispute in Pennsylvania's favor (1782). Organization of a tiny Regular Army to supplement militia levies in protection of the frontier was begun (June 3, 1784). A Navy did not come into being until 1794, when construction of warships to protect commerce—particularly against the pirates of the Barbary coast—slowly began. Meanwhile, internal troubles brought hastily organized levies of militia troops into the field during the abortive **Shays' Rebellion** in New England (August, 1786–February, 1787) and again in the **Whisky Rebellion** in Pennsylvania (July–November, 1794). The principal events were:

1790, October 18–22. Harmar's Defeat. Depredations of the Maumee Indians in the Ohio Valley brought a punitive expedition into the field under Brigadier General **Josiah Harmar.** Of his 1,133 men, only 320 were regulars; the remainder were untrained militia, poorly armed and officered. Leaving Fort Washington (site of Cincinnati, Ohio), the expedition engaged in 3 disastrous clashes in the wilderness, not far from the present site of Fort Wayne, Ind. In each, the militia ran away and the few regulars present were slaughtered. The expedition returned abjectly with losses of 200 men.

1791, November 4. St. Clair's Defeat. General **Arthur St. Clair,** with the entire Regular Army of 600 men—and some 1,500 militia—took the field in October, slowly cutting his way for 100 miles through dense forests north from Fort Washington to the present site of Fort Recovery, Ohio, on the banks of the upper Wabash. Here, after part of his militia had deserted, he was surprised and his force practically destroyed, with great slaughter. The remaining militia decamped, most of the regulars were killed or wounded; more than 900 men and women in all were butchered.

1792, June. New Army; New Leader. Aroused by these reverses, Congress authorized a larger army, which was called the Legion of the United States. President Washington called General Anthony Wayne out of retirement; he began to train this new army near Pittsburgh.

1793–1794. Wayne Prepares. He marched with his command to Greeneville, some 80 miles north of Fort Washington, to establish a new training camp and to continue his rigorous training activities through the following winter.

1794, August. Advance into the Wilderness. Moving north from Greeneville with what was possibly the best-trained command in the history of the United States Army, Wayne set out over St. Clair's ill-fated route.

1794, August 20. Battle of Fallen Timbers. Near present Toledo, Ohio, Wayne's 3,500 troops finally caught up with the main force of the Maumee Indians, gathered in a dense forest slashing. Wayne's infantry now attacked with the bayonet, while his cavalry moved in on both flanks of the Indians in a perfectly executed double envelopment. The result was an overwhelming victory. Wayne lost 33 killed and 100 wounded; the Indian stronghold and nearby villages were destroyed, bringing peace to the frontier for some years. The action took place within view of a British garrison still maintained illegally on American soil.

1798–1800. Quasi War with France. Operations in the West Indies during the Wars of the French Revolution brought strained relations between France and the United States. French interference with American shipping resulted in violence and the threat of war. Washington was called back to command the army, and a Navy Department was established (May 3). When an American schooner was captured by a French warship off Guadeloupe (November 20), U.S. naval vessels moved into West Indian waters. Captain **Thomas Truxton** in U.S.S. *Constellation,* 36 (guns), met and captured the French frigate *Insurgente,* 40, after an hour's engagement off Nevis (February 9, 1799). *Insurgente* served thereafter as a vessel of the U.S. Navy until 1800, when she was lost at sea. A year later (February 1, 1800), Truxton met the French *Vengeance,* 52, off Guadeloupe in a 5-hour night battle. The French ship, much more powerful than the American frigate, was partly dismasted and her guns silenced; she escaped in the night. In all, 85 French vessels, mostly privateers, were taken before peace was made. The last engagement was that of U.S.S. *Boston,* 28, with the French privateer *Berceau.*

LATIN AMERICA

SPANISH AMERICA*

1750. Treaty of Madrid. Portugal agreed to cede Colonia (on the River Plate) to Spain, in return for seven Spanish-Jesuit mission villages (called *reductions*) on the east bank of the Uruguay River. (The treaty also recognized Portuguese sovereignty over the Amazon and Paraná river basins, and Spanish sovereignty over the Philippines.) The Guarani Indians, incited by the Jesuits, refused to accept Portuguese control over the seven ceded *reductions* (see below). Portugal therefore held on to Colonia. Charles III of Spain then annulled the treaty (1761).

1754–1763. The Seven Years' War. (See p. 667.) The war came late to the Iberian Peninsula (see p. 694), and thus to Latin America (see below).

1762. Spanish Invade Portuguese Possessions in the Banda Oriental. Colonia and Portuguese holdings on the lower Uruguay River were captured, and part of southern Brazil was occupied.

* Spain administered the Philippines as an element of her American empire.

1762. British Expeditions to Cuba and the Philippines. Havana was captured and Manila was also occupied by the British.

1763. Treaty of Paris. (See p. 677.) Havana was returned to Spain by Britain; Florida was ceded to Britain. To compensate for the loss of Florida, France ceded Louisiana to Spain. Manila was later returned to Spain by Britain.

1771. Falkland Islands Dispute. Conflicting Spanish and British claims almost led to war. Spain backed down when France refused to support her.

1776–1777. Spanish-Portuguese War. Spanish troops captured Colonia and seized other Portuguese territories in the Banda Oriental and in southern Brazil. The **Treaty of San Ildefonso** (see p. 678) awarded Colonia and the Banda Oriental to Spain. Portugal retained the upper Uruguay River and Brazil.

1779–1783. Spanish Participation in the American Revolutionary War. Spanish forces captured Mobile, Pensacola, and the Bahamas. British efforts to gain control of the Mississippi River were blocked by Spanish forces in Louisiana. The **Treaty of Versailles** (see p. 725) gave Florida to Spain; returned the Bahamas to Britain.

1789. Pacific Coast Dispute with Britain. Spanish forces seized Nootka Island (claimed by both nations) and some British ships in Nootka Sound (between Nootka and Vancouver islands). Again Spain backed down from war when French support was not forthcoming.

1793–1795. Spanish Participation in the War of the 1st Coalition. (See p. 679.) By the **Treaty of Basel** (see p. 682), Spain ceded Santo Domingo to France. Soon afterward, Spain ceded Trinidad to Britain (1797).

PORTUGUESE AMERICA

1750. Treaty of Madrid. (See above.)

1752–1756. War of the Seven *Reductions*. Portugal finally subdued the Guarani Indians and consolidated control over the seven villages ceded by Spain in the Treaty of Madrid (see above).

1754–1763. The Seven Years' War. (See pp. 667, 694, and above.)

1776–1777. Spanish-Portuguese War. (See above.)

AFRICA

NORTH AFRICA

The Barbary States

The internal and external affairs of the Barbary States (Morocco, Algeria, Tunisia, and Tripoli) in this half-century retained the same general pattern of the previous period. Morocco was completely independent; the other 3 were nominally vassals of the Ottoman Empire, but were virtually free from Turk interference during this period. Aside from elementary husbandry, the principal occupations of all 4 states remained piracy and the slave trade, although Tunisia was somewhat less dependent upon these lucrative pursuits than the other 3. During most of the period central authority was fairly strong in Morocco under the benevolent rule of **Sidi Mohammed;** the other 3 countries were less strongly ruled. The principal events were:

1757–1790. Reign of Sidi Mohammed (Mohammed XVI) of Morocco. He did much to establish law and order over his unruly subjects, and was successful in introducing a modicum of Western culture.

1765. French Bombardment of Larache and Salé. These attacks somewhat reduced piratical attacks upon French vessels from these rover bases, and gained some respect for France from Sidi Mohammed.

1767. Treaty with France. Morocco recognized special status of French consuls, and undertook to discourage the pirates from attacking French vessels.

1777. Abolition of Christian Slavery in Morocco. French influence had much to do with this decree by Sidi Mohammed.

1791. Spain Abandons Oran. The Spanish still retained a few small coastal towns in Morocco and western Algeria, of which Ceuta and Melilla were the most important.

Egypt

The effectiveness of Ottoman control over Egypt fluctuated greatly. Even when Turkish sovereignty was most firmly enforced, the Mameluke governors had considerable autonomy. The principal events were:

1750–1769. Rise of Ali Bey. This low-born Mameluke gained ascendancy in Egypt by force of arms, and was recognized as governor by Constantinople. Save for a period when forced to flee the country (1766), he ruled with an iron hand.

1769. Ali Bey Declares Egyptian Independence. After Ali had been ordered to raise a force of 12,000 troops for the war against Russia (see p. 697), Constantinople began to entertain doubts about his loyalty, fearing he would use this force to seize Syria. Secret instructions were sent to Egypt to have Ali assassinated. Ali intercepted the message and, with Mameluke support, declared independence.

[17]69–1770. Conquest of Western Arabia. Ali conquered most of the Red Sea coast and much of the interior of Arabia from nominal Turk rule.

1771–1772. Expedition to Syria. Ali sent a small army under his General **Abu'l Dhahab** into Syria. After arriving at Damascus, Abu'l opened negotiations with the Porte, which commissioned him to overthrow Egypt and replace Ali.

1772, April 8. Flight of Ali. One day before Abu'l's army reached Cairo, Ali fled, seeking support from the Pasha of Acre. At Acre he received money, supplies, and men (3,000 Albanian soldiers) from Russian naval vessels.

1772–1773. Ali's Return to Egypt. En route he recaptured Jaffa and Gaza. He then advanced across the Sinai Desert toward Egypt (February).

1773, April 19–21. Battle of Salihia (Salihiyeh). In a climactic battle with Abu'l, Ali, at first successful, was finally defeated and captured; he died soon afterward.

1785–1786. Revolt in Egypt. This was suppressed by an Ottoman army sent overland and by ship.

1798–1801. Bonaparte's Expedition to Egypt. (**See p. 688.**)

WEST AFRICA

Increasing European attention to the West African coast—stimulated by the slave trade—had relatively little impact upon the continuing turbulence of the interior jungle and upland regions. The remnants of the old Mali Empire persisted around the headwaters of the Niger and Senegal rivers. Farther east in the upland regions were the Kaarta, Mossi, Oyo, Hausa, and Bornu states, of which the Oyo was the only one still flourishing by the end of the century. The others, suffering from internal disorders, disputes with neighbors, and particularly plagued by depredations of the Saharan Tuaregs, were in varying stages of decline, decay, or collapse. Of the many tribal groupings in the intermediate jungle region, the Ashanti continued to prosper and expand until, by the end of the century, they had expanded into the open uplands of the middle Volta region and farther west, and had also approached the Ivory and Gold Coasts. Meanwhile, along the coast, the European wars of France and England were reflected in raid and counterraid. The principal events were:

1752–1781. Reign of Osei Kojo of the Ashanti. This warrior leader greatly expanded the Ashanti dominions in all directions.

1753. Re-establishment of Portuguese Base at Bissan. This was Portuguese Guinea.

1757. British Conquest of French Senegal Posts. The Seven Years' War in Africa.

1763. Treaty of Paris. (**See p. 677.**) Britain returned Goree to France, retaining the remaining posts in the Senegal region.

1776. Rise of Fulani (or Tukulor) Power. This was in northwestern Hausaland, east of the central Niger River, and posed a threat to the hitherto powerful Hausa Empire.

1778–1779. French Reconquest of the Senegal Posts. The African version of the War of the American Revolution (see p. 708).

1783. The Treaty of Paris. (**See p. 722.**) The Senegal posts were divided between England and France; France retained St. Louis.

c. 1785. British Domination of the Slave Trade.

1787. British Acquisition of Sierre Leone.

1792–1800. Renewed Anglo-French Struggle over Senegal Coast. The Wars of the French Revolution in Africa. Under **F. Blanchot de Verly,** the French recovered, then partially lost, the Senegal posts. Verly repulsed repeated British assaults on St. Louis.

c. 1790–1801. Rise of Usman dan Fodio of the Fulani. Originally a religious leader in the area of what is now northern Nigeria, he inspired unrest and then outright revolt against the ruling Hausa, bringing that empire to the brink of collapse.

SOUTH AFRICA

About midway in this half-century the 2 great South African migrations met and began a series of violent clashes. The Dutch settlers who had started from the area of Capetown almost 2 centuries earlier had now become a new colonial peopl[e] known to themselves as **Boers,** or farmers. The spearhead of the movement of th[e] Bantu people was the Xosa tribe, which met the Boers about 400 miles to [the] east and northeast of Capetown. The typical self-reliant Boer tendency toward unruly independence was also beginning to manifest itself along the new frontier, directed first against the administration of the Dutch East India Company and later against the British, after their seizure of the colony during the French Revolutionary Wars. The principal events were:

1750. The Bantu Reach the Keiskama River. This was the Xosa tribe.

1760. The Boers Cross the Orange River. They begin to penetrate the region known as the Great Namaqualand.

1770. The Boers Reach Graaff-Reinet Area. This was 400 miles from Capetown.

c. 1775–1795. Boer Conflicts with Hottentots and Bushmen. Despite desperate native resistance, particularly in the mountains, the Boers had little trouble in overcoming them. Many were slaughtered; many more were enslaved.

1778. Boer and Bantu Meet. There had been long-range contact for several decades, but now the outpost settlements of both peoples came into close contact.

1779–1781. First Kaffir War. This struggle of white Boer against black Bantu (called Kaffir by the Boers) was inconclusive. It led the frontier peoples in the Graaff-Reinet and Swellendam regions to appeal to the company for help.

1793–1795. Second Kaffir War. This was also inconclusive.

1795. Independence Declared by Graaff-Reinet and Swellendam. The frontier Boers were disgusted by lack of support from the company and by the Capetown Boers. Without effective government, these frontier regions were in chaotic condition.

1795, September. British Conquest. There was little opposition, since the Boers accepted the British as enemies of the French, who had conquered Holland.

1796. Order Restored on the Frontier. The British established control over the entire colony, including the two "independent" regions.

1799–1801. Renewed Anarchy on the Frontier. Unrest and chaos resulting from Boer refusal to accept centralized control from Capetown were exploited by Xosa raids and by Hottentot uprisings.

c. 1799. Coalescence of the Zulus Begins. This tribe of the Bantu people had settled in the extensive coastal region since known as Zululand, roughly midway between modern Durban and Lourenço Marques.

EAST AFRICA

By the middle of the 18th century, the Portuguese had abandoned efforts to re-establish control over the East African coast. Moslem Arab-Swahili-Bantu coastal principalities, owing nominal allegiance to the Sultan of Oman, flourished north of Mozambique. The Portuguese held all the coast of modern Portuguese East Africa. Inland, the southern migration of the Bantu was slowly ending as the northernmost tribes closed up into a region extending roughly from Lake Nyasa to the Orange River. Farther north, the unending conflict of Christian Abyssinia (or Ethiopia) continued against the various surrounding Moslem tribes and states (to the north, east, and west) and pagan tribes (to the south). About the middle of the century, the northwestern region of the Tigré, under the leadership of **Mikael Suhul,** broke away from the central control of the Abyssinian emperor and became virtually independent. (Tigré comprised the northwestern part of modern Ethiopia and the southwestern, inland portion of Eritrea.) Imperial authority continued to decline, and the Scottish explorer **James Bruce** reported a state of anarchic rebellion throughout the country (1768–1773).

XVII

THE ERA OF NAPOLEON: 1800–1850

MILITARY TRENDS

In this period military history crossed the second of its three great watersheds. Under the direction or stimulus of Napoleon Bonaparte, the weapons of the age of gunpowder were finally assimilated into consistent patterns of military theory and practice. For the first time since gunpowder had appeared on the battlefield, there was a substantial congruence among weapons, tactics, and doctrine. The bayoneted flintlock musket and the smoothbore cannon had each been perfected to a point closely approaching its maximum potential. After centuries of experimentation, the tactical means of employing these weapons in combination with each other and with cavalry had been refined to the point where a skillful commander could exploit the full potential of his weapons and his arms to achieve decisive results with minimum cost. The last time that commanders had been able to exercise comparable discriminating control over the means available to them had been in the 13th century, in the Mongol and English tactical systems.

Yet just as those two tactical systems had approached perfection in the employment of men and weapons at a time when the systems were doomed to early obsolescence because of the emergence of gunpowder weapons, so the principal tactical systems of the early 19th century (French and English on land, and English at sea) would be equally short-lived under the impact of the Industrial Revolution. (Interestingly, the phenomenon would be repeated again in mid-20th century as weapons and tactics of the Industrial Revolution era approached congruence just as the third great military watershed was reached with the dawn of the Nuclear Age.)

The congruence of weapons, tactics, and doctrine was bound to come during this half-century as a logical result of earlier developments. But the achievement was probably hastened, and certainly made more significant, through the genius of one man: **Napoleon Bonaparte.** No man has more indelibly stamped his personality on an era than did Napoleon. In his own time and for more than a century t come, military theory and practice were measured against his standards and related to his concepts of warmaking.

To a lesser degree, the same kinds of generalizations can be made about the influence of **Horatio Nelson** upon naval thinking and the exercise of the military art at sea. Yet if Nelson's impact upon his time and upon warfare was unquestionably less significant than that of Napoleon, his is the more unique and unchallengeable position with respect to other practitioners of the naval art. There has only been one Nelson; Napoleon's historical greatness as a soldier must always be compared with predecessors like Alexander, Hannibal, and Genghis Khan.

There were other excellent generals during this period, of whom the most outstanding were the Englishmen, **Arthur Wellesley, Duke of Wellington,** and Sir **John Moore,** the Prussian **Gebhard L. von Blücher, Prince of Wahlstatt,** the Austrian **Archduke Charles,** and the French Marshal **Louis Nicolas Davout.** Among Napoleon's marshals, in addition to Davout, at least two others proved themselves capable generals in their own rights: **Nicolas Jean de D. Soult,** and **André Masséna.** Three Americans warrant consideration with this company: **Andrew Jackson, Winfield Scott,** and **Zachary Taylor.**

For reasons noted below, the Industrial Revolution had little direct effect upon the battlefield and upon generalship in this era; that would come in following decades. But it had already had an impact upon manufacturing and upon agriculture which, in combination with the democratization of war that had occurred during the French Revolution, permitted nations to raise, equip, and supply larger armies than had hitherto been possible. And the Industrial Revolution, combined with the stimulation provided by Napoleon, contributed to the development of military theory and military professionalism in this period (see below).

WEAPONS

Great strides were taken in ordnance development. In 1810 **Friedrich Krupp** started the small Prussian forge which would blossom into a great steel and ordnance empire. In the United States, **Robert P. Parrott, John A. Dahlgren,** and **Thomas J. Rodman;** in England, **William G. A. Strong** and **Joseph Whitworth;** in France, **Henri Joseph Paixhans;** and in Sardinia, **Giovanni Cavalli,** in arsenal and foundry were evolving innovations and improvements in cannon manufacture which would begin a revolution in the science of gunnery.

In small arms, the percussion cap would supplant the flintlock, and make possible the invention in 1835 of the revolver. The Minié bullet, with expanding base, an invention of 1849, would improve the accuracy and range of the muzzle-loading rifle, which would then quickly displace the smoothbore musket as the primary infantry weapon.

In practice, however, few of these innovations reached the fighting man on sea or land in this half-century. There was little change in service arms and ammunition. There was one notable exception: the rocket, which emerged as a lethal weapon from its previous long existence as a pyrotechnic oddity, thanks to the efforts of Sir **William Congreve,** English ordnance expert. It found almost immediate favor, both in the United States and in Europe, as an intermediate-range weapon bridging the gap between the still-standard flintlock musket and the 12-pounder field gun. But although its relative economy vis-à-vis conventional ordnance was attractive, its notorious inaccuracy and limited maximum range of about 1,500 yards soon forced its disappearance from the battlefield.

TACTICS

Napoleonic Tactical Concepts

By the end of the 18th century, European warfare was characterized by large-scale formal battle waged primarily on the principles of linear tactics, and sieges conducted according to set patterns. There were no revolutionary new weapons and no major changes in the basic linear organization, although there had been steady development in both. Small arms had improved, and infantry was clearly the dominant arm. Rates of fire had been increased as a result of drill and improvement in firing mechanisms. Rifled firearms had been developed, but were used only by special troops. The flintlock with the bayonet was the standard arm of the infantry. The cavalry primarily used the saber, but some were armed with carbines. Artillery provided support to the extent of its ability. The guns were not yet capable of the rate of fire, accuracy, or trajectory required for close support of troops in the attack. Napoleon did not change these tactical methods so much as he revitalized them, while at the same time integrating his tactics into his broader and more revolutionary strategic concepts.

In war Napoleon always sought a general battle as a means of destroying the enemy's armed force after having gained a strategic advantage by maneuver. Tactically, he usually directed his main blow against the enemy's flank while simultaneously attacking his front; or launched his main thrust against the center of the enemy's battle front with the aim of breaking through, at the same time carrying on an enveloping maneuver against a hostile flank. The divisions attacking important objectives were often supported by massed fire from Napoleon's artillery reserve. Divisions with exposed flanks were protected by corps cavalry or even by the cavalry reserve.

Only after tactical destruction of the main armed force of the enemy did Napoleon bother about occupying the principal strategic and political centers of the enemy's country.

Infantry Tactics

LIGHT INFANTRY

As we have seen, light infantry had been reintroduced into European warfare during the 18th century. It was not a new development; light infantry had been used by all ancient armies and in various forms it had accompanied armies throughout the ages. Almost without exception, however, these had been irregular troops: archers, slingers, javelin men, and various others, who usually opened battles and then moved aside during the main action. With the introduction of gunpowder weapons, similar groups were armed with firearms, but the troops were usually undisciplined and did not form part of a regular army.

The rigid linear tactics of the 18th century had prescribed a fixed and inflexible role for the regular infantry. During the considerable time it took infantry battalions to take up their battle stations, they were vulnerable and needed to be screened from enemy action. In addition, the supply depots and convoys that were needed to support the armies were highly vulnerable to enemy attacks. The regular infantrymen of the enlarged armies, recruited as they were from the rejects of society and subjected to a rigorous discipline, could not be entrusted with detache operations. Consequently, to furnish the necessary support, to carry out operations against the enemy's lines of communications, to raid, and to take prisoners, while at the same time providing for the security of their own depots and convoys, and to screen the main army against surprises, light troops, mainly infantry, were reintroduced into the European armies about midcentury. Within a short time additional functions, above all, individual or group fire missions in advance or on the flanks of the main line, were added to their tasks.

The first large-scale appearance of light troops in Europe had occurred during the War of the Austrian Succession (1740–1748). In 1740, Maria Theresa found herself attacked by the superior strength of Frederick of Prussia and his French and Bavarian allies. She had to muster all the forces at her disposal and did not hesitate to call upon the Borderers, the "wild Croats and Pandours," who had been part of the Austrian frontier defenses against the Turks, to defend her realm. The effectiveness of these light troops impelled the other powers to introduce or augment similar forces. Prussia hastily increased her light cavalry and raised some irregular "free" battalions to counter the Croats, and in France several light regiments as well as a number of combined infantry-cavalry units—usually called "legions"—were raised.

The English Army had no light troops until the line battalions serving in America during the 1750's raised some light companies on an *ad hoc* basis. These units differed significantly from the irregulars, Borderers, free battalions, and free corps by being trained and disciplined troops, usable in the line as well as on detached operations, such as advance guards, assault parties, and also, occasionally, as raiders. They differed in function, but not in equipment and discipline, from the rest of the army, and more often than not were used as line infantry. The inspiration for the formation of these troops derived in part from the painful experiences of the war in America and in part from the continental European developments. After 1770, a light company as well as a grenadier company became part of the permanent establishment in each line battalion. Both companies rapidly assumed elite status and as "flank companies" were often used for special missions during the American Revolution.

However, light infantry never became a dominant element. In Prussia, Frederick II retained his reliance on the massed volleys of the line and spent most of his resources to speed up the fire. Prussia formed a number of fusilier units, but these were trained and equipped as line infantry. The same development took place in Austria, where the regiments of Borderers were drilled in linear tactics. In the British Army, too, there came a sharp reaction against light infantry and a determined attempt to return to the linear system at the turn of the century.

The only country which did not follow this backward evolution was France. Here, even before the Revolution, there was wide agreement that shock action should be delivered by formations having greater depth than the firing line. The main controversy concerned the extent of fire preceding and supporting the assault and whether this fire should be delivered by line, line and skirmishers, or skirmisher swarms. Circumstances and combat leaders together ultimately fashioned that combination of close-order columns and loose-order skirmishers which constituted the new tactics of the Revolutionary and Napoleonic infantry. Skirmishers would so occupy the enemy that the deeper assault formations (see below) could move up without being unduly exposed to the fire of the enemy line.

In the War of the First Coalition (1792–1798), the habit of skirmishing spread throughout the French infantry, and by 1793 all battalions were acting as light infantry, dissolving into skirmisher swarms as soon as action was joined. These fighting methods, sometimes called "horde tactics," were in turn superseded after 1795 by a tendency to return to properly controlled, deeper assault formations, preceded by skirmishers to scout the ground and disturb the enemy by individual aimed fire.

The important point about the French skirmishing action during this period was that it was performed not by special light troops but by integral parts of the regular bodies. Infantry became more flexible and to some observers it appeared as if specialized light troops would soon be eliminated by one all-purpose infantry. But special light troops, not only brought up to the standard of the line but in some cases excelling it in performanace and capable of winning a decision in battle, remained in French service for another 50 years.

In their political implications, the new light-infantry tactics were revolutionary. Both the French Revolutionary armies and the British system abandoned the brutal and degrading discipline of the 18th-century armies. The light infantryman (or the all-purpose infantryman), fighting often as a relatively autonomous individual in small formations in open order, was much less under the direct supervision of his officers. Brutal treatment and close control gave way to appeals to regimental pride, revolutionary *élan,* and the spirit of nationalism.

The character of light infantry and of warfare were greatly changed by the introduction of the rifle. For fighting individually in dispersed order, an accurate missile weapon was particularly valuable to light infantry. Rifles, however, were expensive and, more serious, slow to load. Therefore only select units and select individuals in line companies were thus equipped until well into the 19th century.

THE FRENCH INFANTRY "COLUMN"

The introduction of the so-called attack column as a standard combat formation in the Wars of the French Revolution was in part a result of tactical experimentation begun by Marshal Saxe in the middle of the previous century, and in part a natural formation adopted to make the maximum use of the poorly trained hordes produced by the *levée en masse,* troops that lacked the training and discipline to stand and fight effectively in the then linear system of Frederick.

Nevertheless, this French "column" as developed under Carnot, and perfected by Napoleon, was in no sense a reversion to the phalanx or the Spanish square. It was really an adaptation of the linear system, the deployment of a number of linear units (usually battalions) in depth to provide physical and psychological weight to an attack. The individual units could still operate in a linear formation if desired.

The great tactical value of the column lay in its flexibility and versatility. It permitted the commander to move large numbers of men over the battlefield with better control and far more rapidly than had been possible before. The column could operate in hilly terrain. It could easily change into different formations. The deployment from marching column to attack column, in particular, took far less time than had the development of linear formations from the marching column. Skirmishers could be detached without necessitating major readjustments in the formation. Two- or three-rank firing lines and squares could be formed rapidly. The earlier need to maintain tight flank connections between units in line became less important; the tactical situation opened up and became more dynamic.

The attack column had two main functions. First, it could be used to bring men in close order rapidly to the enemy. The success of such an action was largely dependent on adequate preparation by artillery and skirmishers, and it was they who inflicted most of the casualties rather than the column itself, which possessed little or no fire power once it started to move. Bayonet charges actually driven home against a steady enemy were rare.

The far more common employment of the attack column was as a sustaining force. The column sent out skirmishers to start the fire fight and served as a replacement pool for the skirmishers and as their immediate tactical reserve. If it encountered firm resistance, the column might deploy into lines to carry on the fight with volleys. Once the enemy wavered, these lines could resume the advance, or they might again reduce their front and move forward in column.

THE ENGLISH LINE

The most effective answer to the French system, as well as the most effective form of light infantry, was provided by the British. Their system was largely based on the effects of controlled, aimed musketry, delivered by troops combining as far as possible the mobility of skirmishers with the steadiness of the line. Under Sir John Moore and Sir Arthur Wellesley (later Duke of Wellington), the British began to take advantage of cover, usually crouched behind the crest of a ridge, and then, formed only two deep, arose to deliver a devastating fire against the French columns.

The English light infantry—partially armed with rifles which could deliver rapid fire by the use of subcaliber bullets, or individual aimed fire when using regular-sized bullets—able to operate individually or in close order, represented in essence the all-purpose infantry of the future. The musket of the light infantry was of a special type, a lightweight piece, constructed for this particular purpose. It was somewhat more accurate than the "Brown Bess," with better sights, but shorter in length. The line battalions used the Brown Bess, which was considered superior to muskets used on the Continent. The bayonet was long and triangular, and when fixed made accurate firing difficult. Sergeants did not carry muskets; each had a sword and a pike or a halberd which served as a signaling instrument and a rallying point.

Despite the early successes of the French system, the British retained the two-deep line—in which every man would employ his weapons—to produce a relatively greater volume of fire than could the column. Wellington's success was due undoubtedly in part to this, but it was due also to his tactics. He decided he could overcome Napoleon's tactics by three means: not to expose his line to artillery until the action opened, to protect it against the skirmishers, and to secure his flanks. The first he achieved by placing his infantry whenever possible on reverse slopes; the second by building up his light troops; the third was accomplished by natural obstacles or by his relatively weak cavalry.

In part because of his chronic shortage of cavalry, Wellington paid considerable attention to defense against French cavalry. The steady line and accurate fire of the British infantrymen were usually able to repulse a cavalry charge. On one occasion in the Peninsula, an infantry line advanced against cavalry and drove it from the field. In a square formation, British infantry was practically unbreakable; there is recorded the instance of the Light Division, formed into 5 squares, retreating for 2 miles with only 35 casualties, under attack by 4 brigades of cavalry.

Cavalry Tactics

Calvary remained the shock arm, with lance and saber the principal hand weapons. However, the division between "heavy" cavalry—partly armored men on ig horses—and "light"—more agile troopers on smaller mounts, who could harass well as shock—again became marked during the period.

Napoleon's cavalry, provided with horse artillery and used in great but articulate masses and in surprise operations against the enemy's cavalry and infantry, was very effective. It was usually thrown against the enemy infantry already shaken or shattered by massive artillery fire, or by infantry attacks. It was particularly effective against retreating infantry. It was less successful against fresh infantry which had time to form squares. Under outstanding leaders and by its impetuous charges, French cavalry usually proved superior to the best cavalry of other European nations. By its lightning action in pursuit, French cavalry exploited victory with minimum losses to its own army. Napoleon also used his cavalry very effectively for reconnaissance and for screening.

During the early Napoleonic wars, French cavalry was unexcelled. Later, as casualties and the passage of years took their toll, Napoleon found it difficult to maintain the same high standards of cavalry performance. At the same time, his enemies steadily improved their cavalry, in part by devoting more attention to its organization and training, and in part by copying the French organization, tactics, and methods. In the Peninsula, for instance, cavalry played a minor role in Wellington's campaigns. At Waterloo, however, it was the English cavalry which smashed the final attack of Napoleon's Old Guard.

Artillery Tactics and Techniques

The French Revolutionary Army inherited Gribeauval's excellent field-artillery system from the monarchy. The main feature of this artillery was mobility, obtained by reducing the length and weight of the barrel and the weight of the gun carriage; the latter was also provided with iron axletrees and wheels of large diameter. Range and precision were preserved by more precise manufacture of the projectile (balls of true sphericity and correct diameter, which also made possible a reduction in powder charge). Prefabricated cartridges, which replaced the old loose powder and shot, increased the rate of firing. Draft horses were disposed in double files instead of single. Six horses sufficed to draw the 12-pounder, while 4 were used for smaller guns: 8- and 4-pounders and a 6-inch howitzer.

Napoleon took full advantage of the maneuverability of the French artillery and made out of it the most important tool of his warfare. One of his favorite techniques, particularly employed in later years as the quality of his troops declined, was employment of the *grande batterie,* physically massing a preponderance of artillery fire in support of his main effort on the battlefield, literally blasting the enemy line to shreds to permit his infantry to advance.

Wellington employed his artillery selectively, in small numbers and individual batteries at carefully chosen sites, to be used at critical moments. They were placed all along the front as support for the infantry and played a minor but important role in his defensive-offensive tactics.

MILITARY ORGANIZATION

Origin of the Division and the Corps

The infantry division as a large permanent tactical and administrative formation appeared in France in the 18th century. In 1759, the Duc de Broglie introduced in the French Army a divisional organization, permanent mixed bodies of infantry and artillery.

In 1794, Carnot, the Revolutionary minister of war, developed the divisio embracing all 3 arms, infantry, cavalry, and artillery, and capable of carrying o independent operations. By 1796, the divisional system became universal in the French Army. It was Napoleon Bonaparte, however, who developed all the potentialities of the divisional system and used it in mobile warfare and tactics of fast maneuver. The men were trained in fast marching and the supply system was improved to support them wherever they went. The mobility of the division was also enhanced by artillery which could follow infantry and maneuver on the battlefield.

When army sizes approached 200,000, it became necessary to group divisions into army corps for administration and control. The first such organization was made in 1800, when Moreau grouped the 11 divisions of the Army of the Rhine into 4 corps. It was, however, not until 1804 that Napoleon introduced permanent army corps in the French Army, employing them as he had previously used divisions. However, the division remained the major tactical unit, composed of infantry and artillery, and entrusted with a definite mission. The corps included cavalry as well, which conducted reconnaissance for the whole corps. In addition, Napoleon formed cavalry divisions and cavalry corps.

Napoleon's infantry division consisted of 2 or 3 infantry brigades (each comprising two regiments) and 1 artillery brigade, consisting of 2 batteries, each with 4 field guns and 2 howitzers.

British Organization

The British did not adopt the division until 1807, and Wellington's army in the Peninsula in 1809 was still composed of independent brigades.

The British Army was a volunteer force and necessarily smaller than the French. But it had the advantage of more training and drill. The infantry was also the superior of any other in the excellence of its musketry, an advantage enhanced by its 2-rank line.

During the Peninsular campaigns (1809–1814), Wellington's army at first was organized into 8 brigades of 2 or 3 battalions each. Reorganized as its size increased, it consisted finally of 7 divisions, a light division, and the cavalry under separate command. Although the elements of the divisions varied, they were composed ordinarily of 2 British brigades and 1 Portuguese brigade (usually with 3 battalions), about 6,000 men each. The cavalry was organized as a division of 3 brigades of 2 regiments each. The light division served as a protective screen for the entire army, operating far to the front.

One of the more interesting and important aspects of Wellington's organization grew out of his efforts to secure a strong screen of skirmishers to meet the French *tirailleurs.* Wellington added to every brigade in his army an extra company of light riflemen to reinforce the 3 light companies which were by now standard in the British brigade. Further, each of the brigades of the light division had a number of rifle companies.

LOGISTICS

Napoleon was a master of planned and improvised supply. Logistical planning, which provided, in advance, depots and distribution points for the supply of armies, was brought to a higher and more efficient plane than heretofore envisaged.

Insofar as possible, Napoleon's armies lived off the countryside through which hey were marching or fighting. Troops were often billeted in towns and villages, here the local population was required to provide food. The soldiers and supply lumns following the troops each carried 4 days' provisions, to be consumed only

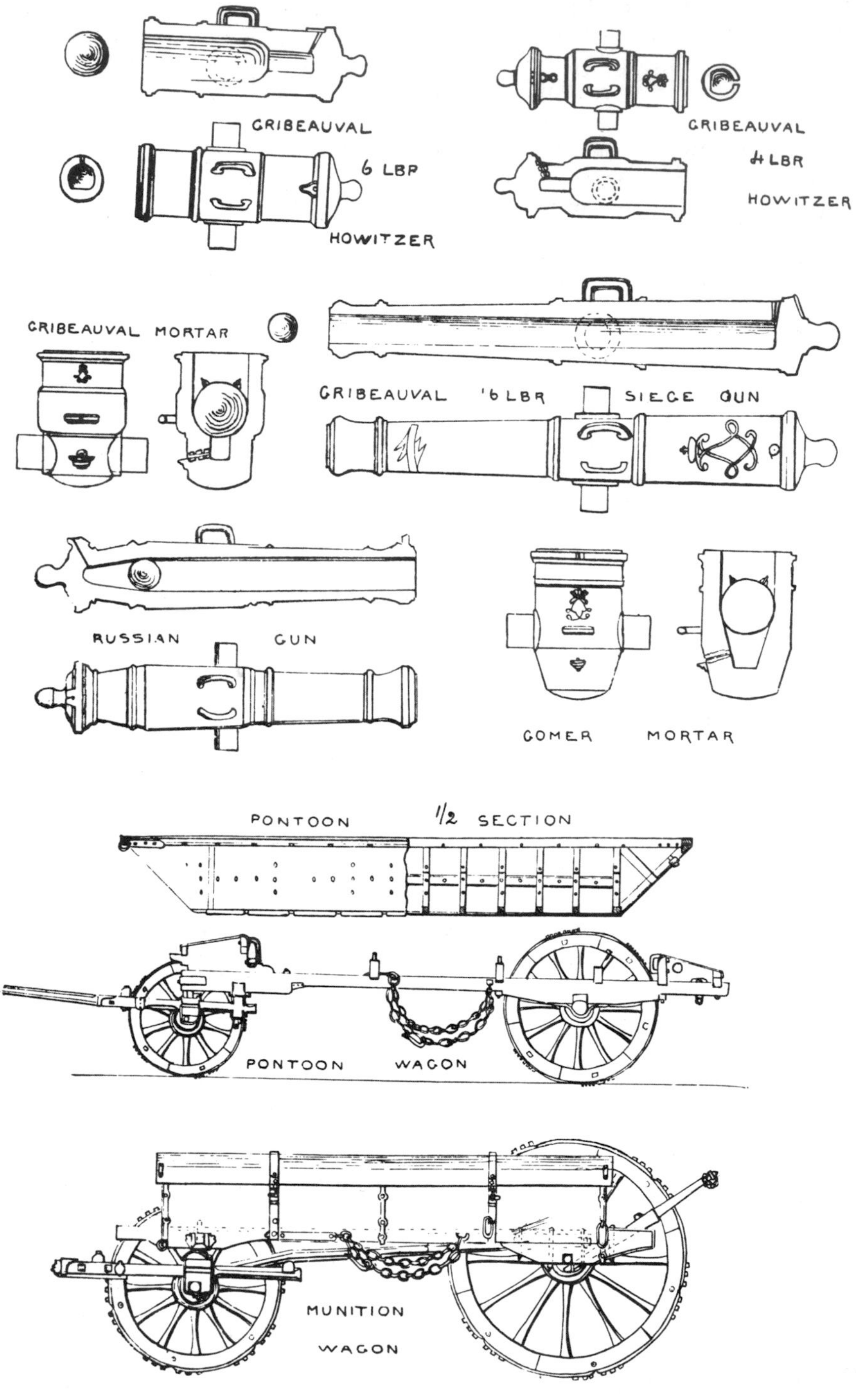

Artillery of the Napoleonic era

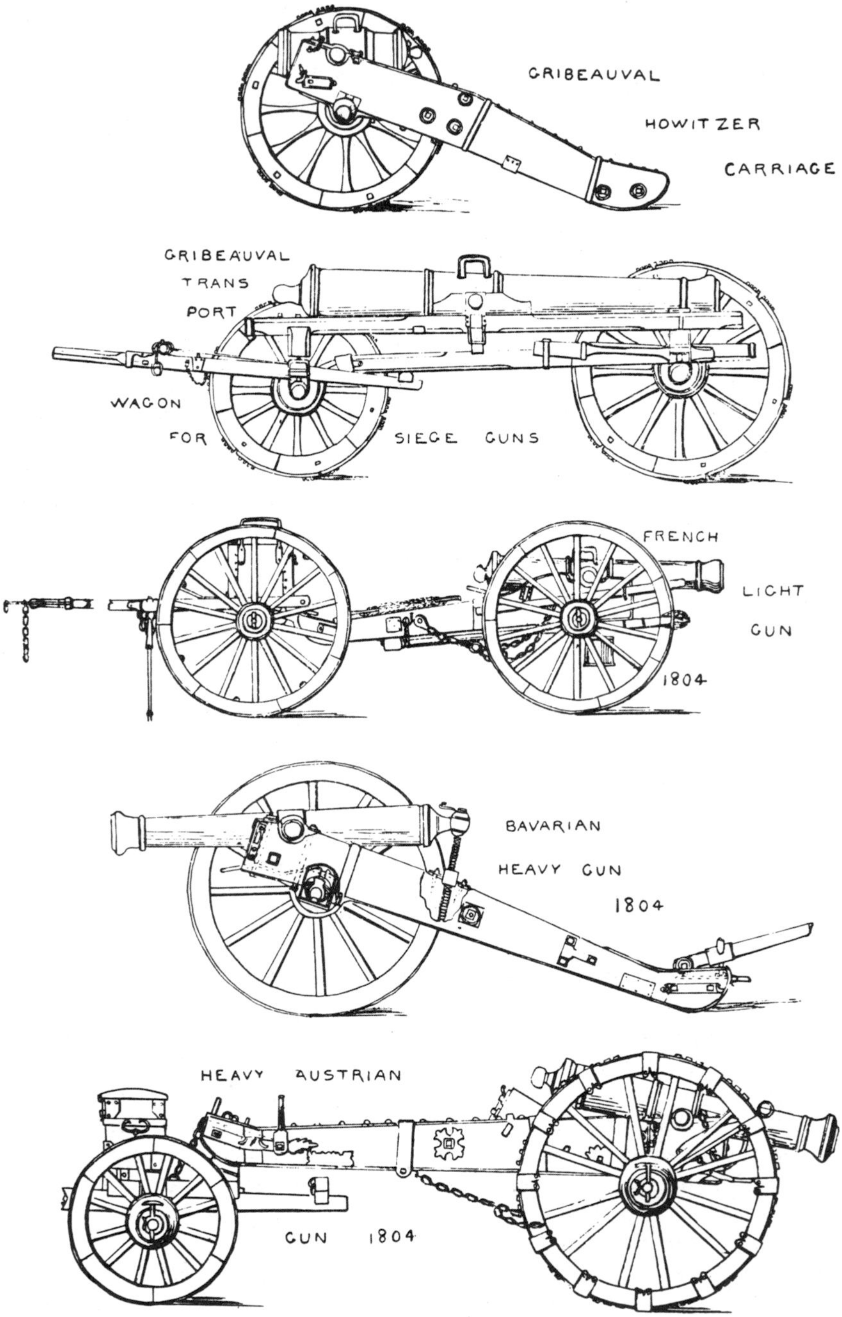

Artillery of the Napoleonic era

in emergency. In addition, provisions were stored at the main base and intermediate depots, the latter moved forward with the advance of the troops.

Through this forethought, French armies moved with amazing rapidity. The most notable instance was the 500-mile march in 1805 from the northern coast of France across Western Europe to Ulm, Vienna, and Austerlitz. A force of nearly 200,000 men kept up an average of 12 to 15 miles per day for 5 weeks, the fastest sustained march of comparable length by an army since the days of Genghis Khan.

This system of logistics proved very satisfactory until the Russian campaign of 1812, when it completely broke down because of bad roads in Russia, the poverty and devastation of the country, and activities of the Russian partisans.

MILITARY THEORY AND STRATEGY

Napoleon

The first coherent new concept of warmaking to manifest itself since Genghis Khan had been demonstrated in the early campaigns of young Napoleon Bonaparte in Italy and Egypt. In his hands it continued to dominate warfare directly for the first decade and a half of this century. Although his enemies copied the Napoleonic system to the best of their abilities, they never fully understood the concept which underlay Napoleon's tremendous revolution in warmaking. Even at the time they were overwhelming him, in 1814, respectful and awed enemies like Blücher or the Duke of Wellington could say (the statement, attributed to both, was probably Blücher's) that Napoleon's mere presence on the battlefield was worth 40,000 men.

Napoleon never committed his concepts to paper in systematic form. From his writings and remarks have been collected a number (varying, but the most authoritative collection has 115) of maxims which, one way or the other, encompass most of his fundamental ideas on strategy and tactics. These maxims are, however, very uneven; sometimes they are merely aphorisms expressing something which is relatively obvious or unimportant; often they deal with tactical and technical details of significance only to the times and places where Napoleon fought.

But Napoleon's methods of warfare and the concepts underlying those methods were deducible from the record of his accomplishments. Friends and enemies began to tackle the task of analysis even before his downfall, and the relatively superficial early insights which his enemies thus derived unquestionably played some part in that downfall. In subsequent decades three great theorists devoted themselves to more systematic and objective analysis, as noted below.

Napoleon avoided stereotypes and attempted to develop his plans for every campaign and every battle in such a way that his enemies could never know what to expect from him. Nevertheless, as he himself remarked, his theories were based upon simple principles, and certain broad patterns of strategic concepts and methods can be discerned from his many campaigns and battles. (One historian has asserted that he fought more battles than Alexander, Hannibal, and Caesar combined; while this depends upon the definition of a "battle," nonetheless it is indicative of the richness of the Napoleonic record.)

Insofar as possible, Napoleon tried to win a campaign before the first battle was fought. Whenever there was an opportunity, he would combine rapid marching and skillful deception to pass around the enemy's flanks to reach the hostile line of communications, and then turn to make the enemy fight at a disadvantage. Outstanding among the campaigns which were thus won before the fighting began were Marengo, Ulm, and Jena.

To deceive and confuse his enemies, whose combined military strength almost always exceeded his, as well as to permit rapidity of movement and efficient foraging, Napoleon kept his forces spread out until the last possible moment. Then, concentrating rapidly, he would bring superior forces to bear at some critical point. Rivoli, Friedland, and Dresden are typical examples. In a favorite variant, Napoleon would endeavor to place his concentrated army between two hostile armies, defeating them in turn. His first and last campaigns are good examples: Montenotte and Waterloo; his failure in the latter was due to the failure of performance (his and his subordinates') to match his superb strategic concept.

Napoleon's Enemies

After the first defeats inflicted on them by Napoleon, other European military leaders tried to imitate him. They gradually introduced divisions and army corps into their armies, replaced linear tactics by deep combat formations (except for the English), applied concentration of forces on the battlefield in general and in its decisive areas in particular, and formed reserves. But although they learned much and greatly improved their military instruments over the years, his opponents could never match the great master and never really grasped the secrets of his genius. They finally overwhelmed him through numerical superiority and the attrition of war on France, both traceable to Napoleon's diplomatic failures.

Jomini

Antoine Henri Jomini, a Swiss by birth (1779), served as a junior officer under Napoleon, being a protégé of courageous (if not brilliant) Marshal **Michel Ney.** An injustice at the hands of Napoleon's chief of staff, Marshal **Louis Alexandre Berthier,** led Jomini to resign and to transfer his allegiance to Russia in the 1813 campaign; he refused, however, to take part directly or indirectly in any operations against Napoleon. For the next 56 years he served with distinction as a general officer in the Russian Army. During those years he devoted himself to study and to writing, mostly based upon his analysis of Napoleonic operations.

Jomini's writings were voluminous. His first book, *Treatise on Great Military Operations,* written while in the French Army, led Napoleon to remark, in alarm, "It teaches my whole system of war to my enemies!" It presented for the first time in writing the fundamental principles of warfare which today are taken for granted by all military men. His *Summary of the Art of War* is his most complete and comprehensive study, and the work most often quoted.

Clausewitz

Karl von Clausewitz was born in Magdeburg, Prussia (1780). He fought with the Prussian Army in all of the campaigns against Napoleon, from disastrous Jena to victorious Waterloo. From 1818 to 1830, he was administrative director of the Kriegsakademie in Berlin, and devoted as much time as possible to writing. Most of his works were studies of military campaigns. His best-known work, however, is *On War,* which embodies his theories and doctrines. It is a book which has cast an indelible stamp on all subsequent military thought. And, as with Jomini, his principal source of inspiration was the genius of his former enemy, Napoleon.

Although Clausewitz believed that he had discovered the fundamental laws of war, he insisted that in practice these are always subject to an almost infinite umber of modifications from external influences, of which psychological and moral fluences are the most important. He was firmly opposed to any effort to codify doctrine on the basis of the laws or principles of war. He was afraid that abstract rules would be applied dogmatically on the battlefield, and with disastrous results.

Clausewitz was the greatest philosopher of war. His inspiration has been strong in every army during the century and more after his death. Probably no other military writer is so widely quoted as he. Even his critics—discarding his basic theories mostly because these theories have been so distorted by German military men in the 20th century—still repeat many of his observations.

Dennis Hart Mahan

The fame of **Alfred Thayer Mahan** as a military and naval theorist (see p. 821) has tended to obscure the reputation of his father: **Dennis Hart Mahan.** The elder Mahan graduated at the top of the class of 1824 at West Point, and was immediately appointed an assistant professor. After 2 years of teaching and 4 years of further study in France, he was appointed Professor of Engineering at West Point (1830). There being no texts available for the courses he taught (there were then no other engineering schools in the United States), he wrote his own, which became the standard American engineering texts for many years.

Nevertheless, it was the art of war which particularly fascinated Mahan. As a scientist, he spent all of his spare time in analyzing military operations of the past, and particularly those of Napoleon. These studies became the basis of a course of lectures on the art of war—the only formal instruction which American officers received in military theory (see below). He wrote several books on the subject, the most important of which was the text for his course at West Point, which was carried and studied by most of the top leaders on both sides in the American Civil War. This book, horrendously entitled *Advanced Guard, Outpost and Detachment Service of Troops, with the Essential Principles of Strategy and Grand Tactics,* was dubbed *"Outpost"* by his students.

Unlike Prussia, the United States had no war college for its officers; their formal education stopped with graduation from West Point. Mahan and his writings became the war college of the American Army.

MILITARY PROFESSIONALISM

The emergence of military professionalism came hand in hand with the appearance of coherent and scientific military theory. This theory became the basis for systematic military education, at graduate and undergraduate level, an essential element for professionalism in the modern sense. The products of this educational system then became members of a highly specialized group of professionals, the practitioners of the theory.

As with the other modern professions, this development was in large part the result of the successive impacts of the Age of Enlightenment and of the Industrial Revolution upon human affairs. It was first manifested by the appearance of military schools for youths preparing themselves for a military life. The British Royal Military College at Sandhurst (1802), the French St. Cyr (1808), and the American West Point (1802) were early examples of this development. Prussia, which had several such cadet schools even earlier, went farther, however, and established a Kriegsakademie, or War Academy (1810). This was to provide the intellectual stimulation for the Prussian General Staff and thus, more than any single factor to spark Prussian (later German) pre-eminence in land warfare for more than century.

WAR AT SEA

Britain continued to dominate the oceans of the world. The trend away from the "formalist" school to the "melee" school was completed by Nelson's dramatically successful adaptation of his means to the circumstances, without regard to custom, tradition, or "Fighting Instructions." His ability to do this was greatly facilitated by a greatly improved signal-flag system developed toward the close of the previous century by Admiral Sir **Home Popham** and officially introduced at the beginning of this period (1800).

Nelson's tactics, combined with Popham's means of control, brought to perfection methods of warfare at sea with sailing vessels. No significant changes or improvements were possible without radical new developments in science and technology. Yet, in fact, these developments were already at hand. The first steamship was launched in France 18 years before the Battle of Trafalgar.

But professional naval men were most reluctant to accept the new technology. Maritime nations, freed from dependence upon the wind for motive power, found themselves hampered by the limitations in cruising range imposed by steam. The necessity for coaling stations stimulated a scramble for colonies. Dubious eyebrows

Ship of the line and frigate at the time of Trafalgar

were raised in the matter of iron hulls versus wood. In a naval era still wedded tactically to the exchange of broadsides, the vulnerability of paddlewheels to gunfire loomed large. **John Ericsson**'s screw propeller, adopted in midperiod, would remove this particular objection, but, except for a few keen-minded and progressive enthusiasts, an overriding fear remained, particularly in England, lest steam propulsion cancel out the advantages of good seamanship as a factor for victory.

The consensus of naval thought was best expressed in the words of the British Admiralty in 1828: "Their Lordships find it their bounden duty to discourage to the best of their ability the employment of steam vessels, as they consider the introduction of steam is calculated to strike a fatal blow at the naval supremacy of the Empire."

THE NAPOLEONIC* WARS, 1800–1815

WAR OF THE SECOND COALITION (continued)

On November 9, 1799, **Napoleon Bonaparte** became dictator of France. By *oup d'état* he placed himself in complete control as First Consul. He offered peace

* Napoleon Bonaparte's accession to power as First Consul is taken as the dividing point ween the Wars of the French Revolution and the Napoleonic Wars.

to the allies, but his gesture was rebuffed. Though Russia had withdrawn, the war continued. He prepared to wage it aggressively.

Operations on Land, 1800–1802

SECOND ITALIAN CAMPAIGN, 1800

The Austrians planned to drive the French from their remaining footholds in Italy. General **Paul Kray von Krajowa,** with 120,000 men, was to hold Germany against any offensive movements by **Moreau,** who had about 120,000 along the upper Rhine in Switzerland and Alsace. Baron **Michael Melas,** with another Austrian army, 100,000 strong, was to overwhelm **Masséna,** who with 40,000 men held the Riviera coast of Italy.

1800, March 8. Bonaparate Raises a New Army. The Army of Reserve assembled at Dijon while he weighed 2 possible courses of action: to combine with Moreau in an offensive through Switzerland into Germany to cut off Kray from his communications with Vienna, or to invade Italy through Switzerland and crush Melas between his army and Masséna's. He decided on the latter plan.

1800, April 6–20. Austrian Victories in Italy. Masséna's army was scattered; he with 12,000 men was driven into Genoa and besieged by General **Karl Ott** with 24,000 men. Melas pursued the remainder of the French, under **Louis Gabriel Suchet,** beyond Nice into the valley of the Var. Bonaparte hastened the concentration of the Army of Reserve at Geneva.

1800, May 14–24. Bonaparte Crosses the Great St. Bernard Pass. He had only 37,000 men. He ordered Moreau to send 15,000 to join him in Lombardy via the Simplon and St. Gotthard passes. To divert Melas' attention, an additional 5,000 men moved through the Mt. Cenis Pass. Bonaparte's advance guard brushed aside Austrian resistance at Fort Bard and Ivrea, and debouched into the Lombardy Plain (May 24). He seized Milan and Pavia and advanced toward Brescia, Cremona, and Piacenza, hoping to relieve Masséna. Melas, hearing of Bonaparte's arrival in Italy, hurried back from Nice.

1800, June 4. Capitulation of Genoa. Masséna, after a protracted and terrible siege, capitulated to Ott, the 7,000 survivors of the French garrison marching out with the honors of war.

1800, June 7. Melas Cut Off from Austria. The Austrian general, at Turin, discovered that Bonaparte was on his line of communication, advancing west against him. Melas moved east, concentrating 34,000 men at Alessandria (June 13).

June 9. Battle of Montebello. General **Jean Lannes,** whose corps numbered 8,000 men, unexpectedly met Ott, who with 18,000 had marched north from Genoa. Lannes attacked furiously; joined by General **Claude Victor**'s corps of 6,000, he drove the Austrians in confusion toward Alessandria.

1800, June 14. Battle of Marengo. Bonaparte, thinking Melas still at Turin, approached carelessly, with his troops widely separated. Unexpectedly he found himself engaged by superior numbers at Marengo, a mile east of Alessandria. He had only 18,000 men—the corps of **Claude Victor** and **Jean Lannes,** and **Joachim Murat**'s cavalry reserve. **Louis C. A. Desaix**'s corps and other units were scattered farther east and south, gathering supplies. Melas enveloped the French right. By 1 o'clock the Austrians had driven the French back 2 miles. Thinking he had won the battle, Melas ordered a march formation, proceeding east leisurely. But Bonaparte, undismayed by apparent defeat, had rallied his troops and had sent for reinforcements—about 14,000, mainly Desaix's corps, only a few miles away. At 5 P.M. he counterattacked; the Austrian advance guard was struck by Desaix from the front, while the French cavalry (under **François E. Kellermann,** son of the hero of Valmy) swept down on the north flank of the Austrian main body, followed by Lannes's corps and the Guard. Mela

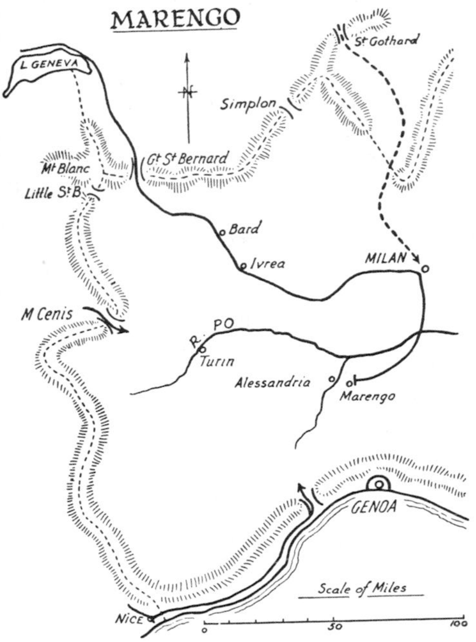

forces crumbled; half of his army was scattered, cut down, or made prisoner. The remainder fled back into Allessandria. Austrian losses were about 9,000, French 4,000. Desaix was among the dead.

1800, June 15. Melas Capitulates. The Second Italian Campaign had virtually ended. Bonaparte returned to Paris, ordering General **Guillaume M. A. Brune** to advance on Mantua to consolidate the victory.

GERMANY, 1800–1801

1800, May–June. Moreau Drives Kray into Bavaria. He won victories at **Stockach** (May 3), **Möskirch** (May 5), **Ulm** (May 16), and **Hochstadt** (June 19). Kray retired behind the Inn. Moreau slowly advanced toward Munich.

1800, July 15–November 13. Armistice. Kray was replaced by the youthful **Archduke John** when operations renewed.

1800, December 3. Battle of Hohenlinden. The 2 armies, each seriously overextended, clashed in mud, snow, and rain. Moreau had about 90,000 men available for battle; John had about 83,000, but committed his forces piecemeal. The superior speed and energy of the French, combined with considerable good luck, enabled them to surround large portions of the Austrian Army, which was completely crushed. Moreau marched eastward toward Vienna; another French army under General **Jacques Macdonald** invaded the Tyrol from Switzerland; Brune's army in Italy advanced toward the passes over the Julian Alps.

1800, December 25. Austrians Sue for Peace.

1801, February 9. Treaty of Lunéville. This reaffirmed the terms of Leoben and Campo Formio. In addition Spain ceded Louisiana to France, which in turn soon sold the vast territory to the United States (1803).

OPERATIONS IN EGYPT, 1800–1801

1800, January 21. Convention of El Arish. Kléber, attacked by both the English and the Turks, agreed to evacuate Egypt on guarantee of free passage of his troops to France. England later disavowing the agreement, Kléber attacked and defeated the Turks at **Heliopolis** (March 20) and recovered Cairo. He was assassinated (June 14), the day Bonaparte was winning at Marengo; **Jacques F. de Menou** assumed command.

1801, March 8. Amphibious Landing at Aboukir. A British-Turkish army (18,000 strong) under Sir **Ralph Abercromby** landed in a brilliant operation.

1801, March 20. Battle of Aboukir. The allies defeated Menou; Abercromby was killed.

1801, April–August. Reconquest of Egypt. The allies took Cairo (July), Alexandria (August). British sea power preventing all French attempts to reinforce the Egyptian expedition, Menou capitulated (August 31). His 26,000 troops were given immediate free passage to France (September). British sea power had wrecked Bonaparte's dream of Oriental conquest.

War at Sea, 1800–1802

1800–1801. Routine Operations. Aside from blockade and convoy operations, the major effort of the Royal Navy was in support of operations against the French in Egypt. The principal exploit was the support of Abercromby's landing at Aboukir by the fleet of Sir **William Keith** (see above).

1801, February. Neutral League. Following the Treaty of Lunéville, Russia, Prussia, Denmark, and Sweden joined to protect their shipping from British belligerent claims.

1801, March. British Reaction. A squadron of 53 sail—18 of them ships of the line—entered the Baltic under command of Admiral Sir **Hyde Parker,** with Sir **Horatio Nelson** as second in command.

1801, April 2. Battle of Copenhagen. Nelson, with 12 ships of the line, boldly sailed into the harbor of Copenhagen. Ignoring orders from Parker, he engaged Admiral ***Fischer's*** Danish flotilla consisting of warships, armed hulks and floating batteries at anchor. In a 5-hour fire fight, fierce Danish resistance was smashed. Nelson hoped to induce Parker to continue to Revel (Tallin) to destroy the Russian fleet, but an armistice suspended further operations. Meanwhile Czar **Paul** had been assassinated (March 24), and his successor, **Alexander I,** signed a convention terminating all necessity for further hostilities (June 17).

1801, July 6 and 12. Naval Battles of Algeciras. Sir **James Saumarez** suffered a setback in an inconclusive action with a small French squadron raiding near Gibraltar (July 6), but retrieved his reputation by a victory against 2-to-1 odds after the French had been reinforced by a much larger Spanish fleet.

Peace of Amiens, 1802–1803

1802, March 27. Treaty of Amiens. Peace between France and England brought general peace to Europe for the first time in a decade.

1802, August 2. Bonaparte Proclaimed Consul for Life.

FRANCO-BRITISH WAR, 1803–1805

1803, May 16. Resumption of Hostilities. Britain imposed a naval blockade of the Continent. Bonaparte began preparations for an invasion of England.

1803–1805. French Threaten Invasion of England. If Bonaparte really intended to invade, all his efforts were thwarted by British sea power. His invasion flotilla gathered at the Rhine mouths was seriously mauled by **Sidney Smith**'s fire and explosion ships (October 2, 1804). British squadrons also balked French naval domination of the Mediterranean, the East Indies, and the West Indies. As **Alfred Mahan** puts it: "Those far distant, storm-beaten ships, upon which the Grand Army never looked, stood between it and the domination of the world."*

1804, December 2. Bonaparte's Coronation as Napoleon, Emperor of the French. He continued concentrating his Grand Army on the northern coast. Numerous landing craft were constructed; there was much apprehension in England. But British diplomatic maneuverings were bringing results.

WAR OF THE THIRD COALITION, 1805–1807

1805. Britain Gains Allies. Austria, Russia, and Sweden prepared to revenge themselves. The bulk of the French Army was assembled near Boulogne; the only other important French concentration was in north Italy: Masséna, with 50,000 men. The allies planned first to destroy Masséna in Italy, then to move westward with overwhelming forces on the northern side of the Alps toward the Rhine and France.

War on Land, 1805

ULM CAMPAIGN

1805, August 31. The Grand Army Marches Eastward. Napoleon, learning of his enemies' intentions, took the initiative, discarding plans for invading England. The Grand Army, totaling more than 200,000 men, secretly began to march eastward from the Boulogne area.

1805, September 2. Austrian Invasion of Bavaria. General **Mack von Leiberich,** knowing nothing of the French movement, marched toward Ulm with 50,000 troops. The **Archduke Charles** with 100,000 men prepared to attack Masséna in Italy. A Russian army of 120,000 began to march westward. An additional contingent was promised by Sweden. When

---

* Alfred T. Mahan, *Influence of Sea Power upon the French Revolution and Empire* Boston, Little Brown, 1893, II, 118.

they joined Mack, the second stage of the allied plan would begin.

1805, September 26. French Cross the Rhine. The advance continued on a wide front. Mack, still unaware that Napoleon had left Boulogne, was between Ulm and Munich; the **Archduke John** with 33,000 Austrians was concentrated at Innsbruck; the Archduke Charles was in the Adige Valley, between Trent and Venice. Far behind them, the Russian generals **Mikhail I. Kutuzov** with 55,000 men and **Friedrich Wilhelm Buxhöwden** with 40,000 more were approaching the Carpathians.

1805, October 6. French Reach the Danube. While Murat's cavalry, thrusting through the Black Forest, demonstrated in front of Mack at Ulm, the Grand Army, in 6 great columns, swept north and east of the Austrian general in a wide concentric arc. Too late Mack realized the French were behind him.

1805, October 17. Capitulation of Ulm. After one futile attempt to break through the encirclement at **Elchingen** (October 14), Mack surrendered with nearly 30,000 men, 40 standards and 65 guns.

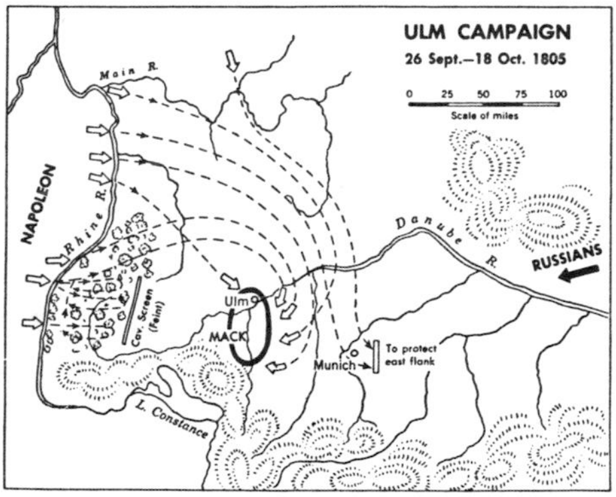

COMMENT. *This campaign opened the most brilliant year of Napoleon's career. His army had been trained to perfection; his plans were faultless. Sweeping through Western Europe on a wide front, he concentrated the magnificent machine on Mack's line of communications in one of the finest historical examples of a turning movement. Ulm was not a battle; it was a strategic victory so complete and so overwhelming that the issue was never seriously contested in tactical combat.*

THE ADVANCE ON VIENNA

1805, October. Napoleon Advances East. He peeled off several army corps to the south to prevent interference by Austrian movements through the Alps from Italy.

1805, October 30. Battle of Caldiero. Masséna in Italy attacked the Archduke Charles, who retired eastward, hotly pursued by Masséna. Joined by Archduke John, retreating from the Tyrol, Charles withdrew across the Julian Alps.

1805, November 1–14. Invasion of Austria. Napoleon, leaving some 50,000 men to guard his line of communications, drove the Russian Kutuzov before him and occupied the Austrian capital. The Russian fought effective delaying actions at **Dürrenstein** (November 11) and **Hollabrünn** (November 15–16).

AUSTERLITZ CAMPAIGN

1805, November 15. Napoleon Advances North. Leaving 20,000 men in Vienna, he began concentrating the major portion of his remaining army near Brünn, some 70 miles from Vienna.

1805, November 20–28. The Strategic Situation. Napoleon with 65,000 men, in the midst of his enemies, waited for them to move. The **Archduke Ferdinand** with 18,000 men lay at Prague, to the northwest; Emperors Alexander of Russia and **Francis II** of Austria at Olmütz, to the northeast (Kutuzov actually commanded) with 90,000 Russians and Austrians. The Archdukes Charles and John, with 80,000 more, were blocked from crossing the Alps (by about 20,000 men of the corps of **Michel Ney** and **Auguste F. L. Marmont,** who guarded the passes) and harassed by Masséna's 35,000 as they withdrew to Austria through Hungary south of the Alps. Napoleon's problem was to prevent the junction of these numerically superior allied forces while preserving his line of communications through Vienna to France. His apparently exposed situation was enticing to his enemies. The emperors and Kutuzov planned to move south from Olmütz, circle his right flank, and cut his communications. This was exactly what he anticipated.

1805, November 28. The Allied Army Begins to Move. The French army lay facing east, about 2 miles west of the vil-

lage of Austerlitz. Deliberately, Napoleon placed his army on low ground and over-extended his right wing—1 division—for 2 miles in plain view of allied scouts, while the bulk of his troops were collected east of Brünn, near the road to **Olmütz.**

1805, December 1, P.M. The Allies Reach Austerlitz. At once they noted the weakened right flank of the French army. They planned to crush it and get between Napoleon and Vienna.

1805, December 2. Battle of Austerlitz. At dawn the weight of the allied main effort fell upon the French right. Although reinforced by the arrival of Louis N. Davout with 8,000 additional men, the French right was forced back. By 9 A.M. fully one-third of the allied army was pressing against this wing, with more troops moving laterally across the French front to join in the assault. Napoleon then sprung his trap. **Nicolas J. Soult**'s corps, in the French center, stormed the heights of Pratzen and split the allied front. Soult then encircled the allied left, rolled it up, and, assisted by Davout, drove it in confused retreat. French artillery fire broke ice on frozen ponds, and many Russians were drowned. Meanwhile, the corps of **Jean Baptiste J. Bernadotte** assaulted the

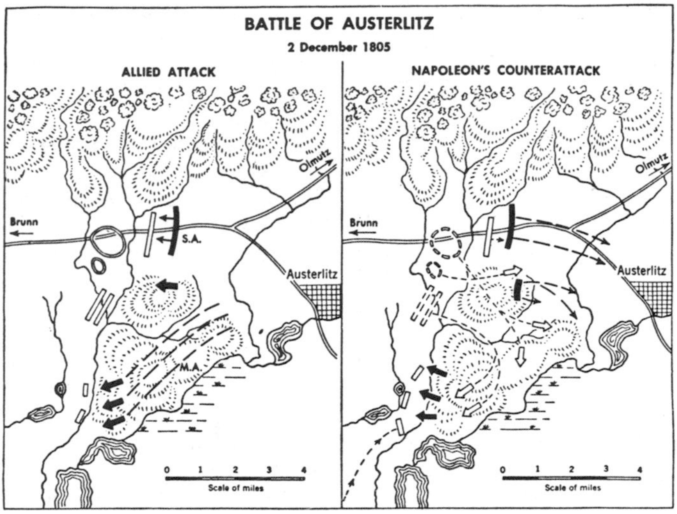

rectly east, through the gap made by Soult, while on the French left Lannes's corps drove full tilt against the allied right, on the Brünn-Olmütz road. The allied right, under Russian Prince **Peter I. Bagration,** resisted fiercely until enveloped by Bernadotte from the south. By nightfall the allied army had ceased to exist. French losses were nearly 9,000 men; the Austro-Russian losses were 26,000 men, 45 standards, and 185 guns; the remnants of the allied army were hopelessly scattered.

COMMENT. *Austerlitz stands as a tactical masterpiece ranking with Arbela, Cannae, and Leuthen.*

1805, December 4. Austrian Capitulation. Emperor Francis agreed to an unconditional surrender. The shattered forces of Czar Alexander retreated to Russia.

1805, December 26. Treaty of Pressburg. Austria withdrew from the war, surrendering territory in Germany and Italy; France gained virtual domination over western and southern Germany. Napoleon had changed the political face of Europe.

War at Sea, 1805

1805, April–July. Nelson's Pursuit of Villeneuve. Admiral **Pierre Villeneuve,** escaping Nelson's blockade of Toulon, sailed into the Atlantic, was joined by a Spanish force, and sailed for the West Indies with about 20 ships. Nelson, who had 10 ships, pursued. After some maneuvering in the West Indies, Villeneuve fled back across the Atlantic, again pursued by Nelson.

1805, July 22. Action off Cape Finisterre. British Sir **Robert Calder**'s squadron of 18 ships clashed with Villeneuve's combined Franco-Spanish fleet, capturing 2 Spanish ships. Villeneuve sailed to Cádiz, where he was reinforced.

1805, August. Napoleon's Naval Plan. Villeneuve was to take his fleet from Cádiz to the Mediterranean. There he would unite with other French ships at Cartagena and move on southern Italy to support Masséna's campaign. Villeneuve knew that Britain's Nelson, now with 29 ships of the line (actually only 27 were present), lay in the offing, a fact unknown to Napoleon; but Villeneuve, smarting under the threat of removal from command for cowardice, complied with his orders (September 27).

1805, October 21. Battle of Trafalgar. Nelson, off Cape Spartel, learned of the allies' move and sailed to meet them. Off Cape Trafalgar the fleets clashed. The Franco-Spanish force of 33 ships turned back toward Cádiz in a 5-mile-long irregular line. In accordance with a prearranged plan, Nelson, in 2 divisions, each in single column, on a course at right angles to his adversary's, drove directly into the center of the long allied column, cut-

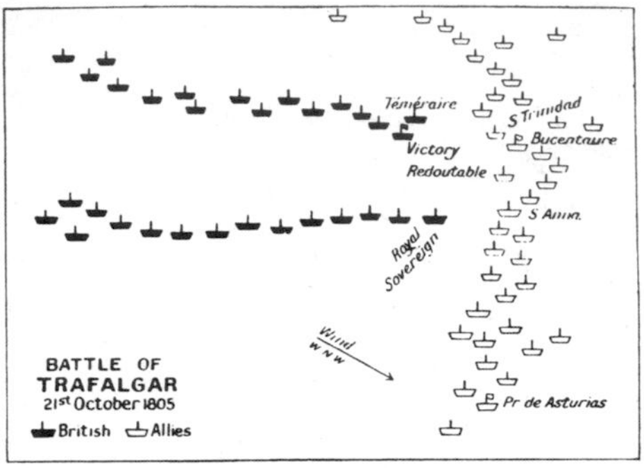

ting it in two. In a 5-hour battle, 18 allied ships were taken; the remainder fled, only 11 reaching Cádiz. No English ship was lost. Nelson was mortally wounded as his flagship *Victory* closed in furious combat with the French *Redoutable.*

COMMENT. *Nelson had destroyed French naval power and established Britain as the mistress of the seas in the most decisive major naval victory—tactically and strategically—of history.*

Jena Campaign, 1806

1806. Napoleon Controls Central and Western Germany. He established the Confederation of the Rhine. By August, the last vestige of German unity, the Holy Roman Empire, expired; its emperor, **Francis II,** becoming **Francis I,** Emperor of Austria. Prussia, which until the French victory of Austerlitz had contemplated joining the coalition against Napoleon, was now so alarmed by the state of events that, with England's encouragement, she secretly prepared for war. Saxony joined Prussia.

1806, September. Opposing Plans. Napoleon's Grand Army of 200,000 was still mostly in southern Germany. He prepared to invade Prussia. Secretly he concentrated far to the east, in northeastern Bavaria, close to the Austrian border, but without violating Austrian neutrality. The Prussian-Saxon field army comprised about 130,000 men under the over-all command of **Karl Wilhelm Ferdinand, Duke of Brunswick.**

1806, October 8. Napoleon Starts North. The rapidity of his strategic concentration and of his advance was remarkable. Preceded by a cavalry screen, the Grand Army moved in 3 parallel columns on a front of about 30 miles at a rate of 15 miles per day. Roughly forming a great square, the army was prepared for tactical concentration in any direction.

1806, October 12. Strategic Turning Movement. The French advance by-passed the Prussian left flank, completely surprising the Prussians. Their first intimation of the situation came when the corps of Marshal Lannes, on the left vertix of the French square, overwhelmed a smaller Prussian force at **Saalfeld** (October 10). Napoleon was now closer to Berlin than they were.

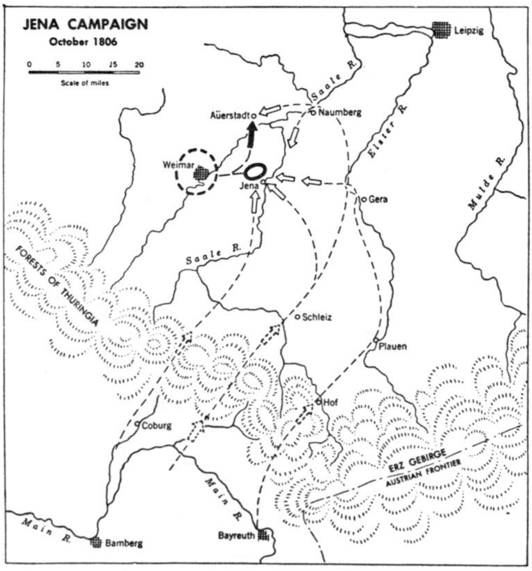

Knowing that the bulk of the Prussian Army was to his left, he ordered Davout and Bernadotte to move west from Naumburg to cut the Prussian line of communications. The remainder of his army advanced toward Jena. Davout responded correctly; Bernadotte, misinterpreting his orders, moved southwest instead of west.

1806, October 14. Battle of Jena. Meanwhile the Prussians, alarmed by news of the French advance, changed their own plans. The **Duke of Brunswick,** with 63,000 men, moved northeast toward Auerstadt, 15 miles north of Jena. Prince **Friedrich Ludwig Hohenlohe,** and 51,000 more were scattered on a 15-mile front between Weimar and Jena to protect Brunswick's rear. Napoleon, shortly after dawn, struck Hohenlohe, concentrating 100,000 men at Jena. By noon, he completely swept the Prussians from the field.

1806, October 14. Battle of Auerstadt. Davout with 27,000 men engaged Brunswick's 63,000. In an epic defensive battle, Davout, on the Prussian line of communications, withstood repeated assaults for more than 6 hours. Brunswick was mortally wounded and King **Frederick William III** assumed command. Prussian morale was weakened by rumors of the French success at Jena. As the Prussian effort slackened, Davout counterattacked. Bernadotte, near Dornburg—far from both battles—now realized something was wrong and marched to the sound of the guns. By 4 P.M. his fresh corps, nearly 20,000 strong, entered the field behind the already routed troops of Hohenlohe and approached the rear of Frederick's wavering command. The entire Prussian Army now disintegrated. They lost 25,000 killed and wounded, and nearly 25,000 more made prisoner. French casualties were approximately 8,000 on both fields.

COMMENT. *Once again Napoleon, by rapidity of movement and skillful combinations, had won a strategic victory before tactical operations ever began.*

1806, October–November. Pursuit. The Grand Army immediately swept northward after the remnants of the Prussian Army. Berlin was seized (October 24). The last element of Prussian resistance, **Gebhard L. von Blücher**'s command, surrendered near Lübeck, nearly 150 miles northwest of Berlin (November 24). Frederick William fled to Russia.

1806, November 30. Advance into Poland. Napoleon moved east with 80,000 men to the line of the Vistula (Wisla) River, occupying Warsaw (Warszawa) to thwart any Russian attempt to sustain Prussia. Count **Lévin A. Bennigsen,** with about 100,000 Russians and some Prussian fragments, lay at Pultusk.

1806, December 30. Winter Quarters. After desperate rear-guard fighting at **Pultusk** (December 26), Bennigsen evaded French attempts to corner him. Napoleon, faced by bitter cold and the exhaustion of his own troops, went into winter quarters. His corps were spread across northern Poland and east Prussia from the Bug River to Ebling (Elblag) on the Baltic.

Eylau Campaign, 1807

1807, January. Russian Offensive. Bennigsen attacked Ney's cantonments south of Königsberg (Kaliningrad) and forced him to withdraw. Pursuing into East Prussia, Bennigsen's communications were menaced by Napoleon's rapid concentration and advance. The Russian withdrew hurriedly. Napoleon caught up with him February 7 at Preussisch-Eylau (Bagrationowski).

1807, February 8. Battle of Eylau. Napoleon hastily attacked, with only part of his army in hand. Russian strength was 67,000 (with a Prussian corps of 10,000 more moving rapidly toward them); Napoleon had less than 50,000 (Ney's and Davout's corps were expected by noon). In a driving snowstorm, a French assault was checked. Davout arrived and turned the Russian left. But he, in turn, was checked by the arrival of **C. Anton Wilhelm Lestocq**'s Prussian corps. Ney now arrived, but neither side could gain a decisive advantage. That night Bennigsen withdrew. Losses on both sides were enormous. Russian casualties were 25,000 men killed and wounded, with some 3,000 men and 23 guns captured. The French lost nearly 18,000 men, with 1,000 more captured. Both armies returned to winter quarters; both brought up reinforcements and refitted.

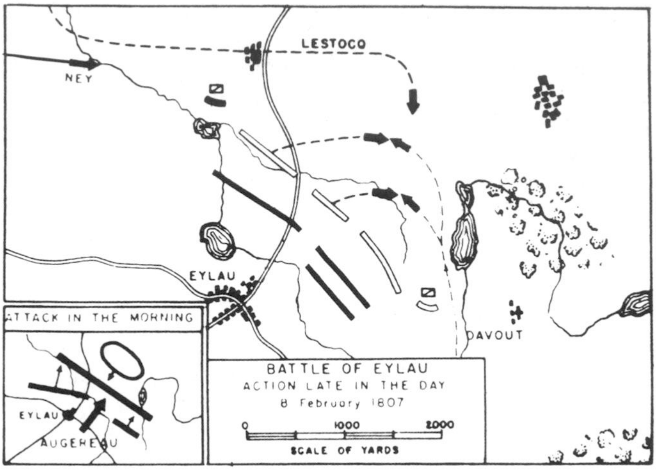

Friedland Campaign

1807, March 15–April 27. Siege of Danzig. The French captured the city, beating off futile Russian and Prussian relief efforts. Napoleon planned a spring offensive to begin June 10.

1807, June 5. Bennigsen Resumes the Offensive. Again he hoped to overwhelm Ney in a surprise assault. Ney withdrew as Napoleon concentrated north of Allenstein.

1807, June 10. Battle of Heilsburg. Napoleon repulsed the Russians, who retreated north. Moving by parallel roads, Napoleon placed the bulk of his army between Bennigsen at Friedland and Lestocq at Königsberg (June 13).

1807, June 14. Battle of Friedland. Napoleon sent Lannes, with 17,000 men, to pin Bennigsen down while the remainder of the army concentrated to the west. The Russian, with 58,000 men in hand and 30,000 more nearby, crossed the Alle River and attacked Lannes with 46,000, leaving the remainder in reserve east of the river. Lannes's delaying action halted the Russians after a 3-mile advance. Napoleon, taking personal command of the battle as his concentrations progressed, launched his main attack at 5 P.M. with 80,000 men. Within 2 hours the Russians' left flank had disintegrated and they were driven back into Friedland. Their resistance stiffened, but by 8 P.M. Napoleon had driven them across the river in great disorder, leaving 25,000 dead and wounded on the

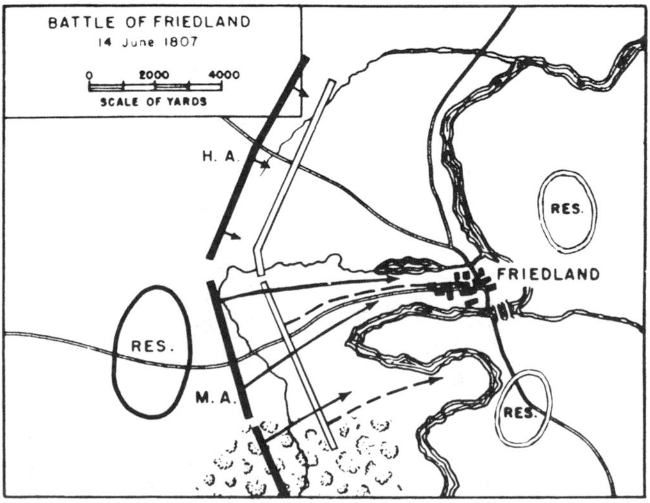

field and 80 guns. French casualties were about 8,000 men.

1807, June 15. Evacuation of Königsberg. Lestocq, who was being pressed by Murat, retreated to Tilsit with 25,000 men when he learned of Bennigsen's defeat.

1807, June 19. Napoleon Occupies Tilsit (Sovetsk). The Russians asked for a truce, which he granted.

1807, July 7–9. Treaties of Tilsit. Napoleon met his enemies—Alexander of Russia and Frederick William III of Prussia—on a raft in the middle of the Niemen (Neman). Prussia gave up to the Grand Duchy of Poland all land taken in the partitions of Poland (see pp. 695 and 696). She gave to Napoleon and the Confederation of the Rhine all her territory between the Elbe and Rhine rivers. Her army was reduced to 42,000 men. She was to pay an indemnity of 140 million francs; until paid, French troops would occupy the country. Russia recognized the Grand Duchy of Warsaw and agreed to an alliance with France against Britain.

COMMENT. *Napoleon was the virtual ruler of Western and Central Europe.*

THE PENINSULAR WAR—CAMPAIGNS OF 1807–1808

1807, July–October. England Alone in Opposition to Napoleon. Her coastline was guarded by her navy; her offensive operations were concentrated in a stringent naval blockade of the entire European coastline. By economic pressures England hoped that internal stresses on the Continent would eventually lead to a new coalition to challenge French control. Napoleon had imposed a counterblockade on Britain—his **Continental System**—aimed to throttle British trade (November 21, 1806). After Tilsit, neutral Portugal was the only access route (save by smuggling) for British trade with the Continent. Napoleon now turned his attention to the Iberian Peninsula.

1807, November–December. French Invasion of Portugal. With Spain's permission, **Andoche Junot** led an army into Portugal, capturing Lisbon (December 1). The Portuguese royal family fled to Brazil.

1807, December 17. Milan Decree. This reaffirmed the Continental System. British trade was forbidden from all Europe. Actually, smuggling became rampant, particularly through Spanish ports.

1808, March. French Invasion of Spain. Under pretext of guarding the Spanish coast, Murat led a French army of 100,000 into Spain. **Charles IV** and his son **Ferdinand** were forced to renounce the throne; Napoleon's brother **Joseph** (who had been King of Naples) was crowned King of Spain. (Murat succeeded him as King of Naples.)

1808, May. Insurrection Flares in Spain. French garrisons became islands in a sea of guerrilla warfare, accompanied by intense cruelty. Murat temporarily fell back to the Ebro. British arms, equipment, and money poured in to help the Portuguese and Spanish peoples. The British government decided to send an expeditionary force to Portugal, commanded by Sir Arthur Wellesley.

1808, June 15–August 15. First Siege of Saragossa. The Spanish garrison, assisted by the aroused population, resisted French attempts to reopen the main line of communications into central Spain and Portugal. After Murat's withdrawal to the Ebro, the French raised the siege.

1808, July 19. Battle of Baylen. General **Pierre Dupont**'s 20,000 men, surrounded by some 35,000 Spanish levies, were forced to capitulate. Promise of safe conduct to France was immediately violated; the unarmed French not butchered on the spot were thrown into prison hulks where most of them perished. The disaster—the first surrender of a Napoleonic army—stimulated Spanish resistance and shocked French morale. Junot's army in Portugal was isolated.

1808, July 20. French Reoccupy Madrid. This partially offset Baylen.

1808, August 1. The Wellesley Expedition. Wellesley landed north of Lisbon.

1808, August 21. Battle of Vimeiro. Wellesley, with 17,000 men, repulsed Junot's attack with 14,000.

1808, August 30. Junot Capitulates. His position had been rendered untenable by a popular uprising in Lisbon; the terms provided that his troops be evacuated to France by sea.

1808, September. British Invasion of Spain. Assisted by 125,000 Spanish irregulars, they drove the French back to the Ebro

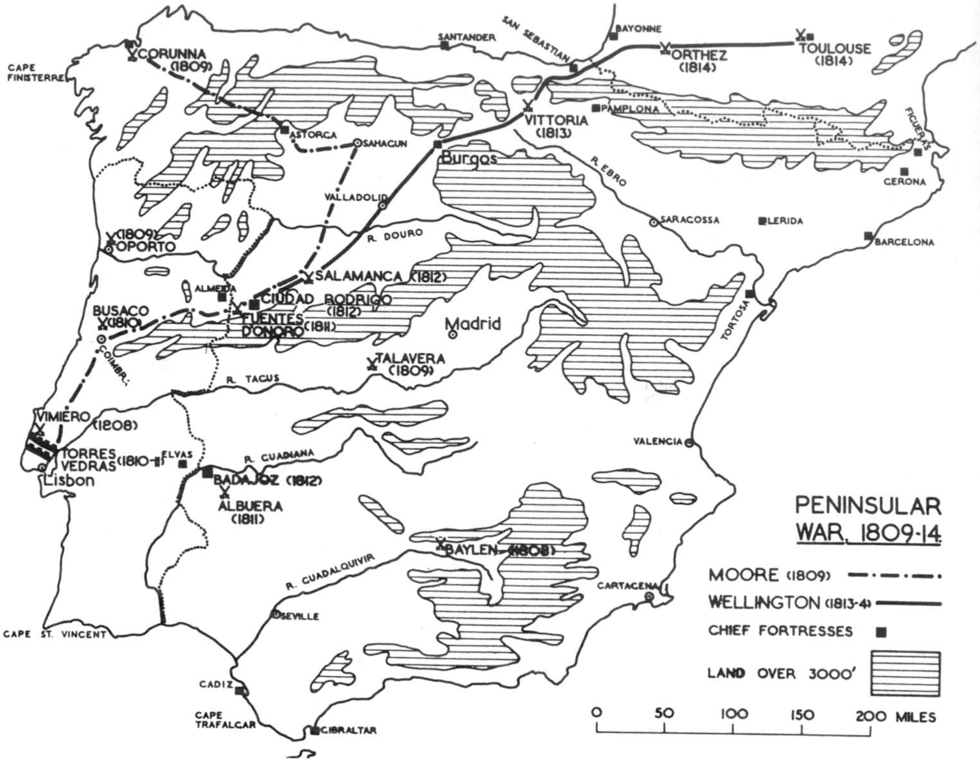

River. Napoleon, in Paris, commented that his army in Spain seemed to be commanded by "post-office inspectors." He sent reinforcements to Spain, and prepared to take the field there himself.

1808, November 5. Napoleon Joins His Army in Spain. He advanced immediately with 194,000 men.

1808, December 4. Capture of Madrid. Napoleon then turned northwest to deal with a British contingent, commanded by Sir **John Moore,** advancing from Corunna in the west. The British retreated skillfully toward the coast, closely pursued by the French.

1808, December 20–1809, February 20. Second Siege of Saragossa. French assaults under Lannes penetrated the defenses (January 27), but desperate resistance continued for three weeks. Finally, those defenders who had survived disease, starvation, and bombardment capitulated.

1809, January 1. Napoleon Returns to Paris. Spain appeared to be pacified and under control. Serious developments in Central Europe demanded his immediate attention (see below). He took much of his army with him, leaving the pursuit of Sir John Moore to Soult.

1809, January 16. Battle of Corunna. Moore reached the coast successfully with 15,000 men. He repulsed Soult's 20,000 in a stiff battle, each side suffering about 1,000 casualties. Moore, mortally wounded, died on the field and was buried on the ramparts of Corunna. The British expedition was safely evacuated by sea.

WAR AGAINST AUSTRIA, 1809

1809, January. Austria Prepares for War. Encouraged by events in Spain, Austria decided to gain vengeance and to liberate Germany from the French yoke. Word of Austrian preparations caused Napoleon to leave Spain.

1809, April 9. Austrian Invasion of Bavaria. The Archduke Charles marched on Ratisbon (Regensburg). Another force moved southwestward from Bohemia.

1809, April. Operations in Italy. An Austrian army of 50,000 men under Archduke

John crossed the Julian Alps to invade Italy. Prince **Eugène de Beauharnais,** Napoleon's stepson, attacked with 37,000 men at **Sacile,** east of the Tagliamento River, but was repulsed (April 16). Eugène retreated behind the Piave.

1809, April–1810, February. Revolt and Guerrilla War in the Tyrol. A popular uprising against the Bavarian garrison (French allies) freed most of the region. Archduke John sent troops to assist the guerrillas. After the Wagram Campaign (see below), French troops under Eugène slowly reconquered the region.

1809, April 16. Napoleon Arrives at Stuttgart. He had rushed from Spain via Paris. He found his armies in Germany—176,000 men ineptly commanded by his chief of staff, **Louis Alexandre Berthier**—had been split by the Austrian invasion forces. Napoleon took command and seized the initiative, while at the same time correcting Berthier's faulty dispositions.

1809, April 19–20. Battle of Abensberg. Having collected more than half of his army west of Ratisbon, Napoleon crossed the Danube River to penetrate the center of the extended Austrian Army—about 186,000 men. The Austrian right flank was forced back toward Ratisbon, while the left was driven back toward Landeshut.

1809, April 21. Battle of Landeshut. The Austrian left wing, under Baron **Johann Hiller,** pursued by the bulk of Napoleon's army, was in danger of being cut off completely by the arrival of Masséna's corps from the west. Masséna's indecision, however, permitted the Austrians to escape eastward across the Isar River after a brisk fight. Napoleon, despite annoyance at less than complete success, immediately turned northward to join Davout, who with 36,000 men had been maintaining pressure against the remainder of the Austrian army, about 80,000 under the Archduke Charles, south of Ratisbon.

1809, April 22. Battle of Eggmühl. Charles attacked the left of Davout's isolated force, planning to cut Napoleon's line of communications. The Austrian attack was lethargic; Davout held firm. Napoleon and the van of his main body arrived on Davout's right early in the afternoon. By midafternoon the Austrian left had been crushed and Charles was retreating, after a loss of 12,000 men. French losses were 6,000. Napoleon was unable to pursue; his troops were utterly exhausted by marching, fighting, and heat.

1809, April 23. Battle of Ratisbon. Charles now devoted every effort to escape northward across the Danube. To cover this retreat, he defended the walled city of Ratisbon. Due to the exhaustion of his troops after a week of hard fighting and marching, Napoleon's pursuit was not energetic. By the time the French fought their way into the town of Ratisbon, most of the Austrian army had escaped. Napoleon was slightly wounded.

COMMENT. *In 7 days of brilliant marching, fighting, and maneuvering, Napoleon had taken a French army from the verge of defeat to brilliant victory. Davout again distinguished himself. Estimated Austrian losses were 30,000 men, including 4,000 prisoners; the French lost some 15,000.*

1809, May 13. Capture of Vienna. There was no opposition. Archduke John withdrew from North Italy, followed closely by Eugene.

1809, May 21–22. Battle of Aspern-Essling. The Austrians having concentrated on the north bank of the Danube, Napoleon attempted to smash his way across at the island of Lobau against fierce resistance. Part of the French army crossed the river, but Napoleon, unable to reinforce it due to insufficient bridges, withdrew. This was his first defeat. Austrian losses were 23,000; French were more than 20,000, including Marshal Lannes, who was killed.

1809, June. Napoleon Makes Detailed Plans. He gathered nearly 200,000 men in the vicinity of Vienna and Lobau, and assembled adequate bridging material. Meanwhile Eugène pursued Archduke John into Hungary against fierce Austrian rearguard resistance. Eugène defeated John at **Raab** (June 14) and marched north to join Napoleon at Vienna. John continued his retreat to Pressburg (Bratislava).

1809, July 4–5. Night Danube Crossing. The French move surprised Charles, who had 140,000 men. Once more Napoleon had placed himself between 2 adversaries, for the Archduke John was approaching from the east with nearly 50,000 men. Napoleon had approximately 140,000 men north of the river; the remainder held his line of communications. Napoleon decided to attack at once before John could arrive with reinforcements.

1809, July 5–6. Battle of Wagram. To prevent Charles from moving eastward to join John, Napoleon made his main attack against the Austrian eastern or left wing. Charles tried to turn Napoleon's left so as to cut him off from his Danube bridgehead. Results were indecisive the first day. On the second day, Napoleon massed his guns against the Austrian center in the greatest concentration of artillery ever made to that time. He launched a heavy infantry assault in the center, while Davout redoubled his efforts to turn the Austrian left. Charles's center was penetrated, his flank thrown back. He withdrew. Although the retreat was made in moderately good order, the defeat was decisive. The Archduke had lost 45,000 men; 24,000 of whom had been killed or wounded. French losses were 34,000 in all.

1809, July 10. Austrians Ask for Armistice. Austrian troops had been driven from the Grand Duchy of Warsaw by Polish troops under Prince **Poniatowski;** Russia had not joined the coalition, as hoped; British landings in Holland and Belgium had been contained and repulsed (see p. 766). It was evident to Emperor Francis that further conflict would be disastrous to Austria.

1809, October 14. Treaty of Schönbrunn. Napoleon's pre-eminence in Europe was reaffirmed. Austria ceded 32,000 square miles of territory, with 3,500,000 inhabitants, to France and her satellites. She agreed to join the Continental System and to break off all connections with England. Except for the fighting still continuing on the Iberian Peninsula (see p. 764) and at sea (see p. 766), and for a few minor rebellions (particularly in the Tyrol), an uneasy peace settled on Europe.

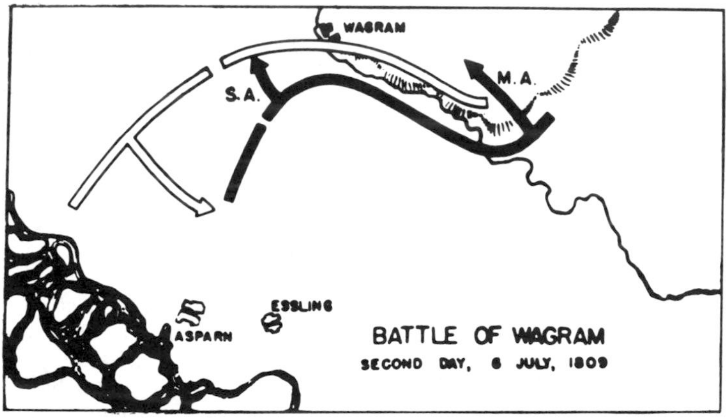

WAR WITH RUSSIA, 1812

Franco-Russian relations had frayed steadily. Czar Alexander, Napoleon's only major rival on the Continent, resented the revival of Poland through the establishment of the Grand Duchy of Warsaw. Napoleon's refusal to join him in trying to drive the Turks out of Southern Europe (see p. 777) made matters worse (1811). England, aware of this situation, made overtures to Russia. She made peace with both Sweden and Russia (June, 1812), and got both nations to renounce the Continental System, a serious economic blow to France.

1812, May–June. Napoleon Prepares for War. He assembled an army group of 450,000 men in Poland. He planned to invade and crush Russia from a base of communications reaching from the Pripet Marshes on the south to the Baltic Sea on the north. His right flank was protected by the Austrian army of Prince **Karl Phil-**

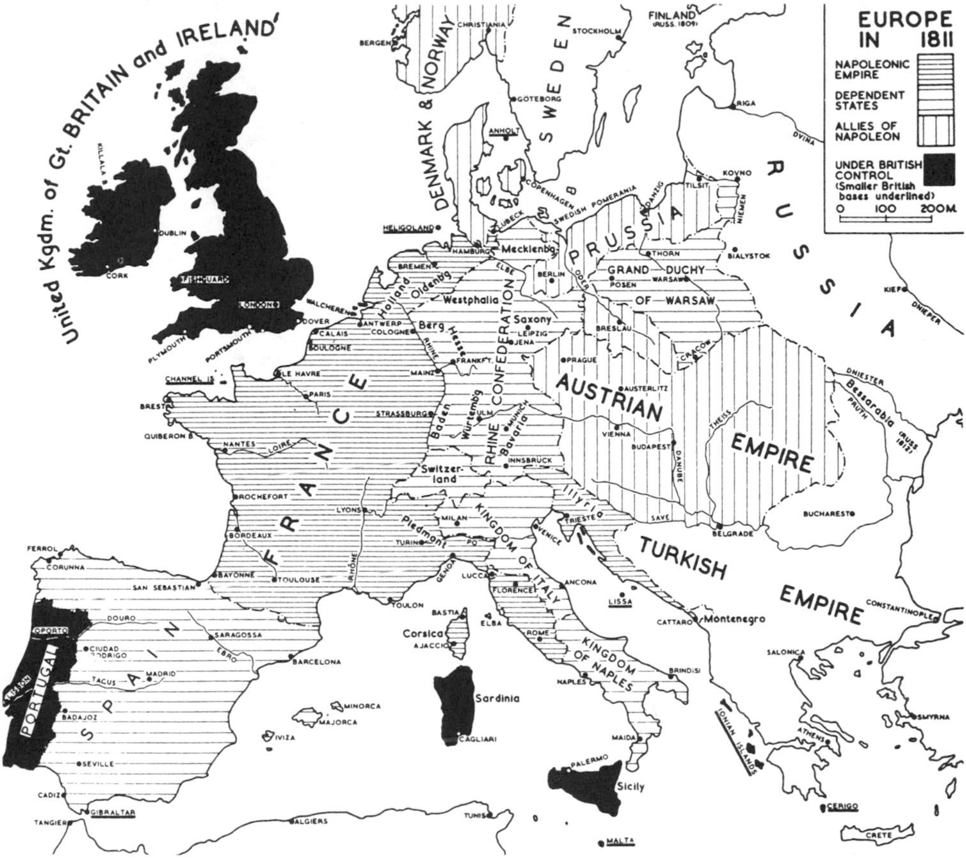

ipp von Schwarzenberg, nearly 40,000 strong. The left flank was covered by Marshal **Jacques E. J. A. Macdonald**'s army, of equal strength, with its principal element a Prussian corps. In the center stood 3 French armies. Napoleon's left wing of 220,000 men was just west of the Niemen (Neman) River, between Kovno (Kaunas) and Grodno. Echeloned to his right rear, to secure the line of communications, were the armies of **Eugène de Beauharnais** and of Napoleon's incompetent brother **Jérôme,** each about 80,000 strong. This Grand Army of 1812 contained less than 200,000 Frenchmen; the remainder were German, Austrian, Polish, and Italian contingents. Napoleon was now depending upon conscripts and upon the soldiery of uneasy allies and seething nations whom he had ground under his heel.

1812, June. Russian Preparations. In a cordon defense along the Russian northwestern frontier were 2 armies: **Barclay de Tolly** (Prince **Michael Andreas Bogdanovich**) with 127,000 men was north of the Niemen; Bagration had 48,000 between the Niemen and the Pripet Marshes. South of the marshes was a third Russian army, 43,000 strong, under General **A. P. Tormassov,** guarding the southwestern frontier. More than 200,000 additional Russian troops were scattered throughout western and central Russia.

1812, June 24. Napoleon Crosses the Niemen. Penetrating between the 2 main Russian armies, he planned to crush them in succession. But Jérôme failed to carry out instructions, unusual heat sapped French strength, and much of the cavalry was incapacitated by a colic epidemic among the horses. Meanwhile Napoleon relieved Jérôme and put Davout in his place. Davout blocked Bagration's effort to join Barclay by a victory at **Mogilev** (July 23), but Bagration retreated east-

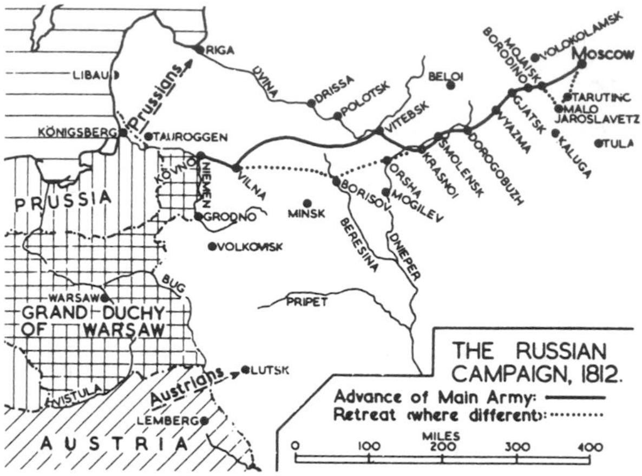

ward across the Dnieper (Dneper) to join Barclay near Smolensk (August 3). Barclay assumed command.

1812, August 7–19. Maneuvers near Smolensk. Barclay planned to fight, but inefficient Russian staff work slowed the Russian movement. Ironically, the errors foiled a turning movement by Napoleon which would have crushed both Russian armies, since he had anticipated their plan. They escaped eastward, with Napoleon—who now had about 230,000 men—again trying to turn their flank by crossing the Dnieper (Dneper) River south of Smolensk. After hard-fought but unsuccessful defensive battles at **Smolensk** (August 17) and nearby **Valutino** (August 19), the Russians escaped Napoleon's trap, largely because of errors by French Marshals Junot and Murat. French casualties were over 10,000; Russian were at least 15,000.

1812, August 29. Kutuzov Commands Russian Armies. He continued to retreat. Reluctantly Napoleon followed. He had planned to spend the winter at Smolensk, but now realized that his supply arrangements were not working as planned. A complete victory in 1812 was essential.

1812, September 7. Battle of Borodino (or of the Moskva). With 120,000 men,

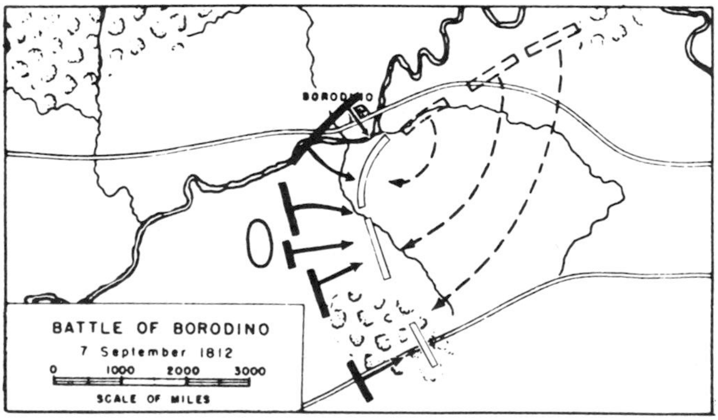

Kutuzov made a stand 60 miles west of Moscow. Napoleon concentrated slightly more than 120,000 men and started enveloping the Russian left flank. In the midst of the fighting, he unaccountably gave up personal control of the battle. This was the first of recurrent seizures, never fully explained medically, which hampered a number of subsequent operations. The bitterly contested struggle continued; by nightfall the Russians had been forced back with nearly 40,000 casualties including the death of Bagration. The French lost some 28,000 men. Kutuzov withdrew to Moscow. There was no energetic pursuit, due to Napoleon's illness.

1812, September 14. Napoleon Enters Moscow. The city, which had been evacuated of its inhabitants, began to burn, set fire by the Russians. Most of the wooden houses were soon in ashes, and the French army had to bivouac in the suburbs. Napoleon had some 95,000 men near Moscow, most of them utterly exhausted. The remainder of his great army was scattered in an elongated triangle with its base on the Niemen River, and extending from Riga through Kovno to Brest Litovsk (Brest). French morale was deteriorating; the allied troops were becoming unreliable. South of Moscow near Kaluga, Kutuzov's army of 110,000 was still intact and full of fight. The entire Russian nation, aroused by needless French cruelty, united in the defense of its homeland. North of Polotsk the French line of communication was threatened by an army under Count **Ludwig Adolf Wittgenstein.** The Russians south of the Pripet Marshes, now under General (or Admiral) **Tshitshagov,** moved west, threatening the French flank at Brest Litovsk. Desperately short of food, and Czar Alexander having ignored peace overtures, Napoleon decided to withdraw to Smolensk (October 19).

1812, October 24. Battle of Maloyaroslavets. Moving southwest from Moscow, Napoleon planned to destroy Kutuzov's army, but was repulsed. Czar Alexander rejected a truce. As winter closed down over central Russia, Napoleon continued to withdraw.

1812, October–December. Retreat from Moscow. Snow, followed by bitter cold, began to impede the march (November 4). Surrounded by swarms of regular and irregular Russian forces, the freezing, starving Grand Army, all of its commissariat broken down, marched through snow to disintegration. Separate French corps fought off repeated attacks. Napoleon decided to continue the retreat from Smolensk (November 12). Most of the army became a disorganized mob.

1812, November 16–17. Battle of Krasnoi (Krasnoye). West of Smolensk, Kutuzov's advance guard, which had circled west of the French, barred the road. Napoleon collected his few effective elements and, in a brilliant display of leadership, drove the Russians off. Ney's corps, reduced to 9,000 men, sacrificed itself in a desperate all-day rear-guard action to save the rest of the army, losing all but 800 men.

1812, November 26–28. Crossing of the Berezina. Near Borisov on the Berezina, Napoleon was cornered between Tshitshagov and Kutuzov, who had 144,000 men between them. French effectives were about 37,000 men. Despite Russian attacks on both sides of the river, pontoon bridges were built across the ice-laden Berezina. By the night of the 27th only Victor's corps remained on the east bank, together with a horde of disorganized stragglers. Oudinot and Ney, on the west bank, were battling desperately against Tshitshagov to keep the bridgehead open. Victor, with 10,000 men, repulsed several attacks of 40,000 Russians with support from French artillery on the west bank. The French disengaged through the night, but thousands of wounded men and stragglers still remained on the far bank when the bridges were blown up at dawn; most of these were massacred by the Cossacks.

1812, December 8. Napoleon Leaves for Paris. For all practical purposes the Grand Army was no more; only 10,000 effectives remained. Napoleon rushed home to raise a new army. Murat, left in command, brought the pitiful remnants—as well as Macdonald's troops from Riga—back to Posen (Posnan) in western Poland. The exhausted Russians stopped their pursuit at the Niemen River. French (and allied) casualties in the campaign exceeded 300,000; Russian losses were at least 250,000.

1813, January 1. Revolt of Prussia. The Prussian contingent of **Hans D. H. Yorck von Wartenburg,** which had been with Macdonald at Riga, broke away to join the Russians. The remainder of Prussia rose, a new army created overnight by General **Gerhard von Scharnhorst** and his new Prussian General Staff. Leaving French garrisons at Danzig (Gdansk) and Thorn (Torun) on the Vistula, and at Stettin (Szczecin), Kustrin (Kostrzyn), and Frankfurt on the Oder, Eugène, who had replaced Murat in command, withdrew to Magdeburg on the Elbe. Late in January reinforcements sent by Napoleon brought his strength to 68,000 men. Meanwhile Schwarzenberg's Austrians had retreated to Warsaw and then turned into Bohemia, one more defection from Napoleon's army.

LEIPZIG CAMPAIGN, 1813

1813, February–March. New Coalition. Russia, Prussia, Sweden, and Britain united to end the Napoleonic grip on Europe. Almost 100,000 veteran allied troops were spread in the Elbe Valley, between Magdeburg and Dresden.

1813, April. Napoleon Returns to Germany. He had a new army 200,000 strong—gathered with amazing speed, but woefully inexperienced. He hastened from the Rhine to join remnants of the old Grand Army.

1813, April 30. Napoleon Crosses the Saale. He moved on Leipzig in 3 columns, preceded by a strong advance guard. Typically, he planned to penetrate the allied cordon and to defeat his enemies in detail. Faulty reconnaissance by his inexperienced cavalry left him unaware that Wittgenstein, with 75,000 allied troops, was concentrating on his south flank.

1813, May 2. Battle of Lützen. The French advance guard was driving a small allied delaying force into the outskirts of Leipzig when Wittgenstein attacked, surprising Ney's corps on the road. Napoleon, hearing the sound of artillery as he stood on the historic battlefield of Lützen (see p. 538), galloped to the scene. He was the Napoleon of old, brilliant and at his best in tactical improvisation on the field. He concentrated his army with a great mass of artillery opposite Wittgenstein's center. Leading an overwhelming counterattack in person, Napoleon split the allied lines. Had his green troops not been exhausted, there might have been a repetition of Austerlitz. Wittgenstein withdrew in fairly good order. Casualties were nearly equal—some 18,000 on each side. Scharnhorst, serving as Wittgenstein's Chief of Staff, was among the wounded; he died of infection.

1813, May 20–21. Battle of Bautzen. Napoleon captured **Dresden** (May 7–8), then followed the retreating allies east of the Elbe. Sending Ney, with nearly half of his army, on a wide turning movement 50 miles north of Dresden, Napoleon pursued Wittgenstein with the remainder. The Russian stood in a formidable position on the east bank of the Spree. Napoleon attacked across the river with 115,000 men, driving the 100,000 allied troops from their defenses. Ney, coming down from the north after dark, was in position to fall on the allied flank and rear next morning. The Napoleonic strategic concept was brilliant. Ney stupidly failed to grasp the situation, attacked late, and made no move toward the enemy rear and his communications. Napoleon, waiting to launch his reserve until Ney had sprung the trap, realized too late that Wittgenstein, in rapid retreat, had gotten safely away eastward into Silesia. There were about 20,000 casualties on each side.

1813, May 22–June 1. Increasing Allied Strength. Napoleon, pursuing east of the Elbe, found his enemies growing stronger. Bernadotte, former marshal of France and now Crown Prince of Sweden, was nearing Berlin with a Prusso-Swedish army 120,000 strong. Austria was about to declare war; Schwarzenberg, with 240,000 Austrians, was in northern Bohemia ominously close to the French line of communications. Blücher, who had taken Wittgenstein's place, was reorganizing that army,checking further French advance.

1813, June 4–August 16. Napoleon Obtains an Armistice. He used this respite to improve training, particularly his cavalry.

1813, August 12. Austria Declares War. The allies, with British subsidies, fielded 3 armies: the Bohemian, 230,000 men under Schwarzenberg; the Silesian, 195,000 under Blücher; and the Northern, 110,000 under Bernadotte. A token British contingent, including a rocket troop, accompanied Bernadotte.

1813, August 16. Opposing Plans. Napoleon had placed Davout's corps at Hamburg, transformed into a fortress, as a permanent threat to allied movements westward through Prussia. Dresden was occupied by **St. Cyr**'s corps as a potential pivot of maneuver. Between these two strong points, the emperor had withdrawn the greater part of his field forces (except **Jean Rapp**'s corps, besieged in Danzig) to positions between the Elbe and the Oder, preparing to operate on interior lines against his enemies. He had now in hand some 300,000 men; the allies totaled more than 450,000. Their strategy was to avoid battle with Napoleon, but to attack his lieutenants wherever possible. Bernadotte drove Oudinot (who had 60,000 troops) south of Berlin in the **Battle**

of Grossbeeren (August 23), and Blücher defeated Macdonald at the **Katzbach** (August 26).

1813, August 26–27. Battle of Dresden. Schwarzenberg's Austrian army (accompanied by the Emperors of Russia and Austria, and the King of Prussia) attacked St. Cyr. Napoleon, arriving rapidly and unexpectedly with reinforcements, repulsed the assault. Next day, although outnumbered 2 to 1, Napoleon attacked, turned the allied left flank, and won a brilliant tactical victory. Then he went into one of his torpors, and left the field. By this time the allies had lost some 38,000 men killed, wounded, and captured and 40 guns. French casualties were about 10,000. Schwarzenberg disengaged hurriedly, narrowly escaping encirclement. Without Napoleon to direct the pursuit, only one of his subordinates, **Dominique René Vandamme,** realized the opportunity. Rapidly crossing the mountains into Bohemia on Schwarzenberg's east flank, he flung his corps across the Austrian line of communications.

1813, August 29–30. Battle of Kulm. No other French corps commander had followed Vandamme. With 30,000 men, he found himself unsupported and pinned between Austrian, Russian, and Prussian forces totaling more than 100,000 men. His corps was virtually annihilated.

1813, September. Blücher Avoids Battle. Having recovered, Napoleon hastened east again, vainly trying to entice Blücher into

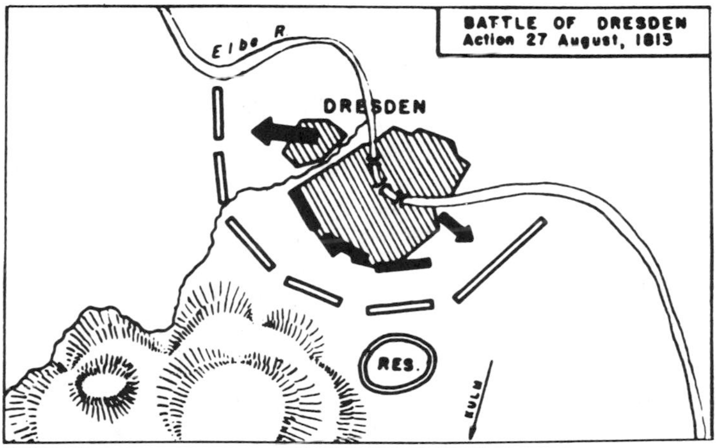

battle in Silesia. The Prussian, however, withdrew rapidly (September 4).

1813, September–October. French Disasters. Ney, who had succeeded Oudinot, attempted to take Berlin, but was defeated by Bernadotte at **Dennewitz** (September 6) when his Saxon divisions fled. Bavaria withdrew from the Rhine Confederation to join the alliance (**Treaty of Ried,** October 8).

1813, October 1–15. The Allies Close In. The French army, tired and discouraged, pressed in between Dresden and Leipzig, had been reduced to 200,000 men. Blücher, abandoning his line of communications, crossed the Elbe north of Leipzig to threaten Napoleon's rear. Schwarzenberg, in coordination, marched north to link with Blücher. Bernadotte, several miles north of Blücher, stood indecisive while French units opposite him joined Napoleon's main army at Leipzig. Napoleon, leaving 2 army corps at Dresden, turned to attack Blücher as Schwarzenberg advanced from the south (15 October).

1813, October 16–19. "Battle of the Nations" (Battle of Leipzig). For 3 days the French fought Prussians on the northwest and both Russians and Austrians on the south. Then Bernadotte moved in on the east, nearly surrounding the French army (October 18). The allies now began massive frontal attacks. Napoleon was driven into Leipzig, though his lines remained intact. The Saxon corps now deserted the French army, ending all possibility of victory. Having been able to keep his line of communications open, despite Blücher's repeated efforts, Napoleon withdrew after a frenzied conflict inside the city (Oc-

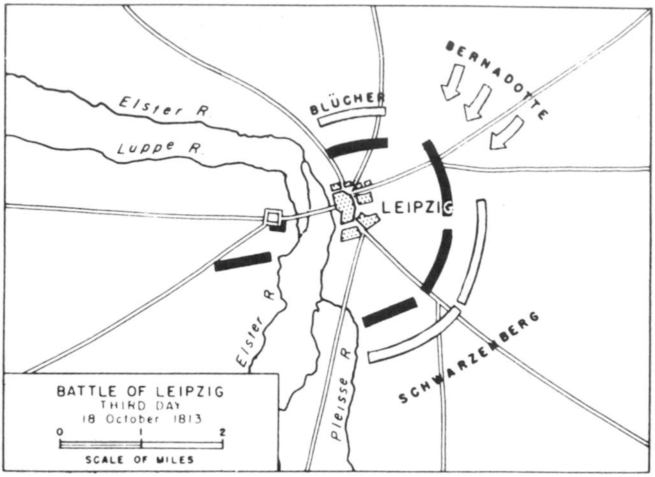

tober 19). The bridge over the Elster River was blown prematurely. Prince **Joseph Anthony Poniatowski** and Marshal Macdonald rode their horses into the river to escape; Poniatowski was drowned; Macdonald got safely across. The allies had won a tremendous victory, but should never have allowed Napoleon to escape the net. As it was, the survivors of the Grand Army, having suffered overall losses of 60,000 men, 150 guns, and 500 wagons, withdrew toward the Rhine. Allied losses had been more than 60,000 men.

1813, October 30–31. Battle of Hanau. A Bavarian army, under Prince **Karl Philipp von Wrede,** 40,000 strong, marched to cut off the French retreat. With the allied armies slowly pursuing from the east, Napoleon was apparently trapped. In a flash of his old spirit, Napoleon, brilliantly maneuvering his artillery in support of the attack, routed the Bavarians, whose losses were 9,000 men and several guns; the French lost less than 5,000. The Grand Army continued on to cross the Rhine (November 1–5).

DEFENSE OF FRANCE, 1814

1813, November 8. Allies Offer Peace. French boundaries would be restricted behind the Alps and the Rhine; Napoleon foolishly rejected this. The allies thereupon decided to invade France (December 1). By this time the Netherlands had revolted and the Rhine Confederation had dissolved (November). The French garrisons of Dresden and Danzig surrendered (November 11, December 30).

1813, December 21. Allies Cross the Rhine at Mannheim and Coblenz.

1814, January 1. French Dispositions and Plans. Some 50,000 men were in German garrisons, most under Davout, at Hamburg. Another 100,000 were in Spain fighting the English and Spaniards. In northeastern Italy, Eugène, with 50,000 men, was facing Austria's Count **Heinrich J. J. Bellegarde** with equal strength. None of these outlying forces, except Oudinot's corps, which would be withdrawn from Spain, would take part in the coming campaign in France. There Napoleon mustered nearly 118,000 men west of the Rhine, from Antwerp to Lyon. Napoleon, operating on interior lines, proved that his strategic brains were unimpaired, but the tactical quality of his troops was low. Except for a small proportion of veterans, the ranks had been filled by boy conscripts and by untrained national guards.

1814, January 1. Allied Dispositions and Plans. There were 3 allied invading armies: Bernadotte, with 60,000, was moving west through the Low Countries; Blücher, with 75,000, was advancing up the Moselle Valley into Lorraine; Schwarzenberg, with 210,000, was crossing Switzerland and moving through the Belfort Gap. Their combined objective was Paris.

1814, January 29–February 1. Operations around La Rothière. Moving with 40,-

000 men to crush Blücher before he could join Schwarzenberg, Napoleon won engagements at **Brienne** (January 29) and **La Rothière** (January 30) but barely escaped a vast allied envelopment as Blücher returned to attack La Rothière (February 1). He lost more than 5,000 men, the allies some 8,000. The allies pushed on toward Paris—Blücher down the Marne Valley, Schwarzenberg down the Seine.

1814, February 10–14. The "Five Days." Napoleon turned on Blücher, defeating him at **Champaubert** (February 10), **Montmirail** (February 11), **Château-Thierry** (February 12), and **Vauchamps** (February 14), a series of brilliant maneuvers directed by the emperor in person. The allies lost in all some 9,000 men in these operations, the French about 2,000. The Prussians retreated north of the Marne.

1814, February 18. Battle of Montereau. Marching rapidly south, Napoleon then attacked Schwarzenberg and drove him back 40 miles despite Austrian superiority of more than 2 to 1. French losses were 2,500, those of the allies 6,000. Blücher meanwhile, regrouping, had pushed on to La Forté (February 27), only 25 miles from Paris. Napoleon turned north to meet this threat, leaving Macdonald on the Aube to contain Schwarzenberg.

1814, March 7. Battle of Craonne. Blücher was driven north, and his rear guard —a Russian corps—was decisively defeated, although each side suffered over 5,000 casualties. Falling back to Laon, Blücher was reinforced by 2 of Bernadotte's army corps. He now had 100,000 to oppose Napoleon's 30,000. Meanwhile Schwarzenberg was forcing Macdonald back toward Paris after a victory at **Bar-sur-Aube** (February 27).

1814, March 9–10. Battle of Laon. Despite the inferiority of his force, Napoleon fell on Blücher in a 2-day fight. Sturdily resisting in strong positions, Blücher finally made a night counterattack which drove 1 French corps from the field in panic. The French lost 6,000 men, the allies about 3,000. Napoleon's reckless assaults had failed; he withdrew to Soissons.

1814, March 13. Battle of Rheims. After a brief rest, Napoleon boldly marched across the front of Blücher's army to smash an isolated Prussian corps at Rheims. He recaptured the city, suffering 700 casualties; the Prussians lost 6,000 men. Napoleon now marched south to strike at Schwarzenberg's line of communications, hoping the Austrian would turn back.

1814, March 20–21. Battle of Arcis-sur-Aube. Schwarzenberg repulsed the French strike and continued westward, as did Blücher. Napoleon ordered the corps of Marmont and Mortier to join him as he prepared for another attack.

1814, March 25. Battle of La Fère-Champenoise. Schwarzenberg's army defeated the greatly outnumbered corps of Marmont and Mortier, and drove them toward Paris. The allied advance continued; Blücher and Schwarzenberg united in front of Paris (March 28), leaving Napoleon's main army far to the east.

1814, March 30. Battle of Paris. Marmont and Mortier, with about 22,000 men, vigorously resisted the advance of the allied army—about 110,000 men. Despite commendable efforts, the French were forced back to Montmartre, bringing allied artillery within range of the city. Marmont agreed to an armistice, surrendering Paris to the allies the next day (March 31). French losses had been 4,000 men, those of the allies 8,000. Napoleon, who had been hurrying to defend his capital, now halted at Fontainebleau.

1814, April 6–11. Abdication of Napoleon. At the urging of his marshals, he abdicated in favor of his son (April 6). The allies rejecting this, he abdicated unconditionally (April 11). He was granted the principality of the little island of Elba, where he retired (May 4). The allies installed **Louis XVIII** (brother of Louis XVI) as King of France.

COMMENT. *Though he was crushingly defeated, Napoleon's military luster had never shone more brilliantly than in the 1814 campaign. Despite recurring bouts of illness and the poor quality of his troops, he postponed the inevitable in a series of maneuvers and battles which aroused the grudging admiration of his opponents.*

1814, May 30. First Treaty of Paris. France was reduced to the frontiers of 1792, and recognized the independence of other areas of Napoleon's empire. England restored most of the colonies seized from France and Holland.

THE PENINSULAR WAR, 1809–1814

The "Spanish Ulcer," as Napoleon termed the war in Spain, was one of the principal factors leading to his downfall. It diverted French military resources badly needed for operations elsewhere. Characterized by appallingly cruel and brutal excesses on both sides, it was a prime example of guerrilla warfare—the almost spontaneous response of a population to invasion and the military problems immediately encountered both by the invaders and the regular foreign forces assisting resistance. The war also emphasized the importance of sea power; for had not England commanded the seas, her troops could neither have landed on the Iberian peninsula nor been maintained to achieve the final victory.

1809, January–February. Guerrilla Warfare in Spain. After the French capture of Saragossa (see p. 754), their position in Spain was re-established. Guerrilla warfare continued throughout the country, however.

1809, March–May. French Invasion of Portugal. Wellesley, in the Lisbon area, had some 26,000 British and Hanoverian troops, plus 16,000 Portuguese under General **William Beresford.** Soult took and sacked **Oporto** (March 29), but was driven out by Wellesley in the **Battle of Oporto** (May 12).

1809, June. Wellesley Invades Spain. In theory he was supported by some 100,000 Spanish irregulars. Actually, jealousies and political jugglings among the junta controlling patriot Spain prevented unified command; Wellesley found the Spaniards poor allies.

1809, July 28. Battle of Talavera. Attacked by the combined 46,000 troops of Victor and King Joseph Bonaparte, Wellesley with 36,000 allied troops fought a drawn battle. Strategically it was a British victory, since the French later retired on Madrid. Allied losses were 6,500—5,300 of them British—the French lost 7,400. Irritable and jealous, Spanish General **Gregorio García de la Cuesta** now withdrew his contingent and Wellesley, his rear menaced by Soult and other French forces, fell back into Portugal. Soon after this he received the title of Viscount Wellington.

1809, November 19. Battle of Ocana. Spanish General **Areizago,** who replaced Cuesta, led an army of 53,000 Spanish troops against 30,000 French under Joseph and Soult. The Spanish were completely defeated, losing 5,000 killed and wounded and 20,000 prisoners; French losses were only 1,700.

1810, February–1812, August. Siege of Cádiz. The Spanish garrison was reinforced by 8,000 men sent by sea by Wellington. The city became the capital of free Spain.

1810. Wellington on the Defensive. Since England was again abandoned by all her allies, during the winter he began the construction of the Torres Vedras defensive lines, north of Lisbon. These constituted a massive 3-line system of field fortifications, mounting 600 guns and stretching for some 30 miles from the Tagus River to the sea. In Spain, Masséna had been placed in command of the Army of Portugal, 65,000 strong. Soult commanded the Army of Andalusia, of equal strength. As Masséna advanced toward the Portuguese frontier, Wellington took a force of 32,000 men (18,000 English, the remainder Portuguese) to confront him. Masséna besieged and captured Ciudad Rodrigo (July 10).

1810, July. French Invasion of Portugal. Wellington withdrew slowly. Meantime, in Spain, Soult solidified French control of Andalusia.

1810, September 27. Battle of Bussaco. To secure his retirement into the Torres Vedras lines, Wellington offered battle from a strong position on high ground. Masséna's attacks were repulsed, and Wellington continued his retreat. French losses were 4,500, those of the English 1,300.

1810, October 10. Wellington Occupies the Torres Vedras Lines. Masséna probed the defenses, but found them impregnable. Running out of food, he retired into Spain with his army in poor condition (November).

1810–1811. Frontier Warfare. During the

bitter winter, both sides strove for possession of the main passes on the Spanish Portuguese frontier—through Ciudad Rodrigo and Badajoz. There were also several flurries of activity outside of besieged Cádiz as a result of British amphibious raids or guerrilla attacks.

1811. French Offensives. Masséna advanced to relieve Almeida, blockaded by Wellington. At the same time, Soult moved toward Badajoz, besieged by a British force under General Beresford.

1811, May 5. Battle of Fuentes de Oñoro. Masséna fought a drawn battle with Wellington, marked by the resistance of British infantry squares to French cavalry, and by the exploit of a British horse artillery battery. Captain **Norman Ramsey,** cut off in the melee, limbered up and charged with his guns through the French horsemen. Allied losses were 1,500 out of 33,000 men engaged; the French lost 3,000 out of 45,000 on the field.

1811, May 16. Battle of Albuera. Soult, with 23,000 men, probing at Badajoz, was defeated by Beresford, with 30,000 men, including 7,000 British. The Spanish contingent on the allied right was driven in, but the British infantry retrieved the day. Allied losses were 7,000, French 8,000.

1811, May–December. Inconclusive Operations. Both French commanders fell back. Masséna was relieved in disgrace; Marmont replaced him. A series of indecisive but hard-fought actions followed, the net result being that at the end of the year the French still held the frontier gateways. Meanwhile, in southern Spain Marshal **Louis Suchet** took **Tarragona** (July 28) and later **Valencia** (January 9, 1812), in a successful antiguerrilla campaign.

1812, January–July. Wellington Takes the Offensive. He stormed **Ciudad Rodrigo** (January 19) and **Badajoz** (April 19). He captured siege and pontoon trains of both Marmont and Soult in his rapid advance.

1812, July 22. Battle of Salamanca. Wellington, with about 46,000 men, met and defeated Marmont, who had 42,000. Wellington cleverly changed position as the French attack developed, and drove Marmont (who was wounded) off the field with losses of nearly 13,000 men. The allies lost about 6,000. Joseph evacuated Madrid.

1812, August 12. Wellington Takes Madrid. He captured 1,700 men, 180 guns, and a quantity of stores.

1812, August–November. Allied Setbacks. After being repulsed at **Burgos** (November), Wellington was forced to fall back as Soult and Marmont concentrated against him. In a bitter retreat to cantonments near Ciudad Rodrigo, the allies lost 7,000 men. But by November, the French, unable to live off the country, were forced to disperse.

1813. Wellington Again Takes the Offensive. He was now in supreme command of allied forces in Spain, with 172,000 men to oppose 200,000 French. In a series of brilliant maneuvers Wellington put the French on the defensive on all fronts. At the same time, in eastern Spain, a British force under Sir **John Murray** forced Suchet back into Tarragona. Joseph abandoned Madrid again (May 17) and fell back to the line of the Ebro. North of that river and south of Vittorio, he occupied an extended position with 65,000 men and 150 guns.

1813, June 21. Battle of Vittorio. Wellington, with 80,000 men and 90 guns, attacked in 4 columns, all within mutual supporting distance. Joseph's center was pierced, both flanks turned. Wellington's left column neared the Bayonne road—the French communication link—and Joseph's army, after a determined defensive stand, broke and fled toward Pampeluna. This was the decisive battle of the Peninsular War. Joseph lost 7,000 men and 143 guns, while his treasury of $5 million and great masses of stores fell into Wellington's hands. Joseph retired across the Pyrenees into France, harried by allied pursuit. Soult took over the French command. Suchet abandoned Tarragona and also slowly fell back into France (March, 1814).

1813, July 26–August 1. Battle of Sorauren. Soult, with 30,000 men, attempting to return to Spain, encountered Wellington with 16,000. After repulsing the initial French attack, Wellington resumed the offensive. Both armies were reinforced, but after 6 days of fighting the French had been driven back across the Pyrenees, having suffered losses of 13,000 men. Wellington had lost 7,000. Soon after this the British captured San Sebastian (August 31). Both sides rested and reorganized.

1814, February 27. Battle of Orthez. Wellington, in an amphibious operation, invested Bayonne and attacked Soult, who fell back to Toulouse to avoid encirclement, losing 4,000 men. Wellington's loss was 2,000. The allies advanced to seize Bordeaux (March 17). Wellington then turned toward Toulouse.

1814, April 10. Battle of Toulouse. Wellington assaulted the city, losing 5,000 casualties. Soult, who had lost 3,000 men, was driven out. Two days later, news of Napoleon's abdication was received, and a convention was agreed to between Wellington and Soult.

WAR AT SEA, 1806–1814

Despite Britain's overwhelming naval supremacy, there were a number of French challenges. At the same time the Royal Navy was busy in supporting the anti-Napoleonic effort on the Continent.

1806, January 8. British Capture of Capetown. Dutch and French defenders were defeated in an amphibious assault by General Sir **David Baird.**

1806, February 6. Battle of Santo Domingo. Sir **John Duckworth**'s British squadron destroyed Admiral **Laissaque**'s French West Indian squadron. Soon after this, halfway around the world in the Indian Ocean, Admiral **C. A. L. Durand Linois** surrendered his 2 ships to a British squadron (March 14).

1806–1807. Operations at Buenos Aires and Montevideo (see p. 812).

1806, June–July. British Amphibious Raid on Calabria. A force of 5,000 troops under General Sir **John Stuart** was put ashore by Admiral **Sidney Smith** to help guerrillas opposing King Joseph Bonaparte. The British defeated a French force of 6,000 under General **E. Reynier** at **Maida** (July 4). The British soon withdrew to Sicily.

1806, October 8. Attack on Boulogne. British Admiral Sidney Smith attacked with rockets.

1807, February–March. British Repulsed at Constantinople. Duckworth's squadron forced a passage through the Dardanelles after a spirited action against the Turkish fleet, Sidney Smith, leading the rear division, taking a prominent part. Duckworth delivered a 24-hour ultimatum to the Porte to make peace with Russia and to dismiss the French ambassador (see p. 777). Sultan **Selim III** decided to resist. Within a day the entire population of Constantinople collected 1,000 guns along the seawall and opened fire on the British fleet. Having suffered considerable damage, Duckworth withdrew to the Mediterranean, receiving further mauling in repassing the Dardanelles.

1807, September 2–7. Second Battle of Copenhagen. Fearful that Denmark and her fleet would join the Franco-Russian alliance after the Treaty of Tilsit, Britain sent a powerful combined force to Zealand under Admiral **James Gambier** and General Lord **William S. Cathcart.** A landing force under Sir Arthur Wellesley invested Copenhagen. When the Danish government refused to negotiate, the British land and naval forces severely bombarded the Danish capital. Congreve rockets were used in great quantities. The Danish fleet surrendered.

1809, June 30. Capture of Martinique and Santo Domingo. French Admiral **Villaret de Joyeuse** surrendered the islands to a Hispano-British expedition after a stout defense. Spain controlled Martinique until 1814, Santo Domingo until 1821.

1809, July–October. Walcheren Expedition. In an effort to divert Napoleon's attention from Central Europe, a British expedition of 35 ships of the line, escorting 200 transports carrying 40,000 men, attempted to take Antwerp. The expedition, commanded by the **Earl of Chatham** (the younger **Pitt**) was a dismal failure, frittered away in the capture of Flushing (August 16), by which time King Louis Bonaparte and Marshal Bernadotte had heavily reinforced Antwerp. Chatham departed, leaving a garrison of 15,000 on Walcheren Island, 7,000 of whom died during an epidemic of malaria. The remnants were later returned to England.

1810–1814, Operations in the West Indies. The British captured **Guadeloupe** and held it until the end of the wars (1816) despite French efforts to recapture (1814).

1810, December. Capture of Mauritius and Réunion. A British naval squadron seized the two French islands, bases for French commerce destroyers operating against British merchant vessels in the Indian Ocean.

WATERLOO CAMPAIGN— "THE HUNDRED DAYS," MARCH–JUNE, 1815

1815, March 1. Napoleon's Return from Elba. He landed at Cannes and marched to Paris, where he resumed power (March 20). At the Congress of Vienna, the allies declared him to be an outlaw (March 13). They renewed their mutual pledges and began gathering forces to **invade France.**

1815, March–June. Napoleon Prepares for War. Displaying once more his amazing efficiency (and at the same time bleeding France white), he extemporized a field force of regulars some 188,000 strong, with another 100,000 in forts and depots. More than 300,000 additional hastily raised levies were in training around the country. Napoleon's own Army of the North, 124,000 men, concentrated around Paris. Other contingents guarded the rest of the frontier. In Italy, to Napoleon's intense annoyance, Murat, who was still King of Naples, declared his support of Napoleon and marched into central Italy. He was defeated by an Austrian army **at Tolentino** (May 2) and fled to France, where Napoleon refused to see him.

1815, June 1. Allied Concentrations on the French Border. In Belgium were Wellington's Anglo-Dutch army of 95,000 men and Blücher's Prussians, 124,000 strong (not including a corps of 26,000 in Luxembourg under General **Friedrich Emil Kleist**). Schwarzenberg, with 210,000 men, lay along the Rhine from Mannheim to Basle. In northeast Italy, Austrian **Johann M. P. von Frimont** had 75,000. In central Germany, a Russian army of 167,000 under Barclay moved slowly westward.

1815, June 1. Napoleon's Plans. Knowing that his enemies could not exercise their full power before mid-July, he decided to take the offensive and to defeat them in detail. He planned to crush the nearest menace first: the allied armies in Belgium. The plan was vigorous and bold, in full Napoleonic brilliance. His ablest subordinate, Davout, Napoleon mistakenly left in command of the defenses of Paris. Murat, in disgrace, was rebuffed when he requested a field command. Soult, a capable field commander, was miscast as chief of staff. So too were brave but flighty Ney and vacillating Marshal **Emmanuel de Grouchy,** selected to command the army's wings.

1815, June 11. Napoleon Leaves Paris. His army, secretly concentrated near Charleroi (June 14), poised to strike Wellington and Blücher before either dreamed that the French had left their cantonments near Paris.

1815, June 15. Seizure of Charleroi. Blücher reacted promptly; by evening 3 of his corps were assembled near Sombreffe, 10 miles northeast of Charleroi. Wellington, more cautious, and fearing for his line of communications, began concentrating 15 miles to the west. The key point was the little crossroads village of Quatre-Bras, linking the two allied armies.

1815, June 16. Battles of Ligny and Quatre-Bras. Napoleon had ordered Ney to seize Quatre-Bras with the left wing of the French army. With the center and right wing (about 77,000 men) Napoleon fell on Blücher's 83,000 at Ligny. By afternoon of the 16th he had rocked the Prussians back and ordered Ney—who he thought had already seized Quatre-Bras—to strike Blücher's right flank and complete the victory.

At **Quatre-Bras,** Ney, procrastinating, had permitted his 25,000 men to be held off by a gallant British brigade until evening of the 16th, while Wellington gathered about 36,000 men. When the English Guards Brigade came hurrying in, a British counterattack threw Ney back. Meanwhile Marshal **Jean Baptiste d'Erlon**'s corps of 20,000 men, moving from reserve toward Ney, through a confusion of orders (for which Ney was responsible) spent the afternoon marching to and fro between the 2 French armies, and aiding neither. Ney and Wellington each lost about 4,500 men.

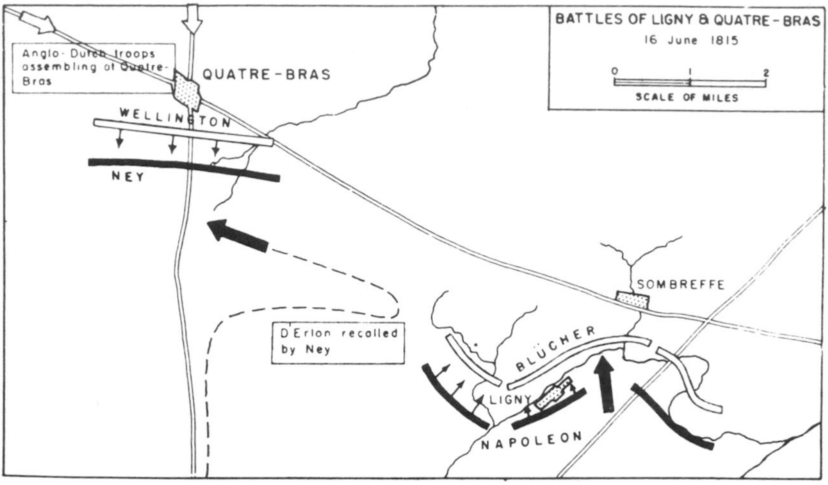

At **Ligny,** Napoleon penetrated Blücher's center, and the Prussians began to retreat. Had aid arrived from Ney, Blücher would have been destroyed, and Napoleon could then have fallen on Wellington's left flank and rolled him up. As it was, defeated Blücher (who had been wounded) retreated to Wavre, with the important assistance of his Chief of Staff, General **August Neidhart von Gneisenau.** In these two battles, allied losses were 19,500; the French lost 14,500.

1815, June 17–18. Delayed French Pursuit. In the morning Napoleon tardily sent Grouchy with the right wing of 33,000 men after the Prussian army. With the remainder of his forces he turned toward Wellington, who had retired from Quatre-Bras toward Brussels, taking up a defensive position south of Waterloo. Ney had failed to pursue, and it was not until mid-afternoon that Napoleon succeeded in getting his forces in movement after the British. A torrential rainstorm hampered the French advance guard in a reconnaissance in force of the strong British position. Napoleon postponed his projected attack until the following morning. In the morning he delayed further for several hours to permit the ground to dry. The delay was fatal, for Grouchy—even more dilatory than Ney—had failed to make contact with Blücher. The Prussian general, unknown to either French commander, had ably rallied his command from its defeat at Ligny and was moving west toward Wellington, less than 9 miles away.

1815, June 18. Battle of Waterloo. Napoleon with 72,000 men attacked Wellington's 68,000 at noon. By 4 P.M., despite obstinate resistance, the Anglo-Dutch army had been pushed back all along the line. The French cavalry, led by Ney in person, charged into the center of the British positions. Had the Imperial Guard infantry supported this cavalry attack, Wellington's center would have been pierced. But Napoleon, worried by the ominous appearance of Prussian elements on his right flank, held the Guards back, and the unsupported horsemen could not break the squares of the magnificent British infantry. About this time, Blücher's strength began to be felt. General Georges Lobau's corps, hurriedly shifted to oppose the Prussians, was driven in. Napoleon made one last effort to break Wellington's line. The Imperial Guard—without cavalry support—struck the British center, made some progress, but was then checked by the "thin red line." Blücher's full strength (61,000) was now engaged, overlapping the French right. As the Guard fell back, Wellington counterattacked. The French army collapsed into a mob of refugees, harassed through the night in their flight by the Prussians. Losses were great on both sides: Wellington, 15,000 men; Blücher, 7,000. The French lost 30,000, of whom 7,000 were captured.

1815, June 18. Battle of Wavre. Grouchy, meanwhile, had caught up with Blücher's rear guard (about 20,000). He was content to fight an unimaginative and partially successful battle while the French

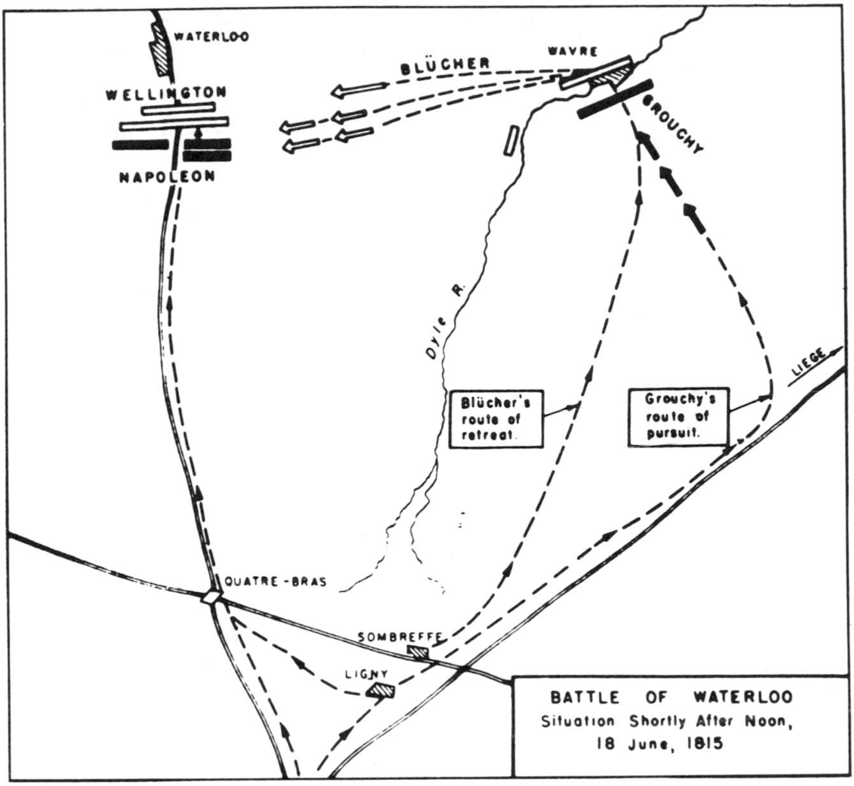

Empire was tumbling into ruins 8 miles to his west.

1815, June 21. Napoleon Abdicates. He then surrendered himself to the British. H.M.S. *Bellerophon* received him on board (July 15) and he started for his exile on the island of St. Helena, where he would die (May 5, 1821).

1815, November 20. Second Peace of Paris. France lost some more territory, her boundary generally that of 1790. She was forced to pay an indemnity.

1815, November 20. Quadruple Alliance. The victors—England, Austria, Prussia, and Russia—agreed to assure the execution of the Peace of Paris. In effect, they established themselves as the arbiters of Europe.

WESTERN EUROPE

BRITISH ISLES

Except for the Napoleonic Wars and the War of 1812, whose respective fringes touched the British Isles and their territorial waters, all of the military and naval operations of the British Empire took place away from the British Isles. These are discussed under their appropriate territorial subheads.

FRANCE

1800–1815. Napoleonic Wars. **(See p. 743.)**

1814–1824. Reign of Louis XVIII.

1823. Invasion of Spain. This was in behalf of **Ferdinand VII** (see p. 770).

1824–1830. Reign of Charles X.

1830, July 28. Revolution in Paris. The monarchy of the Restoration toppled, and **Louis Philippe,** cousin of the deposed king, headed a new constitutional monarchy. The new regime used troops to suppress insurrections in Lyon (1831), and again in both Paris and Lyon (1834).

1830–1848. Conquest of North Africa. **(See p. 781.)**

1848, February 22–24. Revolution in Paris. A series of uprisings culminated in the abdication of Louis Philippe and establishment of the Second Republic, which tottered in a ferment of social and political unrest.

1848, June 23–26. Insurrection of June. A bloody uprising of well-organized Paris workers was suppressed by General **Louis Eugène Cavaignac,** temporary dictator of a provisional government. He executed rebel leaders without mercy, then resigned his dictatorship.

1848, December 20. Prince Louis Napoleon Bonaparte Elected President. He was the nephew of Napoleon I.

1849, April 24. Intervention in Italy. **(See p. 774.)**

IBERIAN PENINSULA

Spain

1807–1814. Peninsular War. **(See pp. 753, 764.)**

1820, January. Mutiny at Cádiz. The revolt, led by Colonel **Rafael del Riego y Núñez,** spread; King Ferdinand VII was taken prisoner.

1822, October. Congress of Verona. The Quadruple Alliance authorized France to intervene to restore peace and the monarchy in Spain.

1823, April 17. French Invasion. An army under Duke **Louis d'Angoulême** crossed the Bidassoa River on the western flank of the Pyrenees, seized Madrid, then marched to Cádiz, where the rebel government had fled.

1823, August 31. Battle of the Trocadero. Riego's rebel forces, defending 2 forts 8 miles from Cádiz, were routed by the French. The revolution was ended; the king, freed, took drastic measures of reprisal.

1834–1839. The Carlist War. Ferdinand, before his death (September 29, 1833), designated his infant daughter **Isabella** as his successor under the regency of his widow, **Maria Christina,** depriving his brother Don **Carlos** of his Salic-law right to the throne. Carlos led a revolution. France, England, and Portugal entered an alliance with the Spanish government to assist in suppressing the revolt (April 22). From England went the so-called Spanish Legion, made up of 9,600 mercenaries recruited under special authority of Parliament and led by Sir **George de Lacy Evans.** France rented her entire Foreign Legion to Spain. Five years of ferocious guerrilla warfare followed; the French Foreign Legion was the backbone of the otherwise ill-handled Spanish loyalist forces. The Legion particularly distinguished itself in the decisive **Battles of Terapegui** (near Pampeluna; April 26, 1836) and **Huesca** (March 24, 1837). When the Legion left Spain after suppression of the revolt (January 17, 1839), it had lost 50 per cent of its initial strength. The war was concluded by the **Convention of Vergara** (August 31, 1839). Don Carlos took refuge in France.

1840–1843. Civil War. General **Baldomero Espartero** led a revolt, seizing dictatorial power and driving Maria Christina and Isabella from the country. He suppressed uprisings (October, 1841; November–December, 1842). A counteruprising under General **Ramón Narváez** was successful (July–August, 1843). Espartero fled, and Isabella was restored to the throne under the guidance of Narváez (1843–1851).

Portugal

1820, August 29. Oporto Revolution. This was sparked by the Spanish revolution (see above). The insurgents expelled the regency established under England's aid during the absence of King **John VI** in Brazil (see p. 816).

1821, July 4. Return of King John. He accepted the insurgents' invitation to return as constitutional monarch.

1823–1824. Civil War. John's second son, **Miguel,** failed in an attempt to restore an absolute monarchy.

1826, March 10. Death of John. His son Dom **Pedro** (now Emperor of Brazil; see p. 817) nominally succeeded him as **Peter IV,** but refused to leave Brazil, handing the Portuguese throne to his infant daughter, **Maria de Gloria,** with Miguel as regent. Civil war flared between the followers of Miguel, who seized Lisbon, and the constitutional government, supported by General **João Carlos de Saldanha** at Oporto.

1827, January. British Intervention. An expeditionary force of 5,000 men under Sir **William Clinton** landed in support of Saldanha's constitutional army. Miguel bowed to force, and the British withdrew (April 28, 1828).

1828, July 7. Miguel Seizes the Throne. Queen Maria was taken to Brazil.

1828–1834. Miguelite Wars. Adherents of the queen organized revolt in the Azores, reinforced by volunteers from Brazil, England, and France. The Miguelite fleet was defeated in **Praia Bay** (August 12, 1828) in an attempt to take the Azores. Maria's supporters, obtaining a British loan, purchased a small squadron in England. Dom Pedro, abdicating in Brazil, joined his daughter's forces (April, 1831). France, following persecution of French subjects in Portugal, seized the Miguelite fleet in the Tagus (July, 1831).

1832, July. Seizure of Oporto. Dom Pedro's "Liberation" expedition from England, 6,500 strong, occupied Oporto, but was besieged by Miguel with 80,000 troops. Britain's Admiral Sir **Charles Napier,** commanding the "Liberation" squadron, defeated a Miguelite flotilla off **Cape St. Vincent** (July 5, 1833), then captured Lisbon (July 24) and held it against the Miguelites. The Quadruple Alliance (see p. 769) solidified anti-Miguel resistance.

1834, May 16. Battle of Santarém. Saldanha's and Dom Pedro's allied liberation forces defeated Dom Miguel, who surrendered 10 days later. His banishment concluded the wars.

THE LOW COUNTRIES

1815, August 24. Unified Kingdom of the Netherlands. Established by the Quadruple Alliance with **William I** (Prince of Orange) as king. Holland and Belgium were joined.

1830, August 25. Belgian Revolution. A revolt against William I started in Brussels with fighting between civilians and Dutch troops.

1830, October 4. Belgian Declaration of Independence.

1830, October 27. Bombardment of Antwerp. The city was held by the Belgian populace, but the citadel was occupied by a Dutch force under General **David Hendryk Chassé.** His bombardment of the city strengthened anti-Dutch feeling among the Belgians.

1830, November 4. Armistice. Ordered by the great-power **Conference of London.**

1830, December 20. Independence of Belgium. The great powers at London declared the dissolution of the Kingdom of the Netherlands.

1831, June 4. Leopold I (of Saxe-Coburg) Elected King of the Belgians.

1831, August 2. Dutch Invasion of Belgium. William led an army of 50,000 troops and was at first successful against extemporized Belgian forces. A French army of 60,000, under Marshal **Étienne Maurice Gérard,** forced the Dutch to retire. Chassé, still holding the citadel of Antwerp, was besieged by the French.

1832, November–December. The French army, assisted by a Franco-British naval squadron, forced Chassé to surrender. An armistice followed (May 21, 1833).

1839, April 19. Dutch Recognition of Belgian Independence.

SCANDINAVIA

1800–1815. Napoleonic Wars. (**See p. 743.**) These resulted in several changes of national status in Scandinavia.

1808. War in Finland. After their alliance at the Treaty of Tilsit, Napoleon and Alexander of Russia called on Sweden to forsake the coalition with England. When Sweden refused to declare war on England, a Russian army under **Count F. W. Buxhöwden** invaded Finland (February). After inconclusive warfare, the Swedes evacuated Finland (December). By the **Treaty of Frederikshavn** (September, 1809) Sweden ceded Finland and the Aland Islands to Russia.

1815. Act of Union. Norway was given the status of an independent kingdom, united with Sweden under one ruler.

1848, March–August. Schleswig-Holstein Revolt. This was inspired by Prussia. Prussian troops under General **Friedrich Heinrich von Wrangel** marched in to occupy the provinces. Sweden sent troops to assist Denmark to re-establish its control; England threatened naval action against Prussia. Austria and Russia also gave diplomatic support to Denmark. The **Convention of Malmo** (August 26, 1848) brought about quasi peace. Desultory operations continued until the **Treaty of Berlin** (1850) restored full Danish rights in the disputed provinces.

AUSTRIA-HUNGARY

1800–1815. Napoleonic Wars. (See p. 743.)

1806, August 6. Dissolution of the Holy Roman Empire. The Austrian Empire took its place (see p. 750). The new empire, a mélange of German, Slav, Magyar, Bohemian, and Latin elements, was dominated by its foreign minister (virtually prime minister) Prince **Klemens W. N. L. von Metternich.** Internal discord boiled in the Italian, Bohemian, and Hungarian provinces, and to some extent in Austria itself.

1810–1850. Austrian Involvement in Italy and the Balkans. (See pp. 773 and 775.)

1848, March 13. Revolt in Vienna. Metternich resigned. Emperor **Ferdinand I** promised constitutional reforms and relaxation of suppressive efforts throughout the empire.

1848, March 18–22. Revolt in Milan. (See p. 773.)

1848–1849. Austro-Sardinian War. (See p. 773.)

1848, April 10. Hungarian Independence. Under the leadership of **Lajos Kossuth,** Hungary became virtually independent.

1848, June 17. Bombardment of Prague. A Czech uprising was quelled by an Austrian force under Marshal **Alfred zu Windischgrätz.** This was followed by martial control over all Bohemia.

1848, September 17. Austrian Invasion of Hungary. Croatian forces under Count **Josef Jellachich** invaded Hungary to suppress the independence movement.

1848, October 3. Hungarian Invasion of Austria. After repulsing Jellachich, the Hungarians advanced toward Vienna.

1848, October 6. Revolt in Vienna. In sympathy with the Hungarians, the populace of the Austrian capital again rose in revolt, but this was promptly suppressed by Windischgrätz (October 31), who then repelled the Hungarians and pursued them. Soon after this Ferdinand abdicated and was succeeded by his nephew, **Franz Josef** (December 2).

1849, January 5. Occupation of Budapest. Windischgrätz captured the Hungarian capital, and drove Hungarian General **Arthur von Görgei** into the mountains north of Budapest. Görgei having broken with Kossuth, Polish General **Henry Dembiński,** was placed in command of Hungarian forces.

1849, February 26–27. Battle of Kápolna. Dembiński was defeated by Windischgrätz.

1849, April 13. Hungarian Republic Established. Kossuth was elected president.

1849, April–May. Hungarian Victories. Görgei, recalled to command, defeated Windischgrätz in a series of smart actions, forcing the Austrians to evacuate Hungary.

1849, June 17. Russian Intervention. Russian troops, led by General **Ivan Paskievich,** assisting Austria, invaded Hungary from the north. At the same time Austrian General **Julius von Haynau,** replacing Windischgrätz, invaded from the west.

1849, June–July. Hungarian Defeats. Görgei was driven southeast, toward Transylvania, where General **Jozef Bem,** a Pole in Hungarian patriot service, had been operating successfully.

1849, July 31. Battle of Segesvar. Bem was badly defeated by Haynau's and Paskievich's converging armies. With the remnants of his troops, Bem joined Görgei for a last stand.

1849, August 9. Battle of Temesvár (Timisoara). Haynau overwhelmed the Hungarians. Görgei managed to withdraw in good order, but recognizing inevitable defeat, surrendered to the Russians (August 11) with 22,000 men. Haynau then ferociously stamped out the last embers of Hungarian rebellion.

GERMANY

Following the dissolution of the Holy Roman Empire, the German states began, with much internal friction, a coalescence around Prussia as a nucleus. The sole external conflict was Prussia's quasi war with Denmark over Schleswig and Holstein (see p. 771).

1805–1807, 1812–1815. Napoleonic Wars. (See p. 746.)

1807–1814. Reorganization of the Prussian Army. Driving spirit in extensive reforms was General Gerhard von Scharnhorst. Principal among his reformer subordinates were August Neidhart von Gneisenau, **Hermann von Boyen, Karl von Grolman,** and Karl von Clausewitz.

1809, March 1. Establishment of Prussian General Staff. Scharnhorst, first Chief of the General Staff, was virtually Minister of Defense in a new War Department.

1821, January 11. General Staff Reorganized. Under General **Karl von Müffling** it took the general form it retained for 120 years.

1847–1848 Unrest in Germany. It was part of the revolutionary ferment in Europe.

1848, March 15–31. March Days in Berlin. A popular uprising, with bloodshed, forced concessions from King **Frederick William IV,** but was suppressed when **General von Wrangel occupied Berlin** (November 10).

1848, April–August. Intervention in Schleswig-Holstein. (See p. 771.)

1849, March 27. Frankfurt Constitution. A federal German state was to be established under a hereditary "Emperor of the Germans." However, Frederick William IV of Prussia rejected the crown.

1850, November 29. Treaty of Olmütz. Prussia abandoned a plan for a new German Confederation excluding Austria; Austrian primacy in Germany was reaffirmed.

ITALY

Revolutionary Ferment, 1814–1847

Following the collapse of the Napoleonic structure, the Italian states—dominated by overt Austrian influence—were reconstituted under their former near-medieval autocratic status. This recrudescence of autocracy was opposed by the popular urge for independence and constitutional government fermenting throughout Europe, and particularly stimulated in the Italian peninsula by Napoleon's enlightened reorganization and government.

1820, July 2. Neapolitan Revolution. General **Guglielmo Pepe** led an army revolt, which was crushed at **Rieti** by an Austrian army coming to the aid of King **Ferdinand IV** (March 7, 1821).

1821, March 10. Sardinian Revolution. This was crushed at **Novara** (April 8) by a combined Austro-Sardinian royalist force.

1831, February–March. Revolts in Modena, Parma, and the Papal States. These were inspired largely by **Giuseppe Mazzini,** and were put down with Austrian military assistance.

1832–1834. Renewed Revolts. Austrian troops occupied Romagna (January, 1832). French troops took Ancona (March). In another Mazzini uprising in Piedmont and Savoy, a young Sardinian sailor, **Giuseppe Garibaldi,** fled when the uprising failed (1834). Matters in Italy went from bad to worse, as abortive revolts flared for several years.

1847, July 17. Austrian Occupation of Ferrara. This united the Italians in growing hatred of Austrian overlordship.

Italian War of Independence, 1848–1849

1848, March 18–22. Milan Revolt. The "Five Days" revolt ended when Austrian Marshal **Josef Radetzky,** 82 years old, withdrew from the city. He concentrated his army of occupation into the fortress "Quadrilateral": Mantua, Verona, Peschiera, and Legnago. He went on the defensive as a coalition of Italian forces gathered in north Italy.

1848, March 22. Sardinian Declaration of War on Austria. King **Charles Albert** of Sardinia took command of the allied Italian forces. Radetzky, with some 70,000 men, fought a brilliant offensive-defensive campaign on interior lines against enemies double his strength, but lacking his skill.

1848–1849. Spread of Italian Independence Movement. Inspired by the Milan Revolt and the Sardinian declaration of war, Italian patriots in Venice, under **Daniele Manin** declared an independent republic (March 26, 1848). The unrest spread to the Papal States, where Giuseppe Mazzini eventually ousted the Pope and declared the independence of a Roman Republic (February 9, 1849).

1848, July 24–25. Battle of Custozza. Massing superior forces against a portion of the Sardinian Army, Radetzky overwhelmed it and drove Charles Albert out of Lombardy. He reoccupied Milan and besieged Venice. Garibaldi, who had formed a volunteer army fighting in the

Alps, fled to Switzerland. Following a brief armistice, hostilities were resumed.

1849, March 23. Battle of Novara. Duplicating Napoleon's maneuver at Marengo, Radetzky with 70,000 men completely defeated Charles Albert and his Polish chief of staff, General **Albert Chrzanowski,** who could put only part of their 100,000 men on the field. Charles Albert abdicated in favor of his son, **Victor Emmanuel II.**

1849, April 24. French Intervention. An expeditionary force, 8,000 strong, under General **Nicolas Oudinot** (son of Napoleon's marshal), landing at Civitavecchia, moved on Rome.

1849, April–June. Siege of Rome. The 20,000 garrison included 5,000 of Garibaldi's red-shirted "Legion." After an initial repulse (April 29), Oudinot persisted, and forced a capitulation (June 29). Garibaldi and his legion retreated toward Venice, hoping to join its defenders, but hot pursuit by French, Austrian, and Italian loyalist forces scattered it. Garibaldi himself fled to America.

1849, May–August. Siege of Venice. Radetzky's army had seized all of Venice's mainland territory after Novara. After terrible suffering from bombardment, starvation, and disease, Manin capitulated (August 24).

1849, August 9. Sardinia Makes Peace. The revolution was quelled; Italy writhed under the cruelty of its conquerors—particularly the Austrian Baron **Julius von Haynau.**

EASTERN EUROPE

RUSSIA

1800–1815. Napoleonic Wars. (**See p. 743.**)
1804–1813. War with Persia. (**See p. 779.**)
1806–1812. War with Turkey. (**See p. 777.**)
1808. Conquest of Finland. (**See p. 771.**)
1825–1828. War with Persia. (**See p. 779.**)

War with Turkey, 1828–1829

1828, April 26. Declaration of War. Russia came to the support of the Greeks in their war for independence (see p. 776). This also was an opportunity for further Russian expansion at Turkey's expense.

1828, May–December. Operations in the Balkans. A 3-pronged offensive under the general direction of Czar **Nicholas I** crossed the Danube, to be checked temporarily by the Turkish fortresses. Silistra was invested. Varna (Stalin) was captured after a siege of 3 months (October 12).

1828, May–December. Operations in the Caucasus. An army under General **Ivan Fedorovich Paskievich** advanced from Tiflis, captured Kars, then moved north to defeat the Turks at **Akhalzic** (Akhaltzikke, August 27), while the Black Sea fleet captured Poti. Fierce Kurdish resistance along the upper Euphrates then checked further Russian advance.

1829. Advance on Adrianople. General **Hans K. F. A. von Diebitsch-Zabalkansky** took over command of the Balkan offensive. He moved south against Turkish Grand Vizier **Mustafa Reshid Pasha,** leaving a force to continue the siege of Silistra (which fell June 30), and defeated Reshid at **Kulevcha** (June 11). Diebitsch then boldly penetrated the passes of the Balkan (Haemus) Mountains, completely outmaneuvering the Turks by the rapidity of his advance. He took Adrianople (August 20). With Constantinople threatened, Turkey sued for peace.

1829, September 16. Treaty of Adrianople. Russia gained the mouth of the Danube River and the eastern coast of the Black Sea.

1830–1832. Polish Insurrection. (**See p. 775.**)

1833. Russian Intervention in Turkey. (**See p. 778.**)

1839–1847. Khivan Conquest. To extend Russian boundaries southward into Turkestan and to open up trade, an army under General **Basil A. Perovsky** moved from Orenburg into the Khanate of Khiva, in what are now the Kazakh, Uzbek, and Turkoman S.S.R.'s. The expedition ended in disaster (1839). The Russians returned to more gradual efforts. A Russian fort was established on the northeastern edge of the Aral Sea, at the Jaxartes (Syr-Darya) River mouth (1847). Other Russian spearheads slowly pushed southeastward toward Tashkent.

1849. Intervention in Hungary. (**See p. 772.**)

POLAND

1815, June 9. New Partition of Poland. The Congress of Vienna divided the Grand Duchy of Warsaw between Prussia, Russia, and Austria, once more dissolving Poland. A tiny fragment—the Cracow (Krakow) area—for a time remained a republic. Russian Poland became the so-called Congress Kingdom, with the czar as its king. There was recurrent friction between the Poles and Russians.

1830, November 29. Polish Insurrection. This began in Warsaw. Polish patriots, among them numbers of veterans of the Napoleonic armies, gathered forces totaling 80,000 men and 158 guns. Russian generals Diebitsch and Paskievich, whose troops totaled 114,000, brought fire and sword throughout the region, while Polish factions fought with one another for supremacy.

1831, February 20. Battle of Grochow. Diebitsch was halted on the outskirts of Warsaw in a sanguinary battle by a Polish army under Prince **Michael Radziwill.** Diebitsch withdrew eastward.

1831, May 26. Battle of Ostrolenka (Ostroleka). Polish General **Jan Zigmunt Skrzneki** fought a long, bloody, but indecisive battle with Diebitsch on the Narew River. The Polish artillery was well handled by General Bem, but the Poles were forced to retreat. Skrzneki gradually fell back on Warsaw, where he was relieved by General Dembiński.

1831, September 6–8. Battle of Warsaw. The capture of the gallantly defended Polish capital by Paskievich's troops was accompanied by great bloodshed. The insurrection was stamped out violently.

1846, February. Cracow Insurrection. A local armed movement against Austria—intended as another general Polish uprising—was speedily suppressed by Austrian troops; the state of Cracow was absorbed by Austria.

THE BALKANS

During this half-century the Balkan Peninsula was in a constant turmoil of war and internal disorder. The Ottoman Empire's decay gave hope of freedom to the oppressed peoples of the peninsula, who as a consequence were ceaselessly engaged in plotting or waging revolutions. And even while fighting or intriguing against the Turks, they were fighting and intriguing among themselves.

Encouraging this internal unrest, and attempting to profit from it both politically and territorially, were the neighboring empires of Russia and Austria, both hoping to inherit all of the Balkan Peninsula and the strategic straits of the Dardanelles and the Bosporus when, as they expected, the Turkish Empire reached an early collapse. The aspirations of both the Hapsburg and Romanoff empires were viewed with alarm and suspicion by both Britain and France. During the Napoleonic Wars, Russia and Austria were somewhat reluctant allies in the Balkans, while Napoleon directly or indirectly supported or encouraged the Porte. For the same reason, Britain—also reluctantly—was frequently allied with Russia and Austria against Turkey, but nonetheless endeavored to direct the main efforts of the alliance against Napoleon. After Napoleon's defeat, Britain continued this policy of maintaining the balance of power in the Balkans, even though, on a few occasions, other policy considerations (such as supporting the independence of Greece) required her to participate in limited military operations against Turkey. The principal events were:

1799. Independence of Montenegro. Achieved by King **Peter I** through his alliance with Russia against Turkey (see p. 698) and support of both Russians and British against French efforts in Dalmatia.

1804–1813. Serbian Insurrection. The Serbs were led by **George Petrovich** (known as **Kara George,** and founder of the Karageorgevich family). Under his leadership Turkish troops were driven from Belgrade and Serb independence proclaimed (December, 1806). Apparently successful, the independent state collapsed when Russia made peace with Turkey (1812) and Turkish armies reoccupied the country; Kara George fled to the mountains.

1812. Bessarabia to Russia. This was a provision of the **Treaty of Bucharest** (see p. 777). The remainder of Moldavia remained under Turkish suzerainty.

1815–1817. Serbian Insurrection. The principal leader was **Milosh Obrenovich,** an opponent of Kara George. The murder of Kara George by Obrenovich adherents resulted in a blood feud between the families which lasted more than a century. The Turks suppressed the revolt, but recognized Obrenovich as hereditary prince of Serbia when he agreed to Turkish suzerainty.

Greek War of Independence, 1821–1832

1821, October 5. Massacre of Tripolitsa. The beginning of revolt in Morea resulted in the massacre of the 10,000-man Turkish garrison. Immediate, savage Turkish reprisals followed, and all Greece flamed.

1822, January 13. Independence Proclaimed at Epidauros.

1822, April–June. Occupation of Chios (Scio). A Turkish squadron under **Kara Ali** took the island, massacring or enslaving its entire population.

1822, June 18–19. Battle of Chios. Greek sailor-patriot **Constantine Kanaris,** with 2 fire ships, sailed into the midst of the Turkish squadron and blew up the Turkish flagship with all on board.

1822, July–1823, January. First Siege of Missolonghi. A Turkish army, invading the peninsula north of the Gulf of Corinth, was stopped before the Greek fort. **Mustai Pasha** hurried with reinforcements for the besiegers.

1822, August 21. Battle of Karpenizi. With 300 men, **Marco Bozzaris** surprised Mustai's advance guard in a night attack. Bozzaris was killed, but the 4,000 Turks were routed, losing most of their leaders.

1823, January. Turkish Withdrawal. Mustai gave up the siege of Missolonghi and retired.

1823–1825. Greek Dissension. Instead of pressing their advantage, the Greeks began quarreling among themselves.

1825, February 24. Egyptian Involvement. Answering Sultan **Mahmud II**'s call for help, **Mohammed Ali** (see p. 778) sent a fleet and an army. **Ibrahim,** son of Mohammed, landed in the Morea, with some 5,000 well-disciplined troops, and quickly overran the peninsula. Meanwhile a new Turkish army, under Reshid Pasha, penetrated from the north and again invested Missolonghi.

1825, May–1826, April 23. Second Siege of Missolonghi. The starving garrison was destroyed in a final desperate sortie.

1825, May–June. Siege of the Acropolis. Reshid moved on Athens and besieged the Acropolis. European interest by now focused on assisting Greek independence; Lord **Byron** had already arrived (1822). He died soon after (1824) but was followed by a number of volunteer adventurers and idealists, the most prominent of whom were Admiral Lord **Cochrane** and General Sir **George Church.** Cochrane was placed in command of the Greek Navy, Church of the Army, but both were paralyzed by Greek internecine intrigue.

1825, June 5. Capitulation of the Acropolis. Greek inefficiency negated the plans of both Cochrane and Church, who fled to the safety of warships in the bay. Reshid accorded the honors of war to the garrison. Continental Greece was again under Turkish control.

1827, July 6. Treaty of London. Forced by pro-Hellenic public opinion, the governments of England, France, and Russia demanded that the Egyptians withdraw and that the Turks agree to an armistice. Both refused. A large Egyptian squadron landed reinforcements at Navarino (September 8), where a Turkish squadron also lay. The 3 allied governments sent naval forces to Greece; they rendezvoused off the harbor of Navarino.

1827, October 20. Battle of Navarino. Learning that Egyptian Ibrahim was carrying out depredations ashore, British Admiral Sir **Edward Codrington,** the senior allied commander, sailed into the harbor where the Egyptian-Turkish fleet was at anchor. Following Codrington's 3 ships of the line and 4 frigates were French Admiral **Henri G. de Rigny**'s 4 ships of the line and 1 frigate. In a second line came Russian Admiral Count **Heiden**'s 4 ships of the line and 4 frigates. **Tahir Pasha**'s 3 ships of the line, 15 frigates, and some 50-odd smaller craft lay in a long horseshoe formation; the flanks were protected by shore batteries. The allied fleet dropped anchor in their midst. A Turkish ship fired on a British dispatch boat, killing an officer and several men. Codrington at once opened fire and his allies joined in. The Turko-Egyptian fleet, heavily outgunned, was destroyed, three-fourths of its vessels either sunk or fired by their own crews. Allied losses were 696 killed and wounded. The Turko-Egyptian loss, never officially reported, must have been great.

COMMENT. *Navarino, which really decided Greek independence, was a gun duel, pure and simple, between floating batteries.*

1828, April 26. Russia Declares War. (See p. 774.)

1828, August 9. Egyptian Evacuation of Greece. This was supervised by a French expeditionary force. The evacuation was completed early next year (1829). This virtually ended the war.

1832, May 7. Treaty of London. This created the independent Kingdom of Greece.

1829. Autonomy of Serbia, Wallachia, and Moldavia. This was a result of the Treaty of Adrianople (see above).

1829–1834. Russian Occupation of Wallachia and Moldavia.

1843, September 14. Revolt in Greece. King **Otto I** was forced to grant constitutional government.

1848. Revolt in Wallachia. This was related to continent-wide political unrest. Russia, with Turkish approval, invaded the principality and subdued the insurrection.

EURASIA AND THE MIDDLE EAST

THE OTTOMAN EMPIRE

The Ottoman Empire, football of France, Russia, and England during the Napoleonic Wars, began to disintegrate.

War with Russia, 1806–1812

A smoldering dispute with Russia over the status of the principalities of Wallachia, Moldavia, and Bessarabia was fanned into flame by the French ambassador to the Porte.

1806, November 6. Turkey Declares War. Russian troops invaded Wallachia and Moldavia.

1807, February–March. British Naval Attack on Constantinople Repulsed. (See p. 766.)

1807, June 30. Battle of Lemnos. A Russian fleet under Admiral **Dmitri Seniavin** defeated a slightly larger Turkish fleet.

1807, August. Armistice. This was largely due to mediation by Napoleon at Tilsit. Russian forces withdrew from Wallachia and Moldavia; the Turkish army retired to Adrianople.

1809–1812. Desultory Warfare. Russia was generally more successful than Turkey.

1812, May 28. Treaty of Bucharest. This resulted from British mediation. Bessarabia went to Russia, but Moldavia and Wallachia remained under Turkish control.

1808–1809. Internal Unrest and Mutinies. Sultan **Selim** was dethroned (1807) and killed (1808) when adherents attempted to reinstate him. His successor **Mustafa IV** was quickly dethroned in turn (1808) and succeeded by **Mahmud II.**

1821–1832. Greek War of Independence. (See p. 776.)

1821–1823. War with Persia. (See p. 779.)

1826, June 15–16. Massacre of the Janissaries. Sultan Mahmud, enraged by the inefficiency of his troops, attempted to displace the Janissaries, who rose in revolt. Loyal troops bombarded their barracks in Constantinople, and Turkish mobs ended the job by a wholesale massacre; more than 6,000 were killed.

First Turko-Egyptian War, 1832–1833

Mohammed Ali demanded control of Syria as reward for his assistance against Greece. This was rejected by the sultan.

1832. Egyptian Invasion of Syria. Ibrahim captured Acre (May 27), Damascus (June 15), and Aleppo (July 16).

1832, December 21. Battle of Koniah (Konya). Invading Anatolia, Ibrahim met and defeated Reshid's main Turkish army, capturing Reshid. Turkey in desperation called on Russia for aid.

1833, February. Defensive Alliance with Russia. A Russian squadron from the Black Sea arrived at Constantinople (February 20, 1833).

1833, May 14. Convention of Kutahya. England and France, alarmed by Russian influence in Turkey, persuaded the sultan to give Syria and Adana to Egypt.

1833–1839. Internal and External Confusion. The great powers then began to squabble among themselves, France siding with Egypt. Turkey, meanwhile, rebuilt its army with Prussian assistance. Captain **Helmuth von Moltke** was one of the advisors (1835–1839).

Second Turko-Egyptian War, 1839–1841

1839. Turkish Invasion of Syria. Hafiz Pasha, accompanied by von Moltke, was in command.

1839, June 24. Battle of Nezib. The Turks were defeated by Ibrahim, partly because Hafiz ignored Moltke's advice. The Turkish fleet went to Alexandria to surrender to Egypt (July 1). With the Ottoman Empire apparently about to disintegrate, the powers—except France—decided to shore it up.

1840, September–November. British and Austrian Intervention. A combined naval force cut Ibrahim's sea communications with Egypt. This was followed by British bombardment and occupation of **Beirut** (October 10) and **Acre** (November 3).

1840, November 27. Convention of Alexandria. British Admiral **Charles Napier** reached an agreement with the Egyptians whereby they abandoned claims to Syria and returned the Turkish fleet.

1841, February. Ibrahim Evacuates Syria. He returned to Egypt.

1841, July 13. Straits Convention. The great powers agreed that the Bosporus and Dardanelles should be closed to all foreign warships in time of peace.

1848, September. Revolt in Wallachia. (See p. 777.)

EGYPT AND THE SUDAN

1805. Rise of Mohammed Ali. The governor of Egypt for the Ottoman Empire, by intrigue and violence he established himself as an independent potentate. Violence continuing, the British decided to intervene in favor of one of his opponents.

1807, March 17. British Expedition. A force of some 5,000 men under General **A. Mackenzie Fraser** occupied Alexandria without resistance, but found their protégé had died. In attempting to take Rosetta and Rahmanieh to secure supplies, a British detachment was badly cut up, retreating to Aboukir and Alexandria with loss of 185 killed and 218 wounded. Another attempt on Rosetta (April 20) failed, with losses of some 900 men out of 2,500 engaged. Many British soldiers were massacred. Alexandria was then evacuated (September 14).

1811, March 1. Massacre of the Mamelukes. Mohammed Ali by treachery wiped out most of the Mameluke chieftains, and then their troops. He consolidated his position; made peace with the Porte, whose suzerainty he recognized; and reorganized the country, building up a powerful army (composed largely of Albanian mercenaries) and a fleet with the assistance of European military advisors. At Turkish command he now instituted a religious war in Arabia.

1811–1818. War with the Wahhabis. This Moslem sect had occupied Mecca, Medina, and Jidda, and threatened Syria. During 7 years of serious combat the Moslem holy places were recovered and the eastern

Red Sea coast placed under Eygptian rule.

1815. Mutiny in Cairo. Mainly by Albanian units, which resented Mohammed Ali's modernization program.

1820–1839. Conquest of the Sudan. Egyptian forces under **Hussein** (son of Mohammed) moved into the eastern Sudan and extended Mohammed's control over a great part of the western Red Sea coast. Egyptian troops pushed up the Nile as far as Gondokoro (modern Uganda).

1823–1827. Operations in Greece. Egyptian warships and troops assisted in checking the Greek struggle for liberty from Turkish rule (see p. 776). As a result, Egypt gained control of Crete.

1832–1833. First Turko-Egyptian War. (**See p. 778.**) This resulted in Egyptian control of Syria and Adana, and extension of Egyptian influence eastward to the Persian Gulf.

1839–1841. Second Turko-Egyptian War. (**See p. 778.**) Although losing both Crete and Syria, Mohammed Ali secured hereditary rule over Egypt.

1848. Death of Ibrahim.

1849. Death of Mohammed Ali.

PERSIA (IRAN)

Russia's policy of expansion to the east and southeast, and the clash of Franco-British interests, as well as internal rebellions, kept Persia in turmoil throughout the period—a striking exemplification of the impact of power politics on underdeveloped regions at the height of European colonial expansion. The unfortunate country was tugged hither and yon by French, British, and Russian interests. The influence of Britain (and the East India Company) was generally predominant. A number of British officers served from time to time in the Persian forces. The principal events were:

War with Russia, 1804–1813

This resulted from Russian annexation of Georgia (1800), which had been nominally under the suzerainty of Persia. Persian assistance to Georgian factions resisting the annexation aroused Russian ire.

1804. Russian Invasion of Persia. The Russian army was under General **Sisianoff.**

1804. Battle of Echmiadzin. An inconclusive 3-day battle. Persian forces were under able Persian prince **Abbas Mirza.**

1804. Siege of Erivan. Shah **Fath Ali** brought up Persian reinforcements, and Abbas Mirza later during the same year relieved the city, forcing the Russians to retire.

1805–1813. Sporadic Warfare. This dragged on throughout the Caucasus and along the Caspian coast.

1812, October 31. Battle of Aslanduz. The Russians surprised and routed Abbas Mirza on the Aras River.

1813, October 12. Treaty of Gulistan. Persia agreed to the cession of Georgia and other trans-Caucasian provinces to Russia.

1816. Persian Invasion of Afghanistan. (**See p. 788.**)

1821–1823. War with Turkey. The conflict was prompted by Russian intrigue and by Turkish protection of rebellious tribes fleeing from Azerbaijan. Abbas Mirza moved west into Turkey (1821) to the Lake Van region. In retaliation, Turkish forces under the Pasha of Baghdad struck east into Persia, but were repelled. The Persian invasion in the north culminated in the **Battle of Erzerum,** where Abbas Mirza with 30,000 men defeated a Turkish army estimated at 52,000 (1821). Peace was finally established by the **Treaty of Erzerum;** both sides agreed to maintain the *status quo* (1823).

1825–1828. War with Russia. Following a boundary dispute, Persian forces were successful along the Caspian littoral, reaching the gates of Tiflis (Tbilisi). Russian General Ivan Fedorovich Paskievich then initiated a brilliant counteroffensive campaign.

1826, September 26. Battle of Ganja (**or Kirovabad**)**.** Abbas Mirza with 30,000 men met Paskievich with 15,000. After initial Persian success, they were routed by the Russians.

1827. Russian Victories. Several indecisive actions were followed by the storming of Erivan by Paskievich and the surrender of Tabriz.

1828, February 22. Treaty of Turkomanchi. This ended the war. It also ended Persia's role as a major power.

1836–1838. War with Afghanistan. Again through Russian intrigue, prompted by British penetration into Afghanistan, Mohammed Shah of Persia undertook to invade that region. Mobilizing his army at Shahrud, he moved slowly through Khorasan (Khurasan) via Meshed into Herat Province, wasting nearly a year in bickerings with the Turkoman tribesmen on his northern flank. Captain **Eldred Potter** of the East India Company's Bombay Army turned up in Herat City, in disguise, as Mohammed's troops began investment of the city (November 23). He offered his services to the Afghan commander, and so organized the defenses that a Persian assault—delivered simultaneously in 5 places—was driven off. After a siege of nearly 10 months, Mohammed withdrew (September 28, 1838).

1849–1854. Russian Conquest of the Syr Darya Valley. This ended nominal Persian suzerainty over this region of Central Asia, and brought Russian power to the northern border of Persian Khorasan.

AFRICA

NORTH AFRICA

The 4 Barbary States—Algiers, Tripoli and Tunis (semi-independent satellites of the Ottoman Empire), and the independent Kingdom of Morocco—continued to afflict the Mediterranean and its Atlantic approaches by their piratical activities. War-torn Europe had found it practical to pay tribute to them for the protection of its commerce. The new United States had followed suit, but undertook punitive action after extreme provocation.

1801–1805. Tripolitan-American War. The Pasha of Tripoli raised his protection ante. He declared war against the United States (May 14) because his demands were not satisfied. President **Thomas Jefferson** sent a punitive expedition to the Mediterranean (July). For the next 2 years a small American naval force blockaded Tripoli, but only lackadaisically and ineffectually (1801–1803).

1803, August. Arrival of Commodore Edward Preble. A more vigorous policy was followed; American warships hunted down Tripolitan corsairs.

1803, October 31. Capture of U.S.S. *Philadelphia*. This frigate, commanded by Captain **William Bainbridge,** pursuing a Tripolitan frigate, ran aground off the harbor. At once surrounded by a score of Tripolitan vessels, Bainbridge was forced to surrender his helpless ship. Later the *Philadelphia* was floated and brought into Tripoli in triumph.

1804, February 16. *Philadelphia* Destroyed. Lieutenant **Stephen Decatur** with 73 officers and men, all volunteers, boldly sailed a small captured Tripolitan vessel into the harbor, boarded, and burned the *Philadelphia* as she lay anchored under the guns of the castle, then escaped. Preble's squadron then systematically bombarded the port, but could not enter through the tortuous, rock-strewn channel.

1804–1805. Eaton's Expedition. U.S. naval agent William Eaton started from Alexandria with 8 Marines, a navy midshipman, and about 100 mercenaries to restore **Hamet Karamanli,** the rightful but dispossessed ruler of Tripoli, to his throne (November 14). After a 600-mile march across the Libyan Desert, he reached and, aided by a naval bombardment, stormed the city of Derna (April 26, 1805). For another 6 weeks Eaton held the city against Tripolitan counterattacks. But Commodore **Samuel Barron,** who had succeeded Preble in command of the Mediterranean squadron, had meanwhile made peace with the reigning Pasha of Tripoli—the usurper **Yusuf Karamanli.** In return for $60,000 cash bounty, the *Philadelphia*'s crew were released from prison and all further ransom payments ceased. Eaton's expedition—America's first overseas land operation—was withdrawn.

1805, August 1. American Peace with Tunis. Commodore **John Rodgers,** in the U.S.S. *Constitution,* sailed into Tunis and forced its bey to make peace. Algiers alone still received American tribute. Trouble, then war, with England delayed American action.

1815, March 3–June 30. American War with Algiers. All U.S. warships having withdrawn from the Mediterranean during the War of 1812, the Dey of Algiers preyed on U.S. commerce. He threw out the U.S. consul, enslaved U.S. nationals, and finally declared war, on the grounds that he was not being paid sufficient tribute. Commodore Stephen Decatur, with a squadron of 10 vessels, entered the Mediterranean, captured 2 Algerian warships, and sailed into Algiers harbor. At cannon mouth he demanded and received cancellation of all tribute and release of all U.S. prisoners without ransom. Cessation of piracy was guaranteed by the dey. Decatur then forced similar guarantees from Tunis and Tripoli, with compensation for U.S. vessels seized by Britain in those waters during the War of 1812. Decatur's forceful action ended U.S. participation in the Barbary Wars.

1816, August 26. Allied Bombardment of Algiers. Following a succession of outrages against British shipping and subjects, a squadron under Admiral **Edward Pellew, Lord Exmouth** destroyed the port fortifications and the Algerian fleet in a 9-hour engagement. A Dutch squadron under Admiral **Theodore F. van der Capellen** assisted. The Algerians surrendered some 3,000 European prisoners.

1819. British Demonstration on the Barbary Coast. This was to discourage recurrent piracy.

1824. Bombardment of Algiers. This was by a British squadron under Admiral Sir **Harry Neal.** Algerian piracy was still not completely suppressed, however.

1826. Independence of Constantine. The city and surrounding region successfully defied the Dey of Algiers.

1827–1829. French Blockade of Algiers. Increasing friction between France and the Algerian pirates culminated when the Dey of Algiers slapped the French consul's face (April 30, 1827). During the subsequent blockade, a French ship bearing negotiators and flying a flag of truce was fired upon by the Algerians (August 3, 1829).

French Conquest of Algeria, 1830–1847

1830, June–July. French Invasion. France sent an army of 37,000 men and 83 guns to Algeria under Marshal **Louis A. V. de Bourmont.**

1830, July 5. Capture of Algiers. The dey was expelled; important ports and key inland towns were occupied.

1832–1837. Wars against Abd el Kader, Emir of Mascara. He emerged as leader of Islam against the Christian invaders. A succession of French generals failed to curb the skillful Algerian warrior.

1837, June 1. Treaty of Tafna. Peace was restored, with France controlling only a few of the major coastal ports. Limited French military operations continued, however.

1837, October. Storming of Constantine. Marshal **C. M. D. Damremont,** leading a final assault on the walled city, which for a year had resisted all French attacks, was killed as his troops won victory. Abd el Kader, claiming a violation of the peace treaty, took the field (December) with a well-trained force of 8,000 infantry and 2,000 cavalry, supplemented by some 50,000 gouma (irregular horse). Indecisive but bitter fighting continued.

1840, December. Arrival of Marshal Thomas R. Bugeaud. He brought large reinforcements. The French army in Africa now amounted to 59,000 men, later to be augmented to 160,000. Bugeaud was the first major French African colonial organizer. His forceful leadership combined great military and administrative qualities. He reorganized the African Army, adding indigenous elements, and established a tactical square combat assault formation which he called the "boar's head." The colorful names and uniforms of Bugeaud's troops —zouaves, voltigeurs, chasseurs d'Afrique, spahis, and the famous Foreign Legion— intrigued and influenced American amateur military organizations and stimulated romantic writers the world over. The French strategic pacification policy initiated by Bugeaud and carried on successfully in North Africa for almost 100 years more consisted of a few fixed bases from which flying columns issued. These mobile elements were as fluid and fast-moving as the Berbers who opposed them.

1843, May 10. Battle of Smala. Duke **Henri d'Aumale,** commanding a flying column of less than 2,000 men, surprised and attacked, headlong, Abd el Kader's army of 40,000, dispersing it.

1843–1844. French Successes. Systematically and progressively Kader was driven west into Morocco. A French squadron dampened Moorish sympathy by bombardment of Tangier and Mogadir, while Bugeaud, with 6,000 infantry, 1,500 cavalry, and some artillery, crossed the border in pursuit.

1844, August 14. Battle of Isly. Adb el Kader, with 45,000 men, was camped on the Isly River. Bugeaud crossed the river and attacked. His "boar's head" square repulsed Kader's counterattacks. Finally the French cavalry, the "boar's tusks," charged in 2 columns, overrunning Kader's camp. After a stubborn struggle Kader's forces gave way. Isly was the decisive battle of the war, although some sharp encounters occurred later.

1844, September 10. Treaty of Tangier. The French withdrew from Morocco.

1847, December 23. Surrender of Abd el Kader.

COMMENT. *Abd el Kader deserves a place in history not only as a chivalrous soldier of great ability but also as one of the great champions of men of letters of the 19th-century Islamic world. Imprisoned by the French for several years, he was later released and returned to the Near East.*

1835–1836. Ottoman Control Re-established in Tripolitania. An Ottoman fleet and army took control.

WEST AFRICA

The related Moslem Fulani and Tukulor peoples became predominant in the western Sudan highlands between the upper Senegal River and Lake Chad. To the south the warlike Ashanti and Dahomey tribes expanded their areas of control in the jungled regions west and east of the Volta River. Meanwhile, along the coast, Britain and France extended their seaport colonial control at the expense of the Portuguese and Danes, as well as the coastal tribes. The principal events were:

1804–1810. Establishment of the Fulani Kingdom of Sokoto. Under the leadership of the semireligious tribal leader **Usman dan Fodio,** the strict Moslem Fulanis overthrew the Hausa Empire. They were repulsed by the Bornu Kingdom, however, south of Lake Chad (1810).

1806–1807. Ashanti Conquest of the Gold Coast. Under their King **Osei Bonsu,** the Ashanti extended their dominions to the coast.

1809. British Capture St. Louis (Senegal) from the French.

1810. Rise of the Tukulor Kingdom. Under Ahmadu Lobo these strict Moslems (like their Fulani kinsmen) conquered the Bambara and Massina peoples in the area around the headwaters of the Niger and Senegal rivers.

1811. Britain Abolishes the Slave Trade. Similar action was taken by Holland (1814), France (1815), and most other European nations.

1816. Britain Returns the Senegal Posts to France.

1818–1858. Reign of Gezo of Dahomey. This able and enlightened ruler greatly expanded his nation's dominions. His principal instrument was a highly trained and efficient army of Amazons, comprising about one-fourth of the nation's adult females.

1822–1847. Establishment of Liberia. Freed slaves from America established a colony, despite constant conflict with neighboring tribes.

1824–1831. First Ashanti War. Sir Charles M'Carthy, governor of British posts on the

Gold Coast, attempted to protect the coastal tribes from the Ashanti, but was defeated and killed. The British sent reinforcements and finally defeated the Ashanti (1827). Peace was established, with the Ashanti surrendering their suzerainty over the coastal region (1831).

1847, July 26. Independence of Liberia. The capital, Monrovia, had originally been founded by a group of freed slaves from the United States (1822).

1842–1843. French Occupation of Ivory Coast Posts.

SOUTH AFRICA

1800–1814. British Annexation of Cape Colony. The Dutch settlement, occupied by the British (1796), was returned to Dutch control (1803), but renewal of the Napoleonic Wars led to its reoccupation (January, 1805). The **Treaty of Paris** (1814) granted the colony to Britain.

1807–1818. Reign of Dingiswayo of Zululand. He began the development of a military system.

1811–1819. Frontier Warfare. The British and Boers drove the Xosa Bantu people beyond the Fish and Keiskama rivers.

1814–1835. Growing Boer-British Friction in the Cape Colony. This was exacerbated by abolition of slavery in the British Empire (1833); the Boers felt they were not adequately compensated for the slaves they freed. Also they felt that British territorial policy was preventing them from occupying frontier lands.

1818–1819. Civil War in Zululand. Dingiswayo was defeated and killed by **Zwide,** who in turn, after fierce fighting, was defeated and killed by **Shaka,** a protégé of Dingiswayo.

1819–1828. Reign of Shaka. One of the greatest African leaders of modern times, this cruel but brilliant man perfected the Zulu military system, and extended his rule greatly, particularly in the area of modern Natal. The local inhabitants were massacred or dispersed.

1828, September 23. Murder of Shaka. The murderers, his half-brothers **Dingaan** and **Mhlangana,** soon quarreled and Dingaan became sole ruler of Zululand.

1834. Boer Frontier War with Bantu. The Bantu tribes (mainly Xosa), enraged by Boer encroachment, invaded the frontier regions and were repulsed with difficulty.

1835–1837. Great Trek of the Boers. Some 12,000 Boers, chafing under British control, decided to make a mass migration northward to establish their own independent states. Some, under **A. H. Potgieter,** headed north toward the Vaal River; the others, under **Piet Retief,** went northeastward toward Natal and Zululand Potgieter and his people, after a fierce struggle, defeated the Matabele Bantu tribe in the Vaal region, and settled down (1837).

1838, February. Durban Massacre. Retief and other Boer leaders were massacred by Dingaan, who then attacked and killed many of the settlers.

1838, December 16. Battle of Blood River. A Boer force under **Andreas Pretorius** decisively defeated Dingaan. The Zulus, beset by internal discord, did not seriously interfere with Boer colonization.

1840, January. Battle of Magango. Boers, allied with **Mpande,** brother of Dingaan, defeated the Zulu ruler, who fled to Swaziland; Mpande took his place and made peace with the Boers, granting them all of southern Natal.

1839. Pretorius Proclaims Boer Republic of Natal.

1842–1843. British-Boer Conflict in Natal. The British barely repulsed a Boer attack on their post at Durban. They then occupied Natal and annexed it (1843). Friction continued.

1846–1847. War of the Ax. Conflict broke out between the British and Kaffirs in the region between the Keiskama and Great Kei rivers. The natives were protesting against both British and Boer colonist encroachment. The British were successful in a 21-month campaign.

1846–1850. British-Boer Friction. There was considerable unrest and some fighting along the frontier near the Great Kei River and in the region between the Orange and Vaal rivers.

1848, August 29. Battle of Boomplaats. Strained relations between Boers in the Orange River colony and the British resulted in an armed clash. A force of British under Sir **Harry Smith** defeated the Boers under Pretorius. The disgruntled Boers retreated across the Vaal River.

EAST AFRICA

The great native migrations continued within the interior of central East Africa. Along the coast the Arabs retained and strengthened their control, while in the highlands of Ethiopia internal chaos continued. The principal events were:

1806–1856. Reign of Seyyid Said, Imam of Muscat and Oman. He consolidated control of the seacoast of East Africa, building up an efficient navy for the purpose. He established a major base at Zanzibar to maintain control (1828).

1813–1847. Reign of Sahla Selassie in Ethiopia. He controlled only Shoa Province, but established peace and order.

1824–1828. British Occupation of Mombassa. This was the result of a dispute with Said.

1839–1845. British Influence around the Horn of Africa. Occupation of Aden (1839) and other ports in Arabia and Somaliland gave them control of the entrance to the Red Sea.

1840. Said Moves His Capital to Zanzibar.

1841–1847. Rise of Theodore of Kwara in Ethiopia. This young chieftain established himself in control of the region west of Lake Tana, repulsing efforts of neighboring provincial rulers to oust him.

MADAGASCAR

The island became a shuttlecock in the Franco-English conflict of the Napoleonic era and later, a situation complicated by the hostility of the natives to both nations. A French force re-established French control at Tamatave (1803), but in 1810 the British seized all French stations on the island. A French effort to regain power (1818–1819) was finally repulsed by the Hovas, the principal tribe (1825); a French squadron bombarded Tamatave (1829) without much effect. In 1846 Franco-British squadrons—now in conjunction—futilely bombarded Tamatave in retaliation for native hostility to all foreigners.

SOUTH ASIA

INDIA

The British conquest of the country progressed under joint crown and East India Company auspices as the British flag followed British trade, and England's leaders parried Bonaparte's thrusts to Egypt and India. Differences with the native rulers were heightened by French intrigue, particularly with the powerful Marathas, whose leaders—**Doulut Rao Sindhia** and **Jaswant Rao Holkar**—had large armies of well-equipped and French-trained soldiers.

1799–1802. Rise of Ranjit Singh. In 3 years of warfare, at the age of 23 he united the Sikhs to control most of the Punjab.

1802. Civil War among the Marathas. Baji Rao II, the Peshwa, hereditary ruler of the Marathas, was defeated and overthrown by Holkar of Indore at the **Battle of Poona.** The British demanded that their ally, the Peshwa, be restored to his throne. Holkar refused.

Second Maratha War, 1803–1805

Simultaneous British offensives into the Deccan and Hindustan were led respectively by Sir Arthur Wellesley (later Duke of Wellington, and not to be confused with his brother, Marquis **Richard C. Wellesley,** then governor general in India) and General **Gerard Lake.**

Deccan Campaign, 1803

1803, March 20. Capture of Poona. Wellesley restored the Peshwa to power without opposition. Meanwhile Sindhia's main army had moved south. When he refused to withdraw, Wellesley's army, some 9,000 regulars and 5,000 additional native contingents, penetrated farther into the Maratha homeland (August 6).

1803, August 11. Capture of Ahmadnagar. Following this, Wellesley continued to the junction of the Jua and Kelna rivers, where he unexpectedly found the army of Sindhia and the Raja of Berar—30,000 horse, 10,000 French-trained infantry, and 200 guns (September 12). Wellesley had with him 4,500 regulars, 2,200 of them cavalry; the remainder of his expedition was beyond supporting distance.

1803, September 23. Battle of Assaye. Wellesley found an unprotected ford over the swollen Kelna. He promptly crossed and attacked Sindhia's army, which faced to its flank to meet him. Wellesley's disciplined infantry—English and Indian—pierced the center of Sindhia's line, only to be attacked on both flanks by the horde of Maratha cavalry. These were repulsed in turn by Wellesley's cavalry, and despite a determined counterattack Sindhia's masses finally broke and ran, leaving 1,200 dead and 98 guns on the field. Wellesley's losses were extremely heavy, more than 2,000 killed and wounded. Wellesley resumed his offensive.

1803, November 28. Battle of Argaon. Sindhia made another stand, but his disheartened troops were easily defeated. The storming of Gawilarh (December 15) ended the campaign.

COMMENT. *This campaign was the first step in Wellington's march to military fame.*

Hindustan Campaign, 1803

Farther north, Lake had commenced operations with the so-called Grand Army, 10,500 strong, mostly East India Company native troops with a small English contingent. He was opposed by a Maratha army of 43,000 men, with 464 guns, under the command of **Pierre Cuillier Perron,** French adventurer, successor to Count **Benoît de Boigne,** who had established European military training. A number of other French adventurers with previous military experience were also in the Maratha forces.

1803, September 4. Capture of Aligarh. The walled city was stormed by the British at a cost of 260 killed and wounded. Maratha losses, while heavy, are unknown. While Lake was proceeding toward Delhi, Perron and some of his French officers rode into Lake's lines and surrendered. **Louis Bourquien** now became the chief foreign officer with the Marathas.

1803, September 16. Battle of Delhi. Lake attacked the Marathas and drove them off the field, capturing 63 guns and much treasure. British losses were 477; again Maratha losses were unknown but heavy. After occupying Delhi, Lake moved south to capture Agra. Anxious to settle the campaign, he pushed rapidly with his cavalry after the retreating Marathas.

1803, November 1. Battle of Laswari. The Maratha army was drawn up behind a line of cannon, linked together by chains. Lake's cavalry charged over the line, but the Maratha infantry rallied. Lake's infantry, which had covered 65 miles in 48 hours, arrived in time to effect the complete destruction of the Maratha army. British losses were 834; Maratha losses again were unknown. This victory, coupled with Wellesley's success in the Deccan, brought Sindhia to submission (December 20).

Holkar's Offensive, 1804

1804, August 24–29. Intervention by Holkar. His troops ambushed a small British detachment under Colonel **William Monson** and wiped it out (August 24–29). Holkar then threatened Delhi (September).

1804, October 1. Relief of Delhi. Lake, who had pulled his army out of summer-monsoon quarters, advanced toward Delhi. Holkar retreated.

1804, November 17. Battle of Farrukhabad. Lake, after a 350-mile cavalry pursuit, dispersed the Maratha cavalry. Holkar fled to the Punjab. Lake continued into Indore to capture Dig (December 25), then turned on Bhurtpore, whose rajah had sided with Holkar.

1805, January–April. Siege of Bhurtpore. Investing the city (January 1), Lake made 4 successive assaults, all of which were repulsed with heavy losses: 103 officers and 3,100 men. The rajah, however, later made peace (April 17). Lake was superseded as commander in chief by Lord **Cornwallis** (July), but returned to command after Cornwallis' death (October).

1805, October–December. Pursuit of Holkar. Lake pursued into the Punjab, and Holkar surrendered at Amritsar (December). An uneasy peace settled over India.

1806. Sepoy Mutiny at Vellore. Religious pressures led to the outbreak—foreshadowing the Great Mutiny (see p. 858). It was quickly suppressed.

1809, April 15. Treaty of Amritsar. Growing friction between the British and Ranjit Singh was settled by agreement on the Sutlej River as the boundary between the Sikh territories and territory the British had seized from the Marathas.

1810–1820. Sikh Conquest of the Punjab. Ranjit Singh conquered all of the Punjab from the Afghans and local princes, consolidating his lands and, with help of French and Italian officers, developing the most powerful and efficient native army in India. He overran Kashmir (1819; see p. 788).

1814–1816. Gurkha War. Expeditionary forces from the British Indian Army were sent into Nepal (November 14) to stop Gurkha raids into northern India. The ferocity of the Gurkhas repelled initial attempts, but General **David Ochterlony** campaigned systematically through the southern portion of the rugged hill country, taking mountain forts one by one (1815). He penetrated the Katmandu Valley and forced peace on the warlike Gurkhas (1816). Since that time the Gurkhas have furnished the British Army with one of its most famous corps.

Third Maratha (and Pindari) War, 1817–1818

A vast horde of Pindaris (outlaws and freebooters of all castes and tribes, mostly former Maratha soldiers) had begun widespread organized depredations in central and southern India. The Maratha chieftains, though giving lip service to Britain, supported the Pindari raids. Two British forces—the Army of the Deccan, under Sir **Thomas Hyslop,** and the Grand Army, under the British commander in chief, Lord General **Francis Rawdon-Hastings of Hastings and Moira,** nearly 20,000 in all—prepared to take the field against the Pindaris, while keeping a watchful eye on the Marathas, who could muster nearly 200,000 men and 500 guns. Meanwhile, several outbreaks against British garrisons occurred, the most notable at Nagpur and Kirkee (a suburb of Poona). Though badly outnumbered, the local garrisons held out, even after Holkar and the Peshwa took the field (November, 1817).

1817, December 21. Battle of Mahidput. Hyslop with 5,500 men crushed Holkar's army of 30,000 horse, 5,000 infantry, and 100 guns.

1818, January–June. Hastings' Campaign. His Grand Army hunted down the Pindaris and remaining Marathas. The campaign ended with the surrender of the Peshwa of the Marathas (June 2, 1818). It marked the end of Maratha political power and the real beginning of the East India Company's paramountcy.

1825–1826. British Intervention in Bhurtpore. Lord **Combermere,** with 1 cavalry and 2 infantry divisions, plus a large artillery train, invested Bhurtpore to settle a disputed succession. Heretofore considered impregnable, the city's strong defenses were successfully assaulted by the British after a desperate conflict (January 18, 1826). The British lost nearly 1,000 killed and wounded; Indian losses were an estimated 8,000.

1839–1842. First Afghan War. (**See p. 789.**)

Conquest of Sind, 1843

There had been increasing friction between the Baluch rulers of Sind and the British during the First Afghan War.

1843, February 15. Attack on the Residency at Hyderabad. Resentful of humiliating terms demanded by British Governor Generals **Auckland** and **Ellenborough,** and outraged by British military threats, 8,000 Baluchis attacked the British residency. The residency was defended by a handful of men under a young British officer, **James Outram.** General Sir **Charles James Napier** immediately initiated a whirlwind campaign to come to the relief of Outram and his gallant garrison.

1843, February 17. Battle of Miani. Napier, with 2,800 men, attacked and defeated 30,000 Baluchis in savage hand-to-hand combat; the 61-year-old general, musket in hand, personally led his troops.

1843, February–March. Advance to Hyderabad. Leaving his transport behind, Napier made a forced march through the desert country in intense heat, with his British infantry mounted 2 men each on camels.

1843, March. Battle of Hyderabad. Napier dispersed the Baluchis at the gates of the city and relieved the British residency.

1843, March–May. Conquest of Sind. Napier, who never had more than 5,000 men, marched 600 miles and fought numerous minor actions and 2 battles to defeat a total of 60,000 enemies. At the conclusion of the campaign he sent his famous message to the governor general: "Peccavi" ("I have sinned").

1843, June–August. Consolidation. Napier marched another 280 miles and dispersed a force of 12,000. Total Baluchi casualties during the campaign are estimated at 12,000. This campaign stabilized India's western frontier, securing the Indus waterway. Napier also constructed the port of Karachi, which replaced Hyderabad as the capital of Sind.

First Sikh War, 1845–1846

Since the death of Ranjit Singh (1839), friction between the British and the Sikhs of the Punjab increased, as did internal disorder in the Punjab.

1845, December 11. Sikh Invasion. An army of 20,000 crossed the Sutlej into British Indian territory. Sir **Hugh Gough** marched to meet them with 10,000 men.

1845, December 18. Battle of Mudki. The Sikhs attacked the British in late afternoon, but were repulsed with heavy losses.

1845, December 21–22. Battle of Ferozeshah. This battle was unique because the British governor general, Sir **Henry Hardinge,** volunteered to serve as second in command under Gough. It was not clear who was giving orders to whom. This was another late-afternoon battle, delayed due to disagreement between the generals. The British finally attacked the well-entrenched army of **Lal Singh,** 50,000 strong, and, after several repulses, finally took the position in one of the most bitterly contested battles ever fought in India. Early next morning Sikh reinforcements under **Tej Singh** attacked halfheartedly and were repulsed. The Sikhs then withdrew across the Sutlej. British losses were 2,400; Sikh casualties were at least 10,000.

1846, January 28. Battle of Aliwal. A raiding Sikh army under **Runjoor Singh** had a brief brush with a British force under Sir **Harry Smith** at **Ludhiana** (January 21). Smith, reinforced, attacked and decisively defeated the Sikhs in another vicious battle.

1846, February 10. Battle of Sobraon. Gough, having crossed the Sutlej with about 20,000 men, attacked the Sikhs, about 50,000 strong, entrenched in a bend of the river. In another sanguinary engagement the British smashed the Sikhs, who lost 10,000 men and 67 guns. Gough had 2,300 casualties. This ended the war. Gough marched to Lahore.

1846, March 11. Treaty of Lahore. The Punjab became a British protectorate.

Second Sikh War, 1848–1849

Knowing they had come closer to victory over the British than had any other Indian forces, the Sikhs wanted revenge. The opportunity came in an incident at Multan (April 20, 1848), in which 2 British officers were killed. The Punjab rose in revolt. At first the Sikh government in Lahore attempted to suppress the revolt, with British assistance, then turned against the British (August).

1848, November–1849, January. Siege of Multan. This was carried out by part of the British Army under General **William S. Whish.**

1848, November 9. Invasion of the Punjab. Gough's main army, about 15,000 men, crossed the Sutlej. The Sikhs under **Shere Singh** moved to meet the British with about 30,000.

1848, November 22. Battle of Ramnagar. Gough's cavalry was repulsed in an effort to cross the Chenab River. After this inconclusive skirmish, Gough decided to wait for Whish to take Multan and join him. When the siege dragged on, he renewed his advance.

1849, January 13. Battle of Chilianwala. Both sides attacked simultaneously. The British had slightly the best of an all-day fight, but lost 2,800 men. The Sikhs lost about 8,000. When the British retired, the Sikhs retook their captured guns. When news of the battle and its losses reached England, Gough was relieved and was to be replaced by Napier.

1849, February 21. Battle of Gujrat. Before his orders arrived, Gough, reinforced by Whish, now had 24,000 men and artillery superiority. He crushed the Sikhs, about 50,000 strong, who were assisted by **Dost Muhammad** of Afghanistan (see below). Preceded by a 2½-hour artillery bombardment, a general British advance overwhelmed the town and camp, capturing all the Sikh guns. Cavalry charges on both flanks completed the victory. British losses were only 96 killed and 700 wounded. Sikh losses were estimated at more than 2,000. Their leaders soon surrendered, and the Punjab was annexed (March 12).

AFGHANISTAN

Harassed by its western neighbor, Persia, and by Sikh invasions from the Punjab on the east, Afghanistan was also torn by internal revolts and violent usurpations of power. The principal antagonists during this period were **Mahmud Shah,** his brother **Shah Shuja,** and Dost Muhammad. In addition, Russian and British intriguers were also working to control the country.

1799–1803. Reign of Mahmud Shah (Brother of Zaman Shah). He overthrew and blinded his brother.

1803–1810. Reign of Shah Shuja (Younger Brother of Mahmud Shah). He overthrew and imprisoned his brother.

1810–1829. Second Reign of Mahmud Shah. Escaping from prison, he defeated Shuja, who fled. Mahmud was greatly assisted by his faithful vizier and general, **Fath Ali.**

1816. Persian Invasion. They captured Herat, but were soon thereafter driven off by local Afghans (see p. 779).

1818. Revolt and Chaos. This was caused by Mahmud's dismissal of Fath Ali.

1819. Sikh Conquest of Kashmir. This province of Afghanistan was conquered by Ranjit Singh, Sikh ruler of the Punjab (see p. 786).

1826. Rise of Dost Muhammad (Brother of

Fath Ali). He captured Kabul, then gradually extended his rule over the rest of the country.

1835–1839. Reign of Dost Muhammad. He became friendly with the Russians, arousing British fears.

1836–1838. Persian Invasion. Their objective was to annex the Herat region (see p. 780).

1838, July 29. Tripartite Treaty. The British East India Company, anxious to block Persian and Russian encroachments, reached an agreement with Ranjit Singh and with Shah Shuja. Shah Shuja was to be restored to the throne of Afghanistan.

First Afghan War, 1839–1842

1839. Opening Campaign. Sir **John Keane** led the Army of the Indus, 21,000 strong, into Afghanistan. He occupied Kandahar (April), stormed Ghazni (July 21), and captured Kabul (August 7). Dost Muhammad was captured and sent to India; Shah Shuja replaced him. Keane returned to India, leaving a garrison at Kabul, to support 2 British civilian envoys: Sir **William Macnaghten** and Sir **Alexander Burnes.**

1841, November. Rising against the British in Kabul. This was led by **Akbar Khan,** son of Dost Muhammad, and resulted in the murder of both British agents. The British garrison, under elderly Major General **William G. K. Elphinstone,** was surrounded.

1842, January 6. British Capitulation at Kabul. Elphinstone's force of 4,500 men and 12,000 refugees was permitted to return to India under safe conduct.

1842, January 13. Gandamak Massacre. Elphinstone's demoralized command was surrounded by Akbar's troops in a defile on the Khyber Pass road. After ineffectual resistance, most of the British and Indian soldiers and noncombatants were massacred; a few were taken prisoner, but only a handful survived in captivity. The small British garrison at Ghazni had also been forced to surrender. Other British detachments at Kandahar and Jalalabad held out.

1842, April. Shuja Assassinated.

1842, April–September. British Invasion. Sir **George Pollock,** with a punitive force from India, stormed the Khyber Pass and relieved Jalalabad (April 16). After reorganizing, he pushed on to Kabul, where he rescued 95 prisoners (September 15). Stern reprisal for the massacre followed. The citadel and central bazaar of Kabul were destroyed. The East India Company decided, however, that continued occupation of Afghanistan would be both unprofitable and dangerous, so the country was shortly evacuated (December), and Dost Muhammad was permitted to resume the throne.

1842–1863. Second Reign of Dost Muhammad.

1848–1849. Second Sikh War. Dost Muhammad allied himself with the Sikhs (see p. 788). His cavalry contingent was routed at the **Battle of Gujrat** (February, 1849). The British annexed the Peshawar territories, but peace was not officially signed until 6 years later (1855).

SOUTHEAST ASIA

BURMA

Militant Burma continued its expansion north, west, and south, encroaching frequently on India and continuing intermittent warfare with Siam.

1811–1815. Arakan Uprising. Arakanese rebels, based in British territory near Chittagong, tried to drive out the Burmese, who protested British failure to stop use of their territory as a rebel base.

1819. Burmese Conquest of Assam. Assamese refugees fled into Manipur, under British protectorate, and again British territory was used as a base for attacks on territory occupied by the Burmese (1820–

1822). Burmese complaints got no satisfaction from the British East India Company.

1822. Burmese Invasion of Manipur and Cachar. This punitive expedition was engaged inconclusively by British forces sent to help the native rulers.

First War with Britain, 1823–1826

1823. Burmese Invasion of India. Infuriated by British action, **Maha Bandula,** Burma's great general, and governor of Assam, planned a 2-pronged attack on Bengal from Assam and Arakan. Burmese troops were soon threatening Chittagong.

1824, March 5. British Declare War on Burma. There were operations in Arakan, Assam, Manipur, and Cachar. The decisive operations were in Burma itself.

1824, April. British Preparations. An expeditionary force of 5,000 British and Indian regular troops, under Major General Sir **Archibald Campbell,** was mobilized in the Andaman Islands.

1824, May 10. Occupation of Rangoon. The city was seized without opposition. The British, soon ravaged by disease, then found themselves ringed by a determined enemy.

1824, May–December. Investment of Rangoon. Savage fighting continued (June–July). Maha Bandula's army arrived from Arakan after a forced march across monsoon-flooded country (August). British reinforcements arrived, including a rocket battery (October–November).

1824, December 1. Burmese Assault. Bandula was decisively repulsed.

1824, December 15. British Assault. They broke Bandula's cordon investment. The Burmese, no match for the British discipline, retreated.

1825, February 13. Advance up the Irrawaddy. Campbell's column of 2,500 men was supported by a flotilla of 60 boats, manned by British sailors, and carrying 1,500 additional troops.

1825, April 2. Battle of Danubyu. Checked by Bandula, Campbell's rockets broke up a Burmese attack; a British counterattack swept the Burmese from the field. Bandula was killed.

1825, April 25. Occupation of Prome. Campbell went into quarters for the monsoon season, behind entrenchments, while the Burmese Army—now under **Maha Nemyo**—again surrounded his position with field fortifications.

1825, November 30–December 2. Battle of Prome. Following repulse of a Burmese attack (November 10), Campbell launched an attack in 2 columns, supported by the flotilla. The Burmese investing lines were ruptured and rolled up; Nemyo was killed and the Burmese army disintegrated after 3 days of intense fighting. The British advance continued upriver to the vicinity of Yandabo (some 70 miles from Ava), the capital, where Burmese envoys, under a flag of truce, sought peace (January).

1826, February 24. Treaty of Yandabo. Burma surrendered Assam, Arakan, and the Tenasserim coast, and paid a large indemnity. Campbell's expedition then withdrew.

COMMENT. *This war ended Burmese military predominance in Southeast Asia.*

1838. Mon Rebellion. This was crushed by King **Tharawaddy.**

1844–1845. Civil War. Misrule by insane Tharawaddy led to revolt, which was suppressed by Tharawaddy's son, **Pagan Min,** who became king.

1845–1850. Deterioration in Anglo-Burmese Relations.

SIAM

Siam continued to be nominally at war with Burma (1785–1826), but this was confined mostly to frontier raids in the Tenasserim area and occasional clashes of expeditionary forces in northern Malaya and on the Kra Isthmus, since Burma was more seriously occupied to the west. Keeping a wary eye on her most dangerous rival, Siam turned her attention mainly to the south, where she coveted Malaya; to the east, where she periodically clashed with Vietnam over control of Cambodia; and to the northeast, where she strengthened her control over most of Laos The principal events were:

1812. Intervention in Cambodia. (See below.)

1821. Invasion of Kedah. Siamese conquest of this Malayan sultanate alarmed the British.

1826, June 20. Treaty with Britain. This established trade relations, and Siam agreed to halt its effort to penetrate farther into Malaya.

1826–1829. War with Vientiane. This ended with Siam virtually sovereign over most of Laos (see below).

1831–1834. Invasion of Cambodia. A Siamese army under able general **P'ya Bodin** was initially successful. The Khmer were defeated at the **Battle of Kompong Chhang.** Cambodian King **Ang Chan** fled to Vietnam. Guerrilla resistance arose in eastern Laos. Intervention of a Vietnamese army of 15,000, combined with a general uprising throughout the country, forced the Siamese to withdraw, leaving Vietnam in virtual control of Cambodia.

1841–1845. War with Vietnam over Cambodia. The Cambodians, revolting against Vietnamese rule, asked Siam for help. Aging P'ya Bodin led another army into Cambodia. The Siamese had somewhat the best of 4 years of fierce warfare. A compromise peace was agreed, with both Siam and Vietnam nominally sharing a protectorate over Cambodia, but with Siam predominant.

LAOS

Able King **Chao Anou** of Vientiane was determined to free himself from Siamese vassalage. He built up a strong army, but maintained friendly relations until Siam's troubles with the British seemed to provide an opportunity to revolt. The principal events were:

1819. Revolt. Chao Anou suppressed this, increasing his own power.

1826. Invasion of Siam. Chao Anou led his army in 3 columns into the heart of Siam, approaching within 30 miles of Bangkok before the surprised Siamese, under P'ya Bodin, halted and repulsed the invaders.

1826–1827. Siamese Invasion. P'ya Bodin led the Siamese Army.

1827. Battle of Nong-Bona-Lamp'on. In a fierce 7-day struggle the Siamese forced their way across the Mekong River. The Laotian Army was destroyed; Chao Anou fled to Vietnam. The Siamese destroyed the capital and devastated the country, deporting entire populations to regions of Siam which had been depopulated in the wars with Burma. They annexed Vientiane (1828).

1829. Return of Chao Anou. The former king and his Vietnamese troops were defeated and scattered by the Siamese. Chao Anou was captured.

1832. Vietnam Conquest of Xieng-Khouang. The Vietnamese annexed this east Laotian kingdom.

CAMBODIA

This weak nation continued to be a football for Siam and Vietnam. The principal events were:

1802–1812. Joint Siamese-Vietnamese Protectorate. King Ang Chan sought to bring peace to his country by paying tribute to both neighbors.

1812. Rebellion and Invasion. Ang Snguon, brother of Ang Chan, revolted, seeking Siamese help. **Rama II** of Siam sent in an army which quickly overran the country. Ang Chan fled to Vietnam. Emperor **Gia Long** of Vietnam immediately sent a large army to restore Ang Chan. The Siamese withdrew without battle. Vietnam became predominant in Cambodia.

1831–1834. Siamese Invasion and Siamese-Vietnamese War. (See above.)

1841–1845. Siamese-Vietnamese War over Cambodia. (See above.)

VIETNAM

Prolonged civil war finally came to an end early in the century, with successful **Nguyen Anh** ascending the throne in Hué as Emperor **Gia-Long** (1802). During the remainder of the period the Vietnamese were occupied with affairs in Cambodia to the west, and with increasing French intervention along the seacoast to the east. The principal events were:

1812. Intervention in Cambodia. (**See p. 791.**)

1824–1847. French Interventions. Persecution of Christians by Emperor **Minh-Mang** prompted several interventions by French naval commanders, with some armed clashes on land and sea. These culminated with an incident at **Tourane,** where 2 French warships destroyed a swarm of attacking Vietnamese vessels (1847).

1831–1845. Involvement in Cambodia. (**See p. 791.**)

MALAYA

1802–1824. Malacca Changes Hands. It was returned by England to the Dutch by the **Treaty of Amiens** (1802), and was repossessed (1811) and used by England as a base for an expedition against Java (see below). Malacca, Java, and Sumatra were restored to the Dutch (1814–1818) by the **Treaty of Vienna.** Malacca again came under English rule—traded by the Dutch (March 17, 1824) in exchange for Benkgulen, on Sumatra.

1819. Founding of Singapore by Sir Stamford Raffles. It soon outstripped the port of Malacca, to become the strategic and commercial center of the area, and Britain's bastion of naval power in the East.

1821–1826. British-Siamese-Burmese Rivalry in Malaya. (**See p. 791.**)

1826, June 20. British Treaty with Siam. (**See p. 791.**)

1826. Establishment of Straits Settlement. Centralization of British colonial holdings in Malaya.

1837–1860. Operations against Pirates. (**See below.**)

INDONESIA

Despite British interference during the Napoleonic Wars, the Dutch were able to consolidate their position in Java and the Spice Islands, and to expand their control over most of the archipelago. The principal events were:

1808. Pacification of Bantam. This brought all of western Java under Dutch sovereignty.

1810–1811. Colonial War with Britain. A large British expedition under Lord **Gilbert Elliot of Minto,** governor general of India, sailed against Java. Batavia was seized (August, 1811). A month later (September 17) the Dutch signed the **Capitulation of Semarang,** in which they ceded Java, Palembang, Timor, and Macassar to the British.

1812. Capture of Palembang. The British seized the town after the local sultan refused to accept the terms of the Capitulation of Semarang.

1816. Britain Returns Indonesian Possessions to the Dutch. This was in accordance with the treaties settling the Napoleonic Wars.

1825–1830. Great Java War. The last native prince, **Dipo Negara,** revolted against Dutch rule. The insurrection was suppressed after 5 years of continuous guerrilla warfare, in which 15,000 Dutch soldiers and an unknown number of Javanese were killed.

1837–1860. Operations against the Pirates. Piratical depredations throughout Indonesia and neighboring waters spurred the Dutch, the British, and the Spanish to action and occasional cooperation.

1841. The White Rajah of Sarawak. S **James Brooke,** leading British effo against the pirates, was granted territ along the west coast of Borneo—and the title of rajah—by the grateful Sultan of Brunei for suppressing a revolt.

1849. Revolt in Java. Suppressed by the Dutch, who increased their control.

1839–1849. Dutch Pacification of Bali.

THE PHILIPPINES

The Philippines had been economically linked with the Spanish colonies in the Americas. Loss of these colonies resulted in stagnation and decadence in the Philippines. There was little of military significance save for operations against the pirates (see above). A French naval expedition, anxious to establish a base for operations against Vietnam, attempted to seize Basilan, in the Sulu Islands, but was ignominiously repulsed (1845). France did not repeat the attempt due to Spanish protests.

EAST AND CENTRAL ASIA

CHINA

Sporadic rebellions and army mutiny, and increasing piratical depredations along the south coast of China, indicated a weakening of central control and a decline of the Manchu Dynasty. The principal events were:

1796–1804. Revolt in Western China. Uprising of the White Lotus Society in Hupei, Szechuan, and Shensi was suppressed with difficulty.

1825–1831. Moslem Invasion of Kashgaria. Inroads from western Turkestan into Kashgaria in western Sinkiang threatened for a time the Chinese hold on that area (captured in 1758). The invaders were finally ejected.

First Opium War, 1839–1842

Disagreements between Chinese officials and British merchants trading at Canton—particularly concerning the importation of opium into China—led to Chinese action against the European community (November, 1839).

1840. British Expedition to China. A force of some 4,000 men—partly English regulars, partly East India Company native troops—under Sir **Hugh Gough** arrived in Chinese waters escorted by a British naval squadron. They occupied the island of Chusan, at the entrance of Hangchow Bay. Moving south, the squadron blockaded Hong Kong and Canton.

1841, February 26. Capture of the Bogue Forts. A British amphibious operation captured the Pearl River fortifications, key to Canton. The flotilla then moved up the Pearl River.

1841, May 24. Capture of Canton. An amphibious assault was followed by the storming of the forts surrounding the city. Temporary peace followed.

1841, August–October. British Coastal Operations. The expeditionary force moved up the China coast. Amoy was bombarded and captured (August 26); Ningpo (Ninghsien) fell (October 13).

1841–1842. British Administrative Mismanagement. Operations halted for the winter, during which the British troops suffered heavily from improper administration and supply. Although British naval and military combat operations were efficient, other arrangements were shockingly poor. At times as many as 50 per cent of the troops were disease-ridden. Many transports were unseaworthy; several foundered in typhoons, with much loss of life. Food and medical attention were unsatisfactory. But China was far away; the stockholders of the British East India Company were profiting; the British

War Office and Admiralty paid little heed.

1842. Yangtze River Operations. The capture of Shanghai (June 19) was followed by a move upriver. The fall of Chingkiang (July 21) menaced Nanking, and China sued for peace.

1842, August 29. Treaty of Nanking. China was required (1) to cede Hong Kong; (2) to open treaty ports—Canton, Amoy, Foochow (Minhow), Ningpo, and Shanghai—to British trade; and (3) to pay an indemnity of $20 million.

1847. Renewed Moslem Invasion of Kashgaria. Incursions from western Turkestan were combined with uprisings among the local Mohammedan population. Severe Chinese reprisals were followed by a mass exodus of Moslems.

JAPAN AND KOREA

Self-isolated Japan continued her efforts to bar foreign contacts, despite several efforts to break down the barrier. Russia's **Nicolai Petrovich de Rezanov** of the Russian-American Company (analogous to Britain's East India Company) reached Nagasaki (1804), but after 6 months of effort failed to obtain a treaty. Raids on Sakhalin and the Kuriles by expeditions of the Russian company were repulsed (1806–1807). Japanese gunfire greeted an American ship attempting to land a party of missionaries and merchants at **Naha** in the Ryukyu Islands (1837). An American naval mission was rebuffed in 1846.

In Korea, no events of military importance transpired during the period.

NORTH AMERICA

THE UNITED STATES, 1800–1812

1801–1805. Tripolitan War. (See p. 780.)

1803. Louisiana Purchase. (See p. 745.)

1810, October 27. Annexation of West Florida. This was proclaimed by President Madison after American frontiersmen seized the Spanish fort at Baton Rouge and neighboring regions and proclaimed the independent State of West Florida. The dispute over whether West Florida was included in the Louisiana Purchase was settled when Spain renounced sovereignty (1819).

1811. Indian Trouble in the Northwest. Tecumseh, chief of the Shawnees, attempted to organize a confederation of tribes to oust the white settlers encroaching on their land. He was supported by British-Canadian fur interests. As friction increased, Brigadier General **William Henry Harrison,** governor of Indiana Territory, moved with 1,000 troops against the Indian capital, "Prophetstown," 150 miles north of Vincennes.

1811, November 7. Battle of Tippecanoe. Harrison's force, bivouacked on Tippecanoe Creek, was attacked at dawn by the Indians, some 700 strong. The assault was repulsed. Harrison's well-trained troops counterattacked and routed the Indians, then destroyed Prophetstown, shattering Tecumseh's power temporarily. American losses were 37 killed and 150-odd wounded. The Indians left 36 dead on the field, with an unknown number of dead and wounded carried off.

1811–1812. Friction with Britain. The Tippecanoe campaign brought to boiling point an ever-increasing anti-British sentiment in the United States, engendered in part by Canadian support of the Indians, in part by American expansionists determined to annex Canada. The tension had been increased by a succession of encroachments on American neutrality by England and France in the continuing Napoleonic Wars. Both nations preyed on American commerce in their mutual blockading efforts. British warships continuously impressed seamen from American merchantmen. (More than 6,200 American citizens were thus handled.) The British frigate H.M.S. *Leopard* opened fire on U.S.S. *Chesapeake* (June 22, 1807) off Norfolk Roads, killed an wounded several men, and then took off 4 alleged deserters. The incident aroused national indignation. Four years later the American frigate U.S.S. *President,* searching for a British frigate which had impressed more American sailors, overhauled the British sloop of war H.M.S. *Little Belt,* disabling her with gunfire and killing or wounding 32 men (May 16, 1811). This retaliation for the *Leopard-Chesapeake* affair was widely acclaimed. Expansionism was in the air; the "War Hawks" urged conquest of Canada while England was busy at war with France.

THE WAR OF 1812 (1812–1815)

1812, June 19. Declaration of War. This was ostensibly to defend the doctrine of "freedom of the seas."

Land Operations, 1812

1812, June. American Plans. A poorly planned 3-pronged invasion of Canada speedily aborted as other events caused Americans to go on the defensive.

1812, July 17. British Capture of Ft. Mackinac.

1812, August 15. British Capture of Ft. Dearborn (Present Site of Chicago). The garrison, a company of infantry, was massacred by the Indians after surrendering.

1812, August 16. Surrender of Detroit. Brigadier General **William Hull** had moved from Dayton, Ohio, to Detroit with some 2,500 men. There he abjectly surrendered, without firing a shot, to British General Sir **Isaac Brock,** who had but 730 Canadians and 600 Indians (under Tecumseh).

1812, October 13. Battle of Queenston. A

force of some 2,270 militia and 900 regulars, under New York militia Major General **Stephen Van Rensselaer,** attempted to invade across the Niagara River at Queenston. Part got across, mostly regulars. But Brock, who had hurried from Detroit to command the defense, brought up reinforcements and pinned them down. The militia contingent still on the American side, refusing to leave the territorial limits of the U.S., stood idly by while Brock's 600 British regulars and 400 Canadian militia overwhelmed their comrades. American losses were 250 killed and wounded and 700 made prisoner. The British lost 14 killed (including Brock) and 96 wounded.

1812, November. Lake Champlain Expedition. The American main effort, 5,000 men under Major General **Henry Dearborn,** moved down the lake from Plattsburg to Rouses Point. The militia contingent now stood on their constitutional rights and refused to cross into Canada (November 19). Dearborn returned to winter quarters.

Naval Actions, 1812

In bright contrast to the dismal army performance, the small but efficient U.S. Navy (14 seaworthy vessels) took to the high seas against overwhelming British sea power (1,048 war vessels) and engaged in a number of brilliant single-ship actions.

1812, August 19. U.S.S. *Constitution* vs. H.M.S. *Guerrière*. Captain **Isaac Hull** in the frigate *Constitution,* 44, after eluding the blockade and escaping from the clutch of a British squadron in a remarkable stern chase, demolished the British frigate *Guerrière,* 38, in a half-hour action off the Nova Scotia coast. Hull arrived at Boston with news of the victory the same day that word was received of his uncle's ignominious surrender at Detroit (see p. 795).

1812, October 18. U.S.S. *Wasp* vs. H.M.S. *Frolic*. These 18-gun sloops of war clashed off the Virginia coast in a 43-minute broadside-to-broadside hammering. When it was over the *Frolic* was a helpless wreck. But the *Wasp's* rigging was so shot up that when H.M.S. *Poictiers,* 74, came over the horizon, the American vessel, unable to make sail, was forced to strike her colors.

1812, October 25. U.S.S. *United States* vs. H.M.S. *Macedonian*. Captain **Stephen Decatur**'s frigate *United States,* 44, off Madeira, systematically smashed the Brittish frigate by long-range gunfire in 90 minutes. Partly dismasted, the *Macedonian,* 38, was brought back to Newport, refitted, commissioned in U.S. service, and took further part in the war against her former flag.

1812, December 29. U.S.S. *Constitution* vs. H.M.S. *Java*. Now under the command of Captain **William Bainbridge,** *"Old Ironsides"* encountered the British frigate off Bahia, Brazil. After a 2-hour contest of maneuver and gunfire, the *Java,* 38, was a total wreck and surrendered.

COMMENT. *Ship for ship and crew for crew the superiority of American design, seamanship, and gunnery was proven. But the strangulating pressure of British sea power was closing in on the Atlantic coastline of the United States. In all, nearly 100 vessels were now engaged in this blockade duty: 11 ships of the line, 34 frigates, and the remainder sloops of war or smaller.*

Land Operations, 1813

ACTION IN THE WEST

1813, January–August. Preliminaries. British General **Henry A. Proctor** with a force of British regulars, Canadian militia, and Indians under Tecumseh (commissioned a British brigadier general) held the initiative. Major General Harrison had received a directive to retake Detroit, but his means were scanty. While he was gathering and training troops, his outposts were attacked by Proctor, who took **Frenchtown** on the Raisin River (January 22). American losses were 197 killed and wounded; another 737 were captured. Many of the wounded were murdered by the Indians. The British also besieged Ft. Meigs on the Maumee River, and Ft. Stephenson on the Sandusky without success.

1813, September. Advance on Detroit. Harrison was now ready with 7,000 well-trained men. But American control of Lake Erie was essential to his plans against Detroit. Soon (September 10) he received a message from Commodore **Oliver Hazard Perry** reporting American victory in the Battle of Lake Erie (see p. 799). Harrison at once started north, sending his cavalry 100 miles overland around the lake, and moving his infantry and artillery in Perry's ships from Ft. Stephenson across to Amherstburg. Both forces converged on Detroit, accompanied by Perry's squadron. Proctor withdrew into Canada.

1813, September 29. Recapture of Detroit. Harrison pushed up the Thames River in pursuit of the British, accompanied by 3 of Perry's lightest ships. When the water shoaled, the commodore came ashore, accompanying Harrison as a volunteer aide.

1813, October 5. Battle of the Thames. Proctor with 800 regulars and 1,000 Indians was brought to bay at Chatham. Harrison, with 3,500 men, attacked methodically. While his infantry assaulted frontally, his cavalry charged the British right. Proctor's command collapsed, losing 12 killed, 22 wounded, and 477 taken prisoner. Tecumseh's Indians held firm until their chief was killed, then they fled, leaving 35 dead. American losses were 29 killed and wounded.

COMMENT. *Highlights of this campaign were the close military-naval cooperation and the prowess of the American cavalry —a regiment of Kentucky mounted riflemen. The victory brought about the collapse of the Indian confederacy, England's allies. It would later bring "Old Tippecanoe" to the White House, but at the moment its fruits were dissipated. The War Department ordered Harrison's militia disbanded and sent home; his regulars were to join the American concentration in the Niagara area. Harrison, enraged, resigned his commission and returned to civil life.*

OPERATIONS ON THE NORTHERN FRONT

On the Niagara front, General **John Armstrong,** Secretary of War, planned an ambitious 2-pronged invasion of Upper Canada. As a preliminary, an amphibious operation on Lake Ontario was mounted by Major General **Henry Dearborn** and Commodore **Isaac Chauncey.**

1813, April–May. Burning of York. A force of 1,600 troops under Brigadier General **Zebulon M. Pike,** embarking in Chauncey's flotilla at Sackets Harbor, captured York (now Toronto), capital of Upper Canada (April 27). The explosion of a powder magazine resulted in killing or wounding 320 of the invaders, Pike being among those killed. Despite Dearborn's orders, the public buildings of York were burned. The expedition returned (May 8), having accomplished nothing except to harden Canadian resentment.

1813, May 27. Capture of Ft. George. During the illness of the ineffectual Dearborn, Colonel **Winfield Scott,** his adjutant general, in cooperation with Perry (then on Lake Ontario under Chauncey), mounted an amphibious operation against Ft. George at the mouth of the Niagara River. Some 4,000 men were landed in the rear of the British post, taking it by assault. As a result of the move, the British garrison of Ft. Erie (opposite Buffalo) withdrew, liberating American vessels bottled up in the Black Rock navy yard. Scott's operation was nullified when British General **John Vincent,** retreating from Ft. George with 700 men, turned on an American pursuing force 3 times his size at **Stony Creek** (June 6) and threw it back. Generals **William H. Winder** and **John Chandler,** political appointees, were bagged in the disaster. The British reoccupied Ft. Erie.

1813, May 28–29. Battle of Sackets Harbor. Amphibious assault by Sir **John Prevost,** governor general of Upper Canada, was repulsed by the small garrison of Brigadier General **Jacob J. Brown.**

1813, September–November. Planned Operation against Montreal. Brigadier General **James Wilkinson,** replacing Dearborn, was to move down the St. Lawrence from Sackets Harbor. Brigadier General **Wade Hampton** would push north from Lake Champlain. Uniting, they were to take

Montreal, defended by some 15,000 British troops.

1813, October 25. Battle of the Chateaugay. Hampton, entering Canada with 4,000 men, moved west to the Chateaugay River and established himself about 15 miles from its mouth (October 22). Attacking a much smaller British force, he entangled himself in a swamp. The British commander caused several bugles to be blown, simulating an envelopment, whereupon Hampton, abandoning any attempt to join Wilkinson—for whom he had a heartily reciprocated antipathy—retreated to Plattsburg and went into winter quarters.

1813, November 11. Battle of Chrysler's Farm. Wilkinson, with 8,000 men, moved down the St. Lawrence by bateaux, with flank guards marching on both banks. A British force of some 800 regulars and Indians under Colonel **J. W. Morrison** menaced his rear about 90 miles from Montreal. Attempting a bungling, piecemeal attack, Wilkinson was routed, losing 102 killed, 237 wounded, and more than 100 others captured. Wilkinson now withdrew to winter quarters at French Mills, on the Salmon River, where his troops suffered great privation.

1813, December 18. British Capture of Ft. Niagara. The Indian allies ravaged the countryside. The fort would remain in British hands for the rest of the war.

1813, December 29–30. Burning of Buffalo. A column of 1,500 men under General **Gordon Drummond** moved south down the Niagara River, burning the city of Buffalo and the Black Rock navy yard, inflicting much damage.

Naval Actions, 1813

AT SEA

The inferiority of American naval strength reduced the U.S. Navy to a policy of commerce destruction, individual ships eluding the British blockade to cruise the oceans. A great number of privateers assisted in the operations.

1813, February 24. U.S.S. *Hornet* vs. H.M.S. *Peacock*. The sloops of war clashed off the Brazilian coast, the British ship being sunk after 11 minutes of combat.

1813, June 1. H.M.S. *Shannon* vs. U.S.S. *Chesapeake*. American Captain **James Lawrence,** unwisely accepting the challenge of Captain Sir **Philip Broke,** took his untried frigate, 38, and newly raised crew out from Boston to meet a vessel reputed to be the most efficient in the Royal Navy. In a few minutes the British frigate, 38, had so raked the *Chesapeake*'s decks that nearly one-third of her crew were killed or wounded. Lawrence, mortally wounded, cried, "Don't give up the ship!" but the Americans surrendered after Broke brought his ship alongside and boarded. In all, 146 Americans, including most of the officers, were casualties; 83 Britishers fell. The *Chesapeake,* brought into Halifax as a prize, would remain on the Royal Navy list for many years to come.

1813, August 14. H.M.S. *Pelican* vs. U.S.S. *Argus*. The sloop of war *Argus,* 18, after a successful cruise in the English Channel, in which she captured and destroyed 20 prizes, was sunk by the British sloop of war, 20.

1813, September 3. U.S.S. *Enterprise* vs. H.M.S. *Boxer*. The American sloop met and captured the *Boxer,* 14, off the New England coast.

OPERATIONS ON THE LAKES

When the war broke out, England possessed several warships on lakes Erie and Ontario, while the U.S. had none. American Commodore Chauncey had begun the construction of vessels at Sackets Harbor on Lake Ontario, and at Erie and Black Rock on Lake Erie. In a remarkably short time, experienced ship carpenters constructed an inland navy, which was manned by seamen sent up from the Atlantic coast. Chauncey retained command of operations on Ontario, but delegated command on Lake Erie to Captain Oliver H. Perry. By early August, Perry had in commission 2 brigs, 6 schooners, and a sloop ready for action in Put in Bay, near Erie. The British flotilla on Lake Erie, under Captain **Robert Barclay,** consisted of 2 ships, 2 brigs, 1 schooner, and a sloop.

1813, September 10. Battle of Lake Erie. The British squadron approached the American anchorage about noon, and Perry went out to meet it. His flagship, the brig *Lawrence,* 20, met the British fire before the rest of his squadron could close, and was put out of action. Perry, in a rowboat, transferred under fire to the brig *Niagara.* In Nelsonian fashion the *Niagara* broke the British line; the remainder of the American squadron closed in. The *Niagara* engaged and put out of action 3 of the British craft, including Barclay's flagship. A detachment of General Harrison's sharpshooting soldiers acted as marines. By 3 P.M. Barclay's entire squadron had struck. British losses were 41 killed and 91 wounded. The Americans lost 27 killed and 93 wounded, most of these (22 killed and 61 wounded) on board the battered *Lawrence.*

COMMENT. *Perry's victory was the turning point in the war in the northwest. His message (beginning "We have met the enemy and they are ours . . .") triggered Harrison's operations leading to the recapture of Detroit* (*see p. 797*).

Land Operations, 1814–1815

NIAGARA FRONT

1814, February–March. Wilkinson Renews the Offensive. He advanced from Plattsburg and Sackets Harbor with 4,000 men.

1814, March 30. Repulse at La Colle Mill. Wilkinson's assault on a small border fort was repulsed by its garrison of 600 men. Wilkinson, who before starting had announced his determination "to return victorious or not at all," at once fell back on Plattsburg. He was summarily relieved of his command (April 12).

1814, April–July. New American Command Team. Jacob Brown, the new commander, at once started reorganizing and training his troops. The task was efficiently performed by Scott, now a brigadier general. Brown's troops were well equipped and newly uniformed—Scott's own brigade was dressed in gray since the contractors could not supply blue cloth.

1814, July 2–3. Invasion of Canada. Brown, with 3,500 troops, crossed the Niagara River, seizing Ft. Erie. He then started north.

1814, July 5. Battle of Chippewa. General **Phineas Riall** with 1,700 British regulars and a small number of Canadian militia and Indians, held a defensive position on the north bank of the unfordable Chippewa River, 16 miles north of Ft. Erie. Brown bivouacked on the south bank of Street's Creek, a mile south of the river (July 4). A flat plain lay between the two forces. Riall crossed the Chippewa next day, driving in a militia and Indian force of Brown's left, only to meet headlong Scott's brigade, 1,300 strong. Riall, noting the gray uniforms of the Americans, believed them to be militia. But when, under fire, they formed line with parade-ground precision and moved to meet him with fixed bayonets, he is said to have exclaimed: "These are regulars, by God!" Scott led a charge that drove the British back in complete defeat across the river and into their entrenchments. British losses were 236 killed, 322 wounded, and 46 captured. Scott's losses were 61 killed, 255 wounded, and 19 captured.

COMMENT. *This was the first time that regular forces of both sides met in close combat on even terms. The gray full-dress uniform of the U.S. Military Academy at West Point commemorates this victory.*

1814, July 25. Battle of Lundy's Lane. Brown moved north to Queenston, Riall falling back before him. But Commodore Chauncey failed to cooperate on the lake with Brown's movement. British reinforcements from Europe having reached Canada, Sir Gordon Drummond took over Riall's command, bringing with him additional troops. Near Niagara Falls the opponents clashed: Brown with 2,600, Drummond with 3,000. A 5-hour sanguinary contest ended in a draw. American losses were 171 killed, 572 wounded, and 110 missing. The British lost 84 killed, 559 wounded, and 235 prisoners and missing. Brown, Scott, and Drummond were wounded; Riall was taken prisoner. Brown fell back on Ft. Erie, which Drummond besieged.

1814, September 17. Battle of Fort Erie. An American sortie from Ft. Erie broke the deadlock. British losses were 609 in all; American, 511. Ft. Erie was later abandoned and with it all further effort to invade Canada (November 5). No further actions of importance occurred on the Niagara front.

LAKE CHAMPLAIN FRONT

1814, August 31. British Invasion. Prevost, with 14,000 of Wellington's veterans just arrived from Europe, advanced on Lake Champlain from Montreal. The only ground force available to oppose him consisted of 1,500 green regulars and about 3,000 raw militia, under General **Alexander Macomb,** manning field fortifications at Plattsburg. Once they had been dispersed, the road would be open all the way to New York, to complete successfully the invasion of the Hudson Valley bungled by Burgoyne 37 years earlier. Prevost planned to assault the fortifications at Plattsburg frontally, while a naval force took care of an American flotilla protecting the lake flank of the American position.

1814, September 11. Battle of Plattsburg. Prevost made his combined ground and naval assault on Plattsburg. The British naval squadron, however, was completely defeated by the American flotilla and was forced to surrender (see p. 803). Prevost thereupon hastily broke off the land action, even though one of his assault columns had made good progress. Believing, with good reason, that his proposed invasion would fail without command of the lake, he retired in some disorder, abandoning a quantity of stores. There was no further action on this front during the war.

CHESAPEAKE BAY AREA

1814, July–August. British Threat to Washington. On the east coast of the United States, Admiral Sir **John Cockburn**'s British squadron, which had been harassing the seacoast (see p. 802), was joined by a force of 5,400 British veteran troops released by the conclusion of the Peninsular War. Under Major General **Robert Ross,** they were landed on the Patuxent and advanced on the American capital, 40 miles away (August 19).

1814, August 24. Battle of Bladensburg. The British advance was opposed by 6,500 untrained militia levies and a minuscule force of 400 sailors and marines, all under incompetent political Major General **William H. Winder.** Ross's advance guard, 1,500 strong, routed them in disgraceful panic. Only the naval contingent, of gunners under Commodore **Joshua Barney** and a handful of regular army troops contested the attack. American losses were 100 killed and wounded and 100 captured. The British had 294 casualties.

1814, August 24–25. British Occupation of Washington. The American government had fled. The British burned the Capitol, the White House, and several other public and private buildings—retaliation for the burning at York. The invaders then marched back to their ships. National indignation resulted in the ousting of War Secretary, General **John Armstrong,** who was replaced by **James Monroe.**

1814, September 12–14. Attack on Baltimore. The British expedition then sailed north, and penetrated the Patapsco River. Ross landed his troops 16 miles from Baltimore, while the naval force attacked Ft. McHenry. Local militia forces, from behind entrenchments, repulsed the land attack. Ross was mortally wounded. Ft. McHenry successfully withstood the bombardment, inspiring **Francis Scott Key** to write "The Star-Spangled Banner." The expedition departed October 14.

SOUTHERN FRONT

1813–1814. The Creek War. The Creek Indians in Alabama allied themselves with England (July, 1813). The militia garrison of Ft. Mims, 35 miles above Mobile, was surprised and more than half of the 550 soldiers and refugees massacred (August 30, 1813). **Andrew Jackson,** then a major general of militia, organized volunteer forces and at **Tallasahatchee** (November 3), and again at **Talladega** (November 9), inflicted severe punishment on the Indians. His force was then disbanded,

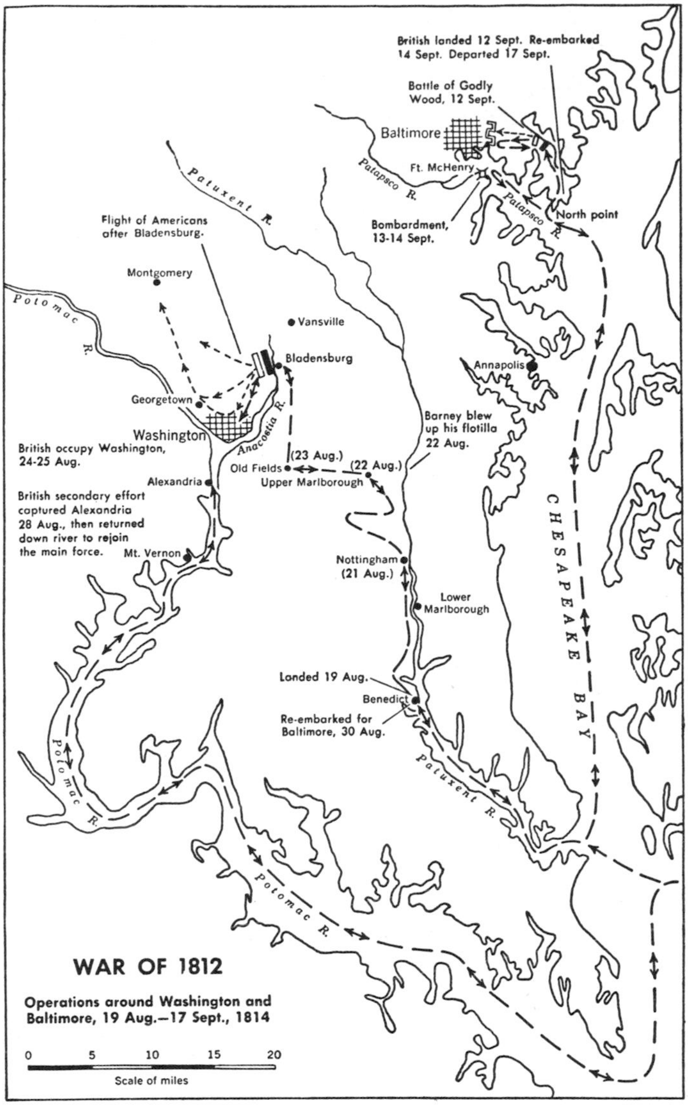

WAR OF 1812

Operations around Washington and Baltimore, 19 Aug.—17 Sept., 1814

however, and the Indians again became a serious menace.

1814, February. Jackson Again Takes the Offensive. He had a reorganized force of volunteers and a small increment of regulars.

1814, March 27. Battle of Horseshoe Bend. The main Creek force of 900 warriors was overwhelmed on the Tallapoosa River by Jackson's 2,000. Some 700 Indians were killed. Jackson lost 201. The Creek War was ended by the **Treaty of Ft. Jackson** (August 9). Jackson, commissioned a major general in the Regular Army (May 22), was put in command of the Gulf Coast area.

1814, November 7. Seizure of Pensacola. Pensacola, in Spanish East Florida, had become a British base, supplying the Creeks. The U.S. administration, fearing that neutral Spain might be brought into the war against the United States, forbade any movement against it. However, when a British-Indian attack mounted from Pensacola struck at Ft. Bowyer, Jackson took matters into his own hands. Invading Spanish Florida, he seized and occupied Pensacola.

NEW ORLEANS CAMPAIGN, 1814–1815

1814, November 22. Jackson Goes to New Orleans. Rumors of a British concentration in the Caribbean–Gulf of Mexico area caused him to go to New Orleans to investigate its defenses.

1814, November 26. British Expeditions against New Orleans. A force of 7,500 Peninsular War veterans, under Major General Sir **Edward Pakenham,** sailed from Jamaica, its objective the seizure of New Orleans and control of the Mississippi River Valley.

1814, December 1. Jackson Arrives at New Orleans. Confirmation of the British preparations at Jamaica led him to prepare a defensive position at Baton Rouge in case he was unable to hold New Orleans.

1814, December 13. British Arrival. They landed in the Lake Borgne area. Jackson concentrated his energies on the defense of New Orleans, where he declared martial law to control the largely anti-American Creole population. Pakenham's advance guard penetrated to within 7 miles of the city. Jackson swiftly organized a defensive line along the Rodriguez Canal, an abandoned waterway south of the city. His right flank rested on the Mississippi, his left on a cypress swamp. His forces consisted of a small core of regulars, his own Tennessee and Kentucky veteran volunteers, and some New Orleans volunteer militia, 3,100 in all. Some 2,000 additional untrained, ill-armed militia were also gathered, but he kept these in the background.

1814, December 23–24. American Night Raid. This reconnaissance in force rocked the British concentration, but was soon repulsed.

1814, December 25–1815, January 7. Opposing Preparations. Jackson continued to strengthen his defenses, piling earth, timbers, and cotton bales along the canal. A British probe of the defenses was hurled back by American artillery and small-arms fire (December 28). Effectiveness and staunchness of American response to a tremendous artillery bombardment (January 1) led Pakenham to wait further action until all of his troops were ready. Attempts by a British naval force to sail up the Mississippi and flank the position were thwarted by the successful defense of **Ft. St. Philip,** 65 miles downstream. Finally, all his troops available, overconfident Pakenham determined to assault Jackson's position, unaware, of course, that the **Peace of Ghent** had been signed (December 24).

1815, January 8. Battle of New Orleans. The British infantry, in serried ranks, twice dared the aimed fire of Jackson's riflemen behind their entrenchments, only to be completely repulsed. Some 2,100 of the attackers were killed or wounded; an additional 500 were captured. Pakenham and his 2 senior subordinates were killed leading their men. The survivors withdrew, Jackson wisely making no attempt at counterattack with his motley command. He lost 7 killed and 6 more wounded. One week later the British force retreated to its boats.

Naval Actions, 1814–1815

1814. British Blockade. The effective restrictions on trade and manufacture brought the U.S. Treasury close to bankruptcy. Depredations of British landing parties brought havoc along the coast. British general orders (July 18) were "to destroy and lay waste such towns and districts upon the coast as you may find assailable."

1814. American Guerre de Course. Although constrained by the blockade, a few U.S. warships and many privateers dared it successfully to prey on British commerce over the world. By midsummer more than 800 British merchantmen had been captured and most traffic about the English and Irish coasts moved only under naval convoy.

1814, April 29. U.S.S. *Peacock* vs. H.M.S. *Epervier*. The American sloop, 18, named to commemorate the British vessel sunk by the *Hornet* (see p. 798) fell in with the *Epervier,* 18, off the coast of Florida. The British vessel struck after a 45-minute gun battle.

1814, March 21. Capture of the *Essex*. Captain **David Porter,** in the frigate U.S.S. *Essex,* 38, had left the Delaware River October 28, 1812, rounding Cape Horn on a fantastic 17-month cruise that terrorized British commerce up and down the Pacific, capturing or destroying more than 40 merchantmen and whalers. Shortly after entering Valparaiso, Chile (February 3), in company with *Essex Junior,* a prize converted into a man of war, Porter was blockaded by a British frigate, H.M.S. *Phoebe,* 36, and *Cherub,* 18, a sloop of war. Porter, leaving his consort, put to sea in a heavy wind, hoping to draw off the slower British vessels. His main topmast snapped in a gust, and Porter returned to the sanctuary of the neutral port. The British ships, standing off his anchorage out of range of *Essex*'s carronades, with their long guns battered the helpless American frigate to a bloody, burning hulk. Porter struck after more than 3 hours, having lost 58 killed, 31 drowned, and some 70 wounded of the ship's 255-man complement. British losses were 5 killed and 10 wounded.

1814, June 28. U.S.S. *Wasp* vs. H.M.S. *Reindeer.* The *Wasp,* 18, cruising in the English Channel, met and virtually destroyed the *Reindeer,* 18, in a half-hour fight. Continuing her cruise, the *Wasp* (second vessel of the name) captured 13 merchantmen.

1814, September 1. U.S.S. *Wasp* vs. H.M.S. *Avon.* The British sloop, 18, was sunk by the American vessel in a night battle.

BATTLE OF LAKE CHAMPLAIN, SEPTEMBER 11, 1814

Paralleling the advance of Prevost's army on Plattsburg (see p. 800) was Captain **George Downie**'s hastily built British squadron of 4 ships and 12 armed galleys. Protecting the lake front of the American position at Plattsburg was the flotilla of Lieutenant **Thomas Macdonough,** who also had 4 ships and 12 galleys, as hastily constructed as their British opponents. The American vessels were anchored close to shore. In weight of metal the 2 squadrons were practically equal, but the Americans had a preponderance in long guns. Prevost's assault on the land side started as the British squadron rounded Cumberland Head and stood in to engage the Americans, ship to ship, taking a galling fire from Macdonough's long guns as they did. A closely contested 2-hour battle ended when Macdonough, whose frigate *Saratoga,* 26, was being badly battered by Downie's flagship, the frigate *Confiance,* 37, cleverly swung his ship by means of a stern anchor and presented a fresh broadside to his enemy. Downie was killed, some 180 of his crew dead or wounded, when the splintered *Confiance* struck her flag. The remainder of the British squadron then surrendered. American losses are estimated at 200, British casualties 300. A British veteran who had been at Trafalgar said it was "child's play" compared to Lake Champlain.

COMMENT. *This battle, ending all danger of British invasion from the north, was undoubtedly the decisive action of the war, saving America from possible conquest or dismemberment. Its influence was strongly felt at the Ghent Peace Conference when the news arrived there (October 21).*

1814, September 26–27. Stand of the *General Armstrong.* This 9-gun privateer brig for 2 days fought off successive boarding parties from a British squadron which attacked her in neutral Fayal, Azores. Captain **Samuel C. Reid** then put his crew ashore and blew up his brig. Portuguese authorities prevented a land assault by the British, who then sailed away.

1814, October. End of the *Wasp.* The *Wasp* was last seen by a Swedish vessel (October 9), then disappeared forever, one of the mysteries of the sea.

1815, January 15. Capture of U.S.S. *President.* Like the following actions, this took place after the peace had been signed. The American frigate, 44, commanded by Decatur, attempted to run the British blockade of New York. Several British vessels chased her. For some hours H.M.S. *Endymion,* 50, and the *President* fought side by side until the Britisher was disabled. By that time 2 more British ships had caught up, and 2 more were in sight. Decatur, his ship crippled and 75 men killed or wounded, surrendered. The *President* became a unit of the Royal Navy.

1815, February 20. U.S.S. *Constitution* vs. H.M.S. *Cyane* and *Levant*. Off Madeira, Captain James Stewart in "Old Ironsides," 44, met the British corvette, 34, and sloop of war, 21. By skillful maneuver, he fought them separately, capturing both.

1815, March 23. U.S.S. *Hornet* vs. H.M.S. *Penguin*. The American sloop, 18, captured the British sloop, 18, off Tristan da Cunha Island in the war's last naval action.

End of the War

1814, December 24. Treaty of Ghent. Ignoring the war's basic issues, it provided for release of prisoners, restoration of territory, and arbitration of boundary disputes. The news reached New York February 11. The treaty was ratified February 15.

COMMENT. *The war decided nothing, and, until the final battle at New Orleans, the British had had somewhat the best of it. They never repeated their highhanded conduct at sea; the Americans never again tried to conquer Canada.*

THE UNITED STATES, 1815–1846

1815. Decatur's Mediterranean Expedition. This concluded U.S. troubles with the Barbary States (see p. 781).

1818. First Seminole War. The Seminoles had sided with the British during the War of 1812. After its end, they continued their depredations. Their so-called Negro Fort (largely manned by escaped slaves) on the Apalachicola River was destroyed by U.S. regular troops (November–December 1817). The Indians in Spanish Florida raided, massacred, and pillaged in U.S. territory. General Jackson moved overland from Nashville with 1,800 regulars and 6,000 volunteers and relieved the besieged garrison of Ft. Scott on the Georgia-Florida border(March 9).

1818, April–May. Invasion of Florida. Jackson, with some 1,200 men, occupied the Spanish post of St. Marks (April 7) and the Spanish capital, Pensacola (May 24). The governor fled to Ft. Barrancas, where Jackson promptly shelled him out and captured the post. Meanwhile, other American columns had been destroying Indian villages, breaking up Seminole power. Two British subjects, traders, found assisting the Indians at St. Marks, were summarily court-martialed, convicted, and executed. The net result was American occupation of Spanish Florida —without authority—and a near war with England. But Seminole depredations had been ended. Jackson's highhanded action was upheld by the government. The posts were returned to Spain, but negotiations were begun to obtain all Florida from Spain.

1819, February 22. Adams–Onís Treaty. Spain surrendered all claims to West Florida, and ceded East Florida to the United States. All Spanish claims to the Pacific Northwest were also canceled. In the southwest, the treaty defined the boundary line of Spanish Mexico from the mouth of the Sabine River in the Gulf of Mexico, northwest to the Pacific Ocean.

1823, December 2. Monroe Doctrine. The declaration of U.S. intention to protect America, for the Americas, and against foreign aggression, was announced.

1825–1832. American Expansion Westward. This steadily encroached on land the Indians considered their own. The Army, in its role of exploration and protection of the settlements, began expansion of its string of frontier posts. Previous treaties with various tribes were nullified, both legally and illegally, and the long process of moving the red man from areas coveted by the white began. This led to a continuous succession of small wars which would last for three-quarters of a century more.

1832, April–August. Black Hawk War. The Sac and Fox tribes, along the Mississippi in Illinois and Wisconsin, led by Chief **Black Hawk,** tried to regain their lands. Colonel **Zachary Taylor,** operating under Brigadier General **Henry Atkinson,** led 400 regulars and 900 militia through swampland to defeat the Indians at the **Battle of the Bad Ax** (August 2).

Second Seminole War, 1835–1843

The Seminoles and Creeks of Georgia, Alabama, and Florida resisted removal to the west. Under **Osceola** they ravaged frontier settlements in Florida. Army garrisons were too small to quell the outbreak.

1835, December 28. Dade Massacre. A detachment of 150 regulars under Major **Francis L. Dade** was ambushed in the Wahoo Swamp of the Withlacoochie River. Only 3 men escaped.

1836, February–April. Scott's Campaign against the Seminoles. Major General Winfield Scott, commanding the Eastern Department, sent to suppress the uprising, rescued his rival, Major General **Edmund P. Gaines,** commanding the Western Department, from a Seminole ambush on the **Withlacoochie River,** where he had come without authority (February 27–March 6). Scott then swept twice through Seminole country with regulars and volunteers until malaria halted operations. He reported that victory would require a large regular force.

1836, June–July. Scott's Campaign against the Creeks. The War Department (in May) ordered Scott to arrange for suppression of the uprising of the Creek Indians of western Georgia and Alabama. Helped by Brigadier General **Thomas S. Jesup,** Scott suppressed it quickly with little loss of life.

1836–1837. Court of Inquiry on Scott and Gaines. Because of a misunderstanding regarding Scott's conduct of these operations and charges brought by Gaines, President Andrew Jackson ordered a court of inquiry, headed by Commanding General **Alexander Macomb.** It commended Scott's performance highly but strongly criticized Gaines (1837, March 14).

1837, December 25. Battle of Lake Okeechobee. Meanwhile Brigadier General Zachary Taylor was placed in command in Florida. Finding the Seminole stronghold in the Everglades, he attacked with about 1,000 men—half regulars, half volunteers—through swampland in 2 lines, the volunteers leading. When the volunteers broke as expected, the regulars held and won the day. Taylor lost 26 killed and 112 wounded. Organized Seminole resistance collapsed, but costly, bloody guerrilla actions continued for 4 years.

1837, December 29. *Caroline* Incident. Canadian militia invaded U.S. territory and seized the steamer *Caroline* on the Niagara River. Troops were concentrated on the border. General Scott's tactful diplomacy averted hostilities with Britain (see Mackenzie's Rebellion, p. 811–2).

1838, February 12. Aroostook "War." Bickering between Maine and New Brunswick over lumbering on U.S. land again roused fears of war. Again Scott's diplomacy brought a settlement. Border disputes were resolved by the **Webster-Ashburton Treaty** (1842).

1844, February 28. The *Princeton* Disaster. On one of the first voyages of U.S.S. *Princeton,* first warship driven by a screw propeller, a gun designed by Commodore **Robert F. Stockton,** commander and co-designer of the ship, exploded, killing the Secretary of State, the Secretary of the Navy, and several congressmen, injuring a number of others. President **John Tyler**, aboard, was uninjured.

1846. June 15. Oregon Treaty. The long-standing Anglo-U.S. argument over Oregon Territory boundaries, which had led to the expansionist slogan, "Fifty-four forty, or fight!" was settled.

WAR OF TEXAN INDEPENDENCE, 1835–1836

1835, June 30. Armed Insurrection. American settlers in Texas revolted against the Mexican government.

1836, February 23–March 6. Siege of the Alamo. General **Antonio López de Santa Anna,** President of Mexico, with a force of 3,000 Mexican regulars, laid siege to 188 Texans in the Alamo, San Antonio. After several repulses, the Mexican troops finally assaulted the place, massacring all within. The Mexicans lost more than 1,500 men. Santa Anna marched eastward, where an insurgent force was gathering.

1836, March 2. Texan Declaration of Independence. Texas was proclaimed a republic; army raised under **Sam Houston.**

1836. Massacre at Goliad. Some 300 Texans defending the place were killed.

1836, April 21. Battle of the San Jacinto. Sam Houston with 740 men surprised and routed Santa Anna's army of 1,600. Santa Anna was captured and recognized the Texan Republic. (This was repudiated by the Mexican government.) Houston was elected president of Texas. U.S. recognition of Texas (July 4, 1836) aroused Mexican resentment.

U.S.-MEXICAN WAR, 1846–1848

After long discussion and negotiations, Texas—which had asked for it—was formally annexed to the United States (March 1, 1845), despite Mexico's threat that this would mean war. Expansionist sentiment in the United States crystallized under the slogan of "Manifest Destiny," referring to the American "right ... to spread over this whole continent." Mexico contended that her territory extended north to the Nueces River; the United States claimed down to the Rio Grande.

Northern Campaign

1846, March 24. American Advance to the Rio Grande. General Zachary Taylor, with 3,500 men (two-thirds of the Regular Army), advanced and established Camp Texas opposite Matamoros, where some 5,700 Mexican troops were concentrated.

1846, April 25. Cavalry Encounter. Mexican cavalry, 1,600 strong, sweeping north of the river near Matamoros, overwhelmed an American reconnaissance force of 63 dragoons. Taylor announced next day that hostilities had commenced and called for volunteers from the governors of Texas and Louisiana. He marched to protect his supply base at the mouth of the Rio Grande from the Mexican cavalry (May 1), leaving his camp opposite Matamoros under command of Major **Jacob Brown.**

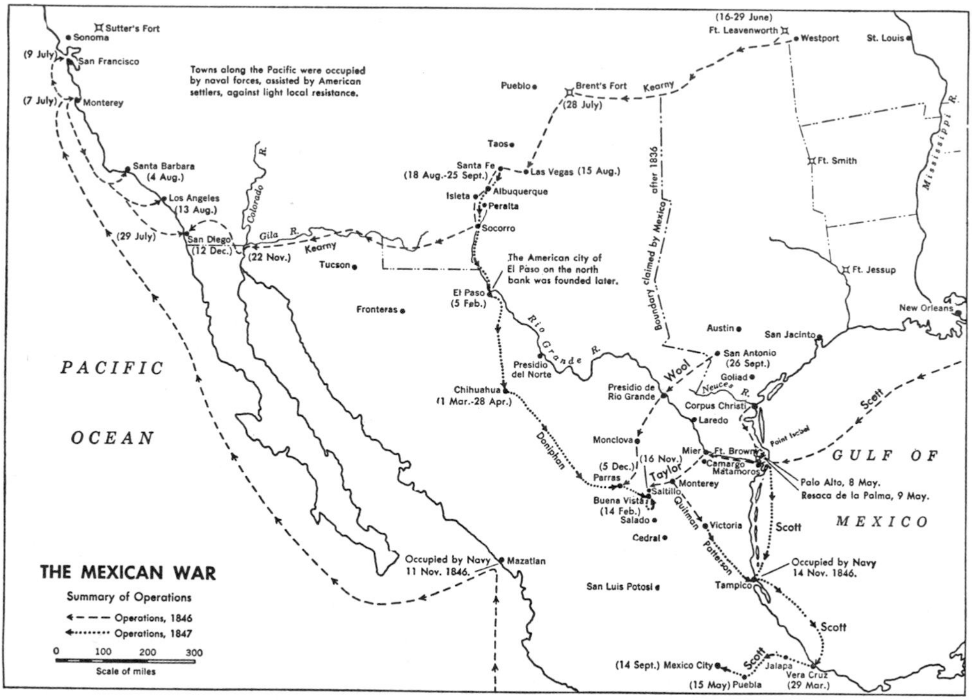

1846, May 1. Mexican Crossing of the Rio Grande. Mexican General **Mariano Arista** led 6,000 troops and advanced on Camp Texas.

1846, May 3–8. Siege of Camp Texas. Major Brown was killed in the successful defense—the site became Brownsville.

1846, May 8. Battle of Palo Alto. Taylor, having fortified his base at Point Isabel, rushed back to relieve Camp Texas. He had 2,200 men. Arista, with about 4,500, moved to meet him on flat, open ground. As the 2 lines faced each other, American artillery caused severe casualties among the Mexicans. A Mexican cavalry charge was repulsed and the shaken Mexicans fled as the American infantry line advanced.

1846, May 9. Battle of Resaca de la Palma. Taylor boldly attacked a strong Mexican defensive position, broke through after a brief but intense fight, and routed Arista's army completely. The Mexicans fled back across the Rio Grande. Mexican losses in the 2 days' battles were about 1,100; American casualties were 170 killed and wounded.

1846, May 13. Declaration of War. The United States declared war on Mexico.

1846, May 18. Taylor Crosses into Mexico.

1846, May–July. Delay in Matamoros. Taylor had to wait 3 months for transportation which had been promised him by the United States Government. Meanwhile he trained volunteer reinforcements hurriedly raised by Congress.

1846, August. Taylor Moves South. He took 6,000 men—half regulars, half volunteers. The remainder of his force—about 6,000 volunteers—he left behind for additional training.

1846, September 20–24. Battle of Monterrey. Mexican General **Pedro de Ampudia,** with 7,000 regulars and 3,000 militia, stood on the defensive, holding the fortified city. In a 3-day battle the Americans, storming position after position, penned Ampudia in the central area of the city. Ampudia capitulated, marching out with the honors of war, but Taylor acceded to a Mexican request for an 8-week armistice. Mexican casualties were 367; American losses were greater: 120 killed, 368 wounded. The armistice was later disapproved by President **James K. Polk.** Taylor thereupon informed the Mexicans, and again advanced south.

1846, November 16. Occupation of Saltillo. There Taylor was joined by Brigadier General **John E. Wool**'s expedition, 3,000 strong, which had marched 600 miles overland from San Antonio (December 21).

1846–1847. American Strategic Debate. General Winfield Scott, commanding the U.S. Army, had planned an invasion of central Mexico via Veracruz. President Polk, a Democrat, was not anxious that Scott, a Whig, should become the war hero. This and other political bickering in Washington delayed matters until Taylor, at Saltillo, declined as militarily unsound the administration's suggestion that he march 300 miles across the desert to San Luis Potosí and then move on Mexico City. Taylor instead recommended a movement via Veracruz along the lines already planned by Scott. Finally Polk ordered Scott to undertake the campaign. Scott left Washington (November 24, 1846). Stopping to gather some of Taylor's troops at Point Isabel, he sailed to Tampico, where he established his headquarters (February 18).

1847, January–March. Scott's Plans and Preparations. The amphibious expedition, mounted in the Tampico area, was 10,000 strong. It included a large proportion of Taylor's veteran troops, leaving the latter with but 5,000 men, of whom only a handful were regulars. Taylor's role was to be defensive, while Scott's mass of maneuver executed a bold turning movement into central Mexico.

1847, January–February. Santa Anna's Plans. The Mexican president, learning of Scott's plans through a captured message, decided to crush Taylor before Scott could land. He moved with 20,000 men across the desert from San Luis Potosí—the very march which Taylor had rightly hesitated to take. Santa Anna's army arrived near Saltillo (February 19) after having lost some 4,000 men in the grueling midwinter desert march.

1847, February 22–23. Battle of Buena Vista. Taylor, though surprised by the Mexican approach, elected to defend, taking position in a narrow mountain gap 8 miles south of Saltillo. Santa Anna, sending a cavalry brigade on a wide northeastern detour to cut Taylor's line of communications, drove in Taylor's outposts on the first day. Next day he attacked the American position with his main body. Initially successful, in a most complicated and disjointed battle, the Mexican attack captured 2 guns, but was held up by magnificent efforts of the American regular artillery after volunteer infantry regiments had recoiled. Here Taylor is supposed to have uttered his historic: "A little more grape, Captain Bragg!"* The gallant Mexican infantry almost reached

* Almost certainly apocryphal; he probably said: "Double shot your guns and give 'em hell!"

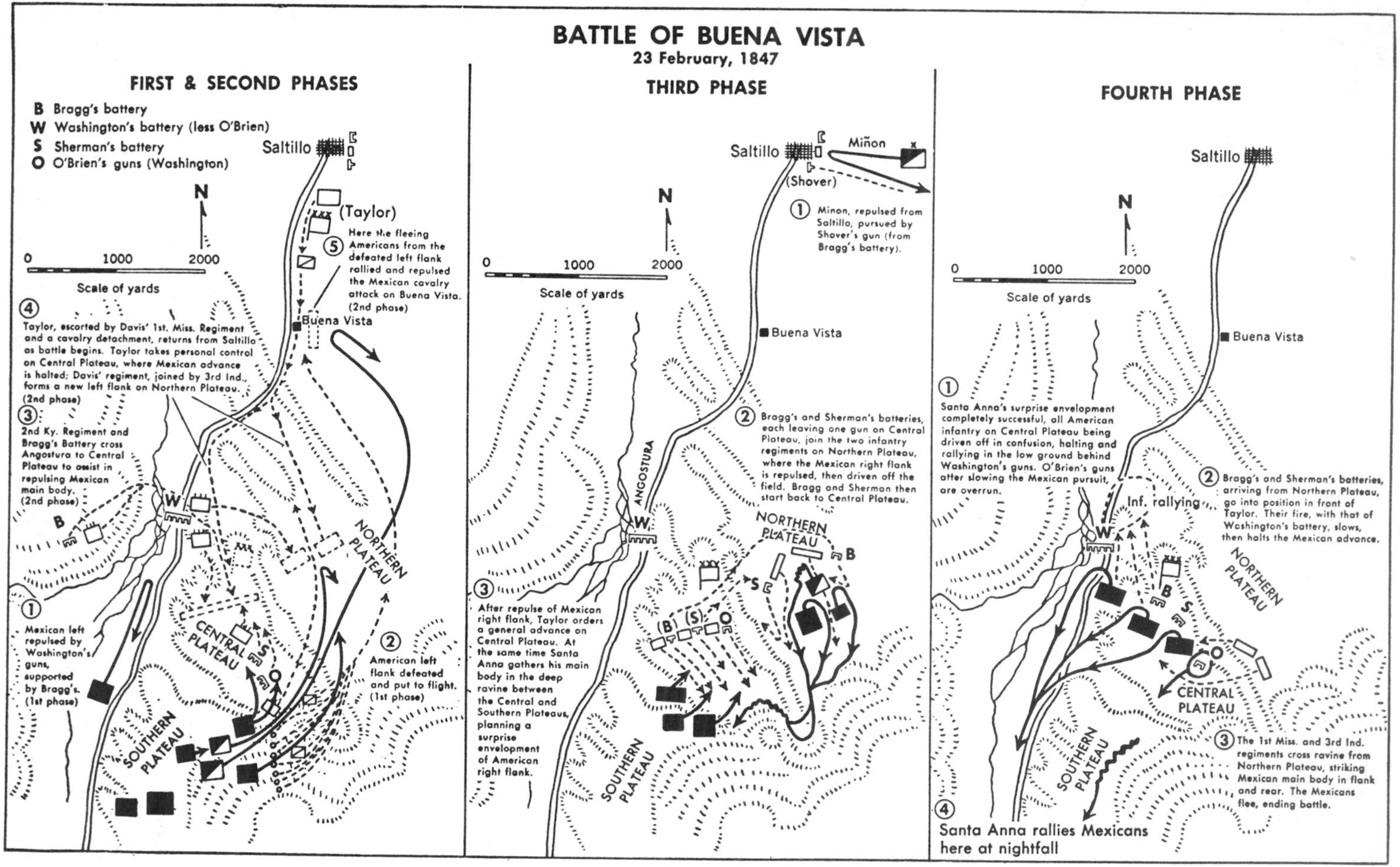
BATTLE OF BUENA VISTA
23 February, 1847
FIRST & SECOND PHASES
B Bragg's battery
W Washington's battery (less O'Brien)
S Sherman's battery
O O'Brien's guns (Washington)
N
0 1000 2000
Scale of yards
Saltillo
(Taylor)
Buena Vista
NORTHERN PLATEAU
CENTRAL PLATEAU
SOUTHERN PLATEAU
④ Taylor, escorted by Davis' 1st. Miss. Regiment and a cavalry detachment, returns from Saltillo as battle begins. Taylor takes personal control on Central Plateau, where Mexican advance is halted; Davis' regiment, joined by 3rd Ind., forms a new left flank on Northern Plateau. (2nd phase)
③ 2nd Ky. Regiment and Bragg's Battery cross Angostura to Central Plateau to assist in repulsing Mexican main body. (2nd phase)
⑤ Here the fleeing Americans from the defeated left flank rallied and repulsed the Mexican cavalry attack on Buena Vista. (2nd phase)
① Mexican left repulsed by Washington's guns, supported by Bragg's. (1st phase)
② American left flank defeated and put to flight. (1st phase)
THIRD PHASE
Saltillo
Miñon
(Shover)
① Minon, repulsed from Saltillo, pursued by Shover's gun (from Bragg's battery).
N
0 1000 2000
Scale of yards
Buena Vista
ANGOSTURA
NORTHERN PLATEAU
SOUTHERN PLATEAU
② Bragg's and Sherman's batteries, each leaving one gun on Central Plateau, join the two infantry regiments on Northern Plateau, where the Mexican right flank is repulsed, then driven off the field. Bragg and Sherman then start back to Central Plateau.
③ After repulse of Mexican right flank, Taylor orders a general advance on Central Plateau. At the same time Santa Anna gathers his main body in the deep ravine between the Central and Southern Plateaus, planning a surprise envelopment of American right flank.
FOURTH PHASE
Saltillo
N
0 1000 2000
Scale of yards
Buena Vista
① Santa Anna's surprise envelopment completely successful, all American infantry on Central Plateau being driven off in confusion, halting and rallying in the low ground behind Washington's guns. O'Brien's guns after slowing the Mexican pursuit, are overrun.
Inf. rallying
② Bragg's and Sherman's batteries, arriving from Northern Plateau, go into position in front of Taylor. Their fire, with that of Washington's battery, slows, then halts the Mexican advance.
NORTHERN PLATEAU
CENTRAL PLATEAU
SOUTHERN PLATEAU
③ The 1st Miss. and 3rd Ind. regiments cross ravine from Northern Plateau, striking Mexican main body in flank and rear. The Mexicans flee, ending battle.
④ Santa Anna rallies Mexicans here at nightfall

the guns before they broke under the American fire. Colonel **Jefferson Davis**' 1st Mississippi Volunteers, supported by regular artillery, meanwhile had checked an attack driving in Taylor's left flank. A vigorous counterattack then drove the Mexicans from the field. Meanwhile the Mexican cavalry envelopment of Taylor's rear collapsed after a short conflict with the American rear guard at Saltillo. Santa Anna withdrew to the south, ending the northern campaign of the war. American losses were 267 killed, 456 wounded, 23 missing, together with the 2 guns captured. Estimated Mexican losses were 500 dead and 1,000 wounded.

Operations in the West

KEARNY'S EXPEDITION

California had been disturbed since U.S. Commodore **Thomas ap C. Jones** had landed a naval force at Monterey (1842). This act had been repudiated by the American government. Upon the outbreak of war, revolts of American settlers were fomented (June) by Army Captain **John C. Frémont,** heading a surveying expedition in the west.

1846, June–December. Kearny's March. Brigadier General **Stephen Watts Kearny** was ordered to occupy New Mexico and California. Marching overland from Ft. Leavenworth with 1,700 men, he established control over New Mexico. He received a message that California had been pacified, and so decided to leave most of his troops to hold New Mexico. Leaving Santa Fe (September 25) with 120 dragoons, Kearny reached southeastern California to learn of the revolts and to find the road to San Diego blocked by about 500 Mexican cavalry.

1846, July 7. Occupation of Monterey. Commodore **John D. Sloat** sent a naval force ashore. His successor, Commodore Robert F. Stockton, expanded the occupation and Frémont was named governor of California. Soon after this the Mexican-Californian populace rose against the Americans and controlled most of the province.

1846, December 6. Battle of San Pascual. This was a violent, inconclusive action in which Kearny held the field, but found his path to San Diego still blocked. However, he made contact with Stockton's sailors and marines, who marched out to meet him (December 10). Kearny's wagon train (the first to cross the Rockies) and a battalion of infantry, under Major **Philip St. George Cooke,** taking another trail, joined him later (January 29, 1847).

1847, January 8. Battle of San Gabriel. Kearny's combined Army-Navy command defeated the main Mexican force outside of Los Angeles.

1847, January 9. Battle of the Mesa. Kearny won a climactic victory, breaking the back of Mexican-Californian resistance. He at once occupied Los Angeles.

DONIPHAN'S EXPEDITION, 1846–1847

An offshoot of Kearny's operations was Colonel **Alexander W. Doniphan**'s march with 850 Missouri mounted riflemen from Santa Fe (December 12) to Chihuahua.

1847, February 28. Battle of the Sacramento River. Near Chihuahua, Doniphan defeated a much larger Mexican force. Mexican losses were 600; American, 7 killed and wounded. Doniphan then continued south.

1847, May 21. Doniphan Arrives at Saltillo. This overland march, like that of Kearny, had been an amazing feat. Each of them marched more than 2,000 miles over desert territory, never previously traversed by organized military forces.

Central Mexican Campaign

1847, March 9. Scott Arrives Near Veracruz. The transports, carrying 10,000 troops, escorted by Commodore **David Connor**'s squadron, began an unopposed landing which completely invested the fortress city.

1847, March 27. Capture of Veracruz. A 5-day bombardment by land and sea brought the surrender of the 5,000-man garrison. Losses on both sides were light: 82 Americans killed and wounded; 180 Mexicans, of whom 100 were civilians. Scott at once moved westward with 8,500 men toward Jalapa to get away from the low coastal area, where yellow fever was feared.

1847, April 18. Battle of Cerro Gordo. Santa Anna, with more than 12,000 men, held the fortified defile, whose flanks were seemingly impregnable. Scott's engineers (who included Captains **Robert E. Lee, George B. McClellan,** and **Joseph E. Johnston,** and Lieutenant **Pierre G. T. Beauregard**) discovered a flanking mountain trail over which Scott hurried his main body, enveloping most of the Mexican force. After a sharp fight the Mexicans were completely routed, losing 1,000 killed and wounded and 3,000 prisoners. Forty-odd guns and 4,000 small arms were captured. American losses were 64 killed and 353 wounded.

1847, May 15. Occupation of Puebla. Here Scott halted, 75 miles from Mexico City. By this time he had but 5,820 men, having had to send home 4,000 others whose enlistments had expired.

1847, May–August. Wait at Puebla. Scott's strength was rebuilt by new troops, hurriedly raised in the United States, to almost 11,000 effectives and an additional 3,000 sick.

1847, August 7. Advance on Mexico City. Leaving his invalids and a small garrison at Puebla, Scott deliberately cut all communications with the outside world. Wellington's comment, when he learned of this, exemplified foreign military opinion: "Scott is lost. He cannot capture the city and he cannot fall back on his base." Santa Anna defended the capital with some 30,000 men. Scott, finding the direct route through Ayutla to be impracticable (August 12), circled to the south, where he discovered strong Mexican concentrations near Contreras and Churubusco, commanding the roads into the city. Scott, with only 4 days' rations left, decided to attack both positions (August 19), his decision guided by the effective reconnaissances of his engineers, who once again had found unmapped trails leading into the Mexican positions.

1847, August 20. Battle of Contreras. The hill position was stormed in a surprise dawn attack and its defenders routed. The 2 guns lost at Buena Vista were recaptured here.

1847, August 20. Battle of Churubusco. Almost simultaneously another American column burst through, storming a fortified convent. Losses were heavy in these 2 battles: 137 Americans killed, 877 wounded and 38 missing; while the Mexicans lost an estimated 4,297 killed and wounded, 2,637 prisoners, and some 3,000 missing. Scott had lost one-seventh of his effectives, Santa Anna one-third of his. The Mexicans retired within the city walls, except for strong detachments in and near the fortress of Chapultepec.

1847, August 25–September 6. Armistice. Discussion of peace proposals ended in disagreement; Scott immediately resumed his offensive.

1847, September 8. Battle of Molino del Rey. Some 12,000 Mexicans garrisoning a gun foundry and an old fort near Chapultepec were finally defeated after a day-long attack in which the Americans lost 116 killed and 665 wounded. Mexican losses were about 2,000 killed and wounded and 700 captured. Scott now had less than 7,500 effectives.

1847, September 13. Battle of Chapultepec. The fortified hill, last major obstacle outside Mexico City, was bombarded (September 12) and taken by storm next day, the rocky slopes and walls being scaled by ladders. Heroic feature of the defense was the resistance of some 100 Mexican Military College cadets on the crest. At the same time other American columns drove along the causeways below the hill to the San Cosmé and Belén gates of the city, under heavy fire. American casualties were 130 killed and 703 wounded. Mexican losses are estimated at 1,800 in and around Chapultepec alone; their total losses are undetermined. Among many Americans distinguishing themselves, Lieutenants **U. S. Grant** and **T. J. Jackson** were outstanding.

1847, September 14. Capture of Mexico City. Scott's troops worked through the night, preparing for a final assault. Santa Anna's main force, however, had with-

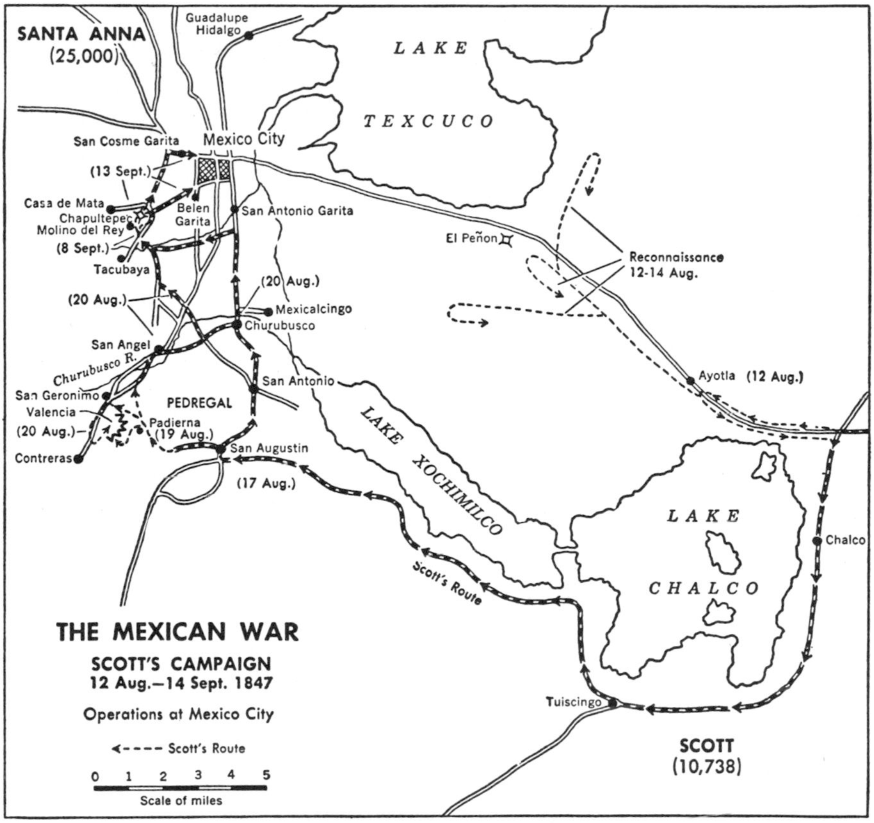

drawn after dark. At dawn, as bombardment was about to begin, the remaining garrison surrendered. Scott immediately occupied the city.

1847, September 14–October 12. Siege of Puebla. A Mexican force besieged the American garrison, but was driven off by troops from Veracruz.

1847, September–1848, February. Peace Negotiations. While these dragged on at Guadalupe Hidalgo, political chicanery in Washington intervened, Scott being summarily removed from command and ordered home to stand trumped-up charges which were later withdrawn. He was received as a hero by the nation, and Congress bestowed a gold medal on him for his successful invasion. Ironically, Polk had to present the medal.

1848, February 2. Treaty of Guadalupe Hidalgo. This confirmed the southern boundary of Texas and transferred to the United States the regions now comprising California, Nevada, Utah, most of Arizona and New Mexico, and parts of Colorado and Wyoming. The U.S. paid Mexico $15 million. U.S. forces evacuated Mexico City (June 12) and Veracruz (August 2). Meanwhile the treaty was ratified (July 4).

CANADA

1812–1815. War of 1812. (See p. 795.)

1837, November. Papineau's Rebellion. French-Canadian leader **Louis Joseph Papineau,** believing that the grievances of French Canadians were being ignored by the British crown, led a brief uprising in Lower Canada (modern Quebec Province) which was suppressed by British forces in a clash at **St. Denis** (November 22). Papineau fled to the United States, and then to France, returning to Canada after a general amnesty (1847).

1837, December. Mackenzie's Rebellion. Advocate of a republican government for Upper Canada (modern Ontario Province) or all of Canada, **William Mackenzie** had been in correspondence with Papineau, although there was evidently no collusion between their entirely separate rebellions. His call for an uprising and establishment of a provisional government was foiled at **Toronto** by Sir **John Colborne** (December 6), and he fled to the United States. In Buffalo he collected a group of Canadian malcontents, and seized Navy Island, in the Niagara River. His followers made a few raids into Canada, but all fled when Canadian forces approached. He returned to Canada after the Amnesty Act of 1849.

1838. Aroostook "War." (See p. 805.)

1840. Act of Union. Upper and Lower Canada were united as a single, partially self-governing colony.

LATIN AMERICA

When the period opened, the greater portion of the Americas roughly south of the Missouri River and 42° latitude belonged to Spain and Portugal. The young United States had as western boundary the line of the Mississippi down to the Floridas. England, Holland, France, and Denmark each claimed some of the West Indies islands. England, too, had a tiny toehold—Belize—on the Caribbean coast just south of Yucatan, and was casting envious eyes on Guiana, where France and Holland held coastal slices. Portugal's share of this rich Latin immensity was Brazil, whose boundaries stand today generally as they were then. The rest was Spain's.

When the period closed, all that remained of these 2 Latin colonial empires were Cuba and Puerto Rico, both Spanish. A group of new nations, self-carved by armed revolution against European overlords and by their own internecine wars, were protected by the Monroe Doctrine (see p. 804) against further overseas encroachments.

The independence movements, ignited by the American Revolution, were further stimulated by the French Revolution, by Napoleon's incursions into Spain and Portugal, and by later revolution in Spain. Turmoil and dissidence, beginning in 1790, smoldered uncertainly until British operations against Spanish South America, in the Napoleonic Wars, kindled the flame.

WARS OF INDEPENDENCE, 1800–1825

Spanish South America

1806, June 17. British Occupation of Buenos Aires. Admiral Sir **Home Popham**'s squadron landed some 500-odd troops under General William Beresford. **Jacques de Liniers** rallied the colonial militia, who forced the capitulation of the invaders (August 12). Popham, who had acted without specific orders, was later court-martialed.

1807, July. British Occupation of Montevideo. An expedition of 8,000 men under General **John Whitelocke** occupied the city, then seized Buenos Aires. Again Liniers led a popular uprising, forcing capitulation of the invaders, after serious street fighting.

1807–1810. Insurrections throughout South America. These were triggered by the 2 successes against foreign soldiery in Buenos Aires. Spanish troops suppressed all except in the River Plate viceroyalty (Argentina), which became practically independent (1810).

1810–1814. Unsuccessful Rebellion in Chile. After a brief struggle Chile won independence under the leadership of **José Miguel Carrera** (1811). Because of incompetence he was replaced by his rival, **Bernardo O'Higgins.** Spanish forces from Peru defeated O'Higgins at **Rancagua** (October 7, 1814) due largely to Carrera's noncooperation. O'Higgins fled to Argentina, and the Spanish reestablished control of Chile.

1811, August 14. Independence of Paraguay. This little inland subdivision of the River Plate viceroyalty declared its independ-

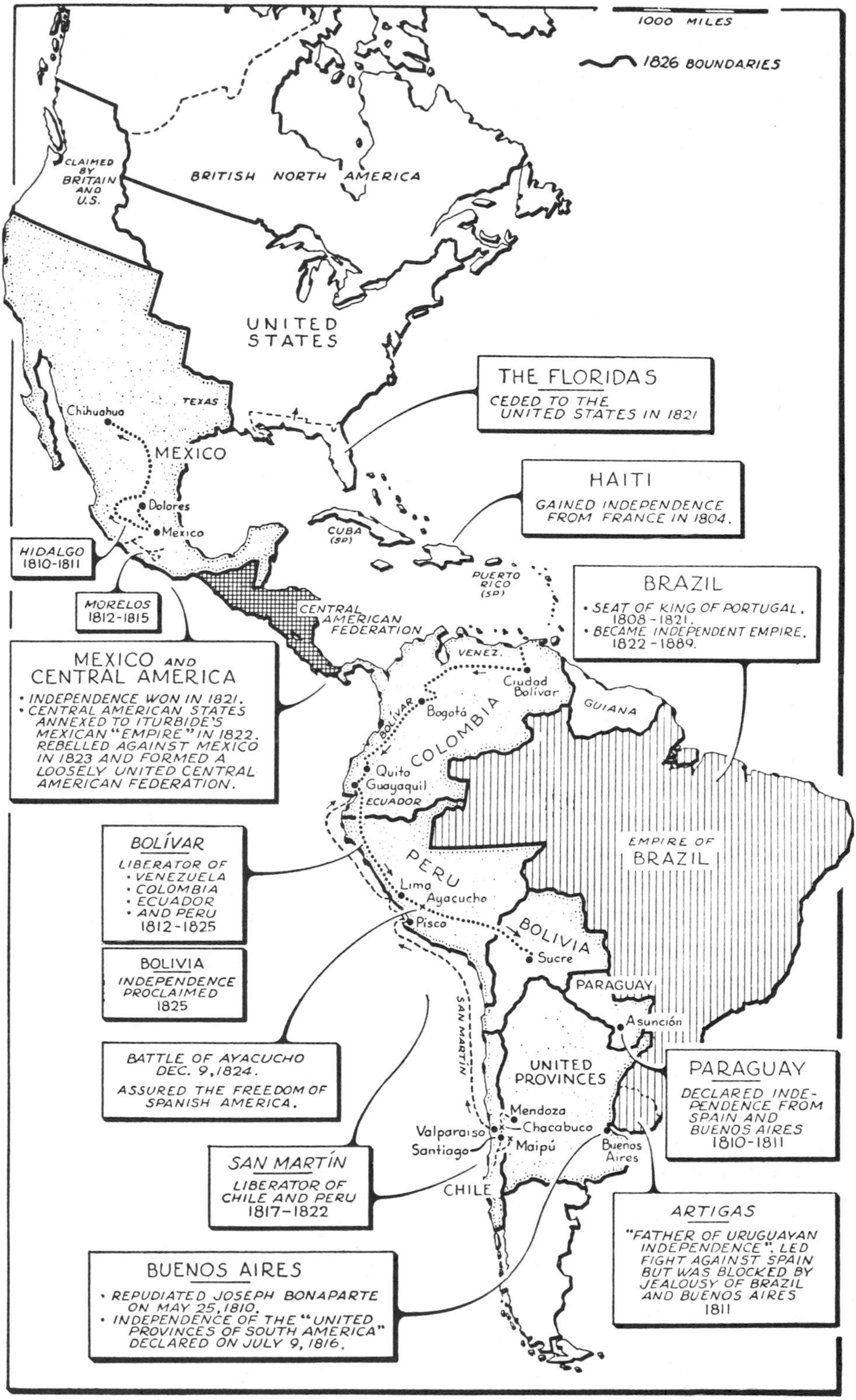
1000 MILES
1826 BOUNDARIES
CLAIMED BY BRITAIN AND U.S.
BRITISH NORTH AMERICA
UNITED STATES
TEXAS
Chihuahua
MEXICO
Dolores
Mexico
THE FLORIDAS
CEDED TO THE UNITED STATES IN 1821
HAITI
GAINED INDEPENDENCE FROM FRANCE IN 1804.
CUBA (SP)
PUERTO RICO (SP)
BRAZIL
• SEAT OF KING OF PORTUGAL, 1808-1821.
• BECAME INDEPENDENT EMPIRE, 1822-1889.
HIDALGO 1810-1811
MORELOS 1812-1815
CENTRAL AMERICAN FEDERATION
MEXICO AND CENTRAL AMERICA
• INDEPENDENCE WON IN 1821.
• CENTRAL AMERICAN STATES ANNEXED TO ITURBIDE'S MEXICAN "EMPIRE" IN 1822. REBELLED AGAINST MEXICO IN 1823 AND FORMED A LOOSELY UNITED CENTRAL AMERICAN FEDERATION.
VENEZ.
Ciudad Bolívar
GUIANA
BOLÍVAR
Bogotá
COLOMBIA
Quito
Guayaquil
ECUADOR
EMPIRE OF BRAZIL
BOLÍVAR
LIBERATOR OF
• VENEZUELA
• COLOMBIA
• ECUADOR
• AND PERU
1812-1825
PERU
Lima
Ayacucho
Pisco
BOLIVIA
Sucre
BOLIVIA
INDEPENDENCE PROCLAIMED 1825
PARAGUAY
Asunción
SAN MARTÍN
BATTLE OF AYACUCHO DEC. 9, 1824.
ASSURED THE FREEDOM OF SPANISH AMERICA.
UNITED PROVINCES
PARAGUAY
DECLARED INDEPENDENCE FROM SPAIN AND BUENOS AIRES 1810-1811
Mendoza
Chacabuco
Valparaiso
Santiago
Maipú
Buenos Aires
SAN MARTÍN
LIBERATOR OF CHILE AND PERU 1817-1822
CHILE
ARTIGAS
"FATHER OF URUGUAYAN INDEPENDENCE". LED FIGHT AGAINST SPAIN BUT WAS BLOCKED BY JEALOUSY OF BRAZIL AND BUENOS AIRES 1811
BUENOS AIRES
• REPUDIATED JOSEPH BONAPARTE ON MAY 25, 1810.
• INDEPENDENCE OF THE "UNITED PROVINCES OF SOUTH AMERICA" DECLARED ON JULY 9, 1816.

Independence movements in Latin America

ence, following a popular uprising, breaking its ties both with Spain and with the revolutionary movement in Buenos Aires. Paraguay was soon under the iron rule of **José Rodríguez de Francia,** who assumed perpetual dictatorship with a policy of armed isolation (1816).

1811–1821. Banda Oriental (Uruguay). The area between the River Plate and the Brazilian border—claimed by Portugal but actually under Spanish control—was liberated by Argentine and local revolutionaries, led by **José Artigas** (1811). He was ousted, in turn, by Brazil (1816–1820), which annexed the Banda.

1811–1825. Bolívar and San Martín. Simón Bolívar in Venezuela and **José de San Martín** in Argentina were 2 strong men who initiated separate and amazing campaigns of liberation from Spanish rule. Bolívar's area of operations in the north was mainly New Granada (Venezuela, Colombia, and Ecuador). San Martín's operations in the south included the River Plate (Argentina), Chile, and Peru. When these leaders met at the equator at Guayaquil (1822), Spain's domination of South America was doomed. Both men were able to enlist foreign soldiery—English, Irish, German, and North American—in their forces. The foreign adventurers included a remarkable British sailor, **Thomas Cochrane,** 10th Earl of Dundonald, perhaps the stormiest petrel the Royal Navy ever produced.

BOLIVAR'S CAMPAIGNS

Simón Bolívar (1783–1830), born in Caracas, spent most of his early life in Europe. He returned to Venezuela (1809) and became involved in the revolutionary movement (1811).

1811, July 5. Venezuelan Independence Declared. Bolívar was put in command of Puerto Cabello, but was driven from it by Spanish General **Juan Domingo Monteverde,** who momentarily crushed the entire revolt, capturing **Francisco Miranda,** its leader. Bolívar fled to Curaçao.

1813, May. Bolívar's Return. He took the field again (May, 1813), defeating Monteverde at **Lastaguanes,** and then capturing Caracas (August 6, 1813). He won another victory over the royalists at **Araure** (December 5, 1813). At **La Victoria** (February, 1814) and **San Mateo** (March, 1814), Bolívar defeated General **José Tomás Boves.** He won another victory at **Carabobo** (May, 1814), but was defeated by Boves at **La Puerta** (July, 1814). With Venezuela again under Spanish control, Bolívar fled to New Granada (Colombia), where he was given another revolutionary command.

1815. Bolívar Defeated. After some preliminary successes, he was defeated by General **Pablo Morillo** at **Santa Mara.** Spanish troops, released by the conclusion of the Napoleonic Wars, now reconquered most of the rebellious provinces. Bolívar fled to Jamaica and Haiti. He led two unsuccessful raids against the coast of Venezuela.

1816, December. Bolívar Returns to Venezuela. He led a new movement against Morillo, winning an important victory near **Barcelona** (February 16, 1817). Now recognized as commander in chief of the patriot forces, Bolívar attempted to raise the country against the Spanish.

1818, March 15. Battle of La Puerta. On the site of an earlier defeat, Bolívar's army was routed by Morillo. Without losing heart, Bolívar continued the insurrection. He decided to try to drive the Spanish from New Granada.

1819, June 11. Crossing of the Andes. Leaving Angostura (Ciudad Bolívar) with 2,500 men, well armed but practically in rags, Bolívar marched across Venezuela, over 7 rivers, and then through the frigid passes of the Andes, debouching in the valley of Sagamose (July 6).

1819, August 7. Battle of Boyaca. Spanish Colonel **Barreiro,** with 2,000 infantry and 400 horse, defended the approaches to Bogotá. Bolívar outmaneuvered him, placing his troops between Barreiro and the capital. While his right drove against the Spanish left flank, Bolívar's British Legion, all veterans, moved in frontal assault, repulsing the Spanish cavalry. Barreiro's troops were completely routed, losing 100 killed, 1,600 prisoners, and all their heavy equipment. This was the decisive battle of the revolution in northern South America. Bolívar entered Bogotá in triumph (August 10), establishing the Republic of Colombia, with himself as its president.

1820–1821. Operations in Northwest Venezuela. Bolívar and other patriot leaders campaigned indecisively against royalist forces. An armistice was effected (November 25, 1820–April 28, 1821) at Trujillo. Upon the conclusion of this truce, Bolívar with 6,000 men once more moved through the Cordillera, this time southeastward.

1821, June 25. Battle of Carabobo. Spanish General **Miguel de La Torre,** with 5,000 men, held the valley of the Carabobo, at the southern foot of the pass. Bolívar, brushing aside Spanish outposts in the pass, found another route through the mountains and sent his cavalry and the British Legion through the detour to fall on the Spanish right flank. La Torre assaulted this force as it debouched with a detachment of his own, but the British Legion held firm and the cavalry broke up the attack. La Torre's error in dividing his force led to defeat in detail. The Spaniards were driven from the field in a 20-mile-long rout. Bolívar entered Caracas. Spanish strength unraveled. **Cartagena** capitulated (October 1) after a 21-month siege, and other garrisons began to fall.

1822. Operations in Quito Province. Bolívar moved south to join his lieutenant, General **Antonio de Sucre,** who, with 2,000 men, had cornered **Melchior Aymerich,** Spanish governor general of Quito, in the mountains near the city. At **Bombоná,** a royalist force of some 2,500 so bitterly contested Bolívar's advance through the mountains that he was forced to halt (April 7).

1822, May 24. Battle of Pichincha. Aymerich turned on Sucre, attempting to storm the slopes of the volcano of Pichincha, where Sucre's forces lay. Although at first successful, the Spanish force was snubbed by a flank attack and driven down the mountain, retreating into Quito, where Aymerich surrendered next day. His losses had been 400 killed, 190 wounded, and 14 guns; Sucre's losses were 200 killed and 140 wounded.

SAN MARTIN'S CAMPAIGNS

San Martín (1778–1850), of Spanish descent, had served in Spain's army during the Peninsular War. He returned to Buenos Aires (1810).

1814–1816. San Martín Commands the Revolutionary Army. For 3 years he organized and trained the Army of the Andes—partly Argentine, partly Chilean—at Mendoza, in preparation for an invasion of the west coast. Meanwhile Argentina declared its independence (July 9, 1816).

1817, January 24. March over the Andes. San Martín led an army of 3,000 infantry, 700 cavalry, and 21 guns across the snowy passes of the Gran Cordillera—a feat never before attempted—debouching into the plain between the coastal range and main Andean chain (February 8). O'Higgins commanded a Chilean contingent.

1817, February 12–13. Battle of Chacabuco. Spanish Colonel **Maroto,** with 1,500 infantry, 500 cavalry, and 7 guns, disputed the advance. San Martín attacked in 2 columns. O'Higgins, moving in the moonlight of early morning, contained the Spanish force while San Martín turned its left, completely routing it. Spanish losses were 500 killed, 600 prisoners, and all their artillery. San Martín lost 12 killed and 120 wounded. Santiago was then occupied (February 15), and Chilean independence became fact (proclaimed a year later, February 12, 1818). Indecisive fighting continued through the remainder of the year, while Spanish General **Mariano Osorio** with 9,000 men moved down from Peru.

1818, March 16. Battle of Cancha-Rayada. San Martín with 6,000 men was defeated by Osorio, losing 120 killed and 22 of his guns. Spanish losses were 200 killed and wounded, and they were much shaken by the encounter.

1818, April 5. Battle of the Maipo. San Martín, regrouping after his defeat, attacked the Spaniards on the bank of the Maipo River. Hurling his main effort against the

Spanish left, San Martín turned it and the royalist army collapsed, losing 1,000 killed, 12 guns, and 2,300 prisoners. San Martín's losses were about 100 killed and wounded. Osorio, giving up further contest, retreated into Peru, and San Martín prepared to follow. But further revolutionary invasion was impossible unless Spanish command of the sea were broken. **Manuel Blanco Encalada,** a Chilean and a former Spanish naval officer, had gathered a squadron of sorts, including a Spanish frigate, cleverly captured.

1818, November 28. Arrival of Cochrane at Valparaiso. After he had resigned from the British Navy under a cloud, the Chilean revolutionary government invited him to command its navy.

1819, January–February. Cochrane Takes to Sea. With 4 ships, he attempted to draw the Spanish squadron based on Callao and Valdivia into action. Unsuccessful in this, he cruised the coast.

1820, June 18. Capture of Valdivia. Cochrane sailed his flagship *O'Higgins,* 50, former Spanish heavy frigate, into the harbor. He bombarded the forts and landed a party to capture the defenses. This broke the last tenuous Spanish hold on the Chilean coast. San Martín now felt able to carry out his proposed invasion of Peru.

1820, September 8. Invasion of Peru. Cochrane's little squadron escorted north 16 transports carrying San Martín's forces. They were landed at Pisco; then Cochrane blockaded Callao, where the Spanish squadron lay.

1820, November 5. Capture of the *Esmeralda*. In a daring cutting-out expedition Cochrane in person took 250 sailors and marines in small boats into the harbor and captured the frigate *Esmeralda.* Had his plans been carried out, all the other Spanish ships would then have been taken in turn, but a subordinate cut the frigate's cable and Cochrane had to be content with his one prize.

1821, July. San Martín Takes Lima. After this, Callao capitulated (September 21) and Peruvian independence was established. San Martín turned his eyes northward again, toward Quito. He apparently decided then to coordinate with Bolívar, who had simultaneously been advancing from the north.

CONCLUDING CAMPAIGNS AGAINST SPAIN

1822, July 26–27. Meeting at Guayaquil. Bolívar and San Martín officially linked their forces. The nature of the conference has always been a mystery, but San Martín turned over control to Bolívar and retired from all further revolutionary activities. The 2 men were completely incompatible: Bolívar with dictatorial ambitions, San Martín a soldier-patriot of high military genius. Bolívar, organizing the Republic of Peru, continued the drive to expel Spanish domination, despite mutinies and vigorous Spanish reaction.

1824, August 6. Battle of Junin. Bolívar and Sucre, with about 9,000 men, met a Spanish army of equal size under General **José Canterac** about 100 miles northeast of Lima. In a purely cavalry battle, about 2,000 men on each side being engaged, and not a shot fired, the revolutionaries were victorious. The Spanish army retreated into the highlands southeast of Lima. Sucre pursued, while Bolívar organized a government at Lima.

1824, December 9. Battle of Ayacucho. Spanish General **José de La Serna** with 10,000 men and 10 guns attacked Sucre with 7,000 and 2 guns. Sucre's left and center contained La Serna's attack, while his right, mostly cavalry, turned the Spanish left. Sucre now threw in a reserve division and the Spanish army collapsed. La Serna, who had received 6 wounds, was captured. Next day General Canterac, La Serna's successor, capitulated. Spanish losses were 1,400 killed and 700 wounded; the republicans lost 300 killed and 600 wounded. Known as the "Battle of the Generals" (14 Spanish generals were captured), Ayacucho ended Spain's grip on South America. All Spanish forces remaining in Peru were withdrawn by the terms of the capitulation. Sucre then moved eastward into the Presidency of Charcas, bordering on Brazil, and established the Republic of Bolivia (August 6, 1825).

Brazil

1807–1821. Brazil Becomes the Seat of Portuguese Government. The Portuguese royal family fled there from the Napoleonic invasion (1807–1808; see p. 753).

The example of revolt in neighboring Spanish America caused an urge for liberty to permeate Brazil. After much dissension, John VI of Portugal returned to his country (1821), leaving his son Dom Pedro as prince regent.

1808. Brazil Occupies French Guiana. This was returned by the Treaty of Paris (1814).

1816–1821. Occupation of Uruguay. **(See p. 814.)**

1822, September 7. Independence of Brazil. This culminated growing tension between Brazil and Portugal and between John and Dom Pedro, who led the independence movement. He was soon crowned emperor (December 1).

1823, March 21. Cochrane Assumes Command of the Brazilian Navy. This was a small squadron of warships obtained by purchase and capture. Portuguese naval strength lay at Bahia, which Cochrane blockaded.

1823, July 2. Portuguese Evacuation of Bahia. Portuguese forces left the port in a convoy of some 60-odd transports escorted by 13 warships—a force far too strong for Cochrane to attack with only 2 frigates. The convoy headed north along the coast for Maranhão (São Luiz).

1823, July. Cochrane Wins the War. In his flagship, the heavy frigate *Pedro Primiero,* 50, the admiral—by superior seamanship—avoided conflict with clumsy Portuguese war vessels while cutting out a number of transports. Then, surmising its destination, he sailed right to Maranhão ahead of the convoy and captured the port, permitting the garrison to embark for Portugal. The main convoy now had no place to go but Portugal. The combined Portuguese convoys were harassed all the way across the Atlantic by several of Cochrane's ships.

1825. Portugal Recognizes Brazilian Independence.

Mexico

1810. Peasant Revolt. The first real revolution in New Spain began with the revolt of **Miguel Hidalgo y Costilla,** a priest interested in social reform. With a horde of 80,000 *paisanos,* he swept through the southern provinces and threatened Mexico City, but his untrained masses were repulsed (November 6) by Spanish General **Félix Calleja.**

1811, January 17. Battle of the Bridge of Calderón. Near Guadalajara, Calleja, with 6,000 men, crushed Hidalgo, who was captured and executed. Hidalgo's lieutenant, **José María Morelos,** also a priest, revived the insurrection, but after 3 years of increasingly hopeless fighting was captured and executed by General **Agustín de Iturbide,** a Mexican-born Spaniard.

1821, January–February. Renewed Rebellion. This time the leader was General Iturbide, who rebelled after the revolution of 1820 in Spain.

1821, February 24. Declaration of Independence. Iturbide occupied Mexico City and was crowned **Agustín I,** Emperor of Mexico (July 21, 1822).

1823, March 19. Republican Revolution. Iturbide was forced from the throne. One of the republican leaders was **Antonio López de Santa Anna.** A federal republic was established (October 4, 1824).

Central America

1821–1823. Mexican Domination. The Spanish captain-generalcy of Guatemala crumbled in a series of revolutions gradually growing in intensity (1811–1821). The uprisings were generally stimulated by the independence movements to the north and south. Following Mexico's independence, the area fell under Mexican domination.

1823, July 1. The United Provinces. After the overthrow of Agustín, a constitutional assembly called by Mexican General **Vicente Filosola** in Guatemala City declared the confederation of Guatemala, El Salvador, Nicaragua, Honduras, and Costa Rica as the United Provinces of Central America.

Haiti and Santo Domingo

1791–1801. Chaos in Haiti. The island of Haiti (Santo Domingo or Hispaniola) was the center of brutal war, revolution, and rapine following a slave rebellion. **Pierre Dominique Toussaint L'Ouverture,** a Negro of military genius, finally restored order (1800), but his efforts aroused the suspicion of Bonaparte, who resolved to restore complete French control over the island and to reinstitute slavery.

1801–1803. French Domination Overthrown. French General **Victor Emmanuel Leclerc,** with 25,000 men, debarked and despite Toussaint's resistance occupied the seaports. He could not, however, compete with the savage resistance of the Negro troops in inland guerrilla warfare. His army wasted by disease, Leclerc offered amnesty, and Toussaint laid down his arms in order to negotiate (June, 1802). He was treacherously seized and taken to France, where he died in prison (1803). Under **Jean Jacques Dessalines,** the Negroes resumed fighting. Leclerc died of yellow fever, and the demoralized French army finally evacuated the island (November, 1803).

1804–1806. Supremacy of Dessalines. He crowned himself Emperor Alexandre I (October 8) and instituted a general massacre of all remaining whites.

1806–1820. Struggle for Power. Following the assassination of Dessalines, the island was divided between **Henri Christophe** in the north and **Alexandre Sabes Pétion** in the south, who warred with one another until Pétion's death (1818). Christophe, a man of undoubted genius, was assassinated (1820). **Jean Pierre Boyer** became President of Haiti.

1808–1809. Revolt of Santo Domingo. With British help, the Spanish eastern portion of the island threw off the control of the French-speaking blacks of the west.

1814. Spanish Control Restored in Santo Domingo.

1822. Haitian Reconquest of Santo Domingo. Boyer drove out the Spaniards to reunite the island under one government.

AFTERMATH OF INDEPENDENCE, 1825–1850

Wars and revolutions raged throughout Latin America as the new republics struggled within and among themselves. Dictators rose and fell.

1825–1828. Brazil-Argentine War. Argentina, assisting a revolt in the Banda Oriental (Uruguay) against Brazil, went to war to acquire the province. At the **Battle of Ituzaingo** (February 20, 1827), Brazilian forces were defeated by an Argentine-Uruguayan combination. Blockade of Buenos Aires by a Brazilian naval squadron brought friction with Europe. British mediation brought peace and the establishment of independent Uruguay.

1827–1829. Peruvian Aggressions. José Lamar, President of Peru, launched his nation on a policy of expansionism. A Peruvian invasion of Bolivia (1827) forced the withdrawal of Sucre, who had become president after the departure of Bolívar. Lamar then invaded Ecuador. A Peruvian naval squadron captured Guayaquil (January, 1829). But Sucre, who had taken **refuge in Ecuador, and Ecuadorian General Juan José Flores led an army which** defeated the invading Peruvians at the **Battle of Tarqui** (February 27, 1829). Guayaquil was recaptured the next day. Lamar's plans for expansion to the north now crumbled.

1829. Spanish Invasion of Mexico. An expedition from Cuba seized Tampico (August 18). Santa Anna promptly led a force against the invaders, who were soon forced to surrender (September 11).

1830. Independence of Ecuador. Flores led this withdrawal from Grañ Colombia, and became first president of Ecuador.

1836–1839. War of the Peruvian-Bolivian Confederation. Bolivian dictator **Andreas Santa Cruz,** with the agreement of Peruvian President **Luis Orbegosa,** established a combination of the two countries (1835). Chile and Argentina opposed the confederation, and Chile declared war (November 11, 1836). A Chilean army, commanded by General **Manuel Bulnes,** decisively defeated Santa Cruz at the **Battle of Yungay** (January 20, 1839), breaking up the confederation.

1838–1839. French Expedition to Mexico. To obtain satisfaction for claims of its citizens, France sent an expedition to Mexico. The French fleet blockaded the Atlantic coast of Mexico and seized Veracruz (April 16, 1838). When the claims were satisfied, the French withdrew (March 9, 1839).

1839–1840. Disintegration of Central American Confederation. Continual internal strife finally caused the dissolution of the confederation into its components. Later attempts at confederation failed.

1841. Peruvian Invasion of Bolivia. President **Agustín Gamarra** of Peru, attempting to annex part of Bolivia, was defeated and killed by the Bolivians under President **José Ballivián** at the **Battle of Ingavi** (November 20).

1844. Independence of Santo Domingo. The predominantly Spanish-speaking inhabitants of the eastern portion of the island of Hispaniola, or Haiti, revolted successfully against the French-speaking rulers of the Republic of Haiti.

1843–1852. Argentine Intervention in Uruguay. A confusing struggle broke out involving internal strife in Argentina and Uruguay, and the intervention of Brazil, France, and England. Argentine dictator **Juan Manuel de Rosas** attempted to take advantage of a civil war in Uruguay to annex that country. He supported **Manuel Oribe** of Uruguay, who for 8 years maintained an ineffective siege of **Fructuoso Rivera** in Montevideo (1843–1851). Giuseppe Garibaldi was among the defenders of besieged Montevideo. To check Rosas, France and England sent forces to occupy parts of Uruguay and to blockade the River Plate (1845–1849). Meanwhile Argentine **Justo José de Urquiza** revolted against Rosas. Brazil, fearful of Argentine annexation of Uruguay, supported Urquiza, who was also encouraged by France and England. At the **Battle of Monte Caseros** (February 3, 1852), Urquiza with a force of Argentines, Brazilians, and Uruguayans defeated Rosas, who fled to England.

1846–1848. U.S.-Mexican War. This war, discussed elsewhere (see p. 806), sharpened the line of political demarcation and distrust between Anglo-Saxon North America and the Latin nations in both the northern and southern divisions of the hemisphere.

AUSTRALASIA

AUSTRALIA

1804. Irish Convict Rebellion. New South Wales had been established (1788) as a penal colony ruled by a military governor —usually an officer of the Royal Navy— and policed by the New South Wales Corps, a military body recruited in England. This "Praetorian Guard" waxed fat on land grants, monopoly of cargoes arriving in the colony, and the rum trade. A considerable proportion of the convicts were Irishmen, political prisoners deported after the suppression of the revolution of 1798. This group rose against the local government, but the mutiny was suppressed with great severity.

1806. Renewed Mutiny. After this was suppressed, Captain **William Bligh,** R.N., of *Bounty* mutiny fame, was appointed governor, the home government expecting that his stern discipline would bring both the N.S.W. Corps and the convicts into line. His drastic methods soon resulted in another mutiny.

1808, January 26. The Rum Rebellion. A group of N.S.W. Corps officers, led by Major **George Johnston,** a regular, arrested Bligh as unfit for office and held him prisoner pending the arrival of a new governor. The home government, while condemning the action, accepted it. Colonel **Lachlin Macquarie,** an able administrator, arrived (1809) and Bligh was sent home (to become a rear admiral). Macquarie broke up the N.S.W. Corps.

NEW ZEALAND

1843–1848. First Maori War. Native resentment of land expropriation broke into conflicts between British settlers and the native Maoris in a guerrilla war that raged for five years.

XVIII

THE EMERGENCE OF THE PROFESSIONAL: 1850–1900

MILITARY TRENDS

A multiplicity of technological developments forced sometimes reluctant military professionals to broaden their horizons and to create new standards. Epitome of this new professionalism was Prussian **Helmuth von Moltke.** He was a competent, sometimes brilliant, soldier who guided rather than led, and his reputation has paled somewhat in the face of growing modern opinion that during the latter half of the 19th century two men alone displayed military genius ranking them among the great captains of the world: **Ulysses S. Grant** and **Robert E. Lee.**

Though neither was completely successful in the effort, these two surpassed their contemporaries in coping in their very different ways with the unprecedented changes in warfare brought about by the Industrial Revolution. The new technological means for waging and supporting warfare meant that for the first time the French Revolutionary concept of the "nation in arms" had been eclipsed by a new concept: the "nation at war." With the national economies on both sides fully integrated into their respective war efforts, the American Civil War was truly the first modern war, and the first "total" war in the modern sense.

It was a period of colonial expansion and conflict of interest among the great powers. War raged practically all over the world, except in the British Isles and in the Scandinavian Peninsula. But the expert juggling of British diplomacy, self-interested in the maintenance of the balance of power, went far to prevent the numerous minor conflicts from spreading into international conflagrations, such as those of the periods immediately preceding and following. Queen Victoria's reign would go down in history as that of the "Pax Britannica."

MILITARY THEORY

The example of Napoleon Bonaparte still dominated military theory on both sides of the Atlantic Ocean. In the United States, **Dennis Hart Mahan** was still the apostle of Napoleonic concepts; more than any other single factor, Mahan's teaching influenced the strategical and tactical thinking of the leading generals on both sides of the American Civil War.

In Europe the seed of the famous—and much misunderstood—Prussian Army General Staff had been planted by Frederick the Great, and its early growth had been nurtured by both Scharnhorst and Clausewitz. But the quiet organizing genius of Moltke brought that staff of its full flower in the second half of the 19th century. The combination in the Prussian General Staff of scholarly research, meticulously detailed planning, and thorough indoctrination in a logical concept of war was the major factor in stunning victories over Austria and France, causing Prussia to be acknowledged as the leading land military power of the world. That Prussia and Germany still held this position at the end of the century was due mainly to Moltke's great successor, **Alfred von Schlieffen.** Military historian Schlieffen's studies of ancient and modern campaigns corroborated the theories of Napoleon and of Clausewitz. He developed a simple, flexible strategic concept for a two-front war against France and Russia. In the hands of a less able successor, this so-called Schlieffen Plan ironically was to become the very epitome of rigidity.

Among the signficant military writings of this period. the works of the French officer **Charles J. J. J. Ardant du Picq** were a major contribution to the development of modern combat theory. Killed in battle at the age of 49 in 1870, Colonel Ardant du Picq was chiefly concerned with the behavorial element in warfare. His masterpiece, *Battle Studies* (published posthumously), had immense influence on the generation of officers who led France in World War I, particularly Marshal **Ferdinand Foch.**

By the end of the century an American sailor was beginning to be acknowledged throughout the world as the leading military theorist of the age. **Alfred Thayer Mahan** had become the Jomini and Clausewitz of naval theory through lucid, logical analyses of the fundamentals of sea power. His theories, which related naval strength to national policy and strategy, were as respected by soldiers, politicians, and emperors as they were by naval colleagues of all nations. Interestingly, his writings were appreciated and respected in Europe before they were thoroughly understood by his own countrymen.

THE IMPACT OF TECHNOLOGY

Steam power became a critical consideration in national strategic planning. This impact of steam power on nautical affairs stimulated Mahan's writings and caused them to be influential in maritime nations.

For such countries the location of a coaling station not only became a limiting factor but also could directly determine the direction and extent of colonial expansion. Two examples were provided in the Spanish-American War. Lacking coaling stations, Admiral **George Dewey** could move his squadron from Hong Kong to Manila only by the outright purchase of British colliers and their cargoes. The long cruise of the U.S.S. *Oregon* from San Francisco around Cape Horn to join the fleet in Cuban waters (nearly 13,000 nautical miles) sparked the later American acquisition of the Panama Canal Zone and the construction of the canal itself.

The railroad became a logistical weapon for both sides during the American Civil War, an example used later to good advantage by the Prussian General Staff in its preparations for the Franco-Prussian War.

Another far-reaching development was the electric telegraph and cable, affecting both strategy and tactics. Beginning with the Crimean War, this was a two-edged sword so far as the over-all direction of war was concerned. Cable and telegraph ensured rapid communication between field commander and government; they also permitted political armchair strategists to hinder field operations. Almost instantaneous transmission of war correspondents' dispatches, immediately appearing in the daily press, brought a new threat to security by revelation of operational plans and moves. This was most pernicious in the American Civil War. But news dispatches also promoted the common soldier from a digit to the status of an individual by emblazoning his hardships for all to see. The result was improvement of the soldier's welfare and of his morale.

Tactically, the field telegraph augmented other improved means of signal communication: the semaphore "wigwag" flags and the heliograph, which already ensured contact between field headquarters and lower commands, and spanned hostile-held terrain to link with isolated elements and reconnaissance detachments. Long before the end of the Civil War the telegraph was in common use in the Union armies and less extensively in Confederate forces. Telegraph wires linked aerial observers in balloons with the ground. The wires also created a communications web, including—as Grant wrote—"each division, each corps, each army and . . . my headquarters."

In addition to the direct effect of new and improved instruments of warfare, industrialization had other significant consequences in the conduct of war. The change from an essentially agricultural economy released a greater percentage of national man power to both the armed forces and to the developing war industries. Larger armies could be raised and supported than had been true in the past, while the development of steam transportation and the electric telegraph facilitated the movement and control of these larger forces.

But it was in the refinement and proliferation of weapons that the new technology had its greatest effect.

WEAPONS AND TACTICS ON LAND

The transition from muzzle-loading to breechloading artillery pieces was complete by the end of the period. So, too, was the refinement of armor-piercing and lighter-walled antipersonnel projectiles. Solid shot became a thing of the past; elongated, streamlined shells, with explosive charges, detonated by improved fuses—both time and impact—were the rule. The smoothbore cannon—which was the predominant artillery type both ashore and afloat as the period opened—had been replaced by the rifled gun, a change made more reluctantly, perhaps, in the world's navies than in their armies. The problem of cannon recoil had been solved, first by ingeniously controlled springs, and later by more sophisticated hydropneumatic apparatus.

For coastal defense the disappearing gun had come into being, its principal protagonist the United States. It rose by means of counterweights to fire from above its parapet and then sank by force of recoil, controlled by pneumatic brakes.

In small arms, the single-shot muzzle-loader was replaced by the repeating magazine rifle, and the Minié ball gave way to the elongated conical bullet. The range, accuracy, and volume of fire of individual weapons were increased manifold. Though its potentialities were still scarcely realized, the machine gun had become an important weapon in the arsenals of all nations. Smokeless powder had become the generally accepted propellant for small arms as well as artillery by the end of the century, facilitating concealment in broken country.

Field mines and booby traps were used in the American Civil War by the Confederates as early as 1862, at the opening of the Peninsula Campaign. Though the ideas were not entirely new, modern prototypes of trench mortars and hand grenades were used by both sides of that conflict in the extended trench warfare of 1863–1865.

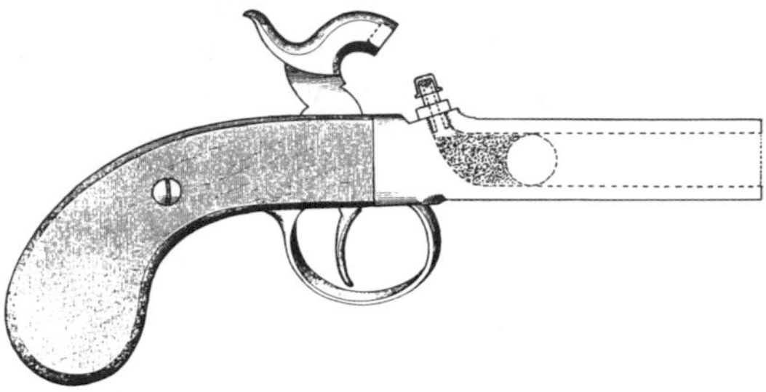

Percussion cap pistol

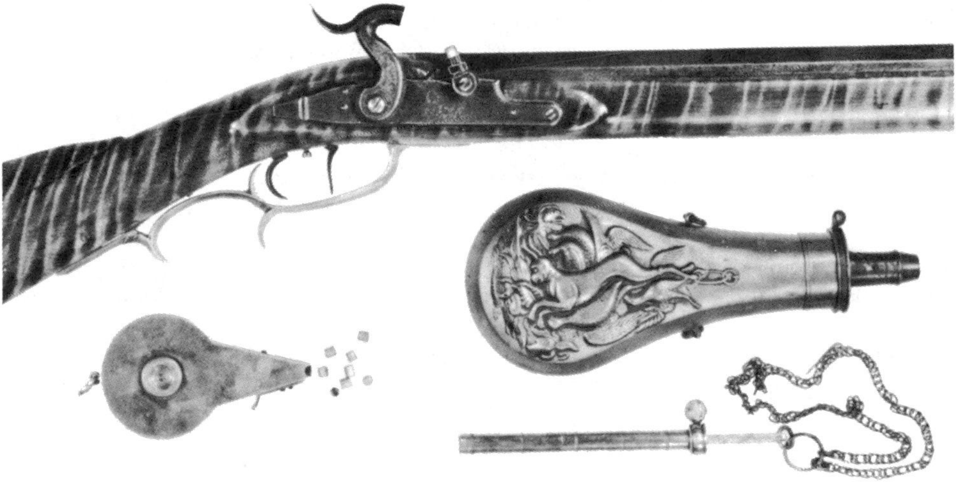

Firing assembly of a percussion cap rifle, with a percussion capper and eight percussion caps (lower left), and a powder flask above a syringe-like powder measure on a chain

The over-all effect of the new weapons was to introduce an entirely different order of fire power on the battlefield, where improved weapons combined with more numerous armies to sweep the front lines with unprecedented hails of iron, steel, and lead missiles. This in turn produced a far-reaching tactical revolution, which was most dramatically and most clearly manifested in the American Civil War.

Neither infantry nor cavalry could attack frontally in the face of the combined fire power of artillery and small arms. There were four immediate effects. First was dispersal; battlefield formations became progressively more spread out and more flexible. Next, maneuver became the order of the day as men sought for decision without suicidal frontal assaults.

Trench warfare was perhaps the most obvious manifestation of this tactical revolution. Field fortifications—heretofore reserved almost exclusively for siege operations—became an integral aspect of infantry tactics. Troops under fire immediately dug in. Foxholes and rifle pits were soon expanded into trench systems which became the bases for maneuver by both sides. It was in the utilization of improvised field fortifications that Lee surpassed all of his contemporaries; most of his victories were the result of his ability to use hasty entrenchments as a base for the aggressive employment of fire and movement.

Another manifestation was in cavalry combat. By the end of the period cavalry shock action had practically disappeared from the battlefield. With frontal charges against infantry unthinkable, mounted cavalry operations were limited almost entirely to screening and reconnaissance missions. The horse, however, provided mobility to mounted riflemen, whose normal mode of combat was as dismounted skirmishers.

The lessons of 1861–1865 were not learned readily elsewhere. It took their own bitter experiences for Europeans to realize the significance of the American example. A decade passed before the old order fell in a welter of broken men and horses during the Franco-Prussian War. The last gasps of the old order came in British colonial wars in Africa. By participating in the climactic cavalry charge at Omdurman, young Winston Churchill experienced the glory of the premodern era. A few years later, as the century was closing, he recognized that the era had ended, when massed British infantry were slaughtered by mobile Boer sharpshooters.

WEAPONS AND TACTICS AFLOAT

At Sinope the Russian Navy first showed the devastating potentialities of improved naval ordnance by smashing a Turkish fleet with shell projectiles. Armored floating batteries were also employed in the Crimean War. A logical evolution led to the creation of the French armor-plated *Gloire*—causing a panic in Britain which forced the reluctant Admiralty to rush construction of its own first armored warship, H.M.S. *Warrior*.

But it was the armor-plated Confederate *Merrimack* (C.S.S. *Virginia*) which tolled the bell for wooden warships; one day later the U.S.S. *Monitor* bowed in the

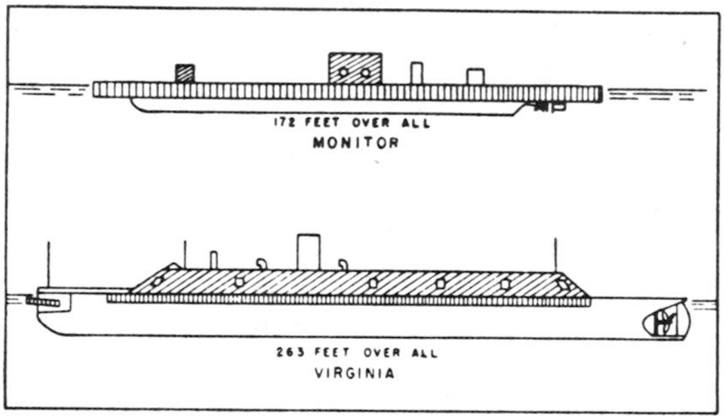

U.S.S. *Monitor* and C.S.S. *Virginia*

age of turret ships. Naval architects here and abroad soon solved the problem of wedding Ericson's revolving battery—introduced on the *Monitor*—to a seaworthy armored hull. By the end of the period the battleship was queen of the seas.

Confederate ingenuity also evolved the submarine, though not until the turn of the century would the gasoline engine and electrical storage battery solve the problem of propulsion. The ram, Civil War rebirth of an old device, enjoyed a fleeting popularity, but soon proved of dubious tactical value, though its vestigial influence lingered long in naval design.

Submarine mines (originally called "torpedoes") came into common use in the Civil War, and were used effectively by the Confederates to protect their ports and coastal defenses from Union warships. The South and North both used such mines offensively by attaching them to the ends of spars or booms attached to submarines or other small craft. By the end of the century, these spar torpedoes had been transformed by compressed-air self-propulsion into a much more lethal threat as prototypes of the modern torpedo. With this development there came into being in the world's navies the fast but fragile torpedo boat, and close on its heels the larger, faster torpedo-boat destroyer.

In combat the line ahead (ships in single file) was still the normal tactical formation and broadside fire was optimum. But the tacticians were toying with "crossing the T," a new version of raking and of Nelsonian massing of forces, in which (by superior speed) a fleet in single file could concentrate its fire upon the lead ships of the slower line. And an important function of the speedy torpedo boat and the destroyer was the disruption of the hostile line by sinking individual ships.

Naval ordnance, striding from the muzzle-loader to the recoil-controlled breech-loader, dallied for a brief moment with the dynamite gun—hurling its charge by compressed air. By 1898, one vessel of the U.S. Navy—the *Vesuvius*—was armed with this novel piece. However, advances in explosives—TNT and similar substances which could be propelled by conventional gunpowder—put the relatively short-ranged dynamite gun in the discard (although on land in the Spanish-American War one such piece was briefly used). All naval ordnance specialists were simultaneously developing the armor-piercing projectile as the answer to armored warships.

MAJOR EUROPEAN WARS

CRIMEAN WAR, 1853–1856

1853. Prelude. A monkish squabble over jurisdiction within the Holy Places of Turkish-ruled Jerusalem brought France (protector of the Catholics) and Russia (protector of the Orthodox clergy) into diplomatic controversy, with Turkey squeezed between. Czar **Nicholas I** saw an opportunity to dominate Turkey and secure entrance into the Mediterranean through the Turkish Straits. A Russian army began occupation of Turkey's Rumanian principalities (July). France had no intention of letting her rival wax more powerful in the Near East, while England opposed any change in the balance of power. Accordingly, British and French fleets arrived at Constantinople to encourage the Turks.

1853, October 4. Turkey Declares War. A Turkish army under **Omar** Pasha (Croatian-born **Michael Lattas,** a good soldier) crossed the Danube.

1853, November 4. Battle of Oltenitza. Omar defeated the Russians in southern Rumania, near the Danube.

1853, November 30. Destruction of Turkish Flotilla at Sinope (Sinop). Russian Admiral **Paul S. Nakhimov,** with 6 ships of the line, 3 frigates, and several smaller craft, attacked Turkish Admiral **Hussein** Pasha's 7 frigates, 3 corvettes, and 2 small steamers lying in the harbor. The Turkish flotilla was destroyed in a 6-hour engagement, the outnumbered and outgunned Turks fighting to the end. Significant aspect of the encounter was the enormous damage done by the Russian shell guns—a new type of naval ordnance making its first bow in warfare.

1854, January 3. Franco-British Fleet in the Black Sea. Both nations, forgetting momentarily their mutual jealousies and suspicions, then allied themselves with Turkey to protect the Turkish coast and shipping (March 12).

1854, March 20. Russians Cross the Danube. A strong Russian army under Marshal **Ivan Paskievich** invaded Bulgaria.

1854, March 28. British and French Declaration of War. They then concluded a mutual alliance (April 10). A Franco-British expeditionary force moved to Varna (Stalin) to assist in repelling the Russian invasion which had now reached and was besieging Silistria (Silistra). The British frigate *Furious* having been fired on while trying to enter Odessa under a flag of truce (April 16), a Franco-British squadron bombarded the shore batteries, inflicting serious damage.

1854, April 20. Threatened Austrian Intervention. Austria massed an army of 50,000 men in Galicia and Transylvania, after entering into a defensive alliance with Prussia against Russia. With Turkish permission, Austria moved into Turkey's Danube principalities. In face of this threat, Russia abandoned the siege of Silistria (June 9) and later withdrew her forces from the area (August 2), but rejected the joint peace conditions set by England, France, Prussia, and Austria (Vienna Four Points, August 8) that Russia must keep hands off the Ottoman Empire.

Crimea and the Siege of Sevastopol

1854, September. Planned Invasion of the Crimea. The Russian evacuation of the Balkans achieved the principal objective of the allied expeditionary force at Varna, which was now rotting with cholera. But London and Paris decided that Russian power in the Black Sea must be broken by crippling the great naval base at Sevastopol. The expedition was decided upon without any consideration of the magnitude of the task, and without any adequate prior reconnaissance. British Major General **Fitzroy James Henry Somerset, Lord Raglan,** 66, and French Marshal **Armand J. L. de Saint-Arnaud,** 53 (who was already seriously stricken by cholera), commanded jointly.

1854, September 7. Departure from Varna. The allied force was transported to the Crimean Peninsula in a great convoy of 150 warships and transports. Typical of the haphazard conduct of campaign was the fact that not until the convoy lay offshore was any decision made as to the point of debarkation. Equally typical was the fact that no attempt was made by Prince **Alexander Sergeievich Menshikov,** Russian commander in the Crimea, to oppose the landing.

1854, September 13–18. Landing at Old Fort. This was on an open beach with no harbor, some 30 miles north of Sevastopol. Bad weather and the weakened condition of the troops combined to delay the debarkation.

1854, September 19. Advance toward Sevastopol. The expeditionary force—51,000 British, French, and Turkish infantry, 1,000 British cavalry, and 128 guns—moved south, the British on the landward flank. The fleet kept pace along the seacoast.

1854, September 20. Battle of the Alma. Menshikov, with 36,400 men, elected to defend on the bank of the Alma River, his left flank refused out of range of the allied fleet, his right anchored on a hill ridge. The allied attack crossed the river without much difficulty, but the British then found themselves faced by a steep slope, which was carried only after a hard fight. Menshikov then withdrew without molestation. Allied losses (mostly British) were about 3,000 men; Russian, 5,709.

1854, September 25–26. Movements around Sevastopol. The allies were in sight of Sevastopol, whose harbor channel had been blocked by sunken ships, rendering naval cooperation in an assault from the north impossible. Without a base, siege was impractical. The only solution was a flank march around the fortress to the south side, and establishment of bases at the ports of Kamiesch and Balaklava. As the allies, abandoning their line of retreat, made the 15-mile circuit with their flank unmolested, Menshikov left a garrison within the works and wisely marched the remainder of his army north to Bakhchisarai to join Russian reinforcements now moving in. Actually, the opponents marched across one another's front without knowing it. The allied army safely made the circuit and regained contact with the fleet, the British based on Balaklava and the French on Kamiesch.

1854, October 8–16. Siege of Sevastopol Opens. The southern defenses of Sevastopol had not yet been fully completed. An immediate assault might have been successful. Instead, while the British contingent and one French army corps covered the operation from attack by the Russian field army, a siege corps was extemporized and investment began. St. Arnaud died of cholera (September 29) and General **François Certain Canrobert** succeeded to command. By October 17, when the first bombardment opened, Colonel **Frants E. I. Todleben,** the Russian chief engineer, had done an amazing job of fortification. The bombardment and counterbattery fire caused serious losses on both sides, but no permanent damage to the works. The port was blockaded by the fleet of Admiral Sir **Edmund Lyons.**

1854, October 25. Battle of Balaklava. Menshikov's field army attempted to drive between the besieging lines and the British base at Balaklava. A penetration was made and some Turkish guns taken. Russian cavalry attempting to exploit the breakthrough were repelled by the British Heavy Cavalry Brigade and the stand of the 93rd Highlanders in "the thin red line." The Light Cavalry Brigade, through circumstances never satisfactorily explained, now charged the Russian field batteries to their front, riding up a narrow, mile-long valley, exposed at the same time to fire from the captured Turkish guns on their right flank and other Russian guns on their left. They reached the guns, rode through them, clashed with Russian cavalry beyond, and then the survivors rode back through the cross fire of the "Valley of Death" made famous by Tennyson's poem. The charge will stand forever as a monument to gallant soldiers doomed to death by the arrant stupidity of Brigadier General **James Thomas Brudenell, Lord Cardigan,** commanding the brigade, and Major General **G. C. Bingham, Lord Lucan,** commanding the Cavalry Division. The return of the survivors was assisted by the equally gallant charge of the 4th French **Chasseurs d'Afrique,** who rode down part of the flanking Russian artillery. Of 673 mounted officers and men entering the 20-minute-long Light Brigade charge, 247 men and 497 horse were lost. Fitting epitaph was the remark of French General **Pierre F. J. Bosquet,** witnessing the charge: "It is magnificent, but it is not war." The Russians retained possession of the Vorontosov ridge, commanding the Balaklava-Sevastopol road. The allies retained Balaklava.

1854, November 5. Battle of Inkerman. Menshikov again tried to break through between the besieging troops and their field support. The brunt of the action fell on the British, in an all-day struggle during which all coordinate control was lost on both sides. The arrival of Bosquet's French division finally tipped the balance, and Menshikov withdrew, with loss of 12,000 men. The allied loss—mostly British—was 3,300 men.

1854, November–1855, March. Dismal Winter. Theoretically, the allies, with sea communications unhindered, should have had little difficulty in their siege operations, whereas the Russians, although their northern line of communications was open, had a long, tenuous overland supply problem. Actually, the allies were totally unprepared for a winter campaign, while a heavy storm (November 14), which wrecked some 30 transports lying at Balaklava, destroyed most of the existing stores of rations, forage, and clothing. To make matters worse, the Russian field army still sat astride the only paved road from Balaklava to the siege lines. Wagon haulage over the muddy plain was almost impossible. The British troops, without shelter or adequate winter clothing, were also actually semistarved. Cholera raged; men died like flies in shockingly inadequate medical facilities. By February, British effectives were down to 12,000. Canrobert, whose administration was much better handled, had 78,000 men in hand, and took over part of the British sector. But the cable and telegraph were pouring out the grim story as seen by **William Howard Russell,** war correspondent for the London *Times.* An outraged British public forced the fall of **George H. Gordon, Lord Aberdeen**'s government, with immediate remedial results, one of the most important being the establishment of proper medical and hospital facilities under **Florence Nightingale.** Meanwhile, despite serious casualties to the working parties from the allied bombardments, Todleben's incessant activity and engineering genius countered the damage done by the allied guns, and the defensive works grew in strength.

1855, January 26. Arrival of a Sardinian Contingent. These 10,000 troops were commanded by General **Alfonso Ferrero di La Marmora.**

1855, January–February. Improved British Logistical Support. A new road and a railroad over the mud plain linked the Balaklava base to the siege corps.

1855, February 17. Battle of Eupatoria (Yevpatoriya). The Russian field army, now commanded by Prince **Michael Gorchakov** (replacing Menshikov), made a halfhearted attempt to interfere. This was repulsed by the Turks. The siege lines drew closer.

1855, April 8–18. Easter Bombardment. A major part of the Russian defenses was destroyed. Russian troops drawn up to meet an expected assault lost more than 6,000 men. But the attack never came. Allied field commanders and home governments were wrangling via telegraph over conduct of the operations. Canrobert, enraged by the interference, resigned his command. His successor, General **Aimable Jean Jacques Pélissier,** a veteran of the Algerian wars like his predecessor, brought new vigor to the allied operations.

1855, May 24. Capture of Kerch. A well-handled joint expedition cleared the Sea of Azov (Azovskoe More) and severed Russian communications with the interior.

1855, June 7. Allied Assault. Part of the Russian outer defenses were seized; there were 8,500 Russian casualties and about 6,900 allied.

1855, June 17–18. Renewed Allied Assault. The objectives were two principal Russian strong points, the **Malakoff** and the **Redan.** Lack of coordination brought utter failure. The French attack on the Malakoff dwindled into an indecisive fire fight, while the British assault on the Redan was caught in the crossfire of 100 heavy guns and thrown back with great loss. The allies lost 4,000 men in this effort, the Russians 5,400. Raglan, heartbroken, died 10 days later, General Sir **James Simpson** succeeding him.

1855, July–August. Attrition. Russian losses through bombardment were draining Sevastopol's strength—some 350 a day during July. The Russian field army decided to make one final effort to break through the allied curtain between Balaklava and the fortress.

1855, August 16. Battle of the Traktir Ridge. Two corps of Gorchakov's army were thrown against some 37,000 French and Sardinian troops on the height above the Chernaya River. A 5-hour combat ended in Russian defeat, ending the last hope for relieving Sevastopol, despite the dogged determination of the Russian infantry. Russian losses were 3,229 dead and some 5,000 wounded. The allies lost about 1,700 killed and wounded.

1855, September 8. Storming of the Malakoff. The one perfectly planned and executed operation of the war. After an intense bombardment (September 5–8) softened the defenses, the French launched a long-prepared mass assault by Bosquet's entire corps. Meticulous attention to detail included a last-minute check by staff officers to ensure that each of the 3 assaulting columns would have easy egress from the trenches, now only 30 yards from the Russian strong point. To preserve secrecy, no signal was given for the assault. Synchronization of watches—for the first time, perhaps, in military history—governed the move. On the stroke of noon the corps surged forward, each column led by its commanding general, while Bosquet established his command post on the outermost French trench. The assault gained the outer wall and swept into the inner defenses, where the Russians disputed every casemate and traverse in hand-to-hand combat. By nightfall the Malakoff was safely in French hands. A simultaneous British assault on the Redan was thrown back, but from the Malakoff the French now turned their fire on the Russians in the Redan and drove them out with heavy loss. That night Gorchakov evacuated Sevastopol, after blowing up the remainder of the fortifications. Next day the allies occupied the city. In all, the allies lost more than 10,000 casualties in this final assault, the Russians 13,000.

1855, October 16. First Appearance of Ironclad Warships. Bombardment of Kinburn, at the mouth of the Bug River, was anticlimactic, but 3 French steam floating batteries made history, demolishing heavy masonry works while Russian round shot and shell spent themselves harmlessly on their iron plates at ranges of 1,000 yards or less.

The Caucasus Front, 1854–1855

Severe but indecisive fighting between Turks and Russians took place in the Caucasus and Transcaucasus. The principal operation of note was the **Siege of Kars** by Russian General **Michael Muraviev.** The Turkish garrison, commanded by Sir **William Fenwick Williams** (Williams Pasha), British commissioner and a lieutenant general in the Turkish Army, repelled a savage Russian assault (September 29, 1855). Omar Pasha, after the fall of Sevastopol, took a force of 15,000 men to the relief of Kars, but the fortress succumbed to starvation and disease before his arrival, Williams surrendering (November 26, 1855).

Naval Operations in the Baltic

1854, August 7–16. Landing on the Alands. A French squadron landed 10,000 men under General **Achille Baraguay d'Hilliers** at Bomarsund, Aland Islands. After an 8-day siege, during which naval gunfire from Sir Charles Napier's allied fleet took joint part, the 2,400-man garrison surrendered and the fortress was destroyed.

1855, August 7–11. Bombardment of Sveaborg. A Franco-British fleet, after demonstrating before the fortress of Kronstadt (Kronshtadt) bombarded Sveaborg (fortress in Helsinki harbor) without success.

1856, February 1. Preliminary Peace Conditions. Agreed to at Vienna. Final ratification took place at the Congress of Paris (February 28–March 30).

COMMENT. *The outstanding aspect of the war was its abysmal mismanagement on both sides, featuring indifference in governments and senility and incompetence on the part of field commanders. Russia, fighting England, France, Turkey, and Sardinia, lost —from all causes—some 256,000 men. The allies lost about 252,600. Actual Russian battle deaths were an estimated 128,700; those of the allies, 70,000. Disease—mainly cholera —accounted for the rest. The combatants themselves displayed raw courage under great handicaps. Revolutionary was the awakening of national interest in the welfare of the troops, particularly so in Great Britain, where war correspondents' accounts spread the news of shocking conditions on the fighting front.*

WAR OF AUSTRIA WITH FRANCE AND PIEDMONT, 1859

1859, March 9. Piedmont (Kingdom of Sardinia) Mobilizes. King **Victor Emmanuel II** and his prime minister, Count **Camillo Benso di Cavour,** saw an opportunity to renew the struggle for Italian independence (see p. 773). They had been assured, by a secret treaty, of French support in a war to expel Austria from north Italy. Austria also mobilized (April 9).

1859, April 23. Austrian Ultimatum. Immediate Piedmontese demobilization was demanded. This provided France an excuse to intervene, and Piedmont rejected the ultimatum.

1859, April 29. Austrian Invasion of Piedmont. The half-hearted movements of General Count **Franz Gyulai** gave time for French troops to arrive.

1859, May 30. Battle of Palestro. This was a Piedmontese victory. The allied forces, under personal command of **Napoleon III,** then invaded Lombardy.

1859, June 4. Battle of Magenta. In a series of blundering meeting engagements, the inept commanders on both sides managed to engage portions of their respective commands: 54,000 French against 58,000 Austrians. The *élan* of the French troops, despite the stupidity of command, brought them victory. French losses were 4,000 killed and wounded and 600 missing. The Austrians lost 5,700 killed and wounded and 4,500 missing. Gyulai retired toward the protection of the famous Quadrilateral: the fortified cities of Mantua, Peschiera, Verona, and Legnago. Napoleon and King **Victor Emmanuel** entered Milan in triumph (June 8).

1859, June 24. Battle of Solferino. Austrian Emperor **Franz Josef,** dismissing Gyulai, assumed personal command and moved to meet the Franco-Piedmontese armies. Both sides were approximately equal in number—about 160,000 strong. Again both blundered into a series of meeting engagements along the Mincio River in which the respective high commands lost all control of their forces. Again the spirit of the French soldiery and the vigor of individual corps commanders—French generals **Marie E. P. M. de MacMahon,** François C. Canrobert, **Adolphe Niel,** and Achille Baraguay d'Hilliers—decided the issue after a sanguinary all-day battle. The Austrian army was saved from total rout by the dogged rear-guard action of General **Ludwig A. von Benedek.** Allied losses totaled 17,191 (5,521 Piedmontese); Austrian, 22,000.

1859, July 11. Conference of Villafranca. Napoleon and Franz Josef agreed that most of Lombardy (save for the fortress cities of Mantua and Peschiera) should go to Piedmont. Austria was to keep Venetia, protected by the Quadrilateral. This was ratified by the **Treaty of Zurich** (November 10). Most Italians, who wanted Venetia under Italian control, were enraged. The entire Italian peninsula continued in revolution, which gradually coalesced about Piedmont (see p. 841).

AUSTRO-PRUSSIAN (SEVEN WEEKS') WAR, 1866

1866, June 14. Austrian Denunciation of Prussian Power Politics. At the Frankfurt Diet, Austria condemned Prussia's occupation of Holstein (see p. 771) and Chancellor **Otto von Bismarck**'s secret treaty with France. Most German states —including Bavaria, Saxony, and Hanover—concurred. Bismarck, who had concluded (April 8) an offensive-defensive treaty with Italy, dissolved the Germanic Confederation and mobilized for immediate war against Austria and her south German supporting states. Italy declared war on Austria (see p. 842 for operations).

1866, June 16. Von Moltke Strikes. Utilizing the railway net to fullest capacity, Moltke caught his opponents off balance. General **Vogel von Falkenstein** with some 50,000 men entered Hanover on the west, while Prussian Crown Prince **Friedrich Wilhelm**'s Second Army (near Landeshut), Prince **Friedrich Karl**'s First Army (near Görlitz) and General **Karl E. Herwarth**

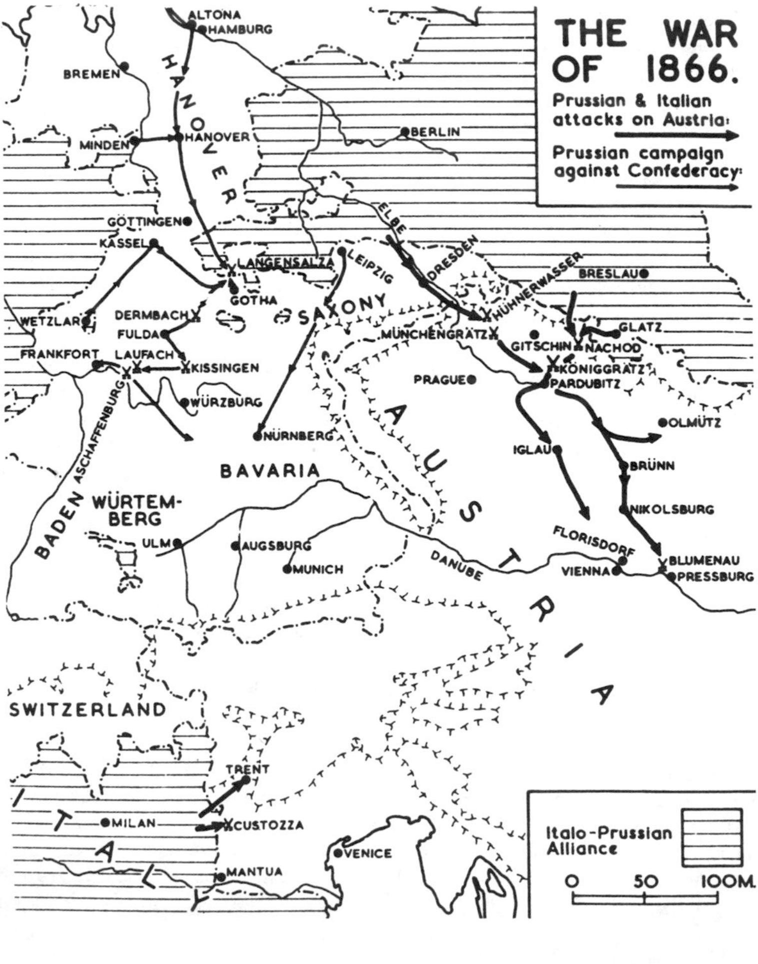

von Bittenfeld's Army of the Elbe (near Torgau) moved south through Silesia and Saxony. Moltke's scheme was to advance on the widest of fronts and concentrate on the battlefield, subordinates being given the greatest latitude in initiative, provided it be offensive. The strategy effected surprise, but had the drawback of a succession of meeting engagements where reinforcements built up piecemeal, moving to the sound of the guns.

1866, June 27–29. Battle of Langensalza. In western Germany, General **Alexander von Arentschildt**'s Hanoverian army, repelling an attack by one of Falkenstein's widespread corps, found itself surrounded by Prussian battlefield concentration and was forced to surrender. Meanwhile, to the southeast, the vital contest of the war was about to take place.

1866, June–July. Converging in Bohemia. Moltke's intelligence reports indicated Austrian intention to concentrate northwest of Olmütz (Olomouc). His eastern armies, nominally under the over-all command of King **Wilhelm I,** converged on Gitschin (Jičin). The Army of the Elbe occupied Dresden (June 19), then advanced to unite with the First Army in the Bohemian mountain passes. The two armies then brushed back advance Austrian elements and retreating Saxons first at **Münchengrätz** (June 27) then at **Gitschin** (June 29). The Second Army engaged in 2 sharp encounters at **Trautenau** (Trutnov) and **Nachod** (both June 27) and halted just east of Gitschin (June 30). General von Benedek, commanding the Austrians, and endeavoring to concentrate along the upper Elbe, north of Königgrätz (Hradec Králové), was more concerned with subsistence than with combat. Moltke, who was in telegraphic touch with all his armies, sought for a Cannae (see p. 65). The Army of the Elbe was ordered to circle to the south and then attack north. The First Army would attack due east, while the Second Army, driving south down the Elbe Valley, would seal the rest of the circle. It did not work out quite that way. The converging Prussian armies totaled about 220,000 men; Benedek's army included 190,000 Austrians and 25,000 Saxons.

Battle of Königgrätz (or Sadowa), July 3, 1866

In a driving rain, the Elbe and First Armies attacked at dawn, but through a telegraphic failure the Second Army had not received Moltke's first attack order and did not move. Overeager, the Elbe Army did not extend its front sufficiently, and its advance crossed the path of the First Army. The confused Prussians were met by a savage Austrian counterattack and massed artillery fire. By 11 A.M. the Prussian advance had been checked and their reserves drawn into what had now become a densely packed frontal attack. Had the Austrians pressed home a cavalry charge at this time, the Prussians might have been driven from the field. But Benedek held his cavalry immobile.

Meanwhile, after a courier had galloped 20 miles to deliver the king's (really Moltke's) peremptory order to the crown prince, the Second Army moved up. At 2:30 P.M. its attack hit the Austrian northern sector, and at the same time the Prussian Guard reserve artillery, pushed forward brilliantly by Prince **Kraft zu Hohenlohe-Ingelfingen,** opened a devastating fire into the Austrian center. The superiority of the Prussian breech-loading needle rifle over the Austrian muzzle-loading rifle musket gave Moltke's infantry a decisive fire superiority. The entire situation changed. Benedek began a dogged withdrawal, covered by his artillery. The Austrians were decisively defeated, but not routed. Prussian losses were nearly 10,000 men; the Austrians lost 45,000, including 20,000 prisoners. Despite the Prussian victory, Königgrätz stands as an example of the dangers to be expected in a battlefield concentration, where success is dependent upon delicate coordination and timing.

1866, July 5. French Mediation. Napoleon III, who had expected both contestants to wear themselves out in a long-drawn-out campaign, now offered mediation, which Bismarck accepted—on his own terms.

1866, August 23. Treaty of Prague. Austria was excluded from other German affairs; the German states north of the Main River would form a North German Confederation under Prussian leadership, the South German states, remaining independent, could form a separate confederation.

FRANCO-PRUSSIAN WAR, 1870–1871

Bismarck's diplomatic rally of the north German states into the anti-French North German Confederation was unexpected by Napoleon III. A Prussian effort to place a Hohenzollern prince on the Spanish throne in mid-1870 threatened France with the possibility of a 2-front war. Napoleon, thinking the French Army invincible, decided to precipitate a war he believed inevitable.

1870, July 15. French Declare War. Immediate mobilization followed in both countries. German mobilization and troop concentrations followed a well-directed plan, using the railway net to the full. French mobilization was haphazard and incomplete.

1870, July 16–17. South German States Join Coalition against France. Bavaria, Baden, and Württemberg began mobilization.

1870, July 31. Prussian Concentration and Plan. Three well-equipped German armies—380,000 men—were concentrated on the frontier west of the Rhine: the First, 60,000, under General **Karl F. von Steinmetz,** between Trier and Saarbrücken; the Second, 175,000, under Prince Friedrich Karl, between Bingen and Mannheim; the Third, 145,000, under Crown Prince Friedrich Wilhelm, between Landau and Germersheim. Nominally commanded by King Wilhelm I, the actual direction was that of General Moltke and his efficient general staff. Prussian intelligence had determined the complete French order of battle. The objective was the destruction of the French armies in the field, to be followed by capture of Paris. An additional 95,000 troops were held back until it was certain that Austria would not intervene.

1870, July 31. French Concentration and Plan. By contrast, the French, some 224,000 men in 8 separate army corps, lay behind the frontier from Thionville to Strasbourg and echeloned back to the fortress line Metz-Nancy-Belfort. Transport was improvised, munitions scanty, units below war strength. Napoleon III, at Metz with his incompetent War Minister Marshal **Edmond Leboeuf,** was in command. The only plan was the cry of the French populace: "On to Berlin!" French intelligence was nonexistent. Napoleon ordered a general advance.

1870, August 2. Battle of Saarbrücken. This skirmish between units of the German First Army and French II Corps alerted the French only to the fact that the enemy was near. Napoleon belatedly directed the grouping of his troops in 2 armies: the Army of Alsace (consisting of the 3 southernmost corps under Marshal MacMahon) and the Army of Lorraine (the remaining 5 corps under Marshal **Achille F. Bazaine**). No army staffs existed; the 2 commanders had to function with their own individual corps staffs.

1870, August 4. Battle of Weissenburg. The crown prince's army, advancing in 4 columns, surprised the leading division of MacMahon's corps in early morning on the Lauter River. The other 2 corps had not yet joined him, although 1 division came up during the day. After a sharp action in which the badly outnumbered French lost 1,600 men killed and wounded and 700 prisoners, against German casualties of 1,550. MacMahon pulled back and concentrated defensively on a wooded plateau fronting on the Lauter.

1870, August 6. Battle of Fröschwiller (Wörth). A German reconnaissance in force was repulsed by MacMahon's right. The crown prince built up his strength, overlapping both French flanks, with the main effort against the right, supported by

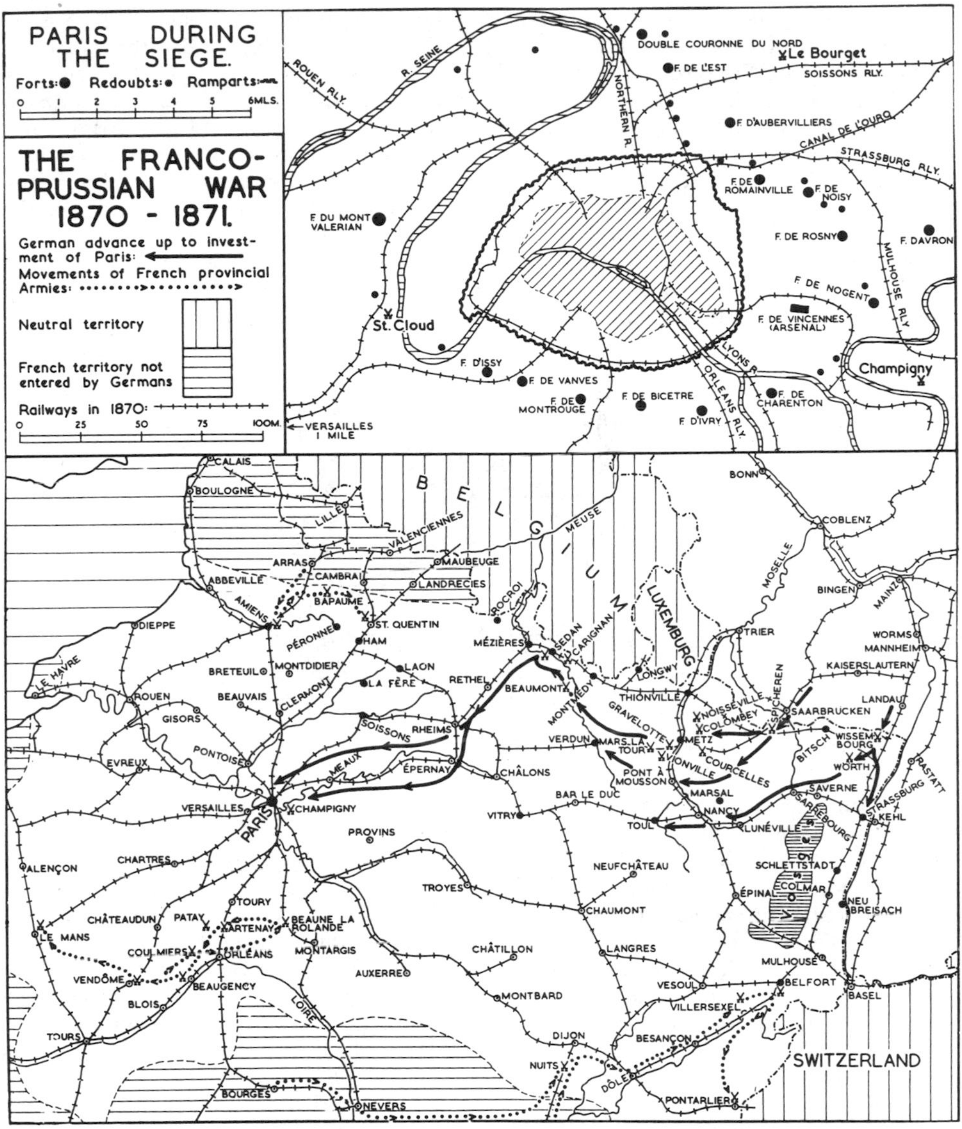

the fire of 150 guns. MacMahon sacrificed his cavalry in gallant, suicidal charges, but was unable to halt the envelopment. He fell back on Fröschwiller, covered by his reserve artillery. There he clung until nightfall, then retreated without interference to Châlons-sur-Marne (August 7–14). Of 125,000 men and 312 guns engaged, German losses amounted to 8,200 killed and wounded and 1,373 missing. The French, of 46,500 men and 119 guns engaged, lost 10,760 killed and wounded and 6,200 prisoners. The Vosges barrier had been pierced, the road to Paris opened. The crown prince's army marched methodically toward the Meuse. The pattern of tactical operation had been set; the French chassepot rifle was superior to the needle gun in accuracy and volume of fire, but the French artillery, thanks to a mistaken reliance on machine guns (mitrailleuses) in place of cannon (about one-fourth of French artillery pieces were mitrailleuses), was far inferior to the German.

1870, August 6. Battle of Spichern. The German First and Second Armies moved into Lorraine, where Bazaine's army was spread in 3 areas, out of mutual supporting distance. Attacked by Steinmetz and a corps of Friedrich Karl's army, General **Charles Auguste Frossard**'s II Corps held the heights of Spichern, southeast of Saarbrücken, for an entire day until threatened by envelopment on both flanks as the German piecemeal attack gradually built up. Bazaine made no attempt to reinforce him. French losses, of 29,980 men engaged, were 1,982 killed and wounded and 1,096 missing. The Germans, who had put 45,000 men into action, lost 4,491 killed and wounded and 372 missing. There was no pursuit by the exhausted Germans.

1870, August 6–15. German Pursuit. Moltke, sending the Third Army after MacMahon, followed hard on Bazaine's trail with the First and Second Armies, on the widest of fronts. The rapidity of the German advance detachments and the boldness of their operations gave the French no respite. The Prussian sweep was a strategic penetration between the two French armies, threatening Bazaine's line of communications.

Mitrailleuse

1870, August 12. Napoleon Relinquishes Command. Shaken by these defeats, he surrendered all initiative and betook himself to Verdun. Leboeuf was relieved, General **Charles G. M. Cousin-Montauban,** Count of Palikao, replacing him. Bazaine, put in full command of a reorganized Army of the Rhine, fell back on the fortress of Metz, while MacMahon regrouped at Châlons.

1870, August 15. Battle of Borny. The Prussian First Army forced Bazaine to retire across the Moselle. He hoped to gain Verdun and a juncture with MacMahon. But the German Second Army, crossing at Pont-à-Mousson, cut him off. Still hoping to break out, Bazaine concentrated between the Orne and the Moselle, facing south with his left resting on Metz.

1870, August 16. Battles of Mars-la-Tour, Vionville, and Rezonville. Friedrich Karl, moving north at dawn across the Verdun-Metz highway, collided with the French. His leading corps at once attacked, while the remainder of the army hurried to the sound of the guns. A French cavalry charge was repulsed with much loss. The German offensive built up in the usual German pattern of concentration on the battlefield, and a piecemeal engagement developed into a full-blown battle. Successive cavalry charges on both sides ended in a cavalry duel in the afternoon; great masses of horsemen mingled in an almost aimless melee for nearly an hour until both sides broke off in exhaustion. Friedrich Karl finally assaulted along his entire front, pushing into Rezonville. Actually, the combat—or series of combats—was a drawn battle, for both sides bivouacked on the field after the hardest-fought engagement of the entire war. German losses were some 17,000; the French lost more than 16,000. Next day Bazaine, giving up hope for a breakout, retired unmolested on Metz, pivoting about his left flank, and his army of 115,000 men took up a new position, some 6 miles long, facing west on a ridge between the Moselle and the Orne. The bulk of the German armies—some 200,000 men, now between Bazaine and Paris—began movement into this area, only a reinforced corps remaining in observation east of Metz.

1870, August 18. Battle of Gravelotte-St. Privat. Moltke, who had taken personal charge of operations, attacked Bazaine, making his main effort on his own left with the Second Army. The walled village of **St. Privat la Montaigne** became the key point of combat. Friedrich Karl squandered the Prussian Guard in a series of charges against the hamlet, which was defended by Marshal Canrobert's VI Corps. From early morning until dusk, Canrobert's 23,000 men held out against 100,000 assailants, while Bazaine ignored his requests for reinforcement. Then a Saxon corps reached Roncourt, to the north, outflanking the French and threatening their rear. After a house-to-house combat through the village, Canrobert pulled the remnants of his troops back into Metz. Meanwhile, on the German right, an almost independent combat was fought. Two German corps battered their way east of Gravelotte, then became entangled in a ravine beyond. Attempts at disengagement turned into panic, and hordes of refugees poured west through Gravelotte. A brilliant French counterattack was checked only by Hohenlohe-Ingelfingen's artillery and the personal efforts of Moltke, who led reinforcements and averted disaster. Not until midnight, when news of the success at St. Privat reached Moltke, were the Germans sure of victory. Had Bazaine made a general counterattack with the forces still at his disposal, he might have broken free. Instead, he remained passive, relinquishing all control to his corps commanders. Moltke, after waiting for a counterattack which never came, proceeded to seal him within his perimeter.

1870, August 21–28. Advance of MacMahon. MacMahon, meanwhile, responding to the frantic appeal of the government, moved out of Châlons with 120,000 men and 393 guns to the relief of Bazaine, his strength and movements widely advertised in the press. Napoleon III accompanied him. MacMahon's stupid choice of a northerly route invited a turning movement. Moltke accepted. While the German First Army and part of the Second—all under Friedrich Karl—invested Metz, the remainder of the Second Army—called the Army of the Meuse, under Crown Prince **Albert** of Saxony—struck west to cooperate with Friedrich Wilhelm, whose Third Army was driving rapidly through the Argonne Forest to bar MacMahon's advance.

1870, August 29–31. Engagements on the Meuse. MacMahon threw part of his army across the Meuse at Douzy. The Prussian Army of the Meuse, advancing on both sides of the river, forced him northward toward Sedan after sharp clashes at **Nouart** (August 29) and **Beaumont** (August 30). Another clash at **Bazeilles** (August 31), where MacMahon was wounded, forced the French into a bend of the river at Sedan itself. Again the Prussians lay between a French army and Paris. The crown prince, arriving from the southeast through Wadlincourt and Donchery on the left bank of the Meuse, crossed the river on ponton bridges and moved into the plain north of Sedan, completing the envelopment of the French army. Meanwhile, Bazaine's halfhearted attempt to break out of Metz was repulsed by Friedrich Karl (August 31).

1870, September 1. Battle of Sedan. General **Auguste Ducrot,** replacing MacMahon in command, found himself with his back to the Belgian frontier, while nearly 200,000 German troops under Moltke pressed in on the south, west, and north. In a desperate attempt to break out, the French cavalry was shattered by German infantry fire, while 426 German guns, ranged in a semicircle on the heights above Sedan, raked the French positions in a day-long bombardment. German cavalry charges were repelled in turn by the French machine guns (mitrailleuses). Thwarted in his northwesterly drive, Ducrot in the afternoon attempted a southerly assault. This was repulsed. By 5 P.M. the day was lost; the French army crowded into the fortress and town, which was pummeled by devastating artillery fire. General **Emmanuel F. de Wimpffen,** who had succeeded to command, urged the emperor to place himself at the head of his troops and make one last charge. Napoleon, refusing to have any more of his men sacrificed, now drove out under a white flag and surrendered as an individual to the King of Prussia. Wimpffen then surrendered the army: 83,000 men and 449 guns. French losses were 17,000; German, 9,000.

1870, September. German Advance on Paris. The war, it seemed, was over. Half of France's regular organized field forces had been captured, the other half immured in Metz. All that remained were the other fortresses studded along the eastern frontier—Strasbourg, Verdun, and Belfort being the most important. While German reinforcements methodically went about reducing these, and the First and Second Armies tightened their iron ring about Bazaine in Metz, the Third Army and the Army of the Meuse rolled on toward Paris. But as they marched, all France flamed in an amazing demonstration of patriotic resiliency.

1870, September 4. The Third Republic. In Paris the empire toppled in popular uprising. A provisional government rose, with **Léon Gambetta** its torchbearer and General **Louis Jules Trochu** its president. Trochu, as military governor of the city, manned its forts with 120,000 hastily recruited soldiers (including many veterans, reservists, and 20,000 regular marine infantry), 80,000 *gardes mobiles* (untrained recruits under 30) and 300,000 highly volatile and anarchistic-minded *gardes nationales* (recruits between 30 and 50).

1870, September 19. Siege of Paris Begins. Moltke had no intention of squandering his troops in assaults upon the deep-sited and massive system of fortifications ringing the city in 2 belts. Elaborate siege works sealed Paris, King Wilhelm established his headquarters at Versailles, and Moltke waited for starvation to bring the great metropolis into his hands. Much to his astonishment, he found his line of communications harassed by *francs-tireurs* (guerrillas) and a new French army gathering in the Loire Valley. Gambetta, escaping from Paris by balloon—the sole link with the outside world—organized nationwide resistance from Tours (October 11), where the provisional government functioned. Moltke now found himself concurrently engaged in 2 major sieges, a field campaign, and a constant guerrilla warfare along a long line of communications—severely straining the efficient German war machine.

1870, October 27. Fall of Metz. Bazaine's army of 173,000 men surrendered after a 54-day siege; it lost more through the vacillation of its commander and by starvation than by force of arms. After the war Bazaine was court-martialed, convicted of treason, and imprisoned.

1870, October–December. French Initiative. Moltke at once utilized the besieging veterans in what had now become a large-scale operation in the Loire and Sarthe valleys as the inexperienced French Army of the Loire made several gallant but unsuccessful attempts to move to the relief of Paris. Fighting continued through the winter, marked also by harsh treatment of the guerrillas on the German line of communications.

1870, October–December. Operations around Paris. Despite famine, Trochu's forces harassed the besiegers. The task was complicated by the mutinous behavior of the *gardes nationales,* whose revolt (October 31) seriously compromised the defense. Two major sorties (November 29–30, December 21) were repulsed after some initial success.

1870, November 9. Battle of Coulmiers. A French victory over a Bavarian corps caused German withdrawal from Orléans, but the French advance was then checked by Prussian reinforcements.

1870, December 2–4. Battle of Orléans. Two days of heavy fighting between General **Louis J. B. d'Aurelle de Paladines'** French Army of the Loire and the army of Friedrich Karl ended with the unwise division of the French forces and reoccupation of Orléans by the Germans. While General **Charles D. S. Bourbaki** hurried to the east to assist the garrison of Belfort, which was under German investment, General **Antoine E. A. Chanzy** with the remainder of the Army of the Loire kept up a constant struggle against much superior force.

1871, January 5. Commencement of Bombardment of Paris. The German shelling caused more resentment than damage, while the war in the provinces continued unabated.

1871, January. Campaign in the North. General **Louis L. C. Faidherbe,** with mixed success, had opposed German efforts to pacify northern France in the **Battle of the Hallue** (December 23). He fought another drawn battle with General **August Karl von Goeben** at **Bapaume**

(January 2–3). At the **Battle of St.-Quentin,** however, he was severely defeated by Goeben (January 19). Faidherbe withdrew in good order and repulsed German pursuit. He immediately prepared to renew his offensive, adding to the alarm of the Germans, now seriously overextended by the unexpectedly effective French resistance in all of the outlying provinces.

Krupp gun

1871, January 10–12. Battle of Le Mans. In the Loire Valley, the Germans repulsed a desperate offensive effort by Chanzy. The untrustworthiness of his troops forced Chanzy to retreat to the west, but he still threatened the German hold on the Loire.

1871, January 15–17. Battle of Belfort. In the east, Belfort was the only important French frontier fortress still resisting. Bourbaki with a woefully inexperienced army of 150,000 men threw General **Karl Wilhelm F. A. L. Werder,** with 60,000 German besiegers, onto the defensive. Bourbaki attacked Werder's positions on the Lisaine River, within cannon shot of the fortress. Thanks to his own ineptness and that of **Giuseppe Garibaldi** (a volunteer fighting for France), Bourbaki was defeated after 3 days of furious fighting. German losses were nearly 1,900, French more than 6,000. Bourbaki failed in attempted suicide and was succeeded by General **Justin Clinchant.** With the arrival of a German reinforcing army under General **Edwin von Manteuffel,** Clinchant found himself pinned between the 2 German armies, with the Swiss frontier at his back. With 83,000 men he moved into Switzerland and hospitable interment at Pontarlier (February 1).

1871, January 26. Armistice at Paris. A third and final sortie of the Paris garrison had been decisively thrown back when the *gardes nationales* treacherously fired at their comrades (January 19). With all hope lost and the population on the verge of starvation, Trochu obtained an armistice.

1871, January 28. Convention of Versailles; Capitulation of Paris. All French regular troops of the garrison, and the *gardes mobiles,* became prisoners of war; the forts around the city were occupied by the Germans. At French request—unwisely, as it turned out—the terms did not include disarmament of the *gardes nationales,* who were supposed to become a police force to control the restive population of Paris. The victors marched triumphantly into the city (March 1).

1871, January–February. Belfort the Invincible. Colonel **Pierre M. P. A. Denfert-Rochereau,** commanding the fortress, had resisted siege since November 3, 1870. An engineer officer who had been in command of the ancient fortress for 6 years, he utilized the existing works, extended an outer line of resistance, and with a garrison of some 17,600 men, mainly *gardes mobiles* and *gardes nationales,* carried on an elastic defense. Not until late January were the Germans established within cannon range of the inner fortress. Even then, their progress was slow. Only upon an imperative order from the French General Assembly at Bordeaux (February 15) did Denfert-Rochereau capitulate. The garrison marched out with the honors of war—under arms, colors flying—with all their baggage and mobile equipment. In a siege of 105 days, French losses were some 4,800, while 336 of the townsfolk had been killed by bombardment. German losses were about 2,000. The defense of Belfort was an epic of the French Army.

1871, May 10. Treaty of Frankfurt. France agreed to cede Alsace and northwestern Lorraine to Germany, and to pay an indemnity of 5 billion francs ($1 billion); a German army of occupation was to remain in France until the indemnity was paid.

WESTERN AND CENTRAL EUROPE

BRITISH ISLES

Great Britain's wars during the period took place overseas; they are noted in the regions directly concerned. Except for the Crimean War (see p. 825) and the Boer War (see p. 852), both of which demanded British man power and logistical support for their successful prosecution, the economy of the British Isles was hardly disturbed. However, British diplomacy and British objectives to maintain an equilibrium in the balance of power were directly concerned in almost every conflict which occurred.

THE LOW COUNTRIES

Neither Belgium nor the Netherlands was directly involved in warfare. Both nations successfully maintained their neutrality.

FRANCE

1851, December 2–4. Coup d'État. President (Prince) Napoleon Bonaparte seized control of Paris with army support. A brief republican uprising was suppressed in the "massacre of the boulevards." Napoleon seized dictatorial powers.

1852, December 2. Accession of Napoleon III. Establishment of the Second Empire brought a resurgence of Napoleonic militaristic spirit.

1854. Crimean War. (See p. 825.)

1859. War of France and Piedmont against Austria. (See p. 829.)

1861–1867. Mexican Expedition. (See p. 909.)

1870–1871. Franco-Prussian War. (See p. 832.)

The Paris Commune, 1871

1871, March 18–May 28. Reign of Terror in Paris. The *gardes nationales* overthrew municipal government and proclaimed the city a free town. Pillage and murder were widespread. The National Assembly fled to Versailles with the disarmed regular troops, and the metropolis was given up to the ravages of the mob. Not until the armies of Sedan and Metz—captured in the Franco-Prussian War (see p. 835 and p. 836)—returned to Versailles and had been rearmed was remedial action possible. Under Marshal MacMahon, the Versailles troops went into action (April 2) from Fort Valerian on the left bank of the Seine. The Communards were swept progressively from the forts they held. The German army of occupation observed without interference.

1871, May 21–28. The Bloody Week. Entering Paris itself, the government troops fought the rebels from street to street, from barricade to barricade. Ruthlessly, as the troops advanced, the Communards murdered hostages they had held, among them the Archbishop of Paris. They burned the Hôtel de Ville and other prominent buildings and attempted to blow up the cathedral of Notre Dame and the Panthéon. The government troops were equally ruthless in suppressing the revolt. An estimated 20,000 Parisians were fusilladed in the grim but not unexpected reprisals.

1873, September 16. German Evacuation. Payment of the war indemnity ended German occupation.

1873–1895. Indochina Expansion. For extension of the French colonial empire in the Far East, see p. 861.

1881. Occupation of Tunis. This was the most significant step of continuing French expansion in Africa.

1886–1889. The Boulanger Crisis. The threatened overthrow of the government by General **Georges Boulanger** never materialized, but widened the existing social fissures in France and in her army.

1894–1906. The Dreyfus Affair. Captain **Alfred Dreyfus,** a Jew, was accused and convicted of treason for espionage actually done by a fellow member of the general staff, Major Count **Charles Walsin-Esterhazy.** When the true facts were discovered, they were suppressed by the aristocratic faction in the army. Finally, thanks largely to the eloquence of **Émile Zola,** the true facts resulted in Dreyfus' exoneration and release from Devil's Island. The French army was almost torn apart in the violent and bitter controversy.

SPAIN

Internal Disorders

1854, July. Revolution. Generals **Leopoldo O'Donnell** and **Baldomero Espartero** overthrew the government of Queen-Mother **Christina,** who was forced to leave Spain. There followed 14 insurrection-wracked years.

1868, September 18. Revolution. The scandalous and despotic reign of Queen **Isabella II** prompted another uprising, led by Admiral **Juan B. Topete.** The rebel army, commanded by General **Francisco Serrano,** defeated loyal troops at **Alcolea** (near Córdova). The queen, fleeing, was formally deposed. The nation seethed in semianarchy while a military junta headed by Generals Serrano and **Juan Prim** attempted to keep order.

1869, February. Meeting of a Constituent Cortes. The delegates voted for continuation of a monarchy. The throne was offered to a number of European royalty, who declined. Germany's efforts to place Prince **Leopold of Hohenzollern-Sigmaringen** on the Spanish throne helped to spark the Franco-Prussian War (see p. 832).

1871–1873. Amedeo I. The Duke of Aosta accepted the crown, but abdicated when the Spanish people refused to acknowledge his rule.

1873–1876. Renewed Carlist War. (See p. 770.) The nation was again torn by civil war, fought with extreme brutality.

1873–1874. Republican Proclamation. The **First Spanish Republic** was proclaimed by the radicals, only to collapse. Serrano returned to power. The Carlist disorders continued.

1874, November 24. Accession of Alfonso XII. The son of Isabella was placed on the throne through a military coup, and a constitutional monarchy was established.

1876, February. Flight of Don Carlos. Spain slowly returned to peace.

External Troubles

1859–1860. War with Morocco. Incidents along the frontiers of Spain's Ceuta enclave caused Spain to declare war on Morocco (1859, October). A Spanish army occupied Tetuan (1860, February). Under British pressure peace was restored (April), with Spain expanding its Ceuta enclave, receiving an indemnity, and gaining vague rights on Morocco's Atlantic coast which eventually became the Ifni enclave.

1861–1862. Intervention in Mexico. (See p. 909.)

1861–1864. Unsuccessful Annexation of Santo Domingo. (See p. 914.)

1864–1865. War with Peru. (**See p. 912.**)

1865–1866. War with Chile. (**See p. 912.**)

1895–1898. Cuban Revolution. This culmination of decades of unrest led directly to the **Spanish-American War** (see p. 907) and Spain's loss of Cuba, Puerto Rico, and the Philippine Islands.

PRUSSIA AND GERMANY

1850–1871. Unification of Germany. Powerful economic, political, and cultural forces within fractionated Germany had long been working toward unification. Realization of this dream of most Germans had been greatly hampered by the polarization of the many petty, jealous German states around the rival powers of Austria-Hungary, Prussia, and neighboring France. The accomplishment of unification, and the resultant emergence of the German Empire, were finally brought about primarily by the joint efforts of 2 Prussian aristocrats: politician Count Otto von Bismarck, chancellor of Prussia, and General Helmuth C. B. von Moltke, chief of the Prussian general staff. Bismarck's careful but bold machinations brought about 3 wars, which were efficiently implemented through the military genius of Moltke. Together, with Bismarck calling the tune, they exemplified Clausewitz' dictum that war is the extension of diplomacy.

Schleswig-Holstein War, 1864

Prussia, with Austria as a somewhat reluctant ally, settled by force the question of Schleswig-Holstein, which had long vexed the great powers (see p. 771).

1864, February 1. Invasion of Denmark. Prussian troops under Prince Friedrich Karl, with some Austrian assistance, swept northward through Schleswig-Holstein. The only major Austrian participation in the war was by the small naval squadron of Admiral **Wilhelm von Tegetthoff,** which broke a Danish blockade of the Elbe and Weser rivers.

1864, March 15–April 17. Siege of Dybböl. Friedrich Karl invested the Danish fortress, finally capturing it by assault. Danish losses were 1,800 killed and wounded and 3,400 prisoners. German losses were negligible. An amphibious assault then captured the island of Als.

1864, April 25–June 25. Truce. British efforts to bring about peace were foiled by Bismarck.

1864, June 26. Renewed Invasion of Denmark.

1864, August 1. Denmark Sues for Peace. She renounced her right to the disputed provinces to Prussia and Austria.

1864, October 30. Treaty of Vienna. This ratified the August agreement.

1865–1866. Friction between Austria and Prussia. Bismarck next moved to gain complete control of the captured provinces and to cement Prussian ascendancy in north Germany. He created a *casus belli* by pressures to oust his former Austrian partner from joint occupation of Schleswig-Holstein. The instrument lay in hand: the Prussian Army, revamped through the efforts of Moltke and Generals **Albrecht T. M. von Roon** (Minister of War) and Manteuffel. It was equipped with breech-loading artillery and small arms (the needle gun), and the brief Danish War had provided its baptism of fire.

1866. Austro-Prussian War. The second of Bismarck's steps toward his dream of a German empire.

1886–1870. Friction between France and Prussia. France was the major obstacle remaining between Bismarck and his dream. The wily chancellor secretly gained the support of the smaller German states, and jockeyed Napoleon III into premature action.

1870–1871. Franco-Prussian War. (**See p. 832.**)

1871, January 18. Foundation of the German Empire. The efforts of Bismarck achieved their goal when King Wilhelm of Prussia was proclaimed emperor of a united Germany (not including Austria) in the Palace of Versailles while the Siege of Paris was still in progress.

1879, October 7. Austro-German Alliance. Bismarck brought about a reconciliation of the 2 major Germanic powers in order to establish a powerful military bloc in Central Europe.

1881, June 18. Alliance of the Three Emperors. This loose alliance of the German, Russian, and Austro-Hungarian empires was anti-British and ostensibly pro-Turkish. The conclusion of the agreements was delayed by the assassination of Czar **Alexander II** (March 13, 1881); Russian association in the alliance was halfhearted.

1882, May 20. Triple Alliance. This treaty, between Germany, Austria, and Italy, was primarily anti-French; it was, however, also anti-Russian and (save for the Italians) anti-British.

1890, March 16. Dismissal of Bismarck. Bismarck's alliance systems were the capstone of his career as empire builder. He was dropped from the Germanic helm by Kaiser **Wilhelm II.** The militarist young kaiser then extended German colonial hold in China, Africa, and—through military and economic assistance to Turkey—the Near East.

1895, June. Completion of the Kiel Canal. This gave Germany a strategic by-pass between the North and Baltic seas and enabled her to avoid the Scandinavian straits.

AUSTRO-HUNGARIAN EMPIRE

1850–1900. Austrian Involvement in the Balkans. Austria expanded her influence and power in the Balkans, generally at the expense of Turkey and, to a lesser extent, of Russia. Austrian influence was great in all of the Balkan nations that became independent during this period (see pp. 843–844).

1859. War with France and Piedmont. (See p. 829.)

1866. Seven Weeks' War. (See pp. 830 and 840.)

ITALY

1850–1870. Unification of Italy. The pressures for unification of Italy were similar to those which were working simultaneously in Germany. A complication—and also a stimulus to cohesion among volatile and suspicious Italian patriots—was the continued occupation of most of north Italy by the Austro-Hungarian Empire, and the consequent political, economic, and military predominance of Austria over the entire Italian peninsula. Piedmont (Kingdom of Sardinia), most stable of the Italian states, became the nucleus of efforts to end Austrian predominance. The premier of Piedmont, Count **Camillo Benso di Cavour,** whose interests initially were solely for increasing the power and prestige of his small country, became the architect of a new state. In this effort he was soon overshadowed in the public mind by his principal instrument, the Italian patriot and soldier of fortune, Giuseppe Garibaldi.

1858, July 20. Alliance of France and Piedmont. Having gained British and French good will by joining with them in the Crimean War (see p. 825), Cavour brought about a secret formal treaty with Napoleon III whereby France would join Piedmont in driving Austria from Italy, if this could be done without opening France to the charge of aggression. Following expulsion of Austria, the Italian states were to be amalgamated into a federation of 4 under the pope's presidency. France, as a *quid pro quo,* would gain Savoy and Nice.

1859, April–July. War of Austria with France and Piedmont. (See p. 829.)

1860, April 4. Uprisings in Naples. Revolts in the Kingdom of Naples were severely suppressed, arousing widespread revulsion in Italy and abroad.

1860, May 11. Garibaldi's Invasion of Sicily. With covert support from Cavour and King Victor Emmanuel II of Piedmont, Garibaldi and his "Thousand Redshirts" landed at Marsala in Sicily, having sailed from Genoa (May 5). He marched inland, rallying the inhabitants to revolt against the Kingdom of Naples. He defeated Neapolitan forces at **Calatafimi** (May 15) and took Palermo (May 27). Marching eastward, he defeated the Neapolitans again at **Milazzo** (near Messina; July 20).

1860, August 22. Passage of the Strait of Messina. With British assistance, Garibaldi crossed to the Italian mainland and marched on Naples.

1860, September 7. Capture of Naples. Seizure of Naples was accomplished against negligible opposition. Garibaldi prepared to march on Rome and Venetia.

1860, September 10. Piedmontese Invasion of the Papal States. Unrest in the Papal States provided an excuse for Cavour to send troops across the border. Papal forces were decisively defeated at **Castelfidardo** (September 18); the Piedmontese marched south to link up with Garibaldi in Neapolitan territory. Meanwhile French troops occupied Rome, and a French fleet took station along the Neapolitan coast, to preclude any Italian attack against the immediate papal domains.

1860, October 26. Battle of the Volturno. After one repulse (October 1), Garibaldi gained another victory over the demoralized Neapolitan forces and advanced on Gaeta.

1860, November 3–1861, February 13. Siege of Gaeta. King **Francis II of Naples,** with 12,000 men, made his last stand against the united Italian forces. The withdrawal of the French fleet (January 19) made it possible for Piedmontese warships to bombard Gaeta from the sea, forcing Neapolitan surrender.

1861, March 17. The Kingdom of Italy. An all-Italian parliament (not including representation from the papal territories around Rome) proclaimed a united Kingdom of Italy, with Victor Emmanuel as its first constitutional monarch. Less than 3 months after the realization of his dream, Cavour died. The hopes of Garibaldi to include all of the Papal States in the kingdom were foiled by continued French occupation of Rome.

1862, March–October. Garibaldi's Operations against Rome. Sporadic and ineffectual attempts to seize Rome were made by Italian patriots—with the covert support of Victor Emmanuel. Garibaldi, rallying volunteers to his standard, marched from the Strait of Messina toward Rome (August 24). The Italian government, unable to countenance an overt act of war against French forces in Rome, ordered its forces to intercept Garibaldi in the toe of Italy.

1862, August 29. Battle of Aspromonte. Regular Italian troops defeated Garibaldi and his volunteers. Garibaldi was wounded and captured. He and his men were soon released.

1866, May 12. Italian-Prussian Alliance. This was concluded with the approval of Napoleon III.

War with Austria, 1866

1866, June 20. Italy Declares War. This followed the outbreak of the Austro-Prussian War (see p. 830).

1866, June 24. Second Battle of Custozza. An Austrian Army, 80,000 strong, under Archduke **Albert,** met the Italian Army, under Victor Emmanuel, 120,000 strong. The Italians, poorly led, were defeated piecemeal. The outstanding feature of the battle was the spirited shock action of 2 improvised Austrian cavalry brigades that broke up repeated Italian assaults. The Italians retreated across the Mincio in disorder, having lost 3,800 killed and wounded and 4,300 missing. Austrian losses were 4,600 killed and wounded and 1,000 missing. The Austrian army was shortly withdrawn for the defense of Vienna against the Prussians.

1866, July. Garibaldi's Alpine Campaign. Leading a small volunteer army, Garibaldi won several minor successes at **Lodrone** (July 3), **Monte Asello** (July 10), **Condino** (July 16), **Ampola** (July 19), and **Bezzecca** (July 21). He was ordered to withdraw when Bismarck made clear to Italy that he would not consent to Italian occupation of the Trentine Tyrol.

1866, July 20. Naval Battle of Lissa. An Italian squadron of 10 ironclads and 22 wooden vessels, under Admiral **Carlo T. di Persano,** was attacked off the island of Lissa (Vis) in the Gulf of Venice by the Austrian squadron of Admiral Count **Wilhelm von Tegetthoff,** 7 smaller ironclads and 14 wooden vessels. The Italians were in a long line-ahead formation. The Austrian commander struck the line in a wedge-shaped formation, ignoring Italian fire until within point-blank range. Breaking through the Italian line, Tegetthoff sank 3 ironclads, with a loss of 1,000 men. The remainder of the Italian squadron broke off action and steamed away.

1866, October 12. Treaty of Vienna. The conclusion of the war resulted in ratification of Italian annexation of Venetia, brought about earlier by the good offices of Napoleon III (July 3).

1866, December. French Troops Withdraw from Rome. Garibaldi seized the opportunity to lead a futile volunteer invasion of the Papal States (January–September, 1867). This, as well as attempts—both overt and covert—by the Italian government to overthrow the papal dominion, led Napoleon III to send French forces back less than a year later.

1867, October 26. French Expedition to Rome. Some 2,000 men under Major General **Charles A. de Failly,** having landed at Civitavecchia, arrived in Rome. Meanwhile Garibaldi, renewing his own invasion, had reached **Monte Rotondo,** where he had defeated a small papal force (October 24).

1867, November 3. Battle of Mentana. Garibaldi's bands, some 4,000 strong, met a combined force of 3,000 papal troops and de Failly's 2,000 French regulars, who were armed with the new **chassepot** rifle. The redshirts were mowed down with heavy losses, and streamed back over the Italian border, leaving 800 prisoners. They were all arrested by the Italian authorities.

1870, September 20. Occupation of Rome. French forces having been withdrawn because of the Franco-Prussian War (see p. 832), an Italian army of 60,000 men under General **Raffaele Cadorna** invested it. After a short bombardment, a breach was effected. The invaders began to stream in and Pope **Pius IX** ordered his troops to cease fire.

1870, October 2. Formal Annexation of Rome by Italy. Following a plebiscite, the city was declared the capital of the nation.

1887–1896. Operations against Ethiopia. (See p. 849.)

EAST EUROPE

RUSSIA

1853–1856. Crimean War. (See p. 825.)

1861, February 2. Warsaw Massacre. Unrest in Russian Poland culminated in a mass demonstration in the Polish capital. Russian troops fired on the mob, killing many. Sporadic uprisings flared through the area.

1863–1864. Second Polish Revolution. Polish guerrilla bands took the field, and the revolt quickly spread into Lithuania and White Russia (January, 1863). Despite protracted resistance, harsh repressive measures finally quelled the uprising (May, 1864).

1864–1876. Conquest of Kokand, Bokhara, and Khiva. Russian colonial expansion followed steady military advances in Central Asia. Subjugation of Kirghiz and Turkoman tribes eventually resulted in the annexation of the entire Transcaspian region (1881).

1877–1878. Russo-Turkish War. (See p. 845.)

1884–1885. Conquest of Merv. The last independent Moslem principality of Central Asia was finally absorbed by Russia, establishing a common frontier with Afghanistan. The result was an increase in British-Russian colonial rivalry and tension.

1885. Frontier Incidents with Afghanistan. Fighting between Russian and Afghan troops came close to full-scale war, and was settled peacefully only after Britain made clear her determination to intervene on the side of Afghanistan (see p. 858).

1891–1894. Franco-Russian Alliance. This was a foil to the Triple Alliance of Germany, Austria, and Italy (see p. 840).

THE BALKANS

Greece

1850, January–March. British Blockade. The purpose was to force Greece to pay interest on an international loan and to pay compensation due some British citizens. A compromise was reached and Britain lifted the blockade.

1854, January–February. Greek Invasion of Thessaly and Epirus. Greece took advantage of Turkish participation in the Crimean War.

1854, April–1857, February. British and French Occupation of the Piraeus. The allies prevented Greece from joining Russia in the Crimean War.

1862, February 13–October 23. Revolution. Otto was deposed. He was replaced, after a long delay, by **George I,** a Danish prince selected by the great powers.

1878, February 2. Greece Declares War on Turkey. Again she was prevented from taking advantage of a Russo-Turkish War (see p. 845) by intervention of the other powers.

1886, May–June. British and Allied Blockade. Again the powers prevented Greece from taking advantage of Turkish troubles.

1896–1897. War with Turkey. (See p. 846.)

Serbia

All internal and external affairs of Serbia were affected by the continuing bitter feud between the Obrenovich and Karageorgevich families. The principal events were:

1862. Turk Bombardment of Belgrade. This was an outgrowth of troubles between Serbians and the Turkish garrisons.

1867, April. Withdrawal of the Turkish Garrisons. This was forced by the great powers.

1876, July. War with Turkey. (See p. 845.) Serbia was quickly overwhelmed. This was one cause of the Russo-Turkish War (see p. 845).

1877, December 14. Renewed War with Turkey. Serbia took advantage of Turk setbacks in the war with Russia.

1878, March 3. Treaty of San Stefano. Turkey recognized Serbian independence and ceded substantial territory (see p. 846).

1878, July 13. Treaty of Berlin. (See below.) Serbian independence was reaffirmed, but territorial cuts caused much bitterness in Serbia, particularly against Austria, which virtually annexed Bosnia and Herzegovina, largely populated by Serbs.

1883, November. Revolt. King **Milan** savagely suppressed it. Unrest continued.

1885–1886. Serbo-Bulgarian War.

1885, November 13. Serbia Declares War. King Milan demanded territory to compensate for Bulgaria's growth after union with Eastern Rumelia. Bulgaria refused so Milan invaded hoping war would unify troubled Serbia.

1885, November 17–19. Battle of Slivnitza. Milan's army was defeated by Bulgarian Prince **Alexander's** hurriedly concentrated forces. The Bulgars then invaded Serbia.

1885, November 26–27. Battle of Pirot. Prince Alexander's outstanding leadership brought another victory after 48 hours of serious conflict between armies each about 40,000 strong. Austrian intervention saved the Serbs (1886, January).

1886, March 3. Treaty of Bucharest. The *status quo* was restored.

Montenegro

1852–1853. War with Turkey. A Turkish army under Omar Pasha invaded Montenegro. Defeated by Prince **Danilo II,** near **Ostrag,** the Turks withdrew in the face of Austrian threats. Border friction erupted in open warfare (1853), and invading Turks were defeated at **Grahovo** by **Mirko Petrovitch,** brother of Danilo; again the Turks withdrew. Montenegro's independence was not recognized abroad.

1861–1862. Renewed War with Turkey. Montenegro supported a revolt in Herzegovina (1860–1861); again Omar Pasha invaded. Despite Mirko's heroic defense of Ostrag, Montenegro was quickly overrun and forced to acknowledge Turkish suzerainty at the **Convention of Scutari** (August 31).

1876–1878. War with Turkey. Montenegro and Serbia shared defeat, triumph, and then disappointment, but gained recognition of independence by the Treaty of Berlin (see above). However, hostilities on the Albanian frontier continued until 1880.

Bulgaria, 1875–1900

1875, September. Bulgarian Revolt. Suppressed by Turkey.

1876, April–August. Bulgarian Revolt. Again suppressed by Turkey. This, however, helped precipitate the Russo-Turkish War, in which Bulgaria was a major battleground (see p. 845).

1878, March 3. Treaty of San Stefano. Bulgarian independence was recognized.

1878, July 13. Treaty of Berlin. Because the other powers feared that Bulgaria would dominate the Balkans and be under Russian influence, the principality was reduced to less than half of the territory recognized in the Treaty of San Stefano. Parts of Macedonia were given to Serbia (in return for lands taken by Austria); most of Macedonia remained Turkish, and much of Thrace was formed into the autonomous Turkish province of Eastern Rumelia. The Bulgarians were bitter against the powers. The treaty also led to friction with Serbia.

1885, November 13. Annexation of Eastern Rumelia. A popular uprising was followed by absorption of the neighboring province. Serbia demanded compensation to offset this increase in Bulgarian power; Bulgaria refused.

1885–1886. Serbo-Bulgarian War. (**See above.**)

Rumania

1853, July. Russian Occupation. This precipitated the Crimean War (see p. 825).

1854, August–1857, March. Austrian Occupation. Russia withdrew under Austrian pressure; the Austrian occupation continued during the Crimean War (see p. 826).

1877–1878. Russo-Turkish War. (See p. 845.) This was precipitated by Russian invasion of Rumania (April 24, 1877).

1877, May 21. Rumanian Declaration of Independence. Rumania immediately entered the war against Turkey, and gave the Russians some assistance at the siege of Plevna (see p. 845).

1878, July 13. Treaty of Berlin. This reaffirmed the terms of the Treaty of San Stefano, so far as Rumania was concerned. She reluctantly surrendered southern Bessarabia to Russia, but received northern Dobruja, to assure an outlet to the sea.

EURASIA AND THE MIDDLE EAST

THE OTTOMAN EMPIRE

1852–1853. War with Montenegro.

1853–1856. The Crimean War. (See p. 825.)

1861–1862. Second Montenegrin War. **(See p. 844.)**

1866–1868. Cretan Insurrection. This uprising, instigated by Greeks, was quelled after furious fighting.

1876. War with Serbia and Montenegro. Cruel Turkish suppression of Christian insurrections in Herzegovina and Bosnia (1875) led to Serbian and Montenegran declarations of war. Serb forces (including Russian volunteers) under Russian leadership were defeated by **Suleiman** Pasha at **Alexinatz** (September 1) and **Djunis** (October 29). Russia, champion of the pan-Slav movement in the Balkans, began to mobilize along her southern frontier.

Russo-Turkish War, 1877–1878

1877, April 24. Russia Declares War. She immediately invaded Rumania, while mobilizing 275,000 men of all arms, plus 850 fieldpieces and 400 siege guns. Another 70,000 invaded Turkey's Caucasian provinces. The Russians expected easy victory over the ill-assorted and scattered Turkish forces of some 135,000 men and 450 guns in Europe and about the same number in Asia. The Grand Duke **Nicholas** (brother of Czar Alexander II) commanded the Russian armies in Europe, **Abdul Kerim** the Turks. The Russian plan was to advance across the Danube, cross the Balkans, and move on Adrianople (Edirne). A flank corps entering the Dobruja would protect the Russian left, while detachments were to mask the Turkish fortress quadrilateral of Ruschuk (Ruse), Silistria (Silistra), Shumla (Kolarovgrad), and Varna (Stalin). Due to Rumania's declaration of independence from Turkey (see p. 844), the Russian advance was made from friendly territory (though Russia delayed recognition of Rumania's independence). From the outset, the operations of the high command on both sides were remarkable for indecision and ineptitude.

1877, June. Clearing the Danube. In a series of combined army-navy operations, Russia quickly seized control of the Danube; bridges were built for the crossing.

1877, June–July. Invasion of Bulgaria. The Russian advance guard of General **Ossip V. Gourko,** with 31 squadrons of cavalry, 10 battalions of infantry, and 32 guns, plunged across the Danube (June 23), followed by the main army. Gourko, learning that the Turks had garrisoned the key Shipka Pass in the Balkans, led his force through the smaller and undefended Khainkoi Pass to the east and forced the immediate retreat (July 18–19) of the Shipka defenders. Meanwhile his patrols raided to within 90 miles of Adrianople, destroying railway and telegraph lines. He had, in fact, penetrated the Turkish cordon defense of the Balkans; a Russian advance in force would probably have resulted in overwhelming victory. Meanwhile the fortresses of **Svistov** and **Nikopol** were seized by the main army.

1877, July 19–December 10. Siege of Plevna. **Osman** Pasha, commanding the fortress of Vidin, well west of the Russian advance, hurried to Plevna (Pleven), whence he threatened the Russian right flank and indirectly threatened the Danube bridges. Instead of merely containing him, the Russians halted to take Plevna, which Osman and his engineer officer, **Tewfik** Pasha, were massively fortifying. Thrice the Russians assaulted (July 20, July 30, and September 11) and were repulsed with total losses of 30,000 men. Young Russian General **Mikhail D. Skobelev** distinguished himself in the last of these attacks, but was not properly supported by his colleagues, while Osman took advantage of the poor Russian coordination. The Russian investment was then put under the command of Todleben (hero of Sevastopol, see p. 826) and systematic siege operations began. Short of provisions, Osman attempted a final sortie (December 9), but was wounded and the effort collapsed. Plevna capitulated (December 10). The Russian advance had been held up for 5 months, completely negating the potentialities of Gourko's brilliant seizure of the Shipka Pass.

1877, July–December. Operations in Central Bulgaria. Meanwhile Abdul Kerim had been replaced as Turkish commander in chief by **Mohammed Ali;** the army of Suleiman Pasha had been recalled from

Montenegro by sea and was opposing Gourko south of the Shipka. The Russians, fearful of overextension while Plevna was still resisting, called Gourko back north of the mountains, but the Shipka Pass was fortified. The Turks established a fortified camp 2 miles to the south, at Senova, under **Vessil** Pasha. The efforts of Mohammed Ali to drive the Russians back to the Danube, and to relieve Plevna, were futile and poorly coordinated; Russian countermoves were no more effective. Gourko, however, assured Russian retention of the initiative by capturing Sofia at the end of the year.

1877, August–1878, January. Operations in the Caucasus. The opposing armies in the east, each about 70,000 men, under the Grand Duke **Michael** and **Mukhtar** Pasha, undertook no major operations until the Russians received sufficient reinforcements to permit an advance. The Russians gained a victory at **Aladja Dagh** (October 15), forcing the Turkish army to fall back on its 2 main fortresses of Kars and Erzerum. The Russians immediately invested **Kars,** which they took by assault a month later in a gallant, well-planned operation (November 18). Despite the bitter cold of winter in the mountains, the Russians continued their advance, and by the end of the year were heavily engaged against the Turkish defenses of **Erzerum.** They were seriously threatening the fortress when operations ceased as a result of an armistice (January 31).

1878, January. Final Campaign in Europe. Deciding upon a winter campaign in the Balkans, the Russians turned on Suleiman Pasha, who now commanded the main Turkish army south of the Shipka. Advancing on a wide front, Russian generals **Fëdor Radetsky,** Skobelev, Gourko, and Prince **Imeretinsky** outmaneuvered the badly extended Turks.

1878, January 8–9. Battle of Senova. Concentrating his columns against Vessil Pasha, south of the Shipka Pass, Skobelev defeated and encircled the entire Turkish force, capturing 36,000 men. The Russians pressed on to Plovdiv and Adrianople (January 17 and 19), cutting off Suleiman, who, with 50,000 men, was still farther west. After some minor engagements, the Turkish general retreated across the mountains to the Aegean at Enos (January 28). His forces went by sea to Constantinople. The Russians had advanced to the Chatalja lines, just outside the Turkish capital (January 30). An armistice immediately followed (January 31).

1878, March 3. Treaty of San Stefano. Turkey paid a large indemnity and conceded independence of Montenegro, Serbia, and Rumania. Bulgaria became an autonomous state under internal Russian control. Russia gained Ardahan, Kars, Batum, Bayazid.

1882. Germany Military Mission Arrives. After the death of the original mission chief, Colonel **Kolmar von der Goltz** headed the mission (1883–1895); his influence on Turkey was significant for the next 33 years.

1896, February. Insurrection in Crete. Local Greeks rose against Turkish rule. Greece intervened, precipitating war.

1897, April 17–September 18. Greco-Turkish War. Greek forces, led by Crown Prince **Constantine,** were consistently defeated by **Edhem** Pasha in parallel campaigns in Thessaly and Epirus. The ineptness of both high commands was remarkable. Through the mediation of the Russian Czar, an armistice was arranged (May 19) and a peace treaty effected (September 18).

PERSIA

1850–1854. Russian Conquests in the Syr Darya Valley. Muscovite influence reached Persia's Central Asian frontier.

1855. Invasion of Afghanistan. After complicated negotiations between Shah **Nasr ed-Din** and local Afghan provincial rulers, and despite British warning, Persian troops occupied Herat, Afghanistan (1856).

1856, November–1857, April. War with Britain. Britain then declared war on Persia (November 1). Britain seized the port of Bushire on the Persian Gulf (January). Sir **James Outram** with 2 Indian Army divisions invaded Persia, which soon sued for peace and evacuated Afghanistan (Treaty of Paris).

1878. Russian Military Influence. A Russian training mission helped establish a Cossack brigade, tangible indication of growing Russian influence in Persia during the conquest of Central Asia (see p. 843).

AFRICA

The powers of Europe were engaged in a bargain-counter rush, each trying to carve out a colonial parcel of the Dark Continent for its own selfish purposes. France and Great Britain were in keen competition not only with one another but also with the newcomers, Germany and Italy. Spain and Portugal, with toeholds long established, strove to maintain those positions. The slowly decaying Ottoman Empire was also clinging—ineffectually—to its possessions in North Africa. Military actions were necessary for these colonial powers to maintain and increase their holdings. A host of little wars flickered around the African periphery throughout the period.

EGYPT AND THE SUDAN

1863–1879. Reign of Khedive Ismail. Nominally a vassal of the Sultan of Turkey, Ismail attempted to modernize Egypt, but in so doing saddled his country with an enormous debt. As a result, Britain and France exerted a dual control, particularly after the British government purchased from Ismail all his interest in the Suez Canal (completed 1869). Ismail, with the aid of British and American army officers in his service, attempted—with mixed success—the conquest of the Red Sea coast (1865–1875) and of the Sudan (1871–1875).

1874–1879. The Upper Nile. Egyptian military control was established as far as Unyoro on Lake Albert Nyanza by a succession of minor expeditions against Arab slave traders and the indigenous tribal kingdoms of the region.

1875–1879. War with Abyssinia. Egyptian expansion eastward, beginning with the occupation of **Suakim** and **Massawa** (1865) by direction of the Ottoman Empire, threatened to cut off Abyssinia from the sea. When the Egyptians militarily occupied **Harar** and adjacent seacoast ports (1872–1875), King **John** of Abyssinia declared war. His troops moved against Ismail's forces, who were almost annihilated at **Gundet** (November 13, 1875). A second Egyptian expedition met defeat at **Gura** (March 25, 1876).

1879, June 25. Deposition of Ismail. The sultan appointed Tewfik, Ismail's son, as his successor.

1881, February 1. Rebellion of Ahmet Arabi. This revolt against Turkish and foreign control spread into an anti-Christian conflict.

1882, May–June. Disorder in Alexandria. French and British naval squadrons converged on Alexandria (May) and were present when some 50-odd Europeans were massacred by a native mob (June 11).

1882, July 11. British Bombardment of Alexandria. The French refused to coöperate with Admiral Sir **Frederick B. P. Seymour**'s reprisal. Britain now landed 25,000 troops at Ismailia under Sir **Garnet Wolseley.**

1882, September 13. Battle of Tell el-Kebir. Arabi's forces—38,000 men and 60 guns—were intrenched along the railway and sweet-water canal. After some preliminary skirmishing, the British launched a surprise night attack, driving the Egyptians off in disorder with losses of 2,000 killed and 500 wounded. British casualties were 58 killed, 379 wounded, and 22 missing. An immediate pursuit resulted in complete collapse and surrender of Arabi's forces. Britain dominated the Egyptian government. All but 10,000 of the British force were now sent home.

1883. Mahdist Uprising. Mahdi **Mohammed Ahmed of Dongola,** announcing himself to be a prophet, led a dervish uprising to set the Sudan in flames. About 10,000 Egyptian troops under General **William Hicks,** a former Indian Army officer, were completely wiped out at **El Obeid** (November 3), while **Osman Digna,** the Mahdi's lieutenant, moved successfully against Egypt's Red Sea ports, wiping out another Anglo-Egyptian force at **El Teb**

(near Suakim; February 4, 1884). Britain ordered Egypt to evacuate the Sudan.

1884, January 18. Gordon to Khartoum. General **Charles ("Chinese") Gordon** (see p. 864) was sent by the British government to Khartoum, at the confluence of the White and Blue Nile rivers, to supervise the evacuation of the Sudan by Egyptian forces. Mahdist forces invested the city (February).

1884–1885. Siege of Khartoum. For nearly a year, Gordon and a small garrison were besieged, while public opinion in England mounted against the British government's indecision in rescuing them. Finally a relief expedition under General Wolseley struck south from Wadi Halfa (October, 1884), too late.

1885, January 26. Fall of Khartoum. The Mahdi's forces swept over the last defenses of Khartoum, massacring the entire garrison. Wolseley's force, after several engagements, reached the city two days later, but was ordered to withdraw.

1885, June 21. Death of the Mahdi. His wild dervish followers under his successor, the Kalifa **Abdullah,** soon completed control of the entire Sudan.

1896–1898. Reconquest of the Sudan. Concerned by increasing French and Italian colonial interest in the Nile Valley, Britain decided to reoccupy the Sudan. Major General Sir **Horatio Kitchener,** sirdar of the Egyptian Army, commenced a methodical reconquest with a mixed force of British and Egyptian troops. Moving up the Nile, escorted by a river gunboat flotilla, he constructed a railway as he went along to ensure his logistical support. Highlights of the step-by-step advance, against fanatical opposition, were the capture of **Dongola** (September 21) and **Abu Hamed** (August 7, 1897) and defeat of Mahdist forces at the **Battle of the Atbara River** (April 8, 1898). Abdullah and Osman Digna concentrated their strength about the strong fortress position of Omdurman on the Nile, just north of Khartoum.

1898, September 2. Battle of Omdurman. Kitchener's army, some 26,000 men—about half British regulars and half well-trained Egyptian troops—were attacked in their fortified encampment at Egeiga, 4 miles from Omdurman, by Abdullah's 40,000 men. The savage bravery of the tribesmen was unavailing against machine guns and modern small arms, and they were repulsed with great slaughter. Kitchener then counterattacked toward Omdurman. The dervishes, rallying, fell on the British right and rear, Sir **Hector A. MacDonald**'s Sudanese brigade repelling 2 successive charges. At almost the same time, a dervish force of some 2,000 men leaped from concealment on Kitchener's right flank. In an old-fashioned cavalry charge, the 21st Lancers swept them away, though losing some 25 per cent of its strength. This ended the battle, the Kalifa's forces streaming from the field. While British and Egyptian cavalry took up pursuit, Kitchener's main body marched into Omdurman. Mahdist losses were more than 10,000 killed, an estimated equal number of wounded, and 5,000 prisoners. Kitchener's casualties amounted to approximately 500 in all.

COMMENT. *Omdurman's importance was twofold: it re-established Anglo-Egyptian influence and control over the vast Nile watershed region, and it was the first real demonstration of the fire power latent in the machine gun (Kitchener's artillery included 20 of them). Kitchener became a British national hero.*

1898, September–November. Fashoda Incident. A small French military and exploratory expedition under Major **Jean B. Marchand** had reached the Nile River at Fashoda in the southern Sudan (July, 1898), apparently assuring France of a foothold on the left bank of the Nile. Kitchener moved up the Nile to Fashoda, while Britain threatened war with France if the expedition did not withdraw. Under orders from Paris, Marchand evacuated Fashoda (November 3).

ETHIOPIA (ABYSSINIA) AND THE RED SEA

1854–1856. Theodore Unifies Abyssinia. After conquering the north, he crowned himself emperor as **Theodore II,** then consolidated most of the nation.

1867–1868. British Abyssinian Expedition. As a result of the imprisonment and murder of consular officials, some 32,000 well-equipped troops under Sir **Robert Napier** landed at Mulkutto (Zula) on the Red

Sea and moved inland. Theodore's troops were defeated at the **Battle of Arogee;** Theodore committed suicide (April 10, 1868). **Magdala,** his capital, was stormed and destroyed (April 13). The expedition, having accomplished its purpose, left the country (May).

1868–1872. Civil War. Finally **John of Tigré** defeated several rivals and unified the country as **John IV.**

1875–1879. War with Egypt. (See p. 847.)

1878. Conquest of Shoa.

1882. War between John and Menelek of Shoa. John, victorious, designated Menelek as his successor.

1882. Italian Colony at Assab, Eritrea. They expanded to Massawa (1885).

1884. War with the Mahdi. John's troops helped the British withdraw from Gallabat and Kassal.

1884. British and French Protectorates on Somali Coast.

1887. War with Italy. Italian penetration from the Red Sea littoral led to war. An Italian force of 500 men was surrounded and most of them killed by John's forces at **Dogali** (January 26). The matter was temporarily composed after an Italian expeditionary force arrived next year. Italy now permanently garrisoned her holdings in Eritrea.

1885–1889. Mahdist Incursions. This resulted in sporadic frontier warfare.

1889, March 12. Battle of Metemma (Gallabat). In response to a Mahdist invasion, Emperor John with a huge force stormed and took Gallabat, defended by 60,000 dervishes under Amir **Zeki Kumal.** The emperor having been killed in the fighting, the Abyssinian army then withdrew.

1889–1909. Reign of Menelek. During the first ten years of this reign there was sporadic civil war with Ras **Mangasha,** illegitimate son of John, who claimed the throne. At the outset of his reign Menelek negotiated the **Treaty of Uccialli** with Italy; the Italians considered that this gave them a protectorate over Abyssinia. Meanwhile Menelek steadily expanded the empire.

1895–1896. War with Italy. This resulted from disagreement over the Treaty of Uccialli, followed by renewed Italian encroachment.

1896, March 1. Battle of Aduwa (Adowa). An Italian force of 20,000 men—Italians and natives—under General **Oreste Baratieri** rashly attacked Emperor Menelek's 90,000 warriors in mountainous country. The leading Italian brigade pushed too far ahead of the main body, was surrounded and destroyed, and the other three brigades then were overwhelmed in detail. Despite the odds and poor leadership, Baratieri's troops fought well. Some 6,500 (4,500 Italian) were killed and wounded; 2,500 prisoners (1,600 Italian) were captured. Despite propaganda of Abyssinian atrocities, Menelek apparently treated his captives humanely.

1896, October 26. Treaty of Addis Ababa. Italy recognized Abyssinian independence.

1899–1905. The Mad Mullah. Mohammed ben Abdullah, claiming supernatural powers, began harassing British and Italian Somaliland, and part of Abyssinia, from his base at Burao, 50 miles south and east of Berbera. Despite all efforts of organized soldiery, mostly British (with considerable Abyssinian assistance), to quell his depredations, Mohammed and his followers kept up a successful guerrilla warfare until he was granted a semi-independent territorial area in Italian Somaliland.

NORTH AFRICA

1859–1860. Spanish-Moroccan War. (See p. 839.)

1865–1880. Franco-Italian Rivalry in Tunisia. France, continuing the pacification of the Algerian hinterland, found Italy her rival in exploitation of Tunisia. Matters came to a head when Tunisian tribesmen began raiding across the Algerian frontier.

1881, April. Seizure of Bizerte. A French naval force occupied Bizerte while French land forces moved across the Tunisian border. The Bey of Tunis was forced to accept a French protectorate (**Treaty of Bardo,** Kasr es-Said, May 19).

1881, June–July. Insurrections in Southern Tunisia and Algeria. These were finally composed by French arms.

1893. Spanish Operations in the Riff. For most of the year incursions of Berber tribesmen from the Riff mountains menaced Spanish Morocco's coastal areas. The Riffians gathered in force around Melilla, then Spain's most important North African port, besieging it on the land side. An expeditionary force of 25,000 Spanish troops finally drove the tribesmen back into the hills.

SOUTH AFRICA

British vs. Boers vs. Blacks, 1850–1880

THREE-WAY STRUGGLE

1850–1878. Kaffir Wars. Britain's development of the Cape Colony was accompanied by a continuation of the tribal outbreaks which had been going on for three-quarters of a century. Most of the operations were those of volunteer units recruited from among the Boer and English settlers. The most serious of these was the **8th Kaffir War** (1850–1853), provoked when the Cape governor, Sir **Harry Smith,** reduced the power of the native chiefs in the eastern regions of the Cape Colony. Shortly after this (1856–1857), the desperate Kaffirs (mainly the Xosa tribes), believing that their actions would call back their ancestral heroes to help drive out the white men, slaughtered their cattle and destroyed their crops. The result was virtual self-destruction of the Kaffirs, about two-thirds of them dying of starvation. Despite this, when their strength had been built up again, after a generation, the Kaffirs rose in the last and **9th Kaffir War** (1877–1878), which was suppressed, and Britain annexed all of Kaffraria.

1852–1856. Emergence of the Boer Republics. Britain renounced sovereignty over the Transvaal region (1852), which later became the South African Republic, with **Marthinus Pretorius** as the first president (December 16, 1856). The Orange Free State was established, and Britain recognized its independence (February 17, 1854).

1854–1877. Zulu-Boer Border Disputes. The Zulus resisted Boer efforts to expand eastward to the sea. There was no overt warfare, but frequent frontier clashes.

1856. Civil War in Zululand. This was the result of a dispute over the succession between **Cetewayo** and **Mbulazi,** sons of **Mpande.** Cetewayo defeated and killed his brother in the decisive **Battle of the Tugela River** (December).

1858–1868. Basuto Wars of the Orange Free State. Under their king, **Mosheshu,** the Basutos resisted and repelled Boer encroachment (1858). A few years later the war was renewed; this time the Boers were successful, and annexed large parts of Basutoland (1864–1866). Friction continued, however, and the Orange Free State annexed more territory after another war (1867–1868). Britain finally annexed Basutoland to prevent further Boer expansion (1868–1871).

1862–1864. Civil War in the Transvaal. The obstreperous Boers, it seemed, could not only not get along with their neighbors; they could not get along with each other. Pretorius and his principal aide, **S. J. Paul Kruger,** finally suppressed the insurgency.

1867. Discovery of Diamonds along the Orange River. This led to British reannexation of the Hopetown region (1871), despite protests of the Orange Free State.

1872. Accession of Cetewayo as Zulu Ruler. The new king immediately began to rebuild Zulu military strength, which had declined somewhat since the death of his uncle, Shaka (see p. 783).

1877, April 12. British Annex Transvaal. This was done in an effort to bring about federation of all of South Africa. The Boers protested vigorously, and began to plan rebellion.

THE ZULU WAR, 1879

After annexation of the South African Republic, the British inherited the Boer border disputes with the Zulus. Cetewayo, rightly convinced that his position was legally and morally sound, was as adamant with the British as he had been with the Boers. At the same time, he continued to develop his nation's fighting power.

1878, December 11. British Ultimatum. Britain demanded a virtual protectorate over Zululand. Cetewayo ignored the British demands.

1879, January 11. British Invasion of Zululand. To force Zulu compliance, General **F. A. Thesiger, Viscount Chelmsford,** led a force of about 5,000 British and 8,200 native troops into Zululand in 3 widely dispersed columns. Cetewayo had a force of 40,000 trained, fanatically brave professional warriors, organized in impis (regiments) and highly disciplined. While some had firearms, the principal Zulu weapon was the assagai, or spear, of which where were two types—throwing and stabbing. The normal Zulu battle formation was a crescent; while the center engaged the enemy, the horns swung in for a double envelopment. All movements were made on foot, at a lope which enabled the warrior to cover ground as fast as a mounted man. Reminiscent of the tactics of the Roman legion, the Zulu attack was carried home with the stabbing assagai, under a shower of throwing assagais.

1879, January 22. Battle of Isandhlwana. Chelmsford's center column—1,800 Europeans and 1,000 natives—established a camp at Isandhlwana. While Chelmsford and about half his men were away, trying to intercept a Zulu force, the camp was hit early in the morning in a surprise attack by 10,000 Zulus. All but 55 Europeans and about 300 natives were killed. Returning next day, Chelmsford discovered the ruined camp and bodies. He fell back through Rorkes-drift to defensive positions. Cetewayo's forces pressed hard against them.

1879, January 22–23. Defense of Rorkes-drift. About half of the Zulu victors of Isandhlwana struck this British base camp, which had a garrison of about 85 able-bodied soldiers, late in the afternoon. In one of the British Army's great epics, the defenders drove off six full-scale Zulu attacks that lasted through the night. Early next day the Zulus withdrew, leaving about 400 dead. The British lost 17 killed and 10 seriously wounded.

1879, January–April. Siege of Eshowe. One of Chelmsford's columns, under Colonel **C. K. Pearson,** was besieged, but finally was relieved after a hard fight at **Gingindlovu** by Chelmsford, who had received some reinforcements.

1879, March 29. Battle of Kambula. Some 20,000 warriors attacked Sir **Evelyn Wood**'s column in a desperate 4-hour attack, but were finally beaten off. Wood lost 100 out of his 400 Europeans engaged; Zulu losses were an estimated 1,000.

1879, April–May. Arrival of Reinforcements. These were hurried out from England. By the end of May, Chelmsford prepared to take the offensive again.

1879, June 1. Death of the Prince Imperial. Young **Louis J. J. Bonaparte,** son of Napoleon III, serving with the British as a volunteer, was killed during a Zulu ambush while out on reconnaissance. His death focused international attention on what up to that time had been just one more of England's innumerable little wars.

1879, July 4. Battle of Ulundi. Chelmsford, with 4,200 Europeans and 1,000 natives, reached the vicinity of Cetewayo's capital. Attacked by more than 10,000 Zulus, the force formed a hollow square, with its 300 cavalry inside. The Zulu charges were broken up by British musketry and bayonets, and the small English cavalry detachment then charged into the disorganized mass. Victory was complete. Cetewayo fled. British casualties were about 100, while the tribesmen lost some 1,500 killed. This action to all intents and purposes ended Zulu power. Cetewayo became a fugitive, but was captured (August 28).

British vs. Boers, 1880–1899

TRANSVAAL REVOLT (OR FIRST BOER WAR), 1880–1881

Diamonds, gold, and greed were the principal factors affecting the fortunes of Boer settlements lying between the Orange and Limpopo rivers in South Africa.

1880, December 30. Boer Republic Proclaimed. The Boers were led by Kruger, **Petrus Jacobus Joubert,** and Pretorius. Several small bodies of British troops were cut up.

1881, January 28. Battle of Laing's Nek. Some 2,000 Boers under Joubert invaded Natal. General Sir **George Colley,** who completely underestimated his opponents, met them at Laing's Nek in the Drakensberg mountains with 1,400 British regulars and was defeated.

1881, February 27. Battle of Majuba Hill. The hill overlooked the principal pass through the mountains. Occupying the hill with part of his force—550 men—Colley was overwhelmed by the Boer riflemen. He and 91 others were killed; 134 more were wounded and 59 captured. Boer casualties were negligible.

1881, April 5. Treaty of Pretoria. This granted independence to the South African Republic, under British suzerainty. Paul Kruger, grim protagonist of Boer independence, became its president (April 16, 1883).

RISING STAKES OF COLONIAL ECONOMICS, 1880–1899

1880–1881. The Gun War. The Basutos revolted when ordered to give up their arms. The revolt was suppressed.

1883–1884. Zulu Civil War. Bickering between rival rulers flared into civil war when Cetewayo was restored (January 29, 1883). After almost a year of fighting, he was overthrown by **Zibelu** (December, 1883), who soon afterward was overthrown by **Dinizulu,** son of Cetewayo.

1884. Establishment of German Colony of Southwest Africa.

1886. Discovery of Gold in the Witwatersrand. This was followed by British diplomatic maneuvers, resulting in annexation of Zululand. The Boers were in fact being cut off from all communication with the sea. While **Afrikanders** and **Uitlanders** (foreigners settled in the area) battled with one another for control of the Transvaal government, **Cecil Rhodes,** then prime minister of the Cape Colony and architect of a plan for British domination of what had now become one of the richest areas in the world, schemed to throttle the Afrikanders. They, on the other hand, were stubbornly resolved to check any foreign aggrandizement.

1887. Zulu Rebellion. After the British annexed Zululand, Dinizulu revolted (June–August), but was defeated.

1893, July–November. Matabele-Mashona War. Lobengula, king of the Matabeles, tried to conquer the Mashonas. The British intervened and defeated the Matabeles near their capital at **Bulawayo** (October 23).

1895–1896. Jameson Raid. Dr. **L. Starr Jameson,** close friend of Rhodes, and 500 adventurers undertook a fantastic dash into the Transvaal to spark an Uitlander uprising in Johannesburg. With 500 men, Jameson rode into Boer territory from Mafeking, 140 miles away (December 29); an *opéra-bouffe* performance, completely lacking in military acumen. Three days later, at Krugersdorp, hard-riding, hard-shooting Boer commandos rounded them up like so many cattle, while the proposed revolt at Johannesburg failed to materialize. Jameson and his men were handed over to the British government, tried and convicted under the Foreign Enlistment Act, and given a slap on the wrist. Conditions worsened in the Transvaal; Boer-British relations grew more strained.

1896, March–October. Matabele Uprising. Suppressed by the British.

1899, October 9. Kruger Ultimatum. Realizing that a British expeditionary force was in the making in Natal, Kruger gave the British government 48 hours to disband all military preparations. The ultimatum was refused. The Orange Free State announced its alliance with the South African Republic.

Boer War, 1899–1902

Boer military organization was extremely sketchy, a localized militia system grouped into so-called commandos varying in strength with the population from which they were recruited. But every individual was a marksman, armed with a modern repeating rifle, and every man was mounted. The riders of the veldt were hunters, trained from childhood to take advantage of cover and terrain. The result was an irregular fire-power capability which could pulverize—from concealed positions—the ranks of any close-order formation. These irregulars were also capable of disappearing from the field when seriously threatened. The Boers also had a small quantity of modern German and French field artillery, on the whole well served. On the other hand, these Boer individuals lacked disciplinary control and most of their leaders had no real concept of tactics and strategy.

1899, October. The Boer Offensive. Fast-moving Boer columns advanced, both east and west. Transwaal General **Piet A. Cronjé** invested **Mafeking** (October 13), valiantly defended by Colonel **Robert S. S. Baden-Powell.** Free State forces besieged **Kimberley** (October 15). The Boer main effort, 15,000 strong, under Transwaal General Joubert, pushed through the Natal Defense Force, equal in number, under General Sir **George White,** at **Laing's Nek** (October 12), and after brushes at **Talana Hill** (October 20), **Elandslaagte** (October 21), and **Nicholson's Nek** (October 30), bottled up White's troops in **Ladysmith** (November 2). British relieving forces were unwisely divided up by General Sir **Redvers Buller,** who tried to check the Boers everywhere at once.

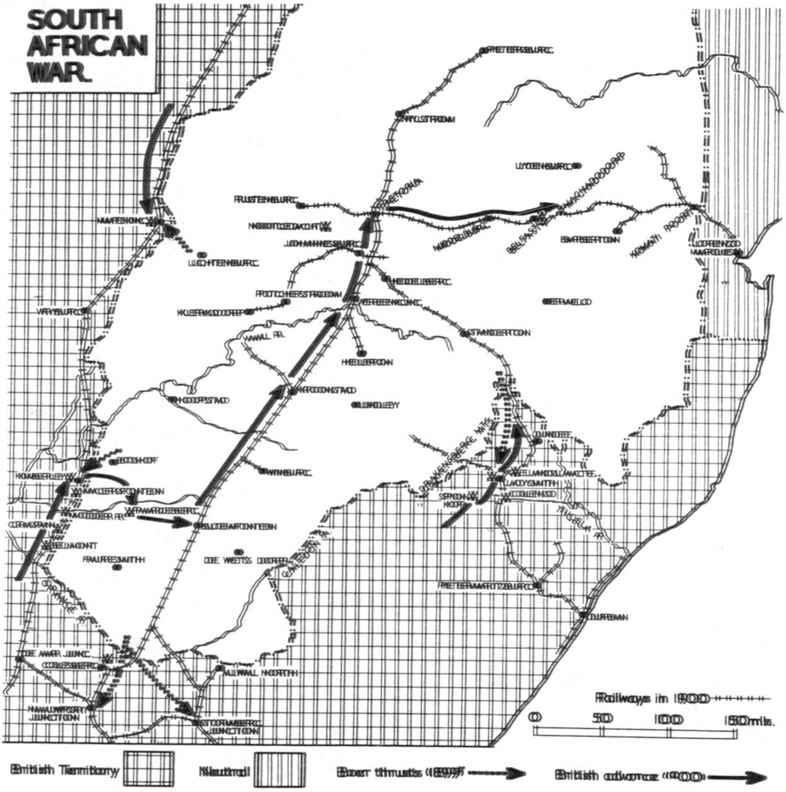

1899, November 28. Battle of the Modder River. General Lord **Paul Methuen**'s column, nearly 10,000 men with 16 guns, moved to the relief of Kimberley. Transwaal and Free State Boer commandos, about 7,000 strong, under Transwaal Generals Cronjé and **Jacobus H. De La Rey,** contested the advance in a series of delaying actions. Methuen finally won through to the Modder River, after losing 72 men killed and 396 wounded, but his troops were so exhausted that he paused to await reinforcements. Boer casualties were negligible.

1899, December 10, Battle of Stormberg. A British force under General Sir **William Gatacre** got lost in a night move against a Boer spearhead 70 miles from Queenstown and was ambushed, losing heavily.

1899, December 10–11. Battle of Magersfontein. The Boers under Cronjé near the Modder River, now about 8,000 strong, occupied an entrenched hill. Methuen attacked frontally, in mass formation, at dawn in the rain. He was defeated with loss of 210 men killed (including one general officer), 675 wounded, and 63 missing. Again, Boer casualties were negligible.

1899, December 15. Battle of Colenso. Buller himself led 21,000 men of all arms to relieve Ladysmith. Crossing the Tugela

River, he attempted to turn the left flank of Free State General **Louis Botha,** entrenched with 6,000 men. The British flank attack, entangled in difficult terrain, was decimated by small-arms fire. British batteries unlimbering to support the frontal attack found themselves at the mercy of a concealed force of Boers. The British were driven back with losses of 143 killed, 756 wounded, and 220 men and 11 guns captured. Boer losses are estimated at not more than 50 men. At the end of Britain's "Black Week" Buller was so badly beaten that he advocated the surrender of Ladysmith. He was at once relieved of the supreme command and replaced by Field Marshal **Frederick Sleigh, Viscount Roberts,** with General Kitchener as his chief of staff.

1900, January 10. Roberts' Reorganization. Realizing at once that mobility was the keynote for success against the Boers, Roberts and Kitchener began revamping British field forces. To meet the Boer fluidity of fire and movement, a progressive build-up of mounted infantry began around the existing yeomanry militia units, a long and arduous task against conservative British military opinion. Brigadier General **John D. P. French,** with 2 small brigades of cavalry, kept up a spirited campaign against De La Rey and Free State General **Christiaan R. De Wet,** who were proving themselves to be natural leaders of light cavalry.

1900, January–February. Buller Repulsed at the Tugela. He failed in 2 successive attempts, **Spion Kop** (January 23) and **Vaal Kranz** (February 5). British losses inflicted by small Boer forces of marksmen were 408 killed, 1,390 wounded, and 311 missing. The Boers lost some 40 killed and 50 wounded.

1900, February 15. Relief of Kimberley. French reached Kimberley, bringing the Boer siege to an end.

1900, February 15. Roberts By-passes Cronjé. Roberts had set out toward Kimberley (late January) with 30,000 men. While French was driving directly on Kimberley, the main British force marched past Cronjé's left flank at Magersfontein, threatening his communications. The Boer leader began a slow withdrawal (February 16).

1900, February 18. Battle of Paardeberg Drift. Cronjé's retreat across the Modder River was blocked by French, rushing back from Kimberley. As the main British army approached, Roberts, temporarily sick, turned his command over to Kitchener, who made a tempestuous frontal piecemeal attack on the Boers' fortified laager (wagon train). The British were repulsed with losses of 320 killed and 942 men wounded.

1900, February 19–27. Siege of Paardeberg. Roberts, recovering, took command again and began a systematic encirclement and bombardment of the Boer laager. Cronjé, who might have broken out with his 4,000 mounted men, stubbornly refused to abandon his wounded and his train. He was starved into surrender (February 27).

1900, February 28. Relief of Ladysmith. Buller, on the Tugela, made a third attack (February 17–18) and succeeded. As he advanced toward Ladysmith, the besiegers withdrew and the relieving force made contact with the garrison. The tide had turned.

1900, March–September. Roberts' Cleanup in the Orange Free State. The British, now heavily reinforced, advanced on all fronts. Roberts took **Bloemfontein,** capital of the Orange Free State (March 13) and reached **Kroonstad** (May 12). Buller in Natal swept Boer resistance away at **Glencoe** and **Dundee** (May 15). The Orange Free State was annexed by Britain (May 24).

1900, May 17–18. Relief of Mafeking. A flying column of cavalry and mounted infantry under Major General **Bryan T. Mahon** relieved the garrison after a siege of more than 7 months.

1900, May–June. Invasion of the Transvaal. Johannesburg fell (May 31), then Pretoria (June 5). Roberts and Buller joined forces at Vlakfontein (July 4), ending all formal resistance. Kruger fled to Portuguese and Dutch protection. Annexation of the Transvaal was announced (September 3). Roberts went home (December), Kitchener being left in command. But the war was far from being over.

1900, November–1902, May. Guerrilla Warfare. De Wet, De La Rey, Botha, and some minor leaders, rallying to their respective commands the disbanded burgher forces, for eighteen months played hob with British communications and defied all attempts to corner them. Erection of a line of blockhouses to protect the rail and other communication lines was the first British remedial action. But the raiders seemed to plunge at will through this cordon defense. Kitchener then copied Spanish procedure in Cuba. The country was swept by flying columns of mounted infantry; the farms on which the Boer raiders depended for sustenance were burned and some 120,000 Boer women and children were herded into concentration camps, in which an estimated 20,000 of them died of disease and neglect. Under these harsh measures, all resistance collapsed. The guerrilla leaders capitulated.

1902, May 31. Treaty of Vereeniging. The Boers accepted British sovereignty. As part of the very lenient terms, Britain granted them £3 million compensation for the destroyed farms. Total British casualties were 5,774 killed and 22,829 wounded. The Boers lost an estimated 4,000 killed; there is no accurate toll of the wounded. About 40,000 Boer soldiers had been captured.

COMMENT. *It took the British Empire 2 years and 8 months to subdue a foe whose man-power potential was 83,000 males of fighting age, and which never had in the field at one time more than approximately 40,000 men. British forces engaged in the beginning totaled not more than 25,000, but before it was ended some 500,000 men were in South Africa—drawn from empire resources around the world. What happened was that the British Army, for the first time since the War of 1812, met hostile mounted riflemen and aimed small-arms fire. The experience of some 85 years of formal and little wars in Europe and around the world went into the discard, and an entire new system of tactics and techniques had to be evolved on the battlefield.*

EAST AFRICA

1862. Increasing British Influence in Zanzibar.

1885. German Protectorate Established over Coast of Tanganyika. Protests of the Sultan of Zanzibar were overcome by German naval demonstrations.

1885–1898. British Wars with Arab Slave Traders in Nyasaland. This was the first, and longest-lasting, of intermittent wars of the various colonial powers with the Arab slave traders in East, West, and Central Africa.

1885–1889. Religious Wars in Uganda. Initially these were mainly between Moslems and the Catholic Christians under King **Mwanga.** The eventual victory of Mwanga over the Moslems (1889) was followed by continuing unrest resulting from Protestant-Catholic disputes.

1887. British Establish Control of Kenya Coast. A 50-year lease was negotiated with the Sultan of Zanzibar, largely to prevent further German expansion along the coast.

1888–1890. Uprising of Coastal Arabs in German East Africa. This was suppressed by the Germans with some naval assistance from Britain.

1890. British Protectorate Established over Zanzibar. This was recognized by Germany and France in return for Britain's cession of Helgoland to Germany and recognition of French claims in Madagascar.

1891–1893. Wahehe War in German East Africa. The rebellion was suppressed by the Germans.

1893. British Protectorate over Uganda.

1896. Uprising in Zanzibar. Suppressed by a British naval bombardment.

1897–1901. Mutiny in Uganda. Continued sporadic unrest in the British protectorate, fomented by rival French interests and religious conflicts, was complicated by the mutiny of British Sudanese troops. King Mwanga was defeated and captured (1899). Not until Indian troops were brought into the area was the outbreak controlled (1900–1901).

WEST AFRICA

1854–1864. French Operations against the Tukulors. General **Louis L. C. Faidherbe** slowly drove **Hajj Omar,** Tukulor ruler, eastward from the upper Senegal to the upper Niger.

1860. German Posts Established on the Cameroon Coast.

1864–1890. Tukulor Civil Wars. These were mainly dynastic conflicts of succession among the sons of Hajj Omar.

1873–1874. Second Ashanti War. Following years of Ashanti raids (1863–1872), British colonial expansion on the Gold Coast precipitated a major Ashanti invasion.

The Gold Coast tribes were overwhelmed, and the small British garrisons were helpless. General Sir **Garnet Wolseley** was appointed governor and given substantial reinforcements. With British regulars and native levies he penetrated to **Kumasi,** the Ashanti capital, and razed it (February, 1874). The British then withdrew from Ashanti lands.

1877–1885. Belgian Explorations in the Congo. Initially these explorations were supported internationally, but the Belgians dominated the region, which was declared an independent state (1885), over which King **Leopold of Belgium** assumed personal sovereignty. The French stepped up their colonial activity to the west and north of the Congo to limit the Belgian-controlled region.

1883–1890. French Expansion. This activity was centered mainly along the frontiers of Dahomey and in the upper Niger, where the Tukulors and other tribes were conquered.

1884. German Protectorates Established. They took control of the Togoland and Cameroon coasts.

1885. Spanish and British Protectorates. The Spanish took control of Rio de Oro and Spanish Guinea. The British proclaimed control of the lower Niger River region, to forestall further French expansion.

1885–1886. First Mandingo-French War. The French defeated **Samori,** warlike ruler of the Ivory Coast tribes. They established a protectorate (1889).

1889–1890. First Dahomey-French War. The victorious French established a protectorate.

1892. Second Dahomey-French War. French General **Alfred A. Dodds** finally defeated the Dahomians, deposed the king, and annexed the country. Uprisings continued, however (1893–1899).

1892–1893. Rising of Arab Slave Traders on the Upper Congo. The sporadic conflicts taking place farther east spread as the Arabs became disturbed by European interference with their trade. Belgian troops finally quelled the disturbances.

1893. Rise of Rabah Zobeir. This half-Arab, half-Negro adventurer, who had fought for and against the British and Egyptians in the Sudan, conquered the ancient Sultanate of Bornu. He then began to expand into nearby regions, and clashed with the French.

1893. French Operations against the Tuaregs on the Niger. The French occupied Jenne and Timbuktu.

1893–1894. Third Ashanti War. Depredations of Ashantis under their new ruler, **Prempeh,** were repulsed, and the Ashantis forced to accept a British protectorate.

1894–1895. Second Mandingo-French War. Samori threw off French control and defeated French efforts to re-establish the protectorate.

1895–1896. Fourth Ashanti War. Prempeh rejected the British protectorate. British troops again took Kumasi, deported the principal Ashanti leaders, dissolved the Ashanti Union, and firmly established their protectorate.

1897. British Conquest of Northern Nigeria. General Sir **George Goldie** defeated the Fula (or Fulani) Empire.

1897–1898. Anglo-French Dispute over Nigeria. The two countries came close to war, but finally resolved their differences, with the British retaining the area of modern Nigeria.

1897–1900. Batetela War on the Upper Congo. This warlike tribe was finally pacified by Belgian troops.

1898. Third Mandingo-French War. The French defeated and captured Samori, and completely broke Mandingo power (September 29).

1399–1900. French Conquest of Chad Region. Forces from the Congo and from Algeria converged to defeat Rabah Zobeir (April 22, 1900) after bitter warfare.

MADAGASCAR

1859. French Protectorate over Coastal Areas.

1863. Revolt in Madagascar. The pro-European king, **Radama II,** was overthrown and killed.

1882. French Claim a Protectorate. This was rejected by the Hova government (see p. 784).

1883–1885. War with France. Majunga and Tamatave were bombarded by a French squadron and troops landed (June 13, 1885). After desultory fighting, the French protectorate was accepted. Unrest pe sisted, however, and Hova troops were trained by and to some extent officered by Englishmen.

1894, June 16. Extended French Claims Rejected. In consequence, Tamatave was again bombarded (December 12). A French expeditionary force of 15,000 men under General **Jacques C. R. A. Duchesne** embarked for Madagascar.

1895, February. French Conquest. Duchesne began landing at Majunga. The French force moved inland slowly, constructing a viable line of communications. **Tananarive,** the capital, was bombarded and at once surrendered (September 30). A violent insurrection then broke out in the interior.

1896, August 6. Madagascar Proclaimed a French Colony. General **Joseph S. Galliéni** set up a military government, deposed Queen **Ranavalona II,** and, actively campaigning, stamped out all revolt. Complete pacification was accomplished by 1905.

SOUTH ASIA

AFGHANISTAN

1850–1855. Recovery of Dissident Regions. Dost Muhammad consolidated control of outlying areas, principal among them Balkh (1850) and Kandahar (1855).

1855. Treaty of Peshawar. This officially concluded Afghan participation in the 2nd Sikh War (see p. 788), confirmed British annexation of the Peshawar territories, and assured British support of Afghanistan against Persian designs on Herat (see p. 846). Persian withdrawal from Herat (1857) having left the region under independent local rule, Dost Muhammad immediately moved to gain control. During the Indian Mutiny (see p. 858), he remained faithful to his alliance with Britain.

1863, May 26. Capture of Herat. After a long-drawn-out local conflict and siege, Herat was brought under central control. Dost Muhammad died shortly afterward (June 9), being succeeded by his son **Sher Ali** Khan.

1863–1879. Internal Disorders. Serious dynastic struggles shook the country as Sher Ali was repeatedly defeated by his warrior cousin **Abdur Rahman** Khan. Sher Ali, courting Russian favor, became increasingly hostile to the British.

Second Afghan War, 1878–1880

1878, November. British Invasion. When Sher Ali ignored British warnings against his pro-Russian stand, British troops, in 3 columns, under Sir **Frederick** (later Lord) **Roberts,** advanced from India and seized the frontier passes, defeating Sher Ali's troops at **Peiwar Kotal** (December 2). Sher Ali fled; his son **Yakub** Khan, replacing him, signed a treaty with Britain (May, 1879). Sir **Louis Cavagnari** was installed as British resident at Kabul.

1879, September 5. Assassination of Cavagnari. In reprisal, a field force under Roberts marched on Kabul from Kurram and Kandahar.

1879, October 6. Battle of Charasia. Roberts' force, 7,500 men and 22 guns, defeated an Afghan army of 8,000, then occupied Kabul (October 12). Yakub Khan, abdicating, fled to British protection.

1879, December 23. Battle of Sherpur. Afghan levies amounting to 100,000 men rallied to the call for a holy war against the infidel British. Roberts' cantonments were surrounded. The British broke out and then Roberts, falling on the Afghan flank, completely dispersed them. Pacification continued, without major opposition, under the over-all command of Sir **Donald Stewart.**

1880, June. Ayub Khan's Offensive. Ayub Khan, brother of Yakub, had seized control of Herat early in the war (January, 1879). Now claiming the throne, he marched on Kandahar with 25,000 men. Lieutenant General **James Primrose,** commanding at Kandahar, sent an Anglo-Indian brigade, 2,500 strong, under Brigadier General **G. R. S. Burroughs,** to **Maiwand,** about 50 miles northwest, to oppose the Afghan advance.

1880, July 27. Battle of Maiwand. Burroughs attacked the Afghan position, but the British artillery expended all its ammunition and a flanking movement by Ayub then shattered the Indian troops, who fled. The one British infantry battalion present was surrounded and practically annihilated; about half the remainder of the command escaped. Ayub now advanced to besiege Kandahar.

1880, August 9. Roberts' March. Roberts moved out of Kabul to intercept Ayub. With him were 10,000 men and a transport corps specifically organized on his own plan. He reached Kandahar in 22 days, covering 313 miles over mountainous country.

1880, September 1. Battle of Kandahar. Roberts at once attacked, completely routing the Afghan army and capturing all its guns and equipage. Ayub fled back to Herat. This action ended the campaign. A pro-British government was established under Abdur Rahman (see p. 857). The British evacuated the country in 1881.

1881. Ayub Khan's Second Bid for Power. With British troops out of the way, Ayub led his followers again on Kandahar, defeating an army sent by Abdur Rahman, and capturing the city (July 27). Abdur Rahman, taking the field in person, crushed the rebels (September 22). Ayub fled to Persia. Abdur Rahman now established a firm, centralized government.

1885, March 30. The Penjdeh Incident. Following the occupation of Merv (1884), Russian troops crossed the disputed Afghan frontier and clashed with Abdur's forces, inflicting heavy losses. The incident brought Britain and Russia close to war (see p. 843).

INDIA

The Great Mutiny, 1857–1858

British military power in India at this time consisted of two elements: the native armies of the East India Company and a comparatively few regular British Army units. This armed force was controlled by the governor general, an official of the company, appointed with crown approval. In 1857 the three company armies—Bengal, Bombay, and Madras—consisted of 233,000 Asians (sepoys) and 36,000 Britishers, commanded by a British officer corps, commissioned by the company. Due largely to poor administration and command, considerable unrest existed among the native contingents. The introduction of the Minié rifle cartridge about this time provided the spark that changed unrest to violence. The paper cartridge, which had to be bitten for loading, was greased. Disaffected elements in the armies claimed—with some truth, as later investigation showed—that the grease used included the fat of cows (sacred to Hindus) and of pigs (unclean to Mohammedans).

1857, May 10. Outbreak at Meerut. The climax came in the Bengal Army garrison at Meerut, some 25 miles from Delhi, after 85 cavalry sepoys who had refused the new cartridge had been disgraced and imprisoned. While the British units were at church, the Indian regiment released the imprisoned soldiers, then killed as many of their European officers and other European men, women, and children as they could find. Before the British troops could take action, the mutineers had fled to Delhi. There was no effective pursuit.

1857, May 11. Massacre at Delhi. Upon arrival at Delhi, the Meerut mutineers were joined by the native garrison, who, with the city rabble, began to butcher all Europeans they could find. All who could escape joined the British garrison, holding cantonments outside of town. In the city a few British officers and men held the arsenal as long as possible, then blew up themselves and the ammunition magazine, causing great damage to the attacking native soldiers and mob. The rebels declared **Bahadur** Shah, last of the decadent Moguls, as their ruler. The surviving Europeans fled to Meerut and Umballa, a large military post in the Punjab, 120 miles northwest of Delhi. Word of the uprising spread throughout India, causing the entire Bengal Army, from Delhi to Calcutta, to revolt against the British.

1857, May–July. British Reaction. Delayed

by the scattering of British units to hill stations for the summer, General **George Anson,** British commander in chief, was unable for several days to get a force together at Umballa to march on Delhi. Shortly after starting the march (May 17), Anson died of cholera (May 27). The British advance ceased briefly. Sir **John Lawrence,** efficient chief commissioner in the Punjab, now assumed control of operations in the north. He immediately rushed a force of 3,000 British troops to besiege Delhi, and promptly gathered more British and loyal Punjabi troops to follow them. At Lucknow, in the center of the dissident area, his elder brother, Sir **Henry Lawrence,** organized the defense of the residency against an ever-increasing rebel force. Sir Henry had 1,720 fighting men, including 712 faithful native troops, plus 1,280 additional noncombatants. At Calcutta, the governor general, Sir **Charles John Canning,** after some temporizing, undertook action to gather British reinforcements.

1857, June 27. Cawnpore Massacre. Dandu **Panth (Nana Sahib),** Rajah of Bitpur, led the rebellious native troops of the garrison in a 3-week siege of the British contingent (June 6–26). He persuaded Sir **Hugh Wheeler,** the British commander, to surrender his handful of British troops and more than 200 noncombatants, mostly English women and children, under promise of safe conduct to Allahabad. As the disarmed British were embarking on river boats, Nana's men murdered the men and imprisoned the women and children.

1857, July 7–16. Havelock Marches toward Lucknow. Sir **Henry Havelock,** with 2,500 men, mostly British, moved from Allahabad to the relief of Lucknow. Marching 126 miles in 9 days, during the hottest season of the year, Havelock met Nana Sahib's forces, defeating them at **Fatehpur** (July 12), **Aong** (July 15), and **Cawnpore** itself (July 16), where Nana's troops were completely shattered. On entering Cawnpore, the British discovered the bodies of the English women and children prisoners, hacked to death and thrown into a well by Nana's orders the day previous. Nana succeeded in escaping the berserk Britishers, although most of his followers were not so fortunate. (Nana's fate is obscure; he fled to Nepal, where he is reported to have died in 1859.) Havelock was now compelled to await reinforcements and supplies before continuing his advance on Lucknow (September 20).

1857, September 14–20. Storming of Delhi. The initial besieging force had taken the Badli-ki-Serai ridge dominating the city (June 8), but not until early August had its strength been sufficient for offensive action. After a 3-day artillery preparation, the assault force, 4,000 strong, moved against the walls in 4 columns, gaining a foothold inside after taking severe losses, including its commander, Brigadier General **John Nicholson,** who was killed. Six days of bitter street fighting followed before the city was finally subdued. Bahadur Shah was captured, and his sons shot out of hand after they had surrendered, in revenge for the murdered women and children of Cawnpore. The British took casualties totaling 1,574 men killed and wounded during the action. The capture of Delhi ended for all time the dream of a revival of the Mogul Empire.

1857, September 25. First Relief of Lucknow. Sir Henry Lawrence had been killed by artillery fire (July 4) and had been succeeded by Brigadier General **John Inglis.** Havelock's relief force, after an arduous campaign up from Cawnpore and bitter street fighting in Lucknow itself, broke through the 60,000 rebels besieging the residency, losing 535 officers and men out of a 2,500 strength. The rebels closed in again. Sir **James Outram,** who had joined the relief force as a volunteer (August 15), took command of the besieged garrison, since he was senior to Havelock. For 6 weeks more the obstinate defense of the residency continued.

1857, November 16. Second Relief of Lucknow. Another relief column, 4,500 strong, under Sir **Colin Campbell,** advanced from Cawnpore (November 12). On the 14th, the defenders heard Scottish bagpipes playing "The Campbells Are Coming." Two days later, the relief column crashed through. The residency was safely evacuated to Cawnpore (November 22), but Havelock was killed during the operation. Campbell decisively defeated a large rebel force outside of **Cawnpore** (December 6).

1858, January–March. Commencement of Central Indian Campaign. Sir **Hugh**

Rose, with 2 brigades (about 3,000 men) from the loyal Bombay Army, in a whirlwind campaign relieved **Saugor** (February 3), forced the pass of **Madanpur** (March 3), and invested **Jhansi,** the rebel stronghold (March 21).

1858, March 16. Recapture of Lucknow. Having been reinforced, Campbell again marched on rebel-held Lucknow. He was joined by **Bang Bahadur,** prime minister of Nepal, with 10,000 Gurkhas. After a week of bitter fighting, the city was finally cleared of the rebels.

1858, April–June. Rose in Central India. While Rose was investing Jhansi, 20,000 rebels under **Tantia Topi,** a lieutenant of Nana Sahib and the most capable military leader of the rebels, arrived on the scene. Rose boldly diverted half of his command to defeat Tantia Topi (April 1), then carried Jhansi itself by assault (April 3). Following this, he defeated rebel forces at **Kunch** (May 1) and **Kalpi** (May 22). In 5 months he had defeated the rebels in 13 actions. Tantia Topi, escaping, rallied another force and with the amazon **Rani of Jhansi** subverted (June 9) the troops of **Sindhia,** who had faithfully kept his treaty with England.

1858, June 19. Battle of Gwalior. Rose overwhelmed Tantia Topi and the Rani, who was killed. Topi escaped to the jungle, where he was later captured and executed (April 18, 1859).

COMMENT. *The victory at Gwalior ended the Mutiny, although mopping-up operations continued. British repressive measures were harsh.*

1858, September 1. End of the Company. The government of India was transferred to the British Crown, ending the century-long rule of the East India Company.

1865. Bhutan War. Long-standing frontier disorders forced the British to send a small force to Bhutan (January). The Bhutanese surprised and drove out the British garrison of **Dewangiri.** Sir **Henry Tombs** pressed a punitive action, resulting in Bhutanese suit for peace (November 11).

1878–1881. Second Afghan War. **(See p. 857.)**

1885. Third Burmese War. **(See below.)**

1896–1897. Malakand Campaign. A British expedition to the Swat Valley suppressed violence resulting from civil war in Chitral.

1897–1898. Tirah Campaign. Afridi tribesmen seized the Khyber Pass and attacked Northwest Frontier forts. The uprising was suppressed after severe fighting.

SOUTHEAST ASIA

BURMA

1852–1853. Second Burmese War. Following continued friction between British interests and the Burmese government, an amphibious expedition of 8,100 men under General Sir **H. T. Godwin** seized Rangoon (April 12). The Burmese army retired northward. Godwin seized Martaban at the mouth of the Salween River and Bassein in the Irrawaddy delta (May). After a halt until the monsoon ceased (October), Godwin occupied Pegu after a sharp engagement at the **Shwe-maw-daw Pagoda,** then seized Prome (October 9).

1852, December 20. Annexation of South Burma. Britain (the East India Company, actually) announced the annexation of Pegu Province. Meanwhile a revolution at Amarapura (Burmese capital, near modern Mandalay) had overthrown King **Pagan Min,** who was replaced by his half-brother, **Mindon Min,** who tacitly acquiesced in the cession of Pegu, though no formal peace treaty was signed.

1878. Accession of Thibaw. One of Mindon's many sons, **Thibaw Min,** ascended the throne on his father's death. Internal order in Burma began to break down under Thibaw's inept rule, while a border dispute with the British flared on the Manipur frontier. Thibaw then tried to offset British influence in Burma by entering into trade and diplomatic negotiations with the French. Burmese interference with the British teak trade became an immediate cause of conflict (1885).

1885. Third Burmese War. A British amphibious force of 9,000 troops and 2,800 native followers, under General **H. N. D. Prendergast,** moved up the Irrawaddy from Thayetmo in 55 river steamers and barges manned by the Royal Navy (November 14). As the expedition rapidly approached his capital, Ava, Thibaw surrendered (November 27). Britain annexed Burma (January 1, 1886).

1885–1895. Guerrilla Warfare. Burma was eventually pacified, although banditry was endemic in the outlying regions.

SIAM

1850–1863. Frontier Incidents in Malaya. Northern Malayan princes attempted to play off Siam and Britain (see p. 862). Firm British military and diplomatic action in the frontier regions blocked Siam's efforts to expand southward.

1863–1867. Siam Ejected from Cambodia. French military intervention in that country forced Siam to choose between war and peace; King **Rama V** reluctantly withdrew his forces from Cambodia.

1871–1872. Expedition to Eastern Laos. Siamese military intervention limited Chinese Black Flag bandit depredations in Luang Prabang, but failed to eject the Chinese from the eastern section (see p. 862).

1883–1887. Renewed Expeditions to Eastern Laos. Concerned by French expansion in Vietnam, Siam sent a second expedition to pacify eastern Laos, so as to eliminate any excuse for French intervention. This force was defeated by the Chinese (1883). A larger army was sent (1885), which eventually pacified much of eastern Laos (1887).

1893. The French Threat. Continued French expansion (see p. 862) led to strained relations and serious incidents in disputed territories in Laos between French and Siamese forces (1892–1893). French warships entered the Menam River, fought their way past the Paknam fort, and anchored off Bangkok (July). This created a serious crisis between Britain and France. Britain, however, unwilling to risk war with France, advised Siam to accept French terms, which included recognition of a French protectorate over Laos and Siamese abandonment of her eastern provinces which had formerly belonged to Cambodia. Siam agreed (October).

INDOCHINA

Vietnam

1851–1857. Clashes with the French. Under King **Tu Duc** a series of repressive measures against Christians, and sporadic murders of French missionaries, inspired French protests and occasional bombardment of Vietnamese ports by French warships.

1858–1862. French Invasion of Cochin China. Murder of the Spanish Bishop of Tongking caused a Franco-Spanish naval task force to bombard and to occupy Tourane (August–September, 1858). Shortages of food caused the allied force to move to Saigon (February, 1859). Sporadic operations continued, the French being primarily engaged in a war with China (see p. 863). A Franco-Spanish garrison of 1,000 held Saigon against a large besieging force for almost a year (March, 1860–February, 1861). A French relief force, under Admiral **Leonard V. J. Charner,** defeated the besiegers at the **Battle of Chi-hoa** (February 25, 1861). The French now steadily expanded their control of Cochin China. Tu Duc sued for peace, and ceded the three eastern provinces of Cochin China to France.

1862–1873. Unrest and Guerrilla War. Tu Duc was plagued by a series of rebellions. French intervention and pacification led to annexation of the 3 southwestern provinces of Cochin China. Internal disorders continued, but French control was strengthened.

1873–1874. Hanoi Incident. Without authority the French governor of Cochin sent a small force to intervene in civil war in Tongking. The French seized Hanoi, but evacuated it after forcing Tu Duc to grant numerous trade and diplomatic concessions. The relative interests of France, Vietnam, and Cochin China in Tongking resulted in continuing tension.

1882–1883. Renewed Vietnamese War with France. French expeditions seized Hanoi and the forts at Hué. Vietnam sued for peace, recognizing a French protectorate, and ceded additional areas to France. China's objections to this soon led to hostilities.

1884. Undeclared War between France and China. (**See p. 864.**)

1885–1895. Widespread Revolts. The Vietnamese population supported Prince **Si Vattha** in an uprising against the French. Order was soon restored in most areas of Vietnam (1886), but the last embers of revolt were not extinguished until Si Vattha surrendered (1892). At the same time, guerrilla warfare engaged the French for several years in Cochin China and Tongking. Relative peace was restored, however, as the result of strenuous French efforts (1895).

1887. Administrative Consolidation of French Indochina. This affirmed the establishment of a permanent French colony.

Cambodia

1861–1862. Dynastic Disorders. King **Norodom** was forced to flee to Siam by a revolt of his brother, **Si Votha.** With Siamese assistance Norodom regained his throne.

1863. Limited French Protectorate. This was established despite the objections of Siam, supported by Britain (see p. 861). France agreed to Siam's retention of some nominal claims to suzerainty over Cambodia (1864).

1866–1867. Revolt of Po Kombo. After some initial success, this pretender was defeated, then chased down by French and Cambodian forces.

1887. Cambodia Part of Indochina. (**See above.**)

1893. French Annexation of Western Cambodia from Siam. (**See p. 861.**)

Laos

1871–1872. Invasion by Chinese Refugees. Bandit refugees from China's internal wars (see p. 864) overran eastern Laos (under Siamese suzerainty) and threatened Luang Prabang. Depredations were limited by Siamese forces, but the Chinese retained their hold on eastern Laos and western Vietnam (roughly the region between Xieng-Khouang and the Black River Valley of Tongking).

1883–1887. Siamese Expedition to Eastern Laos. (**See p. 861.**)

1887–1889. French Influence in Eastern Laos. The French took advantage of disorders in Laos to intervene, and to annex the region between Xieng-Khouang and the Black River Valley, despite Siamese protests (see p. 861).

1893. French Annexation of Laos. After a number of frontier incidents in Laos, probably engineered by local French officials, hostilities broke out between France and Siam (see p. 861). As part of the terms of settlement of the crisis, Siam recognized a French protectorate over Laos, which was then incorporated into Indochina.

MALAYA AND INDONESIA

Both British (in Malaya and parts of Borneo) and Dutch (in Indonesia) were engaged in numerous military activities in their respective colonies, dealing with piracy, native dynastic disputes, and occasional armed revolts. Of these the most serious was a bitter continuing war of the Dutch against the Sultan of Atjeh (1873–1908).

EAST ASIA

CHINA

1850–1860. Taiping Rebellion (First Phase). Accession to the throne of the **Hsien-Feng** emperor was followed by tyranny. Anti-Manchu revolts organized by **Hung Hsiu-ch'uan** broke out in Kwangsi, Hupei, and Hunan provinces. Hung's military leader, **Yang Hsiu-ch'ing,** led rebel armies that swept the Yangtze Valley, capturing **Wuch'ang** and **Nanking.** At the latter city the revolutionary capital was established and a new dynasty—**Taiping T'ien-kuo**—announced with Hung as its ruler. Agrarian unrest aggravated revolt; Shanghai was captured by rebel supporters (September 7, 1853). China was virtually split in two.

1853–1881. Regional Insurrections. Collapse of central authority encouraged widespread insurrections. A bandit regime called **Nien Fei** terrorized Anhwei, northern Kiangsu, and Shantung (1853–1868) before its suppression by a rejuvenated central government. A Mohammedan (Panthay) regime established (1855) at Tali in Yunnan was finally suppressed

(1873). A revolt of the Miao tribe in Kweichow (1855) lasted even longer (1881).

Second Opium War, 1856–1860

1856–1858. Anglo-Chinese Hostilities. Chinese seizure of the British ship **Arrow** at Canton (October, 1856) brought armed reprisal: bombardment of Chinese ports. Later, an Anglo-French force under Admiral Sir **Michael Seymour** occupied Canton (December, 1857), then cruised north to capture briefly the Taku forts near Tientsin (May, 1858).

1858, June 26–29. Treaties of Tientsin. Negotiations between China and England, France, the United States, and Russia theoretically brought peace, China agreeing to open more treaty ports, to receive legations at Peking and missionaries in the interior, to legalize opium importation, and to establish a foreign-inspected maritime customs service. The **Treaty of Aigun (May, 1858)** had already ceded the left bank of the Amur River to Russia. But China soon abrogated the Franco-British treaties.

1859, June 25. Attack on the Taku Forts. Refusal to admit foreign diplomats to Peking was followed by British Admiral Sir **James Hope**'s bombardment of the forts guarding the mouth of the Peiho (Hai) River, below Tientsin. The squadron was severely mauled and British landing parties repulsed by a surprisingly efficient Chinese garrison. Commodore **Josiah Tattnall,** commanding the U.S. Asiatic Squadron, declaring "blood is thicker than water," assisted the British to withdraw. England and France agreed on joint action against China.

1860. Renewed Hostilities. Anglo-French forces gathered at Hong Kong (May 13). A joint amphibious expedition moved north to the Gulf of Chihli (Po Hai), 11,000 British under Lieutenant General Sir **James Hope Grant** and 7,000 French under Lieutenant General **Cousin - Montauban.** Landings, uncontested, were made at Pei-Tang (August 1) and the Taku forts taken by assault (August 21) with the assistance of the naval flotilla. Moving upriver to Tientsin, the expedition started for Peking—the British on the right bank of the Peiho, the French on the left. Chinese pleas for an armistice and parley resulted in the sending of a delegation headed by Sir **Harry Smith Parkes** into their lines. The party was seized (September 18), imprisoned, and—as learned later—horribly tortured. About half of its number died. Meanwhile the expedition pushed ahead, brushing some 30,000 Chinese aside in 2 sharp actions and arriving before the walls of Peking (September 26). Preparations for assault commenced, and the Summer Palace was occupied and looted (October 6).

1860, October 18. Treaty of Peking. Another Chinese bid for peace was accepted; the price was return of the survivors of the Parkes party, surrender of Kowloon on the mainland opposite Hong Kong, and an indemnity of 8 million taels. General Grant then burned the Summer Palace (October 24) in reprisal for the mistreatment of the Parkes party. Leaving a garrison at Tientsin, the expedition withdrew from China.

1860–1861. Russian Expansion. Russia now took advantage of China's prostration to extort from her the Maritime Provinces, where the port of Vladivostok was founded (1860–1861).

Taiping Rebellion (Final Phase), 1860–1864

Following the close of the war with the foreign powers, patriotic Chinese—including particularly **Tseng Kuo-fan** (who became viceroy) and **Li Hung-chang**—led a revitalized government and the Chinese people to organize against the dictatorial Taiping rebel regime in the south.

1860. Appearance of Ward. In the Shanghai area, Chinese merchants financed an army of liberation under **Frederick Townsend Ward,** American merchant marine officer and soldier of fortune from Salem, Mass. Ward won a series of victories which earned for his force the title of "Ever Victorious Army" and for him a commission as brigadier general in the Imperial Chinese forces (1861).

1862, August 20. Battle of Tzeki. Having cleared a 30-mile zone about Shanghai, winning 11 victories in a 4-month period (with the assistance of British and French forces returned from the Peking expedition), Ward attacked the walled city of Tzeki. Here he was mortally wounded while directing the assault.

1863. "Chinese" Gordon. Captain Charles G. Gordon, R.E., was detailed by the British government—at Chinese request—to succeed Ward in command of the Ever Victorious Army. Gordon moved north, along the line of the Grand Canal, taking Soochow (Wuhsien, December 4) and bottling up the Taiping forces in Nanking. Gordon, disgusted by the treacherous murder by Chinese government forces of rebel prisoners who had surrendered to him, threw up the command of his army, which was soon disbanded.

1864, July 10. Fall of Nanking. Chinese forces under Viceroy Tseng ended the Taiping Rebellion, although its last embers were not stamped out until the following year.

COMMENT. *This was perhaps the most destructive war of the entire 19th century. It has been estimated that 20 million people died directly or indirectly due to the war between 1850 and 1864.*

1865–1881. Suppression of Regional Revolts. Tseng supervised the operations of Chinese forces to suppress the revolts of Nien Fei and the Miaos (see p. 862).

1883–1885. Undeclared War with France. This was the result of French expansion in Tongking. Chinese troops, sent to Tongking from Yunnan, were driven out of **Pallen** and **Son-Tay** (1883), following which the French established themselves securely in the lower Black River Valley. Peace negotiations at Peking failed (May, 1884). Chinese troops defeated a French force at **Bac-le** (June 23, 1884). A French naval squadron then entered the harbor of Foochow, destroying a Chinese naval squadron there, as well as the land fortifications and naval arsenal (August 23, 1884). The French then steamed to Formosa, bombarding **Chi-lung** (October 23, 1884). The forts there held out against repeated French attacks, but surrendered (March, 1885), following which the French occupied the port briefly. They demonstrated at Tamsui, captured the Pescadores, and maintained a semiblockade of the island for 7 months. Meanwhile, in Tongking, a major French offensive, after hard fighting, culminated in the capture of **Langson** (February 13, 1885). Six weeks later, however, the French suffered a severe defeat outside Langson and precipitously evacuated the region, abandoning most of their equipment. When news of this reached Paris, the government fell, and its successor instituted peace negotiations. The **Treaty of Tientsin** (June 9, 1885) brought peace, restoring the *status quo;* France restored to China the areas occupied in Formosa and the Pescadores.

Sino-Japanese War, 1894–1895

Chinese and Japanese rivalry over predominance in Korea (semi-independent vassal of the Chinese Empire) had grown intense (see p. 867).

1894, June. Japanese-Fomented Riots in Seoul. China sent troops by sea to Asan (about 40 miles southwest of Seoul) to restore order at the request of the Korean government. Japan responded by rushing troops directly to Seoul through Chemulpo (Inchon). Meanwhile the Korean government suppressed the disorders, but neither China nor Japan would withdraw troops until the other did.

1894, July 20. Japan Seizes Control of the Korean Government.

1894, July 25–29. Preliminary Clashes. Near **Phung-Tao,** on the west coast of Korea, Japanese Admiral **Tsuboi** attacked a Chinese troop convoy bringing reinforcements to Asan, sinking one transport and severely damaging Chinese naval escorts (July 25). At the same time, Major General **Oshima,** commanding Japanese troops in Seoul, advanced on Asan, defeating the Chinese at **Songhwan** (July 29).

1894, August 1. Declaration of War. Both sides declared war and rushed reinforcements to Korea by sea, the Chinese to the

Yalu River and northern ports, the Japanese through Pusan and Chemulpo. Neither navy attempted to interfere with the other's convoys.

1894, September 15. Battle of Pyongyang. General **Michitsura Nozu,** with an army in excess of 20,000 men (partly landed by sea, partly overland from Seoul), attacked and defeated a Chinese force of 14,000 defending Pyongyang. The remnants of Chinese forces withdrew to the Yalu River, where the main Chinese fleet, under Admiral **Ting Ju-ch'ang,** had just escorted a troop convoy with reinforcements.

1894, September 17. Naval Battle of the Yalu (Haiyang). Admiral **Yuko Ito,** with the main Japanese fleet, having convoyed troops to take part in the Pyongyang battle, then headed north to seek Ting's squadron. The two fleets met between the mouth of the Yalu and Haiyang Island. The Chinese squadron consisted of 2 ironclad battleships, 4 light cruisers, and 6 torpedo boats. The Japanese force comprised 4 heavy cruisers, 4 fast light cruisers, and 2 other old armored cruisers. The Japanese had a great preponderance of heavy (over 5″ caliber) quick-firing guns. Japanese gunnery and ship handling were far superior to the Chinese. Five Chinese ships were sunk; the remainder limped into Port Arthur, all severely damaged. The Japanese sustained considerable damage, but lost no ships. Ito, respectful of the 2 powerful Chinese battleships, had failed to close decisively with his defeated enemy, or to pursue aggressively; otherwise the Chinese squadron—out of ammunition at the close of the battle—would have been annihilated.

1894, October 24–25. Passage of the Yalu. After Pyongyang, Nozu's force—advancing to the Yalu—was augmented and reorganized as the First Army, under Marshal **Aritomo Yamagata.** With over 20,000 men, the Japanese crossed the Yalu without opposition.

1894, October 24–November 19. Operations against Port Arthur. The Japanese Second Army (26,000 troops and 13,000 auxiliaries), under Marshal **Iwao Oyama,** was convoyed to the Liaotung Peninsula, landing north of Port Arthur at Pitzuwu (October 24). Opposition to the advance down the peninsula to Port Arthur was negligible. Unaccountably, the Japanese Navy permitted Admiral Ting and his squadron to escape across the Strait of Pohai to Weihaiwei. Oyama's successful dawn attack on the fortifications of Port Arthur (November 19) was led by General **Maresuke Nogi;** the 10,000 defenders made only feeble resistance.

1894, October–1895, January. Operations in Manchuria. After winning some minor actions (of which **Tsao-ho-ku,** November 30, was particularly hard-fought), Yamagata's advance from the Yalu into Manchuria was stopped by a combination of supply problems and cold weather. The Japanese were forced to fight hard to defend their advanced base at **Hai-cheng** against Chinese General **Sung Ch'ing** (December–January).

1895, January. Weihaiwei Campaign. The Japanese decided to eliminate any possibility of further Chinese naval interference. The Third Army—comprising a number of units from the Second Army, and commanded by Oyama—was convoyed to Jungcheng, on the eastern tip of the Shantung Peninsula, about 20 miles east of the Chinese naval base at Weihaiwei (January 19). After an unopposed landing, Oyama promptly marched west and, while the Japanese fleet engaged the fortifications from the sea, captured Weihaiwei and its fortifications in 2 days of bitterly cold winter fighting (January 30–31).

1895, February 2–12. Naval Battle of Weihaiwei. The Chinese squadron (2 battleships, 4 cruisers, 6 gunboats, and 15 small torpedo boats) was now caught between Ito's blockading Japanese fleet and the Japanese Third Army, manning the Weihaiwei forts. Ito commenced a series of night torpedo-boat attacks against the Chinese fleet, while the captured land batteries hammered them by day. Admiral Ting and his men put up the stoutest Chinese resistance of the war, but the situation was hopeless. Torpedo-boat attacks destroyed one of the battleships (February 5). Ting sent his torpedo boats on a dash for freedom, but only 2 escaped (February 7). With most of the fleet destroyed, Ting committed suicide; his remaining men and battered vessels surrendered (February 12).

1895, February–March. Advance into Manchuria. Meanwhile, the Japanese First Army (now under Nozu's command) had made contact with the Second Army in the Liaotung Peninsula, while continuing to beat off repeated Chinese attacks on Hai-cheng. Despite bitter cold, Nozu now advanced, defeating Sung at **Tapingshan** (February 21–23). Chinese forces now began to crumble, and the last effective resistance in Manchuria was eliminated by the Japanese near **Yingkow** (March 9). The Japanese paused for good weather before marching on Peking. Chinese Viceroy Li Hung-chang was sent to Japan to negotiate peace.

1895, April 17. Treaty of Shimonoseki. China recognized Korean independence, agreed to pay a 300-million-tael indemnity, and ceded Formosa, the Pescadores, and the Liaotung Peninsula to Japan. Japan had proven herself a major military power.

1895–1900. Grab for Concessions in China. Russia, France, Germany, and Britain now began a scramble for concessions from supine China and to keep Japan in check. The 3 first-named edged Japan from Port Arthur and the Liaotung Peninsula, which Russia then gobbled up, together with rights for the Chinese Eastern Railway which would link Port Arthur with the trans-Siberian line. Germany occupied Kiaochow (November 14), while Britain secured a 99-year lease of the Kowloon territory on the mainland opposite Hong Kong, and a lease on Weihaiwei—to run so long as Russia occupied Port Arthur.

1899, September 6. The "Open Door" Policy. The United States alone stood firm on its policy of equal commercial opportunity in, and the territorial and administrative integrity of, China, as stated in a note to the other powers from American Secretary of State **John Hay.**

COMMENT. *European imperialist diplomacy sowed the seeds of future war.*

JAPAN

1853–1854. Perry Opens Japan. A U.S. squadron of 4 vessels arrived in Tokyo Bay to negotiate a treaty to end Japan's voluntary isolation from the rest of the world. The Japanese respected Commodore **Matthew C. Perry**'s firmness and conciliation. In the **Treaty of Kanagawa** (March 31, 1854) they agreed to open trade relations with the U.S. and to protect shipwrecked American sailors. Similar treaties were later negotiated by England, Russia, and Holland.

1863, June. Shimonoseki Incidents. Forts of the Choshu clan fired on American, and later on French and Dutch, vessels, bringing immediate American and French reprisal bombardments.

1863, August 15–16. British Bombardment of Kagoshima. Unable to obtain satisfaction from the Satsuma clan for the murder of a British subject (September, 1862), a British squadron bombarded the Satsuma capital.

1863–1868. Internal Strife. The western clans (Choshu and Satsuma) tried to influence the Tokugawa shogun to expel foreigners, and to obtain the emperor's support against the Tokugawas. Repeated demonstrations of Occidental military might caused the western clans to cease their antiforeign efforts (1864), but not their attempts to break the power of the Tokugawa shogunate. The struggle combined intrigue, murder, and civil war, which included clashes at **Kyoto** (September, 1863; August, 1864) and an unsuccessful Tokugawa expedition into Choshu territory (July–October, 1866). The death of **Iemochi,** the old shogun (September, 1866), was followed soon after by that of the emperor (February, 1867). The new shogun, **Keiki,** resigned (November, 1867), but the turmoil continued for another 7 months, when (near Tokyo) the **Battle of Ueno** (July 4, 1868) ended the power of the Tokugawa, leaving the western clans predominant.

1864, September 5–8. Bombardment of Shimonoseki. An allied naval expedition—Dutch, French, British, and American—silenced the forts in reprisal for continued hostility by the Choshu clan. This demonstration of military superiority ended the antiforeign movement in western Japan.

1869, January 3. Restoration of Imperial Power. Emperor **Mutsuhito** (Meiji emperor) assumed control of the government, supported primarily by the western clans. This was the start of Japan's emergence from feudalism.

1874, April–October. Expedition to For-

mosa. Japan, claiming sovereignty over the Ryukyu Islands, sent an expedition to Formosa to punish natives there for the murder of Ryukyu sailors.

1875–1885. Japanese Interventions in Korea. (See below.)

1877, July–September. Satsuma Rebellion. The samurai (feudal warrior class), protesting against modern innovations and particularly against the raising of a national conscript army, rose against the government (but not against the emperor). The most serious threat was the march of 40,000 Satsuma warriors on Tokyo. They were stopped, then defeated, by the new national army at **Kumamoto.**

1879. Annexation of the Ryukyus. Despite Chinese protests, Japan began its overseas expansion.

1894–1895. Sino-Japanese War. (See p. 864.)

KOREA

1866. French Expedition. To punish Korea for the murder of French missionaries, a French naval force occupied **Kanghwa** at the mouth of the Han River. The Korean government refused to negotiate and the French, after inconclusive skirmishes, withdrew.

1871, May. American Expedition. To investigate the imprisonment and murder of some American sailors in earlier years, an American naval force captured the **Kanghwa** forts in a small-scale amphibious assault. After vain efforts to negotiate, the Americans withdrew.

1875–1876. Japanese Intervention. A Japanese vessel having been fired on in Korean waters, a Japanese naval expedition forced Korea to sign a treaty (February 25, 1876) establishing trade relations and opening several ports to Japanese vessels. Significantly, this treaty recognized Korean sovereignty, ignoring nominal Chinese suzerainty. Similar treaties were later concluded (but through Chinese mediation) by the U.S. and other western powers.

1882–1885. Intervention of China and Japan. Several internal disorders culminated in an attack on the Japanese legation. A Japanese milit ry force entered Seoul, obtained reparations, and remained as a powerful legation guard. China then sent troops to re-establish her suzerain position in Korea; **Yuan Shih-k'ai** became the Chinese resident (1883). Renewed disorders led to the dispatch of additional Chinese troops to restore order. At the same time, Japanese troops arrived to protect Japan's interests. War between China and Japan was avoided only by the **Convention of Tientsin** (April 18, 1885) between Chinese Viceroy Li Hung-chang and Japanese Count Ito. Both nations agreed to withdraw troops and to notify each other if further intervention should become necessary.

1894. Tong-hak Rising. An antiforeign society, the Tong-haks, rebelled (March) and for 3 months successfully defied Korean government efforts at suppression. At the request of Korea, Chinese troops entered the country to help restore order. Japan, claiming a violation of the Tientsin Convention, sent a strong force to seize Chemulpo (Inchon) and Seoul. War inevitably resulted.

1894–1895. Sino-Japanese War. (See p. 864.)

1895–1900. Unrest in Korea. Continuing disorders provided Japan and Russia with opportunities to improve their respective positions in Korea. The Russians to some extent supplanted Japanese influence in Seoul; tension between the 2 nations was increasing at the close of the century.

THE PHILIPPINES

1896, August. Insurrection against Spain. The rebellion, led by **Emilio Aguinaldo,** was settled peacefully when Spain promised substantial government and social reforms. Aguinaldo was exiled.

1898, May 1. Dewey's Victory at Manila Bay. (See p. 907.) Aguinaldo, brought to Luzon by Dewey, began to raise a Filipino patriot army to assist the U.S. against Spain.

1898, December 10. Treaty of Paris. The Philippines were sold by Spain to the U.S.

1899, January 20. Aguinaldo Proclaims Filipino Independence. Believing he had been betrayed by U.S. failure to grant independence to the Philippines, Aguinaldo refused to recognize the Treaty of Paris. He called on his compatriots to establish an independent government, under his leadership. His army undertook a virtual siege of Manila, held by U.S. troops at the close of the Spanish-American War.

1899, February 4. Commencement of Philippine Insurrection. Hostilities against the U.S. started when Filipino insurgents fired on an American patrol in the outskirts of Manila. U.S. troops immediately drove the Filipino forces away from the city. The campaign spread through Luzon. Under the field command of Major General **Arthur MacArthur,** punitive columns swept both Luzon and the Visayas as the U.S. poured men and supplies into the islands. The rebellion was still active as the century ended (see p. 1011).

NORTH AMERICA

THE UNITED STATES, 1850–1861

1850–1865. Indian Wars. During this period there were at least 30 separate "wars" or major disturbances involving conflict with the Indians. During the decade before the Civil War nine-tenths of the U.S. Army strength of 16–17,000 troops were spread out over an area of more than 1,000,000 square miles west of the Mississippi, engaged in almost constant patrolling or combat operations against the Indians. Small detachments were also active in Florida, where there were recurrent troubles with the Seminoles. In these operations the Army was engaged at one time or another against Apache, Sioux, Cheyenne, Navajo, Mojave, Arapaho, Kiowa, Comanche, the various tribes of the Pacific Northwest, and others. In the year 1857 alone official records report 37 expeditions or operations involving combat, and many more without fighting. Although the tempo of these small wars subsided somewhat during the Civil War, because the nation's attention was diverted from the West, frontier hostilities continued. There were atrocities on both sides, although the disciplined troops of the Regular Army were rarely guilty of dishonorable treatment of the Indians. The most serious incident involving white treachery was the so-called **Sand Creek Massacre,** in Colorado, where militiamen attacked a village of Cheyenne and Arapaho Indians while their leaders were negotiating a treaty, killing 300 Indians, mostly women and children (November 29, 1864). This disgraceful affair was probably the principal cause of the increasing ferocity of the Plains Indians in the two following decades.

1856, May 21–September 15. Civil War in Kansas. Sacking of **Lawrence** by a proslavery mob (May 21) was followed by abolitionist fanatic **John Brown**'s murderous raid on **Pottawatomie** (May 24–25). **Franklin** was seized (August 13) by Free Staters. Brown and his followers were driven out of **Osawatomie** and the settlement sacked by proslavery guerrillas (August 30). In all, some 20 persons were killed and an estimated $2 million worth of property destroyed before the arrival of Federal troops restored temporary calm in Kansas (September 16).

1857–1858. Mormon Expedition. The Mormons had established a practically independent state in Utah, ignoring government authority, and inciting the Indians against other settlers. A force of less than 1,000 men under Brevet Brigadier General **Albert Sidney Johnston** moved into Utah (October, 1857). Despite provocations by the hostile Mormons, the disciplined troops re-established U.S. Government authority in Salt Lake City and the surrounding countryside without bloodshed (June, 1858).

1859, October 16–18. John Brown's Raid. With 18 followers, Brown seized the Federal arsenal and armory at Harpers Ferry, and captured local citizens as hostages. The slave insurrection he hoped to spark failed to materialize. A detachment of U.S. Marines, commanded by Army Colonel **R. E. Lee,** captured Brown and his men. He and 6 of his men were convicted of treason and criminal conspiracy and hanged (December 2–March 16).

CIVIL WAR, 1861–1865

Election of Republican **Abraham Lincoln** to the Presidency (November 6, 1860) precipitated Southern secession as the only way in which to preserve the southern agricultural economy, based on slave labor. South Carolina seceded (December 20).

1861, January–April. Confederate States of America. In quick succession Mississippi, Florida, Alabama, Georgia, Louisiana, and Texas followed South Carolina's lead. A convention held at Montgomery, Ala., framed a constitution and set up a provisional government (February 8). **Jefferson Davis** was elected Confederate President (February 9). Outgoing U.S. President **James Buchanan** made no attempt to forestall the subsequent general seizure of U.S. military installations throughout the South by seceding state militias, but 4 U.S. Regular Army officers, each acting promptly on his own volition, saved 4 key points on the southern seacoasts—Forts Sumter, Charleston, S.C.; Pickens, Pensacola, Fla.; Taylor, Key West, Fla.; and Jefferson, Dry Tortugas, Fla. Two days after Lincoln's inauguration, Davis, with Confederate congressional authorization, called for 100,000 volunteers for 1 year's military service (March 6). By mid-April the Confederacy had 35,000 men under arms—a force twice as large as the then existing U.S. Army.

1861, April 12–14. Bombardment of Fort Sumter. South Carolinian forces under Major General **Pierre G. T. Beauregard** opened fire on Fort Sumter in Charleston Harbor, commanded by Major **Robert Anderson.** After 34 hours of bloodless bombardment, Anderson, his supplies exhausted, capitulated. He and his garrison, 7 officers and 76 enlisted men, marched out with the honors of war, and were shipped up North.

1861, April 15. Lincoln Calls for Volunteers. He called for 75,000 volunteers for 3 months' service to suppress insurrection.

1861, April 17. Virginia Secedes. She claimed the President's call for volunteers was an act of war against the seceded states. Virginia's secession was followed by Arkansas, Tennessee, and North Carolina. Eleven states were now in armed, open rebellion (May 20). Kentucky declared "neutrality" (May 24).

1861, April–May. Scott's "Anaconda Plan." As a nation *de facto*, the Confederacy had now only to maintain its sovereignty within its own borders. To restore the *status quo ante bellum*, the remainder of the U.S. must invade and destroy all armed resistance. Lieutenant General **Winfield Scott,** General in Chief of the U.S. Army (and a native of Virginia) had foreseen the difficulties and had earlier (October, 1860) advocated adequate reinforcement of all Federal garrisons in the South. Infirm Scott, 74 years old, but still possessing a sound and brilliant mind, now urged immediate blockade of Southern ports and the raising of an army of 300,000 men or more. Once this force was equipped and trained, Scott argued, it should invade the South down the Mississippi Valley to the Gulf of Mexico, thus isolating the Confederacy. This long-range concept of squeezing the South into submission was unpalatable to politicians who wanted quick, cheap victory, and derisively dubbed it the "Anaconda Plan."

1861, April 19. Lincoln Proclaims a Blockade. This was the only part of Scott's plan that was adopted.

The Line-up

The 22 Northern states (including 3 border states with divided loyalties) had a population of some 22 million; the 11 seceding states had 5.5 million whites and 3.5 million Negro slaves. Actually, the available man power—since the Negro slaves performed labor which in the North had to be done by white men—favored the North by a 5:2 ratio. The North was an economic-agricultural entity, potentially capable of supporting a protracted war. The South was agricultural, its crops of tobacco, cotton, and sugar mainly selling abroad; its manufacture was small. To succeed, it must market its produce overseas, and import war materiel.

The U.S. Army strength in 1861 was 16,367 officers and men, scattered along the western frontier and in seacoast forts. Concentration in force was impossible;

recourse was had to militia and volunteers, poorly trained and originally of short enlistment terms. The Confederate Army consisted of men enlisted for 1 year. The 286 U.S. Regular Army officers who resigned and went South were wisely used as leaven for its officer corps. In the North the remaining 780 U.S. Regular officers were mostly kept in their units, instead of being utilized to train the Union armies; political appointees, mostly without previous experience, were substituted instead.

The Confederacy had no naval vessels, but it had 322 of the 1,300 U.S. Navy officer corps and a vigorous Secretary of the Navy—**Stephen R. Mallory** of Florida, who left no stone unturned to build a fighting naval force. The U.S. Navy had some 90 wooden ships—sail and steam—42 of them in commission, and only 4 in Northern waters when the war broke out. **Gideon Welles** of Connecticut, competent U.S. Secretary of the Navy, set about extemporizing an enormous force, backed by the vast maritime resources of the North—resources which did not exist in the South. His assistant, **Gustavus Vasa Fox,** a former U.S. Navy officer, was of tremendous assistance in the task.

Confederate President Jefferson Davis was a West Pointer, a Mexican War hero, and had been Secretary of War; he had also been chairman of the Senate's Military Affairs Committee. He was well qualified for his position as Commander in Chief. U.S. President Abraham Lincoln had had no real military experience. Under political pressure he had rejected the recommendations of his senior military adviser. On the President fell the onus of producing and maintaining in the North the will to win, without which Southern victory would be inevitable. Yet he had no concerted plan of campaign. Lincoln's call for volunteers and his arbitrary immediate strengthening of the Regular Army were countered by Davis' authorization of Confederate privateering. Operations began on both sides of the Appalachians, at first piecemeal, later in force.

War in the East, 1861

1861, April 20. Loss of Norfolk Navy Yard. Virginia militia, seizing this important station, secured for the Confederacy the fine steam frigate *Merrimack,* and a great quantity of naval stores and armament, including 52 modern 9-inch guns.

1861, May 24. Washington Menaced. Virginia militia occupied the Alexandria area and hastily installed Confederate batteries controlled the Potomac approaches.

1861, June. Operations in West Virginia and Virginia. Major General **George B. McClellan** with Ohio volunteers cleared western Virginia of local Confederate forces at **Philippi** (June 3) and **Rich Mountain–Carrick's Ford** (July 11–14). In eastern Virginia, there was a skirmish at **Big Bethel,** near Union-held Fortress Monroe (June 10).

1861, June–July. Focus on Washington and Richmond. The main bodies of both Union and Confederacy gathered between the opposing capitals. Brevet Major General **Irvin McDowell,** with 38,000 Union troops—less than 2,000 professional soldiers among them—moved from Washington (July 19) to attack a Confederate force of 20,000, under Beauregard, near Centerville, Va.

1861, July 21. First Battle of Bull Run. McDowell found his enemy lying along Bull Run. Unaware that General **Joseph E. Johnston** had already arrived with most of his 12,000 men from the lower Shenandoah Valley to reinforce Beauregard, McDowell, who had 28,500 in the field, attempted to turn the Confederate left by a movement too complicated for his untrained troops and staff. After some progress, his attack was checked by the stand of Brigadier General **Thomas J. Jackson**'s Virginia brigade, Jackson winning his sobriquet of **"Stonewall."** Johnston's skillful shift of troops from the original battle front culminated in success with the arrival of his last brigade by rail from Winchester. The Union enveloping force was itself enveloped and most of McDowell's army fled the field in panic, covered only by the dogged rear-guard action of Major

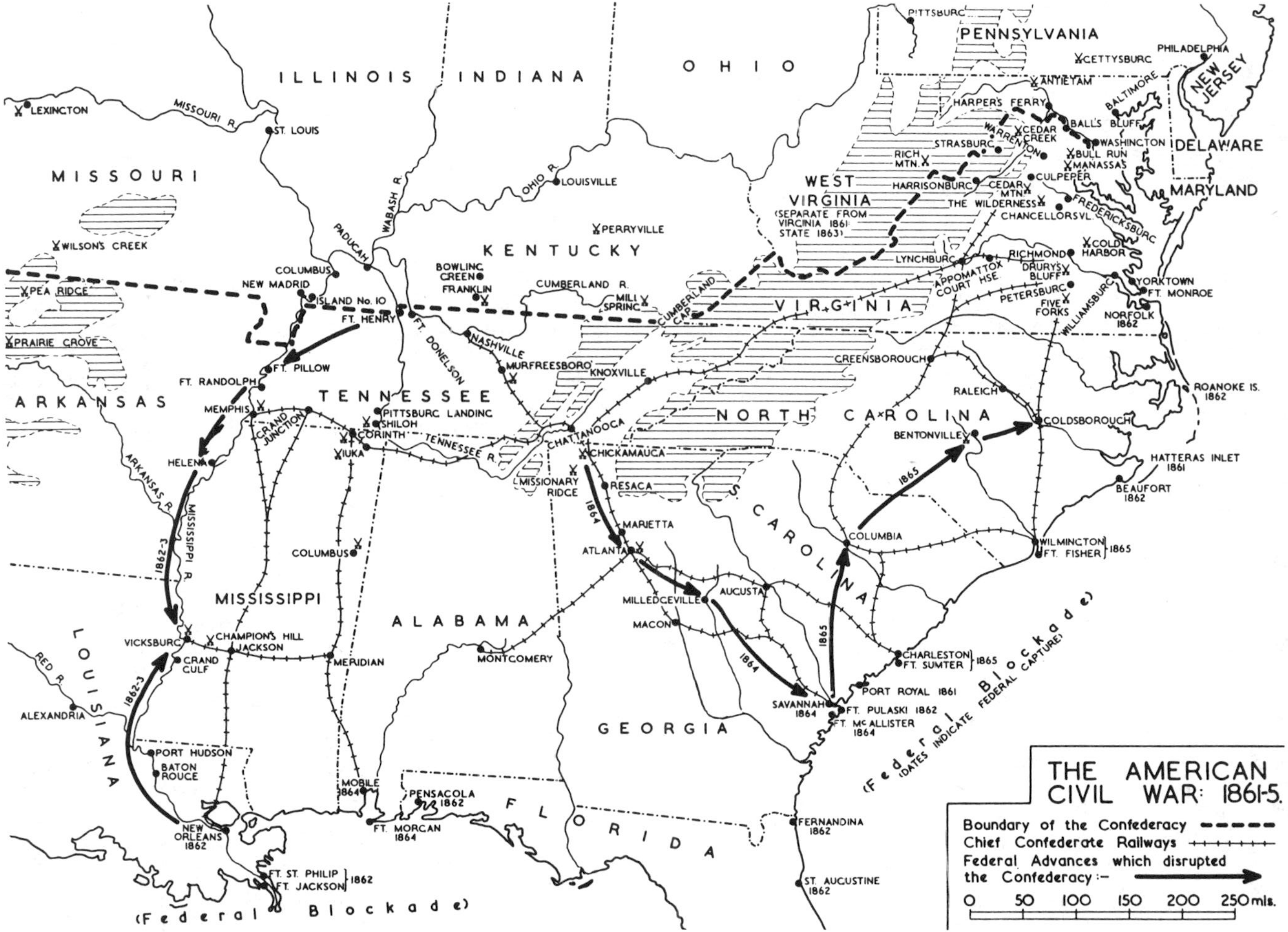
THE AMERICAN CIVIL WAR: 1861-5.
Boundary of the Confederacy
Chief Confederate Railways
Federal Advances which disrupted the Confederacy:—
0 50 100 150 200 250 mls.
(Federal Blockade)
(DATES INDICATE FEDERAL CAPTURE)
ILLINOIS
INDIANA
OHIO
PENNSYLVANIA
NEW JERSEY
DELAWARE
MARYLAND
MISSOURI
KENTUCKY
WEST VIRGINIA
(SEPARATE FROM VIRGINIA 1861: STATE 1863)
VIRGINIA
NORTH CAROLINA
S. CAROLINA
TENNESSEE
ARKANSAS
MISSISSIPPI
ALABAMA
GEORGIA
FLORIDA
LOUISIANA
LEXINGTON
MISSOURI R.
ST. LOUIS
WILSON'S CREEK
PEA RIDGE
PRAIRIE GROVE
COLUMBUS
NEW MADRID
ISLAND No. 10
PADUCAH
WABASH R.
OHIO R.
LOUISVILLE
PERRYVILLE
BOWLING GREEN
FRANKLIN
CUMBERLAND R.
MILL SPRING
CUMBERLAND GAP
FT. HENRY
FT. DONELSON
NASHVILLE
MURFREESBORO
KNOXVILLE
FT. PILLOW
FT. RANDOLPH
MEMPHIS
GRAND JUNCTION
PITTSBURG LANDING
SHILOH
CORINTH
IUKA
TENNESSEE R.
CHATTANOOGA
CHICKAMAUGA
MISSIONARY RIDGE
RESACA
MARIETTA
ATLANTA
MILLEDGEVILLE
MACON
AUGUSTA
SAVANNAH 1864
FT. PULASKI 1862
FT. McALLISTER 1864
PORT ROYAL 1861
CHARLESTON
FT. SUMTER 1865
COLUMBIA
WILMINGTON
FT. FISHER 1865
BENTONVILLE
GOLDSBOROUGH
RALEIGH
GREENSBOROUGH
HATTERAS INLET 1861
BEAUFORT 1862
ROANOKE IS. 1862
NORFOLK 1862
YORKTOWN
FT. MONROE
WILLIAMSBURG
FIVE FORKS
PETERSBURG
DRURY'S BLUFF
RICHMOND
COLD HARBOR
APPOMATTOX COURT HSE.
LYNCHBURG
CHANCELLORSVL.
FREDERICKSBURG
THE WILDERNESS
CEDAR MTN.
HARRISONBURG
CULPEPER
RICH MTN.
STRASBURG
WARRENTON
CEDAR CREEK
MANASSAS
BULL RUN
WASHINGTON
BALL'S BLUFF
BALTIMORE
HARPER'S FERRY
ANTIETAM
GETTYSBURG
PHILADELPHIA
PITTSBURG
HELENA
ARKANSAS R.
MISSISSIPPI R.
1862-3
VICKSBURG
CHAMPION'S HILL
JACKSON
GRAND GULF
COLUMBUS
MERIDIAN
MONTGOMERY
RED R.
ALEXANDRIA
PORT HUDSON
BATON ROUGE
NEW ORLEANS 1862
FT. ST. PHILIP
FT. JACKSON 1862
MOBILE 1864
FT. MORGAN 1864
PENSACOLA 1862
FERNANDINA 1862
ST. AUGUSTINE 1862
1864
1865

George Sykes's infantry battalion and Major **Innis N. Palmer**'s cavalry squadron—both regular units. Union losses were 2,706; Confederate, 1,981. Confederate President Jefferson Davis' refusal to authorize pursuit has been much criticized.

1861, July 22. New Northern Field Commander. McClellan was hurriedly called to Washington to command in place of McDowell.

1861, July–December. McClellan Trains an Army. He began organization and training of what would become the **Army of the Potomac,** while in Virginia across the river the Confederate forces under Johnston remained in the Manassas area.

1861, September 12–13. Battle of Cheat Mountain. Confederate General Robert E. Lee, attempting to recover western Virginia, was repulsed by Union troops.

1861, October 21. Battle of Ball's Bluff. A Union reconnaissance across the Potomac near Leesburg, Va., resulted in disaster when Colonel **Edward D. Baker,** U.S. senator transformed into soldier, foolishly engaged his troops piecemeal against superior Confederate forces led by Colonel **Nathan G. (Shanks) Evans.** Baker was killed. His troops, pinned on a precipitous river bank, were crushed, losing 237 killed and wounded and 714 captured or missing. Confederate losses were 149. Though the battle was minor in tactical importance, political repercussions in Washington were violent. A Joint Congressional Committee on the Conduct of War, headed by abolitionist Senator **Benjamin F. Wade** of Massachusetts, caused Brigadier General **Charles P. Stone,** originator of the reconnaissance, to be imprisoned for 8 months without charges or trial. For the rest of the war, the committee became an incubus on the Union military.

1861, November 1. New Northern General in Chief. McClellan, promoted on the retirement of old General Scott, made no further movement, and the North began to grumble at delay.

War in the West, 1861

1861, June 1. Battle of Booneville. Brigadier General **Nathaniel F. Lyon,** after quelling a Southern threat at St. Louis (May 10), on his own initiative moved on Jefferson City and drove Governor **Claiborne Jackson**'s pro-Southern militia down toward Arkansas. Missouri militia under Brigadier General **Sterling Price** was reinforced by Arkansas militia under Brigadier General **Ben McCullough,** and then attempted to retake Missouri for the Confederates.

1861, August 10. Battle of Wilson's Creek. Lyon, with 4,500 men, attacked McCullough and Price, who now had 11,600. Initial Union success ended when Lyon was killed in a desperate charge. The Northerners retreated in confusion. Confederate losses were 2,084; Union, 1,235.

COMMENT. *Although this was a tactical victory for the South, Lyon's aggressive operations had saved Missouri for the Union. "Neutral" Kentucky now became the target for both sides.*

1861, August–December. Grant and Johnston in Kentucky. Union Brigadier General **Ulysses S. Grant,** learning that General Albert Sidney Johnston, commanding Confederate forces in the West, was sending Major General **Leonidas Polk** to seize key points in Kentucky, forestalled him by occupying Paducah (August 6), thus safeguarding Cairo, the most strategically important spot in the U.S. at that moment. Johnston then established a line across Kentucky to block river movements southward down the Mississippi and up the Tennessee and Cumberland rivers. Western anchor of the line was on the Mississippi at Columbus, Ky., with an outpost at Belmont, Mo., on the west bank of the river.

1861, November 7. Battle of Belmont. Grant, with some 3,000 men, made a successful hit-and-run attack on Belmont to relieve growing Confederate pressure in western Missouri. Federal losses were 498; the Confederates, who had more than 5,000 men on the field, lost some 900.

1861, November 18. Halleck Commands in the West. Major General **Henry W. Halleck** came West to supplant vacillating Major General **John C. Frémont,** but Union command was still divided, with Major General **Don Carlos Buell** commanding in central and eastern Kentucky. As the year ended, Johnston's Confederate cordon from the Mississippi to the Cumberland Gap held firm.

Naval Operations, 1861

1861, May. Appearance of Confederate Privateers. A few hastily converted merchant ships, mounting a few guns, began to prowl the Atlantic coast line.

1861, May. Blockade Begins. An improvised and growing U.S. Navy—converted merchant vessels for the most part—took up the task of blockade from the Potomac River to the Gulf of Mexico.

1861, August 27. Action at Hatteras Inlet. A Union flotilla, under Flag Officer **Silas H. Stringham,** reduced Southern fortifications protecting this back door to the Confederacy, landed 800 troops from Fortress Monroe under Major General **Benjamin F. Butler,** and established a blockade base.

1861, November 7. Action at Port Royal. Flag Officer **Samuel F. du Pont** led a joint expedition to Port Royal Sound, important inland waterway connecting Savannah and Charleston. His 9 warships overwhelmed the defensive forts, and 17,000 troops under Brigadier General **Thomas W. Sherman** were landed. Port Royal became an important naval base for the Union blockading squadrons.

1861, November 8. The *Trent* Affair. Captain **Charles Wilkes** in U.S.S. *San Jacinto* arbitrarily overhauled the British packet *Trent* in the Bahamas, forcibly removing Confederate commissioners **James M. Mason** and **John Slidell,** on their way to England to represent President Davis. The high-handed action almost precipitated war with England, but was composed through diplomacy; Wilkes's action was disavowed by the U.S., and the commissioners were turned over to a British warship to continue their voyage.

War in the East, 1862

1862, January–March. McClellan's Plans. Disturbed by the new General in Chief's lack of aggressiveness, Lincoln finally goaded him to action by an imperative order (March 8). McClellan had about 180,000 men in and near Washington. Misled by reports that J. E. Johnston had over 100,000 men in the Manassas area (actually he had only about 50,000), McClellan decided to turn Johnston's positions by shipping his army down the Chesapeake Bay to Urbana, 45 miles from Richmond. Johnston, informed of the plan, at once countered by retiring behind the Rappahannock. McClellan then decided to move by water to Fortress Monroe, thence overland up the Peninsula—between the York and James rivers—toward Richmond. Lincoln, who doubted the estimates of Johnston's strength, reluctantly approved. Presence of the Confederate ironclad ram *Virginia* (erstwhile steam frigate U.S.S. *Merrimack,* seized at Norfolk Navy Yard and hurriedly armorplated) threatened this proposed water movement.

1862, February–April. North Carolina Coastal Operations. Union troops under Major General **Ambrose E. Burnside,** convoyed by Flag Officer **Louis Goldsborough,** landed on **Roanoke Island** (February 7). After defeating the Confederate garrison (February 8), Burnside captured **New Bern** (March 14) and **Beaufort** (April 26).

1862, March 8. The Battle of Hampton Roads (First Day). The *Virginia,* debouching from Norfolk, attacked the Union blockading squadron—all wooden vessels—awaiting her. The heavily armed, cumbrous ironclad, impervious to Union cannonballs, rammed and sank the U.S.S. *Cumberland* (24), then attacked and sank U.S.S. *Congress* (50). U.S.S. *Minnesota* (50), trying to join the battle, ran aground. The *Virginia* returned to Norfolk before dark to repair superficial damage, as her crew prepared to return next day to finish off 3 remaining Union vessels. That evening U.S.S. *Monitor,* a small, revolutionary armored warship invented by **John Ericsson,** arrived from New York and took station near the helpless *Minnesota.*

1862, March 9. *Monitor* vs. *Virginia* (*Merrimack*). The Confederate ironclad reappeared and the *Monitor* moved to meet her. The *Virginia*'s hull was covered by a heavy iron and oak carapace; she carried 10 large guns, 7- and 9-inch. The *Monitor,* a low-lying, metal "cheesebox on a raft," mounted two 11-inch guns in a heavily armored revolving turret. For 4 hours the ironclads hammered each other unsuccessfully, then the *Virginia* returned to Norfolk. The *Monitor* retained control of Hampton Roads.

COMMENT. *This inconclusive battle revolutionized naval construction by rendering wooden ships obsolete.*

1862, March 10. McClellan Prepares for Action. Satisfied that the *Virginia* was no longer a menace to his transports, McClellan began immediate preparations to move his army to Fortress Monroe.

1862, March 11. Lincoln Assumes Direction of the War. To ensure McClellan's undivided attention to the Richmond theater, Lincoln temporarily relieved him as General in Chief and personally assumed over-all military command. Lincoln's reasoning was sound; the results were disastrous, since neither he nor his Secretary of War, **Edwin M. Stanton,** had the professional experience required.

1862, March 22. McClellan Moves to the Peninsula. McClellan assured Lincoln that after the departure of the Army of the Potomac—130,000 strong—the security of Washington would be maintained by 75,000 men, including 23,000 under General **N. P. Banks,** who was responsible for stopping any threat to Washington through the Shenandoah Valley.

1862, March 23. Battle of Kernstown. Opposed to Banks in the lower Shenandoah Valley was Major General Stonewall Jackson, who had retired south of Strasburg with his 4,300 men. Banks, satisfied that Jackson posed no threat to Washington, left 9,000 men around Winchester under Brigadier General **James Shields** and moved east toward Manassas to cooperate with McClellan's operations in the Peninsula. Jackson, unaware of Shields's strength, attacked him at Kernstown, and was repulsed. So vigorous was the Confederate attack, however, that Shields reported that Jackson must have been reinforced.

1862, March 24. Lincoln Orders Banks Back to the Valley. He also discovered that McClellan had left only 50,000 men to cover Washington, not 75,000. To McClellan's disgust, therefore, Lincoln detained McDowell's corps of 30,000 at Washington as it was about to embark for Fortress Monroe. Lincoln ordered McDowell to join 10,000 Union troops already near Fredericksburg; he assured McClellan that McDowell would be permitted to march overland to join him near Richmond as soon as any possible threat to Washington disappeared. Few minor engagements have had as much significance as the Battle of Kernstown.

1862, April. Lee's Strategic Plan. General Robert E. Lee, military adviser to President Davis, realized that Johnston had only 60,000 men available to protect Richmond against McClellan's 100,000 assembling at Fortress Monroe and McDowell's 40,000 at Fredericksburg. He also knew of Lincoln's sensitivity about Washington. Lee recommended that Jackson—reinforced to nearly 18,000 men—make a demonstration in the Valley so as to divert the largest possible Union forces from McClellan. Johnston agreed, and Davis approved.

THE VALLEY CAMPAIGN

1862, May 1. Jackson's Situation. He was at Swift Run Gap, menaced by 2 threats: Banks coming up the Valley and Frémont with about 15,000 approaching from West Virginia. Leaving Brigadier General **Richard S. Ewell** and 8,000 men to contain Banks, Jackson moved westward into the Alleghenies.

1862, May 8. Battle of McDowell. Jackson surprised and threw back the leading elements of Frémont's army. Frémont halted all further advance. Jackson returned to the valley.

1862, May 9–30. Jackson's Advance. He hurried north, down the Valley. Utilizing the Massanutten Mountain—a 50-mile-long spine bisecting the Shenandoah Valley—as a screen, he turned east through its one pass, then swung northward again.

1862, May 23. Battle of Front Royal. Jackson threw a Federal garrison out of Front Royal and threatened Banks's rear.

1862, May 25. First Battle of Winchester. Jackson pursued Banks to Winchester, defeated him there again, and chased him back across the Potomac. At Harpers Ferry, Banks lost some 3,000 prisoners, 10,000 stands of small arms, some cannon, and a vast quantity of stores. Union casualties were about 1,500; Confederate, 400.

1862, May 26. Lincoln's Reaction. The President diverted McDowell at Fredericksburg from his planned junction with McClellan, and hurried him toward the Valley. Frémont, too, was spurred to re-

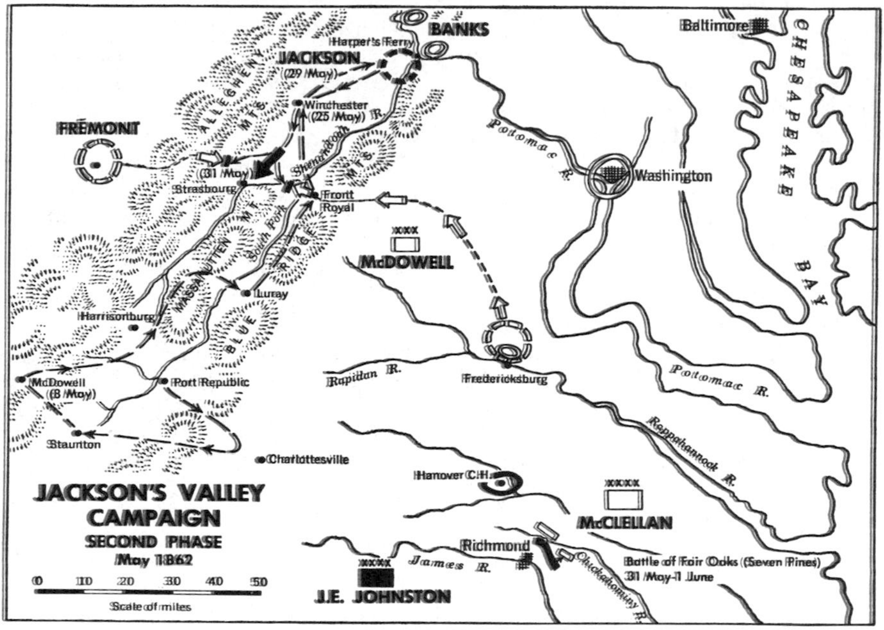

sume his offensive. Jackson, now on the Potomac, thus found himself in a trap. Frémont's 15,000 men were only 25 miles southwest of Winchester, advancing east; Shields, with 10,000 men of McDowell's command, had captured Front Royal and was advancing west with 10,000 more Federals behind him; Banks, across the Potomac, was regrouping and preparing to move south again.

1862, May 30–June 7. Jackson's Withdrawal. With 15,000 men, 2,000 prisoners, and a double column of wagons containing booty, he withdrew rapidly, sending his cavalry ahead to hold Frémont. Clearing Winchester (May 31), he reached Strasburg before the jaws of the trap could close. While Frémont pursued west of the Massanutten and Shields up the east side, Jackson reached Harrisonburg (June 5). Leaving Ewell at Cross Keys to hold Frémont, Jackson turned on Shields with the rest of his command.

1862, June 8. Battle of Cross Keys. Ewell repulsed Frémont's halfhearted attack and burned the one bridge over which the Union general could advance.

1862, June 9. Battle of Port Republic. Jackson fell on Shields at Port Republic. A 5-hour battle ended when Ewell arrived to reinforce Jackson. Shields's force was pushed back some 20 miles. By midnight, Jackson sat safely at Brown's Gap in the Blue Ridge while his wagon train and its booty were rolling on to Richmond. Frémont had retired to Harrisonburg, Shields was rallying at Luray, and McDowell, definitively divorced from McClellan, was occupying Front Royal with orders to remain in the Valley.

COMMENT. *With less than 18,000 men, Jackson—between April 30 and June 9—had stymied 70,000 Federal troops and had changed the complexion of the entire Federal plan of campaign.*

THE PENINSULA CAMPAIGN

1862, April 4–May 4. Siege of Yorktown. McClellan, moving toward Richmond with 90,000 men, was faced by a 10-mile entrenched line, extending across the Peninsula southwest from Yorktown, manned by 15,000 Confederates under Brigadier General **John B. Magruder.** McClellan, deceived by many dummy guns and feigned activity, began a formal investment and ordered siege artillery from Washington. Johnston, arriving from the Rappahannock, brought Confederate strength to 60,000, but retired toward Richmond 2 days before McClellan proposed to open a massive bombardment. McClellan pursued slowly.

1862, May 5. Battle of Williamsburg. The Army of the Potomac was held up by Johnston's rear guard, under Major General **James Longstreet,** in a delaying action. The slow Union advance continued.

1862, May 25. McClellan in Sight of Richmond. McClellan deployed 3 corps north of the Chickahominy River to facilitate the expected junction with McDowell, keeping 3 south of the swollen river, facing Confederate entrenchments in front of Richmond.

1862, May 31–June 1. Battle of Seven Pines (Fair Oaks). Johnston, taking advantage of the division of the Union army, fell on McClellan's isolated left. Poor Confederate staff work turned a planned double envelopment into piecemeal frontal attacks, which were repulsed after Federal reinforcements crossed the river. Johnston was seriously wounded, Major General **Gustavus W. Smith** taking his place. Next day the attacks were again repulsed. Union losses were about 5,000; Confederate, 6,100. McClellan, although he had now learned that McDowell would never join him, only rectified his line in part. Major General **Fitzjohn Porter**'s corps was left on the north side of the Chickahominy.

1862, June 1. Birth of the Army of Northern Virginia. President Davis appointed Lee to replace Johnston.

1862, June 12–15. Stuart's Raid. Brigadier General **J. E. B. Stuart**'s cavalry division circled the entire Federal army, destroying large quantities of stores near McClellan's headquarters at White House, and brought Lee invaluable information on Union dispositions.

The Seven Days' Battles, June 25–July 1, 1862

Lee ordered Jackson to join him and prepared to attack Porter's 30,000 men; the remainder of the Union Army would be contained in front of Richmond by Magruder. Both armies totaled about 90,000.

1862, June 25. Confederate Concentration. Three-fourths of Lee's army concentrated west of Mechanicsville. Jackson reached Ashland Station.

1862, June 26. Battle of Mechanicsville. Inexperience and faulty staff work marred the Confederate assault. Jackson never arrived. Porter threw back piecemeal assaults. Then, learning of Jackson's approach, he retired that night to Gaines's Mill.

1862, June 27. Battle of Gaines's Mill. Lee with 65,000 men again attacked, but Jackson was late and failed to get behind Porter's right flank. Porter was saved by reinforcements sent by other Union corps commanders and fell back in good order. That night, on McClellan's orders he withdrew to the south bank of the Chickahominy. McClellan, convinced the Southern main effort was coming on his left and center, ordered a general withdrawal to the James River (and protection of the Union fleet) despite the objections of Brigadier Generals **Phil Kearny** and **Joseph E. Hooker,** who assured him the thin crust of Magruder's demonstration could be pierced, and that Richmond was his for the taking.

1862, June 29–30. Battles of Peach Orchard, Savage Station, White Oak Swamp, Glendale-Frayser's Farm. Lee, discovering McClellan's withdrawal, pursued. His sharp attacks were rebuffed by the individual Union corps commanders in a series of delaying actions while the Union trains successfully crossed White Oak Swamp. McClellan personally went on ahead to inspect his new base on the James.

1862, July 1. Battle of Malvern Hill. In McClellan's absence, Porter carried out a brilliant defensive action from excellent positions with good fields of fire. Lee's assaults broke down into unco-ordinated attacks which were beaten back with heavy loss—more than 5,000 men in about 2 hours. Malvern Hill was a clear-cut Union success, but McClellan ordered immediate retreat to Harrison's Landing and to the protection of Union gunboats.

COMMENT. *Union losses in the Seven Days were 1,734 killed, 8,062 wounded, and 6,053 missing (mostly prisoners). Southern losses were 3,478 killed, 16,261 wounded, and 875 missing. All Confederate attacks (except at Gaines's Mill) were repulsed. Yet when it was over, the Union Army had been*

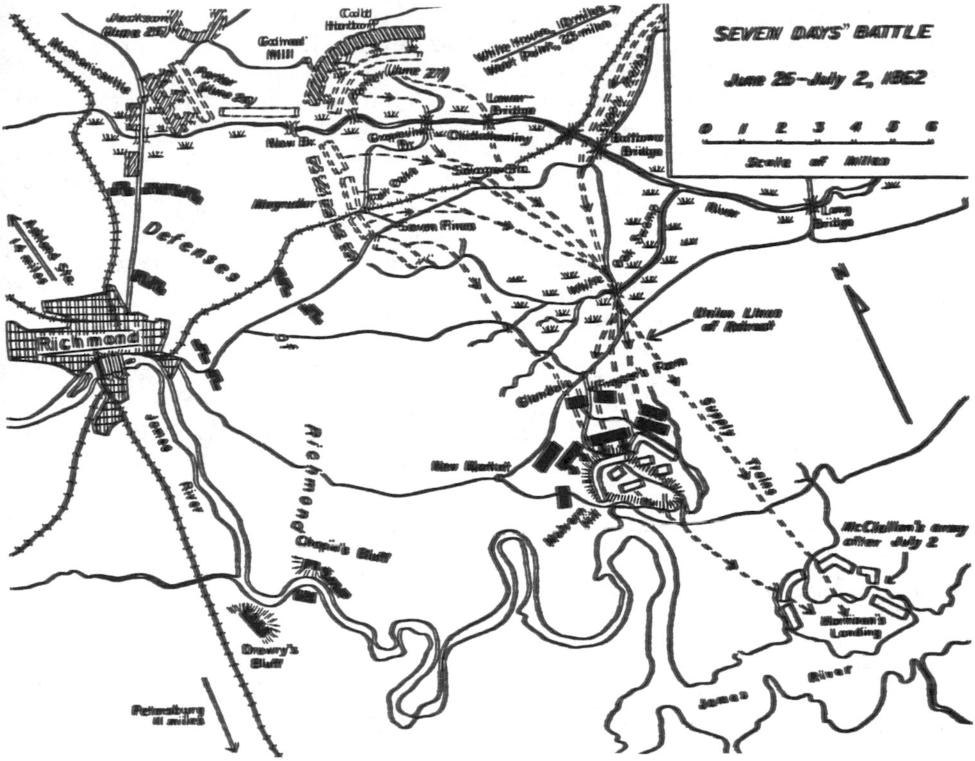

expelled from Richmond's outskirts and huddled in defeat on the banks of the James.

SECOND BULL RUN (MANASSAS) CAMPAIGN

1862, June 26. The Army of Virginia. President Lincoln called Major General **John Pope** from the West to command the new Army of Virginia, comprising the commands of McDowell, Frémont, and Banks.

1862, July 11–August 3. Union Reorganization and Regrouping. Realizing the need for professional generalship, Lincoln brought Halleck from the West to become General in Chief (July 11). The Army of the Potomac was ordered back to Washington (August 3).

1862, July–August. Confederate Reaction. Lee, concerned by these shifts, sent Jackson with 12,000 men to observe Pope in central Virginia. Lee followed slowly, leaving 20,000 to garrison Richmond.

1862, August 9. Battle of Cedar Mountain. Jackson, attempting to halt Pope's movement across the Rappahannock, was impetuously attacked by Banks, commanding the leading Union corps, with some 10,000 men. Jackson's personal efforts saved his troops from defeat; by nightfall he had driven Banks back on Culpeper. Jackson then withdrew across the Rapidan (August 11).

1862, August 24. Lee's Plan. Lee learned that McClellan's army was coming back from the Peninsula to join Pope. The combined Union armies would total 150,000 men against his 55,000. In a daring plan, he determined to crush Pope before such a junction could occur. Jackson was ordered to march north, then east, to get behind Pope's army; Lee, with Longstreet's corps, would follow, to join Jackson and to strike Pope somewhere near Manassas.

1862, August 25–26. Jackson Moves North. He marched 54 miles in 2 midsummer days, falling on Pope's supply depot at Manassas, which was looted and burned (August 27). Jackson then took up a hidden defensive position just west of the old Bull Run battlefield.

1862, August 29–30. Second Battle of Bull Run. Pope, enraged at the raid on his depot, hastened north to hunt the invaders. Finally discovering Jackson's position (when Jackson deliberately attacked a Union division near **Groveton**—August 28—to attract attention from Longstreet's advance), Pope concentrated to destroy him (August 29). Meanwhile, Lee with Longstreet was advancing through Thoroughfare Gap. Pope, refusing to believe Longstreet was near, attacked almost directly north against Jackson, only to be hit in the flank by Longstreet, moving east (August 30). The Union Army was rolled up and thrown back across Bull Run in decisive defeat. The withdrawal to the defenses of Washington, however, was in good order, covered by Sykes's Regular Army division of Porter's corps.

1862, August 31. Battle of Chantilly. Jackson, pursuing, attempted to drive through Union reinforcements covering Pope's retreat. In a blinding rainstorm, Jackson's assault was checked by General Phil Kearny, who was killed in a hand-to-hand combat. Lee made no further attempt to press closer to heavily defended Washington. Confederate losses in the campaign were 9,197. Pope's losses were more than 16,000.

ANTIETAM (SHARPSBURG) CAMPAIGN

1862, September 4–9. Lee's First Invasion of the North. Reinforced to 55,000 men,

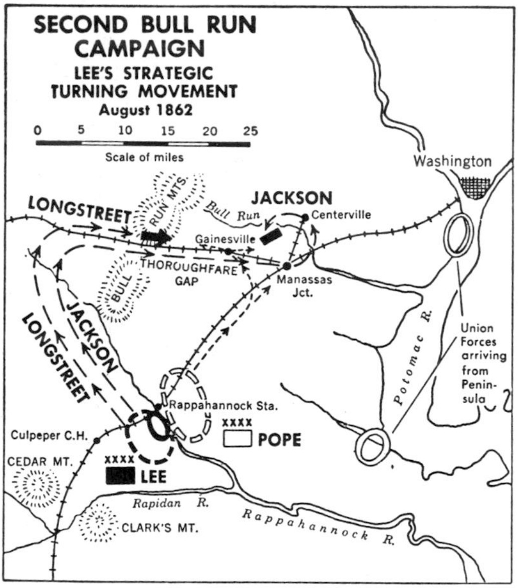

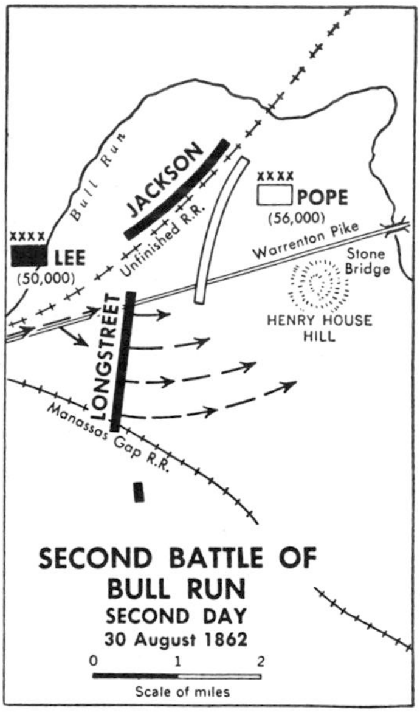

Lee crossed the Potomac near Leesburg. His objective, approved by President Davis, was to carry the war to the North, and by a successful invasion to encourage Britain and France to recognize—and possibly assist—the Confederacy. Screened by Stuart's cavalry, he concentrated at Frederick, Md. (September 7). He decided to move northward into Pennsylvania behind the protection of the Catoctin Mountains. He issued orders (September 9) for Longstreet's corps to advance toward Hagerstown while Jackson returned across the Potomac to capture Harpers Ferry, and to secure a new line of communications through the Shenandoah Valley.

1862, September 7. McClellan Follows Lee. Meanwhile Lincoln had dissolved the Army of Virginia, whose units were absorbed in McClellan's Army of the Potomac, now back in Washington. (Pope was sent to an administrative command in the northwest.) With 97,000 men, McClellan moved out from Washington on Lee's trail.

1862, September 12. The Lost Order. McClellan's advance guard reached Frederick, where a copy of Lee's order of June

9, detailing Confederate dispositions and movements, fell into McClellan's hands.

COMMENT. *Lee's army, spread out over 25 miles and split by an unfordable river, was at McClellan's mercy. Yet it took McClellan 2 days to advance 10 miles from Frederick to the passes over South Mountain.*

1862, September 14. Battle of South Mountain. While covering forces delayed the Union advance through Turner's and Crampton's Gaps, Lee hurriedly concentrated at Sharpsburg.

1862, September 14–15. Battle of Harpers Ferry. After sharp fighting, the Union garrison at Harpers Ferry surrendered to Jackson. Leaving the division of General **A. P. Hill** to secure the 11,000 prisoners and captured stores, Jackson hurried to join Lee at Sharpsburg. McClellan, who could have struck Lee's 20,000 with more than 50,000 on the 15th, incredibly still did not attack on the 16th, permitting the Southerners—now about 45,000 strong—to prepare well-organized defensive positions along Antietam Creek, with the Potomac to their backs.

1862, September 17. Battle of Antietam Creek (Sharpsburg). McClellan planned to roll up Lee's left with 3 corps, while another drove across the creek to pin the Confederate right. Two more corps were in reserve. The Union 3-corps hammer blow degenerated into separate, disjointed attacks against Jackson, with the most sanguinary action along the "Bloody Lane," a sunken road. By midday all Lee's reserves were expended, but the Federal attacks had ground to a halt. The action now shifted to Longstreet's sector. Major General **Ambrose E. Burnside**'s Union corps made three desperate attacks to carry a bridge over the fordable creek. It then took him 2 hours more to reorganize his troops and move to the assault of Sharpsburg. All the while, McClellan had held more than 20,000 men unemployed in reserve. Burnside's final effort had reached the crest of the defense when A. P. Hill's division of Jackson's corps arrived from Harpers Ferry and charged into Burnside's left flank, driving the Federals back across the creek and ending the bloodiest 1-day battle of the entire war.

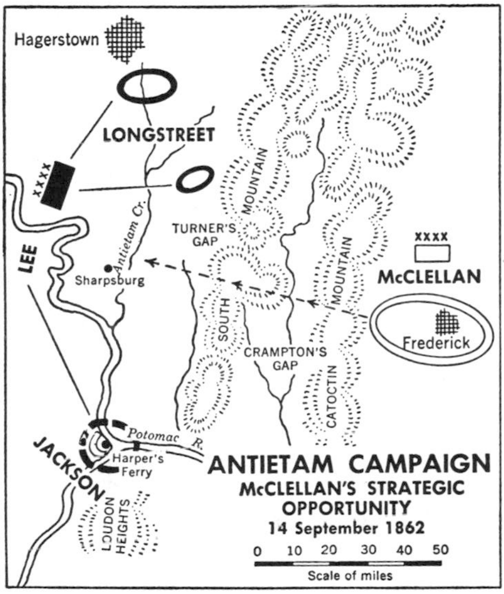

ANTIETAM CAMPAIGN
McCLELLAN'S STRATEGIC OPPORTUNITY
14 September 1862

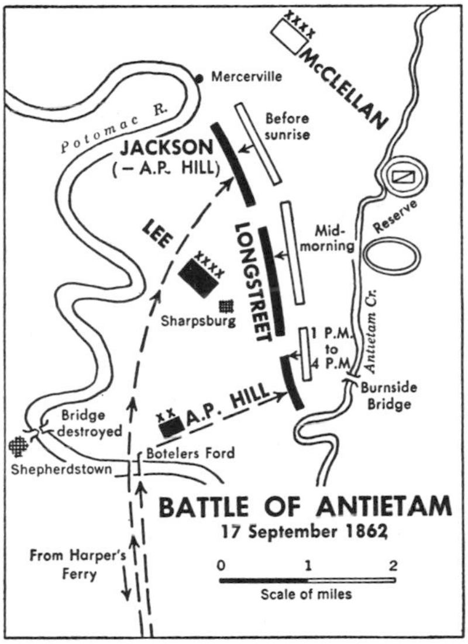

BATTLE OF ANTIETAM
17 September 1862

COMMENT. *With less than 50,000 effectives, Lee had stopped McClellan's 90,000—of whom only 70,000 took part in the battle. Federal losses were 12,400; the Confederates lost 13,700. Lee calmly faced his opponent through that night and through the next day. Then, unmolested, he withdrew across the Potomac (September 19). Tactically, Antietam was a Confederate victory; strategically, since Lee's invasion was stopped, it was a Union victory, which Lincoln used as a springboard for his Preliminary Emancipation Proclamation (September 23).*

FREDERICKSBURG CAMPAIGN

1862, November 7. Relief of McClellan. The Union general did not follow Lee across the Potomac until peremptorily ordered to do so by Lincoln (October 5). He then advanced cautiously to Warrenton, where he was between Longstreet at Culpeper and Jackson in the Valley. When, despite urging, McClellan failed to move further, Lincoln relieved him, placing Burnside in command of the Army of the Potomac.

1862, November–December. Burnside's Plan. He planned another drive upon Richmond. Advancing toward Fredericksburg on the fordable Rappahannock, he waited on the northeast bank for bridging equipment. Lee calmly concentrated on the other side, entrenching his army along the arc of hills overlooking Fredericksburg (from which civilians had been evacuated), Longstreet above the town, Jackson, on the right, farther south.

1862, December 13. Battle of Fredericksburg. Burnside launched a 2-pronged offensive, crossing the river opposite Fredericksburg and south of the town. Jackson threw back the assaulting columns of the Federal left while Stuart's artillery played against their flank. By evening Jackson's position was still intact, the Union troops holding only the river line. On the north, the Federal assault debouched from the ruins of the town to meet devastating artillery and small-arms fire from Longstreet's corps on Marye's Heights beyond. Fourteen successive Union charges melted away under the Confederate fire. Along the entire line, more than 12,500 Union soldiers lay in windrows, 6,000 of them in front of Longstreet's position. Confederate losses were 5,309. Burnside, dissuaded by his corps commanders from making another suicidal attack next day, withdrew across the river (December 15). Burnside blamed his subordinates for the debacle.

1863, January 26. Relief of Burnside. He was removed from command after having made another abortive attempt to cross the Rappahannock above Fredericksburg (January 20), despite Lincoln's order to halt. This "Mud March" bogged down in torrential rains.

War in the West, 1862

WEST OF THE MISSISSIPPI

1862, March 7–8. Battle of Pea Ridge. Confederate Major General **Earl Van Dorn** with 16,000 men tried to encircle the right flank of Union Major General **Samuel R. Curtis,** whose 12,000 men held a defensive position 30 miles northeast of Fayetteville, Ark. Curtis, discovering the movement, spoiled the offensive, and Van Dorn withdrew after 2 days of stubborn fighting. Federal losses were about 1,300; Confederate, upward of 800.

1862, April 15. Battle of Peralta. Confederate Brigadier General **Henry Hopkins Sibley,** moving up the Rio Grande from Fort Bliss, Tex., with some 4,000 Texan volunteers to invade California, had defeated a Union force of equal strength under Colonel **Edward R. S. Canby** at **Valverde,** N.M. (February 21), and occupied in turn Albuquerque and Santa Fe. But lack of food forced Sibley's retirement and Canby, reinforced, fell on him at Peralta, 20 miles south of Albuquerque, and in a series of running fights forced Sibley and his disintegrating force back to Fort Bliss (April–May).

1862, December 7. Battle of Prairie Grove. A Confederate force of 10,000 under Major General **T. C. Hindman** was repulsed by a Union force of equal size under Brigadier Generals **James G. Blunt** and **Francis J. Herron,** leaving northern Arkansas in Union hands.

EAST OF THE MISSISSIPPI

1862, January 19–20. Battle of Mill Springs. In eastern Kentucky a Confederate thrust of 4,000 men from Cumberland Gap, under Generals **Felix Zollicoffer** and **George Crittenden,** was repulsed decisively by an equal number of Union troops under Brigadier General **George H. Thomas,** part of the Army of the Ohio, commanded by Major General **Don Carlos Buell.**

1862, February. Henry-Donelson Campaign. Grant led an amphibious operation from Cairo, Ill., to split A. S. Johnston's cordon defense. Moving up the Tennessee River, Flag Officer **Andrew Foote**'s escorting squadron of ironclad river gunboats' fire overwhelmed low-lying Fort Henry (February 6). Grant then moved overland to

Fort Donelson on the Cumberland River while the gunboats retraced their route and advanced up the Cumberland to support him. Donelson was held by 15,000 men commanded by Major General **John B. Floyd,** assisted by Major Generals **Gideon Pillow** and **Simon Bolivar Buckner.** A Union gunboat attack was repulsed (February 14). Next day the Confederates attacked, almost breaking through the Union encirclement, but Grant's counterattack swept them back into the fort. Floyd and Pillow escaped by water; Buckner's request for an armistice was answered by Grant's famous ultimatum: "No terms except an unconditional and immediate surrender can be accepted." Buckner surrendered (Feb. 16). Union losses were 2,832; Confederate—including prisoners—16,623.

1862, February–March. Collapse of the Confederate Cordon. Attempting to form a new line in Tennessee, Johnston gave up the project when Grant and Buell seized Nashville (February 25). Johnston then

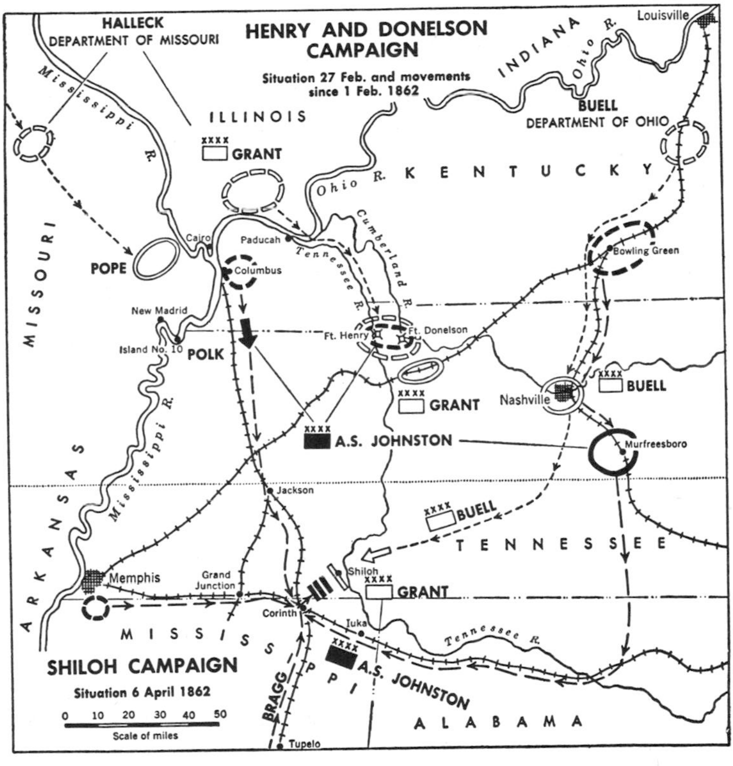

concentrated in the vicinity of Corinth, Miss., with 40,000 men. Grant's planned move on Corinth was halted on the Tennessee River at Savannah, Tenn., by Halleck's order, requiring him to wait until Buell should arrive from Nashville.

1862, April 6–7. Battle of Shiloh. Johnston made a surprise attack on Grant's inadequately outposted bivouacs, in the vicinity of Pittsburg Landing–Shiloh Church, driving in the badly shaken Union forces. Grant's vigorous personal efforts to retrieve the day were finally successful at dusk. The Confederates, all their reserves expended, were first halted by Grant's artillery, then driven back as 2 Union gunboats added their flank fire to the defense. Johnston was killed while leading a last-ditch charge; Beauregard succeeded to command. That night, Buell's army arrived on the east bank of the river and part of it was ferried across. Shortly after dawn next day, Grant counterattacked. By noon Beauregard gave up the struggle and retreated to Corinth. Confederate losses, of some 40,000 men in action, were 10,600. Grant, out of 62,700 engaged, lost 13,000. Criticism of Grant in the North was loud and to a great extent baseless. Lincoln's answer to demands for Grant's relief was: "I can't spare this man. He fights."

1862, May–June. Halleck's Advance. Taking personal command of the combined armies, Halleck moved very slowly to Corinth. Beauregard, falling back in front of him, evacuated it (May 29), retreating to Tupelo, where he reorganized his army. Confederate evacuation of Fort Pillow followed (June 5). Ponderous Halleck now divided his forces. Sending Buell eastward into Tennessee, he restricted Grant to defensive operations in the Mississippi Valley. Meanwhile (June 17), Beauregard was replaced by General **Braxton Bragg** in command of the Confederacy's western campaign. To stop Buell's threat to Chattanooga, Bragg shifted most of his forces rapidly to southeastern Tennessee.

1862, July 11. Halleck to Supreme Command. Halleck, appointed General in Chief, left for Washington (July 17), turning over his western command to Grant and to Buell, in separate commands (Army of the Tennessee and Army of the Ohio).

Grant's Operations, July–November, 1862

1862, July–September. Grant on the Defensive. His slender forces (45,000 men) widespread on a long line of communications to Cairo, Ill., Grant, at Corinth with about 25,000 men, was menaced by Price (17,000 men) and Van Dorn (15,000 men), who attempted to unite against him.

1862, September 19–20. Battle of Iuka. Price was repulsed, but Grant's planned double envelopment was foiled by the error of a subordinate, Brigadier General **William S. Rosecrans.** Price and Van Dorn, uniting, moved against Corinth under the latter's command.

1862, October 3–4. Battle of Corinth. Grant, once again trying for a double envelopment, was again foiled by Rosecrans' laxity. Van Dorn, though defeated, was able to escape. Federal losses were 2,520 (of 23,000 engaged); Confederate, 4,233 (of 22,000 engaged). The net result was firm federal retention of Memphis and Corinth, both strategic outposts. Grant now moved toward Grand Junction, planning an advance against Vicksburg.

Buell and Rosecrans vs. Bragg, July–December, 1862

1862, July–October. Bragg's Invasion of Kentucky. Bragg moved north from Chattanooga while his subordinate, General **Edmund Kirby Smith,** advanced from Knoxville, overwhelming a small Union force at **Richmond** (August 30). The combined Confederate force totaled about 50,000 men. Buell—with about the same number—finding his communications with Nashville menaced, recoiled to the banks of the Ohio River. Bragg now occupied most of Kentucky. Buell, substantially reinforced, and threatened by Washington with replacement, finally advanced from Louisville.

1862, October 8. Battle of Perryville. Buell's advance resulted in a drawn fight with a part of Bragg's army (some 16,000 men) under Generals Leonidas Polk and **William J. Hardee.** The Confederates withstood an all-day attack by 39,000 Federals. Bragg, having concentrated his army, now inexplicably turned and marched back through Cumberland Gap into Tennessee. Buell, equally negligent, failed to pursue him.

1862, October 23. Relief of Buell. Disgusted with Buell's lack of aggressiveness, Lincoln replaced him with Rosecrans, who occupied Nashville (November 6).

1862, November–December. Stalemate. For several weeks Bragg and Rosecrans confronted each other without action between Nashville and Murfreesboro, while both Washington and Richmond berated their procrastinating generals. Meanwhile Confederate cavalry leaders **Nathan Bedford Forrest** and **John H. Morgan** bedeviled both Rosecrans and Grant by raids.

1862, December 31–1863, January 3. Battle of Stones River (Murfreesboro). Spurred to take action, both commanders attacked, each planning to envelop the other's right flank. Bragg, with 38,000 men, struck first, with outstanding initial success, but dilatory and blundering use of his reserve spoiled his exploitation. Rosecrans, who had some 44,000 troops, was able to hold a new defensive line. Both sides bivouacked on the field that night, and held their respective positions next day. Bragg made one more attack, but was repulsed (January 2). He withdrew the next day. The tactically drawn battle was a strategic victory for the North. Federal losses were 12,906; Confederate, 11,740.

UNION ADVANCE DOWN THE MISSISSIPPI, FEBRUARY–JUNE, 1862

1862, February–March. New Madrid and Island No. 10. The northern attack started as an amphibious operation; Major General John Pope, with some 23,000 men, moved on New Madrid and Island No. 10, supported by Flag Officer Foote's gunboats. Pope drove the Confederate garrison out of New Madrid (March 13). Two gunboats made daring runs past the heavy batteries on Island No. 10 (April 4–5, 6–7) and escorted Pope's troops across the river, cutting land communication with the island, whose garrison surrendered (April 8). Sixty miles to the south downriver lay Fort Pillow, north of Memphis. Pope's army, ferried down, invested it, while gunboats and mortar schooners opened bombardment. Halleck withdrew Pope's troops for the Corinth campaign (see p. 882), but the naval bombardment continued. (His success here led to Pope's later appointment to command in the East; see p. 877).

1862, May 9. Battle of Plum Point. A flotilla of Confederate gunboats lying below the fort made a dawn attack on the Federal flotilla, now commanded by Captain **Charles H. Davis,** U.S.N. (Foote, wounded during the Donelson operation, had been evacuated.) After seriously damaging 2 Union gunboats, the Confederate flotilla withdrew. Because of Halleck's advance, Fort Pillow's garrison was withdrawn (June 5).

1862, June 6. Battle of Memphis. The Federal flotilla moved down to attack the southern gunboats off Memphis, destroying all but 1 of the Confederate vessels. Memphis surrendered and Davis' flotilla steamed down to the mouth of the Yazoo River, above Vicksburg.

UNION ADVANCE FROM THE GULF, MARCH–JULY, 1862

1862, March–April. Farragut at the River Mouth. Meanwhile, Commodore **David Glasgow Farragut** had moved into the Mississippi River estuary from the Gulf with 8 steam sloops and corvettes, a 20-ship mortar flotilla, and 9 gunboats. General Butler with 10,000 men accompanied the expedition. The river was defended by **Forts St. Philip** and **Jackson,** mounting between them 115 heavy guns. The Confederate ironclad *Louisiana,* her engines uncompleted, was moored as a floating battery just above St. Philip. A barrier of hulks and logs below the forts barred the river to traffic.

1862, April 24. Naval Battle of New Orleans. While his mortar boats bombarded the forts, Farragut's squadron crashed through the barrier and successfully ran by the forts. Above the forts, 11 Confederate gunboats attacked. Nine of them were sunk. Next day Farragut steamed up and took New Orleans, which had been evacuated by all Confederate troops. Forts St. Philip and Jackson—bombarded by mortar boats and surrounded by Butler's troops—surrendered (April 27). Butler's troops then occupied New Orleans. Farragut moved upriver. Baton Rouge and Natchez surrendered, but Vicksburg, heavily fortified, repelled his squadron (May 23). Returning to New Orleans, Farragut received peremptory orders from Washington to open up the river, and the squadron retraced its steps to Vicksburg, accompanied by mortar boats.

1862, June 28. Run-by at Vicksburg. Farragut's squadron ran a 3-mile gantlet, with some casualties and considerable damage to the vessels, linking with Davis' flotilla off the mouth of the Yazoo River (July 1).

1862, July 15. The *Arkansas* vs. the Union Fleet. The Confederate ironclad ram *Arkansas* debouched from the Yazoo (a strategic error, for so long as she remained in place she menaced Union control of the river) and battered her way to Vicksburg through the entire Union squadron. Farragut ran by the forts again in an unsuccessful attempt to destroy the *Arkansas* (July 21–22) and then returned to the

Gulf, to resume command of the Gulf blockading squadron. The misused *Arkansas* was later destroyed near Baton Rouge.

LAND OPERATIONS AGAINST VICKSBURG, NOVEMBER–DECEMBER, 1862

1862, November–December. Grant's Advance. Grant having concentrated the Army of the Tennessee at Grand Junction, Tenn., started south toward Vicksburg (November 13), pushing back General **John C. Pemberton,** now commanding all Confederate forces in the region. Grant also sent Major General **William T. Sherman** with 40,000 men down toward Vicksburg in an amphibious operation supported by Rear Admiral **David D. Porter,** now commanding naval units in the Memphis area (December 20). But Grant's own advance was harassed by Forrest's raids in northwest Tennessee, and Van Dorn's capture of the Federal supply depot at **Holly Springs,** Miss. (December 20).

1862, December 14. Butler Replaced by Banks. Meanwhile, at New Orleans, General Nathaniel P. Banks had replaced Butler, and in co-ordination with Farragut was moving slowly up the river to threaten Baton Rouge.

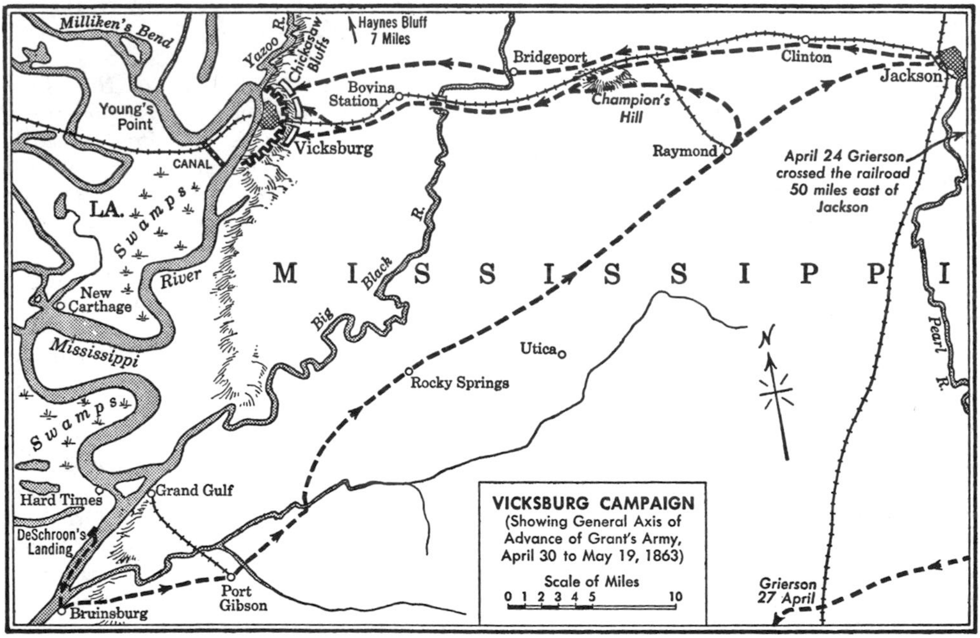

1862, December 25–29. Chickasaw Bluffs Operation. The Sherman-Porter expedition entered the Yazoo River and Sherman attempted unsuccessfully to assault the Chickasaw Bluffs north of Vicksburg, manned by 13,800 of Pemberton's veterans. After a 3-day action (December 27–29), Sherman admitted defeat, retiring to the mouth of the Yazoo. Federal losses were 1,776; Confederate, only 207. Thus the year ended with the Mississippi from Vicksburg to Baton Rouge still under Confederate control.

War in the East, 1863

1863, January 26. Hooker to Command. He was appointed to command the Army of the Potomac in place of Burnside.

CHANCELLORSVILLE CAMPAIGN, APRIL–MAY

1863, April 27–30. Preliminaries to Chancellorsville. Hooker moved to attack Lee from the Federal positions east of the Rappahannock and opposite Fredericksburg. Major General **John Sedgwick** with 40,000 men was to demonstrate by forcing a crossing of the river at Fredericksburg itself. Meanwhile Hooker with 73,000 more would cross the river above, into the Wilderness, and circle Lee's left. The Federal cavalry under Major General **George Stoneman** would ride wide westward, then sweep south to cut Lee's communications with Richmond. Lee's Army of Northern Virginia was reduced to 60,000—high in morale, but short of equipment, rations, and clothing. Longstreet's corps was away, gathering provisions in the lower James River area. Screened by Stuart's cavalry, Lee was well aware of Hooker's movements.

1863, May 1–6. Battle of Chancellorsville. Leaving Major General **Jubal Early** with 10,000 men on Marye's Heights to contain Sedgwick's Fredericksburg attack, Lee moved rapidly west to meet Hooker's main offensive. At first contact (May 1), Hooker, despite his tremendous superiority in numbers, halted and went on the defensive. Early next day, Lee sent Jackson with 26,000 men in a wide envelopment while Lee with only 17,000 held the front. Just before dusk Jackson assaulted—his line perpendicular to the right flank

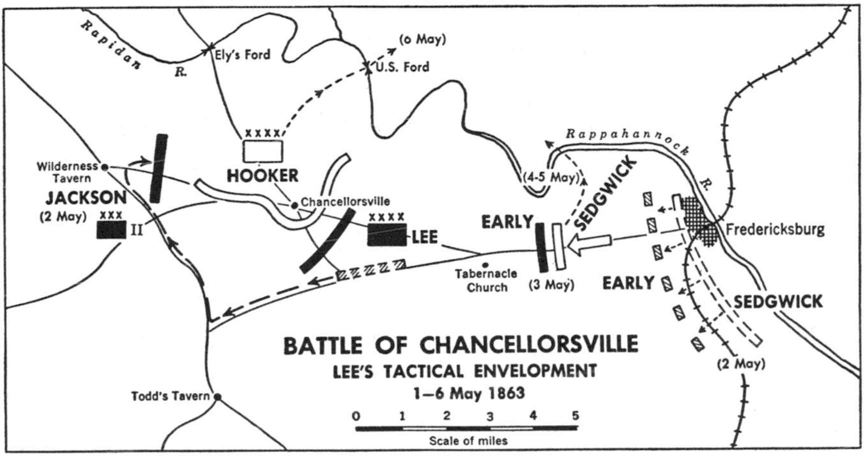

of the Federal entrenchments. He rolled up the Union right flank, completely demoralizing the entire right wing of Hooker's army. Attempting to complete the operation and cut Hooker from his Rappahannock ford communications, Jackson rode into the night in person to reconnoiter and was mortally wounded by the fire of some of his own troops. Next day (May 3) the Confederate attacks resumed, but were slowed by increasing Federal resistance, while at Fredericksburg Sedgwick was driving Early's small force from Marye's Heights. Hooker, with only part of his troops engaged, could still have retrieved the situation, but he had no fight left in him. Leaving Stuart to hold Hooker near Chancellorsville, Lee hastened east to defeat Sedgwick at **Salem Church** (May 4). The Army of the Potomac withdrew across the Rappahannock (May 5–6). Union losses were 16,792 killed, wounded, or captured. The South lost a total of 12,754. Lee had won a tremendous victory, but had lost the one man he could not spare; Jackson died of his wounds (May 10).

GETTYSBURG CAMPAIGN, JUNE–JULY

1863, June 3. Lee Prepares to Invade the North. Determined to maintain the initiative, he moved over to the Shenandoah Valley, leaving Stuart to screen his movements.

1863, June 9. Battle of Brandy Station. Hooker discovered Lee's move when his cavalry, under Major General **Alfred Pleasanton,** crossed the Rappahannock and surprised Stuart's cantonment. Rallying, the Confederates fought the attackers to a standstill in the largest purely cavalry battle of the war. Pleasanton, of 12,000 men engaged, incurred more than 900 casualties. Stuart, out of 10,000, lost some 500 men.

1863, June 13–14. Second Battle of Winchester. Ewell's II Corps (formerly Jackson's) smashed General **Robert H. Mil-**

roy's Union forces in the lower Shenandoah Valley.

1863, June 15–24. Lee Crosses the Potomac. The Southern army—76,000 strong—pushed northward into Pennsylvania through Chambersburg to reach Carlisle and York (June 28).

1863, June 13–27. Hooker Follows Lee. When finally convinced that Lee was making a major movement, Hooker and his 115,000 men began to move north (June 13). He missed repeated opportunities to strike at the stretched-out Confederate Army, and reached Frederick at the same time that he discovered that Halleck (who remembered the discrepancy between Hooker's plan and Hooker's actions at Chancellorsville) had overruled his plan to trap Lee with a 2-pronged strategic envelopment (June 27). Hooker offered his resignation, which—to his surprise—was accepted before dawn next day.

1863, June 26–July 2. Stuart's Raid. Screening Lee's right flank during the crossing of the Potomac, Stuart took advantage of discretionary orders to swing wide on a raid around the rear of the Federal army in central Maryland.

1863, June 28. Major General George C. Meade Takes Command. He was the Army of the Potomac's fifth commander in 10 months. Lee, deprived of reconnaissance intelligence due to Stuart's absence, learned the general whereabouts of the Army of the Potomac—and its change of command—late the same day. Immediately he began concentration near Cashtown.

1863, June 30. Meeting Engagement. Meade, trying to coax the Confederates to give battle south of the Susquehanna, probed cautiously toward Emmitsburg and Hanover. A Confederate infantry brigade, moving southeast toward Gettysburg, met a Union cavalry brigade reconnoitering to the northwest. From that unexpected clash built up, piecemeal, the greatest battle ever to be fought on American soil.

1863, July 1. Battle of Gettysburg (First Day). A. P. Hill's Confederate III Corps opposed **Joseph I. Reynolds**' Union I Corps and **Oliver O. Howard**'s XI Corps, north and northwest of Gettysburg itself. Ewell's II Corps, moving south from Heidlersburg, outflanked the Union right. The Union troops rallied south of the

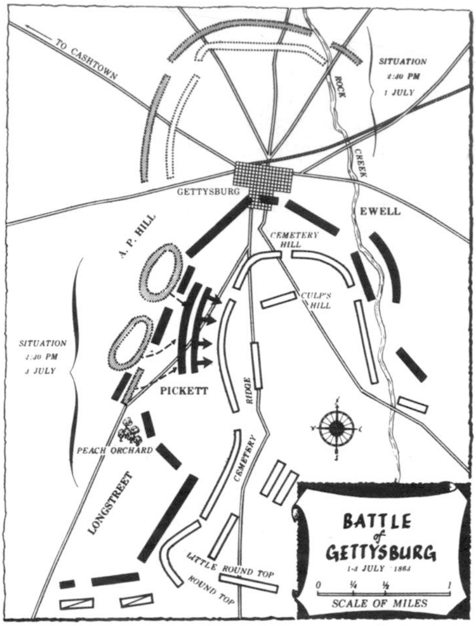

town on Cemetery Hill and Culp's Hill, while the Confederates held Gettysburg and Seminary Ridge to the southwest. Through the night the remainder of the Army of the Potomac marched up and moved into position facing west along Cemetery Ridge. The famous Union "fishhook" was taking shape (see map). Lee decided that he would envelop the Union left next day, using Longstreet's I Corps, which had not yet arrived on the field.

1863, July 2. Battle of Gettysburg (Second Day). Longstreet's attack was delayed until afternoon, but drove back **Daniel E. Sickles**' III Corps from an exposed position in a peach orchard and almost turned the Union left. Brigadier General **Gouverneur K. Warren,** Meade's engineer officer, discovering that Little Round Top was unoccupied, deftly diverted a nearby brigade and artillery battery to this key point and saved the situation. Desperate fighting to the south ended with the Union troops anchored firmly along the ridge from Round Top to Culp's Hill—which latter point Ewell had failed to wrest from Union hands.

1863, July 3. Battle of Gettysburg (Third Day). Lee decided on a penetration of the Union line. Covered by a tremendous artillery bombardment, 10 brigades were launched in the assault known as "Pickett's Charge," although Major General

George E. Pickett was but 1 of 4 division commanders involved. Some 15,500 men pressed for a half-mile through Union cannonading that blew great gaps in their line. Reaching the Union line, the surviving Confederates briefly broke through, only to be thrown back by Meade's reserves. Survivors of the charge (barely half of those who started) reeled back to Seminary Ridge, where Lee, accepting responsibility for the disaster, waited for a counterattack which never came. Union casualties for the 3 days were 3,155 killed, 14,529 wounded, and 5,365 missing. The Confederate army lost 3,903 killed, 18,735 wounded, and 5,425 missing.

1863, July 4–14. Lee's Retreat. This was accomplished without serious hindrance through mud and rain, and despite the swollen Potomac. Meade followed cautiously. Lincoln was gravely disappointed by Meade's failure to exploit his victory.

INCONCLUSIVE OPERATIONS IN THE EAST, AUGUST–DECEMBER

1863, August–September. Stalemate on the Rapidan-Rappahannock.

1863, October 9–14. Lee Advances to Manassas. He jabbed at Meade's left in a long sweep, but was checked at **Bristoe Station** (October 14), and the armies returned to the Rapidan-Rappahannock triangle (November).

1863, November 27–December 1. Mine Run Campaign. Meade made several inconclusive thrusts across the Rappahannock at Lee's position on the west bank of Mine Run in the Wilderness. Union losses were 1,653; Southern casualties, 745.

War in the West, 1863

VICKSBURG CAMPAIGN

1863, January–March. Probing at Vicksburg. The Holly Springs experience (see p. 884) had convinced Grant that, with the forces available to him, overland operations against Vicksburg were impracticable at the end of a long line of communications from Cairo. He distrusted the capabilities of Major General **John A. McClernand,** who, as senior in rank, had superseded Sherman as commander of the river expedition against Vicksburg (see p. 884). McClernand had then gone on a useless diversion up the Arkansas River to capture **Fort Hindman** at **Arkansas Post** (January 11). Ordering McClernand to return to the vicinity of Vicksburg, Grant went down the river to assume personal command at Milliken's Bend, La. (January 30). Through the winter and early spring Grant probed at the increasingly formidable defenses of Vicksburg, keeping his army busy, but accomplishing little else. Actually he was waiting for the cessation of the rains and falling of the flooded rivers.

1863, February–March. Gunboats on the River. Admiral Porter, working closely with Grant in the probes at Vicksburg, also sent the gunboats *Queen of the West* and *Indianola* in daring runs past the Vicksburg batteries to interfere with Confederate river traffic between Vicksburg and Port Hudson. Honors were about even; Confederate river activities were seriously disrupted, but the *Queen* was eventually captured and the *Indianola* destroyed.

1863, March 14. Port Hudson. Carrying out his part of a jointly planned operation with General Banks, Farragut steamed upriver past the powerful defenses of Port Hudson. Only his flagship, U.S.S. *Hartford,* and 1 other vessel were able to fight their way past, all other Union ships being repulsed. Banks failed to co-operate. But Farragut with his 2 ships quickly swept southern shipping off the central Mississippi.

1863, April. Grant Completes His Preparations. Pemberton's forces defending Vicksburg numbered about 50,000, scattered on the east bank of the Mississippi from Haines's Bluff, 10 miles above Vicksburg, to Grand Gulf, 40 miles below. (Farther south, the 15,000-man garrison at Port Hudson was immobilized by the threats of Farragut and Banks.) Grant had about 50,000 men on the west bank. Leaving Sherman's corps above Vicksburg, Grant moved the rest of his army overland to Hard Times, below Vicksburg, opposite Grand Gulf. At about the same time (April 17), in a series of spectacular night actions, Porter began to run gunboats and transports past the Vicksburg batteries to Grant's new base at Hard Times.

1863, April 18–May 3. Grierson's Raid. To

further confuse the Confederates, Grant dispatched Colonel **Benjamin H. Grierson,** with 3 regiments of cavalry, from La Grange, Tenn., on a skillful, destructive ride through the entire length of Mississippi to the Union base at Baton Rouge.

1863, April 30. Crossing the Mississippi. While Sherman's corps and some gunboats demonstrated up the Yazoo, near the Chickasaw Bluffs above Vicksburg, the remainder of Grant's army was ferried unopposed by Porter's vessels to Bruinsburg, 10 miles below Grand Gulf (which Porter's gunboats had bombarded the previous day).

1863, May 1. Battle of Port Gibson. The Confederate Grand Gulf garrison, attempting to resist the Union advance inland, was driven off. Grant then waited while Sherman hurried down from his demonstration to join the remainder of the army east of the Mississippi (May 3).

1863, May 7–19. Big Black River Campaign. In addition to Pemberton's 35,000 in the vicinity of Vicksburg, Joseph E. Johnston (recovered from his wounds and now over-all Confederate commander in the West) had gathered 9,000 men at Jackson, Miss., 45 miles east. Grant, with 41,000 men, now abandoned his communications and marched eastward between these two Confederate forces. While Pemberton probed vaguely for the nonexistent Union line of communications, Grant drove Johnston out of **Jackson** (May 14). Leaving Sherman there to complete destruction of supplies and railroads, and to block Johnston, Grant then turned west again on Pemberton.

1863, May 16. Battle of Champion's Hill. Pemberton, with 22,000 men, held a strong position east of the Big Black. Grant, to rectify errors of McClernand, his leading corps commander, took personal command and drove the Confederates from the field. Pemberton for a few hours held a bridgehead over the Big Black River, but next day McPherson's corps stormed it. At the same time Sherman crossed the river farther north. Pemberton retreated into the Vicksburg defenses (May 19).

COMMENT. *In 19 days, Grant had marched 200 miles, living off the country, and defeated detachments of a numerically superior enemy in 5 distinct engagements and several skirmishes. He had inflicted losses of about 8,000 men at a loss to himself of less than 4,400 casualties. He had now locked up his principal opponent and some 30,000 men in a fortress. The Big Black River campaign was the most brilliant ever fought on American soil.*

1863, May 19–July 4. Siege of Vicksburg. After 2 unsuccessful assaults (May 19 and 22), Grant buckled down to siege operations, leaving Sherman's corps as a mobile force shielding any possible attempt by Johnston to relieve the city. The Federal investment closed in gradually, with continual bombardment from siege guns on land and from Porter's ironclads on the river. Vicksburg's defenders and the civilian population, burrowing in caves and threatened by starvation, kept up a gallant but hopeless fight which excited as much admiration in the North as in the South.

1863, July 4. Surrender of Vicksburg. Learning that Grant was preparing a general assault, Pemberton surrendered. Grant immediately rushed rations to the famished civilians and soldiers in the city. Repulse of a Confederate attack on **Helena,** Ark., that same day was an anticlimax, as was the surrender of Port Hudson to Banks (July 9).

COMMENT. *As Lincoln put it, the Mississippi now "flowed unvexed" to the sea; the Confederacy had been split in two.*

TULLAHOMA, CHICKAMAUGA, AND CHATTANOOGA CAMPAIGNS

1863, June 23–July 2. Tullahoma Campaign. After 6 months of inaction at Murfreesboro, while Bragg sat at Tullahoma—and Grant campaigned near Vicksburg—Rosecrans was finally prodded to action by Halleck's threats to replace him. In a well-planned, well-conducted, bloodless maneuver, Rosecrans forced Bragg to withdraw to Chattanooga.

1863, August 16. Offensives of Rosecrans and Burnside. After another long delay, Rosecrans advanced from Tullahoma. That same day Burnside, with the Army of the Ohio, moved from Lexington, Ky., toward Knoxville. Swinging wide to the southwest, Rosecrans crossed the Tennessee River near Bridgeport, Ala., threatening Bragg's line of communications to Atlanta. The Confederates abandoned Chattanooga (September 7); Rosecrans, with 60,000 men, pursued into northwestern Georgia. President Davis now rushed Longstreet's corps from Virginia by rail; these and other reinforcements brought Bragg's army up to 70,000.

1863, September 19–20. Battle of Chickamauga. Knowing that Rosecrans was widely strung out in pursuit, Bragg attacked across Chickamauga Creek, attempting to turn the Union army's left and cut its line of communications to Chattanooga. Both armies were hampered by the densely wooded terrain; Rosecrans held firm on the 19th. Confederate assaults continued next day. Rosecrans, shifting divisions, left a gap in his center through which Longstreet plunged, cutting the Union army in two and driving its center and right from the field in disorder. Only the resolute resistance of the left, under Major General George H. Thomas (who held the field until nightfall to win the soubriquet of "Rock of Chickamauga"), prevented total disaster. Bragg, irresolute, made no effort to pursue, and Rosecrans' Army of the Cumberland clung to Chattanooga. Federal casualties were 1,657 killed, 9,756 wounded, and 4,757 missing. Bragg's Army of Tennessee lost 2,312 killed, 14,674 wounded, and 1,486 missing.

1863, September–October. Siege of Chattanooga. Bragg invested Chattanooga, cutting Rosecrans off from all communication either with Burnside at Knoxville, Tenn., or with Hooker's 2 corps of the Army of the Potomac, rushed by rail 1,192 miles to reinforce him. Hooker's troops remained at Bridgeport, 30 miles from Chattanooga. The Union-held mountain trails north of the Tennessee River were too rugged to support a supply line. Only a telegraph wire linked Rosecrans' army with the North. Rosecrans' troops and the inhabitants of the city neared starvation.

1863, September–October. Burnside Stalled at Knoxville. His army could not obtain supplies over the atrocious roads back through Cumberland Gap and was unable to advance on Chattanooga.

1863, October 17. Grant to Over-all Command in the West. Lincoln put him over all Union forces between the Mississippi and the Alleghenies.

1863, October 17–27. Relief of Chattanooga. Grant hastened to Chattanooga, en route relieving Rosecrans by telegram, replacing him with Thomas. Arriving by mule trail in Chattanooga (October 23), 4 days later Grant slipped a portion of Thomas' troops on ponton boats past the Confederates on Lookout Mountain and opened a gap in the blockading line. Hooker's troops advanced through this gap, bringing with them an adequate supply of food. At the same time Grant ordered Sherman up from Memphis with the Army of the Tennessee.

1863, November–December. Siege of Knoxville. Bragg, meanwhile, was so confident of the impregnability of his fortifications on Lookout Mountain and Missionary Ridge, overlooking Chattanooga, that he sent Longstreet and 20,000 men to besiege Burnside, whose forces were soon brought to the verge of starvation. Halleck and Lincoln wired frantic appeals to Grant to send relief to Burnside.

1863, November 24. Battle of Lookout Mountain (First Day, Battle of Chattanooga). With the arrival of Sherman—after a month's march—Grant had 61,000 men to oppose Bragg's well-entrenched 40,000. He immediately sent Hooker's 2 corps, on his right, to attack Lookout Mountain, while Sherman—without a pause to rest his weary troops—moved against the northern end of Missionary Ridge. Sherman was repulsed, but Hooker stormed Lookout Mountain in "the battle above the clouds," against light resistance.

1863, November 25. Battle of Missionary Ridge (Second Day, Battle of Chattanooga). Sherman renewed his assaults against the Confederate right, while Hooker somewhat dilatorily advanced against Bragg's left. In the afternoon Thomas' Army of the Cumberland began a limited attack against the front of the 3-tiered Confederate works. Taking the first line, Thomas' men, without orders, swept to the top of the ridge in a spontaneous assault. Bragg's troops, seized with panic, fled. Federal losses in the two days' combat were 753 killed, 4,722 wounded, and 349 missing. The Confederates lost 361 killed, 2,160 wounded, and 4,146 missing. Next day Grant sent Sherman's army to relieve Burnside at Knoxville.

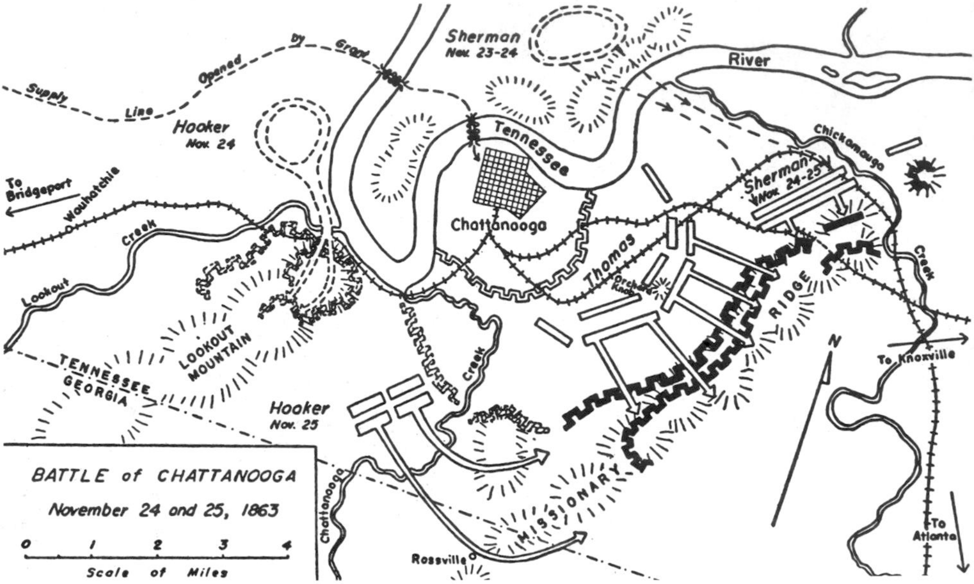

1863, December 6. Relief of Knoxville. Sherman arrived to find that Longstreet had abandoned the siege 2 days previously. With Tennessee now cleared of southern troops, the way was open for the next move—marching into Georgia.

Naval Operations, 1863

COASTAL

By this time the Union naval blockade was slowly strangling the Southern economy, despite the handicaps plaguing the blockaders. Monotonous cruising in all weathers was relieved only by hurried trips to coaling stations. Deep-water ships and sailors had no love for shoal waters and treacherous banks over which shallow-draft blockade runners could slip from hot pursuit. Up to June, 1863, Lincoln's net had bagged 885 runners, but the mesh was wide and blockade running had become big business. Specially built, speedy ships were operating out of Nassau in the Bahamas, Bermuda, Halifax, N.S., and Havana, Cuba. While the Gulf ports took some of this traffic, Charleston and Wilmington, N.C., had become the principal ports of entry. It was evident that to dry up the flood the ports must be occupied. Union interest now centered on Charleston in particular, whose retention had become a symbol in Southern eyes. Its defense was ably planned and vigorously conducted by General Beauregard.

1863, April 7. Repulse at Charleston. Rear Admiral Samuel F. du Pont attacked the fortified harbor with a squadron of 9 Union ironclads, but was decisively repulsed by the forts and shore batteries, bristling with guns.

1863, July–September. Union Bombardment. Rear Admiral **John A. Dahlgren,** succeeding du Pont (July 10), kept up bombardment of the Charleston defenses, in cooperation with land attacks by the troops of Major General **Quincy A. Gillmore.** Fort Wagner, principal target, repulsed several assaults with sanguinary losses (July–August).

1863, September 6. Occupation of Fort Wagner. It was evacuated by the Confederates. Its loss diminished Charleston's value as a blockade-runner's haven.

1863, September–December. Continued

Bombardment. The other fortifications held out. Southern ingenuity now turned to the submarine boat.

1863, October 5. Submarine Attack on *New Ironsides*. C.S.S. *David,* a semisubmersible cigar-shaped craft, steam-driven, manned by a crew of 4 men, approached U.S.S. *New Ironsides* at night and exploded a 60-pound copper-cased torpedo, manipulated on a long spar. Extensive damage was done to the Federal ship. The *David* returned safely to port, though two of her crew, washed off by the spouting water, were captured.

THE HIGH SEAS

Confederate commerce destruction during the period centered principally on the operations of 2 vessels constructed especially for the service in British shipyards and then turned over to Southern crews.

C.S.S. **Florida** had ravaged the Atlantic coast since August, 1862. One of *Florida*'s prizes, converted to a warship, actually sailed into the harbor of Portland, Me., and blew up a Federal revenue cutter before being captured. Finally, *Florida,* a steam corvette, was cornered in Bahia Harbor (October 7) and, in disregard of Brazilian neutrality, was boarded and captured by U.S.S. *Wachusett.*

C.S.S. **Alabama,** single-screw sloop of war, whose career also started in August, 1862, was still ranging the high seas on a history-making cruise under daring Captain **Raphael Semmes** as the year drew to a close.

Total War, 1864

1864, March 9. Grant General in Chief. Already partly choked by the constantly increasing pressure of naval blockade, the South now faced dismemberment by a gigantic co-ordinated turning movement planned by Grant. In the East, Meade's Army of the Potomac (under Grant's immediate supervision) would engage the Army of Northern Virginia while the western armies, under Sherman, swept into the deep South. Grant immediately prepared to bring the war to the speediest possible conclusion. His order (April 17) ending prisoner exchange was a severe blow to Southern man-power capability. Lincoln, realizing that at last he had found a general who could translate political objectives into vigorous, effective military strategy, wrote Grant: "The particulars of your plan I neither know nor seek to know . . . I wish not to obtrude any constraints or restraints upon you."

WAR IN THE EAST, 1864

1864, February 20. Battle of Olustee. In Florida, Confederate General **Joseph Finegan,** with 5,200 men, defeated an invading Union force of equal strength under Brigadier General **Truman Seymour.**

1864, February 28–March 2. Kilpatrick-Dahlgren Raid. An ill-conceived dash on Richmond by Major General **Judson Kilpatrick** with 4,500 cavalrymen ended in disaster. Publication of papers allegedly found on the body of Colonel **Ulric Dahlgren,** indicating intention to burn Richmond and assassinate Jefferson Davis and his cabinet, aroused keen Southern resentment. Meade, queried by Lee under a flag of truce, disclaimed such intentions. The papers were probably forgeries.

Wilderness–Spotsylvania–Cold Harbor Campaign

1864, April–May. Grant's Plan. He intended to lead Meade's Army of the Potomac—almost 105,000 strong—into the dense thickets of the Wilderness, seeking Lee's Army of Northern Virginia—about 61,000 men deployed watchfully along the Rapidan-Rappahannock line. Leaving administrative duties to Halleck, his chief of staff in Washington, Grant planned to operate directly against Lee's army "wherever it may be found," seeking its right flank and dislocating it from Richmond. His own line of communications, based on tidewater Virginian ports, would be secured through the assistance of the Union Navy. Far on the Union flanks—to prevent concentration of outlying Confederate forces against the main effort—Butler (from Fortress Monroe) would move up the James toward Richmond, while Major

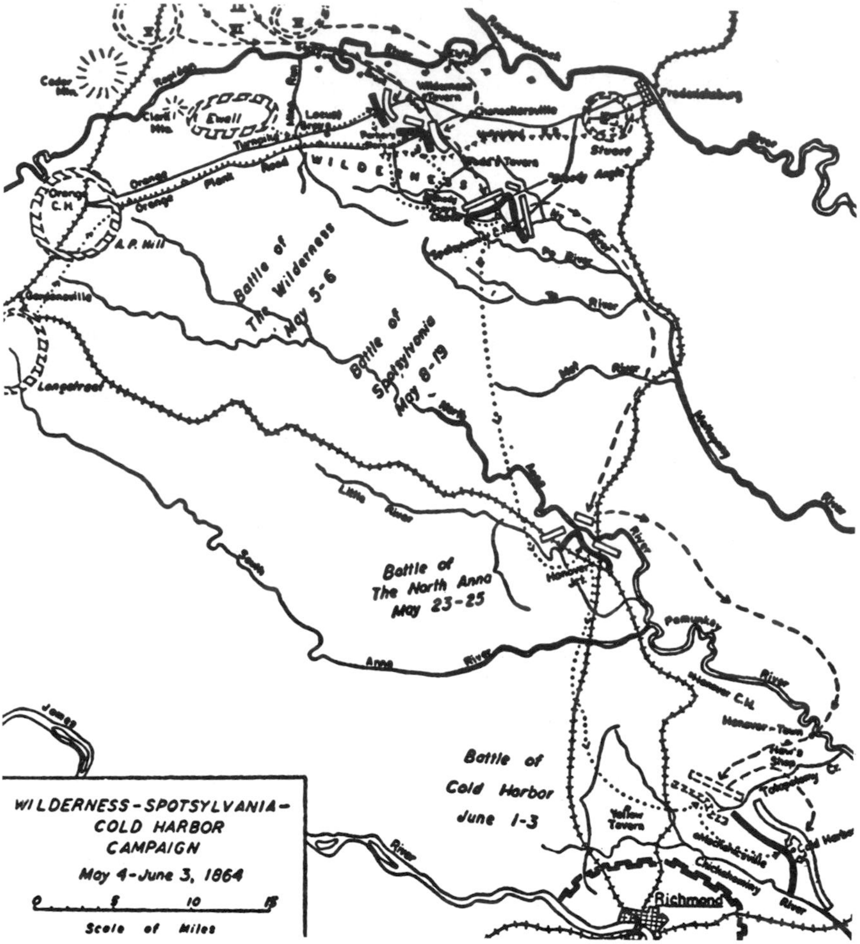

General **Franz Sigel** was to advance southward up the Shenandoah Valley.

1864, May 4. Crossing the Rapidan. Grant began to implement his plan.

1864, May 5–6. Battle of the Wilderness. As soon as Grant moved, Lee began to concentrate. The armies met while Grant was still entangled in second-growth thickets of the Wilderness, 14 miles long by 10 miles wide. The first day's fighting consisted of 2 separate indecisive engagements between bewildered units. Grant forced a general offensive next morning, to be met by determined counterattacks. Longstreet was seriously wounded near the spot where Jackson had fallen a year previously. By nightfall the confused, furious combat was still undecided; the contenders spent the next day quelling forest fires and attempting to rescue wounded trapped in the blazing brush. The Union Army had lost 2,246 killed, 12,037 wounded, and 3,383 missing. Confederate casualties, unrecorded, are estimated at over 12,000.

1864, May 7. Grant Sticks to His Plan. He slipped around Lee's right and moved south. Lee, correctly estimating the situation, had rushed a covering force to Spotsylvania Court House before the Union advance elements arrived at dawn next day.

1864, May 8–18. Battle of Spotsylvania. Now on more maneuverable terrain, both armies struggled for 5 days (May 8–12) in a series of piecemeal engagements, while Lee's position built up into an immense V, with its apex—the "Bloody Angle"—pointing north. A Union grand assault (May 12) was thrown back. Grant, searching for the hostile flanks, was for 6 more days thwarted by Lee's splendid shifting of his reserves. Union losses were 14,267; Confederate, over 10,000.

1864, May 11. Battle of Yellow Tavern. During the Spotsylvania struggle, Major General **Philip H. Sheridan**'s cavalry corps, 10,000 strong, raided south toward Richmond. At Yellow Tavern, on the outskirts of the city's fortifications, he met Stuart, with 4,500 sabers, in pitched battle. The Confederate horsemen were driven from the field and Stuart himself was mortally wounded, a body blow to Lee. Sheridan lost some 400 men; Confederate losses—untabulated—were about 1,000.

1864, May 20. Grant Again Moves South. As before, he went around Lee's right, toward Hanover Junction. Lee, recognizing Grant's stubborn intention to cut him off from Richmond, cleverly shifted from Spotsylvania to a strong position on the North Anna River (May 22) one day before Grant arrived.

1864, May 23–31. North Anna and Haw's Shop. Grant probed the position, but found it too strong for a major assault (May 23). Once more he sidestepped eastward around Lee's right flank. A 2-day delay crossing the Pamunkey River (May 27–29) gave Lee time to interpose once again between Grant and Richmond. Sheridan's cavalry engaged with entrenched Southern horsemen near Haw's Shop (May 28), while Lee was taking new positions south of Totopotomy Creek, near Mechanicsville. Again Grant probed and again he shifted to find Lee's right flank—this time to the vicinity of Cold Harbor, close to the Seven Days' battlefields of 1862.

1864, June 3–12. Battle of Cold Harbor. Grant, reinforced to a strength of 100,000 men, determined to split Lee's army, which he believed to be overextended on a 6-mile line (June 2). Delays in troop movements postponed the attack for 24 hours. Lee, feverishly improving his field fortifications, was himself reinforced by 14,000 men, drawn from the successful opponents of Sigel in the Valley and Butler on the James (see below). Grant's assaults were snubbed by confident, veteran defenders in a well-fortified position, strong in artillery. After losing nearly 7,000 men in less than an hour, Grant called off the attack. The defenders suffered fewer than 1,500 casualties. Other Union probes were also beaten back. Over-all losses in the 10-day battle: Union, 13,078; Confederate, approximately 3,000.

Failures of Butler and Sigel

1864, May 5–16. Bermuda Hundred. Butler, with the Army of the James, 30,000 strong, moved (May 4) from Fortress Monroe upriver by boat. Charged with the occupation of City Point as preliminary to his final objective—Richmond (in co-ordination with Grant's advance)—Butler instead landed at Bermuda Hundred. His timid and vacillating movements now did little more than stimulate the close-in defense of Richmond.

1864, May 15. Battle of Drewry's Bluff. Cleverly defeated by Beauregard, Butler was thrown back to his Bermuda Hundred position, where he remained corked up until Grant advanced south of the James.

1864, May 15. Battle of New Market. In the Shenandoah Valley, Sigel, with 10,000 Union troops, had started south in coordination with Grant's drive (May 4). Advancing from Cedar Creek, he was attacked by Confederate Major General **John Breckenridge,** with 5,000 men. Sigel, who made use of only half his original strength, was driven back and failed to maintain further pressure in the Valley. Noteworthy was the presence in the Confederate line of the cadet corps of Virginia Military Institute.

From Cold Harbor to Petersburg

1864, June 11–12. Battle of Trevilian Station. Grant, determination unshaken, prepared to cross the James River, again circling Lee's right. As a diversion, Sheridan's cavalry raided westward toward Charlottesville with the mission of uniting with old General **David Hunter,** who had replaced Sigel and had pushed up the Valley to Staunton after a successful engagement at nearby **Piedmont** (June 5). The combined force would then drive southeast to meet Grant. Lee matched the threats by sending **Wade Hampton** with 2 cavalry divisions after Sheridan and transferring Early's corps to the Valley to check Hunter. The opposing cavalry forces met (June 11) at **Trevilian Station.** After a confused 2-day conflict, Sheridan withdrew. Hunter, menaced by the arrival of Early, began withdrawal westward across the Alleghenies after some skirmishing near Lynchburg (June 17–18).

1864, June 13–18. Crossing of the James. While Warren's V Corps and Wilson's cavalry demonstrated as if to attack Richmond, the Army of the Potomac faded south from its Cold Harbor positions to the James River. One corps was ferried

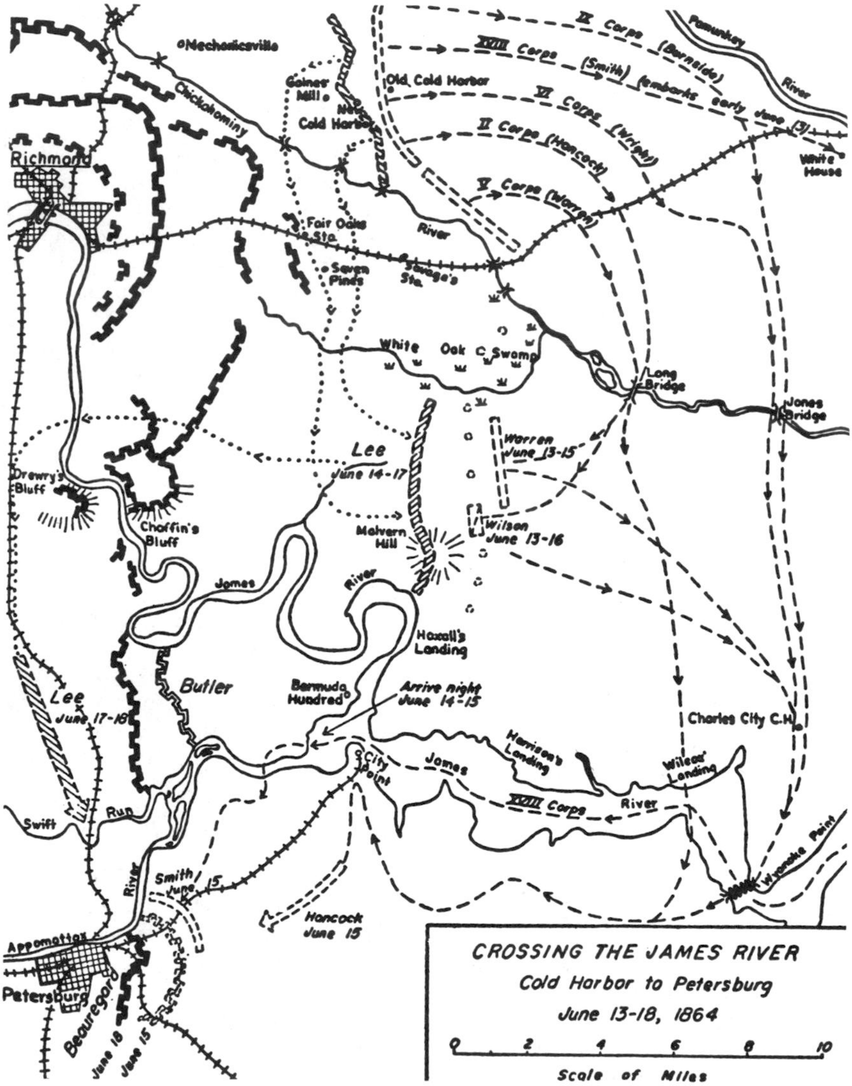

CROSSING THE JAMES RIVER
Cold Harbor to Petersburg
June 13-18, 1864

across by naval transport, another shipped to Bermuda Hundred; but the bulk of the troops crossed on a pontoon bridge erected (June 14) by the Union engineers in 8 hours, a feat unsurpassed in military engineering. Lee was still deployed in expectation of a full-scale Union attack over the old Seven Days' battlefields when the last of the Army of the Potomac had passed south of the James in one of the great feats of the war.

1864, June 15–18. Battle of Petersburg. While the James crossing was in full swing, Grant ordered Butler, with his

Army of the James at Bermuda Hundred to capture fortified Petersburg, 8 miles away and—at the moment—scantily garrisoned. Butler and his subordinate **W. F. Smith** botched the job in 2 piecemeal attempts, while Beauregard, Confederate commander south of the Richmond defenses, rushed all available reinforcements. Grant, arriving on the scene, ordered a major attack as the remainder of the Army of the Potomac began coming up. Meanwhile Lee, finally realizing that Grant had crossed the James, hurried down. Grant, attacking with 65,000 men (June 18), was stopped by 40,000 veterans manning fortified lines. The siege of Petersburg began. This 3-day conflict cost the Union 8,150 casualties. Confederate losses totaled 4,752.

Early's Valley Campaign

1864, July 2. Early Crosses the Potomac. Driving remaining Union forces before him from Winchester to the Potomac, Early's II Corps—Jackson's old command, some 13,000 strong—invaded Maryland; he levied from Hagerstown $20,000, from Frederick $200,000.

1864, July 9. Battle of the Monocacy. Early then struck toward terrified Washington, sweeping out of his way Major General **Lew Wallace**'s extemporized force of 6,000 on the Monocacy River. While Grant hurried the VI and XIX Corps up from the Richmond-Petersburg area to protect Washington, Early reached Fort Stevens, inside the District line (July 11).

1864, July 11–12. Action in Washington's Outskirts. Next day the VI Corps arrived, taking over the defenses from the ill-assorted home guards. Early, after a demonstration, hurriedly retreated, leaving 400 wounded behind him, but carrying his cash booty safely back up the Valley. Procrastinating and contradictory orders from Washington prevented any co-ordinated pursuit.

1864, July 23–30. Early Invades Again. This time he smashed Major General **George Crook**'s Army of West Virginia aside at **Kernstown** and **Winchester** (July 23–24), then he lunged as far as Chambersburg, which he burned (after the town refused to pay $100,000 in gold) as reparation for the burning of Virginia Military Institute by Hunter.

1864, August 7. Sheridan's Army of the Shenandoah. Grant, realizing that so long as a Confederate army stood in the Valley the capital was unsafe, secretly ordered all of Washington's defense forces (48,000 men) concentrated near Harpers Ferry, safe from politicians' meddling. He placed Sheridan in command. Sheridan's mission was to destroy Early's command and to "eat out Virginia clean and clear . . . so that crows flying over it for the balance of the season will have to carry their own provender."

1864, September 19. Battle of Opequon Creek (Third Battle of Winchester). Sheridan's 41,000 men began with cautious probings. Early started north with some 19,000 men, meeting Sheridan headlong. After initial Confederate success, the Union cavalry turned Early's left, while Sheridan's personal leadership sparked the main Federal effort. Early, attempting to stand just outside Winchester, was thrown back to Fisher's Hill, 12 miles south. Union losses were 5,000; Confederate, 4,600.

1864, September 22. Battle of Fisher's Hill. Sheridan assaulted the Southern position in frontal attack, while his cavalry smashed in Early's left. The Confederates were driven back to Waynesboro; they lost about 1,250 men; Union casualties were negligible.

1864, September–October. Devastation in the Valley. Sheridan moved back down the Valley, systematically turning it into a vale of desolation. Confederate guerrillas on his flanks were extremely annoying, but neither they nor Early's troops, hanging on the Union rear, had any effectual result. By mid-October the 31,000-man Army of the Shenandoah, its work completed, bivouacked along Cedar Creek, 20 miles south of Winchester. Sheridan left his command for a conference in Washington about the future disposition of his troops.

1864, October 19. Battle of Cedar Creek. Early, reinforced to 18,400-man strength, sneaked his main effort through the Massanutten Mountain nose to surprise the Federal left and rear at dawn. His cavalry at the same time fell on both Union flanks, and his massed artillery sprayed the front. The daring move was almost successful. The Union VIII Corps stampeded (and would not be rallied for 48 hours). Major General **H. G. Wright,** commanding in Sheridan's absence, fought the XIX and VI Corps in 3 successive delaying positions. By noon, the Union army was defeated, it seemed, but Sheridan, returning from Washington, galloped up the pike from Winchester, "twenty miles away." He rallied his men in an extraordinary display of personal leadership. Regrouping on the battlefield, Sheridan's counterattack drove Early all the way back to New Market. Union casualties were some 5,600. Confederate losses were only 2,900, but the back of Southern resistance in the Shenandoah Valley had been broken. Early's effort, however, had prolonged the war in the East for some 6 months. Most of his troops now returned to Lee at Petersburg.

1865, March 2. Battle of Waynesboro. Early, with but a shadow of his command—some 1,000-odd men—was overrun by Major General **George A. Custer**'s cavalry.

SIEGE OF PETERSBURG—PHASE ONE, 1864

1864, June 19–December 31. Operations South of Petersburg. Grant immediately began to move against the railroads south of Petersburg to isolate Lee from his sources of supply. Operations dragged on through the rest of the year, combining trench warfare with spectacular sorties and maneuvers as Grant slowly extended his partial encirclement of the Richmond-Petersburg complex.

1864, June 22–23. Weldon R.R., Burke's Station, Ream's Station. A Union infantry attack under Generals **D. B. Birney** and H. G. Wright from the Jerusalem Plank Road toward Globe Tavern on the Weldon R.R. was combined with a longer-range cavalry raid of Generals **J. H. Wilson** and **A. V. Kautz** to Burke's Station, 15 miles farther west. The infantry were thrown back by A. P. Hill's counterattack, while the Union cavalrymen, initially successful, were severely handled and barely escaped capture as they returned by way of Ream's Station.

1864, July 30. The Petersburg Mine (Battle of the Crater). A cleverly devised Union mining operation ended with the explosion of 4 tons of gunpowder under the Petersburg defense systems. The blast—a complete surprise—ripped a great crater, through which Burnside's IX Corps was to assault. Shockingly mismanaged, the assaulting troops gathered in the crater without competent leadership. The rallying defenders poured cannon and rifle fire into the milling mass and sealed the break. This operation was one of the great tragic fiascos of the war, comparable to Burnside's previous fiasco at Fredericksburg. Union casualties were 3,793; Confederate (including the victims of the blast), 1,182.

1864, August 14–20. Deep Bottom. To keep the Confederates off balance, Grant tested the Richmond defenses north of the James. Lee shifted troops from Petersburg to meet the threat. Six days of hammering along Bailey's Creek cost the Union 2,900 men. Confederate losses are not recorded.

1864, August 18–21. Globe Tavern. Grant now struck southwest of Petersburg again, overrunning the Weldon R.R., despite A. P. Hill's bitter counterattack. Union losses were 4,455, against Confederate casualties of 1,619, but a vital supply line had been cut.

1864, August 25. Ream's Station. An extemporized Southern railhead farther south was cut off by a Union infantry-artillery force under Hancock. Lee's immediate reaction was a counterattack by Major General Wade Hampton, surprising the Union force as it was wrecking the line. Hancock, rallying, threw him back and completed destruction of a long stretch of railroad.

1864, September 29–30. Chaffin's Bluff. Covered by a demonstration on the southern end of the investment, 2 Union corps attacked the Richmond sector. Lee withdrew forces from Petersburg to counterattack, but Fort Harrison, at the Bluff, fell into Union hands.

1864, September 30. Peeble's Farm. A simultaneous attack southwest of Petersburg inched the Union investment a bit farther east, but could not penetrate the main defensive position.

1864, October 27–28. Boydton Plank Road. Grant's full-scale blow to cut the Southside R.R., last Confederate rail link, was repulsed by Hill. Butler's diversionary demonstration east of Richmond was rebuffed by convalescing Longstreet. Fur-

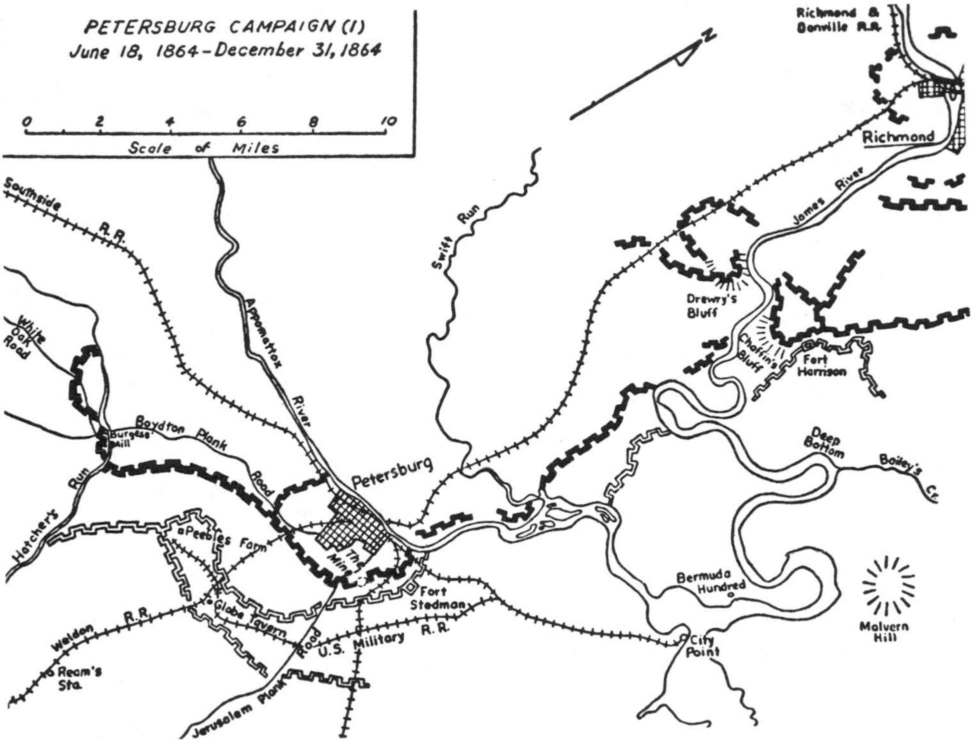

ther mobile operations ceased as winter closed down, and siege became an artillery duel while the semistarved military and civilian population of the Richmond-Petersburg area tightened their belts. Behind the entrenchments of the well-fed, well-housed besiegers, a military railroad belt line, 21 miles long, linked every inch of the front to Grant's huge base at City Point.

WAR IN THE WEST, 1864

West of the Mississippi

1864, March–May. Red River Expedition. Before Grant became General in Chief, Halleck (with Lincoln's approval) ordered General Banks and Admiral Porter to undertake an overland invasion of Texas via the Red River. One objective was to discourage the French (then controlling Mexico; see p. 909) from any intervention through Texas. Porter managed to get 12 of his Mississippi gunboats above the rapids at Alexandria, La., and headed up the winding stream toward Shreveport while Banks with 30,000 men marched along the river bank. At **Grand Ecore,** Banks struck across country toward Shreveport. Ambushed at **Sabine Cross Roads** (April 8), by Generals **Richard Taylor** and Edmund Kirby Smith, Banks retreated hastily to Alexandria, while part of his command delayed Confederate pursuit at **Pleasant Hill** (April 9). Banks lost 3,500 out of 25,000 men engaged in both actions; Southern losses were 2,000 out of 14,300. Porter, abandoned by Banks, steamed back on a falling river, sniped at by Confederate cavalry and artillery. At Alexandria he discovered the water over the rapids was now too low to float his vessels. Banks, bluntly ordered by Grant to remain at Alexandria until Porter got out, assisted in constructing a flume and dam through which the Union gunboats shot to safety. Alexandria was then evacuated (May 14).

1864, September–October. Price in Missouri. During 1863 and 1864, Confederate Major General **Sterling Price** had been operating in Arkansas against Union Major General **Frederick Steele** with mixed success. He now decided to invade Missouri. Crossing the Arkansas River between Little Rock and Fort Smith (September 1), Price with 13,000 veterans and 20 guns headed for St. Louis. Finding that city unexpectedly reinforced, he then struck west toward Kansas City. He defeated Major General **James G. Blunt** at **Lexington** (October 19). Continuing west, Price again drove Blunt back at **Independence** (October 22). But Blunt's stubborn resistance permitted Union troops, pursuing from St. Louis, to reach the scene.

1864, October 23. Battle of Westport. Still engaged with Blunt along the Missouri-Kansas line, Price was struck in the rear by Pleasanton's cavalry and defeated. He was driven back into Arkansas, ending major operations west of the Mississippi.

Operations of N. B. Forrest, February–October, 1864

1864, February 22. Battle of Okolona. Forrest had a handful of Confederate troops in northern Mississippi. Union General **W. Sooy Smith,** with 7,000 cavalry, two to three times Forrest's strength, moved from Memphis (February 11) into northern Mississippi, planning to meet General Sherman at Meridian. Forrest, entrenched amid wooded swamps, stopped Smith, who withdrew (February 20). Forrest pursued, catching the Federals near Okolona, drubbing them in an all-day running fight.

1864, March–April. Raid into Kentucky. Sweeping as far as Paducah, Forrest assaulted and captured **Fort Pillow** on his return (April 12), where his troops have been accused (probably unjustly) of having massacred colored Union soldiers after they surrendered.

1864, June 10. Battle of Brice's Cross Roads. Union Major General Samuel D. Sturgis, under orders from Sherman to find and defeat Forrest, advanced from Memphis with 3,400 cavalry, 2,000 infantry, 12 guns, and a train of 250 wagons. Forrest, who had about 3,000 men, held the Union troops with a thin skirmish line, undertook a double envelopment, and sent a detachment on a wide envelopment to strike the Union rear. The Northerners were routed, abandoning all their wagons and all but 2 guns; they suffered 617 casualties, in addition to 1,623 captured by Forrest, who lost about 500.

1864, July 14–15. Battle of Tupelo. General **A. J. Smith,** with 14,000 troops, undertook another expedition from Memphis against Forrest, who had been reinforced to 10,000. Forrest again seized the tactical offensive in a bitterly contested 2-day drawn battle, but was repulsed. Smith withdrew, having lost 674 men; Forrest's casualties were over 1,300; he was wounded.

1864, August 21. Memphis Raid. Forrest penetrated the Union defenses at dawn, reaching the Union headquarters. The commander, Major General **C. C. Washburn,** escaped in his nightclothes, but Forrest rode off with his uniform.

1864, August–October. Forrest Moves East and North. This was partly due to increased concentration of Federal troops in western Mississippi, and partly in response to the crisis resulting from Sherman's capture of Atlanta (see p. 900). Forrest, in company with young General **Joseph Wheeler,** raided vigorously against Sherman's line of communications from Atlanta back to Nashville, and thence to the Ohio River.

1864, October 29–November 4. Naval Operations on the Tennessee. Raiding into northwestern Tennessee, Forrest ambushed Federal naval forces on the river near Johnsonville, capturing a gunboat and 5 transports. His troops manned these river craft for several days, but abandoned them after the Union Navy concentrated overwhelming force on the lower Tennessee. Forrest was now ordered to go east again to join Hood in the Franklin-Nashville Campaign, in which he again distinguished himself (see p. 901).

Atlanta Campaign, May–August, 1864

1864, May 5. Advance into Georgia. Sherman's army group left Chattanooga: Thomas' Army of the Cumberland, 61,000 strong; **James B. McPherson**'s Army of the Tennessee, 24,500 men; and **John M. Schofield**'s Army of the Ohio, mustering 13,500. In front of Sherman was Johnston's Army of Tennessee, 60,000 strong. In his rear, from the Mississippi to the Appalachians, Confederate cavalrymen **John H. Morgan** and Nathan B. Forrest roamed, hampering communications and bedeviling Union garrisons. Johnston, outnumbered, skillfully opposed Sherman in a series of delaying positions. Sherman, equally skillful, outmaneuvered him by

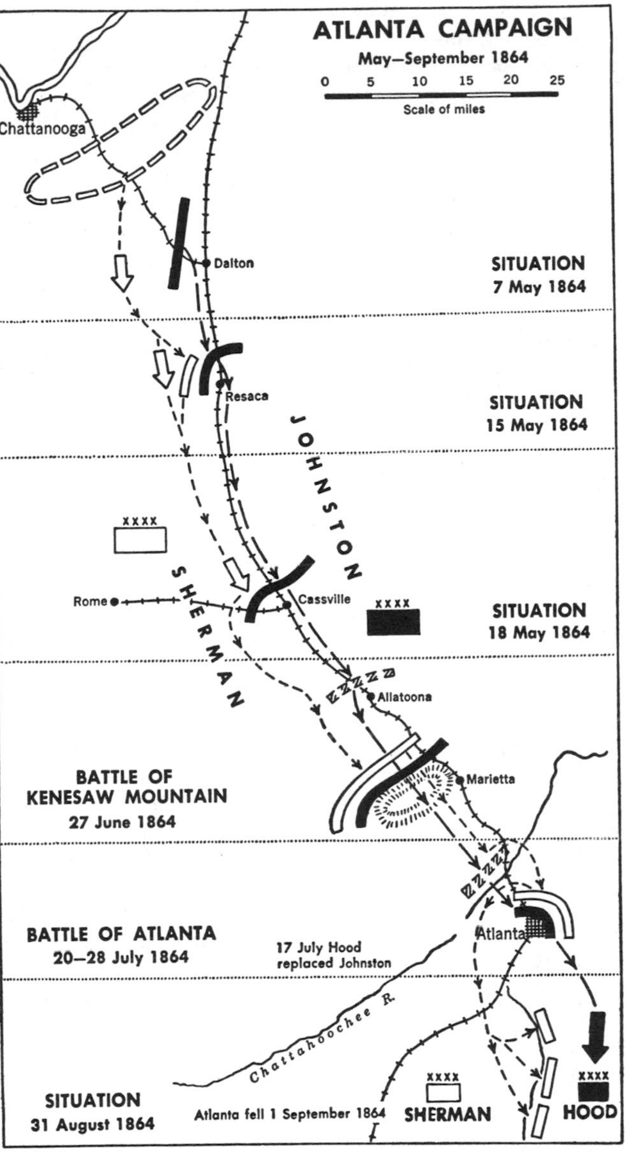

turning movements at **Dalton** (May 9), **Resaca** (May 15), and **Cassville** (May 19). Each time the maneuver was the same: a holding force in front and a wide Union turning movement around the Confederate left. Then Sherman drove due south, by-passing Johnston's position at **Allatoona** (May 24). Johnston, retiring to Marietta, placed himself directly in Sherman's path.

1864, June 27. Battle of Kenesaw Mountain. After a series of indecisive combats near **Dallas** and **New Hope Church** (May 25–28), Sherman made a frontal assault on Kenesaw Mountain, the key to Johnston's positions. The attacks were repulsed at all points, Sherman losing some 3,000 men, while Johnston's losses were only 800. Once again Sherman (July 2) turned his opponent's left, and Johnston (July 4) took up a powerful entrenched line north of the Chattahoochie River.

1864, July 9. Crossing of the Chattahoochie. Again Sherman turned the Confederate position. Johnston fell back on Peachtree Creek, just north of Atlanta, and prepared for a counterattack. He was summarily relieved from command (July 17) as an ungrateful administration's reward for a really remarkable delaying campaign against far superior forces. For 2½ months he had, with a minimum of losses, held Sherman to an average advance of 1 mile per day. Impulsive **John B. Hood** succeeded him.

1864, July 20. Battle of Peachtree Creek. Johnston had already foreseen that Sherman's advance on Atlanta, on a 10-mile front, offered possibility for a successful counterstroke. Hood seized the opportunity, falling on Thomas' army. Although surprised, the Union forces were alert and the attack was repulsed. Some 20,000 men on each side were involved. Southern casualties were about 2,500; Union losses were 1,600. The Union advance continued (July 21), forcing Hood to withdraw into the Atlanta defenses. Sherman, hoping to follow his foe into the city, sent his left-flank cavalry division eastward to cut the railway. Hood, however, had recoiled to strike again.

1864, July 22. Battle of Atlanta. William J. Hardee's corps—the elite of Hood's army—together with **Joseph Wheeler**'s cavalry division hit the open left flank of McPherson's army. Surprise was complete, but the veteran Federal troops reformed, despite the death of McPherson in the melee. The assault was repulsed with Confederate losses of some 8,000 men. Federal casualties were 3,722. Sherman—his strength insufficient for a siege—determined to swing entirely around to the westerly side of Atlanta and operate against the railroads. Sending most of his cavalry raiding south (July 27), he started the move next day.

1864, July 28. Battle of Ezra Church. An assault by Hood was repelled—mainly by the Army of the Tennessee—with 4,300 southern casualties against 632 Union losses.

1864, July 28–August 22. Cavalry Raids. Part of Sherman's cavalry—6,000 strong, moving around both sides of Atlanta—failed in its dual mission: cutting of the railroad and liberation of Union prisoners at Andersonville. Major General **George Stoneman** and some 2,000 men were surrounded and captured (August 4). Meanwhile, Sherman's strength built up on Atlanta's western face. Another Union cavalry raid ended (August 22) in failure to cut rail communication with Atlanta.

1864, August 27–31. Fall of Atlanta. Leaving 1 army corps to guard his own communications, Sherman swung his 3 armies forward in a great wheel toward the railroad lines south of the city, driving Wheeler's cavalry before them. Hood sent Major General **W. J. Hardee,** with half of his army, to hold the railroads, but Hardee was thrown back at **Jonesboro** (August 31). Hood's communications line was cut. Destroying ammunition and supply stores, Hood evacuated Atlanta that night, moving east and south. Next morning Sherman's troops marched in.

The March to the Sea

1864, September–October. Maneuvering around Atlanta. Sherman, making Atlanta a military base, found further movement hampered by the need to protect his 400-mile line of communications to Nashville. In addition to the daring and successful depredations of Forrest and Wheeler, Hood moved west and north with his entire army (October 1) to attack these communications, hoping to force Sherman's withdrawal. After a vain chase of Hood through **Allatoona** (October 5) as far as Baylesville, Ala. (October 22), Sherman came to the conclusion that further efforts to get to grips with the elusive Confederates would nullify Grant's giant pincers concept.

1864, November 15–December 8. March from Atlanta. Sherman solved the problem—with the somewhat reluctant approval of Grant—by sending Thomas' Army of the Cumberland back to Nashville and Chattanooga, while he deliberately abandoned his line of communications and marched eastward from Atlanta toward Savannah with 68,000 veterans. With him were 2,500 wagons and 600 ambulances carrying supplies (mostly ammunition); otherwise, his men lived off the country. With practically no opposition, he cut a 50-mile-wide swath of "scorched earth" to the sea, 300 miles away. He was deliberately making "Georgia howl" as he devastated crops and the war-supporting economy of central Georgia; noncombatants were scrupulously respected. He ignored Hood's efforts to distract him by a full-scale invasion of Tennessee (see below). To his front, Beauregard, assisted by Hardee, endeavored to organize effective resistance to protect Savannah and Charleston.

1864, December 9–21. Operations against Savannah. Arriving in eastern Georgia, Sherman discovered that Hardee held fortified Savannah with 15,000 men. Sherman stormed **Fort McAllister** at the mouth of the Ogeechee River, 15 miles from Savannah (December 13). Then, establishing communications with Union naval forces, he began an investment of the city. With his lines of communication about to be cut, Hardee evacuated, and Sherman moved in at once (December 21), presenting the city (in a ship-borne and telegraph message) as "a Christmas gift" to Lincoln.

Franklin and Nashville Campaign

1864, November 14. Hood Invades Tennessee. Reinforced by Forrest's cavalry, Hood crossed the Tennessee River and moved rapidly north toward Nashville with 54,000 veteran troops. Thomas, building an extemporized army at Nashville about his own hard core of veterans, did not wish to withdraw garrisons from key points in Tennessee; he sparred for time. Major General John M. Schofield, with 2 corps and Wilson's cavalry division—about 34,000 men—was directed to delay the Southern advance. Schofield, slipping away from Hood's attempts to box him in at **Columbia** (November 26–27), and fighting his way through Confederate enveloping forces in a night battle at **Spring Hill** (November 29), stood in previously prepared defenses at Franklin, 15 miles south of Nashville.

1864, November 30. Battle of Franklin. Hood, impetuous, attacked piecemeal, with but two-thirds of his army. He was thrown back with shocking casualties—6,300 out of 38,000 men engaged. Schofield, out of 32,000 men, lost 2,300. Having successfully performed his mission, Schofield retired that night to Nashville.

1864, December 15–16. Battle of Nashville. Hood stood before the Nashville defenses from December 2, while Washington fumed at the seeming procrastination of Thomas, whose numerical strength was superior. But methodical Thomas, busy training his largely recruit army—particularly Wilson's new cavalry corps—would not be budged. Finally he struck, shattering Hood's left flank, exposed because Hood had sent Forrest away raiding toward Murfreesboro. Attempting to continue the fight next day, Hood found Thomas enveloping both his flanks. Wilson's cavalry, striking behind the Confederate left, delivered the final blow. Federal losses, out of 49,773 men engaged, were 3,061; Confederate, 5,350 out of 31,000 on the field, but Hood's army had become a fleeing rabble.

COMMENT. *This was the most decisive tactical victory gained by either side in a major engagement in the war.*

Coastal and High Seas Operations, 1864–1865

1864, February 17. Sinking of U.S.S. *Housatonic*. Submarine warfare claimed its first victim when C.S.S. *H. L. Hunley,* a real submarine boat, torpedoed and sank the steam frigate *Housatonic* of the Federal squadron blockading Charleston Harbor. The *Hunley* sank with her prey.

1864, June 19. *Kearsarge* vs. *Alabama*. Semmes's Confederate sea raider was sunk by U.S.S. *Kearsarge,* off Cherbourg Harbor, after a 1-hour battle. The *Alabama* had just completed a 75,000-mile cruise, practically around the world, in 23 months. She had sunk 1 Federal warship and captured 62 prizes. While the ships were theoretically of nearly equal strength, the *Alabama* was a tired ship and her gun crews lacked practice. The *Kearsarge,* kept in peak condition by Captain **John A. Winslow,** riddled her opponent. Three men only of the *Kearsarge*'s complement were wounded. Forty-odd of sinking *Alabama*'s crew were casualties; 70 were rescued by the *Kearsarge.* The remaining 42, including Captain Semmes, were rescued by a British yacht and avoided capture.

1864, August 5. Battle of Mobile Bay. Lashed to the rigging of his flagship *Hartford,* Admiral Farragut, with 4 ironclad monitors and 14 wooden warships, ran by the cross fire of Mobile Harbor's heavily gunned defenses. When his leading monitor, *Tecumseh,* was blown up by a mine, stopping the fleet under the guns of **Fort**

Morgan, Farragut turned his own ship into the minefield (his "Damn the torpedoes!" has gone down in naval history) to clear the way. The other mines failed to go off and the Union ships passed safely into the bay. There Confederate Commodore **Franklin Buchanan** in the ironclad ram *Tennessee* attempted to take on the entire Union squadron, but was finally pounded into submission. Farragut's victory practically ended blockade running in the Gulf of Mexico.

1864, October 27. Destruction of C.S.S. *Albemarle*. This powerful ironclad ram, constructed up the Roanoke River, had dominated the North Carolina sounds for several months. She took a major part in a successful joint Confederate Army-Navy assault on the Union blockade base at **Plymouth,** N.C., sinking 1 Union gunboat, driving off another, and supporting the land attack (April 18). Later the *Albemarle* dispersed a squadron of 8 Union gunboats (May 5). She was a menace to all Union coastwise operations, since her shallow draft enabled her to evade large warships and she outgunned Union small craft. Lieutenant **William B. Cushing,** U.S.N., in a specially designed launch carrying a powerful torpedo, daringly attacked and sank the *Albemarle* at Plymouth.

1864, December. First Expedition against Fort Fisher. Wilmington, N.C., last remaining Atlantic blockade-runners' haven, had become the overseas supply link of the Army of Northern Virginia. With the *Albemarle* disposed of, Admiral Porter moved against Wilmington's elaborate defenses. A division of Butler's army, under Butler's personal command, took part. An attempt to destroy the principal fortification—Fort Fisher—by exploding a powder ship under its walls failed (December 23).

1864, December 23–25. First Attack on Fort Fisher. Porter's squadron opened a bombardment supposed to cover a landing by Butler's command of 6,500 men, 2,000 of whom went ashore Christmas Day. After a brief demonstration, Butler hurriedly re-embarked and sailed back to Fort Monroe. Porter was furious. Grant sacked Butler and provided Porter with able and co-operative Major General **Alfred H. Terry.**

1865, January 13–15. Assault of Fort Fisher. Terry's force, now augmented to 8,000, landed north of the fort (January 13) and prepared to attack in co-ordination with an intensive naval bombardment. While a Navy-Marine landing force assaulting the sea face was repulsed, Terry's troops swept over the outer works, covered by naval gunfire. Colonel **William Lamb** and his remaining 2,000 men surrendered after 7 hours of bitter fighting. Union losses were 1,341; Confederate, 500-odd. With Fort Fisher's fall, the last sea gate of the Confederacy closed. Richmond and the Army of Northern Virginia were doomed.

Closing Campaigns, 1865

The year opened with Grant still constricting Lee in the Petersburg-Richmond sector, while Sherman started north through the Carolinas from Savannah.

1865, January 31. Abortive Peace Conference. President Lincoln met Confederate peace commissioners, led by Vice President **Alexander H. Stephens,** on a Union warship in Hampton Roads. Lincoln offered complete amnesty if the South rejoined the Union and abolished slavery. The Confederates insisted on independence. The conference failed.

1865, February 3. Lee General in Chief. With the Union pincer jaws closing around the Confederacy, Jefferson Davis (far too late) appointed Lee to supreme command of the Confederate Army. Lee at once restored Johnston to command scattered southern elements in the Carolinas.

CAMPAIGN IN THE CAROLINAS

1865, February 17. Burning of Columbia, S.C. The city was almost entirely destroyed the night that Sherman's troops marched in, probably ignited by cotton stores fired by the departing defenders, but the South blamed Sherman. That same day Hardee abandoned Charleston. (His troops, like those of Bragg and Beauregard, were now placed under Johnston's new command.) Sherman, at Fayetteville, learning of Johnston's return, cut loose from the seacoast (March 15) and marched on Goldsboro to break up the Confederate concentration.

1865, February 22. Fall of Wilmington.

Grant, maintaining unremitting pressure against the collapsing Confederacy and exploiting Union command of the sea, sent Schofield, with troops from Thomas' army, to land at Fort Fisher to operate against Bragg near Wilmington. Driving the Confederates from the city, Schofield began to advance into central North Carolina to join Sherman.

1865, March 19–20. Battle of Bentonville. Sherman, moving north with his 60,000 men on a broad front, was surprised by Johnston, who had only 27,000, but who hoped to defeat the Union left wing before Sherman could concentrate. Sherman's left was driven in, as planned, but Johnston was unable to smash the Union veterans or to fully exploit the success. Sherman concentrated early the next day, and Johnston withdrew. Union casualties were 1,646, Confederate losses probably twice as great. Sherman, continuing the advance, reached Goldsboro (March 23), where he was joined by Schofield. Sherman, whose troops had marched and fought for 425 miles since leaving Savannah, decided to rest for 3 weeks, planning to join Grant near Petersburg in mid-April after muddy roads had dried somewhat.

SELMA CAMPAIGN

1865, March 18. Advance into Alabama. Wilson's cavalry corps—13,500 strong—was sent by Thomas into Alabama to destroy the important Confederate supply depot at Selma. Crossing the Tennessee River at Eastport, Ala., Wilson's swift-moving expedition brushed Forrest's 3,000 men aside from 3 delaying positions. Forrest fell back on Selma, a fortified city ringed by bastioned earthworks. Here he stood, reinforced to a strength of 7,000 by local militia.

1865, April 2. Battle of Selma. Wilson's cavalry assaulted the works. Fighting on foot, they clambered over the earthworks, gained a toehold, and won the town. Forrest, with a few of his men, escaped. Union casualties were some 400; Confederate, including prisoners, were about 4,000. Wilson, after destroying foundries, ammunition dumps, and stores, crossed the Alabama River (April 10). When hostilities ceased, he had already swept through Montgomery into Georgia as far as Macon. His troopers later captured Jefferson Davis (May 10).

PETERSBURG CAMPAIGN (CONCLUSION)

1865, January–March. Grant Increases the Pressure. While supervising the hammer blows his subordinates were dealing around the periphery of the dwindling Confederacy, Grant maintained about 90,000 men in the Armies of the Potomac and of the James around the defenses of Petersburg and Richmond. Lee, who was able to scrape together about 60,000 poorly fed, poorly equipped soldiers, held a front of 37 miles of entrenchments. Their continuing high quality, however, was demonstrated when A. P. Hill threw back still another Union probe on the Southern extreme right flank at **Hatcher's Run** (February 5–7). But it was obvious to Lee that he could not stretch his over-extended forces further.

1865, March 25. Battle of Fort Stedman. Lee, in a desperate gamble to break Grant's grip, threw nearly half his mobile force in a surprise assault on the Union right opposite Petersburg. He hoped that this would force Grant to so weaken his left that the Army of Northern Virginia could slip out, west of Petersburg, to join Johnston in North Carolina. Major General **John B. Gordon** conducted the assault. The fort was taken, but Union veterans promptly rallied and regained the position after a desperate 4-hour battle, in which they also captured several Confederate advanced posts. Lee's situation was now worse than ever. Confederate losses were about 4,000, Union losses half as great.

1865, March 26. Arrival of Sheridan. Next day Sheridan—his work in the Valley completed—joined Grant with his cavalry corps and an infantry corps. Grant now had about 122,000 fighting men, Lee less than 60,000. Grant decided to "end the matter."

1865, March 29–31. Battle of Dinwiddie Courthouse and White Oak Road. While 2 Union infantry corps struck the Confederate right, Sheridan's cavalry corps rode wide to the west to encircle the flank. Lee's brilliant reaction was to encircle the encirclers. Pickett, with 2 divisions and **Fitzhugh Lee**'s cavalry, marched west outside of Sheridan's orbit to attack his left flank at Dinwiddie Courthouse. At the same time A. P. Hill hit the left flank of the Union infantry on White Oak Road. The Union advance was checked, but Sheridan increased his infantry and cavalry pressure against Pickett, who retired to Five Forks and entrenched.

1865, April 1. Battle of Five Forks. Sheridan, with infantry reinforcements, struck Pickett in front and flank with far superior force; the Southern position collapsed in panic, exposing the entire right of the Confederate line. Grant at once ordered a general assault.

1865, April 2. Assault on Petersburg. While Sheridan swept northwest over and behind the vital Southside R.R., 3 Union infantry spearheads broke through Lee's thin lines west of Petersburg. Gallant A. P. Hill was killed trying to rally his men. Only Gordon, at Petersburg itself, was able to hold his positions. Lee rushed Longstreet down from Richmond to bolster Gordon until nightfall. He then commenced an orderly evacuation of the Richmond-Petersburg defenses.

APPOMATTOX CAMPAIGN

1865, April 3. Lee's Withdrawal. The Confederates converged on Amelia Courthouse in abominable weather. Lee's desperate plan was to join Johnston south of Danville, where Jefferson Davis had set up a temporary capital. Grant, blocking the move, marched west—south of and parallel to Lee's movement. Both armies were exhausted, but both responded magnificently to the inspiration of their leaders. Sheridan reached Jeetersville just in time to block Lee's planned movement to the southwest (April 5). Lee, in a night march, continued westward. Sheridan's cavalry harassed the retreat incessantly.

1865, April 6–7. Battle of Sayler's (Saylor's) Creek. Anderson's and Ewell's corps took up a delaying position, hoping to check the pursuit long enough to let the Confederate artillery and trains get safely across the Appomattox River. The halt was fatal. Sheridan's cavalry and horse artillery dashed behind the Confederate position along the creek, while the Union VI Corps pressed frontally. Ewell surrendered his entire corps—barely 4,000 strong —and a third of Anderson's 6,000 was also captured. Lee's strength was now reduced to less than 30,000. Thanks to his foresight, rations were waiting at Farmville for his half-starved men. He resumed the march, pointing for Lynchburg, via Appomattox. Sheridan, realizing Lee's intentions, reached Appomattox as Lee's advanced guard approached Appomattox Courthouse, 2 miles northeast (April 8).

1865, April 9. Battle of Appomattox. Fitzhugh Lee and Gordon, at Lee's orders, attacked the Union cavalry, but the attack was broken off when masses of Union infantry, arriving after an all-night march, deployed for battle. Lee sent a request to Grant for a cease-fire and a conference on terms.

1865, April 9. Lee's Surrender. The leaders met at Appomattox Courthouse, in the home of Wilmer McLean (who had fled from Manassas in 1861 to get out of the path of war). The Army of Northern Virginia, 28,356 strong, was surrendered at 3:45 P.M. To all intents and purposes the war was over.

1865, April 14. Assassination of President Lincoln. Shot by John Wilkes Booth, Lincoln died next day. The outrage curdled Northern sensibilities and interfered with acceptance of Johnston's surrender to Sherman (April 18) until April 26. All other Confederate forces had laid down their arms by May 26.

1865, May 29. Proclamation of Amnesty. President Andrew Johnson's proclamation officially ended the Civil War.

Epilogue

1864–1865. Cruise of the *Shenandoah*. British-built raider C.S.S. *Shenandoah*, turned over to the Confederate Navy at Funchal, Azores (1864, October), under Commander **James I. Waddell,** ranged the high seas around the Cape of Good Hope to Australia, thence north to the Bering Sea. There Waddell destroyed the U.S. whaling industry, capturing 32 whalers and merchantmen, burning 27, and sending the remainder under cartel, with prisoners, to San Francisco. His last 8 victims were destroyed 7 weeks after Appomattox (June 28). Waddell, learning from a British ship off the California coast (August

2) that the war was over, dismounted his guns and sailed for England via Cape Horn. He arrived in Liverpool and surrendered to British authorities 6 months after the war's end (November 6). The *Shenandoah* was turned over to the U.S.; the crew was offered asylum in England.

1872, August 25. Settlement of the *Alabama* Claims. An international arbitration tribunal (representatives of Italy, Switzerland, Brazil, the U.S., and Great Britain) awarded the U.S. $14.5 million in damages from Great Britain in partial reparation for the depredations of British-built raiders (*Florida, Alabama,* and *Shenandoah*) upon the U.S. merchant marine.

THE UNITED STATES, 1865–1900

Wars with the Indians, 1865–1898

National expansion westward brought about incessant clashes between Indian and white man. Between 1865 and 1898, the Regular Army fought 943 actions in 12 separate campaigns and a number of disconnected bickerings. The official campaign listings are:

1865–1868—Southern Oregon, Idaho, northern California, and Nevada.

1867–1875—Against Comanches, Sioux, and confederated tribes in Kansas, Wyoming, Colorado, Texas, New Mexico, and Indian Territory. (Noteworthy were a series of bitter battles near Fort Phil Kearny in northern Wyoming; Captain **William Fetterman** and 82 other soldiers were overrun and massacred near here by 2,000 Sioux under **Crazy Horse** and **Red Cloud** [December 21, 1866]; Red Cloud and 1,500 warriors were repulsed by Captain **James Powell** and 31 men in the "**Wagon Box Fight**" [August 2, 1867]).

1870–1871—Against the Apaches in Arizona and New Mexico.

1872–1873—The Modoc War. (Major General E. R. S. Canby was treacherously murdered during preliminary negotiations.)

1873—Against the Apaches in Arizona. (Major General **George Crook** gained special distinction and won the admiration and respect of the Indians.)

1876–1877—Against the Northern Cheyennes and Sioux (see below).

1877—Nez Percé War (see below).

1878—Bannock War.

1878–1879. Against the Northern Cheyennes.

1879—Against the Sheep-eaters, Piutes, and Bannocks.

1885–1886. Against the Apaches in Arizona and New Mexico (principal leaders were Apache chieftain **Geronimo** and U.S. Generals Crook and **Nelson A. Miles**).

1890–1891. Against the Sioux in South Dakota (see below).

All this was guerrilla-type, fast-moving, light-marching warfare against a savage, brave, and crafty enemy. The Plains Indians—Sioux, Cheyennes, and Comanches—were as good light cavalry as the world has seen. The Apache preferred to fight on foot, using his horse as transportation. All could cover ground at an amazing rate of march. Three campaigns are worthy of specific note.

SIOUX AND NORTHERN CHEYENNE WAR, 1876–1877

1876, February–June. Powder River–Big Horn–Yellowstone Campaign. The refusal of the northern Sioux tribes to go onto their assigned reservations led to the most serious Indian uprising since that of Tecumseh (see p. 794). The uprising was led by Chief Crazy Horse of the Oglala Sioux; a leading instigator was the Prairie Sioux chief and medicine man, **Sitting Bull.** The Sioux were joined by the related Cheyennes. Taking the field with a mounted force of 800 men in bitterly cold weather, Brigadier General George Crook made a long, rapid march through the Big Horn Mountains to mount a surprise attack on Crazy Horse's winter hideout at **Slim Buttes** on the Powder River (March 17). The Indian camp was destroyed and the Sioux scattered, when a panicky subordinate ordered a withdrawal. Crazy Horse rallied his braves and renewed the fight. Seriously outnumbered and short of supplies, Crook was forced to retire. Over-all command of the campaign was now entrusted to Major General Alfred H. Terry, who ordered two other columns to converge with Crook on the Yellowstone River.

1876, June 17. Battle of the Rosebud. Crook again caught up with Crazy Horse, who had now assembled a force of 4,000–6,000 warriors. Against odds of at least 5–1, Crook fought a bitterly contested drawn battle. The Indians, aware of the convergence of Terry's forces, withdrew; Crook also fell back to refit and reorganize his badly mauled command. Terry, out of communication with Crook and unaware of the Rosebud battle, crossed Crazy Horse's trail. He sent Lieutenant Colonel George A. Custer's 7th Cavalry to pursue and to get south of the Indians, to assure that they would be boxed in between the converging columns.

1876, June 25. Battle of the Little Big Horn. Custer impetuously followed the trail and caught up with Crazy Horse, confidently waiting battle. Dividing his small command (about 600 men) into 3 columns, Custer led 1 of these into the center of the Indians. He and the entire column were wiped out (212 officers and men); the remainder of the regiment took refuge in nearby hills and despite heavy losses were able to hold out for 2 days until Terry and the main body caught up. Crazy Horse and his jubilant warriors escaped; Terry's entire campaign had been ruined. For several months, despite intensive efforts, the U.S. forces were unable to regain contact with the elusive Indians.

1876, November 25–26. Battle of Crazy Woman Fork. Crook, discovering a large Indian encampment, sent Colonel **Ranald S. Mackenzie,** with 10 troops of cavalry, to destroy it. Mackenzie, in a surprise night attack in subzero weather, accomplished his mission.

1877, January 8. Battle of Wolf Mountains. Colonel Nelson A. Miles, with some 500 infantrymen and 2 light guns mounted in covered wagons, located Crazy Horse's village, on a commanding bluff. The surprise shelling of the height by Miles's guns stampeded the Indians and ended the campaign, Crazy Horse surrendering shortly afterward.

NEZ PERCE WAR, 1877

1877, June. Defiance of the Nez Percés. Under their young leader, Chief **Joseph** (Thunder-Rolling-Over-the-Mountain), the highly civilized Nez Percés defied government orders to evacuate their rich homeland in the Wallowa Valley, Ore., coveted by greedy whites. Continuing incidents led to the death of 3 whites; a small Army detachment attempted to herd the Nez Percés into a reservation in Idaho. Joseph defeated the white soldiers in **White Bird Canyon** (June 17), then with his entire tribe of 700 people—only 300 warriors—he marched eastward into Idaho and Montana, looking for a new home.

1877, July–August. Battles of the Clearwater and of the Big Hole Basin. After repulsing a pursuing force of soldiers under Brigadier General **Oliver O. Howard** on the Clearwater (July 11), Joseph and his people crossed the Bitterroot Mountains into Montana. In this and other minor engagements, the white soldiers discovered to their surprise that the Nez Percés and their leader fought with the skill and discipline of regular soldiers, while retaining the traditional elusiveness, guile, and stoic courage of Indians. In the Big Hole Basin, Joseph and his people were surprised by the attack of a new white force under Colonel **John Gibbon,** coming unexpectedly from the east. Rallying, in an unparalleled example of Indian discipline, Joseph and his men surrounded and besieged Gibbon's force, withdrawing only when Howard and his men arrived (August 8–11).

1877, August–October. March through Yellowstone and Montana. Joseph now tried to escape to Canada. Eluding or fighting his way past and around more Army forces trying to close in on him, Joseph reached the Bear Paw Mountains, in northern Montana, only 30 miles from the Canadian border. Here, on **Eagle Creek,** after an anabasis of nearly 2,000 miles, he was brought to bay by Generals Nelson A. Miles and Howard. After fighting against

10–1 odds for 4 days, Joseph surrendered (October 5).

COMMENT. *Chief Joseph must be ranked among great American military leaders.*

SIOUX WAR IN SOUTH DAKOTA, 1890–1891

1890, December 15. Death of Sitting Bull. The aging warrior again stirred up unrest among his people against the white man. Trying to escape capture, he was killed in a skirmish on the Grand River.

1890, December 29. Battle of Wounded Knee. Leadership of the Sioux now devolved on Chief **Big Foot.** His braves resisted efforts of Colonel **James Forsythe** of the 7th Cavalry to return them peacefully to the reservation, and were defeated in the ensuing fight—which was *not* a massacre. The 7th Cavalry thus gained revenge for its defeat on the Little Big Horn (see p. 906). This was the last major Indian conflict.

END OF THE INDIAN WARS

1898, October 4–7. Engagement at Leech Lake, Minnesota. This final Indian uprising—a minor disturbance—was suppressed by the U.S. 3rd Infantry.

Spanish-American War, 1898

1898, February 15. Blowing Up of the *Maine*. The American people, already exercised over Spanish cruelty in suppressing a Cuban revolt (see p. 914), were enraged when the battleship U.S.S. *Maine,* moored in Havana Harbor, was blown up and sunk by a mysterious explosion, with the loss of 260 men. A naval court of inquiry asserted the explosion came from outside the battleship's hull (March 21). Spain was blamed.

1898, April 25. American Declaration of War. The U.S. War Department, completely unprepared, increased the Regular Army from 28,000 to 60,000 men, and tried to organize and train these recruits as well as 200,000 volunteers flocking to the colors. The U.S. Navy, ready, immediately went into action.

PACIFIC OPERATIONS

1898, April 27. Dewey Sails for the Philippines. The U.S. Asiatic Squadron —5 cruisers and 2 gunboats—under Commodore **George Dewey,** left China waters and steamed into Manila Bay at night (April 30), ignoring the danger of submarine mines.

1898, May 1. Battle of Manila Bay. Dewey's squadron attacked the Spanish squadron of Admiral **Patricio Montojo**—4 cruisers, 3 gunboats, and 3 other decrepit vessels. The Spanish squadron, inferior in armament, was anchored off the fortified naval yard of Cavite, supported by land batteries. Dewey's squadron completely destroyed the Spanish force, with only 8 men wounded; Spanish losses were 381 sailors killed or wounded. After shelling the shore batteries into submission, Dewey took possession of Cavite. Blockading the City of Manila, he then awaited the arrival of sufficient troops to capture it.

1898, June 30. Arrival of the Army. General **Wesley Merritt,** with 10,000 men—part regulars, part volunteers—arrived in Manila Bay from San Francisco and began debarkation at Cavite.

1898, August 13. Manila Capitulates. Merritt's force, supported by Filipino guerrillas under Emilio Aguinaldo, having invested the city, attacked, supported by the fire of Dewey's squadron. After a short, nominal defense, to satisfy Spanish honor, the city surrendered.

ATLANTIC OPERATIONS

1898, April 29. Cervera Sails for Cuba. Admiral **Pascual Cervera,** with the cream of the Spanish fleet—4 modern cruisers and 3 destroyers—left the Cape Verde islands bound for the Caribbean. Rear Admiral **William T. Sampson,** commanding the U.S. Atlantic Fleet, who had instituted a blockade of Havana, was unsuccessful in intercepting Cervera, who gained the safety of fortified **Santiago de Cuba** (May 19). Sampson had 5 battleships, 2 armored cruisers, and several smaller vessels, including the "Flying Squadron" of Commodore **Winfield Scott Schley.**

1898, May–July. Blockade of Santiago. Sampson at once blockaded the harbor. Lieutenant **Richmond P. Hobson** and a crew of 7 volunteers entered the harbor mouth with the collier *Merrimac,* which they sank there in a gallant but unsuccessful attempt to stopper the channel (June 3).

1898, June 14. Expedition to Cuba. The V Corps, 16,888 strong, consisting of 3 extemporized divisions commanded by Major General **William R. Shafter,** left Tampa under naval escort. The hurriedly mounted expedition included most of the available Regular Army troops (15 regiments), plus 3 regiments of volunteers (including the 1st Volunteer Cavalry, "Roosevelt's Rough Riders"). There were few horses for the 6 cavalry regiments—they would have to fight on foot—and there were serious shortages of equipment.

1898, June 22–25. Debarkation near Santiago. This took place at Daiquirí, an open roadstead, utilizing the small boats of the transports and naval craft. There was no opposition. Shafter then moved on Santiago, after a slight skirmish at **Las Guásimas** (June 23). Shafter and Sampson were unable to agree on co-ordinated action against Santiago, so Shafter decided to attack without naval assistance.

1898, July 1. Battle of San Juan and El Caney. Although there were some 200,000 Spanish troops on the island, less than 35,000 were in the Santiago area, and the actual garrison of the fortified city was but 13,000. General **Arsenio Linares,** passively defensive, made no attempt to concentrate his forces against the American threat. Barring the road to Santiago was the San Juan Ridge, with Kettle Hill in front of it, an organized position manned by 1,200 defenders. Northeast of the city, on the American right, was the isolated position of El Caney, held by 500 men. Shafter's plan was to assault both positions simultaneously. The troops were slow in maneuvering and tardy in assault, but finally took both works. The colorful charge of the "Rough Riders" up Kettle Hill, led by Lieutenant Colonel **Theodore Roosevelt,** would in particular become an American epic, although the assault was delivered with equal gallantry by all units engaged. By evening the Americans held the ridge and the fate of Santiago was sealed. The total cost of both battles was 1,572 Americans killed and wounded. Estimated Spanish losses were 850. Cuban patriot forces in the area took no part in the action. The entire operation was characterized by poor reconnaissance and lack of control, compensated by the raw gallantry of the troops and American unit commanders' reckless and inspiring leadership.

1898, July 3. Battle of Santiago Bay. Cervera led his squadron toward the open sea. Overwhelmed by the fire power of the superior American force, the 4 Spanish cruisers and 2 destroyers were forced ashore. The American ships turned to the work of rescue. Spanish losses: 474 killed and wounded and 1,750 prisoners. U.S. losses: 1 killed, 1 wounded. In the subsequent bitter "Sampson-Schley Controversy," Commodore Schley claimed dubious credit for the victory.

1898, July 17. Santiago Capitulates. General **José Toral,** who had succeeded Linares (wounded in the San Juan battle), surrendered, unaware that the American forces surrounding the city were rapidly disintegrating through yellow fever, malarial fever, and dysentery.

1898, July 25. Landing on Puerto Rico. Major General Nelson A. Miles, with some 5,000 men, landed and, in a well-planned, well-executed operation, had almost eliminated Spanish forces when hostilities ended (August 13).

1898, December 10. Treaty of Paris. Spain relinquished sovereignty over Cuba, ceded Puerto Rico and Guam to the U.S., and sold the Philippine Islands to the U.S. for $20 million.

1899–1902. Philippine Insurrection. (See pp. 868 and 1011.)

CANADA

1866, June 18. Battle of Fort Erie. Fenian raiders into Canada from Buffalo, N.Y., were arrested by U.S. troops but released due to political pressure.

1867, July 1. Federal Union. Canada became fully self-governing, the prototype of later British dominions.

1870, May 25–27. Fenian Raids Fail. U.S. and Canadian troops halted attempts to invade Canada near Frankfort, Vt., and Malone, N.H.

1869–1870. First Riel Rebellion. Louis Riel, French Canadian with Indian blood, led a group, mostly half-breeds, in

armed revolt (October) when the Hudson's Bay Company turned over what is now Manitoba to Canada. They seized **Fort Garry** (Winnipeg; November), and set up a provisional government with Riel as President (December 29). There were occasional clashes with settlers of English descent in the region. An expedition under Colonel Garnet Wolseley captured Fort Garry without opposition (August 24, 1870); Riel had fled. No effort was made to arrest him, and he later became a member of Parliament.

1885, March–May. Second Riel Rebellion. Upon appeal of the frontier half-breeds (who had now moved to the region of Saskatchewan), Riel came to their aid in Western Canada. Again he denounced the authority of the dominion, appealed to the Indians to join his revolt, and set up a provisional government. After several armed clashes and considerable loss of life, the rebellion was suppressed by government troops under General **Frederick Middleton** in a severe action near **Batoche,** Saskatchewan (May 12); Riel was captured (May 15). He was tried and hanged for treason.

LATIN AMERICA

Instability and unrest marked the growth of Latin America during the period, from the Rio Grande down to the tip of Cape Horn. Of the interminable succession of wars, insurrections, and clashes with foreign powers which racked the area, a few are worthy of note.

MEXICO

1857–1860. Civil War in Mexico. Struggle between the Conservative party, under **Félix Zuloaga,** and the Liberal party, under **Benito Juárez.** The Conservatives held the seat of government at Mexico City; the Liberals established a government at Veracruz. Juárez was recognized by the U.S. (April 6, 1859). The Conservative party was defeated at the **Battle of Calpulalpam** and Juárez assumed full control of the country (December 22, 1860). Mexico's finances had been disorganized by the war, and payments of foreign debts were suspended.

1861, December 17. Allied Occupation of Veracruz. To protect their interests and to obtain satisfaction for their debts, Spain, France, and Britain sent a joint expeditionary force to Mexico. The foreign troops moved to Orizaba. Napoleon III, desirous of establishing a puppet Mexican empire, seized the opportunity presented by U.S. involvement in the Civil War to meddle in Mexican politics.

1862, April 8. Spanish and British Withdrawal. This resulted from Napoleon's intrigues and was followed by further French reinforcements.

1862, May 5. Battle of Puebla (or Cinco de Mayo). The French advance toward Mexico City was checked by Mexican Generals **Ignacio Zaragoza** and **Porfirio Díaz.**

1862, September. Reinforcement of the French Expedition. An additional 30,000 French troops, under General **Elie F. Forey,** arrived in Mexico.

1863, February 17. French Offensive. Advancing from Orizaba, the French again moved on Puebla, defended by Zaragoza. Investing Puebla, the French found themselves involved in incessant guerrilla operations on their line of communications from Veracruz.

1863, April 30. Defense of Camerone. Heroic defense of a homestead by a company of the Foreign Legion. For 10 hours, 3 officers and 62 men fought off a Mexican force of some 2,000 men. In contrast to the Alamo massacre (see p. 805), the Mexicans hailed the last three surviving legionnaires as heroes and returned them to French control.

1863, June 12. Enthronement of Maximilian. Having captured Puebla (May 17), Napoleon's troops entered Mexico City (June 7). He placed Archduke **Maximilian,** brother of Austrian Emperor Francis Joseph, on the Mexican throne. The puppet emperor, an honest man, entered on his duties in all sincerity, but the majority of the Mexican people, led by Juárez, wanted none of him.

1863–1865. Continuing Guerrilla War. This was conducted with savagery on both sides. The U.S. refused to recognize Maximilian, and continued to recognize Juárez, who had taken refuge in the United

States, and then returned to Mexico to lead the war with his principal military officer, General **Mariano Escobedo.**

1865–1866. U.S. Demands French Withdrawal. The U.S. threatened to intervene, backing its demand by mobilizing a 50,000-man veteran army under General Sheridan on the Rio Grande. After prolonged negotiations, Napoleon, realizing U.S. determination and impatience, backed down.

1867, February 5. French Withdrawal Begins. Marshal Bazaine, who had superseded Forey, evacuated all French troops, and Maximilian's puppet regime began to crumble.

1867, March–June. Defeat of Maximilian. He refused to abdicate and desert his Mexican followers. Besieged at **Querétaro** by Escobedo he was betrayed by one of his own men, captured (May 14), court-martialed, and executed (June 19). Juárez restored order and reassumed his post as President until his death (1872).

1871–1877. Turmoil in Mexico. A revolt of Díaz against Juárez was almost suppressed when Juárez died. Disorder continued until Díaz, having defeated his principal opponent, **Sebastian Lerdo de Tejada,** at **Tecovac** (November 16, 1876), was elected President (May 12, 1877).

1877–1911. Dictatorship of Díaz. Mexico's "strong man" ruled a prosperous Mexico, maintaining law and order (see p. 1012).

CENTRAL AMERICA

1855–1860. William Walker in Nicaragua and Honduras. Walker, a U.S. soldier of fortune from Nashville, Tenn., with 56 followers, went to Nicaragua on invitation of one of several local factions (May 4). Seizing a U.S. steamer on Lake Nicaragua, he took control of Granada in a surprise move, proclaimed himself president, and opened Nicaragua to slavery. His regime was recognized by President Franklin Pierce (May, 1856). **Cornelius Vanderbilt,** who wanted to monopolize travel to California and its gold across Nicaragua, incited opposition. Walker finally surrendered to U.S. naval control (May 1, 1857). Taken to San Francisco, he soon returned (November 25, 1857) and was again deported. Entering Honduras (August, 1860) in another bid for power, he was arrested by British naval authorities and turned over to Honduran control. He was tried and executed by a firing squad (September 12, 1860).

COMMENT. *The Walker episode was one of the principal instances of meddling by U.S. citizens in Latin American affairs, prime cause for continued resentment against "Yankee" aggression.*

1871. Revolution in Guatemala. Miguel Garcia Granados and **Justo Rufino Barrios** overthrew the government of General **Vicente Cerna.** Granados soon retired, leaving Barrios as President.

1885. Barrios Attempts to Unify Central America. After several peaceful efforts to bring about a Central American union, Barrios tried force. Conflict rose between Guatemala and Honduras on the one hand and Costa Rica, Nicaragua, and El Salvador on the other. Barrios was killed at **Chalchuapa** (April 2) during an invasion of Salvador, and his forces defeated.

SOUTH AMERICA

1843–1852. Argentine Intervention in Uruguay. (See p. 819.)

1860–1861. Civil War in Colombia (New Grenada). Victorious rebel leader **Tomás Cipriano de Mosquera** proclaimed himself president (1861, July).

1863. Ecuador-Colombia War. Long-standing border disputes between Colombia then New Grenada) and Ecuador culminated in war after President Cipriano de Mosquera supported Ecuadorans rebelling against conservative dictator **Gabriel Garcia Moreno.** Elderly General Juan José Flores invaded New Grenada but was repulsed (December 6). Fighting ended; a treaty composed differences.

War of the Triple Alliance (Lopez War), 1864–1870

Francisco Solano Lopez, having become perpetual dictator of Paraguay (1862), turned his country into an isolated despotism. He then plunged into war against Argentina, the Banda Oriental (Uruguay), and Brazil. The war offers no military lesson, but does demonstrate the remarkable bravery of the Paraguayan people. In the end, they were conquered by sheer pressure of numbers and by economic strangulation. Lopez' megalomania reduced the Paraguayan population from about 1,400,000 to some 221,000 (29,000 adult males, 106,000 women, and 86,000 children). His allied opponents lost an estimated 1,000,000 men. The combat area was the Paraguay River Valley from Corrientes north to Coimbra; the principal actions occurred between the confluence of the Paraguay and Paraná Rivers and Asunción.

1864, December 26. Invasion of Brazil. Lopez, who had raised an army 80,000 strong, seized the upper Paraguay River and invaded Brazil at Corumbá, in an area disputed by both nations. This move isolated the Matto Grosso region from communication with eastern Brazil, overland access being impossible across the intervening mountains and marshy jungle land.

1865, March 18. War on Argentina Declared. When Argentina refused to permit Paraguayan troops to cross its territory to invade southern Brazil, Lopez declared war. A Paraguayan river expedition, moving in captured Argentinian vessels, took **Corrientes** (April 13), and Colonel **Antonio L. Estigarribia** then moved overland through Encarnación to invade southern Brazil.

1865, May 1. Establishment of the Triple Alliance. Brazil, Uruguay, and Argentina agreed to destroy the Lopez government and to open the Paraguay and Paraná rivers to free navigation. The 3 nations began organizing new armies for joint operations under Argentina's **Bartolomé Mitre,** Uruguay's **Venancio Flores,** and Brazil's **Louis Osorio.** Naval operations were confided to Brazilian Vice Admiral **Viscount Tamandare.**

1865, July–October. Operations in Southern Brazil. Estigarribia's force reached the Uruguay River and moved south to **Uruguayana,** where it was surrounded by an allied force of 30,000 and a gunboat flotilla; part of his force was destroyed. He surrendered (September 18). The allied army moved north, threatening Paraguayan communications at Corrientes, which was evacuated at once. Lopez concentrated 25,000 men below the Paraguayan fortress of Humaita, in the peninsula between the Paraguay and Paraná rivers.

1866, January–May. Allied Invasion. The allied army, now 45,000 strong, crossed the Paraná and advanced slowly. Lopez attacked (May 2), but was thrown back.

1866, May 24. Battle of Paso de Patria. Surrounded on both flanks by superior force, Lopez' army was shattered after an all-day battle, losing 13,000 casualties. Allied losses were 8,000. No attempt was made to exploit this allied success, and Lopez was enabled to reorganize.

1866, September 22. Battle of Curupayty. After long delay and establishment of a base, the allies attempted to drive Lopez out of his entrenchments at Curupayty, on the Paraguay River, but were repulsed with great loss; 9,000 were killed and wounded. Paraguayan losses were but 54 men. Lopez failed to exploit his victory. For 14 months, operations dragged in stalemate; cholera ravaged both sides.

1867, May. Brazilian Invasion in the North. A Brazilian attempt to invade northwestern Paraguay, through the Matto Grosso, was a complete failure.

1867, July–August. Operations around Humaita. Despite Lopez' efforts, Brazilian monitors moved up the Paraguay, running Humaita's batteries. Asunción was abandoned. Lopez instituted a "scorched earth" policy as he withdrew his mobile forces north from Humaita to Angostura, with his right flank on the river, his left on Lake Ypoa. Humaita, now garrisoned by only 3,000 men, surrendered after an attempt to evacuate proved unsuccessful (August 2). The allied army moved slowly up both banks of the Paraguay, the Brazilians on the east, the Argentines on the west, the gunboat and monitor flotilla accompanying. The advance was stopped by the Angostura defenses, south of Asunción.

1867, August–December. Operations around Angostura. North of Angostura, at Ypacarai, Lopez concentrated his last 10,000 troops. Allied pressure slowly increased. Balloon observation pinpointed the Paraguayan batteries. The allied flotilla turned the Angostura position, while a Brazilian column, passed to the west side by boat, marched up through the Chaco and was then retransported to the east, threatening

Lopez' rear at Ypacarai. A succession of assaults on the Paraguayan position was repelled at great cost to both sides.

1867, December 25. Battle at Ypacarai. A general assault breached Lopez' position and, except for the batteries in Angostura itself, the defense collapsed. Lopez fled north with a handful of cavalry. Angostura surrendered (December 30), and Asunción was occupied and sacked by the Brazilians next day.

1868–1869. Partisan War. Lopez continued a largely partisan campaign, maintaining himself in northern and eastern Paraguay. He rallied several thousand followers in the Cordillera area of eastern Paraguay, briefly threatening Asunción (1869). By this time a provisional government had been organized, and Argentina had withdrawn her forces. The Brazilian army of occupation, under **Gaston de Bourbon, Comte d'Eu,** instituted a mopping-up campaign which slowly drove Lopez north to the Aquidaban River.

1870, March 1. Death of Lopez. The dictator was surrounded by a detachment of Brazilian lancers and killed. Peace came finally through U.S. mediation (June 20). Paraguay ceded some 55,000 square miles of territory to Brazil and Argentina.

Peruvian Hostilities with Spain, 1864–1866

Long-standing differences with Peru, whose independence Spain had not recognized, came to climax when a Spanish squadron under Admiral **Pinzon** seized the Chincha Islands, 12 miles off Pisco on the Peruvian coast, in retaliation for maltreatment of Basque immigrants (April 14, 1864). Spain later (January 27, 1865) concluded a treaty with President **Juan Antonio Perez,** but its provisions aroused Peruvian resentment.

1866, January 14. Peruvian Declaration of War. Perez was driven from office and his successor, General **Mariano Ignacio Prado,** declared war. Defensive alliances were concluded with Chile, Bolivia, and Ecuador. Wholesale deportations of Spanish subjects followed.

1866, March 31. Bombardment of Valparaiso by a Spanish squadron under Admiral **Nuñez** caused considerable damage. The Spaniards lost 1 gunboat to a Chilean cutting-out party.

1866, May 2. Bombardment of Callao. Nuñez attacked the port, but its shore defenses, under Prado's direct command, repelled the attackers. Spain now ceased hostilities (May 9). U.S. mediation brought peace (1871). The net result was a hurried naval program instituted by Chile to modernize and improve her sea power.

War of the Pacific, 1879–1884

This was a struggle for control of the guano- and nitrate-producing provinces of Tacna, Arica, and Tarapacá (Peru) and of Atacama (Bolivia). Atacama was Bolivia's only outlet on the coast. Chilean companies engaging in exploitation of nitrate were so heavily taxed by Peru and Bolivia that Chile went to war.

1879, February 14. Chile Opens Hostilities. A Chilean naval expedition seized Antofagasta; the nearby country was quickly occupied. Chilean blockade of coastal ports followed. Captain **Miguel Grau** in the Peruvian turret ironclad *Huascar* having successfully harassed Chilean warships off Iquique, the entire Chilean Navy hunted him down.

1879, October 8. End of the *Huascar*. Five Chilean warships—2 of them ironclads—surrounded Grau off Antofagasta. In a running fight lasting for 1½ hours, the *Huascar* was battered into submission, with her turret disabled, steering gear shot away, and 64 of her 193-man crew casualties. Among the killed were Grau and the 4 other officers who rapidly succeeded to command in the action. Command of the sea now fell to Chile.

1879, November 1. Chilean Invasion of Bolivia and Southern Peru. Landing an expeditionary force at Pisagua, the Chileans pushed through heavy Bolivian-Peruvian opposition at **Sán Francisco** (November 16). At **Tarapacá** (November 27) they suffered a repulse, but the allies made no attempt to exploit their success. With the Bolivian seacoast and all of Peru's Tarapacá Province in their hands, the Chileans turned their attention northward.

1880, January–June. Blockade of Arica and Callao. Peruvian defensive measures included submarine mines and ineffective torpedos. A Chilean force of 12,000 men landed at Pacocha near Arica and moved inland. At **Questa de Los Angeles** (March 22), Bolivian General **Narciso Campero** with 9,000 allied troops defended a defile until outflanked by Chilean General **Manuel Baquedano.** Allied casualties were 530; Chilean, 687.

1880, May 26. Battle of Tacna. Initial Chilean piecemeal assaults were at first repulsed, but Baquedano finally concentrated his effort against the Peruvian left, and swept the field. Casualties were severe: nearly 3,000 allied and 2,000 Chilean. With allied opposition in this area completely dissolved, the Chilean army moved on **Arica,** taking it in a general assault (June 7).

1880, November–December. Lima Campaign. Disembarking at Pisco (November 18) with more than 22,000 men, Baquedano 6 weeks later began moving up the coast on Lima, where some 22,000 defenders were installed behind 2 successive lines whose flanks could not be turned. In a frontal attack, the Chileans overran **Chorrillos,** the first position, taking losses of 3,000 men. Two days later, while negotiations for peace were in progress, an inadvertent Chilean movement resulted in a daring Peruvian counterattack. The action, hotly contested for 4 hours, ended with complete Chilean victory. Total casualties in the 2 battles: Chilean, 5,443; Peruvian, 9,000. Lima was occupied (December 17). Peruvian resistance having now completely broken down, the Chilean army was withdrawn, leaving only a small occupation force for mopping up.

1883, October 20. Treaty of Ancón. Peru formally ceded Tarapacá Province to Chile and agreed to Chilean occupation of Tacna and Arica for a 10-year period, to be followed by a plebiscite. (Tacna, as it turned out, would be returned to Peru in 1929; see p. 1049.) The **Treaty of Valparaiso** (April 4, 1884) recognized Chile's permanent possession of the Bolivian littoral.

1889, November 15. Brazilian Empire Ended. Led by General **Manuel Deodoro da Fonséca,** a military junta quietly removed Emperor Dom **Pedro II** from his palace and shipped him and his family off to Portugal. A provisional government was quickly followed by establishment of the United States of Brazil. Unrest continued, however, culminating in an insurrection in the province of Rio Grande do Sul (September, 1891).

1893–1895, September 6. Naval Revolt at Rio. Admiral **Custodio de Mello,** commanding Brazilian naval vessels in the harbor of Rio de Janeiro, demanded the resignation of President **Floriano Peixoto.** On refusal, Mello shelled the city. Mediation by foreign ministers prevented further destruction. Mello joined forces with the insurgents in the south, led by **Gumercindo Saraiva.** The government purchased warships abroad and mobilized the national guard. Admiral **Saldanha de Gama,** now commanding the rebellious squadron in Rio Harbor, abandoned his ships to take refuge with his men on board two Portuguese warships, which transported them to Montevideo. Mello and Saraiva fell out. The rebel army was dispersed. Mello, after an unsuccessful attack on the town of Rio Grande do Sul, steamed to Buenos Aires and surrendered to Argentine authorities. Government troops put down the last traces of revolt in the south (July, 1895), de Gama—who had returned from Montevideo—being killed.

1895–1896. Venezuelan-British Boundary Dispute. Disagreements about the boundary between British Guiana and Venezuela led to a crisis between the U.S. and Great Britain (December, 1895). This was settled by negotiations; an international board of arbitration agreed generally with the British claims.

WEST INDIES

Cuba

1849–1851. Lopez Expeditions. Narciso Lopez, a Spanish general and leader of Cuban refugees in the U.S., mounted 3 abortive revolutionary expeditions from the U.S. The first collapsed (August 11, 1849) when U.S. federal authorities intervened. The second, which included a number of Southern volunteers, made a landing at Cárdenas (May 19, 1850), but was driven off. Lopez' third attempt, mounted from New Orleans—again with a number of American volunteers—effected a landing near Havana (August 11–21, 1850), but when no sympathetic Cuban uprising materialized, the filibusters were all captured. Lopez and 51 Americans were tried by court-martial and executed at Havana.

1868–1878. Ten Years' War. Cuban revolts attracted American sympathy and support. The former Confederate blockade runner *Virginius,* sold to a group of Cuban supporters, was captured by the Spanish warship *Tornado* off Morant Bay, Jamaica (October 1, 1873).

1895–1898. Cuban Insurrection. Discontent with the superficial reformation of Spanish colonial policy came to a head when constitutional guarantees were suspended (February 23). Open revolt brought stringent but unsuccessful retaliation; compartmentation of the island by *trochas* —lines of barbed wire, entrenchments, and blockhouses—isolating the insurgents. Finally Spanish Captain General **Valeriano Weyler** established concentration camps in which noncombatants, swept from their homes, were confined under abominable conditions. In the U.S., where sympathy with the rebels ran high, popular indignation was followed by a formal request for Weyler's removal. Spain acquiesced (October, 1897), but rising tension between the U.S. and Spain was climaxed by the still-mysterious blowing up of the battleship U.S.S. *Maine* in Havana Harbor (February 15, 1898; see p. 907).

1898, April 25. Spanish-American War. (See p. 907.)

1898, December 10. Treaty of Paris. Spain relinquished Cuba to the U.S. in trust for its inhabitants. Military government under General **Leonard Wood** began grooming Cuba for permanent independence.

Haiti and the Dominican Republic

Revolutionary ferment continued throughout the entire island. Haiti's successive revolutions—in 1867, 1870, 1874, 1876, and 1888–1889—ended in partial restoration of law and order. In the Dominican Republic, estranged from its western neighbor, fear of Haiti resulted in another Spanish annexation (1861), requested by the people. However, revolution soon broke out (1864) as the result of harsh rule, and Spain then relinquished all claim (1865). A Dominican effort to obtain annexation to the U.S. was rejected by the U.S. Senate (1868–1870). For the remainder of the period, the country was relatively tranquil.

AUSTRALASIA

NEW ZEALAND

1860–1870. Second Maori War. The Maori tribes—sturdy, belligerent, and freedom-loving—rose again against continued encroachments by British settlers on their preserves. The result was a 10-year guerrilla war, reminiscent in principle of the U.S. struggle with the Plains Indians. Both regular British troops and local militia were involved in this wilderness war. In the end it was quelled more through diplomacy than by force of arms. As a result, the Maoris became a respected element of an integrated nation.

XIX

WORLD WAR I AND THE ERA OF TOTAL WAR: 1900–1925

MILITARY TRENDS

GENERAL

The period was one of amazing transitions and sharp contrasts. The Russo-Japanese War (see p. 920) was typical limited war—fought with armies of unprecedented size. World War I, with even larger armies, was total war. The appearance of the gasoline internal-combustion engine, combined with the sharp upward curve of destructiveness of improved weaponry, brought about a quickening of tempo and enlargement of scope that strained man's physical and intellectual capability to wage war.

LEADERSHIP

The quality of leadership developed during the period will always be moot. On the civilian side, France's premier, **Georges Clemenceau**—"the Tiger"—was the embodiment of ferocity and indomitable patriotism, capable of rallying an entire nation in its fight for existence. Outstanding among the military were France's **Joffre** and **Foch**; America's **Pershing**; Britain's **Haig** and **Allenby**; Germany's **Hindenburg, Ludendorff,** and **Falkenhayn**; Russia's **Nicholas** and **Brusilov**; Turkey's **Kemal**; Japan's **Oyama** and **Togo**; and Poland's **Pilsudski.** The administrative and military capability of Soviet Russia's **Leon Trotsky** slowly forged a capable Red Army from a mass of ignorant peasants and disgruntled soldiery. In general terms, the professional standards of military leadership of the German Army were unquestionably the highest in the world in this period. French, British, and American standards, however, were not far behind.

By the time World War I began, all of the major powers had adopted a general-staff system more or less along lines of the concept used so successfully by Prussia and Germany under von Moltke (see p. 821). Both Britain and America had long resisted the introduction of a general staff system, since to many people in the Anglo-Saxon democracies this appeared to be a step toward militarism. But embarrassing evidences of military inefficiency appeared in both countries in relatively minor wars at the turn of the century. In Britain after the Boer War, the Esher Committee and Lord Haldane were able to convince most of their countrymen that a general staff was a military necessity that would not jeopardize the fundamental liberties of a free people (see p. 994). In the United States, at about the same time, Secretary of War Elihu Root achieved a similar result, permitting action to redress the inadequacies so clearly demonstrated in the Spanish-American War (see p. 907).

STRATEGY

The Napoleonic concept of the nation in arms was replaced by that of the nation at war. The ability of the nation to produce and supply its fighting forces with weapons and food became more important than mere man power in uniform. This was demonstrated in World War I by Russia, whose millions of cannon fodder were relatively ineffectual when they could not be armed and maintained on the battlefield. Britain's surface blockade of the Central Powers—and Germany's submarine campaign against the maritime pipelines of Allied supply—equaled, if they did not in fact exceed, the importance of purely military might, since they were intended to strangle the respective populations on whom the armies and navies depended for food and munitions.

This meant that political and economic considerations inevitably dictated military decisions; no longer could war be reserved to the military. Success in total war depended as much on the farmer and the factory worker as on the warrior. That lesson, clear in the American Civil War, was relearned.

As exemplified by the stalemate on the Western Front, strategy in the field was greatly inhibited by weapon power. It would not be correct to conclude from this, however, that the deadlock of trench warfare meant either a decline in competence of military leadership or a decay in the broad strategic concept of maneuver, using both mobility and fire power to effect a decision.

The bloody stalemate on the Western Front was caused as much by territorial limitations as by the tactical effect of improved fire power. The war started in the West with maneuver (the Schlieffen Plan), and its first decisive clash was won by maneuver (Joffre at the Marne). Only when the maneuvering opponents came to the end of the available land mass (after the "Race to the Sea") did the struggle turn into a stalemate, with frontal attack and penetration the only possible solutions.

Through costly trial and error the tactical penetration evolved into a strategic maneuver, employed by both sides, yet never decisively. To be successful against defense in depth required not only the initial power to break through the defense but also the supplemental power, through the use of reserves and continuing fire-power support, to erode the flanks of the gap—much as flood waters enlarge the original break in dam or levee—then to sweep with undiminished ferocity over the countryside beyond. Yet despite several instances of momentary breakthrough, the theoretical analogy to the flood was never fully realized on the Western Front. With existing means of transportation, neither side was able to solve the problems of combat movement, mobile fire-power support, or logistical support in order to carry tactical exploitation to its logical, decisive conclusion before the defender could shift reserves to close the gap. On other major fronts there were comparable stalemates; but because of vast distances, tactical breakthrough and strategic maneuver were more feasible on the Eastern Front.

WEAPONS, DOCTRINE, AND TACTICS ON LAND

Military men had all noted the increasing deadliness of weapons during the latter half of the 19th century. With few exceptions, however, the leading military thinkers of Europe paid inadequate attention to the lessons of the American Civil War (and failed to note that these lessons were corroborated by the Russo-Japanese War). Their attention was focused on European experience, which they generally misinterpreted, due in part to the brevity of European wars during that half-century.

At the outset of the 20th century, the tactical doctrines of the two leading military nations of Europe—Germany and France—stressed the importance of seizing and maintaining the initiative in battle. Their example was followed by most other armies. The *élan,* or offensive spirit, of troops was to be nurtured. The greatest exponent of this doctrine of the offensive was General **Ferdinand Foch,** Commandant of the French École Supérieure de la Guerre, who was convinced that an indomitable will to win was the major ingredient for victory, and that enhanced fire power was as advantageous to attacker as to defender. Foch also insisted upon the importance of high professional standards of training in employment of weapons, use of cover, security, and tactical maneuver. His disciples, however—led by Colonel **Louis Loizeau de Grandmaison**—perverted this concept of the importance of the offensive into a blind doctrine of attack at all costs, at all times, and under any circumstances—*l'offensive à l'outrance.* German doctrine, though also stressing the importance of offensive action, never reached such extremes as existed in France in the years just before World War I.

A few soldiers had some reservations about a doctrine which envisaged mass frontal attacks against modern fire power. American observers of the Russo-Japanese War noted, for instance, that neither the fanatically aggressive Japanese nor the stubbornly stolid Russian could be persuaded to repeat suicidal frontal attacks against field fortifications. As in the American Civil War, a few costly lessons forced commanders to resort to tactical maneuver in seeking a decision.

But most military men ignored the doubts expressed by a civilian—Warsaw banker and economist **Ivan S. Bloch**—in a 7-volume book, *The Future of War in Its Economic and Political Relations: Is War Now Impossible?* This was published in St. Petersburg in 1898, and began to circulate in the West in the early years of the 20th century. After study of the best works on military affairs, the author came to the conclusion that the increased power of modern firearms had made war impossible, "except at the price of suicide." Bloch overestimated the power of the weapons of his day. But he was probably closer to the mark than military men of the Grandmaison ilk.

The deadliness of modern weapons caused vital changes in tactics during World War I—though, as usual, the lessons were not fully digested until after the war was ended. The machine gun and the modern artillery piece, in combination with field fortifications and barbed wire, inhibited frontal attack and ended forever the shock value of horse cavalry. Organization in depth became the *sine qua non* of the defense. Fire and movement—as in the American Civil War—were the fundamental basis of the Hutier tactics (see p. 972), which finally broke the trench stalemate. The infantry-artillery team became the basic tactical element of land warfare in the first half of the 20th century.

The tank—born during the war—emerged as the most important new development in land warfare. Poison gas was another innovation, although prompt countermeasures reduced gas to a weapon of harassment.

French light tank, 1918

Motor transport became of great importance, although horse transport still predominated. In World War I, psychological warfare was for the first time used systematically, although, by present standards, amateurishly. Propaganda campaigns stimulated efforts on the respective home fronts, and subversive leaflets, dropped over enemy lines, were intended to weaken the soldiers' morale. The German long-range gun which bombarded Paris (see p. 978) was a psychological weapon.

War became three-dimensional as the airplane and the dirigible developed from their initial role of reconnaissance into lethal weapons. By the end of the period the air arm had become a major factor in both land and sea combat.

WEAPONS AND TACTICS AT SEA

Britain's *Dreadnought* (see p. 994), (prototype of a class of heavy warships ever afterwards called "dreadnoughts"), combining heavy armor, immense weight of metal hurled by a homogeneous group of large caliber guns, 12-inch or more, and all-around fire capabilities, rendered obsolete all previously constructed battleships. In consequence, the great powers—including England herself—were forced into an armament race. Naval designers, searching to combine fire power and mobility, then brought out the battle cruiser, gunned to near equality with the dreadnought but lacking—a sacrifice to achieve speed—its protective armor belt. But the battle cruiser, like most naval hybrids, proved its inefficiency at Jutland, and by the end of the period was disappearing from the world's navies.

The most significant development in naval warfare, however, was the introduction of the submarine as a weapon of blockade and counterblockade. Although British supremacy on the surface of the waves was only challenged once—and was never seriously jeopardized—the German U-boat offensive against merchant ship

H.M.S. *Queen Elizabeth*, superdreadnought battleship

ping came close to bringing Britain to her knees in 1917. Sinkings by submarines at one point actually threatened to starve England into surrender. The introduction of the convoy system, however, permitted the British to ride out the crisis.

German submarine

THE CONCEPT OF DISARMAMENT

The increasing cost, pervasiveness, and frightfulness of war caused many to consider seriously and hopefully man's age-old dreams of creating an eternally peaceful world. It soon became obvious, however, that the urge for peace was less compelling on nations and statesmen than the prior claims of assuring national security. The **First Hague Peace Conference** (May–July, 1899) had been called by the Czar of Russia, whose interest in disarmament, it soon became clear, was mainly to save economically backward Russia from matching the military expenditures of Germany and Austria. International jealousies and suspicions prevented this, or its successor, the **Second Hague Peace Conference** (June–October, 1907), from doing little more than defining and codifying some of the laws of war and establishing an international court of arbitration. Additional rules, pertaining to naval warfare, were elaborated at the **London Naval Conference** (1908–1909), but the convention agreed to at the conference was never ratified by the participating governments.

The fourth of Wilson's Fourteen Points (see p. 977) gave hope to a war-weary world (January, 1918) that some kind of regulation of armaments would be achieved to establish perpetual peace after World War I. Embodied in the Covenant of the League of Nations, it stimulated the League to a series of disarmament studies in the postwar period. Some regulations on the size and numbers of warships of the leading naval powers were agreed to at the **Washington Conference** (1921–1922).

Realistic statesmen were dubious if true control of armaments would ever be possible. But, heeding popular demands for peace, they tried—just so long as their respective nation's security could be guaranteed absolutely. But, somehow, such guarantees could never be reconciled with arms-control measures satisfactory to potential foes.

MAJOR WARS PRIOR TO 1914

RUSSO-JAPANESE WAR, 1904–1905

Background

Between 1900 and 1903, Japan prepared for a limited war in Korea and Manchuria to crush growing Russian power there, to gain revenge for Russian interference after the Sino-Japanese War (see p. 864), and to ensure her own hegemony over Korea. By 1904 Japan was ready to act. Japanese deployment on the mainland

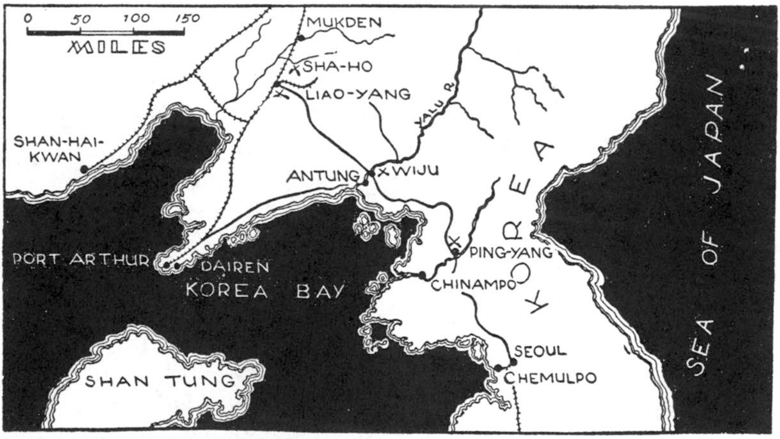

was dependent upon command of the sea, hence it was deemed an essential first step to destroy the Russian Far East Fleet and capture its base, Port Arthur, on the tip of Manchuria's Liaotung Peninsula. Since Port Arthur was Russia's only year-round ice-free port on the Pacific coast, its capture would also deprive the Russians of any winter naval base should they send their Baltic Fleet into the Pacific. The second step in the Japanese plan was to destroy Russian land forces in Manchuria, thus inducing Russia to abandon the war. The Japanese well knew the sole Russian supply line was the Trans-Siberian Railway—a 5,500-mile single-track line between Moscow and Port Arthur. A 100-mile gap in the line at Lake Baikal complicated Russian logistical difficulties. Despite Russia's tremendous man power (the over-all strength of her army was 4,500,000 men), east of Lake Baikal the Russians could dispose immediately only 83,000 field troops with 196 guns, plus some 50,000 garrison troops and railway guards. Given command of the sea, Japan could quickly place on the mainland against this force her entire standing army of 283,000 men and 870 guns, and soon reinforce this with 400,000 trained reserves. Russian naval strength in the Far East consisted of 7 elderly battleships, 9 armored cruisers, 25 destroyers, and some 30-odd smaller craft. The main fleet was based on Port Arthur; 2 cruisers lay at Chemulpo (Inchon), Korea, and 4 more cruisers at Vladivostok. Japanese naval strength consisted of 6 up-to-date battleships, homogeneous in type and carrying 12-inch guns. There were also 1 older battleship, 8 fine armored cruisers, 25 lighter cruisers, 19 destroyers, and 85 torpedo boats, plus 16 smaller craft. The Japanese Army and Navy both were superior to the Russians in doctrine, training, and leadership.

Opening Moves

1904, February 8. The Attack on Port Arthur. Without previous declaration of war, Japanese torpedo boats launched a surprise attack on the Russian fleet at anchor in the harbor of Port Arthur, causing severe damage. At the same time, the main Japanese battle fleet of Vice-Admiral **Heihachiro Togo** appeared off the port to engage the Russian shore batteries and fleet at long range. Togo then instituted a close blockade of the port.

1904, February 9. Naval Action at Chemulpo. The Japanese armored cruiser squadron of Vice-Admiral **Hikonojo Kamimura,** escorting the transports of an expeditionary force, entered the harbor of Chemulpo (Inchon), Korea, and attacked 2 Russian cruisers there. One of these was sunk, the other so severely damaged that it was scuttled by its crew.

1904, February 10. Declaration of War.

1904, February 17. Chemulpo Landing. General **Tamesada Kuroki**'s Japanese First Army began debarkation, followed by a northward advance through Korea to the Yalu River, to cover operations at Port Arthur.

1904, March 8–April 13. Naval Operations off Port Arthur. Energetic and capable Russian Admiral **Stepan Makarov** arrived from Russia to take command of the fleet (March 8). At once he began a series of sorties to harass the blockading Japanese cruisers, while avoiding Togo's battle fleet. Returning from one of these sorties, Makarov's flagship, *Petropavlovsk,* struck a Japanese mine and sank with all on board (April 13). Thereafter the Russian ships remained passively in port. The loss of Makarov was a catastrophe for the Russians.

1904, April–May. Russian Dispositions and Plans. General **Alexei Kuropatkin,** who had been Russian minister of war, and who assumed command of all field forces in the Far East, recognized Russian unreadiness for war. He anticipated Japanese efforts to obtain an early victory. He began concentrating all available forces in 3 groups south of Mukden. General **Stakelberg,** with 35,000 men, lay in the area Hai-cheng-Kaiping, directly north of Port Arthur. General Count **Keller,** who had 30,000, guarded the passes west of the Yalu River, with an advance guard of 7,000 under General **Zasulich** covering the Yalu crossings. Kuropatkin himself, with 40,000 men, lay in reserve at Liaoyang. An additional force of nearly 40,000 under General **Anatoli M. Stësel** comprised the garrison of the powerful fortress of Port Arthur. Recognizing the initial Japanese numerical advantage, Kuropatkin planned to permit the Japanese temporarily to besiege Port Arthur—which he felt sure could hold out for several months—while he fell back slowly toward Harbin, delaying the Japanese advance into Manchuria until reinforcements arrived from Russia. He anticipated that the Trans-Siberian Railway could bring him about 40,000 men per month. By the end of the summer, therefore, he felt he would be strong enough to return southward to relieve Port Arthur, and to drive the Japanese from Manchuria. However, incompetent Admiral **Evgeni Alekseev,** Viceroy of the Far East, appointed as Russian generalissimo by the Czar, insisted upon an immediate offensive, ordering

Kuropatkin to abandon his sound defensive-offensive plan.

1904, April 30–May 1. Battle of the Yalu. Kuroki's First Japanese Army, arriving at the Yalu near Wiju (Uiju or Gishu), was confronted by Zasulich, who stupidly gave battle against overwhelming odds. Zasulich was routed, losing 2,500 casualties; Japanese losses were 1,100 out of the 40,000 engaged. Kuroki advanced into Manchuria.

1904, May 5–19. Japanese Landings on the Liaotung Peninsula. The Second Army, under General **Yasukata Oku,** began landing at Pitzuwu, only 40 miles northeast of Port Arthur. Moving south, he was halted by a powerful Russian defensive position based on Nanshan Hill, at the narrowest part of the peninsula. While this was taking place, the Japanese Fourth Army, under General **Michitsura Nodzu,** began disembarking at Takushan, west of the Yalu River. As the Japanese net tightened around Port Arthur, Admiral Alekseev fled north to Kuropatkin's headquarters at Liaoyang.

The Siege of Port Arthur, 1904–1905

1904, May 25. Battle of Nanshan. Nanshan Hill, outpost of the Port Arthur defenses, was garrisoned by some 3,000 men. Oku's troops, assaulting frontally, were repulsed. Then the Japanese right wing, wading through the surf, turned the Russian left; the defenders were forced to withdraw hastily. In ferocity the fight was a prototype of future Japanese assaults. Oku's losses were 4,500 men out of 30,000 engaged. Russian losses were 1,500. The loss of Nanshan Hill uncovered the port of Dalny (Dairen), which became a Japanese base. Port Arthur was now ringed both by land and by sea. The Japanese Third Army, under General **Maresuke Nogi** (captor of Port Arthur from the Chinese in 1894), began concentrating at Dalny. Nogi was entrusted with the investment of Port Arthur, while Oku's Second Army turned northward to confront Stakelberg's offensive, reluctantly initiated by Kuropatkin on Alekseev's order (see p. 923).

1904, June 1–22. The Opposing Forces at Port Arthur. While Nogi's strength built up, Stësel—a most incompetent man—awaited attack in a dither. The fortress complex consisted of 3 main lines: an entrenchment surrounding the old town itself; the so-called Chinese Wall, some 4,000 yards beyond, composed of a ring of permanent concrete forts linked by a network of strong points and entrenchments; and beyond that, outer works consisting of a series of fortified hills—some fully organized, others still incomplete. The garrison, not counting the fleet personnel, amounted to about 40,000 men and 506 guns. The food supply was insufficient for a long siege, but danger of starvation was far from immediate. Outside the fortress, Nogi's strength was gradually increasing. By the end of July, the Third Army had waxed to more than 80,000 men with 474 field and siege guns, an imposing force, but—given a competent opponent—insufficient for a successful assault against such a formidable fortified position.

1904, June 15. Japanese Naval Losses. Accidents and the loss of 2 battleships to Russian mines left Togo with only 4 battleships and a reduced cruiser force.

1904, June 23. Russian Naval Sortie. Admiral **Vilgelm Vitgeft,** Makarov's successor, whose damaged ships had been repaired, made a sortie, causing Togo some uneasiness due to his weakened strength. He prepared to meet the Russians, but Vitgeft evaded action and returned to port.

1904, June 26. Russian Land Sortie. Stësel attempted a sortie, which was quickly checked.

1904, July 3–4, 27–28. Japanese Probings. These led to heavy but inconclusive fighting along the outer ring of forts.

1904, August 7–8. First Japanese Assault. Spurred by the evidence that the Russian fleet was still capable of action, Nogi attacked the eastern hill masses of the outer defense, which were captured after furious fighting.

1904, August 10. Naval Battle of the Yellow Sea. The Czar now ordered Vitgeft to break out and join the Vladivostok squadron, which was still at large, despite the searches by Kamimura's armored-cruiser squadron. Vitgeft steamed out with 6 battleships, 5 cruisers, and 8 destroyers. Togo closed with him by afternoon.

Japanese gunnery was far superior to the Russian, and his 4 modern battleships threw more metal than their Russian counterparts. Both fleets suffered severe damage. After an hour and a half of action, a 12-inch shell struck Vitgeft's flagship *Czarevich,* killing the admiral. A confusion of orders followed and the Russian ships fled in disorder. One cruiser was sunk; several others ran for neutral ports and were interned. Most of the Russian ships got back into Port Arthur.

1904, August 14. Naval Battle of Ulsan. Kamimura's 4 armored cruisers fell on the 3 remaining ships of Admiral **Jessen**'s Vladivostok squadron in the Korea Strait, sinking the cruiser *Rurik*. The other 2 ships got away. Japan now had complete command of the sea.

1904, August 19–24. Second Assault. In close-packed frontal attack, the Japanese struck both the Chinese Wall fortifications on the northeast and 174 Meter Hill on the northwest. Russian machine-gun fire mowed the attackers down again and again. Much of the fighting was at night, but Russian searchlights and rockets sought out the Japanese. Both sides fought with reckless bravery. Nogi called off the attacks after losing more than 15,000 men. He had captured 174 Meter Hill and one of the outlying batteries of thc eastern defenses. Otherwise the Russian position was unimpaired. Russian losses were but 3,000 men. Nogi, calling for heavy siege artillery, set himself to systematic sapping and mining of the fortifications.

1904, September 15–30. Third Assault. Nogi, having pushed siegeworks close to outlying hill positions on the north and northwestern faces of the fortress, made another close-massed frontal assault. The northern objectives were carried (September 19) and next day one of the northwestern positions. But 203 Meter Hill, the key point of the entire defense system, resisted all attacks. The assault columns were swept away again and again until the hill slopes were covered with Japanese corpses.

1904, October 1. Arrival of Japanese Siege Artillery. This included 19 28-cm. howitzers throwing 500-lb. projectiles 10,000 yards. Continuous bombardment hammered the Russian defenses, while sapping and mining operations lapped about 203 Meter Hill. On the eastern face, Nogi prepared for a mass frontal attack.

1904, October 30–November 1. Renewed Assault. Beginning at 9 A.M., the Japanese struck the northern and eastern works simultaneously. Once more the Japanese infantry, in close columns, attempted to claw through a rain of machine-gun, artillery, and hand-grenade fire. Once more they were repelled with tremendous losses. The same slaughter operation was repeated next day. Within the fortress food was running short, while the sick list mounted, but news that the Russian Baltic Fleet had steamed from Libau (October 15) brought some cheer. The same news spurred the besiegers; at all costs the ships in Port Arthur must be destroyed lest the fleets unite and defeat Togo.

1904, November 26. Fifth General Assault. This was repulsed by the Russians at all points, costing 12,000 more Japanese casualties. Nogi now concentrated on the 203 Meter Hill position, which consisted of a huge redoubt, surrounded by barbed wire and flanked on both sides by smaller hills, also fortified. Some 2,200 men, under Colonel **Tretyakov,** manned the complex, which looked down on the harbor, only 4,000 yards away. In Japanese hands it would seal the fate of the Russian fleet.

1904, November 27–December 5. Capture of 203 Meter Hill. Following an all-day bombardment, the assault troops advanced in the dusk, reaching the barbed-wire entanglements, where they managed to hold all the next day, despite Russian fire. Meanwhile bombardment of the crest continued. Until December 4, in assault after assault, the living attackers came stumbling over the dead in successive waves. Twice Russian counterattacks brushed back detachments that had gained footholds in the fort. The last handful of defenders was overrun after about 11,000 Japanese had died. Next day Japanese artillery fire from the hill began demolishing the Russian fleet in the harbor below. Togo's fleet steamed home to refit, preparatory to meeting the Baltic Fleet.

1905, January 2. Surrender of Port Arthur. Japanese assaults continued against the northern defenses of the fortress, despite freezing weather and heavy snows. The last fort fell on New Year's Day. Stësel surrendered about 10,000 able-bodied but starving survivors of his garrison next day. The Japanese captured a vast quantity of guns, small arms, and foodstuff (a shocking indictment of Stësel's mismanagement). Japanese losses in the siege totaled some 59,000 killed, wounded, and missing, with approximately 34,000 more sick. The Russians had lost 31,000. Nogi prepared to join the other Japanese armies in the north.

Operations in Central Manchuria

1904, June 14–15. Battle of Telissu. Stakelberg's advance toward Port Arthur was halted, and he entrenched, when confronted by Oku's Second Army. Oku attacked. Following a sharp encounter Stakelberg retreated to avoid envelopment. Russian losses were 3,600 out of 25,000 men engaged; Japanese casualties were 1,000 out of 35,000. Oku, advancing, attacked a Russian covering force at **Tashichia** under General **Zarubayev,** who successfully beat off the Japanese in a delaying action (June 24). Oku lost 1,200 men in the fight.

1904, July 17–31. Battle of the Moteinlung River. Keller's defensive group southeast of Liaoyang attacked Kuroki, who was advancing from the Yalu, but was repulsed. Kuroki, attacking in turn (July 31), met sharp opposition.

1904, August 1–25. Russian Retirement. Kuropatkin began pulling back all his advance detachments on Liaoyang, toward which point Kuroki, Nodzu (who had moved up from the coast), and Oku converged.

1904, August 25–September 3. Battle of Liaoyang. Field Marshal **Iwao Oyama,** now commanding all Japanese field forces, gathered his 3 converging armies against Kuropatkin's well-organized positions about Liaoyang. Oyama's strength totaled 125,000 against the 158,000 Russians, who had been reinforced by an army corps from Europe. Kuropatkin took the offensive, but was checked within his own outpost zone. The Russian launched another assault, massing his main effort against Kuroki's First Army, on the Japanese left. Through mismanagement, the stroke was repulsed. As usual, aggressive Japanese tactics overcame preponderance in numbers. The results were indecisive; the Japanese had lost 23,000 men against the Russian 19,000. However, Kuropatkin believed himself defeated and began a systematic, well-managed withdrawal north toward Mukden. Oyama followed, his efforts at pursuit repulsed by effective Russian rear guards.

1904, October 5–17. Battle of the Sha-Ho. Kuropatkin, reinforced to 200,000 men, turned on Oyama's 170,000, concentrating his main effort against Kuroki's First Army, now on the Japanese right. While Kuroki dug in to hold the Russian attack, Oyama threw the weight of his strength violently against the weakened Russian center. The Japanese assault was so severe that Kuropatkin checked his own assault to re-establish his center (October 13). Both sides soon renewed their efforts (October 16–17) without decisive results. Russian losses totaled 40,000 men; the Japanese lost 20,000. Exhausted, both armies dug in.

1905, January 26–27. Battle of Sandepu (Heikoutai). Reinforced to 300,000 men, and with his troops organized in 3 armies —**Linievich, Grippenberg,** and **Kaulbars** —Kuropatkin took the offensive in an effort to crush Oyama's 3 armies, 220,000 strong, before Nogi's Third Army arrived from Port Arthur. Attacking in a heavy snowstorm, the Russians came close to victory. Had Kuropatkin pressed his initial advantage vigorously, the outcome of the war might have been completely different. As it was, after 2 days of most bitter action, Oyama's counterattacks brought a temporary stalemate.

1905, February 21–March 10. Battle of Mukden. The opponents, each entrenched and each about 310,000 strong, faced one another on a 40-mile front. Oyama, seeking an envelopment, attempted to turn the Russian right with Nogi's Third Army. By the end of the first day's fighting, the Russian right—Kaulbars' army—was forced back until it faced west, instead of south. Attack and counterattack followed in quick succession, Kuropatkin shifting his reserves to backstop his crumbling right. Oyama's envelopment was unsuccessful, though Japanese troops actually entered Mukden during two weeks of violent battle. Bringing up his reserves, Oyama reinforced Nogi, permitting him to again try to envelop Kaulbars. After 3 days of fighting (March 6–8), the Russian right flank had been pushed back so far that Kuropatkin feared for his line of communications. He disengaged in workmanlike manner and fell back on Tieling (Teihling) and Harbin, defeated but not routed. Some 100,000 Russians had fallen; much matériel was abandoned. Japanese losses were 70,000 or more. There was no further concerted action on land.

The Naval Campaign of Tsushima

1904, October 15–1905, May 26. Voyage of the Baltic Fleet. Commanded by incapable Admiral **Zinovy P. Rozhdestvenski,** the Baltic Fleet left its home ports of Revel (Tallin) and Libau (Liepaja). It met its first mishap a few days later in the North Sea, where a false alarm of Japanese torpedo attack brought down a hail of Russian gunfire on a British fishing fleet near Dogger Bank. Several British trawlers were damaged, at least 7 fishermen killed. This incident almost brought war with Britain, and British cruisers trailed the Russian armada until it had passed the Bay of Biscay. Two battleships and 3 cruisers were detached to pass through the Suez Canal, while the main body went around the Cape of Good Hope. Problems of coaling and repairs in neutral ports continually vexed the Russians' creaking progress. Reuniting at Madagascar, after a prolonged delay, the fleet finally started across the Indian Ocean (March 16). One last stop was made at Van Fong Bay in French Indochina, where the Russians prepared for battle. Then heading for Vladivostok, and accompanied by supply ships and colliers, the fleet sailed north (May 14). As it approached Tsushima Strait, Rozhdestvenski's fleet comprised 8 battleships, 8 cruisers, 9 destroyers, and several smaller craft. Although imposing in paper strength, the force was a conglomeration of obsolescent or obsolete vessels, whose personnel was inferior in gunnery, discipline, and leadership to Togo's waiting fleet, which consisted of 4 battleships, 8 cruisers, 21 destroyers, and 60 torpedo boats.

1905, May 27. Battle of Tsushima. Rozhdestvenski entered the strait in line-ahead formation. To the northwest, Togo was steaming in similar formation. Both admirals led their respective main bodies—Rozhdestvenski in *Suvorov,* Togo in *Mikasa.* The Japanese turned to head northeast, hoping by superior speed to cross the Russian "T." Rozhdestvenski altered course to the northeast and then east, to avoid being raked. The action opened in early afternoon at 6,400 yards' range. Togo, at 15-knot speed, overhauled the 9-knot Russians and in less than 2 hours put 2 battleships and a cruiser out of action. The toll mounted as Togo brilliantly maneuvered his faster force around the hapless Russians. By nightfall, Rozhdestvenski had been wounded, 3 battleships (including his flagship) were sunk, and the surviving Russians, now under Admiral **Nebogatov,** were fleeing in confusion. Togo turned loose Kamimura's armored cruisers, the destroyers, and the torpedo boats to harry the exhausted Russians through the night. Next day, the destruction was completed. One cruiser and 2 destroyers escaped, to reach Vladivostok; 3 destroyers got to Manila and internment. The remainder of the Russian fleet was sunk or captured. The Japanese lost 3 torpedo boats. Russian casualties mounted to 10,000 killed and wounded; the Japanese lost less than 1,000 men in all.

Conclusions

1905, September 6. Treaty of Portsmouth, N.H. Both sides were ready to make peace. Japan's limited war objectives had been won, while Russia, seething with internal discontent, had no stomach for continuing. Through the efforts of President Theodore Roosevelt, peace negotiations led to a treaty. Russia surrendered Port Arthur and one-half of Sakhalin, and evacuated Manchuria. Korea was recognized as being within Japan's sphere of influence.

COMMENT. *Tactically, the war on land made plain the enormous defensive value of the machine gun and the offensive value of indirect artillery fire. Strangely, western observers failed to grasp fully the lesson of the machine gun. The Russian soldier once more proved his stoic courage in adversity, regardless of the incapacity of most of his officers. The Japanese displayed considerable professional skill and fanatical devotion to duty. The Battle of Tsushima—first and last great fleet action of the ironclad predreadnought era—was also the greatest naval battle of annihilation since Trafalgar. It emphasized that both seamanship and gunnery were still essential to victory at sea. Psychologically and politically, Japan's victory in the war marked a turning point in world history. Asia woke to the fact that the European was not always invincible; "white supremacy," as such, became a shibboleth.*

ITALO-TURKISH WAR, 1911–1912

1911, September 29. Italy Declares War. Italy's objective was to conquer Libya and gain a foothold in North Africa, so as to counterbalance the French colonial empire in Algeria, Tunisia, and Morocco.

1911, September 29–30. Italian Bombardment of Preveza. During the attack on the Epirus coast town, the Italian fleet sank several Turkish torpedo boats.

1911, October 3–5. Italian Bombardment of Tripoli. During the bombardment, Turkish forces evacuated the Libyan capital; an Italian naval landing force then seized the town (October 5). At the same time another naval force was occupying Tobruk (October 4).

1911, October 11. Italian Expeditionary Force Reaches Tripoli. Italian troops took over from the navy. At the same time other landings were made at Homs, Derna, and Benghazi. Turkish resistance was spotty.

1911–1912. Stalemate in Libya. Turkish propaganda so inflamed the Moslem population that cautious Italian General **Carlo Caneva** confined his activities to the coastal zone.

1912, April 16–19. Italian Naval Demonstration off the Dardanelles. The Turks closed the straits and hastily prepared for an invasion; the Italians withdrew without further action.

1912, May. Seizure of the Dodecanese. Italian naval forces occupied Rhodes and other islands.

1912, July–October. Italian Offensive in Libya. Finally pushing out of their coastal enclaves, the Italians began a systematic expansion of their control in Libya, which culminated in clear-cut victories over outnumbered Turkish forces at **Derna** and **Sidi Bilal** (near Zanzur).

1912, October 15. Treaty of Ouchy. The threatened outbreak of the Balkan War (see below) caused Turkey to seek peace, which was concluded after 2 months of negotiations. Libya and (after further negotiations) Rhodes and the Dodecanese Islands were ceded to Italy. The conduct of the war against negligible opposition had not enhanced Italian military prestige.

THE BALKAN WARS, 1912–1913

The First Balkan War, 1912–1913

OUTBREAK OF THE WAR

1912. Formation of the Balkan League. Bulgaria, Serbia, and Greece, seeking to eliminate Turkish power in the Balkans and to increase their own territorial areas, entered into military alliance in the hope of taking advantage of Turkey's war with Italy. Tiny Montenegro was informally associated. The pretext for war was Turkish misrule in Macedonia. Turkey had about 140,000 troops in Macedonia, Albania, and Epirus; another 100,000 were in Thrace. The allies were rightly confident that Greek command of the Aegean would prevent rapid and direct transfer of other Turkish forces to the Balkans. Bulgar active strength was approximately 180,000, Serb 80,000, and Greek 50,000, and each had about an equal number of trained, readily mobilizable reserves. Montenegrin militia strength, capable only of guerrilla operations, was about 30,000. Courage and stamina of the opposing forces were equal, but Turkish tactical leadership was inferior to that of the allies, despite recent German assistance in reorganization of the Ottoman Army.

1912, October 17–20. The Allied Invasions. Almost simultaneously the allies moved into Turkey's European provinces. Three Bulgar armies under General **Radko Dimitriev** invaded Thrace, moving generally on Adrianople. In Macedonia, General **Radomir Putnik**'s 3 Serbian armies from the north and Crown Prince **Con-**

stantine's Greek army from the south converged on the Vardar Valley with the intention of compressing hastily grouping Turkish elements between them.

OPERATIONS IN MACEDONIA

1912, October 20–November 5. Greek Advance. While a small force invaded Epirus in the west, Constantine's main army pressed on to the lower Vardar Valley. He defeated the Turks at **Elasson** (October 23). Most of the Turkish force withdrew toward Monastir, but Constantine did not pursue since, contrary to prior agreements, a Bulgarian division (ostensibly aiding the Serbian invasion) was advancing toward Salonika, which was coveted by both Bulgars and Greeks. Constantine headed eastward to try to forestall the Bulgarians. Turkish resistance in unexpected strength at **Venije Vardar** at first held up the Greek advance (November 2–3). At the same time other Turkish units defeated Constantine's flank detachments at **Kastoria** and **Banitsa.** Despite these setbacks, Constantine finally overwhelmed the Turks at **Venije** (November 5) and pressed on to Salonika. The isolated Turks to his northwest withdrew to Yannina (Ioannina).

1912, October 20–November 4. Serbian Advance. The Serbs met and defeated a Turkish covering force at **Kumanovo** (October 24). Turkish resistance stiffened in the **Babuna Pass,** near Prilep, and checked the Serbs until a threatened double envelopment in the hills forced the Turks to evacuate Skoplje and to retreat on Monastir. There, reinforced to a strength of 40,000, they again gave battle.

1912, November 5. Battle of Monastir. A Serb division impetuously stormed commanding ground to threaten an envelopment of the Turkish left. An Ottoman counterattack, with reinforcements drawn from the center of their line, retook the height, almost annihilating the Serb division. But the Turk center was so weakened that a Serbian frontal attack broke through. Faced with a threatened Greek advance from the south, Turkish resistance collapsed. Nearly 20,000 Turks were killed or captured. The remainder, scattering to the west and south, finally reached the fortress of Yannina, where they were besieged by the Greeks.

1912, November 9. Capture of Salonika. In the face of Greek preparations for an all-out assault, the Turkish garrison of 20,000 surrendered. Constantine occupied the city 1 day before the frustrated Bulgarian division arrived. This incident, and the subsequent dispute over possession of Salonika, worsened relations between the Bulgarians and the Greeks.

1912–1913. Sieges of Yannina and Scutari. By the end of the year, the only Turkish forces still holding out west of the Vardar were the garrisons of Yannina (besieged by the Greeks) and Scutari (Shkodër; besieged by the Montenegrins).

OPERATIONS IN THRACE

1912, October 22–December 3. Bulgarian Advance. The First, Second, and Third Bulgarian armies advanced on a broad front. Simultaneous meeting engagements with Turkish forces under **Abdalla Pasha** took place at **Seliolu** and **Kirk Kilissa** (October 22–25). The fighting at Kirk Kilissa was particularly severe, but the Turks were defeated in both actions. Falling black, Abdalla regrouped, facing west along the 35-mile-long line from Lüle' Burgas (Lüleburgaz) to Bunar Hisar (Pinahisar), with his right anchored in the mountains. The Bulgarian Second Army, on the right, invested Adrianople, while the other 2 armies wheeled eastward against the Turkish position.

1912, October 28–30. Battle of Lüle' Burgas. A Bulgarian piecemeal attack on the north was repulsed, but as the battle spread along the overextended Turkish front, Abdalla was forced to fall back. The Turks reorganized behind the permanent fortifications of the Chatalja (Çatalca) Line, between the Black Sea and the Sea of Marmora, protecting Constantinople.

1912, November–December. Siege of Constantinople. The Bulgars, launching a premature assault, were driven back with heavy loss (November 17–18). A stalemate continued along the Chatalja Line until an armistice temporarily ended hostilities (December 3). Adrianople remained in Turkish possession. Greece and Montenegro ignored the armistice.

CONCLUDING OPERATIONS

1912, December 17–1913, January 13. London Peace Conference. Representatives of the combatants and of the European Great Powers vainly endeavored to settle their conflicting aims with respect to the Balkans and the crumbling Turkish Empire; the conference collapsed.

1913, January 23. Coup d'État at Constantinople. The Turkish government was overthrown by the Young Turk nationalistic group, led by **Enver Bey.** The Young Turks at once denounced the armistice, and hostilities resumed (February 3).

1913, March 3. Fall of Yannina. The Turkish garrison of 30,000 surrendered to Crown Prince Constantine.

1913, March 26. Fall of Adrianople. A combined Bulgar-Serb siege operation ended with a 2-day assault against the eastern face of the fortress, breaching the Turk lines, despite an allied loss of 9,500 men. **Shukri Pasha** surrendered his garrison of 60,000.

1913, April 22. Fall of Scutari. A Serb force had come to the assistance of the irregular Montenegrin besiegers, but left after a month of continuing disagreements (April 16). The Turks then surrendered to the Montenegrins.

1913, May 30. Treaty of London. The Great Powers finally imposed an uneasy peace on the combatants. Turkey lost all of her European possessions save the tiny Chatalja and Gallipoli peninsulas. Bitter squabbles broke out between Bulgaria, on the one hand, and the Greeks and Serbs, on the other, over the division of conquered Macedonia. Montenegro was forced to abandon Scutari to the newly established state of Albania.

Second Balkan War, 1913

Bulgaria's 5 armies were arranged as follows: the First faced the Serbs between Vidin and Borkovitsa, with the Fifth on its left. The Third lay above Kustendil, the Fourth about Koccani and Radaviste (Radovic). The Second faced the Greeks between Strumitsa (Strumica) and Serres (Serrai). The Serb Second Army was on the old Serb-Bulgar frontier; the First, in the center, at Kumanovo and Kriva Palanka. The Third, on the right of the First, was concentrated along the Bregalnica. The Greeks were assembled between the lower Vardar and the mouth of the Struma.

1913, May 30–June 30. Bulgarian Attacks. The Fourth and Third armies, moving to the Vardar, attacked the Serbs without a declaration of war. The Second Army drove in Greek advance elements. Both Serbs and Greeks were disposed in depth, however, and the Bulgar attack lost its momentum.

1913, July 2. Allied Counterattack. Putnik, responsible for the Serbian defensive success, now seized the initiative. While the Third Serbian Army checked the Bulgars on the upper Bregalnica, the First Army broke through, driving on Kyustendil and pushing the Bulgars back in a northeasterly direction. The Greeks (July 3–4) forced the Second Bulgarian Army back, outflanking the Bulgar left (July 7) and driving them north up the Struma Valley. A counteroffensive by the Third and Fourth Bulgarian armies against the Serbian Third, toward the upper Bregalnica, was soon checked (July 10).

1913, July–August. Rumanian and Turkish Intervention. Rumania declared war against Bulgaria (July 15) and moved her troops, practically unopposed, toward Sofia. At the same time the Turks issued from the Chatalja Line and from Bulair (Bolayr) to reoccupy Adrianople. A Bulgar attempt to regroup and attack the Greeks in the Struma Valley was unsuccessful. Bulgaria sued for peace (July 13) and hostilities ended (**Treaty of Bucharest,** August 10).

COMMENT. *Bulgaria's success in the First Balkan War caused her to underestimate her former allies' military capacity. The end result of the Second Balkan War was to deprive the Bulgars of all gains made in the previous conflict.*

WORLD WAR I

THE BACKGROUND

1914, June 28. Assassination of Archduke Franz Ferdinand. The heir to the Austro-Hungarian throne and his wife were murdered by a Serb terrorist in Bosnian (now Yugoslavian) Sarajevo. This toppled the power balance between Europe's 2 armed camps—the Triple Alliance of Germany, Austria-Hungary, and Italy vs. the Triple Entente of France, Russia, and Great Britain. Austria-Hungary, eager to expand in the Balkans and relying on German support, delivered an ultimatum to Serbia (July 23), which was accepted only in part. Serbia mobilized (July 25).

1914, July 28. Austro-Hungarian Declaration of War.

1914, July 28–August 6. The Initial Line-up. Russia ordered mobilization against Austria, whereupon Germany declared war against her (August 1), but (in accordance with her Schlieffen Plan; see p. 931) began invasion to the west through neutral Luxembourg and Belgium, and declared war against France (August 3). Great Britain declared war on Germany because of invasion of neutral Belgium (August 4), Austria-Hungary against Russia (August 6). Italy temporarily remained neutral, cynically pitting her desire to be on the winning side against her obligations to the Triple Alliance, which she claimed were void due to Austrian initiation of the war. Overseas, the United States, stirred by conflicting ancestral urges, became a much-confused spectator.

The Opposing Forces

Except for Britain, the troops of each of the combatants were conscripts, welded by a hard core of career officers and noncoms. Fifty per cent of German youth reaching military age were conscripted for 2 years' service; France, with a smaller population, called 80 per cent of her available youth for 3 years' service. These men remained in reserve cadres after leaving active service; the German system was more highly organized than was the French.

The normal continental infantry division was approximately 16,000 strong, organized in two infantry brigades (4 3-battalion regiments), an artillery brigade of 12 6-gun batteries of light and medium guns, and supporting engineer, signal, medical, and supply units. Usually, 1 cavalry regiment was attached. An army corps consisted of 2 or 3 divisions. Small independent cavalry divisions, normally organized in corps of 2 or more divisions each, were standard in continental armies.

The best-equipped and trained army of 1914 was the German; its preponderance of available medium and heavy artillery was a great advantage. Behind the army was a well-knit industrial organization. Despite an offensive doctrine, units were also trained in defensive tactics.

The French Army, with one vital exception, ranked second to the German in general efficiency. French doctrine of the period was based on complete dedication to the offensive; defensive tactics were almost completely disregarded. The French were unskilled in defensive organization of the ground, field fortification, and defensive application of machine-gun fire.

The French did possess the finest field gun of its time—the famous French 75-mm.—prototype of 20th-century pre-atomic artillery. But, secure in the knowledge that this weapon surpassed anything possessed by their opponents, the French had neglected medium and heavy artillery. Actually, in the beginning there were but some 300 French pieces of larger caliber than 75-mm. to oppose 3,500 German heavier weapons. French battery organization—4 guns against 6—was another handicap.

The Austro-Hungarian Army was patterned on the German, but a poor general staff and the language barrier—75 per cent of the officers were of Germanic origin, while only some 25 per cent of the enlisted men could understand the language—were handicaps. Greatest bar to efficiency was the poor morale of its many discontented Slavic racial groups, with little or no loyalty to the Hapsburg Crown, many of them sympathizing with Russia.

French 75 and American artillerymen

The Russian Army, strong in docile, hardy, and fatalistically brave man power, suffered from severe shortages in matériel and munitions. Its high command, except for the Grand Duke **Nicholas,** who was suddenly made commander in chief on August 3, and a very few others, was careless and incompetent, as was its general staff.

In sharp contrast to the continental forces, the British Regular Army was composed of volunteers enlisted for a 7-year period. Under well-qualified career officers, its morale, discipline, and steadiness were high; individual marksmanship and fire discipline were excellent. The British Expeditionary Force (BEF) of 150,000 men —6 infantry and 1 cavalry divisions, with supporting troops—would play a role in the opening campaign far beyond that indicated by its strength. Behind the regulars was the Territorial Army, a volunteer militia, inadequately trained and equipped.

German machine gun

All these armies entered the war with tactical indoctrination differing little from that of the Franco-Prussian War, but with new and improved weapons. Despite the example of the Russo-Japanese War, the latent power of the machine gun had not been appreciated—2 to each infantry battalion being the general rule. But the thorough Germans had conducted exercises in defense and in the attack and reduction of fortifications. And they had an almost perfect strategical plan, evolved in 1905.

Plans and Preparations

GERMAN PREPARATIONS; THE SCHLIEFFEN PLAN

Germany put into effect a modified version of the plan which had been evolved by General Count **Alfred von Schlieffen,** former chief of the German General Staff (1891–1906), for use in the event of a 2-front war against France and Russia. It was to hold the slowly mobilizing Russians on the east in check with a minimum of force, while the full weight of the German Army would crush France, the more dangerous enemy, in the west.

Schlieffen, who retired in 1906 shortly after his plan was adopted, correctly deduced that upon a declaration of war France would attack immediately; she would not violate the neutral territories of the Low Countries or Switzerland; and French concentration would take place generally between Belfort and Sedan, with the objective of seizing Alsace and German Lorraine.

Schlieffen planned a German feint and then withdrawal in Alsace-Lorraine to further entice the French into a major offensive there. Meanwhile the bulk of the German field forces, 35½ corps in 5 armies, pivoting on the fortified region of Thionville-Metz, would envelop the entire French Army by a wide sickle movement which would drive through Belgium and the Netherlands and whose outer tip would pass well to the west of Paris. The French, thus attacked from the rear behind their left flank, would be rolled up to destruction against the German fortified positions in Alsace-Lorraine, or driven into Switzerland and internment.

Meanwhile, in East Prussia, small forces would withdraw slowly in the face of a Russian advance. By the time these had been forced back to the Vistula, Schlieffen expected that France would be defeated. The main German armies would then be transported eastward by Germany's excellent railroad system to crush the Russians in another lightning campaign.

If carried out as conceived, this plan might have ended the war in a few weeks. However, Schlieffen's successor, General **Helmuth von Moltke** (nephew of the hero of the Franco-Prussian War), began tinkering with it. His first modification was to refrain from violating Dutch neutrality. Thus the 2 northernmost (and strongest) of the 5 enveloping German armies would be crowded and slowed up through the Liége bottleneck in Belgium. Then Moltke, reluctant to surrender any German territory, limited the proposed strategic withdrawal of the left-wing armies before the French advance in Alsace-Lorraine. For similar reasons, he planned diversion of additional forces to East Prussia, which was to be defended near the frontiers, instead of a slow withdrawal to the Vistula in the delaying campaign envisaged by Schlieffen. As a result, the revised plan on which the Germans operated put only 60 per cent of German mobile field forces in the right-wing blow against France instead of Schlieffen's proposed 90 per cent. The right wing totaled about 1,500,000 men; the left-wing armies in Alsace and Lorraine were 500,000 strong; there were about 200,000 men in the army defending East Prussia, and another 200,000 along the remainder of Germany's eastern frontiers.

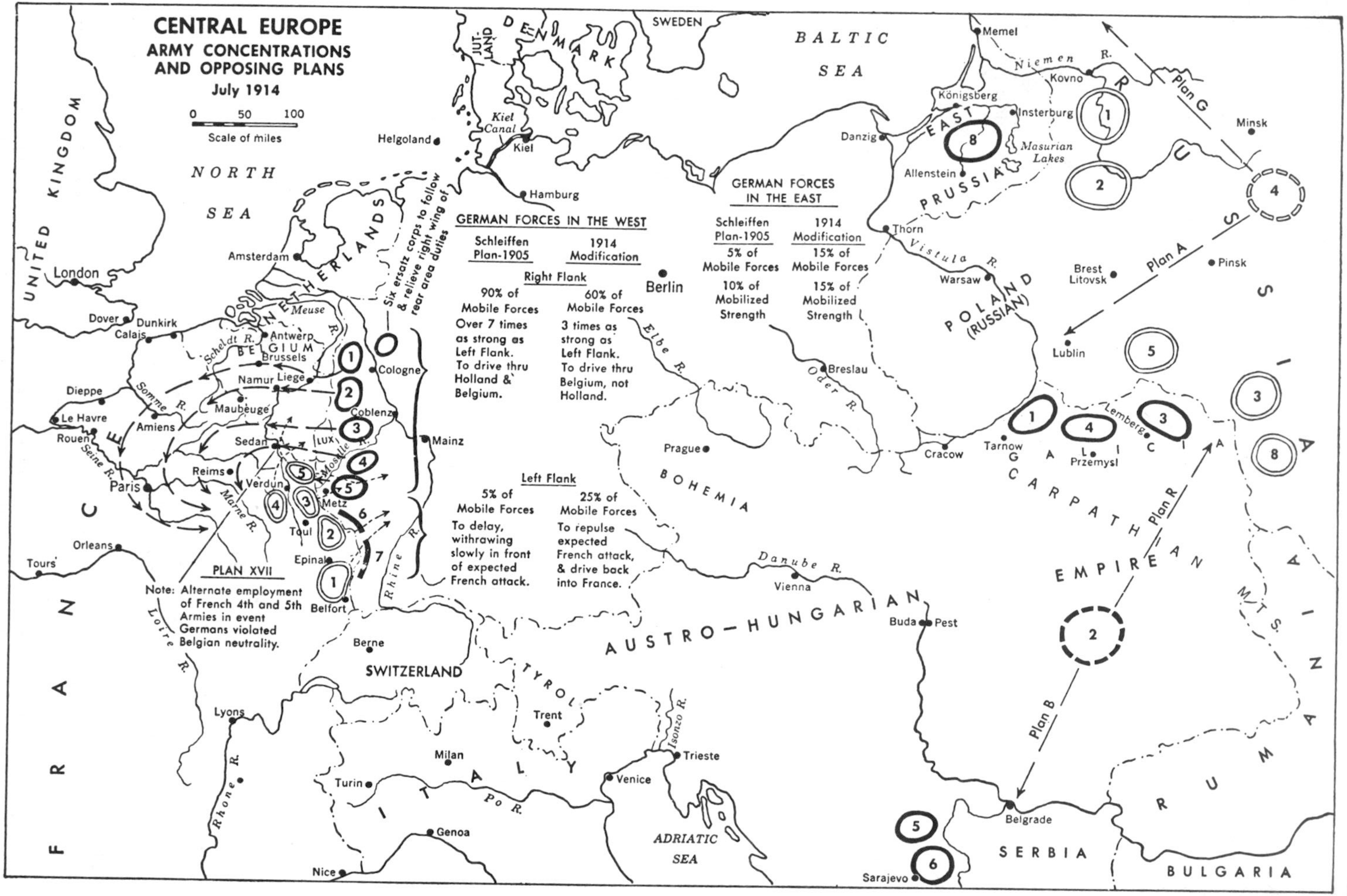

CENTRAL EUROPE
ARMY CONCENTRATIONS AND OPPOSING PLANS
July 1914
0 50 100
Scale of miles
GERMAN FORCES IN THE WEST
Schleiffen Plan-1905
1914 Modification
Right Flank
90% of Mobile Forces
Over 7 times as strong as Left Flank.
To drive thru Holland & Belgium.
60% of Mobile Forces
3 times as strong as Left Flank.
To drive thru Belgium, not Holland.
Left Flank
5% of Mobile Forces
To delay, withrawing slowly in front of expected French attack.
25% of Mobile Forces
To repulse expected French attack, & drive back into France.
GERMAN FORCES IN THE EAST
Schleiffen Plan-1905
5% of Mobile Forces
10% of Mobilized Strength
1914 Modification
15% of Mobile Forces
15% of Mobilized Strength
PLAN XVII
Note: Alternate employment of French 4th and 5th Armies in event Germans violated Belgian neutrality.
Six ersatz corps to follow & relieve right wing of rear area duties
Plan G
Plan A
Plan R
Plan B
UNITED KINGDOM
London
Dover
NORTH SEA
Helgoland
NETHERLANDS
Amsterdam
BELGIUM
Antwerp
Brussels
Namur
Liege
Maubeuge
Dunkirk
Calais
Dieppe
Le Havre
Rouen
Amiens
Somme R.
Seine R.
Scheldt R.
Meuse R.
Paris
Reims
Sedan
Verdun
Metz
Toul
Epinal
Belfort
LUX
Moselle R.
Marne R.
Loire R.
Rhone R.
Orleans
Tours
Lyons
FRANCE
Cologne
Coblenz
Mainz
Rhine R.
JUTLAND
DENMARK
SWEDEN
Kiel Canal
Kiel
Hamburg
Berlin
Elbe R.
BALTIC SEA
Danzig
Königsberg
EAST PRUSSIA
Allenstein
Insterburg
Masurian Lakes
Memel
Niemen R.
Kovno
Thorn
Vistula R.
Warsaw
POLAND (RUSSIAN)
Breslau
Oder R.
Brest Litovsk
Pinsk
Minsk
Lublin
RUSSIA
Cracow
Tarnow
GALICIA
Przemysl
Lemberg
CARPATHIAN MTS.
EMPIRE
AUSTRO-HUNGARIAN
BOHEMIA
Prague
Danube R.
Vienna
Buda Pest
SWITZERLAND
Berne
TYROL
Trent
Isonzo R.
Trieste
Venice
Milan
Turin
Genoa
Nice
Po R.
ITALY
ADRIATIC SEA
Sarajevo
Belgrade
SERBIA
RUMANIA
BULGARIA

FRENCH PREPARATIONS; PLAN XVII

France planned on a concentration along her eastern frontier and an immediate attack through Alsace-Lorraine, exactly as Schlieffen had anticipated. This concept was the essence of French "Plan XVI" in 1911. Then General **Victor Michel,** the new commander in chief of the French Army, believing that any German invasion would come through Belgium rather than across the difficult terrain of Alsace-Lorraine, proposed a radical reorganization. He projected a French invasion through Belgium, regardless of her neutrality, to forestall the Germans. Had the Michel Plan been accepted, the opposing major offensives would have met head on. But this concept was rejected and Michel was relieved of command, General **Joseph J. C. Joffre** replacing him. A watered-down straddle, "Plan XVII," was adopted. The French main effort would be an immediate 2-pronged offensive into Alsace-Lorraine, passing both north and south of the Thionville-Metz area. At the same time, 2 French armies were to be prepared to shift westward if the Germans did in fact violate Belgian neutrality.

Joffre placed too much reliance on the ability of the Russian Army to engage Germany in the east. He relied also on close co-ordination with the BEF, which was expected to reinforce the French left flank. He also gambled—successfully—that Italy would leave the Triple Alliance. But above all, he and his general staff grossly underestimated the immediately available German strength. The French believed the German active Army to be too weak to drive west of the Meuse, and did not believe that they would employ their reserves without some refresher training. Actually, the German reserve elements were in such advanced training that they were immediately available for first-line use, thus giving them a substantial and unexpected 3–2 numerical edge over the 1,300,000 French in the opening battles.

THE RUSSIAN PLAN

This called for immediate, simultaneous offensives against both Germany and Austria, disregarding the fact that slow Russian mobilization could not be completed for 3 months. After the outbreak of war, the Grand Duke **Nicholas,** the Czar's newly appointed commander, was coaxed by pressure from the French high command into speeding up these precipitate offensives. The result was to be disastrous defeat in East Prussia, but the premature Russian offensives into Galicia would be partially successful because of greater Austrian ineptitude.

AUSTRIAN PLANS

General **Franz Conrad von Hötzendorf,** dynamic Austrian Chief of Staff, had evolved two plans: Plan B for war against Serbia alone, Plan R for war against both Serbia and Russia. He chose the former, then changed his mind after concentration began. As a result, 1 of his 6 armies would not be available for action on either front when Conrad ordered advances into Serbia and into Galicia against the Russians. Even if it had been, it is doubtful that Austria would have had sufficient superiority of force to justify 2 simultaneous offensives.

The Naval Situation

The British Navy commanded the seas—28 dreadnoughts and battle cruisers to Germany's 18. Above all, the British Navy was ready to fight, thanks to the foresight of First Lord of the Admiralty **Winston Churchill** and the First Sea Lord, Prince **Louis of Battenberg.** The German Navy had comparable standards of efficiency, but was hampered by deficiencies in bases as well as numbers. The Russian, French, and Austrian navies were limited in strength and were to play only minor roles.

COMPARATIVE NAVAL STRENGTHS—AUGUST, 1914

	British			*German*		
	Total	Home Waters	Grand Fleet[a]	Total	Home Waters	High Seas Fleet
Dreadnoughts[b] (modern battleships)	20	(20)	(20)	13	(13)	(13)
Battle Cruisers[c]	8	(4)	(4)	5	(4)	(4)
Old Battleships[b]	40	(38)	(10)	22	(22)	(10)
Cruisers[d]	102	(48)	(21)	41	(32)	(17)
Destroyers	301	(270)	(50)	144	(144)	(80)
Submarines	78	(65)	(9)	30	(30)	(24)[e]

[a] Numbers of cruisers and destroyers in the Grand Fleet are approximate, and varied considerably during early days of war.

[b] Dreadnoughts were modern, big-gun ships, completely outclassing all old battleships (see discussion in text). Britain had 2 more dreadnoughts completed, but not yet ready for action, and 15 under construction (including 3 that had been intended for other nations). Germany had 3 more completed, but not yet ready for action, and 4 under construction.

[c] Vessels carrying heavy guns similar to dreadnoughts, but with thinner armor and greater speed. Britain and Germany each had one additional battle cruiser completed but not yet ready for action. Britain had 1 building; Germany had 2 building.

[d] Included old armored cruisers and smaller, but faster and better armed, light cruisers.

[e] Records are conflicting on exact number of German submarines in commission. This figure is approximately correct.

Air Power in 1914

Negligible at the outset, aviation gradually would develop from a reconnaissance into a combat role. Lighter-than-air craft, particularly the German Zeppelin rigid dirigibles, were used from the beginning for both reconnaissance and bombing roles. Captive balloons for artillery observation were also used from the outset.

German Zeppelin dirigible

OPERATIONS IN 1914

Western Front

THE OPENING BATTLES

1914, August 3–20. Belgium Overrun. A specially trained German Second Army task force of about 30,000 men under General **Otto von Emmich** crossed the Belgian frontier between the Ardennes and the Dutch border, a narrow corridor guarded by Liége, one of the strongest fortresses of Europe. A night attack (August 5–6) penetrated the ring of 12 outlying forts. Heavy fighting followed, in which German Major General **Erich F. Ludendorff** distinguished himself, as did the Belgian commander, General **Gérard M. Leman.** German bombardment by 42-cm. howitzers (heaviest used to this time) systematically reduced the concrete

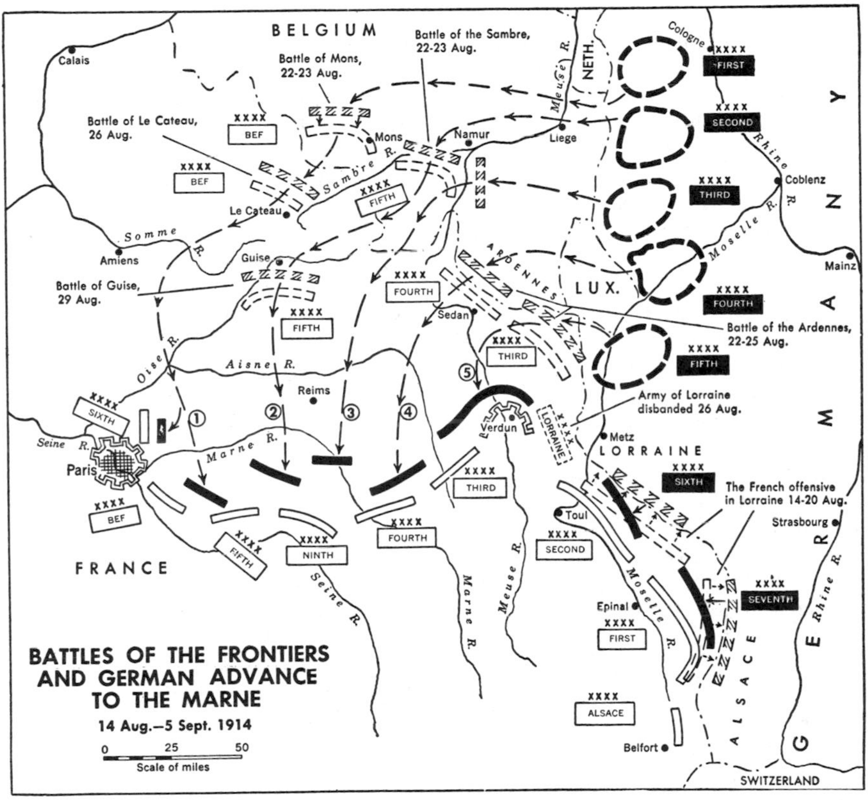

BATTLES OF THE FRONTIERS AND GERMAN ADVANCE TO THE MARNE
14 Aug.—5 Sept. 1914

and steel cupolaed defenses. Liége surrendered (August 16). The German First Army (General **Alexander von Kluck**) and the Second (General **Karl von Bülow**) poured through the Liége corridor and across the Meuse. Hastily mobilized Belgian field forces were brushed aside to the north of **Tirlemont** (August 18–19) and Brussels occupied (August 20). After some skirmishing along the Meuse (August 12–16), the Belgians, personally commanded by King **Albert,** fell back on the fortress of Antwerp.

1914, August 14–25. Battles of the Frontiers. The Germans and the Anglo-French armies met each other head on in 4 almost simultaneous actions:

1914, August 14–22. Battle of Lorraine. An early advance to Mulhouse in Alsace (August 8) by the French right-wing Army of Alsace (General **Paul Pau**) was followed by a full-scale offensive southeast of Metz by the French First (General **Auguste Dubail**) and Second (General **Noël de Castelnau**) armies (August 14–18). After planned withdrawals, the German Sixth

(Prince **Rupprecht** of Bavaria) and Seventh (General **Josias von Heeringen**) armies turned in violent converging counterattacks. The French were thrown back to the fortified heights of **Nancy,** where they barely managed to stop the German drive. The French XX Corps, under General Ferdinand Foch, played a decisive role in holding Nancy.

1914, August 20–25. Battle of the Ardennes. The advancing French Third (General **Pierre Ruffey**) and Fourth (General **Fernand de Langle de Cary**) armies met headlong the German Fourth (Duke **Albrecht of Württemberg**) and Fifth (Crown Prince **Wilhelm**) armies, comprising the pivot of the Schlieffen Plan maneuver. After 4 days of furious fighting, the outnumbered French were repulsed with shocking losses, falling back to reorganize west of the Meuse, with their right flank on the fortress of Verdun.

1914, August 22–23. Battle of the Sambre. To the north, the German First, Second, and Third (General **Max von Hausen**) armies were beginning to sweep west and southwest. In accordance with the contingency provisions of Plan XVII, Joffre ordered the French Fifth Army (General **Charles Lanrezac**) into the Sambre-Meuse angle to meet this unexpected move. The German Second and Third armies struck Lanrezac southwest of Namur, defeating him and forcing him to retreat. The Belgian defenders of **Namur** were hammered into submission by some of Bülow's troops and siege guns after a brief siege (August 20–25).

1914, August 23. Battle of Mons. The British Expeditionary Force (Field Marshal Sir **John French**), 4 divisions and over 100,000 strong, had promptly and efficiently crossed the Channel and concentrated in the vicinity of Le Cateau, left of the French Fifth Army. Upon Joffre's request, the BEF moved into Belgium in co-operation with Lanrezac's advance toward Namur (August 21). Near Mons the British were struck by the full weight of aggressive von Kluck's First German Army. Outnumbered, the British fought back stoutly, their fire discipline taking heavy toll of the close German formations. Sir John French was prepared to continue the fight next day, but the retreat of Lanrezac's Fifth Army from the Sambre left him without support; the BEF therefore withdrew during the night. French was bitter about Lanrezac's unannounced withdrawal, which he believed had jeopardized the existence of his own BEF.

COMMENT. *The French offensive had failed completely—at a cost of some 300,000 casualties. But Moltke overestimated the extent of the German victory. His communications with his armies were poor, his information faulty. Believing that the success in Lorraine was a decisive victory, he ordered his left to continue its offensive against the fortified Nancy heights, hoping thus to obtain a double envelopment of the entire French field forces. The Ardennes and Sambre battles he also considered decisive, and so he renewed the orders for his right-wing armies to continue their sicklelike sweep, with the First Army still to swing west of Paris. He decided to send to the Sixth and Seventh armies reinforcements originally intended for the right-wing armies, to provide more weight to his new offensive in Lorraine. Confident that the French armies were on the verge of destruction, he also detached 2 corps from the right to hasten by railroad to the Eastern Front, where the Russians had shown unexpected initiative. (Ironically, these 2 corps, whose absence would vitally affect the outcome of the Battle of the Marne, were still en route at the time the Battle of Tannenberg made their presence unnecessary in the east.) As a result of these and other detachments to contain the Belgian Army at Antwerp and to besiege the French fortress of Maubeuge, the 3 German right-wing armies had been bled from a total strength of 16 corps to 11. The already watered-down Schlieffen Plan—dependent upon a right-wing hammer blow—was thus still further modified from the concept of its creator.*

Joffre, on the other hand, had kept close touch with his subordinate commanders and was well aware of the actual situation. He knew that, despite tactical defeats, morale of his troops was still high. He was now also aware of the German plan. Seemingly oblivious of the disastrous results of his own Plan XVII, he calmly prepared for a counterattack. This would be a Schlieffen Plan in reverse, pivoting about Verdun and the Nancy heights, where his First and Second armies were ordered to hold on at all costs.

While the Third, Fourth, and Fifth armies and the BEF were to continue their southwesterly withdrawals, Joffre drew units from his embattled right flank and from reserves in the interior of France to create 2 new armies. The Sixth, under General **Michel J. Maunoury,** *was to assemble—first near Amiens, later in and around Paris—west of the German right wing, prepared to attack east. The Ninth, under General Foch, would be gathered in close support behind and between the Fourth and Fifth armies to provide weight for a counterattack against the German main effort. This attack was to be launched when the 4 Allied left-flank armies had fallen back to the general line of the Somme River–Verdun.*

1914, August 25–27. Battle of Le Cateau. Marshal French's BEF, hard-pressed by the German First Army, fought daily rear-guard actions. Attempting a stand (August 27) to relieve his exhausted II Corps troops, General **Horace Smith-Dorrien** became engaged in the biggest battle the British Army had fought since Waterloo. This corps fought off a double envelopment by the full strength of Kluck's army; the survivors successfully disengaged when night fell. The price was high: 7,800 casualties out of 40,000 men engaged.

1914, August 29. Battle of Guise. Joffre, to relieve German pressure on the BEF, ordered the Fifth French Army, itself pressed hard by the German Second Army, to make a 90-degree shift westward to attack the left flank of the German First Army. The initial attack got nowhere, but General **Louis Franchet d'Esperey,** commanding Lanrezac's I Corps, smartly moved from reserve to hit and halt the pursuing German Second Army, thus achieving the first French tactical success in the campaign. Bülow called on Kluck (August 30) for help.

1914, August 30–September 2. Kluck's First Dilemma. The German First Army had driven the BEF from its front; for the time being—as Kluck saw it—the British were out of the picture. On the right, some slight clashes had occurred with French troops (actually part of Maunoury's assembling Sixth Army, but in Kluck's opinion unimportant scattered elements). Bülow on the left had called for help. Aggressive Kluck, thinking the French Fifth Army now to be the left-flank unit of the opposing field forces, and unable to communicate with Moltke, threw the remnants of the Schlieffen Plan into the discard. He shifted his direction of march to the southeast to roll up the Fifth Army (August 31). This change would cause him to pass east of Paris; he knew nothing of the French concentration in the fortified area of the capital. By September 2, Kluck's left flank was on the Marne at Château-Thierry, his right on the Oise, near Chantilly.

1914, September 1–2. Joffre's Reaction. Aware of the German change in direction through air reconnaissance, Joffre ordered the Sixth Army to complete its concentration in the Paris area. He ordered the general retirement to continue until the Fifth Army was out of immediate danger of envelopment. Thus he was forced to abandon his originally planned counterstroke from the Somme-Verdun line. Foch's newly forming Ninth Army continued its concentration between the Fourth and Fifth armies. Joffre was concerned by British lack of responsiveness to his orders, but a visit to Field Marshal French by the British War Minister, Field Marshal **Lord Kitchener,** soon changed Sir John's attitude and he began to co-operate.

1914, September 3–4. Kluck's Second Dilemma. Belatedly Moltke sent a message to Kluck, agreeing to the move east of Paris, but complicating matters by ordering Kluck to guard the right flank of the Second Army, which would thus become the spearhead of the modified German wheel. But Moltke, whose intelligence had informed him of the French concentration near Paris, did not realize that his First Army had been moving at amazing speed under Kluck's driving leadership, and that its advance units were much farther south than those of the slower-moving Second Army. And Moltke failed to explain the reason for his order. For Kluck to have obeyed the order would have meant halting his army for 2 days, which he believed would permit the French either to escape or to rally. Again being unable to communicate directly with his commander, unaware of the situation in Paris, and trying to act in accordance with the apparent intention of Moltke's order, Kluck reasoned that its purpose was to assure that the French were driven southeast of Paris. His own First Army was ideally situated for this task. Accordingly, pugnacious Kluck continued southward, across the Marne, his right flank wide open, just east of Paris.

BATTLE OF THE MARNE, SEPTEMBER 5–10

Joffre's counterattack order (September 4) directed the Sixth Army to attack eastward toward Château-Thierry; the BEF was to move on Montmirail, with the Fifth Army, supported by the Ninth, prepared to conform. The Fourth Army would hold, prepared to advance, and the Third would strike westward from Verdun. On the success of this proposed double envelopment of the German right wing, as Joffre well knew, rested the fate of France. September 6 was to be D day.

Meanwhile Maunoury's Sixth Army, temporarily under the regional command of General **Joseph S. Galliéni,** energetic military governor of Paris, had begun to carry out Joffre's warning orders by an advance from Paris toward the Ourcq River, where Kluck's right flank lay invitingly open. Only the aggressive initiative of the German right-flank corps commander, General **Hans von Gronau,** saved Kluck's army from surprise envelopment (September 5). As it was, Kluck believed that the French activity on his right was only a spoiling attack and merely detached one additional corps to help Gronau to repel it, while pressing southward with the rest of his army in pursuit of the BEF and the French Fifth Army. Not until this **Battle of the Ourcq** had raged for 2 days did Kluck realize the French intentions (September 7). By this time most of his army was south of the Marne. Pulling back north of the river, Kluck rapidly changed his front and turned his entire army westward in savage counterattacks that halted the French and forced Maunoury to fall back on the defensive (September 7–9). Only the arrival of reinforcements rushed from Paris by Galliéni—some in commandeered taxicabs—permitted Maunoury to stem the impetuous German advance.

By this time the action had become general along the entire front west of Verdun. Kluck's westward shift, undertaken on the assumption that the BEF was no longer a threat, widened the already existing gap between his army and that of von Bülow, which was still moving south. Into this gap now moved the BEF, slowly, since Marshal French underrated the recuperative powers of his troops. Franchet d'Esperey's Fifth Army (Lanrezac had been relieved) battered at part of the German Second Army along the **Petit Morin.**

Farther southeast, Foch's Ninth Army, attacking north at **St.-Gond,** found itself confronting the rest of the Second Army while Hausen's Third Army struck its right. A surprise night bayonet attack by 4 divisions of Hausen's army threw part of Foch's army into confusion (September 8). Foch's response was to order an immediate renewal of his own assault; the German advance was halted, but Foch's position was precarious.

At **Vitry-le-François,** Langle de Cary's Fourth Army battled desperately but indecisively with the Duke of Württemberg's Fourth Army and part of the Third. At Revigny in the Argonne Forest, General **Maurice Sarrail**'s Third Army (Ruffey had been relieved) stopped the Crown Prince's Fifth Army, while at **Nancy** and along the Alsace frontier the French First and Second armies—even though attenuated by drafts for Joffre's new formations to the west—clung successfully to the heights, despite a succession of attacks by the reinforced German Sixth and Seventh armies. (Schlieffen had warned against any such attacks.)

Moltke, worried by rumor and pessimistic fragmentary reports from his subordinates, sent a general staff officer, Lieutenant Colonel **Richard Hentsch,** to in-

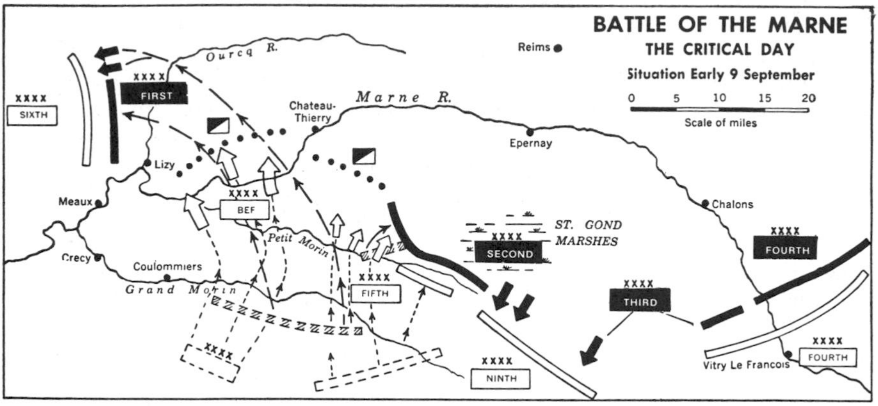

spect the front (September 8). Hentsch's orders were oral; they still remain somewhat of a mystery. He arrived at the Second Army's headquarters just as news was received that its right flank was being turned by a vigorous night attack by Franchet d'Esperey's Fifth Army. This was probably the turning point of the battle. Bülow—personally defeated—was about to retreat. Kluck's First Army was making headway in the northwest against Maunoury's left, but the BEF's advance through the gap threatened Kluck's own left and rear.

Hentsch tacitly approved Bülow's planned retreat and, later the same day, in Moltke's name ordered Kluck also to withdraw (September 9). Moltke, now realizing that his offensive had failed, ordered a general retirement to the line Noyon-Verdun. Within 5 days the Germans, having disengaged without serious interference from the exhausted Allies, were organizing their new positions. The Battle of the Marne thus ended as a strategic Allied victory and Joffre emerged as savior of France. That same day Moltke was relieved, General **Erich von Falkenhayn** replacing him (September 14).

COMMENT. *France's initial offensive plan had failed because it was entirely unrealistic in concept and in execution. The German plan—sound and workable—failed because of the inefficiency of Moltke, who first emasculated the plan, then lost all personal touch with his army commanders and with their progress. Joffre, on the other hand, emerged as a strong and capable leader, who kept in close touch with his subordinates. His reconstruction of a counterattack upon the wreckage of his initial plan was masterful, its execution assisted by the marvelous resiliency of the French Army. The BEF's part was that of a sound professional soldiery. The clash of personalities and mutual distrust existing between Sir John French and Lanrezac prevented better use of the BEF, as did French's excessive caution in the counterattack. Casualties on both sides were enormous: the Allies lost about 250,000 men; German losses were somewhat greater. In 3 weeks of war, each side had lost more than half a million men in killed, wounded, and captured. The Battle of the Marne, tactically indecisive, was a clear-cut strategic victory for the Allies. Had it ended differently, the history of the 20th century would have been altered fundamentally. It was the world's most decisive battle since Waterloo.*

THE "RACE TO THE SEA," SEPTEMBER 15–NOVEMBER 24

1914, September 15–18. First Battle of the Aisne. Slow in their pursuit, the Allied armies, seeking to envelop the German right, were rebuffed from the hastily prepared German field fortifications. Both sides now extended their operations northward, attempting each to outflank the other. Both failed, in bitter fighting in **Picardy** (September 22–26) and **Artois** (September 27–October 10). Meanwhile, behind the German lines, beleaguered **Maubeuge** had fallen (September 8) and the fortress of **Antwerp,** systematically bombarded (October 1–9), surrendered. The Belgian Army fell back to the west along the coast. An extemporized British naval division, rushed to reinforce the Antwerp garrison, also escaped, but with loss of 1 of its 3 brigades.

1914, September 22–25. Verdun and St.-Mihiel. Farther south, repeated German attacks against Verdun were repulsed (September 22–25), but the Germans did seize the strategic **St.-Mihiel** salient (September 24), to which they would cling until 1918.

1914, October 18–November 24. Battles in Flanders. The final actions of the "Race to the Sea" were the **Battle of the Yser** (October 18–November 30) and the bloody **First Battle of Ypres** (October 30–November 24), in which the BEF was nearly wiped out in a successful, gallant defense against a heavily reinforced German drive, ordered by Falkenhayn, who expected to capture the Channel ports. The British were aided by French troops, under Foch, rushed north by Joffre.

French poilus march single file through a dense field of barbed wire

1914, December 14–24. General Allied Attack. From Nieuport to Verdun an allied offensive beat unsuccessfully for 10 red days against the rapidly growing German system of field fortifications. The era of stabilized trench warfare had begun: the spade, the machine gun, and barbed wire ringing down the curtain on maneuver, from the North Sea to the Swiss border. A costly French attempt at breaking through in Champagne—the **First Battle of Champagne** (December 20)—was still in progress as the year ended. By this time, operations on the Western Front had cost the Allies nearly 1 million casualties. German losses were almost as great.

Eastern Fronts

OPERATIONS IN EAST PRUSSIA

The Russian Offensive

1914, August 17–19. Invasions of East Prussia. The Russian Northwest Army Group under General **Yakov Grigorievich Jilinsky,** consisting of General **Pavel K. Rennenkampf**'s First and General **Alexander Samsonov**'s Second armies, advanced into East Prussia. Opposing them was German General **Max von Prittwitz'** Eighth Army, widely disposed from the Baltic south to Frankenau, and based on the fortress of Königsberg (Kaliningrad). Its mission was one of elastic defense and delay in accordance with the modified Schlieffen Plan.

1914, August 17. Battle of Stallupönen. The center of Rennenkampf's widely strung advance met General **Hermann K. von François**'s I German Corps, was badly mauled by the alert François, and was thrown back to the frontier with loss of 3,000 men. François then retired on Gumbinnen.

1914, August 20. Battle of Gumbinnen. Slowly the Russians advanced again. Prittwitz, aware also of the Russian Second Army's advance far to his southern flank, feared envelopment. Aggressive François persuaded him to attack. François's own corps smashed in the Russian right flank, driving it back for 5 miles. Other German attacks were not successful, and a drawn battle resulted.

The Tannenberg Campaign

1914, August 20. German Change in Command. Prittwitz, in near panic after his unsuccessful attack against Rennenkampf, and with Samsonov's army posing a potential threat to his line of communications, telephoned Moltke, at Coblenz, to report his decision to withdraw to the Vistula and to request reinforcements to be able to hold that river line. Moltke at once relieved Prittwitz of command, appointing in his place elderly General **Paul von Hindenburg,** called from retirement, with brilliant General Erich Ludendorff, hero of Liége (see p. 935), as his chief of staff. Thus was created a team destined for world renown.

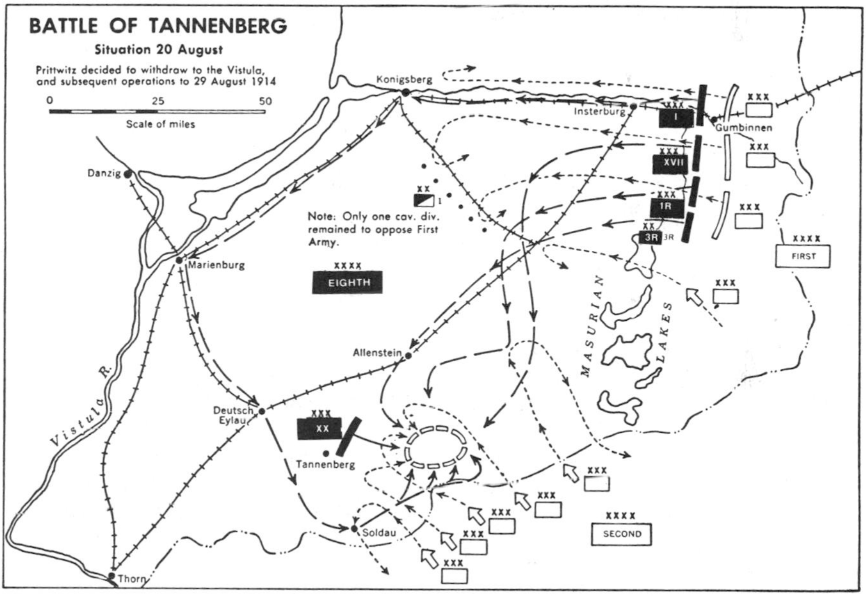

1914, August 22. Ludendorff's Plan. After studying reports from the east, Ludendorff telegraphed orders to the individual corps commanders, directing a concentration against Samsonov's Second Army, while delaying Rennenkampf's First Army farther east. Joining Hindenburg later that day for the rail trip east, Ludendorff reported his actions; Hindenburg approved. When they arrived at Marienburg, Eighth Army Headquarters, next day, they discovered that Lieutenant Colonel **Max Hoffmann,** Prittwitz' capable chief of operations, had already prepared for practically the same movements and dispositions that Ludendorff had ordered (August 20). (The coincidence is especially interesting as evidence of the uniform thought process of the German Army General Staff in dealing with an unexpected situation.) While one lone cavalry division was delaying fumbling Rennenkampf, the bulk of the German army was shifting south, by rail and road, against the equally incompetent Samsonov.

1914, August 24. Battle of Orlau-Frankenau. Advancing without reconnaissance or cavalry screen, Samsonov's central corps suddenly ran into entrenched units of the German XX Corps. Severe fighting raged all day, but the Russian center was unable to advance. Next day, while the Russian army rested, the XX Corps withdrew from Frankenau to Tannenberg, while other units of the Eighth Army hastened up to its right and left. The Germans, who had been listening to Samsonov's uncoded radio messages, now knew the locations of all Russian units, and were aware of their projected moves for the next day.

1914, August 26–31. Battle of Tannenberg. Samsonov's right flank was pushed in from the north by the German XVII and I Reserve Corps; his left was enveloped and turned by François's hard-driving I Corps; his center was struck by the XX Corps. By nightfall of August 29, the encirclement was complete as François stretched his corps across the entire Russian rear. The rest was butchery of disorganized streams of rabble trying to escape the net. Not until the 27th had Jilinsky realized that his Second Army was in real danger; his orders to Rennenkampf to move to its assistance were obeyed only in shadow. Samsonov disappeared the night of the 29th; evidently he committed suicide. Russian losses totaled 125,000 men and 500 guns; the Germans lost between 10,000 and 15,000 men. Aside from its strategic significance, the German victory was a tremendous psychological coup; Allied confidence in Russia was shattered, while the German nation was roused to such a pitch of enthusiasm that the true significance of the Battle of the Marne, which ended 2 weeks later, was overlooked.

1914, September 9–14. First Battle of the Masurian Lakes. Turning northeast, the German Eighth Army promptly moved against the Russian First Army. Again the vigorous François and his I Corps provided the *coup de grâce,* driving in the Russian left. Rennenkampf finally disengaged under cover of a stout 2-division counterattack, spoiling the German effort to gain another double envelopment. The Russians retreated, having lost 125,000 men, 150 guns, and half their transport. German losses were about 40,000.

COMMENT. *Incompetent leadership, faulty reconnaissance, lack of secrecy, and poor communications, added to an astounding state of unpreparedness and shortage of matériel, all contributed to the Russian defeats. Russia never completely recovered from these disasters.*

AUSTRIAN INVASIONS OF SERBIA

1914, July 29. Bombardment of Belgrade. The first military action of the war, this Austrian bombardment of the Serbian capital had little effect other than to enrage the Serbs.

1914, August 12–21. Battle of the Jadar. Austrian forces totaling more than 200,000 men, commanded by General **Oskar Potiorek,** crossed the Save and Drina rivers to invade Serbia from the west and northwest. They were opposed by slightly smaller numbers of tough, hardy Serb troops, inadequately equipped but battlewise from their Balkan Wars experience (see p. 926), commanded by able Marshal **Radomir Putnik.** A Serb counterattack (August 16) punished the Austrians so severely that Potiorek withdrew across the Drina.

1914, September 7–8. Renewed Austrian Invasion. Ignoring a bold, but limited, Serbian invasion of Austrian Bosnia (September 6), Potiorek made a night attack across the Drina. Putnik withdrew his troops from Bosnia and strongly counterattacked the Austrian bridgeheads.

1914, September 8–17. Battle of the Drina. Unable to eliminate the Austrian bridgeheads in 10 days of vicious, bitter fighting, and running short of ammunition, Putnik withdrew to more defensible positions southwest of Belgrade.

1914, November 5–30. Austrian Offensive. In the face of an offensive by the reinforced Austrian armies and short of ammunition, Putnik withdrew slowly and deliberately, planning to counterattack after the Austrians became overextended in the rough mountain country. He evacuated Belgrade, which the Austrians occupied (December 2). At the end of the month, ammunition, sent from France, arrived by rail from Salonika.

1914, December 3–9. Battle of Kolubra. With the Kolubra River, behind the Austrian front, in flood, Putnik launched a vigorous counterattack. The Austrian forces collapsed in the face of determined Serb assaults and were driven from Serbian terrain, their retreat covered by Austrian monitors on the Danube and Save rivers. Belgrade was recaptured (December 15). Potiorek was relieved of his command and replaced by Archduke **Eugene.** Austrian casualties in this savagely fought campaign were some 227,000 out of 450,000 engaged. Serbian losses were approximately 170,000 out of 400,000.

OPERATIONS IN POLAND

The Galician Battles

1914, August 23–September 2. Austrian Offensive. The advance into Russian Poland from Galicia was co-ordinated directly by General Conrad, the Austrian chief of staff. The First, Fourth, and Third armies (from left to right) moved north and east from the vicinity of Lemberg (Lvov) on a 200-mile front, to clash headlong with General **Nikolai Ivanov**'s Southwestern Russian Army Group (the Fourth, Fifth, Third, and Eighth armies) southwest of the Pripet Marshes. At the **Battle of Krasnik** (August 23–24) on the northern flank, the Russian Fourth Army was driven back by the Austrian First. The conflict spread as the Austrian Fourth Army struck and drove back the Russian Fifth in the **Battle of Zamosc-Komarów** (August 26–September 1). But on the southern flank, the Austrian Third Army (with some elements of the Second, belatedly arriving from the Serbian front) was thrown back on Lemberg by the Russian Third and Eighth in the Battle of **Gnila Lipa** (August 26–30). The Austrians, held on the defensive, were defeated again—this time decisively—at **Rava Ruska** (September 3–11), when the Russian Fifth Army penetrated between the Austrian First and Fourth. Abandoning Lemberg, the Austrians fell back 100 miles to the Carpathian Mountains, leaving a garrison in the key fortress of Przemysl. With all the remainder of Galicia now in their hands, the Russians prepared for further advances into the Carpathians. Austrian losses in this campaign amounted to more than 250,000 killed and wounded and 100,000 prisoners. There is no record of Russian losses, which must have been comparable.

Operations in Western Poland

1914, September 17–28. German Movement to Assist Austrians. Falkenhayn ordered Hindenburg to assist the defeated Austrians in Galicia and to prevent a Russian invasion of Silesia. With extraordinary efficiency, 4 corps were transferred by rail in 750 trains from the Eighth Army to the vicinity of the Austrian north flank, near Cracow. There they became the Ninth German Army, commanded directly by Hindenburg. A general Austro-German advance followed (September 28). Meanwhile, as the Germans expected, the Grand Duke Nicholas, reorganizing his armies, was preparing for a general offensive through Poland into Silesia, the heart of Germany's mineral resources. His proposed movement consisted of the Fifth, Fourth, and Ninth armies.

1914, September 28–October 31. Hindenburg's Southwest Poland Offensive. The German Ninth Army hit the Russians west of the Vistula (September 30), attaining the river line south of Warsaw (October 9). Here, with but 18 divisions to oppose the Russian 60, the German offensive was checked (October 12). Hindenburg withdrew skillfully (October 17), leaving behind him a countryside systematically ravaged, vastly impeding fumbling Russian pursuit. Meanwhile, the Austrians to the south had made some advance, but were checked at the River **San.** By the end of October, the Austro-German armies had fallen back to their original line, but had seriously delayed the projected Russian advance.

1914, November 1. Hindenburg Appointed Commander in Chief of the Austro-German Eastern Front. He was told he could expect no reinforcements, despite the fact that the Russians had renewed their forward movement. Skillfully, in accordance with Ludendorff's plan, the German Ninth Army—the only mass of maneuver available—was shifted northwest again to the Posen-Thorn area, leaving another wide gap of "scorched earth" in front of the overwhelming Russian concentration southwest of Warsaw.

1914, November 11–25. Battle of Lódź.

The German Ninth Army, now commanded by General **August von Mackensen,** struck southeast between the First and Second Russian armies, which were protecting the northern flank of the Grand Duke's planned offensive. The Russian First Army (still under Rennenkampf) was crushed and the Second, near Lódź, was embraced by an attempted double envelopment. The key element of the German stroke was the XXV Reserve Corps, commanded by General **Reinhard von Scheffer-Boyadel.** It rolled through the gap between the Russian armies and turned south and west. The movement was foiled by the Grand Duke's prompt counterattack. The Russian Fifth Army from the south and an improvised group from the northern forces checked the German advance. Scheffer's corps was completely surrounded. In an amazing display of leadership, Scheffer not only broke through to safety but also brought back with him 16,000 prisoners and 64 captured guns. This corps marched and fought continuously for 9 days in subzero weather with a net loss of 1,500 killed and 2,800 wounded, who were also brought safely back. While Lódź was tactically a Russian victory, for the Germans it was a strategic success, since the Russian offensive was now called off, Lódź was evacuated, and the Russians fell back in a general retirement, never again to menace the German homeland. German losses in the Lódź campaign were about 35,000 killed and wounded. Russian losses are not known; a conservative estimate would be 90,000 in all. The year ended in stalemate on the Eastern Front.

The War at Sea, 1914

The British Grand Fleet, poised in its bases at Scapa Flow and Rosyth, kept the German High Seas Fleet bottled up behind the highly fortified Heligoland-Jade littoral in the North Sea. Neutral Denmark locked the Baltic gateway to both contestants by mining the Skagerrak.

Germany had 10 major warships at large around the world, based on far-flung colonial ports. Six small British overseas expeditions—4 from England and 2 from Australia and New Zealand—moved (August) to dry up the German naval bases. **Togoland,** the **Cameroons, Southwest Africa, Samoa,** and some of the German Pacific islands were taken in late 1914 or early 1915. In **German East Africa,** however, Colonel (soon General) **Paul von Lettow-Vorbeck** repulsed a British landing effort at **Tanga** (November 3–4) and would carry on an amazing offensive-defensive campaign for 4 years. Except as an example of indomitable leadership, Lettow-Vorbeck's operations were of no significance in the war. Japan, entering the war on the Allied side (August 23), besieged **Tsingtao,** the only German base on the China coast, taking it November 7. Japan also occupied Germany's Marshall, Mariana, Palau, and Caroline island groups.

The 10 scattered German cruisers, deprived of their bases, waged a gallant and aggressive hit-and-run war until overwhelmed or blockaded. The High Seas Fleet at home was limited to sporadic cruiser raids, mine sowing, and submarine warfare.

1914, August 4. The *Goeben-Breslau* Incident. In the Mediterranean, the German battle cruiser *Goeben* and light cruiser *Breslau,* under the command of Vice Admiral **Wilhelm von Souchon,** shelled the French Algerian ports of Bône and Philippeville. Then, in anticipation of a British declaration of war, the German vessels headed east toward Turkey, Germany's secret ally. They met the British battle cruisers *Indomitable* and *Indefatigable* steaming west. The British commander, following instructions from Vice-Admiral Sir **A. Berkeley Milne,** made no effort to stop the Germans, knowing that, although France and Germany were already at war, Britain's ultimatum to Berlin would not expire until midnight. Admiral von Souchon, knowing that the British warships had superior fire power, also refrained from action. The opposing squadrons passed one another at close range without saluting, like two strange dogs; each side was cleared for action,

German cruiser *Emden*

each had shotted guns trained on the other. The British then attempted to follow Souchon, but he skillfully eluded them after a brush with the cruiser squadron of Rear Admiral **E. C. Troubridge** southwest of Greece (August 6–7) and reached the Dardanelles safely (August 10). Both German ships and their personnel then passed into the Turkish Navy, giving that nation naval supremacy in the Black Sea and contributing to her later entry into the war on the side of the Central Powers (October 29; see p. 946).

1914, August 28. Battle of Heligoland Bight. British light cruisers raided into German waters, coaxing a fight. German cruisers emerged, whereupon Vice Admiral Sir **David Beatty**'s battle-cruiser squadron, lurking in support of his light cruisers, drove them back with loss of 4 ships and some 1,000 men.

1914, August–October. Cruise of the *Königsberg*. The German light cruiser, stationed on the East African coast, engaged and sank the British light cruiser *Pegasus* off Mombasa (August 6). She was later cornered by other British naval units and forced to seek refuge up the Rufiji River, German East Africa (October 30), where she remained blockaded.

1914, August–November. Cruise of the *Emden*. This fast light cruiser was detached from the China Squadron of German Admiral **Maximilian von Spee** (August 22). Under daring Captain **Karl von Müller,** she sailed into the Indian Ocean, where she harassed British shipping, taking 21 prizes and destroying ships and cargo valued at over $10 million. She bombarded Madras (September 22). The end of this gallant lone-wolf cruiser came when she was sunk in a hard-fought action with the Australian cruiser *Sydney* at the Cocos Islands (November 9).

1914, September–October. German Submarine Operations. *U-9,* off the Dutch coast, sank in quick succession the British cruisers *Aboukir, Hogue,* and *Cressy,* with a loss of 1,400 lives (September 22). A U-boat raid on Scapa Flow (October 18), while unsuccessful, resulted in the temporary transfer of the British Grand Fleet to Rosyth on the Scottish coast while antisubmarine nets were installed at Scapa. The cruiser H.M.S. *Hawk* was torpedoed and sunk (October 15). The battleship *Audacious* struck a German mine, laid by a submarine off the Irish coast, and sank (October 27).

1914, November 1. Battle of Coronel. After the outbreak of war, Admiral von Spee's China Squadron—2 heavy and 3 light cruisers—crossed the Pacific to the Chilean coast, refueling from colliers. Off the west coast of South America, British Vice Admiral Sir **Christopher Cradock,** with 2 elderly heavy cruisers and 1 light cruiser, plus a converted merchant-ship auxiliary cruiser, searched for the German squadron. Despite Admiralty orders, Cradock had discarded the old battleship *Canopus* as being too slow to hunt the speedy Germans. The 2 squadrons met off Coronel. On paper the fire power of the 2 forces was about equal, but Cradock had only 2 9.2-inch guns (on his flagship, the *Good Hope*), while Spee had 16 8.2-inchers on the *Scharnhorst* and *Gneisenau*. The more numerous British light guns never had a chance to get into the fight because Spee —foiling all efforts of the British ships to close—systematically battered them at long range with his 2 heavy cruisers. He sank the 2 British heavy cruisers with all on board. The light cruiser *Glasgow*, and the auxiliary cruiser *Otranto* obeyed Cradock's orders to run for it and escaped. News of the disaster shocked Britain. The Admiralty feared that Spee would take his squadron around Cape Horn into the South Atlantic. The battlecruisers *Invincible* and *Inflexible,* under Vice Admiral Sir **F. D. Sturdee,** were rushed from home waters to seek Spee.

1914, November 3, December 16. German Coastal Raids against Britain. German cruisers raided the British east coast off Gorleston, but were driven off (November 3). In another raid, German heavy cruisers bombarded Scarborough and Hartlepool (December 16). These "hit-and-run" affairs killed and wounded many civilians.

1914, December 8. Battle of the Falkland Islands. Spee, planning to run into Port Stanley, Falkland Islands, to raid the British wireless and coaling station, discovered Sturdee's squadron there, refueling. The surprised Germans took to their heels. Sturdee, pursuing, destroyed the German ships at long range. The light cruiser *Dresden* escaped and remained at large for 3 more months. Most of the crews of the sunken German ships perished—some 1,800 men—although a few were rescued by the British.

1914, December 25. Loss of the *Jean Bart*. The French battleship was torpedoed by an Austrian submarine in the Straits of Otranto.

SUMMARY. *By year's end, except for the High Seas Fleet in the Jade, and the Baltic command based on Kiel, the German flag had been practically swept from the seas. Allied maritime traffic was uninterrupted, while Germany was already feeling the pinch of naval blockade. The German naval high command now focused its attention on the one major weapon left to it on the high seas: the submarine.*

The Turkish Fronts, 1914

1914, October 29. Turkish Declaration of War against the Allies. This was proclaimed by the guns of the Turkish fleet (including the erstwhile German *Goeben* and *Breslau*), now commanded by German Admiral von Souchon, in a bombardment without warning of Odessa, Sevastopol, and Theodosia on the Russian Black Sea coast. This Turkish alignment with the Central Powers closed the Dardanelles to the Allies, thus physically separating Russia from them.

CAUCASUS FRONT

1914, November–December. Turkish Offensive. Against the sage advice of General **Otto Liman von Sanders,** chief of the German military mission to Turkey, **Enver** Pasha, Turkish war minister, began an invasion of the Russian Caucasus.

1914, December 29. Battle of Sarikamish. The Turkish advance toward Kars was halted and rebuffed with severe losses by Russian General **Vorontsov** in winter snows. The struggle here continued as the year ended.

MEDITERRANEAN REGION

1914, November–December. British Reaction. Britain announced the annexation of Cyprus (November 5). Declaring a protectorate over Egypt (December 18), the British began moving troops there for the defense of the Suez Canal. Meanwhile, British cruisers shelled the Dardanelles forts without effect (November 30).

MESOPOTAMIAN FRONT

1914, October 23. British Landings. British Indian Army troops, who had already been rushed to Bahrein to protect oil refineries there, began an invasion of southern Mesopotamia. Local Turkish garrisons were driven back; **Basra** was captured by the British (November 23).

OPERATIONS IN 1915

The Global Situation

Turkey's entrance had changed the war's complexion. Russia, already shaken by the reverses of 1914, was now almost completely cut off from Franco-British war supplies, upon which she was dependent for a long-continued war. The western Allies, at the same time, were anxious to regain access to the Ukrainian grain fields. These considerations prompted a strategic debate in Britain between "Easterners" and "Westerners." A strident segment of British officialdom, led by capable and energetic Winston Churchill, First Lord of the Admiralty, urged immediate action to seize the Dardanelles and to restore the vital Mediterranean–Black Sea supply route to Russia through the Turkish Straits. British War Minister Field Marshal Horatio Herbert, Lord Kitchener, was equally insistent that a decision be obtained on the Western Front, and deplored any diminution of strength there for a peripheral operation in the east. He was strongly supported in this position by French military and political opinion. Nevertheless, in early January, after lengthy and heated debate in the British War Council, an amphibious operation against the Dardanelles was grudgingly approved.

In the Central Powers' camp also, strategical opinion was divided. The Hindenburg-Ludendorff team urged an all-out effort against faltering Russia. Falkenhayn, though reconciled to the fact that the war had become one of attrition, believed that it would have to be won in the west; he predicted that tactical victories in the east would be meaningless because of the space of Russia and her vast manpower resources. The Kaiser sided with Hindenburg. Accordingly, the Germans adopted a defensive posture in the west, while seeking a decision against Russia.

Western Front

1915, January 1–March 30. Allied Offensive in Artois and Champagne. This, a continuation of the **First Battle of Champagne** (see p. 940), was a major effort by Joffre to liberate the extensive and valuable areas of France held by the Germans. A series of attacks against the western face of the Noyon salient and in the area between Reims and Verdun were unsuccessful. Limited German counterattacks along the La Bassé Canal and near Soissons stabilized the situation (January 8–February 5). Renewed Allied assaults (March) made little headway. The British made an initial breakthrough in a well-planned attack at **Neuve Chapelle** (March 10), but poor management prevented an adequate follow-up; the Germans quickly re-established the line (March 13). French casualties approached 400,000 during this period; British and German losses were also heavy.

1915, January 19–20. First German Air Raids on England. Bombing attacks by Zeppelin dirigible airships (under German Navy control) caused relatively minor casualties and more anger than panic. Eighteen more such raids occurred during the year. The largest of these was a mass attack on London (October 13).

1915, April 6–15. Battle of the Woëvre. Repeated French assaults against the north face of the St.-Mihiel salient were repulsed with heavy losses.

1915, April 22–May 25. Second Battle of Ypres. Allied preparations for another co-ordinated offensive were spoiled by a surprise German attack preceded by a cloud of chlorine gas emitted from some 5,000 cylinders. This was the first use of poison gas in the west. Two German corps drove through 2 terrorized French divisions and bit deeply into British lines, creating a wide gap. The Germans, however, had made no preparations to exploit such a breakthrough and had few reserves available because of their build-up in the east. Local counterattacks by the British Second Army finally stemmed the German advance after bitter fighting. German

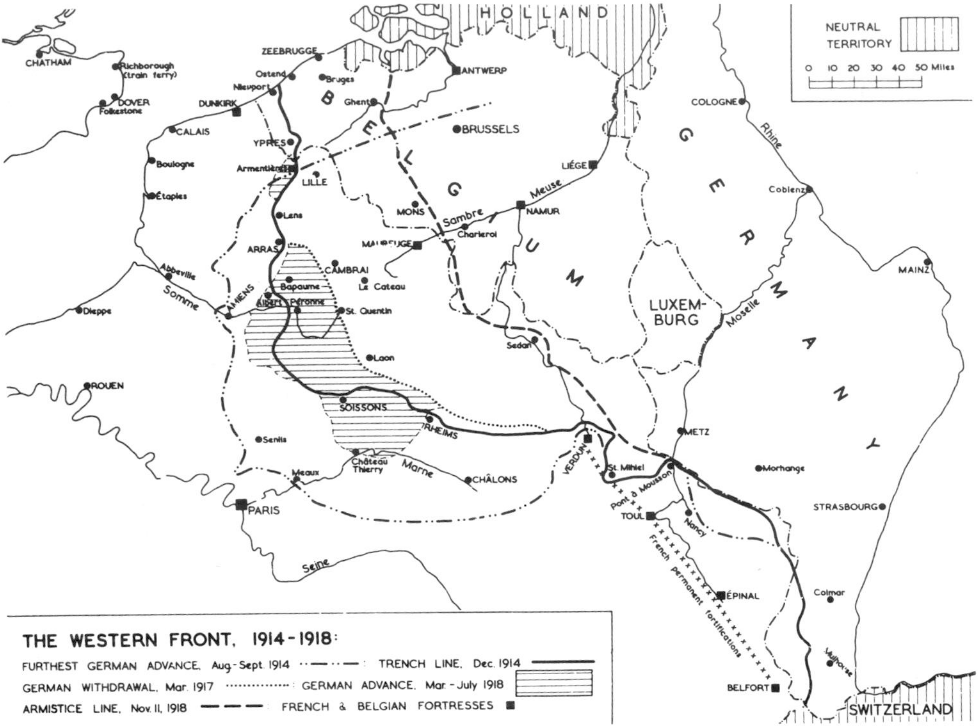

losses were some 35,000 men; the British lost 60,000, the French about 10,000.

1915, May–June. Battles of Festubert and Souchez (Second Battle of Artois). After limited gains, the British were stopped near Festubert (May 9–26). The French did only slightly better in their efforts to seize the commanding height of **Vimy Ridge** near Souchez (May 16–June 30). The Allies, exhausted by their costly and unsuccessful assaults during the first half of the year, spent the rest of the summer in resting, reorganizing, and reinforcing. The Germans, who had also suffered severely, were happy to take advantage of the lull, and by the end of the summer had also reinforced the west with troops from their successful operations in the east. Both sides had come perilously close to expending their ammunition reserves and were now waiting for munitions production to catch up with consumption.

1915, September 25–November 6. Renewed Allied Offensives in Artois and Champagne. This was another major co-ordinated effort planned by Joffre, and was again unsuccessful. In the **Second Battle of Champagne** the French lost more than 100,000 men and the Germans some 75,000. At the same time, in the **Third Battle of Artois,** the French continued their attacks against **Vimy Ridge** (September 25–October 30) while the British, a few miles north, smashed at **Loos** (September 25–October 14). The minor gains made were out of proportion to the casualties suffered: more than 100,000 French, 60,000 British, 65,000 German.

1915, December 17. Change in British Command. Blamed for the failure at Loos, Field Marshal French was relieved and General Sir **Douglas Haig** was placed in command of the BEF, which now comprised 3 armies.

COMMENT. *Increase of lethal fire power, both machine gun and field artillery, had revolutionized combat tactics and had given the advantage to the defense, which was able to bring up reserves to limit a penetration before the attackers could move forward sufficient reserves and artillery to exploit a breakthrough. This was particularly critical on the Western Front, where a continuous battle line prevented classical offensive maneuvers. The Germans, recognizing the change long before the Allies, had adopted an elastic defense, in 2 or more widely separated lines, highly organized with entrenchments and barbed wire, heavy in machine guns, and supported by artillery echeloned in depth. Assaulting troops broke through the first line only to be decimated by the fire from the succeeding lines and pounded by artillery beyond the range of their own guns.*

Appalling losses had been suffered during 1915 on both sides: 612,000 German, 1,292,000 French, and 279,000 British. The year ended with no appreciable shift in the hostile battle lines scarring the land from the North Sea to the Swiss Alps.

The Italian Front

1915, May 23. Italy Declares War on Austria. Adroit Allied diplomacy, offering substantial territorial gains, caused Italy to abrogate the Triple Alliance and to enter the war. The total strength of the Italian Army, commanded by General **Luigi Cadorna,** was about 875,000, but it was deficient in artillery, transport, and ammunition reserves. The Italian plan was to hold the Trentino salient into Italy by offensive-defensive action, while operating eastward offensively in the Isonzo salient projecting into Austrian territory. The immediate objective was Gorizia, but Italian military men dreamed of advancing through Trieste to Vienna.

Austrian Dispositions. Despite the Triple Alliance, Austria had heavily fortified the entire mountain frontier with Italy. Austrian Archduke Eugene was in over-all command of the Italian front. General **Svetozan Borojevic von Bojna,** with some 100,000 men, held the critical Isonzo sector.

1915, June 23–July 7. First Battle of the Isonzo. The Italian Second Army (General **Pietro Frugoni**) and Third Army

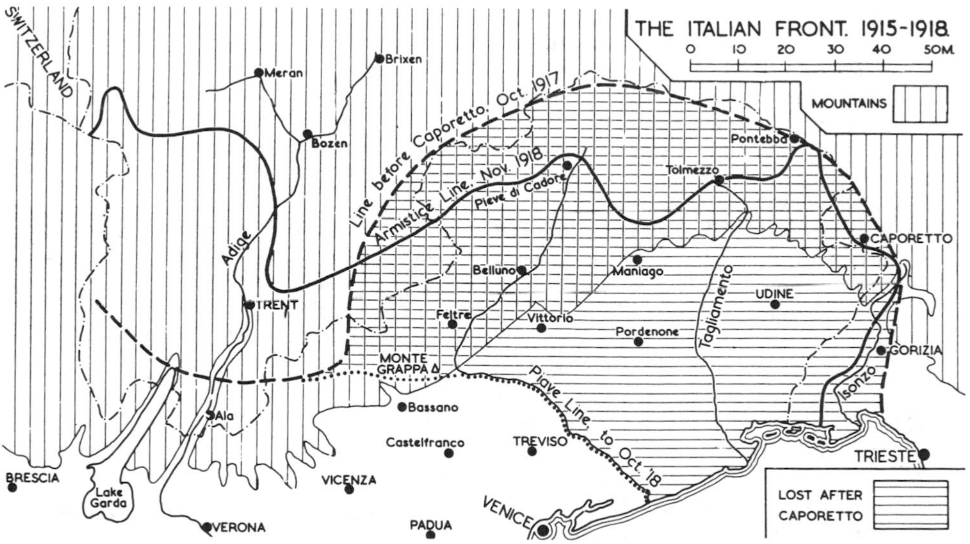

(**Emanuele Filiberto, Duke of Aosta**), totaling approximately 200,000 men and 200 guns, battered in vain against the Austrian defenses.

1915, July 18–August 3. Second Isonzo. Cadorna, bringing up more artillery, tried again. The Austrians, reinforced by 2 additional divisions, held firm. The Italians broke off the struggle when their artillery ammunition gave out. Italian losses in these two battles amounted to about 60,000 men; the Austrian casualties totaled nearly 45,000.

1915, October 18–November 4. Third Isonzo. The Italians, reorganized and strengthened, and supported now by 1,200 guns, struck once more at Gorizia and were again repulsed.

1915, November 10–December 2. Fourth Isonzo. This was really a continuation of the third battle. When the offensive broke off, no material gain had been made to show for the Italian loss of 117,000 men in the 2 battles. The Austrians had lost almost 72,000 men.

COMMENT. *As in France, the invul-*

nerability of highly organized positions to frontal assault had been proven. The Austrian defense was skillful; the Italian offensive tactics were inept, despite the gallantry shown by their infantry on many occasions. The Italian strategic objective—capture of Trieste, thence on the road to Vienna through the Ljubljana Gap and the Danubian Plain—was sound. It was, in fact, the only offensive open to Italy, since successful northern movement of major forces through the Alps not only led nowhere but was patently impossible. Germany took no part in this campaign, since Italy was technically not at war with her; this did not increase Austro-German cordiality.

The Eastern Front

HINDENBURG'S WINTER OFFENSIVE, JANUARY–MARCH

The Central Powers, reinforcing their armies, launched a great double offensive under Hindenburg. The Austro-German South Army (German General **Alexander von Linsingen**) struck northwest through the Carpathians on Lemberg. On its left the Austrian Third Army (General von Borojevic) was to rescue Przemysl from siege, while on the right the Austrian Seventh Army (General **Karl von Pflanzer-Baltin**) supported the main effort. From East Prussia the German Eighth and Tenth armies under Hindenburg's direct control struck east from the Masurian Lakes.

1915, January 31. Battle of Bolimov. This was a feint by the German Ninth Army, aimed at Warsaw, designed to distract Russian attention. Poison gas was used for the first time. The innovation was not impressive; the gas was not very effective in freezing temperatures and the Russians did not report the gas attack to the other Allies (see p. 947).

1915, February 7–21. The Winter Battle (or Masuria, or Second Masurian Lakes). Farther north, the Eighth Army, in a blinding snowstorm, began Hindenburg's offensive by hitting the left flank of Baron **Siever**'s Russian Tenth Army (February 7). Next day the new German Tenth Army (General **Hermann von Eichhorn**), to the north, rolled up the Russian right. Despite desperate defense, the Russians were rapidly driven back into the **Augustow Forest.** There the Russian XX Corps, after resisting heroically, was surrounded and surrendered (February 21); its defense had enabled the other 3 corps of its Tenth Army to escape encirclement. Some 90,000 prisoners were taken. In all, Russian casualties were about 200,000 men in this campaign, an impressive tactical victory for the Germans but without great strategic value. A newly formed Russian army—the Twelfth (General **Wenzel von Plehve**)—counterattacking Hindenburg's right (February 22), halted further German progress after a 70-mile advance.

1915, February–March. Austrian Failure in Galicia. Linsingen's Carpathian advance broke down in freezing snow on a poor road net. Pflanzer-Baltin was initially more successful, capturing **Czernowitz** with 60,000 prisoners (February 17), but his further progress was halted by a Russian counterattack. Borojevic's efforts to relieve Przemysl failed.

1915, March 22. Surrender of Przemysl. After a siege of 194 days, the fortress and its garrison of 110,000 men surrendered to the Russians.

1915, March–April. Russian Counteroffensive. Following these defensive successes, the Russians resumed their advance through the Carpathians, but were checked by the Austro-German South Army (April 2–25).

THE GERMAN SPRING–SUMMER OFFENSIVE, MAY–AUGUST

1915, April. German Build-up in the East. Under instructions from the Kaiser, Falkenhayn now gave full priority to the Eastern Front. Sending reinforcements, he came east to assume direct over-all command. While Hindenburg's army group kept the Russians busy north of Warsaw, the new Eleventh German Army, under General August von Mackensen, supported by Austrian units, was to make the main effort farther south between Tarnow and Gorlice.

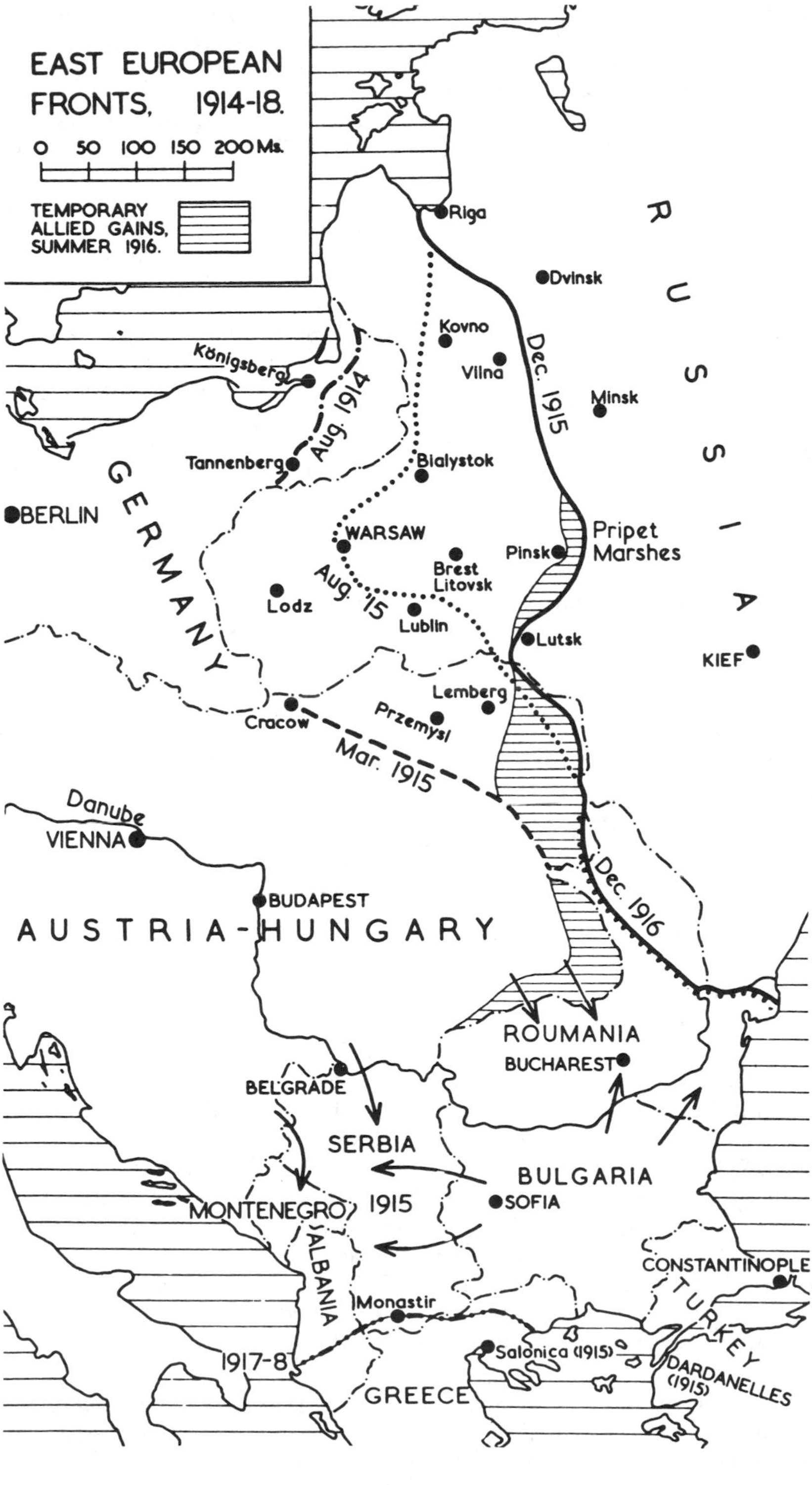
EAST EUROPEAN FRONTS, 1914-18.
0 50 100 150 200 Ms.
TEMPORARY ALLIED GAINS, SUMMER 1916.
RUSSIA
GERMANY
AUSTRIA-HUNGARY
Riga
Dvinsk
Kovno
Vilna
Minsk
Dec. 1915
Königsberg
Aug. 1914
Tannenberg
Bialystok
BERLIN
WARSAW
Pinsk
Pripet Marshes
Brest Litovsk
Lodz
Aug. 15
Lublin
Lutsk
KIEF
Lemberg
Przemysl
Cracow
Mar. 1915
Danube
VIENNA
BUDAPEST
Dec. 1916
ROUMANIA
BUCHAREST
BELGRADE
SERBIA
BULGARIA
1915
SOFIA
MONTENEGRO
ALBANIA
CONSTANTINOPLE
TURKEY
Monastir
Salonica (1915)
1917-8
GREECE
DARDANELLES (1915)

1915, May 2–June 27. The Gorlice-Tarnow Breakthrough. Concentrating superior force for the main effort, the Austro-German armies crashed through the Russian Third Army on a 28-mile front, following a 4-hour bombardment. The southern face of the great Russian Polish-Galician salient began to crumble. Przemysl was retaken (June 3), Lemberg occupied (June 22), and the Dniester crossed (June 23–27).

1915, June–September. Russian Retreat. Thrusting into northern Poland, General **Max von Gallwitz'** new German Twelfth Army advanced toward Warsaw, which was abandoned by the Russians (August 4–7). The entire Russian front was in complete collapse; another Cannae seemed to be inevitable as the salient melted back to the Bug (August 18). Brest Litovsk fell (August 25) and Grodno (September 2). The occupation of Vilna (September 19) marked the high-water mark of the colossal 300-mile advance. Skillfully, however, Grand Duke Nicholas preserved his armies intact, and they withdrew in fairly good order, evading German attempts at envelopment. Autumn rains finally turned roads into quagmires, and the reeling Russians were able to halt the German advance. By year's end the Eastern Front was a line running north and south from Riga on the Baltic to the eastern end of the Carpathians.

COMMENT. *In sharp distinction from the Western Front, this had been a war of movement on a grand scale, part of it in mountainous terrain, all of it hampered by primitive road conditions. The winter campaign was particularly arduous. German operations had been both methodical and brilliant. Excellent staff co-ordination enabled surprise, facilitated by employing short, intensive artillery preparations and by moving assault troops into position only at the last possible moment—usually at night. Austrian operations were spotty, due partly to lower professional standards and partly to friction between the German and Austrian high commands. The Austrians resented German arrogance. On the Russian side, poor troop leadership and lack of weapons, munitions, and supplies were jointly responsible for defeat. Only the marvelous capacity of the Russian soldier to fight while enduring incredible hardships, and the ability of the Grand Duke Nicholas to piece and patch together his baffled, defeated armies, prevented loss of the war in mid-1915. His reward was to be relieved of command (August 21) and banished to the Caucasus front. Czar* **Nicholas II** *assumed personal command of the Eastern Front, with General* **Mikhail Alekseyev** *his chief of staff. Russian casualties on this front in 1915 were more than 2 million men, of whom about half had been captured. Combined German and Austrian casualties were in excess of 1 million.*

The Balkan Front, 1915

Direct communication between Turkey and her allies was essential to the Central Powers if the Turkish Straits were to be held and Russia kept isolated from the western Allies. The direct railway line passing through Serbia had been closed since the beginning of the war; munitions from Germany passed through neutral Rumania until June, when Rumania closed the channel. Both sides pressured Bulgaria to join the war; Germany won when the Gallipoli invasion was repulsed (August 15; see p. 955). The Central Powers at once prepared to renew the attack on Serbia. Her call for assistance was answered by Greek mobilization against threatening Bulgaria; Greece requested 150,000 Allied troops to aid her in assisting Serbia. Small French and British expeditionary forces soon disembarked at Salonika (October 9). On the same day a political upheaval in Greece completely changed the situation; pro-German King **Constantine** dismissed his pro-Allied prime minister, **Eleutherios Venizelos,** and announced he would keep Greece neutral.

1915, October 6. Austro-German-Bulgarian Invasion of Serbia. Meanwhile 2 armies —1 Austrian (General **Hermann Kövess von Kövessháza**) and 1 German (General von Gallwitz)—drove south across the Serbian Save-Danube border. Two Bulgarian armies struck west (October 11); 1 on Nish, the other on Skoplje. Newly promoted Field Marshal von Mackensen was in over-all command of the joint campaign; the plan was Falkenhayn's. Putnik's Serbian Army, struck in front and flank by forces nearly double its strength —330,000 men—escaped envelopment but was rolled up and driven southwest in a series of bitter encounters. General **Maurice P. E. Sarrail,** commanding the French element of the allied force at Salonika, made a tentative stroke up the Vardar Valley to link with the Serbs, but was turned back by superior Bulgarian forces. General Sir **Bryan T. Mahon,** commanding the British element, got no farther than the Bulgarian border.

1915, November 24. Serbian Retreat. While the Allied Salonika forces entrenched against Bulgarian pressure, the Serbian Army withdrew into Montenegro and Albania. After a dismal retreat through the snow-covered mountains, the remnants of the Serbian Army, accompanied by a horde of civilian refugees, reached the Adriatic, pursued by Austrian General Kövess. Serbian losses were more than 100,000 killed or wounded, 160,000 taken prisoner, and 900 guns. The survivors were transferred by Italian and French ships to the island of Corfu (January), where they were refitted by the Allies. Montenegro was also occupied by the Austrians.

COMMENT. *Serbia was doomed when Bulgaria entered the war. Allied intervention attempts were too little, too late, and further complicated by disunity of command. Sarrail and Mahon at Salonika were acting under separate instructions from their respective governments. To make matters worse for them, they were in the unenviable situation of occupying neutral territory, with the Greek Army potentially threatening their rear.*

The Turkish Fronts

THE DARDANELLES AND GALLIPOLI

The Preliminaries

1915, February–March 18. Allied Naval Assault. A Franco-British fleet under British Vice Admiral **Sackville Carden** attempted a systematic reduction of the for-

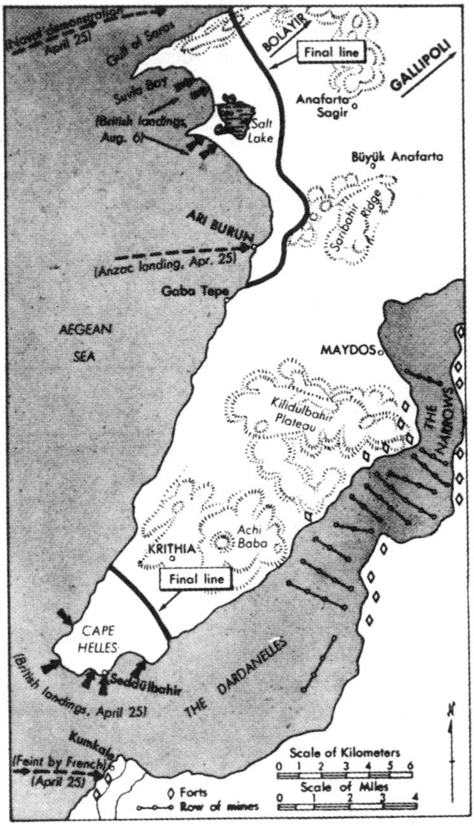

Gallipoli campaign

midable fortifications lining both sides of the narrow straits. More than 100 medium- and heavy-caliber Turkish guns swept the surface in cross fire, with 11 mine belts and an antisubmarine net below the surface. Long-range Allied bombardment of the outer forts (February 19) was followed by a second (February 25), which silenced them. After preliminary shelling and mine sweeping, the principal fortifications at the Narrows were attacked (March 18). Carden having broken down physically, Rear Admiral **John de Robeck** took command. He had, besides smaller craft, 16 battleships—including the *Queen Elizabeth,* most powerful superdreadnought then afloat, carrying 8 15-inch guns. By midafternoon the Turkish Narrows batteries were also silenced. Then 3 old battleships were suddenly sunk in an undetected minefield and 3 others were disabled, 1 of them by gunfire. Actually, at this time, the Turks were at the end of their resources; their ammunition was nearly expended, some batteries had been demolished, and all fire-control communications put out of action. But de Robeck did not know that. He called off the attack and hurried his 10 remaining capital ships out of the Strait.

1915, March–April. Assembling of the Army Expedition. Meanwhile, a hastily gathered British expeditionary force (including 1 French division) under General **Ian Hamilton** was en route from England and Egypt to the Gallipoli Peninsula. Hamilton himself was at this moment an observer on board a British warship. The total strength of his force was 78,000 men. As the first elements gathered at Mudros Bay on the island of Lemnos (mid-March), it was discovered that the contingent from England had been loaded haphazardly, with guns and ammunition on separate ships. The transports had to move (March 25) to Alexandria, Egypt, where they were combat-loaded (by unit) with men, their guns, ammunition, and equipment all on the same ship. This caused a month's delay, while the Turks, fully alerted to the impending landings, improved their dispositions. German General Liman von Sanders, in command, had some 60,000 men on the peninsula, disposed in an elastic defense.

The First Landings, April 25

The plan provided for 2 daylight assaults, with naval gunfire support. One of these landings was to be at Cape Helles on the tip of the peninsula; the other—beyond mutual-support distance—was to be about 15 miles farther north at Ari Burnu, on the western side of the peninsula. At the same time, the French division was to make a diversionary landing on the Asiatic side of the Strait, while a naval demonstration at Bulair—the neck of the peninsula, 50 miles northeast of Helles—distracted Sanders' attention.

At Ari Burnu the Anzacs (Australian and New Zealand Army Corps), landing in force, moved up the slopes toward **Chunuk Bair,** a height dominating the entire peninsula and the Narrows beyond. But a young Turkish reserve division commander with an eye for terrain moved first. Personally leading a battalion, **Mustafa Kemal** rushed for the height, the remainder of his division quickly following. Even though his troops were outnumbered, Kemal's vicious counterattack from the ridge drove the Anzacs back to the beach with a loss of 5,000 men. Here, ordered by Hamilton to hold on, the Anzacs dug in to retain a narrow beachhead.

At Helles, the 29th British Division landed on 5 beaches in a welter of mismanagement, incurring murderous losses. But a part of the division, overwhelming the Turkish beach defense, made its way gallantly almost to its objective, **Achi Baba,** a dominant hill mass. The division commander, safe on his command ship offshore, was not on the spot to handle the situation. Lacking further orders, the British troops stopped to brew tea below the still-unoccupied height. When they renewed their advance, it was too late. The Turks had occupied the hill in force.

Chunuk Bair and Achi Baba would never be taken by the British. Without either of these 2 critical heights the landings were doomed to failure. As the Turks ringed the tiny beachheads with entrenchments, the British found themselves involved in the same kind of trench warfare they had known on the Western Front—but with even less room for maneuver.

The Second Landing, August 6–8

Following 3 months of the bitterest kind of fighting on the rocky slopes of the peninsula, Hamilton, reinforced by 3 more British divisions, attempted a co-ordinated assault. Meanwhile, although British submarines had actually penetrated the Straits and sunk some Turkish craft, German submarines and Turkish destroyers accounted for 3 more British battleships off the Gallipoli coast. The Allied capital ships sought protected harbors; the *Queen Elizabeth* herself was ordered home. So Hamilton's second assault was made without adequate naval gunfire support.

The Anzacs at Ari Burnu were to make the main effort with a night attack, driving for Chunuk Bair and other heights on the Sari Bair ridge. The new divisions, landing at Suvla Bay to the north, were to make a secondary attack. From the Helles position a holding attack was to pin down Turkish reserves.

The holding attack fulfilled its mission, but the Anzac attack bogged down in the darkness. Only the Suvla Bay landing, made without serious opposition, promised success. But General Sir **Frederick Stopford,** the corps commander, lacked vigor and drive. The advance lagged until Turkish reinforcements had time to come up, and again it was too late.

The entire operation had failed. Russia was permanently cut off from her allies. Hamilton was relieved (October 15), General Sir **Charles Monro** taking his place. Monro's recommendation for an evacuation was approved (November 23). Excellent planning, staff co-ordination, and prompt execution did the rest. By December 10, all supplies and many of the troops had been moved out. The remaining crust of 35,000 men slipped away under the eyes of the unsuspecting Turks, completing (January 8–9, 1916) a masterpiece of deception without loss of a single man.

Allied casualties for the entire Dardanelles campaign amounted to 252,000. The Turks lost almost as many: 251,000, but of these 21,000 died of disease.

COMMENT. *With possible exception of the Crimean War, the Gallipoli expedition was the most poorly mounted and ineptly controlled operation in modern British military history. Surprise had been lost even before the inception of the plan, for a premature bombardment of the outer Dardanelles defenses by a British naval force early in the war (November, 1914) had awakened both Turks and Germans to the danger. Under Liman von Sanders' competent direction the fortifications had been vastly strengthened. The prize was a rich one, for success would mean keeping Russia in the war and probably knocking Turkey out; its attainment should have been confided to a single commander, provided with the best of means. Instead, with improvised organizations, both naval and army commanders worked independently.*

De Robeck's decision to break off the naval action (March 18) when success was practically in his hands was particularly questionable. He had suddenly lost 6 of his 16 capital ships. But he knew a supporting expeditionary force was on the way. Under those conditions, if only one battleship had survived to run the gantlet and place Constantinople under its guns, his mission would have been fulfilled. But Nelsons and Farraguts are few and far between.

Back in the War Office, Kitchener failed to assure compliance with logistical, strategic, and tactical fundamentals in mounting the expeditionary force. And he refused Hamilton's requests for adequate forces and staff officers.

Hamilton possibly erred in the landing operations by trying to direct them by remote control from a warship. It has been suggested that he should have been ashore to see for himself and to whip his erring subordinates into decisive action. He should not have put up with the incompetence of some of these. However, it can be argued that he did as competent a job as was possible under the circumstances, and with the limited means and subordinates provided him by Kitchener.

Sharply contrasting with all the previous fumbling was the planning of the evacuation by General Monro and its execution by General **William Birdwood.**

On the Turkish side, German Liman von Sanders conducted a brilliant active defense. Mustafa Kemal, his chief subordinate, shone as an aggressive field commander. The fighting men on both sides performed wonders under most arduous conditions.

THE CAUCASUS FRONT

1915, January 1–3. Battle of Sarikamish (continued). Russian General Vorontsov, with about 100,000 men, lay in the vicinity of Kars to oppose Enver's advance. Colossal mismanagement of a winter campaign had frittered away at least 15,000 of Enver's 95,000 strength through frostbite and desertion before the battle had begun. The Turk's dream of a wide envelopment of the Russians was spoiled by a Russian counterattack which smashed his army (January 3). The Turks lost 30,000 dead, while thousands more froze to death in retreat. Only about 18,000 effectives reached Erzerum. Enver gave up the field command and returned to Constantinople. Vorontsov failed to seize advantage by a pursuit; he was replaced by General **Nikolai Yudenich,** who had more initiative.

1915, April–May. Armenian Revolt. Turkish massacres of Armenians, on suspicion they were aiding the Russians, precipitated an Armenian revolt. The rebels seized the fortress of Van (April 20), holding it until the arrival of the Russians (May 19).

1915, July. Battles of Malazgirt and Kara Killisse (Karakose). The new Turkish commander, **Abdul Kerim,** struck and defeated a Russian corps north of Lake

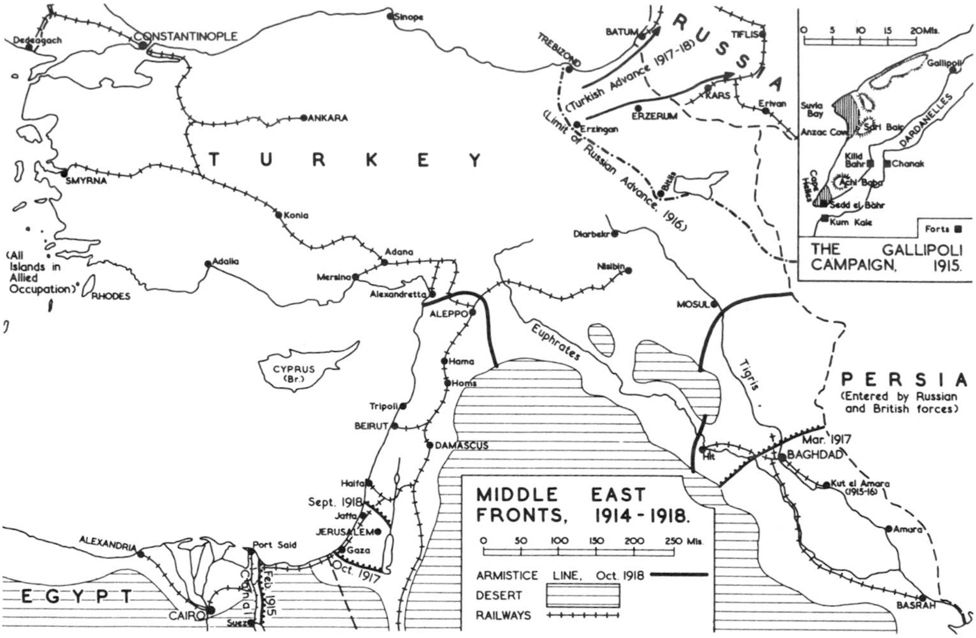

Van (July 16), near the site of the Battle of Manzikert (see p. 303). The Turks cautiously advanced eastward, but Yudenich sent a force of 22,000, mainly Cossacks, under General **N. N. Baratov,** to strike the Turk left, causing Kerim to withdraw after sustaining heavy casualties.

1915, August 5. Turkish Recapture of Van. In the ebb and flow of fighting in the Armenian mountains, the Russians were forced to evacuate Van, which the Turks promptly reoccupied.

1915, September 24. Arrival of Grand Duke Nicholas. Appointed Viceroy of Caucasia, Nicholas retained Yudenich in field command, though taking active part in planning. Preparation for a large-scale offensive began.

EGYPT AND PALESTINE

By the opening of 1915, British defense of the vital Suez Canal was partly organized. However, General Sir **John Maxwell**'s plans utilized the canal more as an obstacle to possible invasion than as a base for future operations to the northeast.

1915, January 14–February 3. Thrust against the Canal. **Djemal** Pasha, Turkish Minister of Marine, personally led a force of 22,000 men secretly across the Sinai Peninsula from Beersheba. German General Baron **Friedrich Kress von Kressenstein,** Djemal's chief of staff, had set up an efficient organization. Advance elements of the force struck across the canal in German-type ponton boats (February 2), but the assault was broken up by the defenders. Djemal retired to Beersheba with a loss of 2,000 men. No further Turkish attack was made against the canal, but the threat held much-needed British reinforcements back from Gallipoli.

MESOPOTAMIAN FRONT, 1915

1915, January–June. Tigris River Expedition.. British forces in the Tigris Valley of lower Mesopotamia were reinforced to a strength of 2 infantry divisions, a cavalry brigade, and some heavy artillery, all commanded by General Sir **John E. Nixon,** at Basra. A Turkish attack on **Qurna,** a fortified post west of Basra, was repulsed (April 12–14). Another Turkish attack on **Ahwaz,** an outpost some 50 miles north of Basra, was driven off (April 24). Nixon, under orders from India to explore the possibility of an advance on Baghdad, sent Major General **Charles V. F. Townshend** with a reinforced division and a small naval flotilla up the Tigris. After overwhelming a Turkish outpost near Qurna in an amphibious assault (May 31), Townshend continued upriver to Amara, occupying it (June 3).

1915, July 24. Battle of Nasiriya. Major General **George F. Gorringe** with a small expeditionary force moved up the Euphrates to protect Townshend's flank and communications by wiping out a Turkish defensive position at **Nasiriya.** Turkish resistance was strong and only after a month of campaigning was Gorringe successful. British casualties were 533; the Turkish unknown. But they left 1,000 prisoners and 17 guns.

1915, August–September. Advance to Kut. Townshend was now reinforced and ordered to take Kut-el-Amara at the confluence of the Tigris and Shatt-el-Hai rivers. By September 16 his attack force was concentrated on the south bank of the Tigris near Sannaiyet, just below Kut. His communications were strained by insufficient river transport over the almost 300-mile winding Tigris, and one of his 2 infantry divisions was scattered downriver to protect the route. **Nur-ud-Din** Pasha, Turkish commander, with 10,000 men and 38 guns, held an entrenched position astride the Tigris below Kut. Townshend had 11,000 men and 28 guns.

1915, September 27–28. Battle of Kut. After receiving supplies, Townshend made a demonstration on the south bank (September 26), then crossed the river, driving the Turks from their positions with the loss of 5,300 men (including 1,300 prisoners) and all their guns. They retreated unmolested to a prepared position at Ctesiphon, midway between Kut and Baghdad. Townshend's troops, lacking land transport, could not pursue, and the naval flotilla was delayed by the shallows of the dry season. British losses were 1,230. After lengthy debate, the British high command finally ordered Nixon and Townshend to continue on to Baghdad, despite Townshend's plaint that his force was inadequate. There were no reinforcements available, however.

1915, November 11–22. Advance to Ctesiphon. Townshend advanced (November 11) with improvised camel and donkey transport supplementing the river boats. Arriving before Ctesiphon he discovered that the Turks had fortified extensively and that Nur-ud-Din had been reinforced to a strength of 18,000 regulars and additional Arabs, with 45 guns. Townshend, having added one of the communications line brigades to his forces, mustered some 10,000 infantry, 1,000 cavalry, and 30 guns. He also had, for the first time in that theater, a squadron of 7 airplanes.

1915, November 22–26. Battle of Ctesiphon. Townshend attacked savagely to turn the Turkish left. But he pressed his luck too far, for he held out no reserve. The first Turkish line was taken and held against repeated counterattacks, but Townshend's troops could do no more. After 4 days of battle, during which more Turkish reinforcements arrived, Townshend decided to withdraw after sending back his wounded. He had lost 4,600 men; the Turks, 6,200. Turkish pursuit was not vigorous, and after a rear-guard action at **Umm-at-Tubal** (December 1) the force arrived at Kut (December 3). Feeling now that his infantrymen were too exhausted to retreat farther, Townshend sent his cavalry away, remaining at Kut to await reinforcements. He had more than 2 months' food supply. Kut was soon invested by the Turks (December 7).

COMMENT. *Townshend's campaign is an example of military "absentee landlordism" at its worst. Operations in Mesopotamia were originally under the direction of the Indian Army. In the last stages the British War Office stepped in. Neither agency was in touch with the situation; both relied on the recommendations of Nixon at Basra, who, to say the least, held an exaggerated view of the capabilities of men in protracted combat at the end of an insufficient supply line.*

Persian Front

At the outset of the war, Russian troops occupied most of northern Persia, despite Persian declaration of neutrality. When Turkey entered the war, the British occupied the northwestern Persian Gulf coast to protect their oil interests and to obtain a base for operations in Mesopotamia. At the same time the Turks seized most of Persian Kurdistan. During the Battle of Sarikamish (see p. 956), Turkish forces seized **Tabriz** from the Russians (January 7), but were soon forced to withdraw (January 30). Sporadic minor fighting continued through the year in western Persia on the flanks of the operations taking place in the Caucasus and Mesopotamia.

The War at Sea

1915, January 24. Dogger Bank Action. The German battle-cruiser squadron under Vice Admiral **Franz von Hipper** moved out (January 23) to raid the English coast and harass the British fishing fleet. Warned by radio intercepts, the Grand Fleet steamed to meet an expected full-dress attack. British Admiral **David Beatty**'s battle-cruiser squadron fell in with Hipper off the Dogger Bank, midway between England and Germany. Beatty had 5 ships, Hipper 3. Both were accompanied by lighter cruisers and destroyers. Hipper wisely fled. Beatty, with superior speed, overhauled him, disabling a heavy cruiser and damaging Hipper's flagship, *Seydlitz*. Then H.M.S. *Lion*, Beatty's flagship, was damaged and fell out of the line. Through misunderstanding of signals, the remainder of the British squadron contented itself with sinking the disabled heavy cruiser, allowing Hipper's remaining ships to get away. The Kaiser ordered his fleet to avoid further risks of losing major warships.

1915, February 4. Initiation of German Submarine Campaign. This was directed against merchantmen in waters surrounding the British Isles. Neutrals were also attacked; a Norwegian ship was sunk (February 19) and—despite American warning to Germany—the American tanker *Gulflight* torpedoed, causing the death of 2 of her crew (May 1).

1915, May 7. Sinking of the *Lusitania*. The British luxury liner was torpedoed without warning by *U-20* off the Irish coast. Among the 1,198 lost were 124 Americans. Feeling in the U.S. ran high, despite the facts that the liner carried a war cargo, including gold and ammunition; was under orders not to halt if hailed; and, prior to her departure from New York, the German Embassy in Washington had publicly warned Americans not to travel in the ship. A vehement U.S. protest was filed.

1915, August 19. Sinking of the *Arabic*. When this British liner was sunk with loss of 4 more Americans, reaction became so hostile that Germany announced (September 1) cessation of unlimited submarine war. However, by year's end German U-boats, operating all over, had accounted for almost one million tons of Allied shipping.

OPERATIONS IN 1916

The Global Situation

The year opened with the Central Powers and the Allies at approximately equal strength, although Germany was perhaps better organized. The man-power drain in France was serious. Britain was on the verge of instituting compulsory service to fill her expanding armies. Unrest in Ireland was approaching rebellion. Russia, with plenty of man power, hoped for time to reorganize and supply it.

In a reversal of the previous year's strategy, Germany now sought decision on the Western Front because, as Falkenhayn told the Kaiser, even if the goal were not reached, France would be "bled white" to prevent it. Germany, too, expected to act aggressively at sea, including submarine warfare.

Joffre, feeling that the Allies' worst failure had been lack of co-ordination, had held a conference at Chantilly (December, 1915) and succeeded in getting agreement from Britain, Russia, Italy, and Rumania that co-ordinated offensives would be launched on the Western, Eastern, and Italian fronts, probably about June, when Russia would be ready. Mutual-support measures were also framed.

In Britain a totally new and revolutionary weapon was being developed: the armored, track-laying tank, conceived partly by Colonel **Ernest Swinton** and partly by imaginative First Lord of the Admiralty Winston Churchill, who supported the new project when the War Office refused to sponsor development.

The Western Front

1916, January–December. Zeppelin Raids on England. The German aerial attacks continued, causing increasing numbers of casualties as their size and effectiveness increased. It was not until late in the year that the first Zeppelin was shot down over England by a British plane (September 3). Two more were soon afterward shot down by antiaircraft fire (September 26). As more were lost to British planes and antiaircraft artillery, German air raids over England were drastically reduced in numbers.

THE BATTLE OF VERDUN, FEBRUARY 21–DECEMBER 18

Both Joffre and Falkenhayn planned great offensives to break the deadlock in the West. But the Germans struck first.

Following an enormous bombardment, the Crown Prince's Fifth German Army attacked the fortified, but lightly garrisoned, region of Verdun, lying in the middle of a salient jutting into the German zone, whose southern face was framed by the countersalient of St.-Mihiel. Through the city ran the Meuse gorge, with the rocky escarpment of the Meuse Heights to the east. Beyond lay the Woëvre, a flat clay plain. The front line itself ran some 3 miles beyond the outer forts on the Meuse Heights.

The German assault, on an 8-mile front, bit through the outlying mobile defense zone on the east. Failure of the retiring French to secure a key position, **Fort Douaumont,** was almost fatal. But Joffre, prohibiting further retreat, determined to hold Verdun at all costs as a symbol of French determination as much as to retain an anchor for his battle lines. He sent General **Henri Philippe Pétain** to assume command and retrieve the situation (February 26). By that time the German assault had reached its first limited objective and halted. Pétain, reorganizing his command, brought up large reinforcements and more artillery.

The next German attack (March 6), launched against the western face of the salient, was at first successful, but was checked when Pétain ordered counterattacks to regain "every piece of ground lost." For the rest of the month a series of attacks and counterattacks heaped the ground with corpses. Rapid rotation of units restored French combat troops exhausted in battle, and Pétain got 2 capable lieutenants: Generals **Robert Nivelle** and **Charles Mangin.** Pétain's watchword for the defense (also attributed to Nivelle) became France's motto for the remainder of the war: *"Ils ne passeront pas!"* ("They shall not pass!")

With all other communications—road and rail—cut off, Verdun's only link with the French rear areas was a 40-mile-long secondary road to Bar-le-Duc. Over it Pétain methodically organized a supply system. Despite persistent German artillery harassment, an endless chain of military trucks moved over this road—called *"La Voie Sacrée"* (Sacred Way)—at 14-second intervals in and out of the salient. Permanent road gangs filled shell craters as fast as they were made.

On April 9 the third German offensive struck both sides of the salient, only to be checked again. Successive attacks and counterattacks followed, until the western German effort petered out (May 29). Pétain, meanwhile, had been promoted to army-group command; he was succeeded by Nivelle at Verdun (April). Savage German assaults continued on the east against **Fort Vaux** and **Thiaumont Farm.** Vaux finally capitulated (June 9) after its water had given out and its interior was churned to rubble. The German Crown Prince personally congratulated its commander, Major **Raynal,** on his heroic defense.

Renewed German assaults on the western salient face in late June and early July almost broke the French line. Phosgene gas was used here for the first time. Pétain recommended abandonment of the western Meuse line, but Joffre refused to permit it. The Somme Offensive was about to begin (see below), and he could not afford to lose the Meuse. The French clung to their positions, and the Germans hesitated. Pressing demands for replacements to meet the Brusilov Offensive on the Eastern Front (see p. 962) then drained 15 German divisions from Verdun. Falkenhayn was relieved of command a little later (August 29) and the Hindenburg-Ludendorff team, replacing him, decided to cut their losses and to go on the defensive in the west.

In the fall the French—now under Mangin—went over to the offensive, retaking Forts Douaumont (October 24) and Vaux (November 2). After a lull of several weeks, Mangin again attacked, pushing the French front forward almost to the lines held in February, capturing over 11,000 prisoners and 115 guns (December 15–18). This brought the campaign to a close. The casualties in this bitterly fought battle were approximately 542,000 French and 434,000 German.

THE FIRST BATTLE OF THE SOMME, JUNE 24–NOVEMBER 13

Joffre's long-planned offensive—delayed for several months by the crisis at Verdun—was finally launched by a stupendous 7-day artillery preparation, but—again due to Verdun—with the British playing the leading role, instead of the joint operation initially planned by Joffre. The main effort was to be made by the British Fourth Army (General **Henry S. Rawlinson**), north of the Somme, with General **Edmund Allenby**'s Third Army farther north also attacking. South of the river, armies of Foch's Army Group of the North would make a holding attack.

On July 1 the British infantry, following a rolling artillery barrage, dashed themselves against the highly organized defensive positions of the German Second Army. Small gains were made, but by nightfall the British had lost about 60,000 men, 19,000 of them dead—the greatest one-day loss in the history of the British Army.* The French, surprisingly, made greater advances, since the Germans had not expected them to take part in the initial assault and so were surprised by the attacks south of the Somme.

Despite the appalling losses of the first day, the British continued to forge ahead in a series of small, limited attacks. Falkenhayn, determined to check the threat, began shifting reinforcements from the Verdun front. To this extent, therefore, Haig had accomplished one objective of the offensive.

A British night attack on July 13 cracked the German second line. British cavalry rode into the gap—the last time horse cavalry was used on a large scale in Western Europe. But other reserves were slow to arrive, and the horsemen were soon mowed down by machine guns, then engulfed by a German counterattack which again sealed the line. The Allied offensive deteriorated into a succession of minor but costly small actions.

Haig launched another major offensive on September 15, southwest of Bapaume. The British tanks had been secretly shipped to the front, and spearheaded the attack. Despite the surprise their appearance caused to the Germans, the tanks were underpowered, unreliable, too slow, and too few in number to gain a decisive victory. (Out of 47 brought up, only 11 got into the battle.) The British made substantial gains, but a breakthrough eluded them. Nevertheless, British and French continued attacks gained small bits of ground through mid-November.

British losses in this campaign were 420,000; French, 195,000. German casualties, which included a great proportion of prewar officers and noncommissioned officers, came to a shocking total of some 650,000.

COMMENT. *The British armies—brave, well-equipped, and gallantly led—could not stand up to machine-gun fire interlacing a defensive zone echeloned in depth for miles. In 4½ months of almost continuous attacks, they were able to advance only a little more than 8 miles. Aerial operations were the most extensive yet seen in war. The British use of tanks was premature, like the German use of gas at Ypres the year before. In both cases the user did not anticipate the effect of a new and fearsome weapon, and so was unprepared to exploit. The German defensive role was magnificent, but repeated German counterattacks proved even more costly than Allied assaults. The Somme bled Germany white in experienced small-unit leaders. That army would never be the same again.*

The Italian Front

1916, March 11–29. Fifth Battle of the Isonzo. Like its predecessors, this was a succession of blunt-nosed inconclusive conflicts. The Italian offensive was broken off when the Austrians attacked elsewhere.

1916, May 15–June 17. Austrian Trentino (Asiago) Offensive. Long planned, the attack caught the Italians unprepared. Archduke Eugene's Eleventh and Third armies overran General **Roberto Brusati**'s First Army. Terrain difficulties and Italian reinforcements finally checked the drive (June 10). An Italian counteroffensive and the need to rush troops eastward to stem the Brusilov Offensive (see p. 962) caused Eugene to withdraw from some of the conquered terrain to defensive positions. Italian losses were more than 147,000 (including 40,000 prisoners), 300 guns, and great stores of supplies. Austrian losses were 81,000 (including 26,000 prisoners).

1916, August 6–17. Sixth Battle of the Isonzo. Cadorna, rapidly shifting forces on interior lines, struck the Austrian Isonzo front, depleted for the Trentino Of-

* A comparison with the Normandy landing, largest assault operation of World War II, reveals that the combined Anglo-American armies fought for 20 days in Normandy before sustaining 60,000 casualties.

fensive. **Gorizia** was taken, but no breakthrough effected. Psychologically, the operation boosted Italian morale, lowered by the previous heavy losses in the Trentino. Italian losses were approximately 51,000 against the Austrians' 40,000.

1916, September 14–November 14. Continued Italian Offensives. Three more Italian assaults, dubbed the **Seventh** (September 14–26), **Eighth** (October 10–12), and **Ninth** (November 1–14) **Battles of the Isonzo,** did little more than to exhaust Austrian powers of resistance. The Italians lost in these operations 75,000, the Austrians 63,000, including more than 20,000 prisoners.

The Eastern Front

1916, March 18. Battle of Lake Naroch. Responding to French appeals, the Russians launched a 2-pronged drive in the Vilna-Naroch area to counter the German Verdun assault in the west. Despite a 2-day preliminary bombardment—the heaviest yet seen on the Eastern Front—the Russian assault broke down in the mud of the spring thaw. Its cost—between 70,000 and 100,000 casualties and 10,000 prisoners—did not improve Russian morale. German losses were about 20,000 men.

1916, June 4–September 20. Brusilov Offensive. The Austrian spring offensive against Italy (see p. 961) brought another appeal to Czar Nicholas for help. In response, capable and courageous General **Alexei A. Brusilov,** commanding the Russian Southwestern Army Group, attacked on a 300-mile front, forgoing any prior massing of troops, or preliminary artillery preparation, in order to gain surprise. Well planned, rehearsed, and executed, his assaults bit through the Austro-German line in 2 places. The Austrian Fourth Army was routed, the Seventh unraveled, 70,000 prisoners were taken, the vital rail junction of Kowel endangered. However, Brusilov received little or no help or co-operation from the 2 other Russian army groups on the front, and a counteroffensive by German General Alexander von Linsingen's army group (June 16) checked his northern thrust. Under orders from Alekseyev, Brusilov renewed the offensive (July 28), making further gains, until slowed down by ammunition shortages. His third assault (August 7–September 20) brought him into the Carpathian foothills. The offensive ended in sheer exhaustion, as German reinforcements hurried from Verdun (see p. 960) bolstered the shattered Austrians. Had it not been for these reinforcements, Austria probably would have been knocked out of the war in 1916.

COMMENT. *The Brusilov Offensive was the most competent Russian operation of World War I. Its strategic consequences may be summed up as weakening the Central Powers' offensives in Italy and at Verdun, contributing to the downfall of Falkenhayn, and eliminating Austria forever as a major military power. But the Russians had lost one million casualties, more even than that populous nation could afford. The Brusilov Offensive did not cause the Russian Revolution, but it probably made revolution inevitable. Austrian losses were even greater, and the defeat contributed more than any other single factor to the disintegration of the Hapsburg Empire.*

1916, August–December. Rumanian Participation in the War. After long haggling with the Allies for a promise of rich territorial gain, Rumania was so impressed by the early success of the Brusilov Offensive that she declared war on Germany and Austria (August 27). Rumanian armies at once invaded coveted Transylvania. Falkenhayn, demoted from Chief of the Imperial German General Staff to army commander, met them with the German Ninth Army and threw them back, while Mackensen, up from the Salonika front with the German-reinforced Bulgarian Danube Army, drove north through the Dobruja and crossed the Danube (November 23). Penned in a salient, Rumanian General **Alexandru Averescu** attempted to envelop Mackensen's left flank with a portion of his forces, while the remainder checked Falkenhayn's advance. Russian co-operation was essential to success, but was not forthcoming. The German armies linked; the Rumanians were disastrously defeated in the **Battle of the Arges River** (December 1–4). Bucharest was occupied (December 6), and by year's end the remnants of the Rumanian armies had been driven north into Russia, holding one tiny foothold in their own country.

The bulk of Rumanian grain- and oil-producing areas were in German hands. Rumanian losses are estimated at from 300,000 to 400,000 (more than half non-battle casualties), and the campaign cost the Central Powers some 60,000 combat casualties and almost the same number of sick.

The Balkan Front, 1916

The Allied forces now held a fortified position—the "Bird Cage"—around Salonika. Sarrail was technically in command, but the British took orders from their home government. The Central Powers' strategy was one of containment. The Greek political situation complicated matters. Sickness decimated the Allied forces. The reconstituted Serbian Army, 118,000 strong, joined (July) and with additional reinforcements the Allied strength rose to more than 250,000. Sarrail decided on an offensive up the Vardar Valley. But the Bulgarians struck first.

1916, August 17–27. Battle of Florina. Bulgar-German attacks drove in the Allied forces to the **Struma River** line.

1916, September 10–November 19. Allied Counteroffensive. Sarrail slowly pushed northward, taking **Monastir** (Bitolje, November 19). Operations dwindled to a stop as Sarrail bickered with his subordinates. The year's campaign had cost the allies some 50,000 men. Bulgar-German losses were approximately 60,000.

1916, July–November. Operations in Albania. During the year an Austrian corps opposed an Italian corps along the Vayusa River in indecisive semi-independent operations. The Italians finally (November 10) pushed the Austrians north and linked with Sarrail's main body at **Lake Ochrida.**

The Turkish Fronts

EGYPT—PALESTINE—ARABIA

1916, January–July. Sinai Bridgehead. British operations in Egypt under General Sir **Archibald Murray** focused upon eastward extension of Suez Canal defenses into the Sinai Desert, a tremendous plan involving water supply, communications, and fortifications. Meanwhile, insurrection of the Senussi tribes in western Egypt necessitated a diversion of force until it was suppressed (March 14). Several minor actions occurred in the Sinai as British covering troops met Turkish resistance.

1916, June 5. Arab Revolt in the Hejaz. This was the result of Franco-British political negotiations with Arab chieftains, aimed at undermining Turkish strength. The Turkish garrison at **Medina** was attacked. **Hussein,** Grand Sherif of Mecca, proclaimed Arab independence. **Mecca**'s garrison surrendered (June 10) and the Turkish forces opposing Murray now found themselves hampered by Arab dissidence threatening their entire line of land communications north through Syria to the Taurus Mountains.

1916, August 3. Battle of Rumani. German General Kress von Kressenstein with 15,000 Turkish troops and German machine gunners struck the British Sinai railhead in a surprise attack. He was repelled, losing more than 5,000 men; British casualties were 1,100. As the year ended, the British had progressed to El Arish.

MESOPOTAMIA

1916, April 29. Fall of Kut-el-Amara. Townshend's besieged force (see p. 958) vainly waited for rescue while British General **Fenton J. Aylmer** with 2 newly arrived Indian divisions battered futilely against the heavy Turkish contravallation (January). General **George F. Gorringe,** succeeding Aylmer, attempted a surprise attack (March 7) on the south bank of the Tigris, but was repulsed by elderly (73) but capable German General **Kolmar von der Goltz,** commanding the Turkish Sixth Army. Continued efforts to break through were unsuccessful. The food supply in Kut failed. With starvation near, Townshend capitulated, surrendering 2,070 British and some 6,000 Indian troops as a half-hearted Russian attempt to move from Persia on Baghdad bogged down. The unsuccessful British relief force suffered more than 21,000 casualties. Von der Goltz died of cholera just prior to the surrender; **Halil** Pasha succeeded him.

1916, December 13. British Advance. British General Sir **Frederick S. Maude,** appointed to the Mesopotamian command (August), had found himself reduced to a defensive role while the War Office and the Indian Army command debated pros and cons of possible British withdrawal from the theater. After chafing on the defensive for more than 2 months, Maude received permission to resume the offensive. He now began movement up both banks of the Tigris with a combat strength of 166,000 men, two-thirds of them Indians.

THE CAUCASUS

1916, January–April. Russian Winter Offensive. General Yudenich (see p. 956), one of the few really capable Russian commanders, advanced from Kars on Erzurum on a broad front (January 11). The Turkish Third Army (Abdul Kerim) was rapidly rolled up at **Köprukoy** (January 18), narrowly escaping envelopment. Kerim retreated to Erzerum, with loss of some 25,000 men—a great number by frostbite in the subzero mountain climate. Yudenich stormed **Erzerum,** rapidly breaking through its ring of forts in a 3-day battle (February 13–16). Meanwhile, he launched a subsidiary offensive along the Black Sea coast, supported by Russian naval craft. **Trebizond** (Trabzon) was captured (April 18), facilitating Russian logistical support.

1916, June–August. Turkish Counteroffensive. Enver Pasha contemplated a dual drive: the Third Army (now under **Vehip** Pasha) along the Black Sea littoral, and a new Second Army (**Ahmet Izzim** Pasha) to advance on Bitlis and turn Yudenich's left. Yudenich, moving with characteristic rapidity and judgment (July 2), split the Third Army at **Erzinjan,** routing it completely (July 25). The Turks lost 34,000 casualties. Yudenich then turned on the Turkish Second Army. Kemal, hero of Gallipoli and now a corps commander, scored the only Turkish successes, capturing **Mus** and **Bitlis** (August 15), but Yudenich retook them (August 24). Both sides went into winter quarters early.

The Persian Front

Russian forces in this area were comparatively small; General N. N. Baratov, with some 20,000 men and 38 guns, moved on Kermanshah to divert Turkish forces from Mesopotamia. Reaching Karind (March 12), he announced his intention to move on Baghdad. The day he started, Kut fell (April 29; see p. 963). **Halil** Pasha thereupon shifted most of his forces from the Kut area to protect Baghdad. Baratov attacked at **Khanikin** (June 1), was repulsed, and withdrew to Karind. Halil took the offensive and by August had retaken Kermanshah. Then this front quieted down again.

The War at Sea, 1916

THE SUBMARINE CAMPAIGNS AND CRUISER RAIDS, JANUARY–MAY

1916, February 21. Extended German Submarine Campaign. Germany proclaimed that after March 1 armed merchantmen would be treated as warships. Sinking of the British passenger liner *Sussex* (March 24), with loss of several American lives, brought vigorous protest from the U.S.

1916, May 10. Sussex Pledge. Germany announced abandonment of the extended campaign, and stated that passenger ships would not be sunk without warning.

1916, April 24–25. German Cruiser Raids. Yarmouth and Lowestoft were bombarded in hit-and-run raids.

THE BATTLE OF JUTLAND, MAY 31–JUNE 1

The German High Seas Fleet under Vice Admiral **Reinhard Scheer** put to sea, cruising north toward the Skagerrak (May 30). Von Hipper's scouting fleet, 40 fast vessels built around a nucleus of 5 battle cruisers, led the way. Well behind was the main fleet of 59 ships, 16 of them dreadnoughts and 6 others older battleships. Warned of the sortie by imprudent German radio chatter, the Grand Fleet under Admiral Sir **John R. Jellicoe** at once put to sea. Leading was Beatty's scouting force

The Fleets—Battle of Jutland

Type	Number at Jutland British	German
Battleships[a]	28	16
Battle Cruisers[b]	9	5
Battleships, Second-Line[c]	0	6
Armored Cruisers	8	0
Light Cruisers	26	11
Destroyer Leaders (Big Destroyers)	5	0
Destroyers	73	61
Minelayers	1	0
Seaplane Carriers	1	0
Submarines	d	d
Total	151	99

[a] These were the modern, fast, heavily armored all big-gun ships known as dreadnoughts, after the first one commissioned by the British in 1906: HMS *Dreadnought.* They carried 8 or 10 guns of 12- to 15-inch caliber.

[b] These were very fast versions of the dreadnoughts, carrying fewer, slightly smaller guns—usually eight 11.5- to 13-inch caliber—and with lighter armor protection to give them more speed.

[c] These were older vessels, still big and powerful, but with fewer big guns, and slower in speed.

[d] The British and Germans each had about 45 submarines available, but none were used.

of 52 ships, including his 6 battle cruisers and Admiral **Hugh Evan-Thomas**' squadron of 4 new superdreadnoughts. Jellicoe's main fleet, following, was composed of 99 vessels, 24 of them dreadnoughts. Over all, the British had 37 capital ships at sea: 28 dreadnoughts and 9 battle cruisers; the Germans had 27 capital ships: 16 dreadnoughts, 6 older battleships, and 5 battle cruisers.

Beatty's 2 divisions steaming east, line ahead, with his battle cruisers on the right and Evan-Thomas' dreadnoughts to the left, next afternoon sighted Hipper's force, also in line ahead, steaming south (he had already sighted Beatty and was returning toward the German main fleet). It was now 3:31 P.M. As Hipper hoped, Beatty turned on a parallel course to the German squadron, signaling Evan-Thomas, whom Hipper had not yet sighted, to follow. Both battle-cruiser forces opened fire at 16,500-yard range, with the German gunnery more accurate. Beatty's flagship, *Lion,* leading, received several hits. Then in succession came mortal blows to the thin-skinned British battle cruisers. A salvo from *Von der Tann* tore into *Indefatigable*'s vitals; she blew up and capsized. *Derfflinger*'s accurate salvos sent *Queen Mary* to the bottom 20 minutes later.

Beatty, with but 4 ships left to oppose the German 5, and Evan-Thomas still out of range, tersely signaled: "Engage the enemy closer." He remarked to his flag captain: "There seems to be something wrong with our bloody ships today. Turn two points to port." And *Lion,* damaged but still fighting, swung closer to the Germans.

Soon afterward, at 4:42, Beatty sighted the German main fleet approaching; he at once turned north to join Jellicoe, in his turn hoping to lead the German fleet

THE PHASES OF THE BATTLE OF JUTLAND

Phase I: The Battle Cruiser Action–the Run to the South.
Phase II: The Run to the North.
Phase III: The Main Fleet Action:
1. Jellicoe's battle line deploys into column.
2. Jellicoe caps Scheer's "T."
3. The Crisis. Jellicoe again caps Scheer's "T."
4. Jellicoe turns away.
Phase IV: The Night Action.

behind him. Hipper had already turned and was firing accurately at Beatty's ships and those of Evan-Thomas, who was slow in turning and was now being pounded by Scheer's main battle line. For over an hour the chase to the north continued, much damage being done on both sides. Shortly after 6 P.M., Beatty sighted Jellicoe's 6 divisions approaching from the northwest in parallel columns, preceded by Rear Admiral Sir **Horace Hood**'s battle squadron—3 battle cruisers and 2 light cruisers. The British main fleet was still over the horizon from the Germans, but Beatty, still heavily engaged, turned generally eastward, in front of the Germans, to get himself into line in front of Jellicoe, whose 6 columns now also turned behind Beatty. Both British admirals were hoping to swing entirely around Scheer and block him from his base. Shortly before 6:30, Scheer sighted Hood's squadron to his right front, just as British dreadnought shells began to fall around the German battle line. Within minutes practically every major ship in both fleets was within range and a furious general engagement was taking place. The German battle cruisers caught the worst of the storm; Hipper's flagship *Lutzow* was hammered out of action. On the British side, at 6:34 Hood's flagship was sunk with all on board by *Derfflinger*'s accurate gunnery, and the cruisers *Defence* and *Warrior* also went down.

The High Seas Fleet was now inside the converging arc of the Grand Fleet and taking heavy punishment. At 6:35, Scheer, under cover of a smoke screen and destroyer attacks, suddenly reversed course by a difficult and perfectly executed simultaneous 180-degree turn, headed west, and in a few minutes his ships were out of range of most of the surprised British. Jellicoe, instead of pursuing, continued southward, since he knew his fleet was now between the Germans and their bases. Then, at 6:55, Scheer made another 180-degree fleet turn back toward the British, apparently thinking Jellicoe had divided his fleet. Suddenly the entire German fleet was again under the guns of the entire Grand Fleet. This time it seemed that the Germans could not escape destruction in the hail of great projectiles.

A second time Scheer made a simultaneous turn away, while the 4 remaining German battle cruisers, under Captain **Hartog** of *Derfflinger,* most gallantly charged toward the British line to cover the withdrawal. (Hipper had transferred to a destroyer and was trying to catch up with his battle cruisers.) *Von der Tann,* her guns already out of action, remained in line only to spread the British fire. Both *Seydlitz* and *Derfflinger* broke into flames but remained in action as the German battle cruisers swung past the British battle line at short range. Then German destroyers sped in toward Jellicoe's battleships to make a torpedo attack and spread a smoke screen. Jellicoe, wary of torpedoes, saved Scheer by himself turning away. By the time he had resumed his battle line, the German High Seas Fleet had disappeared westward into the dusk as Scheer made another 180 degree turn. Amazingly, none of the German battle cruisers had been sunk in their courageous "death ride."

But the battle was not over. Scheer knew that the British fleet was now between his fleet and its home ports, and that Jellicoe was steaming to cover the entrances to those ports. Scheer also knew his fleet could not survive a renewed general battle. After dark he boldly turned to the southeast, deliberately crashing into the formation of light cruisers at the tail of Jellicoe's southbound fleet. He finally battered his way through in a chaotic midnight battle of collisions, sinkings, and gunfire. The British cruiser *Black Prince,* suddenly engulfed in the midst of the Germans, was sunk in 4 minutes. The German predreadnought battleship *Pommern* was cut in two. By dawn, Scheer was shepherding his cripples toward the Jade anchorage, and Jellicoe realized that his quarry had escaped.

The British now turned back to their bases. They had lost 3 battle cruisers, 3 cruisers, and 8 destroyers; they had 6,784 casualties. The Germans lost 1 old battleship, 1 battle cruiser, 4 light cruisers, and 5 destroyers; casualties were 3,039.

COMMENT. *Jutland marked the end of an epoch in naval warfare. It was the last great fleet action in which the opponents slugged it out within eyesight of one another. A drawn battle tactically, it made no change in the strategic situation, other than to make the Germans realize that they had no chance of defeating the Grand Fleet. Of the commanders engaged, Beatty, Hipper, and Hartog stand out, gifted with that "Nelsonian touch" which neither Jellicoe nor Scheer (both able professionals) appeared to have. In general, both sides behaved with the utmost gallantry.*

SUBSEQUENT NAVAL OPERATIONS, JUNE–DECEMBER

The remainder of the year saw one timid sortie of the High Seas Fleet (August 18), which ended as a fiasco, both opponents running home without making contact —Scheer deceived by a false airship report, Jellicoe because he feared a submarine ambush. Two German light-cruiser raids were made on the British coast (August 19 and October 26–27), and several auxiliary cruisers slipped through the British blockade to ravage Atlantic commerce. But in the main, German naval effort was now concentrated on submarine activities. Tremendous toll was taken of Allied shipping: 300,000 tons per month by December.

OPERATIONS IN 1917

Global Situation

Allied strength had grown during 1916. Toward the end of the year, at another Allied conference called by Joffre at Chantilly, there had been general agreement to continue a policy of joint Anglo-French large-scale operations on the Western Front in conjunction with simultaneous Russian and Italian offensives. These would have priority over all operations elsewhere, although new British Prime Minister **David Lloyd George** decided to undertake a major campaign in Palestine as well.

The western Allies at this time did not realize the extent of Russia's instability. The retirement of Joffre (December 31, 1916), who was succeeded by Nivelle, the hero of Verdun, immediately complicated the co-ordination of the Allied operations.

Unity of command was nonexistent. Nivelle, planning a giant joint Anglo-French offensive, to be carried out with "violence, brutality, and rapidity," clashed with Haig on their command relationship. The French government supported Nivelle and the British were divided. British Prime Minister Lloyd George, who distrusted Haig and admired charming, English-speaking Nivelle, placed the BEF under Nivelle's command, to the horror of Haig and of Sir **William Robertson,** the new Chief of the Imperial General Staff. Through this bickering, and Nivelle's own imprudent announcements, secrecy was lost.

Ludendorff, aware of the Allied preparations and particularly fearing for overextended German lines in the west, deliberately chose a defensive attitude on both major fronts while forcing Austria (with German assistance) to take decisive action against Italy, which he believed could be defeated in 1917. The Kaiser approved this strategic concept, and also concurred in the inauguration of unrestricted submarine warfare, regardless of American opinion. He virtually granted unlimited authority to the military high command.

United States Entry

1917, January 31. Germany Proclaims Unrestricted Submarine Warfare. To offset growing hostility in the U.S., covert negotiations were already in process by German diplomats for a German-Mexican-Japanese alliance.

1917, February 3. The U.S. Severs Relations with Germany. This was a protest against unrestricted submarine warfare. Brazil, Bolivia, Peru, and other Latin American nations followed suit, as did China (March 14).

1917, March 1. Zimmermann Note. Publication of a proposed German defensive alliance with Mexico in case of war between Germany and the U.S., with the proviso "that Mexico is to reconquer the lost territory in New Mexico, Texas, and Arizona" caused a wave of American fury. **Alfred Zimmermann,** German Foreign Secretary, had sent the coded proposition, which contained the further suggestion that Mexico urge Japan to join the Central Powers, to **von Eckhardt,** German Minister to Mexico (January 19). British naval intelligence, intercepting and decoding it, gave a copy (February 24) to **Walter Hines Page,** U.S. ambassador to Brittain. He immediately turned it over to the State Department, which released it to the press (March 1). U.S. intelligence sources later verified the authenticity of the note.

1917, March 13. U.S. Merchantmen Armed. President Wilson's decision to arm for self-defense all vessels passing through war zones was announced by the State and Navy departments.

1917, April 6. The U.S. Declares War against Germany. This followed the sinking of several American ships and President Wilson's war message to Congress (April 2). War against Austria-Hungary was not declared until 8 months later (December 7).

1917, April–June. U.S. Preparations. The Army would have to be built. Major General **John J. Pershing** was selected to command the American Expeditionary Force (AEF) and the 1st Division (an amalgamation of existing Regular Army units) was shipped to France (June). Pershing's plan called for a 1-million-man army overseas by May, 1918, with long-range provision for 3 million men in Europe later. A draft law—the Selective Service Act—was passed (May 19) and the nation went into high gear. The Navy was ready (see p. 975).

The Western Front

1917, February 23–April 5. German Withdrawal. Ludendorff had prepared a much shorter, highly organized defensive zone—the Hindenburg Line, or Siegfried Zone—some 20 miles behind the winding, overextended line from Arras to Soissons. Hindenburg approved, and decided to withdraw to the new line, which could be held with fewer divisions, thus providing a larger and more flexible reserve. Behind a lightly held outpost line heavily sown with machine guns lay 2 successive defensive positions, heavily fortified. Behind these again lay the German reserves concentrated and prepared for counterattack. Each successive defensive line was so spaced in depth that, should one be taken, the attackers' artillery would have to displace forward before progressing against the next. Between the original line and the new zone, the countryside had been devastated; towns and villages were razed, forests leveled, water sources contaminated, and roads destroyed. The actual withdrawal, conducted in great secrecy, began February 23 and was completed by April 5.

1917, April 9–15. Battle of Arras. This was the British preliminary to the Nivelle Offensive. The British First (General **H. S. Horne**) and Third (General Sir Edmund Allenby) armies, following a heavy bombardment and gas attack, crashed into the positions of the German Sixth Army (General **L. von Falkenhausen**). British air supremacy was rapidly gained. Canadian troops stormed and took **Vimy Ridge** the first day. The British Fifth Army (**Hubert Gough**), assisting on the south, made little progress. The British advance was finally slowed down in succeeding days of battle. Although this was a British tactical victory, there was no breakthrough. British casualties were 84,000; German, about 75,000.

1917, April 16–20. Nivelle Offensive (Second Battle of the Aisne, Third Battle of Champagne). The French Reserve Army Group (**Alfred Micheler**), heavily reinforced, assaulted on a 40-mile front between Soissons and Reims to take the **Chemin des Dames,** a series of wooded, rocky ridges paralleling the front. The Sixth (Mangin) and Fifth (**Olivier Mazel**) armies were closely supported by the Tenth (**Denis Duchêne**), and backed by the First (**M. E. Fayolle**). French strength in the attacking armies totaled 1,200,000 men and 7,000 guns. The German Seventh (**Max von Boehn**) and First (**Fritz von Below**) armies held the sector, fully cognizant of French plans as a result of Nivelle's confident public boasts of victory. Just before the attack, German flyers swept the sky of French aerial observation and German artillery fire destroyed French tanks still in march column. The French rolling artillery barrage moved too fast for the infantry, who met preplanned artillery and machine-gun fire, and sectional counterattacks. With exceptional gallantry, however, the French managed to reach and take the first German line, but were then stopped. Repeated attacks gained little ground. The whole affair was a colossal failure, costing the French nearly 120,000 men in 5 days. German losses, despite 21,000 captured, were much less. Compared with similar attacks in previous years, such losses might not have seemed excessive, had Nivelle not promised a breakthrough and victory.

1917, April 29–May 20. Outbreak of Mutiny in French Armies. Widespread mutiny followed the Nivelle Offensive disaster. Political repercussions simultaneously shook the nation. Nivelle was replaced by Pétain (May 15). After a 2-week period in which the entire Western Front was nearly denuded of French combat troops, Pétain quelled the mutiny and restored the situation with a combination of tact, firmness, and justice. By amazingly efficient censorship control, French counterintelligence agencies completely blotted out all news of the mutiny. When it finally trickled to Ludendorff, it was too late; renewed British attacks to distract his attention had already drawn German reserves to the northern front. The full extent of the mutiny was not known to the outside world for more than a decade.

1917, June–July. British Offensive in Flanders. Haig, after an abortive renewal of the fighting around Arras to relieve German pressure on the French, had determined to break through between the North Sea and the Lys River. The Ypres salient was selected, but success could only be gained after first taking the dominating Messines Ridge. Plans for an assault had been begun many months earlier by competent, methodical General Sir **Herbert Plumer,** Second Army commander.

1917, June 7. Battle of Messines. After a 17-day general bombardment, British mines packed with 1 million pounds of high explosive tore a wide gap in the German lines on the Ridge. Under cover of this surprise and of British aerial superiority, in a carefully planned and organized attack, Plumer's Second Army successfully gained the position at cost of 17,000 casualties. German losses were 25,000, including 7,500 prisoners. Elbowroom

German pursuit planes attacking
Allied observation planes

had been gained for the main offensive, and the clear-cut victory bolstered British morale.

1917, July 31–November 10. Third Battle of Ypres (Passchendaele). Following an intensive bombardment, the British Fifth Army (Gough) assaulted northeast against the German Fourth Army (**Friedrich Sixt von Armin**). The French First Army (**François Anthoine**), on the left, was the pivot of maneuver; on the right, Plumer's Second Army covered the main effort. The low ground, sodden with rain, had been churned to a quagmire by a 3-day bombardment. Overhead the Allies had won temporary air superiority. All surprise had been lost, however, by the long preparation, and the German defense in depth was well organized. After some early gains, the attack literally bogged down. Haig now placed Plumer in command of the operation. After typical careful planning, a series of limited attacks on narrow fronts began (September 20); the British inched forward against determined counterattacks. Mustard gas was used here by the Germans for the first time, while German planes flew low to strafe British infantry with machine guns. The taking of Passchendaele Ridge and Passchendaele village (November 6) concluded the offensive. The British-held Ypres salient had been deepened for about 5 miles, at great cost—some 300,000 British and 8,528 French casualties. German losses are estimated at 260,000. But Haig, still determined to keep pressure on the Germans to permit the French armies to recover from the mutiny, had another card to play.

1917, November 20–December 3. Battle of Cambrai. General **J. H. G. Byng**'s British Third Army struck General **Georg von der Marwitz'** German Second Army positions in front of Cambrai in complete surprise and under most favorable terrain conditions. At dawn, some 200 tanks followed a sudden burst of artillery fire into the German wire. Behind them moved wave after wave of infantry. The German defense collapsed temporarily and the assault bit through the Hindenburg Line for 5 miles on a 6-mile front, except at **Flesquières,** where German artillery knocked out tanks and the British infantry was unable to close in support. Although 2 cavalry divisions were poised to exploit the breakthrough, infantry reserves were weak, and too many tanks had been put in the first waves. Crown Prince Rupprecht of Bavaria, commanding the defending army group, rushed reinforcements to Marwitz. A large proportion of the British leading tanks became casualties—more from mechanical breakdown than by artillery fire—and the advance slowed down. German counterattacks fell on the salient (November 30) and Haig ordered a partial withdrawal (December 3). Casualties on both sides were approximately equal: about 45,000. The British took 11,000 prisoners; the Germans, 9,000. Cambrai marked a turning point in Western Front tactics on 2 counts: successful assault without preliminary bombardment and the first mass use of tanks.

COMMENT. *The most important lesson emerging from the entire western campaign of 1917 was the necessity for unity of command. Haig and Nivelle between them in two disjointed offensives had squandered more than one-half million men and exhausted the resources of two splendid war machines without appreciable effect. In Haig's defense, however, it should be noted that his persistent costly attacks in Flanders and Artois were largely intended to attract German attention from the weakness of the French armies farther south; in this he was successful, and to him must go at least part of the credit for France's survival through 1917.*

As the year ended, acquisitive eyes in both Britain and France turned to the as yet untouched human resources of the United States.

The Italian Front

1917, April. Allied Planning. Cadorna feared that the Germans would send troops to aid the Austrians in an offensive on the Italian front. Because of this, Nivelle sent Foch to meet Cadorna to work out plans for French and British assistance in such an event. Franco-British-Italian staff officers worked out a program for reinforcements to be rushed into Italy in emergency.

1917, May 12–June 8. Tenth Battle of the Isonzo. Cadorna, despite promises to aid the Allied offensive, did not get started until after the battles of Arras and the Aisne were over. Once again the Italians attempted to batter their way through, over mountainous terrain. After a 17-day battle, gains were small but losses huge: some 157,000 Italian casualties against about 75,000 Austrians. Following some minor give and take on both Isonzo and Trentino fronts, Cadorna decided to make a supreme effort with 52 divisions and 5,000 guns.

1917, August 18–September 15. Eleventh Battle of the Isonzo. The Italian Second Army (General **Luigi Capello**), heavily reinforced, assaulted north of Gorizia, while the Third (Duke of Aosta), to its south, drove into the rocky hills between Gorizia and Trieste. The southern assault was speedily stopped by the left wing of Austrian General Borojevic's Fifth Army, but Capello's Second Army on the north made a clear-cut advance, capturing the strategically important Bainsizza Plateau. Outrunning their artillery and supply, the Italians were then forced to stop. The net result was an incipient collapse of Austrian arms. The Austrians asked for German help.

1917, October 24–November 12. Battle of Caporetto (Twelfth Battle of the Isonzo). A new Fourteenth Austrian Army (7 of its divisions and much of its artillery were German), under German General **Otto von Below,** was concentrated behind the Tolmino-Caporetto-Plezza zone. Using novel "Hutier tactics" (see p. 972), it suddenly crashed against the Italian Second Army. Surprise bombardment, with clouds of gas and smoke shells, disrupted Italian signal communications. Then the German assault elements loomed through mist and rain on the demoralized defenders. Cadorna, having learned of the projected assault, had ordered defense in depth, but Capello—a capable officer—was ill and the acting commander of the Second Army ignored the instructions. By-passing strong points which would be mopped up later by reserves, the German assault elements streamed through the zone, uprooting the Second Army. The Austrian Tenth Army on the right and the Fifth Army on the left supported the main effort. The Italian Third Army withdrew in good order along the coast, but part of the so-called Carnic Force on the northern Alpine fringe was trapped. Farther west the Italian Fourth Army hurriedly fell back to conform with the situation as the battered Second Army was driven in succession from defensive lines along the Tagliamento and Livenza rivers. By November 12, Cadorna managed to stabilize his defense from Mt. Pasubia, south of Trent, to the Piave and along that river to the Gulf of Venice. There the Austro-German offensive slowly ground to a halt, having outdistanced its supply. The catastrophe cost the Italians 40,000 killed and wounded plus 275,000 prisoners, 2,500 guns, and huge stores of goods and munitions. Austro-German losses were about 20,000. By this time French and British reinforcements, in accord with the plan prepared earlier in the year, were moving in, 11 divisions in all, under British General Plumer. Cadorna was now removed from command, being replaced by General **Armando Diaz.**

COMMENT. *Caporetto is a prime example of the military principles (or virtues) of surprise, objective, mass, and economy of force. Below had but 35 divisions in all against the Italian 41, but was far superior in strength at the point of impact. Had he possessed cavalry and armored cars to exploit his success, the battle might have been decisive. As it was, the Italians were badly shaken, but still capable of carrying on the war. A direct result of this disaster to Allied arms was the Rapallo Conference (November 5), which set up a* **Supreme War Council,** *the first attempt to attain over-all Allied unity of command.*

The Eastern Front

1917, March 12. Russian Revolution. Mutiny of the Petrograd garrison (March 10) was followed by establishment of a Provisional Government. Nicholas II abdicated (see p. 998). The new regime, bickering with the Bolshevik-dominated **Petrograd Soviet** (Council of Workers and Soldiers' Deputies), pledged itself to continue war against the Central Powers until an Allied "victorious end" was attained. The Soviet (March 14), fearing counterrevolutionary measures by the officer corps, issued on its own authority the notorious "Order No. 1," depriving officers of disciplinary authority. Broadcast throughout the armed forces, and despite the counterorders of the Provisional Government, it produced the result desired by the Bolsheviks—breakdown of all military discipline. The Russian Army and Navy collapsed like an ice jam in a spring thaw. Mutinous soldiers and sailors murdered many officers; others were simply deposed by soldiers' councils. By mid-April an estimated 50 per cent of the officer corps had been eliminated, among them most of the best men. **Nikolai Lenin** and other Bolshevik agitators were smuggled into Russia by Germany to undermine the Provisional Government. **Leon Trotsky** (Bronstein) joined them. Germany, halting all offensive movements on the Eastern Front lest the Russians reunite in defense of the homeland, took advantage of the lull to send troops to the Western and Italian fronts. Despite all the turmoil, **Alexander Kerensky,** appointed minister of war (May 16), and pressured by the alarmed Allies, attempted to mount an offensive on the Galician front. Brusilov, now chief of staff, commanded.

1917, July 1. Kerensky (or Second Brusilov) Offensive. Brusilov attacked toward Lemberg with the few troops still capable of combat operations. The Eleventh and Seventh Russian armies penetrated German Count **Felix von Bothmer**'s composite South Army (4 German, 3 Austrian, and 1 Turkish division) for 30 miles on a 100-mile front. On the Russian northern flank, the Austrian Second Army was roughly handled. On the south, General **Lavr Kornilov**'s Russian Eighth Army rocked the Austrian Third Army and threatened the oil fields of **Drohobycz** (July 5). But Russian enthusiasm and discipline faded quickly as German resistance stiffened and their own supply system broke down.

1917, July 19. German Counterattack. General **Max Hoffmann,** commanding on the Eastern Front, had quickly obtained reinforcements from the west. Preceded by a most intensive bombardment, the German assault, beginning on the northern flank, rolled up the now demoralized Russian armies in quick succession. They disintegrated; south of the Pripet Marshes no Russian Army now existed. The Germans halted their advance on the Galician border simply because they lacked sufficient reserves and logistical resources to occupy more territory.

1917, September 1. Hutier's Riga Offensive. German General **Oscar von Hutier**'s Eighth Army attacked the northern anchor of the Russian front. While a holding attack on the west bank of the

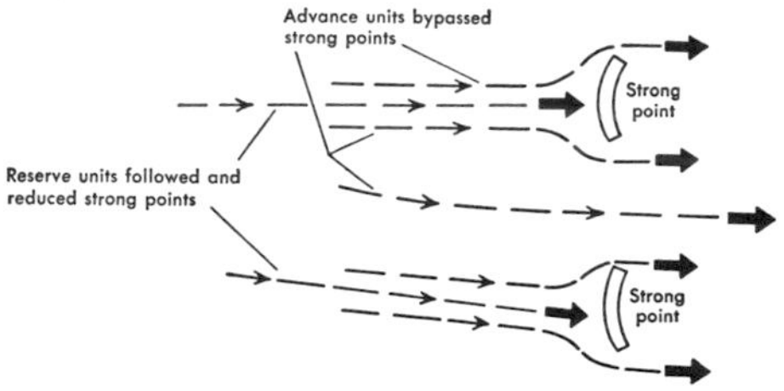

Hutier offensive tactics

Dvina River threatened Riga, 3 divisions crossed the river to the north on ponton bridges, encircling the fortress, while exploiting elements poured eastward. Actually, this highly successful attack was but a dress rehearsal of new German assault techniques to be used again, 6 weeks later, at Caporetto. Long preliminary bombardment was eliminated. Instead, a short, sharp concentration of fire was followed immediately by infantry assaults, both guns and troops being brought into position at the last possible moment to ensure surprise. Heavy concentrations of gas and smoke shells masked known enemy strong points, while infiltrating elements—infantry and light guns—by-passed them. This was the first application of what would become known as "Hutier tactics." The Russian Twelfth Army streamed eastward in complete panic. Only 9,000 prisoners were taken; casualties on both sides were minimal. At this same time a small German amphibious force occupied Osel and Dago islands in the Gulf of Riga, and effected a landing on the mainland.

1917, September–October. Chaos in Russia. The Kerensky government (Kerensky had become head of the Provisional Government July 20) fled Petrograd for Moscow, and the Bolsheviks began to take over. A brief flurry of counterrevolution under General Kornilov petered out (September 9–14).

1917, November 7 (October 25 O.S.) Bolshevik Revolution. Lenin and Trotsky seized power and began dickering for peace with Germany.

1917, December 15. Armistice of Brest Litovsk (Brest). After 12 days of bickering between Bolshevik and German negotiators, armistice terms were agreed, ending hostilities on the Eastern Front. (For further operations, including the Allied invasions of north Russia and Siberia, see p. 1000.) Russia had been permanently erased from the Allied ranks.

The Balkan Front, 1917

1917, January–June. Stalemate. Sarrail, with some 600,000 men on paper, could only muster about 100,000 for combat duty, as malaria and other disease kept the hospitals full. Behind his lines Greece seethed as King Constantine's government continued to conciliate the Central Powers. Several inconclusive Allied attacks failed, at **Monastir** and the **Battle of Lake Prespa (Djoran)** (March 11–17) and the **Battle of the Vardar** (May 5–19). French and British commanders were at cross purposes, while the reconstituted Serbian Army distrusted both. German aerial supremacy added to the Allies' woes.

1917, June 12. Abdication of Constantine. This was the result of Allied pressure. New King **Alexander** appointed pro-Allied **Venizelos** as premier, clarifying the situation (June 26). At the same time, Allied troops moved into Thessaly. A French force occupied the Isthmus of Corinth.

1917, June 27. Greece Enters the War. Greek troops began to swell the Allied strength. However, no real offensive developed.

1917, December 10. Relief of Sarrail. Georges Clemenceau, new French premier, appointed General **M. L. A. Guillaumat,** competent and battle-tried commander, who at once began reorganizing the Allied forces.

The Turkish Fronts

THE CAUCASUS

1917, March. End of Russian Pressure. With the first Russian Revolution in March, Turkish troops were freed to support other fronts.

PALESTINE

1917, January 8–9. Battle of Magruntein. The Sinai Peninsula was cleared of all organized Turkish forces. British losses were 487; they captured 1,600 prisoners and a few guns. Sir Archibald Murray was now authorized to begin a limited offensive into Palestine, where the Turks were established in defensive positions along the ridges between Gaza and Beersheba, the 2 natural gateways to the region.

1917, March 26. First Battle of Gaza. General Sir **Charles M. Dobell** attacked, but, through defective staff work and a communications breakdown between his mounted force and infantry, the attack failed. The British withdrew. Out of forces nearly equal in strength (about 16,000), British losses were 3,967; Turkish, 2,447. Murray's report, unfortunately, presented the action as a British victory. Accordingly, he was ordered to advance without delay and take Jerusalem.

1917, April 17–19. Second Battle of Gaza. Dobell tried again, this time in frontal assault against the now well-prepared defensive Turkish position, and was thrown back, losing 6,444 men against the Turkish loss of about 2,000. Murray relieved Dobell. An exasperated War Office in turn relieved Murray. In his place came General Allenby, fighting cavalryman with the gift of leadership and tactical ability. His instructions were to take "Jerusalem before Christmas." His first step was to move British headquarters from Shepheard's Hotel in Cairo to the fighting front. Insisting on reinforcements, Allenby built up an efficient combat force of 7 infantry divisions and a cavalry element—the Desert Mounted Corps (horse cavalry and camel). Total British strength was 88,000.

Opposing the British was the Turkish Eighth (Kress von Kressenstein) and the incomplete Seventh Army. With some additional German machine-gun, artillery, and technical units, this force totaled 35,000. Basic Turkish weakness was the long and tenuous supply line from Constantinople. Basic British weakness was water supply for the offense; the efficient transport and pipeline extended only to their rear echelon.

1917, October 31. Third Battle of Gaza (Battle of Beersheba). Reversing his predecessor's plans, Allenby left 3 divisions demonstrating in front of Gaza and secretly moved against Beersheba. Surprise was complete, but success was predicated on the ability of the attackers to capture the city's wells; failure would mean collapse of the mounted elements and probably the entire offense. While the infantry assailed Turkish defenses in frontal attack, the Desert Mounted Corps swung wide to the east, then turned on the city. An all-day battle culminated at dusk in the mounted charge of an Australian cavalry brigade through and over the Turkish wire and trenches into Beersheba itself, capturing the coveted water supply. Hastily evacuating, the Turkish Seventh Army now lay with its left flank open. Allenby struck north (November 6), splitting the 2 Turkish armies, and launched the Desert Mounted Corps across country toward the sea. The Turks evacuated Gaza in time to avoid the trap, the Eighth Army retreating up the coast, the Seventh falling back on Jerusalem.

1917, November 13–14. Battle of Junction Station. Pursuing closely, despite logistical difficulties and shortage of water, Allenby struck a hastily established line of the Eighth Army, driving the Turks back north along the railroad. Turning now toward Jerusalem, Allenby was held up by the appearance of Turkish reserves from the Aleppo area (the so-called Yilderim Force) and the arrival of General von Falkenhayn to assume command. Falkenhayn re-established a front from the sea to Jerusalem. A bitter slugging match in the Judean hills followed.

1917, December 9. Fall of Jerusalem. In the face of Allenby's determined attack against Jerusalem (December 8), the Turks evacuated the city, which was occupied by the British next day. A Turkish counterattack was repulsed (December 26). During this campaign Allenby had 18,000 casualties; Turkish losses were about 25,000, including 12,000 captured and 100 guns lost.

MESOPOTAMIA

1917, February 22–23. Second Battle of Kut. Maude skillfully assaulted after preliminary feints against the Turkish left. He crossed the Tigris on the Turkish right and then pressed the attack on both flanks. **Kara Bekr** Bey, Turkish sector commander, fell back to the vicinity of Baghdad, interposing skillful rear-guard resistance to Maude's pursuit. Then the Turkish Sixth Army (Halil Pasha) attempted a stand.

1917, March 11. Fall of Baghdad. After several days of fighting along the **Diyala River,** Maude entered the city, the Turkish forces retreating in some disorder. Maude now launched 3 exploiting columns up the Tigris, Euphrates, and Diyala rivers, securing his hold on Baghdad. A Turkish effort to retake Mesopotamia collapsed when the troops earmarked for the expedition—Yilderim Force—were diverted to bolster the Palestine front (see above).

1917, September 27–28. Battle of Ramadi. As the summer heat subsided, Maude struck sharply northwestward up the Euphrates River. He pursued the Turkish survivors into central Mesopotamia. Brilliant Maude, his objective the oil fields of Mosul, prepared to continue his advance, but died of cholera (November 18), General Sir **William R. Marshall** succeeding to command.

PERSIA

Russian forces in Persia were of concern to the Turks in the beginning of the year, having moved to the vicinity of Saqqiz-Kermanshah, where they were a potential threat to the Mosul oil fields. Maude, in liaison with the Russians, hoped for joint operations against the Turkish Sixth Army, but this hope faded following the Russian Revolution.

War at Sea

THE SUBMARINE CRISIS

1917, February–April. German Unrestricted Submarine Campaign. After careful calculations, the German naval command had come to the conclusion that unrestricted submarine warfare would force Britain to sue for peace in 5 months. The danger of American intervention was recognized (see p. 968), but the potential influence of the U.S. on the war at sea or on land was evaluated as negligible for 2 or more years. By then the submarine campaign, combined with operations on land, was expected to have brought victory to the Central Powers. It almost worked. British shipping losses soared to 875,000 tons per month (April). British and neutral merchant sailors began to refuse to sail. The diversion of most of his light warships from the Grand Fleet for the purpose of seeking and sinking submarines caused great concern to Admiral Beatty (now commanding that fleet) in event of a new sortie of the German fleet, but no such sortie was made. Recommendations for instituting convoys were rejected by the Admiralty as an unsound waste of available cruisers and destroyers. The efforts to sink submarines were disappointing, however. Admiral Jellicoe (now First Sea Lord) calculated that Britain would run out of food and other needed raw materials by July.

1917, May 10. Institution of Convoy System. Insistence of Prime Minister Lloyd George, combined with the strong recommendations of American Admiral **William S. Sims** and of Beatty, finally forced adoption of the convoy system. The results were spectacular. British escort vessels, joined by American destroyers (May), provided adequate protection to merchant ships and at the same time were able to sink more submarines, since these were forced to attack the convoys. Unquestionably the convoys saved Britain. Although shipping losses by the end of the year exceeded 8 million tons, Allied shipbuilding programs more than offset the losses.

OTHER NAVAL ACTIONS

1917, February–April. German Destroyer Raids in the Channel. The first of these 3 raids was uneventful (February 25). In the second the Germans sank 2 British destroyers and a small coastal merchant vessel, with no loss to themselves (March 17). The third was foiled by the gallantry of Commander **E. R. G. R. Evans,** whose destroyer H.M.S. *Broke* sank 2 German destroyers singlehanded in a thrilling sea fight.

1917, May–June. British Raids on Ostend and Zeebrugge. Naval bombardment of the German destroyer and submarine bases caused some damage, but failed to interfere seriously with German U-boat operations.

1917, May 15. Action off Valona. In the Adriatic, Austrian Captain **Miklós Horthy** (later dictator of Hungary) led an Austrian squadron on a raid against Italian transports off the Albanian coast. The Austrians were able to sink 14 of the small merchantmen, and then to escape successfully after a spirited action with British, French, and Italian warships.

1917, July 15. British Raid on German Coastal Shipping. British destroyers sank 2 German merchant ships and captured 4 more off the Dutch coast, stopping coastal trade with Rotterdam.

1917, November 17. Action off Heligoland. Poor British staff work aborted a battlecruiser raid against German minesweeping operations in Heligoland Bight; the German squadron protecting the minesweepers was able to withdraw without damage.

1917, December. German Raids on British Scandinavian Convoys. These inflicted serious losses on British merchant shipping, forcing Beatty to use a squadron of battleships as a covering force for future convoys.

OPERATIONS IN 1918

Global Situation

The Allies entered the year in a state of frustration. The rosy promises of early 1917 had been unfulfilled. Except in the Near East, where Allenby's dynamic leadership had culminated in the capture of Jerusalem—with its tremendous psychological uplift to Christendom—Allied offensives had bogged down in a welter of cross-purpose and disunity of command. Russia had collapsed. The German U-boat campaign still threatened the maritime pipeline of supply from America. Finally, many months would still pass before American armed forces could bolster up lost Allied man power. Both Britain and France were therefore on the defensive. The Supreme War Council did no serious planning. Haig (who had been refused reinforcement by Lloyd George) and Pétain agreed among themselves on mutual support should a German offensive be launched. Some attempt at organization of defense in depth was made.

Nor had the Central Powers been successful. They all felt the strangulation of Allied naval blockade. Austria was at the end of her resources, Turkey and Bulgaria were wobbling, and the burden of the war fell heavier and heavier on Germany. Hindenburg and Ludendorff had established a virtual military dictatorship over Germany, and exercised almost as complete authority over the subservient governments of Austria, Bulgaria, and Turkey.

The American Build-up

Having entered the war without previous preparation, the U.S. was faced with organizing, equipping, training, transporting, and supplying an expeditionary force in Europe. The little Regular Army provided the leaven for 2 successive waves of man power: the National Guard and the draftees produced by the Selective Service Act (May 19, 1917). From a strength of 200,000 men and 9,000 officers (including 65,000 National Guardsmen then serving on the Mexican border), the Army swelled to over 4 million men, including 200,000 officers. Some 2 million in all served overseas. Based on Pershing's recommendations, a divisional organization of approximately 28,000-man strength was adopted. It consisted of 2 infantry brigades of two regiments each, an artillery brigade, an engineer regiment, 3 machine-gun battalions, and trains and supporting services. Forty-two of these divisions, which were nearly double the strength of their European counterparts, reached France. Though Pershing understood the need and importance of entrenchments, he eschewed what he considered to be a defeatist concept of trench warfare. Training was predicated on the spirit of the offensive—mobile combat—with stress on individual marksmanship.

Overseas, the Service of Supply became an empire in itself, manning 9 base sections. Pershing chose the Lorraine area east of Verdun as the American combat zone. The pipeline of supply from the United States went to ports in southwestern France, and movement overland conflicted little with the Allied efforts farther north. Except for small arms, ordnance needs were filled by America's allies. So too with airplanes; American production was limited to the Liberty engine.

Overseas transportation, the province of the U.S. Navy, was in part provided by the German merchant fleet seized in American ports, plus an improvised fleet of the American merchant marine—much of it built with remarkable celerity, some British ships, and neutral shipping sequestrated or leased. The combined fleet carried more than a million American soldiers to France without loss of a single vessel —on eastbound voyages. (The remaining million shipped overseas went on Allied ships, mostly British.)

The Navy, whose personnel waxed to 800,000, was primarily concerned in antisubmarine and convoy activities, though a division of 5 battleships joined the British Grand Fleet and 3 other battleships operated in Irish waters against surface raiders. In all, some 79 American destroyers took part in convoy work, and 135 subchasers also operated in European waters. An important part of U.S. Navy participation was in the laying of 56,000 of the 70,000 mines comprising the North Sea mine belt—from Scotland to Norway. Naval air squadrons took part in bombings of German submarine bases along the Belgian coast. A Marine brigade became part of the AEF.

American combat participation in World War I was based on "co-operation," as Pershing's directive put it. The U.S. was not technically an Ally. Its expeditionary force was to be "a separate and distinct component of the combined forces, the identity of which must be preserved." Pershing's directive ran counter to the Allies' desires. They distrusted the inexperienced Americans' military ability, and they were short of man power. From the beginning Pershing was cajoled, coaxed, and finally threatened, in fruitless efforts to have him turn the AEF over *in toto* as a replacement reservoir for the French and British armies. War Secretary Newton D. Baker and President Wilson upheld Pershing when Clemenceau and Lloyd George went over his head to Washington with their demands.

The Fourteen Points

In an address to Congress on January 8, 1918, President Wilson laid down his "only possible program" for peace. The policy included (1) open covenants, openly arrived at; (2) freedom of the seas in war and peace; (3) removal of trade barriers; (4) national armament reductions; (5) impartial adjustment of colonial claims; (6) evacuation of Russian territory and independent solution by Russia of her political development and national policy; (7) evacuation and restoration of Belgium; (8) evacuation and restoration of all occupied French territory and return of Alsace-Lorraine; (9) readjustment of Italian frontiers on lines of nationality; (10) autonomy for the peoples of Austria-Hungary; (11) evacuation of Rumania, Serbia, and Montenegro, restoration of occupied territories, and Serbian access to the sea; (12) Turkish portions of the Ottoman Empire to be assured secure sovereignty, but other nationalities under Turkish domination to be freed; (13) independence of Poland, to include territories with predominantly Polish population, with free Polish access to the sea; (14) formation of an association of nations ensuring liberty and territorial integrity of great and small alike.

Operations on the Western Front

LUDENDORFF'S OFFENSIVES

During the winter of 1917–1918, Ludendorff realized that Germany's only hope of winning the war lay in a decisive victory in the west in 1918, before the weight of American man power could have a significant effect. With Russia knocked out of the war, he believed that this could be done. Shifting most German forces from the east, he instituted an intensive training program in preparation for an all-out offensive to be launched as early as possible in the spring. The best units were developed into "shock troops," to be spearheads of the planned assaults. His intention was to smash the Allied armies in a series of hammer blows. Recognizing the divergent interests of the French (concerned with protection of Paris) and the British (interested in maintaining their lines of communications with the Channel ports), he intended to drive a wedge between the two Allied armies and then destroy the British in subsequent assaults. Preparations were made with remarkable efficiency.

The Somme Offensive

1918, March 21. The First Offensive. The Germans began their drive at dawn in heavy fog. Three German armies—Seventeenth (Otto von Below), Second (Marwitz), and Eighteenth (Hutier), from north to south—struck the right flank of the British sector—the Third (Byng) and Fifth (Gough) armies—on a 60-mile front between Arras and La Fère. The objective was to break through, dislocate, and roll up the British, wheeling to the north and splitting them from the French on their right. Following a surprise 5-hour bombardment by more than 6,000 cannon, the specially trained German shock elements rolled through the fog, using "Hutier tactics"—infiltration behind a rolling barrage and passing of strong points which would

be later mopped up by reserves, accompanied by artillery neutralization of battery positions and observation posts (see p. 972). No limits were set to the advance; each division pressed as far and as fast as possible, with close-support elements passing through and taking up the advance whenever a local assault should bog down. Gough's Fifth Army, spread thin on a 42-mile front lately taken over from the French, collapsed, exposing the Third Army's right and forcing its withdrawal, but Byng, better organized in depth, held the German Seventeenth and Second armies to limited gains. Hutier, continuing on Gough's heels, reached and passed the Somme. All British reserves were committed to plug the gap and some French units also reinforced. But Pétain was more concerned with protecting Paris than he was with assisting Haig. The British commander hastily appealed to the new British Chief of Staff, General Sir **Henry Wilson,** and the War Minister, Lord **Milner,** for the appointment of "Foch or some other French general who will fight" to take supreme command.

1918, March 23–August 7. Artillery Bombardment of Paris. A remarkable long-range German cannon began a sporadic bombardment of Paris from a position 65 miles away. This amazing achievement of German ordnance technology seriously hurt morale of Parisians and inflicted 876 casualties, but did not significantly affect the war. Actually there were 7 "Paris Guns," with a caliber of about 9 inches, the barrels 117 feet long, with a maximum range of 80 miles.

1918, March 26. Foch Appointed Allied Co-ordinator. In an emergency meeting of the Supreme War Council at Doullens, Foch was appointed co-ordinator for the Western Front.

1918, April 3. Foch to Supreme Command. At Beauvais, the War Council appointed Foch commander in chief of the Allied forces in France. Pershing, who had already (March 27) generously offered his 8 available divisions in France to Foch in the emergency, agreed in principle to the appointment.

1918, April 5. End of the Offensive. Meanwhile the German drive, after gaining a 40-mile-deep salient, lost momentum. Paris had been bombarded by long-range artillery (75 miles; March 21–April 6). Foch's shifting of reserves checked the German assault after it reached Montdidier, and Ludendorff brought it to a halt. Allied losses mounted to about 240,000 casualties (163,000 British, 77,000 French), including 70,000 prisoners and 1,100 guns. German casualties were almost as high, most of them in the specially trained shock divisions. Over Haig's protests, Gough was relieved by the British government; his shattered Fifth Army was taken over by General Sir **Henry Rawlinson**'s Fourth Army headquarters.

COMMENT. *The most serious consequence of the offensive, from the German point of view, had been the institution of an Allied unified command. Thus, despite its initial brilliant tactical success, the offensive was a strategic failure. There were 3 main reasons for this:* (*1*) Lack of logistical mobility. *Once a breakthrough had been made, the Germans found themselves advancing across land devastated by 4 years of war, particularly by their own "scorched earth" measures at the time of the withdrawal to the Hindenburg Line (**see p. 968**). They did not have the means of keeping up a flow of ammunition, food, and other supplies to their troops advancing through a veritable quagmire.* (*2*) Lack of strategic mobility. *The same problem prevented them from fully exploiting the gap with fast-moving mobile forces, or even from providing adequate reinforcements and replacements to the breakthrough troops.* (*3*) Lack of mobile tactical fire support. *Once the breakthrough was made, the front-line infantry quickly outran its artillery, which was unable to advance in any significant numbers through the roadless morass. Thus, when the British were finally able to move reserves into the gap, the Germans lacked sufficient fire power to maintain the momentum of their drive or to deal adequately with the British fighter planes strafing them.*

The Lys Offensive

1918, April 9. Ludendorff's Second Offensive. Again the Germans struck the British sector, this time in Flanders on a narrower front, threatening the Channel ports. The German Fourth Army (Sixt von Armin) struck Plumer's Second Army in a Hutier-type attack. (Plumer had returned from Italy at Haig's request.) **Ferdinand von Quast**'s German Sixth Army on its left clawed through the positions of Horne's First Army, demolishing a Portuguese division.

1918, April 12. "Backs to the Wall." Haig's order forbidding retirement galvanized British resistance. The German drive was halted (April 17) after a 10-mile advance which included recapture of Messines Ridge. Foch, gathering a reserve force behind the British, placed only part of it in the line (April 21), much to Haig's dissatisfaction. After a series of further attacks and counterattacks, Ludendorff finally called the operation off. Again, and for the same reasons as before, he had achieved tactical success but strategical failure. No breakthrough had been effected, and the Channel ports were safe. The cost had been great—another 100,000 British casualties—but again German losses had been almost as great. Ludendorff's carefully trained and prepared shock troops were sadly depleted, the morale of the survivors badly shaken.

The Aisne Offensive

1918, May 27. Third German Offensive. This time Ludendorff struck along the Chemin des Dames, a diversion against the French preparatory to a planned final and decisive blow to be struck against the British in Flanders. The German First (**Bruno von Mudra**) and Seventh (Boehn) armies attacked the French Sixth Army (Duchêne) with 17 divisions in the assault, preceded by tanks. Duchêne's 12 divisions (3 of them British) were surprised in shallow defenses along a lightly held 25-mile front and collapsed. By noon the Germans were crossing the Aisne; by evening they were crossing the Vesle, west of Fismes, and reached the Marne (May 30).

1918, May 28. Battle of Cantigny. Meanwhile, as Pershing was rushing the 2nd (Major General **Omar Bundy**) and 3rd (Major General **J. T. Dickman**) divisions to reinforce the French, the first American offensive of the war took place at **Cantigny,** 50 miles northwest. The 1st U.S. Division (Major General **Robert Lee Bullard**) attacked the village, a strongly fortified German observation point, taking all its objectives, and then repulsed a series of violent German counterattacks (May 28 and 29). While only a local operation, its success, against veteran troops of Hutier's Eighteenth Army, boosted Allied morale.

1918, May 30–June 17. Battles of Château-Thierry and Belleau Wood. The U.S. 2nd and 3rd divisions were flung against the nose of the German offensive along the Marne, moving into position through the retiring troops of the French Sixth Army. The 3rd Division held the bridges at Château-Thierry against German assaults, then counterattacked and, with assistance from rallying French troops, drove the Germans back across the Marne at Jaulgonne. The 2nd Division, taking over the sector of the French XXI Corps between Vaux and Belleau, west of Château-Thierry, checked German attacks. Ludendorff called off his offensive (June 4). The 2nd Division then counterattacked, spearheaded by its Marine brigade. In 6 successive assaults the Germans were uprooted from positions at Vaux, Bouresches, and Belleau Wood, losing some 9,500 men and more than 1,600 prisoners.

COMMENT. *The net result of the third German drive had been to make a serious dent in the Allied front, a salient some 30 miles wide and more than 20 miles deep. Ludendorff determined to exploit this success by another diversionary drive, prior to his proposed Flanders stroke. It would be a 2-pronged affair converging on Compiègne, the Eighteenth Army attacking southwesterly, the Seventh Army westerly.*

Fourth and Fifth German Offensives

1918, June 9–13. Noyon-Montdidier (Fourth) Offensive. Forewarned by German deserters, Foch and Pétain were ready. French defenses were organized in depth. A counterpreparation artillery bombardment disrupted the Eighteenth Army's assault. Some gains were made, but a Franco-American counterattack halted the advance (June 11). The Seventh Army's attack was quickly snubbed (June 12). By this time, 25 American divisions were in France, 7 of them at the front. French and British leaders were making strenuous efforts to incorporate American troops into their respective armies permanently; Pershing was resisting this.

1918, July 15–19. Champagne-Marne (Fifth) Offensive. Ludendorff, clinging to his plan for an all-out drive against the British in Flanders, attempted one more preliminary offensive in Champagne to pinch out the strongly fortified Reims area. Boehn's Seventh Army would advance up the Marne through Épernay to meet Mudra's First Army and **Karl von Einem**'s Third attacking south toward Châlons. Foch, already planning a major counteroffensive, was again warned of the blow by deserters, aerial reconnaissance, and prisoners. German shock troops were tripped by an Allied artillery counterpreparation (night of July 14–15). East of Reims the attack was halted in a few hours by **Henri Gouraud**'s French Fourth Army.

1918, July 15–17. Second Battle of the Marne. West of Reims, where the defenses were neither so strong nor so deep, the German Seventh Army penetration carried to the Marne, some 14 divisions crossing the river. The stout defense of the U.S. 3rd Division again snubbed the attack there. Then Allied aircraft and artillery destroyed the German bridges, disrupting supply and forcing the attack to halt. Ludendorff, admitting defeat, now prepared for a general withdrawal from the Soissons–Château-Thierry–Reims salient to reduce the front held by his depleted forces. In 5 months he had lost half a million casualties. Allied losses had been somewhat greater, but American troops were now arriving at a rate of 300,000 a month.

THE ALLIED COUNTEROFFENSIVE

The Aisne-Marne Offensive

1918, July 18–August 5. Allied Aisne-Marne Offensive. The French Tenth (Mangin), Sixth (**Jean M. J. Degoutte**), and Fifth (**Henri M. Berthelot**) armies, from left to right, assaulted the Marne salient. The Ninth Army (**M. A. H. de Mitry**) was in reserve. In a series of smashing attacks, the Germans were rolled back all along the line, despite desperate resistance and skillful handling. The U.S. 1st and 2nd divisions spearheaded the Tenth Army's attack—the main effort. The 1st Division captured 3,800 prisoners and 70 guns from the 7 German divisions it encountered. Its casualties were 1,000 killed and 6,000 wounded. The 2nd Division, capturing 3,000 prisoners and 75 guns, suffered 5,000 casualties in all. Six other American divisions also took part—the 4th, 26th, and 42nd in Major General **Hunter Liggett**'s I Corps with the French Sixth Army, and the 3rd, 28th, and 32nd in Major General Bullard's III Corps with the Ninth Army (which moved into line between the Sixth and Fifth armies). Ludendorff called off his proposed Flanders drive (July 20), concentrating his efforts to stabilize the situation along the Vesle. The Marne salient no longer existed. In reward for the victory, Clemenceau promoted Foch to Marshal of France (August 6).

COMMENT. *The entire July operation, German offensive and Allied counteroffensive, is sometimes called the* **Second Battle of the Marne.** *Strategically, it was the turn of the tide; the initiative had been wrested from the Germans. Ludendorff's gamble to conclude the war successfully had failed. The front had been shortened by 28 miles, the important Paris-Châlons railway line reestablished, and all menace to Paris ended. On the Allied side, troops of 4 nations—France, Great Britain, the United States, and Italy—had successfully participated in a unified operation. Allied morale soared as German dropped. Ludendorff had lost 30,000 more prisoners, more than 600 guns, 200 mine throwers, and 3,000 machine guns.*

The Amiens Offensive, August 8–September 4

1918, August 8–11. First Phase. Haig, in conjunction with the French Aisne-Marne offensive, threw Rawlinson's British Fourth Army and the French First Army (**M. Eugène Debeny,** attached by Foch to Rawlinson's command) against the German Eighteenth (Hutier) and Second

The Paris gun

(Marwitz) armies. Expecting an Allied attack farther north in Flanders, the Germans were caught off guard by a well-mounted assault secretly prepared. The Canadian and Anzac corps jumped off without preliminary bombardment, preceded by tanks, and bit deep through a dense fog. More than 15,000 prisoners and 400 guns were captured. On their right, the French bombarded first, then advanced. Despite near panic among their front-line troops, the Germans managed to re-establish a position 10 miles behind the former nose of the salient. The French Third Army (**Georges Humbert**), on the right of the First, entered the action (August 10), forcing the evacuation of Montdidier. Haig cautiously paused (August 11) to regroup, despite Foch's wishes to maintain unremitting pressure on the Germans. Both Allied and German air forces took part in the initial fighting after the fog cleared.

1918, August 21–September 4. Second Phase. Progressively, the British Third Army on the left and the French armies on the right took up the assault. The British Fourth Army in the center joined in (August 22), followed by the British First Army (Horne) on the far left. Ludendorff ordered a general withdrawal from both the Lys salient in Flanders and the Amiens area. His plans were disrupted when the Anzacs penetrated across the Somme (August 30–31), taking **Péronne** and threatening **St.-Quentin.** The Canadian corps, shifted to the north flank, broke through near **Quéant** (September 2). The entire German situation deteriorated, necessitating retirement to the final position—the Hindenburg Line. By this time Haig had expended his reserves and could not further exploit his victory. German casualties were more than 100,000, including some 30,000 prisoners. Allied losses were 22,000 British and 20,000 French. Tactically and strategically, the Allies had gained another major victory, cracking German morale.

COMMENT. *Ludendorff's bitter statement that August 8 had been the "Black Day" of the German Army tells the story. He said flatly: "The war must be ended!"*

St.-Mihiel Offensive, September 12–16

Pershing's insistence on a separate and distinct United States Army operating on its own assigned front was reluctantly accepted by Foch (July 24). Reduction of the St.-Mihiel salient was the first mission. The U.S. First Army, with the French II Colonial Corps attached, took over the sector (August 30). Foch, planning an all-out Allied offensive, then attempted to change Pershing's plan and divide part of the American forces between the French Second and Fourth armies. After sharp disagreement, Foch accepted Pershing's position, but the American agreed to shift his army and attack with the French in the Argonne Forest immediately upon conclusion of the St.-Mihiel operation.

Ludendorff, well aware of the threat, started evacuation of the salient (September 8).

Supported by a conglomerate Allied air force of some 600 planes—American, French, Italian, and Portuguese—under American Colonel **William Mitchell,** the First Army attacked both faces of the salient (September 12). The French corps held the nose. The assault—both ground and air—was completely successful; the converging attacks met at Hattonchatel by nightfall on the first day, and the salient was entirely cleared (September 16); more than 15,000 prisoners and some 250 guns were taken. American casualties numbered 7,000. The strategic importance of the victory was great; since 1914 the St.-Mihiel salient in German hands had constituted a standing threat to any Allied movements in Champagne. In addition, the First Army proved itself to both friend and foe to be a competent entity. This was the largest American operation since the Civil War. Pershing at once turned to the tremendous job of shifting his entire army some 60 miles, and entering another major offensive without any rest.

Lieutenant Frank Luke, American ace, with his Spad

FOCH'S FINAL OFFENSIVES

The Concept

Foch planned a double penetration, in 2 major assaults. One of these was to be a Franco-American drive from the Verdun area toward Mézières, a vital German supply center and railroad junction. The other was to be a British offensive between Péronne and Lens, with the railroad junction of Aulnoye as its objective. Seizure of these 2 vital railroad junctions would jeopardize the entire German logistical situation on the Western Front. Supplemental assaults would be made in Flanders by a combined British-Belgian-French army group, and between La Fère and Péronne by another Franco-British force.

The Meuse-Argonne Offensive, September 26–November 11

1918, September 26–October 3. First Phase. Having efficiently shifted by night more than a million men with tanks and guns over an inadequate road and rail net, Pershing launched the First Army—3 corps abreast—in attack at 5:25 A.M. On its left the French Fourth Army (**H. J. E. Gouraud**) attacked also. The American zone lay astride the Meuse Valley, including the Argonne Forest on its left, the Aire Valley, and the heights on both sides of the Meuse. The German defenses (Gallwitz's army group to the east, the Crown Prince's to the west) consisted of 3 heavily fortified lines taking clever advantage of the rugged and heavily wooded terrain. Initial rapid advance was finally slowed in the Argonne Forest and in front of **Montfaucon** as the Germans rushed in reinforcements. The American drive lost momentum on the line **Apremont-Brieulles** (October 3), having penetrated the first 2 German positions.

1918, October 4–31. Second Phase. Replacing a number of his assault divisions by veteran troops from the St.-Mihiel operation, Pershing renewed the offensive. There was no room for maneuver; the First Army battered its way slowly forward in a series of costly frontal attacks, and the actual combat zone was widened to include the east bank of the Meuse, where the Germans had excellent observation from the Heights of the Meuse. The Argonne Forest was cleared, facilitating the advance of the French Fourth Army, on the left, to the Aisne River. Pershing regrouped his forces into a group of 2 armies (October 12). The newly constituted Second Army, commanded by Bullard,

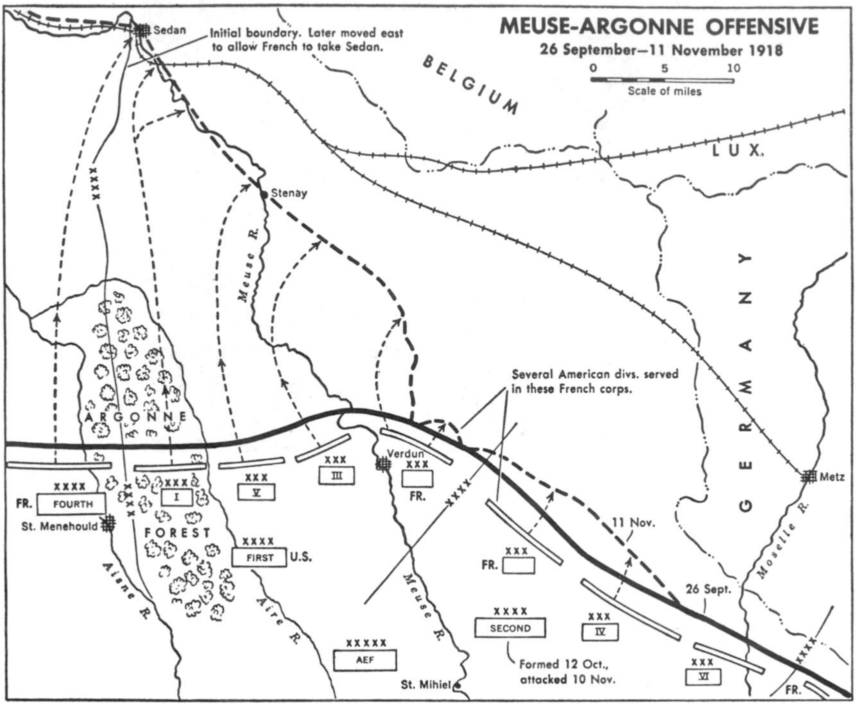

prepared for an offensive northeast, between the Meuse and the Moselle, while the First Army, now under Liggett, continued its slow northward battering-ram progression. Clemenceau, exasperated by the Americans' slow progress, tried unsuccessfully to have Pershing relieved. Foch, aware of the nature of the opposition, well knowing that the American offensive—threatening the part of the front most vital to the Germans—was drawing all available German reserves from elsewhere for its defense, declined to support Clemenceau. As October ended, the First Army had punched through most of the third and final German line.

1918, November 1–11. Final Phase. With rested divisions replacing tired ones, the First Army jumped off again, smashing through the last German positions northeast and west of Buzancy, thus enabling the French Fourth Army to cross the Aisne. In the open now, American spearheads raced up the Meuse Valley, brushing aside last-ditch German defensive stands, reaching the Meuse before Sedan (November 6) and placing destructive artillery fire on the Mézières-Montmédy rail line, vital artery of supply for the entire German front. A spectacular drive on Sedan by the U.S. 1st Division was abruptly checked by orders from higher authority, to permit the French the honor of taking the city and erasing the stain of the 1870 disaster (see p. 835). Bullard's Second Army launched its final attack (November 10), driving for Montmédy. Next day the armistice ended all hostilities.

Final British, French, and Belgian Offensives

1918, September 27–October 17. Storming the Hindenburg Line. One day after the beginning of the American offensive, Haig's army group flung itself against the Hindenburg Line. Trading space for time on this front, Boehn's army group managed to withdraw after a succession of costly and gallant British attacks drove through the last of the Hindenburg Line positions (October 5). To Haig's surprise, he had been unable to achieve a complete breakthrough, and the momentum of his drive slowed down in the face of skillful German defense.

1918, September 28–October 14. Offensive in Flanders. British-Belgian troops of King Albert's army group swept over the Ypres Ridge, but then slowed down as swampy country choked all supply, and Rupprecht's army group fought back grimly.

1918, October 17–November 11. Advance to the Sambre and the Scheldt. Because of American progress in the Meuse-Argonne, a German retreat all along the line became necessary. Ludendorff hoped that he could re-establish a new line west of the German border and by a determined defense through the winter force the Allies to grant generous terms. But his hopes were foiled by the pressure being maintained all along the Allied lines. In a renewed British assault, Rawlinson's Fourth Army broke through German defenses on the Selle River (October 17). Byng's Third Army forced a crossing lower down (October 20). The drive threw back Boehn's army group with the loss of 20,000 prisoners. At the same time the Belgians and British began to move again in Flanders. The German Army began to crack.

The German Collapse

1918, October 6. Request for an Armistice. As the front lines began to crumble, the new German chancellor, Prince **Max of Baden,** sent a message to President Wilson, requesting an armistice on the basis of Wilson's Fourteen Points (see p. 977). An exchange of messages concluded (October 23) with Wilson's insistence that the U.S. (and the Allies) would not negotiate an armistice with the existing military dictatorship.

1918, October 27. Resignation of Ludendorff. Just before formal dismissal, Ludendorff resigned to permit the desperate German government to comply with Wilson's demand. Hindenburg, however, retained his post as German commander in chief, with General **Wilhelm Groener** replacing Ludendorff as Quartermaster General (Chief of Staff).

1918, October 29–November 10. Revolution in Germany. Inspired by the Communists and sparked by a mutiny of the High Seas Fleet, disorders, revolts, and mutinies flared inside Germany. A new Socialist government took power and proclaimed a republic (November 9). The Kaiser fled to Holland (November 10).

1918, November 7–11. Armistice Negotiations. A German delegation, headed by a civilian, **Matthias Erzberger,** negotiated an armistice with Foch in his railway coach headquarters on a siding at Compiègne. Agreement was finally reached at 5 A.M., November 11, 1918. The terms, which were in effect a German surrender, provided that the German Army must immediately evacuate all occupied territory and Alsace-Lorraine; immediately surrender great quantities of war matériel (including 5,000 guns and 25,000 machine guns); evacuate German territory west of the Rhine, and three bridgeheads over the Rhine, to be occupied by the Allies; surrender all submarines; intern all other surface warships as directed by the Allies.

1918, November 11. The Armistice. Hostilities ceased at 11 A.M.; the terms of the armistice immediately became effective.

COMMENT. *Comparisons are invidious. The American Expeditionary Force was the vital factor in the final Allied victory; the Meuse-Argonne offensive was decisive; 6 other American divisions played important spearhead roles elsewhere on the front during the final Allied advances. But the question whether Allied victory could have been achieved without the Americans should not be debated. The American role was to add a final increment of numbers and fresh initiative, permitting the much larger, and more experienced, Allied armies to achieve equally spectacular successes in the final weeks of the war.*

The Italian Front

1918, June 15–22. Austrian Offensive. Germany during the spring transferred her troops in Italy to the Western Front, insisting that the Austrians crush Italy singlehanded. The argument had weight, since Russia was out of the war. Both Conrad (now commanding on the Trentino front) and Borojevic, on the Piave, demanded command of the decisive effort. A compromise decision by Archduke **Joseph** permitted them to attack simultaneously. Since the mountainous terrain and lack of lateral communications would prevent mutual support, the available reserves were split between them. The result was that neither commander had sufficient strength to exploit any initial success.

1918, June 15. Battle of the Piave. Following a diversionary attack in the west at the **Tonale Pass,** which was repulsed (June 13), the twin Austrian drives were launched; Conrad's objective was Verona; Borojevic's, Padua. Forewarned by deserters, Diaz was well prepared. Conrad's Eleventh Army, striking the Italian Sixth and Fourth armies, made some slight gains, but was then checked and thrown back by counterattacks. His troops took little further part in the offensive. Borojevic, attacking along the lower reaches of the Piave, forced a wide crossing and penetrated positions of the Italian Third Army for about 3 miles. The mirage of success failed when unexpected high water and Italian aerial bombing attacks disrupted the Austrian supply line. Diaz, who had kept one entire army in reserve—the Ninth—promptly shifted reinforcements over lateral lines and snubbed the attack. Borojevic, unable to obtain reinforcements from Conrad, withdrew during the night (June 22–23). Diaz, much to Foch's disgust, made no counterattack.

1918, July–October. Italian Counteroffensive Preparations. Diaz, marking time until sure of eventual Allied success on other fronts, finally prepared a double offensive. The Italian Fourth Army was to penetrate the center of the Austrian front. The Eighth Army, supported by the new Tenth and Twelfth armies (mostly containing British and French divisions), was to attack across the Piave on Vittorio Veneto. This diversion of force was based on the demoralized condition of the Austrian forces, whose home government, falling to pieces, was requesting an armistice.

1918, October 23. Battle of Monte Grappo. Showing unexpected determination, the Austrian Belluno Group, defending the key point on the center front, threw back the Italian Fourth Army with heavy loss.

1918, October 24–November 4. The Battle of Vittorio Veneto. The Austrian Sixth Army halted the Italian Eighth on the Piave River line. However, French troops of the Twelfth Army (commanded by French General **Jean Graziani**) clawed a footing on the left, while on the right British troops of the Tenth Army (commanded by British General **Frederic Lambert, Earl of Cavan**) gained a large bridgehead (October 28), throwing back part of the Austrian Fifth Army and splitting the front. One American regiment, the 332nd Infantry, took part in this action. The penetration reached **Sacile** (October 30). Next day, as Italian reinforcements exploited the ever-widening gap, Austrian resistance collapsed. Belluno was reached (November 1) and the Tagliamento (November 2), while in the western zone British and French troops of the Sixth Army drove through to Trent (November 3). Some 300,000 Austrians became prisoners.

1918, November 3. Capture of Trieste. The city was seized by an Allied naval expedition in the Gulf of Venice.

1918, November 3. Armistice Signed. Hostilities were to be concluded the next day (November 4).

The Balkan Front

1918, September 15–29. Battle of the Vardar. Brilliant French General Franchet d'Esperey, who succeeded the capable organizer Guillaumat (July), was given grudging assent by the Supreme War Council to mount a major offensive. He nominally had nearly 600,000 men—Serb, Czech, Italian, French, and British—of whom some 200,000 were available for duty. Opposing him were about 400,000 Bulgars (practically all German troops had been withdrawn except for command and staff). Covered by heavy artillery support, the First and Second Serb armies attacked the center of the front, debouching between elements of the French Orient Army. The penetration was successful, the Serbs pushing north while the French exploited the gap on both flanks. A British diversionary attack (September 18) on the right gained some ground. Gaining momentum, the penetrating assault reached the Vardar (September 25), splitting the Bulgarian front. The British drive reached Strumitsa (September 26), and French cavalry, passing through the main effort, took **Skoplje** (September 29). Allied air forces brought panic to the fleeing Bulgars.

1918, September 29. Bulgarian Armistice. Energetic Franchet d'Esperey kept his Serbian and French troops moving north.

1918, November 10–11. Crossing of the Danube. Franchet d'Esperey had freed the Balkans and was prepared to march on Budapest and Dresden when Germany's armistice halted hostilities.

The Eastern Front

Although hostilities had ended, Russian-German wrangling dragged on for 2 months over the conference tables at Brest-Litovsk. Germany insisted upon autonomy for the former Russian territories of Poland, Finland, Estonia, Latvia, Lithuania, and the Ukraine, all of which were in revolt against the Bolshevik government of Russia (see p. 998). Trotsky, the chief Russian negotiator, refused to accept these terms and to sign a peace treaty. Finally the Germans called the Soviet bluff and marched eastward (February 18). Unable to offer military opposition, the Bolsheviks hastily signed a peace treaty (March 3) whose terms were even stiffer than the Germans had originally offered. German troops continued on to occupy the Ukraine, which provided grain to save the German people from starvation in 1918. As Cyril Falls has written: "Russia lay at the mercy of the Central Powers for the rest of the war. It was Foch and Haig who saved Bolshevik Russia."*

The Turkish Fronts

THE CAUCASUS

1918, January 27. British Advance on Baku. Under Major General **L. C. Dunsterville,** British troops moved northeast from Baghdad, reaching **Enzeli** (Pahlevi) on the Caspian (February 17). An advance battalion crossed the Russian border and entered **Baku** (August 4).

1918, February 24. Turkish Advance into Armenia. The Turks raced the British for possession of the oil wells of western Persia after the Russian collapse. Reoccupying **Trebizond,** the Turks in quick succession reached **Erzerum** (March 12), **Van** (April 5), **Batum** (April 15), and **Kars** (April 27). A German force, landing at **Poti** on the Black Sea (June 12), pressed east to take **Tiflis** (Tbilisi) (June 12), while the Turks reached **Tabriz. Baku** was abandoned by the British after vigorous Turkish attacks (August 26–September 14).

PALESTINE AND SYRIA

1918, January–September. Lawrence of Arabia. While Allenby at Jerusalem was restricted to minor operations because of drafts on his force to the Western Front, Arabia to the south and east was in flames. Colonel **T. E. Lawrence,** with a small group of other British officers, reaped a harvest of Arab rebellion against Turkish rule. Lawrence's guerrillas played hob with the Hejaz Railway, running for some 600 miles from Amman, Palestine, to Medina (Al Madinah) in Arabia, the southernmost Turkish garrison. In all, Lawrence's activities kept more than 25,000 Turkish troops pinned down to blockhouses and posts along this line. By September, Lawrence, with Emir **Faisal,** son of Sherif **Hussein,** self-styled "King of the Hejaz," had isolated Medina by destroying the railway line and was moving north to operate on Allenby's right flank. The Arab strength totaled about 6,000 men. The Arab irregulars had been reinforced with small British armored-car detachments and light guns, and British gold coaxed the fickle Arabs to remain in ranks.

1918, September 18–October 30. Allenby's Offensive. Reinforced during the late summer, Allenby prepared meticulously for what was to be the decisive blow. The Turkish defensive line, skillfully fortified, lay from the Mediterranean, north of Jaffa, to the Jordan Valley. Liman von Sanders, who had replaced Falkenhayn in command, had the Turkish Eighth, Seventh, and Fourth armies in line from right to left, a total of some 36,000 men and 350 guns. Allenby's plan was to mass his main effort on the seashore, burst open a gap, and then let his cavalry corps through while the entire British line swung north

* *The Great War, 1914–1918,* New York, 1959, p. 287.

and east like a gate, pivoting on the Jordan Valley. Utmost secrecy was kept. British planes cleared the sky of all enemy observation. Dummy camps and horse lines indicated to the Turks that the British cavalry was concentrated near Jerusalem. Elaborate plans for a race meet on the day of the offensive were widely publicized. Allenby's strength was 57,000 infantry, 12,000 cavalry, and 540 guns. Of these, 35,000 infantry and 400 guns were concentrated in the main effort against 8,000 Turkish infantry and 130 guns.

1918, September 19–21. Battle of Megiddo. At 4:30 A.M. an artillery concentration fell, followed immediately by the advance of the entire British line. The XXI Corps on the left tore a wide gap along the seacoast, through which the Desert Mounted Corps poured. At the same time the RAF bombed rail junctions and all Turkish army headquarters, completely paralyzing communications. The cavalry raced northward through the disintegrating Turkish Eighth Army, reaching the plain of Esdraelon early next morning. The great eastward wheel of the infantry was completed by dawn (September 20). By this time the Turkish Eighth Army (**Jerad** Pasha) had ceased to exist, and the Seventh (Kemal) was falling back eastward in disorder toward the Jordan. The British cavalry then swept through Nazareth—Sanders himself narrowly escaping capture—and turned east to reach the Jordan just south of the Sea of Galilee (September 21). Alone of the Sanders army group, the German Asia Corps (2 regiments) retained some semblance of order in the rout that followed.

1918, September 22–October 30. The Pursuit. Hordes of fugitives were bombed by the RAF as the Turkish Fourth Army in the Jordan Valley joined the torrent. On the desert flank to the east, Lawrence and Faisal cut the railway line at Deraa (September 27), while Allenby pressed to take Damascus (October 1) and Beirut (October 2). The Desert Mounted Corps continued to spearhead the advance, reaching Homs (October 16) and Aleppo (October 25).

1918, October 30. Turkey Leaves the War. Turkey signed an armistice (October 30) at Mudros.

COMMENT. *Allenby's victory at Megiddo was a set piece of fire and movement, perfectly planned and executed. It was one of the most brilliant operations in the history of the British Army. In 38 days, Allenby's troops had advanced 360 miles, fighting continuously. Three Turkish armies were destroyed, 76,000 prisoners (4,000 of them Germans and Austrians), 360 guns, and a vast amount of other material captured. British casualties—mostly incurred during the initial breakthrough—were 853 killed, 4,482 wounded, and 385 missing.*

MESOPOTAMIA

1918, January–September. Dunsterville Operation against Baku. (See p. 987.)

1918, October 23. Tigris Offensive. A British force of all arms was hurriedly pushed north from Baghdad to secure the Mosul oil fields as a *fait accompli* prior to the expected Turkish collapse. Lieutenant General **A. S. Cobbe** dislodged the Turkish Tigris Group (General **Ismael Hakki**) from its outpost position at Fat-ha. Hakki fell back to the vicinity of **Sharqat,** where Cobbe's forces converged on him after some sharp fighting. A British assault (October 29) was only partially successful, but next day Hakki surrendered, with 11,322 prisoners and 51 guns. British casualties were 1,886. Cobbe now hurried his cavalry to the outskirts of Mosul (November 1). Despite the provisions of the October 30 armistice, Cobbe was ordered to take the place. After some squabbling, the Turkish garrison of Halil Pasha agreed to march out and the British remained (November 14).

COMMENT. *The entire checkered Mesopotamian campaign had hinged upon the oil fields and their protection. The war's end found Britain in possession, at a total cost of 80,007 casualties. Of these 15,814 had been killed in action; an additional 12,807 died from disease.*

1918, November. Capture of Baku. A British flotilla, extemporized on the Caspian Sea, drove the Turks from Baku.

1918, November 12. Envoi. The Allied fleet steamed through the Dardanelles, to arrive off **Constantinople** (Istanbul) next day.

War at Sea

1918, April 23. Zeebrugge and Ostend Raids. The German submarine warfare, contained though it was by this time by the Allied convoy system, was nevertheless still a menace. U-boats operated from bases at Zeebrugge and Ostend, and from the shelter of the canal port of Bruges. British Rear Admiral **R. J. B. Keyes,** commanding the Dover Patrol, organized a raid against the bases, some 75 ships taking part. With the utmost gallantry the light cruiser *Vindictive* (Captain **A. F. B. Carpenter**) dashed into Zeebrugge, with destroyer and submarine escort. The ship laid alongside the mole and demolition parties debarked. At the same time a British submarine loaded with high explosive was blown up against the lock gates and two blockships were also sunk. The *Vindictive* and her landing parties got away after inflicting some damage, but the base was not entirely blocked. A raid against Ostend at the same moment failed. Another raid (May 9) into Zeebrugge was made by the *Vindictive;* the cruiser was deliberately sunk against the lock gates. While not a complete success, these exploits went far to lower German morale.

Several German light cruiser and destroyer raids against the British coast and against North Sea convoys were but minor irritations to the British.

1918, January 20. Sortie from the Dardanelles. The *Goeben* and *Breslau* sailed into the Aegean Sea, but the voyage ended in disaster; the *Goeben* was badly damaged by British mines, and the *Breslau* was sunk. However, the *Goeben,* despite British aerial bombing, was salvaged.

1918, June 9. Austrian Sortie from Pola. This effort against Allied blockading craft was repelled when 2 Italian midget submarines attacked the Austrian squadron, sinking the battleship *Szent-Istvan,* the only dreadnought sunk in action during the war.

1918, October 29. Mutiny of the High Seas Fleet. Hipper (who had succeeded Scheer in August) planned a desperate sortie to bring on a final battle with the British Grand Fleet. The crews mutinied, refused to sail, and seized control of the warships, ending the war at sea.

Operations in East Africa

Despite the most intensive efforts, the British had been unable to overcome elusive and brilliant von Lettow-Vorbeck in 4 years of continuous search and pursuit. They drove him into Portuguese East Africa (1917), where he continued an active and aggressive guerrilla campaign, capturing Portuguese military posts and maintaining his small command by captured supplies. He then re-entered German East Africa and, though he had only 4,000 men and was opposed by forces totaling 130,000, succeeded in capturing several small posts before marching into British Northern Rhodesia. Finally, after the British were able to inform him of the Armistice, he stopped hostilities (November 14) and surrendered his command (November 23).

POSTARMISTICE

1918, November 17. German Evacuation of Allied Territory. Allied troops began to reoccupy those portions of France and Belgium which had been held by the Germans since 1914.

1918, November 21. The Internment of the High Seas Fleet. The German fleet sailed into the Firth of Forth, between the lines of the British Grand Fleet. It later was shifted to Scapa Flow.

1918, December 1. Allied Movement into the Rhineland. In accordance with the Armistice terms, Allied and American troops followed the withdrawing Germans into Germany.

1918, December 9. Bridgehead Occupation. The British were at Cologne, the Americans at Coblenz, the French at Mainz. The bridgeheads were 18 miles deep in radius beyond the Rhine.

1919, May 7–June 28. Treaty of Versailles. The terms as presented to and signed by the German representatives (no discussion was permitted them): (1) admission of German war guilt; (2) Germany was stripped of her colonies, Alsace-Lorraine, the Saar Basin (subject to a plebiscite in 1935), Posen, and parts of Schleswig and

Silesia; (3) reparations were required, later fixed at $56 billion; (4) Germany was disarmed. The Covenant of the proposed League of Nations was attached to the treaty. The U.S. Senate rejected the League Covenant despite the frantic efforts of President Wilson, which resulted in his physical breakdown. Finally (May 20), the Congress by joint resolution declared the end of war with Germany and Austria-Hungary, reserving for the U.S. any rights secured by the Armistice, the Versailles Treaty, or as a result of the war. Separate U.S. treaties concluding peace with Germany, Austria, and Hungary were later ratified (October 18, 1920).

1919, June 21. Scuttling of the High Seas Fleet. Most of the ships of the German fleet were scuttled by their own crews at Scapa Flow, in defiance of the terms of the Versailles Treaty.

1923, January. End of the American Occupation in Germany. The U.S. Occupation Force evacuated Coblenz to return home. The British and French still remained in occupation of the Rhineland as the period ended.

The Cost of the War[a]

	Total Force Mobilized	Military Battle Deaths[b]	Military Wounded	Civilian Dead[c]	Economic and Financial Cost[d] ($ million)
Allies					
France	8,410,000	1,357,800	4,266,000	40,000	49,877
British Empire	8,904,467	908,371	2,090,212	30,633[e]	51,975
Russia	12,000,000	1,700,000	4,950,000	2,000,000[f]	25,600
Italy	5,615,000	462,391	953,886	[g]	18,143
United States	4,355,000	50,585	205,690	[g]	32,320
Belgium	267,000	13,715	44,686	30,000	10,195
Serbia	707,343	45,000[h]	133,148	650,000	2,400
Montenegro	50,000	3,000	10,000	[g]	[g]
Rumania	750,000	335,706	120,000	275,000	2,601
Greece	230,000	5,000	21,000	132,000	556
Portugal	100,000	7,222	13,751	[g]	[g]
Japan	800,000	300	907	[g]	[g]
Total	42,188,810	4,888,891	12,809,280	3,157,633	193,899
Central Powers					
Germany	11,000,000	1,808,546	4,247,143	760,000[i]	58,072
Austria-Hungary	7,800,000	922,500	3,620,000	300,000[j]	23,706
Turkey	2,850,000	325,000	400,000	2,150,000[k]	3,445
Bulgaria	1,200,000	75,844[l]	152,390	275,000	1,015
Total	22,850,000	3,131,889	8,419,533	3,485,000	86,238
Cost to Neutral Nations					1,750
Grand total	65,038,810	8,020,780	21,228,813	6,642,633	281,887

[a] Many of these figures (compiled from various sources) are approximations or estimates, since official figures are often misleading, missing, or contradictory.
[b] Includes only killed in action or died of wounds.
[c] Figures vary greatly; deaths from epidemic disease and malnutrition, probably not completely attributable to the war, are included in some instances and not in others. See specific notes below.
[d] Includes war expenditures, property losses, and merchant-shipping losses.
[e] About two-thirds of these were lost to U-boats, the remainder to naval and aerial bombardment.
[f] Includes approximately 500,000 Poles and Lithuanians.
[g] No reliable figures available; there was relatively small loss.
[h] Approximately 80,000 additional were nonbattle deaths: typhus, influenza, malnutrition, frostbite.
[i] Asserted by German sources to be due to the Allied blockade through 1919; a handful of deaths was caused by Allied air raids.
[j] At least two-thirds of these were Polish; many of the remainder have been attributed to Allied blockade.
[k] More than half of these were Armenian; most of the remainder were Syrian or Iraqi.
[l] At least 25,500 additional were nonbattle deaths.

MAJOR WARS AFTER 1918

RUSSO-POLISH WAR, 1920

1920. Prelude. During the Russian Civil War, Poland (see p. 998) had occupied areas of mixed Polish-Russian population in undefined frontier areas bordering White Russia and the Ukraine. The Soviet government now disputed this Polish action, and began to build up its forces in the west. The Poles decided to attack before the Red Army seized the initiative. North of the Pripet Marshes was Russian Marshal **Mikhail N. Tukhachevski**'s Bolshevik Army of the West, opposed by a smaller Polish army under General **Wladyslaw Sikorski.** South of the Marshes, Russian General **Yegorov**'s Army of the Southwest was opposed by the numerically superior army of General **Józef Pilsudski,** over-all Polish commander. Total forces on each side approached 200,000.

1920, April 25–May 7. Pilsudski's Offensive. The Polish general drove for Kiev, with the support of a mixed force of anti-Bolshevik Ukrainians under Hetman **Simon Petlyura** on his right flank. Capturing **Kiev** (May 7), Pilsudski prepared to swing north, behind the Pripet Marshes, to hit Tukhachevski's left rear. His plan, however, was too ambitious for the force and logistical backup available to him.

1920, May 15. Tukhachevski's Offensive. Striking southwestward, the Russian Army of the North pinned back Pilsudski's left wing. At the same time, General **Semën M. Budënny** of Yegorov's Army of the Southwest drove northwest against Pilsudski's right flank, with a Cossack cavalry corps some 16,000 strong with 48 guns. Budënny reached **Zitomir,** southwest of Kiev, almost bagging Pilsudski's right wing. By June 13, the Polish left was also in full retreat as the Cossack horde swept on to the outskirts of **Lemberg** (Lvov). North of the Pripet area, Tukhachevski advanced (July 4) westerly toward Warsaw. Polish troops fell back on both fronts. Tukhachevski reached Vilna (July 14) and Grodno (July 19), while Budënny's Cossacks kept up pressure on the southern front. By July 25 the Polish forces lay in 2 groups—1 near Warsaw, whose fall appeared imminent (Tukhachevski expected to take it August 14), the other around Lvov. In all, some 180,000 Poles faced approximately 200,000 Russians.

1920, July–August. Polish Counterattack Plan. France's General **Maxime Weygand** arrived at Warsaw to advise Pilsudski, who needed munitions more than advice. Weygand favored a counterattack north of Warsaw against the Russian right, launched from behind the defensive lines of the Vistula. Pilsudski had a better plan. The Bolshevik advance had outrun all supply; the Russians were living off the country, and could not stop. A halt would be disastrous. So, while the seemingly irresistible Russian right lapped westward, passing to the north of Warsaw, Pilsudski prepared a daring counterattack against Tukhachevski's center.

1920, August 16–25. Battle of Warsaw. Its weight concentrated at Deblin, 50 miles south of Warsaw, Pilsudski's assault crashed through the weakly held Russian center, along the axis of the Warsaw-Brest Litovsk road. Pilsudski accompanied it in person. The left of the Russian Sixteenth Army was shattered. Ignoring the Russian elements south of his penetration, Pilsudski turned north, threatening in turn the Third, Fifteenth, Sixteenth, and Fourth armies. At the same time the Polish forces north of Warsaw under Sikorski also advanced, despite desperate Russian resistance. Caught between the Polish pincers, Tukhachevski's command disintegrated. Some 30,000 or more fled north over the East Prussian border and were there disarmed. The remainder reeled eastward, closely pursued. Tukhachevski managed to rally (August 25) along the line Grodno-Brest Litovsk-Wlodawa, where the pursuit ended. The Poles captured 66,000 prisoners and more than 230 guns, 1,000 machine guns, and 10,000 vehicles. Total Russian casualties were approximately 150,000; the Poles lost 50,000 men.

COMMENT. *The Battle of Warsaw ranks among the decisive battles of the 20th century. It was as much a check to Communism's first overt westward thrust as was Charles Martel's victory at Tours a check to the Moslem surge into Europe (see p. 204).*

1920, September 12–October 10. Continued

Polish Offensive. The Poles continued their advance on broad fronts on both sides of the Pripet Marshes. Sikorski, now commanding in the south, reached Tarnopol (September 18). Pilsudski again defeated Tukhachevski in the **Battle of the Niemen** (September 26), driving the Russians from the river-line defensive positions and destroying their Third Army. The Poles next entered Grodno (September 26). Next day, in the **Battle of the Shchara** (Szczara), Pilsudski drove Tukhachevski's beaten troops back to Minsk. In these last 2 battles, the Russians lost some 50,000 prisoners and 160 guns.

1920, October 12. Armistice. Hostilities were brought to a close.

1921, March 18. Treaty of Riga. The Russians conceded all of Poland's territorial claims.

GRAECO-TURKISH WAR, 1920–1922

1918–1919. Allied Disagreements over Turkish Peace Settlement. While the Allies squabbled, Turkey was collapsing in anarchy. A Greek army was landed by the Allies at Smyrna (May 15, 1919) to act as an agent for Allied interests. An Italian force also landed in southwest Anatolia. Long-standing national antipathies precipitated incidents, leading to atrocities against the Turkish civilian population by the Greeks.

1919, June–September. Turkish Nationalist Movement. Aroused by Greek action, a group of patriotic Turks, led by General Mustafa Kemal, banded together to form a new national government. Despite opposition of the Allies (who still occupied Constantinople), Kemal set up his new government in Ankara (April, 1920).

1919, June 22. Greek Offensives in Anatolia and Thrace. Greek Prime Minister Venizelos' offer to act as the Allies' agent in suppressing the Nationalist movement was warmly accepted by British Prime Minister Lloyd George. In Thrace, Greek troops occupied Adrianople (July 25). In Anatolia, a major eastward movement placed the Greeks at Ushaq (Usak), 125 miles from Smyrna (June 29). A flanking operation captured Panderma (Bandirma) and Brusa (Bursa), south of the Sea of Marmora (July 9). There was no effective Turkish opposition.

1919, August 20. Treaty of Sèvres. The Allies imposed terms on the Sultan's government; Turkey again lost all Asiatic possessions outside of Anatolia, and all of European Turkey except the Chatalja Peninsula and Constantinople. Armenia was established as an independent republic. The treaty was not recognized by the Nationalists.

1919, October. Nationalist Offensive against Armenia. Repeated Armenian raids into Anatolia caused the Nationalists to retaliate. A Turkish drive quickly resulted in the capture of **Kars** (October 21) and the massacre of a number of Armenians in counterrevenge for earlier vengeance atrocities against Turks. A truce was soon negotiated with the Armenian and Soviet governments, ending hostilities in northeast Anatolia.

1919, October 25. Political Changes in Greece. The unexpected death of King Alexander of Greece brought his warrior-father **Constantine** (hero of the Balkan Wars, villain of World War I) back to the Greek throne, changing the entire political complexion of the war. Pro-German Constantine was not trusted by the Allies, who withdrew their former support of Greek activities in Turkey. He nevertheless determined to continue operations to gain permanent Greek control of western Anatolia and Thrace.

1921, January. First Battle of Inönü. Greek General **Papoulas,** advancing on Eskisehir, was repulsed at Inönü, 20 miles to the west, by Turk forces under **Ismet** Pasha. The Greek offensive was temporarily halted.

1921, January–March. Kemal's Diplomacy. Negotiations by Kemal resulted in the withdrawal of Italian forces from Anatolia (March 13) and an understanding with the Soviet government (March 16). The Soviets received Batum, and Kemal recognized the independence of the Soviet Armenian Republic in exchange for the return of Kars and Ardahan to Turkey.

1921, March 23. Renewed Greek Offensive. Papoulas' strength had now been built up to 150,000, of whom two-thirds were disposed along his line of communications to Smyrna. He now launched a full-scale attack.

1921, March 28–30. Second Battle of Inönü. Papoulas drove the Turks (**Refet** Pasha) out of **Afyon Karahisar (Afyon).** However, Refet's right, under Ismet Pasha, at Inönü and Eskisehir, held its ground, threatening the Greek left. Three successive Greek attacks were thrown back and Papoulas broke off the offensive (April 2). Kemal replaced Refet by Ismet (who later adopted the name of the victory as his own, and is known to Turkish history as Ismet Inönü).

1921, July 16–17. Constantine's Offensive. The Greek king now assumed personal field command, and moved skillfully against the Turkish positions from Eskisehir to Afyon. A feint at the Turkish right distracted Ismet's attention. The Greek main effort then fell on his left flank at Afyon. The Greeks then shifted direction northward, rolling up the Turkish left and center in a combination of frontal assault and envelopment. Despite Ismet's counterattack, **Eskisehir** fell (July 17). Ismet prepared to fight to the finish, but Kemal sagely ordered a retreat. Ismet's army disengaged at great cost, falling back northward about 30 miles to the Sakkaria (Sakarya) River. As Kemal had expected, the Greeks were too exhausted to pursue. Turkish losses were over 11,000, Greek about 8,000. Constantine regrouped and moved against the Sakkaria line (August 10), which had now been reinforced through Kemal's strenuous efforts.

1921, August 24–September 16. Battle of the Sakkaria. When the attempted Greek turning movement against the Turkish left was stopped, the battle turned into a slugging match. The Greek main effort next shifted to the center, advancing 10 miles in as many days; then the offensive slowed. Kemal, assuming personal command, made a daring enveloping attack with a small force against the Greek left (September 10). Although the success was slight, the psychological effect of the move was immense. With his 350-mile line of communications threatened, his troops facing a deadlock, and the Anatolian winter coming on, Constantine disengaged. The Greeks fell back along the railway line toward Eskishehir and Afyon. Kemal did not pursue closely, undoubtedly fearing this might stimulate Allied intervention in favor of the Greeks.

1921–1922, October–July. Kemal Consolidates Politically and Militarily. While active operations lagged, Kemal built up military strength and mended diplomatic fences; France withdrew her troops from Cilicia (October 20). While the overextended Greek army in the field was weakening, Turkey's internal and international position rapidly improved.

1922, August 18–September 11. Turkish Counteroffensive. Kemal struck, taking **Afyon** (August 30). His main effort then drove westward along the railway toward Smyrna, while a large detachment attacked north, capturing **Brusa** (September 5). The shattered Greek army fell back in confusion, attempting to avenge their defeat in an orgy of burning, pillaging, and murdering. About 1 million Turkish civilians were made homeless, further embittering a conflict already notable for atrocities. Kemal pursued closely, and the Greek army soon disintegrated into a horde of terrified refugees. No arrangements had been made for evacuation by sea; thousands of Greek soldiers were captured—and many massacred—by the Turks. **Smyrna** was captured by assault (September 9–11); the Greek sections of the town were sacked and burned, and many Greek civilians were massacred by the Turks.

1922, September–October. Advance on Constantinople. Kemal, now confident of his own strength, advanced on Constantinople, which was still occupied by a small Allied garrison. The Allies were as anxious to avoid a clash as he was. Diplomatic negotiations at the **Convention of Mudania** (October 3–11) promised the restoration of Thrace and Adrianople to Turkey, and provided for neutralization of the Straits. Kemal proclaimed abolition of the Sultanate; the Sultan fled in a British warship (November 1).

1923, July 24. Treaty of Lausanne. This superseded the Treaty of Sèvres (see p. 1003), formally restoring to Turkey her Thracian territory to the Maritza River. The Allies then evacuated Constantinople (August 23). The Turkish Republic was officially established, with Mustafa Kemal, surnamed Atatürk ("Chief of the Turks"), as its first President (October 29).

COMMENT. *By his charismatic inspiration, firm determination, political skill, and brilliant military genius, Kemal had revived and unified his dismembered, prostrate nation, while at the same time carrying on a victorious war against Greece. Casualty figures for the war are not available. Turkish losses were probably less than 100,000 men. Greek casualties were upward of 200,000, of whom at least half were lost during the flight to Smyrna in August–September, 1922.*

EUROPE, 1900–1925

WESTERN EUROPE

The United Kingdom of Great Britain and Ireland

1904. Committee on Imperial Defense (Esher Committee). An evaluation of the British military system, in the light of Boer War experiences, resulted in recommendations for major reorganization.

1905–1910. Haldane Reforms. Richard Burdon, Viscount Haldane, civilian Secretary for War, achieved a military reorganization generally along the lines recommended by the Esher Committee. As a result, Britain developed the finest army for its size in the world. The vital role of the British Expeditionary Force in the initial Marne Campaign (see pp. 936 and 938) was due in large measure to the Haldane reforms.

1906, February 10. Launching of H.M.S. *Dreadnought*. This new warship, for which First Sea Lord Admiral Lord **John Fisher** was primarily responsible, was the first all-big-gun battleship, carrying 10 12-inch guns. She revolutionized the navies of the world.

1907, August 31. Anglo-Russian Entente. This fused earlier Anglo-French and Franco-Russian military agreements in the Triple Entente, offsetting the Triple Alliance of Germany, Austria, and Italy (see p. 840).

1914, March 20. Curragh "Mutiny." Brigadier General **Hubert Gough** and other officers at the Curragh military base in Ireland submitted their resignations rather than obey orders to force the loyal population of Ulster to accept Home Rule under the separatists of southern Ireland. This incident seriously shook the morale of the British Army on the eve of World War I. All officers were later reinstated, however, and Ulster was permitted to remain directly under the crown.

1914, July 26. Semimobilization of the British Fleet. After the conclusion of normal extended maneuvers in home waters, First Lord of the Admiralty **Winston Churchill** ordered the fleet not to disperse to peacetime stations. As the war clouds rolled over Europe, Churchill and the First Sea Lord, Admiral Prince **Louis of Battenberg,** sent the fleet to the wartime anchorage of Scapa Flow in the Orkneys.

1914, August 4. Britain Declares War on Germany. (See p. 929.)

1914–1918. World War I. (See p. 935.)

1916–1921. Anglo-Irish Civil War. After years of violence and unrest in Ireland, armed rebellion broke out in **Dublin** on Easter Monday (April 24, 1916), largely inspired by Sir **Roger Casement,** Irish nationalist leader, who had been landed on the Irish coast by a German submarine. British action soon suppressed this uprising (May 1); Casement and other leaders were tried and executed (August 3). Sporadic fighting continued throughout the country as the Sinn Fein, Irish patriotic society, fanned the flames of revolt, and later declared Irish independence (January 21, 1919). Open rebellion again broke out later in the year (November 26). As violence spread, the "Black and Tans" (a special British constabulary force) were moved to Ireland, along with British troops (1920). The insurrection continued with increased ferocity, marked by sabotage, arson, and murder, with the illicit Irish Republican Army active in guerrilla warfare against the British forces of law and order. Atrocities were committed by both sides. In all the British employed some 100,000 men—regulars and constabulary—in the conflict. The struggle between the Protestant northern provinces (Ulster) and the Catholic population of southern Ireland continued after peace was formally established (December 6, 1921) upon British promise of dominion status to southern Ireland. The Irish Free State was officially proclaimed a year later.

1919, January 11. Trenchard Appointed Chief of Air Staff. Major General Sir

Hugh Trenchard, who had been first Chief of the Air Staff when the Royal Air Force was established (April, 1918), and who had later commanded the Independent Air Force for the strategic bombardment of Germany (June–November, 1918), returned to the head of the RAF. Trenchard's concepts for the exploitation of air power through strategic bombardment became the basis of RAF doctrine. He was later made the first Marshal of the RAF.

France

1894–1906. Dreyfus Affair. Captain **Alfred Dreyfus,** an officer of the French General Staff, unjustly accused of treason as a German spy, was tried and sentenced to imprisonment on Devil's Island. Important information that would have exonerated him was deliberately withheld from evidence in this and later trials by senior officers of the General Staff who were convinced of Dreyfus' guilt and refused to believe the evidence. The case became a *cause célèbre* within and without the army, involving overtones of anti-Semitism. Eventually it became a major political issue, particularly among liberals eager to sieze an opportunity to smash extreme conservatism and the arrogance of many aristocratic French army officers. With the support of politician **Georges Clemenceau** and the writer **Émile Zola,** the case was finally reopened; Dreyfus was exonerated and restored to duty as a major. The morale and cohesiveness of the French officer corps were severely shaken.

1900–1925. Colonial Wars. These are discussed under various geographic divisions in which the wars took place.

1904, April 8. The Anglo-French Entente. This agreement, which took almost 10 months to negotiate, resolved outstanding differences and colonial rivalries between the 2 traditional enemies, leading later to the Triple Entente (see p. 994).

1906, January 10. Anglo-French Military Conversations. These established the basis for later military collaboration against Germany in World War I.

1911, July. Agadir Incident. The appearance of the German cruiser *Panther* at Agadir, Morocco, almost precipitated war between France and Germany over rival colonial interests in Morocco. Firm British support of France caused Germany to back down.

1914, August 3. Germany Declares War on France. (**See p. 929.**)

1914–1918. World War I. (**See p. 935.**)

Italy

1911–1912. Tripolitan War against Turkey. (**See p. 926.**)

1914, August 3. Italian Declaration of Neutrality. Despite its membership in the Triple Alliance, Italy abjured its understanding with Austria and Germany.

1915, May 23. Italian Declaration of War against Austria. (**See p. 949.**)

1915–1918. World War I. (**See pp. 929 and 949.**)

1919, September 12. Fiume Coup. Gabriele d'Annunzio, Italian World War I hero, writer, and nationalist, with a band of volunteers seized **Fiume.** Italy disavowed his action. Diplomatic wrestling between Italy and Yugoslavia for the disputed area was ended temporarily by the **Treaty of Rapallo** (November 12), granting Fiume independence. D'Annunzio thereupon declared war on Italy. The *opéra bouffe* ended when Italian troops bombarded Fiume and ejected him (December 27).

1921. Retirement of Douhet. Colonel **Giulio Douhet**'s criticisms of the Italian Army in World War I had led to his court martial and imprisonment (1916). The Caporetto disaster (see p. 971) vindicated his criticisms; Douhet was released from prison and made chief of the Italian Army's aviation arm. He was promoted to general shortly before his retirement (1921). After retirement he published his book, *The Command of the Air,* elucidating his doctrine of winning wars by the use of airpower to break the enemy's will through violent and destructive bombardment of enemy cities. In order for airpower to perform its war-winning task, Douhet insisted that it must be completely independent of, and co-equal with, surface forces. Through this and subsequent writings Douhet became the leading theoretician of air warfare, and the apostle of airpower.

1922. Rise of Fascism. Benito Mussolini's "Black Shirt" movement culminated with the **"March on Rome"** (October 28) and grant to him by the king and parliament —under armed pressure—of dictatorial powers (November 25). A virtual Fascist Reign of Terror followed as Mussolini consolidated his power (1923–1925).

1923, August–September. The Corfu Incident. Seizing upon the assassination of Italian members of an international border commission on the Greek-Albanian frontier, Italy sent warships to bombard and to occupy the Greek island of Corfu. After Greek appeal to the League of Nations, Italy withdrew from Corfu under pressure from Britain and other powers.

Spain

Not directly affected by World War I, Spain was involved militarily only in minor colonial operations during the early part of this period. Long-standing unrest in Spanish Morocco, however, broke out into full-scale revolt, in which Spanish arms suffered one disaster and several additional defeats (1921–1925; see p. 1004). One result of these setbacks was to revive internal frictions in Spain itself. A military revolt in Barcelona led to the assumption of dictatorial power by General **Miguel Primo de Rivera,** who was able to restore order temporarily (1923).

Portugal

Portugal was wracked by a series of minor revolts during most of this period. She joined the Allies in World War I (March 9, 1916).

CENTRAL AND NORTHERN EUROPE

Germany

1891–1906. Count Alfred von Schlieffen, Chief of General Staff. (**See p. 931.**)

1900–1913. Colonial Activities. Military operations prior to World War I were confined to colonial areas, and are discussed under the respective geographical sections of this chapter. During this period there were repeated colonial crises in Morocco, leading to the brink of war with France (see p. 1003). Also Germany exerted an intensive, and generally successful, effort to achieve a position of predominating military and civilian influence in Turkey.

1900–1914. Prewar Civil-Military Relations. Militaristic Emperor **Wilhelm II** relied more and more on military advisers, ignoring competent German civilian statesmen. Since the General Staff was not subordinate to or responsible to the chancellor, or the defense minister, or any other element of the parliamentary government, the German Army became a "state within a state." Though most professional German soldiers eschewed politics, their single-minded devotion to the nation's military security had the gravest political implications, which they either did not realize or ignored.

1914–1918. World War I. (**See p. 929.**)

1914–1918. Wartime Civil-Military Relations. The wartime requirements of military necessity still further increased the ascendancy of the military in Germany. Hindenburg and Ludendorff used the special constitutional status of the General Staff, and their own enormous prestige, to create a virtual military dictatorship (1916–1918; see p. 968). Civilian governments were overruled or dismissed by the emperor at their demand. Their threats to resign always caused Wilhelm to comply abjectly with their wishes, thus making himself completely their puppet. Though the motives of these 2 able military men were patriotic and impersonal, their insistence upon military objectives ahead of the over-all political interests of the state contributed greatly to the complete postwar collapse of Germany.

1919–1925. Civil-Military Relations under the Weimar Republic. The shaky government was undermined by a number of revolts, both Communistic and nationalistic. At the same time Allied demands under the Treaty of Versailles strangled the nation financially. During a particularly violent period of revolt and military mutiny, General **Hans von Seeckt** was appointed commander of the army. In effect he thus was Chief of the General Staff, even though this organization had officially been abolished under the terms of the Treaty of Versailles. A typically apolitical, aristocratic Prussian professional, Seeckt was distrustful of the republican regime. He was, however, loyal to Germany, and thus faithfully supported and defended the government. He was able to prevent the civilian chancellor and defense minister from exercising any authority over the army, and virtually recreated the prewar situation of an independent military. He was thus the most powerful figure in Germany, but made no effort to seize personal power. Although he hated Communism, he led Germany toward a *rapprochement* with Soviet Russia as a way eventually to regain the Polish provinces lost under the Treaty of Versailles, and thus to eliminate the hated Polish Corridor (see p. 989). In personal understandings with the Russian commander, Marshal **M. N. Tukhachevski,** he undertook extensive secret military collaboration with the Red Army.

1923, January 11. Occupation of the Ruhr. Because of Germany's default in reparations payments, French and Belgian troops invaded and occupied the heartland of Germany's heavy industry. Britain abstained. Germany, financed by the **Dawes Plan,** met most of her financial obligations and the Ruhr was evacuated (August, 1925). The **Treaty of Locarno** (October 5–16) seemingly guaranteed peace in Europe, but France started feverishly constructing the **Maginot Line** of fortifications along her eastern border for protection against future German aggression.

1923, November 8–11. The "Beer-Hall Putsch." Adolph Hitler, Austrian ne'er-do-well, leading a new German nationalist movement, together with General Ludendorff, representing the reactionary military element, tried to overthrow the Bavarian government in Munich. The rising was crushed and Hitler sent to jail, where he spent nearly a year, writing *Mein Kampf.* On release, Hitler resumed his activities.

1925, April 26. Hindenburg Elected President. With its war hero as its leader, the course of German military rehabilitation was accelerated.

Austria, 1918–1925

This tiny remnant of the once-mighty Hapsburg Austro-Hungarian Empire (dismembered by the **Treaty of St. Germain,** part of the over-all Versailles settlement; September 10, 1919) became a republic after a series of Communist disorders (1919). There was strong sentiment in the country for union with Germany (forbidden by the Treaty of St. Germain), resulting in a quasi alliance with her northern neighbor.

Czechoslovakia, 1918–1925

1918, November 14. Republic Established at Prague. Tomás Masaryk became the first President.

1919, March. Conflict with Hungary. (**See below.**)

1919, May–1920, May. Teschen Dispute with Poland. Clashes between regular and irregular forces of the 2 republics continued sporadically until they agreed to divide the territory.

1920–1921. Creation of the Little Entente. This was an alliance concluded with Yugoslavia (August 14, 1920) and Rumania (April 23, 1921), directed primarily against Hungary and the possibility of a Hapsburg revival. Czechoslovakia built up respectable military strength as the strongest minor European state.

Hungary, 1918–1925

1918, November 16. Proclamation of a Republic. This followed a brief revolution under Count **Michael Karolyi,** who became first President.

1919, March 21. Establishment of Communist Regime. After the resignation of Karolyi, pro-Bolshevik **Béla Kun,** sent from Russia by Lenin, seized power and established a dictatorship.

1919, March 28. Declaration of War with Czechoslovakia. Hungarian troops invaded Slovakia.

1919, April 10. Rumanian Invasion of Hungary. This was begun to forestall threatened Hungarian efforts to reconquer Transylvania, which Rumania had occupied after World War I. With Hungary torn by an anti-Communist counterrevolution, Rumanian troops advanced rapidly.

1919, August 1. Flight of Béla Kun. The Communist leader fled to Vienna just before the Rumanians occupied Budapest (August 4).

1920, June 4. Treaty of Trianon. This confirmed Hungary's acceptance of the Versailles–St. Germain settlements.

1921, March and October. King Charles Attempts to Restore Monarchy. The last Hapsburg emperor failed in 2 abortive military attempts to regain his Hungarian throne. He was permanently exiled.

The Scandinavian States

Untouched by direct impact of World War I, neutral Denmark, Sweden, and Norway confined postwar military efforts to the development of mutual security.

EASTERN EUROPE

Russia

PREREVOLUTIONARY PERIOD, 1900–1917

1904–1905. Russo-Japanese War. (See p. 920.)

1905, December 22–1906, January 1. Moscow Insurrection. Endemic unrest seethed into open, armed violence, largely Communist-inspired, as the Moscow workers revolted in protest against the government inefficiency revealed in the conduct of the Russo-Japanese War. The uprising was quelled by regular troops in a succession of street fights. Later revolutionary movements in the provinces were also put down by vigorous and ruthless army action.

1907–1914. Continuing Unrest. The growing revolutionary movement led to sporadic outbreaks throughout the country, suppressed by the army.

1914–1918. World War I. (See p. 929.)

THE RUSSIAN REVOLUTION, 1917

1917, March 8–15. Overthrow of the Empire. Following the outbreak of strikes and riots in Petrograd (Leningrad, formerly St. Petersburg), the military garrison of the capital mutinied (March 10), joining the revolting workers. A provisional government was established (March 12), and Czar **Nicholas II** abdicated.

1917, March–September. Continuation of the War. The new regime, dominated by the Socialist Minister of War Alexander Kerensky, pledged itself to continue the war against Germany, but suffered severe reverses (see p. 972).

1917, September 9–14. Kornilov Revolt. Alarmed by growing Bolshevik domination of the government, under **Vladimir Lenin** and **Leon Trotsky,** the army commander, General **Lavr Kornilov,** marched against Petrograd. He was defeated by a combination of his own defecting troops and by armed workers.

1917, November 6–7. The Bolshevik Revolution. Under the leadership of Lenin, troops and workers in Petrograd overthrew the Kerensky regime, and established a new Soviet government. (See p. 973.)

THE GREAT RUSSIAN CIVIL WAR, 1917–1922

The General Situation

War seethed both inside Russia and around the periphery of her immense land mass, as the Bolshevik regime strove to establish itself. In the struggle were involved both the residual backwash of World War I (see p. 1000) and a number of serious counterrevolutionary movements, all of them unco-ordinated. The principal areas of unrest were Poland (see pp. 991 and 1002), Finland, southern Russia and the Ukraine, White Russia and the Baltic States, and Siberia.

South Russia and the Ukraine

Here, within a 12,000-mile-long tortuous loop from the Black to the Caspian seas, were fought the major campaigns of the Civil War. The area was embraced within a winding arc from Odessa on the west, through Kiev, Orel, Voronezh, and Tsaritsin (Stalingrad) to Astrakhan and the Volga estuary.

1917, December 9. Revolt of the Don Cossacks. Expropriation of their lands by Bolshevist decree caused the first insurrection. Gathering in force to the standards of Generals **A. M. Kaledin** and Kornilov, the Cossacks moved north through the Kuban and the Don Basin, colliding with Red militia in a number of indecisive fights. Between them Kaledin and Kornilov organized their impromptu armies into a fighting force of sorts, while at the same time Trotsky's efforts were slowly welding the Bolshevik militia into what would become the Red Army.

1918, April–May. The Caucasus. Georgia, Armenia, and Azerbaijan declared their independence (April 22 and May 26). Bolshevik efforts to retain the oil lands of the area brought resentment, then sporadic revolt.

1918, November–December. The Ukraine. German-supported General **Pavel Skoropadski** had been overthrown by Ukrainian socialists under General **Simon Petlyura** after the withdrawal of German troops (November 15). France garrisoned Odessa as a base of supply to feed the growing counterrevolution (December 18).

1919, February 3. Communist Capture of Kiev. Bolshevik forces moving into the vacuum left by the German withdrawal (see p. 989) reached and took Kiev. They then pushed down the valley of the Bug and, lapping westward, drove the French out of Odessa (April 8).

1919, January. The Caucasus. Bolshevik troop movements into the oil fields turned insurrection into full-fledged war. General **Anton Denikin** rallied the White counterrevolutionaries and drove the Bolsheviks out. The conflict had now spread throughout the wide expanse of southern Russia. When, in the central sector, Kaledin committed suicide (February 13) and Kornilov was killed in action (April 13), Denikin came out of the Caucasus to assume —in name at least—command over the entire White fighting front. General **Peter N. Krasnov,** hetman of the Don Cossacks, assisted him.

1919, May. The Line-up. From left to right the Whites were now assembled in 4 groups—the Kiev, Volunteer, Don, and Causasus armies. Against them the Bolshevik array became the Twelfth, Fourteenth, Thirteenth, Ninth, and Tenth Red armies. Trotsky was now faced with a multifront major dilemma, for Kolchak's White offensive (see p. 1000) along the axis of the Trans-Siberian Railway had now penetrated the Urals and reached the line Ufa-Perm. Another White army was assembling in the Baltic provinces under General Nikolai Yudenich (see p. 1001). At the same time Allied forces had landed in some strength in north Russia and eastern Siberia (see p. 1000) with apparent intent to help the White Russians. Considering Kolchak to be the most pressing danger, Trotsky took the offensive in the east, with General Tukhachevski in command, and went on the defensive in south Russia and in the north.

1919, May–October. Denikin Offensive. The 4 White armies pushed northward in an ever-diverging course. **Kiev** was recaptured (September 2). General **Peter Wrangel**'s Caucasus Army drove for Tsaritsin, hoping to make contact with Kolchak. However, Wrangel was delayed by lack of supply, and by the time Tsaritsin fell (June 17), Tukhachevski's Red offensive had rolled Kolchak back through the Urals. The Reds now turned in force against Wrangel, who was in turn forced back. Krasnov's Don Army reached **Voronezh** (October 6), only to be hit in flank and rolled back (October 24) by Tukhachevski, who then drove westward against the Volunteer Army, which had reached Orel (October 13). The White offensive crumbled. The Kiev Army was then pried out of Kiev (December 17) and the disorganized Whites driven back to the Black Sea.

1920, March 27. Evacuation of the White Armies. This was done by sea from Novorossisk, mostly in British ships hurried there for the purpose. Only Wrangel, with a small force, held out in the Crimea.

1920, April. Red Penetration of the Caucasus. Soviet armies reached Baku (April 28). Bolshevik efforts to gain control of the Caspian Sea were temporarily foiled by a British flotilla based on Persian Caspian seaports (see p. 1007).

1920, June–November. Wrangel Offensive and Defeat. Taking advantage of Red preoccupation in the Russo-Polish War (see p. 991), indomitable Wrangel suddenly pressed north from the Sea of Azov, but it was too late. The war with the Poles had ended, and the Reds, concentrating again, drove Wrangel back into the Crimea (November 1). The remnants of his White forces were evacuated—again by the British—by sea to Constantinople (November 14). Soviet Russia had come of age.

COMMENT. *Disunity of command on the White side, and the administrative and strategic ability of Trotsky on the Red, decided the issue. Both sides started as hordes of peasant guerrillas and amateur militiamen. Trotsky welded his masses into a professional fighting force through a process of trial and error. The Whites, lacking competent over-all leadership, and with a command shot through by corruption and stupidity, failed. Wrangel was probably the best of the Whites, and Tukhachevski stood out amid the mediocrity of the Red leadership.*

Siberia and East Russia

1918, June. The Czech Legion. Approximately 100,000 Czech, or Bohemian, prisoners of war from the Austro-Hungarian Army seized control of the Trans-Siberian Railway when their proposed repatriation via Vladivostok was interfered with by the Soviets. Capturing arms from local Bolshevik units, the Czechs organized themselves into an efficient army and marched westward along the railroad into eastern Russia, where they captured **Ekaterinburg** (Sverdlovsk, July 26) just after the massacre of the Czar and his family there. They then opened negotiations with the Soviets and with the liberal anti-Bolshevik government which had been established at Omsk.

1918, November 18. Kolchak Seizes Power in Siberia. Admiral **Alexander Kolchak** of the Imperial Russian Navy seized control of the Omsk government and proclaimed himself "Supreme Ruler of Russia." He allied himself with the Czechs and advanced from Siberia with an army into eastern Russia, capturing Perm and Ufa (December).

1919–1920. Bolshevik Counteroffensive. Under Trotsky's dynamic leadership, the Bolsheviks counterattacked Kolchak's troops and recaptured Ekaterinburg (January 27). Despite the active support of the Czech Legion and the moral support of Britain, France, and Japan, Kolchak's troops were slowly driven back into Siberia. Omsk was captured (November 14); Kolchak lost control of the situation, and was later captured and executed by the Soviets (February 7, 1920). Upon the collapse of the Kolchak regime, the Czechs fought their way eastward along the Trans-Siberian Railway, brushing aside both Red and White Russian units in their way, to reach that portion of eastern Siberia controlled by an American expeditionary force (see below). They were then transported to Vladivostok and evacuated by ship. Though fighting continued, the Bolsheviks gradually consolidated their control over all those parts of Siberia not controlled by American and Japanese forces.

Allied Intervention, 1917–1922

1917, December 30. Japanese Occupation of Vladivostok. A large Japanese force under General **Otani** landed at Vladivostok. The apparent Japanese intention of annexing the Russian Maritime Provinces caused alarm in Washington, London, and Paris.

1918–1919. Allied Invasion of North Russia. Small British-French-American expeditionary forces, under British command, seized Murmansk (June 23, 1918) and occupied Archangel (August 1–2). Their nominal objective was to retrieve Allied supplies and munitions which had been contributed to the Czarist government. Actually the ridiculous underlying concept was that these small forces would invade Russia, striking south and east to link with the Czech Legion at the Urals. This, some Allied visionaries argued, would contribute to a united White Russian counterrevolution and topple the Bolshevik regime. The American contingent was one reinforced infantry regiment. For more than a year of minor but hard-fought undeclared war, the Allied force bickered with Bolshevik troops along the Vologda River. The Americans were then evacuated (August, 1919); the remaining Allied troops left shortly afterward (September–October).

1918, August. American Siberian Expedition. Partly to succor the Czechs, and also to prevent Japan from gobbling the Maritime Provinces, 2 American regiments, under Major General **William S. Graves,** landed at Vladivostok. Graves's instructions were explicit: to refrain from interference with Russian internal affairs, and to rescue the Czechs. He was soon at odds not only with the Japanese but also with British and French military missions, with the Bolsheviks, and with Kolchak's White Russian forces. Continuing tension between Americans and Japanese frequently came close to violence, but conflict was averted by Graves's combined firmness and diplomacy. Britain, France, and Japan all expected the Americans to join in support of Kolchak. Refusing, Graves hewed to his directive. American troops guarded the Trans-Siberian Railway from Lake Baikal to Vladivostok. Several clashes with partisan White and Red Russian forces occurred, the Americans successfully maintaining their control of the railroad in each instance. After the collapse of the Kolchak regime, the Americans held their positions until the arrival of the Czechs, who were evacuated by sea from Vladivostok. The American expedition then left Siberia (April, 1920). This left eastern Siberia, save for the vicinity of Vladivostok, under Soviet control. In the face of the growing strength of the Soviet Far Eastern Republic, the Japanese later evacuated (October 25, 1922).

Finland and the Baltic States

FINLAND

1917, December 6. Independence of Finland.

1918, January 18. Mannerheim to Command. The new Finnish government appointed Baron **Carl Gustaf Mannerheim,** former Russian cavalry general, to organize and command its army. Bolshevik forces had already seized Helsingfors (Helsinki) and a native Red Guard was in process of formation. Vasa (Vaasa), where Mannerheim had his headquarters, contained a Russian garrison.

1918, January 28. Outbreak of Hostilities. A Red revolution broke out throughout Finland, despite the opposition of most of the Finnish people. Mannerheim the same day seized Vasa from the ineffectual Russian garrison and armed his rising levies from its large stock of weapons and munitions. He then moved south with his extemporized army, taking **Tammerfors** (Tampera), but further progress was checked by a large Red Guard force (March 16).

1918, April 3. German Intervention. A force of 10,000 men, under General **von der Goltz,** landed at Hanko (Hangö) in a surprise move. The Germans drove through and seized Helsingfors (April 18), cutting the Red-held area in two, while Mannerheim's rapidly growing forces moved east and cut off the Karelian Isthmus from Russia (April 19). An attempt of the remaining Russian forces to break out near **Vyborg** ended with the surrender (April 29) of 12,000 Reds and much booty. Desultory fighting with Bolshevik forces along the frontier continued.

1920, October 14. Treaty of Dorpat (Tartu). This finally secured Finnish independence.

ESTONIA

1917–1918. Bolshevik and German Occupations. Following its declaration of independence (November 28, 1917), Estonia was trampled first by Bolshevik and then by German troops (see p. 987). The latter were in occupation when the Treaty of Brest-Litovsk was effected (see p. 987).

1918, November 22. Renewed Bolshevik Invasion. Following the German evacuation (November 11), the Soviets returned. Sharp resistance by Estonian forces, assisted by a British naval squadron in the Baltic, caused Russian withdrawal (January, 1919).

1919, October. Yudenich Coup. Capable and energetic White Russian General **Nicolai Yudenich,** who had been gathering a counterrevolutionary army in northeast Estonia, crossed the Russian border (October 6) near Narva in a bold bid to capture Petrograd (Leningrad). Although he had no more than 20,000 men, he reached the outskirts of the city (October 19), causing near panic. Trotsky's frenzied rallying of all available forces, including workers, turned Yudenich back, and he retired into Estonia.

1920, February 2. Treaty of Dorpat. This brought freedom to Estonia through Russian recognition of independence.

LATVIA

1919, January. Russian Invasion. Immediately following Latvian declaration of independence (November 18, 1918), Bolshevik troops moved across the border. Riga was taken (January 4) and a Soviet government set up. With Allied approval, German-Latvian forces drove the Bolshevist invaders back (March). A German attempt to take over the Riga government resulted in confused fighting and occupation of Riga, ending in armistice (April 16–May 22). Fighting broke out again (October 20) between the Latvians and both German and Russian elements. Allied insistence on adherence to the provisions of the Treaty of Versailles (see p. 989) forced German withdrawal (November 20).

1920, January. Russian Withdrawal. The last of the Bolshevik troops were expelled. An armistice with Russia followed (February 1).

1920, August 11. Treaty of Riga. Russia recognized Latvian independence.

LITHUANIA

1918. Bolshevik Invasions. Immediate Soviet invasion followed Lithuanian declaration of independence (February 16), but the Russians were soon driven out by the Germans (see p. 987). However, the evacuation of German troops (November 11) was followed by another Bolshevik invasion.

1919, January 5. Russian Capture of Vilna. This led to Polish intervention and the outbreak of the Russo-Polish War (see p. 991).

1920, July 12. Treaty of Moscow. This ended the Russo-Lithuanian hostilities; Russia recognized Lithuanian independence.

1920, October 9. Polish Seizure of Vilna. (See p. 1003.) League of Nations efforts to mediate and to hold a plebiscite satisfactory to both sides proved unsuccessful. Peace was re-established 7 years later (December, 1927).

1923, January 11. Insurrection in Memel (Klaipeda). A predominantly German city, Memel had been under inter-Allied control since 1918. Upon the outbreak of an uprising sponsored by Lithuania, Lithuanian troops occupied the city, forcing a French garrison to withdraw. The Allies later recognized this highhanded seizure.

Poland, 1914–1925

1914, August 16. Pilsudski's Legions. One of the principal prewar Polish revolutionaries against Russian rule of central Poland, **Józef Pilsudski,** organized Polish legions in Galicia (Austrian Poland) to fight beside the Central Powers against Russia.

1916, November 5. Central Powers Proclaim Polish Independence. This only applied to former Russian Poland. The country remained occupied by German and Austrian troops, however.

1917, March 30. Russia Recognizes Polish Independence. The Provisional Russian Government stated that its recognition applied to all lands with Polish majority populations, thus including German and Austrian Poland.

1918, November 11. De Facto Polish Independence. German troops were disarmed and expelled. Pilsudski, Commander in Chief of all Polish forces, became virtual dictator of the new country. With frontier wars already breaking out in all directions, he devoted all of his energies to building up an effective army; in this he was favored by the many Polish veterans of World War I, who had fought on all fronts and on both sides.

1918, November–1919, May. War with Ukraine. Ukrainian troops entered Galicia to establish a West Ukrainian Republic at Lvov. After 6 months of fighting, the Ukrainians were expelled from Galicia.

1918, December–1919, February. Fighting in Poznan. Theatened outbreak of war between Germany and Poland was halted by Allied pressure.

1919, January–February. Dispute over Teschen. Precipitated by a Czech attack on Polish forces in Teschen, the fighting was quickly ended by Allied pressure.

1919, January–November. Undeclared Conflict with Russia. Poland, insistent upon returning to pre-1772 boundaries, reacted violently when Soviet troops (following the withdrawing Germans) occupied Vilna (January 5) and continued on to the line of the Bug River (February). An undeclared war broke out, and the Poles drove the Russians back, reoccupying **Vilna** (April, 1919). Desultory fighting continued along the front, which brought Polish troops to the Berezina River and into the northern Ukraine. A lull of several months followed.

1919, December 8. The "Curzon Line." The Allied Supreme Council established a provisional eastern frontier for Poland, generally following the Bug River. This line, later called the "Curzon Line," was totally unsatisfactory to Poland. As Soviet forces began to build up in western Russia, the Poles determined to fight for the formerly Polish regions east of the Bug.

1920, April–October. Russo-Polish War. (See p. 991.)

1920, October 9. Polish Reoccupation of Vilna. During the Russo-Polish War, the Soviets had ceded Vilna to Lithuania (July 12). Upon Soviet evacuation, after the Battle of Warsaw, the Lithuanians occupied the city (August 26). This precipitated a dispute between Poland and Lithuania, which led to fighting when Polish General **Lucian Zeligowski** occupied the city. A state of war, without active fighting, persisted between Poland and Lithuania for another 6 years (see p. 1002).

1921. Fighting in Silesia. A dispute between Germany and Poland over the results of the Silesian plebiscite broke out into open fighting (May 3). The Inter-Allied Commission forced a cessation of hostilities (June 24).

Turkey

1900–1909. Disintegration of the Ottoman Empire. The Young Turk nationalistic movement urged constitutional reform and fomented insurrection while the Great Powers and the Balkan States nibbled at the outer fringes of the empire of despotic Sultan **Abdul Hamid II.**

1909, April 13. Military Revolt at Constantinople. The I Army Corps (mostly Albanian) seized control of the capital. The uprising was put down by troops from Macedonia after a 5-hour fight within the city. Other disorders in Anatolia, involving Armenians, were ruthlessly suppressed by Turkish troops, who massacred a number of Armenian demonstrators.

1909, April 26. Deposition of Abdul Hamid. The Young Turks appointed his inept brother, **Mohammed V,** as sultan.

1910, April–June. Albanian Insurrection. The uprising was brutally stamped out by Turkish troops.

1911–1912. War with Italy. (See p. 926.)

1912–1913. The Balkan Wars. (See p. 926.)

1913, January 23. Young Turk Coup d'État. After brief turmoil, "strong men" Enver, **Taalat,** and Djemal came to power. They secretly wooed Germany.

1913, November–December. Liman von Sanders Crisis. The appointment of this German general to reorganize the Turkish Army aroused Russian and French resentment and suspicion.

1914, August 2. Secret Alliance with Germany. This foreshadowed Turkey's entry into the war on the side of the Central Powers.

1914–1918. World War I. (See p. 946.)

1919. Internal Turmoil and Allied Intervention. Defeat in World War I still further weakened the power of the Sultan (now **Mohammed VI**). Increasing nationalist activity resulted from the Sultan's co-operation with the Allies. To curb the Nationalists, Italian troops were landed at Adalia (April 29) and Greek troops at Smyrna (May 14). Atrocities committed by the Greeks aroused Turkish resentment.

1920, March 16. Allied Occupation of Constantinople. An Allied force under British General **George F. Milne** landed to support the Turkish government against the Nationalists, to keep open the straits as a supply line for White Russian counterrevolutionaries, and to protect the Armenians.

1920, April 23. Provisional Nationalist Government at Ankara. Mustafa Kemal, war hero and Nationalist leader, was selected to be President. A military agreement was then reached with Soviet Russia to ensure supplies. (See p. 992.)

1920, June 20. Treaty of Sèvres. This stripped Turkey of all European territory except Constantinople, and gave complete Armenian independence. The terms of the treaty were rejected by the Nationalists, increasing their popular support.

1921–1923. Greco-Turkish War. (See p. 992.)

AFRICA

MOROCCO

1900–1906. Colonial Friction. Rival colonial interests in North Africa of France,

Germany, England, Spain, and Italy were composed to some degree by the **Algeciras Conference** (January 16, 1906–April 7, 1907), recognizing special rights of both France and Spain in Morocco.

1907, July 20. Bombardment of Casablanca. Serious unrest was violently quelled when a French squadron opened fire on the city. French occupation of the Moroccan Atlantic coastal area followed.

1909, July–October. Riff Attacks against the Spanish. Riff Berber tribesmen clashed with the Spanish at **Melilla** on the Mediterranean.

1911, April 26. French Occupation of Fez. This followed a Berber attack on the city.

1911, July 1–November 4. The Agadir Incident. Germany sent the gunboat *Panther* to Agadir, allegedly to protect German nationals and their interests. War was averted by diplomatic horse trading. In return for a free hand in Morocco, France ceded part of her Congo holdings to Germany.

1912, March 30. Treaty of Fez. This established a French protectorate over Morocco. General **Louis H. G. Lyautey,** forceful and tactful, appointed Resident General (May 24), began a successful, progressive program of political and economic betterment cementing French and Moroccan interests.

1912–1921. Troubles in Spanish Mediterranean Zone. In the west, bandit chieftain **Raisuli** (who gained international notoriety by kidnaping an American citizen in 1904) by 1920 was harassing the area south to Tetuán, while a Riff chieftain, **Abd el Krim,** was whipping up hostility south and east of Melilla. Spanish General **Dámaso Berenguer** attained success in pacifying the western area, but in the east General **Fernandes Silvestre** met disaster.

1921, July 21. Battle of Anual. Silvestre, with about 20,000 men, was moving southwest into the Riff mountains. Apparently reconnaissance was inadequate and security dispositions faulty. Abd el Krim's tribesmen had attacked and captured a frontier post at Abaran. The garrison of the next post fled to Anual, to meet Silvestre's column. At the same time the Riffians opened fire on both Silvestre's flanks. The resulting confusion turned to panic and then to slaughter. Silvestre and some 12,000 of his men were killed, several thousand more made prisoner. Dissidence flared throughout the Spanish zone, all frontier posts were either captured or abandoned, and the Spaniards were forced back to fortified coastal zones directly around Melilla and Tetuán. The Anual disaster rocked Spain, leading to the downfall of the government and rise to power (September 13, 1923) of "strong man" General **Primo de Rivera,** who became—with the king's blessing—virtual dictator of Span. Abd el Krim, establishing a "Republic of the Riff," prepared to drive out the French and control all Morocco. Between the tribesmen and a number of foreign adventurers he organized a force of 20,000 men, well armed and provided with artillery and machine guns captured from the Spanish.

1925, April 12. Riffian Advance Southward. Abd el Krim's forces, debouching secretly from the mountain border, swept south to overwhelm the chain of French border posts from Taza to Fez. Forty-three of the 66 blockhouses dotting the 50-mile span were captured and most of their garrisons killed after desperate and gallant resistance. Lyautey had expected attack, but his resources were limited. Skillful handling of his existing reserves checked the Riff advance within sight of Fez. France and Spain, forgetting their former rivalry in Morocco, agreed (July 26) to a joint counteroffensive. Reinforcements raised the French Army strength in Morocco to more than 150,000 men, while Spain prepared an expeditionary force of more than 50,000, commanded by General **José Sanjurjo.**

1925, September 8–9. Joint Counteroffensive. The Spanish expedition began landing in the **Bay of Alhucemas** under cover of French and Spanish warships. Ajdir was captured (October 2). The stage was set for an immense converging movement, with Targuist—Abd el Krim's headquarters—as target. While small Spanish forces struck from the Tetuán and Melilla zones respectively, Sanjurjo's main force advanced almost directly south. At the same time Marshal Pétain, commanding the French field forces, moved 6 converging columns, within mutual supporting distance of one another, into the Riff-held territory between Tafrant and Taza.

1925, September 24. Resignation of Lyautey. Exhausted in health, Lyautey's resignation ended a most brilliant career of pacification and organization. Pétain succeeded him, and General **Boichut** took field command. Despite desperate resistance, Abd el Krim's troops were progressively forced north by the French hammer against the slower-moving Spanish anvil. Delayed by seasonal winter rains, the advance was renewed in the spring.

1926, May 26. Surrender of Abd el Krim. A French spearhead under Colonel **André G. Corap** came thrusting into Targuist, and Abd el Krim gave up the fight.

COMMENT. *The original success of Abd el Krim testifies to the fallacy of cordon defense. Neither the French nor the Spanish frontier could withstand the initial blows, and the loss of one blockhouse led inevitably to the loss of the others. The European counteroffensive, particularly the French operations, consisted of a rapidly moving advance on a wide front, utilizing the terrain and taking advantage of crest lines to avoid ambush. Abd el Krim's own campaigns were an example of development of guerrilla warfare into that of a conventional force. He was overwhelmed by a combination of superior force and sage leadership.*

COLONIAL WARS IN AFRICA

During this period there were almost continuous military operations on the part of the forces of Britain, France, Germany, Italy, and Portugal to stabilize and pacify their colonial empires in Africa. These were generally successful, and by the end of the period most of Africa was relatively peaceful. Listed below, in summary form, are some of these operations.

1899–1920. Operations against the "Mad Mullah" (Somaliland). Somali chieftain **Mohammed ben Abdullah** waged almost constant small war against the Italians, British, and Ethiopians. He and his fierce desert tribesmen proved themselves to be extremely able warriors. His raids ended only with his death.

1899–1902. The Boer War. (**See p. 852.**)

1900, March–November. Ashanti Uprising (Gold Coast, or Ghana). The Ashantis briefly besieged Kumasi before being suppressed by British troops.

1900, April 22. Battle of Lakhta (Kusseri). French troops defeated **Rabah Zobeir,** raider and slave trader, in the eastern French Sudan, or Chad, region. (See p. 856.)

1900, May. French Conquest of Northern Sahara. Culminating protracted desert warfare, the French established themselves firmly in the main oases of the northern Sahara.

1900–1903. British Conquest of North Nigeria. (**See p. 856.**)

1902. Uprising in Angola. Suppressed by the Portuguese.

1903. Hottentot Uprising in German Southwest Africa.

1904. Insurrection in Southern Nigeria.

1904–1905. Insurrection in Cameroons. Suppressed by the Germans.

1904–1908. Uprising in German Southwest Africa. Led by the Herero tribe, this revolt was joined by many of the Hottentots. It was suppressed by the Germans only with difficulty. Its influence spread to Angola.

1905. Uprising in the French Congo.

1905. Insurrection in German East Africa.

1906. Religious Insurrection in Sokoto (Northwest Nigeria).

1907. Uprising in Angola. Largely inspired by the Herero uprising in German Southwest Africa.

1908–1909. French Conquest of Mauretania.

1909–1911. French Conquest of Wadai (mountainous, desert region of eastern Chad or central Sudan).

1914, October–1915, February. Boer Uprising. Boer extremists, led by former Boer General Christiaan De Wet and others, rose in protest against the Union of South Africa's declaration of war against Germany. The rising was suppressed by Prime Minister—and former Boer General—**Louis Botha,** assisted by former Boer commando leader **Jan Smuts.**

SOUTH AND SOUTHWEST ASIA

THE ARAB STATES

Arabia, 1900–1925

1900–1919. Rise of Ibn Saud. A chief of the Wahhabi sect, or tribe, of southern Nejd (central Arabia), **Ibn Saud** established himself as undisputed ruler of the Nejd in a prolonged civil war (1900–1906). He then consolidated his control and annexed outlying regions to establish his authority over all non-Turkish portions of central and northern Arabia. He entered into an alliance with Britain during World War I and fought briefly against the Turks (1915).

1916, June. Arab Revolt against the Turks. Inspired by the British, the Arab tribes of Hejaz (western Arabia) revolted against the Turks under Hashemite Sherif **Hussein.** Under the leadership of his son, Emir **Faisal,** and British Captain (later Colonel) T. E. Lawrence Arab forces fought successfully against the Turks for the remainder of the war (see p. 987).

1919–1925. Struggle for Control of Arabia. A prolonged conflict broke out between Ibn Saud and the Hashemite Dynasty. After a series of Wahhabi victories over the Hashemites and independent Arab chieftains, Hussein abdicated (October, 1924) in favor of his son **Ali.** Ibn Saud captured **Mecca** (October 13, 1924) and continued to press the war. He captured **Medina** (December 5, 1925), Sherif Ali abdicated (December 19), and Ibn Saud then captured **Jidda** to complete his conquest of Hejaz (December 23).

Syria, 1918–1925

1918, October 5. French Occupation of Beirut. A French naval squadron seized the port from the Turks as Allenby's troops were conquering the remainder of Syria (see p. 988). By secret Allied understandings, Syria was to be France's share of the dismembered Ottoman Empire. French claims, however, were soon disputed by Emir **Faisal,** commander in chief of the Arab armies with T. E. Lawrence (see pp. 987 and above).

1919–1920. Dispute between France and Faisal. After the British formally turned the administration of Syria over to France (September, 1919), open fighting broke out between Arabs and French (December). Though Faisal was proclaimed King of Syria (March, 1920), he was unable to obtain support and was forced to flee. French troops occupied Damascus (July, 1920). Faisal, for consolation, was made King of Iraq by the British (see below).

1925–1927. Insurrection of the Druses. An Arab tribe of southeastern Syria, the Druses became restive under French administration. They revolted (July, 1925) and soon seized control of most of southern Syria. Aided by a revolt in Damascus, they forced the French to evacuate the city (October, 1925). As the period closed the French were near defeat in Syria.

Iraq, 1919–1925

1919–1920. Unrest in Mesopotamia. Many Arabs objected to British occupation following the Mesopotamian campaign of World War I (see p. 988).

1920, July–December. Arab Insurrection. Arab nationalists, hoping for the independence of Mesopotamia, rose against the British, who suppressed the uprising, but sought ways to satisfy Arab demands and aspirations.

1921, August 23. British Protectorate over Iraq. The British proclaimed Faisal (former King of Syria) as King of Iraq. The country was given a measure of self-government, but Britain retained control.

1922, June–1924, July. Insurrection in Kurdistan. The Kurds, traditionally semi-independent mountain people of the border region between Iraq, Turkey, and Iran, rose to throw off the control of the British and Arabs. The British, concerned about the rich Mosul oil fields, eventually suppressed the rebellion and granted considerable autonomy to the Kurds.

PERSIA (IRAN)

1905–1909. Persian Revolution. This was a combination of political activity and scattered insurrections against the corrupt and despotic rule of Shah **Mohammed Ali.** Open warfare against the central government was stimulated by a revolt in Tabriz (1908), which was then besieged by the

Shah's army (1908–1909). To protect Russian interests, and nominally to assist the Shah, a Russian army intervened and captured Tabriz, brutally suppressing the revolt (March, 1909). Meanwhile, other rebel forces took the field in northern and central Persia. A rebel army under **Ali Kuli Khan** captured Teheran (July 12, 1909), forcing the abdication of the Shah in favor of his 12-year-old son, Sultan **Ahmad** (July 16).

1911, June 17–September 5. Abortive Return of Mohammed Ali. With Russian connivance, Mohammed Ali landed on the Caspian coast of northeast Persia at Gumish Tepe, and was soon joined by dissident forces. He was quickly defeated by loyal troops and forced to flee again.

1911, November. Russian Occupation of Northern Persia. On the pretext of restoring order in Persia, and to protect their financial interests, Russian forces occupied the northern part of the country and established a virtual protectorate over it. To protect their oil interests, the British occupied much of southwest Persia, but despite strained relations did not break with their Russian allies because of the threat of European war.

1914–1918. World War I. (See p. 929.) The war ended with British troops in occupation of much of western Persia.

1919, May 21. Battle of Alexandrovsk. A British flotilla on the Caspian (see p. 999) defeated a Bolshevik naval force. The British flotilla was later turned over to White Russians, who were then defeated by the Bolsheviks (1920).

1920, May 18. Russian Naval Invasion. A Russian flotilla captured **Enzeli** (Pahlevi) and then seized Resht. British troops withdrew from the Caspian coastal region to avoid a clash. Persian troops briefly recaptured **Resht** (August 24), but were repulsed from Enzeli, then driven south of the mountains.

1921, January. British Withdrawal. Upon negotiation of a treaty between the Soviet government and Persia, British troops began to withdraw from northern Iran.

1921, February 21. Coup d'État of Reza Khan. Widespread disgust with the incompetence and corruption of the oligarchy in Teheran led Persian general **Reza Khan,** commanding the Cossack Brigade, to seize power in Teheran; he soon established himself as virtual dictator. He quickly ratified a treaty with Russia (February 26), whereupon Russian troops began withdrawing from the northern and coastal regions.

AFGHANISTAN

1914–1918. World War I. Neutral Afghanistan was in turmoil as Turkish and German interests provoked anti-Allied religious agitation. England, by subsidies, held the government in line, and after the war Russian interest was resumed.

1919, February. Accession of Amir Amanullah. Placed on the throne by the army and the Young Afghan radical party after the assassination of his father, **Habibullah** (February 19), Amanullah declared the country independent of all foreign control.

1919, May. War with Britain. Amanullah proclaimed a jihad (religious war) against Britain. Afghan levies broke across the Indian border near Landi Khana and occupied **Bagh** (May 3). Immediate mobilization of British Indian troops followed. A punitive expedition moved through the Khyber Pass to **Landi Kotal** and drove the invaders out of Bagh (May 11). The expedition then advanced into Afghanistan, and reached Dakka. British planes bombarded **Jalalabad** and **Kabul.** Amanullah sued for an armistice (May 31), and nominal peace resulted from the **Treaty of Rawalpindi** (August 8). Renewed British recognition of Afghanistan's independence (November 22, 1921), was accompanied by cessation of British subsidies. Sporadic guerrilla warfare continued along the Afghan-Indian border.

1926, August 31. Treaty with Soviet Union. The Soviet Union and Afghanistan signed a neutrality and nonaggression treaty in which they pledged benevolent neutrality and noninterference in each other's domestic politics.

INDIA, 1900–1925

1903–1904. Expedition to Tibet. Under the leadership of Colonel **Francis Younghusband,** a small British expedition entered Tibet to force the **Dalai Lama** to negotiate a treaty to stabilize the northern frontier of India. When the Tibetans refused to negotiate, Younghusband marched to Lhasa, which he reached after several severe engagements (August 3, 1904). A treaty was signed (September 7).

1914–1918, World War I. Indian troops—some 1,400,000 men in all—volunteered for service, taking active part on the Western Front, in the Near East and Africa.

1919, April 13. Amritsar "Massacre." Religious conflicts between Moslems and Hindus, plus **Mahatma Gandhi**'s passive non-cooperation with the government, brought open rebellion in the Punjab. Several Europeans were killed during a riot at Amritsar (April 12). Brigadier General **Reginald Dyer,** commanding the garrison, paraded his troops to enforce order. When an unarmed mob defied orders to disperse, Dyer's troops fired on them, killing 379 and wounding 1,208 others. The incident aroused British public opinion. Dyer was denounced in the Commons, but the House of Lords upheld him on the ground that he had saved British rule in the Punjab. An army council, taking the middle ground, decided his act was "an error of judgment."

1919, May–August. Afghan War. **(See p. 1007.)**

1919, November. Revolt in Waziristan. Excesses committed by Masud tribesmen incited by the Afghans brought a punitive expedition of 30,000 men under General **S. H. Climo.** Concentrating on the **Tank Zam** (December 13), Climo's troops were attacked by the Masuds (December 17), who were repelled. The uprising was quelled (February 1, 1920).

1920–1925. Operations on the Northwest Frontier. Frequent small operations were undertaken to pacify Pathan tribesmen from Afghanistan, who periodically raided across the frontier.

EAST ASIA

CHINA

The Boxer Rebellion, 1900–1901

1899–1900. Rising of the Boxers. Antiforeign elements in the Chinese government, angered by the Great Powers' nibbling of her territory, incited a fanatical secret organization called the Society of the Righteous Harmonious Fists (thus Boxers) to wide-scale depredations against foreign missionaries and their Chinese converts to Christianity. The government of Dowager Empress **Tzu Hsi,** professing inability to control the Boxers, was actually inciting and supporting them. Protests of foreign diplomats brought further violence. Warships of foreign nations began gathering off Tientsin (June, 1900) and military detachments of several nations, totaling 485 men, were sent to Peking to guard the legations.

1900, June 10–26. First Relief Expedition. As the situation worsened, a small allied force of some 2,000 marines and bluejackets, including 112 Americans, was landed under control of British Admiral **E. H. Seymour,** senior officer present. Its movement to Peking was repulsed by much superior Chinese strength at **Tang Ts'u.** The force returned to their ships (June 26), having suffered 300 casualties.

1900, June 17. Capture of the Taku Forts. After receiving an ultimatum, the forts guarding the river gate to Tientsin opened fire on the foreign ships. The fire was immediately returned, and landing parties captured the forts.

1900, June 20–August 14. Siege of the Peking Legations. Mob reaction culminated in the murder of Baron **Klemens von Kettler,** German Minister, and the siege of the legations. Russian, British, French, Japanese, and U.S. detachments were hurried to Taku, where an Allied Expeditionary Force was formed to go to the relief of Peking. (The first American contingent came from the Philippines, with reinforcements sent from San Francisco.)

1900, July 23. Taking of Tientsin. The expeditionary force, now numbering some 5,000 men, stormed the city walls and captured the fortress. The U.S. 9th Infantry Regiment in particular took heavy loss, including its commander, Colonel **E. H. Liscum.** By August 4, the expeditionary force included 4,800 Russians, 3,000 British, 2,500 U.S. (2 infantry and 1 cavalry regiments, a battalion of Marines, and a field battery, under Major General **Adna R. Chaffee**), and 800 French troops. Other detachments brought the total strength to 18,700. No over-all commander was appointed; actions were taken on a co-operative basis.

1900, August 4. Advance on Peking. The Second Relief Expedition began its overland march along the rail and river line. A Chinese force estimated at 10,000 men was driven back at **Yang T'sun** (August 5–6). Here the French contingent remained to protect the line of communications. The other troops pushed on, driving off desultory resistance and arriving before Peking's outer walls (August 13). An immediate and precipitate attack by the Russians, who were in the lead, was thrown back from the Tung Pien Gate.

1900, August 14. Taking of Peking. A Japanese attack on the Ch'i Hua Gate was repulsed. The American force joined the Russians in front of the Tung Pien, and took it. At the same time two companies of the U.S. 14th Infantry assaulted the northeast corner of the outer wall. Bugler **Calvin P. Titus,** first to scale, hoisted the American flag. The defenders were driven off. The British troops waded under the wall through the Water Gate and the combined attack pushed on to relieve the diplomatic group, penned in the British Legation compound. This group of civilian men and women and the legation guards had resisted constant fire and assault for 8 weeks. Casualties among the civilian volunteers were 12 killed and 23 wounded, while the guard detachments lost 4 officers and 49 men killed and 9 officers and 136 men wounded. Rescued also were the defenders of the P'ei Tang, compound of the Catholic cathedral. There 40 French and Italian marines, a handful of priests and nuns, and some 3,000 of their Chinese Christian converts had also held out against incessant Boxer attacks. Seven marines, 4 priests, and an estimated 400 of the Christian Chinese had been killed in the fighting.

1900, August 15. Attack on the Imperial City. American field artillery blasted open the Ch'i Hua Gate, First Lieutenant **Charles P. Summerall** walking under Chinese fire to chalk an aiming spot on its timbers for his gunners. As a diplomatic sop to the Chinese government, the Imperial City was not immediately occupied, but the troops moved in later (August 28).

1900, September 4–October 10. Russian Occupation of Manchuria. This was a further blow to Chinese prestige. The Dowager Empress, from her refuge in Sian, accepted all the Allied demands (December 26).

1900, September–1901, May. Allied Punitive Missions near Peking. Of these, 35 were by German troops under Field Marshal Count **Alfred von Waldersee,** a late arrival (September 12).

1901, September 12. Boxer Protocol. Signed by 12 powers, this laid a crushing penalty on China, the most important item being an indemnity of 450 million taels (approximately $739 million). The United States set aside its share for education of Chinese students in the United States.

COMMENT. *Military operations in China, nominally under a joint command of mutual agreement between the various national commanders, was actually a hit-or-miss affair. Neither the Japanese nor Russian commanders gave more than lip service to joint agreements. Had the Chinese been well trained, well led, and well armed, the expedition would have been doomed to failure. It is interesting to note that the British contingent included a Chinese regiment under British officers; it performed well.*

Turmoil in China, 1901–1925

1904–1905. Russo-Japanese War. This took place mainly on Chinese soil (see p. 920).

1905–1910. Rise of Chinese Nationalism. Pressures of the European powers and of Japan following the Russo-Japanese War resulted in new territorial demands on China. National dissatisfaction with the government flared; revolutionary sentiment was widespread.

1911, October 10. Outbreak of the Chinese Revolution.. Mutiny broke out among troops in Wuch'ang, leading to widespread revolt. Marshal **Yuan Shih-k'ai,** over-all military commander, after some perfunctory moves to suppress the risings, joined the movement (December). This led to the abdication of the child emperor and the establishment of the Republic of China under the presidency of Yuan (February 12, 1912). During this time Tibet rose against Chinese rule and drove the Chinese garrison out of the country. Britain prevented any subsequent Chinese efforts to re-establish authority in Tibet by force.

1913, July–September. The "Summer Revolution." An uprising in the Yangtze Valley was easily suppressed by Yuan.

1915, December–1916, March. Rebellion against Restoration of Empire. In protest against plans of Yuan to re-establish the empire, with himself on the throne, rebellion broke out in Yunnan and spread through China. Yuan's announcement of a change in plans did not completely restore order, but the issue was resolved by his death 3 months later (June 6, 1916). He was succeeded as President by **Li Yuan-hung.**

1917, May–August. Revolt of the Northern Military Governors. Dissatisfied with the parliamentary government operating under President Li, the northern military governors (*tuchuns*) revolted and established a rival government at Tientsin. One of their number, **Chang Hsün,** on the pretense of mediating with Li, overthrew the Peking government and briefly re-established the Manchu Dynasty (July 1–12). He was repudiated by his military colleagues, who occupied Peking, overthrew the empire, forced Li to resign, and installed **Feng Kuo-chang** as the new President.

1917, August 4. China Declares War on Germany and Austria-Hungary. China took no active combat part in the war, but did send labor battalions to France, Mesopotamia, and Africa. In return China secured the termination of all German and Austro-Hungarian concessions and rights in China.

1920–1926. Rise of the War Lords. The military governors and other military leaders became almost completely independent of nominal central authority. They carried out a series of complex internecine struggles while the central government became weaker and weaker.

1924, January 21. Congress of the Kuomintang (National People's Party). Under the leadership of **Sun Yat-sen,** the Nationalists met at Canton to prepare for the liberation and unification of the country. Soviet political and military advisers were prominent. At about this time a new Whampoa Military Academy, with Russian and German advisers, was established by the Kuomintang, under young General **Chiang Kai-shek.**

MONGOLIA

The overthrow of the Manchu Empire in China led Mongolia, under the nominal leadership of the "Living Buddha" of Urga (Ulan Bator) to declare its independence. The following decades were chaotic in Mongolia, which felt the impact of both the Chinese and Russian Revolutions, as well as the tides of Japanese expansionism in East Asia. Russian Communism finally prevailed over the other conflicting forces attempting to take advantage of Mongolian weakness, and the Mongolian People's Republic became the first, and possibly most loyal, of Moscow's satellites. The principal events were:

1911, November 18. Outer Mongolia Proclaims Independence. A theocratic Lamaistic government was established under the *Jebtsun Damba Khutuktu* ("Living Buddha"). Russian influence increased, with Mongolia becoming a virtual Russian protectorate (November 3, 1912).

1919, October. Return of Chinese Control. The warlord government of Peking took advantage of confusion caused by the Russian Civil War to reassert control by sending a small army to occupy Urga.

1920, October–1921, July. White Russian Invasion and Occupation. A force under Baron **Roman von Ungern-Sternberg** invaded Outer Mongolia, and drove the Chinese out of Urga (February 3, 1921). At first welcomed as a liberator from the hated Chinese, sadistic Ungern-Sternberg instituted a reign of terror and aroused popular opposition.

1921, March 13. Establishment of Revolutionary Provisional Government of Mongolia. This was set up at Kiakhta, just inside Siberia, across the border from Mongolia, with Russian Communist support, by Nationalist patriots **Sükhe Bator, Dun-**

zan, and **Khorloghiyn Choibalsan.** A joint Russian-Mongolian military force was assembled; Sükhe Bator led the small Mongolian contingent.

1921, June–July. Russian-Mongolian Invasion of Mongolia. Ungern-Sternberg was defeated, **Urga** was captured (July 6). Later Ungern-Sternberg was captured and executed. Although nominally part of a joint force, the Soviet troops virtually occupied the country. Nevertheless, to avoid undue antagonism to China, the U.S.S.R. professed to recognize Chinese suzerainty over Outer Mongolia (May 31, 1924).

1924, November 26. Proclamation of Mongolian People's Republic. The death of the Living Buddha (May 20) provided the Mongolian Communists and their Soviet masters with an opportunity to complete the transition of Mongolia to a satellite and consolidate control (1924–1928). After the deaths of Sükhe Bator and Dunzan, Choibalsan became the sole leader of Communist Mongolia.

JAPAN

Japan participated in 3 military ventures during the period: Boxer Rebellion (1900–1905; see p. 1008); Russo-Japanese War (1904–1905; see p. 920); and World War I (1914–1918; see p. 944). Her participation in each was coldly calculated for her own aggrandizement. The Russo-Japanese War is particularly important from the standpoint of military history, since it marked the admittance of Japan into the coterie of the Great Powers. Japanese war potential was expanded as rapidly as possible under chauvinistic, expansionist, militaristic leadership.

THE PHILIPPINES

1901–1902. Continuation of Philippine Insurrection. (See p. 868.) The capture of **Aguinaldo** through a ruse, by Brigadier General **Frederick Funston** and a detachment of Filipino troops in U.S. service (1909, March 23), ended the formalized rebellion, though guerrilla warfare continued for more than a year. However, thanks to General **Arthur MacArthur's** wise and just military rule, the Christian Filipinos were gradually won over (1902).

1902–1905. Moro Campaigns. Operations in the southern islands, **Mindanao** and **Jolo** in particular, continued for 3 years. The fanatic Mohammedan tribesmen were not subdued until after serious, though small, campaigns successfully led by Colonel **John W. Duncan** and Captains **John J. Pershing** and **Frank R. McCoy,** among others.

COMMENT. *Suppression of the Philippine Insurrection necessitated the employment of 100,000 American troops, whose casualties amounted to 4,243 killed and 2,818 wounded in action. Filipino losses were some 16,000 killed and approximately 100,000 more died of famine.*

NETHERLANDS EAST INDIES

1900–1908. Continuation of the Achenese War. (See p. 862.) The pacification of Sumatra was finally completed when the Dutch subdued rebellious forces in Acheh (December, 1907).

THE AMERICAS

THE UNITED STATES

1899–1905. Philippine Insurrection. (See p. 868 and above.)

1900, June 17. Boxer Rebellion in China. (See p. 1008.)

1900–1903. Army Reforms. Efforts of **Elihu Root,** secretary of war, brought about establishment of the Army War College (1900), the Command and General Staff School (1901), and the Army General Staff (1903).

1903, November 3. Panamanian Revolt against Colombia. (For U.S. involvement, see p. 1012.)

1906, October 2. Army of Cuban Pacification. (See p. 1013.)

1907–1909. U.S. Fleet Sails Around the World.

1912. Intervention in Honduras and Nicaragua. (See p. 1013.)

1914, April 9–21. Tampico and Veracruz Incidents. U.S. military action against Mexico (see below).

1914, August 4. U.S. Neutrality Declared at Outbreak of World War I.

1915, July 29. Intervention in Haiti. (**See p. 1013.**)

1916–1917. Mexican Border Operations. (**See below.**)

1916, November 29. Intervention in Dominican Republic. (**See p. 968.**)

1917, April 6. Declaration of War on Germany. (**See p. 968.**)

1921, November 12–1922, February 6. Washington Naval Conference. (**See p. 920.**)

MEXICO

1911–1914. Revolutionary Era. Overthrow of President **Díaz** (May 25, 1911) was followed by internecine war between numerous rival leaders. **Francisco Madero,** who succeeded Díaz, was defeated and killed by **Victoriano Huerta** (1913, February 22). Huerta's regime (which was not recognized by the U.S.) was challenged by one of his many rivals, **Venustiano Carranza.**

1914, April 21. American Occupation of Veracruz. Arrest of unarmed U.S. sailors at Tampico (April 9) was followed by the shelling of Veracruz by a U.S. naval force and the landing of a small expeditionary force, which occupied the city. Huerta's government severed relations with the U.S. South American states attempted mediation. U.S. troops were withdrawn later in the year (November 25).

1914, August 15. Carranzists Capture Mexico City. Carranza assumed leadership of Mexico.

1914–1915. Revolt of Zapata and Villa. Emiliano Zapata and **Francisco (Pancho) Villa,** bandit-revolutionist leader who dominated northern Mexico, revolted. Villa briefly captured Mexico City, but was driven out by Carranza's General **Alvaro Obregón,** who won a climactic victory at **Celaya,** (April 13–15). Carranza was recognized by the U.S. as the President of Mexico (1915, October 15). Following a falling-out of Zapata and Villa, each continued separate, small-scale insurgencies until the death of Zapata in a government ambush (1919, April 10) and the surrender of Villa (1920, July 27; see below).

1916, March 9. Villa Raids across the U.S. Border. Villa's band of 500 men made a night attack on **Columbus,** N.M. Surprising the town and its garrison of U.S. cavalry, Villa killed 14 American soldiers and 10 civilians before he was driven off with a loss of 100 men. To prevent repetitions of the outrage, President Wilson sent Regular and National Guard troops to protect the border. (Eventually this force reached a strength of 158,000 men—most of the active military strength of the U.S. at the time.)

1916, March 15. Punitive Expedition. Under President Wilson's directive, Brigadier General **John J. Pershing** with 10,000 troops (mostly cavalry) struck into Mexican territory to pursue Villa. Carranza's reluctant consent soon turned to open antagonism. In addition to several skirmishes with Villistas, the Americans were also engaged on several occasions with regular Mexican troops, notably at **Carrizal** (June 21). Despite all his efforts, Pershing was not able to catch the elusive Villa. The expedition was withdrawn (February 5, 1917).

1916, July 24. The Zimmermann Note. (**See p. 968.**) Though German efforts to exploit Mexican anti-American sentiment failed, coolness between the U.S. and Mexico persisted throughout World War I.

1920, April–July. Renewed Civil War. Carranza was overthrown and killed (May 21) in a revolt led by Generals Obregón, **Adolfo de la Huera,** and **Plutarco Elías Calles.** Villa later surrendered to the victors. Obregón was elected President (September 5) and was later recognized by the U.S. (August 31, 1923). Stabilization of the country began.

CENTRAL AMERICA

1903, November 3. Panama Revolution. U.S. efforts to purchase from Colombia the territory necessary for the proposed and congressionally authorized Panama Canal had been rebuffed (October 31). The Colombian province of Panama rose in revolt (November 3), while U.S. warships stood offshore to discourage effective Colombian reaction. The U.S. recognized Panamanian independence (November

6) and 10 days later received Panama's new Minister to the U.S., **Philippe Bunau-Varilla** (formerly associated with the old Panama Canal Co.). A treaty granting the present Canal Zone to the U.S. was signed November 18. The coup was obviously engineered by U.S. President **Theodore Roosevelt** in the paramount interests of national defense. The canal was intended as a by-pass for strategical shifts of the U.S. navy between the Atlantic and Pacific oceans.

1907, February–December. War between Nicaragua and Honduras. Honduras was defeated and **Tegucigalpa,** Honduran capital, occupied by the victorious Nicaraguans.

1909–1911. Civil War in Honduras. Former President **Manuel Bonilla** led a revolt against President **Miguel Danila.** A stalemate resulted in an armistice (February 8, 1911). Bonilla was elected President (October 29), but disorders continued.

1912, January. U.S. Marines Land in Honduras. Their mission was to protect U.S. property.

1912, July. Civil War in Nicaragua. U.S. Marines were landed to stop hostilities and assure free elections. This small contingent was not withdrawn until 1925.

1917–1918. World War I. All Central American nations declared war upon Germany, following U.S. entrance into the war.

1921, February–March. Panama–Costa Rica Dispute. Armed clashes took place in disputed territory, but U.S. political pressure averted war.

SOUTH AMERICA

During World War I, Argentina, Chile, Paraguay, Colombia, and Venezuela remained neutral. Brazil declared war against Germany (October 26, 1917). Her warships actively co-operated in antisubmarine activities, and much foodstuff was furnished the allies. Uruguay, Bolivia, Peru, and Ecuador severed relations with Germany, but did not declare war. The period was generally quiet in South America, save for civil wars or revolutions in Colombia (1900–1903), Peru (1914), Ecuador (1924–1925), and Brazil (1924).

WEST INDIES

Cuba

1906–1909. American Army of Cuban Pacification. Political unrest which created chaotic conditions caused President **Theodore Roosevelt** to send a force of 5 regiments of infantry, 2 of cavalry, and several field batteries to Cuba. Normal conditions were restored without friction or incident of any sort. The expedition evacuated the island.

1917, February–March. Revolt in Cuba. American forces landed at Santiago to restore order.

Dominican Republic

1916, May. U.S. Intervention. Following internal disorder threatening national bankruptcy, U.S. Marines were landed and U.S. officials took control of fiscal matters. The situation worsening, full military occupation began (November 29). The Marines were withdrawn in 1924.

Haiti

1915, July 3. U.S. Forces Intervention. This followed widespread disorders and economic claims against Haiti by European countries. A protectorate was proclaimed (September 16). Under Marine supervision, a constabulary was organized and conditions quieted.

1918, July 12. Haiti Declares War on Germany.

1918–1919. Revolt against the U.S. Occupation. Disorders were suppressed by the Marines.

XX

WORLD WAR II AND THE DAWN OF THE NUCLEAR AGE: 1925–1945

MILITARY TRENDS

GENERAL

A new era in warfare and a new era in history dawned in the closing days of this period: the nuclear age, ushered in by the first atomic bomb drop, on Hiroshima, August 6, 1945. Its mushroom-shaped cloud became a question mark. Was nuclear power to become arbiter of future world strategy and diplomacy, a possibility indicated by its unprecedented potentiality for cataclysmic destruction, or was this power merely another, more powerful, addendum to military arsenals?

Meanwhile, the dramatic surge of military technology, noted in the two previous periods, continued to accelerate. To mention only a few of the most obvious projects of this trend, one must note the perfections in internal-combustion engines which led to amazingly improved tanks and warplanes; the reappearance of rocket weapons, from the simple, hand-carried "bazooka" to the highly complex long-range German V-2; and, perhaps even more significant, the tremendous burgeoning of electronics, particularly in the form of radar and of improved radio communications.

Thanks to such developments and also to the vertical-assault potentialities of air warfare, the heretofore rigid compartmentalization of land and sea operations disappeared. Three-dimensional warfare multiplied possible strategic and tactical combinations. Success in this new, co-ordinated "triphibious" warfare depended upon ever-closer affiliation of civilian science and industry on the one hand, and military competence and genius on the other. Victory went to the nation which could best combine the disparate elements of such a team in exploitation of all available resources.

Improvements and refinements in weaponry, transport, and communications brought vast changes in tactics and techniques of warfare. However, man and his reasoning power—the ultimate weapons, and also the basic limitations, in warfare—were unchanged, as were the fundamental principles governing the application of force to human conflict.

A most remarkable development was the joint, unified Allied command, epitomized in the Anglo-American alliance of World War II. This encompassed a totally unprecedented pooling, by the British Empire and the United States, of leaders, staffs, troops, and resources. Never before had integrated armies, navies, and air forces entered combat together, willingly subordinating individual national characteristics, doctrine, and training to a unified command directed against common objectives.

Logistics developed into a science in itself, on land and sea. The U.S. Navy's Logistic Support Groups solved one of the most annoying problems of naval warfare: the necessity that vessels return to some land base for fuel, supply, and repair. The necessary withdrawal from action of naval fighting units became a matter of but a few days or even hours, instead of weeks and months, when sea trains of fast cargo ships and floating repair shops became components of each task force. On land, such things as the artificial harbors off the Normandy coast (see p. 1106), flexible fuel pipelines laid under water or along the ground, and the use of cargo planes extended the mobility of combat forces. Organized logistical elements, especially trained—like the Navy's Seabees, the Army's port troops and railroad and airborne Engineers—reduced to routine supply problems which, a short quarter-century before, would have been insuperable obstacles to mobility.

LEADERSHIP

Significant was the propensity of heads of state to exercise more and more the role of strategical military leadership. Britain's **Churchill** and America's **Roosevelt** dominated both their respective national military planners and the Combined Chiefs of Staff, not always for the best. **Stalin** in the U.S.S.R., **Chiang Kai-shek** in China, and Germany's **Hitler** exercised direct over-all command of their respective armed forces. Hitler's frenetic vagaries, as we shall see, assisted greatly in bringing defeat to Germany.

In military leadership we believe that one man—**Douglas MacArthur**—may have risen to join the thin ranks of the great captains of history. Such evaluation is complicated by political and personal controversies which swirled about MacArthur in this and the subsequent period, and we are too close to the events to be certain that we can assess them with sufficient historical objectivity.

Two other excellent Allied soldiers—**Eisenhower** and **Montgomery**—achieved such notable and deserved victories as to present to their people ideal images of the quintessence of charismatic military leadership. We do not believe, however, that they can objectively be ranked above such other superb soldiers as America's **Bradley,** Britain's **Wavell,** and Germany's **Manstein, Model, Rundstedt,** and **Kesselring,** who were outstanding among the numerous leaders of army groups, nor indeed above America's **Patton** and Germany's **Rommel,** who as tacticians shone above all other army commanders.

Given the paucity of revealed evidence, it is impossible to evaluate the leadership of individual Russian commanders; but certainly someone—or some small group of men—possessed sufficient leadership qualities to bring about the remarkable achievements of the armies of the U.S.S.R. There seems to be reason to single out **Zhukov** as the man most responsible.

On the naval side, America's **Nimitz** as an over-all commander, and **Spruance** as a fleet commander, were both outstanding exemplars of the highly competent officer corps of the U.S. Navy, as were superb Admirals **Cunningham** and **Ramsay** for the Royal Navy.

In air warfare, America's **Arnold** was the first individual who had an opportunity actually to apply the theories of long-range strategic air warfare which had been voiced by air prophets Trenchard, Douhet, and Mitchell a few decades earlier. The results were stupendous, though still inconclusive until the atomic bombs presaged weapons of hitherto-unimagined orders of magnitude. Germany's airmen, whose tactical and technical competence was perhaps unsurpassed, failed to visualize the opportunities for long-range strategic warfare which were understood and exploited by British and American airmen like **Harris** and **Spaatz.** Other airmen particularly worthy of mention are Britain's **Dowding** (whose victory in the Battle of Britain was the most decisive of World War II) and **Tedder,** and America's **Kenney,** these latter two demonstrating exceptional competence not only in independent air operations but also in providing support to surface forces.

STRATEGY

Obviously, economic and political considerations dictated major strategy not only in World War II but also in the relatively minor wars which preceded it. The principle of the "nation at war," so clearly demonstrated in World War I (see p. 916), was dominant during 1939–1945. So too were its limitations, though not immediately apparent. Japan, seeking the wherewithal to provide strategic material for prosecution of her aim, overreached herself totally in the advance into the Southern Resources Area. Hitler's preoccupation with the Russian oil fields was equally fatal (see p. 1088). On the Allied side curious contrasts are found. Churchill's determination to dispute control of the Mediterranean even when Britain was seemingly beaten to her knees (see p. 1067) was correct; it proved to be the salvation of the Allied cause. His fascination for attacking the "soft underbelly" of the Axis, which became a bone of contention between American and British planners throughout the war, was politically sound in its aim to curb Russian domination of Eastern Europe. However, the logistical problems would have been stupendous. The question is moot; it will be long debated, as will the opposing, perhaps shortsighted, American strategy, concerned with winning the immediate war rather than with long-range political objectives.

Roosevelt's dictum of "unconditional surrender" in all probability extended the war with Germany far beyond its normal end. Eisenhower's remark, at a press conference (February 28, 1945) that the policy faced the German high command with the choice of being hanged or jumping into a clump of bayonets, was a correct estimate.

Wars of the period were all wars of maneuver; World War II was one of maneuver vast in space, personnel, matériel, and logistics. Air power emerged as a combat force coequal with land power and sea power. Earlier, the Spanish Civil War (see p. 1030) became a testing ground for German, Italian, and Russian theories. The Douhet theory that decision could be attained by air power alone was tested during the siege of Madrid and found wanting, although its efficacy against a primitive nation (Ethiopia; see p. 1040) was high. The citizens of Spain's capital city surmounted their terror, and the decision was reached by ground forces in a war of movement along the Ebro River (see p. 1032).

While the value of fortifications—both fixed and temporary—as springboards for maneuver was again attested throughout the period, sieges *per se* had no appreciable effect other than psychological.

Japan's brilliant and successful opening moves in the Pacific in 1941–1942 (see p. 1127) furnished a lesson of utmost importance to military planners. Consensus of American military thought had been that the Philippines would be the initial target for any Japanese aggression. Defense plans were therefore predicated upon a stout defense of Luzon pending the irresistible counterattack of the U.S. Pacific Fleet. The elimination of that fleet at Pearl Harbor wrecked the entire strategic plan, necessitating an immediate reassessment and readjustment in the midst of war's confusion. British military thought presupposed an initial naval attack on Singapore, essential base for the logistically "short-legged" ships of the Royal Navy and the focal point for successful naval operations in defense of the eastern Indian Ocean and western Pacific areas. The Japanese assault upon the unprotected land side of the fortress (see p. 1133) pricked that balloon.

Both cases were tragic, and almost fatal, instances of the unfortunate tendency of military planners to rely on crystal-ball assumptions of *enemy probable intentions* rather than examining *the worst thing the enemy can do* and providing for such contingency. Proved again, too, was the dictum of Frederick the Great that there is no dishonor in hard-fought defeat, but that there can be no excuse for being surprised.

WEAPONS, DOCTRINE, AND TACTICS ON LAND

We have noted that amazing inventions and refinements in technique emerged from the crucible of World War II. Among these were such things as the proximity fuse, "shaped" charges, bazookas, recoilless rifles, rockets (returning from a century

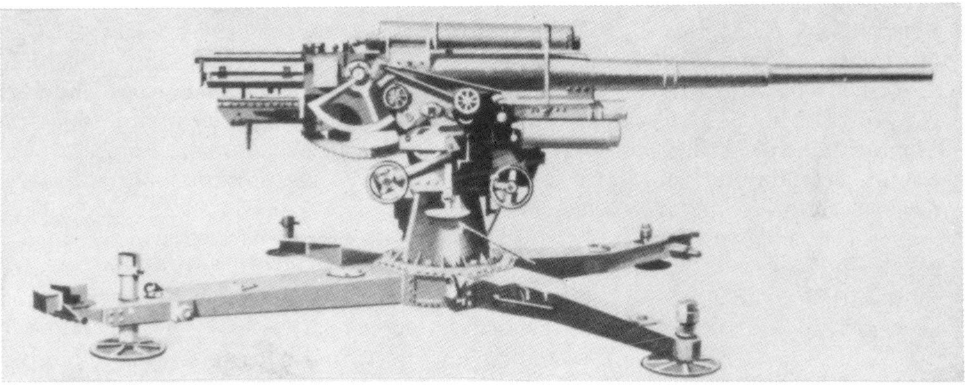

German 88

of oblivion), and concomitant refinements in artillery fire direction and control. Vastly improved mobile ordnance, fast tanks and tank destroyers, and other cross-country vehicles combined to produce a doctrine of mobile warfare at speeds heretofore impossible. With this came wide dispersal of units and elaboration of the "Hutier tactics" of World War I—the sweeping advance which by-passed strong points for later reduction by slower-moving elements; this, in turn, necessitated defensive zones of great depth, so-called "hedgehog" formations which could themselves become points of support for fast counterattack.

Between the World Wars the Germans intensively studied ways and means of overcoming the deficiencies which had stopped their 1918 offensives just short of victory. They came to the conclusion that the tank provided the answer to maintaining the momentum of a breakthrough, and that self-propelled artillery and air support would provide the firepower required when the tanks and other attacking units moved too fast for conventional artillery to keep up. As to resupply and reinforcement, other track-laying vehicles and cross-country trucks were designed to

German tank used by the Afrika Korps

assure resupply and reinforcement to the armored spearheads, while the speed of the advance was expected to avoid the shell-cratered morasses of World War I battlefields. As a result of these studies, when the war began the Germans were far ahead of any other country in tank doctrine. They also enjoyed a slight technical superiority in tank design and construction, which they were able to maintain throughout the war, despite intensive efforts by the British, Americans, and Russians to catch up. The Germans also had a substantial superiority in antitank guns. Almost accidentally they discovered that their high-velocity 88mm antiaircraft gun was the best antitank gun in the world, and was also useful in the normal artillery role in level or rolling areas where its flat trajectory was not a handicap. Probably the most effective use made of the 88mm gun was by General Erwin Rommel in the desert fighting in North Africa, where he aggressively sent batteries of 88's forward with his tanks, to form deadly firepower bases around which his tanks maneuvered rapidly, to the dismay of his British opponents.

While the Germans were rectifying the shortcomings of their 1918 offensives, the major maritime powers were somewhat less intensively studying the Gallipoli campaign as an example of how not to combine land and sea forces in amphibious operations. The British, Americans, and Japanese, quite independently, began to devise weapons, equipment, and techniques to improve assault landings. All three developed shallow-draft, ramp-unloading landing craft that would get troops to the edge of the beach, and enable them to unload rapidly. (It is not known whether Byzantine examples had any influence on these developments.) During the war the British and Americans intensified this effort, even producing ocean-going vessels such as the Landing Ship Tank (LST) and Landing Ship Infantry (LSI) that could carry assault troops across an ocean and land them in combat-ready formation on hostile beaches.

Although inhibited by lack of funds and shortages of personnel, the United States Army was making the most significant development in the enhancement of artillery firepower since the time of Gustavus Adolphus. Elaborating concepts and techniques improvised on the battlefield by Major General **Charles P. Summerall** in the closing days of World War I, the U.S. Field Artillery School developed the technique of massed fires, whereby a single Fire Direction Center could rapidly and accurately shift the fire of many batteries, and sometimes many battalions, across a wide front, multiplying artillery effectiveness many times. This capability, and particularly the massing of the multi-volleyed fires of large numbers of guns on one target in a demoralizing crescendo of destructiveness, gave the Americans a firepower superiority on the battlefield that was not matched by any other nation in the war.

NAVAL WEAPONS, DOCTRINE, AND TACTICS

The effectiveness of bomber and torpedo aircraft against surface warships was so pronounced from the outset of the war—in European waters as well as in the Pacific—that it soon became evident that air superiority also automatically included surface superiority, almost regardless of the relative strength in surface warships of

American LST (Landing Ship Tank) in action

opposing forces. This was demonstrated beyond all doubt in the dramatic American naval victory of Midway (see p. 1146). Thus it was apparent early in the war that carrier-based aircraft were not mere supporters of surface naval forces, but were in fact the primary striking element. The carrier, providing the weapon to destroy enemy surface forces—an extension of fire power—thus quickly displaced the battleship as the capital ship of the fleet, at the very moment that the all-big-gun superdreadnought reached its apogee of firepower and of invulnerability to gunfire in such formidable warships as the German *Bismarck* and the Japanese super-battleships *Yamato* and *Musashi*. The change started with the Japanese carrier blow at Pearl Harbor (see p. 1128). Before the period ended, great fleet actions were con-

Aircraft carrier U.S.S. *Lexington*

tested and won in the air by bombs and torpedoes delivered by airplanes launched from surface vessels which never sighted one another, nor fired other than antiaircraft artillery.

Yet, while the loss of H.M.S. *Renown* and *Prince of Wales* (see p. 1130) early in the Pacific war demonstrated the inability of surface vessels to resist properly delivered air strikes—either land- or carrier-based—the period also saw a number of other naval actions in which surface vessels slugged it out with gunfire. Notable were the Battles of the River Plate (see p. 1053) and the Komandorski Islands (see p. 1163), while the Battle of Surigao Strait, in itself a contest of surface maneuver-*cum*-gunfire, was a component of the large-scale Battle of Leyte Gulf in which carrier air power played the major role (see p. 1179).

The submarine loomed large as a component of sea power, its primary mission being commerce destruction. Germany's U-boat Atlantic campaigns almost, but not quite, weighted the scales in favor of Nazi victory. In the Pacific, where Japan never quite understood the strategic employment of the submarine and ignored antisubmarine procedure, the U.S. submarine campaign strangulated the Nipponese merchant marine. What emerged from the conflict was the sound premise that submarine warfare, in both offense and defense, was a highly specialized affair and—like all military operations of the period, for that matter—demanded professional competence and vision of high order. As a result, despite the fact that at the outset of World War II Japan possessed in the "Long Lance" torpedo, technically the best weapon of its category, her underwater strategy was erroneous.

The use of submarines to evade surface blockade, first attempted by the U.S. Navy during the opening Luzon campaign, became highly developed by the Japanese in the Southwest Pacific. Underwater vessels carried troops and matériel, supplementing the use of fast destroyer-transports for the same purpose.

A striking development in surface operations was the use of naval fire power in support of landing operations. Refinements in fire control and direction enabled

Japanese battleship *Yamato*

U.S. naval craft to put down most effective gunfire support to ground troops during the initial sensitive period prior to debarkation of the assaulters' artillery.

Technological inventions—radar and sonar in particular—played a great part in naval operations. Together with other electronic communications innovations, they constituted a vast and delicate refinement in command control. An important result of this development was the emergence of the command ship in U.S. Navy procedure. In fleet actions, no longer were the admiral and his staff an irritating excrescence on some unfortunate capital ship. In amphibious operations the floating command post enabled close personal co-operation between the naval commander, responsible for putting the ground forces ashore, and the ground commander, who assumed control once the troops gained a toehold on the beach.

WEAPONS, DOCTRINE, AND TACTICS IN THE AIR

The violence and effectiveness of air bombardment, and of close support of ground forces by fighter planes, were clear after the Italian conquest of Ethiopia (see p. 1040) and the Spanish Civil War (see p. 1030). But the full potentialities of air weapons against ground targets were first clearly demonstrated in the German blitzkrieg campaigns in Poland, Norway, the Low Countries, and France in 1939–1940 (see pp. 1050 ff.). Yet for all of the superb tactical efficiency demonstrated by the Luftwaffe in these campaigns, the Germans had not grasped the full implications of air power as a new concept of warfare; they employed their air forces essentially as adjuncts of land forces. The British, though still fumbling in the development of their air doctrine, were nevertheless ahead of the Germans in their air-power concepts. It was this doctrinal advantage—as well as important technical and tactical factors—which more than anything else brought the RAF victory in the Battle of Britain.

As developed by the British, with some later American refinements, by the end of World War II air doctrine had resolved itself to encompass three closely related but nonetheless distinct major functions: command of the air, long-range (so-called "strategic") bombardment directed against the enemy's warmaking potential, and direct support to surface forces.

Command of the air, or "air superiority," was not only essential to effective offensive employment of air units in the other two functions but was also important

Top Messerschmitt ME-Bf109 E-4
A formidable opponent for the RAF's Spitfires and Hurricanes – but over-extended by the long-range flights over Britain, forced to cover ME-110 fighters as well as the bombers, and finally grossly misused as a fighter-bomber. *Speed:* 357 mph. *Max range:* 412 miles. *Armament:* two 20-mm cannons and two 7.92-mm machine-guns.

Middle Junkers JU-87 A-1 Stuka
In close support of the German army during the Blitzkrieg campaigns in Poland and France, the Stuka had made history as 'flying artillery'. It could pinpoint targets with deadly accuracy, but only in the absence of fighter opposition – and it therefore suffered drastic losses in the Battle of Britain. *Crew:* two. *Speed:* 199 mph. Max range: 620 miles. *Bomb load:* 1,100 lbs (pilot only). *Armament:* two 7.92-mm machine-guns.

Bottom Heinkel HE-111 H-3
The Battle of Britain was the first campaign which rammed home Germany's failure to develop a long-range heavy bomber to do the work done by planes such as the HE-111 medium bomber. Like the JU-88, it was also used as an anti-shipping strike aircraft. *Crew:* five. *Speed:* 254 mph. *Max range:* 1,100 miles. *Bomb load:* 4,000 lbs. *Armament:* five 7.92-mm machine-guns, one 20-mm cannon.

Top Messerschmitt ME-Bf110 C-1
Goering hoped that 'destroyer' formations of ME-110s would carve through all fighter opposition, cleaving a path for the bombers – but the 110 was far too heavy and sluggish to 'mix it' with the Spitfire and Hurricane, and suffered accordingly. *Crew:* two. *Speed:* 349 mph. *Max range:* 565 miles. *Armament:* five 7.92-mm machine-guns and two 20-mm cannons.

Middle Junkers JU-88 A-2
Maid-of-all-work for the Luftwaffe, serving as dive-bomber, level bomber, night-fighter, and reconnaissance. It also served with distinction in the torpedo-bombing role against Allied convoys. It suffered – like all German bombers – from a chronic weakness in defensive armament. *Crew:* four. *Speed:* 286 mph. *Max range:* 1,553 miles. *Bomb load:* 3,963 lbs. *Armament:* four 7.92-mm machine-guns.

Bottom Dornier DO-17 Z-2
The DO-17 was a lighter, slimmer plane than the HE-111. Like the Heinkel, it had been blooded in the Spanish Civil War: like all Luftwaffe's bombers, the Battle of Britain forced it to carry out operations which proved the inadequacy of its design. *Crew:* five. *Speed:* 265 mph. *Max range:* 745 miles. *Bomb load:* 2,200 lbs. *Armament:* six 7.92-mm machine-guns.

British Spitfire fighters

in two negative, or defensive, aspects. Command of the air, or at least the capacity to effectively dispute the enemy's control of the air, was important for the defense of a nation's economic strength against long-range bombardment by the enemy, as well as for protecting surface forces against enemy air strikes. And because of the terrorizing effect of air attacks on both civilian and military personnel, command of the air was an important morale factor. Command of the air was achieved in several ways: defensive air combat, attrition of enemy fighter strength through repeated long-range strikes, attacks against air installations and (more slowly, and really as a part of the second function) against aircraft industry.

Strategic bombardment was the function which had been visualized as the decisive role of air power both by Douhet (see p. 995) and by Mitchell (see p. 1047). Long-range bombardment aircraft permitted for the first time military operations against a nation's warmaking capacity by more direct and more rapid means than attrition and the traditional blockade. Despite their substantial numerical inferiority in aircraft, and despite the necessity for concentrating on the development of their

Flying Fortress—B-17F

defensive fighter strength in the early days of the war, the British never lost sight of their objective of offensive air warfare of this sort, and were actually conducting long-range strikes against German industrial and commercial targets even during the Battle of Britain. Quickly improved German fighter defenses, however, forced the British to conduct these attacks at night, when visual conditions were poor, and they had to be content with relatively inaccurate area bombardment of large industrial areas.

American bombers, protected by armor plate and carrying numerous guns—as epitomized in the so-called Flying Fortresses—were better able to bomb in daylight and, thanks also to a more effective bomb sight, were able to strike targets with considerably greater precision. An incidental function of such raids was to entice the German defensive fighters into the air and thus to help reduce German command of the air over Germany by attrition. American losses to the Germans in these daylight raids grew to alarming proportions, however, and could be continued in 1944 and 1945 only because of the development of new longer-range fighter aircraft that could accompany the bombers on their raids into the heart of Germany. Till the end of the war in Europe, therefore, Britain's RAF Bomber Command struck area targets at night, while American long-range units attacked during the day. The Combined Bomber Offensive was a major factor in hastening the collapse of Germany.

Liberators—B-24

Though the details were different (see p. 1196), the development of American strategic bombardment tactics against Japan followed a similar course, with the final effectiveness of the air offensive being in large part due to the ability of long-range fighters to accompany and protect the bomber planes.

The tactical doctrine for close air support of ground forces, as it emerged from World War II, was largely the development of co-operative efforts of Air Marshal Tedder's Desert Air Force and General Montgomery's Eighth Army in 1942. The essential feature of this doctrine was in its command arrangements, whereby the air commander at all times retained full control over all his subordinate units, which were never attached to ground-force commanders. This permitted a degree of flexibility in meeting the ground-force requirements, and in coping with unexpected threats, which was impossible in the German system, for instance, where air units were generally assigned to ground-force command. At the same time, however, it inhibited full integration of air-support units into the land-warfare team.

It is important to note that an essential aspect of this doctrine of support was the dual capability of the fighter-bomber aircraft type. These light, speedy, maneuverable planes were not only the best implements for relatively precise, low-level bombing and strafing attacks against ground targets; they were also the only weapons which could be used with real effectiveness against comparable enemy types. This was why the first mission of these fighter aircraft—assisted by light and medium bombers attacking enemy air installations—had to be the achievement of local air superiority. Otherwise, neither they nor any other aircraft types (reconnaissance, cargo, troop-carrier, etc.) could carry on other missions in support of the ground troops without suffering prohibitive losses from enemy fighters.

At sea the aircraft mission of support of surface forces was similar in concept, though it differed in some important details. This is discussed under naval tactics (see above).

As the period ended, professional opinion upon the capabilities and limitations of air power was widely divided, despite the consensus that it had become an indispensable member of the combat team.

Meanwhile, although various types of aircraft proliferated, the basic categories of combat planes resolved into heavy long-range bombers for offensive purposes, fighters for defense of friendly bombers and use against hostile intruders, fighter-bombers for both air combat and close support, and a variety of reconnaissance, spotting, and other combat auxiliary types.

Airborne operations, initiated in and by the German vertical assault on Norway and Western Europe in 1940 (see pp. 1056 and 1059) and on Crete during 1941 (see p. 1075), became a common practice later of U.S. and British offensives. The troops were transported in planes (to be parachuted to the ground) and towed gliders (for "crash" landings), and were escorted by combat aircraft.

The development of heavy cargo planes permitted logistical air support to ground forces. Allied operations in the Burma and China theaters completely depended upon it.

The weaponry of air combat resolved itself into machine guns, light cannon, bombs, rockets, and torpedoes. Development of a bomb sight of superior accuracy (American) and of radar (mainly British) were twin inventions of enormous importance.

As the war was coming to a close, both Britain and Germany were developing a radically new jet aircraft engine for interceptor aircraft which would be far faster and more powerful than the conventional propeller-driven aircraft. The Germans actually succeeded in producing a number of such interceptors, which proved their effectiveness in combat against Allied bombers over Germany. Their appearance was too late, however, to prevent Germany's over-all military collapse.

DISARMAMENT

During this period was initiated an intensive effort to achieve disarmament (or at least arms control) as a means to assuring world peace. The League of Nations, which had started the effort earlier (see p. 920), continued to take leadership in this field. Although the United States was not a member of the League of Nations, it participated informally in most of the League activities during this period. The results of disarmament efforts were disappointing (see below).

INTERWAR INTERNATIONAL EFFORTS TO MAINTAIN PEACE, 1925–1939

Closely related to the new international attention being focused upon arms control and disarmament in general were the efforts of the major powers—mainly the victors of World War I—to ensure continuation of the postwar peace within the framework established by the Treaty of Versailles (see p. 989). These efforts are summarized as follows:

1925, June 17. Arms Traffic Convention. This was convened by the League of Nations at Geneva in an effort to control international trade in arms and munitions. One result was the **Geneva Protocol,** prohibiting use of poison gas in warfare. The U.S. did not sign.

1925, October 5–16. Locarno Conference. The resulting treaties (signed December 1) included (1) a treaty of mutual guaranty of the Franco-German and Belgo-German frontiers signed by Germany, France, Belgium, and Great Britain, (2) arbitration treaties between Germany and Poland and Germany and Czechoslovakia, (3) arbitration treaties between Germany and Belgium and Germany and France, (4) a Franco-Polish and a Franco-Czechoslovak treaty for mutual assistance in case of attack by Germany. The treaties helped create a sense of security among the European powers.

1925, December. Establishment of Disarmament Preparatory Commission. This was created by the League to prepare for a World Disarmament Conference. The commission wrestled for 7 years with issues that plagued disarmament efforts throughout the interwar period, including France's demand for security guarantees as a prerequisite for arms reduction, Germany's demand for equality in armaments, Great Britain's insistence on arms of the kind and number needed to defend her scattered possessions, and American opposition to the concept of collective security (entangling alliances) and inability to recognize the complexities of disarmament problems faced by other nations.

1927, January 31. Dissolution of Inter-Allied Military Control Commission. Germany had consistently flouted the injunctions of the commission and obstructed its procedures. None of the Allies was willing to use force to obtain compliance. The problem of German armament was henceforth placed under League jurisdiction.

1927, June 20–August 4. Three-Power Naval Conference. Great Britain, the United States, and Japan met at Geneva in an effort to agree on the question of establishing a ratio for strengths in cruisers, destroyers, and submarines as a step beyond the Washington Naval Treaties (see p. 920). The conference failed to reach agreement.

1928, August 27. Kellogg-Briand Pact (Pact of Paris). This was signed at Paris by the United States, France, Great Britain, Germany, Italy, Japan, and a number of other states. This pact renounced aggressive war, but made no provisions for sanctions.

1930, January 21–April 22. London Naval Conference. This led to a treaty signed by Great Britain, the United States, France, Italy, and Japan, regularizing submarine warfare and limiting the tonnage and gun caliber of submarines. The limitation on aircraft carriers provided for by the Washington Treaty (see p. 920) was extended. Great Britain, the United States, and Japan also agreed to scrap certain warships by 1933, and allocated tonnage to other categories. An "escalation clause," permitting an increase over specified tonnages if the national needs of any one signatory demanded it, was included. These agreements were to run until 1936. The treaty gave Britain and the United States equality in over-all cruiser combat effectiveness, which was to be determined by formula. Japan's relative naval position was strengthened. The treaty was to expire at the end of 1936.

1932–1934. World Disarmament Conference at Geneva. The Preparatory Commission's draft treaty included provision for inspection and control, but no relative force ratios had been agreed on. The optimistic atmosphere created by the Kellogg-Briand Pact of 1928, by which all nations had renounced war, and by the London Naval Treaty, had been dissipated by Japan's 1931 invasion of Manchuria (see p. 1046), the international economic depression, and the rising strength of aggressive nationalism in Germany. France's "Tardieu plan," providing for an international police force, stronger security guarantees, and the placing of all powerful weapons "in escrow," to be used only at the direction of the League or to repel an invasion, was too extreme to win acceptance by the other powers. Germany made it clear that she would not accept this or any proposal that did not provide for German equality. Britain introduced a counterproposal providing for proportionate reduction and also "qualitative" reduction—prohibition of aggressive weapons. This proposal failed of adoption, as did a U.S. proposal for the abolition of all "offensive" weapons and another U.S. plan to reduce all armaments by one-third. Failure was certain after Japanese withdrawal from the League of Nations (March, 1933; see p. 1043) and German withdrawal from the conference and the League (October, 1933; see p. 1035). The conference soon adjourned without agreement (June, 1934).

1934, December 19. Japan Denounces Washington and London Naval Treaties. She gave the required 2 years' notice that she was withdrawing from the Washington Naval Treaty of 1922 and assurance that, when the London Treaty expired at the end of 1936, there would be no naval limitations agreement unless a new treaty could be achieved. This followed refusal of the U.S. and U.K. to agree to Japanese demands for equality.

1935, March 16. Germany Denounces Disarmament Clauses of Versailles Treaty. Germany claimed this was due to the failure of other nations to disarm. She announced a massive rearmament program.

1935, December. Five-Power Naval Conference. Representatives of the United States, Great Britain, Japan, France, and Italy met in London with little hope of producing a treaty. Japan soon left the conference. America, Britain, and France did agree to "qualitative" limitation, with restrictions on certain kinds of ships and caliber of guns. Advance notification of construction programs was also to be given, and should one nation build in excess of treaty restrictions, others were freed of restrictions. After 2 years the treaty was discarded, as accelerated Japanese naval construction and the aggressive acts of the revisionist powers forced Great Britain and the United States to rearm as fast as possible.

WESTERN EUROPE BETWEEN WORLD WARS

GREAT BRITAIN

1935, June 18. Anglo-German Naval Agreement. German tonnage (including submarines) would not exceed 35 per cent of British naval tonnage. This separate agreement estranged France from Britain.

1935, September. Britain and the Ethiopian Crisis. (See p. 1040.) Great Britain assumed guidance of the League of Nations in the imposition of sanctions, but shrank from adopting extreme measures (such as oil sanctions) and the League action failed.

1937, January 2. Anglo-Italian Mediterranean Agreement. This affirmed the independence and integrity of Spain, and international freedom of passage through the Mediterranean, but in the long run did not dispel British suspicion aroused by Italian activity in the Mediterranean and Near East.

1938, September 15–28. Chamberlain Attempts to Mediate German-Czech Crisis. (See p. 1038.) The Prime Minister twice flew to Germany to confer with Hitler.

1938, September 29. Munich Agreement. (See p. 1038.) Chamberlain returned with a peace pact with Germany which he rated highly, though it was not universally viewed with such acclaim.

1939, March 31. British Guarantee to Poland. After Hitler seized Czechoslovakia (see p. 1038), the British government pledged aid in case of any aggressive action endangering Poland's independence. Following the Italian conquest of Albania (see p. 1039), similar guarantees were also given to Greece and Rumania, a mutual assistance pact was concluded with Turkey, and the British government began to try to bring Russia into the "peace front."

1939, September 3. Outbreak of War with Germany. **(See p. 1050.)**

IRELAND

1933–1938. Internal Disorder and Conflict.

1935, July. Anti-Catholic Riots in Belfast. They led to expulsion of Catholic families, to reprisals by the Free State government, and to increased friction with Britain.

1938, April 25. Agreement with Great Britain. This resolved a number of outstanding issues for at least 3 years, including turning over to the Free State (Eire) the coast defenses of Cobh, Bere Haven, and Lough Swilly. It improved relations between England and Eire.

FRANCE

1925, April. Beginning of Insurrection in Morocco. **(See p. 1004.)**

1925, July. Rising of the Druses in Lebanon. **(See p. 1041.)**

1935, January 7. Franco-Italian Agreement on Africa. France made several concessions to Italy in the hope of establishing a strong front against increasing German strength.

1935, May 2. Alliance with Russia. The French government, unable to bring Germany and Poland into an eastern pact (which would include Russia) to maintain the *status quo,* hastened to ally itself with Russia, after announcement of German rearmament. There was much opposition from conservative elements in France.

1936, June. France Begins Rearmament. This followed the German reoccupation of the Rhineland, the Italian victory in Ethiopia, the collapse of the League system (on which France had depended heavily), plus the outbreak of civil war in Spain. (See pp. 1035, 1040, 1030.)

1938, September. The German-Czechoslovak Crisis. **(See p. 1038.)** The French Army and Navy were partially mobilized and ready for war. However, the country was strongly in favor of a peaceful settlement and Daladier received a warm reception on his return from Munich. French preponderance on the Continent had been definitely replaced by that of Germany.

1938, December 6. Franco-German Pact. This guaranteed existing frontiers.

1938, December. Franco-Italian Crisis. This arose from Italian demands for French colonies; France took an uncompromising attitude toward any cession of territory.

1939, March. Guarantees to Poland, Rumania, and Greece. France joined Britain in these guarantees, and used all her influence to draw Russia into the nonaggression system.

1939, August 20–September 1. The Danzig-Polish Crisis. **(See p. 1038.)**

1939, September 3. France Declares War on Germany. **(See p. 1051.)**

THE LOW COUNTRIES

Belgium

1936, October 14. Belgium Denounces Military Alliance with France. She resumed liberty of action, following German reoccupation of the Rhineland, in order not to become embroiled against Germany through connection with the Franco-Russian alliance.

1937, October 13. German Guarantee to Belgium. The inviolability and integrity of Belgium were guaranteed so long as the latter abstained from military action against Germany.

1939, August 23. King Leopold Appeals for Peace. This was on behalf of Belgium, Holland, and the Scandinavian states. The appeal was in vain. Belgium mobilized, but proclaimed neutrality in the European war that broke out on September 3.

The Netherlands

1926, November–1927, July. Serious Revolt in Java, Dutch East Indies.

1937–1938. Dutch Naval Forces Increased in Far East. Japan's advance in China exposed the Netherlands East Indies to possible Japanese aggression.

THE IBERIAN PENINSULA

Spain

PRELUDE TO REVOLUTION

1930, January 28. Primo de Rivera Resigns from Quasi Dictatorship. His replacement, General **Dámaso Berenguer,** irritated the Spanish people, who held him responsible for the disaster in Morocco at Anual (see p. 1004).

1930, December 12–13. Mutiny at Jaca. The garrison demanded a republic. The ringleaders were executed, but the virus of revolt spread among the military.

1931, April 14. Overthrow of King Alfonso XIII. After a near-bloodless revolt, **Alcalá Zamora,** Republican leader, set up a provisional government and was elected President (December 10).

1932, August 10. Reactionary Revolt in Seville. This was led by General **José Sanjurjo;** it was speedily suppressed. Regional interests began a tussle for autonomy, fomented by Communist activity.

1933, January 8. Radical Uprising in Barcelona. This quickly spread to other large cities and was repressed only with difficulty by government troops.

1933–1935. Growing Unrest. Communist uprisings in Catalonia and the Asturias brought semichaos to these regions.

1936, February 16. Leftist Coalition Takes Power. Elections gave a majority to a Communist-influenced popular front. The new Socialist Cortes voted to remove Zamora for exceeding his powers, and replaced him with Marxist **Manuel Azaña** (April 10).

THE SPANISH CIVIL WAR, 1936–1939

1936, July 18. Military Revolt. Simultaneously, the military garrisons in 12 cities of the mainland and 5 in Spanish Morocco rebelled, following a clash between a unit of the Spanish Foreign Legion and a Communist-led mob in Melilla, Spanish Morocco. General **Francisco Franco,** erstwhile chief of staff, but exiled by the Socialist government to command of the Canary Islands, flew to Melilla to take command. While Spanish troops in Morocco were air-lifted to Algeciras and La Línea, the garrisons of Burgos, Saragossa, and Huesca in northern Spain concentrated at Burgos, under General **Emilio Mola.** An uprising at Barcelona failed; its leader, General **Manuel Goded,** was cap-

tured by the Loyalists and shot. Madrid, the east-coast seaports, and part of the Basque regions remained loyal to the government, but Seville and Cádiz proclaimed for the rebels, as did the cadets of the military academy at **Toledo,** who rallied around their commander, Colonel **José Moscardo,** in the Alcazar fortress, which was besieged by Loyalists, mostly militiamen (July 20–September 28). Most ships of the Spanish Navy joined the revolt.

1936, July–August. Advance on Madrid. Franco, with some 30,000 regular troops (Spaniards and Moroccans), struck north toward Badajoz; Mola with 15,000 more regulars began moving south. The rebel plan was to converge on Madrid.

1936, August 15. Rebels Capture Badajoz. They then began to advance eastward up the Tagus Valley and through Talavera and Toledo, which was relieved by troops under General **José Varela** (September 28) after a 10 weeks' siege.

1936, September. International Involvements. Soviet Russia supplied and reinforced the Loyalists; Germany and Italy lent material aid to Franco. The first tangible aid to arrive was a contingent of Luftwaffe Junker bombers and pursuit planes. Italian infantry and light tanks followed. Russian air-force contingents, military advisers, artillery, and tanks soon reached the east-coast ports to aid the Loyalists. Soviet propaganda was also directed to enlisting the support of "volunteers," among them a number of Americans who got abroad with false passports to be enrolled in a so-called "Abraham Lincoln Brigade." In all, 12 such "volunteer brigades" materialized from the U.S.S.R. and elsewhere before the war was over.

1936, September 4. Popular Front Government Formed in Madrid. The new Loyalist leader was **Francisco Largo Caballero;** Catalan and Basque Nationalists were represented. Anarchist-Syndicalists later were included in the government (November).

1936, October. Franco Appointed Chief of the Spanish State by the Insurgents. Four rebel columns under Mola continued to converge on Madrid; he said he had a "fifth column" in the city. This was the origin of this as a term for subversive activity.

1936, November 6. Insurgents Lay Siege to Madrid. The Loyalist government moved to Valencia. Despite heavy fighting in the suburbs of the city and intensive air bombardments, Loyalist troops under General **José Miaja** held the capital. After nearly four months of incessant combat, there was a brief lull in the struggle for the city (February–March, 1937).

1936, November 18. Franco Government Recognized by Germany and Italy. France, Great Britain, and the United States continued their policy of nonintervention and nonassistance toward both factions. A nonintervention committee was set up in London; 29 nations, including Italy and Germany, made an attempt to patrol the Spanish coast and limit the war.

1937, February 8. Rebels Capture Málaga. Troops under General **Gonzalo Queipo de Llano** were assisted by Italian troops. However, they were unable to cut the road from Madrid to Valencia. Meanwhile the siege of Madrid continued. Soviet training and "volunteer" reinforcements went far to steady the defense.

1937, March 8–16. Italian Disaster of Guadalajara. Two Italian divisions, accompanied by 50 light tanks, made a surprise penetration of Loyalist lines, in an effort to isolate Madrid. Rain had turned the countryside into a sea of mud, so the Italians advanced in a long road column, with little opposition. Russian dive bombers took them by surprise and after repeated attacks the Italians became a disorganized mob, scattered across the countryside. Most, however, escaped, and eventually returned to their own lines.

1937, March 18. Loyalist Victory over Italians at Brihuega. This was largely a result of Guadalajara. Large stores were captured. The insurgents, frustrated in their efforts to cut off Madrid, turned north.

1937, April 1. Rebels Invest Bilbao. Surrounding Basque Loyalist resistance was soon crushed.

1937, April 25. Guernica Massacre. World opinion was shocked by the ruthless bombing of this northern village by Franco's Luftwaffe pilots with loss of many noncombatant lives. The towns of **Durango** and **Guernica** were occupied (April 28).

1937, April 30. Rebel Battleship *España* Sunk by Loyalist Planes.

1937, May 3–10. Anarchist Uprising in Barcelona. This was put down with considerable bloodshed by Loyalist troops, and caused a crisis in the government.

1937, May 17. The Largo Caballero Regime Falls. A new Loyalist government was formed under **Juan Negrín.**

1937, May 31. German Planes Bomb Almería. This was in retaliation for a Loyalist strike which damaged the German pocket-battleship *Deutschland* at Ibiza in the Balearic Isles.

1937, June 3. Death of General Mola. He died in an air crash.

1937, June 15 and 18. Submarine Attacks on German Cruiser *Leipzig*. These attacks, allegedly by Loyalist submarines, off Oran on the Algerian coast, resulted in Germany and Italy quitting the international patrol.

1937, June 18. Bilbao Captured by Rebels. This followed an 80-day siege. Rebel troops under General **Fidel Dávila** then moved to conquer **Santander** (August 25). By the end of the year all of northwestern Spain was under rebel control.

1937, July 6–25. Loyalist Offensive from Madrid. After some success, this was repulsed by Varela, commanding the investing forces. There was no further serious fighting on this front for nearly two years.

1937, August–September. Loyalist Offensive in Aragon. This was repulsed by the rebels at **Saragossa, Teruel,** and **Huesca.**

1937, September. Nyon Conference. The intense submarine attacks on ships destined for the Loyalists drew protests of piracy from France and England as these ships were supposed to be carrying non-contraband supplies. A 9-power conference was called at Nyon, Switzerland (Germany and Italy abstained). A new system of maritime zone patrols was established. An Anglo-French naval patrol was authorized to attack any submarine, surface vessel, or aircraft illegally attacking a non-Spanish vessel.

1937, October 28. Loyalist Government Moves to Barcelona. It had earlier taken over control of the Catalan government (August 12).

1937, November 28. Franco Announces a Naval Blockade. This covered the entire Spanish coast, and was operated from the island of Mallorca.

1937–1938, December 5–February 20. Battle of Teruel. A Loyalist counteroffensive captured Teruel after a bitter struggle. This diverted the rebels from operations to the northeastward, but the government forces were unable to sustain the offensive. A rebel counteroffensive retook the city (February 15–20).

1938, February–June. Rebel Offensive. Franco's forces drove eastward in great strength, reaching the seacoast at **Vinaroz** (April 15), and isolating Catalonia from the remainder of Loyalist-held territory. An advance on Barcelona was checked by desperate Loyalist resistance along the Ebro River.

1938, July 24–August 1. Loyalist Ebro Counteroffensive. This effort to restore communications between Catalonia and other areas of Republican Spain was repulsed.

1938, August–November. Stalemate. The rebels, who now held most of Spain, prepared for a major offensive to end the war. Meanwhile, in accordance with the Anglo-Italian agreement, Mussolini withdrew some troops from Spain, but kept at least 40,000 troops there.

1938, December 23. Beginning of Rebel Offensive in Catalonia. This cracked the Loyalist defense. Government troops retreated in growing disorder on Barcelona. Both sides were hampered by atrocious weather conditions.

1939, January 26. Rebels Capture Barcelona. They were assisted by Italians. Some 20,000 Loyalist troops, completely routed, fled across the French border, where they were disarmed and interned. Resistance continued at Madrid, Valencia, and in scattered areas of eastern Spain.

1939, February 27. France and Great Britain Recognize Franco Government.

1939, February–March. Internal Disunity among Loyalists. Their grip weakened on their remaining strongholds. Franco launched a new offensive against Madrid (March 26).

1939, March 28. Surrender of Madrid and Valencia. Members of the Loyalist Defense Council fled. The war had cos about 700,000 lives in battle, 30,000 mo executed or assassinated, and another 1

000 killed in air raids. Franco and his government at once set up special tribunals, which convicted and executed hundreds of Loyalist leaders, despite efforts of England and France to ensure moderation.

COMMENT. *The war, prosecuted with the ferocity common to Spanish internecine struggles, presented at least one object lesson to military observers: the transformation in 3 short months of the Loyalist mob of military into reasonably efficient soldiers (at least in defensive combat) thanks to Soviet instruction. The military of Germany, Italy, and the U.S.S.R. learned much from their respective participation—actually dress rehearsals for airing their doctrines and their matériel for the war to come.*

However, the lesson of Madrid, battered, bombed, and wrecked, with heavy loss of noncombatant life during a 28-month siege—all to no appreciable result—was not taken seriously; the Douhet theory of terror bombing as the ultimate weapon of war had been seemingly disproved, but its advocates the world over remained undaunted. The extent of foreign participation in the war was considerable. Foreign contingents in Spain numbered 40,000–60,000 Italian troops, some 20,000 German, and perhaps some 50,000 Soviet and Communist-inspired "volunteers" from various nations.

1939, April 7. Spain Joins the Anti-Comintern Pact. (See p. 1035.)

1939, September 3. Spanish Neutrality Proclaimed.

Portugal

1925–1932. Internal Disorders. This was a period of repeated revolts, military coups, and dictatorships, finally brought under control when **Oliveira Salazar** became premier and dictator (July 5, 1932).

1936, July. Portugal Aids Spanish Rebels. With the outbreak of the Spanish Civil War (see p. 1030), Salazar's government immediately sided with the rebels against the republican government. Portugal became one of the main routes by which supplies reached Franco from Germany and elsewhere. Subsequent British pressure forced Portugal to close her borders (April, 1937), but by that time Franco was able to get his supplies through the north Spanish coast towns.

'9, March 18. Nonaggression Pact with Fascist Spain. Portugal soon after reaffirmed her traditional alliance with Britain (May 22).

1941–1945. Portuguese Neutrality in World War II. While ostensibly neutral during World War II, Portuguese grant of bases in the Azores (October 13, 1943) to Great Britain and the U.S. was of much assistance to the Allies in combating the Atlantic submarine menace (see p. 1091); she finally severed diplomatic relations with Nazi Germany (May 6, 1945).

ITALY

1926–1930. Treaties of Friendship with Spain, Hungary, Greece, Ethiopia, and Austria. This was part of the Fascist policy of rallying the "revisionist" states against the Little Entente and its supporter, France.

1930, April 30. Italy Begins a Great Naval Program. This was the result of failure to secure recognition of Italian parity from France. During the following years, Italian naval and air forces were built up to imposing dimensions.

1934, March 17. Rome Protocols between Italy, Hungary, and Austria. These provided for closer trade relations and established a Danubian bloc under Fascist auspices to counterbalance French influence with the Little Entente.

1934, July. Abortive Nazi Coup in Vienna. (See p. 1036.)

1935–1936. Ethiopian War. (See p. 1040.)

1936, July. Outbreak of the Spanish Civil War. (See p. 1030.) Italian action in Spain aroused the apprehensions of Great Britain and France and served to increase the tension in the Mediterranean. Under these circumstances, Mussolini felt compelled to draw closer to Germany.

1936, October 27. Italian-German Agreement regarding Austria. This served as a foundation for Italo-German co-operation and may be regarded as the beginning of the Rome-Berlin Axis. Germany recognized the conquest of Ethiopia by Italy (October 25).

1937, January 2. Anglo-Italian Agreement. (See p. 1028.)

1937, March 25. Italian-Yugoslav Treaty. This guaranteed existing frontiers and the maintenance of the *status quo* in the Adriatic, ending a long period of friction between the 2 powers. It was a serious blow to the Little Entente structure and to French influence.

1937, November 6. Italy Adheres to the Anti-Comintern Pact. (See p. 1035.) This completed the triangle of states (Rome-Berlin-Tokyo Axis) engaged in upsetting the peace treaties and the *status quo*. In line with this policy, the Italian government announced the withdrawal of Italy from the League of Nations (December 11).

1938, March. Italy Accepts German Annexation of Austria. Italian commitments in Ethiopia, Libya, and Spain made any alternative course impossible. Mussolini was growing increasingly dependent on Germany.

1938, September. German-Czechoslovak Crisis. Mussolini remained in the background until the situation reached critical proportions, when he made a series of threatening speeches; in the final analysis, he appears to have done his utmost to bring about the Munich meeting and the accord which entailed the sacrifice of a large part of Czechoslovakia to Germany.

1938, November 30. Franco-Italian Relations Strained. This resulted from agitated demands in the Italian Chamber for the cession by France of Corsica and Tunisia.

1939, April 7. Italian Invasion and Conquest of Albania. (See p. 1039.)

1939, May 22. Political and Military Alliance with Germany. Much exchange of military men and technical experts followed.

1939, September 1–3. Italy Declares Neutrality. This surprised most of the world, but one motive was evidently the thought of serving Germany as a channel for supplies.

GERMANY

1927, September 18. Hindenburg Repudiates German Responsibility for World War I.

1928, January 29. Treaty with Lithuania. This confirmed frontiers, including the status of Memel as part of Lithuania, and provided for arbitration.

1929, February 6. Germany Accepts the Kellogg-Briand Pact. (See p. 1027.)

1929, June 7. Young Plan Agreement. Germany accepted the plan for stabilizing her finances, subject to promise of complete Allied evacuation of the Rhineland by June, 1930.

1929, September–1930, June. Allied Evacuation of the Rhineland.

1930, September 14. Nazis Gain in Reichstag Elections. This marked the emergence of Hitler's National Socialists as a major party. Hitler's program was opposed to all provisions of the Versailles Treaty, particularly reparations. A period of disorder followed, with numerous clashes between the National Socialists (Nazis) and the Communists.

1931, December 12. Allied Evacuation of the Saar.

1932, April 13. Chancellor Brüning Bans Nazi Storm Troops.

1932, June 16. Ban on Nazi Storm Troops Lifted. The National Socialist movement gained new momentum, thanks to this decision by the new **von Papen** government.

1932, July 20. Coup d'État in Prussia. Von Papen removed the Socialist prime minister and other officials. The cities of Berlin and Brandenburg were put under martial law, the activities of the Nazi Storm Troops having made it almost impossible for the civil authorities to maintain order.

1932, November 17. Resignation of von Papen. This was the result of growing disorders and political unrest.

1932, November 24. Hitler Refuses Chancellorship. Hindenburg offered him the post, but would not grant Hitler's demand for full power.

1933, January 30. Hitler Becomes Chancellor. He accepted the post after 2 months of political crisis.

1933, February 27. Reichstag Fire. Hitler denounced the fire as a Communist plot to disrupt new elections (scheduled for March 5). As a result, President von Hindenburg issued emergency decrees outlawing the Communist party and suspending the constitutional liberties of free speech and free press as well as other liberties. This enabled Nazi Storm Troops to intimidate all opponents without fear of legal opposition. The result was a National Socialist victory in the elections. Later evidence showed that the Nazis were responsible for the fire.

1933–1938. Nazi Dictatorship Firmly Established. All opposing political parties w liquidated under government press

The German state governments were shorn of all effective power, and Germany became a national rather than a federal state. The legal system was radically changed, and dangerously wide powers were given to the People's Court, which was set up in May, 1934. Concentration camps were set up for detainment of political opponents. Racial pressures increased upon the Jewish population and, to a lesser extent, on the Christian churches protesting this racial persecution.

1933, October 14. Germany Withdraws from the League of Nations. (**See p. 1028.**)

1934, January 26. Treaty with Poland. This provided for nonaggression and respect for existing territorial rights for 10 years.

1934, June 30. The Great Blood Purge. Some 77 persons, many of them leaders high in the Nazi party, were executed because of an alleged plot against Hitler and the regime.

1934, July 25. Nazi Putsch in Vienna. (**See p. 1036.**)

1935, March 16. Hitler Denounces Disarmament Terms of Versailles Treaty. (**See p. 1028.**)

1935, June 18. Anglo-German Naval Agreement. (**See p. 1028.**)

1936, March 7. Reoccupation of the Rhineland. Simultaneously, Germany denounced the Locarno Pacts of 1925. France, without support from Britain, decided not to intervene. Later evidence shows that German generals would have deposed Hitler and withdrawn from the Rhineland if France had responded with force.

1936, October 27. Establishment of the Berlin-Rome Axis. (**See p. 1033.**)

1936, November 25. Conclusion of the German-Japanese Anti-Comintern Pact. This was an extension of the Berlin-Rome alignment to counterweight the Franco-Russian Alliance.

1937, November 5. Hitler's Goals. At a top-secret meeting with heads of armed forces and his foreign minister, he announced his intentions of gaining for Germany *Lebensraum* (territorial expansion) in Europe by force of arms. Austria and Czechoslovakia were to be seized, then Poland; finally, Russia. Target date—1938–1943.

1938, March 12–13. The German Invasion and Annexation of Austria. (**See p. 1036.**) This added over 6 million Germans to the Reich and paved the way for future expansion of influence in the Danube River Valley.

1938, September 7–29. The German-Czech Crisis. (**See p. 1038.**) This culminated with the Munich Agreement, annexing over 3 million Sudeten Germans to Germany. Hitler's success made Germany the dominant power on the Continent, politically shattered the Little Entente, and broke down the French alliance system in Eastern Europe.

1939, March 10–16. Annexation of Bohemia and Moravia. This blatant violation of the Munich Agreement obliterated the Czechoslovak state and left Slovakia nominally independent.

1939, March 23. Annexation of Memel. Following this, rigid demands were made on Poland regarding Danzig and Pomorze ("Polish Corridor"). Polish firmness, backed by a pledge of Anglo-French aid (March 31; see p. 1028) deterred immediate German action.

1939, May 23. Hitler Plans Attack on Poland. He informed his military commanders at a secret conference. He discounted danger of a conflict with England and France. A small special staff was set up in the General Staff (OKW) to implement the planning. Secret negotiations were begun for a nonaggression pact with the U.S.S.R. Military and naval preparations included calling of a quarter-million reservists to the colors for "training," and preparation to send the pocket battleships *Graf Spee* and *Deutschland* to sea, together with 21 submarines.

1939, June–August. Tense Relations with Poland. Frequent border incidents caused repeated warnings from France and England.

1939, August 22. Hitler Orders Invasion of Poland. While Foreign Minister **Joachim von Ribbentrop** rushed to Moscow to conclude a nonaggression pact, Hitler gathered his military commanders in a secret meeting at Berchtesgaden to order preparation for war. Troop concentration began behind the Polish border. Warships put to sea.

1939, August 23. German-Russian Pact Signed at Moscow.

1939, August 31. Gleiwitz Incident. A

group of SS men, disguised in Polish uniforms, seized the radio station at Gleiwitz in Upper Silesia, just inside Germany, broadcast threats of invasion in the Polish language, then disappeared. One dying man (actually an inmate of a German concentration camp) was left behind as "evidence" of Polish aggression. The incident, long planned, was Hitler's fig leaf of respectability before world opinion.

1939, September 1. Germany Invades Poland. World War II began (see p. 1050).

1940, September 27. Rome-Berlin-Tokyo Axis. A ten-year mutual assistance alliance.

AUSTRIA

1927. Private Political Armies. The Christian Socialists organized their private army, the Heimwehr, while the Social Democrats organized the Schutzbund.

1930, February 6. Friendship Treaty with Italy.

1933. Nazi Unrest. This was stimulated by the National Socialists' triumphs in Germany. Nazi agitators staged occasional demonstrations until the Nazi party was dissolved (June 19). Campaigns of agitation and terrorism continued.

1935, July 25. Assassination of Prime Minister Engelbert Dollfuss. Growing Austro-German enmity was culminated by a Nazi *Putsch* in Vienna, resulting in the murder of Dollfuss. German intervention was stymied by the mobilization of Italian and Yugoslavian forces on the border. Hitler disavowed connection with the murder and repudiated his Austrian followers.

1936, July 11. German-Austrian Agreement. Mussolini instigated this agreement to assure himself of German support.

1936, October 10. Prime Minister Kurt Schuschnigg Assumes Dictatorial Powers. He dissolved the Heimwehr and established a **Fatherland Front** militia. Renewal of Nazi activity led Schuschnigg to seek pledges of support from France and members of the Little Entente.

1938, March 11–12. German Invasion. Hitler took formal possession in Vienna, annexing Austria to Germany. A reign of terror followed.

THE SCANDINAVIAN AND BALTIC STATES

Denmark, Norway, and Sweden

With the rebirth of Germany as a powerful military state, Scandinavian efforts to achieve mutual co-operation and solidarity were intensified and collective security became a common goal.

Finland and the Baltic States

FINLAND

Finland followed primarily the same policies as the other Scandinavian States. Recognizing the altered situation in the Baltic region after Hitler's ascendancy, she attempted to maintain a balance between Germany and Russia.

THE BALTIC STATES

The successes of Nazi Germany prompted Lithuania, Latvia, and Estonia to improve their relations with Soviet Russia for the purpose of establishing a strong front against possible German intervention in the name of the German minorities. All 3 Baltic states soon adopted some form of dictatorship in order to offer stronger regimes for resistance to Germany.

SOVIET RUSSIA

1924–1926. Power Struggle. Conflicts among Communist party leadership followed the death of Lenin (January 21, 1924).

1926, July–October. Triumph of Stalin. Trotsky, Zinoviev, Radek, and others were expelled from the political bureau of the party. Trotsky was later banished (January, 1929).

1926, August 31. Treaty with Afghanistan. (See p. 1007).

1929, February 9. Litvinov Protocol. This was an analogue of the Kellogg-Briand Pact, signed by Russia, Poland, Rumania, Estonia, and Latvia at Moscow.

1929, December 22. Agreement with China.

This settled disputed claims to the Chinese Eastern Railway (see p. 1045).

1932, July 25. Nonaggression Pacts with Poland, Estonia, Latvia, and Finland. A similar agreement with France followed (November 29). Uneasiness about the deterioration of relations with Japan prompted Stalin's government to amend relations with its European neighbors. Entrance into the world's political arena was further signaled by Russia's active participation in the Disarmament Conference (see p. 1027) and general international cooperation.

1933, November 17. The United States Recognizes the U.S.S.R. Trade relations were opened.

1934, April 4. Extension of Nonaggression Pacts with Poland and the Baltic States. These became 10-year agreements.

1934, September 18. Russia Joins the League of Nations. She became an active exponent of collective security by supporting a French plan for an Eastern European pact.

1935, May 2. Franco-Russian Alliance. This was rightly regarded in Germany as a pact against Hitler's regime.

1935, May 16. Russian-Czechoslovakian Alliance. This further angered the Germans, who feared that the Russians would make Czechoslovakia an air base for operations against Germany.

1935, July 25–August 20. Meeting of the Third International. Russia decided to side with the democracies against the Fascist states. Communist opposition to military appropriations in other countries was to cease and the governments were to be supported.

1936, July. Soviet Support to Loyalist Spain. **(See p. 1031.)**

1938–1939. Undeclared War with Japan. **(See p. 1043.)**

1938, September. German-Czech Crisis. Russia proffered assistance to the Czechs in resisting German demands (see below). Britain and France favored appeasement rather than Communist support and reached a compromise solution at Munich. As a result, the Franco-Russian Alliance was all but abrogated and Russia was almost isolated in Europe.

1939, March–June. Britain Negotiates with Russia. The German annexation of Czechoslovakia and Memel caused this reversal in British policy. Russia was urged to join a common peace front against attack upon Poland and Rumania. The Russians negotiated for a complete offensive alliance as well as for guarantees for the Baltic States.

1939, May 3. Russian Policy Changes. Foreign Minister **Maxim Litvinov,** generally considered to be pro-West, was suddenly replaced by **Vyacheslav Molotov,** whose public criticisms of Britain and France implied that Russia was considering a change of policy. Negotiations with England and France continued, but Russia voiced her distrust of the western powers by rejecting draft after draft at the conference table (June–August).

1939, August 27. Nonaggression Pact with Germany. This confirmed western suspicions of an unbelievable diplomatic union between 2 incompatible enemies.

1939, September 1. German Attack on Poland. Soviet Russia was a benevolent neutral.

1939, September 17. Soviet Invasion of Poland. That country was partitioned with Germany as the result of a secret treaty clause. (See p. 1050.)

1939, November 30. Russia Attacks Finland. **(See p. 1054.)**

1939, December 14. Russia Expelled from League of Nations.

1940, June 15–16. Russian Occupation of Lithuania, Latvia, and Estonia.

1941, April 13. Nonaggression Treaty with Japan. Stalin's desire to assure peace in the East, in light of growing danger of German invasion, coincided with Japanese desires to obtain similar freedom to initiate adventures in Southeast Asia (see p. 1126).

CZECHOSLOVAKIA

1933, February. Reorganization of Little Entente. This was because of the potential danger of the new National Socialist Germany.

1933–1938. Subversion of Sudetenland. The 3 million Sudeten Germans in Czechoslovakia became a hotbed for Nazi agitation.

1935, May 16. Mutual Assistance Pact with Russia. This guaranteed Russian support against attack if it were preceded by French support (see above).

1936, September 10. Beginning of German Propaganda Campaign. Czechoslovakia was accused of basing Soviet planes for operations against Germany. The Czechs intensified their frontier defense program.

1938, March–September. Growing German-Czech Crisis. Recognizing the strategic danger created by the German annexation of Austria, Czechoslovakia undertook partial mobilization and a series of negotiations with the Sudeten German leaders.

1938, September 15. Hitler Demands Cession of Sudetenland. He threatened war otherwise. Chamberlain flew to Berchtesgaden in an attempt to mediate a peaceful settlement.

1938, September 24–29. Czechoslovakian Mobilization.

1938, September 29. Conference and Agreement at Munich. Hitler was accorded practically all his demands as Czechoslovakia was dismembered by Hitler, Ribbentrop, Mussolini, Ciano, Chamberlain, and Daladier. Czechoslovakia was deserted by the Little Entente and the larger powers. Only Russia (not represented at Munich) appeared ready to aid against German aggression. France and Britain, cognizant of their military inadequacies and unpreparedness (especially in air power), acquiesced in a move establishing German hegemony in Central Europe and subsequently the Danubian area.

1939, March 10–16. Hitler Annexes Remainder of Czechoslovakia. Britain and France were shocked by this breach of the Munich Agreement. Yet no resistance was offered; Hitler emerged undisputed victor of a bloodless battle.

HUNGARY

1927, April 5. Friendship Treaty with Italy.

1938, March. German Annexation of Austria. This brought the Reich to the frontier and increased the restlessness of the German minority in Hungary.

1938, September. German-Czech Crisis. Hungary supported the Germans, and was awarded 5,000 square miles of territory in southern Slovakia for her co-operation with Germany (November 2). Occasional conflict in the annexed region continued throughout the winter of 1938–1939.

1939, March 15. Annexation of Carpatho-Ukraine (Ruthenia). This result of co-operation with Germany in the destruction of Czechoslovakia gave Hungary a long-sought-after common frontier with Poland.

1939, April 11. Hungary Withdraws from the League of Nations.

POLAND

1926, May 12–14. Military Coup. Marshal **Jósef Pilsudski** established a dictatorship.

1929, February 9. Litvinov Protocol. (See p. 1036.)

1934, January 26. German-Polish Nonaggression Treaty. (See p. 1035.)

1938, October 2. Occupation of Teschen. Poland settled her old dispute with Czechoslovakia during the German-Czech crisis.

1939, March–April. German Demands for Polish Corridor. The German annexation of Memel (March 23) was accompanied by stiff demands on Poland for annexation of Danzig and the construction of an extraterritorial motor road through Pomorze in return for a German guarantee of Polish independence. These demands provoked the Anglo-French pledge of aid to Poland which later became a pact of mutual assistance (April 6).

1939, April 28. Hitler Denounces the German-Polish Agreement of 1934 and the Anglo-German Naval Agreement of 1935.

1939, June–August. A Period of Rising Tension. (See p. 1035.)

1939, September 1. German Invasion of Poland. (See p. 1050.)

RUMANIA

1926, March 26. Alliance with Poland.

1926, June 10. Treaty of Alliance and Nonaggression with France.

1926, September 16. Friendship Treaty with Italy.

1929, February 9. Litvinov Protocol. (See p. 1036.)

1933, July. Nonaggression Pact with Russia. This implied Russian recognition of the Rumanian possession of Bessarabia.

1934, February 8–9. Balkan Pact. This treaty, concluded between Rumania, Yugoslavia, Greece, and Turkey, bound the signatories to consult with each other if their security was threatened.

1934, June 9. Mutual Guarantees with Czechoslovakia and Russia. They agreed to guarantee each other's frontiers.

1939, April 13. Britain and France Guar-

antee Rumanian Independence. This followed the German annexation of Czechoslovakia. Soon afterward, Rumania straddled the fence and concluded a commercial agreement with Germany.

1939, September 4. Rumania Declares Its Neutrality.

BULGARIA

1925. Greek-Bulgarian Border Clashes. The League of Nations' mediation temporarily settled the crisis (October 21). Further incidents in 1931 (January, February) necessitated intervention by the powers.

1929, March 6. Friendship Treaty with Turkey.

1934, February 9. Bulgaria Rejects the Balkan Pact. She thus indicated that she did not endorse the *status quo* in the Balkans. (See p. 1038.)

1934, May 19. Military Coup d'État. The resulting military dictatorship was soon overthrown by King **Boris,** who established a royal dictatorship.

1937, January 24. Friendship Treaty with Yugoslavia.

1938, July 31. Rearmament Program. Bulgaria's right to rearm was recognized by the Balkan Entente through agreement with Greece. An Anglo-French loan of $10 million financed the program.

YUGOSLAVIA

1926, September 18. Friendship Treaty with Poland.

1927, May. Border Clashes with Albania.

1927, November 11. Treaty of Friendship with France.

1929, January 5. King Alexander Proclaims Dictatorship. This was the result of internal disorders, particularly Croatian nationalistic agitation.

1934, February 9. Balkan Pact (See p. 1036.)

1934, October 9. Murder of King Alexander. The murderer, a Macedonian revolutionary, was believed to be in Hungarian pay, and the slaying brought Yugoslavia and Hungary to the verge of war. The League of Nations arranged a settlement.

1937, January 24. Treaty of Friendship with Bulgaria.

1937, March 25. Nonaggression and Arbitration Pact with Italy. This indicated closer ties with the Axis powers.

GREECE

1925, December 4. Greek-Bulgarian Border Clashes. (**See above.**)

1928, September 23. Friendship Treaty with Italy.

1930, October 30. Treaty of Ankara. This pact with Turkey advocated naval parity in the eastern Mediterranean and the acceptance of territorial *status quo.*

1933, September 15. Ten-Year Nonaggression Pact with Turkey.

1934, February 9. Balkan Pact. (**See p. 1036.**)

1935. Military Coup. King **George II** was restored to the throne.

1939, April 13. British and French Pledge of Support against Aggression. This followed the Italian conquest of Albania.

ALBANIA

1925, January 21. Albania Proclaimed a Republic.

1926, November 20–26. Rebellion in the North. Despite Yugoslavian aid to the rebels, this was suppressed.

1926, November 27. Treaty of Tirana. Italy and Albania pledged themselves to the maintenance of territorial *status quo.*

1927, November 22. Second Treaty of Tirana. This put Albania under Italian protection by establishing a 20-year defense alliance and providing for military co-operation. Italy obtained important rights, especially in oil, road construction, military supervision, and education.

1928, September 1. President Ahmed Bey Zogu Proclaimed King.

1934. Growing Friction with Italy.

1937, May 15–19. Rebellion in the South. This was in protest against the dictatorial measures of King **Zog.** It was suppressed.

1939, April 7. Italian Invasion. Albania was soon occupied and annexed by Italy.

AFRICA

EGYPT AND THE SUDAN

1927. Draft Treaty with Great Britain Rejected. This proposed British military occupation for 10 years, but was rejected by the Egyptian Parliament as inconsistent with Egyptian independence.

1931, April 22. Friendship Treaty between Egypt and Iraq.

1936, August 26. Treaty between Egypt and Great Britain. This granted full independence to Egypt, while retaining the minimum requirements for the strategic security of the British Empire. A 20-year defensive alliance provided for the withdrawal of British troops, except for 10,000 men of land and air forces who would be assigned to the Suez Canal Zone. England was permitted to maintain a naval base at Alexandria for a maximum of 8 years, and Egyptian troops were to return to the Sudan.

1937, May 26. Egypt Admitted to the League of Nations.

ETHIOPIA

1928, August 2. Twenty-Year Friendship Treaty with Italy. This gave Ethiopia a free zone in the Italian-controlled port of Assab in return for the concession of constructing certain roads.

1929. Reorganization of the Ethiopian Army. This was to be done by a Belgian military commission.

1934, December 5. Clash at Ualual. Ethiopian and Italian forces clashed in a disputed zone on the Italian Somaliland border. Approximately 100 Ethiopians and 30 Italian colonial troops were killed in the incident. The Ethiopian government requested an investigation of the incident and the Italians demanded reparation.

1935, September 3. Arbitration by the League of Nations. The arbitral board was unable to establish the responsibility for the clash at Ualual.

Ethiopian-Italian War, 1935–1936

1935, October 3. Outbreak of Hostilities. The Italians invaded Ethiopia without a declaration of war. Well supported by artillery and air forces, they captured Aduwa (October 6).

1935, October 7. Italy Declared to Be an Aggressor. The League debated the imposition of sanctions.

1935, November 8. Italians Capture Fortress of Makalle.

1935, November 18. Sanctions Imposed on Italy. Fifty-one nations joined in embargoes on arms, credit, and raw materials and the restriction of imports. The failure of the League to apply oil sanctions, to deny the movement of Italian troops and matériel through the Suez Canal, or to prevent the German reoccupation of the Rhineland (see p. 1035) gave Mussolini a free hand in Ethiopia with a united Italy backing him.

1935, December–1936, April. Lull in Operations. Field Marshal **Pietro Badoglio** reorganized the expeditionary forces.

1936, April–May. Italy Renews Offensive. Italian air forces, which were unimpeded, systematically spread terror and destruction on a brave but completely outclassed enemy who fought in a medieval style against bombings and poison gas. Badoglio's ground forces advanced.

1936, May 5. Capture of Addis Ababa. Emperor **Haile Selassie I** fled; Ethiopian resistance collapsed.

1936, May 9. Italy Annexes Ethiopia. It was added to Eritrea and Italian Somaliland to make up Italian East Africa. The Italian King assumed the title of "Emperor of Ethiopia." Germany, Austria, and Hungary recognized the conquest at once, England and France a year later.

COMMENT. *The most important result of this war was to give both Mussolini and the Italian nation a much exaggerated opinion of their military prowess.*

NORTH AFRICA (MOROCCO, ALGERIA, TUNISIA, AND LIBYA)

The North African colonies suffered acutely from the economic depression of the 30's. The severity of the situation fostered the growth of unrest and nationalism.

WEST AFRICA

This was a period of consolidation of European colonial administrations.

LIBERIA

1942, March 31. Agreement with the U.S. Only native African state to retain independence during the colonial era, Liberia granted base rights to U.S. forces, both for air transit and for operations against German submarines.

SOUTH AFRICA AND SOUTHWEST AFRICA

In South Africa, the Union was established as a sovereign independent state by the Westminster Statute (1934).

MIDDLE EAST AND SOUTHWEST ASIA

TURKEY

1925, February–April. Insurrection in Kurdistan. Finally suppressed by **Mustafa Kemal.**

1925, December 17. Alliance with Russia. Close political and economic relations were established.

1928, May 30. Five-Year Nonaggression Pact with Italy.

1928, June 15. Treaty with Persia.

1929, March 6. Treaty with Bulgaria.

1929, December 17. Russian Alliance Renewed. But Mustafa Kemal continued firm repression of Communism.

1930, October 30. Treaty of Ankara. After an exchange of populations, Turkey and Greece agreed to territorial *status quo* and naval parity in the eastern Mediterranean.

1930, December 23. Dervish Revolt in Western Anatolia. This protest against Mustafa Kemal's westernization was soon suppressed.

1931, March 6. Russian-Turkish Naval Agreement. This prohibited any changes in the respective Black Sea fleets without 6 months' notice.

1931, October 30. Five-Year Extension of the Turco-Russian Alliance.

1931, May 25. Five-Year Pact with Italy.

1931, July 18. Turkey Joins the League of Nations.

1932, January 23. Agreement with Persia. Outstanding border disputes were settled.

1933, September 15. Ten-Year Turco-Greek Nonaggression Pact.

1934, February 9. Balkan Treaty. A mutual security agreement of Balkan frontiers between Greece, Rumania, and Turkey.

1934, May. Turkish Rearmament. Turkey distrusted Italy's east Mediterranean policy.

1936, July 20. Treaty of Montreux. An international conference approved Turkey's request to refortify the straits.

1937, July 9. Southwest Asian Treaty. A nonaggression pact (**Saadabad** Pact) with Iran, Iraq, and Afghanistan in an Asiatic analogue of the Balkan Pact.

1937, December–1938, July. Alexandretta Crisis. Turk claims to Alexandretta brought tension and threat of war. The crisis ended in agreement to hold elections, which gave Turkey virtual control.

1938, November 10. Death of Kemal Atatürk.

1939, May 12. British-Turkish Mutual Assistance Agreement. This identified Turkey with the British bloc.

1939, June 23. Agreement with France. This resulted in the incorporation of Hatay (Alexandretta) into Turkey.

THE ARAB STATES

Arabia

1925–1930, May 20. Ibn Saud Consolidates Power. He now controlled most of Arabia.

1930, February 22. Peace in Northern Arabia. King Ibn Saud of Hejaz and Nejed made peace with King Faisal of Iraq (former Emir of Hejaz; see pp. 987, 1006) on board H.M.S. *Lupin* in the Persian Gulf, ending part of the Saud-Hashemite dynastic feud.

1932, May–July. Unrest in Northwest Arabia. This came from opposition to the pro-western policies of Ibn Saud.

1932, September 22. Adoption of the Name Saudi Arabia.

1933, July 27. Treaty with Transjordan. This terminated years of dynastic animosity between the Saud and Hashemite families.

1934, February 14. Treaty of Sanaa. A 40-year treaty was signed with Great Britain.

1936, April 2. Nonaggression Treaty with Iraq. This became the basis of efforts to achieve Arab brotherhood and unity.

1936, May 7. Treaty with Egypt. This advanced Pan-Arabism and brought closer political co-operation.

Syria and Lebanon

1925, July 18. Beginning of Druse Rebellion. Under **Sultan el-Atrash** the Druses threatened French control.

1925, October. Bloodshed at Damascus. The French withdrew from the city (October 14). A 2-day bombardment (October 18–19) of the city, with air and tank attacks, took several hundred civilian lives.

1926, July 18. Druse Rebellion Again Sweeps Damascus. French forces, in fortified encampments outside the city, again unleashed a 48-hour period of artillery and aerial bombing, inflicting great damage and loss of life.

1927, June. Collapse of Druse Rebellion. Despite an amazing display of bravery, which included charges of horsemen against French tanks, the rebellious tribesmen were finally subdued, and Druse leaders fled to Transjordan.

1927, May 23. French Declare Lebanon a Republic.

1936, September 9. Franco-Syrian Treaty of Friendship and Alliance. This and a Franco-Lebanon treaty (November 13, 1936) brought comparative peace to the area. Syria and Lebanon were to be independent states after a 3-year period; France was to retain a privileged position for 25 years.

1937, September 8. Pan-Arab Conference in Syria. This was held to organize the defense of Arab interest in Palestine. Syria became a center of Palestine rebel activity.

Palestine and Transjordan

Jewish-Arab enmity kept the area in a turmoil with continuous fighting during this period. In Palestine, Great Britain was trying without much success to satisfy the opposite aspirations of Arabs and Zionists by an implementation of the Balfour Declaration (November 2, 1917) and the establishment of separate Jewish and Arab states.

1923, May 26. Autonomy for Transjordan. This Hashemite kingdom was relatively stable during the years preceding World War II because of the wisdom of King **Abdullah,** and because it was exempted from the clauses in the British mandate dealing with the establishment in Palestine of a national home for the Jewish people.

1936–1939. Arab Revolt. This resulted from opposition to a partition of Palestine. The Arabs controlled the country in most parts outside the large cities and the Jewish settlements. The revolt was suppressed by the British only after the loss of several thousand lives.

Iraq

1930, November 16. Independence of Iraq. Great Britain agreed to support her admission to the League of Nations in 1932. Britain was to obtain a lease on new air bases, the use of Iraqi transportation and communication facilities, and British officers were to train the Iraqi Army.

1930, September 11–1931, April. Kurd Rebellion. Sheikh **Mahmud** led the uprising, which was eventually suppressed with British assistance.

1932, April–June. Renewed Kurd Rising. This was suppressed by the Iraqi forces backed by the British air patrol.

1932, October 3. Iraq Admitted to the League of Nations.

1936, April. Nonaggression Treaty with Saudi Arabia.

1936, October 29. Military Revolt. General **Bakir Sidqi** established a military dictatorship. His assassination (1937) ended the direct intervention of the army in politics.

1937, July 8–9. Treaty of Saadabad. **(See p. 1041.)** Pact with Iran, Turkey, and Afghanistan.

IRAN (PERSIA)

1926, April 22. Treaty with Turkey and Afghanistan.

1930, June–July. Kurd Uprising. This stimulated Persian-Turkish efforts to establish an agreed boundary.

1932, January 23. Treaty with Turkey. The border was revised around Mt. Ararat and relations between Turkey and Persia improved.

1937, July 8–9. Treaty of Saadabad. **(See p. 1041.)** Pact with Iraq, Turkey, and Afghanistan.

SOUTH ASIA

AFGHANISTAN

1928, November. Tribal Insurrection. This forced the abdication of the king.

1929, January–October. Civil War. A bandit leader, **Habibullah Ghazi,** captured Kabul (January), but was defeated and executed by General **Mohammed Nadir Khan,** who took the name **Nadir Shah.** Aided by the British, he reformed his army and restored stability.

1933, November 8. Assassination of Nadir Shah. He was succeeded by his son **Mohammed Zahir Shah.**

1934. Afghanistan Joins the League of Nations.

1937, July 8–9. Treaty of Saadabad. (**See p. 1041.**) Pact with Iran, Iraq, and Turkey.

INDIA

The years 1923–1932 witnessed political assassinations and renewed internationalist terrorist activity. In 1930, Gandhi began a second Civil Disobedience Campaign. This precipitated rioting, violence, and numerous arrests which eventually led to the Government of India Act of 1935: Burma and Aden were separated from India and became crown colonies; Indian local government was reorganized.

EAST ASIA

JAPAN

1925, January 20. Treaty with Russia. Diplomatic relations were established with the U.S.S.R. Japan evacuated North Sakhalin.

1927–1929. Japanese Interventions in Shantung. (**See pp. 1044, 1045.**)

1930, April 22. London Naval Treaty. (**See p. 1027.**) This was finally ratified by Japan, despite strong political and naval opposition (October).

1931, September 19. Mukden Incident. (**See p. 1046.**) Beginning of Japanese conquest of Manchuria.

1932, January–March. First Battle of Shanghai. (**See p. 1046.**)

1932, February 18. Nominal Independence of Manchukuo. This made Manchuria a virtual colony of Japan.

1933, May 27. Japan Withdraws from the League of Nations. (**See p. 1028.**)

1933, May 31. Japanese Invasion of Jehol. (**See p. 1046.**)

1936, February 26. Mutiny. A group of young army officers, impatient at apparent hesitation of politicians to press ahead with the conquest of China, attempted to set up a military dictatorship. Finance Minister **Makoto Saito** and several other high officials were assassinated. The rebellion was promptly suppressed.

1936, November 25. Anti-Comintern Pact with Germany. (**See p. 1034.**)

1937, July 7. Outbreak of War in China. (**See p. 1123.**)

1938, July 11–August 10. Undeclared Hostilities with Russia. Severe fighting broke out because of a dispute over the poorly defined frontier where Manchuria, Korea, and Siberia meet. **Changkufeng Hill,** near the mouth of the Tumen River, had been occupied and fortified by Soviet troops. Japanese efforts to dislodge the Russians failed; a truce ended the episode, with the Russians retaining the hill.

1939, May–September. Nomonhan (Khalkin Gol) Incident. Renewed Japanese–Soviet hostilities resulted from a frontier dispute near the Khalkin Gol (River) claimed by the Japanese as the boundary between Manchuria and easternmost Outer Mongolia. After Soviet troops occupied the disputed territory between the river and Nomonhan, 20 kilometers to the east, the Japanese attacked with a reinforced division and were initially successful. In mid-August a Soviet counteroffensive by 3 divisions, 5 armored brigades, and some Mongolian units—commanded by **General Georgi K. Zhukov**—drove the outnumbered Japanese (28,000 to 65,000) back to Nomonhan. Japanese Kwantung Army commander, General **Kenkichi Ueda** concentrated 3 fresh divisions for a counteroffensive but a ceasefire agreement forced cancellation (September 15). The Soviets admitted 9,824 casualties, but their losses were probably comparable to the Japanese admitted 17,405 casualties. This dispute and the Changkufeng dispute (see above) were settled by treaty (June, 1940).

1939, August 23. Japan Renounces the Anti-Comintern Pact with Germany. This result of outraged reaction to the Nazi-Soviet Treaty (see p. 1035) undoubtedly contributed to the Japanese decision to end hostilities with Russia in Outer Mongolia.

1941, April 13. Treaty with Russia. (See p. 1037.)

CHINA

1925. "May Thirtieth Incident." The British used gunfire to break up student demonstrations in Shanghai (May 30) and Canton (June 23). As a result, a strike and boycott of British goods were in effect for over a year. A wave of antiforeignism swept the country.

1926, July. Nationalists Begin Northern Offensive. The Canton-based National Government sent its army, under General **Chiang Kai-shek,** with the military advice of Russian General **Vasily K. Blücher** (known as **B. K. Galin** to the Chinese), to the north to unify the country. Chiang advanced into the territory of warlord **Wu Pei-fu. Hankow** was captured (Septemer 6); **Wuch'ang** was besieged (later captured, October 10). The National Government moved from Canton to Hankow. Chiang turned east into territory of warlord **Sun Ch'uan-fang,** in the lower Yangtze Valley. **Nanking** was captured by the Nationalists (March 24), amidst Communist-fomented riots. Six foreigners were killed; the Chinese portion of Shanghai was seized by local Communists and trade unionists in the name of the National Government. (The International Settlement was protected by an international force of 40,000, mostly Japanese.)

1927, April 12. Chiang's Seizure of Shanghai. Suspicious of subversive collusion between Communist leaders in Shanghai and the radical elements (Communists and Kuomintang leftists) in the National Government at Hankow, Chiang seized the Chinese portion of Shanghai. All known Communists and trade union leaders (about 5,000) were killed.

1927, April 18. Split in Kuomintang. Denounced for the Shanghai incident by the leftist and Communist-influenced Hankow government, Chiang established a separate National Government at Nanking.

1927, April–May. Nationalist Campaigns against Northern Warlords. Independent campaigns north of Yangtze were fought by Hankow and Nanking regimes, against the northern warlords, now joined by Marshal **Chang Tso-lin,** warlord of Manchuria and northeast China. Hankow troops fought inconclusively against Wu Pei-fu and **Chang Hsueh-liang** (son of Chang Tso-lin) in northern Hupeh and southern Honan. Chiang advanced steadily through Anhwei toward Hsuchow against Sun Ch'uan-fang.

1927, June. Intervention of Feng Yu-hsiang. The so-called "Christian General" advanced southeastward from Shensi through the T'ungkuan Pass. Wu and Chang hastily retreated to northern Honan.

1927, June 21. Alliance of Feng with Chiang. Feng, visiting Chiang at recently captured Hsuchow, agreed to support Chiang's Nationalist regime. Temporary Japanese occupation of Shantung (May–June) blocked Chiang's northward advance.

1927, July. Hankow Nationalist Break with Russia and Communists. Aware of Communist plans to seize control, Kuomintang leaders of the Hankow regime purged Chinese Communists from the government and expelled Russian political and military advisers.

1927, August 1. Nanchang Insurrection. Following the purge at Hankow, Communist elements of Hankow forces mutinied at Nanchang, hoping to spark a nationwide Communist revolution. Leaders were Generals **Yeh T'ing, Ho Lung,** and **Chu Teh.** They were driven out by loyal troops, and pursued by cooperating Hankow and Nanking Nationalist troops to southeast China coast, where the rebels dispersed. Chu Teh escaped to mountains of western Kiangsi with one small organized remnant. This was the real beginning of the 22-year Chinese Civil War.

1927, August–September. "Autumn Harvest Uprising." Attempts of Communist leader **Mao Tse-tung** to organize a peasant revolt in Hunan failed. He fled to the mountains of western Kiangsi, where he was later joined by Chu Teh.

1927, August 8. Chiang Resigns. Despite pleas of his adherents, Chiang refused to seek accommodation with Kuomintang radicals at Hankow. To permit party peace, and a unified front against resurgent northern warlords, he resigned and went to Japan. Soon afterward the Hankow regime moved to Nanking to join the regime there.

1927, September–October. Northern Counteroffensive. Taking advantage of the confusion in the south caused by Communist uprisings and the Kuomintang split, the northern warlords began a southward drive into Yangtze Valley. Sun Ch'uan-fang with 70,000 troops crossed the Yangtze west of Nanking, but was defeated by Nationalist General **Li Tsung-jen,** aided by Nationalist river gunboats, in the 5-day **Battle of Lungtan.** Sun, after losing 20,000 killed and 30,000 prisoners, retreated to Hsuchow. The warlords' offensive was called off.

1927, December 11–15. Canton Commune. A Communist uprising in Canton was ruthlessly suppressed by Nationalist troops.

1928, January 6. Chiang Returns. Reappointed Commander in Chief of the Nationalist Army, and Chairman of the Kuomintang Central Executive Committee, Chiang quickly restored stability, and prepared to renew the northern offensive to unify the nation.

1928, April 7–June 4. Nationalist Northward Drive. Under field commanders Li Tsung-jen, Feng Yu-hsiang, **Pai Ch'eng-hsi,** and **Ho Ying-ch'in,** and the newly allied warlord of Shansi, **Yen Hsi-shan,** the Nationalist armies, some 700,000 strong, defeated the three opposing northern warlords, who had about 500,000 troops, and advanced across the Yellow River. Despite Japanese interference (see below) the Nationalists continued on to capture **Peking** (June 4). The name of the city (which had meant "Northern Capital") was changed to Peiping (meaning "Northern Peace"). Retreating to Manchuria, Chang Tso-lin was assassinated when the Japanese blew up his private train near Mukden (June 4). His son, "Young Marshal" Chang Hsueh-liang, became warlord of Manchuria, and acknowledged Nationalist authority.

1928, May 3–11. Sino-Japanese Clash at Tsinan. The Japanese, again claiming special interests in Shantung, drove out the Nationalists and seized most of the province. Most Japanese troops were withdrawn a year later (May 20, 1929), after an agreement with the Chinese.

1928–1930. Consolidation. Chiang attempted to strengthen China for expected war with Japan. Simultaneously the Communists were recovering strength in the mountain regions of Kiangsi and Fukien.

1929–1930, October–January. Dispute with Russia. As a result of conflicting claims to ownership and control of the Chinese Eastern Railway, Soviet troops invaded Manchuria, forcing China (and in particular the war-lord governor, Chang Hsueh-liang) to acknowledge that the U.S.S.R. retained Imperial Russia's share in control of the line. Russian troops withdrew.

1930, July–August. Li Li-san's Communist Revolt. Communist Party Chairman Li Li-san, believing that the time was ripe for a revolt of the Chinese urban proletariat, ordered the Communist guerrilla forces in Kiangsi and Fukien to seize the principal cities of central China. Mao Tse-tung, believing that Communist success depended upon a peasant uprising rather than an urban revolt, protested, but was overruled. Troops under Communist General **P'eng Teh-huai** briefly seized **Ch'angsha** (July 28), then withdrew. Li ordered a renewed and reinforced offensive against Ch'angsha, but forces under P'eng, Mao Tse-tung, Chu Teh, and Ho Lung were bloodily repulsed by reinforced Nationalist defenders. The Communists retreated to their mountain strongholds. Li was soon recalled to Moscow. Mao's influence increased.

1930–1934. Nationalist Anti-Communist "Extermination Campaigns." (Also called "bandit suppression" campaigns.) The first two efforts (December, 1930–January, 1931; and April–May, 1931) were repulsed by aggressive Communist guerrilla tactics. Chiang personally led the third (July–September, 1931), and Nationalists were converging on the Communist capital of Juichin when word of the Mukden Incident (see p. 1046) caused Chiang to halt the offensive. After agreement was reached with Japan, a peripheral offensive against Oyuwan Soviet (Anhwei-Honan-Hupeh border area) was successful (summer, 1932). The fourth main campaign (April–June, 1933), was also disrupted by need to respond to renewed Japanese activity in the north, and by skillful Communist exploitation of this distraction. The fifth campaign (December, 1933–September, 1934) began after careful preparation, assisted by advice from a German military mission, led by General **Hans von**

Seeckt, recently retired Chief of the German General Staff. This well-coordinated, converging offensive, using entrenchments and a chain of blockhouses, was successful. Communist losses were heavy. The Communist Central Committee approved Mao Tse-tung's recommendation to evacuate the area.

1931, September 19. The Mukden Incident. Alleging that the Chinese had plotted to blow up the railroad from Port Arthur to Mukden, Japan's Kwantung Army in "night maneuvers" seized the arsenal at Mukden and adjacent towns. Chinese troops were forced to withdraw. The Japanese continued their aggressive movements and in a few months all Manchuria was under their domination (February, 1932). The only effective weapon the Chinese had was the boycott, which they invoked at great cost to Japanese trade.

1932, January 28–March 4. First Battle of Shanghai. In a move to stop the Chinese boycott, a Japanese army, 70,000 strong, landed at Shanghai. In a surprisingly effective and valiant resistance, the Chinese 19th Route Army held up the Japanese near the waterfront for about a month, but were finally driven out of their positions in the vicinity of the International Settlement. China agreed to end the boycott.

1932, February 18. Manchukuo (Manchuria) Declared Independent. The Japanese placed **Pu Yi** (former Emperor of China) on the throne of a puppet state, and announced a protectorate over it.

1933–1937. Growing Tension between China and Japan. Chiang Kai-shek attempted to unify and modernize his backward nation (while simultaneously fighting Communist and dissident warlords) in the face of increasingly aggressive Japanese actions.

1933, January–March. Japanese Invasion of Jehol. The pretext was that this Inner Mongolian province was really part of Manchuria. When Peiping (Peking) was threatened, the Chinese signed an armistice at Tangku (May 31) which required their evacuation of the Tientsin area and establishment of a demilitarized zone in eastern Hopei.

1934–1935. The Long March. The Communists, finally driven from their position by Chiang's Nationalist forces, organized a long retreat (October, 1934), marching and fighting (against sporadic opposition) across southern and western China to northern Shensi. The longest distance, 6,000 miles, was covered by Chu Teh's First Front Army—accompanied by Mao Tse-tung as political commissar—in 13 months. This was the longest and fastest sustained march ever made under combat conditions by any army of foot troops, and has been exceeded in rate of march over a long distance only by a few Mongol expeditions of the 13th century. The Second Front Army, commanded by Ho Lung, and the Fourth Front Army, commanded by **Hsu Hsiang-ch'ien,** marched somewhat shorter distances. Total Communist strength at the beginning of the march was about 200,000 troops. They suffered over 100,000 casualties and noncombat losses during the march. About 40,000 men were left behind along the route of march as underground cadres. About 50,000 recruits joined on the march. The total Communist force in Shensi at the end of 1935 was nearly 100,000 men.

1934–1937. Japanese Expansion in Northern China. Japanese troops continued to press westward in the Inner Mongolian province of Chahar into northern Hopei.

1934–1939. Japanese-Soviet Frontier Clashes. **(See p. 1043.)**

1936, Summer. Renewed "Bandit Suppression Campaign." Following a Communist foray into Shansi, Chiang Kai-shek decided to renew efforts to eliminate the Communists. An army of 150,000 was assembled, under Marshal Chang Hsueh-liang, with headquarters at Sian.

1936, December 12–25. Sian Mutiny. Disappointed by inactivity of Chang's "bandit suppression" effort, Chiang flew to Sian (December 7). Chang urged Chiang to call off the campaign; he and his troops wanted to fight the Japanese rather than other Chinese. When Chiang refused, he was taken into "protective custody." The results of the subsequent negotiations, in which Communist **Chou En-lai** participated, have never been revealed. Chiang was released, taking Chang with him as a prisoner. He then called off the anti-Communist campaign.

1937, July 7. Outbreak of Hostilities between China and Japan. **(See p. 1123.)**

MONGOLIA

The Mongolian People's Republic continued to be a satellite of the U.S.S.R., although the Republic of China still stubbornly refused to recognize Mongolian independence from China. The principal events were:

1936, March 12. Soviet-Mongolian Mutual Assistance Pact. This 10-year treaty was a response to the growing Japanese threat in Manchuria and Inner Mongolia. With Soviet assistance, the Mongolian army was maintained at 90,000 men, 10% of the population.

1939, May–September. Border Hostilities with Japan. (**See p. 1043.**) Mongolian forces made up a major portion of the Soviet-Mongolian army which repulsed the Japanese.

1941–1945. Mongolian Neutrality in World War II. Actually Mongolia gave full support to the Soviet Union.

1945, August 10. Declaration of War against Japan. Mongolian troops participated in the successful Soviet invasion of Manchuria and Inner Mongolia (see p. 1188).

1946, January 5. China Recognizes Mongolian Independence. China had promised to do this at the time of signing its treaty of friendship with the U.S.S.R. at the end of World War II (see p. 1305), but had insisted on a plebiscite first. The Mongols had voted virtually unanimously for independence (October 20, 1945).

THE AMERICAS

THE UNITED STATES

1925–1939. Military Retrenchment. The post-World War I reaction against American involvement overseas continued. In a period of pacifism and isolationism, the military services were largely ignored. Dwindling appropriations declined still more rapidly during the period of the Great Depression (1929–1938). Even the Navy, traditional "First Line of Defense," was neglected. In February, 1929, a bill was passed authorizing the construction of 15 cruisers and 1 aircraft carrier in 3 years at a cost of $27 million. By March, 1933, only 8 of the cruisers were completed. Although President **Franklin D. Roosevelt** obtained additional appropriations, construction still lagged far behind America's treaty rights. Once World War II broke in Europe, the U.S. Navy initiated a large-scale building program of warships, merchant ships, landing craft, and planes (1939–1941).

1925, December. Mitchell Trial. An avid crusader for the development of military aviation, Brigadier General **William Mitchell,** chief of the U.S. Army's Air Corps, provoked worldwide repercussions by challenging the traditional American military and naval hierarchy, and by his advocacy of the theories of Douhet (see p. 995). His outspoken criticism of his superiors resulted in his demotion to colonel (April, 1925). Later, Mitchell charged the War and Navy Departments with "incompetency, criminal negligence and almost treasonable administration of the national defense" (September). He was court-martialed by order of President Coolidge, found guilty, and ordered suspended from rank and duty for 5 years. He resigned from the Army (January, 1926) and continued a writing and lecturing campaign in his effort to obtain public support for his concepts of air power.

1929, January 15. Pact of Paris Ratified. (**See p. 1027.**) The Senate did not consider the Kellogg-Briand Treaty to impair the right of self-defense.

1930, January 21–April 22. London Naval Conference. (**See p. 1027.**)

1933, November 17. U.S. Diplomatic Recognition of Russia.

1934–1936. Nye Committee Munitions Investigation. This gave the American public the impression that the entry of the U.S. into World War I had been to save the bankers and to protect the arms trade. These hearings had an appreciable adverse effect on national defense and helped to incite resurgent isolationism.

1935, April. Neutrality Act. This forbade Americans to furnish munitions or loans to foreign belligerents and refused protection to Americans sailing on belligerent ships. Japanese aggression in China, Italian aggression in Ethiopia, and the Spanish Civil War brought the program of neutrality into sharp focus, resulting in a compromise: the War Policy Act (May 1, 1937). The act retained the mandatory provisions of the Neutrality Act, but gave the President wide discretion, especially in determining if the law was to be put into effect by proclamation that a war actually existed.

1939, January 12. End of Military Retrenchment. President Roosevelt asked Congress for $552 million for defense spending.

1939, September 5. U.S. Neutrality Declared. This followed Roosevelt's fireside chat (September 3), stating, "This nation will remain a neutral nation, but I cannot ask that every American remain neutral in thought as well." He proclaimed a limited national emergency (September 8).

1939, November 4. Arms Embargo Lifted. Congress, removing the arms embargo at Roosevelt's urging, authorized "cash and carry" exports of munitions and arms to belligerent nations. The intent was to assist the Allies.

1940. Defense Measures. Roosevelt called for appropriations (January 3 and May 31) totaling approximately $3.4 billion for national defense, and in response to Churchill's call for help released to Britain more than $43 million worth of surplus stocks of arms, planes, and munitions (June 3). A National Defense Research Committee was established, headed by Dr. **Vannevar Bush** (June 15). **Henry L. Stimson** was named Secretary of War and **Frank Knox** Secretary of the Navy (June 20). Congress adopted defense tax measures and raised the national debt limit to $49 billion (June 22). In defense matters Roosevelt particularly relied upon the advice of U.S. Army Chief of Staff, General **George C. Marshall.**

1940, September. The U.S.-British Destroyer Base Agreement. Great Britain received 50 badly needed destroyers (see p. 1066) in return for leases for American naval bases at 8 points on British territory along the Atlantic coast from Newfoundland to British Guiana.

1940, September 16. Initiation of Conscription. The Selective Service Act was passed by Congress.

1940, December 20–29. Roosevelt Speeds Defense. The Office of Production Management was established to extend all aid short of war to Great Britain and all other anti-Nazi belligerents.

1941, March 11. Lend Lease. The act opened mutual aid between all anti-Nazi nations and the U.S.

1941, July 7. Defense of Iceland. American forces landed in Iceland at the invitation of the Danish and Icelandic governments, relieving British troops defending the island.

1941, September. Renewal of Selective Service. The act, violently opposed by isolationists, passed the House of Representatives by one vote.

1941, December 7. Attack on Pearl Harbor. (**See p. 1127.**)

MEXICO

1927, October. Insurrection. A rebellion spread through the provinces, but was crushed within 2 months.

1929, March–April. Renewed Rebellion. Insurrection broke out again in 1929 because of widespread political and religious discontent.

1934. Beginning of Stability. President **Lázaro Cárdenas,** supported by the army, established himself as the undisputed ruler of Mexico and undertook an ambitious program of reforms.

CENTRAL AMERICA (PANAMA, COSTA RICA, NICARAGUA, HONDURAS, SALVADOR, GUATEMALA)

Internal political conditions were unstable and numerous insurrections and depositions occurred. In Nicaragua (1925) a bloody civil war erupted; U.S. intervention resulted in a supervised election and a relatively calm administration until the renewal of rebel activities by General **César Augusto Sandino** (1931). U.S. Marines organized and trained the Guardia Nacional under General **Anastasio Somoza.** After the Marines withdrew (January 2, 1933), Somoza became president (1937) and was virtual dictator until his death (1956).

WEST INDIES (CUBA, HAITI, DOMINICAN REPUBLIC, PUERTO RICO, VIRGIN ISLANDS)

1934, May 29. The Platt Amendment Abrogated. The U.S. lifted limits on Cuba's sovereignty.

1934, August 6. Withdrawal of U.S. Marines from Haiti. The culmination of arrangements between the United States and the Haitian Assembly (see p. 1013).

1937, October. Border Dispute between Haiti and the Dominican Republic. This resulted in the death of many immigrant Haitians. An American-inspired conciliation treaty led to settlement.

1939. Expansion of Military Facilities in Puerto Rico. The island became the keystone of a U.S. Caribbean defense system.

SOUTH AMERICA (ARGENTINA, CHILE, PARAGUAY, URUGUAY, BOLIVIA, PERU, ECUADOR, COLOMBIA, VENEZUELA, BRAZIL)

The Latin American scene was punctuated with jealousy and war between neighbors, widespread internal turbulence, and 2 major international clashes.

1921–1929. Tacna-Arica Dispute. A legacy of the War of the Pacific (see p. 912), Chile's dispute with Peru over this rich nitrate region resulted in several armed clashes. Bolivia, meanwhile, maintained that neither Chile nor Peru was entitled to the provinces. Through United States arbitration, the dispute was solved by compromise: Arica was awarded to Chile; Peru received Tacna. Bolivia's complaints were assuaged somewhat by allocation to her of a railway outlet to the Pacific between La Paz and Arica (1929).

1932, June–August. Disorders in Brazil. The federal government re-established order in São Paulo State.

1932–1935. Chaco War. Armed clashes between Paraguay and Bolivia over the possession of the Chaco region began in 1928 and gradually developed into open war (1932). Efforts of other states and the League to mediate were unsuccessful and the struggle continued despite the economic strain on both sides. The Paraguayans soon gained *de facto* control over much of the region. Bolivia employed a German general, **Hans von Kundt,** to train and command its armies and to establish military posts in territory claimed by Paraguay. When Bolivia captured **Fort Lopez** (Pitiantuta) in central Chaco (June 15, 1932), she seemed to have accomplished her objective of gaining the Paraguay River as an outlet to the ocean. At this point the Paraguayans initiated a remarkable national military effort. While frontier troops recaptured **Pitiantuta** (mid-July), the Paraguayan Army began an expansion from 3,000 to 60,000 men. A supply line was established via Puerto Casado in preparation for a major offensive. This was initiated by Colonel **José Felix Estigarribia,** and the Paraguayans steadily forged their way through the jungle region. In the next year and a half they conquered most of the disputed region, captured the Bolivian headquarters, and took more than 30,000 prisoners. A truce was then signed and active hostilities ceased (June 12, 1935). By the **Treaty of Buenos Aires** (July 21, 1938) an arbitral decision awarded Paraguay three-quarters of the disputed area; Bolivia, however, was provided an outlet to the Atlantic Ocean via the Paraguay River.

1936, December 1–23. Buenos Aires Conference. Meeting of the Pan-American Conference for the maintenance of peace accepted the principle of consultation in case the peace of the continent was threatened. A common policy of neutrality was drawn up in case of conflict between the American states.

1938, December 24. Declaration of Lima. This reaffirmed the absolute sovereignty of the various American states and expressed their determination to oppose "all foreign intervention or activity." This was manifest of a determination to defend Latin-American territory from both external aggression and internal subversion.

WORLD WAR II IN THE WEST

OPERATIONS IN 1939

Polish Campaign, September 1–October 5, 1939

1939, September 1–5. Invasion. Covered by predawn air bombardment, without declaration of war, General **Walther von Brauchitsch**'s 1,250,000 men in 60 divisions—9 of them armored—struck from north, west, and south. The German plan was a double double envelopment, gripping the 6 Polish armies, spread in cordon defense, between pincers closing down first on the Vistula River line, and later on the Bug, farther east. General **Fedor von Bock**'s army group—the Third and Fourth armies—converged from both sides of the Polish Corridor; General **Gerd von Rundstedt**'s group of 3 armies swept eastward and northeastward across Upper Silesia and Galicia. Some 1,600 Luftwaffe planes undertook terror bombings of all principal cities, destruction of air fields and railway centers, systematic sweeping of main highways to dislocate traffic, and close support to the ground troops. With 2 million German sympathizers in the Polish population, fifth-column and intelligence activities were well organized. Flat Poland, with no major terrain obstacles, in the pleasant, dry autumn weather offered ideal terrain for the use of tanks. German armored spearheads slashed through the thin screen of 6 Polish armies, some 800,000 men, commanded by Marshal **Edward Smigly-Rydz,** like knives through butter.

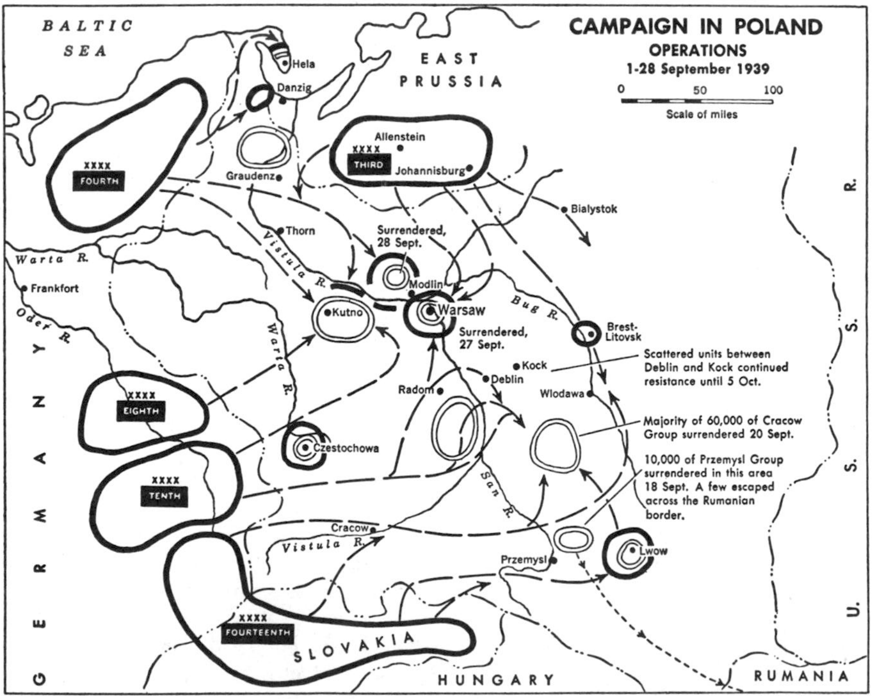

By the third day the Polish air force ceased to exist. All communication between general headquarters and the field armies was ended, further mobilization rendered impossible. Informed by spies, the Luftwaffe learned the location of Polish headquarters and bombed it continuously, even though the Poles moved frequently. In the Gulf of Danzig, a German naval force disposed of the little Polish Navy—4 destroyers, a mine sweeper, and some submarines. Poland was paralyzed, its civilian population terrified.

1939, September 5–17. Battles of Warsaw and Kutno-Lódź. On the north, Bock's left-flank army pressed down on Brest-Litovsk; on the south, Rundstedt's right-flank army streamed northeasterly past Cracow. In the center, Rundstedt's Tenth Army (General **Walther von Reichenau**), with the majority of the armored divisions, approached the Vistula below Warsaw. The interior ring of the double double envelopment was closing on the Vistula River line, the outer ring on the Bug. The Polish armies, fighting with futile gallantry (in some cases horse cavalry charged German tanks), were rolled up in several clusters, each completely surrounded and without any over-all direction. Reichenau's Tenth Army tanks attempted to enter Warsaw (September 8), but local Polish counterattacks drove them off. Principal Polish resistance now centered around Warsaw-Modlin and farther west around Kutno and Lódź. The Polish Kutno-Lódź forces made a gallant but unsuccessful attempt to break out, then, after incessant air and ground attacks—their supplies and ammunition exhausted—surrendered (September 17). Meanwhile the outer encirclement ring had closed, as German Third and Fourteenth armies met, south of Brest-Litovsk.

1939, September 17. Soviet Invasion of Poland. In conformity with the Nazi-Soviet Pact (see p. 1035), Soviet troops swept over Poland's eastern border, north and south of the Pripet Marsh area, ending any Polish hopes of a last-ditch stand in the southeast. The government and the high command took refuge in Rumania.

1939, September 17–October 5. Collapse of Poland. One by one the islands of resistance succumbed. Warsaw, facing starvation and typhoid, fell (September 27); Modlin, just across the Vistula, next day. Up on the Baltic, the naval base of Hel capitulated (October 1). The last organized Polish resistance ended at Kock, where 17,000 Poles surrendered (October 5). Polish losses were about 66,000 killed and at least 200,000 wounded. The greater part of their armed forces was captured—some 694,000 men. A few escaped through Rumania. German losses were 10,570 killed, 30,322 wounded, and 3,400 missing. Germany and Russia divided the country between them, while the German armies slowly recoiled to prepare for a later move against Western Europe.

COMMENT. *The whirlwind campaign was a spectacular demonstration of fire and movement, utilizing the latest developments in weapons, aerial and ground. German adherence to the principles of the offensive, surprise, mass, and maneuver was irresistible. Weak spots or gaps in the Polish defensive ring were exploited by speedy armored columns with unlimited objectives and disregard for flank protection. Fast-moving infantry formations encircled Polish units isolated by the breakthroughs; the demoralized Poles never had time to recover. The pattern of blitzkrieg was set. Contributing factors to German success were the Polish tactical dispositions in cordon defense, and the inertia of France and Britain in the west, permitting undivided German attention to the eastern campaign. Thoroughly documented by scores of cameramen, the film story of the Polish debacle was distributed throughout Europe and the United States—a major weapon in Germany's propaganda war of terror. Hitler—convinced that he, rather than his professional soldiers, had achieved success—began to believe himself to be a military genius. But most western military men, deeply impressed by the German victory, nevertheless wrongly assumed that its magnitude was due mainly to Polish ineptitude.*

War in the West, 1939

Amazing inactivity marked the situation along Germany's western border. France and Great Britain began lethargic mobilization behind the partial shelter of the great concrete, steel-turreted Maginot Line, stretching from the Swiss border northward to Montmédy. From that point to the North Sea, along the Belgian border, extended an outmoded system of unconnected fortresses—relics of pre-World War I defenses. Belgium and Holland both maintained strict neutrality—a fatal concession to political expediency, for it prevented any co-operation with French and British military planners. The British Expeditionary Force, nearly 400,000 strong, was moved across the Channel and concentrated as part of the Allied line in the general area Arras-Lille. Across the German border the Westwall lay quiescent, with supporting mobile troops stripped to a minimum to the benefit of the Polish front. A strong Allied punch might well have broken through and ended Hitler's grandiose scheme of world conquest. Instead, the only overt move was a tentative French probe toward Saarbrücken. The Allies were relying on a policy of blockade, economic strangulation, and defensive fortification to exhaust German strength. From that groundwork, it was believed would eventually come an Allied offensive—as yet only a dream. "Sitzkrieg" and "phony war" were the derisive terms applied to this negation of Germany's blitzkrieg.

The Naval War, 1939

Great Britain proclaimed a naval blockade of Germany immediately after her declaration of war (September 3). The German Navy, under the direction of Grand Admiral **Erich Raeder,** was prepared to prosecute only one type of strategy: commerce destruction. There could be no thought of fleet action against Britain by Germany's small fleet (see table, below). But Germany had 98 submarines against Britain's 70, and the United Kingdom was dependent upon sea transport for both food and war matériel. Already 2 pocket battleships, the *Deutschland* and the *Graf Spee,* were at sea, together with a score of U-boats, with supply ships scattered

COMPARATIVE NAVAL STRENGTHS[a]—SEPTEMBER, 1939

	Britain	*France*	*Germany*[b]	*Italy*
Battleships and Battle Cruisers[c]	18	11	4	6
"Pocket" Battleships[d]	—	—	3	—
Aircraft Carriers	10	1	1	—
Heavy Cruisers (8-inch guns or more)	15	18	4	7
Light Cruisers (6-inch guns or less)	62	32	6	15
Destroyers	205	34	25	59
Destroyer Escorts, Torpedo Boats, etc.	73	30	42	69
Motor Torpedo Boats	39	9	17	69
Submarines	70	72	98	115

[a] Includes ships built or nearing completion.

[b] All German vessels were newly built, and with few exceptions were more modern, faster, bigger, and generally more powerful than comparable types of other nations.

[c] Battle cruisers were as big as battleships and carried the same kind of heavy guns (usually 14- to 16-inch in caliber). But they carried less armor protection, and usually fewer heavy guns, so that, being lighter in weight, they could go faster than battleships. Thus they could hit as hard as battleships, but could not take as much punishment; they sacrificed protection for speed.

[d] Under the provisions of the Versailles Treaty after World War I, Germany was forbidden to build ships larger than 10,000 tons. The pocket battleships were really small battle cruisers; they carried 11-inch guns, were very fast, but did not have much armor, so that they would not exceed the weight limit. They could beat any cruiser in the world, but could not stand up to a real battleship.

strategically around the globe. The first German submarine blow shocked the world, and led immediately to Britain's adoption of the convoy system for her merchant marine.

1939, September 3. Sinking of the *Athenia*. This British passenger liner, bound from Liverpool to Montreal with 1,400 passengers, was sunk without warning by *U-30,* 200 miles west of the Hebrides; 112 died.

1939, September 17. Loss of H.M.S. *Courageous*. Cruising with 4 escorting destroyers off the southwestern coast of England on antisubmarine duty, the carrier was torpedoed at dusk by *U-29,* sinking immediately with loss of 515 lives.

1939, September–December. Cruise of the *Graf Spee*. This German pocket battleship, under Captain **Hans Langsdorff,** cruised the South Atlantic between Pernambuco, Brazil, and Cape Town, South Africa, even venturing into the Indian Ocean, capturing and sinking 9 British merchantmen between September 17 and late November. Making secret rendezvous with the supply ship *Altmark,* she then took on fuel and supplies and transferred to her some 300 prisoners. Resuming his cruise, Langsdorff captured 2 more British ships. Meanwhile, a British aircraft carrier, a battle cruiser, and 6 cruisers, together with 2 French cruisers and some 10 Allied destroyers, were scouring the seas for the *Graf Spee.*

1939, October 14. Sinking of H.M.S. *Royal Oak*. German Lieutenant Commander **Guenther Prien,** commanding *U-47,* at night daringly threaded elaborate antisubmarine defenses and treacherous tide rips to enter Scapa Flow, where the British Home Fleet lay concentrated. Firing 2 spreads of 4 torpedoes each against the nearest large vessel, he scored several hits on the battleship *Royal Oak.* She went down in 2 minutes, taking with her 786 officers and men. Prien then brought his submarine safely out of the harbor, successfully concluding a most gallant exploit.

1939, December 13. Battle of the River Plate. A British squadron—heavy cruiser *Exeter,* 6 8-in. guns, and the light cruisers *Ajax* and *Achilles,* 8 6-in. guns each—under Commodore **Henry Harwood** caught up with the *Graf Spee* off the mouth of the River Plate (early December 13). Langsdorff, confident that his 6 11-in. and 8 5.9-in. guns could blow the lighter British ships out of the water, closed with them, instead of standing off and destroying them with his heavy battery, which outranged their armament by nearly 10,000 yards. Harwood's squadron carried the fight to the German in preplanned maneuvers that prevented the *Graf Spee* from concentrating fire on any one ship. At the end of 80 minutes, the *Exeter* was completely silenced and on fire, the *Ajax* had half of her guns out of action, and the *Achilles* was severely damaged. But the *Graf Spee,* too, had been badly hit, so Langsdorff broke off the fight and made for neutral Montevideo, where he hoped to land his wounded and make emergency repairs. Harwood, following with his 2 serviceable ships (the *Exeter* limped for the Falkland Islands), stood off the port and waited, radioing for reinforcements. Langsdorff was refused more than 72 hours sanctuary by the neutral Uruguayan government. Meanwhile the British heavy cruiser *Cumberland,* 8 8-in. guns, arrived to join Harwood; other British vessels were converging. Langsdorff, leaving most of his crew on board a German merchantman in the harbor, steamed out with a skeleton crew and blew up his vessel. He and his party then returned in their lifeboats to internment. Heartbroken, Langsdorff committed suicide three days later.

1939, mid-December. Other German Raiders. In the North Atlantic the pocket battleship *Deutschland,* after some success in commerce destruction (among her prizes was the neutral American freighter *City of Flint,* whose seizure created an international incident), was forced by engine trouble to make for home. The German Naval Staff sent out the battle cruisers *Scharnhorst* and *Gneisenau* to cover the *Deutschland*'s withdrawal and continue pressure against Atlantic shipping.

1939, December 23. Sacrifice of H.M.S. *Rawalpindi*. The *Scharnhorst* and *Gneisenau* successfully evaded British patrols east of Scotland, but were sighted December 23 between the Faeroe Islands and Iceland by H.M.S. *Rawalpindi,* a merchant liner converted into a cruiser and mounting 4 6-in. guns. Radioing an alarm, the *Rawalpindi* gallantly engaged the giant warships with her popguns, hoping to delay them sufficiently to ensure their interception. Literally blown to bits in a few moments, the *Rawalpindi* and her valiant crew nevertheless had fulfilled their mission, for the German warships returned immediately to port.

FINNISH-RUSSIAN WAR, NOVEMBER 30, 1939–MARCH 1, 1940

Russia, following the division of Poland, and obviously fearful of Germany, began consolidating a Baltic sphere of interest. Mutual defense pacts with Latvia, Estonia, and Lithuania were followed by immediate inrush of Russian troops for their "defense" (October–November). From Finland, Russia demanded a similar agreement, including occupation of the southern portion of the Karelian Isthmus and other island and mainland base areas. Finland, rejecting these demands, mobilized forces along her frontier, under the command of aging, still brilliant Marshal **Baron Carl Mannerheim, veteran of 3 wars. Russia demanded immediate withdrawal of Finnish troops.**

1939, November 30. Bombardment of Helsinki and Viipuri. A Soviet air attack, without declaration of war, initiated hostilities.

1939, November 30–December 15. The Russian Invasion. Armies totaling nearly a million men smashed at Finland from east and southeast, and in amphibious invasions across the Gulf of Finland. They were opposed by Finnish forces totaling 300,000, of which about 80 per cent were mobilized reservists. All the amphibious attacks on the southern coast were repulsed. In the far north a Russian column seized Petsamo, pressed a short distance south, and then was stopped. The main Russian attacking force, driving into the Karelian Isthmus, was hurled back with heavy loss at the Mannerheim Line—a World War I system of field fortifications, all cleverly knitted into the rugged terrain and heavily wooded areas. Other Russian columns pressed into the vast lake and forest region of eastern and central Finland, opposed by mobile defense units of battalion or smaller size habituated to independent action in the forests. The heavy snows and subzero temperature of the Finnish winter had little effect on Finnish troops or their mobility. All were skiers; all were warmly clad. The Russians soon bogged down. Meanwhile, Russian air raids had been ineffective, and Communist fifth-column activities quickly collapsed.

1939, December–1940, January. Battle of Suomussalmi. In eastern Finland, the Russian 163rd Division moved in 2 columns over narrow woods roads which converged at the village of Suomussalmi. Deep snow impeded its advance and temperatures dropping to —40° bit deep into men fresh from the Ukraine and lacking arctic clothing. On the Russian flanks, Finnish civil guard units in white smocks swooped silently on skis, sniping at supply vehicles and field kitchens. The Russian columns joined at the village, but then paused to attempt reconnaissance (December 7–11). Arriving infantry elements of the Finnish 9th Division attacked without waiting for their artillery (December 11). The Russians clung to the village, but both their supply routes were blocked and ambushed, cutting off all supply. The Russian 44th Division, motorized, attempted to cut through to the 163rd's assistance, but was itself immobilized by harassing civil-guard attacks, and dug in on the road some 5 miles east of Suomussalmi. On Christmas Eve both Russian divisions vainly attempted to cut their way out. The Finnish 9th Division, its artillery now up, then made a co-ordinated assault upon the 163rd, and annihilated it (December 27–30). Turning then on the 44th Division, the Finns systematically cut it into smaller groups, each of which was in turn mopped up (January 1–8). Russian losses were about 27,500 killed or frozen to death. Captured were 1,300 others, together with 50 tanks and the entire artillery and equipment of both divisions. Finnish casualties were 900 killed and 1,770 wounded.

1940, January 1–February 1. Russian Regrouping. This followed humiliating repulses. (Russian spearheads had been checked and repulsed in 6 areas along the eastern frontier, with astounding losses—a division and a tank brigade captured; 3 other divisions almost destroyed.) The Russians now prepared to assault the Mannerheim Line, the only sector against which overwhelming strength could be concentrated. Meanwhile, France and England were preparing to mount a strong expeditionary force to Finland's assistance, but neutral Norway and Sweden refused to permit its passage.

1940, February 1–13. Assault on the Mannerheim Line. The Russian Seventh and Thirteenth armies, totaling 54 divisions, began incessant attacks—4 or 5 per day—against the Mannerheim Line, covered by tremendous artillery bombardments and air support. Wave after wave of assault troops dared the devastating defense fire. The Finns were sickened by the slaughter they inflicted. Finally a breakthrough was effected near Summa (February 13). The Finnish right wing and center were rolled back to Viipuri (March 1).

1940, March 12. Finland Capitulates. Her armed forces were exhausted and all hope for foreign assistance was gone. The Russian terms of peace were practically identical with the orginal demands. Stalin had evidently no intention of tempting foreign intervention by further aggression, nor had he any stomach for a future guerrilla war in Finland. Finnish losses in the war were about 25,000 killed and 43,000 wounded. Russian losses have never been published, but they probably were about 200,000 killed and 400,000 more wounded.

COMMENT. *The Finnish defense was conducted by well-led, disciplined soldiers, familiar with the terrain and weather conditions and utilizing tactics geared to those conditions. The Russian offensive was amateurishly planned, without regard to terrain, weather, or the logistical problems involved. It was finally successful only because the Soviet government was willing to utilize cannon fodder in overwhelming masses without regard to casualties. As a result of the Russian blundering, Hitler and his generals assumed that Soviet Russia, inferior in leadership, tactics, and weapons, would be a pushover for the German war machine. This opinion was unfortunately shared by many foreign observers, including the United States War Department.*

OPERATIONS IN 1940

Conquest of Denmark and Norway

Sweden's iron ore, vital to German heavy industry, flowed in 2 channels: via the Baltic Sea and down the coast from Narvik in northern Norway. The latter route was threatened by the British naval blockade. German possession of Norway would permit use of land-based air power against the blockade and provide a springboard for aerial attacks against the British Isles. Hitler determined to seize both Norway and Denmark. Plans were initiated for invasion in early April.

1940, February 16. *Altmark* Incident. British blockaders discovered the *Graf Spee*'s auxiliary heading home along the Norwegian coast with 299 British merchant seamen captured by the *Graf Spee*. The Admiralty ordered their rescue at all costs. Captain **Philip Vian**, in H.M. destroyer *Cossack,* pursued the *Altmark* into Jossing Fjord near Stavanger and despite Norwegian protests boarded and captured her, releasing the prisoners. Norwegian protests of this violation of territorial waters died away in face of British proof that Norway had permitted an armed vessel to take refuge in neutral Norwegian waters.

1940, April 8–10. Naval Actions along the Norwegian Coast. In early April Churchill ordered mines laid in Norwegian territorial waters to deny their use by Germany. British destroyers approaching the Norwegian coast encountered German naval vessels convoying troop transports and warships toward Kristiansand, Stavanger, Bergen, Trondheim, and Narvik. Several violent engagements took place. The German warships successfully protected their convoys, but suffered losses. H.M. destroyer *Glowworm* deliberately rammed the heavy cruiser *Hipper*, damaging her severely, but was herself blown up. In a duel of battle cruisers the German *Gneisenau* was badly damaged by the *Renown*. Two other German cruisers were sunk, and the pocket battleship *Lützow* was damaged near Oslo by British ships and submarines. The German convoys all reached their objectives.

1940, April 9. Conquest of Denmark. German troops dashed across the border into Jutland. A battalion of infantry, hidden on a merchant ship in Copenhagen harbor, landed to seize king and government. Thus fell Denmark, almost without bloodshed.

1940, April 9. Invasion of Norway. The Germans planned simultaneous landings along the coast and parachute assaults at Oslo and Stavanger; they expected to paralyze the nation and to seize king and government by surprise as in Denmark. But the Norwegian armed forces, about 12,000 strong, were more substantial and better prepared than the Danes and had the brief warning provided by distance and size. The Army was a well-trained militia with a small cadre of permanent officers and men, in 6 infantry brigades and supporting artillery, plus local defense units. The Navy, including coast defense artillery, was small and efficient, but ships and equipment were old. Support elements included some fighter and torpedo planes. There were trained reserves of 120,000.

1940, April 9–10. Capture of Oslo. Shore batteries in Oslo Fjord gallantly repulsed the German invasion flotilla; the German cruiser *Blücher* and a smaller vessel were sunk and 2 small craft were damaged. Airborne troops seized Oslo airport, overwhelming the small AA detachment. Norwegian fighter planes shot down 5 Germans before they were driven from the sky. The air-transported troops quickly seized the city, while troops landed from ships overran the coastal defenses.

1940, April 9–10. West Coast Operations. At Kristiansand and Bergen the Germans landed only after suffering heavy casualties at the hands of determined, outnumbered defenders. At Bergen, coast defense guns damaged the cruiser *Königsberg*, which British bombers then sank. Near Stavanger an infantry battalion vainly tried to stop history's first combat airborne assault. Only at Trondheim and Narvik did German efforts at surprise succeed.

1940, April 10–13. Actions at Narvik. Five British destroyers in surprise attack entered the fjord and sank 2 of 10 German destroyers which had carried the assault troops, then withdrew, having also lost 2. H.M. battleship *Warspite* with 9 destroyers went in and wiped out the remaining German destroyers (April 13). Seven U-boats remained.

1940, April 10–30. German Exploitation. With all initial objectives taken, German troops under General **Nikolaus von Falkenhorst** fanned out over the countryside. An intensive airlift brought more troops from Germany. Luftwaffe units from Norwegian airfields attacked British warships off the coast. Overcoming initial surprise and confusion, Norwegian troops under newly appointed Major General **Carl Otto Ruge** fought stubbornly. About 50,000 reservists were mobilized. For three weeks the Norwegians tried to hold south-central Norway. But the Germans were too strong and overwhelmed them or drove them into northern Norway. A small "fifth column" led by traitor **Vidkun Quisling** gave the Germans some help.

1940, April 14–19. Allied Landings. Some 10,000 French and British troops that had been assembled in British ports for a possible attempt to aid Finland (see p. 1055) were hastily embarked and landed at Namsos and Andalsnes to try to take Trondheim and retain a foothold in Norway. A smaller force landed near Narvik (April 14–15).

1940, April 20–May 2. German Reaction. Germans at Trondheim held off the Allies while reinforcements hurried from Oslo. The Luftwaffe struck Allied troops, landing areas, and support ships in continuous violent attacks. Unable to fight effectively, the Allies evacuated Namsos and Andalsnes (May 1–2). King **Haakon VII** and the government meanwhile had moved to northern Norway.

1940, April 24–May 26. Battle for Narvik. While the Allied force hesitated, the Germans prepared hastily for defense (April 14–23). On Churchill's urging, the attack began. Despite powerful naval support, the Allied force, now 25,000 men, was unable to dislodge the stubborn Germans. Norwegian troops, trained for mountain fighting, spearheaded the attack, but co-ordination between the Anglo-French force and the Norwegians was poor. Under Allied pressure the exhausted Germans withdrew and the Allies quickly occupied Narvik (May 28).

1940, June 8–9. Allied Evacuation of Narvik. Because of catastrophe in Western Europe (see below), the Allies evacuated Narvik, which was quickly reoccupied by the Germans, thus completing the conquest of Norway. The Allied force evacuating the area by sea was escorted by H.M. carrier *Glorious* and 2 destroyers. The *Glorious,* surprised by the German battle cruisers *Scharnhorst* and *Gneisenau,* with all her planes on deck, was promptly sunk. So, too, were the destroyers, but one of them succeeded in badly damaging the *Scharnhorst* by a torpedo. A few days later, a British submarine damaged the *Gneisenau.* Both German ships would be out of commission for 6 months. King Haakon and his government accompanied the withdrawing Allies and set up a government in exile in London.

COMMENT. *The German invasion was efficiently and daringly carried out in the face of possible destruction by the Royal Navy. Then speedy operation of the Luftwaffe from the captured bases gave the world its first realization of the value of air power in naval warfare. The net result of the audacious invasion was to loosen the British naval blockade of Germany, ensure the Reich's iron ore supply, and gain tremendous prestige for the German war machine. On the other hand, the German Navy was seriously crippled for several months to come. The performance of the Norwegians was commendable, particularly in their succesful offensive efforts in and near Narvik.*

Campaign in the West, 1940

BACKGROUND

By early May some 2½ million Germans (104 infantry divisions, 9 motorized divisions, 10 armored divisions) had assembled along Germany's western borders. These were organized in 3 army groups: the northernmost—Army Group B, General Fedor von Bock—comprised 2 armies from the North Sea to Aachen. Army Group A, General Gerd von Rundstedt, consisted of 4 armies and a powerful armored (Panzer) group or army, in a relatively narrow zone between Aachen and Sarrebourg. Most of Germany's 2,574 tanks were concentrated in Army Group A. Army Group C, General **Wilhelm J. F. von Leeb,** consisted of 2 armies facing the French defenses in eastern Lorraine and along the Rhine River. Supporting the ground troops were 2 air fleets, consisting of 3,500 combat planes. Over-all command was exercised by Hitler, as commander in chief, with General **Wilhelm Keitel** as his chief of staff. Directly commanding the army was Brauchitsch, who had also been in command of the invasion of Poland.

The opposing Allied forces (over 2 million men, mainly French) were assembled in 3 army groups behind the French borders. The First Army Group (General **Gaston Billotte**), from the English Channel to Montmédy, consisted of 5 armies, including the British Expeditionary Force (General **John Vereker, Lord Gort**). The Second Army Group, General **André Gaston Prételat,** of 3 armies was behind the Maginot Line from Montmédy to Epinal. The Third Army Group, of 1 army (General **Besson**), occupied the Maginot Line defenses. Over-all field commander was General **A. J. Georges,** who in turn was under the Allied commander in chief, General **Maurice G. Gamelin.** Although the Allies had 3,609 tanks (substantially more than the Germans, and many more powerful than the German tanks), these were scattered among 3 armored divisions and a number of separate tank battalions attached to other units. There were exactly 100 other divisions: 9 were British, 1 Polish, and 13 fortress troops incapable of operating outside of their Maginot Line defenses. In support was the French Air Force of some 1,400 combat planes, and about 290 British aircraft. Allied ground and air equipment was generally less modern than that of the Germans.

In the neutral Low Countries, Belgium nominally had some 600,000 men in 22 divisions, under the command of King **Leopold III.** The Dutch Army theoretically comprised some 400,000 men, under the command of General **Henri G. Winkelman.** Neither was assembled in full strength. Both countries had elaborate defensive systems, made more formidable by canal networks, with further arrange-

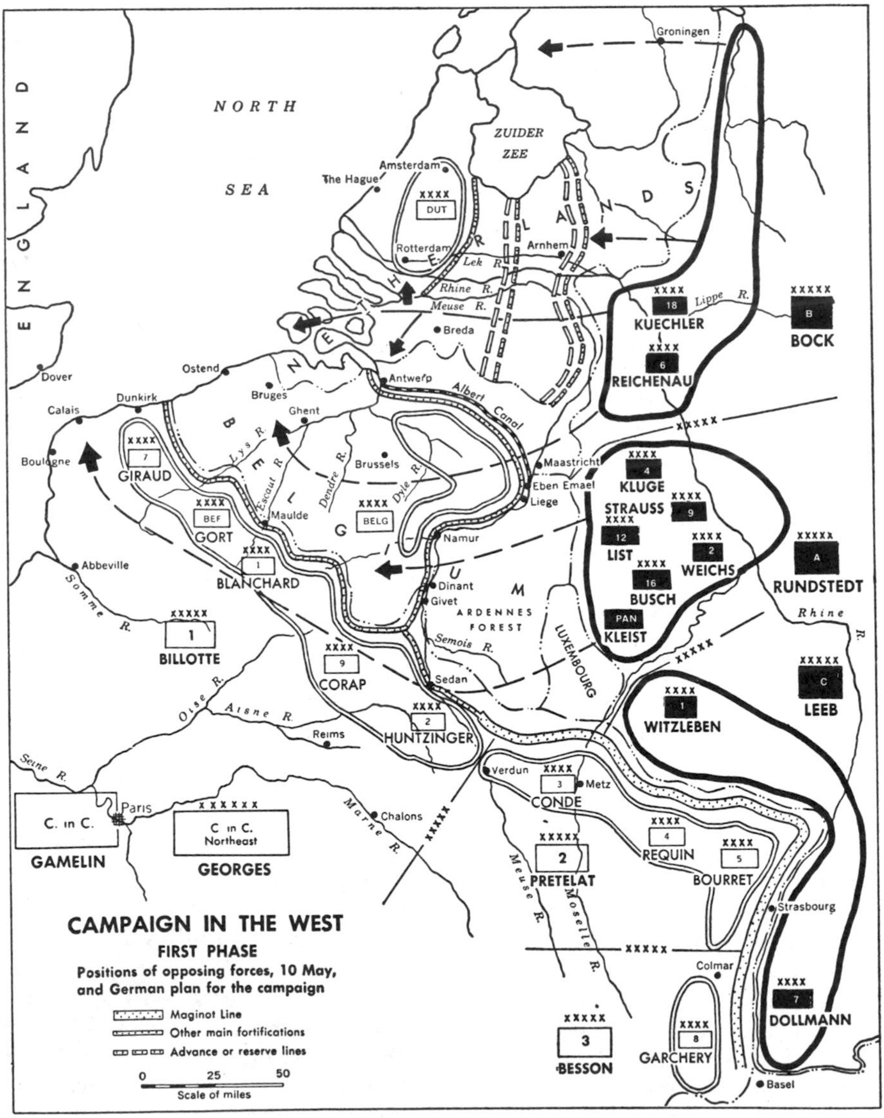

ments for flooding great stretches of country by opening dikes. The troops, however, were not very well trained, and their equipment was less modern and less complete than that of the French and British. The most serious deficiency, however, was lack of adequate defensive plans. In hopes that they could remain neutral, neither Belgium nor the Netherlands had dared to discuss joint defensive plans with the French and British, and had rebuffed every Allied effort to carry on even informal discussions.

German Plans. Following overwhelming terror bombardment, Army Group B would overrun Holland. Moving more slowly into Belgium to encourage the Allied left-flank armies to rush to the assistance of the Low Countries, Army Group A would then hurl an armored drive through the Ardennes Forest and via the Stenay Gap into France. Thus splitting the Allied armies (cutting off those which had advanced into Belgium), Army Group A would continue westward to Calais and roll the northern portion of the Anglo-British forces against the anvil of Army Group B in the Low Countries. Subsequent, prompt southward exploitation of the gap would then roll the southern French armies back upon the Maginot Line, where Army Group C would be waiting.

Allied Plans. The French were still thinking in terms of the Schlieffen Plan of 1914, a southwesterly sickle movement through Belgium. The Allied plan proposed, therefore—just as the Germans expected—to meet the expected invasion on the Dyle Line of Belgium, pivoting the First Army Group about the northern tip of the Maginot Line.

BATTLE OF FLANDERS, MAY 10–JUNE 4

Invasion of the Low Countries

1940, May 10. The German Assault. Following predawn bombardments of all major Dutch and Belgian airfields, Army Groups A and B crossed the Belgian and Dutch frontiers. Initially the main effort was on the right, by Army Group B, in Holland. Paratroop drops in the vicinity of Rotterdam, The Hague, Moerdijk, and Dortrecht quickly paralyzed the interior of the Netherlands. Early in the day, glider and parachute units landed on the top of powerful Fort **Eban Emael,** northern anchor of the main Belgian defense line, neutralizing it, while other German troops crossed the Albert Canal, which should have been defended by Eban Emael's guns. The violence and success of the initial German attacks, combined with terror bombings of the interior regions of both countries, threw their populaces into confusion and panic.

1940, May 10. Churchill Becomes Britain's Prime Minister. News of the early German successes aroused great alarm in Paris and London. Prime Minister Chamberlain, whose government had been tottering because of failures in Norway and general lack of popular support, resigned to permit lionhearted **Winston S. Churchill** to lead a coalition British government in the face of the German avalanche.

1940, May 11–14. Fall of Holland. Pressing its initial advantage, German Army Group B pressed steadily forward, despite frantic Dutch flooding of much of the countryside. By the 13th, German main elements had begun to force their way into the so-called Fortress of Holland, joining up with most of the paratroops, who had seized and held the key bridges over the Rhine estuary. At the same time, German spearheads met advance elements of the French Seventh Army (**Henri Giraud**) near Breda, and drove them back toward Antwerp. The Queen of the Netherlands and her government escaped by ship to England from The Hague. Germany demanded complete surrender, on pain of the destruction of all Dutch cities by aerial bombardment (May 14). As proof of its intentions, the Luftwaffe brutally destroyed the entire business section of **Rotterdam** while negotiations were in process. Winkelman surrendered.

1940, May 11–15. Fall of Belgium. Following a similar pattern of bombings, the German Sixth Army (Reichenau) drove southwest. Fort Eban Emael fell to its audacious attackers. As the Germans poured across the Albert Canal, the Belgian Army retired to the Dyle Line, to be reinforced (May 12) by elements of the BEF and the First French Army (**Georges Blanchard**). By the 15th, some 35 Allied divisions—including most of the BEF—were in the area Namur-Antwerp, with the German Sixth Army probing the Dyle Line in their front and the Eighteenth (**Georg von Kuechler**), now turning southward from Holland, threatening their left flank. At about the same time, these Allied units realized that to their right

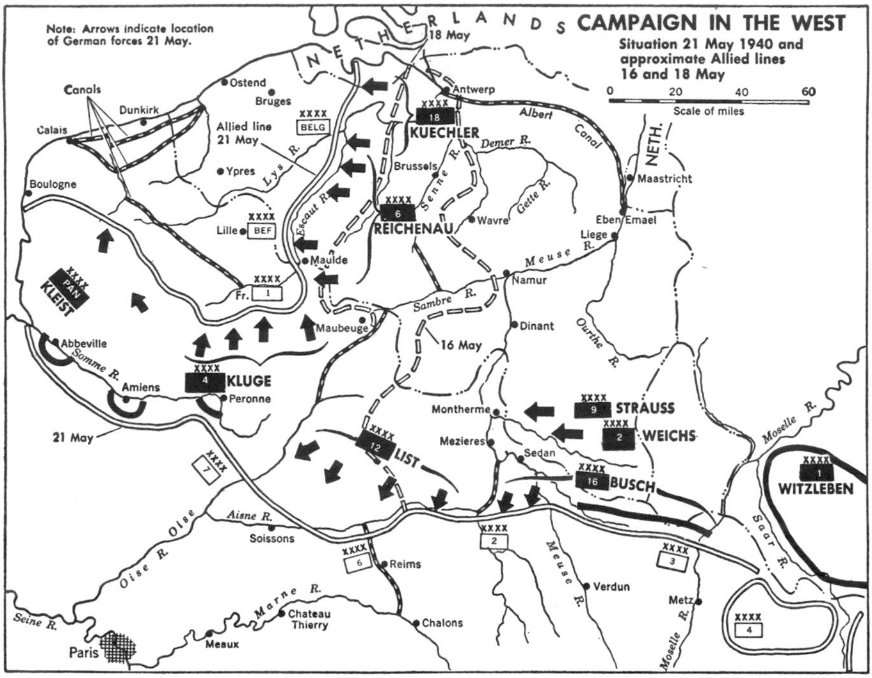

rear the French center was being torn apart.

Northern France

1940, May 10–12. Advance through the Ardennes. The German hammer blow—Rundstedt's Army Group A—moved through the difficult Ardennes simultaneously with the assaults on Holland and Belgium, but by nature of the terrain and road net did not reach the Meuse until May 12. This calculated delay was sufficient to coax the Allied forces north of the Sambre in motion into Belgium. Leading the 3 German invading columns was General **Paul L. E. von Kleist**'s Panzer Group (5 armored and 3 mechanized divisions), to its north General **Hermann Hoth**'s Panzer Corps (2 armored divisions). Never dreaming that the Germans would make their main effort through the hilly, forested Ardennes, General **André-Georges Corap**'s Ninth French Army and General **Charles Huntziger**'s Second had their weakest elements in the Stenay Gap area, while the Ardennes Forest itself was screened only by small French cavalry and Belgian chasseur units, which were quickly brushed aside. With first word of the German advance, both French generals hurried their cavalry forward to cross the Meuse and delay until both armies could establish themselves on the river.

1940, May 13–15. Across the Meuse. But Corap was slow, and Huntziger's cavalry was outflanked. Supported by devastating dive-bombing attacks against accurate French artillery, one of Hoth's armored divisions forced a river crossing at Haux; General **Georg-Hans Reinhardt**'s corps of Kleist's Panzer Group was similarly getting over at Monthermé and General **Heinz Guderian**'s corps at Sedan (May 13). Despite the now frantic efforts of the French, the bridgeheads were quickly expanded. The French Ninth Army was completely shattered, and the Second Army's left pulverized (May 15). The German armor, spearheaded by Stuka dive bombers, roared west on a 50-mile front, while behind them fast-moving German infantry poured through the gap.

1940, May 16–21. The Drive to the Channel. All too late, Gamelin ordered up divisions from the French general reserve, and from the armies south of the German drive, into a new Sixth Army (General **Touchon**) to plug the gap. General Henri Giraud, succeeding the inefficient Corap, attempted to regroup the Ninth Army in the face of the tidal wave, but it was completely routed (May 17), and Giraud was captured. Brigadier General **Charles A. J. M. de Gaulle**'s 4th Armored Division made 3 successive punches into the German south flank from **Laon** (May 17–19), but after limited success (the only successful French attacks of the campaign) his gallant troops were turned back by dive bombers and counterattacks. Gamelin was relieved, General **Maxime Weygand** taking supreme Allied command (May 19). German armor reached the seacoast west of Abbeville, completely splitting the Allied forces and severing communications with the BEF's base port, Cherbourg (May 31). While the French to the south attempted to hold the line of the Somme and Aisne rivers, the severed northern grouping found itself being pinned against the sea.

1940, May 21–25. Exploitation in the North. The German armor wheeled northward in 3 prongs, from the seacoast to Arras, while the Fourth (**Günther von Kluge**), Sixth, and Eighteenth Armies pressed in from the east on the French First Army, the BEF, and the Belgian Army. Lord Gort, on the First Army left, sent a task force south behind the French to bolster the right flank and to counterattack the German armor at Arras, but this effort was repulsed by General **Erwin Rommel**'s 7th Panzer Division (May 21). Guderian's armored corps captured Boulogne and isolated the British garrison of Calais (May 22–23). Dunkirk was chosen as substitute British base. The unbearable pressure of the German attack forced the Allies off the Escault River line into an ever-shrinking perimeter, with the full force of the German armor knocking against the BEF detachment on the Allied right (May 25). Complete and speedy annihilation of the penned-in Allies appeared certain.

1940, May 25–27. The Belgian Surrender. Meanwhile, on the Allied left, the Belgian Army was being pulverized by German attacks. King Leopold, deciding that further resistance was hopeless, surrendered to save further bloodshed, thus exposing the left flank of the Franco-British army to further assault. There could now be no hope of holding any part of Flanders. Churchill ordered the Royal Navy to help evacuate the British troops from Dunkirk.

1940, May 26–28. Hitler's Stop Order. By the Führer's command, the armored attack from the south was halted peremptorily. This incredible order permitted the hasty organization of perimeter defenses around Dunkirk and the equally hasty concentration of evacuation craft from the British Channel ports. The Luftwaffe was given the mission of pulverizing the Dunkirk perimeter. But the Germans in the air met an intensive, continuous attack by the RAF Fighter Command which, from bases in southern Britain, nullified German operations in a series of spectacular air battles.

1940, May 28–June 4. Evacuation from Dunkirk. Hitler rescinded his stop order and the German armor resumed assaults on the Allied right, to be checked by 3 British divisions aligned in deep zonal defense. A conglomeration of some 850 British vessels of every shape, size, and propulsion—most of them manned by civilian volunteers—converged on Dunkirk to begin the most amazing exodus in history. In 8 days, more than 338,000 men—among them 112,000 French and Belgian soldiers—were lifted. The troops streamed in orderly lines over wharves and beaches and through the surf, while overhead Spitfires of the Royal Air Force beat off most of the Luftwaffe's attempts at strafing, and their comrades along the ever-shrinking defensive perimeter held back German assaults. On the final night (June 4), General **Harold Alexander,** commanding the rear guard, personally toured the beaches and the harbor to verify the fact that the last living British soldier had been embarked, then himself got into a boat. Next morning the Germans overwhelmed the fragments of the First French Army gallantly screening the evacuation. The Battle of Flanders had ended.

COMMENT. *Aside from the duplicity and treachery of the Nazi attacks on Holland and Belgium, the actual military operations of the German Army were, with one exception, clear-cut in ruthless efficiency. Hitler's strange stop order, arresting the armored assault on the boxed-in Allied armies in Flanders, cannot be charged against the German commanders. It appears to have been motivated by Goering's plea that the Luftwaffe be permitted to give the* coup de grâce *and thus have full share in the glory of victory. Added, perhaps, was Hitler's fear that miraculously the French might mount a counterattack from the south and wreck his plans of conquest.*

On the other side of the ledger, the Allied operations, having no strong, centralized control, either prior to or during the action, were disjointed and ineffective. The initial French troop distribution, with the weight of forces behind the Maginot Line defenses, was ridiculous. Friction and distrust between British and French commanders complicated the situation. Indecision was the most marked characteristic of the French high command. The over-all handicap was the Allied reliance on fortifications per se, *which throttled the spirit of the offensive. Much has been made of the decay of patriotic fiber in France, sapping the warrior spirit; but the troops of the First French Army, battling without hope in front of Dunkirk while their British comrades were being evacuated, certainly behaved most gallantly.*

THE BATTLE OF FRANCE, JUNE 5–25, 1940

With amazing precision the German armies regrouped for the conquest of France, in accordance—except for minor changes—with previously prepared plans. Bock's Army Group B was poised on the line of the Somme extended east to Bourg. Rundstedt's Army Group A continued east to the Moselle in front of the Maginot Line, and Leeb's Army Group C stretched from there to the Swiss border. Facing it, behind the Somme, the Aisne, and the Maginot Line, the bewildered French forces were regrouping, with Army Group 3 (Besson was now on the left, Billotte having been killed in an auto accident) extending from the sea east to Rheims, Army Group 4 (Huntziger) continuing on to the Meuse and thence to Montmédy, and Prételat's Army Group 2 behind the Maginot Line. The best that Weygand could produce—with half of France's available strength already dissipated and the remainder shaken—was a defense in depth behind the Somme and Aisne. His concentration was hampered by incessant Luftwaffe bombings, dislocating rail centers and blocking troop movements on the roads. He had available only 65 divisions, 3 of them armored units already badly mauled, and 17 others fortress troops or second-line reserve units. All elements were under strength, all lacked equipment, and the general morale was very low.

1940, June 5–13. Renewed German Assault. Army Group B, spearheaded by Kleist's Panzers, struck from the Somme. Smashing through the Tenth French Army (**Félix Altmeyer**), the Germans reached the Seine west of Paris (June 9) and the armor turned westward to pin the French IX Corps and the British 51st Highland Division, one of the few remaining BEF elements still in France, against the sea at St.-Valery-en-Caux. This force surrendered (June 12). The French Seventh Army to the east put up a stiffer fight. But to restore his flank Weygand ordered Army Group 3 to withdraw to the Seine (June 8). Rundstedt's Army Group A launched its main-effort assault next day against the left of the French Group 4, east of Paris. His Panzer spearheads, under Guderian, were reinforced by Kleist's Panzers of Group B, rapidly shifted eastward. Despite valiant resistance in depth by the French Fourth Army (**Edouard Réquin**), and a series of counterattacks, Guderian's tanks crunched through at Châlons and roared southward. Kleist's armor crossed the Marne at Château-Thierry at the same time. The breakthrough was complete. The French government abandoned Paris for Bordeaux, toward which refugees in countless thousands were already pouring (June 10). Paris was declared an open city (June 13) and next day German troops marched in.

1940, June 10. Italy Enters the War. Mussolini, deciding now that France could not win, declared war and ordered an invasion of southern France.

1940, June 13–25. The Pursuit. The French armies disintegrated, while German columns spread west, south, and east. German armor swept the coastal ports from St.-Nazaire north to Cherbourg. Other Germans crossed the Loire (June 17) and

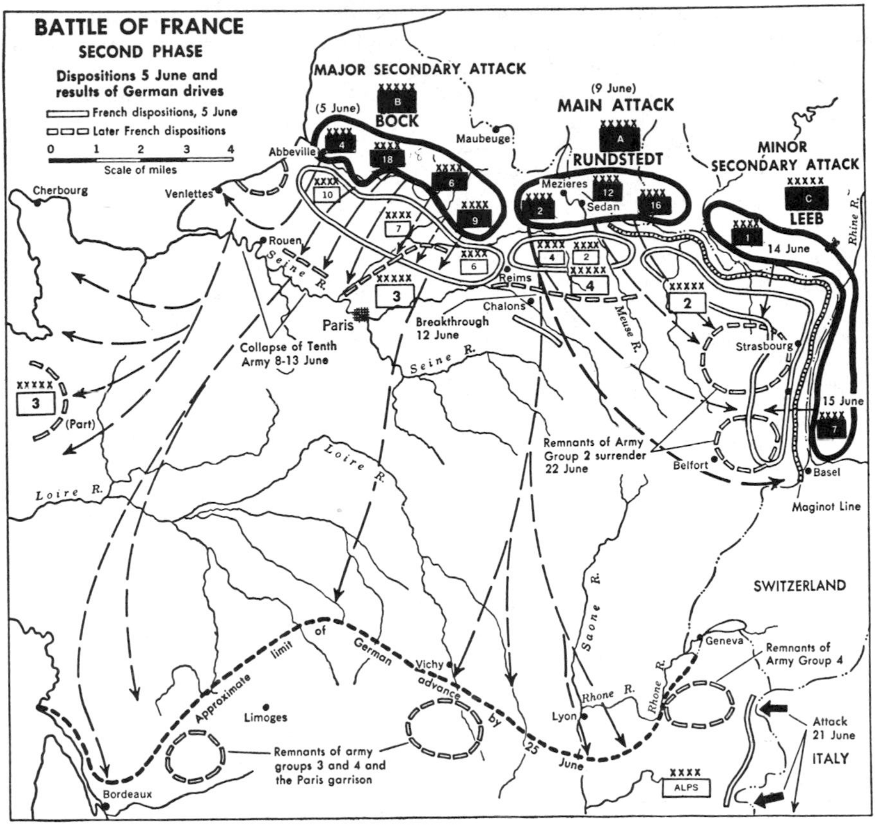

easterly jabs reached the foothills of the French Alps southeast of Besançon, cutting off the French remnants behind the Maginot Line, now shattered by Army Group C's power drive (June 14–15). These isolated French troops soon surrendered (June 22).

1940, June 17. French Governmental Shuffle. After spurning Churchill's offer of an "indissoluble union" of France and Britain—to fight on forever if necessary—the French cabinet voted to sue for terms. Prime Minister **Paul Reynaud** resigned; Marshal **Henri Philippe Pétain** took his place and at once asked for an armistice.

1940, June 21. French Capitulation. General Huntziger, meeting Hitler in the railway car in Compiègne Forest where the 1917 armistice had been signed, capitulated. Hostilities officially ceased June 25. France surrendered three-fifths of her territory to German control; all French troops were disarmed. The one bright spot on France's battered military reputation shone in the Alpes Maritimes, where 6 French divisions threw back a 3-pronged invasion by 32 Italian divisions (June 21).

COMMENT. *Weygand's situation, beginning June 5, was hopeless insofar as the defense of metropolitan France was concerned. Whether he and Pétain should have accepted Churchill's offer of a Franco-English union, and carried on the war from Africa, is a moot question. Certainly the French fleet was intact, as was the French Army of Africa. The fall of France left Hitler the undisputed master of continental Western Europe. He now turned his eyes both northwest and east. Should he carry out his original plan and now conquer Soviet Russia, or should he tarry to invade and overwhelm seemingly helpless England?*

Britain Embattled, June–December, 1940

BRITAIN, FRANCE, AND THE FREE FRENCH

1940, June. Britain Alone. France's fall left the British Empire to face the might of the combined Rome-Berlin Axis powers. Her vital Atlantic sea lanes were menaced by German submarines, her Mediterranean lifeline by Italy's fleet and army, with Soviet Russia an Axis silent partner on the sidelines. Furthermore, there was danger that Hitler would seize the French fleet, which would provide the Axis with a clear preponderance of sea power. The Royal Navy and Royal Air Force were intact though battered, but there were insufficient destroyers in the former to carry out antisubmarine, convoy, and patrolling activities. The British Army at home was in sad state. Although the majority of the BEF personnel had been brought back from Dunkirk, they had left all their arms and other matériel behind them in France, and the remaining army troops in Great Britain (29 divisions, with little armor or artillery) were not yet combat-ready. To most neutrals it appeared that Britain must bow to the inevitable and make peace. Hitler thought so, too, opening the door to a negotiated peace, which Churchill contemptuously slammed shut as Britain girded herself.

1940, June 23. De Gaulle and the Free French. A new element emerged from the debris of fallen France. Brigadier General de Gaulle, exponent of armored warfare, had been called from his division command (June 5) to become Undersecretary of State for National Defense in the short-lived cabinet of Paul Reynaud and had urged continued resistance. When Pétain capitulated, de Gaulle fled to England, calling on all true Frenchmen to rally and fight for freedom. The call was answered by French officers and soldiers from the world over—by driblets at first, then in mounting numbers. De Gaulle at once utilized the best of these men to organize outlying French territories. Captain **Jacques de Hauteclôche**—who protected his family by changing his name to **Jean Leclerc**—was flown to French Equatorial Africa. General **Georges Catroux** went to Cairo as Free French commander in the Middle East. Colonel **Edgard de Larminat** organized the French Congo. In England, Admiral **Émile Muselier** began organization of a Free French Navy. Although supported to great extent by the British government, this Free French movement was as yet regarded with some misgivings by both Britain and the United States, whose leaders underestimated the dynamic driving force of de Gaulle.

1940, June 24. Arms from the U.S. In response to Churchill's urgent purchase request (June 3), a large shipment of small arms, machine guns, light artillery, and ammunition arrived in England.

1940, July 3–4. Seizure of French Warships. A British squadron appeared off **Oran,** Algeria, and demanded that the French squadron there choose (a) to join England and fight Germany, (b) to turn in at an English port for internment, or (c) to sink itself in Oran Harbor. On French refusal, Vice Admiral Sir **James F. Somerville** opened fire. In a short action, 3 French battleships were sunk, a fourth escaped, and 5 destroyers fled to Toulon. British damage was light. That same day the French squadron at Alexandria—1 battleship, 4 cruisers, and 3 destroyers—disarmed itself on orders of Admiral Sir **Andrew B. C. Cunningham,** commanding the British Eastern Mediterranean Fleet. In other English ports were 2 more submarines which, on British summons, joined "Free French" forces and served with the Royal Navy throughout the rest of the war. These coups accounted for a large proportion of the French Navy. Some ships remained at the naval base of Toulon, at Algiers, Casablanca, and Dakar. The conflict at Oran, however, embittered many Frenchmen. Pétain's French Vichy government severed diplomatic relations with Britain (July 5).

1940, September 27. Rome-Berlin-Tokyo "Axis." A 3-power pact was concluded at Berlin, each partner pledging the others total aid for 10 years. The treaty did not, however, require Japan to go to war against Britain or her allies.

THE BATTLE OF BRITAIN

Operation "Sea Lion." Hitler, against the recommendations of his army and navy chiefs, but with the Luftwaffe's enthusiastic support, had decided to invade England (June 5). Control of the sea was essential. Having no adequate surface force to oppose British naval strength, the Luftwaffe's task was first to defeat the RAF and then to neutralize the Royal Navy. French, Low Country, and Norwegian airfields were developed to maximum capability. As prelude, harassing air raids were made daily against British coastal towns and shipping during July. Meanwhile, German armies were regrouping for embarkation, and the Navy was scouring Germany and the occupied countries for landing craft.

1940, August 8–18. First Phase. Goering mustered 2,800 planes, with capability of putting up 900 fighters and 1,300 bombers in 3 fleets—Marshal **Albert Kesselring**'s Air Fleet Two, flying from northern France; Marshal **Hugo Sperrle**'s Three, from Belgian and Dutch bases; and General **Hans-Jürgen Stumpff**'s Five (mainly bombers), based in Norway. Against this force, British Air Marshal Sir Hugh Dowding's Fighter Command mustered but 650 operational fighters in 52 squadrons. German strategy was to coax the British into combat, by strafing seaports and fighter bases, and then shoot them out of the sky. However, aided by Britain's newly developed radar, Dowding was able to concentrate superior force at vital spots and the Luftwaffe's massive daily day and night attacks—1,485 sorties the first day (August 8), rising to 1,786 sorties (August 15)—were roughly handled in combats ranging in a 500-mile arc from southwest to northeast England. In continuous fighting during the rest of the period, Fighter Command still dominated the air over Britain.

1940, August 24–September 5. Second Phase. German attacks were shifted to concentrate against main inland RAF bases. Large groups of bombers, each protected by 100 fighters, crashed through by sheer weight of numbers, inflicting great damage on airfields and communication and control centers. The German high command came close to cracking Fighter Command. More than 450 British fighters were destroyed; 103 pilots were killed and 128 wounded.

1940, August 24–29. Berlin Bombed. In retaliation for a bombing of London, the RAF Bomber Command staged a night raid on Berlin. For 3 hours, 81 British planes hovered unharmed over the fog-shrouded city. Damage was small, but the psychological effect immense. The raid was repeated (August 28 and 29), despite Berlin's 2 rings of antiaircraft batteries; numerous Berliners were killed or injured. Düsseldorf, Essen, and other German cities were also attacked. Hitler and Goering, in blind rage, after undergoing a week of British reprisals, again shifted their strategy. At the moment that British air defense had reached its lowest ebb, and with victory almost in German reach, the Luftwaffe was ordered to drop its assault against British airfields and control centers.

1940, September 7–30. Third Phase. London became the target for tremendous and incessant aerial bombardment. Fighter Command, its task simplified by the German singleness of objective, was thus able to concentrate its dwindling force. The bombing of London reached its crescendo (September 15) when more than 1,000 bombers and some 700 fighters swept all day over the city in wave after wave. By nightfall, 56 assaulting planes had been downed at the expense of only 26 British aircraft. British civilian casualties were heavy during this phase—from 300 to 600 lives lost and from 1,000 to 3,000 persons injured per day in the unrelenting assaults, while a considerable portion of the city was wrecked. But English spirit refused to falter, and the Luftwaffe's losses were so great that daylight bombing had to be dropped. The aerial tide had turned.

1940, September 14–15. British Counterblow. Bomber Command, in conjunction with light naval craft, destroyed nearly 200 barges in French and Low Country ports—one-tenth of the total gathered for the proposed invasion. Hitler suspended Operation Sea Lion—scheduled for September 27. Slowly the German aerial assaults tapered off. The last daylight raid occurred September 30.

1940, October 1–30. Final Phase. Sporadic German hit-and-run raids continued, doing relatively little damage. London was lashed by another intensive air raid (October 10). Hitler now canceled Operation

Sea Lion (October 12). The Battle of Britain had been won by the RAF, of whom Churchill said: "Never, in the field of human conflict, was so much owed by so many to so few." Over-all losses were 1,733 German planes shot down, to 915 British.

COMMENT. *Four factors decided British victory in the air: first was an indomitable will to win; second was radar, which pinpointed enemy presence, routes, and strength; third was a well-organized, efficient ground-control system, which enabled concentration of superior force at the right time and place; and fourth was the Germans' own strategical blunder: dispersion of effort. By mid-September, Luftwaffe losses were so great that decisive victory in the air became impossible, and without air victory there could be no invasion of England.*

1940, November. The Blitz Begins. While the Luftwaffe had given up its effort to gain permanent air control, sporadic night raids continued through the rest of the year. Coventry was struck (November 14–15) by about 500 German bombers and practically demolished. London was again swept by a devastating raid, causing many explosions and fires (December 29). Before the "blitz" ended (May, 1941), more than 43,000 civilians—men, women, and children—had been killed and 51,000 others seriously injured.

Battle of the Atlantic

Despite the convoy system, and the addition to the British merchant marine of a number of Scandinavian vessels (most of these ships had escaped when their countries were overrun), the toll of British shipping sunk by the roving submarines kept mounting. By August 15, 2.5 million tons of shipping had been destroyed. Britain just did not have sufficient light warships to provide adequate protection for her merchant ships from the sea wolves, nor could the shipyards produce sufficient replacements.

1940, September 3. Trading Bases for Destroyers. Churchill expected his urgent shipbuilding program would in a few months produce destroyers in quantity, but until February, 1941, the shortage would be tragic and perhaps fatal to Britain. U.S. President Franklin D. Roosevelt, alive to the worldwide threat imposed by Nazism, agreed to a momentous immediate exchange. For 50 old U.S. destroyers, Britain leased naval and air bases to the U.S. in its Western Hemisphere possessions—Newfoundland, Bermuda, the Bahamas, Jamaica, Antigua, St. Lucia, Trinidad, and British Guiana.

1940, September 22–25. Attack on Dakar. A British–Free French amphibious expedition attempted to take Dakar, French West Africa, to prevent its possible use by Germany as a submarine base for South Atlantic operations. General de Gaulle commanded the Free French force. Due to bad weather and Allied mistakes, the invaders were repelled by the Vichy French defenders. Churchill, hoping to avoid further bitterness between the Vichy French and Britain, ordered the attack canceled.

1940, October–December. The Surface Raiders. In late October the German pocket battleship *Admiral Scheer,* Captain **Theodor Krancke,** slipped through the blockade to pursue commerce destruction in the North Atlantic. She encountered (November 5) a 37-ship British convoy, escorted by the auxiliary cruiser *Jervis Bay,* with 4 6-in. guns, Captain **E. F. S. Fegen.** Fegen, radioing the alarm, ordered his convoy to scatter and deliberately attacked the *Scheer.* For more than an hour the unequal contest kept up until the *Jervis Bay* sank. However, 32 ships of the convoy got away. The German heavy cruiser *Hipper* also got out (November), but engine trouble later forced her into Brest for repairs. The presence of these 2 powerful vessels in the shipping lanes slowed down convoying and necessitated strengthening the escorts. The *Scheer* continued a destructive raid into the South Atlantic and Indian Oceans, returning safely to Germany 4 months later.

Operations in the Mediterranean Area, 1940

1940, June. The Situation. Control of the Mediterranean was vital to Britain.

Through it ran the empire's "life line": the short sea route to India and Australia–New Zealand. Egypt, where both the British Mediterranean Fleet and Middle East Command were based to protect the Suez Canal, was Britain's principal base securing this life line. Mussolini planned to seize the Suez Canal by a pincer movement: from Libya on the west and from Ethiopia and Italian Somaliland on the southeast. At the same time he prepared for invasion of Greece through Albania to secure the northern shore of the Mediterranean opposite Egypt. Recognizing the danger, even though Hitler was threatening to invade Britain, Churchill boldly and wisely rushed Britain's sole remaining armored division to Egypt.

Available British forces were General Sir **Archibald Wavell**'s Middle East Command, with 36,000 troops in Egypt (mostly administrative, plus the understrength armored division), 9,000 in the Sudan, 5,500 in Kenya, 1,475 in British Somaliland, 27,500 in Palestine, 2,500 in Aden, and 800 in Cyprus. His air-force contingent was very small. Admiral Sir Andrew B. C. Cunningham's Mediterranean Fleet consisted of 1 carrier, 3 battleships, 3 heavy and 5 light cruisers, and a number of destroyers. Against these forces were pitted the full strength of the Italian Navy (see table, p. 1052), the land-based Air Force, and much of the Italian Army. Italy itself lay geographically threatening Wavell's westward line of communications, while light Italian naval forces based on Ethiopian and Italian Somaliland coast ports threatened his eastern communications through the Red Sea and Indian Ocean. Mussolini's ground forces in East Africa—Ethiopia, Eritrea, and Italian Somaliland—numbered about 110,000, commanded by **Amadeo Umberto, Duke of Aosta,** while in Libya Marshal **Italo Balbo** had 200,000 men and a sizable air force.

1940, June 11. First Attack on Malta. Immediately upon declaring war, Mussolini launched 2 waves of bombers against the island of Malta—the first of many thousands of such raids.

1940, June–September. Italian Preparations. There were minor border clashes and Italian air raids as the Italians prepared for major operations against Egypt, the Sudan, Kenya, and British Somaliland.

FIRST WESTERN DESERT CAMPAIGN, SEPTEMBER–DECEMBER, 1940

1940, September 13. Graziani's Invasion of Egypt. Marshal **Rodolfo Graziani** (succeeding Balbo, killed in an air crash in June) entered Egypt with 5 divisions, moving on a narrow front along the coast. British covering forces fell back before him. Reaching Sidi Barrani (September 16), the Italians settled down in a series of fortified camps extending over a 50-mile area, while Wavell's forces—now 2 divisions strong—remained at Mersa Matruh, 75 miles east. Both sides received reinforcements. General Sir **Henry M. ("Jumbo") Wilson,** tactical commander in Egypt, made plans for attack, but operations were delayed when Wavell was ordered to occupy Crete and send part of his air force to Greece to assist in countering an Italian invasion there (see p. 1068).

1940, December 9. Wavell's Offensive. After a night approach march, Wavell's Western Desert Force, 31,000 men, 120 guns, and 275 tanks, commanded by Major General **Richard N. O'Connor,** ripped through a gap in the Italian chain of defenses. O'Connor's relatively small force —1 armored and 1 infantry division, 2 additional infantry brigades, and a battalion of the new British "I" tanks—hemstitched its way westward between the desert and the coast, gobbling in turn each Italian fortified area. Air and naval elements assisted. By mid-December, the Italians had been thrown completely out of Egypt, leaving 38,000 prisoners and great quantities of matériel in British hands. As the year ended, the Desert Force, after a pause of 2 weeks, was assaulting the perimeter of Bardia where Graziani's disorganized forces lay.

COMMENT. *This daring assault against a force 4 times its size was well planned and superbly executed. O'Connor's ground forces were ably supported by the RAF under Wing Commander* **R. Collishaw** *and by the long-range naval gunfire of Cunningham's warships along the coast. In principle the operation resembled Allenby's breakthrough in Palestine in 1917 (see p. 974), in which Wavell had played a part. It must be noted, also, that at the time Wavell was launching his westward counterattack in Libya he was* *in process of mounting an equally daring assault into East Africa: a 2-pronged offensive to be launched simultaneously from the Sudan and from Kenya against Italian-held Abyssinia and Italian Somaliland* (*see p. 1071*).

GREECE AND THE BALKANS

1940, October 28. Italian Invasion of Greece. General **Sebastiano Visconti-Prasca,** who had an army of 10 divisions (about 162,000 men) in Albania, advanced into Greece with 8 divisions. The Italians immediately encountered unexpectedly fierce Greek resistance. General **Alexander Papagos,** whose army numbered about 150,000 men, had disposed them in a highly organized defensive zone through the difficult mountainous border area. The Italians were thrown back by determined counterattacks. The ineffective Visconti-Prasca was replaced by General **Ubaldo Soddu** (November 9).

1940, November 22–December 23. Greek Counteroffensive. Beginning with a successful assault on Italian-held Koritza, the Greeks rolled back all opposition. Assisted by Royal Air Force detachments sent by Wavell from Egypt, the Greeks advanced into Albania. As the year ended, the Italians were clinging desperately to the line Valona-Tepelino-Lake Ochrida, immense quantities of Italian war matériel had been captured, Italian military prestige had been degraded, and British naval units were bombarding the Valona base. Marshal Pietro Badoglio, Italian Chief of Staff, was forced to resign.

1940, June–October. Other Balkan Developments. During this year, Soviet Russia seized Bessarabia and northern Bukovina (June 26–28); the Rumanian oil-field area was occupied by "protecting" German troops (October 8), and British troops from Wavell's scanty forces occupied the island of Crete (October 30). The Mediterranean area was shaping up as a major theater of war.

NAVAL OPERATIONS IN THE MEDITERRANEAN, 1940

1940, July 9. Action off Calabria. Aggressive Admiral Cunningham carried the war into enemy waters. Cruising off the Straits of Messina with 3 battleships, an aircraft carrier, 5 light cruisers, and a number of destroyers, he fell in with Admiral **Angelo Campioni**'s squadron of 2 battleships, 6 heavy cruisers, 12 light cruisers, and destroyers, returning from troop convoy to Libya. Cunningham's immediate attack drove the Italians in flight for the Calabrian coast, with serious damage to a battleship and a cruiser. British injuries were negligible, despite the intervention of land-based Italian aviation. Ten days later, H.M. Australian light cruiser *Sydney,* with 4 destroyers, engaged 2 Italian light cruisers off the northwestern coast of Crete, sinking 1. Meanwhile, Malta—Britain's steppingstone for air between Egypt and Gibraltar—was being strengthened, and another battleship, a carrier, and 2 cruisers were added to Cunningham's command.

1940, November 11. Naval Air Assault on Taranto. Admiral Cunningham delivered a crushing attack from carrier H.M.S. *Illustrious* on the Italian naval base of Taranto. Three Italian battleships were left in a sinking condition, 2 cruisers badly damaged, and 2 fleet auxiliaries sunk. The British lost but 2 planes out of 21. The assault re-established British naval supremacy in the Mediterranean. However, Italian aircraft based on Sicily, on Sardinia, and on the African coast continued interfering with British water transport. Italian submarines played a very inefficient part in these operations.

OPERATIONS IN 1941

Battle of the Atlantic

THE SUBMARINE RAIDERS

The Wolf Packs. Under the direction of Admiral **Karl Doenitz,** German operations developed into the "wolf pack" pattern: groups of as many as 15 to 20 U-boats spread over the sea lanes approaching Britain. Any individual merchantmen were attacked at once. Convoys, however, were tracked by the discovering submarine until the pack could be assembled for several simultaneous assaults. Convoy losses mounted; by June, 1941, some 5.7 million tons of British shipping had been sunk, whereas British shipyards could only build 800,000 tons of replacements. When the British intensified their long-range aerial searches, and began to use land-based air escorts in the eastern Atlantic, the wolf packs simply moved out to mid-Atlantic, beyond operational range of aircraft based in Northern Ireland or Great Britain. British bombing reprisals against U-boat bases in Germany, Norway, and France were frustrated by construction of so-called "pens," great roofs of reinforced concrete protecting submarine berths and shore installations.

The German Long-Range Bombers. Working in close co-ordination with the wolf packs were German long-range bombers based in Norway and France. These were able to scour the sea lanes closer to Britain, while still staying beyond the range of RAF fighter planes. Convoys that had been harassed by the wolf packs in mid-ocean suffered further serious losses from these planes as they approached Britain.

1940, September. Introduction of the Escort Carrier. Britain's answer to the combined menace of U-boats and bombers was to develop constant fighter-plane protection for convoys by means of escort carriers. The first of these, H.M.S. *Audacity,* a merchant ship on which a flight deck was constructed, could carry 6 fighter planes. Working with destroyers and other surface warships, these planes somewhat reduced the wolf-pack menace in mid-ocean, and were able to drive off the bombers when the convoys approached the French coast. The *Audacity* was sunk in December, and U-boat sinkings began to mount again. But more escort carriers were being constructed for use in 1942.

THE SURFACE RAIDERS

1941, January–March. *Gneisenau* and *Scharnhorst*. These two battle cruisers under command of Vice-Admiral **Günther Lütjens** entered the North Atlantic. Five unescorted merchantmen were sunk, but the German efforts to find a convoy unescorted by British battleships were unsuccessful until March 18. Falling on a convoy just scattering from a submarine attack, the 2 German surface craft destroyed 16 vessels in a 2-day running chase, then fled for Brest as British battleships converged on the area. An RAF bombing attack found them there in harbor and so severely damaged them that they were out of action for several months.

1941, February–April. *Hipper*. Operating from Brest, the *Hipper* undertook a successful raid into the North Atlantic (February). Later she returned to Germany, slipping past British patrols between Iceland and Scotland.

Cruise of the Bismarck, May 18–28

1941, May 18. The *Bismarck* Leaves Gdynia. This giant new German battleship, largest and most powerful warship in the world at the time, in company with the new heavy cruiser *Prinz Eugen,* sailed to Bergenfjord.

1941, May 21. British Concentration. The *Bismarck* and *Prinz Eugen* were sighted in Bergenfjord by British reconnaissance planes. All available units of the Royal Navy—from Scapa Flow to Gibraltar—concentrated for their destruction.

1941, May 21. The *Bismarck* Puts to Sea. Admiral Lütjens took advantage of foggy weather; his 2 two-ship squadron sailed out, undetected by the British, heading for Denmark Strait.

1941, May 24. Battle of Denmark Strait. British cruisers sighted the German ships entering Denmark Strait (late May 23). Vice-Admiral **Launcelot Holland** in the battle cruiser H.M.S. *Hood,* with the new battleship *Prince of Wales,* intercepted them early next morning. Fire opened at 25,000-yard range. A 15-inch shell from the *Bismarck* penetrated the *Hood*'s vitals and the great ship blew up, taking all but 3 of her 1,500-man crew to the bottom with her. The *Bismarck*'s excellent gunnery then severely damaged the *Prince of Wales,* forcing her to turn out of the fight.

Despite damage to his own ship, Admiral Lütjens continued westward to the open sea. The damaged *Prince of Wales* and the light cruisers *Suffolk* and *Norfolk* trailed the German vessels, while other British warships gathered.

1941, May 24–26. The Chase. Lütjens turned east for Brest, ordering the *Prinz Eugen* to slip away. The British lost contact for more than a day, but a land-based patrol plane sighted the *Bismarck* again during the morning of May 26, 700 miles west of Brest.

1941, May 27–28. Death of the Bismarck. H.M. carrier *Ark Royal* successfully attacked to slow the German ship down and enable the battleships *Rodney* and *King George V* to catch up (May 27). That night a destroyer flotilla closed, inflicting further torpedo damage. Next morning the *Rodney* and *King George V* engaged the *Bismarck* in furious gun battle, finally silencing her. The great helpless, but still defiant, hulk resisted the British 14- and 16-inch shells. Finally, the cruiser *Dorsetshire*—just arrived—sent 2 torpedoes into the blazing *Bismarck* and sank her. Nearly 2,300 German sailors went down, including Admiral Lütjens. Only 110 survivors were picked up by the *Dorsetshire* and a destroyer before the arrival of a German U-boat prevented further rescue efforts.

AMERICAN INVOLVEMENT, 1941

Waning of Isolationism in America. Despite reluctance to become involved in the war, most Americans began to realize the danger to the Western Hemisphere and to the world if Hitler should be able to starve Britain into surrender. President Roosevelt's cautious but deliberate steps to provide all possible assistance to Britain, short of declaration of war, were approved by most of his people.

1941, March 11. Lend Lease Act. The terms of this act empowered the President to provide goods and services to nations whose defense he considered to be vital to the defense of the United States.

1941, April 10. Protection of Greenland. Fearing the possibility that Germany might try to establish a Western Hemisphere base in this Danish possession, President Roosevelt announced that Greenland would be under U.S. protection.

1941, July 7. American Troops to Iceland. This step permitted the garrison which Britain had placed there to be withdrawn for active operations against Germany. It also paved the way for the next planned step.

1941, August 9–12. Atlantic Conference. Roosevelt and Churchill met on American and British warships in Placentia Bay, Newfoundland. In the Atlantic Charter, they pledged their countries to preserve world freedom and to improve world conditions after the war (published August 14). At the same time Roosevelt announced that American warships would escort all North Atlantic convoys west of Iceland.

1941, September 16. Beginning of American Convoys. The U.S. thus became a quasi belligerent in the war, and British warships which had been patrolling and escorting convoys west of Iceland were now free to intensify the antisubmarine war in the eastern North Atlantic. Germany promptly responded to this American quasi belligerency by attacking American warships on convoy duty. Two destroyers (U.S.S. *Kearney* and *Reuben James*) were torpedoed; the *Kearney* limped to safety, the *Reuben James* was sunk (October 17, October 31).

1941, December 24. St. Pierre and Miquelon. Free French Admiral Muselier, with a cockleboat squadron, seized the islands off the Canadian coast, depriving the U-boats of a potential base, but causing some embarrassment to the U.S. government, which was keeping a tenuous link with Vichy.

Operations in the Mediterranean Area, 1941

WAVELL'S OFFENSIVES IN NORTH AND EAST AFRICA

1941, January 1–February 7. Campaign in Cyrenaica. The Western Desert Force resumed the offensive with the opening of the new year. **Bardia** was carried by assault (January 5) after an intensive naval bombardment, while the 7th Armored Division ("The Desert Rats") isolated Tobruk. Land assault against the southern face of **Tobruk**'s perimeter, accompanied by intensive air and naval bombardment, brought capitulation (January 22). The 7th Armored Division raced west across the desert bulge of Cyrenaica to cut off the remaining Italian troops, while the main British force pressed on along the coast road. The British armor closed the trap at **Beda Fomm,** on the Gulf of Sirte (February 5). Two days later, after an abortive effort to break through, General **Bergonzoli**'s demoralized Italians surrendered unconditionally.

COMMENT. *In two months' time, O'Connor's Western Desert Force had advanced 500 miles, destroyed 9 Italian divisions, and taken 130,000 prisoners, 400 tanks, and 1,290 guns. At no time did O'Connor employ more than 2 infantry divisions at once, though the "Desert Rats" were engaged throughout the operation. British casualties amounted to 500 killed and 1,373 wounded. It was a remarkable demonstration of fire and movement, aided by effective naval and air support, against an inept passive defense greatly superior in numbers.*

1941, January. British Plans against Italian East Africa. Simultaneously Wavell launched a pincers offensive against the Duke of Aosta's 110,000 troops in Ethiopia and Italian Somaliland. Lieutenant General **William Platt** with 2 South African divisions and indigenous troops was to strike east from Khartoum in the Sudan; Lieutenant General Sir **Alan A. Cunningham** in Kenya, with 3 South African

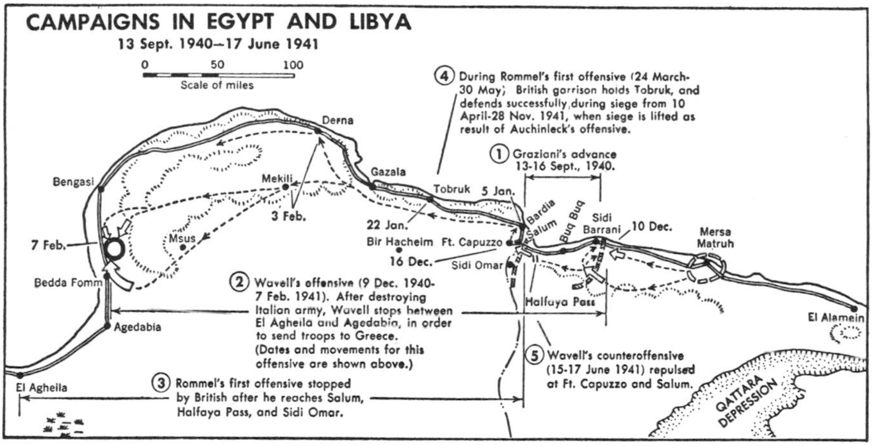

divisions and a conglomeration of indigenous Free French forces, would move northeast. The combined forces totaled some 70,000 men.

1941, January 19–April 20. Invasion of Ethiopia and Eritrea. Platt crossed the frontier (January 19). He caught up with and defeated Italian General **Frusci**'s force at **Agordat** (January 31). He pursued to the defended defile of **Keren,** and broke through after severe fighting (March 3). Asmara and its seaport Massawa were occupied (April 1). Turning south, the British column now faced Amba Alagi, a 1,000-foot conical mountain, where Frusci's command planned a stand.

1941, January 24–March 30. Invasion of Somaliland and Ethiopia. Cunningham moved into Italian Somaliland (January 24), meeting little resistance. Occupying Mogadiscio on the Indian Ocean (February 25), he captured a huge supply depot of gasoline. The Italians began evacuating Somaliland. Reaching Jijiga (March 17), Cunningham pushed on to Harar (March 25).

1941, April 4. Capture of Addis Ababa. Turning southwest, Cunningham occupied the Ethiopian capital while the Duke of Aosta hurriedly retired northward. In an amazing advance of more than 1,000 miles, Cunningham had averaged 35 miles per day, captured 50,000 prisoners, and gained 360,000 square miles of enemy-held terrain at a cost of 135 men killed, 310 wounded, 52 missing, and 4 captured. He now moved north, occupying Dessie, 250 miles from Addis Ababa (April 20), after a brush at the **Combolcia Pass** with the Italian rear guard. Aosta's demoralized forces joined Frusci's at Amba Alagi.

1941, May 5. Return of Emperor Haile Selassie to Ethiopia.

1941, May 18. Italian Capitulation. Aosta surrendered as Platt and Cunningham pressed in.

COMMENT. *Another daring, fast-moving British offensive had resulted in clear-cut victory. As in Libya, the Italian high command had proven to be inept. Wavell's daring strategy securely bolted his back door, eliminating any future threat to the Suez Canal from East Africa, and secured the Red Sea as an Allied supply channel.*

GERMANY REDRESSES THE MEDITERRANEAN BALANCE

1941, January–March. Appearance of the Luftwaffe. Hitler, to bolster Mussolini, sent the Luftwaffe's Air Corps X (500 planes) from Norway to Sicily (January). By the end of February, the long-range German bombers barred use of the port of Benghazi as a base for Wavell's Desert Force. The necessity to send most of his combat troops to Greece and Crete (see p. 1073) had by this time reduced this force to 1 armored division, part of an infantry division, and a motorized brigade.

1941, March. Arrival of Rommel. Hitler sent General Rommel with his Panzer Afrika Korps to Tripolitania, charged with command of Axis operations against Egypt and the Suez Canal. (Titular commander, Italian General **Ettori Bastico,** was a mere figurehead.)

1941, March 24–May 30. Rommel's First Offensive. With the 21st Panzer Division and 2 Italian divisions—1 armored and 1 motorized—Rommel drove back the British covering force at **El Agheila** (March 24), then branched out in reverse of the original British offensive—the Italian column following the coast through Benghazi on Derna, the 21st Panzer cutting across the desert toward Tobruk. The British 2nd Armored Division, attempting to delay, was split; 1 brigade, forced into Derna because of gas shortage, was captured (April 6). Next day, most of the remainder of the division was surrounded and captured. The 9th Australian Division reached Tobruk. Brilliant General O'Connor, reconnoitering on the Barce-Derna road, was captured by a German patrol (April 17).

1941, April–December. Defense of Tobruk. Wavell determined to hold Tobruk at all costs—to deprive Rommel of a base port to support further advance into Egypt, and to threaten the Italo-German flank. By sea he threw in the 7th Australian Division and some tanks to reinforce the Tobruk garrison. Rommel (April 10) mounted an ill-prepared assault and was thrown back after a 3-day attack. Advancing part of his force to the Sollum escarpment east of Tobruk, Rommel invested the fortress, while overhauling his tanks and bringing up reinforcements. His supply problem was now serious, thanks to Wavell's decision to hold Tobruk and to the aggressive operations of the Royal Navy, which took continuous toll of Axis surface transport shuttling between Italy and Tripolitania.

1941, June 15–17. Wavell's Counteroffensive. Forced by political pressure from home to attempt the relief of Tobruk, Wavell launched a shoestring offensive against the Sollum-Halfaya passes held by Rommel—1 infantry division and an armored division participated.. Split into 6 semi-independent task forces and committed piecemeal, the British attack was repulsed by Rommel after some minor successes.

1941, July 1. Wavell Superseded. General Sir **Claude Auchinleck** assumed the Middle East Command. General Wavell was transferred to India.

COMMENT. *Fifty-eight-year-old Wavell, a master of offensive-defensive strategy, was in effect made a scapegoat for the disastrous British intervention in Greece (see below), which had been added to his already monumental task of holding the Middle East for Britain.*

1941, July–October. Opposing Preparations. The Western Desert Force, renamed the Eighth Army, with General Alan Cunningham in command, was reinforced to 7 divisions and 700 tanks and prepared for the offensive. The Desert Air Force was built up to 1,000 planes. Meanwhile Rommel was regrouping the Afrika Korps, which now comprised the 15th and 21st Panzer Divisions and the understrength

90th and 164th Light Infantry Divisions, and 6 weak Italian divisions. Bardia, Sollum, Halfaya, and Sidi Omar were organized into first-line defenses as springboards for invading Egypt. He had 260 German and 154 Italian tanks, and was supported by 120 German and 200 Italian planes.

1941, November 18–December 20. Auchinleck's Offensive. Cunningham's Eighth Army in surprise attack struck northwest from its base at Mersa Matruh. Its new American "Stuart" light tanks sought Rommel's army south of Tobruk, while the main force swung north to isolate the Italo-German Sollum-Bardia defensive zone. In a series of unco-ordinated desert tank battles around **Sidi-Rezegh** (November 19–22), the British were checked, while a sortie from Tobruk was repulsed; seemingly, the British offensive was stalled. Rommel, with reinforced air support, gathered all available tanks and struck over the frontier into the British rear areas. Near panic resulted, and Cunningham contemplated withdrawal. But Auchinleck insisted on a stand. Rommel's momentum was checked, and junction between the Tobruk garrison and a New Zealand division then split the Afrika Korps. The surrounded Germans succeeded in breaking out, and Rommel then withdrew to the west and south of Tobruk (December 7–8). Auchinleck, having retrieved the situation, replaced Cunningham by General **N. M. Ritchie.** Under continued British pressure, Rommel then withdrew his mobile forces all the way back to his original position at El Agheila (December 28–30). The Italo-German garrisons at Bardia and Halfaya were captured (January 2–17, 1942). Italo-German losses were 24,500 killed and wounded and 36,500 prisoners. British losses were about 18,000 in all. But Rommel had also lost 386 tanks and 850 aircraft.

COMMENT. *General Auchinleck's determination had for the moment removed a most serious threat to the Suez Canal and the British Empire itself. Rommel was back where he had started.*

IRAQ AND SYRIA

1941, May. Operations in Iraq. Nazi-stimulated outbreaks in both countries added to General Wavell's troubles in the Middle East. **Rashid Ali,** Prime Minister of Iraq, attacked British garrisons at **Basra** and **Habbaniya** (May 2), threatening the Iraqi oil preserves essential to the Allied war effort. At the same time Hitler sent in munitions, and finally an Italo-German air base was established at Mosul. British reinforcements from India and from Wavell's scanty Palestine garrison—already occupied in Syria (see below)—hurriedly assembled, took the offensive. RAF planes struck the Mosul air base, while ground troops moved on Baghdad. Rashid Ali fled the country, Baghdad was occupied (May 30), and stability was re-established.

1941, June–July. Operations in Syria. Meanwhile the 35,000 pro-German Vichy French forces in Syria, directed by German military and political advisers, threatened from the north. At Churchill's order, Wavell scraped together a 20,000-man force and invaded Syria from Palestine and Iraq (June 8). Free French troops under Catroux's command played an important part in the expedition. Damascus was soon captured (June 21). This caused the surrender of General **Henri Dentz,** French commander in Syria (July 12). Syria and the Lebanon were transferred to Free French control, most of the Vichy French troops volunteering to join Catroux's command.

Operations in the Balkans, 1941

1941, February–March. German Pressure on Yugoslavia. Hitler, planning an invasion of Russia in the summer of 1941, determined to secure his southern flank by first gaining control of Yugoslavia. (Hungary and Rumania were already German satellites.) Under intense diplomatic pressure and threats of force, Yugoslavia's Prince Regent **Paul** reluctantly agreed to join the Axis alliance (March 25).

1941, March 7–27. Arrival of British Troops in Greece. In anticipation of German intervention in the Balkans, and possibly against Greece, the British government had ordered Wavell to send his best Middle East Command troops to Greece. This 4-division force of 57,000 men was commanded by General Maitland Wilson.

YUGOSLAVIA

1941, March 27. Coup d'État. Patriotic anti-German elements in the Yugoslav

Army, encouraged by the presence of British forces in Greece, overthrew Prince Paul, established a new government, and rejected the Axis alliance.

1941, March 27–April 6. German Preparations. Hitler, infuriated by events in Yugoslavia, which he felt resulted from the failure of Italy's invasion of Greece, ordered his military staff to mount an immediate attack against Yugoslavia and Greece. The German planners did so in 10 days—an amazing demonstration of military efficiency. Marshal **List**'s Twelfth Army and Kleist's First Panzer Group (both in Hungary and Rumania preparatory to the Russian invasion) were shifted to southwestern Rumania and Bulgaria, opposite the Yugoslav and Greek borders.

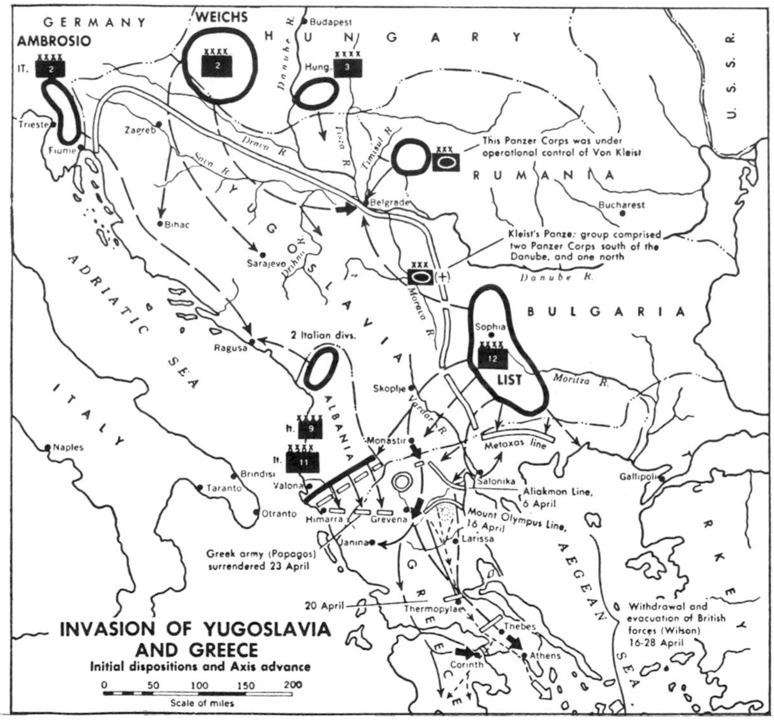

INVASION OF YUGOSLAVIA AND GREECE
Initial dispositions and Axis advance

The hurriedly organized Second Army was assembled in Austria and Hungary opposite northern Yugoslavia. The Italian Second Army, from Trieste, and the Hungarian Third Army were to assist.

1941, April 6–17. Invasion of Yugoslavia. After bombing that concentrated on Belgrade, paralyzing the Yugoslav high command, German armored and infantry forces slashed into the country from north, east, and southeast. Efforts to mobilize the million-man Yugoslav Army were never completed. Zagreb fell (April 10), Belgrade (April 12) and Sarajevo (April 15). Resistance ended in unconditional surrender (April 17). German losses totaled 558 men. Yugoslav losses are unknown; more than 300,000 were captured, perhaps 100,000 killed and wounded.

1941, May–December. Yugoslav Resistance Movements. Many Yugoslav officers and soldiers, refusing to surrender, fled to mountain hideouts from which they harassed the Germans. The principal leader of these refugees, called **Cetnici** (Chetnicks), was Serbian Colonel **Draza Mihailovic.** One of his principal Montenegrin subordinates was Major **Aleksa J. Dujovic.** About the same time, the leader of the Yugoslav Communist Party, **Josip Broz**—known to his followers as **Tito**—established the National Liberation (or Partisan) Movement, operating then in areas other than Serbia and Montenegro. Partisans and Chetnicks hated each other as much as they did the Germans. By the end of the year a bitter, bloody three-way war was raging in Yugoslavia.

GREECE

1941, April 6–9. Invasion of Greece. Simultaneously with the Yugoslav invasion, other elements of List's army smashed against Greece's fortified Metaxas Line, east of the Struma River, where Papagos mistakenly ordered his Second Army to hold. Penetrating quickly, the German spearheads reached the sea at Salonika (April 9). The Second Army, cut off, surrendered. The German Twelfth Army pressed westward toward the British, just arriving and preparing defensive positions between Mt. Olympus and Salonika. Kleist's armored group, driving south from Skoplje, struck through the Monastir Gap, held by a Greek division protecting the British left. The Greeks crumbled; after severe fighting, Wilson withdrew to new positions north of Mt. Olympus.

1941, April 12–20. Battle for Central Greece. German Spearheads forced their way through the rugged mountains of northern Greece between the British and the Greek First Army, now belatedly retreating from Albania. Gallant Papagos, convinced that success was impossible, recommended to Wilson that the British evacuate while he delayed the Germans as long as possible. Meanwhile, Wilson was forced to abandon his Mt. Olympus position, withdrawing to Thermopylae.

1941, April 21–27. Conquest of Greece. Assailed from north, east, and south, the Greek Army, after desperate resistance, was forced to surrender (April 23). Wilson abandoned Thermopylae (April 24), pulling back into the Peloponnesus, as Royal Navy warships, braving violent Luftwaffe attacks, began to move in to pick up British troops by night at eastern Greek ports. A German airborne drop at Corinth (April 26) almost closed the withdrawal route, but Wilson fought his way through with most of his remaining troops. British evacuation was completed on April 27, 43,000 troops being rescued, but all heavy equipment was abandoned. German losses in Greece were slightly over 4,500 men; the British had 11,840 casualties. Greek killed and wounded were more than 70,000; 270,000 were captured.

COMMENT. *The German operations in Yugoslavia and Greece were models of precision and efficiency, marked by bold use of tanks over terrain supposedly impassable to armor.*

CRETE

1941, April 27–May 10. Preparations. About 15,500 of the British troops evacuated from Greece were landed on Crete, expected to be the next German objective. There, joined by 12,000 reinforcements from Egypt and assisted by the 14,000-man Greek garrison, they feverishly prepared the island for defense, despite severe shortages in artillery and other equipment. In command was New Zealand Major General **Bernard C. Freyberg.** The small RAF fighter force on the island was soon forced to withdraw by increasingly severe German air raids, which daily mounted in intensity. In southern Greece, the German XI Airborne Corps, commanded by Lieutenant General **Kurt Student,** prepared for an airborne assault on the island.

1941, May 20–28. The Assault. Following heavy aerial bombardment, units of the German 7th Parachute Division began landing near the principal airports of Maleme, Rethymnon, and Herakleion. The alert defenders inflicted heavy casualties, and by nightfall still controlled the fields, though a few German units had established themselves near Maleme (May 20). Regardless of casualties, the remainder of the 7th Division dropped the next day and gained control of part of Maleme airfield. Student immediately began to send in elements of the 5th Mountain Division by plane. Most of the planes were destroyed, but enough crash-landed safely to permit the determined Germans to hold the field. The most intensive fighting continued in the following days, as German reinforcements continued to come in by plane. Two efforts to send reinforcements by sea were repulsed, with heavy casualties, by the Royal Navy (May 21–22). The airborne elements, however, with very effective air support, were able to force the British and Greeks back. Freyberg was finally forced to withdraw to the south coast (May 28).

1941, May 28–31. Conquest of Crete. Under heavy German pressure, most of the defenders withdrew to Sfakia, whence they were evacuated by the Royal Navy. Remaining elements, cut off by the Germans, were forced to surrender (May 31). British casualties were 17,325 (including 2,011 naval losses and 11,835 prisoners). The **Germans admitted 5,670 casualties, mostly in the 7th Division; this does not include losses in the seaborne convoys.**

COMMENT. *This was the first major airborne assault in history; despite its success, Hitler was so shocked by the losses that he never again ordered a comparable airborne operation.*

NAVAL OPERATIONS IN THE MEDITERRANEAN, 1941

1941, February 9. Surface Raid on North Italy. Daringly, British Admiral Somerville (February 9) with 2 battleships, a carrier, and a cruiser from the Gibraltar naval base swept the northeastern coast of Italy, bombarding Genoa and other ports.

1941, February–March. German Air Intervention. German planes sent to Sicily by Hitler (see p. 1072) established aerial superiority over the central Mediterranean, disrupting Allied surface and air activities. Malta was bombarded incessantly. Shipping from England had to be rerouted via the long Cape of Good Hope route into the Indian Ocean and the Red Sea. The carrier H.M.S. *Illustrious* was badly damaged and a cruiser was sunk.

1941, March 26–27. Sortie of the Italian Fleet. British troop movements from Egypt to Greece led Italian Admiral **Angelo Iachino** to attempt to intercept. The Italian fleet—3 battleships, 8 cruisers, and a number of destroyers and supporting craft—covered by Italian and German air, was divided into 3 detachments. Admiral Cunningham, learning (March 27) that the Italians were threatening several large convoys, ordered the transports back to Egypt and hurriedly steamed to meet the threat. He had 3 battleships, 1 carrier, 4 cruisers, and more than a dozen destroyers.

1941, March 28. Battle of Cape Matapan. Harassed by Cunningham's cruiser-carrier force, the Italians turned away. The battleship *Vittorio Veneto* and heavy cruiser *Pola* were damaged, however, and slowed down. After dark, Admiral Iachino sent 2 cruisers and 4 destroyers back to their assistance. At 10 P.M., Cunningham's pursuing battleship force fell in with the *Pola* and the rescuing Italian vessels, and in surprise attack sank them all. The injured *Vittorio Veneto* and the remainder of the Italian fleet escaped in the darkness. One British cruiser was slightly damaged and 1 airplane lost. From this time to the end of the war, Italian surface naval strength ceased to be an important factor; it remained mostly in port at La Spezia.

1941, April 26–June 1. Evacuation of Greece and Crete. Hitler's conquest of Greece and occupation of Crete (see p. 1075) placed an almost insuperable task on Admiral Cunningham's Mediterranean command: evacuating British troops by sea first from Greece and then from Crete. British surface craft, without air support, were subject to full-scale, determined, and incessant attack by Luftwaffe planes from Italy and Thessaly.

1941, April 26–30. Evacuation from Greece. Using all available shipping and operating under cover of darkness, the Royal Navy lifted some 43,000 of General Wilson's ill-fated Grecian expedition from the Piraeus and from Peloponnesian beaches. Some of the evacuated troops were landed on Crete. Two destroyers and 24 other vessels were lost to German air attacks, and severe damage was inflicted on other British ships.

1941, May 21–June 1. Operations off Crete. A German amphibious operation (May 21–23) to reinforce the airborne assault on Crete met complete disaster. Cunningham's war vessels fell on the small craft attempting to shuttle troops from Greece, sinking most of them. Some 5,000 German troops were lost. Continuous air attacks harassed the British ships in the waters around Crete, sinking 2 cruisers and a destroyer, and damaging 2 battleships and 2 more cruisers. Despite these losses, Cunningham's ships dared the impossible to evacuate more than 15,000 of General Freyberg's Cretan command (May 28 and 31). During this period, 4 cruisers and 6 destroyers were sunk, and 1 carrier and 3 battleships so severely damaged they would be out of action for some time. British naval casualties included 2,000 men killed.

1941, June–December. Other Operations. Arrival of 25 German U-boats in the Mediterranean further complicated the British naval situation. Cunningham's fleet, already crippled by its Greco-Cretan operations, and charged with assuring surface supply to Malta, was put on the defensive. Italian light craft attempted a raid on the Valetta harbor, but were repulsed by British coastal artillery (July). Also, German air attacks on Malta were intensified, for Malta—the "unsinkable aircraft carrier"—was severely punishing German trans-Mediterranean supply to Rommel. The German reinforcements soon made themselves felt. The *Ark Royal,* Cunningham's 1 aircraft carrier in service, was sunk while on escort duty—a disastrous loss (November).

1941, December 19. British Naval Disasters. Three Italian "human torpedo" teams—midget submarines guided by 2 men each—boldly entered Alexandria Harbor and further damaged the battleships *Queen Elizabeth* and *Valiant,* putting them completely out of action for many months. The gallant Italians escaped. That same day, a task force of 3 British cruisers and a destroyer met disaster in a mine field. One cruiser and the destroyer were sunk and the other vessels crippled for months. On Christmas Day, the battleship H.M.S. *Barham,* Cunningham's 1 remaining capital ship, was torpedoed by German submarine *U-331* and sunk with heavy loss of life. Shortly afterward, another British cruiser was torpedoed.

COMMENT. *At year's end Cunningham's fleet, reduced to 3 cruisers and a handful of destroyers, was seemingly impotent. Supply to Rommel was unimpeded. One bold move by the Italian Navy could have swept British sea power from the Mediterranean. But the move never came. Cunningham kept his handful of warships constantly and aggressively at sea and British counterintelligence blacked-out news of the damage to the battleships at Alexandria.*

Invasion of Russia, 1941

German Plans. Hitler considered the dismemberment of Russia as the final step essential to achieving his *Lebensraum* dreams (see p. 1035). Planning for an attack on the U.S.S.R., therefore, began as soon as France was conquered. Time was of the essence, since it was evident that Stalin planned westward expansion, both in the north—Finland—and in the south—Turkey and the Dardanelles. Formal planning began in December, 1940, and troops were shifted to the eastern frontier. Originally set for May 15, 1941, the invasion timetable was seriously disarranged by the necessity for the Balkan campaigns to clear the German southern flank.

In Operation "Barbarossa," Rundstedt's Army Group South—4 armies (1 Rumanian) and Kleist's First Panzer Group—was to drive on Kiev and the Dnieper Valley to envelop and destroy all Russian forces between the Pripet Marshes and the Black Sea. Bock's Army Group Center—2 armies and two Panzer groups (Guderian's Second and Hoth's Third)—was to follow the traditional invasion path: Warsaw-Smolensk-Moscow. Its armored pincers were to meet on the upper Dnieper, then capture Moscow. Leeb's Army Group North—2 armies and Hoeppner's Fourth Panzer Group—was to swing northeast toward Leningrad, pinning the Russians in its zone against the Baltic Sea. Finland allied itself with Germany, and Mannerheim's Finnish army group was to occupy the Karelian Isthmus–Lake Onega front, threatening Leningrad from the north, while still farther north, German General Falkenhorst's Norway Army was to cut the Russians' Murmansk-Leningrad supply line. In all, 162 divisions of ground troops—approximately 3 million men—were involved, 200,000 of them from satellite nations. Hitler envisioned a typical blitzkrieg campaign of not more than 4 months' duration.

Russian Plans. Russian forces were heavily concentrated along the western frontier in the annexed regions of Poland, Bessarabia, and the Baltic States. South of the Pripet Marshes lay Marshal **Semën M. Budënny**'s Southwest Front (Army

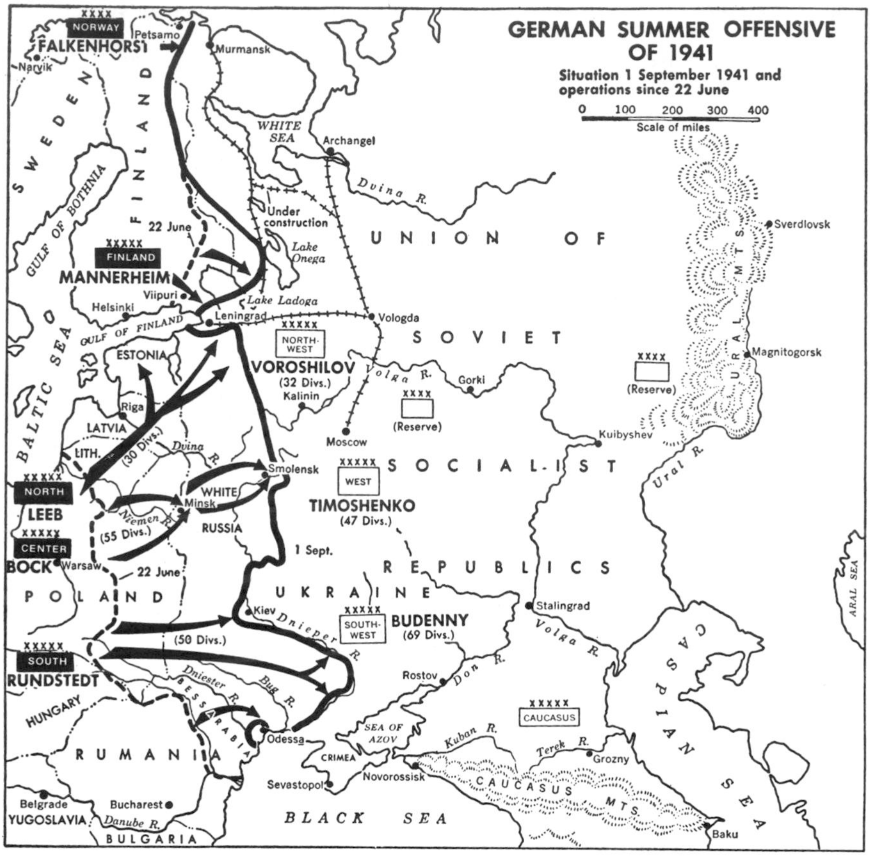

Group), north of the Marshes and up to the Lithuanian border was Marshal **Semën K. Timoshenko**'s Western Front, and Marshal **Kliment Voroshilov**'s Northwest Front was in the Baltic countries. Russian mobilized strength approximated 3 million on the western front, with another million scattered elsewhere. Reserves were available in great quantity. Russian matériel—tanks, cannon, and planes—was plentiful, but inferior in quality to German equipment.

1941, June 22–July 10. The Invasion. Simultaneously, along a 2,000-mile front, the onslaught started at 3 A.M. with the customary preliminary air bombardment. Though the Russians expected an invasion, tactical surprise was complete. Center Army Group advanced spectacularly. Its armored pincers closed on **Minsk** by mid-July, enfolding 290,000 prisoners, 2,500 tanks, and 1,400 guns, then opened in another scoop as the Panzers crossed the Dnieper.

1941, July 10–19. Smolensk. Again the trap snapped, bagging an additional 100,000 prisoners, 2,000 tanks, and 1,900 guns. The remnants of Timoshenko's Western Front recoiled in disorder. One of Bock's spearheads reached Beloj, less than 200 miles west of Moscow. But Rundstedt's Army Group South had made slower progress, while difficult terrain and some errors slowed down Leeb's group on the north. The German supply system was strained to the breaking point by the immense distances, slowing the advance. Tanks and other vehicles were showing the strain of terrific pace and long marches. In all probability, however, these things would not have saved Moscow from the still fast-moving German Army Group Center had Hitler himself not intervened to check its momentum.

1941, July 19–August 21. Hitler's Changes. To bolster the slower-moving flank armies, Hitler detached both Panzer groups and 1 army away from the Army Group Center, despite the vigorous protests of his field commanders. Guderian's Second Panzer Group and the Second Army (**Maximilian von Weichs**) were to support Rundstedt's Army Group South, which by this time had almost reached Kiev. Hoth's Third Panzer Group was to join Army Group North. The immediate results of this unexpected change were favorable.

1941, August 21–September 26. The Kiev "Pocket." Guderian's Panzers from the north, slicing around the eastern edges of the Pripet Marshes, met Kleist's Panzers from the south, to press 5 Russian armies inside the great bend of the Dnieper, near Kiev. German infantry sealed the trap. A period of confused fighting followed as some Russian units battled to break out; others of Buděnny's army group sought to rescue them. Kiev itself fell (September 19), and finally some 665,000 Russian troops surrendered. Buděnny's Southwest Group seemed to have been completely shattered. Meanwhile, on the far southern flank, the Germans reached the Crimean Peninsula, where General **Erich von Manstein**'s newly formed Eleventh Army began a drive for Sevastopol (October). By this time the Luftwaffe had destroyed 4,500 Russian planes, while losing less than 2,000.

1941, October–November. Time, Space, and "General Mud." Rundstedt reached the Don (October 15), threatening Rostov and Kharkov. Leeb slowly progressed toward Leningrad, which was invested (early October). But the Finnish Army, after reaching the original national boundaries, refused to press farther toward Leningrad, and in the far north Falkenhorst, after initial gains, bogged down in the tundra. The Murmansk-Leningrad supply line, though partly disrupted, was never closed entirely. Hitler, meanwhile, had

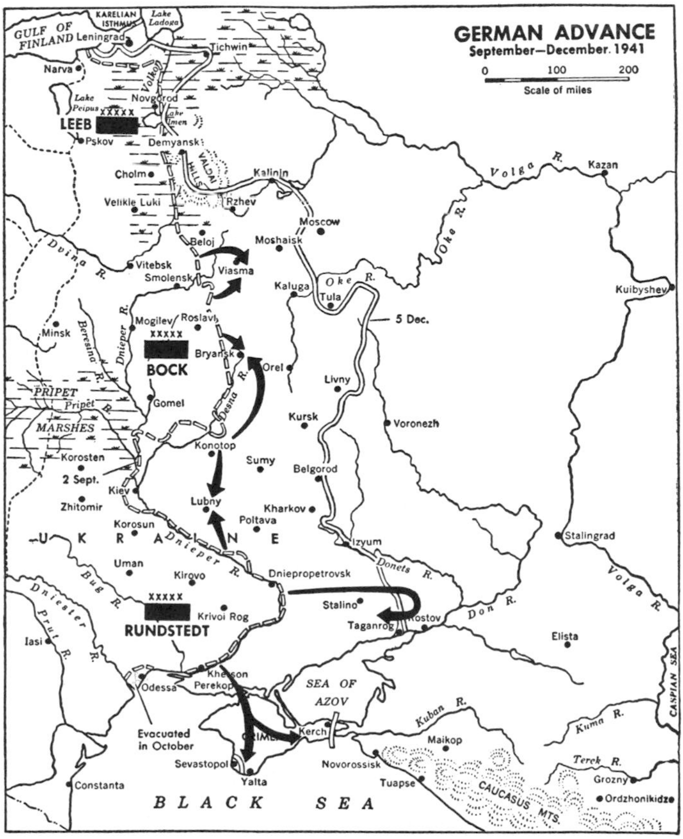

changed plans again and ordered an extreme effort against Moscow. Bock's Army Group Center, reinforced again by the Panzers and Luftwaffe elements taken from it to bolster the flanks, renewed its penetration, winning another tremendous victory at **Vyazma** (September 30–October 7), capturing more than 650,000 prisoners. Although rain now slowed the advance, the drive continued and reached Mozhaisk—40 miles from the Soviet capital (October 20). But the German armies were reaching the limit of their endurance. Armored units were reduced to 50 per cent of their original combat efficiency; infantry divisions were scarcely in better shape. Autumn rains turned the roads into quagmires, and then the fierce Russian winter set in.

1941, November–December. Defense of Moscow. Russian resistance had stiffened. Budënny had been relieved, Timoshenko taking his command, and a newcomer—Marshal **Georgi K. Zhukov**—headed the central Russian forces barring the way to Moscow. These were mostly regular troops assembled from interior and eastern Russia. The losses elsewhere had been made good by newly mobilized but trained reserves, far inferior in quality to the Germans, but fresh, untired, and grimly determined. In the south a Russian counterattack drove Rundstedt's spearheads out of **Rostov** (November 15), and Rundstedt resigned (just as Hitler relieved him), Reichenau taking his place (December 1). Kluge, now commanding the German Army Group Center, reached to within 25 miles of Moscow, and German patrols reached the suburbs in sight of the Kremlin. The Russian government had moved to Kiubyshev. But temperatures had fallen to −40° F. The offensive ground to a halt all along the line. Hitler, infuriated, relieved Brauchitsch, Leeb, and other generals, and took personal command, by radio from Berlin.

COMMENT. *Hitler's decision virtually ruined the famed German General Staff (the Army Supreme Command, or Oberkommando des Heeres, or OKH). He kept General Franz Halder as Chief of Staff of OKH, but supervised it personally, limiting its responsibility to the Eastern Front. His own personal staff (Armed Forces Supreme Command, or Oberkommando der Wehrmacht, or OKW) was augmented and, under Field Marshal* **Wilhelm Keitel** *as Chief of Staff, directed operations in Western Europe and Africa. Thus Hitler had 2 separate general staffs, united only by his personal direction.*

1941, December 6. Russian Counteroffensive. Massively reinforced by 100 fresh divisions, by the year's end the Russian armies were driving into the German armies at Kalinin, north of Moscow; at Tula, south of it; and at Izyum in the Ukraine. Russian troops retook **Kalinin** (December 15) and **Kaluga** (December 26–30) despite desperate and skillful German resistance. As the year ended the stunned and frozen Germans were still yielding ground.

COMMENT. *Between July and November, Hitler's armies had accomplished one of the greatest sustained offensives in military history. About 3 million casualties had been inflicted on the Russians (half of these prisoners), but German losses had also been tremendous—some 800,000. Moreover, the Russian armies had not been destroyed; despite tremendous losses in men and matériel, space had been successfully traded for time. Time was what the Germans lacked, and space consumed their resources. Hitler's offensive was predicated upon quick annihilation of his enemy before the winter set in. No preparations had been made for a winter campaign. Soldiers were freezing to death in summer uniforms; tanks and trucks were immobilized as crankcases froze. German ignorance of Russian capabilities was colossal. Hitler's own actions—the three weeks' delay to accomplish the Balkan sideshow, and his subsequent shifts of objectives when Moscow was almost within his grasp—combined to further handicap his worn generals and armies. Meanwhile, with most of Russia's industrial area overrun or embattled, it was obvious to Britain and the United States that massive assistance in weapons, ammunition, and all kinds of military equipment would be essential to keep Russia in the war against Germany. British convoys to Murmansk started in August. U.S. Lend Lease to Russia was approved (November 6) a month before America became a full belligerent.*

United States Entry into the War, 1941–1942

1941, December 7. Pearl Harbor. Japan's attack on the U.S. base in Hawaii (see p.

1127) was followed by U.S. declaration of war (December 8).

1941, December 11. Germany and Italy Declare War on the U.S.

1941, December. U.S. Mobilization. Congress passed a $10-billion appropriation for defense and for Lend Lease aid (December 15), and 4 days later extended the legal age bracket for compulsory military service to include men from 20 to 44.

1941, December 22–1942, January 14. Arcadia Conference. Prime Minister Churchill and President Roosevelt met in Washington with their senior military advisers who were officially designated as the Combined Chiefs of Staff (CCS). The new CCS began to plan and direct the Allied war effort under the two civilian leaders on February 6. Basic strategy for conducting global war was agreed: priority of effort was to be given to defeating the Western Axis; Japan was to be checked, but her defeat was to be sought only after Germany had been disposed of. Immediate and full cooperation between Britain and the U.S. in prosecuting the war followed, predicated upon the necessity for unity of command in each theater of war.

1942, July 24. Adm. W. D. Leahy, former Chief of Naval Operations, was appointed Chairman, Joint Chiefs of Staff which assured a balance of Army and Naval Officers on the Joint Chiefs of Staff.

OPERATIONS IN 1942

Battle of the Atlantic

1942, January. German Operations against Allied Supply Routes. Immediately upon the entry of the U.S. into the war, German naval efforts concentrated on barring the vital sea lanes to Allied supply. While 64 U-boats went into the Atlantic to carry the war to the American coast, German surface warships gathered along the Norwegian coast to assist the submarine-Luftwaffe blockade of the only remaining sea route to Russia—via Murmansk—from England and the U.S., an essential logistical pipe line if the U.S.S.R. were to be kept in the war. The great new battleship *Tirpitz* (sister ship to the *Bismarck*) went to Trondheim Fjord (January), to be followed later by several other warships. The German vessels at Brest were ordered home, and U-boat construction was intensified.

1942, January–April. The American Coast. The U-boats, supplied by "milch cows"—large cargo- and fuel-carrying submarines—which enabled them to operate for indefinite periods, at first found rich pickings. The U.S. Navy was not yet geared for convoy operations. Hapless merchantmen crowding the coastal sea lanes, silhouetted at night by the glare of lights from coastal ports and resorts, became easy prey. Some 80 merchant ships were destroyed in the first 4 months of 1942.

1942, February 11–13. Run-by in the Channel. The battle cruisers *Scharnhorst* and *Gneisenau* and the heavy cruiser *Prinz Eugen,* under Vice-Admiral **Otto Ciliax,** with destroyer escort and Luftwaffe air cover, daringly swept through heavy fog from Brest through the English Channel into the North Sea despite belated British air and surface efforts to stop them.

1942, February–July. Mounting Losses on the Murmansk Run. Allied convoys to Murmansk (and in summer to Archangel) assembled off Iceland and thence moved eastward past North Cape. Despite strenuous efforts to protect them, German U-boats, surface craft, and land-based aviation from Norway took a grievous toll. Out of 39 convoys—533 ships—participating in 1941–1942, 69 vessels were lost, most during the spring of 1941. The most disastrous trip was that of convoy PQ-17 (June–July); 23 of 37 merchant ships in the convoy were sunk by German submarine, air, and surface attackers, which included the battleship *Tirpitz,* pocket battleship *Scheer,* and heavy cruiser *Hipper.*

1942, May–August. Surface-Submarine Contest off America's Coasts. As air-sea protection—Army, Navy, and Coast Guard—improved, U-boat losses mounted. So the U-boats transferred their operations to the Caribbean, intercepting oil tankers and bauxite carriers from South and Central American ports, and also preying on Panama Canal traffic. The submarines clustered across the Halifax-Iceland-Londonderry run; their operations extended across the South Atlantic to the Cape of Good Hope.

1942, August–December. The Balance Begins to Shift. The German submarine attacks were intensified, but so were Allied countermeasures. In all, Allied merchant losses in the Atlantic and the Arctic

Oceans in 1942 amounted to 1,027,000 tons. But by year's end, some 85 U-boats had been sunk. The menace had not been reduced, but the Battle of the Atlantic was no longer a clear-cut German victory. Also the graph of new American ship construction—both naval and merchant—was coming near to balance with the losses. Meanwhile the American war effort flowed overseas in increasing volume.

Around the Periphery of Fortress Europe

Strategy, Build-up, and Controversy. Anglo-American planning recognized the necessity of keeping Russia in the war by opening a second front. The British Isles would be the springboard, but beyond that the strategic concepts of British and American planners differed widely. The U.S. Chiefs of Staff desired the earliest possible invasion of Western Europe; the British Chiefs of Staff opposed this, fearing failure by premature blows against the efficient German war machine. Churchill believed in attacking the Axis through the "soft underbelly" of the Mediterranean basin. While the planners argued, American strength in the British Isles built up as the convoy system went into high gear. Air and ground troops began moving over in large numbers by mid-1942, and the first American strategic bombing operation began in a small way with the bombing of marshaling yards at Rouen (August 17). Meanwhile embattled Britain was carrying the war to the enemy both by air and sea. Bomber Command's night blows against Germany grew heavier, and a succession of amphibious raids harassed the German-held coast of France. Three of these operations—1 by air and 2 by sea—are notable.

1942, March 28. St.-Nazaire. The destroyer *Campbeltown* (ex-American), loaded with explosives and accompanied by a small group of motor launches carrying commando troops, dashed into the harbor of St.-Nazaire under enemy fire. Despite very severe losses, the attackers wrecked the only dry dock in Europe outside of Germany capable of taking the giant *Tirpitz.*

1942, May 30–31. First 1,000-Plane Raid. A night assault by Bomber Command against the important railroad marshaling yards at Cologne caused heavy damage.

1942, August 19. Dieppe. A major amphibious raid by Anglo-Canadian troops, with some tanks, ended in complete failure after a gallant effort. Of 5,000 men put ashore, the attackers lost 3,350 killed and wounded, 28 tanks, and a number of landing craft. The lessons learned, however, were of immense value in the later Allied large-scale amphibious assaults. The disaster confirmed British views regarding German defensive capabilities and the risk that would result from a major invasion of Western Europe in 1942–1943.

Operations in the Mediterranean

EGYPT AND CYRENAICA

1942, January. Situation. Auchinleck's Eighth Army and Rommel's Italo-German army faced one another at El Agheila in Cyrenaica, 800 miles from Cairo and 450 miles from the Axis base of Tripoli. The weakened British naval forces in the Mediterranean permitted German reinforcements; Rommel's build-up outdid Auchinleck's.

1942, January 21. Rommel's Second Offensive. Attacking on a narrow front, the German drive crashed through the British advanced screen, forcing immediate withdrawal. The Eighth Army, dispersed and still under strength, was rolled back beyond Benghazi and large quantities of stores fell into Rommel's hands.

1942, February 4–June 13. Stalemate at Gazala. Auchinleck made a stand, and Rommel's advance had outrun his supply line. For 4 months more both sides rested, each building up strength. The Eighth Army's fortified and heavily mined defensive positions stretched from Gazala on

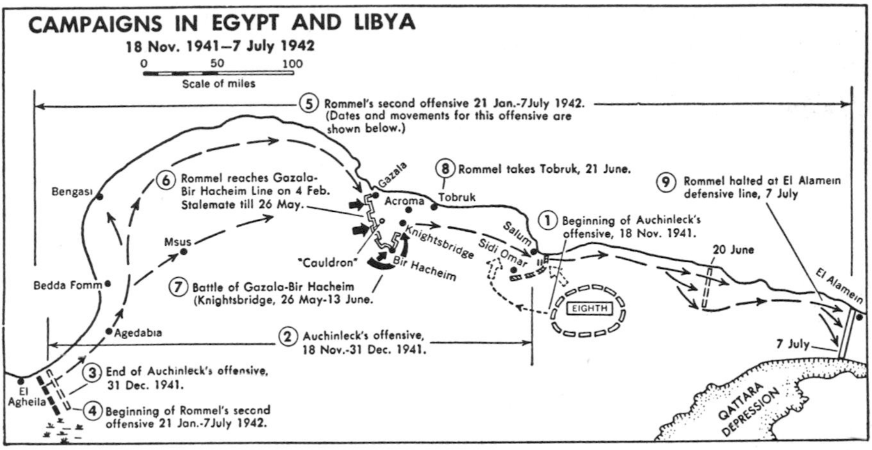
CAMPAIGNS IN EGYPT AND LIBYA
18 Nov. 1941–7 July 1942
0 50 100
Scale of miles
5 Rommel's second offensive 21 Jan.-7July 1942. (Dates and movements for this offensive are shown below.)
Bengasi
6 Rommel reaches Gazala-Bir Hacheim Line on 4 Feb. Stalemate till 26 May.
Gazala
8 Rommel takes Tobruk, 21 June.
Acroma
Tobruk
9 Rommel halted at El Alamein defensive line, 7 July
1 Beginning of Auchinleck's offensive, 18 Nov. 1941.
Salum
Sidi Omar
Knightsbridge
Bir Hacheim
Msus
"Cauldron"
20 June
El Alamein
Bedda Fomm
7 Battle of Gazala-Bir Hacheim (Knightsbridge, 26 May-13 June.
EIGHTH
Agedabia
2 Auchinleck's offensive, 18 Nov.-31 Dec. 1941.
7 July
3 End of Auchinleck's offensive, 31 Dec. 1941.
El Agheila
4 Beginning of Rommel's second offensive 21 Jan.-7July 1942.
QATTARA DEPRESSION

the coast to Bir Hacheim, nearly 40 miles south in the desert, where a Free French light division under General **J. P. Koenig** (up from French Equatorial Africa) held the British left flank. Behind Bir Hacheim, the British armor was concentrated to protect the open-desert left flank. British strength by this time was 125,000 men, with some 740 tanks and 700 aircraft. Rommel had 113,000 troops, with 570 tanks and 500 aircraft.

1942, May 28–June 13. Battle of the Gazala–Bir Hacheim Line. Rommel attacked, hoping to envelop the British desert flank and roll up the position. Italian troops were repulsed from Bir Hacheim by the French. But Rommel's Panzer divisions, circling to the south, turned north inside the British positions, despite vicious attacks by the RAF. The British line held, while behind it German and British armor battled repeatedly around a desert crossroad called Knightsbridge. Just as Rommel's tanks were running out of gas, Italian troops broke through the minefields between Bir Hacheim and the British Gazala positions (May 31), permitting the supply of Rommel's Panzers. Rommel created a fortress in an area called "the Cauldron" inside the British lines. The French had to evacuate Bir Hacheim (June 10–11). Then the German armor debouched from the Cauldron, threatening the rear of the entire Eighth Army. General Ritchie ordered withdrawal (June 13).

1942, June 14–30. Retreat into Egypt. The British fell back to Halfaya on the Egyptian border, leaving the Tobruk fortress menacing the German advance. But **Tobruk** suddenly fell (June 21) to a skillfully co-ordinated ground and air attack by the Afrika Korps. The Eighth Army retreated in disorder as Rommel pursued. Auchinleck, assuming personal command again, rallied his troops and, after a bold delaying action at **Mersa Matruh** (June 28), fell back on the Alam Halfa ridge, a fortified line between El Alamein on the sea and the Qattara Depression some 40 miles inland. Rommel, following, was at the end of his endurance. There, after the entrenched British repulsed some tentative German probes (July), the 2 exhausted adversaries lay again in stalemate, only 60 miles west of Alexandria. Both Auchinleck and Ritchie were relieved by Churchill (August 13), General Harold R. L. G. Alexander taking the Middle East Command and Lieutenant General **Bernard L. Montgomery** the Eighth Army.

COMMENT. *Rommel's advance was a brilliant display of armored force leadership and skillful use of his 88-mm. guns in coordination with his infantry and tanks. The British at Gazala frittered away their own armor in piecemeal counterattacks, losing all but 65 of their tanks. The disaster also cost the British 75,000 casualties (including the 33,000 garrison of Tobruk), the loss of great quantities of stores, and the elimination of Tobruk as a thorn in the side of Rommel's advances. The Germans and Italians lost about 40,000 men. Despite his success, Rommel's logistical situation was worsening as Allied naval and air strength in the Mediterranean again increased (see p. 1087), and Hitler—obsessed with the Russian invasion—urged him to advance to the capture of the Suez Canal, yet failed to provide adequate reinforcement or supply. Meanwhile British strength was rebuilding.*

1942, August 31–September 7. Battle of Alam Halfa. Rommel assaulted to try to gain another victory before British strength became too great. His plan, as at Gazala, was envelopment of the British left by the Afrika Korps. Montgomery was prepared. The Panzers, initially successful despite skillful delay by the British 7th Armored Division, reached the left rear of the British position and then thrust north, to be repulsed by a tank brigade dug in on the Alam Halfa ridge. Short of fuel and harassed by punishing British aerial attacks, Rommel began withdrawing his tanks (September 2). Montgomery refused to risk counterattack and the line stabilized again. But Rommel's failure had been a disaster—he had no further hope of offense; all he could do was defend.

1942, September–October. Preparations. Montgomery prepared methodically for attack. The Mediterranean situation had improved (see p. 1087). By October, the Eighth Army had been built up to an impressive strength—150,000 men organized in 3 army corps—7 infantry and 3 armored divisions, with 7 additional armored brigades (1,114 tanks in all), plus corps and army troops; fuel and ammunition were plentiful. Rommel at this time had 96,000 men (half of them Italians) in 8 infantry and 4 armored divisions (nearly 600 tanks); shortages in fuel, ammunition, and other supplies were severe. Rommel, ill, had temporarily flown back to Germany for medical treatment, leaving General **Hans Stumme** in command. The opponents, each with unturnable flanks, were separated by a broad zone of mine fields. On the north was the Mediterranean, and 40 miles to the south was the Qattara Depression, impassable for either wheeled or tracked vehicles. Montgomery's plan was to effect a penetration, hold off Rommel's armor while eliminating the German infantry, and only then engage in a tank battle. The RAF's Desert Air Force had gained complete air superiority, and subjected Axis forces to intensifying punishment.

1942, October 23–November 4. Battle of El Alamein. At 9:40 P.M., 1,000 British guns opened along a 6-mile front near the sea. Twenty minutes later—under a full moon—the XXX Corps struck the Axis left, while to the south the XIII Corps began a diversionary effort near the Qattara Depression. Four hours later, the X Armored Corps advanced through 2 corridors in the mine fields opened by the XXX Corps infantry. Despite initial surprise, the Italian infantry put up obstinate resistance; an almost immediate counterattack by the 15th Panzer Division nearly stopped British progress. Nor did the diversionary attack of XIII Corps make much gain. Stumme died of a heart attack; Rommel, flying back at first word of the battle, resumed command (October 25). Next day Montgomery, halting further effort on the south, threw his weight against the coastal area, where the 9th Australian Division threatened to pin the German 164th Division against the sea. For a week a ferocious tank battle raged in the mine fields south of the coastal road and railroad, as both sides brought their armored units up from the south. The Axis armor, necessarily thrown in piecemeal, and under continuous aerial bombardment, shrank rapidly. Lack of replacements for damaged vehicles, together with shortages of fuel and ammunition, combined to take cruel toll. Meanwhile the Australians had almost surrounded the German 164th Division along the coast. Rommel, whose existence depended on holding the coast road, committed his last reserve, extricated his infantry from encirclement, and dug in again 3 miles to the west (November 1). Montgomery quickly regrouped, then renewed his attempted breakthrough south of fortified Kidney Hill. The 2nd New Zealand Division, behind a rolling barrage, cleared a corridor through the mine fields for the British tanks (November 2). A desperate Panzer counterattack momentarily snubbed the breakthrough, but by the day's end only 35 German tanks remained in action, while British artillery and aerial bombardment neutralized the deadly German 88-mm. antitank guns.

Rommel, his fuel and ammunition having reached the vanishing point, decided to withdraw, but was halted for 48 hours by Hitler's categorical and senseless command to hold at all costs. Montgomery hurled another assault against the Kidney Hill area, scoring a clean breakthrough. Rommel, disregarding Hitler's order, now disengaged the Afrika Korps, leaving the Italians behind. The entire Axis front crumbled. Cautious Montgomery delayed pursuit for 24 hours. Rommel's losses were enormous: some 59,000 men killed, wounded, and captured (34,000 of them German); 500 tanks, 400 guns, and a great quantity of other vehicles lost. The Eighth Army lost 13,000 killed, wounded, and missing, and 432 tanks had been put out of action.

COMMENT. *Strategically and psychologically, El Alamein ranks as a decisive battle of World War II. It initiated the Axis decline. The victory saved the Suez Canal, was a curtain raiser for the Anglo-American invasion of North Africa 4 days later, and was a prelude to the debacle of Stalingrad. Allied morale soared, particularly in the British Empire, proud to have at long last a victorious army and general; Axis morale correspondingly dipped. Hitler's order that Rommel should stand fast (rescinded 48 hours later, after the "Desert Fox" had already started to withdraw) contributed to the ruin of Rommel's army.*

1942, November 5–December 31. Pursuit. Montgomery's slightly delayed, methodical pursuit, planned to keep unremitting pressure on Rommel's forces, fell somewhat short of its goal. Although forced to stand several times, the Afrika Korps made good its escape. The RAF in particular has been criticized for lackadaisical operation. At **Mersa Matruh** (November 7), the 21st Panzer Division, lacking fuel, made a hedgehog stand, then abandoned its last tanks. At El Agheila (November 23–December 13), Montgomery stopped to open the port of Benghazi and establish a supply line, Rommel withdrawing when again threatened by encirclement. The year ended with another delaying action at the **Wadi Zem Zem,** near Buerat. Again Rommel skillfully evaded entrapment while Montgomery wrestled with the logistical problems of his long communications line.

INVASION OF NORTH AFRICA, 1942

1942, August–November. Preparations for Operation "Torch." This invasion was planned for the purpose of seizing Morocco, Algeria, and Tunis as bases for further operations. It was a compromise between widely differing British and American military strategical concepts (see p. 1082). Roosevelt finally resolved the matter in favor of North Africa. It was the largest amphibious operation attempted to that time. Supreme commander was Lieutenant General **Dwight D. Eisenhower,** then commanding American troops in England. British Admiral Cunningham was Allied naval commander, and Eisenhower had an integrated American-British staff. The operation was divided into 3 main elements. Direct from the U.S. came Major General **George S. Patton**'s Western Task Force—35,000 men in 39 vessels,

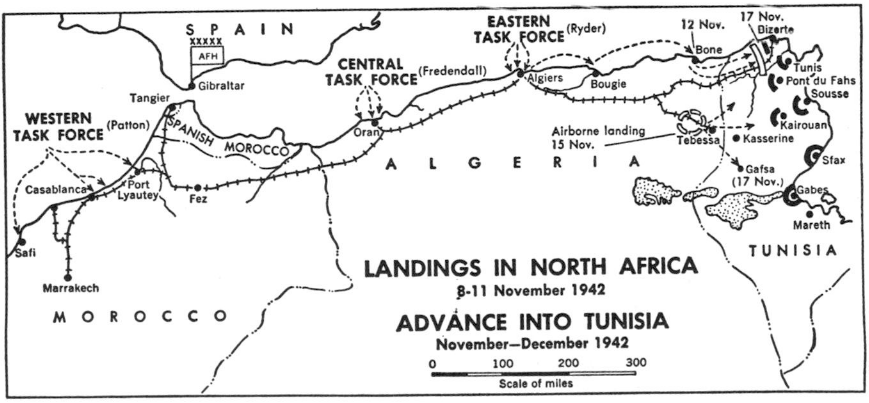

escorted by a powerful squadron under U.S. Rear Admiral **Henry K. Hewitt;** its main target was Casablanca on the Moroccan Atlantic coast. U.S. Major General **Lloyd R. Fredendall**'s Central Task Force, 39,000 men in 47 ships, came from England, its strong naval escort commanded by British Commodore **Thomas H. Troubridge;** the goal was Oran, on the Mediterranean. The Eastern Task Force, under U.S. Major General **Charles W. Ryder,** 33,000 men in 34 ships, also from England, was escorted by a naval force under British Vice-Admiral Sir **Harold M. Burrough;** its objective was Algiers. Except for a British contingent in the Eastern Task Force, all the troops were American, since it was believed that the French would be less favorably disposed toward the British. Prepared and lifted in the greatest secrecy, all 3 assault forces arrived off their respective landing zones after nightfall November 7. Despite some prior clandestine contacts, it was not known whether the French Army of Africa would resist or welcome the invasion.

1942, November 8. The Landings. *Western Task Force.* At 5:15 A.M., landings began at **Safi,** 125 miles southwest of Casablanca; at **Fedala,** 15 miles northeast of it; and at **Mehdia** and **Port Lyautey,** 70 miles to the northeast. Despite surprise, French troops resisted bravely, while at **Casablanca** itself French naval forces made a gallant sortie, promptly crushed by predominant U.S. strength. Despite French opposition, the landings were successful, and the 3 assault forces concentrated for an attack on Casablanca (November 11).

Central Task Force. Landings east and west of **Oran** met determined resistance. An attempt by 2 U.S. Coast Guard cutters at a run-by into the port itself failed dismally. An American airborne assault battalion, flying direct from England, was only partly successful in capturing the nearby airfields. However, the landings progressed; a co-ordinated attack penetrated Oran and the French capitulated (November 10).

Eastern Task Force. Forces landing on both sides of **Algiers** Harbor converged on the city; a frontal naval assault met disaster, as at Oran. Algiers was soon ringed on the land side. The place capitulated (November 10).

1942, November 9–11. Franco-German Reactions. The Pétain regime broke diplomatic relations with the U.S. (November 9) and ordered French African forces to continue resistance. At the same time Hitler ordered immediate military occupation of "unoccupied" France, and began sending German troops by air into Tunisia.

1942, November 11. "Darlan Incident." Admiral Darlan, unexpectedly found in Algiers and taken into protective custody, broke with Vichy, ordered immediate cease-fire by all French troops, and agreed to co-operate with the Allies in driving the Germans out of Tunisia. General **Henri H. Giraud** was put in command of French forces.

COMMENT. *This co-operation with a leading figure in the Vichy regime aroused furore in the U.S. and England, and affronted de Gaulle. From a military viewpoint, the bargain was a major factor in facilitating further Allied operations in North Africa, despite Darlan's later assassination (December 24).*

1942, November 17–December 31. The Race for Tunisia. With 1,000 German troops arriving in northern Tunisia each day, the Allies, unprepared as yet for a major overland operation, attempted a piecemeal eastward rush on Bizerte, while retaining sufficient force to oppose any possible Axis move from Spanish Morocco. British Lieutenant General **Kenneth A. N. Anderson,** with advance elements of what would become the First British Army, moved into the mountainous region southwest of Bizerte, while a screen of U.S. paratroops spread southeast. Aggressive German troops under General **Walther Nehring** checked the British advance, while mud and rain delayed Allied reinforcements from Algiers, 500 miles to the west. Allied spearheads reached to within 20 miles of Tunis (November 28), but were thrown back by German counterattacks. By December, Eisenhower conceded defeat in the race. The year ended with Anderson's First Army and the Fifth Panzer Army, now under General **Jürgen von Arnim,** facing one another in stalemate in north-central Tunisia.

COMMENT. *The invasion of North Af-*

rica succeeded because of strategic surprise, effective joint military-naval planning, and Darlan's check of French resistance. However, the confused French political situation and the prompt German reaction in Tunisia combined to impede the next move. Eisenhower, involved in political repercussions of the "Darlan incident," exercised little command supervision of the eastward thrust, and Anderson's initial moves were pedestrian. There was nothing now to prevent the eventual linking of Rommel, retiring skillfully westward from the Wadi Zem Zem, with von Arnim.

MALTA AND MEDITERRANEAN AIR AND SEA OPERATIONS, 1942

Malta, Britain's "unsinkable aircraft carrier," was the major stumbling block for Axis supply to North Africa. Incessant aerial attacks and Axis surface and submarine operations almost throttled all efforts to supply it. Of 6 convoys in 1942, 2 were repulsed and only parts of the rest reached Malta. The Mediterranean Fleet, from Alexandria, and H Force, from Gibraltar, furnished what escort they could, but until September the situation was precarious. Submarines and 2 speedy minelayers brought driblets of supply. Malta's defenses consisted of fighter planes and antiaircraft artillery. Some 350 fighters were flown in from aircraft carriers—notably the U.S.S. *Wasp*—to replace losses incurred on the open airstrips.

Malta's fighter squadrons played hob with Axis supply throughout the campaign. One-third of Axis supply ships from Italy were sunk in September, and in November British fighters sank three-quarters of the Axis surface craft. This toll of German supply ships was a direct result of the Allies' ability to read German secret radio messages, through a highly classified British code-breaking project known as "Ultra." The Allies profited from these radio intercepts in many operations, beginning with the Battle of Britain, but nowhere was the Ultra information more effectively used than in the sinking of German ships endeavoring to support German operations in North Africa.

Without possession of Malta the Allies could not have made such effective use of the Ultra information. Thus British denial of Malta to the Axis was a major factor in Rommel's defeat. The cost was high: an aircraft carrier, several cruisers and destroyers, hundreds of planes and thousands of men. But the tide had turned. Malta's role of cutting supply by surface ship forced the Germans to send reinforcements by air. By that time much Luftwaffe strength had gone to the Russian front and the rest in this area was supporing Rommel and von Arnim in Tunisia. Futhermore, logistical support for the British Middle East Command through the Indian Ocean–Red Sea–Suez Canal route was now plentiful.

The Eastern Front, 1942

1942, January–February. Continuation of the Russian Counteroffensive. (**See p. 1080.**) Russian attacks along the entire front, from Finland to the Crimea, forced the German armies into a stubborn defensive role. Only in Finland were the Russians repulsed, and the German besiegers of Leningrad still held stubbornly to their lines. Elsewhere, deep penetrations were made at many points. Hitler ordered all of his armies to stand fast. "Hedgehogs" (all-round defensive areas) checked the tide as the Soviet onslaught lost momentum. The danger of possible precipitate retreat, ending in a disaster such as Napoleon's retreat in 1812, was averted.

1942, March–May. Stalemate. Spring thaws and mud stymied movement. The Russians had outrun their supply lines and the exhausted Germans were not yet prepared to resume the offensive.

1942, May 8–June 27. Preliminary German Offensive. Reinforced by 51 satellite divisions (Italian, Rumanian, Hungarian, and Slovak) and 1 Spanish volunteer division, the Germans resumed the offensive, to eliminate salients created by the Russian winter drive. Despite the poor quality of replacements, and shortages of personnel and matériel in the German army units, substantial advances were made. In straightening out the lines, severe casualties were inflicted on the Russians. General Manstein's Eleventh Army swept the Kerch Peninsula, inflicting 150,000 Russian casualties, and renewed the attacks on Sevastopol. Partisan groups hamstringing German movements in the rear areas were partly checked.

1942, June 7–July 2. Capture of Sevastopol. An amphibious assault climaxed the siege; the Russians lost another 100,000 men.

1942, June 28–July 7. Opening of the Summer Offensive. Following plans personally developed by Hitler, Bock's Army Group South smashed eastward from the vicinity of Kursk to capture **Voronezh** (July 6). Hitler now reorganized Army **Group B South; the northern armies,** designated Army Group B, were under General Weichs, the southern armies, designated Army Group A, under General List. It had been originally planned

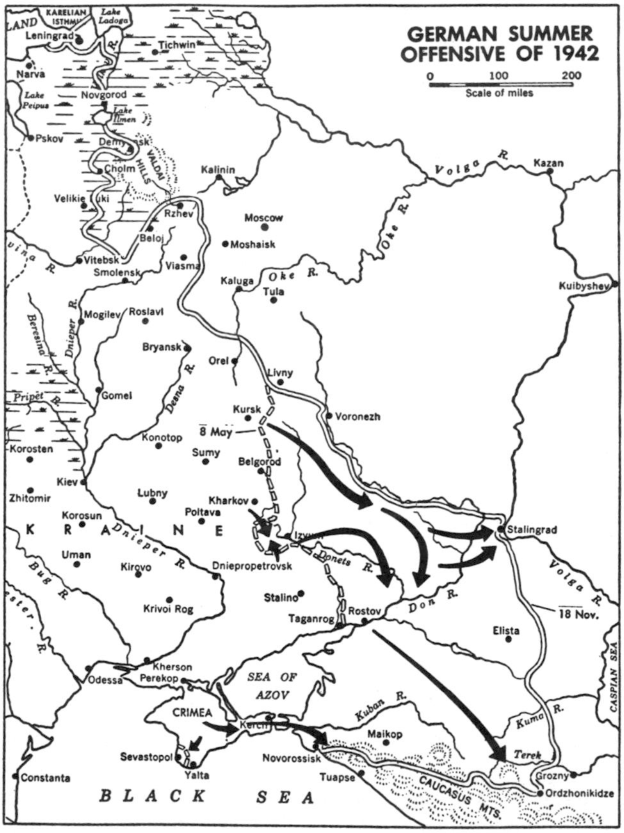

for these 2 groups to cooperate in a powerful and deliberate advance, first to clear the Don and Donets valleys, capturing Rostov and Stalingrad, then to move southward to seize the Caucasus and its rich oil resources.

1942, July 13. Hitler Changes Plans. Hitler now decided to drive for Stalingrad and the Caucasus in simultaneous offensives by Army Groups B and A. This reduced the planned strength for both operations, dangerously overextending both combat and logistical organizations. Furthermore, with diverging objectives, the new plan inevitably would create a gap between the 2 army groups.

1942, July 13–August 23. Drive on Stalingrad. As the powerful attacks progressed, the growing gap between the army groups permitted most of the Russian troops caught in the bend of the Don to escape. Although the German Sixth Army (**Friedrich Paulus**), was approaching Stalingrad, Army Group B's advance was slowed down by Hitler's diversion of Hoth's Fourth Panzer Army to join Army Group A's advance to the south. Nevertheless, with Luftwaffe aid, Group B cleared the bend of the Don, reached the Volga north of Stalingrad (August 23), and threatened the city.

July 13–August 23. Drive on the Caucasus. Army Group A captured **Rostov** (July 23), crossed the Don on a wide front, penetrated deep into the Caucasus Mountains, and had elements within 70 miles of the Caspian Sea near Astrakhan. But Hitler blundered again. Enraged at the relatively slow progress before Stalingrad, he yanked the Fourth Panzer Army back to join the Stalingrad struggle (August 1), leaving Army Group A, badly extended, trying to maintain an offensive in the Caucasus on a 500-mile front. Worse yet, Hitler also ordered Manstein's Eleventh Army—his sole reserve in this area—up north to reinforce the siege of Leningrad. General Franz Halder, OKH Chief of Staff, daring to protest these moves, was relieved. So, too, was List; Hitler took personal command of Army Group A (exercising command from his East Prussian command post more than 1,200 miles distant) in addition to his other responsibilities. The Caucasus campaign inched forward, some German patrols actually reaching the Caspian, but this success was inconsequential.

1942, August 24–December 31. Battle of Stalingrad. Hitler now concentrated on capture of the city's 30-mile perimeter astride the Volga, whose defenses were being strengthened every moment. In a tremendous battle of attrition, the Russian defenders resisted stubbornly from house to house as the Germans gradually closed in and the Russian winter freeze began. Most of Army Group B was now involved in the Stalingrad battle, while Army Group A to the south (now under Kleist) bogged down in stalemate. Between them, 1 single German motorized division held a 240-mile gap, and north of Stalingrad satellite forces screened the Don. German supply was meagerly maintained by a single rail line, completely inadequate for the situation. Hitler bypassed Weichs to issue personal commands to General Paulus, whose Sixth Army was in and around Stalingrad.

1942, November 19–23. Soviet Counterattack. Cleverly planned and timed to coincide with both the frost which enabled cross-country tank movements and the opening of the Allied landings in North Africa, 4 Soviet fronts or army groups, under the over-all command of Zhukov, launched a double envelopment against the Germans crowded about Stalingrad. The Voronezh, Southwest, and Don Fronts slashed in north of the city, the Stalingrad Front on the south. Behind the armored spearheads swept great bodies of cavalry. The overextended German lines gave way, the trap closed. Inside was Paulus' Sixth Army and elements from units on its flanks that had been wrenched aside in the Soviet pincers move. The remainder of Weichs' Army Group B reeled back. Despite Weichs' urging that he fight his way out, Paulus waited for Hitler's command. The Fuehrer demanded he hold in place, assuring him of supply by air, and ordered Manstein, hurriedly rushed from the Leningrad front to Army Group Don (improvised from part of Group A), to recapture immediately the lost ground. The task was impossible. Paulus' situation worsened, the Luftwaffe being unable to deliver more than 70 tons of supply each day. Manstein finally managed to reorganize 3 understrength Panzer divisions and attempted to break through in relief, actually reaching to within 35 miles of Stalingrad (December 19). Manstein radioed Paulus to make a final effort to break out, but Paulus awaited Hitler's authorization. Then the German front collapsed. The year ended with Paulus and his men battling against starvation in an ever-tightening Soviet ring, while Weichs, Manstein, and Kleist fought desperately to maintain themselves as they slowly withdrew westward under constant Russian pressure.

COMMENT. *Hitler's fantastic changes of objective, and his insistence first on an overextended offensive, and later on senseless retention of terrain, had wrecked his eastern armies. Almost 65,000 prisoners were lost (aside from more than 100,000 surrounded in Stalingrad) and some 1,000 tanks destroyed or captured. His satellite forces—Italian and Rumanian—had proved to be unreliable, and his German elements, despite amazing resiliency under appalling conditions, were completely inadequate to oppose the growing Soviet armies. On the Russian side, Marshal Zhukov and his 4 principal subordinates, Marshal* **Konstantin K. Rokossovski** *and Generals* **Nikolai Vatutin, Vasily Chuikov,** *and* **Andrei I. Yeremenko,** *conducted their counterattack efficiently, with several simultaneous penetrations and almost immediate exploitation which never gave the Germans opportunity to re-establish themselves. The defenders of Stalingrad suffered more casualties than the Germans, but proved once again the Russian soldier's ability to endure and to hold ground. Yet absolutely essential to this great Russian victory, one of the decisive battles of history, was the availability of weapons and equipment. Despite the great industrial effort Russia was making, she could not have provided the materials needed for successful defense followed by successful offense without the great quantities of equipment supplied by her Anglo-Saxon allies, particularly the U.S., by the dangerous Murmansk route, and the longer and safer routes across the Pacific and through Iran.*

OPERATIONS IN 1943

Strategy and Policy

1943, January 14–23. Casablanca Conference. Roosevelt, Churchill, and the Combined Chiefs of Staff plotted their future operations. The net result was again a compromise. Britain agreed to U.S. exploitation of the Pacific initiative (see p. 1133). The U.S. agreed to postpone any cross-Channel invasion until 1944, and to the undertaking of another Mediterranean operation, with Sicily the initial objective. With the U-boat menace in the Atlantic again assuming formidable proportions, highest priority was ordered to construction of antisubmarine craft—escorts and carriers. During the conference Roosevelt proclaimed, and the British agreed to accept, nothing but the "unconditional surrender" of their enemies, a policy of dubious expediency.

1943, May 15–25. "Trident" Conference, Washington. Roosevelt, Churchill, and the Combined Chiefs of Staff reaffirmed the basic decision to concentrate primary effort against Germany in agreements (1) to greatly intensify the planned strategic bomber offensive against Germany and German-occupied Europe, and (2) to plan for a cross-Channel invasion of Europe, through France, for May 1, 1944. Other decisions were subsidiary, save for agreement for some further increase in effort against Japan.

1943, August 14–24. "Quadrant" (First Quebec) Conference. The principal decision of this conference was to wage the war against Japan with increasing force, but without relaxation of the war in Europe. Specific decisions relating to Europe were (1) to hasten the invasion of Italy because of the collapse of Mussolini (see p. 1096), (2) to draw the U.S.S.R. into full concert with the western Allies, and (3) to recognize de Gaulle's French Committee of National Liberation as representative of all Free French fighting the Axis.

1943, October 19–30. Moscow Conference. This meeting of the foreign ministers of Russia, the U.K., and the U.S. was called primarily to lay the political groundwork for the forthcoming conference of heads of state at Teheran. They also agreed that China should be the fourth major member of the alliance, and agreed upon a postwar international organization (to become the U.N.).

1943, November–December. "Sextant-Eureka," Cairo-Teheran Conferences. Since the U.S.S.R. was not at war with Japan and was bound by a nonaggression treaty with her (April, 1941), 2 separate heads-of-state conferences were necessary. At Cairo, Roosevelt and Churchill met with Chiang Kai-shek (November 22–26 and December 3–7). At Teheran, they met with Stalin (November 28–30). These were primarily political conferences. Stalin was informed that the cross-Channel invasion would take place in late May or early June, 1944; he agreed to launch a general Russian offensive at the same time.

Battle of the Atlantic, 1943

THE SUBMARINES

1943, January–March. Increasing U-Boat Toll. Admiral Raeder was relieved (early January) by an impatient Hitler. Submarine specialist Admiral Karl Doenitz took his place and stepped up an already-accelerated wolf-pack campaign. The German U-boat operational daily average rose to 116 craft. The U-boats crisscrossed the sea lanes, taking toll of every merchant convoy in a continuous battle. The worst winter storms in many years lashed the Atlantic, increasing the difficulties and dangers for surface craft. By the end of March, with 108 Allied merchantmen sunk, to a loss of only 15 U-boats, the campaign reached its climax. The United Kingdom's larder was reduced to a hand-to-mouth 3-month backlog of supply. The U-boat war was waged with success only against the slow-moving merchant convoys. The 2 other types—fast converted luxury liners operating individually without escort, and the troop convoys—were not touched. The first outran the U-boats; the second, heavily escorted, were too dangerous to attack.

1943, April 28–May 6. Gretton's Convoy. Commander **Peter W. Gretton,** R.N., commanding Convoy ONS-2—42 merchantmen—fought a running battle across the North Atlantic with 51 U-boats. Though he lost 13 of his convoy, 5 U-boats were sunk by Gretton's warships and 2 more were sunk by aircraft. This is considered to be the turning point of the Battle of the Atlantic.

1943, May. Focus on the Bay of Biscay. Air Vice-Marshal Sir **John Slessor** of Britain's Coastal Command put into full operation a scheme of air-sea co-operation against U-boats operating out of French bases. Bombers based on the south of England, in conjunction with R.N. corvettes, and guided by microwave radar, proved to be deadly. In this month 38 U-boats—12 more than Germany could build—were destroyed, and only 41 allied merchantmen lost.

1943, May 26. Doenitz Shifts U-Boat Operational Area. The wolf packs congregated in 3 areas: (1) west of the Azores, athwart the central Atlantic convoy route—life line for the Allied Mediterranean campaigns, (2) in the South Atlantic, and (3) in the Indian Ocean.

1943, June–December. Allied Hunter-Killer Campaign. The U.S. Navy's Tenth Fleet organized "killer groups," each comprising an escort carrier equipped with 24 fighter-bombers using bombs, depth charges, or torpedoes, and accompanied by several old destroyers or new destroyer escorts. Each group commander was given the widest latitude to hunt U-boats whenever a "fix" had been obtained. The result proved catastrophic to the U-boats and their "milch cows" not only along the central transatlantic lane but also in the South Atlantic. The German craft fought back savagely in a number of single-ship and airplane-ship actions. Remarkable was the running gun battle between U.S.S. *Borie* and *U-405,* halfway between Cape Race, Newfoundland, and Cape Clear, Ireland, in which the destroyer rammed the sub, tearing out her own plates. The German finally blew up and sank, the victor following the next day. Remarkable, too, was the raid of *U-516* in the Caribbean (November 5–December 25). The German, despite the efforts of all available American antisubmarine craft in the area, sank 6 vessels, including 2 tankers, then got safely away.

COMMENT. *By year's end the knell was sounding for the German U-boat; Allied "kills" exceeded German replacement ability. Between May and September, 3,546 merchantmen in 62 convoys had crossed the North Atlantic without loss of a single vessel. Allied merchant construction exceeded all enemy destruction by 6 million tons. The food crisis in the British Isles had ended. Acquisition of air bases in Portugal's Azores completed the aerial attack ringing the wolf packs (October 13).*

NAVAL SURFACE WARFARE

1943, January–March. Convoys to Russia. Murmansk convoys, strongly escorted, ran the gantlet during the first 3 months of the year with comparatively little loss. When the Mediterranean later was opened, they were suspended; most supplies for Russia were sent via Iran to avoid exposing Arctic convoys to German air attacks in almost continuous daylight.

1943, March. The *Scharnhorst* Sails North. The battle cruiser, again in commission, slipped through to Norway without detection.

1943, September 6–9. Spitsbergen Raid. The *Tirpitz,* the *Scharnhorst,* and 10 destroyers successfully raided Spitsbergen, bombarding and damaging Allied coal mining and loading installations.

1943, September 21–22. Attack on the *Tirpitz.* The great ship was attacked in Alta Fjord by British midget submarines and again badly damaged.

1943, October–December. Arctic Operations. Harassing Allied carrier-borne aviation sank 9 German coastal vessels near Narvik. As the nights grew longer, Allied convoys to Murmansk resumed.

1943, December 24–26. Last Cruise of the *Scharnhorst*. Accompanied by 5 destroyers, the *Scharnhorst* steamed out of Alta Fjord to attack an Allied convoy, discovered 400 miles northwest of Trondheim. The German flotilla blundered into 2 British task forces west of the North Cape. In a thrilling chase, the *Scharnhorst,* hit at extreme range by the battleship *Duke of York,* was slowed down, battered by heavy gunfire, then finished off by a torpedo attack. Only 36 of her 1,900-man complement could be rescued. This disaster removed the last surface threat to Allied convoys on the Murmansk run.

The Combined Bomber Offensive, 1943

The U.S. Eighth Air Force and Britain's Bomber Command instituted a round-the-clock aerial offensive, codenamed operation "Pointblank", against Germany from British airfields. Bomber Command attacked the economic system and civilian morale by large-scale nighttime saturation bombing; the Eight Air Force concentrated on daylight precision bombing against aircraft industrial targets and the Luftwaffe itself. This was to be followed by later concentration of both forces against vital industries to destroy Germany's ability to make war. Both air forces used new and improved techniques—the "pathfinder," system which located targets by radar and marked them, and "window" (myriad strips of metalized paper released in the air to jam and confuse Germany's electronic defenses).

BRITISH AIR ASSAULT

Bomber Command's night raids rocked German civilian morale by wide devastation of the Ruhr industrial area and of major cities. Highlights included:

1943, June 20–24. First Shuttle Bombing. RAF bombers from England struck Wilhelmshafen outbound, then landed in North Africa. They bombed the Italian naval base of Spezia on the return trip.

1943, July 26–29. Hamburg Incinerated. Two successive mass bombing assaults produced "a catastrophe the extent of which simply staggers the imagination" (Goebbels' diary). Much of the damage came from tornadolike fire storms. Most of the city was reduced to rubble; civilian casualties were enormous and 800,000 survivors made homeless.

1943, August 17–18. Peenemunde Bombed. British intelligence sources had revealed (May) German development of a pilotless jet-propelled aircraft (V-1) and a rocket (V-2). The experimental installation at Peenemunde was bombed, delaying the project.

1943, October–December. Attacks on Mysterious Launching Sites. Aerial reconnaissance revealed the construction of launching sites along the Channel coast, and these, too, were bombed and the majority destroyed (December to spring, 1944), causing a 5-month setback in German plans. Operations against these projects were labeled "Crossbow."

1943, November–December. Battle of Berlin. Bomber Command concentrated its efforts against the German capital in 16 massive raids which continued through the winter and until March, 1944.

U.S. AIR ASSAULT

1943, June 11. Wilhelmshaven Attacked. Eighth Air Force assault on submarine construction works was only partly successful. German interceptors prevented accurate bombing; Allied fighters did not have enough range to accompany the big B-17's and B-24's, a problem plaguing Eighth Air Force operations throughout the year.

1943, July. Attacks on German Aircraft Industrial Targets. This produced a serious, though temporary, setback in German plane production.

1943, August 1. Bombing of Ploesti. Taking off from North African bases, 178 B-24 bombers of the Eighth and Ninth

Air Forces struck deep behind the German lines in the east against the Rumanian oil fields of Ploesti, whence the Axis drew most of its fuel for both Luftwaffe and ground forces. The planes were assembled in secrecy near Benghazi for the 1,000-mile flight, the longest bombing raid yet attempted. Their transit was detected by German radar in Greece, Bulgaria, and Rumania. The bombers, in low-level attack, were met by determined and accurate antiaircraft fire, causing loss of 54 planes, plus 7 damaged planes which landed in Turkey. Extensive but, as it turned out, relatively superficial damage was done to the vast complex of refineries and storage tanks.

1943, October 14. Schweinfurt Raid. Eighth Air Force bombers struck the heart of the German ball-bearing industry a cruel blow. But of the 288 planes (accompanied by short-range fighter escort as far as Aachen), 62 were lost and 138 damaged by antiaircraft and Luftwaffe fighters. Casualties were 599 men killed and 40 wounded. Despite tactical success, the raid was so costly that a temporary halt was called on further daylight bombing until longer-range fighter escorts were available.

1943, December 5. First P-51 Escorts. With these new long-range fighters of the Ninth Air Force to accompany them, the big bombers renewed daylight raids.

COMMENT. *The year ended with the German home-front morale rudely rocked, but industrial production was still potent and the Luftwaffe had improved its defensive tactics.*

The Mediterranean Area, 1943

NORTH AFRICA

1943, January 1–February 13. Stalemate in Tunisia. Allied expeditionary forces, under Anderson's tactical command, were spread thin along the Tunisian Dorsal and Eastern Dorsal ranges from Cape Serrat on the Mediterranean to Gafsa in the south. The British First Army, with a provisional French corps and some U.S. elements, held the line from the north to Fondouk in central Tunisia; the bulk of Fredendall's U.S. II Corps stretched to the south. Arnim's Fifth Panzer Army held northeastern Tunisia; Rommel's Afrika Korps, completing a masterly withdrawal from Egypt, held an old French fortified zone at Mareth, with its left flank on the Gulf of Gabes and its right resting on the almost impassable salt marshes of the Chott Djerid; there they were reequipped. Montgomery slowly began concentrating in front of Mareth. There was no ground communication between Anderson and Montgomery. Arnim, in a series of aggressive blows, kept Anderson off balance, while the Luftwaffe dominated the air.

1943, February 14–22. Battle of Kasserine Pass. Rommel, fearful lest he be caught by an Allied drive in his rear while Montgomery assaulted his Mareth position from the south, launched a 2-pronged surprise attack against the U.S. II Corps sector. His armor thrust through Faid, Sidi-bou Zid, and Sbeitla, driving for Kasserine Pass, while another armored thrust rolled through Gafsa on the south to Feriana (February 17). Elements of the 1st U.S. Armored Division and attached units, scattered through the sector in small packets, were rolled up; a piecemeal counterattack was ambushed. Staged in the best blitzkrieg style, with the Luftwaffe closely supporting by dive bombings and strafings, the drive rolled on. Eisenhower, his vital supply base at Tebessa threatened, rushed reinforcements, while both U.S. and British troops on the front gained their second wind. Rommel's Panzers crashed through the Kasserine Pass (February 18) and fanned northward. Against increasing resistance, his spearheads reached into the Western Dorsal range at Djebel El Hanra, Thala, and Sbiba (February 20–22) before momentum was lost. An expected supporting attack by Arnim in the north failed to materialize. Rommel, unmolested, then retired to his Mareth position as hastily as he had come.

COMMENT. *The attack had accomplished its primary purpose: to wreck Allied plans to divide the German forces by a thrust eastward to the Gulf of Gabes. Had Arnim co-operated, serious damage would have been done, but Hitler had insisted on a divided command in Tunisia; not until February 23 did he place Rommel in overall command. The Allied reverse was what might have been expected from green troops faced by skillful and daring veterans with air superiority. It was compounded by a poorly organized and co-ordinated American air-support system, and by Anderson's faulty terrain appreciation and his patchwork dispositions—a cordon of units divided both in nationality and in tactical formation, with consequent improvisation of command chain. As it was, the American troops put up a remarkably tenacious fight. Eisenhower must share the blame; permitting himself to become too much involved in the Franco-Algerian political turmoil, he had neglected command supervision. His first visit to the front came but 24 hours before the German assault occurred. A shake-up of command followed. All Allied ground forces in Tunisia were combined (February 20) in the 18th Army Group, Alexander commanding, and the organizations were regrouped by nationality. Patton shortly succeeded Fredendall in command of U.S. II Corps (March 6). Upon advice from the RAF's Air Marshal Tedder, and from USAAF officers, the Americans also adopted the British system of air support, which permitted more flexible and more effective employment of available air strength.*

1943, February 26. Arnim's Attack. Belatedly, the Fifth Panzer Army assaulted British First Army's positions in northern Tunisia and gained some ground. However, stubborn resistance cost Arnim much armor, and a British counterattack (March 28) restored the line.

1943, March 6. Rommel Repulsed. Testing Montgomery's positions in front of Mareth, Rommel was decisively repulsed at **Médenine** with much loss in matériel. Still ill, he left Africa. Arnim assumed over-all command in Tunisia; Italian General **Giovanni Messe** took over the Mareth front and General **Gustav von Vaerst** the Fifth Panzer Army in the north.

1943, March 20–26. Battle of Mareth. Montgomery, with greatly superior forces, assaulted the Italo-German position, the XXX Corps making the main effort on his right. Despite heavy bombardment, the 15th Panzer Division counterattacked in the moonlight, checking the British. Montgomery, who had sent the New Zealand Corps on a wide turning movement against the Axis right, now reinforced it with the X Corps. Messe, avoiding encirclement, withdrew to El Hamma. The Allies now held the initiative.

1943, April 1–22. Axis Withdrawal. Patton's II Corps threatened Messe's right; Montgomery lunged north (April 6). When they linked, Messe had escaped and was moving swiftly north. The British IX Corps (First Army) moved east through Fondouk, but Messe was going too fast. This second pincers movement failed also when it closed with Montgomery's pursuing Eighth Army at Kairouan. With Messe's arrival Arnim held a defensive line running generally south and then east from Cape Serrat on the Mediterranean to Enfidaville.

1943, April 22–May 3. Beginning the Final Offensive. Alexander planned a power thrust by First Army with Eighth on the right, and U.S. II Corps on the left, shifted north for this offensive. (Major General **Omar N. Bradley** had relieved Patton to command U.S. forces in the coming Sicilian operation.) Major General **Louis-Marie Koeltz**'s French XIX Corps linked the First and Eighth armies. Vaerst's Fifth Panzer Army held the right, then came the Afrika Korps, then Messe's Italian First Army on the left of the Axis front. The Germans had been reinforced, but the Allies had air superiority. German supplies were desperately short, due largely to "ultra" radio eavesdropping that kept the Allies informed of the sailing of German supply ships, most of which were then sunk. An emergency German air supply effort did not help much, and most of the transports were shot down by Allied fighters. The First and Eighth armies inched forward against determined resistance; the II Corps, probing against the most difficult terrain on the front, moved more rapidly, driving the Germans from Jefna (May 1) and taking Mateur (May 3.)

1943, May 3–13. Battle of Tunisia. Preceded by heavy artillery and air preparation, the Allies penetrated the Axis perimeter, the II Corps north and south of Lake Bizerte, the First Army east from Medjez El Bab. With all reserves committed, and lacking air support (the Luftwaffe was withdrawing to Sicily), Arnim was unable to stem the tide. The U.S. 34th Division entered **Bizerte** (May 7); the 1st Armored Division rolled through Ferryville, cutting the German communications and linking (May 9) with the

British 7th Armored Division, which had already entered **Tunis** (May 7), and turned north. To the south, the French corps and the Eighth Army surrounded the Italian First Army, and British armor cut off the Cape Bon Peninsula (May 11). Thus dislocated and canalized by Allied thrusts, Axis troops began surrendering in droves, Bradley garnering some 40,000 prisoners in his zone. In all, some 275,000 prisoners were taken, including the top commanders. The Italian Navy made no attempt at evacuation. The Axis hold on North Africa was ended.

COMMENT. *Alexander's power punch was well planned and executed. The U.S. II Corps, still stinging from its reverse at Kasserine, aggressively modified its planned secondary role to a major one. The Axis forces put up stout resistance until the last in a situation which they knew could have but one end. The North African victory was prototype for future Allied joint operations. Strategically, it provided a springboard for further Mediterranean operations, including invaluable sites for air bases. Axis losses in casualties and prisoners in the North African campaigns amounted to an estimated 620,000 soldiers, one-third of them Germans. British losses in North Africa—from the beginning of the war—amounted to 220,000 in all. From November, 1942, to May, 1943, French losses were about 20,000, and the Americans suffered some 18,500 casualties.*

SICILY

1943, June 11. Capture of Pantelleria. The Italian garrison of this rocky island surrendered after a week of incessant bombardment by the Northwest African Air Force, as an Allied landing force approached.

1943, July 9–10. Assault on Sicily. Following a month-long bombardment of Axis air bases in Sicily, Sardinia, and Italy, an amphibious assault by Montgomery's British Eighth Army and Patton's U.S. Seventh Army (elements of Alexander's 15th Army Group) gained a toehold on Sicily's southeast coast. Effective support was given by naval gunfire. The Italians, not expecting an attack in stormy weather, were caught by surprise.

1943, July 11–12. Axis Counterattacks. General **Alfred Guzzoni**'s Italian Sixth Army struck back. German divisions, attacking American troops near Gela and Licata, were particularly effective, but were repulsed after nearly driving to the sea. Allied airborne landings were disrupted by bad weather and mistaken Allied antiaircraft fire.

1943, July 15–23. Clearing of Western Sicily. Though determined German resistance stopped Montgomery south of Catania, Patton's army swept through western Sicily, then turned east to assist the British.

1943, July 23–August 17. Advance to Messina. Despite spirited German resistance (now actually directed by one-armed German Colonel General **Hans Hube,** veteran of the Russian front), the Allies pressed steadily forward, aided by several small amphibious operations on the north coast

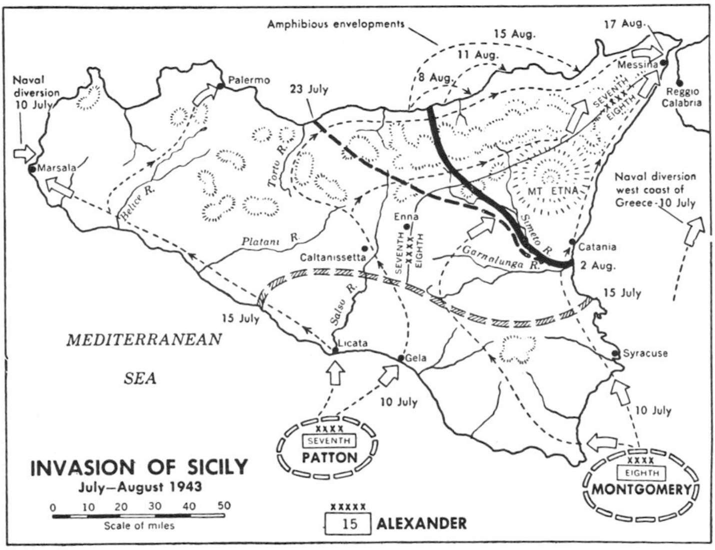

INVASION OF SICILY
July–August 1943

east of San Stefano. The Italians began a mass exodus (August 3–16), followed by a more orderly German withdrawal (August 11–17), which succeeded in evacuating to the mainland over 100,000 men, 9,800 vehicles, and 50 tanks before the Allies occupied Messina (August 17).

COMMENT. *American casualties were 7,319; the British lost 9,353; Axis losses were over 164,000, including some 32,000 Germans. Great quantities of weapons and equipment were captured. Allied operations had been skillfully conducted. German resistance had been professional and tenacious, but the Italians showed little desire to fight. The Allies landed some 160,000 men, who had been transported in 3,000 vessels. Total Axis strength had been about 350,000, of which perhaps one-third were German. The Allies were aided by a great preponderance of air power, 3,700 planes as opposed to 1,600. With the capture of Sicily, the Mediterranean was again opened as an Allied sea route.*

ITALY

1943, July 24. Overthrow of Mussolini. The war-weary Italian nation toppled Mussolini from power during the Sicilian operation. His successor, Marshal Badoglio, though officially declaring intention to continue hostilities, began secret negotiations with the Allies through agents in Lisbon. Hitler, unwitting but suspicious, prepared to control and disarm the Italians, and began movement of German reinforcements into north Italy to protect the Alpine communications. Kesselring, German commander in southern Italy, correctly estimated that the Allies planned an early invasion, and that Salerno was a likely landing site.

1943, September 3. Armistice with Italy. This was signed secretly, to be effective September 8.

1943, September 3. Eighth Army Assault on Calabria. British troops landed on the toe of the Italian boot. Kesselring initiated delaying action in the south while still watching the Salerno area. He was unaware of the armistice.

1943, September 8. Publication of the Armistice. This was timed to coincide with Allied landings at Salerno. At the same time, the Italian fleet fled from Spezia to Allied protection at Malta, severely harassed on its way by the Luftwaffe. The alert Germans began to disarm and imprison all Italian forces.

1943, September 9. Assault at Salerno.* The U.S. Fifth Army, commanded by Lieutenant General **Mark Clark** and comprising the British X and American VI Corps, made assault landings in the Gulf of Salerno before dawn, to be met by alert German defenders, deployed in mobile defense. The British landed north of the Sele River (bisecting the crescent-shaped gulf shoreline), Americans to the south. Due to effective defense, and despite excellent naval gunfire support, by nightfall the Allies only held 4 narrow, unconnected beachheads. Kesselring began moving all available reserves to the Salerno area. To the south, 130 miles away, Montgomery's Eighth Army was slowly consolidating its hold of the Calabrian peninsula; a British division simultaneously landed to seize Taranto.

1943, September 10–14. Struggle for the Beachhead. Though both British and Americans were able to claw their way forward somewhat in their sectors, they still found it impossible to join their beachheads solidly at the Sele. German artillery, with perfect observation from the hills ringing the beaches, was particularly effective. Kesselring, having gathered most of 6 divisions, launched a violent counterattack against the Allied center (September 12). A last-ditch defense by American artillery units, supported by naval gunfire, prevented a breakthrough to the beaches (September 13). The Allied situation was desperate; sufficient reinforcements could not be put ashore to stop the Germans; 3 battalions of the 82nd Airborne Division were parachuted to bolster the crumbling beachhead. All the strength of the Northwest African Air Force and the carrier-based air and all the guns of the naval expedition combined to give close support. Alexander ordered Montgomery (still 50 miles away) to accelerate his advance, but skillful delaying action by a lone German battle group impeded his cautious advance through mountainous country.

1943, September 15–18. Securing the Beachhead. The hasty landing of more Allied reinforcements, combined with superb naval gunfire and air support, checked the

*** Operation "Avalanche."**

German offensive. Montgomery's patrols made contact with the southeastern portion of the beachhead (September 16). Kesselring thereupon began a deliberate disengagement, retiring northward.

COMMENT. *Allied losses exceeded 15,000 men; German casualties were about 8,000. The outstanding feature of the battle had been the foresight, skill, and initiative of Kesselring, and the efficiency of his troops.*

1943, September 18–October 8. Consolidation of Southern Italy. Both Fifth and Eighth armies pressed on. West of the Apennines, the Fifth seized Naples (October 2) and pushed on, to be checked (October 8) by the swollen Volturno River, with all bridges destroyed. To the east, the Eighth Army took Foggia and its great air base (September 27), advancing to Termoli on the Adriatic, captured after a stiff fight (October 3). French troops, assisted by local Resistance elements, seized Corsica (September 11–October 4).

1943, October 12–November 14. Volturno River Campaign. Fifth Army, assaulting across the Volturno with both corps, made foot-by-foot progress over abominable trails in mountainous country drenched by the Italian autumn rains. The Eighth Army, having regrouped, also started north (October 22), forcing the Trigno River. Kesselring had selected the line Garigliano River–Sangro River to bar further Allied advance; his skillful, stubborn delaying actions granted him time to consolidate the position. The Allied armies, exhausted, found themselves facing ever-stiffening opposition. On November 15, Alexander halted to rest and regroup.

1943, November 20–December 31. "Winter Line" Campaign. Alexander's 15th Army Group resumed its advance on Rome. Kesselring by this time had established a formidable defensive zone (called the "Winter Line," or Gustav Line) 10 miles deep, running from the mouth of the swift-running Garigliano River on the Gulf of Gaeta, along its narrow tributary, the Rapido, then over the spine to the

Adriatic north of the Sangro River. This zone was held by the Tenth Army (**Heinrich von Vietinghoff**). On the Mediterranean side the hill masses crowded down on the Liri Valley entrance, backstopped by Monte Cassino with the great Benedictine monastery frowning above the roaring Rapido. Into this zone the Fifth Army attacked. Some progress was made, despite determined resistance, atrociously difficult terrain, and constant rain or snow, but the year ended in blizzard-bound stalemate, with the attackers still 5 miles southeast of the Rapido. The German defense was assisted by the fact that Fifth and Eighth armies alternated in their assaults, thus enabling the defenders to shift forces in opposition.

1943, December. Allied Reorganization. Both Eisenhower and Montgomery left for the coming offensive in Western Europe. British General Sir Henry M. ("Jumbo") Wilson assumed supreme command in the Mediterranean Theater, and General Sir **Oliver Leese** took command of the Eighth Army. Some veteran divisions were drawn off for the European invasion. The VI Corps, too, was out, regrouping for another amphibious operation, and new troops—including Indian, French, Italian, and New Zealand forces—were moving into the now polyglot 15th Army Group.

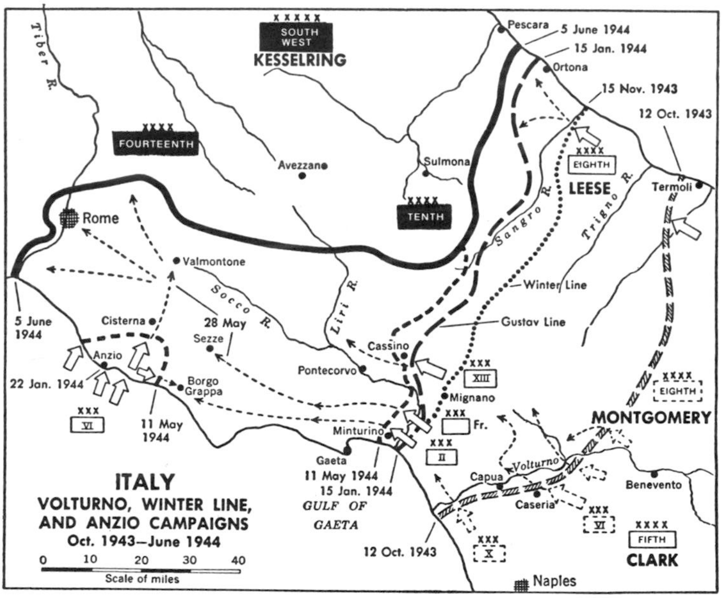

ITALY
VOLTURNO, WINTER LINE, AND ANZIO CAMPAIGNS
Oct. 1943–June 1944

AEGEAN

1943, September 12–November 16. Operations in the Dodecanese. British landings on **Kos, Samos,** and **Leros** (September 12) provoked a prompt German reaction. An airborne assault retook Kos (October 3–4); Samos was then evacuated. Leros was taken by a combined airborne-amphibious assault (November 12–16). British resources were not sufficient to continue operations in the Aegean without interfering with operations elsewhere approved by the Combined Chiefs of Staff.

The Eastern Front, 1943

1943, January–February. Russian Pressure. All German forces in southern Russia were in jeopardy. East of Kharkov, the Hungarian and Italian satellite armies were disintegrating; the Sixth Army at Stalingrad was in death agony; in the Don Valley in front of Rostov, Russian assaults were threatening to cut off Army Group A's thin-spread First Panzer Army, now in retirement from the drive into the Caucasus oil fields.

1943, February 2. The End at Stalingrad. Paulus' Sixth Army, food and ammunition exhausted, surrendered to the relentless pressure of Rokossovski's Don Front (army group) after a last-ditch fight. Hitler's obstinacy had cost him in all 300,000 men. Paulus and 93,000 survivors surrendered. The First Panzer Army reached the Don at Rostov (February 1) to join Manstein's Army Group Don. The remainder of Kleist's Army Group A—Seventeenth Army—established a defensive bridgehead between the Sea of Azov and the Black Sea at Novorossisk.

1943, February 2–20. Russian Drive across the Donets. Russian armor flooded over Kharkov, approaching the Dnieper bend, while partisans harassed the German rear area.

1943, February 18–March 20. Manstein's Counteroffensive. Manstein, skillfully employing reserves and shifting units, slowly checked, then threw back the Soviets, recapturing **Kharkov** (March 14) and restoring the line. Farther north, the line swayed back and forth in a succession of attacks and counterattacks. On the southern flank, Kleist's Army Group A maintained its bridgehead. The spring thaws

THE RUSSO-GERMAN FRONT, 1942-1943

then prohibited further mass movements by either side.

COMMENT. *The great Russian winter offensive was a body blow to Axis power. The Soviets regained most of the territory lost in 1942. German losses are estimated at more than one million. The Soviets claimed capture or destruction of 5,000 aircraft, 9,000 tanks, 20,000 guns, and thousands of motor vehicles, railway cars, and locomotives. Russian losses were at least as great. Hitler's faulty strategy and almost complete incomprehension of logistical factors were his undoing. Large-scale guerrilla activity, engendered by SS atrocities in occupied terrain, greatly assisted Soviet leaders, who themselves had improved in military acumen. The most outstanding military performance had been Manstein's near miracle in halting the Russian drive, despite odds of 7–1, then, amazingly, counterattacking successfully. This was one of the great military achievements of the war.*

1943, March–June. Recuperation and Reinforcement. German strength could no longer support another major offensive, as even Hitler realized. Russian strength was now at least 4 times greater. By this time logistical aid furnished by the U.S. to Russia had mounted to 3,000-odd planes, 2,400 tanks, and 80,000 trucks.

1943, July 5–16. Battle of Kursk. Manstein's plan to strike a limited assault against **the salient west of** Kursk in combination with Kluge's Army Group Center was so long delayed by Hitler that when he finally launched it a Soviet counteroffensive checked it on the ground, while Russian air power smothered Luftwaffe support. German losses were 70,000 killed or wounded, 3,000 tanks, 1,000 guns, 5,000 motor vehicles, and 1,400 planes. Russian losses in this largest of all tank battles were probably slightly less. This battle marked the end of German mass efforts in the east. Alarmed now by the Anglo-American Sicilian invasion (see p. 1095), Hitler broke off the move against Kursk and began transferring a number of Panzer divisions to the west, further weakening his force in the east.

1943, July 12–November 26. Russian Summer Offensive. From Smolensk to the Black Sea, the Russians delivered a series of battering blows, featuring great masses of armor.

1943, August 2. Hitler's Orders to Hold in the East. Partly in reaction to the Soviet offensive, and partly because of fears for the safety of Ploesti created by the American air raid (see p. 1092), Hitler now ordered Manstein, who was conducting a masterly mobile defense, to freeze the defense of the Kharkov sector in place. A Soviet breakthrough (August 3) threatened disaster, and Manstein ignored Hitler's order, abandoning Kharkov (August 23), but kept his lines intact by skillful counterattacks as he fell back to the Dnieper.

1943, September–November. Continuation of the Soviet Offensive. Disregarding losses, the Russians pressed ahead all along the front. When they finally paused, they had pressed Kluge's Army Group Center back to the edge of the Pripet Marshes, had recaptured Kiev (November 6), and Smolensk (September 25), had driven a bridgehead across the Dnieper in Manstein's sector, and had cut off the German Seventeenth Army in the Crimea, since Hitler had refused to follow Manstein's recommendations to evacuate the peninsula.

1943, December. Initiation of Soviet Winter Offensive of 1943–1944. Taking advantage of frozen ground, the Soviets launched a new winter offensive in the Pripet Marsh area and along the Dnieper. Although Manstein's Germans inflicted heavy casualties, they were forced to give up more ground.

THE WAR IN THE WEST, 1944

Strategy and Policy

The year opened with the Axis on the defensive. Hitler's Russian gamble was lost, the eastern front crumbling. Italy was eliminated, North Africa cleared, and the Mediterranean sea lanes opened. In the United Kingdom, American strength was accumulating in astounding abundance. On the other side of the ledger, however, skillful German defense had halted the Allied advance midway up the Italian boot. The U-boats still menaced the Atlantic, Arctic, and Mediterranean sea lanes. Behind *Festung Europa*'s barrier, the embattled German economy was producing war matériel at ever-increasing rates, despite the ravages of Allied bombers. The war was still far from a decision.

The strategic situation in Western and Northern Europe was plain to both Allied and Axis leaders, although never quite understood by their respective peoples. The Allies, from their bridgehead in the British Isles, held the priceless advantage of strategic interior lines. They were free, in principle, to attack Germany at any point in the long arc from Norway's North Cape to Brittany's Cape Finisterre. That they would invade was a foregone conclusion; there was no way to disguise the immense concentration of men and matériel. But where and when and how? This was the situation faced by Hitler, and this was the situation which—thanks to a deceptive cover plan whose details have never been fully revealed—the Allies maintained successfully until they were so firmly established in France that counterattack was futile.

1944, June–December. The V-bomb Threat to England. Soon after the invasion of Normandy, the first V-1 flying bomb struck England (June 13). German scientists had perfected this, the first of Hitler's "secret weapons," despite RAF attacks on the development and test site of Peenemunde (see p. 1092). Terror attacks by these weapons on London severely shook English morale, despite the fact that about half the V-1's were shot down by antiaircraft or fighter defenses. The terror became more serious when the Germans introduced the V-2, the first effective long-range rocket missile (September 8). Because of their speed, these rockets could not be intercepted. The intensity of the attacks, however, was soon drastically reduced by the rapidity of the Allied ground advance along the French and Belgian coasts (see p. 1109). The Germans continued to fire V-2's against London from launching sites in Holland, though intensive Allied air bombardment prevented them from ever mounting a massive assault on England.

1944, July 20. Attempted Assassination of Hitler. A German Army plan to overthrow the Nazi regime failed when Hitler survived the explosion of a bomb in his headquarters. A ruthless purge of army officers ensued, and Hitler took absolute personal control over all military affairs. Rommel, a key figure in the plot, was forced to commit suicide (October 14).

1944, September 12–16. Octagon (Second Quebec) Conference. With Germany finally nearing collapse, principal attention was given to the war against Japan at this meeting of Roosevelt, Churchill, and the military Combined Chiefs of Staff. Despite Churchill's protests, America's increasing preponderance of military strength forced him to accede to American strategic concepts of concentrating all available strength directly against Germany, without consideration of possible "sideshows" in southern Europe, which Churchill felt would put the western Allies in a more favorable bargaining position with the Soviet Union at the time of a peace settlement. Because of such disagreements as to relative importance of political and basic military objectives, questions of postwar territorial settlements were postponed.

Battle of the Atlantic

1944, January–June. Foiling the U-Boats. Protection of the vast quantities of American men and matériel pouring across the seas, both to the United Kingdom and to the Mediterranean basin, became of paramount importance as the time for the cross-Channel invasion neared. German attempts to provide floating bases for the U-boats were scotched: a U.S. Navy hunter-killer group extirpated (February–March) "milch cow" submarines spotted in the Cape Verde Islands. Other groups hunted the elusive craft in both North and South Atlantic areas. The "schnorkel"—a tube providing air for Diesel engines while submerged—assisted the latest German submarines to remain under water for long periods, but improved methods of detection prevailed. By the end of February, more than 1 million American troops had been convoyed to the United Kingdom, and by May the logistical lift had reached the colossal amount of 1.9 million tons per month.

1944, April–November. Target: *Tirpitz*. The British were determined to destroy the *Tirpitz,* hidden in Alta Fjord, Norway, before she could be repaired (see p. 1091). A surprise raid by carrier-based planes scored numerous hits with 1,000-lb. bombs, killing 300 of the *Tirpitz*'s crew, damaging guns and radar equipment, but not harming her armored sides or deck (April 3). Subsequent attacks were less successful, and the Germans pressed on with repairs. A long-range bomber finally (September 15) hit the *Tirpitz* with a 6,000-lb. bomb, causing damage that forced the Germans to move the giant ship to better repair facilities at Tromsö. After several more long-range attacks with 6-ton "blockbusters" against the well-protected ship, she was finally hit by several of these great bombs and sunk, carrying 1,200 men to the bottom (November 12).

1944, November–December. Doenitz Tries Again. As the weather turned wintry and the days longer, Doenitz sent large numbers of his schnorkel-equipped submarines from his Baltic and Norwegian bases (the French bases having all been captured by the Allies) in intensified attacks against Allied shipping, this time trying the new and rather effective technique of operating near Britain in shallow coastal waters where the Allied detection equipment was unreliable. Shipping losses again mounted, though never approaching the serious situation of 1941 and 1942.

The Combined Bomber Offensive

1944, January–May. Unremitting Pressure on Germany. The U.S. Strategic Air Forces (commanded by Lieutenant General **Carl Spaatz** and comprising the Eighth AF, based in England, and the Fifteenth AF, based in Italy) intensified operations, in continuing close co-operation with Air Marshal Harris' RAF Bomber Command. Thousand-plane raids were frequent, with the British bombers continuing to operate at night and the Americans by day, often striking the same targets in pulverizing 1-2 punches.

1944, February 20–26. The "Big Week." The Americans by day, the British by night, ranged over Germany in 5 days of co-ordinated strikes against Germany's airplane and antiaircraft factories and assembly plants, crisscrossing Leipzig, Regensburg, Augsburg, Fürth, and Stuttgart. The Luftwaffe rose to meet them in a last bid for supremacy. American losses alone in these operations were 244 heavy bombers and 33 fighter planes, but the Germans lost 692 planes in the air and many more on the ground.

1944, March–May. Attriting the Luftwaffe. The Germans lost 2,442 fighters in action and another 1,500 through accident or other causes. Although the German aircraft industry recovered from the "Big Week" blows, the loss in trained pilots during the period was irreparable. Allied air supremacy was henceforth unchallenged.

1944, May–June. Preparations for "Overlord." (See p. 1106.) The strategic bombers joined the tactical air forces in operations designed to "isolate the battlefield" over a great arc in France, the Low Countries, and western Germany—too widespread in direction and targets to betray the selected landing area. Bridges, tunnels, marshaling yards, and roads were plastered and the railway system largely paralyzed. All air bases in France in a 130-mile radius from the assault beaches were neutralized. By June 6, Normandy and Brittany were in effect isolated from the remainder of France. In all, some 4 million tons of bombs were dropped during the period, nearly 60 per cent by American aircraft.

1944, June–August. Shuttle Bombing from Russia. To permit American bombers to strike farther east into Germany with greater bomb loads, and also to confuse German air-defense efforts, arrangements were made for them to fly east to bases behind the rapidly advancing Russian front. Despite operational success, the coordination with the Russians was never very effective. Also the Russian air defenses were unable to cope effectively with German counterraids on the American bases in Russia, resulting in severe American losses. The effort was therefore soon abandoned.

1944, July–December. Climax of the Strategic Air Offensive. The long-range bombers returned to their primary mission of attacking Germany's warmaking capacity, save for a few diversionary attacks on tactical targets to assist in the breakout from the Normandy beachhead (July; see p. 1107). The pattern of operations was as before, save that the growing number of planes permitted even more intensive operations. Principal targets were Germany's oil-production facilities and transportation system. All large industrial areas were struck, however, including steel plants, electric-power facilities, and weapon factories. The attacks on oil production drastically reduced the available fuel for airplanes, tanks, trucks, and submarines, thus affecting Germany's ability to fight on land, in the air, and at sea. Lack of fuel reduced the new fighter-pilot training, creating a vicious cycle; inadequately trained German pilots were quickly shot down by the attacking bombers and their fighter escorts. The attack on German transportation also had a wide effect, choking the flow of raw materials to factories, and of finished products to the German fighting forces and population. Finally the curve of German production began to drop sharply; the Combined Bomber Offensive was wrecking Germany's capability to continue the war.

Operations in Italy, 1944

ANZIO-RAPIDO CAMPAIGN

1944, January 5–15. Drive to the Rapido. Stubborn assaults through the mountains, from the confluence of the Liri and Garigliano rivers north to the Apennines, advanced the Fifth Army nearly 7 miles to the final German Gustav Line along the Rapido, with Monte Cassino the key terrain obstacle in the bulge's center. Alexander planned a frontal attack, assisted by an amphibious landing at Anzio (Operation "Shingle"), some 60 miles from the Rapido front. The Anzio force would then advance inland to cut the German communications line. Although the 2 operations were beyond mutual-support capabilities, it was believed the dual operation would force evacuation of the Gustav Line. The Eighth Army, meanwhile, would continue its advance on Pescara, on the Adriatic coast.

1944, January 17–21. Rapido-Cassino Assaults. The X Corps attacked across the Garigliano, attaining a bridgehead. On its right the II Corps U.S. 36th Division attempted to force the Rapido, but was repulsed with heavy loss (January 17–19). The French corps nibbled north of Cassino to make slight but costly gains. As expected, German reserves were drawn to the Rapido front, and the amphibious operation was launched from Naples (January 21).

Anzio Operations, January 22–February 29

1944, January 22. The Landings. Major General **John P. Lucas**' VI Corps—some 50,000 Anglo-American troops, with 5,200 vehicles—began landing without opposition. Forty-eight hours later, most of the troops were ashore, the initial objectives attained, and a beachhead established, 7 miles deep. Lucas, however, made no attempt to drive inland toward the Alban Hills—the vital terrain. Instead, he consolidated his position, awaiting the landing of heavy weapons, tanks, and additional supplies. General Clark, who was present, concurred. But Kesselring's quick reaction brought German reinforcements from the north as well as from quiet sectors of the Gustav Line.

1944, January 23–February 16. German Build-up. Under General **Hans Georg Mackensen** the quickly extemporized Fourteenth Army pinned Lucas to his beachhead.

1944, February 16–29. German Counterattacks. A series of brutal blows drove back the outlying Allied units. Lucas was relieved (February 23) by Clark, Major General **Lucius K. Truscott, Jr.,** U.S. 3rd Division commander, replacing him.

1944, March–May. Stalemate. The amphibious assault became a siege for 3 more months with all the elements of World War I trench warfare. All portions of the narrow beachhead were under continuous observation and fire, while the Luftwaffe swept the harbor area, disrupting supply and reinforcement efforts.

1944, February–May. Operations on the Rapido. Fifth Army battered at the Gustav Line. The U.S. 34th Division assault on Monte Cassino, the so-called **First Battle of Cassino,** was repulsed (February 12). The New Zealand Corps then tried, supported by aerial bombardment (General **Bernard C. Freyburg** mistakenly thought the Germans were using the monastery for observation), in the **Second Battle of Cassino** (February 15–18), and also failed. The Germans quickly occupied the ruined monastery and repulsed the New Zealanders. The most massive close air support attack attempted to date brought no different result in the **Third Battle of Cassino** (March 15–23).

COMMENT. *Since the objective of the Anzio-Rapido operation was to pry the Germans out of the Gustav Line by utilizing Allied sea power to cut their line of communications, Anzio should have been the main effort, the Rapido merely a holding attack. But insufficient sea transportation (because of the demands of the 2 coming amphibious invasions of France) was available to ensure a sledge-hammer blow at Anzio. So the joint operation—and the responsibility must rest on Alexander—became a weak planning compromise: 2 main efforts, entirely incapable of mutual support, neither of them powerful enough to do the job alone. It can be argued that had Lucas immediately and boldly pushed ahead to his final objective—the Alban Hills—the Gustav Line must have collapsed, with Rome quickly occupied. But*

Lucas' commander, General Clark, was ashore on D day and concurred in the decision to consolidate before driving inland. Some 23,860 American and 9,203 British casualties were evacuated during the 4-month hell on the beachhead. In the end the Gustav Line collapsed only as a result of the very type of frontal attack the amphibious operation was designed to avoid.

1944, March 15–May 11. Operation "Strangle." U.S. Major General **Ira C. Eaker**'s Anglo-American Mediterranean Allied Air Forces undertook a systematic air interdiction campaign to cut off supplies to German troops south of Rome. Despite severe punishment, the Germans did not withdraw as Allied air planners had hoped. However, the effect would soon be evident when intensive ground pressure was combined with the air interdiction campaign.

ROME CAMPAIGN

1944, May 11–25. Breakthrough. Regrouped to bring the weight of the 15th Army Group into his main effort, Alexander launched a full-scale surprise assault in the 20-mile zone between Cassino and the sea. The interdiction pressures of "Strangle" were intensified. In the combined air-ground offensive, "Diadem," French, Polish, British, Canadian, and U.S. units smashed through the German lines. The Poles took Cassino (May 17–18). At Anzio the reinforced VI Corps attacked (May 23) toward the Alban Hills; contact was made between the two Allied forces two days later.

1944, May 26–June 4. Advance on Rome. General Clark's shift of the Fifth Army toward Rome now saved the German Tenth Army from possible envelopment. Skillfully handled rear guards checked American advances at Valmontone and Velletri (May 28–June 2), while the remainder of the Tenth Army fell back. Rome was entered (June 4), hot on the heels of a general German retirement.

1944, June–August. Advance to the Arno. The Allies pushed rapidly up the peninsula. But withdrawals of troops—both ground and air—to mount the invasion of southern France (see p. 1108) reduced Alexander's strength, while German reinforcements bolstered Kesselring. In a series of masterly delaying actions the Germans—despite Allied air superiority—retired to the Gothic Line, extending across the peninsula south of Bologna, its outposts running generally from Pisa, through Florence, to Ancona.

1944, August–December. Advance to the Gothic Line. The Fifth Army crossed the Arno (August 26). Leese's Eighth Army took Rimini (September 21), and Clark, committing all his reserves, made an unsuccessful bid for Bologna (October 1–20). Another Italian winter settled on an exhausted Allied army group. Alexander, promoted to Supreme Allied Commander in place of Wilson (transferred to head the British military mission in Washington), was replaced by Clark. Truscott took over the Fifth Army and Lieutenant General **Richard L. McCreery** took over the Eighth from Leese.

The Allied Invasion of Western Europe

THE PRELIMINARIES, MAY, 1943–MAY, 1944

Allied Situation and Plans

At the Trident Conference (see p. 1090), President Roosevelt and Prime Minister Churchill agreed on a major cross-Channel invasion of Europe in 1944. Planning was under Lieutenant General Sir **Frederick Morgan**; the target date was set as the first week of June 1944. A gigantic amphibious operation from southern England to France, with nearly 3 million men, was planned. After all possible landing sites were considered, the area east of the Cotentin Peninsula of Normandy was selected, because of (a) its proximity to Allied fighter bases in England, (b) the short water distance for carrying supplies and reinforcements in limited numbers of landing craft, (c) the nature of the beaches, (d) the nature of the inland area, and (e) the German defenses. In February, General Eisenhower, designated to command the invasion, established Supreme Headquarters Allied

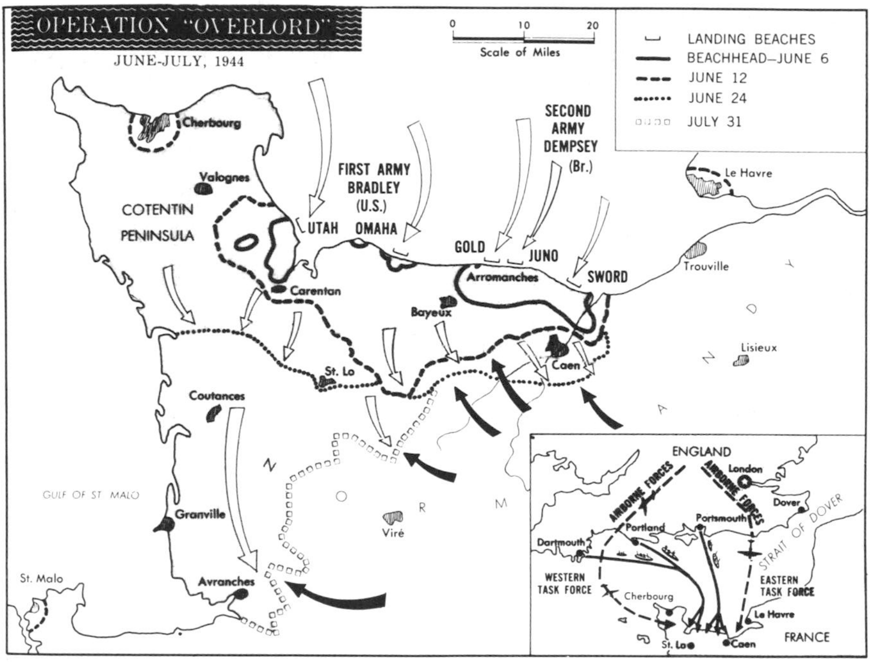

Expeditionary Forces (SHAEF), approved the planning done by General Morgan's staff on Operation "Overlord," as the invasion was designated, and continued plans and preparations. By May, 1944, he reported to the CCS that his force was ready.

In essence, the Allied plan envisaged assault landings on 5 main beaches. Lieutenant General Omar Bradley's First U.S. Army was to land on Utah Beach, northwest of the impassable marshy Carentan estuary, and on Omaha Beach just east of the estuary. The decision to risk defeat in detail on these beaches was made because of the importance of Utah Beach as a base for a quick drive to seize the port of Cherbourg, essential to future logistical support. To reduce the danger of this decision, 2 airborne divisions were to be dropped well inland of the marsh country to facilitate early link-up of the 2 beachheads. Farther east General Sir **Miles Dempsey**'s British Second Army (including a Canadian corps) would land on 3 beaches—Juno, Sword, and Gold—west of the Orne River. Another airborne division was to land just east of the Orne to protect the British left flank. Over-all commander of Allied ground forces was British General Sir **Bernard L. Montgomery.** The total combat strength of the invasion forces gathered in England was 45 divisions, totaling with supporting units about 1 million men (two-thirds American). Almost another million comprised the tremendous logistical and administrative support forces which would sustain the combat units.

The supporting naval and air elements totaled almost another million men. Commanding the invasion armada was British Admiral Sir **Bertram Ramsay.** British and American tactical air forces were commanded by RAF Air Marshal Sir **Trafford Leigh-Mallory.** For the period just before and after the attack, General Spaatz's long-range American bombers were also placed under Eisenhower's command. Eisenhower's deputy commander was RAF Air Chief Marshal Sir **Arthur Tedder.**

German Situation and Plans

Hitler's "Atlantic Wall" stretched from the North Sea coast to Brittany's Atlantic nose and thence southward to the Spanish border—a network of permanent fortifications laced by strong points and field positions, protected by mine fields and underwater obstacles. Inland areas favoring air drops were mined and strewn with obstacles. Manning this complex were 10 Panzer, 15 infantry, and 33 training or coast-defense divisions (of inferior quality) of the Western High Command (von Rundstedt) spread from Norway to the Mediterranean. German troops immediately available in the invasion area were portions of Army Group B (Seventh and Fifteenth Armies), commanded by Rommel—4 coast-defense divisions manning fortifications, 2 infantry divisions, the garrison of Cherbourg, and 3 Panzer divisions in reserve. The remainder of Rommel's troops were frozen, partly because of the disruptive Allied bombing offensive, partly because of Hitler's orders. Obsessed by the idea that the Allied thrust would come over the Pas de Calais—shortest distance from England—the Führer insisted that the Fifteenth Army (east of the designated landing area) rest in place, and that no Panzer divisions be released without his specific order. The brunt of the invasion would thus be borne by the Seventh Army, Colonel General **Friedrich Dollmann**. With the Luftwaffe already swept from the sky by Allied air, and no naval defense except light torpedo craft and submarines, the German situation was precarious, but far from hopeless.

OPERATION "OVERLORD"

1944, June 6. D Day. Preceded by the airborne drops—2 U.S. divisions on the west and 1 British division on the east—the greatest amphibious assault yet known to history began landing on the Normandy coast in complete tactical surprise. Some 4,000 ships and landing craft carried 176,000 troops and their matériel. Escorting the armada were 600 warships. The Allied air forces had earlier drenched the terrain with bombs; 10,000 tons of explosive were dropped by some 2,500 heavy bombers, while 7,000 fighters and fighter-bombers combed the area. Supporting the assault were the guns of the warships, large and small. By nightfall, 5 divisions were ashore and a comfortable toehold had been obtained at all beaches except Omaha, where German resistance had been heaviest and defending artillery fire best directed. There the initial assaults bogged down for a time. Meanwhile, offshore, an amazing conglomeration of concrete floating caissons—"Mulberries," a British invention spurred by Churchill's insistence—was being jockeyed into position to make 2 artificial ports, protected by lines of old vessels scuttled to provide breakwaters. (An unexpected storm of great ferocity was to destroy the American artificial port, June 19, and thereafter supply for both Allied forces moved through the British artificial harbor.)

1944, June 7–18. Expansion. Hitler's fixation that another Allied attack would come in the Pas de Calais area hampered Rundstedt and Rommel in their defensive strategy; reinforcements came in bits and pieces, and part of the Panzer strength was frittered away in piecemeal counterattacks. But the *bocage* (checkerboard of small fields boxed by deep hedgerows) reduced the Allied advance to a crawl. German resistance centered about Carentan and Caen. Montgomery's efforts to take Caen were rebuffed (June 13 and 18), while on the right the U.S. VII Corps, Major General **J. Lawton Collins,** was slowly battering its way across the Cotentin peninsula base. It turned north (June 18) and drove for Cherbourg, while the remainder of Bradley's army took up an aggressive defense.

1944, June 27. Fall of Cherbourg. The garrison surrendered after 5 days of desperate defense, and after demolishing harbor installations. The harbor would not be cleared until August 7, but beach unloading there began immediately. During this time Rommel had attempted to mass armor for a counterattack on the British, but was forced to commit his divisions piecemeal.

1944, July 1–24. Expansion of the Beachhead. Allied strength ashore built up to 1 million men, 150,000 vehicles, and half a million tons of supply. However, progress southward through the *bocage* was disappointngly slow and costly, and the Germans had caught their second wind. Rundstedt was relieved by Hitler, Marshal **Günther von Kluge** taking his place. SS General **Paul Hausser** (Dollmann had been killed) opposed the U.S. First Army's advance with approximately 7 veteran divisions of the Seventh Army, while Panzer Group West, General **Heinrich Eberbach,** barred the British advance with 7 armored and 2 infantry divisions. Montgomery made some progress (July 8) following a heavy bombing attack and renewed his effort, finally taking Caen (July 13). Then, after a costly repulse southeast of Caen (July 20), the attack halted. It had, however, drawn German armored strength to the British front. Bradley prepared for a breakthrough after having slowly crunched his way into St.-Lô (July 18), losing 11,000 casualties. Meanwhile, in the Channel, Allied sea power held open the crossing lanes against 56 German submarines and German light craft operating out of Le Havre. Rommel having been wounded (July 17) when an Allied plane strafed his car, Kluge took over his command in addition to his other duties. Thus far, Allied losses had been some 122,000 men, and the Germans had lost about 114,000, including 41,000 prisoners. The first phase of the invasion was complete.

OPERATION "COBRA"—BREAKOUT FROM THE BEACHHEAD

1944, July 25–31. Breakthrough. Bradley's U.S. First Army assaulted to penetrate the German line west of St.-Lô, with Collins' VII Corps making the main effort. A tremendous bomb carpet by Spaatz's long-range bombers—4,200 tons of explosive—opened a gap, although through miscalculation more than 500 Americans were killed or wounded by "shorts." (General **Lesley J. McNair,** commander of U.S. Army Ground Forces, present as an observer, was killed.) The assault advanced through heavy resistance to Coutances (July 28) and Collins' armor reached Avranches (July 31). Hitler released some Fifteenth Army divisions to Kluge (July 27).

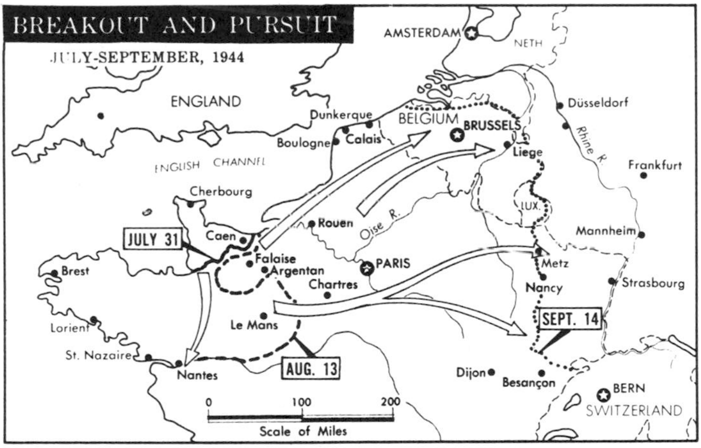

1944, August 1. Allied Reorganization. Unveiled now was the U.S. Third Army, Patton commanding, taking the right of the Allied line. The U.S. 12th Army Group came into existence, Bradley commanding, with Lieutenant General **Courtney Hodges** leading the First Army. In the British zone Montgomery's 21 Army Group also expanded—comprising the Canadian First Army, Lieutenant General **Henry D. G. Crerar,** on the left of Dempsey's Second British Army. Montgomery remained over-all ground-force commander.

1944, August 1–13. Breakout and Exploitation. Patton's Third Army whirled through the Avranches gap. His armor scoured Brittany, then turned south to the Loire and pointed eastward. His infantry curved left toward Le Mans. On the inner ring, the First Army began pivoting to its left.

1944, August 6–10. Counterattack at Avranches. The First Army was momentarily halted by a vicious German counterattack ordered personally by Hitler. Kluge, gathering all available Panzer strength, hurled it westward at Mortain, toward Avranches, hoping to isolate the Third Army and—ultimately—to turn north and crush the Normandy beachhead. Bradley shifted reinforcements and —with the aid of air power, mostly British—Kluge's attack was halted (August 8), although, against his protests, Hitler ordered the effort continued for 2 more days. Meanwhile, oblivious to the threat, the Americans from the southwest and the British from the north bore down on the Germans in a pincers movement.

1944, August 13–19. Falaise-Argentan Pocket. Allied misunderstandings and some timidity contributed to provide a gap through which the now much-disorganized German Seventh and Fifth Panzer (former Panzer Group West) armies fled eastward. As it was, although a goodly part of the German armor got away, some 50,000 Germans were captured and 10,000 more lay dead. These operations cost the U.S. First Army 19,000 casualties; the Third Army suffered about 10,000.

1944, August 20–30. Pursuit. Kluge, in full retreat, made for the safety of the Seine bridges, with all 4 Allied armies in full cry behind him. The Allies advanced to the Seine from Troyes to the Channel (August 25).

1944, August 25. Liberation of Paris. The local population had risen (August 23) and was liberated by the U.S. Fifth Corps, with Leclerc's French 2nd Armored Division spearheading the drive. Kluge's reward for a remarkable salvaging of the German remnants from the Falaise-Argentan gap was to be dismissed by Hitler; General **Walther Model** assumed command of Army Group B. Kluge committed suicide a short time later.

1944, August–September. Germans Isolated in Western France. At Hitler's orders, some German garrisons held French west-coast ports: Brest (captured September 18 after a long siege), Lorient, St.-Nazaire, La Rochelle, and the Gironde estuary (all of which held out for several more months). A wandering German army corps south of the Loire was hunting for Allied troops to surrender to, as the countryside boiled in the French Resistance movement—nominally at least under SHAEF direction.

OPERATION "ANVIL-DRAGOON" —SOUTHERN FRANCE

1944, August 15. The Landings. The U.S. Seventh Army (Lieutenant General **Alexander Patch**), consisting of the U.S. VI and French II corps, with a provisional airborne division, made an amphibious landing and air drop on the Côte d'Azur between Hyères and Cannes. The objective was to free Marseilles (for supply) and protect Eisenhower's southern flank. Mounted in the Mediterranean Theater, the operation was supported by tactical and strategic air forces, while ships of the Western Task Force escorted. Assault landings were made by General Truscott's VI Corps at small cost. By nightfall, some 94,000 men and more than 11,000 vehicles were ashore, the German coastal defense —2 second-line infantry divisions—broken, and over 2,000 prisoners taken. The assault casualties amounted to 183 men killed and wounded, with 49 nonbattle casualties. The French (General **Jean de Lattre de Tassigny**) began landing immediately behind the assault units.

1944, August 16–28. Pursuit. While de Lattre's French troops turned west toward Toulon and Marseille, Truscott's VI Corps boldly thrust north in 2 columns, the main body up the Rhone Valley, the other through the foothills of the Alpes Maritimes. German General **Friedrich Wiese**'s Nineteenth Army was retreating in considerable disorder up the Rhone Valley. German strength consisted of 7 second-rate infantry divisions and the well-handled 11th Panzer Division. Operating on a logistical shoestring, Truscott's fast-moving right column (Task Force Butler and the 36th Division) raced and passed the Germans in the Rhone Valley, then turned west to close the trap at Montélimar (August 22).

1944, August 23–28. Battle of Montélimar. Indecision on the part of the American

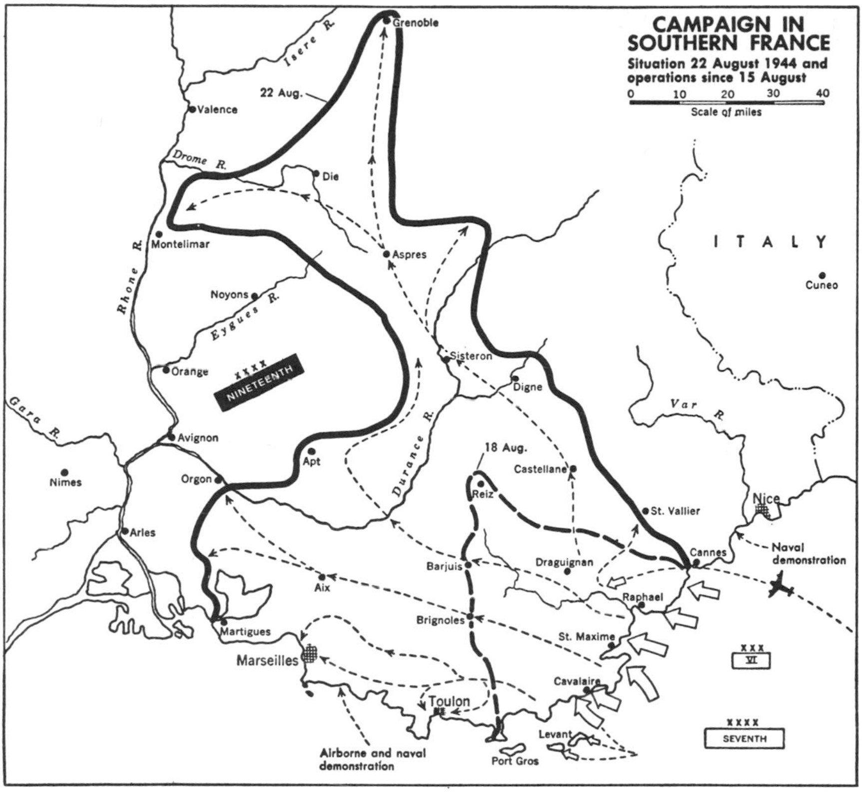

36th Division and a vigorous Panzer counterattack kept the block open long enough to let most of the German Army fight its way past Task Force Butler, whose artillery, supported by tactical air, took a terrible toll. The road from Montélimar north to Loriol became a shambles. More than 15,000 prisoners were taken, while some 4,000 vehicles—tanks, guns, and trucks—were destroyed. The number of German dead is unknown.

COMMENT. *Truscott's Rhone Valley campaign is a shining example of boldness and initiative. In 14 days of incessant drive he had practically destroyed a German army with 1,316 of its 1,481 guns, captured 32,211 prisoners, and advanced some 175 miles, at a cost of 1,395 killed and 5,879 wounded and missing. The French component of the Seventh Army captured Toulon and Marseille (August 28), taking 47,717 prisoners, losing some 1,300 killed and 5,000 wounded and missing. German forces in the south of France had been eliminated.*

1944, August 29–September 15. Advance to the Vosges. Patch's Seventh Army moved north, the U.S. VI Corps leading, with the French I and II corps following on the right and left flanks respectively. Contact with Patton's Third Army was made west of Dijon (September 11). The southern invasion force then became the U.S. 6th Army Group (September 15), under Lieutenant General **Jacob M. Devers,** its components the U.S. Seventh Army and the newly established First French Army, General de Lattre de Tassigny.

ADVANCE TO THE WESTWALL, AUGUST 27–SEPTEMBER 14

1944, August 27–September 4. The British Pursuit. The AEF had crossed the Seine in hot pursuit of the ebbing German tide. But Eisenhower needed possession of Antwerp to provide supply—the 300-mile-long logistical line from the Normandy beaches was stretched almost to breaking point. He thus favored Montgomery's advance into the Low Countries. The British Second Army advanced rapidly. Brussels was entered (September 3) and Antwerp, with port facilities intact, was captured next day.

1944, August 27–September 4. The American Pursuit Falters. Gasoline for Bradley's army group was reduced to a trickle as supplies went to the British. Patton's Third Army crossed the Meuse (August 30), only to be halted there with empty fuel tanks. Hodges' First Army, after bagging 25,000 prisoners at **Mons** (September 3), was also reduced to inchworm progress.

1944, September 3. Eisenhower Assumes Direct Command of Ground Operations. This permitted Montgomery to devote full attention to 21 Army Group.

1944, September 4–14. The Germans Block Antwerp. Hitler ordered General Kurt Student's First Parachute Army to block further advance across the Albert Canal, and General **Gustav von Zangen**'s Fifteenth Army to hold the Scheldt estuary. Until that had been cleared, Antwerp was of no use as an Allied port. Clearing Antwerp became the main mission of the Second Army, while the Canadian First Army, after investing Le Havre, moved up the coast to clear the Channel ports and to overrun the V-1 missile sites in the Pas de Calais area.

1944, September 5. Recall of Rundstedt. Hitler again assigned Rundstedt to supreme command in the west. He prepared a stand along the Westwall fortified zone (Siegfried Line).

1944, September 14. Allies Close on the German Border. The line ran northward from Switzerland, through Lorraine to Aachen, then northwesterly through Maastricht, along the Albert Canal, and west to the Channel at Ostend. Bradley's 12th Army Group had renewed a creeping advance, still hampered by gasoline shortage.

COMMENT. *Since June 6, the Allies had put more than 2.1 million men on French soil, shattered Hitler's dream of a* Festung Europa, *and flung the German forces back to their own border. The stupendous drive through France had cost some 40,000 Allied killed, 165,000 wounded, and 20,000 missing. German losses had been a catastrophic half-million men in the field forces and an additional 200,000 in the coastal fortresses. Chewed, disrupted, and battered, the remnants now stood behind the dilapidated Siegfried Line, seemingly vulnerable to an Allied* coup de grâce. *However, their homogeneous staff structure was still intact, their discipline remained, and replacements were being rushed from Germany and the east. Rundstedt and his principal subordinates provided a high order of leadership. The war was still far from its end.*

INVASION OF GERMANY, 1944

Both Montgomery and Bradley were convinced that a single thrust into Germany, furnished with unlimited support, would end the war, but neither desired to play second fiddle. Eisenhower, straddling, approved Montgomery's plan to turn the northern German flank by seizing a northern bridgehead over the Maas (Meuse) before clearing the water approaches to Antwerp. The First Allied Airborne Army (3 divisions) under Major General **Lewis H. Brereton,** in reserve in England, was attached to Montgomery's command for the operations.

Operation "Market Garden"

Montgomery's bold plan was to drop 3 airborne divisions as steppingstones behind the German lines along a narrow 60-mile causeway over marshy ground, seizing the bridges of three rivers—the Maas (Meuse), Waal (Rhine), and Lek (lower Rhine). The British Second Army—led by XXX Corps—would drive across this "airborne carpet" and turn the northern flank of the Siegfried Line.

1944, September 17. Air Drops at Arnhem, Nijmegen, and Eindhoven. The daylight drops were successful, but German resistance on the ground was stronger than expected. The U.S. 101st Division secured the Wilhelmina Canal crossing near Eindhoven. The U.S. 82nd captured the Maas bridge at Grave, but was unable to gain the Waal bridge at Nijmegen. The British 1st Airborne Division, with a Polish brigade attached, reached the Arnhem area north of the Lek, but at once became involved with unexpectedly strong German forces. The British ground advance, spearheaded by tanks, reached Eindhoven to join the 101st (September 18). The Nijmegen bridge was secured after another 24 hours of bitter fighting by a joint Anglo-American assault. Bad weather and lack of maneuver ground in the flooded countryside hampered further advance, though detachments reached the south bank of the Lek.

1944, September 17–26. Battle of Arnhem. The British 1st Airborne was pocketed by German reinforcements and forced into a small perimeter, though clinging for a while to the Lek bridgehead. Behind them the Germans now completely barred the way to further Allied advance and bad weather prevented dropping of reinforcements or supply. Ringed by close-in artillery and mortar fire, with food and ammunition exhausted, and forced away from the bridge, the defense collapsed. Some 2,200 survivors were evacuated across the Lek in assault boats during the night (September 25–26), leaving 7,000 men behind them killed, wounded, or captured.

COMMENT. *The stand of the 1st Airborne Division at Arnhem ranks high in the annals of the British Army. German reaction was prompt, skillful, and efficient. The Rhine barrier still faced the Allies and the German defense was still intact.*

The Scheldt Estuary Campaign, October–November

Montgomery now turned to the task essential to any further Allied advance—liberation of the water gate to Antwerp. The keys to the Scheldt were the South Beveland peninsula and Walcheren Island at its western tip, both highly fortified.

1944, October 1–November 8. Battle for South Beveland and Walcheren Island. Furious British assaults (some American units participated), plus a small amphibious operation, resulted in capture of the peninsula (October 31) after both sides suffered heavy losses. Walcheren Island fell (November 8) to an amphibious assault, following on the flooding of the defenses by Allied air bombings of the sea dikes. The Scheldt was now free, for the south shore had been cleared already (October 22).

1944, November 4–26. Minesweeping the Scheldt. Even before the last gun was fired at Walcheren, one of the most difficult mine sweeps of the war had begun. The 70-mile channel to Antwerp was combed 16 times by 100 Allied vessels before the first Allied convoy entered the port (November 27).

Breaking the Siegfried Line, October–December

1944, October 1–23. American Advance to the Westwall. Bradley's 12th Army Group pressed against the Siegfried Line from above Maastrich to Lunéville—3 armies now, for the new Ninth U.S. Army, Lieutenant General **William H. Simpson,** had joined (October 3). From Lunéville to the Swiss border, Devers' 6th Army Group penetrated Alsace and the Vosges Mountains. Winter was closing in. German opposition west of the Rhine was strong. Rundstedt's command, OB West, consisted from north to south of Student's Army Group H, from the North Sea to below Roermond; Model's Army Group B, reaching south to the line of the Moselle; and **Hermann Balck**'s Army Group G to Karlsruhe. An SS group, under SS Chief **Heinrich Himmler,** held the remainder of the line to Switzerland. Patton's Third Army reached and closed in on Metz (October 3). Hodges' First Army captured **Aachen** after furious fighting (October 21), the first breach of the Siegfried Line.

1944, October 28. Eisenhower Orders November Offensive. This was to destroy all German forces west of the Rhine, to establish bridgeheads across it, and to advance into Germany.

1944, November 2–7. Repulse at Schmidt. The U.S. 28th Division of the V Corps was repulsed in efforts to take Schmidt, just north of the Roer River dams.

1944, November 16–December 15. Roer River–Hürtgen Forest Operations. Bradley's Ninth and First Armies attacked against heavy opposition, over difficult terrain, enlarging the Aachen breakthrough.

Major obstacle was the Hürtgen Forest. The attack, on a narrow front, reached the Roer River, but crossing could not be attempted until the dams near Schmidt had been seized to prevent the Germans from flooding the valley. A major offensive for this purpose was begun (December 13).

1944, November 16–December 15. Lorraine Operations. Patton's Third Army captured **Metz** (December 13) and battled its way across the Seille River.

1944, November 16–December 15. Alsace Operations. Devers' group made deep gains; Seventh Army's French 2nd Armored Division* thrust through the Saverne Gap of the Vosges Mountains to liberate Strasbourg (November 23), rousing French national morale to a peak. The French First Army overran Mulhouse. Devers was now on the Rhine from Karlsruhe to below Strasbourg, and again from Mulhouse to the Swiss border; but the deep Colmar pocket in between was still firmly held by Wiese's German Nineteenth Army.

* Bitter personal enmity existed between Leclerc and de Lattre de Tassigny; hence, the 2nd French Armored Division was never under the latter's command.

German Ardennes Offensive (Battle of the Bulge), December, 1944–January, 1945

The German Plan. Hitler had prepared a striking force to split the Allies. His armor would rip through to Antwerp, crippling their supply. He hoped to destroy all Allied forces north of the line Antwerp-Brussels-Bastogne, just as in 1940. Success depended on three elements: (1) a breakthrough, (2) seizure of Allied fuel supplies and the key focal points of communication in the area St.-Vith and Bastogne, and (3) widening of the initial gap to increase the flow of invasion. Hitler's commanders, though dubious of success, obeyed orders.

1944, December 16–19. The German Blow. The operation was launched after a period of fog, rain, and snow blanketed Allied aerial observation and hobbled combat capabilities. The striking force, from north to south, consisted of the Sixth SS (General **Sepp Dietrich**) and Fifth (General **Hasso von Manteuffel**) Panzer armies—24 divisions, 10 of them armored. The Seventh Army (General **Ernst Brandenberger**) was to cover the southern flank. The initial wave—8 Panzer divisions—disrupted the U.S. VIII Corps. Tactical and strategic surprise was complete. (SHAEF

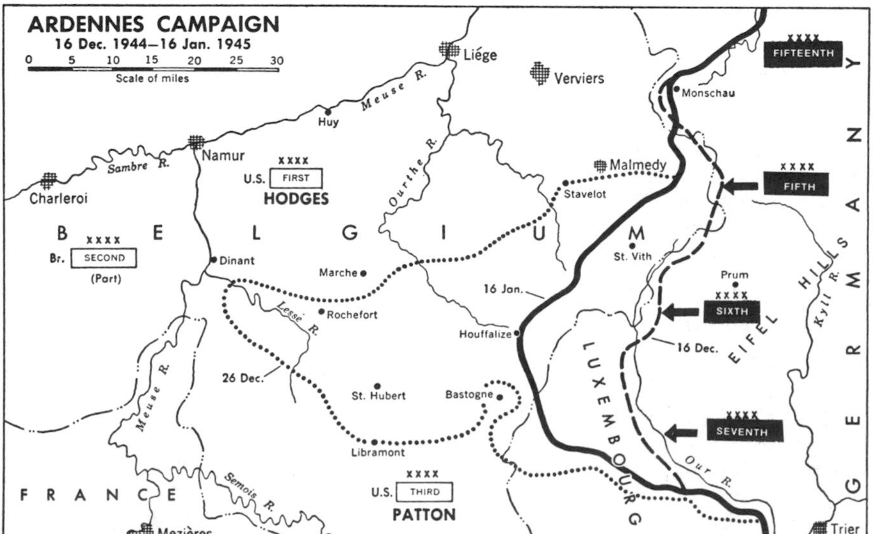

intelligence estimates had dismissed all probability of any immediate major German offensive capability.) The 106th Division, just arrived on the front, and the 28th Division, recuperating from severe fighting at Schmidt, were shattered. A paratroop drop in the area Eupen-Monschau, and a spearhead force of English-speaking German soldiers in American uniforms, added to panic and confusion behind the assault zone. But on the north flank, the U.S. V Corps, halting its own offensive toward the Roer dams, held firm, as did the U.S. 4th Division on the south. Canalized between these shoulders, the attack roared on toward the Meuse. Two U.S. armored divisions were rushed in by Bradley as immediate reinforcement. Eisenhower then committed the SHAEF reserve —the 82nd and 101st Airborne divisions (recuperating near Reims from their Maas operation). Truckborne, they arrived (December 19)—the 101st (under Brigadier General **Anthony C. McAuliffe**) at Bastogne, a check to Fifth Panzer Army's progress, and the 82nd (Major General **Matthew B. Ridgway**) to bolster the northern flank. Montgomery began shifting 1 British corps to backstop the operation along the Meuse. At Bradley's order, Patton (December 18) halted his Third Army's advance in the Saar to begin an amazing 90° shift in direction to the north, to hit the German southern flank.

1944, December 20–26. Allied Recovery. Eisenhower transferred command of all U.S. troops north of the bulge to Montgomery, leaving only Patton's army under Bradley. Despite a desperate defense of **St.-Vith** by the U.S. 7th Armored Division (Brigadier General **R. W. Hasbrouck**), the Sixth Panzer Army forged slowly ahead (December 19–22), but the delay had been fatal to the German plan. The V Corps was still presenting an impenetrable front, while the U.S. VII Corps was hurrying southwest to seal the remainder of the northern flank. At **Bastogne,** the 101st Airborne, with some other units—some 18,000 men in all—resisted all efforts of the Fifth Panzer Army to overrun their perimeter. However, the invading tide, lapping around Bastogne, progressed northwest toward the Meuse. Model, commanding Army Group B, quite properly desired now to shift the weight of the German assault to Manteuffel's Fifth Panzer Army, but Hitler, obstinate and ignorant, insisted the decisive blow be struck by his SS pet, Dietrich. By December 22, Patton was attacking north toward beleaguered Bastogne on a 2-corps front, while Devers' 6th Army Group extended its left to cover his advance. Dietrich's penetration in the Manhay-Stavelot area, and Manteuffel's spearheads—Panzer Lehr and 2nd Panzer divisions—were grinding to a halt with empty fuel tanks at **Celles,** almost in sight of the Meuse, to be struck by American and British counterattacks (December 25–26). Hitler's gamble had failed. Patton's Third Army punched a hole through Manteuffel's troops to reach Bastogne (December 26), and, with the first clear weather, Allied air began pounding German supply trains west of St.-Vith.

1944, December 26–1945, January 2. The Battle for Bastogne. Hitler insisted on the capture of Bastogne, and a furious battle raged for a week while the German tide ebbed elsewhere in the Bulge under Allied pressure. Attempting to disrupt Allied air support, the Luftwaffe made its last offensive strike (January 1), some 800 planes attacking airfields in France, Belgium, and Holland, and destroying 156 Allied planes. The attack was repulsed with heavy losses to the Germans, and the Allied air offensive over the Ardennes area and German rear elements continued.

1945, January 3–16. Allied Counteroffensive. On the northern flank of the German penetration, Montgomery unleashed Hodges' U.S. First Army. German offensive efforts near Bastogne were repulsed, and Patton's increasing efforts, supported by XIX Tactical Air Force, shrank the southern face of the German penetration. Hitler permitted withdrawal of the Sixth Panzer Army (January 8; see p. 1122). The Bulge was eliminated (January 16). Hodges' First Army returned to Bradley's control (January 18), but Simpson's Ninth Army remained in Montgomery's 21st Army Group.

COMMENT. *Hitler's Ardennes offensive was a gamble, pure and simple. The blow was checked first by the resistance of the U.S. elements on both shoulders, next by Hasbrouck's stand at St.-Vith and McAuliffe's epic defense of Bastogne. Hitler's re-*

fusal to shift the weight of the attack to the flank making the best progress was stupid. When the German armor was unable to overrun Allied fuel depots to replenish its tanks, the end was inevitable. The net result was a delay of about 6 weeks to Allied operations in the west, while Hitler had expended the slim reserves with which he otherwise might have checked the coming Russian spring offensive. German losses were some 120,000 men killed, wounded, or missing, 600 tanks and assault guns, 1,600 planes, and 6,000 vehicles. Allied losses (mostly American) were approximately 7,000 killed, 33,400 wounded, 21,000 captured or missing, and 730-odd tanks and tank destroyers. Among the Americans were 86 prisoners captured by the 1st SS Panzer Division at Malmédy on December 17th, then lined up and ruthlessly machine-gunned to death.

The Eastern Front

RUSSIAN WINTER OFFENSIVE

Following a series of probing attacks, the Soviet armies launched a concerted drive as winter hardened roads and froze the waterways.

1944, January 15–19. Liberation of Leningrad. Two Russian army groups fell on the German Eighteenth Army, investing Leningrad. General **L. A. Govorov**'s Leningrad Front, crossing the frozen Gulf of Finland, pierced the German left, while General **Kirill A. Meretzkov**'s Volkhov Front swept over frozen lakes and swamps to penetrate the German right. Novgorod was taken (January 19). German forces under General **Georg Lindemann** escaped annihilation only by rapid withdrawal. A third Russian group—General **M. M. Popov**'s Second Baltic Front—threatened further envelopment and caused the retirement of General von Kuechler's entire

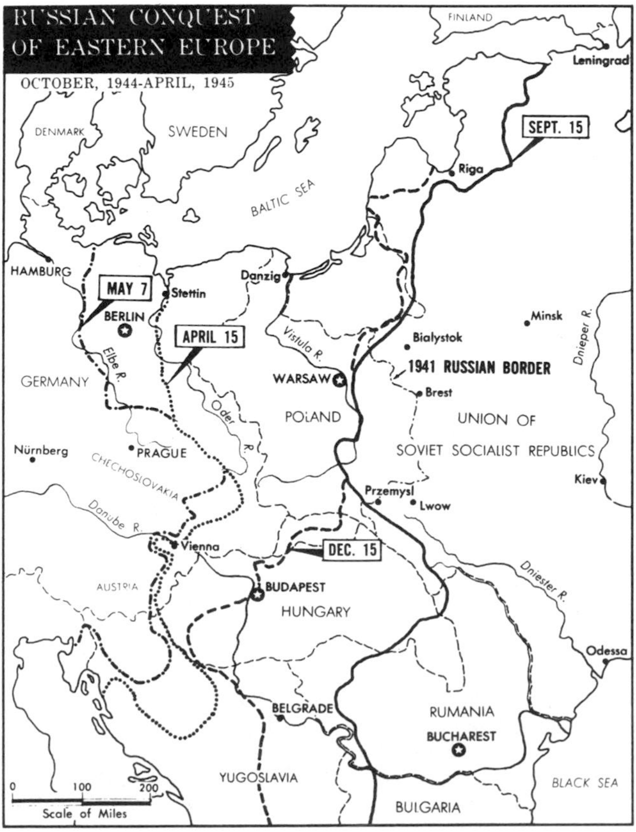

German Army Group North. Model, who replaced Kuechler (January 31), checked the Soviet drive along the line Narva-Pskov-Polotsk (March 1), when the spring thaws impeded further Russian progress.

1944, January 29–February 17. Battle of Korsun. Farther south, the main Russian offensive hit Manstein's Army Group South along the Dnieper River. The First Ukrainian Front (now under Zhukov; Vatutin had been killed) from the north, and Konev's Second Ukrainian Front from the south, encircled the German salient at Korsun, trapping 2 army corps. Manstein's immediate counterattacks bogged down in blizzards and thaws, and attempts of the trapped troops to cut their way out were only partially successful. German casualties were about 100,000. The Russian advance continued southwest across the Bug and Dniester rivers, despite desperate counterattacks by Manstein.

1944, March 10–April 10. Isolation of the First Panzer Army. General Hube, commanding the First Panzer, and operating under instructions from Manstein, kept up a magnificent defensive-offensive behind the Russian lines, playing hob with communications. A hastily-improvised Luftwaffe airlift brought in supply, while the Fourth Panzer Army drove southeast (April 5) below Tarnapol to make contact. Hube attacked westward, fighting defensively to the flanks and rear, and brought out his command practically intact.

1944, March–April. Ukraine and Rumania. Kleist's Army Group A, under pressure both by Konev and by General **Rodion Y. Malinovskiy's** Third Ukrainian Front, was forced back after furious fighting, in which the German Sixth and Eighth armies were badly cut up, and Odessa evacuated (April 10).

1944, March 30. Relief of Manstein and Kleist. Infuriated by these reverses, Hitler relieved both his southern group commanders, Model replacing brilliant Manstein and General **Ferdinand Schoerner** succeeding Kleist. By mid-April, when the thaws and Model's counteroffensive from Lwow had slowed down the Russian advance, the entire western Ukraine had been cleared and Konev's spearheads were threatening the Carpathian passes.

COMMENT. *Several elements in this vast panorama of war of movement stand out: the methodical progression of the Russian masses in a war of attrition closely directed by the Soviet high command; the amazing tenacity and ability of the German commanders, fighting a campaign they all knew was being lost through their Führer's madness; and the simple devotion of the soldiers on both sides. The mobility and efficiency of the Soviet armies were due primarily to Allied logistical assistance provided through Lend Lease.*

THE RUSSIAN SUMMER OFFENSIVE

Hitler's obsession to hold at all costs all occupied terrain prevented any steps to rectify, consolidate, and fortify the Eastern Front during the respite granted by the spring thaws. In consequence, his thin-spread 1,400-mile-long cordon lacked reserves and depth when Stalin launched his next offensive, in step with the Anglo-American invasion of France.

1944, June 22–July 10. Battle for White Russia. Stalin (Marshal Zhukov, now deputy supreme commander, controlled the operation) struck first north of the Pripet Marsh area, after an outburst of guerrilla activity paralyzed General **Ernst Busch**'s communications in rear of Army Group Center (June 22). Supported by an immense mass of artillery (estimated at 400 guns per mile of front), the Russian Third, Second, and First White Russian Fronts assaulted on a 350-mile front along the axis Smolensk-Minsk-Warsaw. Air superiority was complete; the Luftwaffe had been drained for the Western Front. Russian armor tore open a 250-mile-wide gap, encircling German strong points which were then smothered by great masses of infantry. In turn, **Vitebsk** (June 25), **Bobruisk** (June 27), and **Minsk** (July 3) were captured. Army Group Center was completely shattered, some 25 of its 33 divisions trapped. Russian estimates claimed 158,000 Germans captured,

381,000 killed, and the destruction or capture of more than 2,000 tanks, 10,000 guns, and 57,000 motor vehicles. Model was rushed north by Hitler to replace Busch.

1944, July 10–September 19. Defeat of Finland. A Russian drive under Govorov had broken through the Mannerheim Line, capturing **Viipuri** (June 20). Now the eastern Finnish defenses were overrun in the Lake Onega region. Hostilities between Finland and Russia ceased by truce (September 4). The German Twentieth Army still clung in the north around the naval and air bases of Petsamo and Kirkenes.

1944, April 8–May 9. The Crimea. The Germans, after halting the first Russian attack at the Perekop Isthmus, were forced back into Sevastopol's fortifications by General **F. I. Tolbukhin**'s Fourth Ukrainian Front, following an amphibious assault across the Kerch Strait. A 2-day assault, with heavy artillery support, cleared **Sevastopol** (May 9), but most of the German garrison was successfully evacuated by water.

1944, July 10–August 7. Drive into Poland. Methodically advancing on a widening front, Zhukov's masses enlarged both flanks of the gap, at the same time pressing on the main axis toward Warsaw. On the northern flank, a deep penetration toward Riga rolled up German Army Group North, threatening to pin it back against the Baltic Sea. Model scraped up sufficient reserves to counterattack and check the advance of Rokossovski's First White Russian Front just east of Warsaw, but farther south Konev's First Ukrainian Front surged through Lwow (July 27) to reach the upper Vistula at Baranov (August 7). The 450-mile advance by this time had overstrained Russian supply capabilities, and the offensive on this front came to a temporary halt.

1944, August 1–September 30. Warsaw Revolt. Led by General **Tadeusz Bor-Komorowski,** Polish underground forces (anti-Communist) attempted to wrest the city from German control, hoping the Russians, just across the Vistula, would help them. But the Russians lay there idle while a German SS force squelched the revolt in a bloody 2-month house-to-house battle.

1944, August 20–September 14. Conquest of Rumania. The Second and Third Ukrainian Fronts attacked across the Prut River, falling on General **Johannes Friessner**'s Army Group South Ukraine. Two of its 4 armies—Rumanian troops—allied themselves with the Russians when Rumania capitulated (August 23); most of the German Sixth and Eighth armies were trapped. Soviet troops reached the Danube at Bucharest (September 1), having captured about 100,000 prisoners and much matériel. The entire German right flank collapsed, to reform in the Transylvanian mountains.

1944, September 8. Defection of Bulgaria. Bulgaria changed sides in the war when Russian troops crossed the Danube.

1944, October 10–December 15. Drive to the Baltic. Despite efforts of Guderian (now German chief of staff) to pull Schoerner's Army Group North from its dangerous position in Latvia, Hitler delayed the movement until too late. The Russian First Baltic Front drove through to the sea, investing Memel and barring Schoerner's retreat. However, a Russian assault into East Prussia was halted by counterattacks.

1944, October 20–December 31. The Balkans. Russian efforts to block movement of General von Weichs' Army Group F, moving from Greece into Yugoslavia to bolster the German right, were nearly successful. Tolbukhin's Third Ukrainian Front, with a Bulgarian army assisting on its left, took **Belgrade** (October 20), with **Tito**'s (**Josip Broz**'s) partisans fighting beside them. This forced Weichs to move through Sarajevo, to the west. He then linked with Friessner's Army Group South along the Drava, momentarily saving the German flank. The Russians, continuing northwest, reached the Danube and won a bridgehead (November 24). **Budapest,** encircled (December 24), was still holding out as the year ended.

COMMENT. *Again and again, Hitler, despite his generals' entreaties, prevented withdrawals and regroupings which would have improved his defensive capabilities. He resisted evacuating Greece until too late for Army Group F to take any but a minor defensive role in Yugoslavia. He bled white his Panzer strength by transferring its pick to the Western Front for the abortive Ardennes offensive (see p. 1112), and kept the 20 veteran divisions of Army Group North, a splendid reserve mass of maneuver, penned in Latvia. Not the least of his erratic mistakes was to shift generals continuously between commands, as exemplified by transferring Model—his efficient troubleshooter—back to command in the West (August 25).*

WAR IN THE WEST, 1945

Battle of the Atlantic

1945, January–April. U-Boat Resurgence. Doenitz sent his new schnorkel-equipped submarines out into the Atlantic. Germany was producing approximately 27 per month, despite Allied air attacks on the submarine industry. U-boats accounted for the loss of 253,000 tons of shipping, much of it in British waters.

1945, April–May. Allied Countermeasures. A double screen of U.S. destroyer escorts and carriers patrolling the Atlantic north of the Azores stamped out the final German effort. The last action in the Atlantic was the sinking of *U-853* by U.S.S. *Atherton* and *Moberly* off Block Island (May 6).

1945, May 28. Abolition of Convoys. A joint Admiralty–U.S. Chief of Naval Operations announcement so declared, adding that all merchant ships "at night will burn navigation lights at full brilliancy and need not darken ship." The order applied to the North and South Atlantic, the Arctic and Indian oceans. In the Pacific Ocean areas, of course, the war against Japan was still on.

COMMENT. *In all, 781 U-boats were destroyed by Allied naval and air efforts during the war, with loss of 32,000 German sailors. The submarines had taken toll of 2,575 Allied and neutral vessels, causing more than 50,000 Allied casualties, about three-fourths British. At the end, 398 U-boats were still in commission. Of these, 217 were destroyed by their own crews, and the others surrendered.*

The Combined Bomber Offensive

The British and American bombing attacks (alternating night and day as in previous years) mounted in intensity and effectiveness while German air defense efficiency declined as a result of the terrible attrition. Nevertheless, the Luftwaffe continued to fight vigorously, and the appearance of the Messerschmitt 262 twin-jet fighters early in the year partially redressed the balance because of their superior performance. But the German switch to jet fighters came too late to affect the outcome of the air war. Superior numbers of conventional planes, and the superior training and operational efficiency of the Allied pilots—who had no fuel shortage to worry about—prevented the new Messerschmitts from seriously threatening Allied air superiority.

1945, February 13–14. The Dresden Raids. An RAF night attack, followed next day by a massive U.S. Eighth Air Force raid, created uncontrollable fire storms; at least 100,000 people perished in the most destructive bombardment of history.

1945, March 21–24. Crushing the Luftwaffe. Partly in preparation for the Montgomery Rhine crossing at Wesel (see p. 1120), and partly as a culminating blow of the strategic air offensive, Allied strategic and tactical air forces flew a total of 42,000 sorties over Germany from bases in England, France, Italy, and Belgium. More than 1,200 heavy Eighth Air Force bombers smashed German jet bases within range of Wesel, while medium bombers and fighter bombers struck at all other Luftwaffe installations. This, combined with the collapse of the German ground front, ended further effective German air activity.

1945, April–May. Support of the Ground Offensive. The Strategic Air Forces had practically run out of targets. The few remaining operational German factories were within easy range of tactical air forces. Air Chief Marshal Harris and General Spaatz shifted their heavy bombers to direct support of the onrushing British and American armies.

Operations in Italy

1945, January–April. Continued Stalemate. German General **Heinrich S. von Vietinghoff** (Kesselring had been transferred in March to command the defense of western Germany) labored to strengthen the Gothic Line positions of what was now German Army Group Southwest. He wanted to retire north of the Po, but Hitler harshly refused permission. Despite Allied air superiority, reduced strength, and short supplies, German morale remained high in their deep fortified zone across the peninsula. To the west, from Monaco north to the Swiss border, Graziani's Fascist Italian Ligurian Army defended the Alpes Maritimes, a force of doubtful value, except for 2 German divisions.

The polyglot Allied 15th Army Group, reorganized and reequipped, prepared for a vigorous offensive. Alexander (theater commander) and Clark (army group commander) proposed a double penetration of the Gothic Line, British Eighth Army (Richard McCreery) on the right driving on Ferrara and U.S. Fifth Army (Truscott) on Bologna. It was in effect a 1-2 assault, the British jumping off first, the Americans following 5 days later, with air support massed in that same order. Several probing attacks, including an amphibious feint at the mouth of the Po, preceded.

1945, April 9. Eighth Army Assault. Accompanied by massive air and artillery blows, the British infantry attack struck the German Tenth Army, flame-throwing tanks in the lead. A small amphibious assault across Lake Comacchio on the extreme right enveloped the German left, and the assault moved into the Argentia Gap, southeast of Bologna.

1945, April 14–20. Fifth Army Offensive. With the weight of air support now shifted to the west, the Americans sliced into the German position. They soon broke into the open Po Valley (April 20). Vietinghoff, committing his last reserves, failed to stem the tide. German resistance collapsed as American armor pressed forward. While most of the German troops managed to cross the Po, practically all heavy equipment was abandoned.

1945, April 20–May 2. Pursuit. In the Fifth Army zone, Bologna was occupied (April 21). American armor, debouching from the main effort, now reached north through Milan, up to Lake Como, and encircled Lake Garda. Behind the German lines partisans captured Musssolini, attempting to flee to Germany, and killed him (April 28). On the far left the U.S. 92nd Division moved along the coast, occupying Genoa (April 28). It then reached west to meet, near Imperia, French troops advancing from Monaco, and north to take Alessandria (April 28), Turin, and Pavia. The Eighth Army's pursuit reached Verona, Padua, Venice, and crossed the Piave (April 29). Italian Fascist resistance faded, prisoners coming in in droves. Remnants of the German Fourteenth and Tenth Armies streamed north up the Adige and Piave valleys. General Vietinghoff at Caserta agreed (April 29) to unconditional surrender, effective May 2, and American spearheads moved into the Brenner Pass, linking (May 4) at Vipiteno with U.S. Seventh Army elements driving down from the north. New Zealand units of the Eighth Army had already rounded the northern tip of the Adriatic to take Trieste (May 2).

COMMENT. *In marked contrast to all previous operations of the 15th Army Group, the breaching of the Gothic Line and the subsequent pursuit of the broken German armies was tactically superb. Truscott's employment of the Fifth Army was particularly noteworthy.*

The Western Front

ADVANCE TO THE RHINE

1945, January 1–21. German Offensive in Lorraine and Alsace. To take advantage of shifting of Allied troops to meet the German Ardennes offensive, General **Johannes von Blaskowitz'** Army Group G launched a vicious drive against the extended U.S. Seventh Army in Devers' 6th Army Group. Before it was snubbed (January 21), Patch's troops had been forced back from their Rhine Valley salient near Karlsruhe to previously prepared positions stretching from Sarreguemines to Gambs-

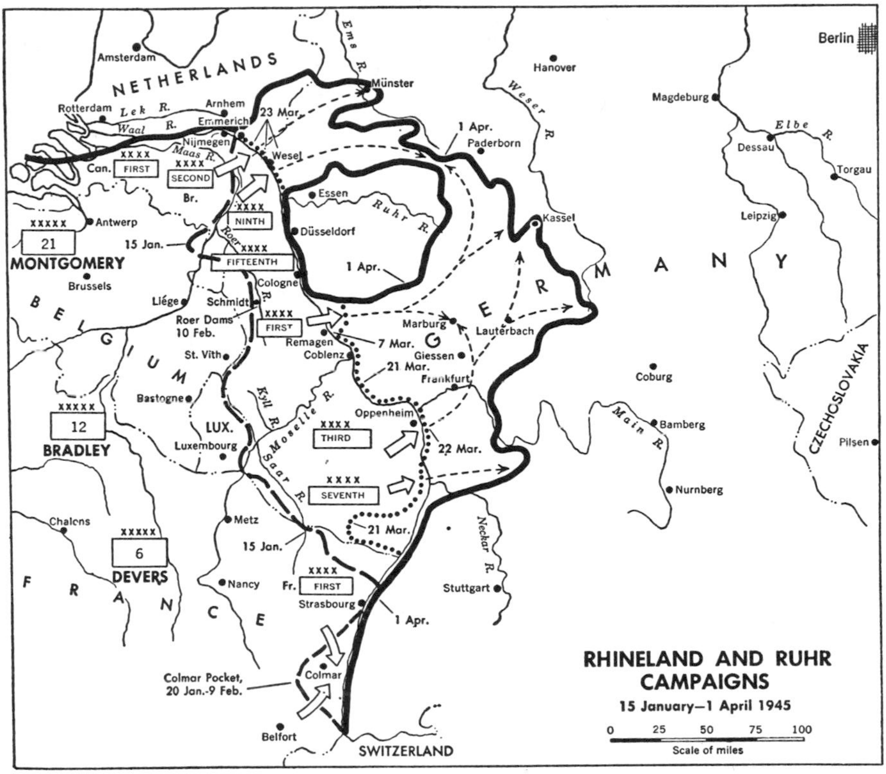

heim, north of Strasbourg. De Gaulle, fearful of the effect on French morale should Strasbourg be evacuated, insisted the city be defended. Accordingly Eisenhower, who was prepared to give ground there, ordered Devers to hold it at all costs. He did. The German advance bogged down.

1945, January 17–February 7. Allied Advances in the North. Eisenhower prepared to resume his offensive to clear the left (west) bank of the Rhine. As preliminary, Montgomery's 21 Army Group pressed into the Roermond area (January 15–26) and Bradley's 12th Army Group approached the upper Roer.

1945, January 20–February 9. End of the Colmar "Pocket." Devers threw the French First Army—reinforced by American divisions—against the Colmar "pocket" in the Vosges. The German Nineteenth Army was pinched out with heavy losses. The Allied southern flank was now solidly on the left bank of the Rhine from the Swiss border to Gambsheim, north of Strasbourg.

1945, February 8–March 10. Clearing the Rhineland—21 Army Group Sector. Montgomery launched a pincers move. Crerar's Canadian First Army attacked (February 8) southeasterly between the Maas (Meuse)—held all the way south to Roermond by Dempsey's Second British Army—and the Rhine. But the Canadians could make only slow progress over water-soaked terrain and in foul weather, and Simpson's Ninth Army attack across the Roer was held up by floods when the Germans suddenly emptied the Roer dams down the valley. His delayed assault (February 23) was most successful. Five days later his troops broke out into the open. The pincers met at Geldern (March 3), and German resistance began collapsing. The last German bridgehead, opposite Wesel, was wiped out (March 10) by the Canadians. Montgomery's armies stood on the Rhine.

1945, February 9–March 10. Clearing the Rhineland—12th Army Group Sector. Hodges' First U.S. Army, pushing through the Hürtgen Forest, protected Simpson's right flank and drove for the Rhine, rolling up Manteuffel's Fifth Panzer Army and remnants of Zangen's Fifteenth Army. Cologne was cleared (March 6–7) and task forces began probing south to contact Patton's Third Army. Patton, construing his mission of "active defense" as one of incessant attacks, had been battering his way through the rugged Eifel region, clearing the Westwall defenses from the Lorsheim Gap south to the Moselle. With Trier captured (March 5), his armored spearheads struck northeastward through disorganized German defense, the U.S. 4th Armored Division reaching the Rhine opposite Neuwied (March 7).

1945, March 7. The Remagen Bridge. A 2-battalion task force of the U.S. 9th Armored Division, probing east as part of the First Army's advance, unexpectedly found the Ludendorff Railroad Bridge over the Rhine, at Remagen, still standing. Daringly seizing it before it could be blown up, these Americans changed the entire course of Eisenhower's planned campaign. By nightfall the First Army held a rapidly swelling bridgehead on the east bank. Hitler, making another inept shuffling, displaced Rundstedt from the western command, putting Kesselring in his place (March 10).

1945, March 11–21. Clearing the Palatinate. While the First Army enlarged the Remagen bridgehead against a series of frantic piecemeal attacks, accompanied by heavy air, artillery, and V-2 bombing strikes against the original span and new bridges being thrown over the Rhine, a dazzling multipronged armored assault crushed the last remaining German forces west of the river. Patton's Third Army, driving southeast across the Moselle, and Patch's Seventh Army of Devers' 6th Army Group, attacking northeast from the Saar, each covered by its tactical air command, destroyed the dazed elements of General Brandenberger's German Seventh Army in an amazingly co-ordinated crisscross operation. Except for a quickly melting bridgehead held by General **Hermann Foertsch**'s German First Army opposite Karlsruhe, the AEF lay solidly along the Rhine from Holland to Switzerland, with its Remagen bridgehead on the east bank now some 20 miles long, 8 miles deep, and linked by 6 bridges. The Rhineland campaign cost the Germans some 60,000 men killed or wounded and 250,000 taken prisoner, together with great quantities of matériel. Allied losses were less than 20,000.

THE RHINE CROSSINGS

Eisenhower, realizing that offensive operations would be much easier in the open North German Plain than in the mountainous region south of the Ruhr, had planned to have Montgomery's 21 Army Group make the main assault into the heart of Germany. Bradley's and Devers' army groups were to play secondary roles. The unexpected Remagen bridgehead had only partly changed this plan. To oppose 85 well-equipped, well-supplied Allied divisions, Kesselring now had east of the Rhine less than 60 half-strength divisions, short of equipment, weapons, fuel, and ammunition. However, they were defending their homeland.

1945, March 22. Oppenheim. Unexpectedly, Patton (who had long planned the move and brought bridging equipment and a Navy detachment with landing craft in his army train) threw the U.S. 5th Division across the Rhine against negligible opposition. Neither air nor artillery support was used in this brilliant surprise assault. His losses were but 34 men killed or wounded. Forty-eight hours later, his bridges were completed, 4 divisions were across, armor was moving over, and another bridge at Boppard, 40 miles to the north, was also in being. Four days later, his spearheads reached Lauterbach, 100 miles east of the Rhine.

1945, March 23. Wesel. One day behind Patton, Montgomery launched his long-planned full-dress Rhine crossing north of the Ruhr. The British Second Army led off, behind the support of some 3,000 guns on a 20-mile front, and a heavy air attack (see p. 1117). The Ninth U.S. Army began its crossing at Dinslaken (March 24), while a daylight drop of 2 airborne divisions—U.S. 17th and British 6th—

landed north of Wesel. German resistance was fierce but relatively ineffective. Montgomery's army group soon was pouring over 12 bridges (March 26) and 2 days later had broken through a final German stand at Haltern on the Lippe River.

1945, March 25. Remagen. Hodges' First Army broke out of its bridgehead and its armored spearheads reached Marburg, some 70 miles to the east (March 28).

1945, March 26. Worms-Mannheim. Devers' 6th Army Group began to move across the river. The Seventh Army crossed in the Worms-Mannheim area. De Lattre de Tassigny's First French Army soon followed at Gersheim (March 31).

THE GERMAN COLLAPSE

1945, March 28. Eisenhower's Change of Plan. Because of the dramatic and unexpected success of Patton's and Hodges' armies, Eisenhower decided to have Bradley's 12th Army Group make the main effort, driving east through central Germany on Leipzig, forgetting Berlin, toward which the Russians were advancing from the east (see p. 1123). Bradley's left and Montgomery's right (U.S. Ninth Army) would encircle the Ruhr, while the remainder of 21 Army Group covered the main advance by moving northeast on Hamburg and the Elbe. The advance would halt on the Elbe. SHAEF was concerned by the threat (later proven a fable) that a Nazi last-ditch guerrilla resistance—the "Werewolves"—would operate from a nebulous "National Redoubt" in the German-Austrian Alps. So while Montgomery and Bradley were to close and await the Russians on the line Elbe-Mulde-Erzgebirge, Devers' 6th Army Group would move down the Danube Valley to squelch all resistance. Eisenhower's decision to turn from what he considered to be a political objective—Berlin—to the apparently more immediate military objective of crushing the last dregs of Nazi armed force was received with bitter criticism by the British. The military and political issues and considerations were complex and confused. In retrospect, Eisenhower's decision appears to have been faulty, but it was evidently consistent with guidance from U.S. Army Chief of Staff General Marshall.

1945, March 28–April 18. Ruhr Encirclement. Armored spearheads of the Ninth and First armies met at Paderborn (April 1). The Ninth Army returned to Bradley's control. Rushing eastward, the Ninth Army reached the Elbe near **Magdeburg** (April 11), and encountered fierce resistance as it closed up to the river to north and south. The First Army's main thrust reached Warburg (April 4). That day Patton's troops were sweeping through the Thuringian Forest, nearly 150 miles east of the Rhine. In Devers' group, the U.S. Seventh Army was on the Main, and the First French Army was reaching through the Black Forest. Behind all, the newly organized U.S. Fifteenth Army, under Lieutenant General **Leonard T. Gerow,** was sealing the western face of the Ruhr area along the Rhine. Inside the 4,000-square-mile area of the Ruhr pocket were crowded more than 300,000 men—mostly the disorganized bulk of Model's Army Group B. To the north Blaskowitz' broken Army Group H was reeling back into Holland and northwest Germany, while to the east and south Army Group G (now under SS General **Paul Hausser**) was putting up disorganized but often bitter resistance. Kesselring watched helplessly, having neither means nor communications to regroup or establish any covering force, while Hitler in Berlin kept thundering his usual senseless "hold in place" directives. Model, inside the pocket, conducted his typical skillful delaying resistance to the closing ring until simultaneous drives from north and south split his forces (April 14). In the face of a preposterous demand from Hitler that he now cut his way out, Model disbanded his troops and disappeared—apparently having committed suicide. Four days later the last resistance dissolved; some 317,000 German soldiers had entered Allied prison camps. The once mighty Wehrmacht was collapsing, although disjointed fanatical opposition was still stiff in places.

1945, April 18–May 7. Final Operations—21 Army Group Sector. In Holland, the Canadian First Army suspended hostilities in a partial truce, Blaskowitz agreeing to cease flooding the country and to permit food to reach the starving population; however, he still refused to surrender. The British Second Army reached the west bank of the Elbe (April 26); Lubeck and Wismar to the north were occupied (May 2); contact with advancing Russians was made the same day. Hamburg surrendered (May 3).

1945, April 18–May 7. Final Operations—12th Army Group Sector. The First Army crushed a determined pocket of resistance in the Harz Mountains area (April 14–21). Closing on the Mulde and Elbe rivers, Hodges's troops made the first contact with Soviet troops from the east at Torgau (April 25). The Allied front now froze on the Mulde-Elbe-Erzgebirge line, while the Third Army swept down the Danube Valley to occupy Linz (May 5). Its left, in Czechoslovakia, reached Pilsen (May 6) and moved on Prague until halted by SHAEF order next day.

1945, April 18–May 7. Final Operations—6th Army Group Sector. The U.S. Seventh Army, after a sharp struggle at Nuremberg, advanced southeast to force a crossing of the Danube, taking Berchtesgaden (Hitler's mountain retreat) and Innsbruck, and meeting in the Brenner Pass elements of the U.S. Fifth Army moving north from Italy. The Seventh Army's movements had been hampered by an annoying clash between Americans and French over Stuttgart. The squabble ended only when U.S. military authorities threatened to cut off further supply to French troops. Meanwhile, de Lattre's spearheads mopped up the Black Forest to the Swiss border.

1945, May 5–7. German Dissolution. Blaskowitz formally surrendered all German forces in Holland, Denmark, Schleswig-Holstein, and northwest Germany, together with the coastal islands, to Montgomery. On the southern flank, General Schulz surrendered Army Group G to Devers. Droves of individual German soldiers fled west over the Elbe from the Russians to surrender to the nearest Anglo-American units. Doenitz, successor to Hitler (see p. 1123), sent emissaries to Eisenhower at Rheims to negotiate final surrender of the Third Reich.

1945, May 7–8. Unconditional Surrender. Admiral **Hans von Friedeburg** and General **Alfred Jodl,** representing Doenitz, surrendered to Eisenhower—represented by his chief of staff, Lieutenant General **Walter Bedell Smith.** Next day, in Berlin, Marshal Keitel, Admiral Friedeburg, and Air General Hans-Jürgen Stumpff ratified the surrender to Soviet Zhukov and Tedder, Eisenhower's Deputy Supreme Commander. World War II in the West officially ended at midnight May 8–9, 1945.

The Eastern Front

RUSSIAN WINTER OFFENSIVE

1945, January 12–February 16. Drive into Germany. From the Baltic to the Carpathians, the front exploded, Konev's First Ukrainian Front on the left leading, the army groups to his right unfolding in turn (Zhukov's First White Russian; Rokossovski's Second White Russian; **Ivan Chernyakovski**'s Third White Russian; **Ivan K. Bagramyan**'s First Baltic; and Andrei Yeremenko's Second Baltic). Vastly outnumbered and lacking any secondary defensive preparations, the Germans fell back, with the isolated fortresses of Torun (Thorn), Poznan (Posen), and Breslau still battling in their rear. Zhukov's First White Russian Front reached the Oder River near Kustrin (January 31) after an advance of nearly 300 miles; Konev, to his left, gained the Oder-Neisse line (February 15). There the advance halted, its long communications lines strained beyond capacity. The invading tide turned north, where the Germans were pinned against the Baltic in 2 isolated areas—Army Group Center in East Prussia and Army Group Kurland (formerly Army Group North) in Latvia.

1945, January 12–April 16. The Danube Valley. South of the Carpathians the advance of the three Russian fronts or army groups (**Ivan Petrov**'s Fourth Ukrainian; Malinovski's Second Ukrainian; and Tolbukhin's Third Ukrainian) was blocked at Budapest for more than a month. Completely surrounded, the city finally fell (February 13). Hitler, in a desperate effort to protect the Lake Balaton oil fields, ordered the rehabilitated Sixth Panzer Army into the area from the Western Front. Its counterattack (in March) checked the valley advance, but died when fuel gave out. Malinovskiy's Second Ukrainian Front then drove into Vienna (April 15).

1945, February 16–April 15. The Baltic

Coast. Zhukov's army group and Rokossovski's Second White Russian Front moved north from the Oder near Stettin up to Königsberg, while Bagramyan, now commanding the Second Baltic Front, blocked the Kurland peninsula. More than 500,000 German troops were cut off, but not isolated, thanks to the German Navy's continuing control of the Baltic Sea. An estimated million and a half fugitives and 4 army divisions were evacuated from Kurland, including 157,000 wounded. In turn, Danzig and Gdynia (March), Königsberg and Pillau (April 25), and Kolberg (mid-April) were successfully evacuated by the German Navy. In these operations Allied air power slowly nibbled away German naval strength. By April only the cruisers *Prinz Eugen* and *Nürnberg* were still afloat. But the task had been accomplished.

COMMENT. *The last stand of the German Navy in the Baltic presents an example of the value of sea power; a small, well-led, and well-trained squadron, in confined waters and without adequate air support, long denied victory to a more powerful enemy unfamiliar with the sea.*

1945, April 16–May 7. The End. For the final offensive against Berlin General **Vassili Sokolovski** took over command of the First White Russian Front from Zhukov, who commanded a super army group of Konev's and Sokolovski's two fronts. The resumed Russian northwest advance, despite desperate but scattered resistance, reached Berlin (April 22) and surrounded it (April 25). That same day, elements of Bradley's 12th Army Group and Konev's First Ukrainian Front made contact at Torgau on the Elbe. Farther north, Rokossovski, who had captured Stettin (April 26), made contact with American units of Montgomery's 21st Army Group at Wismar (May 3). In Berlin, meanwhile, Hitler—after appointing Doenitz as his successor—had committed suicide (April 30) before the Russians, after desperate street fighting, finally stamped out all resistance (May 2). Farther south, Malinovskiy's Second Ukrainian Front was nearing Patton's advance down the Danube near Linz, and at Trieste the British Eighth Army had met Tito's partisans (May 1).

Russian estimates (probably correct) of German losses in the east during the last 3 months of the war were 1 million killed; 800,000 men, 6,000 aircraft, 12,000 tanks, and 23,000 guns were captured.

COMMENT. *Simpson's Ninth U.S. Army was on the Elbe, 60 miles west of Berlin, 5 days before the Russian offensive began, and 2 weeks before they surrounded the city. Since the Ninth Army had moved more than 120 miles in the previous 10 days, many critics assume that it could easily have reached and captured Berlin before the Russians.*

WORLD WAR II IN ASIA AND THE PACIFIC

THE EARLY YEARS, 1937–1941

1931–1937. Background. Japan had been pursuing a policy of aggressive expansion and domination in China (see pp. 1043 and 1044).

1937, July 7. Beginning of the "China Incident." Japanese troops in North China, ostensibly on night maneuvers, clashed with Chinese troops near the Marco Polo Bridge at **Lukouchiao,** near Peiping. This affair initiated a full-scale invasion of China, which the Japanese termed the "China Incident." It may be considered as the start of World War II.

The Opponents. Generalissimo Chiang Kai-shek's National Government Army consisted of approximately 2 million poorly trained, poorly equipped troops. In addition, the Chinese Communist Army, in northwest China, then comprising about 150,000 guerrilla troops, nominally supported Chiang against the Japanese. The National Government supported 45,000 of these in a newly created Eighth Route Army, under Chu Teh. China had no navy, only a handful of outmoded aircraft with relatively inexperienced Chinese and foreign mercenary pilots, and no trained reserves existed. China's industry was incapable of supporting a major war effort.

The regular Japanese Army consisted of about 300,000 soldiers, equipped with the most modern military weapons. There were also about 150,000 moderately well-trained and equipped Manchurian and Mongolian troops under Japanese officers. There were more than 2 million trained reserves in Japan. The Japanese Navy was the third largest in the world and in many respects the most modern. The air forces of both army and navy were equipped with modern aircraft and manned by competent airmen. Japan was a modern industrial nation, capable of turning out great quantities of excellent war matériel.

1937, July–December. Operations North of the Yellow River. Japanese troops quickly captured Peiping (July 28) and Tientsin (July 29). In subsequent months the Japanese advanced west and south against relatively ineffective Chinese opposition to conquer Chahar and part of Suiyuan, reaching the upper bend of the Yellow River at Paotow. Their principal efforts, however, were southward down the railroad lines toward Nanking, Hankow, and Sian. Increasing effectiveness of the Chinese Army, growing unrest and resistance among the Chinese in the heavily populated conquered areas, and the long-distance logistical problems slowed the advance during the fall. The main Japanese drive, however, culminated in the capture of Tsinan, capital of Shantung (December 27). This gave them control of most of the area north of the Yellow River.

1937, August 8–November 8. The Second Battle of Shanghai. **(See p. 1046.)** Chinese resistance against an amphibious Japanese assault was as tenacious as it had been more than 5 years earlier. Japanese reinforcements were rushed to Shanghai to avoid defeat. Despite savage air bombardment and effective naval gunfire support, for several weeks the Japanese were pinned to their beachheads at the outskirts of the city. Finally, after 2 months, additional Japanese reinforcements permitted amphibious landings north and south of Shanghai, and they finally drove out the shattered defenders.

1937, September 25. Battle of P'inghsinkuan. The Japanese 5th Division, under General **Seishiro Itagaki,** was ambushed and defeated in the Wutai Mountains of northern Shansi by the Chinese 115th Division (Communist, of the Eighth Route Army), under General **Nieh Jung-chen.** This victory had great propaganda significance throughout China. It was the first and last division-sized engagement fought by the Chinese Communists during the war.

1937–1940. Communist Consolidation. They spent the next three years expanding and consolidating their control of northwest China, and establishing guerrilla bases behind the Japanese lines. The Eighth Route Army made only a few minor raids against the Japanese front-line forces.

1937, November–December. Japanese Pursuit toward Nanking. The Japanese troops that captured Shanghai advanced up the Yangtze River toward the Chinese capital, meeting ineffectual resistance.

1937, December 12. The *Panay* Incident. Japanese aircraft made an unexpected and unprovoked attack on British and American gunboats moored in the river, near Nanking. The U.S.S. *Panay* was sunk by repeated dive bombings; the British vessel was badly damaged. The American public was outraged, but Japan later apologized and paid an indemnity.

1937, December 13. Fall of Nanking. The city was ravaged by Japanese troops for several days in a senseless orgy of slaughter, rape, and destruction. Chiang Kai-shek had meanwhile moved his capital westward to Hankow. To the surprise of the Japanese and of the rest of the world, the National Government did not collapse; and despite heavy military losses, both the Chinese Army and the Chinese people developed an amazing will to resist, and a moral unity.

1938, January–April. Renewed Offensive in the North. Completing the conquest of Shantung (January), the Japanese resumed their drive down the railroads toward Nanking and Hankow. Their advance was slow but steady; effective action by mobile Chinese regular forces and local guerrillas restricted their control to the vicinity of the railroad.

1938, April. Battle of Taierchwang. Chinese regular forces and guerrillas, under General Li Tsung-jen, probably exceeding 200,000 in numbers, cut off and surrounded a Japanese force of 60,000. Initial Japanese efforts to fight their way out were repulsed, and losses were heavy on both sides. The Japenese finally fought their way out to the north, but left 20,000 dead and large quantities of equipment behind them. This victory greatly bolstered Chinese morale, but had no lasting effects.

1938, May–June. Japanese Recovery. The Japanese quickly regrouped, reorganized, then renewed their attacks from the north, while another column moved up the railroad from Nanking. Hsuchow was captured (May 20); Kaifeng fell soon afterward (June 6). By the end of the month the Japanese had complete control of the Peking-Nanking railroad.

1938, May. Establishment of the New Fourth Army. Chiang Kai-shek agreed to support another Communist army in east-central China, mostly behind the Japanese lines south of the middle Yangtze. The commander was **Yeh T'ing.**

1938, June–July. Japanese Failure at Chengchow. The Japanese now advanced westward from Kaifeng to seize the important railroad junction of Chengchow, preparatory to an advance down the railroad to Hankow. The Chinese broke the Yellow River dikes, flooding the countryside and shifting the entire river course to a former bed, emptying into the Yellow Sea hundreds of miles from its recent mouth in the Gulf of Chihli. The Japanese advance was completely halted by this man-made catastrophe. Many troops were drowned, supplies destroyed, tanks, trucks, and guns covered with water or bogged down in the mud. The offensive was canceled.

1938, July–October. Renewed Advance on Hankow. Shifting their axis of advance farther south, the Japanese again began to threaten Chiang's capital, this time from the east, up the Yangtze River. Determined Chinese resistance resulted in the bloodiest fighting of the war in China. The Japanese, supported by their unopposed air force, captured the city (October 25). Chiang again shifted his capital westward up the Yangtze, this time to Chungking in mountainous Szechwan.

1938, October. Capture of Canton. Japanese amphibious forces landed near Hong Kong (October 12), then advanced inland to seize Canton (October 21). They now controlled China's two principal seaports.

1939. Revised Japanese Strategy. Japan, frustrated by inconclusive war and the problems of controlling a hostile population in occupied China, decided to shift to a strategy of attrition in China, which continued for several years. In 1939 they captured Hainan Island and most of China's remaining seaports, hoping to cut off all foreign supplies from China and thus force the collapse and surrender of Chiang's government. The Chinese, however, were able to keep open 2 supply routes, by means of which they could still obtain a trickle of military supplies. One was along the narrow-gauge railway from Haiphong, in French Indochina, to Kunming. The other was through British Burma, then over the narrow, twisting Burma Road to Kunming.

1940, March 30. Establishment of Puppet Chinese Government. The Japanese installed respected politician **Wang Ching-wei** at Nanking as puppet ruler of occupied China. Their hopes that this government would obtain support of some of Chiang's followers were not fulfilled.

1940, June 25. Preliminary Moves in Indochina. Taking advantage of France's defeat in Europe, Japan demanded and received from the Vichy government the right to land forces. The arrival of Japanese warships in French Indochinese ports soon closed the Haiphong-Kunming supply route.

1940, July 18. Closing of the Burma Road. Hard-pressed by Germany, Prime Minister Churchill's British government acceded to Japanese demands for closing of the Burma Road. China was now virtually isolated, but Chiang and his people remained steadfast.

1940, August 20–November 30. Communist "Hundred Regiments Offensive." An intensive series of small-scale guerrilla raids ordered by Mao Tse-tung was carried out in Shansi, Chahar, Hopeh, and Honan. These attacks against Japanese outposts, roads, and railroads were highly successful, and disrupted the Japanese rear areas.

1940, September 4. American Warning to Japan. Secretary of State **Cordell Hull** warned Japan of the unfavorable reaction which would be aroused in the U.S. by aggressive moves against French Indochina.

1940, September 22. Japan Begins Occupation of Indochina. Japanese troops began to occupy northern Indochina. Air bases were established and ground forces began an offensive into China.

1940, September 26. American Embargo on Steel for Japan. President Roosevelt ordered an embargo on shipment of scrap iron and steel from the United States to Japan. Japan declared this to be an "unfriendly act" (October 8).

1940, September 27. Establishment of the Rome-Berlin-Tokyo Axis. (See p. 1036.)

1940, October 18. Reopening of the Burma Road. With encouragement from the U.S., which wished to be able to ship Lend Lease materials to China, and with the immediate German threat to Britain removed, Churchill reopened the Burma Road.

1941–1943. Japanese Reprisals against the Communists. In reprisal against the "Hundred Regiments Offensive" (see p. 1125) the Japanese began a series of savage punitive raids against the Chinese Communists. During three years, the Communist Eighth Route Army was constantly on the defense and lost about 100,000 casualties.

1941, January 1–7. Anhwei Incident. Chiang Kai-shek had ordered (December, 1940) the Communist New Fourth Army, operating south of the Yangtze in Anhwei, to operate against Japanese troops north of the river. The army commander Yeh T'ing ignored the order, which was apparently not consistent with his instructions from Mao Tse-tung in Yenan. Chiang repeated the order, and threateningly moved Nationalist troops to the vicinity. The Communists slowly began to cross (late December). When only 10,000 of New Fourth Army, including headquarters, remained south of the river, this element was attacked by the Nationalists; all Communists were killed or captured. Yeh T'ing was wounded and captured. Communist-Nationalist relations were greatly embittered by this incident. Mao appointed **Chen Yi** as new commander of New Fourth Army.

1941, April 13. Japanese-Russian Neutrality Treaty. This assured Japan that she would not be involved in a war in Siberia should German threats against Russia materialize, and at the same time assured Stalin that in such an event he would not have to fight a 2-front war.

1941, July 26. "Freezing" of Japanese Assets in the U.S. This was in retaliation for the continuing and spreading Japanese occupation of Indochina. Britain soon followed suit.

1941, August 17. Renewed American Warning. President Roosevelt warned Japan that further attempts to dominate Asia would force the U.S. to take appropriate steps to safeguard American rights and interests. Meanwhile, in Washington, negotiations were going on between the U.S. government and the Japanese ambassador to find ways to reduce the growing tension between the 2 nations.

1941, September–December. The "Flying Tigers." With the tacit approval of the U.S. government, retired U.S. Army Air Force Captain **Claire L. Chennault,** now a colonel in the Chinese Air Force, established a mercenary organization known as the American Volunteer Group for service in China against Japan. The AVG, later dubbed "Flying Tigers," comprised about 100 trained U.S. airmen (formerly Army, Navy, and Marine Corps officers), plus American maintenance personnel, and were equipped with P-40 airplanes provided China under Lend Lease. Chennault trained his group in his own unique, revolutionary air tactical concepts and procedures at an abandoned RAF base at Toungoo in Burma.

1941, October 17. Tojo Becomes Premier. A new militaristic government came into power under Lieutenant General **Hideki Tojo,** supported by Japan's principal military men: Marshal **Hajime Sugiyama,** Chief of the Army General Staff, and Admiral **Osami Nagano,** Chief of the Naval General Staff.

1941, November 5. Promulgation of Secret War Plans. The Japanese Imperial General Headquarters issued a secret plan for simultaneous offensives against the U.S. Pacific Fleet at Pearl Harbor, British Malaya, the American Philippines, and the Netherlands East Indies, to secure the entire Southern Resources Area. The plan was to be implemented only if the continuing negotiations in Washington failed to reach an agreement satisfactory to Japan.

1941, November 15. Arrival of Special Japanese Ambassador Kurusu in Washington. Ambassador (Admiral) **Kichisaburo Nomura,** who had been conducting Japan's negotiations since February, was joined by special envoy **Saburo Kurusu.** They endeavored to obtain American agreement to reopen trade negotiations.

1941, November 26. Secretary Hull's Proposals. Mr. Hull stated that the basis of agreement would have to include Japanese withdrawal from French Indochina and China, and recognition of the National Government of Chiang Kai-shek. This being totally unacceptable to Japan, Tojo's government decided to initiate the war plan as quickly as possible, meanwhile pretending to continue negotiations in Washington to facilitate military surprise.

1941, December 7. Pearl Harbor; War with the U.S. (See below.)

THE WAR AGAINST JAPAN, DECEMBER, 1941

Pearl Harbor and the Central Pacific

1941, November. The Japanese Strategic Plan. Japan realized that she could not match the industrial strength and resources of the Allies, or even of the United States alone. The Japanese believed that they could successfully employ, however, the same basic offensive-defensive strategic concept that had brought them victory over Russia in the Russo-Japanese War (see p. 920). Their plan had three phases: Phase 1, neutralize the U.S. Pacific Fleet—the only major hostile force in the Pacific–East Asia region—by a surprise attack, while simultaneously seizing the Southern Resources Area and also strategic areas permitting establishment of a defensive perimeter around it; Phase 2, consolidate and strengthen the perimeter, so as to make any Allied attacks prohibitively costly; Phase 3, defeat and destroy any Allied efforts to penetrate the perimeter. The Japanese believed that the strength of their defenses, combined with the extremely long and vulnerable Allied lines of communications, would ensure success.

Comparative Naval Strengths in the Pacific

December, 1941	*Japan*[a]	*United States*[b]	*British Empire*[c]	*Netherlands*	*Total Allied*
Battleships and Battle Cruisers	11[d]	9	2	—	11
Aircraft Carriers	11	3	—	—	3
Heavy Cruisers (8-inch guns or more)	18	13	1	—	14
Light Cruisers (6-inch guns or less)	23	11	7	3	21
Destroyers	129	80	13	7	100
Submarines	67	56	—	13	69

[a] Most Japanese ships were newer, faster, and more heavily armed than those of the Allies.
[b] These include the forces of the American Pacific and Asiatic Fleets. In addition, because of the threat of war against Germany's U-boat fleet, in the Atlantic the United States had 8 battleships, 4 carriers, 5 heavy cruisers, 8 light cruisers, 93 destroyers, and 56 submarines.
[c] Includes Australian and New Zealand vessels.
[d] Includes the *Yamato,* largest battleship ever built (with nine 18.1-inch guns, the most powerful in the world), completed in December, 1941. Her sister ship, *Masashi,* was completed in July, 1942.

1941, November 26. Departure of the Japanese First Air Fleet. Including 6 aircraft carriers, supported by battleships, heavy cruisers, and submarines, the fleet of Vice Admiral **Chuichi Nagumo** left the Kurile Islands under conditions of absolute secrecy (November 25, Washington time). He was informed by a code message at sea of the Japanese decision for war, and continued steaming east in accordance with the secret plan to strike the U.S. Fleet at its base at Pearl Harbor.

1941, November 26–December 7. American Readiness and Plans. Japan's preparations for war were well known to U.S. military and civilian authorities, who expected that the blow would fall on Malaya or the Philippines. U.S. intelligence, which had broken the Japanese secret radio code, was aware of the movements and location of most major Japanese army and navy units—with the notable exception of the First Air Fleet, which was moving under strict radio silence, while other radio stations in Japanese home waters simulated the call signals of the vessels of this fleet. (The Japanese did not guess that their secret messages were being decoded, but they knew that the intensity and origins of radio traffic were probably being monitored.)

1941, December 7. Pearl Harbor. In complete surprise, both strategic and tactical, 360 planes of Nagumo's fleet struck Oahu

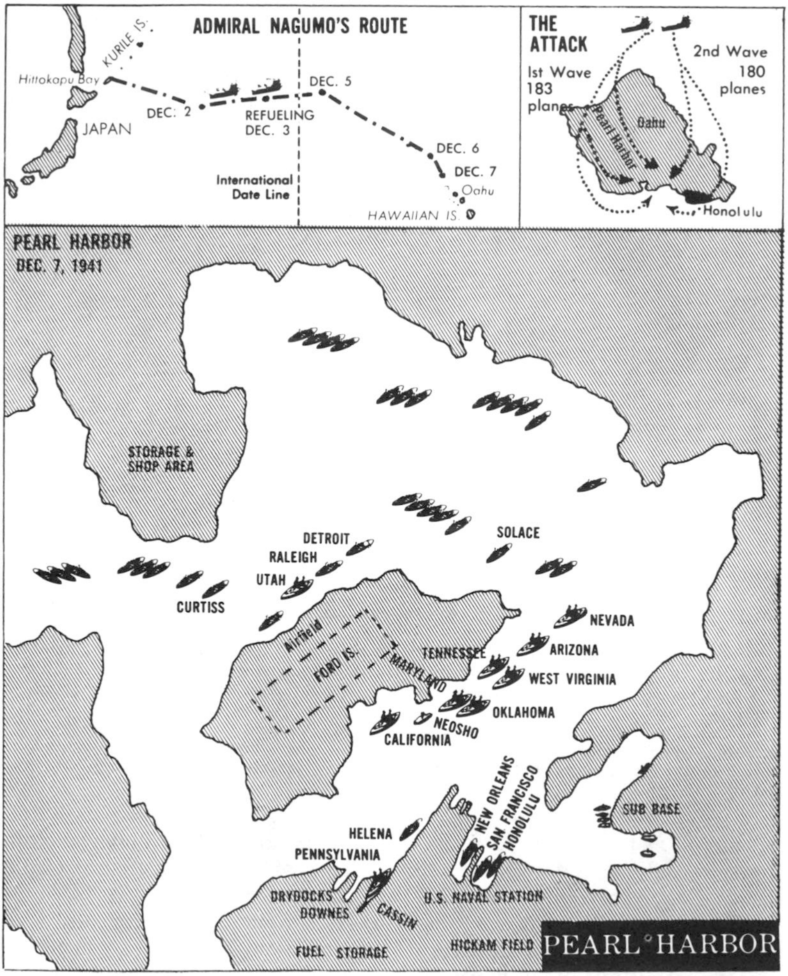

on Sunday morning, their targets the U.S. Pacific Fleet moored in Pearl Harbor and the military airfields on the island. Of the 8 battleships present, 3 were sunk, another capsized, and the remainder seriously damaged. Three light cruisers, 3 destroyers, and other vessels were also sunk or seriously damaged. On land, of 231 Army planes arrayed on airfields, only 166 remained intact or reparable; of Navy and Marine Corps planes, only 54 out of some 250 remained. Despite the surprise, both Navy and Army personnel fought back savagely. More than 3,000 Navy and Marine officers and men were killed and 876 wounded. Army losses were 226 killed and 396 wounded.

COMMENT. *The U.S. Pacific Fleet had been neutralized for at least a year to come. The fortuitous absence from Pearl Harbor of all 3 U.S. carriers of the fleet*—Enterprise, Lexington, *and* Saratoga—*alone prevented a major disaster from assuming the proportions of a national calamity. The issue of responsibility for the disaster has been controversial. However, both the U.S. Army Chief of Staff, General Marshall, and the U.S. Chief of Naval Operations, Admiral* **Harold R. Stark,** *had sufficient information, as a result of U.S. breaking of Japanese codes, to realize that war was imminent, and to recognize that an attack on Pearl Harbor was a distinct possibility. They failed to satisfy themselves that their subordinates in Hawaii were sufficiently alert. On the other hand, those subordinates, Lieutenant General* **Walter C. Short** *and Admiral* **Husband E. Kimmel** *had been alerted; their failure to be ready was inexcusable. Both were relieved of their commands.*

1941, December 8–23. Wake Island. A gallant defense by U.S. Marines and Navy personnel under Major **James Devereux** and Commander **Winfield Cunningham** repulsed one Japanese assault (December 11). A second assault overwhelmed the defenders.

1941, December 10. Guam. A Japanese landing quickly overwhelmed a handful of Marines and sailors.

Operations in Asia

HONG KONG

1941, December 8–10.* Invasion of Kowloon. The Japanese 38th Division smashed its way through the mainland defenses of the Hong Kong Colony. The British withdrew to Hong Kong Island.

1941, December 13. Japanese Demand for Surrender. The British commander, Major General **C. M. Maltby,** rejected the Japanese surrender demand. Japanese artillery, air units, and naval forces began an intensive bombardment of Hong Kong.

1941, December 18–25. The Assault. Amphibious landings on Hong Kong Island were resisted desperately but vainly by the British.

* Note that events west of the International Date Line took place on December 8; that same day, east of the Date Line, was December 7.

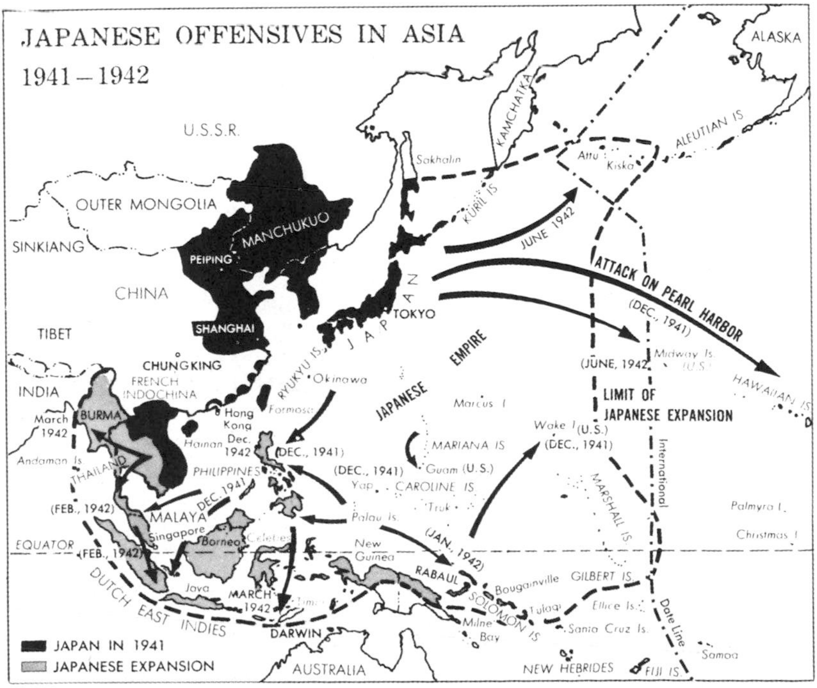

1941, December 25. Surrender. Out of water, and split into small pockets of resistance, the remnants of the 12,000-man British garrison surrendered. Japanese losses totaled fewer than 3,000.

MALAYA

1941, December 8. Invasion of Northern Malaya. Following intensive predawn air attacks against RAF bases in Malaya and Singapore, the Japanese Twenty-fifth Army, commanded by Lieutenant General **Tomoyuki Yamashita,** made amphibious landings at Kota Bharu, near the northeast tip of Malaya, and at nearby Simgora and Patani, at the very southern extremity of Thailand's Kra Isthmus. The invaders, some 100,000 in number, were in 3 divisions, with substantial reinforcements of tanks and artillery. They quickly moved southward, on both sides of the peninsula, sweeping aside relatively light British covering units in the north. The bulk of British forces—slightly more than 100,000 men, also in 3 divisions—had been deployed to meet an anticipated invasion attempt farther south, directed against the great fortress of Singapore. The British commander, Lieutenant General **A. E. Percival,** regrouped to meet the Japanese drives.

1941, December 10. Loss of the *Prince of Wales* and *Repulse*. Admiral **Sir Tom Phillips** had raced north (December 8) from Singapore with H.M. battleship *Prince of Wales,* the battle cruiser *Repulse,* and a few destroyers, seeking to strike and destroy the amphibious armada supporting the Japanese invasion. The RAF, hard hit by Japanese bombings, was unable to provide air support or reconnaissance. Unable to find the Japanese vessels, the British ships were returning south along the Malayan coast, when struck by Japanese aircraft based in southern Indochina. In the subsequent surface-air battle, which raged for about an hour, both great British ships, hit frequently by bombs and torpedoes, sank with heavy loss of life. Survivors were rescued by destroyers. Save for 3 American aircraft carriers, this left the Allies with no remaining serviceable capital ships in the Pacific.

1941, December 10–31. Japanese Drive to Southern Malaya. British troops, unaccustomed to jungle fighting, plagued by serious equipment shortages, and without adequate air support, were rolled up, infiltrated, and pushed back by the well-equipped Japanese—veterans of combat in China and trained for jungle fighting on Hainan Island. British efforts to stop the advance were further discomfited by a number of small amphibious landings, made on both coasts of the peninsula, by Japanese troops using captured fishing vessels. As the year ended, the demoralized British were being driven back relentlessly upon Singapore itself, now a naval base without a naval force.

The Philippines

American Situation and Plan. American and Filipino ground forces in the islands, under General Douglas MacArthur, consisted of some 130,000 men—22,400 U.S. Regulars (including 12,000 Philippine Scouts), 3,000 Philippine Constabulary, and the Philippine Army, 107,000 strong, but only partly organized, trained, and armed. The major portion of this force was on the island of Luzon; other Filipino elements were on the islands of Cebu, the Visayas, and Mindanao. MacArthur's U.S. Far East Air Force, under Major General **Lewis H. Brereton,** comprised about 125 combat planes, including 35 new B-17 "Flying Fortresses." Most of Admiral **Thomas C. Hart**'s U.S. Asiatic Fleet (1 heavy and 2 light cruisers, 13 destroyers, 28 submarines, and other craft) was being withdrawn to Java by Navy Department order; 4 destroyers, the submarines, a squadron of flying boats, and a flotilla of motor torpedo boats remained, together with a regiment of Marines. The major portion of the ground-force strength—Major General **Jonathan M. Wainwright**'s North Luzon Force—was disposed north of Manila to dispute an expected invasion via Lingayen Gulf. Brigadier General **George M. Parker**'s smaller South Luzon Force was south of Manila. MacArthur proposed to meet invasion by counterattack on the ground together with a B-17 strike at Formosa. Last-ditch defense contemplated withdrawal to the mountain jungle of the Bataan Peninsula, northern arm of Manila Bay, supported by the coast-defense complex at the bay mouth, with Corregidor its citadel. This eventuality had long been planned; the successful defense of the Philippines was predicated on the premise that the forces there would hold out until the U.S. Pacific Fleet opened the way for reinforcement.

Japanese Plans. These called for initial paralyzing air attack, mounted from Formosa and followed by amphibious assault by the Fourteenth Army under General **Masaharu Homma** (approximately 50,000 veteran troops). Discounting both the fidelity and the fighting capabilities of the Filipinos, a quick, easy victory was expected. The Japanese high command had allotted Homma 50 days to accomplish the task.

1941, November 27. Alert. With imminence of war with Japan evident to all, the U.S. and Philippine armed forces went on full war alert.

1941, December 8. Disaster at Clark Field. Preceded by minor blows at northern Luzon airfields, the main Japanese aerial attack—108 twin-engined bombers and 34 fighter planes from Formosan bases—struck the Clark Field–Iba airdrome complex in the Manila area at 12:15 P.M., to find the major portion of the American air force grounded, their crews at lunch or servicing their planes. Japanese success was complete and devastating. Eighteen of the 35 B-17's, 56 fighters, and a number of other aircraft were destroyed, together with part of the installations; the 1 U.S. fighter squadron in the air, though it took some toll of the invaders, was almost wiped out. Only 7 Japanese fighters were shot down.

COMMENT. *Responsibility for this tactical surprise has never been definitely fixed. News of the Pearl Harbor disaster had reached Manila at 2:30* A.M. *(8* A.M. *December 7, Hawaiian time) and was confirmed 3 hours later. At 9:30 the northern Luzon airfields had been bombed. Brereton had received a phone call from General H. H. Arnold in Washington, warning him of a likely Japanese attack. Yet, despite knowledge that Japan had struck the first blow, MacArthur's intended B-17 counterblow on Formosa had not materialized and Brereton's planes lay like sitting ducks on their fields at 12:15* P.M.

1941, December 10–20. First Landings on Luzon. While Japanese bombers wrecked the naval base at Cavite, destroying ships, installations, and munitions, small amphibious landings were made at Aparri and Vigan, northern Luzon (December 10), and at Legaspi in the south (December 12). Air bases were established in the north, and planes transferred from Formosa. The remnants of the American air force were transferred to Mindanao; all remaining naval craft except the submarines and a flotilla of motor torpedo boats left for Java.

1941, December 20–31. Mindanao and Jolo. Japanese units gained a toehold on the southernmost island, Mindanao, Philippine Army troops present withdrawing to the hills. The invaders later seized the island of Jolo (December 25). By these moves, air and naval bases were gained for further operations against the Dutch East Indies (see p. 1138). Homma's amphibious force entered Lingayen Gulf and began landing, covered by fighter planes operating from northern Luzon bases.

1941, December 22. Main Invasion of Luzon.

1941, December 23–31. Withdrawal. Driving in the partly trained Philippine Army units opposing them, the Japanese on Luzon advanced rapidly south. Only the gallantry and steadiness of the few American and Philippine Scout units saved Wainwright's troops from disaster as he withdrew in successive positions. In the south, an additional Japanese landing in force at Limon Bay (December 24) threatened the South Luzon Force. MacArthur, between the closing pincer jaws, decided on withdrawal into Bataan. Manila was declared an open city (December 26). A counterattack by rallied Philippine Army units, supported by Regulars, threw back Homma's spearheads long enough to permit the South Luzon Force to withdraw westward across the unfordable Pampanga River. Thus the year ended with MacArthur's troops safe on the Bataan side, thanks to skillful training and excellent troop leading.

COMMENT. *Had MacArthur elected to defend Manila, as the Japanese expected him to do, his entire army would have been irrevocably lost. The Japanese could then have moved their troops southward to aid in seizing the entire Southern Resources Area. As it now stood, they were still confronted by a force in being, which would have to be conquered before the Manila Bay fortifications could be reduced and Manila converted to an advance base. Tactically, Homma had gained a victory; strategically, his campaign had just commenced.*

THE WAR AGAINST JAPAN, 1942

Strategy and Policy

1942, January–March. Struggle for the Malay Barrier. The year opened with Japan moving to victory on all fronts of her "Greater East-Asia Co-Prosperity Sphere." The Dutch East Indies alone remained untouched. There the remnants of Allied forces in the Far East rallied briefly under a short-lived, extemporized command —ABDA (American-British-Dutch-Australian)—authorized at the Arcadia Conference in Washington (see p. 1081) and inaugurated under command of British General Sir **Archibald Wavell** (January 15). His mission was to hold the so-called "Malay Barrier" (the Southeast Asia peninsula, and the projecting island chain of the Netherlands East Indies and New Guinea to northern Australia), while American naval, air, and land forces held open lines of communication across the Pacific to Australia and New Zealand. Hopefully, if the Malay Barrier could be held, Japan would be denied vital raw materials of the Southern Resources Area essential to her war effort.

1942, March. Allied Reorganization. The fall of Malaya, Singapore, and the Dutch East Indies and Japanese successes in the Philippines and Burma caused the collapse of ABDACOM and forced the Allied Combined Chiefs of Staff to reorganize for a last-ditch attempt to hold their most "vital interests" in the Pacific and Asia, while still concentrating primarily against Germany. Britain was to be strategically responsible for the operations in and near India and the Indian Ocean, the United States for the Pacific Ocean; China, under the supreme command of Chiang Kai-shek, was to be within the area of American strategic and logistical responsibility, with American Lieutenant General **Joseph W. Stilwell** to be Chiang's Chief of Staff. (Later, in July, for administrative reasons, the U.S. created the China-Burma-India Command, or Theater, under Stilwell's command, responsible for logistical and combat support to China, for control —under the British—of American and Chinese combat troops in India and Burma; Stilwell was thus simultaneously responsible to the U.S. Joint Chiefs of Staff, to Chiang, and to the British commander in India.) The Pacific Theater was divided into two major commands. General MacArthur's Southwest Pacific Area included Australia, New Guinea, the Netherlands East Indies (save for Sumatra, within the British sphere), and the Philippines. Admiral **Chester W. Nimitz'** Pacific Ocean Areas included the remainder of the ocean, and was in turn divided into three major combat zones: North, Central, and South Pacific Areas.

1942, April–May. Revised Japanese Plan. The second phase of the original Japanese war plan (see p. 1127) had contemplated the consolidation of a defensive perimeter anchored on the mountainous Burma-India border in the west, and in northern New Guinea, the Bismarcks and Gilberts, Wake, and their own Pacific islands on the southeast and east. The ease and rapidity of their first phase conquests, including the seizure of all of the planned island outposts, led them to plan an extension of the perimeter in the central and south Pacific: to seize Midway Island as a base from which to harass Hawaii, and southern New Guinea and the southern Solomon Islands as bases from which to harass Australia and to interfere with the Allied trans-Pacific supply routes from the U.S. and the Panama Canal. Furthermore, they felt that this extension of their perimeter would still further increase the magnitude of any Allied efforts to recover the conquered regions.

1942, May–August. Stemming the Japanese Tide. The failure of the Japanese to gain a victory in the drawn naval Battle of the Coral Sea (see p. 1145), their decisive defeat at the Battle of Midway (see p. 1146), and the repulse of their offensive in southern New Guinea (see p. 1141) prevented the Japanese from achieving any of the new objectives of their revised war plan, save for unopposed occupation of bases in the southern Solomon Islands.

1942, August–December. Limited Allied Offensives. Exploiting their first important successes of the Pacific War, the Allies began local offensives in New Guinea and the Solomon Islands. Since most Allied resources were earmarked for defeat of Germany (see p. 1081), these offensives were limited in scope and objectives, intended primarily to reduce Japanese threats to Allied lines of communication, to seize bases suitable for subsequent offensives, and to subject the Japanese to a war of attrition which they could not afford.

Land and Air Operations in Asia

MALAYA AND SINGAPORE

1942, January 1–31. British Defeat on the Peninsula. Completely outfought and outmaneuvered by Japanese infiltrating and flanking attacks, supported by overwhelming air power, British troops were rapidly forced back to the so-called Johore Line, some 25 miles north of Singapore. This was breached (January 15) and the defenders forced back (January 31) into the island fortress, separated from the mainland by the narrow Strait of Johore —less than a mile wide and bridged by a causeway which the British partly demolished behind them.

1942, February 8–15. Conquest of Singapore. Japanese assaults followed a protracted air bombardment; crossings in armored barges were covered by intense artillery and machine-gun fire. British counterattacks were broken up by dive bombers. Tanks began moving across the causeway, which Japanese engineers had repaired, and despite foot-by-foot resistance the city's reservoirs were captured. The 70,000-man garrison thereupon surrendered unconditionally (February 15). Total casualties were 138,700 British (mostly prisoners) and 9,824 Japanese.

COMMENT. *Two unpardonable deficiencies brought about the fall of this so-called impregnable fortress-naval base: its fixed defenses and artillery were sited to repel naval attack only, and its field forces were shockingly ignorant of the terrain and of jungle fighting. The first was due to poor judgment, the second to inferior preparation and leadership. The high quality of Japanese planning and leadership, evident throughout, was clearly demonstrated by the availability of armored amphibious barges for the final assault across the Strait of Johore.*

BURMA

Land Operations

Simultaneously with the various offensives begun on December 8, 1941, the Fifteenth Japanese Army quietly occupied Thailand. While the main body prepared for an overland invasion of Burma, a detachment seized an air base at Victoria Point, at Burma's southernmost tip, to cut the British air line of communications from India to Malaya (December 23).

1942, January 12–29. Invasion. Lieutenant General **Shojiro Iida**'s Fifteenth Army (initially 2 reinforced divisions, with heavy air support) began a westward advance on Moulmein and Tavoy from Thailand. The Japanese were accompanied by a small group of Burmese revolutionaries, who had been promised Burma's independence from Britain. In subsequent months, **Aung San** and his "Thirty Comrades" had some success in inciting minor uprisings against the British and in sabotage behind the British lines.

1942, January 30–31. Battle of Moulmein. Lieutenant General **Thomas Hutton**'s British forces in Burma (the equivalent of 2 small, ill-equipped divisions of British, Burmese, and Indian troops) were surprised, then driven out of Moulmein with heavy losses and forced to withdraw across the Salween.

1942, February 18–23. Battle of the Sittang.

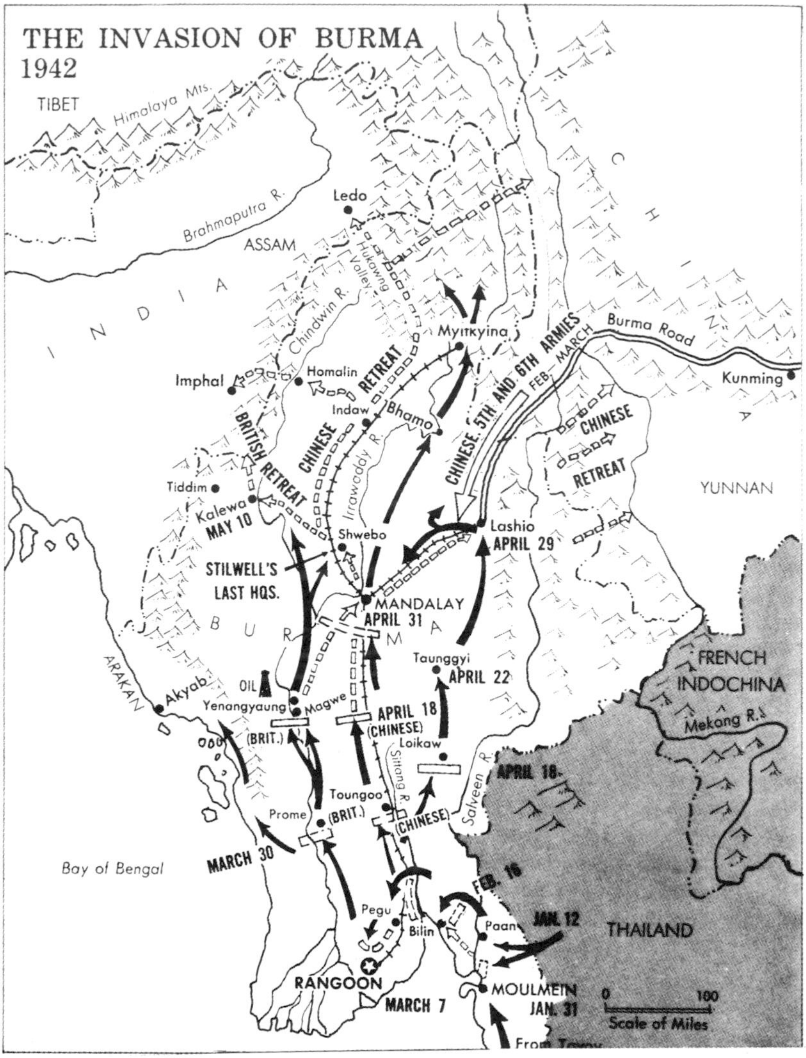

Japanese units crossing the unbridged Salween enveloped the British left, forcing them to withdraw to the Sittang River in a continuous running fight. Approximately half of Hutton's army had gotten across the Sittang's lone bridge when another surprise river-crossing envelopment threatened the bridge from the rear. The British blew up the bridge at once. Most of the cut-off men made their way back across the river on rafts, but all of their heavy equipment was lost.

1942, March 5. Alexander in Command. Lieutenant General Sir Harold R. L. Alexander arrived in Rangoon to replace Hutton. Although the arrival of a number of small reinforcement units from India had brought British ground strength back up to a strength of 2 small divisions, Alexander realized that his scattered and largely demoralized forces could not now hold the onrushing Japanese. He abandoned Rangoon, personally barely escaping capture by converging Japanese columns moving in to seize the capital (March 7). Burma, whose land frontiers were all mountain ranges traversed only by narrow trails, save for the Burma Road, was thus cut off from all the outside world except China.

1942, March 12. Arrival of Stilwell and the Chinese. With their forces in Burma crumbling, the British in February accepted an offer of assistance from Chiang

Kai-shek, who at once sent his Fifth and Sixth Armies marching down the Burma Road. (Chinese and Japanese armies were normally the equivalent of western corps; these 2 were undermanned and very short of artillery, trucks, and other equipment; the Fifth Army, comprising veteran troops, well led, had a combat efficiency comparable to a western or Japanese division; the Sixth was less reliable.) Chiang also sent his new American chief of staff, Lieutenant General Stilwell, to command this expeditionary force in Burma. Stilwell reported to Alexander at Maymyo, Burma's temporary capital.

1942, March 13–20. Reorganizing on the Prome-Toungoo Line. Alexander established a defensive line running generally south of Prome and Toungoo, and thence east to Loikaw, overlooking the Salween River. The British Burma Corps held the right, in the Irrawaddy Valley, covering Prome. The Chinese Fifth Army held the center, traversed by the Rangoon-Mandalay road and railroad; the Chinese Sixth Army held the mountainous, jungled region to the east. Competent British Major General **William Slim** arrived (March 19) to take command of the Burma Corps.

1942, March 21–30. Renewed Japanese Offensive. Iida's troops, reinforced and rested, made their main effort against the Chinese Fifth Army at Toungoo. They cut off the Chinese 200th Division, but determined counterattacks under Stilwell's direction, supported by Slim's British troops, permitted the trapped division to fight its way out. Japanese pressure, however, drove the Chinese slowly back up the railroad, while the British were forced to evacuate Prome.

1942, April 1–9. Reinforcements and Offensive Preparations. The coincidental arrival of reinforcements to both sides now caused a temporary lull. The arrival of part of the Chinese Sixty-sixth Army permitted Stilwell to bolster his troops holding the railroad. With the Japanese apparently stopped, he and Slim began to prepare for a counteroffensive. Iida, however, had just received 2 veteran divisions from the victorious Malaya-Singapore campaign. He prepared for a daring double envelopment; he was ready first.

1942, April 10–19. Battle of Yenangyaung. The Japanese plan called for the first blow to be made against the British Burma Corps while a holding attack kept the Chinese on the railroad occupied; the Sixth Army at Loikaw was temporarily left in peace. Despite a gallant and desperate British effort to hold Magwe and the Yenangyaung oil fields, the Japanese could not be stopped. The 1st Burma Division was cut off, but British counterattacks, combined with an attack by the Chinese 38th Division against the east flank of the Japanese encircling force, permitted Slim to rescue the division.

1942, April 18–23. Collapse of the Chinese Sixth Army. With Allied attention riveted on the desperate battle for the oil fields, the heavily reinforced Japanese 56th Division suddenly struck the Chinese Sixth Army in the Loikaw-Taunggyi area. The surprised Chinese were overwhelmed. Stilwell, personally leading the tough 200th Division, struck at Taunggyi from the west, only to discover that the Japanese had disappeared. Deliberately abandoning its own line of communications, the 56th Division had struck northward along the Salween toward Lashio, terminus of the railroad and starting point of the Burma Road. Meanwhile, the remainder of the Fifteenth Army maintained its pressure against the British and Chinese south of Mandalay, who now began to fall back because of the threat to their left rear.

1942, April 29. Fall of Lashio. Seizing Lashio, the 56th Division then turned southwestward, toward Maymyo and Mandalay. Alexander, who had already decided to abandon Mandalay, now hastened the withdrawal across the Irrawaddy.

1942, April 30–May 1. Fall of Mandalay. Holding off the converging Japanese drives during the night, the remnants of the Allies completed their withdrawal over the Ava railroad bridge, which was then blown up.

1942, May. Retreat from Burma. Pressed closely by the Japanese, Slim and his Burma Corps fell back quickly toward Tiddim and the Indian frontier. After a last desperate defensive battle at **Kalewa** (May 11), Slim got his remaining troops across the Chindwin River and into the border hill region; the retreat continued to Imphal. The Japanese pursuit stopped at the river. To the north and east the

Chinese were also scattering. The survivors of the Sixth Army had already fled to Yunnan. The scattered units of the Fifth and Sixty-sixth armies withdrew as best they could, some across the mountain borders to Yunnan, some to the Himalayan foothills of northern Burma, where they spent a miserable rainy season; a handful moved to the northwest, with a starving stream of civilian refugees, across the mountains to India. Stilwell, gathering his headquarters group, led an aggregation of 100-odd men and women—including American Dr. **Gordon Seagrave** and his Burmese field hospital personnel—on an amazing trek of 400-odd miles, by jeep and foot, across the mountain jungles to Imphal.

COMMENT. *The British had 30,000 casualties among the 42,000 involved in the First Burma Campaign. About half of these were "missing": Burmese who threw down their arms to return to home and family, or refugees who later turned up in India. Chinese losses defy estimation. Of the 95,000 Chinese troops engaged, only 1 division—the 38th, commanded by Major General* **Sun Li-jen** *(VMI and Purdue graduate)—withdrew as a fighting unit, but with heavy losses, cutting its way westward across the path of the Japanese advance and acting as a rear guard for the more demoralized British units retreating from Tiddim to Imphal. Japanese ground losses amounted to 7,000.*

1942, May–December. Japanese Consolidation in Burma. With the monsoon season beginning, the Japanese ended their pursuit and began to consolidate control of Burma, four-fifths of which was in their hands. They had accomplished their major objectives: to cut off China completely from surface communication with her allies, and to seize an area which could be developed into a powerful bastion to protect the western approaches to the Southern Resources Area.

1942, June–December. Allied Reorganization and Planning. Fearful of a possible Japanese invasion of India in the coming dry season, the British feverishly prepared for defense. Wavell, now commanding in India, knew that he could not consider an offensive effort to reconquer Burma for at least another year, until his newly raised British and Indian troops could be adequately equipped and trained. Meanwhile, for training and morale purposes, he planned for a limited invasion of the Arakan region, Burma's northwest seacoast region, isolated from the rest of Burma by mountains. Stilwell, more impatient to reconquer Burma, so as to reopen surface communication with China, was meanwhile building up a Chinese Army in India around the nucleus of the Chinese troops that had escaped from Burma across the Chin Hills. Reinforcements came to the training center at Ramgarh in empty "Hump" planes returning from China (see p. 1137), while equipment was arriving by ship from the U.S. In anticipation of his projected advance through north Burma, Stilwell began construction of a road eastward across the Chin Hills from Ledo, in Assam, generally following the principal northern refugee route from Burma.

Air Operations

1941, December. Deployment of the "Flying Tigers." Upon the outbreak of war in Southeast Asia, Colonel Chennault sent 1 of the 3 squadrons of his American Volunteer Group (AVG, or "Flying Tigers"; see p. 1126) to Kunming to protect the Chinese terminus of the Burma Road from air attack. Another (upon British request) was sent to reinforce the weak RAF force (equipped with obsolescent planes) at Mingaladon Airport near Rangoon. The third squadron, kept in reserve, was rotated regularly with the others after they became involved in active operations. In its first action, the Kunming squadron intercepted Japanese bombers from Indochina on a raid against Kunming, shooting down 6 with no losses to themselves (December 20). Three days later the Japanese mounted their first air raid against Rangoon. Lacking the air warning system Chennault had established in China, the Flying Tigers and RAF fighters at Mingaladon were forced to take off during the raid, but nevertheless shot down several of the attackers with slight loss to themselves (December 23).

1942, January–February. The Air Battle for Rangoon. The effectiveness of the Flying Tigers caused the Japanese to increase the number of fighter escorts for their bombers, but despite heavy losses (compensated by reinforcements from Malaya) they continued to bomb Rangoon regularly. Besides combating air raids on Rangoon, the American fighters frequently flew support missions for hard-pressed British ground forces, easing slightly the merciless pounding these were receiving at the hands of Japanese surface and air units. Meanwhile, RAF bombers based at Magwe made a few raids against the principal Japanese air bases in Thailand, with relatively little effect. By the end of February, the RAF fighters at Mingaladon had all been put out of effective action; but thanks to Chennault's superior aerial tactics, only 15 of his planes had been lost (8 of the pilots walked back to base to fly again), and they had shot down more than 100 Japanese planes. By rotating his squadrons into Mingaladon, he had been able to keep planes and men in good operational condition.

1942, March 1–20. Operations from Magwe. The approach of Japanese ground troops to Rangoon forced Chennault to pull back from Mingaladon to the RAF base at Magwe, whence he continued support of British and Chinese ground troops.

1942, March 21. Japanese Raid on Magwe. A surprise massive Japanese air raid caught most of the American and British planes at Magwe on the ground and destroyed the effectiveness of all air units based there. Chennault, able to salvage only 3 planes from the wreckage, withdrew north to Loiwing just inside the Chinese border. The RAF withdrew to fields in India.

1942, April–May. Long-Range Air Support for Burma. Flying Tigers and RAF fighters continued to give long-range support to the withdrawing Allied troops in Burma, but it was relatively ineffective due to inadequate communications with the ground and to the short time available for action over the battlefield. The arrival of some Spitfires from England, however, permitted the RAF fighter pilots to fight the Japanese on more even terms. With the loss of Burma and the closing of the Burma Road, Chennault, concentrating at Kunming, reduced his activities sharply to conserve his dwindling supplies of fuel and ammunition.

1942, June–December. Flying the "Hump." With ground communications to China severed, the Americans, under Stilwell's direction as commanding general of the China-Burma-India Theater, began a long-range supply airlift from bases in northeastern India to Kunming. Because of Japanese air bases at Myitkyina in northern Burma, the planes were forced to fly over the eastern Himalayas in southeastern Tibet, climbing to 21,000 feet and more to get over the mountains. This route over the world's highest mountains was dubbed the "Hump" by American pilots. Stilwell could get only a few additional transport planes, and so this initial airlift was a feeble and totally inadequate drop in the bucket. The newly activated U.S. Tenth Air Force, Major General **Howard C. Davidson**, was installed on Indian air bases to protect the Hump bases.

CHINA

There was little formal combat activity in China during 1942. The Japanese, engaged elsewhere on an amazing series of peripheral offensives, were content to hold what they had. Guerrilla activity in areas behind the Japanese lines did not seriously threaten their firm occupation hold. The Chinese National Government armies were in no position to take advantage of Japanese inactivity, since the closing of the Burma Road had cut off their already meager supply of matériel and munitions. Stilwell's hitherto good relations with Chiang Kai-shek worsened when the Joint Chiefs of Staff turned down his requests for additional transport planes to increase supply over the Hump. (Other theaters had priority.) At the same time, friction rose between Stilwell and Chennault, now a brigadier general commanding the U.S. China Air Task Force (successors to the Flying Tigers, July 4). Chennault demanded that his fuel and ammunition requirements get priority over all other airlifted supplies, while Stilwell insisted on balance between ground and air forces.

Land and Air Operations in the Pacific Areas

THE NETHERLANDS EAST INDIES

1942, January–February. Japanese Invasion. A 3-pronged Japanese amphibious offensive moved south on the Dutch East Indies, with initial landings at Tarakan, oil-rich island off the east coast of Borneo, and at Menado on northern Celebes (January 11). The Japanese Eastern Force proceeded via Celebes, the Moluccas, and Timor toward Bali and Java. The Central Force advanced down the Macassar Strait along the east coast of Borneo toward Java. The Western Force moved through the South China Sea to north Borneo and Sumatra. Each force comprised a group of heavy cruisers and destroyers escorting transports carrying units of the Sixteenth Army and supported by powerful land-based air units. Admiral Nagumo's First Air Fleet provided additional far-flung air support. To oppose these forces, Wavell's ABDA Command consisted of vastly outnumbered American, British, and Dutch naval units, some 85,000 Dutch troops scattered on the main islands—most of them indigenous and of dubious loyalty—and a small Dutch air force equipped with obsolete planes. Covered by overwhelming and scarcely opposed air support, the Japanese forces moved from one key point to another, establishing new air bases to assure continued air superiority, then pressing generally southward again.

1942, February 25. Dissolution of ABDACOM. The fall of Singapore (see p. 1133) and the rapid decline of Allied naval forces having sealed the doom of the Netherlands East Indies (see p. 1144), Wavell's command was dissolved and he returned to India to supervise the deteriorating situation in Burma. The Dutch retained responsibility for the continuing defense of Java, and remaining American, British, and Australian forces in the area were to continue to assist.

1942, February 28–March 9. Battle for Java. Following intensive air and naval bombardments, the Japanese Western Force landed near Batavia. In subsequent days, units of the Central and Eastern Forces also landed. Determined Dutch resistance was totally incapable of coping with Japanese land superiority and total control of the air. Remaining Dutch forces were finally forced to surrender, virtually completing the conquest of the Netherlands East Indies (March 9).

THE PHILIPPINES

1942, January 7–26. Defense of Bataan. MacArthur's troops lay astride the mountainous jungle at the base of the peninsula. Wainwright's I Corps held the left, Parker's II Corps the right, with the almost impassable height of Mt. Natib in the middle defended only by patrols. The supply situation was deplorable; although dumps had been established on the southern tip of the peninsula and Corregidor, ration reserves had been calculated for a 6-month stand, the mouths to be filled had been increased by more than 20,000 refugees from Manila crowding the area. Japanese command of sea and air precluded relief. The American command went on half-rations at once. Japanese attacks on both flanks were repulsed, but infiltrating elements, crossing Mt. Natib, threatened to split the American position and after bitter fighting MacArthur withdrew to a more easily defended reserve position about 15 miles from the tip of the peninsula.

1942, January 26–February 8. Second Japanese Attack. While vicious assaults on the front were met and thrown back, amphibious landings on the western coast, well behind the battle line, became serious (January 23–26). They were finally repulsed by counterattack, by U.S. motor torpedo boat harassment, and by fire from Corregidor's artillery (January 29–February 13). Homma, withdrawing from the main front, waited for reinforcements from Japan.

1942, March 11. Departure of MacArthur. MacArthur, though unwilling, obeyed a peremptory order from President Roosevelt to leave for Australia and assume command of all Allied forces in the South Pacific. By PT boat and B-17 he arrived safely (March 17).

1942, March 11–April 2. Attrition. Wainwright now commanded, with Major General **Edward P. King** in command on Bataan. Despite good morale resulting from their success in repulsing all Japanese as-

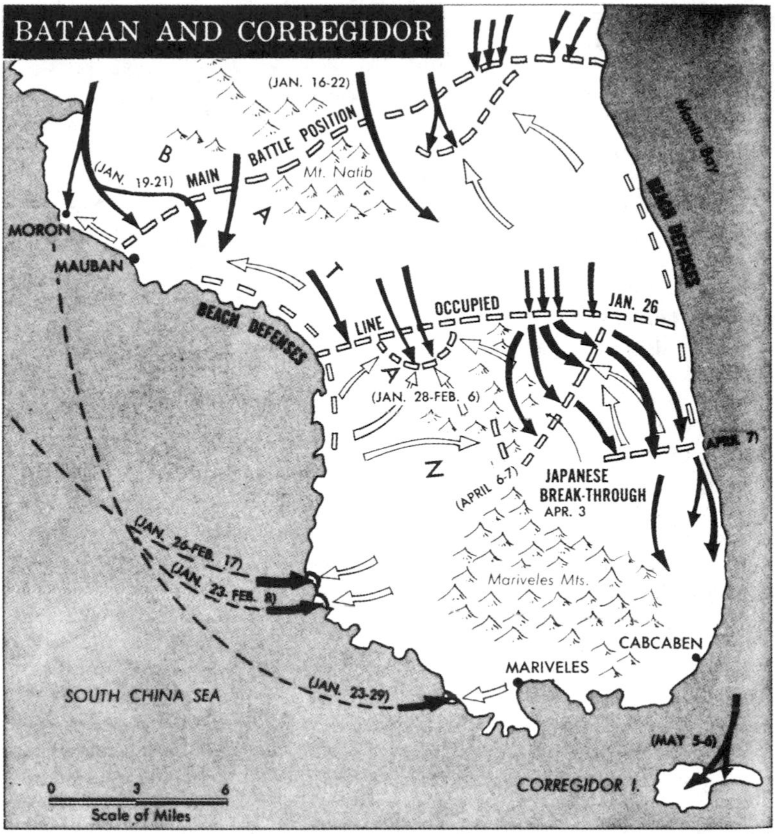

BATAAN AND CORREGIDOR

saults, the efficiency of the troops was now sadly reduced. Rations had been cut to one-quarter, seriously affecting stamina; tropical diseases made great inroads. By the end of March, some 24,000 men were hospitalized or in convalescent areas.

1942, April 3–9. Japanese Breakthrough. Homma, reinforced and refitted, attacked under cover of incessant air and artillery bombardment. Bursting through the left flank of II Corps, the Japanese forced it back 10 miles in 48 hours. On the left, I Corps, bent back toward the sea, attempted counterattacks, but these were easily repulsed. II Corps disintegrated. King surrendered unconditionally (April 9). The Japanese, although permitting many of the Philippine Army personnel to return to their homes, hustled the Regulars, American and Filipino—in callous brutality—on a 90-mile "Death March" to Camp O'Donnell. American and Filipino losses in the Bataan campaign amounted to some 20,000-odd men, discounting deserters, detachments ferried to Corregidor, and those few brave souls who dared the jungle to become the nucleus for a guerrilla warfare which would rage until the end of the war.

1942, April 10–May 3. The Other Islands. Before his departure, MacArthur had left Brigadier General **Bradford G. Chynoweth** in control of forces in Cebu, Panay, Negros, Leyte, and Samar with instructions to prepare for guerrilla operations. Brigadier General **William F. Sharp,** with a larger command, was to oppose any further landings on Mindanao. Homma moved two brigade-size task forces south. One seized Cebu (April 10), the other Panay (April 16), the defending troops retiring to mountain fastnesses. Additional Japanese landings on Mindanao (April 29–May 3) drove Sharp's troops also into the hill country.

1942, April 10–May 6. The Ordeal of Corregidor. The citadel and its satellite island forts at the mouth of Manila Bay had supported the defense of Bataan by the fire of large-caliber fixed armament.

Now the full force of Japanese air and artillery from Bataan and from Cavite swept the complex incessantly. Except for the 14-in. turret guns on Fort Drum—the "Concrete Battleship"—all these emplacements were open to air and plunging artillery fire. The only shelter on Corregidor was a tunnel carved into the rock of Malinta Hill, where the command post and hospital were installed. The bombardments destroyed all other installations.

1942, May 5–6. The Fall of Corregidor. The dazed defenders met Japanese amphibious assaults at the beach, their 155-mm. guns and lighter ordnance inflicting severe damage on the attackers, but a 2-battalion toehold was gained on the southern end of the island. At the end of his resources, with less than 3 days' supply of water remaining, Wainwright surrendered unconditionally. At Homma's imperious demand, the surrender included all U.S. forces in the Philippines. American losses were some 2,000 killed and wounded and 11,500 made prisoner. Japanese losses in the final assault were more than 4,000. In compliance with Wainwright's orders, Sharp surrendered on Mindanao (May 10), and Chynoweth on Panay (May 18). However, individuals and groups of Americans and Filipinos continued guerrilla resistance for the next three years.

COMMENT. *The First Philippine Campaign, its outcome a foregone conclusion from the beginning, was a tribute to the skill, gallantry, and stoic determination of the officers and men involved in the defense. It delayed the Japanese timetable for 5 long months during which the U.S. was rallying its resources. The one glaring error in the otherwise efficient Japanese plan and prosecution of the campaign was a complete miscalculation of the resistance to be expected from the Filipino people. On all other major fronts of the Japanese assaults, the indigenous populations were either indifferent or even disloyal to the defense; the same condition was expected in the Philippines. Homma looked forward to opposition from the small American component of MacArthur's forces only. Instead, the Filipino Regulars, like the Americans, lived up to the finest traditions of the service. The poorly trained and equipped Philippine Army units, after their first panic, quickly settled down, becoming veterans almost overnight. Most of the Filipino people gave loyal support both during the campaign and, as they later showed, in the guerrilla operations which continued to plague the invaders to the end of the war.*

PAPUA, THE BISMARCKS, AND THE SOLOMONS

1942, January–March. Arrival of the Japanese. Amphibious units of the Japanese Fourth Fleet, overcoming brief but stout Australian resistance, seized Kavieng and Rabaul, the latter becoming the principal Japanese naval and air base in the Southwest Pacific. Control of New Britain was consolidated during the following month. Amphibious landings were then made to seize Salamaua and Lae in Papua (March 6), and footholds on Bougainville (March 13).

1942, May–July. Expansion of the Japanese Perimeter. The Japanese expanded their control in the central and southern Solomons, culminating their efforts by establishing a base on Guadalcanal, where they began to build an airfield (July 6). Despite failure to gain naval control of the Coral Sea, Japanese plans to seize Port Moresby, principal city of southern Papua, were initiated by occupation of Gona (July 11) and Buna soon afterward. All land operations in Papua, the Bismarcks, and the Solomons were now under the Eighth Army, commanded by Lieutenant General **Hitoshi Imamura,** with headquarters in Rabaul. In response to repeated Japanese air attacks on Port Moresby, growing Allied air strength harassed Japanese bases.

1942, June–July. Strategic Controversy. Following the great American naval victory at Midway (see p. 1146), both General MacArthur and Admiral **Ernest J. King** (the new Navy chief in Washington) urged an offensive in the Bismarck-New Guinea area as a definite check to the Japanese menace to the U.S.-Australian supply line. King favored Navy-controlled island-hopping up the Solomons to Rabaul, MacArthur a direct thrust—Army-controlled—on Rabaul itself. This clash of personalities and of service jealousies was settled by compromise; the JCS ordered (July 2) a 3-phase operation: seizure of the southern Solomons by Vice Admiral **Robert L. Ghormley** (commanding the South Pacific Area under Nimitz), and seizure of the remainder of the island mass and of the northwest coast of New Guinea by MacArthur, whose final objective was the capture of Rabaul itself. MacArthur's initial move, however, was delayed by a continuation of the Japanese offensive.

Operations in Papua, July, 1942–January, 1943

1942, July 21–September 13. Advance on Port Moresby. Elements of the Japanese Eighteenth Army, under Major General **Tomitoro Horii,** pressed inland from Gona, drove in local Allied troops, and moved up the rugged Kokoda Trail to seize the key pass over the Owen Stanley Mountains (August 12). Pushing ahead, the Japanese reached to within 30 miles of Port Moresby before stiffening Australian and American resistance, under Australian Major General **Edmond F. Hering,** supported by tactical air forces with local air superiority, halted the advance.

1942, August 25–September 5. Operations at Milne Bay. A Japanese regimental-strength amphibious landing was contained and repulsed by Australians.

1942, September–November. The Return Across the Owen Stanley Range. Partly under Allied pressure, and partly in compliance with defensive instructions from Imamura, the Japanese fell back stubbornly over the mountains, followed by the Australian 7th and U.S. 32nd divisions. The Allies were finally halted by a massive jungle fortress, cleverly constructed in the swampy region around the villages of Buna and Gona on the coast of the Solomon Sea (November 19).

1942, November 20–1943, January 22. Battle for Buna-Gona. The Allied offensive bogged down. The Americans and Australians were racked by disease; they were short of artillery and rations, and untrained in jungle warfare. U.S. Lieutenant General **Robert L. Eichelberger,** placed in command by MacArthur (December 1), quickly restored sagging Allied morale and rectified the serious logistical deficiencies. The Australians, on the Allied left, stormed Gona (December 9). More heavily fortified Buna, however, long resisted the American attacks, even after yard-by-yard advances had brought the attackers within sight of the shore. A final converging assault of Americans and Australians overran the defenders, some of whom were able to escape in surface craft, but most of the Japanese died. Total Japanese casualties in the Buna-Gona operation were more than 7,000 dead, an unknown number of wounded evacuated, and 350 wounded prisoners. The Allies lost 5,700 Australians and 2,783 Americans killed and wounded. Both sides lost heavily from disease, the Americans alone having about 60 per cent of 13,646 men incapacitated.

COMMENT. *One of the most important aspects of this relatively small operation was the proof that Allied troops could defeat the hitherto invincible Japanese in the jungle.*

Operations on Guadalcanal, August, 1942–February, 1943

1942, July–August. American Preparations. Word of construction by the Japanese of an airfield on Guadalcanal hurried the planned American amphibious move into the southern Solomons. Admiral Ghormley, at Nouméa, sent an amphibious task force under Rear Admiral **Richmond K. Turner,** carrying Major General **Alexander A. Vandegrift**'s reinforced 1st Marine Division (19,000 men) and an air support force built around Admiral **Frank J. Fletcher**'s 3-carrier task force. Fletcher, as senior officer, commanded the expedition.

1942, August 7. Landings on Tulagi and Guadalcanal. The Marines began landing on Guadalcanal and Tulagi in complete surprise. The small Japanese garrisons—2,200 on Guadalcanal and 1,500 on Tulagi—were quickly scattered. While Vandegrift began a perimeter defense of the still incomplete Guadalcanal airfield, unloading operations commenced from the transports huddled in the sound between Guadalcanal and Florida islands. But prompt and violent Japanese air attacks soon interfered with the unloading.

1942, August 9–19. Departure of the Navy. The combination of the intensive Japanese air attacks and a stunning Japanese night naval victory off Savo Island (see p. 1149) caused Admirals Fletcher and Turner to withdraw their naval forces from the sound and the nearby waters, leaving the Marines, short of supplies,

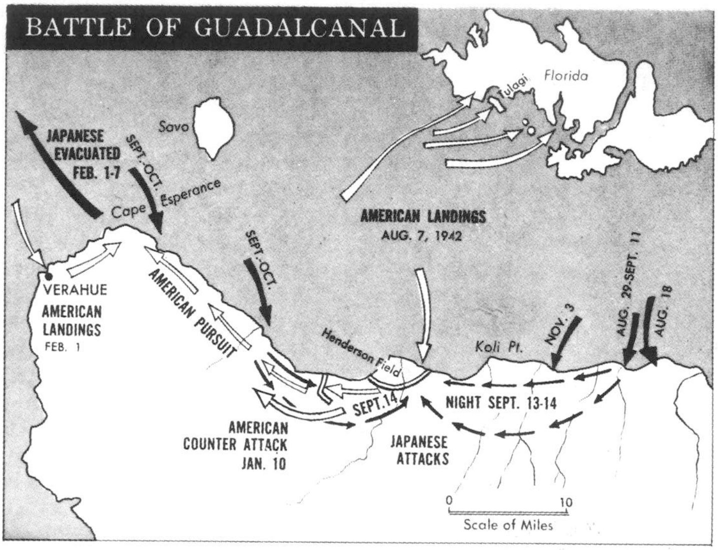

completely isolated on Guadalcanal and Tulagi. However, long-range land-based planes from the New Hebrides flew frequent covering missions overhead, and fast destroyer transports brought additional supplies. Meanwhile, engineers rushed the Guadalcanal airfield, now renamed Henderson Field, to completion. Japanese reinforcements, brought down at night by destroyer, began to assemble near Taivu Point and Kokumbona, east and west of Henderson Field.

1942, August 20. Arrival of Air Support. Upon the completion of Henderson Field, a squadron of 31 Marine planes arrived to give direct support and air cover to the 1st Marine Division. This strength was gradually built up to about 100 aircraft.

1942, August 21–September 12. Skirmishing Around the Perimeter. Clashes between American and Japanese patrols (which had been sporadic since the landings) became more frequent and more intensive. Nightly rushes of Japanese destroyers down "the Slot" (the channel between the northeastern and southwestern chains of the Solomon Islands) brought Japanese reinforcements. In the daytime the waters in the vicinity of Guadalcanal and Tulagi belonged to the American Navy, covered by planes from Henderson Field and from the Hebrides; at night the "Tokyo Express"—Japanese destroyers and light cruisers—dashed into the sound to drop men and supplies on Guadalcanal, and to bombard the Marine positions and airfield.

1942, September 12–14. Battle of Bloody Ridge. Japanese forces, the equivalent of a division, vigorously attempted to seize positions on Lunga Ridge, overlooking the airfield from the south. Combination of infiltration and frontal assaults came close to breaking the Marine lines, but the attacks were repulsed. The Japanese left 600 dead on the field (their total casualties are unknown); American casualties were 143 killed and wounded.

1942, September 15–October 22. Continuing Build-ups on Guadalcanal. While violent air and naval battles took place over and around Guadalcanal, both sides built up their ground strength. By mid-October, Vandegrift's command on Guadalcanal alone had reached a strength exceeding 23,000. The Japanese Seventeenth Army, 2 divisions under Major General **Haruyoshi Hyakutake,** comprised at least 20,000. Patrol skirmishing and probes around the perimeter increased in intensity as the Japanese prepared for another assault.

1942, October 23–25. Land Battle of Guadalcanal. For 3 days the Japanese launched intensive but piecemeal and unco-ordinated attacks at different points of the Marine perimeter. Though fighting was severe, none of the assaults came close to success, and all were repulsed with appalling losses. Japanese dead totaled over 2,000, with numbers of wounded unknown; American casualties were less than 300.

1942, October 26–December 8. Expansion of the Perimeter. Vandegrift immediately extended the American perimeter far enough to prevent Japanese artillery fire from reaching Henderson Field. During the following 6 weeks, the area under American control was gradually extended farther, as units of the 2nd Marine Division landed to reinforce and relieve tired units of the 1st Marine Division. The air and naval battles continued almost without interruption during this period, with Japanese air losses mounting rapidly.

1942, December 9. Relief of the 1st Marine Division. General **Alexander Patch**, commanding the Army Americal Division, relieved General Vandegrift in command of Allied operations on Guadalcanal. The 1st Marine Division was withdrawn.

1942, December 10–1943, January 9. American Build-up. The Japanese were now on the defensive, having established a heavily fortified jungle position about 6 miles west of Henderson Field, extending inland more than 4 miles from Pt. Cruz. This line was held by less than 20,000 Japanese, while American strength built up to 58,000 men in the XIV Corps, commanded by Patch, which included the Americal, 25th, and 2nd Marine divisions. The Japanese were short of supplies and riddled with disease; the Americans were well supplied, in good condition, and high morale, though less experienced in jungle fighting than the Japanese.

1943, January 10–February 7. The American Offensive. A vicious 2-week battle drove the Japanese from their jungle fortifications, which they held with tenacious bravery (January 10–23). Falling back under the cover of a desperate and well-conducted rear-guard action, the Japanese again attempted to stand at **Tassafaronga Point,** but were quickly driven northward toward Cape Esperance (January 31). A small American force was landed behind the Japanese lines west of Cape Esperance in an attempt to encircle the defenders and to prevent evacuation by sea (February 1). The combination of dogged, skillful defense by the starving, defeated Japanese soldiers and brilliant support from the Japanese Navy frustrated the American attempt, however, and approximately 13,000 Japanese were evacuated in night operations (February 1–7).

COMMENT. *Guadalcanal was the first large-scale Allied victory against the Japanese. Both sides made a number of mistakes, but the Japanese, who had a preponderance of land, sea, and air forces at the outset, made more than the Americans. Their greatest failure was in persisting in piecemeal operations, strategically and tactically, instead of attempting to build up local superiority against the Americans, which might have been possible at any time during the first 2 months of the battle.*

Naval Operations in the Pacific

THE NETHERLANDS EAST INDIES

1942, January 11–22. Preliminary Japanese Penetrations. Powerful amphibious forces, under land-based air cover, moved into the northern areas of the Netherlands East Indies (see p. 1138). Supporting the numerous modern screening forces of cruisers and destroyers was Admiral Nagumo's First Air Fleet, veterans of Pearl Harbor. In opposition was a handful of American, British, and Dutch warships, mostly old World War I types. The Japanese air units exercised effective air superiority. The ABDA naval commander, under General Wavell, was American Admiral **Thomas Hart.**

1942, January 23. Battle of Macassar Strait. As the Japanese Central Force approached Balikpapan, it was surprised shortly after dark by 4 American destroyers. In an hour's battle the Americans sank 1 small Japanese warship and 4 heavily loaded troop transports, and damaged several other vessels. Then, having suffered little damage themselves, the Americans raced southward.

1942, January 24–February 3. Continuing Japanese Advance. The setback at Balikpapan did not delay the Japanese advance. Rushing more warships and planes to the Macassar Strait area, all Japanese invasion forces continued to leapfrog southward. The main Dutch naval base at Amboina was captured (January 30).

1942, February 4. Battle of Madoera Strait. Japanese aircraft struck a combined American and Dutch squadron. The Japanese had few losses, but seriously damaged several Allied ships, including the U.S. cruisers *Houston* and *Marblehead.* The latter was forced to limp back to America for repairs, leaving the *Houston* as the only major U.S. ship in the area.

1942, February 13–14. Battle off Palembang. A U.S.-Dutch-British squadron, commanded by Dutch Rear Admiral **Karel Doorman,** attempted to prevent a Japanese landing at Palembang, Sumatra. Intercepted by Japanese planes, they were prevented from reaching the Japanese convoys.

1942, February 14. Change in Naval Command. Admiral Hart was succeeded by Dutch Vice Admiral **Conrad Helfrich.**

1942, February 19–20. Battle of Lombok (Bandoeng) Strait. Admiral Doorman's squadron, attempting to strike spearheads of the Japanese Eastern Force, approaching Java, was engaged by a smaller but skillfully handled Japanese destroyer squadron in a hard-fought night engagement. Damage was heavy on both sides, and 1 Dutch destroyer was sunk.

1942, February 19. Carrier Raid on Darwin. Admiral Nagumo's First Air Fleet struck a crippling blow against Darwin, main port in northern Australia, causing severe damage to shipping and shore installations.

1942, February 27. Battle of the Java Sea. Admiral Doorman's squadron of 5 cruisers and 10 destroyers made a bold but unsuccessful bid to attack the Japanese Eastern Force, which was escorted by Rear Admiral **Takeo Takagi**'s 4 cruisers and 13 destroyers. In a 7-hour running fight of crazy-quilt pattern, with the Dutch admiral gallantly forcing the fight to the end, Doorman's force was crushed; he went down with his flagship, R.N.N.S. *De Ruyter.* Only U.S.S. *Houston,* H.M.A.S. *Perth,* and H.M.S. *Exeter,* with 5 destroyers (4 of them American), survived the battle. Japanese control of air and sea was now undisputed.

1942, February 28–29. Action off Banten Bay. The *Houston, Perth,* and several destroyers, attempting to escape to Australia, encountered a Japanese landing force approaching Java. The Allied ships, despite a hopeless situation, attacked, but were themselves ringed by destroyers and cruisers in point-blank fire and sunk. H.M.S. *Exeter* and a British and an American destroyer, attempting to thread their way to safety through minefields off Surabaya, were all sunk (March 1) by naval gunfire and carrier-based bombers. Four U.S. destroyers escaped to Australia.

1942, February 29–March 9. Conquest of the Indies. The entire Dutch East Indies was formally surrendered (March 9). Japan had gained control of the Southern Resources Area. The Malay Barrier now pierced, the Japanese were free to move west toward India and south toward Australia.

AMERICAN RAIDS IN THE CENTRAL PACIFIC

1942, January. Aftermath of Pearl Harbor. The loss of the U.S. Pacific Fleet battleships at Pearl Harbor meant that there could be no real counteroffensive in the Central Pacific for many months. However, the 3 aircraft carriers, U.S.S. *Lexington, Saratoga,* and *Enterprise,* had escaped the disaster. Admiral Ernest J. King, new Chief of Naval Operations in Washington, ordered Admiral Chester W. Nimitz, new commander of the Pacific Fleet, to use his carriers to harass the Japanese while American naval strength in the Pacific was being rebuilt. The task was complicated by severe damage to the *Saratoga,* struck by a Japanese submarine's torpedo (January 11). However, the U.S.S. *Yorktown* arrived from the Atlantic soon after this to join the Pacific Fleet.

1942, February 1. Attack on Gilbert and Marshall Islands. The carriers *Enterprise* and *Yorktown,* under Vice Admiral **William F. Halsey,** escorted by cruisers and destroyers, sent their planes to attack Japanese bases on the Gilbert and Marshall Islands. Some damage was inflicted. The task force returned safely to Pearl Harbor.

1942, February 20. Aborted Raid on Rabaul. A task force built around the carrier *Lexington,* under Vice Admiral **Wilson Brown,** approached Rabaul through the Solomon Sea in an attempt to strike a surprise blow at Japanese forces concentrating there. Discovered and attacked by Japanese planes, the task force withdrew, but inflicted heavy losses on the Japanese air units.

1942, February 24–March 4. Raids on Wake and Marcus Islands. Halsey's *Enterprise* task force struck Wake (February 24) and Marcus (March 4) islands, inflicting some damage, and returning safely later to Pearl Harbor.

1942, March 10. Strikes at Lae and Salamaua. Brown's *Lexington* task force, joined by the *Yorktown,* sent planes across Papua from the Coral Sea, sinking and damaging several small warships and transports.

1942, April 18. Carrying the War to Japan. Sixteen Army B-25's under Lieutenant Colonel **James H. Doolittle,** carried on the U.S. carrier *Hornet,* escorted by Halsey's *Enterprise* task force, flew 800 miles to bomb Tokyo and other Japanese cities. Little physical damage was done, but the Japanese were greatly alarmed and Americans greatly heartened by the feat. All of the attacking planes were lost or forced to crash land in China, save for one which landed at Vladivostok, where plane and crew were interned. Most of the fliers survived, though 2, falling into Japanese hands, were beheaded. The most important effect of the raid was to influence the Japanese high command to attempt to expand its perimeter in the central and southern Pacific, with disastrous results.

BATTLE OF THE CORAL SEA

1942, May 1. Initiation of the New Japanese Plan. As the first step in the new Japanese plan, Admiral **Shigeyoshi Inouye** (commanding at Rabaul) had been ordered by the commander of the Japanese Combined Fleet, Admiral **Isoroku Yamamoto,** to seize bases in the southern Solomons and to capture Port Moresby. The small carrier *Shoho,* 4 cruisers, and a destroyer escorted an assault force of several transports south through the Solomons toward Tulagi. Meanwhile, a larger force was being assembled at Rabaul to assault Port Moresby by sea. To provide additional support, a striking force built around the large carriers *Shokaku* and *Zuikaku,* under Rear Admiral Takagi, moved south from the Central Pacific to enter the Coral Sea from the east. Unknown to the Japanese, American intelligence was aware of most of these plans because of the breaking of the Japanese code (see p. 1128). Admiral Nimitz sent Admiral Fletcher with a task force built around the carriers *Lexington* and *Yorktown* to block the Japanese plan. Fletcher was joined by a small squadron of American and Australian cruisers and destroyers under Rear Admiral **J. G. Crace,** R.N.

1942, May 3. Occupation of Tulagi. Japanese forces occupied the island without opposition. The *Shoho* task force sailed north to join the Port Moresby assault force, which was leaving Rabaul.

1942, May 4. *Yorktown* Attack on Tulagi. *Yorktown* planes, bombing Tulagi, had minor success.

1942, May 5–6. The Fleets Approach. The *Yorktown* rejoined Fletcher's fleet in the central Coral Sea, just as Takagi's squadron was steaming into the sea from the northeast and as the *Shoho* force and the Port Moresby assault force were approaching the Coral Sea from the Solomon Sea to the north. Both main carrier forces searched for each other without success.

1942, May 7–8. Battle of the Coral Sea. In a confused series of actions marked by serious errors on both sides, the 2 carrier forces found and struck at each other. The *Shoho* was sunk by American planes (May 7). An attempted Japanese night attack (May 7–8) resulted in severe plane losses; American losses were slight. An exchange of strikes the next morning, however, resulted in the sinking of the *Lexington* and some damage to the *Yorktown;* the *Shokaku* was severely damaged, but the *Zuikaku* was unscathed. An American destroyer and oiler were also sunk. Meanwhile, the loss of the *Shoho,* and the threat of Admiral Crace's squadron of 3 cruisers and several destroyers (which survived without damage several Japanese air strikes and a mistaken attack by American land-based planes) moving to intercept the Port Moresby assault force, caused Admiral Inouye to call off the invasion plan. The assault force returned to Port Moresby. Because of the losses they had suffered, Admirals Fletcher and Takagi almost simultaneously decided to withdraw from further action.

COMMENT. *This was the first great carrier battle; no surface ship on either side sighted the enemy. Tactically a draw (the Japanese lost more planes, the Americans more ships), it constituted a major Allied strategic success by halting the proposed assault on Port Moresby.*

THE BATTLE OF MIDWAY

1942, May. Japanese Preparations. While Admiral Yamamoto, commander of the Combined Fleet, was preparing to carry out the revised Japanese strategic plan (see p. 1132), he learned that the American carriers *Enterprise* and *Hornet* were in the South Pacific (where Nimitz had rushed them in an effort to join in the Coral Sea battle). Believing that both the *Yorktown* and the *Lexington* had been sunk in that engagement, he was now certain that his planned blow at Midway would not be opposed by any American carriers. He nevertheless employed 165 warships, all of the available naval might of Japan, in the effort, the greatest armada yet assembled in the Pacific Ocean. Vice Admiral **Boshiro Hosogaya**'s Northern Area Force—2 light carriers, 7 cruisers, and 12 destroyers—was to make diversionary strikes against Alaskan bases just before the main forces struck Midway; after that, Hosogaya was to establish bases in the western Aleutians. The remainder of Yamamoto's fleet headed toward Midway in 3 separate forces: Nagumo's First Air Fleet (sadly missing the 2 carriers put out of action at the Coral Sea by damage or plane loss); the Midway Occupation Force, under Vice Admiral **Nobutake Kondo,** consisting of the powerful Second Fleet of 2 battleships, 1 light carrier, 2 seaplane carriers, 7 cruisers, and 29 destroyers, escorting 12 transports carrying 51,000 troops; and Yamamoto's main body, comprising 7 battleships, 1 light carrier, 4 cruisers, and 12 destroyers. In addition, 18 submarines had been sent to the waters between Midway and Pearl Harbor to report American movements and to attack opportune targets.

1942, May. American Preparation. Nimitz, warned through Navy Intelligence's knowledge of Japanese codes, ordered Halsey's *Enterprise-Hornet* task force to rush back north from the South Pacific; also Fletcher's *Yorktown,* requiring repairs after Coral Sea estimated to take 3 months, was made combat ready in an amazing 48-hour period at Pearl Harbor. These 3 fleet carriers could carry approximately 250 planes, about the same number as on Nagumo's 4 fleet carriers. Nimitz, detaching about one-third of his 76 warships to protect Alaska, planned to fight the main battle within air range of Midway and thus to be able to employ 109 additional Army, Navy, and Marine land-based planes based on that small island. In late May, the Pacific Fleet of some 50 vessels and submarines assembled north of Midway, unsighted by Yamamoto's submarine force, which did not establish its screen until June 1. Halsey was sick in hospital; his *Enterprise-Hornet* force was commanded by Rear Admiral **Raymond A. Spruance.** Fletcher, on the *Yorktown,* was in command at sea under Nimitz' supervision from the Pearl Harbor base.

1942, June 3–7. Operations in the Aleutians. The Japanese Northern Area Force, outmaneuvering Rear Admiral **Robert A. Theobald**'s protective force, bombarded Dutch Harbor twice (June 3 and 4), avoided attacks by American land-based planes, then landed small forces on the islands of Kiska (June 6) and Attu (June 7). Had it not been for the American realization that this was a diversion, these operations would have constituted a great Japanese success. As it was, very little was accomplished except to leave some American military men with red faces, and to arouse further U.S. anger by this seizure of two bits of useless territory in the Western Hemisphere.

1942, June 4, 0300–0700. Battle of Midway—First Phase. Nagumo, confident in Yamamoto's conviction that there were no U.S. carriers in the Central Pacific and that most remaining American warships were rushing north to repel the Aleutian attack, launched half his attack force (108 planes) against Midway in early morning. From Midway, simultaneously, U.S. land-based planes rose both to strike the Japanese carriers and to attack the approaching bombers. Both these American efforts were repulsed with great loss, the American planes being inferior in speed to the Japanese aircraft. While half of the planes attacking the carriers were being shot down by Japanese defensive fighters, with no harm to the carriers, Nagumo's bombers broke through the American screen at 6:30 A.M. and inflicted much damage on the island, sparing the runways, however, for their own expected later use.

1942, June 4, 0700–1700. Battle of Midway—Second Phase. Nagumo, receiving radio word from his Midway strike force

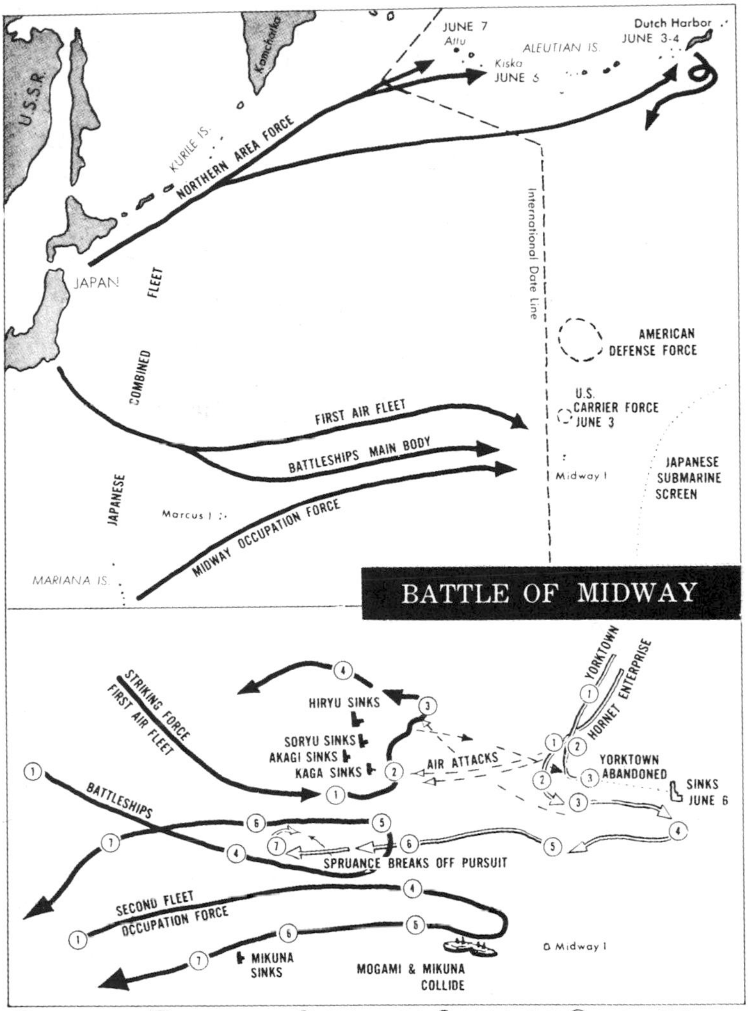

(1) JUNE 4 – 07:00 (2) JUNE 4 – 10:00 (3) JUNE 4 – 15:00 (4) JUNE 5 – 01:00 (5) JUNE 5 – 12:00 (6) JUNE 6 – 07:00 (7) JUNE 6 – 17:50

that a second blow would be needed against the island, now began stripping his reserve planes of armor-piercing bombs and torpedoes, rearming with incendiary and fragmentation bombs—at least an hour's task. At that moment a search plane sighted and reported a formation of large American warships to the northeast. Startled Nagumo began rearming his reserve planes for naval action, while at the same time his Midway force was being retrieved on the carrier decks. He was steaming with his 4 carriers in box formation, each surrounded by protecting battleships, cruisers and destroyers. He shifted course 90° to the east to meet the new threat. Fletcher, meanwhile, had ordered Spruance's *Enterprise* and *Hornet* planes to be launched against the Japanese carriers at 7 A.M. The *Yorktown,* several miles to the east, launched half its planes at 7:30. Spruance's dive bombers, overshooting the new Japanese course, missed Nagumo's carriers in the overcast. But the American torpedo bombers found them and came in, without fighter cover, to be almost completely destroyed by antiaircraft fire and fighter planes at about 9:30. Not a single American hit was scored. Nagumo, assuming victory to be in his grasp, was still feverishly rearming and refueling planes on his carriers' cluttered decks when the American dive-bomber squadrons found him—*Enterprise, Hornet,* and *Yorktown* in turn. By 10:25, 3 Japanese carriers—*Akagi, Kaga,* and *Soryu*—were flaming wrecks. The fourth, *Hiryu,* undamaged, went steaming northeastward, sending her reserve planes to seek the American carriers. They found the *Yorktown* just after noon and hit her with 3 bombs. The *Hiryu,* meanwhile, had rearmed the planes which had struck Midway, and these also attacked the *Yorktown,* scoring 2 fatal torpedo hits. Fletcher abandoned his helpless and listing ship at 3 P.M. But searching American planes had located the Japanese carrier, and from the *Enterprise* a 24-dive-bomber strike—planes hurriedly retrieved from the earlier fight—mortally damaged the *Hiryu,* which burst into flames. It was now 5 P.M., the main battle over. Japan had lost her entire carrier force in being; the U.S. still had two in commission.

1942, June 4–5. Battle of Midway—Third Phase. Yamamoto, thunderstruck by a calamity in part due to his own separation of his fleet into several unsupporting forces, nevertheless hoped to retrieve the disaster. Pushing eastward during the night with all of his big ships, still infinitely superior in surface strength to the Americans, he hoped to lure them into a surface battle. Spruance (to whom Fletcher had relinquished command after the *Yorktown* was abandoned) was aware of this danger, and instead of attempting to pursue had turned eastward during the night. After midnight Yamamoto realized that he could not trap the Americans and, lacking air protection, he ordered a general retirement westward.

1942, June 5–6. Battle of Midway—Closing Actions. For 2 days the Americans pursued the retreating Japanese by day, but avoided possible traps at night. American planes caused additional damage, but no major actions took place. Finally, with fuel running low, Spruance ended the pursuit and turned back toward Pearl Harbor. Meanwhile, the crippled *Yorktown* had remained afloat, and was being slowly towed back to Pearl Harbor when she was sighted and, with an accompanying destroyer, sunk by the Japanese submarine *I-168.* These were the only American vessels lost during the battle. Also lost were 132 land- and carrier-based planes, with a total of 307 Americans killed in the battle. Japanese losses were 4 carriers, 1 heavy cruiser, 275 planes, and 3,500 men killed.

COMMENT. *Midway was one of the decisive battles of history. The loss of her fleet carrier force deprived Japan of the initiative; henceforward she was on the defensive—attempting to hold the great spread of the Southern Resources Area and contiguous regions she had so handily won. The psychological effect on the heretofore ever-victorious Japanese Navy was significant. Tactically, the American operations were almost faultless; Fletcher, the senior officer present, wisely gave Spruance full control over his 2-carrier task force after his own flagship was put out of action. And Spruance made good. Nagumo, on the other hand, was the victim of circumstance and faulty intelligence. His decision to rearm his reserve planes for a second strike at Midway—which resulted in his carriers being caught with their decks crowded with planes—was fatal but perhaps inevitable in view of his lack of vital information. Up to that time he too had conducted his operation faultlessly, and the final strikes of* Hiryu *planes against the* Yorktown *were planned and conducted with skill, gallantry, and determination. Two basic factors led to the result: first and foremost, American knowledge of the Japanese secret codes, which presented Nimitz with an accurate picture of Japanese intentions and dispositions; second, Yamamoto's original dispersion of his tremendous armada to fit his own estimate of probable American intentions and reactions. A minor but interesting sidelight to the battle was the successful transfer of command by both admirals from a sinking flagship to a cruiser: Nagumo from* Akagi *and Fletcher from* Yorktown.

OPERATIONS IN THE SOLOMONS

1942, August 7. Amphibious Landings at Guadalcanal and Tulagi. (For background and land operations, see pp. 1140 and 1141.) Over-all commander of the Allied amphibious invasion of the Solomons was Vice Admiral Ghormley, with headquarters ashore at Nouméa. Commander afloat was Rear Admiral Fletcher, with a task force built round the carriers *Saratoga, Enterprise,* and *Wasp.* The amphibious force itself, comprising 4 U.S. cruisers, 3 Australian cruisers, 19 U.S. destroyers, and 19 troop transports, was commanded by Rear Admiral **R. K. Turner.** Surprise was complete; the Marines were put ashore on Tulagi and Guadalcanal, and within 24 hours had secured their objectives.

1942, August 7–8. Japanese Reaction. Admiral Inouye at Rabaul reacted promptly to reports of the Allied landings. Three separate air raids were made against the invasion force on the first afternoon, and though these caused little damage, they seriously interfered with the landing of supplies and reinforcements to the troops ashore. Meanwhile a naval task force of 7 cruisers and 1 destroyer, under Vice Admiral **Gunichi Mikawa,** rushed southward through the "Slot," or central sound between the central Solomon chains. The following day, Japanese planes continued their intensive attacks, and a series of violent air battles raged over the sound between Guadalcanal and Tulagi, and the seas nearby, as Japanese planes also attempted to hit the American carriers. The carrier planes took a heavy toll of the attackers, but suffered substantial losses themselves. Fletcher decided, therefore, that he would withdraw his carriers from the area, since he feared his losses would make the carriers more vulnerable and would prevent him from providing adequate support to Turner's force and the Marines ashore. As a result of this faulty decision, Turner decided (August 8, evening) that he could not keep his vessels near Guadalcanal without air cover, but decided to continue unloading supplies for 1 more day.

1942, August 9. Battle of Savo Island. Mikawa's force, passing south of Savo Island into the sound between Guadalcanal and Tulagi (later known as Ironbottom Sound), surprised Turner's patrolling cruisers shortly after midnight. In 32 minutes of battle characterized by excellent Japanese gunnery and shiphandling, 4 of the 5 Allied heavy cruisers engaged—1 Australian and 3 U.S.—were sunk and the fifth damaged. Mikawa, fearing American air attack with the dawn (he did not know that Fletcher had withdrawn his carrier force), broke off the engagement and headed for Rabaul, his ships practically unscathed and with only 37 men killed and 57 wounded. Allied casualties were 4 cruisers and 1 destroyer sunk, 1,270 officers and men killed, and 709 wounded. On the way back, an American submarine, *S-44,* took the one substantial toll of Mikawa's command, the heavy cruiser *Kako,* small price for the most humiliating defeat ever suffered in fair fight by the U.S. Navy. Later that day, Admiral Turner departed with the remnant of his warships and all the transports, still only partly unloaded.

COMMENT. *Turner's disposition of his warships in 3 packets to guard all 3 entrances to Ironbottom Sound was faulty, setting up conditions for defeat in detail accomplished later by Mikawa's bold attack. Turner's controversial abandonment of the Marine division, taking with him the greater part of its supply and all heavy ordnance and construction equipment, was justified by Fletcher's prior departure with the carrier force (approved by Ghormley), leaving the amphibious flotilla bare to air attack.*

1942, August 10–23. Force Build-up on Guadalcanal. The Japanese sent in scattered reinforcements and supplies to their small force on Guadalcanal, mostly by fast destroyers which traveled through the Slot only by night. At the same time, the American Marines were receiving supplies by destroyer transport; the captured Japanese airfield (renamed Henderson Field) was completed, and planes brought in (August 20). During this time, long-range air battles were taking place over the island, Japanese planes coming from Rabaul and the northern Solomons, American planes from the New Hebrides. The Japanese failure to take advantage of the withdrawal of the American Navy and undertake an immediate, large-scale land build-up on Guadalcanal, and to make an overwhelming land and naval assault on the Marine positions, was a serious mistake.

1942, August 22–25. Battle of the Eastern Solomons. The next major action was precipitated by a Japanese decision to send a small convoy of destroyers and transports, under Rear Admiral **Raizo Tanaka,** carrying 1,500 reinforcements to Guadalcanal. To provide support and air cover, a Japanese squadron, built around the fleet carriers *Shokaku* and *Zuikaku* and light carrier *Ryujo,* under Admiral **Nobutake Kondo,** steamed toward the Solomons from Truk. The Japanese, because of Midway, had changed their code (although they were not certain that it had been compromised), but increased radio activity warned the Americans of a major operation impending. Ghormley ordered Fletcher's carrier force to intercept. Fletcher, misled by faulty intelligence, permitted the *Wasp* group to leave for a fueling rendezvous, reducing his strength by one-third. On making contact, Fletcher's planes sank the *Ryujo,* which was attacking Henderson Field. In so doing he left himself open to attack by the 2 large Japanese carriers (August 24). The American carriers were operating in independent groups. The Japanese air attack fell first on *Enterprise,* getting through the fighter air cover and doing much damage. No attackers reached *Saratoga,* and the new big battleship *North Carolina*'s antiaircraft fire drove off bombing thrusts. A small flight of *Saratoga*'s planes badly damaged a Japanese seaplane carrier, but the Americans could not find the Japanese fleet carriers. Fletcher now broke off contact, his loss being 17 planes and the damage to the *Enterprise.* Kondo gave up after a short pursuit and called his battleships and cruisers in. Meanwhile Tanaka's destroyers, having put the reinforcements ashore, bombarded Henderson Field. Next day the Marine air group from Henderson Field damaged Tanaka's flagship, and an Army B-17 sank a destroyer. Tanaka withdrew. Technically, the battle was a draw since both naval carrier forces remained intact. The Japanese had accomplished their mission, but the loss of a light carrier and 90 carrier planes was a severe blow.

1942, August 31. Damage to the *Saratoga*. Torpedoed by the submarine *I-26,* the carrier was put out of action for 3 months, leaving only the *Wasp* fit for combat in the South Pacific.

1942, September 15. End of the *Wasp*. Admiral Ghormley had decided to reinforce the 1st Marine Division. His depleted carrier force escorted the 7th Marine Regiment, in 6 transports, leaving Espiritu Santo, New Hebrides (September 14). Japanese submarines *I-15* and *I-19* intercepted the force. The *I-15* damaged the battleship *North Carolina* and sank a destroyer, while *I-19* put 2 torpedoes into the *Wasp,* sending her to the bottom. Admiral Turner boldly continued to Guadalcanal, landing the reinforcements safely (September 18). Both sides now strove to reinforce their troops ashore. Their next efforts met head on.

1942, October 11–13. Battle of Cape Esperance. Admiral Turner with 2 big transports and 8 destroyer transports carried a reinforced regiment of the Army's Americal Division to Guadalcanal. Escorting was Rear Admiral **Norman Scott** with 5 cruisers and 5 destroyers. At the same time, a Japanese transport force—2 seaplane carriers and 6 destroyers carrying men, ammunition, and matériel—was coming down the Slot escorted by 3 heavy cruisers and 2 destroyers. Scott, forewarned, moved to intercept. He surprised the Japanese armada just before midnight, sinking 1 cruiser and a destroyer and crippling 2 more cruisers in gun and torpedo fight illuminated by American search planes. Rear Admiral **T. Joshima** safely landed his troops, losing two destroyers to land-based bombers from Henderson Field as he withdrew. Turner, arriving under cover of the naval battle, also safely landed his reinforcements.

1942, October 13–15. Surface Bombardment of Henderson Field. The battleships *Kongo* and *Haruna,* supported by several cruisers and destroyers, successfully bombarded the Marine perimeter on Guadalcanal, while more Japanese reinforcements were being landed on both sides of the position. A similar bombardment the following night by cruisers under Admiral Tanaka covered the arrival of more Japanese troops. The Japanese had re-established effective control over the seas around Guadalcanal.

1942, October 18. Change in American Command. Vice Admiral Halsey replaced Ghormley as commander of the South Pacific Area. About the same time, Rear Admiral **Thomas C. Kinkaid** relieved Fletcher in command of the carrier force, which now comprised the *Hornet* and the hastily repaired *Enterprise* (this amazingly durable vessel becoming famous as the "Big E").

1942, October 23–25. Yamamoto's Plans. Yamamoto had placed 2 heavy and 2 light carriers under Kondo's command in the South Pacific; with these he expected to defeat the Americans in a climactic naval-air battle for control of the southern Solomons. He was reluctant to risk the precious carriers in action, however, without a good land airfield nearby, from which land-based planes could provide support and where valuable carrier pilots could take refuge if their carrier should be sunk or damaged. Because of their troop build-up on Guadalcanal, the Japanese were confident that Henderson Field could be wrested from the Marines. Once this was done, the carriers could close with the American fleet, while land-based planes rushed down from Rabaul. As the land forces engaged in a bitter battle for control of Henderson Field (see p. 1142), Kondo's fleet moved cautiously south from Truk. Kinkaid's force, with equal caution, circled north of the Santa Cruz Islands.

1942, October 26–27. Battle of the Santa Cruz Islands. While the Japanese land attack on Henderson Field was being repulsed (see p. 1142), Kinkaid obeyed Halsey's radioed orders to carry the fight to the Japanese fleet. In fact, both carrier forces launched simultaneous strikes against each other, the strike forces passing in midair; several American planes were shot down by Japanese escort fighters. The Americans damaged the light carrier *Zuiho* and severely damaged the *Shokaku* (put out of action for 9 months). The *Hornet* was hit even more seriously and had to be towed out of action by a cruiser. The *Enterprise* was hit and badly damaged by a second strike from the 2 remaining Japanese carriers. The Americans were now forced to withdraw. As the pursuing Japanese came closer, the *Hornet* had to be abandoned, and she was sunk by Japanese destroyers. Kondo then withdrew. The Japanese had won a clear-cut victory, but a Pyrrhic one, since they lost 100 planes, about half again as many as the American loss, and this still further depleted their thinning ranks of good carrier pilots. Furthermore, by failing to pursue and possibly to destroy the damaged "Big E," Kondo had made a serious mistake.

1942, November 12–13. Naval Battle of Guadalcanal—First Phase. A reinforcement contingent of 13,000 men in 11 transports, protected by 11 destroyers under Admiral Tanaka, was approaching Guadalcanal. To cover the approach of this reinforcement group, Admiral Kondo sent a powerful squadron of 2 battleships, 2 cruisers, and 14 destroyers under Vice Admiral **Hiroaki Abe** to shell Henderson Field. The carrier force, steaming north of the Solomons, provided air cover. At the same time, American reinforcements arrived at Guadalcanal, convoyed by Admiral Turner, and escorted by 5 cruisers and 8 destroyers under Rear Admiral **Daniel J. Callaghan** (November 12). Learning of the approach of Tanaka's and Abe's forces, Callaghan, with Admiral Turner's approval, moved to intercept, counting on surprise to overcome his serious numerical disadvantage. Kinkaid's carrier force (with only one carrier, the damaged *Enterprise,* with a tender tied alongside actually making repairs as the force steamed toward Guadalcanal to cover Turner's retreating transports) was too far away to take part in the action. Though he had radar (which the Japanese did not), Callaghan misused it and was as surprised as the Japanese when Abe's force entered Ironbottom Sound shortly after midnight and suddenly discovered the Americans. One of the most confused and furious naval actions of history followed. The intermingled forces blazed away at each other in the darkness, sometimes at point-blank range. After 36 minutes, survivors of both sides pulled apart. The battleship *Hiei* was left helpless (to be sunk after dawn by *Enterprise* planes en route to Henderson Field), 2 Japanese cruisers were sunk, and all the other Japanese vessels were damaged. Two American cruisers and 4 destroyers were sunk, another cruiser and a destroyer were close to sinking, and all other American ships save 1 were damaged. Admiral Callaghan and Admiral Scott were both killed. Tactically a draw, this first phase of the battle was strategically an American success, since the planned bombardment of Henderson Field had been repulsed, and Tanaka's convoy had to turn back to the Shortland Islands.

1942, November 13–14. Naval Battle of Guadalcanal—Second Phase. During the following day, air activity was intensive on both sides. Before dark Tanaka again started south with his reinforcement convoy. After dark, 2 Japanese heavy cruisers, part of a cruiser force under Admiral Mikawa, entered Ironbottom Sound, unopposed, to shell Henderson Field. The following morning the air activity stepped up further, with the Americans concentrating on Tanaka's convoy and Mikawa's cruisers. Seven of Tanaka's transports and 2 of Mikawa's cruisers were sunk. Tanaka persevered, however, continuing toward Guadalcanal with his remaining transports, while Admiral Kondo, with the battleship *Kirishima,* 4 cruisers, and 9 destroyers, raced south to cover Tanaka's approach, intending to bombard Henderson Field.

1942, November 14–15. Naval Battle of Guadalcanal—Third Phase. Kinkaid sent Rear Admiral **Willis A. Lee,** with the battleships *Washington* and *South Dakota* and 4 destroyers, to intercept the Japanese. The opponents met at close range in Ironbottom Sound, just south of Savo Island. Two of the American destroyers were quickly sunk and the other 2 put out of action. The 2 battleships, however, closed boldly with the Japanese, who concentrated their fire on the *South Dakota,* causing an electrical power failure and putting her out of action for the rest of the engagement. Briefly it was a battle between the *Washington* and 14 Japanese warships. The odds were quickly lessened, however, as Lee calmly concentrated the *Washington*'s radar-directed guns against the *Kirishima,* leaving her and a destroyer in sinking condition. Kondo now withdrew. The naval Battle of Guadalcanal was ended. Though Tanaka had succeeded in putting 4,000 troops ashore, and rescued 5,000 more on his return to Rabaul, the main result of this 3-day battle was to return to the Americans effective control of the waters around Guadalcanal, thus assuring final victory in this crucial land and naval campaign. The Japanese went on the defensive in the southern Solomons.

1942, November 30. Battle of Tassafaronga. Tenacious Tanaka continued to prove, however, that the victory would not come cheaply. An American force of 5 cruisers and 7 destroyers under Rear Admiral **Carleton H. Wright** moved to meet Tanaka's "Tokyo Express," this time 8 destroyers carrying supplies for the Japanese garrison of the island. Warned by radar of the Japanese approach into Ironbottom Sound, the Americans opened fire and sank the leading destroyer. But Tanaka promptly and skillfully turned his entire squadron toward the Americans, fired several torpedoes each, then scampered north without further loss. They left 1 American cruiser sunk and 3 more badly damaged, with a total of 400 dead sailors.

1943, January 29–30. Battle of Rennell's Island. An American squadron of 6 cruisers, 8 destroyers, and 2 escort carriers, under Rear Admiral **Robert C. Giffin,** was cruising north of Guadalcanal in hopes of enticing gathering Japanese naval forces in the northern Solomons (actually preparing to cover the evacuation of Guadalcanal) into battle. The Japanese did not take the bait; instead, Yamamoto ordered 2 very successful land-based air strikes against the Americans. The first, at dusk, January 20, disabled the *Chicago.* Late the next afternoon, while the Americans were withdrawing southward, the Japanese again hit the *Chicago,* while in tow, and sank her.

1943, February 1–7. Japanese Evacuation of Guadalcanal. Rear Admiral **Koyanagi** (who had replaced Tanaka) brilliantly and skillfully evacuated about 13,000 Japanese troops from Guadalcanal without being detected by the Americans.

COMMENT. *Not since the Anglo-Dutch wars had 2 powerful navies engaged in such a prolonged, intensive, and destructive naval campaign as that which took place for 6 long months around Guadalcanal. Serious mistakes were made on both sides, and the honors were approximately even in skill and gallantry displayed. The margin of the American success was their eventual superiority of numbers and of equipment, both on the surface and in the air.*

Operations in the Indian Ocean

1942, March 23. Seizure of the Andamans. This provided the Japanese with a secure convoy route from Singapore to Rangoon.

1942, March 25. Appearance of the First Air Fleet. Admiral Nagumo with 5 carriers (veterans of Pearl Harbor and Darwin) accompanied by 4 fast battleships and several cruisers and destroyers sailed westward into the Indian Ocean. His mission was to strike British naval bases in Ceylon, and to destroy all British naval and merchant shipping he could find in the ocean and the Bay of Bengal.

1942, March 27–April 2. British Reaction. Admiral Sir James Somerville's British

Far Eastern Force consisted of 5 battleships—4 of them old and slow—3 small carriers, 8 cruisers, and 15 destroyers. Upon learning of Nagumo's approach, Somerville sailed southeast from Ceylon to meet him, but the fleets passed each other without contact. Realizing that he had missed his enemy, Somerville turned back to Addu Atoll, in the Maldives, to refuel. Here he came to the conclusion that it would be suicidal to attempt a formal battle against the superior and faster Japanese fleet; accordingly, he sent his 4 old battleships back to the coast of Africa, attempting to harass the Japanese with his remaining vessels while avoiding a major battle.

1942, April 2–8. Action off the Coasts of Ceylon and India. Japanese carrier aircraft struck the bases of Trincomalee and Colombo, causing damage to the installations, but being heavily engaged by RAF fighter planes. During a week of confused fighting, the Japanese carrier aircraft sank 1 British carrier, 2 cruisers, a destroyer, and several merchant ships. In their several engagements with the RAF and with British carrier aircraft, the Japanese inflicted substantial losses, but suffered heavily themselves as well. Finally, satisfied that he had carried out his mission, and feeling the necessity to rebuild his depleted air strength, the Japanese admiral sailed back toward the Pacific (April 8).

COMMENT. *In 4 months of war, the First Air Fleet had operated across one-third of the globe and had sunk 5 battleships, 1 carrier, 2 cruisers, 7 destroyers, and damaged many more, to say nothing of other destruction, without one of its own vessels having been damaged.*

1942, April–May. British Concern about Africa. Nagumo's demonstration that Japan could control the Indian Ocean at will caused great worry to Churchill and British military leaders regarding the security of the African coast and of the sea routes to India. Fearing that the Japanese might try to gain control of French Madagascar as they had of Indochina, the British decided they would forestall them.

1942, May 5–7. Assault on Diégo-Suarez. A British amphibious force under Rear Admiral **Edward N. Syfret** assaulted and captured the Vichy French port at the northern tip of Madagascar. They hoped no further action on Madagascar would be necessary.

1942, May 29–30. Japanese Activity off Madagascar. A Japanese plane (submarine launched, though this was not known at the time) was sighted over Diégo-Suarez (May 29). The following night a midget submarine (also launched from a large submarine) damaged H.M. battleship *Ramillies* and sank a tanker in the harbor. The British feared that the Japanese were using secret bases elsewhere on Madagascar, and so decided to seize the entire island.

1942, September–November. British Conquest of Madagascar. Following amphibious landings at **Majunga** (September 10) and **Tamatave** (September 18), the British, under Lieutenant General Sir William Platt, moved against the capital, Tananarive. The French were forced to surrender (November 5). The British later turned the island over to the Free French (January 8, 1943).

THE WAR AGAINST JAPAN, 1943

Strategy and Policy

By the end of 1942 the Axis tide was clearly receding in Europe and North Africa, and was ebbing slightly in the Pacific. But the Japanese realized (as did the Allies) that this was merely a shifting from the offensive to the defensive, in accordance with a plan that had been set before they went to war. The setbacks in Papua and Guadalcanal had been unexpectedly costly, but this was attributed primarily to hasty, last-minute modifications in the original strategic plan, and the Japanese intended to make no such error again.

The defeat at Midway had been another matter, however, and the Japanese naval high command was apprehensive about the consequences of the carrier losses in that disastrous battle. These losses, furthermore, had been compounded by extremely heavy casualties among the remaining trained carrier pilots in the air battles around Guadalcanal.

Japanese military leaders hoped, however, that they could make good these losses by initiating an intensive new training program, while the Americans and their allies dashed themselves in costly assaults against the increasingly powerful jungle fortresses rimming the widespread Japanese defensive perimeter. They expected that the U.S. would become discouraged and would make peace, leaving Japan with most of her conquests.

There was no thought of a negotiated peace in America or Britain, however. While concentrating most of their efforts to achieve the defeat of Germany, the Allies were sufficiently encouraged by their limited successes in late 1942 to increase slightly the scale of effort against Japan. Among the Allied leaders, Admiral King was particularly determined to increase the momentum of operations in the Pacific, even though he did not directly question or subvert the primary effort against Germany. But America's naval strength was growing more rapidly than had been expected, both in relative and absolute terms. There were limits to the extent to which naval force could be used against Germany, and so most of this growing naval strength was allocated to the Pacific areas. Because it was obviously uneconomic for this tremendously burgeoning power to remain idle, it was essential to match naval strength, at least to a limited degree, with additional land and air strength—particularly since these categories of military force were also increasing rapidly in America.

Thus, there was at least a partial deviation from the original strategy of remaining on the defensive against Japan, while concentrating full Allied strength against Germany. The increasing American effort was also recognized by a few Japanese as a demonstration of the United States' phenomenal industrial and operational warmaking capability.

Land and Air Operations in Asia

BURMA

General Wavell, commanding Allied forces in India, realized that he would not be ready for a major invasion of Burma until the dry season of late 1943 or early 1944. But he was worried about the psychological effect of the defeats suffered in Malaya and Singapore in 1942, and hoped during the dry season of 1942–1943 to revive the spirit of British troops by success in 2 small, carefully prepared offensives.

The First Arakan Campaign

1942, December–1943, January. Advance into Arakan. The 14th Indian Division* advanced into Arakan, northwest coastal province of Burma, separated from the remainder of Burma by jungled mountains. Moving cautiously, the British gave the outnumbered Japanese time to construct strong defenses north of Akyab.

1943, January–March. Stalemate at Akyab. With the assistance of reinforcements rushed by General Iida, the Japanese repulsed repeated British attacks with heavy losses.

March–May. Japanese Counteroffensive. The Japanese 55th Division counterattacked from Akyab, while other Japanese units worked their way over supposedly impassable mountains to strike the British left and rear (March 13–17). The 14th Division retreated in considerable confusion. Though reinforcements were rushed to the front, the British could not stop the Japanese infiltrating tactics. The campaign

* Elements of the Indian Army included British and Indian units, but were operationally controlled as integral British Army units.

ended where it had started, with the Japanese still occupying Arakan (May 12).

COMMENT. *Instead of rebuilding confidence, the First Arakan Campaign had made British troops still more fearful of Japanese jungle-fighting ability.*

First Chindit Raid

Brigadier **Orde C. Wingate** obtained the approval of General Wavell to demonstrate his concept of "long-range penetration" with his 77th Indian Brigade. It was his belief that small British ground forces, supplied by air, could operate for extended periods deep behind enemy lines, cutting communications, destroying supplies, and creating general confusion. This seemed to him, and to Wavell, a way of beating the Japanese at their own game of infiltration and encirclement.

1943, February 18. Crossing the Chindwin River. Entering Japanese-controlled territory, the 77th Brigade (known later as "Chindits")* split up into several small columns and set out to cut the Mandalay-Myitkyina and Mandalay-Lashio railroads.

1943, March 18. Crossing the Irrawaddy River. Having temporarily interrupted the Mandalay-Myitkyina railroad, Chindit columns pushed on to cross the Irrawaddy. They had now aroused the Japanese, however, and encountered increasing opposition.

1943, April. Withdrawal of the Chindits. As losses mounted, Wingate gave up his plan to cut the Mandalay-Lashio railroad. The Chindits retreated with considerable difficulty back to India in small groups. Losses totaled more than 1,000 men, over one-third of the total force engaged.

COMMENT. *The Chindit raid was a military failure, the losses far too heavy to justify the slight damage inflicted, which was quickly repaired by the Japanese. However, the fact that British troops had successfully raided behind the Japanese lines, then fought their way out again, was hailed by the newspapers as a great Allied victory. Thus, psychologically, the raid went far to offset the discouraging results of the Arakan operation. The total effect of the 2 operations, however, was to convince Wavell and other British leaders that no major British invasion of Burma was possible prior to the dry season of 1944–1945.*

Operations in North Burma

1943, February. Chinese Troops to the India-Burma Border. As Japanese spearheads pressed closer to the India-Burma border in the Hukawng Valley area of north Burma, Stilwell feared that they might attempt to raid into upper Assam (northeast India), where American, Chinese, and Indian engineers were beginning to push a road toward the border from Ledo. He therefore moved most of the rebuilt, retrained Chinese 38th Division from Ramgarh to protect the road-building operations. There were minor clashes of patrols in the mountains just inside Burma. The Japanese withdrew back into the Hukawng Valley.

1943, October–November. Return to Burma. Bitterly disappointed by British and Chinese failure to undertake a major invasion of Burma in 1943–1944 to reopen the land route to China (see above and p. 1156), Stilwell decided that he would initiate the effort with the resources at his disposal. He obtained the reluctant approval of Wavell and Chiang Kai-shek. The 38th Division pushed southeastward through the mountain spine of the India-Burma border into the Hukawng Valley. All supplies were dropped by air. The 22nd Division was moved up from Ramgarh to Ledo and the border area. Work on the road from Ledo intensified as more American engineers arrived, and dry weather permitted more rapid progress.

1943, November 23–December 23. Stalemate. As elements of the Chinese 38th Division advanced in the Hukawng Valley, they were struck by a Japanese counterattack. Three battalions were surrounded and the advance came to a complete halt, though the Japanese were unable to overrun the 3 isolated units, which were maintained by American air supply.

1943, December 24–31. Stilwell Resumes the

* The nickname had two origins: their emblem was a *chinthe,* a mythical Burmese beast resembling a lion; they operated beyond the Chindwin River.

Advance. The arrival of General Stilwell, and also of some light pack artillery, inspired the Chinese to counterattack, relieving the beleaguered battalions and clearing the valley west of the Tarung River.

CHINA

The growing weakness of isolated China was repeatedly demonstrated by easy Japanese successes in minor local offensives. These operations were planned by the Japanese to give experience to newly raised units, and also to seize rice crops in unoccupied China. By these "rice offensives" they were able to get food easily for themselves, while denying it to Chiang's starving people and soldiers. Toward the end of the year, however, with increased American air support (see below) the Chinese repulsed one of these Japanese rice offensives in Hunan by a victory at the **Battle of Changteh** (November 23–December 9).

Although the arrival of additional American transport planes added greatly to the quantity of supplies flowing to China over the Hump during the year, these were totally inadequate to meet the many conflicting needs of China and of the war effort. This led directly to 2 serious disputes involving American leaders in China.

Chennault's China Air Task Force (the only American unit in China; see p. 1137) was having success comparable to that which he had earlier gained with his Flying Tigers, inflicting losses of more than 10 aircraft on the Japanese for every 1 they lost. But because of the restrictions on supplies over the Hump, Chennault felt that he had not had an opportunity to prove the potential of his force, which he believed could win the war in China unaided. He insisted that he should receive all, or most, of the Hump supplies. Stilwell, however, ordered that a substantial proportion of the Hump tonnage should go to the Chinese Army, since it would need supplies to attack north Burma from the east while his troops in India attacked from the west. Chiang, already displeased with Stilwell, supported Chennault, who finally won the argument when he also obtained the support of President Roosevelt. He was promoted to major general, and his command was enlarged and redesignated the Fourteenth Air Force (March 11).

With his increased share of the increasing Hump tonnage, Chennault's growing Fourteenth Air Force was able during the remainder of the year to gain air superiority over most of China. His bombers ranged as far as Formosa, inflicting severe losses on the Japanese.

Because of the diversion of supplies from the Chinese Army to the Fourteenth Air Force, Chiang would not permit Chinese troops in China to participate in Stilwell's planned 2-prong offensive into north Burma. Only with reluctance would he give his assent to the advance of Chinese troops from India, since this would not interfere with Hump supplies to China.

Deteriorating relations between the National Government and the Communist regime at Yenan had, by this time, led Chiang to establish a *de facto* blockade of Communist-held regions of China. This had required the diversion of a substantial number of divisions from the war effort against Japan. Stilwell complained about this diversion, which further increased the tensions between the two men.

Operations in the South and Southwest Pacific

Japanese Defensive Plans. Realizing that their defensive perimeter was threatened by Allied successes on Guadalcanal and Papua, the Japanese began to strengthen Rabaul, the southeastern anchor of their defensive perimeter, with outposts on the Huon Gulf in northeast New Guinea and in the Solomons as far south as New Georgia Island. New Guinea, the Bismarcks, and the Solomons were under navy control, with Vice Admiral **Jinichi Kosaka** commanding. Under him was the 8th Army Area (Lieutenant General **Hitoshi Imamura**), with the Eighteenth Army (Lieutenant General **Hotaze Adachi**) in New Guinea and the Seventeenth (Lieutenant General **Iwao Matsuda**) in the Solomons. Because Allied forces in this region were the most immediate threat to the Japanese perimeter, Admiral Yamamoto, commander of the Combined Fleet, with headquarters at Truk, gave close personal supervision to the defensive measures (see p. 1150).

Allied Offensive Plans. With Rabaul the obvious primary Allied objective, Admiral Halsey's forces of the South Pacific Area, now designated the U.S. Third Fleet, were shifted from the command of Admiral Nimitz to that of General MacArthur for a co-ordinated Allied two-pronged offensive against Rabaul. Halsey's forces were to drive northwestward through the Solomons, while General **Walter Krueger**'s U.S. Sixth Army, under the direct supervision of General MacArthur,

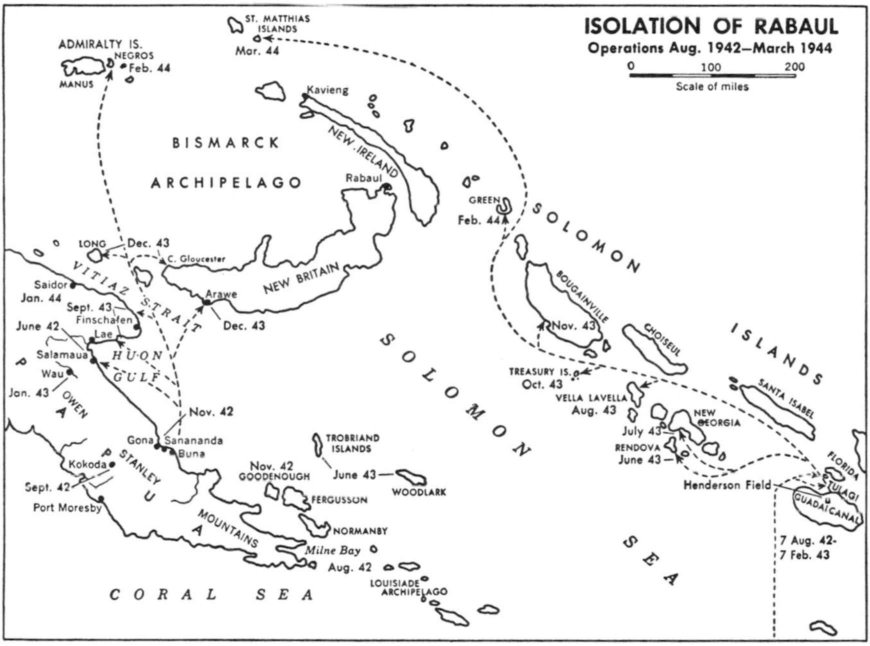

was to advance northward through northeast New Guinea and the island of New Britain toward the Japanese base. Complicating the command arrangements was the fact that Halsey, while under the strategic direction of MacArthur, was still dependent upon his own naval commander in chief, Admiral Nimitz, for ships, troops, aircraft, and the logistic means necessary to operate tactically. That the 2 operations worked smoothly was due to the spirit of co-operation and tolerance displayed by all concerned, with examples set by MacArthur and Halsey.

NEW GUINEA AND NEW BRITAIN, 1943

1943, January 9. Wau. A brigade of Australian General Hering's New Guinea Force, airlifted to a mountain airstrip at Wau, 30 miles west of Salamaua, established a forward base, threatening that Japanese coastal holding while MacArthur built up strength for an offensive.

1943, June 30. Feint at Salamaua. An American amphibious landing at Nassau Bay, south of Salamaua, and demonstrations from Wau indicated a full-scale assault to come. At the same time, MacArthur dispatched elements of Krueger's

Sixth Army to take and occupy the Trobriand-Woodlark island group in the Solomon Sea, north of Papua's eastern tip, securing new airfields.

1943, September 4–16. Lae and Salamaua. Australian General Sir **Thomas Blamey** took over command of the New Guinea Force. American and Australian troops made an amphibious landing east of Lae. Two days later, a U.S. paratroop regiment dropped at Nadzab in the Markham River Valley, to the northwest. The Australian 7th Division was immediately airlifted in to reinforce, and a converging approach began on Lae. Meanwhile, the Allied forces in front of Salamaua increased their activity. The Japanese garrisons began abandoning both places. Salamaua was occupied (September 12) and Lae fell 4 days later.

1943, September 22–October 2. Finschhafen. A quick ground and amphibious advance around the tip of the Huon Peninsula encircled Finschhafen (September 22), which fell October 2. The way was paved for amphibious operations against New Britain.

COMMENT. *This campaign was a splendid example, on a small scale, of combined operations—land, sea and air, featuring deception and surprise. Lieutenant General* **George C. Kenney**'s *U.S. Fifth Air Force isolated the enemy from his strongholds at Madang, Wewak, and Rabaul, while also*

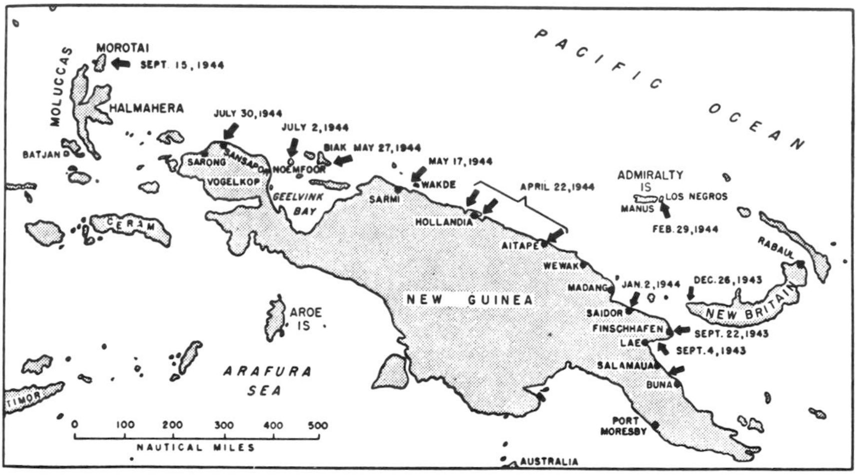

Operations on New Guinea

providing direct support to the ground forces. Of some 10,000 Japanese troops engaged, more than half had been killed, the rest dispersed in the jungle.

1943, October–December. New Britain Toehold. While Blamey's New Guinea Force blocked off the Huon Peninsula, protecting reorganization, Krueger's Sixth Army took over the next task. Elements of the U.S. 1st Cavalry Division* landed (December 15) at Arawe on southern New Britain, where a base was established. The 1st Marine Division, put ashore (December 26) by the Seventh Amphibious Force, secured a successful beachhead and two airfields at Cape Gloucester on the northern side after 4 days of stiff fighting in which more than 1,000 Japanese were killed.

* This division was actually an infantry formation, though retaining its prewar designations and organization.

CENTRAL AND NORTHERN SOLOMONS

1943, February–June. Preparations. Following the conquest of Guadalcanal, there was a lull in surface operations while Halsey reorganized his command and prepared to set in motion the eastern arm of MacArthur's pincers. Elements of the U.S. 43rd Division seized Russell Island (February 11).

1943, June 30. Capture of Rendova Island.

Artillery was quickly landed in range of nearby New Georgia.

1943, July 2–August 25. Assault on New Georgia. Supported by guns from Rendova and by a naval task force, troops of the U.S. 37th and 43rd Divisions, reinforced by Marine battalions, landed near Munda. They were commanded by Major General **John H. Hester** (later by Major General **Oscar Griswold**). Since Munda, commanded by General **Noboru Sasaki,** was now the principal Japanese air base in the Solomons, the attacks were fiercely contested in the bitterest sort of jungle fighting. The U.S. 25th Division was also committed (July 25). Griswold, regrouping his forces, launched a co-ordinated assault on the airfield, which was captured (August 5). All resistance on New Georgia soon ended (August 25).

1943, August 15–October 7. Vella Lavella. A regimental combat team landed on Vella Lavella, leapfrogging Kolombangara, next Japanese airfield of importance, and an American advanced airbase was prepared. Elements of the New Zealand 3rd Division, replacing U.S. troops on Vella Lavella (mid-September), swept away the last remnants of the Japanese garrison. The Japanese began withdrawal from Kolombangara, and the Central Solomons operation came to an end (October 6–7). Allied losses (mostly American) in this campaign were 1,136 killed and 4,140 wounded. More than 2,500 Japanese dead were counted of the 8,000 engaged.

1943, October–December. Bougainville. South of Rabaul, the Japanese grip on the Solomons now included only Choiseul and Bougainville. A feint assault (October 27) on Choiseul by a small Marine expedition (quickly withdrawn) momentarily obscured intentions. That same day the Treasury Islands were seized as staging area for a move on Bougainville, and from it (November 1) the 3rd Marine Division sprang ashore at Empress Augusta Bay against light resistance. By the year's end, Empress Augusta Bay had become an Allied naval base. Three airfields were in operation. All this was embedded in a defensive perimeter some 10 miles wide and 5 miles deep, now under General Griswold's Army control.

NAVAL OPERATIONS

Off the Coast of New Guinea

1943, January–June. The Seventh Fleet. The small American and Australian naval forces in MacArthur's Southwest Pacific Area were reorganized as the Seventh Fleet under the command of Vice Admiral **A. S. Carpender.** The principal missions of this fleet were to gain and keep control of the coastal waters of New Guinea, and to support MacArthur's ground troops in forthcoming amphibious operations. The actual conduct of the amphibious operations was a mission of the subordinate Seventh Amphibious Force (Rear Admiral **Daniel E. Barbey**), a collection of gunfire-support warships, troop transports, amphibious vessels, and landing craft, and including highly trained Army Engineers and Navy Seabees, whose task was to clear beach obstacles and to organize beachhead administration and supply.

1943, June–December. Amphibious Operations. The Seventh Fleet (commanded after August by Vice Admiral Thomas C. Kinkaid) and its Seventh Amphibious Force played key roles in the numerous amphibious operations along the coasts of New Guinea and New Britain (see pp. 1157–1158).

In the Waters of the Solomons

1943, February–June. Reorganization and Preparation. While waiting for reinforcements to permit him to continue operations northward from Guadalcanal, Admiral Halsey reorganized his South Pacific Forces into the Third Fleet. Initially the Third Amphibious Force was commanded by Admiral Turner. Its organization and mission were similar to those of the Seventh Amphibious Force.

1943, June–December. Amphibious Operations. The Third Fleet and Third Amphibious Force (commanded by Rear Admiral **Theodore S. Wilkinson** after July) made leapfrog advances through the Solomons (see above). The Third Fleet was still opposed by substantial Japanese naval forces, leading to numerous surface actions, most of which (at Japanese initiative) took place at night.

1943, July 5–6. Battle of Kula Gulf. An

American light cruiser squadron under Rear Admiral **W. L. Ainsworth** and a Japanese force of 10 destroyers under Rear Admiral **T. Akiyama** met. One U.S. cruiser was sunk; one Japanese destroyer was sunk and another ran aground (and was later destroyed). Despite U.S. superiority in gun power and armor, and the advantage of radar, superior Japanese night-fighting tactics and superior torpedoes gave them the best of this encounter.

1943, July 12–13. Battle of Kolombangara. In another night engagement, in almost the same waters, Japanese Rear Admiral **S. Izaki**'s squadron of 1 cruiser, 5 destroyers, and 4 destroyer transports met Ainsworth's force of 3 light cruisers and 10 destroyers. Again the Japanese inflicted more serious losses than they received: three Allied cruisers damaged and a destroyer sunk, while the Japanese lost their cruiser.

1943, August 6–7. Battle of Vella Gulf. An American squadron of 6 destroyers sank 3 out of 4 destroyers in a Japanese squadron without any loss to themselves.

1943, October 6–7. Battle of Vella Lavella. Rear Admiral **M. Ijuin,** with 9 destroyers, covering smaller craft evacuating Japanese troops from Vella Lavella, was encountered by 6 American destroyers under Captain **F. R. Walker.** One Japanese destroyer was sunk, as were 2 American vessels. With American reinforcements arriving, and with the troops evacuated from Vella Lavella, Ijuin withdrew. This was the last clear-cut Japanese naval success against the Americans.

1943, November 2. Battle of Empress Augusta Bay. This night engagement was the result of an effort by a Japanese squadron of 4 cruisers and 6 destroyers, under Rear Admiral **Sentaro Omori,** to interfere with the amphibious landings on Bougainville (see p. 1159). Rear Admiral **Stanton A. Merrill** with 4 cruisers and 8 destroyers was waiting. Making excellent use of their radar superiority, the Americans attacked Omori's force from front and flanks. The Japanese were assisted by flares dropped by supporting aircraft, but lost 1 cruiser and 1 destroyer, with most of the other vessels damaged. Only 1 American destroyer was badly damaged.

1943, November 5 and 11. Carrier Strikes on Rabaul. Planes of Rear Admiral **Frederick Sherman**'s task force—fleet carrier U.S.S. *Saratoga* and light carrier *Princeton*—severely mauled a powerful cruiser and destroyer force under Vice Admiral **Takeo Kurita,** staging from Truk through Rabaul for refueling in preparation for another blow at the American Bougainville beachhead (November 5). Kurita had 6 cruisers and destroyers badly damaged, and called off his planned attack. A few days later (November 11) another air strike was made by planes from Rear Admiral **A. E. Montgomery**'s task group of the carriers *Essex, Bunker Hill,* and *Independence.* Japanese planes intercepted the attackers, but were overwhelmed, and further severe damage was done to the port and to Kurita's ships, which soon thereafter limped back to Truk.

1943, November 25. Battle of Cape St. George. Captain **Arleigh Burke** with 5 destroyers intercepted 5 Japanese destroyers southeast of New Ireland in early morning darkness, sinking 3 Japanese vessels without damage to his own squadron.

COMMENT. *Having learned from earlier costly experience, the Americans had now established a clear-cut tactical superiority over the Japanese in night naval operations. This, combined with their superiority in all types of equipment save torpedoes, meant that the Americans would never again encounter serious or dangerous opposition in small cruiser and destroyer actions, day or night.*

AIR OPERATIONS

New Guinea and the Bismarcks

1943, January–May. Struggle for Air Superiority. Lieutenant General **George C. Kenney**'s American-Australian Fifth Air Force was engaged during this period in a bitter struggle for air superiority with Japanese naval air units at Rabaul and with heavily reinforced air units of the Eighteenth Army. This resulted in a number of violent air battles and exchanges of strikes between the opposing airfields. By midspring the Allies had gained a clear-cut superiority.

1943, March 2–4. Battle of the Bismarck Sea. This was primarily an air-surface battle between Kenney's medium bombers and a Japanese squadron of 8 destroyers, escorting 8 troop transports with 7,000 soldiers bound from Rabaul to reinforce Lae. Despite persistent fog, which the Japanese had hoped would prevent effective air attack, the Allied planes came down close to the level of the sea to use a newly developed skip-bombing technique. The Allied planes sank 7 transports and 4 destroyers; the other transport was sunk by American PT boats. The 4 destroyers that escaped to Rabaul were badly damaged. The Allies lost 2 bombers and 3 fighters, the Japanese some 25 planes. More than 3,000 Japanese troops were drowned; about an equal number were rescued by the surviving destroyers and by Japanese submarines. The Japanese ceased further efforts to send merchant-ship convoys to New Guinea; all subsequent supply and reinforcement were done by fast destroyer transport.

1943, June–December. Air Support to Land Operations. During this period, Kenney's Fifth Air Force elaborated a pattern of support operations which it continued to follow in general throughout the remainder of the war. *First,* fighter planes and light bombers gained air superiority over the region where the next operation was planned to take place by attacking airfields and by endeavoring always to force Japanese planes to fight at a disadvantage. Simultaneously, longer-range bombers neutralized more distant Japanese air bases, sometimes in co-ordination with land-based or carrier aircraft from the South or Central Pacific areas. *Next,* Allied fighters and light bombers isolated the area to be attacked, making it impossible for Japanese troop transports or warships to land reinforcements. *Finally,* as MacArthur's troops advanced on land, or prepared for an airborne or amphibious operation, air attacks against ground targets in the area were intensified, these attacks continuing throughout the land battle. *In airborne operations,* troop-carrier aircraft flew paratroops to the objective, then shuttled back and forth to airlift supplies and reinforcements to the airborne troops. Meanwhile, engineers with the ground troops were engaged in improving existing airfields, or building new ones if necessary, so that fighter planes could move in to give more effective local air support. These fields also became the advanced bases for supporting the initial long-range air reconnaissance and air strikes for the next advance, the same general cycle of operations being repeated.

The Solomons

1943, January–April. Attrition of Japanese Air Strength. While ground operations in the Solomons temporarily came to a virtual halt after the American conquest of Guadalcanal, air activity continued intensively. The series of naval air losses that had begun at Midway, combined with growing American Army and Navy air strength in the Pacific, put the Japanese at a serious disadvantage. This was further accentuated by damaging Allied air blows from Henderson Field, from New Guinea, and from carrier raids against the complex of air bases around Rabaul.

1943, April 7–12. Japanese Air Counteroffensive. In an endeavor to regain air superiority and the initiative in the Solomons-Bismarcks area, Admiral Yamamoto sent most of the depleted carrier air squadrons to Rabaul from the fleet at Truk to take part in a proposedly devastating aerial offensive against Allied bases in Papua and the Solomons. The attacks, however, inflicted relatively minor damage, while Japanese losses were heavy.

1943, April 18. End of Yamamoto. The Japanese naval commander in chief, visiting the area to inspect conditions personally, flew from Rabaul to Bougainville. Halsey, forewarned by the usual intercept of Japanese communications (the code had again been broken), sent 16 U.S. Army Air Force fighters from Henderson Field to meet him. The 2 bombers carrying the Japanese admiral and his staff were shot down in flames. The death of Yamamoto, Japan's foremost strategist, was tantamount to a major Japanese defeat. Yamamoto was replaced as Commander in Chief of the Combined Fleet by Admiral **Mineichi Koga.**

1943, May–December. Decline of the Japanese Naval Air Force. In a few months the carrier air groups which Yamamoto had sent to Rabaul were practically wiped out. Their replacements were not so well trained and, as pilot experience and ability declined, casualties mounted. Because of this vicious cycle, Japanese air losses became staggering. By the end of 1943,

Japan had lost nearly 3,000 planes and pilots in the Solomons air struggle alone.

The Central Pacific

1943, January–October. American Naval Build-up. Men, ships, and planes in amazing numbers began to assemble in Hawaii, the Fijis, and the New Hebrides as Nimitz prepared for his coming westward offensive across the wide Pacific. By October he had the Fifth Fleet (Vice Admiral **Raymond A. Spruance**), consisting of 7 battleships, 7 heavy and 3 light cruisers, 8 carriers, and 34 destroyers—the largest fleet yet to be put in action by the U.S. He had the Fifth Amphibious Force (Turner), carrying more than 100,000 troops, and the V Amphibious Corps, commanded by Major General **Holland M. ("Howling Mad") Smith,** U.S.M.C. In addition to naval air, Nimitz had the Seventh Army Air Force (Major General **Willis A. Hale**) operating from the Ellice Islands and (when its chore in the Solomons was completed; see p. 1161) the naval and Marine elements which had comprised Halsey's Third Fleet. Nimitz' initial target was the Gilbert Island group, whose seizure would provide advance air bases for the next step—capture of the Marshall Islands. In the Gilberts, Japanese defenses centered on Makin and Tarawa atolls—island clusters each ringed by a coral-reef barrier.

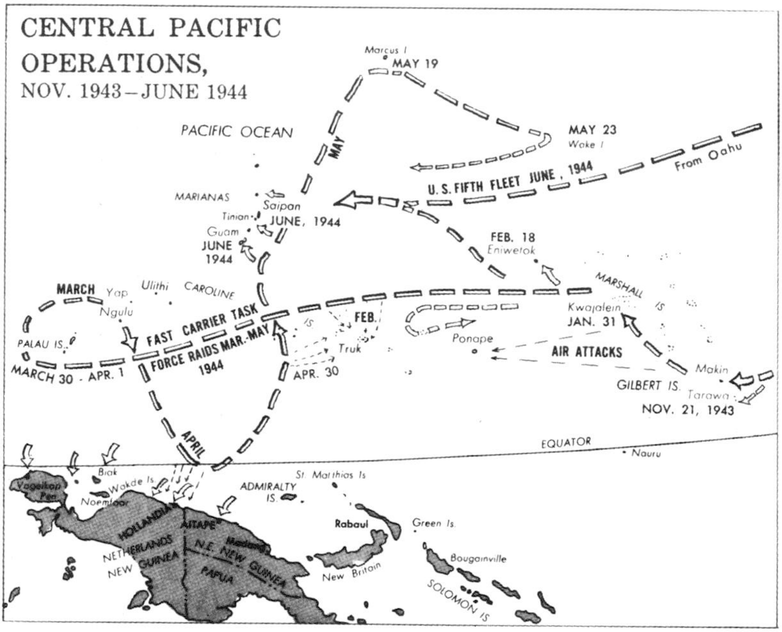

1943, November 13–20. Preassault Bombardment of the Gilberts. Tarawa and Makin were thoroughly strafed by Air Force bombers (November 13–17) and then subjected to heavy naval gunfire before the landing forces were committed.

1943, November 20–23. Makin. The 165th Infantry of the 27th Division, heavily reinforced, found little difficulty in crushing the island's 250 combat troops and several hundred workers, but the advance was too slow to suit General "Howling Mad" Smith. The delay necessitated subjecting the naval forces to counterattack by submarines rushed from Truk. The escort carrier *Liscome Bay* went down, with loss of 640 officers and men, though casualties suffered in the assault were but 66 killed and 152 wounded. Japanese casualties totaled some 500 killed; about 100 prisoners, nearly all of them Korean laborers, were taken.

1943, November 20–24. Tarawa. Betio Island, citadel of the atoll, in area only 300 acres, flat and sandy, had been honeycombed with underground shelters and some 400 concrete pillboxes, bunkers, and strong points. Defending artillery included

8-in. guns brought from Singapore. The island was ringed by a coral reef, its openings studded with submarine mines, and the beaches laced with barbed wire. Insufficient reconnaissance and faulty maps had not disclosed that the inner coral reef of Betio itself was too shallow for landing craft. Despite the heavy preliminary bombing and naval gunfire, 4,700 veteran combat troops under Rear Admiral **Keiji Shibasaki** emerged from underground shelters to man their defenses as the initial assault waves of the 2nd Marine Division approached. While some amphibious tractors reached the beach, most of the assault craft grounded on the inner reef and the assailants were forced to wade several hundreds of yards through crisscross fire, suffering shocking losses. Supporting naval fire ceased shortly after the initial wave hit the beach, lest it hit the Marines, who were thus left clinging to a few yards of terrain swept by artillery, machine-gun, and small-arms fire. Of 5,000 men put ashore by nightfall, some 1,500 were dead or wounded. That night tanks, guns, and ammunition got ashore. Next day the divisional reserve landed, losing 344 officers and men in the withering cross fire. Inch-by-inch frontal assaults—there could be no maneuver in that restricted area—supported now by air and by naval gunfire directed by observers ashore, gradually forced the defenders back to the eastern end of the island. Most of the surviving defenders lost their lives in a suicidal counterattack (night of November 22–23) and the last pocket of resistance was cleaned out next day. Approximately 100 prisoners, only 17 of them combat soldiers, were taken. The remainder of the Japanese garrison were dead. Marine losses were 985 killed and 2,193 wounded. During these operations, Admiral Koga held his crippled fleet at Truk (see p. 1161), fearing the U.S. carrier force, but his land-based planes from Kwajalein twice unsuccessfully attacked warships of the Amphibious Force on Thanksgiving night (November 25).

COMMENT. *Tarawa, in ratio between casualties and troops engaged, ranks among the costliest battles in American military history. Its lessons brought about many improvements in amphibious assault techniques, correcting the manifest mistakes committed there: insufficient reconnaissance and insufficient artillery and air preparation fire, particularly the lack of the high-angle plunging fire necessary to obliterate well-constructed fortifications. Strategically, this epic of Marine Corps gallantry put Nimitz in position to combine land-based air and sea power in assaulting the Marshalls and eliminating or neutralizing Japan's great naval base at Truk.*

The North Pacific Area, 1943

The year opened with Japanese occupation forces on the 2 fortified westernmost Aleutian Islands—Attu and Kiska—supported by land-based aviation from Paramushiro, off the southern tip of Kamchatka. U.S. efforts to dislodge the invaders stemmed from the naval and military base at Dutch Harbor on Umnak in the central Aleutians. Actually, operations in this fog-bound, stormy area had no effect on the war with Japan, other than irritating the U.S. But the North Pacific Theater was the scene of several sporadic clashes while the war was being decided in the momentous struggles of the Southwest and Central Pacific.

1943, March 26. Battle of the Komandorski Islands. Cruising in the mouth of the Bering Sea, Rear Admiral **Charles H. McMorris** with 2 elderly cruisers—1 light and 1 heavy—and 4 destroyers, met Japanese Vice Admiral Hosogaya's Northern Area Force of 2 heavy and 2 light cruisers and 4 destroyers, escorting reinforcements for Attu. In a long-range gun battle, U.S.S. *Salt Lake City* was crippled and the Japanese cruiser *Nachi* severely damaged. But as Hosogaya closed to smother the Americans, 3 of McMorris' destroyers charged in with a desperate torpedo attack. Hosogaya sheered away and then, fearing attack by American air from Dutch Harbor, turned and made for Paramushiro. (His timidity caused his relief from command.) Henceforth the Japanese relied upon submarines alone to resupply their Aleutian bases.

1943, May 11–29. Attu. Admiral Kinkaid's

amphibious task force under Rear Admiral **Francis W. Rockwell** put the U.S. 7th Infantry Division ashore in heavy fog. For 18 days the Americans battled the garrison out of the usual Japanese prairie-dog complex of bunkers and underground shelters. Only 29 of the 2,500-man garrison were captured; the rest died fighting or killed themselves. U.S. losses were 561 killed and 1,136 wounded of the 12,000 men engaged, a costly price for the taking of an island written off by the Japanese high command.

1943, August 15. Kiska. A Canadian-American amphibious landing on Kiska (August 15) found it deserted; its 4,500-man garrison had been skillfully evacuated (July 29) in fog and darkness.

THE WAR AGAINST JAPAN, 1944

Strategy and Policy. In the Pacific, as across the Atlantic, the Axis sun was beginning to set as 1944 opened. U.S. resources—in men and machines—were increasing in strength and infinite technological variety. Japan was beginning to feel the pinch of U.S. submarine operations against her merchant marine, but had no antidote. Nearly 300 of her merchantmen were sunk in 1943 for a total of more than 1,300,000 tons, some 700,000 tons more than Nippon's replacement capability during the same period. U.S. submarine activities would be stepped up in the coming year to drain Japanese tanker strength, still greater than American. But, unwilling to admit overextension, Japan was still a formidable enemy. Her forces continued to strike with much tactical skill and tremendous—though sometimes misdirected—energy on all fronts.

Land and Air Operations in Asia. Both sides girded for offensive moves. Japanese objectives were to conquer all southeast China, eradicating the galling probes of Chennault's Fourteenth Air Force, and to invade India from Burma. The Allied objective was to remove the threat to India by driving the invaders out of Burma and, by opening the land routes of supply to China, to keep that nation in the war. General Stilwell, whose differences with Chiang Kai-shek were rapidly increasing in bitterness, hoped to be able to maintain a successful defense in China while mounting a vigorous offensive in Burma in joint operation with British General Slim's Fourteenth Army.

Burma

Allied Situation and Plans. In October, 1943, the Southeast Asia Command, with Vice Admiral Lord **Louis Mountbatten** as Supreme Allied Commander, became operational, its headquarters at New Delhi (later Kandy, in Ceylon). Mountbatten assumed responsibility for all Allied operations in Burma. General Stilwell was appointed as deputy to Mountbatten, but since he still retained his other duties, spent little time at Kandy. All Allied ground forces operating against Burma from India were grouped under General Slim, including Stilwell's Northern Combat Area Command (2 Chinese divisions), actively engaged in combat in the Hukawng Valley of northern Burma. (Thus Stilwell, who was over Slim as deputy SACSEA, was under him as CG of NCAC, and at the same time was in a purely American chain of command as CG of the China-Burma-India Theater, and also was Chief of Staff to Chiang in the China Theater.)

Mountbatten and Slim felt that British forces in India would not be ready for a major invasion of Burma until the dry season of 1944–1945. They agreed, however, to assist Stilwell's NCAC by minor activities along the entire India-Burma border, as well as by 2 limited thrusts into Burma itself; one of these to be in Arakan, the other an augmented Chindit long-range-penetration effort in north-central Burma under General Wingate. (This raid had been specifically approved by Churchill and the CCS at Quebec.) Stilwell, with 3 (to be increased to 5) Chinese divisions, plus a small American combat unit, hoped to take the major north Burma city of Myitkyina, with its airfields, before the beginning of the 1944 monsoon.

Japanese Situation and Plans. The Japanese also had reorganized their forces in Burma. The new commander of the Burma Area Army was Lieutenant General **Shozo Kawabe,** who was under the over-all command of Field Marshal **Count Terauchi,** with headquarters in Saigon, responsible for military operations in the entire Southern Resources Area. Kawabe had 6 divisions, 2 in southwest Burma, under his direct supervision; the other 4, to the north, were under Lieutenant General **Renya Mutaguchi**'s Fifteenth Army.

Kawabe had directed Mutaguchi to prepare for an offensive across the mountains into eastern India with 3 of his divisions, which, with attached units, totaled nearly 100,000 veteran combat troops. The objective was twofold: first, to seize the Imphal-Kohima plain of Manipur, the logical assembly area and base for any Allied invasion of central Burma from India; second, to cut the railroad line into Assam, which passed through Manipur, and which carried almost all of the supplies ferried to China over the Hump, as well as the supplies for Stilwell's NCAC divisions in north Burma.

THE SECOND ARAKAN CAMPAIGN

1943, December–1944, January. Allied Advance into Arakan. Three divisions of the British XV Corps, advancing toward Akyab, were soon halted by the Japanese 55th Division, which had fortified a mountain spur extending westward to the sea near Maungdaw, blocking the only possible overland route to Akyab. For nearly 2 months the British vainly hammered at this defensive position. Kawabe sent the 54th Division into Arakan as reinforcement.

1944, February 4–12. Japanese Counterattack. Using the same tactics which had defeated the British in the same area a year earlier, the Japanese 55th Division counterattacked, while elements of the 54th circled through the jungles to the east, crossing the mountains behind the British flank and cutting the lines of communication of both British front-line divisions, isolating them from each other and from many of their smaller formations. General Slim, refusing to permit any withdrawal, rushed reinforcements and initiated an emergency air supply to the beleaguered units.

1944, February 13–25. British Counterattack. The Japanese encircling forces now found themselves encircled by determined British and Indian units. The 2 front-line British divisions re-established contact (February 24) and increased pressure on the trapped Japanese, most of whom were wiped out.

1944, March–April. Cracking the Maungdaw Position. In extremely bitter fighting, the British XV Corps fought its way gradually through the Maungdaw position. Having broken through, the corps was about to continue its advance on Akyab, when it was forced to halt and to send reinforcements to the Imphal front (see p. 1169).

1944, May–December. Monsoon Stalemate. No further activities of importance took place on this front until late in the year at the beginning of the 1944–1945 dry season (see p. 1184).

NORTH BURMA

Hukawng Valley Operations, January–April

1944, January–February. Stalemate in the Hukawng Valley. Effective resistance by the Japanese 18th Division, commanded by Major General **Shinichi Tanaka,** brought the advances of the Chinese 38th and 22nd divisions to a virtual standstill. Stilwell's return (late February) brought some increased Chinese activity and a renewal of the advance against determined resistance. At this time there appeared a new American provisional infantry regiment, known to history as "Merrill's Marauders," from the name of its commander, Brigadier General **Frank D. Merrill.**

1944, March 3–7. Battle of Maingkwan-Walawbum. A Chinese frontal attack, combined with an envelopment by Merrill's Marauders, smashed the center of the Japanese 18th Division. Despite heavy losses, Tanaka skillfully extricated his division from near encirclement. The Allies, pressing close behind, were stopped at a new Japanese defensive position established along a jungle ridge separating the Hukawng and Mogaung valleys.

1944, March 28–April 1. Battle of Shaduzup. One battalion of Merrill's regiment and a Chinese regimental task force circled deep behind the Japanese lines to take up a blocking position behind the 18th Division at Shaduzup. Two of Tanaka's regiments were trapped, but fought their way out through obscure jungle trails after suffering severe losses and abandoning much equipment and ammunition. Tanaka, nevertheless, counterattacked and briefly isolated another of Merrill's battalions in the mountains southwest of Shaduzup (March 29–April 8).

The Second Chindit Expedition

1944, January–March. Preparations. For his renewed long-range penetration effort, Wingate was given 6 infantry brigades (only 5 actually participated) organized as the 3rd Indian Division, but more commonly called "Special Forces," or "Chindits" (see p. 1155). Five of these brigades, each divided into two "columns," were to be flown deep into north-central Burma, while the sixth was to march across the mountains, past Stilwell's left flank. Operating separately, but in accordance with a co-ordinated plan, the columns and brigades were to cut the Mandalay-Myitkyina railroad, and generally to disrupt the rear areas of Japanese forces facing Stilwell's NCAC and Slim's Fourteenth Army. The Chindits were to receive combat air support and air logistical support from an American air group commanded by Colonel **Philip C. Cochrane.**

1944, March 5–11. The Chindits Return to Burma. Transported initially in gliders, then in transport planes as a jungle air strip was hastily constructed, 3 brigades of Chindits were flown to preselected, isolated jungle spots dubbed "Broadway" and "Chowringhee." While a few columns spread out over Japanese rear areas to create confusion and to destroy supplies, the main body moved to Mawlu, where a strong defensive position was established, blocking the railroad line (March 16).

1944, March 17–May 6. White City. The blocking position at Mawlu was named "White City" (after a London amusement park) because it was soon strewn with supply parachutes dropped from Cochrane's supporting transport planes. The Japanese did not interrupt their major offensive into India because of this threat to their rear, but a number of determined local attacks were made; all were repulsed. Meanwhile other Chindit columns continued to harass Japanese rear areas.

1944, March 25. Death of Wingate. The Chindit commander was killed in an airplane crash against a jungle mountain. He was replaced by Major General **W. D. A. Lentaigne.**

1944, May 6–25. Blackpool. As newly arrived Japanese reinforcements began to concentrate against White City, Lentaigne decided to abandon the base. Since he had been instructed to join Stilwell's command, a new base, "Blackpool," was established near Hopin, about midway on the rail line between Mawlu and Mogaung. Blackpool was soon attacked by strong Japanese forces, and a violent battle raged. The hard-pressed Chindits, close to exhaustion and having suffered heavy casualties, withdrew again, this time to the relative safety of the mountains farther west.

1944, June–July. Operations with NCAC. The exhausted and battered Chindits gathered in the vicinity of Indawgyi Lake, where British flying boats landed and began to ferry sick and wounded back to India. Meanwhile, the 2 brigades that were least hard hit continued to operate with Stilwell's forces. One of these helped capture Mogaung (see p. 1167), and the other for a while protected the NCAC flank (see p. 1167). Relations between Lentaigne and Stilwell were not good; Stilwell thought the Chindits could have fought more vigorously; Lentaigne felt Stilwell was asking too much in the light of the ordeals they had suffered; both were probably right.

COMMENT. *This was a gallant but largely wasted effort. Although it had somewhat more success than Wingate's first expedition, the same results could have been obtained by smaller commando or guerrilla forces, assisted by air bombardment, without ruining the fighting effectiveness of 5 fine British brigades.*

Myitkyina-Mogaung Operations, April–August

1944, April 28–May 17. Advance on Myitkyina. After a brief pause because of the Japanese threat to his lines of communications through Assam (see p. 1168), Stilwell decided that the British would repulse the Japanese offensive, and continued his efforts to reach Myitkyina before the beginning of the monsoon rains. Merrill's Marauders (now commanded by Colonel **C. N. Hunter,** due to Merrill's protracted illness), reduced by casualties and disease to 1,400 men, were sent with two Chinese regiments in a secret march over the high, extremely rugged ridge between the upper Mogaung and Irrawaddy valleys to take Myitkyina.

1944, May 17–18. Assault on Myitkyina. The American-Chinese attack quickly gained control of Myitkyina's 1 operational airfield, and supplies and reinforcements were rushed there by air while it was still under direct Japanese small-arms fire. Efforts of the exhausted and disease-ridden troops to seize the city were repulsed, however, and the Japanese, with reinforcements arriving from the east bank of the Irrawaddy, also repulsed the fresh air-transported Chinese reinforcements.

1944, May–June. Advance down the Mogaung Valley. Meanwhile Stilwell's veteran Chinese 22nd and 38th Divisions resumed a slow advance down the Mogaung Valley against Tanaka's continued skillful resistance. The 22nd Division (with reinforcements from China) captured **Kamaing** in an old-fashioned bayonet assault (June 16); the 38th, with assistance from a Chindit column (see p. 1166), soon afterward seized **Mogaung** (June 26). Both divisions, which (thanks to Stilwell's inspiration) had fought well and vigorously despite heavy casualties, were now given a rest as monsoon rains made further operations difficult.

1944, May 18–August 3. Siege of Myitkyina. Despite the monsoon, the Allies continued to press against the city, which was never completely invested, the Japanese retaining a line of communications across the Irrawaddy. Co-ordination between Chinese and Americans was poor; the efforts of commanders, staffs, and troops were frequently inept. The Japanese, forced to yield ground inch by inch, exacted a heavy price in Allied casualties. Finally, satisfied that they had imposed sufficient delay on the frustrated Allies, 700 semistarving Japanese survivors crossed the river and made their way south through the jungles to rejoin their main force, just as a final Allied assault, without opposition, swept over the city. Japanese losses were nearly 3,000 dead; the Allies had more than 5,000 casualties.

COMMENT. *The military performance of the Japanese, facing great odds, under constant air and artillery bombardment, was magnificent. But, despite relatively poor performance by his subordinates and troops, Stilwell had successfully completed a campaign which the British, and many Americans, had deemed impossible.*

1944, July–August. The "Railroad Corridor" Campaign. The 3rd West African Brigade of Chindits, now under Stilwell's command to protect his right flank against possible counterattack up the Mandalay-Mogaung railway line, was ordered to advance down the railroad from Mogaung to seize Pinbaw. The Africans were immediately stopped by Japanese defensive positions on the railroad south of Mogaung. The British 36th Division, under Major General **Francis W. Festing,** was transferred (July 7) to Stilwell's command to replace the now exhausted Chindits. Airlifted to Myitkyina, thence by foot to Mogaung, Festing's troops fought down the long, sheltered corridor against determined Japanese resistance, during the height of the monsoon season, to take **Pinbaw,** their objective (August 28). Aggressive Festing, obtaining Stilwell's permission to patrol southward, then struck 50 miles farther down the corridor, driving the Japanese out of a series of hastily prepared delaying positions.

COMMENT. *This 100-mile-long cam-*

paign was the first instance in modern military history of a large-scale offensive in Southeast Asia during the rain and mud of the monsoon season.

Stilwell's Final Offensive, September–December

1944, September–October. Pause and Preparation. Stilwell now had 5 Chinese divisions (3 good, 2 mediocre), the excellent British 36th Division, and the newly organized U.S. "Mars" Brigade (2 U.S. and 1 Chinese regiment and 2 light artillery battalions). He was opposed by the Japanese Thirty-third Army (Lieutenant General **Masaki Honda**) of 3 depleted divisions. As soon as the rains let up, and before the ground had time to fully dry, Stilwell planned a surprise offensive, featured by a sweeping envelopment in which 3 of his Chinese divisions and the American brigade would encircle the entire Japanese Thirty-third Army, which would then be trapped between his army in Burma and the Y-Force in Yunnan (see p. 1172).

1944, October 15. The Offensive Begins. With the 38th and the 30th divisions advancing from Myitkyina toward Bhamo against the main elements of the Thirty-third Army, and the 36th Division continuing down the Railroad Corridor to protect the NCAC right flank and rear, Stilwell's mass advanced southward from the Mogaung area to cross the Irrawaddy River near Shwegu, thence southeastward through the jungle with the objective of reaching the Burma Road near Lashio.

1944, October 15–December 31. Railroad Corridor (Continued). The British 36th Division continued its advance, moving slowly but steadily down the railroad, despite intensifying Japanese resistance. By the end of the year, the division had seized the towns of Indaw and Katha, and halted temporarily because of developments farther east.

1944, October 18. Relief of General Stilwell. (See p. 1172.) The commander of the newly established India-Burma Theater was Lieutenant General **Dan I. Sultan.**

1944, November 6. Crossing the Irrawaddy. The Chinese 22nd Division began the crossing of the Irrawaddy as spearhead of the enveloping hammer blow.

1944, November 14–December 15. Siege of Bhamo. The Chinese 38th Division was held up for a month by the stubborn and determined defense of Bhamo. When further resistance was impossible, 800 surviving Japanese fought their way out at night to rejoin the 56th Division in the mountains between Bhamo and Namkham. The 30th and 38th Divisions pushed slowly after them.

1944, November 30–December 31. Change of Plans in North Burma. Due to disasters caused by a Japanese offensive in China (see p. 1172), Chiang Kai-shek decided to withdraw 2 divisions from Burma to help stop the dangerous Japanese drives in south China. The 22nd and 14th Divisions were flown out of Burma to Kunming in American planes from hastily constructed front-line airfields in the jungle region southeast of the Irrawaddy bend (December 5–10). Sultan was thereupon forced to modify Stilwell's plan of encircling the Japanese Thirty-third Army. The reduced mission was simply to open and secure the road that stretched east from Bhamo through Namkham toward the Burma Road.

CENTRAL BURMA

The Japanese Invasion of India, March–July

1944, March 6. Crossing the Chindwin. Mutaguchi's Fifteenth Army began its projected offensive toward India by crossing the Chindwin River on a broad front. One division headed for Kohima, 2 for Imphal.

1944, March 7–April 5. The Advance to Imphal and Kohima. Although the British had been expecting the offensive, they had underestimated the size of the Fifteenth Army; they were amazed by the speed and power of its advance. British outposts holding the Chin Hills around Tiddim and Fort White were cut off by the Japanese 33d Division, but succeeded in breaking their way through Japanese road blocks to reach Imphal, just before the arrival outside that city of the Japanese 15th Division, which unexpectedly was approaching over rugged mountain trails from the east (April 5). The Japanese 31st Division had begun to invest Kohima the previous day. The British IV

Corps, of 3 divisions, was now almost completely isolated, the bulk of the corps in and around Imphal, with a small garrison holding Kohima.

1944, April 5–20. The Sieges of Imphal and Kohima. While hastily assembled transport planes began an airlift to maintain some 50,000 men in the IV Corps and the 40,000 civilian inhabitants of Imphal and Kohima, General Slim assembled his XXXIII Corps on the railroad at Dimapur. Pushing back Japanese patrols, this corps began a drive to relieve the dangerously pressed garrison of Kohima. At the same time, Slim also began to fly in reinforcements to the IV Corps at Imphal. Bitter fighting flared continuously around both perimeters, and several times Kohima was close to collapse, the margin being air support from American and British fighter planes and medium bombers, which harassed the Japanese mercilessly. The situation became less precarious, however, when the XXXIII Corps broke through to relieve Kohima (April 20).

1944, April 20–June 22. The Siege of Imphal (Continued). Further progress by the XXXIII Corps toward Imphal was painfully slow as the Japanese dug in and held with typical tenacity. Slim flew additional units in to Imphal from Arakan until the IV Corps strength rose to more than 100,000 men. Amazingly, the Japanese held back violent assaults against their lines by both British corps. They had failed, however, to capture the supplies on which they had been counting. The beginning of the monsoon, too, made their situation still more difficult. Because of hunger and disease, their fighting strength finally began to crumble, and the IV and XXXIII Corps were able to hack their way through the last remaining roadblocks (June 22) after a siege of 88 days.

1944, July–September. Collapse of the Fifteenth Army. The Japanese had not foreseen the possibility that the British would refuse to retreat and abandon their supplies. Now that their logistical shoestring was broken, and with the monsoons making large-scale supply operations impossible in the mountain jungles, they had no choice but to retreat. Slowly and stubbornly, they fell back to the Chindwin Valley, harassed from the air and by pursuing British troops; amazingly, they never lost cohesion or combat effectiveness. The army had been virtually ruined, however, by a combination of battle casualties, malaria, and starvation. They lost 65,000 dead, less than half of whom were actual battle casualties.

British Advance into Central Burma, September–December

Allied Plans and Preparations. Pursuit of the Japanese Fifteenth Army had brought Slim's Fourteenth Army again to the edge of the Chindwin Valley. He now prepared for a broad-front crossing of the Chindwin, to take place in November. Over Slim was Lieutenant General Sir Oliver Leese, commanding the newly established headquarters of Allied Land Forces, Southeast Asia (ALFSEA). Under Leese, in addition to Slim, were Stilwell (later Sultan) and his NCAC, and the British XV Corps in Arakan.

Japanese Plans and Preparations. Because of the disaster to the Fifteenth Army, General **Hoyotaro Kimura** had replaced Kawabe in command of the Burma Area Army. He received reinforcements and he devoted the summer to reorganization, and in particular to the rehabilitation of the Fifteenth Army (now under Lieutenant General **Shihachi Katamura**) and the battered 18th Division. By fall his forces of 250,000 men were reorganized into 3 armies: the Thirty-third (3 divisions), holding northeastern Burma; the Twenty-eighth (3 divisions, under Lieutenant General **Seizo Sakurai**), responsible for the coast and Arakan; the Fifteenth (4 divisions), holding the west along the Chindwin. Kimura's strategy was to permit the Allies to reach central Burma, where their logistical difficulties would become increasingly acute, while those of the Japanese would be simplified in the proximity of their bases. Kimura was confident that his 10 divisions could smash the Allies in such circumstances. Accordingly, his orders were to harass and delay the Allied advance, but to avoid a finish fight until the British had been lured across the Irrawaddy near Mandalay.

1944, November 19–December 3. The British Cross the Chindwin. The IV Corps began the crossing at Sittaung; the XXXIII Corps followed soon afterward at Kalewa and Mawlaik. The Japanese fought delaying actions, but in accordance with plan did not attempt a firm defense.

1944, December 14. Linking of NCAC and Fourteenth Army. Patrols of the 19th Indian Division met those of Festing's 36th Division near Indaw. By the end of the year, the Fourteenth Army was approaching the Irrawaddy on a broad front; the stage was set for a climactic struggle long foreseen by both Slim and Kimura.

AIR OPERATIONS OVER BURMA, 1943–1944

Air Combat

1943, January–March. Japanese Raids into India. With unchallenged air superiority over Burma, the Japanese were able to continue long-range bombardment attacks against Calcutta and to undertake a number of raids against the Hump air bases in Assam, in northeastern India. These raids were not very effective and did not do much damage, but they harassed the Allies considerably.

1943, March–June. Arrival of Allied Air Reinforcements. As British and American combat air strength built up in India, the Japanese were forced to abandon their raids across the mountains. The Allies then began to carry the war into Burma, and soon gained air superiority over much of the country.

1943, June–October. Monsoon Lull. Air operations were greatly curtailed by the rainy weather. The Japanese took advantage of the lull to repair damage caused by the Allied raids, to improve their antiaircraft defenses, and to build up their over-all air strength in Burma.

1943, November–1944, May. Struggle for Air Superiority. With the advent of good weather, the Japanese were prepared to challenge Allied air superiority. They began both night and day raids against Calcutta and against the Hump air bases, while their fighters vigorously struck back against Allied air intrusions into Burma. Severe losses were suffered on the ground and in the air by both sides. Slowly, however, the greater numbers and greater skill of the Allied air forces began to assert themselves. By mid-1944, General **George E. Stratemeyer**'s Eastern Air Command completely dominated the skies over Burma; this superiority was never to be relinquished.

Logistical Air Support

General Kimura's strategy for defending Burma in 1944 failed to appreciate Allied air capabilities. The Japanese invasion of India had failed largely because they could not keep up long supply lines through the jungle under the pressure of constant air attack. But the Allies did not depend upon such supply lines to support their troops, or to keep up the advance in the jungle.

Hundreds of Allied transport planes brought food, ammunition, and all manner of supplies directly to the front-line troops. If there were no nearby airfields where they could land, the airmen dropped these supplies into rice-paddy fields or jungle clearings. Anything that might break was dropped by parachute; everything else was free-dropped.

Thus the Allies' only supply line came through the air, which they controlled completely. And, having driven Japanese combat planes from the skies, the Allies had no worries about air strikes against their bases in India.

Combat Air Support

The difficulties of surface transportation in jungle areas meant that ground troops had less artillery support than normal, while the potentialities for defense in the jungle increased their need for it. The Chindits, in particular, needed such support, for they had no artillery. This deficiency was made up, at least in part, by the extensive direct support which British and American fighter-bombers were able to provide, since they had no need to engage the nonexistent Japanese air force.

Most of the supporting missions were flown by fighter-bombers that dive-bombed strong Japanese positions, then strafed them just before ground attacks. In some instances, where Japanese defenses were particularly strong, light and medium bombers were used to support ground attacks.

China

1944–1945. Japanese-Chinese Communist De Facto Truce. The Japanese ended their punitive raids against the Communists. For the last 2 years of the war there was practically no activity on Chinese Communist fronts. Whether this truce was tacit or negotiated is not known. Both sides benefited: The Communists consolidated their control of Northwest China. The Japanese diverted large forces for operations in the south.

1944, January–May. Japanese Plans and Preparations. The punishment they were receiving from Chennault's Fourteenth Air Force led the Japanese to decide to make an all-out effort to capture the American airfields by ground offensives. During the early months of the year, General **Yasuji Okamura**'s China Expeditionary Army, 820,000 strong, undertook preliminary operations to improve its railroad supply lines from northeast China.

1944, January–May. Allied Plans and Preparations. Chiang Kai-shek reconsidered his earlier veto on an advance against northeast Burma from Yunnan in the light of the successes being gained in northwest Burma by Stilwell's Chinese-American forces. He approved an offensive down the Burma Road by a small army group of 2

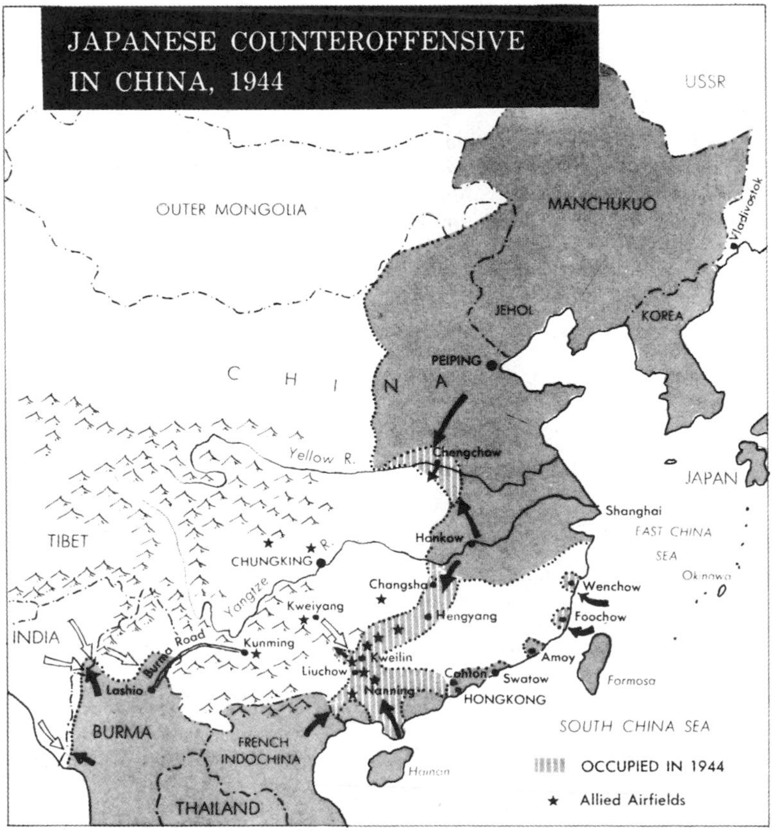

armies (called the "Y-Force"), consisting of 72,000 men commanded by Marshal **Wei Li-huang.** Because of shortages of equipment and weapons, this force was probably not much more powerful than the Japanese 56th Division, about 15,000 men, which held the portion of Yunnan west of the Salween River, its major elements holding the walled cities of Tenchung and Lun-ling (the latter on the Burma Road itself).

1944, May 7–November 30. Japanese East China Offensive. Under Okamura's direct supervision, the Japanese Eleventh Army, 250,000 strong, initiated a southwestward drive from Hankow on Changsha. The Japanese Twenty-third Army, 50,000 strong, that same day thrust west from the Canton area. Chinese resistance was spotty. Ch'ang-sha, abandoned, was occupied (June 19). First stiff Chinese opposition was at **Hengyang,** which fell only after an 11-day siege (July 28–August 9). Chinese resistance began to collapse. Methodically, despite the fierce aerial opposition of Chennault's flyers, 7 of the U.S. Fourteenth Air Force's 12 airfields were captured, and the Japanese movement then turned westward (November 15) to threaten Kunming and Chungking.

1944, May 11–September 30. Operations in Yunnan. The Chinese Y-Force advanced across the Salween in 2 major columns, driving back Japanese outposts. The southern column surrounded **Lun-ling** less than a month after crossing the Salween. A Japanese counterattack drove this column back (June 16). Rallying, the Chinese finally halted the smaller pursuing force and slowly re-established a partial blockade of the city. The northern column was more aggressive. Closely investing **Tenchung** (early July), it penetrated the city walls through a breach made by supporting fighter-bombers of the American Fourteenth Air Force. After a bitter house-to-house battle, the Chinese annihilated the defenders of Ten-chung (September 15). The Japanese thereupon mounted another counterattack at Lun-ling, driving the Y-Force's southern column almost back to the Salween before events in Burma forced them to abandon their pursuit.

1944, October 18. Relief of Stilwell. As Chinese resistance crumbled in the face of the Japanese East China drives, Stilwell vainly recommended to Chiang Kai-shek various measures to reconstitute an effective defense. The American government became alarmed lest China collapse entirely, and President Roosevelt suggested that Chiang grant full command authority over all Chinese forces to Stilwell (October 17). Chiang flatly refused, and in turn demanded the recall of Stilwell. Reluctantly, Roosevelt ordered Stilwell back to the U.S. The China-Burma-India Theater was dissolved. Major General **Albert C. Wedemeyer** replaced Stilwell as commander of a new China Theater and as chief of staff to Chiang.

1944, December. Halting the Japanese Drives. Wedemeyer's tact succeeded where Stilwell's bluntness had failed; he persuaded Chiang to acquiesce in the transfer of only 2 veteran Chinese divisions from the Burma front (see p. 1168); Chiang had demanded the return of all 5. Airlifted, these 2 divisions became the backbone of a revitalized defense. The Japanese advance was blunted by Wedemeyer's reorganized and reinforced Chinese troops, supported by Chennault's air force. Their counterattack east of Kweiyang (December 10) stabilized the situation.

COMMENT. *The Japanese ground offensive disproved the fallacy—vainly disputed by Stilwell when Chennault obtained approval for a Hump-supported air build-up at the cost of Chinese ground troops (see p. 1156)—that air power, unsupported by ground power, could stop Japan in China. The error was costly, since to correct it necessitated abandonment of a full-scale offensive in Burma (see p. 1168) and—by elimination of Chennault's bases—for a time deprived both Nimitz and MacArthur of expected assistance in their respective offensives in the Pacific.*

Land, Naval, and Air Operations in the South and Southwest Pacific Areas, January–August

At the outset of the year, the objective of the combined forces of MacArthur's Southwest Pacific Area and Halsey's Third Fleet was still to isolate, and eventually to assault, Rabaul.

SOUTH PACIFIC AREA, JANUARY–JUNE

1944, January–May. Consolidation in the Solomons. Halsey, still under MacArthur's operational command, was still under Nimitz administratively. In addition to isolating and neutralizing enemy bases in the over-all campaign against Rabaul (see below), Halsey's forces were engaged in hard fighting to contain the Japanese Seventeenth Army in the Solomons, and particularly on Bougainville, where the bulk of that army attempted repeated, uncoordinated assaults against the small Allied perimeter at Empress Augusta Bay. By May, however, when starvation and despair had worked sufficiently on the isolated Japanese forces, the threat declined.

1944, February 15. Green Island. New Zealand troops seized Green Island as a site for an air base to intensify the pounding of Rabaul.

1944, March 20. Emirau. The seizure of this island in the St. Mathias group completed the isolation of Rabaul.

1944, June. Return of the Third Fleet to Nimitz' Command. The isolation of Rabaul and the consolidation of the Solomons virtually ended further combat missions for the South Pacific Area. Halsey reverted to Nimitz' command.

SOUTHWEST PACIFIC AREA

1944, January 2. Saidor. A regimental combat team of the U.S. 32nd Division landed north of Saidor, enveloping the Japanese garrison. The Australians, moving up from Finschhafen, made contact (March 23); the garrison evaporated into the interior. This provided Kenney's Fifth Air Force with a base to support operations on Cape Gloucester.

1944, February 29. The Admiralties. A reconnaissance in force by the U.S. 1st Cavalry Division, accompanied by MacArthur in person, speedily turned into a division-strength invasion of Los Negros Island (cleared March 23) and establishment of advance air bases. In this fighting U.S. casualties were 290 killed and 1,976 wounded. Some 3,000 Japanese were dead, 89 made prisoner.

1944, January–March. New Britain. Across Vitiaz Straits the beachheads of Cape Gloucester and Arawe expanded by mid-March as the 1st Marine and 40th Army divisions moved east along the coasts of the banana-shaped island. U.S. losses were 493 killed, 1,402 wounded; the Japanese left 4,600 dead and 329 prisoners. Later, Blamey's Australians would take over the containment of Rabaul on the land side.

The Hollandia Campaign

The Japanese high command decided to make an all-out effort to hold western New Guinea. The Second Area Army (Lieutenant General **Jo Imura**) had established a major supply and maintenance base at Hollandia, 500 miles west of Saidor and beyond reach of Kenney's fighter aircraft, whose range was about 350 miles. They began to construct airfields for future defensive and offensive air operations. By April, 3 of these were ready, located several miles inland, behind coastal mountains. Knowing that MacArthur had never made an attack beyond the range of fighter aircraft, they had few security troops at Hollandia. Most of Adachi's Eighteenth Army—65,000 strong—was concentrated between Madang and Wewak.

MacArthur, however, had decided to by-pass the Eighteenth Army and to strike at Hollandia itself. With the approval of the JCS, Nimitz agreed to send Admiral **Marc Mitscher**'s Fast Carrier Task Force to provide air support and air cover until land-based air could take over. Because of the danger of operating so near to Japanese air bases in New Guinea and the Carolines, however, Nimitz insisted that the carriers could stay in the coastal waters of New Guinea for only 4 days. Thus it was essential that MacArthur obtain a secure base for land-based fighters, in range of Hollandia, before the carriers withdrew. Yet any earlier attempt to seize such a base would alert the Japanese to the danger to their key base. Accordingly, MacArthur decided to seize Aitape—125 miles east of Hollandia—by amphibious assault at the same time that the main 2-division landing was made at

Hollandia. Aitape was west of the main concentration of the Eighteenth Army, yet it was within extreme range of American airfields at Saidor and thus could be covered by land-based aircraft while the carriers were assisting the main landings. Then, before the carriers withdrew, he planned to shift land-based air units to Aitape to keep adequate air support at Hollandia.

1944, March 30–April 19. Preliminary Air Bombardment. Kenney's long-range bombers struck the Hollandia fields repeatedly as part of an intensified air effort against Japanese coastal installations. Some 120 Japanese planes were shot down and 400 destroyed on the ground; Allied losses were insignificant.

1944, April 1–20. Australian Ground Pressure against Madang. Intensified ground activity against the Eighteenth Army was so successful that reinforcements were drawn from Hollandia, still further weakening the garrison of the air and naval base region.

1944, April 22. Landings at Hollandia and Aitape. The American 24th and 41st divisions landed on beaches 25 miles apart, east and west of Hollandia. At the same time, 2 reinforced American regiments were placed ashore at Aitape, under long-range land-based air support. The Seventh Fleet and Seventh Amphibious Force were responsible for both operations.

1944, April 22–24. Battle for Aitape. A bitter 2-day struggle took place at Aitape, while American engineers hastily prepared an airfield for operational use. American losses were 450 killed and 2,500 wounded; the Japanese lost about 9,000 dead. The area was secure and the air base operational within 2 days (April 24).

1944, April 22–27. Battle for Hollandia. With excellent carrier support, the American divisions converged inland against the Japanese airfields. Japanese resistance was light, due to the complete surprise achieved. When the carriers withdrew (April 26), land-based fighters from Aitape were available to provide support and cover. American losses were about 100 dead and 1,000 wounded; the Japanese lost more than 5,000 dead; about an equivalent number of survivors fled to the jungle.

COMMENT. *The Hollandia operation was one of the most brilliant of World War II. An entire Japanese army was encircled and its effectiveness completely destroyed. Yet because of excellent planning and skillful co-ordination of land, sea, and air forces, the actual combat actions were relatively small, and only insignificant Japanese forces were engaged and defeated.*

1944, May 17. Wakde. An amphibious assault quickly secured this island and its airfields. As at Hollandia, however, the soil proved to be unsuitable to support extensive operations by Kenney's long-range heavy bombers.

1944, May 27–June 29. Biak. This coral and limestone island, already used by the Japanese for an airfield, seemed the most likely spot for a heavy-bomber base in the northern New Guinea area. The amphibious landing of the 41st Division encountered unexpectedly determined resistance. In one of the most bitterly contested battles of the Pacific war, the Americans suffered more than 2,700 casualties, the Japanese nearly 10,000.

1944, June 28–August 5. Operations around Wewak and Aitape. In a series of hard-fought actions, General Blamey's Australians repulsed a Japanese Eighteenth Army offensive against Allied coastal bases of north-central New Guinea. The Japanese army, cut off from supply by land or sea, disintegrated into the jungles of the interior, where its disorganized elements rotted for the remainder of the war.

1944, July 2–7. Noemfoor. Capture of this island, west of Biak, provided additional Allied air strips.

1944, July 30. Sansapor. The unopposed occupation of this cape, on the northwestern tip of New Guinea's Vogelkop Peninsula, brought the campaign to a close. Japan's power in New Guinea had been completely destroyed.

The Central Pacific, January–August

1944, January 29–February 7. Kwajalein. While MacArthur was starting his New Guinea drive, the next target of Nimitz' trans-Pacific offensive was the Marshall group, with Kwajalein atoll its citadel. Admiral Spruance's Fifth Fleet had operational responsibility. As preliminary, Mitscher's Fast Carrier Task Force (Task Force 58: 6 heavy and 6 light carriers, escorted by fast battleships, cruisers, and destroyers) swept ahead in 4 groups to neutralize Japanese air in the Marshalls. Turner's Fifth Amphibious Force, carrying General H. M. Smith's V Amphibious Corps of 1 Army and 2 Marine divisions, carried out the operation. A 3-day preliminary naval and aerial bombardment saturated the atoll. Then (February 1) the 7th Infantry Division was landed on Kwajalein Island, southeastern flank of the lagoon, and the 4th Marine Division was put ashore on Roi and Namur islands, some 50 miles away on the northern rim. As usual, the Japanese garrisons (commanded by Rear Admiral **M. Akiyama**) put up a savage fight, but, thanks to the lessons learned at Tarawa, the defenders were overrun with relatively light losses (February 7). Of 41,000 U.S. troops put ashore, casualties were 372 dead and some 1,000 wounded. Both Japanese garrisons fought to the death, 7,870 of them being killed out of 8,000. Admiral Koga, down at Truk, with no carriers available, dared not risk his Combined Fleet to oppose the assault, but sent up some submarines, which were driven off with loss of 4 of their number. However, a surprise Japanese bomber raid from Saipan later strafed the Roi-Namur complex (February 12), inflicting some damage.

1944, February 17–18. Bombing of Truk. Mitscher's carrier force hit the Japanese naval base. Koga managed to save most of the Combined Fleet by a hurried dispersal, but the attack found 50 merchantmen in harbor and 365 aircraft huddled on airstrips. One Japanese hit was scored on U.S. carrier *Intrepid.* By noon, Mitscher's planes had sunk 200,000 tons of shipping and destroyed 275 Japanese planes. Spruance, combing the vicinity with a battleship, 4 heavy cruisers, and 4 destroyers, sank 1 light cruiser and a destroyer. While the damage to Japanese naval strength was not fatal, the attack proved the vulnerability of Truk. Its usefulness ended, no further attempt was made to occupy the once-formidable naval base, and it was left to wither on the vine. Koga's fleet withdrew to the Philippine Sea behind the Caroline-Marianas islands screen.

1944, February 17. Eniwetok. Turner's amphibious force put the 22nd Marines and army troops ashore on Engebi Island on the northern rim of this atoll without interference by Japanese planes. But Eniwetok Island itself, and Parry Island on the southern rim, were sturdily defended by Major General **Nishida**'s 1st Amphibious Brigade, a veteran combat unit 2,200 strong. Three U.S. battalions fought for and reduced the islands in succession, losing 339 men dead. The Japanese garrisons were annihilated (February 21) in close-in fighting in which Japanese land mines and U.S. flame throwers took heavy toll.

1944, April–May. Operation A-Go. Admiral Koga was killed in an airplane accident (April 1). His successor, Admiral **Soemu Toyoda,** a stronger character, bent all efforts to renew the original Japanese plan to wipe out the Pacific Fleet. Accordingly, he ordered (May 3) Vice Admiral **Jisaburo Ozawa,** commanding both the now somewhat rejuvenated carrier striking force and the First Mobile Fleet, to lure the American naval strength into the area Palaus-Yap-Woleai, where Japanese land-based aviation could assist in its destruction. Ozawa's fleet rendezvoused (May 16) off the southern tip of the Sulu Archipelago, where it was harassed by U.S. submarines, which also later warned Spruance of Ozawa's movement into the Philippine Sea (see p. 1176).

1944, June–August. The Marianas. Turner's V Amphibious Force—530-odd warships and auxiliaries with over 127,000 troops of Smith's V Amphibious Corps aboard—arrived off Saipan (June 15), 1,000 miles from its rendezvous, Eniwetok. Ahead of it, Mitscher's Task Force 58 had softened up the island defenses by fighter and bombing sweeps that cost the Japanese an approximate 200 combat planes and a dozen or more cargo ships (June 11–12). Then Mitscher's battleships and destroyers pounded ground installations at long range. Commanding the Marianas defensive forces was Admiral Chuichi Nagumo (of Pearl Harbor fame), whose Central Pacific Fleet had no major ships; under him was the Thirty-first Army (**Hideyoshi Obata**).

1944, June 15–July 13. Saipan. Landings of 2nd and 4th Marine divisions on 8 beaches, abreast, met instant resistance from Lieutenant General **Yoshitsugo Saito**'s garrison (part of the Thirty-first Army) and Admiral Nagumo's 6,000 sailors ashore. By nightfall, a beachhead had been established, but continued heavy resistance necessitated commitment of the U.S. 27th Division to reinforce the assault. Departure of Mitscher's carriers (June 17) and —later—of all warships (for the Battle of the Philippine Sea; see below) deprived the attackers of much-needed naval air and gunfire support. The ground troops made small but continued progress at heavy cost over accidented terrain skillfully organized and defended by first-class troops. The island's airfield had fallen into U.S. hands by June 18, but not until July 9, following a last-ditch fanatical counterattack by the 3,000 Japanese still surviving, did organized resistance end. American casualties on Saipan were 3,126 killed, 13,160 wounded, and 326 missing. Japanese losses were some 27,000 killed—including hundreds of Japanese civilians who committed suicide by jumping off the cliffs. Only about 2,000 were made prisoner. Both General Saito and Admiral Nagumo committed suicide.

COMMENT. *Slow progress of the 27th Division (committed June 19) particularly aroused "Howling Mad" Smith's ire. He relieved Major General Ralph C. Smith from command (June 24), precipitating an Army-Marine controversy to this day undecided, since it concerned radical difference between Marine and Army doctrine in assault tactics.*

Battle of the Philippine Sea, June 19–21, 1944

Ozawa's fleet had put to sea immediately upon receiving word of the assault on Saipan. Spruance, warned of the movement, gathered the Fifth Fleet under Admiral Mitscher's tactical command (June 18) 160 miles west of Tinian. Ozawa had 5 heavy and 4 light carriers, 5 battleships, 11 heavy and 2 light cruisers, and 28 destroyers. Spruance's fleet, augmented by Turner's Amphibious Force, numbered 7 heavy and 8 light carriers, 7 battleships, 8 heavy and 13 light cruisers, and 69 destroyers. U.S. planes numbered in all 956 to the Japanese 473; however, Ozawa would be giving battle within range of some 100 additional Japanese land-based planes based on Guam, Rota, and Yap. Also, Japanese planes had longer range than the Americans.

Ozawa's search planes picked up the Fifth Fleet by daybreak (June 19), 300 miles from his advance element of 4 light carriers and 500 miles from his main body. The opposing fleets were on southerly courses, Mitscher's carriers some 90 miles northwest of Guam and 110 miles southwest of Saipan in 4 carrier groups backed up by Spruance in the battle fleet. At about the same time, land-based planes from Marianas and Truk bases were repulsed with heavy loss. Following this, Ozawa attacked in 4 successive raids. Mitscher, discovering the first attacking group, loosed his interceptors and then sent the bombers aloft to keep his flight decks clear.

Misfortune struck Ozawa almost immediately. U.S. submarines following his movements picked off *Taiho,* biggest and newest of Japan's carriers, and *Shokaku,* one of the 2 surviving vessels of Pearl Harbor, sinking them both. Mitscher's interceptors took terrible toll of all the raiders, and most of those who did get through were then brought down by antiaircraft fire. The "Great Marianas Turkey Shoot" cost Ozawa 346 planes and 2 big carriers; U.S. losses were but 30 planes and some slight damage to a battleship from the single Japanese bomb which found its target.

Meanwhile, Mitscher's bombers strafed Guam and Rota, neutralizing the airfields. The battle was over by dark (6:45 P.M.). Ozawa had hauled off. Mitscher pursued, but contact was not made again until late afternoon next day. Mitscher launched 216 planes, which sank another carrier and 2 oil tankers and seriously damaged several other vessels. Twenty U.S. planes were lost, and Ozawa lost 65 more of his surviving aircraft. Homeward bound in the dark, the U.S. planes fell into major difficulties despite the fact that Mitscher boldly lighted up his ships to guide his birds home. Some 80 planes out of gas either ditched or crash-landed. Mitscher moved west, his destroyers combing the area to pick up 50-odd flyers floating in the water, reducing U.S. personnel losses that day to 16 pilots and 33 crewmen. Ozawa's crippled fleet made its getaway. The Fifth Fleet returned to Saipan.

COMMENT. *Ozawa's desperate attack in the face of formidable odds cost Japanese naval air power mortal injury. Aside from the material damage suffered in ship and plane losses, the death of more than 460 trained combat pilots was irreplaceable.*

1944, July 21–August 10. Guam. Guam fell to the 3rd Marine and 77th Army divisions and 1st Marine Brigade (August 10) after a tough struggle costing more than 1,400 killed and 5,600 more U.S. personnel wounded. Of the Japanese defenders, some 10,000 were killed during the operation, and several hundred more died rather than surrender during the long mopping-up that followed.

1944, July 25–August 2. Tinian. The island was invaded by the 2nd and 4th Marine divisions, and taken after the usual heavy resistance. U.S. losses were 389 killed and 1,816 wounded.

COMMENT. *Capture of the Marianas and the Battle of the Philippine Sea doomed Japan to defeat. The Tojo cabinet resigned (July 18).*

Return to the Philippines, July–December, 1944

STRATEGIC AND OPERATIONAL BACKGROUND

Strategy of the next move of the war was settled in principle at a conference at Pearl Harbor in July. President Roosevelt weighed 2 different concepts of approach to the final objective: an assault on Japan itself. Admiral Nimitz favored intermediate moves on Formosa or China; General MacArthur insisted on assault first to free the Philippines (for both military and political reasons), then on to Japan. Roosevelt accepted MacArthur's plan. Army and Navy staffs, in close co-operation, plotted progressive moves: MacArthur on Mindanao, Nimitz on Yap, and a joint assault on Leyte. While MacArthur would then invade Luzon, Nimitz would take Iwo Jima and Okinawa.

As soon as the Marianas operation ended, Nimitz set Spruance and his Fifth Fleet staff to planning the future Iwo Jima and Okinawa operations, while Halsey and Third Fleet staff were allotted the immediate task against Yap. Actually, this was a shift in commanders and staffs only; the ships and men were unchanged. What had been the Fifth Fleet was now the Third; Mitscher's Fast Carrier Task Force, TF 58, became TF 38; V Amphibious Force became III Amphibious Force; etc.

PRELIMINARIES

1944, September 15. Morotai and Pelelieu. MacArthur landed troops on Morotai to establish a forward air base; opposition was negligible. Nimitz, in a co-ordinated move, struck Pelelieu in the Palau Islands. Marines of Major General Roy S. Geiger's III Amphibious Corps (part of Vice Admiral **Theodore S. Wilkinson**'s III Amphibious Force) there met tough resistance from tenacious defenders under General **Sadal Inone** (September 15–October 13). Simultaneously Wilkinson, using Army troops, assaulted and captured **Angaur** (September 17–20) and occupied, unopposed, Ulithi Atoll, about 100 miles west of Yap (September 23). Ulithi's magnificent harbor became a fleet base for the Halsey-Mitscher Third Fleet team. Mopping up of scattered resistance continued in the Palaus for several weeks (November 25).

1944, September 15. Change of Plan. In

support of the Morotai-Pelelieu operations, Halsey's Third Fleet carriers had struck Yap, Ulithi, and the Palaus to neutralize nearby Japanese bases and soften the defenses (September 6). They had then swept the Philippine coast (September 9–13). Encountering slight resistance, Halsey sent a message to Nimitz, recommending cancellation of the proposed intermediate landings on Mindanao and Yap, which seemed unnecessary, and urging that the Leyte assault be mounted as soon as possible. Nimitz, agreeing, queried the Joint Chiefs of Staff, then attending the Quebec Conference. Nimitz offered to "loan" MacArthur his III Amphibious Force and his Army XXIV Corps. MacArthur, queried by the JCS if he could step up his Leyte landings to October 20 instead of December 20, as originally planned, immediately agreed (September 15). Accordingly, a directive was issued that day.

COMMENT. *Never had American military men better displayed flexibility and initiative than did Halsey, Nimitz, MacArthur, and the JCS. MacArthur's decision to advance by 2 months the timetable of a full-scale amphibious assault was audacious in light of the monumental logistical problems involved.*

1944, October 7–16. Prelude to Invasion. The Third Fleet moved to paralyze the remnants of Japanese air power. While Army land-based planes—the Fifth AF from New Guinea and the Seventh from the Marianas—attacked all enemy bases within range, long-range B-29's of XX Bomber Command bombed Formosa from bases in China (October 10). Meanwhile, Halsey hit shipping and shore installations in and around Okinawa, then turned south toward Formosa and Luzon (October 11).

1944, October 13–16. The Battle off Formosa. The Japanese air units on Formosa struck back fiercely; 2 cruisers were severely damaged, other vessels hit. Misled by fires on these ships and the flames of many shot-down Japanese planes, Japanese radio reports claimed a great naval victory. Halsey, hoping to decoy the Combined Fleet to action, left 1 carrier group to escort his cripples and took the rest of the Third Fleet east into the Philippine Sea (October 14–15). Toyoda, taking the bait, sent 600 of his carrier planes from Japan to Formosa airfields to complete the "destruction" of the American fleet. Halsey, returning toward Formosa, in 2 days destroyed about half these planes (October 15–16). The total score in these operations was more than 650 Japanese planes destroyed, many others crippled, and numerous shore installations smashed. Most serious was the wrecking of the rebuilt Japanese carrier air squadrons. U.S. losses were 2 cruisers badly damaged, several others hit, and 75 planes lost.

VISAYAS CAMPAIGN

The Philippines were defended by approximately 350,000 Japanese under the command of General Yamashita, conqueror of Malaya and Singapore. General Sosaku Suzuki's Thirty-fifth Army defended the southern and central Philippines.

1944, October 14–19. Approach to Leyte. A vast amphibious armada was closing on the Leyte coast, some 700 vessels, carrying 200,000 men of General Krueger's U.S. Sixth Army, in Admiral Kinkaid's Seventh Fleet. Wilkinson's III and Barbey's VII Amphibious Forces were supported by Rear Admiral **J. B. Oldendorf**'s gunfire-support group—6 battleships (reconditioned survivors of Pearl Harbor), 5 heavy cruisers (including H.M.A.S. *Shropshire*) and 4 light cruisers, and 66 destroyers (including convoy escorts). The air-support group (Rear Admiral **Thomas L. Sprague**) consisted of 16 escort carriers, 9 destroyers, and 11 destroyer escorts. Far in the offing (now neutralizing Luzon air bases and guarding San Bernardino and Surigao straits) was Halsey's Third Fleet, with Mitscher's fast carrier TF 38 its nucleus: 8 heavy and 8 light carriers, 6 fast new battleships, 6 heavy and 9 light cruisers, and 58 destroyers. Mitscher's planes numbered more than 1,000. Four American submarines were engaged.

COMMENT. *One operational blemish marred this magnificent amphibious array:*

command was joint, instead of being unified. MacArthur commanded the ground forces and Kinkaid's Seventh Fleet, while Halsey, still under Nimitz' direction, had a dual mission: first, to destroy the Japanese fleet should it put to sea; and second, to give all possible assistance to Kinkaid and the landings. The Americans had no reason to believe that these 2 missions could be contradictory, but the Japanese had a plan which the Americans had not foreseen.

The "Sho" Plan. *Japan, feeling the effect of continuous air and submarine attacks against her shipping, had long realized that American seizure of the Philippines, Formosa, or the Ryukyus would spilt the empire in two; separate the Southern Resources Area, reservoir for fuel oil and gasoline, from the homeland. Accordingly, the "Sho" (Victory) Plan had been devised as a last-ditch gamble by the Combined Fleet. In principle it embodied use of a portion of the now scattered elements of the fleet to decoy the American carrier force, while the remainder, converging on any new landing area, would overwhelm the amphibious support and isolate the troops ashore. The plan, good in principle, had one major flaw. Without adequate air power it would not work, and the Battle off Formosa had ruined most of Japan's carefully reconstituted naval air strength. Toyoda hoped, however, that land-based air units in the Philippines might make up for this serious deficiency.*

1944, October 20–22. Leyte Landings. Following intensive reconnaissance and a heavy naval bombardment, Sixth Army's X Corps (Major General **Franklin C. Sibert**) and Lieutenant General **John R. Hodge**'s XXIV Corps began landing. The Japanese 16th Division (General **Tomochika**), 16,000 strong, garrisoning the island, gave but little initial opposition. By midnight, 132,400 men and nearly 200,000 tons of supply and equipment were landed, and Kinkaid's combat ships were hurrying south to Surigao Strait to meet a Japanese naval threat. General MacArthur, accompanied by Philippine President **Sergio Osmeña,** came ashore, broadcasting his return (October 22).

The Battle for Leyte Gulf

1944, October 17–23. The Preliminaries. Warned of American intentions, disclosed by the Leyte reconnaissance (October 17), Japan put the **Sho Plan** into immediate effect. The Combined Fleet moved from widely scattered bases. Ozawa's Northern Force (or Third Fleet)—the 4 remaining carriers, 2 battleships, 3 cruisers, and 8 destroyers—steamed from Japan toward Luzon to lure the U.S. Third Fleet away from the landing area; the carriers were phantoms of naval air power, carrying only 116 planes with half-trained pilots. Kurita's Center Force (or First Attack Force)—2 superbattleships, 3 other battleships, 12 cruisers, and 15 destroyers—moving northeast from Malaya, Borneo, and the China Sea, was to traverse the San Bernardino Strait. The Southern Force (or C Force) of Vice Admiral **Shoji Nishimura**'s 2 battleships, 1 heavy cruiser, and 4 destroyers (from Malaya and Borneo), backed up by Vice Admiral **Kiyohide Shima**'s Second Attack Force of 2 heavy and 1 light cruisers and 4 destroyers (from the Ryukyus), moved southeast and east to pass through the Surigao Strait between Mindanao and Leyte. These Center–Southern Force pincers were to destroy all U.S. amphibious forces in Leyte Gulf by a concerted attack, marooning the troops ashore.

1944, October 23–24. Battle of the Sibuyan Sea. U.S. submarines *Darter* and *Dace* discovered Kurita's Center Force as it entered Palawan Passage from the South China Sea. Flashing word to Halsey, the subs sank 2 heavy cruisers and damaged a third. Kurita, continuing into the Sibuyan Sea, was attacked by Mitscher's TF 38. The superbattleship *Musashi* was sunk after 2 days of incessant bombardment and several other vessels damaged. Kurita turned around and headed westward again (late October 24). Halsey assumed he was retreating. Meanwhile, Japanese land-based planes harassed a division of TF 38. Most were shot down, but U.S.S. *Princeton* (light carrier) was sunk and U.S.S. *Birmingham* (cruiser) severely damaged. Unknown to Halsey, after dark Kurita changed course again and headed doggedly for San Bernardino Strait.

1944, October 24–25. Battle of Surigao Strait. Warned of the approach of the Japanese Southern Force, Kinkaid placed Oldendorf's gun-support ships to intercept it. Reconnoitering PT boats picked

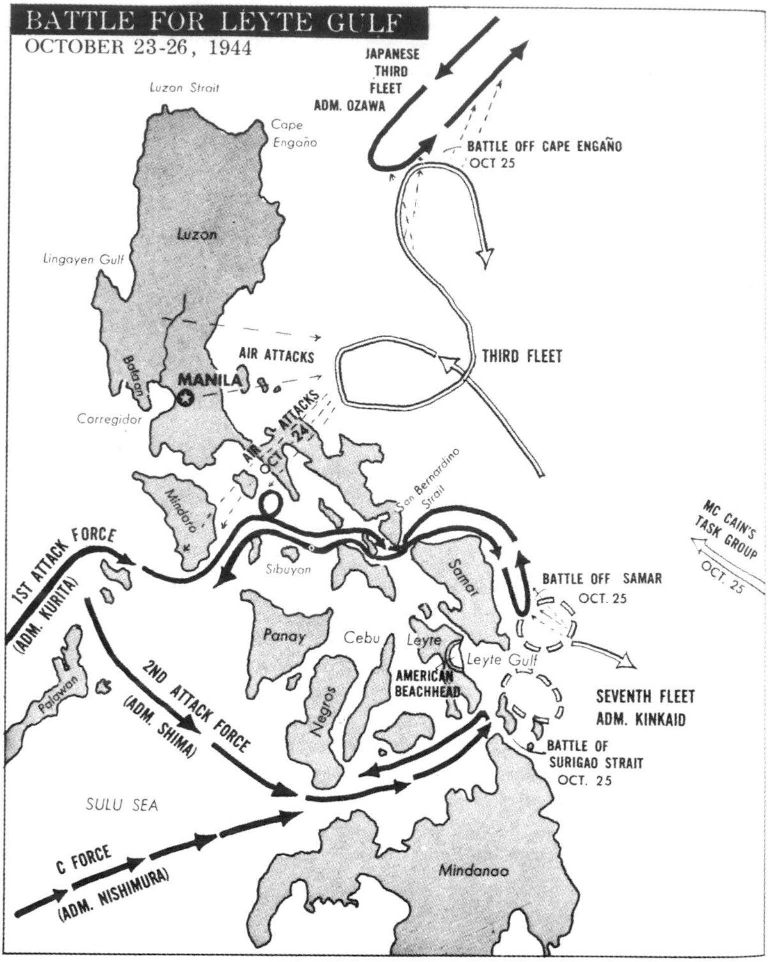

up Nishimura's force that night, moving in single line ahead. Two converging destroyer attacks torpedoed the battleship *Fuso* and 4 destroyers. Nishimura's crippled line then ran into Oldendorf's main force, which crossed his "T." American gunfire and torpedoes sank all except 1 destroyer; Nishimura went down with his flagship, *Yamashiro*. Shima's force, bringing up the rear, now ran the gantlet of PT-boat attack, which crippled 1 light cruiser. Attempting now to retire, Shima's flagship collided with one of Nishimura's mortally wounded vessels. Oldendorf pursued through the strait. Between his fire and planes from Admiral Thomas L. Sprague's escort carriers and land-based Army planes, another Japanese cruiser was sunk. The rest of Shima's force escaped as Oldendorf—his mission accomplished, and knowing he might have to fight another battle immediately—turned back.

1944, October 25, Dawn. San Bernardino Strait. Kurita, hoping still to join Nishimura in Leyte Gulf, debouched unopposed from San Bernardino Strait and turned south. Halsey, with his entire force, was rushing after Ozawa's decoy carrier force, which had been sighted to the far north. Word received of Kurita's retirement in the Sibuyan Sea the previous afternoon, combined with overenthusiastic reports from his flyers, led Halsey to believe Kurita was permanently out of the fight. So—his dual mission in mind—Halsey was rushing northward with all available elements of the Third Fleet to destroy the Japanese carrier force. He failed to inform Kinkaid.

1944, October 25, Early A.M. Battle off Samar. Kurita's southward advance completely surprised Rear Admiral **Clifton A. F. Sprague,** commanding an escort carrier group of Kinkaid's amphibious force, supporting land operations. Sprague, with 6 escort carriers, 3 destroyers, and 4 destroyer escorts, armed only with 5-in. guns, found himself giving battle to 4 battleships, 6 heavy cruisers, and about 10 destroyers. In an amazing running fight, during which his aircraft, armed with relatively harmless fragmentation bombs (for support of land operations), harassed the heavily gunned Japanese ships, while his destroyers nipped boldly at them, Sprague and his escort flattops fought off disaster. One carrier—U.S.S. *Gambier Bay*—was sunk, 2 destroyers and 1 destroyer escort went down, and Kurita's ships were closing in. But planes from other escort-carrier groups—all fleeing south to rejoin Kinkaid's Seventh Fleet—were now attacking Center Force. Kurita, with victory in his hands, hauled off, thinking he was being attacked by TF 38, his decision bolstered by reports that Nishimura's Southern Force had been demolished. At first Kurita thought to reinforce Ozawa, then gave that up and retreated through San Bernardino Strait. He was now harried by American reinforcements—planes from Rear Admiral **John S. McCain**'s task group of Halsey's fleet—rushing back in response to Seventh Fleet calls for help. Meanwhile, Admiral Thomas L. Sprague's escort carriers and Oldendorf's force, returning from the Surigao Strait fight, were assailed by land-based planes—including the first Japanese kamikaze attacks, which sank U.S.S. *St. Lô* and damaged several other ships.

1944, October 25. Battle off Cape Engaño. Halsey's headlong northward rush to catch the Japanese carrier force bore fruit at 2:20 A.M., when Mitscher's search planes picked it up. With dawn came the first of 3 successive plane strikes. Ozawa, who had put nearly all his small force of planes ashore to operate from land bases, had only antiaircraft fire to oppose the U.S. planes and it was not enough. By nightfall, all 4 Japanese carriers were sunk as well as 5 other of the remaining ships. Two battleships, 2 light cruisers, and 6 destroyers escaped. Halsey, infuriated by a query from Nimitz at Pearl Harbor, demanding explanation of his "failure" to help Kinkaid, went steaming southward at "flank speed" (full speed) with most of his fleet.

COMMENT. *The 4-phased naval Battle of Leyte Gulf ended the Japanese fleet as an organized fighting force. Four carriers, 3 battleships, 6 heavy and 4 light cruisers, 11 destroyers, and a submarine were sunk; nearly every other ship engaged was damaged. About 500 planes were lost; some 10,500 Japanese sailors and airmen were dead. American losses were 1 light carrier, 2 escort carriers, 2 destroyers, 1 destroyer escort, and more than 200 aircraft. About 2,800 Americans had been killed, some 1,000 additional wounded. In this, the greatest naval battle ever joined, 282 vessels were involved: 216 U.S.N., 2 R.A.N., 64 Japanese. Estimated man-power strengths were 143,668 U.S.N. and R.A.N., 42,800 Japanese.*

Both Halsey and Kurita may be criticized, the one for abandoning the Leyte Gulf area to chase Ozawa, the other for his timidity in retreating at the moment of victory. In mitigation, one notes that Halsey was on the horns of his dual-mission dilemma; he had no way of knowing that Ozawa's carrier force was only a decoy. As for Kurita, he was bewildered by conflicting reports and already shaken by 2 previous severe joltings. For all he knew, he might be throwing the only Japanese naval strength that remained afloat into the jaws of the overwhelming force of the entire U.S. Navy. So he limped away, victim of an overly complicated plan and of his own fears.

Struggle for Leyte

1944, October 21–December 31. General Yamashita, Japanese commander in the Philippines, recovering from the strategic surprise of the landings, decided to fight for Leyte. While the veteran 16th Division carried on a skillful delaying action, reinforcements were hurried from Luzon and the Visayas to build up the Thirty-fifth Army. Between October 23 and December 11, some 45,000 men and 10,000 tons of supply arrived in small increments, carried mostly by fast-running destroyer transports. U.S. Navy and long-range Army planes then dried up the supply routes, despite fierce Japanese land-based air strikes which only expended a great part of the remaining Japanese air power. Toward the end, only a trickle of sailing craft traversed the Leyte waters. Meanwhile, U.S. Sixth Army made slow progress against desperately defended delaying positions in the central mountain ridge. Progress was further impeded by tropical storms which turned the few dirt roads into quagmires. On the right, X Corps, by overland and amphibious movements, was approaching Limon, the northern anchor of Suzuki's defense line (November 7). On the left, XXIV Corps hammered at the precipitous heights protecting Ormoc, the southern Japanese key point and principal port. An amphibious lift (December 7) threatened Suzuki's southern flank, while at the same time a desperate but ineffective Japanese air drop farther east was repelled. Krueger, reinforced, launched a double envelopment (December 7–8), taking both Limon and Ormoc (December 10). The 77th Division from the south and 1st Cavalry and 24th divisions from the north then met (December 20) at Libungao, surrounding Suzuki's combat elements and cutting him off from his last remaining port, Palompom. All organized resistance collapsed Christmas Day. The Japanese had suffered over 70,000 casualties in the campaign; American losses were 15,584. Meanwhile, a foothold had been gained on adjoining Samar (late October).

1944, December 15. Seizure of Mindoro. A bold amphibious operation put a task force of approximately brigade strength ashore on Mindoro in the northern Visayas, just south of Luzon, to establish an advance air base for MacArthur's coming assault on Luzon.

COMMENT. *Japan's election to force a decision in the Leyte area had cost her a fatally crippled fleet and air force, and a serious reduction in ground-force strength in the Philippines. As the year ended, Japan had lost the war. Her communications with the Southern Resources Area were severed, her merchant fleet reduced from a tonnage of 6 million in 1941 to 2.5 (60 per cent of this loss caused by U.S. submarines). Approximately 135,000 of her soldiers were marooned, helpless, behind the American advance. But as yet Japan would not admit defeat.*

The Strategic Air Offensive

OPERATIONS FROM INDIA AND CHINA

1944, April–May. B-29's to India. With the agreement of Britain and China, new American B-29 "Superfortress" bombers began to arrive at bases near Calcutta. These planes of the XX Bomber Command were to undertake long-range strategic bombardment from India, and were also to strike industrial targets in Manchuria and southern Japan itself from bases in China. These powerful, heavily

B-29 Superfortresses

armed planes could fly over 350 mph, and could carry 20,000 pounds of bombs against targets over 1,500 miles from their bases. They were each armed with 12 .50-cal. machine guns and a 20 mm. cannon.

1944, June 5. First B-29 Combat Mission. This was an attack on railway targets at Bangkok, Thailand.

1944, June 15. First Strike against Japan. Five airfields with extra-long runways had been painstakingly built by coolie labor near Ch'engtu, in western China. Sixty-eight planes, staged to the Ch'engtu bases from Calcutta, hit a steel plant on the Japanese island of Kyushu.

1944, June–December. Continuing Strategic Missions. Because of the limitations on the total amounts of supplies and equipment that could be carried over the Hump, the B-29's were not based permanently in China. Barracks, repair shops, and heavy support equipment were all near the Calcutta bases. The B-29's carried their own fuel and bombs from India to Ch'engtu in preparation for their periodic raids on Kyushu, southern Manchuria, and Formosa. In between these raids, the great planes continued to attack Japanese bases in Southeast Asia from their fields near Calcutta. Under Major General **Curtis E. LeMay,** the XX Bomber Command became increasingly efficient.

OPERATIONS FROM THE MARIANAS

1944, October. B-29's to Saipan. As soon as the Marianas islands of Saipan, Tinian, and Guam had been captured (see p. 1177), Army B-17 and B-24 bombers moved into the captured Japanese airfields to strike at the Bonins and Iwo Jima (August–September). At the same time, Army Engineers began to lengthen existing runways and to build new extra-long airfields on all available areas of the islands. As soon as the first of these was ready, B-29's of the XXI Bomber Command began to arrive.

1944, October 28. First B-29 Mission from the Marianas. This was the first of several operational-training missions against Truk.

1944, November 24. First Marianas Mission against Japan. More than 100 B-29's initiated the final strategic air offensive against Japan by a raid against an aircraft plant near Tokyo.

1944, November–December. Continuing the Strategic Offensive. About once every 5 days, 100 to 120 Superfortresses struck industrial targets in Japan. The raids usually began with a dawn take-off from the Marianas airfields, the planes climbing steadily until they reached an altitude of about 30,000 feet as they crossed the Japanese coast. Resistance was fierce. Fighter planes based on Iwo Jima struck at the bombers as they flew over in the mornings and as they returned in the early afternoons. Over Japan, 200 or more fighters, with the best pilots available, rose to meet them. The Superfortresses shot down many of the attackers, but suffered severely themselves. By the end of the year, XXI Bomber Command was losing about 6 per cent of the planes that started on every raid, exceeding the theoretically acceptable maximum loss rate of 5 per cent.

THE WAR AGAINST JAPAN, 1945

Strategy and Policy

The collapse of Japan's defensive perimeter in the east and south, resulting from the crushing defeats suffered in 1944 by Japan's land, sea, and air forces in the Southwest Pacific and Pacific Ocean Areas, made the outcome of the war against Japan a foregone conclusion to Allied military leadership. Surprisingly, at the outset of the year, it seemed even possible that Japan's defeat might come as early as Germany's. This was the result not so much of the Allies' failing to adhere to their basic strategy of "Germany first"—though the Americans *had* deviated from that strategy to some extent—but was rather the natural consequence of the amazing military might which America had been able to mobilize in 3 short years. No nation in history had ever before been able to exercise so much power over so wide an expanse of the globe, and with such efficiency, as that wielded by the United States at the beginning of 1945. So immense was this power, in fact, and so inevitable the outcome of the war, that the first steps toward U.S. demobilization were actually begun before either Germany or Japan completely collapsed.

Inevitable though the outcome now was, it was also evident that the final subjugation of Japan could be both time-consuming and costly in lives and money. Despite some setbacks, the Japanese hold on Burma had not been seriously impaired, and they still ruled all of the vast Southern Resources Area. And though their sea lines of communication to that rich area had been cut, they had opened a new overland route as a result of their successful campaigns in China in 1944. The American naval blockade of Japan, combined with a relatively small strategic air offensive, was putting a serious strain on Japan's home economy, but the vigorous Japanese air defense effort was already threatening the morale of B-29 airmen. Japanese tenacity, despite their many defeats, caused Allied military leaders to fear that Japan itself, defended by more than 2,000,000 hardy fighting men, could not be conquered without a costly and sanguinary struggle on the 4 main islands themselves. Possibly the most serious danger was that conquest of the home islands might not end the war at all. On the mainland of Asia, Japan controlled Korea, Manchuria, and the richest and most populous areas of China; this vast Asiatic region was garrisoned by a military force well in excess of 1,000,000 undefeated veteran troops. If the Japanese government and a substantial portion of the military strength remaining in Japan should be shifted to the continent, the war might be protracted interminably.

Accordingly, Allied military leaders—and particularly the American JCS—were extremely anxious to draw Russia into the war against Japan at the earliest possible date, solely to hasten the end of the war and avoid probable excessively high casualties. But the agreements reached at Yalta and later at Potsdam were inept and naïve. The Russian week-long participation in the war did not affect the outcome. By that time Japan had not only been brought to the verge of economic and social collapse by physical punishment; she had suffered a psychological shock so severe as to make it easy for a warrior people to acknowledge defeat for the first time in recorded Japanese history. The death of President Roosevelt (April 12) brought Vice President **Harry S Truman** to U.S. leadership, but there were no changes in policy or strategy.

Land and Air Operations in Asia

BURMA

As the year opened, 4 major Allied land forces were converging on Burma. Along the coast of the Bay of Bengal, the British XV Corps was once more pushing through Arakan toward Akyab. Slim's Fourteenth Army was advancing on a broad front through the jungled hills between the Chindwin and Irrawaddy rivers. In north Burma, forces of General Sultan's Northern Combat Area Command were approaching the Burma Road from the west, while Marshal Wei Li-huang's Y-Force was slowly moving down that road from Yunnan toward the Burma-China frontier. Though these Allied forces were encountering minor opposition, it was obvious that the 3 Japanese armies holding Burma were merely conducting delaying actions. Though few of the Allied leaders realized it—with the possible and notable exception of General Slim—General Kimura, over-all commander of Japan's Burma Area Army, was deliberately luring his foes into central Burma for a climactic battle in an area where he expected to have a logistical superiority that would ensure his victory.

Third Arakan Campaign

The renewed advance of the XV Corps had begun on December 12, 1944. In accordance with Kimura's plan, opposition was negligible, and Akyab fell quickly (January 4). The XV Corps prepared for an amphibious invasion of south Burma. Meanwhile, its hold on Arakan was ensured by a number of minor operations to seize and secure the major islands along the Arakan coast.

North Burma and Yunnan

1945, January 1–27. Converging Advances of NCAC and Y-Forces. The Japanese 56th Division withdrew deliberately and skillfully in the face of these 2 converging Chinese drives, making the Chinese fight for every foot of ground. Although units of the 38th Division reached Chinese soil at Loiwing early in the month (January 6), and patrol contacts between the 2 converging forces were continuous from that time, the Japanese stubbornly prevented a link along the road.

1945, January 27. Reopening the Burma Road. The Y-Force pushed across the Shweli River to Burmese soil at **Wanting,** just as troops of the Chinese New First

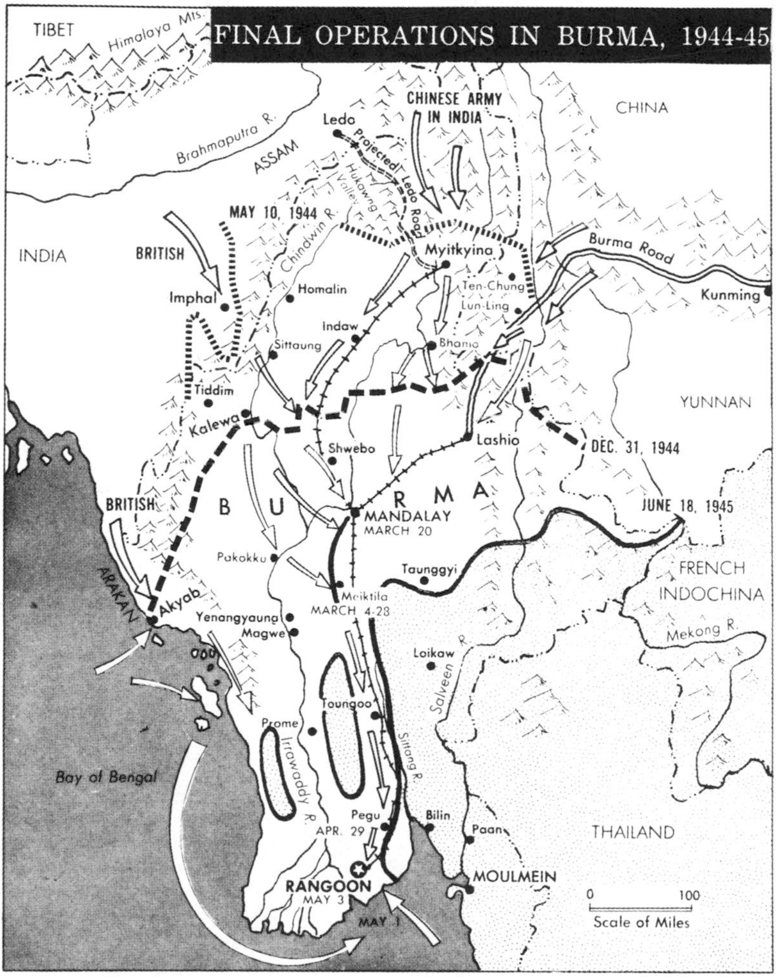

FINAL OPERATIONS IN BURMA, 1944-45

Army (38th and 30th divisions) fought their way to the Burma Road at **Mong Yu;** so skillful was the Japanese withdrawal that the 2 Chinese forces became engaged in a fire fight with each other near Mong Yu before they realized that their elusive enemy had slipped away to new positions blocking further southward advance along the Burma Road toward Lashio.

1945, January 28–February 4. First Land Convoy to China. With great fanfare a truck convoy (manned largely by junketing American newspapermen) left Namkham in Burma for Kunming, arriving amidst rejoicing and celebration. In a magnanimous gesture, Chiang Kai-shek proposed that the combined Burma and Ledo roads be renamed the Stilwell Road, in honor of the man most responsible for breaking the land blockade of China.

1945, January–March. Climactic Operations in North Burma. Although the Chinese and American troops had accomplished their main mission, the war in north Burma was not yet over. Bitter fighting continued along the Burma Road as Allied troops fought their way toward Lashio against typically dogged Japanese resistance. A particularly fierce battle took place when the American Mars Brigade in the vicinity of **Namhpakka** vainly attempted to block the retreat of the Japanese 56th Division to Lashio (January 18–February 3). Equally fierce was the battle fought by the British 36th Division in forcing a crossing of the Shweli River at **Myitson** (January 31–February 21). A few days later, in the center of the NCAC zone, the Chinese 50th Division captured the silver and tin mines of **Namtu** after a sharp engagement (February 27). The Chinese New First Army captured **Lashio** after a desultory 2-day battle (March 6–7). The 50th Division captured **Hsipaw** (March 15), then repulsed Japanese counterattacks until joined by the 30th Division (March 24). The British 36th Division reached the road near Maymyo (March 30), returning to Fourteenth Army control and ending an 8-month period of uninterrupted combat.

Central Burma

1945, January. Slim Sets a Trap. Because of the paucity of resistance to his advance toward the Irrawaddy, Slim divined Kimura's plan to counterattack the Fourteenth Army as it attempted to cross the river north of Mandalay. Accordingly, he left a dummy IV Corps headquarters near Shwebo, on his left flank, maintaining active radio contact with the 19th Indian Division, which continued to advance directly toward the river. Meanwhile, he secretly and rapidly moved the IV Corps and its 2 remaining divisions south, behind the XXXIII Corps, to make a surprise crossing of the Irrawaddy near Pakokku, 100 miles below Mandalay. While the 19th Division and XXXIII Corps were occupying Japanese attention by crossing the river farther north, Slim planned a rapid crossing by the IV Corps, which would then dash eastward, cut Kimura's line of communications to Rangoon, and encircle the Japanese Fifteenth and Thirty-third armies.

1945, January 14. Irrawaddy Crossing of the 19th Division. This crossing at **Kyaukmyaung** was immediately violently counterattacked, confirming Slim's estimate of Japanese intentions. With difficulty the division held its bridgehead, thanks to powerful artillery and air support.

1945, February 12. Crossing of the XXXIII Corps. Having deliberately attracted Japanese attention to their preparations, the divisions of this corps crossed the river against determined resistance just south of Mandalay; losses were heavy, but the bridgehead was established and maintained.

1945, February 13. Crossing of the IV Corps. Slim's planned encirclement got off to a brilliant start with a surprise crossing against negligible opposition. The 7th and 17th Divisions (the latter almost completely armored) established a bridgehead at Pagan and began a quick build-up.

1945, February 21–28. Dash for Meiktila. While the 7th Division held the Irrawaddy bridgehead at Pagan, the tanks of the 17th Division raced to seize the strategic road and railroad junctions at Meiktila and Thazi.

1945, February 28–March 4. Capture of Meiktila. Having seized the town against desperate resistance by surprised, outnumbered Japanese rear-area troops, the British prepared for the inevitable Japanese reaction. Reinforcements were rushed to the 17th Division by air, and an air-supply operation from India was initiated. Kimura, realizing what had happened, began to withdraw his reserves from the Mandalay area and prepared for an all-out assault on Meiktila. Violent, confused fighting raged around that town and Thazi (March 5–15).

1945, March 9–21. Battle of Mandalay. The 19th Division north of Mandalay and the XXXIII Corps to the south broke out of their bridgeheads (February 26) and converged on the old royal capital of Burma. While the XXXIII Corps kept the Japanese busy south of the city, the 19th Division captured it in a dogged house-to-house battle.

1945, March 15–31. The Battle of Meiktila. Elements of 3 Japanese divisions, commanded by capable Major General Tanaka, began an all-out assault on the 17th Indian Division in order to reopen communications with Rangoon. The Japanese closely invested the British and Indian troops, and for a while captured their airfield, forcing them to rely upon parachute drop for supply. Equally determined British counterattacks recovered the airfield, however. With the XXXIII Corps and remainder of the IV Corps moving rapidly toward Meiktila, Kimura realized that he could not fight his way into the town in time to avoid disaster (March 28). He therefore reopened a new line of retreat through Thazi. The IV Corps broke through to relieve the 17th Division, thus ending the climactic battle of the war in Burma.

COMMENT. *Slim's brilliant but simple plan went exactly as he had envisaged it. The plan, and its execution, warrant Slim's inclusion in the list of Britain's greatest generals.*

1945, March 26. Revolt of Aung San. Burmese General Aung San, who had been ordered by the Japanese to take his small Burma National Army from Rangoon to the assistance of the Japanese troops at Meiktila, left the city, ostensibly in compliance with orders, then ordered execution of long-laid plans for a Burmese revolt against the Japanese. Aung San had long been in secret contact with British agents, having become disillusioned with the Japanese. Though the effort was not decisive, nonetheless guerrilla harassment by these Burmese added significantly to the discomfiture of the Japanese.

1945, April 1–May 1. Race for Rangoon. Anticipating early arrival of the monsoon, which would immobilize his tanks, now able to maneuver so easily on the rock-hard, sun-baked rice paddies, Slim turned southward. Several sharp engagements were fought, but the British, spearheaded by the 17th Indian Division, had little difficulty in slashing through confused and unco-ordinated Japanese units. The main problem was to get supplies of fuel and food to the troops by airlift; for the last 10 days of the month the 17th Division was on half-rations. Pegu, only 45 miles from Rangoon, was captured the same day the rains began (May 1).

1945, May 1. Amphibious Landing of the XV Corps. Anxious to beat the Fourteenth Army for the honor of capturing Rangoon, elements of the XV Corps landed at the mouth of the Rangoon River. The Japanese secretly evacuated the city that day.

1945, May 2. Capture of Rangoon. While the 17th Division was trying to push through mud north of the city and the XV Corps was organizing for a short advance upriver to capture the town from the south, an RAF pilot, flying over the city, could see no Japanese. He landed at Mingaladon, walked into the town, and, with the assistance of the local civilian population, released Allied prisoners from the city jail. He had himself rowed down the river to inform the British Army that Rangoon had been captured by the RAF.

1945, May–August. Pursuit and Consolidation. Despite the great difficulties of movement over the flooded countryside, the British pushed after the Japanese elements withdrawing in disorder toward Thailand. There were no further major engagements, though there were frequent patrol clashes between pursuers and pursued. Meanwhile, plans were being made by Admiral Mountbatten's SEAC headquarters for a major amphibious operation against Singapore later in the year.

CHINA

1945, January–February. Renewed Japanese Offensive in Southeast China. Japanese forces made wide gains in the coastal regions between Hankow and the French

Indochina border. Three more U.S. Fourteenth Air Force bases fell.

1945, March 9, Japanese Consolidation in Indochina. French officials, heretofore permitted to retain some internal control despite Japanese occupation, were imprisoned.

1945, March–May. Japanese Offensive in Central China. A drive through the fertile area between the Yellow and Yangtze rivers netted the ripening crops, and the important Fourteenth Air Force base at **Laohokow** was overrun (March 26–April 8). The drive was checked (April 10) by the Chinese, as was a later attempt against **Changteh** and **Chihkiang** (May 8).

1945, April 5. U.S.S.R. Abrogates Treaty with Japan. As war in Europe neared its end, the Kremlin renounced the 1941 neutrality treaty (see p. 1037) which had served Stalin's purpose of avoiding a two-front war.

1945, April–August. Soviet Buildup in East Asia. Commanded by Marshal **Aleksandr M. Vasilevskiy,** the Soviet Far East Command consisted of 11 combined arms armies, 1 tank army, 3 air armies, and 3 air defense armies with a total strength of over 1,500,000 troops, 26,000 guns and mortars, 5,500 tanks, and 3,800 aircraft in three army groups. In Manchuria, Japanese General **Otoza Yamada**'s Kwantung Army had a paper strength of 925,000 men, of which 300,000 were unreliable Manchukuo puppet units with about 6,000 guns and mortars, 1,200 tanks, and 1,900 aircraft. Most veteran troops of the Kwantung Army had been sent to oppose the American offensives in the Pacific.

1945, May–August. Japanese Withdrawals. Realizing he was overextended, General Okamura began movements north to reinforce the Kwantung Army in Manchuria, now menaced by the Soviet threat to enter the war. Chinese counteroffensives cut the corridor to Indochina (May 30). By July 1, more than 100,000 Japanese troops were marooned in the Canton area, while some 100,000 additional had moved back into North China, harassed by the U.S. Fourteenth and Tenth Air Forces. The former American airfield at Kweilin was recaptured (July 27).

1945, August 8. U.S.S.R. Declares War on Japan. The U.S.S.R. declared war following the atomic bombing of Hiroshima to ensure participation in the war before Japan surrendered or collapsed.

1945, August 9–17. Soviet Offensive. Bad weather contributed to Soviet surprise. Marshal **Rodion Y. Malinovskiy**'s 3rd Far Eastern Army Group, making the main effort, swept eastward from Outer Mongolia on a broad front. Marshal **Kirill A. Meretzkov**'s 1st FEAG moved west and south from the line Khabarovsk-Vladivostok. Between these pincers General **Maxim Purkhayev**'s 2nd FEAG advanced south from the Amur River line. Japanese resistance was bitter, except that the bold and unexpected crossing of the almost trackless Khingan Mountains by the Soviet 6th Guards Tank Army was virtually unopposed. When this army, closely followed by the remainder of Malinovskiy's troops, reached the Central Manchurian Plain (August 13), a strategic envelopment of the main forces of the Kwantung Army had been achieved, and Japanese resistance began to collapse. Russian spearheads drove Japanese troops back across the Yalu into Korea. The advance into Korea continued after the official cessation of hostilities (August 15). Scattered fighting throughout Manchuria and northern Korea ended soon after.

1945, August 14. Japanese Surrender. (See p. 1198.)

Operations in the Southwest Pacific Area

THE PHILIPPINES

Yamashita's Defensive Strategy. General Yamashita had 250,000 ground troops on Luzon, deficient to some extent in equipment, but still formidable. His air strength had been dissipated, with little support expected from other sources. He delayed and finally retired to the mountainous central and western regions of Luzon, where formidable defensive works had been prepared. He did not contemplate defense of Manila.

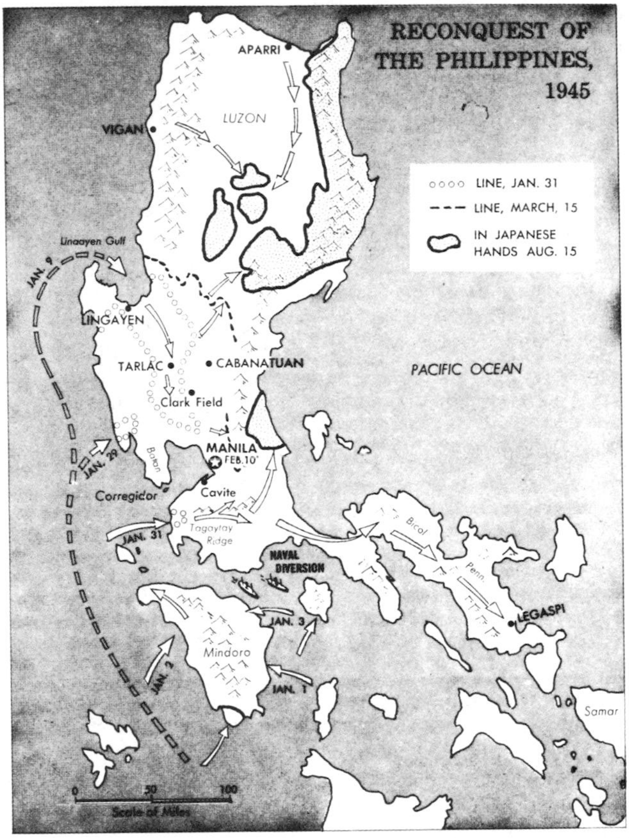

Luzon

1945, January 2–8. The Approach to Luzon. Lifted by the Seventh Fleet, the Sixth Army moved from Leyte through the Surigao Strait and up the western coast of Luzon to Lingayen Gulf. Planes from Halsey's fast carriers were strafing Formosa, as was the China-based XX Bomber Command. Kenney's planes from Leyte and from the new-won base on Mindoro (see p. 1182) attempted to neutralize Japanese aircraft on Luzon, but kamikaze pilots took heavy toll of Admiral Oldendorf's gunfire-support group—both on the way and after it started bombarding the Lingayen shore (January 6). One escort carrier was sunk, another damaged. The battleship *New Mexico,* 1 heavy and 4 light cruisers, and several other vessels were severely damaged. The attacks petered out as the Japanese eliminated themselves by their suicide attacks, while Halsey's and Kenney's planes hammered their bases.

1945, January 9. Lingayen Landing. Krueger's army landed, almost without opposition, on a 2-corps front, 4 divisions abreast. By nightfall 68,000 men were ashore, from Lingayen to Damortis.

1945, January 10–February 2. From Lingayen to Manila Bay. Major General **Oscar W. Griswold**'s XIV Corps, on the right, pushed aside Japanese delaying forces to reach the Camp O'Donnell–Fort Stotsenberg–Clark Field area (January 23), where it turned westward for a week of serious fighting, while 1 regiment pushed down to Calumpit (January 31) and the marshy delta of the Pampanga River. Major General **Innis P. Swift**'s I Corps, on the left, had more difficult going, fighting both to the east and south. Elements of his 1st Cavalry Division met the 37th Division at Plaridel (February 2).

1945, January 30–February 4. Arrival of the Eighth Army. Task forces of Eichelberger's Eighth Army made 2 amphibious landings north and south of Manila, Major General **Charles P. Hall**'s XI Corps in the Subic Bay area (January 30) seizing **Olongapo** to assist in sealing off the Bataan Peninsula, which was quickly occupied to prevent the Japanese from emulating the American defense of 1942. Two regiments of the 11th Airborne Division, under Major General **Joseph M. Swing,** landed at **Nasugbu** (January 31), southwest of Manila. Eichelberger then air-dropped the remaining regiment of the division on Tagaytay Ridge, 30 miles south of Manila (February 3). Next day, advance elements of the division reached Paranaque, on the southern outskirts of the city, where a stiff defense halted them.

1945, February 3–March 4. Recapture of Manila. While the 37th Division battered its way south into the city, the 1st Cavalry Division swung wide to east and then south, linking with the 11th Airborne Division. By February 22, the garrison had been driven into the old walled city (Intramuros) and Manila was isolated from Yamashita's main forces. American military and civilian prisoners held at Santo Tomás University and in Bilibid Prison were released. Inside Intramuros were the survivors of the fanatical Japanese garrison, some 18,000 strong—mainly naval personnel—commanded by Rear Admiral **Mitsuji Iwafuchi.** Ignoring Yamashita's instructions not to defend the city, Iwafuchi embarked on a suicidal defense, ruthlessly demolishing and burning many buildings. Street by street and house by house, the 37th Division now pried the defenders out. When the last resistance ended, historic old Intramuros was a mass of rubble in which at least 16,665 Japanese lay dead.

1945, February 16–April 17. Clearing Manila Bay. Corregidor, "Gibraltar of the East," was assaulted by a skillful paratroop drop on its tiny Topside golf course after intensive air and artillery bombardment (February 16). This was followed by an amphibious landing from Bataan and, after another suicidal defense, the fortress was cleared (February 27). Many of its garrison lay buried in blown-up Malinta Hill tunnel. Counted were 4,417 Japanese dead; 19 prisoners were taken. U.S. casualties were 209 killed and 725 wounded. Cargo began moving into the bay (March 15). **Fort Drum,** the "concrete battleship" on El Fraile rock, fell (April 13) when gasoline and fuel oil were poured down its ventilators and ignited, cooking the garrison. That same day a landing was made on **Caballo Island,** but its garrison was not subdued for 2 weeks. Carabao Island was taken without opposition (April 17).

1945, March 15–August 15. The Mountain Campaign. The weight of the Sixth Army's mass turned east, north, and south in an interminable series of assaults on Yamashita's mountain defenses. In the north, the North Luzon Guerrilla Force and newly reorganized Philippine Army assisted in pocketing the bulk of the Japanese forces in the Cordillera Central and the Sierra Madres. East of Manila, a smaller group held the ridges on the Pacific coast. When Yamashita surrendered at the end of the war (August 15), he still had an organized force of some 50,000 troops.

COMMENT. *The Luzon campaign cost the U.S. 7,933 killed and 32,732 wounded. Japanese losses were more than 192,000 killed and about 9,700 captured in combat. Yamashita, hampered by poor communications and incomplete information from his own high command, was still further impeded by the lack of command unity. It would appear that he did the best that could be expected under the circumstances. On the U.S. side, the ratio of battle deaths—24 Japanese to 1 American, a tremendous exception to the rule that the attacker must expect higher losses than the attacked—is tribute to the genius of MacArthur and the skill of Krueger.*

The Visayas and Southern Islands

1945, February–August. Eichelberger's Campaign. Concurrently with the Luzon campaign, the Eighth Army was charged with the freeing of the remainder of the Philippines, garrisoned by elements of the Japanese Thirty-fifth Army—some 102,000 strong—under General Suzuki. He was directed by Yamashita to delay and defend as long as possible. He decided to concentrate his main defense on Mindanao. Beginning with Palawan, Eighth Army task forces made 50 amphibious landings. Barbey's VII Amphibious Force furnished part of the lifts, supplemented by Army Engineer amphibious special brigades. Air support was provided by Kenney's land-based planes. Each operation followed the same pattern: an assault landing, Japanese withdrawal to the interior, securing of the island, and departure of the troops, leaving mop-up to the extensive native guerrilla forces present.

1945, April 17–July 15. Mindanao. Here, with 2 divisions and some naval troops, Suzuki put up a stiff defense. Concentric landings from the north, east, and south finally pushed the Japanese into 2 groups in the center of the island, where they remained until conclusion of hostilities. Eighth Army casualties during the entire Philippine campaign totaled 2,556 killed and 9,412 wounded. Approximately 50,000 Japanese were killed in the Visayan–Southern Islands Campaign.

NEW GUINEA AND NETHERLANDS EAST INDIES

1945, January–August. The By-passed Areas. Blamey's Australian troops were charged with containing and mopping up Japanese pockets of resistance in New Guinea and the Bismarck and Solomon archipelagos. Contenting himself with containment on New Britain, Blamey undertook aggressive operations on Bougainville in the Solomons and on New Guinea.

1945, May–August. Borneo. Tarakan Island on the northeast coast, Brunei Bay on the southeast coast, and Balikpapan on the northwest were all assaulted in amphibious moves lifted by Seventh Fleet task forces containing also units of the Royal Australian Navy. Air support was furnished by Kenney's air forces (also containing Australian elements).

1945, May 1–June 22. Tarakan. A brigade of the Australian 9th Division, with a detachment of Netherlands troops, was landed. Japanese resistance was determined, but finally overwhelmed.

1945, June 10. Brunei Bay. The Australian 9th Division quickly seized a wide perimeter and established airfields.

1945, July 1–10. Balikpapan. Following heavy naval and air bombardments, the Australian 7th Division landed and seized all major objectives.

COMMENT. *None of the operations in this area had any appreciable effect on the war. The Borneo operations were originally conceived as part of MacArthur's plan to recapture Java and restore the lawful government. As revised, its major objective was seizure of the principal oil-producing areas.*

Operations in the Pacific Ocean Areas

IWO JIMA

American Plans and Preparations. Possession of this pear-shaped rocky island in the Bonin group, only 8 square miles in area, was essential to U.S. advance toward Japan. In Japanese hands it menaced U.S. bombers from Saipan harassing the Japanese mainland at extreme range. In U.S. hands it would become a splendid forward air base. Nimitz's armada, now become the Fifth Fleet, with the Spruance-Turner command team replacing Halsey and his staff, moved against it, lifting Major General **Harry Schmidt**'s Fifth Amphibious Corps—the 3rd, 4th, and 5th Marine divisions.

Japanese Plans and Preparations. Major General **Tadamichi Kuribayashi** commanded more than 22,000 Japanese army and naval troops garrisoning the island. Honeycombed with concealed gun emplacements, concrete pillboxes, and mine fields expertly interlaced, it was one of the most strongly fortified positions to be assaulted during the war. Kuribayashi elected a static defense, his troops protected in an elaborate underground cave system against the incessant bombings long preceding the assault and the 3-day naval bombardment immediately before it.

1945, February 19–March 24. Invasion. Schmidt came ashore (February 19) on the southeast coast, the 4th and 5th Marine divisions abreast and the 3rd in reserve, to be met by intensive fire—front, flank, and enfilade. Taking 2,420 casualties the first day, the Marines cut the island in 2, the 5th Marine Division turning left to assault Mt. Suribachi, the other divisions driving to the right. Naval gunfire gave continuous accurate support as the attackers inched forward through the volcanic dust. Mt. Suribachi was stormed (February 23) and the American flag raised on its crest. By March 11 the remnants of the defenders were pinned on the northern tip of the island. Organized resistance ended (March 16). Next day, 16 B-29's returning from Japan made safe emergency landings, thanks to the U.S. Marine Corps.

COMMENT. *Slight Japanese aerial opposition was encountered. A kamikaze crashed on the carrier* Saratoga *(February 21), destroying 42 planes and killing 123 men; 192 more were wounded. Several other vessels were also damaged that day by kamikazes. Total Marine casualties were 6,891 killed and 18,070 wounded. Only 212 of the Japanese garrison surrendered. Counted dead were more than 21,000; many others were sealed in their underground shelters. Before the war ended, Iwo Jima had proved its usefulness; 2,251 B-29's had made emergency landings, sparing the lives of 24,761 U.S. airmen.*

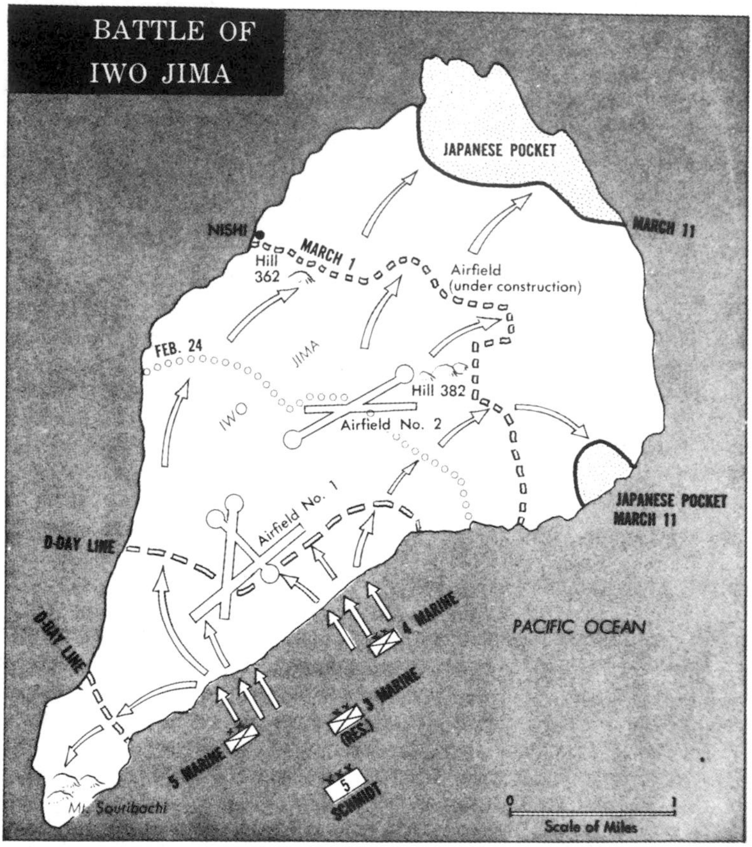

OKINAWA

American Plans and Preparations. Final preliminary to invasion of the Japanese mainland was possession of the Ryukyu group, midway between Formosa and Kyushu, southernmost island of Japan. Operation "Iceberg" was organized for the task, with Okinawa, largest island in the group, the principal objective. Under Nimitz' command, Spruance's Fifth Fleet would lift U.S. Army Lieutenant General **Simon Bolivar Buckner**'s Tenth Army (some 180,000 in the assault force and additional reserves lying in New Caledonia): the XXIV Corps (Major General **John R. Hodge**) and III Marine Amphibious Corps (Major General **R. S. Geiger**). This would be the largest and most complicated amphibious expedition undertaken in the

Pacific. Turner commanded the actual amphibious operation, while Mitscher's fast carrier force sought control of the air. Mitscher's TF 58 was supplemented by the Royal Navy's newly joined carrier force: 4 carriers and 1 battleship under Vice-Admiral **H. B. Rawlings,** R.N. The carrier forces' task was complicated by the fact that while Okinawa was beyond range of American land-based fighter planes, it was within reach of Japanese fighter planes from Formosa and Kyushu. Thus the carriers would have to supply cover from the expected kamikaze attacks, to which Japan was now evidently committed, as well as tactical support for the ground troops.

Japanese Plans and Preparations. On Okinawa was the Japanese Thirty-second Army, under Lieutenant General **Mitsuru Ushijima,** with some 130,000 men. As usual, an extensive defense system had been organized, particularly on the southern part of the island, in the midst of a native civilian population of more than 450,000.

1945, March 14–31. Preliminary Air Operations. To isolate the battlefield, Mitscher's carriers attacked Japanese air bases on Kyushu. Rawlings' British carrier force began neutralization of the Sakishima island group, midway between Formosa and Okinawa, strafing airfields and intercepting strikes destined for the battle area. Army long-range bombers attacked Formosa and industrial targets on Honshu. The big carriers received rough treatment from kamikazes; U.S.S. *Franklin* was so badly crippled that she had to be towed away by the cruiser *Pittsburgh,* and both the *Yorktown* and the *Wasp* were damaged. Special fire-fighting equipment devised by the New York City Fire Department saved all 3 vessels, but 825 officers and men were killed and 534 wounded. Temporary paralysis of the Japanese air bases was accomplished, and 169 of the 193 kamikazes committed were wiped out. (The steel-decked British carriers suffered less from kamikaze strikes than did the American teak-decked ships.)

1945, March 23–31. Preassault Operations. Admiral **W. H. P. Blandy**'s gunfire and escort-carrier ships of the amphibious force closed on Okinawa and began (March 23) continuous air and artillery strafing. At the same time the 77th Division was lifted to the outlying Kerama Retto and Keise Shima island groups to secure a fleet anchorage and seaplane base in the Kerama roadstead and artillery positions on Keise. Capture on Kerama of some 350 small "suicide" boats—each carrying 2 depth bombs and some hand grenades, and manned by a 2- or 3-man crew—removed a potential hazard to the landing operations. The splendid roadstead at once became a valuable repair and supply base for the Navy.

1945, April 1–4. The Landings. While a simulated landing force demonstrated off the southeast coast to distract Japanese attention, an 8-mile-wide column of landing craft disgorged from 1,300 naval vessels assembled off the Hagushi beaches on the western coast. It struck the beaches in 8 successive waves on a bright Easter Sunday morning—under cover of a tremendous air and artillery bombardment—and some 60,000 troops established their beachhead without any ground opposition. The Marine III Amphibious Corps, on the left, turned north; it would receive little opposition in clearing the entire northern area of the island (April 13) and nearby **Ie Shima** Island (April 16–20). The XXIV Corps, turning south, found itself (April 4) suddenly brought up short by the heavily organized **Machinato Line** of the Japanese Shuri Zone: an interlocking system of mountain defenses organized in great depth.

1945, April 6–7. Operation TEN-GO. The Japanese high command decided on a co-ordinated air-naval suicidal attack to check further American advance against the mainland. A kamikaze assault would cripple the amphibious force off Okinawa. The monster battleship *Yamato,* with 1 light cruiser and 8 destroyers, would crush what was left. The vessels, without any air cover, carrying only sufficient fuel for a 1-way trip, but crammed with ammunition, hurried out of the Inland Sea (April 6) on the Japanese Navy's last desperate throw of the dice. Spru-

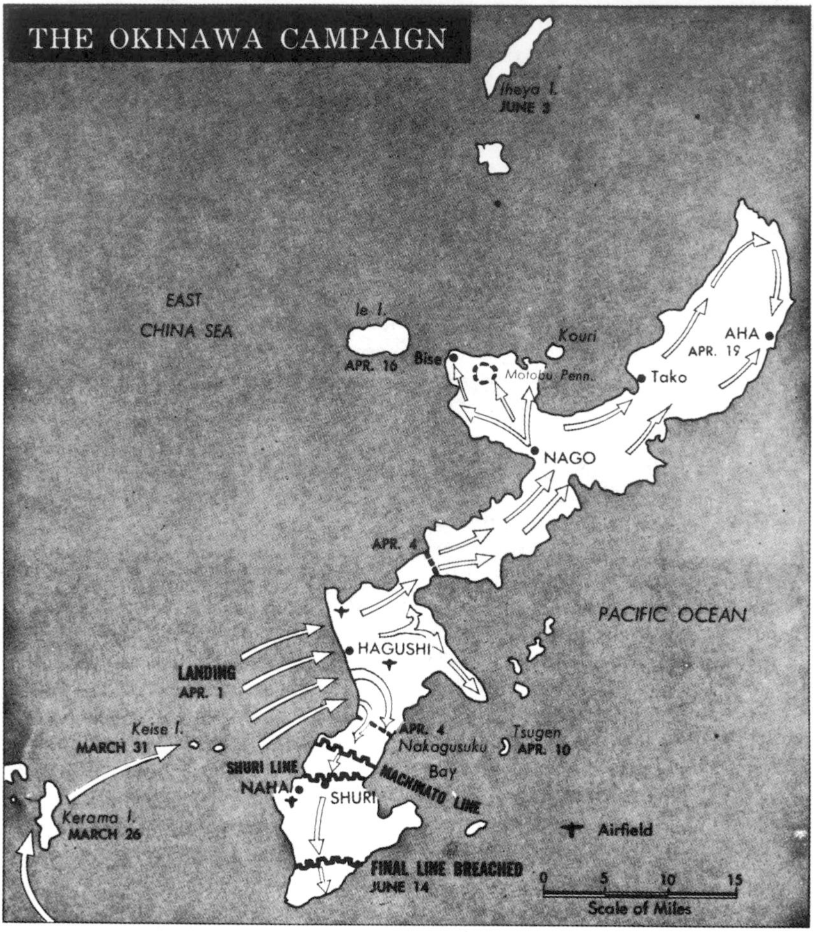

ance, warned by U.S. submarines of the sortie, prepared to meet it with Mitscher's carrier force, backed up by his battle fleet.

1945, April 7. First Kamikaze Assault. Some 355 kamikaze and 340 additional orthodox dive bombers and torpedo planes swept in on the amphibious force. Although 383 of the attackers were lost, when the furious strike ended, 2 U.S. destroyers, 2 ammunition ships, a mine sweeper, and a landing ship had been sunk and 24 other vessels damaged.

1945, April 7. End of the *Yamato*. Vice Admiral **Sejichi Ito,** in the *Yamato,* leading his forlorn hope, was met by Mitscher's carrier planes shortly after noon. Wave after wave of American planes struck home on the monster's topsides with bombs and torpedoes. After nearly 4 hours of constant pummeling, the *Yamato* lay helpless on her beam ends. At 4:23 she slid under, with 2,488 officers and men. The cruiser, too, went down, as did 4 destroyers. The other 4, though damaged, managed to scuttle away. In all, 3,655 Japanese sailors met their deaths in this last fling of the Imperial Navy. U.S. losses were some 15 planes and 84 seamen and pilots.

COMMENT. *Had the Japanese high command concentrated its remaining air power to provide cover for* Yamato *until she reached Okinawa, she might have done severe damage to the amphibious force before her end came. The 42,000-yard range of her 9 18.1-in. guns far exceeded that of American battleships.*

1945, April 6–30. Advance and Stalemate. The XXIV Corps battered its way south against increasing opposition. The Machinato Line was pierced (April 24), but finally the advance was brought to a standstill before the concealed positions of the **Shuri Zone**'s main line of resistance (April 28). General Buckner, with the 77th Division and the 1st and 6th Marine divisions of the III Amphibious Corps still in hand, was faced with a dilemma: to attempt a frontal attack or—as the Marines suggested—effect an envelopment by amphibious landings on the southern tip of the island behind the Japanese. He decided on a double envelopment—frontal attacks piercing both flanks—and reorganized on a 2-corps front, with the Marines on the right.

COMMENT. *The situation was analogous to that in Italy in 1943. The proposed Marine amphibious landing, like the Anzio operation, would have been beyond range of mutual support from the main front. On the other hand, Buckner had relatively more amphibious lift. The Marines and some Army critics believe this was an error of overcaution.*

1945, April 12–13. Renewal of Kamikaze Assaults. Meanwhile, the Japanese suicide air strikes resumed. Nine more separate attacks were launched during the remainder of the campaign, until Japanese air strength had been expended. In all, more than 3,000 suicidal sorties hit the amphibious force and Mitscher's carriers, netting a total of 21 U.S. ships sunk, 43 additional permanently put out of action, and 23 more put out of action for a month or more.

1945, May 3–4. Japanese Counterattack. Ushijima hurled his 24th Division, supported by tanks and artillery, against the U.S. 7th Division on the eastern flank. A minor attack at the same time hit the 1st Marine Division on the western flank. A kamikaze attack from Kyushu supported the thrusts. Caught by American artillery and tactical aircraft, supplemented by naval gunfire, the Japanese offensive was crushed with loss of 5,000 men killed. U.S. losses were 1,066. In addition, the assault had disclosed the positions of heretofore hidden Japanese artillery.

1945, May 11–31. Buckner's Offensive. Under appalling weather conditions and despite bitter resistance, both flanks of the Japanese zone were finally pierced. Disengaging, Ushijima retreated slowly to the hill masses of the southern tip of the island.

1945, June 1–22. Final Operations. A climactic assault brought the 2 American prongs—Marine and Army—around and over the last organized position (June 22) and all resistance ceased. Neither Buckner nor Ushijima lived to see the end. Buckner was killed by an artillery shell as he peered from a Marine observation post on the front line (June 18) and Ushijima committed hara-kiri, just before his headquarters was overrun, 4 days later.

Japanese losses on Okinawa totaled 107,500 known dead and probably 20,000 additional sealed in their caves during the fighting; 7,400 prisoners were taken. Tenth Army casualties were 7,374 killed and 32,056 wounded. Navy losses were some 5,000 killed and 4,600 wounded. About 4,000 Japanese planes had been lost in combat and an equal number destroyed from other causes. U.S. naval aircraft lost totaled 763. The Fifth Fleet lost 36 vessels sunk and 368 damaged.

COMMENT. *The campaign had cost Japan the remainder of her effective navy and much of her air force. Ushijima's tactical decision not to oppose the landings—probably dictated by the high command—was a grievous error. The tactical handling of the Fifth Fleet was brilliant. The logistical support of a great fleet at sea over a protracted period —unprecedented—was a most remarkable demonstration of efficiency.*

The Strategic Air Offensive

1945, January–February. Reappraisal. The B-29 attacks on Japan had not been as successful as the American JCS had hoped they would be. Japanese fighter defense had been more effective than anticipated, and the loss rate of 6 per cent per mission was lowering morale and efficiency of the bomber crews. The weather over Japan at 30,000 feet was worse than had been expected; winds of several hundred miles per hour had thrown bombers off course and decreased effectiveness of their attacks; ice forming on the wings and on the windshields affected plane performance, obscured pilots' vision, and reduced accuracy of instruments and bombsights. Fog often made visual bombing impossible, and radar was not sufficiently accurate for precise concentration of bombs on targets from a small number of planes. Nevertheless, the raids were having some effect on Japan. The strain of frequent alerts reduced worker efficiency and lowered the morale of the whole population. Furthermore, the concentration of attacks on aircraft plants had forced the dispersal of these plants, causing a decline in Japanese aircraft production. Since the operations from the Marianas were more effective and less costly than those through Ch'engtu in China, it was decided to shift the XX Bomber Command from India to the Marianas so as to bring the whole Twentieth Air Force (General **Nathan F. Twining**) together. Meanwhile, General LeMay, because of his experience and success with the XX Bomber Command, was ordered from India to the Marianas to command the XXI Bomber Command.

1945, February–March. Developing New Tactics. The dispersal of Japanese aircraft plants, plus continuing high losses among bomber crews, caused General LeMay and his staff to decide to change the tactics to try a new bombing method that LeMay and Chennault had worked out in joint operations in China: low-level incendiary attacks instead of high-level, high-explosive bombing attacks.

1945, March 9–10. The Tokyo Raid. A night attack by 334 B-29's, flying at about 7,000 feet, initiated the new tactics. A total of 1,667 tons of incendiary bombs was dropped in the most destructive single air raid in history. Widespread fires created a fire storm similar to those which had devastated Hamburg, Dresden, and Darmstadt in Germany. Fifteen square miles of the city were destroyed; more than 83,000 people were killed, nearly 100,000 injured.

1945, March 9–19. Inaugurating the New Phase of Strategic Bombardment. A new pattern of operations was created as the success of the Tokyo raid was repeated 4 times in 10 nights. The low-level attacks permitted the bombers to carry nearly three times heavier bomb loads than those they could lift to 30,000 feet. But because of the danger of Japanese antiaircraft fire and Japanese fighter defense, the raids were made at night. A total of 9,365 tons of incendiary bombs was dropped, 3 times the weight of bombs dropped on Japan during the previous 3½-month period. Thirty-two square miles of the most important industrial areas of Japan were destroyed. Perhaps most important, only 22 B-29's were lost on these raids—1.4 per cent of 1,595 sorties. This dramatic reduction in losses was due to ineffectiveness of Japanese fighters in night operations, plus the use of Iwo Jima as a navigational aid and an emergency landing field. Morale of the Superfortress crews rose, and so did the efficiency of their operations.

1945, April 7. Appearance of American Escort Fighters. The VII Fighter Command, moved to Iwo Jima shortly after its capture, began to send its long-range P-47 Thunderbolt fighters, and its even more effective P-51 Mustangs, as escorts with the B-29's, which now began to mix medium-level daylight bombing raids with the low-level night raids. Losses of Japanese fighter planes mounted rapidly, while those of the B-29's continued to decline. American planes soon had clear air superiority over the heart of Japan (May–August).

1945, May–August. Climax of the Strategic Campaign. The arrival of the planes of the XX Bomber Command from India and China (April) increased the intensity of the raids. This continued to mount steadily as more air strips were built in the Marianas and as more planes arrived from the United States. The industrial areas of Tokyo, Nagoya, Kobe, Osaka, and Yokohama—Japan's 5 largest cities—were completely destroyed. The morale of the Japanese people plummeted. Millions had become homeless, and the government could not provide them with places to sleep. Food became scarce as the effects of the bombing on the transportation system, combined with Allied naval blockade, began to have its effect. And as the B-29's began to drop mines in Japanese ports, the blockade became even more effective. By midsummer the strategic bombing offensive had brought Japan to the verge of economic and moral collapse.

The Collapse of Japan

RELENTLESS PRESSURE

1945, January–August. The Submarines and the Blockade. American submariners had been the first to bring the effects of the war home to the Japanese people through a stringent blockade which began to have some effect in 1943. In these final months of the war, they roamed the waters of the China Sea and the coasts of Japan, making the blockade ever more effective. During the war they sank more than 1,100 Japanese merchant ships, totaling 4,800,000 tons of shipping—over 56 per cent of the total lost by Japan. They also sank 201 warships, totaling 540,000 tons, including 1 battleship and 8 aircraft carriers. Some 52 American submarines were lost, most without a trace, unknown and unsung heroes of the war.

1945, June–August. Preparation for Invasion. The staffs of General MacArthur and Admiral Nimitz completed plans for 2 massive invasions of the main Japanese islands. One, Operation "Olympic" (November), was to strike southern Kyushu. Operation "Coronet" was to follow in March, 1946, the mightiest amphibious force ever assembled, against the Tokyo plain of Honshu. Meanwhile, 3 main forces were setting the stage for these assaults by unrelenting onslaughts against the Japanese Empire: (1) the submarines of the Pacific Fleet (see above), (2) the B-29's of the Twentieth Air Force (see p. 1196), and (3) the Fast Carrier Task Force (see below).

1945, July 10–August 15. Last Raids of the Carriers. After its long ordeal off Okinawa (see p. 1195), Mitscher's Task Force 38 (once more under Halsey) rested briefly at its Ulithi anchorage, repairing damage and taking on supplies and replacements. Mitscher then sped back to the coast of Japan, where his planes added to the terrible punishment being delivered by the B-29's. The Fast Carrier Task Force included more than 1,000 American and 244 British planes. During these 5 final weeks of operations, the Americans lost 290 planes, the British 72, mostly to Japanese antiaircraft fire. During that time, they destroyed more than 3,000 Japanese planes in the air and on the ground.

THE ATOMIC BOMBS

1945, July 16. Explosion at Alamogordo. The first experimental atomic bomb was exploded at Alamogordo, N.M. Meanwhile, the 509th Composite Group of the U.S. Army Air Forces was established, and carried out secret training, in preparation for dropping atomic bombs, in the desert areas of Utah.

1945, July. Debate on Employment of Atomic Weapons. Among the few U.S. officials who knew about the atomic-bomb possibility, a high-level debate took place on whether these terrible weapons should be used and, if so, how. Some felt it would be immoral to use such destructive weapons. Others felt that it would be unnecessary, since they expected Japan to collapse soon anyway because of the blockade and the strategic-bombing offensive. After careful study, however, the JCS and a group of senior officials headed by Secretary of War Henry L. Stimson recommended that the bombs be employed. They believed that the shock of the terrible explosions might convince Japanese military leaders that they could not hope to continue the struggle, and that the very destructiveness of the weapons would give Japanese military men an excuse to surrender. Otherwise, the Americans feared, Japan's 4 million undefeated soldiers would continue fighting in Japan, China, and Manchuria, killing many thousands of Allies as they went down to defeat. Thus, even though these bombs would cause terrible losses, American leaders believed that hastening the end of the war would eventually save more lives than the bombs would take.

1945, July 27. Potsdam Proclamation. At the final war meeting of the heads of state of the U.K., U.S., and U.S.S.R., Truman and Prime Minister **Clement Attlee** (who had just replaced Churchill) issued a virtual ultimatum to Japan. The circumstances indicated that Stalin approved, even though Russia and Japan were not at war. Japan was warned that if she did not surrender at once, it would mean "the inevitable and complete destruction of the Japanese armed forces and . . . the utter devastation of the Japanese homeland." Japan attempted to reply through the U.S.S.R., but the Kremlin did not relay the message. Since Japan seemingly did not reply, President Truman therefore approved the plans for dropping atomic bombs on Japan.

1945, August 6. Hiroshima. This city of more than 300,000 people was an important military headquarters and supply depot. It had not yet suffered severely in the bombing offensive. Early in the morning, an air-raid alert was sounded and most people took cover. Realizing, however, that there were only 2 or 3 planes overhead, many people came out, and so most of the population were unprotected when the bomb exploded over the center of the city. Two-thirds of the city was destroyed; 78,150 people were killed (most outright, in explosion or in fires, though some died later from radiation effects); nearly 70,000 others were injured and most of the remaining population suffered long-term radiation damage.

1945, August 9. Nagasaki. The second bomb was exploded over this seaport and industrial city of 230,000 people. Because hills protected portions of the town, less than half the city was destroyed; nearly 40,000 people were killed, about 25,000 injured.

1945, August 9. Soviet Invasion of Manchuria. (See p. 1188.)

THE SURRENDER OF JAPAN

1945, August 10. Japan Offers to Surrender. The effect of the atomic bombs was what Stimson's group and the JCS had expected. No one knows how long a fanatically militaristic Japan could have continued the war if the bombs had not been dropped. It is clear, however, that these weapons, combined with Soviet entry into the war, convinced the Japanese emperor and government that further resistance was hopeless. After brief negotiations by radio, Japan accepted Allied terms for "unconditional surrender," which actually included conditions the Japanese were eager to accept. They were permitted to retain their imperial form of government, and were assured of the integrity of the 4 main islands of the Japanese Empire.

1945, August 15. Cease-Fire. Japanese forces throughout Asia and the islands of the Western Pacific laid down their arms. General MacArthur and American troops began to fly to Japan (August 28).

1945, September 2. The Official Surrender. Representatives of the Japanese government surrendered on board the battleship U.S.S. *Missouri* in the heart of the Pacific Fleet, anchored in Tokyo Bay, while American planes filled the air overhead. General MacArthur, appointed by the Allied governments as Supreme Commander for the Allied Powers to initiate the occupation of Japan, received the official surrender of Foreign Minister **Mamoru Shigemetsu.** Among the observers of the ceremony were released prisoners American General Wainwright and British General Percival, whose respective commands in the Philippines and Malaya had been overrun at the outset of the war.

The Cost of World War II[a]

Nations	Total Forces Mobilized (million)	Military Dead	Military Wounded	Civilian Dead	Economic and Financial Costs ($ billion)
United States	14.9	292,100	571,822	Negligible	350
United Kingdom	6.2	397,762	475,000	65,000	150
France	6	210,671	400,000	108,000	100
Soviet Union	20	7,500,000	14,012,000	10–15,000,000	200
China	6–10	500,000	1,700,000	1,000,000	No estimate
Germany	12.5	2,850,000	7,250,000	500,000	300
Italy	4.5	77,500	120,000	40–100,000	50
Japan	7.4	1,506,000	500,000	300,000	100
All other participants	20	1,500,000	No estimate	14–17,000,000[b]	350
Total[c]	100	15,000,000	No estimate	26–34,000,000	1,600

[a] Many of these figures are approximations or estimates, since official figures are misleading, missing, or contradictory in many instances.

[b] This includes approximately 6,000,000 Jews of Germany and all occupied European nations, and approximately 4,500,000 Poles.

[c] In economic and financial costs, World War II was about 5 times as expensive as World War I; in military deaths alone, it was almost twice as costly; it was about 3 times as destructive in total deaths.

XXI

SUPERPOWERS IN THE NUCLEAR AGE: 1945–1984*

MILITARY TRENDS

GENERAL HISTORICAL PATTERNS

The period opened at one of the most significant crossroads of world history: inauguration of the Nuclear Age. Man, it seemed, had discovered the power of mass self-destruction (see p. 1197). When the U.S.S.R. in 1949 detonated a nuclear explosion, canceling U.S. monopoly of the secret, the menace chilled the world, threatening as it did mutual annihilation should a general war arise between 2 major powers.

War as the extension of diplomacy, it seemed to many persons, had reached the end of its usefulness. Yet wars, and the threat of war, continued while military men struggled in a fog of experimentation and frustration, seeking on the one hand to harness this new element in weaponry, and on the other to maintain and improve postures of the so-called "conventional" means of warmaking without resort to the use of nuclear fission or fusion.

The confused, tangled, and momentous events of the decades following World War II do not readily yield to systematic historical analysis, partly because they are still too close to be seen in true historical perspective, partly because it was a time of rapid transition. In terms of policy and strategy, and their influence on military affairs, however, 8 major historical patterns seem to have emerged.

Confrontation of the Superpowers

Political and military strategy of all nations was decisively influenced by the confrontation between the United States and the Soviet Union. The two superpowers towered over the other nations of the world, and the most important strategic fact of life for each was the existence and power of the other. The friction, or conflict, which resulted from this confrontation was called the "Cold War." Although, by the end of the period, Cold War grimness had been somewhat ameliorated by determined American and Soviet efforts to achieve a form of "peaceful coexistence" which both sides preferred to call "detente," the confrontation was still the major factor of world affairs, and relations were frequently chilly.

The Technological Revolution

The technological developments of the period may have been even more important historically than the confrontation between the U.S. and the U.S.S.R. In any event, the most significant development strategically was the emergence of nuclear power, although this was hardly more momentous than the beginning of the

* For the period from 1974 to 1984, see Addendum, p. 1346.

human conquest of space. The rocket power propelling a multiplicity of proliferating weapons systems was mainly responsible for thrusting vehicles into outer space. Man-made satellites girdled the globe; the U.S.S.R. and U.S. both put manned space ships into orbit and retrieved them safely; and American astronauts trod the moon in 1969 and subsequent years.

Other major technological developments included electronic communications equipment, enabling telegraph, telephone, and radio to be used in ways earlier undreamed of, reducing the time necessary to transmit ideas and the time available to react to events. The related developments of automation and computerization opened new areas of research and accomplishment; new and improved means of transportation reduced travel time, making the world seem ever smaller.

The Political and Economic Revolutions

The rapid break-up of colonial empires in a very brief span of time created many new states where often there was no group adequately prepared as leaders. Related to the end of colonial rule, and also manifested in countries other than the former colonial dependencies, was the phenomenon of "rising expectations" among the populations of the underdeveloped nations. But the ambitions of those poorer nations were frustrated in many ways. The result was increased unrest and instability in these nations and in vast regions of the globe.

The Conspiracy and Challenge of International Communism

The confrontation of two superpowers would undoubtedly have involved dangers and crises even if the idea of Communism had never existed. Nevertheless, the scope of the Cold War, the violence and the brutality which marked the world political revolution, and a large measure of the bitterness and hatred in the postwar world stemmed directly from the conspiracy of international Communism. There were, of course, a number of basic factors which generated Communism and which made many people susceptible to its doctrines and promises: poverty, political and social injustice, and authoritarian attempts to maintain an intolerable *status quo*. The Soviet Union and, to an increasing extent, Communist China took advantage of the susceptibility to construct a net of Communist parties throughout the world, and to exploit disorders and unrest in the underdeveloped regions.

The Growing Importance of International and Regional Organizations

This was an era of internationalism. Despite its failures and weaknesses, the United Nations enjoyed a number of successes in restoring or maintaining peace in troubled regions of the world. The concept of regional political organization, more or less within the over-all concept of the United Nations but involving only interested nations in problems that are primarily regional and local, was developed in several areas of the world.

The Trend toward Polycentrism

During the latter part of the period, centrifugal forces developed in both of the great sets of alliances which the superpowers built up in the years following World War II. Although both the United States and the Soviet Union were embarrassed and frustrated by this trend, the U.S.S.R. at first suffered more than did the U.S. This was due primarily to the fact that China, under aggressive and militant leadership, had become a leading Asian power and was explicitly challenging the leadership of the U.S.S.R. in the Communist world. The score was at least evened, however, by American loss of prestige in Southeast Asia, where the U. S. was unable to impose its will on a small and relatively underdeveloped nation, North Vietnam,

in hostilities short of a major national effort—which the United States was unwilling to undertake.

Efforts toward Arms Control and Disarmament

Over the previous century there had been a number of attempts to establish controls and limitations on the employment of armed force among nations. There had been nothing to compare, however, with the worldwide intensity, sincerity, and sophistication of the search for arms control of the post-World War II era. This was in large part the result of growing realization by all mankind of the potentialities of nuclear weapons, and a feeling of desperate need to control the use of such weapons before they are allowed to destroy civilization.

New Elements in Military Strategy

If only because of the development of nuclear weapons, military men were faced with the greatest problems of transition in military concepts, doctrines, and strategies that have been known in the history of military affairs.

Weapons—or at least evaluations of weapons—for the first time became determinants of strategy instead of merely implements of strategists, possibly because strategic thinking had not yet reached a comparable development and sophistication. Certainly the very threat or possibility of the use of nuclear weapons was a principal factor in shaping the nature of two of the major clashes of the period—the Korean and Vietnamese wars—and influenced the adjudication of a host of minor wars and crises. In any event, from the availability of these weapons grew a new concept of limiting conflicts through possession of almost unlimited power. The concept of deterrence, known to man since force was first used against another human, achieved new importance, subtlety, and refinement.

Practically all of the other historical patterns noted above affected modern strategic thinking in one way or another. For instance, from the Communist conspiracy emerged a new concept of "wars of liberation," in which an ideology harnessed and modified old and well-known methods of making war. The technological revolution brought a weapon system—the long-range strategic bomber—to perfection and had already made it obsolescent. From the impingement of the technological revolution and the economic revolution upon military affairs emerged an essentially civilian concept of cost effectiveness to affect all modern strategic thinking.

As a result of these changes, the organizational arrangements for co-ordinating the military and political efforts of the nation, and for managing and directing the armed forces, were dramatically changed—particularly in the United States—during these years in an evolutionary process that was not always clearly logical and progressive, but which endeavored to adapt the armed forces and their civilian leadership to the changed environment of conflict.

STRATEGY AND CONFLICT MANAGEMENT

These new elements in military strategy did not seem to alter the fundamental nature of strategy,* but they immeasurably complicated and confused the processes of formulating strategy, and of exercising it in situations of conflict or likely conflict.

---

* Based upon an intensive analysis of conflict experience and theoretical development during the period, in 1966 the Historical Evaluation and Research Organization defined three aspects of strategy as follows: STRATEGY—the art of employing all available resources for the purpose of achieving a successful outcome in a conflict of human wills. NATIONAL STRATEGY—the art of employing all resources available to the highest national authority for the purpose of achieving a successful outcome in a conflict between nations. MILITARY STRATEGY—the art of employing all resources available to a military commander in an actual or anticipated conflict against hostile, or potentially hostile, armed forces in order to carry out requirements established by national strategy.

Because of these complexities, the term "conflict management" began to be used to describe the control or direction of the resources at the disposal of the strategist or "manager of conflict."

The availability of nuclear weapons, and the almost certain catastrophe which would result from their use in any but the most controlled and limited fashion, divided warfare, and the concepts relating to warfare, into two distinct levels: the upper level of conflict, involving a general or "strategic" war of nuclear exchange between the superpowers; and a lower, or "conventional," level in which nuclear weapons would probably not be employed—but their possible use could never be discounted. This lower level, in turn, was considered to have various sublevels, or special forms, of violence. These differentiations were not at all new, but the distinctions took on a new importance not only because of the ever-present possibility of nuclear war but also because of the manner in which Communist theory and practice both exploited and fostered different kinds of violence in support of the nationalistic and international aims of the Communists.

There was not full agreement among military theorists and strategists as to the exact nature of these differentiations and distinctions, but both the significance and the complexities of the concepts can be understood by looking at a "spectrum of conflict" which was produced in one significant theoretical study at the end of the period.

The most significant aspect of strategic theory regarding the upper level of conflict was the concept of **deterrence:** the effort to make the cost of resort to nuclear weapons too high to be profitable. In the United States during this period there was an intensive intellectual effort devoted to the development of theories of deterrence. The result was a series of deterrent strategies. At one extreme, and in vogue in the mid-1950's, was the brutal, direct concept of "massive retaliation": the threat to employ full nuclear force against the instigator of any form of aggression, direct or indirect, conventional or nuclear. The more subtle doctrine of "controlled and flexible response" prevailed in the United States at the close of the period.

The failure of "massive retaliation" demonstrated one of the serious strategic problems posed by the mere availability of nuclear weapons. It is not reasonable to employ truly cataclysmic means to combat threats or dangers which themselves are less than catastrophic. Neither friends nor enemies believed that the U.S. would attack Moscow in response to Kremlin-supported subversion in some remote region of the underdeveloped world. America's friends in Europe were not even certain that if the chips were down they could rely on America's assurances of immediate nuclear response in the event of Soviet aggression in Western Europe. These doubts were affecting both the vigor and stability of the western alliance at the close of the period.

The North Atlantic Treaty Organization (NATO) had emerged early in the period as counterfoil to Soviet aggression in Europe. NATO was unique in that its integrated armed forces, under a single command and backed by U.S. nuclear power controlled by the President of the U.S., constituted the first significant multinational force to arise in peacetime. Effective from the first as a deterrent, its usefulness was marred toward the end of the period by France's intransigent "independent" policy, which included a separate French striking force (*force de frappe*) with equally independent nuclear-power potential.

As the period closed, U.S. strategists had suffered a major defeat in Vietnam in an effort to cope with Communist aggression in an environment in which the existence of nuclear weapons automatically encouraged low-level violence under

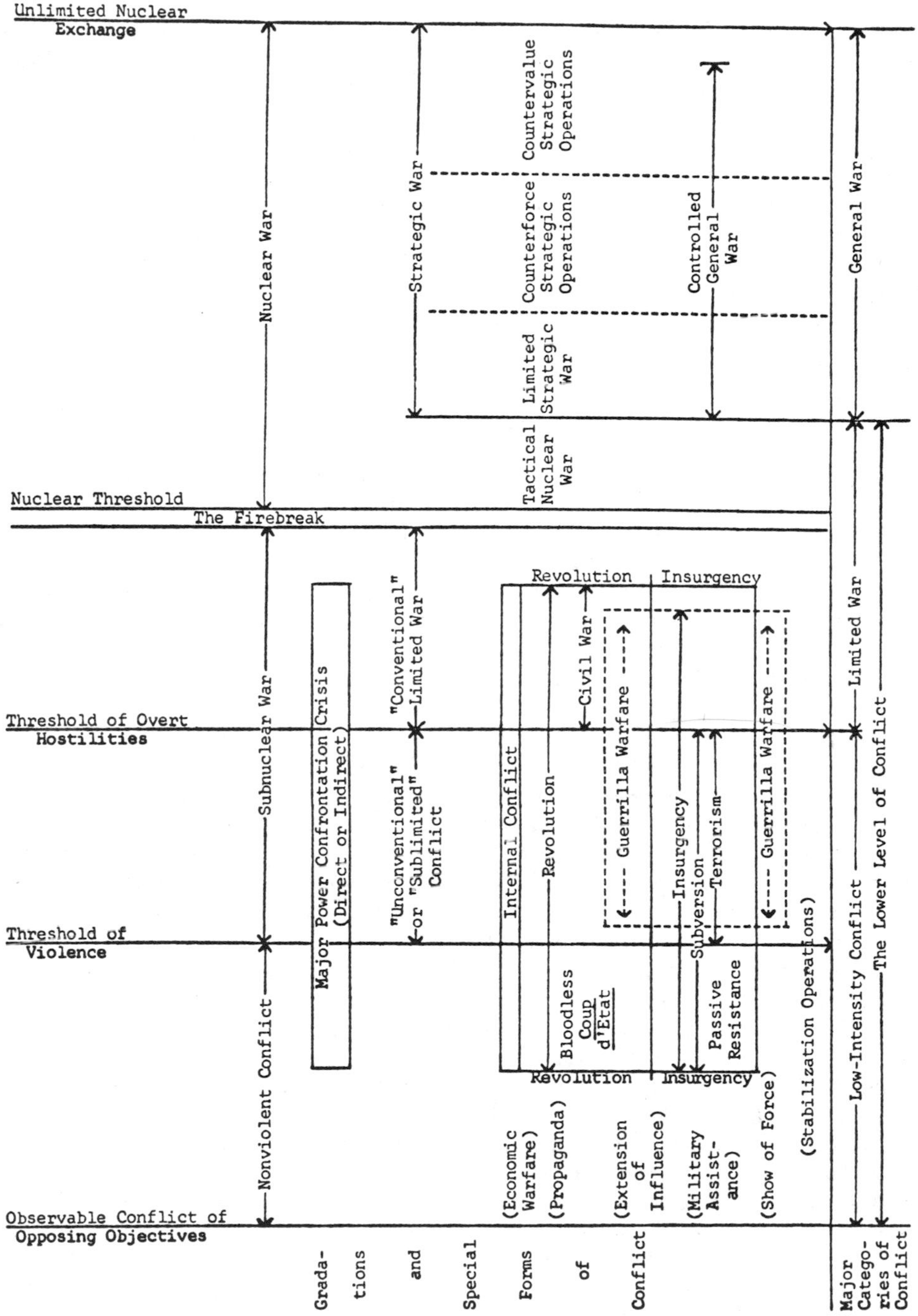

THE SPECTRUM OF CONTEMPORARY CONFLICT

the "umbrella of mutual nuclear deterrence" caused by the nuclear stalemate between the superpowers.

Nevertheless, the United States had developed a strategic policy of military assistance to nations which wished to oppose Communist aggression. Despite the frustrations of Vietnam—and many other frustrations—this policy had been generally successful as a means of projecting U.S. power and influence in the exercise of national strategy in the nuclear age.

On the other hand, the opposing Communist strategy had also enjoyed considerable success. Both the U.S.S.R. and Communist China, exploiting the situation created by the umbrella of mutual nuclear deterrence, kept up incessant thrustings to produce turmoil, expand their respective territorial holdings, and repair damages. In brief, this consisted in exploitation of conflict in three classes: civil wars, wars for "national liberation," and wars in defense of Communist regimes. The possible effect of the Sino-Soviet "split" on this strategy was still unclear at the close of the period.

LEADERSHIP

One the most unique aspects of this period was the manner in which top-level political leadership became more and more involved in the detailed and day-to-day military operations of military forces in the field and at sea. Outstanding examples were President **Truman**'s relief of General MacArthur from command in Korea (see p. 1247), President Eisenhower's assumption of responsibility in the U-2 incident (see p. 1332), French President de Gaulle's intervention in Algeria (see p. 1314), the apparently unfortunate control exercised by President Kennedy and his civilian staff in the Cuban debacle of the Bay of Pigs (see p. 1337), Kennedy's control of the so-called "quarantine" which successfully eliminated the Soviet missile threat in Cuba (see p. 1272), and President Johnson's direction of the employment of air power against North Vietnam (see p. 1297).

These actions in no way suggested a reversion to the old tradition of the king-general. They resulted from political recognition of the fact that any conflict situation had within it the potentiality of escalating to uncontrolled nuclear war. Thus a military man, acting on his own initiative in response to a local military situation in traditional (or unconventional) military fashion, could "escalate" a conflict out of control. Civilian leadership's increasing control over operations in or near conflict situations was merely a reflection of the fact that responsible authority must retain to itself the capability to determine what risks are to be taken, and how.

On the purely military side, in this period, **Douglas MacArthur**'s stature as one of the world's great captains was confirmed by his handling of the early operations of the Korean War, with the Inchon landings the capstone of his career. He was later wrong in disputing strategy with his commander in chief and he must also bear considerable personal responsibility for the subsequent temporary defeat of his U.N. forces by unexpected intervention of Chinese Communist armies in late 1950. This reverse no more detracts from MacArthur's military genius than does Waterloo negate Napoleon's over-all military stature or Gettysburg that of Robert E. Lee. **Matthew B. Ridgway**'s welding of the multinational U.S. Eighth Army in Korea into a competent war machine, and **James A. Van Fleet**'s later control of that army, were outstanding examples of successful troop leadership. The rapid defeat of the Chinese Nationalists by the Chinese Communists in the Chinese Civil War was evidence of **Mao Tse-tung**'s exceptional political-military genius.

Thus, before the period closed, it became quite evident that leadership in this new era of instantaneous decisions and cataclysmic potentialities was being exercised in a totally new way, a leadership linking field commanders to their political overlords in an increasingly complicated mesh of "command and control" systems far removed from Tennyson's "Theirs not to reason why,/Theirs but to do and die." Unless the field commander knew and adhered to the political objectives and directives of the civilian control, a tactical victory, it seemed, might be ephemeral. In other words, imaginative, creative military initiative must wear the harness of political limitation.

How to prevent subsequent galling and chafing from this tight-fitting harness, and still maintain military equilibrium on future battlefields, was at the period's close a basic problem confronting all commanders—from squad leader to generalissimo. One soldier who performed well under these constraints, however, was America's **Creighton W. Abrams** in Vietnam. Also performing well under similar constraints, although for far different reasons, was North Vietnam's brilliant **Vo Nguyen Giap,** the architect of Viet Minh victory over France and of North Vietnam's ultimate triumph over the United States and South Vietnam.

WEAPONS, DOCTRINE AND TACTICS

General

On land, sea, and in the air, rocketry, which had emerged during World War II after a century-long discard, became a major element of artillery. Its projectiles, capable of carrying either nuclear or high-explosive warheads, ranged from the giant intercontinental missile (ICBM), with practically worldwide range, to the one-man "bazooka" type of the foot soldier. Rocket missiles fell into four general classes: surface-to-surface, surface-to-air, air-to-surface, and air-to-air.

During midperiod, the fear of long-range nuclear bombing by long-range bombers or by intercontinental missiles resulted in abortive attempts to preserve the civil populations from holocaust. By the end of the period, the concept of civil defense had seemingly become less important for its potential saving of life—or reduction of catastrophic casualties—than as an element of the psychological considerations relating to nuclear-deterrent strategy.

Another new aspect of the terror of general war was furnished by the threat of contaminating an enemy country, poisoning atmosphere and vegetation by toxic measures: chemical, biological, or radiological. Communist propaganda played loudly on this theme as part of the strategy of terror. Factually, military scientists in all major nations were studying ways and means of prosecuting chemical and biological warfare as the period drew to a close.

On the Ground

Ground combat during the period produced a series of apparent abnormalities and contradictions, none of them vitiating fundamental principles of war, yet necessitating alterations in doctrine and tactics. The Korean War and later operations in Southeast Asia proved the serious limitations of mechanized-warfare operations in jungle and mountain terrain. Mobility of tactical maneuver—the concentration of fire by movement—depended in such regions on the ability of fleet-footed infantrymen to scramble across country.

The threat of nuclear warfare, with its consequent wide devastation, necessitated dispersion, yet ability for rapid concentration remained equally essential, conditions mutually contradictory. Furthermore, the multiplicity of communications essential to command control under such conditions became an enormous problem.

The helicopter, useful for reconnaissance, supply, transport of small packets of troops, and evacuation of wounded, supplanted the jeep as ubiquitous cross-country vehicle. In U.S. combat doctrine, so-called "sky cavalry" units utilized the helicopter to enhance the cross-country capability of the infantryman, and to provide him with flexible combat and logistical support. Through a confusing welter of statistical claims and counterclaims, the mobility of the helicopter, as well as its vulnerability to ground fire, were clearly demonstrated in the guerrilla-warfare operations in Vietnam.

Still another contradiction was to be found in an experimental trend in hand-weapon usage to the theory of the cone of fire rather than the individual aimed fire of the trained marksman. U.S. ordnance theorists seemingly turned the clock back a century and a half by equipping the American rifleman with a lighter weapon capable of firing three different loads: a .22-cal. bullet, lacking the shock action of the heavier calibers; a species of pocket shrapnel (a sheaf of fine steel arrows—*flechettes*); and a cartridge containing two bullets—a throwback to the "buck and ball" loads of smoothbore days. This trend seemed to ignore the fact that a host of electronic and optical improvements were increasing the lethal potential of the individual marksman.

The answer was that increased rates of fire were permitting the application to infantry fire power—consciously or not—of concepts of massed fire already pioneered by American field artillery. Reasonable accuracy, combined with such massing, assured effective neutralization of an enemy, and probably as much or more lethal effect as would have been provided by a smaller volume of more accurately aimed fire. The advantages were undeniable, so long as there was a logistical capability to "feed the battle." There remained, nonetheless, a need for precision, aimed fire among infantrymen as well as in the artillery. There was also evidence that the bayonet, as proven in the Korean War, was still a potential arbiter in hand-to-hand combat.

The days of the elite versus the mass, foreshadowed long ago by the grenadier and the light infantryman, and later by the *Sturmtruppen,* paratroopers, and Special Forces of World War II, seemed to be returning. The green beret of U.S. Special Forces in Vietnam became a status symbol, denoting a superior type of warrior. Whether or not this selectivity would survive cost-effectiveness scrutiny, or whether it might in the long run produce a deleterious inferiority complex in the run-of-the-mill foot soldier, were still moot questions.

The tank, which had emerged from World War II as the major ground battlefield weapon, retained its primacy, actual and potential, in those parts of the world where geography permitted its effective employment. This was demonstrated in the Indian-Pakistani battlefields in the arid Punjab-Kashmir region, as well in the lush farmlands of the Ganges Valley. Tanks dominated the operations of Arabs and Israelis in the Second and Third Arab-Israeli wars. This was only partially modified by the results of the Fourth Arab-Israeli War, in which the dominance was reduced, but not eliminated, by determined infantrymen armed with relatively inexpensive, effective antitank rockets and guided missiles. Despite a partial restoration of balance between infantry and armor in that war, it still seemed that—at least in the mid-1970's—the most effective antitank weapon was still the high velocity gun of a hostile tank.

Nuclear-powered attack submarine

At Sea

The essential importance of sea power and its objectives remained unchanged during the period, as attested by the U.S. Navy's unchallenged control of the high seas. Significant trends were the projection of sea power inland and the logistical utilization of surface traffic, demonstrated during the Korean War and later operations in Southeast Asia and Middle East waters.

Nuclear power, combined with advances in rocketry, brought radical changes in both weaponry and propulsion, necessitating equally radical changes in ship construction. The nuclear-powered vessel, surface and submarine, could remain at sea indefinitely without replenishment of fuel if given periodic replenishment of victuals and ammunition from floating depots—an extension of the logistical use of the sea lanes developed by the U.S. Navy during World War II.

The carrier task force remained the queen of maritime weapons systems, although some observers doubted its survivability in general nuclear war. The nuclear-powered submarine, armed with Polaris-type missiles, launched subsurface, extended sea power inland as never before. To many sailors this was the prototype of the future capital ship.

Freedom of the seas from the always increasing threat of submarine warfare and the *guerre de course,* so menacing in two world wars, necessitated further development of the hunter-killer doctrine—fast, mobile weapons systems of surface and submarine craft, aided by naval air power, utilizing elaborate electronic instrumentation to detect and destroy enemy underwater craft.

During midperiod, rocket launchers appeared to be displacing tube artillery on naval craft. However, as demonstrated both in Korean waters and very definitely later in the South China Sea (see p. 1259), the precision fire of tube artillery was essential both in landing operations and in coastal actions involving small craft; as on land, the theorists were faced with the necessity for establishing proportional quotas of both massed and precision fire power, of both rocket and tube weapons.

Conventional landing operations faced almost certain destruction by nuclear weapons should general war break out. However, for smaller amphibious operations with so-called conventional weapons, the helicopter appeared to be the answer, with vertical assaults largely replacing the surface assaults. But the apparent vulnerability of this item of equipment placed an even greater requirement for control of the air than had been the case in World War II and Korea.

In the Air

Air power's principal problem centered about one crucial question—the respective capabilities of the manned bomber and the missile in delivering nuclear warheads. On the right choice rested, the efficacy of the free world's doctrine of deterrence. As the period ended, opinion was still divided and compromise governed.

Meanwhile, in both missile and manned-aircraft fields, important developments brought more speed and range in all areas of the air-power spectrum. Rate and range of climb increased. Concurrently, technological advances in optics went hand in hand with increased altitude for reconnaissance. The necessity that air and land power become a close-knit tactical team became more apparent. As a result, at least in the U.S., the Tactical Air Force drew closer to ground forces and its separation from the Strategic Air Force became wider.

The problem was far from being solved, however. The tactical use of fixed-wing aircraft in close support was complicated by the fact that the increased speed of jet-propelled combat aircraft restricted its fire-power efficacy to a minimal fleeting moment over the target, thus greatly reducing the pilot's capability for identification and delivery of fire. This same condition also impeded the value of fast-flying aircraft in reconnaissance, while vast refinements in ground-force antiaircraft artillery range, fire control, and direction increased the capabilities of defense against air power, regardless of the speed of the aerial vehicles. The complexities of the problem were increased by controversial attitudes on the type and method of close air support and the necessity for an instantaneous and almost infallible system of command control if air superiority and isolation of the battlefield—an enormous area were nuclear warfare contemplated—could be attained.

Nevertheless, by the end of the period, largely as a result of experimentation in Korea and Vietnam, the United States had developed a variety of techniques of close air support for ground troops involving what was probably the most sophisticated system of interservice teamwork in the history of warfare. Most of this support was provided by the Air Force's Tactical Air Command; some was given by the Army's organic helicopter gunships; and some very effective support came from Navy carrier aircraft. The ability of American aircraft to provide such support, however, had been clearly inhibited in Vietnam by Soviet-made surface-to-air missiles (SAMs) and multiple-barrel, light, automatic AAA guns. The potential of these antiaircraft weapons was further demonstrated by their effective use by Egyptians and Syrians against the Israeli Air Force in the Fourth Arab-Israeli War

There did not appear to be any ground weapon capable of offsetting the tremendous advantage accruing to an interservice team which possessed air superiority.

MAJOR WARS

The period was marked by five major, long-lasting confrontations, of which the most important was the "Cold War" of the superpowers, in which overt hostilities never took place, despite a number of crises and mobilizations. Of these near-conflict situations, the most important were the Berlin crises of 1948 and 1961 (see pp. 1263 and 1333), the Cuban Missile Crisis (see p. 1333), and the 1973 October War alert (see p. 1239).

All four of the more traditional major "hot" shooting wars took place in Asia. Of these, probably the most important was the Chinese Civil War (see p. 1305). The other three major shooting wars—the Indo-China War, the Arab-Israeli Conflict, and the Korean War—are discussed in some detail below.

The 1967 Arab-Israeli War (and to a lesser extent the 1956 war) provides a classic example of **Preemptive War** or **Preventive War** in which one side (in this case Israel), having decided a potential enemy is planning to go to war, and that conflict is virtually inevitable, decides to seize the initiative by starting the war at the time and place of its own choosing.

THE INDO-CHINA WAR, 1945–1975

BACKGROUND

Future historians may refer to the conflict which raged throughout Indo-China from 1945 to 1975 as the **Second Thirty Years' War.*** Although the principal operations took place in Vietnam, both Laos and Cambodia were also extensively involved in conflicts distinct from, yet closely connected with, the fighting in Vietnam. The principal conflict had dragged on, with fluctuating intensity, as a bitter, sanguinary, but basically localized colonial war and civil war when the United States was drawn in as an active participant in 1965. The conflict had reached its conclusion as this edition went to press.

While the pattern was slightly different in Laos and Cambodia, the confused conflict can be considered as having four main periods: **the French Period** (1945–1954), **the Geneva Period** (1954–1965), **the United States Period** (1965–1973), and **the Cease-Fire Period** (1973–1975). Of these, the first two and the last were essentially local, internal conflicts, and are dealt with later in the Southeast Asia region under Vietnam, Laos, and Cambodia (see p.1295). The third period, a major international war, directly involving one of the two superpowers, is discussed below.

THE UNITED STATES WAR IN VIETNAM, 1965–1973

January 1965 was a period of intense Communist activity throughout South Vietnam. Viet Cong and North Vietnamese forces launched assaults on cities, towns, and military bases along the length of the country, causing massive casualties among the South Vietnamese troops and temporarily cutting South Vietnam in two by means of a push eastward to the sea from the central highlands. In early February Viet Cong forces attacked a U.S. installation and helicopter base in the central highlands, and on February 8 President Johnson ordered South Vietnamese and U.S. Air Force and U.S. Navy carrier planes to begin a systematic bombardment of carefully selected military targets north of the demilitarized zone (DMZ) which divided North from South Vietnam. On March 8, the U.S. 9th Marine

* As a possible minor historical footnote, the first known public reference to "thirty years' war" was that of Eric Sevareid, on a CBS news broadcast on April 22, 1975, after this draft had been written.

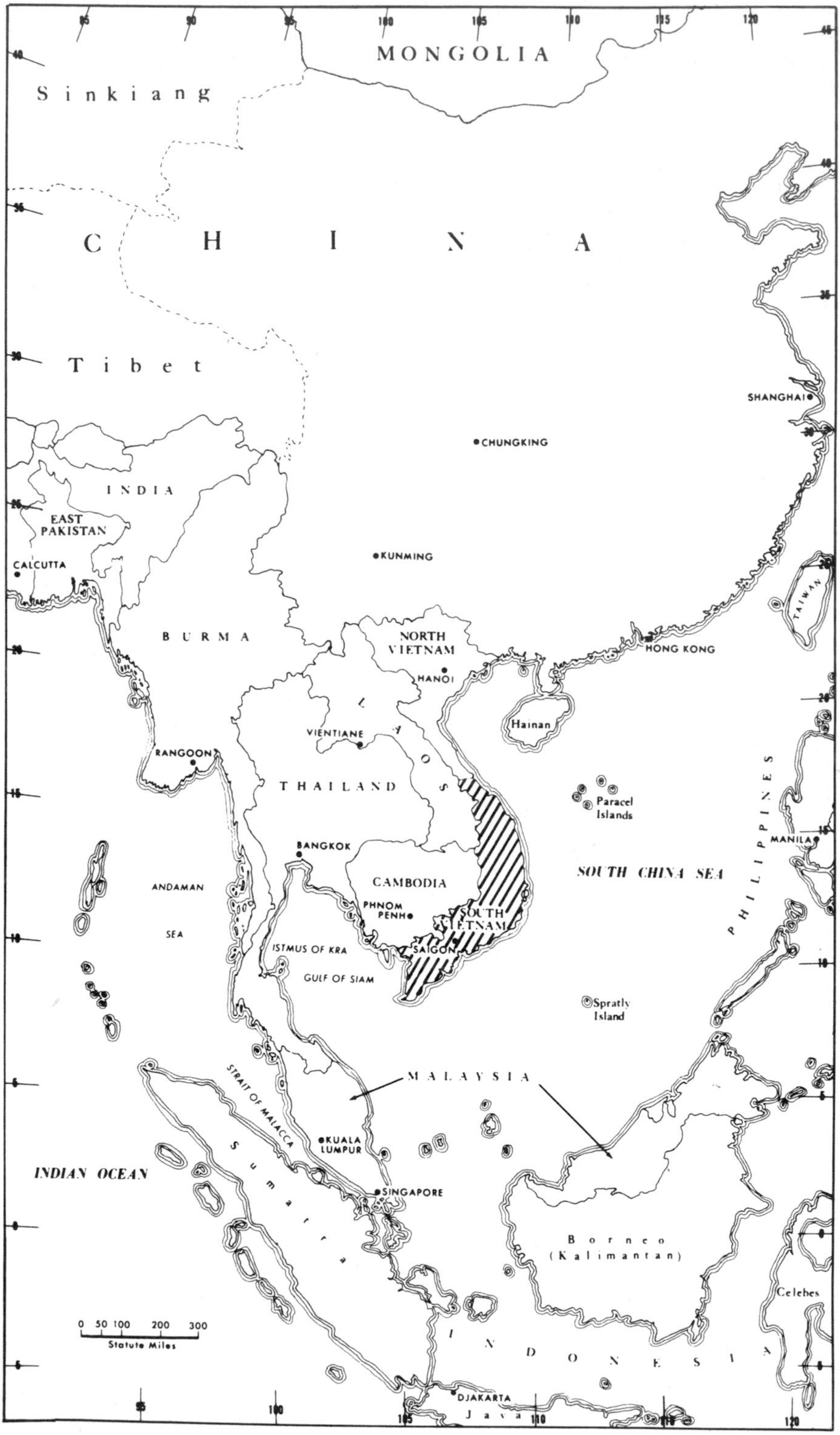

South Vietnam in Southeast Asia

Brigade landed at Danang, second-largest city in South Vietnam, situated 70 miles south of the DMZ on the Tonkin Gulf, and went into immediate action to repulse Communist forces attacking U.S. military assistance installations.

Thus began the pyramiding of American forces pitted against the North Vietnamese and Viet Cong, both supplied by Communist China and the U.S.S.R. (independently and without coordination). The U.S. had entered into the longest, oddest, and by far the most unpopular war in its history. It was a war without a fixed front; the enemy was here, there, and everywhere. The hostile military effort was led by General Vo Nguyen Giap, leader of the Viet units in the earlier successful rebellion against the French; he had made the operations of guerrilla warfare a science. American ground forces held only the soil on which they stood in a war of thousands of savage engagements without a single major battle in the conventional modern sense. The Vietnam war, a phantasmagoria of brutal combat, political and social entanglements, and unceasing frustration, could be viewed on television in American homes; military personnel flew to the area in commercial aircraft; and the military effort was heavily influenced by political considerations in Washington and the frequently overoptimistic views of the Department of Defense, as well as by the State Department, USIA, AID, CIA, and other civilian agencies present in the embattled South Vietnam.

Despite the rapid commitment of some seven additional U.S. ground battalions and an air squadron, and the commencement of raids on Communist bases in South Vietnam by U.S. B-52 bombers, by mid-1965 the military situation showed no improvement, and President Johnson decided that only a massive infusion of American combat troops could prevent the defeat of the Army of the Republic of Vietnam (ARVN).

The U.S. troops operated from fortified bases, carrying out search-and-destroy missions designed to eliminate Communist forces and base areas rather than capture and hold blocks of territory. Combat, except in sieges, consisted of clashes at platoon to no more than battalion strength, even in the occasional large-scale operations. The ubiquitous helicopter—gunship, personnel and cargo carrier, vehicle of rescue and evacuation of wounded—furnished amazing flexibility to the U.S. and allied troops.

In mid-1966 the U.S. forces launched their first prolonged offensive with the goals of locating and destroying major Communist units and bases. The offensive differed from earlier search-and-destroy missions in that it comprised lengthy and continuous sweeps rather than short, swift raids. Operations were carried out in the central highlands and in the provinces around Saigon. But when they were hard pressed, the Communists, relying on their knowledge of the terrain, were generally able to break contact and disappear into the jungle. When the allied sweeps receded, the Communist forces generally moved back into the territory they had held before.

Despite the execution of two massive operations in 1967, "Cedar Falls" and "Junction City," and the completion of the first U.S. base in the Mekong Delta, Communist forces were able to regroup and continue their operations against U.S. bases along the Laotian and Cambodian borders and south of the DMZ. These operations quickly gathered strength and momentum and climaxed in the Tet Offensive of early 1968.

This Communist offensive followed closely on the heels of well-publicized optimistic reports from field commanders; its size, scope, and fury shocked the American public and resulted in demands by many Americans for a U.S. withdrawal from Vietnam. Thus, although the Tet Offensive was a tactical military defeat for the Communists (since they suffered severe casualties and gained neither any substantial new territorial footholds nor increased support among the South Vietnamese) it was a major strategic victory for the North Vietnamese and Viet Cong.

Following the 1968 Communist offensive General **William Westmoreland** stepped down as Commander, United States Military Assistance Command, Vietnam (USMACV), and returned to the United States to become U.S. Army Chief of Staff. General Creighton W. Abrams succeeded him in Vietnam. To exploit heavy Communist losses sustained in the recent offensive and in U.S. operations in the A Shau Valley, and to enhance improved ARVN combat capability, General Abrams undertook a "Vietnamization" program involving the supply of all South Vietnamese units with modern weapons and equipment which would allow American forces to shift the bulk of the combat burden in the defense of their country to the South Vietnamese.

By 1969 the US military presence in Vietnam had grown to the colossal strength of 543,482, supported by the Navy's Seventh Fleet in the Tonkin Gulf, and strategic aircraft flying from bases in Guam and Thailand. Harbors, roads, airfields, cantonments, and warehouses sprang up to supply the needs of more than one million men. Other SEATO nations had joined the US-South Vietnam alliance and when American ground forces in South Vietnam were approaching their peak, troops furnished by Australia, New Zealand, South Korea, Thailand, and the Philipines totalled some 62,000 men, while an Australian cruiser had joined the Seventh Fleet's Tonkin Gulf patrol. (These allies would sustain 8,500 casualties including 2,500 men killed in action.) Non-combatant elements came too from West Germany, Taiwan, and Malaysia. The US furnished logistical support for all allied forces.

Concurrently, an enormous black market developed; South Vietnamese in collusion with corrupt members of the US Armed Forces robbed commissaries, munitions dumps, and post exchanges. Drug traffic boomed, red-light ghettos thrived, venereal rates by 1972 soared to nearly 700 per thousand men. Disillusion with the war grew in the US, yet the war dragged on.

In a major effort to shorten the war and destroy large Communist supply bases in Cambodia, President Nixon ordered US forces to move into the "Parrot's Beak" and "Fishook" areas of Cambodia on April 30, 1970, in conjunction with an operation under execution by South Vietnamese troops. Although vast amounts of equipment were seized in the two-month incursion, supplies continued to reach Communist forces in South Vietnam via the Ho Chi Minh Trail which ran through Laos.

Antiwar sentiment in the U.S. skyrocketed as a result of this "invasion" of Cambodia. The U.S. Government was never successful in justifying this action as part of a widespread war, in which Cambodia had already become involved.) Tens of thousands of young American men joined many others who earlier had dodged the draft, resisted induction, or deserted the ranks of the uniformed services. These protesters fled into exile in Sweden and Canada, went "underground" inside the U.S., or went to jail. The size and scope of antiwar marches, rallies, and organizations grew, drawing into their ranks increasingly diverse segments of American society, ranging from sincere patriots to cynical supporters of international Communist propaganda. Meanwhile, American POWs remained in limbo, the Communists refusing all details of their number, identity, or condition. Peace talks in Paris brought no agreement.

Although by 1972 General Abrams's U.S. and ARVN forces had virtually won the land war in South Vietnam, drastically curtailing Viet Cong and North Vietnamese operations and inflicting unacceptable casualties on their troops, the American public had almost uniformly come to see the U.S. involvement in Vietnam as a tragic mistake. Through secret negotiations conducted since 1969 between presidential advisor **Henry Kissinger** and North Vietnamese envoy **Le Duc Tho,** a peace agreement was signed on January 27, 1973, allowing for the release of U.S. POWs and the withdrawal of all U.S. forces from Vietnam. On March 29, 1973, the last American soldier left South Vietnam.

Included below are a few of the most important actions of the innumerable offensives, counteroffensives, and engagements of this war. See also the Statistical Summary (p. 1221).

OPERATIONS, 1965

1965, February 7. Viet Cong Attack U.S. Support Installations Near Pleiku Air Base. President Johnson considered this a deliberately hostile act. North Vietnam having ignored U.S. warnings to cease its direct assistance to, and control of, the Viet Cong in their insurgency against the legal government of South Vietnam, and having instituted or sponsored a campaign of terrorism and murder against American advisors in South Vietnam, he ordered retaliation against North Vietnam. He also ordered that U.S. dependents be evacuated from South Vietnam.

1965, February 8. U.S. Air War Begins against North Vietnam. U.S. air units, in cooperation with South Vietnamese air forces, carried out joint retaliatory air attacks on bases at Dong Hoi on the coast just north of the Demilitarized Zone (DMZ). This began a systematic but limited offensive against carefully selected military targets in North Vietnam. In response, the Viet Cong intensified its terrorism and sabotage against U.S. installations and personnel.

1965, March 8. First U.S. Ground Combat Force in Vietnam. The 9th Marine Expeditionary Brigade landed at Danang, Quang Nam Province, in the northern coastal area.

1965, May 14. USMACV Authorizes Naval Gunfire Support.

1965, June 28. First Major U.S. Operation. The 173rd Airborne Brigade (arrived South Vietnam May 5) lifted 2 ARVN battalions and 2 battalions of the 503rd Infantry Brigade into battle in Bien Hoa Province, 20 miles northeast of Saigon.

1965, August 18–21. Operation "Star-light." This was the first important victory for U.S. forces. Over 5,000 Marines moved against the Viet Cong 1st Regiment south of Chu Lai, Quang Ngai Province, in the northern coastal region, trapping a large force of Viet Cong and destroying a major stronghold near **Van Tuong,** just south of Chu Lai.

1965, October 23–November 20. Battle of the Ia Drang Valley. The 1st Cavalry Division (Airmobile) defeated North Vietnamese forces which had gathered in western Pleiku Province in the central highlands with the goal of cutting South Vietnam in half. Both sides suffered heavy casualties.

1965, December 15. First U.S. Air Raid on a Major North Vietnamese Industrial Target. This was a thermal power plant at Uongbi, 14 miles north of Haiphong.

1965, December 31. U.S. Military Strength in South Vietnam: 154,000; U.S. combat deaths in Southeast Asia since January 1, 1961: **1,636.**

OPERATIONS, 1966

1966, January 1–8. First American Unit in Mekong Delta. The 173rd Airborne Brigade, in Operation **"Marauder,"** successfully destroyed one Viet Cong battalion and the headquarters of a second in the **Plain of Reeds** area.

1966, January 19–February 21. Operation "Van Buren." The 1st Brigade of the 101st Airborne Division, the 2nd Republic of Korea (ROK) Marine Brigade, and the 4th ARVN Regiment carried out a search-and-destroy action to secure Phu Yen Province in the central coastal region.

1966, January 24–March 6. Operation **"Masher–White Wing."** 20,000 U.S., ARVN, and ROK forces conducted a massive sweep of Binh Dinh Province in

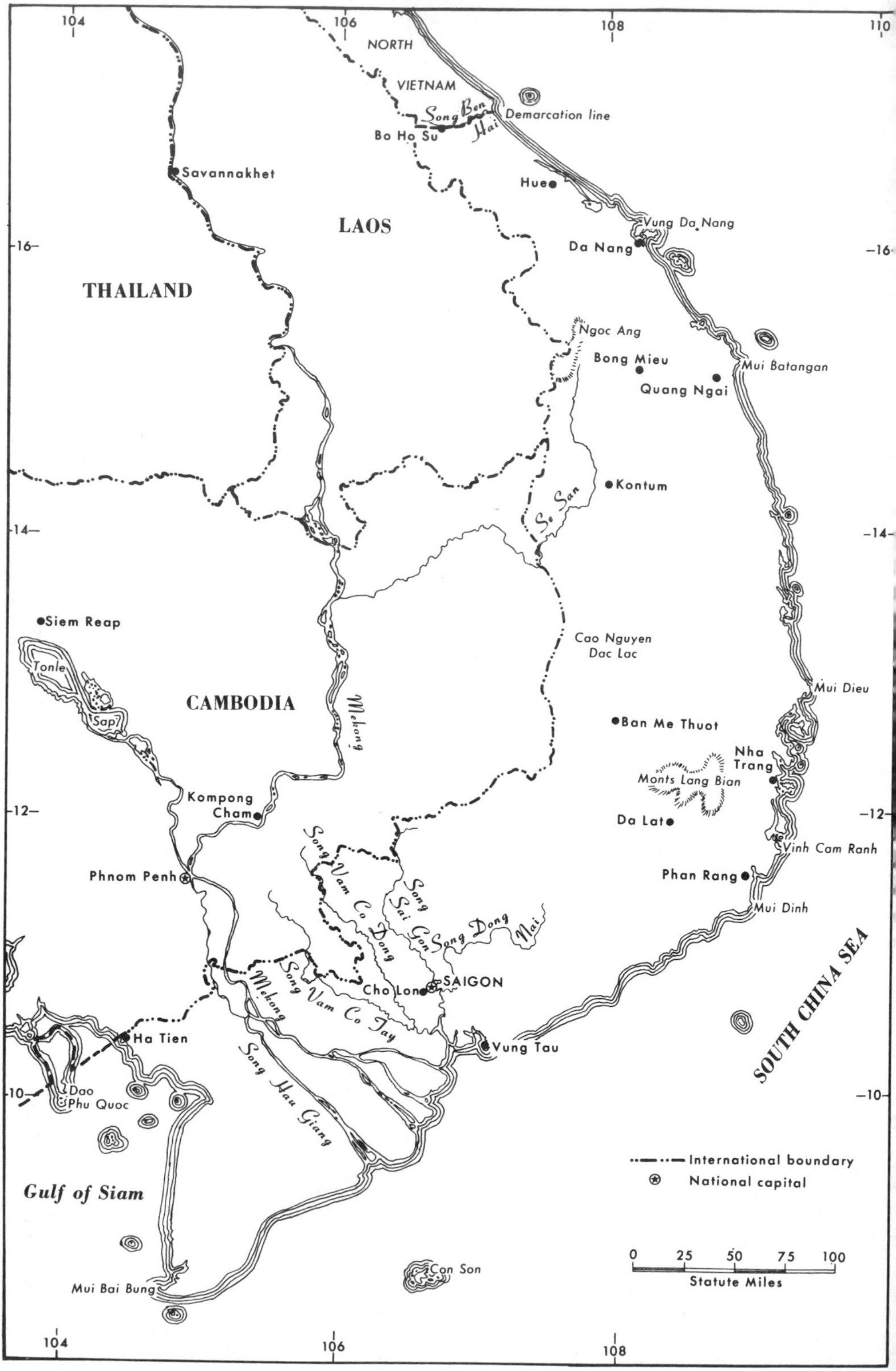

South Vietnam

the central coastal area. Search-and-destroy missions were carried out against two Viet Cong and two North Vietnamese regiments before allied units linked up with U.S. Marine forces moving north from Phu Yen Province.

1966, March–October. U.S. Marines Constantly Engaged in Northern Provinces.

1966, April 12. First Involvement of B-52s Based on Guam. Strikes were carried out against North Vietnamese infiltration routes at the Mugia Pass near the North Vietnam–Laos border.

1966, May 1. First U.S. Combat Operation against Cambodian Territory. U.S. 1st Infantry Division shelled targets on the Cambodian bank of the Caibac River after American troops on the South Vietnam bank came under Communist fire from the Cambodian shore.

1966, May. Beginning of Operation "Game Warden." Naval force of air, sea, and ground units began coastal patrols and inshore surveillance to prevent Viet Cong infiltration into the Mekong Delta.

1966. May–August Operations in Central Highlands. To prevent infiltration from North Vietnam and Cambodia, U.S. 25th Infantry Division, 1st Cavalry Division (Airmobile) and ARVN forces carried out operations in Pleiku Province, while the 101st Airborne Division was heavily engaged in Kontum Province.

1966, June–July. Operations of U.S. 1st Division in Binh Long Province. The American troops were operating with the 5th ARVN Division about 70 miles north of Saigon.

1966, June 29. First U.S. Air Attacks near Hanoi and Haiphong. These were against oil installations.

1966, July. U.S. Aircraft Strike North Vietnamese Positions inside DMZ. The International Control Commission (ICC) said it would act to keep the zone free.

1966, August 3–1967. January 31. Operation "Prairie." The 3rd Marine Division was continuously engaged in the Con Thien–Gio Linh areas near the DMZ.

1966, August 26–1968. February 20. U.S. 1st Cavalry Division in the Central Coastal Region. It conducted a continuous series of one-battalion leap-frogging search-and-destroy operations in Binh Thuan and Binh Dinh provinces.

1966. September 14–November 24. Operation "Attleboro." About 22,000 U.S. troops engaged Viet Cong and North Vietnamese forces in a series of small engagements in Tav Ninh Province next to the Cambodian border northwest of Saigon, with the goal of breaking up a planned Communist offensive. This was the largest U.S. operation to date.

1966, October 18–December 30. Operations in Central Highlands. The 4th Infantry Division and elements of the 25th Infantry and 1st Cavalry Divisions continued operations in Pleiku Province to prevent infiltration.

1966, November 30–1967, December 14. Operations in and around Saigon. One battalion each from the 1st, 4th, and 25th Infantry Divisions were engaged incessantly with Viet Cong forces (1966, November–December). These units were replaced by the 199th Light Infantry Brigade and ARVN troops who secured the area in less intensive combat (1967).

1966, December 31. U.S. Military Strength in South Vietnam: 389,000; U.S. combat deaths in Southeast Asia in 1966; 4,771.

OPERATIONS, 1967

1967, January 6. U.S. Troops Committed to Mekong Delta. Marines landed in Dinh Tuong Province and with the 9th Infantry Division established a base and carried out operations in Long An Province.

1967, January 8–26. Operation "Cedar Falls." The 1st and 25th Infantry Divisions, 173rd Airborne Brigade, 11th Armored Cavalry Regiment, and ARVN forces operated against the Viet Cong regional military headquarters and major Communist base areas in the "Iron Triangle," some 25 miles northwest of Saigon.

1967, February–September. Marine Operations in the North. While the 3rd Marine Division continued operations along the DMZ, the 1st Marine Division was operating in Quang Nam and Quang Tin provinces.

1967, February 22–May 14. Operation "Junction City." In the largest operation of the war to date, 22 U.S. battalions and 4 ARVN battalions moved against Viet Cong and North Vietnamese forces in Tay Ninh and neighboring provinces north of Saigon along the Cambodian border.

1967, February 24. First U.S. Artillery Fire on North Vietnam. Marine gunners shelled antiaircraft positions in the DMZ and North Vietnam.

1967, February 27. U.S. Aircraft Drop First Mines in North Vietnam Rivers.

1967, March 22. Thailand Agrees to Use of U-Tapao Airfield as B-52 Base. The first B-52s arrived in Thailand April 10.

1967, May 3. 3rd Marine Division Seizes High Ground near Khe Sanh. This provided a dominating position over infiltration routes from Laos into the northernmost province of Quang Tri.

1967, May 14–December 7. 25th Infantry Division West of Saigon. Search-and-destroy operations were carried out in Hua Nghia Province.

1967, August–September. Seige of Con Thieu. Marines repelled Viet Cong efforts against a major base in Quang Tri Province near the DMZ.

1967, November 1–1968, March 31. Operations around Khe Sanh. The U.S. 3rd Marine Division probed enemy concentrations along the DMZ in western Quang Tri Province.

1967, November 11–1968, June 10. Americal Division Reinforces Marines in North. This involved search-and-destroy missions in South Vietnam's 5 northern provinces.

1967, December 8–18. U.S. 101st Air Cavalry Division Undertakes Longest and Largest Airlift to Date. 10,024 men and more than 5,300 tons of equipment were carried in 369 C-141 Starfighters and 22 C-133 Cargomasters from Ft. Campbell, Kentucky, directly into combat in Vietnam.

1967, December 31. U.S. Military Strength in South Vietnam: 480,000; U.S. combat deaths in Southeast Asia in 1967; 9,699.

OPERATIONS, 1968

1968, January 21–April 8. Seige of Khe Sanh. About 5,000 U.S. Marines were isolated in **Khe Sanh,** Quang Tri Province (northern sector) by some 20,000 Communist troops (see Operation "Pegasus," below).

1968, January 30–February 29. Communist Tet Offensive. Breaking the Tet holiday truce, an estimated 50,000 Viet Cong and North Vietnamese soldiers launched well-planned and simultaneous attacks on allied bases and major South Vietnamese cities and towns. **Saigon** and **Hue** were the principal targets of the Communist assault. Fighting went on block by block inside the city of Hue until February 25, and in Saigon combat reached inside the American Embassy grounds. All of the assaults were repelled, and fighting subsided in late February with the exception of combat around the U.S. Marine base at Khe Sanh, which remained under siege. Although the offensive was not militarily successful for the Communists, it was a psychological victory since the American and South Vietnamese forces were taken completely by surprise.

1968, February 24. Air Attack on Hanoi. Aircraft from the carrier U.S.S. *Enterprise* struck at the port area.

1968, March 16. My Lai (Song My) Massacre. During a search-and-destroy operation by a task force of the U.S. 23rd (Americal) Infantry Division, C Company, 20th U.S. Infantry, some 200 unarmed civilians—men, women, and children—were murdered in the village of My Lai 4 in Quang Ngai Province (northern sector). This outrage remained unpublicized for more than a year, and when it was disclosed it shocked the Free World and exacerbated antiwar sentiments in the United States.

1968, April 1–15. Operation "Pegasus." A force of 30,000 U.S. and ARVN soldiers, mainly from the 1st Cavalry Division (Airmobile), attacked to free the Marines besieged at Khe Sanh. The North Vietnamese had already begun to withdraw into Laos.

1968, April 8. Operation "Complete Victory." Over 100,000 men from 42 U.S. and 37 ARVN battalions undertook an offensive against Communist forces in 11 provinces around Saigon.

1968, April 19–May 17. Operation "Delaware." An offensive was launched into Communist base areas in A Shau Valley, Quang Tri and Thua Thien provinces (northern sector), by 1st Cavalry Division (Airmobile), 101st Airborne Division, elements of the 196th Light Infantry Brigade, 1st ARVN Division, and ARVN Task Force Bravo (Airborne), designed to prevent an expected attack against Hue.

1968, April. Mobile Riverine Force Begins

Operations. Activities took place along inland waterways of Mekong Delta.

1968, May 5–9. Communist Spring Offensive. Attacks were launched on 122 military installations, airfields, and towns throughout South Vietnam, including Saigon. The attacks were unsuccessful.

1968, May 10. Paris Peace Talks Begin. U.S. and North Vietnamese officials began discussions.

1968, May 19–June 21. Nightly Rocket Attacks Against Saigon. More than 100,000 civilians were left homeless within the city.

1968, July 3. General Creighton W. Abrams Assumes Command. He replaced General William Westmoreland (who became Army Chief of Staff) as Commander of USMACV.

1968, July 14–18. Intensified B-52 Operations. They struck supply bases and troop concentrations 15 miles north of the DMZ (July 14) and North Vietnamese SAM sites for the first time (July 18).

1968, August 17. Third Communist Offensive. This was mounted throughout South Vietnam except the Delta; rocket attacks on Saigon resumed August 21.

1968, September 30. U.S.S. *New Jersey* Begins Combat Operations near DMZ. This was the first combat use of a U.S. battleship since July 1953.

1968, October 18. Operation "Sea Lords." This was launched by three U.S. naval task forces to interdict Viet Cong infiltration routes from Cambodia into the Mekong Delta and coordinate naval operations in the Delta.

1968, October 31. U.S. Ceases Attacks on North Vietnam. President Johnson ordered complete cessation of air, naval, and ground bombardment north of the DMZ, effective at 0800 EST November 1, in an effort to encourage peace negotiations.

1968, December 31. U.S. Military Strength in South Vietnam: 536,040; U.S. combat deaths in Southeast Asia in 1968: 14,437.

OPERATIONS, 1969

1969, January 25. First Substantive Peace Talks in Paris.

1969, February 6. American-Vietnamese Staff Organized to Facilitate "Vietnamization." The combined U.S.–Republic of Vietnam Armed Forces (RVNAF) Joint General Staff was to facilitate increasing Vietnamese responsibility for operations and to improve and modernize the RVNAF.

1969, February 23–March 29. Communist Offensive. This began with a series of rocket and mortar attacks against over 100 cities and bases throughout South Vietnam, including Saigon; attacks peaked on February 26 and March 6 and 16.

1969, April 24. Intensive B-52 Raids. Some 100 B-52s dropped bombs on targets northwest of Saigon near the Cambodian border.

1969, April 26. First "Vietnamization" Transfer. The 6th Battalion 77th Field Artillery completed turnover of equipment to the 213th ARVN artillery Battalion in ceremonies at Can Tho, Phong Dinh Province, in the Mekong Delta.

1969, April 30. Peak U.S. Troops Strength in South Vietnam: 543,482. (See Statistical Summary for additional forces in Thailand and at sea.)

1969, May 8–20. Battle of "Hamburger Hill." As part of an operation against North Vietnamese infiltration routes, U.S. troops took Hill 937 (Ap Bia Mountain or "Hamburger Hill") in the northern A Shau-Valley, Quang Tri Province, after fierce fighting and 10 attempts.

1969, May 11–14. Communist Summer Offensive. This began with coordinated ground attacks throughout South Vietnam.

1969, May 14. President Nixon Announces Planned Withdrawal from Vietnam.

1969, June 5. U.S. Aircraft Resume Bombardment of North Vietnam. Strikes on North Vietnamese targets were the first since the November 1968 bombing halt.

1969, June 17. Communists Retake "Hamburger Hill."

1969, July 8. U.S. Withdrawal Begins. The 3rd Battalion, 60th Infantry Brigade, 9th Infantry Division, left Tan Son Nhut Air Base near Saigon for Ft. Lewis, Washington.

1969, July 25. U.S. Bombing Authorized in Laos. Prime Minister **Souvanna Phouma** announced that he had authorized U.S. bombing along the Ho Chi Minh Trail.

1969, September 3. Ho Chi Minh Dies in Hanoi.

1969, October 1. Vietnamese Forces Assume

Responsibility for Saigon Area Defense.

1969, December 28. Peers in Vietnam. Lieutenant General **William R. Peers** arrived to lead the investigation into the My Lai massacre (see p. 1216).

1969, December 31. U.S. Military Strength in South Vietnam: 484,326; U.S. combat deaths in Southeast Asia in 1969: 6,727.

OPERATIONS, 1970

1970, January 20. United States Protests Execution of Two U.S. POWs. The U.S. Government requested the International Red Cross to investigate the incident, which had occurred on September 30, 1966. The grave of the two soldiers was discovered by Marines (January 17) in Thua Thien Province (northern sector).

1970, January 26. POW Record. Lieutenant **Everett Alvarez, Jr.**, U.S.N., spent his 2,000th day in captivity, marking the longest time any American had spent as a prisoner of war.

1970, February 11. Partial Withdrawal from Thailand. Some 4,200 troops withdrew; 43,800 remained.

1970, February–March. U.S.-ARVN Offensive against Communist Supply Depots near Cambodian Border. Major caches were discovered. During this operation, U.S. troops entered Laos to establish an artillery base and mine the Ho Chi Minh Trail.

1970, March 14. U.S. Ammunition Ship Hijacked. S.S. *Columbia Eagle*, en route to Thailand, was hijacked by two mutineers and taken to Cambodia; the ship was later released by the Cambodian government.

1970, April 1. Communist Spring Offensive. Viet Cong and North Vietnamese forces attacked more than 130 military bases and towns throughout South Vietnam. After three days the force of the assault diminished as the Communist troops encountered supply difficulties.

1970, April 19, U.S. Operations in Laos Acknowledged. A Senate subcommittee released official acknowledgment that U.S. forces had been indirectly involved in conflict in Laos, with 100 American civilians and military personnel killed there since 1962; since 1966 U.S. forces had served as air spotters in Laotian bombers.

1970, April 30–June 30. U.S. Troops Enter Cambodia. President Nixon announced that U.S. troops had begun a ground offensive against Communist bases in Cambodia; the U.S. 1st Cavalry Division and the ARVN Airborne Division, totaling more than 40,000 troops, launched the operation in the "Fish Hook" and "Parrot's Beak" areas immediately across the Vietnamese border in Cambodia. President Nixon later (5 May) announced that U.S. troops would penetrate no more than 21.7 miles into Cambodia and that all U.S. forces would be withdrawn from Cambodia by June 30.

1970, May 1–2. Intensified U.S. Air Raids. These were the largest north of the DMZ since the November 1968 bombing halt.

1970, June 1–7. Fierce Fighting Breaks Out along DMZ. Communist forces began a continuous and concentrated shelling of the U.S. base at **Danang**, Quang Nam Province (northern coastal sector).

1970, June 30. U.S. Troops Withdrawn from Cambodia. The U.S. Command reported capture of 155 tons of weapons, 1,786 tons of ammunition, and 6,877 tons of rice. U.S. forces lost 388 killed and 1,525 wounded; enemy dead were estimated at 4,766.

1970, August 1. U.S. Close Air Support for Cambodians Reported. U.S. air attacks reportedly enabled the Cambodians to free **Kampong Thom** in central Cambodia and the village of Skoun, a suburb of Phnom Penh.

1970, September. Daily B-52 Raids along Laotian Border. This was to prevent further Communist troop build-ups and to disperse the estimated 40,000 troops already gathered and poised for an offensive.

1970, November 21. Son Tay Raid. In an attempt to rescue U.S. POWs, a specially trained volunteer commando force carried out a helicopter raid on the Son Tay POW camp in North Vietnam, 23 miles from Hanoi; however, the camp was found abandoned.

1970, December 31. U.S. Military Strength in South Vietnam: 335,794; U.S. combat deaths in Southeast Asia in 1970: 7,171.

OPERATIONS, 1971

1971, January 12. Vietnamese Navy Convoys Supply Vessels for Cambodia River. This was the beginning of escorting merchant ships carrying fuel and ammunition to Phnom Penh.

1971, January 30. Operation "Dewey Canyon II." This operation by U.S. forces, just south of the DMZ, was to secure that area and establish lines of communication to support a planned South Vietnamese thrust into Laos.

1971, February 3. Renewed South Vietnamese Offensive in Cambodia. USMACV announced that it was providing full air support for the offensive into the Fish Hook and Parrot's Beak areas of Cambodia.

1971, February 8–April 9. South Vietnamese Operation "Lam Son 719" in Laos. This had the objective of disrupting North Vietnamese logistics along the Ho Chi Minh Trail. The U.S. Command in Vietnam announced that no U.S. ground forces or advisors would enter Laos. The South Vietnamese 1st Infantry Division and 1st Armored Brigade seized **Tchepone,** Laos (directly west of Quang Tri City), the main objective of their operation and the primary supply center for forces coming down the Ho Chi Minh Trail (March 6). Preliminary reports at the conclusion of the action on April 9 listed 13,462 Communists killed and 56 captured; 5,066 individual and 1,935 crew-served weapons, 106 tanks, 422 trucks, and 1,250 tons of rice were captured. Friendly losses were listed as 1,707 (176 U.S.) killed, 6,466 (1,042 U.S.) wounded, and 693 (42 U.S.) missing.

1971, July 9. Northern Province Defense Responsibility to Vietnamese Forces. The turnover of "Fire Base Charlie 2," 4 miles south of the DMZ, marked the completion of the transfer of the defense responsibility for that area by U.S. forces.

1971, August 11. All Ground Combat Responsibility Turned Over to South Vietnamese. Defense Secretary **Melvin Laird** announced the completion of the first phase of the Vietnamization program.

1971, December 26–31. U.S. Fighter-Bombers Attack North Vietnamese Targets. Airfields, missile sites, antiaircraft batteries, and supply depots were struck in retaliation for Communist attacks on Saigon, DMZ violations, and attacks on unarmed U.S. reconnaissance planes.

1971, December 31. U.S. Military Strength in South Vietnam: 158,119; U.S. combat deaths in Southeast Asia in 1971: 942.

OPERATIONS, 1972

1972, March 30. Communist Easter Offensive. In the biggest offensive since the 1968 Tet campaign, some 20,000 North Vietnamese forces launched a four-pronged attack into South Vietnam across the DMZ with the goal of taking **Quang Tri City,** capital of South Vietnam's northernmost province, and driving the South Vietnamese 3rd Division from 15 border outposts. In retaliation U.S. aircraft and naval forces began bombing military supply facilities near Hanoi and Haiphong. Some 50,000 Communist troops, poised along the Cambodian and Laotian borders, drove into Binh Long Province north of Saigon (April 5), taking Loc Ninh (April 7) and securing half of **An Loc,** the provincial capital (April 13). In the central coastal region Communist forces attacked Binh Dinh Province in an effort to cut the counrty in two (April 18). Four North Vietnamese divisions attacked in the central highlands in Kontum Province (April 22), taking **Dak To** (April 24) and encircling the provincial capital of **Kontum** (April 29).

1972, April 7. Relief of U.S. Air Commander in Vietnam Announced. General **John Lavelle** was removed as Commander of the U.S. Seventh Air Force in Vietnam in March, retired, and demoted to lieutenant general when it was revealed that he had ordered some 20 unauthorized air strikes against North Vietnamese targets between November 1971 and March 1972.

1972, April 26–May 1. Battle of Quang Tri City. The city fell to North Vietnamese forces as the ARVN 3rd Division retreated to Hue. Heavy fighting continued elsewhere, particularly at An Loc and Kontum.

1972, May 8. President Nixon Orders Mining of North Vietnamese Harbors. Haiphong harbor and the harbors of 6 other North Vietnamese ports were to be mined and all land and sea routes interdicted.

1972, June 28. Appointment of General Frederick C. Weyand to Commander U.S. Forces in Vietnam. He replaced General Creighton W. Abrams.

1972, June 28–September 15. Second Battle

of Quang Tri City. South Vietnamese attacked with 20,000 troops and the heaviest concentration of U.S. air support of the war; by July 26 U.S. and South Vietnamese Air Forces had flown more than 10,000 missions against North Vietnamese forces in support of the ARVN ground action; after Quang Tri City was retaken (September 15) fighting continued elsewhere in the province.

1972, July 19. South Vietnamese Binh Dinh Province Counteroffensive Begins. This was an effort to regain territory lost in the central coastal region during the Communist spring offensive.

1972, July 28. United States Admits Damage to North Vietnamese Dike System. A U.S. government report admitted U.S. bombing damage at 12 locations but maintained that the attacks were on military targets and dike damage had been unintentional.

1972, August 12. End of U.S. Ground Combat Role. This resulted from the withdrawal of the 3rd Battalion, 21st Infantry, from Danang.

1972, October 26. Kissinger Announces That "Peace Is at Hand." In a public report of his secret negotiations with the North Vietnamese Kissinger said that final agreement could be worked out in one more conference.

1972, October 27. Temporary Halt in U.S. Bombing of North Vietnam above 20th Parallel. In recognition of North Vietnamese concessions in the secret negotiations, a bombing halt took effect at 1700 on October 23. (Bombing was continuing in North Vietnam below the 20th parallel, however.)

1972, October 30. U.S. Halts Naval Bombardment North of 20th Parallel. Simultaneously the U.S. stepped up shipment of war materiel to South Vietnam.

1972, December 18. Massive U.S. Air Attack Begins. Since no agreement had been reached, the U.S. resumed bombing strikes against Hanoi and Haiphong; North Vietnamese harbors were also mined. The Pentagon insisted that hits on hospitals and other civilian targets were unintended.

1972, December 30. Renewed Bombing Halt North of the 20th Parallel. This was as a result of North Vietnamese willingness for renewed peace talks.

1972, December 31. U.S. Military Strength in South Vietnam: 24,200; U.S. combat deaths in Southeast Asia in 1972: 531.

OPERATIONS, 1973

1973, January 8. Accidental U.S. Air Attack on Allied Air Base. USMACV acknowledged that U.S. fighter-bombers accidentally hit the base at Danang, Quang Nam Province (northern sector), causing several casualties.

1973, January 15. President Nixon Orders Halt to All Offensive Military Action. This included air strikes, shelling, and mining operations, and reflected progress in recent peace negotiations.

1973, January 23. Cease-fire Agreement Announced. Henry Kissinger and Le Duc Tho initialed a cease-fire agreement to go into effect at 0800 (Saigon time) on January 28. The final agreement was signed at ceremonies in Paris (January 27). Agreement provided for the release of all American POWs, the withdrawal of all remaining U.S. troops, and the establishment of an international force to supervise the truce.

1973, January 27. Defense Secretary Melvin Laird Announces End of Military Draft. He cited the Vietnam cease-fire agreement and the lack of further need for inductions as the reasons behind the decision.

1973, February 12. North Vietnam Releases First U.S. Prisoners. Starting Operation "Homecoming," 142 U.S. POWs were flown to Clark Air Force Base in the Philippines, then to Travis Air Force Base in California.

1973, February 21. Cease-Fire in Laos. The Laotian government and Communist-led Pathet Lao announced a cease-fire agreement to take effect at 1200 (Vientiane time) February 22, thereby ending 20 years of war. The U.S. immediately called on the Pathet Lao to release U.S. prisoners. On February 23 U.S. B-52s raided Communist positions in Laos at the request of the Royal Laotian Army.

1973, March 27. War Continues in Cambodia. The White House announced that the U.S. would continue to bomb in Cambodia until Communist forces suspended military operations and agree to a cease-fire.

1973, March 29. Last American Troops

STATISTICAL SUMMARY: UNITED STATES WAR IN VIETNAM, 1965–1973

	Total U.S. Forces Worldwide	Maximum Deployed Strength	Total Combat Casualties	Killed and Died of Wounds	Wounded	Prisoners or Missing	Non-Battle Deaths
Total	3,300,000	625,866 (3/27/69)	205,023	46,226	153,311	5,486	10,326
Army	1,600,000	440,691 ″	130,359	30,644	76,811	2,904	7,173
Navy	600,000	37,011 ″	6,443	1,477	4,178	788	880
Marines	400,000	86,727 ″	64,486	12,953	51,389	144	1,631
Air Force	400,000	61,137 ″	3,735	1,152	933	1,650	592
RVN Forces		c. 1,000,000	c. 800,000	196,863	502,383	N/A*	N/A
Other Free World**(1969)		72,000	17,213	5,225	11,988	N/A	N/A
North Vietnam and Viet Cong (est.)		c. 1,000,000	c. 2,500,000	c. 900,000	c. 1,500,000	N/A	N/A

* Not available.
** Australia, South Korea, New Zealand, Philippines, Thailand.

Leave Vietnam. Simultaneously North Vietnam released the last 67 U.S. prisoners, bringing the total number of prisoners released to 587. Only 8,500 U.S. civilian technicians remain in Vietnam.

1973, April 16–17. U.S. Air Strikes in Laos. U.S. B-52s and F-111s hit Communist positions at Tha Vieng at the southern end of the Plain of Jars in Laos.

1973, June 13. Supplementary Cease-Fire Agreement.

1973, August 14. U.S. Ceases Bombing in Cambodia. This was in compliance with a June Congressional decision. It officially ended more than nine years of U.S. air combat activity in Indochina.

THE ARAB-ISRAELI WARS

BACKGROUND

The roots of the conflict which has engulfed the Middle East for most of the period since World War II include the Diaspora of the Jews after the Roman subjugation of rebellious Palestine in the 1st century A.D., the Crusaders' conquest of Jerusalem in 1099, the Zionist Movement beginning late in the 19th century, the Balfour Declaration of 1917, the Allies' denial of Arab expectations in the Versailles Treaty, and the Nazi efforts to exterminate the Jews of Europe during World War II. It is beyond the scope of this text to evaluate conflicting interpretations of these emotion-charged events, or to assess responsibility for the conflict. Both the Jewish Israelis and their Arab opponents are convinced of the religious, moral, and legal righteousness of their thus far irreconcilable causes. The military historian can only seek to illuminate what happened, and how it happened, rather than why it happened.

The years since 1945 have been marked by eight distinct periods of hostility: (1) guerrilla warfare sparked by Jewish terrorism, 1945–1948; (2) the First Arab-Israeli War, or Israeli War of Independence, 1948–1949; (3) the Second Arab-Israeli or Sinai-Suez War, 1956; (4) the Third Arab-Israeli War or Six-Day War, 1967; (5) the War of Attrition, 1968–1970; (6) guerrilla warfare sparked largely by Arab terrorism, 1970–1973; (7) the Fourth Arab-Israeli War, or October War,

1973; and (8) strife in Lebanon (1975–1984) marked by two Israeli interventions in 1978 and 1982. The principal events of the four periods of overt or formal international hostilities (2), (3), (4), and (7), above, are covered in this section; the major events of the other four periods will be found in the sections on Palestine, Israel, and neighboring Arab states. For background through 1947, see p. 1276.

FIRST ARAB-ISRAELI WAR, OR ISRAEL'S WAR FOR INDEPENDENCE MAY 14, 1948–JANUARY 7, 1949

Despite previous debate, argument, and violence, it was not until the U.N. partition decision that the Arabs of Palestine and neighboring countries faced the reality of a Jewish state about to be established in their midst. Despite this, the Arabs did not systematically plan or organize to prevent this unacceptable occurrence. The highly organized Jewish Agency, under the leadership of **David Ben-Gurion,** prepared itself for the inevitable struggle. The Jews seized and maintained the initiative in the months of mounting violence that followed the U.N. partition decision. Early in 1948 the British Government decided to withdraw from Palestine on May 14, rather than wait until October 1, the date in the U.N. plan. The Jewish population in Palestine was approximately 650,000, the Arab population approximately 1,200,000.

PRELIMINARY HOSTILITIES, 1948, JANUARY–MAY

1948, January 10. Appearance of the Arab Liberation Army (ALA). Volunteers from all the Arab world, including Palestine, under the loose and vaguely defined leadership of Iraqi General **Ismail Safwat** and Syrian leader **Fawzi Kaukji,** assembled in Syria. A raid from Syria on **Kfar Szold** by a force under Kaukji was repelled by British troops (January 10). Another raid on **Kfar Etzion** (south of Jerusalem) by Arab Palestinians (the Army of Salvation) under **Abdel Kader El-Husseini** was more successful, but was finally halted by troops of Palmach, a small elite striking force of the Haganah, the Jewish Agency's underground army.

1948, January–April. Increasing Violence. A three-way war spread over much of Palestine. British troops attempted to retain order, but were primarily concerned with keeping open their own evacuation routes while incurring minimum casualties. The Jews systematically, and the Arabs in considerable confusion, were jockeying for position to seize areas not garrisoned by the British, and to be ready to move into British-controlled areas after the end of the Mandate. In the north, fighting was almost continuous in and around **Haifa,** despite the effort of British Major General **Hugh Stockwell** to maintain order; the Arab population finally evacuated the city after a climactic battle (April 21–23). The Jews were also successful at **Tiberias** (April 18) and **Safad** (May 6–12). In central Palestine there was continuous fighting along the Tel Aviv–Jerusalem Road, which ran through territory controlled by Arabs, as the Jewish Agency attempted to send weapons, food, and other supplies to the 100,000 Jews in the New City of Jerusalem. In fierce fighting on the road near **Kastel,** Husseini—perhaps the most effective Palestinian Arab leader—was killed (April 9). There was also hard fighting in and around the Arab city of **Jaffa** (April 25–May 13), finally ending in a mass Arab evacuation. South of Jerusalem the Arabs maintained siege lines around four Jewish settlements in the Kfar Etzion area, which was finally overrun by the Arab besiegers (May 14).

1948, April 9. Massacre of Deir Yassin. During the fighting for control of the Tel Aviv–Jerusalem Road, units of 2 Jewish terrorist organizations, the **Irgun Zvai Leumi** and the **Stern Gang,** slaughtered some 254 noncombatant Arab men, women, and children. Although mos

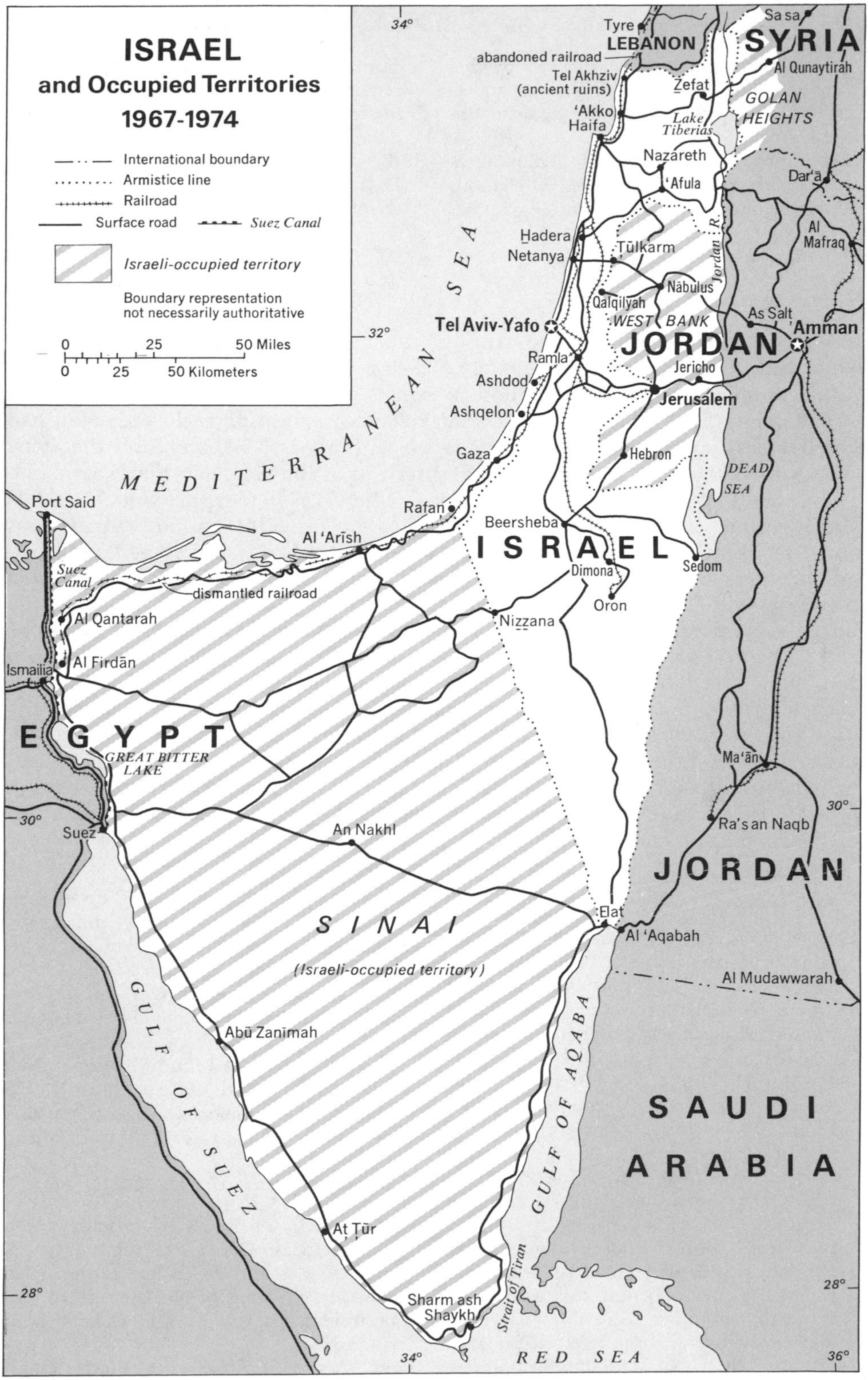

Israel and Occupied Territories, 1967–1974

Palestinian Jews were as shocked by this incident as were the Arabs, it added greatly to Arab bitterness against the Jews and Zionism.

1948, April 25. Neighboring Arab States Agree to Invade Palestine. Lebanon, Syria, Iraq, Transjordan, and Egypt began to prepare for invasion of the Jewish regions of Palestine, under nominal but ineffective over-all command of King Abdullah of Transjordan.

1948, May 14. Independence of Israel. David Ben Gurion became Prime Minister of the new state.

PHASE I: MAY 14–JUNE 11

Opposing Forces

Jewish. The Haganah, the army of the new Jewish state, commanded by **Israel Galili,** mobilized approximately 30,000 men, including about 2,500 in the Palmach under Colonel **Yigael Allon.** Weapons were available for approximately 30,000 more trained men in the Haganah reserve. In addition each settlement had a well-trained armed guard. Both the Irgun with about 3,500 men and the Stern Gang with 500 were under the nominal direction of the Haganah high command.

Arab. The Arab forces were various. The ALA had approximately 4,000 poorly trained troops in 4 major groups. Lebanon provided 4 infantry battalions and 2 artillery batteries, about 2,500 men; Syria 2 infantry brigades, 1 tank battalion, and an air squadron, about 5,000 men; Iraq 4 infantry brigades, an armored battalion, and 2 air squadrons, about 10,000 troops. The Transjordanian Arab Legion, commanded by British General John Glubb, comprised 3 brigade groups and 4 armored car battalions, slightly less than 10,000 men, by far the best trained and most effective of all of the Arab contingents. Egypt provided initially 1 brigade group, 2 or 3 independent battalions, 2 air squadrons, and supporting units, about 7,500 troops. In addition to about 4,000 in the Army of Salvation, there was also an unknown number of armed Palestinian Arabs (at least 50,000) in local units which—despite poor organization and lack of training—were a constant threat to the Jewish community and tied down a substantial proportion of the mobilized Jewish strength.

Operations in the North

1948, May 14–19. Syrian and Lebanese Invasions. Syrian invasion attempts were halted close to the frontier at **Degania** (where Major **Moshe Dayan** distinguished himself), **Zemach,** and **Mishmar Hayarden.** The Lebanese were stopped at **Malkya.**

1948, May 15–June 4. Iraqi Invasion. Advancing from Mafraq, through Irbid, the Iraqis crossed the Jordan south of the Sea of Galilee, but failed in repeated efforts to take **Geshir** (May 16–22). Meanwhile other units moved into Jenin and occupied much of Samaria with armored spearheads approaching Natania (May 30). An Israeli effort to take **Jenin** was repulsed (June 1–4), but this forced the Iraqis to consolidate in the Nablus–Jenin area and withdraw from western Samaria.

1948, May 20. U.N. Mediator Appointed. The U.N. Security Council appointed Count **Folke Bernadotte** of Sweden as mediator between the Jews and Arabs.

1948, June 6–10. Renewed Syrian and Lebanese Offensive. The Syrians failed in their efforts to take **Ein Gev,** but did capture **Mishmar Hayarden.** The Lebanese, with some support from ALA and Syrian units, took **Matka** (June 6), **Ramat Naftali** (June 7), and **Kadesh** (June 7). Exploiting these successes, the ALA was able to overrun much of north-central Galilee.

Operations in the Central Sector

1948, May 15–25. Battle of Jerusalem. In hard fighting, General Glubb's Arab Legion seized and held the eastern and southern portions of New Jerusalem and occupied most of the Old City without opposition.

1948, May 15–28. Siege of the Jewish Quarter of Old Jerusalem. With some assistance from local Arabs, the Arab Legion systematically fought its way through the Jewish Quarter, repelling two Jewish relief attempts. The besieged garrison was finally forced to surrender.

1948, May 18–June 10. Struggle for the Tel Aviv–Jerusalem Road. Jewish forces under American volunteer Colonel **David "Micky" Marcus,** failed to break through the Arab-held road from Tel Aviv to Jerusalem, but succeeded in protecting the builders of a new road through the mountains farther south; this was opened one day before a U.N.-sponsored cease-fire (June 10). A few hours before the cease-fire went into effect, Marcus (who spoke no Hebrew) was killed by a Jewish sentry when he ignored a challenge.

1948, May 25–30. First Battle of Latrun (Bab el Wed). A Legion battalion under Lieutenant Colonel **Habis el Majali** occupied Latrun to secure the Tel Aviv–Jerusalem Road and pose a threat to Tel Aviv. Repeated Jewish efforts to drive them out were repulsed.

1948, June 9–10. Second Battle of Latrun. Again the Arab Legion repulsed Jewish attacks.

Operations in the South

1948, May 15. Egyptian Invasion. Two Egyptian brigade groups advanced into Palestine, under Major General **Ahmed Ali el-Mawawi.** The main force, based at El Arish, advanced up the coast to secure Gaza and threaten Tel Aviv. The smaller force, mostly ALA volunteers, advanced from Abu Ageila via Beersheba toward Jerusalem.

1948, May 16–June 7. Egyptian Coastal Offensive. The Egyptians advanced through Gaza, held by ALA units and local contingents (May 16). After a bitter battle this column captured **Yad Mordechai** (May 19–24), then advanced through Majdal and Ashkelon to seize **Ashdod** (May 29), only 25 miles from Tel Aviv. A Jewish attempt to recapture Ashdod was repulsed (June 2–3). The bypassed settlement of **Nitzanin** was then attacked and taken after a bitter fight (June 7), securing Egyptian communications back to El Arish.

1948, May 16–June 10. Egyptian Inland Offensive. The other column, advancing through El Auja, occupied Beersheba (May 20) and Hebron (May 21), and made contact with the Arab Legion at Bethlehem (May 22).

1948, June 11–July 9. The First Truce. Under U.N. auspices, both sides eagerly accepted the opportunity to rest, reorganize, and regroup. By now the Israelis had mobilized an army of 49,000. The first international police force, 49 uniformed U.N. guards, arrived from New York (June 20).

PHASE II: JULY 9–18, "THE TEN-DAY OFFENSIVE"

Operations in the North

1948, July 9–14. Third Battle of Mishmar Hayarden. A serious Israeli effort failed to drive the Syrians out of their bridgehead west of the upper Jordan River.

1948, July 12–16. Israeli Nazareth Offensive. Israeli units expanded control of the coast north of Haifa, then turned their attention eastward toward Nazareth. An abortive offensive by Kaukji was thrown back, and the Israelis pressed on to seize his Nazareth base.

Operations in the Central Sector

1948, July 9–12. Israeli Lod (Lydda), Ramle Offensive. As part of a major effort to clear the Arab Legion from the coastal plain, and to secure the Tel Aviv–Jerusalem Corridor, the towns of Lydda (Lod) and Ramle and the nearby airport were occupied by the Israelis in tough fighting.

1948, July 9–18. Second Battle for Jerusalem. Israeli offensive efforts were repulsed by the Arab Legion.

1948, July 14–18. Third Battle of Latrun. Repeated Jewish efforts to take **Latrun** were unsuccessful.

Operations in the South

Israeli probes along the entire Egyptian front across central Palestine met with little success.

1948, July 18–October 15. The Second Truce. Once again both sides were eager to take advantage of the truce. The Israelis had taken the initiative in most areas of Palestine with limited success, and they felt the need for more time to prepare for a renewed offensive. The Arabs, shocked by the organization and equipment of the Jews and their ability to undertake major offensives in most regions of Palestine, were anxious to end the fighting as quickly as possible. The Israelis' total mobilized forces at the end of the truce were over 90,000, giving them a substantial numerical superiority over the Arabs.

1948, September 17. Assassination of U.N. Mediator. Confident of success in the war, many Jews were resentful of Count Bernadotte's peace efforts, which would have forced them to relinquish territory which they had conquered or which they hoped to occupy. He was killed by three unidentified men, apparently members of the Stern Gang. Dr. **Ralph Bunche** took over as U.N. mediator.

1948, September 29–October 15. Operations on the Egyptian Front. By mid-September neither side was paying much attention to the cease-fire along the Egyptian front. The Israeli pressure was particularly intense in the Faluja area, as they attempted to cut communications between the Egyptian coastal and inland corridors, and to open a secure line of communications into the Negev.

PHASE III: OCTOBER 6–NOVEMBER 5

Operations in the South

1948, October 15–19, Coastal Offensive. With Arab forces quiescent in the central and northern sectors, the Israelis concentrated their best forces against the Egyptians (now about 15,000 troops) in the south. An intensive effort to drive back the Egyptian forces in the Ashdod-Gaza area had some local successes but failed either to take any major positions or to cut the line of communications through Rafah.

1948, October 19–21. Israeli Beersheba Offensive. A drive to open firm communications with the Negev was successful. After severe fighting **Huleiqat** was taken (October 19) cutting communications between the two Egyptian corridors. Prompt exploitation of this success resulted in the capture of **Beersheba** (October 21). The road to the Negev was open. The Egyptian forces in the Hebron area and an Egyptian brigade group in Faluja were isolated.

1948, October 27–November 5. Egyptian Withdrawal. With their coastal line of communications now seriously threatened, the Egyptians withdrew from Ashdod (October 27) and Majdal (November 5), concentrating their remaining strength (other than forces in the Faluja and Hebron pockets) in the Asluj–Gaza–El Arish area.

Central Sector

1948, October–November. Limited Israeli Offensives. The Israelis succeeded in their efforts to widen the Jerusalem–Tel Aviv axis and to expand their control of regions on the central plateau, north and south of Jerusalem. They were defeated by the Arab Legion, however, in a probe near **Beit Gubrin** (between Faluja and Hebron).

1948, November 30. Israeli-Transjordan Cease-Fire.

1948, December 1. Union of Transjordan and Arab Palestine West of the Jordan. King Abdullah was proclaimed King of Arab Palestine, arousing the ire of most other Arab states. An official union of Arab Palestine and Transjordan was proclaimed in Amman, with the name Hashemite Kingdom of Jordan.

Operations in the North

1948, October 22–31. North Galilee Offensive. Kaukji's ALA probed successfully at **Manara** (October 22), just south of the Lebanese border. In response, the Israelis mounted a major offensive with the dual aim of destroying the ALA and securing all of northern Galilee. After an initial Israeli setback at **Tarshia** (October 28), the ALA was driven back into Lebanon as a result of Israeli successes at **Gish** (October 28) and **Sasa** (October 29). After occupying Tarshia (October 30), the Israelis cleared Arab resistance from the Hula Valley, retook Manara, and seized a strip of southern Lebanon. They then ceased operations to consolidate their gains.

1948, November 30. Cease-Fire in the North. Shaky local cease-fires were arranged by the Israelis with the opposing Syrian and Lebanese commanders.

PHASE IV: NOVEMBER 21–JANUARY 7

1948, November 19–December 7. Egyptian Offensive. Although the Egyptians failed in their effort to relieve the Faluja Pocket, they substantially expanded their holdings east of Gaza and in the Asluj area.

1948, December 20–1949, January 7. Israeli Sinai Offensive. With cease-fires in effect elsewhere around the periphery of Israel, the Israelis mounted a major offensive to force Egypt to withdraw from the war. In a series of encircling maneuvers, **Rafah** was isolated (December 22), then **Asluj** was taken (December 25), and next **Auja** (December 27). While one Israeli column turned west toward Rafah, the other, under Colonel Allon, struck south into the Sinai from Auja and took Abu Ageila after a short fight (December 28). Turning north toward El Arish, the Israelis seized the airfield and outlying villages, but determined Egyptian defense halted the drive east of the road and railroad (December 29). The Israelis turned northeast toward Rafah.

1949, January 7. Israeli-Egyptian Cease-Fire. As the Israelis prepared to attack Rafah, the Egyptians asked for an armistice, which was immediately granted.

THE 1956 WAR (SUEZ OR SINAI WAR) OCTOBER 29–NOVEMBER 6, 1956

BACKGROUND

1956, July 4–26. Tension along Israeli Frontiers. Mounting tension, including a number of armed clashes along the Israeli-Jordan and Israeli-Gaza borders, caused U.N. Secretary General, **Dag Hammarskjöld** to visit the Middle East to attempt to restore the cease-fire.

1956, July 18. United States Withdraws Promised Aid to Egypt for Aswan Dam Project. This announcement by Secretary of State **John Foster Dulles,** shortly after Egyptian President **Gamal Abdel Nasser** had announced that Egypt would receive American and British help for the project, infuriated the Egyptian president. American aid had been conditional upon economic viability, and the rejection was based essentially on economic considerations; however, political considerations also undoubtedly contributed: American unhappiness over increasingly friendly relations of Egypt with the Soviet Union and other states of the Communist Bloc, and pro-Israeli sentiment in the United States.

1956, July 26. Nasser Announces Nationalization of the Suez Canal. In retaliation for the American reneging on Aswan, Nasser announced Canal revenues would be used for the dam's construction. Britain and France raised the issue in the U.N. Security Council and started secret plans for military action (August 3).

1956, August 16–30. New Violence along Israel's Frontiers with Egypt and Jordan. Increasing seriousness of incidents aroused international fears of outbreak of a new Middle East war.

1956, October 5. Security Council Debate Opens on Suez Canal. An Anglo-French proposal for a return to some measures of international control was approved by a majority but vetoed by the U.S.S.R.

1956, October 15. Jordan Accuses Israel of Aggression in U.N. Security Council. This was the result of more shooting incidents and increasing tension on the Israel-Jordan frontier.

1956, October 24. Secret Anglo-French-Israeli Agreement. At Sèvres final agreement was reached on covert coordination of military operations against Egypt.

Opposing Plans

Israeli Plans

Ten brigades (6 infantry, 1 airborne, and 3 armored) were assigned to the Southern Command of Colonel **Asaf Simhoni;** 6 others were held in reserve in the central and northern sectors. Southern Command forces were divided into 4 task groups, each assigned to one of four corresponding land routes. The stated objectives of the Sinai Campaign, code-named Operation "Kadesh," were: to create a military threat to the Suez Canal by seizing the high ground to its east; to capture the Strait of Tiran; to create confusion in the ranks of the Egyptian Army, and to bring about its collapse. These objectives were directly related to an expected Anglo-French operation against the Suez Canal from the north.

Egyptian Plans

Evidence of the massing Anglo-French forces on Malta and Cyprus prompted Nasser to withdraw approximately half the Sinai garrison to the Delta region and the Canal Zone. Remaining in the Sinai were 2 infantry divisions and additional miscellaneous forces totaling some 30,000 men under the Eastern Command of Major General **Ali Amer,** most deployed in static defense positions in the northeast triangle formed by Rafah, Abu Ageila, and El Arish.

Anglo-French Plans

After Egyptian nationalization of the Suez Canal, British General Sir Hugh Stockwell was directed to formulate a plan for seizure of the Suez Canal by a joint Anglo-French expeditionary force. To avoid the appearance of imperialist aggression, the Anglo-French allies entered into secret negotiations with Israel to explore the possibility of relating their planned invasion to a renewed Arab-Israeli war. The modified plans called for Israel to create a threat to the Suez Canal, providing an excuse for Anglo-French intervention. The two governments would call on Israel and Egypt to withdraw 10 miles from the Canal, and when (as expected) the Egyptians refused, the allies would seize the Canal. Code-named "Musketeer," the operation was under the command of British General **Sir Charles Keightley,** with French Vice Admiral **Pierre Barjot** as deputy, General Stockwell commanding the land forces, French General **André Beaufre** as his deputy, Air Marshal **Denis Barnett** in command of air forces, and Admiral **Denis Dunford-Slayter** of naval forces. The necessity for coordination with Israel resulted in a delay of the planned operation from early September to early November.

OPERATIONS

1956, October 29. First Day. As the 1st Battalion of Colonel **Ariel Sharon's** 202nd Paratroop Brigade dropped near the eastern entrance to the **Mitla Pass,** the remainder of the brigade crossed the frontier and took **Kuntilla.** The brigade continued toward Thamad. Near Eilat, the border position of **Ras el-Nagb** was taken by the 9th Infantry Brigade, under Colonel **Avraham Yoffe,** in preparation for an overland march to Sharm el-Sheikh. Egyptian Commander in Chief, General **Abdel Hakim Amer,** ordered an infantry brigade and most of an armored division to cross the Canal to reinforce the Sinai garrison.

1956, October 30, Second Day. The Israeli paratroop battalion near Mitla Pass repulsed Egyptian ground and air attacks. Sharon's main body captured **Thamad** and linked up with the paratroop battalion before midnight. Farther north the Israeli Central Task Group (approximately a division), under Colonel **Yehuda Wallach,** captured **Sabha** and **Kusseima,** then began an attack on the formidable Egyptian defensive position of **Abu Ageila.** The Egyptian 4th Armored Division, having crossed the Canal, advanced to the vicinity of Bir Gifgafa and Bir Rud Salim.

1956, October 30. Anglo-French Ultimatum. At 1800 the British and French governments called on both sides for cessation of hostilities, withdrawal of all forces from the Canal, and approval of temporary Anglo-French occupation of Port Said, Ismailia, and Suez to guarantee freedom of transit in the Canal. Anticipating Egyptian rejection of the ultimatum, the Anglo-French invasion flotilla left Malta.

1956, October 31. Third Day. A large combat patrol of Sharon's paratroopers was ambushed in the **Mitla Pass.** Intense daylong fighting was climaxed by hand-to-hand combat for control of positions in caves in the walls of the Pass. Many of them were taken by the Israelis after dark, but the Egyptians still retained a substantial portion of the defile. A

Abu Ageila, part of the Egyptian defense was overrun, but one Israeli brigade was repulsed with heavy losses. Israeli armored spearheads from the Central Task Group took **Bir Hassnah, Jebel Libni,** and **Bir Hama.**

1956, October 31. Israeli Naval Victory. Following the bombardment of naval and oil installations in Haifa, the Egyptian destroyer *Ibrahim al-Awal* was captured by the Israeli Navy after a running battle at sea and was towed into Haifa harbor.

1956, October 31. Anglo-Egyptian Aerial Bombardment. All major Egyptian air bases were hit. President Nasser ordered a phased withdrawal of all forces in the Sinai to prevent them from being cut off by the expected allied invasion.

1956, November 1. Fourth Day. After another repulse at Abu Ageila, Israeli GHQ suspended further assaults on that stronghold. The Northern Task Group (approximately division strength) commanded by Colonel **Haim Laskov** captured **Rafah,** and Israeli armor advanced along the coastal road toward El Arish. By midnight all the Egyptian forces in the Sinai (except for the garrison at Sharm el-Sheikh, which lacked transportation, and the forces in Gaza, which were completely cut off by Israeli units) had begun to withdraw.

1956, November 2. Fifth Day. The 9th Infantry Brigade advanced down the coast of the Gulf of Aqaba toward Sharm el-Sheikh. Elements of the 202nd Paratroop Brigade and the 12th Infantry Brigade advanced to the Gulf of Suez from Mitla Pass and turned south also toward Sharm el-Sheikh. The Egyptians completed their evacuation of the Abu Ageila defenses and were pursued by the Israelis through Bir Gifgafa to a point 10 miles from the Canal. The 27th Armored Brigade under Colonel **Haim Bar Lev** captured **El Arish** and advanced as far as Romani. The 11th Infantry Brigade of Colonel **Aharon Doron** captured the northern half of the Gaza Strip, including the city of **Gaza.** All Egyptian forces not cut off by the Israelis completed the withdrawal from the Sinai.

1956, November 2. Egypt Accepts U.N. Call for a Cease-Fire with Israel. The Anglo-French bombardment of Egyptian airfields and military installations continued unabated.

1956, November 3. Sixth Day. The Israeli 9th Brigade continued its tortuous progress down the Sinai coast. The paratroopers advancing down the Gulf of Suez coast captured the oil fields at Ras Sudar, Abu Zneima, and El Tur. The 11th Brigade captured Khan Yunis, completing its occupation of the Gaza Strip. The commander of the Sharm el-Sheikh garrison, **Colonel Raif Mahfouz Zaki,** withdrew his forces from Ras Nasrani and consolidated for defense.

1956, November 3–4. Israel Accepts and Rejects the U.N. Call for Cease-Fire. Israel at first assumed that by the time the cease-fire could take effect, Sharm el-Sheikh would have been captured. Cessation of hostilities, however, would reduce Anglo-French justification for intervention at the Canal. Under Anglo-French pressure, therefore, Israeli Prime Minister Ben Gurion withdrew Israel's acceptance by attaching impossible conditions to it.

1956, November 4. Seventh Day. The 9th Brigade continued slowly down the coast over very difficult terrain and passed through Ras Nasrani. Three miles north of Sharm el-Sheikh the brigade came under heavy fire.

1956, November 5. Eighth Day. The first assault on **Sharm el-Sheikh,** just at midnight, was stopped by a minefield and covering fire. At 0530 the attack was renewed with air and mortar support, and at 0930 Sharm el-Sheikh surrendered. The paratroops on the Gulf of Suez road arrived in time to take part in the final assault.

1956, November 5. Anglo-French Air Drop. At 0820, 500 allied paratroopers landed at Gamil Airfield near Port Said, soon followed by over 600 more near Port Fuad. They seized the waterworks and isolated the cities. The Chief of Staff of the Egyptian Eastern Command, Brigadier General **Salah ed-Din Moguy,** arranged a brief truce with Brigadier **M. A. H. Butler,** the paratroop commander, but fighting was renewed at 2230.

1956, November 6. Allied Amphibious Assault. At 0650 the amphibious forces began landing at Port Said. Moguy was captured at 1000, but refused to order a surrender. At 1930 Stockwell received an order to cease fire at midnight. On his order Butler advanced to El-Kap before the ceasefire was effected.

Losses

	Killed	Wounded	Captured	Aircraft
Israel	189	899	4	15
Egypt (in combat with Israel)	(30 officers) 1,000[a]	4,000[b]	6,000	8
Egypt (in combat with Anglo-French)	650[c]	900	185	207[d]
Britain	16	96	0	4[e]
France	10	33	0	1

a. The most widely accepted figure.
b. Estimate.
c. The official estimate. Others run as high as 3,000.
d. Of these, 200 destroyed on the ground.
e. One of these was shot down over Syria by Syrian AA fire.

THE SIX-DAY WAR
JUNE 5–10, 1967

Background

President Nasser of Egypt, who had concluded an alliance with Syria (1966, November), accused Israel of threatening aggression against Syria and promised to come to Syria's aid (May 16). He moved several divisions close to the Israeli-Egyptian border, in the eastern Sinai. On May 18 he demanded the withdrawal of the United Nations Emergency Force (UNEF), which had been patrolling the 1948–1956 cease-fire line. U.N. Secretary General **U Thant** ordered an immediate UNEF withdrawal. On May 22, Nasser, having placed a garrison at Sharm el-Sheikh, announced the blockade of the Strait of Tiran, effectively closing the Israeli port of Eilat. While the United States, within and without the U.N., endeavored to find a formula for peace, both sides seemed bent on war. On May 30 Egypt and Jordan signed a Mutual Security Treaty, and Egypt at once sent General **Abdul Moneim Riadh** to take command of allied Arab forces on the Jordan front. A chronology of prewar events follows:

May 16 Egypt declared a state of emergency.
May 17 Egypt and Syria announced "combat readiness," and Jordan announced mobilization.
May 18 Syria and Egypt placed troops on maximum alert; Iraq and Kuwait announced mobilization.
May 19 UNEF withdrawal.
May 20 Israel completed partial mobilization.
May 23 Saudi Arabian forces prepared to participate.
May 24 Jordanian mobilization completed.
May 28 Sudan mobilized.
May 29 Algerian units moved to Egypt.
May 30 Egypt and Jordan sign mutual security treaty.
May 31 Iraqi troops began moving to Jordan.

Israel had earlier announced that it would go to war under any of the following conditions: closing of the Strait of Tiran; sending of Iraqi troops to Jordan; signing of an Egyptian-Jordanian defense pact; withdrawal of UNEF forces. All of these conditions now existed. War thus was inevitable, although Nasser surprisingly did not think his actions would provoke an Israeli attack.

The Opposing Forces

The following table shows the numerical strengths of the principal participating forces. In most respects the Israeli Army was better trained and much more flexible than any of its opponents, with the possible exception of Jordan. Israeli first-line aircraft were more heavily armed, and the quality and training of Israeli pilots and support units were so much superior to those of the Arab pilots (who were in short supply) that the Israeli Air Force, under Major General **Mordechai Hod,** was at least two or three times more effective than the combined air forces of its Arab opponents.

ESTIMATED MOBILIZATION STRENGTHS
June 5, 1967

	Mobilized Manpower	Division or Equivalent	Tanks	Artillery Pieces	Combat Aircraft	Naval Vessels[a]
Israel	230,000	8	1,100	200	260	22
Egypt	200,000	10	1,200	600	431	60
Syria	63,000	4	750	315	90	15
Jordan	56,000	3⅓	287	72	18	—
Iraq	90,000	5	200	500	110	15[b]

a. Including MTBs.
b. Not available for use against Israel.

OPERATIONS, SINAI FRONT

1967, June 5. Israeli Preemptive Air Strike. With the approval of Prime Minister **Levi Eshkol** and recently appointed Minister of Defense General Moshe Dayan, the Israeli General Staff, under Chief of Staff Lieutenant General **Itzhak Rabin,** decided that since war was inevitable, Israel should obtain the advantage of surprise by launching preemptive attack by air and ground. Early in the morning the Israeli Air Force, flying west over the Mediterranean, then south into Egypt, struck practically every Egyptian airfield and virtually wiped out the Egyptian Air Force. Later in the day, the IAF also destroyed the air forces of Jordan and Syria and—in retaliation for an Iraqi air strike against Israel—inflicted considerable damage on Iraqi air units based in the Mosul area.

1967, June 5. First Day. From north to south the Israeli forces comprised a reinforced mechanized brigade under Colonel **Yehuda Resheff,** a mechanized division commanded by Major General **Israel Tal,** an armored division under Major General **Avraham Yoffe,** a mechanized division under Major General Ariel Sharon; other smaller units were deployed along the frontier down to Eilat. Tal's division initiated the offensive by a drive into the Khan Yunis–Rafah–El Arish area. Resheff's brigade and attached elements drove into the Gaza Strip, and Sharon's division struck southward against the critical fortifications in the Abu Ageila–Kusseima area. Later in the day Yoffe struck southward between the divisions of Tal and Sharon, to penetrate into the heart of the Sinai, to cut off the Egyptian retreat.

1967, June 4–6. Accusations of US Participation. In a radio conversation monitored by the Israelis, King Hussein agreed with President Nasser to accuse the United States of collaborating with Israel, but quickly stopped the accusations after release of the taped radio conversation by Israel. Most Arab nations, except for Jordan, followed Nasser's lead and broke diplomatic relations with the U.S.

1967, June 6. Second Day. Gaza surrendered to Resheff in the afternoon. Tal, having secured Rafah and El Arish, sent a task force down the El Arish–Romani road toward the Suez Canal, and turned inland with the rest of his division and joined Yoffe. Sharon, having quickly captured Abu Ageila, sent part of his force to assist in the mopping up of Rafah and El Arish; with the remainder he struck southward toward Nakhl and Mitla Pass. Yoffe, after a brief engagement east of Bir **Lahfan,** successfully attacked the main Egyptian concentration in the central Sinai at **Jebel Libni** in a night assault. Unknown to the Israelis, Field Marshal Abdel Hakim Amer, the Egyptian commander in chief, had sent orders to all of the Sinai units to withdraw behind the Suez Canal; by this order he completed the demoralization begun by the Israeli attack the day before.

1967, June 7. Third Day. Tal's main body approached Bir Gifgafa; his northern task force moved past Romani. Yoffe's leading brigade reached the eastern end of the Mitla Pass, out of fuel and short of ammunition, and was quickly surrounded by withdrawing Egyptian units. Yoffe's other brigade was en route to relieve this isolated and hard-pressed unit. Sharon approached Nakhl. Other units cleared the northeastern Sinai, and airborne and amphibious forces seized **Sharm el-Sheikh.**

1967, June 8. Fourth Day. Egyptian armored units from Ismailia attempted to cover the general Egyptian withdrawal but were easily repulsed by Tal, who then pressed on to the Suez Canal between Kantara and Ismailia. Yoffe's division, having relieved its isolated brigade, pressed through the Mitla Pass and reached the Canal opposite Port Suez. After a grueling march through the desert Sharon's division took **Nakhl,** then followed Yoffe through the Mitla **Pass.** While there were a number of isolated Egyptian units still intact in the Sinai, for all practical purposes it was completely in the hands of the Israeli Army.

OPERATIONS, JORDANIAN FRONT

Uneasy Neutralists

Israeli strategy called for avoiding operations against Jordan and Syria until a decision had been reached on the Sinai front. At the same time Israel was strongly tempted to eliminate the deep Jordanian West Bank salient into the heart of Israel, and to wrest from the Jordanians control of the holiest places of Judaism in Jerusalem. There were good reasons for King Hussein to remain neutral; but Arab pressures to join in the war, combined with his recent agreement with Nasser, made neutrality difficult. Apparently he hoped that long-range artillery fire by 155mm "Long Tom" guns against Tel Aviv and other places would satisfy his Arab allies without provoking Israel to full-scale hostilities. However, Jordanian long-range artillery fire threatened to close down the runways at Ramot David, Israel's principal northern air base. Israel's leader would not allow this, and in mid-morning, June 5, decided on war against Jordan.

The Battle for Jerusalem

1967, June 5. First Day. Having decided that war against Jordan was unavoidable, Israel decided to take the initiative in Jerusalem, where sporadic firing, mostly by Jordanians, had already begun. Reinforcements were sent to Brig. General **Uzi Narkiss,** commanding Israel's Central Command, permitting him to take the offensive with three brigades, with the main effort by a parachute brigade under Colonel **Mordechai Gur.** The Israelis closed in on the old walled city of Jerusalem, whose garrison of one reinforced brigade was commanded by Jordanian Brigadier **Ata Ali.**

1967, June 6. Second Day. The Israeli advance against the Old City of Jerusalem slowed down in the face of stubborn opposition. Other Israeli units, however, tightened a wider ring around the city. The ridge to the east was seized, and a series of Jordanian relief efforts was smashed by combined ground and air forces. Elements of a tank brigade seized

Ramallah to the north, while another brigade captured Latrun to the west. For the first time since 1947, the old Tel Aviv–Jerusalem Road was open to Jewish traffic.

1967, June 7. Third Day. Colonel Gur stormed into the Old City of **Jerusalem,** as the Jordanian garrison withdrew. **Bethlehem** was taken early in the afternoon, **Hebron** and **Etzion** soon afterward.

The Battle of Jenin-Nablus

1967, June 5. First Day. The Israeli Northern Command, under Major General **David Elazar,** was roughly equivalent to two and a half divisions. Upon receipt of orders to seize Jenin and Nablus, and to push on to the Jordan River, Elazar committed one division and a reinforced armored brigade. By midnight armored and infantry units were approaching Jenin.

1967, June 6. Second Day. Converging Israeli columns took **Jenin** in hard fighting.

1967, June 7. Third Day. Despite repeated Jordanian counterattacks, the Israelis pressed on to **Nablus.** After another hard battle they secured Nablus just before dark. Although badly hurt and seriously depleted, the Jordanian forces withdrew across the Jordan River and were still intact when the Israeli and Jordanian governments agreed to a U.N. call for a cease-fire at 2000 hours.

OPERATIONS, SYRIAN FRONT

1967, June 5–8. First to Fourth Days. The Golan Heights were held by 6 Syrian brigades, with 6 more in reserve east of Kuneitra. For 4 days Elazar was permitted only long-range artillery duels with the Syrians, who obviously had no intention of seizing the initiative.

1967, June 9. Fifth Day. The U.N.-initiated cease-fire agreed to on June 8 was promptly violated by intensive artillery fire from both sides during the night of June 8/9. Elazar was ordered to begin a major offensive early on June 9. He concentrated his available forces for an initial advance through the Dan-Banyas area onto the northern Golan plateau, along the foothills of Mount Hermon. By nightfall these units had fought their way through the first line of Syrian defenses guarding the approaches to the northern Golan, and 3 brigades were poised to debouche onto the plateau early the following morning. Meanwhile, other units were forcing their way up the escarpment north of the Sea of Galilee, and Elazar had sent orders to the units recently engaged against the Jordanians in the Jenin-Nablus area to move north to strike into the Golan south of the Sea of Galilee.

1967, June 10. Sixth Day. The Israelis pushed through the crumbling Syrian defenses on the northern Golan early in the morning, then pressed ahead across the plateau to converge on Kuneitra from the north, west, and southwest. Meanwhile the troops redeployed from the Jordan front had driven northeastward up the Yarmuk Valley to occupy the southern Golan and to threaten Kuneitra from the south. By dark Kuneitra was surrounded, and one armored unit was occupying the city. The cease-fire again became effective at 1830 hours, and this time was observed by both sides.

COMMENT. *This brief three-front campaign clearly demonstrated the combat effectiveness superiority of the Israelis over their more numerous Arab foes. The scope, decisiveness, and speed of the victory was undoubtedly enhanced by the orders of the Egyptian commander, Field Marshal Amer, for a general Egyptian withdrawal on June 6, which turned an inevitable defeat into a disastrous rout. This contributed to an unwarranted Israeli contempt for the Egyptians, and an underestimation of their military potential which would have important consequences a few years later.*

The War at Sea

Naval operations were almost entirely between Egypt and Israel, since there was no naval activity by Jordan and practically none by Syria.

ESTIMATED LOSSES
JUNE 5–10, 1967

	Killed	*Wounded*	*Prisoners and Missing*	*Tanks*	*Combat Aircraft*
Israel	800[a]	2,440	18	100	40[b]
Egypt	11,500[c]	15,000	5,500	700	264
Syria	700	3,500	500	105	58
Jordan	2,000	5,000	4,500[d]	125	22
Iraq	100	300	—	20	24

a. Israel reported 679 dead and 2,563 wounded on June 11; it is assumed that about half of 225 seriously wounded later died.
b. Only 2 in air-to-air combat; an air combat loss ratio of exactly 1–25.
c. More than half were lost in the desert.
d. Many probably were deserters with "West Bank" origins; Israel captured approximately 500 Jordanian prisoners of war.

1967, June 3–4. Israeli Deception. Four landing craft, on huge trucks, were ostentatiously sent by road from the Mediterranean to Eilat, then sent back at night to repeat the ostentatious daylight movement. Egyptian intelligence assumed that at least 8 (and probably more, due to multiple reports) of Israel's 18 LCTs were available for operations in the Gulf of Aqaba. During the night of June 4/5 several Egyptian vessels were sent from the Mediterranean through the Suez Canal to the Red Sea, to counter the anticipated Israeli threat. In this way Israel substantially reduced the imbalance of forces in the Mediterranean.

1967, June 5. Engagement off Port Said. An Israeli destroyer and several MTBs approached Port Said after dark. They were met outside the breakwater by two Egyptian *Osa*-class missile boats. After an inconclusive exchange of fire, with little damage to either side, the Egyptian vessels withdrew into the harbor. Israeli frogmen also entered the harbors of Port Said and Alexandria; some damage was done to Egyptian vessels in Alexandria, but all of the frogmen there were captured.

1967, June 6. Egyptian Withdrawal from Port Said. The intensity of Israeli air attacks, and the threat of General Tal's advance along the northern Sinai coast, caused the Egyptian Navy to withdraw to Alexandria all of its vessels based on Port Said.

1967, June 6–7. Egyptian Coastal Bombardment. Three Egyptian submarines briefly shelled the Israeli coast, near Ashdod, and north and south of Haifa. They submerged and withdrew when attacked by Israeli air and naval forces.

1967, June 7. Israeli Seizure of Sharm el-Sheikh. A task force of 3 MTBs seized the Egyptian fortifications at **Sharm el-Sheikh.** After Israeli paratroops arrived, the naval vessels proceeded through the Strait of Tiran to the Red Sea without interference.

1967, June 8. The *Liberty* Incident. During the afternoon the U.S.S. *Liberty*, electronics surveillance vessel, 14 nautical miles north of El Arish, was attacked and seriously damaged by Israeli fighter-bombers and MTBs. The Israeli government's subsequent apology was accepted by the United States.

Economic Warfare

On June 5, at an Arab League meeting in Baghdad, representatives of Iraq, Saudi Arabia, Qatar, Bahrein, Kuwait, Libya, Algeria, Abu Dhabi, Egypt, Syria, and Lebanon agreed to stop the flow of oil to all nations they believed had attacked any Arab states. This included the United States, whom the Egyptians also accused of participating in the first air attack, Great Britain, and West Germany, as well as Israel. Only Kuwait, Iraq, and Algeria seem to have taken serious measures to carry out this embargo.

THE "OCTOBER WAR"
(YOM KIPPUR WAR OR THE WAR OF RAMADAN)
OCTOBER 6–24, 1973

Background

President **Anwar Sadat** of Egypt apparently decided in November 1972 to go to war on the basis of readiness estimates supplied to him by the Egyptian Minister of War, General (later Field Marshal) **Ahmed Ismail Ali.** Both knew that Egypt had not reached tactical-technical military parity with Israel and that there might be another Israeli victory. Sadat, however, believed that Israel was satisfied with the *status quo*, and its *de facto* annexation of the territories conquered in 1967, and thus would make no moves toward reasonable negotiations without pressure from one or both of the great powers. The only possibility of moving toward a Middle East settlement seemed to be to precipitate action that would force the major powers and the U.N. to pay attention to the "no peace no war" situation in the Middle East.

1973, September 12. Arabs Select D-Day. Sadat, General Ismail, and President **Hafez Assad** of Syria met secretly during an Arab summit meeting in Cairo. Extraordinary and successful measures were taken to preserve secrecy of plans.

1973, September 26. Arab Concentrations; Israeli Alert. Egypt and Syria announced concentrations of troops for routine maneuvers. Although Israeli and U.S. intelligence believed there would be no war, a partial but perfunctory Israeli alert was ordered, including deployment of a second armored brigade to the Golan area (September 29).

1973, October 4–5. Partial Evacuation of Soviet Advisors. The hasty departure of some Soviet advisors and all dependents was noted by Israeli and American intelligence agencies, which again informed their governments that there would be no war (October 5).

1973, October 6, 0400 Hours. War Inevitable. Israeli Director of Intelligence, **General Elihau Zeira,** informed Lieutenant General David Elazar that the Arabs would attack at 1800 hours. Israeli mobilization was ordered at 0930.

SINAI FRONT

1973, October 6, 1405 Hours. Outbreak of War. A massive Egyptian air strike against Israeli artillery and command positions and a simultaneous intensive artillery bombardment of Bar Lev Line fortifications along the Canal achieved complete tactical surprise; Israeli front-line units had been only partially alerted.

1973, October 6–7. Egyptian Assault Crossing of Suez Canal. Egyptian commandos crossed the Canal at 1435, followed by infantry, engineers, and a few amphibious and ferried tanks. Engineers, opening approaches in the Bar Lev Line's sand embankment by demolitions and water jets, had bridges operational in the Second Army area before midnight October 7. In the Third Army area the bridge construction was not completed until the night of October 7/8. About 500 Egyptian tanks crossed the Canal. Two quickly mobilized reserve Israeli armored divisions under Generals Ariel (Arik) Sharon and **Abraham (Bren) Adan** approached the front, Adan near Romani, Sharon near Tasa.

1973, October 8. Israeli Counterattack Repulsed. Counterattacks against the Egyptian Second Army, by Adan's division and Sharon's division (only parts were engaged), were repulsed with heavy losses. The Israelis dug in and the Egyptians consolidated, linking up all their bridgeheads. Israeli close support aircraft suffered heavy losses from Egyptian antiaircraft defense using Soviet missiles and guns.

1973, October 11. Egyptians Plan Offensive. For several days General Ismail rejected subordinates' recommendations to attempt to drive deeper into Sinai. However, following appeals for help from the hardpressed Syrians, he reluctantly ordered an offensive to draw Israeli strength, particularly air power, to the Sinai front.

1973, October 14. Egyptian Offensive Repulsed. The Egyptians were thrown back with heavy losses, particularly in tanks.

1973, October 15–16. Israeli Thrust across Suez Canal. Sharon, hitting the boundary between the Egyptian Second and Third Armies, was able to establish a bridgehead with a brigade of paratroopers near Deversoir about midnight.

1973, October 16–18. Battle of the "Chinese Farm."* The Egyptian Second Army closed the corridor behind Sharon, isolating his division in small bridgeheads east and west of the Canal. In intensive fighting Adan's division broke through, bringing a bridge to the crossing point. The Second Army with some assistance from the Third Army, tried unsuccessfully but repeatedly to close the corridor leading to the Israeli crossing site. Egyptian tank losses again were heavy. Adan's division then crossed (night 17–18 October).

1973, October 18–19. Expansion of Israeli Bridgehead. Despite the Chinese Farm battle and continuing bridging problems, Adan's division pushed westward from Sharon's bridgehead, overrunning Egyptian rear areas, including AA missile sites, and Israeli planes attacked ground targets with less opposition. Sharon's attempt to seize **Ismailia** was repulsed (October 19).

1973, October 20–22. Israeli Breakout from Bridgehead. Repeated thrusts by Sharon to the northwest against Ismailia were contained by paratroop and armored reserves of the Second and Third Army, reinforced from Cairo. Adan's drive south met weaker resistance cutting the main Suez–Cairo road northeast of Suez (October 22).

1973, October 22. First Cease-Fire, 1852 Hours. Both sides promptly claimed violations of the U.N. cease-fire. Israel sent strong reinforcements across the Canal.

1973, October 23–24. Battle of Suez-Adabiya. Despite the cease-fire Adan was ordered to continue his southward drive to the Gulf of Suez, near Suez, isolating the Third Army. At the same time another Israeli division under General **Kalman Magen** followed Adan and continued on to reach **Adabiya** on the Gulf of Suez. The Israelis also endeavored to take Suez, but were repulsed (October 23–24).

1973, October 24. Second Cease-Fire, 0700 Hours. Activity and artillery fire continued, but cease-fire finally came into effect.

COMMENT. *The Egyptian plan for crossing the Suez Canal and its implementation were superb. The Egyptian failure to plan adequately for security of the boundary between the two armies was a costly blunder. The Egyptians have claimed that they had adequate reserves and resources to reopen communications with the Third Army if the fighting had continued. This is doubtful, and had the war lasted a few days longer, the Third Army would probably have been forced to surrender. General Ismail has been severely criticized for failure to exploit his initial successes, particularly after the victory of October 8. Such criticisms fail to recognize that the Israelis retained a tremendous superiority in air power and in the ability to conduct mobile warfare; his decision not to exploit was as sound as that of Andrew Jackson after New Orleans (see p. 802) and Montgomery after Alam Halfa (see p. 1084). Despite some technical and tactical shortcomings, the Israeli crossing of the Canal was also brilliant as a demonstration of flexible improvisation, based upon sound doctrine.*

Perhaps most significant was the return of Egyptian confidence as their infantry stood firm, even though not always successfully, in the face of Israeli tanks. Contributing to this confidence were the Egyptian's simple, reliable Soviet-built antitank missiles—the "Sagger" and the RPG7. It seems, however, that at least as many Israeli tanks were knocked out by tank and antitank guns as by these missiles.

GOLAN FRONT

1973, October 6, 1405 Hours. Outbreak of War. A massive Syrian air strike and

---

* A former Japanese experimental agricultural station; occupying Israeli troops in 1967 had assumed the calligraphy was Chinese.

artillery bombardment against Israeli positions and installations on the Golan achieved complete tactical surprise.

1973, October 6. Fall of Mount Hermon. Syrian commandos, in a ground-helicopter attack, captured the fortified Israeli observation post on **Mount Hermon,** overlooking the Golan Plateau and the Damascus Plain.

1973, October 6–7. Repulse at Amadiye. North of Kuneitra the Syrian 7th Infantry Division was repulsed by the Israeli 7th Armored Brigade; most of the Syrian tanks were destroyed. The 3rd Syrian Tank Division, committed to pass through the 7th Infantry Division, suffered a costly defeat in a renewed major tank battle west of **Amadiye** (October 7).

1973, October 6–7. Breakthrough at Rafid. Taking advantage of weaker opposition and more favorable terrain, the Syrian 5th Mechanized Division broke through the defenses of the Israeli 188th Armored Brigade. In two days of fighting the Israeli brigade was virtually destroyed; the Israeli Golan command post at Khushniye was surrounded. Spearheads of the 5th Mechanized Division, reinforced by the 1st Tank Division, halted near the western escarpment of the Golan, as much by the need for logistical replenishment as by the pressure of recently mobilized Israeli units fed piecemeal into the battle.

1973, October 8–9. Israeli Counterattack. Assisted by units of the 7th Armored Brigade, displaced from the north, newly-arrived Israeli units drove back the Syrian 5th and 1st Divisions, in several places to the original front line. Most of the Syrian tanks were lost, many because they had run out of fuel and ammunition. With difficulty the 7th Brigade halted a renewed Syrian drive north of Kuneitra (October 9).

1973, October 10–12. Israeli Counteroffensive. In a drive generally north of the Kuneitra-Damascus road, 3 Israeli divisions smashed through the first Syrian defensive zone east of the cease-fire line, and into the second zone, near Saassaa, in front of Damascus. The Israelis voluntarily halted their offensive and began to shift units to the Sinai front (October 12). The Iraqi 3rd Armored Division, on the south side of the Israeli salient (October 11), counterattacked but was ambushed and repulsed (October 12).

1973, October 15–19. Arab Counterattacks Repulsed. Another counterattack by the Iraqi 3rd Armored Division was repulsed (October 15). The Jordanian 40th Armored Brigade counterattacked beside the Iraqis but was also repulsed (October 16). Another general Arab counterattack, spearheaded by the Jordanians, was repulsed (October 19). The lines stabilized on the Damascus Plain.

1973, October 22. Israelis Retake Mount Hermon. Two Israeli efforts to retake their **Mount Hermon** position had been repulsed (October 8 and 21). In a final effort, just before the cease-fire became effective, helicopter-borne paratroops seized the original Syrian observation post, higher up than that of the Israelis, and the "Golani" Infantry Brigade finally retook the lost Israeli position.

1973, October 22, 1852 Hours. Save for some fighting continuing briefly on Mount Hermon, an uneasy lull came over the front.

COMMENT. *The Syrian attack was neither as well planned nor as well implemented as that of the Egyptians. Nevertheless Syrian fighting qualities, especially those of the 5th Mechanized Division, impressed the Israelis. Poor logistics, failure to recognize that a complete victory was in their grasp, and the self sacrificing attacks of the Israeli Air Force were all that kept the Syrians from retaking the southern Golan on October 7. The Israelis were also impressed by Syrian tenacity on defense; there was no collapse and rout, as in 1967.*

THE AIR WAR

1973, October 6–8. Preeminence of the SAM. The first Israeli aircraft appeared over the Sinai and Golan fronts about 40 minutes after the Arab H-Hour. They immediately encountered Soviet-made Arab missiles in unexpected quantity and effectiveness. Before dark the Israelis lost more than 30 aircraft. In the following days Egyptian mobile SAM-6s claimed many Israeli planes, and the light, hand-carried Strella (SA-7) made many hits but damaged more planes than it destroyed. Israeli close air support was therefore negligible for several days.

1973, October 8–16. Disputed Skies over the Battlefields. Employing hastily devised tactics and utilizing chaff and other electronic countermeasures (ECM), Israeli aircraft began to make a greater contribution to the ground battles. They claimed hits on Egyptian bridges over the Suez Canal and favorable results in strikes against Arab airfields. The Arabs, however, denied these claims.

1973, October 9–21. The Israeli Strategic Air Offensive against Syria. Claiming retaliation for Syrian "Frog" (long-range surface-to-surface missile) attacks on the Hula Valley, the IAF initiated an intensive and extremely effective strategic air bombardment campaign against targets (mostly industrial) deep within Syria, with a strike against the Syrian Defense Ministry in Damascus. Attacks on Syrian seaports, industrial plants, and fuel storage depots continued until the first ceasefire. The Syrian economy was severely affected.

1973, October 17–24. Israel Regains Air Preeminence over the Suez Canal. As General Adan's advancing tanks captured a number of Egyptian antiaircraft missile batteries and caused the more mobile SAM-6s to be moved hurriedly, a gap was created in the hitherto effective Egyptian antiair network. Israeli aircraft quickly exploited this, and played a major role in the Israeli success in the Chinese Farm battle and in the Israeli breakout south from the west bank bridgehead.

COMMENT. *The SAMs—particularly SAM-6 and Strella—demonstrated that air superiority no longer assured as decisive an effect on the ground battle as had been the case since World War II. Desperate Israeli efforts to deal with the missile threat, particularly in the employment of ECM measures, regained only a slight (but nonetheless significant) measure of air superiority for the Israelis over the battlefield.*

THE WAR AT SEA

1973, October 6–25. Egyptian Blockade. Egypt declared waters of Israel's coasts were a "War Zone" severely curtailing Israeli commerce in the Mediterranean. A blockade by destroyers and submarines at the Strait of Bab el Mandeb stopped all traffic to Eilat.

1973, October 6. Action off Latakia. Israeli "Saar" missile boats striking at night at the Syrian seaport of **Latakia** were engaged by a Syrian squadron. The Israelis sank 4 Syrian vessels without loss to themselves. The surviving Syrians withdrew into the port.

1973, October 7–8. Second Action off Latakia. The results were inconclusive. The Syrian vessels again withdrew.

1973, October 7–8. Scattered Egyptian–Israeli Clashes. These occurred in the Mediterranean and Red seas. The results were inconclusive, with the Egyptians withdrawing in all instances.

1973, October 8–9. Action off Damietta. Egyptian vessels, coming out to meet Israeli raiding missile boats, suffered severe losses, and the survivors withdrew.

1973, October 9–10. Israeli Raids on Syrian Ports. Israeli missile vessels bombarded Latakia, Tartus, and Banias; there was no naval challenge by Syrian vessels.

1973, October 9–10. Action off Port Said. In an encounter between Israeli and Egyptian missile boats, 3 Egyptian vessels were sunk; the others withdrew to Damietta and Alexandria.

1973, October 12–13. Israeli Raids on Syrian Coast. Tartus and Latakia were again bombarded. There were inconclusive clashes with Syrian missile boats, which unsuccessfully attempted hit-and-run tactics.

1973, October 15–16. Nile Delta Raid. Israeli missile vessels sank a number of Egyptian landing craft.

1973, October 21–22. Israeli Attacks on Aboukir Bay and Alexandria. Two Egyptian patrol boats were sunk.

COMMENT. *Israeli "Saar" missile vessels, armed with the Israeli-made "Gabriel" missile, completely dominated the coastal waters off Syria and Egypt. Not a single hostile shell or missile was fired from the sea against the Israeli coast. On the other hand, the Egyptian blockade of the Strait of Bab el-Mandeb (southern entrance to Red Sea) cut off all commerce to and from Eilat, and the declared Egyptian blockade of Israel's Mediterranean coast also severely reduced ship traffic. However, the blockade had no noticeable effect on Israel during the relatively brief war.*

Involvement of the Superpowers

The association of the Soviet Union with Egypt and Syria had been only partially impaired by the Egyptian demand for withdrawal of most Soviet advisors and technicians in mid-1972 (see p. 1279). Both Egypt and Syria were almost completely dependent upon the U.S.S.R. for replacement and repair, equipment and parts. Despite close associations with the Soviet Union, however, the decision to go to war was certainly not dictated by the Soviets, and it is likely that the U.S.S.R. did not learn of the Arab plans to attack Israel until two or three days before the selected D-Day, when the warlike preparations of Egypt and Syria could no longer be concealed.

Israeli technological development was such that there was no need of assistance or advice in using, or maintaining, the wide variety of modern weapons and equipment which Israel had obtained from the United States. There was no collaboration in planning between the two countries. However, they maintained close contact in intelligence affairs, and both were very much aware of the Arab build-up in late September. Both sadly misestimated Arab intentions.

1973, October 6. Soviet Air Flights to Middle East Accelerate. This was primarily to return Soviets to the U.S.S.R. Both Syria and Egypt were so well supplied that resupply presumably seemed unnecessary.

1973, October 8. Israel Begins to Fly Supplies from the United States. The first of a number of flights from the United States to Israel by El Al aircraft took off from Oceana Naval Air Station, Virginia.

1973, October 9. Major Soviet Airlift to Egypt and Syria Begins. Flights went via and/or over Hungary and Yugoslavia. About two-thirds of the flights were to Syria.

1973, October 13. American Airlift Begins. In response to urgent Israeli requests, the United States began to use American planes to supplement the El Al lift. The first 7 American C5A transport aircraft arrived in Israel, flying via the Azores (October 14).

1973, October 14–21. Massive Soviet and U.S. Airlifts Continue. By the time of the cease-fire the Soviets had airlifted about 15,000 tons, the U.S. more than 20,000.

1973, October 24. Alert of Soviet Airborne Troops. A force of about 7 divisions was alerted, presumably for airlift to Egypt if the Israelis did not loosen their stranglehold on the Egyptian Third Army. Apparently because of this alert, there was a decline in the Soviet resupply airlift.

1973, October 25. United States Military Forces Placed on "Precautionary Alert." Secretary of State Henry Kissinger announced that this was because "ambiguous" signs suggested the possibility of unilateral armed Soviet intervention in the Middle East. Unmistakably implied was the United States' determination to act militarily if necessary to prevent or respond to such intervention.

1973, October 27. United Nations Agreement Ends U.S.–Soviet Crisis. The U.N. Security Council, with both the U.S. and the U.S.S.R. voting affirmatively, agreed to establish for 6 months a 7,000-man international peace-keeping force to enforce the cease-fire in the Sinai and on the Golan. No permanent member of the Security Council would participate in this emergency force (UNEF); thus the U.S. and the U.S.S.R. agreed not to commit forces in the Middle East. Simultaneously, conversations were taking place on the west bank cease-fire line at Kilometer 101 (101 kilometers from Cairo) between Egyptian and Israeli military representatives, with the commander of the U.N. Truce Supervision Organization (UNTSO, in existence since 1948). These talks resulted in agreement for Egypt to send noncombat supplies to its Third Army east of the Suez Canal.

1973, November 11. Egyptian–Israeli Prisoner of War Exchange Agreement. Having reached agreement on the location of the cease-fire line, the Egyptian and Israeli military representatives at Kilometer 101 agreed upon a prisoner of war exchange. Involved were 241 Israelis and 8,031 Egyptians. Following the exchange (completed November 22) the talks broke down because of inability of the two sides to agree on a disengagement formula (November 29).

1973, December 21–22. First Meeting of Geneva Peace Conference. Representatives of Egypt, Israel, the U.S. and the U.S.S.R. agreed that Egyptian-Israeli discussion of separation of forces should continue in Geneva (December 26).

1974, January 18. Israeli-Egyptian Disengagement Agreement. This followed a week of intensive "shuttle diplomacy" by Secretary of State Kissinger, flying back and forth between Egypt and Israel (January 11–17). Israeli troops were to withdraw within 40 days from their bridgehead to a line 15 to 20 kilometers east of the Canal. The Egyptians would remain on the East Bank, in a zone 8 to 10 kilometers deep. A buffer zone between the two forces, 5 to 8 kilometers wide, would be patrolled by UNEF. This left the Israelis in control of the Gidi and Mitla passes. The Israeli withdrawal began on January 24 and was completed March 4.

1974, February 28. The U.S. and Egypt Resume Diplomatic Relations. These had been broken since June 6, 1967 (see p. 1231).

1974, February–May. Syrian-Israeli "War of Attrition." Apparently as a tactic to place pressure on Israel to make territorial concessions on the Golan Heights, Syrian forces initiated a protracted artillery and small-arms duel along the entire cease-fire line between Kuneitra and Damascus.

1974, March 18. Arabs End Oil Embargo of the U.S. Libya and Algeria refused to vote with the majority of 7 Arab oil-producing nations (see p. 1284).

1974, April–May. Intensified Palestine Guerrilla Attacks. Palestine guerrillas, attempting to place pressure on Israel, undertook a number of suicide raids across the border from Lebanon into Israel. Most notable were attacks on Qiryat Shemona (April 11) and Maalot (May 15). Israeli aircraft bombed Palestine guerrilla bases and camps in Lebanon in retaliation. Losses of life among the civilian population on both sides further inflamed Arab-Israeli hostilities.

1974, April 18. Egypt Abandons Reliance on Soviet Military Equipment. Announcing that the U.S.S.R. had failed for 6 months to honor Egyptian resupply requests, and that Soviet terms for renewed supply of arms to Egypt were "unacceptable" and an "instrument of policy leverage," President Sadat ended 18 years of Egyptian reliance upon Soviet arms deliveries.

1974, May 31. Israeli-Syrian Disengagement Agreement. After 32 days of shuttle diplomacy by Kissinger between Israel and Syria, Israel gave up all of the territory captured from Syria in the October 1973 war, plus two small strips taken in 1967, including the town of Kuneitra. Military forces were to be limited in zones on either side of the new cease-fire line, and a narrow buffer zone was to be patrolled by units of the UNEF.

THE KOREAN WAR, 1950–1953

BACKGROUND

Korea, annexed by Japan following the Russo-Japanese War (see p. 920), was promised its freedom by the Allies at the Cairo Conference (December 1, 1943). The decision was reaffirmed in the Potsdam Proclamation (July 26, 1945). When Japan surrendered in World War II (see p. 1198), a hurried Allied agreement (August 15, 1945) established the 38th degree of latitude as an arbitrary dividing line, north of which the U.S.S.R. would accept surrender of Japanese forces in Korea; those Japanese south of the line would surrender to U.S. troops. Following the surrender, which took place with little friction, the U.S.S.R. held the 38th parallel to be a political boundary; along it the Iron Curtain dropped.

Two years of unsuccessful attempts to reach agreement were followed by U.S.

referral of the problem to the U.N., which undertook the establishment of an independent Korean government following free nationwide elections. The U.S.S.R. refused to co-operate. In the southern zone, the Republic of Korea was established (August 15, 1947), with Seoul its capital. Declaring the action illegal, the U.S.S.R. set up a puppet government—the Democratic People's Republic of Korea, its capital at Pyongyang—and organized a North Korean Army (NKA). Allegedly, Soviet troops evacuated the north (December, 1948). U.S. troops completed evacuation of the south (June, 1949); a small American military advisory group remained to organize a Republic of Korea (ROK) Army. More than a year of continuous bickering—Communist propaganda, raids, sabotage, terrorism, and guerrilla action—harassed the south without breaking down the ROK government.

THE OPPOSING FORCES

Communist North Korea now had a well-trained and Russian-equipped army: 130,000 men in 10 divisions with a brigade of Russian T-34 medium tanks and supporting troops. Its hard core was composed of some 25,000 veterans of the Chinese Communist campaign in Manchuria (see p. 1306). The air force consisted of some 180 Russian Yak planes of World War II type. There were more than 100,000 trained reserves.

The ROK Army—little more than a national police force—consisted of about 100,000 men in 8 divisions with little supporting artillery. It lacked medium and heavy artillery, tanks, combat aircraft, and reserves.

Naval strength on both sides was negligible.

OPERATIONS, 1950

1950, June 25. Invasion. North Korean forces—7 infantry divisions, the tank brigade, and supporting troops, under Marshal **Choe Yong Gun**—crossed the border in 4 columns, driving on Seoul. Surprise was complete. The power punch, accom-

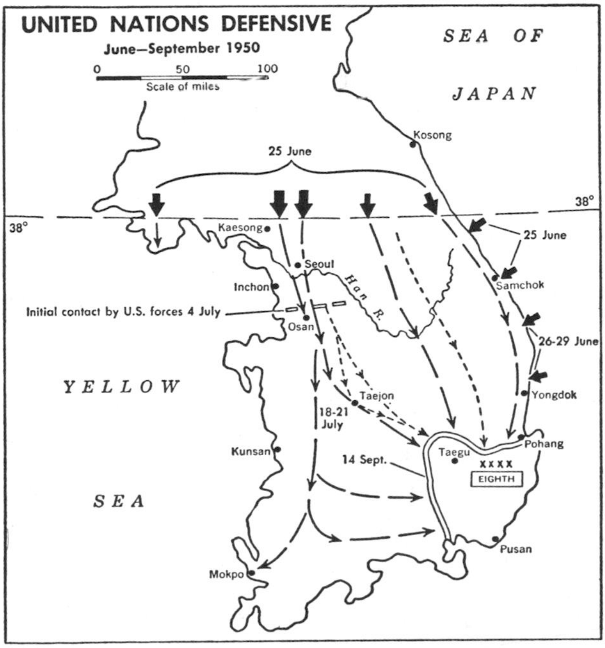

panied by radio broadcasts asserting it to be "national defense" against an alleged ROK "invasion," broke through the scattered resistance of elements of the four ROK divisions in the area. Its objective was to seize the capital and the entire South Korean peninsula, thus presenting the free world with a *fait accompli.*

1950, June 25–30. United Nations and United States Reactions. The Security Council, in emergency session (the U.S.S.R., boycotting the Council, had no representative present to veto the action), called for immediate end to hostilities and withdrawal of the NKA, asking member nations to assist. President **Harry S Truman** (June 27) ordered General MacArthur, commanding U.S. forces in the Far East, to support and cover ROK defense with air and sea forces. MacArthur effected naval blockade of the North Korean coast and furnished air support. Reconnoitering the front in person (June 28), as Seoul fell, he reported the ROK Army to be incapable of stopping the invasion even with U.S. air support. Truman authorized use of U.S. ground troops (June 30).

MacArthur's Resources. Aside from the vessels of the U.S. Seventh Fleet and the Far East Air Force (8½ combat groups), U.S. ground forces—mostly in Japan—consisted of 4 understrength divisions organized in 2 skeleton army corps. Infantry and artillery units were each at two-thirds strength in personnel and cannon, and short of antitank weapons. Corps troops, such as medium tanks, artillery, and other supporting arms, did not exist.

1950, June 30. U.S. Forces Begin Move to Korea. The 24th Division (Major General **William F. Dean**) began movement piecemeal by sea and air into Korea; 2 more divisions were to follow.

1950, July 5. Task Force Smith. One understrength battalion (2 infantry companies) with 1 battery of artillery, under Lieutenant Colonel **Charles B. Smith,** joined the ROK Army near **Osan** (July 4). Next morning an NKA division, with 30 tanks, attacked. The ROK troops fled. Task Force Smith, completely surrounded, held out for 7 hours. Then, ammunition exhausted, the survivors cut their way out, abandoning all matériel.

1950, July 6–21. Dean's Delay. Throwing in the remainder of his division as fast as the units came up, General Dean partly snubbed the NKA advance down the peninsula, trading terrain for time, while the 1st Cavalry and 25th divisions were being rushed from Japan. A 5-day action at **Taejon** (July 16–20) ended when the NKA assaulted the 24th Division from 3 directions. Dean, personally commanding his rear guard while the remainder of the division withdrew, was captured. His battered troops were relieved by the 1st Cavalry Division (July 22), while the 25th Division on its right, together with reorganized ROK divisions, slowed the NKA advance in the center and on the north.

1950, July 7. MacArthur Named Commander in Chief United Nations Command. President Truman made the appointment in response to a Security Council request that a unified command be established under a U.S. officer.

1950, August 5–September 15. The Pusan Perimeter. Lieutenant General **Walton H. Walker,** commanding what had now become U.S. Eighth Army, stabilized his defense on a thinly held line extending along the Naktong River some 90 miles north from Tsushima Strait, thence east for 60 more miles to the Sea of Japan. The area embraced the southeast edge of the Korean peninsula, including Pusan, the one available port. On the north, 5 ROK divisions, re-equipped but still shaken, attempted to contain the invaders, while the western flank, where the weight of incessant NKA attacks fell, was held by U.S. troops, now including 2 additional infantry regiments and a Marine brigade. The Seventh Fleet protected both sea flanks and harassed NKA movements along the coast, while the Far East Air Force (augmented by an Australian group), together with carrier-based naval air, hammered at NKA lines of communication and furnished much-needed close support. Thanks to the advantage of interior lines, Walker was able to shift a mobile reserve from point to point within the perimeter as the NKA attacks nibbled at his front. Several penetrations of the Naktong River line and a 20-mile NKA advance in the north (August 26) were checked. Choe's forces, now estimated at 14 infantry divisions supported by several tank regiments, continued a series of unco-ordinated assaults all around the perimeter. A 3-division attack on the north (September 3) necessitated committing the entire U.N. reserve (the 24th Division) north of Kyongju. Arrival of the U.K. 27th Infantry Brigade (September 14) compensated for the withdrawal of the Marine brigade for duty elsewhere (see below).

1950, September 15–25. The Inchon Landing. At dawn, the U.S. X Corps, Major General **Edward M. Almond** commanding, began landing over the difficult and treacherous beaches at Inchon, on the west coast, more than 150 miles north of the battlefront, and west of Seoul. Strategic surprise was complete, although a 2-day preliminary bombardment had warned the few NKA detachments in and about Seoul. The 1st Marine Division swept through slight opposition, securing Kimpo airport (September 17). The 7th Infantry Division, following the Marines ashore, turned south, cutting the railroad and highway supplying the NKA in the south, and Seoul was surrounded.

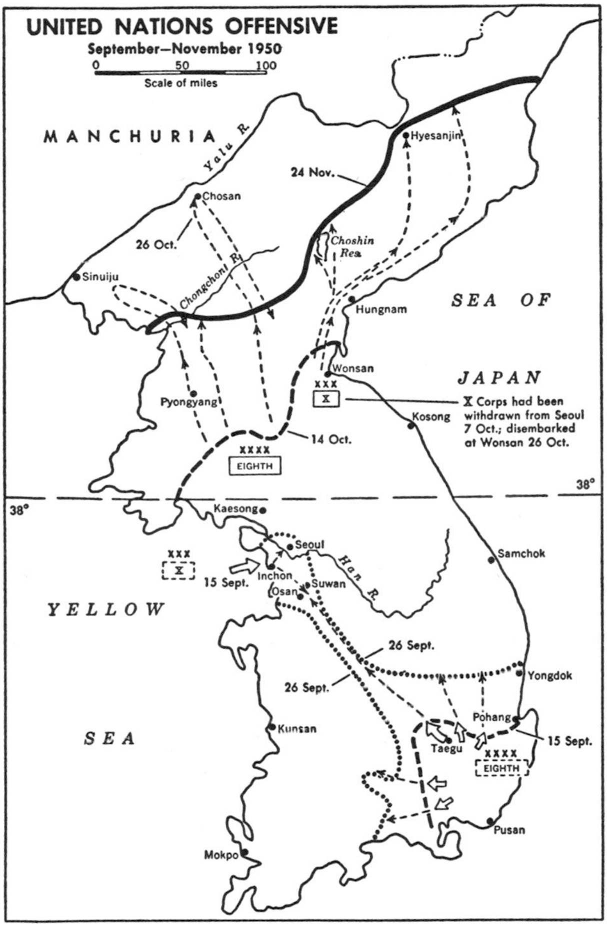

1950, September 15–25. Breakout from the Perimeter. Simultaneously the Eighth Army broke out, the 1st Cavalry Division leading. Choe's NKA, its supplies cut off, and menaced from front and rear, disintegrated. The 1st Cavalry and 7th Infantry divisions met just as Seoul itself was liberated.

1950, September 26. Liberation of Seoul. More than 125,000 prisoners were taken, together with most of its matériel, as the NKA scattered into the roadless, rugged countryside.

COMMENT. *The Inchon landing was one of the great strategic strokes of history, in conception, execution, and results. MacArthur's genius had transformed into a stunning victory a desperate defense seemingly doomed to disaster. The Communist grab at South Korea, which if successful might have meant the eventual absorption of all the Asian mainland, had been thwarted, the North Korean Army crushed. MacArthur's decision was taken while his Eighth Army was still clawing to maintain a toehold at Pusan. On August 12 his staff was ordered to prepare the operation, one month to accomplish what ordinarily would take several. His dynamic insistence overcame the doubts of the U.S. JCS (technically the Inchon area was most disadvantageous for an amphibious operation) and he was provided with the bulk of the 1 division of Marines he demanded. (One of its brigades, already there, came from his own Pusan perimeter.) The 7th Infantry Division was the last of his occupation troops in Japan, its ranks filled by more than 5,000 ROK soldiers hurried to Japan to train with it. Success depended on (a) the ability of the U.S. Navy to provide sufficient water transport, (b) the ability of Walker's hard-pressed Eighth Army to hold the Pusan perimeter until the stroke fell, and (c) perfect timing of the assault (a 30-foot tide variance permitted use of the beaches for only 6 of each 24 hours.)*

1950, October 1–November 24. Advance to the Yalu. As directed by both the U.N. and President Truman, MacArthur pushed north across the 38th parallel. ROK troops crossed the line (October 1); Eighth Army followed (October 9), leaving 2 divisions in the southern area to secure communication lines to Pusan and mop up roving remnants of the NKA. A serious military handicap was the injunction that under no circumstances were U.N. aircraft to fly north of the Yalu River. **Pyongyang,** North Korean capital, was overrun (October 20) by a combined airborne (187th Regimental Combat Team) landing and overland advance. The ROK 6th Division reached the Yalu at Chosan, and other ROK units fanned out behind it. By this time, other U.N. token forces had joined Eighth Army and were integrated in existing U.S. divisional elements: a Turkish brigade, and Canadian, Australian, Philippine, Netherland and Thai battalions.

1950, October 15. Wake Island Conference. President Truman and General MacArthur conferred at Wake Island on the course of the war. This later became an issue in the Senate investigation that followed the relief of General MacArthur (see p. 1271).

1950, October 16–26. Shift of U.S. X Corps to the East Coast. Embarked at Inchon, the corps was moved around to the east coast to Wonsan (October 19), which had already been captured by the ROK I Corps. A 7-day delay in landing was necessary to sweep the harbor clear of latest-type Soviet mines, sown under the direction of Soviet experts with the NKA.

1950, October–November. Threats from Communist China. Peking had threatened intervention should the 38th parallel be crossed by U.N. troops, and heavy concentrations of Chinese Communist (ChiCom) troops were reported north of the Yalu, in Manchuria. Since aerial reconnaissance beyond the Yalu was prohibited, MacArthur knew neither the full strength nor the dispositions of these troops, nor—until his forward ROK divisions were ambushed by them and a U.S. regiment at Unsan was severely mauled (November 1)—was he aware that ChiComs in considerable numbers were already south of the Yalu. Walker, confronted by the presence of this new element in the situation, recalled his leading Eighth Army units and consolidated temporarily along the Chongchon River.

MacArthur's Plans and Problems. His intention was to advance up the entire front of the peninsula, X Corps on the east coast, Eighth Army on the west, and make a sweeping envelopment. X Corps would turn west on reaching the Yalu and drive all enemy forces south of the border into the arms of Eighth Army. Since the rugged, desolate central massif precluded mutual support, these forces acted independently, their control and co-ordination directed by MacArthur in Tokyo. Almond's X Corps now consisted of the U.S. 1st Marine and 3rd and 7th Divisions and the ROK I Corps (3rd and Capital Divisions). The Eighth Army, 9 divisions strong, was grouped in 3 army corps: the U.S. I and IX and the ROK II, from left to right. The total combat strength of the entire command was about 200,000 men, with perhaps 150,000 more in support functions in the rear. In addition to the ROK corps, some 21,000 more Korean troops were attached to or integrated in U.S. units.

MacArthur had believed that Communist China was bluffing; that she would not enter the conflict unless Manchuria itself were invaded. He had expressed this opinion to Truman at Wake Island (see above). The U.S. Central Intelligence Agency was of the same opinion. Yet now Red Chinese troops were in Korea. MacArthur considered that to suspend his advance would be a violation of his directive: "to destroy the North Korean armed forces." Aerial reconnaissance north of the Yalu being still prohibited, he decided the only remaining course was to clarify the situation by a bold advance. The decision was specifically approved by the JCS. Meanwhile X Corps had thrust north, widely distributed over an immense front; the ROK Capital Division had reached Chongjin on the coast; the U.S. 7th Division was on the Yalu at Hyesanjin.

1950, November 24. Eighth Army Advance. MacArthur's "reconnaissance in force" began.

1950, November 25–26. Communist Counteroffensive. After advancing for 24 hours against practically no opposition, the Eighth Army was suddenly struck a massive blow, the main effort being directed against the U.N. force's right flank. Some 180,000 Chinese troops, in 18 divisions, shattered and ripped through the ROK II Corps, hit the U.S. 2nd Division on the right flank of IX Corps, and threatened envelopment of the entire Eighth Army. The 2nd Division, attempting to refuse its right flank, fell into an ambush at **Kunu-ri** as the ChiCom envelopment trapped its columns while passing through a defile in march order. Some 4,000 men and most of the divisional artillery were lost while trying to fight their way out. Walker threw in his reserves, the U.S. 1st Cavalry Division and the Turkish and 27th Commonwealth brigades. They staved off the envelopment, the Turks in particular taking heavy losses, and the Eighth Army managed to disengage in comparatively good order. By December 5, the Eighth Army, its right flank refused, had completely extricated itself, and the Communist drive was beginning to lose momentum; but the central and east-coast area being wide open (see below), a stronger defensive position was essential. Walker accordingly withdrew to the general line of the 38th parallel, slightly north of Seoul and some 130 miles below the November 24 situation. There, as the year ended, the Eighth Army awaited a new Communist offensive.

1950, November 27–December 9. X Corps Withdrawal. In the eastern zone, an additional 120,000 Chinese troops, advancing on both sides of the Chosin reservoir, isolated the 1st Marine Division and drove in elements of the 3rd and 7th divisions. The ROK troops on the coastal flank were hurriedly withdrawn on Almond's order without much molestation. MacArthur ordered evacuation of the entire force, since the Communist drive, directed on the ports of Hungnam and Wonsan, threatened its piecemeal destruction. Navy transports were rushed to both ports. Defensive perimeters were established, manned by elements of the 3rd and 7th divisions, while the 1st Marine Division, under Major General **Oliver Smith,** consolidated south of the Chosin reservoir in subzero weather. Surrounded by 8 Communist divisions, General Smith, announcing to his troops that they were not retreating, but "attacking in another direction," moved southeast on Hungnam, supplied by the Far East Air Force. When a Communist blow destroyed the 1 bridge across a gorge otherwise impassable for the division's trucks and tanks, bridging material was flown in by air and the Marine southward "advance" continued. Thirteen days of running fight ended (December 9) when a relief column of 3rd Division troops met the Marine vanguard outside the Hungnam perimeter.

1950, December 5–15. X Corps Evacuation. Despite continued Communist attacks on the perimeters of both ports, evacuation by air and by sea went smoothly. Air Force and Navy carrier-plane support, together with naval gunfire, facilitated the final embarkation. In all, 105,000 ROK and U.S. troops were lifted by the Navy, together with 98,000 civilian refugees. Some 350,000 tons of cargo and 17,500 vehicles were also carried. The Far East Air Force evacuated 3,600 troops, 200 vehicles, and 1,300 tons of cargo. On arrival at Pusan, the X Corps came under Eighth Army control as a strategical reserve.

1950, December 23–26. Death of Walker; Arrival of Ridgway. Walker, killed in an automobile accident, was replaced by Lieutenant General **Matthew B. Ridgway.** MacArthur gave Ridgway command of all ground operations in Korea, retaining over-all ground, air, and sea command.

COMMENT. *The U.N. forces in Korea had suffered a serious defeat, though disaster was averted through skillful troop leading and stubborn—in some cases phenomenal—resistance. MacArthur's critics were quick to blame his simultaneous advance in 2 independent zones on 1 front, and the inadequate security measures which had permitted the stunning surprise. His supporters, in rebuttal, pointed to the nature of the terrain, which rendered close ground liaison and mutual support between Eighth Army and X Corps impossible. They also blamed the artificial ground rules set up by the U.N. and the JCS prior to the Communist assault prohibiting aerial reconnaissance north of the Yalu. To add to MacArthur's problems, he had been denied his immediate request that he be now permitted to bomb the Yalu bridges and also the important North Korean entry port of Rachin, only 35 miles from Vladivostok, through which Soviet war matériel had long flowed freely to the NKA. Bombing of the southern ends of the Yalu bridges was finally permitted; this was an extremely hazardous and practically futile operation, since to approach them U.N. aircraft had to fly parallel to the river, exposed to antiaircraft fire from Manchuria and to the assaults of Communist attack planes. Communist traffic over the bridges was little interrupted.*

It would appear that MacArthur's original decision to advance—a decision concurred in by the JCS—was proper. But the method may be criticized. The JCS must take much blame for permitting the advance while prohibiting the prior air reconnaissance that was essential. There is no doubt that MacArthur expected that, should the Chinese Communist threat materialize, he would immediately be given full authority to extend his air operations over the border and choke the assault at its source, but the JCS had no intention of giving such authority. Finally, the actual local security measures taken just before and during the Eighth Army's move were inadequate under the circumstances. For this both MacArthur and Walker must share blame.

The most important lesson from this defeat was the necessity that U.N. troops relearn the rudiments of fire and movement on foot. Roadbound, they had found themselves too dependent upon supporting tanks, artillery, or aircraft. The Chinese troops, on the other hand, lightly equipped, utilized fluidity, surprise, and concealment in the rugged regions to compensate for their inferiority in fire power. They moved and attacked by night; lay camouflaged in daylight. Their attacks all followed the same pattern: infiltration, encirclement, and ambush. Frontal assaults were in effect holding attacks in small force, but the penetrations were deep. Each engagement was initially one of small units. It was a platoon commander's war. At no time was the U.N. able to employ its firepower superiority in full force.

OPERATIONS, 1951

1951, January 1–15. Second Communist Invasion. Long prepared and expected, the Communist assault crossed the 38th parallel at daybreak, its main effort in the western zone. Some 400,000 Chinese troops, with an additional 100,000 of the reconstituted NKA, pushed the 200,000-man Eighth Army back almost to Seoul. Then (January 3) a heavy penetration farther east, in the Chungpyong reservoir area, overran the ROK divisions on both flanks of the U.S. 2nd Division, which extricated itself only after serious fighting and the commitment of Ridgway's reserve—the 3rd and 7th divisions.

1951, January 4. Evacuation of Seoul. This was the third time the capital had changed hands. Stubborn resistance of ground troops, plus the Far East Air Force's close support and interdiction of the now exposed Communist lines of communications, slowly checked the momentum of the drive. The U.N. position stabilized some 50 miles south of the 38th parallel, from Pyongtaek on the west coast to Samchok on the east (January 15).

1951, January 25–February 10. U.N. Counteroffensive. Ridgway launched a series of limited-objective attacks, slowly driving north. A Communist counterattack near **Chipyong** and **Wonju** (February 11–18) checked the advance in the center, but on the west U.N. troops reached the outskirts of Seoul.

1951, March 7–31. Operation "Ripper." This was designed primarily to inflict casualties on the enemy, and secondarily to relieve Seoul and eliminate a large Communist supply base now built up at Chunchon. The main effort, in the center, forced the Communists back. The Han River was crossed east of Seoul.

1951, March 14. Reoccupation of Seoul. Patrols of the I Corps found it abandoned. Chinese resistance then stiffened, but an airborne drop by a reinforced regi-

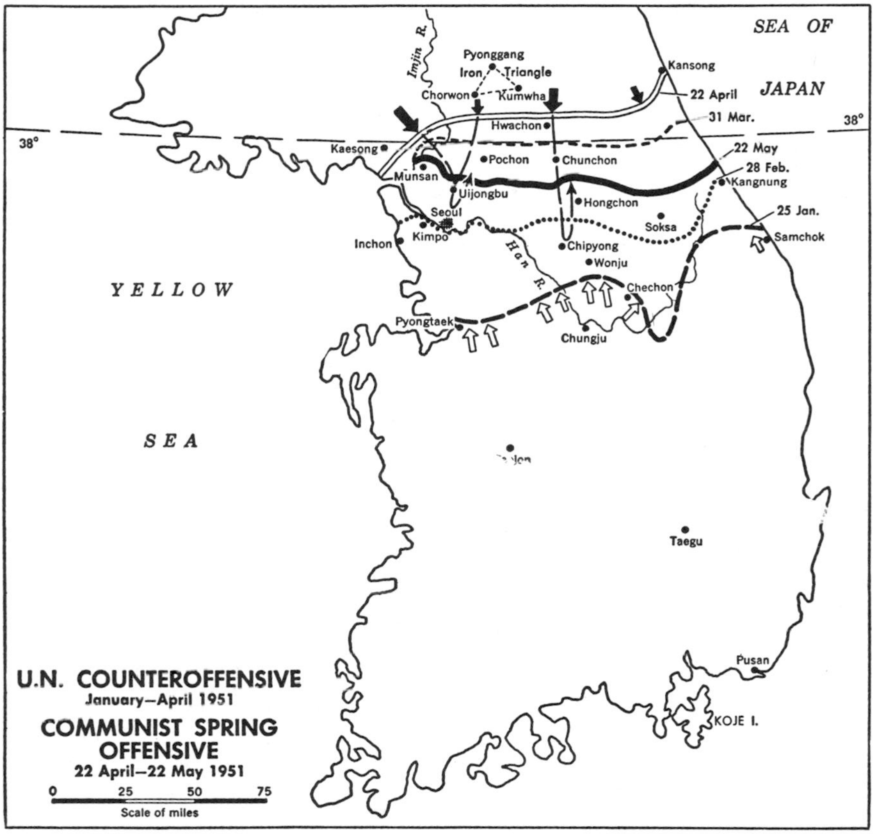

ment (187th Regimental Combat Team) at **Munsan,** 25 miles north of Seoul (March 23), forced a general Communist retirement. The Eighth Army was back roughly along the old 38th-parallel front (March 31). MacArthur and Ridgway decided on further advance, toward the "Iron Triangle"—Chorwan-Kumhwa-Pyonggang, the major assembly and supply area, as well as communications center, for the Chinese.

1951, April 11. MacArthur Relieved. President Truman summarily ousted General MacArthur from his dual command of U.N. forces and of U.S. forces in the Far East. Ridgway was appointed in his place, and Lieutenant General James A. Van Fleet was hurried from the U.S. to command the Eighth Army.

COMMENT. *The President was exercising his legal prerogative as Commander in Chief. MacArthur was not in sympathy with the policy of limiting the war to the Korean peninsula and had not attempted to conceal his dissatisfaction with the restrictions placed on his operations. MacArthur had stated that "in war there is no substitute for victory" in a letter (March 20) to Representative* **Joseph W. Martin, Jr.** *(R., Mass.), which Martin promptly made public. MacArthur was advocating neither the use of the atom bomb nor a land invasion of China. He did want to destroy, by conventional air attack, bases in Manchuria which were being used as springboards for invasion of Korea. He did urge the use of Chinese Nationalist troops in Korea, and also the "unleashing" of Chiang Kai-shek on the Chinese mainland. He believed that the Soviet Union could not afford to risk war by coming to the aid of Red China, but that if it did make such a mistake there could be no better time for the U.S. to face a showdown with the Kremlin. Without consulting Washington, he had called on the ChiCom commander in Korea to surrender (March 25) and hinted that air and naval attacks against Communist China would be the probable consequence if the conflict continued.*

To Truman such opinion and actions were anathema. MacArthur was defying Presidential authority and debating national policy. The United States—listening to an anxious Free World opinion frightened by Soviet possession of the atomic bomb—had deliberately given up the idea of liberating all of Korea and was seeking merely to restore the status quo *in South Korea. So MacArthur had to go. The brusqueness of the ousting—the general learned it first through a news broadcast—offended many people. MacArthur returned to the U.S. to receive a hero's welcome and an invitation to address the Congress in joint session, which he did. A Senate investigation later (May–June 1951) aired all the policy issues; the results of the investigation were inconclusive; in general, however, U.S. policy became tougher subsequently.*

1951, April 12–21. Continued U.N. Advance. Aware of Communist preparations for a counteroffensive to blunt the threat to their "Iron Triangle," General Van Fleet continued forward movement, prepared to fall back, if necessary, to previously prepared defensive positions. There he would contain the enemy by his heavy fire power and then counterattack.

1951, April 22–May 1. Communist Spring Offensive—First Phase. The attack came on a moonlit night; the first assault broke through the ROK 6th Division, west of the Chungpyong reservoir. The U.S. 24th Division on the left and the 1st Marine Division on the right promptly refused their respective flanks, but the penetration compromised Van Fleet's general position and he began withdrawal of his left—the I and IX Corps. The Chinese main effort developed against the I Corps, north of Seoul. Hasty withdrawal by the ROK 1st Division exposed the flank of the U.K. 29th Brigade on its right and a battalion of the Gloucestershire Regiment was cut off. After a heroic defense of their hill position, the survivors attacked *north,* to the momentary confusion of their assailants. Some 40 men escaped; the remainder were killed or captured. As usual, the Communist assault finally lost momentum and came to a pause (April 30). They broke contact, retiring in general beyond U.N. artillery range. Communist losses in this phase were at least 70,000 men, while Eighth Army casualties were about 7,000.

1951, May 14–20. Second Phase of Communist Offensive. Shifting the weight of their attack to the east, more than 20 divisions, with NKA divisions on their right and left, struck the right elements of X Corps—the ROK 5th and 7th Divisions. The U.S. 2d Division, next on the left, stood firm, but the ROK III Corps, farther east, went to pieces under heavy assault. The ROK I Corps, on the extreme right, refused its flank against the Communist surge through this wide corridor. The U.S. 2nd Division (with French and Netherlands battalions attached) and the 1st Marine Division, on the west side, promptly counterattacked. Van Fleet had expected the blow in this area and had already shifted his reserves—the U.S. 3rd Division and 187th Regimental Combat Team. Their combined efforts snubbed the Communist offensive (May 20). Attacks on the west flank, north of Seoul, and in the center, down the Pukhon River, had been repulsed.

COMMENT. *As usual, initial Communist contact was by small units, attempting to infiltrate and terrorize. There were few tanks. The attacks, vigorous at night, ceased with daylight when U.N. artillery and tactical aircraft fire power could intervene. Communist losses in this 7-day phase were estimated at 90,000. They were now overex-*

tended, supplies expended and communications under continuous aerial attack.

1951, May 22–31. U.N. Offensive. Preceded by limited attacks on the far left, anchoring the U.N. position on the Imjim River, north of Munsan, the entire U.N. front moved north. The ROK Capital and 2nd Divisions, on the extreme right, flashed up the east coast with little opposition, reaching Kansong. Advance was slower in the center, but was accelerating by month's end. Van Fleet was now ordered to halt. Despite his plea for approval of "hot pursuit" against an enemy on the verge of collapse, the JCS refused either increased means or permission for another drive northward. The U.S. government was concerned by Soviet threats and by consequent alarm elsewhere in the Free World. It was decided to do nothing to risk World War III.

1951, June 1–15. Consolidation of U.N. Position. With the rainy season on, Van Fleet decided to establish a defensive belt across Korea, from which springboard he could keep the enemy off balance by a succession of JCS-approved limited-objective moves. Some gains were made at the base of the "Iron Triangle"—thus denying its use to the enemy—and on the southern rim of the "Punchbowl," a fortified hill-circle northwest of Sohwa. Meanwhile the Communists were themselves organizing in depth to the north.

1951, June 23. Soviet Cease-Fire Proposal. This was made in the U.N. by Soviet Ambassador Malik. It confirmed that the Chinese had been badly hurt in the previous 6 months' fighting. Estimated enemy losses totaled 200,000 men, together with much matériel. Also, U.N. air attacks had foiled every attempt to install Communist air bases south of the Yalu. Delegations from both sides met at Kaesong.

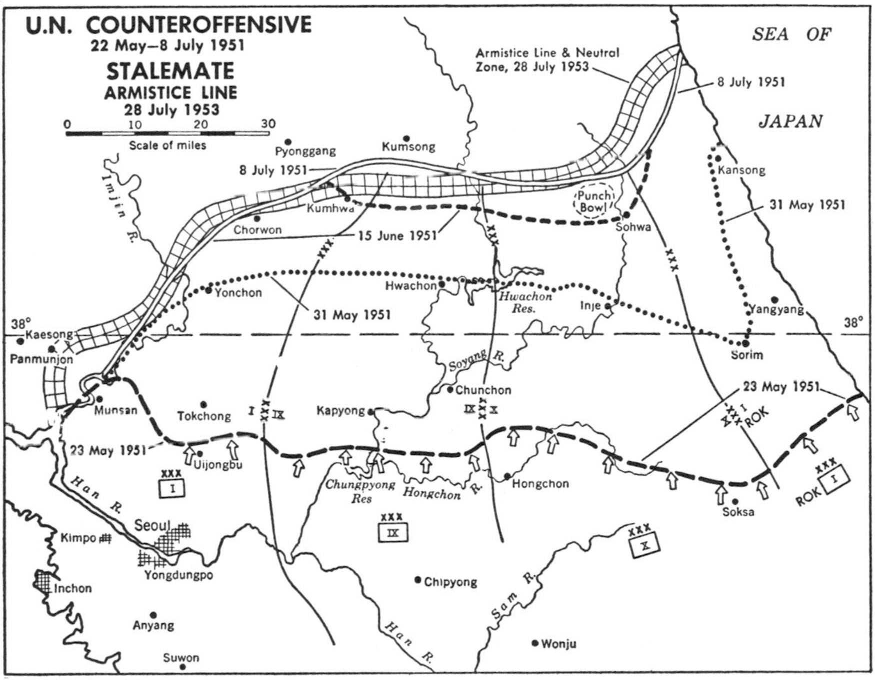

1951, July–August. Negotiations. The Communists, taking advantage of the location of Kaesong just inside their lines, seized every opportunity to insult U.N. negotiators and to delay progress while playing for time to recuperate from their mauling. They used the negotiations as a sounding board for propaganda against the U.N. allies and the U.S. in particular. Meanwhile, clashes between patrols and outposts continued all along the firing line as both sides improved their positions. The Eighth Army improved its hold both on the Iron Triangle and the Punchbowl. The negotiations broke down completely (late August).

1951, August–November. Resumption of U.N. Limited Attacks. Van Fleet's troops cleared the Iron Triangle and the Punchbowl, driving the Chinese back from the Hwachon reservoir and the Chorwan-Seoul railway line. These successes brought prompt Communist requests for resumption of armistice discussions.

1951, November 12. Discussions Begin at Panmunjon. This was a village between the lines in No Man's Land. General Ridgway (November 12) ordered offensive operations stopped, and Eighth Army went on a highly active defense.

OPERATIONS, 1952

While negotiations dragged out interminably at Panmunjon, minor actions flared continually all along the front. General Ridgway, ordered to NATO command (see p. 1224), was replaced (May) by General **Mark W. Clark.** The Communists continued building up their strength. By the year's end an estimated 800,000 Communist ground troops—three-fourths of them Chinese—were in Korea, while heavy shipments of Soviet artillery were brought in, including excellent antiaircraft guns, radar-controlled. However, U.N. command of the air was never seriously threatened, and the Communists were forced to continue their practice of taking shelter during daylight hours in concealed, deep-dug bunkers and other underground installations.

Prisoners of War. Communist wranglings at the Panmunjon conferences centered on the disposition of prisoners of war. About 92,000 U.N. troops had fallen into Communist hands: some 10,000 Americans, 80,000 Koreans, and 2,500 from other U.N. forces. Statistical computation is impossible; no one will ever know how many prisoners died of mistreatment or starvation. Communist boasts in 1951 put their POW bag at 65,000, but at Panmunjon they admitted holding only 11,500. Consensus of reports by returned POW's indicated that about two-thirds of U.S. prisoners died or were killed in the prison camps. No neutral or Red Cross inspections were ever permitted.

Some 171,000 Communist prisoners fell into U.N. hands, more than 20,000 of them Chinese. About 80,000 of them were assembled on the island of Koje, just off Pusan, where they were held under rather haphazard control, due to U.S. anxiety about our own captives in Communist hands, as well as humanitarian, if misguided, efforts to improve their conditions.

At Panmunjon, Communist negotiators insisted on total repatriation of all POW's, but at least 50,000 prisoners in U.N. hands were violently opposed to returning home. The U.N. command had no intention of forcing these unfortunates back into Communist hands. A deliberate build-up of hard-core Communists at Koje—organizers planted to become POW's—produced an organized revolt (May 7) when U.S. Brigadier General **Francis T. Dodd,** naïve camp commander, was captured through a ruse and held as hostage inside his own prison compound. His successor, U.S. Brigadier General **Charles F. Colson,** unwitting that he was abetting a Communist propaganda coup, bartered for Dodd's release by promising in effect that alleged abuses in treatment of Communist POW's (abuses which did not exist in fact) would be "corrected." General Clark ordered U.S. Brigadier General **Haydon Boatner** to clear up the situation. Boatner, combining military firmness with knowledge of the Chinese Communist mentality, swept the Communist hard-core recalcitrants into a separate compound and restored order.

All this while, a dreary succession of attacks and counterattacks—in reality tests of will power—cost both sides great losses in flesh and blood. In October, the negotiations at Panmunjon again broke off, while the war became a political football in the U.S. presidential election. The American people, tired of the struggle, elected **Dwight D. Eisenhower,** who had promised to bring about an honorable conclusion.

OPERATIONS, 1953

1953, March 28. Communist Move for Peace. Unexpectedly, but apparently in tune with internal unrest in the Communist world following Stalin's death (March 5), Premier **Kim Il Sung** of North Korea and General **P'eng Teh-huai,** heading the ChiCom "volunteers," informed General Clark of their agreement to his previously ignored proposal for mutual exchange of sick and wounded POW's. They also urged resumption of the Panmunjon conferences. Unquestionably, indications of extensive U.S. plans to renew offensive operations, and possibly to extend the war, were major factors in the Communist gambit.

1953, April. Operation "Little Switch." This was an exchange of 5,800 Communists for 471 ROK's, 149 Americans, and 64 other U.N. personnel.

1953, May–June. South Korean Intransigence. South Korea's President **Syngman Rhee** flatly refused to become a party to any agreement which left Korea divided. After Communist attacks against his troops (see below), he demanded resumption of the military offensive (June 18). At the same time he released from his own prison camps 27,000 North Korean POW's unwilling to be repatriated.

1953, June 10–31. Chinese Communist Offensive. Massive attacks, mostly against ROK troops, were begun, obviously to bring about U.S. pressure on Syngman Rhee. When he released the prisoners, the Communists, accusing the U.N. of bad faith, again broke off negotiations and launched still another offensive (June 25), against the ROK sector. Some slight gains were made, but quick shifts of U.S. reinforcements and the ChiComs' usual inability to exploit their penetrations brought the attack to a halt, with loss of some 70,000 troops.

1953, July 10. Resumption of Negotiations. Following U.N. assurance to the Communists that no further ROK intransigence would occur, the negotiators hammered out a final armistice.

1953, July 27. Armistice Signed. The *de facto* boundary was the existing battle line. Exchange of prisoners who desired repatriation followed: 77,000 Communists, against 12,700 U.N. men—of whom 3,597 were Americans and 945 Britons.

SUMMARY

The Korean War cost the U.N. 118,515 men killed and 264,591 wounded; 92,987 were captured. (A great majority of these died of mistreatment or starvation.) The Communist armies suffered at least 1,600,000 battle casualties, 60 per cent of them Chinese. An additional estimated 400,000 Communists were nonbattle casualties. U. S. casualties were 33,629 killed and 103,284 wounded (see Statistical Summary). Of 10,218 Americans who fell into Communist hands, only 3,746 returned; the remainder (except 21 men who refused repatriation) either were murdered or died. In all, 357 U.N. soldiers refused repatriation. South Korea's toll—which can only be estimated—came to 70,000 killed, 150,000 wounded, and 80,000 captured. Approximately 3 million South Korean civilians died from causes directly attributable to the war.

This war was significant on several counts. It was the first major struggle of the nuclear age. While no nuclear weapons were employed, the threat of the atom bomb hung heavy over all concerned and throttled exploitation of success.

It was a war between two differing ideologies, a war of stratagem and deceit in which roadbound superior fire power was canceled out by lighter-armed fluidity over desolate, trackless wastes. All ethical standards of western civilization were scorned by the Communists.

STATISTICAL SUMMARY: U.S. FORCES IN THE KOREAN WAR, 1950–1953

	Total U.S. Forces Worldwide	*Maximum Deployed Strength*		*Total Combat Casualties*	*Killed and Died of Wounds*	*Wounded*	*Prisoner or Missing*	*Nonbattle Deaths*
Total	5,764,143	c. 440,000	(Apr-Jul '53)	147,131	33,629	103,284	10,218	20,617
Army	2,834,000	276,581	(July '53)	113,610	27,704	77,596	8,310	9,429
Navy	1,177,000	84,124	(Feb '53)	2,243	458	1,576	209	4,043
Marines	424,000	36,966	(Apr '53)	28,627	4,267	23,744	616	1,261
Air Force	1,285,000	46,388	(Dec '52)	2,651	1,200	368	1,083	5,884

U.N. Participation. Fourteen U.N. member nations besides the U.S. took part in this, the first war in which the U.N. had engaged. Britain and Turkey each contributed a brigade (each about two-thirds of a division). In addition, the U.K. furnished 1 aircraft carrier, 2 cruisers, and 8 destroyers, with Marine and supporting units. Canada sent 1 brigade of infantry, 1 artillery group, 1 armored battalion; Australia, 2 infantry battalions, 1 each air fighter and transport squadrons, 1 aircraft carrier, 2 destroyers, 1 frigate; Thailand, 1 regimental combat team; France, 1 infantry battalion, 1 gunboat; Greece, 1 infantry battalion, 1 air transport squadron; New Zealand, 1 artillery group, 2 frigates; Netherlands, 1 infantry battalion, 1 destroyer; Colombia, 1 infantry battalion, 1 frigate; Belgium and Ethiopia, 1 infantry battalion each; Luxembourg, 1 infantry company; Union of South Africa, 1 fighter squadron. All these elements, though merely token forces, bore themselves well and sustained heavy casualties. In addition, from Denmark, India, Italy, Norway, and Sweden came hospital or field-ambulance noncombat units.

Air Warfare. The conflict reaffirmed the critical importance of air power as an essential ingredient of successful combat; it also was a reminder that air power alone can neither assure adequate ground reconnaissance nor bring about final decision in land warfare. The immediate superiority achieved by the U.N. in the air necessitated bringing in Soviet Mig-15's—then the latest U.S.S.R. jet fighters, quite superior to America's F-84 and surpassing in some respects the F-86. Migs, first seen in Korea in late 1950, increased in number during 1951, but the training and competence of U.N. pilots—mostly American—compensated for any inferiority in matériel. While U.N. pilots were never permitted to hound the Migs across the Yalu in "hot pursuit," they were able to neutralize all Communist efforts to establish bases south of the river. In air-to-air combat, 1,108 Communist planes were destroyed, including 838 Mig-15's; probably destroyed were another 177 and severely damaged were an additional 1,027 planes, against a total U.N. loss of 114 aircraft. As the war drew to a close, U.S. F-86 jets were downing Mig-15's at the rate of 13 confirmed Communist losses to each F-86 shot down. U.N. plane losses to Communist antiaircraft fire—while giving magnificent close support to ground troops—were 1,213.

The Helicopter. The potential of this new means of mobile transportation was clearly demonstrated. It was excellent for reconnaissance, evacuation, and rescue work.

The Navy's Role. American command of the sea was one of the principal handicaps to Communist success. Without this, the U.N. campaign in aid of South Korea would have been impossible. The U.S. Seventh Fleet gave valuable gunfire support along the coast and carried out amphibious operations, while naval and Marine air units participated in Air Force interdiction and close support to ground units. The Navy's blockade of the peninsula prevented any attempts to supply the Communist forces by water. Had it been possible to interdict ground-supply channels from Manchuria and Siberia in similar fashion, the war would have been over in short order.

Brainwashing. Not until the U.N. POW's returned home was the full extent of the Communist ideological warfare realized. Through brutality—physical and psychological torture (some 60 per cent of American and British POW's died from torture or neglect)—many men unraveled. About 15 per cent of Americans in captivity actively collaborated with the enemy; only about 5 per cent of the total resisted categorically all Communist indoctrination and all efforts to use them for propaganda purposes. Consensus in the U.S. and Britain was that their soldiers had been mentally unprepared for such treatment.

INTERNATIONAL PEACEKEEPING

THE UNITED NATIONS

The U.N. Charter, formally ratified by 29 nations, came into force (October 24, 1945; the U.N. was later located in New York), composed of a General Assembly and an elected Security Council of 12, whose 5 permanent members were China, France, Great Britain, the U.S.S.R., and the U.S. Disarmament activities of the U.N. are treated separately below. Important highlights of its other activities during the period were:

1946, April 18. End of League of Nations. The League voted itself out of existence, transferring assets and responsibilities to the U.N.

1946, December 19. Greek Frontiers. A commission was established to investigate violations of the Greek frontiers with Albania, Yugoslavia, and Bulgaria (see p. 1271). A special commission was later established to observe the northern frontier of Greece (October 21, 1947).

1947, May 15. Palestine. A special commission was established to investigate the problem of Palestine (see p. 1276). This led to a plan for establishment of separate independent Jewish and Arabic states, approved by the General Assembly (November 29, 1947).

1947, August 26. Indonesia. A Good Offices Commission was appointed to seek peaceful settlement of the war in Indonesia (see p. 1303).

1948, January 20. Jammu and Kashmir. Attempt was initiated to settle the India-Pakistan dispute by a U.N. mediation commission (see p. 1287).

1948, April 23. Palestine Truce Commission. This was established, after outbreak of Arab-Israeli war (see p. 1224), under the leadership of Count **Folke Bernadotte** of Sweden. An international Palestine U.N. Mediation and Observer Group was later created under Bernadotte's command (May 14). Soon after, Bernadotte was assassinated by Jewish terrorists (see p. 1226).

1948, October 25. Soviet Veto on Berlin. This blocked settlement by the Security Council of the Berlin Blockade (see p. 1263).

1948, December 11. Conciliation Commission for Palestine Established.

1948, December 12. Korea. The General Assembly appointed a commission to aid unification of Korea (see p. 1241).

1949, January 7. Israeli-Arab Armistice. (See p. 1227.) Supervision arrangements were made by the Security Council.

1949, January 28. Indonesia. The Security Council renewed efforts to halt hostilities and settle the Indonesian question; the Good Offices Commission (see above) was reconstituted as the U.N. Commission for Indonesia.

1950, January 3–August 15. Soviet Boycott. The U.S.S.R. boycotted all U.N. bodies on which Nationalist China was represented.

1950, June 27. Korean War. The Security Council voted 7–1 (Russia absent) to assist South Korea in repelling North Korean aggression (see p. 1241).

1950, September 14. U.N. Denounces North Korean Aggression. This was in a report by the Commission on Korea to the General Assembly.

1951, February 1. Communist China Named Aggressor in Korea. This was by General

Assembly vote. Later the Assembly voted an embargo on arms to China (May 8).

1953, April 23. Investigation of Germ-Warfare Charges. The General Assembly adopted by a vote of 51–5 a resolution for impartial investigation of Communist charges that the United States had used germ warfare in Korea.

1953, November 11. U.S. Charges Communist Atrocities in Korea. A U.S. report to the General Assembly charged that at least 6,113 U.S. servicemen and a total of 11,622 U.N. servicemen had been murdered, tortured, or otherwise mistreated.

1954. Egyptian Blockade of Israel. U.S.S.R. vetoed a resolution in the U.N. Security Council to call on Egypt to end restrictions on passage through the Suez Canal of ships bound for Israel.

1955, September 29. Algeria. By 1 vote the General Assembly voted to investigate conditions in Algeria. France withdrew (September 30), but later returned to the Assembly (November 25).

1955, October 12. General Assembly Condemns South Africa's Racial Segregation. South Africa then withdrew from the General Assembly (November 9).

1956, April, July. Hammarskjöld to Middle East. On trips to the tense Middle East at request of Security Council, he attempted to calm down tempers and obtain cease-fire agreements from Israel and Arabs.

1956, October 28. Hungary Crisis. (**See p. 1232.**)

1956, October 29. Suez Crisis. (**See p. 1227.**)

1956, November 4–7. U.N. Emergency Force. At Egypt's request, following Israel's Sinai offensive and the abortive Anglo-French invasion of the Suez Canal area (see p. 1229), the Security Council sent a force of 6,000 men, selected from 10 nations, to supervise cessation of hostilities, protect Egyptian borders, and place a cordon sanitaire across the Negev, separating Israeli and Egyptian forces. The first units arrived in a few days (November 15).

1957, September 14. Soviet Intervention in Hungary Condemned. This was a General Assembly vote.

1958, June 11. Observer Teams for Lebanon and Jordan. (See pp. 1280 and 1283.) These peace-preservation teams facilitated the withdrawal of U.S. and British troops (August 21).

1959, June 20. Korea. The U.N. command in Korea charged North Korea with violating the armistice by building military fortifications in the demilitarized zone.

1959, December 1. Antarctic Treaty. A 12-nation treaty established the continent of Antarctica as being available only for peaceful purposes.

1960, July 14. Establishment of Force for Congo. The Security Council authorized the Secretary General to organize an *ad hoc* military force to help the Congolese government preserve order. These were mainly drafted from African nations into the Congo, under Swedish Major General **Karl Von Horn,** to preserve peace. Some 18,000 strong at its peak, this force actually battled dissident elements (see p. 1321) in hope of bringing about a peaceful settlement of the Congo question. The last U.N. troops left the Congo June 30, 1964, upon which rebellion flared again (see p. 1322).

1961, September 17. Death of Dag Hammarskjöld. The U.N. Secretary General was killed in a plane crash in nearby Northern Rhodesia as he was coming in to land at the airport at Elizabethville, Congo.

1962, September 21. West Irian. A security force was established to supervise transfer of western New Guinea from the Netherlands to Indonesia (see p. 1303).

1963, June 1. U.N. Observer Force for Yemen. (See p. 1280.) This force of 200 observers was established by the Security Council, initially for two months, under Swedish Major General **Karl von Horn.** Soon after the force's life was extended (August 1), von Horn resigned, citing lack of U.S. support and poor administration. He was replaced by Indian Lieutenant General **Prem Singh Gyani** (August 27).

1964, March 4. Cyprus. Establishment of a U.N. force (see p. 1274). A cease-fire was later obtained through U.N. efforts (August 11).

1964, July 3. U.N. Observation Mission in Yemen Extended. Secretary General U Thant announced that the extension to September 4 would facilitate negotiations for mutual withdrawal by the UAR and Saudi Arabia.

1967, May 18. U Thant Agrees to With-

drawal of UNEF from Sinai. **(See p. 1230.)**

1967, July 10. U.N. Observers Agreed for Suez Canal Cease-Fire Supervision. (See p. 1232.)

1973, October 27. UNEF Reestablished in Sinai. (See p. 1239.)

1974, May 31. UN Force Established on Golan Heights. **(See p. 1240.)** This was designated UN Disengagement Observer Force (UNDOF).

DISARMAMENT ACTIVITIES

1945, November 15. U.S., Britain, and Canada Offer Atomic Information to U.N. President Harry S. Truman, Prime Minister **Clement Attlee,** and Prime Minister **Mackenzie King** offered to share information on atomic energy with other members of the U.N.

1946, June 14. Baruch Plan. At the first meeting of the U.N. Atomic Energy Commission, the U.S. Delegate, **Bernard Baruch,** offered a plan whereby the United States would give up its store of atomic bombs and reveal its secrets of controlling atomic energy to an international Atomic Energy Development Authority. There could be no veto power in this international authority.

1946, June 19. Soviet Alternative Plan. The Soviet representative submitted an alternative plan to outlaw all atomic bombs, and insisted on the retention of the veto by the Big-Five Powers in all atomic matters. All atomic weapons would be destroyed within 3 months of ratification of an international agreement. Shortly after this (July 24), the Soviet Union rejected the Baruch Plan. The Russian representative, **Andrei Gromyko,** announced that Russia would not permit any form of inspection of atomic-energy projects within her borders.

1946, December 14. Resolution for World-wide Disarmament. Adopted by acclamation by the General Assembly. This led to the establishment of a U.N. Disarmament Commission, which met sporadically and ineffectively, in subsequent years (1947–1960).

1946, December 30. Baruch Plan Approved. The basic points were adopted by the Atomic Energy Commission and it was referred to the Security Council, where it was killed by Soviet veto.

1958, March 31. Soviet Unilateral Test Ban. The Soviet Union announced that it was halting all tests of atomic and hydrogen bombs. Testing was renewed later, however (September 30).

1958, October 31. U.S. Unilateral Cessation of Nuclear Tests. President Eisenhower announced that this voluntary ban would last for 1 year. After completing a series of tests, the U.S.S.R. tacitly adopted the test ban (December).

1959, August 26. U.S. Extends Unilateral Nuclear Test Ban. A 2-month extension of its 1-year unilateral ban (due to expire October 31) was announced, in view of a 6-week recess in U.S.-British-Soviet nuclear-test talks at Geneva. When no agreement was reached, the U.S. announced that it had dropped its obligation to stop further nuclear-weapons tests (December 31). No tests were made, and it was implied that no atmospheric tests would be conducted so long as the U.S.S.R. refrained from such tests.

1960, March 15. First Meeting of Ten-Nation Disarmament Committee. Results of this effort at Geneva were as fruitless as those of the U.N. commission. It broke up by Soviet action (June 27).

1960, May 7. U.S. Plans to Resume Underground Nuclear Tests. This was for the purpose of improving methods of detecting underground nuclear tests.

1961, September 1. U.S.S.R. Begins Atmospheric Nuclear Tests. This unilateral action, without prior announcement, ended a 2½-year implied atmospheric-test moratorium.

1961, September 5. U.S. Resumes Atmospheric Tests. The U.S. began nuclear tests in response to the Soviet Union's unilateral resumption of testing.

1963, April 5. U.S.-Soviet "Hot Line" Agreement. This direct communications link between Washington and Moscow had been proposed at the 17-nation U.N. Disarmament Committee by the United States (March 15) to reduce the danger of accidental war. This action was inspired by the Cuban missile crisis (see p. 1272).

1963, July 25. Nuclear Test Ban Treaty Signed. This concluded more than 3 years of sporadic discussion. It prohibited all nuclear testing in the atmosphere, but permitted underground nuclear tests to continue. Subsequently, most of the nations of the world also signed the treaty, which went into effect in the fall (October 10).

1963, October 17. Renunciation of Weapons in Space. The U.N. General Assembly confirmed earlier unilateral declarations by the U.S. and the U.S.S.R. It was made binding by a formal **Treaty on the Demilitarization of Outer Space** (January 27, 1967; in force October 10, 1967).

1964, July 21. Denuclearization of Africa. Announced by a declaration of the heads of state and government of the Organization of African Unity at a summit conference at Cairo.

1967, February 14. Denuclearization of Latin America. This treaty, signed in Mexico City by representatives of most Latin American states, was approved by the U.N. General Assembly (December 5, 1967). United States endorsement went into effect May 12, 1971.

1967, March 2. U.S.–U.S.S.R. Agree to Nuclear Arms Limitation Negotiations. (See SALT entries below.)

1968, July 1. Treaty on Nonproliferation of Nuclear Weapons. Most nations of the world agreed to stop the spread of nuclear weapons to nations not yet possessing them. Although many non-nuclear nations protested that this committed them to perpetual second-class sovereignty, most signed the treaty (in force March 5, 1970). Among nations not signing were nuclear powers France and Communist China, and such potential nuclear powers as Argentina, Brazil, India, Israel, Pakistan, South Africa, and Spain.

1969, November 17. Beginning of U.S.–Soviet Strategic Arms Limitation Talks (SALT). Representatives of the two nations met at Helsinki, Finland, for a month to initiate a major effort to establish firm controls over nuclear weapons. Subsequent secret meetings alternated between Helsinki and Vienna.

1969, November 25. United States Renounces Biological Warfare and First Use of Chemical Warfare. President Richard M. Nixon renounced for the U.S. first use of chemical weapons, and all methods of biological warfare. Toxins—weapons on the borderline between chemical and biological agents—were later banned (February 14, 1970). He also requested the U.S. Senate to ratify the Geneva Protocol of 1925 (outlawing chemical warfare), never ratified by the U.S. This was eventually achieved (1974, December).

1971, February 11. Treaty to Denuclearize the Seabed. This treaty prohibited the emplacement of nuclear weapons and other weapons of mass destruction "on the seabed and the ocean floor and in the subsoil thereof."

1971, September 30. U.S.–Soviet Nuclear Accidents Agreement. This was the first published product of the SALT negotiations. To reduce the possible risk of accidental war, both nations pledged themselves to notify each other in the event of (a) an accident that might cause detonation of a nuclear weapon; (b) detection of suspicious activity by either nation's security warning system; or (c) planned missile launches in the direction of the other. The agreement, signed at Washington, entered into force immediately.

1972, May 26. U.S.–Soviet SALT Agreements. At a summit meeting in Moscow President Nixon and Soviet Communist Party Secretary **Leonid Brezhnev** signed the first major results of 3 years of SALT negotiations (see above). The first of these, **Treaty on the Limitation of Anti-Ballistic Missiles,** prohibited nationwide deployment of ABM systems but allowed each nation to establish limited ABM defenses for its national capital and one ICBM site. The problem of verification is not mentioned; both sides tacitly agreed that their observation satellites could assure compliance. The second, **Interim Agreement on Limitation of Strategic Offensive Weapons,** provided for a 5-year moratorium on deployment of strategic offensive rocket launchers; its objective was to freeze ICBM deployments at then-existing levels during the prolonged negotiations anticipated to be necessary to work out a comprehensive agreement limiting strategic nuclear weapons. At that time the U.S. had 1,056 launchers and the Soviets had 1,618 launchers. The interim agreement did not prohibit qualitative improvements (such as accuracy) or the development of multiple independently targeted reentry vehicles (MIRVs).

1973, June 21. Second Round U.S.–Soviet SALT Agreements. At a summit meeting in Washington President Nixon and Secretary Brezhnev signed 2 additional SALT agreements. The first of these, **Basic Principles of Negotiations on the Further Limitation of Strategic Offensive Weapons,** indicated some progress toward the comprehensive treaty needed to replace the Interim Agreement (see above). The second, **Agreement on the Prevention of Nuclear War,** provided that both nations would avoid "situations capable of causing a dangerous exacerbation of their relations, as to avoid military confrontations, and as to exclude the outbreak of nuclear war between them and between either of [them] and other countries."

1973, October 30. NATO-Warsaw Pact Negotiations on Mutual Force Reductions. These discussions began in Vienna.

1974, July 3. ABM Reduction Protocol. The U.S. and the Soviet Union agreed to reduce the number of ABM sites to one each.

1974, November 24. Vladivostok Agreement. A definite limit on all strategic launchers was set at 2,400 and of 1,320 on MIRVed missile launchers. Strategic bombers were to be counted as launchers.

COMMENT. *The SALT I treaty was criticized for a number of reasons, but in particular for limiting ABM development and deployment. Critics believed that the U.S. gave up a substantial advantage in the development of counterforce damage-limiting strategic systems. The treaty was also criticized as an example of a controversial nuclear doctrine of the 1960's–1970's deterrence through mutual assured destruction (MAD). These critics urged the development of a doctrine of deterrence through damage-limiting counterforce capabilities. The criticism seemed to be confirmed when, soon afterward, the U.S. deactivated its sole ABM site protecting missiles at South Forks, South Dakota.*

WESTERN EUROPE

DEFENSE ARRANGEMENTS; NATO 1948–1973

Immediately after World War II, Soviet truculence posed a threat to the postwar recovery of Western Europe. Thanks to American economic assistance through the Marshall Plan, Western Europe avoided the economic chaos which the Communists had hoped to exploit through subversion and revolution. But full economic recovery in these nations was hampered by fears that Soviet Russia, whose armed strength had increased rather than decreased after the war, would take by invasion what Communist agents were unable to subvert from within. Although the U.S. still possessed a nuclear monopoly, Western Europeans feared that a Soviet overland attack could overrun Western Europe in less than a week. They recognized their own military impotence and doubted that America would react in time to prevent a *fait accompli.*

On April 4, 1949, in Washington, a treaty was signed to establish (effective August 24) a North Atlantic Treaty Organization (NATO) by Belgium, Canada, Denmark, France, Iceland, Italy, Luxembourg, the Netherlands, Norway, Portugal, United Kingdom, and the U.S. Greece, Turkey, and West Germany joined later. They agreed to settle disputes by peaceful means, and to develop their individual and collective capacity to resist armed attack, to regard an attack on one as an attack on all, and to take necessary action to repel attack under Article 51 of the U.N. Charter. The principal NATO commands were the European Command (with headquarters at Supreme Headquarters Allied Powers, Europe—SHAPE), Atlantic Command, and a Channel Command. The principal relevant events were:

1948, March 17. Brussels Treaty. A 50-year military and economic assistance treaty between Britain, France, the Netherlands, Belgium, and Luxembourg. Field Marshal Viscount **Bernard L. Montgomery** was appointed to head a permanent "Western Union" defense organization (September 30). The U.S., Canada, and the Brussels Treaty nations began negotiations for a larger North Atlantic Security Treaty (July).

1950, December 19. Eisenhower Appointed Supreme Allied Commander, Europe. As SACEUR, General Eisenhower toured all NATO capitals from his headquarters in Paris to investigate possibilities of creating an effective peacetime force. Later he assumed command of all forces placed at his disposal in Europe by NATO members (April 2, 1951). Montgomery was Deputy SACEUR.

1951, April 27. Defense of Green-

land. The U.S. and Denmark agreed on the joint defense of Greenland for the duration of the North Atlantic Treaty.

1951, September 6. U.S. Rights in Azores. In Lisbon, the U.S. and Portugal agreed on continued U.S. rights in the Azores, within the NATO region.

1951, October 22. Greece and Turkey Admitted to NATO.

1952, April 11. Ridgway to Replace Eisenhower. General **Matthew B. Ridgway** was appointed SACEUR, effective May 30.

1952, May 27. Establishment of European Defense Community. A treaty establishing the EDC between France, West Germany, Italy, Belgium, Luxembourg, and the Netherlands. West Germany would be restored to complete independence, would be a participant in the defense community, and would supply troops to NATO.

1953, April. NATO Plans for Nuclear Weapons. SHAPE Chief of Staff, General **Alfred M. Gruenther,** testified before the Senate Foreign Relations Committee that the NATO defense plans in Europe called for limited use of ground troops and intensive use of atomic weapons.

1953, July 11. Gruenther Replaces Ridgway as SACEUR.

1954, April 16. U.S. Assurances to EDC. President Eisenhower assured the 6 EDC premiers that the U.S. would maintain forces in Europe so long as a threat of Soviet aggression continued to exist.

1954, August 30. France Rejects EDC. This vote of the French National Assembly ruined plans for a new European military pact and the rearmament of Germany.

1954, October 3. New Plan for German Rearmament. The U.S., Britain, France, West Germany, Canada, Italy, Belgium, the Netherlands, and Luxembourg agreed to integrate a rearmed West Germany militarily and politically into the Western European Union and NATO. This was approved by the French National Assembly (October 12) and by the North Atlantic Council (October 22).

1955, April 13. U.S. to Share Atomic Secrets with NATO. President Eisenhower approved an agreement to share information on atomic weapons.

1956, November 20. Norstad Appointed SACEUR. General **Lauris Norstad,** USAF, replaced Gruenther.

1957, January 24. German to Command NATO Ground Forces. General **Hans Speidel** was named commander of NATO forces in Central Europe.

1959, March 13. France Withdraws Fleet from NATO. She notified the North Atlantic Council that one-third of the French Mediterranean Fleet, which had been earmarked for NATO command in wartime, would be retained under French control.

1959, July 8. U.S. Withdraws Planes from France. The decision to move 200 jet fighter bombers to Britain and West Germany was caused by French refusal to permit stockpiling of U.S. nuclear weapons in France unless under French control.

1960, December 16. U.S. Offers Nuclear Submarines to NATO. This offer of 5 nuclear submarines equipped with 80 Polaris missiles was conditional upon agreement by the NATO allies on a multilateral system of control of weapons and on the purchase of 100 additional Polaris missiles by the European NATO states.

1962, May 6. U.S. Commits Nuclear Submarines to NATO. These 5 submarines were to remain under U.S. control since no agreement had been reached on the previous U.S. offer for a multilateral force.

1963, January 2. Lemnitzer Appointed SACEUR. General Lyman L. Lemnitzer, USA, former chairman of the U.S. JCS, succeeded Norstad.

1963, January 14. De Gaulle Rejects U.S. Proposal for a Multilateral Nuclear Force.

1966, March 9. France Announces Military Withdrawal from NATO. The French Government announced withdrawal of its forces and staff officers from the integrated military commands of NATO, and demanded removal of all NATO bases and headquarters installations from French territory within one year. De Gaulle's announced reason was that conditions in 1966 were "fundamentally different from those of 1949." France made clear, however, that it was not withdrawing from the alliance, or from nonmilitary alliance activities. In a joint statement 9 days later, the other 14 members of NATO criticized the French action and reaffirmed their firm commitment to NATO's military structures. Within the next few months the NATO Secretary General's office was moved from Paris to Brussels; SHAPE headquarters was moved from Versailles to Casteau, Belgium; Allied Forces Central Europe headquarters was moved from Fontainebleau to Maastricht; and the NATO Staff College was shifted to Rome. U.S. forces in France, totaling nearly 30,000 troops and 60,000 dependents, began to move to neighboring NATO countries on June 30, 1966.

1969, July 1. Goodpaster Appointed SACEUR. General **Andrew J. Goodpaster,** U.S.A. former Deputy Commander in Vietnam, replaced General **Lemnitzer** as Supreme Commander Allied Powers Europe.

1974, December 15. Haig Appointed SACEUR. General **Alexander M. Haig,** U.S.A., former Chief of Staff for President Nixon, replaced Goodpaster as Supreme Commander Allied Powers Europe.

UNITED KINGDOM

Britain, exhausted and on the verge of national bankruptcy in 1945, began drastic reduction of her international commitments. This was evidenced by dramatic British withdrawal from Greece and from other occupation roles (see p. 1272), as well as the reduction of its occupation force in Germany, and by initiating the liquidation of its vast colonial empire, beginning with India (see p. 1286) and Burma (see p. 1290).

Despite this curtailment, involving a frank though unpalatable acceptance of decline from truly great-power status, Britain still found itself almost continuously involved in military actions of one sort or another around the world throughout the period. The U.K. nevertheless remained the third most powerful nation in the world, despite economic constraint. The major events of military significance:

1945–1947. Pacification in Greece. (See p. 1271.)

1945–1965. Troubles in Arabia. Intermittent frontier conflicts in Aden and Arabian protectorates (see pp. 1284 and 1285).

1947, March 4. Treaty of Dunkirk. A 50-year Anglo-French treaty of alliance in face of the Soviet threat to Western Europe.

1948, March 17. Brussels Treaty. Expansion of the Anglo-French alliance to include the Benelux nations (see p. 1257).

1948–1960. Communist Revolt in Malaya. (See p. 1302.)

1948–1949. Berlin Blockade. RAF units participated in the air shuttle (see p. 1263).

1949, April 18. Independence of Eire. Ireland broke off all ties with Great Britain and became a completely independent republic.

1950, March 29. Churchill Urges Rearmament of Germany. His suggestion that Germans share in defense of Western Europe was called "frightful" by Foreign Minister **Ernest Bevin.**

1950–1953. Korean War. British Commonwealth units (predominantly British) participated (see p. 1252).

1951, May 1. Armed Services Unification. Land, sea, and air forces were placed under the operational control of the 3-man Chiefs of Staff Committee with the ground-force commander, General Sir **Miles Dempsey,** as chairman.

1952–1956. Mau Mau Uprising in Kenya. (See p. 1318.)

1952, September 8. Establishment of Southeast Asia Treaty Organization (SEATO). (See p. 1292.)

1952, October 3. Britain Explodes Atomic Bomb. Through this explosion in northwest Australia, she became the third nation to possess nuclear weapons.

1952–1959. Civil War and Terrorism in Cyprus. (See p. 1273.)

1956, October 31–November 6. Franco-British Attack on the Suez Canal. (See p. 1229.)

1957, April 4. Drastic Change in Defense Policy. Recognizing that protection against nuclear weapons was impossible, Britain concentrated on deterrence by threat of nuclear retaliation. Overseas commitments were drastically reduced and armed forces cut by 40 per cent over 5 years.

1957, May 15. Britain Explodes Its First Hydrogen Bomb.

1957, July–August. Assistance to Muscat and Oman (see p. 1285).

1960, February 16. New Defense Policy. The government announced a shift from reliance on ground-based nuclear weapons to ballistic nuclear missiles launched from aircraft and nuclear submarines.

1960, April 13. Britain Abandons Ballistic-Missile Development. A government decision was announced to abandon the military development of a fixed-site medium-range "Bluestreak" ballistic missile, and to rely on the RAF strategic V-bombers and the U.S.-designed "Skybolt" missile. This was formally agreed by the U.S. (June 6).

1960, November 1. U.S. Nuclear Submarine Base in Scotland. Prime Minister **Harold Macmillan** announced to the House of Commons an agreement for basing U.S. nuclear-powered Polaris missile submarines at Holy Loch, on the Firth of Clyde, in Scotland.

1962. Commonwealth Troops to Thailand. This was to fulfill a SEATO commitment, resulting from civil war in Laos (see p. 1300).

1962, December 21. Collapse of "Skybolt" Program. After discussions between President Kennedy and Prime Minister Macmillan at Nassau, Bahamas, it was announced that the U.S. had decided to cancel the "Skybolt" program (upon which British nuclear defense and deterrence plans were based), but had agreed on the development of a multilateral NATO nuclear force (see p. 1258).

1963–1965. Malaysia-Indonesia Crisis. Commonwealth forces (primarily British) supported the Federation of Malaysia against Indonesian encroachments.

1964, January. British Intervention in East Africa. Troops were dispatched to Tanzania, Kenya, and Uganda (at request of local governments) to suppress antigovernment uprisings (see p. 1319).

1964, September 21. Independence to Malta. The tiny republic remained in the British Commonwealth.

1965, February 9. Retrenchment in Development of Weapons Systems. Aviation Minister **Roy Jenkins** told Parliament that Britain could not afford to develop its own expensive new weapons systems and in future must cooperate, particularly in aircraft projects, with other nations, primarily the United States.

1966, December 3. Reinforcement of Zambia. Britain sent a squadron of RAF jets, plus a ground force protective contingent from the RAF Regiment, in response to an appeal from President **Kenneth Kaunda** of Zambia, who feared an attack by Rhodesia on the Kariba Dam on the Zambia River.

1967, July–August. Violence in Hong Kong. Communist-inspired violence, bordering on insurrection, was suppressed by British troops after much bloodshed.

1967, November 2. Withdrawal from Arabia. Foreign Secretary **George Brown** announced that Britain would withdraw all forces (some 5,000 troops) from Aden and south Arabia, calling this "the end of the imperial era." Two months later (1968, January 16) it was announced that all British bases east of Suez would be closed by 1971; simultaneously Britain announced canceling an order of 50 F-111 jets from the United States.

1968, May 10. Britain Increases Forces "Earmarked" for NATO. Because of the withdrawal from east of Suez, Britain's share in land, sea, and air forces for NATO was increased by 40 per cent.

Civil War in Northern Ireland, 1969–1974

1969–1974. Continuous Violence in Ulster. Catholic-Protestant terrorism kept the province in a bloody turmoil barely controlled by the equivalent of a British division plus local police. The Irish Republican Army (IRA) terrorist group, outlawed in Eire, was nonetheless based in Eire and attempted to force the British to agree to cession of Ulster to Eire. Some violence, in the form of bombings, spread to Britain. Ostensibly religious, the real issues were economic, social, and political.

1969, April 21. British Troops Protect Key Installations in Ulster. As a result of increased violence, more than 1,000 troops were deployed to protect reservoirs, telephone exchanges, and power stations.

1969, August 19. British Army Assumes Responsibility for Ulster Security. This was a response to increased violence in Ulster and to a suggestion from Eire that a British-Irish force, or a U.N. force, assume responsibility for security in Northern Ireland. The British Government rejected the Irish proposal.

1971, November 1. ANZUK Force Replaces British Garrison in Singapore. **(See p.1303.)**

1972–1973. Dispute with Iceland. The unilateral extension of Iceland's coastal fishing rights area from 12 to 50 miles (July 14) led to British protests, supported by the International Court of Justice (August 17). Iceland refused to recognize the ruling, and Icelandic police gunboats drove away British trawlers, leading to the bloodless collision of an Icelandic gunboat and a British frigate (1973, September 10). Temporary British acceptance of the new limit did not settle the dispute.

1972, January 30. "Bloody Sunday" in Londonderry. Thirteen unarmed civilians were killed by British troops attacked by Catholic demonstrators. In response, an Irish mob in Dublin stormed and burned the British Embassy.

1972, July 28. British Army Occupies Catholic Areas of Belfast and Londonderry. Barricaded enclaves previously considered too dangerous to enter were swept in a 3-day operation. British forces in Northern Ireland were at a 17,000-man peak.

IRELAND

1956, December–1957, November. IRA Terrorist Campaign. Efforts by the outlawed Irish Republican Army to obtain the support of the Irish Government in efforts to unite Ireland and Ulster were partially successful and led to fruitless discussions between President **Eamon de Valera** and the British Government (1958, March).

THE LOW COUNTRIES

Belgium and the Netherlands both assumed Western Union and NATO (see p. 1257) commitments. Other Belgian military action has been limited to occasional commitment in the Congo (see p. 1321), and the Netherlands has been involved in military action in Indonesia (1945–1949) and in defending New Guinea against Indonesian encroachments (1949–1963; see p. 1303). All three contributed combat units to the U.N. Command in Korea (see p. 1252).

FRANCE

The nation was plunged into political turmoil following World War II. General de Gaulle, elected president of the provisional government of the Fourth Republic (November 13, 1945), resigned in disgust as the feuding factions refused to compose their differences (January 20, 1946). He returned to power 12 years later, averting likely civil war. The following are the major events of military significance:

1946–1954. Indochina War. (See p. 1295.)

1947, March 4. Anglo-French Treaty of Alliance. (See p. 1259.)

1948, March 17. Brussels Treaty. (See p. 1257.)

1948, October 21–28. Revolution in Mahe (French India). A pro-Indian revolt was suppressed by French troops.

1949, April 4. NATO Treaty. (See p. 1257.)

1950–1953. Korean War. (See p. 1252.)

1954. Geneva Conference. (See p. 1296.) End of French rule in Indochina.

1954–1962. Algerian Revolt. (See p. 1314.)

1956, October 31–November 6. Franco-British Attack on the Suez Canal. (See p. 1229.)

1957–1958. To the Brink of Civil War. France slipped to the verge of civil war as increasingly impotent political leadership proved unable to cope either with the problems of the revolt in Algeria or the pressing political and economic issues at home.

1958, June 1. De Gaulle Returns to Power. With the French army in Algeria virtually in a state of mutiny against the government (see p. 1314), de Gaulle was recalled to power by popular clamor and the Fifth Republic was established with him as its first president (December 21).

1960, January–November. France Gives Up Colonial Empire. (See p. 1314.) De Gaulle offered the newly independent countries economically attractive terms to remain members of the French community. Most accepted.

1960, February 13. France Explodes Nuclear Weapon in the Sahara. She became the world's fourth nuclear power.

1960, December 6. France to Be Militarily Independent of U.S. De Gaulle formally announced a plan for establishing an independent French nuclear striking force. By development of its own independent military power, exemplified by the small nuclear-capable air bombardment striking force, or *force de frappe,* de Gaulle emphasized French military and political independence of the U.S. and NATO, while retaining a consistently western-oriented strategy (1960–1965).

1961, April 22–26. Army Mutiny in Algeria. This was forcefully suppressed by de Gaulle (see p. 1314).

1961, July 19–21. Clash with Tunis. Tunisian violence, caused by Algerian border dispute, erupted against French bases in Tunisia; Bizerte was besieged by Tunisian forces. Massive French counterattacks, by land, sea, and air, overwhelmed Tunisian besiegers; both sides accepted a U.N. cease-fire (see p. 1316).

1963, January 22. Franco-German Treaty of Friendship. This pledged co-operation between the 2 countries in foreign policy, defense, and cultural affairs.

1964, February 18. French Intervention in Gabon. (**See p. 1267.**)

1963, August 15. French Troops to Congo (Brazzaville). The French unit in the Congo was reinforced by troops airlifted to Chad during disorders related to a coup d'état (see p. 1324). President de Gaulle refused, however, to have French troops support ousted President **Fulbert Youlou.**

1965, July 14. Mirage IV Jet Bombers Revealed. Twelve flew over the Bastille Day Parade, demonstrating a French long-range nuclear weapon delivery capability.

1966, March 9. French Military Withdrawal from NATO. (See p. 1258.)

1966, July–October. French Nuclear Weapons Tests in the Pacific. Between July 2 and October 4, France exploded 5 weapons, up to 400 kilotons in size, at Mururoa Atoll, 750 miles southeast of Tahiti. France ignored protests from Australia, New Zealand, Japan, and 5 South American nations.

1967, November 16. Intervention in Central African Republic. (See p. 1320.)

1968, August 24. France Explodes Thermonuclear Weapon in the Pacific. The 2-megaton device, suspended from a balloon above Mururoa Atoll, made France the world's fifth thermonuclear power. A second H-bomb was detonated on September 8.

1968, August 28. French Troops to Chad. The French contingent of 1,000 troops was ordered to assist the Chad Government in putting down a rebellion in the northwest corner of the country. Approximately one battalion of French paratroopers was airlifted in to participate.

1970, January 9. Sale of Aircraft to Libya. (**See p. 1315.**)

1973, July. Nuclear Tests in Pacific.

WEST GERMANY

Threat of war between the U.S.S.R. and her satellites on the one hand and the nations of the Free World on the other hung over divided Germany throughout the period. The Federal Republic of Germany, with its capital at Bonn, was proclaimed May 23, 1949, the puppet Communist German Democratic Republic on October 7. Meanwhile, friction intensified in Berlin, lying within the Soviet zone of occupation but divided in a quadripartite Kommandatura, and access—except by air—was never established by formal agreement.

1945, November 20. Nuremberg War Crimes Trials Begin. Twenty-two Nazi leaders were convicted of war crimes, 11 being condemned to death by the International Military Tribunal (October 1, 1946): Hermann Goering, Joachim von Ribbentrop, Ernst Kaltenbrunner, Marshal Wilhelm Keitel, Alfred Rosenberg, Hans Frank, Wilhelm Frick, Julius Streicher, Fritz Sauckel, General Alfred Jodl, and Arthur Seyss-Inquart. Rudolph Hess, Walther Funk, and Admiral Erich Raeder were sentenced to life imprisonment. Baldur von Schirach and Albert Speer were sentenced to 20 years imprisonment, Konstantin von Neurath to 15 years, Admiral Karl Doenitz to 10. Hjalmar Schacht, Franz von Papen, and Hans Fritsche were acquitted. Ten of the convicted war criminals were hanged (October 15, 1946); Goering committed suicide by swallowing poison 2 hours before scheduled to be hanged.

1947, January 14. Beginning of Talks for

German and Austrian Peace Treaties. In London, deputies of the Big-Four foreign ministers opened preliminary talks.

Berlin Blockade, 1948–1949

1948, March–June. Soviet Harassment of Western Powers in Berlin. This began when the Soviet delegation walked out of the Allied Control Council (March 20). Soon thereafter, the Soviets began interference and harassment of American and British access to Berlin from West Germany (April 1). The Soviet representative walked out (June 16) of the Kommandatura (4-power military commission in Berlin), virtually cutting off the Soviet military command in Berlin from the 3 western powers.

1948, June 22. Beginning of the Blockade. Soviet occupation authorities halted all railroad traffic between Berlin and the west. There was less than 1 month's food supply for the 2 million inhabitants of the western sectors of Berlin. U.S. General **Lucius D. Clay**, commanding U.S. occupation forces in Germany, urged that the Western Allied garrisons stay put, and that Berlin be supplied by air. His recommendations were upheld.

1948–1949, June 26–September 30. Operation "Vittles." Immediate mobilization of all Western Allied military aircraft available began, while Clay rallied Berlin civilian help to expand the 2 available airfields. (A third was soon built.) Air Lift Task Force (Provisional), commanded by U.S. Major General **William H. Tunner** and composed mainly of U.S. planes and pilots, with smaller increments of British and French air forces, accomplished the most extraordinary military peacetime effort in history. Running on split-second schedule, through all sorts of weather, and harassed from time to time by "buzzing" of Soviet fighter planes, 277,264 flights were made, lifting a total of 2,343,315 tons of food and coal. The record day's lift was on Easter Sunday, April 16, 1949, when 1,398 flights brought 12,940 tons into Berlin. The operation cost the lives of 75 American and British airmen, including a collision when a Soviet pilot, bedeviling a passenger-loaded British plane, misjudged his distance and brought both aircraft down in the crash.

1948, July 26. Western Powers Halt All Trade with East Germany. This was retaliation for the blockade.

1949, May 12. Soviets End Blockade. Soviet authorities, conceding defeat, officially lifted the blockade, but the air supply operation continued until September 30.

1949, April 14. End of the Nuremberg War Crimes Trials.

1949, September 7. The Federal Republic of Germany Established. Its capital was at Bonn. Dr. **Konrad Adenauer** was elected chancellor (September 15). The U.S., Britain, and France guaranteed the defense of West Germany (September 19) and ended their military government (September 21).

1949–1965. Intermittent Berlin Incidents. The U.S.S.R. and the East German Communist regime frequently tested Western Allied will and determination, and attempted to erode the occupation and access rights of the Western Allies to Berlin.

1952, March 1. Britain Returns Heligoland to West Germany.

1953, March. Allied-Soviet Air Incidents. An American plane was shot down over the U.S. zone (March 10), and a British bomber was shot down over the British zone (March 12). The U.S. ordered 25 of its latest Sabrejets to Germany, to counter the threat, while secret conciliation talks began between Britain and Russia (March 31) which later were attended by France and the U.S.

1954, October 23. Rearmament of Germany within NATO. The NATO Council admitted Germany to NATO. Next day, France specifically recognized the sovereignty of West Germany.

1955, May 5. Federal Republic of Germany Becomes a Sovereign State.

1961, July. Renewed Berlin Crisis. Prime Minister **Nikita Khrushchev,** renewing demands for Allied withdrawal from Berlin, announced suspension of planned troop reduction and an increase in the Soviet military budget (July 8). Britain, France, and the U.S. rejected Khrushchev's terms for the settlement of the Berlin and German questions (July 17). President Kennedy directed a build-up of U.S. military strength and mobilized 4 National Guard divisions (see p. 1333).

1961, August 12–13. The Wall. The East

German government closed the borders between East and West Berlin to East Germans. A wall, built overnight, split the city. The Soviet Union rejected western protests against the sealing of the border (September 11). Soviet and U.S. tanks confronted one another at "Checkpoint Charlie," but tension died. The division continued at the end of the period.

1965, February 12. Germany Suspends Arms Shipments to Israel. This was in response to UAR warning that it would sever diplomatic relations if shipments were not halted.

1966, December 6. Luftwaffe's F-104G Starfighters Grounded. This action was taken by General **Johannes Steinhoff** as a result of the Luftwaffe's 65th Starfighter crash since 1962. American airmen said that the German crashes were due to the German practice of putting more equipment into these aircraft than they were designed to carry.

1970, August 12. German-Soviet Nonaggression Treaty. This was signed in Moscow by German Chancellor **Willy Brandt** and Soviet Premier **Alexei Kosygin.**

1970, December 7. Treaty with Poland. This recognized the post-World War II boundary imposed by the Allies, along the Oder-Neisse rivers. It confirmed cession of 40,000 square miles, one-fourth of Germany, to Poland.

1971, August 23. New Agreement on Berlin. The U.S., Britain, France, and the U.S.S.R. signed a new agreement on access to Berlin and passage of West Berliners into East Germany. The agreement was endorsed by both East and West Germany. East Germans were not authorized to visit West Germany or West Berlin. This was followed (December 17) by an agreement between the two Germanies, authorizing West Germany free access to West Berlin.

1972, December 21. Treaty between East and West Germany. Although the possibility of future unity was left open, this meant full recognition by each of the sovereignty of the other.

SCANDINAVIAN STATES

All Scandinavian states were preoccupied during the period with the question of national security against Communist infiltration or outright aggression. While Denmark, Norway, and Iceland became members of NATO, Sweden maintained a strict—though western-oriented—neutrality. Finland—which clearly demonstrated an equally pro-western orientation—also maintained a neutral status, but was forced by geography and power realities to maintain closer relations with the U.S.S.R. (For Iceland's dispute with Britain, see p. 1260.)

AUSTRIA

After 10 years of Allied occupation marked by inability of the Big Four to agree on a peace treaty, the nation regained its independence by a treaty signed at Vienna by the U.S., U.K., France, and U.S.S.R. (May 15, 1955), restoring Austria's frontiers existing January 1, 1938. Under the treaty a small army and air force (about 60,000 strong) were permitted. The treaty requirement for neutrality was confirmed by Austria's official proclamation of permanent neutrality (act of October 26, 1955).

ITALY

1946, May 9. Abdication of King Victor Emmanuel III. He abdicated in favor of his son, **Humbert II.**

1946, June 2. Italian People Vote to End the Monarchy. The Italian government declared Italy a republic (June 2). After some outbreaks of violence between royalists and republicans, King Humbert left the country (June 13).

1946, July 29. Peace Conference Opens in Paris. Treaties were negotiated between the World War II victors and Italy, Hungary, Bulgaria, Rumania, and Finland. These allied peace treaties were eventually signed in Paris (February 10, 1947).

1947, September 16. Crisis at Trieste. A

Yugoslav military force, menacing Trieste, was deterred by the deployment of an American battalion for combat. Tension remained high; incidents, including occasional small-arms fire, were frequent.

1947, December 14. End of Allied Occupation of Italy. British and U.S. units remained in Trieste, however, to prevent Yugoslav seizure.

1948, July 14–16. Communist Riots. These were sparked by an assassination attempt against Communist leader **Palmiro Togliatti.** Police and troops restored order after considerable bloodshed.

1952, March 20. Civil Disorder in Trieste. Pro-Italians attacked American and British installations in protest against continued Allied occupation of Trieste.

1953, August 29–31. Border Clash with Yugoslavia. Italy's dispute with Yugoslavia escalated as both sides held maneuvers near Trieste, and Yugoslav antiaircraft fired at Italian planes over the border. Shots also were fired between Yugoslav troops and the Anglo-American force occupying Trieste.

1953, October 8–December 5. De Facto Settlement at Trieste. Britain and the U.S. announced that they would withdraw their occupation forces (4,000 U.S. and 3,000 British) and return Zone A of Trieste to Italy. After an increase of tension between Italy and Yugoslavia, the 2 nations agreed to withdraw their troops from the border (December 5). An agreement was later signed between them (October 5, 1954).

1963, January. Nuclear Weapons Agreement with U.S. (See p. 1273.)

SPAIN

1949, August 4. Spain's Application for Marshall Plan Aid Rejected. The U.S. Senate refused to include such aid in the Marshall Plan appropriations.

1953, September 26. Ten-Year Defense Agreement with U.S. This gave the U.S. rights to Spanish naval and air bases in return for economic and military aid. The bases were to be: air bases near Madrid, Albacete, Valencia, and Seville; naval facilities at Ferrol, Cadiz, Cartagena, Valencia, and Port Mahon on Minorca.

1965, September 26. Renewal of Base Agreement with the United States. This provided for the continued lease of air and naval bases to the U.S., in exchange for economic and military aid.

1970, August 8. Renewal of Base Agreement with United States. In return the U.S. was to provide $153 million in economic and military aid, including the lease of 12 naval vessels.

PORTUGUAL

1946, October 11. Unsuccessful Revolt Attempt. Most military rebels against the regime of dictator **Antonio de Oliveira Salazar** were captured in Estarreja or Lisbon.

1961, January 22–February 2. *Santa Maria* Incident. Portuguese rebels, planning a revolt against the Salazar government, seized the Portuguese passenger ship S.S. *Santa Maria.* The rebel leader was former Navy Captain **Henrique Malta Galvao** and former General **Humberto da Silva Delgado** (ashore in Brazil). After warnings from the U.S. and British navies, Galvao took the *Santa Maria* to Recife and accepted asylum in Brazil.

1961–1974. Rebellion in Angola. **(See p. 1323.)**

1962, January 1. Unsuccessful Revolt Attempt. Loyal troops quickly suppressed an uprising by a small military unit in Beja.

1962–1974. Rebellion in Portuguese Guinea. **(See p. 1325.)**

1962–1974. Rebellion in Mozambique. **(See p. 1327.)**

1967, July–August. Violence in Macao. Communist-inspired violence, bordering on insurrection, was suppressed by local police only after the major center of violence, on Hong Kong, was eliminated by British troops (see p. 1260).

1970, November 22–24. Portuguese-Supported Invasion of Guinea. **(See p. 1324.)**

1974, March 16. Military Revolt Fails. Young officers, leading a small motor march on Lisbon, surrendered when other military units failed to join them. Reportedly they were supporters of General **Antonio de Spinola,** who was dismissed as Deputy Chief of Staff (March 14) as a result of a recent book critical of Portugal's military, diplomatic, economic, and colonial policies.

1974, April 25. Coup d'État. The government of Premier **Marcello Caetano** (successor to Salazar) was overthrown by a military uprising. General Spinola was the leading member of a six-officer junta which pledged liberal freedom to Portugal after 40 years of repressive dictatorship. Spinola became provisional president (May 15).

1974, September 30. Spinola Resigns. This was because of his inability to control leftist tendencies in his new government represented by Premier (former general) **Vasco Gonçalves.** Spinola was replaced by General **Francisco da Costa Gomes,** who reappointed Gonçalves as premier.

EASTERN EUROPE

SOVIET BLOC AND WARSAW PACT NATIONS

1947, July. Communist Nations Reject the Marshall Plan. Although Poland and Czechoslovakia initially indicated an interest in joining in the Marshall Plan, they later rejected the offer, obviously under Soviet pressure, as did the other East European nations: Hungary, Rumania, Albania, Bulgaria, Yugoslavia, and Finland.

1947, October 5. Establishment of the Cominform. At a meeting in Moscow of the Communist parties of 9 European nations, a new Communist International, the Cominform, was established.

1955, May 14. The Warsaw Pact. The Soviet Union and its satellites—Poland, Czechoslovakia, Hungary, Rumania, Bulgaria, East Germany, and Albania—signed a treaty of mutual friendship and defense at Warsaw. Yugoslavia refused to join. This nominally mutual-defense treaty was the Communist bloc's answer to NATO and the remilitarization of West Germany. This actually caused no changes in the relationship between Soviet and satellite forces.

SOVIET UNION

Despite near-catastrophic losses of man power, materials, and production facilities, at the close of World War II the U.S.S.R. was without question the second great power in a bipolar world. Soviet armies occupied all of Eastern Europe, much of Central Europe, northern Iran, Manchuria, and northern Korea. While the Western Allies demobilized their armies as quickly as possible after the war, Soviet military forces were maintained close to their wartime strength. At the same time, the Soviets were increasingly truculent in and out of the U.N., refused to carry out postwar agreements for the liberation of Eastern Europe, and were obviously determined to extend Soviet power and influence in any direction at any opportunity. This threatening and aggressive attitude was combined with the Soviet-directed efforts of international Communism to take advantage of postwar chaos and dislocation to gain control of the governments of many nations in Europe and Asia.

It soon became evident that the combination of Soviet threats of external aggression and of internal subversion by indigenous Communists was creating pressures that few of the war-weakened nations in the world could withstand by their own individual efforts. Subservient Communist satellite governments were established throughout East Europe. Britain's sudden and unexpected decline caused the U.S. to undertake economic and military measures to assist nations threatened by Soviet Communist aggression (Truman Doctrine, Marshall Plan). This U.S. response to Soviet moves, with the aim of blocking Soviet expansion, triggered the so-called Cold War.

Thwarted by American counteraction—initially supported by the American monopoly of nuclear weapons and long-range bombardment capability—the U.S.S.R. devoted itself to unceasing efforts to improve and modernize its military capability in an effort to offset and, if possible, surpass that of the U.S. The result was unexpectedly early Soviet detonation of atomic and hydrogen bombs. Again the potentially more powerful U.S. slowly reacted to meet the armament challenge and Soviet-inspired aggression of North Korea against South Korea (see p. 1208). As a result, despite rapid modernization and sophistication of its weapons and armed forces, by the end of the period the Soviet Union had failed to achieve its aim of military parity or superiority over the U.S. (save possibly in the fields of rocket power and space exploration). Nevertheless, its substantial capability in nuclear weapons, and possession of long-range missiles to deliver such weapons, had brought the U.S.S.R. to a position of nuclear stalemate with the U.S., and permitted continuation of its policy of encouraging and supporting Communist subversion in underdeveloped nations throughout the world.

In the development of its nuclear capability, the U.S.S.R. had obviously come to understand the unprecedented destructive power of nuclear weapons, and apparently realized that an all-out nuclear exchange would result in the virtual destruction of the U.S.S.R. This, combined with serious ideological and nationalistic differences with increasingly powerful Communist China, had led to some diminution in the intensity of the Cold War (particularly after the Cuban missile crisis), though there was no evidence of any change in basic Soviet Communist objectives. The undeclared conflict continued at lower levels, and in different forms, as Communist agents fomented and carried on low-intensity "wars of national liberation" wherever the opportunity presented itself around the world. The principal military events of the period were:

1945, August 14. Treaty with China. (**See p. 1305.**)

1945–1946. Intervention in Azerbaijan. (**See p. 1286.**) This was the real beginning of the Cold War.

1945–1947. Soviet Bloc Established. Despite World War II agreements at Yalta and Potsdam, and subsequent peace treaties with Nazi East European satellite states, the U.S.S.R. established its own satellite governments in areas occupied by its forces: Albania, Bulgaria, Czechoslovakia, Hungary, Poland, Rumania, eastern Austria, and East Germany (including the eastern sector of Berlin). Yugoslavia, under Tito's Communist government, was initially included in this East and Central European Communist satellite bloc.

1947, March 4. Norway Rejects Soviet Demands on Spitsbergen. The U.S.S.R. had requested rights to establish a military base.

1947, July 7. Russia Rejects the Marshall Plan.

1948, April 6. Treaty with Finland. A 10-year alliance was agreed.

1948–1949. Berlin Blockade. (**See p. 1263.**)

1948, June. Dispute with Yugoslavia. Amidst violent denunciation and counter-denunciation, Yugoslavia withdrew from the Soviet Bloc (see p. 1270).

1949, September 23. Russia Explodes Its First Atomic Bomb. This ended the U.S. nuclear monopoly.

1950–1953. Korean War. The U.S.S.R. supported North Korea and (later) Communist China in the Korean War (see p. 1240).

1953, March 5. Death of Stalin. He was succeeded by a triumvirate of **Georgi Malenkov, Lavrenti Beria,** and **Nikita Khrushchev.** Beria, who apparently contemplated seizing power, was later overthrown (July) by his colleagues (with army support) and executed (December 23).

1953, June 16–17. Suppression of Uprising in East Berlin. (**See p. 1269.**)

1953, August 12. U.S.S.R. Detonates Its First Hydrogen Bomb.

1955, May 14. Establishment of the Warsaw Pact. (**See p. 1266.**)

1955, December 28. Soviet Defense Budget Reduction Announced. Later (May 14, 1956) it was announced that armed forces would be cut by 1,200,000 men over the following year.

1956, February 14–25. De-Stalinization. At the 20th Party Congress in Moscow, Khrushchev, by now unquestioned leader of the U.S.S.R., attacked the memory of Stalin, and to some extent liberalized life and governmental policy in the U.S.S.R. and in the satellites. This revived hopes of personal liberty which created a wave of unrest in the U.S.S.R. and in the satellites.

1956, June 6. Bulganin Demands Reduction

of Western Forces in Germany. President Eisenhower rejected the Soviet premier's demand (August 7).

1956, June 28. Unrest in Poland. **(See p. 1269.)**

1956, July 10. Charges of U.S. Military Aircraft Violation in Korea. A complaint was made to the U.N. Security Council. The U.S. denied the charges.

1956, October 23–November 4. Hungarian Revolt Suppressed by Soviet Forces. **(See p. 1269.)**

1957, October 4. Soviet Space Triumph. Soviet artificial satellite, Sputnik I, made the first successful penetration of space. It established Soviet pre-eminence in space exploration, which was being challenged, and perhaps overtaken, at the end of the period by belated American efforts to catch up. It also evidenced a Soviet military pre-eminence in long-range rocketry, and particularly in the power of its rocket boosters.

1958, March 27. Khrushchev Seizes Control. Ousting Bulganin as premier, he became virtual dictator.

1960, January 20. Soviet Ballistic Missile Achievement. The U.S.S.R. claimed it fired a missile 7,752 nautical miles to within 1.24 miles of its target in the Central Pacific.

1960, May 1. U-2 Incident. Soviet air-defense missiles in central Russia shot down an American U-2 reconnaissance plane piloted by **F. G. Powers,** employee of the U.S. CIA. (See p. 1332.)

1960, May 17. Khrushchev Wrecks Summit Conference. **(See p. 1332.)**

1961, April 12. First Manned Space Flight. Soviet Major **Yuri Gagarin** became the first human to travel in space. He landed safely in the Soviet Union after 1 circuit of the globe.

1961, August 12–13. The Berlin Wall. **(See p. 1263.)**

1961, December 9. Soviet Superbombs. At the close of the Soviet Union's post-moratorium test series (see p. 1255), Khrushchev publicly boasted that the Soviet Union had nuclear bombs more powerful than 100 megatons. American analysis of fallout seemed to substantiate the claim.

1962, October 17. Khrushchev Reveals Soviet-Sino Rift. During the 22nd Soviet Communist Party Congress in Moscow, Khrushchev revealed the existence of a Soviet-Sino ideological rift, mainly by attacking Albania, ideological ally of Communist China.

1962, October–November. Cuban Missile Crisis. **(See p. 1333.)**

1963, July 25. Limited Nuclear Test Ban Treaty. **(See p. 1255.)**

1964, October 12. First Multimanned Space Flight. The Soviet Union orbited a spacecraft, carrying 3 men, for 16 orbits.

1964, October 14–15. Khrushchev Deposed as Soviet Leader. He was replaced by **Leonid I. Brezhnev** and **Aleksei N. Kosygin.**

1964–1974. Border Clashes With Communist China. (See p. 1310.)

1967, November 3. Soviet Fractional Orbital Bombardment System. **The development of this system was revealed in a statement by US Defense Secretary Robert S. McNamara, who said that it would permit firing a nuclear weapon from an orbiting position at a target on the earth. McNamara said that the US had rejected such a system, and did not believe that it would give the USSR any advantage.**

HUNGARY

Despite overwhelming anti-Communist popular sentiment, a Communist satellite government was installed with the assistance and protection of Soviet occupation forces (1945–1947). Communist control was unchallenged until a wave of unrest swept over Eastern Europe in 1956, following Khrushchev's de-Stalinization speech (see p. 1267).

1947, May 30. Communist Coup. The government of Premier **Ferenc Nagy** was overthrown.

1956, July 18–22. Shake-up in Communist Government. This was evidence of serious internal unrest in the party and the nation.

1956, October 23. Outbreak of Popular Revolt against Communism. This followed security police attempts to suppress a popular demonstration in Budapest. Soviet occupation forces fired on demonstrators (October 24–25). Revolutionary Councils sprang up throughout the country. The Communist government was toppled in a surprising constitutional parliamentary upheaval (October 25). Erstwhile moderate Communist **Imre Nagy** established a pro-western government. **Erno Gero,** ousted party secretary, called for Soviet troops. Fighting involving Hungarian Communist forces and Soviet troops spread across the country.

1956, October 28. Nagy Announces Soviet Agreement to Withdraw Troops. A lull in the fighting followed.

1956, November 1–4. Soviet Suppression of Revolt. By a combination of treachery and surprise, Soviet forces—with some 200,000 troops and 2,500 tanks and armored cars—surrounded Budapest. Nagy appealed for U.N. aid. The Soviets attacked, captured Nagy and his government (November 4), and swept through Budapest despite the valiant resistance of Hungarian troops and civilians. Approximately 25,000 Hungarians and 7,000 Russians were killed. One unfortunate aspect of the debacle was the stimulus of American broadcasting programs that led the patriots to believe that the U.S. would come to their aid.

1956, November 5–30. Unrest and Flight. Resistance and strikes persisted despite ruthless Soviet suppression. By the end of the month over 100,000 refugees had fled to the West.

POLAND

A Communist people's republic since 1947, when Stalin's repudiation of the free election promised at the Potsdam Conference brought a Communist puppet government into being, under the protection of Soviet occupation forces, Poland was an uneasy satellite of the U.S.S.R. during the period. Persecution of the Catholic Church and imprisonment—until 1956—of **Stefan Cardinal Wyszynski** added to the tension between the Polish people and their government.

1949. Russian Commands Army. Soviet Marshal **Konstantin Rokossovski** was appointed Minister of Defense and Commander in Chief of the Polish army.

1950, June 7. Frontier Agreement with East Germany. The Oder-Neisse line was accepted as the official boundary.

1956, June 28–29. Workers' Revolt in Poznan. This was suppressed by Russian troops and brought death to over 50, injury to hundreds more, and imprisonment of more than 1,000 persons. Unrest in Poland continued and tension mounted between people and Soviet occupation army.

1956, October. Wladyslaw Gomulka Becomes Premier. The moderate Polish Communist leader was released from jail and restored to party leadership. This reduced tension and unrest, brought amelioration of conditions, and slackening of Soviet restrictions. Gomulka defied Khrushchev's warnings that democratization was too rapid. Cardinal Wyszynski was released; cultural and financial relations with the West were initiated. Soviet Marshal Rokossovski was dismissed as Polish defense minister.

1956, November 18. Agreement with U.S.S.R. Poland was given greater independence.

1957, October 3. Riots in Warsaw. Suppressed by police and troops.

1970, December 15–20. Civil Disturbance. Widespread disorders throughout much of Poland, particularly in the north, caused the death of more than 300 people in clashes between mobs and troops. Communist Party Secretary **Wladyslaw Gomulka** resigned and was replaced by **Edward Gierek,** who ended the disturbances by promising revised economic policies.

EAST GERMANY

1949, October 7. Establishment of German Democratic Republic. Otto Grotewohl was established as Chancellor of this new Soviet satellite.

1953, June 16–17. Anticommunist Riots in East Berlin and East Germany. These were suppressed by the Soviet Army.

1953, August 23. Soviet Moves to Strengthen Ties with East Germany. This included release of war prisoners, lowering of occupation costs, and an intensive propaganda campaign. The U.S.S.R. returned to East Germany 30 factories which had been seized as reparations after World War II (December 31). It was announced that all reparations were ended, and that further occupation costs would be limited to 5 per cent of East Germany's national income.

1954, March 26. U.S.S.R. Announces East German Sovereignty. Soviet troops were to remain only for security functions and for the fulfillment of Soviet obligations under the Potsdam Agreement.

1955, January 10. Defections to West. The West German Refugee Ministry reported that 184,198 persons had left East Germany for the West in 1954.

1956, January 18. East Germany Rearms. Parliament approved creation of a defense ministry and a people's army.

1964, January–March. Air Incidents. Soviet aircraft shot down an unarmed U.S. reconnaissance plane (March 10) and an Air Force jet training plane which by mistake flew over East Germany (January 28). Both the U.S. and the U.S.S.R. protested.

1972, December 21. Treaty with West Germany. (See p. 1264.)

CZECHOSLOVAKIA

1948, February 24. Communist Coup d'État. President **Eduard Beneš** was forced to accept an ultimatum of Premier **Klement Gottwald,** putting Communists in charge of all branches of the government except the Foreign Ministry, where **Jan Masaryk** remained Foreign Minister, but all his aides were Communists.

1948, March 10. Death of Jan Masaryk. The Communist government announced this was suicide. There is little doubt that he was murdered by the Communists.

1968, July 15. Czechoslovakia Demands Revision of Warsaw Pact. Increasing coolness between the Kremlin and the "democratic" Communist government of Prime Minister **Alexander Dubcek** led the Czechs to request assurances that the treaty would not be used for political purposes, but only for the defense of Eastern Europe against foreign military aggression. A subsequent meeting of Czech and Soviet political leaders in the border town of Cernia did not reduce the tension.

1968, August 20. Warsaw Pact Invasion. Soviet, East German, Polish, Bulgarian, and Hungarian forces in overwhelming strength (at least 500,000 men) met little resistance as they occupied the country and deposed the government of Prime Minister Dubcek. After a safely pro-Soviet Communist government was firmly installed in power, most of the invading trops were withdrawn (beginning in October), but a garrison of several Soviet divisions (totaling more than 65,000 troops) remained.

YUGOSLAVIA

1946, March 24. Capture of General Draja Mikhailovich. He was tried and executed by a firing squad in Belgrade (July 17).

1946–1948. Intervention in Greece. Yugoslavia supported the rebels in the Greek Civil War (see p. 1271).

1947–1953. Crises over Trieste, (See pp. 1264–1265.)

1948, June 28. Yugoslav-Soviet Rift. The Cominform denounced Marshal **Tito** and the Yugoslav Communist party for putting national interests above party interests. Tito and the Yugoslav Communist party, insisting that they were still Communists, also insisted that they were Yugoslav Communists and not Russian satellites. This marked the end of Yugoslavia's role as a Soviet satellite and the beginning of completely independent existence, although under President Tito the nation remained definitely, although individualistically, Communist.

1949, August–September. Yugoslav-Soviet Crisis. Each nation accused the other of preparing for war, and Russia denounced the 1945 treaty of friendship and mutual assistance with Yugoslavia (September 29).

1953, June 1. Political Commissars Abolished in the Armed Forces. This was announced by Marshal Tito personally.

1956, October 15. U.S. Assistance. Eisenhower authorized continuance of U.S. economic aid to Yugoslavia, but withheld heavy military equipment pending further study.

1956, November 11. Renewed Difficulties with U.S.S.R. This resulted from a Tito speech at a party meeting.

1961, October 13. U.S. Military Assistance. The U.S. confirmed that it was granting military aid to Yugoslavia, to include 130 jet fighter planes, and the training of Yugoslav fighter pilots in the United States.

ALBANIA

1946, October 22. Corfu Channel Incident. Two British destroyers were damaged by Albanian mines in the Corfu Channel, with 40 men killed or missing. (Earlier in the year, Albanian shore batteries had fired at British and Greek warships in the channel.) Britain cleared the mines from the channel, under naval protection, despite Albanian protests to the U.N. (November 12–13). The U.S.S.R. vetoed a Security Council resolution blaming Albania for the damage (March 25, 1947). In subsequent litigation before the Court of International Justice, Albania was found at fault (April 9, 1949).

1961, December 19. Diplomatic Relations with U.S.S.R. Broken. This was a protest against de-Stalinization. Albania became the first European satellite of Communist China.

RUMANIA

1966, May 10. Soviet–Rumanian Tension over Warsaw Pact. Cautious Rumanian moves toward a policy independent of the U.S.S.R., and suggestions that the terms of the Warsaw Pact be changed, led to a visit to Bucharest by Soviet Communist Party First Secretary Leonid Brezhnev for discussions with independence-minded Rumanian First Secretary **Nicholas Ceausescu.** The result was a reduction in the stridency of Rumanian assertions of independence.

1968, August 20. Rumanian Nonparticipation in Invasion of Czechoslovakia. Apparently the Rumanian Government was not informed of the Warsaw Pact plan.

MEDITERRANEAN AND SOUTHEASTERN EUROPE

GREECE

1944, December 3–January 11, 1945. Guerrilla Warfare. Communist resistance groups attempted to overthrow the reestablished legal government of Greece, then under the protection of British occupation forces. British troops suppressed the uprisings and established an uneasy truce between the rival factions.

1945, September 1. Monarchy Restored. The Greek people voted to return King **George II** to the throne.

1946, May–1949, October. Greek Civil War. Communist rebels under General **"Markos" Vafiades,** with support from Albania, Yugoslavia, and Bulgaria, seized control of major northern border regions, while fighting flared throughout the nation. The Greek government received some support from Britain at the outset, but was barely able to maintain control of major cities and some portions of the countryside. Fighting was particularly intensive in the Vardar Valley.

1946, December 10. U.N. Begins Investigation. The Security Council began an investigation into Greek charges that Yugoslavia, Bulgaria, and Albania were supporting guerrilla forces on Greece's northern frontier. The Balkans Investigating Committee reported to the Security Council (May 23, 1947) that Yugoslavia, Bulgaria, and Albania had violated the U.N. Charter by aiding guerrilla uprisings in Greece.

1947, March 12. Truman Doctrine. Britain, close to economic collapse, was forced to suspend its assistance to Greece. President Truman announced American determination to assist Greece and Turkey against internal and external Communist threats. This resulted in extensive economic aid and provision of military equipment to the strife-torn nation. An American military advisory group trained the Greek Army in employment of U.S. military equipment, and also rendered combat advice. The Greek Army slowly regained the initiative, and suppressed the revolt throughout all of Greece (1947) save in the northern border regions, where rebels obtained direct assistance from the neighboring Soviet satellites.

1948, January 1. Relief of Konitsa. Greek government troops relieved Konitsa, long under rebel siege, driving the defeated guerrilla forces into Albania. A subsequent rebel effort to capture Konitsa was repulsed (January 25).

1948, June 19. Greek Army Offensive Begins. Greek efforts to capture the rebel stronghold of Vafiades were partially successful. Intensive fighting continued for several months in the **Mt. Grammos** region.

1948, November 27. U.N. Condemns Greece's Neighbors. The General Assembly condemned Albania, Bulgaria, and Yugoslavia for continuing to give assistance to the Greek guerrillas. In fact, however, Yugoslav assistance had declined rapidly after her expulsion from the Cominform (see p. 1270). This greatly facilitated the task of government troops.

1949. General Markos Replaced. Markos Vafiades was replaced as commander of the Greek guerrillas by **John Ioannides.**

1949, June 25. U.N. Charges against Bulgaria. The U.N. Special Committee on the Balkans accused Bulgaria of permitting Greek guerrillas to establish fortifications within Bulgaria from which to fire on Greek troops in Greek territory.

1949, August 28. Greek Troops Clear Mt. Grammos. The principal rebel resistance in Greece was broken by a government assault which captured the northern ridge of Mt. Grammos.

1949, October 16. End of the Civil War.

1951, September 20. Greece Joins NATO.

1954, August 9. Treaty with Turkey and Yugoslavia. This was a 20-year treaty for military assistance and political co-operation, and marked a remarkable *rapprochement* among old enemies.

1955–1965. Strained Relations with Turkey. This was due to the Cyprus issue (see p. 1273).

1955–1959. Strained Relations with Britain. This was due to Cyprus (see pp. 1273–1274).

1967, April 21. Military Coup d'État. A junta of right-wing army officers, led by Colonel **George Papadopoulos,** seized control of the government to prevent elections which might have brought a leftist government to Greece under **George Papandreou.** The military leaders set up a puppet civilian government and claimed the support of King **Constantine,** who appeared unenthusiastic about the coup.

1967, December 13. Failure of King Constantine's Attempted Countercoup. A broadcast appeal failed to arouse popular and military support to overthrow the junta; Constantine fled by air to exile in Rome. Papadopoulos, with junta approval, appointed himself prime minister of a completely military government.

1973, June 1. Greece Becomes a Republic. Papadopoulos proclaimed himself president. A popular referendum, held under strict military control, approved (July 29).

1973, November 25. Military Coup d'État Ousts Papadopoulos. A period of popular unrest, in which President Papadopoulos made some concessions to demonstrators, led militant right-wing military leaders, under secret police chief, Brigadier General **Demetrios Ioannides,** to seize control. Papadopoulos was placed in house arrest and replaced as president by Lieutenant General **Phaidon Gizikis.**

1974, July. Tension over Cyprus. (See p. 1274.)

1974, July 24. End of Military Dictatorship. The military junta turned control over to former Premier **Constantine Karamanlis,** who returned to Greece from self-imposed exile.

MALTA

1964, September 21. Independent Malta Guarantees British Bases. Becoming independent, Malta joined the British Commonwealth and guaranteed bases for British forces for ten years.

1972, March 26. Treaty Renews British Base Rights. After demanding British and NATO withdrawal from Malta, and threatening to allow Soviet military forces to use facilities on Malta, Prime Minister **Dom Mintoff** agreed to a treaty extending limited British base rights for 7 years in return for $260 million.

TURKEY

1945–1947. Tension between Turkey and U.S.S.R. The Soviets unsuccessfully used diplomatic pressure and threats of force to gain concessions from Turkey in the Straits area and in Turkish Caucasus regions.

1946, August 12. Soviet Demands Dardanelles Rights. The U.S.S.R. demanded joint control of military bases along the Dardanelles, and proposed to Turkey that only Black Sea countries share in the administration of the Turkish Straits. Turkey rejected the Soviet demands (October 18).

1947, March 12. Truman Doctrine. American economic assistance and military equipment greatly strengthened Turkish resistance to Russian pressures.

1950, September 20. Korean War. Turkey sent a major contingent (initially 4,500 men, later increased to about 8,000) to join the U.N. forces in Korea.

1951, September 20. Turkey Joins NATO.

1955–1965. Strained Relations with Greece over Cyprus. **(See below.)**

1955, September 6. Anti-Greek Riots. Riots against the Greeks broke out in Istanbul and Izmir as a result of troubles between the Greek and Turkish inhabitants in Cyprus and anti-Turkish demonstrations in Greece.

1957, October 8. Border Clash with Syria. This, like several previous incidents, arose from Syrian smuggling. This incident heightened tension which already existed, and was followed by other clashes (November 4, 9).

1960, April 28–May 21. Civil Disorder. Widespread rioting by students was put down by police and army with some bloodshed. Martial law was declared, but protests continued. Students from the Military Academy joined in protests, defying martial law (May 21).

1962, February 27. Attempted Coup. A Military Academy mutiny was suppressed without bloodshed.

1963, January 21. Nuclear Weapons Agreement with U.S. Turkey accepted U.S. offers to station Polaris missiles submarines in the Mediterranean Sea to replace Jupiter missiles stationed on Turkish soil. (Italy simultaneously agreed to the withdrawal of Jupiter missiles from Italian soil.)

1963, May 20. Attempted Coup. A Military Academy mutiny was suppressed with some bloodshed.

1964, August 7–9. Air Force Intervention in Cyprus. (See p. 1274.)

1966–1967. Intermittent Tension with Greece over Cyprus.

1971, March 12. Army Ultimatum Forces Government Change. Military leaders threatened to take over the government unless a strong coalition government was established to replace that of Prime Minister **Suleyman Demirel,** who had been unable to control sporadic unrest and violence. At the same time, several high-ranking officers who had favored an immediate coup were forced to retire. Prime Minister **Nihat Erim** established a coalition government two weeks later.

1974, July 20. Turkish Invasion of Cyprus. **(See p. 1274.)**

CYPRUS

For more than 70 years Cyprus was a British dependency or colony. The population of this east-Mediterranean island is about 80 per cent Greek and nearly 20 per cent Turkish. Long before World War II, there was a strong sentiment among the Greek population for *enosis,* or union with Greece. This was bitterly opposed by the Turkish minority, who believed that if under Greek control they would be deprived of the rights they enjoyed under British rule.

1952–1959. Guerrilla Warfare. Greek agitation for *enosis* was translated into terrorism directed against the Turkish minority, and guerrilla warfare combined with terrorism waged against the British occupation forces. Principal guerrilla leader was a Greek war hero, Colonel **Grivas.** Complete support to the *enosis* movement was given by Greek Orthodox Archbishop **Makarios,** who was exiled by the British.

1959, March 13. Cease-Fire in Cyprus.

This followed an agreement between the British government and the Greek and Turkish communities on Cyprus, with the approval of Greece and Turkey (February 19). An independent republic of Cyprus was to be established, in which the rights of the Turkish minority would be clearly and constitutionally protected. Britain was to retain military bases on the island.

1959, December 14. Makarios Elected First President of Cyprus.

1960–1963. Agitation for *Enosis* Continues. Tension increased between the Greek and Turkish communities.

1963, December 21. Outbreak of Conflict. As a result of Makarios' efforts to reform the constitution and thus reduce the rights of the Turkish minority, armed clashes between Greeks and Turks spread throughout the island. Britain sent reinforcements to attempt to restore order, but widespread fighting continued.

1964, January–February. Unsuccessful Mediation. British and American efforts to establish an international peace-keeping force, under NATO or the U.N., were all rejected by Makarios, who meanwhile was building up his military forces.

1964, March 4. U.N. Intervention. After an impasse had been reached in U.N. discussion, the Security Council authorized Secretary General **U Thant** to establish a peace force and to appoint a mediator.

1964, March 27. A U.N. Peace Force Becomes Operational.

1964, August 7–9. Turkish Air Attacks. Following Greek Cypriote attacks on Turkish Cypriote villages, Turkish planes attacked Greek Cypriote positions. With Greece and Turkey close to war, the U.N. was able to get agreement of the Turkish and Cypriote governments to a cease-fire.

1966, August. Renewed Threats of Turkish Intervention. Unhappy over the condition of Turkish Cypriots in the uneasy stalemate on Cyprus, Turkey again threatened military intervention. Upon appeal from U.N. Secretary General U Thant, President Archbishop Makarios lifted restrictions which had been imposed upon Turkish Cypriots.

1967, November. Greek–Turkish Tension over Cyprus. Danger of war was averted by American mediation and strong pressures on Greece and Turkey. Greece began to withdraw its troops from Cyprus following the resultant agreement.

1974, July 15. Military Coup d'État. The Greek Cypriot National Guard, under leadership of Greek officers from Greece, and obviously abetted by the Greek military government, seized power. Archbishop Makarios (who had been reelected president on February 8, 1973) fled the country.

1974, July 20. Turkish Invasion. To forestall expected plans of the new Greek Cypriot government for "Enosis" (union) with Greece, Turkey seized the north coast of the island. Greece mobilized, but the military government of that country recognized its military weakness, combined with lack of popular support at home, and returned the government of Greece to civilian control (see p. 1273).

1974, July–August. Turkish Occupation Zone Expanded. Paying little attention to a series of cease-fire arrangements negotiated in the United Nations, Turkish forces expanded their control over the northeastern third of the island, establishing a *de facto* division of Cyprus into Greek and Turkish zones.

THE MIDDLE EAST

Unrest permeated the entire area, due to a unique combination of powerful and emotional forces: Cold War pressures, manifested in all parts of the world, particularly intense in this region due to its strategic geographic location and the untold wealth of vast oil reserves; aspirations of new nations breaking away from western colonialism; and the particularly virulent and irreconcilable strife between Israel and the Arab world. Least affected by these swirling tides within the region were the 2 non-Arab Moslem states of the region, Iran and Turkey.

THE ARAB LEAGUE

The Arab League was established shortly before the end of World War II (March 22, 1945) by the governments of Egypt, Iraq, Jordan, Lebanon, Saudi Arabia, Syria, and Yemen. The principal purpose was to prevent the British mandate in Palestine from becoming a separate and independent Jewish state. Later the League was joined by Algeria, Kuwait, Libya, Morocco, the Sudan, and Tunisia. Cairo has been the headquarters for the Secretary General of the League.

1947, January 5. Palestinian Talks. The Arab League accepted a British proposal to participate in a conference on the Palestinian problem to begin on January 26.

1948–1949. War with Israel. (See p. 1238.)

1950, June 17. Collective Security Pact. Egypt, Saudi Arabia, Syria, Lebanon, and Yemen signed a collective security pact in Alexandria. Iraq and Jordan did not join.

1954, June 11. Egypt and Saudi Arabia Reject Baghdad Pact. Under the terms of the Arab League Collective Security Pact, Egypt and Saudi Arabia agreed to pool defenses and military resources, rejecting western plans for a Middle East Defense Treaty against Communism (see below).

1956, March 3–11. Egypt, Syria, and Saudi Arabia Plan United Defense. Plans for combined action against Israel were agreed on by the heads of state at Cairo. King Hussein of Jordan refused to give up British subsidy.

1964, January 13–17. Arab League Conference. Leaders of the 13 Arab League nations met in Cairo and agreed to set up a joint military command for possible action against Israel.

1965, May 13. Severance of Diplomatic Relations with Germany. This was in protest over West Germany's recognition of Israel. Ten states (out of 13) participated: UAR, Jordan, Iraq, Syria, Lebanon, Yemen, Saudi Arabia, Algeria, Kuwait, and Sudan. Tunisia, Libya, and Morocco abstained.

1966, March 14. Arab League Conference in Cairo. Twelve of 13 members were represented; Tunisia was boycotting Arab League activities because of failure to consider compromise accommodations with Israel. The meeting agreed: (1) to continue severance of diplomatic relations with West Germany because of its recognition of Israel; (2) to denounce U.S. arms shipments to Israel as endangering U.S.–Arab relationships; and (3) to raise money for a project to divert the Jordan River from Israel.

1966, December 10. Arab League Defense Council Agreements. Saudi Arabian and Iraqi troops, with Jordanian approval, were to be deployed in Jordan to bolster defenses against Israel. Jordan simultaneously announced that this agreement was conditioned upon UAR troops replacing U.N. forces in the Sinai and Gaza Strip, which in turn would require UAR withdrawal from Yemen. Jordan refused to permit Syrian troops or Palestine Liberation Organization (PLO) guerrillas in Jordan.

CENTRAL TREATY ORGANIZATION OF THE MIDDLE EAST

The Central Treaty Organization of the Middle East is a successor organization to the Middle East Treaty Organization, or Baghdad Pact, established (1955) as a result of initiatives begun by the United States (1954).

1954, April 2. Turkey-Pakistan Treaty. Signing a 5-year mutual-defense pact, the 2 nations invited neighboring nations, particularly Iraq and Iran, to join.

1955, February 24. Turkey-Iraq Treaty. A 5-year mutual-defense pact with a 5-year renewal clause, joined by Britain (April 4), to establish so-called Baghdad Pact.

1955, November 21. First Meeting of the Baghdad Pact. Representatives of Iran, Iraq, Pakistan, Turkey, and Great Britain met in Baghdad to establish the Middle East Treaty Organization (METO). The U.S. did not join, but sent official observers to the meeting.

1956, April 19. U.S. Partial Participation. At a meeting in Teheran, the U.S. agreed to establish a permanent liaison office, and to help support the permanent METO secretariat.

1959, March 5. U.S. Treaties with the "Northern Tier." The U.S. signed separate defense treaties with Iran, Turkey, and Pakistan, in Ankara, to assure the nations of the Baghdad Pact that the U.S. would come to their support in need of any Communist aggression.

1959, October 7. Reorganization of the Alliance. In view of the withdrawal of Iraq (see p. 1282), the remaining members—Britain, Turkey, Pakistan, and Iran—changed its name to Central Treaty Organization (CENTO).

PALESTINE AND ISRAEL

1945–1948. Guerrilla Warfare in Palestine. This bitter and bloody struggle was waged mainly by Jewish Zionists against the Arab population and against British occupation forces, in their efforts to achieve an independent Jewish nation. U.N. efforts to solve rival aspirations of Jews and Arabs proved futile.

1947, November 29. U.N. Decision to Partition Palestine. The General Assembly approved a plan presented to it by a special committee to partition Palestine into separate Jewish and Arab states effective October 1, 1948. The Arab states refused to accept the decision, and announced their determination to fight if necessary.

1948–1949. Arab-Israeli War. (See p. 1222.)

1948, May 14. Independence of Israel. Britain surrendered her mandate over Palestine and withdrew her armed forces. The Israeli nation, immediately recognized by the U.S., was at once attacked and invaded by troops of Egypt, Iraq, Lebanon, Syria, and Transjordan (or Jordan).

1950, May 19. Egypt Closes Suez Canal to Israel. Israeli ships and Israeli commerce were banned.

1951, April 5–16. Border Hostilities with Syria. A cease-fire was later re-established (May 8).

1953–1956. Intermittent Frontier Clashes. Both sides appear to have been responsible for these various small and large outbreaks along the entire length of Israel's frontiers. However, the initiative appears in most cases to have been with the Arabs. Israeli punitive reprisals were largely stimulated by Arab breaches of the truce or by clandestine raids of Arab terrorists into Israel.

1955, December–1956, October. Increasing Tension along Israel's Borders. Raids of Arab terrorists and guerrillas were met by stern Israel punitive strikes at Egyptian, Syrian, and Jordanian border positions. Arab states, supported by the U.S.S.R., complained in the U.N., as tempers and emotions rose (see p. 1227). Both Israel and Arabs complained of U.S. arms shipments to the other side.

1956, October 29. Israel Strikes First. Hastily mobilized Israeli forces, commanded by General **Moshe Dayan,** plunged into the Sinai. Efficient mechanized columns scattered 4 Egyptian divisions in dismal, headlong rout. At cost of 180 men killed, the Israeli invasion pushed toward the Suez Canal, halting only 30 miles away when France and Britain gave both Egypt and Israel a 12-hour ultimatum to end hostilities (October 30), and then intervened (see p. 1240). U.N. denunciation of Israel, Britain, and France followed. Egyptian losses reported by Israel were 7,000 prisoners and an estimated 3,000 dead. Practically all the Egyptian equipment and matériel (worth $50 million) in the Sinai fell into Israeli hands.

1956, November 15. U.N. Intervention. (See p. 1254.) A curtain of U.N. troops moved into the Sinai between the adversaries. The Israeli invaders slowly retired to the

Negev (March 1957), only after U.S. assurances of rights to use the Gulf of Aqaba as an international waterway. A U.N. unit occupied Sharm el Sheikh, overlooking the gulf entrance, which had been captured by the Israelis.

1956–1965. Continuing Tension. Frontier skirmishing continued along Israel's frontiers, with the economic boycott of the Arab League continuing, and growing threat of war over water rights in the Jordan River system. The Arab states, particularly Egypt, were already building up strength in hopes of revenge, obtaining plentiful Soviet equipment.

1962, September 26. U.S. Assistance to Israel. The State Department announced that the United States had agreed to sell defensive missiles to Israel in order to restore the threatened balance of power in the Middle East.

1965, January 30. German Military Equipment to Israel. As part of an agreement between West Germany and Israel, following German recognition of Israel, shipment began of some $80 million worth of military equipment, including helicopters, submarines, antiaircraft guns, and U.S.-made M48 "Patton" tanks. There were strong complaints by the Arab states, which threatened to recognize Communist East Germany if the shipments continued. Germany stopped the shipments, but not before most of the Arab states had broken diplomatic relations (see p. 1275).

1966, February 5. United States Assumes Responsibility for Arms to Israel. The U.S. took over the former West German obligation, to maintain arms "stabilization" in the Middle East, in the light of continuing Soviet arms shipments to Egypt and Syria. Included in the American shipments would be 200 M48 tanks. Soon afterward (May 20) the U.S. revealed that, in accordance with its stabilization policy, it was also providing A-4 Skyhawk tactical aircraft to Israel.

1969, December 25. Israeli Seizure of Embargoed Gunboats from France. Five fast missile gunboats, being constructed in France under contract with Israel, were held by the French Government following President de Gaulle's embargo on all arms shipments to Israel as a result of the 1967 Arab-Israeli War. In a daring feat, Israeli crews secretly seized the vessels and took them to Haifa, arriving New Year's Eve.

1970, January 9. Israel Protests French Aircraft Sale to Libya. (See p. 1315.)

1972, January 13. U.S.–Israeli Arms Assistance Agreement Revealed. By this agreement (1971, November) Israel was authorized to manufacture various kinds of American weapons and equipment, as part of the U.S. stabilization policy.

EGYPT—UNITED ARAB REPUBLIC

1945–1952. Internal and Anti-British Unrest. Egypt called for an end to British military occupation and abrogated its treaties with Britain (October 27, 1951). The U.K. acquiesced and began withdrawal, but rioting at Port Said and Ismailia, endangering Suez Canal operations, necessitated British military action and continued occupation.

1948–1949. Arab-Israeli War. (See p. 1222.)

1949–1956. Continuous Friction and Incidents along Israeli Border. (See above.)

1952, July 22. Military Coup d'État. King **Farouk** was dethroned by a military uprising under the leadership of General **Mohammed Naguib,** his right-hand man being Colonel **Gamal Abdal Nasser.**

1953, June 18. Egypt Proclaimed a Republic. Naguib became first president and premier.

1954, February 25–November 14. Naguib-Nasser Struggle for Control. After considerable internal maneuvering, Naguib was finally ousted and replaced by Nasser (November 14).

1955, September 27. Agreement with Czechoslovakia. Nasser announced a commercial agreement to exchange Egyptian cotton for armaments. He stated that western nations had refused Egyptian requests for arms and that Israel was buying French warplanes.

1955, October 20. U.S. Offers to Finance Aswan Dam. Egypt accepted financing by the International Bank for Reconstruction and Development and the U.S. (December, 1955–February, 1956), rejecting Soviet offers to supply more than one-third of the $.6- to $1.2-billion cost.

1956, June 13. Britain Completes Withdrawal from Egypt. This ended 74 years of British military occupation in Egypt.

1956, June 18. Soviet Renews Offer to Finance Aswan Dam. This time the U.S.S.R. agreed to furnish about $1.0 billion at 2 per cent interest. President Nasser began to reopen bargaining with the U.S., Britain, and IRDB to get better terms.

1956, July 19. U.S. Withdraws Offer to Finance Aswan Dam. Disgusted by Egyptian anti-U.S. propaganda and negotiations with the U.S.S.R., Secretary **Dulles** withdrew the offer; Britain supported the U.S. action.

1956, July 26. Nationalization of Suez Canal. Egypt seized control of the canal from the private (primarily British) Suez Canal Corporation, announcing its nationalization. Hot debate in and out of the U.N. followed; France and Britain particularly considered the action as a threat to world peace. The U.S. was gravely concerned and began negotiations to achieve international control. The Communist bloc supported the Egyptian seizure. Nasser turned down western proposals and began to operate the canal (September 14).

1956, October 29. Israeli Invasion of Sinai. (**See p.** 1228.)

1956, October 31. Franco-British Intervention. Following Israel's assault in the Sinai, France and Britain issued an ultimatum calling on Israel and Egypt to cease fire in 12 hours. Israel accepted subject to Egyptian acceptance (October 30). Egypt rejected the ultimatum. Franco-British air forces began bombardment of Egyptian air bases.

1956, November 5–7. Franco-British Invasion of Canal Zone. British paratroops, flown by helicopter from Cyprus, made vertical combat landings at Port Said while Franco-British warships bombarded the port and landed troops in an amphibious assault. One day of street fighting brought the port into the attackers' hands, and the advance continued along the canal. Egyptian resistance concentrated on the sinking of stone-laden barges and other vessels in the canal itself, completely blocking it. Immediate U.N. reaction followed, with the U.S. and U.S.S.R. for once in agreement. A cease-fire demand was reluctantly obeyed by France and Britain (November 7). By this time the northern half of the canal, from Port Said to Ismailia, had fallen into the invaders' hands. Allied losses were 33 dead and 129 wounded; Egyptian losses are unknown. Following U.N. pressure and unilateral U.S. efforts, the Franco-British forces evacuated Egyptian territory (November 19–December 22).

COMMENT. *While U.S. denunciation of this bilateral assault, and the threats of the U.S.S.R. to use missiles against Britain and France and to furnish a "volunteer" army for the relief of Egypt, both played dominant roles in causing France and Britain to withdraw, a very practical military reason also underlay the decision. What might have become a* fait accompli, *had the operation been properly prepared, became a disastrous fumble when, due to inadequate warning and preparation, 5 inactive days elapsed between the initial air bombings and the amphibious assault. World opinion had time to react. The net result was a strengthening of Nasser's domination in Egypt and his affiliation with the U.S.S.R., and a weakening of accord amongst NATO members.*

1957, March 7. Suez Canal Reopens. U.N. salvage crews took only 69 days to clear hulks from the channel, sunk there by Egyptians during the crisis.

1958, February 1. Union with Syria. The United Arab Republic was established with Yemen as another partner. This was Nasser's next move to dominate the Middle East by a powerful Arab state. Anti-Egyptian opposition in Syria broke up the short-lived partnership (September 30, 1961), but Nasser's Egypt continued as the United Arab Republic.

1961–1967. Involvement in Yemen. Breaking relations with the monarchical government of Yemen (December 26, 1961), Egypt began subversive support of a republican movement, followed by active military support of the republican government against the Imam (see below). Egyptian losses were heavy; the experience was frustrating and costly to Egypt. Egyptian troops were withdrawn after the Sinai defeat at the hands of Israel, to bolster Egypt's defense of the Suez Canal.

1964, May 26. Planned Unification with Iraq. President Nasser and Iraq's President **Abdel Salim Arif** signed an agreement in Cairo to establish a joint Egyptian-Iraqi military command in time of war, and to appoint immediately a joint presidential council to study ways of unifying the two governments.

1967, June. War with Israel. (See p. 1230.)

1970, September 28. Death of Nasser. This was the result of a heart attack.

1970, October 7. Sadat Appointed President. Vice President Anwar Sadat, a loyal assistant of Nasser, was appointed president by Egypt's National Assembly. This was confirmed by a national plebiscite (October 14).

1971, May 13. Sadat Purges Opponents. A coalition of militant anti-Israel and pro-Russian politicians, disappointed by Sadat's political moderation and skillful consolidation of government control, had been plotting to replace him when the President quickly dismissed and jailed dissident government leaders.

1971, May 28. Treaty of Friendship and Cooperation with the U.S.S.R. Signed in Cairo by President Sadat and President **Nikolai Podgorny** of the U.S.S.R., this assured continuing Soviet military assistance, but without the danger of a Communist takeover after Sadat had consolidated his political power by purging pro-Russian elements from his government (see above).

1971, August 20. Agreement for Union with Syria and Libya. This agreement theoretically went into effect when referenda in the three countries enthusiastically confirmed the agreement (September 1). Since each nation retained its national sovereignty, the agreement was virtually meaningless.

1972, July 18. Sadat Orders Withdrawal of Soviet Advisors. Sadat said that the decision to "terminate the mission of the Soviet military advisors and experts" was due to Soviet failure to provide arms for renewed war with Israel. Moscow announced that the withdrawal was by mutual agreement. Not all Soviet advisors were withdrawn, however.

1972–1973. Agreements for Union with Libya. (See p. 1315.)

YEMEN

1948, February 19. Revolt. King **Hamid** was overthrown and replaced by Imam **Ahmed.**

1950, June 17. Yemen Joins Arab League Collective Security Pact. (See p. 1275.)

1954, May. Border Clashes with Aden.

1955, April 2–5. Military Revolt. Imam **Seif el-Islam Ahmad** and Crown Prince **al Badr Mohammed** and loyal tribesmen defeated an army revolt led by Emir **Seif al-Islam Abdullah.**

1956, April 3. Claim to Britain's Aden Protectorate. The nebulous boundary line became theater of a sporadic war continuing to the end of the period.

1957–1962. Communist Arms Provided to Yemen. This was through negotiations with the U.S.S.R. and later with Red China. The U.S.S.R. began extensive port construction at Hodeiya (Port Ahmed).

1961, December 26. U.A.R. Breaks Relations with Yemen. (See above.)

1962, September 19. Death of Imam Ahmed. Crown Prince **Saif al-Islam Mohammed al Badr** assumed the crown. A republican uprising followed.

1962, September 27. Proclamation of "Free Yemen Republic." The rebel government, supported by the U.A.R., was also recognized by Communist-bloc nations (September 29). Heading the rebels was Colonel **Abdullah al-Sallal** (proclaimed president, October 31).

1962–1965. Civil War. The rebel government was assisted by the U.A.R. Egyptian troops entered the country to assist the rebels. With Egyptian forces waxing to some 60,000 strength by 1965, Yemen became a battleground for pro- and anti-Communist Arabs. Saudi Arabia provided active military support to the monarchical faction, while British forces resisted a republican Yemenite invasion of Aden.

1965, August 24. Saudi-Egyptian Agreement and Cease-Fire. For the third time in two years President Nasser and King **Faisal** agreed to end their support of the republicans and royalists, who also agreed to a cease-fire and to a plebiscite to determine the future government.

1966, February 22. Egypt Supports Republicans in Renewed Fighting. A republican attack on a royalist tribe was supported by UAR aircraft. That same day, in a response to Faisal's appeal to withdraw, President Nasser announced that his troops would stay in Yemen until a plebiscite was held. In the outburst of renewed fighting Saudi Arabia accused UAR planes of bombing Saudi towns near the Saudi–Yemen frontier.

1967, November 5. Coup d'État in Republican Government. President **Abdullah el-Salal** was overthrown by dissident republicans under **Rahman al-Iryani,** who assumed title of Chairman of Presidential Council. Despite Iryani's apparent intention of seeking an understanding with the royalists, the war dragged on. UAR troops had been withdrawn after Egypt's disastrous defeat in the Sinai (see p. 1231).

1968, February. Southern Yemen Intervenes. Participation of troops from Southern Yemen in attacks on royalist troops was announced by both the Southern Yemen and the Yemen republican government (February 19).

1968, February 28. Saudi Arabia Renews Aid to Royalists. The Saudi Government announced that this was needed to offset assistance to the republicans from the U.S.S.R., Syria, and Southern Yemen.

1970, April 14. Agreement with Saudi Arabia Ends Civil War. King Faisal's government agreed to recognize the republican government of Yemen, in return for the inclusion of a number of royalists in the government.

1972–1973. Border Clashes with South Yemen.

1974, June 13. Military Coup d'État. Colonel **Ibrahim al-Hamidi** was the leader of an army group seizing control.

LEBANON

1945–1956. Precarious Existence. The republic strove to maintain independent status despite the coaxing and threats of its neighbors to force its participation in the Pan-Arab movement. There was constant friction with Syria.

1949, July 8. Brief Rebellion Suppressed.

1956, January 13. Military Defense Treaty with Syria.

1958, April 14–July 14. Insurrection. This was inspired by the U.A.R. Fighting spread to the streets of Beirut (June 14). U.N. observers, with **Dag Hammarskjöld,** secretary general, arrived.

1958, July 14. Lebanese Appeal for Help. President **Camille Chamoun** appealed to the U.S., Britain, and France, urging troop aid to seal the Syrian border as the revolution in Iraq (see p. 1281) set the Middle East aflame and stimulated renewed unrest in Lebanon.

1958, July 15. U.S. Intervention. Responding to Chamoun's appeal, a U.S. force of Marines and Army troops arrived by sea and by air from Europe and the U.S. to protect Lebanon from U.A.R. or Communist invasion.

1958, August 21. U.S. Begins Withdrawal. Stabilization of the situation having been effected, withdrawal of 14,300 U.S. troops began (completed October 25).

1961, December 31. Attempted Coup. Rightist elements, including some troops, were crushed by prompt reaction of the Army.

1969, October. Lebanese Army Clashes with Palestinian Commandos. A six-month period of tension and occasional outbreaks of violence between Palestinian guerrillas and the Lebanese Army flared into virtual civil war. During three weeks of sporadic fighting the Palestinians seized control of 14 of 15 U.N.-operated refugee camps in Lebanon.

1969, November 3. Cease-Fire Agreement Signed in Cairo. The Lebanese Government virtually accepted extraterritorial sovereignty of the Palestinian commandos. Following one more clash (November 20) an uneasy peace returned to most of Lebanon, with the Palestinian guerrillas free to continue their terrorist operations against Israel.

1973, May 2–8. Renewed Army Conflict with Palestinian Commandos. Confused fighting intensified when the Lebanese Army intercepted 1,000 guerrillas trying to cross into Lebanon from Syria. An uneasy cease-fire was finally arranged by representatives of Egypt, Iraq, and Algeria. Syria closed the border with Lebanon, denouncing the Lebanese Government for conspiring with "foreign" powers in an anti-Palestinian conspiracy.

SYRIA

1946, April 15. Independence of Syria. A former League of Nations mandated territory under French control, Syria was granted independence in accordance with the United Nations Charter.

1948–1949. Arab-Israeli War. (See p. 1222.)

1949, March 30. Coup d'État.

1949, August 18. Coup d'État.

1949, December 17. Coup d'État.

1951, November 28. Coup d'État.

1953–1954, December–February. Jebel Druze Uprising. Suppressed by the Syrian Army after extensive fighting.

1954, February 25. Coup d'État.

1958, February 1. Union with Egypt. (See

1961, September 28. Coup d'État. Elements opposed to the union with Egypt seized power.

1961, September 30. Dissolution of Union with Egypt. This was the result of the recent coup d'état.

1962, March 28. Coup d'État.

1962, April 1. Unsuccessful Military Revolt at Aleppo.

1963, March 8. Coup d'État.

1964, February 8–25. Civil Disorders. Bloody riots in Banias and Homs marked general unrest.

1964, April 13–15. Unsuccessful Insurrection in Hama. There was severe loss of life in the uprising, which apparently was aimed at overthrow of the government.

1966, February 23. Coup d'État. Premier **Salal al Bitar**, moderate leader of the Ba'ath Party, was overthrown by left-wing military dissidents of the party led by Major General **Salal Jedid.**

1967, June. War with Israel. **(See p. 1230.)**

1969, February 28. Coup d'État.

1970, September 19–23. Invasion of Jordan Repulsed. **(See p. 1283.)**

1970, November 13. Coup d'État. Right-wing Army officer members of the Ba'ath Party, led by Defense Minister Lieutenant General **Hafez el-Assad,** seized power.

1971, March 12. Assad Elected President. This was for a term of 7 years. Assad gave the country the most stable government it had had since independence.

1971, September 1. Union with Egypt and Libya. **(See p. 1279.)**

1973, October 6–22. War with Israel. **(See p. 1235.)**

IRAQ

Internal affairs in Iraq were chaotic throughout the period. The central government (in its various manifestations) was more or less constantly at war with the Kurdish minority in the northwestern mountain region. Principal military events of the period were:

1946, April. Uprising in Kurdistan. The Kurd rebellion had not been suppressed by the close of the period.

1948–1949. Arab-Israeli War. **(See p. 1222.)**

1955, November 21. Baghdad Pact. **(See p. 1275.)**

1958, July 14. Army Revolt. An army officer revolt, led by Brigadier General **Abdul Karim el Kassim,** overthrew the monarchy. King **Faisal II** and Premier **Nuri es Said** were brutally murdered. Initially closely tied to the U.A.R. and pan-Arab unity, Kassim's Republic of Iraq soon diverged from policies followed by Nasser's U.A.R.

1958, December. Iraq-Soviet Agreement

Verified. U.S. sources determined that Premier Kassim had accepted Soviet arms and had entered into a working agreement with the U.S.S.R.

1959, March 8–9. Revolt Suppressed. This was an attempt by a group of officers in **Mosul.**

1959, March 24. Iraq Withdraws from the Baghdad Pact. Soon after this, Iraq abrogated her agreements with the U.S. and refused further U.S. military aid (June).

1959, July 14–20. Unsuccessful Rebellion. A confused uprising of Kurds, Communists, Moslem factions, and Army troops in the Kirkuk region was put down with heavy loss of life by loyal troops.

1961, December 27. Britain Supports Kuwait. Britain dispatched naval reinforcements to the Persian Gulf to deter Kassim's threatened annexation of Kuwait (December 24).

1961–1970. Kurd Rebellion. Refusal of the Iraqi Government to provide autonomy to their mountainous home land, in the region where Iraq, Iran, and Turkey meet, led to Kurdish defiance of the central government, and the outbreak of virtual civil war (1961, September 17). The Kurds were led by Mullah **Mustafa Barzani.**

1963, February 8. Revolt. Kassim was deposed and executed; his estranged partner in the 1958 revolt, **Abdul Salam Arif,** became the new president.

1963, November 18. Military Coup. The government was overthrown; President Arif, who had been a figurehead, seized control and pledged support to Nasser of Egypt.

1965, September 17. Partial Coup d'État. General **Abdel Rahman Arif** suppressed a revolt against his brother, President **Abdel Salim Arif,** then seized control of the government himself.

1968, July 17. Coup d'État. Major General **Ahmed Hassan al Bakr** led a group of Army officers of the right wing of the Ba'ath Party overthrowing President Abdel Rahman Arif.

1969–1975. Border Clashes with Iran. These began with a dispute over Iraqi control of navigation of the Shatt-al-Arab (see p. 1286), and with Iranian support of the Kurds.

1970, January 20. Attempted Coup d'État. The government said the crushed rebel forces were supported by Iran.

1970, March 11. Peace with the Kurds. Iraq agreed to grant autonomy and to make constitutional reforms to grant the Kurds a major role in the central government.

1972, April 9. Treaty with the U.S.S.R. This 15-year friendship pact carried with it a promise of more Soviet arms for Iraq.

1973, March 20–21. Border Clashes with Kuwait. Iraq again backed down in the long-standing dispute after the arrival of 20,000 Saudi Arabian troops to help Kuwait.

1973, June 30. Unsuccessful Coup Attempt.

1974–1975. Renewed Kurd Rebellion. The Kurd rebellion collapsed when Iran withdrew support as a result of a resolution of its border dispute with Iraq (1975, March).

JORDAN

1946, March 22. Independence of Transjordan. This former League of Nations mandate was granted independence by Britain. Emir **Abdullah** became the first king.

1948–1949. Arab-Israeli War. Transjordan, due mainly to its British-trained Arab Legion, was the only Arab state to perform creditably against the Jewish Army of Israel (see p. 1222).

1949, June 2. Hashemite Kingdom of Jordan Established. This change of name was a step in the process of annexation of Arabic Palestine (April 24, 1950), occupied by the Arab Legion during the Arab-Israeli War. This annexation was strongly protested by most other Arab League states.

1951, July 20. Assassination of Abdullah. Murder of this moderate ruler by an Arab extremist was applauded in many other Arab countries. They feared that he was moving to an accommodation with Israel. He was briefly succeeded by his eccentric son, Emir **Tallal** (September 5).

1952, May 2. Accession of King Hussein. This young king (only 17 when he came to the throne) proved himself a wise, tough, durable ruler, who maintained control over his volatile nation (with the help and support of his Arab Legion), despite continued and overt efforts of Nasser and most other Arab League leaders to have him overthrown or assassinated (1955–1962). By the end of the period, Hussein and Nasser, however, had temporarily resolved their differences and were at least nominally in accord on their strong anti-Israel policies.

1954, May 2. Jordan Rejects British Suggestion of Peace Talks with Israel.

1956, March 2. Dismissal of Glubb. British Lieutenant General **John Bagot Glubb,** commander of the British-subsidized Arab Legion, was dismissed by Hussein for failure to prepare for an Israeli attack. Upon his return to Britain, Glubb was knighted (March 9).

1958, July 17–October 29. British Support to Hussein. Following the revolt in Iraq, and as combined U.A.R. and Communist pressure and threats against Hussein and Jordan mounted, British paratroops landed in Jordan, at Hussein's request, shortly after the landings of U.S. forces in Lebanon (see p. 1280). This strong Anglo-American co-operation restored comparative stability to the Middle East.

1962. Military Co-ordination of Jordan and Saudi Arabia. Merger of the armed forces of the 2 countries was announced as a show of strength and unity against the U.A.R. and other Arab League members. Though never officially abrogated, this merger was apparently never fully activated and was quickly ignored.

1967, June 5–10. War with Israel. **(See p. 1232.)**

1967, November 6. Hussein Suggests Peace Negotiations with Israel. The King said he was ready to recognize Israel if the boundary questions could be negotiated satisfactorily. He also suggested that Egypt was ready to permit Israeli ships in the Suez Canal, once a general agreement was reached. Egypt denied this latter statement, amid a storm of protests from most Arab nations.

1968, March 21. Battle of Kerama. An Israeli raid against Palestine guerrilla bases in the Jordan Valley was met by Jordan Army units, who claimed success in driving the Israelis off after a sharp fight.

1970, February 10–12. Fighting Between Jordanian Army and Palestinian Commandos. This resulted from Palestinians' refusal to obey a Jordanian directive forbidding them to carry arms openly in public, and ordering the surrender of arms and ammunition. Both sides backed down under pressure from other Arab states.

1970, June 7–11. Renewed Fighting with Commandos. A virtual 5-day civil war was again brought to a conclusion by pressure from other Arab states and appeals to the guerrillas from King Hussein and **Yasser Arafat**, leader of Al Fatah, the largest commando group. The Jordanian Army had the better of the fighting, but losses were heavy on both sides; each accused the other of numerous atrocities.

1970, September 17–26. Open Warfare with Palestinian Commandos. Apparently believing his monarchy could not survive if the commandos continued to defy his authority and Jordanian sovereignty, Hussein ordered an all-out attack on the commando bases. Despite interference from Syria (see below), the Jordanian Army was successful and commando losses severe. A cease-fire was arranged in Cairo (September 27), with the guerrilla survivors accepting practically all of the King's demands.

1970, September 19–23. Undeclared War with Syria. Following a day of artillery fire across the border, Syrian troops, mostly armored units, invaded northern Jordan and, with Palestinian commando assistance, captured Irbid, Jordan's second-largest city. A major tank battle took place near Irbid between Jordanians and Syrians (September 22). The Jordanians completely defeated the Syrians, who retreated across the border (September 23). Jordanian close support aircraft contributed largely to the victory. Syria broke diplomatic relations with Jordan. The Syrians were deterred from further action by a partial Israeli mobilization and clear indications that Israel would attack if the Syrians renewed the war.

1971, June 13–19. Final Suppression of Palestinian Commandos. Not satisfied with the commandos' adherence to the cease-fire terms, the Jordanian Army captured some 2,000 commandos and drove the remainder out of the country into Israel and Syria. Syria again fired artillery across the border, but made no further aggressive move.

1971, November 28. Palestinians Assassinate Jordanian Prime Minister. While attending an Arab League Defense Council meeting in Cairo, Prime Minister **Wafsi Tal** was killed by three Palestinian gunmen, who later said they were members of the Black September Organization, a Palestinian terrorist group whose name commemorated the Jordanian 1970 attack against the commandos.

SAUDI ARABIA

Involved like all the other nations in the Middle East in pan-Arab, anti-Jewish movements, Saudi Arabia, one of the great oil centers of the area, could be considered as at least partly amenable in policy to the **Arabian American Oil Company** (ARAMCO), which operated the fields and was the sole source of financial revenue. The death (November 9, 1953) of King **Ibn Saud,** a firm supporter of the West, momentarily loosed its ties with the Free World. His sons, **Saud Ibn Aziz** (1953–1965) and Faisal (who deposed his brother in 1964), continued, however, in attempts to maintain at least neutrality in the Cold War.

1952. Saudi Forces Invade the Buraimi Oasis. This territory was also claimed by the Sultan of Muscat and Oman. A clash with British interests in that area ended with the ousting of the invaders (October 26, 1955) by British-led troops of Muscat and Oman.

1956. Military Alliance with Egypt and Yemen. (See p. 1275.)

1957–1962. Friction with U.A.R. This brought about closer ties between Saudi Arabia and Jordan (see above).

1962–1970. Saudi Arabian Support of Royalists in Yemen. (See p. 1280.) This intensified friction with the U.A.R.

1964, March 28. King Saud II Stripped of Royal Power. This was by decree of a royal council, led by his younger brother, Prince Faisal, who became virtual regent, with Saud a figurehead.

1964, November 2. Saud Deposed; Faisal Named King.

1969, November 26–December 5. Border Clashes with Southern Yemen. (See p. 1285.)

1973, March 21. Troops Sent to Support Kuwait against Iraq. (See p. 1282.)

1973, October. Saudi Leadership in Oil Embargo. Supporting Egypt and Syria in the October War (see p. 1235), Faisal led the Arab oil-producing states in a highly successful embargo against all nations directly or indirectly supporting Israel.

ARAB GULF STATES

Britain retained a shaky hegemony over the southern and southeastern regions of Arabia, from Aden to the Persian (or Arabian) Gulf. British troops were involved in frontier fighting between Yemen and the Aden Protectorate, in suppressing internal disorders in Aden, and on the southeastern fringes of the Arabian Desert in desultory warfare between the Sultanate of Muscat and Oman and Saudi Arabia, centering around the disputed Buraimi Oasis. British troops also helped the Sultan of Muscat and Oman suppress a serious revolt (July–August, 1957).

1952–1955. Muscat, Abu Dhabi, Saudi Arabia Dispute over Buraimi Oasis. (See above.)

1967, November 2. Britain Announces Planned Withdrawal from Arabia. This was to take place in 1971 (see p. 1260).

1971, July 18. Establishment of United Arab Emirates. At a meeting in Dubai, six Persian Gulf emirs agreed to form a federation before the planned British withdrawal at the end of the year. Participants: Abu Dhabi, Sharjah, Ajman, Umm al Qaiwain, Fujairah, and Dubai.

1971, August 14. Independence of Bahrain.

1971, September 21. Independence of Qatar.

1971, November 30. Iranian Troops Seize Persian Gulf Islands. Ras al Khaimah, which claimed the Greater and Lesser Tunb Islands, protested the seizure. Abu Musa, also seized, was claimed by Sharjah, but the Iranian Government agreed to respect Sharjah's sovereignty in return for base rights on the island.

1972, January 24. Unsuccessful Coup in Sharjah. Sheikh **Khalid bin Mohommed al Qasmi** was killed and was succeeded as emir by his brother, Sheikh **Saqr bin Mohommed al Qasmi.**

1972, February 11. Ras al Khaimah Joins United Arab Emirates. This brought membership to 7 states.

1972, February 22. Coup d'État in Qatar. Sheikh **Ahmed bin Ali al-Thani** was deposed and replaced by his cousin, Sheikh **Khalifa bin Hammad al-Thani.**

OMAN (MUSCAT AND OMAN)

1952–1955. Buraimi Oasis Dispute. (See p. 1284.)

1955, December 15. Sultan Reestablishes Authority over Oman. Sultan **Said bin Taimur** suppressed a conspiracy by the Imam of Oman, who was exiled.

1957, July–August. Imam Revolt against Sultan. The exiled Imam of Oman led a revolt against the Sultan's British-led army. After serious fighting near **Nizwa** (July 15), the Sultan requested British assistance, which was provided, mostly in air support, resulting in suppression of the rebellion (mid-August). An Arab League effort to censure Britain in the U.N. Security Council failed (August 20).

1968–1974. Revolt in Dhofar. Separatist rebels, Marxist and supported by the People's Republic of Yemen (Southern Yemen), waged constant guerrilla war against the government. Oman employed British officers to command counterinsurgency units. This buildup and Iranian assistance (beginning 1973) suppressed the insurgency.

1970, July 23. Palace Coup. Sultan Said bin Taimur was overthrown and replaced by his son, **Qabus bin Said,** on the basis of the former's "inability" to use the newfound oil "wealth of the country for the needs of the people." The new Sultan changed the name of the country to "Sultanate of Oman."

SOUTHERN YEMEN (PEOPLE'S DEMOCRATIC REPUBLIC OF YEMEN)

1945–1967. British Aden Protectorate. Violence and unrest in the protectorate, beginning in December 1963, resulted in virtual civil war, with the British and local sheikhs fighting leftist revolutionaries. Britain decided to withdraw.

1964, July 4. Britain Pledges Independence to the Federation of South Arabia. At a constitutional conference in London this was promised to take place "not later than 1968." Britain planned to retain its base in Aden, one of the 13 federated states. The leftist revolutionaries continued guerrilla warfare. Britain decided to withdraw completely.

1967, November 30. Independence of the People's Democratic Republic of Yemen. Violence and unrest continued, as rival factions vied for power.

1968–1974. Guerrilla Warfare against Oman in Dhofar. **(See above.)**

1968, March 20. Attempted Army Coup.

1968, May 13–16. Unsuccessful Revolt. This was led by dissident leaders of the ruling National Liberation Front.

1968, July 26–August 9. Unsuccessful Rebellion. Tribesmen south of Yemen rose under the leadership of members of the Front for Liberation of South Yemen. The rebellion was suppressed after fierce fighting. The Government said the rebels were aided by Saudi Arabia.

1969, June 22. Coup d'État. A militant leftist government seized power.

1969, November 26–December 5. Border Clashes with Saudi Arabia. Saudi Arabia claimed victory in fierce fighting for the disputed oasis of **Al Wadeiah.**

1972–1973. Border Clashes with Yemen. **(See p. 1280.)**

1974, August 28. U.S. Alleges Soviet Naval Base in South Yemen. President Gerald Ford stated that the Soviet Union had a naval base in South Yemen. The Soviets denied this accusation.

IRAN

At the close of World War II, the U.S., British, and Soviet governments agreed to withdraw their forces from Iranian territory. The withdrawals were to be completed by March 2, 1946.

1945, November 18. Rebellion in Azerbaijan. A Communist-inspired revolt by the Tudeh party broke out. Efforts of the government to repress it were hampered by Soviet troops still in Iran. Prime Minister **Qavam** protested to the U.N. Security Council (January 19, 1946). The firm stand of the U.S. government in support of Iran brought withdrawal of Soviet troops (May 6), and the rebellion was later put down (December 6–11).

1946, September 15–October 7. Rebellion in Southern Iran. This was settled by agreement between government and rebellious tribesmen.

1951, April 29. Nationalization of Oil Industry. Mohammed Mossadegh, new Iranian premier, ordered nationalization of the oil industry. Violent repercussions in Britain and the U.S. followed, and oil production virtually ceased.

1953, August 19. Mossadegh Overthrown. The pro-Communist dictatorial prime minister was ousted and imprisoned by a coup supported by Shah **Mohammed Reza Pahlavi,** who became virtual prime minister himself.

1954, August 5. Iranian Oil Production Renewed. European and American oil interests agreed to operate the former Anglo-Iranian oil plant on a new royalty basis.

1955, November 21. Baghdad Pact. (See p. 1275.)

1969, April 19. Iran Abrogates Treaty with Iraq on Navigation of Shatt-al-Arab. Claiming that Iraq had violated provisions of a 1937 treaty giving most of the river to Iraq (and claiming the treaty was based on a series of unequal treaties imposed by Great Britain since 1847), Iran announced that it would enforce its claim to sovereignty up to the middle of the river (Arand-Rud in Iranian). Iraq massed troops on the border, as did Iran; Iran sent ships under armed escort to the ports of Abadan and Khorramshahr. There were no immediate hostilities, but this was the basis of later border clashes (see p. 1282 and below).

1969, September. Border Clashes with Iraq. (See p. 1282.)

1970–1974. Modernization of Iranian Army. A major program of military modernization, improvement, and build-up was undertaken by Shah Mohammed Reza Pahlavi.

1970, January 20. Border Clash with Iraq.

1971, November 30. Iran Seizes Persian Gulf Islands. (See p. 1285.)

1973–1974. Iranian Troops Assist Oman in Dhofar. (See p. 1285.)

1974, February 6–15. Border Clashes with Iraq. This ended a lull caused by the Arab-Israeli War.

1974, March 5–6. Border Clash with Iraq. Some 180 incidents occurred in 1973–1974.

1975, January–March. Border Clashes with Iraq. Iranian aid to the Kurds ended with signature of a boundary agreement (March 5).

SOUTH ASIA

BRITISH INDIA

The post-World War II events in South Asia were shaped almost entirely by the division of the Indian subcontinent on religious lines at the time Britain relinquished her colonial Empire of India in 1947: the essentially Hindu Dominion of India and the essentially Moslem Dominion of Pakistan, the latter being divided into 2 separate portions, about 1,000 miles apart, separated by Hindu India. Strife and bloodshed occurred across the country during the year before partition, and intensified immediately upon independence and partition. The principal events were:

1946–1947. Violence and Unrest Sweep India. With Britain clearly preparing to give independence, violence flared intermittently across all of India between Hindus and Moslems. The fighting was particularly intense and bloody in the Punjab, almost equally divided between Mohammedan and Hindu inhabitants. During one 4-month period (July–October, 1946), the British government announced that 5,018 persons had been killed and 18,320 injured in the Hindu-Moslem rioting. The toll was even heavier in the early months of 1947.

1947, August 14. Independence of India and Pakistan. India and Pakistan both received their independence simultaneously, and both became dominions within the British Commonwealth of Nations. Rioting, violence, and death increased throughout both nations, and particularly in the Punjab. Mobs of religious majorities in both nations began to terrorize, rob, and murder the minority groups, most of whom took refuge beyond the partition frontier. After about 6 weeks of slaughter, relative peace returned, mostly because the persecuted minorities had been wiped out or chased away. No reliable statistics exist, but it is probable that close to a million people were massacred, while 10–15 million people were forced to flee from their homes.

KASHMIR DISPUTE, 1947–1965

1947, October. Moslem Uprising in Kashmir. The decision of the Hindu Raja of Kashmir to have his state join India (October 26) precipitated an uprising of the predominantly Moslem population, who wished to join Pakistan. Afridi and Mahsud tribesmen who had crossed into Kashmir from Pakistan joined in a march on Srinagar. Indian troops were flown into Kashmir to quell the uprising (October 27). Intensive fighting broke out between air and ground forces of the Indian government and the rebellious Moslems and their supporters from Pakistan. (October 28–30.)

1947, November–1949, December. Undeclared War in Kashmir. Pakistani troops crossed the border into Kashmir to assist the Moslem rebels, precipitating an undeclared war between India and Pakistan.

1948, February 8. Pathan Uprising in Kashmir. This was suppressed by Indian troops.

1949, January 1. Cease-Fire. U.N. mediation brought about an uneasy truce along the fighting front in Kashmir, ending 14 months of warfare.

1949–1954. Intermittent Negotiations Between India and Pakistan. No firm agreements were reached.

1953, August 20. Plebiscite Agreement. Sheikh **Mohammad Abdullah,** prime minister of Kashmir, and **Jawaharlal Nehru,** prime minister of India, agreed to a plebiscite to settle the dispute over the state of Jammu in Kashmir. India later withdrew its agreement and imprisoned Mohammed Abdullah.

1954, February 6. Kashmir Ratifies Accession to India. Pakistan protested.

1954, October 4. Pakistan White Paper. This declared that negotiations with India had failed and asked the Security Council to settle the problem.

1957, January 26. India Annexes Kashmir. Pakistan protested; the U.N. disapproved. Henceforward Kashmir was merely one (although one of the most important) of a number of issues between India and Pakistan.

INDIA, 1947–1961

1947, August 14. Independence.

1948, January 30. Assassination of Gandhi in New Delhi. Rioting broke out across India.

1948, September 15–17. Indian Occupation of Hyderabad. After the Nizam of Hyderabad had refused to join the Dominion of India, Indian troops invaded and forced unconditional surrender.

1949, June–July. Disorders and Violence in Kerala. The Indian Government intervened to dismiss the Communist government of Kerala State and to take direct control after widespread, bloody, antigovernment riots.

1950, January 25. India Becomes a Republic. She retained membership in the British Commonwealth.

1950. Medical Unit to Korea. This was in support of the U.N. war effort (see p. 1252).

1953. Revolt in Nepal. Indian troops assisted in the suppression of a Communist-inspired revolt in Nepal.

1954–1974. Naga Revolts. India consistently refused demands for autonomy by these primitive tribesmen of the Northeast Frontier.

1954, April 29. Nonaggression Treaty with Communist China. This was *de facto* recognition of the Chinese seizure of Tibet (see p. 1311).

1954, July–August. India-Pakistan Dispute over Indus Valley Water. The dispute was settled by mediation by the International Reconstruction and Development Bank (August 5).

1954, July 22–1955, August 15. Border Clashes around Goa. Indian nationalists attempted to seize parts of the Portuguese possession, but were ejected by Portuguese troops (July–August, 1954). After further violence around Goa (August 1955), India broke off diplomatic relations with Portugal.

1959, February 25. US Arms Aid Rejected. Since Pakistan accepted proferred American assistance, Nehru demanded the withdrawal of U.S. members of the UN Ceasefire Commission in Kashmir.

1959, April 3. Arrival of the Dalai Lama in India. He was seeking refuge from Chinese persecution of Tibetans (see p. 1311).

1959, August 28. Border Dispute with China. Prime Minister Jawaharlal Nehru reported Chinese violations of India's frontiers with Tibet and China in the Longju and Ladakh areas.

1960, June 10. Himalayan Border Clash. India claimed Chinese troops were occupying Indian territory.

1961, March 14. Troops to the Congo. India sent troops to join the U.N. effort in the Congo (see p. 1322). The Indians were airlifted by U.S. cargo planes.

1961, December 18. Seizure of Goa. India seized the Portuguese enclaves of Goa, Damao, and Diu, which had been Portuguese possessions for four and a half centuries. There was little opposition.

Hostilities with China, October–November, 1962

1962, October 20. Chinese Invasion. Chinese troops in massive surprise attacks defeated Indian frontier forces in Jammu and in the northeastern frontier region, on fronts 1,000 miles apart. The eastern drive, in particular, was spectacularly successful, and all Indian resistance north of the Brahmaputra Valley was overrun.

1962, November 21. Chinese Unilateral Cease-Fire. Having gained all of the border regions they had claimed, the Chinese suddenly declared a unilateral cease-fire and withdrew to lines which would assure their retention of these regions. Nehru rejected the Chinese terms for settling the dispute, but since the defeated Indians had no desire to renew the war, informal truce prevailed along the Himalayan frontiers at the end of the period.

1962–1965. Military Reform. India, receiving considerable military assistance from the U.S. and from other Commonwealth nations, attempted to revitalize her armed forces and remedy the many defects disclosed in the disastrous war with China.

Hostilities with Pakistan, May–September, 1965

1965, April–May. Undeclared War in the Rann of Kutch. A frontier dispute with Pakistan, in a desolate region where the frontier had not been clearly defined, broke into full-scale hostilities for approximately 2 weeks. The Pakistanis seem to have had slightly the better of the struggle before monsoon rains ended operations.

1965, August 5–23. Border Clashes in Kashmir and Punjab. Following Pakistan's initiative in Kashmir, military and irregular infiltrators on both sides crossed the Kashmir cease-fire line and the nearby Punjab border in raids and counterraids.

1965, August 24. Indian Raid. Indian troops crossed the cease-fire line in considerable force; fighting raged along the northern frontier. U.N. truce observers in Kashmir brought about a temporary cease-fire.

1965, September 1–25. Major Hostilities. In retaliation for the Indian raid, Pakistan initiated a major invasion across the cease-fire line in Kashmir (September 1). Both sides undertook minor air raids against nearby Punjab cities, as well as against Karachi and New Delhi. Indian troops launched a major attack against Lahore (September 6). The attacks on both sides soon bogged down. In large-scale armored battles, Indian units achieved marginal success over Pakistani tanks. On balance, however, a stalemate resulted.

1965, September 7–8. U.S., U.K., and Australia Halt Arms Shipments to India and Pakistan. The British and Australian announcements followed that of the U.S. by one day.

1965, September 8. Communist China Threatens India. In the face of quiet but determined American and British diplomacy, China failed to carry out threatened actions against Indian border positions in the Himalayas.

1965, September 27. U.N. Cease-Fire Demands Honored. After accepting, then ignoring, an earlier U.N. demand (September 22), both sides agreed to abide by a Security Council cease-fire and began withdrawal to lines held on August 5. A new U.N. India-Pakistan Observation Mission (independent of the U.N. Observer Group in Kashmir) was established (September 25), and 75 observers from 8 nations came to the Punjab to supervise the cease-fire. Cease-fire violations by both sides were reported in the following weeks, but there were no further major hostilities.

1966, January 10. Declaration of Tashkent. India and Pakistan agreed to withdraw their troops from frontier confrontation positions. This pullback was completed on February 25.

1967, September 11–14. Clashes with Chinese on Sikkim–Tibet Frontier. Both India and China accused the other of border violations. However, the clashes were limited to exchanges of rifle and artillery fire, and no substantial movement was made into either Tibet or the Indian protectorate of Sikkim.

1971, August 9. Treaty of Friendship with the U.S.S.R. This 20-year pact greatly strengthened India's hand in the increasingly tense relations with Pakistan resulting from unrest in East Pakistan.

1971, December 3–17. War with Pakistan. **(See p. 1290.)**

1972, March 12. Last Indian Troops Withdraw from Bangladesh.

1972, March 19. Treaty of Friendship with Bangladesh. The provisions were very similar to those in the 1971 India–U.S.S.R. friendship treaty.

1972, July 3. Peace Treaty with Pakistan. **(See p. 1291.)**

1973, April 8. India Assumes Administrative Control of Sikkim. This was in response to a plea from Chogyal (Prince) Palden Thondup Namgyal of the protectorate, following two weeks of antigovernment violence in Sikkim. This arrangement was ratified in an agreement between India and Sikkim one month later.

PAKISTAN

The military history of Pakistan during this period has been essentially that of her continuing friction with India. There have also been sporadic border disputes with Afghanistan. Pakistan is a member of the Central Treaty Organization (see p. 1275) and Southeast Asia Treaty Organization (see p. 1292).

1947, August 14. Independence. Viscount Mountbatten turned over the government of Pakistan to **Mohammed Ali Jinnah** in a ceremony in Karachi, as rioting, violence, and death spread through the Punjab and elsewhere along the border regions of India and Pakistan (see p. 1287).

1948, January 8. Unrest and Rioting in Karachi. A result of popular dissatisfaction with the government, the economic and political unrest generally increased during the following 10 years.

1954, May 19. U.S. Military Aid. Agreement between the U.S. and Pakistan for America to provide military supplies and technical assistance. Pakistan agreed to use the aid only for defense and participation in U.N. collective-security arrangements; India, however, proclaimed bitterly that this was giving Pakistan assistance for possible war with India.

1955, September 19. Pakistan Joins Baghdad Pact. (See p. 1276.)

1956, March 23. Pakistan Becomes a Republic. It remained in the British Commonwealth.

1958, October 7–27. Bloodless Coup d'État. Acting through President **Iskander Mirza,** General **Ayub Khan** dismissed the government, annulled the constitution, and established a "benign martial law." He immediately began sweeping economic and political reforms, re-establishing stability. Mirza soon resigned (October 27). Ayub Khan was elected president under a new constitution (February 17, 1960).

1959, February 25. U.S. Arms Aid Accepted. President Eisenhower reported that Pakistan would receive arms aid from the U.S. to strengthen the defensive capabilities of the Middle East. India rejected a comparable offer (see p. 1288).

1965, May–September. Hostilities with India. (See p. 1288.)

1969, March 25. Ayub Khan Resigns. As a result of increasing violence and unrest throughout the country, he turned over the government to General Agha **Mohommed Yahya Khan,** commander in chief of the Army.

1970, December 7. First General Election. This was to elect a National Assembly, which early in 1971 was to formulate a new constitution for the country. An absolute majority of Assembly seats was won by the Awami League of East Pakistan, headed by Sheikh **Mujibur Rahman.** Sheikh Mujibur and his League had long struggled to gain autonomy for East Pakistan. This was totally unacceptable to the dominant, but less numerous, people and administrators of West Pakistan.

1971, March 24. President Yahya Khan Proclaims Martial Law. In response to violence in East Pakistan after the President postponed the first scheduled session of the National Assembly. Sheikh Mujibur undertook a nonviolent civil disobedience campaign, giving him virtual control of the eastern province. President Yahya Khan flew to Dacca to negotiate with Sheikh Mujibur, but left abruptly after 11 days (March 24). He called the Sheikh a traitor, and outlawed the Awami League.

1971, March 25. Outbreak of Civil War. Initiation of suppressive action by Pakistani forces (almost all from West Pakistan) led Sheikh Mujibur to proclaim the independence of East Pakistan as Bangladesh (March 26). Mujibur was seized early in the struggle, and the well-equipped Pakistani Army brutally suppressed the revolt in about five weeks (by May 5). The number of East Pakistani casualties is unknown, but probably exceeded 100,000. During the fighting about 3 million refugees fled from East Pakistan into India, complicating the already serious food problem of that country. During the next month another 3 million Bengali refugees from East Pakistan fled into India. A few of the refugees attempted to harass the East Pakistan frontiers, with little success, until they began to receive covert Indian support (fall, 1971). The result was increasing frontier incidents and intensified Pakistani suppression of unrest in East Pakistan.

1971, June–November. Growing Tension with India. There were frequent instances of artillery fire across the border, and small raids by both sides. India gave considerable assistance to East Pakistan rebels based in eastern India.

1971, November 8. Cancellation of U.S. Arms Shipments to Pakistan. Although described as an action of "mutual consent," this was really the result of increasing American unhappiness about the use of American weapons to suppress the Bengalis of East Pakistan.

HOSTILITIES WITH INDIA, DECEMBER 3–16, 1971

1971, December 3. Outbreak of War. The Indian tactic of increasing aid to the Bangladesh rebels, while avoiding an overt Indian-Pakistani confrontation, finally accomplished the result India had obviously been seeking: goading Pakistan into taking the first hostile action. This was a massive air strike by the Pakistani Air Force against most major Indian air bases, in hopes of achieving the kind of result accomplished by Israel at the outbreak of the 1967 Middle East War (see p. 1231). The Indians, aware that their policy of goading Pakistan to war demanded complete alertness, were ready, and the Pakistani air strikes were generally unsuccessful.

1971, December 3. Indian Invasion of East Pakistan. Fully prepared for the outbreak of hostilities, Indian forces at least triple the strength of the 90,000-man Pakistani garrison of East Pakistan began a major two-pronged invasion of the province, from the north and the west, with 3 subsidiary attacks from north, west, and east.

1971, December 4. Pakistani Invasion of Indian Kashmir. The Pakistanis made minor gains, some as much as 10 miles, but their advance was soon halted by the alert Indians, who had expected this move.

1971, December 5–6. Soviets Veto U.N. Security Council Cease-Fire Resolutions. In support of their Indian allies, who were advancing rapidly into East Pakistan, the Soviets refused to agree to a cease-fire which would have halted the advance. Pakistan Foreign Minister **Zulfikar Ali Bhutto** at once took the issue to the slow-moving General Assembly.

1971, December 6. India Recognizes Bangladesh.

1971, December 14–16. Battle for Dacca. This began when Indian ground troops, only 7 miles from the capital, advanced under cover of artillery fire and air attacks against the defenders in the city. The East Pakistani government resigned and took refuge in a neutral zone in the city, established by the Red Cross.

1971, December 15. U.N. General Assembly Demands Cease-Fire in East Pakistan. By this time most Pakistani resistance had collapsed in East Pakistan. Having piously called for a cease-fire, and having no enforcement authority, the General Assembly prepared to turn to other business. Foreign Minister Bhutto, denouncing the United Nations' "miserable, shameful" failure to take positive action, walked out of the building and flew home.

1971, December 15. Indian Attacks in the West. In intensified fighting the Indians recovered some captured territory on the India-Pakistan border in Kashmir and the Punjab and advanced into Pakistan at some points in Hyderabad and the Punjab.

1971, December 16. Pakistani Surrender in Dacca. Lieutenant General **A. A. K. Niazi** surrendered to General **S. H. F. J. Manekshaw,** Indian Army Chief of Staff. This virtually ended the war.

1971, December 17. Cease-Fire Accepted by Both Sides. Indian losses were approximately 2,400 killed, 6,200 wounded, and 2,100 captured; India lost 73 tanks and 45 aircraft. Pakistani losses were more than 4,000 dead and 10,000 wounded; most of the wounded were included among 93,000 prisoners of war.

1971, December 20. Yahya Khan Resigns; Bhutto Becomes President. As his first official act Bhutto dismissed the senior military leaders and put them and the former president under arrest.

1972, July 3. Interim Peace Settlement. President Bhutto and Prime Minister **Indira Gandhi** of India, after a 5-day meeting at Simla, India, agreed to a troop withdrawal along most of their joint frontier, but postponed action on the more difficult problems of the Kashmir frontier and the return of 93,000 Pakistani prisoners of war held by India.

1972, December 7. Agreement on Kashmir Truce Line. Both sides began to withdraw their troops.

1973, August 8. India Agrees to Release Pakistani Prisoners of War. Return was completed in April 1974.

AFGHANISTAN

1949–1965. Strained Relations with Pakistan. Pakistani refusal to honor Afghan claims for frontier revision resulted in tension and occasional border clashes.

1956, August–October. Soviet Military Aid. The U.S.S.R. provided guns, ammunition, and airplanes.

1973, July 17. Coup d'État. During the absence of King **Mohammed Zahir Shah,** his brother-in-law and Army commander, Lieutenant General **Mohammed Daoud Khan,** seized power and declared the country a republic with himself as President and Premier.

(CEYLON) SRI LANKA

1948, February 4. Independence of Ceylon. It became an independent dominion within the British Commonwealth.

1953, August 12–19. Communist Terrorism. The government suppressed the disorders after receiving emergency powers from Parliament.

1956–1961, Sporadic "Language Riots." These stemmed from the desire of the minority Tamils to have their language accepted as an alternative to Sinhalese. These bloody riots intensified in 1958 (February–July) but were ended when limited official status was granted Tamil (1961, August 5).

1962, January 29. Attempted Coup.

1971, April 5–June 9. Rebellion of the People's Liberation Front. The PLF, impatient with the slow social progress of the leftist government of Prime Minister Mrs. **Sirimavo Bandaranaike,** attempted to seize control of Colombo and other cities. A plot to assassinate the Prime Minister failed. The revolt was soon suppressed in the cities (April 13), but fierce fighting continued in rural and jungle areas. The U.S.S.R. provided Ceylon with fighter aircraft and pilot training personnel, to help the government reestablish control. Both India and Pakistan provided helicopters and crews. Britain shipped weapons and ammunition. The rebellion was officially declared to be suppressed, and the nation's schools were reopened, 2 months after the outbreak of civil war (June 9).

1972, May 22. Ceylon Becomes Republic of Sri Lanka.

BANGLADESH

1971, March 26. Independence of Bangladesh Proclaimed. Following disputes with West Pakistan, and resentful of West Pakistan's domination, Sheikh Mujibur Rahman, political leader of East Pakistan, declared the independence of the province as Bangladesh. This resulted in prompt action by the Government of Pakistan to reestablish firm control (see p. 1290).

1971, March–December. War for Independence. This was largely unsuccessful until intervention by India (see p. 1290).

1971, December 17. Independence Effective. This was the result of India's victory over Pakistan (see p. 1291).

NEPAL

1950, November 11–20. Insurrection. King **Tribhubarra Bir Bikram,** deposed by the government of Premier **Mohan Shumshere** (November 7), was supported by an uprising of the reform-minded Congress Party. Loyal Gurkha troops defeated the rebels. The king was later invited back to resume his reign.

1952, January 24. Unsuccessful Revolt. The Communist Party was outlawed.

1952, August 13. King Tribhubarra Takes Control. This was in an effort to end the unrest which had been plaguing the country. He restored parliamentary rule in 1953 (April 13).

1960, June 28. Border Incident with China. China apologized for "carelessness" in attacking Nepalese troops, but said they were on Tibetan territory.

1960, December 15. Royal Coup. King **Mahendra Bir Bikram** seized power, with army support, ousting the regime of Premier **B. P. Kirala.**

1961, March–December. Civil War. The revolt was suppressed.

SOUTHEAST ASIA

The area became the eastern battleground for the warring ideologies—Communism vs. the Free World. The Communists, checked at least temporarily by the armistice in Korea, shifted their efforts to support existing, indigenous struggles already under way in Indochina, Malaya, and Indonesia. After the collapse of French colonial rule in Indochina (1954; see below), the U.S. took the lead in sponsoring an anti-Communist regional organization to prevent further Communist gains in the area.

SOUTHEAST ASIA TREATY ORGANIZATION (SEATO)

This treaty was established as part of the American effort to create a group of mutual-security pacts around the world after the 1954 Geneva Conference (see

p. 1296). The 8 members were Australia, France, New Zealand, Pakistan, the Philippines, Thailand, the United Kingdom, and the United States. The treaty was set up for the purpose of providing for collective defense and economic co-operation in Southeast Asia, and to protect the weak nations of the region against aggression. Theoretically patterned after NATO, SEATO has been relatively helpless and ineffective, due to 3 major factors: lack of widespread support among Southeast Asian nations fearful of angering Communist China; skillful Communist subversion, diplomacy, and "agitprop"; and French foot-dragging.

1954, September 8. Manila Treaty. The defense treaty for Southeast Asia was signed in Manila by representatives of the participating governments. This followed diplomatic initiatives by the ANZUS nations (Australia, New Zealand, and the U.S., beginning June 30).

1955, February 19. Southeast Asia Defense Treaty into Effect.

1964, April 15. SEATO Supports South Vietnam. The Ministerial Council of SEATO, meeting in Manila, issued a declaration of support of South Vietnam military efforts against the Viet Cong guerrillas. France abstained.

BURMA

Independence sentiment among the people, combined with results of Burmese independence activities during the war, directed against both the British and the Japanese (see pp. 1133 and 1187), led to British agreement to grant independence to Burma.

1945–1946. Guerrilla Warfare. British troops were forced to wage a sporadic guerrilla warfare against armed dissidents, most of whom were bandits, throughout Burma.

1947, January 28. Britain Announces Plans for Burma's Independence.

1947, July 19. Assassination of General Aung San. The premier of Burma, the nation's war hero, and 5 members of his cabinet were assassinated by intruders during a cabinet meeting in Rangoon. The assassins were apprehended, tried, and executed (December 30).

1948, January 4. Independence of the Union of Burma. Burma, under Prime Minister **U Nu,** refused to join the British Commonwealth.

1948, March. Outbreak of Communist Revolt. This began in south-central Burma, mainly in the Irrawaddy Delta.

1948, August. Outbreak of Karen Revolt. The objective was to achieve an autonomous Karen state. At first successful, the Karens, in somewhat reluctant co-operation with the Communists, gained control of much of south-central Burma. They proclaimed their independence (June 14, 1949), with capital at Toungoo.

1949, January–February. Karen Rebels at Outskirts of Rangoon. They cut the Rangoon-Mandalay railroad and were within artillery range of parts of the area within Rangoon city limits.

1949–1950. Government Counteroffensive.

1950, March 19. Government Forces Capture Toungoo. The Karen revolt began to collapse. The Burmese government reestablished control over most of central Burma.

1950, May 19. Government Forces Capture Prome. This was the main Communist center of south-central Burma.

1950–1974. Continuous Guerrilla Warfare in Burma. After barely surviving collaboration between nationalistic and communistic rebels (1948–1949), loyal Burmese forces under General **Ne Win,** in methodical guerrilla warfare, re-established law and order in most parts of the country (1954). Endemic rebellion and guerrilla warfare continued throughout many of the outlying provinces, however.

1953, April 23. U.N. Calls for Withdrawal of Chinese Nationalists. These were Chinese Nationalist refugee troops who were defying Burmese government authority in the northeastern portions of Burma, where they had withdrawn after the defeat of the National Government in China. Burma had complained to the U.N. (1950). The refugees refused to withdraw and the National Government of China refused to recognize them. However, after considerable U.S. pressure, some 2,000 of these Chinese Nationalist guerrillas were evacuated from Burma to Formosa (November). Early next year, 6,400 guerrillas and dependents were evacuated to Formosa (May). It was estimated, however, that at least 6,000 remained in the jungle region.

1956, July 31. Border Dispute with Communist China. Chinese troops seized 1,000 square miles of territory in northeast Burma.

1958, September 26. Military Coup. Deterioration of government control and a threatened Communist coup led General Ne Win to seize control of the government. He restored civil rule after national elections (February 6, 1960), after signing a nonaggression treaty with Communist China (January 28).

1962, March 2. Second Military Coup. Deterioration of civilian government again led Ne Win to establish a military dictatorship.

THAILAND

Despite considerable political turbulence, leading to several coups d'état and the murder of a king, Thailand as a nation has remained relatively stable, more so than any other in the region. It has been steadfastly anti-Communist, and is a member of SEATO (see p. 1292). As the period ended, Thailand was giving substantial assistance, including base rights, to the U.S. effort in Vietnam.

1946, May 26–30. Franco-Thai Frontier Dispute. After clashes along the Mekong River, Thailand appealed to the U.N. Security Council to halt French aggression, but France insisted that the so-called military activity was simply pursuit by Chinese troops of bandits from the Siamese side of the river that had been raiding east of the river.

1946, June 9. King Ananda Dies Under Suspicious Circumstances. He was succeeded by his brother, **Phumiphon.**

1947, November 9. Military Coup d'État. Field Marshal **Luang Pibul Songgram** seized control of the government in Bangkok. Prime Minister **Pridi Phanomyong** fled the country.

1949, February 26–27. Insurrection. During a state of emergency caused by Communist activity along the Malayan border, units of the Thai Army and Navy accused each other of plotting a coup against the government of Premier **Pibul Songgram,** and extensive fighting took place in and around Bangkok.

1951, June 29–July 1. Naval Revolt Suppressed.

1951, November 29. Military Uprising Suppressed. In the confusion, however, a political coup forced Pibul to amend the constitution.

1957, September 17. Bloodless Coup d'État. Field Marshal **Sarit Thanarat** seized control; Field Marshal Pibul fled to Cambodia. Sarit later retired, establishing a caretaker government (April, 1958).

1958, October 20. Sarit Seizes Control Again. He retained power and became prime minister (January, 1959).

1958, November–December. Border Clashes with Cambodia.

1964–1970. Repeated Border Incidents with Cambodia. Thailand wanted to recover eastern frontier territory long disputed with France (see above, 1946, May 26–30).

1964–1974. Sporadic Communist Terrorism. This violence was confined to the extreme northern and southern areas of the country.

1967, March 22. U.S. B-52 Bomber Bases Permitted in Thailand. This enabled the U.S. to shift some heavy bombers from Guam to Thai bases much closer to targets in Vietnam.

1967, September. Thai Troops Committed to Combat in Vietnam. Their participation was financed by the U.S., under the terms of an executive agreement between Thailand and the U.S. (1965).

1967, December 1. Martial Law Declared in Five Provinces. This was the result of increased Communist guerrilla activity, and brought to 12 the number of provinces under martial law in the extreme north and south of the country.

1969, July 7. Secret Military Agreement with U.S. Revealed. U.S. Senator **J. W. Fulbright** revealed the agreement, which permitted stationing 47,000 U.S. military men in Thailand.

1970, February 2. Withdrawal of 4,200 American Military Personnel Announced. This left 43,800 American troops in Thailand.

1971, November 17. Government Coup. Prime Minister, General **Thanom Kittikachorn,** ended constitutional rule, seized full power, and declared martial law.

1972, February 4. Thai Troops Withdrawn from Vietnam.

1973, October 14. Resignation of Prime Minister Kittikachorn. This was the culmination of increasing unrest and popular dissatisfaction with the military dictatorship, which had erupted a few days earlier in bloody violence. King **Phumiphol Adulet** appointed **Sanya Dhamasakti,** Dean of Thammasat University (center of student protests against Kittikachorn) as Prime Minister.

INDOCHINA, 1945–1954

By the close of World War II, the guerrilla forces of Vietnamese nationalists and Communists, combined in an organization known as the Viet Minh, under the over-all political leadership of Communist **Ho Chi Minh** and the military leadership of initially nationalist guerrilla leader Vo Nguyen Giap, had gained control of much of the jungle region of north Vietnam. This success had been achieved with the largely unwitting assistance of the Chinese National Government and of the U.S., both happy to receive assistance from the Vietnamese against Japan, and both willing to see France eliminated from Indochina, but neither fully realizing the international Communist ties of Ho. The Viet Minh declared their independence when Japan collapsed at the close of the war but the French, through their own efforts, and with some British assistance, moved immediately to re-establish their colonial rule over the area. The resultant conflict touched off the most prolonged warfare of the entire period since World War II.

1945, September 2. Vietnam Republic Proclaimed by Ho Chi Minh.

1946, March 6. France Recognizes Independence of Vietnam Republic. This was only as a free state within the Indochinese Federation and the French Union. Meanwhile, French military strength built up rapidly. French-imposed limitations on independence proving unacceptable to the Viet Minh, guerrilla warfare broke out, mostly in northern Vietnam, later in the year.

1947, January–February. Siege of Hué. After a siege of several weeks, French troops relieved the besieged garrison of Hué, driving off the Viet Minh guerrillas surrounding the ancient capital of the country.

1950, January. Viet Minh Recognized by Communist China and the U.S.S.R. Increasing military assistance was given to the Viet Minh guerrillas by China. Viet Minh troops received intensive training in southern China. American military aid to French Vietnam increased with the intensity of guerrilla warfare.

1950, October. French Setbacks. Well-trained, well-equipped Viet Minh troops, operating partly from China and partly from the jungled highlands of northern Vietnam, mounted a major assault against the French cordon of defenses in northern Tonkin, covering the Chinese border. French troops were badly defeated at **Fort Caobang,** near Langson (October 9). This, combined with increased activity by the Communist Pathet Lao insurgents in Laos (see p. 1299), forced the French to abandon most of northern Vietnam (October 21) and to establish a fortified perimeter around the Red River Delta in the north (December). The situation in southern and central Vietnam was not much better, with much of the Mekong Delta in Communist hands.

1950, December. De Lattre de Tassigny to Command. France sent her leading soldier to try to restore the situation. He soon re-established French morale, regained the initiative, and reoccupied most of the areas lost in late 1950.

1950, December 23. Vietnam Sovereign within French Union. A treaty was signed at Saigon.

1951–1953. Continued Guerrilla Warfare. This was combined with anti-French terrorism in the major cities. Despite De Lattre's military successes, French control could be asserted only where major French forces were stationed.

1952, September. De Lattre Relieved. Seriously ill, he returned to France via the U.S., where he pleaded for more aid. He died a few months later.

1953, January–February. Intensified French Operations. In the biggest naval operation of the war, French troops (now under General **Raoul Salan**) seized **Quinhon,** a rebel base, and destroyed several Viet Minh war factories concealed in the jungles of south Vietnam.

1953, March–September. Increased U.S. Aid to France for the Indochina War.

1953, May 8. Navarre Relieves Salan. Pedestrian General Salan was relieved by pedestrian General **Henri-Eugène Navarre.**

1953, July 6. Increased Independence for Vietnam and Laos. They accepted a French offer to negotiate for greater self-government in the Associated States of Indochina. Cambodia refused.

1953, August–October. Negotiations between France and Cambodia. France gave the government of King **Norodom Sihanouk** almost complete military, political, and economic sovereignty, although France retained operational control of some military forces in eastern Cambodia for purposes of prosecuting the war against the Viet Minh.

1953, October–1954, April. Intensified Viet Minh Operations. French premier **Joseph Laniel** said his government would accept "any honorable" solution to the war in Indochina, and was not trying to force the Viet Minh to unconditional surrender (November 12).

1953, November 20–1954, May 7. Siege of Dienbienphu. General Navarre, hoping to decoy the Communists into one large pocket and then crush them, permitted Brigadier General **Christian de la Croix de Castries,** with some 15,000 men—French regulars, Foreign Legion, and indigenous troops—to fortify and hold the village and an airstrip, situated 220 miles west of Hanoi and near the Laotian border. General Giap, with 4 divisions of Chinese-trained Viet Minh troops, surrounded Dienbienphu with 2 divisions while the remainder of his force sealed it off and swept into Laos. Against the French artillery—24 105-mm. and 4 155-mm. howitzers—Giap assembled the overwhelming fire power of over 200 guns, including antiaircraft artillery and rocket launchers. A trickle of supply by air from Hanoi, little enough when the defenders still held the air field, ceased with its capture (March 27). Attempts at air drop failed; the Viet Minh antiaircraft artillery was too good. Of 420 French aircraft available for this purpose, 62 were shot down and 107 others damaged. One by one the outlying strong points of the Dienbienphu defense complex fell to a combination of mining, well-directed artillery fire, and direct assault. A final assault overran the starving defenders as their last ammunition was expended (May 7). Only 73 of the 15,094-man garrison escaped. Some 10,000—half of them wounded—were captured; the remainder were dead. Viet Minh losses were estimated at 25,000.

COMMENT. *The fall of Dienbienphu virtually ended French control over Indochina. At the same time, it proved the fallacy of cordon defense in jungle warfare, particularly when the opponents are well trained, armed, and supplied. French military thought in this instance was still clinging to methods used against guerrillas in North Africa and, in 1882–1885, in this very area. (See p. 864; the French garrison of Tuyen-Quang successfully resisted besiegement by "Black Flag" indigenous guerrillas from November 23, 1884, to February 28, 1885. But the "Black Flags," while fanatically brave, had neither discipline nor resources, and were unable to hold up the French relief column advancing from Hanoi, only 50 miles away.)*

1954, April 26–July 21. Geneva Conference. The Conference on Far Eastern Affairs of 19 nations (including Communist China) resulted in an agreement for a cease-fire and divided Tonkin and Annam into North (Communist) and South (anti-Communist) Vietnam as independent nations divided at the 17th parallel of North Latitude. Cambodia, which had proclaimed its independence of France (November 9, 1953), and Laos, its independence proclaimed (July 19, 1949), were both recognized as neutral independent states. The United States accepted the agreements, but refused to sign them, and reserved the right to take whatever action was necessary in the event that the agreements were breached. France withdrew her troops from Indochina, but continued military direction and instruction in South Vietnam, Laos, and Cambodia, while the U.S. assumed the chore of providing military equipment and instruction as well as economic aid.

1954, December 29. Independence of Indochina. Vietnam, Laos, and Cambodia signed agreements with France, giving them economic independence and virtually ending foreign control. The states granted each other freedom of navigation on the Mekong River.

VIETNAM

1954, July 7. Ngo Dinh Diem Appointed Premier.

1954, October 11. Communist Viet Minh Takes Control of North Vietnam.

1955, January 20. U.S. Military Aid. The U.S., France, and South Vietnam agreed to reorganize the Vietnamese Army with 100,000 active troops and 150,000 reserves. The U.S. was to send a training mission to operate under the direction of General **Paul Ely**, new French commander in Indochina.

1955, October 26. Republic Proclaimed. Diem was inaugurated president.

1956–1964. Continuous Insurrection. This was sponsored by the Communist bloc, despite efforts of the government to control rebellious factions (Viet Cong) supported by troops and equipment from North Vietnam in turn aided and supported by Communist China. U.S. efforts to strengthen the South Vietnamese military force consistently increased, without retrieving the situation.

1956, April 28. U.S. Military Assistance Advisory Group (MAAG) Assumes Responsibility for Training.

1960, November 11. Military Revolt against Diem. This was suppressed.

1961, October 11. U.S. Assistance Pledged. The U.S. agreed to support the government of South Vietnam against attacks by Communist Viet Cong guerrillas. General **Maxwell D. Taylor** was sent to Vietnam by President **John F. Kennedy** to determine the most effective means of help. President Kennedy sent a personal message to President Diem with a pledge to continue assistance (October 26).

1961, December 11. First U.S. Support Units Arrive. Two U.S. Army helicopter companies, the first direct military support for South Vietnam, arrived in Saigon aboard a U.S. aircraft carrier.

1962, February 8. U.S. Military Assistance Command Established. The purpose was to demonstrate U.S. determination to prevent a Communist takeover.

1962, March 22. Operation "Sunrise" Begins. This was designed to eliminate the Viet Cong. Operations began in Binh Duong Province.

1963, November 1–2. Military Coup d'Etat. The government of President Diem was overthrown; he and his brother were killed. A provisional government was established under former Vice-President **Nguyen Ngoc Tho,** and was recognized by the U.S. Actual control was under a military junta led by Major General **Duong Van Minh.**

1964, January 30. Military Coup d'État. The government was overthrown by Major General **Nguyen Khanh.**

1964, February 4–6. Viet Cong Launches Offensive in Tay Ninh Province and Mekong Delta.

1964, August 2–4. Action in the Gulf of Tonkin. Three North Vietnamese PT boats attacked a U.S. destroyer. The PT boats were repelled and damaged or sunk by the destroyer and U.S. planes. A similar incident occurred 2 days later (August 4).

1964, August 5. U.S. Air Strikes against North Vietnam. American carrier-based strikes against naval bases were ordered by President Johnson in retaliation for the PT-boat attacks.

1964, August 7. Gulf of Tonkin Resolution. Congress approved a resolution giving President **Lyndon B. Johnson** authority to take "all necessary measures to repel any armed attack" against U.S. armed forces. It also authorized him to take "all necessary steps, including the use of armed forces," to help any nation requesting aid "in defense of its freedom" under the Southeast Asia Collective Defense Treaty.

1964, August–September. Political Turmoil. The government of General Khanh survived riots and demonstrations, but only by promising to give early control to a civilian government and suppressing an attempted military revolt (September 13).

1964, November 1. Communist Guerrilla Attack on U.S. Support Base at Bien Hoa. Four Americans and 2 Vietnamese were killed; 12 Americans and 5 Vietnamese wounded. Several American and Vietnamese aircraft and helicopters were destroyed or damaged.

1964, November 4. Civilian Regime Installed. General Khanh resigned as **Tran Van Huong** became premier.

1964, December 19. Military Uprising. A Military Council retained Premier Huong in nominal control.

1965, January 27. Khanh Returns to Power. The Armed Forces Council deposed Premier Huong and returned General Nguyen Khanh to the head of the government.

1965–1973. The United States War in Vietnam. (See p. 1209.)

1965, February 21. Khanh Deposed. After a complicated series of moves, in which civilian **Phan Huy Quat** was installed as premier, with Khanh retaining behind-the-scenes control, the Armed Forces Council voted to oust Khanh as council chairman and armed forces commander. Quat remained premier.

1965, June 12–19. Bloodless Government Upheaval. Premier Quat resigned as a result of religious turmoil involving Buddhists and Catholics. The military took over and elected Air Vice-Marshal **Nguyen Cao Ky** (age 36) as premier. This was the eighth government since the overthrow of Diem (November, 1963).

1967, September 3. Nguyen Van Theiu Elected President. He was inaugurated the first president of South Vietnam's Second Republic (October 31).

1973, January 23. Cease-Fire Agreement. (See p. 1220.)

1973, March 29. Departure of Last American Troops from Vietnam. (See p. 1220.)

1973, April 7. International Peace-Keeping Helicopter Shot Down by Communists. Attempting to investigate one of the increasingly numerous and serious ceasefire violations throughout South Vietnam, an international peace-keeping force team was shot down by a Communist missile in northern Quang Tri Province. All 9 aboard were killed.

1973, June 13. New Cease-Fire Agreement. Representatives of the U.S., North Vietnam, South Vietnam, and the Viet Cong signed a 14-point agreement calling for an end to all cease-fire violations. Among its provisions: U.S. reconnaissance flights over North Vietnam would end; U.S. minesweeping operations would be resumed in North Vietnamese waters; commanders of opposing troops in contact would meet to prevent further outbreaks of hostilities and to assure adequate medical supplies and care. For a while there was some reduction in the intensity of fighting, but the local ground commanders failed to meet, and fighting continued.

1973–1975. Widespread Combat. Fighting continued in many areas despite the cease-fire.

1975, January 1–7. Communists Capture Phuoc Binh. The capital of Phuoc Long fell after a 7-day siege.

1975, January 17. ARVN Counteroffensive in the Mekong Delta. About 2,000 troops attacked along the Cambodian border.

1975, February 24–March 2. Visit of U.S. Congressional Delegation. Eighty-one members went to Indochina to review the situation as a basis for action on requests for additional aid.

1975, March 5. Communists Launch Offensive in the Central Highlands. Major fighting by strong North Vietnamese forces resulted in the capture of many towns, cutting of highways, and isolating of garrisons in the Communist advance, and the fall of **Ban Me Thuot** after a fierce battle (March 5–13). In Quang Tri and Thua Thien provinces North Vietnamese forces also made important gains.

1975, March 18–20. ARVN Collapse in the North and West. Government troops withdrew in the face of a growing North Vietnamese offensive. President **Nguyen Van Thieu** announced (March 20) the government's intention to evacuate 2 provinces in the northwest and 9 in the central highlands.

1975, March 25. Hue Falls. The former imperial capital was abandoned, giving the Communists control of Thua Thien Province.

1975, April 1. Danang Falls. Despite plans to hold the city, second-largest in South Vietnam, ARVN troops offered little resistance. The third-largest city, Qui Nhon, was similarly abandoned the following day (April 2).

1975, April 9–22. Battle of Kuon Loc. After fierce fighting in which both sides took heavy casualties and the town changed hands several itmes, it was finally abandoned by the ARVN.

1975, April 21. Thieu Resigns as President. Vice President Tran Van Huong was appointed to replace him.

1975, April 27. Huong Resigns as President. Unacceptable to the Communists for negotiations, he resigned in favor of Lieutenant General **Duong Van Minh.**

1975, April 30. South Vietnam Surrenders to the Communists.

LAOS

Its independence proclaimed (July 19, 1949), and recognized as a neutral nation by the Geneva Conference (see p. 1296), Laos nevertheless became the center of a maelstrom of Communist-inspired outbreaks by the indigenous Pathet Lao, supported by both the U.S.S.R. and Communist China. U.S. support of the Royal Laotian Army (July 9, 1955) was temporarily suspended (October, 1960) as the country seethed in a 3-cornered conflict—rightist forces under General **Phoumi Nosavan,** neutralist troops under Premier Prince **Souvanna Phouma,** and the Communist Pathet Lao under Souvanna's half-brother, Prince **Souphanouvong.**

The Plaine des Jarres area in north-central Laos was the arena for most of the fighting, an endless series of inconclusive clashes. Stepped-up assaults by the Pathet Lao brought a concentration of 5,000 U.S. troops into Thailand (May 19, 1962) to protect that nation's border. This force was withdrawn (July 30), its mission accomplished. U.S. military advisers to the Laotian Army were withdrawn by October 7. During 1962, Laotian territory became a convenient communications channel for North Vietnamese troops infiltrating South Vietnam in support of the Viet Cong. On May 17, 1964, the U.S. instituted a continuous aerial reconnaissance sweep of Laos by jet planes. The principal events were:

1953, April 14. Viet Minh Invades Laos. They seized a base abandoned by the French at Samneua. Joining with rebel Laotians, the Viet Minh advanced toward the capital of Luang Prabang, capturing **Xiengkhouang** (April 20). Laos mobilized military forces, and the U.S. rushed military aid. Vietnamese forces began to retreat (early May). French forces retook Xiengkhouang.

1953, October 22. Independence of Laos. France and Laos signed a treaty giving the state full independence and sovereignty within the French Union.

1953–1954. Anti-French Insurgency. This was accompanied by complicated maneuvering by Communist and anti-Communist factions.

1954, July 21. Geneva Accord. (See p. 1296.)

1959, July 30–31. Communist-Led Guerrillas Attack Laotian Army Posts. Communist-led Pathet Lao guerrillas, armed by North Vietnam, attacked Laotian Army posts throughout northern Laos.

1959, September 7. U.N. Investigation. The Security Council voted to inquire into the Laos government's charges of aggression by North Vietnam.

1960, August 9. Coup d'État. The government of Premier **Tiao Samsonith** was overthrown by a military rebellion led by Captain **Kong Le,** a parachute battalion commander. Under Kong Le's sponsorship, neutralist leader Prince **Souvanna Phouma** became premier. Kong Le, soon to become a general, was to play an important, ambiguous, neutralist, but anti-Communist role in subsequent years of the complex civil war.

1961, March 23. U.S. Warnings. President Kennedy announced that the U.S. would not stand idly by and permit Laos to be taken over by advancing externally supported pro-Communist rebel forces. A previous warning had been made without effect by the Eisenhower administration (December 31).

1961, April 3. Cease-Fire between Government and the Pathet Lao.

1962, May 12. U.S. Troop Deployments. As a result of Pathet Lao violation of the 1961 cease-fire agreement and the overrunning of most of northern Laos, President Kennedy ordered a task force of the U.S. Seventh Fleet to move toward the Indochina peninsula. He then ordered 4,000 more U.S. troops to Thailand (where some 1,000 U.S. troops were already stationed, May 15).

1962, July 23. Geneva Agreement on Laos. Fourteen nations guaranteed the neutrality and independence of Laos.

1962, October 5. Withdrawal of U.S. Military Advisers. This was in compliance with the Geneva Agreement. There were approximately 800 U.S. advisers and technicians withdrawn.

1963, April. Renewed Conflict. Major fighting between neutral and Pathet Lao forces stopped after 3 weeks by a cease-fire agreement. Small-scale warfare continued.

1964, May 16–24. Communist Pathet Lao Forces Seize the Plain of Jars. Kong Le's forces were defeated.

1964–1973. Constant Warfare in Laos. The Pathet Lao, supported by strong North Vietnamese forces, ranging in size from 10,000 to 40,000 troops, held the eastern, southern, and northern portions of the country and posed intermittent threats to the government of Prime Minister **Souvanna Phouma** in Vientiane.

1964, April 19. Coup d'État. Prime Minister Souvanna Phouma was ousted by a right-wing military committee led by Brigadier General **Kouprasith Abhay,** which seized control of Vientiane. However, after a typical Laotian political ballet, Souvanna Phouma was restored to power, after agreeing to accept the rightist demands for modification of government policy in a merger of rightist and neutralist factions (May 2). This development was denounced by the Pathet Lao.

1965, January 31–February 4. Unsuccessful Army Revolt. Loyal troops cleared rebels from Vientiane, after much fighting. The leader, General **Phoumi Nosavan,** Deputy Prime Minister, fled to Thailand.

1965, March 28–30. Unsuccessful Army Revolt. This was suppressed without bloodshed.

1965, April 16–30. Army Mutiny. Supporters of exiled Deputy Prime Minister Phoumi Nosavan again attempted a revolt, but were crushed.

1969, April–May. Laotian Troops Recapture Plain of Jars from Communists. The offensive was greatly aided by U.S. close air support. Communist troops still held part of the rim of the plain and were unhindered when they initiated simultaneous operations in southern and central Laos.

1970, February 2. Communists Complete Recapture of Plain of Jars. The region was secured by Pathet Lao troops, supported by North Vietnamese, in an 11-day operation.

1970, April 29–30. North Vietnamese Troops Capture Attopeu.

1972, February 7–March 6. Plain of Jars Battle. Offensive by 4,000 Laotian troops with U.S. air support made some gains. These were all lost to a Communist counteroffensive (February 22).

1973, February 21. Cease-Fire in Laos. The agreement provided for: immediate cessation of hostilities by all Laotian and foreign forces; a new provisional coalition government within 30 days; removal of all foreign troops within 60 days after formation of a government; repatriation of all prisoners within 60 days; supervision by the International Control Commission until a new system could be worked out by the Laotians. The cease-fire was not very effective at first, and at the request of the Vientiane Government U.S. B-52 bombers on 2 occasions in the next few days hit Communist positions.

1973, September 14, Renewed Cease-Fire Agreement. This was the most effective cease-fire in Laos in more than 20 years, although sporadic outbreaks of violence continued.

1975, April. Combat Intensity Rises. Pathet Lao forces in Laos began an offensive following major Communist victories in Cambodia and South Vietnam.

CAMBODIA

After its recognition by the Geneva Conference (see p. 1296) as a "neutral" state, Cambodia was in continual friction with her neighbors and with the U.S.

as the country veered ever more strongly toward the Communist bloc under its head of state (and ex-king) Prince Norodom Sihanouk. Sihanouk accepted military aid from the Communist bloc, while placing restrictive conditions upon the reception of U.S. aid. Early (February 18, 1956) he renounced the protection of SEATO. Border clashes with South Vietnam were frequent; free movement through Cambodia of Viet Cong guerrillas was apparently permitted or condoned. Relations with Thailand were equally bad throughout the period.

1950–1954. Widespread Anti-French Insurgency.

1953, June 14. King Norodom Sihanouk into Voluntary Exile. He went to Thailand to promote his fight for complete independence from the French Union.

1963, November 12. Cambodia Refuses U.S. Assistance.

1963, December 12. Cambodia Withdraws Embassy from Washington.

1964–1970. Repeated Border Incidents with Thailand. **(See p. 1294.)**

1965–1970. Peripheral Involvement in Vietnamese War. Despite the reiterated denials of Chief of State Prince Norodom Sihanouk, practically constant use was made of Cambodian territory by the North Vietnamese, sending reinforcements and supplies to southern South Vietnam via the Ho Chi Minh Trail, and reinforcements by sea through Sihanoukville. The North Vietnamese and the Viet Cong established sanctuary regions and supply depots just inside the Cambodian frontier with South Vietnam. Sihanouk repeatedly denounced U.S. and South Vietnamese pursuit of Communists across the frontier, and occasional U.S. bombings of the sanctuary areas and supply routes.

1969–1970. Guerrilla Warfare against Communist Insurgents. There was increasing violent opposition to the government by Cambodian Communist Party (**Khmer Rouge**) guerrillas throughout the country. Collaboration of these antigovernment forces with North Vietnamese and Viet Cong forces was a source of embarrassment as well as a threat to Sihanouk.

1970, March 15. Prime Minister Lon Nol Demands Withdrawal of Communist Forces. In the absence of Prince Sihanouk, the Prime Minister, General **Lon Nol,** responded to anti-Communist demonstrations (which he may have engineered) throughout Cambodia by demanding the immediate withdrawal of North Vietnamese and Viet Cong forces from Cambodian territory. Both refused.

1970, April 30. U.S. Forces Enter Cambodia. **(See p. 1218.)**

1970, November 1. End of Cambodian Monarchy. Following unanimous legislative action on October 9, Cambodia became the Khmer Republic, ending the 2,000-year-old monarchy.

1972, March 10. Lon Nol Assumes Full Power as Head of State. Sihanouk, who was abroad, went to Peking.

1972, March 21. Communist Bombardment of Phnom Penh. More than 200 rocket and artillery projectiles hit the capital, in the heaviest assault to date.

1972, December. Rocket and Artillery Attacks on Phnom Penh Begin. Shelling by Khmer Rouge communist forces occurred sporadically, with many civilian casualties, until the end of the war.

1973, March–April. Phnom Penh under Virtual Siege. With all roads to the capital blocked by Communist forces, and the Mekong River supply route also cut by strong forces deployed along the river banks, the capital was in danger of starvation and of running out of necessary military supplies for its hard-pressed garrison. However, strongly protected convoys broke the river blockade (April 8–9), and after the main supply route to the port of Kampong was opened, a large truck convoy reached the city (April 11).

1973, March 17. Lon Nol Declares a State of Emergency. This followed the bombing of the Presidential Palace by a single Cambodian Air Force plane.

1973, August 14. Final U.S. Air Bombardments in Cambodia. (See p. 1221.)

1975, January 1. Rebels Launch Major Drive. In a concerted attack on three fronts around **Phnom Penh,** rebel troops, joined by North Vietnamese and Viet Cong, came within 2 miles of the city's defense line (January 2). All land routes were soon cut. U.S. Government-contracted airlift was increased to 10 planes a day.

1975, January 1. Siege of Neak Luong Begins. On the Mekong River, the town commanded the river approach to Phnom Penh.

1975, January 17. Two Convoys Fail to Reach Neak Luong. Both lost ships with ammunition to rebel artillery.

1975, January 23. Ship Convoy Reaches Phnom Penh. Passing through heavy rebel fire, 23 ships arrived from South Vietnam.

1975, February. U.S. Increases Airlift. Flights with arms and ammunition for Phnom Penh were increased to 22–24 a day on February 12 and again 3 days later. Deliveries of food by air were begun on February 27.

1975, February 25. President Ford Requests $222 Million Supplemental Aid. Report edly less than a month's supply of ammunition remained.

1975, February 28–March 12. Shelling of Phnom Penh's Airport. Intermittent shelling disrupted the airlift, as rebel forces approached within 5 miles of the center of the city.

1975, February 29. U.S. Congressional Delegation Visits Cambodia.

1975, March 11. Military Command Changes. Lieutenant General **Sosthene Fernandez** was removed as commander of the Armed forces. Lieutenant General **Saksut Sakhan** replaced him as chief of staff.

1975, April 1. Lon Nol Leaves Cambodia. A collective leadership replaced him.

1975, April 1. Insurgents Capture Neak Luong. The 3-month siege had left the naval base in total ruin. With rebel forces closing in on Phnom Penh and the airport under repeated fire, air traffic was suspended temporarily several times.

1975, April 16. Khmer Rouge Victorious. The government of President Lon Nol (who fled on April 1) surrendered to the Communists, who occupied Phnom Penh.

MALAYSIA

1948, February 1. Federation of Malaya Established. This comprised British colonies on the Malay Peninsula.

1948, February–May. Communist Revolt Begins. This was mainly among the predominantly Chinese element of the population.

1948, June 16. State of Emergency Proclaimed. Guerrilla warfare flared through the Federation. U.K., Australian, and New Zealand troops reinforced the garrison. Terrorism became endemic.

1952, February 7. British Offensive Begins. General Sir **Gerald Templer,** High Commissioner and commander of government forces in the Federation, instituted a concerted, well-planned anti-insurgency campaign. Some 45,000 troops—regulars and special local forces—began warfare against the rebels, combat and psychological.

1954, February 8. Communist High Command Withdraws. British authorities in Kuala Lumpur announced that the Communist party's high command in Malaya had moved to Sumatra. While this was a victory for Britain in their 6-year war, it was also an indication of an attempt to establish a Communistic Indonesian front.

1957, August 31. Federation Becomes a Constitutional Monarchy. It remained within the Commonwealth. By this time, the revolt had been suppressed for all practical purposes, though a few pockets of resistance remained in remote jungle areas.

1960, July 31. Emergency Officially Ended. The government announced that the crushing of revolt was completed. Total casualties: Communist rebels, 6,705 killed, 1,286 wounded, 2,696 surrendered; government troops, 2,384 killed, 2,400 wounded.

1962, December 8. Revolt in Borneo. This Indonesian-supported rebellion was quickly suppressed.

1963, September 16. Federation of Malaysia Proclaimed. This included Singapore, Sabah, and Sarawak added to the Federation of Malaya. The new state, a Free World bastion against Communist aggression and encroachments in Southeast Asia, at once became target for attack by Communist-oriented Indonesia (see p. 1255). British military support bolstered the Malaysian defense against interior terrorism and Indonesian raids.

1963–1966. Undeclared War with Indonesia. **(See pp. 1303–1304.)**

1964, May 3. Sukarno Announces Intent to Crush Malaysia.

1964, July 21–23. Communal Rioting in Singapore. The Communists incited Chinese rioting against Malaysia. Disorders were suppressed by police and troops.

1964, July 22. U.S. Pledges Support for Malaysia. This was to bolster the new nation against Indonesian threats.

1965, August 9. Independence for Singapore. By mutual agreement, the city of Singapore withdrew from Malaysia. Initially a British garrison remained responsible for the defense of Singapore.

1971, November 1. ANZUK Force Replaces British Garrison. Units from Australia, New Zealand, and the U.K. made up the new garrison. Singapore began to raise substantial armed forces to share this responsibility in a 5-power defense pact with Malaysia and the other 3 Commonwealth nations.

INDONESIA

1945, August 17. Independence of Republic of Indonesia. This was declared by **Achmed Sukarno** and **Mohammed Hatta** after the collapse of Japan, in an effort to forestall Dutch reoccupation.

1945, September 29. British and Dutch Troops Arrive in Batavia. They began to disarm and repatriate Japanese forces, and to re-establish Dutch control over Netherlands East Indies.

1945, October 14. Hostilities Begin. The Indonesian People's Army declared war against occupying British and Dutch forces.

1945, November 6. Negotiations Rejected. Indonesian republicans rejected the Dutch offer of dominion status and home rule.

1945, November 29. Fall of Surabaya. British troops captured the rebel capital after an intensive battle with Indonesian nationalists.

1946, November 13. Cheribon Agreement. The Dutch recognized the Indonesian Republic (Java, Sumatra, and Madura) and U.S. of Indonesia—to include Borneo, Celebes, Sunda, and Molucca Islands—all under the Netherlands Crown. Clashes with the Dutch continued.

1947, May 4. Nationalists Proclaim Independence of West Java.

1947, July 20. Dutch Offensive on Java. U.N. intervention called for a cease-fire (August 4), but fighting went on despite continuing mediation efforts of the U.N. committee and of U.S. diplomats (1947–1948).

1948, December 19. Dutch Airborne Troops Capture Jogjakarta. This was the capital of the Indonesian rebels. The Dutch soon gained effective control of the entire island of Java (December 25).

1948, December 21. Cease-Fire.

1949, January 28. U.N. Security Council Orders Transfer of Sovereignty. The Netherlands refused, and sporadic hostilities continued.

1949, May 7. Cease-Fire. Dutch troops withdrew from Jogjakarta and Djakarta, new capital of the Indonesian Republic (June 30).

1949, November 2. The Netherlands Grants Full Sovereignty.

1950, August 15. Republic of Indonesia Is Proclaimed.

1950–1961. Endemic Civil War. Unrest, turmoil, and revolt throughout Indonesia, particularly on Sumatra and Celebes.

1955, April 18–27. Bandung Conference. Delegates from 29 Asian and African nations met at Bandung, and announced their aims as elimination of colonialism, independence and self-determination for all peoples, and membership for all nations in the U.N.

1957–1963. Indonesian Harassment against West New Guinea. The Indonesians claimed that this territory (called by them West Irian) should be given to them by the Dutch.

1962, January–August. Sporadic Hostilities. Indonesian torpedo boats off the coast of Dutch New Guinea were attacked by Netherlands forces (January 16). Soon afterward, a guerrilla campaign on Netherlands New Guinea was started by Sukarno (February 20).

1962, August 15. The Netherlands Agrees to Abandon West New Guinea. Formal transfer to Indonesia followed (May 1, 1963).

1962, December. Indonesian-sponsored Revolt in Brunei. The insurgency was suppressed by British troops.

1963, May 18. Sukarno Named President for Life.

1963, September 15. Harassment of Malaysia Begins. Following proclamation of the Federation of Malaysia, Sukarno refused to recognize the new federation, saying "we will fight and destroy it." Continual diplomatic and guerrilla harassment followed, with frequent infiltrations of Indonesian guerrillas into Malaysian territory (see p. 1302).

1965, January 21. Indonesia Withdraws from U.N. This was in protest at Malaysia's being given a seat on the Security Council.

1965, October 1. Communist Coup Effort. The Indonesian Army defeated the Communist effort, and a wave of anti-Communist, anti-Chinese violence swept the islands. The Army, under the leadership of Chief of Staff General **Abdul Haris Nasution** (who became Defense Minister), attempted to break up the Indonesian Communist Party (PKI).

1965, October–December. Massacre of the Communists. The Army and anti-Communist groups killed up to 100,000 PKI members. (Some estimates are much higher.) The result was considerable diminution of the power of President Sukarno, who had been supported by the PKI.

1966, February 21. Sukarno Dismisses Anti-Communist Members of Government. In Sukarno's effort to restore his own power, General Nasution was one of 15 anti-Communist cabinet members dismissed and replaced by left-wingers. There was an immediate violent reaction. Three students, demonstrating outside the Presidential Palace, were killed by police; rioting spread through Djakarta and Java (February 24). Thousands more suspected Communists were killed.

1966, March 12. Military Seizes Control; Sukarno a Figurehead. Leader of the military partial coup d'état was Lieutenant General **Suharto.** The PKI was outlawed; pro-Communists were purged from the government. Sukarno's few remaining powers were later taken by Suharto (1967, February 20).

1966, June 1. End of Hostilities with Malaysia. This was announced after four days of peace talks in Bangkok, although the status of Sabah and Sarawak on Borneo remained unresolved.

1966, August 11. Treaty With Malaysia. Signed in Djakarta, this formally ended the undeclared hostilities.

1966, September 28. Indonesia Rejoins the U.N. The U.S. resumed economic aid.

1968, March 27. Suharto Named President. This was proclaimed by the Consultative Assembly, formally ending the regime of Sukarno. Five years later Suharto was re-elected (1973, March).

PHILIPPINES

1946, July 4. Republic of the Philippines Established.

1946–1954. Hukbalahap Rebellion. This Communist-led peasant party, dominating central Luzon, conducted civil war against government troops for nearly a decade before being subdued. Primary responsibility for success of the antiguerrilla operations was that of **Ramon Magsaysay,** minister of defense.

1947, March 14. Agreement with U.S. Ninety-nine-year base agreement between the United States and the Philippines.

1952, April 15. Huk Leader Captured. Philippine troops captured **William J. Pomeroy,** leader of the Communist-led Hukbalahaps.

1954. The Philippines Join SEATO. (See p. 1292.)

1962, June 22. The Philippines Claim Sabah Province, North Borneo. This was based upon prior ownership by the Sultan of Sulu before Sabah was seized by Britain in the 19th century. The claim created subsequent tension with Malaysia.

1964–1974. Guerrilla War against Communist "Huks." Recovering from defeat in the early 1950's (see above), the Philippine Communist Party created a new military arm, successor to the Hukbalahap, called Hukbong Magagpalaya Nang Bayan (People's Liberation Army), operating mainly in central Luzon. The tactics of these new "Huks" were similar to those of the Viet Cong, combining terror and assassination with selective measures to gain local good will. Government suppressive activities prevented the Huks from major success but were unable to destroy the guerrillas.

1966, September 16. Agreement Reduces U.S. Base Lease. The term of U.S. leases on bases in the Philippines was reduced from 99 to 25 years.

1966, September 25. Philippine Construction Battalion Reaches Vietnam. The force, eventually reaching 2,000 men, was initially 1,000 strong. It was sent to demonstrate adherence to SEATO policy.

1970–1974. Moslem Insurgency in Southern Islands. Low-level warfare was waged, the Communist-supported New People's Army (NPA) taking advantage of traditional Moslem-Christian hostility.

1972, September 23. Martial Law in the Philippines. Proclaimed by President **Ferdinand Marcos** as a "last desperate step" to save the islands from Communist-inspired insurgency and chaos, because of the Huk and NPA insurgencies in Luzon and Mindanao. Political opponents claimed this was merely an excuse for dictatorship.

EAST ASIA

ASIAN AND PACIFIC COUNCIL

The Asian and Pacific Council (ASPAC) was established by 9 anti-Communist nations, meeting in Seoul (1966, July 14–16). The members were: Japan, South Korea, the Republic of China (Taiwan), South Vietnam, Thailand, Malaysia, the Philippines, Australia, and New Zealand. At this first meeting the new organization announced its determination to preserve "integrity and sovereignty" in the face of Communist threats, particularly from the People's Republic of China. Other than occasional statements of general support for the efforts of South Vietnam against its Communist enemies, ASPAC has had little influence and has not figured prominently in the policies of any of its members.

CHINA (NATIONAL REPUBLIC)

The civil war between the National Government (of the Kuomintang party) and the Chinese Communist party, which began in 1926, and which was only partially interrupted by the war against Japan, burst into even fiercer flames at the time of the Japanese surrender. **Chiang Kai-shek**'s National Government, decisively defeated, withdrew from the mainland to Formosa (1949), where with U.S. support it defiantly continued to claim to be the legal government of China, now ruled from Peking by **Mao Tse-tung.** The principal events were:

1945, August 14. Treaty with U.S.S.R. This pledged friendship and alliance between Soviet Russia and Chiang Kai-shek's Nationalist Government (see p. 1267). The Manchurian Railway and the port of Dairen were to be held in joint ownership for 30 years. Port Arthur was to become a Soviet-Chinese naval base and the independence of Outer Mongolia recognized.

1945, August. Renewed Chinese Civil War. Chinese Communist forces moved to take over as much of the Japanese-occupied areas as possible, ignoring Chiang's orders to halt. To permit Nationalist compliance with agreed Allied terms of Japanese surrender, and to forestall Communist takeover of all North China, General **Albert C. Wedemeyer,** still Chiang's Chief of Staff, provided American sea and air lift (August–October) to move Nationalist forces to Central and North China. By mid-October about 500,000 Nationalist troops had been so moved.

1945, August 28. American-Sponsored Nationalist-Communist Negotiations. After persuading Chiang to issue an invitation, U.S. Ambassador **Patrick J. Hurley** personally escorted Mao to Chungking for a peace conference. After nearly two months, this broke down, when Nationalists discovered that a large Communist force under General **Lin Piao** was quietly moving into southwest Manchuria.

1945, September 30. Arrival of U.S. Marines. To prevent an expected clash of Nationalist and Communist forces, the U.S. First

Marine Division and other units were landed in eastern Hopei and Shantung. This force soon grew to about 53,000 men. They occupied Peiping, Tientsin, and coastal areas of both provinces.

1945, November 15. Nationalist Offensive in Southwest Manchuria. Nationalist requests to move troops into Manchuria by sea through the Liaotung Peninsula were rejected by Soviets, who occupied the region under agreed Allied terms for Japanese surrender. Nationalist troops were landed at Chinwangtao, in the area held by U.S. Marines. They attacked across the Great Wall into regions held by Communists, outside the Russian zone of occupation. The well-trained, well-equipped Nationalists pushed aside the Communists and soon held the region as far as Chinchow (November 26).

1945, November 30. Communist Offensive in Shantung. Chen Yi's New Fourth Army occupied much of the province not already held by U.S. Marines.

1945, December 5. Hurley Accuses Foreign Service Officers. Disappointed by failure of his negotiation efforts, Hurley had resigned (November 26). He now charged that his failure had been largely due to obstructive efforts of pro-Communist American Foreign Service officers.

1945, December 14. Marshall as Mediator. U.S. General of the Army George C. Marshall, recently retired as U.S. Army Chief of Staff, was sent to China as personal representative of President Truman, with mission of mediating the dispute.

1946, January 14. Truce in China. Achieved as a result of Marshall's mediation. Despite frequent violations, and nonapplication in Manchuria, this truce remained in effect in most of China for nearly six months.

1946, February 25. Nationalist-Communist Accord. National Government and Communist representatives, meeting with General Marshall and other U.S. mediators, agreed to unify the Chinese armed forces into one national army with 50 Nationalist and 10 Communist divisions. This agreement broke down within a few weeks.

Operations in Manchuria, 1946–1948

1946, March 1. Soviet Forces Begin Withdrawal from Manchuria. Chinese Communist troops, scattered about the countryside, moved toward the cities, as Nationalist troops advanced up the main roads and railroads from the southwest. The Soviets had completely dismantled all Japanese-built factories and industrial facilities, and moved the equipment to Siberia. Vast stores of captured Japanese military equipment, however, were left behind by the Russians where they could be seized by the Chinese Communists, enough to equip the entire Chinese Communist Army.

1946, March 10–15. Battle for Mukden (Shenyang). The day following the Russian withdrawal from the city, a battle broke out for control. The Nationalists were successful; they pushed northward.

1946, March 17. First Battle of Szeping. A massive Chinese Communist counterattack drove Nationalist spearheads back. The Communists entrenched this important rail center.

1946, April 14–18. First Battle of Ch'angch'un. A Nationalist contingent of 4,000, airlifted into Ch'angch'un, was driven out by numerically superior Communists.

1946, April 16–May 20. Second Battle of Szeping. The Nationalist New First Army, 70,000 veterans of the Burma Campaigns under **Sun Li-jen,** drove out 110,000 well-entrenched Communists, who claimed they had been attacked by American planes. The Nationalists immediately pushed north toward Ch'angch'un.

1946, April 25–28. Communists Seize Harbin and Tsitsihar. The National Government made no effort to seize these northern cities as the Russians completed their withdrawal from Manchuria (May 3).

1946, May 22. Communists Evacuate Ch'angch'un. Nationalist troops seized the city and continued their northward drive against ineffectual resistance.

1946, June 1. Crossing the Sungari. The Nationalists continued their drive toward Harbin, as Communist resistance stiffened.

1946, June 7–30. Cease-Fire in Manchuria. Brought about by efforts of General Marshall. The Nationalists halted at Shuangcheng. When negotiations broke down, hostilities resumed.

1946, June-December. Stalemate in Manchuria. During the truce the Communists had strengthened their defenses south of Harbin; the Nationalist advance was stalled. The Nationalists, now over 200,000 strong, held the principal centers of southern and central Manchuria, a bridgehead north of the Sungari, and controlled the railroads. The drain of garrisoning these areas precluded assembling and supporting forces large enough to continue the drive toward Harbin. The Communists, who had recruited the disbanded Manchukuan army, had a strength of over 500,000 and held the countryside, but were unable to mount effective attacks against the Nationalists. After cessation of U.S. military assistance (see below), Nationalist forces in Manchuria went completely on the defensive, to conserve supplies and to permit Nationalist offensives elsewhere in China (see below).

1947, January–March. Communist Sungari River Probes. General Lin Piao, commanding Communist forces in Manchuria, launched three offensives across the Sungari, southwest of the Nationalist bridgehead. All were repulsed.

1947, May–June. Sungari River Offensive. Some 270,000 Communists converged on Ch'angch'un, Kirin, and Szeping. All three cities were isolated, and supplied by air. The Nationalists evacuated their bridgehead. Two Nationalist armies were rushed north from Liaotung.

1947, June–July. Third Battle of Szeping. The Communists briefly occupied the rail center (June 16), but were finally repulsed. A lull followed, as both sides prepared for further action (July–August).

1947, September 20. Communists Begin Liaosi Corridor Offensive. The purpose was to cut off Mukden from overland communications to North China. Counteroffensive by Nationalist field commander in Manchuria, **Cheng Tung-kuo,** finally secured the corridor (October 10).

1948, January–February. Renewed Liaosi Corridor Offensive. Chiang Kai-shek flew to Mukden to take personal command. Nationalist counterattacks again secured the corridor. Chiang returned to Nanking.

1948, March–September. Nationalist Erosion. Steady Communist pressure eroded the Nationalist defenses. Nationalists evacuated Kirin to strengthen isolated Ch'angch'un. The defensive attitude and psychology adversely affected Nationalist morale.

1948, September 12. Renewed Liaosi Corridor Offensive. The Communists seized the corridor, repulsing all Nationalist efforts to reopen the line of communications to the south. Chiang flew to Peking to assume command. Finding the situation in Manchuria to be hopeless, he ordered the garrisons to withdraw, fighting their way south. Ch'angch'un was evacuated (October 21).

1948, October 27–30. Battle of Mukden-Chinchow. Retreating Nationalist columns, 3 armies, were struck by a massive Communist counteroffensive. All were killed, captured, or dispersed. The Nationalist commander, General **Liao Yueh-hsiang,** competent Burma veteran, was killed.

1948, November 1. Fall of Mukden. The small remaining Nationalist garrison surrendered. By the end of the year the Communists held all of Manchuria. The Nationalists had lost 300,000 of their best troops.

Operations in North and Central China, 1946–1949

1946, May 1. National Capital to Nanking. The Chinese Government officially returned to Nanking from Chungking.

1946, May 5. Hostilities at Hankow. This was one of many breakdowns in the cease-fire established in January (see p. 1306).

July–November. Nationalist North China Offensive. Claiming the provocation of frequent Communist truce violations, Chiang ordered a major offensive to seize North China, hoping to prevent Communists from entrenching themselves. The offensive was highly successful. The Nationalists recovered most of Kiangsu, reopened the Tsinan-Tsingtao railway in Shantung, occupied Jehol and much of Hopeh. The Communists undertook minor counteroffensives, winning temporary successes along the Lung-Hai Railway (Sian-Kaifeng-Hsuchow) and in north Shansi.

1946, July 29. U.S. Halts Military Equipment Assistance. General Marshall, annoyed by the Nationalist offensive, and under strong Communist propaganda attack for U.S. assistance to the Nationalists, ordered an embargo of all U.S. military assistance to both sides. This actually only affected the U.S.-equipped armies of the National Government. Chiang ordered units in Manchuria to go on the defensive, but continued the North China offensive in belief he could win before supplies ran out. This U.S. action had serious psychological as well as practical effects on the National military situation.

1946, September. U.S. Marines Begin Withdrawal. This was interpreted by many Chinese as further evidence of U.S. abandonment of the National Government.

1946, November 8. Chiang Orders Nationalist Cease-fire. He informed General Marshall that he was willing to resume negotiations. Nationalist overtures and U.S. mediation efforts were rejected by the Communists.

1947, January 6. Failure of the Marshall Mission. At Marshall's request, he was recalled by President Truman. Marshall left China, criticizing both sides (January 7). Remaining U.S. Marines in North China (about 12,000) were ordered to withdraw, save for one regiment left in Tientsin under terms of 1901 Boxer Protocol.

1947, January–December. Nationalists on the Defensive. They held the towns and main railroads. Elsewhere the Communists seized the initiative, save for one continuing Nationalist offensive in Shensi.

1947, March 19. Nationalists Capture Yenan. The Nationalist offensive in Shensi captured the Communist capital; Mao Tse-tung was forced to flee. Elsewhere the Communists held the initiative, and Mao refused to call back any troops from more important theaters of the war to defend his capital.

1947, October. Communist Offensives. Coordinated with offensives in Manchuria, **Liu Po-ch'eng**'s Central Plains Army and Chen Yi's East China Field Army were active in the area between the Yangtze River and the Lung-Hai Railway and in Shantung. Chen Yi's forces cut the railroad line north of Kaifeng, cutting the main line of communications of Nationalist armies in North China.

1948, March–April. Communist Offensive in Shensi. Troops of General **P'eng Teh-huai** recaptured Yenan (April).

1948, May–September. Communist Offensives in Yellow River Valley. Armies of Chen and Liu steadily reduced Nationalist holdings north of Yellow River. This offensive culminated in the **Battle of Tsinan** (September 14–24), in which 80,000 Nationalist troops defected or were captured.

1948–1949, November–January. Battle of the Hwai Hai. Under over-all command of Chen Yi, his army and Liu Po-ch'eng's attacked the Nationalist Seventh and Second Army groups, deployed along the Lung-Hai Railway generally east of Kaifeng. About 500,000 troops were involved on each side. While the East China Field Army pinned down the Seventh Army Group, between Hsuchow and the sea, the Central Plains Field Army smashed into and through the flank of the Second Army Group, west of Hsuchow toward the Hwai River. Efforts of the Seventh and Second Army Groups to retreat to the Hwai were blocked. Much of the Second Army Group broke through, but the Seventh Army Group was destroyed. Total Nationalist casualties exceeded 250,000 men; among those killed were the commanders of both Nationalist Army groups.

1949, January 21. Chiang Resigns. Vice President **Li Tsung-jen** became Acting President.

1949, January 22. Fall of Peking. Nationalist General **Fu-Tso-yi** surrendered to the Communists after a long siege. Mao Tse-tung soon thereafter moved the Communist capital to Peking from Yenan.

1949, February. Evacuation of Last U.S. Troop Contingent. Withdrawal of the U.S. 3d Marine Regiment from Tientsin was considered by both sides to indicate American abandonment of the National Government.

1949, April 1. Nationalist Peace Effort. Li Tsung-jen sent a delegation to Peking to seek Communist agreement to a division of China at the Yangtze. The Communists rejected this, insisting upon Nationalist surrender.

1949, April 20. Communists Cross the Yangtze River. Liu Po-Ch'eng's redesignated Second Field Army and Chen Yi's Third Field Army crossed on a broad front between Nanking and Wuhan. During the crossing two British warships on the Yangtze were attacked and severely damaged by Communist artillery. As Communist troops approached Nanking, the movement of the National Government capital to Canton (begun January 19) was completed.

1949, April 22. Fall of Nanking. This was

followed by the capture of Hsuchow (April 26), Wuhan (May 17), Nanchang (May 23), and Shanghai (May 27). Two other important beleaguered cities north of the Yangtze also surrendered: Taiyuan (April 24) and Sian (May 20).

1949, May–December. Nationalist Collapse. Many Nationalist commanders and troop units defected to the Communists. As the Communist armies approached Canton (October), the capital was shifted to Chungking.

1949, August 5. U.S. White Paper. This State Department document, criticizing the Nationalist Government, formally announced cutoff of all further military aid.

1949, October 15. Fall of Canton. Chinese Communist troops occupied Canton without opposition. Chiang returned to head the collapsing National Government.

1949, November 30. Fall of Chungking. Chiang established a new capital at Ch'engtu.

1949, December 7. Withdrawal to Formosa. Chiang's government and all his remaining troops successfully completed withdrawal from the mainland as Communist columns approached Ch'engtu. Nationalist troops retained offshore islands of Quemoy, Tachen, and Matsu.

1950. National Government Reforms. Following institution of social and political reforms of the sort promised while the government was still on the mainland, the U.S. resumed economic and military assistance.

1950, June 25. Chiang Offers Military Assistance to U.N. in Korea. Favorably considered by General MacArthur, the offer was turned down by President Truman, who (June 27) ordered the U.S. Seventh Fleet to prevent either Red Chinese attack on Formosa or Nationalist assault against the mainland.

1950, July 24. Intensive Artillery Bombardment of Quemoy.

1951, January 30. U.S. Military Assistance Group Established.

1952, February 1. U.S.S.R. Censured by U.N. General Assembly. A resolution was approved charging Russia with obstructing the efforts of the National Government of China to retain control of Manchuria following Japan's surrender, and giving military assistance to the Chinese Communists.

1953, February 2. Chiang "Unfettered." President Eisenhower declared that the Seventh Fleet would no longer "serve as a defensive arm of Communist China."

1954, August 17. Communist Threats against Formosa. President Eisenhower said that the Seventh Fleet would go to the defense of Formosa if the Chinese Communists should attempt to invade.

1954, September 3. Heavy Bombardment of Quemoy. Increased activity threatened an invasion of Formosa, and the Seventh Fleet moved to take up positions to defend it.

1954, December 2. Mutual Defense Treaty with the United States. Fear of further involvement of the U.S. in Asian war led to new restrictions on Nationalist China, whose territorial limits were described in the treaty (signed March 3, 1955) as "Formosa and the Pescadores." Communist bombardment of Quemoy and Matsu continued.

1955, January. Tachen Islands Threatened. Intense Chinese Communist pressure against the islands by airplane raids and small-craft raids. The U.S. Seventh Fleet helped to evacuate 25,000 military and 17,000 civilians from the islands (February 6–11). Meanwhile, President Eisenhower asked Congress for emergency powers to permit U.S. armed forces to protect Formosa and the Pescadores islands, and to assist the National Government in defending the islands (January 24).

1955, June 7. "De Facto" Cease-Fire. An uneasy truce settled over Quemoy and Matsu.

1958, August 23. Blockade of Quemoy by Communist Artillery. Continuous bombardment interrupted supply to the islands for both garrison and civilian population. Strenuous effort of Seventh Fleet, convoying supply by water and air, defeated the Red plan (September). The blockade fire gradually died down (October), dwindling to almost nothing (June, 1958).

1962, March 24. Chinese Communist Planes over Quemoy. Rumors of pending invasion and heavy mainland troop concentrations produced another tense situation. Once again U.S. sea-power potential asserted itself. Chinese Nationalist planes shot down several Communist aircraft. The U.S. warned the Communists to keep hands off Quemoy and Matsu (January 22). All threat of invasion soon ended.

1962–1974. Civil War Continues. For several years tension between Formosa and the mainland was undiminished, with sporadic guerrilla operations by the Nationalists harassing the Chinese mainland. This tension abated, however, in the later 1960's, with only occasional, prepublicized, shellings of Quemoy reminding both sides that nominally, at least, they were still at war. Severe blows were struck at hopes of Nationalist return to the mainland first by the replacement of the Republic of China in the United Nations by the People's Republic (1972), and second by the United States' recognition of the rival government in Peking (1973).

CHINA (PEOPLE'S REPUBLIC)

1949, September 21. People's Republic Proclaimed at Peking. Mao Tse-tung was named chairman of the Central People's Government; **Chou En-lai,** premier. Immediate recognititon was granted by the U.S.S.R. and its satellites, also by India, Burma, and Ceylon. Great Britain soon recognized the new state (January 6, 1950).

1950, February 15. Treaty of Friendship and Alliance with U.S.S.R.

1950, April 23. Communist Conquest of Hainan Island Completed.

1950, October 7. Invasion of Tibet. (See below.)

1950, October 26. Intervention in Korean War. (See p. 1245.)

1954–1964, September 3. Bombardments of Quemoy. (See p. 1309.)

1957–1965. Rift with U.S.S.R. Increasing ideological differences and mutually conflicting power ambitions by the end of the period widened the crack in the "monolithic" structure of world Communism.

1959, August 29. Indian Border Violated by Chinese Troops. (See p. 1288.)

1960, January 28. Sino-Burmese Treaty. (See p. 1294.)

1960, June 3. Anti-Chinese Revolt in Tibet. (See below.)

1960, June 29. Border Friction with Nepal.

1962, October 20–November 21. India-China Border War. (See p. 1288.) Before the fighting ended, some 3,213 Indian soldiers and 800 Indian civilians had been made prisoner; total casualties are unknown. Prisoners were later returned (April, 1963).

1963–1965. Chinese Support of North Vietnamese Aggression. (See p. 1297.) This became another issue exacerbating strained relations between the U.S.S.R. and Communist China.

1964–1974. Intermittent Border Violence along Sino-Soviet Frontiers. This was the result of tensions created by Chinese demands for return to China of vast areas of Soviet East Asia taken by Czarist Russia in the 19th century. Most incidents seem to have occurred at places where border demarcation was unclear.

1964, October 16. China Explodes Its First Atomic Bomb. She became the world's fifth nuclear power.

1966–1969. "Cultural Revolution." Unrest and violence spread throughout much of mainland China, apparently to some extent deliberately inspired by Chairman Mao Tse-tung for the purpose of rejuvenating the revolutionary spirit among members of the Communist Party and the people. Initially the Army seems to have supported, or at least endured, excesses of Communist youth, but as the unrest continued unabated, Army leaders seem to have taken the lead in restoring order, apparently with the somewhat reluctant approval of Mao.

1966, October 27. China Reports Firing a Nuclear Missile. This was China's fourth nuclear explosion, the first in which actual weaponry was tested.

1967, June 17. China Explodes Its First Hydrogen Bomb. China's fifth nuclear explosion, like the others, was conducted at the test site at Lop Nor, in Sinkiang.

1969, March 2–15. Undeclared Combat Between Chinese and Soviet Troops. These clashes took place at different points along the Manchurian frontier. Although there had been no previous public announcements, these were mainly intensifications of armed clashes between Chinese and Soviet forces that had been going on for at least 5 years. Clashes occurred frequently in subsequent months, with both sides accusing the other of provocation.

TIBET

1949, November 24. Communist "Liberation" of Tibet Urged. This was a radio appeal from Peking by the **Panchen Lama**—refugee rival of Tibet's nominal ruler, the **Dalai Lama.** The Chinese Communist government soon announced its intention of doing just this (January 1, 1950).

1950, October. Chinese Communist Invasion. A large Chinese force swept across the frontiers despite a Tibetan appeal to the U.N. (November 10), soon overrunning the entire country. The Dalai Lama was permitted to remain as a figurehead ruler in Lhasa. Widespread revolt continued despite fierce Communist repressive measures (1950–1954).

1954, Spring and Summer. Widespread Revolt. This was suppressed by Chinese Communist troops. Most of the 40,000 rebels were killed or executed.

1956–1959. Renewed Unrest. Mass deportations, Chinese infiltrations, and forced Tibetan labor on the military highway connecting Lhasa and Chungking stirred the population.

1959, March 10–27. Rebellion. This was suppressed by Chinese Communist troops. The Dalai Lama fled from Lhasa to India, where political asylum was afforded. He formally accused Communist China of genocide and suppression of human rights, asserting that 65,000 Tibetans had been killed in the revolt, 10,000 young people and children deported to China, and 5 million Chinese moved into Tibet in a resettlement project.

1959–1974. Continued Guerrilla Warfare. Resistance was sporadic, weak, and relatively ineffective.

MONGOLIAN PEOPLES REPUBLIC

1945, October 20. Mongolia Votes for Independence from China. This was the overwhelming result of a plebiscite required under the terms of the Sino-Soviet treaty of friendship and alliance (1945, August 14; see p. 1305).

1946, February 27. Treaty with the U.S.S.R. This treaty of friendship, for 10 years, has been regularly renewed.

1947, June 5–8. Mongolian Raid into Sinkiang. Mongolian troops attacked Peitashan to rescue Mongols captured by Chinese in prior border skirmishes.

KOREA

1945, December 27. Moscow Declaration. The U.S., Soviet, British, and French foreign ministers announced the establishment of a U.S.-Soviet Joint Commission for the purpose of unifying Korea in accordance with the terms of the Cairo Agreement (see p. 1240).

1946–1947. Failure of the U.S.-Soviet Joint Commission. No agreement could be reached on the establishment of an interim government for all Korea.

NORTH KOREA

1948, May 1. Soviets Proclaim North Korean Independence. By establishing the Democratic People's Republic, the U.S.S.R. defied a planned U.N. plebiscite for all Korea. The president was veteran Communist **Kim Il Sung.**

1948, October 19–December 25. Russian Troops Withdraw. A large Soviet training mission remained in North Korea.

1950–1953. Korean War. (See p. 1241.)

1961, July 6. Treaty with the U.S.S.R. Soviet Russia provided assurance of defense protection, plus financial and military equipment assistance.

1968, January 23. *Pueblo* Incident. The The U.S.S. *Pueblo,* a Navy electronic intelligence vessel, was attacked and seized by North Korean gunboats, on the pretext that the vessel had violated the territorial waters of North Korea. U.S. naval forces, including the nuclear-powered carrier U.S.S. *Enterprise,* took station off the coast of North Korea, but no reprisals were taken.

1968, December 22. Release of the Crew of the *Pueblo*. This was the result of a complicated agreement with North Korea, whereby the United States representative on the Mixed Armistice Commission in Panmunjon signed a "confession" that the vessel had been engaged in "espionage," then immediately, and with the agreement of the North Koreans, denounced the document as false.

1969, April 15. North Koreans Shoot Down U.S. Reconnaissance Plane. The attack by North Korean aircraft took place about 100 miles off the coast of North Korea. Again U.S. naval forces threatened North Korea, but no action was taken.

SOUTH KOREA

1948, August 15. Proclamation of the Republic of Korea. This was the result of U.N.-supervised elections early in 1948. The first president of the new republic was **Syngman Rhee.**

1948, October 20–27. Communist-Inspired Army Revolt. A Communist cell in a military unit sparked an uprising which briefly controlled the cities of Yosu and Sunchon in southern South Korea. After vicious fighting, in which at least 1,000 were killed on both sides, loyal troops and police suppressed the insurrection. Another revolt in Taegu was quickly subdued (November 3).

1948–1950. Tension in Korea. Border incidents, Communist infiltration across the border, and Communist-inspired disorders throughout South Korea continued and intensified.

1949, June 29. Withdrawal of U.S. Occupation Forces Completed. **(See p. 1241.)**

1950, June 25. North Korean Invasion of South Korea. **(See p. 1241.)**

1950–1953. Korean War. **(See p. 1241.)**

1953–1971. Continued Tension. Deliberate Communist violations of armistice force limitations in North Korea caused the U.S. and South Korea to announce a compensatory build-up of forces and weapons (beginning June 21, 1957). North Korean raids intensified during the period 1967–1971, but no large-scale hostilities occurred.

1960, April 6–27. Korean Violence Forces Resignation of Rhee. Demonstrations and protests by students against the repressive regime of President Syngman Rhee led to widespread riots and disorders. Rhee's efforts to reorganize the government failed to satisfy the protesters, and Rhee resigned, apparently in part as a result of pressure from the United States. Foreign Minister **Huh Chung** became the acting president under the constitution.

1961, May 16. Coup d'État. General **Chung Hee Park** seized power and dismissed the existing government. Later Park was formally elected president (1963, October 15).

1965, February 25. First South Korean Troops Arrive in South Vietnam. A contingent of 600 troops arrived, scheduled to be increased to 2,000. By early 1966 this force had risen to 21,000, and by late October, 1966, to 41,000, including 2 divisions organized as a corps. This was a demonstration of solidarity with the United States.

JAPAN

1945–1950. MacArthur as Supreme Commander for the Allied Powers. Under the firm control and guidance of MacArthur's military government, the Japanese government and nation began recovery from the devastation of the war.

1946, November 3. New Constitution. This became effective May 3, 1947. Among its provisions was a renunciation of the right to wage war.

1951, September 8. Peace Treaty with the Allies. Unable to obtain Soviet agreement to negotiate a peace treaty, the U.S. and 48 other non-Communist nations signed a treaty with Japan (effective April 28, 1952). At the same time, the U.S. signed a bilateral defense agreement with Japan.

1951–1954. Japan Begins Limited Rearmament. Despite apparently sincere devotion to the war-renunciation clause of the constitution, it became apparent to Japan that internal and external security required military forces. With U.S. encouragement, Japan began to develop small "self-defense forces."

1954, March 8. Mutual Defense Agreement with U.S. Under this the U.S. was to give Japan about $100 million in subsidies for production of munitions and food.

1954, July 1. Official Rearmament Approved. After prolonged national and legislative debate, Japan enacted legislation authorizing new armed forces.

1956, October 19. State of War with Russia Terminated. A joint Japanese-Soviet declaration.

1960, January 19. Renewed Mutual Defense Treaty with the U.S.

1972, May 15. Okinawa Returns to Japanese Control. This was a result of a treaty with the United States (1971, June 17).

1972, September 29. Peace Treaty with Communist China. Signed by Japanese Prime Minister **Kakuei Tanaka** and Chinese People's Republic Prime Minister **Chou En-lai,** this ended the state of war which had technically existed between Japan and China since 1937. Simultaneously Japan severed relations with the Republic of China (Formosa).

AFRICA

Before World War II, Africa, the second largest continent in land area, included but one truly independent nation: tiny, unimportant Liberia. The Union of South Africa, in fact independent, as a dominion was a part of the British Empire. Egypt, nominally independent, was actually under British protection and influence. Ethiopia, which had been truly independent, had recently been conquered by Italy (see p. 1040). In the 20 years after World War II, complete independence was achieved by all nations and regions of Africa, save for a few insignificant Spanish coastal colonies and the large Portuguese colonies of Angola and Mozambique. This achievement of independence, however, did not in the slightest halt the working of the forces of nationalism (and related anticolonialism) in the independent nations or in the few remaining colonial areas. Revolution, new nationalism, new and indigenous imperialism, Communist subversion (of two varieties, one directed from Moscow and the other from Peking), racial antagonisms, and sweeping technological change kept most of Africa in constant turbulence for the entire period. There were internal and external military actions and hostilities of one sort or another in practically every nation and colonial region of the continent. Only the most important will be noted here.

ORGANIZATION OF AFRICAN UNITY

The Organization of African Unity (OAU) was formed in 1963 through the efforts of the leaders of Nigeria, Ethiopia, and Guinea and was the culmination of earlier efforts to form a broad-based continental organization. All African countries are members except South Africa and Rhodesia. The charter prescribes noninterference in the internal affairs of states, observance of sovereignty and territorial integrity of members, peaceful settlement of disputes, condemnation of political assassination and subversive activities, nonalignment with power blocs, and emancipation of the white-ruled African territories. (The OAU Liberation Committee supports the various liberation movements directed against the white-dominated regimes.)

The OAU succeeded in arbitrating the Algerian-Moroccan border war of 1963 and in helping Tanzania replace with African troops the British troops which had quelled its 1964 army mutiny. However, it was ineffective in assisting Zaire (then Democratic Republic of the Congo) during its rebellion in 1964–1965, in resolving the Nigerian-Biafran civil war in 1969, in reconciling various rival liberation movements, or in successfully prosecuting a war of liberation in Southern Africa or Rhodesia. Following an allegedly Portuguese-inspired mercenary raid on Guinea (1970, December) consideration was given to establishment of a common African army, but nothing came of that. At a meeting of African leaders at Cairo, July 21, 1964, it was agreed that nuclear weapons would be banned from Africa.

AFRICAN AND MALAGASY COMMON ORGANIZATION

The African and Malagasy Common Organization (OCAM) was formed in 1965 as an outgrowth of earlier attempts at cooperation among French-speaking states, including the African and Malagasy Union and the Regional Council of France, Ivory Coast, Niger, and Dahomey. Aside from political and economic motives, the prime factors were establishment of a common front to meet Ghana's then subversive activities, Chinese Communist infiltration and subversion, and endemic chaos in the former Belgian Congo (now Zaire). OCAM is largely consultative, and no common defense staff or organization exists. Most members have bilateral defense treaties with France, which ensures their immediate internal and external security when threatened beyond their means to cope. The 14 members are: Cameroon, Central African Republic, Chad, Congo (People's Republic of the Congo), Dahomey, Gabon, Ivory Coast, Malagasy Republic, Niger, Rwanda, Senegal, Togo, Upper Volta, and Zaire.

NORTH AFRICA

Algeria

1945–1954. Autonomy Demanded. The first clash (May 8, 1949) between nationalists and French caused the death of 88 French and more than 1,000 Algerians.

1954–1962. Open Rebellion. The FLN (Front de Libération Nationale, organized 1951) started organized warfare, which was to continue until freedom had been attained. Use of Tunisian bases by the FLN strained French relations with Tunisia (see p. 1316). The insurrection drew nearly one-half of the entire French Army into Algeria, with resulting casualties of 10,200 French soldiers and some 70,000 Algerian insurgents killed.

1958, May 13. French Officer Uprising. Brigadier General **Jacques Massu** established a Committee of Public Safety, protesting against political leadership in the war. This started the chain of political events in France that brought de Gaulle to power (see p. 1261).

1958, June 1. De Gaulle Offers Self-Determination by Referendum. This was opposed by the *pieds noirs* (Algerians of French descent). Rioting and terrorism were manipulated by the "Secret Army" (or OAS, an extremist group organized by *pieds noirs* and French military men). De Gaulle visited Algeria and demanded dissolution of the Committee of Public Safety, restoring French government control in Algeria.

1960, January 22–February 1. Uprising of French Rightists in Algiers. They were opposed to de Gaulle's policy of self-determination for Algeria. This was suppressed by loyal French troops under General **Maurice Challe.**

1961, January 6–8. French Voters Support de Gaulle's Algerian Program. An overwhelming majority approved a referendum to permit Algerian self-determination.

1961, April 22–26. French Military Revolt. A mutiny headed by Generals Challe and **Raoul Salan** was quickly put down (April 25) by loyal French troops on de Gaulle's order (see p. 1262). Salan escaped and directed intensified OAS terrorism in France and Algeria.

1961, May 20. Peace Talks Begin. These took place at Evian-les-Bains in France between representatives of the French government and the rebel Algerian provisional government.

1962, March 7–18. Cease-Fire. Evian negotiations brought a cease-fire between Moslem nationalists (FLN) and French Army. **Ahmed Ben Bella** was chosen as premier.

1962, July 3. Algerian Independence.

1962–1965. Continuing Internal Unrest. There was widespread opposition to Ben Bella's relatively inefficient and dictatorial government, closely aligned with the U.S.S.R. and with the U.A.R. There were several mutinies, revolts, and uprisings around the country.

1963, October 6–12. Berber Revolt. Under the leadership of a dissident Army officer, Colonel Mohand ou el Hadj, Berber tribesmen of the Kabylin Mountains region rose against the government. President Ben Bella claimed the insurgency was incited by Morocco, as a result of tense relations over a border dispute (see below). The defeated rebels were forced to flee into the mountains. Colonel Mohand soon ended his revolt and joined in the war against Morocco (October 24).

1963, October 13–30. Border War with Morocco. (See p. 1316.)

1965, June 19. Overthrow of Ben Bella. Control of the nation was seized in a near-bloodless *coup d'état* by the army commander, Communist-trained Colonel **Houari Boumedienne,** a hero of the revolution against France, who was soon installed as president (July 5).

1967, December 13. Attempted Coup d'État. The uprising, involving Army officers, was suppressed.

1967, June. Algeria Sends Contingent to Support Egypt. (See p. 1230.)

Libya

1949–1951. Anticolonial Rioting. This was directed at both British occupation authorities and Italian administration.

1951, December 24. Independence of Libya.

1953, July 29. Treaty with Britain. This gave Britain 20-year rights to maintain military establishments in Libya, in return for which Britain was to pay Libya £1 million a year for 5 years for economic development and £2.75 million a year to aid in balancing the Libyan budget.

1954, September 9. Agreement with the U.S. An agreement was signed in Benghazi, giving the United States use of air bases in Libya in return for payment of $5 million in 1954, $2 million yearly for 20 years.

1969, September 1. Coup d'État. King **Mohammed Idris Al Mahdi as-Sanusi** was overthrown, while out of the country, by a military uprising led by young officers, of whom the leader was Captain **Muammar el Qaddafi.**

1969, December 10. Unsuccessful Coup Attempt. Qaddafi blamed "invisible foreign hands."

1970, January 21. Sale of French Aircraft to Libya. The sale of 100 French Mirage-III supersonic fighter jets to Libya was seen by most of the world as a transparent French evasion of their own embargo on weapons for the warring nations of the Middle East, since it was generally assumed (despite French denials) that these planes would be turned over by Libya to Egypt.

1970, June 11. Departure of Last Americans. As a result of pressure from the government of President Qaddafi, the United States abandoned Wheelus Air Force Base in Libya.

1971, September 1. Loose Union with Egypt and Syria. (See p. 1279.)

1972, August 2. Agreement to Unite with Egypt. This was the result of three days of conversations between Presidents Sadat of Egypt and Qaddafi of Libya at Tobruk and Benghazi.

1973, August 29. Reaffirmation of Unification with Egypt. The joint announcement by Sadat and Qaddafi made it clear that the unification would be a slow and gradual process, despite the obvious desire of Qaddafi for immediate union.

1974, January 12–14. Plan for Union with Tunisia. Joint announcement of the merger (January 12) was soon followed by a Tunisian announcement (January 15) that it would be delayed, probably indefinitely.

Morocco

1947–1953. Nationalistic Unrest. Sultan **Mohammed V** gave his support to the nationalist movement, in defiance of the French administration.

1953, August 15–20. French-Inspired Uprising. Tribal leaders in Marrakesh rose against the sultan, under the influence of pro-French leader **Thami Al-Glaoui.** The sultan was deposed and sent into exile by the French.

1953–1955. Increased Unrest. Terrorism and guerrilla operations of nationalists spread throughout Morocco.

1955, August 19–November 5. Intensified Guerrilla Hostilities. French efforts to suppress the risings of Berber tribes and the terrorism in the countryside and in the cities were not very successful.

1955, November 5. France Agrees to Independence. Mohammed V was restored to power.

1956, March 2. Protectorate Status Ceases. France and Morocco by mutual agreement terminated the Treaty of Fez (March 30, 1912). Spain relinquished her protectorate over Spanish Morocco (April 17), and the international status of the Tangier zone later ended (October 29).

1957–1964. Foreign Troops and Bases Withdrawn. Morocco called for evacuation of foreign troops. The last of a large complex of U.S. air bases was returned in 1964; French and Spanish forces had been previously withdrawn. As the period ended, the enclave of Spanish Sahara still remained *in statu quo.*

1957, November–December. Border Clashes at Ifni. Moroccan irregulars were repulsed by Spanish troops after seizing much of the colony. Later Spain ceded Ifni to Morocco (April 1, 1958).

1958, October 21. Pro-Monarchist Revolt. Army units, supporting King Mohammed V in his dispute with the Istiqlal Party, were attacked by loyal troops. Although disowned by the King, they were soon joined by Rif tribesmen in the Tasa area (November).

1959–1960. Revolt in Rif. Antigovernment operations in the Rif continued (see above) despite severe rebel defeats (1959, January) until the region was finally pacified (1960, April). Leader of the government troops was Crown Prince **Montay Hassan.**

1963, October 13–30. Border War with Algeria. Large-scale hostilities broke out along a disputed frontier area in the Atlas Mountains–Sahara Desert region after prolonged tension and a number of incidents. A cease-fire was arranged through the mediation of Emperor **Haile Selassie** of Ethiopia and President **Modibo Keita** of Mali.

1963, October 13–November 4. Border War with Algeria. Large-scale hostilities broke out along a disputed frontier area in the Atlas Mountain–Sahara Desert region after prolonged tension and a number of incidents. A cease-fire was arranged through the mediation of Emperor **Haile Selassie** of Ethiopia and President **Modibo Keita** of Mali. The Moroccans had the better of the fighting in the Hassi-Beida, Tindouf, Figuig area.

1971, July 10. Attempted Coup. The revolt was suppressed in bloody fighting which began when insurgents attacked the royal palace during a birthday party for King **Hassan II.**

1972, August 17. Attempted Coup. The leader of the revolt, trusted General **Mohommed Offkir,** Minister of Defense since the previous coup attempt, committed suicide when an attempt to shoot down the King's plane failed.

1973, March 2–7. Guerrilla Activity. Guerrillas, apparently from outside the country, disrupted at least 2 towns in southern Morocco. They were defeated and more than 100 were captured, some admitting support from Libya.

Tunisia

1952, March. Violence and Unrest. National self-determination came to a boiling point in disorders and riots directed against French rule.

1955, June 3. Full Internal Autonomy Granted by France. This was effective September 1.

1956, March 17. Independence. All former treaties and conventions were abrogated. **Habib Bourguiba** was chosen premier (March 25). France retained several military bases.

1956, July 25. Republic Proclaimed. Bourguiba became president. Despite disagreements—and one subsequent conflict—with France, Bourguiba kept his nation oriented to the West.

1957, May 26–June 7. Clashes with France. These were the result of activities of French and Tunisian troops in the vicinity of the Algerian border. Similar incidents occurred sporadically until the end of the insurgency in Algeria (see p. ???).

1958, February–June. Clashes with France. These sporadic border incidents were mostly French punitive action in response to Tunisia-based operations of Algerian nationalists.

1961, July 19–22. Hostilities with France. (**See p. 1262.**) Tunisian attacks against French military posts brought prompt retaliation. French troops occupied Bizerte. Hostilities were ended by U.N. mediators.

1962, June. French Evacuation Completed. Air-base rights were retained by France.

1962, December 22. Unsuccessful Coup Attempt.

1965, April 28. Tunisia Boycotts Arab League Meetings. This was because the other states refused to consider President Bourgiba's proposals for peace negotiations with Israel.

1966, October 3. Tunisia Breaks Relations with United Arab Republic. This was a result of continued disagreement about peace negotiations with Israel.

1974, January 12–15. Plan for Union with Libya. (**See p. 1315.**)

EAST AFRICA

Ethiopia

1952, September 11. Union with Eritrea. Moslem Eritrea and Christian Ethiopia were united in a federation.

1954, May 14. Agreement with the U.S. Ethiopia gave the United States 99-year military base rights.

1960, December 13–17. Military Revolt. During the absence of Emperor Haile Selassie, members of the Imperial Guard seized control of Addis Ababa and proclaimed Crown Prince **Asfa-Wossen** the new emperor. Loyal troops suppressed the rebellion. The emperor pardoned his son, who had apparently acted under duress.

1964. Frontier Warfare with Somalia. (See p. 1318.)

1965–1974. Revolt in Eritrea. Eritrea's Assembly had voted unanimously for permanent union with Ethiopia (1962, November 14). However, nationalist, Communist, and pan-Arab elements had joined forces to compel dissolution of the union. This dissidence, apparently financed by neighboring Arab states (primarily Sudan and Somalia), flared into guerrilla war.

1971–1974. Intensification of Eritrean Revolt. The Eritrean Liberation Front (ELF) stepped up guerrilla-terrorist activities against the government that spread to Addis Ababa.

1974, February 26–28. Army Mutiny. This spread from Asmara to Addis Abada. In an effort to retain control, Emperor Haile Selassie formed a new cabinet and raised Army pay. The nation remained, however, under virtual military control.

1974, June 28. Army Seizes Control. The Emperor became a figurehead, and his remaining power was soon reduced (August 16).

1974, September 12. Army Deposes Haile Selassie. Crown Prince **Asfa Wossen,** in Geneva, said he would serve as a constitutional monarch, as the Army demanded, but he didn't return. General **Aman Michael Andom,** chairman of the Provisional Military Government, became virtual head of state.

1974, November 22–24. Coup d'État. A power struggle among leaders of the Military Council ruling Ethiopia led to the ouster of General Aman (November 22), who was killed the next day during, or executed after, an armed clash of rival forces near his home. This was followed by the execution of about 60 former officials, including 32 military officers as well as cabinet ministers, provincial governors, and members of the nobility, including at least one royal prince. One reason for the power struggle was differences in philosophy and policy with respect to the continuing Eritrean separatist insurrection.

Kenya

1945–1952. Unrest and Violence. This British crown colony became a hotbed of revolution. A secret native organization—the Mau Mau—began a campaign of dissidence which finally erupted in an appalling area-wide blood bath, white colonists and native negroes alike, men, women, and children, being murdered under conditions of terror and treachery.

MAU MAU REVOLT

1952, October 20. Britain Declares a State of Emergency. Britain sent a warship and troops to Kenya to restore order and to suppress the Mau Mau uprising. Guerrilla war spread.

1953, January–May. British Military Measures. Major military and punitive measures were initiated. Leading Kikuyu tribe nationalist leaders, known or suspected to have connections with the Mau Mau Society, were arrested, tried, and convicted, including a 7-year prison sentence for **Jomo Kenyatta** (October 20). Central Kenya was sealed off from the rest of the country, and a separate East African command comprising Kenya, Uganda, and Tanganyika was set up under General Sir **George Erskine.**

1953, June 15. British Victory in the Aberdare Forest. More than 125 Mau Mau were killed, bringing the total of terrorists killed since October to approximately 1,000. Meanwhile, the colonial government undertook measures to improve housing conditions in Nairobi, and soon afterward dropped leaflets over known Mau Mau strongholds promising lenient treatment to all who surrendered and who were not guilty of murder or serious crimes.

1955, February–June. Climactic Campaign Begins. Some 10,000 troops dispersed about 4,000 terrorists in the Mt. Kenya and Aberdare areas.

1955, September 2. Britain Begins to Reduce

Forces. Since October, 1952, almost 10,000 terrorists had been killed, 1,538 had surrendered, and over 24,000 had been captured or were held as suspects. The campaign against the remaining scattered dissidents continued into early 1956.

1961, August 14. Kenyatta Released from Prison. He immediately became leader of the principal political independence party and began negotiations with the British for independence.

1963, March. Frontier Clashes with Somalia. Somali claims to frontier regions of northern Kenya led to border hostilities. Somalia broke relations with Britain (March 14).

1963, June 1. Kenyatta Prime Minister of Kenya.

1963, December 12. Independence of Kenya. She became an independent state within the British Commonwealth of Nations. Assured by the new status, and under promise of amnesty, Mau Mau adherents began surrendering en masse.

1963, December. Diplomatic Relations Broken with Somalia. Serious border warfare broke out.

1964, January. Unrest and Violence. Communist-inspired violence spread from Zanzibar and Tanganyika.

1964, January 25. British Troops Restore Order in Kenya. British intervention was requested by Kenyatta to suppress Communist-inspired native uprisings. The period ended with the nation threatened by internal turmoil and external war.

1968, January 31. Peace with Somalia. An informal understanding of October 1967 was affirmed by the resumption of diplomatic relations.

Malagasy Republic (Madagascar)

1947–1948. Revolt against France. A nationalist uprising, centering on the east coast, was suppressed by French troops after much bloodshed.

1960, June 25. Independence. The Malagasy Republic elected to remain a member of the French community.

1971, April 1. Rebellion Suppressed. Leftist rebels in Tulear Province, southern Madagascar, were overwhelmed by loyal troops.

1972, May 18. Military Coup d'État. The government of President **Philibultsiranana** was ousted following 4 days of violence. General **Gabriel Pomanantsoa became head of state.**

Somalia

1948–1960. Anticolonial Disorders. These were directed against British occupiers and Italian administrators.

1960, July 1. Independence of Somalia. Italian and British Somaliland were combined as a single state. Somalia almost immediately claimed substantial regions of Ethiopia and Kenya, where Somali populations had been placed by arbitrary colonial frontiers.

1960, August 14. Border Clashes along Ethiopian Frontier. (See p. 1317.)

1961, December 10. Unsuccessful Army Revolt.

1963–1968. Hostilities with Kenya. **(See p. 1317.)**

1964, February 8. Renewed Ethiopian-Somalian Hostilities. Despite a truce resulting from mediation of the Organization of African States, frontier warfare continued.

1968, January 31. Peace with Ethiopia. **(See p. 1317.)**

1968, September 20. Peace with France. Frontier violence by Somali intruders into the French Territory of the Afars and Issas was ended by agreement.

1969, October 21. Coup d'État. Army and police officers joined to overthrow the regime and to establish a Supreme Revolutionary Council, under Army control.

1970, April 21. Unsuccessful Coup Attempt.

1971, May 25. Unsuccessful Coup Attempt.

Sudan

1953, February 12. Self-Government. Egypt and Great Britain signed an agreement providing for self-government in the Anglo-Egyptian Sudan.

1955, August 16. British and Egyptian Withdrawal Demanded. The parliament of Sudan asked Britain and Egypt to evacuate their troops from the Sudan in 90 days. Britain with 900 troops and Egypt with 500 agreed to be out by November 12.

1955–1972. Revolt in Southern Sudan. The black inhabitants of southern Sudan, in the jungled swamps of the Upper Nile, rebelled against the Arab-Moslem ruling group in Khartoum. Small-scale but bitter fighting continued for eight years.

1956, January 1. Independent Republic Proclaimed.

1958, November 17. Military Coup. Control of the government of Sudan was seized by **Lieutenant General Ibraham Abboud.**

1959, November 10. Unsuccessful Coup Attempt.

1964, October–November. Violence Forces Overthrow of Abboud Government. Unable to quell mounting disorders, and faced with a possible military coup, General **Abboud** resigned as president. He was replaced by a council under Premier Sir **el-Khatim el-Khalifa.**

1966, December 28. Unsuccessful Coup Attempt. Loyal army troops subdued insurgents in a training center, after a sharp fight.

1967, June. Sudan Sends Units to Support Egypt in Sinai.

1969, May 25. Coup d'État. The government of Prime Minister **Mohommed Ahmed Mahgoub** was overthrown by a leftist military coup headed by Colonel **Mohommed Gafaar al-Nimeiry.**

1970, March 30–31. Unsuccessful Coup Attempt. In bloody fighting rebel leader Imam **el-Hadi Ahmed el-Mahdi** was killed by troops loyal to President Nimeiry.

1971, July 19–21. Coup and Countercoup. A group of Communist-oriented officers, apparently with covert Soviet support, briefly seized control of the government in a bloodless coup d'état. President Nimeiry, however, apparently with support from Egypt and Libya, staged a countercoup and regained power.

1972, March 27. Agreement Ends North-South Civil War. The Arab-Moslem government of northern Sudan reached an accommodation with the black Christians and pagans of the south, ending 17 years of strife.

1973, March 2. Palestinian Terrorists Assassinate American and Belgian Diplomats. The Black September terrorists were convicted of murder (1974, June), but freed by the government and released to the Palestine Liberation Organization (PLO) in Cairo. The U.S. at once recalled its new ambassador.

Tanganyika, Zanzibar, and Tanzania

1961, December 9. Independence of Tanganyika. It remained in the British Commonwealth.

1963, December 10. Independence of Zanzibar. It remained in the British Commonwealth.

1964, January 12. Zanzibar Rebellion. The government was overthrown by African nationalist rebels, some of whom had been trained in Communist China. Nationalist unrest, stirred up by Communists, spread to nearby mainland nations; widespread mutinies resulted.

1964, January 25. British Intervention. At the request of local governments, British troops suppressed mutinies of African troops in Tanganyika, Kenya, and Uganda.

1964, April 26. Establishment of Tanzania. This resulted from the merger of Tanganyika and Zanzibar.

1971, August 24–30. Border Clashes with Uganda. President Amin's pretext for attacks on Tanzanian troops was the accusation that Tanzania was assisting Ugandan rebels (see p. 1320).

Uganda

1949–1962. Anticolonial Disorders.

1962, October 9. Independence of Uganda. Freedom was granted by Great Britain to the kingdom, under King **Mutesa II,** Kabaka of Buganda. The new state was initially governed as a dominion, with a loose federal relationship between Uganda proper and the kingdom of Buganda.

1963, October 9. Uganda a Republic. King Mutesa II was elected president (as **Edward Mutesa**) under a new constitution, under which Uganda became a sovereign state within the British Commonwealth. Prime Minister was **Milton Obote,** principal Ugandan politician.

1966, March 3. Obote Deposes President Mutesa. The President fled to Kampala, Buganda, where he was still the Kabaka, and began a separatist movement, demanding withdrawal of Uganda troops by May.

1966, May 23–24. Uganda Suppresses Bugandan Separatist Movement. In 2 days of fighting in Kampala, federal troops seized the Kabaka's palace and restored federal control to Buganda. Mutesa escaped to England. Obote became president.

1971, January 25. Bloody Coup d'État. While Obote was attending a Commonwealth conference in Singapore, a group of officers, headed by Major General **Idi Amin,** seized control of the government and overwhelmed loyal troops. Obote took refuge in Tanzania.

1971, August 24–30. Border Skirmishes with Tanzania. Tense situations between Tanzania and Uganda following Amin's coup resulted in a protracted outburst of hostilities along the border west of Lake Victoria.

CENTRAL AFRICA

Union of Central African States

This loose federation for defense and economic cooperation was established by Zaire (then still known as Congo–Kinshasa), Chad, and the Central African Republic (1968, April 2–3). It has not played an important role in the policy.

Burundi

1962, July 1. Independence of Burundi. A former German colony and later Belgian mandate and trusteeship, Burundi became an independent monarchy under King **Mwami Mwambutsa,** of the dominant but minority Watusi (Tutsi) tribe. The first years of independence were extremely shaky.

1966, July 8. Coup d'État. Prince **Charles Ndizeye** overthrew his father and proclaimed himself King **Mwami Ntare V.**

1966, November 28. Coup d'État. The new King was overthrown by his appointed Prime Minister, Colonel **Michael Micombero,** who proclaimed himself president. Burundi became a republic.

1970, October 19–20. Unsuccessful Army Mutiny and Coup Attempt. Army officers from the majority, but suppressed, Bahutu (or Hutu) tribe, aided by some Watusi soldiers and police, staged an abortive coup attempt. Bahutu tribesmen revolted and massacred several thousand Watusis. The fierce and bloody Watusi reprisal eliminated all of the Bahutu leaders in and out of the government and army.

1972, April 29–July 31. Civil War and Massacres in Burundi. An effort by Bahutu tribesmen and some Watusi monarchists to free former King Mwami Ntare V failed. Mwami was killed, but armed rebellions spread throughout the country. At least 100,000 people were killed in the first 2 months, largely in reprisal massacres by official and unofficial Watusi organizations. The reprisal killings ended in August, with the government of President Micombero firmly in control.

Central African Republic

1960, August 13. Independence of the Central African Republic. A former French colony, the CAR had been self-governing since 1958. Its President, **David Dacko** established strong ties with Communist China.

1966, January 1. Coup d'État. Military officers, led by Colonel **Jean Bedel Bokassa,** ousted the Dacko Government. Bokassa became chief of state and immediately broke relations with Communist China.

1967, November 16. French Troops Support Regime. They were airlifted into the capital, Bangui, to help President Bokassa suppress a threatened uprising.

Republic of Chad

1960, August 11. Independence of Chad. A former French colony, Chad had been autonomous since 1958.

1968–1971. Rebellion of Northern Arabs. This was initiated by a fierce battle in the Tibesti Desert region (1968, March 15). The revolt was suppressed by the central government with the assistance of French troops (see p. 1262). French troops were later withdrawn (1971, June).

1971, August 27. Unsuccessful Coup Attempt. The rebels apparently were supported by Libya. Chad broke diplomatic relations with Libya. Relations were resumed in 1973 when Chad broke relations with Israel.

Malawi

1959–1964. Anti-Colonial Disorders in Nyasaland.

1964, July 6. Independence of Malawi. This was granted by Great Britain to the former self-governing colony of Nyasaland. The new republic joined the British Commonwealth.

Rwanda

1959–1961. Civil War in Belgian Rwanda. Shortly after self-government was granted by Belgium, and following U.N.-supervised elections, the suppressed Bahutu (or Hutu) majority rose in revolt against the minority but dominant Watusi (or Tutsi) tribesmen and seized control after bloody tribal warfare against the giant Watusis.

1962, July 1. Independence of Rwanda. A former German colony and later Belgian mandate and trusteeship, Rwanda became a republic, with the majority Bahutu tribe controlling the country.

Zaire

1949–1960. Widespread Unrest and Disorder in Belgian Congo. Colonial authorities were only partially successful in maintaining order.

1960, June 30. Belgium Grants Independence to the Congo. The first president, **Joseph Kasavubu,** appointed leftist **Patrice Lumumba** as premier. The new republic was unprepared for independence and chaos followed; soldiers and civilians rioted, looted, raped, and murdered. The white population fled the country, taking their expertise with them and adding further to the chaos. Central control disappeared from remote provinces. A few pockets of order were kept by some 10,000 Belgian troops remaining in the Congo, mostly in Katanga, where they were protecting the extensive manufacturing complex created by Belgium to process Katanga's great natural wealth.

1960, July 11. Katanga Proclaims Independence. Moise Tshombe, leader of Katanga, refused Lumumba's demands to submit to central control and to oust Belgian troops; he proclaimed secession of Katanga from the Congo and requested more Belgian military assistance to meet threatened Congo invasion. Lumumba appealed to the U.N. for military assistance in suppressing the Katanga revolt.

1960, July 14. International Crisis. The U.N. Security Council approved establishment of a U.N. security force by Secretary General Dag Hammarskjöld to restore order in the Congo (see p. 1254). The first contingent (from Tunisia) reached Leopoldville the next day, as Khrushchev was threatening military intervention on behalf of Lumumba. Eventual strength of the force was 20,000 men.

1960, July 22. U.N. Demands Belgian Troop Withdrawal. The Belgians complied partially (July 31), save for a few local security detachments and a garrison in Katanga remaining at Tshombe's request.

1960, August 12. Katanga Crisis. Hammarskjöld and 240 Swedish U.N. troops arrived at the Elizabethville airport in Katanga. He repeated earlier demands that all Belgian troops be withdrawn and replaced by U.N. troops. Tshombe refused to permit the U.N. force entry into Elizabethville and threatened to use force if necessary. Erratic Lumumba denounced Hammarskjöld for using white troops, for conniving with Tshombe, and for not placing U.N. forces under his command.

1960, August 24. Revolt in Kasai. Lumumba sent a military force to Kasai to suppress revolt of Buluba chief **Albert Kalonji.** Results were inconclusive.

1960, August 30. Belgium Announces Combat Troop Withdrawal. Hammarskjöld insisted that some still remained on in Katanga.

1960, September 14. Lumumba Overthrown. Colonel **Joseph Mobutu,** Army Chief of Staff, seized virtual control of the government. Kasavubu named **Joseph Ileo** as premier. Lumumba, at first arrested, then fled to east-central Congo.

1960, September 20. U.N. Votes Confidence in Hammarskjöld. Following Soviet representative **Valentin A. Zorin**'s bitter denunciation of Hammarskjöld's policies and action in the Congo, the U.N. overwhelmingly voted its confidence in the Secretary General.

1960, October–November. Widespread Violence and Disorders. These were largely the responsibility of undisciplined Congo troops; there were some clashes with U.N. troops.

1960, December 1. Lumumba Arrested. Government troops seized him and flew him to Leopoldville.

1960, December 14. Stanleyville Revolt. Antoine Gizenga, who had been Lumumba's vice-premier, proclaimed himself premier and established a pro-Communist government in Stanleyville. His adherents began to expand their control over much of east-central Congo.

1961, February 9. Lumumba Murdered. Kasavubu ordered Lumumba transferred to a "more secure" prison in Katanga (January 17). Soon afterward, under circumstances not clear, Lumumba was murdered. Tshombe has been accused, probably correctly, of responsibility.

1961, February 21. Katanga Mobilization. This was ordered by Tshombe in response to U.N. threats to force integration of Katanga with the Congo.

1961, February 24. U.N. Action against Stanleyville Requested. Premier Ileo asked for help after Gizenga forces seized Luluabourg, capital of Kasai province.

1961, March 12. Proclamation of a New Congo Federation. This was a reorganization of the government, proclaimed at a meeting in Tananarive, Malagasy, of President Kasavubu, Premier Ileo, and all regional leaders except Gizenga.

1961, April 17. Congo-U.N. Agreement. This document, signed by Congolese President Joseph Kasavubu, authorized the U.N. to use force if necessary to prevent civil war in the Congo.

1961, April 26–June 2. Tshombe Arrested. Following a "unity" conference in Leopoldville, Tshombe was seized and detained by the Congo government. After promising to bring Katanga into the Congo, he was released by Mobutu. Tshombe thereupon repudiated his agreements made under duress.

1961, August 1. New Government. The reconvened Congo parliament elected **Cyrille Adoula** as premier; Gizenga was named vice-premier.

1961, August 21. U.N. Action in Katanga. After a gradual force build-up, U.N. troops in Katanga seized communications centers in and around Elizabethville to force Tshombe to dismiss white mercenary officers. Reluctantly, he complied, but began measures for the defense of Elizabethville.

1961, September 13–21. Hostilities in Katanga. U.N. forces, attempting to seize control of Elizabethville, were unsuccessful; they lost face while Tshombe and his army gained prestige. Tragically, Hammarskjöld, flying in to bring about a cease-fire, was killed in a plane crash near Ndola, Northern Rhodesia (September 18).

1961, November. Congolese Invasion of Katanga Repulsed. Congolese forces were repelled by the Katanga Army.

1961, December 18. U.N. Capture of Elizabethville. This led to an agreement between Tshombe and Premier Adoula to restore the unity of the Congo (December 21). Tshombe again failed to comply and retained autonomy.

1962, January. Renewed Stanleyville Revolt. Gizenga again attempted an uprising from Stanleyville, but his troops were defeated by Congo Army troops; he was dismissed from the government by Adoula.

1962, December 29–1963, January 15. U.N. Offensive in Katanga. Operations against Elizabethville were begun in response to Katangese provocations, and with the objective of ending Katanga's secession from the Congo. Katanga forces were completely defeated, and Tshombe forced to flee. After accepting the integration of his province with the central government (January 15), he went into exile.

1963–1964. Steady Reduction of U.N. Forces. This was largely because of lack of funds to support them. Unrest and revolt continued throughout the country, particularly in the northeastern region.

1964, June 16. American Civilians Fighting as Mercenaries. The U.S. State Department conceded, after several denials, that "some American civilian pilots under contract with the Congolese Government have flown T-28 sorties in the last few days in the eastern part of the Congo." This was part of the central government's effort to suppress a revolt of Bafulero tribesmen in Kivu Province.

1964, June 30. Last U.N. Troops Leave the Congo.

1964, July 9. Moise Tshombe Named Premier. This was obviously a last desperate effort to achieve stability in the Congo. Returning from exile, he immediately began a campaign of combined conciliation and threat of force with the various rebel groups. He also strengthened the Congo Army by bringing in white mercenary troops and officers to help train it. Further training assistance was given by a U.S. military-aid mission. Tshombe, considered a traitor to Africans (even by many moderate African leaders) because of his history in Katanga and his more recent recruiting of white troops, was bitterly denounced throughout Africa, and particularly in Communist-bloc states.

1964, August 30. Congolese Army Retakes Albertville. This had been in rebel hands for 2 months.

1964, September–October. Rebel Gains in East-Central Congo. The alarming increase in strength was largely due to assistance from Communists, and from the U.A.R., through Sudan and Uganda.

1964, November. Congo Army Prepares Offensive against Stanleyville. The rebels then seized some 2,000 white hostages and threatened massacre if Congolese troops approached the rebel capital.

1964, November 25–27. Belgian-U.S. Intervention. A surprise airborne landing by a Belgian paratroop battalion, flown by U.S. air units from Belgium via Ascension Island, seized Stanleyville and rescued some 1,650 white hostages. Violent outcries from the Communist bloc and from anti-Tshombe Africans led to the overly quick withdrawal of the Belgian troops and American planes. As a result, other planned rescue missions were abandoned, and several hundred white hostages were brutally massacred.

1965, October 13. Tshombe Ousted from Office. In a power struggle, the Prime Minister was defeated by President Kasavubu.

1965, November 25. Coup d'État. General Mobutu, Commander in Chief of the Army, ousted Kasavubu in a bloodless coup and named himself president. (He later changed his name to Mobutu Sese Seho.)

1966, May 30. Unsuccessful Coup Attempt. Mobutu gained more strength.

1967, June–November. Revolt by Katangese and Foreign Mercenaries. Belgian and French mercenaries attempted to seize control of Katanga and Kivu provinces. Lack of local support, and prompt counteraction by Mobutu, soon resulted in collapse of the revolt. The mercenaries fled the country.

1967, August 9. Rebels Capture Bukava. The capital of Kivu Province was seized by 1,500 Katangese rebels and 160 mercenaries. The rebels failed to receive expected local support and were soon attacked by forces of the central government.

1967, November 5. Rebels Flee to Rwanda; Revolt Collapses. After recapturing Bukava, Congolese troops pursued some 2,000 rebels and mercenaries across the border of neighboring Rwanda.

1968–1974. Stability Returns to the Congo.

1971, October 27. Congo's Name Changed to Republic of Zaire. This was part of the policy of President Mobutu to replace with African names those brought in by colonists in the 19th and 20th centuries.

Zambia

1952–1964. Anticolonial Disorders in Northern Rhodesia.

1964, January 22. Independence of Zambia. This was granted by Britain to the former self-governing protectorate.

1965–1974. Zambia Becomes a Base for Anticolonial Forces. While scrupulously avoiding incidents with Portuguese Angola and Mozambique, and with Rhodesia, Zambia did allow insurgent forces to operate from its territory. The result was strained relations, and some border clashes with Portuguese and white Rhodesian frontier forces.

WEST AFRICA

Angola

1961, February 4–7. Antigovernment Riots. These were apparently connected with the *Santa Maria* incident (see p. 1265).

1961–1974. Rebellion against Portugal. The efforts of separatist rebels to throw off Portuguese colonial rule were generally unsuccessful. Portuguese military repression eliminated most of the rival groups from Angolan territory. Raids against the Portuguese continued, however, from insurgent bases in Zaire and Zambia.

1974, October 15. Cease-fire Agreed. After the coup in Portugal (see p. 1266), the new Portuguese government moved rapidly to grant autonomy, and the opportunity for independence, to its African colonies. The problem was complicated by the rivalries of different insurgent groups. Unrest and violence continued, mostly between the rival national groups.

Cameroon

1956–1959. Anticolonial Terrorist Activities.

1960, January 1. Independence of East Cameroon. This former French mandate and trusteeship (the eastern part of the former German colony of Cameroons) had been autonomous for two years.

1961, October 1. Establishment of the Federal Republic of Cameroon. Following a referendum, most of West Cameroon, a former British mandate and trusteeship (the western part of the old German colony), joined East Cameroon to form a federal union. (The northern part of West Cameroon voted to join Nigeria).

1962–1971. Insurgent Rebellion. Communist insurgents, based in Congo (Brazzaville), kept up a low-keyed rebellion against the central government until the capture and execution of their leader (1971).

People's Republic of the Congo

1960, August 15. Independence of Congo (Brazzaville). A former French colony, Congo had for 2 years been autonomous. Taking the name of Republic of Congo, the new nation was generally referred to as Congo (Brazzaville), to distinguish it from the Democratic Republic of Congo, known as Congo (Kinshasa). This need to distinguish the two Congos by means of their capitals became unnecessary when Congo (Kinshasa) changed its name to Zaire (see p. 1323).

1963, August 15. Coup d'État. The government of President **Fulbert Youlou** was overthrown by a trade-union coup (see also p. 1262). The new President, **Alphonse Massamba-Debat,** established close relations with Communist China.

1966, June 28–29. Coup d'État.

1968, September 4. Coup d'État. Military officers led by Major **Marien Ngoubai** ousted the former government, after fierce fighting between the Army and Cuban-trained militants. Ngoubai soon became president (1969, January 1). The pro-Peking orientation was not changed. The following year the name of the state was changed to People's Republic of the Congo (1970, January).

Dahomey

1960, August 1. Independence of Dahomey. Self-governing since 1958, Dahomey was granted independence by France.

1963, October 28. Coup d'État. The government of President **Hubert Maga** was overthrown by a group of officers under General **Christophe Soglo,** who installed a civilian government.

1965, December 22. Coup d'État. Again General Soglo led a military coup. This time he retained power as president.

1967, December 17. Coup d'État. A military junta under Major **Maurice Kouandete** overthrew President Soglo.

1969, July 12. Unsuccessful Coup Attempt.

1969, October 21. Unsuccessful Coup Attempt.

1969, December 10. Coup d'État. In the sixth coup or coup attempt since independence, the Army overthrew the government of President **Emile D. Zinsou.**

1972, October 26. Coup d'État. Major **Mattneu Kerekou** became president.

Gabon Republic

1960, August 17. Independence of Gabon. Granted by France, the former colonial power.

1964, February 17–18. Unsuccessful Coup Attempt. The government of President **Leon Mba** was briefly overthrown by the Army, but was restored the next day when French troops flew in and routed the revolutionaries.

The Gambia

1965, February 18. Independence of The Gambia. Granted by Britain. The Gambia changed its government from dominion status to a republic within the Commonwealth (1970, April).

Ghana

1948–1956. Anticolonial Disorders.

1957, March 6. Independence of Ghana. Initially with dominion status, Ghana became a republic within the Commonwealth, with **Kwame Nkrumah** as president (1960, July 1).

1966, February 24. Coup d'État. The armed forces seized power during the absence of Nkrumah on a visit to Communist China. Leader of the revolt was Lieutenant Colonel (soon General) **Joseph Ankrah.**

1966, March–April. Invasion Threat from Guinea. President **Sekou Toure** of Guinea, after welcoming Nkrumah (March 10), threatened to use force to restore his old friend to power. He backed down in the face of mobilization by Ghana and Ivory Coast.

1972, January 13. Coup d'État. Prime Minister **Kafi A. Busia** was deposed by Army officers while he was in London for medical treatment. The military men, under Colonel **Ignatius Kutu Acheampong,** suppressed a countercoup (January 15).

Guinea

1958, October 2. Independence of Guinea. Under the leadership of Prime Minister Sekou Toure, Guinea refused to participate in a French plan for gradual independence of its former African colonies, and proclaimed independence. Toure became president.

1966, March–April. Threat of War with Ivory Coast and Ghana. (See above.)

1970, November 22–24. Portuguese-Supported Invasion Attempt. Dissident

Guineans, with some Portuguese support, attempted a seaborne invasion but were repulsed. The Portuguese support was in retaliation for Toure's support of rebels in Portuguese Guinea. Portugal was censured by the United Nations.

Guinea-Bissau

1962–1974. Rebellion against Portugal. Rebels in Portuguese Guinea were the most successful of the African nationalists opposing Portuguese rule. By the time of the coup in Portugal (see p. 1266), the rebel organization—African Independence Party of Guinea and Cape Verde (PAIGC)—held at least 50 per cent of the countryside.

1974, July 27. Independence of Guinea-Bissau. Portuguese Guinea was the first of Portugal's dissident African colonies to receive independence.

Ivory Coast

1950–1960. Sporadic Anticolonial Disorders.

1960, August 7. Independence of the Ivory Coast. Granted independence by France after a two-year period of autonomy, under the leadership of President **Felix Houphouet-Boigny.**

1966, March–April. Threat of War with Guinea. When President Sekou Toure of Guinea threatened to invade Ghana, to reinstate Nkrumah as president (see p. 1324), he planned to march through the Ivory Coast. President Houphouet-Boigny refused passage and mobilized his army. Toure backed down.

Liberia

1963, February 5. Unsuccessful Coup Attempt.

Mali (Sudanese Republic)

1959, January 17. The Mali Federation Established. The Sudanese Republic, former French Sudan, elected in 1958 to accept French assistance in reaching independence through progressive autonomy. The region joined with Senegal to establish a new federation.

1960, June 20. Independence of the Sudanese Republic. Despite increasing internal strains, the federation with Senegal continued.

1960, August 20. The Sudanese Republic Withdraws from Federation with Senegal. The new state officially adopted the name Republic of Mali (September 22).

1968, November 19. Coup d'État. The socialist government of President **Mobido Keita** was overthrown by a military group under Lieutenant **Moussa Traore,** who became president (December 6).

1971, April 7. Unsuccessful Coup Attempt.

Mauritania

1957, February 15. Unsuccessful Efforts to Annex Mauritania to Morocco. A so-called Moroccan Army of Liberation, based in Morocco, although disavowed by the Moroccan Government, raided into Mauritania in an unsuccessful attempt to incite rebellion and to join Mauritania to Morocco, which claims sovereignty. The effort was suppressed by French troops.

1960, November 28. Independence of Mauritania. Granted by France.

1962, April 1. Rebel Invasion Attempt from Morocco. The rebels were driven out, again preventing efforts to reunite Morocco and Mauritania.

Niger

1960, August 3. Independence of Niger. Granted by France.

1961–1974. Endemic Unrest. This was exacerbated by famine in the early 1970's.

Nigeria

1960, October 1. Independence of Nigeria. It became a republic within the British Commonwealth. Internal tensions soon appeared, based largely on regional tribal allegiance and jealousies.

1966, January 16. Coup d'État. The government of Prime Minister Sir **Abudakar Tafawa Balewa** was overthrown by dissident Army officers. Balewa was killed. Following a power struggle among the officers, the Army commander, General **Johnson Aguyi-Ironsi,** took control and established a provisional federal military government.

1966, July 29. Coup d'État. A group of mutinous army officers, mostly from the northern Hausa tribe, kidnapped the Chief of State, General Aguyi-Ironsi, and killed him. During another confused power struggle among officers with regional ties, a group of northern officers led by Colonel **Yakubu Gowon** seized control. Bloodshed continued in the country, with most of the victims members of the industrious southeastern Ibo tribe, predominantly Christians, who had achieved coveted positions in government or commerce in other regions. Most of the Ibo survivors moved from the Moslem northern regions back to their own area.

1967, May 30. Secession of Biafra from Nigeria. Southeastern Nigeria, inhabited mostly by Ibos and rich in agricultural and mineral resources, primarily petroleum, declared independence from Nigeria, under the leadership of Army Lieutenant Colonel **Chukwuemeka Odumegwu Ojukwu,** who became president of the Republic of Biafra.

Civil War

1967, June 7–1970, January 12. Nigeria-Biafra Civil War. Colonel Gowon's federal government refused to accept the secession of Biafra and moved to subdue the rebellious region by force. Initial efforts of federal troops—about 12,000 strong—to move into Biafra were repulsed. Biafran forces, hastily recruited, invaded the midwestern region and captured the capital, **Benia** (1967, August 9).

1967, September–1968, May. Federal Invasion of Biafra. With substantial superiority in numbers and quality of equipment, the expanded military forces of the federal government slowly occupied almost half of Biafra, but were halted on a defensive line protecting the Biafran capital of Umuahia. Tentative peace negotiations in London (May) and Kampala (June) were fruitless.

1968, September. Renewed Nigerian Offensive. Federal troops captured **Aba** (September 4) and **Owerri** (September 16). Again the Biafran defenses stiffened and halted the invading forces. Biafra had lost direct access to the sea but maintained contact with the outside world through a tenuous airlift to Fernando Po, a Spanish colony.

1969, February–March. Biafran Counteroffensive. In a surprise counteroffensive, Biafran troops pushed southward in an effort to reopen a seaport. They reached the outskirts of Aba before being halted (March 3). A stalemate followed, during which Nigerian aircraft repeatedly bombed Biafran military targets and civilian centers.

1969, June–December. Final Nigerian Offensive. In a slow but steady offensive, the enlarged, well-equipped Nigerian Army—now about 180,000 strong—overwhelmed the desperate Biafran defense.

1970, January 12. Surrender of Biafra. The last organized defense collapsed. Colonel Ojukwa fled by air to seek refuge in the Ivory Coast. The population of Biafra, which had been about 12 million at the start of the revolt, had suffered approximately 2 million dead (many of these children), mostly from starvation. The region, which had been one of the best-developed in Africa before the war, was devastated

Senegal

1959, January 17. Senegal and Sudan Form the Mali Federation. These colonial regions, which had been granted autonomy by France in 1958, joined to form a federated republic.

1960, June 20. Independence of Senegal Granted by France. The federal union with the Sudanese Republic continued.

1960, June 20. Collapse of the Mali Federation. The Sudanese Republic adopted the name of Mali (see p. 1325); Senegal continued an independent status.

1962, December 17. Unsuccessful Coup Attempt.

Sierra Leone

1955–1960. Anticolonial Disturbances.

1961, April 27. Independence of Sierra Leone. It assumed dominion status within the British Commonwealth.

1967, March 23. Coup d'État. A military junta seized power without bloodshed, under the leadership of Majors **Charles Blake** and **Andrew T. Juxon-Smith.**

1968, January 25. Coup d'État. Military insurgents seized power.

1968, April 18. Coup d'État. A group of noncommissioned officers overthrew the government of Colonel **Juxon-Smith.** They called back from exile Colonel **John Bangura** to head a new junta, which installed **Siaka Stevens** as Prime Minister.

1968, November 21–25. Violence Suppressed by Government.

1970, October 5. Unsuccessful Coup Attempt.

1971, January 21. Unsuccessful Coup Attempt.

1971, April 19. Sierra Leone Becomes a Republic. Prime Minister Stevens became president. The nation remained in the Commonwealth.

Togo

1960, April 27. Independence of Togo. Granted by France, following 2 years of autonomy.

1963, January 13. Coup d'État. A military junta of noncommissioned officers seized power after killing President **Sylvanus Olympio.**

1967, January 13. Coup d'État. The government of President **Nicholas Grunitzky** was overthrown without bloodshed by Army Chief of Staff Lieutenant Colonel **Etienne Eyadema.**

1970, August 8. Unsuccessful Coup Attempt.

Upper Volta

1960, August 5. Independence of Upper Volta. Granted by France, following 2 years of autonomy.

1966, January 3. Coup d'État. Army Chief of Staff Lieutenant Colonel **Sangoule Lamizana** bloodlessly overthrew the government of President **Maurice Yameogo.** Lamizana proclaimed himself chief of state.

SOUTHERN AFRICA

Botswana

1966, September 30. Independence of Botswana. The former British colony of Bechuanaland remained in the Commonwealth.

Lesotho

1966, October 4, Independence of Lesotho. The former British protectorate of Basutoland, completely surrounded by the Union of South Africa, remained in the Commonwealth.

1970, January 30. Coup d'État. In a bloodless and apparently reasonably amicable action, the Prime Minister, Chief **Jonathan,** placed King **Moshoeshoe II** in house arrest and seized power. The King left the country for 6 months, returned, took an oath not to get involved in politics, and was returned to the throne.

Mozambique

1962–1974. Rebellion against Portugal. A number of minor separatist movements united under the Frente de Liberatacao de Mocambique (FRELIMO), which established its headquarters in Dar es Salaam. Although other rival groups were organized, FRELIMO carried most of the burden of sporadic guerrilla war against the Portuguese Army and was able to establish control in a number of regions of the country, operating mainly from bases in Tanzania and (to a lesser extent) Zambia.

1974, September 7. Independence from Portugal Agreed. After the coup in Portugal (see p. 1266), the new Portuguese government moved promptly to grant independence to its African colonies. By agreement signed by Portuguese and FRELIMO representatives in Lusaka, Zambia, a cease-fire was initiated. Formal independence followed (June 25, 1975).

Rhodesia

1960, July–October. Rioting in Southern Rhodesia.

1965, November 11. Unilateral Declaration of Independence. The white population (270,000) of the British colony of Southern Rhodesia, fearful of British policies that seemed directed toward placing political power in the hands of the majority black population (5,400,000), declared independence from Great Britain, under Prime Minister **Ian D. Smith.** Economic sanctions were announced by Great Britain, the U.S., and most African nations.

1968, May 9. United Nations Security Council Orders Trade Embargo on Rhodesia. This action was taken after the failure of repeated British peaceful efforts to get Rhodesia to grant political rights to the black population.

1970, March 2. Rhodesia Proclaims Itself a Republic.

1971–1974. Low-Level Insurgency. Although no immediately serious threat to the stability of the Rhodesian Government, incursions of black insurgents, based in neighboring countries, particularly Zambia, aroused fears and tension in the white population.

Republic of South Africa

1949–1962. Sporadic Race Riots. Of these the most significant were at Durban (1949, January; 1959, June; 1960, January), Kimberley (1952, November), and Sharpeville (1960, March). They were suppressed ruthlessly by government police and troops.

1949, July 13. The United Nations Defied. The Union of South Africa rejected a

U.N. Trusteeship Council demand that Southwest Africa become part of the trusteeships system.

1950–1953. Korean War. South Africa provided an air unit to the U.N. command.

1960, March 21. Sharpeville Race Riot. Police opened fire on a crowd of 20,000 blacks attacking a police station; 56 were killed, 162 wounded. Other riots, breaking out throughout the country, were quickly suppressed. There was a wave of international revulsion against South Africa and its racial policy of *apartheid* (apartness).

1961, May 31. South Africa Becomes a Republic. The new republic withdrew from the British Commonwealth.

1966, October 27. United Nations Resolves an End to South African Mandate over South West Africa. This was a League of Nations mandate, after World War I, over the former German colony. South Africa refused to recognize the authority of the U.N. to interfere with its authority over the territory.

1970, July 23. United Nations Security Council Arms Embargo. This was in response to repeated South African defiance of the authority of the U.N. over South West Africa.

1974, November 25. U.N. General Assembly Votes to Suspend South Africa from Membership.

NORTH AMERICA

UNITED STATES

1945, September 14. Pearl Harbor Investigation. A Joint Congressional Committee was appointed to investigate the Pearl Harbor disaster. The investigation opened two months later (November 15), and submitted an inconclusive report (July 20, 1946).

1945, December 19–1947, July 26. Military Unification Controversy. President Truman sent a special message to Congress outlining a program of unification for the Army and the Navy and the establishment of the new Air Force in a single Department of Defense. Senior naval officers testifying before the Senate Military Affairs Committee had already expressed violent opposition to the unification concept. Despite this opposition, President Truman later submitted to Congress a specific plan for the merger of the Army and Navy and a new Air Force in a Department of National Defense (June 15, 1946).

1945–1947. The Marshall Mission to China.

1946, January–March. Crisis in Iran. (See p. 1286.)

1946, March 5. Churchill Speech at Fulton, Mo. In an address at Westminster College, Churchill advocated a fraternal association between the U.S. and Great Britain to deter Soviet aggression. He coined the expression "Iron Curtain."

1946, April 4. Horse Cavalry Abolished. Remaining cavalry units and individuals were merged with armored forces; cavalry disappeared as a separate service.

1946, July 1–25. Bikini Nuclear Tests. First peacetime weapons tests in history were carried out at Bikini Atoll in the Marshall Islands in the Pacific.

1946, December 16. Establishment of Unified Overseas Commands. This was ordered by President Truman on the advice of the Joint Chiefs of Staff.

1947, January 1. Civilian Control of Nuclear Affairs. The U.S. Atomic Energy Commission formally took command of all U.S. atomic-energy affairs.

1947, January 7. General Marshall Appointed Secretary of State. The State Department made public his report on his mission to China, in which he criticized both reactionaries in the Nanking government and the Chinese Communists.

1947, March 12. Truman Doctrine. This proposed economic and military aid to nations threatened by Communist aggression. Specifically, President Truman asked Congress for $400 million to give economic and political aid to Greece and Turkey, both seriously threatened by the possibility of Soviet aggression and both further endangered by Britain's recent decision to withdraw forces from Greece. This was approved by Congress (May 15) and signed by the President (May 22).

1947, March 31. The Selective Service Act Expired.

1947, June 5. Marshall Plan. In a speech at Harvard, Secretary of State Marshall suggested American economic assistance to help Europe recover and to gain the strength necessary to avoid internal subversion and external aggression.

1947, June 5. Satellite Peace Treaties. The Senate ratified peace treaties with Italy, Hungary, Rumania, and Bulgaria.

1947, July 26. The National Security Act of 1947. This was based upon the unification plan submitted a year earlier by President Truman. Three armed services were unified within a National Military Establishment. Secretary of the Navy **James Forrestal** was appointed the first Secretary of Defense.

1947, September 26. Establishment of the U.S. Air Force. Pursuant to the Act of July 26 (see above).

1948, March 27. Key West Agreement. Publication of an agreement between the 3 armed services to resolve disputes regarding their respective roles and missions in the national defense of the U.S.

1948, April 3. Marshall Plan in Operation. President Truman signed the first foreign-aid bill for $6.98 billion.

1948, June–1949, May. Berlin Blockade. **(See p. 1263.)**

1948, June 11. Vandenberg Resolution. A resolution sponsored by Senator **Arthur H. Vandenberg** proclaimed U.S. policy to give military aid to defensive alliances among the free nations of the world.

1948, June 19. New Selective Service Act. Conscription was reinstated by Congress.

1948, August 23. Newport Agreement; New Roles and Missions. At a meeting at Newport, R.I., Secretary of Defense Forrestal and the Joint Chiefs of Staff agreed on further revision of the roles and missions of the armed forces.

1949, April 23. Construction Stopped on Supercarrier. Secretary of Defense Johnson ordered abandonment of construction on the 65,000-ton U.S.S. *United States.*

1949, June 3–August 25. B-36 Controversy. This began with accusations and rumors in the press (by Navy adherents in an interservice controversy) that the B-36 bomber had been chosen as the principal Air Force weapon for personal and political reasons. Secretary of Defense **Louis Johnson** and Secretary of the Air Force **Stuart Symington** were anonymously accused of having personal-gain motives in the decision. After a 2-month investigation, the House Armed Services Committee cleared top-ranking government officials and Air Force officers of "charges and insinuations that collusion, fraud, corruption, influence, or favoritism played any part whatsoever in the procurement of the B-36 bomber."

1949, July 21. North Atlantic Treaty Ratified. This was signed by President Truman (July 25) after Senate ratification. The treaty went into effect after ratification by all 12 signatories (August 24).

1949, August 2. Military Reorganization. Congress approved military recommendations suggested by the Hoover Committee and by Secretary of Defense Forrestal (December, 1948). The National Military Establishment was renamed the Department of Defense with increased powers for the Secretary of Defense. The Departments of Army, Navy, and Air Force were reduced from cabinet to departmental rank, and a Chairman was provided for the Joint Chiefs of Staff.

1949, August 5. State Department White Paper on China. **(See p. 1309.)** Secretary of State **Dean Acheson** blamed Generalissimo Chiang Kai-shek for the defeats of the National Government. Dr. **Wellington Koo,** Chinese Ambassador to the U.S., acknowledged that China might have made some errors, but insisted that mistakes were not confined to his country (August 7).

1949, October 3–27. "Revolt of the Admirals." This was a continuation of the B-36 controversy. Senior Navy officers publicly and privately charged that the Army and Air Force were trying to destroy naval aviation in order to reduce Navy influence in the military establishment. The Chief of Naval Operations, Admiral **Louis Denfeld,** and Admiral **Arthur Radford,** Commander in Chief of the Pacific Fleet, wrote strong letters criticizing unification of the armed forces. In a subsequent Navy Department investigation, it was ascertained that the instigator of this controversy was Captain **John G. Crommelin,** U.S.N. During a House Armed Services Committee investigation, Admiral Radford attacked the B-36 and the concept of nuclear war as advocated by the Air Force. In subsequent testimony before the House Armed Services Committee, Admiral Denfeld accused the other services of not accepting the Navy "in full partnership." General **Clifton B. Cates,** Commandant of the Marine Corps, personally attacked Secretary of Defense Johnson and the Chiefs of Staff of the Army and Air Force (October 16). Army Chief of Staff General **Omar Bradley,** in testifying before the committee, declared that the Navy admirals were "fancy Dans" "in open rebellion" against civilian authority. Following an investigation, Navy

Secretary **Francis P. Matthews** recommended that Truman relieve Admiral Denfeld as Chief of Naval Operations; this effectively ended the revolt (October 27).

1949, October 29. Controversy on Air Force Build-up. President Truman impounded more than $600 million earmarked by Congress for a 58-group Air Force; he instructed Secretary of Defense Johnson not to build more than 48 groups.

1949, December 7. Secretary of Defense Johnson "Cuts Fat." He announced that by more efficient operation the 1949–1950 budget of $15.7 billion had been cut to $13.0 billion for 1950 without reducing preparedness. Most military men believed preparedness was dangerously impaired, an opinion seemingly corroborated by early results in Korea (see p. 1242).

1950, January 5. Truman Announces Continued Economic Aid to Nationalist China. No more military assistance was contemplated.

1950, May 5. Enactment of Uniform Code of Military Justice.

1950, June 25. Korean War Begins. **(See p. 1240.)**

1950, June 30. Partial Mobilization; Selective Service Extended. President Truman signed a bill extending the Selective Service Act until July 9, 1951. The measure also authorized the President to call the National Guard and Organized Reserves for 21 months of active service.

1950, September 18. Congress Approves General Marshall as Secretary of Defense. Legislation was necessary, since he had recently been a Regular Army officer.

1950, December 8. Truman Confers with British Prime Minister Attlee. Attlee had come to Washington to convey British hopes that the atomic bomb would not be used first by the United States in the Korean War. President Truman stated that he hoped that world conditions would never call for the use of the atomic bomb. They agreed to support the U.N. in attempts to achieve a free and independent Korea.

1950, December 16. Truman Proclaims State of National Emergency. This was to facilitate prosecution of the war in Korea.

1951, May 1. Publication of Wedemeyer Report. This controversial report on China and Korea had been submitted to President Truman, on September 9, 1947, by retiring General Albert C. Wedemeyer. It had been partially described in the State Department's White Paper on China (August 5, 1949).

1951, May–June. Senate Investigates Relief of General MacArthur. **(See p. 1247.)**

1951, September 1. Security Treaty with Australia and New Zealand (ANZUS Pact).

1952, March 4. Universal Military Training. The House of Representatives defeated a proposal for universal military training, based upon recommendations of an advisory commission to President Truman (June 1, 1947) and of former Army Chief of Staff Eisenhower (February 15, 1948).

1952, July 13. Military Aid to Yugoslavia Approved. **(See also p. 1270.)**

1952, August 4. ANZUS Pact. The U.S., Australia, and New Zealand established a Pacific Council. At the first meeting in Washington, the ANZUS Council pledged to guard against the threat of Communism and maintain peace in the Pacific (September 9–10, 1953).

1952, November. First Hydrogen Weapon. The U.S. exploded a thermonuclear weapon at Eniwetok. President Truman had broken an AEC controversy earlier by ordering the development (January 31, 1950).

1953, April 3. Military Reorganization Plan. President Eisenhower proposed to give civilian officials in the Defense Department more control. The plan was approved by Congress (June 27).

1953, December 19. Emphasis on Air Power. President Eisenhower and the National Security Council supported plans for the Department of Defense to emphasize air power and continental defenses by increasing Air Force strength and budget, decreasing the Navy and Marine Corps by 15 per cent, and decreasing the Army by one-third. The next budget request (January 21, 1954) provided for an Army budget of $10.198 billion, Navy $10.493 billion, and Air Force $16.209 billion. Later General Ridgway, in a magazine article, denied President Eisenhower's statement that the JCS had approved Army cuts (January, 1956).

1954, March 8. President Eisenhower's Report on the Mutual Security Act. The U.S. had shipped $7.7 billion of arms and other military equipment to allies since October, 1949, and about $3.8 billion in 1953. Almost $6 billion had gone to Western European nations alone, who themselves had spent over $35 billion to build up NATO defenses, of which $11.5 billion had been spent in 1953. Since 1949, military aid to Greece and Turkey totaled $761 million; Far East aid totaled $1.18 billion.

1954, March 16. Presidential Authority under NATO aud Rio Treaties. Secretary of State John Foster Dulles said the President had authority to order instant retaliation without consulting Congress in the event of an attack against the U.S., its western European allies, or the Western Hemisphere.

1954, May 7. U.S. Rejects Russian Application to NATO. Britain and France had been consulted prior to the rejection.

1954, September 30. First Atomic-Powered Submarine. The U.S.S. *Nautilus* was commissioned.

1955, January 12. "Massive Retaliation" Concept. Secretary of State Dulles announced that the President and the National Security Council had taken a basic decision "to depend primarily upon a great capacity to retaliate instantly [against aggression anywhere] by means and at places of our choosing."

1955, January 17. Defense Budget Controversy. The national defense budget of $34 billion included $15.6 billion for the Air Force, $9.7 billion for the Navy, and $8.85 billion for the Army. General **Matthew B. Ridgway,** Army Chief of Staff, subsequently testified before the House Armed Services Committee that this budget, and planned cuts in Army armed forces, jeopardized the safety and security of the U.S.

1955, July 11. Opening of U.S. Air Force Academy. Temporarily at Lowry Air Force Base, Denver, Colorado, it was permanently located at Colorado Springs (1958, September).

1956, May 18. Outbreak of "Colonels' Revolt." Newspaper publication of "leaked" Army and Air Force staff papers revealed bitter interservice rivalry, with Army jealousy and suspicion of the Air Force particularly outspoken in a paper challenging Air Force doctrine that national security lay mainly in air power. Newspapermen, remembering the "Revolt of the Admirals" (see p. 1329), noted that the Army papers had been prepared by a small staff group composed primarily of colonels. Secretary of Defense **Charles E. Wilson** called a special press conference of the Joint Chiefs of Staff to try to demonstrate interservice solidarity (May 21). The Army officers involved were reprimanded and ordered away from the Pentagon.

1956, October 28. Eisenhower Warns Israel. He warned against taking any "forceful initiative in the Middle East." When Israel attacked Egypt the following day (see p. 1228) and Britain and France subsequently became involved at Suez (see p. 1229), Eisenhower forcefully opposed their "aggressions" directly and in the U.N.

1956, November 26. Army Roles and Missions Curtailed. Secretary Wilson gave the Air Force control of all missiles with a range of more than 200 miles. He also severely restricted the Army's planned aviation program.

1956, February 12. Army Opposes Force Levels. Chief of Staff General M. D. Taylor said that 19 authorized divisions were inadequate; 27 or 28 were required to back up U.S. international commitments.

1957, March 9. "Eisenhower Doctrine." The President signed bills authorizing him to use armed forces in Middle East if necessary.

1956, December. End of an Era. The Army announced deactivation of the last mule unit (December 1) and the end of carrier pigeons in the Signal Corps (December 4).

1957, September 24–25. Eisenhower Sends Troops to Little Rock. This ended local defiance of court-ordered school integration.

1958, January 31. First U.S. Satellite. Designed and developed by the U.S. Army, this was "Explorer I." Later, after several more successful launchings, the Army Ballistic Missile Agency was transferred to the newly created National Aeronautics and Space Administration, taking the Army out of space exploration (October 21, 1959).

1958, March 8. Deactivation of Last U.S. Battleship. This was the U.S.S. *Wisconsin.*

1958, May 12. NORAD Established. Formal establishment of the Joint Canadian-U.S. North American Air Defense Command confirmed measures already initiated through informal agreement of the 2 governments (October, 1957). NORAD Headquarters was established at Colorado Springs.

1958, May 20. Strategic Army Corps Established. The Pentagon announced that 4 combat-ready divisions, comprising (with supporting troops) 150,000 men, were being combined into a force capable of action at short notice "to meet or reinforce any initial emergency requirements throughout the world."

1958, July 15. U.S. Intervention in Lebanon.

1958, August 6. Department of Defense Reorganization Act. This was the result of a plan submitted to Congress by President Eisenhower (April 16), to (1) stop "unworthy and sometimes costly [interservice] bickering"; (2) assure "clear-cut civilian responsibility, unified strategic planning and direction and completely unified commands"; (3) stop "inefficiency and needless duplication"; and (4) assure "safety and solvency." The Act (a) substantially strengthened the position and authority of the Secretary of Defense in relation to the service departments; (b) authorized a limited general staff type organization for the Joint Staff, capable of more efficient and more comprehensive service to the Joint Chiefs of Staff; and (c) removed service elements in unified commands from the command jurisdiction of the service secretaries and chiefs of staff.

1959, March 3. Warning of Submarine Menace. Admiral **Arleigh A. Burke,** Chief of Naval Operations, warned of the ever-present danger to U.S. warships and commercial shipping posed by Soviet submarines in international waters.

1959, December 10. Withdrawal of U.S. Troops from Iceland.

1959, December 30. First Operational Polaris Nuclear Submarine. U.S.S. *George Washington* was commissioned.

1960, January 19. No Missile Gap. Defense Secretary **Thomas S. Gates** told the Senate Armed Services Committee that previously announced Pentagon estimates of a "missile gap," or "deterrent gap," were based on evaluation of Soviet production potentiality, rather than actual Soviet production. He later (March 16) told the Senate Preparedness Subcommittee that the U.S. had, and would maintain, a nuclear destructive power "several times" greater than that of the U.S.S.R.

1960, May 7. U-2 Reconnaissance Plane Shot Down over Russia. Khrushchev made the announcement to the Supreme Soviet that the plane had been shot down from an altitude of 65,000 feet near Sverdlovsk.

1960, May 10. First Submerged Circumnavigation of the Earth. U.S. nuclear-powered submarine *Triton* went 41,519 miles in 84 days.

1960, May 17. Summit Conference Collapses in Paris. Khrushchev, angrily denouncing American spying by the U-2 plane over Russia, broke up the meeting. President Eisenhower later reported on TV to the people on the U-2 incident and the failure of the summit conference (May 25).

1960, June 13. Soviet Spy Net. Senator **J. William Fulbright** made public a U.S. State Department report that the Soviet bloc maintained a network of 300,000 spies throughout the world.

1960, July 14. U.S. Reaffirms Monroe Doctrine. A response to Khrushchev's threats to retaliate with missiles if the U.S. should intervene militarily in Cuba.

1960, July 20. First Successful Polaris Firing. This was from the submerged nuclear submarine U.S.S. *George Washington.*

1960, September 24. Launching of U.S.S. *Enterprise.* This was the largest ship ever built and the world's first nuclear-powered aircraft carrier.

1960, November 1. Nuclear Submarine Base Agreement with United Kingdom.

1960, November 14. First Polaris Patrol Mission. The U.S.S. *George Washington,* armed with 16 thermonuclear Polaris missiles, sailed from Charleston, S.C.

1961, January. Kennedy Reappraises U.S. Defense Posture. In his first State of the Union Message, he said that he had ordered an appraisal of U.S. strategy, and had directed action to increase U.S. airlift capacity, to step up the Polaris submarine program, and to accelerate the missile program. Shortly thereafter, in a revised budget (March 28), President Kennedy requested $1.954 billion more in defense appropriations than the $41.84-billion budget submitted by Eisenhower.

1961, April 15–20. Bay of Pigs Incident in Cuba. (See p. 1337.)

1961, May 5. First U.S. Manned Space Flight. This was a suborbital flight made by Navy Commander **Alan B. Shepard, Jr.,** launched from Cape Canaveral, Fla., and landed safely in the Atlantic after reaching an altitude of 116.5 miles.

1961, June 3–4. Kennedy-Khrushchev Meeting at Vienna. No agreement was reached, and Kennedy left the meeting apparently with grave doubts as to a peaceful future.

1961, July 10. Berlin Crisis. (See p. 1263.)

The United States rejected a Soviet proposal that the U.S., Britain, and France withdraw their forces from West Berlin, to be replaced by a smaller U.N.-supervised force.

1961, September 26. Establishment of the Arms Control and Disarmament Agency.

1962, January 3. Army Increase. President Kennedy announced an increase from 14 to 16 divisions. The Army soon thereafter (February 23) announced an increase in the size of the Strategic Army Corps from 3 to 8 divisions, and its strength had gone from 90,000 to 160,000 men in 6 months since the beginning of the Berlin crisis.

1962, May 6. First Polaris Nuclear Warhead Test. The missile was fired from the nuclear submarine U.S.S. *Ethan Allen* and exploded in the Christmas Island testing area.

CUBAN MISSILE CRISIS, SEPTEMBER–NOVEMBER, 1962

1962, September 4. Soviet Military Aid to Cuba. President Kennedy announced that Cuba's military strength had been increased by deliveries of Soviet equipment, but that there was no evidence of significant offensive capability in Cuba. A few days later, despite prodding from members of Congress (particularly Senator **Kenneth Keating**), President Kennedy said that he opposed any invasion of Cuba (September 12). Next day he warned the U.S.S.R. and Cuba against any build-up of offensive strength.

1962, October 22. Crisis Begins. President Kennedy announced to the nation on TV that U.S. surveillance had "established the fact that a series of offensive missile sites is now in preparation" in Cuba that could menace most of the major cities of the Western Hemisphere, and that jet bombers capable of carrying nuclear weapons were being uncrated. He said he had ordered a naval and air quarantine of Cuba that would not be lifted until all offensive weapons were dismantled and removed from Cuba under U.N. supervision. He declared that the launching of any nuclear missile from Cuba against any Western Hemisphere nation would be considered an attack on the U.S. "requiring a full retaliatory response upon the Soviet Union." U.S. forces were placed on alert, and preparations were begun to invade Cuba if necessary.

1962, October 23. Action in U.N. and OAS. A U.S. demand for dismantling of the bases was lodged in the U.N. Security Council. The Council of the Organization of American States approved a resolution authorizing the use of force to carry out the quarantine.

1962, October 23. Soviet Alert. Alerting its armed forces, the Soviet government challenged the U.S. right to quarantine its shipments to Cuba. U.S. invasion preparations continued.

1962, October 24–29. Secret U.S.-Soviet Negotiations. Prime Minister Khrushchev backed down after an exchange of letters with President Kennedy. He agreed to halt construction of bases in Cuba, to dismantle and remove Soviet missiles there under U.N. supervision. In turn Kennedy agreed to lift the quarantine when the U.N. had taken the necessary measures, and pledged that the U.S. would not invade Cuba.

1962, November 2. Quarantine Lifted. President Kennedy reported to the nation that the Soviet missile bases were being dismantled, and "progress is now being made for the restoration of peace in the Caribbean." The U.S. Defense Department later announced that the U.S.S.R. had begun withdrawal of its jet bombers from Cuba, as pledged by Khrushchev (December 3). In response to congressional criticism, Secretary of Defense **Robert S. McNamara** proved by photographs that offensive weapons had been fully removed from Cuba (1963, February 6). The U.S. and U.S.S.R. later reported to U.N. Secretary General Thant that the crisis was ended (1963, January 7).

1962, December 19. Missile Inventory. The Air Force announced that the U.S. had 200 operational ICBM's: 126 Atlas, 54 Titan, and 20 solid-fuel Minuteman.

1963, May 9. Russians Remain in Cuba. The Defense Department estimated that 17,500 Russians were still in Cuba, including 5,000 combat troops.

1963, August 30. Opening of the "Hot Line." Direct communications were provided between White House and Kremlin.

1963, October 22–24. Operation Big Lift. Fifteen thousand men in a U.S. division were airlifted 5,600 miles in 63 hours and 20 minutes from the U.S. to West Germany.

1964, February 6. Cuba Cuts off Supply of Water to Guantánamo Base. A U.S. distillation plant made the base self-sufficient.

1964, August 7. Gulf of Tonkin Resolution. (See pp. 1297–1298.)

1964, September 17. Announcement of Perfection of U.S. Antimissile Defense Systems. President Johnson also announced that U.S. weapons could intercept and destroy hostile armed satellites in orbit. Secretary of Defense McNamara described 2 rocket systems: the Army's 3-stage solid-fueled "Nike Zeus" and the Air Force's liquid-fueled "Thor."

1964, December 12. Defense Secretary McNamara Proposes to Combine Army Reserve and National Guard. After violent public and Congressional protest the plan was dropped.

1965, February 7–1973, January 23. Vietnam War. (See p. 1209.)

1965, April 28. U.S. Intervention in the Dominican Republic. (See p. 1338.)

1965, September 30. Reorganization of Army Reserve and National Guard. Secretary McNamara achieved part of his objective of reserve component reorganization by eliminating a number of Reserve units and increasing the readiness of the remaining Reserve and National Guard units. Additional reorganization to this same end was accomplished 2 years later (1967, June 2).

1967, July 12–17. Race Riots in Newark, N.J. National Guard troops were employed to restore order.

1967, September 18. McNamara Announces Plans for Antiballistic Missile System. "Nike-X" (later called "Sentinel") would be a "light" system employing "Sprint" and "Spartan" missiles, capable of countering any long-range missile that Communist China might deploy in the next 10 years. A system to prevent Soviet missiles from reaching this country would be impossibly expensive. Congress failed to approve.

1968, January 23. *Pueblo* Incident. **(See p. 1311.)**

1968, March 2. C-5A "Galaxy" Displayed. This jet transport was the world's largest aircraft.

1968, March 30. NORAD Renewed. The U.S. and Canada agreed to extend the treaty against long-range bombing attack (see p. 1331) for another 5 years. Canada was not committed to involvement in continental defense against missiles.

1968, March 31. President Johnson Announces Cessation of Bombing of North Vietnam. (See p. 1217.)

1968, May 29. Disappearance of Nuclear Submarine U.S.S. *Scorpion*. This was announced after the vessel was 2 days overdue from a 3-month training exercise. There was a crew of 99 aboard.

1969, March 14. President Nixon Announces the "Safeguard" Antiballistic Missile System. This modification of the "Sentinel" system plan was approved by Congress (November 6).

1969, March 29–1970, March 17. Investigation of Alleged 1968 Massacre of Vietnamese Civilians at My Lai. (See p. 1216.) The allegation was made in a published letter to Secretary of Defense McNamara and several members of Congress by a former soldier, **Ronald L. Ridenhour.** An investigating committee headed by Lieutenant General **William R. Peers** was appointed by Secretary of the Army **Stanley Resor.** Nearly one year later Resor announced that the Peers investigation report had been submitted to him (March 14), that it established that a massacre had in fact occurred, and that information about the incident had been "kept from being passed up the chain of command" by "several individuals."

1969, July 20. First Men Reach Surface of Moon. Astronauts **Neil Armstrong** and Colonel **Edwin Aldrin, Jr.**, U.S.A.F., were carried to the moon by the Apollo 11 spacecraft.

1969, October 15. Vietnam War "Moratorium." Hundreds of thousands of Americans participated in an antiwar demonstration. In a similar demonstration 250,000 "marched on Washington" a month later (November 15).

1969, November 24. Nuclear Nonproliferation Treaty Signed. Signing by President Richard M. Nixon and Soviet President Nikolai V. Podgorny took place on the same day. The Senate had ratified it March 13.

1970, May 4. Kent State University Incident. Ohio National Guard troops, called out to control disorders at Kent State, fired into students with insufficient provocation, killing four.

1970, May 25. Announcement of Deployment of MIRV Missiles. Multiple Individual Reentry Vehicles, or multiple warheads, were fixed on U.S. intercontinental ballistic missiles (ICBMs).

1970, August 28. Successful Test of Safeguard ABM System. A "Spartan" ABM missile launched from Kwajalein inter cepted the nose cone of a "Minuteman" ICBM, launched from Vandenburg Air Force Base, 4,200 miles away.

1970, November 23. U.S. Coast Guard Returns Defector to Soviet Control. When a member of a crew of a Russian fishing trawler jumped from his vessel to the U.S.C.G.C. *Vigilant*, Soviet sailors were allowed to board and seize him. The *Vigilant*'s Commander **Ralph W. Eustis** was subsequently relieved of command, and the First Coast Guard District commander and his chief of staff were retired.

1971, March 29. Lt. William H. Calley Convicted by Court-martial of Murder of Civilians at My Lai. This ended more than 4 months of frequently interrupted proceedings and 13 days of deliberation by the military court. Because of discrepancies in testimony, Calley was found guilty of only 22 of the 102 murders with which he had been charged. Four days later he was sentenced to life imprisonment. Although Calley's guilt in the taking of innocent lives was clear, paradoxically the verdict was opposed by as many liberal "dove" opponents of the war (who thought Calley an unfortunate victim of a cover-up by superiors who were responsible for the war and its alleged atrocities) as it was by ardent "hawk" supporters of the war (who thought he had merely been trying to do his duty in obedience to orders as he understood them). The resulting public furor assured lenient treatment for Calley and his eventual release from a few months' confinement in prison three and a half years after his conviction (December 1974). Also contributing to sympathy for Calley was the fact that only 4 people had been tried for the incident and the alleged cover-up, and only Calley had been convicted. (See pp. 1216 and 1334.)

1971, April 12. Largest "Conventional" Bomb Announced. This was the 15,000-pound "daisy cutter," being used in Vietnam to clear jungle areas the size of a baseball park, when set to explode 7 feet above ground.

1971, April 19–24. Antiwar Demonstrations. Vietnam veterans were prominent among the demonstrators in Washington and San Francisco.

1971, May 19. Defeat of the Mansfield Amendment. Senator **Mike Mansfield's** proposal for a 50 per cent reduction of the 300,000 U.S. combat troops in Europe was defeated 61–36.

1971, June 13. New York *Times* Publishes "Pentagon Papers." A highly classified official record of U.S. involvement in Vietnam, prepared in the late 1960's at direction of Secretary of Defense McNamara, was covertly delivered to the New York *Times* by **Daniel Ellsberg,** a former Government official and later a research analyst with the Rand Corporation, who was authorized access to the closely guarded documents. Ignoring the official classification stamps on the documents, the *Times* began publishing excerpts from the 47-volume collection until prohibited by Government injunction two days later. The *Times* appealed the case to the Supreme Court, which ruled in favor of the newspaper. Publication was renewed, and selections were published in book form. Ellsberg was later tried for violation of Government security legislation, but the case was dismissed on technical grounds.

1971, June 17. Treaty with Japan on Okinawa. The island was returned to Japan, but U.S. bases were to remain.

1971, November 6. Explosion of 5-Megaton H-Bomb under Amchitka Island. This was the last of some 20 underground tests for a "Spartan" missile warhead. Efforts by environmentalists and antiwar protesters to block the test were rejected by the Supreme Court. There were none of the immediate effects prophesied by the protesters.

1972, May 27. Cessation of Work on "Safeguard" ABM System. This was the result of a "summit" agreement between President Richard M. Nixon and Soviet Chairman Brezhnev (see p. 1256).

1972, June 3. Partial Release of Peers Report on My Lai Massacre. The report of Peers' investigating committee charged that some 300 civilians had been slaughtered in the My Lai incident, and that there was serious misconduct on the part of Americal Division Commander, Major General **Samuel W. Koster,** and his assistant division commander, Brigadier General **George H. Young, Jr.,** in their failure to investigate the affair or to take disciplinary action against subordinates who had been obviously guilty of misconduct either in the operation which led to the massacre or in subsequent failure to take corrective or investigative action. General

Koster was demoted and reprimanded (1971, May 19) and allowed to retire; General Young was also reprimanded and allowed to retire. The full report was released 2 years later (1974, November 13; see above and pp. 1216 and 1334.)

1972, September 14. U.S. Senate Approves U.S.–Soviet Offensive Nuclear Missile Agreement. (See p. 1256.) By the "Jackson Amendment," proposed by Senator **Henry M. Jackson,** Senate approval was contingent upon U.S. reservation that the accord should not limit the U.S. "to levels of intercontinental strategic forces inferior to the limits provided for the Soviet Union." The agreement had permitted the U.S.S.R. to have about 1,618 ICBMs, including some 300 massive SS-9s, compared to 1,054 American ICBMs, generally smaller, but mostly with multiple warhead (MIRV) capability, in addition to a substantially larger fleet of U.S. long-range bombers.

1973, January 23. Vietnam Peace Accord. (See p. 1220.)

1973, January 27. End of U.S. Conscription. It was announced by Defense Secretary **Melvin Laird,** 6 months earlier than expected, principally because of the end of the Vietnam War. Legislation remained in effect for use in event of an emergency.

1973, May 14–June 22. First Orbiting Space Station. A Navy crew manned the station, "Skylab."

1973, November 7. Congress Limits Presidential Authority to Commit Forces to Hostilities Abroad. Congress passed, over President Nixon's veto, legislation requiring (1) the President to inform Congress within 48 hours of committing any U.S. forces to a foreign conflict, or of "substantially" enlarging the size of a combat force already in a foreign country, and (2) the end of such commitment within 60 days unless its continuation was specifically authorized by Congress.

1974, December 14. U.S. Senate Ratifies Geneva Protocol. After a delay of nearly 40 years the Senate Foreign Relations Committee agreed to U.S. adherence to the Protocol on prohibition of gas and biological warfare (see pp. 1027 and 1256).

CANADA

1950–1953. Korean War (see p.1240). Canada contributed 1 brigade of infantry, 1 artillery group, and an armored battalion to U.N. forces.

1953, January 8. Agreement on Radioactive Resources. Agreement between Britain, U.S., and Canada to share in uranium ore produced in Australia.

1954, May 13. St. Lawrence Seaway Approved by U.S. President Eisenhower signed legislation authorizing the U.S. to join Canada in constructing the Seaway. This was later dedicated by Queen Elizabeth and President Eisenhower (June 26, 1959).

1954, November 19. Joint Hemisphere Defense. The U.S. and Canada announced plans to construct a Distant Early Warning (DEW) radar line across Arctic Canada.

1958, May 19. NORAD Established. (See p. 1331.)

1963, May 11. U.S. Nuclear Warheads to Canada. Canada accepted U.S. nuclear warheads for missiles installed on Canadian soil and used by Canadian NATO forces.

1963, August 16. Joint Control of Nuclear Air Defense Weapons. U.S. and Canada signed an agreement under which the U.S. would arm the Canadian Air Defense System.

1968, March 30. NORAD Extended for Five Years. (See p. 1334.)

1969, September 19. Canada Announces Reduction of NATO Force in Europe. Following a previous announcement (1969, April 3), Prime Minister **Pierre Elliott Trudeau**'s government announced that Canadian forces in Europe were to be reduced from 9,800 to 5,000 men in 1970, and that Canada would end its nuclear role in NATO by 1972.

LATIN AMERICA

ORGANIZATION OF AMERICAN STATES

1947, September 2. Treaty of Rio de Janeiro. The Inter-American Defense Treaty, transforming the old Pan American Union into the Organization of American States, was signed by all nations of the Western Hemisphere except Canada. This was ratified by the U.S. Senate (December 8) and became effective when ratified by the fourteenth nation, Costa Rica (December 3, 1948).

1948, April 26. Charter for the Organization of American States. This was established at a conference in Bogotá.

1954, March 1–28. Caracas Resolution. The Tenth Inter-American Conference of Foreign Ministers, at Caracas, declared that control of the political institutions of any American state by the Communist movement, an extension of the political system of a Continental power outside the Western Hemisphere, would be a threat to the peace of America.

1959, August 12–18. Emergency OAS Session. This was in response to Cuban threats of invasion or infiltration in the Caribbean area.

1962, February 14. Cuba Excluded from the Organization of American States.

1964, July 26. OAS Votes Sanctions against Cuba. This action was sparked mainly by Cuban subversion efforts in Venezuela in 1963. OAS members were to sever all diplomatic and consular relations with Cuba; all trade and transportation to Cuba was banned, save for food and medicine.

1964, August 3. Mexico Refuses to Adopt Sanctions against Cuba. **(See p. 1338.)**

1968, May 6. OAS Establishes Peace Force for the Dominican Republic. **(See p. 1338.)**

MEXICO

1964, August 3. Mexico Refuses to Adopt Sanctions against Cuba. **(See above.)** Mexico was thus the only state in the hemisphere retaining diplomatic relations and normal trade connection with Cuba.

1968, July 26–October 2. Student Disorders at National University. In an effort to end 7 weeks of sporadic violence, the Mexican Army seized the university (September 18). Student protests erupted into bloody battles, mostly involving students against police (September 19–24). There were several deaths. Two months of unrest climaxed in a major battle between the Army and students, in which about 50 students were killed. The result, however, was an end to the disorders.

CARIBBEAN REGION

Anguilla

1967, July 11. Independence of Anguilla. The tiny island withdrew from confederation with St. Kitts and Nevis, and vainly sought association with Britain, Canada, or the U.S.

1969, March 19. British Occupation. Unrest and economic troubles led Britain to send a mixed force of 100 paratroops, Marines, and policemen to take control. They were soon withdrawn (September 15), but the island remained virtually a British dependency.

Cuba

1952, March 10. Coup d'État. General **Fulgencio Batista** seized control of the country and established a dictatorship.

1953, July 26–27. Uprising in Santiago and Bayamo Suppressed. An effort by **Fidel Castro** to seize a government armory was defeated; Castro and his brother Raúl were captured and imprisoned.

1956, April 29. Rebellion Suppressed. The uprising occurred at Matanzas.

1956, December 2. Cuba Claims Castro Killed. Castro, who had been released from prison, went to Mexico and led an insurgent group landing in Oriente Province (November 30), was defeated and presumed (erroneously) to have been killed. Actually he and his followers fled to safety in the Sierra Maestra Mountains.

1957–1958. Insurrection. Revolutionaries under Fidel Castro carried out a successful guerrilla campaign from the Sierra Maestra Mountains of Oriente Province, gaining increasing popular support. Castro took the offensive and moved out of the mountains (October, 1958).

1959, January 1. Castro Victorious. Batista fled the country as the revolutionaries swept through the country and seized Havana (January 8).

1959, January 7. U.S. Recognizes Castro Government.

1960, May 7–Sept. 25. Cuba Joins Soviet Bloc. This was initiated by resumption of diplomatic relations (May 7) which had been broken in 1952; culminated by Khrushchev's threat to use intercontinental rockets to support Cuba if attacked by U.S. (September 25).

1960, November 1. Castro Rebuffed. President Eisenhower, in response to Castro's threats against Guantánamo, said the U.S. would "take whatever steps are necessary to defend" the base.

1961, January 3. U.S. Breaks Diplomatic Relations.

1961, April 15–20. Bay of Pigs Incident. An attempted invasion of Cuba by approximately 1,400 anti-Castro Cuban revolutionaries clandestinely supported by the U.S. Central Intelligence Agency, who did not receive the air naval support from U.S. forces which they had been promised, was defeated by Castro forces. This failure was a serious blow to American prestige.

1961, May 1. Castro Proclaims Cuba a So-

cialist Nation. Secretary of State **Dean Rusk** next day said that Cuba had become a full-fledged member of the Communist bloc.

1962, September 11. Soviet Threatens War in Support of Cuba. The U.S.S.R. accused the U.S. of preparing for an invasion of Cuba, and warned that any U.S. attack on Cuba or on Soviet ships bound for Cuba would mean war.

1962, September–December. Missile Crisis. (See p. 1333.)

1963, March 30. U.S. Bans Exile Raids Against Cuba.

1964, July 26. OAS Sanctions against Cuba.

1965, November 6. Cuba Permits Refugees to Fly to United States. These flights continued until August 1971, during which time 246,000 Cubans flew from Havana to Miami.

1966, February 6. Castro Accuses Communist China of "Betraying" Cuban Revolution. He denounced Chinese propaganda efforts in Cuba and failure of China to provide promised assistance.

Dominican Republic

1949, June 20–21. Revolt Suppressed.

1959, June 23. Cuban Invasion. Cuban-supported invasion of the Dominican Republic by 86 men was crushed by forces of dictator **Leonidas Trujillo.**

1961, May 30. Assassination of Trujillo. This ended the repressive dictatorial regime which had lasted for 31 years.

1962, January 13. Unsuccessful Coup Attempt.

1963, April 27–30. Dispute with Haiti. This resulted from a raid by Haitian police into the Dominican embassy in Port au Prince. The OAS mediated the dispute.

1963, September 25. Military Coup d'État. The leftist government of President **Juan Bosch** was overthrown by military leaders. Later the government was returned to civilian control (October).

1965, April 24–25. Military Coup d'État. The civilian triumvirate was overthrown. A bloody civil war broke out between leftist and military adherents of former President Bosch and Army and Air Force units under the command of Brigadier General **Elias Wessin y Wessin.** Although Wessin gained control of much of the capital and the country, fighting continued.

1965, April 28. United States Intervention. President Johnson sent in a force of Marines to protect Americans. These were followed by U.S. Army airborne units, as the fighting continued, with the pro-Bosch "rebels" regaining some lost ground, and the adherence of previously uncommitted army units.

1965, May 5. Truce Agreement. Under pressure from the U.S. and the OAS, a cease-fire was agreed upon between the rebel units, under the provisional President, Colonel **Francisco Caamans Deno** and a newly established 3-man military junta led by Brigadeir General **Antonio Imbert Barreras.** U.S. forces in the country were 12,439 Army troops and 6,924 Marines. More than 2,000 Dominican deaths were reported in the confused fighting.

1965, May 6. OAS Agrees to Establish Interamerican Peace Force. This would replace the United States force. Participating countries were Venezuela, Brazil, Guatemala, Costa Rica, Honduras, Paraguay, and the U.S.

1965, May 13–19. Renewed Civil War. The junta attacked the rebel forces and drove most of them from the capital. U.S. forces, attempting to hold open an International Security Zone, were accused of aiding both sides. Under U.S. pressure a new truce was agreed.

1965, May 23. OAS Interamerican Armed Force Becomes Operational. The United States began to reduce its 21,000-man force, which had had 19 men killed during the hostilities.

1965, August 31. Provisional Government Approved. Following resignation of the 3-man junta, the rival factions agreed with an OAS Peace Committee to establish a government under Provisional President **Hector Garcia-Godoy.** Sporadic violence continued in the country, however, for several months, becoming more intense in early 1966.

1966, June 3. Election of President Joaquin Balaguer. A centrist, he defeated left-wing candidate Juan Bosch and a right-wing candidate.

1966, June 28. Withdrawal of OAS Force Begins. The first units of the 6,000-man U.S. contingent of the 8,200-man force began to leave the country following an OAS resolution (June 24).

Haiti

1946, January 11. Military Coup d'État President **Élie Lescot** was overthrown. Th military junta selected **Dumarsais Estimé** as president (August 16).

1950, April. Military Coup. Estimé was ousted and replaced by Colonel **Paul Magloire** (October 23).

1956–1958. Chaos in Haiti. Magloire was forced to resign (December 13, 1956) and **François Duvalier** was elected president (September 22, 1957). By ruthless repression he restored order (July, 1958).

1959, August 12–18. Emergency session of the Organization of American States was called to ease tensions in the Caribbean area.

1959, August 13. Cuban Invasion. The invading force of 30 armed men was crushed.

1960, November 22. Duvalier Proclaims Martial Law. The dictator took advantage of disorders at the University of Haiti to increase his control over the country.

1962–1963. Border Incidents with Dominican Republic.

1963, August 5–7. Rebel Invasion from the Dominican Republic. A force of Haitian exiles, hoping to overthrow the government of dictator President François Duvalier, landed by sea in northern Haiti, having embarked in the Dominican Republic. The rebels were defeated and fled across the border into the Dominican Republic, which was charged with complicity by Haiti.

1969, June 4. Unidentified Aircraft Attacks Port-au-Prince. Six homemade incendiary bombs dropped from a transport plane caused 3 deaths. Haiti accused **Cuba**.

Trinidad-Tobago

1962, August 31. Independence Granted by Great Britain.

1970, April 21–25. Riots and Army Mutiny. Racial tension between blacks (47 per cent of population) and East Indians (36 per cent) flared into violence, which became more serious when perhaps one-fourth of the 800-man army mutinied in support of black-power rioters. Loyal troops suppressed the rebellion after much shooting but negligible bloodshed.

CENTRAL AMERICA

Costa Rica

1948, April 13–20. Revolution. The dictatorial government of President **Teodoro Picado** was overthrown by rebels led by Colonel **José Figueres.**

1948, December 12. Invasion by Armed Rebels from Nicaragua. This was repelled; strained relations with Nicaragua resulted.

1949, April 3. Unsuccessful Coup Attempt.

1955, January 11. Invasion and Rebellion Suppressed. President José Figueres again accused Nicaragua of aggression and asked the OAS Council for aid. An OAS committee set up as a result of this complaint reported (February 17) that the rebels were mostly Costa Ricans who had been based in Nicaragua, and called for conciliation of the dispute between the 2 nations.

1956, January 9. Agreement with Nicaragua. It provided for effective co-operation in joint surveillance of borders.

1960, November 9–14. Clash with Nicaraguan Rebels. (See p. 1340.)

El Salvador

1948, December 12. Military Revolt. President **Castaneda Castro** was overthrown, and replaced by a revolutionary junta.

1960, October 26. Coup d'État. The government of President **Jose Maria Lemus** was overthrown by a military junta led by Colonel **Cesar Yanes Urias.**

1969, June 24–28. War with Honduras. Long-smoldering economic and territorial border disputes (1967–1969) were sparked to war by rioting over a series of soccer games. El Salvadoran troops had occupied considerable Honduran territory when both sides accepted a cease-fire arranged by the OAS. Sporadic fighting continued for more than a month, however, with the advantage remaining with El Salvador.

1972, March 25. Attempted Coup d'État. Troops loyal to the President, General **Fidel Sanchez Hernandez,** suppressed a military revolt in brief but bloody fighting; more than 300 were killed on both sides.

Guatemala

1949, July 16–18. Rebellion Suppressed.

1954, June 18–29. Revolution. Anti-Communist forces under Lieutenant Colonel **Carlos Castillo Armas** invaded the country and called on the people to overthrow leftist President **Jacobo Arbenz Guzmán.** Arbenz sought asylum in the Mexican embassy (June 27). A cease-fire was effective after about 100 casualties had been incurred on both sides. Castillo Armas became leader of a junta, and shortly afterward was declared president (July 1).

1955, January 20. Revolt Suppressed. Continuing Communist-inspired insurgency.

1957, October 25. Coup d'État. President **Luis Arturo Gonzalez Lopez** was ousted by a military junta headed by Colonel **Oscar Mendoza.** Colonel **Guillermo Flores Anendaño** was proclaimed president (October 26).

1960, November 16. Threatened Cuban Invasion. U.S. warships protected Guatemala and Nicaragua, threatened by invasion from Cuba.

1963, March 30. Coup d'État. Colonel **Enrique Peralta Azurdia** proclaimed himself president. Low-level, Communist-inspired insurgency continued to cause sporadic violence throughout the country.

1968, August 18. Communist Guerrillas Kill U.S. Ambassador. John Gordon Mein was slain in an apparent kidnap attempt.

1970, April 5. Communist Guerrillas Kill West German Ambassador. Count **Karl von Spreti** was kidnapped, then assassinated.

Honduras

1956, October 21. Military Coup. A junta took control after charges of election fraud against President **Julio Lozano Diaz** caused violence and bloodshed (October 7).

1957, May 2–3. Border Clashes with Nicaragua. (See below.)

1961, January 27. Invasion Attempt from Nicaragua. Honduran rebels, possibly encouraged by Nicaragua, were repulsed.

1963, October 3, Coup d'État. President **Ramon Villeda Morales** was ousted after sharp fighting between rebel and loyal troops by Colonel **Osvaldo Lopez Arellano,** chief of the armed forces, who proclaimed himself President.

1969, June 24–28. War with El Salvador.

Nicaragua

1947, May 26. Coup d'État. General **Anastasio Somoza** overthrew the government of President **Leonardo Argüello.**

1948–1955. Disputes with Costa Rica (see p. 1339).

1956, September 21. Assassination of President Somoza. His son, **Luís,** was elected by Congress to complete his term.

1957, May 2–3. Border Clashes with Honduras. Troops of both sides withdrew following OAS mediation.

1959, May 30–June 14. Attempted Insurgent Invasion. Air-transported rebels were defeated by forces of General **Anastasio Somoza Debayle** (brother of President **Luis A. Somoza Debayle**), who accused Cuba of fomenting insurrection.

1960, January–May. Insurgent Border Raids. These were from Honduras (January 2, February 29, and May 14) and Costa Rica (January 9).

1960, November 11–15. Insurgent Invasion from Costa Rica. This was defeated by Nicaraguan troops, aided by Costa Rican troops (November 9–14). Cuba was blamed for supporting the insurgency.

1961, July 26. Sandinista National Liberation Front (FSLN). Nicaraguan insurgents, trained and indoctrinated in Cuba, established the new organization in Honduras, named in honor of the 1920–1930s revolutionary leader, César Augusto Sandino (see p. 1098).

1963. Sandinista Base Established in Nicaragua. The FSLN began guerrilla operations in the northern mountains of Matagalpa, but failed to rally the local peasants to the cause of armed insurrection. Sporadic raids continued.

1967, January 22–23. Attempted Coup d'État. A coalition of civilians and dissatisfied military officers attempted a coup that was suppressed by the National Guard, commanded by Anastasio Somoza Debayle; this youngest son of Anastasio Somoza was elected president (February 5).

1972–1974. Civil Unrest. The increasingly despotic rule of dictator Somoza and his ruthless National Guard alienated much of the population.

Panama

1949, November 26. Coup d'État. Dr. **Arnulfo Arias** was installed as president by the national police.

1951, May 10. Coup d'État. President **Arnulfo Arias** was overthrown in violent fighting. He was succeeded by Vice President **Alicibiades Arosmena.**

1955, January 25. Treaty with the U.S. Yearly payments for the Canal Zone were increased from \$430,000 to \$1,930,000.

1959, April 24–May 1. Cuban-Based Insurgent Invasion. More than 100 invaders, many Cuban, were defeated, and most killed or captured.

1959, November 3. Anti-U.S. Riots in Panama.

1964, January 9–10. Anti-U.S. Riots. Panama broke diplomatic relations with the U.S. because of riots in the Canal Zone.

1964, April 3. Resumption of Diplomatic Relations with the U.S.

1968, October 11. Coup d'État. Recently inaugurated President Arnulfo Arias was overthrown by the National Guard. A military junta elected two of its members, Colonel **Bolivar Urrutia** and Colonel **Jose M. Pinella,** as president and vice president, respectively.

1969, December 15. Coup d'État. Brigadier General **Omar Torrijos,** who had been a principal leader in the October 11 coup against President Arias, ousted the two colonels who had outmaneuvered him to gain power after the coup.

SOUTH AMERICA

Argentina

1948, March 4. Agreement with Chile against Britain. The 2 nations agreed on joint defense of their rights in the Antarctic and the Falkland Islands against British claims and occupation.

1951, September 28. Revolt Suppressed. President **Juan Perón** blamed the military revolt, suppressed by loyal troops, on the activities of former U.S. Ambassador **Spruille Braden.** A state of virtual martial law was declared which gave Perón dictatorial powers.

1955, June–September. Violence, Disorders, Unrest. Minor military and civilian revolts were ruthlessly suppressed by the Perón regime. Perón was excommunicated by the Catholic Church for suppressing Catholic schools and imprisoning priests.

1955, September 16–19. Perón Overthrown. As disorders spread, Perón declared a state of siege (September 11). The armed forces then rose in a brief revolt. Perón fled. A junta under Major General **Eduardo Leonardi** took control.

1955, November 13. Military Revolt. Leonardi, accused of being "fascist," was overthrown and replaced by Major General **Pedro Aramburu.**

1956, June 10–14. Peronist Revolt Suppressed. Later Peronist plots were discovered and smashed (August 15, November 22).

1960, June 13. Unsuccessful Revolt. An Army unit in San Luis surrendered without bloodshed when no other military unit responded to radio appeals for a national uprising.

1962, March 29. Military Coup d'État. President **Arturo Frondizi** was ousted by the armed forces.

1962, August 8–11. Army Mutiny. President **Jose Maria Guido** accepted Army demands for a change in the War Secretary and Army commander in chief.

1962, December 11–12. Military Revolt. This was suppressed by loyal troops.

1963, April 2–5. Military Mutiny and Rebellion. The rebels, mostly naval, were defeated after brief fighting at scattered locations.

1966, June 28. Coup d'État. A military junta ousted President **Arturo Illia** and installed Lieutenant General **Juan Carlos Ongania** as provisional president.

1970–1975. Growth of Terrorist Violence. The country was plagued by a rash of kidnappings and assassinations.

1970, June 8. Coup d'État. A military junta ousted President Ongania and installed Brigadier General **Roberto Marcelo Levingston** as president.

1971, March 23. Coup d'État. A military junta, headed by Army Commander General **Alejandro Augustin Lanusse,** ousted President Levingston.

1971, July 1. Britain and Argentina Agree to Disagree on the Falkland Islands. Although neither side relinquished its claim to sovereignty (Malvinas Islands to Argentina), they agreed to resolve outstanding issues by negotiation.

1973, July 13. Return of Peron. He was elected president, with his second wife, **Isabel,** vice president. She succeeded him upon his death (1974, July 1).

Bolivia

1946, July 17–21. Popular Revolution. President **Gualberto Villaroel** was killed and succeeded by a liberal government.

1949, May–September. Unrest and Rebellion in the Tin Mines. Suppressed by the army, but left the nation on the verge of bankruptcy.

1950, January 14. Unsuccessful Coup Attempt.

1950, May 18–19. Unsuccessful Coup Attempt.

1951, May 16. Military Coup. A 10-man military junta, led by General **Hugo Ballivián,** seized control in Bolivia.

1952, April 8–11. Revolution. The junta was overthrown by a popular revolt under **Hernán Siles Zuazo.** Doctor **Victor Paz**

Estenssoro was proclaimed president (April 16).

1953, November 9. Unsuccessful Revolt.

1958, May 16–22. Unsuccessful Revolt. Uprising in Santa Cruz, suppressed by troops.

1958, October 21. Revolt Suppressed.

1959, April 19. Unsuccessful Revolt in La Paz.

1959, June 26. Unsuccessful Revolt in Santa Cruz.

1960, March 19. National Police Revolt. Crushed by the army.

1964, November 3–4. Military Revolt. President Paz Estenssoro was overthrown by Army General **Alfredo Ovando Candia** and Air Force General **René Barrientos Ortuno.** Ovando soon resigned, leaving popular Barrientos in control.

1966–1967. Cuban-Sponsored Insurgency. Guerrilla activity intensified after arrival of **Ernesto (Che) Guevara** from Cuba (1966, November 7).

1967, October 8–16. Elimination of Che Guevara and His Guerrillas. Military forces commanded by Brigadier General **Juan Jose Torres,** an anti-Communist officer with socialist political views, methodically tracked down, surrounded, then annihilated Che and his small band of followers. Guevara, wounded, was captured (October 8) and died the next day.

1969, April 27. Death of President Barrientos. He was killed in a helicopter crash. He was succeeded by Vice President **Adolfo Siles Salinas.**

1969, September 26. Coup d'État. General Ovando seized control in a bloodless coup and named himself president.

1970, October 6–7. Coup d'État and Countercoup. President Ovando resigned under pressure from right-wing military officers. During the confusion, however, leftist General Torres seized control and proclaimed himself president.

1971, August 19–22. Coup d'État. Right-wing military officers, led by Colonel **Hugo Banzer Saurez,** ousted President Torres after a brief and not very intensive struggle.

Brazil

1954, August 8–25. Civil Disorder. Unable to restore order, President **Getulio Vargas** resigned under military pressure, then committed suicide (August 24).

1955, November 11. Coup d'État. Military officers, led by Lieutenant General **H. B. D. Teixeira Lott,** deposed Acting President **Carlos Coimbra da Luz,** who was accused of fostering a coup to cancel the election of **Juscelino Kubitschek** as president. Kubitschek took office as scheduled (1956, January 31).

1961, August 26. Military Coup.

1963, September 12. Military Revolt Suppressed.

1964, March 31. Military Revolution. President **Joao Goulart** was deposed and a military dictatorship was established.

1969, August 31. Military Junta Takes Control. Leaders of the 3 armed forces assumed authority after President **Artur da Costa e Silva** was incapacitated by a stroke.

Chile

1973, September 11. Coup d'État. The Chilean tradition of military subordination to civilian political authority ended when a four-man military junta seized power from President **Salvador Allende Gossens,** an avowed Marxist, after three years of increasing chaos under his presidency. (It is not clear to what extent this chaos was the result of Allende's inefficiency, of obstructionism by right-wing civilian and military elements, and of subversion prompted by the U.S. Central Intelligence Agency.) During brief but bitter fighting for the Presidential Palace, Allende was killed, apparently by suicide.

Colombia

1945–1965. Endemic Civil War Continues. **(See p. 1050.)**

1948, April 9–10. Uprising in Bogotá. This revolt, embarrassing to the government because it occurred during a meeting of the Inter-American Conference, was suppressed.

1948–1958. La Violencia; Low-Scale Guerrilla Insurrection. A variety of local and national issues and problems were exploited by Colombian Communists to stir up a constant state of revolt and insurrection in rural areas of the country. At least 250,000 violent deaths occurred during this decade of violence.

1953, June 13. Military Coup d'État. President **Laureano Gomez** was overthrown by the military under Lieutenant General **Gustavo Rojas Pinilla.**

1957, May 10. Military Coup d'État. Rojas Pinilla overthrown by junta.

Ecuador

1947, March 14. Unsuccessful Coup Attempt.

1947, August 23. Military Coup d'État. President **Jose Maria Velasco Ibarra** was overthrown in a bloodless revolt by Colonel **Carlos Mancheno.** (Velasco Ibarra had also been ousted in 1935.)

1947, September 1–3. Successful Counterrevolution. Mancheno was overthrown and replaced by **Carlos Julio Arosemena Monroy.**

1951–1955. Dispute with Peru. This was due to disputed frontier locations in an area which had been in dispute for over a century. There were intermittent border clashes and arguments before the International Court of Justice.

1961, November 7–9. Coup d'État. Antigovernment riots led to the overthrow of the government of President Jose Maria Velasco Ibarra and clashes between military units supporting rival candidates to replace Velasco. After brief fighting, Army and Air Force leaders agreed to install Vice President **Carlos Julio Arosemena Monroy** as president.

1963, July 11. Coup d'État. Military leaders ousted President Arosemena, who was replaced by a 4-man military junta.

1966, March 29. Antimilitary Coup. The junta resigned as a result of antigovernment riots.

1971, January 18. United States Suspends Arms Aid to Ecuador. This was a result of numerous incidents (28 since 1966) of Ecuadoran seizure of American tuna fishing boats, more than 12 miles off shore but within Ecuador's claimed territorial waters, extending 200 miles from shore. Ecuadoran seizures continued.

1972, February 15. Military Coup d'État. President Jose Maria Velasco Ibarra was ousted by a military junta, which named General **Guillermo Rodriguez Lara** as President. This was the fourth time Velasco had been ousted as president by a military coup.

Guyana

1953, October 9. British Intervention. The left-wing government of Prime Minister **Cheddi Jagan** was ousted by British troops to prevent a Communist takeover of the self-governing colony.

1962–1966. Endemic Violence. Promised independence in 1966, the colony was torn by disorders, riots, and bloodshed, primarily because of racial and political strife between East Indians (49 per cent of the population) and blacks (32 per cent).

1966, May 26. Independence of Guyana. Despite the continuing explosive internal situation, Britain granted the promised independence, leaving a military garrison in the country. Following national elections Guyana became a republic, but remained in the British Commonwealth (1970, February 23).

1969, January 2–4. Rebellion Crushed. Rebels from Brazil, apparently supported by large ranch owners and possibly by Venezuela (because of a long-standing border dispute) were driven out; some were killed and captured.

1969, August 19–September 10. Border Clash with Surinam. This resulted from Dutch occupation of territory in a disputed border region. It ended when the Dutch withdrew.

Paraguay

1947, March 30–August 20. Civil War. Efforts by former President **Rafael Franco** to seize control were defeated by the government of President General **Higinio Morínigo.**

1948–1949. Chaos. After the retirement of Morínigo the nation had 5 presidents in 5 months.

1954, May 5. Army Revolt. President **Frederico Chaves** was deposed. General **Alfredo Stroessner,** commander of the armed forces, later was installed as president (August 15).

1959–1960. Rebel Invasions. About 1,000 rebels, based in Argentina, invaded and were crushed (December, 1959). President Stroessner blamed the action on Cuba. Six smaller invasions were also crushed (1960).

1963–1974. Stability under Relaxed Dictatorial Control. President Stroessner, allowing limited opposition political activity, was thrice reelected president (1963, 1968, 1973).

Peru

1948, October 27–29. Military Revolt. The government of President **José Bustamante** was overthrown by a military junta under General **Manuel Odría.**

1951–1955. Disputes with Ecuador. (See above.)

1956, February 16–25. Revolt at Iquilas. The military uprising collapsed when all army units failed to join.

1962, July 18. Military Coup d'État. President **Manuel Prado Ugarteche** was overthrown. A military junta took over, under the leadership of General **Ricardo Perez Godoy.**

1963, March 3. Coup d'État. Chief of State Perez was ousted by the junta following 2 months of internal violence. He was succeeded as chief of state by General **Nicholas Lindley Lopez.**

1964–1965. Communist Revolt. A very minor state of revolt was maintained by Castroite Communist agents in remote Andes regions.

1968, October 3. Coup d'État. The government of President **Fernando Belaunde Terry** was ousted without bloodshed; Army Chief of Staff General **Juan Velasco Alvarado** proclaimed himself president.

Uruguay

1961, January 11–12. Riots and Street Fighting. The government blamed these on Cuban and Soviet agitation.

1967–1973. Era of the Tupamaros. This leftist guerrilla organization, including members of many prominent families and a large number of professionals, terrorized the nation with large-scale robberies and kidnappings their specialty. Victims included U.S. police advisor Dan A. Mitrione, kidnapped, then killed (1970, August 10), and British Ambassador Geoffrey Jackson, kidnapped and held for 8 months (1971, January 8–September 9).

1973, February 10. Military Control Granted by President. Under great pressure from rebellious military leaders, President **Juan Maria Bordaberry** ceded practically all governmental authority to military commanders, to permit them to marshal the resources of the nation against the Tupamaro guerrillas.

1973, February–December. Elimination of the Tupamaros. The Army conducted a wholesale campaign, arresting and imprisoning hundreds of members. Some fled to Argentina, where they led an antigovernment group.

Venezuela

1945, October 18. Military Revolt.

1948, November 24. Bloodless Coup d'État. Colonel **Carlos Delgado Chalbaud** seized control. He was later assassinated (November 13, 1950) and replaced by **Germán Suárez Flámerich.**

1951, October 13. Revolt Suppressed.

1952, December 2. Coup d'État. Colonel **Marcos Perez Jimenez,** a member of the junta, seized power "by decision of the armed forces," nullifying the results of a national election 3 days earlier.

1958, January 1–23. Revolt. President **Marcos Pérez Jiménez** suppressed the first revolutionary actions, but was ousted by a military junta in a renewed revolt (January 21–23).

1958, July 23. Counter-revolt Suppressed.

1958, September 7. Unsuccessful Coup Attempt.

1960–1974. Communist Insurgency. Continuous small-scale harassment of the central government through the period.

1961, June 26. Military Uprising Suppressed.

1962, May 4–5, June 4. Military Uprisings Suppressed. President **Romulo Betancourt** became more firmly seated in control.

1963, November. Castro Plot Discovered. Cuban agents and large quantities of arms were captured by government troops.

AUSTRALASIA

Australia

1950–1953. The Korean War. (See p. 1240.) Australia contributed two infantry battalions, one air fighter squadron, one air transport squadron, one aircraft carrier, two destroyers, and a frigate to the United Nations forces.

1965–1972. The Vietnam War (See p. 1209). As a member of SEATO, Australia contributed forces ranging from a battalion to a brigade group and supporting elements (about 7,500 troops) to the allied forces supporting the government of South Vietnam.

1965, June 3. First Australians Arrive in Vietnam. A contingent of more than 100 infantrymen arrived, soon followed by 400 more (June 8).

1966, March 8. Conscription Adopted. This was the first peacetime draft in Australia's history, provoking antigovernment demonstrations. The purpose was to send draftees to an augmented Australian contingent in Vietnam.

1971, November 1. ANZUK Force Established at Singapore. (See p. 1303.)

1972, December 5. End of Conscription. The newly elected government of Prime Minister **Gough Whitlam** carried out its electoral campaign promises of ending the peacetime draft and withdrawing from Vietnam.

1972, December 18. Last Unit Withdraws from Vietnam.

1973, January 21–22. Australia and New Zealand Reaffirm Ties with SEATO and the United States. Announcements were made by Prime Ministers Gough Whitlam and **Norman Kirk** at a meeting in Wellington, N.Z.

NEW ZEALAND

1950–1953. The Korean War. (See p. 1240). New Zealand contributed an artillery group and 2 frigates to the United Nations forces.

1965–1972. The Vietnam War. As a member of SEATO, New Zealand contributed an artillery battery (later increased to a battalion of 550 men) to the allied forces supporting the government of South Vietnam. (See p. 1209.)

1971, November 1. ANZUK Force Established at Singapore. (See p. 1303.)

1973, January 21–22. New Zealand and Australia Reaffirm Ties with SEATO and the United States. (See p. 1345.)

1973, July 21–29. New Zealand Warship Enters French Nuclear Test Zone. As a protest against French nuclear tests near Tahiti (see p. 1262), a New Zealand frigate cruised just outside the 12-mile limit of the territorial waters of Mururoa Atoll, where the French were conducting their tests.

ADDENDUM

THE 1982 WAR IN LEBANON*

1982, June 6. Operation "Peace for Galilee." At 11 A.M., 3 division-size Israeli task forces crossed the border into Lebanon. Their immediate objective was to entrap and destroy PLO forces in southern Lebanon. On the left, Task Force A, with support from a small amphibious force that landed north of Tyre, moved rapidly along the narrow coastal plain bypassing or smashing PLO strongpoints. By nightfall they had surrounded Tyre. In the center, Task Force C captured key Litani River bridgeheads, took Beaufort Castle, secured the Arnoun Heights, and encircled Nabatiye. On the right Task Force H advanced up the Bekaa Valley toward Hasbaiya to secure the eastern flank of Task Force C. Although Task Force H at first experienced no serious resistance, upon entering the Hasbaiya area the Israelis came under fire from Syrian artillery. A fourth task force, Task Force B, composed of naval commandos, paratroops, armor, and artillery, made a surprise amphibious landing north of Sidon at the mouth of the Awali River at 11 P.M. They overran several PLO units and isolated PLO forces in Sidon.

1982, June 7. Second Day, Western Sector. While elements of Task Force A moved into Tyre and eliminated PLO resistance south of the Litani River, others approached Sidon from the south. Reserves mopped up areas that had been bypassed. Near Tyre, Task Force A units surrounded and attacked the PLO base at the Rashidiye refugee camp. Meanwhile, Task Force B broke into 3 battle groups. One moved north within 7 kilometers of Damour, south of Beirut; another enlarged the beachhead to the east, forcing the PLO defenders to retreat into the mountains; the third blocked Sidon from the north. Elements of Task Force C took Nabatiye and cleared the Arnoun-Nabatiye plateau of pockets of resistance while other elements pushed northwest toward Sidon to link up with detachments of Task Force A and B to encircle Sidon. Task Force D now entered Lebanon in Task Force C's sector, and by evening approached the Bessri Bridge north of Jezzine to cut off the coastal plain area from the Bekaa Valley. This task force received fire from Syrian artillery as forward elements approached the Bessri River. Although careful to avoid battle with the Syrians, the Israelis returned fire to silence the Syrian artillery.

1982, June 7. Second Day in the Bekaa Valley. Task Force H did not advance, but exchanged fire with PLO and Syrian elements. During the day Task Force H was joined by task forces V and Z to form the Bekaa Forces Group (BFG), about two divisions in strength, commanded by Maj. Gen. **Avigdor Ben Gal.** The mission of BFG was to gain control of the Bekaa Valley and the flanking mountains: the western slopes of the Anti-Lebanon Mountains and Mount Hermon on the east, and the Lebanon Mountains on the west. The BFG would then cut the Beirut-Damascus highway.

1982, June 8. Third Day, Western Sector. Task Force A carried out mop-up operations in Tyre and the Rashidiye refugee camp, and captured Sidon. The Israelis were careful to avoid casualties to Lebanese or Palestinian civilians. Task Force B (reinforced by a battle group

* See map, p. 1366.

from Task Force A) and elements of Task Force C continued to advance slowly on Damour. Opposition was light. Meanwhile Task Force D reached the Bessri River Bridge where it met and defeated the Syrian 85th Brigade. Toward evening the task force reached Beit el Dine and Ain Zhalta about ten miles south of the Beirut-Damascus highway.

1982, June 8. Third Day in the Bekaa Valley. Task Force Z attacked the Syrian right flank which, with PLO units, held Jezzine. The combined infantry and armor attack crushed the Syrian defenders, destroying 32 tanks and inflicting heavy casualties. To the east Task Force H captured the village of Mimes and by evening was about 15 kilometers from the main Syrian defense zone in the Rashaiya area.

1982, June 9. Fourth Day on the Coast. Elements of Task Force B attacked Damour which, despite fierce PLO resistance, was taken by evening. Task Force C and elements of Task Force A and remaining units of Task Force B bypassed Damour and drove north reaching the southern suburbs of Beirut by nightfall.

1982, June 9. Fourth Day; Israeli Air Victory. The Israeli Air Force attacked Syrian SAM missile batteries in the Bekaa Valley destroying 17 out of 19 in a 3-hour battle without loss of a single plane. Twenty-nine Syrian MiGs were shot down.

1982, June 9. Fourth Day in the Bekaa Valley. Task Force H advanced up the Valley and through the Anti-Lebanon Mountains to envelop the Syrian–PLO left flank. Resistance was substantial, but progress was rapid. Task Force Z advanced north from Jezzine toward the Syrian Kara defense zone. Task Force V was committed to combat in the center of the Bekaa Valley and by evening reached the village of Dneibe.

1982, June 10. Fifth Day on the Coast. Task Force A continued to mop up in southern Lebanon, including Sidon and the El Hilweh refugee camp where there was considerable resistance, but proceeded slowly to avoid civilian casualties. Task Force B advanced toward the mountain town of Kfar Matta while Task Force C, reinforced by elements of Task Force A, reached the outskirts of Khalde about 3 miles from the Beirut international airport. Task Force D mopped up in Ain Zhalta, approached Ain Dara and came to within 2 miles of the Beirut-Damascus highway.

1982, June 10. Fifth Day in the Bekaa Valley. The Israelis approached the Syrian main defense area in 3 task forces on a broad front. In the center Task Force H drove up the Valley and cleared out PLO and Syrian units deployed between the Litani River on the west and the Hasbani River to the east. To the west Task Force Z advanced as far as Zalia, within 10 miles of the Beirut-Damascus highway. On the east, in very mountainous terrain, Task Force V also advanced well into the main Syrian defense zone, south of the Beirut-Damascus road. In the air the Israeli Air Force knocked out 2 more SAM batteries.

1982, June 11. Sixth Day; Israelis Close on Beirut and the Beirut-Damascus Highway. Khalde, on the outskirts of Beirut, fell to Task Force C and Israeli troops took up positions on hills overlooking the Beirut Airport. Task Force D approached the Beirut-Damascus highway, which it could control with fire from the dominating hills. To the east in the Bekaa Valley, the Israelis probed the new Syrian defense line just below the Beirut-Damascus highway.

1982, June 11. Sixth Day; Cease-Fire. The fierce fighting of the two previous days had cost the Syrians heavy losses in both men and armor. Both they and the Israelis agreed to a cease-fire as of noon. However fighting with the PLO continued.

COMMENT: *In six days of fighting, the Israelis had destroyed the military forces of the PLO in Lebanon and captured enormous quantities of equipment. They had also decisively defeated the Syrians and had artillery in position within range of Damascus.*

1982, June 12–15. Mop-Up; Resistance at El Hilweh Refugee Camp. The Israelis continued to battle remnants of the PLO in the Sidon area, particularly at the El Hilweh refugee camp. The PLO held thousands of Palestinians hostage in their stronghold, hoping at least for a propaganda victory. The Israelis surrounded the camp and advanced slowly, minimizing casualties to civilians and to their own troops. They gradually squeezed the PLO fighters into the center of the camp and finally overwhelmed the survivors (June 15).

1982, June 12–13, Battle of Ain Aanoub. The Israelis, attempting to link up with Christian Lebanese Phalangist forces near Beirut, battled PLO units and Syrian commandos deployed with the PLO. The Syrians and Palestinians were forced to retreat. They lost many tanks and APCs and suffered heavy casualties. The Israelis then linked up with the Phalangists. PLO and Syrian troops in Beirut were cut off from the Syrian forces to the east.

1982, June 14. Israelis Reach Beirut. Advancing to the eastern and southeastern suburbs of Beirut, the Israelis closed on the Syrian and PLO forces trapped in Beirut. They also took control of the southern part of the international airport. The Israelis subsequently deployed along the "green line," separating Christian eastern Beirut from the Moslem western sector of the city (June 18). The Israelis had effectively invested Beirut.

1982, June 22–26. Final Israeli Offensive. The Israelis launched a combined arms offensive toward the Beirut-Damascus highway just east of Beirut. Combat raged for four days. By June 25, the Syrians were driven from the outskirts of Beirut. The Israelis controlled the Beirut-Damascus highway from east Beirut to Sofar, 10 miles to the east of the city, and most of the ridges north and south of the highway. Only the Dahr el Baider Ridge separated the Israeli forces in the western sector from the Syrians in the northern Bekaa Valley.

1982, June 26. New Cease Fire. With a new cease-fire in effect major offensive combat operations were complete; however, the Israelis continued to besiege Beirut in order to assure the withdrawal of the PLO and Syrians from the city.

1982, June 26–September 3. Siege of Beirut. Having trapped the PLO and Syrians in west and southwest Beirut, the Israelis determined to coerce the PLO to leave on terms favorable to Israel rather than assault the city. Wishing to minimize civilian casualties the IDF had pilots drop leaflets warning civilians to leave the city along the coastal road controlled by Christian militamen or by the Israeli-controlled Beirut-Damascus highway (June 27). The Israelis then began aerial, naval, and artillery bombardment of the Moslem sectors of the city. The Israelis demanded the PLO surrender their arms and leave Lebanon. While the Israelis were conducting their siege operations, U.S. Special Envoy **Philip Habib,** with the aid of King **Fahd** of Saudi Arabia, conducted multilateral negotiations between the Israelis, the PLO, the government of Lebanon, and the Syrians. The Israelis tightened the noose around West Beirut, by turning off essential utilities and prohibiting food and medical supplies from being sent into the besieged sectors of the city (July 3). They later eased these restrictions (July 7). Habib won PLO approval of a withdrawal plan (August 6). The Israeli Cabinet agreed to the Habib plan (August 19) and the PLO and Syrians began withdrawing 2 days later (see below). The Israelis lifted the siege as the last PLO fighters departed the city (September 3).

1982, August 21–28. Deployment of Multinational Peacekeeping Force. With the agreement of the governments of Israel, Syria, and Lebanon, a multinational peacekeeping force with independent contingents of about 1,200 men each from the United States (U.S. Marines), France, and Italy was deployed in Beirut to ensure safe withdrawal of the PLO and Syrian forces besieged in Beirut by Israeli forces.

1982, September 16–18. Massacre at Sabra and Shatilla Refugee Camps. Phalangist militiamen slaughtered at least 400 men, women, and children while con-

THE 1982 WAR IN LEBANON (JUNE 6–SEPTEMBER 3): STRENGTHS AND LOSSES

	Strengths	Killed	Wounded	Missing or Prisoners	Tanks Lost	Aircraft Lost
Israeli Armed Forces	65,000	305	1,230	2	40	2
Palestine Liberation Organization	18,000	1,100	2,350	5,100	20	–
Syrian Armed Forces	45,000	1,350	4,800	220	420	92
Total Syrian & PLO Forces	63,000	2,450	7,150	5,320	440	92

ducting an operation in search of PLO fighters. Israeli troops in the vicinity had permitted the Phalangists to enter the camp to search for PLO soldiers, and apparently did nothing to prevent these massacres.

1982, September 28. Kahan Commission of Inquiry Established. The Israeli government announced that **Yitzhak Kahan,** president of the Supreme Court, would head a commission which would conduct an official inquiry to determine whether or not the IDF or the government of Prime Minister **Menachem Begin** could be held responsible for the massacre of Palestinian refugees at the Sabra and Shatilla camps. The inquiry began several weeks later (October 16) and was completed 3 months later (January 16).

1983, February 8. Israeli Report on Massacre. An official Israeli government inquiry conducted by the Kahan Commission into the Sabra and Shatilla camp massacres concluded that Phalangist militiamen bore all direct responsibility for the massacres. However, Israeli officials were charged with indirect responsibility for failure to heed information that Lebanese Christian Phalangists were likely to seek revenge on Palestinians for the assassination of Lebanon's President-elect **Bashir Gemayel** (see p. 1365). Israeli Prime Minister Menachem Begin and Defense Minister Ariel Sharon were held to be indirectly responsible for the massacres, as were IDF Chief of Staff Lt. Gen. **Rafael Eytan,** Director of Military Intelligence Maj. Gen. **Yehoshua Saguy** and Brig. Gen. **Amos Yaron,** commander of the Israeli division deployed in Beirut.

1983, November 24. Israeli-PLO Prisoner Exchange. The Israelis and PLO agreed to exchange 4,500 PLO prisoners of war held by the Israelis for 6 Israelis held by the PLO since their capture more than a year before.

INTERNATIONAL PEACEKEEPING

THE UNITED NATIONS

1975–1984. United Nations Force in Cyprus (UNIFCYP). The U.N. Security Council maintained a peacekeeping force in Cyprus.

1975–1984. United Nations Emergency Force (UNEF) in Sinai. The U.N. Security Council continued to extend the mission of the UNEF in the Sinai until faced with the prospect of a Soviet veto. The Security Council voted (1979, July 24) to eliminate this force, and to rely solely upon observers from the United Nations Truce Supervision Organization (UNTSO). (See pp. 1239.)

1975–1984. Golan Heights U.N. Disengagement Observer Force (UNDOF). The U.N. Security Council continued to deploy a peacekeeping force in the Golan Heights. (See p. 1240.)

1978, March 19. U.N. Peacekeeping in Lebanon. The U.N. Security Council passed a resolution (March 19) calling for Israeli troop withdrawal from southern Lebanon and their replacement with a United Nations Interim Force in Lebanon (UNIFIL). The UNIFIL troops began to replace the Israelis soon after the passage of the resolution (April) and have remained in Lebanon to date (1984). (See p. 1362.)

INTERNATIONAL PEACEKEEPING

1975, July 30–August 2. Helsinki Security Conference. Representatives of 35 countries met in the Finnish capital to discuss security arrangements for Europe, including the sanctity of national borders, the free passage of citizens across national borders, exchange of information on military maneuvers, and human rights. The Helsinki Accord accepted by the conference was a political triumph for the Soviet Union. Although not a binding agreement, the Accord in effect ratified the existing boundaries of Europe and legitimized Soviet dominance of Eastern Europe. However, the human rights section of the agreement, clearly not being observed in the U.S.S.R., has become a significant political embarrassment to the U.S.S.R.

1975, July 22. OAU Arbitration Effort in Angola. The Organization of African Unity sent appeals to the warring factions in Angola (see p. 1387) calling for a cease-fire and asking them to send representatives to Kampala—where the OAU was holding its 12th summit meeting. The appeal was unheeded. On the basis of a report by a special OAU commission (October 1–4) President **Idi Amin Dada** of Uganda, OAU chairman, recommended that an OAU peacekeeping force be sent to Angola (November 15). The Popular Movement for the Liberation of Angola (MPLA), the *de facto* government and one of the factions, cited the presence of South African troops in Angola as a basis for rejecting the OAU peacekeeping effort (December 18). Because of deadlock in an emergency meeting (1976, January 10–13) no OAU actions were taken.

1977, August 5–9. OAU Attempts to Achieve Peace in Ogaden. The OAU's Border Mediation Committee called on Ethiopia and the Somalia-backed Ogaden rebels to stop fighting. There was no response to this by the participants, or to a later mediation effort (1978, February 9).

1979, March 2. Arab League Mediation of Yemen Conflict. The Arab League accepted a role as a mediator in the border conflicts of Yemen and South Yemen (see pp. 1371).

1981, December 17–1982, June 30. OAU Peacekeeping Force in Chad. (See p, 1386.)

1982, August 26. OAU Offers Cease-Fire Plan in Moroccan-Sahara War. The OAU proposed a cease-fire plan which called for a bilateral withdrawal of belligerents and a referendum to decide the future of the Western Sahara. There was no response. (See p. 1391.)

1982, October 4. Proposal for Central America Peace Forum. The United States and six other American nations (Costa Rica, Belize, El Salvador, Honduras, Jamaica, and Colombia) agreed to a peace plan calling for (1) a "verifiable and reciprocal" regional treaty, banning arms supplies to warring factions, subversion of national governments, and foreign military advisers in any nation in the region; and (2) development of a "Peace Forum" in which regional states would work to assure democratic elections. The immediate objective of the plan was to end fighting between Honduras and Nicaragua and end internal hostilities in El Salvador and Nicaragua. It was rejected by Nicaragua because of the role of the U.S. in its formulation (November 3). (See p. 1397.)

1983, January 7–9. Contadora Group Peace Initiatives. In an effort to bring peace to Central America, the foreign ministers of four Latin American nations (Mexico, Panama, Venezuela, and Colombia) met on the Panamanian island of Contadora. There were no results from this or subsequent meetings (April 10–12 and July 17).

DISARMAMENT ACTIVITIES

1975–1984. The Geneva Conference on Disarmament. The Conference on Disarmament (founded in 1962 as the 18-Nation Disarmament Committee) continued to meet annually; China became the fortieth nation to join (1980). The Conference was attempting to negotiate a comprehensive ban on nuclear testing and on production and use of chemical weapons in warfare, and was negotiating a ban on development or production of radiological fissionable materials. Soviet Union and United States each prepared versions of a treaty for ban on chemical weapons (1984).

1975, March 26. Biological Weapons Ban Takes Effect. The 1972 Convention banning the production and stockpiling of biological and toxin weapons went into effect. There were subsequently charges that the Soviet Union and its ally Vietnam had violated this treaty and the earlier (1925) Geneva Protocol (see pp. 1359 and 1379).

1979, June 18. SALT II Agreement Signed. U.S. President **Jimmy Carter** and Soviet President **Leonid Brezhnev,** in Vienna, Austria, signed a treaty designed to fill certain loopholes not covered by SALT I: to provide additional verification of compliance; to prohibit the deployment of mobile ICBMs or ALCMs (air-launched cruise missiles); and to prohibit flight testing of mobile ICBMs. The new treaty set limits on the numbers of warheads and on the numbers of launchers. Limits on new systems were also set by allowing only one new type of sea-based ICBM and one new type of land-based ICBM. Also the treaty prohibited the controversial Soviet "Backfire" bomber from increasing its radius of action, so it could not threaten the U.S. without refueling. American critics of the treaty charged that even with the limitations on warheads, the Soviets would have a sufficient number—when combined with their existing advantage in "throw weight" (explosive power) and improved accuracy—to threaten U.S.

landbased missiles in the early 1980s. The critics also charged that the treaty was not verifiable, and that it would place the U.S. in a position of strategic inferiority without achieving strategic stability. Because of these criticisms the U.S. Senate refused to ratify the treaty. However, President Carter pledged to abide by its terms as long as the Soviets did likewise.

1979, December 12. NATO Proposes MNF Negotiations. The foreign and defense ministers of the member states of NATO agreed to deploy United States medium-range nuclear missiles to replace 1,000 obsolete U.S. tactical missiles which would be removed (see p. 1352). They also agreed that negotiations between the United States and the Soviet Union on the reduction of medium-range nuclear forces (MNF) should begin at the earliest possible date.

1981, September 30. Proposal for Nuclear Weapons "Freeze." Scientists from 40 countries at the 31st "Pugwash" meeting agreed that nuclear weapons should be frozen at current levels. This idea was picked up and became the basis for nuclear weapons "freeze" movements in many countries. Legislation was introduced into both houses of the U.S. Congress (1982, May 4 and October 31).

1981, November 30. Medium-Range Nuclear Force Talks Begin. U.S. and Soviet negotiating teams met in Geneva to discuss reductions of medium-range nuclear forces (MNF) in Europe. The principal issue was the reduction or elimination of Soviet SS-20 missiles in the western U.S.S.R., and of U.S. Pershing II missiles and cruise missiles which NATO planned to deploy in Western Europe. **Paul Nitze** was the chief U.S. negotiator; his Soviet counterpart was **Yuli A. Kvitsinsky.** In a so-called "zero based option," the U.S. offered not to deploy its planned missiles if the U.S.S.R. destroyed all of its SS-20s. One reason for Soviet rejection was that this would allow the U.K. and France to retain in their strategic deterrent forces some 167 missiles capable of reaching the U.S.S.R.

1982, March 16. Brezhnev Announces Freeze on SS-20 Deployment. Soviet leader Leonid Brezhnev announced that the Soviet Union was freezing MRBM forces at present levels and that some missiles would be dismantled. At that time the U.S.S.R. had about 280 SS-20 missiles deployed in the western U.S.S.R. The missiles to be dismantled were presumably older SS-4 and SS-5 missiles.

1982, May 31. START Talks Set to Begin; U.S. Adheres to SALT Treaties. The Soviet Union and the United States announced that the two superpowers had agreed to begin Strategic Arms Reduction Treaty (START) negotiations. U.S. President **Ronald Reagan** also asserted that the U.S. would continue to abide by the existing strategic arms treaties (SALT I and II) as long as the Soviet Union continued to honor those treaties.

1982, June 29. START Negotiations Begin. The chief of the U.S. negotiating team was retired Lt. Gen. **Edward Rowny.** The Soviet team was headed by **Victor Karpov.**

1982, December 21. Andropov's MNF Proposal. New Soviet leader **Yuri Andropov** proposed to reduce the Soviet SS-20 force from 280 to 162 missiles, establishing parity with the missiles of the U.K. and France, in return for a U.S. commitment not to deploy the Pershings or cruise missiles in Europe. The U.S. refused to consider British and French missiles in bilateral talks, particularly since these were national deterrent strategic missiles, and not part of NATO's forces. The U.K. and France announced their refusal to have their missiles considered in bilateral talks. However, British Prime Minister **Margaret Thatcher** (January 18) and Germany's Premier **Helmut Kohl** (March 12) suggested that the U.S. retreat somewhat from its negotiating position (zero-based option) and make a counterproposal to break the impasse.

1983, March 29–30. U.S. and NATO's Interim MRBM Solution. In response to the urging of NATO allies, President Reagan offered an alternative to the U.S. zero-based option plan on the reduction of medium-range ballistic missiles: he called for equality in warheads between the two superpowers. Reagan pointed out that the Andropov plan (see above), with 162 SS-20 missiles, would still leave the U.S.S.R. with 486 warheads because each SS-20 carried three warheads. The Soviet negotiating team subsequently rejected the Interim Solution (June 24).

1983, November 23. Soviet Walkout from MNF Talks. In protest of the NATO deployment of the first medium-range missiles in West Germany and England (see below) the Soviet negotiators withdrew from the negotiations in Geneva. Also the Soviet negotiators at both the START (Strategic Arms Reduction Treaty) and the MBFR (Mutual Balanced Force Reductions) negotiations used the deployment as a reason for halting negotiations.

1984, January 23. United States Alleges Soviet SALT and Geneva Violations. President Reagan presented to the U.S. Congress charges of Soviet violations: of the Interim SALT Agreement and the unratified SALT II Treaty. He also charged violations of the 1925 Geneva Protocol and 1972 Geneva Convention by production and stockpiling of biological weapons. The U.S.S.R. promptly countered with its own list of U.S. violations.

WESTERN EUROPE

WESTERN EUROPEAN DEFENSE ARRANGEMENTS: NATO, 1975–1983

1977, June 9. Soviet SS-20 Missile Deployment Reported to NATO. NATO Secretary General **Joseph Luns** reported that NATO intelligence had determined that the Soviet Union had deployed SS-20 MRBMs in the western regions of the Soviet Union. The SS-20 had three warheads and a 5,000-kilometer range. The NATO countries of Western Europe were all within the range of the SS-20.

1979, December 11–12. NATO Decides to Deploy MRBMs. Meeting in Brussels the NATO foreign ministers agreed to deploy 108 Pershing II IRBMs and 464 land-based cruise missiles in Western Europe to counter the Soviet deployment of SS-20 MRBMs. At the same time it was agreed that the U.S. would pursue negotiations with the Soviets on the reduction of medium-range nuclear missiles in Europe. This "two track" approach became the basis for subsequent NATO and U.S. negotiating positions regarding the reduction of medium-range nuclear forces in Europe (see p. 1351).

1975–1983. Mutual Balanced Force Reduction (MBFR) Talks. The NATO countries and the Warsaw Pact countries continued MBFR negotiations but no real progress was made in reaching agreement on the reduction of the size of the conventional forces that each alliance has deployed in Europe. The major problem was the inability of the participants to agree on the strength of ground forces deployed by the Warsaw Pact. NATO estimates of Warsaw Pact troop strength were consistently higher than that acknowledged by the Warsaw Pact.

1981–1983. Western European Disarmament Movement. There were numerous large-scale disarmament protests in England, the Netherlands, and West Germany against the impending installation of Pershing II and cruise missiles in Western Europe.

1983, November 22–28. NATO Begins Deploying MRBMs. The first Pershing IIs and land-based cruise missiles were deployed in NATO member countries England and the Federal Republic of Germany.

UNITED KINGDOM

1975–1984. Continuing Civil War in Northern Ireland. Despite the deployment of substantial British Army forces in the area, violence, bloodshed, and property destruction plagued Northern Ireland, spilling over into the Irish Republic and Great Britain. The hatred and intransigence of both radical Protestants and the outlawed Irish Republican Army (IRA) prevented any compromise. Authorities of the U.K. and the Irish Republic agreed to punish political terrorists on either side of the border between Northern Ireland and the Republic of Ireland. Most notable incidents were the assassinations of the British ambassador to Ireland and his secretary (July 21, 1976) and of Lord Mountbatten of Burma (August 27, 1979).

1975, November 17. "Cod War" with Iceland. Following expiration of a 2-year interim fishing agreement between the United Kingdom and Iceland, harassment of British fishermen was begun by Icelandic Coast Guard vessels within Iceland's declared 200-mile territorial limit. Three British frigates were dispatched to Icelandic waters (November 24). Iceland closed its ports and airports to British traffic. Following mediation by NATO Secretary General Joseph Luns, the British frigates withdrew (1976, January 19). Continued clashes led the British to send two frigates back into the fishing area (February 5). Diplomatic relations were severed (February 19). However, negotiations continued. As a result of agreement on British fishing rights, the British warships withdrew (May 30). The agreement was signed (June 1) and diplomatic relations were restored (1976, June 3).

1982, January. Dispute with Argentina on Falklands Issue. *La Prensa,* a major Buenos Aires newspaper, reported that Argentine General **Leopoldo Galtieri,** President and leader of the ruling junta, had pledged to return the Falkland Islands—called the Malvinas by the Argentinians—to Argentine control by January 1, 1983. The history of the Falkland/Malvinas dispute between Argentina and Britain can be summarized as follows: In 1829 the first Argentinian settlers arrived at the Falklands but found British settlers already on the islands. Clashes between British and Argentinian settlers led to the establishment of a British administration over the islands in 1833. Argentinian settlers were expelled. Although Argentina did not attempt to establish any more settlements, it never relinquished its claim. More recently (July 1, 1971) the two countries agreed to settle their dispute by negotiations (see p. 1341). These efforts were unsuccessful (see Argentina, p. 1398).

1982, March 19. South Georgia Incident. A crew of Argentinian workers landed at Leith in South Georgia (part of the Falklands colony) to salvage scrap metal from 3 abandoned whaling stations. Britain sent a diplomatic protest alleging that the crew had illegally entered British territory. Argentina sent 5 warships to the area and issued a communiqué asserting that Argentinian workers did not need permission from the British to be on native soil. The British Foreign Minister informed Parliament that a potentially dangerous situation prevailed in the Falklands (March 30).

Britain–Argentina Falkland Islands War

1982, April 2. Argentina Invades the Falklands. A 2,000-man task force landed at Port Stanley. The 84-man Royal Marine garrison surrendered after a 3-hour fight.

1982, April 3. Argentinians Seize South Georgia. A small task force landed at Grytviken, South Georgia, and took control of the island after a 7-hour battle with a 22-man detachment of Royal Marines.

1982, April 3. U.N. Declares Argentina Aggressor. The British took the case to the U.N. Security Council, which voted to declare Argentina an aggressor and demanded immediate withdrawal (Resolution 502). Argentina rejected the resolution, but offered to negotiate with Britain. The British refused to negotiate until Argentina withdrew from the Falklands.

1982, April 5. Falkland Task Force Leaves Britain. Two light aircraft carriers (HMS *Hermes* and HMS *Invincible*) and 28 other vessels sailed from Portsmouth for the Falklands. The naval task force included an amphibious task force of 2,000 Royal Marine commandos. The commander of the Falkland Islands Task Force, Rear Admiral **Sir John Woodward,** sailed from Gibraltar with seven warships and Royal Fleet Auxiliary (RFA) support vessels for Ascension Island where they joined the ships sailing from Britain. Approximately 2,000 additional troops sailed from Southhampton soon after on the passenger cruise ship *Canberra,* refitted to be used as a troop and supply ship (April 9.) By this time the RAF had deployed Hercules and VC-10 Air Transport aircraft at Ascension Island, 3,750 miles northeast of the Falklands. Ascension became a vital supply base for the Falklands Task Force, which would receive tons of stores from Ascension transported by the RAF transport aircraft and by ships of the Royal Fleet Auxiliary (RFA) and Merchant Navy. Ascension also served as a base for RAF bombers and reconnaissance aircraft.

1982, April 8–28. U.S. Attempts Diplomatic Solution. Secretary of State **Alexander Haig** carried on shuttle diplomacy by flying back and forth between Buenos Aires and London in an attempt to reach a peaceful solution to the crisis. Both sides refused to budge from their positions. The U.S. then announced support for Britain (April 30).

1982, April 12. Britain Announces Falklands Quarantine. Britain announced that as of April 28 any Argentine vessel

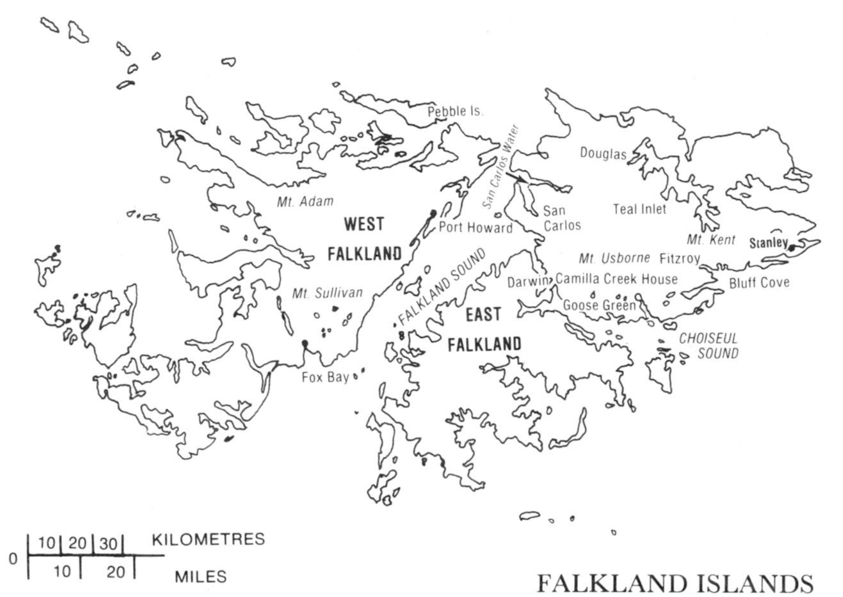

FALKLAND ISLANDS

within 200 miles of the Falklands would be considered an aggressor and be treated accordingly.

1982, April 18. British Reconnaissance Units Land. Special Boat Service (SBS) troops (Royal Marines) and Special Air Service (SAS) troops (Army) began secret landings on the Falklands to carry out intelligence operations which later proved invaluable to the invasion force.

1982, April 25–26. British Recapture South Georgia. British helicopter machine-gun and rocket fire forced an Argentine submarine to run aground at Grytviken Harbor. The next morning a contingent of Royal Marines overcame the Argentine detachment at Grytviken and SAS troops easily recaptured Leith, taking 156 Argentines captive. This concluded operations in South Georgia. The recapture of South Georgia was not only a psychologically important victory, but was of strategic value as well, giving British ships a staging area.

1982, April 28. British Blockade Goes into Effect.

1982, May 1–3. British Air and Naval Successes. A British Vulcan bomber from Ascension Island, and Harrier jump jets from the task force's light carriers, pounded Port Stanley's airfield (May 1). The field was effectively closed. (There were four additional Vulcan bombing attacks in the course of the campaign.) Harriers also bombed a smaller airfield at Goose Green while Sea King helicopters strafed Argentine positions at Darwin. That same day a British Harrier shot down an Argentine Mirage with a Sidewinder air-to-air missile. Naval combat intensified when Britain's nuclear-powered submarine HMS *Conqueror* hit the World War II vintage cruiser *General Belgrano* with two wire-guided torpedos (May 2). The *General Belgrano* sank in less than an hour; 368 men were lost.

1982, May 4. Argentine Reprisal. An Argentinian Super Etendard fighter-bomber fired an Exocet air-to-sea missile, hitting HMS *Sheffield* 30 miles away. Although the *Sheffield* did not sink, the damage was too extensive to warrant salvaging, and she was scuttled.

1982, May 12. *Queen Elizabeth 2* Sails for Falklands. Refitted for service as a troop transport, the liner left for the Falklands carrying the 5th British Army Brigade, composed of Welsh Guards, Scots Guards, and the 7th Gurkhas.

1982, May 14–15. Pebble Island Raid. In a daring night raid, SAS troops with destroyer naval gunfire support severely damaged the Argentine base at Pebble Island, destroying 11 aircraft, the base radio station, and fuel and ammunition dumps.

1982, May 21. San Carlos Beachhead Established. The 3rd Marine Commando Brigade, reinforced with 2 battalions from the Army's Parachute Regiment, established a beachhead at San Carlos on the west coast of East Falkland. British Harriers downed 15 Argentine planes, while losing one Harrier. However, 3 British ships were hit by Argentine planes and one, the HMS *Ardent,* was lost. By the end of the day 3,000 British troops were ashore.

1982, May 23–25. Argentine Air Attacks and British Buildup. Argentine aircraft continued to mount strong attacks against British ships. The British lost one ship on May 23 and two on May 25. Nonetheless, the British continued their buildup and by May 24 they had 5,000 men and 5,000 tons of ordnance and supplies ashore. British Harriers and surface-to-air missiles fired from ships and by troops ashore shot down 36 Argentinian planes.

1982, May 26–27. Advance on Port Darwin. The British plan was to strike at Port Stanley as quickly as possible. But first it was determined to secure the southern flank and lines of communication by eliminating Argentine positions at Goose Green and Darwin approximately 20 miles southeast of the San Carlos beachhead. The 2nd Battalion of the Parachute Regiment moved south at night from San Carlos toward Darwin.

1982, May 28. British Take Darwin. At 0200, with supporting naval gunfire from British ships offshore, the attack on Darwin began. The 2nd Battalion also got air support from Harriers. The Argentines offered staunch resistance but were pushed out of their positions into the settlement. They surrendered the following afternoon and the paratroops pushed on to Goose Green (May 28).

1982, May 28–29. Goose Green Seized. The Argentines were well dug in and a bitter fight continued into the night. Early in the morning the last Argentinian position surrendered to the paratroops. The British loss was 17 killed, with 31 wounded. The Argentine loss was 250 killed and 121 wounded. The British took 1,000 prisoners.

COMMENT: *The British victories at Darwin and Goose Green secured the British southern flank, and lines of communication to the beachhead at San Carlos. They also gave the British ground forces a decided psychological advantage over the Argentinians.*

1982, May 27–June 1. Advance on Stanley. While the 2nd Battalion of the Parachute Regiment was advancing on Darwin (see above), the 3rd Marine Commando Brigade's 45th Royal Marine Commando and the Parachute Regiment's 3rd Battalion marched northeast from the San Carlos beachhead to Douglas and thence southeast to Teal Inlet, a 50-mile journey over rough terrain (May 27–30). Major General **Jeremy Moore** assumed direct control of the land operations from San Carlos. Meanwhile a small task force of SAS troops had been dropped by helicopter on Mount Kent, ten miles west of Stanley (May 28). They were joined by the 42nd Royal Marine Commando and a supporting light artillery unit (June 1–2).

1982, June 1. 5th Infantry Brigade Establishes Beachhead. The 5th Infantry Brigade (Scots Guards, Welsh Guards, and Gurkha Rifles) began landing at San Carlos. At the same time, the 2nd Battalion of the Parachute Regiment advanced from Goose Green to Fitzroy (18 miles southwest of Stanley), which had been abandoned by the Argentinians.

1982, June 6–8. Advance to Bluff Cove. Elements of the 5th Brigade moved forward to Goose Green and were then transported by sea to Bluff Cove northeast of Fitzroy to take up position for the attack on Port Stanley. Disembarkment operations were hindered by air attacks from Argentine Mirages. Two British troop transport ships were hit and abandoned with heavy losses (June 8). British Harriers downed four Mirages. British ships and planes began to soften up Argentinian positions at Port Stanley.

1982, June 11–12. British Take Heights Overlooking Stanley. The 3rd Royal Marine Commando Brigade launched a night attack on three key Argentine strong points: Mount Longdon, Two Sisters, and Mount Harriet. Despite surprise, resistance was substantial at Mount Longdon on the north flank and Two Sisters in the center. Mount Harriet, enveloped from the rear, fell quickly.

1982, June 13–14. Final Night Assault. The 2nd Parachute Battalion (victors at Darwin and Goose Green) made a surprise night attack on Wireless Ridge 3 miles east of Mount Longdon. To the south a battalion of Scots Guards took Tumbledown Mountain after a tough fight with Argentine Marines. Gurkhas then passed through the Scots Guards to take Mount William less than 4 miles west of Port Stanley. A planned third phase of the operation proved unnecessary as Argentinian resistance collapsed.

1982, June 14. Argentine Surrender. The Argentine military governor of the Falklands, General **Mario Benjamin Menendez,** surrendered to General Moore.

1982, June 14. Surrender of South Thule. An Argentine naval detachment that had maintained a research facility at South Thule since 1976 surrendered to a small task force of Royal Marine Commandos without a struggle.

COMMENT: *The British successfully carried out a very difficult operation on short notice over very long lines of communication (over 8,000 miles). The war was an excellent proving ground for modern high technology weaponry. However, the principal lesson was that wars are still won by well-trained, determined soldiers, sailors, and airmen.*

THE NETHERLANDS

1981, February 28. Dutch Parliament Approves the Deployment of MRBMs. The Dutch Parliament voted to permit deployment of U.S. medium-range cruise missiles and Pershing II missiles on Dutch soil as part of NATO's deterrent.

FRANCE

1975, March 4–December 15. French Military Personnel Unrest. Public protest marches by French military draftees led to a substantial pay increase. Later the French government established a new and relaxed code of discipline (July 16). However, unrest continued. Army units attempted to form unions (November 3 and 4 and December 9). Following an inquiry, ringleaders were arrested (December 15).

1975, April 13. French Intervention in Chad. **(See p. 1386.)**

1975–1977, French Activity in Afars and Issas. **(See p. 1384.)**

1976, February 4. French-Somali Troops Clash. **(See p. 1384.)**

1978, May 19. French Intervention in Zaire.

1978–1983. French Interventions in Chad. **(See p. 1386.)**

1980, June 26. French Announce Neutron Bomb Test. French President **Valéry Giscard d'Estaing** announced that France had tested enhanced radiation weapons (the so-called "neutron bomb") in the South Pacific. The decision on whether or not to deploy it would be deferred until a later date.

1982–1984. French Peacekeeping Contingent in Beirut. **(See pp. 1365–86).**

1982, October 7. Nuclear Force Modernization Plan Announced. French Defense Minister **Charles Hernu** said that France intended to give "absolute priority" to the development of improved nuclear capability and that conventional ground forces would be cut 10%. This plan subsequently drew fire from French military leaders. General **Jean Delaunay** (Army Chief of Staff) protested that Hernu's plan would reduce the French Army by more than 30,000 men and that reduced spending on conventional forces would result in equipment obsolescence. French Air Force officials also complained that the French Air Force would lose 3,000 badly needed combat aircraft. French Foreign Minister **Claude Cheysson** defended Hernu's plan, asserting that the basis of effective deterrence is nuclear forces. Hernu also answered the critics by saying that conventional capabilities would be increased through a "rapid action and assistance command" able to intervene quickly in any European conflict. He also pointed out that the plan contemplated construction of a nuclear-powered aircraft carrier, a nuclear-powered submarine, and three hunter-killer submarines.

1983, May 18. France Supports NATO MNF Deployment. French President **François Mitterand** and German Chancellor Helmut Kohl formally announced support for the scheduled deployment of Pershing and cruise missiles in Western Europe. Mitterand reaffirmed this position at a meeting of NATO's Atlantic Council (June 10), while also reaffirming retention of the French *force de frappe* (independent nuclear deterrence force).

1983, October 23. Suicide Attack on French Peacekeeping Force in Lebanon. (See p. 1366).

1983, November 8. French Catholic Bishops Support Concept of Deterrence. In a position differing from that of American Catholic bishops (see p. 0000), the French bishops issued a pastoral letter defending nuclear deterrence as being consistent with the Just War doctrine of the Catholic Church. Rejecting pacifism, the French bishops stated that the argument for peace at any price would lead to a situation in which the West would not have the means to defend itself, and would only serve to encourage aggression.

WEST GERMANY

1979, June 7. Schmidt Warns of Dangers of Soviet Missiles. In a speech at Harvard University's commencement exercises, German Chancellor **Helmut Schmidt** warned that NATO must respond to the Soviet deployment of the SS-20 medium-range ballistic missiles (MRBMs).

1981, May 17. Schmidt Threatens Resignation over MNF Deployments. Defying the opposition of his Social Democratic Party (SPD), Chancellor Schmidt threatened to resign if the party failed to support his approval of the deployment of U.S. medium-range nuclear missiles in Germany as part of the NATO deterrent.

1981, May 26. German Parliament Approves Deployment of Pershing and Cruise Missiles. Despite opposition in his own party, Schmidt won parliamentary approval for the deployment of U.S. cruise missiles and Pershing IIs in West Germany as part of the NATO tactical nuclear force.

1983, April 18. West German Bishops Issue Pastoral Letter on War and Peace. The Roman Catholic bishops of West Germany issued a pastoral letter strongly endorsing nuclear deterrence as a necessary but regrettable means of keeping the peace.

1983, July 4–7. Kohl Negotiates with Soviets about MNF Deployment and Reductions. German Chancellor Helmut Kohl unsuccessfully attempted to persuade Soviet leaders to reconsider their position at the MNF (medium-range nuclear force) reduction talks in Geneva and to accept the NATO interim reduction plan. Later, Soviet Premier **Nikolai Tikhonov** warned that if the West German parliament did not reverse its position on the MNF deployment, the Soviet Union would have to deploy additional missiles and that in the event of war, West Germany would suffer devastation.

1983, November 22, West German Parliament Votes Approval of MRBMs. The West German Bundestag voted to permit the scheduled deployment of U.S. medium-range ballistic missiles on West German soil. This vote assured the Soviet walkout from the Geneva negotiations on MNF reduction. (See p. 1352).

SWEDEN

1981, October 27–November 6. Soviet Submarine Grounded in Swedish Territorial Waters. (See Soviet Union, p. 1359.)

DENMARK

1983, December 1. Danish Parliament Opposes MNF Deployment. The Danish Parliament voted against NATO deployment of U.S. Pershing IIs and ground-launched cruise missiles in Denmark (December 1). Subsequently Parliament voted to withhold from NATO funds that were to be allocated for deployment of the missiles (December 7).

ITALY

1981–1982, December 17–January 28. American General Held Hostage by Terrorists. Brigadier General **James L. Dozier** was seized in his Verona apartment (December 17) and held by terrorists for 42 days. After an extensive search a special Italian police Anti-Terrorist Task Force stormed the building where Dozier was being held and rescued him.

1982–1984. Italian Peackeeping Contingent in Beirut. (See pp. 1365–68).

1983, March 30. Italy Backs Medium-Range Missile Deployment. The Italian government endorsed the U.S.–NATO interim solution on the reduction of medium-range nuclear missile forces in Europe. The Italians later specifically endorsed deployment of Pershing IIs and ground-launched cruise missiles (May 29).

SPAIN

1975. Spanish Withdrawal from Rio de Oro. (See p. 1391.)

1975, November 22. Restoration of Spanish

Monarchy. After the death of Generalissimo Francisco Franco, his protégé, **Juan Carlos de Borbón,** was proclaimed king. Almost immediately he began to change Spain into a parliamentary democracy.

1979–1983. Terrorism by Basque Separatists. Terrorism by radical Basque separatists increased in frequency and intensity. Spanish military officers became targets of many attacks. A home-rule bill sponsored by King Juan Carlos was approved by Basque voters in a popular referendum (October 25, 1980). The radicals, however, wanted total independence and continued their violence. The government deployed troops in the Basque region (March 23, 1981). Violence and defiance continued both in the Basque provinces and in other parts of Spain.

1981, February 23. Attempted Coup. Dissatisfaction with Spain's parliamentary democracy led to an attempt by senior military officers to seize power and overthrow the government. One conspirator led civil guards in seizing and holding hostage the cabinet and 350 members of the lower house of the legislature. The commander in Valencia declared martial law, while a principal military adviser to the King, General **Alfonso Armada Comyn,** urged the King to seize control and establish military rule. Juan Carlos refused, and by telephone calls and a radio address persuaded the army to remain loyal to the government. The conspirators surrendered and were arrested (February 24–26). They were later tried by court-martial and sentenced to prison terms.

1982, May 30. Spain Enters NATO. Following the approval of each NATO member nation, Spain became the sixteenth member of the alliance.

1982, October 2. Coup Foiled. Spanish authorities loyal to the King and the democratic regime discovered plans for a coup to take place just before the national elections scheduled for October 27. Three senior officers were arrested.

1983, February 24. Base Protocol with the United States. Spain and the U.S. signed an agreement which permitted the U.S. to retain its bases in Spain.

1983, June 2. Spain Declines to Sign Medium-Range Missile Deployment Agreement. The Spanish government rejected a NATO agreement permitting future deployment of Pershing II and ground-launched cruise missiles on Spanish soil.

PORTUGAL

1975. Portuguese Mediation in Angola. **(See p. 1387.)**

1975, March 11. Rightist Coup Fails. Troops loyal to the ruling Armed Forces Movement (MFA) thwarted a coup attempt. Former provisional President General Antonio de Spinola was accused of leading the coup but denied complicity.

1975, November 25–28. Leftist Coup Fails. Following more than a month of political unrest, military and civilian leftists attempted to overthrow the new moderate government of Vice Admiral **José Pinheiro de Azevedo.** Rebellious air force troops seized 4 air bases, the Air Force Command Center, and the national radio and television stations. Army commandos suppressed the revolt in hard fighting.

1982, August 12. Council of Revolution Eliminated. The transition from military to civilian rule was completed when the Portuguese Parliament voted the Revolutionary Council out of existence.

SOVIET UNION

1975–1983. Soviet Military Advisers in Africa, Asia, and Latin America. The Soviet Union gave military and technical aid and sent military advisers to a number of Third World countries (see Cuba, Angola, Ethiopia, South Yemen, Yemen, Afghanistan). In addition to military advisers in client nations, the Soviets were able to project power by greatly upgrading their naval capabilities and obtaining naval and air base rights at a number of strategically located areas around the world including Cuba and Vietnam.

1976, December 26. Soviets Strive for Strategic Nuclear Superiority. The *New York Times* reported that the CIA's latest national intelligence estimate (NIE) was far more pessimistic than in preceding years. The estimates indicated that the U.S.S.R. was trying to achieve strategic superiority.

1977, September 26. Soviet–Warsaw Pact Ground Force Troop Strength Increase Reported. Newspaper reports asserted that in 10 years the U.S.S.R. had increased its ground forces by 30 divisions, to a total strength of 170 divisions.

1979, May 30. Soviet Union Purportedly Seeks First-Strike Capability. United States Secretary of Defense **Harold Brown** speaking at the U.S. Naval Academy in Annapolis, Md., declared that the Soviets were seeking to develop a "first-strike" capability. This would be an ability to destroy all U.S. retaliatory capabilities in one preemptive strike.

1979, December 17. Mission of Soviet Navy Enlarged to Include Global Role. U.S. Navy specialists asserted that the Soviet Union was building a navy with the capability of projecting Soviet power anywhere on the globe. This buildup was being performed under the direction of Admiral **Sergey G. Gorshkov,** chief of the Soviet Navy.

1979, December 25–28. Soviets Invade Afghanistan. (See p. 1376.)

1980, January 3. Soviet Union Rejects MNF Talks with NATO. The Soviets rejected a NATO offer to negotiate the reduction of MRBMs. They claimed that the NATO decision (1979, December 12) to deploy new Pershing II and ground-launched cruise missiles "destroyed the basis for negotiation" (see p. 1351).

1980, March 20. Soviets Deny Biological Weapons Violation. The Soviets denied that an anthrax epidemic (April 1979) in the city of Sverdlosk was due to an accident that occurred in the manufacture of biological weapons.

1980, April 18. Soviets Test-Launch Killer Satellite. The Soviets launched a killer satellite, Cosmos 1174. The target, Cosmos 1171, had been launched earlier (April 3).

1980, September 18. Reported Improvement in Strategic and ABM Capabilities. London's International Institute for Strategic Studies (I.I.S.S.) reported that Soviet ICBMs were now "significantly more accurate" than earlier generation missiles, thus weakening U.S. deterrence. U.S. intelligence sources had also ascertained that the Soviets had improved their ABM capabilities with a phased-array radar to direct interceptor rockets. The U.S. government did not consider this to be a violation of SALT I because each side was allowed one ABM site under the terms of the treaty.

1980, October 2. *Kirov* Guided Missile Cruiser in Service. The nuclear-powered guided missile cruiser *Kirov* was reported in active service, giving the Soviet Union substantially increased offensive and defensive strategic naval capability.

1981, January 9. Soviets Launch New Attack Submarine. The new submarine class, called *Oscar* by U.S. Naval Intelligence, was 10,000 tons and could attain speeds up to 40 knots.

1981, September 23. Soviet MNF Superiority Reported. London's I.I.S.S. reported that the U.S.S.R. had more than 3 times as many warheads in their MNF than did NATO.

1981, September 29. Soviet Military Capabilities Enhanced Through Technology Transfers. A U.S. Defense Department booklet on Soviet military capabilities reported that the Soviet Union had used a variety of means, legal and illegal, to acquire Western technology to improve military capabilities.

1981, October 27–November 6. Soviet Submarine Grounded in Swedish Territorial Waters. A Soviet submarine ran aground near the Karlskrona Naval Base. The U.S.S.R. maintained this was due to poor weather and faulty navigational equipment, but this explanation was rejected by Sweden. Swedish investigation discovered radiation near the submarine's torpedo tubes. Sweden pointed out that this was incompatible with Soviet efforts to persuade Sweden to agree that Scandinavia and the Baltic should be a nuclear-free zone. The Soviets insisted there was no radiation in the submarine.

1983, September 1. Soviets Down Korean Commercial Aircraft. Soviet pilots shot down Korean Air Lines plane Flight 007 near Sakhalin Island. The plane bound for Seoul had apparently strayed off course. After tracking the plane for several hours a Soviet aircraft shot down the plane with a missile, killing all 269 passengers and crew.

1983, November 23. Soviets Walk Out from MRBM (MNF) Reduction Talks. (See p. 1351.)

1983, December 8. START Talks Recess without Resumption Date. (See p. 1352.)

1983, December 15. MBFR Talks Adjourn without Setting New Date. (See p. 1352.)

POLAND

1980–1981. Labor Unrest in Poland. Months of labor unrest and strikes led to the establishment of a national labor union, Solidarity, reluctantly accepted by the Polish government to avoid increased violence (1980, August 30). However, unrest continued.

1981, February 9. Military Government Installed. The inability of the civilian government to restore stability led the Communist Party, presumably to forestall Soviet military intervention, to install the defense minister, General **Wojciech Jaruzelski,** as Prime Minister. Despite strong military leadership and repressive measures, unrest continued throughout the country.

1981, September 4–11. Soviets Conduct War Games near Polish Border. Over 100,000 Soviet troops participated in combat exercises near the Polish border in violation of the Helsinki Accord (see International Peacekeeping, p. 1349) since the Soviets did not reveal the number of troops involved in the games until the U.S. accused them of the violation. The size and timing of the war games, coinciding with the Polish Solidarity national congress, led observers to believe that this was intended to intimidate the Poles.

1981, October 18. Jaruzelski Becomes Head of Polish Communist Party. In an attempt to strengthen the hand of the government, the Polish Communist Party appointed General Jaruzelski as First Secretary of the Polish Communist Party.

1981, December 13. Jaruzelski Imposes Martial Law. Worsening conditions in Poland and the continuing threat of armed Soviet intervention led Jaruzelski to impose martial law. Restrictions on civil and personal liberties were directed particularly against the activities of the Solidarity labor movement.

1982, March 13. Warsaw Pact Military Maneuvers in Northern Poland. The Soviet Union, Poland, and East Germany conducted Warsaw Pact military exercises in northern Poland. These exercises were again seen as an attempt to intimidate the Poles, who were restive under martial law which had been imposed three months earlier (December 13).

1983, July 21–23. End of Martial Law in Poland. General Jaruzelski announced the end of 19 months of martial law (July 21) effective noon the next day. However, living conditions did not improve, since a number of harsh and oppressive laws were left intact.

GREECE

1980–1983. Strained Relations with NATO Allies. The socialist government of Greece opposed NATO's planned MNF deployment in Western Europe. The unresolved problem of a partitioned Cyprus with 25,000 Turkish troops deployed in northern Cyprus further strained Greek–NATO relations. Prime Minister **Andreas George Papandreou** repeatedly threatened to force the U.S. to give up military bases in Greece. Papandreou did, however, renew the base agreement with the U.S. for an additional five years (August 20, 1983).

TURKEY

1975–1984. Continued Deployment of Turkish Troops in Cyprus. Turkey continued to deploy 25,000 troops in Cyprus. But after the Cypriot Turkish Federal State declared its independence and permanent separation from Cyprus, the Turks made a token withdrawal of 1,500 troops (see p. 1361).

1978, December 26. Martial Law Enacted in Thirteen Provinces. In an effort to bring about a halt to internal religious violence between Sunni and Shi'ite Moslems, the government (with the approval of parliament) imposed martial law in 13 of Turkey's 67 provinces (including Ankara and Istanbul). Later this was extended to six additional provinces (April 25, 1979).

1980, September 12. Military Coup d'État. Following months of violence due to political and religious rivalry, the Chief of General Staff, General **Kenan Evren,** established a military dictatorship. He pledged a return to democratic government when public order was restored.

1981, January 15. Constituent Assembly Date Selected. General Evren announced his intention to convene a Constituent Assembly to draft a new democratic constitution. This was done June 30.

1982, July 17. Constituent Assembly Submits Draft Constitution. This was approved by a 90% vote in a national referendum (November 7).

1983, December 13. End of Military Rule. Following parliamentary elections (November 6) General Evren and his junta resigned (December 11) and a civilian government took office under Premier **Turgut Ozal** (December 13).

CYPRUS

1975, February 13. Turkish Cypriot Federal State Established. Greek Cypriot President **Archbishop Makarios III** refused to recognize the new state. Only Turkey recognized the legitimacy of the new state. Negotiations between the two Cypriot factions made no progress in solving the partition issue. **Rauf Denktash** was chosen President of Turkish Cyprus (1976, June 20).

1977, February 12. Partition Negotiations. The Turkish Cypriots accepted territorial concessions in exchange for recognition of their Turkish Cypriot Federated State. However, talks broke down when the Greek Cypriots alleged that the Turkish Cypriots reneged on their part of the bargain.

1983, November 15. Turkish Cyprus Declares Independence. Turkey continued to deploy troops in Cyprus but made the first troop withdrawal since the 1974 invasion.

THE ARAB LEAGUE

1976, June 10. Arab League Establishes Peacekeeping Force in Lebanon. The Arab League voted to establish an Arab League peacekeeping force with troops from Algeria, Libya, Saudi Arabia, and Sudan. Syria, which already had nearly 16,000 troops in Lebanon, was also to participate. The force was dominated by the Syrians who continued to maintain their strong presence in Lebanon (see p. 1365).

1976, September 6. PLO Granted Full Membership in the Arab League. The Arab League unanimously approved an Egyptian-sponsored motion to grant full membership to the Palestinian Liberation Organization (PLO).

1976, October 17. Arab League Deterrent Force for Lebanon. Since Syria either would not or could not bring a cessation of civil war in Lebanon, the leaders of Lebanon, Egypt, Syria, Saudia Arabia, Kuwait, and PLO chief **Yasir Arafat** met at Riyadh, Saudia Arabia, and agreed to establish an Arab League Deterrent Force in Lebanon. The Deterrent Force would be under the personal leadership of President **Elias Sarkas** of Lebanon. The new Deterrent Force was still largely made up of Syrians. Saudi Arabia, the United Arab Emirates (UAE), Sudan, and North Yemen sent small troop contingents, but withdrew them when it became clear that Syria intended to continue its dominance of the Arab League Force (1979, June). The Syrians continued to maintain large forces in Lebanon nominally under the auspices of the Arab League. Later the Arab League chose not to renew the mandate for its Deterrent Force in Lebanon (1982, July 17) (see p. 1365).

1978, November 1. Arab League Denounces Camp David Accords. The Arab League denounced the Camp David Accords and the agreement of Egypt and Israel to negotiate a treaty (see p. 1364).

1979, March 31. Arab League Imposes Sanctions on Egypt. Because of the Israeli-Egyptian peace treaty, the leaders of 18 of the member nations of the Arab League imposed a boycott of Egyptian goods and agreed to sever diplomatic ties with Cairo. However, two member states, Sudan and Oman, retained relations with Egypt and absented themselves from the meeting (see p. 1364).

ISRAEL

1976, June 27–28. Entebbe Incident. PLO guerrillas hijacked an Air France commercial aircraft en route to Paris from Athens and diverted it to Entebbe Airport, Uganda. They held the crew and passengers hostage. The hijackers demanded the release of 53 PLO political prisoners in Israel, West Germany, Switzerland, France, and Kenya. The hijackers released 47 passengers but continued to hold hostage 98 passengers and the crew. Uganda's President Idi Amin cooperated with the hijackers, deploying troops to help guard the hostages who were held in the airport terminal. The Israeli government expressed a willingness to negotiate while secretly planning an armed rescue operation.

1976, July 3–4. Entebbe Rescue Mission: Operation "Jonathan." In a daring, meticulously planned and executed rescue operation, Israeli commandos under Lt. Col. **Jonathan Netanyahu** landed at the Entebbe airport, overcame Ugandan and PLO resistance, and freed the hostages. To assure a safe exit the Israelis also destroyed Ugandan air force MiGS based at the airport. The Israelis killed the 7 PLO guerrillas and 20 Ugandan soldiers in the fighting. Three hostages and the Israeli commander, Colonel Netanyahu, were killed; 3 Israeli soldiers were wounded.

1978, March 11. The Coastal Road Massacre. Operating out of Lebanon, 11 seaborne PLO guerrillas landed south of Haifa, killed 1 U.S. civilian on the beach, and attacked a taxi, killing 6 more civilians. The guerrillas commandeered a bus bound for Haifa and made the driver take them toward Tel Aviv. They stopped another northbound bus and opened fire, killing several passengers. They continued south coming within 10 miles of Tel Aviv when they were halted by Israeli troops. In the ensuing fire fight, 9 guerrillas were killed and 2 captured; 35 Israeli civilians were killed and 75 wounded.

1978, March 14–21. The Litani River Operation. In retaliation for the Coastal Road Massacre, the Israeli Defense Force (IDF) launched an invasion of southern Lebanon. The mission was to destroy PLO forces south of the Litani River. Because of the Israeli Cabinet's insistence that casualties be kept to a minimum, the IDF advance was deliberate, enabling most of the PLO fighters to escape beyond the Litani River. Nonetheless, the Israelis were able to secure all of southern Lebanon. They avoided Tyre and the Palestinian refugee camp at Rashidiye.

1978, April 11–June 13. Israeli Withdrawal and the Establishment of a United Nations Force in Lebanon. In accordance with U.N. Security Council Resolution 425, the Israelis withdrew from Lebanon. A United Nations Interim Force in Lebanon (UNIFIL) replaced Israeli troops in southern Lebanon. However, the Israelis insisted that the Lebanese troops and militia commanded by Lebanese Army Major **Saad Haddad** be given control over a strip of land averaging 8 miles in depth just north of the Israeli-Lebanese border. Haddad subsequently named this territory the Independent Republic of Free Lebanon (April 18, 1979). The PLO, however, derisively referred to it as Haddadland.

1978, April–1981, April. PLO Buildup in Lebanon. Following the Litani River Operation, the Israeli withdrawal, and the establishment of the UNIFIL peacekeeping force, the PLO resumed its policy of harassment of Israel. Despite the presence of the UNIFIL forces and Major Haddad's force in southern Lebanon, the PLO made numerous attempts to infiltrate over land and by sea. There were more than 50 artillery and mortar shelling incidents. As a result of these actions 10 Israelis were killed and 57 were wounded. This was a much smaller casualty rate than that before the Litani River Operation, but was considered unacceptable by Israel and the people of northern Galilee. The Israelis carried out numerous air and ground retaliatory attacks upon the PLO in Lebanon, inflicting many casualties. The PLO leaders began reorganizing and changing tactics. They fortified base areas in southern Lebanon. At the same time they began to build up a conventional military force with the assistance of large quantities of arms from the U.S.S.R., including tanks, artillery, and multiple rocket launchers.

1978–1979. Camp David and Peace Treaty with Egypt (see p. 1364).

1981, June 7. Israeli Air Attack Destroys Iraq Nuclear Reactor. Israeli aircraft bombed and destroyed Iraq's sole nuclear power plant, under construction and nearing completion outside of Baghdad, at Osirak. Prime Minister Menachem Begin justified the preemptive raid because Israel believed that Iraqis intended to produce atomic weapons in the plant and to use them against Israel.

1981, July–1982, May. Uneasy Cease-Fire with PLO. Following a cease-fire arranged by U.S. mediator, Ambassador Philip Habib (July 24), an uneasy truce ensued. The PLO, apparently convinced that any retaliatory Israeli offensive would be limited, like the 1978 Litani River Operation, continued its terrorism against Israeli civilian targets, inside Israel, on the West Bank, and in foreign countries. Israel built up forces just south of the border.

1982, June 3. Israeli Diplomat Wounded. The attempted assassination of Israel's ambassador to England culminated a series of PLO terrorist attacks that prompted a massive Israeli reprisal three days later.

1982, June 6. Israeli Invasion of Lebanon (see p. 1346).

1983, February 8. Kahan Commission Report (see p. 1349).

1983, May 17. Agreement with Lebanon (see p. 1365).

EGYPT

1975, March 29. Reopening of Suez Canal. Egyptian President **Anwar Sadat** announced that Egypt had reopened the Suez Canal. Israeli ships were barred from using the canal. Sadat also announced that he would renew the mandate of the U.N. Sinai peacekeeping force (see U.N., p. 1349).

1975, July–1976 August. Tense Relations with Libya. Egypt charged Libya with numerous acts of terrorism and plans for terrorist acts in Egypt.

1975, September 1. Egypt and Israel Agree on Sinai Disengagement. After a summer of negotiating, Israel and Egypt reached agreement on Sinai troop withdrawals. The Israelis agreed to withdraw from the Mitla and Gidi passes and return the Abu Rudeis oil fields to Egypt. Egypt agreed to allow Israel to ship nonmilitary goods through the Suez Canal. Both sides agreed to limit the number of troops in the Sinai Peninsula to 8,000. Americans were to operate an early warning system in the passes.

1975, November 30. Israeli Withdrawal. In accordance with the Sinai disengagement agreement, the Israelis withdrew from a 90-mile strip, including the oil fields.

1976, March 14. Sadat Ends Soviet Friendship Treaty. Citing Soviet refusal to rebuild Egyptian military capability after the 1973 Arab-Israeli War and the Soviet unwillingness to reschedule debts, Egyptian President Sadat renounced the 1971 Friendship Treaty with the Soviet Union. Sadat was harshly critical of the Soviets for preventing India from supplying Egypt with MiG parts from a Soviet-licensed MiG plant in India. Sadat later signed an arms deal with China to procure the spare parts for the MiGs (April 21).

1976, July 13–18. Egyptian-Sudanese-Saudi Arabian Cooperation Pacts Signed. Egyptian President Anwar Sadat and Sudanese President **Gaafar al-Nimeiry** agreed to a nonagression pact to deter Libyan aggression against Sudan. The two leaders flew to Jiddah where they met Saudi Arabia's King **Khalid** and concluded a trilateral agreement on military, political, and economic cooperation. Sadat and Nimeiry were convinced that Libya's Qaddafi had been behind an aborted coup attempt in Sudan earlier that month (see p. 1384).

1976, December 18–21. Joint Political Command Established Between Syria and Egypt. Talks between Egypt's President Anwar Sadat and Syria's President Hafez Assad concluded with an agreement to coordinate the defense and foreign policies of their two countries.

1977, January 16–19. Troops Used to Quell Food Riots. Egyptian troops suppressed riots resulting from government approved rises in food prices.

1977, July 12–19. Border Incidents with Libya. Relations between Libya and Egypt worsened as Egyptian authorities arrested Libyan saboteurs in the border region (July 12). Libyan officials responded by arresting 10 Egyptians (July 16). These incidents culminated in an armed clash.

1977, July 21–24. Egypt–Libya: Border Conflict. Egyptian troops turned back a Libyan combined arms attack across the Egyptian-Libyan border. The Egyptians claimed to have shot down 2 Libyan aircraft and knocked out 40 tanks. Egyptian losses were light. The Egyptians retaliated by launching a counterattack across the Libyan border and an air attack against a Libyan air base. Satisfied that Libyan dictator **Muammar Qaddafi** had for the time being learned his lesson, Sadat called a cease-fire (July 25). Sadat warned that "that maniac [Qaddafi] is playing with fire."

1977, November 10–18. Sadat Offers to Go to Israel. In a series of dramatic announcements, President Sadat declared he was ready to visit Jerusalem to discuss peace. Prime Minister Begin reciprocated by inviting Sadat.

1977, November 20–22. Sadat Visits Jerusalem. Sadat boldly visited the Israeli capital and addressed the Knesset. Sadat and Begin pledged that they would work for peace and that they would end the enmity between their two countries. A peace process was begun. However, leading Arab nations, especially Libya and Syria, expressed indignation at Sadat's visit and efforts to bring an end to hostilities with Israel. Libya severed diplomatic ties with Egypt.

1977, December 2–5. Arab States Form Anti-Egyptian Front. Representatives of Libya, Syria, Iraq, Algeria, South Yemen, and the PLO met in Tripoli and agreed to form an anti-Egyptian front. Although they condemned Sadat's peace initiative as an act of "high treason," they did not eliminate hopes for eventual rapprochement. The relative mildness of the condemnation prompted a break between Iraq and the other Arab members of the new anti-Egyptian front, causing the Iraqi representative to leave the conference early. Sadat promptly recalled his ambassadors from the five member nations (December 5).

1978, February 23. Egyptian Raid on Cyprus. Arab terrorists claiming to be PLO attacked and killed an Egyptian newspaper editor in Nicosia, Cyprus (February 19), and took 30 hostages. Sadat sent Egyptian commandos on a rescue mission. The commandos killed the terrorists but then were attacked themselves by a unit of the Cypriot National Guard. Fifteen commandos were killed in the ensuing battle. Others were captured. Egyptian officials were furious and subsequently broke off diplomatic relations with Cyprus.

1978, September 7–17. Camp David Talks and Accords. U.S. President Jimmy Carter arbitrated negotiations between Sadat and Begin for over a week until they agreed on a working plan for a peace treaty. They agreed that the West Bank would have autonomy and that Egypt and Israel would sign a peace treaty within 3 months of the signing of the Camp David Accords.

1979, March 20. U.S. Agrees to Provide Arms to Egypt and Compensation to Israel. As a preliminary to signature of the Egyptian-Israeli Peace Treaty, the U.S. pledged to provide Egypt with warplanes and weapons worth $2 billion and to compensate Israel for its withdrawal from the Sinai with $3 billion.

1979, March 26. Egyptian-Israeli Peace Treaty Signed. After months of difficult negotiations, Egyptian President Sadat and Israeli Prime Minister Begin signed a peace treaty between their two countries at Washington. Both leaders gave U.S. President Jimmy Carter credit for his vital role in the negotiations. Under the terms of the treaty, the Israelis pledged a staged withdrawal of troops and settlers from the Sinai Peninsula, to be completed in 3 years. Israel would use the Suez Canal and pledged to begin negotiations for Palestinian self-rule a month after ratification.

1979, March 27. Israel Starts Withdrawal. Israeli troops began the first stage of withdrawal.

1979, September 8. Egypt Helps Morocco Battle Polisario. Egyptian arms were received by Morocco to assist in the war with Polisario (see p. 1391).

1979, October 6. First U.S. Arms Shipment to Egypt. In a parade commemorating the sixth anniversary of Egypt's crossing of the Suez Canal to begin the October War (1973) Egypt displayed the first new weapons systems received from the United States. The recent Egyptian acquisitions displayed at the parade were F-4 Phantom Jet fighter-bombers and M-113 armored personnel carriers (APCs).

1980, January 8. U.S. and Egypt Joint Training Exercises. It was announced that U.S. and Egyptian air forces had recently concluded joint training exercises at Egyptian Air Base at Luxor.

1981, October 6. Sadat Assassinated. President Anwar Sadat was assassinated while he was reviewing a parade commemorating the Egyptian crossing of the Suez Canal at the beginning of the 1973 War with Israel. The assassins, one a soldier, were Moslem fundamentalists opposed to Sadat's peace with Israel and his liberal interpretation of Islamic law. He was replaced by former Vice President Hosne Nubarak.

1981, November 14. Operation Bright Star Begins. Egypt began joint maneuvers with Sudan, Somalia, Oman, and U.S.

1982, April 25. Israelis Complete Withdrawal from the Sinai.

1983, August 18–September 18. Operation Bright Star 83. Over 5,000 U.S. troops participated with Egyptian troops in joint maneuvers.

YEMEN (NORTH YEMEN)

1977, October 10. Assassinations of President and Vice-President. President **Ibrahim al-Hamdi** and his brother Colonel **Abdullah Mohammed al-Hamdi** were assassinated. The assassins apparently hoped to prevent planned discussions with South Yemen regarding a possible merger of the two countries.

1978, June 24. President Assassinated. The new President, **Ahmed Hussein al-Ghashmi,** was killed when the briefcase of an envoy from South Yemen President **Salem Rubaya Ali** exploded. The South Yemen envoy was also killed in the blast. North Yemen authorities charged that the assassination was planned by Rubaya. Other Arab sources said that the bomb was planted by North Yemen political opponents of Ghashmi. A 3-man military council replaced Ghashmi.

1979, February 24–26. Border Fighting with South Yemen. North Yemen officials alleged that South Yemeni troops had attacked across the border. South Yemen officials denied the charge and claimed they were responding to an invasion of their territory by North Yemen. Both countries agreed to let the Arab League mediate (February 28).

1979, March 17. Cease-Fire. Both North and South Yemen agreed to a cease-fire.

1979, March 29, National Unification Agreement. Following the cease-fire, reconciliation talks were held between North and South Yemen. Despite apparent agreement, the unification did not take place.

1980, May–June. Renewed conflict with Southern Yemen. (See p. 1371.)

LEBANON

1975–1984. Lebanese Civil War. The establishment of the PLO in Lebanon exacerbated tensions between various Moslem and Christian factions. Full-scale civil war broke out (April 13, 1975). This conflict continued to rage throughout the remainder of the decade and into the 1980s. The PLO, whose objective was the destruction of Israel, used Lebanon as a staging area from which to conduct raids into Israel and to use long-range artillery and rockets to shell Israeli territory.

1976, March. Syrian Intervention. Under the pretext of acting as a peacemaker between warring Lebanese factions, Syria dispatched troops to Lebanon, initially to prevent the PLO and Moslem Lebanese factions from defeating the Christians.

1978, March 14–21. Israeli Invasion of Southern Lebanon: The Litani River Operation. (See p. 1371.)

1978, April 11–June 13. Israeli Withdrawal and the Establishment of United Nations Interim Force in Lebanon. (See p. 1371.)

1978, April–1981, June. PLO Buildup in Lebanon. The PLO built an extensive military/political infrastructure in Lebanon. They received large shipments of arms and equipment from the Soviet Union (see p. 1362).

1982, June–August. Israeli Invasion of Lebanon. (See p. 1346.)

1982, August 21–28. Deployment of Multinational Peacekeeping Force. (See p. 1348.)

1982, August 27–September 3. Evacuation of PLO and Syrian Forces from Beirut. All 15,000 Syrian and PLO forces were evacuated, most by sea; the Syrians and a small Palestine Liberation Army (PLA) contingent went overland through Israeli lines to Damascus. The multinational force contingents withdrew shortly after this (September 10).

1982, September 13. Assassination of President-elect Bashir Gemayel. Lebanese President-elect Gemayel was assassinated by terrorists allegedly backed by Syria. Israeli troops occupied Beirut for the declared purpose of keeping order and preventing bloodshed.

1982, September 16–19. Sabra and Shatilla Refugee Camp Massacres. (See p. 1348.)

1982, September 20–22. Multinational Peacekeeping Force Redeployed in Beirut. This was in response to world horror because of the Sabra and Shatilla massacres. The U.S. Marine position was just east of the airport. The Italian contingent was further north, closer to Beirut. The French contingent was still further north, on the outskirts of West Beirut. They were later joined by a token British contingent of about 150 men, who took position near the U.S. Marines.

1982–1983. Buildup of PLO in Northern Lebanon. Despite their defeat, the PLO were able to reorganize and began rebuilding their forces in Lebanon.

1983, May 17. Lebanon-Israel Agreement. With the diplomatic aid of the United States, Israel and the Lebanese government of President **Amin Gemayel** reached an agreement which was, in effect, a treaty between the two nations, ending a war which had existed since 1947. Israel was recognized by the Lebanese government and relations between the two countries were at least partially normalized.

1983, September 3. Partial Israeli Withdrawal. Against the wishes of the United States, which wanted the Israelis to remain in the Chouf Mountains to

maintain order, the Israelis withdrew their forces (about 10,000 troops) from the Beirut area and the Chouf Mountains to new positions south of the Awali River.

1983, September 4–25. Civil War in the Chouf Mountains. As the Israelis were completing their withdrawal, Phalangist troops and the Lebanese Army began to move into the areas evacuated. The local Druze Moslem militia began immediately attacking both Phalangist and Lebanese Army forces. The Druze attacked major strongholds at Aley (Alieh) ten miles east of Beirut and Bhamdun south of the Beirut-Damascus highway (September 4–6). In subsequent fighting, the Druze militiamen surrounded Deir al Qamar (September 10), and attacked Suk al Gharb, which directly overlooked the President's palace (September 10–11). A Druze armored assault was turned back from Suk al Gharb with the help of U.S. naval gunfire support from offshore (September 19). The warring Lebanese factions agreed to a cease-fire arranged by Saudi mediator Prince **Bandar bin Sultan** (September 25). During this fighting considerable fire from the Druze guns landed in and near the multinational force positions, mostly near the U.S. Marines. Much of this was fire from stray rounds. Much of it was deliberate. The cease-fire was subsequently broken on a number of occasions.

1983, September 10–October 20. U.S. Navy Supports Marine Peacekeeping Efforts in Beirut. The U.S. government authorized air strikes and gunfire support from the U.S. Navy squadron offshore near Beirut, to help defend the Marine positions near the Beirut Airport. The Navy was also authorized to fire in support of nearby Lebanese Army positions if these were believed to contribute to the security of the Marine positions. The result was occasional fire from U.S. ships against nearby positions of Druze and other antigovernment militia, and against their supporting artillery in the Syrian occupied zone further east. U.S. carrier aircraft began to fly reconnaissance missions over west-central Lebanon.

1983, October 23. Suicide Attack on U.S. and French Peacekeeping Force. An Arab terrorist allegedly belonging to a pro-Iranian and pro-Syrian terrorist organization drove a truck loaded with explosives into a combined headquarters and barracks building in the U.S. Marine compound; 241 servicemen were killed. This led to widespread demands in the United States that the Marines be brought home. An official inquiry determined that inadequate security precautions had been taken, and blamed security failures on the local Marine commander, and Navy and Army senior officers in the chain of command. President Ronald Reagan assumed responsibility and no officers were court-martialed. Simultaneously a similar attack on the French peacekeeping force compound killed 58 French soldiers and wounded 15.

1983, November 13–14. Renewed Fighting between Druze Forces and Lebanese Army. After a number of cease-fire violations in weeks following the September 25 cease-fire agreement, fighting erupted at Suk al Gharb in the mountains just east of and overlooking Beirut. The Druze militia began shelling Christian East Beirut. Intense combat ensued between the militias and the Lebanese Army. Again U.S. Marine positions at the airport came under fire. Fighting continued until a new cease-fire was arranged (December 27).

1983, December 4. Two U.S. Planes Shot Down by Syrian SAMs. Following Syrian firing on U.S. reconnaissance planes (December 3) U.S. Navy carrier planes carried out attacks against Syrian air defense positions in the Bekaa Valley. In the attack 2 planes were shot down by Syrian SAMs. One crew was rescued; in the other the pilot was killed, and the navigator, Lt. **Robert Goodman,** captured. The Syrians held Goodman as a prisoner of war.

1983, December. Continued Shelling of Marine Position. The U.S. Marine positions were repeatedly shelled. The Marines returned fire.

1983, December. Pro- and Anti-Arafat PLO Forces Battle in Tripoli Area. PLO dissidents, dissatisfied with Yasir Arafat's leadership, had been fighting against PLO forces loyal to Arafat for several months. The dissidents, supported by Syria, drove the loyalist contingents back to the port city of Tripoli. A cease-fire was finally arranged between the PLO combatants; Arafat and troops loyal to him were allowed to leave Lebanon by ship. Israeli ships at first barred Arafat's departure, but eventually (after pressure from the U.S.) permitted him to escape (December 20).

1983, December–1984, January 3. Jesse Jackson Wins Goodman's Release. Rev. **Jesse Jackson,** a Democratic Party candidate for President of the United States, appealed personally to Syrian President Hafez Assad in Damascus and won the release of Navy flyer Lt. Robert Goodman. The Syrians announced that the release was for humanitarian reasons.

1984, January 15. Death of Haddad. Major **Saad Haddad,** commander of Lebanese troops and militia in southern Lebanon, died after a lengthy illness (see p. 1362). Haddad, who had been expelled from the Lebanese Army by the pro-Syrian government in 1979, was reinstated to his rank just before his death by the Lebanese State Court, Lebanon's highest judicial body. The Court, composed of 1 Christian and 2 Moslems, held that Haddad's dismissal had been unjust and prompted by international pressure. He had, in fact, been continuously paid by the Lebanese Army, and had received regular logistical support from Lebanon, through Haifa. The Israelis praised Haddad for his courage and sense of soldierly duty. Haddad, a Christian, was admired and praised by fellow officers of the Lebanese Army, Moslem and Christian.

1984, January 6–March 5. Druze and Shi'ite Moslems Defeat Lebanese Army. Intense fighting again erupted between Druze and Shi'ite militiamen and Lebanese Army units (January 6). After a brief lull, the fighting intensified (January 13), and the Syrian-backed Shi'ite and Druze forces won a complete victory over the Army east and south of Beirut. At the same time, Shi'ite militiamen drove the Lebanese Army out of West Beirut. President Gemayel tacitly acknowledged the changed milieu by going to Damascus to conduct talks with Syrian President Assad (February 29–March 1) in order to strike the best deal he could and retain some power in Lebanon. Upon returning to Lebanon at the conclusion of the negotiations (March 5) he renounced the Lebanese agreement with Israel (see p. 1365).

1984, February 7–March 31. Withdrawal of the Multinational Peacekeeping Force from Lebanon. President Reagan ordered the withdrawal of the U.S. Marine peacekeeping force from Beirut. The next day the British contingent of the multinational peacekeeping force was withdrawn and the Italian government likewise announced the withdrawal of their peacekeeping contingent (February 8). The Marines began withdrawing to ships offshore two weeks later (February 21). The withdrawal of the U.S. peacekeeping force was complete some five weeks later when President Reagan announced that the U.S. peacekeeping role was at an end (March 31). That same day the French completed the withdrawal of their peacekeeping force.

SYRIA

1975, June 3–July 8. Increased Tensions and Border Incidents with Iraq. (See below.)

1975, June 12–August 22. Coordination of Military Policy with Jordan. (See p. 1369.)

1975, December 25–31. Joint Jordanian-Syrian Military Exercises. (See p. 1369.)

1976–1981. Syrian Buildup in Lebanon. Syria moved into Lebanon under the pretext of being a peacemaker between Christian militia on one side and the PLO and its Lebanese Moslem leftist allies on the other (March 1976; see pp. 1361 and 1365). The Syrians subsequently received approval from the Arab League to contribute troops to an Arab League Deterrent Force (October 17–18, 1976; see p. 1361). The Syrians gradually increased the size of their forces in Lebanon to about 20,000 troops and shifted their support from the Lebanese Christians to the Moslem factions. The Syrians were deployed in Beirut and south of the Damascus-Beirut highway, along the western slopes of Mount Hermon and in the Bekaa Valley.

1976, June–December. Strained Relations with Iraq. (See p. 1369.)

1977, February 4. Joint Political Command Established between Syria and Egypt. (See p. 1363.)

1977, December 2–5. Arab States Form Anti-Sadat Front at Tripoli Conference. (See p. 1363.)

1978, January 11. Syrian-Soviet Arms Deal. President Hafez Assad made an arms deal with the Soviet Union in which Syria was to receive additional SAMs, tanks, and planes.

1978, October 24–26. Syria and Iraq Agree on Political and Military Coordination. In response to the Israeli-Egyptian Camp David Accords the governments of Syria and Iraq put aside their serious policy differences and pledged to establish a bilateral committee to coordinate military strategy, defense, and foreign policies in order to "serve as the basis for a full military union."

1979, June 19. Joint Political Command with Iraq Established. In accordance with their earlier agreement Syria and Iraq established a Joint Political Command to coordinate defense, foreign, and economic policies.

1979, August 8. Assad Charged with Supporting Attempted Coup in Iraq. Saddam Hussein, new chairman of Iraq's Revolutionary Command, accused Syrian President Assad of supporting a recent coup attempt in Iraq (see p. 1369). This ended all planning for policy coordination.

1982, February 2–24. Syrian Troops Crush Hama Revolt. Efforts by the Syrian Army to suppress the illegal Moslem Brotherhood in Hama led to a full-scale revolt by Sunni Moslem fundamentalists. Fighting was bitter and thousands of Hama residents were killed. Eventually the troops employed armor to destroy whole sections of the city.

1982, March 7. Assad Blames Iraq for Hama Revolt. Syrian President Assad accused Iraq of arming the Moslem Brotherhood, enabling them to revolt against Syrian authority.

1982, June 6–26. War with Israel in Lebanon. (See p. 1346.)

1982, September–December. Syria Rebuilds Armed Forces with Soviet Aid. Syria, with the aid of the Soviet Union, rebuilt the forces shattered in the recent war with Israel. The U.S.S.R. not only replaced the arms and equipment the Syrians had lost in Lebanon but supplied additional weaponry as well.

1983, December 4. Syrian SAMs Shoot Down American Planes. (See p. 1367.)

1984, February 29–March 1. Assad Receives Gemayel. Lebanese President Amin Gemayel traveled to Damascus to meet Syrian President Hafez Assad. Syria had gained virtual domination over all of Lebanon except the southern area occupied by Israel.

IRAQ

1975, June 3–July 8. Strained Relations with Syria. Within weeks of settling a dispute over Syrian control of the flow of water of the Euphrates River (June 3), relations again became strained. Iraq charged Syria with violating Iraqi air space and with armed incursions of Syrian troops into Iraq. Iraq also claimed that Syria was aiding Kurdish rebels in their attempt to win autonomy (see p. 1282). Syria countered by ousting the Iraqi military attaché from Damascus and closing its military attaché's office in Baghdad (July 8).

1976, May 1–30. Kurd Revolt Renewed. Hostilities with Kurd tribesmen in northeast Iraq flared up. The new fighting was caused by the Iraqi policy of forcing Kurds to relocate. The Kurd insurgents were apparently receiving aid from Syria.

1976, June–December Increased Tension with Syria. Syrian intervention in Lebanon further strained relations between Iraq and Syria. Claiming that Syria posed a grave threat to its security Iraq called up its reserves and massed troops on its border with Syria (June 9–12). Syria responded by concentrating forces in the border region. Relations were further strained by Syrian acknowledgment of aid to Kurd rebels (July 4). Syria accused Iraq of closing the common border in order to cover large-scale troop movements (November 2). Relations remained tense as Syrian Foreign Minister **Abdel Halim Khaddam** was wounded in an assassination attempt traced to the radical Palestinian Black June movement, based in Iraq (December 2), while Iraq blamed Syria for attempting to assassinate Saddam Hussein, Deputy Chairman of the Iraqi Revolutionary Command Council (December 14).

1977, July–October. Continued Strained Relations with Syria. (See p. 1368.)

1977, December 2–5. Arab States Form Anti-Sadat Front at Tripoli Conference. (See p. 1363.)

1978, October 24–26. Syria and Iraq Agree on Joint Political-Military Command. (See p. 1368.)

1979, March 1. Kurdish Guerrilla Chieftan Dies. General Mustafa Barzani, leader of the Kurdish Democratic Party (KDP) and the Kurdish struggle for autonomy, died in Washington, D.C. (see p. 1282). Barzani's sons continued the struggle for autonomy.

1979, June 4–14. Iraqi Counterinsurgency Operations into Iran. Iraqi troops in pursuit of Kurd guerrilla fighters raided Iranian territory, and Iraqi jets strafed Iranian villages (June 4–5). These attacks evoked a warning from the Iranian government (June 14).

1979, June 19, Joint Syrian-Iraqi Command Established. (See p. 1368.)

1979, July 20–August 8. Attempted Coup Foiled; Syrian Involvement Charged. An attempted coup against the new regime of President Saddam Hussein was foiled and one of the major conspirators allegedly confessed to receiving Syrian support. Syrian President Assad denied the charge (August 6). Twenty-two co-conspirators, including five members of the Revolutionary Command Council, were executed by firing squad (August 8). The allegations against Assad ended any chance for the implementation of the two nations' plans for a joint political and military command (see p. 1368).

1979, September 1. Iran Accuses Iraq of Aiding Kurd Rebels. (See p. 1372.)

1980, September–1984. Iran-Iraq Gulf War. (See p. 1372.)

1980, October 1. Kurds Escalate Guerrilla Activities. A London-based spokesman for the Kurd Democratic Party said that the guerrillas fighting for Kurd autonomy had escalated their insurgency efforts against the Iraqi government. The guerrillas, led by **Massoud** and **Idris Barzani,** sought to take advantage of the war between Iraq and Iran in order to win autonomy from Iraq.

1981, June 7. Israeli Air Attack Destroys Iraq's Nuclear Reactor. (See p. 1362.)

JORDAN

1975, August 22. Joint Jordanian and Syrian Political-Military Command Formed. Jordan's King Hussein and Syrian President Hafez Assad issued a joint communiqué, announcing the establishing of a joint high command to formulate, coordinate, and execute political and military initiatives against Israel.

1975, December 25–31. Joint Military Exercises with Syria. Two Jordanian brigades of about 10,000 troops joined Syrian forces for maneuvers in Syria, simulating defensive operations against a hypothetical Israeli invasion.

1978–1980. Cooling Relations between Syria and Jordan.

1980, November 26–December 11. Border Tension with Syria. Apparently irritated by King Hussein's announcement of support for Iraq in the Iran-Iraq War, pro-Iranian President Assad of Syria ordered a troop buildup on the Jordanian-Syrian border. Hussein placed his forces on alert, and ordered several units to the border area. The two leaders bitterly denounced each other in radio addresses to their nations. Israeli Prime Minister Begin announced that Israel would not tolerate a Syrian invasion of Jordan. Syria issued a list of demands on Jordan, including a call for Jordan to reassert its pledge recognizing the PLO as the only legitimate representative of the Palestinian people (December 2). Hussein rejected the Syrian demands. The crisis was eased by Saudi Arabian mediation. The Syrians withdrew their troops from the border (December 11); next day the Jordanians followed suit.

1982, January 28–March 3. Hussein Reaffirms Jordanian Support of Iraq War Effort; Calls for Volunteers. The Jordanian volunteer contingent was to be called the Yarmuk Force, in honor of the Arab victory over the Byzantines (636 A.D.; see p. 230). In his plea for volunteers Hussein denounced Iran as a threat to the Arab world.

SAUDI ARABIA

1978, February 14. Saudi Arabia Buys F-15 Fighters from the U.S. The U.S. agreed to sell Saudia Arabia 60 F-15 fighter planes for $2.5 billion as part of a larger deal involving the sale of planes to Israel and Egypt (see p. 1364). The sale was later approved by the U.S. Senate (May 15) with the provision that the planes not be deployed near Israel.

1979, March 9. U.S. Sends AWACs to Saudi Arabia. The 2 Airborne Warning and Control reconnaissance planes were intended to help both the U.S. and Saudi Arabia improve intelligence capabilities in the Persian Gulf area, threatened by revolution in Iran. These were American planes, with American crews, but providing information to the Saudi armed forces. The U.S. government believed that this would help the U.S. retain Saudi Arabian friendship. Some observers, particularly in Israel, believed this was naïve.

1980, September 30. More AWACs to Saudis. The U.S. government shipped 4 more U.S. AWAC reconnaissance planes to Saudi Arabia to bolster American interest, influence, and capability in the Persian Gulf area in the aftermath of the Iranian Revolution.

1981, August 8. Saudi Crown Prince Offers Peace Plan for Middle East. Crown Prince Fahd's plan provided for Israeli withdrawal from all occupied territory, the removal of all Israeli West Bank settlements, the establishment of a Palestine State, and the right of all peoples to live in peace. Some Israelis thought the plan offered some hope for peace because of the clause calling for the right of all peoples to live in peace, which was implicit admission of Israeli's right to exist as a sovereign nation. However, the Israeli government rejected the plan, as did the PLO.

1981, October 29. U.S. Senate Approves Sale of AWAC Aircraft to Saudi Arabia. This was achieved only after a bitter parliamentary debate forced by supporters of Israel, which objected strongly to the sale. The Reagan Administration apparently hoped that this might influence Saudi Arabia to agree to the establishment of U.S. bases in Saudi Arabia.

1982, January 26. Regional Defense Agreement. Saudi Arabia, Kuwait, Bahrain, Qatar, Oman, and the United Arab Emirates agreed to establish a joint military command and an interlinked air defense system. Prompting this decision were the security challenges posed by the Iranian Revolution, the Gulf War, and the Soviet invasion of Afghanistan.

OMAN (MUSCAT AND OMAN)

1975–1983. Dhofar Separatist Movement Continues Guerrilla Struggle. Oman continued to battle against the Dhofar separatist movement insurgents. The Dhofar rebels, who had been assisted by Southern Yemen, now also received aid from Libya.

1975, February 2. Defense Pact with Iran. Iran agreed to give Oman air and naval support against foreign aggression. Iranian troops also assisted the Omani Army against the Dhofar rebels.

1980, June 4. Assistance and Base Agreement with the United States. Oman agreed to permit U.S. access to selected naval and air bases in exchange for U.S. military and economic aid.

1982, January 26. Regional Defense League Established. (See above.)

SOUTHERN YEMEN (PEOPLE'S DEMOCRATIC REPUBLIC OF YEMEN)

1975, November 30. Cuban Military Advisers in South Yemen. Press reports were subsequently confirmed by the U.S. State Department.

1978, June 25–27. President Deposed and Executed. It is not clear whether President **Salem Rubaya Ali** was overthrown—after a brief battle—because of his reported role in the assassination of President al-Ghashmi in North Yemen (see p. 1364) or because he was suspected by Communist colleagues of possibly reducing his links with the Soviets and improving relations with the U.S. and Saudi Arabia. The Arab League, suspecting the South Yemeni leadership of involvement in Ghashmi's death, suspended economic and cultural ties with South Yemen (July 2).

1980, April 23. President Resigns. Abdel Fattah Ismail was pressured to resign as president of South Yemen because of serious policy differences with Premier **Ali Nasser Mohammed al-Hasani.** Ismail was apparently too eager to bring about the proposed unification with North Yemen.

1980, May 1–June 1. Fighting Intensifies between North and South Yemen. There was a significant rise in armed conflict between North and South Yemen.

1980, June 9. Increase in Soviet-Cuban Presence in South Yemen. The number of Soviet advisers in South Yemen had reportedly risen to more than 1,000 and the number of Cubans to 4,000. The internal security and intelligence systems were allegedly headed by East Germans.

1981, August 19. Treaty with Libya and Ethiopia. The 3 countries pledged reduction of U.S. influence in the region.

IRAN

1975–1978, Unrest Becomes Rebellion. The Shah combined repression with concessions. Arbitrary arrests were made by the secret police (Savak). Opposition political parties were abolished. Nevertheless opposition to the Shah's rule increased. Political reforms and the release of political prisoners (1978, September–October) failed to satisfy the opposition.

1978, November 5–6. Military Rule Imposed; National Elections Promised. The Shah established martial law while seeking national reconciliation by promising elections no later than by June 1979. Again repression combined with concessions failed to satisfy the National Front opposition; civil unrest continued.

1978, December 29. Shah Names New Premier for Civilian Government. In a last attempt to satisfy his opponents, the Shah named opposition leader **Shahpur Bakhtiar** to head a civilian government. Bakhtiar accepted and established a government (January 6). However, the response of the National Front opposition was to demand the Shah's abdication and to label Bakhtiar a traitor.

1979, January 13. Khomeini Demands Establishment of Islamic Republic and Shah Departs Iran. In Paris the exiled **Ayatollah Ruhollah Khomeini,** senior Iranian Islamic (Shi'ite) clergyman, demanded that Iran become an Islamic republic. He established a Revolutionary Council.

1979, January 16. Departure of the Shah. Although the Shah did not formally give up his throne, his departure was tantamount to abdication.

1979, January 16–February 11. Bakhtiar-Khomeini Power Struggle. In an effort to restore order and preserve his government Bakhtiar temporarily closed Iran's airports to prevent Khomeini's return. When the airports were reopened (January 29) Khomeini immediately flew to Teheran from Paris (February 1), proclaimed the establishment of an Islamic republic and named **Mehdi Bazargan** premier of a provisional government. Armed civilians and rebel soldiers battled government troops in a climactic 3-day struggle which ended with the overthrow of the Bakhtiar government (February 9–11).

1979, February 12. Khomeini's Islamic Republic Established. Although Khomeini himself had no official cabinet portfolio, he exercised virtually unlimited power.

1979, February 14. First Invasion of U.S. Embassy. Iranian "students" broke into the diplomatic compound of the U.S. Embassy and took a U.S. Marine hostage, but later freed him (February 21).

1979, February 26–December 30. Rebellion and Civil Strife in Provinces. A wave of civil unrest, violence, and in some cases outright rebellion swept through several

Iranian provinces. Uprisings began in Azerbaijan, where an army barracks was seized (February 22). In response to unrest in Kurdistan, the Kurds were granted limited autonomy (March 25). This did not satisfy them and armed clashes continued throughout the summer.

1979, August–October. Civil War in Kurdistan. Khomeini mobilized the armed forces in order to wipe out the Kurdish rebellion (August 19). The Iranian government also accused Iraq of assisting the Kurdish rebels. A determined offensive by government troops drove the Kurds from their strongholds and across the border into Iraq (September 6). But guerrilla warfare continued. The Kurds regained a key stronghold, Mehabad (October 20), then called for a cease-fire (October 22), which was subsequently granted.

1979, November 3. Seizure of U.S. Embassy. Militant Iranian "students" broke into the U.S. Embassy compound and seized some 90 hostages, including 62 (later 66) Americans. Of these, 13 were soon released because they were black and/or women (November 19–20). The 53 remaining Americans were held as prisoners, and were subjected to abuse and mistreatment by their captors. One hostage was eventually released because he was severely ill (July 11, 1980).

1979, December 5. Renewed Hostilities in Kurdistan and Azerbaijan. Following a national plebiscite and a new constitution the Kurds rose again in rebellion. In Azerbaijan the Moslem People's Party took almost complete control of the province, but the central government soon regained authority.

1980–1984. Kurd Revolt Continues. Despite numerous offensives the Iranian Armed Forces were unable to suppress the Kurd rebellion. The Iranian Kurds received aid from Iran's arch enemy Iraq, while Iraq's rebellious Kurds allied themselves with Iran (see p. 1369).

1980, April 24–25. U.S. Efforts to Rescue Hostages: "Desert One." After repeated diplomatic efforts had been rebuffed, an American Joint Service rescue mission was mounted. Helicopters and transport planes with assault troops met in an isolated spot in central Iran ("Desert One"). The breakdown of three helicopters forced cancellation of the mission. During withdrawal 8 Americans were killed when a helicopter collided with a transport plane loaded with fuel. An official U.S. investigating board later severely criticized planning and command arrangements for the mission.

COMMENT: *The hostage crisis had already hurt American international prestige; the U.S. government appeared to all the world as being weak and irresolute. The failed rescue mission reinforced these assessments.*

1981, January 20. Release of the U.S. Hostages. The 52 Americans held hostage in Iran were released in return for U.S. agreement to free Iranian assets frozen in the U.S. following seizure of the U.S. Embassy in Teheran.

1982, April 7–19. Plots Uncovered: Attempted Coup Foiled. Foreign Minister **Sadegh Ghotbzadeh** and several Iranian Army officers were arrested for planning a coup and the assassination of Ayatollah Khomeini. They were subsequently tried and executed.

Iran–Iraq Gulf War

1980, September 9. Iraq Invades Iran. Sensing military weakness in Iran because of the Iranian revolution, Iraq launched a major offensive to resolve the long-standing border dispute (see p. 1286). The Iraqis at first met slight resistance. However, they were very cautious and failed to exploit opportunities for quick victory. The Iranians recovered from the initial defeats and a stalemate ensued along a battle line penetrating into Iran more than 30 miles in some places. The city of Khorramshahr was captured by the Iraqis.

1980–1982. Stalemate. Both sides made repeated efforts to break through the opposing lines. Casualties were heavy, but little was accomplished.

1982, January 23–March 3. Jordanian Volunteers Aid Iraqi Gulf War Efforts. **(See p. 1370.)**

1982, March 22–30. Iranian Counteroffensive. The Iranians began a determined attempt to drive the Iraqi forces from Iranian soil, and pushed Iraqi forces back as much as 24 miles in some places.

1982, April 30–May 20. Renewed Iranian Offensive. The Iranians again pushed the Iraqis back. The Iranians drove until they approached the Iraqi defenses near the port city of Khorramshahr, which the Iraqis had captured early in the war.

1982, May 22–23. Recapture of Khorramshahr. In the night attack the Iranians encircled the Iraqi force in Khorramshahr, which surrendered. The Iranians captured large quantities of Soviet arms, apparently supplied by Syria. The Iranians, ebullient because of their victory, proclaimed as their war aim and "greatest right" the deposition of Iraqi President Saddam Hussein (May 26).

1982, June 10–20. Iraq Offers Truce and Troop Withdrawal. Iraq proposed a truce and promised to withdraw all Iraqi troops from Iranian soil within 2 weeks of an Iranian acceptance of the truce. Iraq also declared a unilateral cease-fire. Iran responded by reiterating its demand for Hussein's removal from office (June 11, June 20).

1982, July 14–30. Iranian Offensive. Iran launched another offensive. The Iranians made some headway, but suffered heavy casualties for minimal gains.

1982, July 21–August 30. Air War Escalates. Iranian planes attacked Baghdad (July 21). Iraq retaliated with air attacks on Khargh Island, striking Iran's oil shipping facilities and sinking 2 merchant ships (August 18–30).

1982, September–November. New Iranian Offensives. The Iranians regained some territory on the northern front near the border town of Sumar, which Iraq had taken early in the war (October 1). The Iranians again attacked west of Dezful and advanced 3 miles into Iraqi territory near the town of Mandali (November 2). Iraqi troops counterattacked and drove the Iranians back to the border. To the south the Iranians advanced to within artillery range of the stategically important Baghdad-Basra highway (November 17).

1982, December 21. Arab Peace Initiative. The leaders of Algeria, United Arab Emirates, and Saudi Arabia attempted to mediate between the two warring Gulf states.

1983, February 2–March 9. Iraqi Air Attacks Cause Massive Oil Spill. Iraqi air attacks on Iranian Persian Gulf oil-producing facilities resulted in the largest oil spill in Persian Gulf history.

1983, February 7–16. Al Amarah Offensive. Iranians advanced toward the Baghdad-Basra road in an attempt to cut that road at Al Amarah. They reached within 30 miles of Al Amarah before being halted and thrown back by an Iraqi counterattack. The Iraqis claimed they knocked out 100 Iranian tanks and took 1,000 POWs.

1983, April–October. Repeated Iranian Offensives. Attacks west of Dezful failed to make significant gains (April 11–14). Next the Iranians launched an offensive into northern Iraq (July 23). Advances were negligible. Iranian troops then tried to break the Iraqi line west of Dezful in a major offensive (July 30). The Iraqis repulsed a number of Iranian thrusts, then counterattacked, but were repulsed in turn (August 6–12). Casualties were severe on both sides. The Iranians launched still another offensive on the northern front and closed a salient that had been opened by Iranian Kurdish rebels (October 20).

1983, July 20. Iraq again Attacks Iranian Oil Centers. Iraqi planes struck Iranian oil industry facilities.

1984, February 11–22. Renewed Iranian Offensive. Iran tried to carry the war deeper into Iraq by resuming the offensive on both the northern and central fronts (February 11). Iraq claimed that on the central front its troops had approached the Baghdad-Basra highway. The Iranians renewed attacks toward Basra in the south (February 22). The Iraqis repulsed the attack, only after severe loss of troops and some territory. Their counterattacks to recapture undeveloped Iraqi oil fields on Majnoon Island also failed. The Iranians claimed that Iraq used poison gas in these battles. International observers confirmed that mustard gas was apparently employed. During this battle Iraqi planes attacked Iranian oil installations near Kargh Island.

SOUTH ASIA

INDIA

1975, February 25. Sheik Mohammed Abdullah Reinstated as Chief Minister of Kashmir. The Indian government reinstated the "Lion of Kashmir" as the senior official in the Indian sector of the disputed province 22 years after removing him from power (see p. 1287). Pakistan claimed that this abrogated a 1972 agreement to maintain the status quo (see p. 1291).

1975–1979. Tribal Revolts in Northeast India. Government troops carried out counterinsurgency operations against tribal rebels seeking independence for Mizoram and Nagaland. The Nagas ended their 20-year rebellion in exchange for a general amnesty (November 11). Despite losses exceeding 1,000 per year the Mizos continued their guerrilla war against India.

1975–1976. Border Incidents and Strained Relations with Bangladesh. (See p. 1377.)

1975, October 20. Border Clash with China. Both India and China claimed the other side had violated the frontier.

1979, January 5. Resumption of Naga Insurgency. Nagas raided from Nagaland into neighboring Assam state. They demanded that parts of Assam should be ceded to Nagaland.

1979, April 20. Parliamentary Request for Atomic Weapons Rejected. The Indian government turned down a request from its parliament to produce atomic weapons to meet the possible threat of Pakistan's manufacture of these weapons.

1981, April 26. India Threatens Nuclear Weapons Production and Deployment. K. Subrahmanyam, a military adviser to the Indian government, stated that the threat posed by a possible Pakistani deployment of nuclear weapons warranted India's production of these weapons.

1981, November 3–23. India-Pakistan Border Incidents. There was an increase of border incidents as tensions rose because of military aid received by Pakistan from the U.S. and because of Indian fear of Pakistan achieving nuclear capabilities.

1979–1982. Indian Troops Battle Insurgents in States. Indian Army units carried out widespread counterinsurgency or riot suppression operations in Assam, Gujerat, Manipur, Mizo, Tripura, and Bombay.

1982, May 17–20. Indian-Sino Border Talks Held. India and China held border talks concerning disputed territories in the Ladakh region of Kashmir, which was under control of the Chinese, and along the border of Bhutan under Indian control.

1983, April 6. Troops Restore Order in Assam. Indian Army troops were needed to restore order in Assam, racked by struggles between Assamese and Bengali immigrants.

1983, June 7. Punjab Disturbances Require Paramilitary Troops Intervention. Civil disturbances caused by rival Sikh and Hindu groups required the intervention of central government paramilitary troops to maintain order.

PAKISTAN

1975, February 5–28. U.S. Military Aid Strains India-Pakistan Relations. U.S. President **Gerald Ford** lifted a 10-year arms embargo to Pakistan. India protested that this would encourage Pakistan's Prime Minister **Zulfikar Ali Bhutto** in a bellicose anti-Indian policy. India was not placated when subsequently the U.S. lifted its arms embargo against India (February 24).

1975, February 8–March 4. Unrest in Northwest Frontier Province Charged to Afghanistan. Pakistan alleged that Afghanistan was responsible for subversion and collusion with Pakistani dissidents.

1976, February 25. Pakistan Purchases French Nuclear Reprocessing Plant. Foreign arms control analysts interpreted this as a reaction to India's successful nuclear detonation (May 18, 1974). (See p. 1291.)

1976, September 3–10. Kohistani Tribal Revolt Smashed. More than 10,000 troops with armor and air support were necessary to suppress the revolt.

1977, April 21. Martial Law Imposed in Three Cities. Prime Minister Ali Bhutto, who was being accused of election corruption, responded to increased violence and unrest by imposing martial law in Karachi, Lahore, and Hyderabad. The martial law decree was later declared unconstitutional by the Supreme Court of Pakistan (June 3) and was lifted 3 days later (June 6).

1977, July 5. Military Coup d'État. Growing unrest, and the election corruption charges, led to a military takeover by Army Chief of Staff General **Mohammed Zia ul-Haq.** Prime Minister Bhutto, as well as opposition party leaders, were jailed; martial law was imposed. Bhutto was soon released. Zia promised to hold elections in October, but soon reneged on this pledge.

1977, September 5. Bhutto Arrested and Charged with Murder. The former Prime Minister was tried and convicted of ordering the murder of a political foe (March 18, 1978).

1979, April 4. Execution of Ali Bhutto. General Zia rejected foreign appeals for clemency.

1979, April 6. U.S. Cuts Military Aid to Pakistan. This was based upon evidence that Pakistan was attempting to develop a nuclear weapons capability. Pakistan denied the charge, asserting only an interest in development of nuclear power for peaceful purposes (April 18). Subsequent talks failed to persuade the U.S. to change its position (Oct. 17–18).

1980, January 15. U.S. Reverses Position on Military Aid. The Soviet Union's invasion of Afghanistan prompted a reversal of the U.S. position on military aid to Pakistan. Despite misgivings about Pakistan's nuclear development intentions, the U.S. offered $400 million in military aid to Pakistan. The U.S. also announced its intent to invoke a 1959 Security Treaty permitting the U.S. to intervene militarily if Pakistan were invaded by the U.S.S.R. Pakistan's President Zia welcomed the pledge but rejected the military aid offer as insignificant.

1980, September 26. Soviet Helicopters Violate Pakistan Border. Pakistani authorities charged that Soviet helicopter gunships violated Pakistani territory and attacked Pakistani troops. Pakistan asserted that this was only one of several such violations since the Soviet invasion of Afghanistan.

1981, March 23–April 21. U.S. Renews Military Aid to Pakistan. The U.S. government offered Pakistan $500 million in military aid to meet the security challenge posed to Pakistan by the Soviet invasion of Afghanistan.

1981, October 16. Pakistan Offers Renunciation of War Treaty with India. India rejected the offer by President Mohammed Zia ul-Haq, dismissing it as a propaganda move (November 11).

1981, November 25. Pakistan Threatens to Develop Nuclear Weapons Capacity. Western press sources reported that Pakistan's President Mohammed Zia ul-Haq told visiting Turkish journalists that Pakistan was striving to develop nuclear weapons because this was the only way to survive militarily and politically in the present international milieu.

1982, January 29–31. Treaty Talks with India. The Indian government reversed its opposition to Pakistan's proposal for a nonaggression treaty and began negotiations with Pakistan in the hopes of arriving at a genuine rapprochement. However, India withdrew from the negotiations because of anti-Indian remarks made by a Pakistani diplomat at the U.N. (February 25).

AFGHANISTAN

1975, August 30. Economic Assistance Agreement with the U.S.S.R. Under this agreement Afghanistan was to receive economic aid for 30 years.

1978, January 1–March 1. Cooled Relations with Soviets. President Daoud became concerned about growing Soviet influence and drastically reduced the number of Soviet advisers from about 1,000 to 200.

1978, April 27–28. Marxist Coup. Daoud was overthrown and killed in a Soviet-backed coup by **Noor Mohammad Taraki,** who began a forced modernization and reeducation program. This program was resented and opposed by most Afghans. Between 8,000 and 12,000 opponents were ruthlessly killed.

1979, February 14. U.S. Ambassador Killed. Ambassador **Adolph Dubs,** taken hostage by Moslem extremists, was killed in a gun battle when Soviets and Afghan authorities stormed the hotel where Dubs was being held. The U.S. State Department, which had urged caution, protested the role the Soviets played in the affair.

1979, March 27. Amin Becomes Premier. President Taraki named **Hafizullah Amin** as Premier. Although the Communist Party tightened control over the government, popular resistance grew into full-scale rebellion. Many deserters from the Afghan Army joined rebel groups (called *mujahedeen* freedom fighters or holy warriors), who gained control of 22 of Afghanistan's 28 provinces.

1979, September 16–18. Taraki's Downfall. Amin overthrew Taraki, who was slain in a gun battle. Amin's coup was apparently accomplished without Soviet approval. Friction grew between Amin and his Soviet advisers.

Soviet Invasion of Afghanistan

1979, December 1–16. Soviet Buildup. The Soviets increased the size of their garrisons at the two air bases in Kabul, and began secret preparations for the ouster of Amin. A partial mobilization of Soviet troops just north of Afghanistan was quietly initiated. The Kremlin apparently feared that the mujahedeen would overthrow Amin and end Soviet influence in Afghanistan, and were determined to prevent this at any cost.

1979, December 24. Soviet Seizure of Kabul Airport. This was done by special Soviet forces, directed by First Deputy Minister of Internal Affairs (MVD) Lt. General **V. S. Paputin.**

1979, December 25–28. Occupation of Kabul. A massive airlift of Soviet troops began Christmas Day. Three airborne divisions—103rd, 104th, and 105th—were flown in while 4 motorized rifle divisions invaded Afghanistan overland from the north. The 105th Division occupied Kabul against considerable resistance from elements of the Afghan Army and the local population. Amin and his ministers were islolated in his palace. A Soviet task force attacked the palace and Amin was killed, either in the fighting or by execution. General Paputin was also killed during the battle.

1979, December 28. Karmal Installed As President. Amin's former Vice President, **Babrak Karmal,** now ambassador to Czechoslovakia, was recalled by the Soviets to become President.

COMMENT: *The Soviet invasion of Afghanistan inflamed world public opinion. The Soviet move assured that the U.S. Senate would refuse to ratify the Strategic Arms Limitation Treaty (SALT II Treaty) that had been signed by presidents Carter and Brezhnev the preceding spring (see p. 1350). President Carter enacted a grain embargo against the Soviet Union and canceled U.S. participation in the 1980 Summer Olympics, which were to be held in Moscow.*

1980, January–February. Popular Resistance Intensifies. Following the initial success of the December coup, opposition to the Soviets became widespread and fierce. Convoys were ambushed and numerous armored vehicles were destroyed. Several towns held by the Soviets were surrounded and besieged by mujahedeen. Soviet activities were constrained by the severe weather conditions that prevailed in Afghanistan in January and February.

1980, February 21–23. Uprising in Kabul. This was crushed by Soviet troops. About 500 Afghans were killed and another 1,200 jailed.

1980, March–April. Soviet Offensive. Soviet objectives were: (1) beseiged towns would be relieved, (2) the mujahedeen were to be driven from the fertile valleys and the strategic roadways that traversed them, (3) a security zone would be established on the border near the Khyber Pass, the route by which the mujahedeen were getting supplies and arms from Pakistan, (4) all of the bases of resistance in the mountainous regions of Afghanistan were to be eliminated.

1980, March 1. Phase One. The Soviets employed MiG-21s to strafe rebel positions with napalm and rockets. Then MiG-24 helicopters showered mujahedeen positions with more napalm and rocket fire. Next MiG-6 helicopters dropped airborne assault troops on the positions. All Soviet garrisons were soon relieved and the remaining mujahedeen driven into the hills.

1980, April–May. Phases Two and Three. In order to drive the mujahedeen from the valleys and win control of strategic roadways the Soviets used combined arms, air-land attacks, featuring MiG-24s. Although these attacks met with strong resistance and the mujahedeen were able to inflict heavy casualties on the Soviets, they were forced to withdraw to the hills with heavy losses. A security zone was soon established, but the Soviets were unable to prevent the movement of supplies and arms from Pakistan, nor were they able to prevent mujahedeen raids in the strategic valleys.

1980–1984. Continued Afghan Resistance. Gradually the Soviets increased the size of their forces from 85,000 to 105,000, but were unable to break the resistance movement. The rebels continued to attack Soviet convoys and supply lines with considerable success. These attacks enabled the mujahedeen to acquire badly needed arms and ammunition, in addition to supplies from Pakistan. The Soviets mounted numerous offensives, inflicting heavy casualties on the Afghan resistance fighters, but themselves suffered severe casualties from guerrilla attack and ground operations. The Soviets not only were not able to pacify the mountain areas but were unable to maintain uninterrupted control of the rural valleys. Afghanis alleged that the Soviets used chemical and biological weapons in Afghanistan, in violation of the 1925 Geneva Protocol and the 1972 Geneva ban on the manufacture of biological weapons. The U.S. Department of State also alleged Soviet use of illegal biochemical weapons. The mujahedeen were hampered by religious and tribal rivalries and shortages of arms, equipment, and ammunition. They were unable to create a single political opposition group or a unified command structure. The Soviets, despite setbacks and high casualties (estimates of Soviet casualties by 1984 were about 15,000), showed no signs of giving up in Afghanistan. They expanded the runways at 19 airports and constructed new airports at Kandahar, Herat, Dadadhshan and Mazarree Sharif, as well as a base in the Wakhan corridor near the Chinese border. In 1984, the air bases, in easy range of the Persian Gulf and the Indian Ocean, held an estimated 400 planes, including MiG-23s and Ilyushin-38s.

SRI LANKA

1977, February 15. State of Emergency Ended. A state of emergency, which had been imposed during the PLF revolt 6 years earlier, was lifted (see p. 1292).

1981–1984. Racial Violence, Civil Disturbance, and Insurgency. Racially motivated violent clashes between the Sinhalese majority and the Tamil minority intensified. A state of emergency was declared (August 17, 1981). However, violence continued, and Tamil insurgents frequently attacked government troops.

BANGLADESH

1975, August 15. Coup d'État. Minister of Commerce **Khandakar Mushtaque Ahmed,** supported by army officers, led a successful coup which toppled the government of Sheik **Mujibur Rahman,** President and founder of Bangladesh. (See p. 1292.) Mujibur was killed. Martial law was established (August 20).

1975, November 3–6. Military Coup d'État. Major General **Ziaur Rahman** overthrew President Moshtaque. Rahman appointed former Bangladesh Supreme Court Chief Justice **Abu Sadat Mohammed Sayem** president, who appointed a 3-man advisory Council of Armed Forces Chiefs. Continuing internal unrest and border violations were blamed on India, which denied complicity.

1976, November 29–30. Martial Law Proclaimed. General Ziaur Rahman became virtual dictator.

1977, April 21–May 29. Rahman Consolidates Power. Bangladesh President Sayem resigned, and named General Rahman to succeed him. A national referendum approved Rahman's martial law government by a 99% majority (May 29).

1977, October 2. Coup Attempt Fails. Rahman's troops defeated dissident insurgents in a brief but bloody battle. Leaders of the coup were tried and executed (October 27).

1979, April 7. Martial Law Ends. Bangladesh President Ziaur Rahman announced the end of martial law, and promised the return to civilian rule.

1979, April 18. Accord with India Reached. Bangladesh reached an agreement with India on a number of issues that had caused strained relations between the two countries.

1981, May 30–June 2. Rahman Murdered in Coup Attempt. President Ziaur Rahman was killed in Chittagong. However, loyal troops put down the revolt led by General **Manzur Ahmed,** who was killed. Other leading conspirators were tried later. Vice-president **Abdus Sattar** took office as President and later won a national presidential election (November 15).

1982, March 25. Coup d'État. Army Chief of Staff General **Hossein Mohammed Ershad** seized power in a bloodless coup. He later assumed the office of President (December 11).

SOUTHEAST ASIA

BURMA

1975–1984. Continuous Guerrilla Warfare in Burma. Burmese government troops continued to battle Communist and tribal insurgents (see p. 1293). The People's Republic of China supplied rebels with arms and equipment while maintaining tolerable relations with Burma.

1983, October 9. Korean Officials Killed in Terrorist Bombing. A bomb explosion during a state visit by South Korean President Chun Doo Hwan killed 4 members of his cabinet and 13 other South Korean officials. Chun, apparently the target, arrived just after the explosion. A Burmese investigation found North Korea responsible. Burma severed relations with North Korea.

THAILAND

1975–1980. Border Clashes with Laos. There were a number of border clashes with Laos varying in size and intensity.

1975–1978. Border Clashes with Cambodia. **(See p. 1380.)**

1975–1976. Thai Troops Battle Communist Insurgency. Government troops continued to carry out counterinsurgency operations against Thai guerrillas, mostly in southern Thailand, but also in the northeast. The government claimed that the guerrillas had been trained and were receiving aid from China, Cambodia, and Vietnam.

1975, May 14–19. Thai Protest against American Use of Thai Bases. Thai officials were furious because the U.S. used Thai bases as a staging area for the *Mayaguez* rescue operations (see p. 1380). The U.S. government issued a formal apology which Thailand accepted (May 19).

1975–1976. U.S. Withdrawal from Thailand. The U.S. began to withdraw planes and troops (June 6–7). All U.S. planes were withdrawn from Thailand before the end of the year (December 19). All troops were withdrawn the following year (June 20).

1976, October 8. Military Coup. The return of exiled former Premier **Thanom Kittikachorn** (September 19) led to demonstrations and riots by university students (October 4–6). To restore order, a military coup was led by Admiral **Sangad Chaloryu. Thanin Kraivichien** (a civilian) was appointed premier, but Admiral Chaloryu retained control as defense minister.

1975–1977. Thai-Malaysian Counterinsurgency Cooperation. Thailand and Malaysia agreed to cooperate in counterinsurgency efforts against Communist insurgents in the Kra Isthmus (April 11, 1975). After initial cooperative successes, the two countries later agreed that forces of either country could cross their common border to pursue guerrillas and pledged to continue joint counterinsurgency operations (March 4, 1977). Another major success was achieved later in the year in southern Thailand near the Malaysian border (July–August).

1977, March 26. Attempted Coup. General **Chalard Hiranyasiri** failed in his attempt to gain power.

1977, October 20. Military Coup. Defense Minister Admiral Sangad Chaloryu seized control in a bloodless coup.

1978, July 15. Thailand and Cambodia Agree to End Border Hostilities. After neary 4 years of numerous armed border clashes of varying size and intensity, the Thai and Cambodian governments agreed to end their border conflict and exchange envoys.

1979–1984. Vietnamese Incursions into Thailand. Vietnamese troops clashed with Thai troops on a number of occasions while pursuing Cambodian guerrillas. (See p. 1379).

1980, June 15–July 23. Border Clashes with Laos. Despite earlier agreements to end hostilities, incidents continued, mostly provoked by the Laotians.

VIETNAM

1975–1977. Border War with Cambodia. Vietnamese troops clashed repeatedly with troops of the Khmer Rouge Communist regime in Cambodia.

1976, July 2. North and South Vietnam Officially Reunited. The North Vietnamese Communist regime completed the reunification of the country, establishing the Socialist Republic of Vietnam.

1977, November–December. Vietnamese Invasion of Cambodia. Vietnam forces crushed a Cambodian division at Snoul (November 18–19) then halted its advance 10 miles inside the Cambodian border (December 3). The Vietnamese soon resumed the offensive and drove 70 miles into southern Cambodia before halting (December 21). At the same time, Vietnam denounced the atrocities the Khmer Rouge had committed against the population of Cambodia (see p. 1380).

1979, January 2–15. Renewed Vietnamese Invasion of Cambodia. In reaction to the Pol Pot regime's war of extermination against the Kampuchean rebels and the Cambodian civilian population, Vietna invaded Cambodia. The Vietnamese quickly smashed Cambodian forces in 6 provincial capitals and captured Phnom Penh, the Cambodian capital, where they established a puppet regime. Pol Pot's forces were crushed, but maintained several pockets of resistance in the Cambodian countryside.

1979, February 17–March 15. Chinese Invasion of Vietnam. Before dawn, 25,000 Chinese troops and 1,200 tanks crossed the Vietnamese border and penetrated Vietnamese territory from 12 to 20 miles deep. But then the drive slowed. It is however unclear whether the Chinese slowed their offensive because of effective Vietnamese resistance or because the Chinese deliberately stopped their advance (as they claimed). No further major actions were fought. The Chinese began to withdraw, proclaiming they had accomplished their mission (March 5). They announced that the withdrawal was completed 10 days later. No reports of losses were given by either side, but Vietnamese losses probably exceeded those of the Chinese.

1979–1984. Vietnamese Counterinsurgency Operations in Cambodia. Vietnamese forces and their Cambodian allies conducted largely successful counterinsurgency operations against the forces of Pol Pot's deposed Khmer Rouge regime, taking a major headquarters and driving many Khmer Rouge troops into Thailand (1979, March 16–31). Nonetheless, strong pockets of guerrilla resistance remained, both Khmer Rouge guerrilla forces of Pol Pot and forces loyal to Prince Norodom Sihanouk as well (see p. 1380).

1979–1984. Strained Relations with Thailand. Because of the Vietnamese invasion of Cambodia, large numbers of Cambodians fled to neighboring Thailand. Vietnam charged Thailand with aiding rebels, while Thai officials charged Vietnam with genocide in Cambodia. Vietnamese incursions into Thailand caused tensions between the two nations (see p. 1378).

1979, April 9–1980, March 6. Chinese-Vietnamese Reconciliation Talks. No real progress was made; relations remained strained.

1979, July–1983, April. Border Incidents with China.

1980–1984. Low-Level Insurgency in South Vietnam. Soldiers of the former Army of the Republic of Vietnam continued to conduct small-scale guerrilla operations against the Communist regime.

LAOS

1975, May–August. Pathet Lao Consolidates Power. The Pathet Lao continued to be successful in the long civil war in Laos (see p. 1300). After securing key positions around Vientiane, the Pathet Lao agreed to a cease-fire (May 7). Soon after this, Pathet Lao troops took control of all of southern Laos (May 16–20). Prime Minister Souvanna Phouma ordered government troops to cease resistance to the Pathet Lao (May 23). The Royal Laotian Army and the Pathet Lao were unified (June 17). Two months later the Pathet Lao assumed control in Vientiane Province, giving them complete control of Laos (August 23).

1975–1980. Border Incidents with Thailand. **(See p. 1378.)**

1975–1977. Insurrection of Meo Tribesmen. Some 5,000 Meo tribesmen, formerly armed and trained by the U.S. Central Intelligence Agency, undertook guerrilla operations against Pathet Lao troops. The Meos inflicted heavy casualties on the Pathet Lao, despite Vietnamese assistance to the Pathet Lao.

1975, December 1–3. Laos Becomes a Socialist Republic. The ancient monarchy was ended and the rule of the Pathet Lao legitimatized.

1977, July 18. Friendship and Assistance Treaties with Vietnam. These legitimatized the presence of 40,000 Vietnamese troops already stationed in Laos.

1978, February 10–March 28. Counterinsurgency Operations Against Meo Tribesmen. Laotian troops and some 30,000 Vietnamese troops eliminated most resistance by Meo tribesmen and other dissidents. Nonetheless, strong pockets of guerrilla resistance remained.

1979, March 7–15. Chinese Border Incidents. Laotian authorities reported several incursions into Laos by Chinese troops.

1979–1983. Meo Accusations of Laotian and Vietnamese Use of Chemical Weapons. Meo tribesmen who had fled Laos charged that Pathet Lao and Vietnamese troops had used poison gas and biochemical weapons against them (November 3). These reports were repeated as guerrilla resistance continued.

CAMBODIA (KAMPUCHEA)

1975–1978. Khmer Rouge Massacres. Conducting what was tantamount to a war on the entire population, the Khmer Rouge government of Premier **Pol Pot** was responsible for the deaths of over 2 million people in its attempts to wipe out resistance to its rule.

1975–1978. Border Clashes with Thailand. There were numerous border clashes with Thailand varying in size and intensity. In part these stemmed from the large numbers of refugees seeking to escape the Khmer Rouge massacres. The 2 countries signed an agreement pledging to pacify their borders (July 19, 1978; see p. 1378).

1975, May 12–14. *Mayaguez* Incident. While in international waters some 60 miles off the coast of Cambodia, the American merchant ship S.S. *Mayaguez* was captured and its 39 crewmen taken prisoner by a Cambodian gunboat, then transported to the Cambodian port of Sihanoukville. Failing to win the release of the crew through diplomatic means, President Gerald Ford ordered U.S. Marines to conduct a rescue mission. After being airlifted to Thailand from bases in Okinawa and the Philippines, the Marines conducted a helicopter attack on Tang Island (off Sihanoukville) where the *Mayaguez* was thought to be held. At the same time, carrier aircraft attacked a nearby Cambodian air base and gunboats in Sihanoukville. In the course of the rescue operations, the Cambodians released the *Mayaguez* crewmen in a captured Thai fishing boat. The U.S. losses were 18 killed in action and 50 wounded. The Cambodians lost 17 aircraft and 3 gunboats and an unknown number of personnel.

1975–1979, December. Border War with Vietnam. (See p. 1378.)

1976–1978. Resistance to Khmer Rouge Builds. Defectors from the Cambodian Army, with Vietnamese support, formed a resistance movement called the Movement for Khmer National Liberation (April 21, 1976).

1979–1984. Vietnamese Invasion and Counterinsurgency Operations in Cambodia (see p. 1378).

1979, October 4. Sihanouk Announces Formation of New Resistance Movement. Prince Norodom Sihanouk, former Cambodian chief of state in exile in Peking, announced the formation of a new resistance movement in opposition to both the Khmer Rouge guerrillas and the Vietnam-backed Kampuchean regime. The resistance movement was to be called the Confederation of the Khmer Nation. Later nominal coordination was established between the Confederation and Khmer Rouge guerrillas (1982, June).

MALAYSIA

1977, January 14–17. Combined Thai-Malaysian Guerrilla Operations. (See p. 1378.)

1977, March 4. Border Pact Signed with Thailand. (See p. 1378.)

1977, July–August. Combined Thai-Malaysian Guerrilla Operation. (See p. 1378.)

INDONESIA

1975–1984. Guerrilla Warfare in Timor. Indonesian troops battled guerrillas in East Timor after the Revolutionary Front for Independent East Timor declared its independence from Portugal (November 28, 1975).

1975, November 29. Annexation of Timor. The Timor Democratic Union (UDT) declared that Timor had become part of Indonesia.

PHILIPPINES

1975–1984. Moslem Rebellion Continues in Southern Islands. (See p. 1305.)

1976, February 20. SEATO Disbanded. The Southeast Asia Treaty Organization (SEATO), founded after the 1954 Geneva Conference (see pp. 1292–1293) in order to provide collective security for the region, formally came to an end with ceremonies in Manila.

1981, January 17. Marcos Pronounces End to Martial Law. President Ferdinand Marcos ended martial law which had been in effect over 9 years (p. 1305).

1983, August 21. Assassination of Aquino. President Marcos's main political foe, **Benigno Aquino,** was assassinated upon his return to Manila from a period of self-exile. Popular indignation flared in the Philippines because of suspicion that Aquino had been killed by soldiers on order of Marcos.

PAPUA, NEW GUINEA

1975, September 16. Independence from Australia.

1975–1976. Bougainville Separatist Movement. Island leader **John Momis** led a secessionist movement which conducted attacks on Papuan government installations and committed other acts of sabotage before arriving at a negotiated settlement with New Guinea Premier **Michael Somare** (March 26, 1976).

EAST ASIA

CHINA (PEOPLE'S REPUBLIC)

1976, September 9. Death of Mao Zedong. The death of the original leader of China's Communist Party, theoretician of guerrilla warfare, and founder of the People's Republic of China, provided an opportunity for the emerging pragmatic leadership of the Communist Party to turn away from idealism to practicality in the affairs of the most populous nation on earth. The most powerful man in the New China soon became **Deng Xiaoping,** whose position of strength was finally consolidated when he forced Mao's immediate successor, **Hua Guofeng,** to resign as Premier (1980, September 4).

1979, January 1, Diplomatic Relations with the United States. This was a major diplomatic triumph for the P.R.C. The U.S. agreed to withdraw diplomatic recognition from the Nationalist Government of Taiwan, and to abrogate its defense treaty with the N.R.C. The U.S. accepted the status of Taiwan as a province of China, and the P.R.C. agreed that it would not use force to regain control over Taiwan.

1979, February 17. Invasion of Vietnam. (See p. 1379.)

1980, May 18. China Test-Launches ICBM. The Chinese made their first successful test-launch of an ICBM; the missile traveled 6,200 miles.

TAIWAN (NATIONAL REPUBLIC OF CHINA)

1975, April 5. Death of Chiang Kai-shek. He was succeeded as President of the N.R.C. by his son, **Chiang Ching-kuo.**

1979, January 1. Abrogation of Diplomatic Relations and Treaties with United States. The United States took this step in order to establish diplomatic relations with the People's Republic of China (see above). But semidiplomatic relations were retained through liaison offices, and the practical effect of the change was initially negligible.

1982, July 17. U.S. Fighter Plane Co-production Agreement with Taiwan. U.S. President Ronald Reagan signed an agreement with Nationalist China extending the co-production of F-5E fighter planes by the two countries. The People's Republic of China promptly protested that this was a violation of the agreement by which diplomatic relations had been established.

1982, August 18. U.S. to Reduce Arms Supply to Nationalist China. U.S. President Reagan assured the P.R.C. that the United States would continue to reduce arms supplies to the N.R.C. on Taiwan.

TIBET

1975–1984. Continued Guerrilla Warfare. There was continued low-level insurgency against Chinese rule in Tibet (see p. 1311).

NORTH KOREA

1975–1984. Naval Incidents and Continued Tense Relations Along Border with South Korea. (See below.)

1976, August 18. North Korean Assault on South Korean–U.S. Work Crew. North Korean soldiers, armed with metal pikes and axes, assaulted a South Korean-U.S. military personnel work team in the DMZ while they were trimming a tree in order to improve surveillance. Two U.S. Army officers were killed and five U.S. enlisted men were wounded. Another South Korean-U.S. work crew returned 3 days later and cut the tree down.

SOUTH KOREA

1975–1984. Clashes with North Korea. There were a number of border incidents and clashes between the North and South Korean navies.

1976, August 18. North Korean Assault on South Korean–U.S. Work Crew. (See above.)

1977, March 9. Planned U.S. Troop Withdrawal. (See p. 1391.)

1978, April 28. South Korean Airliner Attacked over Soviet Territory. Soviet fighter plane fired on and forced a Korean commercial plane to land in Soviet territory. Two passengers were killed and 13 were injured during the incident. The Soviet Union claimed that the airliner was attacked only after the Korean pilot had failed to respond to warning signals. Korea claimed that the Soviets had failed to warn the pilot.

1979, December 12–13. Martial Law Chief Arrested. General **Chung Seung Hwa** was arrested by subordinates for complicity in the slaying of President Park. Chung was subsequently tried and sentenced to 10 years in prison for his role in the assassination (March 13, 1980).

1980, May 18. Martial Law Imposed. Following rioting and antigovernment demonstrations by students and others throughout South Korea, total martial law was imposed by General **Lee Hi Song.**

1981, January 24. Martial Law Decree Lifted. In fulfillment of a promise made upon his accession to the presidency (September 1, 1980) **Chun Doo Hwan** announced the end of martial law in South Korea. South Korea had been under some form of martial law since the assassination of South Korean President Chung Hee Park.

1983, September 1. Soviets Down Korean Commercial Aircraft. (See p. 1359.)

1983, October 9. Korean Officials Killed in Terrorist Bombing. (See p. 1378.)

JAPAN

1982–1983. Five-Year Military Buildup Plan. The Japanese government announced a five-year plan of military development with the objective of developing a capability to defend 1,000 miles beyond its seacoast (1982, July 23). The plan was the first attempt at providing for its own national security since its defeat in the Second World War, and the establishment of the National Self-Defense Force (see p. 1312). The Japanese Diet voted funds for this buildup (December 30, 1982; July 12, 1983).

AFRICA

EAST AFRICA

Ethiopia

1975, January 31–July 31. Civil War Escalates in Eritrea. Ethiopian forces continued to battle Eritrean secessionist rebels in Asmara and north of the provincial capital. The rebels were unsuccessful in their attempt to cut the main road between the Ethiopian capital, Addis Ababa, and the deep-water port of Assab on the Red Sea. The rebels also failed to capture Asmara and Keren, northwest of Asmara. Although the rebels failed to capture any key urban center, they did control most areas near Asmara. The two principal rebel factions, the Eritrean Liberation Front–Revolutionary Command (ELF–RC) and the Eritrean Popular Liberation Front (EPLF), joined forces for these operations.

1976, May 16. Ethiopian Peace Offer. Brigadier General **Tafari Banti,** Ethiopian chief of state and nominal head of the Military Council, offered amnesty to Eritrean political prisoners, economic aid to the Eritrean province, and also held out the possibility of regional autonomy for the Eritreans if they would cease fighting.

1976, May 18–22. Ethiopian Peasant Volunteer Offensive. While the Ethiopian government was offering peace, it was raising a volunteer army of as many as 50,000 peasants to launch an offensive against the Eritrean rebels. The drive bogged down almost immediately when the Eritreans blew up a key bridge. The peasant militia was soon disbanded (June 13).

1976, December, Ethiopians Sign Soviet Assistance Pact. Ethiopian leaders signed a long-term military aid treaty with the Soviet Union.

1977, January 5–August 25. Eritrean Successes. The EPLF won an important psychological victory by taking the town of Karora (January 5). Soon after they captured Naqfa, a district capital (March 23). Keren, the second largest city in Eritrea and the key to control of the north and west of the province, was captured (July 3). Taking advantage of Ethiopian involvement in Ogaden, the Eritreans attacked the deep-water port of Massawa on the Red Sea, 45 miles east of Asmara (July 15). Massawa was encircled and almost the entire northern part of the province was in rebel hands (August 25).

1977, January–June. Rebellion in Ogaden Province. A majority of the sparse population of Ethiopia's desert Ogaden Province were Somalis. Undoubtedly encouraged by the Soviet-supported Somalia government, the Western Somalia Liberation Front (WSLF) took up arms to throw off Ethiopian rule and to join Somalia

Ethiopian forces in the province were forced to retreat to fortified mountain bases at Jijiga, Harar, and Diredawa.

1977, February 3. Mengistu Seizes Power. Colonel **Mengistu Haile Mariam** and his followers bested Brigadier General Tafari Banti in a bloody gun battle in Addis Ababa in which Banti was killed. Mengistu ruled virtually unopposed.

Ogaden War with Somalia

1977, July 13. Somalian Invasion of Ogaden. Encouraged by Soviet economic and military assistance, and by Ethiopia's involvement in Eritrea, Somali President **Siad Barre** sent troops into Ogaden Province from northwest Somalia to help the WSLF, with the ultimate objective of annexing Ogaden to Somalia. Barre insisted, however, that the invasion troops were volunteers, and denied any regular Somali troop involvement. Barre's action was embarrassing to the U.S.S.R., which had also begun to provide military assistance to Ethiopia.

1977, August 16–19. Battle of Diredawa. Ethiopia troops repulsed attacks by Somali and WSLF troops to take their fortified positions at Diredawa. The extent to which this Ethiopian success was due to the presence of Soviet advisers and a small contingent of Cuban combat troops is unclear. The Somalis, however, were able to block the railroad from Addis Ababa to Djibouti on the Red Sea.

1977, September 4–14. Battle of Jijiga. Somalis and WSLF defeated Ethiopian forces, destroying or capturing 50 tanks. Casualties were heavy on both sides. The Somalis seized the Kara Marda Pass (September 23–27) and advanced from north and east to blockade Harar. Ethiopian troop buildup, assisted by Soviet advisers and Cuban combat troops, halted further Somali advance, and a stalemate ensued. The Soviets attempted to arrange a settlement between their warring clients.

1977, November 13. Soviets Expelled from Somalia. Infuriated by the fact that his presumed Soviet allies were also assisting his Ethiopian enemies, Siad Barre expelled his Soviet military and technical advisers, and required them to evacuate their naval and submarine bases at Mogadishu and elsewhere on the Indian Ocean coast. Soviet Colonel General **Grigory Borisov,** who commanded the Soviet mission in Somalia, went to Ethiopia.

1977, November–1978; January. Soviet and Cuban Buildup in Ethiopia. Soviet adviser strength increased from a handful to about 1,500; Cuban troop strength increased from about 500 to about 11,000. The Soviet mission was commanded by Army General **Vasily Petrov,** who had been First Deputy Commander of Soviet ground forces. He was assisted by General Borisov after he arrived from Somalia. A combined Ethiopian-Cuban offensive into the Ogaden was planned.

1978, February 6. Relief of Harar. Ethiopian and Cuban troops, assisted by air support provided by Soviet and Cuban pilots, drove the Somalis from their positions around Harar. They were repulsed, however, by Somali and WSLF troops dug in near Babile and the Kara Marda Pass (February 14).

1978, March 2–5. Battle of Diredawa–Jijiga. An Ethiopian-Cuban offensive was spearheaded by a Cuban paratroop battalion airlifted to the vicinity of Diredawa, and routed the Somali forces blocking the railroad. The Ethiopian 10th Division, advancing along the railroad, enveloped the principal Somali positions around Jijiga from the north and east. The Cuban paratroops moved against the rear of the Somali positions, while 3 Cuban infantry regiments and an armored regiment drove southward and eastward through the Kara Marda Pass. The Somalis, virtually surrounded, collapsed after suffering heavy casualties.

1978, March 8. Somali Withdrawal from Ogaden. President Barre asked for a cease-fire, and withdrew his forces. WSLF resistance continued, but was easily controlled by the victorious Ethiopians, who were now able to turn their major attention to the rebellion in Eritrea (see above).

1978, April 6–30. Ethiopian Buildup in Eritrea. Mengistu was determined to seek a military solution with or without Soviet-Cuban aid in Eritrea, despite Soviet advice to seek a diplomatic settlement. He began massing 100,000 troops along the Eritrean border.

1978, July–November. Ethiopian Offensive in Eritrea. Ethiopian troops advanced into Eritrea between Tigre and Bagemdir (July 26). They drove the Eritreans away from Massawa and advanced toward

Keren. They took Keren after a number of bloody battles (November 27). The Eritreans retreated to the northwest corner of the province.

1979–1984. Eritrean Guerrilla War Drags On. The Ethiopians were unable to destroy the stubborn Eritrean rebels.

Seychelles

1976, June 28. Seychelles Granted Independence from Great Britain.

1977, June 5. Coup d'État. The new Socialist government of **France Albert René** established friendly ties with the Soviet Union, granting access to Seychelles naval facilities.

1978, April 29. Coup Attempt Fails. Officials loyal to President France Albert René uncovered a plot to overthrow René and replace him with former President **James Mancham.**

1981, November 25. Coup Attempt Fails. A band of 50 mercenaries, veterans of the Katanga insurrection in the Congo (Zaire, 1961–1967; see pp. 1322–23) led by soldier of fortune "Mad Mike" Hoare, failed to oust President René's regime by force of arms. Hoare and his band arrived in the Seychelles disguised as rugby players but fighting broke out when a customs guard noticed that one member had an automatic weapon. A 20-hour gun battle ended with the capture of 5 of the mercenaries, one killed in the course of the action, while Hoare and 43 others made their escape on a comandeered Air India airliner and landed in South Africa. Subsequently, the mercenaries were tried in South African court but received light sentences, fueling the speculation that the South African government had authorized the operation.

1982, August 18–19, Army Revolt. An uprising by dissident army troops was suppressed with the assistance of Tanzanian forces.

Somalia

1975, July 6. Soviet Base in Somalia Confirmed. A U.S. congressional delegation concluded, despite Soviet denials, that the Soviet Union had established a base for naval refueling and storage of weapons at Berbera.

1976, April 5. Soviet Advisers in Somalia. Foreign observers reported the presence of more than 2,000 Soviet military advisers in Somalia, as well as 600 Cubans.

1977, January–June. Involvement in Ogaden. President Siad Barre encouraged ethnic Somali insurgents in Ethiopia's Ogaden Province (see p. 1382).

1977–1978. Ogaden War with Ethiopia. (See p. 1383.)

1978, April 9. Army Revolt Suppressed. Troops loyal to Somali President Siad Barre easily suppressed a revolt of dissident army officers, who blamed the political leadership for the defeat in the Ogaden Desert War.

1980, August 21. U.S.-Somalia Military Cooperation Agreement. Somalia signed an agreement which permitted the U.S. to use Somali naval and air force facilities at Mogadishu on the Indian Ocean and Berbera on the Gulf of Aden. The agreement provided the Somalis with $25 million in military assistance for 1 year (1981) and additional aid in following years.

Djibouti (French Somaliland)

1975–1977. Unrest in French Somaliland (Territory of Afars and Issas. Internal unrest was compounded by border incidents between French troops and Ethiopian and Somali forces, resulting from hostilities between those countries and insurgency in Ethiopia of separatist Afars and Issas tribesmen.

1977, June 27. Independence of Djibouti. The new nation—renamed Djibouti—began with tension and strained relations with neighboring Ethiopia and Somalia.

Sudan

1975, September 5. Coup Attempt Fails. Troops loyal to President Gaafar al-Nimeiry crushed rebel army officers who had seized a radio station and announced the overthrow of the government.

1976, July 2–3. Coup Attempt Fails. Rebel soldiers attempting to overthrow the Nimeiry government were overwhelmed by loyal troops.

1976, July 13–19. Egyptian, Sudanese, and Saudi Defense Pacts. (See p. 1363.)

1977–1978. Border Skirmishes with Ethiopia. Occasional small-scale fighting occurred due to Sudan's support of the Eritrean separatists.

1977, February 2–6. Separatists Defeated. Elements of the air force, attempting to set up a separate government in the southern portion of the country, were crushed by government troops.

1977, February 27–28. Sudan Enters Joint Command with Egypt and Syria. **(See p. 1363.)**

1977–1984. Continued Insurgency in the South. Despite earlier agreements (see p. 1319) the dissident Christians and pagans of the south continued their resistance.

1983, May 15–16. Army Mutiny Crushed. Local government troops suppressed a mutiny of disgruntled Sudanese Army enlisted personnel and noncommissioned officers.

Uganda

1976, July 4. Israeli-Entebbe Operation. **(See p. 1361.)**

1977–1978. Tension with Tanzania. (See below.)

1978, October 30–November 27. Ugandan Invasion of Tanzania. Ugandan troops penetrated 20 miles into northwestern Tanzania. Tanzania launched counterattacks (November 11). The Ugandans withdrew (November 27).

1979, January–June. Tanzanian Invasion. Tanzanian troops entered Uganda in support of Ugandan exiles attempting to overthrow President Idi Amin Dada. Libyan ruler Colonel Muammar Qaddafi flew troops to aid Amin but the Libyans and Ugandans were routed by the Tanzanians. A provisional government was formed (April 11–13). Tanzanian forces occupied Kampala and systematically wiped out remaining pockets of resistance (April 18–June 3). Tanzanian troops remained in Uganda for the next 2 years.

1980, May 11. Military Coup d'État. Brigadier General **David Oyite Ojok** deposed the civilian President **Godfrey Binaisa** and established a ruling military junta. Tanzanian troops in Uganda did not intervene. The junta reinstated political parties, then relinquished control of the government (September 17).

1980, October 7–15. Amin Supporters Invade Uganda. Ugandan rebels, loyal to former President Idi Amin, invaded Uganda from Zaire and Sudan. They captured Arua and Koboko, but fled Uganda when Tanzanian troops arrived.

1981. Civil Unrest and Guerrilla Warfare. Following national elections (1980, December 10–11) civil unrest and guerrilla warfare began in opposition to the government of President **Milton Obote.**

1981, June 30. Tanzanian Troops Withdraw. Tanzanian troops concluded a 2-year peacekeeping mission. President Milton Obote protested the departure of the Tanzanian troops because of guerrilla activity in Uganda.

Tanzania

1977–1978. Tension with Uganda. Uganda's President Idi Amin made repeated charges of Tanzanian plans to invade Uganda. President **Julius Nyerere** of Tanzania denied the charges.

1978, October 30–November 27. Ugandan Invasion of Tanzania. (See above.)

1979, January–June. Tanzanian Invasion of Uganda. (See above.)

1979–1981. Tanzanian Peacekeeping Force in Uganda. (See above.)

1982, August 18–19. Tanzanian Intervention in Seychelles. **(See p. 1384.)**

CENTRAL AFRICA

Burundi

1976, November 1. Coup d'État. The government of President **Michel Micombero** was overthrown in a bloodless military coup led by Lt. Col. **Jean-Baptiste Bagaza.**

Central African Empire (Central African Republic)

1976, December 4. Empire Proclaimed. President Jean-Bedel Bokassa officially renamed the Central African Republic the Central African Empire and proclaimed himself Emperor Bokassa I.

1979, January 20–21. Student Riots Suppressed. A governmental order that university students wear state uniforms resulted in rioting and looting in the capital city of Bangui. Troops from neighboring Zaire helped put down the riots.

1979, September 20. Coup d'État. Emperor Bokassa I was overthrown by former President David Dacko with French help in a bloodless coup d'état. The country was renamed Central African Republic.

1981, September 21. Coup d'État. President Dacko was overthrown in a bloodless coup by the Army Chief of Staff, General **André Lolingoa,** who named himself president.

Chad

1975, April 13–15. Coup d'État. General **Noel Odingar** led a successful coup against the government of Chad's first president, **N'garta Tombalbaye,** who was killed. General **Felix Malloum,** commander of the armed forces, was named head of the Military Council (April 15).

1975, September 27. Malloum Orders French Troops Out of Chad. President Malloum ordered France to withdraw its troops from Chad because France had been negotiating for the release of French nationals held hostage by a Moslem rebel movement, Frolinat, led by **Hissen Habre.**

1975, October 13–October 27. French Withdrawal. This ended 78 years of French military presence in Chad.

1976, April 13. Attempted Coup. Frolinat guerrillas failed in an attempt to assassinate Malloum.

1976–1977. Libyan Intervention. Libyan leader Muammar Qaddafi provided aid for Frolinat rebels in northern Chad and claimed 37,000 square miles of northern Chad (September 9, 1976).

1977, July 18. French Military Assistance. At the request of Chad's government, French transport planes airlifted Chad troops to the battle front in northern Chad. France also sent a few military advisers.

1978, February 1–February 24. Rebel Success. A Frolinat offensive overran nearly 80% of the country (February 7). President Malloum agreed to a cease-fire (February 20), then met with the leaders of Libya, Niger, and Sudan to negotiate a peaceful solution (February 24). But the Frolinat broke the cease-fire by launching a major offensive (April 15).

1978, April 26–June 6. French Intervention. At the request of President Malloum, about 500 troops of the French Foreign Legion intervened on behalf of the government and combined with 1,500 government troops to stop the rebel offensive (June 6). Additional French Foreign Legionnaires soon raised the total of French troops to around 2,500.

1978, August 29. Habre Named Premier. Malloum named guerrilla chieftain Hissen Habre as premier after his faction split with Frolinat.

1979, February 12–17. Attempted Coup. Prime Minister Habre attempted to overthrow President Malloum. French troops helped the government quell the insurrection. Habre fled to the north where he kept his rebellion alive.

1979, March 16–23. National Coalition Government Formed. An agreement was reached between the government, Habre's Frolinat faction, and the rival Frolinat faction headed by **Goukouni Oueddi** to halt civil war and form a coalition provisional government (March 16). It was also agreed that all French troops would be withdrawn. A new government was established with Oueddi at its head (March 23).

1979, April 20. Libyan Invasion Repulsed. Under the pretext of aiding the rebels in northern Chad, Libyan troops invaded. They were repulsed with French assistance. The French began a slow troop reduction.

1980, January 18. Congolese Peacekeepers Arrive. Under the auspices of the Organization of African Unity (OAU), a Congolese peacekeeping force arrived in Chad.

1980, March 22–December 16. Renewed Revolt. Fighting erupted in Ndjamena, the capital city, after Malloum was succeeded as president by Oueddi. The revolt was finally suppressed with the assistance of Libyan troops requested by Oueddi. Habre fled to Cameroon.

1981, January 7. Quaddafi Proclaims Unity of Chad and Libya. This announcement of complete unity was endorsed by Oueddi. Chad was initially occupied by about 6,000 Libyan troops.

1981, October 31. Agreement for Libyan Withdrawal. Oueddi's request for withdrawal was supported by the OAU. Qaddafi reluctantly complied; the Libyan troops were replaced by a smaller OAU peacekeeping force (December 17).

1982, March 21–June 8. Renewed Civil War. After the Libyan departure Habre renewed his rebellion and overthrew Oueddi (June 8).

1983, June–July. Oueddi Renews Civil War. The former President, assisted by

Libyan troops, gained control of most of the northern half of the country.

1983, July 30. Government Resurgence. After the rebels seized the Faya-Largeau oasis, Habre directed a counteroffensive to recapture the oasis.

1983, August 3–10. Libyan Intervention. Following a savage air bombardment by Soviet-built Libyan planes, Oueddi's rebels recaptured Faya-Largeau.

1983, August 9–13. France Intervenes. Some 1,000 French paratroopers landed at Ndjamena, then advanced north to Salaland Arada, in the middle of the country. A nonshooting stalemate ensued.

1983, August 17. Cease-Fire. The rival Chad factions agree to a French-arranged cease-fire.

WEST AFRICA

Angola

1975, January 15. Alvor Agreement. The 3 major opposing factions in Angola met at Alvor, Portugal: Dr. **Agostinho Neto**'s Popular Movement for the Liberation of Angola (MPLA); **Holden Alvaro Roberto**'s National Front for the Liberation of Angola (FNLA); and **Jonas Savimbi**'s National Union for the Total Independence of Angola (UNITA). They agreed upon a coalition government. Despite this, fighting continued through the spring and summer, punctuated by cease-fires and truces.

1975, March–April. Soviet Support to MPLA. Massive shipments of arms arrived for Neto's faction. Several hundred Cuban military "advisers" also arrived to support Neto.

1975, August 9. Coalition Government Collapses. UNITA and FNLA withdrew from the government, leaving Neto and MPLA in control. Intensified civil war resumed.

1975, August 14. South African Intervention. P. W. Botha, defense minister of the Republic of South Africa, seeking to assure the defeat of Neto's MPLA faction, sent an armored task force into southern Angola. The South Africans twice defeated Cuban troops.

1975, December 12. Battle of Bridge 14. Despite a 3-to-1 advantage in troop strength, Cuban troops were again decisively defeated by the South Africans. By this time there were approximately 7,500 Cuban combat troops in Angola.

1976, February 8. FNLA Crushed. Neto's troops and their Cuban allies defeated FNLA forces and took their major stronghold, Huambo. Roberto and many of his followers fled to neighboring Zambia.

1976, April 30. South Africans Withdraw from Angola. The South African government reached an agreement with MPLA guaranteeing protection of South African economic interests in Angola, provided South African combat troops were withdrawn from Angola. This was a major setback for Savimbi's UNITA.

1976, June–August. Cuban Offensive. Cuban troops launched a combined arms offensive against Savimbi troops hoping to crush UNITA as a rival force in Angolan politics (June 3). The Cubans drove Savimbi's troops from central Angola into the southeast corner of Angola.

1976, September–November. Renewed Cuban Offensive. In an attempt to end all resistance to MPLA rule of Angola, an estimated 15,000 Cuban combat troops launched an offensive against UNITA strongholds in southern Angola. They had only limited success and withdrew.

1977–1981. Savimbi's War of Insurgency. MPLA forces and their Cuban allies were frustrated by UNITA's guerrilla warfare. Savimbi's troops successfully attacked supply routes and MPLA camps. Their efforts were aided by South African intervention in southern Angola against bases from which SWAPO guerrillas were operating against South African controlled Namibia (see p. 1390). Savimbi's UNITA guerrillas had a number of successes and won effective control over much of southern Angola, cutting the railroad from Benguela to Zaire, the country's major east-west axis. The Cubans apparently took a less active role in counterinsurgency operations, leaving most of the heavy fighting to MPLA troops and SWAPO guerrillas.

People's Republic of Benin (Dahomey)

1975, January 21. Attempted Coup. A brief rebellion led by the minister of labor was put down by government troops.

1975, October 18. Coup Plot Thwarted. Security forces discovered and suppressed a plot to overthrow President Mathieu Kerekou.

1977, January 16. Attempted Coup.

Cameroon

1976, November 16. Border Clash with Gabon. (See below.)

People's Republic of the Congo (Congo, Brazzaville)

1978, August 14. Attempted Coup. Plans to overthrow the military government of President **Joachim Yombi Opango** were thwarted.

Gabon Republic

1976, November 17. Border Clash with Cameroon. Gabon's common border with Cameroon was closed following a Cameroon rocket attack launched on a police post.

1978, June 6–1979, August 14. Peacekeeping Force Sent to Zaire.

Gambia

1981, July 30. Attempted Coup. A coup attempted by paramilitary police and armed civilians enjoyed initial success until Senegalese troops intervened to put down the revolt.

Ghana

1975, December 23. Attempted Coup.

1978, July 5. Coup d'État. Ghana's head of state, General Ignatius Kutu Acheampong, was deposed by his deputy, Lieutenant General **Fred Akuffo.**

1979, May 15. Attempted Coup. A coup attempt by Flight Lieutenant **Jerry Rawlings** was unsuccessful, resulting in Rawlings's imprisonment.

1979, June 4. Coup d'État. After being freed from prison by rebels, Rawlings led a successful coup against General Akuffo's government. A civilian government was installed.

1981, December 31. Coup d'État. Rawlings seized complete control from the civilian government, claiming corruption and incompetence.

Guinea

1979, April 17. Troops Sent to Liberia. (See below.)

1980, January 18. Peacekeeping Forces Sent to Chad.

Guinea-Bissau

1975, March 30. Attempted Coup.

1980, November 14. Coup d'État. President **Luis de Almeida Cabral** was ousted by Premier **Joao Bernardo Vieira.**

Liberia

1979, April 14–15. Price Increase Riots. Following the government's proposed increase in the price of rice, demonstrations and riots flared in the capital of Monrovia. Order was restored with the help of 200 troops from neighboring Guinea.

1980, April 12. Coup d'État. Sergeant **Samuel K. Doe,** leading enlisted men of the Liberian Army, overthrew President **William R. Tolbert,** promising an end to corruption in government. Tolbert and 27 others were killed while soldiers went on a looting spree in Monrovia for several days.

Mauritania

1975, December 10. Mauritania Seizes Southern Sahara. While Moroccan troops were seizing the northern two-thirds of the former Spanish colony of Sahara (see p. 1391) Mauritanian troops seized Southern Sahara. They were immediately attacked by indigenous guerrilla forces seeking independence for Sahara: the Popular Front for the Liberation of Saqiat al Hamra and Rio de Oro (Polisario). A fierce three-way struggle for the control of Sahara ensued, with Polisario guerrillas fighting both Mauritanians and Moroccans.

1978, July 10. Coup d'État. President **Moktar Ould Daddah** was overthrown in a bloodless coup led by Army Chief of Staff Col. **Mustapha Ould Salek.** Salek began negotiating with the Polisarios for a cease-fire in Sahara. A peace treaty was signed the following year and all Mauritanian troops were withdrawn from the Sahara (August 5, 1979).

1980, January 4. Coup d'État. President **Mohammed Mahmoud Ould Luly** was overthrown by Premier **Mohammed**

Khouna Ould Haidalla in a bloodless coup. Luly had been in power for only 6 months following Salek's resignation (June 4, 1979).

1981, March 16. Attempted Coup. A coup attempt by Mauritanian military exiles was put down by the military government. Morocco was blamed for the attempt because of anger over Mauritania's backing out of the Polisario war.

Niger

1976, March 15. Attempted Coup.

1983, October 6. Attempted Coup. Easily suppressed by troops loyal to President **Seyni Kountche.**

Nigeria

1975, July 29. Coup d'État. General **Yakubu Gowon** was deposed in a bloodless military coup, and replaced by Brigadier **Muritala Rufai Mohammed.**

1976, February 13. Attempted Coup. A military coup was suppressed, but rebels assassinated Nigerian head of state General Muritala Rufai Mohammed. Lieutenant General **Olusegun Obsanjo** was chosen as the new chief of the Supreme Military Council.

1983, December 31. Coup d'État. President **Shehu Shagari** was overthrown in a military coup by Major General **Mohammed Buhari,** ending 4 years of civilian rule.

Senegal

1981, July 30. Assistance to Gambia. Senegalese troops assisted Gambia in the suppression of a coup attempt (see p. 1388).

Togo

1978, June 19–1979, August 14. Peacekeeping Force in Zaire.

Upper Volta

1980, November 25. Coup d'État. President Sangoule Lamizana was overthrown in a military coup and replaced by Colonel **Saye Zerbo.**

1982, November 17. Coup d'État. Zerbo was overthrown by dissident soldiers led by Major General **Jean-Baptiste Ouedraogo.**

1983, August 5. Coup d'État. Ouedraogo was ousted by former Premier **Thomas Sankara.**

SOUTHERN AFRICA

Mozambique

1975–1983. Guerrilla War. Mozambique troops carried out counterinsurgency operations against the National Resistance Movement, which was receiving substantial aid from South Africa. At the same time, Mozambique provided bases for guerrilla operations of the South African National Congress (ANC) (see p. 1390).

1975, December 17–19. Coup Attempt. An attempted coup by dissatisfied army officers and policemen was thwarted after 2 days of bloody fighting.

1984, January 17–March 16. Pact with South Africa. (See p. 1390.)

Lesotho

1982, December 9. South Africa Raids ANC Base. (See p. 1390.)

Zimbabwe-Rhodesia

1975–1976. Guerrilla Warfare Intensifies. There were two main forces operating in Rhodesia against Prime Minister Ian Smith's minority white government: **Joshua Nkomo**'s Zimbabwe African People's Union (ZAPU) and **Robert Mugabe**'s Zimbabwe African National Union (ZANU). Nkomo negotiated with Smith throughout 1975, but when no progress was made he renewed guerrilla activities, operating out of neighboring Zambia. Continued pressure was also maintained by Mugabe's insurgents operating out of Mozambique. Both Mugabe's and Nkomo's groups received substantial aid from the Soviet Union. Economic sanctions and diplomatic pressures from Western democracies forced Ian Smith to accept in principle the concept of majority rule for Rhodesia, and to schedule elections. Bishop **Abel Muzorewa,** leader of moderate opposition to Smith's minority white government, returned to bolster support before elections (1976, October).

1979, April 17–24. Muzorewa Wins Election. In an election boycotted by both Mugabe and Nkomo, Bishop Muzorewa emerged the clear winner. But ZAPU and ZANU continued guerrilla warfare.

1979, September 10–24. London Conference—British Rule Established. In an effort to defuse the situation in Rhodesia, the government of Prime Minister Margaret Thatcher intervened. Agreement of all parties was reached to return Rhodesia to colony status, and elections were scheduled on terms accepted by Mugabe and Nkomo.

1980, February 27–29. Mugabe Wins Election. Robert Mugabe's ZANU party won a huge majority of votes and seats in the new parliament.

Republic of South Africa

1975–1982. South African Operations in Angola and Namibia. South African troops carried out several large-scale interventions in the Angolan civil war on behalf of Jonas Savimbi's UNITA forces (see p. 1387), as well as continuing counterinsurgency operations against SWAPO bases in northern Namibia and Angola (see p. 1391).

1981–1982. Counterinsurgency Raids into Mozambique. South African commandos staged a number of successful raids on South African National Congress bases in Mozambique.

1982, December 9. Counterinsurgency Raids into Lesotho. South African commandos raided suspected ANC bases in Lesotho. The headquarters was discovered in a residential area, and a number of civilians were killed as well as ANC guerrillas.

1983, May 20–23. Terrorist Attack and Retaliatory Air Strike. A bomb explosion outside the South African Air Force headquarters killed 18 civilians and wounded 200 others (May 20). South Africa retaliated by an air attack on a suspected ANC base in Matola, a suburb of Maputo, Mozambique. Mozambique charged that the attack had hit only civilian businesses and homes. South Africa disputed this claim, asserting that they had hit an ANC guerrilla base.

1983, December 6–1984, January 8. Counterinsurgency Operations in Angola. South Africa troops attacked SWAPO positions in southern Angola, smashing the staging area for a planned guerrilla operation in Namibia. They continued their offensive. At Cuvelai the South Africans defeated a combined Cuban, Angolan, and SWAPO force, killing 324, while suffering only 21 casualties (January 3–5).

1984, January 17–March 16. Pact with Mozambique. Representatives from South Africa and Mozambique met at Komatiport on the Komati River and after extensive negotiations agreed that they cease supporting insurgents in the others' country.

1984, January 31. South Africa Begins Withdrawal from Angola.

1984, February 23. SWAPO Truce Set. The government of South Africa and SWAPO leader **Sam Nujoma** agreed to a truce in Namibia.

Namibia (Southwest Africa)

Britain's League of Nations Mandate over the former German colony of Southwest Africa after World War I was administered by the Union of South Africa, which later became the Republic of South Africa. South Africa continued to administer the region when the former mandates became U.N. trusteeships after World War II. Popular dissatisfaction with South African rule, and doubts whether South Africa would ever grant independence to the region, led to the establishment of the Southwest African People's Organization (SWAPO) by independence-minded local leaders (1960, June). SWAPO began to conduct local guerrilla activities against the South African administration, receiving considerable assistance and training from the U.S.S.R. Despite stern repressive measures, insurgency grew and guerrilla warfare continued during the 1960's and early 1970's.

1975, September 1–12. Turnhalle Conference. As a step toward autonomy, and presumably ultimate independence, the South African government convened a constitutional conference at Turnhalle. Participants were tribal leaders and other local leaders (including representatives of ethnic black groups and of the tiny white community). Multi-ethnic political parties (obviously including SWAPO) were excluded, thus effectively barring most educated and westernized blacks. The results were totally unsatisfactory to SWAPO; guerrilla war continued.

1978, December 4–8. Elections Held. In preparation for independence, South African-supervised elections were held. There were large turnouts, as tribal members did their chiefs' bidding and voted. SWAPO boycotted the elections. The SWAPO boycott assured the electoral triumph of the South African-backed Democratic Turnhalle Alliance.

1978–1983. Insurgency. South Africa continued to operate effectively against the insurgents and administer Namibia in preparation for complete independence. SWAPO guerrillas carried out hit-and-run raids into northern Namibia from bases in southern Angola. This led to repeated South African operations in Angola (see p. 1388).

NORTH AFRICA

Algeria

1976–1978. Tension with Morocco and Mauritania. Algeria's support of the Polisarios resulted in sporadic border skirmishes with Morocco and Mauritania (see p. 1388).

Libya

1977, July 12–24. Border Conflict with Egypt. (See p. 1363.)

1981, August 20. U.S. Planes Down Libyan Planes. During U.S. Sixth Fleet naval exercises in the Gulf of Sidra, in the southern Mediterranean, two U.S. navy F-14s were attacked by two Libyan SU-22s. The Americans shot down both Libyan planes.

1981–1983. Libyan Intervention in Chad. (See pp 1386–87.)

Morocco

1975, December 11. Morocco Moves into West Sahara. Moroccan troops occupied West Sahara (former Spanish colony of Rio de Oro). The Moroccan government laid claim to the northern two thirds of the former colony. Morocco's claims were violently disputed by an indigenous movement, the Popular [Front] for the Liberation of Saqiat al-Hamra and Rio de Oro (Polisario). At the same time Mauritania occupied the southern portion of Sahara (see p. 1388).

1976–1984. Moroccan-Polisario War Continues. The Moroccan-Polisario conflict continued unabated. The Moroccans, despite a commitment of 90,000 troops, were unable to suppress the Polisario, while the Polisario were not able to establish effective rule over the region.

NORTH AMERICA

UNITED STATES

1975, February–June. Middle East Peace Efforts. Secretary of State **Henry Kissinger** made a concentrated effort to work out a Sinai Peninsula troop disengagement scheme between Israel and Egypt while also trying to get the two countries and other Middle East nations to convene a general Middle East peace conference in Geneva. Kissinger made a number of trips to the Middle East and also met with Soviet Foreign Minister Andrei Gromyko in an effort to involve the Soviet Union in the planned Middle East Geneva Conference (February 16–17). It was largely through Kissinger's efforts that Israel and Egypt eventually worked out a Sinai Disengagement plan (see p. 1363).

1975, February 16–July 21. Mutual Balanced Force Reduction (MBFR) Talks. This was the begining of an effort to achieve equivalent reductions of NATO and Warsaw Pact forces in Central Europe.

1975, May 12–14. *Mayaguez* Incident. (See p. 1380.)

1977–1979. U.S. Efforts Toward Middle East Peace. U.S. President **Jimmy Carter** devoted considerable attention to efforts to bring about peace in the Middle East. High points of these efforts were the Camp David Accords and the subsequent Egypt-Israel Peace Treaty–Treaty of Washington (see p. 1364).

1977, March 9. Planned U.S. Troop Withdrawal from Korea. President Carter announced that all U.S. ground troops (32,000) would be withdrawn from South Korea within four or five years. Soon after this, Army Chief of Staff General **Bernard W. Rogers** announced that the U.S. had begun removing tactical missiles from South Korea and that South Koreans had begun manning some U.S. air defense missiles deployed in South Korea (April 14). The Carter announcement touched off a controversy involving Major General **John K. Singlaub,** chief of staff of U.S. forces in South Korea, who criticized Carter's plan. Singlaub was recalled to Washington and reassigned (May 27). The planned troop withdrawal began later in the year but was canceled by President Carter after the Soviet Union invaded Afghanistan (see p. 1376).

1977, June 30. Production of the B-1 Bomber Stopped. President Carter canceled production plans for the proposed B-1 strategic bomber because he thought it was not cost-effective and because he and Secretary of Defense **Harold Brown** thought the cruise missile would be a more effective and cheaper deterrent.

1978, April 7. Carter Defers Production of the Neutron Bomb. Following months of urging NATO allies to declare that they would deploy enhanced radiation nuclear weapons ("neutron bomb"), President Carter announced he would not produce the controversial weapon. Proponents of the weapon argued that its radiation would be very effective in penetrating Soviet tanks and stopping a Soviet combined armed offensive on NATO's central front, while causing little damage to nearby structures. Critics questioned this and claimed that radiation from the weapon would threaten civilians in NATO countries. Later that same year (October 18), Carter partially reversed his decision on the neutron bomb and gave the go-ahead to manufacture some parts of the weapon.

1979, January 22. Carter Budgets MX Missile, Trident Submarine, and Cruise Missile. Under growing criticism of his defense policies from influential critics such as Senator Henry Jackson, President Carter requested $675.4 million for the MX (Missile Experimental) mobile ICBM. The proponents of adding the MX to the U.S. strategic arsenal argued that it would strengthen the strategic triad (land-based ICBMs, nuclear missile armed submarines, and long-range strategic bombers) which was seen as increasingly vulnerable because of qualitative improvements in the Soviet ICBM force (see p. 1350). In addition to the MX, President Carter requested funding for one submarine armed with Trident nuclear missiles and low-altitude cruise missiles and hardening of the silos for the existing ICBM force. Critics faulted Carter for denying Navy requests for a new supercarrier and for deciding to phase out the large carrier force. Critics also scored Carter for considering submarines as a possible basing mode for the MX because greater accuracy could be achieved from the land-based mode. Carter later decided upon the controversial horizontal "racetrack" basing mode in which the missiles would be shuttled from point to point along five oval concourses with a number of the underground silos always remaining vacant. This so-called "shell-game" approach was to complicate targeting for the Soviets.

1980, March 1. Development of a Rapid Deployment Force. The Rapid Deployment Task Force (RDTF) was to be a 100,000-man force composed of units from the Army and Marine Corps, whose mission was to respond and deploy quickly, with naval and air support, to crisis situations around the world.

1980, May 6. MX Basing Mode Changed. The Carter Administration abandoned the controversial racetrack basing mode for a straight track basing mode because of the opposition of environmentalists and residents of Utah and Nevada. This did not silence opponents, and the problem of finding the proper basing mode was not resolved.

1980, August 5. Change in U.S. Plans for Nuclear Targeting. In Presidential Directive 59 (PD 59), the emphasis in targeting for the U.S. strategic nuclear force was changed from a countervalue to counterforce strategy. Countervalue calls for targeting industrial facilities and population centers, whereas counterforce is directed against Soviet nuclear missiles.

1980, August 20. Development of "Stealth" Bomber Revealed. The Defense department revealed planned development of a new, long-range strategic bomber capable of penetrating Soviet defenses by evading radar. The aircraft would not be operative until the 1990s. Republican presidential candidate Ronald Reagan charged that the Carter Administration had compromised national security by a premature leak of sensitive information for political gain, and that the announcement was made to offset Reagan's criticism of cancellation of the B-1 bomber (September 4).

1981, August 10. U.S. Reversal on Neutron Bomb. U.S. Secretary of Defense **Caspar Weinberger** announced President Reagan's decision to proceed with full production of enhanced radiation weapons. They could be deployed as warheads for Lance missiles or as 8-inch artillery shells. Reagan, however, decided not to ship it to Europe until a later date, when the Allies would not object to its deployment or when it was needed in a crisis situation.

1981, October 2. New Strategic Missile Deployment Plan. President Reagan announced that he was reversing former President Carter's cancellation of the B-1 bomber. Production of 100 of these strategic bombers would serve to replace the aging B-52 force until the "Stealth" strategic bomber was operational in the 1990s. He also announced a new basing mode for the MX missile (see p. 1392). The first 36 of the 100 planned missiles would be deployed in existing superhardened silos (reinforced with concrete and steel). The decision on how to deploy the remaining missiles would be deferred until completion of further study. The Reagan program called for the development of improved Trident nuclear missile submarines with more accurate and more powerful missiles. Also the plan called for improved strategic defenses and for improved command, control, and communications systems.

1982, June 2–5. Conference on "Military Reform Movement." Widespread criticism of U.S. and NATO doctrine and strategy among members of Congress (who had established an informal "Reform Caucus") and many Defense intellectuals culminated in a 3-day conference at West Point, N.Y. The "Reformers" had been asserting for several years that U.S. doctrine, particularly in the army, was based upon a concept of "attrition warfare," in contrast to the ideas of the Reformers, who favored "maneuver warfare." The Reformers were also opposed to the "Forward Defense" concept in NATO. Although few opinions were changed among the participants, the ferment unquestionably influenced changes in doctrine in the U.S. Army, which appeared about this time, putting emphasis on maneuver, defense in depth, offensive warfare concepts, and long-range strikes by deep interdiction with weapons of increasing range, in a modified doctrinal concept which the army called "Air Land Battle."

1982–1984. U.S. Peacekeeping Contingent in Beirut. (See p. 1365.)

1982, November 27. "Dense Pack" Basing Planned for MX Missiles. This provided for basing the silos of the new ICBMs close together, on the assumption that the attacking Soviet missiles would be rendered ineffective because of the principle of "fratricide." Under this concept, incoming missiles would have to be targeted so close together that the explosion of the first missiles destroys the following missiles before they hit the counterforce target. Advocates of the plan said that only one fourth to one third of the U.S. missiles would be destroyed by a Soviet first-strike attack; this was believed to be a rate of survivability so high as to deter a Soviet attack. The Joint Chiefs of Staff were divided on the dense pack basing mode. But public and Congressional opposition was vociferous. Congress voted to withhold funds (December 20).

1983, January 3. Bipartisan MX Basing Commission Appointed. In an attempt to depoliticize and resolve the MX basing mode controversy, President Reagan appointed a commission, headed by Lt. Gen. **Brent Scowcroft,** U.S.A.F. Retired, to study and make recommendations regarding possible basing modes for the controversial missile.

1983, March 23. ABM Research and Development. In an address to Congress, derided by critics as the "Star Wars Speech," President Reagan announced that the United States would pursue the feasibility of perfecting an antiballistic missile (ABM) defense from outer space. Supporters applauded the speech, saying it was an important step in overcoming the mutual-assured destruction (MAD) mentality that had dominated strategic thinking from the late 1960's to the late 1970's. The project to implement this concept was termed "The Strategic Defense Initiative" (SDI).

1983, April 11. Scowcroft Commission Report. The commission recommended that 100 MX missiles with 10 warheads each be deployed in existing Minuteman silos in Wyoming and Nebraska. The MX would be supplemented by a large, but as yet undetermined, number of smaller single-warhead mobile missiles ("Midgetmen"). The Commission also stressed "vigorous research and development of an antimissile defense system." President Reagan approved, finding this consistence with his "Star Wars" concept, and endorsed the Commission's recommendations (April 19)

1983, May 3. United States Bishops' Pastoral Letter. The Catholic bishops of the U.S. published a pastoral letter in which they condemned any use of nuclear weapons as immoral, regardless of circumstances, and equally condemned the planned or threatened use of such weapons, thus also proscribing deterrence through threat of employing nuclear weapons.

1983. October 30. Suicide Attack on U.S. Peacekeeping Force in Beirut. (See p. 1366.)

1983. October 25–30. Invasion of Grenada. (see p. 1395.)

CANADA

1975, May 9. NORAD Pact Renewed. The North American Air Defense treaty, originally signed in 1958, was renewed. The revised treaty gave Canada responsibility for its own air defense for the first time.

1977, July. Armed Forces Enlargement and Modernization Plan Announced. Scheduled to begin in 1978, the plan would add 4,700 men to the 78,000-member Canadian armed forces over a 5-year period, at a $100-million-a-year increase in the yearly budget. The armed forces equipment was to be completely modernized. West German Leopard tanks would replace the Centurions while 20 new destroyers were to be purchased to replace some of the aging Canadian ships.

1981, March 11. NORAD Extended for Five Years. (See above.)

LATIN AMERICA

ORGANIZATION OF AMERICAN STATES

1976, October 6. Arbitration of Honduran-Salvadoran Border Disputes. Representatives of the two countries signed a 14-point agreement concerning disputed territory and submitted the dispute to OAS arbitration (see p. 1396).

1977, October 26. OAS Investigates Nicaragua-Costa Rica Border Dispute. A 3-member OAS team arrived in Managua to investigate charges of border violations stemming from attacks by Sandinista rebels across the Costa Rican border (see p. 1395).

MEXICO

1979, January 26. Mexico Supports Guatemala against Insurgents. Mexican troops cooperated with Guatemalan troops in Chiapas, helping them to fight Guatemalan insurgents (see p. 1396).

1982, February 21. Lopez Proposes Central American Peace Plan. Warning against U.S. military intervention in the Central American region, Mexican President **José Lopez Portillo** proposed a plan for ending strife in Central America. This called for: The U.S. to end intervention in Nicaragua; a reduction in the size of Nicaraguan armed forces; and signing of a nonagression pact among Nicaragua, her Central American neighbors, and the U.S. (see Contadora Group, p. 0000).

CARIBBEAN REGION

Cuba

1975–1984. Armed Intervention Abroad and the Proliferation of Revolution. Cuba has intervened militarily in a number of countries throughout the period, most notably Angola 1975–1984 (see p. 1387), South Yemen 1978–1984 (see p. 1371), and Ethiopia 1977–1984 (see p. 1383). Fidel Castro's regime also helped Marxist-Leninist political movements such as in Grenada, Nicaragua and El Salvador (see pp. 1395–97).

1983, October 25–30. Cuban Troops Defeated in Grenada. (See below.)

Grenada

1979, March 13. Coup d'État. Maurice Bishop seized power and established a socialist dictatorship on the Caribbean island which had earlier been granted independence by Britain (1973, February 7). Bishop sought close ties with Cuba and the Soviet Union. Construction began on a new airport, with a 2-mile runway, supposedly to accommodate tourists, also suitable for military planes. Cuban troops and construction workers as well as Soviet advisers arrived on the island.

1983, October 10–19. Coup d'État. Bishop was suspected by his Marxist colleagues of planning to shift allegiance from the Soviet Union to the United States. He was placed under arrest by his Deputy Prime Minister, **Bernard Coard,** who assumed power. Bishop was temporarily freed by his supporters, but he and many of them were killed by the new regime (October 19). Chaos reigned on the island.

1983, October 23. Caribbean Nations Appeal to U.S. for Help. Noting the chaos on the island, and that the new regime controlled armed forces larger than the combined military strength of all neighboring Caribbean states, the Eastern Caribbean States (a regional grouping including Jamaica, Dominica, Trinidad, Barbados, Tobago, and Belize) formally requested the U.S. to intervene militarily in Grenada to restore order. Since the U.S. government was concerned for the safety of some 1,000 Americans on the island (mostly medical students), President Reagan directed the Defense Department to intervene.

1983, October 25–30. Invasion of Grenada. Hastily planned Operation "Urgent Fury" provided for the landing on Grenada of some 6,000 U.S. troops (U.S. Marines, Army Rangers, and elements of the U.S. Army 82nd Airborne Division), plus token forces (about 500 troops) from the neighboring Caribbean states. Defending the island were approximately 1,000 troops of the Grenadian Army and about 600 Cuban combat engineers. The U.S. forces came ashore at three points in amphibious and airborne assaults. The resistance of the Grenadian troops ranged from slight to negligible; the Cubans fought fiercely. U.S. forces secured the island in about 60 hours. Total U.S. casualties: killed 18, wounded 83. Casualties of the defenders: killed in action 36, wounded in action 66, captured 655.

Haiti

1982, January 9–17. Revolution Thwarted. An attempt to overthrow the government of President **Jean-Claude Duvalier** (son of François Duvalier; see p. 1339) was suppressed.

CENTRAL AMERICA

Costa Rica

1977, October 14–17. Border Dispute with Nicaragua. Costa Rica closed its borders and moved constabulary troops to the Nicaraguan border following the pursuit of Sandinista rebels by Nicaraguan National Guardsmen into Costa Rican territory. Both nations appealed to the OAS, accusing the other of border violations (see p. 1394).

El Salvador

1976. July. Border Clashes with Honduras. (See p. 1396.)

1979, January 20–March 20. Increase in Violence and Guerrilla Activity. Smoldering leftist unrest exploded into violent insurgency as a result of failure of the government to implement a satisfactory land redistribution program. An investigation by the Inter-American Commission of Human Rights resulted in charges that human rights violations were being committed by the El Salvadoran government against its political enemies.

1979, April–October. Continuing Violence. Efforts to suppress the insurgency by President **Carlos Romero** were unsuccessful. The new government of Nicaragua was suspected by the U.S. government of supporting the insurgency, as part of a policy of fomenting revolution and using force of arms to overturn all existing governments in Central America.

1979, October 15. Coup d'État. Disgruntled army officers staged a successful coup, overthrowing Romero.

1979, October–1980, December. Violence and Chaos. Efforts of the new junta to stabilize the country and satisfy the dissidents failed completely, and alienated much of the population. A land reform program was announced (February 11), disavowed (February 20), then a new program was announced (March 6).

1979, March 26. Assassination of Archbishop Romero. Outspoken and much-beloved Bishop Romero was assassinated by a gang while saying Mass (1980, March 24). Leftist rebels and right wing extremists were suspects in the crime.

1980, May 2. Attempted Coup d'État. The effort by former President Romero and disgruntled military officers failed.

1980, December 13. Duarte Named President. The junta appointed moderate Christian Democrat **José Napoleon Duarte** as president, and directed him to reorganize the government.

1981–1984. Continuing Civil War. Despite massive financial and military assistance from the U.S., the Salvadoran Army was unable to suppress the insurgents, who were receiving comparable support from the U.S.S.R. and Cuba, via Nicaragua. Atrocities continued, committed not only by adherents of the leftist guerrillas but also by rightist extremists operating in so-called "death squads" believed to be composed of members of the armed forces, and operating under the direction of military officers. Among the victims were 7 Americans: 4 female missionaries (1980, December 3), 2 labor leaders advising the Salvadoran government (1981, January 2), and a naval officer military adviser (1983, May 25).

1982, March 28. Election. Despite a guerrilla boycott and active efforts to frighten people not to vote, there was a large turnout in an election that international observers considered very fair. Duarte's party won a 40% plurality of the vote, but a coalition of the right wing parties, with a majority of right wing representatives under the leadership of former National Guard officer **Roberto D'Aubuisson,** formed a government. D'Aubuisson, rumored to be one of those responsible for the death squads, failed, however, in his effort to be appointed president. Despite the election, violence and atrocities by both sides continued unabated.

1982, November 12–17. El Salvadoran Counteroffensive. The Salvadoran Army carried out a major counteroffensive in an effort to envelop the guerrilla strongholds and block their escape to Honduras. The Honduran Army also deployed along the common border of the two countries in order to apprehend elements of the guerrilla forces who escaped. The offensive was only partially successful.

1984, May 6. Duarte Elected President. Duarte defeated D'Aubuisson. He promised to seek reconciliation with leftist rebels, without compromising democratic institutions. He also promised to eliminate death squads.

1984, May 24. Military Men Convicted of Death Squad Murders. Largely as a result of pressure from the U.S., the Salvadoran government brought to trial 5 National Guardsmen suspected of murdering the four female missionaries (see above). The 5 were tried and convicted of murder.

Guatemala

1976–1983. Guerrilla Attacks. A political movement called the Guerrilla Army of the Poor (EGT) staged a number of raids in various parts of the country destroying farm equipment and on one occasion killing two land owners (1976, November 13). They were especially active in the mountainous El Quiche region north of Guatemala City.

1982, March 25. Coup d'État. Brigadier General **Efrain Rios Montt** headed a successful coup. Combining religious fervor with ruthlessness, Rios Montt reduced unrest, but alienated the army.

1983, August 8. Rios Montt Overthrown in Coup. Military officers, headed by Defense Minister General **Oscar Humberto Mehia Vitores,** ousted Rios Montt after a brief struggle.

Honduras

1976, July 14–22. Border Clashes with El Salvador. There were a number of armed clashes on the disputed border between El Salvador and Honduras.

1977. Staging Area for Sandinista Forays into Nicaragua. Honduras permitted Nicaraguan Sandinista immigrants of the National Liberation Front (NLF) to conduct operations in Nicaragua from bases in Honduras.

1981–1982. Strained Relations with Nicaragua. Anti-Sandinista guerrilla activity emanating from Honduras led to increased tensions between Nicaragua and Honduras. The Sandinista regime in Nicaragua alleged that the Honduran government had given aid to anti-Sandinista forces within Honduras. Nicaragua increased forces along the border. Honduras received increased military aid from the United States. By early 1982 there were 100 U.S. military advisers in Honduras. Relations deteriorated until both countries withdrew their ambassadors (April 4). Honduran President **Roberto Suazo Cordova,** concerned about Nicaraguan and Cuban subversion in his own country, asked for and received more aid from the U.S. (July 16).

1982, October 4. Latin American Peace Forum. Honduras participated in a peace forum with other South and Central American nations in an attempt to end hostilities in the region (see International Peacekeeping, p. 1350).

1982. November 12. Honduran Troops Aid El Salvadoran Counteroffensive. Honduras supported an El Salvadoran counteroffensive against rebel strongholds by posting 2,000 troops along the Honduran-El Salvadoran border in an attempt to block the rebel passage into Honduras.

1983, August 5. U.S. begins Honduras Military Maneuvers. The U.S. began large-scale military exercises in Honduras. These were to last as long as 8 months. Ostensible objectives included training Hondurans in counterinsurgency tactics, coordinating with Honduran troops, and training them in amphibious operations and in U.S. field artillery procedures and tactics. The obvious unstated objective was to impose caution on Nicaragua, particularly in its support of the insurgency in El Salvador.

Nicaragua

1975–1976. Successful Counterinsurgency. The National Guard appeared to be winning their counterinsurgency war, and guerrilla activities subsided. However, harsh repressive measures aroused much resentment in the population.

1977. Somoza Under Fire. At home Somoza lost the support of the Catholic Church and much of the middle-class business population. In the international press, the Sandinistas' campaign of violence and terror was ignored, while the Carter Administration's citation of Nicaragua as a violator of human rights was widely applauded.

1977, October. Border Dispute with Costa Rica. (See p. 1395.)

1978, January–September. Violence and Anarchy. Taking advantage of widespread public disobedience and largely effective strikes, the Sandinistas stepped up attacks and also were able to gain many new recruits, including foreigners from East Germany, the PLO, and Cuba.

1978, September 9. Full-Scale Sandinista Offensive Launched. The Sandinistas successfully attacked several large towns and cities. National Guard counteroffensives drove the rebels into the mountains with great difficulty. But the cost was enormous; many civilian casualties were suffered, further alienating the population. The Sandinistas continued their pressure.

1979, May 29–July 17. Sandinista Final Offensive. The rebels resumed the offensive, easily winning control of most of the cities and the countryside in a matter of weeks, and surrounded Managua (July 10). Certain of victory, they named a 5-man ruling junta (July 17). They rejected a belated U.S. request that they share power with more moderate elements of the opposition. At U.S. insistence, Somoza left Managua for Miami.

1979, July 19. Sandinistas Enter Managua in Triumph. The new regime was established with the entry of the Sandinistas into the capital city.

1979–1984. Sandinista Rule and New Revolution. Once in power, the Sandinistas squelched domestic opposition, cracked down on freedom of the press and speech, while postponing elections until at least 1985. The regime carried out a brutal forced relocation of the Misquite Indians. In the international sphere, the junta established warm relations with the Soviet Union, Cuba, and the PLO. Cuba sent 5,000 advisers to Nicaragua, which became an important conduit in the flow of Soviet arms and munitions from Cuba to the various Central American countries, and particularly El Salvador. By 1982 two large groups of insurgents (Contras) were operating in the northern part of the country, with a smaller group operating in the south. The northern-based insurgents were made up of various elements of the old regime's national opposition but included some former supporters of Somoza. The southern-based insurgents were composed of disaffected Sandinistas who claimed that they were the true Sandinistas and that the revolution had been betrayed. These groups were receiving aid from the U.S.

Panama

1977, September 7. Preliminary Draft Canal Treaties Signed. U.S. President Jimmy Carter and Panamanian leader

General Omar Torrijos Herrera signed preliminary draft treaties for turning the administration and ownership of the Canal over to Panama. The treaties were ratified by a 2–1 majority in a Panamanian plebiscite (October 23).

1978, March 16, April 18. U.S. Senate Ratifies Panama Canal Treaties. The U.S. Senate ratified the two Panama Canal treaties. President Carter and General Torrijos signed the final draft of the treaties (June 16).

SOUTH AMERICA

Argentina

1976, January 14. Argentina Places Ambassador to Britain on Indefinite Leave. As a protest against Britain's renewed interest in the Falkland Islands (called Malvinas Islands by Argentinians) the Argentinian government placed their ambassador on indefinite leave. The British reciprocated (January 19).

1976, February 4. Argentinian Ship Fires on British Research Ship. An Argentinian destroyer fired two rounds at the British scientific research ship *Shackleton* after requesting that the *Shackleton* be escorted to Tierra del Fuego. The *Shackleton* proceeded to Port Stanley with the Argentinian destroyer giving chase. Six miles from Port Stanley the Argentinian ship fired the two warning rounds.

1976, March 24–25. Military Coup d'État. President **Maria Estela "Isabel" Perón,** widow of Juan Perón, was ousted by the Armed Forces Chiefs of Staff, who immediately formed a ruling junta and imposed martial law on Argentina. The junta outlawed 5 extremist parties and initiated a counterinsurgency campaign against guerrilla and political extremists who had terrorized Argentina for several years.

1976, March 25–1982, July 16. "The Dirty War." Argentina's military junta carried out a relatively successful counterinsurgency war against radical leftist guerrilla forces and political parties, most notably the People's Revolutionary Army (ERP), but in the process carried on a ruthless and indiscriminate campaign of counterterror, committing flagrant violations of the Argentinian citizenry's human rights. During this "Dirty War," as many as 20,000 to 25,000 people "disappeared." Following the defeat of Argentina by Britain in the Falkland Islands War (see p. 1353) the discredited military junta restored civil liberties (July 15) and political parties were allowed to function (July 16).

1977–1978, British and Argentinian Representatives Resume Falkland Negotiations. British and Argentinian diplomats met in New York and carried on negotiations about the future of the Falkland Islands (December 15–18). British and Argentinian negotiators again met in Lima, Peru, to discuss control of the Falkland Islands (February 15–17). The talks took on new meaning because of the discovery of large undersea deposits of oil in the vicinity of the islands.

1979, November 16. Argentina and Britain Resume Exchange of Ambassadors. The British and Argentinian governments sent new ambassadors to each other's capitals. Chargé d'affaires had been the chief officers since Argentina placed its ambassador on indefinite leave (see above).

1980, January–June. Falklands Crisis and War. (See United Kingdom, p. 1363.)

Bolivia

1976. Guerrilla Activity. The National Liberation Army (ELN), founded by Ché Guevara (see p. 1342), launched a number of raids throughout the year. They were allegedly aided by a Chilean group, the Revolutionary Left Movement.

1978, July 21. Military Annulment of Election Results. Bolivia's first election in 12 years (July 19) was annulled by the candidate of the ruling military government, Air Force General **Juan Pereda Asbun.**

1978, November 24. Military Coup d'État. After 4 months in power, General Pereda was overthrown by fellow junta member Army General **David Padilla Arancibia,** who promised new elections.

1979, July 1–August 6. Return to Civilian Rule. None of the 8 candidates for president achieved a majority in the promised election (July 1). Congress finally selected a provisional president, **Walter Guevara Arce,** bringing a temporary end to military rule.

1979, November 1. Military Coup d'État. Colonel **Alberto Natusch Busch** led a successful coup, overthrowing President Guevara and seizing the presidency. However, he was opposed by other military officers and was forced to resign. The military leaders then selected **Lydia Gueiler Tejada** provisional president (November 16).

1980, July 17. Military Coup d'État. Following a presidential election in which no candidate received a majority, officers under General **Luis García Meza** seized power.

1981, January–August. Continued Civil and Military Unrest. A power struggle within the armed forces led to an armed revolt of senior cadets at the national military academy (March 17). A coup attempt ended in a military stalemate but forced the resignation of García (August 4). A 3-man military junta dominated by former president Natusch took power.

Chile

1973–1980. Junta Rule and Domestic Unrest. The military junta, under the leadership of Army General **Augusto Pinochet Ugarte,** established firm control over the country. There was, however, much internal unrest, and the Revolutionary Left Movement attempted to foment insurrections throughout the period.

1980, September 11. Voters Approve Pinochet's Transition Constitution and Continued Rule. By a better than two-thirds margin the voters approved General Pinochet's constitution, which included his accession to the presidency and the continuation of at least 8 more years of military rule. Pinochet formally assumed the office of president the following year (March 11, 1981).

1983–1984. Civil Unrest. Opposition to Pinochet's rule resulted in a number of riots and some leftist guerrilla activity in rural areas.

Colombia

1975–1978. Social Unrest and Insurgency. Colombia suffered from domestic unrest and several insurgency efforts against the government. One of the two major guerrilla movements, the Revolutionary Armed Forces (FARC), attempted to disrupt the national elections (February 26, 1978). Later that year FARC and the second leading revolutionary group, National Liberation Army (ELN), joined forces (August 24).

1979, January 9–November 14. Successful Counterinsurgency Campaign. This effort resulted in the elimination of 2,000 guerrillas and enabled President **Julio Cesar Turbay Ayala** and Defense Minister General **Luis Carlos Camacho Leyva** to pacify the country.

1980–1983. Continuing Guerrilla Activity. Despite setbacks the Colombian insurgents continue to carry on low-level guerrilla activities.

Ecuador

1975, September 1. Attempted Coup. Armed Forces Chief of Staff General **Raul Gonzalez Alvear** was defeated by troops loyal to President Guillermo Rodriguez Lara.

1976, January 11. Military Coup d'État. The armed forces commanders ousted President Rodriguez in a bloodless coup.

1978, January 16–17. Border Incident with Peru. Brief hostilities broke out along the disputed Marañón River border in the Cordillera del Condor Mountains.

1981, January 28–February 2. Renewed Border Hostilities with Peru. The long-standing border dispute erupted into hostilities when Ecuadoran troops pushed 13 kilometers into Peruvian territory. Peruvian counterattacks were partially successful, too. In Washington the OAS helped negotiate a cease-fire (February 2).

1981, March 6. Truce with Peru. Both sides announced an "immediate peace" along the disputed border and agreed to mediation by the U.S., Chile, Brazil, and Argentina.

Paraguay

1975–1978. Low-Level Insurgency. Army units carried out counterinsurgency operations against Marxist-Leninist guerrillas and police also conducted operations against leftist guerrillas in Asunción.

1978, May 5. State of Siege Lifted in Three Departments. A state of siege, which had been present since 1947 in the departments of Itapua and Central and Alto Paraná, was lifted. Asunción, the capital, still remained under a state of siege because of the threats posed by Marxist-Leninist guerrillas.

Peru

1975–1984. Communist Insurgency. A self-proclaimed Maoist organization, the Shining Path, centered in and around Ayacucho, terrorized much of the country's south-eastern region. Although successful in carrying out bombings in Cuzco and Lima (1983), it failed in its efforts to overthrow the government.

1975, August 29. Military Coup d'État. The commander of Peru's five military districts issued a joint communiqué removing President Velasco from office and proclaiming General **Francisco Morales Bermúdez Cerrutti** president.

1976, July 9. Attempted Coup d'État. Troops loyal to President Morales crushed a barracks rebellion.

Surinam

1980, February 25. Military Coup d'État. Premier **Henck A. E. Arron** was ousted from power in a coup led by two army sergeants.

1980, August 13. Military Coup d'État. The military leadership removed President **Johan Ferrier,** who had survived the earlier coup which had ousted Premier Arron.

1982, February 5. Military Coup d'État. The military leadership ousted the civilian government and then imposed military rule.

Uruguay

1976, June 12. Coup d'État. President **Juan Maria Bordaberry** was removed by the armed forces in a bloodless coup. Vice-President **Alberto Demichelli** temporarily assumed the presidency.

1982, September 28. Military Government Lifts Ten-Year Ban on Political Parties. In preparation for November elections and the restoration of democracy the government lifted a 10-year ban on political parties.

Venezuela

1975–1984. Continued Communist Insurgency. Government troops continued to combat low-level Communist insurgency.

BIBLIOGRAPHY*

GENERAL**

Albion, Robert G. *Introduction to Military History.* New York: 1929.
Almirante, Gen. D. José. *Bosquejo de la historia militar de España hasta la fin del siglo XVIII España.* 4 vols. Madrid: 1923.
Ardant du Picq, Charles J.J.J. *Battle Studies.* Harrisburg: 1947.
Ballard, George A. *Rulers of the Indian Ocean.* London: 1927.
Belloc, Hilaire. *The Battleground; Syria and Palestine.* Philadelphia: 1936.
Bodart, Gaston. *Losses of Life in Modern Wars.* Oxford: 1916.
———. *Militär-historisches Kriegs-Lexicon, 1618–1905.* Vienna and Leipzig: 1908.
Bretnor, Reginald. *Decisive Warfare.* Harrisburg: 1969.
Brodie, Bernard. *Seapower in the Machine Age.* Princeton: 1943.
Brodie, Bernard, and Brodie, Fawn. *From Crossbow to H-Bomb.* New York: 1962.
Cady, John F. *Southeast Asia.* New York: 1964.
Churchill, Winston. *A History of the English-Speaking Peoples.* 4 vols. New York: 1956–1958.
Clausewitz, Carl von. *On War.* Washington: 1956.
Crafts, Alfred, and Buchanan, Percy. *A History of the Far East.* London: 1958.
Craig, Gordon A. *The Politics of the Prussian Army.* New York: 1956.
Creasy, Sir Edward S. *The Fifteen Decisive Battles.* London: 1908.
———. *History of the Ottoman Turks.* 2 vols. London: 1878.
Creswell, John. *Generals and Admirals.* London: 1952.
Delbrueck, Hans. *Geschichte der Kriegskunst im Rahmen der Politischen Geschichte.* 7 vols. Berlin: 1900–36.
Dodge, Theodore Ayrault. *Great Captains.* Boston: 1895.
Dupuy, R. Ernest. *The Compact History of the United States Army.* New York: 1961.
———. *Men of West Point.* New York: 1951.
———. *Where They Have Trod.* Philadelphia: 1940.
Dupuy, R. Ernest, and Dupuy, Trevor N. *Brave Men and Great Captains.* New York: 1959.
———. *Military Heritage of America.* New York: 1956.†
Dupuy, Trevor N. *A Genius for War: The German Army and General Staff, 1807–1945.* New York: 1977.
———. *Numbers, Predictions, and War.* New York: 1979.
———. *The Evolution of Weapons and Warfare.* New York: 1980.
Earle, Edward M., *et al. Makers of Modern Strategy.* Princeton: 1943.
Edmonds, James E. *Fighting Fools.* New York: 1938.
Eggenberger, David. *A Dictionary of Battles.* New York: 1967.
Esposito, Vincent J. (ed.) *The West Point Atlas of American Wars.* New York: 1959.
Falls, Cyril. *The Art of War from the Age of Napoleon to the Present Day.* New York: 1961.
———. *A Hundred Years of War, 1850–1950.* New York: 1962.
Fortescue, John W. *A History of the British Army.* 13 vols. New York: 1930.

* This list does not by any means include all of the works consulted during twenty years of intensive research. It does, however, include most of those that we believe have sufficient importance to be listed as references for further study and reading.

** Apply to three or more historical periods.

† Contains additional bibliography.

Fuller, J. F. C. *Armament and History*. New York: 1945.
———. *The Conduct of War, 1789–1961*. New Brunswick: 1961.
———. *A Military History of the Western World*. 3 vols. New York: 1954.
Ganoe, William A. *The History of the United States Army*. New York: 1942.
Goerlitz, Walter. *History of the German General Staff, 1857–1945*. New York: 1953.
Hall, D. G. E. *A History of Southeast Asia*. London: 1955.
Harbottle, Thomas B. *A Dictionary of Battles*. New York: 1905. (Republished Detroit: 1966.)
Hazard, Harry W. *Atlas of Islamic History*. Princeton: 1954.
Heinl, Robert D., Jr. *Soldiers of the Sea: The United States Marines Corps, 1775–1962*. Annapolis: 1962.
———. *Dictionary of Military and Naval Quotations*. Annapolis: 1966.
Herrin, Hubert. *A History of Latin America*. New York: 1962.
Historical Evaluation and Research Organization. *Historical Trends Related to Weapon Lethality*. Washington: 1964.
Hitti, Philip K. *The Near East in History*. New York: 1961.
Hittle, James D. *The Military Staff*. Harrisburg: 1949.
Langer, William L. *An Encyclopedia of World History*. Boston: 1952.
Larousse Encyclopedia of Modern History. New York: 1964.
Latourette, Kenneth S. *The Chinese: Their History and Culture*. New York: 1934.
Lawford, James, ed. *The Cavalry*. New York: 1976.
Leeb, Wilhelm von. *Defense*. Harrisburg: 1943.
Lewis, Michael. *The Navy of Britain*. London: 1948.
Liddell Hart, Basil H. *The Decisive Wars of History*. London: 1929.
Mahan, Alfred T. *The Influence of Seapower upon History, 1660–1783*. Boston: 1890.
Manucy, Albert. *Artillery Through the Ages*. Washington: 1949.
McNeil, William H. *The Rise of the West*. Chicago: 1963.
Mitchell, William A. *Outlines of the World's Military History*. Washington: 1931.
Montross, Lynn. *War Through the Ages*. New York: 1946.
Morris, Richard B. *Encyclopedia of American History*. New York: 1953.
Morison, Samuel E. *The Oxford History of the American People*. New York: 1965.
Mrazek, James. *The Art of Winning Wars*. New York: 1968.
New Cambridge Modern History. 12 vols. Cambridge, Eng.: 1951.
Oliver, Roland, and Fage, J. D. *A Short History of Africa*. London: 1962.
Palmer, John M. *Washington, Lincoln, Wilson*. New York: 1930.
Payne, L. G. S. *Air Dates*. New York: 1957.
Peterson, Harold L. *A History of Firearms*. New York: 1961.
Phillips, Thomas R. (ed.) *Roots of Strategy*. Harrisburg: 1940.
Potter, E. B., and Nimitz, Chester W. (eds.). *Sea Power*. New York: 1960.
Preston, Richard A.; Wise, Sydney F.; and Werner, Herman O. *Men in Arms*. New York: 1962.
Reischauer, Edwin O., and Fairbank, John. *A History of East Asian Civilization*. Boston: 1960.
Richardson, Lewis Fry. *Statistics of Deadly Quarrels*. Pittsburgh: 1960.
Ropp, Theodore. *War in the Modern World*. Durham: 1959.
Schlieffen, Alfred von. *Cannae*. Leavenworth: 1931.
Shepherd, William R. *Historical Atlas*. New York: 1929.
Spaulding, Oliver L. *The United States Army in War and Peace*. New York: 1937.
Spaulding, Oliver L.; Nickerson, Hoffman; and Wright, John W. *Warfare: A Study of Military Methods from the Earliest Times*. Washington: 1937.
Spear, Percival. *India*. Ann Arbor: 1961.
Sprout, Harold, and Sprout, Margaret. *The Rise of American Naval Power*. Princeton: 1939.
———. *Toward a New Order of Sea Power*. Princeton: 1940.
Stacy, C. P. *Military History for Canadian Students*. Ottawa: 1953.
Starr, Chester, *et al*. *A History of the World*. Chicago: 1960.

Steele, Matthew F. *American Campaigns.* Washington: 1909.
Todd, Frederick P., and Kredel, Fritz. *Soldiers of the American Army, 1775–1954.* Chicago: 1954.
Toynbee, Arnold. *A Study of History.* Somervell abridgment. 2 vols. New York: 1947–1957.
Turner, Gordon. *A History of Military Affairs in Western Society Since the Eighteenth Century.* New York: 1953.
Upton, Emory. *The Military Policy of the United States.* Washington: 1917.
United States Army. *The Army Almanac.* Washington: 1950.
United States Military Academy. *Summaries of Selected Military Campaigns.* West Point: 1952.
Wright, Quincy. *A Study of War.* 2 vols. Chicago: 1942.

ANCIENT WARFARE
(Chapters I–VII, to A.D. 600)

Adcock, Frank E. *The Greek and Macedonian Art of War.* Berkeley: 1957.
———. *The Roman Art of War under the Republic.* Cambridge, Mass.: 1940.
Caesar, Julius. *Commentaries.* (Edited and translated by John Warrington.) London: 1953.
Cambridge Ancient History. 12 vols., with 5 vols. of plates. Cambridge, Eng.: 1923–1939.
Cottrell, Leonard. *Hannibal, Enemy of Rome.* New York: 1961.
Diodorus Siculus. *Bibliotheca Historica.* (English translation by C. H. Oldfather. Loeb Series.) 12 vols. Cambridge, Mass.: 1933–1957.
Dodge, Theodore Ayrault. *Alexander the Great.* Boston: 1890.
———. *Hannibal.* Boston: 1891.
———. *Julius Caesar.* Boston: 1892.
Fuller, J. F. C. *The Generalship of Alexander the Great.* New Brunswick: 1958.
———. *Julius Caesar.* New Brunswick: 1965.
*Gibbon, Edward. *Decline and Fall of the Roman Empire.* 3 vols. New York: 1953.
Holy Bible, The. Various versions and editions.
**Larousse Encyclopedia of Ancient and Medieval History.* New York: 1963.
Liddell Hart, Basil H. *A Greater Than Napoleon—Scipio Africanus.* Edinburgh: 1926.
Livy. *History of Rome.* (English translation by B. O. Foster, E. T. Sage, and A. C. Schlesinger. Loeb Series.) 14 vols. Cambridge, Mass.: 1919–1957.
Mommsen, Theodor. *History of Rome.* 5 vols. New York: 1895.
Plutarchus. *Lives of Themistocles, etc.* New York: 1937.
Polybius. *Histories.* (English translation by W. R. Paton. Loeb Series.) Cambridge, Mass.: 1922–1927.
Robinson, Charles Alexander, Jr. *Alexander the Great.* New York: 1963.
Starr, Chester G. *A History of the Ancient World.* New York: 1965.
Sun Tzu. *The Art of War.* (Translated by Samuel B. Griffith.) New York: 1963.
Tarn, William W. *Alexander the Great.* Cambridge, Eng.: 1948.
Thucydides. *History of the Peloponnesian War.* London: 1954.
Vegetius. *The Military Institutions of the Romans.* In T. R. Phillips (ed.). *Roots of Strategy.* Harrisburg: 1940.
Xenophon. *Anabasis.* (English translation of complete works by W. Miller, *et al.* Loeb Series.) Cambridge, Mass.: 1914–1925.
———. *Cyropaedia.* (English translation of complete works by W. Miller, *et al.* Loeb Series.) Cambridge, Mass.: 1914–1925.

MEDIEVAL WARFARE
(Chapters VIII–XII, 600–1500)

Cambridge Medieval History. 8 vols. Cambridge, Eng.: 1924–1936.
Charol, Michael (pseud.: Michael Prawdin). *The Mongol Empire.* London: 1952.
Costain, Thomas B. *The Last Plantagenets.* New York: 1962.

* Signifies applicability to more than one historical period.

Grousset, René. *Conqueror of the World: The Life of Chingis Khan.* New York: 1966.
———. *The Epic of the Crusades.* New York: 1971.
Kendall, Paul Murray. *The Yorkist Age.* New York: 1962.
Lamb, Harold. *Charlemagne.* New York: 1954.
———. *The Crusades.* New York: 1931.
———. *The Earthshakers.* New York: 1949.
———. *Genghis Khan, Emperor of All Men.* New York: 1927.
Oman, Charles. *A History of the Art of War in the Middle Ages.* London: 1924.
Prescott, William Hickling. *History of the Reign of Ferdinand and Isabella.* 2 vols. New York: 1837.
Waley, Arthur (ed.). *The Secret History of the Mongols.* London: 1964.
Wise, Terence. *Medieval Warfare.* New York: 1976.

EARLY MODERN WARFARE

(Chapters XIII–XV, 1500–1750)

Dodge, Theodore Ayrault. *Gustavus Adolphus.* Boston: 1890.
MacMunn, George. *Gustavus Adolphus.* New York: 1931.
Mattingly, Garrett. *The Armada.* New York: 1959.
Oman, Charles. *A History of the Art of War in the Sixteenth Century.* New York: 1937.
Prescott, William H. *The History of the Conquest of Mexico.* New York: 1843.
Thompson, James Westfall. *The Wars of Religion in France.* New York: 1958.
Wedgewood, C. V. *The Thirty Years' War.* New York: 1961.

THE CENTURY OF REVOLUTION

(Chapters XVI and XVII, 1750–1850)

Ballard, Colin. *Napoleon: An Outline.* New York: 1924.
Camon, Hubert. *Deux grands chefs de guerre du XVIIe siecle: Condé et Turenne.* Paris: 1899.
Chandler, David. *The Art of Warfare in the Age of Marlborough.* New York: 1976.
———. *Marlborough as Military Commander.* New York: 1973.
Dodge, Theodore Ayrault. *Gustavus Adolphus.* Boston: 1890.
Godley, Eveline. *The Great Condé.* London: 1915.
Heilmann, Johann Ritter von. *Das Kriegswesen der Kaiserlichen und Schweden zur Zeit des dreissigjaehrigen Krieges.* Leipzig: 1850.
Machiavelli, Niccolò. *The Art of War.* Albany: 1815.
MacMunn, George. *Gustavus Adolphus.* New York: 1931.
Mattingly, Garrett. *The Armada.* New York: 1959.
Oman, Charles. *A History of the Art of War in the Sixteenth Century.* New York: 1937.
Prescott, William H. *The History of the Conquest of Mexico.* New York: 1843.
Sweden, Armen Generalstaben. Krigshistoriska avdelningen. *Sveriges Krig, 1611–1632.* 6 vols. Stockholm: 1936–39.
Taylor, Frederick Louis. *The Art of War in Italy, 1494–1529.* Reprint. Westport: 1973.
Thompson, James Westfall. *The Wars of Religion in France.* New York: 1958.
Villermont, Antoine Charles Hennequin, comte de. *Tilly; ou La guerre de trente ans de 1618 à 1632.* 2 vols. Paris: 1860.
Wedgewood, C. V. *The Thirty Years' War.* New York: 1961.

Dodge, Theodore Ayrault. *Napoleon.* 4 vols. Boston: 1904.
Duffy, Christopher. *The Army of Frederick the Great.* New York: 1974.
Dupuy, R. Ernest. *Battle of Hubbardton.* Montpelier: 1960.

Jacobs, James R., and Tucker, Glenn. *Compact History of the War of 1812.* New York: 1969.
Johnson, Curtis J. *Battles of the American Revolution.* London: 1975.
Ludwig, Emil. *Napoleon.* New York: 1926.
Mahan, Alfred T. *The Influence of Seapower on the French Revolution.* Boston: 1893.
———. *Life of Nelson.* 2 vols. Boston: 1900–1907.

Mitchell, Lt. Col. Joseph B. *Decisive Battles of the American Revolution.* New York: 1962.
Napier, Sir Williams. *History of the War in the Peninsula and in the South of France from the Year 1807 to the Year 1814.* London and New York: n.d. (First English edition 1828–1840.)
Parkman, Francis. *Montcalm and Wolfe.* Boston: 1905.
Reiners, Ludwig. *Frederick the Great.* New York: 1960.
Roosevelt, Theodore. *The Naval War of 1812.* New York: 1894.
Runciman, Sir Walter. *The Tragedy of St. Helena.* New York: 1911.
Scheer, George F., and Rankin, Hugh F. (eds.). *Rebels and Redcoats.* Cleveland: 1957.
Simon, Edith. *The Making of Frederick the Great.* Boston: 1963.
Smith, Justin H. *The War with Mexico.* 2 vols. New York: 1919.
Thaddeus, Victor. *Frederick the Great, the Philosopher King.* New York: 1930.
Trevelyan, George O. *The American Revolution.* 4 vols. London: 1921.
Tucker, Glenn. *Poltroons and Patriots.* 2 vols. Indianapolis: 1954.
Ward, Christopher. *The War of the Revolution.* 2 vols. New York: 1952.
Yorck von Wartenburg, Maximilian. *Napoleon as a General.* 2 vols. London: 1897.

THE EMERGENCE OF THE PROFESSIONAL
(Chapter XVIII, 1850–1900)

Ballard, Colin. *The Military Genius of Abraham Lincoln.* Cleveland: 1965.
Burke, John G. *On the Border with Crook.* New York: 1891.
Catton, Bruce. *The Army of the Potomac.* 3 vols. New York: 1962.
———. *Centennial History of the Civil War.* 3 vols. New York: 1965.
Churchill, Winston S. *The River War.* London: 1899.
Commager, Henry S. *The Blue and the Gray.* 2 vols. Indianapolis: 1950.
Downey, Fairfax. *Indian-Fighting Army.* New York: 1941.
Dupuy, R. Ernest, and Dupuy, Trevor N. *The Compact History of the Civil War.* New York: 1960.
Farwell, Byron. *Queen Victoria's Little Wars.* New York: 1972.
Freeman, Douglas S. *Lee's Lieutenants.* 3 vols. New York: 1944.
———. *R. E. Lee.* 4 vols. New York: 1949.
Fuller, J. F. C. *The Generalship of Ulysses S. Grant.* New York: 1929.
———. *Grant and Lee.* London: 1933.
Furneaux, Rupert. *The Breakfast War.* New York: 1958.
Gibbs, Peter. *Crimean Blunder.* New York: 1960.
Grant, Ulysses S. *Personal Memoirs.* New York: 1895.
Henderson, George F. R. *Stonewall Jackson and the American Civil War.* London: 1898.
Howard, Michael. *The Franco-Prussian War.* New York: 1962.
Johnson, Robert Underwood, and Buel, Clarence Clough (eds.). *Battles and Leaders of the Civil War.* 4 vols. New York: 1884–1888.
Livermore, Thomas L. *Numbers and Losses in the Civil War.* Boston: 1901.
Mahan, Alfred T. *Lessons of the War with Spain.* Boston: 1899.
Millis, Walter. *The Martial Spirit: A Study of Our War with Spain.* Boston: 1931.
Nye, W. S. *Carbine and Lance.* Norman: 1942.
Sandburg, Carl. *Abraham Lincoln.* New York: 1959.
Whease, K. C. *Lincoln.* New York: 1948.
Williams, Kenneth P. *Lincoln Finds a General.* 5 vols. New York: 1959.
Williams, T. Harry. *Lincoln and His Generals.* New York: 1952.
Woodham-Smith, Cecily. *The Reason Why.* New York: 1953.
Wyeth, John A. *That Devil Forrest: Life of General Nathan Bedford Forrest.* New York: 1959.

WORLD WAR I AND THE ERA OF TOTAL WAR
(Chapter XIX, 1900–1925)

Ayres, Leonard P. *The War with Germany: A Statistical Summary.* Washington: 1919.
Baldwin, Hanson. *World War I.* New York: 1963.

Balfour, Patrick, Baron Kinross. *Ataturk*. New York: 1965.
Barnett, Corelli. *The Swordbearers: Supreme Command in the First World War*. New York: 1964.
Bloch, Ivan S. *The Future of War . . . Is War Now Impossible?* St. Petersburg: 1898.
Buchan, John. *A History of the Great War*. Boston: 1922.
Churchill, Winston. *The World Crisis*. 6 vols. New York: 1932.
Clubb, O. Edmund. *Twentieth-Century China*. New York: 1964.
*Dornbusch, Charles E. *Histories of American Army Units*. Washington: 1956.
Dupuy, R. Ernest. *Five Days to War*. Harrisburg: 1967.
———. *Perish by the Sword*. Harrisburg: 1939.
Dupuy, R. Ernest, and Baumer, William H. *Little Wars of the U.S.* New York: 1969.
Dupuy, Trevor N., *et al. Military History of World War I*. 12 vols. New York: 1967.
Falls, Cyril. *The Great War, 1914–1918*. New York: 1959.
Fischer, Fritz. *Germany's Aims in the First World War*. New York: 1967.
Fuller, J. F. C. *Machine Warfare*. Washington: 1943.
Hamilton, Ian A. S. *A Staff Officer's Scrap Book*. London: 1905.
Hayes, Grace P. *Compact History of World War I*. New York: 1972.
Higgins, Trumbull. *Winston Churchill and the Dardanelles*. New York: 1957.
Hindenburg, Paul von. *Out of My Life*. 2 vols. New York: 1921.
Hoffmann, Max. *The War of Lost Opportunities*. New York: 1925.
James, Robert R. *Gallipoli*. London: 1965.
*Kennan, George F. *Russia and the West*. Boston: 1962.
———. *Soviet Foreign Policy, 1917–1941*. Princeton: 1960.
Landor, A. H. S. *China and the Allies*. 2 vols. New York: 1901.
Lawrence, T. E. *Seven Pillars of Wisdom*. New York: 1926.
Liman von Sanders, Otto V. K. *My Five Years in Turkey*. Annapolis: 1927.
*Liu, F. F. *A Military History of Modern China*. Princeton: 1956.
Ludendorff, Erich. *Ludendorff's Own Story*. New York: 1920.
MacArthur, Douglas. *Reminiscences*. New York: 1964.
McEntee, Gerard L. *Military History of the World War*. New York: 1937.
Millis, Walter. *The Road to War*. Boston: 1935.
Moorehead, Alan. *The Russian Revolution*. New York: 1958.
———. *Gallipoli*. New York: 1945.
Pitt, Barrie. *1918—The Last Act*. New York: 1963.
Sexton, William T. *Soldiers in the Philippines*. Harrisburg: 1939.
Stamps, T. Dodson, and Esposito, Vincent J. *A Short History of World War I*. West Point: 1950.
Taylor, Edmond. *The Fall of the Dynasties*. Garden City: 1963.
The Times, London. *The Times Diary and Index of the War, 1914 to 1918*. London: 1921.
Tschuppik, Karl. *Ludendorff: The Tragedy of a Military Mind*. Boston: 1932.
Tuchman, Barbara. *The Guns of August*. New York: 1962.
U.S. War Department. *Reports of the Chief of Staff*. Washington: 1913–1915, incl.
Wheeler-Bennett, John W. *Nemesis of Power: The German Army in Politics, 1918–1945*. 2nd ed. New York: 1964.
———. *Wooden Titan: Hindenburg in Twenty Years of German History, 1914–1934*. New York: 1936.
Wavell, Archibald. *Allenby—A Study in Greatness*. New York: 1941.

WORLD WAR II AND THE DAWN OF THE NUCLEAR AGE
(Chapter XX, 1925–1945)

Auphan, Paul, and Mordal, Jacques. *The French Navy in World War II*. Annapolis: 1959.
Baldwin, Hanson W. *Battles Lost and Won: Great Campaigns of World War II*. New York: 1966.
Blumenson, Martin. *Anzio: The Gamble That Failed*. Philadelphia: 1963.
———. *The Duel for France*. Boston: 1963.

* Signifies applicability to more than one historical period.

Bryant, Arthur. *Triumph in the West*. New York: 1959.
———. *The Turn of the Tide*. New York: 1957.
Bullock, Alan. *Hitler: A Study in Tyranny*. New York: 1962.
Bush, Vannevar. *Modern Arms and Free Men*. New York: 1949.
Churchill, Randolph. *Winston S. Churchill*. 2 vols. Boston: 1967.
Churchill, Winston S. *The Second World War*. 6 vols. Boston: 1948–1953.
Clark, Alan. *Barbarossa: The Russian-German Conflict, 1941–45*. New York: 1965.
Cowles, Virginia. *Winston Churchill*. New York: 1953.
Craven, Wesley F., and Cate, James L. (eds.). *The Army Air Forces in World War II*. 6 vols. Chicago: 1948–1955.
De Gaulle, Charles. *War Memoirs*. 3 vols. London: 1959.
Dupuy, R. Ernest. *St. Vith—Lion in the Way*. Washington: 1949.
*Dupuy, Trevor N. *Military History of the Chinese Civil War*. New York: 1969.
———. *Military History of World War II*. 19 vols. New York: 1966.
Dupuy, Trevor N., and Martell, Paul. *Great Battles of the Eastern Front*. New York: 1982.
Eisenhower, Dwight D. *Crusade in Europe*. New York: 1948.
Freiden, Seymour, and Richardson, William. *The Fatal Decisions*. New York: 1956.
Fuller, J. F. C. *The Second World War*. New York: 1949.
Gilbert, Felix. *Hitler Directs His War: The Secret Records of His Daily Military Conferences*. New York: 1950.
Glubb, Sir John B. *War in the Desert*. London: 1960.
Griffith, Samuel B. *The Chinese People's Army*. New York: 1967.
Guderian, Heinz. *Panzer Leader*. New York: 1952.
Higgins, Trumbull. *Winston Churchill and the Second Front*. New York: 1957.
History of the Second World War; United Kingdom Military Series. 24 vols. London: 1956–1969.
The Illustrated London News. *Winston Churchill, the Greatest Figure of Our Time*.
Isely, Jeter A., and Crowl, P. A. *The U.S. Marines and Amphibious War*. Princeton: 1951.
Jackson, W. G. F. *The Battle for Italy*. New York: 1967.
Liddell Hart, Basil H. *The German Generals Talk*. London: 1968.
———. *The Liddell Hart Memoirs*. 2 vols. New York: 1966.
Manstein, Eric von. *Lost Victories*. Chicago: 1958.
Marshall, George C.; Arnold, Henry H.; and King, Ernest J. *The War Reports*. . . . Philadelphia: 1947.
Marshall, Samuel L. A. *Men Against Fire*. Washington: 1947.
Moran, Lord. *Churchill from the Diaries of Lord Moran*. Boston: 1966.
Morison, Samuel E. *History of United States Naval Operations in World War II*. 15 vols. Boston: 1962.
———. *The Two-Ocean War*. Boston: 1963.
Pitt, Barrie (ed.). *History of the Second World War*. London: 1966–1969.
Pogue, Forrest C. *George C. Marshall*. 3 vols. New York: 1969.
Prittie, Terence. *Germans Against Hitler*. Boston: 1964.
Ruge, Friedrich. *Der Zeekrieg: The German Navy's Story, 1939–1945*. Annapolis: 1957.
Shirer, William L. *The Rise and Fall of the Third Reich*. New York: 1960.
Slim, William J. *Defeat into Victory*. London: 1956.
Smyth, Henry D. *Atomic Energy for Nuclear Purposes*. Princeton: 1945.
Snyder, Louis L. *Hitler and Nazism*. New York: 1961.
Spears, Edward L. *Assignment to Catastrophe*. 2 vols. New York: 1955.
Speer, Albert. *Inside the Third Reich*. New York: 1970.
Stamps, T. Dodson, and Espostio, Vincent J. *Military History of World War II*. 2 vols. West Point: 1953.
Thomas, Hugh. *The Spanish Civil War*. New York: 1961.
Trevor-Roper, H. R. *The Last Days of Hitler*. New York: 1947.
Truscott, Lucian. *Command Missions*. New York: 1954.
*Tsou Tang. *America's Failure in China*. Chicago: 1963.

* Signifies applicability to more than one historical period.

U.S. Army, Office of the Chief of Military History. *The U.S. Army in World War II*. 80 vols. Washington: 1950–1968.
U.S. Strategic Bombing Survey. *Overall Report (European War), etc.* Washington: 1945–1947.
*Wedemeyer, Albert C. *Wedemeyer Reports*. New York: 1958.
*Werth, Alexander. *France, 1940–1955*. New York: 1956.
———. *Russia at War, 1941–1945*. New York: 1964.
White, Theodore H., and Jacoby, Annalee. *Thunder out of China*. New York: 1946.
*Willoughby, Charles A., and Chamberlain, John. *MacArthur, 1941–1951*. New York: 1954.
Wilmot, Chester. *The Struggle for Europe*. New York: 1952.
Ziemke, Earl. *From Stalingrad to Berlin*. Washington: 1968.

SUPERPOWERS IN THE NUCLEAR AGE
(Chapter XXI, 1945–1984)

Badri, Hassan el, Magdoub, Taha el, and Zohdy, Mohommed Dia el Din. *The Ramadan War*. Dunn Loring: 1978.
Blackett, Patrick. *Studies of War, Nuclear and Conventional*. New York: 1962.
Brodie, Bernard. *Strategy in the Missile Age*. Princeton: 1959.
Dunn, Frederick; Brodie, Bernard; *et al. The Absolute Weapon*. New York: 1946.
Dupuy, Trevor N. *Elusive Victory: The Arab-Israeli Wars, 1947–1974*. New York: 1980.
Fall, Bernard B. *Street Without Joy*. Harrisburg: 1964.
Fehrenbach, T. R. *This Kind of War*. New York: 1963.
Halberstam, David. *The Best and the Brightest*. New York: 1972.
Herzog, Haim. *The War of Atonement*. Tel Aviv: 1975.
Hsieh, Alice L. *Communist China's Strategy in the Nuclear Era*. Englewood Cliffs: 1962.
Kahn, Herman. *On Thermonuclear War*. Princeton: 1960.
Kissinger, Henry. *Nuclear Weapons and Foreign Policy*. New York: 1957.
Leckie, Robert. *Conflict: The History of the Korean War*. New York: 1962.
Marshall, S. L. A. *The Military History of the Korean War*. New York: 1963.
———. *The River and the Gauntlet*. New York: 1953.
———. *Sinai Victory*. New York: 1958.
Osgood, Robert. *Limited War*. Chicago: 1957.
Pinson, Koppel S. *Modern Germany: Its History and Civilization*. 2nd ed. New York: 1966.
Scott, William F., and Scott, Harrier F. *The Armed Forces of the USSR*. Boulder: 1979.
Slessor, John. *Strategy for the West*. New York: 1954.
Smith, Jean E. *The Defense of Berlin*. Baltimore: 1963.
Trager, Frank N. *Marxism in Southeast Asia*. Stanford: 1959.
U.S. Army, Office of Chief of Military History. *The U.S. Army in the Korean War*. 5 vols. Washington: 1951–1966.

* Signifies applicability to more than one historical period.

GENERAL INDEX

INDEX TO ADDENDUM

(pages 1346–1400)

INDEX OF BATTLES AND SIEGES

INDEX OF WARS

(Including Civil Wars, Colonial Wars, Rebellions, etc.)*

* *Note:* 1. Wars commonly known by name (e.g., of the Chiogga, Hundred Years', Seven Years', Napoleonic, World Wars, etc.) are so listed and do not appear under names of individual nations.

2. Periods of protracted or recurrent warfare are not included, unless specifically identified in the text; for such periods look under the appropriate entries in the General Index.

3. Internal Wars include civil wars, insurrections, mutinies, rebellions, revolts.